P9-CKX-892

REFERENCE GUIDE TO AMERICAN LITERATURE

St. James Reference Guides

American Literature

English Literature, 2 vols. (in preparation)

World Literature (in preparation)

REFERENCE GUIDE TO AMERICAN LITERATURE

SECOND EDITION

INTRODUCTIONS BY
LEWIS LEARY AND WARREN FRENCH

EDITOR
D.L. KIRKPATRICK

St J

ST. JAMES PRESS
CHICAGO AND LONDON

ST. JAMES PRESS
425 North Michigan Avenue
Chicago 60611, U.S.A.
or
3 Percy Street
London W1P 9FA, England

First published in the U.S.A. and U.K. in 1987

British Library Cataloguing in Publication Data

Reference guide to American literature.—
2nd ed.—(St. James Press reference guides).
1. American literature—Dictionaries
I. Kirkpatrick, D.L.
810′.3′21 PS21

ISBN 0-912289-61-9

Typeset at BookMasters, Ashland, Ohio
Printed at The Bath Press, Avon

CONTENTS

EDITOR'S NOTE

The main part of *Reference Guide to American Literature* consists of the entries in the Writers section. The entry for each writer includes a biography, a complete list of the writer's published books, a selected list of bibliographies and critical studies on the writer, and a signed critical essay.

In the biography, details of education, military service, and marriage(s) are given before the usual chronological summary of the writer's life; awards and honors are given last.

The Publications list includes all separately published books, though as a rule broadsheets, single sermons and lectures, minor pamphlets, exhibition catalogs, etc., are omitted. Under the heading Collections we have listed the most recent collection of the complete works and of the individual genres (verse, plays, novels, stories, and letters); only those collections that have some editorial authority and were issued after the writer's death are cited; on-going editions are indicated by a dash after the date of publication; often a general selection from the writer's works or a selection from the individual genres mentioned above is included.

Titles are given in modern spelling; often titles are "short." The date given is that of the first book publication, which often followed the first periodical or anthology publication by some time; we have attempted to list the actual year of publication, sometimes different from the date given on the title page. No attempt has been made to indicate which works were published anonymously or pseudonymously, or which works of fiction were published in more than one volume. We have listed plays that were produced but not published; librettos and musical plays are listed along with the other plays. Reprints of books (including facsimile editions) and revivals of plays are not listed unless a revision of text or a change of title is involved. The most recent edited version of an individual work is listed if it supersedes the collected edition cited. Introductions, memoirs, editorial matter, etc., in works cited in the Publications list are not repeated in the Critical Studies list.

Some of the entries in the Writers section are supplemented in the Works section, which includes a selection of essays on the best known works in American literature, as well as on some works important chiefly for historical reasons. When appropriate to the writer concerned, a single representative poem or story is the subject of an essay.

The *Reference Guide* concludes with a brief Chronology of literary and social history, and a Title Index to the Publications lists in the Writers section.

We would like to thank the contributors, and, in particular, our advisers Warren French and Lewis Leary, for their patience and help.

CONTRIBUTORS

M.J. Alexander
Walter Allen
David D. Anderson
James Angle
Robert D. Arner
Leonard R.N. Ashley
Alvin Aubert
James C. Austin
Jonathan Barker
Samuel Irving Bellman
George N. Bennett
Alice R. Bensen
Dominic J. Bisignano
Jean Frantz Blackall
Lynn Z. Bloom
Joseph Blotner
Walter Bode
Mary Weatherspoon Bowden
Neville Braybrooke
Lawrence R. Broer
Ashley Brown
Martin Bucco
R.A. Burchell
Richard J. Calhoun
Guy A. Cardwell
Frederic I. Carpenter
Humphrey Carpenter
Paul Christensen
William Claire
Hennig Cohen
Ruby Cohn
William J. Collins
Neil Corcoran
Martha Heasley Cox
Richard H. Crowder
Eugene Current-Garcia
Tish Dace
Curtis Dahl
James M. Drayton
Louise Duus
Clayton L. Eichelberger
Chester E. Eisinger
Patrick Evans
Charles Fanning
Philip José Farmer
M.J. Fitzgerald
Ian Fletcher
Joseph M. Flora
Edward Halsey Foster
G.S. Fraser
Warren French
Jane S. Gabin
Sally M. Gall
John C. Gerber
Donald B. Gibson
R. Barbara Gitenstein
Clarence A. Glasrud
Lois Gordon
George Grella
John Heath-Stubbs
William J. Heim
Geof Hewitt
Jack Hicks
William Higgins
Bert Hitchcock
Thomas E. Hockersmith
Jacqueline Hoefer
Daniel Hoffman
Robert Hogan
Jan Hokenson
Jonathan Holden
C. Hugh Holman
Robert N. Hudspeth
M. Thomas Inge
Mary Jarrett
Estelle C. Jelinek
Robert K. Johnson
Nancy Carol Joyner
Zoë Coralnik Kaplan
Bruce Kellner
Kimball King
Keneth Kinnamon
John G. Kuhn
Chirantan Kulshrestha
Lewis Leary
James A. Levernier
Naomi Lewis
Bruce A. Lohof
George C. Longest
John Lucas
Townsend Ludington
Brent MacLaine
Frank MacShane
David Madden
Suzanne Marrs
Margaret B. McDowell
Howard McNaughton
Walter J. Meserve
Jordan Y. Miller
Christian H. Moe
George Monteiro
Jack B. Moore
Rayburn S. Moore
Katharine M. Morsberger
Robert E. Morsberger
I.B. Nadel
Francis M. Nevins, Jr.
Brady Nordland
Thomas F. O'Donnell
William Peden
Barbara M. Perkins
George Perkins
Margaret Perry
John B. Pickard
Jan Pilditch
Sanford Pinsker
Helen Houser Popovich
Peter Quartermain
David Ray
John Q. Reed
James Reeves
John M. Reilly

Sylvia Lyons Render
Robert F. Richards
Donald A. Ringe
Earl Rovit
Glenn Richard Ruihley
Geoff Sadler
Carol Lee Saffioti
Stewart F. Sanderson
Mollie Sandock
George Brandon Saul
Arnold T. Schwab
Catherine Seelye
Per Seyersted
J.N. Sharma
Alan R. Shucard
Amritjit Singh
Esther Marian Greenwell Smith
Stan Smith
Eric Solomon
Louis Charles Stagg
Donald E. Stanford
Jane W. Stedman
Madeleine B. Stern
David Stouck
W.J. Stuckey
Joseph H. Summers
G. Thomas Tanselle
Ann Thwaite
Derek A. Traversi
Richard C. Turner
Linda W. Wagner
Marshall Walker
Mark I. Wallach
Richard Walser
George Walsh
Val Warner
R.J.C. Watt
Harold H. Watts
Gerald Weales
Sybil B. Weir
Perry D. Westbrook
T.J. Winnifrith
James Woodress
Kenneth Young
Thomas Daniel Young

REFERENCE GUIDE TO AMERICAN LITERATURE

WRITERS

Henry Adams
George Ade
James Agee
Conrad Aiken
Edward Albee
Louisa May Alcott
Horatio Alger
Nelson Algren
James Lane Allen
A.R. Ammons
Maxwell Anderson
Sherwood Anderson
Timothy Shay Arthur
John Ashbery
Gertrude Atherton
Louis Auchincloss

James Baldwin
Joseph G. Baldwin
Amiri Baraka
James Nelson Barker
Joel Barlow
Djuna Barnes
Philip Barry
John Barth
Donald Barthelme
L. Frank Baum
S.N. Behrman
David Belasco
Edward Bellamy
Saul Bellow
Ludwig Bemelmans
Robert Benchley
Stephen Vincent Benét
William Rose Benét
John Berryman
Ambrose Bierce
Robert Montgomery Bird
Elizabeth Bishop
John Peale Bishop
Robert Bly
Maxwell Bodenheim
Louise Bogan
George Henry Boker
Paul Bowles
James Boyd
H.H. Boyesen
Kay Boyle
Hugh Henry Brackenridge
Roark Bradford
William Bradford
Anne Bradstreet
Louis Bromfield
Gwendolyn Brooks
Charles Brockden Brown
Sterling A. Brown
William Wells Brown
William Cullen Bryant
Pearl S. Buck

Ed Bullins
Kenneth Burke
Frances Hodgson Burnett
Edgar Rice Burroughs
William S. Burroughs
William Byrd II

James Branch Cabell
George Washington Cable
Abraham Cahan
James M. Cain
Erskine Caldwell
Hortense Calisher
Truman Capote
Willa Cather
Raymond Chandler
William Ellery Channing
Paddy Chayefsky
John Cheever
Charles Waddell Chesnutt
Thomas Holley Chivers
Kate Chopin
Winston Churchill
Walter Van Tilburg Clark
George M. Cohan
Marc Connelly
Ebenezer Cooke
John Esten Cooke
James Fenimore Cooper
James Gould Cozzens
Hart Crane
Stephen Crane
F. Marion Crawford
Robert Creeley
Rachel Crothers
Countée Cullen
E.E. Cummings

Edward Dahlberg
Augustin Daly
Richard Henry Dana, Jr.
Donald Davidson
Rebecca Harding Davis
Richard Harding Davis
John William De Forest
Margaret Deland
Floyd Dell
John Dewey
James Dickey
Emily Dickinson
Ignatius Donnelly
Hilda Doolittle
John Dos Passos
Frederick Douglass
Joseph Rodman Drake
Theodore Dreiser
W.E.B. Du Bois
Paul Laurence Dunbar
Robert Duncan

William Dunlap
Finley Peter Dunne
Timothy Dwight

Richard Eberhart
Jonathan Edwards
Edward Eggleston
T.S. Eliot
Ralph Ellison
Ralph Waldo Emerson

James T. Farrell
William Faulkner
Kenneth Fearing
Edna Ferber
Eugene Field
Vardis Fisher
Clyde Fitch
F. Scott Fitzgerald
John Gould Fletcher
Hannah Foster
Stephen Collins Foster
Waldo Frank
Benjamin Franklin
Harold Frederic
Mary E. Wilkins Freeman
Philip Freneau
Robert Frost
Henry Blake Fuller

William Gaddis
Zona Gale
Erle Stanley Gardner
John Gardner
Hamlin Garland
William Gillette
Allen Ginsberg
Ellen Glasgow
Susan Glaspell
Michael Gold
Paul Goodman
Caroline Gordon
Paul Green
Horace Gregory
Zane Grey
Louise Imogen Guiney
Ramon Guthrie

Fitz-Greene Halleck
Dashiell Hammett
Lorraine Hansberry
Edward Harrigan
George Washington Harris
Joel Chandler Harris
Moss Hart
Bret Harte
John Hawkes
Nathaniel Hawthorne
John Hay
Robert Hayden
Paul Hamilton Hayne
Lafcadio Hearn
Ben Hecht
Joseph Heller
Lillian Hellman

Ernest Hemingway
O. Henry
Joseph Hergesheimer
James A. Herne
Robert Herrick
DuBose Heyward
Charles Fenno Hoffman
Oliver Wendell Holmes
Johnson Jones Hooper
Francis Hopkinson
Richard Hovey
Bronson Howard
Sidney Howard
E.W. Howe
William Dean Howells
Langston Hughes
Richard Hugo
James Huneker
Zora Neale Hurston

William Inge
Joseph Holt Ingraham
Washington Irving

Helen Hunt Jackson
Shirley Jackson
Henry James
William James
Randall Jarrell
Robinson Jeffers
Thomas Jefferson
Sarah Orne Jewett
James Weldon Johnson
James Jones

George S. Kaufman
George Kelly
John Pendleton Kennedy
Jack Kerouac
Sidney Kingsley
Joseph Kirkland
Arthur Kopit
Jerzy Kosinski
Stanley Kunitz

Oliver La Farge
Sidney Lanier
Ring Lardner
Arthur Laurents
John Howard Lawson
Denise Levertov
Sinclair Lewis
Vachel Lindsay
Ross Lockridge
Jack London
Henry Wadsworth Longfellow
Augustus Baldwin Longstreet
H.P. Lovecraft
Amy Lowell
James Russell Lowell
Robert Lowell
Andrew Lytle

Charles MacArthur
Ross Macdonald

Percy MacKaye
Archibald MacLeish
Norman Mailer
Bernard Malamud
Edwin Markham
John P. Marquand
Don Marquis
Edgar Lee Masters
Cotton Mather
Mary McCarthy
Carson McCullers
Claude McKay
Herman Melville
H.L. Mencken
James Merrill
W.S. Merwin
Edna St. Vincent Millay
Arthur Miller
Henry Miller
Joaquin Miller
Donald Grant Mitchell
Langdon Mitchell
Margaret Mitchell
S. Weir Mitchell
William Vaughn Moody
Marianne Moore
Christopher Morley
Wright Morris
Willard Motley
Anna Cora Mowatt
Mary Noailles Murfree

Vladimir Nabokov
Petroleum V. Nasby
Ogden Nash
John Neal
Howard Nemerov
Anaïs Nin
Frank Norris

Fitz-James O'Brien
Flannery O'Connor
Clifford Odets
Frank O'Hara
John O'Hara
Charles Olson
Eugene O'Neill

Thomas Nelson Page
Thomas Paine
Dorothy Parker
Francis Parkman
Kenneth Patchen
James Kirke Paulding
John Howard Payne
Walker Percy
S.J. Perelman
David Graham Phillips
Sylvia Plath
Edgar Allan Poe
Katherine Anne Porter
Ezra Pound
J.F. Powers
James Purdy
Thomas Pynchon

Ellery Queen

John Crowe Ransom
Marjorie Kinnan Rawlings
Kenneth Rexroth
Elmer Rice
Adrienne Rich
Conrad Richter
Laura Riding
James Whitcomb Riley
Mary Roberts Rinehart
Elizabeth Madox Roberts
Kenneth Roberts
Edwin Arlington Robinson
Theodore Roethke
O.E. Rølvaag
Henry Roth
Philip Roth
Mary Rowlandson
Susanna Rowson
Muriel Rukeyser
Damon Runyon

J.D. Salinger
Edgar Saltus
Carl Sandburg
George Santayana
William Saroyan
Delmore Schwartz
Catharine Maria Sedgwick
Samuel Sewall
Anne Sexton
Karl Shapiro
Henry Wheeler Shaw
Sam Shepard
Robert E. Sherwood
William Gilmore Simms
Louis Simpson
Upton Sinclair
Isaac Bashevis Singer
Seba Smith
W.D. Snodgrass
Gary Snyder
Jean Stafford
William Stafford
Wilbur Daniel Steele
Gertrude Stein
John Steinbeck
Wallace Stevens
Trumbull Stickney
Rex Stout
Harriet Beecher Stowe
T.S. Stribling
William Styron
Ruth Suckow

Booth Tarkington
Allen Tate
Bayard Taylor
Edward Taylor
Sara Teasdale
Augustus Thomas
Henry David Thoreau
Thomas Bangs Thorpe
James Thurber

Henry Timrod
Melvin B. Tolson
Jean Toomer
Albion W. Tourgée
B. Traven
Lionel Trilling
John Trumbull
Frederick Goddard Tuckerman
Mark Twain
Royall Tyler

John Updike

Mark Van Doren
John van Druten
Carl Van Vechten
Jones Very
Gore Vidal
Kurt Vonnegut, Jr.

Alice Walker
Lew Wallace
Edward Lewis Wallant
Artemus Ward
Charles Dudley Warner
Mercy Warren
Robert Penn Warren
Booker T. Washington

Eudora Welty
Glenway Wescott
Nathanael West
Edith Wharton
Phillis Wheatley
John Wheelwright
E.B. White
Walt Whitman
John Greenleaf Whittier
Michael Wigglesworth
Richard Wilbur
Thornton Wilder
Tennessee Williams
William Carlos Williams
Nathaniel Parker Willis
Edmund Wilson
Yvor Winters
Owen Wister
Thomas Wolfe
Constance Fenimore Woolson
James Wright
Richard Wright
Elinor Wylie

Frank Yerby

Louis Zukofsky

WORKS

Absalom, Absalom!, novel by William Faulkner, 1936

Adventures of Huckleberry Finn, novel by Mark Twain, 1884

The Adventures of Tom Sawyer, novel by Mark Twain, 1876

All the King's Men, novel by Robert Penn Warren, 1946

The Ambassadors, novel by Henry James, 1903

Ariel, poems by Sylvia Plath, 1965

The Assistant, novel by Bernard Malamud, 1957

Awake and Sing!, play by Clifford Odets, 1935

The Awakening, novel by Kate Chopin, 1899

"Because I could not stop for Death," poem by Emily Dickinson, written 1863

The Big Sleep, novel by Raymond Chandler, 1939

"Big Two-Hearted River," story by Ernest Hemingway, 1925

Billy Budd, novel by Herman Melville, 1924 (written 1888–91)

The Bridge, poem by Hart Crane, 1930

The Call of the Wild, novel by Jack London, 1903

The Cantos, poems by Ezra Pound, from 1925

The Catcher in the Rye, novel by J.D. Salinger, 1951

Catch-22, novel by Joseph Heller, 1961

The Cathedral, poem by James Russell Lowell, 1870

Common Sense, essay by Thomas Paine, 1776

The Country of the Pointed Firs, novel by Sarah Orne Jewett, 1896

The Damnation of Theron Ware, novel by Harold Frederic, 1896

The Day of the Locust, novel by Nathanael West, 1939

Death of a Salesman, play by Arthur Miller, 1949

"The Death of the Hired Man," poem by Robert Frost, 1914

Democracy, novel by Henry Adams, 1880

The Dream Songs, poems by John Berryman, from 1964

The Education of Henry Adams: An Autobiography, 1907

"Ethan Brand," story by Nathaniel Hawthorne, 1850

"The Fall of the House of Usher," story by Edgar Allan Poe, 1839

The Federalist, essays by Alexander Hamilton, James Madison, and John Jay, 1788

Four Quartets, poems by T.S. Eliot, 1943

"Gifts of the Magi," story by O. Henry, 1905

The Glass Menagerie, play by Tennessee Williams, 1944

Go Tell It on the Mountain, novel by James Baldwin, 1953

Gods Determinations, poem by Edward Taylor, written 1680's (?)

The Grapes of Wrath, novel by John Steinbeck, 1939

Gravity's Rainbow, novel by Thomas Pynchon, 1973

The Great Gatsby, novel by F. Scott Fitzgerald, 1925

"Haircut," story by Ring Lardner, 1925

Herzog, novel by Saul Bellow, 1964

The House of Mirth, novel by Edith Wharton, 1905

Howl, poem by Allen Ginsberg, 1956

Invisible Man, novel by Ralph Ellison, 1952

John Brown's Body, poem by Stephen Vincent Benét, 1928

The Jungle, novel by Upton Sinclair, 1906

The Last of the Mohicans, novel by James Fenimore Cooper, 1826

Leaves of Grass, poems by Walt Whitman, 1855 (and later revisions)

"The Legend of Sleepy Hollow," story by Washington Irving, 1820

Life Studies, poems by Robert Lowell, 1959

The Little Foxes, play by Lillian Hellman, 1939

Little Women, novel by Louisa May Alcott, 1868–69

Lolita, novel by Vladimir Nabokov, 1955

Long Day's Journey into Night, play by Eugene O'Neill, 1956

Look Homeward, Angel, novel by Thomas Wolfe, 1929

Looking Backward 2000–1887, novel by Edward Bellamy, 1888

Losing Battles, novel by Eudora Welty, 1970

"The Luck of Roaring Camp," story by Bret Harte, 1868

Main Street, novel by Sinclair Lewis, 1920

Main-Travelled Roads, stories by Hamlin Garland, 1891

"The Man That Corrupted Hadleyburg," story by Mark Twain, 1899

Margret Howth, novel by Rebecca Harding Davis, 1862

The Maximus Poems, by Charles Olson, from 1953

The Member of the Wedding, novel by Carson McCullers, 1946

Moby-Dick, novel by Herman Melville, 1851

Modern Chivalry, fiction by Hugh Henry Brackenridge, 1792–1805 (and later revisions)

Murder in the Cathedral, play by T.S. Eliot, 1935

"The Murders in the Rue Morgue," story by Edgar Allan Poe, 1841

My Ántonia, novel by Willa Cather, 1918

The Naked and the Dead, novel by Norman Mailer, 1948

Naked Lunch, novel by William S. Burroughs, 1959

Native Son, novel by Richard Wright, 1940

Nature, essay by Ralph Waldo Emerson, 1836

The Octopus, novel by Frank Norris, 1901

"Old Mortality," story by Katherine Anne Porter, 1938

On the Road, novel by Jack Kerouac, 1957

"One of the Missing," story by Ambrose Bierce, 1888

Our Town, play by Thornton Wilder, 1938

Paterson, poem by William Carlos Williams, 1946–63

Picnic, play by William Inge, 1953

"Poetry," poem by Marianne Moore, 1919 (and later revisions)

The Portrait of a Lady, novel by Henry James, 1881

The Recognitions, novel by William Gaddis, 1955

The Red Badge of Courage, novel by Stephen Crane, 1895

The Rise of Silas Lapham, novel by William Dean Howells, 1885

The Scarlet Letter, novel by Nathaniel Hawthorne, 1850

"The Secret Life of Walter Mitty," story by James Thurber, 1939

Sister Carrie, novel by Theodore Dreiser, 1900

Snow-Bound, poem by John Greenleaf Whittier, 1866

"Somewhere i have never travelled, gladly beyond," poem by E.E. Cummings, 1931

The Song of Hiawatha, poem by Henry Wadsworth Longfellow, 1855

Souls of Black Folk, essays by W.E.B. Du Bois, 1903

The Sound and the Fury, novel by William Faulkner, 1929

Strange Interlude, play by Eugene O'Neill, 1928

A Streetcar Named Desire, play by Tennessee Williams, 1947

The Sun Also Rises, novel by Ernest Hemingway, 1926

"Sunday Morning," poem by Wallace Stevens, 1923

"The Swimmer," story by John Cheever, 1964

Tender Is the Night, novel by F. Scott Fitzgerald, 1934

The Tenth Muse, poems by Anne Bradstreet, 1650

"Thanatopsis," poem by William Cullen Bryant, 1821

Tobacco Road, novel by Erskine Caldwell, 1932

The Tooth of Crime, play by Sam Shepard, 1972

The Turn of the Screw, story by Henry James, 1898

U.S.A., novels by John Dos Passos, 1930–36

Uncle Remus, stories and sketches by Joel Chandler Harris, 1880

Uncle Tom's Cabin, novel by Harriet Beecher Stowe, 1852

The Virginian, novel by Owen Wister, 1902

Walden, prose by Henry David Thoreau, 1854

The Waste Land, poem by T.S. Eliot, 1922

The Weary Blues, poems by Langston Hughes, 1926

Who's Afraid of Virginia Woolf?, play by Edward Albee, 1962

Winesburg, Ohio, stories by Sherwood Anderson, 1919

Winterset, play by Maxwell Anderson, 1935

Wise Blood, novel by Flannery O'Connor, 1952

The Wonderful Wizard of Oz, novel by L. Frank Baum, 1900

INTRODUCTION

AMERICAN LITERATURE TO 1900

Literature *of* America began with accounts of adventurers who, exploring its coasts, spoke of the perils and possibilities of the new found land. Literature *from* America was written by colonists who described for their countrymen in England their experiences, satisfactions, and hardships in making a home in the wilderness, or, more often than not, attempting to inform or reform people in England whose religious ideas were unlike their own. Literature *in* America, meant for American readers, came later, after Stephen Day had set up a printing press in Cambridge in 1638, but especially almost a century after that when newspapers, and then magazines, provided an outlet for colonial writers.

The various adventures of Captain John Smith, especially his spectacular, self-certified rescue by the Indian Princess Pocahontas, have become part of American lore. William Bradford's *Of Plimmoth Plantation* (not published until 1896) is admired for its placid homespun simplicity, and Thomas Morton's rakish account of roistering with Indians to the displeasure of his Puritan neighbors has made his *New English Canaan* (1637) a source of continuing delight. Captain Edward Johnson's *The Wonder-Working Providence of Sion's Saviour in New-England* (1654), an epic in prose that rises to rhythms of poetry, is among many a cherished book, as is Nathaniel Ward's whimsical *The Simple Cobler of Aggawam* (1647) that grumbles delightfully about, among other matters, the unpredictable silliness of women. But justice prevailed, for it may have been Ward himself who carried to England, without her knowledge, the manuscript of Anne Bradstreet's *The Tenth Muse Lately Sprung Up in America* (1650), a cumbersome and derivative, but effective reminder that inherited culture did survive in the American colonies. When published in Boston (1678), the volume contained later poems presenting scenes and sorrows of the new world, "Contemplations" she called them, and it is on these and on the aphoristic "Meditations" in prose on her spiritual and workaday life that her reputation rests.

Far more popular was Michael Wigglesworth whose jingling and horrendous *The Day of Doom* (1662), the first volume of verse to be published in the colonies and America's first bestseller, remained a reminder to many generations that damnation and hell-fire inevitably await those who succumb to the allure of sin. Equally religious but less condemnatory was Edward Taylor, an inconspicuous clergyman, extracts from whose *Poetical Works* (1939) were not published until more than two centuries after his death. A more comprehensive edition appeared in 1960, and a series of sermons prefaced with preparatory meditations in verse two years later. His *Diary* (1964) and *Metrical History of Christianity* (1962) have been transcribed for publication, but to the delight of scholars who rush to the task, he has not been revealed complete. Here, at last, was a voice rising above the dreary desert of theological dispute to speak with self-abnegating sweetness of the glory of God and the insignificance of man, "a crumb of earth," in such striking imagery that Taylor has been somewhat loosely compared with Richard Crashaw, George Herbert, and Francis Quarles. "God's Determinations Touching His Elect" is a long dramatic poem, speaking with tenderness and compassion of what Wigglesworth had made a nightmare vision. Taylor's "Meditations," though repetitious in theme, are deftly phrased, and his occasional secular poems are a refreshing proof that in colonial America literary artistry was not moribund.

For colonial Americans wrote busily, and none more so than doughty Cotton Mather whose colossal *Magnalia Christi Americana* (1702), often ridiculed, is now regarded with increasing respect. A multi-faceted man, the bibliography of whose writings requires three large volumes, he straddles, a giant, the tight-minded theological certainty of New England's 17th century and its entry into the age of the enlightenment. Mather's *Essays to Do Good* (1710) provided his young neighbor Benjamin Franklin with a title, though not the content, for "The Dogood Papers" (1721–23), contributed to the *New-England Courant* as America's first series of periodical essays. Franklin was to make a career of being first, in establishing (1741) the first successful magazine in America, in "The Speech of Polly Baker" (1747) presenting what may be thought of as its first short story, and in "Advice to a Young Man on Choosing a Mistress" (1745) its first manual of sex. His *Autobiography* (written 1771–89) created the prototype of the self-made, opportunistic, and self-reliant American, and his *The Way to Wealth* (1757) provided a handbook on how others might achieve that end. He was colloquial, iconoclastic, alternately jovial and bitter in satire, warm in praise of conviviality but a champion of frugality, a facile versifier and caustic critic of doggerel. To paraphrase, and perhaps improve, what Ernest Hemingway once said of Mark Twain, all American literature can be thought to have begun with this multi-faceted man.

But not quite all. Among Franklin's 18th-century contemporaries were other writers who helped form part of what can be thought of as a distinctively American view. First among them was William Byrd II of Virginia, educated in England and familiar with its fashionable spas and London literary circles, who wrote much in the fashionable patois of the time, but, returning to play an inherited role in colonial government, had occasion to survey or inspect backcountry areas that had not been described before. Urbane and witty, with an eye for scene and comic situation, he wrote between 1729 and 1733 the accounts "History of the Dividing Line," "Journey to the Land of Eden," and "Progress to the Mines," which he polished carefully and showed to a few friends, but which were not publicly revealed until almost two centuries after his death. A gentle satirist and a stylist of practised skill, aloof but observant, he represents a kind of writing, patrician but penetrating, that has become another characteristic of literature in America. Of coarser but more ebullient kind was Ebenezer Cooke, first transient, then colonist in Maryland, who in *The Sot-Weed Factor* (1708) and *Sotweed Redivivus* (1730) wrote boisterous doggerel condemning, then damning with faint praise, tobacco (sot-weed) growers and other colonial settlers among whom he found few men honest, or women chaste. His descendants also thrive.

Jonathan Edwards may be thought of as representative of another prominent strand woven to the American pattern. Remembered for such things as his hell-fire sermons, like *Sinners in the Hands of an Angry God* (1741) and his logical masterwork denying *Freedom of the Will* (1754), he is better represented as a person who saw in all physical objects images and shadows of the majesty of God, a concept on which 19th-century Transcendentalists would play a variety of changes. His *A Treatise Concerning Religious Affections* (1746) is written with charming simplicity and his posthumous *The Nature of True Virtue* (1765) is a rhapsodic celebration of moral beauty upheld by love as a goal for God-directed people. Even with inherited religion in his way, Edwards blazed trails that others would follow—in several directions.

Literature for literature's sake, however, emerged slowly in the American colonies. Richard Lewis, a schoolmaster in Maryland, wrote in the 1730's landscape poetry that was printed with approval in London periodicals. During the 1760's there was a brief flurry of activity in Boston, where Mather Byles, Joseph Green, and other young men amused themselves and honored visiting dignitaries with occasional verse. But the first concerted surge of activity came from young men in Philadelphia under the leadership of William Smith, Provost of its college. Thomas Godfrey presented in *The Prince of Parthia* (written 1759) the first play by an American to be performed on the professional stage. His *Juvenile Poems* (1765) were posthumously edited by his friend Nathaniel Evans, whose *Poems on Several Occasions* (1772) were in turn posthumously edited by their mentor Smith. Thomas Coombe and Jacob Duché, active among the group, when the colonies rose in revolt, fled to England, there to publish writings begun at home. Best remembered among them, however, is Francis Hopkinson, poet, essayist, musician, and lawyer and, until his death in 1791, as graceful and disarming a political satirist as his time produced. His *A Pretty Story* (1774) was an Arbuthnotian satire about a new farm (the colonies) that had trouble in adhering to restrictions set by the nobleman owner of the old farm (Great Britain). In *The Battle of the Kegs* (1779) he made great fun of British soldiers who fired at floating barrels, thinking them to be filled with armed rebels. During times of stress, Hopkinson's good-natured satire kept his countrymen laughing.

In New England was also gathered a group of young men remembered as the Connecticut Wits. Their leader was John Trumbull, who in *The Progress of Dulness* (1772–73) told in jovial Hudibrastic couplets of the misadventures of two collegians, Tom Brainless and Dick Hairbrain, and of a local belle, Harriet Simper, who, in choosing between them, chose perforce the duller. Two years before, on graduation from Yale College, Trumbull had in "Prospect of the Future Glory of America" looked to the time when his "land her Steele and Addison shall view" and a "future Shakespeare charm a rising age." To hasten this, he gathered about him a group of young men, students or tutors at the college. Each would engage in large literary activity. Trumbull, again in Hudibrastics, in a mock-epic *M'Fingal* (1775–82) pointed to absurd activities among his countrymen in revolt against or loyal to the Crown. Though his writings long remained popular, Trumbull was too prudent to risk reputation by continued satire, and turned aside from further major literary excursions. But not his friends Timothy Dwight and Joel Barlow. Each had for years been working over a long poem. Dwight's *The Conquest of Canaan* (1785), celebrating the leading of the Israelites to their promised land, was interpreted as an allegory (though Dwight insisted that it was not) of George Washington leading Americans to freedom. Barlow's *The Vision of Columbus* (1787) tells in cumbrous, often unrelated, detail what the purported discoverer of the new world saw in a dream of its future, in accomplishment and promise. David Humphreys, a soldier, later turned diplomat and successful man of commercial affairs, wrote with more enthusiasm than skill verses that called for industry and frugality among his countrymen. Perhaps more useful than any of these were the spellers and readers put together by Barlow's classmate Noah Webster, so that the new United States, he said, would not have to depend on English texts "to learn our children."

Dwight continued to write, and Barlow also, the first in *The Triumph of Infidelity* (1788), a vitriolic attack on heresies offered by attractive tempters like Voltaire, in *Greenfield Hill* (1794) in which he borrowed English manner and meter to describe the quiet virtues of a New England village, and then in tracts, sermons, and *Travels* (1821–22). Barlow seemed to his friends a traitor to conservative New England ways when, crossing to Europe, he joined Thomas Paine—whose *The Rights of Man* (1791–92) and *The Age of Reason* (1794–95) were attacked as heretical—by publishing *Advice to the Privileged Orders* (1792–93) in prose and *The Conspiracy of Kings* (1792) in verse. Best remembered for his charming little homesick poem about a favorite New England dish, *The Hasty-Pudding* (1796), late in life he expanded and revised *The Vision of Columbus* to *The Columbiad* (1807), a handsomely printed book remembered now chiefly by title.

To harass loyalists in Boston, Mercy Warren wrote satirical closet dramas, *The Adulateur* (1773) and *The Group* (1775). Later, she would contribute occasional verse to periodicals, and publish her *Poems, Dramatic and Miscellaneous* (1790). But the principal scourge of the British was Philip Freneau, a young gentleman from Princeton, who on graduating collaborated with his classmate Hugh Henry Brackenridge in writing *A Poem on the Rising Glory of America* (1772) that looked with ebullient optimism to a time when America would discover a new Homer, a new Milton to sing its spacious charms and wondrous prospects. His activities as a patriotic propagandist, notably in *General Gage's Confession* (1775) and *American Liberty* (1775), earned him the title "Poet of the American Revolution." But he was more than that. Both early and late he wrote verses of unusual merit, like "The House of Night" (1779), "The Wild Honey Suckle" (1786), and "To a Caty-did" (1815). His *Poems* (1786) reveals him a poet of many facets, whose early aspiring "The Power of Fancy" (written 1770) suggests promise never fully achieved, and his *Miscellaneous Works* (1788) reveals him also deft in prose, humorous, satirical, even philosophical. But much of his active career was spent as a political propagandist, his poetical talent unrealized. Though editions of his *Poems* appeared in 1795, 1809, and 1825, and though he continued to publish verse into the late 1820's, he died in obscurity.

Brackenridge did little better. During the Revolution he wrote patriotic plays for amateur production, *The Battle of Bunkers-Hill* (1776) and *The Death of General Montgomery* (1777). Moving after the war to the Pennsylvania frontier where he was unsuccessful as a politician, he wrote his disappointment into *Modern Chivalry* (1792–1805) in which the peripatetic Captain Farrago and various Sancho Panzas, notably an illiterate Irishman named Teague O'Regan, wandered the countryside through a series of quizzical adventures that revealed democratic processes as not always effective. Other instructive novels had now begun to attract attention, many warning of the danger of reading novels because novels render young ladies easy prey to men of evil intention. Often called America's first novel is William Hill Brown's *The Power of Sympathy* (1789), followed in rapid succession by such instructive fictions as Susanna Rowson's *Charlotte Temple: A Tale of Truth* (1791) and Hannah Foster's *The Coquette* (1797), all moral guides. But not until the last years of the decade did America's first important novelist appear.

Charles Brockden Brown, Quaker born and bred, is often remembered as America's first professional man of letters. From the publication of *The Rhapsodist* (1789), a series of periodical essays, until his death at 39, he wrote verse, literary criticism, and a substantial number of tales and essays. His career came to an astounding climax as the century ended, with *Alcuin: A Dialogue* (1798), advocating the rights of women, followed in rapid succession by the novels for which he is best remembered: *Wieland* (1798), *Arthur Mervyn* (1799), *Ormond* (1799), and *Edgar Huntly* (1799), gothic tales written under the liberalizing influence of William Godwin, but proudly with American settings. With *Clara Howard* (1801) and *Jane Talbot* (1801) his effective literary career ended. Illness, poverty, and hackwork occupied much of the rest of his brief life. Admired by Shelley and Scott, an influence on Edgar Allan Poe, his *Novels* (1827) were reprinted in Boston, at which time they were read with interest by Henry Wadsworth Longfellow and Nathaniel Hawthorne. In technique, Brown was experimental, often cumbersome, but there is vigor in what he wrote, a sense of scene and situation, and an ability to create characters, often introspective, that certify his writings as more than historical artifacts. *Wieland* explores the sad consequences of religious fanaticism, *Arthur Mervyn* details the adventures of a young man in search of himself, *Ormond* glances at the international conspiracy of Illuminati who would reform the world to their pattern, and *Edgar Huntly* is a murder mystery, brim-filled with terror and suspense, Indians, panthers and backwoods villainy. Together, they contain seeds that, cultivated by surer hands, would later more effectively flower.

Brown's friend and biographer, William Dunlap, also began a career in the 1790's that for him would extend for almost half a century. Painter, dramatist, theatrical manager, novelist, biographer, and historian, brother-in-law of Timothy Dwight, friend and adviser to James Fenimore Cooper, like Franklin he was a jack of many trades. Returning to the United States in the fall of 1787 after three years of study in the London atelier of Benjamin West, he had just missed seeing the production of Royall Tyler's *The Contrast* (1787) in New York that spring, the first play by a citizen of the United States to be produced professionally. Tyler's play, leaning heavily on English sources for much of its dialogue and action, had nonetheless donned native garb in its presentation of Captain Manly, truly a manly veteran of the Revolution who spurned the foppish Chesterfieldian airs of many of his countrymen, urging them to patriotic frugality, but especially in the Captain's servant Jonathan, the ancestor of many later native country bumpkins who would continue to fascinate American audiences. Tyler, a young man about town, a soldier, then successful as a jurist, was a better writer of light verse than he was a playwright. He would produce other plays, like *May Day in Town* (1787) and *The Georgia Spec* (1797), and even biblical drama in verse, and a rambling novel, *The Algerine Captive* (1797), but *The Contrast*, by reason of its being an American first, provides the fragile base on which his reputation rests.

Dunlap, not conspicuously successful as a painter, seems to have been sure that as playwright he could do better. *The Father; or, American Shandy-ism* (1789) did well enough to persuade him over the next twenty-some years to write or translate, often to produce as theatrical manager, some fifty more, among the best remembered of which are *André* (1798) and *The Italian Father* (1799). But Dunlap's most lasting contribution is in the reminiscences of people he had known, in his *Diary* (1930), his *Life* (1815) of Brown, his *A History of the American Theatre* (1832), his *A History of New York* (1837), and in a remarkably good, usually unnoticed work, *Thirty Years Ago; or, The Memoirs of a Water Drinker* (1836). If he accomplished nothing of primary importance, he was there, he recorded, providing sustenance to every historian of early American literature.

He knew and admired Washington Irving, whom everyone remembers for two stories, "Rip Van Winkle" (1819) and "The Legend of Sleepy Hollow" (1820), both included in *The Sketch Book of Geoffrey Crayon* (1819–20), which appeared as if in reply to Sydney Smith's somewhat surly question, "Who reads an American book?" Though most of the sketches were of English countryside and manners, urbane, witty, in cautiously patterned prose, they seemed to offer proof in plenty that here at last was an American who wrote with skill and grace. But a younger Irving, less cautious, had done better in his sacrilegious burlesque *A History of New-York* (1809), supposed to have been the product of a crotchety Dutchman named Diedrich Knickerbocker who wrote boldly, with light flashes of humor, about events of the past that foreshadowed contemporary foolishments. Then, after seventeen years abroad, delightedly a companion of Campbell and Scott, and including a sentimental pilgrimage to Spain that he chronicled in *The Conquest of Granada* (1829) and *The Alhambra* (1832), Irving returned to America and American scenes in *A Tour on the Prairies* (1835) and *Astoria* (1836). Though the effective force of his early writing was diminished, no one of his time wrote more gracefully than he, and his imitators were legion. Among the better were John Pendleton Kennedy in *Swallow Barn* (1832), Nathaniel Parker Willis in *Pencillings by the Way* (1835), and Charles Fenno Hoffman in *A Winter in the West* (1835).

James Fenimore Cooper was of a different sort, a burly man who came to writing late. A former naval officer become country squire, he never achieved felicity in prose. Author of more than thirty novels, some like *The Spy* (1821) of the American Revolution, some like *The Pilot* (1823) of the sea, others of corrupt European traditions as *The Bravo* (1831) or of corruption in America as *Home as Found* (1838), Cooper was a forthright and contentious man, often embroiled in libel suits brought against his critics, and scolding their kind in *A Letter to His Countrymen* (1834) and *The American Democrat* (1838). Among his better writings is the trilogy *Satanstoe* (1845), *The Chainbearer* (1845), and *The Redskins* (1846) that tells of rent-wars against patroons of the Hudson River Valley. But in his "Leatherstocking Tales"—*The Pioneers* (1823), *The Last of the Mohicans* (1826), *The Prairie* (1827), *The Pathfinder* (1840), and *The Deerslayer* (1841)—he created in the woodsman Natty Bumppo a character who has become in various avatars permanently a part of native lore, the ancestor of many Indian-fighting or Indian-protecting stalwarts in film or fiction.

John Neal also wrote sympathetically of the Indian in *Logan* (1822), of the Revolution in *Seventy-Six* (1823), and of early life in New England in *Brother Jonathan* (1825). In the south William Gilmore Simms wrote romances of frontier life in *Guy Rivers* (1834), of adventure during the American Revolution in *The Partisan* (1835), of Indian warfare in *The Yemassee* (1835), and dozens of other well-wrought volumes. John Pendleton Kennedy's *Horse-Shoe Robinson* (1835) and John Esten Cooke's *Leather Stocking and Silk* (1854) continued the tradition of native romance. Robert Montgomery Bird's *Nick of the Woods* (1837) is a thrilling account of bloodthirsty revenge against bloodthirsty Indian attack. But none of these succeeded, as Cooper did, in setting forth in mythic terms the gradual encroachment of civilization on wilderness.

Irving's friend James Kirke Paulding wrote in verse of the expanding west in *The Backwoodsman* (1818) and William Cullen Bryant of "The Prairies" (1832), but Paulding's later writings would be in fiction of the Hudson River Valley, and Bryant, after a brilliant early career that produced "Thanatopsis" (first version 1817) and "To a Waterfowl" (1821), spent much of the rest of a long life as a prominent newspaper editor in New York, respected for the simple dignity of his writings in prose and verse. His early contemporaries, Fitz-Greene Halleck and Joseph Rodman Drake, highly praised in their lifetime, are now virtually forgotten, though the former's *Fanny* (1819) is amusing satire of New York society and his "Alnwick Castle" (1817) remains a favorite anthology piece. Drake's "The Culprit Fay" (written 1816), a pretty little tale in verse of the adventures of a small elf assigned to deeds of derring-do, was severely criticized by Edgar Allan Poe as he made his distinction between fancy and imagination.

America's first prominent bohemian, as graceful with his pen as clumsy in managing his personal affairs, Poe was also its first complete man of letters. Poet, essayist, editor, a critic so severe that he was called "the tomahawk man," a pioneer in the short story, master of detective fiction and the mystery thriller, he liked cryptograms, puzzles, and bewilderments, so that tales like "Ligeia" (1838) and poems like "Ulalume" (1847) offer a variety of interpretations, and poems like "The Raven" (1845) seem designed to create more of mood than meaning. Poe was a runaway boy, troubled through much of his life by misfortunes, many of his own making; his first volume of verse, *Tamerlane* (1827), appeared when he was eighteen, followed by *Al Aaraaf* (1829) and *Poems* (1831), all printed at his own expense. *The Raven and Other Poems* (1845) was his only collection of poetry that found a regular publisher. He had great trouble also in finding someone to underwrite collections of his sketches and stories. *Tales of the Grotesque and Arabesque* (1840) and *Tales* (1845), however, cemented his reputation as a writer as dexterous and devious in prose as in verse. His novel, *The Narrative of Arthur Gordon Pym* (1838), is sometimes read with interest as foreshadowing some elements in Melville's *Moby-Dick*. A nimble writer, of large influence on other writers in his country and abroad, Poe has been considered by many to have fallen short of genuine greatness.

Yet he was overshadowed by writers less talented than he. Perhaps no poet writing in English has been more universally popular during his lifetime than Henry Wadsworth Longfellow from New England, whose simple verse narratives and songs of aspiration or quiet revery were everyone's favorites. He was the great literary educator of his countrymen, introducing them to rhythms and stanzaic forms drawn from many languages, adapting them to simple native situations. *Evangeline* (1847), *Hiawatha* (1855), and *The Courtship of Miles Standish* (1858) were all bestsellers. Such poems as "The Village Blacksmith" (1841), "The Children's Hour" (1860), and "Paul Revere's Ride" (1861) have long remained favorite recitation pieces. But though still remembered with affection, Longfellow is less highly thought of now. With John Greenleaf Whittier, Oliver Wendell Holmes, and James Russell Lowell he is recalled as one of "the schoolroom poets" whose portraits, once gracing each classroom, are now turned face to the wall.

Everyone remembers that Whittier was a great and good man, who hated slavery, wrote *Snow-Bound* (1866), and verses about childhood and country customs. Holmes, physician, essayist, novelist, witty raconteur, and occasional poet is remembered for a few recitation pieces like "Old Ironsides" (1830), "The Chambered Nautilus" (1858), and "The Deacon's Masterpiece; or, The Wonderful 'One-Hoss Shay' " (1858). His once popular essays collected in *The Autocrat of the Breakfast-Table* (1858) and its sequels are now seldom read. His "medicated novels" like *Elsie Venner* (1861) and *A Mortal Antipathy* (1885) are curious antecedents of "psychological" fiction, seldom removed from the library shelves. Lowell, perhaps the most influential literary figure of his generation, ready to supply verse for any occasion, is hardly remembered at all, except perhaps for portions of *The Vision of Sir Launfal* (1848) that ask "what is so rare as a day in June?", and his *A Fable for Critics* (1848) that good-naturedly satirizes his literary contemporaries.

Each of these was a genteel man, writing impeccably well in inherited forms, expressing inherited notions. In the south, Henry Timrod and Paul Hamilton Hayne, each fragile, wrote fragile lines, often of infinite sweetness and lingering charm, and later Sidney Lanier, who combined music and poetry, sometimes to the detriment of both, fought courageously against disease to produce dulcet rhythms celebrating scenery and chivalry. Frederick Goddard Tuckerman, who published little during his lifetime, has since the collection of his *Complete Poems* (1965) risen in critical esteem. Skilled craftsmen all, and read with appreciative reverence, they nevertheless look more often to the past than to the workaday world of expanding America.

Sharing center stage with Longfellow, Holmes, and Lowell was Ralph Waldo Emerson who probably had more influence on his and succeeding generations than any writer in America. His was the voice of independence. Rely on yourself, he counselled. Think your own thoughts. Forget the dogma of your fathers. Today is today, and each day can provide its own fresh, new revelation. His "The American Scholar" (1837) has been called his country's literary declaration of independence. His essay "Self Reliance" in *Essays* (1841) seemed to catch and encourage the buoyant spirit of the United States as it reached toward wealth. But essays like "Experience" in *Essays: Second Series* (1844) and "Fate" in *The Conduct of Life* (1860) showed him to be more than simply an ebullient advocate of confidence as he spoke in them of the terror of living, and of man's fearsome responsibilities. For what purpose, he challenged, are people allowed the privilege of living? And he answered, to be themselves, to realize whatever potential was available. Believing that there was a method of apprehending truth that transcended what senses could apprehend, he was called a Transcendentalist. There was one spirit common to, within, and available to all persons, which, if listened to with care, with knowledge that fate or experience might distort its voice, was a person's best guide. Follow, but with caution, the voice within, confident that what is true for each is true for all. In *Representative Men* (1850) he called on his countrymen to be prepared for the challenge of their time.

And then suddenly, as if in response or rebuttal to what Emerson seemed to have been saying, there appeared in rapid succession four books that stand high among America's masterworks. Nathaniel Hawthorne's *The Scarlet Letter* (1850) and Herman Melville's *Moby-Dick* (1851) dealt with what Emerson had spoken of as the mischances or terrors of life. Henry David Thoreau's *Walden* (1854) and Walt Whitman's *Leaves of Grass* (1855) have been thought of as extensions or applications of his more ebullient pleas. It has sometimes seemed convenient to capsulize America's writers of the mid-19th century as those of the party of memory—such as Longfellow, Whittier and their kind; those of the party of hope—Emerson, Thoreau, Whitman; and those of the party of doubt—Hawthorne and Melville. But this, however convenient, is a deceptive simplification. Each was in his own degree a Transcendentalist, searching beneath appearances for truths surpassing understanding.

This is why Hawthorne called his fictions romances. They sought below surfaces for what words could not tell—a characteristic, many believe, of that which is best in American, perhaps in any, literature. His *Twice-Told Tales* (1837, enlarged 1842) seemed simple nostalgic narrative sketches, but *Mosses from an Old Manse* (1846) introduced troublesome, ambiguously teasing allegories, defying precise explanation. Until the publication of *The Scarlet Letter*, Hawthorne had been largely a coterie writer, admired by a discriminating few. The popularity of that small book, partly because it seemed a scandalous tale, tempted him to further book-length stories. *The House of the Seven Gables* (1851) owed in externals much to the then pervasive influence of Charles Dickens, but carried within it seeds of symbolic meaning which seem to bear new fruit for each critical generation. With *The Blithedale Romance* (1852), a tale that may in part be sardonic autobiography, Hawthorne's effective career was over. *The Marble Faun* (1860), which tells of Americans abroad, is perhaps more revealing of themes hidden subtly in his earlier writings than successful in its own right. During his later years, his creative powers declined, and the fragments of fiction published posthumously do little to add to his literary stature.

Hawthorne's reputation among his contemporaries came to him after years of apprentice work. Melville's first fiction, however, brought him almost instant fame. After some years footloose at sea, he wrote of exotic escapades in the South Seas in *Typee* (1846) and *Omoo* (1847), books that were well received. But Melville was not satisfied with admiration for his books of adventure. He would be remembered, he hoped, as something more than a man who had lived among savages. So in *Mardi* (1849) he put together a narrative so tangled with emblematic meanings that few in his time or since have been able to unravel them. He followed it with two more simply devised books, *Redburn* (1849) and *White Jacket* (1850), partly winning back some share of popularity. But then he published *Moby-Dick* (1851) and followed it with *Pierre* (1852). A madman certainly, it was thought, had put these books together, each recounting a quest after great emblematic phantoms representing who knows what. A discouraged and apparently seriously distraught Melville retreated then from public exposure with two parting shafts, *The Piazza Tales* (1856), which included such tantalizing gems as "Bartleby," "Benito Cereno," and "The Encantadas," and *The Confidence-Man* (1857), which anticipated Mark Twain in exposing cupidities of the "damned human race." In retirement, Melville wrote poetry. His *Battle-Pieces* (1866) shares with Whitman's *Drum-Taps* (1865) the distinction of presenting the best verse to emerge from the United States' struggle in the early 1860's to remain united. *Clarel* (1876), a long, musing poem based on travels in the Holy Land, *John Marr and Other Sailors* (1888), and *Timoleon* (1891) were all privately printed. After Melville's death the manuscript of a short narrative, *Billy Budd* (1924), was discovered, seeming to epitomize in some part what he had brilliantly suggested in his earlier, once spurned, great parables of whales and walls. Only then, more than three decades after his death, was he recognized as a writer of whom his countrymen could be, and continue to be proud.

Even less universally appreciated during his lifetime was Henry David Thoreau. Then, as now, people were likely to admire him greatly or think him a pretentious humbug. Thoreau published only two books, *A Week on the Concord and Merrimack Rivers* (1849) and *Walden; or, Life in the Woods* (1854). An adventurer in forest and meadowland, he wandered, notebook in hand, to record what he found valuable. He is often thought of as a hermit who lived in a little house built with his own hands on land owned by Emerson beside Walden Pond. But he was no hermit. He was chanticleer, he said, crowing loudly to wake his neighbors from their daily stupor, so busy were they at being good that they were, he told them, finally good for nothing. Thoreau was a rebel in word and action, and his essay "Civil Disobedience" (1849) provided a rallying cry for people in rebellion, in his time, in the time of Mahatma Gandhi, and in ours. All who reverence wildness or wilderness or nature, including the unpredictable nature of man, reverence Thoreau. His posthumously published volumes of travel and his journals remain continuously a delight—to his admirers. (To others, he is self-centered, man-centered, and a bore.)

Much the same must be said of Whitman, that gigantic superman poet who soars in imagination aloft above his country, admiring it, describing it and its people in loving detail, missing nothing, embracing all. His one great work was of America as choreographed by Walt Whitman, and he called it *Leaves of Grass*. From 1855 to 1897 it went through many editions, expanding and rearranging itself as America expanded into new arrangements of land and people. Whitman's outspoken boldness that battered through traditions of form and content attracted many, particularly among the younger persons of his time, but many respectable contemporaries found him far too outspoken about matters of which respectable people do not speak. And yet here, as in Emerson, Thoreau, and Melville also, was the true voice of an emerging new nation. They had their female counterpart in Emily Dickinson, quietly a recluse, who published only a handful of verses during her lifetime, whose *Poems* (1890) appeared posthumously, and were not collected complete until 1955. Dickinson spoke more softly than her male contemporaries, but her brief, often gnomic, lines examine nature and aspiration, and other such mysteries, including death. The critic mistakes his purpose in attempting to explain her. She must be read in order to understand how a person who spoke with such hesitation to her own contemporaries speaks so clearly now to ours.

At mid-century the United States, in politics as in literature, was at a turning point. Civil war loomed on the horizon. Tempers flared, and indignation ran high. Thoreau went to jail rather than pay taxes to support what he thought to be an unjust war against Mexico. Whittier wrote militantly in prose and verse against the injustice of the slavery of blacks. Even mild Emerson was aroused. But none spoke more effectively than Harriet Beecher Stowe whose *Uncle Tom's Cabin* (1852), combining sentiment with realism, exposed the evils of slavery. More than 300,000 copies were sold within a year—no American book had done as well. It was made immediately into a play, and as presented on stage or as story has become part of American lore. Propagandistic and perhaps overwrought, violently attacked and zealously defended, it remains both a sociological and a literary monument.

When in 1865 the Civil War was over, literature in the United States took new directions. Before 1860 it had derived almost entirely from the eastern seaboard. But after the war as the country expanded westward, new voices rose. Though the older poets—Longfellow, Lowell, Whittier, and Whitman, and, though unheard, Emily Dickinson also—still wrote, the new literature of the later decades of the century was largely in prose, much of it about sections of the expanding country seldom written of before. Bret Harte presented in "The Luck of Roaring Camp" (1868) and "The Outcasts of Poker Flat" (1869) frontier types in the mine fields of California. John Hay's *Pike County Ballads* (1871) presented dialect verse accounts of the Illinois frontier, George Washington Cable in *Old Creole Days* (1879) introduced bilingual Louisiana, and Joel Chandler Harris told stories of plantation life in Georgia in *Uncle Remus* (1880) and its popular sequels. Mary Noailles Murfree as Charles Egbert Craddock wrote of people *In the Tennessee Mountains* (1884). Thomas Nelson Page wrote sentimentally of plantation life *In Ole Virginia* (1887). New England rural life was revealed in Harriet Beecher Stowe's *Oldtown Folks* (1869), in Mary E. Wilkins Freeman's *A New England Nun* (1891), and with greater artistry in Sarah Orne Jewett's *The Country of the Pointed Firs* (1896). Lafcadio Hearn, meticulously a stylist, wrote descriptive sketches of urban Ohio, of New Orleans, most effectively in *Chita* (1889), then of the West Indies, and finally of Japan.

These people who revealed uncommon characters in simple, often romantic situations in areas not well known to ordinary readers have been called local colorists. Closely linked to them were novelists often intent on reform like Rebecca Harding Davis, whose *Margret Howth* (1862) reveals sordidness in the life of a northern mill town, much as Albion W. Tourgée in *A Fool's Errand* (1879) and *Bricks Without Straw* (1880) reveals problems in rebuilding the war-torn south, as do John William De Forest in *Miss Ravenel's Conversion from Secession to Loyalty* (1867) and Constance Fenimore Woolson in *Rodman the Keeper* (1880). Life in the middle west was realistically presented by Edward Eggleston in *The Hoosier School-Master* (1871), by E. W. Howe in *The Story of a Country Town* (1883), and with some bitterness by Joseph Kirkland in *Zury, The Meanest Man in Spring County* (1887). Helen Hunt Jackson's *Ramona* (1884) is a romantic tale of Spaniards and Indians in southern California. James Lane Allen in *A Kentucky Cardinal* (1895) and *The Choir Invisible* (1897) wrote of local scenes sentimentally in beautifully cadenced prose. For in spite of what has been called the rise of realism in the late 19th century, romance, sentimentality, and optimism stalwartly held their own, in the dozens of exemplary tales by Horatio Alger, each proving that indeed, in America, goodness and diligence inevitably bring success, in Timothy Shay Arthur's horrendous experiences in *Ten Nights in a Bar-Room* (1854), in Martha Finley's guide to obedience and good manners in *Elsie Dinsmore* (1868), in Louisa May Alcott's happy family accounts in *Little Women* (1868) and its popular sequels, and in Frances Hodgson Burnett's *Little Lord Fauntleroy* (1886) who represented, in contradistinction to Mark Twain's *Huckleberry Finn*, everything that every good boy should be. From the 1880's well into the 20th century F. Marion Crawford, Edgar Saltus, and many another provided in romance the thrill and chill of escape to adventure.

Though the theater remained active, not only in larger cities, but increasingly in smaller towns visited by travelling companies, few plays of lasting interest were produced during the 19th century. Samuel Woodworth, better known for his song of "The Old Oaken Bucket" (1823), and James Nelson Barker wrote now forgotten plays with native settings, while John Howard Payne, whose major claim to fame is his nostalgic song "Home, Sweet Home" (1823), wrote equally unremembered romantic dramas with settings abroad. Everyone flocked to see dramatizations of *Rip Van Winkle* and *Uncle Tom's Cabin*, each done with melodramatic flair. Augustin Daly produced melodramas like *Under the Gaslight* (1867), problem plays like *Divorce* (1871), and romantic dramas of the west, like *Horizon* (1871). Later in the century audiences seemed satisfied with the timely though quite undistinguished society-oriented dramas of Bronson Howard and Clyde Fitch. The slapstick comedy of the minstrel show delighted many audiences.

For native American humor, present since the jocularities of Franklin and Ebenezer Cooke, surged toward popularity at mid-century. Seba Smith had used rustic New England dialect in detailing the *Life and Writings of Major Jack Downing* (1833). Augustus Baldwin Longstreet's sketches in *Georgia Scenes* (1835) had told of raucous backcountry shenanigans, as had Joseph G. Baldwin's *The Flush Times of Alabama and Mississippi* (1853). Johnson Jones Hooper in *Some Adventures of Captain Simon Suggs* (1845) had revealed peccadilloes of a backwoods gambler in the old southwest, and James Russell Lowell had moved beyond conventional verse in *The Biglow Papers* (1848–62) turning dialect and humor to the service of politics and reform. Fabulous tales were told of Mike Fink, the riverboat man, and of Paul Bunyan, the giant lumberjack. Thomas Bangs Thorpe's whopper about "The Big Bear of Arkansas" (1841) became a classic among native tall tales. George Washington Harris had great fun in detailing the often scandalous misadventures of that "nat'ral born durn'd fool" *Sut Lovingood* (1867). David Ross Locke as Petroleum V. Nasby distorted grammar and spelling in presenting the escapades of a renegade clergyman in *The Nasby Papers* (1864). Henry Wheeler Shaw as *Josh Billings* (1866) poked down-to-earth good-natured fun at backsliding in politics, home-life, and morals. None was more popular than Charles Farrar Browne who as Artemus Ward captured the fancy of the public, especially as a lecturer whose laconic humor brought both fame and fortune. It was he who started Mark Twain in the same profitable business.

For dominating the latter years of the 19th century were three men beside whom most of these others may seem Lilliputian indeed. Samuel Clemens came roaring in from the west as Mark Twain, to take the country by storm. William Dean Howells, a more precise man from Ohio, moved into New England and then New York to take over from native sons command of their literary establishments. Henry James, born to wealth in the east and largely educated abroad, did most of his writing in England. Clemens and James can be thought to represent extremes, in simplified terms one proudly plebeian, the other with equal pride patrician. As far as is known, they never met, nor did either comment more than casually on the writings of the other. Howells stood in the middle, friend and counsellor to both. That was characteristic of Howells, to be a middleman, neither too far out nor in too deep. Each of these three continued in activity and influence into the 20th century when Clemens was an embittered scold and James was read with decreasing enthusiasm, but when Howells was esteemed, except by younger men who thought him to have been too long in office, as the dean of American letters.

Samuel Clemens become Mark Twain: had there ever been another like him? Mountebank and sage, he played a part, and provided himself costume and legend to create an image unique. Journeyman printer, steamboat pilot, speculator, journalist, raconteur, world traveller, a man of few ties and little apparent literary ambition, except as literature secured worldly comfort, he seemed specially favored by fortune. Quite by chance his "The Celebrated Jumping Frog of Calaveras County" (1865), written in California at the suggestion of Artemus Ward, took the east by storm, and when the letters that he wrote as a newspaper correspondent on a cruise ship to the Mediterranean were gathered as *The Innocents Abroad* (1869), his reputation was secure, his profitable career as a public lecturer guaranteed to keep audiences aroar with laughter well underway. He ventured first into the novel in collaboration with Charles Dudley Warner in *The Gilded Age* (1873), a light-handed exposé of political and economic chicanery, which gave a name to the era in which Mark Twain, and many another entrepreneur, flourished. Then he certified himself as a novelist in his own right with *The Adventures of Tom Sawyer* (1876), *The Prince and the Pauper* (1881), and *A Connecticut Yankee in King Arthur's Court* (1889), stories designed to appeal to readers of almost every age. He wrote popular books of travel in humorously peculiar countries like England, Germany, and South Africa, and a nostalgic account of his *Life on the Mississippi* (1883). In *The Tragedy of Pudd'nhead Wilson* (1894) and *The Man That Corrupted Hadleyburg* (1899) he wrote again of .varieties of human corruption. But his single masterwork is *Adventures of Huckleberry Finn* (1884), the book with which Ernest Hemingway was later to testify all American literature begins. This saga of a boy at war with his conscience as he floats down a great river tells much of Samuel Clemens and his time, but even more of conditions that face people, inevitably conscience-ridden, at any time.

Mark Twain's genius was in control of language, colloquial and formal, and in a view of the world as a place roiled by the sometimes well-meaning misdeeds of people. As he grew older, he pointed with increasing despair, less lightened by humor, at the hideous malefactions of what he called, not without affection, the damned human race. To his friend Howells, however, people seemed susceptible to redemption, and he wrote some forty novels to demonstrate that human decency might somehow prevail. There are not large heights nor great depths in Howells's writings, not in the fiction, the plays, the essays, the travel books, or the occasional poems that for more than half a century he diligently produced. He pleaded for realism in literature. Life should be presented as neither worse nor better than it is. He was wholly dedicated, a good man, interested in social causes and, however despairing he may sometimes seem in private correspondence, confident in his public statements that right will prevail.

A generous man, as editor of the *Atlantic Monthly* from 1871 to 1881 Howells encouraged many new young writers, notably the local colorists. His eventual move to New York was taken as a visible sign that that city had replaced Boston as the literary capital of the nation. There as elder statesman, he continued as patron and adviser to young men like Stephen Crane, Hamlin Garland, and Frank Norris who ventured even further than he in realistic detail. His own novels *The Rise of Silas Lapham* (1885) and *A Hazard of New Fortunes* (1889) are worthy of shelfroom beside any of America's best. They are books to which the historian may turn in confidence to learn how people lived and spoke in those late Victorian times.

To some Henry James is without question America's foremost writer of fiction, who in depth of perception and subtle skill with words produced more novels of excellence than any other. They would argue that while Hawthorne, Melville, and even Mark Twain are remembered, each for one superlatively fine book, James is represented by perhaps half a dozen or more of equal excellence. Each admirer will set forth his own favorites, but most will agree that in, at very least, *The Portrait of a Lady* (1881), *The Princess Casamassima* (1886), *The Aspern Papers* (1888), and the three novels representative of what has been called his major phase, *The Wings of the Dove* (1902), *The Ambassadors* (1903), and *The Golden Bowl* (1904), he reached heights unscaled before. Each of these examines Americans in Europe, faced with a culture different from their own, to which they become victims or over which they triumph. Others may prefer his two principal novels with American settings, *Washington Square* (1881) and *The Bostonians* (1886). Still others, however, consider James an unmitigated bore, only to be tolerated in his early, more simply devised stories of *The American* (1877) or *Daisy Miller* (1878).

There is little action, still less of overt adventure in the writings of Henry James. His interest is in the friction of personality on personality, and in the complications that arise when several distinct personalities grope toward understanding of the complex relationships that bind them together or keep them apart. Specifically, his concern was with the culture, the fine things in manners and art, that Europe offered, and how they might be received, assimilated, or rejected by intelligent representatives of the new America where culture, when it existed, was borrowed or bought. Most of his Americans do well, whether trapped within or rising above inherited transatlantic patterns. Decency and honesty override tradition, so that James, for all his foreign settings and subtle discriminations, can be thought of, as much as Walt Whitman, as a champion of the probity and promise of his countrymen.

As the century ended, new writers appeared, some of whom, like Hamlin Garland, who in *Main-Travelled Roads* (1891) began presentation of hardships of Iowa and South Dakota farm life, and Henry Blake Fuller, who in *The Cliff-Dwellers* (1893) told a story of romance and intrigue in a Chicago skyscraper, would write well into the 20th century, as would Harold Frederic, who in *The Damnation of Theron Ware* (1896) told of the downfall of a well-intentioned but misguided young clergyman, and S. Weir Mitchell whose historical romances like *Hugh Wynne, Free Quaker* (1897) made him long a popular favorite. Robert Herrick began a novel-writing career that would extend for more than thirty years with *The Man Who Wins* (1897) and *The Gospel of Freedom* (1898), introducing an increasingly pessimistic view of the inevitable influence of capitalism and political corruption on well-meaning people. Ambrose Bierce, newspaperman and iconoclast, leaped to prominence with short narratives of horror and suspense in *Tales of Soldiers and Civilians* (1891), setting a standard that he would not quite reach again. Encouraged by Howells, Norwegian-born H.H. Boyesen in *The Golden Calf* (1892) wrote of the downfall of a young man in search of easy wealth. Needing encouragement from no one, the populist reformer Ignatius Donnelly in *Caesar's Column* (1890) looked with jaundiced eye toward the 20th century when the rich would get richer and the poor poorer.

These were all worthy writers, popular in the best sense. But as the 19th century moved toward a close fresh new voices arose, harbingers each of better things. Frank Norris at 21 published a long romantic poem, *Yvernelle: A Legend of Feudal France* (1891). But then, first influenced by Emile Zola and later encouraged by Howells, he turned abruptly to realism of the starkest kind. He is sometimes held forth as America's first naturalistic novelist, secured in certainty that people were playthings of fate. His first attempt at fiction of this kind was *Vandover and the Brute*, a gruesome tale of moral disintegration, not published until 1914, twelve years after its author's death. In *Moran of the Lady Letty* (1898) naturalism skirts close to melodrama in a lurid tale of violence and intrigue in adventure at sea. *McTeague* (1899), though tinged with melodrama also, presents a more effective account of how greed and inexperience, and the inexorable hand of fate, can lead to the destruction of people of good intentions. Norris's brief career came to a climax with the publication of *The Octopus* (1901) and then, posthumously, of *The Pit* (1903), novels which he had intended to be part of a trilogy (the final volume to be called *The Wolf*) that would tell of the problems in growing, the chicanery in selling, and, in the third volume, the consumption of American wheat in poverty-stricken Europe. For all his early accomplishment, Norris remains one of the great might-have-beens of American fiction. In *The Responsibilities of the Novelist* (1903), a volume put together the year after his death, he gives stalwart indication that had he lived he would certainly have seriously contended for success.

Even younger than Norris, and with a career more brief, was Stephen Crane, who brought a new dimension to the realism of his contemporaries. At 22 he borrowed money to pay for the publication of *Maggie, A Girl of the Streets* (1893); it found few readers, but with it modern American fiction was born. With great economy in words, with impressionistic imagery, and with tremendous sympathy Crane presented the fateful circumstances that propelled an attractive innocent toward degradation and destruction. No reinforcement of commentary was necessary. Crane's images created a panoramic backdrop against which characters, often as if in pantomime, moved toward predestined ends. Crane saw with a poet's eye. His own verse as presented in *The Black Riders* (1895) and *War Is Kind* (1899) seemed stark indeed to a generation nourished on Longfellow and Whittier, and responding to the whimsical songs of Eugene Field, the nostalgic sentimentalities of James Whitcomb Riley, and invitations to romantic adventure in Richard Hovey's *Songs from Vagabondia* (1894). Crane's were sharp cryptic poems, stark in imagery, suggesting acquaintance with the poems of Emily Dickinson that had been publicly revealed only five years before, and with them pointing toward the imagist movement that would rise in America a quarter of a century later.

The Red Badge of Courage (1895) is Crane's best known, most often discussed novel. Some critics have placed it beside Hawthorne's *The Scarlet Letter*, Melville's *Moby-Dick*, and James's *The Portrait of a Lady* as among the best produced in America's 19th century. It is a story of war, of the advance and retreat of armies, in which a young man faces death, first with terror but finally with assurance that a person can accept and withstand, however briefly, its awesome inevitability. But Crane's health, never robust, broke after service as a war correspondent in Cuba and Greece during the later 1890's, and he spent his later years in Europe, closely associated with Henry James and Joseph Conrad. During the remaining years of his active career, he wrote a dozen further volumes of fiction or reminiscence, none of which was completely a popular or artistic success. But his short stories "The Blue Hotel," "The Open Boat," and "The Bride Comes to Yellow Sky" identify him as anticipating Ernest Hemingway in mastery of that form.

Black voices, though often raised in protest by such militant advocates of equal rights as the orator Frederick Douglass, and by autobiographical slave narratives such as those by Nat Turner and William Wells Brown (the latter also, in *Clotel; or, The President's Daughter*, 1853, used fiction to suggest miscegenation in high places), during much of the 19th century had been only unobtrusively represented, except as distorted in sentimental song or story most often composed by whites. Booker T. Washington spoke perhaps too optimistically of *The Future of the American Negro* (1899) anticipating his biographical *Up from Slavery* that would appear two years later. Paul Laurence Dunbar's *Lyrics of Lowly Life* (1896) and his sketches in *Folks from Dixie* (1898) and *The Strength of Gideon* (1900) combine pathos with humor in picturing the life of blacks in America. More realistic were the stories of blacks in slavery collected in *The Conjure Woman* (1899) by Charles Waddell Chesnutt and the comparison between a black woman enslaved and a black woman free presented in *The Wife of His Youth* (1899).

Women until recently have not fared well in the discussion of literature in the United States before 1900. A nod in passing has been directed toward Anne Bradstreet as, curiously, America's first poet, and toward Phillis Wheatley who in the late 18th century somehow miraculously became its first black poet. But many Americans have grumbled as Hawthorne did about the "damned tribe of scribbling women." Margaret Fuller, who never feared to correct Emerson or Thoreau, or anyone else, when convinced, as she often was, that the person, usually male, was wrong, has been largely remembered as a strange woman, perhaps not completely moral, when she was in truth one of the more able literary critics in English of the 19th century. Emily Dickinson through her own choosing remained unhonored and unknown, but the posthumous publication of her verse revived interest in poetry that was more than merely metronomically melodious, not only in people like Stephen Crane, but in greater poets—one of whom, Edwin Arlington Robinson, had already begun to publish as the century ended—who during the first decades of the new century would open even more expansive territories for poetry to explore. And Harriet Beecher Stowe, once condescended to as simply a sentimental propagandist, is increasingly recognized as a writer of superior skill, while Sarah Orne Jewett, rising high above others who have sometimes been dismissed as mere local colorists, is almost universally recognized as an artist complete. But not until the 20th century was almost halfway over did many Americans remember that there had been in their grandparents' time a woman in the United States who had written more candidly than any other about women, their rights and rightful aspirations.

Like *Moby-Dick, Walden*, and *Leaves of Grass*, Kate Chopin's *The Awakening* (1899) was not well received by most readers of its time. Like *The Scarlet Letter*, it spoke of matters that many contemporaries thought indelicate. For more than ten years Chopin had been a popular local colorist, collecting her tales of Creole and Acadian life in Louisiana into *Bayou Folk* (1894) and *A Night in Acadie* (1897). Many of her stories are about spirited girls restive under restrictions of convention. Others, not selected for either volume, tell of married women, tempted toward freedom from bonds imposed by society. *The Awakening* reveals a woman who does break those bonds to search for self-realization unallowed by convention. She fails, as does the ghetto waif in Stephen Crane's *Maggie*, but not for the same reasons. Edna Pontellier of *The Awakening* is not simply a victim. She makes choices, and whether she chooses rightly or wrongly is not subject to authorial comment. Whether Edna's failure to achieve the freedom she seeks is her fault or results from the rigidity of custom is something each reader must determine. In *The Awakening*, Chopin for the first time in the literature of her country presented a candid woman's view of a woman's problem. Beside it, the man's view of a not unsimilar seeking for freedom presented a year later in Theodore Dreiser's *Sister Carrie* has been said to seem shallow indeed. Chopin published nothing further, but with *The Awakening* left testimony that in literature at the very least the voice of the woman would increasingly be heard over the land.

—LEWIS LEARY (1980)

AMERICAN LITERATURE SINCE 1900

"In your rocking-chair, by your window, shall you dream such happiness as you may never feel." Thus ends Theodore Dreiser's *Sister Carrie*, the first outstanding American novel of the twentieth century, published in 1900, though largely ignored for the next ten years. Dreiser's description of Carrie's fate is uncannily prophetic of what awaits the protagonists of the major American literary works for the next eight decades that we can now recognize as the Age of Modernism. Dreiser brought to a reluctant United States a Modernist sensibility characterized by a feeling of isolation and alienation from an urbanized, mechanized society.

Dreiser was ahead of his time, however, even though he had conceived all of the novels that he would publish—including his Cowperwood trilogy about a corrupt businessman—by 1914. The "pre-Modernists," conventionally labeled "realists," gave up slowly and grudgingly the struggle to dominate American taste with the dogma that William Dean Howells had pronounced—that the writer "can no longer expect to be received on the ground of entertainment only; he assumes a higher function, something like that of a physician or priest," working within established society to adjust the individual to its institutions. While the Modernists were not content, either, only to entertain, they saw themselves as enemies of oppressive social institutions, presenting the individual's only hope as lying in flight.

1. The Age of Innocence, 1900–19

The beginning of the 20th century was more than an arbitrary chronological dividing line in American literature. Few established writers of the previous century produced significant work after 1900; and the early death of Stephen Crane, who envisioned the individual transcendence of society in *The Red Badge of Courage* and his bitterly ironic poems, deprived us of a key transitional figure. Howells bravely attempted to maintain the status quo in *The Son of Royal Langbrith* (1904); but his subsequent work retreated to the midwest of his own childhood before the Civil War. Mark Twain's writings became so angry and bitter that readers shunned *What Is Man?* (1906) and *The Mysterious Stranger* (1916). Only Henry James produced triumphant curtain calls—*The Wings of the Dove* (1902), *The Golden Bowl* (1904), and *The Ambassadors* (1903), in which Lambert Strether's last eloquent speech—"That, you see, is my only logic. Not, out of the whole affair, to have got anything for myself"—definitively enunciates just as the voices of the pre-Modernists were fading into silence the altruistic principles their age failed to realize in practice.

Except for Booth Tarkington, who offered an indulgent criticism of the middle class in *The Magnificent Ambersons* (1918) and the Penrod stories, the novelists who flourished during the first years of the 20th century were "muckrakers" concerned about the social breakdown resulting from persons in responsible positions seeking to get everything for themselves. These writers continued, however, to try to work within the Establishment, hoping that it might yet prove capable of reform. *The Thirteenth District* (1902) by Brand Whitlock, who became a reform mayor of Toledo, Ohio, was less successful than David Graham Phillips's exposure of New York City corruption in novels like *Susan Lenox: Her Fall and Rise* (1917). Winston Churchill (no relation to the British political leader) explored such problems against American historical backgrounds in novels like *The Crisis* (1901) and *Coniston* (1906).

By far the most popular and successful of the novelists who indicted American business ethics, however, was Upton Sinclair, whose *The Jungle* (1906) led to reform of the meatpacking industry. Although Sinclair continued to expose corruption for another thirty years and even ran for governor of California, he never equaled his early success until during World War II when he began a series of eleven novels about a kind of cosmopolitan superhero, Lanny Budd. Most critics, however, found the premise that altruistic and patriotic supermen could take over and redeem the international military/industrial complex old-fashioned.

The Modernist concept of escape began to dominate American writing with the fiction of Jack London. Though presumably a socialist who predicted the return of a primitive Golden Age following a fascist revolution in *The Iron Heel* (1908), London praised the Nietzschean superman in *The Sea-Wolf* (1904) and, in his most self-revelatory tale, *Martin Eden* (1909), portrayed a hero driven at last to suicide by the personal and political problems that he sought vainly to solve. George Cabot Lodge's even more bleakly cynical "The Genius of the

Commonplace," suppressed by the Howells consistory and only recently published, dramatizes the disillusionment as the century began of even Boston's traditionalist Brahmin society, as does also the posthumously published *The Education of Henry Adams* (1918, privately printed in 1907) by the scholarly scion of one of the nation's most famous families. The collapse of the venerated role of the aristocrat as guardian of public morals finds its ultimate statement in philosopher George Santayana's novel *The Last Puritan* (1935).

The transition to Modernism was made most importantly but much less violently in the works of three distinguished women novelists who tempered their traditional conservatism with an awareness that the past was irretrievable in a changing world. Edith Wharton, one of the few American writers born into the wealthy international set, symbolically provided the name for the period that ended exactly with the appearance of her novel in *The Age of Innocence* (1920), which depicts the cost in human happiness of the rigid rules regulating New York Victorian society. Earlier, in *The House of Mirth* (1905), she had shown the suicidal cost of attempting to play society's games. Most of her other fiction portrayed ironically international society, except for *Ethan Frome* (1911), which disposed of dreams of primitive virtue by showing how bad things could be in backwoods New England. Ellen Glasgow offered a similarly cheerless picture of another traditional society in her native Virginia.

More complex and most important is the fiction of Willa Cather, which seemed to offer fresh hope in two epic tributes to the passing frontier, *O Pioneers!* (1913) and *My Ántonia* (1918). Later, however, after she made the statement that her world fell apart in 1922 (the year of Eliot's *The Waste Land*), her fiction, especially *A Lost Lady* (1923) and *The Professor's House* (1925), reflected a bitter disillusionment with contemporary materialistic society. Her increasing desire to escape into memories of a more glorious past colors two of her finest works, *Death Comes for the Archbishop* (1927) and *Shadows on the Rock* (1931).

The Modernist sensibility also manifested itself in American poetry almost exactly at the turn of the century, when the genteel influence of New England's "fireside poets" was ebbing. About the only traditional poet active at the turn of the century likely to be anthologized today is William Vaughn Moody, whose "An Ode in Time of Hesitation" (1901) exactly captures in its title the bankruptcy of America's genteel dream in the face of a growing imperialism. Moody's Harvard friends, Trumbull Stickney and George Cabot Lodge, were already sounding in their poetry the notes of alienation and the rejection of American culture that would characterize Modernist expatriate writings; but both men died—like Stephen Crane—early in the century. Even Moody turned principally to drama before his death in 1910.

At first a dark new vision manifested itself in American poetry through the ironic regionalism of Edwin Arlington Robinson's *The Children of the Night* (1897) and Edgar Lee Masters's *Spoon River Anthology* (1915). Robert Frost's *A Boy's Will* (1913) and *North of Boston* (1914) exhibit a wider range of sympathies; but all are unprecedented psychological probings of determined and frustrated villagers and farmers from New England and the midwest. Vachel Lindsay's attempt to promote "the higher vaudeville" through his "Gospel of Beauty," as exemplified by *General William Booth Enters into Heaven and Other Poems* (1913) also emphasized the use of small town figures and native legends in a new "public poetry."

The triumph of an urban, cosmopolitan, elitist viewpoint was signaled, however, by the most important event in the development of 20th-century American poetry, Harriet Monroe's founding in Chicago in 1912 of *Poetry: A Magazine of Verse*, which still remains the journal in which poets courting recognition wish to be published. An indifferent poet herself, Monroe helped re-establish the Whitman strain in American poetry by her early support of Carl Sandburg's Chicago songs; but her influence was more widely felt when she became allied with the international Imagist movement, led by Bostonian heiress Amy Lowell and her cohort and later bitter foe, Ezra Pound. Pound had removed to Europe in 1908 and had begun to develop an international reputation as a translator; but he was to loom largest when he turned to bitter social criticism after World War I.

The American drama made less progress than other native arts between 1900 and World War I. At the peak of its popularity during these years before it was seriously challenged by the cinema, the American theater was also at the nadir of its never previously very impressive artistic power. Turn of the century audiences favored exotic romantic works produced with elaborate naturalistic scenery, like David Belasco's *Madame Butterfly* (1900) and *The Girl of the Golden West* (1905), which live on as the basis for Puccini's operas. Genteel longings for a theater that combined high art with high seriousness were vainly focused upon William Vaughn Moody's idealistic appeals for human dignity in *The Great Divide* (1906) and *The Faith Healer* (1909) and Percy MacKaye's spectacular historical dramas like *The Scarecrow* (1908). Almost none of the hundreds of American dramas produced between 1900 and 1915 are revived today, even as period curiosities; the event that was to prove the equivalent for American drama of what the founding of *Poetry* magazine had been for American poetry was the establishment in 1915 of the Provincetown Players, which began in 1916 to produce the one-act plays of Eugene O'Neill, subsequently grouped as *The Long Voyage Home*.

Memorable American humor was also in short supply early in the century. Many of Mark Twain's later and bitter works were withheld from the public, while Finley Peter Dunne and George Ade did not repeat their initial successes with folksy humor in *Mr. Dooley in Peace and in War* (1898) and *Fables in Slang* (1900). Vaudeville and film clowns like W.C. Fields, Charlie Chaplin, and the Keystone Cops had taken over.

2. The Triumph of Modernism, 1919–29

Just as the decade of boom and bust really began with the end of World War I, so 1919 also marked the Modernist breakthrough in American fiction with the publication of Sherwood Anderson's *Winesburg, Ohio* and James Branch Cabell's *Jurgen*. These were joined the next year by Edith Wharton's *The Age of Innocence*, F. Scott Fitzgerald's *This Side of Paradise*, Eugene O'Neill's first full-length plays, and the collected lyrics of Edna St. Vincent Millay. Above all 1920 brought Sinclair Lewis's *Main Street*, which lambasted the ugliness, complacency and vulgarity of the small midwestern town and satirized the death of the pioneering spirit. These set the tone for the decade; sympathetic novels about rural America, like Rølvaag's immigrant epic, *Giants in the Earth* (1927), were rare.

Although Anderson's subsequent stories and Cabell's further legends of the mythical Poictesme were not widely read, Sinclair Lewis became the country's most famous novelist with *Babbitt* (1922), which provided the derogatory tag still attached to the kind of fatuous community booster it depicted; *Arrowsmith* (1925), about the persecution that drives a genuinely idealistic doctor into exile; *Elmer Gantry* (1927), about the hypocritical religious revivalists who save souls for the preacher's profit; and *Dodsworth* (1929), Lewis's first sympathetic international novel about a retired businessman who goes abroad to find a decent life. These confirmations of the European intelligentsia's view of the parvenu excesses of the United States led to Lewis's becoming in 1930 the first American to win the Nobel Prize for literature.

None of Lewis's novels so well epitomizes, however, the reaction of a Modernist sensibility to a demoralized United States as F. Scott Fitzgerald's *The Great Gatsby* (1925), which presents Jay Gatsby, born James Gatz, who "springs from his Platonic conception of himself," as the possessor of "some heightened sensitivity to the promises of life," which, in his innocence and ignorance, he puts at "the service of a vast, vulgar, and meretricious beauty," only to be destroyed by "what foul dust floated in the wake of his dreams." Although he became a legendary figure himself, Fitzgerald never matched *The Great Gatsby*. His novel about expatriate society, *Tender Is the Night* (1934), never found its final form; and his tale of Hollywood, *The Last Tycoon* (1941), is only a collection of brilliant fragments.

Fitzgerald's accomplishment in *Gatsby* was not quickly recognized because it was overshadowed in 1925 by the long-awaited publication of Dreiser's *An American Tragedy*. Though the novel does in a way epitomize the decadence of 20th-century American society by portraying the inexorable way in which the appeal of quick material rewards ultimately destroys an attractive, impressionable, but not too bright youth, readers of a faster-paced age began to lose patience with Dreiser's lumbering style and heavy-handed moralizing.

Fitzgerald's reputation was also for years overshadowed by that of his sometime friend, often bitter foe and critic, the fellow expatriate Ernest Hemingway. Hemingway leaped to fame as the principal spokesman for the "lost generation" in his novels *The Sun Also Rises* (1926), about an aimless group of American expatriates in Europe after World War I, and *A Farewell to Arms* (1929), with its tragic message, set against the background of an Italian retreat during the war, that even the man who wishes to make "a separate peace" is at the mercy of a nature that man's puny dreams cannot control.

Like Hemingway, John Dos Passos began his literary career after serving as an ambulance driver in World War I and became subsequently involved in the Spanish Civil War. His *One Man's Initiation—1917* (1920) and *Three Soldiers* (1921) rank with *A Farewell to Arms* as the classic American accounts of World War I. Dos Passos then went on to develop the technique of the montage novel in order to present first a cross-section of the chaos of New York City life in *Manhattan Transfer* (1925), and then an epic portrait of the decay of American life and values in the three novels constituting the *U.S.A.* trilogy—*The 42nd Parallel* (1930), *1919* (1932), and *The Big Money* (1936), which portrays the spectacular excesses leading to the stock market crash through a variety of factual and fictional materials.

The famous appellation "lost generation" for those morally disoriented by World War I has been attributed to Gertrude Stein's impatience with a Parisian auto mechanic. Whether or not she can be credited with the phrase, this redoubtable avant-garde writer, an expatriate since 1902, when she began to feel stifled by American conventionality, was the center of the American literary community in France between the World Wars. Her experimental works are also both thematically and formally at the very center of the Modernist tradition because of their attempt, on one hand, to adapt for literary purposes the techniques of the cubist painters like Picasso and, on the other, to portray the pointlessness and frustration of women's lives, from the clearly delineated portrayals of long-suffering women in *Three Lives* (1909) through the mazes of the massive *The Making of Americans* (1925) to the mysterious *Ida* (1941) and her opera librettos like *Four Saints in Three Acts* (1934, with music by Virgil Thomson). Despite the range and variety of her incessant experiments, however, Stein's reputation with the general public rested on *The Autobiography of Alice B. Toklas* (1933), her account of her life with her long-time companion.

Few other expatriates or experimentalists shared her fame. Djuna Barnes is known almost entirely for *Nightwood* (1936), a stream-of-consciousness novel about disturbed people; none of Glenway Wescott's other works enjoyed the popularity of his early *The Grandmothers* (1927), about a pioneering Wisconsin family as seen through the eyes of an expatriate descendant; and the lives of writers like Robert McAlmon, Harry and Caresse Crosby, and Charles Henri Ford remain better known than their works. Not all the uprooted went to Paris. The still mysterious B. Traven wrote social protest novels like *The Death Ship* in Mexico for initial publication in Germany. Americans preferred, however, the exoticism of one of Gertrude Stein's friends, Thornton Wilder, whose *The Bridge of San Luis Rey* (1927), about an inscrutable tragedy in 18th-century Peru, became one bestselling novel of permanent value.

Some writers like Maxwell Bodenheim (*Replenishing Jessica*, 1925) and Carl Van Vechten (*Peter Whiffle*, 1922) simply fled the midwest for Greenwich Village, where they joined poets like E.E. Cummings and Edna St. Vincent Millay in turning out highly stylized and wittily cynical works about the jazz age that are valued today principally as period pieces. Van Vechten, however, achieved a more enduring reputation through his association with the Harlem Renaissance, which he depicted with sympathetic realism in *Nigger Heaven* (1926).

This Harlem Renaissance of the 1920's provided the first serious opportunity for black writers to depict a developing black culture in a black community, in the hope of cultivating a black audience; but their contemporary audiences were largely sympathetic white patrons. Black writers had been producing notable novels since late in the 19th century; but the works of Charles Waddell Chesnutt, like *The Wife of His Youth* (1899), and James Weldon Johnson's *The Autobiography of an Ex-Colored Man* (1912) dealt principally with the problems of light-skinned blacks "passing" for whites to overcome the handicaps of racial prejudices. Encouraged, however, by the freedom of "jazz age" Harlem, blacks like sociologist-educator W.E.B. Du Bois and Claude McKay began to produce distinguished novels about the problems of aspiring members of a black community that would be fragmented again by the Depression.

Most striking of these novels was the long-neglected but now much discussed *Cane* (1923) by Jean Toomer, a mysterious figure of uncertain origins who abandoned a promising career to devote himself to the teachings of philosopher G.I. Gurdjieff. A collage of stories, songs, and plays, *Cane* has often been the subject of pointless controversy over its form; what matters is that Toomer uses all the means at his disposal to dramatize the plight of blacks alienated twice—by race and by the common neglect of artists in the 20th century.

Although Langston Hughes wrote one of the finest novels about black life, *Not Without Laughter* (1930), he is best known for his stories of a black folk-philosopher, Simple, and the poetry in which he experimented with the use of black folksong and jazz rhythms. Countée Cullen also experimented with lyrical forms in *The Ballad of the Brown Girl* (1927) and *The Black Christ* (1929), but he used traditional English forms and, as Gerald Moore explains, "attacked the whole notion of an American-Negro school of poetry and urged the importance of the Anglo-American poetic tradition upon his fellow black writers."

Cullen's attitude was closely in tune with the most respected poets of the decade who viewed their dissolute period with dismay. Ezra Pound launched the attack in 1920 with his "Mauberley" poems. The opening stanza of *Hugh Selwyn Mauberley* epitomizes the Modernist poet's state of mind: "For three years, out of key with his time, / He strove to resuscitate the dead art / Of poetry; to maintain 'The sublime' / In the old sense. Wrong from the start—." Pound's increasing displeasure took the form of a long series of "Cantos," collages of miscellaneous erudition drawn from cultures of all times and all places mixed with the rantings against modern economic and political systems that became the substance also of his increasingly frequent prose polemics. While a small cult of ultra-elitists has admired these works hysterically, most readers have found them too cryptic, dogmatic, or offensive. Pound ultimately became much more a political symbol than a poetic force when, after making propaganda broadcasts for Italy's fascist government during World War II, he was arrested for treason and confined for some years in an insane asylum.

Pound's place in the poetic hierarchy was early usurped, however unintentionally, by his major discovery, T.S. Eliot, an American expatriate in London, whose *The Waste Land* (1922) became the most quoted and imitated poem of the century—the high-water mark of the Modernist era. It is entirely possible to take at face value the statement attributed to Eliot that to him the poem was "only the relief of a personal and wholly insignificant grouse against life" and yet to maintain as I have in *The Twenties* that it is "the embodiment of a world-view widely characteristic of thoughtful and sensitive individuals during the 1920's." Eliot's personal protest happened to give voice to the feelings of the sensitive persons of a generally gross age.

Yet, despite the idolization of Eliot, there were vigorous dissenters from his view. Chief among these were Hart Crane and William Carlos Williams, who could only begin to win proper recognition when Eliot's influence began to wane after World War II. As Donald Pease points out, Hart Crane felt that it was Eliot who had to be transcended in creating *The Bridge* (1930), his "epic of modern consciousness." Although scholars still debate the "unity" of Crane's mystical epic with some finding it only a chaos of fragments like the age it mirrors, others find its vast structure a coherent reinvigoration of the lapsed tradition of Walt Whitman (whom Eliot greatly mistrusted).

Williams even more indignantly protested that "Eliot returned us to the classroom just at the moment when I felt that we were on the point of escape . . . to a new art form . . . rooted in the locality which should give it fruit." As Robert K. Johnson points out, Williams put forward, against Eliot's increasingly metaphysical concerns, a creed based on the beauty contained in physical reality that is best illustrated by his own epic of the commonplace, *Paterson* (1946–58), based on impressions of his home city in New Jersey.

Another dissenting voice took an even bleaker view than Eliot's of the contemporary world and the entire human experience. Also going against the grain of an age that cultivated principally the brief lyric by writing long blank verse narratives about the forbidding California coast near Big Sur, where he lived, Robinson Jeffers in works like *Tamar* (1924) and *Roan Stallion* (1925) shocked readers with his misanthropic legends of violent, amoral people bent on courses leading to self-destruction.

Although Jeffers considered protest only a bubble "in the molten mass," some surfaced in Greenwich Village in the typographically eccentric satires of E.E. Cummings like "Poem, or Beauty Hurts Mr. Vinal" and "Next to Of Course God America I," which are still unmatched vignettes of empty-headed pomposity. One other New York writer who managed to maintain a unique stability in the midst of madness was Marianne Moore, editor of the revived *The Dial* (1926-29), who persisted throughout the years in viewing poets as "liberators of the imagination."

A once enormously admired poem that has been virtually forgotten over a half century is Stephen Vincent Benét's *John Brown's Body* (1928), an epic account of the Civil War from a Union point of view. Americans have lost their taste for historical epics, for the fate of Benét's work was shared by Archibald MacLeish's narration of Cortez's conquest of Mexico, *Conquistador* (1932), though MacLeish's shorter "Ars Poetica" has continued to be regarded, perhaps wrongly, as a statement of the Modernist aesthetic, just as his much anthologized "You, Andrew Marvell" sums up a cyclical theory of destiny.

The United States developed a drama of truly international importance for the first time in the 1920's in the plays of Eugene O'Neill, whose first full-length offering in New York, *Beyond the Horizon* (1920), carried off the Pulitzer Prize. O'Neill won two more Pulitzer Prizes during the decade for *Anna Christie* (1921) and *Strange Interlude* (1928) and presented four other major productions in New York during the decade. While all his plays are Modernist statements of the need of individuals to escape the deadly constraints of monotonous lives or oppressive institutions, they are written in two strikingly different styles. While some are sombre dramas of personal frustration in the prevailing naturalistic mode of the period (*Beyond the Horizon, Desire under the Elms*), others are practically the only important American examples of the European Expressionist drama that sought to suggest interior states of mind through stylized sets and actions (*The Emperor Jones, The Hairy Ape, The Great God Brown*). In his greatest triumph during his lifetime, the nine-act *Strange Interlude*, he combined naturalistic action with expressionist revelation through a double set of speeches that allow the audience to hear both what the characters are saying and what they are thinking.

Most of even the other Pulitzer prize-winning plays of the decade pale beside O'Neill's work. The few foreshadowings of a generally brilliant decade ahead included Sidney Howard's *The Silver Cord* (1926), an archetypal picture of a mother fixation, and the only other important American expressionist play besides O'Neill's, Elmer Rice's *The Adding Machine* (1923), a devastating picture of dehumanization. Audiences enjoyed especially, however, two rollicking farces that caught the bumptious pseudo-sophisticated tone of the decade, Maxwell Anderson and Laurence Stallings's *What Price Glory?* (1924) and Ben Hecht and Charles MacArthur's *The Front Page* (1928). But the biggest hit of all was Anne Nichols's ethnic farce, *Abie's Irish Rose* (1922).

American humor generally made a great comeback during years of careless laughter. H.L. Mencken had been delighting the "smart set" with his iconoclastic attacks on the "booboisie" and defenses of American authors like Theodore Dreiser since 1914; but he and the outrageous drama critic George Jean Nathan scored their greatest successes after founding the *American Mercury* in 1923. Its cynical wit was soon overshadowed by that of the *New Yorker*, founded in 1925 by editor Harold Ross, "not for the old lady in Dubuque." The magazine attracted the sophisticated funsters who became members of the Algonquin Round Table (named for the hotel where they met for lunch)—James Thurber, poet and short-story writer Dorothy Parker, essayist E.B. White, monologuist Robert Benchley, popular book reviewer Alexander Woollcott. They did not have the New York scene to themselves, however, for even more popular were the ironically comic short stories of Ring Lardner (*The Big Town*, 1921) and the poems that Don Marquis attributed to a newspaper-office cockroach madly in love with a fickle cat (*Archy and Mehitabel*, 1927).

3. Alienation Vindicated—Depression and World War, 1929–45

If American writings of the 1920's were not equalled in brilliance by those of the 1930's, they were surpassed in profundity by the outpouring of moving responses to the human condition inspired by the international depression and the rise to power of the authoritarian regimes that precipitated World War II.

Apparently traumatized by the end of the world they had known, few established American novelists matched their earlier accomplishments after 1929. Sinclair Lewis's satirical portraits of pretentious Americans began to resemble comic strips. Only *It Can't Happen Here* (1935), a warning about the possibility of a fascist takeover by popular demagogues in the United States, and *Kingsblood Royal* (1947), an early attack on anti-Negro prejudice outside the south, won great attention, but even these were overstated, two-dimensional tracts. After publishing *U.S.A.*, John Dos Passos became embittered by his experiences with both sides in the Spanish Civil War and became increasingly a right-wing isolationist stressing the American values of the founding fathers. The Spanish Civil War, however, brought Ernest Hemingway out of a long slump to find a new voice in praising the individual whose dreams exceed the squalid possibilities of the world about him in *For Whom the Bell Tolls* (1940) and again in his very popular fable, *The Old Man and the Sea* (1952).

The most enduring novelists of the 1930's, however, were those who found their inspirations rooted in their localities, as William Carlos Williams had hoped poets would. After making a false start with the stylized history of a pirate (*Cup of Gold*, 1929), John Steinbeck found his locality in the rural valleys of central California in the mystical *To a God Unknown* (1933) and the ironic *The Pastures of Heaven* (1932). After revealing a gift for humorous allegory in *Tortilla Flat* (1935) and naturalistic tragedy (*Of Mice and Men*, 1937), he published what both public and critics have acclaimed as the greatest work of American social protest since *Uncle Tom's Cabin, The Grapes of Wrath* (1939), a novel about the sufferings of the dispossessed "Okies" from the Dust Bowl on Highway 66 and in an unfriendly California, in which his hitherto morbidly Modernist irony gives way to a transcendent faith in the ultimate triumph of simple people. Also noteworthy are his story cycle of a boy's coming of age after the passing of the frontier in a diminished America, *The Red Pony* (1937), and his denunciation of middle-class smugness and praise of "outcasts" in his tribute to his friend Ed Ricketts, *Cannery Row* (1945).

The long depressed south, however, was the region that would really experience a Renaissance while long-favored lands sank into lethargy. Beginning in 1929 with *Look Homeward, Angel*, Thomas Wolfe turned the memories of his childhood in Asheville, North Carolina, and his adult journeyings throughout the United States and in Europe into epic fiction, especially in *Of Time and the River* (1935). Erskine Caldwell devastatingly satirized the rednecks of the southern backwoods in *Tobacco Road* (1932) and *God's Little Acre* (1933), while

Elizabeth Madox Roberts paid tribute to the heroically sacrificial life of the pioneers in Kentucky in *The Great Meadow* (1930). The most important southern writer of this period, however, a figure of international stature, was William Faulkner.

After an unpromising start in two "jazz age" novels influenced by Sherwood Anderson, Faulkner found his "little postage stamp of territory" in Yoknapatawpha County, modeled on the region where he lived in the red clay hills of northeast Mississippi. In *Sartoris* (1929), he relates a late chapter in the history of the aristocratic family that becomes the foil for the upstart, white trash Snopeses, whose tale is told in the trilogy *The Hamlet* (1940), *The Town* (1957), and *The Mansion* (1959). Other novels and short stories, including his four supreme achievements—*The Sound and the Fury* (1929), *As I Lay Dying* (1930), *Light in August* (1932) and *Absalom, Absalom!* (1936)—fill in the story, pieces of which have been brilliantly arranged into a chronological history by Malcolm Cowley in *The Portable Faulkner*. The typical Modernist concept that underlies the whole cycle of the human loss of innocence that accompanies the destruction of the wilderness comes into sharpest focus in two companion stories of the *Go Down, Moses* cycle (1942)—"The Bear," in which the isolated Ike McCaslin protests greedy man's destruction of his bond with nature, and "Delta Autumn," in which a dying Ike thinks to himself, "No wonder the ruined woods I used to know don't cry for retribution. . . . The people who have destroyed it will accomplish its revenge."

Perhaps inspired by Faulkner's example, James Agee paid what remains the most sympathetic tribute to the hard life of southern poor whites in *Let Us Now Praise Famous Men* (1941), and southern fiction flourished as never before. Four women novelists made especially distinguished contributions to the movement. Caroline Gordon was directly associated with the influential southern agrarian poets and in novels from *Penhally* (1931) to *The Malefactors* (1956) was a most outspoken critic of the region's departure from its traditional culture, as was her husband, Allen Tate, in his one novel, *The Fathers* (1938). More impressive, however, were Katherine Anne Porter's tales of her native Texas, like *Noon Wine* (1937), and of Mexico. Late in the period the changing life in small southern rural communities became the subjects of stories by Carson McCullers and Eudora Welty. McCullers published her first novel, *The Heart Is a Lonely Hunter* in 1940, and Welty's fantastic novelette *The Robber Bridegroom* appeared in 1942. McCullers, however, quickly reached the peak of her career with her third novel, *The Member of the Wedding* (1946) and her play version of it (1949), while Welty did not produce her most ambitious work, *Losing Battles*, until 1970. The most popular novel ever to come out of the south, however, was Margaret Mitchell's mammoth *Gone with the Wind* (1936), a mythical evocation of life in the plantation south during the Civil War that was made into what has remained the country's favorite motion picture.

The fiction that bulked largest, however, in the United States during the depression years was the work of the "tough guy" proletarian writers. The most prolific of these, James T. Farrell, was never able to equal the success of his first naturalistic stories about growing up on Chicago's South Side, the *Studs Lonigan* trilogy (1932–35), and many other prolific writers of the time like Josephine Herbst have been largely forgotten. Edward Dahlberg proved an exception when he developed a belated reputation for the autobiographical *Because I Was Flesh* (1964). James M. Cain, however, won a wide following for his tales of the seedy elements of society in glamorous southern California like *The Postman Always Rings Twice* (1934) and *Double Indemnity* (1944).

The grimmest work about decadent movieland, however, was Nathanael West's hallucinatory prediction of the destruction of Los Angeles, *The Day of the Locust* (1939), which followed his other powerful indictments of the American myth of the self-made man (*A Cool Million*, 1934) and the Christ complex developed by an advice-to-the-lovelorn columnist (*Miss Lonelyhearts*, 1933). Another cynical attack on the shoddiness of American middle-class values was John O'Hara's *Appointment in Samarra* (1934). The most outrageous novels about the period, however, were Henry Miller's *Tropic of Cancer* (1934) and *Tropic of Capricorn* (1939), curious melanges of turgid philosophizing and explicit pornography that were banned from the United States for decades until they were the subject of a court battle in the 1960's.

An even more telling indictment of social injustices was Richard Wright's *Native Son* (1940), an account of the corruption and destruction of an ambitious but ill-educated Chicago black boy, modeled after Dreiser's *An American Tragedy*. Wright was the first black novelist to win major critical and public recognition for both his novel and his harrowing autobiography, *Black Boy* (1945).

The poets who dominated the American academies beginning in the mid-1930's came, like Wright, from the south; but they represented not its belligerent black fugitives, but conservative white "fugitives" from the 20th century's urban society. The group at Vanderbilt University who had styled themselves the "Fugitives" attracted national attention when they identified themselves as Agrarians and called for a return to traditional values in an essay collection, *I'll Take My Stand* (1930). Although the reputation of their leader, Donald Davidson, arch-foe of TVA, has declined, three of the group have heavily influenced American literary culture generally. Allen Tate's "Ode to the Confederate Dead" overshadowed his more ambitious efforts to give a peculiarly southern cast to T.S. Eliot's concept of the value of traditional orthodoxy. John Crowe Ransom won distinction as a poet, but is best known as the theorist in *The World's Body* (1938) of the "New Criticism" that dominated American universities from the late 1930's to the 1960's. The most prominent of the group, however, has been Robert Penn Warren, who has won distinction not only as a poet, for works like *Brother to Dragons* (1953), but as a novelist, especially for *All the King's Men* (1946), a cautionary tale about a southern demagogue resembling Louisiana's Huey Long, and particularly—along with his Yale colleague Cleanth Brooks—as the principal popularizer of New Criticism techniques in the uniquely influential *Understanding Poetry* (1938).

Despite this southern offensive, the center of poetic activity began to shift back during the 1930's to New England, where Robert Frost—his important writing behind him—was just beginning to make his impact as a lecturer and embodiment of Yankee tradition. The most telling satirical poetry of the decade was Archibald MacLeish's *Frescoes for Mr. Rockefeller's City* (1933), inspired by the controversy over Mexican muralist Diego Rivera's designs for the Rockefellers' Art Deco Radio City. The caustic "Empire Builders," which tells of the "making of America in five panels" by Harriman, Commodore Vanderbilt, J.P. Morgan, Andrew Mellon, and Bruce Barton, concludes with the observation that there is "nothing to see of America but land." MacLeish's subsequent pioneering in radio dramas like *The Fall of the City* (1937) set a model not yet equalled for this aborted form.

MacLeish's polemics have been overshadowed, however, by those of the theorist of the "Supreme Fiction," the Hartford, Connecticut, insurance executive Wallace Stevens. Stevens's complex and subtle work defies brief synthesis. Perhaps one can only be as cryptic as Stevens himself in "Notes Toward a Supreme Fiction" (1942) by specifying that the three requirements for its achievement are that "It must be abstract," "It must change," and "It must give pleasure." To suggest how such contradictory demands may be reconciled, one turns back to Stevens's early "Sunday Morning," in which the narrator specifies, "We live in an old chaos of the sun," and then leap forward to the very late "Final Soliloquy of the Interior Paramour," whose narrator tells us that "The world imagined is the ultimate good"—a world like that of "the single artificer of the world in which she sang" in "The Idea of Order at Key West," who "knew that there never was a world for her / Except the one she sang and, singing, made." It is impossible to go beyond this point in celebrating the rejection of the world of received opinion for the one that the artist creates. If American literature appears static since 1945, it is because the Modernist frame of reference had been by then established; and no important breakthrough has been made in another direction.

Within this framework, however, the drama achieved an unparalleled effectiveness. O'Neill no longer dominated the stage. After capping his great decade with a trilogy audaciously transplanting the sole surviving Greek trilogy, Aeschylus's *Oresteia*, to 19th-century New England in *Mourning Becomes Electra* (1931), O'Neill withdrew from the scene after his one nostalgic comedy, *Ah, Wilderness!* (1933), not to be heard from again until the long, cheerless drama of the triumph of dreams over life, *The Iceman Cometh*, reached Broadway in 1946.

An unprecedented number of other dramatists, however, commanded attention. Most honored at the time was Maxwell Anderson for his commercial success with a blank verse play, *Winterset* (1935), inspired by the notorious Sacco-Vanzetti case that had outraged many American artists. Even more popular at the time were Robert E. Sherwood's serio-comic responses to the fascist march to European war in *Idiot's Delight* (1936) and *There Shall Be No Night* (1940). Politics also influenced the radical critique of the depravity of American bourgeois society in Clifford Odets's *Awake and Sing!* (1935) and *Golden Boy* (1937) and especially in Lillian Hellman's bitter and controversial *The Children's Hour* (1934), *The Little Foxes* (1939) and the anti-Nazi *Watch on the Rhine* (1941). Comparable pieces were offered by the subsidized Federal Theatre Project, which also provided the start for Orson Welles's Mercury Theater.

An antidote to the grim exposures of the failure of the American dream like Sidney Kingsley's *Dead End* (1935) and John Steinbeck's *Of Mice and Men* (1937) were the comic collaborations of George S. Kaufman and Moss Hart, especially *You Can't Take It with You* (1936), which championed individualist rejection of pressures toward social conformity in a way that delighted depression-weary Americans. William Saroyan also achieved his one enduring success with *The Time of Your Life* (1939), a zany reversal of O'Neill's tragedies about defeated dreamers. The most heartening plays of the period—and even perhaps of the world's theater—were Thornton Wilder's two internationally acclaimed meditations on the value of every moment of human experience and of the struggle to preserve the often threatened race in *Our Town* (1938) and *The Skin of Our Teeth* (1942). These were also important experimental efforts to break away from the dominant naturalistic tradition of the proscenium-arch stage in theatrical production.

4. The Harvest of Modernism, 1946–57

Relatively few new writers published their first works during World War II. John Cheever published a short story collection, and Mary McCarthy, Wright Morris, Saul Bellow, and Jean Stafford, novels; but wartime paper shortages and the absence in military service and other war work of promising young writers precluded the development of a new generation of fictionists influenced by the war until 1946.

Gore Vidal, who was to become one of our most prolific writers, was the first soldier-author to break into print with *Williwaw* (1946), a fictional account of his experiences on the little-known Alaskan front; but he was to become most famous for one of the first American novels to broach the forbidden subject of homosexuality (*The City and the Pillar*, 1948) and for the outrageously camp *Myra Breckinridge* (1968). His works were overshadowed, however, by Norman Mailer's *The Naked and the Dead* (1948), an episodic novel, influenced by John Dos Passos's *U.S.A.*, about one Army squad's role in the taking of a Pacific island from the Japanese. Mailer made his dozen men, however, representative of a cross-section of American life and their story a powerful indictment of the power in the United States and its army of the very fascism that we expended our resources and lives to defeat. The novelist subsequently became, in less celebrated works, culminating in the hallucinatory account of the moral disintegration of the country, *Why Are We in Vietnam?* (1967), a controversial critic of American political life, before abandoning fiction for the journalistic "non-fiction novel."

Another large-scale novel also attacked the depravities of the American military establishment—James Jones's *From Here to Eternity* (1951)—but other forms of decadence began to command even more attention. In a novel (*Other Voices, Other Rooms*, 1948) and short stories (*A Tree of Night*, 1949), Truman Capote presented a south even more degenerate than Faulkner's before also turning to the "non-fiction novel" to present in *In Cold Blood* (1966) a minutely detailed account of the senseless murder of a family by two drifters. An even more appallingly grotesque picture of the south emerged in the novels (*Wise Blood*, 1952, and *The Violent Bear It Away*, 1960) and the short stories (*A Good Man Is Hard to Find*, 1955) of Flannery O'Connor. Less gothic in its excesses, but equally critical of the hypocrisy of decadent southern aristocrats was *Lie Down in Darkness* (1951) by William Styron.

The south had no monopoly on decadence, however. Two of the most shocking novels of the post-war period to still tender-minded Americans seeking to preserve a few ideals were Paul Bowles's tale of Morocco, *The Sheltering Sky* (1949), and John Hawkes's surrealist account of occupied Germany, *The Cannibal* (1949). Certainly not coincidentally, the years following the war saw the development of a cult of admirers for the earlier writings of H.P. Lovecraft, who in horror fantasies principally published in the pulp magazine *Weird Tales* had created a mythology about the once dispossessed minions of the god Cthulu attempting to take over our planet by subversion.

It was the still inconceivable decadence of the Nazi holocaust in Europe, too, that in part accounted for the rise after the war of a group of Jewish-American novelists keenly aware of their people's ancient traditions and recent persecutions. Saul Bellow, the most remarkable of the group and the Nobel Prize winner in 1976, began to publish during the war, but first gained international recognition for *The Adventures of Augie March* (1953), a picaresque account of the *Wanderjahren* of a young opportunist from the Chicago slums. Bellow's cryptic *Henderson the Rain King* (1959) has attracted much speculation; but his most powerful work is *Herzog* (1964), the self-revelation of a typically alienated, overly ambitious modern man who is at last able to make peace with himself (even if the world thinks him mad) through his imaginary conversations with the living and the dead.

The most impressive of Bernard Malamud's novels remains *The Assistant* (1957), in which the novelist most directly deals with racial and religious problems through the touching account of the relationship between an aggressive young Italian and his employer, a poor Jewish grocer. Growing to be even more respected, however, are the many works, originally written in Yiddish, by Isaac Bashevis Singer, particularly stories of life before World War I in the *shtetls* in Czarist Russia from which the ancient Jewish communities were driven. (Malamud also deals with a gruesome incident involving the Jews in Russia in *The Fixer*, 1966.) The most troubling tale to involve recollections of a direct involvement with the Nazi persecution, however, is Edward Lewis Wallant's *The Pawnbroker* (1961).

Another oppressed group, blacks, also began to win greater recognition for their fiction after World War II. Although Richard Wright's later works, written in exile in France and heavily influenced by existentialist philosophy, were disappointing, Ralph Ellison's *Invisible Man* (1952), a brilliant *Bildungsroman* about the transformation of a naive, ambitious southern black boy into a sophisticated fugitive living off a society that he rejects as a result of his disillusioning experiences with both whites and other blacks, conservatives and reformers, businessmen and religious revivalists, transcends any racial bounds to stand beside James Joyce's *A Portrait of the Artist as a Young Man* as a prototypical account of the creation of a Modernist sensibility. More limited in scope but deeply revealing of the sufferings of a sensitive young black are James Baldwin's *Go Tell It on the Mountain* (1953) and the related non-fictional *The Fire Next Time* (1963), based on recollections of the indignities and illuminations he experienced while growing up in Harlem.

The most popular novel of this period, especially with young readers, however, concerns the indignities and illuminations also experienced by a boy growing up during the same years as Baldwin a few miles south of Harlem in the upper-middle-class high-rise apartment district of Manhattan—J.D. Salinger's *The Catcher in the Rye* (1951). Although Salinger had been publishing short stories since 1941, he first attracted attention with a short story in the *New Yorker*, "A Perfect Day for Bananafish," about the suicide of Seymour Glass, who with his six siblings was to be the subject of most of the only thirteen other stories that Salinger has allowed to be published in book form. He received almost hysterical adulation for his one novel, a colloquial monologue about the traumatic experiences of a seventeen-year-old boy seeking to maintain an innocence doomed to adulteration in the corrupted world of New York at Christmas.

Despite the popular triumph of this culmination of "waste land" thinking in *The Catcher in the Rye* and the Glass family stories, the Modernist sensibility remained under attack from some able traditionalists who sought the rejuvenation of 19th-century moral codes. John P. Marquand had begun a sentimental satirization of a vanished culture in *The Late George Apley* (1937) and *Wickford Point* (1939). James Gould Cozzens was writing at the same time, but did not attract great attention until his *Guard of Honor* (1948), about problems of command in a Florida training camp, was cited by the conservative forces of the *New York Times Book Review* as the best American novel about World War II, its sober judgments providing a counter to Norman Mailer's violent excesses. Even as late as 1957, Cozzens's mammoth *By Love Possessed* was hailed as a kind of nine-day's-wonder by critics alienated by Modernism, but its reputation faded quickly. The novels of socialite-lawyer Louis Auchincloss, like *The Rector of Justin* (1964), however, have continued to be well received; and even as late as 1977 a rabid attack on Modernist decadence, especially southern, attracted interest in Walker Percy's austere *Lancelot*. John Steinbeck in his later works, especially his most ambitious novel, *East of Eden* (1952), also argued for a return to traditional values; but these writings failed to match the artistry of his earlier stories. A serious call for a rediscovery of the principal of "sacrality" in life also underlies the delicately-wrought fictions of Walter Van Tilburg Clark, beginning with his effort to create a new kind of "western" in *The Ox-Bow Incident* (1940).

Traditional values exerted, for a time at least, a greater force than they did in fiction after World War II in the poetry of Robert Lowell, the only poet to emerge during those years whose place in American literary history seems, even after more than three decades, indisputably fixed. Critical consensus is wanting. Gay Wilson Allen, Walter B. Rideout and James K. Robinson's bulky anthology *American Poetry* (1965) includes of the poets who became prominent then only Lowell, Theodore Roethke, Karl Shapiro, Randall Jarrell, John Berryman, and Richard Wilbur; and they are widely separated both by birthdates and dates of first publication from Allen Tate and James Dickey on either side of them. But this list is overselective. While other anthologies omit some of this half dozen (except Lowell) and propose a bewildering variety of substitutes, a substantial number include Robert Duncan, Richard Eberhart, Howard Nemerov, Charles Olson, and Kenneth Patchen.

Of the dozen that must be seriously considered, two—Jarrell and Shapiro—began their careers with poems about their participation in the war, a paltry number in view of the millions of American servicemen. Even this link was soon broken: Shapiro became increasingly contentious as he adopted prosy stances as "bourgeois poet" and "Jewish poet"; Jarrell withdrew to an academic life, writing, like many of his contemporaries, several works for children. Berryman and Roethke also became college teachers, but led increasingly troubled lives. Richard Wilbur, a model of style and sanity among his contemporaries, has devoted himself increasingly to witty translations from the French. Eberhart, another of the hardiest, has become a grand old man at Dartmouth College. Nemerov has written, besides his introspective poems, several competent novels. Patchen also wrote novels, but they proved too extreme for most American readers, and after a long and painful illness, he died in obscurity, celebrated only by the youngsters of the Beat Generation, with which Robert Duncan was briefly associated. Duncan has consistently shunned the spotlight, however, something that cannot be said of Charles Olson, who, as founder of the influential Black Mountain group and theorist for "projective verse," sought more than any other recent poet to develop a school based on his own often adumbrated theories that some anthologists find more important than his Maximus poems.

A most curious feature of the treatment by anthologists of the years under consideration is the entire neglect of women poets. One responsible anthology of American literature does include, along with selections from the work of only four of the men mentioned, extensive selections from the work of Elizabeth Bishop and Gwendolyn Brooks, the first black woman poet of distinction in this century.

While it is apparent that there is no agreement about what may have been poetically significant during these years beyond Lowell's "confessional" poetry, one thing that is clear is that the long narrative poem, which had been going out of fashion since the end of the 19th century, had been almost totally replaced by short, highly personal, and often cryptic lyrics like John Berryman's "Dream Songs." Yet curiously the only earlier poet who added substantially to his reputation during these years was William Carlos Williams, whose narrative evocation of his home town, *Paterson*, appeared in five sections between 1946 and 1958.

The situation in post-World War II American drama was as clear-cut as it was fuzzy in poetry. Our stage was dominated not by just two playwrights, but by two plays. Not even O'Neill's works have created as much speculation and controversy as Tennessee Williams's *A Streetcar Named Desire* (1947) and Arthur Miller's *Death of a Salesman* (1949), which are often paired in discussions of whether "tragedy" is possible in modern secular terms. Both Williams's Blanche DuBois and Miller's Willy Loman dream such happiness as they will never feel. They are models of the Modernist vision, for both have made complete shambles of their real worlds in their frantic pursuits of impossible dreams.

In an important sense, *Streetcar* is Williams's only play (despite the popularity of the earlier *The Glass Menagerie*), for all of his steadily less successful works dealt with the inability of a sensitive individual to adjust to the demands of a crass, materialistic world, especially its sexual demands on the spiritualized idealist. Miller's work has been much more varied, since most of his frustrated heroes have been victims of society rather than of their own fantasies. Only in *After the Fall* (1964), based on Miller's troubled marriage to his second wife, the film star Marilyn Monroe, has his work become as richly personal as O'Neill's and Williams's. Williams's quarrel with the world was, of course, haunted by problems of sexual orientation, while Miller's grew from his ambiguous feelings about an economic system that he deplores, but that has rewarded him well.

A third playwright, William Inge, enjoyed popularity as long as he avoided or sublimated his personal sexual problems in plays like *Picnic* (1953); but when he confronted problems of homosexuality directly in his later plays, audiences rejected them, leading to a despondency that resulted in his suicide.

The ghost to Eugene O'Neill returned also to promote him to an even higher place than he had hitherto occupied in the hierarchy of world dramatists, not through his long study of the hopeless state of alcoholic dreamers, *The Iceman Cometh* (1946), but through the posthumous *Long Day's Journey into Night* (1956), in which by facing squarely at last the love-hate relationships within his own family, he made his greatest contribution to the theater. O'Neill's characters in this play, which he withheld during his lifetime, are doomed by neither external social nor cosmic forces, but by their own lack of self-knowledge and self-criticism; as such they make the play, like Eliot's *The Waste Land* and Ralph Ellison's *Invisible Man*, not "a personal grouse," but a synecdoche for a culture seemingly irreversibly set on a course that will lead to its own destruction.

As the drama, like the novel, became increasingly despairing and preoccupied with decadence, humor as an art form declined in the United States. Even the *New Yorker* became less funny and more threatening, though it did sponsor the dazzling word play of S.J. Perelman: but even most of his short comic sketches, however, contemptuously belittled the present or evoked, as in "Cloudland Revisited," the superficialities of an innocent past.

5. Modernist Decadence, 1957–79

The year 1959 is remarkable in that it saw the first important publications of fiction by an unusually large group destined to become some of our most prominent writers, a larger group than would appear in any subsequent year for at least the next two decades. These modern scriptures were preceded by two prophetic novels that subsequently became idols of cult worship.

William Gaddis's *The Recognitions* (1955) is a monstrously long tale with many bizarre characters and plot lines that has attracted a small band of avid readers. Jack Kerouac's *On the Road* (1957), which circulated for years in manuscript until it became the best known unpublished novel in the country, is an epic of the frenzied cross-country travels of the progenitors of the Beat Generation. Gaddis has subsequently published two more big, puzzling novels, *JR* (1975) and *Carpenter's Gothic* (1985), and remains himself a mysterious figure. Kerouac published many more books during the decade after *On the Road* (many of them written during his earlier days of obscurity), before his sudden death—apparently from the ravages of too high living—in 1969. Dissimilar as the novels are, they share important characteristics. Both are rambling works that ignore and even mock traditional forms, and both feature characters who live unplanned lives, often involving hysterical fantasies and deceptive behavior. They depict a world in which individuals lack any frame of reference but their own self-indulgent delusions.

This is the world also of the novelists who began to achieve recognition in 1959. The world of William S. Burroughs's *Naked Lunch* is, in fact, the most chaotic that a drugged vision could convey to paper at all. While the worlds of James Purdy (*Malcolm*), Philip Roth (*Goodbye, Columbus*), and John Updike (*The Poorhouse Fair*) are tersely mapped in better disciplined fables, they all deal with characters caught up in their own fantasies and only spasmodically in touch with the external realities of their situations (if indeed *Malcolm* has a geographical reality at all). The same comments can be applied to the works of a number of other contemporaries. John Barth had published *The Floating Opera* in 1956 (though not in its original form until 1967), but his reputation was established by a historical fantasy (*The Sot-Weed Factor*, 1960) and an allegorical tour-de-force about a computerized culture (*Giles Goat-Boy*, 1966). Donald Barthelme's short stories in *Come Back, Dr. Caligari* (1964) and his "novel" *Snow White* (1967) presented figures from folklore and contemporary media against artificial backgrounds reminiscent of the Pop Art painting of the period. Joseph Heller's anti-war *Catch-22* (1961) dealt with characters whose private fantasies made more sense than the public world that oppressed them. Thomas Pynchon's *V.* (1963) seemed, like Vladimir Nabokov's *Lolita* (1955) and *Pale Fire* (1962), elaborate and masterfully inventive word games that shuffled the same deck of cards as *Alice in Wonderland* to suggest the ultimate unreality of all human action.

These tendencies had begun to manifest themselves as early as 1952 in the relatively thin apprentice works of the man who was eventually to have the last word in such matters, Kurt Vonnegut, Jr. Although *Player Piano* seemed only a kind of comic strip spinoff from the increasingly popular science fiction that had begun to win serious critical attention, Vonnegut's work became increasingly serious in its portraits of paranoid self-destruction (*Mother Night*, 1962) and universal destruction (*Cat's Cradle*, 1963). *Slaughterhouse-Five* (1969) combined the historical horror of the fire raid on Dresden during World War II with science-fiction fantasy to suggest that the only possible hope for humanity lay beyond our own corrupted planet; but Vonnegut returned to the confines of this planet to deliver in *Breakfast of Champions* (1973) a damning indictment of every facet of American society, in which existence becomes tolerable only when the author-narrator withdraws into his own head "where the big show is" and ultimately "sets at liberty" all his literary characters.

Vonnegut's erasing of the line that reputedly exists between external and internal realities completes the withdrawal begun in American literature by Sister Carrie's passive dreaming in her rocking chair; but his action is only the most flamboyant execution of a step already taken by Nabokov, Barth, and Purdy, among others. Some critics have recently tended to regard these writers as "post-Modernist"; but I think that the use of this terminology is premature. While some critics have suggested that the Modernist Age ended as early as 1930 or as late as 1960, the characters in our most respected recent fiction have not behaved fundamentally differently from Henry Fleming and Sister Carrie; they have only been more blatant and extreme in their alienation. The fables that critics sometimes described as "post-Modernist" are still concerned with the complete and irrevocable divorce of the utterly disillusioned individual from an irredeemably corrupt and demoralized society. Such a movement is not in a new direction; it is rather a milling about at the end of a road that goes no further.

Sporadic lamentations beginning in the 1960's of "the death of the novel" appeared justified by the lack of anything to write about following the apocalypse prophesied by Thomas Pynchon in the short story "Entropy" (1960) and limned in excruciating detail and with flabbergasting erudition in *Gravity's Rainbow* (1973)—a happening which would see the world of T.S. Eliot's waste land come to its end with both a bang and a whimper.

The continued absence of critical consensus about the worth of American poets proved not a bad thing. At least poets generally escaped one of the plagues besetting bestselling novelists by producing works unprofitable enough to escape sensational commercial exploitation. With rare exceptions poets after World War II were driven into the subsidized refuge of college teaching. Although a rather often attenuated "academic verse" resulted and a new elitism developed in writers workshops, like the famous one presided over by Paul Engle at the University of Iowa, poets were left to their own devices and not required to pander to the confectionary tastes of a public that, when it read poetry at all, preferred the imported effusions of Kahlil Gibran.

While there have probably never been so many technically competent poets at work as at present, only Allen Ginsberg, a non-academic, with a single poem, *Howl* (1956), has made a striking impression on the general public. The importance of *Howl* is that, as James E. Miller, Jr., has pointed out, it established Ginsberg, one of the charter members of the Beat Generation, as the last spokesman for a national audience in the tradition of Whitman, Hart Crane, and Carl Sandburg. Ginsberg was one of six poets who participated at a legendary reading at San Francisco's Six Gallery in the autumn of 1955 that launched the brief San Francisco Renaissance, the last literary movement with large public support, especially among dissident youths who later became increasingly politicized. *Howl* became notorious through the efforts of the police and customs officials to suppress it; but it is the only Beat poem to attain enduring popularity. Of Ginsberg's fellow readers at the Six Gallery—older sponsor Kenneth Rexroth, Michael McClure, Philip Lamantia, Philip Whalen, and Gary Snyder—only Snyder remains almost universally respected for his deeply sensitive nature poetry inspired by his years of study of oriental religions. The movement itself as a newsworthy phenomenon was exhausted by 1960, but the attack on conventional respectability that it launched has continued to affect American lifestyles.

A question that continues to divide critics is whether even *Howl* is a classic or obscene trash, as traditionalists maintain. The issue has polarized opinion particularly because of the failure of any subsequent work to attract anything like comparable attention. The heart of the problem is that the opening line of the poem, "I saw the best minds of my generation destroyed by madness, starving hysterical naked . . .," sums up histrionically the fundamental reason for the Modernist rejection of materialist culture, so that the poem leaves little room except for others to imitate it or to refute it convincingly, as none has so far succeeded in doing.

A few poets also gained nearly legendary status by focusing upon newly fashionable fields of speculation that did not appeal to our more polite academics. Robert Bly, after developing a considerable reputation as an editor and translator, became the idol of sensitive youthful dissidents through his outspoken political leadership of the artistic protest against the Vietnam war. More recently Bly has explored the role of archetypes from Jungian psychology in creating a poetry of universal consciousness. James Dickey imported into poetry the macho persona of fiction's Norman Mailer and film's Marlon Brando. Although more often judged as a poet than a novelist, Dickey in his novel *Deliverance* (1970) captures more vividly and hauntingly than his concerned contemporaries the ambiguous feelings of those who seek to escape civilization and its discontents in the primitive purity of the wilderness only to find that their retreat is both corrupted and threatened with extinction.

An even stronger hold on the American imagination than Dickey's was achieved by Sylvia Plath, whose brief and troubled life ended in suicide even before the appearance of her most remarkable works. Like Dickey she complemented confessional poetry (*Ariel*, 1965) with a self-revelatory novel (*The Bell Jar*, 1963). Another poet who died tragically young, but accidentally, Frank O'Hara was both a leader of the New York school closely associated with young painters of the period and a hero of the gay activist movement because of his frank revelation of his homosexual sensibility. Both movements have since languished because of the failure of any adequate successor to O'Hara to emerge.

Other talented poets have tended to develop cultist followings. Denise Levertov, Adrienne Rich, and Diane Wakowski have been strongly supported by feminists. Levertov is represented along with W.D. Snodgrass and W.S. Merwin in Rideout and Robinson's *American Poetry*, but Poirier's anthology omits them and includes James Merrill, John Ashbery, and LeRoi Jones (Amiri Baraka). But where are others, equally deserving, such as A.R. Ammons, Louis Simpson, and William Stafford?

The year 1959 proved as important to American drama as to the American novel, for it saw the first off-Broadway production of the first playwright since the end of World War II to rank with O'Neill, Williams, and Miller. Like O'Neill, Edward Albee first won attention with electrifying one-act plays, *The Zoo Story* (1959) and *The American Dream* (1961), the latter managing in only a few minutes to justify its pretentious title by stripping the façade of respectable success from a stereotyped American family. Doubts about Albee's ability to follow up these dramatic vignettes with a full-length play were triumphantly set to rest with *Who's Afraid of Virginia Woolf?* (1962), the Walpurgis night exorcism of the decadent dreams of a childless and professionally sterile American couple. Albee failed, however, to match this initial success with either the engrossingly experimental *Tiny Alice* (1964) or his later plays; and he has devoted much of his subsequent effort to touring with his own productions of his early works. Like the contemporary novelists, Albee and his generation of playwrights seem stymied by the problem of where to go beyond the dead end of the Modernist sensibility reached in the international absurdist drama of Eugène Ionesco's *Rhinoceros* and Samuel Beckett's *Endgame*.

Black American drama has also failed to sustain its promise of the 1960's. Amiri Baraka scored a spectacular success with *Dutchman* (1964), a two-character play about a confrontation between a black man and a white woman on a New York subway train; but *The Toilet* (1962) and *The Slave* (1964) proved too gross for even off-Broadway's blasé audiences. Lorraine Hansberry did enjoy a heartening public and critical success with her first full-length play, *A Raisin in the Sun* (also that last magical year of 1959), a 1930's-type realistically staged inspirational drama about a Chicago black family's aspirations to own its own home in a segregated suburb; but her subsequent plays, some left unfinished at her early death, proved too heavily freighted with ideological talk to come to life on the stage.

By far the most financially successful playwright of the last third of this century has been Neil Simon, whose works also return to the 1930's manner of the well-made farce; even Simon, however, has been becoming increasingly serious and nostalgic, returning to the years between the World Wars for his subject matter and style. Lanford Wilson, who launched his career as an off-off-Broadway writer of brief evocations of doomed figures like the monologuist in *The Madness of Lady Bright* (1964) has also turned back to the past in rural America for his greatest success with a series of plays about a southwestern American family, including the Pulitzer Prize-winning *Talley's Folly* (1979) and *5th of July* (1978).

Similar nostalgia is also creeping into the recent works of the most admired comic writer of the decadent years, Woody Allen; but this change seems only part of a larger one underway as an exhausted Modernist sensibility runs out of fresh inspirations even for its proclamations of doom.

6. Minimalism, 1980–

It is not yet apparent that any overlooked literary landmark precisely fixes the turning point that marked the "exhaustion," to borrow John Barth's term, of the Modernist vision of flight—even to death—from a world too much with us. But certainly 1979 brought the several-years delayed revelation of the mammoth finale in what has become the dominant "literary" medium—film—that marked not just the end, but in a sense the defeat of Modernism as the seminal cultural force—Francis Ford Coppola's *Apocalypse Now*. As even the clouded-crystal-ball finality of Coppola's title calls to attention, the very apocalypse long heralded in both fiction and film has been, if by no means surely averted, at least indefinitely postponed. America's prophetic artists are left much in the position of the 19th-century Millerites, who had to come back down the mountain to make a fresh start, when the world failed to come to an end as their schedule advertised.

In retrospect, one begins to see that the situation had materialized when the national bicentennial in 1976 failed to bring either a much prayed for renewal of the pioneering spirit that had made the nation great or a widely anticipated day of doom. Coppola's allegory—obscured by the auteur's uncertainty about whether to conclude it with a world-consuming conflagration—ironically marked as clearly as had its turn-of-the-century inspiration, Joseph Conrad's *Heart of Darkness*, the dissipation of an age's illusion. The "horror" encountered by Conrad's Kurtz had shattered the expectation that the white man's bearing his burden would illuminate the dark corners of the world. The "horror" experienced by Coppola's Kurtz forced the realization that flight from a fallen world could not be achieved even by its extermination.

As from any point that marks the end of a frustrated journey, the troops dispersed in several directions. The title of poet-prophet that once seemed might have been bestowed on either Walt Whitman/Allen Ginsberg or T.S. Eliot should be, it seems, at least tentatively awarded (as indeed it had been by President Kennedy at his 1960 inauguration) to Robert Frost. Frost posed the problem that the shapers of American myth would face in the nation's third century of independence, in his modest ovenbird's inquiry about "What to make of a diminished thing?"

Hard-core Modernists clung to escape. J.D. Salinger had lapsed into silence as early as 1965, hiding out in the same New Hampshire wilds from which Frost had earlier derived inspiration. Thomas Pynchon has pursued the same course to the extreme point of disappearing even as a person. After earlier disavowing the novel, Norman Mailer and Kurt Vonnegut, Jr., have returned to fiction, but Mailer's venturing back to the distant Egypt of *Ancient Evenings* (1983) and Vonnegut's returning to the squalor and cuteness of an earlier American midwest in *Deadeye Dick* (1982) have not enlarged their reputations.

As during any such period of soul-searching there has been some literary backtracking in the ever-repeated effort to locate where we took the wrong turning. John Steinbeck had launched this effort as far back as 1952; but *East of Eden* failed to prescribe a probable pattern for regenerating one's life. *The Winter of Our Discontent* (1961), his last novel, came closer to foreshadowing a new tendency in fiction, but Steinbeck lacked the energy to follow up on a fresh start and fell back in *America and Americans* (1966) on lambasting his countrymen for their lack of respect for the kind of law and order that had gotten Conrad's Kurtz in his fix. Hemingway also in 1952 provided a model for a stripped-down portrayal of self-fulfillment in *The Old Man and the Sea*, but had left things at that at a time when such an about-face was viewed as a sign of sentimentality if not senility. Ralph Ellison's invisible man, who had gone underground to await a new day, has not yet re-emerged. The exhuming of a rotten past has, however, at least not only promoted the sales of hundreds of bulky "historical" novels and TV miniseries, but has generated considerable literary and extra-literary debate through William Styron's pointing the finger at slavery and racial warfare in *The Confessions of Nat Turner* (1967) and the Nazi holocaust in *Sophie's Choice* (1979); but Styron still seems to see no way out short of apocalypse. The most successful effort to present fictionally a new sense of direction has been James Purdy's largely ignored *Mourners Below* (1981), in which he moves from his gruesome indictments of selfish, loveless parents in *The House of the Solitary Maggot* (1974) and *Narrow Rooms* (1978) to envision a new sense of family as a nurturing force.

Literary critics, including such acute analysts of post-Modernist tendencies as Jerome Klinkowitz, have been strenuously promoting the virtues of a new generation of avant-garde novelists including Walter Abish, Don DeLillo, Frederick Exley, Raymond Federman, Kenneth Gangemi, Clarence Major, Gilbert Sorrentino, and Ronald Sukenick; but their experiments in furthering the exploration of language as both subject and theme appear still in the tradition of Joyce's flight from the phenomenal world in *Finnegans Wake*, and their writings have not so far attracted much attention from readers or reviewers beyond academic journals.

Much wider interest has been stimulated by a group of writers associated with a resurgence of the influence on the American literary scene of the *New Yorker* magazine. For some years the only general circulation magazine in the United States that continued to promote the development of new writers of fiction, the *New Yorker*, following the deaths of such principal contributors as John O'Hara and John Cheever and the self-silencing of J.D. Salinger, failed to develop during the years of enthusiasm for Mailer, Vonnegut, and Pynchon others as generally well esteemed. Within the last decade, however, the magazine has fostered the talents of recently emerged writers like Anne Tyler, Raymond Carver, and Ann Beattie, as it moves to the forefront once more as a tastemaker.

What links the writers just named is their return to what Willa Cather described as "the unfurnished novel," simple stark "chilly scenes of winter," as Ann Beattie titles one of her books, not steeped in the contemplation of impending apocalypse, but rather portraying characters, striving, like Frost's ovenbird, to accept the world as they find it and trying, like the title character in Cather's *The Professor's House* (who rejected in 1925 the tempting prospect of suicide), to make something of a life devoid of joy. After a succession of novels that attracted increasing attention, Anne Tyler appears to have formulated the prototype of a new quest novel attuned to the times in *Dinner at the Homesick Restaurant* (1982). Although he has not yet produced a novel and may, like Salinger, work best in shorter forms, Raymond Carver has won both many literary awards and devoted readers with grim, brilliantly executed short stories and poems well suited to his sculptor's name. Ann Beattie in several novels and short story collections seems to have become the literary spokeswoman for the increasingly influential, prosperous but aimless Yuppies. Sparing with words, guarded in feelings, avoiding the rich allusiveness of Modernist writing, these writers look upon America's suburban ghetto not with the elegant spite of O'Hara, Cheever and Salinger, but with a bewilderment shared with the characters, employing techniques analogous to those the minimalist painters and sculptors introduced in the 1960's. It will be interesting to observe if, as so often in the past, the visual artists will blaze the trail that the writers will follow.

One tremendous difference between the advent of Modernism at the end of the 19th century and the apparent shift toward a new literary sensibility as we near the end of the 20th is the diminished role of poets in leading the transition. If there are successors to Pound and Eliot, Frost and Williams and Stevens, they have yet to be heard from, nor does there seem to be any fresh inspiration from abroad like that earlier provided by the French symbolists and Yeats. Robert Creeley's work probably introduced the term "minimalism" into American criticism of poetry, but his "minimalism" is closer to the compressed emotional intensity of Paul Klee's tiny forms than to the arid geometry of the recent illuminati. The influence of the New York school of the 1960's continues to be felt only in the metaphysical complexities of John Ashbery's poems, and no perceptible important new "schools" seem to have formed.

From the exciting avant-garde theater off-Broadway during the 1970's Sam Shepard alone seems to have survived and flourished. Although Shepard's work is rarely produced on an increasingly traditional Broadway, it has won plaudits in Greenwich Village and in many regional theaters emerging throughout the country; these theaters have decentralized, and, one hopes, will reinvigorate native drama. Exceptionally prolific and with a growing reputation as a screenwriter and actor, Shepard has employed a variety of settings, but often returns to the vanishing west of his early *Cowboys* (1964). Clearly related to the minimalists by the staccato Pinteresque dialogue of characters barely able to communicate with each other and by his squalid settings, Shepard remains a transitional figure, still haunted by a vision of apocalypse that provides a spectacular ending for *Fool for Love* (1983) as translated to the screen by director Robert Altman with Shepard playing a leading role.

Despite the nostalgia for the 1930's coloring some of Woody Allen's recent films, Allen as both dramatist and humorist has employed minimalist techniques and themes in two of his most admired films, the earth-toned *Interiors* (1978) and the colorless *Manhattan* (1979). Allen may well be the artist to watch to see whether the new sensibility is a passing trend or a growing tendency, for film's combination of image and language may become a dominant form in shaping our culture if others possess Allen's native talents and can acquire his auteurist control in an expensive medium.

—WARREN FRENCH

READING LIST

Bibliographies, handbooks, etc.

American Literary Scholarship 1963— (annual review), 1965—

Bain, Robert, Joseph M. Flora, and Louis D. Rubin, Jr., editors, *Southern Writers: A Biographical Dictionary*, 1979.

Blanck, Jacob, *Bibliography of American Literature*, 1955—

Brooks, Cleanth, R.W.B. Lewis, and Robert Penn Warren, editors, *American Literature: The Makers and the Making*, 2 vols., 1973.

Bryer, Jackson R., editor, *Sixteen Modern American Authors: A Survey of Research and Criticism*, 1973.

Bufkin, E.C., *The Twentieth-Century Novel in English: A Checklist*, 1967.

Clark, Harry Hayden, *American Literature: Poe Through Garland*, 1971.

Cohen, Hennig, *Articles in American Studies 1954–1968*, 1972.

Contemporary Writers series (*Poets, Novelists, Dramatists, Literary Critics*), 1970— (each volume revised every 5 years).

Dargan, Marion, *Guide to American Biography 1607–1933*, 2 vols., 1949–52.

Davis, Richard Beale, *American Literature Through Bryant 1585–1830*, 1969.

Dictionary of American Biography, 20 vols., 1928–37; supplements, 1944, 1958, 1973, 1974, 1977, 1980, 1981; concise edition, 1964; 3rd concise edition, 1980.

Dictionary of Literary Biography, 1978—

Faust, Langdon Lynne, editor, *American Women Writers: A Critical Reference Guide from Colonial Times to the Present*, 2 vols., 1983.

Gerstenberger, Donna, and George Hendrick, *The American Novel: A Checklist of Twentieth-Century Criticism*, 2 vols., 1961–70.

Gohdes, Clarence, editor, *Bibliographical Guide to the Study of the Literature of the U.S.A.*, 1959; 5th edition, 1984.

Hart, James D., *The Oxford Companion to American Literature*, 1941; 5th edition, 1984.

Havelice, Patricia, *Index to American Author Bibliographies*, 1971.

Herzberg, Max J., and others, *The Reader's Encyclopedia of American Literature*, 1962.

Holman, C. Hugh, *The American Novel Through Henry James*, 1966; 2nd edition, 1979.

Inge, M. Thomas, editor, *Black American Writers*, 2 vols., 1978.

Inge, M. Thomas, editor, *Handbook to American Popular Culture*, 3 vols., 1979–81.

Jones, Howard Mumford, and Richard M. Ludwig, editors, *Guide to American Literature and Its Backgrounds since 1890*, 1959; revised edition, 1972.

Kolb, Harold H., Jr., *A Field Guide to the Study of American Literature*, 1976.

Kunitz, Stanley J., and Howard Haycraft, *American Authors 1600–1900: A Biographical Dictionary of American Literature*, 1938.

Leary, Lewis, *Articles on American Literature 1900–1950*, 1954; *1950–1967*, 1970; *1968–1975*, 1979.

Leary, Lewis, *American Literature: A Study and Research Guide*, 1976.

Long, E. Hudson, *American Drama from Its Beginnings to the Present*, 1970.

Mainiero, Lina, editor, *American Women Writers*, 4 vols., 1979–82.

Mottram, Eric, and Malcolm Bradbury, editors, *U.S.A.*, in *The Penguin Companion to Literature 3*, 1971.

Myerson, Joel, editor, *The Transcendentalists: A Review of Research and Criticism*, 3 vols., 1984.

Nevius, Blake, *The American Novel: Sinclair Lewis to the Present*, 1970.

Nilon, Charles H., *Bibliography of Bibliographies of American Literature*, 1970.

Parker, Patricia L., *Early American Fiction: A Reference Guide*, 1984.

Rees, Robert A., and Earl N. Harbert, editors, *Fifteen American Authors Before 1900: Bibliographic Essays on Research and Criticism*, 1971; revised edition, 1984.

Robbins, J. Albert, editor, *American Literary Manuscripts*, 1960; revised edition, 1977.

Rubin, Louis D., Jr., *A Bibliographical Guide to the Study of Southern Literature*, 1969.

Ryan, Pat M., *American Drama Bibliography: A Checklist of Publications in English*, 1969.

Salzman, Jack, editor, *The Cambridge Handbook of American Literature*, 1986.

Spiller, Robert E., and others, editors, *Literary History of the United States: Bibliography*, 1948; 4th edition, 1974.

Stovall, Floyd, editor, *Eight American Authors: A Review of Research and Criticism*, revised by James Woodress, 1971.

Tanselle, G. Thomas, *Guide to the Study of United States Imprints*, 2 vols., 1971.

Turner, Darwin T., *Afro-American Writers*, 1970.

Twentieth-Century Writers series (*Children's Writers, Crime and Mystery Writers, Science-Fiction Writers, Romance and Gothic Writers, Western Writers*), 1978— (each volume revised every 5 years).

Weixlmann, Joe, *American Short-Fiction Criticism and Scholarship 1959–1977: A Checklist*, 1982.

Woodress, James, *Dissertations in American Literature*, 1962.

Woodress, James, editor, *American Fiction 1900–1950: A Guide to Information Sources*, 1975.

Wright, Lyle H., *American Fiction: A Contribution Toward a Bibliography 1774–1850*, 1948, revised edition, 1966; *1851–1875*, 1965, revised edition, 1966; *1876–1900*, 1966.

Yanella, Donald, and John H. Roch, *Prose to 1820: A Guide to Information Sources*, 1979.

General histories

Attebery, Brian, *The Fantasy Tradition in American Literature from Irving to Le Guin*, 1980.

Baker, Houston A., Jr., *Singers of Daybreak: Studies in Black American Literature*, 1974.

Bercovitch, Sacvan, editor, *Reconstructing American Literary History*, 1986.

Blair, Walter, and Hamlin Hill, *America's Humor: From Poor Richard to Doonesbury*, 1978.

Bogard, Travis, and others, *American Drama*, 1977.

Bridgman, Richard, *The Colloquial Style in America*, 1966.

Brooks, Van Wyck, *Makers and Finders: A History of the Writer in America 1800–1915*, 5 vols., 1936–52.

Budd, Louis J., Edwin H. Cady, and Carl L. Anderson, editors, *Toward a New American Literary History*, 1980.
Clark, Harry Hayden, editor, *Transitions in American Literary History*, 1953.
Cowie, Alexander, *The Rise of the American Novel*, 1948.
Cowley, Malcolm, *A Many-Windowed House: Collected Essays on American Writers and American Writing*, edited by Henry Dan Piper, 1970.
Cunliffe, Marcus, *The Literature of the United States*, 1954; 3rd edition, 1970.
Feidelson, Charles, *Symbolism and American Literature*, 1953.
Fiedler, Leslie A., *Love and Death in the American Novel*, 1960.
Fiedler, Leslie A., *The Inadvertent Epic: From Uncle Tom's Cabin to Roots*, 1979.
Gelpi, Albert, *The Tenth Muse: The Psyche of the American Poet*, 1975.
Habegger, Alfred, *Gender, Fantasy, and Realism in American Literature*, 1982.
Handlin, Oscar, and others, *Harvard Guide to American History*, 1954 (and later editions).
Hart, James D., *The Popular Book: A History of America's Literary Taste*, 1950.
Hicks, Granville, *The Great Tradition: An Interpretation of American Literature since the Civil War*, 1933; revised edition, 1935.
Howard, Leon, *Literature and the American Tradition*, 1960.
Hughes, Glenn, *A History of the American Theatre 1700–1950*, 1951.
Jones, Howard Mumford, *The Theory of American Literature*, 1948; revised edition, 1965.
Kazin, Alfred, *On Native Grounds: An Interpretation of Modern American Prose Literature*, 1942.
Kazin, Alfred, *An American Procession: The Major Writers from 1830–1930*, 1984.
Kronick, Joseph G., *American Poetics of History: From Emerson to the Moderns*, 1984.
Leisy, Ernest E., *The American Historical Novel*, 1950.
Lewis, R.W.B., *Trials of the Word: Essays in American Literature and the Humanistic Tradition*, 1965.
Lindberg, Gary, *The Confidence Man in American Literature*, 1982.
Liptzin, Solomon, *The Jew in American Literature*, 1966.
McIlwaine, Shields, *The Southern Poor-White from Lubberland to Tobacco Road*, 1939.
Meserve, Walter J., *An Outline History of American Drama*, 1965.
Moses, Montrose J., and John Mason Brown, editors, *The American Theatre as Seen by Its Critics 1752–1934*, 1934.
Mott, Frank Luther, *Golden Multitudes: The Story of Best Sellers in the United States*, 1947.
Mott, Frank Luther, *American Journalism 1690–1960*, 1962.
Nye, Russel B., *The Unembarrassed Muse: The Popular Arts in America*, 1970.
Parrington, Vernon Louis, *Main Currents in American Thought: An Interpretation of American Literature from the Beginnings to 1920*, 3 vols., 1927–30.
Pearce, Roy Harvey, *The Continuity of American Poetry*, 1961; revised edition, 1965.
Peden, William, *The American Short Story*, 1964; revised edition, 1975.
Quinn, Arthur Hobson, *A History of American Drama*, 3 vols., 1923–27; revised edition, 2 vols., 1936–43.
Quinn, Arthur Hobson, *American Fiction: An Historical and Critical Survey*, 1936.
Quinn, Arthur Hobson, editor, *The Literature of the American People: An Historical and Critical Survey*, 1951.
Rubin, Louis D., Jr., editor, *The History of Southern Literature*, 1985.
Spiller, Robert E., and others, editors, *Literary History of the United States*, 3 vols., 1948; 4th edition, 2 vols., 1974.
Spiller, Robert E., *The Cycle of American Literature*, 1955; revised edition, 1967.
Spindler, Michael, *American Literature and Social Change: William Dean Howells to Arthur Miller*, 1983.
Stauffer, Donald Barlow, *A Short History of American Poetry*, 1974.
Stovall, Floyd, *The Development of American Literary Criticism*, 1955.
Tanner, Tony, *The Reign of Wonder: Naivety and Reality in American Literature*, 1965.
Tebbel, John, *A History of Book Publishing in the United States*, 4 vols., 1972–81.
Voss, Arthur, *The American Short Story: A Critical Survey*, 1973.
Wagenknecht, Edward, *Cavalcade of the American Novel*, 1952.
Waggoner, Hyatt H., *American Poets from the Puritans to the Present*, 1968; revised edition, 1984.
Walcutt, Charles Child, *American Literary Naturalism: A Divided Stream*, 1956.
Watts, Emily Stipes, *The Poetry of American Women from 1632 to 1945*, 1977.
Whitlow, Roger, *Black American Literature: A Critical History*, 1973.
Winters, Yvor, *In Defense of Reason*, 1947; revised edition, 1960.

American Literature to 1900: Critical Studies

Aaron, Daniel, *The Unwritten War: American Writers and the Civil War*, 1973.
Anderson, Quentin, *The Imperial Self: An Essay in American Literary and Cultural History*, 1971.
Auchincloss, Louis, *Pioneers and Caretakers: A Study of 9 American Women Novelists*, 1965.
Baker, Houston A., Jr., *The Journey Back: Issues in Black Literature and Criticism*, 1980.
Baritz, Loren, *City on a Hill: A History of Ideas and Myths in America*, 1964.
Baym, Nina, *Women's Fiction: A Guide to Novels by and about Women in America 1820–1870*, 1978.
Bell, Michael Davitt, *The Development of American Romance: The Sacrifice of Relation*, 1983.
Bercovitch, Sacvan, editor, *Typology and Early American Literature*, 1972.
Bercovitch, Sacvan, editor, *The American Puritan Imagination: Essays in Revaluation*, 1974.
Bercovitch, Sacvan, *The Puritan Origins of the American Self*, 1975.
Bercovitch, Sacvan, *The American Jeremiad*, 1978.
Bercovitch, Sacvan, and Myra Jehlen, editors, *Ideology and Classic American Literature*, 1986.
Berthoff, Warner, *The Ferment of Realism: American Literature 1884–1919*, 1965.

Bewley, Marius, *The Complex Fate: Hawthorne, Henry James, and Some Other American Writers*, 1952.

Bewley, Marius, *The Eccentric Design: Form in the Classic American Novel*, 1959.

Bigelow, Gordon E., *Rhetoric and American Poetry of the Early National Period*, 1960.

Bode, Carl, *The Anatomy of American Popular Culture 1840–1861*, 1959.

Boller, Paul F., Jr., *American Transcendentalism 1830–1860: An Intellectual Inquiry*, 1974.

Brown, Herbert Ross, *The Sentimental Novel in America 1789–1860*, 1940.

Buell, Lawrence, *Literary Transcendentalism: Style and Vision in the American Renaissance*, 1973.

Cady, Edwin H., *The Light of Common Day: Realism in American Fiction*, 1951.

Carter, Everett, *The American Idea: The Literary Response to American Optimism*, 1977.

Charvat, William, *Literary Publishing in America 1790–1850*, 1959.

Charvat, William, *The Profession of Authorship in America 1800–1870*, edited by Matthew J. Bruccoli, 1968.

Chase, Richard, *The American Novel and Its Tradition*, 1957.

Daly, Robert, *God's Altar: The World and the Flesh in Puritan Poetry*, 1978.

Davis, Richard Beale, *Intellectual Life in the Colonial South 1585–1763*, 3 vols., 1978.

Donovan, Josephine, *New England Local Color Literature: A Women's Tradition*, 1983.

Dormon, James H., Jr., *Theater in the Ante-Bellum South 1815–1861*, 1967.

Douglas, Ann, *The Feminization of American Culture*, 1977.

Earnest, Ernest, *The American Eve in Fact and Fiction 1775–1914*, 1974.

Elliott, Emory, editor, *Puritan Influences in American Literature*, 1979.

Elliott, Emory, *Revolutionary Writers: Literature and Authority in the New Republic 1725–1810*, 1982.

Emerson, Everett, editor, *Major Writers of Early American Literature*, 1972.

Emerson, Everett, editor, *American Literature 1764–1789: The Revolutionary Years*, 1977.

Emerson, Everett, *Puritanism in America 1620–1750*, 1977.

Falk, Robert, *The Victorian Mode in American Fiction 1865–1885*, 1965.

Fiedler, Leslie A., *No! In Thunder: Essays on Myth and Literature*, 1960.

Fussell, Edwin, *Frontier: American Literature and the American West*, 1965.

Gaustad, E.S., *The Great Awakening in New England*, 1957.

Gilbert, Sandra M., and Susan Gubar, *The Madwoman in the Attic: The Woman Writer and the Nineteenth-Century Literary Imagination*, 1979.

Gilmore, Michael T., editor, *Early American Literature: A Collection of Critical Essays*, 1980.

Goddard, Harold Clarke, *Studies in New England Transcendentalism*, 1908.

Granger, Bruce, *Political Satire in the American Revolution 1763–1783*, 1960.

Granger, Bruce, *American Essay Serials from Franklin to Irving*, 1978.

Green, Martin, *Re-appraisals: Commonsense Readings in American Literature*, 1963.

Gura, Philip F., *The Wisdom of Words: Language, Theology, and Literature in the New England Renaissance*, 1981.

Hoffman, Daniel, *Form and Fable in American Fiction*, 1961.

Holman, C. Hugh, *The Roots of Southern Writing: Essays on the Literature of the American South*, 1972.

Holman, C. Hugh, *The Immoderate Past: The Southern Writer and History*, 1977.

Howard, Leon, *The Connecticut Wits*, 1943.

Howe, Irving, *The American Newness: Culture and Politics in the Age of Emerson*, 1986.

Hubbell, Jay B., *The South in American Literature 1607–1900*, 1954.

Inge, M. Thomas, *The Frontier Humorists: Critical Views*, 1975.

Israel, Calvin, editor, *Discoveries and Considerations: Essays on Early American Literature and Aesthetics*, 1976.

Jones, Howard Mumford, *O Strange New World: American Culture: The Formative Years*, 1964.

Jones, Howard Mumford, *The Age of Energy: Varieties of American Experience 1865–1915*, 1971.

Jones, Howard Mumford, *Revolution and Romanticism*, 1974.

Kagle, Steven E., *American Diary Literature 1620–1799*, 1979.

Kammen, Michael, *A Season of Youth: The American Revolution and the Historical Imagination*, 1978.

Keiser, Albert, *The Indian in American Literature*, 1933.

Kolb, Harold H., Jr., *The Illusion of Life: American Realism as a Literary Form*, 1969.

Kolodny, Annette, *The Lay of the Land*, 1975.

Kolodny, Annette, *The Land Before Her: Fantasy and Experience of the American Frontiers 1630–1860*, 1984.

Lawrence, D.H. *Studies in Classic American Literature*, 1923.

Leary, Lewis, editor, *Soundings: Some Early American Writers*, 1975.

Levin, Harry, *The Power of Blackness: Hawthorne, Poe, Melville*, 1958.

Lewis, R.W.B., *The American Adam: Innocence, Tragedy, and Tradition in the Nineteenth Century*, 1955.

Love, Glen A., *New Americans: The Westerner and the Modern Experience in the American Novel*, 1982.

Lowance, Mason I., Jr., *The Language of Canaan: Metaphor and Symbol in New England from the Puritans to the Transcendentalists*, 1980.

Martin, Jay, *Harvests of Change: American Literature 1865–1914*, 1967.

Martin, Ronald E., *American Literature and the Universe of Force*, 1981.

Martin, Terence, *The Instructed Vision: Scottish Common Sense Philosophy and the Origins of American Fiction*, 1961.

Marx, Leo, *The Machine in the Garden: Technology and the Pastoral Ideal in America*, 1964.

Matthiessen, F.O., *American Renaissance: Art and Expression in the Age of Emerson and Thoreau*, 1941.

McGiffert, Michael, editor, *Puritanism and the American Experience*, 1969.

McKay, Janet Holmgrin, *Narration and Discourse in American Realistic Fiction*, 1982.

Meserve, Walter J., *An Emerging Entertainment: The Drama of the American People to 1828*, 1977.

Miller, Perry, *The New England Mind*, 2 vols., 1939–53.

Miller, Perry, *Errand into the Wilderness*, 1956.

Miller, Perry, *The Raven and the Whale: The War of Words and Wits in the Era of Poe and Whitman*, 1956.

Miller, Ruth, editor, *Backgrounds to Blackamerican Literature*, 1971.

Morgan, Edmund S., *Visible Saints: The History of a Puritan Idea*, 1963.

Murdock, Kenneth B., *Literature and Theology in Colonial New England*, 1949.

Nye, Russel B., *The Cultural Life of the New Nation 1776–1830*, 1960.

Nye, Russel B., *American Literary History 1607–1830*, 1970.

Nye, Russel B., *Society and Culture in America 1830–1860*, 1974.

Pattee, Fred Lewis, *The First Century of American Literature 1770–1870*, 1935.

Petter, Henri, *The Early American Novel*, 1971.

Pizer, Donald G., *Realism and Naturalism in Nineteenth-Century American Literature*, 1961; revised edition, 1984.

Poirier, Richard, *A World Elsewhere: The Place of Style in American Literature*, 1966.

Porte, Joel, *The Romance in America: Studies in Cooper, Poe, Hawthorne, Melville, and James*, 1969.

Richardson, Robert D., Jr., *Myth and Literature in the American Renaissance*, 1978.

Ringe, Donald A., *American Gothic: Imagination and Reason in Nineteenth-Century Fiction*, 1982.

Rourke, Constance M., *American Humor: A Study of the National Character*, 1931.

Rowe, John Carlos, *Through the Custom-House: Nineteenth-Century American Fiction and Modern Theory*, 1982.

Rubin, Louis D., Jr., editor, *The Comic Imagination in American Literature*, 1973.

Rusk, Ralph Leslie, *The Literature of the Middle Western Frontier*, 2 vols., 1925.

Seelye, John D., *Prophetic Waters: The River in Early American Life and Literature*, 1977.

Shea, Daniel B., Jr., *Spiritual Autobiography in Early America*, 1968.

Silverman, Kenneth, *The Cultural History of the American Revolution*, 1976.

Simpson, Lewis P., *The Man of Letters in New England and the South*, 1973.

Slotkin, Richard, *Regeneration Through Violence: The Mythology of the American Frontier 1600–1860*, 1973.

Smith, Henry Nash, *Virgin Land: The American West as Symbol and Myth*, 1950.

Smith, Henry Nash, *Democracy and the Novel: Popular Resistance to Classic American Writers*, 1978.

Spencer, Benjamin T., *The Quest for Nationality: An American Literary Campaign*, 1957.

Spengemann, William C., *The Adventurous Muse: The Poetics of American Fiction 1789–1900*, 1977.

Stafford, John, *The Literary Criticism of "Young America": A Study of the Relationship of Politics and Literature 1837–1850*, 1952.

Sundquist, Eric J., editor, *American Realism: New Essays*, 1982.

Taylor, Walter Fuller, *The Economic Novel in America*, 1942.

Tyler, Moses Coit, *A History of American Literature During the Colonial Period*, 2 vols., 1878; *The Literary History of the American Revolution*, 2 vols., 1897; abridged by Archie H. Jones, as *A History of American Literature 1607–1783*, 1967.

von Frank, Albert J., *The Sacred Game: Provincialism and Frontier Consciousness in American Literature 1630–1860*, 1985.

Walker, Cheryl, *The Nightingale's Burden: Women Poets and American Culture Before 1900*, 1983.

Warren, Austin, *Rage for Order: Essays in Criticism*, 1939.

Warren, Austin, *New England Saints*, 1956.

Warren, Austin, *The New England Conscience*, 1966.

Westbrook, Perry D., *Acres of Flint: Writers of New England 1870–1900*, 1951; revised edition, 1981.

White, Peter, editor, *Puritan Poets and Poetics: Seventeenth-Century American Poetry in Theory and Practice*, 1985.

Wilson, Edmund, *Axel's Castle: A Study in the Imaginative Literature of 1870–1930*, 1931.

Wilson, Edmund, editor, *The Shock of Recognition: The Development of Literature in the United States Recorded by the Men Who Made It*, 1943; enlarged edition, 1955.

Wilson, Edmund, *Patriotic Gore: Studies in the Literature of the American Civil War*, 1962.

Wright, Louis B., *The Cultural Life of the American Colonies 1607–1763*, 1957.

Yates, Norris W., *William T. Porter and the Spirit of the Times: A Study of the Big Bear School of Humor*, 1957.

Young, Philip, *Three Bags Full: Essays in American Fiction*, 1972.

Ziff, Larzer, *The American 1890's: Life and Times of a Lost Generation*, 1966.

Ziff, Larzer, *Puritanism in America: New Culture in a New World*, 1973.

Ziff, Larzer, *Literary Democracy: The Declaration of Cultural Independence in America*, 1981.

(List prepared with the assistance of Thomas E. Hockersmith.)

American Literature since 1900: Critical Studies

Aaron, Daniel, *Writers on the Left: Episodes in American Literary Communism*, 1961.

Aiken, Conrad, *Scepticisms: Notes on Contemporary Poetry*, 1919.

Aldridge, John, *After the Lost Generation: A Critical Study of the Writers of Two Wars*, 1951.

Aldridge, John, *In Search of Heresy: American Literature in the Age of Conformity*, 1956.

Allen, Donald M., and Warren Tallman, *The Poetics of the New American Poetry*, 1974.

Allen, Walter, *Tradition and Dream: The English and American Novel from the Twenties to Our Time*, 1964; as *The Modern Novel in Britain and the United States*, 1964.

Atkinson, Brooks, *Broadway*, 1970.

Baumbach, Jonathan, *The Landscape of Nightmare: Studies in the Contemporary American Novel*, 1965.

Beach, Joseph Warren, *American Fiction 1920–1940*, 1941.

Beach, Sylvia, *Shakespeare and Company*, 1959.

Beidler, Philip D., *American Literature and the Experience of Vietnam*, 1982.

Bentley, Eric, *The Dramatic Event: An American Chronicle*, 1954.

Berthoff, Warner, *Fictions and Events*, 1971.
Berthoff, Warner, *A Literature Without Qualities: American Writing since 1945*, 1979.
Bigsby, C.W.E., *Confrontation and Commitment: A Study of Contemporary American Drama 1959–1966*, 1967.
Bigsby, C.W.E., editor, *The Black American Writer*, 2 vols., 1969.
Bigsby, C.W.E., editor, *The Second Black Renaissance*, 1980.
Bigsby, C.W.E., editor, *A Critical Introduction to Twentieth-Century American Drama*, 3 vols., 1982–85.
Blotner, Joseph, *The Modern American Political Novel 1900–1960*, 1966.
Bogan, Louise, *Achievement in American Poetry 1900–1950*, 1951.
Bone, Robert A., *The Negro Novel in America*, 1958; revised edition, 1965.
Boyers, Robert, editor, *Contemporary Poetry in America*, 1974.
Bradbury, John M., *The Fugitives: A Critical Account*, 1958.
Bradbury, John M., *Renaissance in the South: A Critical History of the Literature 1920–1960*, 1963.
Bradbury, Malcolm, and David Palmer, editors, *The American Novel and the Nineteen Twenties*, 1971.
Bradbury, Malcolm, *The Modern American Novel*, 1983.
Brooks, Cleanth, *Modern Poetry and the Tradition*, 1939.
Brooks, Cleanth, *The Hidden God*, 1963.
Broussard, Louis, *American Drama: Contemporary Allegory from Eugene O'Neill to Tennessee Williams*, 1962.
Brown, John Mason, *Two on the Aisle: Ten Years of the American Theatre in Performance*, 1938.
Bryant, Jerry H., *The Open Decision: The Contemporary American Novel and Its Intellectual Background*, 1970.
Charters, Samuel, *Some Poems/Poets: Studies in American Underground Poetry since 1945*, 1971.
Clurman, Harold, *The Fervent Years: The Story of the Group Theatre and the Thirties*, 1945.
Coffman, Stanley K., Jr., *Imagism: A Chapter for the History of Modern Poetry*, 1951.
Cohen, Sarah Blacher, *Comic Relief: Humor in Contemporary American Literature*, 1978.
Cohn, Ruby, *Dialogue in American Drama*, 1971.
Cooperman, Stanley, *World War I and the American Novel*, 1967.
Cowan, Louise, *The Fugitive Group: A Literary History*, 1959.
Cowley, Malcolm, *Exile's Return: A Narrative of Ideas*, 1934; revised edition, as *Exile's Return: A Literary Odyssey of the 1920's*, 1951.
Cowley, Malcolm, editor, *After the Genteel Tradition: American Writers since 1910*, 1937; revised edition, 1964.
Cowley, Malcolm, *A Second Flowering: Works and Days of the Lost Generation*, 1973.
Cowley, Malcolm, *—And I Worked at the Writer's Trade: Chapters of Literary History 1918–1978*, 1978.
Davis, Arthur P., *From the Dark Tower: Afro-American Writers (1900 to 1960)*, 1974.
Dembo, L.S., *Conceptions of Reality in Modern American Poetry*, 1966.
Deutsch, Helen, and Stella Hanau, *The Provincetown: A Story of the Theatre*, 1951.
Dickey, James, *Babel to Byzantium: Poets and Poetry Now*, 1968.
Donoghue, Denis, *Connoisseurs of Chaos: Ideas of Order in Modern American Poetry*, 1965.
Downer, Alan S., *Fifty Years of American Drama 1900–1950*, 1951.
Duberman, Martin, *Black Mountain: An Exploration in Community*, 1972.
Edel, Leon, *The Psychological Novel 1900–1950*, 1955; as *The Modern Psychological Novel*, 1959; revised edition, 1964.
Eisinger, Chester E., *Fiction of the Forties*, 1963.
Fabre, Geneviève, *Drumbeats, Masks, and Metaphors: Contemporary Afro-American Theatre*, translated by Melvin Dixon, 1983.
Fiedler, Leslie A., *Waiting for the End: The American Literary Scene from Hemingway to Baldwin*, 1964.
Fitch, Noel Riley, *Sylvia Beach and the Lost Generation: A History of Literary Paris in the Twenties and Thirties*, 1983.
Flanner, Janet, *Paris Was Yesterday 1925–1939*, edited by Irving Drutman, 1972.
Folsom, James K., *The American Western Novel*, 1966.
Folsom, James K., editor, *The Western: A Collection of Critical Essays*, 1979.
Fredman, Stephen, *Poet's Prose: The Crisis in American Verse*, 1984.
French, Warren, *The Social Novel at the End of an Era*, 1966.
French, Warren, editor, *The Twenties [Thirties, Forties, Fifties]: Fiction, Poetry, Drama*, 4 vols., 1967–75.
Friebert, Stuart, and David Young, editors, *A Field Guide to Contemporary Poetry and Poetics*, 1980.
Frohock, Wilbur M., *The Novel of Violence in America*, revised edition, 1958.
Fussell, Edwin, *Lucifer in Harness: American Meter, Metaphor, and Diction*, 1973.
Gaines, James R., *Wit's End: Days and Nights of the Algonquin Round Table*, 1977.
Galloway, David, *The Absurd Hero in American Fiction*, 1966; revised edition, 1970.
Gass, William H., *Fiction and the Figures of Life*, 1970.
Gassner, John, *Theatre at the Crossroads: Plays and Playwrights of the Mid-Century American Stage*, 1960.
Gayle, Addison, Jr., editor, *Black Expression: Essays by and about Black Americans in the Creative Arts*, 1969.
Gayle, Addison, Jr., *The Way of the New World: The Black Novel in America*, 1975.
Geismar, Maxwell, *Writers in Crisis: The American Novel Between Two Wars*, 1942.
Geismar, Maxwell, *The Last of the Provincials: The American Novel 1915–1925*, 1947.
Geismar, Maxwell, *Rebels and Ancestors: The American Novel 1890–1915*, 1953.
Geismar, Maxwell, *American Moderns: From Rebellion to Conformity*, 1958.
Gelfant, Blanche Housman, *The American City Novel*, 1954.
Gibson, Donald B., *The Politics of Literary Expression: A Study of Major Black Writers*, 1981.
Glicksberg, Charles I., *The Sexual Revolution in Modern American Literature*, 1971.
Gould, Jean, *American Women Poets: Pioneers of Modern Poetry*, 1980.
Gould, Jean, *Modern American Women Poets*, 1985.
Graff, Gerald, *Literature Against Itself: Literary Ideas in Modern Society*, 1979.
Gregory, Horace, and Marya Zaturenska, *A History of American Poetry 1900–1940*, 1946.
Guttmann, Allen, *The Wound in the Heart: America and the Spanish Civil War*, 1962.

Guttmann, Allen, *The Jewish Writer in America: Assimilation and the Crisis of Identity*, 1971.
Hall, Donald, *Remembering Poets*, 1978.
Handy, William, *Modern Fiction: A Formalist Approach*, 1971.
Hardwick, Elizabeth, *A View of My Own: Essays on Literature and Society*, 1962.
Harriman, Margaret Case, *The Vicious Circle: The Story of the Algonquin Round Table*, 1951.
Hassan, Ihab, *Radical Innocence: Studies in the Contemporary American Novel*, 1961.
Hassan, Ihab, *Contemporary American Literature 1945–1972*, 1973.
Hilfer, Anthony Channell, *The Revolt from the Village 1915–1930*, 1969.
Hill, Errol, editor, *The Theater of Black Americans: A Collection of Critical Essays*, 2 vols., 1980.
Hoffman, Daniel, editor, *Harvard Guide to Contemporary American Writing*, 1979.
Hoffman, Frederick J., *The Modern Novel in America 1900–1950*, 1951.
Hoffman, Frederick J., *The Twenties: American Writing in the Postwar Decade*, 1955; revised edition, 1962.
Holman, C. Hugh, *Windows on the World: Essays on American Social Fiction*, 1979.
Howard, Richard, *Alone with America: Essays on the Art of Poetry in the United States since 1950*, 1969; revised edition, 1980.
Huggins, Nathan, *Harlem Renaissance*, 1971.
Jackson, Blyden, *The Waiting Years: Essays on American Negro Literature*, 1976.
Jarrell, Randall, *Poetry and the Age*, 1953.
Jones, Peter G., *War and the Novelist: Appraising the American War Novel*, 1976.
Juhasz, Suzanne, *Naked and Fiery Forms: Modern American Poetry by Women*, 1976.
Kalstone, David, *Five Temperaments: Elizabeth Bishop, Robert Lowell, James Merrill, Adrienne Rich, John Ashbery*, 1977.
Karolides, Nicholas J., *The Pioneer in the American Novel 1900–1950*, 1967.
Kazin, Alfred, *Contemporaries*, 1962.
Kazin, Alfred, *Bright Book of Life: American Novelists and Storytellers from Hemingway to Mailer*, 1973.
Kenner, Hugh, *The Pound Era*, 1971.
Kenner, Hugh, *A Homemade World: The American Modernist Writers*, 1975.
Kerr, Walter, *Journey to the Center of the Theatre*, 1979.
Klein, Marcus, *After Alienation: American Novels in Mid-Century*, 1964.
Klein, Marcus, *Foreigners: The Making of American Literature 1900–1940*, 1981.
Klinkowitz, Jerome, *Literary Disruptions: The Making of a Post-Contemporary American Fiction*, 1975; revised edition, 1980.
Kostelanetz, Richard, *The End of Intelligent Writing: Literary Politics in America*, 1974.
Kramer, Dale, *Chicago Renaissance: The Literary Life in the Midwest 1900–1930*, 1966.
Krutch, Joseph Wood, *The American Drama since 1918: An Informal History*, 1939; revised edition, 1957.
Lacey, Paul A., *The Inner War: Forms and Themes in Recent American Poetry*, 1972.
Langner, Lawrence, *The Magic Curtain*, 1951.
Lee, Robert Edson, *From West to East: Studies in the Literature of the American West*, 1966.
Lehan, Richard, *A Dangerous Crossing: French Literary Existentialism and the Modern American Novel*, 1973.
Levertov, Denise, *The Poet in the World*, 1973.
Lieberman, Laurence, *Unassigned Frequencies: American Poetry in Review 1964–77*, 1977.
Lowell, Amy, *Tendencies in Modern American Poetry*, 1917.
Madden, David, editor, *Tough Guy Writers of the Thirties*, 1968.
Madden, David, editor, *Proletarian Writers of the Thirties*, 1968.
Madden, David, editor, *American Dreams, American Nightmares*, 1970.
Malin, Irving, *New American Gothic*, 1962.
Malin, Irving, *Jews and Americans*, 1965.
Malkoff, Karl, *Escape from the Self: A Study in Contemporary American Poetry and Poetics*, 1977.
Margolies, Edward, *Native Sons: A Critical Study of Twentieth-Century Negro American Authors*, 1968.
Mariani, Paul, *A Usable Past: Essays in Modern and Contemporary Poetry*, 1984.
Mathews, Jane DeHart, *The Federal Theatre 1935–1939: Plays, Relief, and Politics*, 1967.
McCarthy, Mary, *Sights and Spectacles 1937–1956*, 1956; augmented edition, as *Theatre Chronicles 1937–1962*, 1963.
Miller, J. Hillis, *Poets of Reality: Six Twentieth-Century Writers*, 1965.
Miller, James E., Jr., *The American Quest for a Supreme Fiction: Whitman's Legacy in the Personal Epic*, 1979.
Millgate, Michael, *American Social Fiction: James to Cozzens*, 1964.
Mills, Ralph J., Jr., *Contemporary American Poetry*, 1965.
Mordden, Ethan, *The American Theatre*, 1981.
Nemerov, Howard, *Figures of Thought: Speculations on the Meaning of Poetry and Other Essays*, 1978.
Olderman, Raymond M., *Beyond the Waste Land: A Study of the American Novel in the Nineteen-Sixties*, 1972.
Parkinson, Thomas, editor, *A Casebook on the Beat*, 1961.
Perkins, David, *A History of Modern Poetry: From the 1890's to the High Modernist Mode*, 1976.
Phillips, Robert, *The Confessional Poets*, 1963.
Pinsker, Sanford, *The Schlemiel as Metaphor: Studies in the Yiddish and American-Jewish Novel*, 1971.
Pinsky, Robert, *The Situation of Poetry: Contemporary Poetry and Its Traditions*, 1976.
Pizer, Donald G., *Twentieth-Century American Literary Naturalism*, 1982.
Podhoretz, Norman, *Doings and Undoings: The Fifties and After in American Writing*, 1964.
Poirier, Richard, *The Performing Self: Compositions and Decompositions in the Language of Contemporary Life*, 1971.
Quinn, M. Bernetta, *The Metamorphic Tradition in Modern Poetry*, 1955.
Rabkin, Gerald, *Drama and Commitment: Politics in the American Theatre of the 1930's*, 1964.
Rahv, Philip, *Essays on Literature and Politics 1932–72*, edited by Arabel J. Porter and Andrew J. Dvorsin, 1978.
Ransom, John Crowe, *The New Criticism*, 1941.
Rexroth, Kenneth, *American Poetry in the Twentieth Century*, 1971.
Rideout, Walter B., *The Radical Novel in the United States 1900–1954*, 1956.
Rosenblatt, Roger, *Black Fiction*, 1974.

Rosenthal, M.L., *The Modern Poets: A Critical Introduction*, 1960.
Scholes, Robert, *The Fabulators*, 1967.
Shapiro, Karl, *The Poetry Wreck: Selected Essays 1950–1970*, 1975.
Simpson, Louis, *A Revolution in Taste: Studies of Dylan Thomas, Allen Ginsberg, Sylvia Plath, and Robert Lowell*, 1978.
Singal, Daniel J., *The War Within: From Victorian to Modernist Thought in the South 1919–1945*, 1982.
Solotaroff, Theodore, *The Red Hot Vacuum and Other Pieces on the Writing of the Sixties*, 1970.
Spears, Monroe K., *Dionysus and the City: Modernism in Twentieth-Century Poetry*, 1970.
Spiller, Robert E., editor, *A Time of Harvest: American Literature 1910–1960*, 1962.
Stanford, Donald E., *Revolution and Convention in Modern Poetry*, 1983.
Stewart, John L., *The Burden of Time: The Fugitives and Agrarians*, 1965.
Sutton, Walter, *American Free Verse: The Modern Revolution in Poetry*, 1973.
Swados, Harvey, *The American Writers and the Great Depression*, 1966.
Tanner, Tony, *City of Words: American Fiction 1950–1970*, 1971.
Taubman, Howard, *The Making of the American Theatre*, 1965; revised edition, 1967.
Taylor, Gordon O., *Chapters of Experience: Studies in Twentieth-Century American Autobiography*, 1983.
Thorp, Willard, *American Writing in the Twentieth Century*, 1960.
Thurber, James, *The Years with Ross* (on the *New Yorker* magazine), 1959.
Thurley, Geoffrey, *The American Moment: American Poetry in the Mid-Century*, 1977.
Tuttleton, James W., *The Novel of Manners in America*, 1972.
Tytell, John, *Naked Angels: The Lives and Literature of the Beat Generation*, 1976.
Valgemae, Mardi, *Accelerated Grimace: Expressionism in the American Drama of the 1920's*, 1972.
Vendler, Helen, *Part of Nature, Part of Us: Modern American Poets*, 1980.
Weales, Gerald, *American Drama since World War II*, 1962.
Weales, Gerald, *The Jumping-Off Place: American Drama in the 1960's*, 1969.
Weatherhead, A. Kingsley, *The Edge of the Image*, 1967.
Werner, Craig Hansen, *Paradoxical Resolutions: American Fiction since James Joyce*, 1982.
West, Ray B., *The Short Story in America 1900–1950*, 1952.
Widmer, Kingsley, *The Literary Rebel*, 1965.
Williams, Ellen, *Harriet Monroe and the Poetry Renaissance: The First Ten Years of "Poetry" 1912–1922*, 1977.
Williamson, Alan, *Introspection and Contemporary Poetry*, 1984.
Wilson, Edmund, *The Shores of Light: A Literary Chronicle of the Twenties and Thirties*, 1952.
Wilson, Edmund, *Classics and Commercials: A Literary Chronicle of the Forties*, 1960.
Wilson, Edmund, *The Bit Between My Teeth: A Literary Chronicle of 1950–1965*, 1965.
Winters, Yvor, *On Modern Poets*, 1959.
Witham, W. Tasker, *The Adolescent in the American Novel 1920–1960*, 1964.
Writers at Work: The Paris Review Interviews, 1958—

WRITERS

ADAMS, Henry (Brooks). Born in Boston, Massachusetts, 16 February 1838; great grandson of John Adams, grandson of John Quincy Adams, and son of the writer Charles Francis Adams. Educated at Harvard University, Cambridge, Massachusetts, 1854–58, A.B. 1858; studied law at the University of Berlin, 1858–59. Married Marian Hooper in 1872 (died, 1885). Lived in Dresden, 1859–60; traveled in Italy, writing for the Boston *Courier*, 1860; private secretary to his father, when Congressman from Massachusetts, in Washington, D.C., 1860–61, and when Minister to the Court of St. James, London, 1861–68; lived in Washington, D.C., and again in London, contributing to various American periodicals, 1869; editor, *North American Review*, Boston, and Assistant Professor of History, Harvard University, 1870–77; settled in Washington, D.C.; in later life spent six months in each year in France. President, American Historical Society, 1894. Recipient: Loubat Prize, for history, 1893; Pulitzer Prize, for autobiography, 1919. LL.D.: Western Reserve University, Cleveland, 1892. Member, American Academy of Arts and Letters. *Died 27 March 1918.*

PUBLICATIONS

Collections

Letters, edited by Worthington Chauncey Ford. 2 vols., 1930–38.
A Henry Adams Reader, edited by Elizabeth Stevenson. 1958.
The Education of Henry Adams and Other Selected Writings, edited by Edward N. Saveth. 1965.
Letters, edited by J.C. Levenson and others. 1983—
Novels, Mont Saint Michel, The Education (Library of America), edited by Ernest and Jayne N. Samuels. 1983.

Fiction

Democracy: An American Novel. 1880.
Esther. 1884.

Other

Chapters of Erie and Other Essays, with Charles Francis Adams, Jr. 1871.
Essays in Anglo-Saxon Law, with others. 1876.
The Life of Albert Gallatin. 1879.
John Randolph. 1882; revised edition, 1883.
History of the United States of America During the Administration of Jefferson and Madison. 9 vols., 1889–91; abridged version, edited by Herbert Agar, as *The Formative Years*, 2 vols., 1947; complete edition, edited by Earl Harbert (Library of America), 2 vols., 1986.
Historical Essays. 1891.
Memoirs of Marau, Last Queen of Tahiti. 1893; as *Memoirs of Arii*, 1901; edited by Robert E. Spiller, as *Tahiti: Memoirs of Arii Taimai*, 1947.
Recognition of Cuban Independence. 1896.
Mont-Saint-Michel and Chartres. 1904; revised edition, 1912.
The Education of Henry Adams: An Autobiography. 1907; edited by Ernest Samuels, 1974.
A Letter to American Teachers of History. 1910.
The Life of George Cabot Lodge. 1911.
The Degradation of the Democratic Dogma. 1919.
Letters to a Niece and Prayer to the Virgin of Chartres, edited by Mabel La Farge. 1920.
The Great Secession Winter of 1860–61 and Other Essays, edited by George Hochfield. 1958.

Editor, *Documents Relating to New England Federalism 1800–1815*. 1877.
Editor, *The Writings of Albert Gallatin*. 3 vols., 1879.
Editor, with Clara Louise Hay, *Letters of John Hay and Extracts from Diary*. 3 vols., 1908.

*

Bibliography: *Adams: A Reference Guide* by Earl Harbert, 1978.

Critical Studies: *The Young Adams, Adams: The Middle Years*, and *Adams: The Major Phase* by Ernest Samuels, 3 vols., 1948–64; *Adams: Scientific Historian* by William H. Jordy, 1952; *Adams: A Biography* by Elizabeth Stevenson, 1955; *The Mind and Art of Adams* by J.C. Levenson, 1957; *Adams* by George Hochfield, 1962; *The Suspension of Adams: A Study of Manner and Matter* by Vern Wagner, 1970; *A Formula of His Own: Adams's Literary Experiment* by John Conder, 1970; *Symbol and Idea in Adams* by Melvin E. Lyon, 1970; *The Circle of Adams: Art and Artists* by Ernst Scheyer, 1970; *Adams* by Louis Auchincloss, 1971; *Adams* by James G. Murray, 1974; *The Force So Much Closer Home: Adams and the Adams Family* by Earl Harbert, 1977, and *Critical Essays on Adams* edited by Harbert, 1981; *Adams* by R.P. Blackmur, edited by Veronica A. Makowsky, 1980; *Adams: The Myth of Failure* by William Dusinberre, 1980; *Adams and the American Experiment* by David R. Contesta, 1980; *Power and Order: Adams and the Naturalist Tradition in American Fiction* by Harold Kaplan, 1981; *The Virgin of Chartres: An Intellectual and Psychological History of the Work of Adams* by Joseph F. Byrnes, 1981; *Both Sides of the Ocean: A Biography of Adams, His First Life 1838–1862* by Edward Chalfant, 1982; *The Ironies of Progress: Adams and the American Dream* by William Wasserstrom, 1984.

* * *

Standing in much the same relation to American culture in the latter half of the 19th century that Emerson did to the earlier period, Henry Adams might be said to have made a distinguished and melancholy career out of being the right sensibility for the wrong time and place. Dedicated to public service but shunted to the sidelines, genuinely committed to the orderly development of democratic processes but disillusioned by the post-Civil War expansionism that has been called "The Big Barbecue," Adams gradually contracted the sphere of his idealism, his sociality, and the generosity of his responses to a diminished center of bleak pessimism. Even so, this proved to be a sufficient base on which was built a noteworthy career as teacher (Harvard University), editor (*North American Review*), novelist (*Democracy* and *Esther*), and historian. The two novels deal with pressing issues of the period, the growth of business in government and the strength of science in terms of religious dogma. It is, however, in his twin meditations, *Mont-Saint-Michel and Chartres* and *The Education of Henry Adams*, that his erudition and mastery of the ironic mode fuse with a sombre lyricism to produce a pair of eccentric masterpieces that combine autobiography, philosophy of history, and saturnine prophecy.

Respectively subtitled "A Study of Thirteenth-Century Unity" and "A Study of Twentieth-Century Multiplicity," the books establish the figures of the virgin and the dynamo as the historically dominant symbols of forces that shape the values, the social organization, and the concepts of personality in both time-periods. The replacement of the former by the latter, in Adams's view, exemplifies what he believed to be the scientific principle of the acceleration of history. In these terms he attempts to understand and explain the loss of stable certitudes, the increased fragmentation of social groups, and the new burden of impotence and isolation on the individual psyche. Adams doubtless believed that his own shattered private life was an accurate reflection of this larger social and metaphysical explosion, and this personal despair lends a tone of mordant authority to his prose which almost precisely counters the accents of Emerson's optimism. Brilliant, acerbic, and unsparing in its effort to conduct a grim cultural biopsy. Adams's work consummately articulates the outrage of the Genteel Tradition and stands as a major formulation of the ideology that would later be expressed by such alienated writers as Eliot and Pound.

—Earl Rovit

See the essays on *Democracy* and *The Education of Henry Adams*.

ADE, George. Born in Kentland, Indiana, 9 February 1866. Educated at local schools, and Purdue University, Lafayette, Indiana, 1883–87 (editor, *Purdue*), B.S. 1887. Reporter, Lafayette *Morning News*, 1888, and Lafayette *Call*, 1888–90; advertising writer, 1888; worked for Chicago *Morning News*, later *News-Record*, then the *Record*, 1890–1900: from 1893 collaborated with cartoonist John T. McCutcheon on a daily illustrated column about Chicago life ("Stories of the Street and of the Town"); settled on a farm near Brook, Indiana, 1904. Delegate, Republican National Convention, 1908; trustee, Purdue University, 1908–15, and promoted the Ross-Ade Stadium at Purdue, 1923–24; Grand Consul, Sigma Chi fraternity, 1909; publicity director, Indiana State Council of Defense, 1917–18; member, Indiana Commission for the Chicago World's Fair, 1933. L.H.D.: Purdue University, 1926; LL.D.: Indiana University, Bloomington, 1927. Member, American Academy, 1908. *Died 16 May 1944.*

PUBLICATIONS

Collections

The Permanent Ade, edited by Fred C. Kelly. 1947.
The America of Ade: Fables, Short Stories, Essays, edited by Jean Shepherd. 1961.
Letters, edited by Terence Tobin. 1973.
The Best of Ade, edited by A.L. Lazarus. 1985.

Fiction

Stories of the Street and of the Town. 8 vols., 1894–1900; collected edition, 1941; as *Chicago Stories*, 1963.
What a Man Sees Who Goes Away from Home. 1896.
Circus Day. 1896.
Stories from History. 1896.
Artie. 1896.
Pink Marsh. 1897.
Doc' Horne. 1899.
Fables in Slang. 1900.
More Fables. 1900.
Forty Modern Fables. 1901.
Grouch at the Game. 1901.
The Girl Proposition. 1902.
People You Know. 1903.
Circus Day. 1903.
Handsome Cyril. 1903.
Clarence Allen. 1903.
In Babel. 1903.
Rollo Johnson. 1904.
Breaking into Society. 1904.
True Bills. 1904.
In Pastures New. 1906.
The Slim Princess. 1907.
I Knew Him When—. 1910.
Hoosier Hand Book. 1911.
Knocking the Neighbors. 1912.
Ade's Fables. 1914.
Hand-Made Fables. 1920.
Single Blessedness and Other Observations. 1922.
Stay with Me Flagons. 1922.
Bang! Bang! 1928.

Plays

The Back-Stair Investigation (produced 1897).
The Night of the Fourth (produced 1901).
The Sultan of Sulu, music by Alfred G. Wathall (produced 1902). 1903.
The County Chairman (produced 1903). 1924.
Peggy from Paris, music by William Loraine (produced 1903).
Bird Center: Cap Fry's Birthday Party (produced 1904).
The Sho-Gun, music by Gustav Luders (produced 1904).
The College Widow (produced 1904). 1924.
Just Out of College (produced 1905). 1924.
The Bad Samaritan (produced 1905).
Marse Covington (produced 1906). 1918.
Artie (produced 1907).
Father and the Boys (produced 1908). 1924.
Mrs. Peckham's Carouse (produced 1908).
The Fair Co-ed, music by Gustav Luders (produced 1909).
The City Chap (produced 1910).
U.S. Minister Bedloe (produced 1910).
The Old Town (produced 1910).
The Mayor and the Manicure (produced 1912). 1923.
Nettie (produced 1914). 1923.
Speaking to Father. 1923.
The Persecuted Wife, in *Liberty*, 4 July 1925.
The Willing Performer, in *The Country Gentleman*, February 1928.
Aunt Fanny from Chautauqua. 1949.

Screenplays: many short films, and the following: *Our Leading Citizen*, with Waldemar Young, 1922; *Back Home and Broke*, with J. Clarkson Miller, 1922; *Woman-Proof*, with Tom Geraghty, 1923; *The Confidence Man*, with others, 1924; *Old Home Week*, with Tom Geraghty, 1925; *Freshman Love*, with Earl Felton and George Bricker, 1936.

Verse

Verses and Jingles. 1911.

Other

The Old-Time Saloon (essays). 1931.
Revived Remarks on Mark Twain, edited by George Hiram Brownell. 1936.
One Afternoon with Mark Twain. 1939.

Editor, *An Invitation to You and Your Folks, from Jim and Some More of the Home Folks*. 1916.

*

Bibliography: *A Bibliography of Ade* by Dorothy R. Russo, 1947.

Critical Studies: *Ade, Warmhearted Satirist* by Fred C. Kelly, 1947; *Ade* by Lee Coyle, 1964; "Ade: The City Uncle" by Edmund Wilson, in *The Bit Between My Teeth*, 1965; *Small Town Chicago: The Comic Perspective of Finley Peter Dunne, Ade, and Ring Lardner* by James DeMuth, 1980.

* * *

Born in a small Indiana town in 1866, George Ade grew up fascinated with the talk around main-street shops and country stores. While attending Purdue College (later University) he became an avid theater-goer, rarely missing a minstrel show or musical comedy at the Lafayette Opera House. Not surprisingly, transcribing speech and writing plays became his lucrative livelihood. Following a stint as a hometown newspaper man, Ade went up to Chicago in 1890 to join his friend, the cartoonist John T. McCutcheon, on the Chicago *Morning News*.

In 1893 these two collaborated on a daily illustrated column, "All Roads Lead to the World's Fair," a potpourri of interviews and observations centered on the Columbian Exposition. After the Fair closed, their column continued as "Stories of the Streets and of the Town." Taking all Chicago as their province, Ade and McCutcheon described urban life and common speech in hundreds of vivid sketches. Stylistically, Ade experimented in the "Stories" with straight narrative, light verse, dramatic dialogue, and various ethnic dialects. The pieces were popular enough to be saved and sold in eight paperback collections between 1894 and 1900. Ade also extracted three recurring characters, stitched their scattered appearances into sustained narratives, and published the results as *Artie*, *Pink Marsh*, and *Doc' Horne*. The title characters were, respectively, a brash street-wise office worker, a black shoeshine boy in a basement barbershop, and a genial yarn-spinner living at the Alfalfa European Hotel. Not coherent enough to be considered novels, these books remain important as pioneering realistic transcriptions of urban vernacular voices—particularly Artie's colorful slang and Pink's northern Negro dialect.

Ade's best work is in his "Fables in Slang," the first of which appeared in the "Streets and Towns" column in 1897 after Ade had asked himself, "why not retain the archaic form and the stilted manner of composition (of the fable) and, for purposes of novelty, permit the language to be 'fly,' modern, undignified, quite up to the moment?" The fables became a regular Saturday feature, and were soon syndicated and collected into book form. Nine additional collections followed, the last in 1920. Most of Ade's fables were gently satiric exempla of pretension and folly, set in midwestern small towns or in Chicago, and capped by incongruous, undercutting moral tag lines. They follow his earlier work in reproducing familiar character types and common street talk. His master stroke was the use of capital letters for comic and ironic emphasis of the tendency of such talk toward platitudes and slang: "One morning a Modern Solomon, who had been chosen to preside as Judge in a divorce Mill, climbed to his Perch and unbuttoned his Vest for the Wearisome Grind." The fables brought to literary visibility a host of ordinary people: the bombastic preacher and the travelling salesman, college students, bohemian writers and fast-talking vaudevillians, and numbers of country folk lost in the city. They are valuable as a microcosm of midwestern middle-class life at the turn of the century. More important, Ade's use of the vernacular instead of genteel-academic English provided a shot of vitality to the language, and helped make it more flexible for the next generation of American writers.

During his most productive decade, 1900–10, Ade also wrote over a dozen plays. Three were very successful on Broadway: *The Sultan of Sulu*, a musical-comedy satire on American assumption of the "white man's burden" in the South Pacific: *The County Chairman*, a comedy-drama about politics in the rural midwest; and his best play, *The College Widow*, which introduced college life and football to the American stage.

—Charles Fanning

AGEE, James (Rufus). Born in Knoxville, Tennessee, 27 November 1909. Educated at St. Andrews School, Sewanee, Tennessee, 1919–24; Knoxville High School, 1924–25; Phillips Exeter Academy, Exeter, New Hampshire, 1925–28; Harvard University, Cambridge, Massachusetts (editor, *Harvard Advocate*), 1928–32, A.B. 1932. Married 1) Olivia Saunders in 1933 (divorced, 1937); 2) Alma Mailman, one son; 3) Mia Fritsch in 1946, one daughter. Staff writer, *Fortune* and *Time* magazines, New York, 1932–48: film reviewer for *Time*, 1939–48; film critic, *Nation*, New York, 1942–48. Co-director of film *In the Street*, 1948. Recipient: American Academy award, 1949; Pulitzer Prize, 1958. *Died 16 May 1955.*

PUBLICATIONS

Collections

Collected Poems and *Collected Short Prose* (includes excerpt of screenplay *Man's Fate*), edited by Robert Fitzgerald. 2 vols., 1968.

Fiction

The Morning Watch. 1951.
A Death in the Family. 1957.
Four Early Stories, edited by Elena Harap. 1964.

Plays

Agee on Film 2: Five Film Scripts (includes *The Blue Hotel, The African Queen, The Bride Comes to Yellow Sky, The Night of the Hunter, Noa Noa*). 1960.

Screenplays: *The Quiet One* (documentary), 1949; *The African Queen*, with John Huston, 1951; *Genghis Khan* (English commentary), 1952; *The Bride Comes to Yellow Sky* (episode in *Face to Face*), 1953; *White Mane* (English commentary), 1953; *Green Magic* (English commentary), 1954; *The Night of the Hunter*, 1955.

Television Scripts: for *Omnibus* series, 1953.

Verse

Permit Me Voyage. 1934.

Other

Let Us Now Praise Famous Men: Three Tenant Families, photographs by Walker Evans. 1941.
Agee on Film: Reviews and Comments. 1958.
Letters to Father Flye. 1962; revised edition, 1971.
A Way of Seeing: Photographs of New York, photographs by Helen Levitt. 1965.
Selected Journalism, edited by Paul Ashdown. 1985.

*

Bibliography: by Genevieve Fabre, in *Bulletin of Bibliography 24*, 1965; *John Hersey and Agee: A Reference Guide* by Nancy Lyman Huse, 1978; *Agee: An Annotated Bibliography of Published Primary and Secondary Sources 1925–1985* by Nancy Jane Richards, 1986.

Critical Studies: *Agee* by Peter H. Ohlin, 1966; *Agee: Promise and Fulfillment* by Kenneth Seib, 1969; *Agee* by Erling Larsen, 1971; *A Way of Seeing: A Critical Study of Agee* by Alfred T. Barson, 1972; *Remembering Agee* edited by David Madden, 1974; *Irony in the Mind's Life: Essays on Novels by Agee, Elizabeth Bowen, and George Eliot* by Robert Coles, 1974; *Agee* by Victor A. Kramer, 1975; *Agee: A Study of His Film Criticism* by John J. Snyder, 1977; *The Restless Journey of Agee* by Genevieve Moreau, 1977; *Tell Me Who I Am: Agee's Search for Selfhood* by Mark A. Doty, 1981; *Agee: A Life* by Laurence Bergreen, 1984; *Agee: His Life Remembered* edited by Ross Spears and Jude Cassidy, 1985; *American Silences: The Realism of Agee, Walker Evans, and Edward Hopper* by J.A. Ward, 1985.

* * *

In 1941 James Agee and the photographer Walker Evans published *Let Us Now Praise Famous Men*. A long, journalistic piece that would become the central fixture of Agee's critical fame, the book was the result of eight months that he and Evans had spent in Alabama sympathetically chronicling in prose and photographs the daily lives of sharecropper families in the deep South.

Prior to the appearance of *Let Us Now Praise Famous Men*, Agee had published a book of poetry, *Permit Me Voyage*, as well as many magazine articles—most of them anonymously—as a member of the staff of *Fortune*. He had also begun writing film criticism for *Time*, an activity which he continued for *The Nation* and which signaled the beginnings of a deep involvement with cinema, not only as an outspoken critic of the medium but also as a writer of highly detailed screenplays.

Let Us Now Praise Famous Men and his film work aside, Agee is best remembered for his novels, *The Morning Watch* and *A Death in the Family*, the latter published two years after his death, earning him a posthumous Pulitzer Prize. Largely autobiographical, both novels reveal the influence in Agee's life and work of two elemental facts of his childhood: the death of his father when Agee was six years old, and the religious piety of his mother, a piety with which he would constantly struggle. *The Morning Watch*, for instance, is the story of a young student at a religious school who grows away from orthodoxy toward self-awareness and, eventually, alienation. And in *A Death in the Family* the young protagonist's father has been killed in an automobile accident—as Agee's own father had been killed—leaving the boy and his family to cope with his absence, even as had the Agee family.

Many critics have felt that Agee failed to reach the artistic achievement for which he seemed destined. Never one to settle on a particular genre, they point out, he chose instead to try it all: poetry, journalism, fiction, criticism, screenplays. And never one to care for his own health, he lived, as film director John Huston wrote, as though "body destruction was implicit in his make-up." Still, Agee achieved much in his 45 years, and his premature death meant, finally, that his greatest fame would have to come posthumously.

—Bruce A. Lohof

AIKEN, Conrad (Potter). Born in Savannah, Georgia, 5 August 1889. Educated at Middlesex School, Concord, Massachusetts; Harvard University, Cambridge, Massachusetts (President, *Harvard Advocate*), 1907–10, 1911–12, A.B. 1912. Married 1) Jessie McDonald in 1912 (divorced, 1929), one son and two daughters, the writers Jane Aiken Hodge and Joan Aiken; 2) Clarissa M. Lorenz in 1930 (divorced, 1937); 3) Mary Hoover in 1937. Contributing editor, *The Dial*, New York, 1916–19; American correspondent, *Athenaeum*, London, 1919–25, and London *Mercury*, 1921–22; lived in London, 1921–26 and 1930–39; Instructor, Harvard University, 1927–28; London correspondent, *New Yorker*, 1934–36; lived in Brewster, Massachusetts, from 1940, and Savannah after 1962. Fellow, 1947, and Consultant in Poetry, 1950–52, Library of Congress, Washington, D.C. Recipient: Pulitzer Prize, 1930; Shelley Memorial Award, 1930; Guggenheim fellowship, 1934; National Book Award, 1954; Bollingen Prize, 1956; Academy of American Poets fellowship, 1957; American Academy Gold Medal, 1958; Huntington Hartford Foundation award, 1960; Brandeis University Creative Arts Award, 1967; National Medal for Literature, 1969. Member, American Academy, 1957. *Died 17 August 1973.*

PUBLICATIONS

Collections

Selected Letters, edited by Joseph Killorin. 1978.

Verse

Earth Triumphant and Other Tales in Verse. 1914.
The Jig of Forslin: A Symphony. 1916.
Turns and Movies and Other Tales in Verse. 1916.
Nocturne of Remembered Spring and Other Poems. 1917.
The Charnel Rose, Senlin: A Biography, and Other Poems. 1918.
The House of Dust: A Symphony. 1920.
Punch: The Immortal Liar. 1921.
The Pilgrimage of Festus. 1923.
Priapus and the Pool and Other Poems. 1925.
(*Poems*), edited by Louis Untermeyer. 1927.
Prelude. 1929.
Selected Poems. 1929.
John Deth: A Metaphysical Legend, and Other Poems. 1930.
Preludes for Memnon. 1931.
The Coming Forth by Day of Osiris Jones. 1931.
Landscape West of Eden. 1934.
Time in the Rock: Preludes to Definition. 1936.
And in the Human Heart. 1940.
Brownstone Eclogues and Other Poems. 1942.
The Soldier. 1944.
The Kid. 1947.
The Divine Pilgrim. 1949.
Skylight One: Fifteen Poems. 1949.
Collected Poems. 1953.
A Letter from Li Po and Other Poems. 1955.
The Flute Player. 1956.
Sheepfold Hill: Fifteen Poems. 1958.
Selected Poems. 1961.
The Morning Song of Lord Zero: Poems Old and New. 1963.
A Seizure of Limericks. 1964.
Preludes. 1966.
Thee. 1967.
The Clerk's Journal, Being the Diary of a Queer Man: An Undergraduate Poem, Together with a Brief Memoir of Dean LeBaron Russell Briggs, T.S. Eliot, and Harvard, in 1911. 1971.
Collected Poems 1916–1970. 1970.
A Little Who's Zoo of Mild Animals. 1977.

Play

Mr. Arcularis (produced 1949). 1957.

Fiction

Bring! Bring! and Other Stories. 1925.
Blue Voyage. 1927.
Costumes by Eros. 1928.
Gehenna. 1930.
Great Circle. 1933.
Among the Lost People (stories). 1934.
King Coffin. 1935.
A Heart for the Gods of Mexico. 1939.
Conversation; or, Pilgrims' Progress. 1940; as *The Conversation*, 1948.
The Short Stories. 1950.
The Collected Short Stories. 1960.
The Collected Novels. 1964.

Other

Scepticisms: Notes on Contemporary Poetry. 1919.
Ushant: An Essay (autobiography). 1952.
A Reviewer's ABC: Collected Criticism from 1916 to the Present, edited by Rufus A. Blanshard. 1958; as *Collected Criticism*, 1968.
Cats and Bats and Things with Wings (for children). 1965.
Tom, Sue, and the Clock (for children). 1966.

Editor, *Modern American Poets*. 1922; revised edition, 1927; revised edition, as *Twentieth Century American Poetry*, 1945; revised edition, 1963.
Editor, *Selected Poems of Emily Dickinson*. 1924.
Editor, *American Poetry 1671–1928: A Comprehensive Anthology*. 1929; revised edition, as *A Comprehensive Anthology of American Poetry*, 1944.
Editor, with William Rose Benét, *An Anthology of Famous English and American Poetry*. 1945.

*

Bibliography: *Aiken: A Bibliography (1902–1978)* by F.W. and F.C. Bonnell, 1982; *Aiken: Critical Recognition 1914–1981: A Bibliographic Guide* by Catherine Kirk Harris, 1983.

Critical Studies: *Aiken: A Life of His Art* by Jay Martin, 1962; *Aiken* by Frederick J. Hoffman, 1962; *Aiken* by Reuel Denney, 1964; *Lorelei Two: My Life with Aiken* by Clarissa M. Lorenz, 1983.

* * *

Characteristically, Conrad Aiken himself raises the essential critical problem in a note he wrote in 1917: "It is difficult to place Conrad Aiken in the poetic firmament, so difficult that one sometimes wonders whether he deserves a place there at all" (*Collected Criticism*). The problem is further complicated by the fact that Aiken was not only a poet, but also a respected novelist and critic. The list of his admirers is persuasive: R.P. Blackmur, Allen Tate, Malcolm Lowry all find in him one of the central voices of his age. Yet to the contemporary reader such claims are likely to seem excessive.

About the scope of his ambition there can be no doubt. Five long, complicated novels; many lengthy poetic sequences, or "symphonies," dealing with themes as varied, and as large, as the history of America (*The Kid*), the importance of his Puritan heritage ("Mayflower"), the problems of the self encountering the realities of love and death (*Preludes for Memnon* and *The Coming Forth by Day of Osiris Jones*): all testify to the courageous attempt to convey a rich, complex life in a wide-ranging, always technically experimental, art.

The centre of this art lies in maintaining the difficult balance between aesthetic purity and formal perfection on the one hand, and the menacing chaos of terrifying experience on the other. It is tempting to relate this to Aiken's very early experience as a child when he discovered the bodies of his parents after a mutual suicide pact: this moment is placed at the centre of his long autobiographical essay *Ushant*. This deeply buried memory may also have encouraged Aiken's passionate interest in Freud. The five novels show this interest everywhere: the hero of *Blue Voyage*, Demarest, is on a voyage of self-discovery through journey, quest, and dream. This novel, like *Great Circle*—which Freud himself admired—is an elaborate metaphor for the author's psychic search, the exploration of his own consciousness. At their best, the novels find a language for disturbing, hidden states of the psyche: the combination of thriller form and psychoanalytic imagery in *King Coffin* is uniquely memorable. But too often the novels slip into vagueness and imprecision. As Frederick J. Hoffman has observed, their separate parts fail *quite* to cohere. The lack of adequate characterisation, and the over-literariness of the enterprise, are at odds with our valid expectations of prose fiction. It is significant, then, that Aiken's "autobiography," *Ushant*, should seem to so many of his critics his finest achievement in prose. Here, Aiken as writer, and his literary friends, including Eliot and Pound, are at the centre of a "fictionalised" account of the author's life. Apart from its other intrinsic interests, this quite extraordinary, unclassifiable work is justified, almost alone, by the majestic sweep and lyrical seductiveness of Aiken's rhetoric.

It is this majestic rhetoric that one also recognises in the poetry: Malcolm Lowry referred to Aiken as "the truest and most direct descendant of our own great Elizabethans." This quality is immediately apparent in *Preludes for Memnon*:

> What dignity can death bestow on us,
> Who kiss beneath a street lamp, or hold hands
> Half hidden in a taxi, or replete
> With coffee, figs and Barsac make our way
> To a dark bedroom in a wormworn house?

The combination here of the common and quotidian—street lamp, taxi, coffee—with noble, "Elizabethan" cadences, is the characteristic Aiken manner. It is a manner that frequently skirts parody and pastiche, but equally often rises to a rich, solemn verbal music. In poem after poem in his enormous output, Aiken sustains a long, flowing musical line, celebrating, as in "Landscape West of Eden," the capacity of language to order the chaos of the unaccommodated self. What one misses, however, in too much of this poetry, and what contributes to a certain lack of *energy* in the verse, is any intense verbal particularity, or, often, the sense of real feeling significantly expressed. In *Time in the Rock*, one of his most ambitious pieces, there is little sense of any real pressure or urgency behind the words; they have a tendency, as it were, to slip off the edge of the page as we read; nothing seems to make it all *cohere*.

His more objective, "dramatic" poems, like *The Kid* and "Mayflower," with their incorporation of historical and legendary material and their evocations of New England landscape and geography, are perhaps more valuable, in the end, than his lyrical self-communings. The contemporary reader is also likely to be more drawn to the lighter side of Aiken: in a poem like "Blues for Ruby Matrix" the rhetoric remains, but allied now to a delightful sexiness and tenderness.

Whatever the mode, however, there is always in Aiken, even if only residually, that sense of horror, of terror, and of death—"The sombre note that gives the chord its power," as he puts it in "Palimpsest"—that gives the best poetry its capacity to hurt and wound us. When, in *Preludes for Memnon*, he defines the role of the poet, Aiken finds a definition that takes full note of this fundamental ground-bass of his own work: the poet is one who

> by imagination [apes]
> God, the supreme poet of despair . . .
> Knowing the rank intolerable taste of death,
> And walking dead on the living still earth.

—Neil Corcoran

ALBEE, Edward (Franklin, III). Born in Virginia, 12 March 1928; adopted as an infant. Educated at Lawrenceville School; Valley Forge Military Academy, Pennsylvania; Choate School, Connecticut, graduated 1946; Trinity College, Hartford, Connecticut, 1946–47. Served in the U.S. Army. Radio writer, WNYC, office boy, Warwick and Legler, record salesman, Bloomingdale's, book salesman, G. Schirmer, counterman, Manhattan Towers Hotel, messenger, Western Union, 1955–58, all in New York; producer, with Richard Barr and Clinton Wilder, New Playwrights Unit Workshop, later Albarwild Theatre Arts, and Albar Productions, New York; also a stage director. Founder, William Flanagan Center for Creative Persons, Montauk, Long Island, New York, 1971. U.S. cultural exchange visitor to the U.S.S.R. Recipient: Berlin Festival award, 1959, 1961; Vernon Rice Award, 1960; Obie award, 1960; Argentine Critics award, 1961; Lola D'Annunzio Award, 1961; New York Drama Critics Circle award, 1964; Outer Circle award, 1964; London *Evening Standard* award, 1964; Tony award, 1964; Margo Jones Award, 1965; Pulitzer Prize, 1967, 1975; American Academy Gold Medal, 1980; Brandeis University Creative Arts Award, 1983, 1984. D. Litt.: Emerson College, Boston, 1967; Litt. D.: Trinity College, 1974. Member, American Academy, 1966. Lives in Montauk, Long Island, New York.

PUBLICATIONS

Plays

The Zoo Story (produced 1959). In *The Zoo Story, The Death of Bessie Smith, The Sandbox*, 1960.
The Death of Bessie Smith (produced 1960). Included in *The Zoo Story, The Death of Bessie Smith, The Sandbox*, 1960.
The Sandbox (produced 1960). In *The Zoo Story, The Death of Bessie Smith, The Sandbox*, 1960.
The Zoo Story, The Death of Bessie Smith, The Sandbox: Three Plays. 1960; as *The Zoo Story and Other Plays* (includes *The American Dream*), 1962.
Fam and Yam (produced 1960). 1961.
The American Dream (produced 1961). 1961.
Bartleby, with James Hinton, Jr., music by William Flanagan, from the story by Melville (produced 1961).
Who's Afraid of Virginia Woolf? (produced 1962). 1962.
The Ballad of the Sad Café, from the story by Carson McCullers (produced 1963). 1963.
Tiny Alice (produced 1964). 1965.
Malcolm, from the novel by James Purdy (produced 1966). 1966.
A Delicate Balance (produced 1966). 1966.
Breakfast at Tiffany's, music by Bob Merrill, from the story by Truman Capote (produced 1966).

Everything in the Garden, from the play by Giles Cooper (produced 1967). 1968.
Box and Quotations from Chairman Mao Tse-tung (as *Box-Mao-Box*, produced 1968; as *Box and Quotations from Chairman Mao Tse-tung*, produced 1968). 1969.
All Over (produced 1971). 1971.
Seascape (produced 1975). 1975.
Counting the Ways (produced 1976). In *Two Plays*, 1977.
Listening (broadcast 1976; produced 1977). In *Two Plays*, 1977.
Two Plays: Counting the Ways and Listening. 1977.
The Lady from Dubuque (produced 1980). 1980.
Lolita, from the novel by Vladimir Nabokov (produced 1981).
Plays 1-4. 4 vols., 1981-82.
The Man Who Had Three Arms (produced 1982).
Envy, in *Faustus in Hell* (produced 1985).

Screenplay: *A Delicate Balance*, 1975.

Radio Play: *Listening*, 1976.

*

Bibliography: *Albee at Home and Abroad: A Bibliography 1958–June 1968* by Richard E. Amacher and Margaret Rule, 1970; *Albee: An Annotated Bibliography 1968–1977* by Charles Green, 1980.

Critical Studies: *Albee: Tradition and Renewal* by Gilbert Debusscher, translated by Anne D. Williams, 1967; *Albee* by Richard E. Amacher, 1969, revised edition, 1982; *Albee* by Ruby Cohn, 1969; *Albee: Playwright in Protest* by Michael E. Rutenberg, 1969; *Albee* by C.W.E. Bigsby, 1969, and *Albee: A Collection of Critical Essays* edited by Bigsby, 1975; *Albee* by Ronald Hayman, 1971; *From Tension to Tonic: The Plays of Albee* by Anne Paolucci, 1972; *Albee: The Poet of Loss* by Anita Maria Stenz, 1978; *Who's Afraid of Albee* by Foster Hirsch, 1978; *Albee: An Interview and Essays* edited by Julian N. Wasserman, 1983; *Albee* by G. McCarthy, 1986.

* * *

Critics are divided as to whether Edward Albee is a realist or absurdist. Critics and public are divided as to the quality of his writing after *Who's Afraid of Virginia Woolf?* Actors and directors are divided as to whether he is wise to direct his own plays. Never one to soar above the battle, Albee wittily attacks his attackers.

The Zoo Story, completed in 1958 when he was thirty years old, played in New York City on the same bill as Beckett's *Krapp's Last Tape*, and Albee was immediately pigeonholed as absurdist. Rather than dramatize a metaphysical impasse, however, Albee creates a protagonist who is a martyr to brotherly love and cultural vigor. In arousing smug Peter to enact a zoo story, Jerry strikes hard at complacent conformity, and Albee strikes hard at conventional theater.

Albee's next few plays in the next few years are more traditionally satiric. *The Death of Bessie Smith* lacerates white racism; *The American Dream* and *The Sandbox* ridicule American materialism and mindlessness. *Fam and Yam*, a slight piece, confronts an old established playwright with a bright young novice.

For all the energetic idiom of *The Zoo Story* and the satiric verve of his other short plays, Albee remained a fringe playwright until *Who's Afraid of Virginia Woolf?* The play has been misunderstood as a marital problem play, a campus satire, or veiled homosexuality, but, even misunderstood, its verbal pyrotechnics attracted audiences. Slowly, its symbolic import has seeped through an apparently realistic surface. George and Martha, ostensibly an American academic couple but related by name to the father (and mother) of the United States, have based their union on the illusion of a child. On the eve of the child's twenty-first birthday, the fantasy parents return home from a campus party. Drinking heavily, the older couple uses a younger couple for "flagellation." As in O'Neill's *Long Day's Journey into Night* alcohol proves confessional and penitential for all four characters. In the play's third act "Exorcism" George kills their imaginary son. The middle-aged couple, alone at daybreak, has to learn to live with naked reality.

Albee continues the corruscating dialogue of *Virginia Woolf* into the first scene of *Tiny Alice* but then shifts to slower rhythms of mystery—both murder and metaphysics. As in *The Zoo Story* and *Virginia Woolf*, the protagonist of *Tiny Alice* seeks the reality beneath the surface, and the surface glitters theatrically with such devices as a model castle, a Cardinal who keeps caged cardinal-birds, a beautiful woman disguised as an old crone, an operatic staircase, and visual reminders of the Pietà and Crucifixion. Brother Julian claims to be "dedicated to the reality of things, rather than the appearance." Abandoned on his wedding day by his bride Alice and her entourage. Julian finally lies in cruciform posture, clinging to illusion as he really dies.

A Delicate Balance returns to a more realistic surface; as in *Virginia Woolf* a love relationship in one couple is explored through the impact of another couple. In Friday's Act I terrorized friends seek refuge with Tobias and Agnes; in Saturday's Act II Tobias welcomes them, but his daughter Julia reacts hysterically. In Sunday's Act III the friends know they are not welcome, know that they would not have welcomed, and they leave. The passion leads not to resurrection but restitution of a delicate family balance.

After two related and exploratory plays, *Box-Mao-Box*, Albee returns in *All Over* to the upper-middle-class American milieu that he stylizes deftly. He brings to the center of this play a theme at the periphery of his other plays—the existential impact of death. In spite of the title, "all" is not quite "over," for a once powerful man is dying behind a stage screen. Waiting for his death are his wife, mistress, best friend, son, and daughter, whose mannered conversation traces the man's presence everywhere or "all over." Death precariously joins these people, only to sunder them again, as each is suffused in his/her own unhappiness.

Between *A Delicate Balance* and *All Over*, upper-middle-class plays in credible settings, Albee wrote "two inter-related" and experimental plays, *Box* and *Quotations from Chairman Mao Tse-tung*. In *Box*, "a parenthesis around *Mao*," a brightly lit cube usurps the whole stage while the audience hears nearby an associational monologue of a middle-aged woman. Apparently rambling, the speech is carefully structured: "When art hurts. That is what to remember." *Quotations* theatricalizes art hurting. Within the cube appears a steamship deck with four characters on it—a silent minister. Chairman Mao speaking only in the titular quotations, a shabby old woman speaking only doggerel verse of Will Carleton, and a middle-class, middle-aged, long-winded lady whose discourse further develops the themes of art and suffering. Skillfully counterpointed, the three voices dramatize the frailty of art—how it is nourished by suffering and how it suffers.

After the jejune lapse of *Seascape* Albee created another two short experimental plays, *Listening* and *Counting the Ways*. *Listening*, "a chamber play" translated from radio, resembles a chamber quartet in its blend of four voices. Grouped about a fountain pool, the three visible characters engage in non-linear dialogue on the theme of listening. The girl charges: "You don't listen. . . . Pay attention, rather, is what you don't do." Though the characters seem to speak in a limbo beyond life, the play is climaxed by a shocking suicide and a last reiteration of the girl's charge countered by the fifty-year-old woman: "*I* listen." Less resonant is the two-character *Counting the Ways*, "A Vaudeville" in 21 scenes varying the moods of a love affair as Bergman does that of a marriage.

The Lady from Dubuque was first performed in New York in 1980, but rather than usher in a new theater decade, the play reflects earlier Albee accomplishments: witty repartee, preoccupation with death, skepticism about identity. Albee's eight characters (his largest cast) are centered on a wife in her thirties, who is dying of cancer. Neither she, her husband Sam, nor the two couples they know is adequate to deal with the fear and pain. Enter a mysterious couple, black Oscar and Elizabeth, who claims to be both the invalid's mother and the lady from Dubuque. Despite interference from the rest of the cast, the strange couple not only ease the sick woman into death, but they confront the other characters with their deepest selves.

The corpus of Albee's work shows stylistic variety and close attention to the nuances of language. Rarely facile, never clumsy, recently mannered, Albee continues to dramatize deep themes in distinctive theatrical forms.

—Ruby Cohn

See the essay on *Who's Afraid of Virginia Woolf?*

ALCOTT, Louisa May. Born in Germantown, Philadelphia, Pennsylvania, 29 November 1832; daughter of the philosopher Amos Bronson Alcott; grew up in Boston, and later in Concord, Massachusetts. Educated at home by her father, with instruction from Thoreau, Emerson, and Theodore Parker. Began to write for publication, 1848; also worked as a teacher, seamstress, and domestic servant to support her family; army nurse at the Union Hospital, Georgetown, Washington, D.C., during the Civil War, 1862–63; visited Europe, 1865–66; editor of the children's magazine *Merry's Museum*, 1867; visited Europe, 1870–71, then settled in Boston. *Died 6 March 1888.*

PUBLICATIONS

Collections

Glimpses of Louisa: A Centennial Sampling of the Best Short Stories, edited by Cornelia Meigs. 1968.
Works, edited by Claire Booss. 1982.

Fiction

Flower Fables. 1855.
The Rose Family: A Fairy Tale. 1864.
On Picket Duty and Other Tales. 1864.
Moods. 1865; revised edition, 1882.
Morning-Glories and Other Stories. 1867; revised edition, 1868.
The Mysterious Key and What It Opened. 1867.
Proverb Stories. 1868; as *Three Proverb Stories*, n.d.
Kitty's Class Day. 1868.
Aunt Kipp. 1868.
Psyche's Art. 1868.
Little Women; or, Meg, Jo, Beth, and Amy. 2 vols., 1868–69; as *Little Women and Good Wives*, 1871; vol. 2 as *Little Women Wedded*, 1872, *Little Women Married*, 1873, and *Nice Wives*, 1875.
An Old-Fashioned Girl. 1870.
Will's Wonder Book. 1870.
V.V.; or, Plots and Counterplots. 1870.
Little Men: Life at Plumfield with Jo's Boys. 1871.
Aunt Jo's Scrap-Bag: My Boys, Shawl-Straps, Cupid and Chow-Chow, My Girls, Jimmy's Cruise in the Pinafore, An Old-Fashioned Thanksgiving. 6 vols., 1872–82.
Work: A Story of Experience. 1873.
Beginning Again, Being a Continuation of "Work." 1875.
Eight Cousins; or, The Aunt-Hill. 1875.
Silver Pitchers, and Independence: A Centennial Love Story. 1876; as *Silver Pitchers and Other Stories*, 1876.
Rose in Bloom: A Sequel to "Eight Cousins." 1876.
A Modern Mephistopheles. 1877.
Under the Lilacs. 1877.
Meadow Blossoms. 1879.
Water-Cresses. 1879.
Jack and Jill: A Village Story. 1880.
Proverb Stories. 1882.
Spinning-Wheel Stories. 1884.
Jo's Boys and How They Turned Out. 1886.
Lulu's Library: A Christmas Dream, The Frost King, Recollections. 3 vols., 1886–89; vol. 3 as *Recollections of My Childhood Days*, 1890.
A Garland for Girls. 1887.
A Modern Mephistopheles, and A Whisper in the Dark. 1889.
Louisa's Wonder Book: An Unknown Alcott Juvenile, edited by Madeleine B. Stern. 1975.
Behind a Mask: The Unknown Thrillers, edited by Madeleine B. Stern. 1975.
Plots and Counterplots: More Unknown Thrillers, edited by Madeleine B. Stern. 1976.

Plays

Comic Tragedies Written by "Jo" and "Meg" and Acted by the "Little Women," edited by A.B. Pratt. 1893.

Other

Hospital Sketches. 1863; revised edition, as *Hospital Sketches and Camp and Fireside Stories*, 1869.
Nelly's Hospital. 1865.
Something to Do. 1873.
A Glorious Fourth. 1887.
What It Cost. 1887.
Jimmy's Lecture. 1887.
Alcott: Her Life, Letters, and Journals, edited by Ednah D. Cheney. 1889.
A Sprig of Andromeda: A Letter on the Death of Henry David Thoreau, edited by John L. Cooley. 1962.

Transcendental Wild Oats, and Excerpts from the Fruitlands Diary. 1981.

*

Bibliography: in *Bibliography of American Literature* by Jacob Blanck, 1955; in *Louisa's Wonder Book* edited by Madeleine B. Stern, 1975; *Alcott: A Reference Guide* by Alma J. Payne, 1980.

Critical Studies: *Alcott* by Madeleine B. Stern, 1950, and *Critical Essays on Alcott* edited by Stern, 1984; *Miss Alcott of Concord* by Marjorie Worthington, 1958; *Alcott and the American Family Story* by Cornelia Meigs, 1970; *Louisa May: A Modern Biography of Alcott* by Martha Saxton, 1977; *The Alcotts: Biography of a Family* by Madelon Bedell, 1980; *Alcott* by Ruth MacDonald, 1983; *The Promise of Destiny: Children and Women in the Short Stories of Alcott* by Joy A. Marsella, 1983; *A Hunger for Home: Alcott and Little Women* by Sarah Elbert, 1984; *Victorian Domesticity: Families in the Life and Art of Alcott* by Charles Strickland, 1985.

* * *

Louisa May Alcott's reputation as one of America's best-loved writers is based upon *Little Women*, a domestic novel for girls which is also appealing to adults. *Little Women* reflects the Alcott family background of high-minded idealism while it glosses over the Alcott family problems. Its characters, the four March girls, were drawn from those of the author and her sisters, its scenes from the New England where she had grown up, and many of its episodes from those she and her family had experienced, although the literary influence of Bunyan, Dickens, Carlyle, Hawthorne, Emerson, Theodore Parker, and Thoreau may be traced.

In the creation of *Little Women*, Alcott was something of a pioneer, using her own life as the basis of a novel for children and achieving a realistic but wholesome picture of family life with which readers could readily identify. The Alcott poverty was sentimentalized, the eccentric Alcott father was an adumbrated shadow; yet the core of the domestic drama was apparent. Reported simply and directly in a style that applied her injunction, "Never use a long word, when a short one will do as well," the narrative embodied the simple facts and persons of a family, and so filled a gap in the literature of adolescence and domesticity.

There is no doubt that *Little Women* was the author's masterpiece. It had been preceded by a succession of literary efforts and experiments that gave Alcott a wide range of professional experience before she undertook her domestic novel. Her first published book, *Flower Fables*, consisted of "legends of faery land" and was dedicated to Emerson's daughter Ellen, for whom the tales were originally created. Her first novel, *Moods*, was a narrative of stormy violence, death, and intellectual love in which she attempted to apply Emerson's remark "Life is a train of moods like a string of beads." On and off she worked on an autobiographical, feminist novel, *Success*, subsequently renamed *Work: A Story of Experience*.

The Alcott bibliography encompasses nearly 300 books, articles, novels, short stories, and poems, many of which appeared in the periodicals of the day. They were written in a variety of literary genres: stories of sweetness and light; dramatic narratives of strong-minded women; realistic episodes of Civil War life based upon her experience as a nurse; pseudonymous blood-and-thunder thrillers of revenge and passion whose leading character was usually a manipulating and vindictive woman. From the exigencies of serialization she developed the skills of cliff-hanger and page-turner. By 1868, when she began *Little Women*, Alcott had produced a broad spectrum of stories from tales of virtue rewarded to tales of vice unpunished.

Little Women was followed by a succession of wholesome domestic narratives, the so-called *Little Women Series*, in which the author continued to supply a persistent demand. More or less autobiographical in origin, perceptive in their characterizations of adolescents, all are in a sense sequels of *Little Women* though none quite rises to its level. *An Old-Fashioned Girl* is a domestic drama in reverse, exposing the fashionable absurdities of one home in contrast with the wholesome domesticity of another. *Eight Cousins* exalts the family hearth again, and *Jack and Jill* enlarges upon the theme of domesticity, describing the home life of a New England village rather than of a single family.

An exception to this preoccupation with domestic life was *A Modern Mephistopheles*. Here Alcott exploited a theme of Goethe in a novel that reverted to the sensationalism of her earlier thrillers. "Enjoyed doing it," she wrote in her journal, "being tired of providing moral pap for the young." Actually, this novel had first been written during the 1860's, and rejected as "too sensational."

Alcott was a far more complex writer than has been recognized. Drawn to a variety of literary themes and techniques, she eschewed most of them in favor of the domestic novel she had perfected. Motivated by the "inspiration of necessity," she became a victim of her own success. She has inevitably achieved fame as the "Children's Friend" and the author of a single masterpiece. Thanks to its psychological perceptions, its realistic characterizations, and its honest domesticity, *Little Women* has become an embodiment of the American home at its best. As the Boston *Herald* commented after her death: "When the family history, out of which this remarkable authorship grew, shall be told to the public, it will be apparent that few New England homes have ever had closer converse with the great things of human destiny than that of the Alcotts." Imbedded in the domestic novel *Little Women* are "the great things of human destiny," for there the particular has been transmuted into the universal.

—Madeleine B. Stern

See the essay on *Little Women*.

ALGER, Horatio (Jr.). Born in Chelsea, Massachusetts, 13 January 1832. Educated at Chelsea Grammar School; Gates Academy, Marlborough, Massachusetts, 1845–47; Harvard University, Cambridge, Massachusetts (Bowdoin Prize, 1851), 1848–52, A.B. 1852 (Phi Beta Kappa); Harvard Divinity School, 1853, 1857–60, graduated 1860: ordained 1864. Assistant editor, Boston *Daily Advertiser*, 1853–54; schoolteacher, East Greenwich, Rhode Island, 1854–55; principal, Deerfield Academy, Massachusetts, 1856; tutor, and editorial writer, *True Flag*, Boston, 1856–57; traveled in Europe, 1860–61; private tutor in Cambridge and Nahant, Massachusetts, 1861–64; minister, First Unitarian Church, Brewster, Massachusetts, 1864–66; lived in New York, 1866–96, and private tutor from 1869; lived in South Natick, Massachusetts, 1896–99. *Died 18 July 1899.*

PUBLICATIONS

Collections

Alger Street: The Poetry, edited by Gilbert K. Westgard II. 1964.

Fiction

Bertha's Christmas Vision: An Autumn Sheaf (stories and verse). 1856.
Frank's Campaign; or, What Boys Can Do on the Farm for the Camp. 1864.
Paul Prescott's Charge. 1865; as *Paul Prescott the Runaway*, 1867.
Helen Ford. 1866.
Timothy Crump's Ward; or, The New Years Loan, and What Came of It. 1866; revised edition, as *Jack's Ward; or, The Boy Guardian*, 1875.
Charlie Codman's Cruise. 1866; as *Bill Sturdy; or, The Cruise of Kidnapped Charlie*, 1887.
Fame and Fortune; or, The Progress of Richard Hunter. 1868.
Ragged Dick; or, Street Life in New York with the Boot-Blacks. 1868.
Luck and Pluck; or, John Oakley's Inheritance. 1869.
Mark, The Match Boy; or, Richard Hunter's Ward. 1869.
Rough and Ready; or, Life among the New York Newsboys. 1869.
Ben, The Luggage Boy; or, Among the Wharves. 1870.
Rufus and Rose; or, The Fortunes of Rough and Ready. 1870.
Sink or Swim; or, Harry Raymond's Resolve. 1870; as *Paddle Your Own Canoe*, 1887.
Paul the Peddler; or, The Adventures of a Young Street Merchant. 1871; as *Plucky Paul*, 1888.
Strong and Steady; or, Paddle Your Own Canoe. 1871.
Tattered Tom; or, The Story of a Street Arab. 1871.
Phil, The Fiddler; or, The Story of a Young Street Musician. 1872.
Slow and Sure; or, From the Street to the Shop. 1872.
Strive and Succeed; or, The Progress of Walter Conrad. 1872.
Bound to Rise; or, Harry Walton's Motto. 1873.
Try and Trust; or, The Story of a Bound Boy. 1873; as *Trials and Adventures of Herbert Mason*, 1887.
Brave and Bold; or, The Fortunes of a Factory Boy. 1874.
Julius; or, The Street Boy Out West. 1874.
Risen from the Ranks; or, Harry Walton's Success. 1874.
Herbert Carter's Legacy; or, The Inventor's Son. 1875; as *George Carter's Legacy*, 1887.
The Young Outlaw; or, Adrift in the Streets. 1875.
Sam's Chance, and How He Improved It. 1876.
Shifting for Himself; or, Gilbert Greyson's Fortunes. 1876; as *How His Ship Came Home*, 1887.
Wait and Hope; or, Ben Bradford's Motto. 1877.
The New Schoolma'am. 1877; as *A Fancy of Hers*, 1981.
The Western Boy; or, The Road to Success. 1878; as *Tom, The Bootblack*, 1880.
The Young Adventurer; or, Tom's Trip Across the Plains. 1878.
The Young Miner; or, Tom Nelson in California. 1879.
The Telegraph Boy. 1879; as *The District Telegraph Boy*, n.d.
The Young Explorer; or, Among the Sierras. 1880.
Tony, The Hero. 1880; as *Tony, The Tramp*, 1910(?).
Ben's Nugget; or, A Boy's Search for Fortune: A Story of the Pacific Coast. 1882.
The Train Boy. 1883.
The Young Circus Rider; or, The Mystery of Robert Rudd. 1883.
Dan, The Detective. 1884; as *Dan the Newsboy*, 1893; as *Dutiful Dan, The Brave Boy Detective*, 1895.
Do and Dare; or, A Brave Boy's Fight for Fortune. 1884.
Hector's Inheritance; or, The Boys of Smith Institute. 1885; as *Never Despair!*, 1887.
Helping Himself; or, Grant Thornton's Ambition. 1886.
Joe's Luck; or, A Boy's Adventure in California. 1887.
Frank Fowler, The Cash Boy. 1887.
Number 91; or, The Adventures of a New York Telegraph Boy. 1887.
The Store Boy; or, The Fortunes of Ben Barclay. 1887; as *The Fortunes of Ben Barclay*, 1896; as *Ben Barclay's Courage*, 1904.
Ben Stanton, The Explorer (includes *The Young Explorer* and *Ben's Nugget*). 1887.
Bob Burton. 1888; as *The Young Ranchman of the Missouri*, 1888.
The Errand Boy; or, How Phil Brent Won Success. 1888.
The Merchant's Crime. 1888; as *Ralph Raymond's Heir*, 1892.
Tom Temple's Career. 1888.
Tom Thatcher's Fortune. 1888.
Tom Tracy; or, The Trials of a New York Newsboy. 1888.
The Young Acrobat of the Great North American Circus. 1888; as *He Would Be a Mountebank*, 1888.
Luke Walton; or, The Chicago Newsboy. 1889.
Mark Stanton; or, Both Sides of the Continent. 1890.
Ned Newton; or, The Fortunes of a New York Bootblack. 1890.
A New York Boy. 1890.
The Odds Against Him; or, Carl Crawford's Experience. 1890; as *Driven from Home*, n.d.
Struggling Upward; or, Luke Larkin's Luck. 1890.
Dean Dunham. 1890; as *Wait Till the Clouds Roll By*, 1890.
The Erie Train Boy. 1890; as *The Straight Ahead*, 1891.
$500; or, Jacob Marlowe's Secret. 1890; as *Uncle Jacob's Secret*, 1890; as *The Five Hundred Dollar Check*, 1891.
Digging for Gold: A Story of California. 1892.
The Young Boatman of Pine Point. 1892.
Facing the World; or, The Haps and Mishaps of Harry Vane. 1893.
In a New World; or, Among the Gold-Fields of Australia. 1893; as *The Nugget Finders*, 1894; as *Val Vane's Victory; or, Well Won*, 1903(?).
Only an Irish Boy; or, Andy Burke's Fortunes and Misfortunes. 1894.
Victor Vane, The Young Secretary. 1894.
Adrift in the City; or, Oliver Conrad's Plucky Fight. 1895.
The Disagreeable Woman: A Social Mystery. 1895.
Frank Hunter's Peril. 1896.
The Young Salesman. 1896.
Walter Sherwood's Probation. 1897.

Frank and Fearless; or, The Fortunes of Jasper Kent. 1897.
The Young Bank Messenger. 1898.
A Boy's Fortune; or, The Strange Adventures of Ben Baker. 1898.
Rupert's Ambition. 1899.
Mark Mason's Victory: The Trials and Triumphs of a Telegraph Boy. 1899.
Jed, The Poorhouse Boy. 1900.
A Debt of Honor: The Story of Gerald Lane's Success in the Far West. 1900.
Out for Business; or, Robert Frost's Strange Career, completed by Edward Stratemeyer. 1900.
Falling in with Fortune; or, The Experiences of a Young Secretary, completed by Edward Stratemeyer. 1900.
Ben Bruce: Scenes in the Life of a Bowery Newsboy. 1901.
Lester's Luck. 1901.
Making His Mark. 1901.
Nelson the Newsboy; or, Afloat in New York, completed by Edward Stratemeyer. 1901.
Striving for Fortune; or, Walter Griffith's Trials and Successes. 1901; as *Walter Griffith*, 1901.
Tom Brace: Who He Was and How He Fared. 1901.
Young Captain Jack; or, The Son of a Soldier, completed by Edward Stratemeyer. 1901.
Andy Grant's Pluck. 1902.
A Rolling Stone; or, The Adventures of a Wanderer. 1902; as *Wren Winter's Triumph*, 1902.
Tom Turner's Legacy: The Story of How He Secured It. 1902.
The World Before Him. 1902.
Bernard Brook's Adventures: The Story of a Brave Boy's Trials. 1903.
Chester Rand; or, A New Path to Fortune. 1903.
Forging Ahead. 1903; as *Andy Gordon*, 1905.
Adrift in New York. 1903; revised edition, 1904.
Finding a Fortune. 1904; as *The Tin Box* 1905(?).
Jerry, The Backwoods Boy; or, The Parkhurst Treasure, completed by Edward Stratemeyer. 1904.
Lost at Sea; or, Robert Roscoe's Strange Cruise, completed by Edward Stratemeyer. 1904.
From Farm to Fortune; or, Nat Nason's Strange Experience, completed by Edward Stratemeyer. 1905.
Mark Manning's Mission; or, The Story of a Shoe Factory Boy. 1905.
The Young Book Agent; or, Frank Hardy's Road to Success, completed by Edward Stratemeyer. 1905.
Joe the Hotel Boy; or, Winning Out by Pluck, completed by Edward Stratemeyer. 1906.
Randy of the River; or, The Adventures of a Young Deckhand, completed by Edward Stratemeyer. 1906.
The Young Musician. 1906.
In Search of Treasure: The Story of Guy's Eventful Voyage. 1907.
Wait and Win: The Story of Jack Drummond's Pluck. 1908.
Ben Logan's Triumph; or, The Boys of Boxwood Academy, completed by Edward Stratemeyer. 1908.
Robert Coverdale's Struggle; or, On the Wave of Success. 1910.
Silas Snobden's Office Boy. 1973.
Cast upon the Breakers. 1974.
Hugo, The Deformed. 1978.
Madeline, The Temptress. 1981.
The Secret Drawer. 1981.
The Cooper's Ward. 1981.
Herbert Selden. 1981.
Manson, The Miser. 1981.
The Gipsy Nurse. 1981.
The Discarded Son. 1981.
The Mad Heiress. 1981.
Marie Bertrand. 1981.

Verse

Nothing to Do: A Tilt at Our Best Society. 1857.
Grand'ther Baldwin's Thanksgiving with Other Ballads and Poems. 1875.

Other

From Canal Boy to President; or, The Boyhood and Manhood of James A. Garfield. 1881.
From Farm Boy to Senator, Being the History of the Boyhood and Manhood of Daniel Webster. 1882.
Abraham Lincoln, The Backwoods Boy. 1883.

*

Bibliography: *Alger: A Comprehensive Bibliography* by Bob Bennett, 1980; *Alger: An Annotated Bibliography of Comment and Criticism* by Gary Scharnhorst and Jack Bales, 1981.

Critical Studies: *Alger: A Biography and Bibliography* by Frank Gruber, 1961; *Horatio's Boys: The Life and Works of Alger* by Edwin P. Hoyt, 1974; *Alger* by Gary Scharnhorst, 1980, and *The Lost Life of Alger* by Scharnhorst and Jack Bales, 1985.

* * *

In 1867 Horatio Alger, failed preacher and school master, entered upon a literary career which eventually produced more than a hundred so-called boys' novels, thereby becoming one of the most successful writers in history. Indeed, so successful was he that his name has entered the language to signify the rags-to-riches American hero who, though born in dire straits, follows a virtuous and diligent life to a position of respectability, and sometimes wealth and influence.

So prodigious an output necessarily dictated that Alger's characters were little more than caricatures, heroes with faces that "indicated a frank, sincere nature" (as in *The World Before Him*), and villains "with shifty black eyes and thin lips, shaded by a dark moustache" (*Adrift in New York*). His plots also inevitably located an impoverished but ingenuous lad, often an orphan, in a hostile environment, usually the city. There, possessed of those virtues which have become synonymous with the Alger myth—optimism, ambition, thrift, and self-reliance—the lad matured toward an adulthood of power, affluence, and respectability.

This conventional reading of the Alger stories and the myth to which they gave birth is, however, somewhat misleading. For to the more careful reader Alger's novels carry a more ambiguous message. First, it is not simply individual virtue but virtue in the face of good fortune that brings success to Alger's boys. Thus, as the typical story unfolds, the hero chances to save the millionaire's grandson from drowning or to find and return the lost bag of bank notes. In a sense, then, the cultivation of virtue is really a ritual of purification which prepares Alger's hero for the providential moment when he will be tried and found not wanting. Luck, no less than pluck—not to mention virtue—figures deeply in the success of the Alger hero. Second, the Alger hero's virtues are often compromised by their countervailing vices. Thrift, for instance, routinely gives way to a profligate visit to the theater or a spendthrift ride on a ferry boat, and self-reliance is often submerged in the desire for security and dependence.

Alger's heroes, in short, are not of the unalloyed virtue that the myth would have one believe. And virtue itself, compromised as it is, is routinely abetted by dumb luck. Still, Alger's name lives in the language as a synonym for virtue rewarded. And Alger himself, a novelist of admittedly modest abilities, has been eclipsed by his own name in the minds of the millions who have never read his work.

—Bruce A. Lohof

ALGREN, Nelson. Born Nelson Ahlgren Abraham in Detroit, Michigan, 28 March 1909. Educated at schools in Chicago; University of Illinois, Urbana, 1928–31, B.S. in journalism 1931. Served in the U.S. Army Medical Corps, 1942–45: Private. Married 1) Amanda Kontowicz in 1936 (divorced, 1939); 2) Betty Ann Jones in 1965 (divorced, 1967). Worked as salesman, migratory worker, carnival shill, and part owner of a gas station, 1931-35; editor, Illinois Writers Project, WPA (Works Progress Administration), 1936–40; worked for the Venereal Disease Program of the Chicago Board of Health, 1941–42. Teacher of creative writing, University of Iowa, Iowa City, 1967, and University of Florida, Gainesville, 1974. Editor, with Jack Conroy, *New Anvil*, Chicago, 1939–41; columnist, Chicago *Free Press*, 1970. Recipient: American Academy grant, 1947, and Award of Merit Medal, 1974; Newberry Library fellowship, 1947; National Book Award, 1950; National Endowment for the Arts grant, 1976. *Died 9 May 1981.*

PUBLICATIONS

Fiction

Somebody in Boots. 1935; as *The Jungle*, 1957.
Never Come Morning. 1942.
The Neon Wilderness (stories). 1946.
The Man with the Golden Arm. 1949.
A Walk on the Wild Side. 1956.
The Last Carousel (stories). 1973.
Calhoun (in German), edited by Carl Weissner. 1980; as *The Devil's Stocking*, 1983.

Other

Chicago: City on the Make. 1951.
Who Lost an American? Being a Guide to the Seamier Sides of New York City, Inner London, Paris, Dublin, Barcelona, Seville, Almería, Istanbul, Crete and Chicago, Illinois. 1963.
Conversations with Algren, with H.E.F. Donohue. 1964.
Notes from a Sea-Diary: Hemingway All the Way. 1965.

Editor, *Algren's Own Book of Lonesome Monsters*. 1962; as *Algren's Book of Lonesome Monsters*, 1964.

*

Bibliography: *Algren: A Checklist* by Kenneth G. McCollum, 1973.

Critical Study: *Algren* by Martha Heasley Cox and Wayne Chatterton, 1975.

* * *

Four novels, some fifty short stories, numerous sketches, essays, poems, travel books, book reviews and other literary criticism produced over a period of more than forty years assure Nelson Algren a place in American literature. Chicago, where Algren lived for much of his life, is the setting for most of his work. Characters, themes, symbols, and imagery, as well as the Chicago settings, recur throughout his canon as he becomes the spokesman for the derelicts, professional tramps, prostitutes, addicts, convicts, prize-fighters, and baseball players who inhabit his city jungle, "The Neon Wilderness," as he titled one of his collections of short stories. While most of Algren's characters speak the dialogue of the gutter, his style varies from staccato reporting to the rich passages that have gained him the title "the poet of the Chicago slums." His books contain much offbeat information revealed with satire, irony, humor, and farce.

His first novel, *Somebody in Boots*, is a "Depression novel," a chronicle of poverty and failure dedicated to "those innumerable thousands: the homeless boys of America." His second, *Never Come Morning*, is a story of rape and murder with a doomed Chicago Polish boxer as its hero. His best known work, however, is his third novel *The Man with the Golden Arm*, which won him the first National Book Award. In this book, written two decades before drug addiction became a national dilemma, Algren fictionalized the world of the drug addict with as yet unsurpassed authority and impact.

His last novel, *A Walk on the Wild Side*, the result of an attempt to rework *Somebody in Boots*, was Algren's favorite work as well as that of most of his later critics. Though Algren once maintained that no one understood *A Walk on the Wild Side*—a book, he said, of a kind never before written, "an American fantasy—a poem written to an American beat as truly as *Huckleberry Finn*"—the novel is now acclaimed for its prophetic qualities and for its influence on later novels and films such as *Midnight Cowboy* and *Easy Rider*.

—Martha Heasley Cox

ALLEN, James Lane. Born near Lexington, Kentucky, 21 December 1849. Educated at Transylvania Academy, Lexington, 1866–68; Kentucky University (now Transylvania University), Lexington, 1868–72, 1875–77, B.A. (honors) 1872, M.A. 1887. Teacher at a district school in Fort Springs, Kentucky, 1872–73, and at a high school in Richmond, Missouri, 1872–74; teacher at his own school in Lexington, Missouri, 1875; principal, Transylvania Academy, 1878–80; Professor of Latin, Bethany College, West Virginia, 1880–83; opened and taught at a private school in Lexington, Kentucky, 1883–85; thereafter full-time writer; moved to New York, 1893; lived in Europe, 1894, 1900, 1909. M.A.: Bethany College, 1880; LL.D.: Kentucky University, 1898. *Died 18 February 1925.*

PUBLICATIONS

Collections

A Kentucky Cardinal, Aftermath, and Other Selected Works, edited by William K. Bottorff. 1967.

Fiction

Flute and Violin and Other Kentucky Tales and Romances. 1891.
John Gray: A Kentucky Tale of the Olden Time. 1893.
A Kentucky Cardinal. 1895.
Aftermath. 1896.
Summer in Arcady: A Tale of Nature. 1896.
The Choir Invisible. 1897; revised edition, 1898.
The Reign of Law: A Tale of the Kentucky Hemp Fields. 1900; as *The Increasing Purpose*, 1900.
The Mettle of the Pasture. 1903.
The Bride of the Mistletoe. 1909.
The Doctor's Christmas Eve. 1910.
The Heroine in Bronze; or, A Portrait of a Girl: A Pastoral of the City. 1912.
The Last Christmas Tree: An Idyll of Immortality. 1914.
The Sword of Youth. 1915.
A Cathedral Singer. 1916.
The Kentucky Warbler. 1918.
The Emblems of Fidelity: A Comedy in Letters. 1919.
The Alabaster Box (stories). 1923.
The Landmark (stories). 1925.

Other

The Blue-Grass Region of Kentucky and Other Kentucky Articles. 1892.
Chimney Corner Graduates. 1900.

*

Bibliography: in *Bibliography of American Literature* by Jacob Blanck, 1955.

Critical Studies: *Allen* by John Wilson Townsend, 1927; *Allen and the Genteel Tradition* by Grant C. Knight, 1935; *Allen* by William K. Bottorff, 1964.

* * *

James Lane Allen was ideally suited to purveying the kind of story and novel demanded by the popular reading audience of the 1890's. Because of his evangelical religious orthodoxy, his innate southern chivalry, and his readings in Hawthorne, Eliot, Thackeray, and Dickens, he demonstrated the rigorous moral control so often admired by conservative readers of the *fin de siècle*.

Although Allen wrote during an era of fiction that is generally regarded as realistic, he himself is remembered as a romantic local colorist under the influence of Wordsworth, Thoreau, and Audubon, who tended to idealize Nature by pointing out the "spiritual sustenance" nature offers (William K. Bottorff). Allen's settings were often in the central Kentucky landscape he knew so well.

There are essentially four groups of works in the Allen canon (see H.A. Toulmin, Jr., *Social Historians*). The first group sprang naturally from the disposition of a local colorist: a distinctive, sympathetic treatment of Kentucky life (*Flute and Violin and Other Kentucky Tales* and *The Blue-Grass Region of Kentucky*). The second group shows a certain philosophical growth in its treatment of nature (*A Kentucky Cardinal* and *Aftermath*). The third group champions the doctrines of evolution and the consequences of circumstance (*Summer in Arcady, The Reign of Law*, and *The Mettle of the Pasture*). The fourth vein of Allen's writings is the historical problem novel (*The Choir Invisible*).

It is to *Flute and Violin and Other Kentucky Tales* that the avid Allen reader returns. Three distinct weaknesses, however, become apparent in this early collection—sentimentality, an excessively adorned style, and a puritanic point of view that weaves, as Grant C. Knight says, "allegories and symbols into the pattern of the narratives." The title story has enjoyed considerable popularity owing to its sentimental portrayal of the Reverend James Moore who communes on his flute with the fatherless waif David, who plays the violin. The influence of Dickens is marked.

A Kentucky Cardinal is a love story set against the beauties of the rural Kentucky landscape just outside Lexington. The hero, Adam Moss, may well be Allen's finest and most Thoreau-like character. *The Choir Invisible*, a poorly unified work, sought to create a gentleman "in buckskins." The novel, set in Kentucky in 1795, brings to mind Eliot and Thackeray in its morality, humor, and pathos.

Allen's work began a marked decline early in the 20th century. *The Mettle of the Pasture* had a mixed critical reception. *The Bride of the Mistletoe* and *The Doctor's Christmas Eve* met with indifference and disapproval, and his later works are all but forgotten.

Today's readers and critics will find it difficult to agree with Edmund Gosse's opinion that Allen's was "A pen possessed of every accomplishment." The contemporary literary historian will agree, however, that Allen's writings constitute some of the best moments of American local color. Allen may be regarded as the supreme southern Victorian in his medievalism, in his moral and didactic inclination, in his desire to experiment, and in his eclecticism. As Bottorff notes, from Hawthorne Allen drew his psychology, morality, and complexity, from Thoreau he learned his transcendentalism, and from James the complexity of his psychological probings.

—George C. Longest

AMMONS, A(rchie) R(andolph). Born in Whiteville, North Carolina, 18 February 1926. Educated at Wake Forest College, North Carolina, B.S. 1949; University of California, Berkeley, 1950–52. Served in the U.S. Naval Reserve, 1944–46. Married Phyllis Plumbo in 1949; one son. Principal, Hatteras Elementary School, North Carolina, 1949–50; Executive Vice-President, Friedrich and Dimmock, Inc., glass manufacturers, Millville, New Jersey, 1952–62; Assistant Professor, 1964–68, Associate Professor, 1969–71, since 1971 Professor of English, and since 1973 Goldwin Smith Professor of English, Cornell University, Ithaca, New York. Visiting Professor, Wake Forest University, 1974–75. Poetry editor, *Nation*, New York, 1963. Recipient: Bread Loaf Writers Conference scholarship, 1961; Guggenheim fellowship, 1966; American Academy traveling fellowship, 1967, and award, 1977; National Book Award, 1973; Bollingen Prize, 1975; MacArthur fellowship, 1981; National Book Critics Circle award, 1982. D.Litt.: Wake Forest University, 1972; University of North Carolina, Chapel Hill, 1973. Fellow, American Academy of Arts and Sciences, 1982. Lives in Ithaca, New York.

PUBLICATIONS

Verse

Ommateum, with Doxology. 1955.
Expressions of Sea Level. 1964.
Corsons Inlet. 1965.
Tape for the Turn of the Year. 1965.
Northfield Poems. 1966.
Selected Poems. 1968.
Uplands. 1970.
Briefings: Poems Small and Easy. 1971.
Collected Poems 1951–1971. 1972.
Sphere: The Form of a Motion. 1974.
Diversifications. 1975.
The Snow Poems. 1977.
The Selected Poems 1951–1977. 1977.
Highgate Road. 1977.
For Doyle Fosco. 1977.
Poem. 1977(?).
Six-Piece Suite. 1979.
Selected Longer Poems. 1980.
A Coast of Trees. 1981.
Worldly Hopes. 1982.
Lake Effect Country. 1983.

*

Bibliography: *Ammons: A Bibliography 1954–1979* by Stuart Wright, 1980.

Critical Studies: "Ammons Issue" of *Diacritics*, 1974; *Ammons* by Alan Holder, 1978.

* * *

A.R. Ammons is one of the most prolific poets of his generation, amassing to date more than twenty books of verse that have won him the National Book Award in 1973, for his *Collected Poems 1951–1971*, and several other important prizes. The earliest poems, searching boldly for a center of self from which to project his persona, achieve their best effect from his recklessly strewn imagery and the pressure of his imagination to find the edges and furthest barriers of experience. The excellent *Selected Poems* of 1968, a winnowing of all the early work, dramatizes this search with varied, often profoundly moving language.

Ammons's attention ranges from intricately detailed portraits of the landscape of upper New York state, to travels throughout the southwestern United States, and memories of his childhood growing up on a farm in North Carolina, where he is fresh and original. His reminiscence of the partly mute woman who raised him as a child, "Nelly Myers," is a minor classic of the modern elegy, with its lilting rhythms and its quiet, loving tribute to her wisdom and imperfections.

Much of Ammons's poetry depends upon a texture of rapid, rambling speech that precipitates a poem within often lush formations. The edge of his poem is not silence but the banter and commentary in which it lies embedded. This pointedly risky strategy of creating a lyric can, when it is not in control, produce tracts and harangues that run on tediously. When inspired, however, the language gives way to a charged form of words partly submerged in the verbal undergrowth. His poems are like statues half perceived lying in high grass.

His verbal felicity has, however, occasioned more dry commentary than inspired lyricism. In an experiment with writing on adding machine tape, which imposed a narrow frame on the poet, Ammons wrote a seemingly endless discourse on the minutiae of his life during the winter of 1964–65, published as *Tape for the Turn of the Year*. As a professor teaching at Cornell University and living in Ithaca, New York, the persona lacks adventure and change, and the poet's journal suffers from the uneventful pace of his days. In succeeding volumes, *Northfield Poems* and *Uplands*, the style is noticeably more clipped and abrupt, approaching Imagist concision. The poet is clearly inspired by natural phenomena, particularly in the latter volume where his attention to mountain scenery is keenly alert. In *Briefings* he continues to experiment with short, sudden articulations of feeling and momentary perceptions. But in *Sphere* the style changes again into a long sequential discourse patterned by sections of four triplets where language is only partly sculpted. *The Snow Poems* returns to the mode of shorter poems and is a large collection devoted to the poet's favorite landscape, the snowladen terrain of the northeast.

Ammons's most recent work, collected in *A Coast of Trees, Worldly Hopes*, and *Lake Effect Country*, resolves all the earlier conflicts between form and language in poems that vigorously foreground a key figure and draw from it the inferences of an inner life beyond materiality. The language is now more reflexive and paradoxical, but it is Ammons's genius to preserve the natural speech of conversation in these richer, more demanding explorations of experience. Notable here is a quality of sombre reflection upon mortality, and upon the elusive but omnipresent spirit in ordinary things. Ammons, like Robert Frost before him, has insisted upon modest subjects and situations for his poetry, but his claims upon them reach to metaphysical conclusions.

—Paul Christensen

ANDERSON, Maxwell. Born in Atlantic, Pennsylvania, 15 December 1888; grew up in North Dakota. Educated at Jamestown High School, North Dakota, graduated 1908; University of North Dakota, Grand Forks, 1908–11, B.A. 1911; Stanford University, California, 1913–14, M.A. in English 1914. Married 1) Margaret C. Haskett in 1911 (died, 1931), three sons; 2) Gertrude Anthony in 1933 (died, 1953), one daughter; 3) Gilda Oakleaf in 1954. Principal and English teacher, Minnewaukan High School, North Dakota, 1911–13; English teacher, Polytechnic High School, San Francisco, 1914–17; Professor and Head of the English Department, Whittier College, California, 1917–18; staff member, *New Republic* magazine, New York, 1918–19, New York *Evening Globe*, 1919–21, and New York *World*, 1921–24; founding co-editor, *Measure* magazine, New York, 1921–26; founder, with Robert E. Sherwood, Elmer Rice, S.N. Behrman, Sidney Howard, and John F. Wharton, Playwrights Company, 1938. Recipient: Pulitzer Prize, 1933; New York Drama Critics Circle award, 1936, 1937; American Academy Gold Medal, 1954. Litt.D.: Columbia University, New York, 1946; University of North Dakota, 1958. Member, American Academy, 1955. *Died 28 February 1959.*

PUBLICATIONS

Collections

Dramatist in America: Letters 1912–1958, edited by Laurence G. Avery. 1977.

Plays

White Desert (produced 1923).
What Price Glory?, with Laurence Stallings (produced 1924). In *Three American Plays*, 1926.
First Flight, with Laurence Stallings (produced 1925). In *Three American Plays*, 1926.
The Buccaneer, with Laurence Stallings (produced 1925). In *Three American Plays*, 1926.
The Feud. 1925.
Outside Looking In, from the novel *Beggars of Life* by Jim Tully (produced 1925). With *Gods of the Lightning*, 1928.
Forfeits (produced 1926).
Saturday's Children (produced 1927). 1927.
Gods of the Lightning, with Harold Hickerson (produced 1928). With *Outside Looking In*, 1928.
Gypsy (produced 1929). Shortened version in *The Best Plays of 1928–29*, edited by Burns Mantle, 1929.
Elizabeth the Queen (produced 1930). 1930.
Night over Taos (produced 1932). 1932.
Sea-Wife (produced 1932).
Both Your Houses (produced 1933). 1933.
Mary of Scotland (produced 1933). 1933.
Valley Forge (produced 1934). 1934.
Winterset (produced 1935). 1935.
The Masque of Kings (produced 1937). 1936.
The Wingless Victory (produced 1936). 1936.
High Tor (produced 1937). 1937.
The Feast of Ortolans (broadcast 1937; produced 1938). 1938.
The Star-Wagon (produced 1937). 1937.
Knickerbocker Holiday, music by Kurt Weill (produced 1938). 1938.
Key Largo (produced 1939). 1939.
Eleven Verse Plays 1929–1939. 1940.
Second Overture (produced 1940). 1940.
Journey to Jerusalem (produced 1940). 1940.
The Miracle of the Danube (broadcast 1941). In *The Free Company Presents*, edited by James Boyd, 1941.
Candle in the Wind (produced 1941). 1941.
The Eve of St. Mark (produced 1942). 1942; revised edition, 1943.
Your Navy, in *This Is War!* 1942.
Letter to Jackie, in *The Best One-Act Plays of 1943*, edited by Margaret Mayorga. 1944.
Storm Operation (produced 1944). 1944.
Joan of Lorraine (produced 1946). 1946.
Truckline Cafe (produced 1946).
Anne of the Thousand Days (produced 1948). 1948.
Joan of Arc (screenplay), with Andrew Solt. 1948.
Lost in the Stars, music by Kurt Weill, from the novel *Cry, The Beloved Country* by Alan Paton (produced 1949). 1950.
Barefoot in Athens (produced 1951). 1951.
Bad Seed, from the novel *The Bad Seed* by William March (produced 1954). 1955.
A Christmas Carol, music by Bernard Heermann, from the story by Dickens (televised 1954). 1955.
The Masque of Pedagogues, in *North Dakota Quarterly*, Spring 1957.
The Day the Money Stopped, from the novel by Brendan Gill (produced 1958).
The Golden Six (produced 1958). 1961.

Screenplays: *All Quiet on the Western Front*, with others, 1930; *Rain*, 1932; *We Live Again*, with others, 1934; *Death Takes a Holiday*, with Gladys Lehman and Walter Ferris, 1934; *So Red the Rose*, with Laurence Stallings and Edwin Justus Mayer, 1935; *Joan of Arc*, with Andrew Solt, 1948; *The Wrong Man*, with Angus MacPhail, 1957.

Radio Plays: *The Feast of Ortolans*, 1937; *The Bastion Saint-Gervais*, 1938; *The Miracle of the Danube*, 1941; *The Greeks Remember Marathon*, 1944.

Television Play: *A Christmas Carol*, 1954.

Fiction

Morning, Winter, and Night. 1952.

Verse

You Who Have Dreams. 1925.
Notes on a Dream, edited by Laurence G. Avery. 1971.

Other

The Essence of Tragedy and Other Footnotes and Papers. 1939.
The Bases of Artistic Creation: Essays, with Rhys Carpenter and Roy Harris. 1942.
Off Broadway: Essays about the Theatre. 1947.

*

Bibliography: *A Catalogue of the Anderson Collection at the University of Texas* by Laurence G. Avery, 1968; *Anderson and S.N. Behrman: A Reference Guide* by William Klink, 1977.

Critical Studies: *Anderson, The Man and His Plays* by Barrett H. Clark, 1933; *Anderson: The Playwright as Prophet* by Mabel Driscoll Bailey, 1957; *Life among the Playwrights* by John F. Wharton, 1974; *Anderson*, 1976, and *The Life of Anderson*, 1983, both by Alfred S. Shivers.

* * *

Maxwell Anderson became a playwright by accident, but once committed to a career in the theater, he set out to base his work on carefully wrought principles of composition. His dramatic theories were based on the practices of ancient Greece and the Elizabethan period, and he was fiercely dedicated to the ideal of the theater as the democratic cultural institution.

He reintroduced the idea of poetic tragedy and attracted large audiences to his historical verse plays though there are few striking passages of poetry in his work.

For Anderson the theater was both a spiritual experience and a commercial medium. While he agreed with Aristotle that the audience should be led by the playwright to experience strong emotions, he was sure that the proper mark of success was ticket sales. He accepted the maxim that no playwright deserves or will get posthumous adulation who has not attracted an enthusiastic audience during his lifetime. He attacked the New York critics for short-circuiting the gleaning process with their first-night reviews, but was personally willing to accept the audience's spontaneous judgment. He rejected the notion of government subsidization because he thought it would interfere with the natural selection process and resisted the lure of off-Broadway production on the grounds that only the more rigorous Broadway circuit was an ample test. Anderson successfully countered the commercial forces of Broadway for more than a quarter of a century and dominated American theater in the 1930's.

Anderson believed in theater of ideas. In an essay called "Keeping the Faith" he enunciated as rule number one the necessity of having a central idea or conviction which cannot be excised without killing the play. His *Joan of Lorraine* dramatizes the process of making concessions to the realities of play production while trying to protect the central core of the play's integrity. Though his convictions changed markedly during his career, his use of the stage to express them did not. He attacked big government, defended democracy, preached pacifism, and urged commitment to war. As his ideas about war, for instance, changed from the cynicism of *What Price Glory?* (written with Laurence Stallings) to the patriotic fervor of *The Eve of St. Mark* and *Storm Operation*, he presented each new certainty with as much strength as the one before.

Anderson's overriding theme is the spiritual victory of humanity. In his essay "Off Broadway" he defined theater as "a religious institution devoted entirely to the exaltation of the spirit of man." He tried through the disillusionment of the 1920's, the depression of the 1930's, and the global war of the 1940's to present the triumphant human spirit. He has been accused of being a pessimist, but his view is essentially that of an optimistic humanist. He emphasized the importance of individual choice and the necessity of commitment. King McCloud of *Key Largo*, for instance having failed to make a stand in the last days of the Spanish Civil War, finds it hard to stop running. His spirit triumphs only when he finds something for which he is willing to die. Mio of *Winterset*, emotionally crippled by lust for revenge, becomes a complete person only when he accepts love.

In many plays Anderson used the lives of historical characters to illumine broad questions of power and choice. He wrote plays about Christ, Socrates, Elizabeth I, Mary Stuart, George Washington, and Peter Stuyvesant. A comparison of *Elizabeth the Queen* with *The Masque of Kings* illustrates the major problem in Anderson's method of historical tragedy. He is able to delineate Elizabeth's choice to have her lover Essex beheaded as a triumph of wise government over personal weakness, but Rudolph's suicide will not fit into such a neat pattern. As a result the third act of *The Masque of Kings* takes a different direction from the one we might reasonably expect after the recognition scene of Act II, and the ending is weak and inappropriate.

The high seriousness of his subject matter is often a mistake. It is unfortunate that he did not leaven his work with comedy more often. In *High Tor* and *Knickerbocker Holiday* (music by Kurt Weill) he demonstrated a rich gift for humor. *Both Your Houses*, a play about Congressional corruption, makes excellent use of satire and was highly praised by critics.

Anderson's deficiencies as a playwright seem to be related to conflicts between his intellectual approach to form and his spontaneous ideas for content. He wanted to emphasize the primacy of individual choice, for instance, but Aristotelian tragedy, which he chose to emulate, best communicates the powerful forces that neutralize free will. He wanted to write plays constructed around a second act recognition scene followed by spiritual triumph in physical defeat, but some of the historical characters he chose do not fit this pattern. He wanted to show the triumph of the human spirit, but one of his most successful plays, *Bad Seed*, demonstrates the victory of congenital evil. He wanted to treat universal themes, but in plays such as *Gods of the Lightning* and *The Wingless Victory* he gets bogged down in heavy social commentary.

Anderson has been criticized for lack of innovation, and that is a fair criticism. His approach and subject matter are quite traditional. Echoes of *Medea* are clear in the plot of *The Wingless Victory*, and the parallels between *Winterset* and *Romeo and Juliet* are obvious. His concern is less with striking out into new territories than with re-vitalizing the old. The actors in *Elizabeth the Queen* actually use Shakespeare's lines, for instance, but the effect is to illuminate the Queen's character and judgment.

Anderson was a prolific writer whose work attracted audiences and made money; by his own criteria he was a success. In comparison with his fellow writers in the American theater he must also be rated a success; only O'Neill outshone him in his time. Anderson did not always overcome the problems posed by his own methods, but he did illuminate the mazes of power, freedom, and faith he set out to explore. For over a quarter of a century, especially with works such as *Elizabeth the Queen*, *High Tor*, and *Winterset*, he dramatized the human condition in some striking scenes and created some high moments in American theater.

—Barbara M. Perkins

See the essay on *Winterset*.

ANDERSON, Sherwood (Berton). Born in Camden, Ohio, 13 September 1876. Educated at a high school in Clyde, Ohio; Wittenberg Academy, Springfield, Ohio, 1899–1900. Served in the U.S. Army in Cuba during the Spanish-American War, 1898–99. Married 1) Cornelia Pratt Lane in 1904 (divorced, 1916), two sons and one daughter; 2) Tennessee Claflin Mitchell in 1916 (divorced, 1924); 3) Elizabeth Prall in 1924 (separated, 1929; divorced, 1932); 4) Eleanor Copenhaver in 1933. Worked in a produce warehouse in Chicago, 1896–97; advertising copywriter, Long-Critchfield Company, Chicago, 1900–05; President, United Factories Company, Cleveland, 1906, and Anderson Manufacturing Company, paint manufacturers, Elyria, Ohio, 1907–12; free-lance copywriter, then full-time writer, Chicago, 1913–20; visited France and England, 1921; lived in New Orleans, 1923–24; settled on a farm near Marion, Virginia, 1925: publisher, *Smyth County News* and Marion *Democrat* from 1927; travelled extensively in the

U.S. in mid-1930's reporting on Depression life. Member, American Academy, 1937. *Died 8 March 1941.*

PUBLICATIONS

Collections

Anderson Reader, edited by Paul Rosenfeld. 1947.
The Portable Anderson, edited by Horace Gregory. 1949; revised edition, 1972.
Letters, edited by Howard Mumford Jones and Walter B. Rideout. 1953.
Short Stories, edited by Maxwell Geismar. 1962.
Selected Letters, edited by Charles E. Modlin. 1984.

Fiction

Windy McPherson's Son. 1916; revised edition, 1922.
Marching Men. 1917; edited by Ray Lewis White, 1972.
Winesburg, Ohio: A Group of Tales of Ohio Small Town Life. 1919; edited by John H. Ferres, 1966.
Poor White. 1920.
The Triumph of the Egg: A Book of Impressions from American Life in Tales and Poems. 1921.
Many Marriages. 1923; edited by Douglas G. Rogers, 1978.
Horses and Men (stories). 1923.
Dark Laughter. 1925.
Alice, and The Lost Novel (stories). 1929.
Beyond Desire. 1932.
Death in the Woods and Other Stories. 1933.
Kit Brandon: A Portrait. 1936.

Plays

Winesburg (produced 1934). In *Winesburg and Others*, 1937.
Mother (produced ?). In *Winesburg and Others*, 1937.
Winesburg and Others (includes *The Triumph of the Egg*, dramatized by Raymond O'Neil; *Mother, They Married Later*). 1937.
Above Suspicion (broadcast 1941). In *The Free Company Presents*, edited by James Boyd, 1941.
Textiles, in *Anderson: The Writer at His Craft*, edited by Jack Salzman and others. 1979.

Radio Play: *Above Suspicion*, 1941.

Other

Mid-American Chants. 1918.
A Story Teller's Story. 1924; edited by Ray Lewis White, 1968.
The Modern Writer. 1925.
Notebook. 1926.
Tar: A Midwest Childhood. 1926; edited by Ray Lewis White, 1969.
A New Testament. 1927.
Hello Towns! 1929.
Nearer the Grass Roots. 1929.
The American County Fair. 1930.
Perhaps Women. 1931.
No Swank. 1934.
Puzzled America. 1935.
A Writer's Conception of Realism. 1939.
Home Town. 1940.
Memoirs. 1942; edited by Ray Lewis White, 1969.
Return to Winesburg: Selections from Four Years of Writing for a Country Newspaper, edited by Ray Lewis White. 1967.
The Buck Fever Papers, edited by Welford Dunaway Taylor. 1971.
Anderson/Gertrude Stein: Correspondence and Personal Essays, edited by Ray Lewis White. 1972.
The Writer's Book, edited by Martha Mulroy Curry. 1975.
France and Anderson: Paris Notebook 1921, edited by Michael Fanning. 1976.
Anderson: The Writer at His Craft, edited by Jack Salzman and others. 1979.
Letters to Bab: Anderson to Marietta D. Finley 1916–1933, edited by William A. Sutton. 1985.

*

Bibliography: *Anderson: A Bibliography* by Eugene P. Sheehy and Kenneth A. Lohf, 1960; *Merrill Checklist of Anderson*, 1969, and *Anderson: A Reference Guide*, 1977, both by Ray Lewis White; *Anderson: A Selective, Annotated Bibliography* by Douglas G. Rogers, 1976.

Critical Studies: *Anderson: His Life and Work* by James Schevill, 1951; *Anderson* by Irving Howe, 1951; *Anderson* by Brom Weber, 1964; *Anderson* by Rex Burbank, 1964; *The Achievement of Anderson: Essays in Criticism* edited by Ray Lewis White, 1966; *Anderson: An Introduction and Interpretation* by David D. Anderson, 1967, and *Anderson: Dimensions of His Literary Art*, 1976, and *Critical Essays on Anderson*, 1981, both edited by David D. Anderson; *The Road to Winesburg: A Mosaic of the Imaginative Life of Anderson* by William A. Sutton, 1972; *Anderson: A Collection of Critical Essays* edited by Walter B. Rideout, 1974; *Anderson: Centennial Studies* edited by Hilbert H. Campbell and Charles E. Modlin, 1976; *Anderson* by Welford Dunaway Taylor, 1977.

* * *

In an interview for the *Paris Review* (Spring 1956), William Faulkner stated that Sherwood Anderson was "the father of my generation of American writers and the tradition of American writing which our successors will carry on." Anderson's importance in literary history is accurately summed up in Faulkner's statement, for Anderson is a seminal figure whose prose style has had a significant impact on the direction of American literature in the 20th century. As a boy from a small town in Ohio Anderson fell under the spell of Twain's *Huckleberry Finn* with its innocent narrator and non-literary, vernacular style. Later, as an aspiring writer in Chicago and New York, he became fascinated with Gertrude Stein's attempt to use language as a plastic medium, the way an artist uses paints. These influences on Anderson resulted in the development of a simple, concrete style close to the rhythms of American speech, a style which left an indelible imprint on the prose of Hemingway and his followers.

Anderson also developed a number of characteristically American themes in his fiction. The celebration of youth and innocence is one of those distinguishing features of American writing, and Anderson, raised in the midwest before the turn of the century, celebrates small-town life in the days of the horse and buggy. A boy's wonder and innocent joy in rural life, his love of horses and the open countryside, his admiration for the craftsmen of the village are all part of a nostalgic vein running through Anderson's writing. But Anderson, raised in poverty, was intimate with another side of American life, one which he eventually termed "grotesque." As a young man he observed the people of his town caught in a struggle for material wealth and cowed by a repressive Puritan ethic, and consequently wrote with great feeling about people like his parents whose lives were made wretched by their society's values. Anderson is very sensitive in his fiction to movement, to the restlessness of the individual and to the movements of peoples within the ever-changing fabric of society. He documents America's transition from a rural to an industrial society, and in several books he represents Americans, working in factories, as trapped in a form of living death. He saw the great masses of working Americans as alienated from creative work, and he pondered the artist's role in reawakening his countrymen to more meaningful forms of life.

Anderson's influence and reputation, however, outweigh his actual achievement as a writer. He published seven novels, but critics are not agreed that any one of the novels is wholly successful. The first, *Windy McPherson's Son*, which at the outset effectively recreates something of Anderson's own youth, particularly his relation to his father, becomes a rambling, incoherent narrative about a man's quest for a family and meaningful work. *Marching Men* is an ideological novel with a cranky and finally incoherent vision of men marching for the betterment of humankind. *Poor White*, which dramatizes the industrialization of America, is usually considered the best of the novels, but the charges of diffuseness and unnecessary repetition are not without some justification. Critics generally feel Anderson's worst novel is *Many Marriages*, the story of a man on the point of giving up his business and family in order to escape what has become for him a living death. Anderson himself walked out on his family and a successful career in order to become a writer, which explains perhaps his own fondness for *Many Marriages*. The other novels, *Dark Laughter, Beyond Desire*, and *Kit Brandon* all contain interesting variations on the theme of the individual's quest for a more vital existence, but none of these books succeeds completely in terms of characterization and especially plot. More valuable and interesting are Anderson's autobiographical writings, *A Story Teller's Story, Tar: A Midwest Childhood*, and the posthumous *Memoirs*, all of which fictionalize to a degree the actual events of Anderson's life and reveal the contrary and powerful impulses of the writer's imagination.

Anderson's success as a fiction writer, however, is undisputed in the short story form, and all the collections he published contain at least one or two first rate pieces. Stories such as "I Want to Know Why," "I'm a Fool," and "The Man Who Became a Woman" in which he employs an innocent narrator and a simple, direct style have a unified purpose and effect that is lacking in all the longer fictions. These are initiation stories wherein a youth, usually an innocent boy from the country who loves horses, is awakened to fear, sexual guilt, and a knowledge of his own limitations. "Death in the Woods" is another short masterpiece; it describes a peasant woman's work-burdened existence with a simplicity and sureness of craft that have made critics compare it with the best of Turgenev's stories.

But the book for which Anderson will always be best known is *Winesburg, Ohio*, a cycle of stories about lonely people in a small midwestern town. Anderson originally titled it "The Book of the Grotesque" and in these stories he portrays with both compassion and clinical accuracy the secret lives of people who have been irreparably thwarted and frustrated in different ways. The narrator explains by means of a dream vision that the characters have become grotesque because they have chosen to believe in a single truth. Whether they believe in love, virginity, or godliness, the truth becomes a lie because such a narrow view distorts reality and tragically cuts people off from each other. The grotesques, caught up in their obsessive beliefs, are unable to communicate their ideas and feelings to each other. For example, a farmer consumed with the idea of being a biblical patriarch so confuses and terrifies his only grandson in a ritual of sacrifice that the boy runs away forever. A young man, obsessed with the idea that he is "queer," hopelessly different from other people, breaks into a frantic dance and physically strikes out at his one sympathetic listener. A shy woman, who has waited many years for the return of her lover, one night in desperation runs naked across her front lawn in the rain. Appearing in several stories is the young newspaper reporter, George Willard, to whom some of the grotesques tell their stories. George's mother, one of the aliens of the town, finds an ultimate release from her frustration and loneliness through death, but before she dies she prays that some day her son will "express something" for them both, that he will redeem their lives through art. The mother gives the book a tragic cast, for her prayer cannot be answered. The artists in *Winesburg, Ohio* are ineffectual figures, often persons the least capable of expressing themselves. George Willard at the end of the book leaves Winesburg and we can assume he has written the stories we have read, but he has not been able to "save" his people because the underlying insight in his book is that each man lives by a truth and no one can fully understand or express that truth for someone else.

Anderson once described himself as "the minor author of a minor masterpiece," and one recognizes here an author's startlingly accurate self-assessment. But what Anderson's statement does not comprehend is the powerful influence he had on writers like Hemingway and Faulkner and on the course of American literature as a whole.

—David Stouck

See the essay on *Winesburg, Ohio*.

ARTHUR, Timothy Shay. Born near Newburgh, New York, 6 June 1809; moved with his family to Baltimore, 1817. Educated at public schools in Baltimore. Married Eliza Alden in 1836; five sons and two daughters. Apprentice, possibly for a tailor, then clerk in a counting room, Baltimore, 1830–33; western agent, Susquehanna Bridge and Banking Company, Baltimore, 1833; member of the editorial staff of various Baltimore journals, including *Athenaeum*, 1833–36, and *Saturday Visiter*, 1837–40; co-editor, Baltimore *Literary Monument*, 1836–39; editor, Baltimore *Merchant*, 1840; moved to Philadelphia, 1841, and became writer for *Saturday Courier*, *Graham's Magazine*, and *Godey's Lady's Book*; founder, *Arthur's Ladies' Magazine*, 1845; founder and publisher, *Arthur's Home Gazette Weekly* (*Arthur's Home Magazine* monthly, from 1853), 1850–85; publisher, *Children's Hour*, 1867–74, *Workingman*, 1869, and *Once a Month*, 1869–70. Wrote for children as Uncle Herbert. Member of the Executive Committee,

Centennial Exhibition, Philadelphia, 1876. *Died 6 March 1885.*

PUBLICATIONS

Fiction

Insubordination: An American Story of Real Life. 1841.
The Widow Morrison. 1841; as *Mary Ellis; or, The Runaway Match*, with *Alice Mellville; or, The Indiscretion*, 1850.
Tired of Housekeeping. 1842.
Six Nights with the Washingtonians (stories). 1842; revised edition, as *The Tavern-Keeper's Victims*, 1860.
The Ladies' Fair. 1843.
The Story Book. 1843.
Bell Martin; or, The Heiress. 1843; revised edition, 1849.
Fanny Dale; or, The First Year after Marriage. 1843.
The Tailor's Apprentice: A Story of Cruelty and Oppression. 1843.
The Little Pilgrims: A Sequel to The Tailor's Apprentice. 1843.
Madeline; or, A Daughter's Love, and Other Tales. 1843.
Making a Sensation and Other Tales. 1843.
The Ruined Family and Other Tales. 1843; as *Temperance Tales*, 1843.
Swearing Off and Other Tales. 1843.
The Seamstress. 1843.
The Stolen Wife. 1843.
Sweethearts and Wives; or, Before and after Marriage. 1843.
The Two Merchants. 1843.
The Village Doctors and Other Tales. 1843.
Cecilia Howard; or, The Young Lady Who Had Finished Her Education. 1844.
Pride or Principle—Which Makes the Lady? 1844.
Family Pride; or, The Palace and the Poor House. 1844.
Hints and Helps for the Home Circle; or, The Mother's Friend. 1844.
Hiram Elwood, The Banker; or, Like Father Like Son. 1844.
The Martyr Wife. 1844.
Prose Fictions Written for the Illustration of True Principles. 1844.
The Ruined Gamester; or, Two Eras in My Life. 1844.
The Two Sisters; or, Life's Changes. 1844.
Alice; or, The Victim of One Indiscretion. 1844.
The Maiden. 1845.
The Wife. 1845.
Anna Milnor, The Young Lady Who Was Not Punctual, and Other Tales. 1845.
The Heiress. 1845.
The Club Room and Other Temperance Tales. 1845.
Married and Single; or, Marriage and Celibacy Contrasted. 1845.
Lovers and Husbands. 1845.
Tales from Real Life. 1845.
The Two Husbands and Other Tales. 1845.
The Mother. 1846.
Random Recollections of an Old Doctor. 1846.
The Beautiful Widow. 1847.
Improving Stories for the Young. 1847.
Keeping Up Appearances. 1847.
Riches Have Wings. 1847.
The Young Lady at Home. 1847.
The Young Music Teacher and Other Tales. 1847.
Agnes; or, The Possessed: A Revelation of Mesmerism. 1848.
Debtor and Creditor. 1848.
The Lost Children. 1848.
Retiring from Business; or, The Rich Man's Error. 1848.
Love in a Cottage. 1848.
Rising in the World. 1848.
Stories for My Young Friends [*Parents, Young Housekeepers*]. 3 vols., 1848–51.
Temptations. 1848.
Lucy Sanford: A Story of the Heart. 1848.
Making Haste to Be Rich. 1848.
The Three Eras of a Woman's Life (includes *The Maiden, The Wife, The Mother*). 1848.
Love in High Life. 1849.
Mary Moreton; or, The Broken Promise. 1849.
Sketches of Life and Character. 1849.
Our Children: How Shall We Save Them? 1849.
All for the Best; or, The Old Peppermint Man. 1850.
The Debtor's Daughter. 1850.
The Divorced Wife. 1850.
Golden Grains from Life's Harvest Field. 1850.
Illustrated Temperance Tales. 1850; revised edition, as *The Lights and Shadows of Real Life*, 1851.
The Orphan Children. 1850.
Pride and Prudence; or, The Married Sisters. 1850.
Tales of Domestic Life. 1850.
True Riches and Other Tales. 1850.
The Two Brides. 1850.
The Young Artist; or, The Dream of Italy. 1850.
The Two Wives. 1851.
The Banker's Wife. 1851.
Lessons in Life for All Who Will Read Them. 1851.
Off-Hand Sketches. 1851.
Seed-Time and Harvest (stories). 1851.
The Way to Prosper; or, In Union There Is Strength and Other Tales. 1851.
Woman's Trials (stories). 1851.
Words for the Wise (stories). 1851.
Home Scenes and Home Influence. 1852.
The Tried and the Tempted. 1852.
Cedardale. 1852.
Pierre the Organ-Boy and Other Stories. 1852.
The Poor Wood-Cutter and Other Stories. 1852.
Jessie Hampton. 1852.
Uncle Ben's New-Year's Gift. 1852.
The Ways of Providence (stories). 1852.
Confessions of a Housekeeper. 1852; revised edition, as *Trials and Confessions of an American Housekeeper*, 1854; as *Ups and Downs*, 1857.
Who Are Happiest? and Other Stories. 1852.
Who Is Greatest? and Other Stories. 1852.
Haven't-Time and Don't-Be-in-a-Hurry and Other Stories. 1852.
The Last Penny and Other Stories. 1852.
Maggy's Baby and Other Stories. 1852.
The Wounded Boy and Other Stories. 1852.
Married Life: Its Shadows and Sunshine (stories). 1852.
The Lost Children and Other Stories. 1852.
Trials of a Needlewoman. 1853.
Before and After the Election; or, The Political Experiences of Mr. Patrick Murphy. 1853.
Finger Posts on the Way of Life. 1853.
The Fireside Angel. 1853.
Heart-Histories and Life-Pictures. 1853.

Home Lights and Shadows. 1853.
The Home Mission. 1853.
The Iron Rule; or, Tyranny in the Household. 1853.
The Lady at Home. 1853.
Leaves from the Book of Human Life. 1853.
The Old Man's Bride. 1853.
Sparing to Spend; or, The Loftons and Pinkertons. 1853.
The Old Astrologer. 1853(?).
Ten Nights in a Bar-Room and What I Saw There. 1854; edited by C. Hugh Holman, with *In His Steps* by Charles M. Sheldon, 1966.
The Angel of the Household. 1854.
Shadows and Sunbeams. 1854.
Leaves from the Book of Human Life. 1855.
The Good Time Coming. 1855.
Trial and Triumph. 1855.
What Can Woman Do? 1856.
The Withered Heart. 1857.
The Hand But Not the Heart; or, The Life-Trials of Jessie Loring. 1858.
The Angel and the Demon: A Tale of Modern Spiritualism. 1858.
The Little Bound-Boy. 1858.
Lizzy Glenn; or, The Trials of a Seamstress. 1859.
The Allen House; or, Twenty Years Ago and Now. 1860.
Aunt Mary's Preserving Kettle. 1863.
Nancy Wimble. 1863.
Hidden Wings and Other Stories. 1864.
Light on Shadowed Paths. 1864.
Out in the World. 1864.
Sunshine at Home and Other Stories. 1864.
Sowing the Wind and Other Stories. 1865.
Home-Heroes, Saints, and Martyrs. 1865.
Nothing But Money. 1865.
What Came Afterwards. 1865.
Life's Crosses and How to Meet Them. 1865.
Our Neighbors in the Corner House. 1866.
The Lost Bride; or, The Astrologer's Prophecy Fulfilled. 1866.
Blind Nelly's Boy and Other Stories. 1867.
The Son of My Friend. 1867.
After the Storm. 1868.
The Peacemaker and Other Stories. 1869.
After a Shadow and Other Stories. 1869.
Not Anything for Peace and Other Stories. 1869.
Heroes of the Household. 1869.
Rainy Day at Home. 1869.
The Seen and the Unseen. 1869.
Anna Lee. 1869.
Beacon Lights. 1869.
Tom Blinn's Temperance Society and Other Tales. 1870.
Idle Hands and Other Stories. 1871.
Orange Blossoms, Fresh and Faded (stories). 1871.
The Wonderful Story of Gentle Hand and Other Stories. 1871.
Grace Myers' Sewing Machine and Other Tales. 1872.
Three Years in a Man-Trap. 1872.
Cast Adrift. 1873.
Comforted. 1873.
Woman to the Rescue: A Story of the New Crusade. 1874.
The Power of Kindness and Other Stories. 1875.
Danger; or, Wounded in the House of a Friend. 1875.
The Latimer Family. 1877.
The Wife's Engagement Ring. 1877.
The Bar-Rooms at Brantley. 1877.
The Mill and the Tavern. 1878.
The Strike at Tivoli Mills and What Came of It. 1879.
Window Curtains. 1880.
Saved as by Fire. 1881.
Death-Dealing Gold. 1890.
The Little Savoyard and Other Stories. 1891.
Two Little Girls and What They Did. 1899.
Won by Waiting. N.d.

Other

The Young Wife's Book. 1836.
Hints and Helps for the Home Circle; or, The Mother's Friend. 1844.
A Christmas Box for the Sons and Daughters of Temperance. 1847.
Advice to Young Men [Ladies] on Their Duties and Conduct in Life. 2 vols., 1847.
Wreaths of Friendship: A Gift for the Young, with Francis Channing Woodworth. 1849.
A Wheat Sheaf, Gathered from Our Own Field, with Francis Channing Woodworth. 1851.
Our Little Harry and Other Poems and Stories. 1852.
The History of Georgia, Kentucky, Virginia, New Jersey, New York, Ohio, Vermont, Connecticut, Pennsylvania, Tennessee, Illinois, with W.H. Carpenter. 11 vols., 1852–57.
The String of Pearls for Boys and Girls, with Francis Channing Woodworth. 1853.
Steps Towards Heaven (sermons). 1858.
Growler's Income Tax. 1864.
Talks with a Philosopher on the Ways of God and Man. 1871.
Strong Drink: The Curse and the Cure. 1877; as *Grappling with the Monster*, 1877.
Feet and Wings; or, Among the Beasts and Birds. 1880.
Adventures by Sea and Land. 1890.
Sow Well and Reap Well: A Book for the Young. N.d.
Story Sermons. N.d.
Talks with a Child on the Beatitudes. N.d.

Editor, with W.H. Carpenter, *The Baltimore Book*. 1838.
Editor, *The Sons of Temperance Offering*. 2 vols., 1849–50.
Editor, *The Brilliant: A Gift-Book*. 1850.
Editor, *The Crystal Fount for All Seasons*. 1850.
Editor, *The Temperance Gift*. 1854.
Editor, *The Temperance Offering*. 1854.
Editor, *Friends and Neighbors; or, Two Ways of Living in the World*. 1856.
Editor, *The Mother's Rule*. 1856.
Editor, *Our Homes*. 1856.
Editor, *The True Path and How to Walk Therein*. 1856.
Editor, *The Wedding Guest*. 1856.
Editor, *Words of Cheer for the Tempted, The Toiling, and the Sorrowing*. 1856.
Editor, *Orange Blossoms*. 1857.
Editor, *Little Gems from the Children's Hour*. 1875.
Editor, *The Prattler*. 1876.
Editor, *The My Book*. 1877.
Editor, *The Budget*. 1877.
Editor, *My Pet Book*. 1877.
Editor, *My Primer*. 1877.
Editor, *The Playmate*. 1878.
Editor, *The Boys' and Girls' Treasury*. 1879.
Editor, *Pleasant Stories and Pictures*. 1880.

Editor, *Lucy Grey and Other Stories*. 1880.
Editor, *Sophy and Prince*. 1881.
Editor, *Uncle Herbert's Speaker*. 1886.
Editor, *Friendship's Token*. N.d.

* * *

Timothy Shay Arthur is likely to be recalled today as the author of *Ten Nights in a Bar-Room*, the popular melodrama about a small-town miller turned saloon-keeper who brings misfortune upon his family and community, until the killing of his daughter by drunken brawlers saves him and the town for temperance (which to Arthur meant total prohibition). Actually he did not write the play, which was one of the most often performed on the American stage during the late 19th century and which still survives, though now it is usually burlesqued; the dramatization was prepared by William W. Pratt from Arthur's novel. Nor did Arthur devote himself before the Civil War exclusively to the temperance cause, although he enjoyed his first success with *Six Nights with the Washingtonians*, tales about the work of this noble band that sought to redeem drunkards through "moral suasion." After gaining experience as a contributor to literary magazines and then as co-editor of several short-lived publications in Baltimore from 1834 to 1840, he moved to Philadelphia, where, after several earlier experiments in finding the profitable format for a journal devoted to "the good, the true, and the beautiful," he founded in 1853 *Arthur's Home Magazine*, which he edited until his death.

During these years he wrote about a hundred novels and uncounted short stories, most of which appeared first either in his magazines or in the many gift-books that he edited. Before the Civil War, the majority of these tales were thinly fictionalized guides to young people getting married and setting up a home and business. *The Three Eras of a Woman's Life* was only the most ambitious of about two dozen that advised maiden, wife and mother on the woman's proper "sphere" and duties. *Debtor and Creditor* was one of many that warned against unsound business practices; but Arthur was also one of the first American novelists, even before the age of the Robber Barons, to condemn unscrupulous business practices growing out of a greed for gain in an unexpectedly bleak and cynical novel like *Nothing But Money*. Arthur was also a member of the Church of the New Jerusalem, as the followers of Emmanuel Swedenborg called themselves; and he expounded the doctrines of the church in novels like *The Good Time Coming*, an attempt to dissuade egotistical people from reckless courses. He also, surprisingly, pioneered in fiction dealing with divorce—then a scandalous subject. *The Hand But Not the Heart, After the Storm*, and *Out in the World* castigate hasty marriage and easy divorce, but grant that legal separation may be necessitated by a spouse's philandering or intemperance.

After the Civil War left him disheartened about his fellow Americans, he devoted his fiction largely to the temperance crusade, growing through *Three Years in a Man-Trap, Woman to the Rescue*, and *The Bar-Rooms at Brantley* constantly more hysterical in his denunciation of the evils of drink and shriller in his demands for legal prohibition rather than a reliance upon self-reform. These works in print or on the stage, however, failed to enjoy the success of his earlier writings.

—Warren French

ASHBERY, John (Lawrence). Born in Rochester, New York, 28 July 1927. Educated at Deerfield Academy, Massachusetts; Harvard University, Cambridge, Massachusetts (member of the editorial board, *Harvard Advocate*), A.B. in English 1949; Columbia University, New York, M.A. in English 1951; New York University, 1957–58. Copywriter, Oxford University Press, New York, 1951–54, and McGraw-Hill Book Company, New York, 1954–55; co-editor, *One Fourteen*, New York, 1952–53; art critic, European Edition of New York *Herald Tribune*, Paris, 1960–65, and *Art International*, Lugano, Switzerland, 1961–64; editor, *Locus Solus* magazine, Lans-en-Vercors, France, 1960–62; editor, *Art and Literature*, Paris, 1963–66; Paris correspondent, 1964–65, and executive editor, 1965–72, *Art News*, New York; since 1974 Professor of English, Brooklyn College; poetry editor, *Partisan Review*, New Brunswick, New Jersey, 1976–80; art critic, *New York* magazine, 1978–80; since 1980 art critic, *Newsweek*, New York. Recipient: Fulbright fellowship, 1955, 1956; Poets Foundation grant, 1960, 1964; Ingram Merrill Foundation grant, 1962, 1972; Guggenheim fellowship, 1967, 1973; National Endowment for the Arts grant, 1968, 1969; American Academy award, 1969; Shelley Memorial Award, 1973; Frank O'Hara Prize, 1974; Harriet Monroe Poetry Award, 1975; National Book Critics Circle award, 1976; Pulitzer Prize, 1976; National Book Award, 1976; Rockefeller grant, for playwriting, 1978; English Speaking Union prize, 1979; Bard College Charles Flint Kellogg Award, 1983; Academy of American Poets fellowship, 1983; Bollingen Prize, 1984. D.Litt.: Long Island University, Southampton, New York, 1979. Member, American Academy, 1980; American Academy of Arts and Sciences, 1983. Lives in New York City.

PUBLICATIONS

Verse

Turandot and Other Poems. 1953.
Some Trees. 1956.
The Poems. 1961(?).
The Tennis Court Oath. 1962.
Rivers and Mountains. 1966.
Selected Poems. 1967.
Three Madrigals. 1968.
Sunrise in Suburbia. 1968.
Fragment. 1969.
Evening in the Country. 1970.
The Double Dream of Spring. 1970.
The New Spirit. 1970.
Penguin Modern Poets 19, with Lee Harwood and Tom Raworth. 1971.
Three Poems. 1972.
The Vermont Notebook. 1975.
The Serious Doll. 1975.
Self-Portrait in a Convex Mirror. 1975.
Houseboat Days. 1977.
As We Know. 1979.
Shadow Train. 1981.
A Wave. 1984.
Selected Poems. 1985.

Plays

The Heroes (produced 1952). In *Three Plays*, 1978.

The Compromise (produced 1956). In *Three Plays*, 1978.
Three Plays. 1978.
The Philosopher (produced 1982). In *Three Plays*, 1978.

Fiction

A Nest of Ninnies, with James Schuyler. 1969.

Other

Ashbery and Kenneth Koch (A Conversation). 1965(?).
R.B. Kitaj: Paintings, Drawings, Pastels, with others. 1981.
Fairfield Porter: Realist Painter in an Age of Abstraction. 1983.

Editor, *Penguin Modern Poets 24*. 1973.
Editor, *Muck Arbour*, by Bruce Marcus. 1975.
Editor, *The Funny Place*, by Richard F. Snow. 1975.

Translator, with Lawrence G. Blochman, *Murder in Montmartre*, by Noël Vexin. 1960.
Translator, *Melville*, by Jean-Jacques Mayoux. 1960.
Translator, with Lawrence G. Blochman, *The Deadlier Sex*, by Geneviève Manceron. 1961.
Translator, *Alberto Giacometti*, by Jacques Dupin. 1963(?).
Translator, *Fantomas*, by Marcel Allain and Pierre Souvestre. 1986.

*

Bibliography: *Ashbery: A Comprehensive Bibliography* by David K. Kermani, 1976.

Critical Studies: *Ashbery: An Introduction to the Poetry* by David Shapiro, 1979; *Beyond Amazement: New Essays on Ashbery* edited by David Lehman, 1980.

* * *

John Ashbery was originally associated with the New York school of poets, whose central figure is Frank O'Hara, and whose poetic style is noted for its painterly emphasis on setting, luxurious detailing, and leisurely meditative argument. This group closely identified itself with the abstract expressionist painters and with the Museum of Modern Art; some of these poets wrote for *Art News*. Ashbery was directly connected with all three spheres, and from the painters learned a curious collage-like style of poetry made of bits and pieces of lyric phrasing. This mode of speech, lacking transition between leaps of thought and reflection, early marked Ashbery as difficult, if not impenetrable. As he remarked in a later poem,

> I know that I braid too much my own
> Snapped-off perceptions of things as they come to me.
> They are private and always will be.

The root of Ashbery's lyric style may be traced back to the Symbolists, and to the allusive poems of T.S. Eliot, whose echo is frequently heard in Ashbery's work. At his best, Ashbery can give uncanny immediacy to his language; his stance of uncertainty before life draws him to the appearance of the phenomenal world which he contemplates in a delicate, sinewy language.

Some Trees is Ashbery's first work of note, and contains one of his most anthologized poems, "The Instruction Manual." His second major book of poems, *The Tennis Court Oath*, in particular emphasizes the style of pastiche. Beginning with *Rivers and Mountains*, Ashbery introduced his specialty, the long discursive meditation running to many pages in which the effort is made to piece together the fragments of experience into a sensible whole, "The Skaters" makes up half of the book. The meditative style is pursued most fully in *Three Poems*, prose poems that are linked like the moments of dialectical reason, in which the speaker loses himself in the metaphysical and spiritual ambiguities of his existence.

Much of the poetry of these books is suffused with a restrained melancholy. Ashbery is articulating the post-existential awareness, in which existence is a palpable but unknowable dimension. That stance is succinctly phrased in "Poems in Three Parts":

> One must bear in mind one thing.
> It isn't necessary to know what that thing is.
> All things are palpable, none are known.

No faith or hope can fully support the speaker, and he is recurrently plunged into reflection to discover the purpose of his life. *Self-Portrait in a Convex Mirror* continues this self-analysis and metaphysical exploration, particularly in the brilliant long title poem and in "Grand Galop." In recent books, there is a perceptible effort to take up subjects beyond the self, but the poems are still deeply absorbed with the absence of a philosophical and religious context in which to value or understand life. Ashbery's innovative and sophisticated humor is clear in *The Double Dream of Spring*, particularly in such surreal high jinks as his "Variations, Calypso and Fugue on a Theme of Ella Wheeler Wilcox."

Ashbery has been deconstructing philosophical arguments throughout his canon, writing parodies of such efforts that reduce the metaphysical quest to subtle absurdity. In his latest work, beginning with *As We Know, Shadow Train*, and *A Wave*, the poems seem to drift, to follow the flow of thought without will or purpose, and as such, appear to trace the metabolism of mental life. "Litany," in *As We Know*, takes both sides of an inner dialog and plays them out to no conclusion, though one feels that there are peaks and valleys to the chatter, a landscape of dreams and passing notions that illuminates a curious recess of subjectivity heretofore uncharted. In these works especially, one sees Ashbery as forerunner to the present movement of American poetry which calls itself L=A=N=G=U=A=G=E poetry. A rigorously edited version of the canon now appears as *Selected Poems*.

—Paul Christensen

ATHERTON, Gertrude (Franklin, née Horn). Born in San Francisco, California, 30 October 1857. Educated in private schools in California and Kentucky. Married George H. Bowen Atherton in 1876 (died, 1887). Moved to New York, 1888, then traveled extensively and lived in Europe; lived in San Francisco after 1932. Trustee, San Francisco Public Library; member, San Francisco Art Commission; President, American National Academy of Literature, 1934; Chairman of Letters, League of American Pen Women, 1939; President, Northern

California Section of PEN. Recipient: International Academy of Letters and Sciences of Italy Gold Medal. D.Litt.: Mills College, Oakland, California, 1935; LL.D.: University of California, Berkeley, 1937. Chevalier, Legion of Honor (France), 1925; member, American Academy, 1938. *Died 14 June 1948.*

PUBLICATIONS

Fiction

What Dreams May Come. 1888.
Hermia Suydam. 1889; as *Hermia, An American Woman*, 1889.
Los Cerritos: A Romance of the Modern Time. 1890.
A Question of Time. 1891.
The Doomswoman. 1893.
Before the Gringo Came. 1894; revised edition, as *The Splendid Idle Forties: Stories of Old California*, 1902.
A Whirl Asunder. 1895.
His Fortunate Grace. 1897.
Patience Sparhawk and Her Times. 1897.
American Wives and English Husbands. 1898; revised edition, as *Transplanted*, 1919.
The Californians. 1898.
The Valiant Runaways. 1898.
A Daughter of the Vine. 1899.
Senator North. 1900.
The Aristocrats. 1901.
The Conqueror, Being the True and Romantic Story of Alexander Hamilton. 1902.
Heart of Hyacinth. 1903.
Mrs. Pendleton's Four-in-Hand. 1903.
Rulers of Kings. 1904.
The Bell in the Fog and Other Stories. 1905.
The Travelling Thirds. 1905.
Rezánov. 1906.
Ancestors. 1907.
The Gorgeous Isle: A Romance: Scene, Nevis, B.W.I., 1842. 1908.
Tower of Ivory. 1910.
Julia France and Her Times. 1912.
Perch of the Devil. 1914.
Mrs. Balfame. 1916.
The White Morning: A Novel of the Power of the German Women in Wartime. 1918.
The Avalanche: A Mystery Story. 1919.
The Sisters-in-Law: A Novel of Our Time. 1921.
Sleeping Fires. 1922; as *Dormant Fires*, 1922.
Black Oxen. 1923.
The Crystal Cup. 1925.
The Immortal Marriage. 1927.
The Jealous Gods: A Processional Novel of the Fifth Century B.C. (Concerning One Alcibiades). 1928; as *Vengeful Gods*, 1928.
Dido, Queen of Hearts. 1929.
The Sophisticates. 1931.
The Foghorn: Stories. 1934.
Golden Peacock. 1936.
Rezánov and Doña Concha. 1937.
The House of Lee. 1940.
The Horn of Life. 1942.

Play

Screenplay: *Don't Neglect Your Wife*, with Louis Sherwin, 1921.

Other

California: An Intimate History. 1914; revised edition, 1927.
Life in the War Zone. 1916.
The Living Present (essays). 1917.
Adventures of a Novelist (autobiography). 1932.
Can Women Be Gentlemen? (essays). 1938.
Golden Gate Country. 1945.
My San Francisco: A Wayward Biography. 1946.

Editor, *A Few of Hamilton's Letters, Including His Description of the Great West Indian Hurricane of 1772*. 1903.

*

Bibliography: "A Checklist of the Writings of and about Atherton" by Charlotte S. McClure, in *American Literary Realism 1870–1910*, Spring 1976.

Critical Studies: *Atherton* by Joseph Henry Jackson, 1940; *Atherton*, 1976, and *Atherton*, 1979, both by Charlotte S. McClure.

* * *

Gertrude Atherton was a popular and prolific writer, publishing nearly forty novels, several volumes of short stories, three collections of essays, a history of California, two books about San Francisco, a selection of Alexander Hamilton's letters, and numerous uncollected articles. Although her novels lack great artistic merit, they are significant for the literary historian because they helped to free American literature from the shackles of Victorian prudery. From the beginning of her career Atherton rejected the Victorian myths about woman's moral superiority and sexual imbecility. Her heroines are sensual, egotistical, and intellectually ambitious. They seek an identity based on their own needs and talents rather than on the attributes ascribed to women by society. Her treatment of female sexuality in particular gained her considerable critical attention both in America and in England; liberal critics singled her out for her "fearless treatment of the problems of sex," while conservatives screamed that she exalted "the morals of the barn-yard into a social ideal" and accelerated "the corruption of private life and the destruction of the family relation."

Atherton's California fiction is of particular interest to the cultural historian, focusing, as it does, on the effects of the "gringo" coming to power at the expense of the Mexican aristocracy. Her best novel, *The Californians*, effectively analyzes the conflict between the heritages of Hispanic indolence and pride and Yankee shrewdness and pragmatism. In this novel Atherton's conception of her heroine is firmly rooted in her knowledge of the patriarchal, restrictive Spanish tradition as well as the shallow ambiance of San Francisco society. However, in many of her other California novels, Atherton romanticizes her subject matter. As Kevin Starr points out in *Americans and the California Dream*, Atherton speaks for the California elite which, on the one hand, mourned the loss of the Arcadian existence of other Hispanic settlers, but, on the other, repudiated that existence as inimical to the progress of the state.

In most of her fiction Atherton sensationalized her material. Thus, the heroine of *Patience Sparhawk and Her Times* is wrongly convicted of her husband's murder, the heroine of *Black Oxen* is a rejuvenated 58-year-old woman who falls in love with a man in his thirties, and the heroine of *The Immortal Marriage* is Aspasia, whom Atherton presents not as a prostitute, but as Pericles's beloved wife, supremely beautiful and intelligent enough to provoke admiration from men such as Sophocles and Socrates. Despite Atherton's artistic shortcomings, her lifelong concern with the contribution of women to civilization as well as her fictional observation of fifty years of America's social history suggest that her work deserves further examination by literary and cultural historians.

—Sybil B. Weir

AUCHINCLOSS, Louis (Stanton). Born in Lawrence, New York, 27 September 1917. Educated at Groton School, Massachusetts, graduated 1935; Yale University, New Haven, Connecticut, 1935–38; University of Virginia Law School, Charlottesville, LL.B. 1941; admitted to the New York bar, 1941. Served in the U.S. Naval Reserve, 1941–45: Lieutenant. Married Adèle Lawrence in 1957; three sons. Associate Lawyer, Sullivan and Cromwell, New York, 1941–51; Associate, 1954–58, and since 1958 Partner, Hawkins Delafield and Wood, New York. President, Museum of the City of New York, since 1966; trustee, Josiah Macy Jr. Foundation, New York; former member of the Executive Committee, Association of the Bar of New York City. Recipient: New York State Governor's award, 1985. D.Litt.: New York University, 1974; Pace College, New York, 1979. Member, American Academy. Lives in New York City.

PUBLICATIONS

Fiction

The Indifferent Children. 1947.
The Injustice Collectors (stories). 1950.
Sybil. 1951.
A Law for the Lion. 1953.
The Romantic Egoists: A Reflection in Eight Minutes (stories). 1954.
The Great World and Timothy Colt. 1956.
Venus in Sparta. 1958.
Pursuit of the Prodigal. 1959.
The House of Five Talents. 1960.
Portrait in Brownstone. 1962.
Powers of Attorney (stories). 1963.
The Rector of Justin. 1964.
The Embezzler. 1966.
Tales of Manhattan. 1967.
A World of Profit. 1968.
Second Chance (stories). 1970.
I Come as a Thief. 1972.
The Partners. 1974.
The Winthrop Covenant. 1976.
The Dark Lady. 1977.
The Country Cousin. 1978.
The House of the Prophet. 1980.
The Cat and the King. 1981.
Watchfires. 1982.
Narcissa and Other Fables. 1983.
Exit Lady Masham. 1983.
The Book Class. 1984.
Honorable Men. 1985.
Diary of a Yuppie. 1986.

Play

The Club Bedroom (produced 1967).

Other

Edith Wharton. 1961.
Reflections of a Jacobite. 1961.
Ellen Glasgow. 1964.
Pioneers and Caretakers: A Study of 9 American Women Novelists. 1965.
Motiveless Malignity (on Shakespeare). 1969.
Henry Adams. 1971.
Edith Wharton: A Woman in Her Time. 1971.
Richelieu. 1972.
A Writer's Capital (autobiography). 1974.
Reading Henry James. 1975.
Persons of Consequence: Queen Victoria and Her Circle. 1979.
Life, Law, and Letters: Essays and Sketches. 1979.
Three "Perfect Novels" and What They Have in Common. 1981.
Unseen Versailles. 1981.
False Dawn: Women in the Age of the Sun King. 1984.

Editor, *An Edith Wharton Reader*. 1965.
Editor, *The Warden, and Barchester Towers*, by Anthony Trollope. 1966.
Editor, *Fables of Wit and Elegance*. 1975.
Editor, *Maverick in Mauve: The Diary of a Turn-of-the-Century Aristocrat*, by Florence Adele Sloane. 1983.

*

Bibliography: *Auchincloss and His Critics: A Bibliographical Record* by Jackson R. Bryer, 1977.

Critical Studies: *The Novel of Manners in America* by James W. Tuttleton, 1972; *Auchincloss* by Christopher C. Dahl, 1986.

* * *

Louis Auchincloss is a successor to Edith Wharton as a chronicler of the New York aristocracy. In this role he necessarily imbues his novels with an elegiac tone as he observes the passing beauties of the city and the fading power of the white Anglo-Saxon Protestants of old family and old money who can no longer sustain their position of dominance. His principal subject is thus the manners and morals, the money and marriages, the families and houses, the schools and games, the language and arts of the New York aristocracy as he traces its rise, observes its present crisis, and meditates its possible fall and disappearance. The point of vantage from which he often observes the aristocracy is that of the lawyer who serves and frequently belongs to this class.

The idea of good family stands in an uneasy relation to money in Auchincloss's fiction. Auchincloss dramatizes the dilemma of the American aristocracy by showing that it is necessary to possess money to belong to this class but fatal to one's standing within the class to pursue money. People who have connections with those who are still in trade cannot themselves fully qualify as gentlemen, as the opportunistic Mr. Dale in *The Great World and Timothy Colt* shows. On the other hand, Auchincloss is clearly critical of those aristocrats like Bertie Millinder or Percy Prime who do nothing constructive and are engaged simply in the spending of money. Auchincloss recognizes that the family is the most important of aristocratic institutions and that its place in its class is guaranteed by the conservation of its resources. This task of preserving the family wealth falls to the lawyers, and his fiction is rich in the complexities, both moral and financial, of fiduciary responsibility; *Venus in Sparta* is a novel in point.

Auchincloss fully exploits the conflict between the marriage arranged for the good of the family, often by strong women, and romantic or sexual impulses that are destructive of purely social goals, as *Portrait in Brownstone* illustrates. Sex and love are enemies to the organicism of conservative societies, in which the will of the individual is vested in the whole. Auchincloss observes the workings of this organic notion in the structure of family and marriage as well as in institutions like the school and the club. Such institutions preserve a way of life and protect those who live by it from those on the outside who do not.

Auchincloss's fiction does more than present us with a mere record of the institutions that support the American aristocracy. The dramatic interest in his novels and whatever larger importance may be accorded them lies in his recognition that the entire class is in jeopardy and that individual aristocrats are often failures. Sometimes Auchincloss sees problems arising within the context of aristocracy itself, as when individual will or desire comes in conflict with the organicism; perhaps Reese Parmalee, in *Pursuit of the Prodigal*, makes the most significant rebellion of all Auchincloss's characters, but he is rejecting a decadent aristocracy and not aristocracy itself. But the real failures are those aristocrats who suffer, as so many of Auchincloss's male characters do, from a sense of inadequacy and insecurity that leads them to self-destructiveness. They are not strong and tough-fibred, as so many of the women are; they seem too fastidious and over-civilized, and they are failing the idea of society and their class. *A World of Profit* is the most explicit recognition of this failure.

Auchincloss has made his record of the New York aristocracy in a style which is clear and simple, occasionally elegant and brilliant, and sometimes self-consciously allusive. He has a gift for comedy of manners, which he has not sufficiently cultivated, and a fine model in Oscar Wilde. Yet among his faults as a novelist, especially evident because of the particular genre he has chosen, is a failure to give the reader a richness of detail. Furthermore, he sometimes loses control of his novels and permits action to overwhelm theme. The most serious criticism to be made of his work is that while he does indeed pose moral dilemmas for his characters, he too easily resolves their problems for them. He has given us, on balance, a full enough record of upper-class life in New York, but he has fallen short of the most penetrating and meaningful kinds of social insight that the best of the novelists of manners offer.

—Chester E. Eisinger

BALDWIN, James (Arthur). Born in New York City, 2 August 1924. Educated at Public School 139, Harlem, New York, and DeWitt Clinton High School, Bronx, New York, graduated 1942. Worked as handyman, dishwasher, waiter, and office boy in New York, and in defense work, Belle Meade, New Jersey, in early 1940's; full-time writer from 1943; lived in Europe, mainly in Paris, 1948–56. Member, Actors Studio, New York, National Advisory Board of CORE (Congress on Racial Equality), and National Committee for a Sane Nuclear Policy. Recipient: Saxton fellowship, 1945; Rosenwald fellowship, 1948; Guggenheim fellowship, 1954; American Academy award, 1956; Ford fellowship, 1958; National Conference of Christians and Jews Brotherhood Award, 1962; George Polk Award, 1963; Foreign Drama Critics award, 1964; Martin Luther King, Jr., Award (City University of New York), 1978. D.Litt.: University of British Columbia, Vancouver, 1963. Member, American Academy, 1964. Lives in New York City and St.-Paul, near Vence, France.

PUBLICATIONS

Fiction

Go Tell It on the Mountain. 1953.
Giovanni's Room. 1956.
Another Country. 1962.
Going to Meet the Man (stories). 1965.
Tell Me How Long the Train's Been Gone. 1968.
If Beale Street Could Talk. 1974.
Just above My Head. 1979.

Plays

The Amen Corner (produced 1955). 1968.
Blues for Mister Charlie (produced 1964). 1964.
One Day, When I Was Lost: A Scenario Based on "The Autobiography of Malcolm X." 1972.
A Deed from the King of Spain (produced 1974).

Screenplay: *The Inheritance*, 1973.

Verse

Jimmy's Blues: Selected Poems. 1983.

Other

Notes of a Native Son. 1955.
Nobody Knows My Name: More Notes of a Native Son. 1961.
The Fire Next Time. 1963.
Nothing Personal, photographs by Richard Avedon. 1964.
A Rap on Race, with Margaret Mead. 1971.
No Name in the Street. 1972.
A Dialogue: Baldwin and Nikki Giovanni. 1973.
Little Man, Little Man (for children). 1976.
The Devil Finds Work: An Essay. 1976.
The Price of a Ticket: Collected Nonfiction 1948–1985. 1985.
Evidence of Things Not Seen. 1985.

*

Bibliography: "Baldwin: A Checklist 1947–1962" by Kathleen A. Kindt, and "Baldwin: A Bibliography 1947–1962" by Russell G. Fischer, both in *Bulletin of Bibliography*, January–April 1965; *Baldwin: A Reference Guide* by Fred L. and Nancy Standley, 1979.

Critical Studies: *The Furious Passage of Baldwin* by Fern Eckman, 1966; *Baldwin: A Critical Study* by Stanley Macebuh, 1973; *Baldwin: A Collection of Critical Essays* edited by Keneth Kinnamon, 1974; *Baldwin: A Critical Evaluation* edited by Therman B. O'Daniel, 1977; *Baldwin* by Louis H. Pratt, 1978; *Baldwin* by Carolyn W. Sylvander, 1980; *Baldwin: Three Interviews* by Kenneth B. Clarke and Malcolm King, 1985; *Black Women in the Fiction of Baldwin* by Trudier Harris, 1985.

* * *

James Baldwin's major theme has always been identity or its denial. He develops the complex personal and social dimensions of this theme in four main subjects: church, self, city, and race. The result is a substantial body of writing in fiction, drama, and the personal essay characterized by intense feeling, stylistic eloquence, and social urgency.

As Baldwin was making his first adolescent efforts to write, he was simultaneously preaching in store-front churches in Harlem. Of brief duration, his religious vocation both satisfied his need to prove his worth to his father and complicated his intellectual development. Seeming to simplify personal problems, his religious commitment actually generated tensions that were to make Baldwin an eloquent critic of Christianity, especially its pernicious social effects, as well as a witness of its emotional power and richness. The enduring fictional achievement of Baldwin's involvement with the church is his brilliant first novel, *Go Tell It on the Mountain*. By means of a carefully crafted tripartite structure, rich characterizations, and a distinctive stylistic voice, Baldwin tells the story not only of John Grimes, a Harlem youth undergoing a personal and religious crisis, but also of his stepfather, Gabriel; his stepfather's sister, Florence; and his mother, Elizabeth. With historical scope as well as personal immediacy, the author shows how sex, race, and religion affect the lives of these worshippers in the Temple of the Fire Baptized. Religious experience is conveyed to the reader with overwhelming emotional power, but he is also forced to recognize how it erodes social reality or even, in the case of Gabriel, becomes a means of oppression. The critique of the church is carried further in the play *The Amen Corner*, in which a fanatical woman preacher substitutes her small church for the love of her husband. Narrowly fulfilling, but in the final analysis life-denying, religion must be abandoned, Baldwin implies, if the self is to be realized.

Many of Baldwin's best early essays and stories—"Autobiographical Notes," "Notes of a Native Son," "Stranger in the Village," "The Discovery of What It Means to Be an American," "Previous Condition," "The Rockpile," "The Outing"—concern his search for self. His second novel, *Giovanni's Room*, explores the theme mainly as it relates to love and sexuality. David, an American expatriate in France, must choose between his mistress Hella and his lover Giovanni. By rejecting Giovanni, David denies his true homosexual self and his deepest feeling for another person in favor of socially sanctioned heterosexuality. As Baldwin develops it, the choice is also between America and Europe, conformity and freedom, safety and the risks necessary to realize love. In search of psychological security, David instead precipitates chaos and tragedy for himself, Hella, and Giovanni.

Both *Go Tell It on the Mountain* and *Giovanni's Room* express social concerns, but their emphasis is on psychological conflict. In his third novel, *Another Country*, Baldwin gives greater attention to the city itself as both the arena and the cause of personal problems. The New York setting of this novel, seething with hatred, corruption, and moral disarray, dooms the characters who inhabit its inhuman confines. The most obvious victim is Rufus Scott, a disconsolate black jazz musician who commits suicide at the end of the long first chapter, but the other seven major characters also suffer as they struggle to assuage their guilt and satisfy their craving for love in the unloving urban environment. Some of these concerns appear in the splendid earlier story, "Sonny's Blues" (1957), where, however, racial suffering in the northern city is controlled, expressed, and thus to some degree transcended through music. In *If Beale Street Could Talk*, Baldwin again tries to transcend the hostility of urban life, this time through a story of young love, but his effort is vitiated by sentimentality and problems of fictional technique.

With few exceptions, most of Baldwin's books have dealt in one way or another with race and racism. From youthful disengagement he has moved through commitment to interracial efforts to achieve civil rights to black nationalism to bitter prophecies of racial vengeance on the white West. *The Fire Next Time* is an eloquent statement of militant intergrationism, but the play *Blues for Mister Charlie* expresses a deeper racial outrage and a diminished but not entirely abandoned hope for improvement. The social pathology revealed in this drama of race relations in the South derives from psychosexual origins much more than from political or economic causes. The shift from the nonviolent mode of resistance to racism to the advocacy of violence as the appropriate means of black self-defense begins in the play, and receives a stronger endorsement in the idealized portrait of Christopher, a fierce young black nationalist, in the novel *Tell Me How Long the Train's Been Gone*. The protagonist of this novel, a middle-aged actor named Leo Proudhammer, is an autobiographical character whose experience Baldwin sentimentalizes tiresomely, but in the autobiographical material of the tough-minded *No Name in the Street* the author avoids self-pity. Shifting back and forth between private experience and the public history of the violence-wracked 1960's, Baldwin offers in this work a sad and embittered testimony on race and racism. Quite different in its restrained tone and deliberately flat rhetoric from the hortatory *The Fire Next Time*, it is equally impressive.

By comparison Baldwin's more recent books are minor efforts. He may yet produce the genuinely major novel for which stylistic resources, his capacity for feeling, and his thematic breadth equip him. In any event, as a master of the personal essay, as racial commentator, and as a gifted if uneven novelist and short story writer, Baldwin has been one of the indispensable writers of the third quarter of the 20th century.

—Keneth Kinnamon

See the essay on *Go Tell It on the Mountain*.

BALDWIN, Joseph G(lover). Born in Friendly Grove Factory, Virginia, 21 January 1815. Educated at schools in Staunton, Virginia, 1825–27; Staunton Academy, 1827–29; studied law, 1833–35; licensed 1835. Married Sidney White in 1840; six children. Deputy clerk, Old Chancery Court, Staunton, 1829–32; lawyer, DeKalb, Mississippi, 1836, and Gainesville, 1837–50, and Livingston, 1850–54, both Alabama; law partner of Philip Phillips, Mobile, Alabama, 1853; moved to San Francisco, 1854, and practiced law there; Associate Justice, California Supreme Court, 1858–62, then returned to private practice. Whig member, Alabama House of Representatives, 1843; delegate, Whig Convention, Philadelphia, 1848; candidate for U.S. House of Representatives, 1848, and U.S. Senate, 1860. Co-publisher, Lexington *Gazette* (later *Union*), 1835, and Buchanan *Advocate and Commercial Advertiser*, 1835–36, both Virginia. *Died 30 September 1864.*

PUBLICATIONS

Fiction

The Flush Times of Alabama and Mississippi: A Series of Sketches. 1853; edited by William A. Owens, 1957.
The Flush Times of California, edited by Richard E. Amacher and George W. Polhemus. 1966.

Other

Party Leaders: Sketches of Jefferson, Hamilton, Jackson, Clay, Randolph of Roanoke. 1854.

*

Bibliography: in *Bibliography of American Literature* by Jacob Blanck, 1955.

Critical Studies: "Baldwin: Humorist or Moralist?" by Eugene Current-Garcia, in *The Frontier Humorists: Critical Essays* edited by M. Thomas Inge, 1975.

* * *

Although well known to American literary scholars for *The Flush Times of Alabama and Mississippi*, Joseph G. Baldwin has been little studied. As the title itself suggests, *Flush Times* constitutes an attempt to re-create in the *native* American tradition of the Old Southwest humorists a day and age with which Baldwin was well acquainted: an "age of litigation in a lawless country," as Eugene Current-Garcia says. A closer examination both of the author's life and the text of his work, however, suggests that Baldwin, in addition to being a frontier humorist, is a serious "moralist" who employs traditional conventions such as satire and irony in his exposure of the vices and weaknesses of mankind, thus bridging the gap between native Southwest humor and the older literary conventions of Europe.

Baldwin's purpose was doubtlessly moral, and his generic forte was essays and sketches rather than short stories. His literary models were, in all probability, Lamb and Dickens. His best character types remain self-important Virginians, inexperienced lawyers, and garrulous narrators. Two characters in particular are notable. Ovid Bolus, Esq., a truly artful liar, and Colonel Simon Suggs, Jr., to Current-Garcia the "symbol of his time, the epitome of a lawless, acquisitive society which had raised fraud and corruption to the level of 'super-Spartan roguery.' "

19th-century sensibilities extended, by contemporary standards, odd shadows. As a practising attorney, Baldwin no doubt felt some sense of embarrassment over his authorship of *Flush Times*, a work which many American Victorians would have considered inconsequential. In order to demonstrate his talents for more "serious" writing, Baldwin published in 1854 *Party Leaders*, which is rarely read today. Containing sketches of political leaders like Jefferson, Hamilton, Jackson, Clay, and Randolph, the book is motivated by the author's biographical and historical impulse and emphasizes moral instruction at the expense of humor.

Had Baldwin not died as suddenly as he did, he might well have become, as his wife believed, the Thucydides of the Civil War. In any event, his accomplishments as frontier humorist, moralist, and essayist continue to be admired by readers.

—George C. Longest

BARAKA, Amiri. Born Everett LeRoi Jones in Newark, New Jersey, 7 October 1934; took name Amiri Baraka in 1968. Educated at Central Avenue School, and Barringer High School, Newark; Rutgers University, New Brunswick, New Jersey, 1951–52; Howard University, Washington, D.C., 1953–54, B.A. in English 1954. Served in the U.S. Air Force, 1954–57. Married 1) Hettie Cohen in 1958 (divorced, 1965), two daughters; 2) Sylvia Robinson (now Amini Baraka) in 1966, five children; also two step-daughters and one other daughter. Teacher, New School for Social Research, New York, 1961–64, and summers, 1977–79, State University of New York, Buffalo, Summer 1964, and Columbia University, New York, 1964 and Spring 1980; Visiting Professor, San Francisco State College, 1966–67, Yale University, New Haven, Connecticut, 1977–78, and George Washington University, Washington, D.C. 1978–79; since 1980 Assistant Professor of African Studies, State University of New York, Stony Brook. Founder, *Yugen* magazine and Totem Press, New York, 1958–62; editor, with Diane di Prima, *Floating Bear* magazine, New York, 1961–63; founding director, Black Arts Repertory Theatre, Harlem, New York, 1964–66; director of several of his own plays. Since 1966 founding director, Spirit House, Newark; involved in Newark politics: member of the United Brothers, 1967, and Committee for Unified Newark, 1969–75; Chairman, Congress of Afrikan People, 1972–75. Recipient: Whitney fellowship, 1961; Obie award, for drama, 1964; Guggenheim fellowship, 1965; Dakar Festival prize, 1966; Rockefeller grant, 1981; Before Columbus Foundation award, 1984. D.H.L.: Malcolm X College, Chicago, 1972. Member, Black Academy of Arts and Letters. Lives in Newark, New Jersey.

PUBLICATIONS (earlier works as LeRoi Jones)

Plays

A Good Girl Is Hard to Find (produced 1958).
Dante (produced 1961; as *The 8th Ditch*, produced 1964). In *The System of Dante's Hell*, 1965.
The Toilet (produced 1962). In *The Baptism, and The Toilet*, 1967.

Dutchman (produced 1964). In *Dutchman, and The Slave*, 1964.
The Slave (produced 1964). In *Dutchman, and The Slave*, 1964.
Dutchman, and The Slave. 1964.
The Baptism (produced 1964). In *The Baptism, and The Toilet*, 1967.
Jello (produced 1965). 1970.
Experimental Death Unit No. 1 (produced 1965). In *Four Black Revolutionary Plays*, 1969.
A Black Mass (produced 1966). In *Four Black Revolutionary Plays*, 1969.
The Baptism, and The Toilet. 1967.
Arm Yrself or Harm Yrself (produced 1967). 1967.
Slave Ship: A Historical Pageant (produced 1967). 1967.
Madheart (produced 1967). In *Four Black Revolutionary Plays*, 1969.
Great Goodness of Life (A Coon Show) (produced 1967). In *Four Black Revolutionary Plays*, 1969.
Home on the Range (produced 1968). In *Drama Review*, Summer 1968.
Police, in *Drama Review*, Summer 1968.
The Death of Malcolm X, in *New Plays from the Black Theatre*, edited by Ed Bullins. 1969.
Four Black Revolutionary Plays. 1969.
Insurrection (produced 1969).
Junkies are Full of (SHHH . . .), and Bloodrites (produced 1970). In *Black Drama Anthology*, edited by Woodie King and Ron Milner, 1971.
BA-RA-KA, in *Spontaneous Combustion: Eight New American Plays*, edited by Rochelle Owens. 1972.
Columbia the Gem of the Ocean (produced 1973).
A Recent Killing (produced 1973).
The New Ark's a Moverin (produced 1974).
The Sidnee Poet Heroical (produced 1975). 1979.
S-1 (produced 1976). In *The Motion of History and Other Plays*, 1978.
The Motion of History (produced 1977). In *The Motion of History and Other Plays*, 1978.
The Motion of History and Other Plays (includes *S-1* and *Slave Ship*). 1978.
What Was the Relationship of the Lone Ranger to the Means of Production? (produced 1979).
At the Dim'crackr Convention (produced 1980).
Boy and Tarzan Appear in a Clearing (produced 1981).
Weimar 2 (produced 1981).
Money: A Jazz Opera, with George Gruntz, music by Gruntz (produced 1982).
Primitive World (produced 1984).

Screenplays: *Dutchman*, 1967; *A Fable*, 1971.

Fiction

The System of Dante's Hell. 1965.
Tales. 1967.

Verse

Spring and Soforth. 1960.
Preface to a Twenty Volume Suicide Note. 1961.
The Dead Lecturer. 1964.
Black Art. 1966.
A Poem for Black Hearts. 1967.
Black Magic: Poetry 1961–1967. 1969.
It's Nation Time. 1970.
In Our Terribleness: Some Elements and Meaning in Black Style, with Fundi (Billy Abernathy). 1970.
Spirit Reach. 1972.
Afrikan Revolution. 1973.
Hard Facts. 1976.
Selected Poetry. 1979.
AM/TRAK. 1979.
Reggae or Not! 1982.

Other

Cuba Libre. 1961.
Blues People: Negro Music in White America. 1963.
Home: Social Essays. 1966.
Black Music. 1968.
Trippin': A Need for Change, with Larry Neal and A.B. Spellman. 1969(?).
A Black Value System. 1970.
Gary and Miami: Before and After. N.d.
Raise Race Rays Raze: Essays since 1965. 1971.
Strategy and Tactics of a Pan African Nationalist Party. 1971.
Beginning of National Movement. 1972.
Kawaida Studies: The New Nationalism. 1972.
National Liberation and Politics. 1974.
Crisis in Boston!!!! 1974.
Afrikan Free School. 1974.
Toward Ideological Clarity. 1974.
The Creation of the New Ark. 1975.
Selected Plays and Prose. 1979.
Spring Song. 1979.
Daggers and Javelins: Essays 1974–1979. 1984.
The Autobiography of LeRoi Jones. 1984.

Editor, *Four Young Lady Poets*. 1962.
Editor, *The Moderns: New Fiction in America*. 1963.
Editor, with Larry Neal, *Black Fire: An Anthology of Afro-American Writing*. 1968.
Editor, *African Congress: A Documentary of the First Modern Pan-African Congress*. 1972.
Editor, with Diane di Prima, *The Floating Bear: A Newsletter, Numbers 1–37*. 1974.
Editor, with Amini Baraka, *Confirmation: An Anthology of African American Women*. 1983.

*

Bibliography: *Jones (Baraka): A Checklist of Works by and about Him* by Letitia Dace, 1971.

Critical Studies: *From Jones to Baraka: The Literary Works* by Theodore Hudson, 1973; *Baraka: The Renegade and the Mask* by Kimberly W. Benston, 1976, and *Baraka (Jones): A Collection of Critical Essays* edited by Benston, 1978; *Baraka/Jones: The Quest for a Populist Modernism* by Werner Sollors, 1978; *Baraka* by Lloyd W. Brown, 1980; *To Raise, Destroy, and Create: The Poetry, Drama, and Fiction of Baraka (Jones)* by Henry C. Lacey, 1981; *Theatre and Nationalism: Wole Soyinka and Jones* by Alain Ricard, 1983; *The Poetry and Poetics of Baraka: The Jazz Aesthetic* by William J. Harris, 1986.

* * *

Amiri Baraka (originally LeRoi Jones) says he has "always tried to be a revolutionary." That is the consistent quality in a thirty-year career which has included writing in every literary genre and representing contradictory points of view.

The rebel in Baraka led him in his youth to prefer running with the ghetto gangs to remaining in his respectable middle-class home. At Howard University, which he found distastefully bourgeois, it led him to quit college after his junior year to join the Air Force. In New York in the late 1950's, it prompted him to become a Greenwich Village bohemian and a disciple of Allen Ginsberg and Jack Kerouac, to turn out lyric poetry and surreal fiction expressing the romantic angst and waggish frivolity which permitted publication under titles such as *The System of Dante's Hell* and *Preface to a Twenty Volume Suicide Note*: "My wife is left-handed. / which implies a fierce de- / termination. ITS WEIRD BABY. / The way some folks are always trying to be / different. A sin & a shame."

Jones in the late 1950's and early 1960's possessed a boundless energy and an extraordinarily diverse talent. He was still speaking to white people and writing for a racially mixed audience. He founded periodicals with two white women, the magazine *Yugen* with his wife Hettie Cohen and the newsletter *The Floating Bear*—its title derived from an A.A. Milne Winnie the Pooh story—with the poet Diane di Prima. His saturation in the western literary tradition (William Carlos Williams, Whitman, Eliot, Yeats, Pound, and the Black Mountain poets) was clearly discernible in his poetry and novel. At that time Jones did not write specifically ethnic literature. Indeed, he alleged in 1959 that "Negro writing" can at best be folklore, for what is written out of racial consciousness cannot achieve literary status. In 1961 his poetry muses "Africa / is a foreign place. You are / as any other sad man here / american."

Yet even in the early work techniques analogous to black music—jazz and the blues—are evident, and Jones was also writing music criticism and essays expressing an increasingly inflammatory political consciousness. He was becoming politicized as early as 1960, when he visited Cuba and wrote the essay *Cuba Libre* in praise of Castro and that island's revolution. His verse became edgy, uneasy with his white life, and his essays and plays began to express an urgency which was turning, by 1964, to racial militancy.

Although a portion of his novel and the play *The Toilet* had been produced earlier, 1964 was the year that Baraka really won attention as a playwright. In March *The Eighth Ditch* (his *Dante* play) opened and was quickly closed by police on grounds of obscenity. Within a week *The Baptism*, an equally startling play, this one a religious satire which drew charges of both obscenity and blasphemy, jarred and amused its spectators. The very next day *Dutchman* opened, and later that year a double bill of *The Toilet* and *The Slave* further solidified Baraka's reputation. (A full-length play, *A Recent Killing*, which was written in this year but not produced until a decade later, dramatizes an inter-racial cooperation in which Jones was already losing faith.)

These plays are blistering in their dramatization of raw racial tensions on a realistic level, but they also function on an allegorical plane. *Dutchman*, in particular, is generally acknowledged to be his finest achievement. The Flying Dutchman constitutes one of the more obvious symbolic references in this play about a woman picking up a man on a New York City subway, but critical opinion has been divided over whether white Lula or black Clay embodies the legendary captain who is doomed to roam until his final peace can be purchased by a lover willing to die with him. Perhaps it is white racism, as exemplified by the murderous Lula, that won't die, or possibly the swallowing of pride and suppression of rage which the superficially assimilated Clay practices represents what Jones had in mind. Whatever the parallel, a double death does not occur, so the spectre of racism is not exorcised.

Dutchman can also be interpreted as a modernization of the Adam and Eve story in which Lula—who keeps eating and offering apples—is a corrupter of the innocent, natural man of Africa and the cause of his expulsion from the paradise of the American dream. Other religious parables which have been discerned include that of Clay as Christ and Lula as Satan (with the young man at the end representing the resurrection) and the idea that Clay is being baptized in hell-fire. *Dutchman* can therefore be viewed as a reference to disguise and the voluntary assumption of roles. Lula is an author creating a series of characters for herself. When Clay stops concealing his blackness behind white clothes, intellectual interests, and a courteous demeanor, Lula rewards his self-assertion with murder.

Equally playable and nearly equally subject to glosses (sometimes more arcane than illuminating), *The Toilet* and *The Slave* take somewhat different approaches to racial conflict. The earlier play, *The Toilet*, depicts interracial relations in a fashion which Baraka later came to regard as more sentimental than realistic, for the black gang leader really loves the white boy who is beaten up in the lavatory, and he returns to comfort Karolis when the bullies have left. A major factor in the play's appeal is Baraka's embodiment in his protagonist of a universal conflict between the gentle, nurturing, reflective aspect of the character (the "Ray" side of us) and the belligerent, aloof, authoritative aspect (the "Foots" side). The split in this particular temperament, of course, sets up a conflict between the assimilationist with aspirations to white goals (Ray, the good student who is attracted to Karolis) and the true black man (Foots, the natural leader).

Although *The Toilet* is milder than *Dutchman, The Slave* finds its protagonist has progressed beyond the birth of militance, which Clay barely reaches, to full leadership in a race war. Walker has left the insurgents just long enough to visit a white couple, his ex-wife and her new husband, the latter a college professor who represents the western culture to which Walker has bidden farewell. That he would pay such a call at all suggests that Walker is still something of a slave to the white liberal heritage, and the old slave whom Walker becomes in a long monologue reinforces that notion. Still, Walker is wiping out, literally, the old associations, and he, like Jones himself at this time of his life, sets a new, independent course.

Jones's drama had been by and large realistic and by and large addressed to a white or racially mixed audience. But the radical changes in his life—his departure in 1965 for Harlem and soon thereafter for the Newark ghetto, his divorce (subsequent to the prophetic *The Slave*) from the white wife (who now felt she was the enemy) and his marriage to a black woman, his conversion to the Kawaida sect of Muslim and his adoption of an African name, Amiri (prince) Baraka (blessedness), preceded for a time by the religious title Imamu (spiritual leader)—all reflect an ideological transformation which had a profound effect upon all his writing. The essays grew violent, the poetry took on the dialect of black speech, and the plays increasingly spoke only to blacks and were presented in segregated theatres. Realism was generally rejected in favor of a technique sometimes expressionistic and sometimes a montage of brief episodes, cinematic juxtapositions.

The first plays of this black militant period, including *Experimental Death Unit No. 1, Jello, A Black Mass*, and *Madheart*, explicitly proclaim the superiority of black to white, of black revolutionist to assimilationist, and of male to female. *Jello* is also a quite funny parody of Jack Benny's radio show in which Rochester stops serving Benny and starts asserting his new-found black manhood, and *A Black Mass* is a lyrical evocation of a misguided black man's creation of the white race. While some later black nationalist plays by Baraka—*Arm Yrself or Harm Yrself*, for instance—are simple didactic dramas with lines which preach the point, others make considerable use of nonverbal techniques and are theatrical in ways Antonin Artaud would have appreciated. *Slave Ship*, for instance, forces its spectators to feel they themselves are manacled in the hold of that ship, and it employs Swahili and moans and groans quite as much as English dialogue. The play's spectacle of human suffering is marvelously powerful drama. Some other plays of the late 1960's are cinematic or surreal, and some experiment with language in ways outside the tradition of mainstream American drama.

A recent resurgence of the polemical in Baraka's dramaturgy has followed another political change. The creator of and foremost writer in the black arts movement by 1973 had become a Communist leader and had rejected his nationalist rage and rancor toward whites as racist. Therefore, *S-1* and *The Motion of History* employ agit-prop techniques, in the former to attack a proposed senate bill which opponents felt would have abridged freedom of speech and assembly, and in the latter to urge the solidarity of blacks and whites in a revolution to overthrow their oppressors. *The Motion of History* dramatizes instances from the past four centuries in which the ruling class has pitted poor blacks and whites against each other so as to obscure their common interests in ending exploitation. This play even ridicules the black militant, who is represented as a mindless robot chanting "the white man is the devil."

In 1961, LeRoi Jones was president of the Fair Play for Cuba Committee. He strayed far afield from such politics, but has returned now to a Marxist-Leninist-Maoist stance. Whatever his particular affiliation, he continues to be one of the foremost of contemporary committed writers.

—Tish Dace

BARKER, James Nelson. Born in Philadelphia, Pennsylvania, 17 June 1784; son of General George Barker. Educated at schools in Philadelphia. Commissioned Captain in the 2nd U.S. Artillery, 1812; Assistant Adjutant-General, U.S. Army, rising to the rank of Major, 1814–17. Married Mary Rogers in 1811; one daughter. Playwright, Philadelphia, 1804–08; studied government, Washington, D.C., 1809–10; returned to Philadelphia and resumed writing for the stage, 1812; contributed "The Drama" series to *Dramatic Pieces*, 1816–17; member, Board of Aldermen, Philadelphia, 1817–19, 1822–29: Mayor, 1819–21; Collector of the Port of Philadelphia, 1829–38; controller, U.S. Department of the Treasury, Washington, D.C., 1838–41, and served various administrations as clerk in the office of the Chief Clerk of the Treasury, 1841–58. *Died 9 March 1858.*

PUBLICATIONS

Plays

Tears and Smiles (produced 1807). 1808; edited by Paul H. Musser, in *Barker*, 1929.
The Embargo; or, What News? (produced 1808).
Travellers; or, Music's Fascination, from a work by Andrew Cherry (produced 1808).
The Indian Princess; or, La Belle Sauvage, music by John Bray (produced 1808). 1808; revised version, as *Pocahontas* (produced 1820).
Marmion; or, The Battle of Flodden Field, from the poem by Scott (produced 1812). 1816.
The Armourer's Escape; or, Three Years at Nootka Sound (produced 1817).
How to Try a Lover (as *A Court of Love*, produced 1836). 1817.
Superstition; or, The Fanatic Father (produced 1824). 1826.

Other

Delaplaine's Repository of the Lives and Portraits of Distinguished American Characters, vol. 1, part 2. 1817.
Sketches of the Primitive Settlements on the River Delaware. 1827.

*

Critical Study: *Barker* by Paul H. Musser, 1929 (includes bibliography).

* * *

James Nelson Barker, Democratic mayor of Federalist Philadelphia and amateur historian, wrote for the Chestnut Street Theatre. His historical researches, political commitments, and talent for allegorical verse are all evident in his plays. His critical articles, such as "Tragedy of Character," examined the problems of adapting and performance, and the social function of drama. Barker intended his earliest, unproduced "mask" (*America*, with "Liberty" singing) to conclude an unfinished dramatization of John Smith's 1624 history of Virginia. Instead, his popular but comically melodramatic opera *The Indian Princess* (John Bray's music) introduced the frequently repeated Pocahontas figure to the stage.

The stage for Barker addressed and shaped the partisan energies that preceded the War of 1812. *Tears and Smiles*, his clever sentimental comedy, marshalled early Yankee types, a patriotic sailor, fops, an Irishman, and mysterious European fugitives to question commercial aristocracy and praise domestic products in fashions, morals, and persons. *The Embargo*, written for a benefit performance, supported Jefferson's controversial ban on trade with Britain and France. After the war Barker's "melo-dramatic sketch" *The Armourer's Escape* let the Indian-captured sailor Jewitt play himself, to capitalize on current (1817) interest in the Oregon boundary dispute.

How to Try a Lover, a singularly unpolitical gem in prose, was produced as *A Court of Love*. It celebrates blinding love, from insatiable lust to courtly and impractical idealism. Love's confusing possibilities are drawn, with literary parodies ("Almanzor" as hero-lover's pseudonym; conventional allegories of love/honor), through the neoclassically comic dance of a picaresque plot, while carefully described settings develop from dark gothic vault toward brilliant court. Movements and situations belie the spoken words. Barker's balancing of his characters and their antithetical dialogue intensify the skeptical-romantic counterpoint in this play, the "only dream" that "satisfied" him as artist.

Barker's verse tragedies explored what politicians considered resolved. *Marmion* and *Superstition* are historical tragedies of personal and national character. "*The* American playwright" (New York review) and best adaptor of Scott's poem (London critic) reexamined Scott's sources, tightened the narrative, and alternated scenes for deeper psychological effect, with a view toward rallying sentiment for war against Britain—though in 1811–12 victory seemed unlikely. *Marmion* presents determining destiny against individual responsibility. In *Superstition* manifest destiny and liberty are threatened by public hysteria. The inspired leadership of the Puritan Unknown (a fugitive regicide) saves a New England community from Indian attack; but the perverting religious fervor of witch-hunts and narrow-mindedness, part of the colonial heritage, leave a Columbia-figure and the young lovers of a New World dead. The play also features spying courtiers who supply objectifying comedy. Behind the play's action loom the New England fathers and the war for independence from the mother country, as well as the current themes of Greek and South American struggles for independence, Philadelphia's epidemics and religious riots, and Barker's campaigning for Andrew Jackson (Hero of the People) against New England's Adams ("John the Second"). Though Barker the politician honored "The People," *Superstition* questions their readiness for genuine democracy and implies a vision of rational, tolerant, effective, and affective leadership, fatalistic action, and individual heroism. Allegory becomes symbolic and moving in these tragedies, the finest of early America.

—John G. Kuhn

BARLOW, Joel. Born in Redding, Connecticut, 24 March 1754. Educated at Moor's School, Hanover, New Hampshire; Dartmouth College, Hanover 1773–74; Yale University, New Haven, Connecticut, 1774–78, B.A. 1778, M.A. 1781; admitted to the bar, 1786. Served in the Massachusetts Brigade, 1780–83: Chaplain. Married Ruth Baldwin in 1781. Lawyer after the Revolution; also schoolteacher and proprietor of a bookshop, Hartford, Connecticut; founding editor, with Elisha Babcock, *American Mercury*, 1784; lived in Europe, 1788–1805: European agent (to sell land in Ohio to Europeans), Scioto Associates, 1788–90; lived in London (friend of Thomas Paine), 1790–92, and in Paris after 1792: made honorary French citizen, became involved in French radical politics, and ran for National Assembly deputy (representing Savoy), 1793; shipping agent, Hamburg, 1794–95; U.S. Consul, Algiers, 1796; lived at his home Kalorama, near Washington, D.C., 1805–11; sent by President James Madison to negotiate with Napoleon, 1811–12. *Died 24 December 1812*.

PUBLICATIONS

Collections

Works (facsimile edition), edited by William K. Bottorff and Arthur L. Ford. 2 vols., 1970.

Verse

The Prospect of Peace. 1778.
A Poem, Spoken at the Public Commencement at Yale College. 1781.
An Elegy of the Late Titus Hosmer. 1782.
Doctor Watts's Imitation of the Psalms of David, Corrected and Enlarged. 1785; supplement, 1785.
The Vision of Columbus. 1787; revised edition, as *The Columbiad*, 1807.
The Conspiracy of Kings. 1792.
The Hasty-Pudding. 1796.
The Anarchiad: A New England Poem, with others, edited by Luther G. Riggs. 1861.

Other

Advice to the Privileged Orders in the Several States of Europe. 2 vols., 1792–93.
A Letter to the National Convention of France. 1793(?).
Lettre adressée aux habitans du Piémont. 1793; as *A Letter to the People of Piedmont*, 1795.
The History of England, 1765–95. 5 vols., 1795.
The Political Writings. 1796.
To His Fellow Citizens. 2 vols., 1799–1800.

Editor, *M'Fingal: A Modern Epic Poem*, by John Trumbull. 1792.

Translator, *New Travels in the United States of America in 1788*, by J.P. Brissot de Warville. 1792; revised edition, 1794.
Translator, *The Commerce of America with Europe*, by J.P. Brissot de Warville. 1794.
Translator, with Thomas Jefferson, *Volney's Ruins; or, Meditations on the Revolution of Empires*. 2 vols., 1802.

*

Critical Studies: *Life and Letters of Barlow* by Charles Burr Todd, 1886; *The Early Days of Barlow, A Connecticut Wit: His Life and Works from 1754 to 1787* by Theodore Albert Zunder, 1934 (includes bibliography); *The Connecticut Wits* by Leon Howard, 1943 (includes bibliography); *A Yankee's Odyssey: The Life of Barlow* by James Woodress, 1958; *Barlow* by Arthur L. Ford, 1971.

* * *

Although Joel Barlow had hoped to be remembered as an epic poet, only one mock-epic poem and a short bitter piece of satiric verse give him what enduring interest he has as a poet. At the same time, however, he holds a secure place as a political pamphleteer in the early national period and as a minor figure in American history. He is a character of considerable interest, for his life touches many of the significant historical events between the Revolution and the War of 1812, and he stands as a representative figure of the American Enlightenment.

Going from a Connecticut farm to Yale on the eve of the Revolution, Barlow versified his way through college, and, after serving as a chaplain in Washington's army, he set about writing his epic, *The Vision of Columbus*, a poem in nine books of heroic couplets celebrating the history of America, past, present, and future. The poem was a considerable success in its day, but it seems unreadable in the 20th century. Twenty years later Barlow brought out an expanded and revised version that he called *The Columbiad*. It appeared as a large quarto, leather bound and handsomely illustrated, the most beautiful book yet produced in America—but still unreadable.

The Hasty-Pudding, on the other hand, is a delightful piece of mock-heroic verse occasioned by Barlow's visit to Savoy in 1793 when he was running unsuccessfully for the French National Assembly. It was inspired by his being served a dish of corn meal mush (polenta, hasty pudding), which reminded him of his Connecticut boyhood. This poem has been reprinted many times and is often anthologized. The other notable piece of verse, "Advice to a Raven in Russia," was occasioned by Barlow's sharp reaction to Napoleon's campaign in Russia in 1812. It was written in the last month of Barlow's life when he had gone to Vilna in an effort to negotiate a treaty with Napoleon. To a Jeffersonian American the slaughter and carnage all about him evoked bitter criticism, and in a sense Barlow himself some days later was one of Napoleon's victims, for he caught pneumonia on the precipitous return to Paris from Lithuania after Napoleon's debacle.

During the years that Barlow was living in Europe (1788 to 1805), he plunged into political controversy. His tract *Advice to the Privileged Orders* was one of the important answers to Burke's *Reflections on the Revolution in France*, and it was proscribed in England, along with Paine's *The Rights of Man*. He also wrote political polemics in support of France and the Jeffersonians during the contentious days of Adams administration, and as a result made himself unpopular with the conservative Federalists he had grown up with in Connecticut. Of all that group of writers known as the Connecticut Wits, who flourished in and about Hartford after the Revolution, Barlow was the only one who became a political liberal.

—James Woodress

BARNES, Djuna (Chappell). Born near Cornwall-on-Hudson, New York, 12 June 1892. Educated privately; studied art at Pratt Institute, Brooklyn, New York, 1911–12, and Art Students' League, New York, 1915. Married Courtenay Lemon c. 1917 (divorced, c. 1919). Journalist and illustrator, 1913–31: with Brooklyn *Daily Eagle*, 1913, and *Press, World*, and *Morning Telegraph*, all New York, 1914; actress in New York, 1920–22; columnist, *Theatre Guild Magazine*, New York, 1929–31; lived in Paris, 1922–37 (with periods in New York, 1922–23, 1926–27, 1929–31), London, 1937–39, and New York, 1940–82. Also an artist: exhibition at Art of This Century Gallery, New York, 1946. Trustee, New York Committee of Dag Hammarskjöld Foundation. Member, American Academy. *Died 18 June 1982.*

PUBLICATIONS

Fiction

A Book (stories, verse, and plays). 1923; augmented edition, as *A Night among the Horses*, 1929; shortened version (stories only), as *Spillway*, 1962.
Ryder. 1928.
Nightwood. 1936.
Vagaries Malicieux: Two Stories. 1974.
Smoke and Other Early Stories, edited by Douglas Messerli. 1982.

Plays

Three from the Earth (produced 1919). In *A Book*, 1923.
Kurzy of the Sea (produced 1919).
An Irish Triangle (produced 1919). In *Playboy*, 1921.
To the Dogs, in *A Book*. 1923.
The Dove (produced 1926). In *A Book*, 1923.
She Tells Her Daughter, in *Smart Set*, 1923.
The Antiphon (produced 1961). 1958; revised version, in *Selected Works*, 1962.

Verse

The Book of Repulsive Women: Eight Rhythms and Five Drawings. 1915.
Creatures in an Alphabet. 1982.

Other

Ladies Almanack. 1928.
Selected Works. 1962.
Greenwich Village as It Is. 1978.
Interviews, edited by Alyce Barry. 1985.
I Could Never Be Lonely Without a Husband (interviews). 1987.

*

Bibliography: *Barnes: A Bibliography* by Douglas Messerli, 1976.

Critical Studies: *A Festschrift for Barnes on Her 80th Birthday* edited by Alex Gildzen, 1972; *Barnes* by James B. Scott, 1976; *The Art of Barnes: Duality and Damnation* by Louis F. Kannenstine, 1977; *Djuna: The Life and Times of Barnes* by Andrew Field, 1983, as *The Formidable Miss Barnes*, 1983; *Silence and Power: A Re-evaluation of Barnes* edited by Mary Lynn Broe, 1986.

* * *

Djuna Barnes was one of the original members of the Theater Guild and acted in New York in plays by Tolstoy and Paul Claudel in the early 1920's. By the late 1930's the publication of her novel *Nightwood*, with an enthusiastic introduction by T.S. Eliot, had led to her being considered the most important woman novelist living in Paris. In the fiction of Anaïs Nin she appears frequently as "Djuna," and David Gascoyne's poem "Noctambules" carries the dedication "Hommage à Djuna Barnes." When her play *The Antiphon* was published, Edwin Muir declared that it was "one of the greatest things written in our times." Yet, despite such high praise, her books were for many years available only in small editions.

Nightwood is about the obsession of two American women for each other in the 1920's. Their Paris is not the Paris of Scott Fitzgerald, but that of Romaine Brooks, Natalie Clifford Barney, and the circle of "Amazonians" which surrounded them. Norah Flood, one of the protagonists of the novel, arranges publicity from time to time for the Denckman Circus, and she also runs a *salon*. Some thirty years before, Dr. Matthew O'Connor assisted at her birth; now living in Paris, he has given way to his homosexual-transvestite urges. He is called one night from a café to a nearby hotel to attend Robin Vote, a boyish young woman who has had a collapse. The doctor takes along with him his drinking companion, Baron Felix Volkbein, who falls in love with Robin and subsequently marries her. In due course Robin bears him a son, but she cannot stand the course of marriage and starts an affair with Norah. A passionate and tempestuous sequence of events follows and Robin's promiscuity nearly unhinges Norah's mind. Her old friend the doctor sits with her through the night boozing and pouring forth great streams of disconnected thoughts on life, literature, and the vagaries of the human heart. Had the novel been adapted for radio, the role of the doctor was one that Dylan Thomas aspired to play.

The Antiphon, written in blank verse, recalls a Jacobean closet drama:

> You have such sons
> Would mate the pennies on a dead man's eyes
> To breed the sexton's fee.

But the setting is modern and takes place in England during World War II. Augusta Burley betrays her aristocratic lineage by marrying a coarse, uncultivated Mormon from Salem, by whom she has three sons and a daughter. Now a widow, she arranges a reunion at Burley Hall for the whole family. Yet nothing is what it seems. For as two of the brothers and their sister await their third brother, he enjoys himself at their expense disguised as "a coachman." Recriminations and suppressed violence cause the two identified sons to plan a matricide, while their sister acts as inquisitor to her mother for marrying her father. Finally incensed by the desertion of her two sons, the mother turns on her daughter to kill her and brings about her own death at the same time. The original production of this powerful play—by the Royal Dramatic Theatre of Stockholm in 1961—was in a translation by Dag Hammarskjöld.

Barnes also illustrated books and wrote poems, short stories, plays, journalism, and essays. Her *Ladies Almanack*, published anonymously in Paris, created a minor *succès de scandale* in the 1920's. In it a number of lesbians are gently mocked—among them Radclyffe Hall (Lady Buck-and-Balk). Natalie Clifford Barney (Evangeline Musset), and Lady Una Troubridge (Tilly-Tweed-in-Blood).

—Neville Braybrooke

BARRY, Philip. Born in Rochester, New York, 18 June 1896. Educated at East High School, Rochester; Yale University, New Haven, Connecticut (editor, *Yale Review*), 1913–17, 1919, A.B. 1919; studied with George Pierce Baker at Harvard University, Cambridge, Massachusetts, 1919–21. Worked in the code department of the U.S. Embassy, London, 1918–19. Married Ellen Semple in 1922; two sons and one daughter. Worked in advertising, New York, 1921; full-time playwright from 1922; wrote for M.G.M., Hollywood, after 1934; lived in France, 1938–39. Member, American Academy. *Died 3 December 1949.*

PUBLICATIONS

Collections

States of Grace: Eight Plays, edited by Brendan Gill. 1975.

Plays

Autonomy (produced 1919).
A Punch for Judy (produced 1921). 1922.
You and I (as *The Jilts*, produced 1923; as *You and I*, produced 1923). 1923.
God Bless Our Home. 1924.
The Youngest (produced 1924). 1925.
In a Garden (produced 1925). 1926.
White Wings (produced 1926). 1927; revised version, music by Douglas Moore (produced 1935).
John (produced 1927). 1929.
Paris Bound (produced 1927). 1929.
Cock Robin, with Elmer Rice (produced 1928). 1929.
Holiday (produced 1928). 1929.
Hotel Universe (produced 1930). 1930.
Tomorrow and Tomorrow (produced 1931). 1931.
The Animal Kingdom (produced 1932). 1932.
The Joyous Season (produced 1934). 1934.
Bright Star (produced 1935).
Spring Dance, from a play by Eleanor Golden and Eloise Barrangon (produced 1936). 1936.
Here Come the Clowns (produced 1938). 1939.
The Philadelphia Story (produced 1939). 1939.
Liberty Jones (produced 1941). 1941.
Without Love (produced 1942). 1943.
Foolish Notion (produced 1945). Abridged version in *The Best Plays of 1944–45*, edited by Burns Mantle, 1945.
My Name Is Aquilon, from play by Jean Pierre Aumont (produced 1949).
Second Threshold, completed by Robert E. Sherwood (produced 1951). 1951.

Fiction

War in Heaven. 1938.

Other

The Dramatist and the Amateur Public. 1927.

*

Critical Studies: *The Drama of Barry* by Gerald Hamm, 1948; *Barry* by Joseph Patrick Roppolo, 1965.

* * *

American theater has never been particularly congenial to that honorable but somewhat amorphous genre *high comedy*. Philip Barry is one of the very few American playwrights who is a celebrated practitioner of the form. In plays like *Paris Bound, The Animal Kingdom, Without Love*, and—most famously—*Holiday* and *The Philadelphia Story*, he places articulate and well-to-do people in well-appointed homes and forces them to face domestic crises—usually a marriage in danger—with an equanimity that might be called courage and a wit which demands—but does not always get—audiences willing to listen for the precise meaning of lines which will direct them to the seriousness which lies at the heart of all the plays. That Barry is not simply an elegant entertainer can be seen in the variety of work in his canon—in which the successful comedies share space with a satirical extravaganza (*White Wings*), a biblical play more concerned with theology than anecdote (*John*), a mood play in which characters find spiritual regeneration through psychodrama (*Hotel Universe*), a parable of good and evil among vaudevillians (*Here Come the Clowns*, based on Barry's own novel *War in Heaven*), a symbolic political drama (*Liberty Jones*), and a mixture of the real and the imaginary (*Foolish Notion*).

The comedies tend to be more effective than the overtly earnest plays, in which art sometimes loses out to exposition. But the important thing about Barry as a serious playwright is that, light or heavy, his work is informed by a major theme. Most of his plays, from *You and I* to *Second Threshold*, deal with man's need to be faithful to himself and his possibilities, personal and professional. The Barry protagonists have to escape the rigidities dictated by family (*The Youngest*), convention (*The Animal Kingdom*), society (*Holiday*). Sometimes, as with John and Herodias in *John*, the characters are trapped by their own preconceptions, and the luckier among them learn to live by discovering that, however benign their intentions, they too are manipulators (Nancy in *The Youngest*, Linda in *Holiday*) or by accepting their own imperfect, human condition (Tracy Lord in *The Philadelphia Story*). Barry's central concern is supported by recurrent minor themes—marriage as a bond of love, not a legal or religious ritual; work as a self-fulfilling activity, not a social imposition—and by the implicit religious assumptions that mark him even at his most secular. That *Holiday* and *The Philadelphia Story* are likely to remain Barry's most popular plays should not hide the fact that a number of the others—particularly the neglected *In a Garden*—deserve a place in the working American repertory.

—Gerald Weales

BARTH, John (Simmons). Born in Cambridge, Maryland, 27 May 1930. Educated at Cambridge High School, graduated 1947; Juilliard School of Music, New York, 1947; Johns Hopkins University, Baltimore, A.B. 1951, M.A. 1952. Married 1) Anne Strickland in 1950 (divorced, 1969), one daughter and two sons; 2) Shelly Rosenberg in 1970. Junior Instructor in English, Johns Hopkins University, 1951–53; Instructor 1953–56, Assistant Professor, 1957–60, and Associate Professor of English, 1960–65, Pennsylvania State University, University Park; Professor of English, 1965–71, and Butler Professor, 1971–73, State University of New York, Buffalo; since 1973 Centennial Professor of English and Creative Writing, Johns Hopkins University. Recipient: Brandeis University Creative Arts Award, 1965; Rockefeller grant, 1965; American Academy grant, 1966; National Book Award, 1973. Litt.D.: University of Maryland, College Park, 1969. Member, American Academy, 1977, and American Academy of Arts and Sciences, 1977. Lives in Chestertown, Maryland.

PUBLICATIONS

Fiction

The Floating Opera. 1956; revised edition, 1967.
The End of the Road. 1958; revised edition, 1967.
The Sot-Weed Factor. 1960; revised edition, 1967.
Giles Goat-Boy; or, The Revised New Syllabus. 1966.
Lost in the Funhouse: Fiction for Print, Tape, Live Voice (stories). 1968.
Chimera (stories). 1972.
Letters. 1979.
Sabbatical: A Romance. 1982.

Other

The Literature of Exhaustion, and The Literature of Replenishment (essays). 1982.
The Friday Book: Essays and Other Nonfiction. 1984.
Don't Count on It: A Note on the Number of the 1001 Nights. 1984.

*

Bibliography: *Barth: A Descriptive Primary and Annotated Secondary Bibliography* by Joseph Weixlmann, 1976; *Barth: An Annotated Bibliography* by Richard Allan Vine, 1977; *Barth, Jerzy Kosinski, and Thomas Pynchon: A Reference Guide* by Thomas P. Walsh and Cameron Northouse, 1977.

Critical Studies: *Barth* by Gerhard Joseph, 1970; *Barth: The Comic Sublimity of Paradox* by Jac Tharpe, 1974; *The Literature of Exhaustion: Borges, Nabokov, and Barth* by John O. Stark, 1974; *Barth: An Introduction* by David Morrell, 1976; *Critical Essays on Barth* edited by Joseph J. Waldmeir, 1980; *Passionate Virtuosity: The Fiction of Barth* by Charles B. Harris, 1983.

* * *

Highly susceptible to the sport of metaphysical games and passionately attracted to the conundrums of self-consciousness, John Barth has moved steadily away from the objective and realistic toward myth and unashamed fable. His first two novels, *The Floating Opera* and *The End of the Road*—novels which he has claimed to be twin explorations of the comic and tragic aspects of philosophical nihilism—fall well within the conventions of realism. But his next novel, *The Sot-Weed Factor*, takes an entirely different direction. It is framed on a gigantic scale of multiple plots, disguises, coincidences, intrigues, and deceptions, and it is written in an exuberant and constantly inventive pastiche of 17th-century prose style. Mingling history, legend, fiction, and outrageous lie in a bawdy, funny, and learned parody of the initiation-and-quest novel, *The Sot-Weed Factor* purports to chronicle the life and career of Ebenezer Cooke, Poet-Laureate of Maryland. Partly a reinterpretation of the primal fall from innocence, and partly a reexamination of the rich ambiguities in the archetypal American experience, it is both a dazzling tour de force and a major contribution to the novel of fabulation.

Barth is even more ambitious in scope and substance in *Giles Goat-Boy*. In this gargantuan spoof, he attempts to fuse myth, allegory, satire, parody, and the conventions of science-fiction to produce a comically revised New Testament which will expose the fictive sources of all myths while leaving a new one in their place. Although the novel inevitably falls short of its excessive aims, its relative failure—it goes on too long and its plot becomes mechanical—is still a significant and startling achievement. In *Lost in the Funhouse* and *Chimera*, he has withdrawn into an increasingly abstract and cerebral style, deliberately focusing on the naked process of story-telling itself as a subject—if not a substitute—for telling stories. *Letters* features many of the characters in his previous fictions. The results are curiously mixed: over-clever, strained, whimsical, desperate, terrifying, boring, and funny. Whether these works represent a temporary exhaustion of Barth's imaginative energies or are, instead, a necessary and courageous phase in his development as a major writer, there is little doubt that his literary intelligence and mastery of language place him in the forefront of his generation of writers.

—Earl Rovit

BARTHELME, Donald. Born in Philadelphia, Pennsylvania, 7 April 1931; brother of the writer Frederick Barthelme. Educated at the University of Houston. Served in the U.S. Army, 1953–55. Married 1) Birgit Barthelme; 2) Marion Knox in 1978; two daughters. Reporter, Houston *Post*, 1951, 1955–56; worked on public relations and news service staff, and founding editor of the university literary magazine *Forum*, University of Houston, 1956–59; director, Contemporary Arts Museum, Houston, 1961–62; managing editor, *Location* magazine, New York, 1962–64; Visiting Professor, State University of New York, Buffalo, 1972, and Boston University, 1973; since 1974 Distinguished Visiting Professor, City College, New York; since 1981 Visiting Professor, University of Houston. Recipient: Guggenheim fellowship, 1966; National Book Award, 1972; American Academy Morton Dauwen Zabel Award, 1972. Member, American Academy. Lives in Houston.

PUBLICATIONS

Fiction (stories)

Come Back, Dr. Caligari. 1964.
Snow White (novel). 1967.
Unspeakable Practices, Unnatural Acts. 1968.
City Life. 1970.
Sadness. 1972.
Guilty Pleasures. 1974.
The Dead Father (novel). 1975.
Amateurs. 1976.
Great Days. 1979.
The Emerald. 1980.
Presents, collages by the author. 1980.
Sixty Stories. 1981.
Overnight to Many Distant Cities. 1983.
Paradise (novel). 1986.

Play

Great Days, from his own story (produced 1983).

Other

The Slightly Irregular Fire Engine; or, The Thithering Dithering Djinn (for children). 1971.

*

Bibliography: *Barthelme: A Comprehensive Bibliography and Annotated Secondary Checklist* by Jerome Klinkowitz, Asa Pieratt, and Robert Murray Davis, 1977.

Critical Studies: "Barthelme Issue" of *Critique*, vol. 16, no. 3, 1975; *Barthelme* by Lois Gordon, 1981; *Barthelme* by Maurice Courturier and Régis Durand, 1982; *The Metafictional Muse: The Works of Robert Coover, Barthelme, and William H. Gass* by Larry McCaffery, 1982; *Barthelme's Fiction: The Ironist Saved from Drowning* by Charles Molesworth, 1982; *The Shape of Art in the Short Stories of Barthelme* by Wayne B. Stengel, 1985.

* * *

Since the American publication of two volumes of fictions by Argentinian Jorge Luis Borges in 1962, an interest in short, highly self-conscious, directly philosophical fiction has become apparent in the United States. Donald Barthelme is perhaps the best exemplar of this strain of fiction. His best work to date has been in the short story (for lack of a more expansive term), particularly in the sub-strain "metafiction," a term coined by William H. Gass. Like Borges, the Americans John Barth, Gass, and Robert Coover, and the Italian Italo Calvino, Barthelme has little interest in mimetic fiction which works from the bedrock of the "real" world. Instead of protracted social or psychological studies, he busies himself with very short, often truncated and discontinuous, literary pieces that depend on other literary works, philosophy, film, pop culture, and high art for their fictional matrices. There is throughout his work a suspicion of received morality or attitude, indeed of any unself-conscious and sustained human construct—including fiction. Thus his works are brief, constantly shifting in tone and style, evincing as much the juxtaposition and reverberation of image and language in modern poetry and the open randomness and "objectness" of the collage and much modern art as they do traditional fictional technique.

Barthelme's first work, *Come Back, Dr. Caligari*, was very well-reviewed, but one notes the bewilderment of critics who searched for "meaning" in his work. His best works have been collections of short fiction; of these, *City Life* and *Sadness* are most sustained in imagination and execution.

While Barthelme has little interest in miming reality, he does have a recurrent interest in modern consciousness, particularly as manifested in urban Americans. He issues elegant fictional reports on the state of consciousness in "The City," and, indeed, the daily sorrowful, maddening minutiae of city life—tattered marriages, the loss of innocence, the failure of love, the absurd hope of social or political "progress," the torrent of stimulation by the media—comprise the stuff of his reports. "The City" is dangerous and confusing, and is finally a configuration of human consciousness: "It heaves and palpitates. It is multi-dimensional and has a mayor. To describe it takes many hundreds of thousands of words. Our muck is only a part of a much greater muck—the nation state—which is itself the creation of that muck of mucks, human consciousness" ("City Life").

Indeed, the human urban condition is Barthelme's major subject, and like his city, his vision can certainly appear bleak and pessimistic. Endlessly self-conscious (his narrators offer clues to the significance of their tales), satiric and parodic (Barthelme's liberated *Snow White* is hilarious), a mournful connoisseur of the many flavors of metaphysical malaise and angst of our time (a character "pickets" the human condition in an early story: "THE HUMAN CONDITION: WHY DOES IT HAVE TO BE THAT WAY?"), he can often seem depressing and negative. Yet his wit and humor are a delight, and his stylistic command is among the most deft of writers in English in our time.

Barthelme demands a creative reader, and he offers his own best apologia in writing on the work of Samuel Beckett: "His pessimism is the premise necessary to a marvelous pedantic high-wire performance, the wire itself supporting a comic turn of endless virtuosity. No one who writes as well as Beckett can be said to be doing anything but celebrating life."

—Jack Hicks

BAUM, L(yman) Frank. Born in Chittenango, New York, 15 May 1856. Educated at schools in Syracuse, New York, and Peekskill Military Academy, New York, 1868–69. Married Maud Gage in 1882; four sons. Reporter, New York *World*, 1873–75; founding editor, *New Era*, Bradford, Pennsylvania, 1876; actor (as Louis F. Baum and George Brooks), manager, Baum's Opera House, Richburg, New York, 1881–82, and producer, New York and on tour, 1881–83; poultry farmer and editor, *Poultry Record*, 1880's; salesman, Baum's Castorine axle grease, 1884–88; owner, Baum's Bazaar general store, Aberdeen, Dakota Territory, 1888–90; editor, *Saturday Pioneer*, Aberdeen, 1890–91; reporter, Chicago *Post*, buyer, Siegel Cooper and Company, Chicago, and salesman, Pitkin and Brooks, Chicago, 1891–97; founder, National Association of Window Trimmers, 1897, and founding editor and publisher, *Show Window* magazine, Chicago, 1897–1902; founding director, Oz Film Manufacturing Company, Los Angeles, 1914. *Died 6 May 1919.*

PUBLICATIONS

Fiction

A New Wonderland. 1900; as *The Surprising Adventures of the Magical Monarch of Mo*, 1903.
The Wonderful Wizard of Oz. 1900; as *The New Wizard of Oz*, 1903; *The Annotated Wizard of Oz*, edited by Michael Patrick Hearn, 1973.
Dot and Tot of Merryland. 1901.
The Master Key: An Electrical Fairy Tale. 1901.
The Life and Adventures of Santa Claus. 1902.
The Enchanted Island of Yew. 1903.
The Marvelous Land of Oz. 1904.
Queen Zixi of Ix. 1905.
The Woggle-Bug Book. 1905.
The Fate of a Crown. 1905.
Daughters of Destiny. 1906.
John Dough and the Cherub. 1906.
Annabel. 1906.
Sam Steele's Adventures on Land and Sea. 1906; as *The Boy Fortune Hunters in Alaska*, 1908.
Aunt Jane's Nieces [*Abroad, at Millville, at Work, in Society, and Uncle John, on Vacation, on the Ranch, Out West, in the Red Cross*]. 10 vols., 1906–15.
Twinkle Tales. 6 vols., 1906; as *Twinkle and Chubbins*, 1911.
Tamawaca Folks. 1907.
Ozma of Oz. 1907; as *Princess Ozma of Oz*, 1942.
Sam Steele's Adventures in Panama. 1907; as *The Boy Fortune Hunters in Panama*, 1908.
Policeman Bluejay. 1907; as *Babes in Birdland*, 1911.
The Last Egyptian. 1908.
Dorothy and the Wizard in Oz. 1908.
The Boy Fortune Hunters in Egypt [*China, Yucatan, the South Seas*]. 4 vols., 1908–11.
The Road to Oz. 1909.
The Emerald City of Oz. 1910.
The Sea Fairies. 1911.
The Daring Twins. 1911.
The Flying Girl [*and Her Chum*]. 2 vols., 1911–12.
Sky Island. 1912.
Phoebe Daring. 1912.
The Patchwork Girl of Oz. 1913.
The Little Wizard Series. 6 vols., 1913; as *Little Wizard Stories of Oz*, 1914.
Tik-Tok of Oz. 1914.
The Scarecrow of Oz. 1915.
Rinkitink in Oz. 1916.
The Snuggle Tales. 6 vols., 1916–17; as *Oz-Man Tales*, 6 vols., 1920.
Mary Louise [*in the Country, Solves a Mystery, and the Liberty Girls, Adopts a Soldier*]. 5 vols., 1916–19.
The Lost Princess of Oz. 1917.
The Tin Woodman of Oz. 1918.
The Magic of Oz. 1919.
Glinda of Oz. 1920.
Jaglon and the Tiger Fairies. 1953.
A Kidnapped Santa Claus. 1961.
The Purple Dragon and Other Fantasies, edited by David L. Greene. 1976.

Plays

The Maid of Arran, music and lyrics by Baum, from the novel *A Princess of Thule* by William Black (produced 1882).
Matches (produced 1882).
Kilmourne; or, O'Connor's Dream (produced 1883).
The Wizard of Oz, music by Paul Tietjens, lyrics by Baum, from the story by Baum (produced 1902; revised version, as *There Is Something New under the Sun* produced 1903).
The Woggle-Bug, music by Frederic Chapin, from the story *The Marvelous Land of Oz* by Baum (produced 1905).
The Tik-Tok Man of Oz, music by Louis F. Gottschalk, from the story by Baum (produced 1913).
Stagecraft: The Adventures of a Strictly Moral Man, music by Louis F. Gottschalk (produced 1914).
The Uplift of Lucifer; or, Raising Hell, music by Louis F. Gottschalk (produced 1915). Edited by Manuel Weltman, 1963.
The Uplifters' Minstrels, music by Byron Gay (produced 1916).
The Orpheus Road Company, music by Louis F. Gottschalk (produced 1917).

Screenplays: *The Fairylogue and Radio-Plays*, 1908–09; *The Patchwork Girl of Oz*, 1914; *The Babes in the Wood*, 1914; *The Magic Cloak of Oz*, 1914; *The Last Egyptian*, 1914; *The New Wizard of Oz*, 1915.

Verse

By the Candelabra's Glare. 1898.
Father Goose, His Book. 1899.
The Army Alphabet. 1900.
The Navy Alphabet. 1900.
The Songs of Father Goose, music by Alberta N. Hall. 1900.
Father Goose's Year Book: Quaint Quacks and Feathery Shafts for Mature Children. 1907.
The High-Jinks of Baum (songs for Uplifters). 1959.

Other

The Book of the Hamburgs: A Brief Treatise upon the Mating, Rearing, and Management of the Different Varieties of Hamburgs. 1886.
Mother Goose in Prose. 1897.
The Art of Decorating Dry Goods Windows and Interiors. 1900.
American Fairy Tales. 1901; augmented edition, 1908.
Baum's Juvenile Speaker (miscellany). 1910; as *Baum's Own Book for Children*, 1912.
Our Landlady (*Saturday Pioneer* columns). 1941.
Animal Fairy Tales. 1969.

*

Bibliography: in *The Annotated Wizard of Oz* edited by Michael Patrick Hearn, 1973.

Critical Studies: *The Wizard of Oz and Who He Was* edited by Russel Nye and Martin Gardner, 1957; *To Please a Child: A Biography of Baum* by Frank Joslyn Baum and Russell P. MacFall, 1961; *Wonderful Wizard, Marvelous Land* by Raylyn Moore, 1974.

*   *   *

L. Frank Baum's *The Wonderful Wizard of Oz*, illustrated by W.W. Denslow, is his masterpiece. It made him famous and, with its 13 sequels, has established him as a classic writer of children's stories.

The Wonderful Wizard of Oz was a novelty in children's books at the time it was published, lacking the didactic, moralizing, and stilted tone so common. Its characters spoke the American vernacular; its plot was simple but intriguing and well-structured. Moreover, Baum created five characters worthy to stand with Lewis Carroll's Alice and J.M. Barrie's Peter Pan. Dorothy and the Wizard, and the three non-human characters (the Tin Woodman, the Scarecrow, and the Cowardly Lion), are all archetypes yet sharply distinguished individuals. The quest of the Scarecrow for brains, the Woodman for a heart, and the Lion for courage, qualities they already possessed but did not know how to use, is the stuff of which classics are made.

The Wizard was also Baum's most successful, though not his best, example of what he called the American or modernized fairy tale. Responding to ideas expressed by Hamlin Garland and others, he intended to write fantasies which would be distinct from the European and New England tradition. They would recognize the existence and importance of the industry, technology, and social concepts of the dawning 20th century. He incorporated mechanical gadgets (particularly electricity, which fascinated him) into his works—*The Master Key: An Electrical Fairy Tale* is the best example—and dealt with such modern concepts as Populism. But in general his ambition to create a new genre was only partly successful. Though the visitors to Oz were American, the country itself was as foreign as James Branch Cabell's Poictesme or Swift's Lilliput. Furthermore, he often used such traditional fairy tale paraphernalia as witches, gnomes, talking animals, and wishing caps. What many consider his best book, *Queen Zixi of Ix*, is entirely derived from European children's literature, though it contains many imaginative novelties.

Baum tired of his Oz series. But just as public demand kept Doyle writing his Sherlock Holmes stories when he would have preferred to concentrate on his more "serious" works, so it kept Baum at his Oz tales, though he did write many other children's books, few of them fantasies. Though written "to please a child" (Baum's phrase), the Oz books have also been popular with adults, who recognize subtleties which escaped them as children. *The Wonderful Wizard of Oz* is still popular, and now seems to have passed the judgment of time.

—Philip José Farmer

See the essay on *The Wonderful Wizard of Oz*.

BEHRMAN, S(amuel) N(athaniel). Born in Worcester, Massachusetts, 9 June 1893. Educated at Providence Street School, and Classical High School, both Worcester; Clark College (now Clark University), Worcester, 1912–14; Harvard University, Cambridge, Massachusetts, A.B. 1916 (Phi Beta Kappa); Columbia University, New York, M.A. 1918. Married Elza Heifetz in 1936; one son and two step-children. Advertising writer and book reviewer, *New York Times*, 1917–18; reviewer, *New Republic*, New York, and free-lance publicist until early 1920's; columnist, *New Yorker*, from 1927. Founder, with Robert E. Sherwood, Elmer Rice, Maxwell Anderson, Sidney Howard, and John F. Wharton, Playwrights Company, 1938. Trustee, Clark University. Recipient: American Academy grant, 1943; New York Drama Critics Circle award, 1944; Writers Guild of America West award, for screenplay, 1959; Brandeis University Creative Arts Award, 1962. LL.D.: Clark University, 1949. Member, American Academy, 1943, and American Academy of Arts and Sciences. *Died 9 September 1973.*

PUBLICATIONS

Plays

Bedside Manners: A Comedy of Convalescence, with J. Kenyon Nicholson (produced 1923). 1924.
A Night's Work, with J. Kenyon Nicholson (produced 1924). 1926.
The Man Who Forgot, with Owen Davis (produced 1926).
The Second Man (produced 1927). 1927.
Love Is Like That, with J. Kenyon Nicholson (produced 1927).
Serena Blandish, from the novel by Enid Bagnold (produced 1929). In *Three Plays*, 1934.
Meteor (produced 1929). 1930.
Brief Moment (produced 1931). 1931.
Biography (produced 1932). 1933.

Love Story (produced 1933).
Three Plays: Serena Blandish, Meteor, The Second Man. 1934.
Rain from Heaven (produced 1934). 1935.
End of Summer (produced 1936). 1936.
Amphitryon 38, with Roger Gellert, from a play by Jean Giraudoux (produced 1937). 1938.
Wine of Choice (produced 1938). 1938.
No Time for Comedy (produced 1939). 1939.
The Talley Method (produced 1941). 1941.
The Pirate, from a play by Ludwig Fulda (produced 1942). 1943.
Jacobowsky and the Colonel, from a play by Franz Werfel (produced 1944). 1944.
Dunnigan's Daughter (produced 1945). 1946.
Jane, from a story by W. Somerset Maugham (produced 1946; as *The Foreign Language*, produced 1951). 1952.
I Know My Love, from a play by Marcel Achard (produced 1949). 1952.
Let Me Hear the Melody (produced 1951).
Fanny, with Joshua Logan, music by Harold Rome, from a trilogy by Marcel Pagnol (produced 1954). 1955.
Four Plays: The Second Man, Biography, Rain from Heaven, End of Summer. 1955.
The Cold Wind and the Warm (produced 1958). 1959.
The Beauty Part (produced 1962).
Lord Pengo: A Period Comedy, based on his book *Duveen* (produced 1962). 1963.
But for Whom Charlie (produced 1964). 1964.

Screenplays: *Liliom*, with Sonya Levien, 1930; *Lightnin'*, with Sonya Levien, 1930; *The Sea Wolf*, with Ralph Block, 1930; *The Brat*, with others, 1931; *Surrender*, with Sonya Levien, 1931; *Daddy Long Legs*, with Sonya Levien, 1931; *Delicious*, 1931; *Rebecca of Sunnybrook Farm*, with Sonya Levien, 1932; *Tess of the Storm Country*, with others, 1932; *Brief Moment*, 1933; *Queen Christina*, with Salka Viertel and H.M. Harwood, 1933; *Cavalcade*, 1933; *Hallelujah, I'm a Bum* (*Hallelujah, I'm a Tramp, Lazy Bones*), with Ben Hecht, 1933; *My Lips Betray*, 1933; *As Husbands Go*, with Sonya Levien, 1934; *The Scarlet Pimpernel*, with others, 1934; *Anna Karenina*, with others, 1935; *A Tale of Two Cities*, with W.P. Lipscomb, 1935; *Conquest* (*Marie Walewska*), with others, 1937; *Parnell*, with John van Druten, 1937; *The Cowboy and the Lady*, with Sonya Levien, 1938; *Waterloo Bridge*, with others, 1940; *Two-Faced Woman*, with others, 1941; *Quo Vadis*, with others, 1951; *Me and the Colonel*, with George Froeschel, 1958; *Stowaway in the Sky* (English narration), 1962.

Fiction

The Burning-Glass. 1968.

Other

Duveen. 1952.
The Worcester Account (*New Yorker* sketches). 1954.
Portrait of Max: An Intimate Memoir of Sir Max Beerbohm. 1960; as *Conversation with Max*, 1960.
The Suspended Drawing Room. 1965.
People in a Diary: A Memoir. 1972; as *Tribulations and Laughter: A Memoir*, 1972.

*

Bibliography: *Maxwell Anderson and Behrman: A Reference Guide* by William Klink, 1977.

Critical Studies: *Life among the Playwrights* by John F. Wharton, 1974; *Behrman* by Kenneth T. Reed, 1975; *Behrman: The Major Plays* by William Klink, 1978.

* * *

It is now sixty years since S.N. Behrman's *The Second Man* was produced by the Theatre Guild and made him famous. Even by the 1950's the material was old-hat, and writers of comedies of manners (even better ones, such as Philip Barry) are now quite out of date. Behrman's work after the 1930's was fairly unimportant, largely adaptations. His sophisticated comedy belongs to an earlier generation. A recent revival of *The Second Man* looked very old-fashioned. It, of course, lacked the Lunts, who created roles in it (and Noël Coward and Raymond Massey, who played it in London), and it needed them.

In his time Behrman also had the assistance of stars like Greta Garbo, Ina Claire, Katherine Cornell, and Laurence Olivier. He, like the blasé and aphoristic writer Clark Storey in *The Second Man*, said "(*Seriously*) Life is sad. I know it's sad. But I think it's gallant to pretend that it isn't." In the 1930's this approach made him an American Noël Coward and gave him "perhaps the most considerable reputation" among young playwrights (A.H. Quinn). But soon proletarian and "socially significant drama" was to render inoperable the approach of the heroine of *Biography*, which was to laugh at injustice because nothing could be done about it, and the hero of *No Time for Comedy*, who chose to write light comedy instead of propagandist melodrama. The depression and World War II wiped out Behrman's impassive, indifferent, intellectual sophisticates who gracefully soared above reality. In *Rain from Heaven*, even though it revolves around Fascists and German refugees, the sophisticates are still doing arabesques on the thin ice of political problems.

Behrman wrote a number of screenplays, including such movies as *Queen Christina* and *Anna Karenina* (both with Garbo), *Waterloo Bridge*, and *Quo Vadis*. For the *New Yorker* he wrote the sketches that became *Duveen* (about the art dealer who became Lord Millbank) and *The Worcester Account* (about his boyhood in Worcester, Massachusetts). These, I think, surpass his original comedies of manners, his adaptation of Giraudoux (*Amphitryon 38*) or Franz Werfel (*Jacobowsky and the Colonel*), his dramatization of stories by Enid Bagnold (*Serena Blandish*) and W. Somerset Maugham (*Jane*), all his theatre work, and his cinema writing. It is unfortunate that he did not find time in his 80 years to write a work for the stage about the sort of people who enliven *The Worcester Account*. His cosmopolitan intellectuals may be well observed for a "brief moment" (as a 1931 play of his was called), but they are seen by a stranger, however clever. The people of Providence Street in Worcester, Behrman knew.

—Leonard R.N. Ashley

BELASCO, David. Born in San Francisco, California, 25 July 1853; moved with his family to Victoria, British Columbia, 1858. Educated at a monastery in Victoria, 1858–62; in various schools in San Francisco, where his family returned in 1865; Lincoln Grammar School, San Francisco, graduated 1871. Married Cecilia Loverich in 1873 (died, 1925); two daughters. Actor in repertory, touring California; acted at Piper's Opera House in Virginia City, Nevada, where he was employed briefly by Dion Boucicault as a secretary, 1873; stage manager, Maguire's Theatre, San Francisco, 1874; assistant to the manager, 1875–78, and stage manager, 1878–82, Lucky Baldwin's Academy of Music, San Francisco; began writing for the stage in the late 1870's; lighting manager, then stage manager, Madison Square Theatre, New York, 1882–86; manager, with David Frohman, Lyceum Theatre, New York, 1886–90; independent actor/manager, New York, 1890–1906; owner, Stuyvesant Theatre, later Belasco Theatre, New York, 1906–31. Produced over 350 plays for Broadway and stock companies. Chevalier, Legion of Honor (France), 1924. *Died 14 May 1931.*

PUBLICATIONS

Collections

The Plays of Henry C. DeMille and Belasco (includes *The Senator's Wife, Lord Chumley, The Charity Ball, Men and Women*), edited by Robert Hamilton Ball. 1941.

The Heart of Maryland and Other Plays (includes *The Stranglers of Paris, La Belle Russe, The Girl I Left Behind Me, Naughty Anthony*), edited by Glenn Hughes and George Savage. 1941.

Plays

Jim Black (produced 1865).
The Doll Master (produced 1874–75?).
Sylvia's Lovers (produced 1875?).
The Creole, from a play by Adolphe Belot (produced 1876–77?).
Olivia, from the novel *The Vicar of Wakefield* by Goldsmith (produced 1878).
Proof Positive (produced 1878).
Within an Inch of His Life, with James A. Herne, from a play by Emile Gaboriau (produced 1879). Edited by Arthur Hobson Quinn, in *The Early Plays of Herne*, 1940.
A Fast Family, from a play by Sardou (produced 1879).
The Millionaire's Daughter (produced 1879).
Marriage by Moonlight, with James A. Herne, from the play *Camilla's Husband* by Watts Phillips (produced 1879).
Drink, from a novel by Zola (produced 1879).
Hearts of Oak, with James A. Herne (as *Chums*, produced 1879; as *Hearts of Oak*, produced 1879). Edited by Mrs. James A. Herne, in *Shore Acres and Other Plays*, by Herne, 1928.
Paul Arniff; or, The Love of a Serf (produced 1880).
True to the Core, from the play by A.R. Slous (produced 1880).
La Belle Russe, from the plays *Forget-Me-Not* and *New Magdalen* (produced 1881). 1914; in *The Heart of Maryland and Other Plays*, 1941.
The Stranglers of Paris, from a novel by Adolphe Belot (produced 1881). In *The Heart of Maryland and Other Plays*, 1941.
The Curse of Cain, with Peter Robinson (produced 1882).
American Born, from the play *British Born* (produced 1882).
May Blossom (produced 1884). 1883.
Valerie, from a play by Sardou (produced 1886).
The Highest Bidder, from the play *Trade* by John Maddison Morton and Robert Reece (produced 1887).
Baron Rudolph, with Bronson Howard, revised version (produced 1887). Edited by Allen G. Halline, in *The Banker's Daughter and Other Plays*, by Howard, 1941.
Pawn Ticket 210, with Clay M. Greene (produced 1887).
The Senator's Wife, with Henry C. DeMille (as *The Wife*, produced 1887; as *The Senator's Wife*, produced 1892). In *The Plays of DeMille and Belasco*, 1941.
Lord Chumley, with Henry C. DeMille (produced 1888). In *The Plays of DeMille and Belasco*, 1941.
The Charity Ball, with Henry C. DeMille (produced 1889). In *The Plays of DeMille and Belasco*, 1941.
The Marquis, from a play by Sardou (produced 1889).
Men and Women, with Henry C. DeMille (produced 1890). In *The Plays of DeMille and Belasco*, 1941.
Miss Helyett, from a play by Maxime Boucheron (produced 1891).
The Girl I Left Behind Me; or, The Country Ball, with Franklin Fyles (produced 1893). In *The Heart of Maryland and Other Plays*, 1941.
The Younger Son, from a play by O. Vischer (produced 1893).
The Heart of Maryland (produced 1895). In *The Heart of Maryland and Other Plays*, 1941.
Under the Polar Star, with Clay M. Greene (produced 1896).
Zaza, from a play by Pierre Berton and Charles Simon (produced 1898).
Naughty Anthony (produced 1899). In *The Heart of Maryland and Other Plays*, 1941.
Madame Butterfly, from the story by John Luther Long (produced 1900). In *Six Plays*, 1928.
Du Barry (produced 1901). In *Six Plays*, 1928.
The Darling of the Gods, with John Luther Long (produced 1902). In *Six Plays*, 1928.
Sweet Kitty Bellairs, from the novel *The Bath Comedy* by Agnes and Egerton Castle (produced 1903).
Adrea, with John Luther Long (produced 1904). In *Six Plays*, 1928.
The Girl of the Golden West (produced 1905). In *Six Plays*, 1928.
The Rose of the Rancho, from the play *Juanita* by Richard Walton Tully (produced 1906). 1936.
A Grand Army Man, with Pauline Phelps and Marion Short (produced 1907).
The Lily, from a play by Pierre Wolff and Gaston Leroux (produced 1909).
The Return of Peter Grimm (produced 1911). In *Six Plays*, 1928.
The Governor's Lady, with Alice Bradley (produced 1912).
The Secret, from a work by Henri Bernstein (produced 1913).
Van Der Decken: A Legendary Play of the Sea (produced 1915).
The Son-Daughter, with George Scarborough (produced 1919).
Timothy Shaft, with W.J. Hurlbut (produced 1921).
Kiki, from the play by André Picard (produced 1921).
The Merchant of Venice, from the play by Shakespeare (produced 1922). 1922.
The Comedian, from a play by Sacha Guitry (produced 1923).
Laugh, Clown, Laugh!, with Tom Cushing, from a play by Fausto Martini (produced 1923).
Salvage. 1925.

Fanny, with Willard Mack (produced 1926).
Mima, from a play by Molnar (produced 1928).
Six Plays (includes *Madame Butterfly, Du Barry, The Darling of the Gods, Adrea, The Girl of the Golden West, The Return of Peter Grimm*), edited by Montrose J. Moses. 1928.

Other

The Theatre Through Its Stage Door, edited by Louis V. Defoe. 1919.
A Souvenir of Shakespeare's Merchant of Venice. 1923.

Editor, with Charles A. Byrne, *Fairy Tales Told by Seven Travellers at the Red Lion Inn*. 1906.

*

Bibliography: *Plays Produced under the Stage Direction of Belasco*, 1925.

Critical Studies: *The Life of Belasco* by William Winter, 2 vols., 1918; *The Bishop of Broadway: The Life and Work of Belasco* by Craig Timberlake, 1954; *Belasco: Naturalism in the American Theatre* by Lise-Lone Marker, 1975.

* * *

The parents of David Belasco came to San Francisco from England during the Gold Rush, and his early theatrical experience was gained entirely in the American and Canadian west. Humphrey Abraham Belasco was a harlequin turned shopkeeper, and his son at the age of eleven played the Duke of York to Charles Kean's Richard III. At twelve, he wrote and produced his first melodrama. He supered, prompted, played Hamlet, Uncle Tom, and Armand on tour, and in 1876 was secretary to Dion Boucicault, whose "sensation dramas" heavily influenced the would-be playwright.

While stage manager at Baldwin's Academy of Music, Belasco began to experiment with spectacle and stage lighting as well as adapting and collaborating on several plays, one of which, *La Belle Russe* was a success in New York. Its derivative plot involves a woman's impersonation of her virtuous twin sister, even to the sister's titled husband. Here Belasco began treating "strong," sometimes demonic, always sexual female characters and tense situations. The sketchy good twin also foreshadows Belasco's virtuous, suffering heroines such as Adrea and Cho-Cho-San.

In 1882 Belasco came east, where he was at times associated with the Frohmans, and in the late 1880's collaborated with Henry C. DeMille on four very popular but unmemorable plays. Belasco's real success as a playwright began with *The Heart of Maryland* in 1895, in which Mrs. Leslie Carter swung on the clapper of a bell to save her soldier-sweetheart, Belasco having been inspired by the Civil War and "Curfew Shall Not Ring Tonight!" Mrs. Carter, the star of a scandalous divorce trial, was taught to act by Belasco, who later wrote *Zaza, Du Barry*, and *Adrea* for her. Too high in voice and too low in stature to be effective on stage himself, he acted through the players he coached and in his own off-stage character as the silver-haired, clerical-collared "Bishop of Broadway."

In 1900 Belasco collaborated with John Luther Long on *Madame Butterfly*, from which Puccini derived his opera, and when the same composer set Belasco's *The Girl of the Golden West*, the playwright directed Caruso and the Metropolitan Opera cast for its 1910 premiere. Belasco's later work was largely as director and deviser of scenic effects, and the plays he dealt with were inconsequential except for his productions of Sacha Guitry's *Deburau, The Merchant of Venice* with David Warfield as Shylock, and Molnar's *Mima*—unsuccessful but stupendous.

It is doubtful that David Belasco did anything which could be called truly original, but he improved all he touched and he touched almost everything in the theatre of his day. A master of the exciting plot, he developed from the physical sensationalism of Boucicault to the emotional sensationalism of Sardou. In *The Girl I Left Behind Me*, for example, he used elements of Boucicault's *Defense of Lucknow* for a situation which John Ford would adapt for his film *Stage Coach*. Belasco heroines such as Du Barry, Minnie, and Yo-San face Tosca's dilemma of proscribed lover and lascivious authority, while *Adrea* with its blind princess, wicked sister, exotic kingdom, disloyal lover, and tower of death recalls the extravagant costume dramas Sardou created for Sarah Bernhardt. Yet Belasco could also devise plays of quiet sentiment such as *The Return of Peter Grimm* with its affectionate ghost *ex machina* (and its only partly-acknowledged debt to the young Cecil B. DeMille). As Belasco explained in *The Theatre Through Its Stage Door*, his plays appealed because he tried "to tug at the hearts of my audience." He also made those heart-strings zing with excitement, part of which arose from his extraordinary scenic effects.

Dion Boucicault had blown up steamboats on stage; Belasco created battlefields. Later, working in the tradition of realistic *mise en scène* introduced by Tom Robertson, Belasco used a real switchboard and telephone booths in his production of William C. DeMille's *The Woman* and re-created the interior of a Childs Restaurant on stage in *The Governor's Lady* by Alice Bradley. The theatres which he built (the Belasco and the Stuyvesant) contained the most sophisticated stage equipment of their day, and he experimented endlessly with electricity, first used by W.S. Gilbert at the Savoy Theatre.

Belasco believed that color and light could "communicate to audiences the underlying symbolism of a play." Cho-Cho-San's pathetic vigil was accompanied by fourteen minutes of mood lighting in which twilight darkened to night, stars appeared, lamps were lighted and flickered out one by one, and dawn broke. The River of Souls in *The Darling of the Gods* was composed of shadowy spirits "floating across and disappearing," an anticipation of back projection. For *The Girl of the Golden West*, Belasco spent three months designing a sunset, only to reject it—"It was a good sunset, but it was not Californian."

Although Belasco's meticulous realism is no longer fashionable, it is still significant in the *verismo* operas which Puccini based on his plays and productions. Moreover, like his predecessors Robertson and Gilbert, Belasco played a part in turning the stage from a star-dominated playhouse to a director's theatre. Finally, the exciting motifs which he developed or adapted are still part of the vocabulary of American melodrama.

—Jane W. Stedman

BELLAMY, Edward. Born in Chicopee Falls, Massachusetts, 26 March 1850. Educated in local schools; at Union

College, Schenectady, New York, 1867–68; traveled and studied in Germany, 1868–69; studied law in Springfield, Massachusetts: admitted to the Massachusetts bar, 1871, but never practised. Married Emma Sanderson in 1882; one son and one daughter. Staff member, New York *Evening Post*, 1871–72; editorial writer and reviewer, Springfield *Union*, 1872–77; founder with his brother, Springfield *Daily News*, 1880; after 1885 writer and lecturer in support of the Nationalist movement (in favor of nationalization); founder, *New Nation*, Boston, 1891–96. *Died 22 May 1898.*

PUBLICATIONS

Fiction

Six to One: A Nantucket Idyl. 1878.
Dr. Heidenhoff's Process. 1880.
Miss Ludington's Sister: A Romance of Immortality. 1884.
Looking Backward 2000–1887. 1888; edited by John L. Thomas, 1967.
Equality. 1897.
The Blindman's World and Other Stories. 1898.
The Duke of Stockbridge: A Romance of Shays' Rebellion, edited by Francis Bellamy. 1900; edited by Joseph Schiffman, 1962.

Other

Bellamy Speaks Again! Articles, Public Addresses, Letters. 1937.
Talks on Nationalism. 1938.
The Religion of Solidarity, edited by Arthur E. Morgan. 1940.
Selected Writings on Religion and Society, edited by Joseph Schiffman. 1955.

*

Bibliography: in *Bibliography of American Literature* by Jacob Blanck, 1955.

Critical Studies: *Bellamy*, 1944, and *The Philosophy of Bellamy*, 1945, both by Arthur E. Morgan; *The Year 2000: A Critical Biography of Bellamy*, by Sylvia E. Bowman, 1958, and *Bellamy Abroad: An American Prophet's Influence* by Bowman and others, 1962; *Bellamy, Novelist and Reformer* by Daniel Aaron and Harry Levin, 1968; *Authoritarian Socialism in America: Bellamy and the Nationalist Movement* by Arthur Lipow, 1982; *Alternative America: Henry George, Bellamy, Henry Demarest Lloyd, and the Adversary Tradition* by John L. Thomas, 1983.

* * *

Edward Bellamy is known chiefly for his Utopian romance *Looking Backward 2000–1887*, which within a short time after its publication sold over one million copies. The purpose of the book was to offer a blueprint of what Bellamy considered to be an ideal society. To make his presentation more palatable to the general reader, he encased it in a romantic plot: A young Bostonian after a hypnotic sleep of 113 years awakens in the year 2000 to discover a totally transformed social and economic order. Falling in love with a girl descended from his fiancée of 1887, he learns from her father, a physician, the details of the state socialism that has replaced the laissez-faire capitalism that obtained before his long sleep. Under the new order all commerce, industry and other economic and professional activities have been nationalized into one vast interlocking enterprise. All men and women between the ages of 21 and 45 are required to engage in work suitable to their abilities and, when possible, to their tastes; and all, no matter what occupation they may be in, receive the same wages. Superior ability and productivity are rewarded by social recognition and by assignment to positions of leadership. After the age of 45 all are retired and are free to do what they wish.

Looking Backward is one of a number of books expressing the dissatisfaction of many Americans with the conditions of labor, the rise of monopolies, and the political corruption that characterized the second half of the 19th century. But Bellamy's book enjoyed a greater popularity and exerted a stronger influence than any other, with the possible exception of Henry George's *Progress and Poverty* (1879). Bellamy called his program Nationalism, and in the 1890's many Nationalist Clubs were formed and began to wield a political influence, most notably on the newly formed and temporarily quite powerful Populist Party. As a sequel to *Looking Backward*, Bellamy wrote *Equality*, which he finished shortly before his death. But by this time the Nationalist movement was losing its momentum, though Bellamy's ideas continued to be an influence on later reform efforts. Bellamy's most lasting contribution, as one critic has put it, was in fostering "an attitude toward social change." For example, many of the innovations of the New Deal had been suggested and made familiar to the public by Bellamy's book.

Bellamy's literary career was not confined solely to reformist writing. He was an able newspaper and magazine editor and the author of nonpolitical fiction. Several of his novels, among them *Dr. Heidenhoff's Process* and *Miss Ludington's Sister* received favorable notice in their day; and his *The Duke of Stockbridge* (serialized 1879) has been called, perhaps extravagantly, "one of the greatest historical novels." Dealing with the revolt in 1786 and 1787 of Massachusetts farmers who were overburdened with debt and taxes and ruthlessly exploited by lawyers, merchants, and bankers, this book provides early evidence of Bellamy's concern with social and economic injustice—a concern that doubtless had its origin in his early awareness of the exploitation of workers in the Massachusetts mill town in which he grew up.

—Perry D. Westbrook

See the essay on *Looking Backward 2000–1887*.

BELLOW, Saul. Born in Lachine, Quebec, Canada, 10 June 1915; grew up in Montreal; moved with his family to Chicago, 1924. Educated at Tuley High School, Chicago, graduated 1933; University of Chicago, 1933–35; Northwestern University, Evanston, Illinois, 1935–37, B.S. (honors) in sociology and anthropology 1937; did graduate work in anthropology at University of Wisconsin, Madison, 1937. Served in the U.S. Merchant Marine, 1944–45. Married 1) Anita Goshkin in 1937 (divorced), one son; 2) Alexandra Tschacbasov in 1956 (divorced), one son; 3) Susan Glassman in 1961 (divorced), one son; 4) Alexandra Ionescu Tulcea in 1975. Teacher, Pestalozzi-Froebel Teachers College, Chicago, 1938–42; member of the editorial department, "Great Books" project, *Encyclopaedia Britannica*, Chicago, 1943–44; free-lance editor and reviewer, New York, 1945–46; Instructor, 1946, and Assistant Professor of English, 1948–49, University of Minnesota, Minneapolis; Visiting Lecturer, New York University, 1950–52; Creative Writing Fellow, Princeton University, New Jersey, 1952–53; member of the English faculty, Bard College, Annandale-on-Hudson, New York, 1953–54; Associate Professor of English, University of Minnesota, 1954–59; Visiting Professor of English, University of Puerto Rico, Rio Piedras, 1961; since 1962 Professor, and Chairman, 1970–76, Committee on Social Thought, University of Chicago; now Grunier Distinguished Services Professor. Co-editor, *Noble Savage*, New York, then Cleveland, 1960–62. Fellow, Academy for Policy Study, 1966; Fellow, Branford College, Yale University, New Haven, Connecticut. Recipient: Guggenheim fellowship, 1948, 1955; American Academy grant, 1952, and Gold Medal, 1977; National Book Award, 1954, 1965, 1971; Ford grant, 1959, 1960; Friends of Literature Award, 1960; James L. Dow Award, 1964; International Literary Prize, 1965; Jewish Heritage Award, 1968; Formentor prize, 1970; Nobel Prize for Literature, 1976; Pulitzer Prize, 1976; Neil Gunn International Fellowship, 1977; Brandeis University Creative Arts Award, 1978; Malaparté Award (Italy), 1984. D.Litt.: Northwestern University, 1962; Bard College, 1963; Litt.D.: New York University, 1970; Harvard University, Cambridge, Massachusetts, 1972; Yale University, 1972; McGill University, Montreal, 1973; Brandeis University, Waltham, Massachusetts, 1974; Hebrew Union College, Cincinnati, 1976; Trinity College, Dublin, 1976. Member, American Academy, 1970; Chevalier, Legion of Honor, 1983, and Commander, Order of Arts and Letters, 1985 (France). Lives in Chicago.

PUBLICATIONS

Fiction

Dangling Man. 1944.
The Victim. 1947.
The Adventures of Augie March. 1953.
Seize the Day, with Three Short Stories and a One-Act Play (includes *The Wrecker*). 1956.
Henderson the Rain King. 1959.
Herzog. 1964.
Mosby's Memoirs and Other Stories. 1968.
Mr. Sammler's Planet. 1970.
Humboldt's Gift. 1975.
The Dean's December. 1982.
Him with His Foot in His Mouth and Other Stories. 1984.

Plays

The Wrecker (televised 1964). In *Seize the Day*, 1956.
Scenes from Humanitas: A Farce, in *Partisan Review*, Summer 1962.
The Last Analysis (produced 1964). 1965.
Under the Weather (includes *Out from Under, A Wen*, and *Orange Soufflé*) (produced 1966; as *The Bellow Plays*, produced 1966). *A Wen* and *Orange Soufflé* in *Traverse Plays*, edited by Jim Haynes, 1966.

Television Play: *The Wrecker*, 1964.

Other

Dessins, by Jesse Reichek; text by Bellow and Christian Zervos. 1960.
Recent American Fiction: A Lecture. 1963.
Like You're Nobody: The Letters of Louis Gallo to Bellow, 1961–62, Plus Oedipus-Schmoedipus, The Story That Started It All. 1966.
Technology and the Frontiers of Knowledge, with others. 1973.
The Portable Bellow, edited by Edith Tarcov. 1974.
To Jerusalem and Back: A Personal Account. 1976.
Nobel Lecture. 1977.

Editor, *Great Jewish Short Stories*. 1963.

*

Bibliography: *Bellow: A Comprehensive Bibliography* by B.A. Sokoloff and Mark E. Posner, 1971; *Bellow, His Works and His Critics: An Annotated International Bibliography* by Marianne Nault, 1977; *Bellow: A Bibliography of Secondary Sources* by F. Lercangée, 1977; *Bellow: A Reference Guide* by Robert G. Noreen, 1978.

Critical Studies: *Bellow* by Tony Tanner, 1965; *Bellow* by Earl Rovit, 1967, and *Bellow: A Collection of Critical Essays* edited by Rovit, 1975; *Bellow: A Critical Essay* by Robert Detweiler, 1967; *The Novels of Bellow* by Keith Michael Opdahl, 1967; *Bellow and the Critics* edited by Irving Malin, 1967, and *Bellow's Fiction* by Malin, 1969; *Bellow: In Defense of Man* by John Jacob Clayton, 1968, revised edition, 1979; *Bellow* by Robert R. Dutton, 1971, revised edition, 1982; *Bellow* by Brigitte Scheer-Schäzler, 1972; *Bellow's Enigmatic Laughter* by Sarah Blacher Cohen, 1974; *Whence the Power? The Artistry and Humanity of Bellow* by M. Gilbert Porter, 1974; *Bellow: The Problem of Affirmation* by Chirantan Kulshrestha, 1978; *Critical Essays on Bellow* edited by Stanley Trachtenberg, 1979; *Bellow, Drumlin Woodchuck* by Mark Harris, 1980; *Quest for the Human: An Exploration of Bellow's Fiction* by Eusebio L. Rodrigues, 1981; *Bellow* by Malcolm Bradbury, 1982; *Bellow's Moral Vision: A Critical Study of the Jewish Experience* by L.H. Goldman, 1983; *Bellow: Vision and Revision* by Daniel Fuchs, 1984; *Bellow and History* by Judie Newman, 1984; *A Sort of Columbus: The American Voyages of Bellow's Fiction* by Jeanne Braham, 1984; *On Bellow's Planet: Readings from the Dark Side* by Jonathan Wilson, 1985.

* * *

Since receiving the Nobel Prize Saul Bellow has been assured of an important position in American literature; but this position is not really a new one. For more than thirty years, at least since the publication of his popular *The Adventures of Augie March*, Bellow has been heralded as the major spokesman of realism in America, as the most articulate voice for humanism in America, as the most sophisticated comedian of the modern predicament, and even as the one on whose shoulders has fallen the mantle of genius previously worn by William Faulkner. No matter how exaggerated these evaluations might seem, Bellow is surely one of the major postwar American novelists.

It is as a novelist that he assumes his important position. However, Bellow also writes essays, short stories, and plays. Most of his non-fiction is a clarification of his view of the duties of novelist and human being. For Bellow fiction should be basically realistic; it should not obscure the human condition, but should delve deeply into the psychological idiosyncrasies that explain an individual act. *To Jerusalem and Back* relates a visit to Israel less for the purpose of providing an answer to the Middle East question than for the fascinating personalized portraits of individuals. It is not sociology, but psychology.

Most of the short pieces that appear in journals are sections of novels in progress, but some of these short pieces have remained as short stories, the best of which have been collected in *Mosby's Memoirs*. Perhaps the best of these tales in relation to his major work is "The Old System," a short story that approaches one of Bellow's significant themes: the conflict between modern Jewish man and his ageless ties to a Jewish past. His plays, especially the one-act sketches, barely hint at the power of his novels, *The Last Analysis*, a full-length work, is his best attempt in this genre. The fragmentation, confusion, and discomfort of modern life color the play as much as they do the novels.

Bellow's first novel, *Dangling Man*, is a diary of a young man awaiting induction into the army during World War II. Joseph quits his job, planning to relax and read before being subjected to the rigors of army life. Instead, the period becomes one of inaction and meaninglessness. Joseph begins to question the value of his friendships, the meaning of his family, and finally even the goodness of life. After months of stultification, existence seems absurd; relief comes in the promise of the regimentation of military life. Joseph no longer awaits induction; he enlists.

The Victim is similar to *Dangling Man* in atmosphere and tone, but dissimilar in form. Asa Leventhal is plagued by family responsibilities, human responsibilities, and anti-Semitism. He is the victim. But in his treatment, or rather his acceptance, of his major tormentor, Kirby Allbee. Asa victimizes his tormentor and himself. The bleak picture of human irrationality, death, and sorrow is broken only by the end of an unbearably hot summer, the return of Asa's wife, and the philosophy of humanism that is spoken by the Yiddishist Schlossberg. These reprieves assure Asa's escape.

The Adventures of Augie March was the novel that thrust Bellow before the American public. An exuberant picaresque tale of a Chicago boy, born to a retarded mother, *Augie March* asserts an American innocence and joy in existence that Bellow seemed shy of in his first novels. This joyousness is not, however, unadulterated. Augie is a Jewish bastard who must learn to fend for himself in the confused and constantly changing world that was America in the 1940's: he encounters abortion, political manipulation, the black market, and sexual perversion. In the face of all of this, Augie can still laugh.

Seize the Day, a novella, tells how middle-aged Wilky Adler is forced to recognize the aimlessness of his life. Always a failure in his father's eyes, Wilky tries to establish an independent identity by attaining what his father most admires—wealth. Wilky is, of course, an abysmal failure, though he learns the valuelessness of money. His epiphany comes with the recognition of his shared humanity with all man. The beauty of humanity is not revealed in the predatory stalking for materialistic gain, but rather in the prayer over the corpse of a stranger.

Henderson the Rain King is a fantasy of a trip to an Africa of the spirit. Here in the continent that saw the first man evolve, Eugene Henderson tries to return to essentials. Henderson leaves America as a man who feels his soul gnawed at by a demanding voice crying "I want! I want!" By the time he returns from Africa, after encountering the primitive power that is in a lion and in an African tribal king, he assumes the status of human being, with human grace and goodness. His desire to do good for others, his love for his family and wife, are directed now so that he can accept the joy of existence. Suffering is no longer his only means of definition.

In *Herzog* Bellow created a character who caught the consciousness of the American intellectual of the 1960's. Moses Elkanah Herzog, on the brink of divorce (for the second time) and professional suicide, begins to develop his naturally reflective nature to the point of insanity. He writes letters—letters to his friends, to his family, to famous people both dead and alive, even notes to himself. These attempts to come to terms with his changing self-image center especially on his feeling for his Jewish past. During his adult life Moses has been a Jew totally assimilated into the Christian intellectual world; he has learned the history of the Christian West; he has accepted the precepts of the Christian philosophers and theologians; and he has taken a Christian wife. Suddenly, this life begins to disintegrate. Before Herzog can attain any equanimity he must learn how to balance his present individuality with his past tradition.

In *Mr. Sammler's Planet* the conflict between past and present is again a concern, but with many added ambiguities. Arthur Sammler, representative of the Old World, survivor of the Holocaust, is divorced from his Jewish past. He is one who admires and studies the Christian ideals of the West. In America, his benefactor and nephew, Elya Bruner, a gynecologist who got rich by doing illegal abortions for the Mafia, is the representative of the Old World patterns. He is the one who, despite his flaws, follows the humanistic ideals that were the backbone of the East European *shtetl*. Only at the end of the novel can Sammler articulate the beauty that he sees in his nephew. In most of the novel, Sammler is suffering life in New York, dodging nymphomaniacs, pickpockets, exhibitionists, violent madmen, and schizophrenics. In the face of such disruption of morals, his own delicacy is not the answer; Elya's goodness is the only philosophy that provides order.

Humboldt's Gift relates the growth of a dilettante writer, Charlie Citrine, who must learn the true value of his mad mentor, Von Humboldt Fleischer (a personalized portrait of the poet Delmore Schwartz). As a young man, Charlie worships the charismatic Humboldt. Moving east to follow his god, Charlie becomes a friend and colleague of the poet. Only after Charlie's success on Broadway do the two writers part—Humboldt accusing Charlie of stealing his personality for the hero of his play. This big, funny, and poignant novel centers on the young man's reflections on Humboldt and on his true value as an artist and mentor. Through flashbacks Citrine reveals the despair and paranoia that destroy his idol. The persistence of Humboldt's spiritual presence in Charlie's later life, long after the poet's death, bespeaks the importance of Humboldt to Charlie. The gift that the mentor leaves is really twofold. The most obvious gift is the absurd play that will probably become a great success as a film. But, more importantly, Humboldt serves as a model for Charlie's own life. The reflection of later years gradually reveals that Humboldt was indeed mad; he was a genius who was driven insane and finally killed by his own unwritten poems. He was one who misused his talents. After this realization Charlie is able to accept the memory of Humboldt. The reburial of the poet's body is a significant rite of passage for Charlie: no longer is he possessed by his mentor's personality.

The variety and power of Bellow's novels (including his most recent, *The Dean's December*, which focuses on a character who has some of the qualities of both Herzog and Sammler) are unquestioned. When Bellow resists the term "Jewish writer," it is because his art is not a chauvinistic and narrow one. But as readers we must not be misled by his resistance to this term: he is most assuredly a writer whose style, characters, form, and humor derive in large part from his Jewish past.

—R. Barbara Gitenstein

See the essay on *Herzog*.

BEMELMANS, Ludwig. Born in Meran, Austria (now Merano, Italy), 27 April 1898; moved to the U.S. in 1914; became citizen, 1918. Educated at schools in Regensburg and Rothenburg, Bavaria. Served in the U.S. Army during World War I. Married Madeline Freund in 1935; one daughter. Worked in hotels and restaurants, 1914–17 and 1919–24; owner, Hapsburg House Restaurant, New York, 1925–35; writer for *New Yorker*; also an artist: exhibitions in galleries in the U.S. and abroad. Recipient: American Library Association Caldecott Medal, for children's book, 1954. *Died 1 October 1962.*

PUBLICATIONS

Collections

Tell Them It Was Wonderful: Selected Writings, edited by Madeline Bemelmans. 1985.

Fiction

I Love You, I Love You, I Love You (stories). 1942.
Now I Lay Me Down to Sleep. 1943.
The Blue Danube. 1945.
Dirty Eddie. 1947.
The Eye of God. 1947; as *The Snow Mountain*, 1950.
The Woman of My Life. 1957.
Are You Hungry, Are You Cold. 1960.
The Street Where the Heart Lies. 1963.

Other (for children)

Hansi. 1934.
The Golden Basket. 1936.
The Castle Number Nine. 1937.
Quito Express. 1938.
Madeline. 1939.
Fifi. 1940.
Rosebud. 1942.
A Tale of Two Glimps. 1947.
Sunshine. 1950.
The Happy Place. 1952.
Madeline's Rescue. 1953.
The High World. 1954.
Parsley. 1955.
Madeline and the Bad Hat. 1956.
Madeline and the Gypsies. 1959.
Welcome Home! 1960.
Madeline in London. 1961.
Marina. 1962.
Madeline's Christmas, completed by Madeline and Barbara Bemelmans. 1985.

Other

My War with the United States. 1937.
Life Class. 1938.
Small Beer. 1939.
At Your Service: The Way of Life in a Hotel. 1941.
Hotel Splendide. 1941.
The Donkey Inside. 1941.
Hotel Bemelmans. 1946.
The Best of Times: An Account of Europe Revisited. 1948.
How to Travel Incognito. 1952.
Father, Dear Father (autobiography). 1953.
To the One I Love the Best. 1955.
The World of Bemelmans. 1955.
My Life in Art. 1958.
How to Have Europe All to Yourself. 1960.
Italian Holiday. 1961.
On Board Noah's Ark. 1962.
La Bonne Table (writings and drawings), edited by Donald and Eleanor Friede. 1964.

Editor, *Holiday in France*. 1957.

* * *

William McFee once wrote of Ludwig Bemelmans, the writer, stage designer, illustrator and painter, that he was "one of those fortunate writers who have all the reviewers ranged on one side, rooting for him." I must confess myself one of that number. Whether chronicling the adventures of Madeline, the irrepressible little French *gamine*, or reporting his own adventures as "El Señor Bnelemaas" in Ecuador (*The Donkey Inside*) or as a waiter (in *Hotel Splendide*), he is delightful. He always wanted to be a painter (despite his family's belief that all artists are "hunger candidates") and only wrote because he had insomnia, but in his acerb and risible little essays, even more than in his drawings, every line is precisely *right*.

To him happen all the most fabulous things. He meets "Mr. Sigsag" of the Hotel Splendide and a host of other charming eccentrics. Just for him a war breaks out (*My War with the United States*) to galvanize a gallery of characters into action. He encounters a little girl who contrives to make her schoolmates livid with jealousy by having an appendix operation. For him tables and chairs have something droll about them. For him people do the most ludicrous things. The world ("I regard it as a curiosity") is funny and he has only to report it (*I Love You, I Love You, I Love You*). He claimed he had no imagination.

Bemelmans is always satirical, but at his best when his unquenchable good humor is given free play, as in the novel *Now I Lay Me Down to Sleep* or the collection of *New Yorker* essays *Small Beer*. It is hard not to gush when mentioning his works, but his delightful humor disarms criticism.

—Leonard R. N. Ashley

BENCHLEY, Robert (Charles). Born in Worcester, Massachusetts, 15 September 1889. Educated at Worcester High School, 1904–07; Phillips Exeter Academy, New Hampshire, 1907–08; Harvard University, Cambridge, Massachusetts (President of the Board of Editors, *Harvard Lampoon*), 1908–12, A.B. 1913. Married Gertrude Darling in 1914; two sons, including the writer Nathaniel Benchley. Staff member, Boston Museum of Fine Art, 1912, and Curtis Publishing Company, 1912–14 (editor of the house journal *Obiter Dicta*); welfare worker in Boston and New York, 1914; worked in advertising, then reporter, New York *Tribune* and *Tribune* magazine, 1916–17, and editor, *Tribune Graphic* Sunday supplement, 1918; drama critic, *Vanity Fair*, New York, and press agent for theatrical producers, 1917; news censor, Aircraft Board, Washington, D.C., 1918; promoter, Liberty Loan drive, 1919; managing editor, *Vanity Fair*, 1919–20; columnist, New York *World*, 1920–21; drama critic, 1920–24, and editor, 1924–29, *Life* magazine, New York; contributor, 1925–40, and drama critic 1927–40, *New Yorker*; columnist, King Features Syndicate, 1933–36. Founder, with Dorothy Parker, Robert E. Sherwood, and others, Algonquin Hotel Round Table, 1920. Also an actor: stage debut, 1923; starred in numerous films (mainly shorts), 1928–45; radio broadcaster from 1938. Recipient: Oscar, for acting in short film, 1935. *Died 21 November 1945.*

PUBLICATIONS

Essays and Sketches

Of All Things! 1921.
Love Conquers All. 1922.
Pluck and Luck. 1925.
The Early Worm. 1927.
The Bridges of Binding. 1928.
20,000 Leagues under the Sea; or, David Copperfield. 1928.
The Treasurer's Report and Other Aspects of Community Singing. 1930.
No Poems; or, Around the World Backwards and Sideways. 1932.
From Bed to Worse; or, Comforting Thoughts about the Bison. 1934.
Why Does Nobody Collect Me? 1935.
My Ten Years in a Quandary and How They Grew. 1936.
After 1903—What? 1938.
Inside Benchley (selection). 1942.
Benchley Beside Himself. 1943.
One Minute Please. 1945.
Benchley—or Else! 1947.
Chips Off the Old Benchley. 1949.
The "Reel" Benchley, edited by George Hornby. 1950.
The Bedside Manner; or, No More Nightmares. 1952.
The Benchley Roundup, edited by Nathaniel Benchley. 1954.
Benchley Lost and Found: 39 Prodigal Pieces. 1970.
Benchley at the Theatre (reviews). 1985.

Plays

Screenplays: *The Treasurer's Report*, 1928; *The Sex Life of the Polyp*, 1928; *The Spellbinder*, 1928; *Furnace Trouble*, 1929; *Lesson Number One*, 1929; *Stewed, Fried and Boiled*, 1929; *Sky Devils*, with others, 1932; *The Sport Parade*, 1932; *Your Technocracy and Mine*, 1933; *Murder on a Honeymoon*, with Seton I. Miller, 1935; *Foreign Correspondent*, with others, 1940; *No News Is Good News*, 1943; *Important Business*, 1944; *Why, Daddy?*, 1944.

*

Critical Studies: *Benchley: A Biography* by Nathaniel Benchley, 1955; *Benchley* by Norris W. Yates, 1968; *Benchley: His Life and Good Times* by Babette Rosmond, 1970; *Starring Benchley: Those Magnificent Movie Shorts* by Robert Redding, 1973.

* * *

After the customary false starts, forays into advertising and personnel work, Robert Benchley, like most of the American humorists of his generation, found his way to journalism. He began as a reporter for the New York *Tribune* in 1916, and within a few years became editor, columnist, or occasional contributor to *Collier's, Vanity Fair*, the New York *World, Life*, the *Bookman*, and the *New Yorker*. Aside from his comic writing, his most sustained work in the magazines was as a drama reviewer, primarily for *Life* and the *New Yorker*, and as a press critic, in which capacity he used a pseudonym, Guy Fawkes, and initiated "The Wayward Press" department in the *New Yorker*. His first book, *Of All Things!*, was published in 1921 and between that time and his death in 1945, some dozen more volumes appeared, all of them collections of pieces written for magazines or newspapers. Some of the later ones, like *Benchley Beside Himself*, cannibalize earlier collections.

In a letter to his mother written in 1922, E.B. White called *Of All Things!* "about as funny as anything there is on the market today," and, in a letter to Walter Blair in 1964, he admitted that he imitated Benchley in his early work. That writers like White and James Thurber, who so early found their own authentic voices, were influenced by Benchley is evidence not simply of the pervasiveness of his subject matter—the little indignities of daily life which have always beset humorists—but of the quality of his prose. Benchley could, like Frank Sullivan, rise to complete nonsense, but most of the time he wrote simple, deceptively rational sentences in which a judicious choice of adjective or a demanding parenthesis could turn the sentence, the whole piece, a conventional way of thinking inside out.

Benchley early developed a firm comic personality, created a character who sometimes appears in the pieces, is more often the voice that creates them. His persona became a Benchley after-image, through the Gluyas Williams illustrations for his books and the bumbling character he played in movie shorts and in feature films. As he emerges in Benchley's writing, the character is more than the conventional little man so loved by humorists, cartoonists, and politicians. He is both vain and ponderous, using his own self-esteem as the banana peel on which to slip; he is easily embarrassed, but he will snarl—a bit tentatively—if he is cornered by too preposterous as assault from social usage. His ordinary antagonists are things like pigeons, roadmaps, ocean liners, Christmas, but there are hints of darker enemies, as in "My Trouble" in which he asks, "Do all boys of 46 stop breathing when they go to bed?" This disquieting undertone emerges infrequently in Benchley's work; for the most part, his confused and confusing other self is satisfied to worry a pomposity or a platitude to death and in the process leave the reader laughing.

—Gerald Weales

BENÉT, Stephen Vincent. Born in Bethlehem, Pennsylvania, 22 July 1898; brother of William Rose Benét, *q.v.* Educated at Hitchcock Military Academy, Jacinto, California, 1910–11; Summerville Academy; Yale University, New Haven, Connecticut (Chairman, *Yale Literary Magazine*, 1918), 1915–18, 1919–20, A.B. 1919, M.A. 1920; the Sorbonne, Paris, 1920–21. Married Rosemary Carr in 1921; one son and two daughters. Worked for the State Department, Washington, D.C., 1918, and for advertising agency, New York, 1919; lived in Paris, 1926–29; during 1930's and early 1940's was an active lecturer and radio propagandist for the liberal cause. Editor, Yale Younger Poets series. Recipient: Poetry Society of America prize, 1921; Guggenheim fellowship, 1926; Pulitzer Prize, 1929, 1944; O. Henry Award, 1932, 1937, 1940; Shelley Memorial Award, 1933; American Academy Gold Medal, 1943. Member, 1929, and Vice-President, National Institute of Arts and Letters. *Died 13 March 1943.*

PUBLICATIONS

Collections

Selected Poetry and Prose, edited by Basil Davenport. 1960.
Selected Letters, edited by Charles A. Fenton. 1960.

Verse

The Drug-Shop; or, Endymion in Edmonstoun. 1917.
Young Adventure. 1918.
Heavens and Earth. 1920.
The Ballad of William Sycamore 1790–1880. 1923.
King David. 1923.
Tiger Joy. 1925.
John Brown's Body. 1928.
Ballads and Poems 1915–1930. 1931.
A Book of Americans, with Rosemary Benét. 1933.
Burning City. 1936.
The Ballad of the Duke's Mercy. 1939.
Nightmare at Noon. 1940.
Listen to the People: Independence Day 1941. 1941.
Western Star. 1943.
The Last Circle: Stories and Poems. 1946.

Plays

Five Men and Pompey: A Series of Dramatic Portraits. 1915.
Nerves, with John Farrar (produced 1924).
That Awful Mrs. Eaton, with John Farrar (produced 1924).
The Headless Horseman, music by Douglas Moore (broadcast 1937). 1937.
The Devil and Daniel Webster, music by Douglas Moore, from the story by Benét (produced 1938). 1939.
Elementals (broadcast 1940–41). In *Best Broadcasts of 1940–41*, edited by Max Wylie, 1942.
Freedom's a Hard Bought Thing (broadcast 1941). In *The Free Company Presents*, edited by James Boyd, 1941.
Nightmare at Noon, in *The Treasury Star Parade*, edited by William A. Bacher. 1942.
A Child Is Born (broadcast 1942). 1942.
They Burned the Books (broadcast 1942). 1942.
All That Money Can Buy (screenplay), with Dan Totheroh, in *Twenty Best Film Plays*, edited by John Gassner and Dudley Nichols. 1943.
We Stand United and Other Radio Scripts (includes *A Child Is Born*, *The Undefended Border*, *Dear Adolf*, *Listen to the People*, *Thanksgiving Day—1941*, *They Burned the Books*, *A Time to Reap*, *Toward the Century of Modern Man*, *Your Army*). 1945.

Screenplays: *Abraham Lincoln*, with Gerrit Lloyd, 1930; *Cheers for Miss Bishop*, with Adelaide Heilbron and Sheridan Gibney, 1941; *All That Money Can Buy*, with Dan Totheroh, 1941.

Radio Plays: *The Headless Horseman*, 1937; *The Undefended Border*, 1940; *We Stand United*, 1940; *Elementals*, 1940–41; *Listen to the People*, 1941; *Thanksgiving Day—1941*, 1941; *Freedom's a Hard Bought Thing*, 1941; *Nightmare at Noon*; *A Child Is Born*, 1942; *Dear Adolf*, 1942; *They Burned the Books*, 1942; *A Time to Reap*, 1942; *Toward the Century of Modern Man*, 1942; *Your Army*, 1944.

Fiction

The Beginning of Wisdom. 1921.
Young People's Pride. 1922.
Jean Huguenot. 1923.
Spanish Bayonet. 1926.
The Barefoot Saint (stories). 1929.
The Litter of Rose Leaves (stories). 1930.
James Shore's Daughter. 1934.
Thirteen O'Clock: Stories of Several Worlds. 1937.
The Devil and Daniel Webster. 1937.
Johnny Pye and the Fool-Killer (stories). 1938.
Tales Before Midnight. 1939.
Short Stories: A Selection. 1942.
O'Halloran's Luck and Other Short Stories. 1944.

Other

A Summons to the Free. 1941.
Selected Works. 2 vols., 1942.
America. 1944.
Benét on Writing: A Great Writer's Letter of Advice to a Young Beginner, edited by George Abbe. 1964.

Editor, with others, *The Yale Book of Student Verse 1910–1919*. 1919.
Editor, with Monty Woolley, *Tamburlaine the Great*, by Christopher Marlowe. 1919.

*

Bibliography: by Gladys Louise Maddocks, in *Bulletin of Bibliography 20*, September 1951 and April 1952.

Critical Studies: *Benét* by William Rose Benét, 1943; *Benét: The Life and Times of an American Man of Letters* by Charles A. Fenton, 1958; *Benét* by Parry Stroud, 1962.

* * *

Stephen Vincent Benét occupies a curiously equivocal position in American letters. One of America's best known and rewarded poets and storytellers, he has at the same time been virtually ignored in academic discussions of major 20th-century writers, and seldom anthologized. In light of the greater critical success enjoyed by his student friends at Yale—Thornton Wilder, Archibald MacLeish, and Philip Barry, themselves often unremarked among "major" writers—Benét's reputation seems thin indeed.

Benét's permanent place in the history of American fiction is nevertheless assured by the fact that among his many volumes of prose and verse there are several minor classics that are widely read and admired. His early light and ironic verse, such as "For City Spring" and "Evening and Morning," and such frolicking ballads as "Captain Kidd," "Thomas Jefferson," "The Mountain Whippoorwill," and "The Ballad of William Sycamore" are highly regarded. His long narrative poem about the Civil War, *John Brown's Body*, dramatized by Charles Laughton in 1953 and called by Henry Steele Commager "not only the best poem about the Civil War, and the best narrative, but also the best history," won Benét his first Pulitzer Prize. Benét's best known short story, "The Devil and Daniel Webster," which combines the author's flare for fantasy and old folktale traditions, shares an equally prominent place in the tall-tale genre of American storytelling. Finally, *Western Star*, another long narrative poem about the heroic pioneering of America, begun in 1934 and incomplete at his death, won for Benét a second Pulitzer Prize in 1944.

Among the notes for the continuation of *Western Star* found after Benét's death, the following quatrain was saved:

> Now for my country that it still may live,
> All that I have, all that I am I'll give.
> It is not much beside the gift of the brave
> And yet accept it since tis all I have.

What Benét had—an unbounded, 19th-century faith in the promises of American democracy, and an expansive, Whitmanesque love for what seemed the nation's special attributes, diversity, amplitude, self-sufficiency, frankness, innocence—he poured into every poem, story, and novel he wrote. He praised New York as the communal achievement of the spirit of man, and America because there every man could most freely become what God meant him to be. "Out of your fever and your moving on," he said in the "Prelude" to *Western Star*, "Americans, Americans, Americans . . . I make my song."

Both in sentiment and in style, Benét's work attempts to embody the very democratic virtues it is about. Like Sandburg, Hart Crane, and Vachel Lindsay, he uses the zesty tempos, conversational rhythms, and laconic vernacular to capture the spirit of greatness in the strength and simplicity of the nation's common people. In his book of 56 verses about famous American men and women, great and small, *A Book of Americans*, Benét says of the greatest and humblest of American native sons:

> Lincoln was a long man
> He liked out of doors.
> He liked the wind blowing
> And the talk in country stores.

Just as *John Brown's Body* projects Benét's sensitive feeling for half a dozen countrysides, racial strains, and political attitudes, so this book stands in praise of the nation's heroic ability to reconcile its opposites among that "varied lot" who "each by deed and speech / Adorned our history."

Despite the warmth, genuineness, and impish charm with which Benét celebrates the country's democratic potential, his failure to win wider critical respectability is clearly attributable to the fact that his breadth of sympathy and deep-rooted patriotism seem parochial and old-fashioned to today's audiences, and that even his best work, viewed alongside the more realistic and richly inventive fiction of such contemporaries as Crane, Joyce, Proust, and Eliot, appears lacking in depth, subtlety, and originality. The pastoral rebellion of the earth against machines, against the "Age of Steam," which pervades so many of his poems, and his use of conventional verse forms and technical devices that have made him dear to school teachers, seem, in the words of one critic, "all too clear and all too facile." It is significant that Benét's writing has been praised more for its lively evocation of American history than for its aesthetic value.

—Lawrence R. Broer

See the essay on *John Brown's Body*.

BENÉT, William Rose. Born in Fort Hamilton, New York, 2 February 1886; brother of Stephen Vincent Benét, *q.v.* Educated at Albany Academy, Albany, New York, graduated 1904; Yale University, New Haven, Connecticut (Chairman, *Yale Courant*; editor, *Yale Record*), 1904–07, B.Phil. 1907. Served in the U.S. Army Signal Corps, 1918: Second Lieutenant. Married 1) Teresa Frances Thompson in 1912 (died, 1919), one son and two daughters; 2) Elinor Wylie, *q.v.*, in 1923 (died, 1928); 3) Lora Baxter in 1932 (divorced, 1937); 4) the writer Marjorie Flack in 1941. Ship's clerk, 1908; lived in California, 1909–10; clerk and reader, 1911–14, and assistant editor, 1914–18, *Century* magazine, New York; advertising writer, 1918; assistant editor, *Nation's Business*, Washington, D.C., 1918–19; associate editor, *Literary Review* supplement of New York *Evening Post*, 1920–24; founder, with Christopher Morley, 1924, associate editor, 1924–29, columnist ("The Phoenix Nest"), 1924–50, and contributing editor, 1929–50, *Saturday Review of Literature*, New York; editor, Brewer and Warren, publishers, New York, 1929–30. Recipient: Pulitzer Prize, 1942. Secretary, National Institute of Arts and Letters. *Died 4 May 1950.*

PUBLICATIONS

Verse

Merchants from Cathay. 1913.
The Falconer of God and Other Poems. 1914.
The Great White Wall. 1916.
The Burglar of the Zodiac and Other Poems. 1918.
Perpetual Light: A Memorial. 1919.
Moons of Grandeur. 1920.
Man Possessed: Selected Poems. 1927.
Sagacity. 1929.
Rip Tide: A Novel in Verse. 1932.
Starry Harness. 1933.
Golden Fleece. 1935.
Harlem and Other Poems. 1935.
A Baker's Dozen of Emblems. 1935.
With Wings as Eagles: Poems and Ballads of the Air. 1940.
The Dust Which Is God: A Novel in Verse. 1941.
Adolphus; or, The Adopted Dolphin and the Pirate's Daughter (for children), with Marjorie Flack. 1941.

Day of Deliverance. 1944.
The Stairway of Surprise. 1947.
Timothy's Angels (for children). 1947.
Poetry Package, with Christopher Morley. 1950.
The Spirit of the Scene. 1951.

Play

Day's End, in *The Best One-Act Plays of 1939*, edited by Margaret Mayorga. 1939.

Fiction

The First Person Singular. 1922.

Other

Saturday Papers (essays), with Henry Seidel Canby and Amy Loveman. 1921.
The Flying King of Kurio (for children). 1926.
Wild Goslings: A Selection of Fugitive Pieces. 1927.
The Prose and Poetry of Elinor Wylie. 1934.
Stephen Vincent Benét: My Brother Steve. 1943.

Editor, *Poems for Youth: An American Anthology*. 1925.
Editor, with John Drinkwater and Henry Seidel Canby, *Twentieth-Century Poetry*. 1929.
Editor, *Collected Poems*, by Elinor Wylie. 1932.
Editor, *Fifty Poets: An American Auto-Anthology*. 1933.
Editor, *Guide to Daily Reading*. 1934.
Editor, *The Pocket University*. 13 vols., 1934.
Editor, with others, *Adventures in English Literature*. 1936.
Editor, *Mother Goose: A Comprehensive Collection of the Rhymes*. 1936.
Editor, *From Robert to Elizabeth Barrett Browning* (letters). 1936.
Editor, with Norman Holmes Pearson, *The Oxford Anthology of American Literature*. 1938.
Editor, with Adolph Gillis, *Poems for Modern Youth*. 1938.
Editor, *Supplement to Great Poems of the English Language*, edited by Wallace Alvin Briggs. 1941.
Editor, with Conrad Aiken, *An Anthology of Famous English and American Poetry*. 1945.
Editor, with Norman Cousins, *The Poetry of Freedom*. 1945.
Editor, *The Reader's Encyclopedia*. 1948.

Translator, with Teresa Frances, *The East I Know*, by Paul Claudel. 1914.

*

Critical Study: in *Elinor Wylie, A Life Apart: A Biography* by Stanley Olson, 1979.

* * *

William Rose Benét has perhaps been more remarked upon in recent American literary history as the "older brother" of the writer Stephen Vincent Benét, and as husband of Elinor Wylie, than as an accomplished poet in his own right. Serious attention to his verse has also been diverted by his prominence as a reviewer, critic, and anthologist, and by his numerous activities as a promoter of the arts. But despite this dispersion of energies, Benét managed to publish many volumes of verse whose value has not properly been acknowledged.

The obvious unevenness of Benét's creative output is hinted at by the fact that one critic rated him no better than a mere "journeyman of letters," while another claimed that he was a "builder [whose] strongest rhythms have the certitude of an arch. . . ." Certainly Benét's weakest poems are unapologetically romantic and lacking in intensity. When he announces his poetic intentions in his most celebrated work, *The Dust Which Is God*, as "I will be plain at least," he does more than alert us to what he hopes will be a poetic voice free of bombast and ornamentation; unwittingly, he indicts a good number of poems whose over-statedness results in an absence of color or emotional vitality. "Throw wide / The gates of the heart," he counsels in his poem "Study of Man," "Taking your part / In percipient life . . . Ever Extend / Your boundaries, and be / Inwardly free!"

Such direct statement issues from the poet's almost passionate reverence for the freedom and dignity of man, and for the ample spirit of God and nature, which he finds so abundantly manifest in his native America, as in "Men on Strike":

> The Country of the Free! Yes, a great land.
> Thank God that I have known it East to West
> And North to South, and still I love it best
> Of all the various world the seas command.

From the point of view of the wise primitivist, Benét celebrates the democratic virtues of common men, and envisions portents of disaster in the encroachments of the machine age. In "The Stricken Average," he writes:

> Little of brilliance did they write or say.
> They bore the battle of living, and were gay.
> Little of wealth or fame they left behind.
> They were merely honorable, brave, and kind.

He yearns for the "pristine creation / Unsullied by our civilization," ("Young Girl") whose elemental harmonies are forever threatened by factories, corporations, "towers of glass and steel" ("Shadow of the Mountain Man").

Such romantic attitudes were bound to lessen the appeal of Benét's work in an age whose best literary efforts were in direct opposition to such simple and sentimental verse. Yet there are indisputable qualities in Benét's best work, perhaps most forcibly realized the *The Dust Which Is God*, which in 1942 won him a Pulitzer Prize. An autobiographical verse narrative, it demonstrates a remarkable range of interests and intellect, and admirable versatility in the use of changing forms and rhythms to capture the diverse and sprawling nature of his subject—the birth and growth of the country, which he treats as synonymous with his own life. The poetry here reveals a lively and sophisticated grasp of cultural ideas, and often achieves a rich synthesis of opposites: classical and modern, noble and banal, holy and sensual, lyrical and prosaic. At their best, these "vignette illustrations" project for us a poetic talent of greater potential stature than that of the author's more celebrated brother—more original, more sensuous, and more varied and universal in scope.

—Lawrence R. Broer

BERRYMAN, John. Born John Allyn Smith, in McAlester, Oklahoma, 25 October 1914; took step-father's surname, 1926. Educated at schools in Oklahoma, Florida, and New York City; South Kent School, Connecticut, 1928–32; Columbia University, New York (Rensselaer Prize, 1935), 1932–36, A.B. 1936 (Phi Beta Kappa); Clare College, Cambridge (Kellett Fellow, 1936–37; Oldham Shakespeare Scholar, 1937), 1937–38, B.A. 1938. Married 1) Eileen Patricia Mulligan in 1942 (divorced, 1956); 2) Elizabeth Ann Levine in 1956 (divorced, 1959), one son; 3) Kathleen Donahue in 1961, two daughters. Instructor in English, Wayne State University, Detroit, 1939–40, and Harvard University, Cambridge, Massachusetts, 1940–43; Instructor in English, 1943, Associate in Creative Writing, 1946–47, Resident Fellow, 1948–49, and Hodder Fellow, 1950–51, Princeton University, New Jersey; Lecturer in English, University of Washington, Seattle, 1950; Elliston Professor of Poetry, University of Cincinnati, 1952; teacher of creative writing, University of Iowa, Iowa City, 1954; Assistant Professor, 1955–56, Associate Professor, 1957–62, Professor, 1962–72, and Regents' Professor of Humanities, 1969–72, University of Minnesota, Minneapolis. U.S. Information Service Lecturer, India, 1957; Visiting Professor, University of California, Berkeley, 1960, and Brown University, Providence, Rhode Island, 1962–63. Poetry editor, *Nation*, New York, 1939. Recipient: Rockefeller fellowship, 1944–46, 1956; Shelley Memorial Award, 1949; Guggenheim fellowship, 1952, 1966; Harriet Monroe Award, 1957; Brandeis University Creative Arts Award, 1959; Ingram Merrill Foundation grant, 1964; Loines Award, 1964; Pulitzer Prize, 1965; Academy of American Poets fellowship, 1967; National Endowment for the Arts award, 1967, and senior fellowship, 1971; Bollingen Prize, 1969; National Book Award, 1969. D.Let.: Drake University, Des Moines, Iowa, 1971. Member, American Academy; American Academy of Arts and Sciences; Academy of American Poets. *Died (suicide) 7 January 1972.*

PUBLICATIONS

Collections

Collected Poems 1934–1972, edited by Charles Thornbury. 1986.

Verse

Five Young American Poets, with others. 1940.
Poems. 1942.
Two Poems. 1942.
The Dispossessed. 1948.
Homage to Mistress Bradstreet. 1956; as *Homage to Mistress Bradstreet and Other Poems*, 1959.
His Thought Made Pockets & the Plane Buckt. 1958.
77 Dream Songs. 1964.
Two Dream Songs. 1965.
Berryman's Sonnets. 1967.
Short Poems. 1967.
I Have Moved to Dublin. . . . 1967.
His Toy, His Dream, His Rest: 308 Dream Songs. 1968.
The Dream Songs. 1969.
Two Dream Songs. 1969.
Two Poems. 1970.
Love and Fame. 1970; revised edition, 1972.
Delusions, Etc. 1972.
Selected Poems 1938–1968. 1972.
Henry's Fate and Other Poems 1967–1972, edited by John Haffenden. 1977.

Fiction

Recovery. 1973.

Other

Stephen Crane (biography). 1950.
The Freedom of the Poet (miscellany). 1976.
One Answer to a Question. 1981.
Stephen Crane: The Red Badge of Courage. 1981.

Editor, with Ralph Ross and Allen Tate, *The Arts of Reading* (anthology). 1960.
Editor, *The Unfortunate Traveller; or, The Life of Jack Wilton*, by Thomas Nashe. 1960.

*

Bibliography: *Berryman: A Checklist* by Richard J. Kelly, 1972; *Berryman: A Descriptive Bibliography* by Ernest C. Stefanik, Jr., 1974; *Berryman: A Reference Guide* by Gary Q. Arpin, 1976.

Critical Studies: *Berryman* by William J. Martz, 1969; *Berryman* by James M. Linebarger, 1974; *A Tumult for Berryman: A Homage* edited by Marguerite Harris, 1976; *The Poetry of Berryman* by Gary Q. Arpin, 1977; *Berryman: An Introduction to the Poetry* by Joel Conarroe, 1977; *Berryman: A Critical Commentary*, 1980, and *The Life of Berryman*, 1982, both by John Haffenden; *Poets in Their Youth* by Eileen Simpson, 1982; *The Stock of Available Reality: R.P. Blackmur and Berryman* by James D. Bloom, 1984; *The Soul under Stress: A Study of the Poetics of Berryman's Dream Songs* by Bo Gustavsson, 1984.

* * *

John Berryman spent his childhood on a farm in Oklahoma under the sombre and difficult aegis of a father whose improvidence finally led to his suicide, an event which haunted and disturbed the poet for the rest of his life. From these dark beginnings, he leapt into the brighter world of his education, first at a private school in Connecticut, and then at Columbia University, where his immense energies and brilliance were manifested. A scholarship to Cambridge University led to his studies in Shakespeare and the English Renaissance, the stylistic exuberance of which was to influence his own discordant, richly embellished mode of verse. At Princeton University, he began a frenzied pace of writing that led to his first full-length collection of short poems, *The Dispossessed*. He had also completed much of the cycle of poems later published as *Berryman's Sonnets*. In both volumes Berryman is a mature craftsman of traditional forms and meters, which he renewed with his energetic speech.

Berryman's major work begins with *Homage to Mistress Bradstreet*, which includes poems from *The Dispossessed*. The title poem, a sequence of 57 eight-line stanzas, evokes the life and hardships of this American poet through an original strategy of merging the narrator's voice with his subject's, in which all the details of her sickness, frailty, and harsh family life are rendered with powerful immediacy. The poet's speech slips into the Colonial tongue and out again into a flinty modern colloquialism with masterful control. Berryman etches the character of Bradstreet and holds her up as an instance of the artist's eternal struggle against adversity:

> Headstones stagger under great draughts of time
> after heads pass out, and their world must reel
> speechless, blind in the end
> about its chilling star: thrift tuft,
> whin cushion—nothing. Already with the wounded flying
> dark air fills, I am a closet of secrets dying,
> races murder, foxholes hold men,
> reactor piles wage slow upon the wet brain rime.

Included in *Homage* is the series "The Nervous Songs," where he again inhabits other strained minds and articulates their emotions. They are important, however, chiefly for their form; each poem is cast in three six-line stanzas, the form employed throughout his greatest work, *The Dream Songs*.

The persona of the *Dream Songs* is variously referred to as Henry, Pussy-Cat, and Mr. Bones, and the poems evoke his daily inner life as he struggles through the routines of teaching, drying-out from chronic alcoholism, and writing ambitious books of poems. His deepest dilemma is with his own identity, which fits him in the middle of every extreme of life: he is middle-aged, of the middle-class, and of middling talent. Against all these middlings he struggles to find an edge, by occasionally daubing burnt cork on his face, by heavy drinking, and by hard working, but each time falls back into the slough of his middleness depressed and exhausted:

> He lay in the middle of the world, and twicht.
> More Sparine for Pelides,
> human (half) & down here as he is,
> with probably insulting mail to open
> and certainly unworthy words to hear
> and his unforgivable memory.

Or again, "Henry felt baffled, in the middle of the thing," which is a refrain of his efforts and sufferings.

The desire to transcend his undefined existence wears down into defeat in later sections of this sequence, until "Henry hates the world. What the world to Henry / did will not bear thought." The despair deepens into rejection: "This world is gradually becoming a place / where I do not care to be any more." He broods upon death in all its forms and nightmare possibilities, including the frequent lamentations for other poets who have died recently, and who seem to share his dark view of the world:

> I'm cross with God who has wrecked this generation.
> First he seized Ted [Roethke], then Richard [Blackmur],
> Randall [Jarrell], and now Delmore [Schwartz].
> In between he gorged on Sylvia Plath.
> That was a first rate haul. He left alive
> fools I could number like a kitchen knife
> but Lowell he did not touch.

In a later, grimmer juncture of the *Songs*, Henry remarks bitterly, "The world grows more disgusting dawn by dawn." The poems then take up a plot of sorts with a residence in Ireland, followed by a return to the United States and the long attempt to recover from alcoholism, a turn that also involves Henry in religious conversion.

The whole work, including the posthumous additions, *Henry's Fate*, amounts to a vast mosaic of pieces of Henry's life and character, without transforming such pieces into a unified vision. The work is discordant throughout, in its language and in its jagged progression of themes and motifs. It is essentially a long and despairing examination of a poet's alienation from the post-war world, in which his brilliance and cultural inheritance appear to have no place or value. The grave, devoted artist founders and ultimately destroys himself, lamenting throughout the cursed and crooked fate of his fellow poets. This tragedy is lifted above self-pity and sentimentality by the essential good character of Henry, whose complications give us a Hamlet for this age.

Berryman's later works, *Love and Fame, Delusions, Etc.*, and the novel *Recovery*, turn away from the *Dream Songs* to treat more directly of the poet's life. *Love and Fame* is unabashed autobiography of the poet's education and rise to prominence, delivered in a flat, narrative style unlike his earlier verse. In *Delusions, Etc.* his religious turning is expressed in a section of liturgical poems where Berryman is again the effortless master of sonorous lyrics. *Recovery*, unfinished at the poet's death, exposes the torment of the alcoholic and eloquently pleads for understanding of this disease from which the poet suffered much of his life.

—Paul Christensen

See the essay on *The Dream Songs*.

BIERCE, Ambrose (Gwinnet). Born in Horse Cave Creek, Meigs County, Ohio, 24 June 1842. Educated at a high school in Warsaw, Indiana; Kentucky Military Institute, Franklin Springs, 1859–60. Served in the 9th Indiana Infantry Regiment of the Union Army during the Civil War, 1861–65: Major. Married Mollie Day in 1871 (separated, 1888; divorced, 1905); two sons and one daughter. Printer's devil, *Northern Indianan* (anti-slavery paper), 1857–59; U.S. Treasury aide, Selma, Alabama, 1865; served on military mapping expedition, Omaha to San Francisco, 1866–67; night watchman and clerk, Sub-Treasury, San Francisco, 1867–68; editor and columnist ("Town Crier"), *News Letter*, San Francisco, 1868–71; lived in London, 1872–75: staff member, *Fun*, 1872–75, and editor, *Lantern*, 1875; worked in the assay office, U.S. Mint, San Francisco, after 1875; associate editor, *Argonaut*, 1877–79; agent, Black Hills Placer Mining Company, Rockerville, Dakota Territory, 1880–81; editor and columnist ("Prattle"), *Wasp*, San Francisco, 1881–86; columnist, San Francisco *Examiner*, 1887–1906, and New York *Journal*, 1896–1906; lived in Washington, D.C., 1900–13: Washington correspondent, New York *American*, 1900–06; columnist, *Cosmopolitan*, Washington, 1905–09; traveled in Mexico, 1913–14: served in Villa's forces and is presumed to have been killed at the Battle of Ojinaga. *Died* (probably 11 January) *in 1914.*

PUBLICATIONS

Collections

Collected Works, edited by Walter Neale. 12 vols., 1909–12.

Letters, edited by Bertha Clark Pope. 1921.
Complete Short Stories, edited by Ernest Jerome Hopkins. 1970.
Stories and Fables, edited by Edward Wagenknecht. 1977.

Fiction

The Fiend's Delight. 1873.
Nuggets and Dust Panned Out in California. 1873.
Cobwebs from an Empty Skull. 1874.
The Dance of Death, with Thomas A. Harcourt. 1877; revised edition, 1877.
Tales of Soldiers and Civilians. 1891; as *In the Midst of Life*, 1892; revised edition, 1898.
The Monk and the Hangman's Daughter, from a translation by Gustav Adolph Danziger of a story by Richard Voss. 1892.
Can Such Things Be? 1893.
Fantastic Fables. 1899.
A Son of the Gods, and A Horseman in the Sky. 1907.
Battlefields and Ghosts. 1931.

Verse

Black Beetles in Amber. 1892.
Shapes of Clay. 1903.

Other

The Cynic's Word Book. 1906; as *The Devil's Dictionary*, 1911; revised edition, by Ernest Jerome Hopkins, as *The Enlarged Devil's Dictionary*, 1967.
The Shadow on the Dial and Other Essays, edited by S.O. Howes. 1909; revised edition, as *Antepenultimata* (in *Collected Works 11*), 1912.
Write It Right: A Little Black-List of Literary Faults. 1909.
Twenty-One Letters, edited by Samuel Loveman. 1922.
Selections from Prattle, edited by Carroll D. Hall. 1936.
Satanic Reader: Selections from the Invective Journalism, edited by Ernest Jerome Hopkins. 1968.

*

Bibliography: *Bierce: A Bibliography* by Vincent Starrett, 1929; in *Bibliography of American Literature* by Jacob Blanck, 1955; *Bierce: Bibliographical and Biographical Data* edited by Joseph Gaer, 1968.

Critical Studies: *Bierce: A Biography* by Carey McWilliams, 1929; *Bierce, The Devil's Lexicographer*, 1951, and *Bierce and the Black Hills*, 1956, both by Paul Fatout; *Bierce* by Robert A. Wiggins, 1964; *The Short Stories of Bierce: A Study in Polarity* by Stuart C. Woodruff, 1965; *Bierce: A Biography* by Richard O'Connor, 1967; *Bierce* by M.E. Grenander, 1971; *Critical Essays on Bierce* edited by Cathy N. Davidson, 1982, and *The Experimental Fictions of Bierce: Structuring the Ineffable* by Davidson, 1984.

*   *   *

Though not widely read today, Ambrose Bierce is a familiar name in American letters. After several years of distinguished soldiering in the Civil War, the almost completely self-taught Bierce turned to journalism and ended up being one of the most colourful figures in late 19th- and early 20th-century journalism in America. In San Francisco, where he spent most of his life, he was a newspaper editor and columnist, and delighted in exposing hypocrisy and stupidity in private and public life. Besides his witty and pungent journalistic writing, Bierce produced a sizeable body of short stories and essays, and also some verse, chiefly occasional and satiric. His literary reputation, however, must depend upon the stories collected in *Tales of Soldiers and Civilians*. In "An Occurrence at Owl Creek Bridge" Bierce skilfully uses suspense not as a mere melodramatic device but as a logical and calculating means of rendering believable the bizarre plot, which concerns a young man about to be executed. In other stories, like "One of the Missing," there is perhaps a heavier use of coincidence than most readers will accept without protest.

If young Bierce dealt in the tall tale and broad western humour, the older Bierce was a master of sardonic humour and mordant but often sparkling wit. The best specimen of these qualities as well as of Bierce's life-long cynicism is to be found, outside his journalism, in *The Devil's Dictionary*, a book quoted universally even though many that quote from it may not be aware of the author's identity. As a serious literary writer Bierce belongs to—and has helped perpetuate (in a small measure)—the tradition of the absurd and grotesque in American writing. There is in his work a marked interest in abnormal or intensified psychological states and a persistent hostility to the realistic mode. One will look in vain for a range of emotional experience in his writing and the depth of serious feeling found in great literature. But for his picturesque personality and his contribution as a committed and hard-hitting journalist, and as a writer of some excellent stories, Bierce is an enduring figure in the history of American literature.

—J.N. Sharma

See the essay on "One of the Missing."

BILLINGS, Josh. See **SHAW, Henry Wheeler.**

BIRD, Robert Montgomery. Born in New Castle, Delaware, 5 February 1806. Educated at Germantown Academy, Philadelphia; University of Pennsylvania, Philadelphia, 1824–27, M.D. 1827. Married Mary Mayer in 1837; one son. Practised as a physician in Philadelphia for one year, then gave up medicine to become a writer; wrote plays for the actor-producer Edwin Forrest, 1831–34; wrote novels, 1835–40; suffered a breakdown and retired to a farm in Maryland, where he subsequently recovered, 1840; Professor, Institutes of Medicine and Materia Medica, Pennsylvania Medical College, Philadelphia, 1841–43; literary editor and part owner, *North American*, Philadelphia, 1847–54. Honorary member, English Dramatic Authors Society. *Died 23 January 1854.*

PUBLICATIONS

Collections

The Life and Dramatic Works (includes *Pelopidas, The Gladiator, Oralloossa*), edited by Clement E. Foust. 1919.

The Cowled Lover and Other Plays (includes *Calidorf; or, The Avenger; News of the Night; or, A Trip to Niagara; 'Twas All for the Best; or 'Tis All a Notion*), edited by Edward O'Neill. 1941.

Plays

The Gladiator (produced 1831; also produced as *Spartacus*). In *The Life and Dramatic Works*, 1919.
Oralloossa (produced 1832). In *The Life and Dramatic Works*, 1919.
The Broker of Bogota (produced 1834). Edited by Arthur Hobson Quinn, in *Representative American Plays*, 1917.
News of the Night; or, A Trip to Niagara (produced 1929). In *The Cowled Lover and Other Plays*, 1941.
The City Looking Glass: A Philadelphia Comedy, edited by Arthur Hobson Quinn (produced 1933). 1933.

Fiction

Calavar; or, The Knight of the Conquest. 1834; as *Abdalla the Moor and the Spanish Knight*, 1835.
The Infidel; or, The Fall of Mexico. 1835; as *Cortez*, 1835; as *The Infidel's Doom*, 1840.
The Hawks of Hawk-Hollow: A Tradition of Pennsylvania. 1835.
Sheppard Lee. 1836.
Nick of the Woods; or, The Jibbenainosay: A Tale of Kentucky. 1837; edited by Cecil B. Williams, 1939.
Peter Pilgrim; or, A Rambler's Recollections. 1838.
The Adventures of Robin Day. 1839.

*

Bibliography: in *Bibliography of American Literature* by Jacob Blanck, 1955.

Critical Studies: *Life of Bird* by Mary Mayer Bird, edited by C. Seymour Thompson, 1945; *Bird* by Curtis Dahl, 1963.

* * *

One of the truly remarkable men of his time, Robert Montgomery Bird boasted sufficiently varied interests and equally responsive talents to lead his active mind through the fields of medicine, science, music, art, history, politics, pedagogy, and literature. Early in life he outlined a literary career in which he would begin with poetry and drama, turn next to novels, and finally write history. A scholarly man, widely read in the classics, he was also very much a product of and a part of the Romantic tradition which was being revealed in the idealism of Emerson and Thoreau, the gothic qualities in Hawthorne and Poe, and the concern for nature which distinguished the novels of Cooper, John Pendleton Kennedy and William Gilmore Simms. Indeed, Bird was a significant force in bringing Romanticism to American literature, particularly the drama.

For his career as a dramatist Bird projected at least 55 plays, and in response to the play contests which Edwin Forrest established in 1828 he began to write in earnest. Four of Forrest's nine prize plays were written by Bird—*Pelopidas, The Gladiator, Oralloossa*, and *The Broker of Bogota*—but it did not prove to be a completely happy arrangement. For his efforts Bird received $1,000 for each play; Forrest, on the other hand, made hundreds of thousands of dollars. When Bird realized that plays such as *The Gladiator* and *The Broker of Bogota* would become permanent in Forrest's repertory, he complained, received no satisfaction, and stopped writing for the stage. "What a fool I was to think of writing plays!" he confided in his *Secret Records*. In all he completed only nine of his projected plays.

As a consequence of the events surrounding his relations with Forrest, Bird turned to politics, journalism, and novels. Two of his most popular novels are *The Hawks of Hawk-Hollow* and *Nick of the Woods*. Bird's loss to American drama, however, must be considered significant. An imaginative man, keenly aware of the forces working upon his culture, he espoused theories of dramaturgy which not only reflected the Romanticism of his day but were ideally suited to the style of acting then popular. The idealized hero was the central force in his plays. All other dramatic elements—the plot, the dramatic incidents and spectacle, the poetic speech, the passions of the characters, the theme of the play—contributed to the creation of the hero and led to the climax of the play. Bird obviously had the energy and the skill to write good romantic melodrama. An early play, *The City Looking Glass* (written in 1828), also showed considerable potentiality for comedy. Unfortunately, all of this talent was shelved when his indignation was righteously ignited, and the help that copyright laws might have provided was years in the future.

—Walter J. Meserve

BISHOP, Elizabeth. Born in Worcester, Massachusetts, 8 February 1911. Educated at Walnut Hill School, Natick, Massachusetts, 1927–30; Vassar College, Poughkeepsie, New York, 1930–34, A.B. 1934. Lived in Key West, Florida, in late 1930's and 1940's, and in Brazil, 1951–66. Consultant in Poetry, Library of Congress, Washington, D.C., 1949–50; Poet-in-Residence, University of Washington, Seattle, 1966, 1973; Lecturer in English, Harvard University, Cambridge, Massachusetts, 1970–79. Recipient: Guggenheim fellowship, 1947; American Academy grant, 1951; Shelley Memorial Award, 1953; Pulitzer Prize, 1956; Amy Lowell traveling fellowship, 1957; Chapelbrook fellowship, 1962; Academy of American Poets fellowship, 1964; Rockefeller fellowship, 1967; Ingram Merrill Foundation grant, 1969; National Book Award, 1970; Harriet Monroe Poetry Award, 1974; Neustadt prize, 1976; National Book Critics Circle award, 1977. LL.D.: Smith College, Northampton, Massachusetts, 1968; Rutgers University, New Brunswick, New Jersey, 1972; Brown University, Providence, Rhode Island, 1972. Chancellor, Academy of American Poets, 1966; Member, American Academy, 1976. Order of Rio Branco (Brazil), 1971. *Died 6 October 1979*.

PUBLICATIONS

Collections

Complete Poems 1927–1979. 1983.
Collected Prose, edited by Robert Giroux. 1984.

Verse

North and South. 1946.
Poems: North and South—A Cold Spring. 1955.
Poems. 1956.
Questions of Travel. 1965.
Selected Poems. 1967.
The Ballad of the Burglar of Babylon (for children). 1968.
The Complete Poems. 1969.
Geography III. 1977.

Other

Brazil, with the editors of *Life.* 1962.

Editor, with Emanuel Brasil, and Translator, *An Anthology of Twentieth-Century Brazilian Poetry.* 1972.

Translator, *The Diary of Helena Morley*, by Alice Brant. 1957.

*

Bibliography: *Bishop: A Bibliography 1927–1979* by Candace W. MacMahon, 1980; *Bishop and Howard Nemerov: A Reference Guide* by Diana E. Wyllie, 1983.

Critical Studies: *Bishop* by Anne Stevenson, 1966; *Bishop and Her Art* edited by Lloyd Schwartz and Sybil P. Estess, 1983.

* * *

Elizabeth Bishop's autobiographical "In the Village," a story which moves towards poetry and was originally included at the center of *Questions of Travel*, shows how the sounds and sights and textures of a Nova Scotia village enable a child to come to terms with the sound of the scream which signified her mother's madness and, ultimately, with human isolation, loss, mortality: the child's capacity for meticulous attention serves not merely as a method of escaping from intolerable pain, but also as an opening from the prison of the self and its wounds to a rejoicing in both human creativity and the things and events of an ordinary day. The story, with its nod of homage to Chekhov, provides an accurate anticipation of the peculiar virtues of Bishop's poetry: her fantastic powers of observation, her impeccable ear, and her precise and often haunting sense of tone.

Her first volume, *North and South*, was a rigorous selection from earlier work. Although some of its poems are set in New York or Paris or New England or have no localized geographical setting, a number of the best ones are firmly placed in Nova Scotia or Florida. *A Cold Spring* continued the emphasis on place: a farm in Maryland, Nova Scotia again, Washington, D.C., Key West and New York, and, with "Arrival at Santos," Brazil, which was to be her home for a number of years. The poems in *Questions of Travel* are divided into two groups: "Brazil" and "Elsewhere." (Another result of her residence of Brazil was her beautiful translation of *The Diary of Helena Morley.*) The 1969 *Complete Poems* included new poems set in Brazil as well as translations from Carlos Drummond de Andrade and João Cabral de Melo Neto. The 1983 *Complete Poems* contained more translations from the Portuguese, Spanish, and French, and previously uncollected poems.

The title and some of the directions of *Geography III* were anticipated in the final line of "The Map," the first poem in her first volume: "More delicate than the historian's are the map-maker's colors." The map-maker (not the tourist) who comes truly to know differing peoples and their places for himself can see with fresh and multiple perspectives, and his discriminations may well be finer than the historian's if his powers of observation are intense, his sympathies wide, his moral judgments delicate, and his imagination that of a poet.

Bishop's geography is also of the imagination and the soul. Her poems treat their readers with unusual consideration. With the beginning of each poem we know that we *are* somewhere interesting (whether in a real or a surreal or a dream world), and we hear immediately a recognizable human voice: the poems make absorbing sense on a simple or naturalistic level. She is interested in, and asks our respectful attention for, everything that she puts into her poems; ultimate and "large" significances come only (and naturally) out of our experience of the whole.

The consideration is real, and one of its chief instruments is an unusual purity of diction. On a number of occasions one may be surprised to discover an image or detail or even a quoted phrase from the poetry of George Herbert. She found Herbert's example thoroughly congruent with one of the things she admired most about modernist poetry of the early 20th century: the rejection of familiar public rhetoric and the consciously poetic for a language closer to that of a conversation between literate friends. Bishop consistently sustained her own high version of that standard: no inversions and no inflations, no Ciceronian periods, no elevated "poetic diction." Her indebtedness to Marianne Moore's imaginative precision was handsomely acknowledged in "Invitation to Miss Marianne Moore" (the poem also owes something to Pablo Neruda). Her uses of other writers are markedly individual: her few epigrams are from Bunyan, Hopkins, and Sir Kenneth Clark; the poignant "Crusoe in England" owes as much to Charles Darwin as to Defoe.

Also like Herbert, Bishop seemed to seek a unique form for almost every poem. Her range extended from prose poems such as "Rainy Season; Sub-Tropics" and "12 O'Clock News" through relatively "free" and blank verse and unrhymed Horatian forms to strict quatrains and elaborately "counter-pointed" stanzas, a double sonnet ("The Prodigal," one of her best poems), sestinas and a villanelle, including along the way the lengthening triplets of "Roosters," derived from Crashaw's "Wishes to his (supposed) Mistress," "Visits to St. Elizabeths," modelled on "The House that Jack Built," a true ballad, "The Burglar of Babylon," and the songs that she wrote for Billie Holiday. Whatever the forms, they provide opportunities rather than limitations, and their art is self-effacing: the lines of "Sestina" end with the words *house, grandmother, child, stove, almanac*, and *tears*. Her use of assonance and slant-rhymes and variable line lengths and rhyme patterns promised a useful freedom. Her example suggested to Robert Lowell the "way of breaking through the shell of my old manner" indicated by his "Skunk Hour."

Although Bishop's poetry is collected in a single volume of moderate size, Lowell remarked some years before her death, "When Elizabeth Bishop's letters are published (as they will be), she will be recognized as not only one of the best, but also one of the most prolific writers of our century." Most of her letters and papers have been collected by the Vassar College Library. David Kalstone's essay, "Prodigal Years: Elizabeth Bishop and Robert Lowell, 1947–49" (*Grand Street*, Summer 1985), provides a tantalizing promise of the riches still to come.

As a poet Bishop remained remarkably independent of schools or movements, religious, political, or literary. One modern practice that proved fruitful for her was that of the collage, in which the artist discovers subject and form in ordinary or unexpected materials and objects. ("Objects and Apparitions," Bishop's translation of "Octavio Paz's poems for Joseph Cornell, suggests the relation between collage and all art—as do her poems on the pictures of her great-uncle George.) Although the fictional speakers of her poems are often moving or witty (the Trollope of the Journals, a Brazilian friend in "Manuelzinho," Crusoe, a giant snail, a very small alien who reports on the writer's desk as a foreign landscape—all remarkable observers), in most of the poems the poet speaks in a voice recognizably her own. That the poems remain deeply personal rather than confessional may owe something to how firmly they are rooted in the "found": "Trouvée" in the flattened white hen on West 4th Street, "The Man-Moth" in a newspaper misprint for *mammoth*, "The Burglar of Babylon" in the fact that on the hills of Rio the rich and poor live their melodramas and lives within sight and sound of each other, "The Moose" in the Nova Scotia bus ride, "In the Waiting Room" in the events of late afternoon, "the fifth / of February, 1918." Almost every poem by Bishop represents a human discovery both of the world and of an angle of vision. It is only superficially paradoxical that such creative novelty returns us, like "The Prodigal," to a familiar place and life: "But it took him a long time / finally to make his mind up to go home."

—Joseph H. Summers

BISHOP, John Peale. Born in Charles Town (now Charleston), West Virginia, 21 May 1892. Educated at Charles Town Academy; Washington County High School, Hagerstown, Maryland; Mercersburg Academy, Pennsylvania; Princeton University, New Jersey, 1913–17 (managing editor, *Nassau Literary Magazine*), Litt.B. 1917 (Phi Beta Kappa). Served in the U.S. Army Infantry, 1917–19: First Lieutenant; director of the Publications Program, 1941–42, and special consultant, 1943, Office of the Coordinator of Inter-American Affairs, Washington, D.C. Married Margaret Grosvenor Hutchins in 1922; three sons. Managing editor, *Vanity Fair*, New York, 1920–22; free-lance writer from 1922; lived in Paris and Sorrento, 1922–24, New York, 1924–26, France, 1926–33, Connecticut and Louisiana, 1933–37, and South Chatham, Massachusetts, 1937–44. *Died 4 April 1944.*

PUBLICATIONS

Collections

Collected Poems, edited by Allen Tate. 1948; *Selected Poems*, 1960.
Collected Essays, edited by Edmund Wilson. 1948.

Verse

Green Fruit. 1917.
The Undertaker's Garland (poems and stories), with Edmund Wilson. 1922.
Now with His Love. 1933.
Minute Particulars. 1935.
Selected Poems. 1941.

Fiction

Many Thousands Gone (stories). 1931.
Act of Darkness. 1935.

Other

The Republic of Letters in America: The Correspondence of Bishop and Allen Tate, edited by Thomas Daniel Young and John J. Hindle. 1981.

Editor, with Allen Tate, *American Harvest: Twenty Years of Creative Writing in the United States*. 1942.

*

Bibliography: "Bishop: A Checklist" by J. Max Patrick and R.W. Stallman, in *Princeton University Library Chronicle 7*, 1946.

Critical Studies: *A Southern Vanguard: The Bishop Memorial Volume* edited by Allen Tate, 1947; "The Achievement of Bishop" by Joseph Frank, in *The Widening Gyre*, 1963; *Bishop* by Robert L. White, 1966; "Bishop and the Other Thirties" by Leslie Fiedler, in *Commentary 43*, 1967; "Bishop" by Allen Tate, in *Essays of Four Decades*, 1968; *Bishop: A Biography* by Elizabeth Carroll Spindler, 1980.

* * *

John Peale Bishop seems to owe his posthumous reputation to Allen Tate and Edmund Wilson, whose editing of the *Collected Poems* and *Collected Essays* in 1948 brought his most important work to the attention of a small audience. These books have long been out of print, but he continues to attract critics as different as Joseph Frank and Leslie Fiedler, and no account of American literary life between the two world wars is complete without his name. He was at Princeton with Wilson and F. Scott Fitzgerald and consequently has associations with the milieu popularized by Fitzgerald's early novels; indeed he is the original for a character in *This Side of Paradise*. During the 1930's, especially after his return to America, he was thought of as a southerner, partly because of his friendship with Tate. His two works of prose fiction are set in the "lost" part of West Virginia where he spent his boyhood and certainly have something in common with the southern tradition of Faulkner, Caroline Gordon, and others.

Bishop, however, must be thought of mainly as a poet, and it is the verse of his last decade that is most impressive. His regional allegiances count for very little here, though his residence on Cape Cod after 1938 was surely responsible for such late poems as "A Subject of Sea Change" and the group called "The Statues." These meditations on the sea and the destiny of civilizations carry forward the strongly pictorial qualities of such earlier poems as "The Return." Eventually one should see Bishop as an American poet who is descended from a great tradition of European humanism, and his criticism of the American scene is conducted from this point of view. One of his finest poems, "The Burning Wheel," sets the American pioneers beside the figure of Aeneas:

They, too, the stalwart conquerors of space,
Each on his shoulders wore a wise delirium
Of memory and age: ghostly embrace
Of fathers slanted toward a western tomb.

A hundred and a hundred years they stayed
Aloft, until they were as light as autumn
Shells of locusts. Where then were they laid?
And in what wilderness oblivion?

This refined yet deeply felt humanism is perhaps not characteristic of American writers, and Bishop was a writer on a small scale, but his best work in poetry and criticism survives very well.

—Ashley Brown

BLY, Robert (Elwood). Born in Madison, Minnesota, 23 December 1926. Educated at St. Olaf College, Northfield, Minnesota, 1946–47; Harvard University, Cambridge, Massachusetts, A.B. (magna cum laude) 1950; University of Iowa, Iowa City, M.A. 1956. Served in the U.S. Naval Reserve, 1944–46. Married 1) Carolyn McLean in 1955 (divorced, 1980), four children; 2) Ruth Counsell Ray in 1981. Founding editor, since 1958, *The Fifties* magazine (later *The Sixties* and *The Seventies*), and the Fifties Press (later The Sixties and The Seventies Press), Madison, Minnesota. Recipient: Fulbright fellowship, 1956; Amy Lowell traveling fellowship, 1964; Guggenheim fellowship, 1964, 1972; American Academy grant, 1965; Rockefeller fellowship, 1967; National Book Award, 1968. Lives in Moose Lake, Minnesota.

PUBLICATIONS

Verse

The Lion's Tail and Eyes: Poems Written Out of Laziness and Silence, with James Wright and William Duffy. 1962.
Silence in the Snowy Fields. 1962.
The Light Around the Body. 1967.
Chrysanthemums. 1967.
Ducks. 1968.
The Morning Glory: Another Thing That Will Never Be My Friend: Twelve Prose Poems. 1969; revised edition, 1970; complete version, 1975.
The Teeth Mother Naked at Last. 1970.
Poems for Tennessee, with William Stafford and William Matthews. 1971.
Water under the Earth. 1972.
Christmas Eve Service at Midnight at St. Michael's. 1972.
Jumping Out of Bed. 1973.
Sleepers Joining Hands. 1973.
The Dead Seal near McClure's Beach. 1973.
The Hockey Poem. 1974.
Point Reyes Poems. 1974.
Grass from Two Years, Let's Leave. 1975.
Old Man Rubbing His Eyes. 1975.
The Loon. 1977.
This Body Is Made of Camphor and Gopherwood: Prose Poems. 1977.
This Tree Will Be Here for a Thousand Years. 1979.
Visiting Emily Dickinson's Grave and Other Poems. 1979.
The Man in the Black Coat Turns (includes prose). 1981.
Finding an Old Ant Mansion. 1981.
The Eight Stages of Translation. 1983.
Four Ramages. 1983.
Out of the Rolling Ocean. 1984.
Loving a Woman in Two Worlds. 1985.
Selected Poems. 1986.

Other

A Broadsheet Against the New York Times Book Review. 1961.
Talking All Morning: Collected Conversations and Interviews. 1979.
Selected Essays of Literary Imagination. 1985.

Editor, with David Ray, *A Poetry Reading Against the Vietnam War*. 1966.
Editor, *The Sea and the Honeycomb: A Book of Poems*. 1966.
Editor, *Forty Poems Touching on Recent American History*. 1970.
Editor, *Leaping Poetry: An Idea with Poems and Translations*. 1975.
Editor, *Selected Poems*, by David Ignatow. 1975.
Editor, *News of the Universe: Poems of Twofold Consciousness*. 1980.
Editor, *The Winged Life: The Poetic Voice of Henry David Thoreau*. 1986.

Translator, *The Illustrated Book about Reptiles and Amphibians of the World*, by Hans Hvass. 1960.
Translator, with James Wright, *Twenty Poems of Georg Trakl*. 1961.
Translator, *The Story of Gösta Berling*, by Selma Lagerlöf. 1962.
Translator, with James Wright and John Knoepfle, *Twenty Poems of César Vallejo*. 1962.
Translator, with Eric Sellin and Thomas Buckman, *Three Poems* by Tomas Tranströmer. 1966.
Translator, *Hunger*, by Knut Hamsun. 1967.
Translator, with Christina Paulston, *I Do Best Alone at Night*, by Gunnar Ekelöf. 1967.
Translator, with Christina Paulston, *Late Arrival on Earth: Selected Poems of Gunnar Ekelöf*. 1967.
Translator, with others, *Selected Poems*, by Yvan Goll. 1968.
Translator, with James Wright, *Twenty Poems of Pablo Neruda*. 1968.
Translator, *Forty Poems of Juan Ramón Jiménez*. 1969.
Translator, *Ten Poems*, by Issa Kobayashi. 1969.
Translator, with James Wright and John Knoepfle, *Neruda and Vallejo: Selected Poems*. 1971.
Translator, *Twenty Poems of Tomas Tranströmer*. 1971.
Translator, *The Fish in the Sea Is Not Thirsty: Versions of Kabir*. 1971.
Translator, *Night Vision*, by Tomas Tranströmer. 1971.
Translator, *Ten Sonnets to Orpheus*, by Rainer Maria Rilke. 1972.
Translator, *Lorca and Jiménez: Selected Poems*. 1973.
Translator, *Elegy, Some October Notes*, by Tomas Tranströmer. 1973.

Translator, *Basho*. 1974.
Translator, *Friends, You Drank Some Darkness: Three Swedish Poets, Henry Martinson, Gunnar Ekelöf, Tomas Tranströmer*. 1975.
Translator, *Grass from Two Years*, by Kabir. 1975.
Translator, *Twenty-Eight Poems*, by Kabir. 1975.
Translator, *Try to Live to See This! Versions of Kabir*. 1976.
Translator, *The Kabir Book*. 1977.
Translator, *The Voices*, by Rainer Maria Rilke. 1977.
Translator, with Lewis Hyde, *Twenty Poems of Vicente Aleixandre*. 1977.
Translator, *Twenty Poems of Rolf Jacobson*. 1977.
Translator, *Mirabai Versions*. 1980.
Translator, *I Am Too Alone in the World*, by Rainer Maria Rilke. 1980.
Translator, *Canciones*, by Antonio Machado. 1980.
Translator, *Truth Barriers*, by Tomas Tranströmer. 1980.
Translator, *Selected Poems*, by Rainer Maria Rilke. 1981.
Translator, with Coleman Barks, *Night and Sleep*, by Rumi. 1981.
Translator, with Will Kirkland, *Selected Poems and Prose*, by Antonio Machado. 1983.
Translator, *Times Alone: Selected Poems of Antonio Machado*. 1983.

*

Bibliography: "Bly Checklist" by Sandy Dorbin, in *Schist 1*, Fall 1973.

Critical Studies: *Alone with America* by Richard Howard, 1969, revised edition, 1980; *Four Poets and the Emotive Imagination* by Ronald Moran and George Lensing, 1976; *Moving Inward: A Study of Bly's Poetry* by Ingegerd Friberg, 1977; *Of Solitude and Silence: Writings on Bly* edited by Kate Daniels and Richard Jones, 1982; *Bly: An Introduction to the Poetry* by Howard Nelson, 1984; *Bly: When Sleepers Awake* edited by Joyce Peseroff, 1984.

* * *

The spirited presence of Robert Bly is felt throughout the realms of modern poetry and literary criticism; he emerged from the early 1960's as one of the more stubbornly independent and critical poets of his generation, bold to state his positions against war and commercial monopoly, the spread of federal government, and crassness in literature wherever a forum was open to him. He was a dominating spokesman for the anti-war circles during the course of the Vietnam war, staging readings around the United States and compiling (with David Ray) the extraordinary poetic protests in the anthology, *A Poetry Reading Against the Vietnam War*. Throughout his career, he has been a cranky but refreshing influence on American thought and culture for the very grandeur of his positions and the force he has given to his artistic individuality.

Although his output of poetry has been relatively small in an era of prolific poets, his books follow a distinctive course of deepening conviction and widening of conceptions. *Silence in the Snowy Fields*, his first book, is a slender collection of smooth, mildly surreal evocations of his life in Minnesota and of the landscape, with its harsh winters and huddled townships. Bly's brief poems animate natural settings with a secret, wilful life-force, as in this final stanza from "Snowfall in the Afternoon":

> The barn is full of corn, and moving toward us now,
> Like a hulk blown toward us in a storm at sea:
> All the sailors on deck have been blind for many years.

Silence in the Snowy Fields has an immediacy of the poet's personal life that reflects the inward shift of poetry during the late 1950's and early 1960's, a direction that Bly then actively retreated from, claiming poetry deserved a larger frame of experience than the poet's own circumstances and private dilemmas.

The Light Around the Body moves into the political and social arena, with poems against corporate power and profiteering, presidential politics, and the Vietnam war. Here the poems are charged with greater flight of imagination and a more intensely surreal mode of discourse. The poems wildly juxtapose the familiar with the bizarre, in "A Dream of Suffocation"—"Accountants hover over the earth like helicopters, / Dropping bits of paper engraved with Hegel's name"—and "War and Silence"—

> Filaments of death grow out.
> The sheriff cuts off his black legs
> And nails them to a tree

To explain his poetic and to give it context, Bly edited a volume of poems entitled *Leaping Poetry* in which he argued that consciousness had now expanded to a new faculty of the brain where spiritual and supralogical awareness is stored. His commentary is wonderfully speculative and vivid, but bluffly assertive of its premise. Building on this provocative thesis, he commented in an essay, "I Came Out of the Mother Naked," part of his volume *Sleepers Joining Hands*, that society is now returning to a matriarchal order, where sensuousness of thought and synthetic reason are replacing the patriarchal emphasis on rationality and analytic thinking. *The Kabir Book*, Bly's translations of the 15th-century Indian poet, is an effort to present the work of a figure who both "leaps" in his poetry and illustrates the kind of thinking Bly has argued for recently.

In the preface to *This Tree Will Be Here for a Thousand Years* Bly talks of "a consciousness *out there* among plants and animals," which is the "ground tone" of his new poems. Indeed, this duality is the theme of not only this book, but succeeding ones as well, especially his provocative and sombre collection *Loving a Woman in Two Worlds* in which a figure moves freely between his own subjectivity and the brooding mind that surrounds him. The two worlds are like the realms of Martin Buber's I and Thou, an internal reality of the ego, and the lost sense of collective spirit belonging to the ancient world. Bly's poems are efforts to regain that lost sense of a vital universe in which selfhood is only an atom, though a necessary and participatory one. Bly's usual inventiveness is present throughout these poems, but his prose sketches in *The Man in the Black Coat Turns* are notable for their clarity, simplicity, and powerful evocation of this sense of doubleness.

—Paul Christensen

BODENHEIM, Maxwell. Born Maxwell Bodenheimer in Hermanville, Mississippi, 26 May 1892. Educated at Hyde Park High School, Chicago. Served in the U.S. Army, c. 1908–11: jailed for desertion and discharged. Married 1)

Minna Schlein in 1918 (divorced, 1938), one son; 2) Grace Finan in 1939 (died, 1950); 3) Ruth Fagan in 1951(?). Traveled in southwest U.S., 1911–12; lived in Chicago, 1912–15; settled in New York, 1916; writer for Chicago *Literary Times*, 1923–24; lived in Paris, 1929; worked for Federal Writers Project (Works Progress Administration), 1939–40 (fired for presumed association with Communist Party). *Died (murdered) 7 February 1954.*

PUBLICATIONS

Fiction

Blackguard. 1923.
Crazy Man. 1924.
Cutie, A Warm Mamma, with Ben Hecht. 1924.
Replenishing Jessica. 1925.
Ninth Avenue. 1926.
Georgie May. 1928.
Sixty Seconds. 1929.
A Virtuous Girl. 1930.
Naked on Roller Skates. 1931.
Duke Herring. 1931.
6 A.M. 1932.
Run, Sheep, Run. 1932.
New York Madness. 1933.
Slow Vision. 1934.

Plays

Knot Holes (produced 1917).
The Gentle Furniture Shop (produced 1917). In *Drama 10*, 1920.

Verse

Minna and Myself (includes play *The Master Poisoner* by Bodenheim and Ben Hecht). 1918.
Advice. 1920.
Introducing Irony: A Book of Poetic Short Stories and Poems. 1922.
Against This Age. 1923.
The Sardonic Arm. 1923.
Returning to Emotion. 1927.
The King of Spain. 1928.
Bringing Jazz! 1930.
Lights in the Valley. 1942.
Selected Poems 1914–1944. 1946.

Other

My Life and Loves in Greenwich Village (attributed to Bodenheim; ghostwritten by Sam Roth). 1954.

*

Critical Study: *Bodenheim* by Jack B. Moore, 1970.

* * *

Maxwell Bodenheim's slow but steady and determined pursuit of self-destruction, and the frequently giddy capers he cut while parading (at first) and then lurching around New York's literary scene, have almost completely obscured his solid if inconsistent achievements as a writer. Easily forgotten, because buried under an avalanche of anecdotes, novels, and plays by other writers about his escapades during the Jazz Age and Depression years, is the undoubted evidence that he was sometimes a very powerful, often an innovative, and nearly always a fascinating poet-novelist of the world that ultimately passed him by.

Bodenheim's social and literary criticism are perhaps the least well known of his writings. Ezra Pound wanted to have published Bodenheim's "whole blooming book" on aesthetics although (or perhaps because) Pound claimed only he and a few other writers would understand it. In fact only a few chapters of the book were ever printed, and these were published separately as essays. As a reviewer for many of the leading journals of the 1920's, he championed the work of such contemporaries as Conrad Aiken, Wallace Stevens, and William Carlos Williams: lambasted what he considered the sham pastoralism in modern fiction where "young men lie upon their backs in cornfields and feel oppressed by their bodies"; and tilted with the very popular and he felt often fake Freudianism of his times for trumpeting that "sex underlies all human motives and is the basis of all creations." He also sought out new writers. When he was one of the editors of the avant-garde little magazine *Others* he went out of his way to praise and secure publication for the very young Hart Crane.

From 1923 to 1934 he published some dozen novels, which, together with the poetry he wrote around the same period, refute the idea that he crippled himself as a writer simply through dissipating his resources in sordid adventures. He was by no means a major novelist, for his works lack artistic control. Too often he used the form as a way to settle personal scores, or, worse, did not attend strictly enough to technical details of his craft. He sometimes seemed more intent upon setting down striking phrases than in constructing a coherent and compelling story. But most of the novels display solid and significant attainments: the touching comic (and autobiographic) portrait of the young artist in *Blackguard*; the sad, sordid decline of the prostitute Georgie May; the urban nightmare of *Ninth Avenue*; the parade of numbed derelicts that sleepwalk through *Slow Vision*, his Depression novel.

Bodenheim's artistic reputation rests most solidly upon his poetry, and his ultimate failure to become a first-rate poet is probably the saddest element of his professional career. Bodenheim was early considered one of the most promising writers taking part in the American literary renaissance of the 1910's: Harriet Monroe and Margaret Anderson, editors of the two most influential literary magazines of the day, both strove to be the first to announce the arrival of his genius. Conrad Aiken and William Carlos Williams were only two of the many writers who, though sometimes appalled by his antics, highly praised his poetry. Among his chief virtues as a poet were his ability to compose beautiful and exotic images and to weave them harmoniously into the texture of a unified poem, such as "Death." He could also write harshly and effectively about the ugliness of modern city life, as in "Summer Evening: New York Subway Station." His jazz poems, such as those in *Bringing Jazz!*, were interesting experiments in a form one critic said had been successfully employed only by one other poet—T.S. Eliot.

Bodenheim's artistic death, which long preceded his physical death, was lamentable, for he never came close to attaining the greatness his early promise and ability seemed to predict. Yet he accomplished far more than his relatively obscure reputation today would suggest.

—Jack B. Moore

BOGAN, Louise. Born in Livermore Falls, Maine, 11 August 1897. Educated at Mount St. Mary's Academy, Manchester, New Hampshire, 1907–09; Girls' Latin School, Boston, 1910–15; Boston University, 1915–16. Married 1) Curt Alexander, 1916 (died, 1920), one daughter; 2) Raymond Holden in 1925 (divorced, 1935). Free-lance writer in New York, 1919–25; poetry editor, *New Yorker*, 1931–69. Fellow, 1944, and Consultant in Poetry, 1945, Library of Congress, Washington, D.C.; Visiting Professor, University of Washington, Seattle, 1948, University of Chicago, 1949, University of Arkansas, Fayetteville, 1952, Salzburg Seminar in American Studies, 1958, and Brandeis University, Waltham, Massachusetts, 1964–65. Recipient: Guggenheim grant, 1933, 1937; Harriet Monroe Poetry Award, 1948; American Academy grant, 1951; Bollingen Prize, 1955; Academy of American Poets fellowship, 1959; Brandeis University Creative Arts Award, 1961; National Endowment for the Arts grant, 1967. L.H.D.: Western College for Women, Oxford, Ohio, 1956; Litt.D: Colby College, Waterville, Maine, 1960. Member, American Academy, 1951, and Academy of American Poets, 1954. *Died 4 February 1970.*

PUBLICATIONS

Collections

What the Woman Lived: Selected Letters 1920–1970, edited by Ruth Limmer. 1973.

Verse

Body of This Death. 1923.
Dark Summer. 1929.
The Sleeping Fury. 1937.
Poems and New Poems. 1941.
Collected Poems 1923–1953. 1954.
The Blue Estuaries: Poems 1923–1968. 1968.

Other

Works in the Humanities Published in Great Britain 1939–1946: A Selected List. 1950.
Achievement in American Poetry 1900–1950. 1951.
Selected Criticism: Prose, Poetry. 1955.
Emily Dickinson: Three Views, with Archibald MacLeish and Richard Wilbur. 1960.
A Poet's Alphabet: Reflections on the Literary Art and Vocation, edited by Robert Phelps and Ruth Limmer. 1970.
Journey Around My Room: The Autobiography of Bogan: A Mosaic, edited by Ruth Limmer. 1980.

Editor and Translator, with Elizabeth Roget, *Journal*, by Jules Renard. 1964.
Editor, with William Jay Smith, *The Golden Journey: Poems for Young People*. 1965.

Translator, with Elizabeth Mayer, *The Glass Bees*, by Ernst Jünger. 1961.
Translator, with Elizabeth Mayer, *Elective Affinities*, by Goethe. 1963.
Translator, with Elizabeth Mayer and (verse only) W.H. Auden, *The Sorrows of Young Werther, and Novella*, by Goethe. 1971.

*

Bibliography: by Jane Couchman, in *Bulletin of Bibliography 33*, 1976.

Critical Studies: *Bogan: A Woman's Words* by William Jay Smith, 1972; *Bogan: A Portrait* by Elizabeth Frank, 1985.

* * *

Louise Bogan's collected poems, *The Blue Estuaries*, make up a slender volume that brings together work published from 1923 to 1968. She rarely wrote poems longer than a page, and all her earlier published books are brief and cut to the bone. She was a relentless reviser of her work and a slow, cautious craftsman who refused publishers' urgings to increase her output.

Although she was keenly aware of the revolutions in poetic technique throughout her life, her poems adhered to rhyme and set meter and treated the themes of love, regret, death, memory, and landscape meditation in subtly alliterative language. Her style shows the influence of Emily Dickinson and perhaps the wit of Metaphysical poetry, but the essential charm of her best work is the quiet, feminine perception she expresses in her strict, tightly framed forms, as in "Second Song," an early poem:

I said out of sleeping:
Passion, farewell.
Take from my keeping
Bauble and shell.

Black salt, black provender.
Tender your store
To a new pensioner,
To me no more.

Although she relaxes into a certain lyric frankness of feeling in her later work, her style of spare restraint remains consistent throughout her work. In several of her poems a more strident feminine consciousness flares, as in "Women," with its sardonic portrayal of woman caught in her stereotype of the put-upon mate:

Their love is an eager meaninglessness
Too tense, or too lax.

They hear in every whisper that speaks to them
A shout and a cry.
As like as not, when they take life over their door-sills
They should let it go by.

Bogan regarded the poem as a deliberate and highly worked distillation of thought, and was perhaps too strict with her own imagination. The fire and wit of her mind are muted in most of her poetry but luxuriously displayed in her brilliant correspondence, collected in *What the Woman Lived*, where her sarcasm and acute critical nature are shared with a circle of notable literary figures of her time, including Edmund Wilson, Morton Dauwen Zabel, Rolfe Humphries, and Theodore Roethke.

Like her poetry, her critical writing eschewed partisanship and fashion in favor of a classical standard of moderation, balance, and form. As the poetry critic for the *New Yorker*, she was well known for her honest and abrasive judgments of the work of even her close friends, and her essays of these years, published in *A Poet's Alphabet*, endure in their accuracy and acumen. A brief treatise on modern poetry, *Achievement in American Poetry 1900–1950*, though merely a sketch of the main trends of these years, argues a provocative thesis that female poets of the late 19th century were chiefly responsible for revitalizing poetry with their sensuous, daring imaginations.

—Paul Christensen

BOKER, George Henry. Born in Philadelphia, Pennsylvania, 6 October 1823. Educated at the College of New Jersey, now Princeton University (one of the founders of the *Nassau Monthly*, 1842), graduated 1842; also studied law. Married Julia Mandeville Riggs in 1844; one son. Writer from 1845; playwright from 1848; founding member, 1862, Secretary, 1862–71, and President, 1879, Union Club, later Union League, Philadelphia; U.S. Ambassador to Turkey, 1871–75, and to Russia, 1875–78; President, Philadelphia Club, 1878; President, Fairmount Park Commission, Philadelphia, 1886–90. *Died 2 January 1890.*

PUBLICATIONS

Collections

Glaucus and Other Plays (includes *The World a Mask, The Bankrupt*), edited by Sculley Bradley. 1940.

Plays

Calaynos (produced 1849). 1848.
Anne Boleyn (produced 1850). 1850.
The Betrothal (produced 1850). In *Plays and Poems*, 1856.
The World a Mask (produced 1851). 1856; in *Glaucus and Other Plays*, 1940.
The Widow's Marriage (produced 1852). In *Plays and Poems*, 1856.
Leonor de Guzman (produced 1853). In *Plays and Poems*, 1856.
Francesca da Rimini (produced 1855). In *Plays and Poems*, 1856.
The Bankrupt (produced 1855). In *Glaucus and Other Plays*, 1940.
Nydia, edited by Sculley Bradley. 1929; revised version, as *Glaucus*, in *Glaucus and Other Plays*, 1940.

Verse

The Lesson of Life and Other Poems. 1848.
The Podesta's Daughter and Other Miscellaneous Poems. 1852.
Poems of the War. 1864.
Our Heroic Themes. 1865.
Königsmark: The Legend of the Hounds and Other Poems. 1869.
The Book of the Dead: Poems. 1882.
Sonnets: A Sequence of Profane Love, edited by Sculley Bradley. 1929.

Other

Plays and Poems. 2 vols., 1856.

*

Bibliography: in *Bibliography of American Literature* by Jacob Blanck, 1955.

Critical Studies: *Boker, Poet and Patriot* by Sculley Bradley, 1927; *Boker* by Oliver H. Evans, 1984.

* * *

In keeping with his aspiration to live the life of the poet, George Henry Boker's first publication, *The Lesson of Life*, was a book of verse. The scion of a wealthy and aristocratic family who was classically educated at what would become Princeton University, Boker followed this first book with poems on public affairs, with patriotic verse, and with sonnets—a form with which he enjoyed particular felicity—on love and statesmanship. He subsequently collected many of these pieces into *Plays and Poems*, whose two volumes have been reprinted many times and are today the most accessible source of Boker's verse. Despite his love for poetry, however, Boker is remembered primarily as a dramatist, having written nearly a dozen plays between his first, *Calaynos*, a tragedy in blank verse, and his last, *Nydia*, which he rewrote as *Glaucus* in 1886.

Surely the most famous of Boker's plays is *Francesca da Rimini*, completed in 1853 and first produced in New York two years later. Based on the tragic love story of 13th-century Italy which Dante celebrated in *The Inferno* and which had been reworked by so many other authors, Boker's *Francesca* consists of more than 3,500 lines of neo-Elizabethan verse, so befitting its author's poetic urges as well as the day's theatrical tastes. In these lines Boker chronicled once again the unhappy triangle of Francesca, a noblewoman of Ravenna, Paolo, a nobleman of Rimini to whom she had given her heart, and Lanciotto, Paolo's equally noble but sadly deformed brother to whom she had given her hand in marriage. A stirring success, *Francesca* ran on the New York and Philadelphia stage in 1855, and was reproduced for longer runs in 1882–83 and again in 1901–02.

As the corpus of his work reveals, Boker was a playwright whose sense of the literary matched his sense of the theatrical. Understandably, then, he is among the best remembered of America's 19th-century dramatists.

—Bruce A. Lohof

BOWLES, Paul (Frederick). Born in New York City, 30 December 1910. Educated at the School of Design and Liberal Arts, New York, 1928; University of Virginia, Charlottesville, 1928–29; studied music with Aaron Copland in New York and Berlin, 1930–32, and with Virgil Thomson in Paris, 1933–34. Married Jane Sydney Auer (i.e., the writer Jane Bowles) in 1938 (died, 1973). Music critic, New York *Herald-Tribune*, 1942–46; also composer. Recipient: Guggenheim fellowship, 1941; American Academy award, 1950; Rockefeller grant, 1959; Translation Center grant, 1975; National Endowment for the Arts grant, 1977. Since 1947 has lived in Tangier, Morocco.

PUBLICATIONS

Fiction

The Sheltering Sky. 1949.
The Delicate Prey and Other Stories. 1950.
A Little Stone: Stories. 1950.
Let It Come Down. 1952.
The Spider's House. 1955.
The Hours after Noon. 1959.
A Hundred Camels in the Courtyard (stories). 1962.
Up above the World. 1966.
The Time of Friendship (stories). 1967.
Pages from Cold Point and Other Stories. 1968.
Three Tales. 1975.
Things Gone and Things Still Here (stories). 1977.
Collected Stories 1939–1976. 1979.
Midnight Mass (stories). 1981.

Play

Senso, with Tennessee Williams, in *Two Screenplays*, by Luigi Visconti. 1970.

Screenplay: *Senso* (*The Wanton Countess*, English dialogue, with Tennessee Williams), 1949.

Verse

Scenes. 1968.
The Thicket of Spring: Poems 1926–1969. 1972.
Next to Nothing. 1976.
Next to Nothing: Collected Poems 1926–1977. 1981.

Other

Yallah (travel). 1956.
Their Heads Are Green (travel). 1963; as *Their Heads Are Green and Their Hands Are Blue*, 1963.
Without Stopping: An Autobiography. 1972.
In the Red Room. 1981.
Points in Time (on Morocco). 1982.

Translator, *No Exit*, by Jean-Paul Sartre. 1946.
Translator, *Lost Trail of the Sahara*, by Roger Firson-Roche. 1956.
Translator, *A Life Full of Holes*, by Driss ben Hamed Charhadi. 1964.
Translator, *Love with a Few Hairs*, by Mohammed Mrabet. 1967.
Translator, *The Lemon*, by Mohammed Mrabet. 1969.
Translator, *Mhashish*, by Mohammed Mrabet. 1969.
Translator, *The Boy Who Set the Fire and Other Stories*. 1974.
Translator, *For Bread Alone*, by Mohamed Choukri. 1974.
Translator, *Jean Genet in Tangier*, by Mohamed Choukri. 1974.
Translator, *The Oblivion Seekers*, by Isabelle Eberhardt. 1975.
Translator, *Hadidan Aharam*, by Mohammed Mrabet. 1975.
Translator, *Harmless Poisons, Blameless Sins*, by Mohammed Mrabet. 1976.
Translator, *Look and Move On*, by Mohammed Mrabet. 1976.
Translator, *The Big Mirror*, by Mohammed Mrabet. 1977.
Translator, *Five Eyes: Short Stories by Five Moroccans*. 1979.
Translator, *Tennessee Williams in Tangier*, by Mohamed Choukri. 1979.
Translator, *The Beach Café, and The Voice*, by Mohammed Mrabet. 1980.
Translator, *The Chest*, by Mohammed Mrabet. 1983.
Translator, *She Woke Me Up So I Killed Her*. 1985.
Translator, *The Beggar's Knife*, by Rodrigo Rey Rosa. 1985.

Published Music: *Tornado Blues* (chorus); *Music for a Farce* (chamber music); *Piano Sonatina*; *Huapango 1* and 2; *Six Preludes for Piano*; *El Indio*; *El Bejuco*; *Sayula*; *La Cuelga*; *Sonata for Two Pianos*; *Night Waltz* (two pianos); *Songs: Heavenly Grass*; *Sugar in the Cane*; *Cabin*; *Lonesome Man*; *Letter to Freddy*; *The Years*; *Of All the Things I Love*; *A Little Closer, Please*; *David*; *In the Woods*; *Song of an Old Woman*; *Night Without Sleep*; *Two Skies*; *Que te falta?*; *Ya Llego*; *Once a Lady Was Here*; *Bluebell Mountain*; *Three*; *On a Quiet Conscience*; *El Carbonero*; *Baby, Baby*; *Selected Songs*, Santa Fe, Soundings Press, 1984.

Operas: *Denmark Vesey*, 1937; *The Wind Remains*, 1941.

Ballets: *Yankee Clipper*, 1937; *Pastorella*, 1941; *Sentimental Colloquy*, 1944; *Blue Roses*, 1957.

Incidental Music, for plays: *Horse Eats Hat*, 1936; *Dr. Faustus*, 1937; *My Heart's in the Highlands*, 1939; *Love's Old Sweet Song*, 1940; *Twelfth Night*, 1940; *Liberty Jones*, 1941; *Watch on the Rhine*, 1941; *South Pacific*, 1943; *Jacobowsky and the Colonel*, 1944; *The Glass Menagerie*, 1945; *Twilight Bar*, 1946; *On Whitman Avenue*, 1946; *The Dancer*, 1946; *Cyrano de Bergerac*, 1946; *Land's End*, 1946; *Summer and Smoke*, 1948; *In the Summer House*, 1953; *Edwin Booth*, 1958; *Sweet Bird of Youth*, 1959; *The Milk Train Doesn't Stop Here Anymore*, 1963; for films: *Roots in the Soil*, 1940; *Congo*, 1944.

Recordings: *The Wind Remains*; *Café Sin Nombre*; *Sonata for Two Pianos*; *Night Waltz*; *Scènes d'Anabase*; *Music for a Farce*; *Song for My Sister*; *They Cannot Stop Death*; *Night Without Sleep*; *Sailor's Song*; *Rain Rots the Wood*; *Sonata for Flute and Piano*; *Six Preludes*; *Huapango 1* and 2; *A Picnic Cantata*, lyrics by James Schuyler, 1955; *El Bejuco* and *El Indio*; *Blue Mountain Ballads*; *Concerto for Two Pianos, Winds and Percussion*; *Once a Lady Was Here*; *Song of an Old Person*; *Six Latin American Pieces*, 1984; *Five Songs*, 1984.

*

Bibliography: *Bowles: A Descriptive Bibliography* by Jeffrey Miller, 1986.

Critical Studies: *Bowles: The Illumination of North Africa* by Lawrence D. Stewart, 1974; *Bowles: Staticity and Terror* by Eric Mottram, 1976; *The Fiction of Bowles: The Soul Is the Weariest Part of the Body* by Hans Bertens, 1979; "Bowles Issue" of *Review of Contemporary Fiction*, vol. 2, no. 3, 1982; *Bowles: The Inner Geography* by Wayne Pounds, 1985.

* * *

A prolific writer of music, Paul Bowles did not commit himself seriously to writing fiction until after World War II, when he was in his mid-thirties and living in New York after many years spent in North Africa. He has described the period as "the Atomic Age" (*The Sheltering Sky*), and his characters are appropriate to a period of fear and desolation—most are empty, deracinated, and hopeless, the hollow men of T.S. Eliot, as Chester E. Eisinger has described them (*Fiction of the Forties*, 1963).

His first novel, *The Sheltering Sky*, may be taken as typical of most of his fiction. In it, three young Americans, a married couple and a male friend, have left fashionable New York for adventure in North Africa. There, they move steadily into the Sahara, leaving their morality, sense of purpose, and identities further behind them as they move from town to town. They become separated: Porter Moresby dies of typhoid after a horrifying vision of blood and excrement: his wife, Kit, a neurotic socialite, eventually loses her sanity after living with Arabs. Only their companion, Tunner, survives, left with the task of escorting the remnant of the woman he loves back to civilization. Some critics would agree with the reaction of Doubleday, the publishers who commissioned but then rejected the novel on the grounds that it lacked coherence and purpose. It is a charge that could be brought against several of his stories, which seem full of gratuitous violence and emptiness, as well as his second novel, *Let It Come Down*, which follows the steady degeneration of a single American, Dyar, in North Africa—he too moves steadily away from civilization and morality and toward murder and violence, ending with nothing but confirmation of his basic nature.

But what such a critical response ignores is the virility and vigour of the native life that is so central to Bowles's writing; his apathetic Europeans and Americans make a telling contrast to his vision of authenticity. Every native in his fiction is as much an individual as each European and American is not. His third novel, *The Spider's House*, is probably more successful than the first two because it gives considerable weight to such a native—Amar, the Moroccan youth who shares the story with a couple of Americans. Details and rituals of native life come into the foreground and the novel is given a liveliness and colour that are rather lacking in the others. His fourth novel, *Up above the World*, although set in Central America, again charts disintegration into violence and death. More satisfying are Bowles's recent translations of stories told by pre-literate Moroccan storytellers, in which the patterns of native life are once more dominant.

—Patrick Evans

BOYD, James. Born in Harrisburg, Pennsylvania, 2 July 1888. Educated at Hill School, Pottstown, Pennsylvania, 1901–06; Princeton University, New Jersey 1906–10, B.A. 1910; Trinity College, Cambridge, 1910–12. Served in the New York Infantry, 1916, as a Red Cross volunteer, 1917, and in the U.S. Army Ambulance Service, in Italy and France, 1917–19: Lieutenant. Married Katharine Lamont in 1917; two sons and one daughter. Staff writer and cartoonist, Harrisburg *Patriot*, 1910; teacher of English and French, Harrisburg Academy, 1912–14; member of the editorial staff, *Country Life in America*, New York, 1916; settled on a farm in Southern Pines, North Carolina, 1919: owner and editor, Southern Pines *Pilot*, 1941–44. Founder and first National Chairman, Free Company of Players, 1941. Honorary degree: University of North Carolina, Chapel Hill, 1938. Member, American Academy, 1937; Society of American Historians, 1939. *Died 25 February 1944.*

PUBLICATIONS

Fiction

Drums. 1925.
Marching On. 1927.
Long Hunt. 1930.
Roll River. 1935.
Bitter Creek. 1939.
Old Pines and Other Stories. 1952.

Play

One More Free Man (broadcast 1941). In *The Free Company Presents*, 1941.

Verse

Eighteen Poems. 1944.

Other

Mr. Hugh David MacWhirr Looks after His $1.00 Investment in the Pilot Newspaper (sketches). 1943.

Editor, *The Free Company Presents: A Collection of Plays about the Meaning of America*. 1941.

*

Critical Study: *Boyd* by David E. Whisnant, 1972.

* * *

In the 1920's James Boyd was in the forefront of those who set about revitalizing and reconditioning the American historical novel, which had lapsed into romantic clichés and suspect authenticity. His deliberate apprenticeship in professional writing consisted of a series of experimental short stories testing his ability to master such techniques as dialogue, mood, and setting. Though his research for sketching in the Revolutionary milieu of *Drums* was facilitated by the availability of archival depositories then being developed and enlarged, he went a step further by uncovering period documents on his own and by visiting the scenes about which he would write. His authoritative historicity was never questioned. But Boyd's principal contribution to the historical novel was an emphasis on a "psychological realism" in addition to the romantic conventions and accuracy of detail. For example, in *Drums*, Boyd's most highly acclaimed work, the ambivalent loyalties of the backwoodsman Johnny Fraser during the dislocations of the American Revolution, and his slow development from an acceptance of British rule in the Colonies to his realization that change is inevitable, are never subsidiary to events, which instead are used to support the demands of characterization and motivation. From the hinterlands of North Carolina to the famed battle between the *Serapis* and John Paul Jones's *Bonhomme Richard*, the incidents of history are mere background to the novelist's multi-dimensional portrait of his hero.

In *Marching On*, it is from the point of view of the Confederate infantryman James Fraser, descendant of Johnny Fraser, that the Civil War is seen as "a rich man's war but a poor man's fight." In addition to such climactic chapters as that narrating James's participation in the Battle of Antietam, the novel provides social commentary in depicting and contrasting the lower segments of southern life, Fraser's middle class, and the landed aristocrats. Often criticized is Boyd's yielding to romantic practice in allowing his hero at war's end to marry the planter's daughter. *Long Hunt*, though it required as much research is gathering historical minutiae as did Boyd's first two books, is more properly defined as a frontier novel of the 1790's when settlers moved from North Carolina across the mountains into Indian territory and on to the Mississippi River. *Roll River* was a change in pace. In it Boyd wrote from personal observation of the shifting values among four generations of a proud, wealthy family in the city of Midian (the author's native Harrisburg, Pennsylvania). *Bitter Creek* is a cowboy western to which Boyd, as in the other books, applied his gift for psychological analysis.

His biographer wrote that Boyd saw man as "first of all a creature of history whose problems had to be understood in historical depth." His books, especially the two war novels which profited from his battlefield experience in World War I, were so highly regarded as exemplary of the "new" American historical novels that their other virtues have been for the most part overlooked by readers and critics alike.

—Richard Walser

BOYESEN, H(jalmar) H(jorth). Born in Frederikvaern, Norway, 21 September 1848; emigrated to the U.S. in 1869. Educated at the Latin School, Drammen; Christiania Gymnasium; Royal Fredriks University, post-graduate degree 1868; University of Leipzig, 1873. Married Elizabeth Keen in 1874. Tutor in Latin and Greek, Urbana University, Ohio, 1869–70, 1871; editor, Norwegian weekly *Fremad* (Forward), Chicago, 1870; Professor of German, Cornell University, Ithaca, New York, 1874–80; member of the German Department, 1880–82, Gebhard Professor of German, 1882–90, and Professor of Germanic Languages and Literatures, 1890–95, Columbia University, New York. *Died 2 October 1895*.

PUBLICATIONS

Fiction

Gunnar: A Tale of Norse Life. 1874.
A Norseman's Pilgrimage. 1875.
Tales from Two Hemispheres. 1876.
Falconberg. 1879.
Ilka on the Hill-Top and Other Stories. 1881.
Queen Titania (stories). 1881.
A Daughter of the Philistines. 1883.
The Light of Her Countenance. 1889.
Vagabond Tales. 1889.
The Mammon of Unrighteousness. 1891.
The Golden Calf. 1892.
Social Strugglers. 1893.

Play

Alpine Roses, from his own story *Ilka on the Hill-Top* (produced 1884). 1884.

Verse

Idyls of Norway and Other Poems. 1882.

Other

Goethe and Schiller: Their Lives and Works. 1879.
The Story of Norway. 1886.
The Modern Vikings: Stories of Life and Sport in the Norseland (for children). 1887.
Against Heavy Odds: A Tale of Norse Heroism (for children). 1890.
Essays on German Literature. 1892.
Boyhood in Norway: Stories of Boy-Life in the Land of the Midnight Sun (for children). 1892; as *The Battle of the Rafts and Other Stories*, 1893.
Norseland Tales (for children). 1894.
A Commentary on the Writings of Henrik Ibsen. 1894.
Literary and Social Silhouettes. 1894.
Essays on Scandinavian Literature. 1895.

*

Bibliography: in *Bibliography of American Literature* by Jacob Blanck, 1955.

Critical Studies: *Boyesen* by Clarence A. Glasrud, 1963; *Boyesen* by Robert S. Frederickson, 1980; *From Norwegian Romantic to American Realist: Studies in the Life and Writings of Boyesen* by Per Seyersted, 1984.

* * *

H.H. Boyesen published his first novel, *Gunnar*, in 1874, five years after he came to the United States and mastered English. This romantic Norwegian idyl was influenced by Bjørnstierne Bjørnson's early fiction; Boyesen's success with this first effort was due in large part to his friendship with William Dean Howells, who helped polish the manuscript and serialized the story in the *Atlantic Monthly*. But though he was unquestionably a romantic by nature and early influence, Boyesen became a realist by conviction; with Howells he read and admired Turgenev and Tolstoy. Boyesen met Turgenev in Paris in 1873, with an introduction from a German critic; and Boyesen's second novel, *A Norseman's Pilgrimage*, was dedicated to Turgenev. Howells declined this romantically autobiographical story, warning the author that he was too hungry for publication; ten years elapsed before Turgenev approved one of the realistic stories Boyesen sent him ("A Dangerous Virtue").

Boyesen became one of America's best known teachers and lecturers. His *Goethe and Schiller*, essentially an English reworking of German scholarship and criticism, went into ten editions. His three collections of essays on German and Scandinavian literature published in the 1890's are magazine pieces, usually reprinted without revision. Boyesen was a literary journalist and popularizer, not a scholar and critic. But he was an important European-American liaison man who argued persuasively that Americans were so subservient to British literature that they ignored Goethe and Ibsen.

Boyesen's hundreds of articles, essays, and short stories reveal him as a magazinist who depended on the income from such writing, but they also reflect his changing experience and convictions. His articles and stories on Norwegian-Americans, including the novel *Falconberg*, are not convincing because he had little contact with his fellow immigrants. Boyesen lived in New York for fifteen years, on Fifth Avenue and at Southampton; and he was both fascinated and repelled by the social world of the newly rich.

He became sharply critical of American political and financial corruption, arguing that the American novelist was duty-bound to document and criticize American problems; and he tried to do this in such novels as *The Golden Calf* and *Social Strugglers*. For such efforts he was berated as an ungrateful foreigner and blamed for abandoning the idyllic vein of *Gunnar*. But Boyesen was consistent in his views, whether they were expressed in novels, essays, or speeches: when he died suddenly and unexpectedly in 1895, he was arguing vehemently for more realistic and responsible American fiction, citing the "high water mark" of realism established by the new Scandinavian writers.

In his long battle with the "purveyors of romance," Boyesen identified the American girl as the enemy of serious writing. She was "the Iron Madonna" who strangled the American novelist in her fond embrace, because magazine editors and book publishers knew she was the reader and arbiter they must satisfy. The beautiful, vivacious, and independent girls Boyesen found in America had fascinated him from his first arrival. He married one of them, and his subsequent efforts to augment a professor's salary by ceaseless writing and lecturing dissipated his talents and shortened his life. It seems significant that such girls frustrate their Norwegian-born admirers in his earliest fiction, dominate their parents in later stories (*A Daughter of the Philistines*), and victimize their husbands, notably in his most ambitious work, *The Mammon of Unrighteousness*.

—Clarence A. Glasrud

BOYLE, Kay. Born in St. Paul, Minnesota, 19 February 1902. Educated at the Cincinnati Conservatory of Music, 1916; Ohio Mechanics Institute, 1917–19. Married 1) Richard Brault in 1922 (divorced, 1932), one daughter by Ernest Walsh; 2) Laurence Vail in 1932 (divorced, 1943), three daughters; 3) Baron Joseph von Franckenstein in 1943 (died, 1963), one daughter and one son. Lived in Europe, 1923–41 and 1947–53; foreign correspondent, *New Yorker*, 1946–53; Professor of English, San Francisco State University, 1963–80, since 1980 Professor Emerita. Lecturer, New School for Social Research, New York, 1962; fellow, Wesleyan University, Middletown, Connecticut, 1963; director, New York Writers Conference, Wagner College, New York, 1964; fellow, Radcliffe Institute for Independent Study, Cambridge, Massachusetts, 1964–65; Writer-in-Residence, University of Massachusetts, Amherst, 1967, Hollins College, Virginia, 1970–71, and Eastern Washington University, Cheney, 1984. Recipient: Guggenheim fellowship, 1934, 1961; O. Henry Award, 1935, 1941; San Francisco Art Commission award, 1978; National Endowment for the Arts grant, 1980; Before Columbus Foundation award, 1983; Celtic Foundation award, 1984. D.Litt: Columbia College, Chicago, 1971; Southern Illinois University, Carbondale, 1982; D.H.L.: Skidmore College, Saratoga Springs, New York, 1977. Member, American Academy, 1979. Lives in San Francisco.

PUBLICATIONS

Fiction

Short Stories. 1929.
Wedding Day and Other Stories. 1930.
Plagued by the Nightingale. 1931.
Year Before Last. 1932.
The First Lover and Other Stories. 1933.
Gentlemen, I Address You Privately. 1933.
My Next Bride. 1934.
The White Horses of Vienna and Other Stories. 1936.
Death of a Man. 1936.
Monday Night. 1938.
The Crazy Hunter: Three Short Novels. 1940; as *The Crazy Hunter and Other Stories*, 1940.
Primer for Combat. 1942.
Avalanche. 1944.
Thirty Stories. 1946.
A Frenchman Must Die. 1946.
1939. 1948.
His Human Majesty. 1949.
The Smoking Mountain: Stories of Post War Germany. 1951.
The Seagull on the Step. 1955.
Three Short Novels. 1958.
Generation Without Farewell. 1960.
Nothing Ever Breaks Except the Heart. 1966.
The Underground Woman. 1975.
Fifty Stories. 1980.

Verse

Landscape for Wyn Henderson. 1931.
A Statement. 1932.
A Glad Day. 1938.
American Citizen: Naturalized in Leadville, Colorado. 1944.
Collected Poems. 1962.
Testament for My Students and Other Poems. 1970.
This Is Not a Letter and Other Poems. 1985.

Other

The Youngest Camel (for children). 1939; revised edition, 1959.
Breaking the Silence: Why a Mother Tells Her Son about the Nazi Era. 1962.
Pinky, The Cat Who Liked to Sleep (for children). 1966.
Pinky in Persia (for children). 1968.
Being Geniuses Together 1920–1930, with Robert McAlmon. 1968; revised edition, 1984.
The Long Walk at San Francisco State and Other Essays. 1970.
Four Visions of America, with others. 1977.
Words That Must Somehow Be Said: Selected Essays 1927–1984, edited by Elizabeth S. Bell. 1985.

Editor, with Laurence Vail and Nina Conarain, *365 Days*. 1936.
Editor, *The Autobiography of Emanuel Carnevali*. 1967.
Editor, with Justine Van Gundy, *Enough of Dying! An Anthology of Peace Writings*. 1972.

Translator, *Don Juan*, by Joseph Delteil. 1931.
Translator, *Mr. Knife, Miss Fork*, by René Crevel. 1931.
Translator, *The Devil in the Flesh*, by Raymond Radiguet. 1932.
Translator, *Babylon*, by René Crevel. 1985.

Ghostwriter: *Relations and Complications, Being the Recollections of H.H. the Dayang Muda of Sarawak* by Gladys Palmer Brooke, 1929; *Yellow Dusk* by Bettina Bedwell, 1937.

*

Bibliography: by Roberta Sharp, in *Bulletin of Bibliography* 35, October 1978.

Critical Studies: *Boyle: Artist and Activist* by Sandra Whipple Spanier, 1986; *Four Lives in Paris* by Hugh Ford, 1986.

* * *

What is most memorable in Kay Boyle's fiction are specific scenes—the sight of the sea tide building and crashing through the mouth of a river; a young man, sick with tuberculosis, leaning over a basin to vomit blood; a bus-driver arguing recklessly with his passengers while the bus careens along a cliff road; a run-over dog pulling itself forward, as its spilled-out entrails drag and turn white in the dust; Americans and Germans waiting over real fox holes in a German forest, ready to club the young foxes as they come out, and underground, moving through the tunnels, now near, now distant, the sound of the yelping pack and pursuing dog.

Boyle's concern here is to heighten our responses to these events. She asks us not only to respond to the vivid and extreme sensations which they present, but to see them in sharp moral and aesthetic terms, as beautiful or dangerous or agonizingly brutal. She offers very little neutral ground on which we may look at these scenes on our own. The youthful idealists, who play a major role in her novels, give us the right emotional cues for appreciating her work. Inexperienced in the ways of the world, their feelings are open and unmitigated; they do not quite believe in evil and yet they are deeply troubled by pain and injustice. Bridget, Victoria John, Mary Farrant, Milly Roberts—young Americans whose destinies are connected with Europe—are such figures. If the fictional situation would seem to echo James, there are major differences in its development, for Boyle's morality is active rather than introspective.

Indeed, whether her heroes are young Americans in Europe or former German soldiers, they express themselves in concrete acts. What her heroes have in common is the courage to act—it is the only thing people ever remember, one character says. But action is, of course, no guarantee of success. Involved in every human venture, it would seem, are elements that bring about its destruction. Those elements may be in nature—not malevolent but merely indifferent—stupid accident, or man's incapacity to make a social world that is supportive and helpful.

Thus, in *Plagued by the Nightingale*, the closely bound world of a French family becomes so destructive that three daughters and a son wait desperately for an escape. Only Charlotte, the fourth daughter, loves her richly domestic life and her place within the family; and only Charlotte is deprived of it by death. In *Year Before Last*, Martin, a young poet, dying of tuberculosis, and Eve, his aunt, are bound together by their dedication to art. Yet the emotion that shapes their lives is Eve's cruel jealousy of Hanah, whom Martin loves and who would shield him from the agonies of poverty and illness. In *My Next Bride*, the artist, Sorrel, uses the common funds of the art colony to buy a magnificent and expensive automobile. In this shallow attempt to escape poverty and ugliness, he betrays the destitute craftsmen who work for him, as well as the artistic creed he has professed to live by.

The qualities of her strongest characters—courage to act as a counter to failure, energy rather than hopeless despair—admit the possibility of tragedy. Very often these qualities seem wasted, for although Boyle insists upon courageous action, the possible choices she sees in such action are limited. Also, perhaps equally harmful, these choices do not necessarily grow out of the fictional situation; they are fixed from the beginning. It is for this reason, perhaps, that her characters adopt unreal positions—in *Avalanche*, the mountain men are total in their dedication to a good cause, the German agent, total in his dedication to a bad one; in *The Seagull on the Step*, the doctor commits melodramatic villainies, the teacher-reformer, heroic deeds; in *Generation Without Farewell*, the American colonel is brutal and gross, his wife and daughter are gentle and sensitive. Such extreme divisions in realistic novels fail to convince.

But what gives her work strength is her understanding that our human connections lie finally in our limitations, most of all in our common mortality. This understanding is sometimes expressed with startling clarity. In *Plagued by the Nightingale* Charlotte's family is hastily called to her bedside. Those who have waited through the day—Charlotte's young children, her sisters—make their way through the dark, wet autumn night, to Charlotte's house, up the great stairs and to her room. There, they wait in silence until the door is opened, and the children walk "calmly into the roar of Charlotte's death." In *Generation Without Farewell* a power shovel in downtown Frankfurt accidentally unearths an underground air raid shelter and releases a single survivor, entombed there since the war. As the mad, tattered figure runs wildly across the upturned ground, bewildered by his resurrection, any ideals we may hold about nationality, military success, moral justification, diminish into nothingness. Only a sense of our common inhumanity persists.

—Jacqueline Hoefer

BRACKENRIDGE, Hugh Henry. Born in Kintyre, near Campbeltown, Argyll, Scotland, in 1748; emigrated with his family to a farm in York County, Pennsylvania, 1753. Educated at Slate Ridge School and Fagg's Manor; College of New Jersey (now Princeton University), 1768–71, B.A. 1771, M.A. 1774; studied law under Samuel Chase in Annapolis, Maryland, 1780: admitted to Philadelphia bar 1780. Served in George Washington's army during the Revolutionary War, 1777–78: Chaplain. Married 1) Miss Montgomery in 1785 (died, 1788), one son; 2) Sabina Wolfe in 1790, two sons and one daughter. Teacher in a public school, Gunpowder Falls, Maryland, 1763–67, and at Somerset Academy, Back Creek, Maryland, 1772–76; founding editor, *United States Magazine*, Philadelphia, 1779; founder, *Tree of Liberty* newspaper, 1780; moved to Pittsburgh, and practised law there, 1781–99: founder, Pittsburgh *Gazette*, 1786; Pennsylvania State Assemblyman, 1786–88; established Pittsburgh Academy, 1786, and the first bookshop in Pittsburgh, 1789; Justice of the Pennsylvania Supreme Court, 1799–1816. *Died 25 June 1816.*

PUBLICATIONS

Collections

A Brackenridge Reader, edited by Daniel Marder. 1970.

Fiction

Modern Chivalry. 6 vols., 1792–1805; revised edition, 1815, 1819; edited by Claude Milton Newlin, 1937.
Father Bembo's Pilgrimage to Mecca 1770, with Philip Freneau, edited by Michael Davitt Bell. 1975.

Plays

The Battle of Bunkers-Hill. 1776.
The Death of General Montgomery at the Siege of Quebec. 1777.

Verse

A Poem on the Rising Glory of America, with Philip Freneau. 1772.
A Poem on Divine Revelation. 1774.
An Epistle to Walter Scott. 1811(?).

Other

Six Political Discourses Founded on the Scriptures. 1778.
An Eulogium of the Brave Men Who Have Fallen in the Contest with Great Britain. 1779.
Incidents of the Insurrection in the Western Parts of Pennsylvania in 1794. 1795; edited by Daniel Marder, 1972.
The Standard of Liberty. 1802.
Gazette Publications (miscellany). 1806.
Law Miscellanies. 1814.

Editor, *Narratives of a Late Expedition Against the Indians*. 1783.

*

Bibliography: in *Bibliography of American Literature* by Jacob Blanck, 1955; *A Bibliography of the Writings of Brackenridge* by Charles F. Heartman, 1968.

Critical Studies: *The Life and Writings of Brackenridge* by Claude Milton Newlin, 1932; *Brackenridge* by Daniel Marder, 1967.

* * *

Although Hugh Henry Brackenridge wrote in a number of different genres—poetry, drama, and non-fictional prose—his one real claim to our attention today is for the first part of *Modern Chivalry*, an extended piece of satiric fiction published in four volumes between 1792 and 1797. It can hardly be called a novel. The narrative line is thin, merely holding together a series of episodes involving a modern American Quixote, Captain John Farrago, and his Irish servant, Teague O'Regan, as they travel together on the western frontier and later visit the city of Philadelphia. It moves toward no climax in either plot or meaning, but merely illustrates through their adventures various failings of American democracy.

But if *Modern Chivalry* is weak in both narrative and thematic development, it is strong in its realistic pictures of frontier life and manners—exaggerated though they may be for satiric purposes—and in the simple, straightforward style through which both the incidents and the authorial discussions of them are presented. Various kinds of dialect—Irish, Scotch, and Negro—are well reproduced in its pages, and, though the characters may not be fully developed, they are sharply and skillfully sketched through their language and actions. Thus, the book has often been justly praised as an early piece of American realism.

It is also important for what it has to say about the theory and practice of American democracy. Most of the satire is directed against the Teague O'Regans, ignorant and ambitious men who are eager to accept honors and positions for which they are not qualified, and against an electorate that will put such men in office. But the book is not anti-democratic. It attacks as well those men of wealth or inherited position who are no more suited to rule, and members of organizations who admit unqualified persons to their ranks. What the book affirms is the basic principle of democracy: that positions of leadership should be given only to men of ability and integrity, qualities that may appear at any level of society, but which must be developed through education.

Only this first part is wholly successful. Brackenridge published the second in 1804–05 and extended the work yet again in the edition of 1815. His satiric touch was gone, however, and with it much of the charm of the book. The second part even lacks the narrative line of the first and becomes, in effect, an endlessly redundant lecture. It more than doubles the size of *Modern Chivalry*, but it does not add appreciably to what Brackenridge had accomplished in the 1790's.

—Donald A. Ringe

See the essay on *Modern Chivalry*.

BRADFORD, Roark. Born in Lauderdale County, Tennessee, 21 August 1896. Educated in local schools. Served in the

Artillery Reserve of the U.S. Army, 1917–20: Lieutenant; U.S. Naval Reserve, assigned to the Bureau of Aeronautics Training Literature Division, Navy Department, Washington, D.C., 1942–45. Married Mary Rose Himler; one son. Reporter, Atlanta *Georgian*, 1920–22, Macon *Telegraph*, Georgia, 1923, and Lafayette *Daily Advertiser*, Louisiana, 1923; night city editor, later Sunday editor, New Orleans *Times Picayune*, 1924–26; full-time writer from 1929. Recipient: O. Henry Award, 1927. Member, American Academy. *Died 13 November 1948.*

PUBLICATIONS

Fiction

Ol' Man Adam an' His Chillun. 1928.
This Side of Jordan. 1929.
Ol' King David and the Philistine Boys. 1930.
John Henry. 1931.
Kingdom Coming. 1933.
Let the Band Play Dixie and Other Stories. 1934.
The Three-Headed Angel. 1937.

Plays

How Come Christmas: A Modern Morality. 1930.
John Henry, music by Jacques Wolfe, from the story by Bradford. 1939.

Other

The Green Roller (miscellany). 1949.

* * *

To read the stories and novels of Roark Bradford is to enter into a world separated from us by time, space, and especially by temperament. In his depiction of the life on southern plantations, the white man's world fades into the background, becoming no more nor less important than the plowing of fields or the picking of cotton. Bradford wrote of the southern black out of a deep respect and love, which, coupled with his uncanny gift for imitating dialectical speech, makes his writing altogether unique in a white man.

Bradford turned to writing full-time in 1929, concerning himself not with philosophical or moral evaluations of the Negro's life, but rather with the reality of his situation, and the problems of coping with it. His prose, like his characters, is simple and direct, even childlike, but never sentimental. Death can come quickly and unromantically to them, and when it does, they face it with the deep faith that was a part of the author himself, up until his death in 1948.

Above all, Bradford was a storyteller. His work vibrates with the strong, simple rhythms of speech, whether in his realistic novels or in his modern myths like *John Henry*: "The night John Henry was born the moon was copper-colored and the sky was black. . . . Forked lightning cleaved the air and the earth trembled like a leaf. The panthers squalled in the brake like a baby and the Mississippi ran upstream a thousand miles."

Bradford won the O. Henry Award in 1927 with his second published short story, "Child of God." His retelling of biblical stories, *Ol' Man Adam an' His Chillun*, was adapted for the stage by Marc Connelly, and became the highly successful play *The Green Pastures*.

—Walter Bode

BRADFORD, William. Born in Austerfield, Yorkshire, England; baptized 19 March 1590. Joined a non-conformist congregation at age 12, and a church in Scrooby, Nottinghamshire (which met at the house of William Brewster), 1606; moved with this congregation to Holland, 1608. Married 1) Dorothy May in 1613 (died, 1620), one son; 2) Alice Carpenter Southworth in 1623, one daughter, two sons, and two stepsons. Silkworker, Amsterdam, 1608–09; fustian worker, Leyden, 1609–20; sailed from Delftshaven and Plymouth on ship *Speedwell* (later transferred to the *Mayflower*), signed Mayflower Compact, and was member of Miles Standish's initial exploring expeditions that decided to settle at Plymouth, 1620; Governor, Plymouth Colony, 1621, and re-elected 30 times, 1622–56 (served as Assistant Governor, 5 years); principal judge and treasurer until 1637; with other Plymouth leaders bought out the London colonial investors, 1627. *Died 9 May 1657.*

PUBLICATIONS

Collections

Collected Verse, edited by Michael G. Runyan. 1974.

Prose

A Relation or Journal of the Beginning and Proceedings of the English Plantation Settled at Plymouth (Mourt's Relation), with Edward Winslow. 1622; edited by Dwight B. Heath, 1963.
Of Plymouth Plantation (facsimile edition), edited by John A. Doyle. 1896; as *History of Plymouth Plantation*, edited by Worthington Chauncey Ford, 2 vols., 1912; edited by Samuel Eliot Morison, 1952.

*

Critical Studies: *Saints and Strangers, Being the Lives of the Pilgrim Fathers and Their Families* by George F. Willison, 1945; *Bradford of Plymouth* by Bradford Smith, 1952; *Bradford* by Perry D. Westbrook, 1978; *Style as Structure and Meaning: Bradford's Of Plymouth Plantation* by Floyd Ogburn, Jr., 1981.

* * *

William Bradford was a man of enormous energy and diverse talents. He was governor of Plymouth Plantation during most of his life after 1620, and his leadership, business acumen, and general good sense contributed vitally to the survival of the colony. He was also the historian of the colony—the author of a work now known as *History of Plymouth Plantation* (titled *Of Plimmoth Plantation, 1620–1657* by him). Bradford had a flare for writing and his pages are seldom dull. He was self-educated, acquiring over the years some mastery of Latin, Greek, and Hebrew. In England and Holland, as well as in America, he had access to the rather extensive library of his good friend and mentor, William Brewster, who had attended Cambridge University. Both by inclination and by his studies, Bradford was prepared for authorship.

But behind Bradford's writing there is another compelling motive—a sense of duty. The early colonists in New England, whether Puritan or Separatist, were Calvinists. As such, they believed that their venture in the wilderness was under the close guidance and scrutiny of God. Indeed, they thought of themselves as a chosen people, fleeing from the Egyptian darkness of Europe, entrusted with the founding of a New Jerusalem where God's will for His people could finally be fulfilled. The leader of such an undertaking would obviously feel obligated to record the events in the struggle to accomplish what God had mandated. Thus, historians abounded in New England. They called themselves "God's rememberancers," chroniclers for future generations of the what Cotton Mather called *Magnalia Christi Americana*—the great works of Christ in America.

Bradford was the first "God's remembrancer" in New England, but during his lifetime only one of his writings was published. This was a section of a book titled *A Relation or Journal of the Beginning and Proceedings of the English Plantation Settled at Plymouth* (commonly known as *Mourt's Relation*, after its supposed editor, G. Mourt), published in London in 1622. Bradford's contribution to the book, it is generally agreed, was a lengthy account of the settlers' landing at Cape Cod, their exploration of the area, and their first winter at Plymouth. The narrative is swift-paced and concrete and pleasantly colloquial in language. Since the purpose of the book was to interest others in coming to New England, the authors either omitted or toned down many of the difficulties and hardships endured by the colonists during their first year.

In *Mourt's Relation* the religious motif is less pervasive than in Bradford's major work, *History of Plymouth Plantation*. In the latter Bradford recounts many "special providences," events that demonstrate God's hand in the progress of the colony. Thus the Indian Squanto, who taught the newcomers how to plant maize, was put on the scene by God. Similarly, God intervened when, during the Atlantic voyage, He afflicted with a fatal disease a young man who planned to throw half of the *Mayflower* passengers overboard. On the other hand, unfavorable events were taken as signs of divine displeasure. Bradford, indeed, regarded the Plymouth venture as nothing less than a crucial episode in the rise of Protestantism, crucial to its eventual triumph over the Church of Rome; and in the first part of the *History* he develops this idea by relating the adventures of his group of Separatists during the years before 1620. The second and by far the larger part of the *History* is in the form of annals, recording in graphic, at times amusing detail the daily life of the colonists as well as the political and military events that shaped their destiny. It gives character sketches of various persons, both saintly and disreputable, who visited or lived in the colony. Bradford himself announced that his writing would be in the "plain style" favored by the Puritans over the ornate style that they associated with orthodox Anglican authors, but his style is not plain to the point of dullness. Its almost chatty tone and diction and its imagery drawn from everyday life and the fast pace of the narrative sections make the book very readable. Most appealing to modern readers would be Samuel Eliot Morison's edition (1952) in which spelling and punctuation have been modernized.

The manuscript of the *History* was mined for material by New England historians throughout the colonial period. After being lost for 75 years following the American Revolution, the manuscript turned up in the Fulham Palace Library in London. It was then first published in its entirety by the Massachusetts Historical Society (1856). A small body of additional writing by Bradford—some undistinguished verse and two religious dialogues—have been published. The reader who ignores them will miss nothing. Bradford's very considerable and well deserved literary reputation rests on his *History*.

—Perry D. Westbrook

BRADSTREET, Anne (née Dudley). Born probably in Northampton, England, in 1612 or 1613. Educated privately. Married Simon Bradstreet, later Governor of Massachusetts, in 1628(?) (died, 1697); four sons and four daughters. Emigrated to Massachusetts, with the Winthrops, 1630; lived in Salem and near Boston, 1630–35, Ipswich, 1635–45, and North Andover, 1645–72. *Died 16 September 1672*.

PUBLICATIONS

Collections

Works, edited by Jeannine Hensley. 1967.
Poems, edited by Robert Hutchinson. 1969.
Complete Works, edited by Joseph R. McElrath, Jr., and Allan P. Robb. 1981.
A Woman's Inner World: Selected Poetry and Prose, edited by Adelaide P. Amore. 1982.

Verse

The Tenth Muse Lately Sprung Up in America. 1650; revised edition, as *Several Poems Compiled with Great Variety of Wit and Learning*, 1678.

*

Bibliography: "A List of Editions of the Poems of Bradstreet" by Oscar Wegelin, in *American Book Collector 4*, 1933; "Bradstreet: An Annotated Checklist" by Ann Stanford, in *Bulletin of Bibliography 27*, 1970.

Critical Studies: *Bradstreet and Her Time* by Helen S. Campbell, 1891; *Bradstreet* by Josephine K. Piercy, 1965; *Bradstreet: The Tenth Muse* by Elizabeth Wade White, 1971; *Bradstreet, The Worldly Puritan* by Ann Stanford, 1974, and *Critical Essays on Bradstreet* edited by Stanford and Pattie Cowell, 1983; *An American Triptych: Bradstreet, Emily Dickinson, Adrienne Rich* by Wendy Martin, 1984.

* * *

Anne Bradstreet has long been recognized as the first genuine poet to develop in the English-speaking New World. A recent biographer, Elizabeth Wade White, maintains further that she "was also the first significant woman poet of England." The one volume that appeared during her lifetime as *The Tenth Muse Lately Sprung Up in America*—published in England without her knowledge and with a title she did not supply—was the first collection of poetry to come out of the New England colonies, to which Bradstreet had emigrated as a young wife in 1630.

Paradoxically, Bradstreet continues to attract an appreciative audience not for the poetry in *The Tenth Muse* but for a considerable number of poems that were first published in 1678, six years after her death. Of the thirteen poems in *The Tenth Muse*, only one, the 48-line "Prologue," appeals to the modern reader; the others are lengthy and tedious exercises in imitation of various poets—chiefly Guillaume du Bartas (as rendered into English by Joshua Sylvester), Spenser, and Sidney. Their works, together with Ralegh's *The History of the World*, she first read as a precocious child in the library of her indulgent father. Thomas Dudley, for many years steward to the Earl of Lincoln. Bradstreet's obvious indebtedness to these authors suggests that she carried her favorite books aboard the *Arbella* and into the New England wilderness in 1630.

Life in that wilderness however—rather than her father's books—prompted the poetry that has won for her a modest but permanent place in English-American literature. Her *Several Poems* contained—in addition to the pieces in *The Tenth Muse*—almost a score of poems that show her abandoning her old models and striking out with nuances, texture, and techniques that are her own. One of these is "The Author to Her Book," a well-controlled sustained metaphor that dramatizes her chagrin on first seeing the poorly printed *The Tenth Muse*. "Contemplations," often regarded as her best poem, anticipates the romantic view of nature and hints at her discomfort lest her physical reactions be at odds with her spiritual convictions. A number of love poems written for her devoted husband, Simon Bradstreet—a busy colonial official often away from home—reveal a healthy sensuality and suggest that, although she was a Puritan, she was not puritanical. In other poems to and about her children and about the fortunes and misfortunes of her family, she avoids sentimentality and brings to her work the same quiet strength that helped her to survive for 42 years in remote Massachusetts.

—Thomas F. O'Donnell

See the essay on *The Tenth Muse*.

BROMFIELD, Louis. Born in Mansfield, Ohio, 27 December 1896. Educated at Cornell University Agricultural College, Ithaca, New York, 1914–15; School of Journalism, Columbia University, New York, 1916, honorary war degree 1920. Served in the American Ambulance Corps, with the 34th and 168th divisions of the French Army, 1917–19: Croix de Guerre. Married Mary Appleton Wood in 1921 (died, 1952); three daughters, Reporter, City News Service and Associated Press, New York, 1920–22; editor and/or critic, *Musical America*, *The Bookman*, and *Time*, also worked as an assistant to a theatrical producer and as advertising manager of Putnam's, publishers, all New York, 1922–25; lived in Senlis, France, 1925–38; lived on a farm in Richland County, Ohio, 1939–56. President, Emergency Committee for the American Wounded in Spain, 1938. Director, U.S. Chamber of Commerce. Recipient: Pulitzer Prize, 1927. LL.D: Marshall College, Huntington, West Virginia; Parsons College, Fairfield, Iowa; Litt.D.: Ohio Northern University, Ada. Chevalier, Legion of Honor (France), 1939; member, American Academy. *Died 18 March 1956.*

PUBLICATIONS

Fiction

The Green Bay Tree. 1924.
Possession. 1925; as *Lilli Barr*, 1926.
Early Autumn. 1926.
A Good Woman. 1927.
The Strange Case of Miss Annie Spragg. 1928.
Awake and Rehearse (stories). 1929.
Tabloid News (stories). 1930.
Twenty-Four Hours. 1930.
Modern Hero. 1932.
The Farm. 1933.
Here Today and Gone Tomorrow: Four Short Novels. 1934.
The Man Who Had Everything. 1935.
It Had to Happen. 1936.
The Rains Came: A Novel of Modern India. 1937.
It Takes All Kinds (omnibus). 1939; selection, as *You Get What You Give*, 1951.
Night in Bombay. 1940.
Wild Is the River. 1941.
Until the Day Break. 1942.
Mrs. Parkington. 1943.
Bitter Lotus. 1944.
What Became of Anna Bolton. 1944.
The World We Live In: Stories. 1944.
Colorado. 1947.
Kenny. 1947.
McLeod's Folly. 1948.
The Wild Country. 1948.
Mr. Smith. 1951.

Plays

The House of Women, from his novel *The Green Bay Tree* (produced 1927).
DeLuxe, with John Gearnon (produced 1934).
Times Have Changed (produced 1935).

Screenplays: *One Heavenly Night*, with Sidney Howard, 1930; *Brigham Young—Frontiersman*, with Lamar Trotti, 1940.

Other

The Work of Robert Nathan. 1927.
England, A Dying Oligarchy. 1939.
Pleasant Valley. 1945.
A Few Brass Tacks. 1946.
Malabar Farm. 1948.
Out of the Earth. 1950.
The Wealth of the Soil. 1952.
A New Pattern for a Tired World. 1954.
From My Experience: The Pleasures and Miseries of Life on a Farm. 1955.
Animals and Other People. 1955.
Walt Disney's Vanishing Prairie. 1956(?).

*

Critical Studies: *Bromfield and His Books* by Morrison Brown, 1956; *The Heritage: A Daughter's Memories of Bromfield* by Ellen Geld, 1962; *Bromfield* by David D. Anderson, 1964.

* * *

One of the most promising young American novelists of the 1920's, Louis Bromfield fell into critical disfavor in the early 1930's, a condition that prevailed until his death in 1956, in spite of a continued prodigious production of novels and short stories and a remarkable popular success. To assess his contributions to American literature is not difficult; the many literary shortcomings that prevented the fulfillment of his early literary promise are sufficient to keep him out of the first rank of American novelists. But at the same time he deserves a better literary fate than he has received: his effective style, his character portrayal, and his narrative technique are consistently strong, and his interpretations of American life are effective and intelligent.

The themes with which he dealt are significant: the decline of American individualism and agrarian democracy and the growth of industrialism; the unique role of the strong woman in American life; the egalitarian philosophy that permits a young person to rise above his origins. In his use of them in his work he came close to the essence of American life as thoughtful Americans know it. That he did not go on to chronicle the rise of an industrial democracy, as the Marxist critics of the 1930's demanded, but attempted instead to return to the past, contributed to the demise of his reputation, but it resulted in some of his best works, those in which he develops his major themes effectively as he reiterates the values upon which the country was built and emphasizes the need to return to those values in an increasingly materialistic age.

Among his substantial literary contributions must be included his four panel novels, *The Green Bay Tree, Possession, Early Autumn*, and *A Good Woman*, which document in human terms the impact of sweeping social changes and perverted values in the early years of this century. These novels also illustrate his literary talents: a forthright, literate style; characters who are human and intense; and strong narratives. To these novels must be added *The Farm*, his best single work, *Twenty-Four Hours*, a remarkably controlled work in spite of its lapses, and *The Rains Came*, the most dramatic and philosophically unified of his books. Of his later work, *Mrs. Parkington* is an intensely human portrait of a magnificent American woman, and *The Wild Country* comes close to a definitive expression of the American midwestern experience in transition from frontier to civilization.

Also worth noting are Bromfield's contributions to the literature of nature, folklore, and agriculture. Most of the best of his folklore and nature writing is included in *Animals and Other People*, while *Pleasant Valley* and *Malabar Farm* indicate what technical writing may achieve when it is lively, imaginative, and literate.

Unfortunately, Bromfield still suffers from the fact that he has received little objective criticism. The unfair criticisms of the early 1930's have discouraged later critics from looking at his work clearly and coherently. He wrote too well too easily, and his early critical and commercial successes ultimately worked to his disadvantage. But in almost all of his work he wrote well and he constructed memorable characters and situations—uncommon abilities in any age.

—David D. Anderson

BROOKS, Gwendolyn. Born in Topeka, Kansas, 7 June 1917. Educated at Wilson Junior College, Chicago, graduated 1936. Married Henry L. Blakely in 1939 (divorced); one son and one daughter. Publicity director, NAACP Youth Council, Chicago, 1930's. Taught at Northeastern Illinois State College, Chicago, Columbia College, Chicago, Elmhurst College, Illinois, and University of Wisconsin, Madison; Distinguished Professor of the Arts, City College, City University of New York, 1971. Editor, *Black Position* magazine. Consultant in Poetry, Library of Congress, Washington, D.C., 1986. Recipient: Guggenheim fellowship, 1946; American Academy grant, 1946; Pulitzer Prize, 1950; Anisfield-Wolf Award, 1968; Shelley Memorial Award, 1976. L.H.D.: Columbia College, 1964; D.Litt.: Lake Forest College, Chicago, 1965; Brown University, Providence, Rhode Island, 1974. Poet Laureate of Illinois, 1969. Lives in Chicago.

Publications

Verse

A Street in Bronzeville. 1945.
Annie Allen. 1949.
Bronzeville Boys and Girls (for children). 1956.
The Bean Eaters (for children). 1960.
Selected Poems. 1963.
In the Time of Detachment, In the Time of Cold. 1965.
In the Mecca. 1968.
For Illinois 1968: A Sesquicentennial Poem. 1968.
Riot. 1970.
The Wall. N.d.
Family Pictures. 1970.
Aloneness. 1971.
Aurora. 1972.
Beckonings. 1975.
To Disembark. 1981.

Fiction

Maud Martha. 1953.

Other

A Portion of That Field, with others. 1967.
The World of Brooks (miscellany). 1971.
Report from Part One: An Autobiography. 1972.
The Tiger Who Wore White Gloves; or, What You Are You Are (for children). 1974.
A Capsule Course in Black Poetry Writing, with Don L. Lee, Keorapetse Kgositsile, and Dudley Randall. 1975.
Young Poets' Primer. 1981.
Very Young Poets. 1983.

Editor, *A Broadside Treasury*. 1971.
Editor, *Jump Bad: A New Chicago Anthology*. 1971.

*

Bibliography: *Langston Hughes and Brooks: A Reference Guide* by R. Baxter Miller, 1978.

Critical Study: *Brooks: Poetry and the Heroic Voice* by D.H. Melhem, 1986.

* * *

Gwendolyn Brooks solves the critical question of whether to judge black poetry in America by standards different from those applied to white poetry: she simply writes so powerfully and universally out of the black American milieu that the question does not arise. Her poems may sometimes be bitter, angry, or threatening, but always they are poems and never mere propaganda. She may personally feel caught between racial allegiance and the need for social action on the one hand and purer and higher art on the other, but in her work the distinction dissolves.

Indeed, *In the Mecca*, published in 1968, and especially the poems published since, reflect the conversion from deep racial pride to a harsher militancy that she experienced under the tutelage of a group of young blacks at a meeting at Fisk University in 1967. Thus she speaks in "Young Africans" (from *Family Pictures*) of "our black revival, our black vinegar, / our hands and our hot blood," and warns in the acerbic *Riot*, "Cabot! John! You are a desperate man, / and the desperate die expensively today. But nearly always she finds the tight poetic structure, the *things* in which to embody the idea, so that the reader comes away with that sense of surprise and delight at the insight—in addition to any other emotion—that means that the work was a poem, and that the poem was a fine one.

Brooks has devoted much of her time since the late 1960's to helping young black Americans, and especially writers. But she speaks out of the American consciousness and to the American conscience, and it is the color-blind America that has rightly given her a Pulitzer Prize and other testaments to her great lyrical voice.

—Alan R. Shucard

BROWN, Charles Brockden. Born in Philadelphia, Pennsylvania, 17 January 1771. Educated at the Friends' Latin School, Philadelphia, 1781–86; studied law in the office of Alexander Wilcocks, Philadelphia, 1787–92, but never practised. Married Elizabeth Linn in 1804; three sons and one daughter. Lived in New York and was associated with the Friendly Society there, 1798–1801: editor of the society's *Monthly Magazine and American Review*, 1799–1800; returned to Philadelphia, and worked in his brother's importing business, 1800–06, and as an independent trader, 1807–10. Editor, *Literary Magazine*, 1803–07, and *American Register*, 1807–10. *Died 21 February 1810.*

PUBLICATIONS

Collections

Novels. 7 vols., 1827.
Novels and Related Works, edited by Sydney J. Krause. 1977—

Fiction

Wieland; or, The Transformation: An American Tale. 1798.
Ormond; or, The Secret Witness. 1799.
Arthur Mervyn; or, Memoirs of the Year 1793. 2 vols., 1799–1800.
Edgar Huntly; or, Memoirs of a Sleep-Walker. 1799; edited by David Lee Clark, 1928.
Clara Howard. 1801; as *Philip Stanley; or, The Enthusiasm of Love*, 1807.
Jane Talbot. 1801.
Carwin the Biloquist and Other American Tales and Pieces. 1822.
Memoirs of Stephen Calvert, edited by Hans Borchers. 1978.

Other

Alcuin: A Dialogue. 1798; edited by Lee R. Edwards, 1971.
An Address to the Government on the Cession of Louisiana to the French. 1803; revised edition, 1803.
Monroe's Embassy. 1803.
An Address on the Utility and Justice of Restrictions upon Foreign Commerce. 1809.
The Rhapsodist and Other Uncollected Writings, edited by Harry R. Warfel. 1943.

Translator, *A View of the Soil and Climate of the United States of America*, by C.F. Volney. 1804.

*

Bibliography: in *Bibliography of American Literature* by Jacob Blanck, 1955; "A Census of the Works of Brown" by Sydney J. Krause and Jane Nieset, in *Serif 3*, 1966; *Brown: A Reference Guide* by Patricia Parker, 1980.

Critical Studies: *The Life of Brown* by William Dunlap, 2 vols., 1815, as *Memoirs of Brown*, 1822; *Brown, American Gothic Novelist* by Harry R. Warfel, 1949; *Brown, Pioneer Voice of America* by David Lee Clark, 1952; *Brown* by Donald A. Ringe, 1966; *Rational Fictions: A Study of Brown* by Arthur G. Kimball, 1968; *Critical Essays on Brown* edited by Bernard Rosenthal, 1981; *The Coincidental Art of Brown* by Norman S. Grabo, 1981; *Brown: An American Tale* by Alan Axelrod, 1983; *A Right View of the Subject: Feminism in the Works of Brown and John Neal* by Fritz Fleischmann, 1983.

* * *

When Charles Brockden Brown began to write fiction in the latter half of the 1790's, he turned for his models to the popular novels of his time: the gothic romances of England and Germany, the sentimental tale of seduction, and the novel of purpose. All of these types of fiction had a strong influence on the young American, and each of his six novels can be classified under one or more of these headings. But however much he may have learned from his wide reading, Brown was no mere imitator. He shaped his models to his own artistic ends and turned even such unpromising forms as the gothic and sentimental romance into vehicles for the development of important themes. He left his indelible mark on everything he wrote.

A major characteristic of Brown's fiction is its intense intellectuality. Though *Wieland* and *Ormond* may both be viewed as tales of seduction, and *Wieland* and *Edgar Huntly* as tales of terror, all three carry a weight of thematic meaning not commonly found in the sentimental or Gothic romance. Sensationalist psychology, theories of education, and the sources of mania are major concerns in *Wieland*; utopian theories, the proper training for women, and the place of religion in education in *Ormond*; and benevolist principles in *Edgar Huntly*. Other of Brown's books are equally intellectual. Benevolist theory also appears in *Arthur Mervyn*, a book modeled on William Godwin's *Caleb Williams*, and Godwinian rationalism clashes with religion in *Jane Talbot*, a sentimental romance.

This is not to say that Brown is a propagandist. He used his fiction, as one critic has observed, not for the exposition, but for the discovery of ideas, which he puts to the test through the actions of his characters. The mistakes that the mad Theodore Wieland, the distraught Clara Wieland, and the rationalistic Henry Pleyel make in attempting to act on the basis of misinterpreted sensations, and the disaster that Edgar Huntly causes by acting on benevolist principles well illustrate Brown's technique. He forces the reader to examine the ideas in the context of the action, but he draws no conclusion himself. Indeed, since all of his books are first-person narrations, told through the voices of one or more characters or through a series of letters, the reader must often penetrate the psychology of the narrator before he can discover the thematic meaning embodied in the action.

In *Ormond* the point of view causes relatively little trouble, for the story is told in a straightforward manner by a rational character who, throughout most of the book, plays no major role in the action. In other novels, however, where the protagonists tell their own stories, the problem can be difficult. Blessed with an innocent face and a glib tongue, Arthur Mervyn always presents himself in a favorable light, but he exists in a world where appearances are often deceiving, and his actions seem to belie the purity of motive that he consistently attributes to himself. He is, therefore, extremely difficult to penetrate, and critics are divided over the meaning of his experience. The protagonists in *Wieland* and *Edgar Huntly* present a different problem, for both are mentally disturbed. Clara Wieland lapses into madness in the course of her narrative, and Edgar Huntly is driven by strange compulsions from the very first pages of the book. Both narrators are, presumably, brought back to sanity by the close of their stories, but neither is easy for the reader to plumb.

In both of these gothic tales, however, Brown found effective means for revealing the mental state of his disturbed narrators. Through the use of enclosures in *Wieland*—the temple, the summer house, and Clara's room and closet—he suggests the isolation and introspection of all the Wielands, including Clara; through the labyrinthine paths and deep cave in *Edgar Huntly*, he projects his protagonist's mental journey and withdrawal into himself. Other devices, too—Clara's dream, Edgar Huntly's somnambulism, and the appearance of his double, Clithero Edny—help the reader to understand their psychology. All of these were excellent inventions that function well in their respective books. Through them, Brown helped to establish the kind of psychological gothic that became so popular throughout the 19th century in the works of Poe, Hawthorne, and even James.

Brown's position at the head of that tradition accounts for part of the interest he generates among readers today, but his historical importance is not his only claim to attention. Though he never wrote a wholly satisfactory novel—even his best books are marred by structural flaws and a defective style—he achieved so great an intellectual and imaginative intensity in such works as *Wieland, Edgar Huntly*, and *Arthur Mervyn* that one can forgive the weaknesses for the strengths. All are told by protagonists whose psychological state fascinates, and the tales they recount appeal to both the intellect and the emotions of the reader. The ideas Brown explores are always interesting, and the means he found to reveal the psychology of the narrators and to advance the action are absorbing. Though a hasty and careless writer—he hurried all six of his novels through the press in about three years—Brown instilled in the best of his books a vitality yet apparent almost two centuries after they were written.

—Donald A. Ringe

BROWN, Sterling A(llen). Born in Washington, D.C., 1 May 1901. Educated at Dunbar High School, Washington, D.C.; Williams College, Williamstown, Massachusetts, 1918–22, A.B. 1922 (Phi Beta Kappa); Harvard University, Cambridge, Massachusetts, A.M. 1923. Married Daisy Turnbull in 1927. Teacher at Virginia Seminary and College, Lynchburg, 1923–26, Lincoln University, Jefferson City, Missouri, 1926–28, and Fisk University, Nashville, Tennessee, 1929; since 1929 Professor of English, Howard University, Washington, D.C. Visiting Professor, New York University, New School for Social Research, New York, Vassar College, Poughkeepsie, New York, and University of Minnesota, Minneapolis. Literary editor, *Opportunity* magazine, Washington, D.C., 1930's; editor of *Negro Affairs* for the Federal Writers Project, 1936–39; staff member, *American Dilemma*. Recipient: Guggenheim fellowship, 1937; Lenore Marshall Prize, 1981. Honorary degrees: Atlanta University; Boston University; Brown University, Providence, Rhode Island; Harvard University; Howard University; Lewis and Clark College, Portland, Oregon; Lincoln University, Pennsylvania; University of Maryland, College Park; University of Massachusetts, Amherst; Northwestern University, Evanston, Illinois; University of Pennsylvania, Philadelphia; Williams College; Yale University, New Haven, Connecticut. Poet Laureate of the District of Columbia, 1984. Lives in Washington, D.C.

PUBLICATIONS

Verse

Southern Road. 1932.
The Last Ride of Wild Bill and Eleven Narrative Poems. 1975.
The Collected Poems, edited by Michael S. Harper. 1980.

Other

Outline for the Study of the Poetry of American Negroes (study guide for James Weldon Johnson's *The Book of American Negro Poetry*). 1931.
The Negro in American Fiction. 1937.
Negro Poetry and Drama. 1937.
James Weldon Johnson, with A.B. Spingarn and Carl Van Vechten. 1941(?).
The Negro in Washington, with *Negro Newcomers in Detroit*, by George Edmund Haynes. 1969.

Editor, *The Negro in Virginia*. 1940.
Editor, with Arthur P. Davis and Ulysses Lee, *The Negro Caravan: Writings by American Negroes*. 2 vols., 1941.

*

Bibliography: by Robert G. O'Meally, in *The Collected Poems* edited by Michael S. Harper, 1980.

Critical Studies: "Brown Issue" of *Callaloo*, February–March 1982.

* * *

Essentially a traditional song-maker and storyteller, Sterling A. Brown has witnessed cross-currents of American literature, and chooses in his poetry to depict blacks and the clash of their roles with those of whites in the variegated society of the American South, particularly in the time caught between two world wars.

His poetry was collected in anthologies as early as James Weldon Johnson's *The Book of American Negro Poetry* (1922), and, like Johnson himself and Langston Hughes, he set about disrupting the patently false and banal image of the docile American Negro with his charming *patois*, artificially stylized and mimicked by the whites in the minstrel shows still popular in the 1920's and 1930's. Johnson says in his preface of Hughes and Brown that they "*do* use a dialect, but it is not the dialect of the comic minstrel tradition or the sentimental plantation tradition; it is the common, racy, living, authentic speech of the Negro in certain phases of real life."

Brown uses original Afro-American ballads such as "Casey Jones," "John Henry," and "Staggolee" as counterpoint for his modern ones, but the portent of his ironic wit should not be underestimated, for it is actually a tool to shape an ironic, infernal vision of American life as Hades: "The Place was Dixie I took for Hell," says Slim in "Slim in Hell." The American Negro is heralded not as Black Orpheus but as modern tragic hero Mose, a leader of *all* people while futilely attempting to save his own: "A soft song, filled with a misery / Older than Mose will be." In "Sharecropper" he is broken as Christ was broken; his landlord "shot him in the side" to put him out of his misery; he is lost and wild as Odysseus in "Odyssey of a Big Boy"; and found again:

> Man wanta live
> Man want find himself
> Man gotta learn
> How to go it alone.

Though small in quantity, Brown's poetry is epic in conception; his ballad, blues, and jazz forms are the vehicles for creative insight into themes of American life.

—Carol Lee Saffioti

BROWN, William Wells. Born on a plantation near Lexington, Kentucky, in 1813; son of a slave owner and one of his slaves. Married Elizabeth Schooner in 1834; three daughters. Taken to St. Louis as a boy and hired out on a steamboat; worked in the printshop of the editor of the St. Louis *Times*; then again hired out on a steamboat; escaped from slavery to Cincinnati, 1834 (assumed the name of a man who befriended him); moved to Cleveland, then to Monroe, Michigan, where he ran a barbershop and set up a bank; steamboat steward on Lake Erie and helped fugitive slaves escape to Canada; moved to Buffalo, 1836, and became active in abolitionist activities: lecturer for abolitionist movement, New York and Massachusetts, 1843-49, and England, 1849–54; also associated with other reform movements: represented the American Peace Society at the Peace Congress, Paris, 1849; studied medicine and had medical practice in Boston for many years. *Died 6 November 1884*.

PUBLICATIONS

Fiction

Clotel; or, The President's Daughter: A Narrative of Slave Life in the United States. 1853; other versions published as *Clotelle: A Tale of the Southern States*, 1864, and *Clotelle; or, The Colored Heroine*, 1867; edited by William Edward Farrison, with *Narrative of Brown*, 1969.

Play

The Escape; or, A Leap for Freedom. 1858.

Other

Narrative of Brown, A Fugitive Slave. 1847; revised edition, 1848, 1849; edited by William Edward Farrison, with *Clotel*, 1969.
Three Years in Europe; or, Places I Have Seen and People I Have Met. 1852; revised edition, as *The American Fugitive in Europe*, 1855.
The Black Man: His Antecedents, His Genius, and His Achievements. 1863; revised edition, 1863.
The Negro in the American Rebellion: His Heroism and His Fidelity. 1867.
The Rising Son; or, The Antecedents and Advancement of the Colored Race. 1874.
My Southern Home; or, The South and Its People. 1880.

Editor, *The Anti-Slavery Harp: A Collection of Songs for Anti-Slavery Meetings*. 1848.

*

Bibliography: *Brown and Martin R. Delany: A Reference Guide* by Curtis W. Ellison and E.W. Metcalf, 1978.

Critical Studies: *Brown, Author and Reformer* (includes bibliography) by William Edward Farrison, 1969; *Brown and Clotelle: A Portrait of the Artist in the First Negro Novel* by J. Noel Heermance, 1969; *My Chains Fell Off: Brown, Fugitive Abolitionist* by L.H. Whelchel, Jr., 1985.

* * *

Born a slave in Kentucky, William Wells Brown was schooled by the "peculiar institution" for life-long work as a reformer. Within two years of his own escape from bondage in 1834, he was conducting others to freedom on the underground railroad, and by the 1850's he was among the most famous abolitionists in Europe as well as America.

Crusaders then as now employed every medium available to their talents to advance their cause. In this company, Brown was remarkable, for besides oration and documentary reports he also produced a novel, a European travel book, plays, several historical studies, and reflective memoirs. The novel, *Clotel*, the travel book, *Three Years in Europe*, and the five-act drama, *The Escape*, are first examples of their type written by a black American. Together with the range of his other writings they assure Brown a place in American literary history.

Brown's narrative of life in slavery was a bestseller. His novel found a broad audience by virtue of its appearance in several versions, and his histories and recollections went through multiple editions. Their contemporary appeal seems to have been due largely to their reaffirmation of standard arguments in their use of familiar literary conventions.

Yet it is the evident redundancy in his work that accounts for Brown's present significance. In his autobiography, Brown's first published book, he describes his master as stealing him as soon as he was born. His mother, he explains, bore seven children by seven different men, including a white relative of the master, who fathered William. Each infant was claimed by the master as his property without regard to lineage or paternal affection. William and his mother tried to escape slavery but were caught, and his mother sold into the deep South "to die on a . . . plantation!" Later, when he made his way alone to freedom in Ohio, he joined the name his mother had given him with that of Wells Brown, his first white friend and surrogate father. These autobiographical facts reveal the terms in which Brown saw destiny. Thus, his fiction centers upon mulatto characters whose very existence images violation and relates incidents where neither blood, race, nor intimacy prevent subjugation. Carried into non-fiction, where he argued the case for equality on the basis of achievement and service, Brown adapts his motifs into a plea for reconciliation within the human family.

It is repeated examination of fate in an America where essential humanity is divided by brutal practice that gives Brown continued importance. For this first black man of letters established in literature the prevalent Afro-American concern with identity.

—John M. Reilly

BROWNE, Charles Farrar. See **WARD, Artemus.**

BRYANT, William Cullen. Born in Cummington, Massachusetts, 3 November 1794. Educated privately, and at Williams College, Williamstown, Massachusetts, 1810–11; studied law under Elias Howe, Worthington, Massachusetts, 1811–14, and in the office of William Baylies, Bridgewater, Massachusetts, 1814–15: admitted to the Massachusetts bar, 1815. Married Frances Fairchild in 1821 (died, 1866); two daughters. Lawyer, Plainfield, 1816, and Great Barrington, 1817–25, both Massachusetts; editor, with Henry J. Anderson, *New York Review and Athenaeum Magazine*, 1825–26; assistant editor, *United States Review*, 1826–27; assistant editor, 1826–29, and editor and part owner, 1829–78, New York *Evening Post*. President, American Free Trade League, 1865–69. *Died 12 June 1878.*

PUBLICATIONS

Collections

Poetical Works, Prose Writings, edited by Parke Godwin. 4 vols., 1883–84.
Poetical Works, edited by Henry C. Sturges and Richard Henry Stoddard. 1903.
Selections, edited by Samuel Sillen. 1945.
Letters, edited by William Cullen Bryant II and Thomas G. Voss. 1975—

Verse

The Embargo; or, Sketches of the Times: A Satire. 1808.
The Embargo and Other Poems. 1809.
Poems. 1821.
Poems. 1832; London edition, edited by Washington Irving, 1832; revised edition, 1834, 1836, 1850.
The Fountain and Other Poems. 1842.
The White-Footed Deer and Other Poems. 1844.
Poems. 2 vols., 1855.
Thirty Poems. 1864.
Hymns. 1864; revised edition, 1869.
Poems. 1871.
Poems. 3 vols., 1875.
Poems. 1876.

Other

Letters of a Traveller; or, Notes of Things Seen in Europe and America. 1850; as *The Picturesque Souvenir*, 1851.
Reminiscences of The Evening Post. 1851.
Letters of a Traveller, Second Series. 1859.
A Discourse on the Life, Character, and Genius of Washington Irving. 1860.
Letters from the East. 1869.
Some Notices of the Life and Writings of Fitz-Greene Halleck. 1869.
Orations and Addresses. 1873.

Editor, *Tales of Glauber-Spa*. 2 vols., 1832.
Editor, *Selections from the American Poets*. 1840.
Editor, *The Berkshire Jubilee*. 1845.
Editor, *A Library of Poetry and Song*. 1871; revised edition, as *A New Library*, 1876(?).
Editor, with Oliver B. Bunce, *Picturesque America; or, The Land We Live In*. 2 vols., 1872–74.
Editor, *A Popular History of the United States*, vols. 1-2, by Sydney Howard Gay. 1876–78.
Editor, with Evert A. Duyckinck, *Complete Works of Shakespeare*. 25 vols., 1888.

Translator, *The Iliad and The Odyssey of Homer*. 4 vols., 1870–72.

*

Bibliography: in *Bibliography of American Literature* by Jacob Blanck, 1955; *A Bibliography of Bryant and His Critics 1808–1972* by Judith T. Phair, 1975.

Critical Studies: *A Biography of Bryant* (includes letters) by Parke Godwin, 2 vols., 1883; *Gotham Yankee: A Biography of Bryant* by Harry Houston Peckham, 1950; *Politics and a Belly-Full: The Journalistic Career of Bryant* by Curtiss S. Johnson, 1962; *Bryant* by Albert F. McLean, Jr., 1964; *Bryant* by Charles H. Brown, 1971; *Bryant and His America* edited by Stanley Brodwin and Michael D'Innocenzo, 1983.

* * *

When in his poem "The Poet" William Cullen Bryant urges a writer to eschew the "empty gust / Of passion" but to express "feelings of calm power and mighty sweep, / Like currents journeying through the windless deep," he is making an apt comment on his own best work. For though in "A Fable for Critics" James Russell Lowell goes too far in joking at Bryant for his coldness, his lack of enthusiasm, his "supreme *ice*olation," Bryant's strong points are indeed not passion, not delicacy, not soaring imagination, but dignity and power. Even through his lighter poems sound a strong didactic note that reminds one that his literary forebears were New England Puritans, his work also has overtones of the sober 18th-century neoclassicism of Gray and Collins. He is at his best when with stately force he depicts the grand sweeping cycle of life which carries all away with its resistless current.

Thus his first major poem, "Thanatopsis," written in the tradition of the British Graveyard Poets in grave, resounding lines, pictures man, even new American man, living on the tombs of countless races. When we too join the caravan to the inevitable tomb, Bryant says, may we face our fate with stoic dignity. "The Journey of Life," "The Ages," "The Past," and "The Flood of Years," though with a more specifically Christian hope of immortality, similarly emphasize with stately resonance and images the cyclical patterns of human existence. The same theme is effectively voiced in such poems as "The Prairies," "Monument Mountain," and "An Indian at the Burial Place of His Fathers," which delineate the successive destruction of America's aboriginal races and remind the white man that he too may disappear. Because of such epic grandeur in his own themes it is not surprising that Bryant was a highly successful translator of Homer.

But the classic dignity of much of Bryant's best work is nicely balanced by his Romantic sense of the soothing power and divinity of nature. Bryant was America's first major Romantic poet. Poems like "A Forest Hymn," "Green River," and "Inscription for the Entrance to a Wood" earnestly inculcate the creed that nature can give solace to the weary heart. Some of these poems verge on pantheism and foreshadow Emerson's doctrine that the divine creation has never ceased. Throughout even the simple nature poems, such as "The Yellow Violet" and "To a Fringed Gentian," Bryant preaches sometimes somberly, sometimes wittily; his favorite lyric form is a series of descriptive stanzas followed by one or two of moral. Though he is playful in "A Meditation on Rhode Island Coal" and "Robert of Lincoln," he rarely writes for fun. Yet in such a poem as "To a Waterfowl" he can so superbly blend his moralism with telling imagery and restrained emotion that it becomes an integral part of a powerful work of art, indeed one of America's finest lyrics.

Though Bryant was intensely concerned with mutability and nature, he was also acutely awake to American life around him. His first published volume, *The Embargo*, was a satire against the Jeffersonians. Not only was he the writer of powerful liberal editorials in the New York *Evening Post*, of which for many years he was editor, but he also wrote many effective and graceful occasional poems such as his elegy on Lincoln. Like the Hudson River School painters with whom he was closely associated (see "To Cole, The Painter, Departing for Europe"), he patriotically celebrated American landscape, American nature, and American history and legend. He even edited a collection of essays and engravings entitled *Picturesque America*. He wrote on popular causes such as slavery ("The African Chief") and Greek independence ("The Massacre at Scio"). Sometimes, as in "The Death of the Flowers," he verged toward the mawkish sentimentalism that was the bane of America's "Feminine Fifties," but his lack of pretentiousness, quiet integrity, and basic good sense, seen also in his anthologies of American poetry and especially in his first-rate critical essays on poets and poetry, ordinarily saved him from banality. Like so many American authors of his time he also wrote hymns.

With some justice Bryant's poetry has been derogated as bloodless, undramatic, too orotund, too much concerned with death and mutability, out of touch with vivid life, even morbid. To read his verse, Marius Bewley says, is "a little like listening to a harmonium with the pedal stuck," and his poetry gives the impression of "a best parlor filled with marmoreal statuary." But such comment is unfair. Bryant is a significant pioneer in American literature. His best work is also still worthy to be read for what Lowell calls "the grace, strength, and dignity" of his art and for the quiet depth and earnestness of his vision of the ever-flowing stream of nature and human life. His was surely the most powerful poetic voice in America between Edward Taylor and Poe.

—Curtis Dahl

See the essay on "Thanatopsis."

BUCK, Pearl S(ydenstricker). Born in Hillsboro, West Virginia, 26 June 1892; daughter of Presbyterian missionaries in China. Educated at boarding school in Shanghai, 1907–09; Randolph-Macon Woman's College, Lynchburg, Virginia, B.A. 1914 (Phi Beta Kappa); Cornell University, Ithaca, New York, M.A. 1926. Married 1) John Lossing Buck in 1917 (divorced, 1935), one daughter; 2) Richard J. Walsh in 1935 (died, 1960); eight adopted children. Psychology teacher, Randolph-Macon Woman's College, 1914; English teacher, University of Nanking, 1921–31, Southeastern University, Nanking, 1925–27, and Chung Yang University, Nanking, 1928–31; returned to the U.S., 1935; co-editor, *Asia* magazine, New York, 1941–46; founder and director, East and West Association, 1941–51; founder, Welcome House, an adoption agency, 1949, and Pearl S. Buck Foundation, 1964; member of the Board of Directors, Weather Engineering Corporation of America, Manchester, New Hampshire, 1966. Recipient: Pulitzer Prize, 1932; American Academy Howells Medal, 1935; Nobel Prize for Literature, 1938; National Conference of Christians and Jews Brotherhood Award, 1955; President's Commission on Employment of the Physically Handicapped citation, 1958; Women's National Book Association Skinner Award, 1960; ELA award, 1969. M.A.: Yale University, New Haven, Connecticut, 1933; D.Litt.: University of West Virginia, Morgantown, 1940; St. Lawrence University, Canton, New York, 1942; Delaware Valley College, Doylestown, Pennsylvania, 1965; LL.D.: Howard University, Washington, D.C., 1942; Muhlenberg College, Allentown, Pennsylvania, 1966; L.H.D.: Lincoln University, Pennsylvania, 1953; Woman's Medical College of Philadelphia, 1954; University of Pittsburgh, 1960; Bethany College, West Virginia, 1963; Hahnemann Medical College, Philadelphia, 1966; Rutgers University, New Brunswick, New Jersey, 1969; D.Mus.: Combs College of Music, Philadelphia, 1962; D.H.: West Virginia State College, Institute, 1963. Member, American Academy. *Died 6 March 1973.*

PUBLICATIONS

Fiction

East Wind: West Wind. 1930.
House of Earth. 1935.
The Good Earth. 1931.
Sons. 1932.
A House Divided. 1935.
The First Wife and Other Stories. 1933.
The Mother. 1934.
This Proud Heart. 1938.
The Patriot. 1939.
Other Gods: An American Legend. 1940.
Today and Forever: Stories of China. 1941.
China Sky. 1942.
Dragon Seed. 1942.
The Promise. 1943.
China Flight. 1945.
The Townsman. 1945.
Portrait of a Marriage. 1945.
Pavilion of Women. 1946.
The Angry Wife. 1947.
Far and Near: Stories of Japan, China, and America. 1948.
Peony. 1948; as *The Bondmaid*, 1949.
Kinfolk. 1949.
The Long Love. 1949.
God's Men. 1950.
The Hidden Flower. 1952.
Satan Never Sleeps. 1952.
Bright Procession. 1952.
Come, My Beloved. 1953.
Voices in the House. 1953.
Imperial Woman. 1956.
Letter from Peking. 1957.
Command the Morning. 1959.
Fourteen Stories. 1961; as *With a Delicate Air and Other Stories*, 1962.
Hearts Come Home and Other Stories. 1962.
The Living Reed. 1963.
Stories of China. 1964.
Death in the Castle. 1965.
The Time Is Noon. 1967.
The New Year. 1968.
The Good Deed and Other Stories of Asia, Past and Present. 1969.
The Three Daughters of Madame Liang. 1969.
Mandala. 1970.
The Goddess Abides. 1972.
All under Heaven. 1973.
The Rainbow. 1974.
Book of Christmas (stories). 1974.
East and West (stories). 1975.
Secrets of the Heart (stories). 1976.
The Lovers and Other Stories. 1977.
The Woman Who Was Changed and Other Stories. 1979.

Plays

Flight into China (produced 1939).
Sun Yat Sen: A Play, Preceded by a Lecture by Dr. Hu-Shih. 1944(?).
China to America (radio play), in *Free World Theatre*, edited by Arch Oboler and Stephen Longstreet. 1944.
Will This Earth Hold? (radio play), in *Radio Drama in Action*, edited by Erik Barnouw. 1945.
The First Wife (produced 1945).
A Desert Incident (produced 1959).
Christine, with Charles K. Peck, Jr., music by Sammy Fain, from the book *My Indian Family* by Hilda Wernher (produced 1960).
The Guide, from the novel by R.K. Narayan (produced 1965).

Screenplays (with Ted Danielewski): *The Big Wave*, 1962; *The Guide*, 1965.

Verse

Words of Love. 1974.

Other (for children)

The Young Revolutionist. 1932.
Stories for Little Children. 1940.
When Fun Begins. 1941.
The Chinese Children Next Door. 1942.
The Water Buffalo Children. 1943.
The Dragon Fish. 1944.
Yu Lan: Flying Boy of China. 1945.
The Big Wave. 1948.
One Bright Day. 1950; as *One Bright Day and Other Stories for Children*, 1952.
The Man Who Changed China: The Story of Sun Yat Sen. 1953.
The Beech Tree. 1954.
Johnny Jack and His Beginnings. 1954.
Christmas Miniature. 1957; as *The Christmas Mouse*, 1958.
The Christmas Ghost. 1960.
Welcome Child. 1964.
The Big Fight. 1965.
The Little Fox in the Middle. 1966.
Matthew, Mark, Luke, and John. 1967.
The Chinese Storyteller. 1971.
A Gift for the Children. 1973.
Mrs. Starling's Problem. 1973.

Other

Is There a Case for Foreign Missions? 1932.
East and West and the Novel: Sources of the Early Chinese Novel. 1932.
The Exile (biography). 1936.
Fighting Angel: Portrait of a Soul (biography). 1936.
The Chinese Novel. 1939.
Of Men and Women. 1941.
American Unity and Asia. 1942; as *Asia and Democracy*, 1943.
What America Means to Me. 1943.
Talk about Russia, with Masha Scott. 1945.
Tell the People: Talks with James Yen about the Mass Education Movement. 1945.
How It Happens: Talk about the German People, 1914–1933, with Erna von Pustau. 1947.
American Argument, with Eslanda Goode Robeson. 1949.
The Child Who Never Grew. 1950.
My Several Worlds (autobiography). 1954.
Friend to Friend, with Carlos P. Romulo. 1958.
The Delights of Learning. 1960.

A Bridge for Passing (autobiography). 1962.
The Joy of Children. 1964.
The Gifts They Bring: Our Debts to the Mentally Retarded, with Gweneth T. Zarfoss. 1965.
Children for Adoption. 1965.
The People of Japan. 1966.
For Spacious Skies: Journey in Dialogue, with Theodore F. Harris. 1966.
My Mother's House, with others. 1966.
To My Daughters, With Love. 1967.
The People of China. 1968.
The Kennedy Women: A Personal Appraisal. 1970.
China as I See It, edited by Theodore F. Harris. 1970.
The Story Bible. 1971.
China Past and Present. 1972.
A Community Success Story: The Founding of the Pearl Buck Center. 1972.
Oriental Cookbook. 1972.

Editor, *China in Black and White: An Album of Woodcuts by Contemporary Chinese Artists.* 1945.
Editor, *Fairy Tales of the Orient.* 1965.

Translator, *All Men Are Brothers*, by Shui Hu Chan. 2 vols., 1933.

*

Bibliography: by Lucille S. Zinn, in *Bulletin of Bibliography 36*, 1979.

Critical Studies: *Buck* by Paul A. Doyle, 1965, revised edition, 1980; *Buck: A Biography* by Theodore F. Harris, 2 vols., 1969–71; *Buck: A Woman in Conflict* by Nora Stirling, 1983.

* * *

The amount and variety of Pearl S. Buck's writing and the strong correlation between her writing and her life make critical analysis complex. She admired the work of such naturalists as Zola and Dreiser and often emphasized the power of nature and culture, but she was never sordid nor pessimistic, and her realistic details of places, events, and people are organized around such romantic tenets as individuality, the nobility of common people, the corrupting influence of wealth and cities, and the universal interest in "love." Her years in China, her missionary connections, her exposure to many forms of domestic life, and her humanitarian projects furnished both the material and the themes of her stories. And while her masterpiece, *The Good Earth*, and the biographies of her parents, *The Exile* and *Fighting Angel*, are widely regarded as classics, much of the rest of her work is of uneven artistic merit.

The Good Earth achieves a perfect blending of appropriate diction, informative detail, epic structure, and universal themes. Such semi-biblical lines as "I am with child," and such "Chinese" lines as "There is this woman of mine," are held together with such thematic lines as: "He had no articulate thought of anything; there was only this perfect sympathy of movement, of turning this earth of theirs over and over to the sun, this earth which formed their home and fed their bodies and made their gods." Occasionally there are poetic lines as delicate as a Chinese painting: "A small soft wind blew gently from the east, a wind mild and murmurous and full of rain." While she used a similar style in her other Chinese books, she both modernized and Americanized the language when appropriate.

The Good Earth is the "epic" of a "rags-to-riches" farmer-hero of Old China, practicing his native customs but experiencing the universal drama of birth and death, prosperity and famine, work and sex, tradition and change. The plot is structured by Wang's relationship to three wives—and to his land. The "good" wives sympathize with his love of the land; the "bad" wife hates the land. Like nearly all of Buck's male characters, Wang is inept in human relations, controlled by forces he never understands, yet capable of resisting social pressure and remaining loyal to personal qualities of honesty and kindness. In contrast, nearly all of her female characters are wiser, or craftier, than the men they are destined to serve—an "autobiographical" point of view especially apparent in *This Proud Heart, Pavilion of Women, Peony*, and *Letter from Peking*.

Throughout her writing Buck portrays religion, slavery, economic tyranny, war, and government as capable of being manipulated by individuals. And although she occasionally generalizes about settings or classes, her character development is consistent, the variety of her "solutions" credible. Certainly her informative depiction of cultural conflicts served her overriding aims—freedom and reconciliation.

—Esther Marian Greenwell Smith

BULLINS, Ed. Born in Philadelphia, Pennsylvania, 2 July 1935. Educated in Philadelphia public schools; at William Penn Business Institute, Philadelphia; Los Angeles City College; San Francisco State College. Served in the U.S. Navy, 1952–55. Married to Trixie Bullins. Playwright-in-Residence and associate director, New Lafayette Theatre, Harlem, New York, 1967–73; since 1974, producing director, The Surviving Theatre, New York; Mellon Lecturer, Amherst College, Massachusetts, from 1977. Editor, *Black Theatre* magazine, New York, 1969–74. Recipient: Rockefeller grant, 1968, 1970, 1973; Vernon Rice Award, 1968; American Place grant, 1968; Obie award, 1971, 1975; Guggenheim grant, 1971, and fellowship, 1976; Creative Artists Public Service grant, 1973; National Endowment for the Arts grant, 1974; New York Drama Critics Circle award, 1975, 1977. D.L.: Columbia College, Chicago, 1976. Lives in Brooklyn, New York.

PUBLICATIONS

Plays

Clara's Ole Man (produced 1965). In *Five Plays*, 1969.
How Do You Do? (produced 1965). 1965.
Dialect Determinism; or, The Rally (produced 1965). In *The Theme Is Blackness*, 1973.
The Theme Is Blackness (produced 1966). In *The Theme Is Blackness*, 1973.
It Has No Choice (produced 1966). In *The Theme Is Blackness*, 1973.
A Minor Scene (produced 1966). In *The Theme Is Blackness*, 1973.

The Game of Adam and Eve, with Shirley Tarbell (produced 1966).
In New England Winter (produced 1967). In *New Plays from the Black Theatre*, edited by Bullins, 1969.
In the Wine Time (produced 1968). In *Five Plays*, 1969.
A Son, Come Home (produced New York, 1968). In *Five Plays*, 1969.
The Electronic Nigger (produced 1968). In *Five Plays*, 1969.
Goin' a Buffalo: A Tragifantasy (produced 1968). In *Five Plays*, 1969.
The Gentleman Caller (produced 1969). In *Illuminations 5*, 1968.
The Corner (produced 1968). In *The Theme Is Blackness*, 1973.
Five Plays. 1969; as *The Electronic Nigger and Other Plays*, 1970.
We Righteous Bombers, from a work by Camus (produced 1969).
The Man Who Dug Fish (produced 1969). In *The Theme Is Blackness*, 1973.
Street Sounds (produced 1970). In *The Theme Is Blackness*, 1973.
The Helper (produced 1970). In *The Theme Is Blackness*, 1973.
A Ritual To Raise the Dead and Foretell the Future (produced 1970). In *The Theme Is Blackness*, 1973.
The Fabulous Miss Marie (produced 1970). In *The New Lafayette Theatre Presents*, edited by Bullins, 1974.
Four Dynamite Plays: It Bees Dat Way, Death List, The Pig Pen, Night of the Beast (produced 1970). 1971.
The Duplex: A Black Love Fable in Four Movements (produced 1970). 1971.
The Devil Catchers (produced 1971).
The Psychic Pretenders (produced 1972).
You Gonna Let Me Take You Out Tonight, Baby (produced 1972).
Next Time, in *City Stops* (produced 1972).
House Party, music by Pat Patrick, lyrics by Bullins (produced 1973).
The Theme Is Blackness: The Corner and Other Plays (includes *Dialect Determinism, or The Rally; It Has No Choice; The Helper; A Minor Scene; The Theme Is Blackness; The Man Who Dug Fish; Street Sounds*; and the scenarios and short plays *Black Commercial No. 2, The American Flag Ritual, State Office Bldg. Curse, One-Minute Commercial, A Street Play, A Short Play for a Small Theatre*, and *The Play of the Play*). 1973.
The Taking of Miss Janie (produced 1975).
The Mystery of Phyllis Wheatley (produced 1976).
I Am Lucy Terry (produced 1976).
Jo Anne!!! (produced 1976).
Home Boy, music by Aaron Bell, lyrics by Bullins (produced 1976).
Daddy (produced 1977).
Sepia Star; or, Chocolate Comes to the Cotton Club, music and lyrics by Mildred Kayden (produced 1977).
Storyville, music and lyrics by Mildred Kayden (produced 1977; revised version, produced 1979).
Michael (produced 1978).
C'mon Back to Heavenly House (produced 1978).
Leavings (produced 1980).
Steve and Velma (produced 1980).

Screenplays: *Night of the Beast*, 1971; *The Ritual Masters*, 1972.

Fiction

The Hungered One: Early Writings. 1971.
The Reluctant Rapist. 1973.

Verse

To Raise the Dead and Foretell the Future. 1971.

Other

Editor, *New Plays from the Black Theatre*. 1969.
Editor, *The New Lafayette Theatre Presents: Plays with Aesthetic Comments by 6 Black Playwrights*. 1974.

*

Bibliography: in *Black Image on the American Stage* by James V. Hatch, 1970.

Critical Studies: "The Polished Reality: Aesthetics and the Black Writer" in *Contact Magazine*, 1962; "The Theatre of Reality" in *Black World*, 1966; "Up from Politics" in *Performance*, 1972.

* * *

Ed Bullins is the most original and prolific playwright of the American Black Theatre movement. To quote him: "To make an open secret more public: in the area of playwriting, Ed Bullins, at this moment in time, is almost without peer in America—black, white or imported." Written in 1973, the statement exaggerates little. It appears in *The Theme Is Blackness*, a title that polemically reduces Bullins's actual thematic range; he dramatizes many relationships of black people—family, friendship, business, the business of crime. From urban black ghettos Bullins draws characters who speak with humor, obscenity, and sophistication. Whereas Langston Hughes had to strain to capture underworld idiom in Harlem, Bullins modulates a language that ignores the black as well as the white middle-class.

As ambitious as O'Neill, Bullins has embarked on a Twentieth Century Cycle of twenty plays, to depict the lives of certain Afro-Americans between 1900 and 1999. The first five plays very loosely trace the experiences of the Dawsons—it would be inaccurate to call them a family, since the men found households, abandon them, disappear, reappear. Even incomplete, the cycle stresses the necessarily fragmentary nature of relationships of black urban males in 20th-century America. Each of the plays focuses on a complete action, free in dramatic form, often embellished with song and dance, rich in rhythmic speech and terse imagery which Bullins crafts so beautifully. Indefatigable, Bullins has also written agit-prop Dynamite Plays, in which his anti-white rage is indistinguishable from that of Amiri Baraka. Other extra-cycle plays resemble Chekhov in their evocation of a dying class, e.g., *Clara's Ole Man* and *Goin' a Buffalo*. Like Chekhov, Bullins dramatizes the foibles of his people, endearing them to us through a poignant humor.

—Ruby Cohn

BURKE, Kenneth (Duva). Born in Pittsburgh, Pennsylvania, 5 May 1897. Educated at Peabody High School, Pittsburgh; Ohio State University, Columbus, 1916–17; Columbia University, New York, 1917–18. Married 1) Lillian Mary Batterham in 1919 (divorced), three daughters; 2) Elizabeth Batterham in 1933, two sons. Lived in New York City, 1918–21, and Andover, New Jersey since 1921; co-editor, *Secession*, 1923; research worker, Laura Spelman Rockefeller Memorial, New York, 1926–27; music critic, *Dial*, New York, 1927–29, and *The Nation*, New York, 1934–35; editor, Bureau of Social Hygiene, New York, 1928–29; Lecturer, New School for Social Research, New York, 1937; University of Chicago, 1938, 1949–50; Bennington College, Vermont, 1943–61; Princeton University, New Jersey, 1949, 1975; Kenyon College, Gambier, Ohio, 1950; Indiana University, Bloomington, 1953, 1958; Drew University, Madison, New Jersey, 1962, 1964; Pennsylvania State University, University Park, 1963; Regents' Professor, University of California, Santa Barbara, 1964–65; Lecturer, Central Washington State University, Ellensburg, 1966; Harvard University, Cambridge, Massachusetts, 1967–68; Washington University, St. Louis, 1970–71; Wesleyan University, Middletown, Connecticut, 1972; University of Pittsburgh, 1972; University of Washington, Seattle, 1976; University of Nevada, Reno, 1976. Recipient: Guggenheim fellowship, 1935; American Academy grant, 1946, and Gold Medal, 1975; Princeton Institute for Advanced Studies fellowship, 1949; Stanford University Center for Advanced Study in Behavioral Sciences fellowship, 1957; Rockefeller grant, 1966; Brandeis University Creative Arts Award, 1967; National Endowment for the Arts award, 1968; New School for Social Research Horace Gregory Award, 1970; Ingram Merrill Foundation award, 1970; American Academy of Arts and Sciences award, 1977; National Medal for Literature, 1981; Bobst Award, 1983. D.Litt: Bennington College, 1966; Rutgers University, New Brunswick, New Jersey, 1968; Dartmouth College, Hanover, New Hampshire, 1969; Fairfield University, Connecticut, 1970; Northwestern University, Evanston, Illinois, 1972; University of Rochester, New York, 1972; Indiana State University, Terre Haute, 1976; Kenyon College, 1979. Member, American Academy; American Academy of Arts and Sciences; Honorary Fellow, Modern Language Association.

PUBLICATIONS

Verse

Book of Moments: Poems 1915–1954. 1955.
Collected Poems 1915–1967. 1968.

Fiction

The White Oxen and Other Stories. 1924.
Towards a Better Life, Being a Series of Epistles or Declamations. 1932; revised edition, 1966.
The Complete White Oxen: Collected Short Fiction. 1968.

Other

Counter-Statement. 1931; revised edition, 1968.
Permanence and Change: An Anatomy of Purpose. 1935; revised edition, 1954.
Attitudes Towards History. 2 vols., 1937; revised edition, 1959.
The Philosophy of Literary Form: Studies in Symbolic Action. 1941; revised edition, 1957.
A Grammar of Motives. 1945.
A Rhetoric of Motives. 1950.
The Rhetoric of Religion: Studies in Logology. 1961.
Perspectives by Incongruity (includes *Terms for Order*), edited by Stanley Edgar Hyman. 1964.
Language as Symbolic Action: Essays on Life, Literature and Method. 1966.
Dramatism and Development. 1972.
Ideas for Environment [*Reading and Writing, Science, Spelling and Phonics, Sports, American History, Americans—All, Consumer Education, Men and Women of the World, World History*], with Julie Kranhold. 10 vols., 1973–74.
William Carlos Williams (lectures), with Emily H. Wallace. 1974.

Translator, *Death in Venice*, by Thomas Mann. 1925; revised edition, 1970.
Translator, *Genius and Character*, by Emil Ludwig. 1927.
Translator, *Saint Paul*, by Emile Baumann. 1929.

*

Critical Studies: *Critical Moments: Burke's Categories and Critiques* by George Knox, 1957; *Burke and the Drama of Human Relations* by William H. Rueckert, 1963, revised edition, 1982, and *Critical Responses to Burke 1924–1966* edited by Rueckert, 1969 (includes checklist by Armin and Mechtchild Frank); *Burke* by Armin Frank, 1969; *Burke* by Merle E. Brown, 1969; *Representing Burke* edited by Hayden White and Margaret Brose, 1982.

* * *

In his poem "The Momentary, Migratory Symptom" (*Book of Moments*) Kenneth Burke as narrator makes a curious remark that happens to contain the formula for his broadly based literary criticism, which encompasses rhetorical and verbal analysis, psychology, politics, economics, philosophy, logic, theology, history, and music—to say nothing of literature itself. It also contains the formula for his general attitude toward life, now and in the hereafter. He went to see a doctor about a recurrent shooting pain, Burke confesses: "I wanted him to help me track it down/With every verb and adjective and noun." Here then are the formulaic elements in his thinking: the belief that the right words, strategically used, can solve all or most problems; the revelation of motives by means of rhetoric; the representation of symbolic action through the strategic use of words; the (potential) "dramatistic" schematization of a situation, for the purpose of clarification, whereby one of five essential elements (act, scene, agent, agency, purpose) is shown to predominate, and whose importance in relation to the other elements can be studied. Burke's skill in rhetoric analysis, his remarkably wide reading in the ancients and moderns, and his powers of association have astounded many literary scholars. Still, there is a dismaying deeply-rooted tendency in Burke to float impractical, frivolous sounding ideas and to indulge in nonsensical and occasionally tasteless wordplay.

A few examples of Burke's over-reliance on abstractions, cloud-castle theorizing, and negligible associations of meaning may be given. "War is a disease of cooperation which should be curable by means of 'creative and peaceful verbal acts' " (to paraphrase William H. Rueckert in his essay "Some of the

Many Kenneth Burkes" in *Representing Kenneth Burke*). Burke, in the essay "Literature as Equipment for Living" (*The Philosophy of Literary Form*), instead of discussing the vital, down-to-earth application of literature to human problems and needs, "throws away his line" and lapses into woolly generalizations and constructs. Using a series of proverbs and their extension into literary works, he suggests the formation of a "sociological criticism" for codifying and classifying the strategies that artists have formulated for "the naming of situations." And, in *Attitudes Towards History* Burke traces James Joyce's punning to his guilt for having rejected Catholicism and his thereby being caught in an incongruous situation. This leads Burke to the American "Knock, knock, who's where?" game of pun-making in the 1930's (whose popularity Burke sees as a reflection of national uncertainty about authority-symbols in business). Next Burke leaps to Thomas De Quincey's discussion of the guilt-symbol of the knocking at the gate in *Macbeth*; he goes from there to the Negro spiritual "Somebody's Knocking at Your Door," and finally to Poe's "The Raven," with its tapping and rapping at the chamber door.

On the other hand, though Burke has not been closely identified with any one group of critics—despite his Marxist leanings in the 1930's and 1940's—his ongoing intense concern with the complexities of language and meaning in the text has linked him with the newer and more fashionable schools of criticism. According to Hayden White, in his Preface to *Representing Kenneth Burke*, Burke had already by 1977 begun working on deconstructive criticism (wherein meaning in a text is no longer an absolute, no longer subject to a rank-order of importance), and it was obvious at that time that he had anticipated both the structuralist and post-structuralist movements before they had come into existence. This restlessly inquiring, penetrating approach (fueled by Burke's close familiarity with the history of Western philosophy and with Greek and Latin rhetorical modes) makes for very exciting reading, *when* he sticks to literature. Two examples of how well "he illuminates texts" (I am borrowing Howard Nemerov's apt expression) are the article on Mark Antony—"Antony in Behalf of the Play," and his discussion of Coleridge and "The Rime of the Ancient Mariner" (both in *The Philosophy of Literary Form*). Important as rhetorical analysis and dialectical exposition are to Burke, his intense concern with naming, renaming, and classifying critical concepts and categories must also be included among his accomplishments—although this particular concern can be quite wearying. A good, concise overview of this situation is given by Rueckert, in "Some of the Many Kenneth Burkes": one instance of Burke's seemingly gratuitous word-coinages is his shifting from "dialectics" to "logologic" and then to a more encompassing term, "logology."

Burke's poems and his overly academic and philosophical attempts at fiction (*The White Oxen* and *Towards a Better Life*) will not be dealt with here. His first non-fiction book, *Counter-Statement*, written during the 1920's, reflects Burke's interest in political forces and deals with the status of art in society—and the various ways in which art has been regarded. A long "set-piece," "Lexicon Rhetoricae," shows Burke already embarked on a naming and classifying project. His aim, in exemplifying 39 terms ("Patterns of experience," "The Symbol," " 'Priority' of forms," "Ideology," etc.), is to explain the foundations of literature's appeal, the way that writers produce their effects. *Permanence and Change*, written at the beginning of the Depression, when it seemed to Burke that there might be more than a major change to come in the "traditional ways"—in fact "a permanent collapse"—seeks an alleviation of the fear and anxiety felt by Burke and people like him. Though the book contains an intriguing section on Burke's fruitful concept of "perspective by incongruity," it unmistakably reads as though Burke were living in a private universe and spinning out happy, idealistic theories to keep his spirits up. Communication problems in society, viewed through Burke's tinted lenses, constitute the subject matter of *Permanence and Change*; Burke even posits an "Ideal New Order," following his examination of old, modified, and outworn meanings and signs.

Attitudes Towards History is another therapeutic attempt to deal with the "troubled thirties"—this time by examining the way people have felt about "life in political communities." Burke first examines the positions of "Acceptance and Rejection"; next he creates a five-act drama, "The Curve of History," which moves from the emergence of Evangelical Christianity to Collectivism; then he deals with rituals and routines; finally he generates a "Dictionary of Pivotal Terms"—"attitudinal" expressions such as "Discounting," "Efficiency," "Problem of Evil," "Rituals of Rebirth"—used to confront dilemmas at various periods in history. *The Philosophy of Literary Form*, subtitled "Studies in Symbolic Action," consists of writings also produced during the 1930's, fascinatingly written attempts to relate somehow "political programs and cultural concerns in general." Any verbal act, according to Burke, may be taken as a "symbolic action"—the *act* being "the *dancing of an attitude*" (a concept Burke adapts from I.A. Richards's original idea), in such a way as to involve the entire body, and to evoke the tenets of behavioristic psychology.

A Grammar of Motives deals at length with Burke's system of "dramatism," and is considered one of his most important contributions to literary criticism. The book also includes an extensive section on the dialectic process, as well as an appendix consisting of four articles. One of these, "Four Master Tropes," shows Burke once more renaming and classifying: metaphor, metonymy, synecdoche, and irony become, respectively, perspective, reduction, representation, and dialectic (in the narrow sense). A sequel, *A Rhetoric of Motives*, continues to reflect Burke's social concerns. By discovering rhetorical motives in unsuspected places and by developing a "philosophy of rhetoric" while emphasizing the key terms "identification" and "persuasion," he seeks to promote tolerance and contemplation, thereby (as he so fondly hopes) reducing the ill-will so widespread at the time—the end of the 1940's. *The Rhetoric of Religion* pursues the matter of rhetoric-as-persuasion into the field of religion, just far enough to deal with nomenclature: specifically, the individual's "relationship to the *word* 'God.' " For this reason, Burke explains, he has subtitled the book "Studies in Logology"; the subject matter is "words-about-words."

Despite Burke's many accomplishments the reader is tempted to raise a few questions. They have to do with matters dearest to Burke's heart: rhetoric, dialectic, symbolic action, motives. Has it never occurred to him, in all the decades he has been writing, that he has continued to describe individuals in the abstract *only as males*, just as if females who are not designated by legal names do not exist, or as if he did not want them to exist? Has he never been aware that his voluminous body of esoteric, highly specialized writings, reflecting his ongoing desire to move society "towards a better life" (to borrow the title of his anti-novel), could not possibly have the intended effect—on grounds both of practicality and probability? Few could digest his abstruse arguments, fewer still could act on them in any meaningful way. Ergo: have not his lifelong efforts at literary-political writing really been motivated by the desire to take the easy way out, while at the same time assuaging a chronically-nagging social conscience?

—Samuel Irving Bellman

BURNETT, Frances (Eliza) Hodgson. Born in Cheetham Hill, Manchester, England, 24 November 1849; emigrated with her mother to New Market, Tennessee, 1865; became citizen, 1905. Educated in schools in Manchester. Married 1) Dr. Swan Moses Burnett in 1873 (divorced, 1898), two sons; 2) Stephen Townesend in 1900 (separated, 1901; died 1914). Lived in Knoxville, 1869–74, Europe, 1875–76, and Washington, D.C., 1877–87; after 1887 traveled frequently between the U.S. and Europe. *Died 29 October 1924.*

PUBLICATIONS

Fiction

Surly Tim and Other Stories. 1877.
Theo: A Love Story. 1877.
Pretty Polly Pemberton: A Love Story. 1877.
That Lass o' Lowrie's. 1877.
Dolly: A Love Story. 1877; as *Vagabondia*, 1883.
Kathleen: A Love Story. 1878.
Miss Crespigny: A Love Story. 1878.
Earlier Stories. 1878; second series, 1878.
A Quiet Life, and The Tide on the Moaning Bar. 1878.
Our Neighbour Opposite. 1878.
Jarl's Daughter and Other Stories. 1879.
Natalie and Other Stories. 1879.
Haworth's. 1879.
Louisiana. 1880.
A Fair Barbarian. 1881.
Through One Administration. 1883.
Little Lord Fauntleroy. 1886.
A Woman's Will; or, Miss Defarge. 1887.
Sara Crewe; or, What Happened at Miss Minchin's. 1887.
Editha's Burglar. 1888.
The Fortunes of Philippa Fairfax. 1888.
The Pretty Sister of José. 1889.
Little Saint Elizabeth and Other Stories. 1890.
Children I Have Known. 1892; as *Giovanni and the Other: Children Who Have Made Stories*, 1892.
Piccino and Other Child Stories. 1894; as *The Captain's Youngest, Piccino and Other Child Stories*, 1894.
Two Little Pilgrims' Progress: A Story of the City Beautiful. 1895.
A Lady of Quality. 1896.
His Grace of Osmonde. 1897.
In Connection with the De Willoughby Claim. 1899.
The Making of a Marchioness. 1901; revised edition, 1901.
The Methods of Lady Walderhurst. 1901.
In the Closed Room. 1904.
A Little Princess, Being the Whole Story of Sara Crewe Now Told for the First Time. 1905.
Racketty-Packetty House. 1906.
The Dawn of a To-morrow. 1906.
Queen Silver-Bell. 1906; as *The Troubles of Queen Silver-Bell*, 1907.
The Cozy Lion, as Told by Queen Crosspatch. 1907.
The Shuttle. 1907.
The Spring Cleaning, as Told by Queen Crosspatch. 1908.
The Good Wolf. 1908.
Barty Crusoe and His Man Saturday. 1909.
The Land of the Blue Flower. 1909.
The Secret Garden. 1911.
My Robin. 1912.
T. Tembarom. 1913.
The Lost Prince. 1915.
The Way to the House of Santa Claus: A Christmas Story. 1916.
Little Hunchback Zia. 1916.
The White People. 1917.
The Head of the House of Coombe. 1922.
Robin. 1922.

Plays

That Lass o' Lowrie's, with Julian Magnus, from the novel by Burnett (produced 1878).
Esmeralda, with William Gillette (produced 1881; as *Young Folks' Ways*, produced 1883). 1881.
The Real Little Lord Fauntleroy, from her own novel (produced 1888).
Phyllis, from her novel *The Fortunes of Philippa Fairfax* (produced 1889).
Editha's Burglar, with Stephen Townesend, from the novel by Burnett (produced 1890; as *Nixie*, produced 1890).
The Showman's Daughter, with Stephen Townesend (produced 1891).
The First Gentleman of Europe, with Constance Fletcher (produced 1897).
A Lady of Quality, with Stephen Townesend, from the novel by Burnett (produced 1897).
A Little Princess, from her own novel *Sara Crewe* (as *A Little Unfairy Princess*, produced 1902; as *A Little Princess*, produced 1903). In *Treasury of Plays for Children*, edited by Montrose J. Moses, 1921.
The Pretty Sister of José, from her own novel (produced 1903).
That Man and I, from her novel *In Connection with the De Willoughby Claim* (produced 1903).
Dawn of a Tomorrow, from her own novel (produced 1909).
Racketty-Packetty House, from her own novel (produced 1912).

Other

The Drury Lane Boys' Club. 1892.
The One I Knew Best of All: A Memory of the Mind of a Child (autobiography). 1893.
In the Garden. 1925.

*

Critical Studies: *Mrs. Ewing, Mrs. Molesworth, and Mrs. Burnett* by Marghanita Laski, 1950; *Happily Ever After: A Portrait of Burnett* by Constance Buel Burnett, 1969; *Waiting for the Party: The Life of Burnett* by Ann Thwaite, 1974; *Burnett* by Phyllis Bixler, 1984.

* * *

When Frances Hodgson Burnett died in 1924, *The Times'* obituary writer praised her work in helping to bring about the 1911 Copyright Act but decided that it was almost solely by her "idyll of child life" *Little Lord Fauntleroy* that Burnett would be remembered. *Times* readers rushed to deny that her claims to permanence were so limited. Some of her adult novels were mentioned and, of course, *The Secret Garden*. In fact, since her death, her three major children's books, *Fauntleroy, A Little Princess*, and *The Secret Garden*, have never been out of print. *Fauntleroy* made an immediate impact on its first publication. Along with *King Solomon's Mines* and *War and Peace* it was one of the bestselling novels of 1886 in America, read by old and young alike. The descriptions of the "handsome, blooming, curly-headed little fellow" may be nauseating to today's taste but it remains an excellent story.

Its wild success changed Burnett's career. Up till this time, she had been gradually establishing herself as a serious and important novelist. In 1877 her American publisher, Scribner, wrote to her English publisher, Warne, "She is considered by good judges as the 'Coming Woman' in literature." The Boston *Transcript* wrote of her first full-length novel, *That Lass o' Lowrie's*: "We know of no more powerful work from a woman's hand in the English language, not even excepting the best of George Eliot." Both this novel and *Haworth's* were set in industrial Lancashire with a liberal use of the dialect which had fascinated her even as a young child in Manchester.

Through One Administration, her last adult novel before *Fauntleroy*, is a considerable achievement, proving that Burnett was indeed much more than the romantic middle-brow novelist her later books suggest. It was not the love between Bertha Amory and Tredennis that interested her; it was the lack of love between Bertha and Richard Amory. And the novel's picture of Washington lobbying, of machinations and intrigues, is vivid and convincing. It was at this time (in an article in the July 1883 issue of the *Century*) that Burnett was named as one of the five writers in America "who hold the front rank today in general estimation." Then came *Fauntleroy*, a great deal of money and a pattern of writing which had to keep pace with her new way of life—large houses, numerous crossings of the Atlantic, and a constant demand for her talents.

The most interesting of her later adult books are *A Woman's Will*, her autobiography, *The One I Knew the Best of All, The Shuttle*, and *The Making of a Marchioness*, In Marghanita Laski's words, the last is a "fairy story diluted with unromantic realism," and it is that realistic treatment of its period which gives it its special appeal today.

Much of the appeal of her children's story *A Little Princess* is its period charm. But its incredible coincidences do not conceal Burnett's understanding of children. Sara is real in an unreal story. *The Secret Garden* has real children in a real story. Two unhappy children are convincingly transformed, not by outside intervention but by their own determination. It is a book which made no great impact on publication, but it has steadily established itself as one of the few real classics of children's literature.

—Ann Thwaite

BURROUGHS, Edgar Rice. Born in Chicago, Illinois, 1 September 1875. Educated at the Harvard School, Chicago, 1888–91; Phillips Academy, Andover, Massachusetts, 1891–92; Michigan Military Academy, Orchard Lake, 1892–95; Served in the U.S. 7th Cavalry, 1896–97; Illinois Reserve Militia, 1918–19. Married 1) Emma Centennia Hulbert in 1900 (divorced, 1934), two sons and one daughter; 2) Florence Dearholt in 1935 (divorced, 1942). Instructor and Assistant Commandant, Michigan Military Academy, 1895–96; owner of a stationery store, Pocatello, Idaho, 1898; worked in his father's American Battery Company, Chicago, 1899–1903; joined his brother's Sweetser-Burroughs Mining Company, Idaho, 1903–04; railroad policeman, Oregon Short Line Railroad Company, Salt Lake City, 1904; manager of the Stenographic Department, Sears Roebuck and Company, Chicago, 1906–08; partner, Burroughs and Dentzer, advertising contractors, Chicago, 1908–09; office manager, Physicians Co-Operative Association, Chicago, 1909; partner, State-Burroughs Company, salesmanship firm, Chicago, 1909; worked for Champlain Yardley Company, stationers, Chicago, 1910–11; manager, System Service Bureau, Chicago, 1912–13; free-lance writer after 1913; formed Edgar Rice Burroughs, Inc., publishers, 1913, Burroughs-Tarzan Enterprises, 1934–39, and Burroughs-Tarzan Pictures, 1934–37; lived in California after 1919; Mayor of Malibu Beach, 1933; also United Press correspondent in the Pacific during World War II, and columnist ("Laugh It Off"), Honolulu *Advertiser*, 1941–42, 1945. *Died 19 March 1950.*

PUBLICATIONS

Fiction

Tarzan of the Apes. 1914.
The Return of Tarzan. 1915.
The Beasts of Tarzan. 1916.
The Son of Tarzan. 1917.
A Princess of Mars. 1917.
Tarzan and the Jewels of Opar. 1918.
The Gods of Mars. 1918.
Jungle Tales of Tarzan. 1919.
The Warlord of Mars. 1919.
Tarzan the Untamed (stories). 1920.
Thuvia, Maid of Mars. 1920.
Tarzan the Terrible. 1921.
The Mucker (stories). 1921; as *The Mucker* and *The Man Without a Soul*, 2 vols., 1921–22.
The Chessmen of Mars. 1922.
At the Earth's Core. 1922.
Tarzan and the Golden Lion. 1923.
The Girl from Hollywood. 1923.
Pellucidar. 1923.
Tarzan and the Ant Men. 1924.
The Land That Time Forgot (stories). 1924; selections, as *The Land That Time Forgot, The People That Time Forgot*, and *Out of Time's Abyss*, 3 vols., 1963.
The Bandit of Hell's Bend. 1925.
The Eternal Lover (stories). 1925; as *The Eternal Savage*, 1963.
The Cave Girl (stories). 1925.
The Mad King (stories). 1926.
The Moon Maid (stories). 1926; selection, as *The Moon Men*, 1962.
The Tarzan Twins (for children). 1927.
The Outlaw of Torn. 1927.
The War Chief. 1927.

Tarzan, Lord of the Jungle. 1928.
The Master Mind of Mars. 1928.
Tarzan and the Lost Empire. 1929.
The Monster Men. 1929.
Tarzan at the Earth's Core. 1930.
Tanar of Pellucidar. 1930.
Tarzan the Invincible. 1931.
A Fighting Man of Mars. 1931.
Tarzan Triumphant. 1932.
Jungle Girl. 1932; as *The Land of Hidden Men*, 1963.
Tarzan and the City of Gold. 1933.
Apache Devil. 1933.
Tarzan and the Lion-Man. 1934.
Pirates of Venus. 1934.
Tarzan and the Leopard Men. 1935.
Lost on Venus. 1935.
Tarzan and the Tarzan Twins, with Jad-Bal-Ja, The Golden Lion (for children). 1936.
Tarzan's Quest. 1936.
Swords of Mars. 1936.
The Oakdale Affair; The Rider. 1937.
Back to the Stone Age. 1937.
Tarzan and the Forbidden City. 1938.
The Lad and the Lion. 1938.
Tarzan the Magnificent (stories). 1939.
Carson of Venus. 1939.
The Deputy Sheriff of Comanche County. 1940.
Synthetic Men of Mars. 1940.
Land of Terror. 1944.
Escape on Venus. 1946.
Tarzan and the Foreign Legion. 1947.
Llana of Gathol (stories). 1948.
Beyond Thirty. 1955; as *The Lost Continent*, 1963.
The Man-Eater (story). 1955.
Savage Pellucidar (stories). 1963.
Escape on Venus (stories). 1964.
Tales of Three Planets. 1964.
John Carter of Mars (stories). 1964.
Beyond the Farthest Star. 1964.
Tarzan and the Castaways (stories). 1964.
Tarzan and the Madman. 1964.
The Girl from Farris's. 1965.
The Efficiency Expert. 1966.
I Am a Barbarian. 1967.
Pirate Blood. 1970.
The Wizard of Venus. 1970.

Other

Official Guide of the Tarzan Clans of America. 1939.

*

Critical Studies: *Edgar Rice Burroughs, Master of Adventure*, 1965, revised edition, 1968, and *Barsoom: Burroughs and the Martian Vision*, 1976, both by Richard A. Lupoff; *Tarzan Alive: A Definitive Biography of Lord Greystoke* by Philip José Farmer, 1972; *Burroughs' Science Fiction* by Robert R. Kudlay and Joan Leiby, 1973; *Burroughs, The Man Who Created Tarzan* (includes bibliography) by Irwin Porges, 1975; *Guide to Barsoom* by John Flint Roy, 1976; *The Burroughs Bestiary: An Encyclopaedia of Monsters and Imaginary Beings Created by Burroughs* by David Day, 1978; *Tarzan and Tradition: Classical Myth in Popular Literature* by Erling B. Holtsmark, 1981.

* * *

When he was almost 36 years old, with a wife and three children, disappointed in his military and various business careers, Edgar Rice Burroughs decided to try writing fiction. His first sale, later printed in hardcovers as *A Princess of Mars*, was serialized in *All-Story Magazine* in 1912. The first of a series still immensely popular, the novel illustrates most of the strengths and weaknesses of Burroughs's works. Fast-paced, colorful, and strikingly imaginative, it stimulates the sense of wonder, especially of children and adolescents. But the characters are one-dimensional, either evil or good, and coincidences abound. Though Burroughs presents the "Barsoomian" cultures vividly, he does not develop them in depth. The historical novel *The Outlaw of Torn* and his "realistic" stories, notably those of crime and corruption in Chicago and Hollywood, illustrated his failure to be convincing at anything other than fantasy. He dealt much more effectively with the never-never lands of Mars, darkest Africa, the earth's center—worlds that neither he nor his readers knew much about.

Burroughs is best known as the creator of Tarzan, son of an English peer, Lord Greystoke, raised from the age of one in the African jungle by language-using great apes. Critics have maintained that Burroughs wrote *Tarzan of the Apes* to demonstrate his belief in the superiority of heredity over environment, and especially of the superior heredity of the British upper classes. In one sense they are correct. Tarzan's human genes gave him an intelligence superior to the apes'; they gave him an innate curiosity and drive which would have taken him out of any lowly station into which he had been born. But in the end it is the environment that molds Tarzan's character. Raised as a feral child, he is a classic example of the outsider, one who has an objective view of human society because he has not imbibed its irrationalities along with his mother's milk. Through Tarzan's eyes Burroughs satirizes Homo sapiens, as he did through some of his other heroes, notably Carson Napier of the "Venus" series.

However, Burroughs's ape-man is neither a Voltairean observer nor a noble savage. He regards pre-literates as superior in their way of life to civilized peoples, and he himself is never quite human. He is, when in the jungle, free of the mundane, drab, wearing, and often tragic restrictions of civilized, social life. Tarzan's being a law unto himself and his closeness to nature are part of his appeal. But Burroughs, though unconsciously, also gave him most of the attributes of the pre-literate and classical hero of fairy tale, legend, and mythology, including the Trickster. Tarzan is the last of the Golden Age heroes, a literary character who reflects the archetypal images and feelings of the unconscious mind noted by Carl Jung and Joseph Campbell.

Like Arthur Conan Doyle, Burroughs had the gift of writing adventure stories with an indefinable quality that made them endure while thousands of similar works dropped into oblivion. Like Doyle he created a classical fictional character of whom he wearied. The later Tarzan novels, in fact all of his works written in the latter part of his career, show a flagging invention, repetitiveness of plot and incident, excess of coincidences and improbabilities, and failure to develop promising themes.

Burroughs never thought of himself as anything but a commercial writer of romances. His works betray the bias, conservatism, and timidity of his social class and time, and his style is old-fashioned. With the exception of Tarzan and a few others, his characters are cardboard. His genius was in the creation of an archetypal feral man and the writing of many pseudoscientific romances which have enthralled generations of young—and not so young—readers.

—Philip José Farmer

BURROUGHS, William S(eward). Born in St. Louis, Missouri, 5 February 1914. Educated at John Burroughs School and Taylor School, St. Louis; Los Alamos Ranch School, New Mexico; Harvard University, Cambridge, Massachusetts, A.B. in anthropology 1936; studied medicine at the University of Vienna; Mexico City College, 1948–50. Served in the U.S. Army, 1942. Married Jean Vollmer in 1945 (died, 1951); one son (deceased). Worked as a journalist, private detective, and bartender; then full-time writer; heroin addict, 1944–59. Recipient: American Academy award, 1975. Member, American Academy, 1983. Lived for many years in Tangier; now lives in New York City.

PUBLICATIONS

Fiction

Junkie: Confessions of an Unredeemed Drug Addict. 1953; complete edition, 1977; as *Junky*, 1986.
The Naked Lunch. 1959; as *Naked Lunch*, 1962.
The Soft Machine. 1961.
The Ticket That Exploded. 1962; revised edition, 1967.
Dead Fingers Talk. 1963.
Nova Express. 1964.
The Wild Boys: A Book of the Dead. 1971; revised edition, 1979.
Exterminator! (stories). 1973.
Short Novels. 1978.
Blade Runner: A Movie. 1979.
Port of Saints. 1980.
Cities of the Red Night: A Boy's Book. 1981.
Early Routines (stories). 1981.
The Streets of Chance (stories). 1981.
The Place of Dead Roads. 1983.
Ruski (story). 1984.
Queer. 1985.

Play

The Last Words of Dutch Schultz. 1970.

Other

The Exterminator, with Brion Gysin. 1960.
Minutes to Go, with others. 1960.
The Yage Letters, with Allen Ginsberg. 1963.
Roosevelt after Inauguration. 1964.
Valentine Day's Reading. 1965.
Time. 1965.
Health Bulletin: APO-33: A Metabolic Regulator. 1965; revised edition, as *APO-33 Bulletin*, 1966.
So Who Owns Death TV?, with Claude Pelieu and Carl Weissner. 1967.
The Dead Star. 1969.
Ali's Smile. 1969.
Entretiens avec Burroughs, by Daniel Odier. 1969; translated as *The Job: Interviews with Burroughs* (includes *Electronic Revolution*), 1970.
The Braille Film. 1970.
Brion Gysin Let the Mice In, with Brion Gysin and Ian Somerville, edited by Jan Herman. 1973.
Mayfair Academy Series More or Less. 1973.
White Subway, edited by James Pennington. 1974.
The Book of Breeething. 1974; revised edition 1980.
Snack: Two Tape Transcripts, with Eric Mottram. 1975.
Sidetripping, with Charles Gatewood. 1975.
The Retreat Diaries, with *The Dream of Tibet*, by Allen Ginsberg. 1976.
Cobble Stone Gardens. 1976.
The Third Mind, with Brion Gysin. 1978.
Roosevelt after Inauguration and Other Atrocities. 1979.
Ah Pook Is Here and Other Texts (includes *The Book of Breeething, Electronic Revolution*). 1979.
A Burroughs Reader, edited by John Calder. 1982.
Letters to Allen Ginsberg 1953–1957. 1982.
Sinki's Sauna. 1982.
New York Inside Out, photographs by Robert Walker. 1984.
The Burroughs File. 1984.
The Adding Machine: Collected Essays. 1985.

*

Bibliography: *Burroughs: An Annotated Bibliography of His Works and Criticism* by Michael B. Goodman, 1976; *Burroughs: A Bibliography 1953–73* by Joe Maynard and Barry Miles, 1978.

Critical Studies: *Burroughs: The Algebra of Need* by Eric Mottram, 1971; *Contemporary Literary Censorship: The Case History of Burroughs' Naked Lunch* by Michael B. Goodman, 1981; *With Burroughs: A Report from the Bunker* edited by Victor Bokris, 1981; "Burroughs Issue" of *Review of Contemporary Fiction*, vol. 4, no. 1, 1984; *Burroughs* by Jennie Skerl, 1985.

* * *

There are two fields of experience central to the life and work of William S. Burroughs. They mark points at which criticism of his work must begin, and around which controversy has swirled. Scion of the Burroughs Adding Machine family, he travelled for much of adult life (only recently settling in New York), during which he became addicted to heroin in 1944, remaining so across three continents and fourteen years. His addiction and cure (the last and presumably final in 1957) have provided the controlling metaphor for an *oeuvre* of cosmic dimensions.

The second area of concern is, like Burroughs's opiate addiction, an extended series of drug experiences. In 1953, he journeyed to the Peruvian Amazon expressly for the purpose of taking *yage*, a mescaline-like natural hallucinogen used sacramentally by the Indians of the region. These and subsequent psychedelic experiences provided not only primary materials for *Naked Lunch, The Soft Machine*, and *The Ticket That Exploded*, but served to expand and intensify his vision beyond the relative solipsism of "junk."

For Burroughs's most fervent admirers he has become a cult figure: an international underworld traveller, a gifted teacher, a universal personage reborn, at least partially, from innumerable deaths, returned to speak and write of his experiences. For this group, his life is an example and his writing is a report, a formal statement of an entire life-style. He is a beatific figure, the madman-saint, like de Sade, Artaud, Céline and his contemporary Genet. His life is a message, as Alan Ansen writes unabashedly: "In the case of Burroughs, the writing is only a by-product, however brilliant, of a force. What I am writing is not only a paean to a writer; it is also a variant of hagiography." His detractors are equally enthusiastic: George Garrett speaks for John Wain, George Steiner, Anaïs Nin, and others when he complains: "Do we have to become connoisseurs of vomit? Is the world doing so badly a job at tearing itself apart that it needs the aid of gifted writers to finish it off?"

The indelible image of the heroin addict is presented in Burroughs's first work, *Junkie*— the addict slumped nodding in his chair or out on the street, waiting, making his ruins public. The rhetoric of this small book has the economy and force of needle and spoon, and its initial sociological value is as reportage, in the lucid pictures of the addict world. But more, in the linking of the heroin addict with the metaphysical condition of the "enslaved" condition of modern man, it establishes the single radical image from which Burroughs's "new mythology for the space age" develops.

Naked Lunch is Burroughs's most famous work. Admitted for publication to the United States after several famous obscenity trials, "composed" with aid from his friends Allen Ginsberg and Jack Kerouac, the novel is a series of fantastic episodes arranged in collage form, the whole being held together by a mantic and comic narrative voice that turns matters inevitably to the theme of human control. *Naked Lunch* becomes increasingly disjointed and surrealistic in technique, and it displays the misogynist-homosexual concerns and the satiric comic vision that have become Burroughs's signatures.

Subsequent longer works, especially *The Soft Machine* and *The Ticket That Exploded*, have ranged from anthropological pre-history to the uncertain future of dystopian science fiction, but share a predilection for radical linguistic and textual experiment: the "cut-up," the "fold in," and similar dislocations. As revealed in *The Job* (interviews with Daniel Odier), Burroughs's recent interests have been less in fiction than in the possibilities for human growth—evidenced especially in his fascination with out-of-body experience and psychobiology. *Exterminator!* and *The Wild Boys* are more accessible than much of his previous work, but no less unsettling. John Tytell, for one, suggests that *The Wild Boys* is Burroughs's best work since *Naked Lunch*.

The piercing of flesh by the needle, the body by the phallus, the rending of language and—finally—the physical cosmos itself, these are transformations. William Burroughs's endless, cranky linguistic experiments—with cut-ups, fold-ins, the shattering of images, sentences and words, with nightclub routines and carnival "drums" and surreal war and sex fantasies—flawed and confusing as they can be, I see as an attempt to use The Word itself to negate its own power, to lay bare the multiple prisons of corporeal existence, the passage of time, the deceits of language, the illusions of individual consciousness, the endless charades of mass social and political existence.

—Jack Hicks

See the essay on *Naked Lunch*.

BYRD, William, II. Born in Westover, Virginia, 28 March 1674. Educated at Felsted Grammar School, Essex, England; trained in business, London, 1690–91; studied at Middle Temple, London, 1692–95; called to the bar, 1695. Married Lucy Parke in 1706 (died, 1716), two daughters and two sons; 2) Maria Taylor in 1724, three daughters and one son. Returned to Virginia, 1696; elected to House of Burgesses, Williamsburg, for Henrico County, 1696; represented Virginia Assembly in London, 1697, and colonial agent, 1698–1705; returned to Virginia and appointed Receiver-General, 1705; member, Virginia Council, 1709–44: represented Council against Lieutenant-Governor Spotswood in London, 1715–19, and as agent, 1721–26; President of Council, 1743. Commissioner in boundary dispute between Virginia and North Carolina, 1728, and crown representative in survey of Northern Neck of Virginia, 1735-36; re-built his estate at Westover, 1730–31. Member, Royal Society (London), 1696. *Died 26 August 1744.*

PUBLICATIONS

Collections

Prose Works, edited by Louis B. Wright. 1966.
The Correspondence of the Three William Byrds of Westover, Virginia 1684–1776, edited by Marion Tinling. 2 vols., 1977.

Prose

A Discourse Concerning the Plague, With Some Preservations Against It (possibly not by Byrd). 1721.
Description of the Dismal Swamp and a Proposal to Drain the Swamp, edited by Earl Gregg Swem. 1922.
A Journey to the Land of Eden and Other Papers, edited by Mark Van Doren. 1928.
Histories of the Dividing Line Betwixt Virginia and North Carolina, edited by William K. Boyd. 1929.
Natural History of Virginia; or, The Newly Discovered Eden (probably not by Byrd), edited and translated (from 1737 German version) by Richmond Croom Beatty and William J. Mulloy. 1940.
The Secret Diary 1709–1712, edited by Louis B. Wright and Marion Tinling. 1941; selection, as *The Great American Gentleman: Byrd of Westover in Virginia*, 1963.
Another Secret Diary 1739–1741, edited by Maude H. Woodfin and Marion Tinling. 1942.
The London Diary 1717–1721, and Other Writings, edited by Louis B. Wright and Marion Tinling. 1958.

*

Bibliography: *John and William Bartram, William Byrd II and St. John de Crèvecour: A Reference Guide* by Rose Marie Cutting, 1976.

Critical Studies: *Byrd of Westover* by Richmond Croom Beatty, 1932; *The Byrds of Virginia* by Alden Hatch, 1969; *Byrd of Westover 1674–1744* by Pierre Marambaud, 1971.

* * *

The reputation of William Byrd II of Westover has grown steadily in importance among scholars and historians of American culture during the last few decades. Critics have labelled him a belated Restoration cavalier and satirist, a Queen Anne wit, a pamphleteer, a promoter, an American Pepys, a travel writer, a naturalist, and a historian. He was all of these things, but he was also a model for what would become the southern gentleman-planter and a founder of the southern school of letters.

Some have questioned Byrd's position as a writer since he published so little. It is true that his only published works during his lifetime were a scientific paper in the *Philosophical Transactions* of the Royal Society in 1698, the anonymous pamphlet *A Discourse Concerning the Plague* in 1721, and a few poems attributed to him, but he was writing constantly. He produced almost without fail daily entries in his diary and wrote four complete travel narratives, love poetry and occasional verse, character sketches, satiric essays, translations, literary exercises, and a large body of correspondence—business, family, and love letters. Writing was an integral part of his life, and he expressed himself with all the rhetorical skills of the published writer.

Byrd clearly had some theories of composition and understood the importance of style and audience. Many of his ideas might have been absorbed from his contemporaries and colleagues in England—William Congreve, Nicholas Rowe, John Oldmixon, and William Wycherley were among his friends—and he frequently attended the theatre at Drury Lane and Lincoln's Inn when in residence. We know that Byrd prepared a second version of his *History of the Dividing Line* specifically for publication, although he never submitted it to the printer. A comparison of both versions shows that he was aware of audience—the first was witty and satirical of things Virginians would understand, and the second is more serious and directed to a British audience with a distinct promotional slant. The manuscripts of his narratives *A Progress to the Mines in the Year 1732* and *A Journey to the Land of Eden Anno 1773* were copied out apparently with publication in mind, and there exist fair-hand copies of other pieces which seem to have been intended for the printer. Most of his writings, however, were known only to the friends among whom they circulated.

The diaries, the least literary of Byrd's manuscripts, were not written with the assumption that anyone would read them, thus his use of a cryptic shorthand. We need not exclude the possibility, however, that he entertained the notion of writing an autobiography some day for which the entries would provide an outline. There is, in any case, little of the refined wit and bawdy humor one finds in Byrd's public writings, but once the reader adjusts to the routine of the daily formula for entries, little nuggets of insight and activity appear which flesh out Byrd's life and personality. We observe the skills necessary for the management of a large estate; the political duties of a prominent Virginia aristocrat; Byrd's pursuit of learning and literature as a scholar and author; his reading habits; his private dreams and superstitions; his religious beliefs; his interest in other women besides his wife; his drinking, gambling, horse-play, and lewd language; his bowel movements and practice of masturbation; and the quality of his domestic life, including his wife's moods, their marital arguments, and even where they had sex ("In the afternoon my wife and I had a little quarrel which I reconciled with a flourish. Then she read a sermon in Dr. Tillotson to me. It is to be observed that the flourish was performed on the billiard table."—30 July 1710). In short, Byrd emerges from these pages a broad-minded, engaging, and warmly human individual.

Throughout Byrd's writings, both public and private, satire and irony remained central to his perspective and style. "Satire is much the easier work of the understanding," he once noted, "because Nature is always at hand to assist us, when we attempt to sink the character of our neighbor below our own. . . ." This implies his theory of humor—that comedy depends on viewing others as inferior to one's self. His comic sense is nowhere more evident than in the *History of the Dividing Line*, where he chronicles the habits and peculiarities of the inhabitants of North Carolina, which he calls condescendingly "Lubberland." In such passages lies the genesis of a mainstream of southern humor populated by a series of opportunists and disreputable poor white trash, such as Sut Lovingood, Simon Suggs, Flem Snopes, and Snuffy Smith.

Much of the myth and idea of the American south originated with Byrd in the colonial period. Long before the Revolution and the formal organization of several of the states into a southern political bloc, as a writer and a man Byrd anticipated many of the characteristics of what would become known as southern culture. Because of the wide range of his work in style, sophistication, and subject matter, Byrd may also be entitled to recognition as the south's first man of letters.

—M. Thomas Inge

CABELL, James Branch. Born in Richmond, Virginia, 14 April 1879. Educated at the College of William and Mary, Williamsburg, Virginia, 1894–98, A.B. 1898. Married 1) Priscilla Bradley Shepherd in 1913 (died, 1949), one son; 2) Margaret Waller Freeman in 1950. Instructor in Greek and French at the College of William and Mary while an undergraduate, 1896–97; staff member, Richmond *Times*, 1898, New York *Herald*, 1899–1901, and Richmond *News*, 1901; engaged in genealogical research in America and Europe, 1901–11; office worker at coal mine in West Virginia, 1911–13; genealogist, Virginia Society of Colonial Wars, 1916–28, and Virginia Sons of the American Revolution, 1917–24; editor, Virginia War History Commission, 1919–26; silent editor, *Reviewer*, Richmond, 1921; an editor, *American Spectator*, 1932–35. President, Virginia Writers Association, 1918–21. Member American Academy. *Died 5 May 1958.*

PUBLICATIONS

Collections

The Letters, edited by Edward Wagenknecht. 1975.

Fiction

The Eagle's Shadow. 1904; revised edition, 1923.
The Line of Love (stories). 1905; revised edition, 1921.
Gallantry (stories). 1907; revised edition, 1922.
Chivalry (stories). 1909; revised edition, 1921.
The Cords of Vanity. 1909; revised edition, 1920.
The Soul of Melicent. 1913; revised edition, as *Domnei*, 1920.
The Rivet in Grandfather's Neck. 1915.
The Certain Hour (stories). 1916.
The Cream of the Jest. 1917; revised edition, 1923.
Beyond Life. 1919.
Jurgen. 1919.
Figures of Earth. 1921.
The High Place. 1923.
The Silver Stallion. 1926.
The Music from Behind the Moon (stories). 1926.

Something about Eve. 1927.
The Works (Storisende Edition; includes "The Biography of the Life of Manuel": revised editions of earlier works, plus new material). 18 vols., 1927–30.
The White Robe (stories). 1928.
The Way of Ecben. 1929.
Smirt: An Urbane Nightmare. 1934.
Smith: A Sylvan Interlude. 1935.
Smire: An Acceptance in the Third Person. 1937.
The King Was in His Counting House. 1938.
Hamlet Had an Uncle. 1940.
The First Gentleman of America. 1942; as *The First American Gentleman*, 1942.
There Were Two Pirates. 1946.
The Witch-Woman (includes revised editions of *The Music from Behind the Moon, The Way of Ecben, The White Robe*). 1948.
The Devil's Own Dear Son. 1949.

Play

The Jewel Merchants. 1921.

Verse

From the Hidden Way. 1916; revised edition, 1924.
Ballades from the Hidden Way. 1928.
Sonnets from Antan. 1929.

Other

Branchiana (genealogy). 1907.
Branch of Abingdon. 1911.
The Majors and Their Marriages. 1915.
The Judging of Jurgen. 1920.
Jurgen and the Censor. 1920.
Taboo: A Legend Retold from the Dirghic of Saevius Nicanor. 1921.
Joseph Hergesheimer. 1921.
The Lineage of Lichfield: An Essay in Eugenics. 1922.
Straws and Prayer-Books. 1924.
Some of Us: An Essay in Epitaphs. 1930.
Townsend of Lichfield. 1930.
Between Dawn and Sunrise: Selections, edited by John Macy. 1930.
These Restless Heads: A Trilogy of Romantics. 1932.
Special Delivery: A Packet of Replies. 1933.
Ladies and Gentlemen: A Parcel of Reconsiderations. 1934.
Preface to the Past. 1936.
The Nightmare Has Triplets: An Author's Note on Smire. 1937.
On Ellen Glasgow. 1938.
The St. Johns: A Parade of Diversities with A.J. Hanna. 1943.
Let Me Lie. 1947.
Quiet, Please. 1952.
As I Remember It: Some Epilogues in Recollection. 1955.
Between Friends: Letters of Cabell and Others, edited by Padraic Colum and Margaret Freeman Cabell. 1962.

*

Bibliography: *Cabell: A Complete Bibliography* by James N. Hall, 1974; *Cabell: A Reference Guide* by Maurice Duke, 1979.

Critical Studies: *No Place on Earth: Ellen Glasgow, Cabell, and Richmond-in-Virginia* by Louis D. Rubin, Jr., 1959; *Cabell* by Joe Lee Davis, 1962; *Jesting Moses: A Study in Cabellian Comedy* by Arvin R. Wells, 1962; *Cabell: The Dream and the Reality* by Desmond Tarrant, 1967; *Cabell: Three Essays* by Carl Van Doren, H.L. Mencken, and Hugh Walpole, 1967; *Cabell under Fire: Four Essays* by Geoffrey Morley-Mower, 1975; *Cabell: The Richmond Iconoclast* by Dorothy B. Schlegel, 1975; *In Quest of Cabell: Five Exploratory Essays* by William Leigh Godshalk, 1976; *Cabell: Centennial Essays* edited by M. Thomas Inge and Edgar E. MacDonald, 1983.

* * *

Regarded as belonging in the top echelon of American writers throughout the 1920's, James Branch Cabell has never regained the prestige he then knew. But even during the decade of his greatest fame, Cabell was outside the mainstream. While his contemporaries found increasing fascination with life in their period and used the standard of critical realism to treat the immediate, Cabell's preference was for romance and myth. He defined his preference brilliantly in *Beyond Life* and reiterated it in essays and romances throughout his long career. He avowed "The auctorial virtues of distinction and clarity, of beauty and symmetry, of tenderness and truth and urbanity."

Cabell's tastes, like his ancestry, were aristocratic and mannered. The elegant prose style he perfected was appropriate to his Virginia roots and his subject matter. It is ironic that so cultivated a writer with a specialized appeal became so popular. One important reason was that Cabell was almost the only sign of hope H.L. Mencken could find that the culture of the post-Civil War South was not to be damned totally, and Mencken made very loud noises about Cabell's work. More important was *Jurgen*, the tale of a medieval pawnbroker in Cabell's mythical kingdom of Poictesme. Jurgen was ever willing to do the gentlemanly thing, and word got around that Cabell's book was lascivious. It was suppressed in 1920, but Cabell's cause rallied the foes of censorship, ensuring booming sales. The novel, which certainly has it Rabelaisian touches, was exonerated in court in 1922.

Jurgen is a part of Cabell's most ambitious and most important work, the eighteen-volume "Biography of the Life of Manuel." Dom Manuel is the founder of Poictesme, and his followers and offspring (legitimate and otherwise) inherit his legend and face the same tensions between the dream (the dynamic illusion) and the frustrating reality of everyday life. The most brilliant of the Romances besides *Jurgen* are *Figures of Earth, The Silver Stallion, The High Place*, and *Something about Eve*. Cabell revised his earlier Romances of Virginia as later volumes of the Biography because they, too, were illustrative of the attitudes of Chivalry, Gallantry, and Poetry treated in the more famous books. Virginia and Poictesme have much in common.

After the completion of the Biography, Cabell published for a time under the name Branch Cabell, to symbolize the completion of his grand design and perhaps in recognition of the end of the era of his greatest fame. During the years of the Depression and World War II, Cabell tenaciously followed his own ideals and eschewed the contemporary. A trilogy of high satire (*Smirt, Smith, Smire*) treated the dream life of the writer, mirroring the dream experience more fully than anything Cabell had written previously. Another trilogy dealt with murder, conquest, and intrigue in Hamlet's Denmark, the family circle of Cosimo dei Medici, and the Virginia of Nemattanon, an Indian prince during the time of the Spanish conquests. A final trilogy explored Florida's legendary past.

Cabell then focused attention on his own life with several volumes of reminiscences and assessments of his career and those of many of his contemporaries. He viewed his progress with humor and detachment. His professed goal was to write beautifully of beautiful happenings. Although he can certainly sting his readers with a sense of reality, it seems clear that writing gave him great joy. He wrote mainly for himself, he tells us, but he did so with such humor and insight that he insures himself a loyal group of enthusiasts.

—Joseph M. Flora

CABLE, George Washington. Born in New Orleans, Louisiana, 12 October 1844. Educated at New Orleans public schools until 1859. Served in the 4th Mississippi Cavalry during the Civil War, 1863–65. Married 1) Louisa Stewart Bartlett in 1869 (died, 1904), six children; 2) Eva C. Stevenson in 1906 (died, 1923); 3) Hanna Cowing in 1923. State surveyor in Louisiana, 1865–66; incapacitated by malaria, 1866–68; reporter and columnist ("Drop Shot") New Orleans *Picayune*, 1870; accountant and correspondence clerk, A.C. Black and Company, cotton factors, New Orleans, 1869–79; accountant with cotton exchange, 1879–81; full-time writer from 1881; after 1884 made yearly tours of the U.S. reading his own works; lived in Northampton, Massachusetts, from 1885; organized the Home-Culture Club, Northampton, 1886 (renamed Northampton People's Institute, 1909); published the journals *Letter*, 1892–96, and *Symposium*, 1896. A.M.: Yale University, New Haven, Connecticut, 1883; D.Litt.: Washington and Lee University, Lexington, Virginia, 1882; Yale University, 1901; Bowdoin College, Brunswick, Maine, 1904. Member, American Academy. *Died 31 January 1925.*

PUBLICATIONS

Collections

Creoles and Cajuns: Stories of Old Louisiana, edited by Arlin Turner. 1959.

Fiction

Old Creole Days (stories). 1879.
The Grandissimes: A Story of Creole Life. 1880.
Madame Delphine. 1881.
Dr. Sevier. 1884.
Madame Delphine, Carancro, Grande Pointe. 1887.
Bonaventure: A Prose Pastoral of Acadian Louisiana. 1888.
Strange True Stories of Louisiana. 1889.
John March, Southerner. 1894.
Strong Hearts. 1899.
The Cavalier. 1901.
Père Raphaël. 1901.
Bylow Hill. 1902.
Kincaid's Battery. 1908.
"Posson Jone'" and Père Raphaël. 1909.
Gideon's Band: A Tale of the Mississippi. 1914.
The Amateur Garden. 1914.
The Flower of the Chapdelaines. 1918.
Lovers of Louisiana (Today). 1918.

Other

The Creoles of Louisiana. 1884.
The Silent South. 1885; revised edition, 1889.
The Negro Question. 1890.
A Busy Man's Bible. 1891.
A Memory of Roswell Smith. 1892.
A Southerner Looks at Negro Discrimination: Selected Writings, edited by Isabel Cable Manes. 1946.
Twins of Genius: Letters of Mark Twain, Cable, and Others, edited by Guy A. Cardwell. 1953.
The Negro Question: A Selection of Writings on Civil Rights in the South, edited by Arlin Turner. 1958.
Mark Twain and Cable: The Record of a Literary Friendship, edited by Arlin Turner. 1960.

*

Bibliography: *Cable: An Annotated Bibliography* by William H. Roberson, 1982.

Critical Studies: *Cable: His Life and Letters* by Lucy Leffingwell Cable Biklé, 1928; *Cable: A Study of His Early Life and Work* by Kjell Ekström, 1950; *Cable: A Biography* by Arlin Turner, 1956, and *Critical Essays on Cable* edited by Turner, 1980; *Cable: The Northampton Years*, 1959, and *Cable*, 1962, both by Philip Butcher; *Cable: The Life and Times of a Southern Heretic* by Louis D. Rubin, Jr., 1969; *The Grandissimes: Centennial Essays* edited by Thomas J. Richardson, 1981.

* * *

George Washington Cable was one of the first progressive writers of the "New South." His father's German background and his mother's New England protestantism contributed to his own sense of isolation in a community whose leaders were primarily French and Catholic. Cable's position as an outsider may have stimulated his interest in sociological problems and made him more sensitive to the needs of minorities, especially southern blacks. His father's untimely death and the Civil War prevented him from completing his formal education, but he was always an avid reader and enjoyed writing. In his late twenties he took a part-time job on the New Orleans *Picayune*, where his "Drop Shot" column, though occasionally controversial, was well received. At this time Cable began writing a series of short stories and was discovered by Scribner's Edward King, who was touring Louisiana in search of materials for his "Great South" series. Although Scribner's rejected "Bibi," Cable's story of a tormented slave-prince, on the grounds of its unpleasant subject matter, they published his character sketch of an old Creole, "'Sieur George," in 1873. Richard Watson Gilder, editor of *Scribner's Monthly* and the *Century*, considered Cable one of his leading local colorists, who would contribute to Gilder's plan for reconciling the North and South through literature. H.H. Boyesen also took an interest in Cable's writing and initiated a correspondence helpful to the latter's career.

In 1879 Cable's *Old Creole Days*, a collection of short stories, was published, and the first installments of *The Grandissimes*, which incorporated the "Bibi" materials, appeared in

Scribner's Monthly. In 1880 *The Grandissimes* was published in book form, as was *Madame Delphine*, a novella. These two books represent Cable's highest achievement, anticipating the complex drama of Faulkner's works. Each deals with racial injustice, the continuing problems caused by exploitation of the black community, and the Creoles' resistance to social change. He described the lush, exotic world of the deep South unknown to most Americans. Topics considered off limits to the genteel authors of the Tidewater region or the wholesome humorists of the Piedmont are insightfully probed: miscegenation, the cruelties of the *Code Noire*, and the arrogance and indolence of the aristocracy.

By 1882 Cable began a full-time career as a writer, completing *Dr. Sevier*, a serious novel dealing with prison reform, which was followed by a *Century* exposé, "The Convict Lease System in the Southern States," and a history, *The Creoles of Louisiana*. These three works, openly polemical, offended Gilder and caused tremendous resentment throughout the South. A reading tour with Mark Twain brought Cable some additional income and popularity, but his increasingly fervent publications on the Negro's dilemma, especially "A Freedman's Case in Equity" and *The Silent South*, made him notorious in New Orleans, and he eventually settled in Northampton, Massachusetts.

There Cable organized the Home-Culture clubs, racially integrated reading groups designed to raise the educational level of average citizens. The success of the movement was due in part to the national atmosphere of self-improvement and upward mobility in the last quarter of the 19th century.

When Cable was fifty he published *John March, Southerner*, an ambiguous portrait of a Southern aristocrat during the reconstruction era. As in his earlier fiction he examined outmoded conceptions of chivalry and honor, racial injustice, and anachronistic social and political attitudes. This was his last attempt at social satire. He continued to be an outspoken essayist, but his fiction became unashamedly romantic. The public taste of the period and his editors reinforced his tendency toward sentimentalism. *The Cavalier* was Cable's greatest popular success. He even overcame his Calvinistic distrust of the stage and authorized a dramatic version of the novel, starring Julia Marlowe. Energetic until the end, he wrote three novels in his seventies and shaped an optimistic vision of technological progress in the New South and the eventual integration of the races.

Perhaps because he remained too dependent on the family magazine audience and the taste of his editors, Cable did not live up to his early potential as a major southern writer. Nevertheless, in his best fiction he transcended the limitations of the local color genre and revealed a daring and prophetic intelligence.

—Kimball King

CAHAN, Abraham. Born in Podberezy, near Vilna, Lithuania, 7 July 1860; emigrated to the U.S. in 1882; later became citizen. Educated at the Vilna Teachers Institute, 1877–81; later attended law school in New York. Married Anna Bronstein in 1887. Settled in New York: worked in a cigar factory, and as tutor and free-lance writer, from 1882; co-editor, *Neie Tseit* (New Era) Yiddish socialist paper, 1886; editor, *Arbeiter Zeitung*, 1891–94, and *Die Zukunft*, 1893–94; reporter, *Commercial Advertiser*, New York, 1897–1901; helped found, 1897, and editor, 1902 and 1903–51, *Vorwärts* (*Jewish Daily Forward*) Yiddish newspaper, New York. *Died 31 August 1951*.

PUBLICATIONS

Fiction

Yekl: A Tale of New York Ghetto. 1896.
The Imported Bridegroom and Other Stories of the New York Ghetto. 1898.
The White Terror and the Red: A Novel of Revolutionary Russia. 1905.
Rafael Naarizokh (story). 1907.
Neshoma Yesorah; Fanny's Khasonim (Fanny's Suitors; novellas). 1913(?).
The Rise of David Levinsky. 1917.
Yekl and the Imported Bridegroom and Other Stories of the New York Ghetto. 1970.

Other

Social Remedies. 1889.
Historia fun di Fareingte Shtaaten (History of the United States). 2 vols., 1910–12.
Bleter fun Mein Leben. 5 vols., 1926–31; vols. 1 and 2 as *The Education of Cahan*, 2 vols., 1969.
Palestina. 1934.
Rashel: A Biografia. 1938.
Grandma Never Lived in America: The New Journalism of Cahan, edited by Moses Rischin. 1986.

Editor, *Hear the Other Side: A Symposium of Democratic Socialist Opinion*. 1934.

*

Bibliography: *Cahan: A Bibliography* by Ephim H. Joshurin, 1941; by Sanford E. Marovitz and Lewis Fried, in *American Literary Realism 1870–1910*, no. 3, 1970.

Critical Study: *From the Ghetto: The Fiction of Cahan* by Jules Chametzky, 1977.

* * *

Abraham Cahan is perhaps more notable for his leadership in Yiddish-speaking community of the Lower East Side than he is for any of his English prose. For more than forty years he was the editor of the popular Yiddish newspaper the *Jewish Daily Forward*. As such he guided the immigrant Jewish populace in their Americanization. His editorials, his Yiddish fiction, and his work as a union organizer all bespoke his socialist goals and didactic prejudices.

It was not until 1895 that he published his first short story in English. However, at least as early as the 1880's he was contributing non-fiction prose to the New York *World* and the New York *Sun and Press*. In these pieces Cahan introduced the East Side ghetto to non-Jewish America. In the career of Cahan, however, these articles are not as important as the writing he did in the offices of the *Commercial Advertiser* (1897–1901). The relationship between Cahan and his colleagues on the English newspaper was mutually beneficial: Hutchins Hapgood and Lincoln Steffens learned of the intellectual turmoil and excitement of the Lower East Side; Cahan learned more sophisticated techniques of journalism.

Before his tenure on the *Commercial Advertiser*, Cahan had published only two short stories and a novella in English. These three pieces are local color treatments of immigrant life, reflecting Cahan's strong moralizing temperament and his socialist criticism of the dehumanization of capitalism.

Cahan never abandoned this socialist didacticism, but his later fiction is more successful in keeping it under aesthetic control. Cahan grew more interested in presenting the dilemma of his old world immigrants in modern America, whose struggles result from the conflict between the teachings and expectations of the past and the realities and threats of the present. In short story form, Cahan's most successful treatment of this conflict is "The Imported Bridegroom," a tale of the repercussions of the modern world vision on Jews in different stages of alienation from their Jewish past.

It is, however, the novel *The Rise of David Levinsky* that assures Cahan his significance in American literature. Past ideals and present desires plague the rise of this Silas Lapham. The title clearly alludes to the famous novel of William Dean Howells, Cahan's favorite American writer and his staunch supporter in the American literary establishment. The story of David is different from that of Silas: unlike the Protestant version of the rags to riches hero, Cahan's hero never effects a moral rise, never learns to balance his present reality with his past expectations.

Cahan's novel is one of the most powerful about immigrant life in America and one of the most telling portraits of the joylessness of the moneyed life without spiritual fulfilment. After this great success, Cahan seemed to have finished his discourse with English-speaking America. The rest of his career was centered on the *Jewish Daily Forward* and his autobiography in Yiddish.

—R. Barbara Gitenstein

CAIN, James M(allahan). Born in Annapolis, Maryland, 1 July 1892. Educated at Washington College, Chesterton, Maryland, B.A. 1910, M.A. 1917. Served in the U.S. Army during World War I (editor-in-chief of *Lorraine Cross*, 79th Division newspaper). Married 1) Mary Rebecca Clough in 1920 (divorced, 1923); 2) Elina Sjösted Tyszecha in 1927 (divorced, 1942); 3) Aileen Pringle in 1944 (divorced, 1945); 4) Florence Macbeth Whitwell in 1947 (died, 1966). Reporter, Baltimore *American*, 1917–18; Baltimore *Sun*, 1919–23; Professor of Journalism, St. John's College, Annapolis, 1923–24; editorial writer, New York *World*, 1924–31; screenwriter, 1932–48. Recipient: Mystery Writers of America Grand Master Award, 1970. *Died 27 October 1977.*

PUBLICATIONS

Fiction

The Postman Always Rings Twice. 1934.
Serenade. 1937.
Mildred Pierce. 1941; edited by Albert J. LaValley, 1980.
Love's Lovely Counterfeit. 1942.
Career in C Major and Other Stories. 1943.
Three of a Kind: Career in C Major, The Embezzler, Double Indemnity. 1944; *Career in C Major* and *The Embezzler* published as *Everybody Does It*, 1949.
Past All Dishonor. 1946.
The Butterfly. 1947.
Sinful Woman. 1947.
The Moth. 1948.
Three of Hearts (omnibus). 1949.
Jealous Woman. 1950.
The Root of His Evil. 1952; as *Shameless*, 1958.
Galatea. 1953.
Mignon. 1962.
The Magician's Wife. 1965.
Rainbow's End. 1975.
The Institute. 1976.
The Baby in the Icebox and Other Short Fiction, edited by Roy Hoopes. 1981.
Cloud Nine. 1984.
The Enchanted Isle. 1985.
Career in C Major and Other Fiction, edited by Roy Hoopes. 1986.

Plays

Hero; Hemp; Red, White, and Blue; Trial by Jury; Theological Interlude; Citizenship; Will of the People (short plays), in *American Mercury 6* to *29*, 1926–29.
The Postman Always Rings Twice, from his own novel (produced 1936).
Algiers (screenplay), with John Howard Lawson, in *Foremost Films of 1938*, edited by Frank Vreeland. 1939.

Screenplays: *Algiers*, with John Howard Lawson, 1938; *Stand Up and Fight*, with others, 1939; *When Tomorrow Comes*, with Dwight Taylor, 1939; *Gypsy Wildcat*, with others, 1944; *Everybody Does It*, with Nunnally Johnson, 1949.

Other

Our Government. 1930.
Sixty Years of Journalism, edited by Roy Hoopes. 1986.

Editor, *79th Division Headquarters Troop: A Record*, with Malcolm Gilbert. 1919.
Editor, *For Men Only: A Collection of Short Stories*. 1944.

*

Critical Studies: "Man under Sentence of Death: The Novels of Cain" by Joyce Carol Oates, in *Tough Guy Writers of the Thirties* edited by David Madden, 1968, and *Cain*, 1970, and *Cain's Craft*, 1985, both by Madden; *Cain: The Biography* by Roy Hoopes, 1982.

* * *

James M. Cain is the twenty-minute egg of the hard-boiled school. The tough-guy novel made a lasting impact on "serious" American and European fiction; for instance, Albert Camus admitted that *The Postman Always Rings Twice* was a model for *The Stranger*.

Cain said he had only one story to tell: a love story. "I write of the wish that comes true, for some reason a terrifying concept . . . I think my stories have some quality of the opening of a forbidden box." The act of forcing the wish to come true isolates Cain's obsessed lovers from society and places them on what he calls a "love-rack."

If Cain's "heels and harpies" are to consummate and prolong their sexual passion, they must commit a crime. Frank Chambers and Cora in *The Postman* must murder Cora's husband; in *Serenade* Juana must slaughter Winston Hawes, a homosexual symphony conductor, to ensure the sexual salvation of her lover, Howard Sharp, an opera singer; sex and money are the motives in Walter's and Phyllis's murder of her husband in *Double Indemnity*; in *The Butterfly*, when his apparently incestuous lust for his daughter Kady is threatened, Jess Tyler, a West Virginia farmer, shoots Moke Blue.

In his novels dealing with criminal love, even in his romances *Career in C Major* and *Galatea* and his historical novels *Past All Dishonor* and *Mignon*, Cain effectively dramatizes profound insights into the American character and scene and into the way American dreams degenerate into nightmares. In his novels of character, *Mildred Pierce* and *The Moth*, set in the depression years, his scrutiny is most direct. Physically and often intellectually aggressive, Cain's audacious American male is an inside-dopester equipped with great know-how in many areas (even food, music, and the art of biography); but self-dramatizing inclinations, a suppressed sentimentality, and a misconceived American romanticism and optimism often defeat him. The female is realistic, ruthless, materialistic, and sensitive to minor social taboos even while violating major laws. A deadly pair, they are more often destroyed by their own sexual and materialistic overreaching than by the police. In their total commitment to each other, severing all ties to other people, Cain's lovers experience a blazing, self-consuming flash of self-deceptive purity and hideous innocence.

Without style and technique, Cain's rich and fascinating subject matter, energized by imagination and controlled by formula, would lack sustaining power. A few characters and a simple plot with a first-person narrator—that is the magic combination of a Cain "natural," producing a style like the "metal of an automatic," a pace like "a motorcycle," and a sense of immediacy that hypnotizes the reader. The first person narration enables Cain to use basic technical devices with special skill and appropriateness. His distinctive dialog is especially powerful when it is all of a piece with the cold objectivity and immediacy of the arrogant, commanding first-person voice. Cain, whose conscious intention was to "cast a spell on the beholder," stated that he developed "the habit of needling a story at the least hint of a breakdown," striving for a "rising coefficient of intensity."

Cain would never have used the term "existential," but as a consequence of his primary intention to tell a story superbly well, he created an objective, disinterested, often pessimistic view of life that is simultaneously terrifying and starkly beautiful.

—David Madden

CALDWELL, Erskine (Preston). Born in Moreland, Georgia, 17 December 1903. Educated at Erskine College, Due West, South Carolina, 1920–21; University of Virginia, Charlottesville, 1922, 1925–26; University of Pennsylvania, Philadelphia, 1924. Married 1) Helen Lannigan in 1925 (divorced, 1938), two sons and one daughter; 2) the photographer Margaret Bourke-White in 1939 (divorced, 1942); 3) June Johnson in 1942 (divorced, 1955), one son; 4) Virginia Moffett Fletcher in 1957. Played professional football, Wilkes-Barre, Pennsylvania, 1920's; reporter, Atlanta *Journal*, 1925–26; free-lance writer from 1926; ran a bookstore in Portland, Maine, 1928; screenwriter, Hollywood, 1930–34, 1942–43; foreign correspondent in Mexico, Spain, Czechoslovakia, Russia, and China, 1938–41; editor, American Folkways series (25 vols.), 1941–55. Recipient: Order of Cultural Merit (Poland), 1981. Member, National Institute of Arts and Letters, 1942, and American Academy, 1984; Commander, Order of Arts and Letters (France), 1984. *Died 11 April 1987.*

PUBLICATIONS

Fiction

The Bastard. 1930.
Poor Fool. 1930.
American Earth (stories). 1931; as *A Swell-Looking Girl*, 1951.
Mama's Little Girl (story). 1932.
Tobacco Road. 1932.
A Message for Genevieve (story). 1933.
God's Little Acre. 1933.
We Are the Living: Brief Stories. 1933.
Journeyman. 1935; revised edition, 1938.
Kneel to the Rising Sun and Other Stories. 1935.
The Sacrilege of Alan Kent (story). 1936.
Southways: Stories. 1938.
Trouble in July. 1940.
Jackpot: The Short Stories. 1940; abridged edition, as *Midsummer Passion*, 1948.
All Night Long: A Novel of Guerrilla Warfare in Russia. 1942.
Georgia Boy (stories). 1943.
A Day's Wooing and Other Stories. 1944.
Stories by Caldwell: 24 Representative Stories, edited by Henry Seidel Canby. 1944; as *The Pocket Book of Caldwell Stories*, 1947.
Tragic Ground. 1944.
A House in the Uplands. 1946.
The Caldwell Caravan: Novels and Stories. 1946.
The Sure Hand of God. 1947.
This Very Earth. 1948.
Where the Girls Were Different and Other Stories, edited by Donald A. Wollheim. 1948.
A Woman in the House (stories). 1949.
Place Called Estherville. 1949.
Episode in Palmetto. 1950.
The Humorous Side of Caldwell, edited by Robert Cantwell. 1951; as *Where the Girls Were Different and Other Stories*, 1962.
A Lamp for Nightfall. 1952.
The Courting of Susie Brown (stories). 1952.
The Complete Stories. 1953.
Love and Money. 1954.
Gretta. 1955.
Gulf Coast Stories. 1956.
Certain Women (stories). 1957.

Claudelle Inglish. 1959; as *Claudell*, 1959.
When You Think of Me (stories). 1959.
Men and Women: 22 Stories. 1961.
Jenny by Nature. 1961.
Close to Home. 1962.
The Last Night of Summer. 1963.
Miss Mama Aimee. 1967.
Summertime Island. 1968.
The Weather Shelter. 1969.
The Earnshaw Neighborhood. 1971.
Annette. 1973.
Stories. 1980.
Stories of Life: North and South. 1983.
The Black and White Stories of Caldwell. 1984.

Plays

Screenplays: *A Nation Dances* (documentary), 1943; *Volcano*, 1953.

Other

In Defense of Myself. 1930.
Tenant Farmer. 1935.
Some American People. 1935.
You Have Seen Their Faces, photographs by Margaret Bourke-White. 1937.
North of the Danube, photographs by Margaret Bourke-White. 1939.
Say! Is This the U.S.A.?, photographs by Margaret Bourke-White. 1941.
All-Out on the Road to Smolensk. 1942; as *Moscow Under Fire: A Wartime Diary 1941*, 1942.
Russia at War, photographs by Margaret Bourke-White. 1942.
Call It Experience: The Years of Learning How to Write. 1951.
Molly Cottontail (for children). 1958.
Around About America. 1964.
In Search of Bisco. 1965.
The Deer at Our House (for children). 1966.
In the Shadow of the Steeple. 1967.
Writing in America. 1967.
Deep South: Memory and Observation (includes *In the Shadow of the Steeple*). 1968.
Afternoons in Mid-America: Observations and Impressions. 1976.

*

Critical Studies: *The Southern Poor White from Lubberland to Tobacco Road* by Shields McIlwaine, 1939; *Caldwell* by James Korges, 1969; *Black Like It Is/Was: Caldwell's Treatment of Racial Themes* by William A. Sutton, 1974; *Critical Essays on Caldwell* edited by Scott MacDonald, 1981; *Caldwell* by James E. Devlin, 1984.

* * *

The degenerate side of life that Erskine Caldwell exploited so successfully in 1932 in *Tobacco Road* extends back some 200 years in southern life, suggesting some kinship between his work and that of the frontier humorists. A hallmark of Caldwell's exploitation of southern folk and folkways is his use of what Shields McIlwaine calls "idiotic gravity," emanating from characters who are in dead earnest in their sometimes misguided, if not perverted, commitment.

Caldwell's humorous approach to the seaminess and poverty of southern life, whether in *Tobacco Road, God's Little Acre*, or *Georgia Boy*, accounts for his avoidance of the melodramatic and banal. As Robert Cantwell suggested, Caldwell's comic treatment of materials makes the poverty of his characters "unforgettable."

In terms of literary tradition, it is Caldwell's Chaucerian treatment of sex that places his novels in the mainstream of the *fabliau*, McIlwaine noting that the author's poor whites like Ty Ty Walden (*God's Little Acre*) and Jeeter Lester (*Tobacco Road*) enjoy the "game of sex without self consciousness." Cantwell, moreover, points out that Caldwell's sexual scenes normally have witnesses—visitors, Negroes peering over fences, etc.—thus suggesting an initiation process. Caldwell's frank treatment of sex marks in the 1930's a major shift in popular literature. After the success of *Tobacco Road*—especially in resisting suppression—similar works by later writers became a staple of commercial fiction. But, with the exception of *Trouble in July* (1940), few of Caldwell's own novels after *God's Little Acre* add to his stature as a creative artist.

In an equally important sense the Caldwell canon owes much to the tradition of naturalism in American writing. Thus Caldwell's characters—oppressed by barren land, mill life, heredity, or other circumstances beyond their control—fail to perceive any solution in flight. The author, moreover, creates with some consistency character after character who is a victim of his heredity and/or environment. Jeeter Lester (*Tobacco Road*), for example, is but the inevitable outcome of 100 years of family degeneration and disintegration, whereas Ty Ty Walden's degeneracy (*God's Little Acre*) is owed to a "perverted idealism" (McIlwaine).

Current criticism of Caldwell's work, however, places it in the American gothic vein. The author's use of deformed and sometimes mentally deficient and perverted characters defines his purpose. In *Tobacco Road* one is confronted by a grandmother consumed by pellagra, in *God's Little Acre* by Pluto's obesity, and in *Tragic Ground* by Bubber's permanent grin. Whereas 18th- and 19th-century gothicists exploited setting and the supernatural as vehicles, both Caldwell and Faulkner turned southern sociology and misshapen personalities into effective gothic pronouncements concerning the quality of modern life.

The Complete Stories reveals the author's true métier: southern settings, disenfranchised blacks and poor whites, a depression background. "Candy-Man Beechum," his most frequently anthologized story, presents the artist at his best: passionate in his commitment to social values, primitive in his rhythmic articulation, and genuine in the sense of uncontrolled fate that he evokes.

—George C. Longest

See the essay on *Tobacco Road*.

CALISHER, Hortense. Born in New York City, 20 December 1911. Educated at Hunter College High School, New

York; Barnard College, New York, A.B. in philosophy 1932. Married 1) H.B. Heffelfinger in 1935, one daughter and one son; 2) Curtis Harnack in 1959. Worked for Department of Public Welfare, New York, 1933–34; Adjunct Professor of English, Barnard College, 1956–57; Visiting Professor, University of Iowa, Iowa City, 1957, 1959–60, Stanford University, California, 1958, Sarah Lawrence College, Bronxville, New York, 1962, and Brandeis University, Waltham, Massachusetts, 1963–64; Writer-in-Residence, 1965, and Visiting Lecturer, 1968, University of Pennsylvania, Philadelphia; Adjunct Professor of English, Columbia University, New York, 1968–70 and 1972–73; Clark Lecturer, Scripps College, Claremont, California, 1969; Visiting Professor, State University of New York, Purchase, 1971–72; Regents' Professor, University of California, Irvine, Spring 1976; Visiting Writer, Bennington College, Vermont, 1978; Hurst Professor, Washington University, St. Louis, 1979; National Endowment for the Arts Lecturer, Cooper Union, New York, 1983; Visiting Professor, Brown University, Providence, Rhode Island, 1986. Recipient: Guggenheim fellowship, 1952, 1955; Department of State American Specialists grant, 1958; American Academy award, 1967; National Endowment for the Arts grant, 1967. Litt.D.: Skidmore College, Saratoga Springs, New York, 1980. Member, American Academy, 1977. Lives in New York City.

Publications

Fiction

In the Absence of Angels: Stories. 1951.
False Entry. 1961.
Tale for the Mirror: A Novella and Other Stories. 1962.
Textures of Life. 1963.
Extreme Magic: A Novella and Other Stories. 1964.
Journal from Ellipsia. 1965.
The Railway Police, and The Last Trolley Ride (two novellas). 1966.
The New Yorkers. 1969.
Queenie. 1971.
Standard Dreaming. 1972.
Eagle Eye. 1973.
The Collected Stories. 1975.
On Keeping Women. 1977.
Mysteries of Motion. 1983.
Saratoga, Hot (stories). 1985.
The Bobby-Soxer. 1986.

Other

What Novels Are (lecture). 1969.
Herself (memoir). 1972.

Editor, with Shannon Ravenel, *The Best American Short Stories 1981*. 1981.

* * *

Hortense Calisher may be too demanding to find a wide audience, despite her remarkable perceptions and formidable talent. She marks an elliptical narrative with subtle, verbal humor and penetrating examinations of the heart. The patient reader is always richly rewarded.

Her shorter fiction is probably more successful than her full-length novels. The mandarin precision in the telling is better sustained in "an apocalypse, served in a very small cup," in Calisher's own definition of a story. Her range is astonishing: as serious as children confronting death by way of professional mourners; as levitous as a dinner party at which the women suddenly decide to remove their blouses. In *Extreme Magic* two people suffering from the intensity of emotional scars find solace in each other's pain and memory, singled out for the implication in the title of this novella. In another, *The Railway Police*—which is, perhaps, Calisher's most powerful work—a woman abandons the artificial identity represented by her collection of elaborate wigs in order to face the world with a bald skull.

Textures of Life, an early novel, represents Calisher at her most accessible: a conventional, even romantic plot salvaged from the ordinary by a vast intelligence and compassion. *False Entry* and *The New Yorkers*, loosely connected novels of rich complexity in both plot and narrative, contain brilliant set pieces—the Ku Klux Klan section in the former, the childhood story of a Hungarian immigrant in the latter—but are probably too prolix for most readers. *Journal from Ellipsia*, which "only the uninitiate still call science fiction," has an interplanetary Gulliver as heroine and sometime narrator; it anticipates *Mysteries of Motion* a decade later, Calisher's interplanetary epic that weaves the lives of several contemporary types together for a first civilian flight into space, too many of them in a prose too complex for easy access. *On Keeping Women* and *The Bobby-Soxer* are modern novels of marital and non-marital relationships, spun out in her customary elegance; and *Saratoga, Hot*, "little novels," as she has termed them, contains some of her best stories to date, notably "Gargantua," as painful as any she has written, and "The Passenger," one of her autobiographical pieces, its cruel self-assessment cut with her deadpan humor and rich compassion. *Queenie* is perhaps the best example of her delicious wit, a verbal tour de force in the disguise of a sexual fable in answer to Portnoy, by way of Colette, and a 1970's bawdy of immaculate taste.

Calisher's autobiography, *Herself*, discloses less about the author than about her view of art, including, in "Pushing Around the Pantheon," an entertaining and enlightening discussion of sexuality in literature in relation to the masculine and feminine roles tradition has imposed on writers. "The magic is in her writing," Marya Mannes has written, "the marvel is in her range."

—Bruce Kellner

CAPOTE, Truman. Born Truman Streckfus Persons in New Orleans, Louisiana, 30 September 1924; took step-father's surname. Educated at Trinity School and St. John's Academy, New York; Greenwich High School, Connecticut. Worked in the art department, and wrote for "Talk of the Town," *New Yorker*, early 1940's; then full-time writer. Recipient: O. Henry Award, 1946, 1948, 1951; American Academy grant, 1959; Mystery Writers of America Edgar Allan Poe Award, 1966; Emmy award, for television adaptation, 1967. Member, American Academy. *Died 25 August 1984*.

PUBLICATIONS

Collections

A Capote Reader. 1987.

Fiction

Other Voices, Other Rooms. 1948.
A Tree of Night and Other Stories. 1949.
The Grass Harp. 1951.
Breakfast at Tiffany's: A Short Novel and Three Stories. 1958.
A Christmas Memory (story). 1966.
Answered Prayers (unfinished novel). 1986.

Plays

The Grass Harp, from his own novel (produced 1952). 1952.
House of Flowers, music by Harold Arlen, lyrics by Capote and Arlen (produced 1954; revised version, produced 1968). 1968.
The Thanksgiving Visitor, from his own story (televised 1968). 1968.
Trilogy (screenplay, with Eleanor Perry), in *Trilogy*. 1969.

Screenplays: *Beat the Devil*, with John Huston, 1953; *Indiscretion of an American Wife*, with others, 1954; *The Innocents*, with William Archibald and John Mortimer, 1961; *Trilogy*, with Eleanor Perry, 1969.

Television Plays and Films (includes documentaries): *A Christmas Memory*, with Eleanor Perry, from the story by Capote, 1966; *Among the Paths to Eden*, with Eleanor Perry, from the story by Capote, 1967; *Laura*, from the play by Vera Caspary, 1968; *The Thanksgiving Visitor*, from his own story, 1968; *Behind Prison Walls*, 1972; *The Glass House*, with Tracy Keenan Wynn and Wyatt Cooper, 1972; *Crimewatch*, 1973.

Other

Local Color. 1950.
The Muses Are Heard: An Account of the Porgy and Bess Tour to Leningrad. 1956.
Observations, photographs by Richard Avedon. 1959.
Selected Writings, edited by Mark Schorer. 1963.
In Cold Blood: A True Account of a Multiple Murder and Its Consequences. 1966.
Trilogy: An Experiment in Multimedia, with Frank and Eleanor Perry. 1969.
The Dogs Bark: Public People and Private Places. 1973.
Then It All Came Down: Criminal Justice Today Discussed by Police, Criminals, and Correction Officers with Comments by Capote. 1976.
Music for Chameleons. 1980.
One Christmas (memoir). 1983.
Conversations with Capote, with Lawrence Grobel. 1985.
Capote: Conversations, edited by M. Thomas Inge. 1987.

*

Bibliography: *Capote: A Primary and Secondary Bibliography* by Robert J. Stanton, 1980.

Critical Studies: *The Worlds of Capote* by William L. Nance, 1970; *Capote* by Helen S. Garson, 1980; *Capote* by Marie Rudisill and James C. Simmons, 1983; *Footnote to a Friendship: A Memoir of Capote and Others* by Donald Windham, 1983; *Capote: Dear Heart, Old Buddy* by John Malcolm Brinnin, 1986; *Capote: A Biography* by Gerald Clarke, 1987.

* * *

Few contemporary writers have projected a public image as compelling or as enduring as that of Truman Capote. John W. Aldridge in *After the Lost Generation*, for example, compared the popular image of Capote to that of Hemingway and Byron, noting that the author's publishers exploited him in order to reinforce the reader's "impression of fragile aestheticism" evident in his works. Certainly Capote's personal idiosyncrasies and the superficial effects of the style and atmosphere of his work did much to enhance his popular following.

Although the art of Capote speaks directly to his own day and age, the best of it is rooted in 19th-century American literary traditions reflected in Hawthorne and James. Like Hawthorne, for example, his work focuses upon the dichotomy of good and evil, light and dark. Capote's craft, moreover, is that of the romance as defined by James. Dream symbolism adds to the gothic impact of the author's resonance.

Recent critics have tended to divide Capote's works into two fictional modes, the nocturnal and the daylight, or the dark and the light. The light Capote fiction tends to take place in a public world (*The Grass Harp*) and reveals an often aggressive social order. The daylight fiction, moreover, is marked by a realistic, colloquial, often funny, first-person narrative (*Breakfast at Tiffany's*). The nocturnal, by contrast, is manifest in the dreamlike, detached, inverted, third-person narrative focusing on an inner complex world, often approaching the surreal as in *Other Voices, Other Rooms*.

Because of the romance tradition implicit in his work, Capote's characters are rooted in gothic narcissism. As an instance of that narcissism, a major Capote theme is the discovery of one's *real* identity. In a supernatural context a character often confronts his alter ego, as in *Other Voices, Other Rooms*. The tree house in *The Grass Harp* becomes a place for wish fulfilment, a refuge for fighting off the hypocrisy of the social order. Even Holly Golightly's rebellion in *Breakfast at Tiffany's* suggests a degree of self-love. *In Cold Blood* emphasizes the nocturnal motif, the use of the modern gothic, and the skillful manipulation of narcissus. This experiment with what has been called the non-fiction novel, is an excellent example of Capote's skillful penetration of the nightmarish enigma of evil, suggesting again his kinship to Hawthorne, Melville, and James.

—George C. Longest

CATHER, Willa (Sibert). Born in Back Creek Valley, near Winchester, Virginia, 7 December 1873; moved with her family to a farm near Red Cloud, Nebraska, 1883. Educated at Red Cloud High School, graduated 1890; Latin School, Lincoln, Nebraska, 1890–91; University of Nebraska, Lincoln, 1891–95, A.B. 1895. Columnist, Lincoln *State Journal*, 1893–95; member of the editorial staff, *Home Monthly*, Pittsburgh,

1896–97; telegraph editor and drama critic, Pittsburgh *Daily Leader*, 1897–1901; Latin and English teacher, Central High School, Pittsburgh, 1901–03; English teacher, Allegheny High School, Pittsburgh, 1903–06; editor, *McClure's* magazine, New York, 1906–11; full-time writer from 1912. Recipient: Pulitzer Prize, 1923; American Academy Howells Medal, 1930, and Gold Medal, 1944; Prix Fémina Américaine, 1932. Litt.D.: University of Nebraska, 1917; University of Michigan, Ann Arbor, 1922; Columbia University, New York, 1928; Yale University, New Haven, Connecticut, 1929; Princeton University, New Jersey, 1931; D.L.: Creighton University, Omaha, Nebraska, 1928; LL.D.: University of California, Berkeley, 1931; L.H.D.: Smith College, Northampton, Massachusetts, 1933. Member, American Academy. *Died 24 April 1947.*

PUBLICATIONS

Collections

Novels and Stories 1896–1922 (Library of America), edited by Sharon O'Brien. 1986.

Fiction

The Troll Garden (stories). 1905; variorum edition, edited by James Woodress, 1983.
Alexander's Bridge. 1912; as *Alexander's Bridges*, 1912.
O Pioneers! 1913.
The Song of the Lark. 1915.
My Ántonia. 1918.
Youth and the Bright Medusa (stories). 1920.
One of Ours. 1922.
A Lost Lady. 1923.
The Professor's House. 1925.
My Mortal Enemy. 1926.
Death Comes for the Archbishop. 1927.
Shadows on the Rock. 1931.
The Fear That Walks by Noonday (stories). 1931.
Obscure Destinies (stories). 1932.
Lucy Gayheart. 1935.
Novels and Stories. 13 vols., 1937–41.
Sapphira and the Slave Girl. 1940.
The Old Beauty and Others. 1948.
Early Stories, edited by Mildred R. Bennett. 1957.
Collected Short Fiction 1892–1912, edited by Virginia Faulkner. 1965.
Uncle Valentine and Other Stories: Uncollected Fiction 1915–1929, edited by Bernice Slote. 1973.

Verse

April Twilights. 1903.
April Twilights and Other Poems. 1923; revised edition, 1933; edited by Bernice Slote, 1962; revised edition, 1968.

Other

The Life of Mary Baker G. Eddy, and the History of Christian Science, by Georgine Milmine (ghostwritten by Cather). 1909.
My Autobiography, by S.S. McClure (ghostwritten by Cather). 1914.
Not Under Forty. 1936.
On Writing: Critical Studies on Writing as an Art. 1949.
Writings from Cather's Campus Years, edited by James R. Shively. 1950.
Cather in Europe: Her Own Story of the First Journey, edited by George N. Kates. 1956.
The Kingdom of Art: Cather's First Principles and Critical Principles 1893–1896, edited by Bernice Slote. 1967.
The World and the Parish: Cather's Articles and Reviews 1893–1902, edited by William M. Curtin. 2 vols., 1970.

Editor, *The Best Stories of Sarah Orne Jewett*. 2 vols., 1925.

*

Bibliography: *Cather: A Bibliography* by Joan Crane, 1982.

Critical Studies: *Cather: A Critical Introduction* by David Daiches, 1951; *Cather: A Critical Biography* by E.K. Brown, completed by Leon Edel, 1953; *The Landscape and the Looking Glass: Cather's Search for Value* by John H. Randall III, 1960; *The World of Cather* by Mildred R. Bennett, 1961; *Cather's Gift of Sympathy* by Edward and Lillian Bloom, 1962; *Cather* by Dorothy Van Ghent, 1964; *Cather and Her Critics* edited by James Schroeter, 1967; *Cather: Her Life and Art*, 1970, and *Cather: A Literary Life*, 1987, both by James Woodress; *Cather* by Dorothy McFarland Tuck, 1972; *Cather: A Pictorial Memoir* by Bernice Slote, 1973, and *The Art of Cather* edited by Slote and Virginia Faulkner, 1974; *Five Essays on Cather*, 1974, and *Critical Essays on Cather*, 1984, both edited by John J. Murphy; *Cather's Imagination* by David Stouck, 1975; *Cather* by Philip L. Gerber, 1975; *Chrysalis: Cather in Pittsburgh 1896–1906* by Kathleen D. Byrne and Richard C. Snyder, 1982; *Willa: The Life of Cather* by Phyllis C. Robinson, 1983; *Cather's Short Fiction* by Marilyn Arnold, 1984; *The Voyage Perilous: Cather's Romanticism* by Susan Rosowski, 1986; *Cather: The Emerging Voice* by Sharon O'Brien, 1986.

* * *

Willa Cather, who now can be ranked among the most important American writers of the first half of this century, is best known for her novels and stories depicting the early years of Nebraska. Her range is considerably broader, however, and also includes notable work set in the American southwest, Quebec, and Virginia. Her reputation is based on an extraordinary ability to capture the sense of place and a meticulous craftsmanship that combines a very clear prose style with effective use of myth and symbol. In an age when authors were increasingly able to exploit their literary talents in the marketplace Cather displayed an awesome dedication to her art. She wrote slowly and carefully, consistently refused to allow her works to be anthologized, dramatized, or sold in paperback editions, and when she died she had produced twelve novels and at least 55 stories of consistently high quality.

Cather served a long literary apprenticeship before she was able to cut loose from journalism and devote her time exclusively to writing. Her ideas and values, however, were formed early, as the volumes of her early newspaper writings show. During her early years of journalism and teaching she wrote mostly short fiction, producing 45 stories before 1912, when she resigned from her editorship of *McClure's*. These stories, which show a slowly maturing talent, explore themes and subjects that she later employed in her novels. Her first book, however, was *April Twilights*, a volume of verse published while she was teaching high school in Pittsburgh. Her first fiction was a collection of stories, *The Troll Garden*. These stories deal in various ways with the artist and society and show a strong Jamesian influence. They also make use of western material, particularly "A Sculptor's Funeral" and "A Wagner Matinee," but the tone of these last is more akin to the revolt-from-the-village strain in early 20th-century American literature than Cather's later work celebrating the land in novels like *O Pioneers!* and *My Ántonia*.

In 1911 Cather took a leave from *McClure's* and wrote "The Bohemian Girl," a long story that uses for the first time in a nostalgic and affirmative manner the memories of her early years on a Nebraska farm and in the prairie village of Red Cloud. She blends a realistic use of detail with a romantic sensibility in a very successful story that encouraged her to plunge into full-length novels of the same genre. Even before writing "The Bohemian Girl," however, she had published her first novel, *Alexander's Bridge*, but, despite the fact that it is a well-written work of considerable interest, she later deprecated the book and regarded it as a false start. The novel is very Jamesian, takes place in Boston and London, and concerns a bridge-builder whose bridge, like his character, contains a fatal flaw. The story ends with the collapse of the bridge and the death of the protagonist.

O Pioneers!, *The Song of the Lark*, *My Ántonia*, *One of Ours*, and *A Lost Lady* are set entirely or in part in Nebraska, and form the basis for Cather's identification with that part of the United States. It is important to note that she began using this material nearly two decades after she had left Nebraska to live in the east. By then the youthful experience was ripe and ready for artistic employment. In a 1925 introduction to the stories of Sarah Orne Jewett, who had been her friend and a literary influence, she quoted from a letter from Jewett: "The thing that teases the mind over and over for years, and at last gets itself put down rightly on paper—whether little or great, it belongs to literature." This was a literary principle in which Cather thoroughly believed, and it places Cather closer to Wordsworth with his view of poetry as "emotion recollected in tranquility" than it does to the realists or naturalists of the late 19th and early 20th centuries like Howells, Garland, or Dreiser, who "worked up" their materials.

O Pioneers! is the story of Alexandra Bergson, a Swedish immigrant who tames the wild land in the pioneer days of Nebraska. Alexandra's life is a success story told with a loving affirmation of the beauty of the land and the value of the pioneer struggle. The novel is not all light, however, as two of Alexandra's brothers turn out to be mean-spirited materialists and her beloved younger brother dies at the hand of a Czech farmer whose wife he has fallen in love with. *The Song of the Lark* combines Cather's memories of her young life in Red Cloud with her great interest in music and in particular the Wagnerian soprano Olive Fremstad, who had grown up in an immigrant family in Minnesota. Thus the youth of the singer is Cather's own youth and the career of the artist is a fictionalized biography of Olive Fremstad. *My Ántonia*, regarded by many readers as Cather's best novel, creates a memorable character in a Bohemian immigrant heroine who had her prototype in a childhood friend. This story is told retrospectively by a male narrator whose experience growing up on a farm and in the town of Black Hawk (Red Cloud) parallels Cather's own life. Again the same sense of place is evoked memorably, and the land and its pioneer settlers are presented with a haunting nostalgia. The book is episodic in character, which is typical of Cather, and contains stories within stories. The novel is carefully constructed, however, and given an organic form that suits the material.

One of Ours is less successful, though the early parts of the novel set in Nebraska create a vivid picture of life on a Nebraska farm and in a college town like Lincoln where Cather attended the university. The story was suggested by the life of her cousin who was killed in France during the First World War. Ironically, this novel won a Pulitzer Prize and brought Cather handsome royalties for the first time. She returned to an all-Nebraska setting in *A Lost Lady*, and again evoked childhood memories in the creation of Captain and Mrs. Forrester, the chief characters. The setting is again a fictionalized Red Cloud, and the story of the lost lady, lost only to the point-of-view character, is told from the perspective of a boy growing up in the small town. This novel demonstrates the literary technique that Cather explains in her essay "The Novel Démeublé." It is a work of about 50,000 words in which all the excess detail is stripped away. "The higher processes of art are all processes of simplification," she wrote. She also was fond of quoting Dumas *père*, who once had said that to make a drama all "a man needed [was] one passion, and four walls."

The Professor's House is a different sort of novel from the Nebraska stories, the tale of a middle-aged professor of history who loses the will to live and barely escapes death. Although he had won an important literary prize and apparently had everything to live for, he is profoundly depressed by the materialism of his family and his culture. There is a good deal of autobiography in this novel, for Cather, too, felt that for her "the world broke in two in 1922 or thereabouts." There is a long tale inserted in the middle of this novel, "Tom Outland's Story," that evokes the ancient civilization of the Mesa Verde Indians in sharp contrast to the 1920's and also reflects Cather's growing interest in the southwest.

Her most significant use of the southwest came two years later in *Death Comes for the Archbishop*, the novel that she thought her best. It creates in episodic form the life of Jean Latour, the first bishop of New Mexico. She long had been fascinated by the story of the Catholic church in the southwest, and had begun visiting the area as early as 1912. When she ran across a letter collection that gave her a clear account of the real Bishop Lamy's career in New Mexico in the 19th century, she found her story and produced a distinguished historical novel. Much of the detail is fiction and it is romanticized, but the material does not do violence to history or to the historical characters it recreates. The work represents Cather at the peak of her creative powers.

Two more historical novels followed, *Shadows on the Rock* and *Sapphira and the Slave Girl*, and Cather after 1927 seemed to take refuge in writing about the past. *Shadows* is a story of Quebec at the end of the 17th century, a novel that is dramatically thin but pictorially rich. *Sapphira*, the only novel Cather ever wrote about her native Virginia, takes place in the Shenandoah Valley before the Civil War and deals with an incident of family history, her grandmother's successful efforts to help a slave escape to Canada. *Lucy Gayheart*, one of Cather's lesser novels, returns to the use of Red Cloud and a musician's life in Chicago.

—James Woodress

See the essay on *My Ántonia*.

CHANDLER, Raymond (Thornton). Born in Chicago, Illinois, 23 July 1888; moved to England with his mother: became British citizen, 1907; again became American citizen, 1956. Educated in a local school in Upper Norwood, London; Dulwich College, London, 1900–05; studied in France and Germany, 1905–07. Served in the Gordon Highlanders, Canadian Army, 1917–18, and in the Royal Air Force, 1918–19. Married Pearl Cecily Hurlburt in 1924 (died, 1954). Worked in supply and accounting departments of the Admiralty, London, 1907; reporter, London *Daily Express* and Bristol *Western Gazette*, 1908–12; returned to the U.S., 1912; worked in St. Louis, then on a ranch and in a sporting goods firm in California; accountant and bookkeeper, Los Angeles Creamery, 1912–17; worked in a bank in San Francisco, 1919; staff member, Los Angeles *Daily Express*, 1919; bookkeeper, then auditor, Dabney Oil Syndicate, Los Angeles, 1922–32; full-time writer from 1933. President, Mystery Writers of America, 1959. Recipient: Mystery Writers of America Edgar Allan Poe Award, for screenplay, 1946, for novel, 1954. *Died 26 March 1959*.

PUBLICATIONS

Collections

Selected Letters, edited by Frank MacShane. 1981.

Fiction

The Big Sleep. 1939.
Farewell, My Lovely. 1940.
The High Window. 1942.
The Lady in the Lake. 1943.
Five Murderers (stories). 1944.
Five Sinister Characters (stories). 1945.
Finger Man and Other Stories. 1946.
Red Wind (stories). 1946.
Spanish Blood (stories). 1946.
The Little Sister. 1949; as *Marlowe*, 1969.
The Simple Art of Murder (stories). 1950; as *Trouble Is My Business*, *Pick-Up on Noon Street*, and *The Simple Art of Murder*, 3 vols., 1951–53.
The Long Goodbye. 1953.
Smart Aleck Kill (stories). 1953.
Pearls Are a Nuisance (stories). 1953.
Playback. 1958.
Poodle Springs (unfinished novel), in *Chandler Speaking*. 1962.
Killer in the Rain (stories), edited by Philip Durham. 1964.
The Smell of Fear. 1965.
The Midnight Chandler (omnibus), edited by Joan Kahn. 1971.

Plays

Double Indemnity, with Billy Wilder, in *Best Film Plays 1945*, edited by John Gassner and Dudley Nichols. 1946.
The Blue Dahlia (screenplay), edited by Matthew J. Bruccoli. 1976.
Chandler's Unknown Thriller: The Screenplay of Playback. 1985.

Screenplays: *And Now Tomorrow*, with Frank Partos, 1944; *Double Indemnity*, with Billy Wilder, 1944; *The Unseen*, with Hagar Wilde and Ken Englund, 1945; *The Blue Dahlia*, 1946; *Strangers on a Train*, with Czenzi Ormonde and Whitfield Cook, 1951.

Other

Chandler Speaking, edited by Dorothy Gardiner and Kathrine Sorley Walker. 1962.
Chandler Before Marlowe: Chandler's Early Prose and Poetry 1908–1912, edited by Matthew J. Bruccoli. 1973.
The Notebooks of Chandler, and English Summer: A Gothic Romance, edited by Frank MacShane. 1976.
Chandler and James M. Fox: Letters. 1979.

*

Bibliography: *Chandler: A Descriptive Bibliography* by Matthew J. Bruccoli, 1979.

Critical Studies: *Down These Mean Streets a Man Must Go: Chandler's Knight* by Philip Durham, 1963; *The Life of Chandler* by Frank MacShane, 1976; *The World of Chandler* edited by Miriam Gross, 1977; *Chandler* by Jerry Spier, 1981; *Chandlertown: The Los Angeles of Philip Marlowe* by Edward Thorpe, 1983; *Something More Than Night: The Case of Chandler* by Peter Wolfe, 1985.

* * *

Raymond Chandler first attempted a literary career in London in his early twenties, when he unsuccessfully tried to establish himself as a poet and critic. Twenty years later, after losing his important job with an oil company because of his drinking, he tried again, writing stories for pulp magazines, notably *Black Mask*. This time he was immediately successful, and, along with Dashiell Hammett, became the principal champion of the "hard-boiled" school of detective fiction.

Chandler was scornful of the English school of detective fiction which, as he said in a famous remark, was an "affair of the upper classes, the week-end house party and the vicar's rose garden." He believed that crime fiction should deal with real criminals and should employ the language actually used by murderers and policemen. Chandler used what he called the "objective method" which assures authenticity. At the same time, his work has a strong emotional center that is capable of illuminating "an utterly unexpected range of sensitivity."

In 1939 he published *The Big Sleep*, his first novel. In quick succession he published *Farewell, My Lovely*, *The High Window*, and *The Lady in the Lake*, reworking material from his earlier stories. Chandler's novels are narrated by the central character, Philip Marlowe, an idealistic and romantic detective who is also tough and cynical. The books are dramatic and funny: Chandler's prose is formal but his vocabulary is full of the slang of his characters. The prose is a mirror of the political and financial corruption that lies under the bland surface of California life. Chandler was the first to give Los Angeles a literary identity.

During the 1940's and early 1950's Chandler wrote movie scripts in Hollywood, notably *Double Indemnity* (with Billy Wilder), *The Blue Dahlia*, and *Strangers on a Train*. Chandler disliked Hollywood, but earned enough money to retire with his wife, Cissy, to La Jolla, where he returned to fiction, writing *The Little Sister* and his most ambitious novel, *The Long Goodbye*. This book is a conscious effort to stretch the conventions of the detective novel so as to convert it into a general work of fiction. It brings crime fiction to the highest level it has attained in modern times. Chandler also wrote an essay, "The Simple Art of Murder," which places his work in the context of other crime novelists. It attempts to justify his blend of idealism and realism and may be considered his literary testament. He also wrote incisively about Hollywood.

Following the death of his wife, Chandler spent much time in England, where he became a celebrity, acknowledged as a master of contemporary fiction. Nevertheless, he was lonely and withdrawn, and succeeded in writing only one further novel, *Playback*. Since his death his stature has continued to grow, and he is now generally considered to be among the most important American novelists of his time.

—Frank MacShane

See the essay on *The Big Sleep*.

CHANNING, William Ellery. Born in Boston, Massachusetts, 29 November 1817; nephew of the writer William Ellery Channing. Educated at Round Hill School, Northampton, Massachusetts; Boston Latin School; Harvard University, Cambridge, Massachusetts, 1834. Married Ellen Fuller in 1842 (died, 1856); five children. Farmer, Woodstock, Illinois, 1839–40; tutor and journalist, Cincinnati, 1840–41; settled in Concord, Massachusetts, to be near Emerson, 1842: associated with other members of the Concord community, especially Thoreau; lived in New York, writing for the *Tribune*, 1844; visited France and Italy, 1846; editor, New Bedford *Mercury*, Massachusetts, 1855–58. *Died 23 December 1901.*

PUBLICATIONS

Collections

Poems of Sixty-Five Years, edited by F.B. Sanborn. 1902.
Collected Poems (facsimile edition), edited by Walter Harding. 1967.

Verse

Poems. 1843; second series, 1847.
Conversations in Rome: Between an Artist, A Catholic, and a Critic. 1847.
The Woodman and Other Poems. 1849.
Near Home. 1858.
The Wanderer: A Colloquial Poem. 1871.
The Burial of John Brown. 1878.
Eliot. 1885.
John Brown and the Heroes of Harper's Ferry. 1886.

Other

Thoreau, The Poet-Naturalist. 1873; revised edition, 1902.
Editor, with Sophia Thoreau, *The Maine Woods*, by Henry David Thoreau. 1864.
Editor, with Sophia Thoreau, *Cape Cod*, by Henry David Thoreau. 1865.
Editor, with Sophia Thoreau, *A Yankee in Canada, with Anti-Slavery and Reform Papers*, by Henry David Thoreau. 1866.

*

Bibliography: in *Bibliography of American Literature* by Jacob Blanck, 1957.

Critical Studies: *Channing of Concord: A Life* by Frederick T. McGill, 1967; *Channing* by Robert N. Hudspeth, 1973.

* * *

When Emerson helped found *The Dial* in 1840, it was just such a poet as William Ellery Channing for whom he intended the new magazine. Channing was a young man with a talent but with no readily available place for his verses. Under Emerson's sponsorship, Channing went on to publish not only poems in *The Dial*, but two books of lyrics and four book-length poems later in his life. These early lyrics are in many ways most characteristic of him. His themes were beauty, self-reliance, and nature. He was hostile to the development of urban America, and in such poems as "Reverence" and "Walden Spring" he gave voice to his fears and to his longings for a pastoral life which was quickly vanishing in the 1840's. What he wanted was the union of nature and self such as he imaged in "Wachusett":

> It went within my inmost heart,
> The overhanging Arch to see,
> The liquid stream, became a part
> Of my internal Harmony.

Typical of his time and place, he insisted on a union of art and life. To write well was to live well; to *be* a poet was itself a creation of supreme importance.

His increasing awareness of his own loneliness and his isolation was most apparent in two of his book-length poems, *Near Home* and *The Wanderer*. The first of these is a charming hymn to New England as a place of healing power.

> Perpetual newness and the health in things.
> This, is the startling theme, the lovely birth
> Each morn of a new day, so wholly new,
> So absolutely penetrated by itself,
> The fresh, the fair, the ever-living grace. . . .

In *The Wanderer*, Channing completed his journey from the simplicity of his lyrics to a more complex recognition of the tensions between man's love of nature and the forces working against the fulfillment of his pastoral idealism. The poem counterpoises a reverence for the land with a stark awareness of the destructive forces of death and technology. A poetic career beginning in enthusiasm ends in a mature perception of frustration.

Beyond the achievement of his poetry, Channing's career included the first biography of Thoreau, who had been Channing's close friend from 1841. *Thoreau, The Poet-Naturalist* is a narrative built on extensive quotations from Thoreau's journal, which was then unpublished. The book had the virtue of thus putting before the public quite a bit of Thoreau's little-known writing, and it also offered a cogent commentary by Channing who rightly emphasized the ethical strictness and the aesthetic craftsmanship in Thoreau's writing. Appearing at a time when Thoreau was all but unknown, the biography had the virtue of keeping his name alive and making his work more readily accessible.

Finally, it is as a friend that Channing may be best remembered. He was the only close friend of Thoreau; he was a constant companion of Emerson for forty years; he was a frequent visitor in the homes of Alcott and Hawthorne; he was Margaret Fuller's brother-in-law. Channing was a brilliant talker, full of wit and spontaneity. The universal report from his contemporaries was that he spoke better than he wrote. Emerson was convinced that "In walking with Ellery you shall always see what was never before shown to the eye of man." For his part, Hawthorne wrote in *Mosses from an Old Manse*, "Could he have drawn out that virgin gold [of his conversation] and stamped it with the mint mark that alone gives currency, the world might have had the profit, and he the fame." In a narrow society such as New England was, the vitality of Channing's conversation was not to be ignored. He showed his gifted friends how they might see better; he was a receptive audience, a sympathetic and shrewd critic, one who made it possible for men such as Emerson and Thoreau to act on their talent.

—Robert N. Hudspeth

CHAYEFSKY, Paddy. Born Sidney Chayefsky in the Bronx, New York, 29 January 1923. Educated at DeWitt Clinton High School, Bronx, graduated 1939; City College, New York, B.S. in social science 1943. Served in the U.S. Army, 1943–45: private; Purple Heart. Married Susan Sackler in 1949; one son. Worked for a printer, New York, 1946; writer in Hollywood, late 1940's; gag writer for Robert Q. Lewis, New York, 1950. President, Sudan Productions, 1956, Carnegie Productions, 1957, S.P.D. Productions after 1959, Sidney Productions after 1967, and Simcha Productions after 1971, all New York. Council member, Dramatists Guild, from 1962. Recipient: Screen Writers Guild award, 1954, 1971; Oscar, for screenplay, 1955, 1971, 1976; New York Film Critics award, 1956, 1971, 1976; British Academy award, 1976. *Died 1 August 1981.*

PUBLICATIONS

Plays

No T.O. for Love, music by Jimmy Livingston (produced 1945).
Printer's Measure (televised 1953). In *Television Plays*, 1955.
Middle of the Night (televised 1954; revised version, produced 1956). 1957.
Television Plays (includes *The Bachelor Party*, *The Big Deal*, *Holiday Song*, *Marty*, *The Mother*, and *Printer's Measure*). 1955.
The Bachelor Party (screenplay). 1957.
The Goddess (screenplay; stage version produced 1971). 1958.
The Tenth Man (produced 1959). 1960.
Gideon (produced 1961). 1962.
The Passion of Josef D. (produced 1964). 1964.
The Latent Heterosexual (produced 1968). 1967.

Screenplays: *The True Glory* (uncredited), with Garson Kanin, 1945; *As Young as You Feel*, with Lamar Trotti, 1951; *Marty*, 1955; *The Bachelor Party*, 1957; *The Goddess*, 1958; *Middle of the Night*, 1959; *The Americanization of Emily*, 1964; *Paint Your Wagon*, with Alan Jay Lerner, 1969; *The Hospital*, 1971; *Network*, 1975; *Altered States*, 1979.

Radio Plays: *The Meanest Man in the World*, *Tommy*, and *Over 21* (all in *Theater Guild of the Air* series), 1951–52; scripts for *Cavalcade of America*.

Television Plays: scripts for *Danger* and *Manhunt* series; *Holiday Song*, 1952; *The Reluctant Citizen*, 1952; *Printer's Measure*, 1953; *Marty*, 1953; *The Big Deal*, 1953; *The Bachelor Party*, 1953; *The Sixth Year*, 1953; *Catch My Boy on Sunday*, 1953; *The Mother*, 1954; *Middle of the Night*, 1954; *The Catered Affair*, 1955; *The Great American Hoax*, 1957.

Fiction

Altered States. 1978.

*

Critical Study: *Chayefsky* by John M. Clum, 1976.

* * *

"I write out of social necessity," Paddy Chayefsky once explained, but he might have said with equal candor, "I write out of personal conviction." A determined idealist who believed the message of his plays, Chayefsky wrote about men—*The Man Who Made the Mountains Shake* (an earlier title of the unproduced *Fifth from Garibaldi*), *The Tenth Man*, *The Latent Heterosexual*, *Marty*, *Gideon* and *Josef D.*—and about the agony man suffers in the *Middle of the Night* and the doom he senses when lost in *The Hospital* or inhumanly controlled within the *Network*. "I write a call to disaster," Chayefsky also once said, and the echoes of that "call," early and late, presented in stage plays, screenplays and plays for television, detail Chayefsky's progress from a writer with a wholesome faith in man and his power to love to a man who found in his despair that love was not enough.

Chayefsky's early work clearly illustrates his positive approach to the world, the world of the common man whose urgent search for values in his real and spiritual existence absorbed the playwright. Chayefsky's overwhelming sympathy for poor, trapped, and self-defeated people drove him to explore post-war urban society in America and, with his own abundant faith, to boost their self-esteem. Mario Fortunato, the ditch digger in the Boston Navy Yard who once "made the mountains shake," must recognize his own worth, not through wealth or his son's activities but as a man loved by his sons. How does one find meaning in life? That was Chayefsky's question, and in the personal dramas he created for television during the 1950's he contrived the simple and sentimental answers that first made him popular. His secret was a combination of distinctive craftsmanship, a belief in his art and a medium (television) which he found most suitable for his talents in creating a sense of reality among everyday crises. With a natural ear for human speech which earned him the reputation of the best writer of realistic dialogue in America, Chayefsky created a memorably poignant sense of frail humanity within the television framework of 53 minutes. In the early years his work was an affirmation of faith, revealed in such teleplays as *Holiday Song* and *The Reluctant Citizen*. Marty was just an ordinary, fat, ugly man with certain values and many conflicts who at the end of 53 minutes began a new and purposeful life.

The three best and most successful plays of Chayefsky's career epitomize the playwright of faith whose balanced approach to the frailties of man was buttressed by an empyreal sense of humor. In *Middle of the Night* a 53-year-old widowed manufacturer and a 24-year-old girl, both beset by greedy and insensitive people, decide that "even a few years of happiness you don't throw away. We'll get married." They are gentle and likeable people who flaunt social conventions with a nervous laugh and a calculated gamble. Arthur Landau in *The Tenth Man* has a terrifyingly perceptive view of modern life that underscores his assertion that he believes in nothing. This is his dybbuk. When he is commandeered to help fulfill the requirement for Jewish worship and discovers his fondness for a girl whose more conventional dybbuk arouses the Jews and their Cabalist to perform an exorcism, Arthur finds himself purged. It is a tender tale, realistically told, and the urban hero, feeling the power of love—or God, if you will—asserts himself and takes the girl away. According to Chayefsky, Gideon tests the God he knows, once again illustrating the playwright's very human view of man's relationship to his Old Testament God whose patience is indeed tried by this "vain ass" whose power to contemplate God evokes only his ingenuous but reasonable request that he be allowed to believe in himself. And God agrees—he loves Gideon—but with a cosmic sense of mocking humor; let man try to be God if he can.

Although Chayefsky's thoughtful concern for man remained prominent in his work, his convictions changed. His faith in the power of love to free a trapped mankind was replaced by fears for humanity. In *The Passion of Josef D.* belief in God becomes no longer possible. "Nothing is real," says Lenin; the gods that men create for themselves are illusions. Although *The Latent Heterosexual* is undeniably a serious play showing the wretched horror of the times, it is also frequently crude and brutal with a hero whose ego denies him real emotions, serious thoughts, or any recognizable values. After these plays, Chayefsky wrote only screenplays. *The Hospital* shows "the whole wounded madhouse of our times," a sick society in which the hero, struggling to regain his sense of purpose, finally recognizes a need "to be responsible." *Network* also pictures a grotesque and dehumanized world where there is no hope for man. The craftsmanship that was a hallmark of Chayefsky's work remained but he now dramatized a total disillusionment where sentimental faith had become a fearful bitterness, and hope had changed to horror in the world around him.

—Walter J. Meserve

CHEEVER, John (William). Born in Quincy, Massachusetts, 27 May 1912. Educated at Thayer Academy, South Braintree, Massachusetts. Served in the U.S. Army Signal Corps, 1943–45: Sergeant. Married Mary M. Winternitz in 1941; one daughter and two sons. Full-time writer in New York City, 1930–51, Scarborough, New York, 1951–60, and Ossining, New York, after 1961; teacher at Barnard College, New York, 1956–57, Ossining Correctional Facility (Sing Sing prison), 1971–72, and University of Iowa Writers Workshop, Iowa City, 1973; Visiting Professor of Creative Writing, Boston University, 1974–75. Recipient: Guggenheim fellowship, 1951, and second fellowship; Benjamin Franklin Award, 1955; O. Henry Award, 1956, 1964; American Academy grant, 1956, and Howells Medal, 1965; National Book Award, 1958; National Book Critics Circle award, 1979; Pulitzer Prize, 1979; MacDowell Medal, 1979; American Book Award, for paperback, 1981; National Medal for Literature, 1982. Litt.D.: Harvard University, Cambridge, Massachusetts, 1978. Member, American Academy, 1958. *Died 18 June 1982.*

PUBLICATIONS

Fiction

The Way Some People Live: A Book of Stories. 1943.
The Enormous Radio and Other Stories. 1953.
Stories, with others. 1956; as *A Book of Stories*, 1957.
The Wapshot Chronicle. 1957.
The Housebreaker of Shady Hill and Other Stories. 1958.
Some People, Places, and Things That Will Not Appear in My Next Novel (stories). 1961.
The Brigadier and the Golf Widow (stories). 1964.
The Wapshot Scandal. 1964.
Bullet Park. 1969.
The World of Apples (stories). 1973.
Falconer. 1977.
The Stories. 1978.
The Day the Pig Fell into the Well (story). 1978.
The Leaves, The Lion-Fish and the Bear (story). 1980.
Oh, What a Paradise It Seems. 1982.

Plays

Television Plays: scripts for *Life with Father* series; *The Shady Hill Kidnapping*, 1982.

*

Bibliography: *Cheever: A Reference Guide* by Francis J. Bosha, 1981.

Critical Studies: *Cheever* by Samuel Coale, 1977; *Cheever* by Lynne Waldeland, 1979; *Critical Essays on Cheever* edited by R.G. Collins, 1982; *Cheever: The Hobgoblin Company of Love* by George W. Hunt, 1983; *Home Before Dark: A Biographical Memoir of Cheever* by Susan Cheever, 1984.

* * *

John Cheever made his mark as a chronicler of a modern American sensibility that is well-educated, disoriented, and generally bitter toward the situations, sexual and cultural, in which it finds itself. That sensibility is usually represented as able to look back on an earlier generation in which moral codes were fixed and confident; that fixity and confidence almost constitute a romantic backdrop against which the frustrations of current life play out their inconclusive courses. These courses are often presented in short stories which combine the irony of sheer event with Cheever's own comments on what is happening—happening to persons who endure the events rather than understand them. For example, one story, "The Swimmer" (in *The Brigadier and the Golf Widow*), illustrates the texture and scope of many a Cheever tale. A man decides, for reasons that he does not clearly understand, to reach his home by swimming through all the private pools that extend toward his own home and pool. In the course of his feat, no more sensible than climbing the Himalayas, the swimmer has contact, ironic for Cheever and his readers, with several aspects of the swimmer's society. And at the end, the swimmer arrives at his own pool, only to find his house empty; there is no explanation of this shocking conclusion. The man's dismay is but an intensification of the pressures that set him on his way.

Novels allowed Cheever to explore at greater length destinies no more controlled and intelligible than the afternoon efforts of the swimmer. Two closely related novels, *The Wapshot Chronicle* and *The Wapshot Scandal*, represent the decline of a "good family" in a small New England community; the modest certainties of an older generation unravel in the adventures of two sons as they wander from job to job and from one sexual relation to another. Stories loosely connected with the fates of the two young men ornament the novels and illustrate the impact of conspicuous wealth. American go-getting, scientific research, and the soft life that lies in wait for most Cheever characters. *Bullet Park* presents these themes with more rigor as they apply to two men, Hammer and Nailles. In Nailles appears a man who is fairly content with the disintegrating Zion where he finds himself. In Hammer, Cheever offers a man whose wealth and success create in him only a nameless bitterness. It is a bitterness that leads Hammer to an envy of the complacent Nailles, whose unconsidered contentment he tries to destroy; Hammer attempts to crucify Nailles' son.

Is this the end of the road? *Falconer* seems to say "Not necessarily." Farragut, the hero of this novel, has one of the bitterest experiences that Cheever ever contrived. The man is a drug addict who has been sent to prison for the murder of his brother. In a highly unified narrative, Farragut experiences the heartless pressures of the prison system, goes through the routine inhumanity, homosexuality, and sheer boredom of prison life—and has enough energy left to contrive his escape into a world whose qualities are not necessarily superior to the concentrated hell of the prison. Farragut's will to persist, to continue in a life made up of the absurdities that society and fate and Cheever contrive, sums up the counsel that Cheever offers.

Counsel less definite appears in Cheever's last book, *Oh, What a Paradise It Seems*. In this brief tale, a suitable coda to Cheever's work, several persons are briefly stirred to action by a commercial threat to a local pond. But the encounter of the persons at the village meeting is brief, and it is clear that all the participants will go their separate ways. And such dispersion is enough, at least for Cheever. For the mark of a superior intelligence is to be able to look down on the minds and deeds of others.

So once more advice is offered with a skill that is ingenious and deft. It is advice that comes from an authorial consciousness that is condescending rather than sympathetic.

—Harold H. Watts

See the essay on "The Swimmer."

CHESNUTT, Charles Waddell. Born in Cleveland, Ohio, 20 June 1858; moved with his family to Fayetteville, North Carolina, 1866. Educated privately, and in local schools. Married Susan U. Perry in 1878; four children. Teacher, North Carolina public schools, 1873–77; assistant principal, 1877–79, and principal, 1880–83, Howard Normal School, Fayetteville; reporter, New York *Mail and Express*, 1883; clerk for railway company, Cleveland, 1883, then stenographer for the company's lawyer and studied law (admitted to Ohio bar, 1887); owned a stenographic business, mid-1880's–1899 and after 1902. Recipient: NAACP Spingarn Medal, 1928. *Died 15 November 1932*.

PUBLICATIONS

Collections

The Short Fiction, edited by Sylvia Lyons Render. 1974.

Fiction

The Conjure Woman (stories). 1899.
The Wife of His Youth and Other Stories of the Color Line. 1899.
The House Behind the Cedars. 1900.
The Marrow of Tradition. 1901.
The Colonel's Dream. 1905.

Other

Frederick Douglass. 1899.

*

Bibliography: "The Works of Chesnutt: A Checklist" by William L. Andrews, in *Bulletin of Bibliography*, January 1976; *Chesnutt: A Reference Guide* by Curtis W. Ellison and E.W. Metcalf, Jr., 1977.

Critical Studies: *Chesnutt, Pioneer of the Color Line* by Helen M. Chesnutt, 1952; *Chesnutt: America's First Great Black Novelist* by J. Noel Heermance, 1974; *An American Crusade: The Life of Chesnutt* by Frances Richardson Keller, 1978; *The Literary Career of Chesnutt* by William L. Andrews, 1980; *Chesnutt* by Sylvia Lyons Render, 1980.

* * *

Charles Waddell Chesnutt, a "voluntary Negro," reflects in his writings major inter- and intraracial tensions of the 19th-century United States. Beginning and ending his life in Cleveland, Ohio, and from age seven to 25 living in North Carolina, he found the major motivations and materials of his works in his own life and that of contemporaries or immediate forebears on both sides of the Mason-Dixon line. Chesnutt's preoccupations with the problems of powerless blacks and poor whites is doubtless a reflection not only of the trauma which marked his own poverty-stricken youth but also of the resultant resolve to improve the quality of life for all those denied access to the fullness of American life because of color and/or class.

Chesnutt's fiction ranges in form from simple tale to highly plotted novel, in mood from comic to tragic. The subject matter reflects the major contemporary concerns of black Americans. However, the general reading public, primarily white, rejected Chesnutt's increasingly explicit advocacy of equal rights for blacks and other under-privileged citizens. Consequently, after *The Colonel's Dream* in 1905, Chesnutt terminated his writing career.

By that time, however, Chesnutt had won a permanent place in American literary history, especially for his short fiction. His serious consideration as a conscious, accomplished author by critics such as William Dean Howells and George Washington Cable was unprecedented for a black American prose writer. His works, usually presented from a black perspective, are historically and sociologically accurate as well as aesthetically satisfying and ethically admirable. Chesnutt is recognized as "the first real Negro novelist," "the pioneer of the color line," and the first American writer not only to use the folk tale for social protest but also extensively to characterize black Americans.

After he stopped writing Chesnutt used in other ways his increasing influence to improve the status of his fellow blacks. In recognition of his achievements, the National Association for the Advancement of Colored People awarded him its annual Spingarn Medal in 1928. Upon Chesnutt's death in 1932, a friend summed up accurately: "His great contribution in letters is a monument to our race and . . . to our national life."

—Sylvia Lyons Render

CHIVERS, Thomas Holley. Born near Washington, Georgia, 18 October 1809. Educated at a preparatory school in Georgia; Transylvania University, Lexington, Kentucky, M.D. (honors) 1830. Married 1) his cousin Frances Elizabeth Chivers in 1827, one daughter; 2) Harriette Hunt in 1837, two sons and two daughters. Practised medicine briefly, then full-time writer: contributed to numerous periodicals throughout his life; corresponded with Poe from 1840, met him in 1845, and was later involved in a controversy about plagiarism of Poe's work. *Died 18 December 1858.*

PUBLICATIONS

Collections

Chivers: A Selection, edited by Lewis Chase. 1929.
Correspondence 1838–1858, edited by Emma Lester Chase and Lois Ferry Parks. 1957.

Verse

The Path of Sorrow; or, The Lament of Youth. 1832.
Nacoochee; or, The Beautiful Star, with Other Poems. 1837.
The Lost Pleiad and Other Poems. 1845.
Eonchs of Ruby: A Gift of Love. 1851; revised edition, as *Memoralia; or, Phials of Amber Full of the Tears of Love*, 1853.
Virginalia; or, Songs of My Summer Nights: A Gift of Love for the Beautiful. 1853.
Atlanta; or, The True Blessed Island of Poesy: A Paul Epic in Three Lustra. 1853.
Birth-Day Song of Liberty: A Paean of Glory for the Heroes of Freedom. 1856.

Plays

Conrad and Eudora; or, The Death of Alonzo. 1834.
The Sons of Usna: A Tragi-Apotheosis. 1858.
The Unpublished Plays (includes *Count Julian*, *Osceola*, *Charles Stuart*, *Leoni*), edited by Charles M. Lombard. 1980.

Other

Search after Truth; or, A New Revelation of the Psycho-Physiological Nature of Man. 1848.
Life of Poe, edited by Richard Beale Davis. 1952.

*

Bibliography: in *Bibliography of American Literature* by Jacob Blanck, 1957; by John O. Eidson, in *A Bibliographical Guide to the Study of Southern Literature* edited by Louis D. Rubin, Jr., 1969.

Critical Studies: *Chivers, Friend of Poe* (with selections) by S. Foster Damon, 1930; *Chivers: His Literary Career and His Poetry* by Charles H. Watts, 1956; *Chivers* by Charles M. Lombard, 1979.

* * *

Unlike many of his American and southern contemporaries, Thomas Holley Chivers was free to devote himself to poetry since he had independent means, and, though he could hardly be called a professional man of letters, he took literature seriously and developed a theory of poetry and an aesthetic. Over a period of 25 years he published, usually at his own expense, a great deal of verse and a smattering of prose in periodicals in Washington and Decatur, Georgia, as well as occasionally in the *Knickerbocker* and *Graham's*, and in book form in Macon, Georgia, and Franklin, Tennessee, as well as in New York and Philadelphia.

Chivers's theory of poetry as expressed in his prefaces to his collections of poems, especially *Nacoochee*, *Memoralia*, and *Atlanta*, and in his unpublished and incomplete articles and lectures is, according to Edd Winfield Parks, that true poetry is "divinely inspired" and the poet is "at once the mediator and the revelator of God." "Poets," Chivers says in "The Beauties of Poetry," "are the apostles of divine thought, who are clothed with an authority from the Most High, to work miracles in the minds of men." The poet sees all things with "*internal*, or spiritual eyes," though, admittedly, celestial beauty can only be partially glimpsed on earth. Still, the inspired writer can recognize transcendental truth and can "convey the idea of a heavenly truth by an earthly one."

In his own practice Chivers tried the usual forms—drama, ode, sonnet, narrative—but he gradually became fascinated with rhythm, diction, sound, and with the lore and melodies of the Indian, the Negro, and the folk tradition of Georgia. His experimentation with ballad-like forms, refrains, and language led him to a special vocabulary and declamatory style that manifest themselves in, among others, "Lily Adair," "Avalon," "Apollo," and "Rosalie Lee."

The first and last of these poems, to be sure, suggest the work of Poe, as do such earlier pieces as "Isadore" and "To

Allegra Florence." Still, despite a certain amount of critical attention in recent decades, Chivers's work is largely of interest because of its relationship to Poe's. The thorny problems of precedence and influence have not yet been fully resolved, despite recent efforts by scholars interested in each poet. Even if it is established that Chivers provided Poe with hints concerning rhythm, meter, and refrain, the disinterested critic can only conclude with Jay B. Hubbell in *The South in American Literature* that Poe's supposed "borrowings" are "all assimilated and transformed into something original and Poesque." This, of course, is to say nothing of Chivers's borrowings from Poe, nor to mention that nothing was said of plagiarism until Poe was dead.

Whatever one may say, however, of the Poe-Chivers matter, one must also conclude that Chivers's work, erratic and uneven as it may be, is fascinating in its own right and deserves more critical consideration than it has hitherto received.

—Rayburn S. Moore

CHOPIN, Kate (Katherine Chopin, née O'Flaherty). Born in St. Louis, Missouri, 8 February 1851. Educated at the Academy of the Sacred Heart, St. Louis, graduated 1868. Married Oscar Chopin in 1870 (died, 1883); five sons and one daughter. Lived in New Orleans, 1870–79, on her husband's plantation in Cloutierville, Louisiana, 1880–82, and in St. Louis after 1884; began writing in 1888. *Died 22 August 1904.*

PUBLICATIONS

Collections

Complete Works, edited by Per Seyersted. 2 vols., 1969.

Fiction

At Fault. 1890.
Bayou Folk (stories). 1894.
A Night in Acadie (stories). 1897.
The Awakening. 1899; edited by Margaret Culley, 1976.
The Awakening and Other Stories, edited by Lewis Leary. 1970.
Portraits: Short Stories, edited by Helen Taylor. 1979.
The Awakening and Selected Stories, edited by Sandra M. Gilbert. 1984.

Other

A Chopin Miscellany, edited by Per Seyersted and Emily Toth. 1979.

*

Bibliography: in *Bibliography of American Literature* by Jacob Blanck, 1957; *Edith Wharton and Chopin: A Reference Guide* by Marlene Springer, 1976.

Critical Studies: *Chopin and Her Creole Stories* by Daniel S. Rankin, 1932; *The American 1890's: Life and Times of a Lost Generation* by Larzer Ziff, 1966; *Chopin: A Critical Biography* by Per Seyersted, 1969; *Chopin* by Barbara C. Ewell, 1985; *Chopin* by Peggy Skaggs, 1985.

* * *

In 1894, when Kate Chopin published *Bayou Folk*, a collection of Louisiana stories, she was greeted as an outstanding local color writer. In 1899, when she brought out *The Awakening*, a novel which in certain respects is an American *Madame Bovary*, she so shocked the public that some libraries banned the book. As a result, her creative spirit was stifled, and, when she died in 1904, she was forgotten. But in 1969, when *The Complete Works of Kate Chopin* appeared, the time was ripe for a reassessment and revival of this writer. Today she is recognized both as a literary artist of the American realist movement and as a particularly significant commentator on the female experience.

Chopin grew up in the French atmosphere of her mother's family in St. Louis, and she married a Creole, and lived in New Orleans and on a Louisiana plantation for thirteen years. Her *oeuvre* consists of two novels and about 100 stories. Nearly all she wrote is set in Louisiana, and she makes the atmosphere of this picturesque state vivid, with the enchanting physical setting and the charming peculiarities of the Creoles, Cajuns, and blacks of the region.

But she used local color discreetly, never as an end in itself; rather, her interest was general human nature. As a child she had been taught to face life without fear and embarrassment and to observe people without judging them. She did not believe in idealism, and she disliked moral reformers. In her first novel, *At Fault*, she lets a woman (who has forced a man to remarry his divorced drunkard wife in order to redeem her) come to the conclusion that no one has the right to submit others to the "exacting and ignorant rule of . . . moral conventionalities."

From an early age Chopin was an avid reader, with a particular interest in books dealing with women's position. She was especially influenced by Maupassant, probably because she felt he spoke secretly to her with his frank treatments of the hidden life of women. This fitted in with her own ambition, which was to portray especially the lives of women, as truthfully and openly as America would permit. Her first extant story deals with a "feminine" or traditional heroine who submissively leaves it to the man to decide her fate, and the second with an "emancipated" woman who insists on deciding for herself about her own life. Most of her later heroines are variations on these two types. She often wrote about them in pairs, thus keeping up a kind of balanced dialogue between traditional and emancipated women.

As Chopin gained in self-confidence, she became more daring in her descriptions of unconventional women. When she had just been nationally praised for *Bayou Folk* she wrote "The Story of an Hour," a tale about a woman who, when told that her husband has suddenly died, whispers "free, free, free!" A few weeks later the author in a sense answered this extreme example of the self-assertive woman with an entry in her diary, where she wrote that could she get her husband back, she would have been willing to give up "the past ten years of my growth—my real growth."

Chopin's ultimate examples of the feminine and the emancipated woman are found in *The Awakening*. Adèle Ratignolle strikingly illustrates the patriarchal ideal of the self-forgetting woman. A Creole and a Catholic, she is likened to a "Faultless

Madonna" and described as a "mother-woman," that is, one who lives for and through her family and who considers it "a holy privilege to efface themselves as individuals." She is a perfect foil for Edna Pontellier, an American married to a New Orleans Creole and the mother of two, who says: "I would give up the unessential; I would . . . give my life for my children; but I wouldn't give myself." What she means by this becomes clear as she gradually awakens to a self-assertion both in the physical and spiritual field. Like Emma Bovary, she becomes estranged from her husband, neglects her children, has lovers, and finally takes her life. But while Emma acts out roles inherited from romantic literature and gains little self-knowledge, Edna outgrows her romantic notions and learns "to look with her own eyes [and] to apprehend the deeper undercurrents of life."

She realizes that the physical side of love can live apart from the spiritual one, and that sex is a basic force which—in the guise of romantic emotions—drives us blindly on toward procreation. She understands that, for her, a return to the submission and self-delusion of the past is impossible. She refuses to let the children "drag her into the soul's slavery for the rest of her days," but she finally accepts a responsibility not to give them a bad name and takes her life. While defeated by her environment, she is also victorious: finally understanding her own nature and her situation as a woman, she exerts her inner freedom by assuming sole responsibility for her life.

The critics had to concede that, artistically, *The Awakening* is a small masterpiece. But just as with Dreiser's *Sister Carrie* a year later, they could not accept an author who in no way condemns such a heroine. Larzer Ziff has said of Chopin's silence after this setback that it was "a loss to American letters of the order of the untimely deaths of Crane and Norris." Today *The Awakening* is available in numerous editions, and with this novel and her best stories Kate Chopin seems assured a permanent place in American literature.

—Per Seyersted

See the essay on *The Awakening*.

CHURCHILL, Winston. Born in St. Louis, Missouri, 10 November 1871. Educated at Smith Academy, St. Louis, 1879–88; U.S. Naval Academy, Annapolis, Maryland, 1890–94; naval cadet on the cruiser *San Francisco*, New York Navy Yard, 1894. Married Mabel Harlakenden Hall in 1895 (died, 1945); one daughter and two sons. Editor, *Army and Navy Journal*, New York, 1894; managing editor, *Cosmopolitan*, New York, 1895; full-time writer from 1895; Republican member for Cornish, New Hampshire Legislature, 1903–05; delegate for New Hampshire, Republican National Convention, Chicago, 1904; Progressive Party candidate for the New Hampshire governorship, 1912; toured European battle fronts, and wrote for *Scribner's*, New York, 1917–18. President, Authors League of America, 1913. *Died 12 March 1947.*

PUBLICATIONS

Fiction

The Celebrity: An Episode. 1898.
Richard Carvel. 1899.
The Crisis. 1901.
Mr. Keegan's Elopement (stories). 1903.
The Crossing. 1904.
Coniston. 1906.
Mr. Crewe's Career. 1908.
A Modern Chronicle. 1910.
The Inside of the Cup. 1913.
A Far Country. 1915.
The Dwelling-Place of Light. 1917.
The Faith of Frances Craniford (story). 1917.

Plays

The Title-Mart (produced 1905). 1905.
Dr. Jonathan. 1919.

Other

A Traveller in War-Time, with an Essay on the American Contribution and the Democratic Idea. 1918.
The Green Bay Tree. 1920.
The Uncharted Way: The Psychology of the Gospel Doctrine. 1940.

*

Bibliography: *Churchill: A Reference Guide* by Eric Steinbaugh, 1985.

Critical Studies: *The Romantic Compromise in the Novels of Churchill* by Charles C. Walcutt, 1951; *Churchill* by Warren I. Titus, 1963; *Novelist to a Generation: The Life and Thought of Churchill* by Robert W. Schneider, 1976.

* * *

Winston Churchill (no relation to the British statesman) was a gifted storyteller who became very popular with well-researched but episodic romances concerning the American Revolution in *Richard Carvel*, the Civil War in *The Crisis*, and the settlement of Tennessee and Kentucky in *The Crossing*. Drawing upon his personal experience as a legislator and candidate for gubernatorial nomination in New Hampshire, Churchill then became a more serious social critic in *Coniston*, a novel about political bossism. The boss, Jethro Bass (based on a real political figure, Ruel Durkee), is a complex mixture of good and evil who in part manipulates the system, and is in part a product of it. He is probably Churchill's best developed and most human character. *Mr. Crewe's Career* does not so much concern the bumbling political efforts of the amateur politician Humphrey Crewe (said by Churchill to be a self-satire) as it concerns the corrupting influence of the railroad and other industries on the state legislature and the courts. Churchill mars these two novels by resolving the conflicts with a marriage between a daughter and a son of the opposing major figures. Although this device was supposed to show how the dynamism of industry could be combined with the idealism of politics, it actually leaves the essential differences of the two views unsettled, and reflects Churchill's mild "Progressive" approach in these novels (he was a friend and admirer of Roosevelt's).

Churchill first evidenced in his fiction a concern for religion in *The Inside of the Cup*, a novel which concerns a clergyman of an unspecified persuasion (Churchill was an active Episcopal layman) who comes to see the necessity for preaching a social gospel rather than a purely "spiritual" one. Although he meets resistance from a slum landlord in his congregation, the minister makes many converts to his position and remains in the good graces of his church. The novel is therefore less hard-hitting than, say, Charles Monroe Sheldon's *In His Steps*. *A Far Country* deals even more forcefully with the conflict Churchill saw between Christianity and capitalism and with society's ill-treatment of unwed mothers. Churchill lent his pen to the propaganda effort during World War I, but immediately afterward returned in *Dr. Jonathan* to call for more social justice and a more equitable distribution of wealth.

Churchill's popularity declined gradually after he forsook the historical romance, but in 1920 he found himself almost without an audience. He then devoted twenty years to research in psychology and theology before publishing a non-fiction re-interpretation of the world and of the Bible, *The Uncharted Way*. Churchill did not think his analysis of history as the conflict between the "moral" self and the "technical" self, the generous and selfish side of each man, would be immediately understood, but looked to future generations for vindication.

—William Higgins

CLARK, Walter Van Tilburg. Born in East Orland, Maine, 3 August 1909. Educated at Reno High School, Nevada, graduated 1926; University of Nevada, Reno, 1926–31, B.A. 1931, M.A. 1932; University of Vermont, Burlington, M.A. 1934. Married Barbara Frances Morse in 1933 (died); one daughter and one son. English teacher and basketball coach, Cazenovia Central School, Cazenovia, New York, 1933–45, and a school in Rye, New York, 1945–46; Lecturer, 1950–53, and Writer-in-Residence, 1962–71, University of Nevada; Rockefeller Lecturer, 1953; Associate Professor of English, University of Montana, Missoula, 1953–56; Professor of English and Creative Writing, San Francisco State College, 1956–62; Fellow in Fiction, Center for Advanced Studies, Wesleyan University, Middletown, Connecticut, 1960–61. Recipient: O. Henry Award, 1945. Litt.D.: Colgate University, Hamilton, New York, 1958; University of Nevada, 1969. *Died 10 November 1971.*

PUBLICATIONS

Fiction

The Ox-Bow Incident. 1940.
The City of Trembling Leaves. 1945; as *Tim Hazard*, 1951.
The Track of the Cat. 1949.
The Watchful Gods and Other Stories. 1950.

Verse

Christmas Comes to Hjalsen, Reno. 1930.
Ten Women in Gale's House and Shorter Poems. 1932.

Other

Editor, *The Journals of Alfred Doten 1849–1903*. 3 vols., 1973.

*

Bibliography: "Clark: A Bibliography" by Richard W. Etulain, in *South Dakota Review*, Autumn 1965.

Critical Studies: *Clark* by Max Westbrook, 1969; *Clark* by L.L. Lee, 1973; *Clark: Critiques* edited by Charlton Laird, 1983.

* * *

The place of Walter Van Tilburg Clark in literary history rests on two of his three novels, *The Ox-Bow Incident* and *The Track of the Cat*. If that perch is narrow, it is also firm, not merely because both were made into memorable films, but, more importantly, because both are sensitive psychological studies of great impact.

Taken as a parable of fascism at the time of its writing, *The Ox-Bow Incident*, set in the American west, is a powerful examination of leadership and mob violence. Against a dry-tinder backdrop of lassitude reminiscent of the setting of Faulkner's "dry September," the men of Bridger's Wells need only an act of violence and the imposition of a strong will to be ignited into a flaming mob. The point is that violence triumphs by default; that a single-minded person can take charge and use the vast energy latent in boredom and resentment for evil as long as no one will take steps sufficient to stop him.

Four years after his jejune second novel, *The City of Trembling Leaves*, Clark published his second successful novel, *The Track of the Cat*. Much more self-consciously artistic than *The Ox-Bow Incident*, the novel uses as its focus a mountain lion that becomes, literally and symbolically, the *bête noire* of the men who are tracking it. In the death of the two men, there is penetrating insight into human character: one, the overbearing realist, cannot cope with the mythic dimensions of the cat and falls from a cliff in fear of it; the other, the arch romantic, forgets the cat's deadly reality and is struck down.

Clark's problem as a novelist resides in his inability to proportion characters appropriately to plot. He invests no one in *The Track of the Cat*, for example, with stature commensurate with the great task of hunting the real and mythic beast. His characters are sometimes sententious. But in his two fine western novels, he largely overcomes the problem by sheer narrative force and by showing his audience some revealing habits of the human animal.

—Alan R. Shucard

CLEMENS, Samuel Langhorne. See **TWAIN, Mark.**

COHAN, George M(ichael). Born in Providence, Rhode Island, 3 July 1878; son of the vaudevillians Jerry and Helen Cohan. Briefly attended two elementary schools in Providence; received no formal education after age 8. Married 1) Ethelia Fowler (the actress Ethel Levey) in 1899, one daughter; 2) Agnes Nolan in 1907, two daughters and one son. Traveled with his parents as a child, and made his stage debut with them in 1887; thereafter regularly appeared with his parents and sister as The Four Cohans; appeared as an actor in *Peck's Bad Boy*, in New York, 1890; toured the U.S. with The Four Cohans, throughout the 1890's, and was appearing with them in leading vaudeville houses in New York and Chicago by 1900; produced first musical for the New York stage, starring The Four Cohans and his wife, in 1901; formed producing partnership with Sam Harris, 1904, and wrote, presented, and starred in a number of musical hits on Broadway; presented plays, with Harris, at the New Gaiety Theatre, New York, 1908–10, and at the George M. Cohan Theatre, New York, 1910–20; lived in semi-retirement after 1920, occasionally appearing on the New York stage. Produced 150 plays, and wrote more than 500 songs. Recipient: U.S. Congress gold medal, 1940. *Died 5 November 1942*.

PUBLICATIONS

Plays

The Governor's Son (produced 1901). Songs published 1901(?).
Running for Office (produced 1903); revised version, as *The Honeymooners* (produced 1907).
Little Johnny Jones (produced 1904).
Popularity (produced 1906).
Forty-Five Minutes from Broadway (produced 1906).
George Washington, Jr. (produced 1906).
Fifty Miles from Boston (produced 1907).
The Talk of New York (produced 1907).
The American Idea (produced 1908). 1909.
The Yankee Prince (produced 1908).
The Man Who Owns Broadway (produced 1909). Songs published 1909(?).
Get-Rich-Quick Wallingford, from a story by George Randolph Chester (produced 1910).
The Little Millionaire (produced 1911). 1911.
Broadway Jones (produced 1912). 1923; revised version, music by the author, as *The Two of Us* (as *Billie*, produced 1928), 1928.
Seven Keys to Baldpate, from the novel by Earl Derr Biggers (produced 1913). 1914.
The Miracle Man, from a story by Frank L. Packard (produced 1914).
Hello, Broadway!, music by the author (produced 1914).
What Advertising Brings, with L. Grant (produced 1915).
Hit-the-Trail Holliday (produced 1915). 1916.
The Cohan Revue 1916 (produced 1916).
Honest John O'Brien (produced 1916).
The Cohan Revue 1918 (produced 1918).
The Voice of McConnell (produced 1918).
The Fireman's Picnic. 1918.
A Prince There Was, from the novel *Enchanted Hearts* by Darragh Aldrich (produced 1918). 1927.
The Royal Vagabond, with Stephen Ivor-Szinny and William Cary Duncan, music by Anselm Goetzl (produced 1919). 1919.
The Farrell Case: A One Act Mystery (produced 1919).
Madeleine and the Movies (produced 1922).
Little Nelly Kelly (produced 1922).
The Song and Dance Man (produced 1923).
The Rise of Rosie O'Reilly (produced 1923). Songs published 1923(?).
American Born (produced 1925).
The Home-Towners (produced 1926).
The Baby Cyclone (produced 1927). 1929.
The Merry Malones (produced 1927).
Whispering Friends (produced 1928).
Gambling (produced 1929).
Friendship (produced 1931).
Confidential Service. 1932.
Pigeons and People (produced 1933). 1941.
Dear Old Darling (produced 1935).
Fulton of Oak Falls, from a story by Parker Fennelly (produced 1936).
The Return of the Vagabond (produced 1940). 1940.

Verse

Songs of Yesteryear. 1924.

Other

Twenty Years on Broadway, and the Years It Took to Get There. 1925.

*

Critical Study: *Cohan, The Man Who Owned Broadway* by John McCabe, 1980.

* * *

Cohan the dramatist? Surely not. Cohan the Yankee Doodle Dandy, the song and dance man, the song writer (not only "Yankee Doodle Dandy" but also "Mary's a Grand Old Name" and "Give My Regards to Broadway"). But Cohan the playwright is as unknown today as Cohan the vaudevillian and Cohan the movie star. The only play of his that is still remembered is probably *Seven Keys to Baldpate*, a comedy thriller filmed five times.

In his own time, however, Cohan was significant not only as an actor but as a playwright. As Alan S. Downer puts it (in *Fifty Years of American Drama*, 1951), "Out of the variety houses and into the legitimate theatre came George M. Cohan, the apostle of rampant Americanism. With a sharp ear for the colloquial speech of New York . . ., with his single-minded devotion to the color combination in Old Glory, he created a wise-cracking, quick-footed, dashing young hero who could instantaneously declare and prove his superiority to all lesser mortals, 'reubens' or 'limeys' or both." From his success derive plays such as those of Winchell Smith and George Kelly, the tough talk of the 1930's films, the snappy wisecracks of Kaufman and Dorothy Parker.

The best of the plays are probably *Little Johnny Jones*, *Forty-Five Minutes from Broadway*, *Get-Rich-Quick Wallingford*, *Seven Keys to Baldpate*, *The Miracle Man*, and *Gambling*. Cohan learned his craft in the 1880's and 1890's and seldom went beyond what he learned. He used theatrical tricks in many of the plays, shocked the audience by putting Billy Sunday on the stage in *Hit-the-Trail Holliday*, kept the title character offstage in *The Miracle Man*, had no intermission in *Pigeons and People*, revealed the identity of the robber in the first act of *Confidential Service*, always with an eye on theatrical effect. His one rule was to "wow them."

—Leonard R.N. Ashley

CONNELLY, Marc(us Cook). Born in McKeesport, Pennsylvania, 13 December 1890. Educated at Trinity Hall, Washington, Pennsylvania, 1902–07. Married Madeline Hurlock in 1930 (divorced, 1935). Reporter and drama critic, Pittsburgh *Press* and *Gazette-Times*, 1908–15; moved to New York, 1915: free-lance writer and actor, 1915–33; reporter, New York *Morning Telegraph*, 1918–21; helped found the *New Yorker*, 1925; wrote screenplays and directed in Hollywood, 1933–44; Professor of Playwriting, Yale University Drama School, New Haven, Connecticut, 1947–52. U.S. Commissioner to Unesco, 1951; adviser, Equity Theatre Library, 1960. Council member, Dramatists Guild, from 1920; member of the Executive Committee, U.S. National Committee for Unesco. Recipient: Pulitzer Prize, 1930; O. Henry Award, for short story, 1930. Litt.D.: Bowdoin College, Brunswick, Maine, 1952; Baldwin-Wallace College, Berea, Ohio, 1962. President, Authors League of America; President, National Institute of Arts and Letters, 1953–56. *Died 21 December 1980.*

PUBLICATIONS

Plays

$2.50 (produced 1913).
The Lady of Luzon (lyrics only), book by Alfred Ward Birdsall, music by Zoel Parenteau (produced 1914).
Follow the Girl (lyrics only, uncredited; produced 1915).
The Amber Empress, music by Zoel Parenteau (produced 1916; as *The Amber Princess*, produced 1917).
Dulcy, with George S. Kaufman (produced 1921). 1921.
Erminie, revised version of the play by Henry Paulton (produced 1921).
To the Ladies!, with George S. Kaufman (produced 1922). 1923.
No, Sirree!, with George S. Kaufman (produced 1922).
The 49ers, with George S. Kaufman (produced 1922).
West of Pittsburgh, with George S. Kaufman (produced 1922; revised version, as *The Deep Tangled Wildwood*, produced 1923).
Merton of the Movies, with George S. Kaufman, from the story by Harry Leon Wilson (produced 1922). 1925.
A Christmas Carol, with George S. Kaufman, from the story by Dickens, in *Bookman*, December 1922.
Helen of Troy, New York, with George S. Kaufman, music and lyrics by Harry Ruby and Bert Kalmar (produced 1923).
Beggar on Horseback, with George S. Kaufman, music by Deems Taylor, from a play by Paul Apel (produced 1924). 1925.
Be Yourself, with George S. Kaufman, music and lyrics by Lewis Genzler and Milton Schwarzwald, additional lyrics by Ira Gershwin (produced 1924).
The Wisdom Tooth: A Fantastic Comedy (produced 1926). 1927.
The Wild Man of Borneo, with Herman J. Mankiewicz (produced 1927).
How's the King? (produced 1927).
The Green Pastures: A Fable Suggested by Roark Bradford's Southern Sketches "Ol' Man Adam an' His Chillun" (produced 1930). 1929.
The Survey (skit), in *New Yorker*, 1934.
The Farmer Takes a Wife, with Frank B. Elser, from the novel *Rome Haul* by Walter D. Edmonds (produced 1934). Abridgement in *Best Plays of 1934–1935*, edited by Burns Mantle, 1935.
Little David: An Unproduced Scene from "The Green Pastures." 1937.
Everywhere I Roam, with Arnold Sundgaard (produced 1938).
The Traveler. 1939.
The Mole on Lincoln's Cheek (broadcast 1941). In *The Free Company Presents*, edited by James Boyd, 1941.
The Flowers of Virtue (produced 1942).
The Good Earth, with others, in *Twenty Best Film Plays*, edited by John Gassner and Dudley Nichols. 1943.
A Story for Strangers (produced 1948).
Hunter's Moon (produced 1958).
The Portable Yenberry (produced 1962).
The Green Pastures (screenplay), edited by Thomas Cripps. 1979.
The Stitch in Time (produced 1981).

Screenplays: *Whispers*, 1920; *Exit Smiling*, with others, 1926; *The Bridegroom*, *The Burglar*, *The Suitor*, and *The Uncle* (film shorts), 1929; *The Unemployed Ghost* (film short), 1931; *The Cradle Song*, 1933; *The Little Duchess* (film short), 1934; *The Green Pastures*, 1936; *The Farmer Takes a Wife*, 1937; *Captains Courageous*, with John Lee Mahin and Dale Van Emery, 1937; *The Good Earth*, with others, 1937; *I Married a Witch*, with Robert Pirosh, 1942; *Reunion* (*Reunion in France*), with others, 1942; *The Imposter* (additional dialogue), 1944; *Fabiola* (English dialogue), 1951; *Crowded Paradise* (additional scenes), 1956.

Radio Play: *The Mole on Lincoln's Cheek*, 1941.

Fiction

A Souvenir from Qam. 1965.

Other

Voices Off-Stage: A Book of Memoirs. 1968.

*

Critical Study: *Connelly* by Paul T. Nolan, 1969.

* * *

Born to parents who had both had stage careers, Marc Connelly early became dedicated to the theatre. As a young child, he says in his memoirs, he got the "feeling that going to the theater is like going to an unusual church, where the spirit is nourished in mystical ways, and pure magic may occur at any moment." Connelly spent his life as a man of the theatre seeking to produce that pure magic—as actor, director, and playwright.

Convinced that there was much to be enjoyed in life, Connelly as a young man fell in naturally with the famed "Round Table" of the 1920's at New York's Algonquin Hotel. His first New York stage venture had been the lyrics for the musical *The Amber Empress* (1916), but success did not come until the collaborations with George S. Kaufman. In 1921 their *Dulcy*, a mixture of gentle satire and fun, helped to set the standard for the Broadway comedy of the 1920's. They collaborated on six other plays. Their *Merton of the Movies*, based on the story by Harry Leon Wilson, inaugurated an era of Broadway satires on

Hollywood. The play's success was marked by Hollywood's turning it into a movie.

The most important play of the Kaufman-Connelly collaboration was *Beggar on Horseback*, a masterpiece of American expressionism and a fitting symbol of the *joie de vivre* the collaborators consistently sought to bring to the stage. The play is based on Paul Apel's *Hans Sonnestössers Höllenfahrt*, but it is no slavish copy of the German play—the expressionism has been completely Americanized in technique and in its satiric ends. Framed by scenes of comic realism, the visual and audial effects of the expressionism, helped by cinematic techniques, are more varied than those of Elmer Rice's *The Adding Machine* (1923).

After the success of *Beggar on Horseback*, the collaborators decided to pursue their careers apart. Connelly wrote musicals and plays (most successfully *The Wisdom Tooth*) and wrote short stories for the *New Yorker* (he was on the editorial board of the struggling new magazine), but it was not until he read Roark Bradford's *Ol' Man Adam an' His Chillun* that he wrote the play that insured his unique position in 20th-century drama. In Bradford's rendering of Old Testament stories from the viewpoint of uneducated Louisiana Negroes, Connelly immediately perceived the basis of a drama where pure magic might nourish the human spirit. The result was *The Green Pastures*, a work which, while it contained much of the fun of Bradford, gave it a greater dignity and a greater vision. Connelly's Lawd is a growing protagonist; his play's action concerns man's search for God and God's search for man. Connelly enhanced his episodically structured play through the use of Negro spirituals, suggesting other aspects of the folk longings. By framing the play with a children's Sunday School, Connelly conveyed the value of his material: unless one becomes as a little child, the play's vision would be beyond him. Broadway had long been without a religious play, and an all-Negro cast was also unusual. Connelly had difficulty getting backing for the play, but the production (directed by himself) proved the sceptics wrong. The play ran for five years, totalling 1642 performances.

Connelly was in Hollywood often in the 1930's, writing screenplays (some of the best of the period) and directing. (He would later act in *Our Town* and in other plays.) Although Connelly wrote some scripts and other plays, none matched his earlier successes. *A Souvenir from Qam*, his only novel, satirizes spy stories. He reminisced about his many years on the stage and in the movies in *Voices Off-Stage*, which gives brief glimpses of famous contemporaries but is most valuable for its account of *The Green Pastures*.

—Joseph M. Flora

COOKE, Ebenezer. Surname also spelled Cook. Born in London, England, c. 1667. First came to Maryland c. 1694; returned to London c. 1700 and again before 1708; in Maryland after 1712, when he inherited a family estate in Dorchester County; Deputy Receiver-General, Cecil County, after 1720; also land agent; admitted to Prince George's County bar, 1728. *Died c. 1732*.

PUBLICATIONS

Verse

The Sot-Weed Factor; or, A Voyage to Maryland. 1708; edited by Brantz Mayer, 1865.

Sotweed Redivivus; or, The Planter's Looking-Glass. 1730.

The Maryland Muse (includes *The Sot-Weed Factor* and *The History of Colonel Nathaniel Bacon's Rebellion in Virginia*). 1731.

*

Critical Studies: *Men of Letters in Colonial Maryland* by J.A. Leo Lemay, 1972; *Cooke: The Sot-Weed Canon* by Edward H. Cohen, 1975; "Cooke: Satire in the Colonial South" by Robert D. Arner, in *Southern Literary Journal 8*, 1975.

* * *

Known as the self-proclaimed "Poet Laureate" of colonial Maryland, Ebenezer Cooke was among the first American poets to write satire about the colonies from the point of view of a disgruntled colonist. He is also recognized as the most popular and successful of America's early southern poets and a precursor of the frontier humorists of the 19th century.

While little is known for certain about Cooke's early life, he is thought to have been born in England, to have spent a brief period of time in Maryland in 1694, and to have migrated there sometime after 1712. His first visit to the "Western Shoars" is thought to have inspired his most famous work, *The Sot-Weed Factor*, published in London in 1708 but believed to have been written much earlier. About the experiences of a British tobacco merchant who comes to America to trade with the colonists and who is cheated and insulted during the course of his visit, *The Sot-Weed Factor* is biting satire on the manners and mores of the people who lived in the colony of Maryland at the beginning of the 18th century. Written in hudibrastic couplets, the poem burlesques the escapades of drunken lawyers, inept physicians, illiterate and often dishonest planters, crude and debased women, and degenerate Indians, all of whom are said to typify New World culture, or the lack thereof. Omitted in the American edition of 1731, the final lines of the poem are a "Curse," delivered by the narrator as he departs from America for England, on the "Inhospitable Shoar" which he has just visited, "Where no Man's Faithful, nor a Woman Chast."

A sequel to *The Sot-Weed Factor*, once attributed to an imitator but now correctly attributed to Cooke, was published in Maryland in 1730 by William Parks under the title *Sotweed Redivivus*. By the time of the poem's publication, Cooke had permanently established himself in Maryland, where he had become a respected member of the community. As a result, *Sotweed Redivivus* is less a satire of colonial manners than an attempt to write serious didactic poetry on the necessity of remedying the economic woes of Maryland through legislative reform. According to Cooke, the standard of living in Maryland would be greatly improved if its people would endorse legislation to control inflation, limit the production of tobacco for which there was no market, curtail the slave trade, and halt the indiscriminate waste of natural resources, particularly the wanton destruction of forests.

Other poems in the Cooke canon which merit critical analysis are "The History of Colonel Nathaniel Bacon's Rebellion in Virginia," published along with *The Sot-Weed Factor* in *The*

Maryland Muse, and a series of elegies on the deaths of public figures with whom Cooke associated. A mock-heroic epic of the type then popular in England, "The History of Colonel Nathaniel Bacon's Rebellion" reflects Cooke's conservative thinking on the subject of revolution and colonial self-government. Far from praising Nathaniel Bacon, the popular American hero who in 1676 had led the people of frontier Virginia to revolt against the tyrannical administration of Governor William Berkeley, Cooke's stated aim in writing a history of the rebellion was to "Cooke *this* Bacon" whose "dire . . . Wars" he considered a threat to civilization and an act of extreme folly. Although they lack the clever wit and polished charm of his other poems, Cooke's elegies are numbered among the finest surviving examples of colonial American elegiac verse. Particularly noteworthy is "An Elegy on the Death of the Honourable William Lock" (1732), in which Cooke uses the death of a local dignitary as the occasion for poetic commentary on the universality of death.

After 1732 Cooke stopped writing poetry, and because nothing is known about his subsequent activities, scholars have assumed that he died at this time. Cooke attracted the attention of John Barth, whose novel *The Sot-Weed Factor* (1960) alone earned Cooke a lasting reputation in the annals of American literary history.

—James A. Levernier

COOKE, John Esten. Born in Winchester, Virginia, 3 November 1830. Educated at schools in Charleston and Richmond, Virginia; studied law with his father: admitted to Virginia bar, 1851. Served in the Confederate Army during the Civil War, 1861–65: Captain. Married Mary Frances Page in 1867 (died, 1878); three children. Lawyer in Richmond, 1851–52 and intermittently, 1853–54; temporary editor, *Southern Literary Messenger*, Richmond, 1851 and 1854, and Richmond *Express*, 1854; full-time writer from 1854; moved to an estate near Millwood, Virginia, 1868; thereafter writer and farmer. *Died 27 September 1886.*

PUBLICATIONS

Fiction

Leather Stocking and Silk; or, Hunter John Myers and His Times: A Story of the Valley of Virginia. 1854; as *Leather and Silk*, 1892.
The Virginia Comedians; or, Old Days in the Old Dominion. 1854; as *Beatrice Hallam* and *Captain Ralph*, 2 vols., 1892.
Ellie; or, The Human Comedy. 1855.
The Last of the Foresters; or, Humors on the Border: A Story of the Old Virginia Frontier. 1856.
Henry St. John, Gentleman, of "Flower of Hundreds" in the County of Prince George, Virginia: A Tale of 1774–'75. 1859; as *Bonnybel Vane*, 1883; as *Miss Bonnybel*, 1892.
Surry of Eagle's-Nest; or, The Memoirs of a Staff-Officer Serving in Virginia. 1866.
Fairfax; or, The Master of Greenway Court: A Chronicle of the Valley of the Shenandoah. 1868; as *Lord Fairfax*, 1888.
Mohun; or, The Last Days of Lee and His Paladins: Final Memories of a Staff Officer Serving in Virginia. 1869.
Hilt to Hilt; or, Days and Nights on the Banks of the Shenandoah in the Autumn of 1864. 1869.
The Heir of Gaymount. 1870.
Hammer and Rapier. 1870.
Out of the Foam. 1871; as *Westbrooke Hall*, 1891.
Doctor Vandyke. 1872.
Her Majesty the Queen. 1873.
Pretty Mrs. Gaston and Other Stories. 1874.
Justin Harley: A Romance of Old Virginia. 1875.
Canolles: The Fortunes of a Partisan of '81. 1877.
Professor Pressensee, Materialist and Inventor. 1878.
Stories of the Old Dominion from the Settlement to the End of the Revolution. 1879.
Mr. Grantley's Idea. 1879.
The Virginia Bohemians. 1880.
Fanchette, by One of Her Admirers. 1883.
My Lady Pokahontas: A True Relation of Virginia. 1885.
The Maurice Mystery. 1885; as *Col. Ross of Piedmont*, 1893.

Other

The Youth of Jefferson; or, A Chronicle of College Scrapes at Williamsburg, in Virginia, A.D. 1764. 1854.
The Life of Stonewall Jackson. 1863; revised edition, as *Stonewall Jackson: A Military Biography*, 1866.
Wearing of the Gray, Being Personal Portraits, Scenes, and Adventures of the War. 1867; edited by Philip Van Doren Stern, 1960.
A Life of Gen. Robert E. Lee. 1871.
Virginia: A History of the People. 1883.
Poe as a Literary Critic, edited by N. Bryllion Fagin. 1946.
Stonewall Jackson and the Old Stonewall Brigade, edited by Richard Barksdale Harwell. 1954.
Outlines from the Outpost, edited by Richard Barksdale Harwell. 1961.
Autobiographical Memo, edited by John R. Welsh. 1969.

*

Bibliography: *A Bibliography of the Separate Writings of Cooke* by Oscar Wegelin, 1925, revised edition, 1941; in *Bibliography of American Literature* by Jacob Blanck, 1957; by Theodore L. Gross, in *A Bibliographical Guide to the Study of Southern Literature* edited by Louis D. Rubin, Jr., 1969.

Critical Study: *Cooke, Virginian* by John O. Beaty, 1922.

* * *

Although John Esten Cooke, the younger brother of Philip Pendleton Cooke (1816–1850) and cousin of John Pendleton Kennedy (1795–1870), was best known in his own time and afterwards as a writer of long fiction, he was also something of a poet, one of whose fugitive pieces—"The Band in the Pines"—is still occasionally anthologized; a biographer, whose lives of Lee and Stonewall Jackson are worthy of attention but more as accounts of battles than as biography; and a historian, whose *Virginia*, though hardly scholarly according to modern standards, is a pleasant narrative of the early days of the Commonwealth.

Along with stories, sketches, essays, verse, and other contributions to periodicals, Cooke produced at least five novels before the Civil War, four of which are actually historical romances—*Leather Stocking and Silk*, *The Virginia Comedians*, *Henry St. John, Gentleman*, and *Fairfax* (serialized in 1859). The second of these is, according to the author, "intended to be a picture of our curiously graded Virginia society just before the Revolution" and included portraits of Patrick Henry and Lewis Hallam's actors in the Williamsburg area. It remains his best work of historical fiction, despite the fact that many of his numerous books on the war are based on his own first-hand experience.

Surry of Eagle's-Nest, the most notable of the war novels and his most popular long fiction, and its sequel, *Mohun*, cover many of the great battles of Lee's army, military actions in which Cooke participated, from the first engagement at Bull Run to Appomattox—priceless material for a novelist. Cooke found it difficult, nevertheless, to fuse fact and fiction in these novels and to refrain, any more than had his predecessors Scott, Cooper, Irving, and Simms, from introducing extraneous materials into his structure, in these particular instances gothic characters, melodrama, and sub-plots in works that are essentially historical or even realistic. But when, for example, the narrative focuses on Surry and military adventure, it moves swiftly and with eyewitness authority. Though much of Cooke's long fiction now seems romantic and dated, some of it anticipates Mary Johnston (*Canolles*) and Ellen Glasgow (*The Heir of Gaymount*), and his style remains charming and graceful; his appreciation of the past manifests itself in the antebellum work, and his military experience lends authenticity to the best of the Civil War romances.

—Rayburn S. Moore

COOPER, James Fenimore. Born in Burlington, New Jersey, 15 September 1789; moved with his family to Cooperstown, New York, 1790. Educated in the village school at Cooperstown; in the household of the rector of St. Peter's, Albany, New York, 1800–02; Yale University, New Haven, Connecticut, 1803–05: dismissed for misconduct; thereafter prepared for a naval career: served on the *Sterling*, 1806–07; commissioned midshipman in the U.S. Navy, 1808; served on the *Vesuvius*, 1808; for a brief time in command on Lake Champlain, also served on the *Wasp* in the Atlantic, 1809; resigned commission, 1811. Married Susan Augusta DeLancey in 1811; five daughters and two sons. Lived in Mamaroneck, New York, 1811–14, Cooperstown, 1814–17, and Scarsdale, New York, 1817–21; began to write in 1820; lived in New York, 1821–26, and Europe, 1826–33; returned to New York, 1833, and lived in Cooperstown, 1834–51. M.A.: Columbia University, New York, 1824. *Died 14 September 1851.*

PUBLICATIONS

Collections

Works. 33 vols., 1895–1900.
Representative Selections, edited by Robert E. Spiller. 1936.
Letters and Journals, edited by James Franklin Beard. 6 vols., 1960–68.
Writings, edited by James Franklin Beard. 1980—

Fiction

Precaution. 1820.
The Spy: A Tale of the Neutral Ground. 1821.
The Leatherstocking Tales (Library of America), edited by Blake Nevius. 2 vols., 1985.
  The Pioneers; or, The Sources of the Susquehanna: A Descriptive Tale. 1823.
  The Last of the Mohicans: A Narrative of 1757. 1826.
  The Prairie: A Tale. 1827.
  The Pathfinder; or, The Inland Sea. 1840.
  The Deerslayer; or, The First War-Path: A Tale. 1841.
Tales for Fifteen; or, Imagination and Heart. 1823.
The Pilot: A Tale of the Sea. 1823.
Lionel Lincoln; or, The Leaguer of Boston. 1825.
The Red Rover: A Tale. 1827; edited by Warren S. Walker, 1963.
The Borderers: A Tale. 1829; as *The Wept of Wish Ton-Tish*, 1829; as *The Heathcotes*, 1854.
The Water Witch; or, The Skimmer of the Seas: A Tale. 1830.
The Bravo: A Venetian Story. 1831.
The Heidenmauer; or, The Benedictines. 1832.
The Headsman; or, The Abbaye des Vignersons: A Tale. 1833.
The Monikins: A Tale. 1835.
Homeward Bound; or, The Chase: A Tale of the Sea. 1838.
Home as Found. 1838; as *Eve Effingham; or, Home*, 1838.
Mercedes of Castile; or, The Voyage to Cathay. 1840.
The Two Admirals: A Tale of the Sea. 1842.
The Jack O'Lantern (Le Feu-Follet); or, The Privateer. 1842; as *The Wing-and-Wing; or, Le Feu-Follet*, 1842.
Le Mouchoir: An Autobiographical Romance. 1843; as *The French Governess; or, The Embroidered Handkerchief*, 1843; edited by George F. Horner and Raymond Adams, as *Autobiography of a Pocket Handkerchief*, 1949.
Wyandotté; or, The Hutted Knoll. 1843.
Afloat and Ashore; or, The Adventures of Miles Wallingford. 1844.
Lucy Harding: A Second Series of Afloat and Ashore. 1844; as *Afloat and Ashore*, vols. 3–4, 1844.
Satanstoe; or, The Family of Littlepage: A Tale of the Colony. 1845; as *Satanstoe; or, The Littlepage Manuscripts*, 1845; edited by Robert E. Spiller and Joseph D. Coppock, 1937.
The Chainbearer; or, The Littlepage Manuscripts. 1845.
Ravensnest; or, The Redskins. 1846; as *The Redskins; or, Indian and Injin, Being the Conclusion of the Littlepage Manuscripts*, 1846.
Mark's Reef; or, The Crater: A Tale of the Pacific. 1847; as *The Crater; or, Vulcan's Peak*, 1847; edited by Thomas Philbrick, 1962.
Captain Spike; or, The Islets of the Gulf. 1848; as *Jack Tier; or, The Florida Reef*, 1848.
The Bee-Hunter; or, The Oak Openings. 1848; as *The Oak Openings*, 1848.
The Sea Lions; or, The Lost Sealers. 1849; edited by Warren S. Walker, 1965.
The Ways of the Hour: A Tale. 1850.
The Lake Gun, edited by Robert E. Spiller. 1932.

Other

Notions of the Americans, Picked Up by a Travelling Bachelor. 2 vols., 1828; as *America and the Americans*, 1836.

Letter to Gen. Lafayette. 1831.
A Letter to His Countrymen. 1834.
Sketches of Switzerland. 2 vols., 1836; as *Excursions in Switzerland*, 1836.
A Residence in France with a Second Visit to Switzerland. 2 vols., 1836; as *Sketches of Switzerland, Part Second*, 1836.
Recollections of Europe. 2 vols., 1837; as *Gleanings in Europe*, 1837.
England, with Sketches of Society in the Metropolis. 2 vols., 1837; as *Gleanings in Europe: England*, 1837.
Excursions in Italy. 2 vols., 1838; as *Gleanings in Europe: Italy*, 1838.
The American Democrat. 1838; edited by George Dekker and Larry Johnston, 1969.
The Chronicles of Cooperstown. 1838.
The History of the Navy of the United States of America. 2 vols., 1839.
The Battle of Lake Erie. 1843.
Ned Myers; or, A Life Before the Mast. 1843.
Lives of Distinguished American Naval Officers. 2 vols., 1846.
The Works, revised by the author. 12 vols., 1849–51.
New York, edited by Dixon Ryan Fox. 1930.
Early Critical Essays 1820–1822, edited by James Franklin Beard. 1955.

Editor, *Elinor Wyllys*, by Susan A. Fenimore Cooper. 1845.

*

Bibliography: *A Descriptive Bibliography of the Writings of Cooper* by Robert E. Spiller and Philip C. Blackburn, 1934; in *Bibliography of American Literature* by Jacob Blanck, 1957.

Critical Studies: *Cooper, Critic of His Times*, 1931, and *Cooper*, 1965, both by Robert E. Spiller; *Cooper* by James Grossman, 1949; *Cooper and the Development of American Sea Fiction* by Thomas Philbrick, 1961; *Cooper* by Donald A. Ringe, 1962; *Cooper: An Introduction and Interpretation*, 1962, and *Plots and Characters in the Fiction of Cooper*, 1979, both by Warren S. Walker; *Cooper's Americans* by Kay House, 1966; *Cooper the Novelist* by George Dekker, 1967, as *Cooper, The American Scott*, 1967, and *Cooper: The Critical Heritage* edited by Dekker and J.P. McWilliams, 1973; *Cooper: The Last of the Mohicans* (study guide) by Jack B. Moore, 1971; *Cooper's Landscapes: An Essay on the Picturesque Vision* by Blake Nevius, 1976; *A World by Itself: The Pastoral Moment in Cooper's Fiction* by H. Daniel Peck, 1977; *Cooper: A Study of His Life and Imagination* by Stephen Railton, 1978; *Cooper: A Collection of Critical Essays* edited by Wayne Fields, 1979; *The New World of Cooper* by Wayne Franklin, 1982; *Plotting America's Past: Cooper and the Leatherstocking Tales* by William P. Kelly, 1983; *Early Cooper and His Audience* by James D. Wallace, 1986; *Cooper: New Critical Essays* edited by Robert Clark, 1986.

* * *

James Fenimore Cooper will always be remembered first for his Leatherstocking tales: *The Pioneers*, *The Last of the Mohicans*, *The Prairie*, *The Pathfinder*, and *The Deerslayer*. These five books recount the experiences of an American frontiersman, variously named Deerslayer, Hawkeye, Pathfinder, Leatherstocking, and the trapper, between the early 1740's, when British America was a line of settlements along the Atlantic coast, and 1805–06, when the Lewis and Clark expedition crossed the continent. Though the books were not written in the order of the events they portray, they form, nonetheless, a kind of American epic, concerned not only with the opening of the West, but also with the costs involved in the process: the cutting of the forests, the killing of the game, and the displacement of the Indian. Leatherstocking, a man of the woods, wants to preserve the natural environment and use it only as needed, but by acting as hunter and scout, he opens the wilderness to the very settlers whose wasteful ways he abhors.

Cooper details both the social and moral consequences of the process, and though he laments the fate of the Indian and warns his countrymen against the destruction of their resources, he does not place his values in Leatherstocking alone. He consistently affirms, rather, the Christian civilization that must supplant the wilderness. The problem America faces, these books seem to say, is to insure that the new society will be a just and democratic one, ruled by the most talented and virtuous men who will not needlessly destroy the bounties of nature. To develop the social aspects of his theme, Cooper includes a wide range of characters, both white and Indian, who illustrate the various attitudes that men have toward God, nature, and society, and he uses his physical setting—both dense woods and desolate prairie—to reveal the moral state of his characters and their relation to a transcendent system of value revealed in the landscape—one that Leatherstocking always recognizes, but which too many of his fellow countrymen fail to perceive.

The neutral ground in *The Spy*, where contending irregulars fight during the American Revolution, typifies well a moral world where motives and identities are masked and loyalties are uncertain. The isolated frontier settlements in *The Wept of Wish Ton-Tish* and *Wyandotté* clearly represent the islands of peace and order that the colonists try to establish in a moral chaos. Even the sea in the maritime novels functions in a similar fashion. In the two series of *Afloat and Ashore*, it serves a dual purpose as a testing ground for men. Here the right to rule, by virtue of character, training, and knowledge, may be established in the handling of a ship, but here too the weakness of even the most capable men before the power of God may be starkly revealed. Indeed, in *The Crater*, Cooper uses both the sea and the isolated settlement, some islands in the Pacific, to establish the relation between the moral basis of a society and its ability to survive.

Much of Cooper's success as an artist derives from his ability to project his meaning through setting, whether it be a frontier fort in America, a ship at sea, or a part of the European scene: the city of Venice in *The Bravo*, an isolated valley in Germany in *The Heidenmauer*, or the breathtaking landscape of Switzerland in *The Headsman*. That meaning, moreover, is always both moral and social. At times, of course, one or the other aspect may dominate, and, especially in the social criticism, the moral basis may be muted or unexpressed, but it is never completely absent. His attacks on aristocracy in his three European novels and on the excesses of American democracy in the books that followed derive from his consistent belief that the evils of society are caused by the fallen nature of men, who must humble themselves before God and act, not from economic, but from moral motives if society is ever to escape the wrongs and injustices that have plagued it in the past.

Cooper detested aristocracy wherever he found it and wrote the European novels not merely to attack it in the abstract, but also to make clear the evils of such societies wherever they might appear. Though Cooper was thinking of contemporary

England and of the France of Louis Philippe when he wrote these books, he also wished to warn his countrymen that a similar oligarchy, based on commerce, could develop in the United States and subvert its political principles. When he viewed American democracy, on the other hand, he saw a quite different problem. The leveling democrat is impelled by an economic motive no less strong than that of the aristocrat; he wishes to remove all distinctions among men and rule, not through a governing class, but through the manipulation of the electoral process. In place of the aristocrat, there appears the demagogue.

Cooper never found a completely suitable means for presenting his criticism of American democracy, and most of his novels attacking the failings of contemporary America do not succeed as fiction. Yet all of them are interesting. In *The Monikins*, he satirized English, American, and French society through a race of monkeys who live in Antarctica, and in *Homeward Bound* and *Home as Found*, he attempted to depict a cross section of American life through the experience of the Effingham family, descendants of the founder of Templeton in *The Pioneers*, who are returning home after a sojourn in Europe. The device gave him the opportunity to attack the leveling democrats and the social climbers, the Anglophiles and the super-patriots of America, while affirming through the Effinghams what true Americans should be. His major characters are rather wooden, however, and though each book has its interest—the adventure parts of the former are very well done—both are rather weak novels.

Cooper did better in some of his later works: the Littlepage series and his final book, *The Ways of the Hour*. Critics have sometimes set the Littlepage series against the Leatherstocking tales to illustrate a bifurcation in Cooper's fiction, but the two series actually complement each other. The Leatherstocking tales, after all, have much to say about American society, and the first two Littlepage books, *Satanstoe* and *The Chainbearer*, contain major frontier episodes. They portray the rise of the Littlepage family during the 18th century and their successful struggle to maintain their possessions against both French and Indian invaders and New England squatters. The third book, *The Redskins*, shows them defending their property against insurgent radical democrats in contemporary New York, but the book is too polemical to work as fiction. *The Ways of the Hour*, focused upon a jury trial for murder, is a far more effective treatment of the failings of American democracy.

Not all of Cooper's novels fit into the two main categories for which he is best known: frontier romance and social criticism. A third major type is one he created, the tale of the sea. Cooper's maritime novels cover a wide range, from delightful romantic fictions, like *The Red Rover* and *The Water Witch*, to serious explorations of moral problems, like *The Two Admirals* and *The Wing-and-Wing*. They include the patriotic *The Pilot*, the grim *Jack Tier*, in which all value seems to have been lost, and the deeply religious *The Sea Lions*, which, like *The Oak Openings*, a late tale of the wilderness, makes a strong affirmation of Christian faith. These tales of the sea may appear diverse in theme and tone, but, seen in the broad pattern of Cooper's thirty-year career as a novelist, their relation to his other work is clear. His successful sailors are men who, like Leatherstocking, submit to the God they perceive in the natural setting. Those who fail to do so cause the many evils and injustices that, Cooper believed, always result when men act from selfish motives in this fallen world.

Cooper also wrote a significant amount of good non-fiction. *Notions of the Americans* and *The American Democrat* are sound statements of American beliefs and principles; his five travel volumes (1836–38) not only describe his sojourn abroad, but also make sharp observations on European society; and *The History of the Navy of the United States of America* and *Lives of Distinguished American Naval Officers* are sound historical works. Though Cooper's claim to our attention must always rest on his fiction, these miscellaneous works made a real contribution to 19th-century American thought and are still of interest to serious readers today.

—Donald A. Ringe

See the essay on *The Last of the Mohicans*.

COZZENS, James Gould. Born in Chicago, Illinois, 19 August 1903. Educated at the Kent School, Connecticut, 1916–22, graduated 1922; Harvard University, Cambridge, Massachusetts, 1922–24. Served in the U.S. Army Air Force, 1942–45: Major. Married Sylvia Bernice Baumgarten in 1927. Tutor, Santa Clara, Cuba, 1925, and in Europe, 1926–27; librarian, New York Athletic Club, 1927; guest editor, *Fortune* magazine, New York, 1938. Recipient: O. Henry Award, 1936; Pulitzer Prize, 1949; American Academy Howells Medal, 1960. Litt.D.: Harvard University, 1952. Member, American Academy, 1943. *Died 9 August 1978.*

PUBLICATIONS

Collections

Just Representations: A Cozzens Reader, edited by Matthew J. Bruccoli. 1978.

Fiction

Confusion. 1924.
Michael Scarlett: A History. 1925.
Cock Pit. 1928.
The Son of Perdition. 1929.
S.S. San Pedro: A Tale of the Sea. 1931.
The Last Adam. 1933; as *A Cure of Flesh*, 1933.
Castaway. 1934.
Men and Brethren. 1936.
Ask Me Tomorrow; or, The Pleasant Comedy of Young Fortunatus. 1940.
The Just and the Unjust. 1942.
Guard of Honor. 1948.
By Love Possessed. 1957.
Children and Others (stories). 1964.
Morning Noon and Night. 1968.
A Flower in Her Hair (stories). 1974.

Other

A Rope for Dr. Webster (essay). 1976.
Some Putative Facts of Hard Record. 1978.
A Time of War: Air Force Diaries and Pentagon Memos 1943–45, edited by Matthew J. Bruccoli. 1984.
Selected Notebooks 1960–1967, edited by Matthew J. Bruccoli. 1984.

*

Bibliography: *Cozzens: A Descriptive Bibliography* by Matthew J. Bruccoli, 1981.

Critical Studies: *The Novels of Cozzens* by Frederick Bracher, 1959; *Cozzens: Novelist of Intellect* by Harry John Mooney, Jr., 1963; *Cozzens* by D.E.S. Maxwell, 1964; *Cozzens* by Granville Hicks, 1966; *Cozzens* by Pierre Michel, 1974; *Cozzens: A New Acquist of True Experience*, 1979, and *Cozzens: A Life Apart*, 1983, both by Matthew J. Bruccoli.

* * *

James Gould Cozzens is a writer whose work offers, with a quiet persistence, an account of American life that is not really duplicated elsewhere. After tentative starts in novels which were modish when they were published, Cozzens found a stride that carried him off in a more personal direction. The early novel *Confusion* played off the refinement of Europe against the crudity of America, as many novelists of the time were doing. The somewhat later novel, *The Last Adam*, stridently celebrated the lusty and primitive energy of the hero as if he were cousin to the gamekeeper in *Lady Chatterley's Lover*.

But these novels—and *The Last Adam* is excellent in its own right—were apprentice exercises: a cutting-away of underbrush that kept Cozzens from reaching his own territory. This territory is kept strictly to in novels like *The Just and the Unjust* and *By Love Possessed*. It is only apparently departed from in *Men and Brethren*, Cozzens's "clerical" novel with a big-city setting, and *Guard of Honor*, a "war" novel with an army base for its background. Cozzens's domination of his territory has not been difficult; few other American writers have wanted to enter it. Of those who seem to, it is Louis Auchincloss who comes closest to Cozzens; both Auchincloss and Cozzens depict the lives of a privileged minority. But Auchincloss's characters are both more wealthy and more powerful than Cozzens's, "big city" and mobile. In contrast, Cozzens's "right people" are provincial and fixed in their habitations and their careers.

The typical Cozzens heroes, most fully displayed in *The Just and the Unjust* and *By Love Possessed* but represented elsewhere, are the latest members of families that have enjoyed privilege, education, and position for several generations in American towns of medium size. The heroes are at the center of the web of custom and law which continues to hold together the communities they serve, often as lawyers and always as thoughtful and responsible citizens. Both men have fathers who speak of the order they supported in *their* days; the fathers encourage their sons to continue the quiet battle of preserving a way of life that is already old, shadowed by elms and dominated by court-house domes and the law-courts beneath those domes. It is a way of life best enjoyed by people of substance and privilege—a way both misunderstood and resented by those who are "outside the law": Poles, Irish Catholics, and blacks. For these persons, whose drunkenness and violence often take them into the lawyers' offices, the lawyers (and Cozzens the novelist) offer sympathy and comprehension but hardly acceptance; the clients' disorder is part of a more general confusion which is always threatening not just the privileged but the entire community.

This confusion—as most of Cozzens's narratives suggest—can be held back by law and custom; it will not cease. So, in face of the disorder in "alien" behavior and the outbreaks of lust and malice in their own beings, the Cozzens heroes fight and learn while they fight. Their battles are related by Cozzens in such a way that all events, all human deliberations, are bathed in a rationality that is calm and unmilitant; absent from the novels is the self-righteousness of many a novelist whose orientation is liberal. Cozzens has faith in what he says, but the faith is not excessive. Absent also are the transcendental hopes of novelists who have heard a gospel. Cozzens and his heroes are committed to a kind of dubiety, a dubiety both provincial and shrewd. It is a world in which expectations of happiness are both clear and quite modest.

Cozzens's analysis of human motive is sharp. Cozzens and his most perceptive characters—he is not easily to be separated from them—are armed with generations of common sense and desultory talk rather than with the Freudian or Jungian strategies that are useful to many of Cozzens's contemporaries. Cozzens was—differences being allowed for—the Anthony Trollope of the recent American day, judging the life he knew with sharp intelligence rather than dismissing it with contempt or violence.

—Harold H. Watts

CRADDOCK, Charles Egbert. See **MURFREE, Mary Noailles.**

CRANE, (Harold) Hart. Born in Garrettsville, Ohio, 21 July 1899. Educated at East High School, Cleveland, 1914–15. Lived in New York, 1916–17; worked in munitions plant, Cleveland, 1918; reporter, Cleveland *Plain Dealer*, 1918–19; advertising manager, *Little Review*, and clerk, Rheinthal and Newman, both New York, 1919; worked for his father in Akron, Ohio, and Cleveland, 1920–21; advertising copywriter, Cleveland, 1922–23; worked at office jobs in advertising and sales, New York, 1923–25; given money by financier Otto Kahn, 1925 and 1927; traveled in Europe, 1928–29, and Mexico, 1931–32. Recipient: Guggenheim fellowship, 1931. *Died (suicide) 27 April 1932.*

PUBLICATIONS

Collections

Letters 1916–1932, edited by Brom Weber. 1952.
Complete Poems and Selected Letters and Prose, edited by Brom Weber. 1966; revised edition, 1984.
Poems, edited by Marc Simon. 1986.

Verse

White Buildings. 1926.
The Bridge. 1930.
Seven Lyrics. 1966.
Ten Unpublished Poems. 1972.

Other

Twenty-One Letters to George Bryan, edited by Joseph Katz and others. 1968.

Robber Rocks: Letters and Memories of Crane 1923–1932 edited by Susan Jenkins Brown. 1969.

Letters of Crane and His Family, edited by Thomas S.W. Lewis. 1974.

Crane and Yvor Winters: Their Literary Correspondence, edited by Thomas Parkinson. 1978.

*

Bibliography: *Crane: A Descriptive Bibliography* by Joseph Schwartz and Robert C. Schweik, 1972, and *Crane: A Reference Guide* by Schwartz, 1983.

Critical Studies: *Crane: A Biographical and Critical Study* by Brom Weber, 1948; *Crane: An Introduction and Interpretation* by Samuel Hazo, 1963, revised edition, as *Smithereened Apart: A Critique of Crane*, 1978; *Crane* by Vincent Quinn, 1963; *Crane* by Monroe K. Spears, 1965; *The Poetry of Crane* by R.W.B. Lewis, 1967; *The Crane Voyages* by Hunce Voelcker, 1967; *Crane: An Introduction to the Poetry* by Herbert A. Leibowitz, 1968; *Voyager: A Life of Crane* by John Unterecker, 1969 (*Notes*, 1970); *The Broken Arc: A Study of Crane* by R.W. Butterfield, 1969; *Hart's Bridge* by Sherman Paul, 1972; *Crane: The Patterns of His Poetry* by Margaret Dickie Uroff, 1974; *Crane's Bridge: A Description of Its Life* by Richard P. Sugg, 1977; *Vision of the Voyage: Crane and the Psychology of Romanticism* by Robert Combs, 1978; *Crane's Divided Vision: An Analysis of The Bridge* by Helge Nilsen, 1980; *Crane's Holy Vision: White Buildings* by Alfred Hanley, 1981; *Crane: A Collection of Critical Essays* edited by Alan Trachtenberg, 1982; *Critical Essays on Crane* edited by David R. Clark, 1982; *Splendid Failure: Crane and the Making of The Bridge* by Edward Brunner, 1984; *Crane: The Contexts of The Bridge* by Paul Giles, 1986.

* * *

It is difficult to give a final and objective estimate of Hart Crane's place as a poet. He is important, on more than one count, for what he set out to do, but critics have differed widely as to his actual achievement. Furthermore, there is the legend, as we may call it, of his life. We are presented with the picture of a man driven by compulsive and self-destructive urges, both alcoholic and homosexual, culminating in a spectacular suicide. Crane himself identified with such doomed and outcast figures as Christopher Marlowe and Arthur Rimbaud, and it is easy to make him into the romantic scapegoat of American civilisation. On the other hand, a critic like Yvor Winters can too readily move from a moral disapproval of the undisciplined life to a total dismissal of the work.

The Bridge is Crane's longest and clearly his most important poem. In form it is modelled on Eliot's *The Waste Land*, and it is generally agreed that Crane intended his own poem as a kind of riposte, giving a positive rather than a negative view of the modern metropolitan city. In *The Waste Land*, and in Joyce's *Ulysses*, the protagonist moves about the city—London or Dublin—which becomes a symbolic landscape, crowded with mythical and heroic archetypes. Past splendours contrast with modern squalor. *The Bridge* follows the same plan. The setting is New York. The protagonist wakes in the morning, passes over Brooklyn Bridge, wanders about the city and returns in the evening by the subway under the Hudson River. Crane tries to create a mythology for America out of scraps of literature, history, and tradition. Columbus, Rip Van Winkle, and the Wright brothers appear, as well as Whitman, Poe, Emily Dickinson, and Isadora Duncan. In the section entitled "Powhatan's Daughter" Pocahontas represents the American earth itself and its Indian past: "Lie to us. Dance us back our tribal dawn." In "The Tunnel," through the suffocating atmosphere of a rush hour subway, Crane encounters the ghost of Edgar Allan Poe:

> And why do I often meet your visage here,
> Your eyes like agate lanterns—on and on
> Below the toothpaste and the dandruff ads?
> —And did their riding eyes right through your side,
> And did their eyes like unwashed platters ride?
> And Death, aloft,—gigantically down
> Probing through you—toward me, O evermore!

In this remarkable passage, Crane shows that he is aware that the American dream of materialistic, technological progress has its reverse side of neurotic nightmare, and that Poe represents this nightmare. But it is Brooklyn Bridge itself which is the unifying symbol of the poem. The bridge unites the two halves of the city, and by the railroad that it carries unites the city with the country and thus its present with its past. As a feat of engineering it denotes human achievement, and in its clean functional beauty the union of aesthetics and technics.

We may thus consider Crane, as does Harold Bloom, as standing in the succession of Romantic, myth making, and visionary poets. He is one of the explorers of what Charles Williams called "the Image of the City." But as an urban poet he differs sharply from his American and British successors of the 1930's in that his poetry is almost devoid of social and political comment. He has indeed been reproached by left-wing critics for his unreflecting celebration of the American capitalist system. Indeed, the sudden collapse of that system in the Depression was one of the factors contributing to his despair and his suicide.

Crane may also be considered, at least in part, as the most notable representative in the English-speaking world of the Futurist movement founded in 1909 and extending through the 1920's. The term "Futurism" was coined by the Italian Marinetti, a figure more notable for self-publicity than literary genius. But his claim that art should celebrate the achievements and imitate the rhythms of a machine civilisation influenced poets better than himself. These included Apollinaire in France and Mayakovsky in Russia. The latter, like Crane, found his new faith inadequate to sustain him and ended in suicide. But Crane, as we have seen, did not regard the traditions of the past as irrelevant. He suffered, however, from a certain paucity in his own cultural background: it really does seem that he thought the phrase "Panis angelicus" which he quotes in the "Cape Hatteras" section of *The Bridge* meant "angelic Pan" and could be applied to Walt Whitman. And some may feel that the only religious tradition he seems to have been acquainted with, his mother's Christian Science, lacked a richness compared with the theological currents which fertilised the work of Eliot and Joyce.

Although Whitman's populist rhetoric represents one of Crane's stances, his free verse is not in the least Whitmanesque. Like that of Eliot, it is based on an extension of principles already found in the blank verse of Shakespeare's contemporaries. But while Eliot's is founded upon that of Webster and his generation, that of Crane is to be related to the practice of Marlowe, with its strongly stressed iambic rhythm and its terminal pause. As in Marlowe there is an element of bombast in Crane, and a certain degree of rhythmical monotony. At his best he sweeps us along by the sheer energy of his writing, in spite of the frequent difficulty of grasping the exact sense of what he is saying. Crane is undeniably often very obscure. But his much quoted letter to Harriet Monroe, defending his poem, "At Melville's Tomb," shows that he was very much intellectually in control. The poem consists in fact of a series of compressed conceits, rather different from the extended metaphysical conceits of Donne and his school. At times it is difficult to translate these into completely logical terms. These lines (from "Voyages") are typical—"In all the argosy of your bright hair, I dreamed / Nothing so flagless as this piracy"—yet their haunting quality is manifest. As a visual poet Crane is remote from Pound and the Imagists; instead of a clear pictorial impression of a scene or object we get a kind of kaleidoscope of sense impressions. His style might best be described as manneristic, and in this respect his affinities are less with his contemporaries and immediate predecessors than with certain poets who came into prominence a decade later, such as George Barker and Dylan Thomas. Crane has indeed been claimed as an influence on the latter poet, but this is difficult to determine.

When Crane moved from the early short poems of *White Buildings* to the elaborately planned *The Bridge* he was attempting to encompass something in the nature of an epic style. What he in fact achieved might more properly be described as quasi-Pindaric or dithyrambic lyric. This dithyrambic quality is even more marked in "For the Marriage of Faustus and Helen." This sequence of three poems continues some of the themes of *The Bridge*. Faustus's evocation of the shade of Helen is, of course, one of the most memorable moments in Marlowe's *Doctor Faustus*; and Marlowe, as we have seen, was one of Crane's heroes. The marriage of Faust and Helena, in the second part of Goethe's *Faust*, was a symbol of the union of the modern with the antique spirit. Crane may have taken his cue from this, since the theme of these three poems is the union of American technological civilization with the traditional idea of beauty. Crane here forces language almost to the breaking point as he strives to evoke Helen first from a vision of the metropolitan city, second (it would seem) from a scene of jazz revelry at the summit of a skyscraper, and third from the airman's conquest of distance:

> Capped arbiter of beauty in this street
> That narrows darkly into motor dawn,—
> You, here beside me, delicate ambassador
> Of intricate slain numbers that arise
> In whispers, naked of steel;
> religious gunman!
> Who faithfully, yourself, will fall too soon,
> And in other ways than as the wind settles
> On the sixteen thrifty bridges of the city:
> Let us unbind our throats of fear and pity.

In contrast to this, the series of poems entitled "Voyages" represents Crane's return to a purer and more personal lyricism. These may in the end constitute his most enduring, though not his most ambitious achievement. In these poems Crane thinks of himself united with one of his lovers, a merchant seaman, as he voyages through imaginary seascapes. The verse of these poems has a new kind of music, and they are less rhetorically accentuated. Crane now uses enjambment with effect, especially a characteristic trick of ending a line with a grammatically unimportant word as in the second line of the following quotation:

> O minstrel galleons of Carib fire,
> Bequeath us to no earthly shore until
> Is answered in the vortex of our grave
> The seal's wide spindrift gaze toward paradise.

Crane's final days were spent in Mexico. He had gone there on a grant from the Guggenheim Foundation, with a project to compose a long poem on the Spanish Conquest of Mexico. This historical theme, almost too highly charged with imaginative potential, has more than once proved a trap for poets. What Crane might have made of it we can only conjecture. In fact his Mexican days were a disaster, and, before he committed suicide by drowning on his return voyage, he knew that he had no work on the project to show and in the light of the changed economic situation it was unlikely his grant would be renewed. Nevertheless, some of the last poems, such as "The Idiot" and "Bacardi Spreads the Eagle's Wings," give a compassionate view of the poor and outcast which hints at a grasp of reality previously somewhat wanting in Crane's poetry.

—John Heath-Stubbs

See the essay on *The Bridge*.

CRANE, Stephen. Born in Newark, New Jersey, 1 November 1871. Educated at schools in Port Jervis, New York, 1878–83, and Asbury Park, New Jersey, 1883–84; Pennington Seminary, 1885–87; Claverack College, and Hudson River Institute, Claverack, New York, 1888–90; Lafayette College, Easton, Pennsylvania, 1890; Syracuse University, New York, 1891. Lived with Cora Taylor from 1897. News agency reporter, New York *Tribune*, 1891–92; wrote sketches of New York life for New York *Press*, 1894; travelled in the western U.S. and Mexico, writing for the Bacheller and Johnson Syndicate, 1895; sent by Bacheller to report on the insurrection in Cuba, 1896: shipwrecked on the voyage, 1897; went to Greece to report the Greco-Turkish War for New York *Journal* and *Westminster Gazette*, London, 1897; lived in England after 1897; reported the Spanish-American War in Cuba for the New York *World*, later for the New York *Journal*, 1898. *Died 5 June 1900.*

PUBLICATIONS

Collections

Letters, edited by R.W. Stallman and Lillian Gilkes. 1960.
The Portable Crane, edited by Joseph Katz. 1969.
Works, edited by Fredson Bowers. 10 vols., 1969–76.
Prose and Poetry (Library of America), edited by J.C. Levenson. 1984.

Fiction

Maggie, A Girl of the Streets (A Story of New York). 1893; revised edition, 1896.
The Red Badge of Courage: An Episode of the American Civil War. 1895.
George's Mother. 1896.
The Little Regiment and Other Episodes of the American Civil War. 1896.
The Third Violet. 1897.
The Open Boat and Other Tales of Adventure. 1898.
Active Service. 1899.
The Monster and Other Stories. 1899; augmented edition, 1901.
Whilomville Stories. 1900.
Wounds in the Rain: War Stories. 1900.
Last Words. 1902.
The O'Ruddy: A Romance, with Robert Barr. 1903.
The Sullivan County Sketches, edited by Melvin Schoberlin. 1949; revised edition, edited by R.W. Stallman, as *Sullivan County Tales and Sketches*, 1968.

Play

The Blood of the Martyr. 1940.

Verse

The Black Riders and Other Lines. 1895.
A Souvenir and a Medley: Seven Poems and a Sketch. 1896.
War Is Kind. 1899.

Other

Great Battles of the War. 1901.
Et Cetera: A Collector's Scrap-Book. 1924.
A Battle in Greece. 1936.
Uncollected Writings, edited by Olov W. Fryckstedt. 1963.
The War Despatches, edited by R.W. Stallman and E.R. Hagemann. 1964.
The New York City Sketches and Related Pieces, edited by R.W. Stallman and E.R. Hagemann. 1966.
Notebook, edited by Donald J. and Ellen B. Greiner. 1969.
Crane in the West and Mexico, edited by Joseph Katz. 1970.
The Western Writings, edited by Frank Bergon. 1979.

*

Bibliography: *Crane: A Critical Bibliography* by R.W. Stallman, 1972; *Crane: An Annotated Bibliography* by John C. Sherwood, 1983.

Critical Studies: *Crane*, 1950, and *Crane: The Red Badge of Courage*, 1981, both by John Berryman; *The Poetry of Crane* by Daniel Hoffman, 1957; *Crane* by Edwin H. Cady, 1962, revised edition, 1980; *Crane in England*, 1964, and *Crane: From Parody to Realism*, 1966, both by Eric Solomon; *Crane: A Biography* by R.W. Stallman, 1968; *The Fiction of Crane* by Donald B. Gibson, 1968; *A Reading of Crane* by Marston LaFrance, 1971; *Cylinder of Vision: The Fiction and Journalistic Writing of Crane* by Milne Holton, 1972; *Crane: The Critical Heritage* edited by Richard Weatherford, 1973; *Crane's Artistry* by Frank Bergon, 1975; *Crane and Literary Impressionism* by James Nagel, 1980; *The Anger of Crane: Fiction and the Epic Tradition* by Chester L. Wolford, 1983; *Crane* by James B. Colvert, 1984.

* * *

Stephen Crane was a descendant of Methodist ministers and of Revolutionary soldiers. One ancestor was a founder of the city of Newark, New Jersey; a grandfather was a bishop and founder of Syracuse University. His father was a parson, his mother a journalist for religious newspapers. This ancestry of military and civic virtue and literate religious vocation influenced Stephen's responses to experience.

Crane's life was brief; he was dead of tuberculosis before his thirtieth birthday. His career as an author lasted only from 1892 to 1900. Yet he wrote the first naturalistic novel of city life in the U.S. (*Maggie, A Girl of the Streets*); the greatest novel of the American Civil War, perhaps the best fictional study in English of fear (*The Red Badge of Courage*); and poems which in their avoidance of debilitated Victorian verse conventions seem heralds of the modernist movement (*The Black Riders*, *War Is Kind*). He wrote incomparable short stories—of shipwreck and survival ("The Open Boat"), of violence in the American west ("The Bride Comes to Yellow Sky," "The Blue Hotel"); a volume of unsentimental local-color stories of a village childhood (*Whilomville Stories*); and a novella ("The Monster") comparable to Ibsen's *An Enemy of the People* in its treatment of alienation and the callousness of society. In addition to these works he was a prolific journalist whose sketches—of war in the Caribbean and the Balkans, of the underside of New York City life, of travels in the American west and Mexico—are stylistically distinguished and raise journalistic occasions to an imaginative intensity close to that in his fiction. Crane was the doomed boy wonder of American literature.

As varied as his subjects were his fictional modes. Critics still debate whether Crane was an impressionist, a realist, a naturalist. With little formal education—he dropped out of college after two semesters, during which he played on the baseball team, smoked cigarettes, and wrote the draft of *Maggie*—he was a natural writer who absorbed from the literature around him the then dominant methods of writing and transformed these with imaginative energy into the instrument of his own purposes. At the time he wrote *Maggie*, his only literary acquaintance was the midwestern realist Hamlin Garland. On its appearance William Dean Howells recognized and encouraged the genius of this youth whose work differed so greatly from his own. *The Red Badge of Courage* made Crane famous overnight; he was sent by a newspaper syndicate to cover the Cuban insurrection and the Spanish-American War; later, he reported the war between Greece and Turkey. He went, he said, to test his knowledge in *The Red Badge of Courage*. This novel about a conflict that had ended seven years before Crane's birth had been grounded on his experience on the football field, where "the opposing team is the enemy tribe." After seeing war up close, "*The Red Badge*," Crane concluded, "is all right." In fact there were other models beside football: Crane had read Zola's *The Downfall* (*La Débacle*) and Tolstoy's *Sebastopol*; he had studied the reminiscences and memoirs in the *Century* series "Battles and Leaders of the Civil War"; and he had absorbed and internalized the creed of aesthetic realism held by the war correspondent in Kipling's *The Light That Failed*.

These influences were welded together by a sensibility that found in war the externalization of its obsessive psychological conflicts. There is war everywhere in Crane's work. *Maggie* shows family life in perpetual conflict, the social environment as hostile there as Nature is to the men adrift in "The Open Boat." In "The Blue Hotel," the immigrant Swede, stranded by a blizzard, brings to a frontier outpost the mental image of the violence he expects to find in the west. Crane encapsulated the theme in a brief poem:

> A man feared that he might find an assassin;
> Another that he might find a victim.
> One was more wise than the other.

One of his ironic war tales is titled "The Mystery of Heroism." Crane was possessed by that mystery; he called *The Red Badge of Courage* "a study of fear." His life was such a study, and a conquest of its subject.

He brought to all of his writings a style at once metaphoric, animistic, striated with color, dense with implication. "An artist," he once wrote, "is nothing but a powerful memory that can move itself at will through certain experiences sideways and every artist must be in some things powerless as a dead snake," thus granting his vocation at once freedom from and subjection to necessity. His influence on later American writers is considerable. His theme of grace under pressure in a masculine world of conflict provided Hemingway with a model, while Crane's metaphoric, ironic style anticipates Flannery O'Connor.

As a poet Crane's work was too fragmentary and his career too brief to affect the glib versifiers of the American 1890's, but after 1912, when the imagist movement had begun and the conventions Crane avoided were being defied by the new modernists, he was revived and remembered as a forerunner. His theme is the alienation of man in an uncaring universe. He rebels against the pieties of conventional Christianity, overthrows the rule of its vengeful God, proposes a kinder deity. Certain of his poems, such as "War Is Kind" and "A Man Adrift on a Slim Spar," crystallize the themes of his fiction. This one typifies his parabolic brevity:

> A man said to the universe:
> "Sir, I exist!"
> "However," replied the universe,
> "The fact has not created in me
> A sense of obligation."

Crane's personal life in the decade of his authorship was as vivid as any of his fictions. As a reporter he frequented the Bowery in New York City, seeking subjects for his sketches. He befriended a woman whom he saw being entrapped by police on a charge of soliciting; after testifying in her defense he was run out of town by the police department. On his way to Cuba to sail aboard the gun-running tug whose shipwreck led him to write "The Open Boat," he met in Jacksonville, Florida, the undivorced wife of a son of the British Governor General of India. Cora Taylor was then the madame of a pleasure parlor. She and Crane lived together as man and wife until his death. Cora went with Stephen to the Balkans as the first woman war correspondent. While in England, as tenants of Morton Frewen's manor house, Brede Place, in Surrey, they entertained Henry James, Joseph Conrad, H.G. Wells, and other notable writers. The preacher's son Stephen Crane lived in notoriety and scandal. He and Cora were spendthrift, always in need of money. His last two years, while sick and dying, were spent desperately in hack work.

Crane remains the most interesting American writer of the 1890's. His work is of lasting value; what is local and dated in it (his struggle against the dour God of his fire-eating, Evangelistic background) is subsumed in what anticipates the spiritual negation of the war-torn 20th century: his sense of the world as a juggernaut of impersonal force against which the precious values of the individual life must be precariously maintained by heroic struggle.

—Daniel Hoffman

See the essay on *The Red Badge of Courage*.

CRAWFORD, F(rancis) Marion. Born in Bagni di Lucca, Tuscany, Italy, 2 August 1854; son of the sculptor Thomas Crawford. Educated privately in Rome, 1860–66; at St. Paul's School, Concord, New Hampshire, 1866–69; privately in Hatfield Broad Oak, Essex, England, 1870–73; Trinity College, Cambridge, 1873; Technische Hochschule, Karlsruhe, Germany, 1874–76; University of Heidelberg, 1876; University of Rome, 1878. Married Elizabeth Berdan in 1884; two daughters and two sons. Correspondent, London *Daily Telegraph*, late 1870's; editor, *Indian Herald*, Allahabad, 1879–80; convert to Roman Catholicism, 1880; full-time writer from 1881; lived in Boston, 1881–83, Rome, 1883–84, and Sorrento, Italy, after 1885. *Died 9 April 1909.*

PUBLICATIONS

Collections

Novels. 30 vols., 1919.

Fiction

Mr. Isaacs: A Tale of Modern India. 1882.
Doctor Claudius: A True Story. 1883.
To Leeward. 1883.
A Roman Singer. 1884.
An American Politician. 1884.
Zoroaster. 1885.
A Tale of a Lonely Parish. 1886.
Saracinesca. 1887.
Marzio's Crucifix. 1887.
Paul Patoff. 1887.
With the Immortals. 1888.
Greifenstein. 1889.
Sant' Ilario. 1889.
A Cigarette-Maker's Romance. 1890.
Khaled: A Tale of Arabia. 1891.
The Witch of Prague. 1891.
The Three Fates. 1892.
Don Orsino. 1892.
The Children of the King. 1893.
Pietro Ghisleri. 1893.
Marion Darche. 1893.
Katharine Lauderdale. 1894.
The Upper Berth (stories). 1894.
Love in Idleness. 1894.

The Ralstons. 1895.
Casa Braccio. 1895.
Taquisara. 1896.
Adam Johnstone's Son. 1896.
A Rose of Yesterday. 1897.
Corleone. 1897.
Via Crucis: A Romance of the Second Crusade. 1899.
In the Palace of the King: A Love Story of Old Madrid. 1900.
Marietta, A Maid of Venice. 1901.
Cecilia: A Story of Modern Rome. 1902.
Man Overboard! 1903.
The Heart of Rome: A Tale of the "Lost Water". 1903.
Whosoever Shall Offend. 1904.
Soprano: A Portrait. 1905; as *Fair Margaret*, 1905.
A Lady of Rome. 1906.
Arethusa. 1907.
The Little City of Hope: A Christmas Story. 1907.
The Primadonna: A Sequel to Soprano. 1908.
The Diva's Ruby: A Sequel to Soprano and Primadonna. 1908.
The White Sister. 1909.
Stradella: An Old Italian Love Tale. 1909.
The Undesirable Governess. 1910.
Uncanny Tales. 1911; as *Wandering Ghosts*, 1911.

Plays

Doctor Claudius, with Harry St. Maur, from the novel by Crawford (produced 1897).
Francesca Da Rimini (produced 1902). 1980.
The Ideal Wife, from a work by M. Prage (produced 1912).
The White Sister, with Walter Hackett, from the novel by Crawford. 1937.

Other

Our Silver. 1881.
The Novel: What It Is. 1893.
Constantinople. 1895.
Bar Harbor. 1896.
Ave, Roma Immortalis: Studies from the Chronicles of Rome. 2 vols., 1898; revised edition, 1902.
The Rulers of the South, Sicily, Calabria, Malta. 2 vols., 1900; as *Southern Italy and Sicily, and The Rulers of the South*, 1905.
Salve Venetia: Gleanings from Venetian History. 2 vols., 1905; as *Venice, The Place and the People*, 1909.

*

Critical Studies: *My Cousin Crawford* by Maud Howe Elliott, 1934; *Crawford* by John Pilkington, Jr., 1964; *The American 1890's: Life and Times of a Lost Generation* by Larzer Ziff, 1966; *A Crawford Companion* by John C. Moran, 1981.

* * *

F. Marion Crawford was America's most successful novelist at the end of the 19th century. He sometimes published three novels a year, simultaneously in New York and London, and Macmillan paid him $10,000 in advance for each of them in the 1890's. All of his 42 novels are marred by haste and a kind of contempt for the esthetics of fiction. In *The Novel: What It Is* Crawford argued that the novel is "an intellectual artistic luxury" that had one essential ingredient, "a story or romance," and one purpose—to entertain. Crawford knew exotic and lowly places in many lands. He could tell a story easily and naturally, and his fast-moving romances are not impeded by subtleties or significance. He held to traditional values and opposed social, political, and economic change; he upheld the genteel, moral, and ideal in literature and the chivalric code of honor of Christian gentlemen.

The glamor of "the magnificent Marion Crawford," the "Prince of Sorrento," was a factor in his success. He was born in Rome, son of a New England heiress (the sister of Julia Ward Howe) and the Irish-American expatriate sculptor Thomas Crawford, whose circle Hawthorne pictured in *The Marble Faun* (1860). His mother gave her son an international education, designed for an aristocratic genius: private tutors in Rome, St. Paul's School in New Hampshire (which he hated), and additional schooling in England and Germany in preparation for brief periods at Cambridge and Heidelberg. He considered himself both a Roman and an American. He was a linguistic genius and reputedly knew 16 languages. His wide travels gave him a "special and accurate knowledge that created a perfect illusion" (Van Wyck Brooks) of such places as Constantinople (where he was married). St. Petersburg, Munich (where he wrote *A Cigarette-Maker's Romance* and *The Witch of Prague* in 1890), of Iceland and India—as well as Paris, London, and Rome. To a wide audience, many of them attaining great wealth and seeking easy sophistication, Crawford seemed the most cosmopolitan of writers: in a letter to Howells Henry James petulantly called Crawford "a six-penny humbug"—and begged Howells not to betray his jealous outburst!

His first novel, *Mr. Isaacs*, is the fictional portrait of an enormously wealthy and powerful Persian diamond merchant Crawford had met two years before when he edited a newspaper in Allahabad. With this novel, which anticipated Kipling in its vivid pictures of Indian life, Crawford made himself world famous; Gladstone called it a "literary marvel." Within the same year Crawford published a second semi-biographical novel, *Doctor Claudius*: a Swedish-born Heidelberg Ph.D. inherits an American fortune and marries a Russian countess after saving her inheritance. *A Roman Singer* is based on Crawford's own attempts to become an opera singer. His weakest efforts are the American novels: *An American Politician*, *Katharine Lauderdale*, and *The Ralstons*. His best are *Saracinesca* and its three sequels, which deal with the Roman social world of his childhood; the others are *Sant' Ilario, Don Orsino*, and *Corleone*. Literary historians exempt these novels from their general condemnation of 19th-century melodramatic costume romances and note some other Crawford successes: the English countryside in *A Tale of a Lonely Parish* and the evocation of Phillip II of Spain in *In the Palace of the King*.

—Clarence A. Glasrud

CREELEY, Robert (White). Born in Arlington, Massachusetts, 21 May 1926. Educated at Holderness School, Plymouth, New Hampshire; Harvard University, Cambridge, Massachusetts, 1943–44, 1945–47; Black Mountain College, North Carolina, B.A. 1956; University of New Mexico, Albuquerque, M.A. 1960. Served in the American Field Service in India and Burma, 1944–45. Married 1) Ann MacKinnon in

1946 (divorced, 1955), two sons and one daughter; 2) Bobbie Louise Hall in 1957 (divorced, 1976), three daughters; 3) Penelope Highton in 1977, one son and one daughter. Farmer near Littleton, New Hampshire, 1948–51; lived in France, 1951–52, and Mallorca, 1952–53; Instructor, Black Mountain College, Spring 1954, Fall 1955; teacher in a boys school, Albuquerque, 1956–59, and on a finca in Guatemala, 1959–61; Visiting Lecturer, 1961–62, and Visiting Professor, 1963–66, 1968–69, 1978–80, University of New Mexico; Lecturer, University of British Columbia, Vancouver, 1962–63; Visiting Professor, 1966–67, Professor 1967–78, and since 1978 Gray Professor of Poetry and Letters, State University of New York, Buffalo. Visiting Professor, San Francisco State College, 1970–71. Operated the Divers Press, Palma de Mallorca, 1953–55; editor, *Black Mountain Review*, North Carolina, 1954–57, and associated with *Wake*, *Golden Goose*, *Origin*, *Fragmente*, *Vou*, *Contact*, *CIV/n*, and *Merlin* magazines in early 1950's, and other magazines subsequently. Recipient: D.H. Lawrence fellowship, 1960; Guggenheim fellowship, 1964, 1971; Rockefeller grant, 1965; Shelley Memorial Award, 1981; National Endowment for the Arts grant, 1982; DAAD fellowship, 1983. Lives in Waldoboro, Maine.

PUBLICATIONS

Verse

Le Fou. 1952.
The Kind of Act of. 1953.
The Immoral Proposition. 1953.
A Snarling Garland of Xmas Verses. 1954.
All That Is Lovely in Men. 1955.
Ferrini and Others, with others. 1955.
If You. 1956.
The Whip. 1957.
A Form of Woman. 1959.
For Love: Poems 1950–1960. 1962.
Distance. 1964.
Two Poems. 1964.
Hi There! 1965.
Words. 1965.
About Women. 1966.
Poems 1950–1965. 1966.
For Joel. 1966.
A Sight. 1967.
Words. 1967.
Creeley Reads (with recording). 1967.
The Finger. 1968.
5 Numbers. 1968.
The Charm: Early and Uncollected Poems. 1968.
The Boy. 1968.
Numbers. 1968.
Divisions and Other Early Poems. 1968.
Pieces. 1968.
Hero. 1969.
A Wall. 1969.
Mazatlan: Sea. 1969.
Mary's Fancy. 1970.
In London. 1970.
The Finger: Poems 1966–1969. 1970.
For Betsy and Tom. 1970.
For Benny and Sabina. 1970.
As Now It Would Be Snow. 1970.
America. 1970.
Christmas: May 10, 1970. 1970.
St. Martin's. 1971.
Sea. 1971.
1.2.3.4.5.6.7.8.9.0. 1971.
For the Graduation. 1971.
Change. 1972.
One Day after Another. 1972.
A Day Book (includes prose). 1972.
For My Mother. 1973.
Kitchen. 1973.
His Idea. 1973.
Sitting Here. 1974.
Thirty Things. 1974.
Backwards. 1975.
Away. 1976.
Selected Poems. 1976.
Myself. 1977.
Thanks. 1977.
The Children. 1978.
Hello: A Journal, February 23—May 3, 1976. 1978.
Later. 1978.
Desultory Days. 1978.
Later: New Poems. 1979.
Corn Close. 1980.
The Collected Poems 1945–1975. 1982.
Echoes. 1982.
A Calendar. 1983.
Mirrors. 1983.
Memories. 1984.
Memory Gardens. 1986.

Play

Listen (produced 1972). 1972.

Fiction

The Gold Diggers. 1954.
The Island. 1963.
Mister Blue. 1964.
The Gold Diggers and Other Stories. 1965.

Other

An American Sense (essay). 1965(?).
Contexts of Poetry. 1968.
A Quick Graph: Collected Notes and Essays. 1970.
A Day Book. 1970.
Notebook. 1972.
A Sense of Measure (essays). 1972.
The Creative. 1973.
Contexts of Poetry: Interviews 1961–1971, edited by Donald Allen. 1973.
Inside Out: Notes on the Autobiographical Mode. 1973.
Presences: A Text for Marisol. 1976.
Mabel: A Story, and Other Prose. 1976.
Was That a Real Poem or Did You Just Make It Up Yourself. 1976.
Was That a Real Poem and Other Essays, edited by Donald Allen. 1979.
Charles Olson and Creeley: The Complete Correspondence, edited by George F. Butterick. 5 vols., 1980–83.
The Collected Prose. 1984.

Editor, *Mayan Letters*, by Charles Olson. 1953.
Editor, with Donald Allen, *New American Story*. 1965.
Editor, *Selected Writings*, by Charles Olson. 1966.
Editor, with Donald Allen, *The New Writing in the U.S.A.* 1967.
Editor, *Whitman*. 1973.

*

Bibliography: *Creeley: An Inventory 1945–1970* by Mary Novik, 1973.

Critical Studies: *Three Essays on Creeley* by Warren Tallman, 1973; *Measures: Creeley's Poetry* by Ann Mandel, 1974; "Creeley Issue" of *Boundary 2*, Spring-Fall 1978; *Creeley's Poetry: A Critical Introduction* by Cynthia Edelberg, 1978; *Creeley* by Arthur L. Ford, 1978; "A Creeley Chronology" by Mary Novik, in *Was That a Real Poem and Other Essays* by Creeley, edited by Donald Allen, 1979; *The Lost America of Love: Rereading Creeley, Edward Dorn, and Robert Duncan* by Sherman Paul, 1981; *Creeley: The Poet's Workshop* edited by Carroll F. Terrell, 1984.

* * *

In his 1967 Berlin lecture, "I'm Given to Write Poems," Robert Creeley acknowledged his indebtedness to William Carlos Williams for teaching him the use of an American speech in poetry and for the emotional perception he has achieved, as well as his debt to Charles Olson for "the *freedom* I have as a poet." This freedom lies not in the lyric itself, which is tightly restrained from committing verbal excess, but in the flow of the thought which ranges freely over a complex psychological interior. Creeley's best poems contain remarkable articulation of shades and hues of mood, often achieved by the subtle word play of the discourse. The poems, brief seizures of attention, are a chronicle of his two marriages, in which the self undergoes remorseless scrutiny and analysis. The larger canon of these miniature self-portraits reveals a life of emotional isolation as a man attempts both to possess and submit to women who are repelled by his profound vulnerability.

The early poems, collected in *For Love: Poems 1950–1960*, are intensely formal in their compactness and closure. Many tend toward epigram in their brevity and pithy advice. A typical instance is "The Warning":

> For Love—I would
> split open your head and put
> a candle in
> behind the eyes.
>
> Love is dead in us
> if we forget
> the virtue of an amulet
> and quick surprise.

But the best of the short poems define the self from an oblique but penetrating angle of insight, as in the three couplets of "The End":

> When I know what people think of me
> I am plunged into my loneliness. The grey
> hat bought earlier sickens.
> I have no purpose no longer distinguishable.
>
> A feeling like being choked
> enters my throat.

Creeley's marital theme is expressed in the majority of poems in *For Love*, but "The Whip," "A Form of Women," "The Way," "A Marriage," and "Ballad of the Despairing Husband" capture its dilemmas with deep poignance. Other poems in this large collection depict the female as not only a sexual partner, but as a force or element to sustain male consciousness. "The Door," among the longest and most ambitious of these poems, explores the female in her divine and archetypal aspect.

More recently Creeley has dissolved the formalism of his verse in order to create verse fields in book-length serial compositions, in the manner of Charles Olson and Robert Duncan. He has abandoned the structural neatness of his earlier verse, but the more fluid compositions of *Words*, *Pieces*, and *A Day Book* tend to be lax and to include much trivial detail of his daily life.

In *Later*, as the title suggests, Creeley has made reassessments of his outlook; the style may not have changed, but the attitude is now one of reconciliation with life, with ordinary events, with the nature of experience. His tone here is one of serene resignation to the will of his surroundings, which he surmises with appreciation. More importantly, this and later books make stark contrast between the exaggerations of a mercantile society that sells everything with excessive flair, and these quietly accurate, penetrating descriptions of life simply as it is. As he remarks in "Prayer to Hermes" near the end of *Later*, "Imagination / is the wonder / of the real. . . ." It is his defense against the "cheapshit world of / fake commerce, *buy and sell*," a point made in *Mirrors*, which features some of his most expansive lyric. *Mirrors*, with its suggestion of a new reflectiveness, comes after his massive *The Collected Poems 1945–1975*, which sums up a corpus of rigorously taciturn poetry.

His prose work follows the themes of his verse. The novel *The Island* deals with his first marriage. Creeley's prose is unique in modern fiction: his use of detail is extraordinarily delicate and precise, producing an uncanny perceptiveness in his narrators. Self-absorption in *The Island* is all the more compelling as the narrator dismantles his own thinking process to inspect the deterioration jealousy causes in him. Although Creeley is a highly provocative writer of prose, his poetry has had a more pervasive influence.

In his criticism *A Quick Graph*, in interviews, collected in *Contexts of Poetry*, and in *Was That a Real Poem and Other Essays*, Creeley has proved an astute chronicler of modern poetry, particularly on the work and influence of Charles Olson, with whom he launched the movement now known as Black Mountain poetry.

—Paul Christensen

CROTHERS, Rachel. Born in Bloomington, Illinois, 12 December 1878. Educated at Illinois State University Normal High School, Bloomington, graduated 1891; New England School of Dramatic Instruction, certificate 1892; Stanhope-

Wheatcroft School of Acting, New York, 1897. Elocution teacher, Bloomington, 1892–96; teacher, Stanhope-Wheatcroft School, 1897–1901; directed and staged her own plays. Founder, Stage Women's War Relief Fund, 1917; President, Stage Relief Fund, 1932–51; founder and first President, American Theatre Wing, and organized American Theatre Wing for War Relief, 1940. Recipient: Megrue prize, 1933; Chi Omega award, 1939. *Died 5 July 1958.*

PUBLICATIONS

Plays

Elizabeth (produced 1899).
Criss-Cross (produced 1899). 1904.
Mrs. John Hobbs (produced 1899).
The Rector (produced 1902). 1905.
Nora (produced 1903).
The Point of View (produced 1904).
The Three of Us (produced 1906). 1916.
The Coming of Mrs. Patrick (produced 1907).
Myself, Bettina (produced 1908).
Kiddie. 1909.
A Man's World (produced 1910). 1915.
He and She (as *The Herfords*, produced 1912; as *He and She*, produced 1920). 1932.
Young Wisdom (produced 1914). 1913.
Ourselves (produced 1913).
The Heart of Paddy Whack (produced 1914). 1925.
Old Lady 31, from the novel by Louise Forsslund (produced 1916). In *Mary the Third . . .*, 1923.
Mother Carey's Chickens, with Kate Douglas Wiggin, from the novel by Wiggin (produced 1917). 1925.
A Little Journey (produced 1918). In *Mary the Third . . .*, 1923.
Once upon a Time (produced 1918). 1925.
39 East (produced 1919). In *Expressing Willie . . .*, 1924.
Everyday (produced 1921). 1930.
Nice People (produced 1921). In *Expressing Willie . . .*, 1924.
Mary the Third (produced 1923). In *Mary the Third . . .*, 1923.
Mary the Third, Old Lady 31, A Little Journey: Three Plays. 1923.
Expressing Willie (produced 1924). In *Expressing Willie . . .*, 1924.
Expressing Willie, Nice People, 39 East: Three Plays. 1924.
Six One-Act Plays (includes *The Importance of Being Clothed, The Importance of Being Nice, The Importance of Being Married, The Importance of Being a Woman, What They Think, Peggy*). 1925.
A Lady's Virtue (produced 1925). 1925.
Venus (produced 1927). 1927.
Let Us Be Gay (produced 1929). 1929.
As Husbands Go (produced 1931). 1931.
Caught Wet (produced 1931). 1932.
When Ladies Meet (produced 1932). 1932.
The Valiant One. 1937.
Susan and God (produced 1937). 1938.

Screenplay: *Splendor*, 1935.

*

Critical Study: *Crothers* by Lois C. Gottlieb, 1979.

* * *

Rachel Crothers was that rarity, a total woman of the theatre. Seldom had such complex personal supervision over an entire theatrical production been seen: she exercised complete control over her plays which were generally directed, and occasionally even acted in, by her. Most extraordinary was the fact that it was a woman who had such a multi-leveled theatrical success and over so long a period of time. Altogether, the career of Rachel Crothers was unparalleled.

As a writer, she was a playwright and a playwright only, and the singlemindedness of her literary style also became the singlemindedness of her essential theme, that of woman emerging from the oppressions of society. Her "problem comedies"—which were notable for their witty and natural dialogue—dealt with such themes as career versus marriage (*He and She*), the "liberated" girl of the 1920's (*Nice People*), the generation gap (*Mary the Third*), divorce (*Let Us Be Gay*), adultery (*When Ladies Meet*), and emotional-cum-spiritual restlessness (*Susan and God*).

Crothers was critically and popularly acclaimed as America's foremost woman playwright for over thirty years. Always concerned with human dignity, Crothers organized war relief committees in both world wars. This patriotism carried into her work, for, in addition to her depiction of her theme of the feminine view of life in many variations, she was a very endemically American playwright. Speaking of her play on love firmly rooted in Yankee soil (*Old Lady 31*), a *New York Times* article compared her to Booth Tarkington, saying "Rachel Crothers must be admitted to the small and select group of those who tend to reveal America to the Americans."

In her time she was enormously successful, and perhaps the wholesomeness of her approach and the sound common sense and decency of spirit underlying all her plays (which stand up theatrically because of their timely situations and excellent dialogue) are the essential reasons behind this resounding success. Her interest in the "balanced or everyday life" was epitomized in her work: it is her plea for "sanity in all art," as she herself termed it, which her plays so ably exemplify.

—Zoë Coralnik Kaplan

CULLEN, Countée. Born Countée Leroy Porter in Louisville, Kentucky, 30 May 1903; adopted by Frederick Asbury Cullen, 1918. Educated at De Witt Clinton High School, New York, graduated 1922; New York University, 1922–25, B.A. 1925 (Phi Beta Kappa); Harvard University, Cambridge, Massachusetts, A.M. in English 1926. Married 1) Yolande Du Bois (daughter of W.E.B. Du Bois) in 1928 (divorced, 1930); 2) Ida Mae Roberson in 1940. Assistant editor and columnist ("From the Dark Tower"), *Opportunity*, magazine of the National Urban League, 1927; lived in France, 1928–30; French teacher, Frederick Douglass Junior High School, New York, 1934–46. Recipient: Guggenheim fellowship, 1928. *Died 9 January 1946.*

PUBLICATIONS

Collections

On These I Stand: An Anthology of the Best Poems of Cullen. 1947.

Verse

Color. 1925.
Copper Sun. 1927.
The Ballad of the Brown Girl: An Old Ballad Retold. 1927.
The Black Christ and Other Poems. 1929.
The Medea and Some Poems. 1935.
The Lost Zoo (A Rhyme for the Young, But Not Too Young). 1940.

Plays

St. Louis Woman, with Arna Bontemps, from novel *God Sends Sunday* by Bontemps (produced 1946). In *Black Theater*, edited by Lindsay Patterson, 1971.
The Third Fourth of July, with Owen Dodson, in *Theatre Arts*, August 1946.

Fiction

One Way to Heaven. 1932.
My Lives and How I Lost Them (for children). 1942.

Other

Editor, *Caroling Dusk: An Anthology of Verse by Negro Poets*. 1927.

*

Bibliography: *A Bio-Bibliography of Cullen* by Margaret Perry, 1971.

Critical Studies: *Roots of Negro Racial Consciousness: Three Harlem Renaissance Authors* by Stephen H. Bronz, 1964; *Cullen and the Negro Renaissance* by Blanche E. Ferguson, 1966; *In a Minor Chord* (on Cullen, Hurston, and Toomer) by Darwin T. Turner, 1971; *A Many-Colored Coat of Dreams: The Poetry of Cullen* by Houston A. Baker, Jr., 1974; *Cullen* by Alan R. Shucard, 1984.

* * *

Countée Cullen, a black American, was a lyricist who found his inspiration among the 19th-century Romantic poets, especially Keats. As Cullen himself said in 1928, "good poetry is a lofty thought beautifully expressed" (*St. Louis Argus*, 3 February 1928). Even though Cullen wrote poetry that was racially inspired, he was, first of all, a poet consciously in search of beauty.

Cullen was described frequently as being the least race-conscious among the early modern black poets who achieved fame in the 1920's during the period labelled the Harlem Renaissance. Cullen suffered in his efforts to pay homage to Beauty and his race, and critics were divided about the effect of this conflict of universal vs. black experience (few then, including Cullen, speculated on aesthetic value from a strictly black point of view). When Cullen's first book, *Color*, appeared, one reviewer wrote, "Countée Cullen is a supreme master of Beauty." What a reader of Cullen's poetry must understand, however, is that Cullen was trying to place all of his poetry on the same level of achievement, rather than have his "racial" poetry (e.g., "Heritage," "Shroud of Color") judged by one set of standards and his "non-racial" poetry (e.g., "Wisdom Cometh with the Years," "To John Keats, Poet. At Spring Time") judged upon another, more universal, academic set.

As a black man, Cullen was not insensitive to the genre of music and sound indigenous to black Africa. The influence on Cullen's poetry, in most cases, is extremely subtle. Indeed, there is an interesting combination of black sensuousness and Romantic language in such lines as "Her walk is like the replica / Of some barbaric dance / Wherein the soul of Africa / Is winged with arrogance" ("A Song of Praise"). In his poetry Cullen was consistently absorbed by the themes of love (both its joy and sorrow), beauty, and the evanescence of life as well as racial sorrow and racial problems; and he also revealed a romantic evocation of the African heritage he shared with his fellow poets in Harlem.

In his one novel, *One Way to Heaven*, Cullen displayed deftness at characterization and symbolism. His novel was, in Cullen's words, a "two-toned picture" of the upper and lower classes of blacks in Harlem during the 1920's.

Cullen never achieved the heights many felt he was destined to reach when the reading public was exposed to his famous poem "Heritage" in March 1925. But he may have been restrained by the poignant last lines of this particular poem—"Yet do I marvel at this curious thing / To make a poet black and bid him sing!"

—Margaret Perry

CUMMINGS, E(dward) E(stlin). Born in Cambridge, Massachusetts, 14 October 1894. Educated at a private school in Cambridge; Cambridge High and Latin School; Harvard University, Cambridge, 1911–16 (co-founder, Harvard Poetry Society, 1915), A.B. (magna cum laude) in Greek 1915, A.M. 1916. Served in the Norton-Harjes Ambulance Group, 1917; interned in France, 1917–18; served in the U.S. Army, 1918–19. Married 1) Elaine Orr Thayer in 1924 (divorced, 1924), one daughter; 2) Anne Barton in 1929 (divorced, 1932); 3) Marion Morehouse in 1934(?).Worked at P.F. Collier and Company, mail order books, New York, 1917; lived in Paris 1921–23; writer, *Vanity Fair*, New York, 1925–27. Artist: paintings included several times in group shows at the Society of Independent Artists, Paris; individual shows include Painters and Sculptors Gallery, New York, 1932; American British Art Center, New York, 1944, 1949; Rochester Memorial Art Gallery, New York, 1945, 1950, 1954, 1957. Charles Eliot Norton Professor of Poetry, Harvard University, 1952–53. Recipient: Guggenheim fellowship, 1933; Shelley Memorial Award, 1945; Academy of American Poets fellowship, 1950; Harriet Monroe Poetry Award, 1950; National Book Award, 1955; Bollingen Prize, 1958; Ford Foundation grant, 1959. *Died 3 September 1962*.

PUBLICATIONS

Collections

Three Plays and a Ballet, edited by George James Firmage. 1967.
Poems 1905–1962, edited by George James Firmage. 1973.
Complete Poems 1910–1962, edited by George James Firmage. 2 vols., 1981.

Verse

Tulips and Chimneys. 1923; complete edition, 1937; edited by George James Firmage, 1976.
Puella Mea. 1923.
XLI Poems. 1925.
&. 1925.
Is 5. 1926.
Christmas Tree. 1928.
(No Title). 1930.
VV (Viva: Seventy New Poems). 1931; edited by George James Firmage, 1979.
No Thanks. 1935; edited by George James Firmage, 1978.
1/20 (One Over Twenty). 1936.
Collected Poems. 1938.
50 Poems. 1940.
1 x 1. 1944.
Xaipe. 1950; edited by George James Firmage, 1979.
Poems 1923–1954. 1954.
95 Poems. 1958.
100 Selected Poems. 1959.
Selected Poems 1923–1958. 1960.
73 Poems. 1963.
Etcetera: The Unpublished Poems, edited by George James Firmage and Richard S. Kennedy. 1983.
Hist Whist and Other Poems for Children, edited by George James Firmage. 1983.

Plays

Him (produced 1928). 1927.
Tom: A Ballet. 1935.
Anthropos; or, The Future of Art. 1945.
Santa Claus: A Morality. 1946.

Fiction

The Enormous Room. 1922; edited by George James Firmage, 1978.

Other

CIOPW (drawings and paintings). 1931.
Eimi (travel). 1933.
i: Six Nonlectures. 1953.
A Miscellany, edited by George James Firmage. 1958; revised edition, 1965.
Adventures in Verse, photographs by Marion Morehouse. 1962.
Fairy Tales (for children). 1965.
Selected Letters, edited by F.W. Dupee and George Stade. 1969.

Translator, *The Red Front*, by Louis Aragon. 1933.

*

Bibliography: *Cummings: A Bibliography* by George James Firmage, 1960; *Cummings: A Reference Guide* by Guy L. Rotella, 1979.

Critical Studies: *The Magic-Maker: Cummings* by Charles Norman, 1958, revised edition, 1964, 1972; *Cummings: The Art of His Poetry*, 1960, and *Cummings: The Growth of a Writer*, 1964, both by Norman Friedman, and *Cummings: A Collection of Critical Essays* edited by Friedman, 1972; *Cummings and the Critics* edited by S.V. Baum, 1962; *Cummings* by Barry Marks, 1964; *The Poetry and Prose of Cummings* by Robert E. Wegner, 1965; *Cummings* by Eve Triem, 1969; *Cummings: A Remembrance of Miracles* by Bethany K. Dumas, 1974; *Cummings and Ungrammar: A Study of Syntactic Deviance in His Poems* by Irene R. Fairley, 1975; *I Am: A Study of Cummings' Poems* by Gary Lane, 1976; *Cummings: An Introduction to the Poetry* by Rushworth M. Kidder, 1979; *Dreams in the Mirror: A Biography of Cummings* by Richard S. Kennedy, 1980.

* * *

Edward Estlin Cummings, better known in lower case as e.e. cummings, is a major poet of the modern period, who grew up in a comfortable, liberal household in Cambridge, Massachusetts, where ingenuity was energetically cultivated. The neighborhood of the Irving Street home was populated by Harvard faculty; his father had taught at Harvard before becoming a Unitarian minister of considerable renown in Boston. Cummings's parents had been introduced to each other by the distinguished psychologist and writer William James, also a neighbor. Summers were spent on the family farm in New Hampshire, where the young Cummings spent his hours musing in a study his father had built him; another was situated in a tree behind their Cambridge house. Both father and mother encouraged the gifted youth to paint and write, and, by their excessive indulgence, perhaps nurtured his diffident character. At Harvard, Cummings distinguished himself and graduated with honors in Greek and English studies, and delivered a commencement address entitled "The New Art," his survey of Cubism, new music, the writings of Gertrude Stein and Amy Lowell, all of which he defended with insight and daring before his proper Bostonian audience. It was an early declaration of Cummings's bold taste and artistic direction.

At Harvard, Cummings wrote and published poems in the undergraduate reviews, but most of them were conventional and uninspired, except for a brief collection of poems issued in a privately printed anthology, *Eight Harvard Poets* (1917). After a brief stint of work in a mail-order publishing house, the first and only regular employment in his career, Cummings quit and volunteered for service in the Norton-Harjes Ambulance Group in France. Soon after, he and a friend, William Slater Brown, were interrogated by security police regarding Brown's correspondence with a German professor at Columbia University, and both were incarcerated in a French concentration camp. Cummings was freed after three months, but only after his father had written to President Wilson requesting special attention to his son's internment. From that experience, Cummings wrote *The Enormous Room*, a World War I classic, at the insistence of his father who viewed the incident as a sinister act of an ally. The long autobiographical account sparkles with reportorial details, insight, and comic invention, and asserts a theme of anti-authoritarianism throughout.

Cummings submitted his first book of poems to Boni, the

publisher of *The Enormous Room*, but was refused there and at other houses. The large manuscript, entitled *Tulips and Chimneys*, contained 152 poems ranging from a long, rambling epithalamion and other derivative exercises to short, pithy works of explosive energy and significant innovation. As a last resort, Cummings's old classmate John Dos Passos found a publisher for a shortened version of 60 poems in 1923. Two years later 41 more poems were issued as *XLI*, and Cummings printed the remaining poems with some additions in *&*. In 1937 the original manuscript was issued in its entirety under its first title and now stands as one of the great classics of Modernist poetry.

For lyric energy, imagination, and verve, few books of poems compare with it. Even Cummings's later books do not have the vigor of this first work. Among the poems in the collection are "All in green went my love riding," "In Just," "O sweet spontaneous," "Buffalo Bill's / defunct." The work is astounding for its variety of voice, tone, technique, and theme, and the content ranges widely from outrageous satire to jazzy lyrics, from naive rhymes to sexually explicit portraits. Cummings caught the irreverent, slapdash tonality of the jazz age in his sprawling, sensuous lyrics. The old decorums were exploded and replaced by a humor Cummings had absorbed from vaudeville shows, burlesque houses, and music halls of the day.

But there is more to these experiments than we might suspect. The young Cummings was fascinated with the asyntactic language of Stein and the grotesque, paralogical imagery of Amy Lowell, and in the dismantled shapes of Cubist paintings, all of which seemed to liberate the artist from traditional logic. The new art made spontaneous perception the basis of expression. This was equally the force of jazz itself: the soloist departed from the melodic pattern to perform his own spontaneous variations according to his mood. Cummings attacked the conventional lyric with the lesson of these other arts. He took the formal lyric apart and redistributed each of its components: punctuation becomes a series of arbitrary signals he sometimes uses even as words. The function of nouns, pronouns, adverbs, and adjectives could all be interchanged in verbal flights. The barrel shape of the standard lyric could simply be blown open, as though the staves had all been unhooped. Language drips, spills, dribbles, runs over the frame in one of Cummings's Cubist-style poems. The genius in the experiment is that Cummings evolved a series of innovations that seemed to Americanize the European-born lyric poem: in his irreverent care, the poem had become a display of verbal energy and exuberance, a vehicle of melting-pot humor and extravagance, a youthfully arrogant jazz variation of an old standard form. The modern lyric has continued to sprawl whimsically down the page ever since Cummings first scattered it in *Tulips and Chimneys*.

Cummings's innovations in other forms and media are less sure and significant, but he is nonetheless a refreshing influence. In the play form, he was drawn to over-subtle psychological comedy, as in *Him*, but he was far ahead of his time in his absurdist dialogue and surreal sets and costumes. Cummings was also a prolific graphic artist who worked in most media. Some of this work was published in *CIOPW*. Cummings strained the immediacy of prose with his massive account of a visit to Russia entitled *Eimi*, in which he assails the Marxist state and the regimented condition of Soviet citizens. The book offended the American left at home, which dominated the publishing field during the first years of the depression, and for several years Cummings published little work. A volume entitled *No Thanks*, the title directed at publishers who had rejected the manuscript, appeared in 1935, followed three years later by his first *Collected Poems*.

The many books of poems that succeeded *Tulips and Chimneys* sustained the nervous energy of his first experiments, but Cummings did not advance in new techniques so much as refine and consolidate his discoveries from the first book. As Norman Friedman points out, Cummings experimented with different aspects of his style in the years after 1923. In the 1930's, in *VV* and *No Thanks*, Cummings sought the limits of typographical experiment, extending to the curious strategy known as *tmesis*, or, the breaking up and mingling of words to achieve intense immediacy. The dismantled language of his poems focused attention on the individual word and its component letters, and often gave expressiveness to the word through its spatial arrangement. A famous poem of his later years, "l(a," is an arrangement of letters that plummet abruptly down the page, emblematic of a falling leaf and of autumn.

Over the span of his career, Cummings moved slowly away from the simple delight in love, in the seasons, in nature and simplicity, to more urgent and didactic poems that finally came to preach the virtues of naive existence, as in *Xaipe* and *95 Poems*. His argument against science, which he sometimes equated with "death," may have turned him too much against the modern world and toward pastoral themes. As a result; he is a poet of a large canon of work that is marked by much repetition of theme and perspective, but his status as a major poet is secure; one has only to "look" at an anthology of new poems to see his pervasive influence.

—Paul Christensen

See the essay on "Somewhere i have never travelled, gladly beyond."

DAHLBERG, Edward. Born in Boston, Massachusetts, 22 July 1900. Educated at schools in Kansas City; Jewish Orphan Asylum, Cleveland, 1912–17; University of California, Berkeley, 1922–23; Columbia University, New York, 1923–25, B.S. in philosophy 1925. Served in the U.S. Army, 1918: Private. Married 1) Fanya Fass in 1926 (divorced); 2) Winifred Sheehan Moore in 1942, two sons; 3) Rlene LaFleur Howell in 1950; 4) Julia Lawlor in 1967. Messenger, Western Union, Cleveland, 1917–18; stockyard drover, Kansas City, 1918; traveled and worked at odd jobs in western U.S., 1919–20; lived in Europe, 1926–28; teacher, Boston University, 1947; lecturer, School of General Education, New York University, 1961–62; Cockefair Professor, 1964–65, and Professor of Language and Literature, 1966, University of Missouri, Kansas City; teacher, Columbia University, 1968. Recipient: Longview Foundation award, 1961; American Academy award, 1961; Rockefeller grant, 1965; Ariadne Foundation award, 1970; Cultural Council Foundation award, 1971. Member, American Academy, 1968. *Died 27 February 1977.*

PUBLICATIONS

Fiction

Bottom Dogs. 1929.
From Flushing to Calvary. 1932.

Kentucky Blue Grass Henry Smith (story). 1932.
Those Who Perish. 1934.
Because I Was Flesh. 1964.
The Olive of Minerva; or, The Comedy of a Cuckold. 1976.
Bottom Dogs, From Flushing to Calvary, Those Who Perish, and Hitherto Unpublished and Uncollected Works. 1976.

Verse

Cipango's Hinder Door. 1965.

Other

Do These Bones Live. 1941; as *Sing, O Barren*, 1947; revised edition, as *Can These Bones Live*, 1960.
The Flea of Sodom. 1950.
The Sorrows of Priapus. 1957.
Truth Is More Sacred: A Critical Exchange on Modern Literature, with Herbert Read. 1961.
Alms for Oblivion: Essays. 1964.
Reasons of the Heart: Maxims. 1965.
The Dahlberg Reader, edited by Paul Carroll. 1967.
Epitaphs of Our Times: The Letters of Dahlberg. 1967.
The Leafless American, edited by Harold Billings. 1967.
The Carnal Myth: A Search into Classical Sensuality. 1968.
The Confessions of Dahlberg. 1971.

Editor, *The Gold of Ophir: Travels, Myths and Legends in the New World*. 1972.

*

Bibliography: *A Bibliography of Dahlberg* by Harold Billings, 1971.

Critical Studies: *Dahlberg: American Ishmael of Letters* edited by Harold Billings, 1968; *Dahlberg: A Tribute* edited by Jonathan Williams, 1970; *Dahlberg* by Fred Moramarco, 1972; *The Wages of Expectation: A Biography of Dahlberg* by Charles DeFanti, 1978; *Charles Olson and Dahlberg: A Portrait of a Friendship* by John Cech, 1982.

* * *

Edward Dahlberg was the illegitimate son of a lady barber whose hardships and endurance were to be a central subject in his work.

His first book, *Bottom Dogs*, was published with a preface by D.H. Lawrence. Based on his own experience of poverty, it shows the influence of his left-wing politics. His next two novels, *From Flushing to Calvary* and *Those Who Perish*, were reportorial pieces of social realism, the first affected by the hardships of the depression, the second by anti-Nazi sentiments, the result of a trip to Germany. For a while, Dahlberg was associated with the Communist Party, but he abandoned politics for aesthetic reasons. He then entered a long period of silence broken only by occasional works of literary criticism such as *Do These Bones Live* and *Sing, O Barren* that examine the heritage of Poe, Thoreau, Melville and other writers, as well as the sexlessness of American literature. Dahlberg's years of study and rumination bore fruit in *Because I Was Flesh*, an autobiography in fictional form. The book is a rewriting of *Bottom Dogs*, but the events and characters are related to literary and mythical antecedents. The prose is aphoristic and affects classical and biblical overtones. *Because I Was Flesh* is Dahlberg's most universal book and is already considered a masterpiece of contemporary prose.

In 1965 Dahlberg returned to America after living abroad for many years, mainly in Spain and Ireland. In the last decade of his life he made up for his long silence by publishing on average of a book a year—poems, a collection of aphorisms, essays, fiction, a selection of letters and a literary autobiography entitled *The Confessions of Edward Dahlberg*. Writing in a style reminiscent of Sir Thomas Browne, Dahlberg was a literary Jeremiah, attacking materialism and lamenting the loneliness of human existence. He was also a steadfast foe of modernism, opposed to the work of Faulkner, Hemingway, Pound, Eliot, and Joyce. He felt kinship with Anderson, Dreiser, and William Carlos Williams.

Dahlberg's writing is extremely individualistic, purposefully unfashionable. He thought our age desiccated; he wanted flesh and blood in life as well as literature. He influenced many of his contemporaries but remained an isolated nay-sayer.

—Frank MacShane

DALY, Augustin. Born in Plymouth, North Carolina, 20 July 1838; grew up in New York City. Educated in local schools. Married Mary Dolores Duff in 1869; two sons. Worked for house furnishers in mid-1850's; writer, New York *Sunday Courier*, 1859–67; drama critic, *Express*, 1864–67, *Sun*, 1866–67, *Citizen*, 1867, and *Times*, 1867–69, all New York; professional playwright from 1862; manager for Batemans, Philadelphia, 1863; manager of the Fifth Avenue Theatre, New York, where he established his own company of actors, 1869 until the theatre burned down in 1873; took over the New York Theatre and reopened it as Daly's Broadway Theatre, 1873; also formed the first professional organization of theatrical managers in New York, 1873; managed the Grand Opera House, New York, 1873, and the New Fifth Avenue Theatre, 1873–77; visited Italy and England, 1878–79; returned to New York and converted Wood's Museum into Daly's Theatre, where he assembled a new company of actors, and subsequently became internationally known for his productions of Shakespeare: managed the theatre and company, 1879–99; toured London, 1884, 1886 (also Germany and Ireland), 1888, 1890, 1891, 1896, 1897, and Paris, 1888, 1891; ran Daly's Theatre, London, 1893–95. *Died 7 June 1899*.

PUBLICATIONS

Collections

Man and Wife and Other Plays (includes *Divorce*, *The Big Bonanza*, *Pique*, *Needles and Pins*), edited by Catherine Sturtevant. 1942.
Plays (includes *A Flash of Lightning*, *Horizon*, *Love on Crutches*), edited by Don B. Wilmeth and Rosemary Cullen. 1984.

Plays

Leah the Forsaken, from a play by S.H. von Mosenthal (produced 1862). 1863.

Taming a Butterfly, with Frank Wood, from a play by Sardou (produced 1864). 1867; revised version, as *Delmonico's; or, Larks up the Hudson* (produced 1871).
Lorlie's Wedding, from a play by C. Birchpfeiffer (produced 1864).
Judith, The Daughter of Merari, with Paul Nicholson (produced 1864).
The Sorceress (produced 1864).
Griffith Gaunt; or, Jealousy, from the novel by Charles Reade (produced 1866). 1867(?).
Hazardous Ground, from a play by Sardou (produced 1867). 1868.
Under the Gaslight; or, Life and Death in These Times (produced 1867). 1867; revised version (produced 1881); edited by Michael Booth, in *Hiss the Villain: Six English and American Melodramas*, 1964.
A Legend of "Norwood"; or, Village Life in New England, with Joseph W. Howard, from the novel *Norwood* by Henry Ward Beecher (produced 1867). 1867.
The Pickwick Papers, from the novel by Dickens (produced 1868).
A Flash of Lightning (produced 1868). 1885; in *Plays*, 1984.
The Red Scarf; or, Scenes in Aroostock (produced 1868).
Fernanda, with Hart Jackson, from a play by Sardou (produced 1870).
The Red Ribbon (produced 1870).
Frou-Frou, from a play by Henri Meilhac and Ludovic Halévy (produced 1870). 1870(?).
Man and Wife, from the novel by Wilkie Collins (produced 1870). 1885; in *Man and Wife and Other Plays*, 1942.
Come Here; or, The Debutante's Test, from a play by F. von Elsholtz (produced 1870).
Divorce, from the novel *He Knew He Was Right* by Trollope (produced 1871). 1884; in *Man and Wife and Other Plays*, 1942.
Horizon (produced 1871). 1885; in *Plays*, 1984.
No Name, from the novel by Wilkie Collins (produced 1871).
Article 47, from a play by Adolphe Belot (produced 1872).
King Carrot, from a play by Sardou, music by Offenbach (produced 1872).
Round the Clock; or, New York by Dark (produced 1872).
Alixe, from a play by Théodore Barrière and A. Régnauld de Prébois (produced 1873).
Roughing It! (produced 1873).
Uncle Sam; or, The Flirtation, from a play by Sardou (produced 1873).
Madelaine Morel, from a play by S.H. von Mosenthal (produced 1873). 1884.
The Parricide, from a play by Adolphe Belot (produced 1873).
Folline, from a play by Sardou (produced 1874).
Monsieur Alphonse, from a play by Dumas fils (produced 1874). 1886.
What Should She Do? or, Jealousy, from a novel by E. About (produced 1874).
The Two Widows, from a play by F. Mallefille (produced 1874).
The Critic, from the play by Sheridan (produced 1874; as *Rehearsing the Tragedy*, produced 1888). 1889.
Yorick, from a play by M. Tamayo y Baus (produced 1874).
The School for Scandal, from the play by Sheridan (produced 1874). 1891.
The Big Bonanza; or, Riches and Matches, from a play by Gustav von Moser (produced 1875). 1884; in *Man and Wife and Other Plays*, 1942.
Pique (produced 1875; as *Only a Woman*, produced 1882; as *Her Own Enemy*, produced 1884). 1884; in *Man and Wife and Other Plays*, 1942.
Life (produced 1876).
The American, from a play by Dumas fils (produced 1876).
Lemons; or, Wedlock for Seven, from a play by Julius Rosen (produced 1877). 1877.
Blue Grass, from a play by J.B. von Schweitzer (produced 1877).
The Princess Royal, from a play by J. Adenis and J. Rostaing (produced 1877).
Vesta, from a play by D.A. Parodi (produced 1877).
The Dark City! and Its Bright Side, from a play by T. Cogniard and L.F. Nicolaïe (produced 1877).
The Assommoir, from a novel by Zola (produced 1879).
Love's Young Dream, from a French play (produced 1879). In *Three Preludes to the Play*, n.d.
An Arabian Night in the Nineteenth Century, from a play by Gustav von Moser (produced 1879). 1884.
Needles and Pins, from a play by Julius Rosen (produced 1880). 1884; in *Man and Wife and Other Plays*, 1942.
The Royal Middy, with Frederick Williams, from an opera by F. Zell, music by R. Genée (produced 1880).
The Way We Live, from a play by A. L'Arronge (produced 1880).
Tiote; or, A Young Girl's Heart, from a translation by Frederick Williams of a play by M. Drach (produced 1880).
Zanina; or, The Rover of Cambaye, from an opera by A. West and F. Zell, music by R. Genée (produced 1880).
Quits; or, A Game of Tit for Tat (produced 1881).
Royal Youth, from a play by Dumas père and fils (produced 1881).
The Passing Regiment, from a play by Gustav von Moser and Franz von Schönthan (produced 1881). 1884.
Odette, from a play by Sardou (produced 1882).
Mankind, from the play by P. Merritt and G. Conquest (produced 1882).
Our English Friend, from a play by Gustav von Moser (produced 1882). 1884.
She Would and She Would Not, from the play by Colley Cibber (produced 1883). 1884.
Serge Panine, from a play by G. Ohnet (produced 1883).
7-20-8; or, Casting the Boomerang, from a play by Franz von Schönthan (produced 1883). 1886.
Dollars and Sense; or, The Heedless Ones, from a play by A. L'Arronge (produced 1883). 1885.
The Country Girl, from Garrick's adaptation of the play *The Country Wife* by Wycherley (produced 1884). 1898.
Red Letter Nights; or, Catching a Croesus, from a play by E. Jacobson (produced 1884).
A Woman Won't, from a play by M. Röttinger (produced 1884).
A Wooden Spoon; or, Perdita's Penates, from a play by Franz von Schönthan (produced 1884).
Love on Crutches, from a play by H. Stobitzer (produced 1884). 1885; in *Plays*, 1984.
Nancy and Company, from a play by Julius Rosen (produced 1886). 1884.
A Night Off; or, A Page from Balzac, from a play by Franz and P. von Schönthan (produced 1885). 1885.
The Recruiting Officer, from the play by Farquhar (produced 1885). 1885.
Denise, from a play by Dumas fils (produced 1885).
Living for Show, from a German play (produced 1885).
The Merry Wives of Windsor, from the play by Shakespeare

(produced 1886). 1886.
A Wet Blanket, from a play by P. Bilhaud and J. Lévy (produced 1886). In *Three Preludes to the Play*, n.d.
A Sudden Shower, from a play by F. Beissier (produced 1886). In *Three Preludes to the Play*, n.d.
After Business Hours, from a play by Oscar Blumenthal (produced 1886). 1886.
Love in Harness; or, Hints to Hymen, from a play by Albin Valabrègue (produced 1886). 1887.
The Taming of the Shrew, from the play by Shakespeare (produced 1887). 1887.
The Railroad of Love, from a play by Franz von Schönthan and G. Kadelburg (produced 1887). 1887(?).
A Midsummer Night's Dream, from the play by Shakespeare (produced 1888). 1888.
The Lottery of Love, from a play by A. Bisson and A. Mars (produced 1888). 1889.
The Undercurrent (produced 1888).
The Inconstant; or, The Way to Win Him, from the play by Farquhar (produced 1889). 1889.
An International Match, from a play by Franz von Schönthan (produced 1889). 1890.
Samson and Delilah, from a play by A. Bisson and J. Moineaux (produced 1889).
The Golden Widow, from a play by Sardou (produced 1889).
Roger la Honte; or, A Man's Shadow, from the play by R. Buchanan (produced 1889).
The Great Unknown, from a play by Franz von Schönthan and G. Kadelburg (produced 1889). 1890.
As You Like It, from the play by Shakespeare (produced 1889). 1890.
Miss Hoyden's Husband, from the play *A Trip to Scarborough* by Sheridan (produced 1890).
The Last Word, from a play by Franz von Schönthan (produced 1890). 1891.
The Prodigal Son, from a play by M. Carré fils, music by A. Wormser (produced 1891).
Love's Labour's Lost, from the play by Shakespeare (produced 1891). 1891.
A Sister's Sacrifice, in *Werner's Readings and Recitations 4*, edited by Elsie M. Wilbor. 1891.
Love in Tandem, from a play by H. Bocage and C. de Courcy (produced 1892). 1892.
Little Miss Million, from a play by Oscar Blumenthal (produced 1892). 1893.
A Test Case; or, Grass Versus Granite, from a play by Oscar Blumenthal and G. Kadelburg (produced 1892). 1893.
The Hunchback, from the play by Sheridan Knowles (produced 1892). 1893.
The Belle's Stratagem, from the play by Hannah Cowley (produced 1892). 1893.
The Foresters, from the play by Tennyson, music by Arthur Sullivan (produced 1892).
Twelfth Night, from the play by Shakespeare (produced 1893). 1893.
The Wonder. 1893.
The Orient Express, from a play by Oscar Blumenthal and G. Kadelburg (produced 1895).
Two Gentlemen of Verona, from the play by Shakespeare (produced 1895). 1895.
A Bundle of Lies, from a play by K. Laufs and W. Jacoby (produced 1895).
The Transit of Leo, from a play by B. Köhler and Oscar Blumenthal (produced 1895).
The Countess Gucki, from a play by Franz von Schönthan and F. Koppel-Ellfeld (produced 1896). 1895.
Much Ado about Nothing, from the play by Shakespeare (produced 1896). 1897.
The Wonder! A Woman Keeps a Secret, from the play by Susanna Centlivre (produced 1897). In *Two Old Comedies*, 1897.
The Tempest, from the play by Shakespeare (produced 1897). 1897.
Number Nine; or, The Lady of Ostend, with F.C. Burnand, from a play by Oscar Blumenthal and G. Kadelburg (produced 1897).
Cyrano de Bergerac, from a translation by G. Thomas and M.F. Guillemard of a play by Rostand (produced 1898).
The Merchant of Venice, from the play by Shakespeare (produced 1898). 1898.

Other

Woffington: A Tribute to the Actress and the Woman. 1888.

*

Critical Studies: *Memories of Daly's Theatres* by E.A. Dithmar, 1896; *The Life of Daly* by Joseph F. Daly, 1917; *Daly's: The Biography of a Theatre* by D.F. Winslow, 1944; *The Theatre of Daly* by Marvin Felheim, 1956.

* * *

The career of Augustin Daly is particularly difficult to summarize. A man of tremendous energies and almost total dedication to the theatre, he became the most powerful man in American theatre during his lifetime. A drama critic, theatre manager, playwright, and adapter of foreign plays, he was also the manager of a company of actors that successfully performed Shakespearean drama in England and Europe. In the modern sense of the term he was the first stage director in America, and the strict control he exercised over all aspects of a theatrical production, even the lives of his actors, suggests both his tyranny and his devotion.

The two most important trends in late 19th-century American drama were an interest in social comedy and realism. Daly contributed to both, while illustrating in his plays that he was living in the age of spectacular melodrama as well as the rise of realism. Both *Divorce* and *Pique* suggest the slowly developing social comedy. *Under the Gaslight* was his first successful melodrama and boasted such realistic scenes as the Blue Room at Delmonico's, the New York pier, and the famous railroad scene in which the heroine switches the train and saves the life of the hero who is tied to the tracks. His other spectacular melodramas included *A Flash of Lightning* with its water and fire thrills, and *The Red Scarf*, in which the hero was tied to a log and sent to the saw mill.

A strong-minded impresario, Daly was primarily interested in giving audiences what they wanted. Although he tried to encourage playwriting, even tried to work with Mark Twain and William Dean Howells, he was not an innovator. Realism was spectacle to him, not a theory of living and writing. Plays by Shaw and Ibsen were never produced on his stages, and his encouragement to playwrights was always governed by the limitations which he felt the public dictated. As for his own plays, either original or adaptations, there is still some mystery concerning the part that his brother Joseph Daly contributed to their writing. Because he understood the requirements of the theatre he was able to inject the right ingredients into his plays and meet the demands of commercial theatre. But for this same reason he did not contribute markedly to the development of American drama and, in some ways, considering the force of his standing in theatrical circles, was a negative influence. Mainly he was a contriver of effects, a bold and ingenious creator of theatrical magic from his position as a *regisseur*. But in his best commercial successes, in both the manner of production and the material dramatized, he suggested certain truths about the society that melodrama may reflect.

—Walter J. Meserve

DANA, Richard Henry, Jr. Born in Cambridge, Massachusetts, 1 August 1815; son of the writer Richard Henry Dana, Sr. Educated at Harvard University, Cambridge, Massachusetts, 1831, 1832; sailor on the brig *Pilgrim*, and on the *Alert*, 1834–36; returned to Harvard, 1836–37, graduated 1837; attended Harvard Law School, 1837–40, and taught elocution at Harvard, 1839–40; admitted to Massachusetts bar, 1840. Married Sarah Watson in 1841; six children. Lawyer, specializing in maritime cases, Boston, 1840–78; a founder, Free Soil Party, 1848; member of the convention for the revision of the Constitution of Massachusetts, 1853; visited England, 1856 and 1866; U.S. District Attorney for Massachusetts, 1861–66; Lecturer, Harvard Law School, 1866–68; member, Massachusetts House of Representatives, and counsel for the U.S. in the proceedings against Jefferson Davis, 1867–68; candidate for U.S. House of Representatives, 1868; nominated ambassador to England by President Grant, 1876 (appointment not confirmed by the Senate); senior counsel for the U.S. before the Fisheries Commission at Halifax, 1877; lived in Europe, studying and writing on international law, 1878–82. Overseer, Harvard University, 1865–77. LL.D.: Harvard University, 1866. *Died 6 January 1882.*

PUBLICATIONS

Prose

Two Years Before the Mast: A Personal Narrative of Life at Sea. 1840; revised edition, 1869; edited by Thomas Philbrick, 1981.
The Seaman's Friend. 1841; as *The Seaman's Manual*, 1841.
To Cuba and Back: A Vacation Voyage. 1859; edited by C. Harvey Gardiner, 1966.
Speeches in Stirring Times, and Letters to a Son, edited by Richard Henry Dana, 3rd. 1910.
An Autobiographical Sketch (1815–1842), edited by Robert F. Metzdorf. 1953.
Journal, edited by Robert F. Lucid. 1968.

Editor, *Lectures on Art, and Poems*, by Washington Allston. 2 vols., 1850.
Editor, *Elements of International Law*, 8th edition, by Henry Wheaton. 1866.

*

Bibliography: in *Bibliography of American Literature* by Jacob Blanck, 1957.

Critical Studies: *Dana* by Samuel Shapiro, 1961; *Dana* by Robert L. Gale, 1969.

* * *

Richard Henry Dana, Jr., was the author of the best known of three outstanding 19th-century travel books dealing with what were then largely unexplored sections of the American continent. *Two Years Before the Mast* has won a reputation as an adventure story for boys, while the other books, Francis Parkman's *The Oregon Trail* and Lewis Hector Garrard's *Wah-to-yah and the Taos Trail*, survive principally because of their historical, as well as literary, value. Dana would surely have preferred a similar fate for his book; its popularity among boys was a reputation he neither sought nor welcomed.

This popularity is curious, for the book's complex, if precise, prose might make it seem less accessible than, in particular, *Wah-to-yah*, characterized as it is by a rather colloquial and flowing style. Undoubtedly the major reason for the popularity of Dana's book is its series of high adventures, vividly and objectively described. Parkman and Garrard lived with Indians—but Dana did that and much more. His realistic narrative deals effectively with a wide range of adventures that include not only life on shipboard but also life in what is today the American southwest, then a seemingly exotic region known to most Americans only through rumor. *Two Years Before the Mast* still makes Dana's adventures seem exciting and unique, long after the type of customs and way of life he experienced have vanished.

After the publication of *Two Years Before the Mast* Dana became a lawyer and was never able to duplicate its success. He published a travel book based on a trip to Canada, and wrote a popular handbook for sailors, *The Seaman's Friend*, but neither book has literary interest for readers today.

—Edward Halsey Foster

DANNAY, Frederic. See **QUEEN, Ellery.**

DAVIDSON, Donald (Grady). Born in Campbellsville, Tennessee, 18 August 1893. Educated at Branham and Hughes School, Spring Hill, Tennessee, 1905–09; Vanderbilt University, Nashville, Tennessee, 1910–11, 1914–17, A.B. 1917, M.A. 1922. Served in the 324th Infantry, 81st Division of the U.S. Army, in France, 1917–19: First Lieutenant. Married Theresa Sherrer in 1918; one daughter. Teacher at schools in Cedar Hill and Mooresville, 1910–14, and Pulaski, 1916–17, all Tennessee; Head of the English Department, Kentucky Wesleyan College, Owensboro, 1919–20; Instructor, 1920–24, Assistant Professor, 1924–27, Associate Professor, 1927–36, Professor of English, 1937–64, and Professor Emeritus from 1964, Vanderbilt University. Teacher, Bread Loaf School of English, Middlebury College, Vermont, summers 1931–68.

Staff member, 1920, and columnist ("Spyglass") and book page editor, 1924–30, Nashville *Tennessean*; member of the Fugitive group of poets: co-founder, *The Fugitive*, Nashville, 1922; advisory board member, *Modern Age* and *Intercollegiate Review*. Chairman, Tennessee Federation for Constitutional Government, 1955–59. Litt.D.: Cumberland College, 1946; Washington and Lee University, Lexington, Virginia, 1948; L.H.D.: Middlebury College, 1965. *Died 25 April 1968.*

PUBLICATIONS

Verse

Avalon, with *Armageddon* by John Crowe Ransom, and *A Fragment* by William Alexander Percy. 1923.
An Outland Piper. 1924.
The Tall Men. 1927; revised version in *Lee in the Mountains*, 1938.
Lee in the Mountains and Other Poems. 1938.
The Long Street. 1961.
Poems 1922–1961. 1966.

Play

Singin' Billy, music by Charles Faulkner Bryan (produced 1952).

Other

I'll Take My Stand: The South and the Agrarian Tradition, with others. 1930.
Who Owns America? A New Declaration of Independence, with others, edited by Herbert Agar and Allen Tate. 1936.
The Attack on Leviathan: Regionalism and Nationalism in the United States. 1938.
American Composition and Rhetoric. 1939; revised edition, with Ivar Lou Myhr, 1947, 1953.
The Tennessee. 2 vols., 1946–48.
Twenty Lessons in Reading and Writing Prose. 1955.
Still Rebels, Still Yankees, and Other Essays. 1957.
Southern Writers in the Modern World. 1958.
The Spyglass: Views and Reviews 1924–1930, edited by John Tyree Fain. 1963.
Concise American Composition and Rhetoric. 1964.
It Happened to Them: Character Studies of New Testament Men and Women. 1965.
The Literary Correspondence of Davidson and Allen Tate, edited by John Tyree Fain and Thomas Daniel Young. 1974.

Editor, *British Poetry of the Eighteen-Nineties*. 1937.
Editor, with Sidney Erwin Glenn, *Readings for Composition, From Prose Models*. 1942; revised edition, 1957.
Editor, *Selected Essays and Other Writings of John Donald Wade*. 1966.
Editor, with Mary C. Simms Oliphant, *Voltmeier; or, The Mountain Men*, by William Gilmore Simms. 1969.

*

Critical Studies: *The Fugitive Group*, 1959, and *The Southern Critics*, 1971, both by Louise Cowan; *The Fugitive Poets* edited by William Pratt, 1965; *Davidson: An Essay and a Bibliography*, 1965, and *Davidson*, 1971, both by Thomas Daniel Young and M. Thomas Inge; *Essays on Davidson: Actions and Events* edited by Bruce Vermazen and Merrill B. Hintikka, 1985.

* * *

An original member of the group of poets who published the *Fugitive*, Donald Davidson published some of his first poems in that journal. From 1924 to 1930 he was literary editor of the Nashville *Tennessean* and produced what one critic has called the "best literary page ever published in the South." He contributed to both agrarian symposia, *I'll Take My Stand* and *Who Owns America?*, and was widely known and respected as poet, essayist, editor, historian, and critic.

Davidson's reputation as a poet must stand on *The Tall Men*, "Lee in the Mountains" (1934), and a half dozen poems from *The Long Street*. *The Tall Men*, a book-length narrative, is organized around a young man's search for a meaningful tradition, a heritage of heroism and humanism. The exploration of Davidson's protagonist, a modern southern American, is not a vague, nostalgic meandering into a far distant past. Instead, his excruciating self-analysis is an attempt "to name and set apart from time / One sudden face" and to understand his present situation by discovering how he is related to the history and history makers of his own section of the country. He finally becomes aware not only of his traditional heritage but of the forces that would destroy it. "Lee in the Mountains," Davidson's most widely anthologized poem, presents his art at its best. In its epic dignity, its purity of form, its dramatic presentation of theme, it demonstrates as no other poem of his does the totality of his vision and the range of his imagination. The force and clarity of his presentation in this and many other of his poems give him a place almost unique among the poets of his generation. For Davidson, however, prose was the dominant means of expression throughout his career. As literary critic and social and political philosopher he offered cogent and convincing arguments in a prose that was lucid, smooth, and supple. As a prose stylist Davidson has few peers in contemporary American literature.

—Thomas Daniel Young

DAVIS, Rebecca (Blaine) Harding. Born in Washington, Pennsylvania, 24 June 1831; moved with her family to Alabama, then to Wheeling, West Virginia. Married L. Clarke Davis in 1863 (died, 1904); two sons (including Richard Harding Davis, *q.v.*) and one daughter. Professional writer from 1861; lived in Philadelphia, 1863–1910; member of the editorial staff, New York *Tribune* from 1869. *Died 29 September 1910.*

PUBLICATIONS

Fiction

Margret Howth: A Story of Today. 1862.
Dallas Galbraith. 1868.
Waiting for the Verdict. 1868.

Kitty's Choice (stories). 1874(?).
John Andross. 1874.
A Law unto Herself. 1878.
Natasqua. 1886.
Kent Hampden (for children). 1892.
Silhouettes of American Life. 1892.
Dr. Warrick's Daughters. 1896.
Frances Waldeaux. 1897.
Life in the Iron Mills; or, The Korl Woman. 1972.

Other

Pro Aris et Focis: A Plea for Our Altars and Hearths. 1870.
Bits of Gossip. 1904.

*

Critical Studies: *The Richard Harding Davis Years: A Biography of a Mother and Son* by Gerald Langford, 1961; afterword by Tillie Olsen to *Life in the Iron Mills*, 1972.

* * *

When Rebecca Harding Davis died in 1910, she was remembered in the New York *Times* obituary primarily as the mother of Richard Harding Davis, secondarily as a novelist who had, in 1861, written a story about the "grinding life of the working people" that was so stern in its realism that "many thought the author must be a man." Nearly eighty years after her death, aside from an occasional mention of that story, "Life in the Iron Mills," in literary histories, her work is almost entirely unknown, although in recent years feminist critics such as Tillie Olson have sought to reclaim her from obscurity. Davis was not a prolific writer—some dozen works, novels, short stories, and improving essays during a writing career of forty years—and not a particularly good one. Her plots are slipshod, her prose awkward. Her chief gift lies in the creation of character. But having acknowledged her limitations, a critic must recognize her achievement. She lived for her first 32 years the proper life of a middle-class spinster in the frontier industrial town of Wheeling, West Virginia, out of touch with literary circles, restricted in her social contacts. Yet she wrought out of this limited life a coherent theory of literary realism that preceded by a quarter of a century the admonition of William Dean Howells that fiction ought to be true to the life of actual men and women.

In her first, and most important, novel, *Margret Howth: A Story of Today*, she attacks her readers' preference for "idylls delicately tinted." She wants them instead to "dig into this commonplace, this vulgar American life and see what is in it." She finds "a new and awful significance" in the grim underlife of the industrial city where workers live thwarted lives amidst the "white leprosy of poverty." Her heroine, Margret, has been deserted by her fiancé and has gone to work as a bookkeeper in a woolen mill to support her ill and aging parents. The novel is a romance, and ultimately her fiancé is restored to his senses and her arms, but in the course of the narrative, as in "Life in the Iron Mills," Davis provides a fully realized image of the oppressive noise, stench, and grime of industrial work. In addition, she creates in Margret a new kind of heroine—plain, blunt, occasionally pettish about the sacrifices she is required to make. Margret is the first of a series of Davis heroines who are, as one is described in a later novel, "built for use and not for show."

Davis always wrote about contemporary issues—the Civil War, the problem of the free black, and, in *John Andross* (probably her strongest work), political corruption. Contemporary critics were not kind to her. They found her subjects disagreeable, her prose mawkish, her attitude overly didactic. But one critic, writing in the *Nation* in 1878, acknowledged that despite these flaws she contrived in her "grim and powerful etchings" to evoke the American atmosphere, "its vague excitement, its strife of effort, its varying possibilities." That is a more apt summary of her contribution to American letters than the *Times* obituary.

—Louise Duus

See the essay on *Margret Howth*.

DAVIS, Richard Harding. Born in Philadelphia, Pennsylvania, 18 April 1864; son of Rebecca Harding Davis, *q.v.* Educated at the Episcopal Academy, Swarthmore, Pennsylvania; Ulrich's Preparatory School, Bethlehem, Pennsylvania; Lehigh University, Bethlehem, 1882–85; Johns Hopkins University, Baltimore, 1885–86. Married 1) Cecil Clark in 1899 (divorced, 1910); 2) Elizabeth Genevieve McEvoy in 1912, one daughter. Journalist from 1886: reporter, Philadelphia *Record*, 1886, Philadelphia *Press*, 1886–89, and New York *Sun*, 1889–90; managing editor, *Harper's Weekly*, New York, 1890–95; correspondent for various newspapers and journals, including *Harper's Monthly*, New York *Sun*, *Collier's Weekly*, New York *Journal*, New York *Herald*, London *Times*, and London *Daily Mail* from 1890; covered Queen Victoria's Jubilee in London, Spanish War in Cuba, the Greco-Turkish War, Spanish-American War, Boer War, and World War I; most widely known reporter of his generation. Fellow, Royal Geographical Society (UK). *Died 11 April 1916.*

PUBLICATIONS

Collections

From "Gallegher" to "The Deserter": The Best Stories, edited by Roger Burlinghame. 1927.

Fiction

Gallegher and Other Stories. 1891.
Stories for Boys. 1891.
Van Bibber and Others (stories). 1892.
The Exiles and Other Stories. 1894.
Cinderella and Other Stories. 1896.
Soldiers of Fortune. 1897.
The King's Jackal. 1898.
Episodes in Van Bibber's Life. 1899.
The Lion and the Unicorn. 1899.
In the Fog. 1901.
Ranson's Folly. 1902.
Captain Macklin, His Memoirs. 1902.
The Bar Sinister. 1903.
Real Soldiers of Fortune. 1906.
The Scarlet Car. 1907.
Vera the Medium. 1908.

The White Mice. 1909.
Once upon a Time. 1910.
The Man Who Could Not Lose (stories). 1911.
The Red Cross Girl (stories). 1912.
The Lost Road (stories). 1913.
The Boy Scout (stories). 1914.
Somewhere in France (stories). 1915.
Novels and Stories. 12 vols., 1916.

Plays

The Other Woman (produced 1893).
The Disreputable Mr. Reagan (produced 1895).
The Princess Aline. 1895.
Soldiers of Fortune (produced 1902).
The Taming of Helen (produced 1903).
Ranson's Folly (produced 1904).
The Dictator (produced 1904). In *Farces*, 1906.
The Galloper (produced 1905). In *Farces*, 1906.
Miss Civilization, from a story by James Harvey Smith (produced 1906). 1905.
Farces: The Dictator, The Galloper, Miss Civilization. 1906.
A Yankee Tourist, music by Alfred G. Robyn, lyrics by Wallace Irwin (produced 1907). Music published 1907.
Vera, The Medium (produced 1908).
The Seventh Daughter (produced 1910).
The Consul. 1911.
Blackmail (produced 1913).
Who's Who (produced 1913).
The Trap, with Jules Eckert Goodman (produced 1914).
The Zone Police (produced 1916). 1914.
Peace Manoeuvres (produced 1917). 1914.

Other

The Adventures of My Freshman. 1884.
The West from a Car-Window. 1892.
The Rulers of the Mediterranean. 1894.
Our English Cousins. 1894.
About Paris. 1895.
Three Gringos in Venezuela and Central America. 1896.
Dr. Jameson's Raiders vs. the Johannesburg Reformers. 1897.
Cuba in War Time. 1897.
A Year from a Reporter's Note-Book. 1897; as *A Year from a Correspondent's Note-Book*, 1897.
The Cuban and Porto Rican Campaigns. 1898.
With Both Armies in South Africa. 1900.
The Congo and Coasts of Africa. 1907.
Notes of a War Correspondent. 1910.
With the Allies. 1914.
The New Sing Sing. 1915.
With the French in France and Salonika. 1916.
The Adventures and Letters, edited by Charles Belmont Davis. 1917.

*

Bibliography: *Davis: A Bibliography* by Henry Cole Quinby, 1924; in *Bibliography of American Literature* by Jacob Blanck, 1957; "Davis: A Checklist of Secondary Comment," by Clayton L. Eichelberger and Ann McDonald, in *American Literary Realism 4*, 1971.

Critical Studies: *Davis: His Day* by Fairfax D. Downey, 1933; *The Davis Years: A Biography of a Mother and Son* by Gerald Langford, 1961; *Davis* by Scott C. Osborn and Robert L. Phillips, Jr., 1978.

* * *

Although the close connection between journalistic and fictional writing in the late 19th century in America has never been adequately analyzed, critics have often claimed that Richard Harding Davis failed as a writer of fiction because he excelled as a journalist. Such a judgment may be less than accurate, for Davis incorporated in his fiction the best qualities of his journalism—his quick recognition of the picturesque, his unerring selection of interest-arousing features, his keen eye for external detail, his easy phrasing of remarkably lively impressionistic passages, his youthful appreciation of adventure and movement. These qualities explain his immense contemporary popularity.

But beneath the pace and vivid detail and youthful verve of Davis's fiction, a certain emptiness bothered the serious critics. Journalistic superficiality and haste were blamed. "Smart and shallow," Ludwig Lewisohn briefly intoned in *Expression in America* (1932); and others had said much the same thing. Davis wrote too much too rapidly. He never probed beneath the surfaces. Although clever, he was unconvincing; although satisfying, never profound. At his best he exhibited impressive dramatic power, but too often the drama drifted into theatricality. His stories always charmed, but they were rarely memorable. Those who waited for Davis's exceptional promise to be fulfilled, waited in vain. "Like many handsome and idolized American college men," wrote Francis Hackett in the *New Republic* (2 March 1918), Davis "never quite graduated." Although his fiction excited, it did not confront or deal meaningfully with those issues of humanity that contribute timelessness to a literary work.

Despite the reluctant acknowledgment of serious literary critics, however, and despite their occasional condescending tributes to Davis as the best of the journalistic novelists, his work was not without value in his own time, nor is it in ours. He was the very symbol of achievement for the mass of Americans at the turn of the century, and so serves as an index to a cultural state. Not only was he the visible embodiment of the exuberant life style of the Strenuous Age, but he was also a vocal exponent of ideals that for many readers pointed direction in their dreams. Further, in both his journalistic and his fictional work, he, perhaps better than any other writer, preserved "for all ages," as Thomas Beer noted in *Liberty* (October 1924), "the adventurous, expansionist spirit of the decades that ushered in the twentieth century, the world war, and our own times."

—Clayton L. Eichelberger

DE FOREST, John William. Born in Humphreysville (now Seymour), Connecticut, 31 March 1826. Educated in local schools. Married Harriet Silliman Shepard in 1856 (died, 1878); one son. Lived in Syria, 1846–48, and in Florence and Paris, 1850–55; writer from 1856; active soldier during the Civil War: recruited and became Captain of Company I, 12th

Connecticut Volunteers, 1862–64; Inspector-General, 1st Division, XIX Corps of the U.S. Army; commissioned Major, United States Volunteers, 1865; also wrote descriptions of battle scenes for *Harper's Monthly* during the war; Commanding Captain, Veterans Reserve Corps of Company I, 14th Regiment, Washington, D.C., 1865; commander of a district of the Freedman's Bureau, Greenville, South Carolina, 1866–68; full-time writer, mainly for magazines, New York and New Haven, Connecticut, 1868–81; inactive as writer after 1880's; invalid, in hospital, from 1903. A.M.: Amherst College, Massachusetts, 1859. *Died 17 July 1906.*

PUBLICATIONS

Fiction

Seacliff; or, The Mystery of the Westervelts. 1859.
Miss Ravenel's Conversion from Secession to Loyalty. 1867; revised edition, 1939.
Overland. 1871.
Kate Beaumont. 1872.
The Wetherel Affair. 1873.
Honest John Vane. 1875.
Playing the Mischief. 1875.
Justine's Lovers. 1878.
Irene the Missionary. 1879.
The Bloody Chasm. 1881; as *The Oddest of Courtships*, 1882.
A Lover's Revolt. 1898.
Witching Times, edited by Alfred Appel, Jr. 1967.

Verse

The Downing Legends: Stories in Rhyme. 1901.
Poems: Medley and Palestina. 1902.

Other

History of the Indians of Connecticut from the Earliest Known Period to 1850. 1851.
Oriental Acquaintance; or, Letters from Syria. 1856.
European Acquaintance. 1858.
The De Forests of Avesnes (and of New Netherland): A Huguenot Thread in American Colonial History 1494 to the Present Time. 1900.
"The First Time under Fire" of the 12th Regiment, Connecticut Volunteers. 1907.
A Volunteer's Adventures: A Union Captain's Record of the Civil War, edited by James H. Croushore. 1946.
A Union Officer in the Reconstruction, edited by James H. Croushore and David Morris Potter. 1948.

*

Bibliography: in *Bibliography of American Literature* by Jacob Blanck, 1957; "De Forest: A Critical Bibliography of Secondary Comment" by James F. Light, in *American Literary Realism 4*, 1968.

Critical Studies: *Patriotic Gore: Studies in the Literature of the American Civil War* by Edmund Wilson, 1962; *De Forest* by James F. Light, 1965; *Critical Essays on De Forest* edited by James W. Gargano, 1981.

* * *

John William De Forest was in his own day a prolific but little-read author. Despite the praise of William Dean Howells, 19th-century readers, with their love for melodrama and romance, could not accept De Forest's realism. Yet unquestionably De Forest deserves the credit as an innovator that literary critics such as Edmund Wilson and Van Wyck Brooks have accorded him. Three of his novels, *Miss Ravenel's Conversion from Secession to Loyalty*, *Kate Beaumont*, and *Playing the Mischief*, are particularly fine examples of realistic fiction.

In his first published work, *History of the Indians of Connecticut from the Earliest Known Period to 1850*, he demonstrated the objectivity and the penchant for debunking romantic myths which characterize his fictional style. By the time the Civil War began he had written two novels. *Witching Times* is set during the hysteria of the Salem witch trials. *Seacliff*, a country-house novel with a mystery theme, presents Mrs. Westervelt, the first of his wealthy, bored, neurotic middle-aged women. The story is told from a limited first-person point of view, a technique later perfected by Henry James. De Forest also published two travel books, *Oriental Acquaintance* and *European Acquaintance*, during this pre-war period.

The author and his family left Charleston, South Carolina just before Fort Sumter was fired on. In 1862 De Forest, a successful author and a family man of 36, became captain of a company of Connecticut volunteers. This Civil War service became the raw material for a series of magazine articles collected and published posthumously under the title *A Volunteer's Adventures*, and for his most famous novel, *Miss Ravenel's Conversion*. His post-war stint in the Freedmen's Bureau gave him local settings for *Kate Beaumont* and *The Bloody Chasm* and the materials for essays in *A Union Officer in the Reconstruction*.

De Forest's descriptions of war are unemotional, graphic and vivid. Perhaps his maturity at the time he had his wartime experience accounts in part for his dispassionate style, but the same objectivity and ironic detachment characterize all his best fiction. Though the fever pitch of the early war years had been lessened by the tragedy of Bull Run, the war was for most Northern readers still the great crusade; the notion that promotions were ruled by political patronage or that generals caused needless deaths through incompetence were unwelcome dashes of cold water. Descriptions of grim field hospitals with amputated limbs and coagulating blood under the operating table or the dead blackening and bloating in the hot Louisiana sun were too strong for the mass audience.

Howells blamed De Forest's lack of success on the female reader. Certainly it is true that De Forest does not romanticize many female figures in his work. Mrs. La Rue of *Miss Ravenel's Conversion* and Mrs. Chester of *Kate Beaumont* are fading flirts still trying to attract young men. Though Mrs. Chester ultimately goes mad, Mrs. La Rue succeeds in captivating Miss Ravenel's first husband and, after his death, finding another influential lover who helps her to recoup her fortunes lost in the war. Josie Murray of *Playing the Mischief* and Olympia Smiles Vane of *Honest John Vane* manipulate men for material gain with complete success; there may be storm clouds in their futures, but they are secure as the novels end. Even the chaste ingenues like Lily Ravenel and Clara Van Dieman of *Overland* respond passionately to the sexual aspects of the men they marry. The Howells theory has, no doubt, an element of truth in it, but other factors enter in as well.

De Forest suffered as Melville, Hawthorne and others did from the unfavorable conditions of American publishing in their day. With no international copyright protection from European rivals and the high volume of sales needed to turn a profit, one after another of De Forest's publishers went bankrupt. De Forest approached his work with the detachment of a scientist; even when exposing the scandal and malfeasance of the war and the Grant era, his tone is clinical and detached. His post-war work eschews sermonizing and he either lets the scene speak for itself or comments with ironic indirection. This lack of passion and subtlety of point of view may have been too demanding for his readers. Moreover, the author's cynicism may have disturbed some readers. There are no gods in his pantheon. Democracy is failing in his Washington novels; the women's suffrage movement produces humor but no greatness; romantic love is a delusion better buried, as in *A Lover's Revolt*, in more compelling public issues.

Although occasionally De Forest could not resist the lure of popular taste—*Overland* and *The Bloody Chasm* have highly contrived melodramatic plots—at his best he carefully deflates romantic situations. Josie Murray entraps two Congressional lovers, but the man she really admires escapes one romantic embrace after another, coolly appraising the dangers of commitment to an enticing but amoral woman. Nelly Armitage, Kate Beaumont's sister, lured by passion into marriage with a handsome drunkard, is praised for her fortitude in staying with him. She replies, "It is mere hardened callousness and want of feeling. I ceased some time ago to be a woman. I am a species of brute." Captain Colburne, the hero of *Miss Ravenel's Conversion*, is bored during the bombardment of Port Hudson and finds his freed servant is not saintly Uncle Tom, but a pilferer who must be constantly watched. De Forest's last novel, *A Lover's Revolt*, demonstrates the conflict between the romantic plot elements he knew the mass audience wanted and the realistic passages he wrote so successfully. The book contains the required love story, but the author's prime concern is the military situation in Boston of 1775–76; the love triangle is mechanically and scantily disposed of.

De Forest wrote many fine stories and novels in the years immediately following the war, and he explored new ground with almost every effort, but his books did not sell. He hoped to leave a standard edition of his work as a "little monument," but no publisher would agree to the venture. Finally this accomplished writer gave up in discouragement; he wrote little during the last two decades of his life.

—Barbara M. Perkins

DELAND, Margaret(ta Wade, née Campbell). Born near Allegheny, Pennsylvania, 23 February 1857; orphaned: raised by her aunt and uncle in Manchester, Pennsylvania. Educated in local schools, and at Pelham Priory, New Rochelle, New York, 1873–75; studied art and design at Cooper Union, New York, 1875–76. Married Lorin F. Deland in 1880 (died, 1917). Assistant Instructor of Drawing and Design, Normal College of the City of New York (later Hunter College), 1876–80; lived in Boston from 1880; with her husband created a hostel, in their home, for unmarried mothers, 1880–84; full-time writer from 1886. Honorary degrees: Rutgers University, New Brunswick, New Jersey, 1917; Tufts College, Medford, Massachusetts, 1920; Bates College, Lewiston, Maine, 1920; Bowdoin College, Brunswick, Maine, 1931. Member, American Academy, 1926. *Died 13 January 1945.*

PUBLICATIONS

Fiction

John Ward, Preacher. 1888.
A Summer Day. 1889.
Sidney. 1890.
The Story of a Child. 1892.
Mr. Tommy Dove and Other Stories. 1893.
Philip and His Wife. 1894.
The Wisdom of Fools. 1897.
Old Chester Tales. 1898.
Good for the Soul. 1899.
Dr. Lavendar's People. 1903.
The Awakening of Helena Richie. 1906.
An Encore. 1907.
R.J.'s Mother and Some Other People. 1908.
The Way to Peace. 1910.
The Iron Woman. 1911.
The Voice. 1912.
Partners. 1913.
The Hands of Esau. 1914.
Around Old Chester. 1915.
The Rising Tide. 1916.
The Promises of Alice. 1919.
An Old Chester Secret. 1920.
The Vehement Flame. 1922.
New Friends in Old Chester. 1924.
The Kays. 1926.
Captain Archer's Daughter. 1932.
Old Chester Days. 1937.

Play

Screenplay: *Smouldering Fires*, with others, 1925.

Verse

The Old Garden and Other Verses. 1886.

Other

Florida Days. 1889.
The Common Way. 1904.
Small Things. 1919.
If This Be I, As I Suppose It Be (autobiography). 1935.
Golden Yesterdays (autobiography). 1941.

* * *

In 1888 Margaret Deland, who had previously written only one book of poetry, *The Old Garden and Other Verses*, published a novel, *John Ward, Preacher*. A complex, thesis-ridden saga of Puritan zealotry gone rigid and perverse, the book became an infamous bestseller and made its author a celebrity. John Ward, an unreconstructed Calvinist, is married to an Episcopalian woman who, as Percy H. Boynton has written (in *America in Contemporary Fiction*) "is so devoted to her husband that she can ignore his bigotry if only he will permit her to. He believes, however, that the salvation of her soul is more imperative than the survival of his home, sends her away, breaks down under the strain, and dies."

In the years that followed the publication of *John Ward*, Deland moved from the infamous and realistic to the conventional and placid. Her Old Chester pieces—many of which were collected in *Old Chester Tales* and *Dr. Lavendar's People*—for which she is best remembered, told of life in the turn-of-the-century village. Old Chester, a fictionalized Manchester, the small Pennsylvania town in which Deland had spent a part of her childhood, was not drawn with the cynicism of Lewis's Gopher Prairie or the grotesquery of Anderson's Winesburg or even with the zeal of Deland's own *John Ward*. Hers, rather, was an image of small-town Americana both peaceful and homiletic.

Reminiscences of her earlier realism were signaled now and again in Old Chester, however. In *The Awakening of Helena Richie*, for instance, the protagonist comes to the village to escape the drunkenness of her husband and her own adulterous past, only to be revealed by Dr. Lavendar and subsequently shown the path of penitence. And in a sequel, *The Iron Woman*, the awakened Helena leads the next generation away from the realistically portrayed pitfalls of adultery and divorce.

Born before the Civil War, Deland was a sometimes outspoken defender of marriage, family, and community. But by the time of her death in 1945 one could scarcely imagine that so benign a spokesman had ever been thought provocative. Indeed, the very virtues which she had stood for seemed to be in disarray.

—Bruce A. Lohof

DELL, Floyd. Born in Barry, Illinois, 28 June 1887. Educated at schools in Barry and Quincy, Illinois, and Davenport High School, Iowa. Served in the U.S. Army, 1918. Married 1) Margery Curry in 1909 (separated, 1913; divorced, 1916); 2) Berta Marie Gage in 1919, two sons. Reporter, Davenport *Times*, 1905; editor, *Tri-City Workers' Magazine*, Davenport, 1906; reporter, Davenport *Democrat*, 1906, and Chicago *Evening Post*, 1909, and assistant editor, 1909–10, associate editor, 1910–11, and editor, 1911–13, *Evening Post Friday Literary Review*; moved to New York, 1913: managing editor, *The Masses*, 1914–17, and associate editor of its successor, *The Liberator*, 1918–20; tried for sedition for his pacifist writings, 1917; full-time writer from 1921; editor for the WPA (Works Progress Administration), Washington, D.C., 1935–47. *Died 23 July 1969.*

PUBLICATIONS

Fiction

Moon-Calf. 1920.
The Briary-Bush. 1921.
Janet March. 1923; revised edition, 1927.
This Mad Ideal. 1925.
Runaway. 1925.
Love in Greenwich Village (stories and poems). 1926.
An Old Man's Folly. 1926.
An Unmarried Father. 1927; as *Little Accident*, 1930.
Souvenir. 1929.
Love Without Money. 1931.
Diana Stair. 1932.
The Golden Spike. 1934.

Plays

Human Nature (as *A Five Minute Problem Play*, produced 1913). In *King Arthur's Socks . . .*, 1922.
The Chaste Adventures of Joseph (produced 1914). In *King Arthur's Socks . . .*, 1922.
Ibsen Revisited (produced 1914). In *King Arthur's Socks . . .*, 1922.
Enigma (produced 1915). In *King Arthur's Socks . . .*, 1922.
Legend (as *My Lady's Mirror*, produced 1915). In *King Arthur's Socks . . .*, 1922.
The Rim of the World (produced 1915). In *King Arthur's Socks . . .*, 1922.
King Arthur's Socks (produced 1916). In *King Arthur's Socks . . .*, 1922.
The Angel Intrudes (produced 1917). 1918.
A Long Time Ago (produced 1917). In *King Arthur's Socks . . .*, 1922.
Sweet and Twenty (produced 1918). 1921.
Poor Harold! (produced 1920). In *King Arthur's Socks . . .*, 1922.
King Arthur's Socks and Other Village Plays. 1922.
Little Accident, with Thomas Mitchell, from the novel *An Unmarried Father* by Dell (produced 1928).
Cloudy with Showers, with Thomas Mitchell (produced 1931).

Other

Women as World Builders: Studies in Modern Feminism. 1913.
Were You Ever a Child? 1919.
Looking at Life. 1924.
Intellectual Vagabondage: An Apology for the Intelligentsia. 1926.
The Outline of Marriage. 1926.
Upton Sinclair: A Study in Social Protest. 1927.
Love in the Machine Age: A Psychological Study of the Transition from Patriarchal Society. 1930.
Homecoming: An Autobiography. 1933.
Children and the Machine Age. 1934.

Editor, *Poems*, by Wilfrid Scawen Blunt. 1923.
Editor, *Poems of Robert Herrick*. 1924.
Editor, *Poems and Prose of William Blake*. 1925.
Editor, with Paul Jordan-Smith, *The Anatomy of Melancholy*, by Robert Burton. 1927.
Editor, *Daughter of the Revolution and Other Stories*, by John Reed. 1927.

*

Bibliography: *Dell: An Annotated Bibliography of Secondary Sources 1910–1981* by Judith Nierman, 1984.

Critical Study: *Dell* by John E. Hart, 1971.

* * *

In a writing career running from 1908 to 1935, Floyd Dell published more than twenty books and roughly one thousand periodical pieces. They, like his life, fall into several distinct periods and reflect his connection with many of the important literary movements and intellectual concerns in the U.S. during the first quarter of the century.

In his Chicago period (1908–13), his output consisted chiefly of book reviews and essays for the *Friday Literary Review* of the Chicago *Evening Post*, which during his editorship found itself at the heart of what has come to be known as the Chicago Renaissance. His brisk and often highly personal discussions for the *Review* championed the "new" literature, introduced the work of many continental novelists, and surveyed current books on socialism and sex; one of his series of articles, "Modern Women," taking up the views of ten feminists, became his first book, *Women as World Builders*.

His Greenwich Village years (1913–20, chronicled nostalgically in prose sketches, short stories, and poetry in *Love in Greenwich Village*), coincided with a period of intense creative and intellectual activity there, and he became one of the leading figures both through his participation in the the little theatre movement—several of his short plays gently satirizing the intellectual concerns of the Villagers were collected as *King Arthur's Socks and Other Village Plays*—and his writings as an editor of the socialistic journals *The Masses* and its successor, *The Liberator*. The books that resulted from this writing reflect the dualism both of Dell and of these magazines, which were concerned with art as well as politics and were often as conservative in the former as they were radical in the latter. *Looking at Life* draws together forty short pieces, largely unconnected with socialism; they display an acute intelligence playing lightly and entertainingly, but seldom profoundly, over a wide range of subjects. *Were You Ever a Child?*, based on a series in *The Liberator*, is a plea for educational reform, popularizing the ideas of John Dewey and other educational theorists and presenting them with humor and playfulness (and often in dialogue form). *Intellectual Vagabondage*, based on another series written for *The Liberator* (but after Dell left the Village), is the most important of the three, and is Dell's most ambitious effort at interpreting literature from a social and economic standpoint; with characteristic lightness of touch he traces the historical role of the intelligentsia and then, more significantly, sets forth the "spiritual autobiography" of his own generation, depicting, among other things, the idealistic revolt of youth against the restraints of a commercial world.

This perennial theme of Dell's runs through the novels that he produced during what may be regarded as his third period, the years when he lived at Croton-on-the-Hudson, New York (1920–35). His first—and most famous and best—novel, *Moon-Calf*, draws heavily on his own pre-Chicago years and describes with great sensitivity the intellectual development of a young dreamer and poet; with it he made the analysis of moon-calves, and their adjustment to reality, his own special province. In ten succeeding novels he continued to explore the predicaments of youthful idealists, who in the end find happiness by accepting conventions; like his other writings, these novels are facile and exhibit a keen sense of irony and humour, but they do not fulfill the promise suggested by *Moon-Calf*. The interest in psychological and social problems manifested in the novels reaches its climax in Dell's substantial study of adolescent adjustment, *Love in the Machine Age*, a well-written exposition of the thesis that the neuroses of the modern world are the result of outmoded but still operative patriarchal conventions.

For psychological insight, however, readers are likely to prefer his autobiography, *Homecoming*, especially the first half dealing with the years covered fictionally in *Moon-Calf*. As the title implies, the movement of the book and of his life is toward the stability finally found in marriage and a home; but he never lost the ability to write perceptively of youthful rebellion, and the book contains some of his best work. The dust jacket calls it "not Floyd Dell's autobiography but your own," a remark that points to Dell's importance as a representative figure. He will be best remembered as an intelligent and articulate commentator on the characteristic concerns of a sizable segment of his literary generation.

—G. Thomas Tanselle

DEWEY, John. Born in Burlington, Vermont, 20 October 1859. Educated at schools in Burlington; University of Vermont, Burlington, 1875–79, B.A. 1879; Johns Hopkins University, Baltimore, 1882–84, Ph.D. 1884. Married 1) Alice Chipman in 1886 (died, 1927), three sons, three daughters, and one adopted son; 2) Roberta L. Grant in 1946, one son and one daughter, both adopted. High school teacher, Oil City, Pennsylvania, 1879–81; Assistant Professor, 1886–88, and Professor of Philosophy, 1889–94, University of Michigan, Ann Arbor; Visiting Professor of Philosophy, University of Minnesota, Minneapolis, 1888–89; Professor of Philosophy and Chairman of the Department of Philosophy, Psychology and Pedagogy, University of Chicago, 1894–1904 (founder, Laboratory School, 1896; Director, School of Education, 1902–04); Professor of Philosophy, 1904–30, Professor Emeritus in Residence, 1930–39, and Professor Emeritus, 1939–52, Columbia University, New York. Lecturer, Imperial University of Tokyo, 1919, and National Universities of Peking and Nanking, 1919–21; Clifford Lecturer, University of Edinburgh, 1929; William James Lecturer, Harvard University, Cambridge, Massachusetts, 1930; Dwight Harrington Terry Lecturer, Yale University, New Haven, Connecticut, 1934. Conducted surveys of education in Turkey, 1924, Mexico, 1926, and the Soviet Union, 1928; Chairman, Commission of Inquiry into the Charges Made Against Leon Trotsky in the Moscow Trials, 1937. President, American Psychological Association, 1899, and Eastern Division of American Philosophical Association, 1905–06; a founder and first President, American Association of University Professors, 1915. Honorary degrees: University of Wisconsin, Madison, 1904; University of Vermont, 1910; University of Michigan, 1913; Johns Hopkins University, 1915; University of Peking, 1920; University of St. Andrews, Scotland, 1929; Columbia University, 1929; University of Paris, 1930; Harvard University, 1932; University of Pennsylvania, Philadelphia, 1946; University of Oslo, 1946; Yale University, 1951. Member, National Academy of Sciences, 1910. *Died 1 June 1952.*

PUBLICATIONS

Collections

The Early Works 1882–1898, edited by Jo Ann Boydston. 5 vols., 1967–72.
The Middle Works 1899–1924, edited by Jo Ann Boydston. 15 vols., 1976–83.
The Later Works 1925–1953, edited by Jo Ann Boydston. 1981—
The Poems, edited by Jo Ann Boydston. 1977.

Prose

Psychology. 1887; revised edition, 1889, 1891.
Leibniz's New Essays Concerning the Human Understanding: A Critical Exposition. 1888.
The Ethics of Democracy. 1888.
Applied Psychology: An Introduction to the Principles and Practices of Education, with J.A. McLellan. 1889.
Outlines of a Critical Theory of Ethics. 1891.
The Study of Ethics: A Syllabus. 1894.
The Psychology of Number and Its Applications to Methods of Teaching Arithmetic, with J.A. McLellan. 1895.
My Pedagogic Creed, with *The Demands of Sociology upon Pedagogy*, by Albion W. Small. 1897.
The Significance of the Problem of Knowledge. 1897.
Psychology and Philosophic Method. 1899.
The School and Society. 1899; revised edition, 1915; edited by Jo Ann Boydston, 1980.
Psychology and Social Practice. 1901.
The Child and the Curriculum. 1902.
The Educational Situation. 1902.
Studies in Logical Theory, with others. 1903.
Logical Conditions of a Scientific Treatment of Morality. 1903.
The School and the Child, Being Selections from the Educational Essays of Dewey, edited by J.J. Findlay. 1907.
Ethics (lecture). 1908.
Ethics, with James H. Tufts. 1908; revised edition, 1932; selection, as *Theory of the Moral Life*, 1960.
Moral Principles in Education. 1909.
How We Think. 1910; revised edition, 1933.
The Influence of Darwin on Philosophy and Other Essays in Contemporary Thought. 1910.
Educational Essays, edited by J.J. Findlay. 1910.
Interest and Effort in Education. 1913.
Some Dangers in the Present Movement for Industrial Education. 1913.
German Philosophy and Politics. 1915.
Schools of To-morrow, with Evelyn Dewey. 1915.
Democracy and Education: An Introduction to the Philosophy of Education. 1916.
Essays in Experimental Logic. 1916.
Creative Intelligence: Essays in the Pragmatic Attitude, with others. 1917.
Enlistment for the Farm. 1917.
Vocational Education in the Light of the World War. 1918.
Letters from China and Japan, with Alice Chipman Dewey, edited by Evelyn Dewey. 1920.
Reconstruction in Philosophy. 1920; revised edition, 1948.
China, Japan and the U.S.A.: Present-Day Conditions in the Far East and Their Bearing on the Washington Conference. 1921.
Human Nature and Conduct: An Introduction to Social Psychology. 1922.
Experience and Nature. 1925; revised edition, 1929.
The Public and Its Problems. 1927.
The Philosophy of Dewey, edited by Joseph Ratner. 1928.
Progressive Education and the Science of Education. 1928.
Impressions of Soviet Russia and the Revolutionary World: Mexico, China, Turkey. 1929.
Characters and Events: Popular Essays in Social and Political Philosophy, edited by Joseph Ratner. 2 vols., 1929.
Art and Education, with others. 1929.
The Quest for Certainty: A Study of the Relation of Knowledge and Action. 1929.
The Sources of a Science of Education. 1929.
Individualism, Old and New. 1930.
Construction and Criticism. 1930.
Context and Thought. 1931.
Philosophy and Civilization. 1931.
The Way Out of Educational Confusion. 1931.
American Education Past and Future. 1931.
The Place of Minor Parties in the American Scene. 1932.
The Educational Frontier, with others. 1933.
Steps to Economic Recovery. 1933(?).
Education and the Social Order. 1934.
The Meaning of Marx: A Symposium, with others. 1934.
Art as Experience. 1934.
A Common Faith. 1934.
Liberalism and Social Action. 1935.
The Teacher and Society, with others. 1937.
The Case of Leon Trotsky: Report of the Hearings of the Charges Made Against Him in the Moscow Trials, with others. 1937.
Not Guilty: Report of the Commission of Inquiry into the Charges Made Against Leon Trotsky in the Moscow Trials, with others. 1938.
Logic: The Theory of Inquiry. 1938.
Experience and Education. 1938.
Democracy and Education in the World of Today. 1938.
Intelligence in the Modern World: Dewey's Philosophy, edited by Joseph Ratner. 1939.
Freedom and Culture. 1939.
Theory of Valuation. 1939.
What Is Democracy?, with others. 1939.
Education Today, edited by Joseph Ratner. 1940.
Problems of Men. 1946.
Knowing and the Known, with Arthur F. Bentley. 1949.
The Wit and Wisdom of Dewey, edited by A.H. Johnson. 1949.
David Dubinsky: A Pictorial Biography. 1951.
Dewey: His Contribution to the American Tradition, edited by Irwin Edman. 1955.
Dewey on Education, edited by Martin S. Dworkin. 1959.
Dictionary of Education, edited by Ralph B. Winn. 1959.
On Experience, Nature, and Freedom: Representative Selections, edited by Richard J. Bernstein. 1960.
Philosophy, Psychology, and Social Practice: Essays, edited by Joseph Ratner. 1963.
Dewey and Arthur F. Bentley: A Philosophical Correspondence 1932–1951, edited by Sidney Ratner and Jules Altman. 1964.
Dewey on Education, edited by Reginald D. Archambault. 1966.
Lectures in the Philosophy of Education 1899, edited by Reginald D. Archambault. 1966.
Selected Educational Writings, edited by F.W. Garforth. 1966.
(*Selections*), edited by Malcolm Skilbeck. 1970.
The Philosophy of Dewey: The Structure of Experience and *The Lived Experience*, edited by John J. McDermott. 2 vols., 1973.
Lectures in China 1919–1920, edited and translated by Robert W. Clopton and Tsuin-chen Ou. 1973.
Lectures on Psychological and Political Ethics 1898, edited by Donald F. Koch. 1976.
The Moral Writings, edited by James Gouinlock. 1976.
The Essential Writings, edited by David Sidorsky. 1977.

Editor, *New York and the Seabury Investigation*. 1933.
Editor, *The Living Thoughts of Thomas Jefferson*. 1940.
Editor, with Horace M. Kallen, *The Bertrand Russell Case*. 1941.

*

Bibliography: *Dewey: A Centennial Bibliography* by Milton Halsey Thomas, 1962; *Checklist of Writings about Dewey 1887–1977* by Jo Ann Boydston and Kathleen Poulos, 1978.

Critical Studies: *Dewey: An Intellectual Portrait* by Sidney Hook, 1939, and *Dewey, Philosopher of Science and Freedom: A Symposium* edited by Hook, 1967; *The Philosophy of Dewey* edited by Paul Arthur Schilpp, 1939; *The Logic of Pragmatism: An Examination of Dewey's Logic* by H.S. Thayer, 1952; *The Nihilism of Dewey* by Paul K. Crosser, 1955; *Dewey in Perspective* by George R. Geiger, 1958; *Dewey: His Thought and Influence* edited by John Blewett, 1960; *Dewey as Educator: His Design for Work in Education 1894–1904* by Arthur G. Wirth, 1966; *Guide to the Works of Dewey* edited by Jo Ann Boydston, 1970; *Dewey* by Harry M. Campbell, 1971; *Dewey's Philosophy of Value* by James Gouinlock, 1972; *The Life and Mind of Dewey* by George Dykhuizen, 1973; *Dewey and His Influence* by Robert C. Whittemore, 1973; *Young Dewey: An Essay in American Intellectual History* by Neil Coughlan, 1975; *Dewey's Aesthetic Philosophy* by Philip M. Zeltner, 1975; *Dewey Reconsidered* edited by R.S. Peters, 1977; *New Studies in the Philosophy of Dewey* edited by Steven M. Cahn, 1977; *Dewey: Recollections* edited by Robert Bruce Williams, 1982; *The Politics of Dewey* edited by Gary Bullert, 1984.

* * *

John Dewey's writings are a notable exception to the frequently expressed despair that Philosophy affords no answers to problems of living. Dewey's greatness as a philosopher derives from his recognition that this despair articulates a need to transcend the Western philosophical tradition, to advance a view that "re-understands" the human condition, a view that in Dewey's words (in *Reconstruction in Philosophy*) "would have an active share in the work of construction of a moral human science which serves as a needful precursor of reconstruction of the actual state of human life toward order and toward other conditions of a fuller life than man has yet enjoyed." So, what conceptual disease explains the impotence of traditional philosophy in the face of life's perils? What therapy is there? What philosophical outlook can ground this "moral human science"?

Dewey's therapy resembles that prescribed by such thinkers as Wittgenstein and Heidegger. Dewey recommends reflection upon the natural and socio-cultural history of those dualisms which have preoccupied the Western tradition: Mind-Matter, Subject-Object, Certainty/Knowledge-Belief/Doing, Experience-Nature, Contemplation-Action—a "naturalistic Hegelianism," as it were. Dewey contends that these dualisms are rooted in certain primitive evaluations of remote antiquity, according an inherently "higher" value to "religious" over "technological" attempts at securing human existence.

"Philosophy inherited the realm with which religion had been concerned" and rationally justified the value-distinction between its inherited realm and the realm of technics. Technics comprised "bodies of information that corresponded to the everyday arts, the store of matter-of-fact knowledge, . . . things men knew because of what they did" (*The Quest for Certainty*). Philosophy, however, sought genuine knowledge of a realm "higher" than the earthly realm of technics. It aspired accurately to represent an immutable, eternal Reality.

These conceptions—of Philosophy as genuine knowledge, of genuine knowledge as representation of Reality, of Reality as eternal and thus independent of human existence—engendered a picture of Mind's relation to Reality that is pivotal in the Western tradition, what Dewey calls the "spectator theory of knowledge." It portrays Mind as metaphysically removed from Reality, as beholding Reality through a conceptual veil.

The theory motivates the concern over whether we shall ever know if Thought truthfully represents Reality. We cannot "hold up" our moral and scientific theories in comparison with Reality—we cannot wedge Thought between Mind and Reality. Indeed, our scientific theories demonstrate that various qualities ascribed to Reality—colors, sounds, etc.—are effects on sensory receptors, merely subjective experiential representations of Reality; and as a measure of the Real, such theories cast moral and aesthetic values as ontologically aberrant. Seeking comfort in a Kantian bastion of transcendental deduction is illusory: assimilating the empirically real to the transcendentally ideal.

According to Dewey, we must reject the spectatorial separation of Mind from Reality. We must recognize Mind as part of Reality: Thinking and Knowing are activities, things we do. Their fruits are simply further ways of dealing with life's perils. We must recognize "Doing" as the heart of "Knowing," "regard knowings and reasonings and mathematical and scientific adventurings even up to their highest abstraction, as activities . . ." (*The Quest for Certainty*).

Philosophy must attempt to integrate "our cognitive beliefs, our beliefs resting upon the most dependable methods of inquiry, with the practical beliefs about the values, the ends and purposes, that should control human action in the things of large and liberal human import" (*Experience and Nature*). The integration is to be conducted methodologically: our "most dependable methods" being the experimental methods characteristic of physical science, Philosophy must advance a framework for introducing these methods into the "human sciences."

Initially such a framework seems incoherent. Physical science cannot be unified with human science. The latter countenances mental, moral, and aesthetic entities; these are not entities physical science can countenance. However, Dewey asserts we should not construe physical science as the measure of Reality. Following the pragmatic instrumentalism of Charles Sanders Peirce and William James, he maintains that physical science should not be construed as true by virtue of successful reference to an objective Reality whose nature is antecedent to observation and inquiry. Physical science is an "instrument" that helps explain regularities governing phenomena observable in everyday life; its "truth" is gauged by its consequences in life.

The project introduces tensions. Dewey urges that we abandon traditional metaphysics. However, he aspires toward an account "of the generic traits manifested by existence of all kinds without regard to their differentiation into physical and mental . . ." (*Experience and Nature*). Why do we need such an account? Does it resolve the above tension? However, a thoroughgoing instrumentalism does that. But can such an instrumentalism be coherently maintained? It is a problem in the theory of meaning whether one can distinguish "theoretical" from "observational" as instrumentalism requires. Finally, it is questionable whether Dewey's diagnosis of the tradition is adequate; in this he stands trial with Wittgenstein and Heidegger.

These difficulties aside, Dewey's philosophical view at least outlines a framework in which all fields of human endeavour can buttress each other towards creating "conditions of a fuller life than man has yet enjoyed."

—James M. Drayton

DICKEY, James (Lafayette). Born in Atlanta, Georgia, 2 February 1923. Educated at Clemson College, South Carolina, 1942; Vanderbilt University, Nashville, Tennessee, B.A. (magna cum laude) 1949 (Phi Beta Kappa), M.A. 1950. Served as a pilot in the U.S. Army Air Force during World War II and as a training officer in the Air Force during the Korean War. Married 1) Maxine Syerson in 1948 (died, 1976), two sons; 2) Deborah Dodson in 1976, one daughter. Teacher at Rice University, Houston, 1950, 1952–54, and University of Florida, Gainesville, 1955–56; Poet-in-Residence, Reed College, Portland, Oregon, 1962–64, San Fernando Valley State College, Northridge, California, 1964–66, and University of Wisconsin, Madison, 1966; Consultant in Poetry, Library of Congress, Washington, D.C., 1966–68; since 1969 Professor of English and Writer-in-Residence, University of South Carolina, Columbia. Recipient: Vachel Lindsay Prize, 1959; Longview Foundation award, 1960; Guggenheim fellowship, 1961; Melville Cane Award, 1966; National Book Award, 1966; American Academy grant, 1966; Médicis Prize, for novel, 1971. Member, American Academy. Lives in Columbia, South Carolina.

PUBLICATIONS

Verse

Into the Stone and Other Poems. 1960.
Drowning with Others. 1962; selection, as *The Owl King*, 1977.
Helmets. 1964.
Two Poems of the Air. 1964.
Buckdancer's Choice. 1965.
Poems 1957–1967. 1967.
The Achievement of Dickey: A Comprehensive Selection of His Poems, edited by Laurence Lieberman. 1968.
The Eye-Beaters, Blood, Victory, Madness, Buckhead and Mercy. 1970.
The Zodiac. 1976; revised edition, 1976.
The Strength of Fields. 1977; revised edition 1979.
Veteran Birth: The Gadfly Poems 1947–1949. 1978.
Head-Deep in Strange Sounds: Free-Flight Improvisations from the UnEnglish. 1979.
Falling, May Day Sermon, and Other Poems. 1981.
The Early Motion. 1981.
Puella. 1982.
The Central Motion: Poems 1968–1979. 1983.
False Youth—Four Seasons. 1983.

Plays

Deliverance: A Screenplay, edited by Matthew J. Bruccoli. 1981.

Screenplay: *Deliverance*, 1972.

Television Play: *The Call of the Wild*, from the novel by Jack London, 1976.

Fiction

Deliverance. 1970.

Other

The Suspect in Poetry. 1964.
A Private Brinksmanship (address). 1965.
Spinning the Crystal Ball: Some Guesses at the Future of American Poetry. 1967.
Metaphor as Pure Adventure (lecture). 1968.
Babel to Byzantium: Poets and Poetry Now. 1968.
Self-Interviews, edited by Barbara and James Reiss. 1970.
Sorties (essays). 1971.
Exchanges . . . : Being in the Form of a Dialogue with Joseph Trumbull Stickney. 1971.
Jericho: The South Beheld, paintings by Hubert Shuptrine. 1974.
God's Images: The Bible: A New Vision, illustrated by Marvin Hayes. 1977.
Tucky the Hunter (for children). 1978.
The Enemy from Eden. 1978.
In Pursuit of the Grey Soul (on fishing). 1979.
The Water-Bug's Mittens: Ezra Pound, What We Can Use (lecture). 1980.
Scion. 1980.
The Starry Place Between the Antlers: Why I Live in South Carolina. 1981.
The Eagle's Mile. 1981.
The Poet Turns on Himself. 1982.
How to Enjoy Poetry. 1982.
For a Time and Place. 1983.
Night Hurdling: Poems, Essays, Conversations, Commencements, and Afterwords. 1983.

Translator, *Stolen Apples*, by Yevgeny Yevtushenko. 1971.

*

Bibliography: *Dickey: A Bibliography 1947–1974* by Jim Elledge, 1979; *Dickey: A Bibliography* by Stuart Wright, 1982.

Critical Studies: *Dickey: The Expansive Imagination: A Collection of Critical Essays* edited by Richard J. Calhoun, 1973, and *Dickey* by Calhoun and Robert W. Hill, 1983; "Dickey Issue" of *South Carolina Review*, April 1978; *Dickey: Splintered Sunlight* edited by Patricia De La Fuente, 1979; *The Imagination as Glory: Essays on the Poetry of Dickey* edited by Bruce Weigl and T.R. Hummer, 1984; *Understanding Dickey* by Ronald Baughman, 1985; *Dickey: The Poet as Pitchman* by Neal Bowers, 1985.

* * *

James Dickey emerged as an important American poet and as a still underrated literary critic through an astonishing period of creative productivity from 1957 to 1967. He was regarded so much as a poet without imitators and without specific social or political concerns that his important contributions to post-modernism both as a poet and critic were not adequately recognized. But Dickey should be seen as a post-modernist romantic—because of his desire to make imaginative contact with natural forces which have been lost to modern man, because of his romantic faith in the power of his imagination, and because of the expansive affirmative character of most of his poems.

Dickey has always violated the modernist practice of impersonality in his poetry for there has always been a close correspondence between the chronology of his poems and his life. In his earliest poems he drew from such autobiographical data as the death (before Dickey was born) of his brother Eugene and his experiences as a fighter pilot in two destructive wars, as well as from his love for hunting, archery, and the southern landscape. Many of these poems feature encounters leading to vividly imagined exchanges of identity between the living and the dead, between men and "unthinking" nature, for the purpose of understanding through the imagination what reason alone cannot comprehend.

Dickey early declared himself an affirmative poet, with an acknowledged affinity for the poetry of his friend and mentor Theodore Roethke; but his affirmations are from the knowing perspective of a grateful survivor of two wars. His poems have always portrayed those who were *not* survivors and affirmed the risk inherent in an exchange of identity. In later poems, especially in *The Eye-Beaters*, Dickey has exhibited a fascination with fantasy, with what he has called his "country surrealism," blurring distinctions between reality and dreams, even suggesting hallucinations. His intention has been to produce a poetry that releases the unconscious and the irrational, with results that are both life affirmative and life threatening.

Two poems that might serve as transitions from earlier to later themes are "Power and Light" and "Falling," both from *Poems 1957–1967*. There is a shift of emphasis from a celebration of "more life" through the imaginative comprehension of nature to the necessity of confronting destructive forces and of finding spiritual resources for that confrontation. Dickey's formal interests likewise shifted from regular towards more irregular forms, from the directness of "the simple declarative sentence" to the intimations of open and "big forms," and to such devices as split space punctuation within lines—effective in a tour de force like "Falling," but less effective in some recent poems.

In the 1970's Dickey's production of poetry lessened with a developing interest in the novel, television and film scripts, and in a form of literary criticism, the self-interview. His successful novel *Deliverance* shares with his poetry a concern with the cycle of entry into "unthinking nature," followed by a return to the world, perhaps having become while in nature "another thing." The return to the human realm is just as important as the entry into the natural. Dickey also became engaged in writing coffee-table sized prose-poem celebrations of the southern landscape (*Jericho*) and of the King James version of the Bible (*God's Images*). He produced one book of poetic "imitations" to mixed reviews from his critics, *The Zodiac*, his versions of the poems of a drunken Dutch sailor-poet of the 1940's. This book seemingly exhausted wildness and madness in Dickey's poetry. *The Strength of Fields* marked a change in tone towards acceptance and kindness. He offered additional translations, or, more properly, imitations. There are new war poems, but these are not poems about death and Dickey as survivor but more positive poems of acceptance of war and death. *Puella* displays an even more radical experiment in poetic voice. As the title suggests, Dickey adopts not his usual very masculine voice but the perspective of a girl, "male imagined." He traces the development of the girl Deborah from girlhood to womanhood and shows her relationship to the four traditional elements, fire, air, water, earth.

Dickey is by birth and residence a southern poet, with academic credentials from the stronghold of agrarianism, Vanderbilt University. Yet he has always made it clear that he is no "latter-day Agrarian." Still, like John Crowe Ransom, who feared the loss of "the world's body," and Allen Tate, who feared the loss of "complete knowledge" of man and his universe in an era dominated by science and technology, Dickey has his own version of agrarian fears of technology and urbanization. He has always been "much more interested in man's relationship to the God-made world, or the universe made than to the man made." He has made his best poetic subject clear: "The relationship of the human being to the great natural cycles of birth, the seasons, the growing up of seasons out of dead leaves, the generations of animals and of men, all on the heraldic wheel of existence is very beautiful to me." (*Self-Interviews*).

—Richard J. Calhoun

DICKINSON, Emily (Elizabeth). Born in Amherst, Massachusetts, 10 December 1830. Educated at Amherst Academy; Mount Holyoke Female Seminary, South Hadley, Massachusetts, 1847. Lived a secluded life in Amherst except for brief visits to Washington, D.C., Philadelphia, and Boston; semi-invalid, 1884–86. *Died 15 May 1886.*

PUBLICATIONS

Collections

The Poems, edited by Thomas H. Johnson. 3 vols., 1955.
Letters, edited by Thomas H. Johnson and Theodora Ward. 3 vols., 1958; *Selected Letters*, 1971.
Complete Poems (single version of all poems), edited by Thomas H. Johnson. 1960; *Final Harvest* (selections), 1961.
The Manuscript Books, edited by R.W. Franklin. 2 vols., 1981.

Verse

Poems, edited by Mabel Loomis Todd and T.W. Higginson. 1890; *Second Series*, 1891; *Third Series*, edited by Todd, 1896.
The Single Hound: Poems of a Lifetime, edited by Martha Dickinson Bianchi. 1914.
The Complete Poems, edited by Martha Dickinson Bianchi. 1924.
Further Poems, edited by Martha Dickinson Bianchi and Alfred Leete Hampson. 1929.

Unpublished Poems, edited by Martha Dickinson Bianchi and Alfred Leete Hampson. 1935.
Bolts of Melody: New Poems, edited by Mabel Loomis Todd and Millicent Todd Bingham. 1945.

Other

Letters (includes some poems), edited by Mabel Loomis Todd. 2 vols., 1894.

*

Bibliography: *Dickinson: An Annotated Bibliography: Writings, Scholarship, Criticism, and Ana 1850–1968* by Willis J. Buckingham, 1970; *The Poems of Dickinson: An Annotated Guide to Commentary Published in English 1890–1977* by Joseph Duchac, 1979.

Critical Studies: *The Life and Letters of Dickinson* by Martha Dickinson Bianchi, 1924; *Dickinson* by Richard Chase, 1951; *Dickinson: An Interpretative Biography* by Thomas H. Johnson, 1955; *The Years and Hours of Dickinson* edited by Jay Leyda, 2 vols., 1960; *Dickinson's Poetry: Stairway of Surprise* by Charles R. Anderson, 1960; *Dickinson: A Collection of Critical Essays* edited by Richard B. Sewall, 1963, and *The Life of Dickinson* by Sewall, 2 vols., 1974; *The Recognition of Dickinson: Selected Criticism since 1890* edited by Caesar R. Blake and Carlton F. Wells, 1964; *The Long Shadow: Dickinson's Tragic Poetry* by Clark Griffith, 1964; *Dickinson: The Mind of the Poet* by Albert J. Gelpi, 1965; *The Editing of Dickinson: A Reconsideration* by R.W. Franklin, 1967; *Dickinson: An Introduction and Interpretation* by John B. Pickard, 1967; *The Poetry of Dickinson* by Ruth Miller, 1968; *The Voice of the Poet: Aspects of Style in the Poetry of Dickinson* by Brita Lindberg-Seyersted, 1968; *Circumference and Circumstance: Stages in the Mind and Art of Dickinson* by William R. Sherwood, 1968; *Dickinson* by Denis Donoghue, 1969; *After Great Pain: The Inner Life of Dickinson* by John J. Cody, 1971; *Dickinson's Poetry* by Robert Weisbuch, 1975; *Dickinson and the Image of Home* by Jean McClure Mudge, 1975; *Dickinson* by Paul J. Ferlazzo, 1976, and *Critical Essays on Dickinson* edited by Ferlazzo, 1984; *The Only Kangaroo among the Beauty: Dickinson and America* by Karl Keller, 1979; *Dickinson's Imagery* by Rebecca Patterson, edited by Margaret H. Freeman, 1979; *Lyric Time: Dickinson and the Limits of Genre* by Sharon Cameron, 1979; *Dickinson: The Modern Idiom* by David Porter, 1981; *Dickinson and the Romantic Imagination* by Joanne Feit Diehl, 1982; *Dickinson: When a Writer is a Daughter* by Barbara A.C. Mossberg, 1983; *The Marriage of Dickinson: A Study of the Fascicles* by William Shurr, 1983; *Feminist Critics Read Dickinson* edited by Suzanne Juhasz, 1983, and *The Undiscovered Continent: Dickinson and the Space of the Mind* by Juhasz, 1984; *Dickinson: The Anxiety of Gender* by Vivian R. Pollak, 1984; *Dickinson: A Voice of War* by Shira Wolosky, 1984; *Dickinson and Her Culture: The Soul's Society* by Barton Levi St. Armand, 1985; *Dickinson: Strategies of Limitation* by Jane Donahue Eberwein, 1985; *Dickinson* by Helen McNeil, 1986; *Dickinson and the Life of Language: A Study in Symbolic Poetics* by E. Miller Budick, 1986; *Dickinson: The Lives of a Poet* edited by Christopher Benfey, 1986; *Dickinson* by John Robinson, 1986; *Dickinson: A Biography* by Cynthia Griffin Wolff, 1986.

* * *

Emily Dickinson's importance as a poet is not in any doubt. Her cause may have been damaged by injudicious partisanship during the 1930's, but a longer retrospect sets her firmly among the major poets who have written in English. She never prepared her poems for publication, and had she done so must in all probability have rejected many of those which are now in print. It follows from this that the general reader is likely to read no more than a selection of her work; and yet nothing that she wrote is without interest, and even the "failures" take their place in an *oeuvre* which is marked by a distinctive union of style and sensibility. In this respect, then, she satisfies T.S. Eliot's criterion (see his "What Is Minor Poetry?," *On Poetry and Poets*) by which all the work of a major poet should be read. Nor can we deny that her work possesses "significant unity," another of Eliot's desiderata; and if we accept his third point, that a poet's majority does not depend on his having written lengthy works, then Dickinson's status cannot be in doubt.

Even the most enthusiastic appreciations of her work have tended, however, to contain a note of reservation. She has been reproached for faults of technique, and her idiosyncratic sensibility has been criticised on account of the alleged whimsicality of its perceptions. The technical objections fall, insofar as they are not merely general, into three categories. First there is the question of her "bad grammar" (Yvor Winters wrote, in his *Maule's Curse*, of her "habitual carelessness"). The chief issue here is that of her very frequent use of a sort of subjunctive mood, of which the following lines provide an instance:

> Time is a test of trouble
> But not a remedy.
> If such it prove, it prove too
> There was no malady.

The usage here is surely justified, at least in the case of the first "prove," insofar as the subjunctive mood expresses an awareness that the statement is provisional: time may or may not "prove" a remedy. And the second "prove" contains a similar elliptical suggestion: "may prove" or "will prove" are implied. At all events, this feature of Dickinson's poetry occurs far too often to be ascribed to "carelessness," and is better seen as a (largely successful) attempt to express linguistically the poet's tentative and scrupulous searching for the truth, which she could never see as straightforward or self-evident. Nor should we forget that there are, especially during the period of Dickinson's greatest creative power in the early 1860's, many poems of confident assertion, strongly indicative in mood, like "Because I could not stop for Death."

Other critics speak of failings in metre and in rhyme. It is certainly difficult to find any consistent explanation for the irregularities of Dickinson's verse, any principle on which they can be said deliberately to occur. This does not, however, oblige us to consider such irregularities as weaknesses. Dickinson composed by instinct (which is not to say automatically), adapting the basic rhythms of the hymns she had heard from childhood; and her instinct told her that mechanical regularity would make for monotony. Her poems are a great deal more varied than their appearance on the page might suggest. Generalisation is inappropriate in this connection, for her rhythms, considered as personal variations on a rigid pattern, are to be acclaimed or found wanting according to the shapes and sounds of particular poems. To my ear, at least, her rhythmic sense is seldom absolutely deficient, and often inspired.

In the matter of rhyme, it is probably equally misconceived

to search for a uniform pattern, although some have tried to show that her use of assonance in place of full rhyme is always deliberate artistry. It would be truer to say that full rhyme usually, though not invariably, accompanies moods of confidence, while assonance implies uncertainty. But there are significant exceptions to this rule. All we can safely assert is that she felt no compulsion to find exact rhymes, and that the use of assonance also helped her to get away from the mechanical jingle of hymn-forms.

Those who object to the quality of Dickinson's sensibility cannot, of course, be answered "in good set terms." This is inevitably a subjective matter; moreover, the idiosyncratic vision of which we are speaking is not evident only intermittently, in this image or that turn of phrase, but informs every line, so that despite their differences Dickinson's poems are always unmistakably hers. One can do no more here than offer a brief sketch of her sensibility, hoping to counter the charge of whimsicality or childishness—as opposed to what might be called child*like*ness which certainly is present in her work, and helps to account for the immediacy as well as the strangeness of such an image as "Great streets of silence led away / To neighborhoods of pause." Immediacy of perception; a predominantly spatial (rather than temporal) apprehension; a direct and yet uncanny confrontation with natural phenomena—these qualities, epitomised in poems such as "A narrow fellow in the grass" or "I started early, took my dog" go to make up the distinctive atmosphere of her work. But, although these qualities might in themselves be called childlike or naif, those epithets would quite fail to characterize Dickinson's poetry as a whole. In the following, for instance, we find indeed a physical image, but this is no more than the beginning of the poem, the vivid introduction to the metaphor whose meaning the lines develop:

> It dropped so low in my regard
> I heard it hit the ground
> And go to pieces on the stones
> At bottom of my mind;
>
> Yet blamed the fate that fractured less
> Than I reviled myself
> For entertaining plated wares
> Upon my silver shelf.

This is scarcely the observation of a child. The poem, moreover, is typical in this respect of its author's work. The clarity of physical image serves above all to enforce what we must call the poem's abstract meaning, which in this case is moral and psychological. Similarly, the poem "Presentiment is that long shadow on the lawn" does not describe any particular lawn at dusk so much as it invokes, with wonderful economy, the essential nature of all presentiment and all nightfalls. The same, finally, is true of many of those poems whose theme is death. If we think of the graphic spareness of "There's been a death in the opposite house," of the more exuberant images of "As far from pity as complaint," or of the triumphantly bold conceit which ends "Ample make this bed" ("Let no sunrise' yellow noise / Interrupt this ground"), we recognize that the poet has not only made alive for us an unfamiliar world of the senses, but in doing so has created a new awareness of the experience underlying the phenomena which she has described.

The underlying common quality which especially characterizes Dickinson's poetry is best denoted by her own term "awe." Awe is fear divested of its physical attributes and raised to the status of a mental attitude. It is the spiritual form of fear, or the corporeal form of reverence, and defines the nature of the childlike sensibility's response to the wonder and ecstasy of simple existence. This sense of awe is clearly present in a poem like "I know some lonely houses off the road," but it is also a general presence, found to some degree even in so brief and seemingly impersonal a poem as this:

> How still the bells in steeples stand
> Till swollen with the sky,
> They leap upon their silver feet
> In frantic melody.

The sensibility which perceived bells in this way was not, it goes without saying, "normal"—any more than were the sensibilities of John Clare or Vincent van Gogh. But the intensity of the vision defies the charge of eccentricity, and the perception, although so wholly personal, is at the same time universal. The analogy with van Gogh can be pursued, for in the case of the poet as of the painter an initial sense of strangeness gives way to a recognition that we too have known just such experiences as are being depicted, but could never acknowledge them as ours until they were articulated for us by another's art.

In order further to apprehend, if not to understand, the success of this articulation, we have to consider Dickinson's language. To examine her use of words in constructing the world in which she lived out her poems is a long and rewarding study which cannot be undertaken here. One might usefully begin with a consideration of her undoubted sensitivity to the quality which makes English unique among European languages as a poetic medium, its contrasting and complementary Saxon and Romance elements. Not all poets have recognized the exceptional resources of this vocabulary, but the greatest, of whom Chaucer and Shakespeare are the pre-eminent examples, have undoubtedly done so. Dickinson, as a close reading of her poems will confirm, is to be counted among their number.

—James Reeves

See the essay on "Because I could not stop for Death."

DONNELLY, Ignatius. Born in Philadelphia, Pennsylvania, 3 November 1831. Educated at Central High School, Philadelphia, graduated 1849; read law in the office of Benjamin Harris Brewster, Philadelphia, 1850–52: admitted to Pennsylvania bar, 1852. Married 1) Katharine McCaffrey in 1855 (died, 1894), three children; 2) Marian Hanson in 1898. Practiced law and active in Democratic politics, Philadelphia, 1852–56; moved to Minnesota, 1856; involved in unsuccessful attempt to develop Nininger City, Minnesota, 1857; left Democratic Party over slavery issue, 1857, and joined Republican Party; Lieutenant Governor of Minnesota, 1859–63; member (Republican, Minnesota), U.S. House of Representatives, Washington, D.C., 1863–69; lobbyist for railroad interests and correspondent for St. Paul *Dispatch*, Washington, D.C., 1869–70; President, National Anti-Monopoly Convention, 1872, and editor, *Anti-Monopolist* newspaper, 1874–79; member of the Minnesota Senate, 1874–78; Greenback-Democrat candidate for House of Representatives, 1878 (also candidate in 1884 and 1889); farmer and writer after 1878; Farmers Alliance member, Minnesota State Legislature, 1887; President, State

Farmers Alliance of Minnesota, 1890, and helped turn Alliance into Populist Party, 1891–92 (wrote preamble to Populist Party's "Omaha Platform," 1892); Populist candidate for Governor of Minnesota, 1892, and nominee for U.S. Vice-President, 1898; founding editor, St. Paul *Representative*, from 1895. After 1878 developed theory that Francis Bacon wrote Shakespeare's plays. *Died 1 January 1901*.

PUBLICATIONS

Fiction

Caesar's Column: A Story of the Twentieth Century. 1890; edited by Walter B. Rideout, 1960.
Doctor Huguet. 1891.
The Golden Bottle; or, The Story of Ephraim Benezet of Kansas. 1892.

Verse

The Mourner's Vision. 1850.

Other

Nininger City. 1856.
The Sonnets of Shakespeare: An Essay. 1859.
Atlantis: The Antediluvian World. 1882; edited by Egerton Sykes, 1949.
Ragnarok: The Age of Fire and Gravel. 1883.
The Great Cryptogram: Francis Bacon's Cipher in the So-Called Shakespeare Plays. 1888.
In Memoriam Mrs. Katharine Donnelly. 1895.
The American People's Money. 1895; revised edition, as *The Bryan Campaign for the American People's Money*, 1896.
The Cipher in the Plays and on the Tombstone. 1899.

*

Bibliography: in *Bibliography of American Literature* by Jacob Blanck, 1957.

Critical Studies: *North Star Sage: The Story of Donnelly* by Oscar M. Sullivan, 1953; *Donnelly: Portrait of a Politician*, by Martin Ridge, 1962; *Donnelly* by David D. Anderson, 1980.

* * *

Ignatius Donnelly's works are imaginative, eccentric, and occasionally startling in their perceptions. *Atlantis: The Antediluvian World* is an attempt to demonstrate and expand upon Plato's myth of a great civilization that once supposedly existed near the mouth of the Mediterranean long before any similarly high culture, an island society suddenly destroyed by the gods because of its decadence. In his stupifyingly data-crammed book, Donnelly argued not only that Atlantis actually existed, but that it was "the region where man first rose from a state of barbarism to civilization." Furthermore, Atlantis was the source of most of the world's gods, legends, inventions, languages, architectural styles, plants, and animals.

The book was extremely popular, running through over twenty editions, and it inspired countless imitators and followers to publish their corroborative findings. Since, as Martin Gardner says in *Fads and Fallacies*, there is "not a shred of reliable evidence, geological or archeological, to support" the myth, this popularity seems a testament to Donnelly's ability to immerse his readers in an impressively assembled mass of highly interesting but nearly totally misleading information. Donnelly's argument is dense and the farrago of seemingly expert testimony he scraped together from a wide variety of library nooks and crannies is mountainous: his own literary style is far from ornate, however, and though assertive seems simply the straight-from-the-shoulder truth of a no-nonsense scholar. The work is fun to read, filled with arcane stories and ingenious, wild yoking of disparate cultural phenomena. He advances all his evidence quite seriously, including parallel lists showing the similarities between the Sioux and Danish languages, and hilarious drawings of skulls from Central America and Egypt artificially deformed in the same fashion. In *Ragnarok: The Age of Fire and Gravel* he theorized that long ago the Earth passed through the tail of a giant comet, producing world-wide catastrophe, "rearings, howlings, . . . hissings," and great heat. When the fires from this heat subsided, an Age of Darkness began, followed by the Ice Age. In *The Great Cryptogram* he produced a thousand pages of cipher analyses and lists of parallel quotations to prove that Francis Bacon wrote Shakespeare's plays. One critic used Donnelly's de-coding formula to demonstrate that a passage from *Hamlet* really read "Dou-nill-he, the author, politician, and mountebanke, will work out the secret of this play. The sage is a daysie."

But it would be a mistake to dismiss Donnelly as a crank. He was, according to David W. Noble in *The Progressive Mind 1890–1917*, "one of the most important critics who represented and expressed the . . . fears which ultimately found political expression in the Populist Party of the 1890's." He is frequently fascinating and his forays into scientific theory or literary criticism display impressive if ill-digested and misguided learning, and sensitivity to literary values. Both *Ragnarok* and *Atlantis*, in some ways freakish books, also contain attacks upon the harsher aspects of social Darwinism, and *Atlantis* argues for the simpler virtues and systems of the early Jeffersonian Republic. Furthermore, in his fiction he seriously addressed social problems such as agricultural decay and the political weakness of the poor in *The Golden Bottle*, and racial intolerance in *Doctor Huguet*, a novel tracing complications following exchanges in racial identity. *Caesar's Column* is a minor anti-Utopian classic predicting class warfare between the economic oppressors and oppressed, forces equally matched in their brutality. Marred only by two silly love stories, the novel accurately depicts many technological horrors of the future—such as air raids—and, more importantly, discusses specific social reforms such as an eight-hour work day and socialized medicine. The book's central image is a grotesque symbol of modern civilization: Caesar's column is a gigantic pillar of dead bodies from both sides killed in the slaughter of war.

—Jack B. Moore

DOOLITTLE, Hilda. Wrote as H.D. Born in Bethlehem, Pennsylvania, 10 September 1886. Educated at Gordon School, and Friends' Central School, 1902–04, both Philadelphia; Bryn Mawr College, Pennsylvania, 1905–06. Married the writer Richard Aldington in 1913 (separated, 1918; divorced, 1938); one daughter by Cecil Gray. Lived in Europe after 1911; closely associated with the Imagist movement after 1912; editor, *Egoist* magazine, London, 1916–17 (took over editorship from Aldington); began long relationship with the writer Bryher (Annie Winifred Ellerman) in 1919; joint founder, *Close Up* film journal, Territet, Switzerland, 1927–33. Recipient: Brandeis University Creative Arts Award, 1959; American Academy Award of Merit Medal, 1960. *Died 27 September 1961.*

PUBLICATIONS

Collections

Collected Poems 1912–1944, edited by Louis L. Martz. 1983.

Verse

Sea Garden. 1916.
Choruses from the Iphigenia in Aulis by Euripides. 1916.
The Tribute, and Circe: Two Poems. 1917.
Choruses from the Iphigenia in Aulis and the Hippolytus by Euripides. 1919.
Hymen. 1921.
Heliodora and Other Poems. 1924.
Collected Poems. 1925.
(*Poems*), edited by Hughes Mearns. 1926.
Red Roses for Bronze. 1931.
The Usual Star. 1934.
What Do I Love. 1943(?).
Trilogy. 1973.
The Walls Do Not Fall. 1944.
Tribute to the Angels. 1945.
The Flowering of the Rod. 1946.
By Avon River. 1949; revised edition, 1986.
Selected Poems. 1957.
Helen in Egypt. 1961.
Two Poems. 1971.
Hermetic Definition. 1972.
The Poet and the Dancer. 1975.
Priest, and A Dead Priestess Speaks. 1983.

Plays

Hippolytus Temporizes. 1927; revised version, 1985.
Ion, from the play by Euripides. 1937; revised version, 1985.

Fiction

Palimpsest. 1926; revised edition, 1968.
Hedylus. 1928; revised edition, 1980.
Kora and Ka. 1934.
Nights. 1935.
The Hedgehog (for children). 1936.
Bid Me to Live: A Madrigal. 1960; revised edition, 1983.
HERmione. 1981; as *Her*, 1984.

Other

Borderline. 1930.
Tribute to Freud, with Unpublished Letters by Freud to the Author. 1956; revised edition, 1974.
Temple of the Sun. 1972.
End to Torment: A Memoir of Ezra Pound (includes poems by Pound), edited by Norman Holmes Pearson and Michael King. 1979.
The Gift (memoir). 1982.
Notes on Thought and Vision, and The Wise Sappho. 1982.

*

Bibliography: "H.D.: A Preliminary Checklist" by Jackson R. Bryer and Pamela Roblyer, in *Contemporary Literature 10* ("H.D. Issue"), 1969.

Critical Studies: *The Heart of Artemis: A Writer's Memoirs* by Bryher, 1962; *The Classical World of H.D.* by Thomas Burnett Swann, 1962; *Doolittle/H.D.* by Vincent Quinn, 1967; *Psyche Reborn: The Emergence of H.D.* by Susan Stanford Friedman, 1981; *H.D.: The Life and Work of an American Poet* by Janice S. Robinson, 1982; *Herself Defined: The Poet H.D. and Her World* by Barbara Guest, 1984; *H.D.: Woman and Poet* edited by Michael King, 1986; *H.D.: The Career of That Struggle* by Rachel Blau DuPlessis, 1986.

* * *

Hilda Doolittle, whose works were published under the initials H.D., was a poet of considerable significance. Her work itself is precise, careful, sharp, and compressed; it gives one the sense that the poet is excluding much more than she expresses. Natural objects (e.g., "Oread," "Pear Tree") are presented in lines that are free of conventional poetic rhythms and that are yet as carefully shaped as a piece of Greek statuary. So the immediate pleasure of much of H.D.'s work is a response to an object that is created by a few carefully chosen phrases: phrases that exist in the presence of easy and facile language that has been excluded. As painters say, the "negative space"—the area around a represented object—is as important as the object itself.

Doolittle's work has an air of being isolated, of being simply her considered and purified record of what has stirred her senses and her emotions: the natural world with, for human context, the ancient Greek world as Doolittle remembers it. Birds fly through air that is radiantly Greek, love intensifies its expression in the presence of Helen and Lais, and the mysteries of life and death bring into view satyrs and not Christian saints.

But Doolittle's work did not actually proceed in isolation; she was closely associated with the Imagist movement from 1913 onwards. Ezra Pound, John Gould Fletcher, Amy Lowell, and others thought of their poetic effort as a realization of Walt Whitman's demand for new words that would bring poetry closer to the object it was "rendering" and free poetic expression from the abstractions and the overt moral purposes which had made much 19th-century poetry vague and imprecise. Poetry—and this was a main drive of Imagist theory—was a medium in which could appear the poet's direct apprehension of physical entities and the poet's immediate reaction to those entities. In pursuit of object and emotion, the poet should be free to discard both conventional rhythms and shop-worn poetic diction. Much of Doolittle's poetry achieves these aims. Thus, the emotion in many a poem is coerced, to be recreated in the mind of the reader, by the carefully selected physical details—details which pass before the reader following a syntax that is simple and uninvolved and expressed in words that are familiar and unmysterious. But the poems, in the long run, are not free of general impressions or even abstractions although they state very few. The impressions and abstractions must vary from reader to reader, but they concern the beneficence that reaches the human mind through the senses; it is a beneficence unsullied by ancient dogma and more recent social purpose. Poets like Shelley and Tennyson did not hesitate to offer "gospels." If there is some sort of message in much of Doolittle's work, it is very neatly fused with the external world she duplicates.

A modification of these effects appears in a late work like *The Walls Do Not Fall*. This work, using the techniques of the writer's previous verse, moves beyond the innocent and "natural" invocations of Greek health—health which is also of the physical world. But the destruction of World War II make the Greek health an insufficient corrective to modern chaos. *The Walls Do Not Fall* becomes quite specific about the sources of human health. Those sources find expression not only in halcyon flight and the play of light on the Aegean Sea. They can be traced in the essence of all great religions, and it is particularly the work of Egyptian gods that allows us to see the physical world achieving completion in myths and rituals. In such a body of faith as the Egyptian are myth and "Vision" coming into a focus of great human relevance. H.D. sees the Egyptian Amen and the later "Christos" as identical. They and other august entities are the symbols if not the ultimate élan of the eternal cycles of excellence and health which modern insanity—in its pursuit of power and inferior sorts of knowledge—has ignored.

This concluding attitude in the work of H.D. may strike some readers as going beyond the confines of the early Imagism. The attitude can also be regarded as an effort to defend and exploit the initial stance of Imagist simplicity and directness. These are opposing judgments. At any rate, in her late work Doolittle's implications intensify and complicate themselves. But the modes of expression do not change. Perhaps their persistence indicates an essential continuity in the entire body of her poetry.

—Harold H. Watts

DOS PASSOS, John (Roderigo). Born in Chicago, Illinois, 14 January 1896. Educated at Choate School, Wallingford, Connecticut, 1907–11; Harvard University, Cambridge, Massachusetts (editor, *Harvard Monthly*), 1912–16, A.B. (cum laude) 1916; studied in Castile, 1916–17. Served in the Norton-Harjes Ambulance Group in France, 1917, and the American Red Cross Ambulance Corps in Italy, 1918; served in the U.S. Medical Corps, 1918–19. Married 1) Katharine F. Smith in 1929 (died, 1947); 2) Elizabeth Hamlin Holdridge in 1949, one daughter. Lived in Spain and Portugal, 1919; traveled in the Near East with the Near East Relief Organization, 1921; lived in New York, 1922; traveled in Spain, 1923; cofounder, *New Masses*, New York, 1926, and contributor until early 1930's; director, New Playwrights Theatre, New York, 1927–29; visited the U.S.S.R., 1928; contributor, *Common Sense*, 1932; screenwriter in Hollywood, 1934; war correspondent in the Pacific, and at Nuremberg, 1945, and in South America, 1948, for *Life* magazine, New York. Treasurer, National Committee for the Defense of Political Prisoners, 1931; chairman, National Committee to Aid Striking Miners, 1931; treasurer, Campaign for Political Refugees, 1940; U.S. delegate, International PEN Club Congress, England, 1941. Artist: individual show of sketches, New York, 1937. Recipient: Guggenheim fellowship, 1939, 1940, 1942; American Academy Gold Medal, 1957; Feltrinelli prize (Italy), 1967. Member, American Academy, 1947. *Died 28 September 1970.*

PUBLICATIONS

Fiction

One Man's Initiation—1917. 1920; as *First Encounter*, 1945; complete edition, 1969.
Three Soldiers. 1921.
Streets of Night. 1923.
Manhattan Transfer. 1925.
U.S.A. 1938.
  The 42nd Parallel. 1930.
  1919. 1932.
  The Big Money. 1936.
District of Columbia. 1952.
  Adventures of a Young Man. 1939.
  Number One. 1943.
  The Grand Design. 1949.
Chosen Country. 1951.
Most Likely to Succeed. 1954.
The Great Days. 1958.
Midcentury: A Contemporary Chronicle. 1961.
Century's Ebb: The Thirteenth Chronicle. 1975.

Plays

The Garbage Man: A Parade with Shouting (as *The Moon Is a Gong*, produced 1925; as *The Garbage Man*, produced 1926). 1926.
Airways, Inc. (produced 1927). 1928.
Fortune Heights (produced 1933). In *Three Plays*, 1934.
Three Plays. 1934.
USA: A Dramatic Review, with Paul Shyre. 1963.

Screenplay: *The Devil Is a Woman*, with S.K. Winston, 1935.

Verse

A Pushcart at the Curb. 1922.

Other

Rosinante to the Road Again. 1922.
Orient Express. 1927.
Facing the Chair: The Story of the Americanization of Two Foreignborn Workmen (on Sacco and Vanzetti). 1927.
In All Countries. 1934.
The Villages Are the Heart of Spain. 1937.
Journeys Between Wars. 1938.
The Ground We Stand On: Some Examples from the History of a Political Creed. 1941.
State of the Nation. 1944.
Tour of Duty. 1946.
The Prospect Before Us. 1950.
Life's Picture History of World War II. 1950.
The Head and Heart of Thomas Jefferson. 1954.
The Theme Is Freedom. 1956.

The Men Who Made the Nation. 1957.
Prospects of a Golden Age. 1959.
Mr. Wilson's War. 1962.
Brazil on the Move. 1963.
Thomas Jefferson: The Making of a President (for children). 1964.
Occasions and Protests: Essays 1936–1964. 1964.
The Shackles of Power 1801–1826: Three Jeffersonian Decades. 1966.
The Best Times: An Informal Memoir. 1966.
The Portugal Story: Three Centuries of Exploration and Discovery. 1969.
Easter Island: Island of Enigmas. 1971.
The Fourteenth Chronicle: Letters and Diaries, edited by Townsend Ludington. 1973.

Editor, *The Living Thoughts of Tom Paine*. 1940.

Translator, *Metropolis*, by Manuel Maples Arce. 1929.
Translator, *Panama: or, The Adventures of My Seven Uncles*, by Blaise Cendrars. 1931.

*

Bibliography: *A Bibliography of Dos Passos* by Jack Potter, 1950; *Dos Passos: A Reference Guide* by John Rohrkemper, 1980; *Dos Passos: A Comprehensive Bibliography* by David Sanders, 1986.

Critical Studies: *Dos Passos* by John H. Wrenn, 1961; *Dos Passos* by Robert Gorham Davis, 1962; *The Fiction of Dos Passos* by John D. Brantley, 1968; *Dos Passos, The Critics, and the Writer's Intention* edited by Allen Belkind, 1971; *Dos Passos' Path to U.S.A.: A Political Biography 1912–1936* by Melvin Landsberg, 1972; *Dos Passos: A Collection of Critical Essays* edited by Andrew Hook, 1974; *Dos Passos* by George J. Becker, 1974; *Dos Passos and the Fiction of Despair* by Iain Colley, 1978; *Dos Passos: Artist as American* by Linda W. Wagner, 1979; *Dos Passos: A Twentieth Century Odyssey* by Townsend Ludington, 1980; *Dos Passos: Politics and the Writer* by Robert C. Rosen, 1981; *Dos Passos: A Life* by Virginia Spencer Carr, 1984.

* * *

John Dos Passos was involved in many of the episodes that have played an important part in 20th-century literary history; not surprisingly, these had an important effect on his writing. After a lonely childhood living in Europe and then being a bookish student among advocates of the strenuous life at the Choate School in Wallingford, Connecticut, he went through Harvard University with a number of the writers who became part of the artistic renaissance that started during the period just before World War I. T.S. Eliot was still at Harvard while Dos Passos was there; E.E. Cummings, Robert Hillyer, and Stewart Mitchell were among his close friends. He drove an ambulance during World War I, then roamed the Continent afterward and passed frequently through the Paris expatriate scene, though he was never truly a part of it. He was a friend of writers such as Scott Fitzgerald, Upton Sinclair, Van Wyck Brooks, and a close friend of Archibald MacLeish, Edmund Wilson, and—for a while—Ernest Hemingway, among others. He became deeply involved in political radicalism during the 1920's but was never the activist that his writings made him seem; he interviewed and wrote about the Italian anarchists Sacco and Vanzetti, who had been found guilty of murder on dubious evidence; he worked as a director of a left-wing, experimental drama group, the New Playwrights, in the late 1920's; he traveled to Russia in 1928; he visited the Harlan County, Kentucky, coal mines with Theodore Dreiser in 1931; he experienced the "big money" briefly as a screenwriter in Hollywood in 1934; and he went to Spain many times, returning in 1937 with Hemingway to report on the Civil War. During World War II he wrote about the domestic scene, visited the Pacific, and reported on Europe and the war-crimes trials in Germany after the war. In the 1940's and subsequently he took an interest in capitalism—this time viewing it favorably—in Jeffersonian liberalism, and in the development of Latin America.

Although his reputation is not what it was in 1938 when Jean-Paul Sartre declared, "I regard Dos Passos as the greatest writer of our time," his works of fiction, which he came to call chronicles, and his non-fiction continue to be read widely. He is one of the two or three most important political novelists the United States has produced, and certain of his books—in particular *Three Soldiers*, *Manhattan Transfer*, and the three volumes of *U.S.A.*—are landmarks in the nation's literary history. *Three Soldiers* was the first of the significant novels to come from an American writer's experiences during World War I. *Manhattan Transfer* represents Dos Passos's innovative application to literature of the artistic theories and techniques which emerged during the decades before and after the turn of the century, when a veritable revolution in the arts occurred in Europe and then in the United States. This chronicle of the city incorporates impressionism, expressionism, montage, simultaneity, reportage, and other techniques of "the new" in the arts and is important also for its themes of alienation and loss, as well as for its satiric treatment of the urban scene.

The three volumes of *U.S.A.* are Dos Passos's attempt to employ his techniques of art to chronicle American civilization from 1900 to the beginning of the Great Depression in 1929. While he was writing *U.S.A.* from 1927 to 1936, he was far to the left politically, although he began turning toward the center by 1934. The trilogy, a panorama of the nation's life from his political perspective, is deeply satiric about business and the materialistic society it had created. The period he was chronicling, he wrote the critic Malcolm Cowley, was a time when the country moved from "competitive" to "monopoly" capitalism.

From being a political leftist, Dos Passos moved toward the right after believing himself personally betrayed by the Communists, a feeling culminating with the execution—he claimed at the hands of the Communists—of his close friend José Robles in Spain in 1937. Betrayal by the Communists became the fate of the hero in his next novel, the distinctly anti-left *Adventures of a Young Man*. Dos Passos's own adventure with the left was over by then; his subsequent chronicles, which extended through the 1960's, were increasingly strident satires, most of them about the modern liberalism and government bureaucracy that he saw to be the heritage of Franklin Roosevelt's New Deal administration. A single exception is *Chosen Country* where, through the adventures of an autobiographical hero, Jay Pignatelli, Dos Passos told of his gradual allegiance to the United States and his romance with his first wife, Katharine Smith.

But Dos Passos was not only a novelist. He wrote numerous books of reportage describing his world travels and analyzing the life and politics of his own and other nations. After 1937, he began also to write histories, repeatedly considering the origins of the United States in books such as *The Ground We Stand On, The Men Who Made the Nation, Prospects of a Golden Age*, and *The Shackles of Power: Three Jeffersonian Decades*. He became fascinated by Thomas Jefferson, who was, in fact, a sort of hero for him; he wrote a biography—*The Head and Heart of Thomas Jefferson*—as well as several studies of the man and his era. In addition to all these works he wrote a volume of poetry, several plays, and many articles about politics, drama, and art, among other subjects.

In the early 1950's he sympathized with Senator Joseph McCarthy's efforts to ferret Communists out of the government, but did not support McCarthy's methods. In 1964 he supported Senator Barry Goldwater for the Presidency; yet Dos Passos's conservatism was never the simplistic matter his critics took it to be. Always critical rather than doctrinaire, Dos Passos wanted to remain independent, something of the anarchist, in his works supporting individual freedoms against bureaucracies and monoliths wherever he saw them while portraying the swirl of life in his chosen country. Granting Dos Passos his political perspectives, the reader can get from his works a remarkably broad chronicle of the 20th-century United States.

—Townsend Ludington

See the essay on *U.S.A.*

DOUGLASS, Frederick. Born Frederick Augustus Washington Bailey in Tuckahoe, Talbot County, Maryland, 1818; took name Douglass upon escape from slavery. On plantation until 1825; house servant, Baltimore, 1825–33 (learned to read and write); inherited by new owner and worked as field hand, St. Michael's, Maryland, 1833–36: unsuccessfully conspired to escape, 1836; sent to Baltimore and trained as ship's caulker (allowed to do some free-lance work), 1837–38; escaped to New York, 1838. Married 1) Anna Murray in 1838, one daughter and three sons; 2) Helen Pitts in 1884. Shipyard laborer, New Bedford, 1838–41, and Lynn, 1842, both Massachusetts; agent, Massachusetts Anti-Slavery Society from 1841, and central figure in the New England anti-slavery campaigns, and, after 1848, in the women's rights movement; lectured in Britain and Ireland, 1845–47; British friends bought his freedom, 1847; founder, *North Star* abolitionist paper (became *Frederick Douglass' Paper*, 1851), Rochester, New York, 1847–60, and *Frederick Douglass' Monthly*, 1858–63; escaped to Canada, 1859, and lived in Britain, 1859–60, when named as accomplice to John Brown in Harper's Ferry raid; recruited black regiments (Massachusetts 54th and 55th), 1863, and worked for civil rights during Reconstruction; owner, *New National Era* newspaper, Washington, D.C., 1870–74; assistant secretary, Santo Domingo annexation commission, 1871; President, Freedman's Savings and Trust Company, 1873–74; U.S. marshal, 1877–81, and recorder of deeds after 1881, Washington, D.C.; U.S. minister to Haiti, 1889–91. *Died 20 February 1895.*

PUBLICATIONS

Collections

Life and Writings, edited by Philip S. Foner. 4 vols., 1950–55.

Papers, edited by John W. Blassingame. 1979—

The Narrative and Selected Writings, edited by Michael Meyer. 1984.

Prose

Narrative of the Life of Douglass, An American Slave. 1845, edited by Houston A. Baker, Jr., 1982; revised edition, as *My Bondage and My Freedom*, 1855; as *Life and Times of Douglass*, 1881, revised edition, 1892.

Douglass on Women's Rights, edited by Philip S. Foner. 1976.

A Black Diplomat in Haiti: The Diplomatic Correspondence of U.S. Minister Douglass from Haiti 1889–1891, edited by Norma Brown. 2 vols., 1977.

*

Critical Studies: *Douglass* by Charles Waddell Chesnutt, 1899; *Douglass* by Booker T. Washington, 1907; *Douglass* by Benjamin Quarles, 1948, and *Douglass* edited by Quarles, 1968; *Douglass: A Biography* by Philip S. Foner, 1964; *Free at Last: The Life of Douglass* by Arna Bontemps, 1971; *Young Douglass: The Maryland Years* by Dickson J. Preston, 1980; *Slave and Citizen: The Life of Douglass* by Nathan Irvin Huggins, edited by Oscar Handlin, 1980; *The Mind of Douglass* by Waldo E. Martin, Jr., 1986.

* * *

Born a slave on a plantation in Maryland, Frederick Douglass escaped to freedom in the North at age 21 and eventually rose to international prominence as a lecturer, journalist, editor, autobiographer, and political activist. Although he was almost totally a self-educated man, his brilliant rhetorical powers as well as tireless efforts on behalf of the oppressed made Douglass a forceful leader in the abolitionist movement of the late 1840's and 1850's, earning him the title in the 20th century of "Father of the Civil Rights Movement."

As a writer Douglass is primarily remembered today for the *Narrative of the Life of Frederick Douglass*. An autobiographical account of Douglass's life as a slave, this work has been called a "landmark in the literary crusade against slavery" and "one of the most influential pieces of reform propaganda in American literature." Unlike many other works in the subgenre of American writing known as the "slave narrative," the Douglass *Narrative* has never ceased to attract an audience. Within just a few months of its publication in 1845, some 5,000 copies had been sold. More than thirty thousand copies are estimated to have been printed during the ten years that followed; revised and enlarged editions were published in 1855 under the title *My Bondage and My Freedom* and in 1881 under the title *Life and Times of Frederick Douglass*. During the 20th century, Douglass's autobiography has been almost continually in print.

Several factors have been noted as contributing to the *Narrative*'s appeal as a lasting work of literature. Unlike many of the other works of its kind, the Douglass *Narrative*, as its introductions by William Lloyd Garrison and Wendell Phillips attest, was written by Douglass himself, without the assistance of an editor or ghostwriter. As such, the *Narrative* possesses the genuine force of eyewitness conviction that was often lost in similar accounts whose editors and transcribers could not resist the impulse to sentimentalize or fictionalize for the sake of stylization and emotional effect. Throughout the *Narrative*, Douglass remains true to the facts of his experience, and those facts themselves provide a relentless condemnation of slavery and its supporters. Clear and direct, the style of Douglass's writing is one that the average individual can easily assimilate, and its clarity and directness only tend to underscore the barbarities and inhumanities described in the book: the separation of families, a total disregard on the part of slaveowners and overseers for the human rights of their slaves, and brutal beatings meant to dehumanize the slaves and rob them of their personal identities and dignity. Moreover, as recent scholarship has shown, carefully developed patterns of animal and maritime imagery reinforce tensions and themes present in the *Narrative* as a whole, making it, in the words of one commentator, "the first native American autobiography to create a black identity in style and form adequate to the pressures of historic black experience."

As editor of and contributor to the *North Star, Douglass' Monthly*, and the *New National Era*, Douglass further distinguished himself in literary and political circles. For his work on the *North Star* Douglass has been called a "champion of literary taste." Although the major editorial philosophy behind Douglass's weekly was the furtherance of the cause of emancipation and civil rights, he nonetheless published works of literature on a variety of topics and by a variety of authors, including Emerson, Coleridge, Tennyson, and Dickens. As a result his paper has been praised as one of the most "respected guides to cultural and literary taste in the nineteenth century" and "a source of lasting pride" for both black and white Americans.

—James A. Levernier

DRAKE, Joseph Rodman. Born in New York City, 7 August 1795. Studied medicine at a school on Barclay Street, New York, and qualified 1816. Married Sarah Eckford in 1816. Toured Europe, 1816–19; partner, with William Langstaff, in a drugstore in New York, 1819–20. *Died 21 September 1820.*

PUBLICATIONS

Collections

Life and Works: A Memoir and Complete Text of His Poems and Prose, by Frank Lester Pleadwell. 1935.

Verse

Poems, with Fitz-Greene Halleck. 1819; revised edition, as *The Croakers*, 1860.
The Culprit Fay and Other Poems. 1835.

*

Bibliography: in *Bibliography of American Literature* by Jacob Blanck, 1957.

* * *

Joseph Rodman Drake is an American member of the brotherhood of poets whose small measure of lasting fame depends on one or two popular successes. His fanciful 639-line poem "The Culprit Fay"—written in 1816 but not published until long after his death—continues to please many readers. "The American Flag," written and published pseudonymously in 1819, was widely admired in America and set to music by numerous composers (including Dvorak). His memory also survives because of the monody "On the Death of Joseph Rodman Drake," written by his friend Fitz-Greene Halleck, that opens with the well known quatrain:

> Green be the turf above thee,
> Friend of my better days!
> None knew thee but to love thee,
> Nor named thee but to praise.

Otherwise, Drake is remembered only by some historical critics who—following the example set by Edgar Allan Poe in the 1830's—are still outraged by the vogue that Drake's work enjoyed in America after his death.

Except for one excursion abroad, Drake lived out his short life in New York City. Trained as a physician, he never aspired to literary fame; he published little during his lifetime, and he reportedly requested on his deathbed that his poetry manuscripts be burned as "valueless." The request was ignored, however, and when his verse appeared in 1835 he was revealed as one of the authors (the other was his friend Halleck) of the "Croaker" poems that had titillated readers of New York newspapers during the summer of 1819. This revelation, together with the appearance of Drake's only long poem, "The Culprit Fay," prompted extravagant praise that Poe deplored (*Southern Literary Messenger*, April 1836), as did later critics. More recently, a biographer of Poe (Vincent Buranelli, *Edgar Allan Poe*, 1961) labeled Drake "a third-rate versifier."

Despite such judgments, Drake's poetry reflects a promising if aborted talent. A number of his "Croaker" poems—"To Ennui," "The National Painting," "To John Minshull, Esquire," to name only a few—poke healthy fun at an America that was already beginning to take itself too seriously. In "The Culprit Fay"—reportedly written in three days—Drake anticipated both Washington Irving and James Kirke Paulding in experimenting with fantasy; the poem tells the story of a Hudson River fairy who, for having fallen in love with "an earthly maid," is sentenced by his "lily-king" to perform herculean tasks in miniature. Derivative as it is, "The Culprit Fay" reflects not only Drake's perceptive reading of great masters—ranging from Shakespeare and Michael Drayton to his own contemporaries Coleridge and Keats—but an exciting young imagination that was too soon stilled by death.

—Thomas F. O'Donnell

DREISER, Theodore (Herman Albert). Born in Terre Haute, Indiana, 27 August 1871. Educated at public schools in

Warsaw, Terre Haute, Sullivan, and Evansville, all Indiana; Indiana University, Bloomington, 1889–90. Married 1) Sara Osborne White in 1898 (separated 1914; died, 1942); 2) Helen Patges Richardson in 1944. Worked in a restaurant and for a hardware company, in Chicago, 1887–89; real estate clerk and collection agent, Chicago, 1890–92; reporter, Chicago *Globe*, 1892; dramatic editor, St. Louis *Globe-Democrat*, 1892–93; reporter, St. Louis *Republic*, 1893; columnist, Pittsburgh *Dispatch*, 1894; moved to New York, 1894; editor, *Ev'ry Month*, New York, 1895–97; free-lance magazine writer, 1897–99; had no settled job or home, 1900–03; editor, *Smith's Magazine*, 1905–06, and *Broadway Magazine*, 1906–07, both New York; managing editor, Butterick Publications, New York, and editor of Butterick's *Delineator*, 1907–10; editor, *Bohemian* magazine, 1909–10; full-time writer from 1911; lived in Los Angeles, 1919–23 and after 1938; co-editor, *American Spectator*, 1932–34; applied for membership of the Communist Party, 1945. Chairman, National Committee for the Defense of Political Prisoners, 1931. Recipient: American Academy Award of Merit Medal, 1944. *Died 28 December 1945.*

PUBLICATIONS

Collections

Letters: A Selection, edited by Robert H. Elias. 3 vols., 1959.
A Dreiser Reader, edited by James T. Farrell. 1962.
Selected Poems, edited by Robert P. Saalback. 1969.
Works (Pennsylvania Edition), edited by Neda Westlake and James L.W. West III. 1981—

Fiction

Sister Carrie. 1900.
Jennie Gerhardt. 1911.
The Financier. 1912; revised edition, 1927.
The Titan. 1914.
The "Genius." 1915.
Free and Other Stories. 1918.
Twelve Men. 1919.
An American Tragedy. 1925.
Chains: Lesser Novels and Stories. 1927.
A Gallery of Women. 1929.
Fine Furniture (stories). 1930.
The Bulwark. 1946.
The Stoic. 1947.

Plays

Laughing Gas (produced 1916). In *Plays*, 1916.
Plays of the Natural and the Supernatural (includes *The Girl in the Coffin, The Blue Sphere, Laughing Gas, In the Dark, The Spring Recital, The Light in the Window, The Old Ragpicker*). 1916; augmented editions, 1926 (includes *Phantasmagoria* and *The Count of Progress*) and 1927 (includes *The Dream*); as *Plays, Natural and Supernatural* (includes *The Anaesthetic Revelation*), 1930.
The Girl in the Coffin (produced 1917). In *Plays*, 1916.
The Old Ragpicker (produced 1918). In *Plays*, 1916.
The Hand of the Potter (produced 1921). 1919; revised version, 1927.

Verse

Moods, Cadenced and Declaimed. 1926; revised edition, 1928; as *Moods Philosophic and Emotional, Cadenced and Declaimed*, 1935.
The Aspirant. 1929.
Epitaph. 1930.

Other

A Traveler at Forty. 1913.
A Hoosier Holiday. 1916.
Life, Art, and America. 1917.
Hey Rub-a-Dub-Dub: A Book of the Mystery and Wonder and Terror of Life. 1920.
Autobiography. 2 vols., 1965.
A Book About Myself. 1922; as *Newspaper Days*, 1931.
Dawn: A History of Myself. 1931.
The Color of a Great City (on New York City). 1923.
Dreiser Looks at Russia. 1928; shortened version, as *Dreiser's Russia*, 1928.
My City. 1929.
The Carnegie Works at Pittsburgh. 1929(?).
Tragic America. 1931.
Tom Mooney. 1933.
America Is Worth Saving. 1941.
Letters to Louise, edited by Louise Campbell. 1959.
Notes on Life, edited by Marguerite Tjader and John J. McAleer. 1974.
A Selection of Uncollected Prose, edited by Donald Pizer. 1977.
Selected Magazine Articles of Dreiser: Life and Art in the American 1890's, edited by Yoshinobu Hakutani. 1986.

Editor, *The Living Thoughts of Thoreau*. 1939.

*

Bibliography: *Dreiser: A Primary and Secondary Bibliography* by Donald Pizer and others, 1975.

Critical Studies: *Dreiser, Apostle of Nature* by Robert H. Elias, 1949, revised edition, 1970; *Dreiser* by F.O. Matthiessen, 1951; *The Stature of Dreiser* edited by Alfred Kazin and Charles Shapiro, 1955, and *Dreiser: Our Bitter Patriot* by Shapiro, 1962; *Dreiser*, 1964, and *Plots and Characters in the Fiction of Dreiser*, 1977, both by Philip L. Gerber; *Dresier* by W.A. Swanberg, 1965; *Dreiser: A New Dimension* by Marguerite Tjader, 1965; *Dreiser: An Introduction and Interpretation* by John J. McAleer, 1968; *Two Dreisers* by Ellen Moers, 1969; *Dreiser: His World and His Novels* by Richard Lehan, 1969; *Dreiser: A Collection of Critical Essays* edited by John Lydenberg, 1971; *Homage to Dreiser* by Robert Penn Warren, 1971; *Dreiser* by W.H. Frohock, 1972; *Dreiser: The Critical Reception* edited by Jack Salzman, 1972; *Dreiser* by James Lundquist, 1974; *The Novels of Dreiser: A Critical Study* by Donald Pizer, 1976, and *Critical Essays on Dreiser* edited by Pizer, 1981; *Young Dreiser: A Critical Study* by Yoshinobu Hakutani, 1980; *Dreiser and His Fiction: A Twentieth-Century Quest* by Lawrence E. Hussman, 1983; *The Small Canvas: An Introduction to Dreiser's Short Stories* by Joseph Griffin, 1985; *Dreiser: At the Gates of the City 1871–1907* (vol. 1 of biography) by Richard Lingeman, 1986.

*   *   *

The first major writer to emerge from America's "melting pot" population (his father was a German-Catholic weaver), Theodore Dreiser almost single-handedly created and made respectable a socially oriented fiction that surprisingly complements the romance tradition of Hawthorne and Melville, while expanding the narrowly focused realism of Howells and James. His achievement is vast, paradoxical, and, considering the conditions of his birth and the poverty of his youth, highly unlikely. Personally ungainly, erratically educated, and possessing an unusually shoddy conception of aesthetics, he succeeds through a combination of passionate integrity and a brutal determination to exhaust his material completely. For the first time in American fiction he introduced on an epic scale a literary effort in which the social environment was given a detailed attention equal to, if not greater than, that which was focused on the individual protagonist. His heroes are neither orphans set adrift in a bewildering chaotic world, nor are they archetypal symbols occupying spaces in a moral or allegorical diagram. Instead they are begotten out of concrete family relationships within particular socio-economic situations. And although Dreiser's characters are never the mere pawns of their social and biological circumstances, still they can only be understood in terms of those circumstances. Sex and money have ever been the twin thematic strands out of which novels are built, but Dreiser is the first American novelist to scrutinize these concerns with a consistently unashamed and unaverted gaze. His reluctance to apply moralistic judgments and the spacious compassion with which he views the behavior of his characters infuse his fiction with a vitality and a sense of wonder that transcend by far the mechanical operations of the naturalistic formulas that are sometimes invoked to explain—or explain away—his work.

Partly influenced by Herbert Spencer's interpretation of evolution and excited by the honesty he found in the novels of Balzac, Tolstoy, Zola, and Hardy, Dreiser is, of course, far less intellectual than his intellectual influences. Nearer to the bone he drew upon chequered adventures of his own large family and his personal experiences as an ill-favored ambitious young man struggling to make good in the big blustering city. With the successes and failures of his brothers and sisters in mind, he had no need of philosophical theory to perceive the sharp disparity between the sanctimonious cant of the pulpit and the popular press and the actual practices of life in the booming economy of the last years of the 19th century. And, perhaps most important, his capacity to project himself autobiographically into such different personalities as Carrie Meeber, Hurstwood, Drouet, Jennie Gerhardt, Frank Cowperwood, and Clyde Griffiths makes his novels both impersonal and personal—widescale renderings of American life as viewed from a detached brooding perspective and intimately felt transcriptions of the loneliness, frustration, and burning desire to succeed that torment the sensibilities of the American temperament.

His first novel, *Sister Carrie*, already shows Dreiser in full possession of his powers. The pilgrimage of the eighteen-year-old country girl to Chicago and then later to stardom on the New York stage follows the hackneyed scenario of the sentimental fiction (the Horatio Alger-Cinderella fairy tale) that Dreiser knew well as an editor for Butterick publications. But Dreiser does more than simply refuse to disapprove of his amoral heroine; he transforms these stock melodramatic materials into a dispassionate dissection of the factors that conjoin for success and failure in a society where "making" and "being" good are sometimes in radical disalignment. Carrie's rise, Drouet's complacent survival, and Hurstwood's fall are complementary elements in the turbulence of a collective life-force surging and ebbing in accord with its own laws of movement. Man may attempt to resist or try to ride along with the current, but, in terms of his most profoundly cherished ideals, he is alien to the purposes of life and doomed to recurrent and ultimate dissatisfaction.

Sister Carrie introduces the themes that were to preoccupy Dreiser throughout his career and also displays his novelistic techniques in full maturity. Although he has been frequently condemned by critics as a wretched stylist, it might be more accurate to suggest that he simply had no personal style at all. Instead, he absorbed the highly detailed, prolix, occasionally ornate but usually lucid magazine-style of the Mauve Decade and employed it as an impersonal instrument in the fashioning of his fiction. In Dreiser's case, his personal style may be more fruitfully sought in his characteristic use of structure. He built his novels in large narrative blocks, each of them composed of simple sequences of action; these he relates unhurriedly, setting minutely observed detail upon detail like a workman laying bricks. These narrative sequences succeed one another in ponderous waves of relentless motion suggesting a sense of the irrevocable passage of time, a cumulative weight of authenticity, and a rhythm of inevitability. With the writing of *Sister Carrie*, Dreiser's development as a novelist was complete. In his subsequent novels he might intensify, broaden, or polish aspects of his ideas and craftsmanship, but his work would remain within the same methodology and frame of bemused compassion that constitute his signature in *Sister Carrie*.

After *Jennie Gerhardt*—a curiously neglected novel that turns *Sister Carrie* inside-out, as it were, and presents in its title character the nearest approach to a saint that Dreiser ever made—he produced his study of an American "robber baron" in *The Financier* and *The Titan*. Modeling his protagonist, Frank Cowperwood, on the millionaire Charles T. Yerkes, Dreiser's intention is to show the obverse side of the Darwinian coin—the ruthless Superman, coolly aware of the amoral rules of the game, who stakes his formidable energies in a singleminded drive for power. Utterly persuasive in its grasp of the political and financial minutiae of stock transfers and bond issues, Dreiser's treatment of Cowperwood's career is easily the authoritative—if caricatured—portrait of the American businessman, relentless in his pursuit of wealth and power, but destined to the same frustration as the weak and victimized whom he manipulates.

The last of Dreiser's major novels and perhaps his single most impressive work is *An American Tragedy*. Here Dresier is at the very peak of his ability, identifying closely with his protagonist, Clyde Griffiths, even as he broods with Olympian resignation over the wretched banality of Clyde's life. Dreiser reveals that life with magisterial authority, piece by painstaking piece, from Clyde's beginnings as a small embarrassed boy walking the city streets with his missionary parents to his final state execution for murder. More like a massive monument that turns in slow-motion before the reader than a literary portrait, *An American Tragedy* patiently and inexorably amasses evidence to show how a weak malleable personality can be so thoroughly molded by his circumstances and by the shallow values of his culture as to become virtually negligible as a generative force in himself. By the end of the novel, the reader so fully understands the elements that have created Clyde that the character himself almost recedes into the landscape of the novel as merely one more passive factor. And although—or because—every relevant fact in his life has been clearly illumined, the reader can no more determine to what extent Clyde is a murderer and to what extent a victim than can Clyde himself.

Dreiser not only wrote long novels, but he was prolific in many genres. Of the poetry, short stories, plays, and nonfiction as well as other novels, we might cite as of special interest *A Book About Myself* and *Dawn*, two volumes of memoirs. *Hey Rub-a-Dub-Dub*, a characteristic volume of essays, and *The "Genius"*, his least successful but most nakedly autobiographical novel. Dreiser's stature in American letters is huge, stubborn, and undeniable. As the 19th-century Russian novelists are supposed to have climbed out from under Gogol's overcoat, so one might suggest that Dreiser must bear a similar paternal responsibility for the fiction of the 1920's (Anderson, Faulkner, Fitzgerald, Hemingway, Lewis, Wolfe), the 1930's (Farrell, Steinbeck, Wright), and even the 1940's (Bellow, Mailer). There is a sense in which his achievement may seem crude, I suppose, but it required something stronger than gentility to clear a continent in which his successors could pursue their visions of truth unimpeded by the barriers of hypocrisy, reticence, and prudential caution. The momentum of history was in this direction, of course, but yet some of the richness and power of the modern American novel is due to Dreiser's sweeping redefinition of the novelist's task.

—Earl Rovit

See the essay on *Sister Carrie*.

DU BOIS, W(illiam) E(dward) B(urghardt). Born in Great Barrington, Massachusetts, 23 February 1868; emigrated to Ghana, 1961; became citizen, 1963. Educated at public schools in Great Barrington; Fisk University, Nashville, Tennessee (editor, *Fisk Herald*), 1885–88, A.B. 1888; Harvard University, Cambridge, Massachusetts, 1888–90, A.M. 1891, Ph.D. 1895; University of Berlin, 1892–94. Married 1) Nina Gomer in 1896 (died, 1950), one son and one daughter; 2) Shirley Graham in 1951. Professor of Greek and Latin, Wilberforce University, Ohio, 1894–96; Assistant Instructor in Sociology, University of Pennsylvania, Philadelphia, 1896–97; Professor of Economics and History, Atlanta University, 1897–1910; editor, *Moon Illustrated Weekly*, Memphis, Tennessee, 1906, and *Horizon*, Washington, D.C., 1907–10; a founder of the National Association for the Advancement of Colored People, 1910, and director of publicity and research for the NAACP and editor of the NAACP's magazine *Crisis*, New York, 1910–34; editor, with A. G. Dill, *Brownies' Book*, 1920–22; columnist ("A Forum of Fact and Opinion"), Pittsburgh *Courier*, 1936–38 and ("As the Crow Flies"), *Amsterdam News*, New York, 1939–44; editor, *Phylon*, Atlanta, 1940–44; director of the Department of Special Research, NAACP, New York, 1944–48; columnist ("The Winds of Time"), Chicago *Defender*, 1945–48, and *People's Voice*, 1947–48. Founder, Pan-African Congress, 1900, and Niagara Movement, 1904; Vice-Chairman, Council on African Affairs, 1949–54; candidate for U.S. Senate, from New York, 1950. Recipient: Spingarn Medal, 1920; International Peace Prize, 1952. Knight Commander, Liberian Order of African Redemption; fellow, American Association for the Advancement of Science; member, American Academy. *Died 27 August 1963*.

PUBLICATIONS

Collections

The Seventh Son: The Thought and Writings of Du Bois, edited by Julius Lester. 2 vols., 1971.
Correspondence, edited by Herbert Aptheker. 3 vols., 1973–78.
Writings (Library of America), edited by Nathan Huggins. 1986.

Fiction

The Quest of the Silver Fleece. 1911.
Dark Princess: A Romance. 1928.
The Black Flame
The Ordeal of Mansart. 1957.
Mansart Builds a School. 1959.
Worlds of Color. 1961.

Plays

The Star of Ethiopia (pageant, produced ?). 1913.
Haiti, in *Federal Theatre Plays*, edited by Pierre de Rohan. 1938.

Verse

Selected Poems. 1965.

Other

The Suppression of African Slave-Trade to the United States of America 1638–1870. 1896.
The Conservation of Races. 1897.
The Philadelphia Negro: A Social Study, with *A Report on Domestic Service* by Isabel Eaton. 1899.
Possibilities of the Negro: The Advance Guard of Race. 1903.
Souls of Black Folk: Essays and Sketches. 1903; revised edition, 1953.
Of the Wings of Atlanta. 1904.
The Black Vote of Philadelphia. 1905.
The Negro South and North. 1905.
The Negro in the South: His Economic Progress in Relation to His Moral and Religious Development, with Booker T. Washington. 1907; as *The American Negro (Southern States)*, 1909.
John Brown (biography). 1909.
The Social Evolution of the Black South. 1911.
Disfranchisement. 1912.
The Negro. 1915.
Darkwater: Voices from Within the Veil. 1920.
The Gift of Black Folk: Negroes in the Making of America. 1924.
Africa: Its Geography, People, and Products. 1930.
Africa: Its Place in Modern History. 1930.
Black Reconstruction in America: An Essay. 1935.
A Pageant in Seven Decades 1868–1938. 1938.
Black Folk Then and Now: An Essay in the History and Sociology of the Negro Race. 1939.
The Revelation of Saint Orgne, The Damned. 1939.
Dusk of Dawn: An Essay Toward an Autobiography of a Race Concept. 1940.

Encyclopedia of the Negro: Preparatory Volume. 1945; revised edition, 1946.
Color and Democracy: Colonies and Peace. 1945.
The World and Africa. 1947; revised edition, 1965.
In Battle for Peace: The Story of My 83rd Birthday. 1952.
The Story of Benjamin Franklin. 1956.
Africa in Battle Against Colonialism, Racialism, Imperialism. 1960.
An ABC of Color. 1963.
Autobiography. 1968.
The Black North in 1901: A Social Study. 1969.
Du Bois Speaks: Speeches and Addresses 1890–1963, edited by Philip Foner. 2 vols., 1970.
Du Bois: A Reader, edited by Meyer Weinberg. 1970.
A Du Bois Reader, edited by Andrew D. Paschal. 1971.
The Crisis Writings, edited by Daniel Walden. 1972.
The Emerging Thought of Du Bois: Essays and Editorials from The Crisis, edited by Henry Lee Moon. 1972.
The Education of Black People: Ten Critiques 1906–1960, edited by Herbert Aptheker. 1973.
Book Reviews, edited by Herbert Aptheker. 1977.
Du Bois on Sociology and the Black Community, edited by Dan S. Green and Edwin D. Driver. 1978.
Prayers for Dark People, edited by Herbert Aptheker. 1980.
Selections from The Crisis, edited by Herbert Aptheker. 1983.
Against Racism: Unpublished Essays, Papers, Addresses 1887–1961, edited by Herbert Aptheker. 1985.

Editor, *An Appeal to the World*. 1947.
Editor, *Atlanta University Publications* (pamphlets published in 1898–1913). 2 vols., 1968–69.

*

Bibliography: *Annotated Bibliography of the Published Writings of Du Bois* by Herbert Aptheker, 1973; *Du Bois: A Bibliography of His Published Writings* by Paul G. Partington, 1979, supplement, 1984.

Critical Studies: *Du Bois* by Elliott M. Rudwick, 1960; *His Day Is Marching On: A Memoir of Du Bois*, 1971, and *Du Bois: A Pictorial Biography*, 1978, both by Shirley Graham; *Du Bois: A Profile* by Rayford W. Logan, 1971; *The Art and Imagination of Du Bois* by Arnold Rampersad, 1976; *Du Bois* by Jack B. Moore, 1981; *The Social Thought of Du Bois* by Joseph P. DeMarco, 1983; *Critical Essays on Du Bois* edited by William L. Andrews, 1985.

* * *

At the age of 35, in 1903, W. E. B. Du Bois took intellectual leadership of those within the Afro-American world who preferred liberal idealism to compensatory realism. Du Bois was prepared for his role by rigorous training in the traditional liberal arts as well as the newer empirical social sciences. But it was confidence in the moral absolute of truth and a poetic imagination that were to prove the sources of his effectiveness.

Souls of Black Folk, the book in which Du Bois publicly announced his differences with Booker T. Washington, is constructed from first-hand observation, historical research, and reasoned analysis. Its power, however, derives from the images of divided consciousness (souls), a culturally united black nation (folk), and the veil behind which black remained nearly invisible. In a time when Jim Crow shaped perception as much as policy, Du Bois's metaphors represented intellectual liberation, giving blacks a profoundly dignified way of conceiving their own lives and history. The cultural nationalism of *Souls of Black Folk* had been implicit in the earlier study *The Philadelphia Negro*, in which Du Bois documented class structure and shared institutions. It reappeared as motivation for the utopian vision of agricultural cooperatives in *The Quest of the Silver Fleece* and the romantic narrative of worldwide organization for colored people in *Dark Princess*.

Du Bois's well-known commitment to the idea of leadership by a talented tenth has its counterpart in the learned rhetoric of his essays and the grandiose design of his novels. It is no wonder that writing as a critic in Crisis he was unsympathetic to the experimentation and modern realism of the younger generation in the Negro Renaissance. Still, he made his own characteristic contribution to the "new Negro." His book *The Negro*, anticipating anti-colonial conferences organized after World War I, corrected popular impressions that American blacks were without roots by celebrating the African past. Then *Black Reconstruction in America*, written out of Du Bois's new enthusiasm for Marxism in the 1930's, recovered the significance of black people in the history of the south. Despite limitations of style, these historical re-evaluations initiated a scholarly revisionism comparable to the re-direction of thought in the book *Souls of Black Folk*.

Nearing the end of his life, Du Bois published his most comprehensive treatment of America, *The Black Flame*, a trilogy binding into one narrative an historical account of the years corresponding roughly to his own life and a fictional account of Manuel Mansart. That the plots are meant to inter-relate goes without saying. More to the point is the observation that Du Bois's career, capped by the trilogy, was his most important dialectical demonstration. Seeking to write as truthfully as possible, he became not only a scribe of history but its maker.

—John M. Reilly

See the essay on *Souls of Black Folk*.

DUNBAR, Paul Laurence. Born in Dayton, Ohio, 27 June 1872; son of a former slave. Educated at Dayton High School, graduated 1891. Married Alice Ruth Moore in 1898. Elevator operator, Dayton, 1891–93; worked at the Haiti Building, World's Columbian Exposition, Chicago, 1894; encouraged in his writing by prominent Dayton men, and by William Dean Howells, at whose instigation he joined the Pond Lecture Bureau, 1896; attained great popularity throughout the U.S. as a reader of his own works, and visited England, 1897; assistant in the Library of Congress, Washington, D.C., 1897–98. Suffered from tuberculosis. *Died 9 February 1906.*

PUBLICATIONS

Collections

Complete Poems. 1913.
The Dunbar Reader, edited by Jay Martin and Gossie H. Hudson. 1975.

Verse

Oak and Ivy. 1893.
Majors and Minors. 1895.
Lyrics of Lowly Life. 1896.
Lyrics of the Hearthside. 1899.
Poems of Cabin and Field. 1899.
Candle-Lightin' Time. 1901.
Lyrics of Love and Laughter. 1903.
When Malindy Sings. 1903.
Li'l' Gal. 1904.
Chris'mus Is A-Comin' and Other Poems. 1905.
Howdy, Honey, Howdy. 1905.
Lyrics of Sunshine and Shadow. 1905.
Joggin' Erlong. 1906.
Speakin' o' Christmas and Other Christmas and Special Poems. 1914.
I Greet the Dawn, edited by Ashley Bryan. 1978.

Plays

The Gambler's Wife, in *Dayton Tattler*, Ohio, 13, 20, and 27 December 1890.
African Romances, music by Samuel Coleridge Taylor. 1897.
Clorindy; or, The Origin of the Cakewalk, music by Will Marion Cook. 1898.
Dream Lovers, music by Samuel Coleridge Taylor. 1898.
Jes Lak White Fo'ks (lyrics only, with others), music by Will Marion Cook. 1900.
Uncle Eph's Christmas, music by Will Marion Cook. 1900.
Plantation Melodies, Old and New (lyrics only, with others), music by H. T. Burleigh. 1901.
In Dahomey (lyrics only, with others), music by Will Marion Cook. 1903.
My Lady (lyrics only, with others), music by Will Marion Cook. 1914.

Fiction

The Uncalled. 1898.
Folks from Dixie (stories). 1898.
The Love of Landry. 1900.
The Strength of Gideon and Other Stories. 1900.
The Fanatics. 1901.
The Sport of the Gods. 1902; as *The Jest of Fate*, 1902.
In Old Plantation Days (stories). 1903.
The Heart of Happy Hollow (stories). 1904.

*

Bibliography: *Dunbar: A Bibliography* by E. W. Metcalf, Jr., 1975.

Critical Studies: *The Life and Works of Dunbar*, biography by Lida Keck Wiggins, 1907; *Dunbar and His Song* by Virginia Cunningham, 1947; *Oak and Ivy: A Biography of Dunbar* by Addison Gayle, Jr., 1971; *A Singer in the Dawn: Reinterpretations of Dunbar* edited by Jay Martin, 1975.

* * *

There were, in truth, two Paul Laurence Dunbars. One was the writer supported by the interest of white Americans because some of his work was sufficiently faithful to black stereotypical images designed and demanded by white Americans. The other, in a sense the more "real" Dunbar, was the writer of genuine literary talent and dramatic sensibility, whose true literary worth could not be widely assessed until a wide range of his work was gathered and published as late as 1975 in *The Dunbar Reader*.

In his first manifestation, that of dialect poet, Dunbar was not so much pandering to the demands of white editors and a white reading public as indulging his own natural affinity for the rhythms of common speech and often for comedy; dialect in literature was, after all, very much *à la mode* with the interest in local color in late 19th-century America. That he had a gift as a dialect poet is undeniable, but it is rather too bad that his white audience could not accept him as anything more.

Much more he was, as William Dean Howells recognized early. As a writer of fiction and essays, he used the stuff of black lore to greater effect than any previous black writer, and at least as well as such whites as Joel Chandler Harris had done. Particularly noteworthy in his work is the reflection of religion in black American life and of the implications of the black migration to American cities. As a poet, Dunbar often superbly starched his ready lyricism with a keen sense of drama. It is a truism to say that while his material was mainly black, his insights were universal.

Dunbar did not choose to be the exemplar of the white view of black America in his time—but he was, and he made a sturdy pivot. He managed to entertain and enlighten whites while helping to imbue fellow blacks with a sense of history and importance, making him a close spiritual ancestor of Countée Cullen, Langston Hughes, James Baldwin, and the other powerful 20th-century black American voices.

—Alan R. Shucard

DUNCAN, Robert (Edward). Born Edward Howard Duncan in Oakland, California, 7 January 1919; adopted in 1920 and given name Robert Edward Symmes; took original surname, 1942. Educated at the University of California, Berkeley, 1936–38, 1948–50. Editor, *Experimental Review*, 1938–40, *Phoenix*, and *Berkeley Miscellany*, 1948–49, all in Berkeley; lived in Mallorca, 1955–56; teacher at Black Mountain College, North Carolina, 1956; assistant director of the Poetry Center (Ford grant), 1956–57, and lecturer in the Poetry Workshop, 1965, San Francisco State College; lecturer, University of British Columbia, Vancouver, 1963. Recipient: Guggenheim fellowship, 1963; National Endowment for the Arts grant, 1966 (two grants); Shelley Memorial Award, 1984; Cody award, 1985; Before Columbus Foundation award, 1985. Lives in San Francisco.

PUBLICATIONS

Verse

Heavenly City, Earthly City. 1947.
Poems 1948–1949. 1950.
Medieval Scenes. 1950.
The Song of the Border-Guard. 1952.
Fragments of a Disordered Devotion. 1952.
Caesar's Gate: Poems 1949–50. 1955.

Letters. 1958.
Selected Poems. 1959.
The Opening of the Field. 1960.
Roots and Branches. 1964.
Writing, Writing: A Composition Book of Madison 1953, Stein Imitations. 1964.
Wine. 1964.
Uprising. 1965.
A Book of Resemblances: Poems 1950–1953. 1966.
Of the War: Passages 22–27. 1966.
The Years as Catches: First Poems 1939–1946. 1966.
Boob. 1966.
Epilogos. 1967.
The Cat and the Blackbird. 1967.
Christmas Present, Christmas Presence! 1967.
Bending the Bow. 1968.
My Mother Would Be a Falconess. 1968.
Names of People. 1968.
The First Decade: Selected Poems 1940–1950. 1968.
Derivations: Selected Poems 1950–1956. 1968.
Play Time, Pseudo Stein. 1969.
Achilles' Song. 1969.
Poetic Disturbances. 1970.
Bring It Up from the Dark. 1970.
Tribunals: Passages 31–35. 1970.
In Memoriam Wallace Stevens. 1972.
Poems from the Margins of Thom Gunn's Moly. 1972.
A Seventeenth Century Suite. 1973.
An Ode and Arcadia, with Jack Spicer. 1974.
Dante. 1974.
The Venice Poem. 1975.
Veil, Turbine, Cord, and Bird. 1979.
The Five Songs. 1981.
Ground Work: Before the War. 1984.

Plays

Faust Foutu (produced 1955). Published as *Faust Foutu: Act One of Four Acts: A Comic Mask*, 1958; complete edition, as *Faust Foutu: An Entertainment in Four Parts*, 1960.
Medea at Kolchis: The Maiden Head (produced 1956). 1965.

Other

The Artist's View. 1952.
On Poetry (radio interview), with Eugene Vance. 1964.
As Testimony: The Poem and the Scene. 1964.
The Sweetness and Greatness of Dante's Divine Comedy 1265–1965. 1965.
Six Prose Pieces. 1966.
The Truth and Life of Myth: An Essay in Essential Autobiography. 1968.
65 Drawings: A Selection of 65 Drawings from One Drawing-Book: 1952–1956. 1970.
Notes on Grossinger's Solar Journal: Oecological Sections. 1970.
An Interview with George Bowering and Robert Hogg, April 19, 1969. 1971.
Fictive Certainties: Five Essays in Essential Autobiography. 1979.
Towards an Open Universe. 1982.

*

Critical Studies: "Duncan Issue" of *Origin*, June 1963, *Audit 4*, 1967, and *Maps 6*, 1974; *Godawful Streets of Man* by Warren Tallman, 1976; *Duncan: Scales of the Marvelous* edited by Robert J. Bertholf and Ian W. Reid, 1979; *The Lost America of Love: Rereading Robert Creeley, Edward Dorn, and Duncan* by Sherman Paul, 1981.

* * *

The poet, Robert Duncan has said, is akin to the paranoiac: everything seems to belong to the plot. Raised in a Theosophist environment, in much of his work Duncan seeks, like the paranoiac but without his fear, for something that does *not* belong to the coherent cosmic plot. Duncan, therefore (as he expounds it most clearly in the sections of the incomplete "The H.D. Book"), lives in a world in which "things strive to speak," where the poet seems to read "the language of things," where "the poet must attend not to what he means to say but to what what he says means" (*Caterpillar 7*). The poet is, then, subject not to "inspiration" so much as he is to "possession," where he may be had by an idea, and poetry is—in Duncan's language—an Office: the text the poet writes is part of a larger text: the Poem, and the office of poet is subsumed in the larger Office, of Poet.

It is thus perhaps to be expected that Duncan, of all poets associated with Black Mountain College and with post-modernism, should be the American writer most closely associated with the great tradition of English poetry and of mystical poetry, while at the same time he is the one who seems most consistently and perversely to be at odds with the traditions and conventions of English poetry. Such apparent perversity arises in part from Duncan's insistence, drawn from Heraclitus that "an unapparent connexion is stronger than an apparent": it derives also, in part, from "the strongest drive of my life, that things have not come to the conclusions I saw around me, and this involved the conclusions that I saw shaping in my own thought and actions" (*Caterpillar 8/9*). Thus, "A Poem Beginning with a Line by Pindar" (1958) is a combination of traditional devices, forms, and sources with the unexpected and unconventional. The synecdoche of "the light foot *hears*," quoted from Pindar's First Pythian Ode, involves the breaking of things "normal" in the language; this in turn suggests a range of possible meanings for "*light* foot." The poem, an extended meditation and discovery on—among other things—the notion of Adulthood, proposes a world in which the Real is found, not in a landscape, but "in an obscurity"—hidden, that is to say, from normal, familiar, conventional (or mortal) sight. In two essays central to his work, "Ideas of the Meaning of Form" (*Kulchur 4*) and "Man's Fulfillment in Order and Strife" (*Caterpillar 8/9*), Duncan insists that "to the conventional mind" form is "what can be imposed," and, in all of his writing, conventional syntax and language are a part of conventional form, and man is a creature of language. In section two of the "Pindar" poem the language, individual words and syllables, breaks down, loses its articulation, becomes almost nonsense. The breakdown is triggered by the word "stroke" which—initially of a brush, painting, or of a pen, writing—becomes a medical stroke (Eisenhower's?), and the poem, which at that point seems to be struggling to a halt, moves into a firm political rhetoric which reveals adulthood as a condition of nations as well as of individuals, and the condition itself as a process. Reading the poem, we witness the testimony of the poet discovering the world as it reveals itself to him through language. Meaning, in such poems as this, is to be found in the play of possible meanings, rather than in the conventionally ordered exposition of rational or reasonable thought. Duncan's insistence "not to reach a conclusion but to keep our exposure to what we do not know" has led to "Passages," a series of rhetorical poems which, resting on the Julian motto "The even is bounded, but the uneven is without bounds," explores all possible voices as its testimony to What Is.

—Peter Quartermain

DUNLAP, William. Born in Perth Amboy, New Jersey, 19 February 1766. Educated in local schools until his family moved to New York in 1777; then studied painting with a New York artist. Married Elizabeth Woolsey in 1789; one son and one daughter. Clerk in his father's store, then portrait painter, New York, 1782–84; studied art with Benjamin West in London, 1784–87; returned to New York and abandoned painting to write for the stage; manager and part owner, Old American Company, at the John Street Theatre, later at the Park Theatre, New York, presenting his own plays as well as current French and German plays in translation, 1796 until he went bankrupt, 1805; itinerant painter of miniatures, 1805–06; general assistant to the new manager of the Park Theatre, 1806–11; freelance writer and editor, 1811–15; founder, *Monthly Record*, New York, 1813; Assistant Paymaster-General, New York Militia, 1814–16; painter of miniatures, portraits, and religious commissions, 1816–mid-1830's. Founder member, 1826, and Vice-President, 1831–38, National Academy of Design. *Died 28 September 1839*.

PUBLICATIONS

Collections

Four Plays (1789–1812) (includes *The Father of an Only Child, Leicester, The Italian Father, Yankee Chronology*), edited by Julian Mates. 1976.
Musical Works (includes *Darby's Return, The Archers, The Wild-Goose Chase, The Glory of Columbia*), edited by Julian Mates. 1980.

Plays

The Father; or, American Shandy-ism (produced 1789). 1789; revised version, as *The Father of an Only Child*, in *Dramatic Works*, 1806; in *Four Plays*, 1976.
Darby's Return (produced 1789). 1789; edited by Walter J. Meserve and William R. Reardon, in *Satiric Comedies*, 1969; in *Musical Works*, 1980.
The Miser's Wedding (produced 1793).
Leicester (as *The Fatal Deception; or, The Progress of Guilt*, produced 1794). In *Dramatic Works*, 1806; in *Four Plays*, 1976.
Shelty's Travels (produced 1794).
Fountainville Abbey (produced 1795). In *Dramatic Works*, 1806.
The Archers; or, Mountaineers of Switzerland, music by Benjamin Carr (produced 1796). 1796; in *Musical Works*, 1980.
Ribbemont; or, The Feudal Baron (as *The Mysterious Monk*, produced 1796). 1803.
The Knight's Adventure (produced 1797). 1807.
The Man of Fortitude, with John Hodgkinson (produced 1797). 1807.
Tell Truth and Shame the Devil, from a play by A. L. B. Robineau (produced 1797). 1797.
The Stranger, from a play by Kotzebue (produced 1798). 1798.
André (produced 1798). 1798.
False Shame; or, The American Orphan in Germany, from a play by Kotzebue (produced 1798). Edited by Oral Sumner Coad, with *Thirty Years*, 1940.
The Natural Daughter (produced 1799).
The Temple of Independence (produced 1799).
Don Carlos, from the play by Schiller (produced 1799).
Indians in England, from a play by Kotzebue (produced 1799).
The School for Soldiers, from a play by L.S. Mercier (produced 1799).
The Robbery, from a play by Boutet de Monval (produced 1799).
The Italian Father, from the play *The Honest Whore* by Dekker (produced 1799). 1810; in *Four Plays*, 1976.
Graf Benyowsky, from a play by Kotzebue (produced 1799).
Sterne's Maria; or, The Vintage (produced 1799).
Lovers' Vows, from a play by Kotzebue (produced 1799). 1814.
The Force of Calumny, from a play by Kotzebue (produced 1800).
The Stranger's Birthday, from a play by Kotzebue (produced 1800).
The Knight of Guadalquiver (produced 1800).
The Wild-Goose Chase, music by J. Hewitt, from a play by Kotzebue (produced 1800). 1800; in *Musical Works*, 1980.
The Virgin of the Sun, from a play by Kotzebue (produced 1800). 1800.
Pizarro in Peru; or, The Death of Rolla, from a play by Kotzebue and the version by Sheridan (produced 1800). 1800.
Fraternal Discord, from a play by Kotzebue (produced 1800). 1809.
The Soldier of '76 (produced 1801).
Abee de l'Epee, from a play by Jean Bouilly (produced 1801).
Where Is He?, from a German play (produced 1801).
Abaellino, The Great Bandit, from a play by J. H. D. Zschokke (produced 1801). 1802.
The Merry Gardener, from a French play (produced 1802).
The Retrospect; or, The American Revolution (produced 1802).
Peter the Great; or, The Russian Mother, from a play by J. M. Babo (produced 1802). 1814.
The Good Neighbor: An Interlude, from a work by A. W. Iffland (produced 1803). 1814.
Blue Beard: A Dramatic Romance, from the play by George Colman the Younger. 1803.
The Voice of Nature, from a play by L. C. Caigniez (produced 1803). 1803.
The Blind Boy, from a play by Kotzebue (produced 1803).
Bonaparte in England (produced 1803).
The Proverb; or, Conceit Can Cure, Conceit Can Kill (produced 1804).
Lewis of Monte Blanco; or, The Transplanted Irishman (produced 1804).
Nina, from a play by Joseph Marsollier (produced 1804).
Chains of the Heart; or, The Slave of Choice, from a play by Prince Hoare (produced ?). 1804.

The Wife of Two Husbands, from a play by Pixérécourt (produced 1804). 1804.
The Shipwreck, from a play by Samuel James Arnold (produced ?). 1805.
Dramatic Works. 3 vols., 1806–16.
Alberto Albertini; or, The Robber King (produced 1811).
Yankee Chronology; or, Huzza for the Constitution! (produced 1812). 1812; in *Four Plays*, 1976.
The Glory of Columbia: Her Yeomanry! (produced 1813). 1817; in *Musical Works*, 1980.
The Flying Dutchman (produced 1827).
A Trip to Niagara; or Travellers in America (produced 1828). 1830.
Thirty Years; or, The Gambler's Fate, from a play by Prosper Goubaux and Victor Ducange (produced 1828). Edited by Oral Sumner Coad, with *False Shame*, 1940.

Other

Memoirs of the Life of George Frederick Cooke. 2 vols., 1813; revised edition, as *The Life of Cooke*, 1815.
A Record, Literary and Political, of Five Months in the Year 1813, with others. 1813.
The Life of the Most Noble Arthur, Marquis and Earl of Wellington, with Francis L. Clarke. 1814.
A Narrative of the Events Which Followed Bonaparte's Campaign in Russia. 1814.
The Life of Charles Brockden Brown, with Selections. 2 vols., 1815; as *Memoirs of Charles Brockden Brown*, 1822.
A History of the American Theatre. 1832.
History of the Rise and Progress of the Arts of Design in the United States. 2 vols., 1834; revised edition, edited by Alexander Wyckoff, 1965.
Thirty Years Ago; or, The Memoirs of a Water Drinker. 2 vols., 1836.
A History of New York, for Schools. 2 vols., 1837.
History of the New Netherlands, Province of New York, and the State of New York. 2 vols., 1839–40.
Diary: The Memoirs of a Dramatist, Theatrical Manager, Painter, Critic, Novelist, and Historian, edited by Dorothy C. Barck. 3 vols., 1930.

*

Bibliography: in *False Shame, and Thirty Years* edited by Oral Sumner Coad, 1940; in *Bibliography of American Literature* by Jacob Blanck, 1957.

Critical Studies: *Dunlap: A Study of His Life and Works and of His Place in Contemporary Culture* by Oral Sumner Coad, 1917; *Arts of the Young Republic: The Age of Dunlap* by Harold E. Dickson, 1968; *Dunlap* by Robert H. Canary, 1970.

* * *

"The American Vasari" and "Father of American Theatre" are phrases which honor William Dunlap as the first historian of United States arts. But his *Rise and Progress of the Arts*, though richly anecdotal, is a moralistic, opinionated source of biographical sketches. His *American Theatre* concentrates on 1787 to 1811 when Dunlap, as a playwright and manager, knew everyone in the business and contributed to its growth from a British "provincial" company to a theatre bragging of native-born stars and playwrights. Dunlap proposed federal subsidies, questioned the star-system, and despised the new Scribean play-factories—despite having translated the lurid *Thirty Years*.

This democratic abolitionist and artist saw himself as an anti-partisan reconciler. Because the best European models required an indefinable purification of "old world vices," Dunlap was left without dependable aesthetic grounds for resisting commercial standardization. He became the compromiser who packaged the acceptable best. Over half of his plays introduced fashionable continental dramatists into the American repertory. After successfully adapting *The Stranger*, Dunlap depended particularly upon the popularity of Kotzebue's plays (twelve translations) with their affecting sentimentality coupled with, admittedly, "false philosophy and unsound morals." *False Shame* typically puts all major characters through set-piece confessions of "false shame" before redeeming them by intermarriage or new-found family relationships. It conforms in kind to Dunlap's own sentimental comedies.

Dunlap's first produced play, *The Father*, uses the stock comic doctor and country maidservant to give some savor to its purposeful actions: an American patriot's reunion with his son, an English officer; the redemption of a mildly rakish husband; a pallid literary borrowing from Sterne. Art, politics, and business "now in Virtue's cause engage/And rear that glorious thing, a *Moral Stage*." For benefit performances or historical occasions Dunlap framed narrative songs. In *Yankee Chronology* a sailor returns to tell and sing of the 1812 victory of the (parable-pun) U.S.S. Constitution. Contradicting the travel-writers, *A Trip to Niagara* frames a moving diorama with interesting American (and British) types to persuade an English snob of some American virtues.

Only an unsophisticated audience could tolerate the ghastliness, disguises, and mistaken identities of the gothic *The Mysterious Monk* and the romantic *The Fatal Deception*—harmlessly abstract figures justified by much talk in verse about honor. But idea and theme, finally, make *André* a substantial and significant tragedy. General Washington and Major André are its heroic figures, while young Bland tries to be Otway's Pierre. Captain Bland and the other American officers play out their neoclassic alternatives of mind or heart, and the poetic drama gathers relevant force in their debate of the modes, moralities, and reconciliations necessary for an independent country in 1780, or in 1798 (the year of production).

Dunlap fashioned his controversial, unpopular, but finest play into a popular celebration. Incoherent and delightful, *The Glory of Columbia: Her Yeomanry!* wraps pieces of *André* with a despicable Benedict Arnold, some honest Yankee soldiers who capture André, a singing sister Sal in uniform, and a canny Irishman. He changes sides for a final victory pageant at Yorktown and a chorale to "Columbia's Son, Immortal Washington!"

—John G. Kuhn

DUNNE, Finley Peter. Born Peter Dunne in Chicago, Illinois, 10 July 1867. Educated at West Division High School, Chicago, graduated 1884. Married Margaret Abbott in 1902; three sons and one daughter. Journalist from 1885; city editor, *Times*, 1888–89, editor, *Tribune* Sunday edition, 1890–91, editorial page editor, *Evening Post*, 1892–97, and managing editor, *Journal*, 1897–1900, all Chicago; editor, New York *Morning Telegraph*, 1902–04; writer, *Collier's*, 1902, and editor, *Collier's Weekly*, 1917–19, both New York; editor, with Ida Tarbell and Lincoln Steffens, 1906, and contributor, 1906–15, *American Magazine*, New York. Member, American Academy. *Died 24 April 1936.*

PUBLICATIONS

Collections

Mr. Dooley and the Chicago Irish, edited by Charles Fanning. 1976.

Prose

Mr. Dooley in Peace and in War. 1898.
Mr. Dooley in the Hearts of His Countrymen. 1899.
What Dooley Says. 1899.
Mr. Dooley's Philosophy. 1900.
Mr. Dooley's Opinions. 1901.
Observations by Mr. Dooley. 1902.
Dissertations by Mr. Dooley. 1906.
Mr. Dooley Says. 1910.
New Dooley Book. 1911.
Mr. Dooley on Making a Will and Other Necessary Evils. 1919.
Mr. Dooley at His Best, edited by Elmer Ellis. 1938.
The World of Mr. Dooley, edited by Louis Filler. 1962.
Mr. Dooley Remembers: The Informal Memoirs of Dunne, edited by Philip Dunne. 1963.

*

Critical Studies: *Mr. Dooley's America: The Life of Dunne* by Elmer Ellis, 1941; *Mr. Dooley's Chicago* by Barbara C. Schaaf, 1977; *Dunne and Mr. Dooley: The Chicago Years* by Charles Fanning, 1978; *Small Town Chicago: The Comic Perspective of Dunne, George Ade, and Ring Lardner* by James DeMuth, 1980; *Dunne* by Grace Eckley, 1981; *Mr. Dooley and Mr. Dunne: The Literary Life of a Chicago Catholic* by Edward J. Bander, 1981.

* * *

Finley Peter Dunne is best known for having created Mr. Martin Dooley, an aging Irish saloonkeeper from Chicago, who began appearing in a weekly column in the Chicago *Evening Post* in October 1893. Dunne's own parents had been Irish immigrants to Chicago, and he began his journalistic career there in 1884 at age seventeen. After working on several different newspapers, he settled as precocious editorial chairman at the *Post* in 1892. The last in a series of dialect experiments for his creator, Mr. Dooley succeeded Colonel Malachi McNeery, a downtown Chicago barkeep modeled on a friend of Dunne's, who had become a popular *Post* feature during the World's Fair of 1893. Unlike McNeery, Mr. Dooley was placed on Chicago's South Side, in the Irish working-class neighborhood of Bridgeport. Between 1893 and 1898, 215 Dooley pieces appeared in the *Post*. Taken together, they form a coherent body of work, in which a vivid, detailed world comes into existence—that of Bridgeport, a self-contained immigrant culture, with its own customs and ceremonies and a social structure rooted in family, geography, and occupation. Included are memories of Ireland and emigration, descriptions of the daily round of Bridgeport life, and inside narratives of rough-and-tumble politics in a city ward. In addition, other pieces contain wholly serious treatments of suffering and starvation among the poor, the divisive scramble for middle-class respectability, and conflict between immigrant parents and their American children. In these Bridgeport pieces, Dunne contributed to the development of literary realism in America. In depicting this immigrant community and its working-class inhabitants through the medium of Irish vernacular dialect, he gave Chicagoans a weekly example of the realist's faith in the potentiality for serious fiction to use common speech and to show everyday life.

Dunne's career took a sharp turn in 1898, when Mr. Dooley's satirical coverage of the Spanish-American War brought him to the attention of readers outside Chicago. Beginning with his scoop of "Cousin George" Dewey's victory at Manila, Mr. Dooley's reports of military and political bungling during the "splendid little war" were widely reprinted, and national syndication soon followed. By the time Dunne moved to New York in 1900, Mr. Dooley was the most popular figure in American journalism. From this point until World War I, Dunne's gadfly mind ranged over the spectrum of newsworthy events and characters, both national and international: from Teddy Roosevelt's health fads to Andrew Carnegie's passion for libraries; from the invariable silliness of politics to society doings at Newport; from the Boer and Boxer Rebellions to the Negro, Indian, and immigration "problems." Mr. Dooley's perspective was consistently skeptical and critical. The salutary effect of most pieces was the exposure of affectation and hypocrisy through undercutting humor and common sense. The most frequently quoted Dooleyisms indicate this thrust: Teddy Roosevelt's egocentric account of the Rough Riders is retitled, "Alone in Cubia"; Henry Cabot Lodge's imperialist rationale becomes "Take up th' white man's burden an' hand it to th' coons"; a fanatic is defined as "a man that does what he thinks th' Lord wud do if He knew th' facts iv th' case." Although he joined Ida Tarbell and Lincoln Steffens in taking over the *American Magazine* in 1906, Dunne was not himself a progressive reformer. He viewed the world as irrevocably fallen and unimproveable, and many Dooley pieces reflect their author's tendency toward cynicism, pessimism, and fatalism. More pronounced in the early Chicago work than in the lighter national commentary, Dunne's darker side may be explained by his Irish background and his journalist's education into the realities of 19th-century urban life.

Mr. Dooley was the first Irish voice in American literature to transcend the confines of "stage Irish" ethnic humor. Dunne's accomplishment divides (at 1898) into two parts: the Chicago pieces, which contain pioneering realistic sketches of an urban immigrant community, and the pieces written for a national audience, which contain some of the best social and political satire ever penned in America.

—Charles Fanning

DWIGHT, Timothy. Born in Northampton, Massachusetts, 14 May 1752. Educated at Yale University, New Haven, Connecticut, 1766–69, 1771–72, B.A. 1769, M.A. 1772. Served in General Parson's Connecticut Brigade during the Revolutionary War, 1777–79: Chaplain. Married Mary Woolsey in 1777; eight sons. Headmaster, Hopkins Grammar School, New Haven, Connecticut, 1769–71; tutor, Yale University, 1771–77; licensed to preach, 1777; member, Massachusetts Legislature, 1781–82; ordained to the ministry of the Congregational Church, 1783; pastor, Greenfield Hill Congregational Church, Connecticut, 1783–95 (also schoolmaster in Greenfield); Professor of Divinity, and President, Yale University, 1795–1817 (founder of the medical department). Helped establish the Andover Theological Seminary and Missionary Society of Connecticut; member, American Board of Commissioners for Foreign Missions. LL.D.: Harvard University, Cambridge, Massachusetts, 1810. *Died 11 January 1817.*

PUBLICATIONS

Verse

America; or, A Poem on the Settlement of the British Colonies. 1780(?).
The Conquest of Canaan. 1785.
The Triumph of Infidelity. 1788.
Greenfield Hill. 1794.
The Psalms of David, by Watts, altered by Dwight. 1801.

Other

The Nature, and Danger, of Infidel Philosophy. 1798.
Remarks on the Review of Inchiquin's Letters. 1815.
Theology Explained and Defended in a Series of Sermons. 5 vols., 1818–19; abridged edition, as *Beauties of Dwight*, 4 vols., 1823.
Travels in New-England and New-York. 4 vols., 1821–22; edited by Barbara Miller Solomon, 4 vols., 1969.
An Essay on the Stage. 1824.
Sermons. 2 vols., 1828.

*

Bibliography: in *Bibliography of American Literature* by Jacob Blanck, 1957.

Critical Studies: *A Sketch of the Life and Character of Dwight* by Benjamin Silliman, 1817; *Dwight: A Biography* by Charles E. Cunningham, 1942; *Dwight* by Kenneth Silverman, 1969; *Calvinism versus Democracy: Dwight and the Origins of American Evangelical Orthodoxy* by Stephen E. Berk, 1974.

* * *

In his own time Timothy Dwight was a figure of towering significance, president of Yale University, foremost among the Hartford Wits, educator, and theologian. Today, however, he is in the main remembered as a staunch advocate of Federalist and Calvinist orthodoxies in a world of change, and as a poet who made modest if seminal contributions to the growth of an indigenous American literature.

Dwight's reputation for obstinacy originates mostly in his crabbed and dogmatic prose works. In 1798, for instance, with Deism and Thomas Jefferson on the rise, he announced in his sermon "The Duty of Americans, at the Present Crisis" that a return to Calvin and to Federalism was mandatory. In *The Nature, and Danger, of Infidel Philosophy*, published that same year, he castigated the liberal politics of John Locke, David Hume, and Thomas Paine. As for his own hero he would go on record two years later with a laudatory "Discourse on the Character of George Washington." And his *Theology Explained and Defended*, a five-volume collection of sermons which he had delivered to his students at Yale, was an apologia for the theocracy which he sought to maintain.

Dwight's orthodoxy also informed some of his verse. For example, *The Conquest of Canaan*, an epic in eleven books reminiscent of Milton, was a veiled allegory of the American War for Independence, with Joshua in the role of Washington. And his most venomous verse, *The Triumph of Infidelity*, recounted in heroic couplets the sins of Voltaire, Hume, and other expositors of liberalism. Still other of his poems, however, revealed another, softer, side of Dwight. In his most famous poem, *Greenfield Hill*, for instance, he spoke in seven different sections—now as narrator, now as rural mother or clergyman or farmer—of the virtues of pastoral life in the new nation in ways which are actually Jeffersonian in intonation.

It was also in *Greenfield Hill*, and to a lesser degree in *The Conquest of Canaan*, that Dwight made an important contribution to the growth of an indigenous literature by employing landscapes and personalities of an indubitably American nature. Unfortunately, the more reactionary of Dwight's writings, together with the prevailing view that the setting of poetry should be other than American, conspired to hide Dwight's attempts at a native literature. In another generation, however, the authors of the American Renaissance would build a successfully native literature upon the earlier efforts of poets such as Dwight.

—Bruce A. Lohof

EBERHART, Richard (Ghormley). Born in Austin, Minnesota, 5 April 1904. Educated at the University of Minnesota, Minneapolis, 1922–23; Dartmouth College, Hanover, New Hampshire, B.A. 1926; St. John's College, Cambridge, B.A. 1929, M.A. 1933; Harvard University, Cambridge, Massachusetts, 1932–33. Served in the U.S. Naval Reserve, 1942–46: Lieutenant Commander. Married Helen Butcher in 1941; two children. Tutor to the son of King Prajadhipok of Siam, 1930–31; English teacher, St. Mark's School, Southboro, Massachusetts, 1933–41, and Cambridge School, Kendal Green, Massachusetts, 1941–42; assistant manager to Vice-President, Butcher Polish Company, Boston, 1946–52; now honorary Vice-President and member of the Board of Directors; Visiting Professor, University of Washington, Seattle, 1952–53, 1967, 1972; Professor of English, University of Connecticut, Storrs, 1953–54; Visiting Professor, Wheaton College, Norton, Massachusetts, 1954–55; Resident Fellow and Gauss Lecturer, Princeton University, New Jersey, 1955–56; Professor of English and Poet-in-Residence, 1956–68, Class of 1925 Professor, 1968–70, and since 1970 Professor Emeritus, Dartmouth College; Elliston Lecturer, University of Cincinnati, 1961; Visiting Professor, University of Florida, Gainesville, winter term, 1974–82, Columbia University, New York, 1975, and University of California, Davis, 1975; Wallace Stevens Fellow, Timothy Dwight College, Yale University, New Haven, Connecticut, 1976. Founder, 1950, and first President, Poets' Theatre, Cambridge, Massachusetts; member, 1955, and since

1964, director, Yaddo Corporation; Consultant in Poetry, 1959–61, and Honorary Consultant in American Letters, 1963–69, Library of Congress, Washington, D.C. Recipient: New England Poetry Club Golden Rose, 1950; Shelley Memorial Award, 1952; Harriet Monroe Poetry Award, 1955; American Academy grant, 1955; Bollingen Prize, 1962; Pulitzer Prize, 1966; Academy of American Poets fellowship, 1969; National Book Award, 1977; President's Medallion, University of Florida, 1977; Sarah Josepha Hale Award, 1982. D.Litt: Dartmouth College, 1954; Skidmore College, Saratoga, New York, 1966; College of Wooster, Ohio, 1969; Colgate University, Hamilton, New York, 1974; D.H.L.: Franklin Pierce College, Rindge, New Hampshire, 1978. Poet Laureate of New Hampshire, 1979. Since 1972 Honorary President, Poetry Society of America. Member, American Academy, 1960, and American Academy of Arts and Sciences, 1967. Lives in Hanover, New Hampshire.

PUBLICATIONS

Verse

A Bravery of Earth. 1930.
Reading the Spirit. 1936.
Song and Idea. 1940.
A World-View. 1941.
Poems, New and Selected. 1944.
Rumination. 1947.
Burr Oaks. 1947.
Brotherhood of Men. 1949.
An Herb Basket. 1950.
Selected Poems. 1951.
Undercliff: Poems 1946–1953. 1953.
Great Praises. 1957.
The Oak: A Poem. 1957.
Collected Poems 1930–1960, Including 51 New Poems. 1960.
The Quarry: New Poems. 1964.
The Vastness and Indifference of the World. 1965.
Fishing for Snakes. 1965.
Selected Poems 1930–1965. 1965.
Thirty One Sonnets. 1967.
Shifts of Being. 1968.
The Achievement of Eberhart: A Comprehensive Selection of His Poems, edited by Bernard F. Engel. 1968.
Three Poems. 1968.
Fields of Grace. 1972.
Two Poems. 1975.
Collected Poems 1930–1976, Including 43 New Poems. 1976.
Poems to Poets. 1976.
Hour, Gnats. 1977.
Survivors. 1979.
Ways of Light: Poems 1972–1980. 1980.
New Hampshire: Nine Poems. 1980.
Four Poems. 1980.
Florida Poems. 1981.
In the Fourth World. 1983.
The Long Reach: New and Uncollected Poems 1948–1983. 1984.
Snowy Owl. 1984.
Throwing Yourself Away. 1984.

Plays

The Apparition (produced 1951). In *Collected Verse Plays*, 1962.
The Visionary Farms (produced 1951). In *Collected Verse Plays*, 1962.
Triptych (produced 1955). In *Collected Verse Plays*, 1962.
Devils and Angels (produced 1956). In *Collected Verse Plays*, 1962.
The Mad Musician (produced 1962). In *Collected Verse Plays*, 1962.
Collected Verse Plays (includes *Triptych, The Visionary Farms, The Apparition, The Mad Musician, Devils and Angels, Preamble I and II*). 1962.
The Bride from Mantua, from a play by Lope de Vega (produced 1964).
Chocurua. 1981.

Other

Poetry as a Creative Principle (lecture). 1952.
Of Poetry and Poets. 1979.

Editor, with others, *Free Gunner's Handbook*, revised edition. 1944.
Editor, with Selden Rodman, *War and the Poet: An Anthology of Poetry Expressing Man's Attitude to War from Ancient Times to the Present*. 1945.
Editor, . . . *Dartmouth Poems*. 12 vols., 1958–59, 1962–71.

*

Critical Studies: *Eberhart* by Ralph J. Mills, Jr., 1966; *Eberhart: The Progress of an American Poet* by Joel Roache, 1971; *Eberhart* by Bernard F. Engel, 1972; *Eberhart: A Celebration* edited by Sydney Lea and Jay Parini, 1980.

* * *

"Poetry is a recognition of man's estate and of his fate, and ultimately, poetry is praise."

Even Richard Eberhart's most ardent admirers admit the striking unevenness of his work—stirring and exquisite poems published alongside lines marred by sentimentality, pedantic diction, and banal abstractions. That his work is so uneven derives from Eberhart's personal definition of poetry, as well as his method of composition: "Poetry is dynamic, Protean," he writes. "In the rigors of composition . . . the poet's mind is a filament, informed with the irrational vitality of energy as it was discovered in our time in quantum mechanics. The quanta may shoot off any way." Eberhart rewrites little. His is an inspirational verse; through it he discovers life's significances: "You breathe in maybe God," and at those moments, "the poet writes with a whole clarity."

Unlike many of his contemporaries during the 1930's, Eberhart never worked for the hard, spare line; he rejected the ironic mode and created no personae. He wrote a personal poetry, much in the vein of the Romantics, especially Blake, Wordsworth, and Whitman—a poetry concerned with understanding and transcending concrete experience. Regardless of the inevitable problems such an aesthetic might invite, there remains a large body of inspired and original verse wherein Eberhart has been able to "aggravate" perception into life. His best work results from his success in transforming keenly felt sense perceptions, through the language of the experience itself, into meaning—moral, metaphysical, mystical, even religious. His most impressive work retains the urgency and radiance of the felt experience, as it simultaneously transforms it into the significant; Eberhart is epiphanic, much like Gerard Manley Hopkins. "The poet," he states, "makes the world anew; something grows out of the old, which he locks in words."

In Eberhart's first volume, *A Bravery of Earth*, he writes about the three types of "awareness" one must gain in the progress toward maturity—of mortality, mentality, and men's actions. These goals have been reflected throughout his career. Particular subjects have also persisted, such as the poet's sheer wonder in nature and the fierce exhilaration inspired by "lyric" and "lovely" nature within which "God" "incarnate" resides. Intimate involvement with physical nature involves the poet in its cycles of growth and decay, and Eberhart, always aware of his own mortality, searches for intimations of immortality.

Eberhart's compassion extends toward all living things which share a common fate. "The Groundhog," one of his best known poems, evokes a wild, extravagant transcendence in the face of physical decay. The poet now experiences an exhilaration not through an awareness of nature's eternal, recurrent cycles but rather through his creative articulation of the fact of decay. Returning year after year to the dead groundhog, he wishes for its absorption within nature's processes but instead witnesses its transformation from simple decay—"I saw a groundhog lying dead. / Dead lay he"—to something aesthetically moving, its few bones "bleaching in the sunlight / Beautiful as architecture." Eberhart moves from a sense of "naked frailty" to "strange love," "a fever," "a passion of the blood." Elsewhere, Eberhart has said: "Poetry is a spell against death," and he concludes "The Groundhog" with:

> I stood there in the whirling summer,
> My hand capped a withered heart,
> And thought of China and of Greece,
> Of Alexander in his tent;
> Of Montaigne and his tower,
> Of Saint Theresa in her wild lament.

Eberhart comes to identify with the mighty figures of the past who transcended the ravages of time through the very energy of their creative living and through the legacy of historical memory and art. The poet has transcended through the creation of his poem.

He writes about the variety of experiences associated with death. In "Imagining How It Would Be to Be Dead" and "When Golden Flies upon My Caracass Come," he tries to apprehend his own death. It may be the moment of revelation and transcendence, of "worldless Ecstasy/Of mystery." But death may also be "merely death"—"This is a very ordinary experience. / A name may be glorious but death is death" ("I Walked over the Grave of Henry James"). In "The Cancer Cells," he expresses an aesthetic glee in the artistic design of malignant cells: "They looked like art itself . . . / I think Leonardo would have in his disinterest / enjoyed them precisely with a sharp pencil."

Poems like "If I Could Only Live at the Pitch That Is Near Madness" represent another theme in Eberhart's poetry—his desire to retain the intensity of childhood, "the incomparable light," "when everything is as it was in my childhood / Violent, vivid, and of infinite possibility." But Eberhart accepts, indeed embraces, the "moral answer," the awareness that one cannot leave the world of men and maturity, and, as he returns "into a realm of complexity," there is a sense of new wonder and exaltation, as of joyful paternity, in his acceptance of the responsibilities of adulthood. One must not just feel experience; one must understand and articulate it.

Also recurrent are the variety of images of man's fallen state, his cruelty to his fellow man, the varieties of human suffering that grow out of social, political, and family strife. One is under obligation, implies Eberhart in his famous "Am I My Neighbor's Keeper," to care for his fellow man. Perhaps best known among this group is "The Fury of Aerial Bombardment," one of his many poems concerned with the inhumanity of war, where the poet ultimately wonders what sort of God would permit the barbarism of war: "You would feel that after so many centuries / God would give man to relent."

Familiar themes recur in *Ways of Light*, poems written between 1972 and 1980: man's relation to nature, his fate, and the larger themes of life, such as "love and the challenge of time." The poet listens, once more, to the owl cry ("Who") and returns to the rowboat of his youth to contemplate the seals and the "loon's cry far beyond the human." These shake his "sense to worldlessness" and make a "mystical matter of his involvement." Although he would seem to repeat that the ways of light remain through love, he admits that neither age and love nor honor and fame have brought him wisdom or certitude. Wonder and mystery remain in a world forever rich and unfathomable. *The Long Reach* intensifies Eberhart's sense of the fragility of life and immutability of death. Once again, confronting experience in his typically non-ironic, direct, and occasionally naive terms, he accepts the variegated conditions of life and the oblivion of death.

Throughout his nearly sixty years of writing, Eberhart has emphasized the need for a transcending credo—a personal belief structure created through both personal and concrete experience. As intensely aware of man's existential condition as many of his contemporaries, Eberhart has always focused on life and its creative possibilities. (In his speech accepting the 1977 National Book Award he lamented the suicides of some of his contemporaries and said: "Poets should not die for poetry but live for it.") For him, words lead to "joy" and "ecstasy": "The only triumph is some elegance of style."

But each person is a poet, in a sense, for everyone is, in everyday life, the creator of any meaning that life can have. Everyone must "make [his] own myth," because nature remains benignly indifferent. As one of his reviewers put it, the owl's cry tells man nothing unless one goes "somewhere beyond realism" and learns to "listen to the tune of the spiritual. Nature does not love or heed us. We are the lovers of nature."

—Lois Gordon

EDWARDS, Jonathan. Born in East Windsor, Connecticut, 5 October 1703. Educated at home, and at Yale University, Wethersfield, later New Haven, Connecticut, 1716–20, B.A. 1720; studied theology, 1720–22. Married Sarah Pierpont in

1727; 11 children. Presbyterian minister, New York, 1722–23; tutor, Yale University, 1724–25; assistant minister, later minister, Congregational church, Northampton, Massachusetts, 1726–50 (dismissed by congregation); missionary to Mohican Indians and minister, Stockbridge, Massachusetts, after 1751; President, College of New Jersey (now Princeton University), 1757–58. *Died 22 March 1758.*

PUBLICATIONS

Collections

Works (Leeds Edition), edited by Edward Williams and Edward Parsons. 8 vols., 1806–11; revised edition, 10 vols., 1847.
Representative Selections, edited by Clarence H. Faust and Thomas H. Johnson. 1935; revised edition, 1962.
Works, edited by Perry Miller. 1957—
Basic Writings, edited by Ola Elizabeth Winslow. 1966.

Prose

God Glorified in the Work of Redemption. 1731.
A Divine and Supernatural Light. 1734.
A Faithful Narrative of the Surprising Work of God in the Conversion of Many Hundred Souls in Northampton. 1737.
A Letter to the Author of the Pamphlet Called An Answer to the Hampshire Narrative. 1737.
Discourses on Various Important Subjects. 1738.
The Distinguishing Marks of a Work of the Spirit of God. 1741.
The Resort and Remedy of Those That Are Bereaved by the Death of an Eminent Minister. 1741.
Sinners in the Hands of an Angry God. 1741.
Some Thoughts Concerning the Present Revival of Religion in New England. 1742.
The Great Concern of a Watchman for Souls. 1743.
The True Excellency of a Minister of the Gospel. 1744.
Copies of the Two Letters Cited by Rev. Mr. Clap. 1745.
An Expostulatory Letter. 1745.
The Church's Marriage to Her Sons and to Her God. 1746.
A Treatise Concerning Religious Affections. 1746; in *Works 2*, 1959.
True Saints, When Absent from the Body, Are Present with the Lord. 1747.
An Humble Attempt to Promote Explicit Agreement and Visible Union of God's People in Extraordinary Prayer. 1747.
A Strong Rod Broken and Withered. 1748.
An Account of the Life of the Late Reverend Mr. David Brainerd. 1749; in *Works 7*, 1984.
An Humble Inquiry into the Rules of the Word of God Concerning . . . Communion. 1749.
Christ the Great Example of Gospel Ministers. 1750.
A Farewell Sermon Preached at the First Precinct in Northampton. 1751.
Misrepresentations Corrected and Truth Vindicated. 1752.
True Grace Distinguished from the Experience of Devils. 1753.
A Careful and Strict Enquiry into . . . Freedom of Will. . . . 1754; in *Works 1*, 1957; as *Freedom of the Will*, edited by Arnold S. Kaufman and William K. Frankena, 1969.
The Great Christian Doctrine of Original Sin Defended. 1758.
Two Dissertations: Concerning the End of Which God Created the World; The Nature of True Virtue. 1765.
The Life and Character of Edwards, with a Number of His Sermons, edited by Samuel Hopkins. 1765.
A History of the Work of Redemption. 1774.
Sermons, edited by Jonathan Edwards the Younger. 1780.
Practical Sermons, edited by Jonathan Edwards the Younger. 1788.
Miscellaneous Observations. 1793.
Remarks on Important Theological Controversies. 1796.
Charity and Its Fruits, edited by Tryon Edwards. 1852.
Selections from the Unpublished Writings, edited by Alexander B. Grosart. 1865.
Observations Concerning the Scripture Economy of the Trinity and Covenant of Redemption, edited by Egbert C. Smyth. 1880.
An Unpublished Essay on the Trinity, edited by George P. Fisher. 1903.
Selected Sermons, edited by H. Norman Gardiner. 1904.
Images; or, Shadows of Divine Things, edited by Perry Miller. 1948.
Puritan Sage: Collected Writings, edited by Vergilius Ferm. 1953.
The Philosophy of Edwards from His Private Notebooks, edited by Harvey G. Townsend. 1955.
Sermon Outlines, edited by Sheldon B. Quincer. 1958.
The Mind: A Reconstructed Text, edited by Leon Howard. 1963.
Treatise on Grace and Other Posthumously Published Writings, edited by Paul Helm. 1971.

*

Bibliography: *The Printed Writings of Edwards: A Bibliography* by Thomas H. Johnson, 1940; *Edwards: A Reference Guide* by Milton X. Lesser, 1981; *Edwards: Bibliographical Synopses* by Nancy Manspeaker, 1981.

Critical Studies: *Edwards* by Arthur Cushman McGiffert, Jr., 1932; *Edwards: A Biography* by Ola Elizabeth Winslow, 1940; *Edwards* by Perry Miller, 1949; *Edwards* by Alfred Owen Aldridge, 1964; *Edwards: The Narrative of a Puritan Mind* by Edward H. Davidson, 1966; *Edwards and the Visibility of God* by James Carse, 1967; *Beauty and Sensibility in the Thought of Edwards* by Roland André Delattre, 1968; *Edwards: A Profile* edited by David Levin, 1969; *Edwards* by Edward Griffin, 1971; *Edwards: His Life and Influence* edited by Charles Angoff, 1975; *The Writings of Edwards: Theme, Motif, and Style* by William J. Scheik, 1975, and *Critical Essays on Edwards* edited by Scheik, 1980; *Edwards, Pastor: Religion and Society in Eighteenth-Century Northampton* by Patricia Tracy, 1980; *Edwards: Art and the Sense of the Heart* by Terrence Erdt, 1980; *Edwards's Moral Thought and Its British Context* by Norman Fiering, 1981.

* * *

Jonathan Edwards is legendary in American history and letters not just as a Calvinist minister of fire and brimstone but, more importantly, as a revolutionary thinker who incorporated contemporary psychological and scientific ideas into his discourses on the human mind, natural science, and religion. A man who epitomized the mystical and practical (the evangelical and Puritan) tendencies of his time, Edwards was instrumental in the mid-18th-century revival of American Calvinism known as the Great Awakening. Edwards strove to destroy the increasingly popular Arminianist propositions which rejected the doctrines of predestination and the enslavement of the will. Arminianism asserted a doctrine of universal redemption based on the *election*, rather than the *predetermination*, of salvation. Edwards was unyielding in his strict adherence to the absolute primacy of deity and the utter subordination of man, to the Calvinist concept of the depravity of man and grace of the Gospel—to a belief system focusing on God as an inscrutable power that, while constituting humanity and nature, lacked complete identification with either. Throughout his life, despite the growing religious liberalism, Edwards repudiated all modern claims to man's natural rights and free will: "The unconverted are guilty and deserve the punishment awaiting them; this punishment is given by an infinite God in His justice; and the only hope of escape is by the gift of salvation which cannot be won by man's effort."

According to Perry Miller, Edwards's reading of John Locke's *An Essay Concerning Human Understanding* was the major event in his intellectual life. From it, Edwards refined his idea that whatever the mind knows as idea depends upon sensation, rather than reason or speculation. As such, through a series of light images in *A Divine and Supernatural Light*, he discusses religious certainty in empirical terms: one intuits or feels grace (the loveliness of God's holiness) through supernatural illumination. One "does not merely rationally believe that God is glorious but he has a sense of the gloriousness of God in his heart." Religious conversion is an overwhelming intuition.

"Justification of Faith Alone" (1734) amplifies Edwards's thesis that the covenant between God and man is one of grace, not works; but "faith actualizes grace." Again, consonant with the science of his day, Edwards incorporates Newton's causation theory, that effect exists, regardless of cause (atoms adhere not because of their inherent physical properties but because of an undefined Cause). To Edwards, as gravity adheres in matter, so God inheres in gravity and gives being and oneness to all. Man is therefore not justified just through faith. He has faith because he is first justified through God's grace. Man's state is not prior but posterior to God's grace.

"Personal Narrative" details his conversion 20 years earlier. Grace is a "Divine and Supernatural Light" that gives the regenerate a "new apprehension and disposition to love divine decrees." He traces his regeneration out of the "swamp" into the "meadow" of experience, how he saw divine beauty in everything and experienced "vehement longings of soul after God and Christ and after more holiness." The mention of a single word in the Bible caused his heart to burn with the "ardency of soul" and a "flood of tears and weeping aloud." Edwards yearned to "be nothing before God . . . that God might be all." For the saved, there is a mystical-aesthetic intuition of divine beauty through supernatural illumination.

Despite growing resentment toward his frightening portraits of the unredeemed, Edwards delivered the famous sermon *Sinners in the Hands of an Angry God* in Enfield, 8 July 1741. In a formidable examination of the blackness of death and the emptiness of non-being, he amplified how man is subject to spiritual disintegration. Expounding upon Deuteronomy 32:35 ("their foot shall slide in due time"), the sermon speaks of damnation, "The wrath of God is like great waves . . . [that] increase more and more, and rise higher and higher." By convincing the sinner that only divine mercy will protect him, Edwards hoped to convey a "new sense of the heart." "On Virtue" had already stated that all creation continuously depends on God's action, in which all goodness is constituted.

Edwards's many essays on the psychology of religion include *The Distinguishing Marks of a Work of the Spirit of God*, which separates "true signs" and "false signs," and *A Treatise Concerning Religious Affections*, which distinguishes understanding and will. The first is related to reason, judgment, and perception; the latter to feeling, the heart, and the more essential experience of religion. One of his most virulent adversaries, Charles Chauncey, continued to argue that God's presence could not be proved by experience, that Christianity is rational, and that emotionalism should be equated less with holiness than Satan. Nevertheless, *An Humble Inquiry* reiterated Edwards's insistence that church membership could only be open to those with visible evidence of grace.

Because of this kind of singlemindedness, Edwards was dismissed, in 1750, from his prestigious Northampton, Massachusetts, pulpit. From the frontier settlement at Stockbridge, he wrote the great *Freedom of the Will* and posited that will is not separate from mind but indissolubly connected to intellect: man *chooses* what he understands to be the greatest good. One will do only the "greatest good," and God is man's most apparent good. Furthermore, if the will and intellect are inseparable, then the true inner man (and "morality") will be manifest in man's actions. Edwards also argued that although man is free to gratify his will, he is not free to determine what he chooses. Prior to will is divine determination. *A History of the Work of Redemption* is his apocalyptic view of divine and human history from the creation to the final judgment; *The Great Christian Doctrine of Original Sin Defended* posits that we are all corrupted offspring of Adam, damned to utter alienation. The more positive *The Nature of True Virtue* argues that virtue is a kind of moral beauty that is love—benevolence toward Being, one's neighbor, and God. It also exemplifies Edwards's typical tripartite sermon structure: text (thesis, with biblical passage and commentary); doctrine (thematic implications, the heart of the essay); sermon or application (the bulk of the essay).

—Lois Gordon

EGGLESTON, Edward. Born in Vevay, Indiana, 10 December 1837. Educated in Indiana country schools, and at Amelia Academy, Virginia, 1854–55. Married 1) Lizzie Snider in 1858 (died, 1890), three daughters; 2) Frances E. Goode in 1891. Teacher, Madison, Indiana, 1855; entered the Methodist ministry, 1857: circuit rider in southeast Indiana, 1856–57; preacher, Traverse and St. Peter, 1857–58, St. Paul, 1858–60, Stillwater, 1860–61, St. Paul, 1862–63, and Winona, 1864–66, all Minnesota; associate editor, *Little Corporal* magazine, and columnist, Chicago *Evening Journal*, 1866–67; editor, *National Sunday School Teacher*, Chicago, 1867–69; literary editor, 1870, and superintending editor, 1871, New York *Independent*; editor, *Hearth and Home*, New York, 1871–72; left the Methodist ministry, 1874; founder and pastor of the non-sectarian Church of the Christian Endeavor, Brooklyn, New York, 1874–79. Co-founder, Authors' Club, 1882; President, American Historical Association, 1900. D.D.: University of Indiana, Bloomington, 1870; D.H.L.: Allegheny College, Meadville, Pennsylvania, 1893. *Died 2 September 1902.*

PUBLICATIONS

Fiction

Mr. Blake's Walking-Stick: A Christmas Story for Boys and Girls. 1870.
The Book of Queer Stories, and Stories Told on a Cellar Door. 1871.
The Hoosier School-Master. 1871; revised edition, 1892.
The End of the World: A Love Story. 1872.
The Mystery of Metropolisville. 1873.
The Circuit Rider: A Tale of the Heroic Age. 1874.
The Schoolmaster's Stories for Boys and Girls. 1874.
Roxy. 1878.
The Hoosier School-Boy. 1882.
Queer Stories for Boys and Girls. 1884.
The Graysons: A Story of Illinois. 1888.
The Faith Doctor: A Story of New York. 1891.
Duffels (collected stories). 1893.

Other

Sunday School Conventions and Institutes. 1867; revised edition, 1870.
The Manual: A Practical Guide to the Sunday-School Work. 1869.
Improved Sunday School Record. 1869.
Tracts for Sunday School Teachers. 1872(?).
Tecumseh and the Shawnee Prophet, with Lillie Eggleston Seelye. 1878; as *The Shawnee Prophet*, 1880.
Pocahontas, with Lillie Eggleston Seelye. 1879; as *The Indian Princess*, 1881.
Brant and Red Jacket, with Lillie Eggleston Seelye. 1879; as *The Rival Warriors, Chiefs of the Five Nations*, 1881.
Montezuma and the Conquest of Mexico, with Lillie Eggleston Seelye. 1880; as *The Mexican Prince*, 1881.
A History of the United States and Its People, for the Use of Schools. 1888.
A First Book in American History. 1889.
Stories of Great Americans for Little Americans: Second Reader Grade. 1895.
Stories of American Life and Adventures: Third Reader Grade. 1895.
The Beginners of a Nation. 1896.
The Transit of Civilization from England to America in the Seventeenth Century. 1901.
The New Century History of the United States, edited by G.C. Eggleston. 1904.

Editor, *Christ in Literature*. 1875.
Editor, *Christ in Art*. 1875.
Editor, with Elizabeth Eggleston Seelye, *The Story of Columbus*. 1892.
Editor, with Elizabeth Eggleston Seelye, *The Story of Washington*. 1893.

*

Bibliography: in *Bibliography of American Literature* by Jacob Blanck, 1959; "Eggleston" by William Peirce Randel, in *American Literary Realism 1*, 1967.

Critical Studies: *Eggleston, Author of "The Hoosier School-Master,"* 1946, and *Eggleston*, 1963, both by William Peirce Randel.

* * *

In 1871 Edward Eggleston, a former Methodist clergyman from Indiana who had become a successful editor of popular magazines for children and adults, published *The Hoosier School-Master*, thereby launching the first of two literary careers which made him an important—if decidedly minor—figure. In the adventures of a fictional frontier Indiana schoolteacher, Eggleston the novelist created a pioneering piece of western dialect fiction, and also contributed seminally to the growth of a midwestern realism, a genre which would subsequently be developed by Hamlin Garland.

Written initially for serialization in Eggleston's magazine *Hearth and Home*, with the early installments in print well before the later portions were in outline, *The Hoosier School-Master* has rightly been criticized for its many structural flaws. But Eggleston soon followed with a series of finer though curiously less famous novels in the same realistic vein: *The End of the World*, based upon the Millerite delusion of the 1840's; *The Mystery of Metropolisville*, a poorly constructed but equally realistic saga of boom and bust on the midwestern frontier; *The Circuit Rider*, a novel of remembrance, as the erstwhile preacher Eggleston wrote in its dedication, for his "Comrades of Other Years . . . with whom I had the honor to be associate in a frontier ministry"; and *Roxy*, the story of a small-town Ohio girl, thought by some to be Eggleston's best fictional work. Throughout his novels Eggleston sought to portray the commonplace in 19th-century American life. As he stated in *The Mystery of Metropolisville*, a novel "needs to be true to human nature in its permanent and essential qualities, and it should truthfully represent . . . some form of society."

Given the realistic character of his fiction, it was a short step for Eggleston to his next and final career, that of historian. In 1888 he published *A History of the United States and Its People*. And in 1896 appeared *The Beginners of a Nation*, the first of a projected multi-volume "History of Life in the United States." True to his proclivities as a realist, Eggleston had planned, as he said in 1880, for his history to be "a history of . . . the life of the people, the sources of their ideas and habits, the course of their development from beginnings." And had he been able to complete his series he surely would have joined Moses Coit Tyler and John Bach McMaster as one of the great founders of American social history. Unfortunately he came to history too late in life and with too expansive a plan; after publishing the second volume in the series, *The Transit of Civilization*, he died in 1902.

—Bruce A. Lohof

ELIOT, T(homas) S(tearns). Born in St. Louis, Missouri, 26 September 1888; became British citizen, 1927. Educated at Mrs. Lockwood's school, St. Louis; Smith Academy, St. Louis, 1898–1905; Milton Academy, Massachusetts, 1905–06; Harvard University, Cambridge, Massachusetts (board member, *Harvard Advocate*, 1909–10; Sheldon Traveling Fellowship, 1914), 1906–10, 1911–14, A.B. 1909, A.M. in English

1910; the Sorbonne, Paris, 1910–11; Merton College, Oxford, 1914–15. Married 1) Vivien (born Vivienne) Haigh-Wood in 1915 (separated, 1933; died, 1947); 2) Esmé Valerie Fletcher in 1957. Teacher, High Wycombe Grammar School, Buckinghamshire, 1915–16, and Highgate Junior School, London, 1916; tutor, University of London Extension Board, Southall, 1916–19; clerk in the Colonial and Foreign Department, then in charge of the Foreign Office Information Bureau, Lloyd's Bank, London, 1917–25; editor, later director, Faber and Gwyer, 1925–28, and Faber and Faber, publishers, London, 1929–65. Assistant editor, *The Egoist*, London, 1917–19; regular contributor, *Times Literary Supplement*, London, from 1919; founding editor, *The Criterion*, London, 1922–39; member of the editorial board, *New English Weekly*, London, 1934–44, and *Christian News Letter*, Oxford, 1939–46. Clark Lecturer, Trinity College, Cambridge, 1926; Charles Eliot Norton Professor of Poetry, 1932–33, and Theodore Spencer Memorial Lecturer, 1950, Harvard University; Page-Barbour Lecturer, University of Virginia, Charlottesville, 1933; Visiting Fellow, Institute for Advanced Studies, Princeton University, New Jersey, 1948. Joined Church of England, 1927. Recipient: Nobel Prize for Literature, 1948; New York Drama Critics Circle award, 1950; Hanseatic-Goethe Prize (Hamburg), 1954; Dante Gold Medal (Florence), 1959; Order of Merit (Bonn), 1959; Emerson-Thoreau Medal, 1960; U.S. Medal of Freedom, 1964. Litt.D.: Columbia University, New York, 1933; Cambridge University, 1938; University of Bristol, 1938; University of Leeds, 1939; Harvard University, 1947; Princeton University, 1947; Yale University, New Haven, Connecticut, 1947; Washington University, St. Louis, 1953; University of Rome, 1958; University of Sheffield, 1959; University of Bologna, 1967; LL.D.: University of Edinburgh, 1937; St. Andrews University, Fife, Scotland, 1953; D.Litt.: Oxford University, 1948; D.Lit.: University of London, 1950; D. ès L.: University of Paris, 1951; University of Aix-Marseille, 1959; University of Rennes, 1959; D.Phil.: University of Munich, 1959. Honorary Fellow, Magdalene College, Cambridge, 1948, and Merton College, Oxford, 1949. O.M. (Order of Merit), 1948; Officer, Legion of Honor, and Commander, Order of Arts and Letters (France), 1950; Honorary Member, American Academy; Foreign Member, Accademia dei Lincei (Rome) and Akademie der Schönen Künste. *Died 4 January 1965.*

PUBLICATIONS

Collections

Selected Prose, edited by Frank Kermode. 1975.

Verse

Prufrock and Other Observations. 1917.
Poems. 1919.
Ara Vos Prec. 1920; as *Poems*, 1920.
The Waste Land. 1922; *A Facsimile and Transcripts of the Original Drafts Including the Annotations of Ezra Pound*, edited by Valerie Eliot, 1971.
Poems 1909–1925. 1925.
Journey of the Magi. 1927.
A Song for Simeon. 1928.
Animula. 1929.
Ash-Wednesday. 1930.
Marina. 1930.
Triumphal March. 1931.
Words for Music. 1935.
Two Poems. 1935.
Collected Poems 1909–1935. 1936.
Old Possum's Book of Practical Cats. 1939.
The Waste Land and Other Poems. 1940.
East Coker. 1940.
Later Poems 1925–35. 1941.
The Dry Salvages. 1941.
Little Gidding. 1942.
Four Quartets (includes *Burnt Norton, East Coker, The Dry Salvages, Little Gidding*). 1943.
A Practical Possum. 1947.
Selected Poems. 1948.
The Undergraduate Poems. 1949.
Poems Written in Early Youth, edited by John Hayward. 1950.
The Cultivation of Christmas Trees. 1954.
Collected Poems 1909–1962. 1963.

Plays

Sweeney Agonistes: Fragments of an Aristophanic Melodrama (produced 1933). 1932.
The Rock: A Pageant Play (produced 1934). 1934.
Murder in the Cathedral (produced 1935). 1935; revised version, in *The Film of Murder in the Cathedral*, with George Hoellering, 1952.
The Family Reunion (produced 1939). 1939.
The Cocktail Party (produced 1949). 1950; revised edition, 1950.
The Confidential Clerk (produced 1953). 1954.
The Elder Statesman (produced 1958). 1959.
Collected Plays: Murder in the Cathedral, The Family Reunion, The Cocktail Party, The Confidential Clerk, The Elder Statesman. 1962; as *The Complete Plays*, 1969.

Other

Ezra Pound: His Metric and Poetry. 1918.
The Sacred Wood: Essays on Poetry and Criticism. 1920.
Homage to John Dryden: Three Essays on Poetry in the Seventeenth Century. 1924.
Shakespeare and the Stoicism of Seneca. 1927.
For Lancelot Andrewes: Essays on Style and Order. 1928.
Dante. 1929.
Charles Whibley: A Memoir. 1931.
Thoughts after Lambeth. 1931.
Selected Essays 1917–1932. 1932; revised edition, 1950.
John Dryden: The Poet, The Dramatist, The Critic. 1932.
The Use of Poetry and the Use of Criticism: Studies in the Relation of Criticism to Poetry in England. 1933.
After Strange Gods: A Primer of Modern Heresy. 1934.
Elizabethan Essays. 1934; as *Elizabethan Dramatists*, 1963; selection, as *Essays on Elizabethan Drama*, 1956.
Essays Ancient and Modern. 1936.
The Idea of a Christian Society. 1939.
Points of View, edited by John Hayward. 1941.
The Classics and the Man of Letters. 1942.
The Music of Poetry. 1942.
Reunion by Destruction: Reflections on a Scheme for Church Unity in South India Addressed to the Laity. 1943.
What Is a Classic? 1945.

Die Einheit der Europäischen Kultur. 1946.
On Poetry. 1947.
Milton. 1947.
From Poe to Valéry. 1948.
A Sermon Preached in Magdalene College Chapel. 1948.
Notes Towards the Definition of Culture. 1948.
The Aims of Poetic Drama. 1949.
Poetry and Drama. 1951.
The Value and Use of Cathedrals in England Today. 1952.
An Address to the Members of the London Library. 1952.
The Complete Poems and Plays. 1952.
Selected Prose, edited by John Hayward. 1953.
American Literature and the American Language. 1953.
The Three Voices of Poetry. 1953.
Religious Drama, Mediaeval and Modern. 1954.
The Literature of Politics. 1955.
The Frontiers of Criticism. 1956.
On Poetry and Poets. 1957.
Geoffrey Faber 1889–1961. 1961.
George Herbert. 1962.
Knowledge and Experience in the Philosophy of F. H. Bradley (doctoral dissertation). 1964.
To Criticize the Critic and Other Writings. 1965.

Editor, *Selected Poems*, by Ezra Pound. 1928; revised edition, 1949.
Editor, *A Choice of Kipling's Verse*. 1941.
Editor, *Introducing James Joyce*. 1942.
Editor, *Literary Essays of Ezra Pound*. 1954.
Editor, *The Criterion 1922–1939*. 18 vols., 1967.

Translator, *Anabasis: A Poem*, by Saint-John Perse. 1930; revised edition, 1938, 1949, 1959.

*

Bibliography: *Eliot: A Bibliography* by Donald Gallup, 1952, revised edition, 1969; *The Merrill Checklist of Eliot* by B. Gunter, 1970; *Eliot: A Bibliography of Secondary Works* by Beatrice Ricks, 1980.

Critical Studies: *The Achievement of Eliot: An Essay on the Nature of Poetry* by F.O. Matthiessen, 1935, revised edition, 1949, with additional material by C.L. Barber, 1958; *Four Quartets Rehearsed* by R. Preston, 1946; *Eliot: A Symposium* edited by Richard March and Tambimuttu, 1948; *Eliot: The Design of His Poetry* by Elizabeth Drew, 1949; *The Art of Eliot*, 1949, *Eliot and the English Poetic Tradition*, 1965, and *The Composition of Four Quartets*, 1978, all by Helen Gardner; *The Poetry of Eliot* by D.E.S. Maxwell, 1952; *A Reader's Guide to Eliot* by George Williamson, 1953, revised edition, 1966; *Eliot's Poetry and Plays: A Study in Sources and Meaning*, 1956, revised edition, 1975, and *The Waste Land*, 1983, both by Grover Smith; *Eliot: A Symposium for His Seventieth Birthday* edited by Neville Braybrooke, 1958; *The Invisible Poet: Eliot* by Hugh Kenner, 1959, and *Eliot: A Collection of Critical Essays* edited by Kenner, 1962; *Eliot's Dramatic Theory and Practice* by Carol H. Smith, 1963; *Eliot* by Northrop Frye, 1963, revised edition, 1968; *Notes on Some Figures Behind Eliot* by Herbert Howarth, 1964; *Eliot* by Philip Headings, 1964, revised edition, 1982; *Eliot: The Dialectical Structure of His Theory of Poetry* by Fei-pai Lu, 1965; *Eliot: The Man and His Work* edited by Allen Tate, 1966; *Eliot: Movements and Patterns* by Leonard Unger, 1966; *A Student's Guide to the Selected Poems of Eliot* by B.C. Southam, 1968, revised edition, 1981; *Twentieth-Century Interpretations of The Waste Land* edited by Jay Martin, 1968; *The Waste Land: A Casebook* edited by C.B. Cox and Arnold P. Hinchliffe, 1968; *Eliot's Four Quartets: A Casebook* edited by Bernard Bergonzi, 1969, and *Eliot* by Bergonzi, 1972, revised edition, 1978; *The Making of Eliot's Plays* by E. Martin Browne, 1969; *Eliot: Poems in the Making* by Gertrude Patterson, 1971; *Eliot's Intellectual Development 1922–1939* by John D. Margolis, 1972; *Eliot: Poet and Dramatist* by Joseph Chiari, 1972, revised edition, 1979; *Critics on Eliot* edited by Sheila Sullivan, 1973; *Eliot in His Time: Essays on the Occasion of the Fiftieth Anniversary of The Waste Land* edited by A. Walton Litz, 1973; *Eliot's Impersonal Theory of Poetry* by Mowbray Allan, 1974; *Eliot: A Collection of Criticism* edited by Linda W. Wagner, 1974; *Eliot* by Stephen Spender, 1975; *Eliot: The Pattern in the Carpet* by Elisabeth W. Schneider, 1975; *Eliot: The Longer Poems* by Derek A. Traversi, 1976; *Eliot's Personal Waste Land: Exorcism of the Demons* by James E. Miller, Jr., 1977; *Eliot's Early Years* by Lyndall Gordon, 1977; *The Literary Criticism of Eliot: New Essays* edited by David Newton-De Molina, 1977; *Eliot: Poet* by A.D. Moody, 1979; *Eliot and the Romantic Critical Tradition* by Edward Lobb, 1981; *Eliot: The Poet and His Critics* by Robert H. Canary, 1982; *Eliot* by Burton Raffel, 1982; *Eliot: The Critical Heritage* edited by Michael Grant, 2 vols., 1982; *Eliot: A Chronology of His Life and Works* by Caroline Behr, 1983; *Eliot and the Poetics of Literary History* by Gregory S. Jay, 1983; *Eliot: A Study in Character and Style* by Ronald Bush, 1984; *Eliot: A Life* by Peter Ackroyd, 1984; *Critical Essays on Eliot: The Sweeney Motif* edited by Kinley Roby, 1985; *An Eliot Companion: Life and Works* edited by F.B. Pinion, 1986.

* * *

T.S. Eliot's influence was predominant in English poetry in the period between the two world wars. His first small volume of poems, *Prufrock and Other Observations*, appeared in 1917. The title is significant. Eliot's earliest verse is composed of *observations*, detached, ironic, and alternately disillusioned and nostalgic in tone. The prevailing influence is that of French poetry, and in particular of Jules Laforgue; the mood is one of reaction against the comfortable certainties of "Georgian" poetry, the projection of a world which presented itself to the poet and his generation as disconcerting, uncertain, and very possibly heading for destruction.

The longest poem in the volume, "The Love Song of J. Alfred Prufrock," shows these qualities, but goes beyond them. The speaker is a kind of modern Hamlet, a man who after a life passed in devotion to the trivial has awakened to a sense of his own futility and to that of the world around him. He feels that some decisive act of commitment is needed to break the meaningless flow of events which his life offers. The question, however, is whether he really dares to reverse the entire course of his existence by a decision the nature of which eludes him:

> And indeed there will be time
> To wonder, "Do I dare?" and, "Do I dare?"
> Time to turn back and descend the stair,
> With a bald spot in the middle of my hair . . .
> Do I dare
> Disturb the universe?

The answer, for Prufrock, is negative. Dominated by his fear of life, misunderstood when he tries to express his sense of a possible revelation, Prufrock concludes "No! I am not Prince Hamlet, nor was meant to be," refuses to accept the role which life for a moment seemed to have thrust upon him, and returns to the stagnation which his vision of reality imposes.

Eliot's earliest poems are American in theme and inspiration, and reflect his experiences there, especially while studying philosophy at Harvard. The outbreak of war in 1914 found him in England, where he eventually made his home and where his conception of his art underwent a considerable change. After a second small volume, published in 1919, which shows, especially in its most impressive poem, "Gerontion," a notable deepening into tragedy, came the publication in 1922 of *The Waste Land*. Written in part in Switzerland, while Eliot was recovering from a period of deep depression, the poem underwent considerable changes at the suggestion of Ezra Pound, before bursting upon its readers with the effect of a literary revolution. Many of its first readers found it arid and incomprehensible, though it was in fact neither. The poet tells us that he is working through "a heap of broken images." He does this because it is a world of dissociated fragments that he is describing; but his aim, like that of any artist, is not merely an evocation of chaos. The poem is built on the interweaving of two great themes: the broken pieces of the present, as it presents itself to a disillusioned contemporary understanding, and the significant continuity of tradition. These two strains begin apart, like two separate themes in a musical composition, but the poem is animated by the hope, the *method*, that at the end they will converge into some kind of unity. Some critics, reading it in the light of Eliot's later development, have tried to find in the poem a specifically "religious" content, which however is not there. At best, there is a suggestion at the close that such a content, were it available, might provide a way out of the "waste land" situation, that the life-giving rain *may* be on the point of relieving the intolerable drought; but the poet cannot honestly propose such a resolution and the step which might have affirmed it is never rendered actual.

For some years after 1922, Eliot wrote little poetry and the greater part of his effort went into critical prose, much of it published in *The Criterion*, the literary quarterly which he edited until 1939. Eliot's criticism, which profoundly affected the literary taste of his generation, contributed to the revaluation of certain writers—the lesser Elizabethan dramatists, Donne, Marvell, Dryden—and, more controversially, to the depreciation of others, such as Milton (concerning whom, however, Eliot later modified his views) and some of the Romantic poets. It was the work of a poet whose interest in other writers was largely conditioned by the search for solutions to the problems raised by his own art; and, as such, it was marked by the idiosyncracies which constitute at once its strength and its limitation.

In 1928, in his preface to the collection of essays *For Lancelot Andrewes*, Eliot declared himself Anglo-Catholic in religion, royalist in politics, classicist in literature: a typically enigmatic statement which indicated the direction he was to give to the work of his later years. *Ash-Wednesday*, published in 1930, was his first considerable poem of explicitly Christian inspiration: a work at once religious in content and modern in inspiration, personal yet without concession to sentiment. The main theme is an acceptance of conversion as a necessary and irretrievable act. The answer to the question posed by Prufrock—"Do I dare / Disturb the universe?"—is seen, in the translation of the first line of the Italian poet Guido Cavalcanti's ballad, "Because I do not hope to turn again," as an embarkation, dangerous but decisive, upon the adventure of faith.

The consequences of this development were explored in the last and in some respects the most ambitious of Eliot's poetic efforts: the sequence of poems initiated in 1935 and finally published, in 1943, under the title of *Four Quartets*. The series opens, in *Burnt Norton*, with an exploration of the *possible* significance of certain moments which seem to penetrate, briefly and elusively, a reality beyond that of normal temporal experience. "To be conscious," the poem suggests, "is not to be in time": only to balance that possibility with the counter-assertion that "Only through time time is conquered." The first step towards an understanding of the problems raised in the *Quartets* is a recognition that time, though inseparable from our human experience, is not the whole of it. If we consider time as an ultimate reality, our spiritual intuitions are turned into an illusion: whereas if we seek to deny the reality of time, our experience becomes impossible. The two elements—the temporal and the timeless—need to be woven together in an embracing pattern of experience which is, in fact, the end to which the entire sequence points.

The later "quartets" build upon this provisional foundation in the light of the poet's experience as artist and human being. The impulse to create in words reflects another, still more fundamental, impulse which prompts men to seek *form*, coherence, and meaning in the broken intuitions which their experience offers them. The nature of the search is such that it can never be complete in time. The true value of our actions only begins to emerge when we abstract ourselves from the temporal sequence—"time before and time after"—in which they were realized; and the final sense of our experience only reveals itself when the pattern is completed, at the moment of death. This moment, indeed, is not properly speaking a single final point, but a reality which covers the whole course of our existence.

These reflections lead the poet, in the last two poems of the series, *The Dry Salvages* and *Little Gidding*, to acceptance and even to a certain optimism. The end of the journey becomes the key to its beginning, and this in turn an invitation to confidence: "Not fare well, / But fare forward, voyagers." The doctrine of detachment explored in the second poem, *East Coker*, becomes an "expanding" one of "love beyond desire." The conclusion stresses the continuity between the "birth" and "death" which are simultaneously present in each moment, in each individual life, and in the history of the human race. It is true, as the closing section of *Little Gidding* puts it, that "we die with the dying"; but it is equally true that "we are born with the dead." We die, in other words, as part of the tragedy which the fact of our humanity implies, but we are born again when, having understood the temporal process in its true light, we are ready to accept our present position within a still-living and continually unfolding tradition.

Eliot's poetic output was relatively small and intensely concentrated: a fact which at once confirms its value and constitutes, in some sense, a limiting factor. It should be mentioned that in his later years he devoted himself to the writing of verse plays, in an attempt to create a contemporary mode of poetic drama. The earlier plays, *Murder in the Cathedral* and *The Family Reunion*, which are also the best, take up the themes which were being explored at the same time in his poetry and develop them in ways that are often interesting and dramatically effective. *The Cocktail Party*, though still a skilful work, shows some decline in conception and execution, and the later plays—*The Confidential Clerk* and *The Elder Statesman*—

while they seem to show that he was arriving towards the end of his life at a more accepting view of the world, can safely be said to add little to Eliot's achievement.

—Derek A. Traversi

See the essays on *Four Quartets*, *Murder in the Cathedral*, and *The Waste Land*.

ELLISON, Ralph (Waldo). Born in Oklahoma City, Oklahoma, 1 March 1914. Educated at a high school in Oklahoma City, and at Tuskegee Institute, Alabama, 1933–36. Served in the U.S. Merchant Marine, 1943–45. Married Fanny McConnell in 1946. Writer from 1936; Lecturer, Salzburg Seminar in American Studies, 1954; Instructor in Russian and American Literature, Bard College, Annandale-on-Hudson, New York, 1958–61; Alexander White Visiting Professor, University of Chicago, 1961; Visiting Professor of Writing, Rutgers University, New Brunswick, New Jersey, 1962–64; Whittall Lecturer, Library of Congress, Washington, D.C., 1964; Ewing Lecturer, University of California, Los Angeles, 1964; Visiting Fellow in American Studies, Yale University, New Haven, Connecticut, 1966; Albert Schweitzer Professor in the Humanities, New York University, 1970–79, now emeritus. Chairman, Literary Grants Committee, American Academy, 1964–67; member, National Council on the Arts, 1965–67; member, Carnegie Commission on Educational Television, 1966–67; member of the editorial board, *American Scholar*, Washington, D.C., 1966–69; Honorary Consultant in American Letters, Library of Congress, Washington, D.C., 1966–72; trustee, John F. Kennedy Center of the Performing Arts, Washington, D.C., New School for Social Research, New York, Bennington College, Vermont, Educational Broadcasting Corporation, and Colonial Williamsburg Foundation. Recipient: Rosenwald fellowship, 1945; National Book Award, 1953; National Newspaper Publishers Association Russwarm Award, 1953; American Academy Rome Prize, 1955, 1956; U.S. Medal of Freedom, 1969; National Medal of Arts, 1985. Ph.D. in Humane Letters: Tuskegee Institute, 1963; Litt.D.: Rutgers University, 1966; University of Michigan, Ann Arbor, 1967; Williams College, Williamstown, Massachusetts, 1970; Long Island University, New York, 1971; College of William and Mary, Williamsburg, Virginia, 1972; Wake Forest College, Winston-Salem, North Carolina, 1974; Harvard University, Cambridge, Massachusetts, 1974; L.H.D.: Grinnell College, Iowa, 1967; Adelphi University, Garden City, New York, 1971; University of Maryland, College Park, 1974. Commander, Order of Arts and Letters (France), 1970; member, American Academy, 1975. Lives in New York City.

PUBLICATIONS

Fiction

Invisible Man. 1952.

Other

The Writer's Experience, with Karl Shapiro. 1964.
Shadow and Act (essays). 1964.
The City in Crisis, with Whitney M. Young and Herbert Gnas. 1968.
Going to the Territory (essays). 1986.

*

Bibliography: "A Bibliography of Ellison's Published Writings" by Bernard Benoit and Michel Fabre, in *Studies in Black Literature*, Autumn 1971; *The Blinking Eye: Ellison and His American, French, German and Italian Critics 1952–1971* by Jacqueline Covo, 1974.

Critical Studies: *Five Black Writers: Essays* by Donald B. Gibson, 1970; *Twentieth-Century Interpretations of Invisible Man* edited by John M. Reilly, 1970; "Ellison Issue" of *CLA Journal*, March 1970; *The Merrill Studies in Invisible Man* edited by Ronald Gottesman, 1971; *Ellison: A Collection of Critical Essays* edited by John Hersey, 1974; *Invisible Man's Literary Heritage: Benito Cereno and Moby-Dick* by Valerie Bonita Gray, 1978; *Folklore and Myth in Ellison's Early Works* by Dorothea Fischer-Hornung, 1979; *The Craft of Ellison* by Robert G. O'Meally, 1980; *Ellison: The Genesis of an Artist* by Rudolf F. Dietze, 1982.

* * *

A bookish as well as a musical child, Ralph Ellison began to read some of the classics of modern literature, including *The Waste Land*, while a student at Tuskegee. His literary education was accelerated after he met Richard Wright in 1937. In addition to providing an example of commitment to social and racial justice, Wright helped to persuade Ellison to direct his creative energies to writing, encouraging him to turn to "those works in which writing was discussed as a craft . . . to Henry James' prefaces, to Conrad, to Joseph Warren Beach and to the letters of Dostoievsky" (*Shadow and Act*). Despite some later disavowals, Ellison was deeply influenced by Wright's own fiction as well as by his literary tutelage. Such early short stories as "Slick Gonna Learn" and "Mister Toussan'," for example, reveal how carefully Ellison had read Wright's *Uncle Tom's Children*.

When one looks at *Invisible Man*, however, one sees that Ellison's creative consciousness encompasses a vast range of the world's literature. Such modern giants as Eliot, Joyce, Malraux, Hemingway, Pound, Stein, and Faulkner are clearly part of his literary inheritance, but so are the writers of the Harlem Renaissance; the Continental (especially Dostoevsky), British, and American (especially Melville and Twain) masters of 19th-century fiction; and his namesake Emerson and other Transcendentalists. Some critics have argued for *The Odyssey* or *The Aeneid* as major influences on Ellison's novel. However allusive, Ellison is also profoundly original, putting his sophisticated technique and literary education to the service of his vision of the racial and human condition in America.

Invisible Man concerns the quest of an unnamed young black man for personal identity and racial community as he travels from South to North, from innocence to experience, from self-deception to knowledge, from a spurious visibility to an existential invisibility. These journeys take place in the immediate context of the late depression, but, as they unfold, their implications extend backward in time to the Reconstruction, slavery, and the founding of the Republic, and outward from the protagonist's self to the social situation of black America and to the very nature of the democratic experiment.

Framed by a prologue and an epilogue set in an underground chamber to which the protagonist has retreated from the chaos of life above ground, the narrative proper begins in the deep South with his initiation rite into the social order of white supremacy as he graduates from high school and prepares to matriculate at a black college closely resembling Tuskegee Institute, where he hopes to learn to become a black leader. There the idyllic setting and his personal ambition are disrupted by his naivety, by a northern white capitalist's ambiguous "philanthropy," and by the ruthless self-aggrandizement of Dr. Bledsoe, the black president of the institution. Expelled from college and from the South, the protagonist travels to New York to seek employment in a white-collar position. Unsuccessful in that effort, he undergoes a still more disastrous experience as an industrial worker in the Liberty Paint plant. After these repeated failures in his personal pursuit of success, the protagonist becomes involved with the Brotherhood, a radical political organization paralleling the Communist Party. Here, he hopes, he can achieve self-realization while contributing to social amelioration. But political radicalism fails him—and his race—just as completely as southern segregation and northern employment, and for similar reasons of personal and racial exploitation. When his very physical existence is threatened in a Harlem race riot, he goes underground for sanctuary and reassessment. Ending in the epilogue where it began in the prologue, the narrative completes its circular ("boomerang") structure. Whatever one thinks of the rather forced optimism concerning a possible resurrection and return to the world above ground, the success of which may be viewed as problematical given his repeated rebuffs, the protagonist has at last and at least achieved for himself and for the reader the kind of self-actualization that knowledge of self and society can bring. To that extent he is no longer an invisible man.

Shadow and Act, is a prose miscellany deriving some unity from its tripartite arrangement: "The Seer and the Seen"—topics in literature (especially his own career) and folklore; "Sound and the Mainstream"—topics in music, especially the blues and jazz; and "The Shadow and the Act"—black American social and cultural conditions in the context of national patterns. This organization emphasizes the lifelong interests of the author: books, music, and race.

Ellison's long second novel on religion and politics, published excerpts from which indicate high quality, has been in progress for three decades. It is clear that Ellison's reputation as a novelist will rest not on an ample *oeuvre* but on the brilliance, verbal dexterity, and mythic and social dimensions of one or two books.

—Keneth Kinnamon

See the essay on *Invisible Man*.

EMERSON, Ralph Waldo. Born in Boston, Massachusetts, 25 May 1803. Educated at Boston Latin School; Harvard University, Cambridge, Massachusetts (class poet), A.B. 1821; Harvard Divinity School. Married 1) Ellen Louisa Tucker in 1829 (died, 1831); 2) Lydian Jackson in 1835, two sons and two daughters. Schoolmaster in 1820's; assistant pastor, then pastor, Old Second Church (Unitarian), Boston, 1829-32 (resigned); visited Europe, 1832–33; lyceum lecturer after 1833; moved to Concord, Massachusetts, 1834; a leader of the Transcendental Club from 1836, and contributor to the club's periodical *The Dial*, 1840–44 (editor, 1842–44); lectured in England, 1847–48; active abolitionist in 1850's. LL.D.: Harvard University, 1866. *Died 27 April 1882.*

Publications

Collections

Complete Works. 12 vols., 1883–93; edited by Edward Waldo Emerson, 12 vols., 1903–04.
Letters, edited by Ralph L. Rusk. 6 vols., 1939.
Collected Works, edited by Alfred R. Ferguson. 1971—
Essays and Lectures (Library of America), edited by Joel Porte. 1983.

Verse

Poems. 1847.
Selected Poems. 1876.

Other

Nature. 1836.
Essays. 1841; revised edition, as *Essays: First Series*, 1847; *Second Series*, 1844; revised edition, 1850.
The Young American. 1844.
Nature: An Essay, and Lectures of the Times. 1844.
Orations, Lectures, and Addresses. 1844.
Nature: Addresses and Lectures. 1849.
Representative Men: Seven Lectures. 1850.
English Traits. 1856.
The Conduct of Life. 1860.
Complete Works. 2 vols., 1866.
May-Day and Other Pieces. 1867.
Prose Works. 3 vols., 1868–78(?).
Society and Solitude. 1870.
Letters and Social Aims. 1876.
The Preacher. 1880.
The Correspondence of Carlyle and Emerson 1834–1872, edited by Charles Eliot Norton. 2 vols., 1883; supplement, 1886; edited by Joseph Slater, 1964.
The Senses and the Soul, and Moral Sentiment in Religion: Two Essays. 1884.
Two Unpublished Essays: The Character of Socrates, The Present State of Ethical Philosophy. 1896.
Journals 1820–76, edited by Edward Waldo Emerson and Waldo Emerson Forbes. 10 vols., 1909–14.
Uncollected Writings, edited by Charles C. Bigelow. 1912.
Uncollected Lectures, edited by Clarence Gohdes. 1932.
Young Emerson Speaks: Unpublished Discourses on Many Subjects, edited by Arthur Cushman McGiffert, Jr. 1938.
The Portable Emerson, edited by Mark Van Doren. 1946; revised edition, edited by Carl Bode and Malcolm Cowley, 1981.
Selections, edited by Stephen E. Whicher. 1957.
Early Lectures, edited by Stephen E. Whicher, Robert E. Spiller, and Wallace E. Williams. 3 vols., 1959–72.
Journals and Miscellaneous Notebooks, edited by William H. Gilman and Ralph H. Orth. 16 vols., 1960–83; selection, as *Emerson in His Journals*, edited by Joel Porte, 1982.
Literary Criticism, edited by Eric W. Carlson. 1979.
Selected Essays, edited by Larzer Ziff. 1982.
Poetry Notebooks, edited by Ralph H. Orth and others. 1985.

Editor, *Essays and Poems*, by Jones Very. 1839.
Editor, with James Freeman Clarke and W.H. Channing, *Memoirs of Margaret Fuller Ossoli*. 2 vols., 1852.
Editor, *Excursions*, by Henry David Thoreau. 1863.
Editor, *Letters to Various Persons*, by Henry David Thoreau. 1865.
Editor, *Parnassus* (poetry anthology). 1875.

Translator, *Vita Nuova*, by Dante, edited by J. Chesley Mathews. 1960.

*

Bibliography: *Emerson and the Critics: A Checklist of Criticism 1900–1977* by Jeanetta Boswell, 1979; *Emerson: A Descriptive Bibliography* by Joel Myerson, 1982, and *Emerson: An Annotated Secondary Bibliography* by Myerson and Robert E. Burkholder, 1985.

Critical Studies: *The Life of Emerson* by Ralph L. Rusk, 1949; *Spires of Form: A Study of Emerson's Aesthetic Theory* by Vivian C. Hopkins, 1951; *Emerson's Angle of Vision: Man and Nature in American Experience* by Sherman Paul, 1952; *Emerson Handbook* by Frederic I. Carpenter, 1953; *Freedom and Fate: An Inner Life of Emerson* by Stephen E. Whicher, 1953, *Emerson: A Collection of Critical Essays* edited by Whicher and Milton R. Konvitz, 1962, and *The Recognition of Emerson: Selected Criticism since 1837* edited by Konvitz, 1972; *Emerson and Thoreau: Transcendentalists in Conflict*, 1966, and *Representative Man: Emerson in His Time*, 1979, both by Joel Porte, and *Emerson: Prospect and Retrospect* edited by Porte, 1982; *Emerson among His Contemporaries* edited by Kenneth Walter Cameron, 1967; *Emerson: A Portrait* edited by Carl Bode, 1968; *Emerson's Nature: Origin, Growth, Meaning* edited by Merton M. Sealts, Jr., and Alfred R. Ferguson, 1969, revised edition, edited by Sealts, 1979; *Emerson: Portrait of a Balanced Soul* by Edward Wagenknecht, 1974; *Emerson as Poet* by Hyatt H. Waggoner, 1974; *Emerson: Prophecy, Metamorphosis, and Influence* edited by David Levin, 1975; *The Slender Human Word: Emerson's Artistry in Prose* by William J. Scheik, 1978; *Emerson and Literary Change* by David Porter, 1978; *Emerson and the Orphic Poet in America* by R.A. Yoder, 1978; *Emerson: An Interpretive Essay* by Lewis Leary, 1980; *The Trans-Parent: Sexual Politics in the Language of Emerson* by Eric Cheyfitz, 1981; *Emerson: A Biography* by Gay Wilson Allen, 1981; *Emerson's Fall: A New Interpretation of the Major Essays* by B.L. Packer, 1982; *Emerson, Whitman, and the American Muse* by Jerome Loving, 1982; *Emerson* by Donald Yannella, 1982; *Apostle of Culture: Emerson as Preacher and Lecturer* by David Robinson, 1982; *Emerson Centenary Essays* edited by Joel Myerson, 1982, and *Critical Essays on Emerson* edited by Myerson and Robert E. Burkholder, 1983; *Emerson's Romantic Style* by Julie Ellison, 1984; *Emerson: Days of Encounter* by John J. McAleer, 1984.

* * *

Ralph Waldo Emerson was the most distinguished of the New England Transcendentalists and one of the most brilliant American poets and thinkers of the 19th century. Although Transcendentalism as a mode of Romantic thought has been largely discredited by modern scientific theory, Emerson's essays and poems remain remarkably provocative—and much more tough-minded than they have frequently been given credit for being.

Emerson was not a highly systematic philosopher. His thought was an amalgam from a wide variety of sources: 1) New England religious thought and related English writings of the 17th and 18th centuries; 2) Scottish realism, which he absorbed principally while at Harvard; 3) French and English skepticism, the lasting effects of which should not be underestimated; 4) Neo-Platonism, the dominant element in his thought, especially as it was interpreted by the English Romantic poets and the German and French Idealists; 5) Oriental mystical writings, even though he never accepted their fatalism or their concept of transmigration; 6) Yankee pragmatism, which was latent in almost all of his work and which muted his Romantic Idealism, especially in his essays on political and economic affairs. In Coleridge's explanation of Platonic dualism Emerson found the ordering principle for these disparate strands of thought. The discovery of Coleridge's distinction between the Reason and the Understanding brought such a surge of confidence in him that it is hardly an exaggeration to say that it transformed Emerson's life. Certainly it transformed his thinking.

Within one great Unity, he came to believe, there are two levels of reality, the supernatural and the natural. The supernatural is essence, spirit, or Oversoul as Emerson most frequently called it. It is an impersonal force that is eternal, moral, harmonious, and beneficent in tendency. The individual soul is a part of the Oversoul, and man has access to it through his intuition (which like Coleridge Emerson called the Reason, thereby confusing his readers then and now). One of the tendencies of the Oversoul is to express itself in form, hence the world of nature as an emanation of the world of spirit. The individual has access to this secondary level of reality through the senses and the understanding (the rational faculty). To explain the relation between the spiritual and physical levels of being Emerson used such oppositions as One and Many, cause and effect, unity and diversity, object and symbol, reality and appearance, truth and hypothesis, being and becoming. Since laws of correspondence relate the two levels of being, the study of physical laws can generate intuitions of spiritual truths. What especially delighted Emerson about this dualism was that it allowed him to entertain both faith and doubt: to accept the promptings of the intuition without question and yet to view the hypotheses of the understanding as only tentative and hence constantly open to question.

In his earlier essays, Emerson particularly stressed the unlimited potential of the individual. The most notable of these, *Nature*, argues that, although nature serves as commodity, beauty, language, and discipline, its most important function is to excite the intuition so that the individual through a mystical experience becomes aware of the power of the Oversoul residing within him. "Nature always speaks of Spirit. It suggests the absolute." "The American Scholar" (1837) warns that books and scholarship can divert one from seeking the spiritual power within, and the "Divinity School Address" (1838) suggests that historical Christianity can do the same. "Self Reliance" (1844), in metaphor after metaphor, challenges the reader to seek the truths of the Reason: "Trust thyself; every heart vibrates to that iron string." In many respects "Self Reliance" is the capstone of American Romanticism. Later essays are more guarded in announcing the individual's limitless potential. In "Experience" (1844), for example, Emerson admits that such this-world elements as health, temperament, and illusion can prevent one from exploiting all of the vast possibilities asserted in *Nature*. The enormous confidence of his earlier essays dwindles to "Patience and Patience, we shall win at last."

On subjects of public interest, Emerson's philosophical liberalism had to contend with his pragmatism. At most he was a cautious liberal. The Democrats, he thought, had the better causes, the Whigs the better men. Following Adam Smith, he believed that "affairs themselves show the best way they should be handled." So he was for *laissez-faire* and free trade, though he was more of an agrarian than Smith. Of the followers of Smith he rejected the utilitarians and the pessimists, and approved of only the optimists, particularly such members of the American school as Daniel Raymond, A.H. Everett, and Henry C. Carey. Emerson had nothing against wealth *per se*, but was against rule by the wealthy because the wealthy were too likely to be nothing more than materialists, persons without intuitive insight. Rule by an upper class, however, was agreeable to him so long as the upper class consisted of persons wise, temperate, and cultivated, persons with the insight and courage necessary to protect the poor and weak against the predatory. Clearly his thinking did not drift far in the direction of Marxism. Nor was he willing to admit that the socialistic experiments of Owen and Fourier, though he admired their objectives, had the magic key to Utopia. Even the Transcendental experiments at Fruitlands and Brook Farm he believed impractical. Bereft of their romance, he said, they were projects that well might make their participants less intuitive and self-reliant rather than more so. Of the other major reforms of his day, Emerson lectured only in favor of child labor legislation, a public land policy, and the abolition of slavery. The passage of the Fugitive Slave Bill in 1850 made him as angry as he probably ever became on a public issue. More practical than most abolitionists, however, he argued that slavery was basically an economic matter, and that if the Northern church people really wanted to emancipate the slaves they should sell their church silver, buy up the slaves, and themselves set them free. He saw the Civil War not only as necessary for liberating the slave but "a hope for the liberation of American culture."

Emerson's aesthetic theory, to the extent that he had one, is a direct outgrowth of his Idealistic philosophy. As he conceived of it, the great work of art is not an imitation of nature but a symbolization of Truth realized intuitively. It is the result of resigning oneself to the "divine *aura* which breathes through forms." In his most quoted statement on the subject he put it this way: "It is not metres, but a metre-making argument that makes a poem—a thought so passionate and alive that like the spirit of a plant or animal it has an architecture of its own, and adorns nature with a new thing." Thus the poet (or any great artist) must first of all be the Seer, intuitively experiencing the absolutes of the Oversoul, and secondly the Sayer, communicating those absolutes so compellingly that readers are stimulated to have intuitions of their own. Emerson was realistic enough to realize that such a process is not easy. Intuitions fade quickly. And words, being but symbols of symbols, are inadequate even at best to convey them. The most that a writer can do is to suggest his intuitions by a series of half-truths. The greatest writing, therefore, must be provocative, not descriptive or explanatory. Such a conviction lies behind Emerson's epigrammatic prose style and the liberties he takes with poetic conventions.

There is a good reason for considering Emerson as primarily a poet even though one must go to his journals and essays to realize the fullness of his thought. His concentration on the concrete image, the simplicity of his symbols and words, and his willingness within limits to let form follow function were practices that profoundly influenced such widely divergent followers as Whitman and Dickinson and through them much of modern poetry. Many of Emerson's best-known poems, such as "Concord Hymn" and "The Snow Storm," celebrate local events. But his more notable ones give expression to elements of his philosophy. Through the voice of the cosmic force, "Brahma" suggests the enclosure of all diversity in the one great Unity; so does "Each and All" in which the beauty and meaning of "each" is seen to be dependent upon its context, or the "all." "The Problem" contrasts the unlimited freedom of the poet's imagination with the stultifying routine of the "cowed churchman." Perhaps Emerson's most poignant poem is "Threnody," written in two periods after the death of his young son Waldo. The first part, composed immediately after Waldo's death, describes the poet's disillusionment with nature, indeed with the cosmic scheme, which he had spent so many years celebrating. The second part, written several years later, asserts his resurgent confidence. Nathaniel Hawthorne probably spoke for some modern readers when he said that he "admired Emerson as a poet of deep beauty and austere tenderness, but sought nothing from him as a philosopher." Yet his philosophy cannot be dismissed so summarily. It resulted in a freedom of spirit, a respect for the individual human being, a sense of awe and wonder before the inexplicable that many modern readers still find stirring and reassuring.

—John C. Gerber

See the essay on *Nature*.

FARRELL, James T(homas). Born in Chicago, Illinois, 27 February 1904. Educated at St. Anselm Grammar School, and St. Cyril High School, both Chicago; DePaul University, Chicago, 1924–25; University of Chicago, 1926–29; New York University, 1941. Married 1) Dorothy Butler in 1931 (divorced); 2) Hortense Alden (divorced, 1955), one son; 3) remarried Dorothy Butler in 1955 (separated, 1958). Clerk for an express company, Chicago, 1922–24; writer from 1930; lived in Paris, 1931–32; Adjunct Professor, St. Peter's College, Jersey City, New Jersey, 1964–65; Writer-in-Residence, Richmond College, Virginia, 1969–70, and Glassboro State College, New Jersey, 1973. Chairman, National Board, Workers Defense League. Recipient: Guggenheim fellowship, 1936; Emerson-Thoreau Medal, 1979. D.Litt.: Miami University, Oxford, Ohio, 1968; Columbia College, Chicago, 1974. Member, American Academy, 1941. *Died 22 August 1979.*

PUBLICATIONS

Fiction

Studs Lonigan. 1935.
Young Lonigan: A Boyhood in Chicago Streets. 1932.
The Young Manhood of Studs Lonigan. 1934.
Judgment Day. 1935.
Gas-House McGinty. 1933.
Calico Shoes and Other Stories. 1934; as *Seventeen and Other Stories*, 1959.
Guillotine Party and Other Stories. 1935.

Danny O'Neill pentalogy
A World I Never Made. 1936.
No Star Is Lost. 1938.
Father and Son. 1940; as *A Father and His Son*, 1943.
My Days of Anger. 1943.
The Face of Time. 1953.
Can All This Grandeur Perish? and Other Stories. 1937.
The Short Stories. 1937; as *Fellow Countrymen: Collected Stories*, 1937.
Tommy Gallagher's Crusade. 1939.
Ellen Rogers. 1941.
$1000 a Week and Other Stories. 1942.
Fifteen Selected Stories. 1943.
To Whom It May Concern and Other Stories. 1944.
When Boyhood Dreams Come True. 1946.
More Fellow Countrymen. 1946.
Bernard Carr trilogy
Bernard Clare. 1946; as *Bernard Clayre*, 1948; as *Bernard Carr*, 1952.
The Road Between. 1949.
Yet Other Waters. 1952.
The Life Adventurous and Other Stories. 1947.
Yesterday's Love and Eleven Other Stories, edited by Donald A. Wollheim. 1948.
A Misunderstanding (story). 1949.
A Hell of a Good Time and Other Stories, edited by Donald A. Wollheim. 1950.
An American Dream Girl (stories). 1950.
This Man and This Woman. 1951.
French Girls Are Vicious and Other Stories. 1955.
An Omnibus of Short Stories. 1956.
A Dangerous Woman and Other Stories. 1957.
Saturday Night and Other Stories. 1958.
The Girls at the Sphinx (stories). 1959.
Looking 'em Over (stories). 1960.
Side Street and Other Stories. 1961.
Boarding House Blues. 1961.
Sound of a City. 1962.
A Universe of Time
The Silence of History. 1963.
What Time Collects. 1964.
When Time Was Born. 1966.
Lonely for the Future. 1966.
A Brand New Life. 1968.
Judith. 1969.
Invisible Swords. 1971.
Judith and Other Stories. 1973.
The Dunne Family. 1976.
The Death of Nora Ryan. 1978.
Olive and Mary Anne (stories). 1978.
New Year's Eve/1929. 1967.
Childhood Is Not Forever and Other Stories. 1969.
Sam Holman. 1983.

Verse

The Collected Poems. 1965.

Other

A Note on Literary Criticism. 1936.
The League of Frightened Philistines and Other Papers. 1945.
The Fate of Writing in America. 1946.
Literature and Morality. 1947.
The Name Is Fogarty: Private Papers on Public Matters. 1950.
Poet of the People: An Evaluation of James Whitcomb Riley, with Horace Gregory and Jeannette Covert Nolan. 1951.
Reflections at Fifty and Other Essays. 1954.
My Baseball Diary: A Famed Author Recalls the Wonderful World of Baseball, Yesterday and Today. 1957.
It Has Come to Pass (on Israel). 1958.
Dialogue with John Dewey, with others. 1959.
Selected Essays, edited by Luna Wolf. 1964.
Literary Essays 1954–1974, edited by Jack Alan Robbins. 1976.
On Irish Themes, edited by Dennis Flynn. 1982.
Hearing Out Farrell (lectures), edited by Donald Phelps. 1985.

Editor, *Prejudices: A Selection*, by H.L. Mencken. 1958.
Editor, *A Dreiser Reader*. 1962.

*

Bibliography: *A Bibliography of Farrell's Writings 1921–1957* by Edgar M. Branch, 1959, supplements in *American Book Collector 11*, 1961, *17*, 1967, and *26*, 1976.

Critical Studies: *Farrell* by Edgar M. Branch, 1971; *Farrell: The Revolutionary Socialist Years* by Alan M. Wald, 1978.

* * *

The son and grandson of Irish Catholic working-class laborers, James T. Farrell was raised in a South-Side Chicago neighborhood that became the source for much of his remarkable body of work, which constitutes the greatest sustained production in 20th-century America of uncompromisingly realistic fiction. Filling, to date, some fifty volumes, this corpus includes four large fictional cycles, three of which are further connected as progressive explorations of their main characters' varying responses to an urban ethnic environment similar to Farrell's. Published between 1932 and 1953, these three related groups are the Studs Lonigan trilogy, the O'Neill-O'Flaherty pentalogy, and the Bernard Carr trilogy.

Begun with Farrell's first novel, *Young Lonigan*, the first group traces the downward drift to death at 29 of its weak-willed, misguided protagonist. A normally inquisitive boy, Studs shows signs of intelligence, even imagination, in early scenes. And yet he assumes the facile and corrupting "tough guy" values of the Chicago street-corner society to which he is drawn after graduation from eighth grade. As a partial explanation of the boy's failure of judgment, the trilogy chronicles the breakdown in the 20th-century city of the previously directing institutions of family, school, and church, and Studs's origin in a well-fixed, middle-class family makes the indictment of urban "spiritual poverty" (Farrell's phrase) all the more severe. The result is a powerful narrative, terrifying in its seemingly inexorable progress to *Judgment Day*, an American tragedy in the Dreiserian mold.

In the O'Neill-O'Flaherty novels, Farrell uses his own family history much more directly. The main figure is Danny O'Neill, a slightly younger contemporary of Studs Lonigan who takes an opposite road—out of Chicago and toward understanding and control of his own life. More intelligent than Studs, Danny is driven by a persistent dream of accomplishment that crystallizes into the desire to be a writer. On the other hand, he also sometimes slips into aimless idling and drinking, and his economic and family situations are potentially dangerous to his normal development. The O'Neills are so poor that some of the children, including Danny, have had to be raised by his mother's parents, the O'Flahertys. This arrangement alienates Danny but provides the pentalogy with a large number of major characters, including his grandfather, Tom O'Flaherty, an aging immigrant teamster, fully evoked in *The Face of Time*, and his grandmother, an archetypal Irish-American matriarch, strong-willed and fiercely maternal, who dominates the early novels of the series. Danny's father, Jim O'Neill, works his way from teamster to shipping clerk, only to be dealt a cruel, decisive blow by a series of paralyzing strokes. His hysterical, hyper-religious wife, Lizz, is no help to him, and in *Father and Son* Jim faces inutility, boredom, and approaching death—but with lonely courage and dignity that make him one of the most memorable characters in Farrell's fiction. Painful attempts at closeness between "father and son," Danny's high school graduation, and Jim's death bring the novel to its climax. In *My Days of Anger*, Danny begins to find his way, through attendance at the University of Chicago, great gulps of reading, and a final decision in 1927 to leave Chicago for New York and a writing career.

Instead of the tight, fatalistic narrative drive of the Lonigan trilogy, the five O'Neill-O'Flaherty novels are diffused and episodic; and in this looser structure is embodied a broader, more open and optimistic, but still unsentimentalized view of urban society. Moreover, in his complex creation of the interrelated lives of the O'Neills and O'Flahertys, Farrell has provided the most thoroughly realized immigrant-ethnic community in American literature.

The Bernard Carr trilogy, published between 1946 and 1952, continues the action of the O'Neill novels in dealing with the young manhood of a working-class Chicago Irishman with literary ambitions who has fled to New York in search of experience and perspective. His ambition is akin to that of Joyce's Stephen Dedalus, with whom Farrell's O'Neill/Carr figure has much in common. In these novels of education, Bernard Carr learns to reject the Catholic Church, his own naive appropriation of Nietzsche, and the Communist Party, all of which he comes to find as threatening to his artistic integrity. His emergence as a successful writer rounds out the Lonigan-O'Neill-Carr connected cycles. The Carr trilogy lacks the rootedness in place and community of the previous Chicago-based novels, but it compensates by providing a vivid rendering of the lives of New York left-wing intellectuals in the 1930's, with particular attention given to their passionate engagement with the question of the relationship between the artist and society.

In addition to his large cycles and a few isolated novels, Farrell published about 250 short stories and novelettes, in which his presentation of 20th-century life became even more inclusive. Many stories concern the protagonists of his novels (there are fifty about Danny O'Neill alone); others place new characters in familiar Chicago or New York settings, and still others are set in Europe, especially Paris. True to Farrell's realistic aesthetic, the stories are strong on character revelation and spurn machinations of plot.

Farrell's critical writings also fill several volumes; these contain useful explanations of the relationship between his life and his work, appreciations of writers who have been important to him, including Dreiser, Joyce, and Sherwood Anderson, and declarations of his position as a realist who writes "as part of an attempt to explore the nature of experience."

In 1963 Farrell published *The Silence of History*, his sixteenth novel, and the first of *A Universe of Time*, his fourth fictional cycle, which, in his heroic projection, would have run to thirty volumes. Integrated by the central recurrent character of Eddie Ryan, another Chicago writer, born, like his creator, in 1904, the *Universe* cycle embodies a reassessment of Farrell's life-long concern with the experience of the artist in the modern world, as well as a continuation of the "lifework" that he defined, in an introduction to the new cycle's sixth unit, *Judith*, as "a panoramic story of our days and years, a story which would continue through as many books as I would be able to write."

Farrell was first and foremost an American realist: fiercely and scrupulously honest, immune to sentimentality, and, in the earlier novels especially, pioneering in his commitment to giving serious literary consideration to the common life in an urban-immigrant-ethnic community. In his later fiction he often went beyond Chicago and the Irish to explore more widely his most important themes—the possibilities in modern life for self-knowledge, growth, and creativity. Farrell died in 1979, leaving much fiction in manuscript. His first posthumously published work, *Sam Holman*, is a novel of New York intellectual life in the 1930's.

Farrell's great strengths as a novelist are his development of convincing characters, the firm placement of these characters in a detailed, realistic urban setting, and the ability to conceive and carry through monumental fictional cycles. In addition, he perfected an urban American plain style, an appropriate mode for registering the self-consciousness of ordinary people living relatively uneventful lives. In his best work, a hard-won, minimal eloquence emerges from the convincingly registered thoughts of such characters as Jim O'Neill and Old Tom O'Flaherty. Farrell achieved what he declared to be "my constant and major aim as a writer—to write so that life may speak for itself." In this vein, his fullest and most compassionate creation remains Chicago's Irish Catholic South Side, which emerges in his fiction as a realized world, as whole and coherent as Faulkner's Mississippi.

—Charles Fanning

FAULKNER, William. Born William Cuthbert Falkner in New Albany, Mississippi, 25 September 1897; moved with his family to Oxford, Mississippi, 1902. Educated at local schools in Oxford, and at the University of Mississippi, Oxford, 1919–20. Served in the Royal Canadian Air Force, 1918. Married Estelle Oldham Franklin in 1929; two daughters. Bookkeeper in bank, 1916–18; worked in Doubleday Bookshop, New York, 1921; postmaster, University of Mississippi Post Office, 1921–24; lived in New Orleans and contributed to New Orleans *Times-Picayune*, 1925; traveled in Europe, 1925–26; returned to Oxford, 1927; thereafter a full-time writer; screenwriter for Metro-Goldwyn-Mayer, 1932–33, 20th Century-Fox, 1935–37, and Warner Brothers, 1942–45; Writer-in-Residence, University of Virginia, Charlottesville, 1957, and part of each year, 1958–62. Recipient: O. Henry Award, 1939, 1949; Nobel Prize for Literature, 1950; American Academy Howells Medal, 1950; National Book Award, 1951, 1955; Pulitzer Prize, 1955, 1963; American Academy of Arts and Letters Gold Medal, 1962. Member, National Institute of Arts and

Letters, 1939, and American Academy, 1948. *Died 6 July 1962.*

PUBLICATIONS

Collections

The Portable Faulkner, edited by Malcolm Cowley. 1946; revised edition, 1967.
The Faulkner Reader, edited by Saxe Commins. 1954.
Selected Letters, edited by Joseph Blotner. 1977.
Letters, edited by Louis Daniel Brodsky and Robert W. Hamblin. 1984.
Novels 1930–35 (Library of America), edited by Joseph Blotner and Noel Polk. 1985.

Fiction

Soldiers' Pay. 1926.
Mosquitoes. 1927.
Sartoris. 1929; original version, as *Flags in the Dust*, edited by Douglas Day, 1973.
The Sound and the Fury. 1929.
As I Lay Dying. 1930.
Sanctuary. 1931.
These 13: Stories. 1931.
Idyll in the Desert. 1931.
Light in August. 1932.
Miss Zilphia Gant. 1932.
Doctor Martino and Other Stories. 1934.
Pylon. 1935.
Absalom, Absalom! 1936.
The Unvanquished. 1938.
The Wild Palms (includes *Old Man*). 1939.
The Hamlet. 1940; excerpt, as *The Long Hot Summer*, 1958.
Go Down, Moses, and Other Stories. 1942.
Intruder in the Dust. 1948.
Knight's Gambit (stories). 1949.
Collected Stories. 1950.
Notes on a Horsethief. 1950.
Requiem for a Nun. 1951.
A Fable. 1954.
Big Woods (stories). 1955.
Faulkner County. 1955.
Jealousy and Episode: Two Stories. 1955.
The Town. 1957.
Uncle Willy and Other Stories. 1958.
The Mansion. 1959.
Selected Short Stories. 1961.
The Reivers: A Reminiscence. 1962.
Barn Burning and Other Stories. 1977.
Uncollected Stories, edited by Joseph Blotner. 1979.
Father Abraham, edited by James B. Meriwether. 1984.

Plays

The Marionettes (produced 1920). 1975; edited by Noel Polk, 1977.
Requiem for a Nun (produced 1957). 1951.
The Big Sleep, with Leigh Brackett and Jules Furthman, in *Film Scripts One*, edited by George P. Garrett, O.B. Harrison, Jr., and Jane Gelfmann. 1971.
To Have and Have Not (screenplay), with Jules Furthman. 1980.
The Road to Glory (screenplay), with Joel Sayre. 1981.
Faulkner's MGM Screenplays, edited by Bruce F. Kawin. 1983.
The DeGaulle Story (unproduced screenplay), edited by Louis Daniel Brodsky and Robert W. Hamblin. 1984.
Battle Cry (unproduced screenplay), edited by Louis Daniel Brodsky and Robert W. Hamblin. 1985.

Screenplays: *Today We Live*, with Edith Fitzgerald and Dwight Taylor, 1933; *The Road to Glory*, with Joel Sayre, 1936; *Slave Ship*, with others, 1937; *Air Force* (uncredited), with Dudley Nichols, 1943; *To Have and Have Not*, with Jules Furthman, 1945; *The Big Sleep*, with Leigh Brackett and Jules Furthman, 1946; *Land of the Pharaohs*, with Harry Kurnitz and Harold Jack Bloom, 1955.

Television Play: *The Graduation Dress*, with Joan Williams, 1960.

Verse

The Marble Faun. 1924.
Salmagundi (includes prose), edited by Paul Romaine. 1932.
This Earth. 1932.
A Green Bough. 1933.
Mississippi Poems. 1979.
Helen: A Courtship, and Mississippi Poems. 1981.
Vision in Spring. 1984.

Other

Mirrors of Chartres Street. 1953.
New Orleans Sketches, edited by Ichiro Nishizaki. 1955; revised edition, edited by Carvel Collins, 1958.
On Truth and Freedom. 1955(?).
Faulkner at Nagano (interview), edited by Robert A. Jelliffe. 1956.
Faulkner in the University (interviews), edited by Frederick L. Gwynn and Joseph Blotner. 1959.
University Pieces, edited by Carvel Collins. 1962.
Early Prose and Poetry, edited by Carvel Collins. 1962.
Faulkner at West Point (interviews), edited by Joseph L. Fant and Robert Ashley. 1964.
The Faulkner-Cowley File: Letters and Memories 1944–1962, with Malcolm Cowley. 1966.
Essays, Speeches, and Public Letters, edited by James B. Meriwether. 1966.
The Wishing Tree (for children). 1967.
Lion in the Garden: Interviews with Faulkner 1926–1962, edited by James B. Meriwether and Michael Millgate. 1968.
Mayday. 1978.
Sherwood Anderson and Other Famous Creoles. 1986.

*

Bibliography: *The Literary Career of Faulkner: A Bibliographical Study* by James B. Meriwether, 1961; *Faulkner: A Reference Guide* by Thomas L. McHaney, 1976; *Faulkner: A Bibliography of Secondary Works* by Beatrice Ricks, 1981; *Faulkner: The Bio-Bibliography* by Louis Daniel Brodsky and

Robert W. Hamblin, 1982; *Faulkner: An Annotated Checklist of Recent Criticism* by John Earl Bassett, 1983.

Critical Studies: *Faulkner: A Critical Study* by Irving Howe, 1952, revised edition, 1962, 1975; *Faulkner* by Hyatt H. Waggoner, 1959; *The Novels of Faulkner* by Olga W. Vickery, 1959, revised edition, 1964; *Faulkner* by Frederick J. Hoffman, 1961, revised edition, 1966; *Faulkner: The Yoknapatawpha Country*, 1963, *Faulkner: Toward Yoknapatawpha and Beyond*, 1978, and *Faulkner: First Encounters*, 1983, all by Cleanth Brooks; *Faulkner's People* by Robert W. Kirk and Marvin Klotz, 1963; *A Reader's Guide to Faulkner* by Edmond L. Volpe, 1964; *Faulkner: A Collection of Critical Essays* edited by Robert Penn Warren, 1966; *The Achievement of Faulkner* by Michael Millgate, 1966; *Faulkner: Myth and Motion* by Richard P. Adams, 1968; *Faulkner of Yoknapatawpha County* by Lewis Leary, 1973; *Faulkner's Narrative* by Joseph W. Reed, Jr., 1973; *Faulkner: Four Decades of Criticism* edited by Linda W. Wagner, 1973, and *Hemingway and Faulkner: Inventors/Masters* by Wagner, 1975; *Faulkner: A Collection of Criticism* edited by Dean M. Schmitter, 1973; *Faulkner: The Abstract and the Actual* by Panthea Reid Broughton, 1974; *Faulkner: A Biography* by Joseph Blotner, 2 vols., 1974, revised and condensed edition, 1 vol., 1984; *A Faulkner Miscellany* edited by James B. Meriwether, 1974; *Doubling and Incest/Repetition and Revenge: A Speculative Reading of Faulkner* by John T. Irwin, 1975; *Faulkner: The Critical Heritage* edited by John Earl Bassett, 1975; *A Glossary of Faulkner's South* by Calvin S. Brown, 1976; *The Most Splendid Failure: Faulkner's The Sound and the Fury* by André Bleikasten, 1976, and *Faulkner's The Sound and the Fury: A Critical Casebook* edited by Bleikasten, 1982; *Faulkner's Heroic Design: The Yoknapatawpha Novels* by Lynn Levins, 1976; *Faulkner's Craft of Revision* by Joanne V. Creighton, 1977; *Faulkner's Women: The Myth and the Muse* by David L. Williams, 1977; *Faulkner's Narrative Poetics* by Arthur F. Kinney, 1978, and *Critical Essays on Faulkner: The Compson Family*, 1982, and *The Sartoris Family*, 1985, both edited by Kinney; *The Fragile Thread: The Meaning of Form in Faulkner's Novels* by Donald M. Kartiganer, 1979; *Faulkner's Career: An Internal Literary History* by Gary Lee Stonum, 1979; *Faulkner: The Transfiguration of Biography* by Judith Wittenberg, 1979; *Faulkner's Yoknapatawpha Comedy* by Lyall H. Powers, 1980; *Faulkner: His Life and Work* by David Minter, 1980; *The Heart of Yoknapatawpha* by John Pilkington, 1981; *Faulkner's Characters: An Index to the Published and Unpublished Fiction* by Thomas E. Dasher, 1981; *Faulkner: The Short Story Career: An Outline of Faulkner's Short Story Writing from 1919 to 1962*, 1981, and *Faulkner: The Novelist as Short Story Writer*, 1985, both by Hans H. Skei; *A Faulkner Overview: Six Perspectives* by Victor Strandberg, 1981; *Faulkner: Biographical and Reference Guide* and *Critical Collection* edited by Leland H. Cox, 2 vols., 1982; *The Play of Faulkner's Language* by John T. Matthews, 1982; *The Art of Faulkner* by John Pikoulis, 1982; *Faulkner's "Negro": Art and the Southern Context* by Thadious M. Davis, 1983; *Faulkner: The House Divided* by Eric J. Sundquist, 1983; *Faulkner's Yoknapatawpha* by Elizabeth M. Kerr, 1983; *Faulkner: New Perspectives* edited by Richard Brodhead, 1983; *The Origins of Faulkner's Art* by Judith Sensibar, 1984; *Uses of the Past in the Novels of Faulkner* by Carl E. Rollyson, Jr., 1984; *Faulkner's Absalom, Absalom! A Critical Casebook* edited by Elizabeth Muhlenfeld, 1984; *A Faulkner Chronology* by Michel Gresset, 1985; *Faulkner* by Alan Warren Friedman, 1985; *Genius of Place: Faulkner's Triumphant Beginnings* by Max Putzel, 1985; *Faulkner's Humor* and *Faulkner and Women* both edited by Doreen Fowler and Ann J. Abadie, 1986; *Figures of Division: Faulkner's Major Novels* by James A. Snead, 1986; *Heart in Conflict: Faulkner's Struggles with Vocation* by Michael Grimwood, 1986.

* * *

William Faulkner often said that he regarded poetry as the most difficult genre and himself as a "failed poet." Although he wrote prose quite early, he devoted most of his energy as a beginning writer to verse, imitating Housman and Swinburne, translating French Symbolist poets, and coming under the spell of Pound and Eliot. *The Marble Faun*, however, was a cycle of pastoral poems, and one of the keys to both the complexity and power of his mature prose is the carryover of poetic techniques and pastoral imagery into his realistic fiction. In his Waste Land novel, *Soldiers' Pay*, he struck the contemporary note of postwar disillusionment, but in his third, *Sartoris*, he set his scene in Mississippi and began to mine the resources of his native region. Conventional in technique, this novel drew upon his own family, especially Colonel William C. Falkner, in the creation of Colonel John Sartoris and his troubled descendants. Placed in opposition to them were the Snopeses, a family of landless whites. In their craft, rapacity, and savagery, they represented the negative aspects of the rise of the new man in the New South but also perennial facets of human nature castigated by literature's classic moralists and satirists.

By the time Faulkner began his next novel he had not only read Joyce and imitated Eliot, he had also composed highly experimental drama and prose tales. All of this exploration and maturation, together with the frustration he felt at repeated rejections of the manuscript of *Sartoris*, combined to produce in his new work a novel of extraordinary power and poetic sensibility. In *The Sound and the Fury* he told the story of the tragic Compson family from four different points of view, employing complex patterns of image and symbol and exploiting the stream of consciousness technique quite as much as Joyce had done. This novel, showing him suddenly at the height of his powers, would later be studied and explicated almost as much as Joyce's *Ulysses*.

In his next two works he employed the Chickasaw name he had chosen for his apocryphal county: Yoknapatawpha. One of these, *Sanctuary*, seemed *grand guignol* to some readers, updated Greek tragedy to others. Its violence and atrocities in a gangland setting, combined with ribald humor and poetic sensibility, constituted a virtuoso performance which gained Faulkner the mass attention which had eluded him. But books such as *As I Lay Dying* repelled many readers, not only because their poor southern whites seemed strange and often violent, but also because of the technical complexity with which Faulkner presented them, employing 59 separate interior monologues to tell the story of the Bundrens and their disaster-plagued journey undertaken to bury their mother in her family plot.

In novels such as *Light in August* Faulkner continued his exploration of the range of human possibility, not only "the human heart in conflict with itself," but also man in conflict with society, as in the case of Joe Christmas, who does not know whether he is white or black and cannot come to terms with life in either of these worlds. Here Faulkner continued his probing into the psychologies of his characters, their lives deeply determined by their past. Increasingly he employed flashbacks, shifts in chronology, and poetic renderings of perception combined with vivid factual narration and scrupulous use of dialects both black and white.

Now clearly a master of prose fiction, Faulkner published his second and last book of verse, *A Green Bough*, comprising poems written over a decade or more. Embodying several different styles, they showed his versatility but justified his earlier judgment that he was primarily a fiction writer and not a poet. One critic, however, would aptly call him an epic poet in prose.

When *Absalom, Absalom!* appeared (the novel which would challenge *The Sound and the Fury* for pre-eminence), it revealed not only the further exploration of Yoknapatawpha County and its people but also Faulkner's use of the mystery story genre in his attempts to understand history. In part a narrative of the Civil War, it went beyond the regional and the particular to constants in human experience. Like *The Sound and the Fury*, it left some questions unanswered in a kind of aesthetic expression of a principle of indeterminacy in human life. Continuing his work in shorter fiction, Faulkner depicted his county in the days before the white man came in a sequence of Indian stories which showed his imaginative grasp of another people's culture. Other short stories were later reworked, deepened, and augmented to form novels: *The Unvanquished*, a further tale of the Sartoris family and the south; *The Hamlet*, an account of country people and particularly the Snopeses, whose rise would be further chronicled in *The Town* and *The Mansion*; and *Go Down, Moses*, a narrative of the relations between black and white in Yoknapatawpha County.

A striking quality in his fiction was the interrelationships from book to book, as though the whole panorama of his creation was there in his mind at once, with people, places, and events to be summoned up at will, at times even seeming to obsess him, demanding his creative efforts whether he willed it or not. Nearly twenty years after *Sanctuary* he brought back the ill-starred Temple Drake in a work which explored her partial atonement and that of her husband for their sins in *Sanctuary*. Begun as a play, *Requiem for a Nun* refused to coalesce for Faulkner, and so he turned to narrative prose, introducing each act with a long prologue which set this new drama of passion and murder against the history of Yoknapatawpha County, beginning in the dawn of time and coming up to the present.

Faulkner did not, however, limit himself to settings in Yoknapatawpha, as *A Fable*, set in France during the Great War, testified. More than ten years in the writing, this book was the only one, Faulkner would say, that he had ever written from an idea: what would happen if Christ were to return, giving man his last chance not only for salvation but for survival? His retelling of the story of Christ's Passion and Death during the false armistice on the Western Front was in its way his most explicit statement of his own humanistic faith, using conventional Christian lore as a metaphor. The novel was an ambitious if not wholly successful attempt at a kind of summary statement.

But it was in the Yoknapatawpha novels that his genius found its fullest expression. *The Town* and *The Mansion* completed his chronicle of the rise of the Snopeses and the decline of the Sartoris class, reflecting social changes in the south over the better part of a century yet at the same time remaining faithful to such patterns in other times and other societies. Though these novels had in them something of the same quality of family chronicle as had the earlier *Sartoris*, he continued his technical experimentation, passing the narration from one major character to another and intervening in an omniscient narrative voice when his strategy demanded it. In this latter part of his career, a volume of detective stories and a volume of hunting stories testified to his continuing vigor and versatility. One book, *Intruder in the Dust*, had begun as a detective story turned into a novel, and evolved as well into a study of racial prejudice and conflict in the south and the process by which a young white boy came to see the humanity of the innocent Negro whom he helped to save from lynching. Faulkner's last book, a kind of valedictory, was a retrospective and often mellow novel, a story of a boy's initiation which was amusing and touching by turns. *The Reivers* showed him once more as master of this domain he had created and exploited as no one had done since Balzac.

Thus it is that he can be called the greatest of modern American novelists. To his strongest admirers he is the greatest of American novelists, a claim that rests upon his prodigious creativity and productivity, his extraordinary mastery of literary techniques, and a breadth of characterization and insight into the human condition which made Yoknapatawpha County a paradigm for the larger world beyond its forests and rivers.

—Joseph Blotner

See the essays on *Absalom, Absalom!* and *The Sound and the Fury*.

FEARING, Kenneth (Flexner). Born in Oak Park, Illinois, 28 July 1902. Educated at public schools in Oak Park; University of Wisconsin, Madison, B.A. 1924. Married 1) Rachel Meltzer in 1933, one son; 2) Nan Lurie in 1945 (divorced, 1958). Reporter in Chicago; free-lance writer in New York from 1925: contributor to poetry magazines, and staff writer, *Time* magazine. Recipient: Guggenheim fellowship, 1936, 1939; American Academy award, 1945. *Died 26 June 1961*.

PUBLICATIONS

Verse

Angel Arms. 1929.
Poems. 1935.
Dead Reckoning. 1938.
Collected Poems. 1940.
Afternoon of a Pawnbroker and Other Poems. 1943.
Stranger at Coney Island and Other Poems. 1948.
New and Selected Poems. 1956.

Fiction

The Hospital. 1939.
Dagger of the Mind. 1941; as *Cry Killer!*, 1958.
Clark Gifford's Body. 1942.
The Big Clock. 1946.
John Barry, with Donald Friede and Henry Bedford-Jones. 1947.
Loneliest Girl in the World. 1951; as *The Sound of Murder*, 1952.
The Generous Heart. 1954.
The Crozart Story. 1960.

*

Critical Study: "The Meaning of Fearing's Poetry" by M.L. Rosenthal, in *Poetry*, July 1944.

* * *

Poet, novelist, and editor, Kenneth Fearing is associated with the literature of disillusionment written in America during the 1930's and 1940's when technological achievements and social institutions appeared incapable of remedying the profound evils of economic depression. Severely affected by the senseless suffering he perceived in his environment, Fearing became disillusioned with capitalistic systems of government and industry, espousing instead a Marxist belief in the inherent goodness of common men, whom he hoped would unite and lead the world into a new era of utopian humanism.

Into this crusade for social justice Fearing enlisted his talents as a writer. His poetry earned him the admiration of his contemporaries and a lasting position of respect in modern literature. The deft ironic tone which characterizes much of Fearing's poetry, and which undercuts the optimism of the Whitmanesque lines in which he wrote, is admirably suited to capturing his anger and bitterness at the disregard of institutions for the liberties of the individual, and his sympathy and pity for those people who were trapped by social circumstance in sterile urban environments where they were forced by industrial and political taskmasters to lead mechanical lives of quiet desperation.

But if the economic and social conditions of the 1930's provided Fearing with the subject matter for his poetry, they also limited the scope of his poetic growth. In many respects, Fearing's hatreds and fears shackle his imagination to themes and obsessions which do not sustain repeated or extended treatment. As a result, the reader who indulges in more than one volume of Fearing's poems receives the impression that while the setting and characters of his poems may vary from volume to volume the ideas which they embody remain the same. In his best poems, however, Fearing captures the anxieties, hopes, and frustrations of his generation with sensitivity and depth. At least two of Fearing's books of poetry, *Dead Reckoning* and *Afternoon of a Pawnbroker*, repay close reading.

As a novelist Fearing specialized in pulp thrillers into which he interjected social commentary. His first novel, *The Hospital*, is replete with scandals and intrigues which expose the machinations behind the workings of the medical profession. Equally shocking and equally involved are *Clark Gifford's Body*, a murder mystery which explores the possibility of revolution in America, and *The Generous Heart*, a novel which depicts the graft and greed involved in the misappropriation of funds by a charitable organization. Another novel, *The Big Clock*, proved so popular that it became the subject of a film. Ostensibly about a murder, *The Big Clock* also analyzes the ruthlessness of journalistic rivalry and muckraking. Fearing excelled in the use of multiple, first-person narrators, and while this technique sometimes detracted from the movement of his plots it allowed him the opportunity to develop in his many detective and mystery novels considerably more psychological complexity than most of his predecessors in these genres had been able to accomplish.

—James A. Levernier

FERBER, Edna. Born in Kalamazoo, Michigan, 15 August 1885. Educated at Ryan High School, Appleton, Wisconsin, graduated 1902. Reporter, Appleton *Daily Crescent*, 1902–04, Milwaukee *Journal*, 1905–08, and Chicago *Tribune*; full-time writer from 1910; lived in New York after 1912; served with the Writers War Board and as a war correspondent with the U.S. Army Air Force during World War II. Recipient: Pulitzer Prize, 1924. Litt.D.: Columbia University, New York; Adelphi College, Garden City, New York. Member, American Academy. *Died 16 April 1968.*

PUBLICATIONS

Fiction

Dawn O'Hara, The Girl Who Laughed. 1911.
Buttered Side Down (stories). 1912.
Roast Beef, Medium: The Business Adventures of Emma McChesney and Her Son, Jock. 1913.
Personality Plus: Some Experiences of Emma McChesney and Her Son, Jock. 1914.
Emma McChesney & Co. 1915.
Fanny Herself. 1917.
Cheerful, By Request (stories). 1918.
Half Portions (stories). 1920.
The Girls. 1921.
Gigolo (stories). 1922; as *Among Those Present*, 1923.
So Big. 1924.
Show Boat. 1926.
Mother Knows Best. 1927.
Cimarron. 1930.
American Beauty. 1931.
They Brought Their Women (stories). 1933.
Come and Get It. 1935.
Nobody's in Town (includes *Trees Die at the Top*). 1938.
No Room at the Inn (stories). 1941.
Saratoga Trunk. 1941.
Great Son. 1945.
One Basket: Thirty-One Stories. 1947.
Giant. 1952.
Ice Palace. 1958.

Plays

Our Mrs. McChesney, with George V. Hobart (produced 1915).
$1200 a Year, with Newman Levy. 1920.
Minick, with George S. Kaufman, from the story "Old Man Minick" by Ferber (produced 1924). In *Old Man Minick: A Short Story . . . Minick: A Play*, 1924.
The Eldest: A Drama of American Life. 1925.
The Royal Family, with George S. Kaufman (produced 1927). 1928; as *Theatre Royal* (produced 1935), 1936.
Dinner at Eight with George S. Kaufman (produced 1932). 1932.
Stage Door, with George S. Kaufman (produced 1936). 1936.
The Land Is Bright, with George S. Kaufman (produced 1941). 1941.
Bravo!, with George S. Kaufman (produced 1948). 1949.

Screenplay: *A Gay Old Dog*, 1919.

Other (autobiography)

A Peculiar Treasure. 1939.
A Kind of Magic. 1963.

*

Critical Studies: *Women and Success in American Society in the Works of Ferber* by Mary Rose Shaughnessy, 1977; *Ferber: A Biography* by Julie Goldsmith Gilbert, 1978.

* * *

Although many of Edna Ferber's novels were very big best-sellers, she acquired among some critics the reputation of being more than an entertainer. Grant Overton, for instance, called her a social critic. It is primarily as a social historian, however, that she made her critical reputation. William Allen White said of her books that there is "no better picture of American in the first three decades of this century." And it is this aspect of her work—appearing to tell the unvarnished truth about American life—that has most appealed to her serious readers.

Whatever the final judgment about Ferber's work, there is no doubt that her finger was always on the pulse of what many American readers felt or wanted to feel about American life. She had the journalist's gift of "working up" her subject with a minimum of research and often no first-hand experience, though doubtless her earliest books about shrewd, hard-driving working girls came out of her own early career. Books like *Dawn O'Hara*, *Roast Beef, Medium*, and *Emma McChesney & Co.* helped establish her reputation as a writer who knew the facts about American life. She won the Pulitzer Prize in 1924 for *So Big*, a novel dealing with farm life, a subject, she confessed, about which she knew nothing first-hand. Later books were written after quick trips to the locale to get the feel of the territory and gather a few facts.

Cimarron purported to deal with the opening of the Oklahoma Territory and the discovery of oil, *Saratoga Trunk* with the career of a 19th century self-made millionaire (whose exciting life story newspaper reporters refused to believe). *Giant* dealt with the fabulous excesses of the Texas new-rich. These books, as well as Ferber's two dozen or so others, are movie-like romances about the lure of money and big-time success, presented with a clever blend of voyeuristic fascination and a satirical undercutting which permits the reader to luxuriate in the fantasy but at the same time feel superior to it.

In addition to romances about working girls, farmers, Oklahoma roustabouts, Indians, and self-made millionaires, Ferber also published several collections of short stories, two autobiographical volumes, and several plays (most written in collaboration with George S. Kaufman). A number of her novels have also been turned into successful stage musicals and motion pictures, *Show Boat* and *Saratoga Trunk* being perhaps the best known. Ferber's popularity and the critical attention she has received suggest that when the definitive study of popular taste in America is written her novels, plays, and short stories will have to be reckoned with.

—W.J. Stuckey

FIELD, Eugene. Born in St. Louis, Missouri, 2 (or 3) September 1850. Educated at a school in Monson, Massachusetts; Williams College, Williamstown, Massachusetts, 1868–69; Knox College, Galesburg, Illinois, 1869–70; University of Missouri, Columbia, 1870–71. Married Julia Sutherland Comstock in 1873; eight children. Traveled in Europe, 1872–73; reporter and city editor, St. Louis *Evening Journal*, 1873–75; city editor, St. Joseph *Gazette*, Missouri, 1875–76; editorial writer, St. Louis *Times-Journal*, 1876–80; managing editor, Kansas City *Times*, 1880–81, and Denver *Tribune*, 1881–83; columnist ("Sharps and Flats"), Chicago *Morning News* (later called Chicago *Record*), 1883–95. *Died 4 November 1895.*

PUBLICATIONS

Collections

Writings in Prose and Verse. 10 vols., 1896.
Hoosier Lyrics, edited by Charles Walter Brown. 1905.
Poems, Complete Edition. 1910.

Verse

A Little Book of Western Verse. 1889; revised edition, 1890.
Echoes from the Sabine Farm, Being Certain Horatian Lyrics, with Roswell M. Field. 1891; revised edition, 1893.
Second Book of Verse. 1892.
Love-Songs of Childhood. 1894.
Songs and Other Verse. 1896.
A Little Book of Tribune Verse: A Number of Hitherto Uncollected Poems, Grave and Gay, edited by Joseph G. Brown. 1901.
A Little Book of Nonsense, edited by Edward B. Morgan. 1901.
John Smith U.S.A., edited by Charles Walter Brown. 1905.

Fiction

A Little Book of Profitable Tales. 1889.
The Holy-Cross and Other Tales. 1893.
The House: An Episode in the Lives of Reuben Baker, Astronomer, and of His Wife Alice. 1896.
Second Book of Tales. 1896.
How One Friar Met the Devil and Two Pursued Him. 1900; as *The Temptation of Friar Goncol*, 1900.
The Stars: A Slumber Story, edited by Will M. Clemens. 1901.

Other

Tribune Primer. 1881.
The Model Primer. 1882.
Culture's Garland, Being Memoranda of the Gradual Rise of Literature, Art, Music, and Society in Chicago and Other Western Ganglia. 1887.
With Trumpet and Drum. 1892.
The Love Affairs of a Bibliomaniac. 1896.
Field to Francis Wilson: Some Attentions. 1896.
Florence Bardsley's Story: The Life and Death of a Remarkable Woman. 1897.
The Field Book: Verses, Stories, and Letters, edited by Mary E. Burt and Mary B. Cable. 1898.
Sharps and Flats, edited by Slason Thompson. 2 vols., 1900.

Clippings from Denver Tribune 1881–1883, edited by Willard S. Morse. 1909.
Verse and Prose from the George H. Yenowine Collection, edited by Henry H. Harper. 1917.
Some Love Letters. 1927.

*

Bibliography: in *Bibliography of American Literature* by Jacob Blanck, 1959.

Critical Studies: *Field: A Study in Heredity and Contradictions*, 2 vols., 1901, and *Life of Field, The Poet of Childhood*, 1927, both by Slason Thompson; *Field's Creative Years* by Charles H. Dennis, 1924; *The Gay Poet: The Story of Field* by Jeannette Covert Nolan, 1940; *Field Days: The Life, Times, and Reputation of Field* by Robert Conrow, 1974.

* * *

Eugene Field's was a motley genius, for he was a modern jester, the man and his works being a puzzling combination of perverse contrasts. Field is generally remembered as a children's writer of charming if dated bits of verse like "Little Boy Blue" and "Wynken, Blynken, and Nod," yet he still enjoys a sub rosa reputation for off-color lines, his "Little Willie" perhaps the best known of these naughty verses. Field openly professed a dislike for children—other than his own—and his *Tribune Primer*, written in sardonic imitation of grade-school readers, encourages young folks to cultivate the acquaintanceship of wasps and gluepots. While capable of turning out in apparent sincerity the most pious of verses like "The Divine Lullaby," Field was the libidinous originator of pornographic exercises which, like "Bangin' on the Rhine," enjoyed a long underground life even before seeing formal (if surreptitious) print.

Commencing his career as a newspaper columnist of the humorous one-liner breed, Field, despite his New England birth and education, was fond of identifying himself with the west, hence with the vital western tradition of journalism that produced Mark Twain, Ambrose Bierce, and (closer in generation and region to Field) James Whitcomb Riley. It is a tradition that accommodates Field's many sides, his love of hoaxes, his use of public print to roast friends and enemies alike, his fierce (in all senses) loyalties, his displays of saccharine sentimentality, and his airing of public dislikes and private passions. Most of what he wrote did not outlive him, and he died relatively young, at the height of his career and powers. Though he was a skillfull and witty occasional poet, that alone doomed his work to ephemerality. The best of his writing is the early dialect verse which in its masculine vitality and mining-camp settings anticipates Robert Service and parallels in chronology and spirit Kipling's barrack-room voice.

Field possessed a genuinely comic sense, which from his inveterate love of practical jokes to his humorous verse and prose, was thoroughly of his times and did not transcend them. He was a classic instance of Victorian madness, in which dilettantism took on a thoroughly middle-class, cigar-smoking, feet-on-desk pose, and self-conscious archaicism gained a popular audience. Born in 1850, he was absolutely in synchronization with his half-century, and died, most timely, five years before it ran out.

—Catherine Seelye

FISHER, Vardis (Alvero). Born in Annis, Idaho, 31 March 1895. Educated at Rigby High School, Idaho, graduated 1915; University of Utah, Salt Lake City, B.A. 1920; University of Chicago, A.M. 1922, Ph.D. (magna cum laude) 1925. Served in the U.S. Army Artillery Corps, 1918: Corporal. Married 1) Leona McMurtrey in 1917 (died, 1924), two sons; 2) Margaret Trusler in 1928 (divorced, 1939), one son; 3) Opal Laurel Holmes in 1940. Assistant Professor of English, University of Utah, 1925–28, and New York University, 1928–31; full-time writer from 1931; teacher at Montana State University, Bozeman, summers 1932–33; director, Idaho Writers' Project and Historical Records Project (Works Progress Administration), 1935–39; syndicated columnist ("Vardis Fisher Says") in Idaho newspapers, 1941–68. Recipient: Western Writers of America Spur Award, for novel, 1966, for non-fiction, 1969. *Died 9 July 1968.*

PUBLICATIONS

Fiction

Toilers of the Hills. 1928.
Dark Bridwell. 1931; as *The Wild Ones*, 1952.
Vridar Hunter tetralogy
In Tragic Life. 1932; as *I See No Sin*, 1934.
Passions Spin the Plot. 1934.
We Are Betrayed. 1935.
No Villain Need Be. 1936.
April: A Fable of Love. 1937.
Odyssey of a Hero. 1937.
Forgive Us Our Virtues: A Comedy of Evasions. 1938.
Children of God. 1939.
City of Illusion. 1941.
The Mothers. 1943.
Darkness and the Deep. 1943.
The Golden Rooms. 1944.
Intimations of Eve. 1946.
Adam and the Serpent. 1947.
The Divine Passion. 1948.
The Valley of Vision. 1951.
The Island of the Innocent. 1952.
Jesus Came Again: A Parable. 1956.
A Goat for Azazel. 1956.
Pemmican: A Novel of the Hudson's Bay Company. 1956.
Peace Like a River. 1957; as *The Passion Within*, 1960.
My Holy Satan: A Novel of Christian Twilight. 1958.
Tale of Valor: A Novel of the Lewis and Clark Expedition. 1958.
Love and Death: The Complete Stories. 1959.
Orphans in Gethsemane. 1960; as *For Passion, For Heaven* and *The Great Confession*, 2 vols., 1962.
Mountain Man. 1965.

Verse

Sonnets to an Imaginary Madonna. 1927.

Other

The Neurotic Nightingale. 1935.
The Caxton Printers in Idaho: A Short History. 1944.
God or Caesar? The Writing of Fiction for Beginners. 1953.

Suicide or Murder? The Strange Death of Governor Meriwether Lewis. 1962.
Thomas Wolfe as I Knew Him and Other Essays. 1963.
Gold Rushes and Mining Camps of the Early American West, with Opal Laurel Holmes. 1968.
Three West: Conversations with Fisher, Max Evans, Michael Straight, by John R. Milton. 1970.

Editor, *Idaho: A Guide in Word and Picture*. 1937.
Editor, *The Idaho Encyclopedia*. 1938.
Editor, *Idaho Lore*. 1939.

*

Bibliography: "Fisher: A Bibliography" by George Kellogg, in *Western American Literature*, Spring 1970.

Critical Studies: "Fisher Issue" of *American Book Collector*, September 1963; *Fisher* by Joseph M. Flora, 1965; *Fisher: The Frontier and Regional Works* by Wayne Chatterton, 1972; *Fisher: The Novelist as Poet* and *A Solitary Voice: Vardis Fisher* both by Dorys C. Grover, 1973; *The Epic of Evolution: Its Ideology and Art: A Study of Fisher's Testament of Man* by Alfred K. Thomas, 1973; *The Past in the Present: Two Essays on History and Myth in Fisher's Testament of Man* by Lester Strong, 1979.

* * *

Vardis Fisher is usually placed with the naturalists in American literature and among the strident voices of protest in the 1930's. Although his greatest fame came in the Depression years—reaching its height in 1939 with *Children of God*—he was a prolific writer whose work spanned four decades. He wore no labels easily and relished defying definition. Not interested in literary trends, he stuck doggedly to the goals he set himself. He survived numerous battles with publishers and lived to see a modest but genuine revival of interest in his work.

Fisher's youth in an isolated area along the Snake River in Idaho was lonely and terrifying. Alfred Kazin called him America's last authentic novelist of the frontier. More important, Fisher was the first to write significant novels of the Rocky Mountain west. His passionate, sometimes violent and ambiguous, response to his mountain country produced his best work. His first published novel, *Toilers of the Hills*, gave a poignant rendering of pioneer efforts to farm the difficult Antelope Hills bordering the South Fork of the Snake. The sense of place and people was even stronger in his second novel, *Dark Bridwell*—his most satisfying work of fiction. Fisher seemed on the way to founding a western counterpart to Faulkner's Yoknapatawpha County, for he was also writing short stories and poems about the people of the Antelope Hills. Vridar Hunter, the protagonist of *In Tragic Life*, had already appeared as a minor character in *Dark Bridwell*; and Dock Hunter, the farmer of *Toilers of the Hills*, is Vridar's uncle.

But Vridar was not simply a character who had played a part in the earlier novel. As his name indicates, he was also an autobiographical figure. *In Tragic Life* renders Fisher's first eighteen, largely agonized, years forcefully. The book became the first volume of an autobiographical tetralogy—and as the other volumes appeared Antelope became less significant. It became clear that Fisher was intent on exploring his own agonies more than a region. His first wife had committed suicide while he was a graduate student, and there were major psychological problems he had to work out. The confessional aspect of his work is large. Vridar made an unusual hero, for Fisher was often castigating him. Hence, the tetralogy becomes increasingly intellectual and loaded with indictments of a world Vridar never made—the final volume being decidedly a novel of ideas.

Not overly concerned with critical objections to his tetralogy, Fisher felt that his autobiographical searches had not led him to understand Vridar as he would have liked. Even as he finished the tetralogy, Fisher made plans for his *Testament of Man* novels—a series to be based on extended research into man's evolutionary development, particularly his ideas about divinity. Beginning with *Darkness and the Deep*, when man is little more than an ape and possessed only the simplest speech, Fisher traces man's "progress" until he eventually retells Vridar's story as the final volume in the series of twelve. The most successful books are the first two and the final one. The later volumes become increasingly discursive and the presentation of research as experience less successfully integrated.

Still, Fisher has an important place among the American writers of historical novels. The impetus behind his famous *Children of God* was a search into his most immediate religious heritage—Mormonism. He focuses directly on the lives of Joseph Smith and Brigham Young for the major part of his long novel. His intention was to be as accurate as possible. The success of *Children of God* led Fisher to pursue other aspects of the western American past, with the goal of accurate rendering a prime consideration. He also wrote non-fictional works about the west as well as about writing.

Fisher's final novel, *Mountain Man*, is vastly different from his other historical novels of the west. Although based on an actual mountain man, "Liver-eating" Johnson, the novel is markedly unlike such factual novels as *Children of God* or *The Mothers*. It is patterned on music and highlights the romantic spirit more carefully hidden in his other work.

—Joseph M. Flora

FITCH, (William) Clyde. Born in Elmira, New York, 2 May 1865. Educated at Hartford Public High School, Connecticut; Holderness School, New Hampshire; Amherst College, Massachusetts (editor, *Student*), 1882–86, B.A. 1886, M.A. 1902. Free-lance writer and tutor, New York, 1886: wrote for *Life* and *Puck*; visited Paris and London, and met writers in the aesthetic movement, 1888; returned to New York, and wrote children's stories for *Churchman, Independent*, and other magazines; full-time playwright and producer/director of his own plays from 1898. *Died 4 September 1909*.

PUBLICATIONS

Collections

Plays (includes *Beau Brummell, Lovers' Lane, Nathan Hale, Barbara Frietchie, Captain Jinks of the Horse Marines, The Climbers, The Stubbornness of Geraldine, The Girl with the Green Eyes, Her Own Way, The Woman in the Case, The Truth, The City*), edited by Montrose J. Moses and Virginia Gerson. 4 vols., 1915.

Plays

Beau Brummell (produced 1890). 1908; in *Plays*, 1915.
Frédérick Lemaitre (produced 1890). Edited by Oscar Cargill, in *The Social Revolt*, 1933.
Betty's Finish (produced 1890).
Pamela's Prodigy (produced 1891). 1893.
A Modern Match (produced 1892; as *Marriage*, produced 1892).
The Masked Ball, from a play by Alexandre Bisson and Albert Carré (produced 1892).
The Moth and the Flame (as *The Harvest*, produced 1893; revised version, as *The Moth and the Flame*, produced 1898). 1908; edited by Montrose J. Moses, in *Representative Plays*, 1921.
April Weather (produced 1893).
A Shattered Idol, from a novel by Balzac (produced 1893).
The Social Swim, from a play by Sardou (produced 1893).
An American Duchess, from a play by Henri Lavedan (produced 1893).
Mrs. Grundy, Jr., from a French play (produced 1893).
His Grace de Grammont (produced 1894).
Gossip, with Leo Ditrichstein, from a play by Jules Claretie (produced 1895).
Mistress Betty (produced 1895; revised version, as *The Toast of the Town*, produced 1905).
Bohemia, from a play by Théodore Barrière and Henri Murger (produced 1896).
The Liar, from a play by Alexandre Bisson (produced 1896).
A Superfluous Husband, with Leo Ditrichstein, from a play by Ludwig Fulda (produced 1897).
The Head of the Family, with Leo Ditrichstein, from a play by Adolph L'Arronge (produced 1898).
Nathan Hale (produced 1898). 1899; in *Plays*, 1915.
The Merry-Go-Round, with F. Kinsey Peile (produced 1898).
The Cowboy and the Lady (produced 1899). 1908.
Barbara Frietchie, The Frederick Girl (produced 1899). 1900; in *Plays*, 1915.
Sappho, from the play by Daudet and Belot, based on the story by Daudet (produced 1899).
Captain Jinks of the Horse Marines (produced 1901). 1902; in *Plays*, 1915.
The Climbers (produced 1901). 1906; in *Plays*, 1915.
Lovers' Lane (produced 1901). In *Plays*, 1915.
The Marriage Game, from a play by Emile Augier (produced 1901).
The Last of the Dandies (produced 1901).
The Way of the World (produced 1901).
The Girl and the Judge (produced 1901).
The Stubbornness of Geraldine (produced 1902). 1906; in *Plays*, 1915.
The Girl with the Green Eyes (produced 1902). 1905; in *Plays*, 1915.
The Bird in the Cage, from a play by Ernst von Wildenbruch (produced 1903).
The Frisky Mrs. Johnson, from a play by Paul Gavault and Georges Beer (produced 1903). 1908.
Her Own Way (produced 1903). 1907; in *Plays*, 1915.
Algy (produced 1903).
Major André (produced 1903).
Glad of It (produced 1903).
The Coronet of the Duchess (produced 1904).
Granny, from a play by Georges Michell (produced 1904).
Cousin Billy, from a play by Labiche and Martin (produced 1905).
The Woman in the Case (produced 1905). In *Plays*, 1915.
Her Great Match (produced 1905). Edited by Arthur Hobson Quinn, in *Representative American Plays*, 1917.
Wolfville, with Willis Steell, from a novel by Alfred Henry Lewis (produced 1905).
Toddles, from a play by Godferneaux and Bernard (produced 1906).
The House of Mirth, with Edith Wharton, from the novel by Wharton (produced 1906). Edited by Glenn Loney, 1981.
The Girl Who Has Everything (produced 1906).
The Straight Road (produced 1907).
The Truth (produced 1907). 1907; in *Plays*, 1915.
Miss McCobb, Manicurist (produced 1907).
Her Sister, with Cosmo Gordon-Lennox (produced 1907).
The Honor of the Family, from a play by Emile Fabre based on a novel by Balzac (produced 1908).
Girls, from a play by Alexander Engel and Julius Horst (produced 1908).
The Blue Mouse, from a play by Alexander Engel and Julius Horst (produced 1908).
A Happy Marriage (produced 1909).
The Bachelor (produced 1909).
The City: A Modern Play of American Life (produced 1909). In *Plays*, 1915.

Fiction

The Knighting of the Twins and Ten Other Tales (for children). 1891.
A Wave of Life. 1909.

Other

Some Correspondence and Six Conversations. 1896.
The Smart Set: Correspondence and Conversations. 1897.
Fitch and His Letters, edited by Montrose J. Moses and Virginia Gerson. 1924.

*

Critical Study: *The Fitch I Knew* by Archie Bell, 1909.

* * *

No playwright in the history of American drama has been able to match the commercial success of Clyde Fitch and at the same time achieve the international reputation that his work brought him. Many have written better plays; probably some have made more money; but none has equalled his cumulative success. Clearly aided by the copyright law of 1891 and his membership in the "Syndicate School," Fitch produced a considerable body of work (more than 50 plays, including many adaptations of foreign works), became the first millionaire dramatist in America, and showed himself to be not just an extremely colorful man of the theatre but a dramatist of some sensitivity whose plays were produced in several countries.

His theory of playwriting reflected the prevailing 19th-century attitudes toward literature and art. "Try to be truthful," Fitch explained: true to the details of life and environment which he saw, true to every emotion, every motive, every occupation, every class. Fitch himself was most successful in portraying the upper levels of society which in a few plays occasionally reflected the realistic and truthful detail of noteworthy drama. In most instances, however, his concern for truth lacked the necessary perspective, and he simply imitated the popular melodramatic caricature of life with an excess of what became recognized as "Fitchian detail."

As a flamboyant man-about-town Fitch enjoyed the places frequented by New York society. The problems of married life, the peculiarities of individuals, the faults and foibles of a rapidly changing society—these were the aspects of life which appealed to Fitch and which he tried to picture truthfully in his plays. His first full-length social drama was *A Modern Match*, concerned with a selfish woman who refused to assume the responsibilities of marriage. *The Climbers* is one of his better social melodramas, ridiculing the hypocrisy and materialism of New York society. *The Stubbornness of Geraldine* and *Her Great Match* reflect the international social scene. In *The Truth*, concerned with a pathological liar, and *The Girl with the Green Eyes*, which dramatized what he termed an "inherited" jealousy, Fitch was at his melodramatic best, using the particular personal insight which distinguished the plays. In his final play, *The City*, he attempted to present a serious view of city life disintegrating under a weight of moral, economic, and political problems, but the lighter and satiric view of high society was his proper métier.

As one who prepared the way for an established social comedy in America Fitch deserves attention. He was above all a man of that society, and a craftsman of the commercial theatre whose interest in truthfulness in drama helped him create some believable characters and memorable social scenes against a background of melodrama.

—Walter J. Meserve

FITZGERALD, F(rancis) Scott (Key). Born in St. Paul, Minnesota, 24 September 1896. Educated at the St. Paul Academy, 1908–11; Newman School, Hackensack, New Jersey, 1911–13; Princeton University, New Jersey, 1913–17. Served in the U.S. Army, 1917–19: 2nd Lieutenant. Married Zelda Sayre in 1920; one daughter. Advertising copywriter, Barron Collier Agency, New York, 1919–20; full-time writer from 1920; lived in Europe, 1924–26, 1929–31; screenwriter for Metro-Goldwyn-Mayer, Hollywood, 1937–38. *Died 21 December 1940.*

PUBLICATIONS

Collections

The Bodley Head Fitzgerald, edited by Malcolm Cowley and J.B. Priestley. 6 vols., 1958–63.
The Fitzgerald Reader, edited by Arthur Mizener. 1963.
Correspondence, edited by Matthew J. Bruccoli and Margaret M. Duggan. 1980.

Fiction

This Side of Paradise. 1920.
Flappers and Philosophers (stories). 1920.
The Beautiful and Damned. 1922.
Tales of the Jazz Age. 1922.
John Jackson's Arcady, edited by Lilian Holmes Stack. 1924.
The Great Gatsby. 1925; *A Facsimile of the Manuscript* edited by Matthew J. Bruccoli, 1973; *Apparatus* edited by Bruccoli, 1974.
All the Sad Young Men (stories). 1926.
Tender Is the Night: A Romance. 1934; revised edition, edited by Malcolm Cowley, 1951.
Taps at Reveille (stories). 1935.
The Last Tycoon: An Unfinished Novel, Together with The Great Gatsby and Selected Writings, edited by Edmund Wilson. 1941.
The Stories, edited by Malcolm Cowley. 1951.
The Mystery of the Raymond Mortgage (story). 1960.
The Pat Hobby Stories, edited by Arnold Gingrich. 1962.
The Apprentice Fiction of Fitzgerald 1909–1917, edited by John Kuehl. 1965.
Dearly Beloved. 1969.
Bits of Paradise: 21 Uncollected Stories, with Zelda Fitzgerald, edited by Matthew J. Bruccoli and Scottie Fitzgerald Smith. 1973.
The Basil and Josephine Stories, edited by Jackson R. Bryer and John Kuehl. 1973.
The Price Was High: The Last Uncollected Stories of Fitzgerald, edited by Matthew J. Bruccoli. 1979.

Plays

Fie! Fie! Fi-Fi! (plot and lyrics only), book by Walker M. Ellis, music by D.D. Griffin, A.L. Booth, and P.B. Dickey (produced 1914). 1914.
The Evil Eye (lyrics only), book by Edmund Wilson, music by P.B. Dickey and F. Warburton Guilbert (produced 1915). 1915.
Safety First (lyrics only), book by J.F. Bohmfalk and J. Biggs, Jr., music by P.B. Dickey, F. Warburton Guilbert, and E. Harris (produced 1916). 1916.
The Vegetable; or, From President to Postman (produced 1923). 1923.
Screenplay for Three Comrades, edited by Matthew J. Bruccoli. 1978.

Screenplays: *A Yank at Oxford* (uncredited), with others, 1937; *Three Comrades*, with Edward E. Paramore, 1938.

Radio Play: *Let's Go Out and Play*, 1935.

Verse

Poems 1911–1940, edited by Matthew J. Bruccoli. 1981.

Other

The Crack-Up, with Other Uncollected Pieces, Note-Books, and Unpublished Letters, edited by Edmund Wilson. 1945.
Afternoon of an Author: A Selection of Uncollected Stories and Essays, edited by Arthur Mizener. 1957.
Thoughtbook, edited by John Kuehl. 1965.
Fitzgerald in His Own Time: A Miscellany, edited by Matthew J. Bruccoli and Jackson R. Bryer. 1971.
Dear Scott/Dear Max: The Fitzgerald-Perkins Correspondence, edited by John Kuehl and Jackson R. Bryer. 1971.
As Ever, Scott Fitz—: Letters Between Fitzgerald and His Literary Agent Harold Ober 1919–1940, edited by Matthew J. Bruccoli and Jennifer Atkinson. 1972.
Ledger, edited by Matthew J. Bruccoli. 1973.

The Cruise of the Rolling Junk (travel). 1976.
The Notebooks, edited by Matthew J. Bruccoli. 1978.

*

Bibliography: *The Critical Reception of Fitzgerald: A Bibliographical Study* by Jackson R. Bryer, 1967, supplement 1984; *Fitzgerald: A Descriptive Bibliography* by Matthew J. Bruccoli, 1972, supplement 1980; *The Foreign Critical Reception of Fitzgerald: An Analysis and Annotated Bibliography* by Linda C. Stanley, 1980.

Critical Studies: *The Far Side of Paradise* (biography) by Arthur Mizener, 1951, revised edition, 1965, and *Fitzgerald: A Collection of Critical Essays* edited by Mizener, 1963; *The Fictional Technique of Fitzgerald* by James E. Miller, Jr., 1957, revised edition, as *Fitzgerald: His Art and His Technique*, 1964; *Beloved Infidel: The Education of a Woman* (with Gerold Frank), 1958, and *The Real Fitzgerald: Thirty-Five Years Later*, 1976, both by Sheilah Graham; *Fitzgerald* by Andrew Turnbull, 1962; *The Composition of Tender Is the Night*, 1963, *Scott and Ernest: The Authority of Failure and the Authority of Success*, 1978, and *Some Sort of Epic Grandeur: The Life of Fitzgerald*, 1981, all by Matthew J. Bruccoli, and *New Essays on The Great Gatsby* edited by Bruccoli, 1985; *Fitzgerald* by Kenneth Eble, 1963, revised edition, 1977, and *Fitzgerald: A Collection of Criticism* edited by Eble, 1973; *Fitzgerald and His Contemporaries* by William F. Goldhurst, 1963; *Fitzgerald: A Critical Portrait* by Henry Dan Piper, 1965; *The Art of Fitzgerald* by Sergio Perosa, 1965; *Fitzgerald and the Craft of Fiction* by Richard D. Lehan, 1966; *Fitzgerald: The Last Laocoön* by Robert Sklar, 1967; *Fitzgerald: An Introduction and Interpretation* by Milton Hindus, 1968; *Zelda: A Biography* by Nancy Milford, 1970, as *Zelda Fitzgerald*, 1970; *The Illusions of a Nation: Myth and History in the Novels of Fitzgerald* by John F. Callahan, 1972; *Fitzgerald: The Critical Reception*, 1978, and *The Short Stories of Fitzgerald: New Approaches in Criticism*, 1982, both edited by Jackson R. Bryer; *Candles and Carnival Lights: The Catholic Sensibility of Fitzgerald* by Joan M. Allen, 1978; *Fitzgerald* by Rose Adrienne Gallo, 1978; *Fitzgerald: Crisis in an American Identity* by Thomas J. Stavola, 1979; *The Achieving of The Great Gatsby: Fitzgerald 1920–1925* by Robert Emmet Long, 1979; *Fitzgerald and the Art of Social Fiction* by Brian Way, 1980; *Fitzgerald: A Biography* by André Le Vot, 1983; *Fool for Love: Fitzgerald* by Scott Donaldson, 1983, and *Critical Essays on Fitzgerald's The Great Gatsby* edited by Donaldson, 1984; *Invented Lives: The Marriage of F. Scott and Zelda Fitzgerald* by James R. Mellow, 1984.

* * *

Like so many modern American writers, F. Scott Fitzgerald created a public image of himself as a representative figure of his times, which may have been a part of the promotional campaign to sell his fiction. It worked for a while, with such success that any effort to evoke the Jazz Age or the Roaring Twenties is inevitably accompanied by a reference to or a photograph of Fitzgerald. But the public memory is fickle, and after he and Zelda had left the big stage and the gossip columnists no longer had their reckless antics to report, people forgot that he was once considered a writer of great promise and talent, and few realised that he had produced a body of work that bids well to bring him status as a writer for all times.

When Fitzgerald appeared on the literary scene in 1920 with *This Side of Paradise*, a semi-autobiographical guide to life at Princeton and the story of a sensitive young man who is trying to find his place in society, the critics were taken with its sophisticated style, its use of the social milieu, its honest treatment of emotional experience, and its somewhat bold portrayal of the younger generation. His readers, then, looked for even better writing in the following five years, but few would agree that he fulfilled his promise. Neither the two collections of intriguing, skillful, but often uneven short stories, *Flappers and Philosophers* and *Tales of the Jazz Age*, nor the weak play *The Vegetable* seemed to satisfy their expectations. His second novel, *The Beautiful and Damned*, was looked to more eagerly and was more widely reviewed than any other work by the author. The hero, Fitzgerald said in a letter to his publisher, was intended as "one of those many with the tastes and weaknesses of an artist but with no actual creative inspiration," and the novel related how he and his beautiful young wife were "wrecked on the shoals of dissipation." The use of autobiographical details again occasioned some speculation and caused the book to sell well, but many critics found it an unsuccessful effort at a somber tragedy of a typical American sensibility and thought that it lacked organization or focus. Some recent critics, however, have felt it to be a better novel than contemporary readers realized.

Whatever faults one may find in Fitzgerald's early work, with the publication of *The Great Gatsby* he fulfilled his highest promise and gave to American literature one of its masterworks. On the surface, of course, *The Great Gatsby* is much a part of its age as a brilliant dramatization of the social and economic corruptions of the jazz age, marked by Prohibition, gangsterism, blasé flappers, and uprootedness. American morality was marked by questionable business ethics, commercial criteria for success, and ultraconservatism in social and political thinking. Historians like Charles Beard were insisting that materialistic and economic factors rather than idealistic motives had determined the course of American history. Through character and theme, Fitzgerald dealt in one way or another with all of these historic factors with such a sensitivity that one can even intuit in the text slight prophetic reverberations of the stock market crash of 1929 and the Great Depression in the offing.

Beyond these surface concerns, the novel deals symbolically with the failure of the American dream of success, which in Fitzgerald's time was still best-known through the Horatio Alger novels. Like Benjamin Franklin before him, Horatio Alger expounded, by way of his dime novels, the possibility of rising from rags to riches through industry, ambition, self-reliance, honesty, and temperance. In this myth, and the frontier tradition of self-reliance, lies the genesis of what impels Gatsby. Behind his simple and touching study and work schedule in the copy of *Hopalong Cassidy* cherished by his father lies the childhood dreams of a Franklin or a Thomas Edison, the lectures on self-improvement of a Russell Conwell or a Dale Carnegie, the lessons on bodily development of a Charles Atlas, and the tradition that every American boy could make a million dollars or become President. But what an ironic reversal! By imitating the great American moralists, Gatsby rises to be a rich and powerful criminal.

A second significant thematic concern of the novel relates to its symbolic use of the midwest as a contrast with the east. In his nostalgic reverie on the midwest near the end of the novel, Nick Carraway concludes, "I see now that this has been a story of the West, after all—Tom and Gatsby, Daisy, Jordan, and I, were all Westerners, and perhaps we possessed some deficiency in common which made us subtly unadaptable to Eastern life." This last line is ironic, because Nick left his Minnesota home originally because it "seemed like the ragged edge of the universe," but by the end of the novel it is the place to which he returns to regain a sense of balance and moral equilibrium. Fitzgerald is playing with the traditional American dichotomy between the east as a model of European sophistication and corruption and the west as a repository of the fundamental decencies and virtues derived from contact with the American soil, the new Garden of Eden.

A figure who lurks in the background of the novel is Dan Cody, whose name suggests the mythic traditions surrounding Daniel Boone and Buffalo Bill Cody. Cody had helped settle the nation and made a fortune besides, and therefore he represents the energies that sparked the western frontier movement. But as Frederick Jackson Turner had reminded everyone in 1893, the frontier had been closed and no longer carried the significance it once had as the source of sudden wealth and the place of refuge for those seeking a second chance. By the time Gatsby met him, Dan Cody had degenerated into a senile old man subject to the advances of opportunists and gold-diggers. Gatsby takes him as his ideal, nevertheless, and, like the romantic that he is, he refuses to let historic circumstance stand in his way. Rather than wrest his fortune from the raw earth, he pioneers eastward and conquers the urban wilderness through adapting its devious means to the romantic end of recapturing the past. But history cannot be repeated, and the historic promise that Gatsby learned from Cody was, Nick notes, "already behind him, somewhere back in that vast obscurity beyond the city, where the dark fields of the republic rolled on under the night."

Jay Gatsby, then, is the ultimate American arch-romantic. Because he lacked the wealth and timing, he missed the girl on whom he had focused what Nick calls his "heightened sensitivity to the promises of life." After obtaining the wealth through corrupt means, he returns five years later to fulfill his "incorruptible dream" by attempting to repeat the one golden moment of his life when he possessed that "elusive rhythm," that "fragment of lost words" which we all seek to recall in this mundane existence from a former life, time or world. Not since Don Quixote's pursuit of Dulcinea has literature seen such a noble, heartbreaking, and impossible quest.

Adopting a modified first-person narrative form from Conrad, Fitzgerald unfolds Gatsby's tragedy for us through the eyes of the narrator, Nick Carraway. What we learn through Nick is that pure will power divorced from rationality and decency leads to destruction, and that a merely selfish dream or notion is insufficient to justify the enormous amount of energy and life expended by Gatsby. It is a lesson that this nation would not learn for almost another fifty years, and a suggestion that Fitzgerald's prophetic vision saw farther into the future than the Depression years. When Gatsby is viewed against the moral decadence and cowardly conduct of the Buchanans—"You're worth the whole damn bunch put together," Nick tells him—his unassailable romanticism makes him appear heroic. As an individual, then, who dreams higher than he can achieve, whose reach exceeds his grasp, Gatsby is at the heart of the tragic condition and thus shares certain characteristics with Oedipus, Hamlet, and other tragic heroes of Western literature. Unlike Arthur Miller's modern tragic figure, Willy Loman, Gatsby doesn't evoke mere pity and disgust at the end, as he faithfully waits for a phone call that will never come.

Aside from its concern with social and moral questions of continuing consequence, *The Great Gatsby* is one of the most carefully constructed and precisely written novels in American literature. The subtle complexity of the language; the calculated use of colors, references, and connotations; the striking configurations of verbal patterns and repetitions—all lead the reader to read and reread sentences time and time again to catch the multi-level nuances of meaning. The style is poetic and repays the application of the techniques of studied explication.

Because of the disarray of his personal life, his dwindling financial resources, and his increasing self-doubts as a writer, Fitzgerald was unable to bring his artistry to such a perfect pitch again. His numerous short stories written primarily for pay (some of which were collected in *All the Sad Young Men* and *Taps at Reveille*) and his indifferent work for Hollywood only occasionally encouraged his best talents. His next novel, *Tender Is the Night*, which came nine years after *Gatsby*, used European locales and his experiences with his wife's mental illness, another foray into autobiographical materials. What some critics felt was an unresolved problem in structure and a failure to provide clear character motivation caused many to overlook its impressive sweep of characters and its admirable effort to deal with significant psychological and social themes. After his death, the fragments of a novel, *The Last Tycoon*, were found, many pages of which suggest that Fitzgerald was regaining control of his creative skills at the last. Despite his lapses and occasional self-indulgence, the high quality of his best work, and most certainly the striking achievement in *The Great Gatsby*, has brought his work the esteem which eluded Fitzgerald himself during his own lifetime.

—M. Thomas Inge

See the essays on *The Great Gatsby* and *Tender Is the Night*.

FLETCHER, John Gould. Born in Little Rock, Arkansas, 3 January 1886. Educated at Little Rock High School, 1899–1902; Phillips Academy, Andover, Massachusetts, 1902–03; Harvard University, Cambridge, Massachusetts, 1903–07. Married 1) Florence Emily Arbuthnot in 1916 (divorced, 1936); 2) Charlie May Hogue Simon in 1936. Lived in Italy, 1907–08, and England, 1909–14 and 1916–33: associated with the Imagist movement; returned to the U.S. and settled in Arkansas, 1933; founder, Arkansas Folk Lore Society, 1935. Recipient: Pulitzer Prize, 1939. LL.D.: University of Arkansas, Fayetteville, 1933. Member, American Academy. *Died (suicide) 10 May 1950.*

PUBLICATIONS

Verse

The Book of Nature 1910–1912. 1913.
The Dominant City (1911–1912). 1913.
Fire and Wine. 1913.
Fool's Gold. 1913.
Visions of the Evening. 1913.
Irradiations: Sand and Spray. 1915.
Goblins and Pagodas. 1916.

Japanese Prints. 1918.
The Tree of Life. 1918.
Breakers and Granite. 1921.
Preludes and Symphonies. 1922.
Parables. 1925.
Branches of Adam. 1926.
The Black Rock. 1928.
XXIV Elegies. 1935.
The Epic of Arkansas. 1936.
Selected Poems. 1938.
South Star. 1941.
The Burning Mountain. 1946.

Other

La Poésie d'André Fontainas. 1919.
Some Contemporary American Poets. 1920.
Paul Gauguin: His Life and Art. 1921.
John Smith—Also Pocahontas. 1928.
The Crisis of the Film. 1929.
The Two Frontiers: A Study in Historical Psychology (on Russia and America). 1930; as *Europe's Two Frontiers*, 1930.
I'll Take My Stand: The South and the Agrarian Tradition, with others. 1930.
Life Is My Song (autobiography). 1937.
Arkansas. 1947.

Editor, *Edgar Allan Poe*. 1926.

Translator, *The Dance over Fire and Water*, by Elie Faure. 1926.
Translator, *The Reveries of a Solitary*, by Rousseau. 1927.
Translator, with others, *Jean sans terre/Landless John*, by Yvan Goll. 1944.

*

Bibliography: *Fletcher: A Bibliography* by Bruce Morton, 1979.

Critical Studies: *Fletcher* by Edna B. Stephens, 1967; *Fletcher and Imagism* by Edmund S. de Chasca, 1978.

* * *

Although most often linked with the Imagist movement because of his early association with Amy Lowell, John Gould Fletcher belongs to no one "school" of poetry; his work covers a wide range of styles and themes. But in all of his work an emphasis upon the visual is a reflection not only of his interest in art but of his early experience with Imagist philosophy. In 1907, at the age of 22, Fletcher left America for Europe, and spent the next 25 years moving between the two continents. In 1913, having published, at his own expense, five volumes of poetry, he went to Paris where he came under the influence of Impressionist art, new music, and Ezra Pound. But it was with Amy Lowell that he aligned himself, joining her Imagist circle in 1914; Lowell included some of Fletcher's poems in her anthologies, he dedicated some of his work to her, and together they formulated a poetic style of "polyphonic prose."

Of Fletcher's many works, the most famous are his "symphonies"; these are expressions of mood symbolized by a distinct color, one for each symphony. They are all divided into movements (the poems of *Irradiations: Sand and Spray* are even given tempo markings), each reflecting another aspect of the color stressed in the imagery of the poem. The result is an effective synaesthetic blend of verbal, visual, and musical elements. In "White Symphony," for instance, mood is reflected in white peonies "like rockets in the twilight," the "white snow-water of my dreams," and a "white-laden" snowy landscape. Fletcher retains the idea of symphonic form in later poems as well. Orientalism, so influential upon the Imagists, also had a profound effect upon Fletcher; Chinese philosophy and Japanese poetry (especially *haiku*) were important to the writing of the symphonies, and Fletcher's viewing of Oriental art exhibited in America in 1914 and 1915 is reflected in *Goblins and Pagodas* and *Japanese Prints*. The subjects of the latter volume are not necessarily Japanese, as Fletcher notes in his preface, "but all illustrate something of the charm I have found in Japanese poetry and art." Here he seeks "to universalize our emotions," to show "that the universe is just as much in the shape of a hand as it is in armies, politicians, astronomy, or the exhortations of gospel-mongers; that style and technique rest on the thing conveyed and not the means of conveyance." This emphasis upon the concrete remains constant throughout all of Fletcher's poetry, which, in general, is fairly traditional in form.

In the 1920's, traveling through the American south, Fletcher met the writers of the agrarian "Fugitive" movement, in whom he had been interested for several years. Although he did not embrace the Fugitives' belief in purely intellectual poetry, he did share their concept of southern agrarian culture as a bastion against modern industrialism. His contribution to the 1929 Fugitive symposium was a discussion of "Education, Past and Present" (published in 1930 in *I'll Take My Stand*), in which he stressed the importance of encouraging folk education to help the south maintain its distinct culture. In 1933, Fletcher returned to his native Little Rock, and from that point he can be considered a southern regional writer.

—Jane S. Gabin

FOSTER, Hannah (Webster). Born in Salisbury, Massachusetts, 10 September 1758. Educated at a boarding school after 1762. Married the Reverend John Foster in 1785; six children. Lived in her husband's parish of Brighton, Massachusetts, until his death, then settled with her daughters in Montreal. *Died 17 April 1840.*

PUBLICATIONS

Fiction

The Coquette; or, The History of Eliza Wharton. 1797.
The Boarding School; or, Lessons of a Preceptress to Her Pupils. 1798.

*

Bibliography: in *Bibliography of American Literature* by Jacob Blanck, 1959.

Critical Study: "Flirting with Destiny: Ambivalence and Form in the Early American Sentimental Novel" by Cathy N. Davidson, in *Studies in American Fiction*, Spring 1982.

* * *

Two of the earliest essays into American fiction were designed to "expose the dangerous consequences of seduction." William Hill Brown's *The Power of Sympathy* and Hannah Foster's *The Coquette* are cut from the same Richardsonian pattern. Of the two the more convincing and more durable is the Foster book. Better constructed and more single-minded in its purpose, it can still appeal to readers today.

Moreover, *The Coquette* is based on fact and thus achieves a kind of realism more becoming to American than English taste. Eliza Wharton, the heroine, was in reality Elizabeth Whitman and her lover was Pierpont Edwards, both of good Massachusetts families. The newspaper accounts tell of her elopement with him and of her death in the Bell Tavern in Danvers, Massachusetts. A secret marriage is hinted at, but that part of the story remains a mystery. These events took place ten years before the appearance of the novel; but even more compelling is the fact that Foster's husband was the cousin of the wife of Deacon John Whitman of Stow, himself a cousin of Elizabeth Whitman's father. It seems probable that Foster, through these family connections was in possession of the facts.

The Coquette is an imitation of Richardson's *Clarissa*, but it is one of the most successful in a long series of seduction novels written in its period. The characters of Major Peter Sanford, the seducer, and Eliza Wharton are convincing and straightforward. The other characters are skillfully used to build the plot and comment on the unfortunate lovers, so that the reader's attention never moves away from the unfolding tragedy. The motivation is real and the moments of tortured self-revelation raise the novel above the sensationalism and sentimentality of many novels of this genre. Moreover, Foster does not fall into the obvious excesses of the epistolary form; she does not tax the credulity of the reader, nor does she intrude with tedious editorializing.

—Dominic J. Bisignano

FOSTER, Stephen Collins. Born in Pittsburgh, Pennsylvania, 4 July 1826. Educated privately, Allegheny, and at Towanda Academy, Athens Academy, Tioga Point, 1840–41, and Jefferson College, Canonsburg, 1841, all in Pennsylvania. Married Jane McDowell in 1850; one daughter. Bookkeeper for his brother, Cincinnati, 1847; then songwriter: contracted to Firth Pond and Company from 1849. *Died 13 January 1864.*

PUBLICATIONS

Collections

The Melodies. 1909.
Foster's Forgotten Songs, edited by Hamilton A. Gordon. 1941.
A Treasury of Foster. 1946.

*

Bibliography: *A Pictorial Bibliography of the First Editions of Foster* by James J. Fuld, 1957.

Critical Studies: *Foster, America's Troubadour*, 1935, and *The Literature of Foster*, 1944, both by John T. Howard; *Foster, Boy Minstrel* by Helen B. Higgins, 1944; *The Songs of Foster* by William W. Austin, 1975.

* * *

While Stephen Collins Foster's literary output is inextricably linked to the music to which he set it, he must nevertheless be considered as a poet, and more influential in his writing of words than of music. The abstract art of his music surrounds and complements his lyrics in an inimitable Bellinian "simplicity of genius," but his carefully crafted words ultimately reflect and refine the mores of American society in the pre-Civil War period: optimistic, sentimental, patriotic, and proudly unsophisticated.

Foster has been criticised as too sentimental, as having embodied the patronising racism of his time, and of having been not a poet at all but a musician who wrote some of his own lyrics. About a third of Foster's 180-odd songs were, it is true, written to the texts of others, but only two or three of these have survived among the forty and more Foster songs with which most Americans are familiar. As a musician, he responded best to himself as poet.

Of Foster's own lyrics, most, and the most important, form two groups: the sentimental ballad and the Negro dialect song. His few political, patriotic, and non-dialect comic lyrics are neither greatly distinguished in themselves nor sources of memorable musical accompaniments. The sentimental ballads, such as "Beautiful Dreamer," "Come Where My Love Lies Dreaming," and "Jeannie with the Light Brown Hair" are comparable in intensity of emotion to, and less pretentious stylistically than, the sentimental poetry of such contemporaries as Poe and Lanier. At the same time, his lyrics are more metrically and verbally sophisticated than those of his contemporaries who wrote not as poets but only as lyricists.

The Negro-dialect lyrics, or "Etheopian Songs" as they were popularly known, demonstrate Foster's keen ear for the rhythms and patterns of black speech. In his earliest efforts, such as "Oh Susanna" and "Old Folks at Home," some crudities and a tendency to see the black, slave or free, as a happy buffoon, can be traced. But the poet's close observation of blacks for both poetic and musical veracity resulted in a gradual and progressive move away from stereotype to the image of the black person as dignified, sensitive, and empathetic rather than simple and ridiculous. He jettisoned objectionable words commonly descriptive of blacks, leading to later lyrics such as "Old Black Joe" in which dialect disappears entirely, though by then his grasp of it, in "Nelly Bly," "My Old Kentucky Home," and "Massa's in de Cold Ground" demonstrate a command equal to Sidney Lanier's of the contemporary white southerner.

The Civil War, which abolished black servitude and replaced sentimentality with expansionism and urbanism, cut off the possibility of Foster's being an influence on the poetry which followed his death, and froze him into the posture of a spokesman for a vanished age. The strong American sense of nostalgia has thus deified him, and the mythic figure thus created has so far repelled any serious study of his considerable talents as a poet.

—William J. Collins

FRANK, Waldo (David). Born in Long Branch, New Jersey, 25 August 1889. Educated at De Witt Clinton High School, New York, 1902–06; Les Chamettes Pensionnat, Lausanne, Switzerland, 1906–07; Yale University, New Haven, Connecticut, B.A. and M.A. 1911. Married 1) Margaret Naumberg in 1916 (divorced, 1926), one son; 2) Alma Magoon in 1927 (divorced, 1943), two daughters; 3) Jean Klempner in 1943, two sons. Theatre critic, New Haven *Courier-Journal*, 1910–11; reporter, New York *Evening Post*, 1911–12, and New York *Times*, 1912; lived abroad, 1913–14; associate editor, *Seven Arts*, New York, 1916; conscientious objector during World War I; staff member, *Ellsworth County Leader*, Kansas, 1919; contributing editor, *New Republic*, New York, 1925–40, and *New Masses*, New York, 1926; lecturer, New School for Social Research, New York, 1927; Honorary Professor, Central University of Ecuador, 1949. Chairman, Independent Miners' Relief Committee, 1932; first Chairman, League of American Writers, 1935. Litt.D.: Universidad Nacional de San Marcos, Lima, Peru, 1929. Member, American Academy, 1952. *Died 9 January 1967*.

PUBLICATIONS

Fiction

The Unwelcome Man. 1917.
The Dark Mother. 1920.
Rahab. 1922.
City Block. 1922.
Holiday. 1923.
Chalk Face. 1924.
The Death and Birth of David Markand: An American Story. 1934.
The Bridegroom Cometh. 1938.
Summer Never Ends. 1941.
Island in the Atlantic. 1946.
The Invaders. 1948.
Not Heaven. 1953.

Play

New Year's Eve. 1929.

Other

The Art of the Vieux Colombier: A Contribution of France to the Contemporary Stage. 1918.
Our America. 1919; as *The New America*, 1922.
Salvos: An Informal Book about Books and Plays. 1924.
Time Exposures, By Search-Light. 1926.
Virgin Spain: Scenes from the Spiritual Drama of a Great People. 1926; revised edition, 1942.
Five Arts, with others. 1929.
The Re-Discovery of America: An Introduction to a Philosophy of American Life. 1929.
America Hispana: A Portrait and a Prospect. 1931.
Dawn in Russia: The Record of a Journey. 1932.
In the American Jungle 1925–1936. 1937.
Chart for Rough Water: Our Role in a New World. 1940.
South American Journey. 1943.
The Jew in Our Day. 1944.
Birth of a World: Bolívar in Terms of His Peoples. 1951.
Bridgehead: The Drama of Israel. 1957.
The Rediscovery of Man: A Memoir and a Methodology of Modern Life. 1958.
Cuba, Prophetic Island. 1961.
Memoirs, edited by Alan Trachtenberg. 1973.

Editor, *Tales from the Argentine*, translated by Anita Brenner. 1930.
Editor, *The Collected Poems of Hart Crane*. 1933; revised edition, as *The Complete Poems*, 1958.
Editor, with others, *America and Alfred Stieglitz: A Collective Portrait*. 1934.

Translator, *Lucienne*, by Jules Romains. 1925.

*

Critical Studies: *The Novels of Frank* by William Bittner, 1958; *The Shared Vision of Frank and Hart Crane* by Robert L. Perry, 1966; *Frank* by Paul J. Carter, 1967.

* * *

Although Waldo Frank produced a large and varied body of work in prose—history, fiction, essays—he considered himself a poet. In his memoirs, he refers to himself as a poet, describes his novels as lyrical, and says that *Virgin Spain* represents a subjective, lyrical expression of the author. The memoirs provide a useful introduction to the man and to the genesis and the attitudes informing some of his important books.

Surprisingly, his important books are history, not fiction or essays. Frank's essays were written for periodicals, and consist principally of commentary on literature, the theatre, the current American scene, and the position of the Jew in the modern world. Occasionally they are listed as criticism, but Frank lacked the tools of criticism. He also lacked wit and humor, as is painfully evident in a collection of brief "Profiles," first published in the *New Yorker*. Like his history and fiction, his essays offer a poet's vision and use of language. In the best, in the introduction to Hart Crane's poems, for example, this vision enlarges the reader's understanding. It tends to vitiate much of his other writing, especially his fiction.

At the heart of Frank's work is his vision of a social and personal Whole—variously termed Cosmos or Being or The Great Tradition—achieved in western Europe in the middle ages by the church, through the teaching of Jesus. In succeeding ages, according to Frank, this very teaching—that the Kingdom of God is within man—gave rise to an ego which, particularly in America, replaced the Ptolemaic universe with a secular, mechanistic multiverse. The chaos of the multiverse is but a stage, however, in man's history, which must culminate in the Whole once more, the knowledge that God, the universal, is within man, whose life therefore has purpose and direction.

The timeless, spaceless nature of this vision of the Whole precludes the development of character and situation in Frank's fiction, as he himself asserts. Consequently, his short stories are made up essentially of moments of epiphany, and his novels contain inert ideological and symbolic material. Like a poet, he attempts to re-create language, using nouns as verbs and adjectives as nouns. These usages and his poetic descriptions unhappily abound to the point of embarrassment in his writing.

On account of his vision, his histories of North and South America, Russia, and Spain must be accepted on his terms, as works of art. His considerable research gives substance to some that otherwise would amount to little more than poetic travel books. As history, *Birth of a World* is his best, undoubtedly in part because it was commissioned by the Venezuelan Government and because Bolívar, not Frank, is at the center of the narrative. Most important for the reader's comprehension and intelligent assessment of Frank's work is *The Re-Discovery of America*. For it presents his vision, interpreting religion and history from a poet's perspectives, with a poet's insights.

—Robert F. Richards

FRANKLIN, Benjamin. Born in Boston, Massachusetts, 17 January 1706. Educated at Boston Grammar School, 1714; George Brownell's School, Boston. Married Deborah Read in 1730 (died, 1774); one son and one daughter; also an illegitimate son (William Franklin, loyalist governor of New Jersey) and daughter. Worked in his father's tallow chandler business, Boston, from age 10; apprenticed as printer to his half-brother James, 1718; worked on James's *New-England Courant*: contributed "Silence Dogood" articles, 1721–23, and published paper during James's imprisonment, 1722; moved to Philadelphia, 1723; worked for printer Samuel Keimer, 1723–24; sent to London to buy printing equipment and worked for printers Palmer, then Watt, 1724–25; clerk for Denham, a merchant, Philadelphia, 1726–27, and Keimer, 1728; established own printing business, Philadelphia, 1729: publisher, 1729–48, and co-publisher, 1748–66, *Pennsylvania Gazette*; publisher, *Philadelphische Zeitung*, 1732; editor, *General Magazine*, Philadelphia, 1741; retired and turned over running of business to partner, 1748. Clerk, 1736–51, member for Philadelphia, 1751–64, and Speaker, 1764, Pennsylvania Assembly: London agent for the Assembly, chiefly on taxation matters, 1757–62 and 1764–75 (involved in passage and repeal of the Stamp Act); also colonial agent for Georgia, 1768, New Jersey, 1769, and Massachusetts, 1770; deputy postmaster, Philadelphia, 1737–53, and joint deputy postmaster of the colonies, 1753–74 (dismissed by British; elected postmaster general of the colonies by Continental Congress, 1775); delegate, Albany Congress (to unite colonies in French and Indian War), 1754. Returned to America from London and delegate to Second Continental Congress, 1775–76; member of the drafting committee and signatory, Declaration of Independence, 1776; sent by Congress as one of three commissioners to negotiate with the French, 1776, and became sole commissioner, 1778 (treaty of commerce and defensive alliance signed, 1778); lived at Passy, near Paris, and established a press there, 1776–85; member, with John Jay and John Adams, of commission to negotiate peace with Britain, from 1781 (treaty signed, 1783); returned to Philadelphia, 1785; President, Pennsylvania Executive Council, 1785–87; delegate, Constitutional Convention, Philadelphia, 1787 (helped arrange the compromise on representation incorporated into the Constitution); President, Pennsylvania Society for the Abolition of Slavery, 1787. Involved in Philadelphia community affairs: worked on projects to establish police force and street paving and cleaning schemes; helped found Library Company of Philadelphia (first circulating library in America), 1731, Union Fire Company, 1736, American Philosophical Society, 1743, Academy for the Education of Youth (later University of Pennsylvania), 1751, and Philadelphia City Hospital, 1751. Invented "Franklin Stove" or "Pennsylvania Fireplace," 1739; studied electricity after 1746: performed kite experiment to test identity of lightning and electricity, and invented lightning rod, 1752. Recipient: Royal Society Copley Medal, 1753. M.A.: Harvard University, Cambridge, Massachusetts, 1753; Yale University, New Haven, Connecticut, 1753; College of William and Mary, Williamsburg, Virginia, 1756; LL.D.: University of St. Andrews, Fife, Scotland, 1759; D.C.L.: Oxford University, 1762. Fellow, Royal Society (London), 1756; member, French Academy of Sciences, 1772. *Died 17 April 1790.*

PUBLICATIONS

Collections

Writings, edited by Albert Henry Smyth. 10 vols., 1905–07.
Representative Selections, edited by Frank Luther Mott and Chester E. Jorgenson. 1936; revised edition, 1962.
Papers, edited by Leonard W. Labaree and William B. Willcox. 1959—
Collected Works (Library of America), edited by J.A. Leo Lemay. 1987.

Prose

A Dissertation on Liberty and Necessity, Pleasure and Pain. 1725.
A Modest Enquiry into the Nature and Necessity of a Paper-Currency. 1729.
Poor Richard: An Almanack 1733 [through *1747*]. 1732–46; as *Poor Richard Improved 1748* [through *1763*], 1747–64; *The Complete Poor Richard Almanacks*, edited by Whitfield Bell, Jr., 2 vols., 1970.
A Defense of the Rev. Mr. Hemphill's Observations. 1735.
A Letter to a Friend in the Country. 1735.
Some Observations on the Proceedings Against the Rev. Mr. Hemphill. 1735; as *Some Sermons*, 1735.
A Proposal for Promoting Useful Knowledge among the British Plantations in America. 1743.
An Account of the New Invented Pennsylvania Fire-Places. 1744.
Reflections on Courtship and Marriage. 1746.
Plain Truth. 1747.
Proposals Relating to the Education of Youth in Pennsylvania. 1749.
Experiments and Observations on Electricity. 1751; *Supplemental Experiments*, 1753; *New Experiments and Observations*, 1754; revised edition, 1769, 1774.
Idea of the English School. 1751.
Some Account of the Pennsylvania Hospital. 1754.
Some Account of the Success of Inoculation for the Small-Pox. 1759.
A Parable Against Persecution. 1759 (?).
Father Abraham's Speech. 1760; as *The Way to Wealth*, 1774.
The Interest of Great Britain Considered, with Regard to Her Colonies. 1760.
Cool Thoughts on the Present Situation of Our Public Affairs. 1764.
A Narrative of Late Massacres, in Lancaster County, of a Number of Indians, Friends of This Province, by Persons Unknown. 1764.
Remarks on a Late Protest Against the Appointment of Mr. Franklin an Agent for This Province. 1764.
The Examination of Doctor Franklin, Relative to the Repeal of the American Stamp Act. 1766.
Physical and Meteorological Observations and Suppositions. 1766.

Oeuvres (in French), edited by Jacques Dubourg. 2 vols., 1773.
Political, Miscellaneous, and Philosophical Pieces, edited by Benjamin Vaughan. 1779.
Remarks Concerning the Savages of North America. 1784.
Information to Those Who Would Remove to America. 1784(?).
Philosophical and Miscellaneous Papers, edited by Edward Bancroft. 1787.
Observations on the Causes and Cure of Smoky Chimneys. 1787.
Rules for Reducing a Great Empire to a Small One. 1793.
The Art of Swimming. 1816 (?).
The Private Correspondence, edited by William Temple Franklin. 2 vols., 1817.
A Collection of the Familiar Letters and Miscellaneous Papers, edited by Jared Sparks. 1833.
Autobiography, edited by John Bigelow. 1868; edited by Leonard W. Labaree and others, 1964; *The Autobiography: A Genetic Text*, edited by J.A. Leo Lemay and P.M. Zall, 1981.
An Address to the Good People of Ireland, on Behalf of America . . . 1778, edited by Paul Leicester Ford. 1891.
Franklin's Contribution to Medicine, edited by Theodore Diller. 1912.
Letters to Madame Helvétius and Madame La Freté, edited by Luther S. Livingston. 1924.
My Dear Girl: The Correspondence of Franklin with Polly Stevenson, Georgiana and Catherine Shipley, edited by James Madison Stifler. 1927.
Account Books, edited by George Simpson Eddy. 2 vols., 1928–29.
Advice to a Young Man on Choosing a Mistress, edited by Harold D. Carew. 1930.
The Ingenious Dr. Franklin: Selected Scientific Letters, edited by Nathan G. Goodman. 1931.
Satires and Bagatelles, edited by Paul McPharlin. 1937.
The General Magazine and Historical Chronicle for All the British Plantations in America (issued 1741), edited by Lyon N. Richardson. 1938.
Autobiographical Writings, edited by Carl Van Doren. 1945.
A Franklin Reader, edited by Nathan G. Goodman. 1945; as *The Franklin Sampler*, 1956.
Letters and Papers of Franklin and Richard Jackson 1753–1785, edited by Carl Van Doren. 1947.
Memoirs: Parallel Text Edition, edited by Max Farrand. 1949.
The Will of Franklin 1757, edited by Carl Van Doren. 1949.
Franklin and Catharine Ray Greene: Their Correspondence 1775–1790, edited by William Greene Roelker. 1949.
Letters of Franklin and Jane Mecom, edited by Carl Van Doren. 1950.
Letters to the Press 1758–1775, edited by Verner W. Crane. 1950.
Franklin's Wit and Folly: The Bagatelles, edited by Richard E. Amacher. 1953.
Mr. Franklin: A Selection from His Personal Letters, edited by Leonard W. Labaree and Whitfield J. Bell, Jr. 1956.
Franklin on Education, edited by John Hardin Best. 1962.
The Political Thought of Franklin, edited by Ralph L. Ketcham. 1965.
The Bagatelles from Passy, edited by Claude-Anne Lopez and Willard F. Trask. 1967.
Franklin Laughing: Anecdotes from Original Sources by and about Franklin, edited by P.M. Zall. 1980.

*

Bibliography: *Franklin Bibliography* by Paul Leicester Ford, 1889; *Franklin's Philadelphia Printing 1728–1766: A Descriptive Bibliography* by C. William Miller, 1974; *Franklin 1721–1906: A Reference Guide* by Melvin H. Buxbaum, 1983.

Critical Studies: *Franklin* by Carl Van Doren, 1938, and *Meet Dr. Franklin* edited by Van Doren, 1943; *Franklin: His Contribution to the American Tradition* by I. Bernard Cohen, 1953; *Franklin* by Richard E. Amacher, 1962; *Franklin: An American Man of Letters* by Bruce Ingham Granger, 1964; *Franklin, Philosopher and Man*, 1965, and *Franklin and Nature's God*, 1967, both by Alfred Owen Aldridge; *Franklin* by Ralph L. Ketcham, 1965; *The Private Franklin: The Man and His Family* by Claude-Anne Lopez and Eugenia W. Herbert, 1975; *Franklin* by David Freeman Hawke, 1976; *The Oldest Revolutionary: Essays on Franklin* edited by J.A. Leo Lemay, 1976, and *The Canon of Franklin: New Attributions and Reconsiderations* by Lemay, 1986; *Franklin: A Collection of Critical Essays* edited by Brian M. Barbour, 1979; *Franklin: A Biography* by Ronald W. Clark, 1983; *Cotton Mather and Franklin: The Price of Representative Personality* by Mitchell Robert Breitwieser, 1984; *Franklin of Philadelphia* by Esmond Wright, 1986.

* * *

Benjamin Franklin is an American idol. One of the founders of the American political tradition and a distinguished scientist, diplomat, and humanitarian, Franklin was also, to quote David Hume, the "first great man of letters" for whom Europe was beholden to America.

In his every accomplishment, Franklin epitomized the American Enlightenment. Possessed of an infinitely curious mind fixed on understanding and improving the world around him, he sought a better life for people of all classes and situations. A Deist, he tried to reconcile rationalism and science with the belief in God, urging faith and good will and always advocating the application of faith based on intelligence; he never spared humor in meeting the contingencies of the human condition.

He brought to his writing this broad humanism and selflessness, and a grace and wit that made him one of America's greatest writers. He gave an American flavor to the epistolary and essay forms, mastered the use of persona in creating the first memorable American comic character, and left for succeeding generations to emulate a crackerbarrel and homey humor. Always, Franklin's work appeals to human reason and retains as its purpose social and moral betterment. "No Piece can properly be called good . . . which is void of any tendency to benefit the [Reader's] . . . Virtue or his Knowledge."

His essays include the "Do-Good Papers," "Busy-Body Papers," and *Bagatelles*. The first—fourteen essays that appeared in his half-brother's *New-England Courant* and written under the name of Silence Dogood—is the essential Franklin. His persona, a parson's widow writing of both the serious and ridiculous—provides the author distance for irony and satire. Her subjects include "Pride and Hoop Petticoats," women as the cause of men's sins, and the more serious problems of excessive religious zeal, alcoholism, and the plight of widows (this was written shortly after the smallpox epidemic and Indian wars of 1722); "The Temple of Learning" is a hearty satire of Harvard University; there are also essays of literary criticism, one on Arminianism, and many on other topical matters. The essays represent early social criticism in American journalism. The "Busy-Body Papers" comprises 32 letters addressed to a competing newspaper, the *American Weekly Mercury*. On subjects like religion, morality, and various social issues, Franklin accomplishes his retaliation against the publisher Samuel Keimer, who shortly thereafter went bankrupt. The fifteen *Bagatelles*, short and urbane essays written in his seventies, cover a broad range of subjects and include "The Ephemera," "Parable Against Persecution," and "The Whistle." Some are in the vein of Swift's *A Modest Proposal*. "Rules by Which a Great Empire May Be Reduced to a Small One," for example, contains 20 rules by which the British empire may be reduced, like a cake. "I would propose that all the Capitals of the several Provinces should be burnt to the Ground, and that they cut the throats of all the inhabitants: Men, Women, and Children, and scalp them, to serve as an Example." Franklin also wrote a prodigious number of letters.

Poor Richard's Almanack, the early work that brought him great success in the colonies and then abroad, epitomizes Franklin's passion for improving himself and others: "I write Almanacks with no other View than that of the publick Good." Like the popular almanacs of the time, Franklin's includes weather predictions, short sayings, a history of European kings and dates of courts, tides, fairs, recipes, maxims, movements of planets and eclipses, a calendar of meetings, and the distance between towns. Unique is Franklin's fictional character, his persona Richard Saunders who, married to the proud and talkative Bridget, is shamed into writing because she can't stand his obsessive gazing at the stars. Franklin dramatizes a very funny battle between the sexes and once again utilizes the persona device to distinguish his work from the tired, moralizing pieces popular at the time. The self-denying Richard frequently illustrates the dangers of frugality.

The book is filled with maxims that Franklin gathered from a vast number of sources, many of which he adapts to the circumstances of his impoverished Richard. Franklin gives a homespun flavor to the gospel of American folk wisdom. He alters, for example, "Fresh fish and poor friends become soon ill sav'd [savored]" to "Fresh fish and visitors stink in three days." Other sayings include:

> Early to bed, early to rise, makes a man healthy, wealthy, and wise.
> It is hard for an empty sack to stand upright.
> Neither a fortress nor a maidenhead will hold out long after they begin to parley.
> Men and Melons are hard to know.

The first *Almanack* sold so well that "as poor Richard says" became a household phrase on thrift. *The Way to Wealth*, Father Abraham's speech on the nature of the times, contains 90 maxims on "industry, frugality, and prudence," many of which are from *Poor Richard's Almanack*.

The very popular *Autobiography* was dedicated to Franklin's son, on how "from the poverty and obscurity in which I was born . . . I have raised myself to a state of affluence and some degree of celebrity in the world." Although unfinished, these "Memoirs," in four sections, portray both the didactic and witty Franklin. They expound the thirteen virtues of his self-improvement course: Temperance, Silence, Order, Resolution, Frugality, Industry, Sincerity, Justice, Moderation, Cleanliness, Tranquility, Chastity, and Humility. The book is appealing not only as a guide to morality but as an early Horatio Alger tale, a story about the American dream and Franklin's particular application of common sense in the brave new world of opportunity.

Franklin wrote over 20,000 works; his stylistic goals were clarity, precision, and propriety. He was extraordinarily well-read: his major literary influences were Addison, Locke, Swift, Bunyan, and Defoe. In his many political tracts, letters, satires, essays, fables, pamphlets, and even hoaxes, he made clear his belief in God and man's capabilities and responsibilities: "I believe in one God, Creator of the Universe. That He governs it by his Providence. That the most acceptable service we render to Him is doing good to His other children. That the soul of man is immortal and will be treated with justice in another life respecting its conduct in this."

—Lois Gordon

FREDERIC, Harold. Born in Utica, New York, 19 August 1856. Educated at the Advanced School, Utica, graduated 1871. Married Grace Williams in 1877, two daughters and two sons; also had two daughters and one son by Kate Lyon. Photographer's assistant and retoucher, Utica, 1871–73, and Boston, 1873–74; proofreader, Utica *Morning Herald*, 1875; reporter, 1875–80, and editor, 1880–82, Utica *Observer*; editor-in-chief, Albany *Evening Journal*, 1882–84; London correspondent, *New York Times*, 1884–98. *Died 19 October 1898.*

PUBLICATIONS

Collections

Stories of York State, edited by Thomas F. O'Donnell. 1966.
(*Works*), edited by Stanton Garner. 1977—

Fiction

Seth's Brother's Wife: A Study of Life in the Greater New York. 1887.
The Lawton Girl. 1890.
In the Valley. 1890.
The Return of the O'Mahony. 1892.
The Copperhead. 1893.
The Copperhead and Other Stories of the North During the American War. 1894.
Marsena and Other Stories of the Wartime. 1894.
The Damnation of Theron Ware. 1896; as *Illumination*, 1896; edited by Everett Carter, 1960.
Mrs. Albert Grundy: Observations in Philistia. 1896.
March Hares. 1896.
In the Sixties (stories). 1897.
Gloria Mundi. 1898; abridged version, as *Pomps and Vanities*, 1913.
The Deserter and Other Stories: A Book of Two Wars. 1898.
The Market-Place. 1899.

Other

The Young Emperor William II of Germany: A Study in Character Development on a Throne. 1891.
The New Exodus: A Study of Israel in Russia. 1892.

*

Bibliography: *A Bibliography of Writings by and about Frederic* by Thomas F. O'Donnell, Stanton Garner, and Robert H. Woodward, 1975; *The Literary Manuscripts of Frederic: A Catalogue* by Noel Polk, 1979.

Critical Studies: *Frederic* by Thomas F. O'Donnell and Hoyt C. Franchere, 1961; *The Novels of Frederic* by Austin Briggs, Jr., 1969; *Frederic* by Stanton Garner, 1969.

* * *

Two distinct strains, realistic and romantic, mix in Harold Frederic's fiction. He regarded Erckmann-Chatrian and Hawthorne as the principal influences on his own work. His reading of popular romance, together with qualities inherent in his temperament and the pattern of his career, manifests itself in certain romantic effects. He lapses into melodrama and sentimentality and recurrently draws central figures who are young, hopeful, naive, and embarked on fairy-tale adventures of personal fulfilment. Frederic's romanticism matures in the brief course of his writing career, however, from an initial school-boy emulation of Erckmann-Chatrian in the earliest stories towards a Hawthorne-like probing of the ambiguities manifest in human character, and of the inner and outer pressures that determine behavior. Frederic's reputation and his distinctive character as a writer depend primarily on his talents as a realist who exploited materials pertaining to the Mohawk Valley region of New York. In the autobiographical derivation of his fiction, in his faithful representation of everyday language, behavior, and scene, and in his dramatic method (i.e., his letting the tale tell itself rather than interpreting it for the reader) Frederic has been compared to William Dean Howells, whom he greatly admired. His essentially comic vision also associates him with Howells and with an underlying American optimism ultimately deriving from Emerson.

Frederic's first novel, *Seth's Brother's Wife*, his masterwork *The Damnation of Theron Ware*, and his best stories are all realistic. They draw upon his childhood experiences in a working-class, Methodist home during the Civil War era and upon his subsequent observations as a photographer's apprentice and a journalist in upstate New York. Seth is a young journalist variously involved with his job, politics, and his brother's wife, his story enacted against the dreary background of a poor upstate farming district. Theron Ware is a small-town Methodist minister whose intellectual, aesthetic, and sexual initiations under the influence of town sophisticates paradoxically result in both *éclaircissement* and moral degeneration. Here as elsewhere Frederic's overt treatment of sexuality and his preoccupation with the type of the modern woman are manifest. The Civil War stories are highly original, dealing with ambivalent attitudes toward the war and with its effects upon civilians at home rather than celebrating military heroics. Written in 1892–93 these have been collected in a modern edition as *Stories of York State*. *The Lawton Girl*, a moderately successful sequel to *Seth*, and *In the Valley*, a historical romance of the Revolutionary War, are also set in the Mohawk Valley.

Frederic was a highly successful foreign correspondent, and his fiction writing represented a second career in part motivated by financial objectives. All his fiction except the early stories was written in England, and he initially attempted to assimilate European materials in *The Return of the O'Mahony*. This far-fetched, comical, trivial romance is Frederic's deepest plunge into Irish folk materials, although folklore, legend, and genealogy interested him throughout his career, and his interest in the New York Irish predated his journalistic immersion in Irish politics. *March Hares*, set in London, is believed to be a fictional celebration of Frederic's liaison with Kate Lyon. Its deft, urbane, and comic tone, characteristic of Frederic's mature voice, is reminiscent of that of his bachelor narrator in *Mrs. Albert Grundy*, a series of fictionalized satirical sketches originally published in the *National Observer* in 1892 as "Observations in Philistia."

In his last two novels, *Gloria Mundi* and *The Market-Place*, Frederic makes his most serious attempts to discover European materials of sufficient richness to replace the New York regionalist material that he had substantially worked through. Of these *Gloria Mundi*, a Cinderella tale of a young man's coming into a dukedom and an inheritance, is the less successful. Frederic was ill-advised to attempt the depiction of a social milieu inaccessible to him, and the novel lacks the authenticity that characterizes his scene-painting of rural New York. In *The Market-Place*, however, a romance of commercial enterprise dealing with life in the City and with the interaction of political and philanthropic motives, Frederic opens up a vein of material that he might easily have exploited thereafter. Taken together, the central figures of *Theron Ware*, *Gloria Mundi*, and *The Market-Place* manifest a deepening psychological insight and an ever-increasing subtlety and ambiguity in rendering the relationships between character and environment. The peculiar strength of *Theron Ware*, which is generally regarded as a minor classic, may in fact derive from its bringing together the New York regionalist material at which Frederic was a sure hand, with his increasingly subtle probing into the forces that shape and thwart human development.

Frederic's novels reveal curious mixtures of disparate treatment, material, and attitudes within individual works. A sort of intellectual omnivorousness characterizes him, though some of the inconsistencies may result from lack of time for revision. In any case, the diversity of his talents, attitudes, and experiments is in itself remarkable. His novels characteristically reveal multiple perspectives, a tendency to view experience from more than one point of view. The problem of distinguishing between mere inconsistencies and calculated ironies is a crux in assessing individual works fairly and in forming a conclusive judgment of his achievement as a novelist.

—Jean Frantz Blackall

See the essay on *The Damnation of Theron Ware*.

FREEMAN, Mary E(leanor) Wilkins. Born in Randolph, Massachusetts, 31 October 1852; brought up in Randolph, then in Brattleboro, Vermont; returned to Randolph, 1883. Educated at Brattleboro High School, graduated 1870; Mount Holyoke Female Seminary, South Hadley, Massachusetts, 1870–71; Glenwood Seminary, West Brattleboro, 1871. Married Charles M. Freeman in 1902 (died, 1923). Lived in Metuchen, New Jersey, after 1902. Recipient: American Academy Howells Medal, 1925. Member, American Academy, 1926. *Died 13 March 1930.*

PUBLICATIONS

Collections

Selected Stories, edited by Marjorie Pryse. 1983.
The Infant Sphinx: Collected Letters, edited by Brent L. Kendrick. 1985.

Fiction

A Humble Romance and Other Stories. 1887; as *A Far-Away Melody and Other Stories*, 1890.
A New England Nun and Other Stories. 1891.
Jane Field. 1892.
Pembroke. 1894; edited by Perry D. Westbrook, 1971.
Madelon. 1896.
Jerome, A Poor Man. 1897.
Silence and Other Stories. 1898.
The People of Our Neighborhood. 1898; as *Some of Our Neighbours*, 1898.
The Jamesons. 1899.
In Colonial Times. 1899.
The Heart's Highway: A Romance of Virginia in the Seventeenth Century. 1900.
The Love of Parson Lord and Other Stories. 1900.
Understudies (stories). 1901.
The Portion of Labor. 1901.
Six Trees (stories). 1903.
The Wind in the Rose-Bush and Other Stories of the Supernatural. 1903.
The Givers (stories). 1904.
The Debtor. 1905.
"Doc" Gordon. 1906.
By the Light of the Soul. 1907.
The Fair Lavinia and Others. 1907.
The Shoulders of Atlas. 1908.
The Winning Lady and Others. 1909.
The Butterfly House. 1912.
The Yates Pride. 1912.
The Copy-Cat and Other Stories. 1914.
An Alabaster Box, with Florence Morse Kingsley. 1917.
Edgewater People (stories). 1918.
The Best Stories, edited by Henry Wysham Lanier. 1927.

Play

Giles Corey, Yeoman. 1893.

Other (for children)

Goody Two-Shoes and Other Famous Nursery Tales, with Clara Doty Bates. 1883.
Decorative Plaques (verse), designs by George F. Barnes. 1883.
The Cow with Golden Horns and Other Stories. 1884(?).
The Adventures of Ann: Stories of Colonial Times. 1886.
The Pot of Gold and Other Stories. 1892.
Young Lucretia and Other Stories. 1892.
Comfort Pease and Her Gold Ring. 1895.
Once Upon a Time and Other Child-Verses. 1897.
The Green Door. 1910.

*

Bibliography: in *Bibliography of American Literature* by Jacob Blanck, 1959.

Critical Studies: *Freeman* by Edward Foster, 1956; *Freeman* by Perry D. Westbrook, 1967.

* * *

Mary E. Wilkins Freeman, who wrote almost exclusively about rural and village life in New England, ranks among the foremost American local colorists or regionalists. Brought up in a family of modest means and station in the small towns of Randolph, Massachusetts, and Brattleboro, Vermont, she drew the material for her fiction from her own experience; and when she started, in her early twenties, to write stories with New England settings she was hailed as an expert in the dialect, customs, and character traits of the people of her region. Thus she won a place among the early realists in American literature, receiving praise from William Dean Howells, a leader in the realist movement.

Freeman's keenest personal interest and her greatest strength were in the psychological analysis of characters representative of the final phase of Puritanism. In her day the old religion and culture lingered in the back country, but in an advanced state of decay. This was a period in the rural areas that one literary historian felicitously described as "the terminal moraine of New England Puritanism." Among the people the old Puritan strengths had degenerated into eccentricity, neurosis, and worse; and these warpings of personality are portrayed unforgettably in Freeman's works. Especially fascinating to her was the transformation of the Puritan will—once considered to be under God's direction—into pathological compulsions and obsessions: a man who will not enter his church but sits on its porch for ten years during Sabbath services because of a minor doctrinal difference with the minister ("A Conflict Ended"); a village seamstress who faints from hunger rather than receive payment for two patchwork quilts because she keeps misplacing one rag and forces herself to redo her work twice ("An Honest Soul"); a woman who waits fifteen years for her lover to return from Australia, finds on his return that he is in love with another girl, and lives out the rest of her life in self-imposed solitude ("A New England Nun"); a young farmer who breaks his engagement with his fiancée because of an insignificant political disagreement with her father and postpones reconciliation for ten years (*Pembroke*).

Freeman's best writing is in the form of short fiction, which from the beginning of her career found ready acceptance in periodicals like *Harper's New Monthly*. The best known among the many volumes of her tales were the first two to be published—*A Humble Romance and Other Stories* and *A New England Nun and Other Stories*. Freeman also wrote a number of novels, the most notable of which are *Jane Field* and *Pembroke*, both dealing with New England village life. The latter is a powerful novel, which received high praise from Arthur Machen and Arthur Conan Doyle. In all her writing Freeman's style is simple and direct, though at times she proves herself adept at using symbols (the chained dog and caged canary in "A New England Nun"). Recently, because of her sympathetic and realistic fictional treatment of women, she has aroused considerable interest among feminist critics in America.

—Perry D. Westbrook

FRENEAU, Philip (Morin). Born in New York City, 2 January 1752. Educated privately, and at the College of New Jersey (now Princeton University), 1768–71, B.A. 1771. Enlisted in New Jersey militia and served as crew member on blockade runners, 1778–80: captured by the British, 1780. Married Eleanor Forman in 1790. Teacher on Long Island, New York, 1772, and at Somerset Academy, Back Creek, Maryland, 1773–74; lived in New York, 1775; planter's secretary and sailor, Santa Cruz, West Indies, 1776–78; editorial staff member, *Freeman's Journal*, Philadelphia, 1781–84; post office clerk, Philadelphia, 1782–84; master of a brig bound for Jamaica, 1784, and officer on ships in the Caribbean and Atlantic coast trade, 1785–89; editor, New York *Daily Advertiser*, 1790–91; translating clerk, U.S. Department of State, and editor, *National Gazette*, Philadelphia, 1791–93; bookseller and farmer, 1795, and editor, *Jersey Chronicle*, 1795–96, Mount Pleasant, New Jersey; editor, *Time-Piece*, New York, 1796–98; managed his New Jersey farm, 1799–1801 and after 1808; sailor, 1802–07. *Died 18/19 December 1832.*

PUBLICATIONS

Collections

Poems, edited by Fred Lewis Pattee. 3 vols., 1902–07.
Poems, edited by Harry Hayden Clark. 1929.
Prose, edited by Philip M. Marsh. 1955.
A Freneau Sampler, edited by Philip M. Marsh. 1963.

Verse

A Poem on the Rising Glory of America, with Hugh Henry Brackenridge. 1772.
The American Village. 1772.
American Liberty. 1775.
A Voyage to Boston. 1775.
General Gage's Soliloquy. 1775.
General Gage's Confession. 1775.
The British Prison-Ship. 1781.
The Poems. 1786; as *Poems on Various Occasions*, 1861.
A Journey from Philadelphia to New-York. 1787; as *A Laughable Poem*, 1809.
The Village Merchant. 1794.
Poems Written Between the Years 1768 and 1794. 1795.
Poems, Written and Published During the American Revolutionary War. 2 vols., 1809.
A Collection of Poems on American Affairs. 2 vols., 1815.
Some Account of the Capture of the Ship Aurora, edited by Jay Miller. 1899.
Last Poems, edited by Lewis Leary. 1946.

Fiction

Father Bembo's Pilgrimage to Mecca 1770, with Hugh Henry Brackenridge, edited by Michael Davitt Bell. 1975.

Other

Miscellaneous Works. 1788.
Letters on Various Interesting and Important Subjects. 1799.
Unpublished Freneauana, edited by Charles F. Heartman. 1918.
The Writings of Hezekiah Salem, edited by Lewis Leary. 1975.

Editor, *An Historical Sketch of the Life of Silas Talbot*. 1803.

Translator, *New Travels Through North America*, by Abbé Claude Robin. 1783.

*

Bibliography: *A Bibliography of the Separate and Collected Works of Freneau* by Victor Hugo Paltsits, 1903; in *Bibliography of American Literature* by Jacob Blanck, 1959; *Freneau's Published Prose: A Bibliography* by Philip M. Marsh, 1970.

Critical Studies: *That Rascal Freneau: A Study in Literary Failure* by Lewis Leary, 1941; *Freneau and the Cosmic Enigma* by Nelson F. Adkins, 1949; *The Prose of Freneau*, 1955, *Freneau, Poet and Journalist*, 1967, and *The Works of Freneau: A Critical Study*, 1968, all by Philip M. Marsh; *Freneau: Champion of Democracy* by Jacob Axelrad, 1967; *Freneau* by Mary Weatherspoon Bowden, 1976; *Land and Sea: The Lyric Poetry of Freneau* by Richard C. Vitzthum, 1978.

* * *

Philip Freneau's poetry and prose reflect his life and times: he gloried in matching the image of the Enlightened gentleman-scholar, one who could be as content administering his estate as intriguing in the latest political uproar, as happy translating the classics as being the master of a ship safely brought into port. Current politics, the latest scientific discovery, the newest philosophy, the recent misfortune of a neighbor, the chance observation of a terrapin: Freneau thought all fit subjects for his pen.

Many of his poems were propaganda, either for political party or for the United States during the two wars against Great Britain. In his poems of the Revolution, he moved from personal attacks on the British ("Cain, Nimrod, Nero—fiends in human guise, / Herod, Domitian—these in judgment rise, / And, envious of his deeds, I hear them say / None but a George could be more vile than they") to calls for greater exertion by the patriots ("Rouse from your sleep, and crush the thievish band, / Defeat, destroy, and sweep them from the land"). But his War of 1812 verse is more urbane: both sides are pictured with wit and humor. Freneau was also involved in other causes: for the Revolution in France, against the American lack of support for poetry ("An age employed in edging steel / Can no poetic raptures feel"), against the dislocation of the Indians, against debtors' prisons. Much of this occasional verse, written in the heat of the moment, deserves to be forgotten, but sometimes, as in "Stanzas to an Alien" or "Stanzas on the Decease of Thomas Paine," he achieves lasting feeling.

Freneau's best known prose is that in his several series of essays. In the early series, the major characters, "The Pilgrim" and "The Philosopher of the Forest," tend to be preachy and fuzzily drawn. The Indian "Tomo-Cheeki" of another series voices the expected noble-savage statements in elegant prose: he is but a device for social criticism through the contrast of cultures. Used somewhat similarly is "Hezekiah Salem," the chief character of a light series that appeared in New York. As a New Englander, Salem is an early progenitor of American humor based on regional differences. But Freneau's greatest prose creation was Robert Slender, spokesman of an electioneering series. Robert Slender is the common man: he speaks as one, he feels as one, his fears are those of one. He views government from the point of view of everyday life, as here where he talks to himself on the way to a tavern:

> Had I, said I, (talking to myself all the while) the disposal of but half the income of the United States, I could at least so order matters, that a man might walk to his next neighbour's without splashing his stockings, or being in danger of breaking his legs in ruts, holes, gutts, and gullies. I do not know, says I to myself, as I moralized on my splash'd stocking, but money might with more profit be laid out in repairing the roads, than in marine establishments, supporting a standing army, useless embassies, exorbitant salaries, given to many flashy fellows that are no honour to us, or to themselves, and chartering whole ships to carry a single man to another nation.

Freneau's best prose pieces are those in which he speaks in this colloquial, common style.

But the works of Freneau which are read today are not the occasional verse which made him famous, nor his prose, but poems which capture the melancholy so admired by the pre-Romantics. Best known of this type is "The Wild Honeysuckle," which presents the inevitable decay of the flower's beauty: "Smit with those charms, that must decay, / I grieve to see your future doom." The emotion is restrained, is never permitted to become more than a pleasing melancholy:

> From morning suns and evening dews
> At first thy little being came
> If nothing once, you nothing lose,
> For when you die you are the same;
> The space between, is but an hour,
> The frail duration of a flower.

As Freneau revised the last couplet several times, so he revised his best poems frequently, polishing them as a craftsman. One of his best is "Ode to Fancy," a late revision of his very early "The Power of Fancy." The poem begins with Fancy's origin and nature: "Wakeful, vagrant, restless thing, / Ever wandering on the wing, / Who thy wondrous source can find, / Fancy, regent of the mind." The poet then presents the analogy between the creations of man's fancy and the elements of the universe, "Ideas of the Almighty mind!" After a description of Fancy's power, the poem ends with this plea: "Come, O come—perceiv'd by none, / You and I will walk alone." The whole is a unified, satisfying poem. As, later in life, Freneau became a better poet, he also became a more philosophical one, often presenting in verse his views on nature and the universe, still clinging to that most cherished virtue of the Enlightenment—moderation. In one of his last poems, "Winter," he again emphasizes this virtue:

> Happy with wine we may indulge an hour;
> The noblest beverage of the mildest power.
> Happy, with Love, to solace every care,
> Happy with sense and wit an hour to share;
> These to the mind a thousand pleasures bring
> And give to winter's frosts the smiles of spring.

These virtues appear also in Freneau's works: they show wit and sense, and feeling.

—Mary Weatherspoon Bowden

FROST, Robert (Lee). Born in San Francisco, California, 26 March 1874. Educated at Lawrence High School, Massachusetts, graduated 1892; Dartmouth College, Hanover, New Hampshire, 1892; Harvard University, Cambridge, Massachusetts, 1897–99. Married Elinor Miriam White in 1895; one son and three daughters. Mill worker and teacher, Lawrence, 1892–97; farmer, Derry, New Hampshire, 1900–12; English teacher, Pinkerton Academy, Derry, 1905–11; conducted course in psychology, State Normal School, Plymouth, New Hampshire, 1911–12; sold his farm, and lived in England, 1912–15; returned to America and settled on a farm near Franconia, New Hampshire, 1915; Poet-in-Residence, Amherst College, Massachusetts, 1916–20; subsequently Visiting Lecturer at Wesleyan University, Middletown, Connecticut; University of Michigan, Ann Arbor, 1921-23, 1925–26; Dartmouth College; Yale University, New Haven, Connecticut; and Harvard University. A founder, Bread Loaf School, Middlebury College, Vermont, 1920. Poetry Consultant, Library of Congress, Washington, D.C., 1958. Recipient: Pulitzer Prize, 1924, 1931, 1937, 1943; New England Poetry Club Golden Rose, 1928; Loines award, 1931; American Academy Gold Medal, 1939; Academy of American Poets fellowship, 1953; Sarah Josepha Hale Award, 1956; Emerson-Thoreau Medal, 1959; U.S. Senate Citation of Honor, 1960; Poetry Society of America Gold Medal, 1962; MacDowell Medal, 1962; Bollingen Prize, 1963. Litt.D.: Cambridge University, 1957; D.Litt.: Oxford University, 1957. Member, American Academy. *Died 29 January 1963.*

PUBLICATIONS

Collections

The Poetry, edited by Edward Connery Lathem. 1969.
Selected Letters, edited by Lawrance Thompson. 1964.
Selected Prose, edited by Hyde Cox and Edward Connery Lathem. 1966.

Verse

Twilight. 1894.
A Boy's Will. 1913.
North of Boston. 1914.
Mountain Interval. 1916.
Selected Poems. 1923.
New Hampshire: A Poem with Notes and Grace Notes. 1923.
West-Running Brook. 1928.
The Lovely Shall Be Choosers. 1929.
Collected Poems. 1930; revised edition, 1939.
The Lone Striker. 1933.
Three Poems. 1935.
The Gold Hesperides. 1935.
From Snow to Snow. 1936.
A Further Range. 1936.
Selected Poems. 1936.
A Considerable Speck. 1939.
A Witness Tree. 1942.
Come In and Other Poems, edited by Louis Untermeyer. 1943; revised edition, as *The Road Not Taken*, 1951.
A Masque of Reason. 1945.
The Courage to Be New. 1946.
Poems. 1946.
Steeple Bush. 1947.
A Masque of Mercy. 1947.

Complete Poems. 1949.
Hard Not to Be King. 1951.
Aforesaid. 1954.
Selected Poems. 1955.
Dedication: The Gift Outright. 1961.
In the Clearing. 1962.
One Favored Acorn. 1969.

Plays

A Way Out (produced 1919?). 1929.
The Cow's in the Corn. 1929.

Other

Two Letters. 1931.
Frost and John Bartlett: The Record of a Friendship, edited by Margaret Bartlett Anderson. 1963.
Letters to Louis Untermeyer. 1963.
Frost: Farm-Poultryman, edited by Edward Connery Lathem and Lawrance Thompson. 1963.
Frost: Life and Talks—Walking, edited by Louis Mertins. 1965.
Frost and the Lawrence, Massachusetts "High School Bulletin": The Beginning of a Literary Career, edited by Edward Connery Lathem and Lawrance Thompson. 1966.
Interviews with Frost, edited by Edward Connery Lathem. 1967.
Family Letters of Robert and Elinor Frost, edited by Arnold Grade. 1972.
Frost on Writing, edited by Elaine Barry. 1973.
A Time to Talk, edited by Robert Francis. 1973.
Frost and Sidney Cox: Forty Years of Friendship, edited by William R. Evans. 1981.
Stories for Lesley (for children), edited by Roger D. Sell. 1984.

*

Bibliography: *A Descriptive Catalogue of Books and Manuscripts in the Clifton Waller Barrett Library, University of Virginia* by Joan St. C. Crane, 1974; *The Critical Reception of Frost: An Annotated Bibliography of Secondary Comment* by Peter VanEgmond, 1974; *Frost: A Bibliography 1913–1974* by Frank and Melissa C. Lentricchia, 1976.

Critical Studies: *Human Values in the Poetry of Frost: A Study of a Poet's Convictions* by George W. Nitchie, 1960; *The Pastoral Art of Frost* by John F. Lynen, 1960; *Frost: A Collection of Critical Essays* edited by James M. Cox, 1962; *An Introduction to Frost* by Elizabeth Isaacs, 1962; *The Major Themes of Frost* by Radcliffe Squires, 1963; *The Poetry of Frost: Constellations of Intention* by Reuben Brower, 1963; *Frost* by Elizabeth Jennings, 1964; *Frost* by James Doyle, 1965; *Frost* by Philip L. Gerber, 1966, revised edition, 1982, and *Critical Essays on Frost* edited by Gerber, 1982; *Frost: The Early Years*, 1966, *The Years of Triumph*, 1970, and *The Later Years*, 1977, by Lawrance Thompson and R.H. Winnick (one vol. edition, edited by Edward Connery Lathem, 1982); *Frost* by Elaine Barry, 1973; *Frost* by Reginald Cook, 1974; *Frost: The Poet and His Critics* by Donald J. Greiner, 1974; *Frost: Centennial Essays 1-3* edited by Jac Tharpe, 3 vols., 1974–78; *Frost: Modern Poetics and the Landscapes of Self* by Frank Lentricchia, 1975; *Frost's Imagery and the Poetic Consciousness* by Dennis Vail, 1976; *Frost: The Critical Reception* edited by Linda W. Wagner, 1977; *Frost: The Work of Knowing* by Richard Poirier, 1977; *Frost and New England: The Poet as Regionalist* by John C. Kemp, 1979; *Frost: Studies of the Poetry* by Kathryn Gibbs Harris, 1979; *Frost Handbook* by James L. Potter, 1980; *Frost: Contours of Belief* by Dorothy Judd Hall, 1984; *Frost: A Literary Life Reconsidered* by William H. Pritchard, 1984; *Frost and the Opposing Lights of the Hour* by Richard Wakefield, 1984; *Frost Himself* by Stanley Burnshaw, 1986.

* * *

In 1959, at a dinner celebrating Robert Frost's 85th birthday, Lionel Trilling gave an after-dinner address that was later incorporated in "A Speech on Robert Frost: A Cultural Episode." Trilling announced his antipathy for those poems by Frost which expressed a "distaste for the life of the city" and for "the demand that is made upon intellect to deal with whatever are the causes of complexity, uncertainty, anxiety." Then Trilling specified poems he did admire, poems that led him to define Frost as a "terrifying poet" who depicted a "terrifying universe." The speech confused Frost (who was not sure whether he had been attacked or praised), outraged many of his friends, and caused quite a furor.

It would seem ludicrous that as late as at the time of Frost's 85th birthday there could be so much confusion concerning what constituted his basic point of view. Yet several factors make this situation plausible. For one thing, although such critics as John Crowe Ransom and Randall Jarrell praised Frost's poetry, his work gained comparatively little critical attention in the decades when the practitioners of the New Criticism reigned supreme. Further complications were caused by many of the critics who did laud his work. These admirers touted precisely the glib, sentimental, shallow poems by Frost that Trilling disliked. The main source of the confusion, however, was Frost himself. Because Frost hungered so insatiably for popularity and esteem, he meticulously created a "folksy" public image of himself that his audiences would be entranced by. He never read any of his somber poems in public. He saw to it that his unattractive traits—his obsessive need to win at everything, his violent temper, his delight in back-biting, his race prejudices—remained totally unknown to the public. With equal skill, he hid his family misfortunes—his sister's insanity, his severe marital problems, his son's suicide, a daughter's insanity.

It is no wonder, then, that although Frost began writing in the late 19th century, we are still only beginning to formulate an intelligent evaluation of his poetry. Yet, despite all the obfuscations, such an evaluation is well worth pursuing, for Frost's best poems—and there are many of them—are of a very high quality. Frost was a consummate craftsman. He mastered a variety of forms; he wrote excellent sonnets, heroic couplets, and blank verse poems. His rime patterns are deftly wrought. He was even more adroit in matters of meter and rhythm. He proved repeatedly that there is no reason to believe that traditional rhythmical patterns inevitably lead to monotony.

What ultimately makes Frost's best poems valuable, however, is their dynamic view of our daily life. Frost believed that we live in a God-directed universe, but despite all his religious meditations Frost found God's ways absolutely inscrutable. At his most grim, as represented in "Design," Frost not only acknowledges the presence of the appalling in physical reality, but wonders if there is any cosmic design at all. It is certain in any case, as "Nothing Gold Can Stay" states, that no purity can abide in physical reality. What is pure is almost immediately contaminated. Nature is lovely at times, yet its very loveliness can prove fatally alluring, as the speaker in "Stopping by Woods on a Snowy Evening" testifies. Nor can we imitate the animal world and rely on our instincts; "The White-Tailed Hornet" reports that nature's creatures, acting on pure instinct, often blunder ridiculously.

Man experiences no clarifying visions. "The Fear" insists that we live surrounded by a literal and metaphorical darkness which harbors the hostile and the terrifying ambiguous. Weariness and loneliness define the archetypal human being who narrates "Acquainted with the Night." Isolation and poverty can crush a person physically, mentally, and spiritually, as they do characters in "A Servant to Servants" and "The Hill Wife." Moreover, man is badgered by his suppressed desires—the point of "The Sound of the Trees." Yet "The Flood" states that man cannot always control his destructive urges.

Frost also makes it clear that people cannot easily offer each other solace. The difficulty of understanding another human being is sometimes insurmountable. In "Home Burial," a husband and wife attempt to cope with the death of their child in two different ways. Neither can understand the other's attitude or behavior; neither can in any way help the other.

In his essay " 'The Death of the Hired Man': Modernism and Transcendence," Warren French pinpoints why Frost's poetry is especially valuable today. French remarks that, aware of modern man's grim situation, Frost—unlike the pre-modernists—did not proclaim the need for every individual to retreat at all costs to the safety of society; nor did Frost adopt or advocate the lifestyle lauded by modernist writers—the deliberate withdrawal on the part of the individual from society. Instead, Frost concentrated on what marks him—in French's term—as a "post-modernist." He struggled to discover what positive course is possible for a man who wants to maintain his individuality without exiling himself from society.

The affirmative albeit starkly limited goal Frost strove for and suggested to others is best indicated by his statement that his poems offer "a momentary stay against confusion." A series of momentary stays, created by the individual, is all man can hope for. As Lawrance Thompson wrote in his introduction to Frost's *Selected Letters*, Frost "bluntly rejected all the conventional stays which dogmatists call permanent"; they are too inflexible to contend successfully with physical reality's ever-shifting conditions. Frost was equally uninterested in trying to transcend the physical—material—world. He thought that the label "materialist" was used too quickly as a pejorative term. He said that it was "wrong to call anybody a materialist simply because he tried to say spirit in terms of matter, as if that were a sin." Nor did Frost fall back on the Romantic belief that man is basically good. He spurned the view that because man and nature are God's creations, they can do no wrong.

According to Frost, in order to achieve a momentary stay against confusion the first thing man needs is courage. A character in *A Masque of Mercy* says, "The saddest thing in life / Is that the best thing in it should be courage." Man must also try to maintain his equilibrium. Again and again, as in "The Vantage Point," "Goodbye and Keep Cold," and "To Earthward," Frost underscores the need to have the right perspective on all things, including oneself. Men should focus on the facts—and not daydream. In "Mowing," he declares that "The fact is the sweetest dream that labor knows." "Labor" is another key word. In "Two Tramps in Mud Time," he states that we should work and that our work should be motivated simultaneously by "love" and "need."

In some ways, nature can be supportive. "The Onset" and "The Need of Being Versed in Country Things" remind us that many things on earth are cyclical; this means that although evil comes to us, it will not last. So, too, nature is a revitalizing force, and sometimes awesomely beautiful, as described in "Iris by Night." It can also startle us out of a black mood created by too much self-centeredness—the development recorded in "Dust of Snow." It should also be remembered, as "Our Hold on the Planet" points out, that nature is at least "one fraction of one per cent" in "favor of man"—otherwise we would never have been able to thrive on earth.

Finally, Frost specifically advises us to preserve our individual integrity, but to link ourselves to society. Frost's emphasis on the value of society (often symbolized by the home) is coupled with his emphasis on the value of love. Love can be tenderly lyrical, as described in "Meeting and Passing." "Putting In the Seed" proclaims that love can be dynamically fertile. Love can alter reality—the point in "Never Again Would Birds' Song Be the Same." Love, breeding forgiveness and acceptance, provides a home against adversity. This is what Mary, in "The Death of the Hired Man," knows to be so, and what her husband Warren comes to realize. They decide to nurse Silas, their old hired man, but also to allow him his self-respect. Perhaps the finest example of Frost's stress on the importance of a viable balance between the individual and society is "The Silken Tent." Here, the woman described is a vibrant individual, yet held—willingly—by "countless ties of love and thought / To everything on earth."

—Robert K. Johnson

See the essay on "The Death of the Hired Man."

FULLER, Henry Blake. Born in Chicago, Illinois, 9 January 1857. Educated at South Division High School, Chicago, 1872, 1875–76, and Allison Classical Academy, Oconomowoc, Wisconsin, 1873–74. Worked at Ovington's Crockery, 1875–76, and Home National Bank, 1877–78, Chicago; toured Europe, 1879–80; free-lance writer in Chicago, 1880–82 and after 1885, Rome, 1883, and Boston, 1884–85: wrote for Chicago *Tribune*, 1884, and book review section of Chicago *Evening Post*, 1901–02; editorial writer, Chicago *Record-Herald*, 1911–13. Member of the advisory committee, *Poetry*, Chicago, 1912–29. *Died 28 July 1929.*

PUBLICATIONS

Fiction

The Chevalier of Pensieri-Vani (stories). 1890; revised edition, 1892.
The Chatelaine of La Trinité. 1892.
The Cliff-Dwellers. 1893.
With the Procession. 1895.
From the Other Side: Stories of Transatlantic Travel. 1898.
The New Flag: Satires. 1899.
The Last Refuge: A Sicilian Romance. 1900.
Under the Skylights (stories). 1901.

Waldo Trench and Others: Stories of Americans in Italy. 1908.
Lines Long and Short: Biographical Sketches in Various Rhythms (stories). 1917.
On the Stairs. 1918.
Bertram Cope's Year. 1919.
Gardens of This World. 1929.
Not on the Screen. 1930.

Plays

O, That Way Madness Lies: A Play for Marionettes, in *Chapbook 4*, December 1895.
The Puppet-Booth: Twelve Plays. 1896.
The Coffee-House, and *The Fan*, from plays by Goldoni. 2 vols., 1925–26.
The Red Carpet, in *Fuller: A Critical Biography* by Constance Griffin. 1939.

Other

Editor, *The So-Called Human Race*, by Bert Leston Taylor. 1922.

*

Bibliography: *Fuller and Hamlin Garland: A Reference Guide* by Charles L.P. Silet, 1977.

Critical Studies: *Fuller: A Critical Biography* by Constance Griffin, 1939; *Fuller* by John Pilkington, 1970; *Fuller of Chicago: The Ordeal of a Genteel Realist in Ungenteel America* by Bernard R. Bowron, Jr., 1974.

* * *

A writer whose work suggests Henry James or William Dean Howells, but without the former's strength and without the latter's variety, Henry Blake Fuller strikes his admirers as subtle and his detractors as dull. In his best novels the style is elegant and spare, distinguished by a dry wit; in verse and drama, and in his last two novels, however, the performance is uncertain and even embarrassing. An "unconquerable reticence," in Harriet Monroe's phrase, and the "deliberate flatness" which Edmund Wilson observed do not encourage many readers to pursue this decorous writer. Three novels and several stories, however, do not deserve their present neglect.

Fuller's fictions pass in Italy or in Chicago. In the first group, somewhat vulgar Americans encounter sophisticated Europeans in a series of books beginning with *The Chevalier of Pensieri-Vani*. An elderly American woman, for example, longs to escape her crass new country for the older, presumably better one; an Italian nobleman is persuaded to alter his family's villa to suit the whims of tasteless Americans; on a train, an American encounters a travelling theatrical troupe and mistakes it for royalty. These ironic miniatures are finely honed and atmospheric, but they are less persuasive than the best of the Chicago novels.

With the Procession traces a middle-class family's pathetic attempts to social climb. An older generation has made the modest family fortune which a younger one wastes. The son is a posturing dilettante, the daughter a fatuous spinster, each aspiring to join Chicago's social "procession." *On the Stairs* follows the equally mediocre lives of two boys, the rise of one and the fall of the other, through two generations that blur the social distinctions which separated them in youth and separate them through economic ones.

Fuller's preoccupation with failures—despite his wry humor—may account, in part, for the indifference with which his best novel was greeted. *Bertram Cope's Year* attempts to overcome Fuller's "unconquerable reticence" in dealing with homosexuals, but in a manner sufficiently elliptical to obscure its intentions. Cope, an androgynous young man of surpassing good looks, attracts everyone despite his seeming diffidence and lack of marked intellect, but the attraction is only superficial. Cope is the *beau ideal* with little to offer, and his catastrophic effect on a variety of people is emotional rather than physical, spun in Fuller's most indirect manner. Critics seem to have misunderstood the novel, and Fuller's friends were embarrassed by it. A decade later he wrote two other novels, but at the time of the failure of *Bertram Cope's Year* he said, "No further novels likely: too much effort and too little return—often none." It deserves attention.

—Bruce Kellner

GADDIS, William. Born in New York City in 1922. Educated at Harvard University, Cambridge, Massachusetts. Has one son and one daughter. Staff member, *New Yorker*, 1946–47; lived in Latin America, Europe, and North Africa, 1947–55; free-lance speech and filmscript writer, 1956–1970's. Recipient: American Academy grant, 1963; National Endowment for the Arts grant, 1966, 1974; National Book Award, 1976; Guggenheim fellowship, 1981; MacArthur Prize, 1982. Member, American Academy, 1984.

PUBLICATIONS

Fiction

The Recognitions. 1955.
JR. 1975.
Carpenter's Gothic. 1985.

*

Critical Studies: *City of Words* by Tony Tanner, 1971; *A Reader's Guide to Gaddis's The Recognitions* by Steven Moore, 1982, and *In Recognition of Gaddis* edited by Moore and John Kuehl, 1984; "Gaddis Issue" of *Review of Contemporary Fiction*, vol. 2, no. 2, 1982; *American Fictions 1940–1980* by Frederick Karl, 1983.

* * *

William Gaddis's novels are, without exception, works long and complex, and all are marked by technical departures from ordinary conventions of narrative. The esteem for these works may testify to a widespread impatience with old fashions of narrative and a thirst for other ways of presenting experience. Among these "other ways"—ways that can also be observed in John Barth, Thomas Pynchon, Richard Brautigan, and others—are the modes of transmuting reality, perhaps of getting at its essence by stringent rearrangement, which the reader meets in *The Recognitions* and *JR*.

JR is, as a story, an account of the fraudulent manipulation of stocks by a sixth-grader in a Long Island school for delinquents. The boy (JR) uses adults as agents and exploits for his own benefit the fatuities and self-deceptions of the great American world of trade and "development." An amusing anecdote. But Gaddis opens it out to deal with all that takes place in the universe that is composed of stock flotation, management of industry, manipulation of bequests, and even in the arts, which are not independent of the commercial textures that surround them. In these tossing seas, the little craft of the boy JR often vanishes from view to reappear a hundred pages later.

All this is presented in a way that leaves a realistic copying of the world to one side. Interminable conversations, by telephone or face-to-face, blend with other conversations, and one learns by osmosis rather than by explicit statement which characters are speaking on a certain page. Moreover, many characters are endowed with knowledge they would not have in "real life"; obscure Christian heresies or references to Eliot's *The Waste Land* occasionally sum up what a fumbling speaker is trying to say. To some readers, the result of all this is just confusion; others will find *JR* an often comic and revealing view of a world in which conventional pieties, familial and sexual, conform to the laws of trade. From this point of view, the novel is a confident innovation that refines a reader's awareness and encourages his detachment from what the bulk of mankind regard as important.

The earlier novel, *The Recognitions*, also views a great variety of persons and settings, but under the sign of religion rather than money. Persons try to see the sum of human meaning expressed by the various religions of the world and express some of these meanings in works of art and, even, in personal involvements. If Gaddis himself has an attitude toward the motley adventures and aspirations he reports, it is perhaps indicated by several references to Frazer's *Golden Bough*, where the effort of a scholar's mind to free itself from delusion is displayed. But such a firm center to *The Recognitions* becomes dim as endless inconsequence and violence mingle, undoing the "noble" hope of this character or that one. Scenes of great comic power alternate with interminable discussion.

Carpenter's Gothic has a plot. But, as is usual with Gaddis, the course of events comes to us filtered through a thick-mashed screen. The screen, in this novel, is the way in which the characters usually speak. Now and then a man called McCandless is allowed to express himself rather clearly on fundamentalism and other evils. But otherwise each utterance is a blend of what the particular character is saying and what that character might well be thinking. This is particularly true of the utterances of the scatter-brained heroine, Liz. Each new topic that enters her mind is obscured by the ferment of the topics that are already present. And Liz's habit of thought is for the most part the mode of expression with which Gaddis endows all the other characters.

In short, Gaddis's presentation in *Carpenter's Gothic* is once more unconventional and difficult. But the plot, unlike that of *JR* and *The Recognitions*, is as full of conventional surprises as a thriller. McCandless is no tower of sense, but is actually insane. Liz's best friend Edie not only discovers Liz's body but drives off with Liz's husband, both well content. However, it is not in these events that the interest of *Carpenter's Gothic* lies but in the dense texture of spoken discourse, of conversations where minds, as often as not, do not meet.

Such, indeed, in this novel and the other two is the ordinary texture which persons weave when their hands reach out to each other, and do not touch.

—Harold H. Watts

See the essay on *The Recognitions*.

GALE, Zona. Born in Portage, Wisconsin, 26 August 1874. Educated in Portage public schools, and at the University of Wisconsin, Madison, 1891–95, B.L. 1895, M.L. 1899. Married William L. Breese in 1928; one adopted daughter. Reporter, Milwaukee *Evening Wisconsin*, 1895–96, Milwaukee *Journal*, 1896–1901, and New York *Evening World*, 1901–03; returned to Portage, 1904; thereafter a full-time writer. Member, Wisconsin Library Commission, 1920–32; member, Board of Regents, 1923–29, and Board of Visitors, 1936–38, University of Wisconsin; Wisconsin delegate, International Congress of Women, Chicago, 1933. Recipient: Butterick Prize, 1911; Pulitzer Prize, for drama, 1921. D.Litt.: Ripon College, Wisconsin, 1922; University of Wisconsin, 1929; Rollins College, Winter Park, Florida, 1930. *Died 27 December 1938.*

PUBLICATIONS

Fiction

Romance Island. 1906.
The Loves of Pelleas and Etarre (stories). 1907.
Friendship Village (stories). 1908.
Friendship Village Love Stories. 1909.
Mothers to Men. 1911.
Christmas: A Story. 1912.
Neighborhood Stories. 1914.
Heart's Kindred. 1915.
A Daughter of the Morning. 1917.
Birth. 1918.
Peace in Friendship Village (stories). 1919.
Miss Lulu Bett. 1920.
Faint Perfume. 1923.
Preface to a Life. 1926.
Yellow Gentians and Blue (stories). 1927.
Borgia. 1929.
Bridal Pond (stories). 1930.
Papa La Fleur. 1933.
Old-Fashioned Tales. 1933.
Light Woman. 1937.
Magna. 1939.

Plays

The Neighbours (produced 1912). 1926.
Miss Lulu Bett, from her own novel (produced 1920). 1921.
Uncle Jimmy. 1922.
Mister Pitt (produced 1925). 1925.
Evening Clothes. 1932.
Faint Perfume, from her own novel. 1934.
The Clouds. 1936.

Radio Play: *Neighbors*, with Marian de Forest, from stories in *Friendship Village* by Gale, 1933.

Verse

The Secret Way. 1921.

Other

Civic Improvement in Little Towns. 1913.
When I Was a Little Girl. 1913.
What Women Won in Wisconsin. 1922.
Portage, Wisconsin, and Other Essays. 1928.
Frank Miller of Mission Inn. 1938.

*

Bibliography: "Gale" by Harold P. Simonson, in *American Literary Realism 3*, 1968.

Critical Studies: *Still Small Voice: The Biography of Gale* by August Derleth, 1940; *Gale* by Harold P. Simonson, 1962.

* * *

"There is no contemporary author," wrote Joseph Wood Krutch in 1929, "whose evolution is more interesting than that of Zona Gale." Although she lived most of her life in the village of her birth—Portage, Wisconsin—and wrote largely in the village vein that attracted the talents of so many other writers of her generation, she was nevertheless a child of her age who responded to the astonishing variety of its pressures.

After four years in New York, during which she wrote *Romance Island* and *The Loves of Pelleas and Etarre*, two works of saccharine sentimentality, Gale returned to Portage to write a series of novels and tales, including *Friendship Village*, *Friendship Village Love Stories*, *Neighborhood Stories*, and *Peace in Friendship Village*. Unlike the meanness of Lewis's Gopher Prairie, the grotesquery of Anderson's Winesburg, or the enervation of Garland's Middle Border, Gale's Friendship Village, though not so sentimentally drawn as her earlier Romance Island, was an idyllic and hospitable town dedicated to children, family, and community.

However, her pastoral rendering of Friendship Village obscured her growing concerns with the issues and movements of her day—pacifism, women's rights, prohibition, civil liberties, progressivism, and others—even as it did her labors in their behalf: writing pamphlets and delivering speeches, campaigning for the progressive La Follettes of her native Wisconsin, joining the ill-fated protest against the execution of Sacco and Vanzetti. In truth, Gale's increasingly realistic image of the world found its way even into the Friendship Village tales, which by the decade's end had begun to compromise the idyll with an occasional suggestion of reform. More important, her growing politicization was signaled in three novels of social relevance, all written during the Friendship Village period. *Heart's Kindred*, a pacifist piece; *A Daughter of the Morning*, a portrait of the working woman's plight; and what is perhaps her best work, *Birth*. In the last of these three, readers found a vision of small-town Americana whose acerbity approaches that of the better-known realist writers of her time. Indeed, *Birth*, along with *Miss Lulu Bett*, an equally acerbic novel of village life for which, after dramatization, Gale was awarded the Pulitzer Prize, nearly established their author as an authentic if minor realist writer.

Gale soon moved on, however. Prompted on a personal level by the death of her doting mother and more generally by the rise of a variety of New Thought movements in which she took an interest, Gale moved from realism to spiritualism and the occult, a vantage point from which she wrote a number of short stories and also *Preface to a Life*, a novel whose major character, though living on some higher astral plane, is understood by his fellow villagers to be insane.

Her talent having been a modest one, Gale has fallen into the obscurity which most critics agree she deserves. Still, she was in tune with many of the social currents of her day. And had her powers of imagination been greater, had her artistic control been stronger, her contribution to American letters might well have been of a high rank.

—Bruce A. Lohof

GARDNER, Erle Stanley. Born in Malden, Massachusetts, 17 July 1889. Educated at Palo Alto High School, California, graduated 1909; Valparaiso University, Indiana, 1909; studied in law offices and admitted to the California bar, 1911. Married 1) Natalie Talbert in 1912 (separated, 1935; died, 1968), one daughter; 2) Agnes Jean Bethell in 1968. Lawyer, Oxnard, California, 1911–18; salesman, Consolidated Sales Company, 1918–21; lawyer, Ventura, California, 1921–33; contributed hundreds of stories, often under pseudonyms, to magazines, 1923–32; self-employed writer after 1933. Founding member, Court of Last Resort (now the Case Review Committee), 1948–60; frequent reporter on criminal trials; founder, Paisano Productions, 1957. Honorary Life Member, American Polygraph Association. Recipient: Mystery Writers of America Edgar Allan Poe Award, 1952, and Grand Master Award, 1961. Honorary alumnus: Kansas City University, 1955; D.L.: McGeorge College of Law, Sacramento, California, 1956. *Died 11 March 1970.*

PUBLICATIONS

Fiction

The Case of the Velvet Claws. 1933.
The Case of the Sulky Girl. 1933.
The Case of the Howling Dog. 1934.
The Case of the Curious Bride. 1934.
The Case of the Lucky Legs. 1934.
The Case of the Counterfeit Eye. 1935.
The Case of the Caretaker's Cat. 1935.
The Clew of the Forgotten Murder. 1935.
This Is Murder. 1935.
The Case of the Sleepwalker's Niece. 1936.
The Case of the Stuttering Bishop. 1936.
The Case of the Dangerous Dowager. 1937.
The Case of the Lame Canary. 1937.
The D.A. Calls It Murder. 1937.
Murder up My Sleeve. 1937.
The Case of the Shoplifter's Shoe. 1938.
The Case of the Substitute Face. 1938.
The D.A. Holds a Candle. 1938.

The Case of the Perjured Parrot. 1939.
The Case of the Rolling Bones. 1939.
The D.A. Draws a Circle. 1939.
The Bigger They Come. 1939; as *Lam to the Slaughter*, 1939.
The Case of the Baited Hook. 1940.
Gold Comes in Bricks. 1940.
Turn On the Heat. 1940.
The Case of the Silent Partner. 1940.
The D.A. Goes to Trial. 1940.
The Case of the Haunted Husband. 1941.
The Case of the Turning Tide. 1941.
The Case of the Empty Tin. 1941.
Double or Quits. 1941.
Spill the Jackpot! 1941.
Bats Fly at Dusk. 1942.
Owls Don't Blink. 1942.
The Case of the Careless Kitten. 1942.
The Case of the Drowning Duck. 1942.
The D.A. Cooks a Goose. 1942.
The Case of the Buried Clock. 1943.
The Case of the Drowsy Mosquito. 1943.
The Case of the Smoking Chimney. 1943.
Cats Prowl at Night. 1943.
Give 'em the Ax. 1944; as *An Axe to Grind*, 1951.
The D.A. Calls a Turn. 1944.
The Case of the Crooked Candle. 1944.
The Case of the Black-Eyed Blonde. 1944.
The Case of the Half-Wakened Wife. 1945.
Over the Hump. 1945.
The Case of the Golddigger's Purse. 1945.
The Case of the Borrowed Brunette. 1946.
The Case of the Backward Mule. 1946.
The D.A. Breaks the Seal. 1946.
Crows Can't Count. 1946.
Fools Die on Friday. 1947.
The Case of the Fan-Dancer's Horse. 1947.
The Case of the Lazy Lover. 1947.
Two Clues: The Clue of the Runaway Blonde, The Clue of the Hungry Horse. 1947.
The D.A. Takes a Chance. 1948.
The Case of the Vagabond Virgin. 1948.
The Case of the Lonely Heiress. 1948.
The Case of the Dubious Bridegroom. 1949.
The D.A. Breaks an Egg. 1949.
Bedrooms Have Windows. 1949.
The Case of the Cautious Coquette. 1949.
The Case of the Musical Cow. 1950.
The Case of the Negligent Nymph. 1950.
The Case of the One-Eyed Witness. 1950.
The Case of the Angry Mourner. 1951.
The Case of the Fiery Fingers. 1951.
The Case of the Moth-Eaten Mink. 1952.
The Case of the Grinning Gorilla. 1952.
Top of the Heap. 1952.
Some Women Won't Wait. 1953.
The Case of the Green-Eyed Sister. 1953.
The Case of the Hesitant Hostess. 1953.
The Case of the Runaway Corpse. 1954.
The Case of the Fugitive Nurse. 1954.
The Case of the Restless Redhead. 1954.
The Case of the Glamorous Ghost. 1955.
The Case of the Sun Bather's Diary. 1955.
The Case of the Nervous Accomplice. 1955.
The Case of the Terrified Typist. 1956.
The Case of the Gilded Lily. 1956.
The Case of the Demure Defendant. 1956.
Beware the Curves. 1956.
Some Slips Don't Show. 1957.
You Can Die Laughing. 1957.
The Case of the Daring Decoy. 1957.
The Case of the Lucky Loser. 1957.
The Case of the Screaming Woman. 1957.
The Case of the Long-Legged Models. 1958.
The Case of the Foot-Loose Doll. 1958.
The Case of the Calendar Girl. 1958.
The Count of Nine. 1958.
Pass the Gravy. 1959.
The Case of the Singing Skirt. 1959.
The Case of the Mythical Monkeys. 1959.
The Case of the Deadly Toy. 1959.
The Case of the Waylaid Wolf. 1960.
The Case of the Shapely Shadow. 1960.
The Case of the Duplicate Daughter. 1960.
Kept Women Can't Quit. 1960.
Bachelors Get Lonely. 1961.
Shills Can't Cash Chips. 1961; as *Stop at the Red Light*, 1962.
The Case of the Bigamous Spouse. 1961.
The Case of the Spurious Spinster. 1961.
The Case of the Reluctant Model. 1962.
The Case of the Blonde Bonanza. 1962.
The Case of the Ice-Cold Hands. 1962.
Try Anything Once. 1962.
Fish or Cut Bait. 1963.
The Case of the Amorous Aunt. 1963.
The Case of the Mischievous Doll. 1963.
The Case of the Stepdaughter's Secret. 1963.
The Case of the Phantom Fortune. 1964.
Up for Grabs. 1964.
The Case of the Horrified Heirs. 1964.
The Case of the Daring Divorcee. 1964.
The Case of the Beautiful Beggar. 1965.
Cut Thin to Win. 1965.
The Case of the Troubled Trustee. 1965.
Widows Wear Weeds. 1966.
The Case of the Worried Waitress. 1966.
The Case of the Queenly Contestant. 1967.
Traps Need New Bait. 1967.
The Case of the Careless Cupid. 1968.
The Case of the Murderer's Bride and Other Stories, edited by Ellery Queen. 1969.
The Case of the Fabulous Fake. 1969.
All Grass Isn't Green. 1970.
The Case of the Crimson Kiss (stories). 1971.
The Case of the Crying Swallow (stories). 1971.
The Case of the Fenced-In Woman. 1972.
The Case of the Irate Witness (stories). 1972.
The Case of the Postponed Murder. 1973.
The Amazing Adventures of Lester Leith (stories), edited by Ellery Queen. 1981.
The Human Zero: The Science Fiction Stories, edited by Martin H. Greenberg and Charles G. Waugh. 1981.
Whispering Sands: Stories of Gold Fever and the Western Desert, edited by Charles G. Waugh and Martin H. Greenberg. 1981.
Pay Dirt and Other Whispering Sands Stories, edited by Charles G. Waugh and Martin H. Greenberg. 1983.

Other

The Land of Shorter Shadows. 1948.
The Court of Last Resort. 1952.
Neighborhood Frontiers. 1954.
The Case of the Boy Who Wrote "The Case of the Missing Clue" with Perry Mason. 1959.
Hunting the Desert Whale. 1960.
Hovering over Baja. 1961.
The Hidden Heart of Baja. 1962.
The Desert Is Yours. 1963.
The World of Water. 1965.
Hunting Lost Mines by Helicopter. 1965.
Off the Beaten Track in Baja. 1967.
Gypsy Days on the Delta. 1967.
Mexico's Magic Square. 1968.
Drifting Down the Delta. 1969.
Host with the Big Hat (on Mexico) 1970.
Cops on Campus and Crime in the Street. 1970.

*

Critical Studies: *The Case of Gardner* by Alva Johnston, 1947; *Gardner: The Case of the Real Perry Mason* by Dorothy B. Hughes, 1978 (includes bibliography by Ruth Moore); *Murder in the Millions: Gardner, Mickey Spillane, Ian Fleming* by J. Kenneth Van Dover, 1984.

* * *

Erle Stanley Gardner spent much of his childhood traveling with his mining-engineer father through the remote regions of California, Oregon, and the Klondike. In his teens he not only boxed for money but promoted a number of unlicensed matches. Soon after entering college he was, by his own account, expelled for slugging a professor. But in the practice of law he found the form of combat he seemed born to master. He was admitted to the California bar in 1911 and opened an office in Oxnard, where he represented the Chinese community and gained a reputation for flamboyant trial tactics. In one case, for instance, he had dozens of Chinese merchants exchange identities so that he could discredit a policeman's identification of a client. In the early 1920's he began to write western and mystery stories for magazines, and eventually he was turning out and selling the equivalent of a short novel every three nights while still lawyering during the business day. With the sale of his first novel in 1933 he gave up the practice of law and devoted himself to full-time writing, or more precisely to dictating. Thanks to the popularity of his series characters—lawyer-detective Perry Mason, his loyal secretary Della Street, his private detective Paul Drake, and the foxy trio of Sergeant Holcomb, Lieutenant Tragg and District Attorney Hamilton Burger—Gardner became one of the wealthiest mystery writers of all time.

The 82 Mason adventures from *The Case of the Velvet Claws* (1933) to the posthumously published *The Case of the Postponed Murder* (1973) contain few of the literary graces. Characterization and description are perfunctory and often reduced to a few lines that are repeated in similar situations book after book. Indeed virtually every word not within quotation marks could be deleted and little would be lost. For what vivifies these novels is the sheer readability, the breakneck pacing, the involuted plots, the fireworks displays of courtroom tactics (many based on gimmicks Gardner used in his own law practice), and the dialogue, where each line is a jab in a complex form of oral combat.

The first nine Masons are steeped in the hardboiled tradition of *Black Mask* magazine, their taut understated realism leavened with raw wit, sentimentality, and a positive zest for the dog-eat-dog milieu of the free enterprise system during its worst depression. The Mason of these novels is a tiger in the social-Darwinian jungle, totally self-reliant, asking no favors, despising the weaklings who want society to care for them, willing to take any risk for a client no matter how unfairly the client plays the game with him. Asked what he does for a living, he replies: "I fight!" or "I am a paid gladiator." He will bribe policemen for information, loosen a hostile witness' tongue by pretending to frame him for a murder, twist the evidence to get a guilty client acquitted and manipulate estate funds to prevent a guilty non-client from obtaining money for his defense. Besides *Velvet Claws*, perhaps the best early Mason novels are *The Case of the Howling Dog* and *The Case of the Curious Bride* (both 1934).

From the late 1930's to the late 1950's the main influence on Gardner was not *Black Mask* but the *Saturday Evening Post*, which serialized most of the Mason novels before book publication. In these novels the tough-guy notes are muted, "love interest" plays a stronger role, and Mason is less willing to play fast and loose with the law. Still the oral combat remains breathlessly exciting, the pace never slackens and the plots are as labyrinthine as before, most of them centering on various sharp-witted and greedy people battling over control of capital. Mason, of course, is Gardner's alter ego throughout the series, but in several novels of the second period another author-surrogate arrives on the scene in the person of a philosophical old desert rat or prospector who delights in living alone in the wilderness, discrediting by his example the greed of the urban wealth- and power-hunters. Among the best cases of this period are *Lazy Lover*; *Hesitant Hostess*, which deals with Mason's breaking down a single prosecution witness; and *Lucky Loser* and *Foot-Loose Doll* with their spectacularly complex plots.

Gardner worked without credit as script supervisor for the long-running *Perry Mason* television series (1957–66), starring Raymond Burr, and within a few years television's restrictive influence had infiltrated the new Mason novels. The lawyer evolved into a ponderous bureaucrat mindful of the law's niceties, just as Burr played him, and the plots became chaotic and the courtroom sequences mediocre, as happened all too often in the TV scripts. But by the mid-1960's the libertarian decisions of the Supreme Court under Chief Justice Earl Warren had already undermined a basic premise of the Mason novels, namely that defendants menaced by the sneaky tactics of police and prosecutors needed a pyrotechnician like Mason in their corner. Once the Court ruled that such tactics required reversal of convictions gained thereby, Mason had lost his *raison d'être*.

Several other detective series sprang from Gardner's dictating machine during his peak years. The 29 novels he wrote under the by-line of A.A. Fair about diminutive private eye Donald Lam and his huge irascible partner Bertha Cool are often preferred over the Masons because of their fusion of corkscrew plots with fresh writing, characterizations, and humor. The high spots of the series are *The Bigger They Come* and *Beware the Curves*. And in his nine books about small-town district attorney Doug Selby Gardner reversed the polarities of the Mason series, making the prosecutor his hero and the defense lawyer the oft-confounded trickster. But most of

Gardner's reputation stems from Perry Mason, and his best novels in both this and his other series offer abundant evidence of his natural storytelling talent, which is likely to retain its appeal as long as people read at all.

—Francis M. Nevins, Jr.

GARDNER, John (Champlin, Jr.). Born in Batavia, New York, 21 July 1933. Educated at DePauw University, Greencastle, Indiana, 1951–53; Washington University, St. Louis, A.B. 1955; University of Iowa (Woodrow Wilson Fellow, 1955–56), M.A. 1956, Ph.D. 1958. Married 1) Joan Louise Patterson in 1953, one son and one daughter; 2) Liz Rosenberg in 1980. Teacher at Oberlin College, Ohio, 1958–59; California State University, Chico, 1959–62, and San Francisco, 1962–65; Southern Illinois University, Carbondale, 1965–74; Bennington College, Vermont, 1974–76; Williams College, Williamstown, Massachusetts, and Skidmore College, Saratoga Springs, New York, 1976–77; George Mason University, Fairfax, Virginia, 1977–78; Member of the English Department, State University of New York, Binghamton, 1978–82. Visiting Professor, University of Detroit, 1970–71, and Northwestern University, Evanston, Illinois, 1973. Editor, *MSS* and Southern Illinois University Press Literary Structures series. Recipient: Danforth fellowship, 1970; National Endowment for the Arts grant, 1972; American Academy award, 1975; National Book Critics Circle award, 1976. *Died 14 September 1982.*

PUBLICATIONS

Fiction

The Resurrection. 1966.
The Wreckage of Agathon. 1970.
Grendel. 1971.
The Sunlight Dialogues. 1972.
Jason and Medeia (novel in verse). 1973.
Nickel Mountain: A Pastoral Novel. 1973.
The King's Indian: Stories and Tales. 1974.
October Light. 1976.
In the Suicide Mountains. 1977.
Vlemk, The Box-Painter. 1979.
Freddy's Book. 1980.
The Art of Living and Other Stories. 1981.
Mickelsson's Ghosts. 1982.
Stillness, and Shadows, edited by Nicholas Delbanco. 1986.

Plays

William Wilson (libretto). 1978.
Three Libretti (includes *William Wilson, Frankenstein, Rumpelstiltskin*). 1979.

Verse

Poems. 1978.

Other

The Gawain-Poet. 1967.
Le Mort Darthur. 1967.
The Construction of the Wakefield Cycle. 1974.
Dragon, Dragon and Other Timeless Tales (for children). 1975.
The Construction of Christian Poetry in Old English. 1975.
Gudgekin the Thistle Girl and Other Tales (for children). 1976.
A Child's Bestiary (for children). 1977.
The Poetry of Chaucer. 1977.
The Life and Times of Chaucer. 1977.
The King of the Hummingbirds and Other Tales (for children). 1977.
On Moral Fiction. 1978.
On Becoming a Novelist. 1983.
The Art of Fiction: Notes on Craft for Young Writers. 1984.

Editor, with Lennis Dunlap, *The Forms of Fiction*. 1962.
Editor, *The Complete Works of the Gawain-Poet in a Modern English Version with a Critical Introduction*. 1965.
Editor, with Nicholas Joost, *Papers on the Art and Age of Geoffrey Chaucer*. 1967.
Editor, *The Alliterative Morte Arthure, The Owl and the Nightingale, and Five Other Middle English Poems, in a Modernized Version, with Comments on the Poems, and Notes*. 1971.
Editor, with Shannon Ravenel, *The Best American Short Stories 1982*. 1982.

Translator, with Nobuko Tsukui, *Tengu Child*, by Kikuo Itaya. 1983.
Translator, with John Maier, *Gilgamesh*. 1984.

*

Bibliography: *Gardner: A Bibliographical Profile* by John M. Howell, 1980; *Gardner: An Annotated Secondary Bibliography* by Robert A. Morace, 1984.

Critical Studies: *Gardner: Critical Perspectives* edited by Robert A. Morace and Kathryn VanSpanckeren, 1982; *Arches and Light: The Fiction of Gardner* by David Cowart, 1983; *A World of Order and Light: The Fiction of Gardner* by Gregory L. Morris, 1984; *Thor's Hammer: Essays on Gardner* edited by Jeff Henderson and Robert E. Lowrey, 1985.

* * *

In his treatise *On Moral Fiction* John Gardner is quite specific: a good book is "one that, for its time, is wise, sane, and magical, one that clarifies life and tends to improve it." His best works give testimony to this belief. Gardner was not only a fine novelist, but also a critic, historian, and respected medieval and classical scholar. The canon renders these pursuits inseparable. This integrity is unsurprising in view of his general thesis that "We recognize true art by its careful, thoroughly honest search for and analysis of values." Art, it is said, seeks that which is "good," and such a search entails a wholeness of vision; an account taken of all the possibilities. It is this honest search for, and examination of values which characterizes Gardner's fiction. It promotes the dualisms so often remarked upon as typical and provides his recurring theme.

Against an existential world, Gardner posits the transcending power of love and imagination.

The theme becomes apparent in *Grendel* in which Gardner, turned modern fabulator, re-creates the story of Beowulf from the monster's point of view. When Grendel begins his story he has already been at war with the Hrothgars for twelve years and, in a retrospective first-person narrative, must already be bleeding to death. His story is a tragi-comic lament to brute existence, inspired by the nihilism he has acquired from the Dragon. The Dragon, borrowing from Sartre and others, has told Grendel everything that an existentialist would. You are the "brute existent—the blunt facts of their mortality." Grendel, pointless ridiculous monster that he is, becomes an archetypal absurd hero. His monstrous set of values threaten civilization and form an ironic commentary on Hrothgar's attempts to live the Anglo-Saxon heroic ideal. Opposing the brute existence with a belief in the holy and miraculous, is the high priest Ork. Gardner, it seems, believed neither. At the end of the book, he tells us, is another Dragon whose opinions oppose those of the first. This "dragon" is Beowulf, whispering to Grendel that "Time is mind, the hand that makes (fingers on harpstrings, heroswords, the acts, the eyes of queens). By that I kill you." Civilization is redeemed by an act of imagination.

The constant search for value lends a quality of literary evolution to the canon. The last "dragon" in *Grendel*, says Gardner, expresses the views of William Blake. *Nickel Mountain*, rightly subtitled *A Pastoral Novel*, finds Henry Soames coming to a "mariner"-like awareness of the holiness of all things, so that, at the end of the novel, he sees life "less as a yarn told after dinner," and more as "a kind of church service—communion say, or a wedding." In *The King's Indian* one hears the voice of Melville and others, and *October Light* is coloured by the gentle wisdom of Matthew Arnold. Style, likewise, matches content.

In *Mickelsson's Ghosts*, Gardner's last and most demanding novel, the lyricism found in *Grendel* and the naturalism of *October Light*, give way to a hard-edged contemporary prose. This, with the modern setting and the novel's sheer complexity, suggests some attempt to culminate ideas in what is, necessarily, an open-ended form. The novel follows Gardner's recurrent pattern. A philosopher of ethics, Mickelsson is brought to the brink of insanity and despair by a multiplicity of sorrows. He must, in common with other Gardner characters, travel an anguished road toward self-regeneration. The book is, in essence, a modern morality play. Ghosts, merely evocative in previous novels, visibly haunt the protagonist of this one. Mickelsson faces the living ghosts of family and friends whom he feels he has failed, and the ghosts of dead philosophers whom he blames for the modern world's insanity. A modern "everyman," Mickelsson must wrestle with their ideas. Heidegger, Luther, Nietzsche, Wittgenstein, and others are evoked to create the dualisms which negate the obvious, and force Mickelsson to a recognition of his common humanity. The resolution, when it comes, takes place on the very brink of possibility. Surrounded by all of life, Mickelsson makes love: "oblivious to the tumbling, roaring bones and blood . . . pitiful empty-headed nothings complaining to be born."

Gardner does not expect his contemporary heroes to slay monsters. A clumsy affirmation of love, or some small gesture towards responsible action may be all that denies what, in *October Light*, is called "gravity." Even language, low speech, it is understood, suffers gravity. "Everything decent supported the struggle upward." Such affirmation is unusual in the 20th century, but since his death, Gardner's stature as a major American writer has been confirmed. His influence is likely to be lasting.

—Jan Pilditch

GARLAND, (Hannibal) Hamlin. Born near West Salem, Wisconsin, 14 September 1860. Educated at Cedar Valley Seminary, Osage, Iowa, 1876–81. Married Zulime Taft in 1899; two daughters. Taught at a country school, Grundy County, Ohio, 1882–83; homesteader in McPherson County, Dakota Territory, 1883–84; student, then teacher, Boston School of Oratory, 1884–91; full-time writer from 1891: lived in Chicago, 1893–1916, New York, 1916–30, and Los Angeles, 1930–40. Founding President, Cliff Dwellers, Chicago, 1907. Recipient: Pulitzer Prize, for biography, 1922; Roosevelt Memorial Association Gold Medal, 1931. D.Litt: University of Wisconsin, Madison, 1926; Northwestern University, Evanston, Illinois, 1933; University of Southern California, Los Angeles, 1937. Member, 1918, and Director, 1920, American Academy. *Died 5 March 1940.*

PUBLICATIONS

Fiction

Main-Travelled Roads: Six Mississippi Valley Stories. 1891; revised edition, 1899, 1922, 1930; edited by Thomas A. Bledsoe, 1954.
A Member of the Third House. 1892.
Jason Edwards: An Average Man. 1892.
A Little Norsk; or, Ol' Pap's Flaxen. 1892.
A Spoil of Office. 1892.
Prairie Folks (stories). 1893; revised edition, 1899.
Rose of Dutcher's Coolly. 1895; revised edition, 1899; edited by Donald Pizer, 1969.
Wayside Courtships (stories). 1897.
The Spirit of Sweetwater. 1898; revised edition, as *Witch's Gold*, 1906.
The Eagle's Heart. 1900.
Her Mountain Lover. 1901.
The Captain of the Gray-Horse Troop. 1902.
Hesper. 1903.
The Light of the Star. 1904.
The Tyranny of the Dark. 1905.
Money Magic. 1907; as *Mart Haney's Mate*, 1922.
The Moccasin Ranch. 1909.
Cavanagh, Forest Ranger. 1910.
Other Main-Travelled Roads (includes *Prairie Folks* and *Wayside Courtships*). 1910.
Victor Ollnee's Discipline. 1911.
The Forester's Daughter. 1914.
They of the High Trails (stories). 1916.

Play

Under the Wheel. 1890.

Verse

Prairie Songs. 1893.
Iowa, O Iowa! 1935.

Other

Crumbling Idols: Twelve Essays on Art. 1894; edited by Jane Johnson, 1960.
Ulysses S. Grant: His Life and Character. 1898.
The Trail of the Goldseekers: A Record of Travel in Prose and Verse. 1899.
Boy Life on the Prairie. 1899; revised edition, 1908.
The Long Trail (for children). 1907.
The Shadow World. 1908.
A Son of the Middle Border. 1917; edited by Henry M. Christman, 1962.
A Daughter of the Middle Border. 1921.
A Pioneer Mother. 1922.
Commemorative Tribute to James Whitcomb Riley. 1922.
The Book of the American Indian. 1923.
Trail-Makers of the Middle Border. 1926.
The Westward March of American Settlement. 1927.
Back-Trailers from the Middle Border. 1928.
Prairie Song and Western Story (miscellany). 1928.
Roadside Meetings. 1930.
Companions on the Trail: A Literary Chronicle. 1931.
My Friendly Contemporaries: A Literary Log. 1932.
Afternoon Neighbors: Further Excerpts from a Literary Log. 1934.
Joys of the Trail. 1935.
Forty Years of Psychic Research: A Plain Narrative of Fact. 1936.
The Mystery of the Buried Crosses: A Narrative of Psychic Exploration. 1939.
Diaries, edited by Donald Pizer. 1968.
Observations on the American Indian 1895–1905, edited by Lonnie E. Underhill and Daniel F. Littlefield, Jr. 1976.

*

Bibliography: *Garland and the Critics: An Annotated Bibliography* by Jackson R. Bryer and Eugene Harding, 1973; *Henry Blake Fuller and Garland: A Reference Guide* by Charles L.P. Silet, 1977.

Critical Studies: *Garland: A Biography* by Jean Holloway, 1960; *Garland's Early Work and Career* by Donald Pizer, 1960; *Garland: L'homme et l'oeuvre* by Robert Mane, 1968; *Garland: The Far West* by Robert Gish, 1976; *Garland* by Joseph B. McCullough, 1978; *Critical Essays on Garland* edited by James Nagel, 1982; *The Critical Reception of Garland 1891–1978* edited by Charles L.P. Silet and Robert E. Welch, 1985.

* * *

Hamlin Garland played an important role in the development of realism in America, but the work of enduring significance that he bequeathed to the last half of the 20th century is modest. One volume of stories, one novel, and his autobiography are all that a contemporary reader need bother about. Garland is one of the most uneven of American writers, for the gulf is wide between the stories in *Main-Travelled Roads* and the popular fiction he later turned out for the *Saturday Evening Post*. His fall from realism into sentimental romance is simply embarrassing.

After Garland left the midwest and went to Boston to become a writer, he was encouraged by Joseph Kirkland, a realist writer, to make use of his farm background. No authentic farmer yet had appeared in American literature, and the subject was virgin. This advice came in 1887 as Garland was returning from a visit to see his mother, who had had a stroke, and he was burning with indignation over the privations and injustices of farm life. In addition, the 1880's were a period of farm depression, for too much new land had been opened up too fast and the invention of farm machinery had over-stimulated production. Out of this context came the six stories that made up the original edition of *Main-Travelled Roads*. They are "A Branch-Road," "Up the Coulé," "Among the Corn Rows," "The Return of a Private," "Under the Lion's Paw," and "Mrs. Ripley's Trip." Some take place in Wisconsin where Garland was born, some in Iowa where the Garlands homesteaded after the Civil War, and one makes use of the Dakotas where Garland homesteaded himself before leaving for Boston to become a writer. The general theme is the hard lot of the farmer, and especially the farm wife, but the stories are not all somber. "Mrs. Ripley's Trip" is bucolic comedy, and "Among the Corn Rows" ends with an elopement and high hopes. All of the stories, however, are filled with closely observed detail that make them good examples of literary realism. There are some naturalistic elements in the victimization of the characters by forces beyond their control, but Garland is not really a naturalist. It is above all the intensity of his feeling that carries these stories.

That Garland's compulsion to write these stories lay mostly in his anger of the moment and not in deeply held convictions is shown by subsequent developments. After he settled his mother in Wisconsin and began to prosper, he lost his zeal for social criticism. He was not dishonest, but he saw the world in terms of himself and later lapsed into a terrible respectability. He continued to write stories, however, and the six stories in *Main-Travelled Roads* eventually grew to twelve, but the later tales are inferior and lapse into sentimentality. He also produced another volume of somber tales, *Prairie Folks*, before his indignation abated, and he wrote four novels worth mentioning. The first, *A Little Norsk*, has something of the hard Dakota farm life in it, but it is marred by sentimentality. His best novel, and one that still can be recommended, is *Rose of Dutcher's Coolly*, the story of a farm girl who goes to the state university and then to Chicago to pursue a career. The detail is good, especially the childhood and adolescence of Rose on the farm, and it deals with feminist problems of the 1890's. *Jason Edwards* is single-tax propaganda written after Garland had met Henry George and become a supporter of the single-tax panacea for economic ills. *A Spoil of Office* is a populist novel attacking political corruption and reminding modern readers who stumble on it that 1892 was the year that James Weaver led the United States' most successful third party movement.

Garland made a literary comeback in 1917 when he wrote his autobiography, *A Son of the Middle Border*. This is a first-rate work that ranks with the best that Garland accomplished in the 1890's. He followed this with three other volumes of family history: *A Daughter of the Middle Border*, *Trail-Makers of the Middle Border* (this one fictionalized), and *Back-Trailers from the Middle Border*, but these are less interesting than the first. Because Garland lived a long time and made a point of meeting writers and public figures, students of literary history will find considerable interest in his literary reminiscences: *Roadside Meetings*, *Companions on the Trail*, *My Friendly Contemporaries*, and *Afternoon Neighbors*. Also noteworthy is Garland's one venture into literary criticism, *Crumbling Idols*, in which he makes a strong defense of realism.

—James Woodress

See the essay on *Main-Travelled Roads*.

GILLETTE, William (Hooker). Born in Hartford, Connecticut, 24 July 1853. Educated at Hartford High School, graduated 1873; Monroe School of Oratory, Boston University, 1875–76. Married Helen Nickles in 1882 (died, 1888). Debut as actor, St. Louis and New Orleans, 1873–74; acted in New York and Boston, 1875; appeared with Boston Museum Company, 1876, and Bernard Macauley's company, Cincinnati and Louisville, 1876–78; returned to New York and from 1881 was one of the most prominent actors on the New York and London stage; appeared in most of his own plays: especially noted for his portrayal of Sherlock Holmes; retired in 1919 to an estate in Connecticut, but later came out of retirement to appear in various of his early roles in New York and on U.S. tours; retired again in 1936. Recipient: American Academy Gold Medal, 1931. M.A.: Yale University, New Haven, Connecticut, 1930; Trinity College, Hartford, Connecticut, 1930; LL.D.: Dartmouth College, Hanover, New Hampshire, 1930; Columbia University, New York, 1930. Member, National Institute of Arts and Letters, 1898, and American Academy, 1915. *Died 29 April 1937.*

PUBLICATIONS

Collections

Plays (includes *All the Comforts of Home*, *Secret Service*, *Sherlock Holmes*), edited by Rosemary Cullen and Don B. Wilmeth. 1983.

Plays

Ballywingle the Beloved (produced 1873).
The Professor (produced 1881; as *The Professor's Wooing*, produced 1881).
Esmeralda, with Frances Hodgson Burnett (produced 1881; as *Young Folks' Ways*, produced 1883). 1881.
Digby's Secretary, from play by Gottfried von Moser (produced 1884; revised version, as *The Private Secretary*, produced 1884).
Held by the Enemy (produced 1886; revised version, produced 1886). 1898.
She, from the novel by Rider Haggard (produced 1887).
A Legal Wreck (produced 1888). 1900.
Robert Elsmere, from the novel by Mrs. Humphry Ward (produced 1889).
All the Comforts of Home, with H.C. Duckworth, from a play by Carl Lauf (produced 1890). 1897; in *Plays*, 1983.
Mr. Wilkinson's Widows, from a play by Alexandre Bisson (produced 1891).
Settled Out of Court, from a play by Alexandre Bisson (produced 1892).
Ninety Days (produced 1893).
Too Much Johnson, from a play by Maurice Ordonneau (produced 1894). 1912.
Secret Service (produced 1895). 1898; revised version, in *Representative American Plays*, edited by Arthur Hobson Quinn, 1917; in *Plays*, 1983.
Because She Loved Him So, from a play by Alexandre Bisson and Adolphe Leclerq (produced 1898).
Sherlock Holmes, with Arthur Conan Doyle, from works by Doyle (produced 1899). 1922; revised version, 1935; in *Plays*, 1983.
The Painful Predicament of Sherlock Holmes (produced 1905). 1955.
Clarice (produced 1905; revised version, produced 1905).
That Little Affair at Boyd's (produced 1908; as *Ticey*, produced 1908).
The Red Owl (as *The Robber*, produced 1909). 1924.
Among Thieves (produced 1909). In *One-Act Plays for Stage and Study 2*, 1925.
Electricity (produced 1910). 1913.
Diplomacy, from translation of play by Sardou (produced 1914).
The Dream Maker, from story by Howard E. Morton (produced 1921).
Winnie and the Wolves, from stories by Bertram Akey (produced 1923).
How Well George Does It! 1936.

Fiction

A Legal Wreck. 1888.
The Astounding Crime on Torrington Road. 1927.

Other

The Illusion of the First Time in Acting. 1915

Editor, *How to Write a Play: Letters from Augier, Banville, Dennery, Dumas, Gondinet, Labiche, Legouvé, Pailleron, Sardou, and Zola*, translated by Dudley Miles. 1916.

*

Critical Studies: *Sherlock Holmes and Much More; or, Some Facts about Gillette* by Doris Cook, 1970.

* * *

William Gillette was one of the first to profess that an actor should build his characterization on the dominant qualities of his own personality; his first major performance, with an assist from Mark Twain, was in *Faint Heart Ne'er Won Fair Lady* in 1875. He appeared in several stock companies before opening his own play, *The Professor*, at Madison Square Garden in 1881. Thereafter, except for roles in *Samson*, *Diplomacy*, *The Admirable Crichton*, *A Successful Calamity*, and *Dear Brutus*, he appeared in his own plays, in which he did his best work. He was at his best portraying the "cool man of action," whether it was the title role in *Sherlock Holmes* (he played the part for 30 years), Brant in *Held by the Enemy* (a melodrama, but the first successful play about the Civil War), or *Secret Service* (his most popular Civil War play). Notable among his other plays are *A Legal Wreck*, set in a coastal New England town, and *The Painful Predicament of Sherlock Holmes*, an hysterically funny mini-play sequel to *Sherlock Holmes* featuring a bumbling, loquacious, accident-prone escapee from a nearby mental hospital who, while appealing for help to the always silent Holmes, accidentally destroys his violin, violin bow, lamp, cocaine pot, crime notes, and photographs, before Holmes's servant can summon sanatorium assistance.

Gillette's best claim to fame today lies in *Sherlock Holmes* (written with Arthur Conan Doyle), revived gloriously by the Royal Shakespeare Company in 1974 at the Aldwych and transferred in triumph to New York. The play skillfully blends dialogue and the most dramatic moments directly from Doyle's "A Scandal in Bohemia" and "The Final Problem," though the melodramatic tension is Gillette's own. He not only demonstrates Holmes's great skill against Moriarty, the Napoleon of Crime, but also shows Holmes falling in love with the heroine, Alice Faulkner, though one sometimes wonders whether he will shoot Moriarty or cocaine. A good script editor can easily keep the play's many dramatic turns from becoming too intricate, and its melodramatic turns from becoming maudlin, since Holmes, besottedly in love, could have provided a deadly melodramatic element, especially when coupled with Alice's innocence and naivety. Romance spurs interest in the triumph of good, however. Holmes quickly solves the mystery, foils the thugs, recovers the blackmail papers (50% honestly), jails Moriarty, and, to the audience's delight, has Alice fall ecstatically into his arms at the final curtain.

—Louis Charles Stagg

GINSBERG, Allen. Born in Newark, New Jersey, 3 June 1926. Educated at Paterson High School, New Jersey; Columbia University, New York, 1943–45, 1946–48, A.B. 1948. Served in the Military Sea Transport Service. Book reviewer, *Newsweek*, New York, 1950; market researcher, New York, 1951–53, and San Francisco, 1954; free-lance writer: participant in many poetry readings and demonstrations; since 1971 Director, Committee on Poetry Foundation, New York; co-founder, 1974, and director, Kerouac School of Poetics, Naropa Institute, Boulder, Colorado. Recipient: Guggenheim fellowship, 1965; National Endowment for the Arts grant, 1966; American Academy grant, 1969; National Book Award, 1974; National Arts Club Gold Medal, 1979; Los Angeles *Times* award, 1982. Member, American Academy, 1973. Lives in New York City.

PUBLICATIONS

Verse

Howl and Other Poems. 1956; revised edition, 1971.
Siesta in Xbalba and Return to the States. 1956.
Empty Mirror: Early Poems. 1961.
Kaddish and Other Poems 1958–60. 1961.
A Strange New Cottage in Berkeley. 1963.
Reality Sandwiches 1953–60. 1963.
Penguin Modern Poets 5, with Lawrence Ferlinghetti and Gregory Corso. 1963.
The Change. 1963.
Kral Majales. 1965.
Prose Contribution to Cuban Revolution. 1966.
Wichita Vortex Sutra. 1966.
T.V. Baby Poems. 1967.
Wales—A Visitation, July 29, 1967. 1968.
Scrap Leaves, Hasty Scribbles. 1968.
Message II. 1968.
Planet News 1961–1967. 1968.
Airplane Dreams: Compositions from Journals. 1968.
Ankor Wat. 1968.
The Moments Return. 1970.
Notes after an Evening with William Carlos Williams. 1970.
Iron Horse. 1972.
The Fall of America: Poems of These States 1965–1971. 1972.
The Gates of Wrath: Rhymed Poems 1948–1952. 1972.
Open Head, with *Open Eye*, by Lawrence Ferlinghetti. 1972.
New Year Blues. 1972.
Bixby Canyon Ocean Path Word Breeze. 1972.
Sad Dust Glories. 1975.
First Blues: Rags, Ballads, and Harmonium Songs 1971–1974. 1975.
Mind Breaths: Poems 1972–1977. 1978.
Poems All Over the Place: Mostly Seventies. 1978.
Mostly Sitting Haiku. 1978; revised edition, 1979.
Careless Love: Two Rhymes. 1978.
Straight Hearts' Delight: Love Poems and Selected Letters 1947–1980, with Peter Orlovsky, edited by Winston Leyland. 1980.
Plutonian Ode: Poems 1977–1980. 1982.
Collected Poems 1947–1980. 1984.
White Shroud: Poems 1980–1985. 1986.

Plays

Don't Go Away Mad, in *Pardon Me, Sir, But Is My Eye Hurting Your Elbow?*, edited by Bob Booker and George Foster. 1968.
Kaddish (produced 1972).

Other

The Yage Letters, with William S. Burroughs. 1963.
Notes on an Interview with Ginsberg, by Edward Lucie-Smith. 1965.
Indian Journals: March 1962—May 1963: Notebooks, Diary, Blank Pages, Writings. 1970.
Improvised Poetics, edited by Mark Robison. 1971.
Declaration of Independence for Dr. Timothy Leary. 1971.
Gay Sunshine Interview, with Allen Young. 1974.
Allen Verbatim: Lectures on Poetry, Politics, Consciousness, edited by Gordon Ball. 1974.
The Visions of the Great Rememberer (on Jack Kerouac). 1974.
Chicago Trial Testimony. 1975.
To Eberhart from Ginsberg. 1976.
The Dream of Tibet, with *The Retreat Diaries*, by William S. Burroughs. 1976.
As Ever: The Collected Correspondence of Allen Ginsberg and Neal Cassady, edited by Barry Gifford. 1977.
Journals: Early Fifties—Early Sixties, edited by Gordon Ball. 1977.
Composed on the Tongue: Literary Conversations 1967–1977, edited by Donald Allen. 1980.

*

Bibliography: *A Bibliography of Works of Ginsberg October 1943-July 1, 1967* by George Dowden, 1970; *Ginsberg: An Annotated Bibliography 1969-1977* by Michelle P. Kraus, 1980.

Critical Studies: *Ginsberg in America* by Jane Kramer, 1968, as *Paterfamilias*, 1970; *Ginsberg* by Thomas F. Merrill, 1969; *Scenes Along the Road*, edited by Ann Charters, 1971; *Ginsberg in the 60's* by Eric Mottram, 1972; *The Visionary Poetics of Ginsberg* by Paul Portugés, 1978; *Cometh with Clouds (Memory: Ginsberg)* by Dick McBride, 1983; *Great Poet's Howl: A Study of Ginsberg's Poetry 1943-1955* by Glen Burns, 1983; *On the Poetry of Ginsberg* edited by Lewis Hyde, 1984.

* * *

Like Whitman, his forebear, Allen Ginsberg is a prolific poet who writes too much: some of his work is, like Whitman's, unfocused, emotionally scattered, and prone to large abstractions unrelated to any concrete particularity. And, like Whitman, Ginsberg insists that any subject is a fit one for poetry. And so, like Whitman, he has been attacked for his vulgarity, for his failure to be "proper" or dignified; yet at the same time, like both Whitman and Blake (from whom he has learned much), he appeals to the young, to those who do not think that poetry and the business of daily life are essentially grave matters whose languages have to be separated from one another. Ginsberg is a World-Poet, like Neruda and Yevtushenko, and like Gibran, Tagore, Whitman, and Blake in previous times. And, like each of these, he has written a quantity of slight but interesting occasional verse, of which "Portland Coloseum" (in *Planet News*), about a Beatles concert, is representative.

In *Improvised Poetics* Ginsberg talks about writing this poem. "I changed things," he said, "like *Hands waving* LIKE *myriad snakes of thought* to *Hands waving myriad / snakes of thought*. Ah . . . *The million children* OF *the thousand worlds*, so I just changed *The million children, / the thousand worlds*." These apparently minor revisions are significant: Ginsberg talks about his "paragraphal" mode of composition and explains, "when I'd get three or four [phrases] that made an apposition I'd start a new paragraph." In taking out "a lot of syntactical fat" and thus "putting two short lines together that had just images in them," Ginsberg prunes the lines of prepositions which express relationship and embraces the technique of juxtaposition, learned from Pound. The danger of such technique is that the poem can degenerate into a mere list (although, as Emerson remarked in *The Poet*, "bare lists of words are found suggestive to an imaginative and excited mind"). The value of such appositional language is that it can *imply* cause-and-effect relationships, but it does not state them: cause and effect are not to be assumed in or about the world of event; it is a world of immediacy. That is to say, the reader is moved into a world of event, a place *where things happen*, for (to quote Emerson again) "the quality of the imagination is to flow, and not to freeze." Ginsberg's reader can, therefore, often be overwhelmed by a rush of sensory, social, political and/or intellectual data to very good effect, as in poems like *Howl* or *Kaddish*.

The concern of the poet is for registering the precise nature of the occurrence (his thought, his feeling, the particularities from which they arise) in the here and now. So Ginsberg, like other modernists, finds crucial the accuracy of the poem as notation of the spoken voice or as notation of the process of thought. The notation is exact: in *Airplane Dreams* the lines of the long poem "New York to San Fran" are, in Ginsberg's words, "hung out on the page a little to the right . . . A little bit like diagramming a sentence, you know, the old syntactical diagrammatic method of making a little platform and you put the subject and object on it and hang adjectives and adverbial clauses down" (*Improvised Poetics*). Here is a short sequence from "Portland Coloseum":

> The million children
> the thousand worlds
> bounce in their seats, bash
> each other's sides, press
> legs together nervous
> Scream again & claphand

Like Olson's, Ginsberg's line-breaks serve an emphatic, syntactic purpose, in which the slight hesitancy at the end of the line provides for unexpected semantic conjunctions and emphases, while at the same time they direct the reader's voice into the (in this case slightly nervous) rhythm and rhetorical inflection of the verse.

Such a line, the unit of thought or the unit of speech, reinforces the air of spontaneous improvisation characteristic of much of Ginsberg's work. The publication of *Howl* in 1956, brought Ginsberg to prominence and gave wide currency to the notion that poetry might be a spontaneous art, requiring little or no skill or revision. Deceptively simple in appearance, *Howl* rests on an extensive apprenticeship in rhymed verse (some of which has been published in *The Gates of Wrath*) and in conscious craftsmanship. As Ginsberg wrote to Richard Eberhart, the "general ground plan" of the poem, "quite symmetrical, surprisingly," structures the three sections of the poem round three main devices: the fixed base of "who" and a long line; the repetition and variation of the fixed base "Moloch"; and the "fixed base / reply / fixed base / longer reply" of the final section. Such writing is not always done, of course, in a single extended burst of composition (the result of a fairly extended gestation): Ginsberg's compositions are often leisurely and deliberative, and very often, in revising a poem, Ginsberg in effect composes a completely new one. "Sunflower Sutra," for example, is a revised version of "In Back of the Real." It is fundamentally a different poem that came about as the result of "re-seeing" the same event. With its long lines, its introduction of a second person into the poem, and its focus on the *perceiver* of the flower, "Sunflower Sutra" is both less general and more immediate in its effect. At the same time it is, as is much of Ginsberg's work, more a celebration and affirmation of the individual, of the personal, and of nature than a denunciation of the world of man. Ginsberg's great strengths as poet are to be found in such visionary poems as this, with its long and carefully controlled lines juxtaposed against shorter lines, leading the poem to a crescendo which is not rhetorical only but quite literally *physical*: Ginsberg's long interest in yoga and in the breath as a measure in verse has led him to speculate on the correlations in Sanskrit poetry between prosody and human physiology, and has led him to attempt similar correlations in his own work. At the same time, the unabashed frankness of his words and the declarative nature of much of his writing have made the work accessible to the casual reader, and have thus given Ginsberg a wide following.

—Peter Quartermain

See the essay on *Howl*.

GLASGOW, Ellen (Anderson). Born in Richmond, Virginia, 22 April 1873. Educated at home, and in private schools in Richmond; began to lose her hearing at age 16, and eventually went deaf. Writer from 1896; lived in New York, 1911–16. President, Richmond Society for the Prevention of Cruelty to Animals, 1924–25. Recipient: American Academy Howells Medal, 1941; Pulitzer Prize, 1942. Litt.D.: University of North Carolina, Chapel Hill, 1930; LL.D.: University of Richmond, 1938; Duke University, Durham, North Carolina, 1938; College of William and Mary, Williamsburg, Virginia, 1939. Member, American Academy, 1938. *Died 21 November 1945.*

PUBLICATIONS

Collections

Letters, edited by Blair Rouse. 1958.
Collected Stories, edited by Richard K. Meeker. 1963.

Fiction

The Descendant. 1897.
Phases of an Inferior Planet. 1898.
The Voice of the People. 1900; edited by William L. Godshalk, 1972.
The Battle-Ground. 1902.
The Deliverance. 1904.
The Wheel of Life. 1906.
The Ancient Law. 1908.
The Romance of a Plain Man. 1909.
The Miller of Old Church. 1911.
Virginia. 1913.
Life and Gabriella. 1916.
The Builders. 1919.
One Man in His Time. 1922.
The Shadowy Third and Other Stories. 1923; as *Dare's Gift and Other Stories*, 1924.
Barren Ground. 1925.
The Romantic Comedians. 1926.
They Stooped to Folly: A Comedy of Morals. 1929.
The Sheltered Life. 1932.
Vein of Iron. 1935.
In This Our Life. 1941.
Beyond Defeat: An Epilogue to an Era, edited by Luther Y. Gore. 1966.

Verse

The Freeman and Other Poems. 1902.

Other

Works (Old Dominion Edition). 8 vols., 1929–33.
Works (Virginia Edition). 12 vols., 1938.
A Certain Measure: An Interpretation of Prose Fiction (prefaces to Virginia Edition). 1943.
The Woman Within (autobiography). 1954.

*

Bibliography: *Glasgow: A Bibliography* by William W. Kelly, edited by Oliver L. Steele, 1964.

Critical Studies: *On Glasgow* by James Branch Cabell, 1938; *No Place on Earth: Glasgow, James Branch Cabell, and Richmond-in-Virginia* by Louis D. Rubin, Jr., 1959; *Glasgow and the Ironic Art of Fiction* by Frederick P.W. McDowell, 1960; *Glasgow* by Blair Rouse, 1962; *Glasgow* by Louis Auchincloss, 1964; *Glasgow's American Dream* by Joan Foster Santas, 1966; *Three Modes of Modern Southern Fiction: Glasgow, Faulkner, and Wolfe* by C. Hugh Holman, 1966; *Without Shelter: The Early Career of Glasgow*, 1971, and *From the Sunken Garden: The Fiction of Glasgow 1916–1945*, 1980, both by J.R. Raper, 1971; *Glasgow's Development as a Novelist* by Marion K. Richards, 1971; *Glasgow and the Woman Within* by E. Stanly Godbold, Jr., 1972; *Glasgow: Centennial Essays* edited by M. Thomas Inge, 1976; *The Social Situation of Women in the Novels of Glasgow* by Elizabeth Gallup Myer, 1978; *The End of a Legend: Glasgow's History of Southern Women* by Barbro Ekman, 1979; *Glasgow* by Marcelle Thiébaux, 1982; *Glasgow: Beyond Convention* by Linda W. Wagner, 1982.

* * *

Ellen Glasgow was the first clear voice in the movement that became known as the Southern Literary Renaissance. She was the first writer to apply the principles of critical realism and a detached and ironic point of view to the people, the region, and the problems of the American south. Beginning with her first novel, *The Descendant*, in 1897, and ending with *Beyond Defeat*, posthumously published in 1966, she produced twenty novels in which with varying degrees of success she brought to Virginia and the south what she felt it most needed, "blood and irony." In addition to these novels, she published a volume of critical introductions to a collected edition of her novels, *A Certain Measure*; a volume of undistinguished verse, *The Freeman and Other Poems*; and a collection of mediocre short stories, *The Shadowy Third*.

Her first two novels, both set in New York, point to her later work only in attempting a clear-eyed realism and in having southern characters. But beginning in 1900, with *The Voice of the People*, and continuing through *The Battle-Ground*, *The Deliverance*, *The Romance of a Plain Man*, *The Miller of Old Church*, *Virginia*, and *Life and Gabriella*, Glasgow constructed a fictional social history of the Commonwealth of Virginia from the Civil War to World War I, placing a particular emphasis upon the transition from a ruling aristocracy to the rise of the middle class to political and economic power. In this series of novels, she traced the petrifaction of the aristocratic ideals of pre-war Virginia and recorded through the lives of fictional characters the major social revolution which the rise of the middle class produced. These novels are historical only in the sense that all historical novels deal with issues of manners, politics, and economic forces in an earlier age; they do not deal with historical personages or actual events. She treated social history with detachment, irony, and a self-consciously witty style. In 1925 she published *Barren Ground*, a novel of a lower-middle-class country woman, Dorinda Oakley, in her struggle with self, circumstance, and the soil. In this novel Glasgow reached the highest expression of her historical view, although there are no historical events as such in the novel. *Barren Ground* is a grim story, reminiscent of the works of Thomas Hardy, whom she greatly admired. It recounts, she declared, events that could happen "wherever the spirit of fortitude has triumphed over the sense of futility." She also said that it demonstrated that "one may learn to live, one may even learn to live gallantly without delight." Though she was acquainted with modern scientific, social, and anthropological views of man and society, her fundamental view of life remained shaped, as this statement suggests, by a firm but non-theological Calvinistic determinism.

Barren Ground not only summed up the first period in her active career—a period which had seen, in addition to the works named, the publication of four minor novels and her short stories and poetry—it also launched the most productive and artistically successful period in her career. In 1926 she published *The Romantic Comedians*, an almost perfectly constructed novel of manners, laid in Queenborough, her name for her native city of Richmond. The novel, centered in the marriage of an old man to a young girl, is a witty and amusing attack upon the social customs of the surviving Virginia aristocracy. She followed *The Romantic Comedians* with *They Stooped to Folly*, another comedy of manners laid in Queenborough, which plays amusing variations on the idea of the ruined woman through three generations of a Virginia family. *The Sheltered Life*, a tragi-comedy which concludes the Queenborough trilogy, ranks with *Barren Ground* as one of her two best works. *The Sheltered Life* is particularly noteworthy for its treatment of time and memory. "The Deep Past," a section of the novel consisting of the recollections of a very old man, is her finest single piece of work. The last two novels published during her lifetime portray the growing darkness of her view of life. *Vein of Iron* is a grim picture of life in the Virginia mountains, a story which she called "a drama of mortal conflict with fate." *In This Our Life*, a Pulitzer Prize-winner, is a despairing view of modern life in Queenborough, a book which, she said, shows "that character is an end in itself." *Beyond Defeat*, written as a sequel to it, strongly supports this view.

Glasgow was a committed realist with a tragic view of human potentialities. Her world view was strongly shaped by a sense of imperfection and failure in all human efforts. Supremely the novelist and fictional historian of her native Virginia, she maintained toward the places in which she lived and the people whom she loved an ironic detachment largely the result of her witty and polished and consciously fashioned style. A half-dozen of her novels, including *Virginia, Barren Ground*, the Queenborough trilogy, and *Vein of Iron* are works of considerable distinction. In her own time, she enjoyed both popular and critical respect. Since her death she has received little attention, but she deserves to be better known and more widely read.

—C. Hugh Holman

GLASPELL, Susan (Keating). Born in Davenport, Iowa, 1 July 1882 (possibly 1876). Educated in Davenport schools; at Drake University, Des Moines, Iowa, Ph.D. 1899; University of Chicago, 1902. Married 1) the writer George Cram Cook in 1913 (died, 1924); 2) the writer Norman Matson in 1925 (divorced, 1932). Reporter, Des Moines *Daily News* and *Capital*, 1899–1901; free-lance writer in Davenport, 1901–11; founder, with George Cram Cook, Provincetown Players, 1915, and wrote for the company in Provincetown, Massachusetts, and New York, 1915–22; lived in Greece, 1922–24; director, Midwest Play Bureau of the Federal Theater Project, Chicago, 1936–38. Recipient: Pulitzer Prize, 1931. *Died 27 July 1948.*

PUBLICATIONS

Plays

Suppressed Desires, with George Cram Cook (produced 1915). In *Plays*, 1920.
Trifles (produced 1916). In *Plays*, 1920.
The People (produced 1917). 1918.
Close the Book (produced 1917). With *The People*, 1918.
The Outside (produced 1917). In *Plays*, 1920.
Woman's Honor (produced 1918). In *Plays*, 1920.
Tickless Time, with George Cram Cook (produced 1918). In *Plays*, 1920.
Bernice (produced 1919). In *Plays*, 1920.
Plays. 1920; as *Trifles and Other Short Plays*, 1926.
Inheritors (produced 1921). 1921.
The Verge (produced 1921). 1922.
Chains of Dew (produced 1922).
The Comic Artist, with Norman Matson (produced 1928; revised version, produced 1933). 1927.
Alison's House (produced 1930). 1930.

Fiction

The Glory of the Conquered. 1909.
The Visioning. 1911.
Lifted Masks: Stories. 1912.
Fidelity. 1915.
A Jury of Her Peers (stories). 1927.
Brook Evans. 1928; as *The Right to Love*, 1930.
Fugitive's Return. 1929.
Ambrose Holt and Family. 1931.
The Morning Is near Us. 1940.
Cherished and Shared of Old. 1940.
Norma Ashe. 1942.
Judd Rankin's Daughter. 1945; as *Prodigal Giver*, 1946.

Other

The Road to the Temple (on George Cram Cook). 1926.

Editor, *Greek Coins* (verse), by George Cram Cook. 1925.

*

Critical Study: *Glaspell* by Arthur E. Waterman, 1966.

* * *

When the Provincetown Players opened a subscription theatre in Greenwich Village in 1916, their two major playwrights were Eugene O'Neill and Susan Glaspell. With her husband, George Cram "Jig" Cook, Glaspell was a founder of the Provincetown Players and, before his dissatisfaction with the direction the theatre was taking and their departure for Greece in 1922, she was a substantial contributor to the success of the group. Although she lacked O'Neill's theatricality at this time, she was much closer to O'Neill in his concern for intense, meaningful drama than any of their contemporaries.

An intelligent and perceptive person, confident in her art and the values she found meaningful, she was most impressive in her thoughtful and theatrically effective one-act plays. *Suppressed Desires* (written with Cook) is a clever satire on the idea of complete freedom in self-expression. *Trifles* combines mystery with a penetrating understanding of a woman's character in a single tense scene. Other one-act plays performed by the Provincetown Players were *The People*, *The Outside*, and *Woman's Honor*.

Her full-length plays, all of which reveal a liberal woman's approach with force and dignity, never quite reached the quality she seemed capable of producing. *Bernice*, although too conversational and contrived, shows the power and thoughtful ingenuity of a loving wife to effect a dramatic and sustaining change upon her husband after her death. One of her most popular plays from this period is *Inheritors*, which dramatizes the problems of a midwestern college in carrying on the liberal ideas of its founder over the conservatism of its present Board of Trustees. It is in *The Verge* that Glaspell came closest to portraying the emotional struggles that were central to O'Neill's plays. Searching for an understanding of herself, the heroine is on the "verge" both of insanity and that answer which eludes her. In language and idea the play suggests a power which was never completely dramatized.

After her husband's death in Greece Glaspell wrote *The Road to the Temple*, a moving and interesting biography-autobiography of their work together in theatre and of his last years. She also produced a number of short stories and novels which did little for her reputation as a writer. Her single outstanding work of this later period was the Pulitzer Prize-winning *Alison's House*, a thought-provoking and beautifully expressed play based on Emily Dickinson's life. Her major contribution to American drama and theatre, however, rests almost entirely on those years of the Provincetown Players, an extremely important time in the growth of American drama.

—Walter J. Meserve

GOLD, Michael. Born Itzok Granich in New York City, 12 April 1893. Educated at private high schools in New York; New York University, 1912–13; Harvard University, Cambridge, Massachusetts, 1914. Married. Driver, Adams Express Company, New York, and worked at various other jobs in New York and Boston until 1918; lived in Mexico, 1918–20; member of the editorial board, *Liberator*, New York, 1920–22; assistant editor, *Masses*, and co-founder, 1926, and editor, 1928–47, *New Masses*; also contributing editor, *Masses and Mainstream*; columnist, *Daily Worker*, New York, 1933–66. *Died 14 May 1967.*

PUBLICATIONS

Collections

Gold: A Literary Anthology, edited by Michael Folsom. 1972.

Fiction

The Damned Agitator and Other Stories. 1926.
Jews Without Money. 1930.

Plays

Down the Airshaft (produced 1916).
Ivan's Homecoming (produced 1917).
Money (produced 1920). 1930.
Hoboken Blues (produced 1928). In *The American Caravan* edited by Van Wyck Brooks and others, 1927.
Fiesta (produced 1929).
Battle Hymn, with Michael Blankfort (produced 1936). 1936.

Other

Life of John Brown. 1924.
120 Million. 1929.
Charlie Chaplin's Parade (for children). 1930.
Change the World! 1937.
The Hollow Men (*Daily Worker* articles). 1941.
The Gold Reader. 1954.

Editor, with others, *Proletarian Literature in the United States: An Anthology*. 1935.

*

Critical Studies: "The Education of Gold" by Michael Folsom, in *Proletarian Writers of the Thirties* edited by David Madden, 1968; *Gold: Dean of American Proletarian Writers* by John Pyros, 1979.

* * *

Michael Gold's passion for the flowering of a truly proletarian culture grew from his familiarity with the life of the ghetto, though he himself had a lower-middle-class upbringing. "When I hope it is the tenement hoping . . .," he reminisced in his celebrated essay "Towards Proletarian Art," "I am all that the tenement group poured into me during those early years of my spiritual travail." His semi-autobiographical novel, *Jews Without Money*, which poignantly evoked the suffocating reality of the ghetto, with its stench and filth, hoodlums and prostitutes, bugs, sweatshops, and swarming immigrants, was itself intended as a model for the kind of art he envisioned. A proletarian movement in art could take root, he felt, only if there was a spontaneous resurgence of creativity among workers at all levels—when "in every American factory there is a dramatic group . . . when mechanics paint in their leisure, and farmers write sonnets." It was, therefore, necessary that preference in art be given to the sufferings of the hungry and persecuted masses over the "precious silly little agonies" of bourgeois writers. Workers, he maintained, must employ "swift action, clear form, the direct line, cinema in words" to create an art imbued with social purpose and detailing the nuances of their lives. *New Masses*, which Gold helped to start in 1926 with the aim of publishing and popularising the contributions of working men and women, did succeed, to a limited extent, in providing a forum of artistic expression to obscure worker-poets such as H.H. Lewis and Martin Russak, but the experiment could not be sustained for long. Gold's plays, *Hoboken Blues*, which intimately describes the Harlem poor in the jazz age, and *Fiesta*, which provides a picture of peasants and patricians in the countryside of Mexico, though not successful commercially, attested to his earnestness.

Gold, never a perfectionist in matters of style, put his trust in the absolute sovereignty of the "message" of art, and, in spite of his fondness for Shakespeare and Schiller, often insisted that the artists of the working class had nothing to learn from the great literature of the bourgeois past. In his poetry he employed direct statement: dramatising a predicament in "Vanzetti in the Death House" or celebrating the raw pleasures of ordinary life in "Bucket of Blood". In his prose Gold inclined, Whitmanlike, toward lyricism and prophetic bursts of eloquence to invoke the grandeur of the Marxist apocalypse awaiting the decay of the old economic order: "For out of our death shall arise glories, and out of the final corruption of this old civilization we have loved shall spring the new race—the supermen." Despite his political fervour, he could display real objectivity and candour in his literary criticism. His admiration for Upton Sinclair, for instance, was always tempered by his awareness that Sinclair's vision was limited by a fuzzy and unrealistic idealising of the working class and an inbred puritanism that grudged "the poor little jug of wine and hopeful song of the worker." Likewise, his criticism of Hemingway's "colorful if sterile world . . . completely divorced from the experience of the great majority of mankind" never overlooked that great writer's stylistic and narrative accomplishments.

Though faded in appearance, Gold's writings today serve as a powerful reminder of the often forgotten truth that artistic possibilities can be discovered even in the most neglected sections of society and that it is mostly the writers "corrupted by all the money floating everywhere" that find it "unfashionable to believe in human progress . . . to work for a better world."

—Chirantan Kulshrestha

GOODMAN, Paul. Born in New York City, 9 September 1911. Educated at City College, New York, B.A. 1931; University of Chicago, Ph.D. 1940 (received, 1954). Married twice; two daughters and one son. Reader, Metro-Goldwyn-Mayer, 1931; Instructor, University of Chicago, 1939–40; teacher of Latin, physics, history and mathematics, Manumit School of Progressive Education, Pawling, New York, 1942; also teacher at New York University, 1948, Black Mountain College, North Carolina, 1950, and Sarah Lawrence College, Bronxville, New York, 1961; Knapp Professor, University of Wisconsin, Madison, 1964; teacher at Experimental College of San Francisco State College, 1966, and University of Hawaii, Honolulu, 1969, 1971. Editor, *Complex* magazine, New York; film editor, *Partisan Review*, New Brunswick, New Jersey; television critic, *New Republic*, Washington, D.C.; editor *Liberation* magazine, New York, 1962–70. Recipient: American Council of Learned Societies fellowship, 1940; American Academy grant, 1953. *Died 3 August 1972.*

PUBLICATIONS

Collections

Collected Poems, edited by Taylor Stoehr. 1974.
Collected Stories, edited by Taylor Stoehr. 4 vols., 1978–80.

Fiction

The Grand Piano; or, The Almanac of Alienation. 1942.
The Facts of Life (stories). 1945.
The State of Nature. 1946.
The Break-Up of Our Camp and Other Stories. 1949.
The Dead of Spring. 1950.
Parents Day. 1951.
The Empire City. 1959.
Our Visit to Niagara (stories). 1960.
Making Do. 1963.
Adam and His Works: Collected Stories. 1968.
Don Juan; or, The Continuum of the Libido, edited by Taylor Stoehr. 1979.

Plays

Childish Jokes: Crying Backstage. 1938.
The Tower of Babel, in *New Directions in Prose and Poetry 5*. 1940.
2 Noh Plays (produced 1950). In *Stop-Light*, 1941.
Stop-Light: 5 Dance Poems (Noh plays: *Dusk: A Noh Play*, *The Birthday*, *The Three Disciples*, *The Cyclist*, *The Stop Light*). 1941.
Faustina (produced 1949). In *Three Plays*, 1965.
Theory of Tragedy, in *Quarterly Review of Literature*, Winter 1950.
Jonah (produced 1950; revised version, produced 1966). In *Three Plays*, 1965.
Abraham (cycle of Abraham plays; produced 1953). *Abraham and Isaac* in *Cambridge Review*, November 1955.
The Young Disciple (produced 1955). In *Three Plays*, 1965.
Little Hero (produced 1957). In *Tragedy and Comedy: Four Cubist Plays*, 1970.
The Cave at Machpelah, music by Ned Rorem (produced 1959). In *Commentary*, June 1958.
Three Plays. 1965.
Tragedy and Comedy: Four Cubist Plays (includes *Structure of Tragedy, After Aeschylus*; *Structure of Tragedy, After Sophocles*; *Structure of Pathos, After Euripides*; *Little Hero, After Molière*). 1970.

Verse

Ten Lyric Poems. 1934.
12 Ethical Sonnets. 1935.
15 Poems with Time Expressions. 1936.
Homecoming and Departure. 1937.
A Warning at My Leisure. 1939.
Five Young American Poets, with others. 1942.
Pieces of Three, with Meyer Liben and Edouard Roditi. 1942.
The Copernican Revolution. 1946; revised edition, 1947.
Day and Other Poems. 1954(?).
Red Jacket. 1955.
Berg Goodman Mezey, with Stephen Berg and Robert Mezey. 1957.
The Well of Bethlehem. 1957.
Ten Poems. 1961.
The Lordly Hudson: Collected Poems. 1962.
Hawkweed. 1967.
North Percy. 1968.
Homespun of Oatmeal Gray. 1970.
Two Sentences. 1970.

Other

Art and Social Nature (essays). 1946.
Kafka's Prayer. 1947.
Communitas: Means of Livelihood and Ways of Life, with Percival Goodman. 1947; revised edition, 1960.
Gestalt Therapy: Excitement and Growth in the Human Personality, with Frederick S. Perls and Ralph F. Hefferline. 1951.
The Structure of Literature. 1954.
Censorship and Pornography on the Stage, and Are Writers Shirking Their Political Duty? 1959(?).
Growing Up Absurd: Problems of Youth in the Organized System. 1960.
Drawing the Line. 1962.
The Community of Scholars. 1962.
Utopian Essays and Practical Proposals. 1962.
The Society I Live in Is Mine. 1963.
Compulsory Mis-Education. 1964; revised edition, 1971.
People or Personnel: Decentralizing and the Mixed System. 1965.
Mass Education in Science. 1966.
Five Years: Thoughts During a Useless Time. 1966.
The Moral Ambiguity of America. 1966; revised edition, as *Like a Conquered Province: The Moral Ambiguity of America*, 1967.
The Open Look. 1969.
New Reformation: Notes of a Neolithic Conservative. 1970.
Speaking and Language: Defence of Poetry. 1972.
Little Prayers and Finite Experience. 1972.
Drawing the Line: The Political Essays, edited by Taylor Stoehr. 1977.
Nature Heals: The Psychological Essays, edited by Taylor Stoehr. 1977.
Creator Spirit, Come! The Literary Essays, edited by Taylor Stoehr. 1977.
The Black Flag of Anarchism. 1978.

Editor, *Seeds of Liberation*. 1964.

*

Bibliography: *Adam and His Work: A Bibliography of Sources by and about Goodman* by Tom Nicely, 1979.

Critical Studies: *The Literary Rebel*, 1965, and *Goodman*, 1980, both by Kingsley Widmer; *Toward an Effective Critique of American Education* by James E. MacLellan, 1968; *The Party of Eros: Radical Socialist Thought and the Realm of Freedom* by Richard King, 1972; *Goodman et le reconquête du présent* by Bernard Vincent, 1976.

* * *

Towards the end of his life Paul Goodman became a cult figure among young, disaffected Americans. His writings were in favour of sexual liberation (he was avowedly bi-sexual) and freedom from planners' control, and they passionately protested against the American involvement in Vietnam—these were all causes that could be and were embraced by a large number of students and their sympathisers. Goodman became suddenly famous, his books went into paperback, he led marches, received many offers to speak on and off campus; and in a sense he wore himself out trying to make the armies of the night into an efficient fighting force against corporation America.

Cult figures rise and fall. But Goodman is a far more substantial figure than his brief celebrity status might make him appear. Probably comparatively few of those who began buying his books in the 1960's managed to work their way through them. And this is not because the books are poor, or badly written, but because Goodman was a tough-minded thinker, a man of real intellectual distinction, who refused to be caught out in simplistic postures, and who never pandered to popular demands that he should become a generation's guru. In short, Goodman is in no way to be blamed for the odd, upward turn of his reputation during those last hopeful, bewildering, and finally sad years of his life. (The sadness was caused by a series of heart attacks and more grievously by the death of his beloved son, Matty, about which he writes in a series of moving poems in *Homespun of Oatmeal Gray*.)

Perhaps the single work that did most to endear him to the young was *Growing Up Absurd*, which he subtitled "Problems of youth in the organized system." Yet this is not a glib tract for the times: on the contrary, it clearly grew out of Goodman's lifelong dedication to his own particular brand of intellectual anarchism, his deeply held and passionately argued belief that the life of the individual was being more and more threatened by the state. Goodman is really a descendant of John Stuart Mill and Walt Whitman: he longs to invite his soul to loaf, but he fears that the time for loafing may well be past. The themes of *Growing Up Absurd* are also presented in fictional form in many of his stories, in *The Empire City*, and, particularly, in *Making Do*.

Behind *Growing Up Absurd* is a quite magnificent study of the American city as it is and as it might be, *Communitas*, written with his brother Percival. Wonderfully well-written, rigorous in method, argument, and detailed application, *Communitas* is a deeply sane and wise book. And the same may be said for most of the essays in *Utopian Essays and Practical Proposals*. Goodman is indeed an extraordinarily good essayist, better, I would say, than Orwell; he is also a minor poet of some distinction (his posthumous *Little Prayers and Finite Experience* is an interesting experiment in intercutting small lyrical prayers-in-verse with longer prose meditations); and also, though not so successfully, a writer of fiction. Reviewing *Growing Up Absurd*, Webster Schott pointed out that Goodman is "a rational Utopian who has most of the analytical apparatus and theoretical formulations of modern sociology, psychology, historiography and aesthetics at his finger tips."

This almost terrifying breadth and depth—along with his warm and loving heart—help give Goodman his distinction.

—John Lucas

GORDON, Caroline. Born in Todd County, Kentucky, 6 October 1895. Educated at Bethany College, West Virginia, A.B. in Greek 1916. Married Allen Tate, *q.v.*, in 1924 (divorced and remarried, 1946; separated, 1955; divorced, 1959); one daughter. High school teacher, 1917–19; reporter, Chattanooga *News*, Tennessee, 1920–24; secretary to the writer Ford Madox Ford, New York, 1926–28; lived in Europe, 1928–29 and 1932–33; writer-in-residence, University of North Carolina Woman's College, Greensboro, 1938–39; Lecturer in Creative Writing, School of General Studies, Columbia University, New York, from 1946; Visiting Professor of English, University of Washington, Seattle, 1953; Writer-in-Residence, University of Kansas, Lawrence, 1956, University of California, Davis, 1962–63, and Purdue University, Lafayette, Indiana, 1963; teacher of creative writing, University of Dallas, after 1973. Joined Catholic Church, 1947. Recipient: Guggenheim fellowship, 1932; O. Henry Award, 1934; American Academy grant, 1950; National Endowment for the Arts grant, 1966. D.Litt.: Bethany College, 1946; St. Mary's College, Notre Dame, Indiana, 1964. *Died 11 April 1981.*

PUBLICATIONS

Collections

Collected Stories. 1981.

Fiction

Penhally. 1931.
Aleck Maury, Sportsman. 1934; as *The Pastimes of Aleck Maury: The Life of a True Sportsman*, 1935.
None Shall Look Back. 1937.
The Garden of Adonis. 1937.
Green Centuries. 1941.
The Women on the Porch. 1944.
The Forest of the South (stories). 1945.
The Strange Children. 1951.
The Malefactors. 1956.
Old Red and Other Stories. 1963.
The Glory of Hera. 1972.

Other

How to Read a Novel. 1957.
A Good Soldier: A Key to the Novels of Ford Madox Ford. 1963.

Editor, with Allen Tate, *The House of Fiction: An Anthology of the Short Story*. 1950; revised edition, 1960.

*

Bibliography: *Flannery O'Connor and Gordon: A Reference Guide* by Robert E. Golden and Mary C. Sullivan, 1977.

Critical Studies: *Gordon* by Frederick P.W. McDowell, 1966; *Gordon* by W.J. Stuckey, 1972; *The Short Fiction of Gordon: A Critical Symposium* edited by Thomas H. Landess, 1972; *Gordon as Novelist and Woman of Letters* by Rose Ann C. Fraistat, 1984.

* * *

Caroline Gordon is rightly grouped with writers of the so-called Southern Literary Renaissance, but is sometimes inappropriately called a regionalist. Most of her novels and short stories are set in her native Kentucky and in other nearby regions of the south, but her fiction strives toward the kind of universality achieved by the writers she most admired: Flaubert, Henry James, and James Joyce. She was an artist of the "dramatic" school, that is, she attempted to efface herself as author and allow her fiction to speak for itself. In addition to her nine novels and two short story collections, *The Forest of the South* and *Old Red and Other Stories*, Gordon wrote a critical book, *How to Read a Novel*, in which she set down the theoretical basis for her own fiction. With Allen Tate she edited *The House of Fiction*, an anthology of the short story with critical commentary on the craft and teaching of the short story form.

Gordon was a novelist, however, not a critic. Her life-long theme was the quest for heroic paradigms, a search that led her back to pioneer Kentucky (*Green Centuries*), to the pre-Civil War south (*Penhally*), to the war itself (*None Shall Look Back*) and, in modern times, to a southern plantation in the 1930's (*The Garden of Adonis*) ruined by drought and the Depression. Gordon's heroes are men or women who, on principle or out of commitment to a cause, stand up for what they believe to be right. This quest, as her fictions moved toward the 20th century, necessarily involved her with the widespread modern preference for the anti-hero and its attendant cultural implications, particularly with the view that meaningful action is impossible to an intellectually aware individual. In *The Women on the Porch*, set in New York and Kentucky, she took as her hero a deracinated intellectual-poet and "saved" him from emotional detachment through a final reconciliation with his estranged wife, a resolution that points toward the next stage in Gordon's development. In *The Strange Children*, narrated by a young girl, the hero—also an intellectual—comes to the realization that what is missing from his life is religious faith. *The Malefactors* carries this resolution a step further: the hero, Thomas Claiborne, cures his emotional paralysis by entering the Catholic Church. In *The Glory of Hera*, Gordon returned once more to the past, finding her hero and her heroic paradigm in Hercules; she set forth his story with all the sharpness of detail and dramatic enactment that characterized her earlier work.

The fiction of Gordon has much in common with the major fiction of the modern period, particularly with Hemingway's tightly controlled, dramatic, impersonal symbolic novels and stories, and reflects the same attachment to the natural world and traditional values to be found in southern writers generally and Faulkner in particular. The chief difference, perhaps, between the work of Gordon and that of her contemporaries is in her lack of moral ambiguity. Her fiction is less a discovery of acceptable shades of meaning than a bodying forth in enigmatic form of timeless moral truths.

—W.J. Stuckey

GREEN, Paul (Eliot). Born near Lillington, North Carolina, 17 March 1894. Educated at Buies Creek Academy (now Campbell College), North Carolina, graduated 1914; University of North Carolina, Chapel Hill, 1916–17 and 1919–21, A.B. 1921 (Phi Beta Kappa), graduate study, 1921–22; Cornell University, Ithaca, New York, 1922–23. Served in the U.S. Army Engineers, 1917–19: Lieutenant. Married Elizabeth Atkinson Lay in 1922; one son and three daughters. School principal, Olive Branch, North Carolina, 1914–17; Lecturer, then Associate Professor of Philosophy, 1923–39, Professor of Dramatic Art, 1939–44, and Professor of Radio, Television and Motion Pictures, 1962–63, University of North Carolina. Editor, *Reviewer* magazine, Chapel Hill, 1925. President, National Folk Festival, 1934–45, National Theatre Conference, 1940–42, and North Carolina State Literary and Historical Association, 1942–43; member, U.S. Executive Committee, and National Commission, Unesco, 1950–52; Rockefeller Foundation lecturer in Asia, 1951; director, American National Theatre Company, 1959–61; delegate, International Conference on the Performing Arts, Athens, 1962. Recipient: Pulitzer Prize, 1927; Guggenheim fellowship, 1928, 1929; Claire M. Senie Drama Study Award, 1937; Freedoms Foundation George Washington Medal, 1951, 1956, 1967; Yale School of Drama award, 1964; Susanne M. Davis Award, 1966; National Theatre Conference citation, 1974; American Theatre Association award, 1978. Litt. D.: Western Reserve University, Cleveland, 1941; Davidson College, North Carolina, 1948; University of North Carolina, 1956; Berea College, Kentucky, 1957; University of Louisville, Kentucky, 1957; Campbell College, Buies Creek, North Carolina, 1969; Duke University, Durham, North Carolina, 1980; D.F.A.: North Carolina School of the Arts, Winston-Salem, 1976; L.H.D.: Moravian College, Bethlehem, Pennsylvania, 1976. Member, American Academy, 1941. *Died 4 May 1981.*

PUBLICATIONS

Plays

Surrender to the Enemy (produced 1917).
Souvenir (produced 1919).
The Last of the Lowries (produced 1920). In *The Lord's Will and Other Carolina Plays*, 1925.
The Long Night, in *Carolina Magazine*, 1920.
Granny Boling, in *Drama*, August-September 1921.
Old Wash Lucas (The Miser) (produced 1921). In *The Lord's Will and Other Carolina Plays*, 1925.
The Old Man of Edenton (produced 1921). In *The Lord's Will and Other Carolina Plays*, 1925.
The Lord's Will (produced 1922). In *The Lord's Will and Other Carolina Plays*, 1925.
Blackbeard, with Elizabeth Lay Green (produced 1922). In *The Lord's Will and Other Carolina Plays*, 1925.
White Dresses (produced 1923). In *Lonesome Road*, 1926.
Wrack P'int (produced 1923).
Sam Tucker, in *Poet Lore*, Summer 1923; revised version, as *Your Fiery Furnace*, in *Lonesome Road*, 1926.
Fixin's, with Erma Green (produced 1924). 1934.
The No 'Count Boy (produced 1925). In *The Lord's Will and Other Carolina Plays*, 1925; revised (white) version, 1953.
In Aunt Mahaly's Cabin: A Negro Melodrama (produced, 1925). 1925.
The Lord's Will and Other Carolina Plays (includes *Blackbeard, Old Wash Lucas (The Miser), The No 'Count Boy, The Old Man of Edenton, The Last of the Lowries*). 1925.
Quare Medicine (produced 1925). In *In the Valley and Other Carolina Plays*, 1928.
The Man Who Died at Twelve O'Clock (produced 1925). 1927.
In Abraham's Bosom (produced 1926). In *The Field God, and In Abraham's Bosom*, 1927.
Lonesome Road: Six Plays for the Negro Theatre (includes *In Abraham's Bosom*, one-act version; *White Dresses*; *The Hot Iron*; *The Prayer Meeting*; *The End of the Row*; *Your Fiery Furnace*). 1926.
The Hot Iron, in *Lonesome Road*, 1926; revised version as *Lay This Body Down* (produced 1972), in *Wings for to Fly*, 1959.
The Field God (produced 1927). In *The Field God, and In Abraham's Bosom*, 1927.
The Field God, and In Abraham's Bosom. 1927.
Bread and Butter Come to Supper. 1928; as *Chair Endowed* (produced in *Salvation on a String*, 1954).
In the Valley and Other Carolina Plays (includes *Quare Medicine, Supper for the Dead, Saturday Night, The Man Who Died at Twelve O'Clock, In Aunt Mahaly's Cabin, The No 'Count Boy, The Man on the House, The Picnic, Unto Such Glory, The Goodbye*). 1928.
Supper for the Dead (produced in *Salvation on a String*, 1954). Included in *In the Valley and Other Carolina Plays*, 1928.
Unto Such Glory (produced 1936). In *In the Valley and Other Carolina Plays*, 1928.
The Goodbye (produced 1954). In *In the Valley and Other Carolina Plays*, 1928.
Blue Thunder; or, The Man Who Married a Snake, in *One Act Plays for Stage and Study*. 1928.
Old Christmas, in *Wide Fields*. 1928.
The House of Connelly (produced 1931). In *The House of Connelly and Other Plays*, 1931; revised version (produced 1959), in *Five Plays of the South*, 1963.
The House of Connelly and Other Plays (includes *Potter's Field* and *Tread the Green Grass*). 1931.
Potter's Field (produced 1934). In *The House of Connelly and Other Plays*, 1931; revised version, as *Roll Sweet Chariot: A Symphonic Play of the Negro People*, music by Dolphe Martin (produced 1934), 1935.
Tread the Green Grass, music by Lamar Stringfield (produced 1932). In *The House of Connelly and Other Plays*, 1931.
Shroud My Body Down (produced 1934). 1935; revised version, as *The Honeycomb*, 1972.
The Enchanted Maze: The Story of a Modern Student in Dramatic Form (produced 1935). 1939.
Hymn to the Rising Sun (produced 1936). 1939.
Johnny Johnson: The Biography of a Common Man, music by Kurt Weill (produced 1936). 1937; revised version, 1972.
The Southern Cross (produced 1936). 1938.
The Lost Colony (produced 1937). 1937; revised version, 1939, 1946, 1954, 1980.
Alma Mater, in *The Best One-Act Plays of 1938*, edited by Margaret Mayorga. 1938.
Out of the South: The Life of a People in Dramatic Form (includes *The House of Connelly, The Field God, In Abraham's Bosom, Potter's Field, Johnny Johnson, The Lost Colony, The No 'Count Boy, Saturday Night, Quare Medicine, The Hot Iron, Unto Such Glory, Supper for the Dead, The Man Who Died at Twelve O'Clock, White Dresses, Hymn to the Rising Sun*). 1939.
The Critical Year: A One-Act Sketch of American History and the Beginning of the Constitution. 1939.
Franklin and the King. 1939.
The Highland Call: A Symphonic Play of American History (produced 1939). 1941; revised version, 1975.
Native Son (The Biography of a Young American), with Richard Wright, from the novel by Wright (produced 1941). 1941; revised version, 1980.
A Start in Life (broadcast 1941). In *The Free Company Presents*, edited by James Boyd, 1941; as *Fine Wagon*, in *Wings for to Fly*, 1959.
The Common Glory: A Symphonic Drama of American History

(produced 1947). 1948; revised version, 1975.
Faith of Our Fathers (produced 1950).
Peer Gynt, from the play by Ibsen (produced 1951). 1951.
The Seventeenth Star (produced 1953).
Serenata, with Josefina Niggli (produced 1953).
Carmen, from the libretto by H. Meilhac and L. Halévy, music by Bizet (produced 1954).
This Declaration. 1954.
Salvation on a String (includes *Chair Endowed*, *The No 'Count Boy*, *Supper for the Dead*) (produced 1954).
Wilderness Road: A Symphonic Outdoor Drama (produced 1955; revised version, produced 1972). 1956.
The Founders: A Symphonic Outdoor Drama (produced 1957). 1957.
The Confederacy: A Symphonic Outdoor Drama Based on the Life of General Robert E. Lee (produced 1958). 1959.
The Stephen Foster Story: A Symphonic Drama Based on the Life and Music of the Composer (produced 1959). 1960.
Wings for to Fly: Three Plays of Negro Life, Mostly for the Ear But Also for the Eye (includes *The Thirsting Heart*, *Lay This Body Down*, *Fine Wagon*). 1959.
The Thirsting Heart (produced 1971). In *Wings for to Fly*, 1959.
Five Plays of the South (includes revised versions of *The House of Connelly*, *In Abraham's Bosom*, *Johnny Johnson*, *Hymn to the Rising Sun*, *White Dresses*). 1963.
Cross and Sword: A Symphonic Drama of the Spanish Settlement of Florida (produced 1965). 1966.
The Sheltering Plaid. 1965.
Texas: A Symphonic Outdoor Drama of American Life (produced 1966). 1967.
Sing All a Green Willow (produced 1969).
Trumpet in the Land (produced 1970). 1972.
Drumbeats in Georgia: A Symphonic Drama of the Founding of Georgia by James Edward Oglethorpe (produced 1973).
Louisiana Cavalier: A Symphonic Drama of the 18th Century French and Spanish Struggle for the Settling of Louisiana (produced 1976).
We the People: A Symphonic Drama of George Washington and the Establishment of the United States Government (produced 1976).
The Lone Star: A Symphonic Drama of Sam Houston and the Winning of Texas Independence from Mexico (produced 1977).
Palo Duro: A Sound and Light Drama (produced 1979).

Screenplays: *Cabin in the Cotton*, 1932; *State Fair*, with Sonya Levien, 1933; *Dr. Bull*, 1933; *Voltaire*, with Maude T. Howell, 1933; *The Rosary*, 1933; *Carolina*, 1934; *David Harum*, 1934; *Time Out of Mind*, 1947; *Roseanna McCoy*, 1949; *Red Shoes Run Faster*, 1949.

Radio Play: *A Start in Life*, 1941.

Fiction

Wide Fields (stories). 1928.
The Laughing Pioneer: A Sketch of Country Life. 1932.
This Body the Earth. 1935.
Salvation on a String and Other Tales of the South. 1946.
Dog on the Sun: A Volume of Stories. 1949.
Words and Ways: Stories and Incidents from My Cape Fear Valley Folklore Collection. 1968.
Home to My Valley (stories). 1970.
Land of Nod and Other Stories: A Volume of Black Stories. 1976.

Verse

Trifles of Thought. 1917.
The Lost Colony Song-Book. 1938.
The Highland Call Song-Book. 1941.
Song in the Wilderness, music by Charles Vardell. 1947.
The Common Glory Song-Book. 1951.
Texas Song-Book. 1967.
Texas Forever. 1967.

Other

Contemporary American Literature: A Study of Fourteen Outstanding American Writers, with Elizabeth Lay Green. 1925; revised edition, 1927.
The Hawthorn Tree: Some Papers and Letters on Life and the Theatre. 1943.
Forever Growing: Some Notes on a Credo for Teachers. 1945.
Dramatic Heritage (essays). 1953.
Challenge to Citizenship (address). 1956.
Drama and the Weather: Some Notes and Papers on Life and the Theatre. 1958.
The University in a Nuclear Age (address). 1963.
Plough and Furrow: Some Essays and Papers on Life and the Theatre. 1963.

*

Critical Studies: *Green* by Barrett H. Clark, 1928; *Green of Chapel Hill* by Agatha Boyd Adams, 1951; *Green* by Walter S. Lazenby, 1970; *Green* by Vincent S. Kenny, 1971; *The Green I Know* by Elizabeth Lay Green, 1978.

* * *

Paul Green's career as a playwright can be divided conveniently into four overlapping periods. In the first he used the history, dialect, superstitions, customs, and beliefs of both white and black inhabitants of his native region in eastern North Carolina, and began by writing short realistic folkplays, comedies as well as tragedies. Noticeable from the outset was a compassion for society's expendibles, those cast-offs who, though victims of social injustice, held within them the dreams and hopes common to all mankind. The full-length *In Abraham's Bosom*, its protagonist a luckless black schoolteacher, was an extended treatment of a one-act play. It was followed on Broadway by *The Field God*, dealing with the oppressive religious orthodoxy among back-country whites.

Tread the Green Grass, a deliberate experiment, turned from realism toward a mythic non-realistic folk drama, but retained the kind of rustic characters who were now his special province. Green's stylized blend of pantomime, dance, ritual, dream sequences, puppetlike movements, fantasy and legend, with music an integral part of the play as with the Greeks, expanded, he believed, the accepted concepts of time and space on the stage. For those of his plays synthesizing the theatrical arts—plays like *Roll Sweet Chariot* (earlier title, *Potter's Field*), *Shroud My Body Down*, and *Sing All a Green Willow*—Green coined the term "symphonic drama," intending apparently to devise an American *Gesamtkunstwerk*.

Meanwhile he did not abandon the commercial theater. *The House of Connelly*, a dramatization of the fluctuating conditions among aristocrats and "poor whites" in the post-Civil War south, conformed to Broadway standards of what a well-made play should be. The anti-war musical *Johnny Johnson* was a collaborative effort with Kurt Weill, and *Native Son* an adaptation of Richard Wright's tragic story of a black misfit in Chicago. For the New York stage he provided an English version of *Peer Gynt*, and for an opera theater in Colorado a translation of Carmen.

The fourth phase began in 1937 with *The Lost Colony*, an "outdoor symphonic drama" produced on the very spot where Sir Walter Ralegh's colonists landed in 1587. Applying the elements of his experimental plays, and superimposing upon an event in history a tightly drawn plot, Green was finally permitted, on the huge open-air stage, the freedom of sweeping folk dances, large choruses, and broad movements of men, women, and children. The throngs of unsophisticated ticket-buyers who attended *The Lost Colony* inspired him to establish away from Broadway a "theater of the people." In 1947 came *The Common Glory* for Virginia, then *Faith of Our Fathers* (Washington, D.C.), and other plays like *Wilderness Road* (Kentucky), *Cross and Sword* (Florida), *Texas*, and *Trumpet in the Land* (Ohio). Green and his followers used his "formula" for more than sixty similar works, spread out from the Atlantic coastline to California and Alaska. Never satisfied with his last versions, Green constantly revised the annual summertime repetitions of his outdoor plays.

—Richard Walser

GREGORY, Horace (Victor). Born in Milwaukee, Wisconsin, 10 April 1898. Educated at the Milwaukee School of Fine Arts, summers 1913–16; German-English Academy, Milwaukee, 1914–19; University of Wisconsin, Madison, 1919–23, B.A. 1923. Married the poet Marya Zaturenska in 1925 (died, 1982); one daughter and one son. Free-lance writer, New York, 1923–33; Member of the English Department, 1934–60, and Professor Emeritus, 1960–82, Sarah Lawrence College, Bronxville, New York. Lecturer, New School for Social Research, New York, 1955–56. Associate editor, *Tiger's Eye* magazine, New York. Recipient: Russell Loines Award, 1942; Guggenheim fellowship, 1951; Academy of American Poets fellowship, 1961; Bollingen Prize, 1965; Horace Gregory Foundation award, 1969. D.Litt.: University of Wisconsin, Milwaukee, 1977. Member, American Academy, 1964. *Died 11 March 1982*.

PUBLICATIONS

Verse

Chelsea Rooming House. 1930; as *Rooming House*, 1932.
No Retreat. 1933.
A Wreath for Margery. 1933.
Chorus for Survival. 1935.
Poems 1930–1940. 1941.
Selected Poems. 1951.
Medusa in Gramercy Park. 1961.
Alphabet for Joanna (for children). 1963.
Collected Poems. 1964.
Another Look. 1976.

Other

Pilgrim of the Apocalypse: A Critical Study of D.H. Lawrence. 1933; revised edition, 1957.
The Shield of Achilles: Essays on Beliefs in Poetry. 1944.
A History of American Poetry 1900–1940, with Marya Zaturenska. 1946.
Poet of the People: An Evaluation of James Whitcomb Riley, with James T. Farrell and Jeannette Covert Nolan. 1951.
Amy Lowell: Portrait of the Poet in Her Time. 1958.
The World of James McNeill Whistler. 1959.
The Dying Gladiators and Other Essays. 1961.
Dorothy Richardson: An Adventure in Self-Discovery. 1967.
The House on Jefferson Street: A Cycle of Memories. 1971.
Spirit of Time and Place: Collected Essays. 1973.

Editor, with Eleanor Clark, *New Letters in America*. 1937.
Editor, *Critical Remarks on the Metaphysical Poets*, by Samuel Johnson. 1943.
Editor, *The Triumph of Life: Poems of Consolation for the English-Speaking World*. 1943.
Editor, *The Portable Sherwood Anderson*. 1949; revised edition, 1972.
Editor, *The Snake Lady and Other Stories*, by Vernon Lee. 1954.
Editor, *Selected Poetry*, by Robert Browning. 1956.
Editor, with Marya Zaturenska, *The Mentor Book of Religious Verse*. 1957.
Editor, with Marya Zaturenska, *The Crystal Cabinet: An Invitation to Poetry*. 1962.
Editor, with others, *Riverside Poetry 4: An Anthology of Student Verse*. 1962.
Editor, *Evangeline and Selected Tales and Poems of Longfellow*. 1964.
Editor, *Selected Poems*, by E.E. Cummings. 1965.
Editor, with Marya Zaturenska, *The Silver Swan: Poems of Romance and Mystery*. 1966.
Editor, *Selected Poems of Lord Byron*. 1969.

Translator, *The Poems of Catullus*. 1931.
Translator, *Poems*, by Catullus. 1956.
Translator, *The Metamorphoses*, by Ovid. 1958.
Translator, *Love Poems of Ovid*. 1964.

*

Critical Studies: "Gregory Issue" of *Modern Poetry Studies*, May 1973.

* * *

Horace Gregory was perhaps best known as the translator of Catullus and Ovid. But he also wrote studies of Amy Lowell, D.H. Lawrence, James McNeill Whistler and others, as well as collaborating with his wife, the poet Marya Zaturenska, on *A History of American Poetry 1900–1940*.

Elizabeth Drew wrote that his "emotional range is perhaps the most comprehensive among modern poets," and Louis Untermeyer wrote that Gregory "does not share Eliot's disillusions or Crane's disorganization," a statement that is unfair to all three poets. However, poems like "Valediction to My Contemporaries" compare interestingly with Hart Crane's *The Bridge* in language, idealism, purposes; and many of Gregory's efforts to recapture in monologues the pathos and cacophony of life in the modern city remind one of Eliot. In the final analysis, however, authenticity and integrity may not be enough; subtleties of syntax, powers of condensation, originality of imagery, distinguish Eliot and Crane from those who wrote with comparable verve.

Gregory is academic, ordered, descriptive, even-paced; he might be quite properly compared with MacLeish for his intellectual ambition, rhetorical power, and sense of American history. Most of his poems are based on classical subjects in one way or another, though he often juxtaposes classical imagery with modernistic impressions; he also has many poems about paintings, European scenes, and—like MacLeish—his country's cultural history. His well-known poem on Emerson recapitulates Emerson's life in an investigation of the intellectual's role ("To know too well, to think too long") in a land where action and immortality are even more akin than rhetoric and relevance. Gregory, like MacLeish, bears a heavy weight of idealism at all times, perhaps more than his country's history can support. Because the idealism is more muted in his Chelsea rooming house poems, they are perhaps more appealing than his poems with more epic ambition. In poems like "McAlpin Garfinkel, Poet" and "Time and Isidore Lefkowitz", Gregory seems to have absorbed the influence of Edwin Arlington Robinson and to have looked forward to the work of poets like Kenneth Fearing:

> Look at Isidore Lefkowitz,
> biting his nails, telling how
> he seduces Beautiful French Canadian
> Five and Ten Cent Store Girls,
> beautiful, by God, and how they cry
> and moan, wrapping their arms
> and legs around him
> when he leaves them. . . .

In an age when we have come to think of poems as the swiftly captured sound of madness, Gregory's work stands as a celebration of order, with the glimpsed backstreet life crying out to have a part of that order and the consideration due to it.

> How can I unlearn
> the arts of love within a single hour:
> How can I close my eyes before a mirror,
> believe I am not wanted, that hands, lips, breast
> are merely deeper shadows behind the door
> where all is dark?

—David Ray

GREY, Zane. Born Pearl Zane Gray in Zanesville, Ohio, 31 January 1872. Educated at Moore High School, Zanesville; University of Pennsylvania, Philadelphia, D.D.S. 1896. Married Lina Elise Roth in 1905; two sons and one daughter. Dentist in New York, 1896–1904; thereafter a full-time writer; traveled in the western U.S., 1907–18; settled in California, 1918. *Died 23 October 1939.*

PUBLICATIONS

Fiction

Betty Zane. 1903.
The Spirit of the Border. 1906.
The Last of the Plainsmen. 1908.
The Last Trail. 1909.
The Heritage of the Desert. 1910.
Riders of the Purple Sage. 1912.
Desert Gold. 1913.
The Light of Western Stars. 1914.
The Rustlers of Pecos County. 1914.
The Lone Star Ranger. 1915.
The Rainbow Trail. 1915.
The Border Legion. 1916.
Wildfire. 1917.
The U.P. Trail. 1918; as *The Roaring U.P. Trail*, 1918.
The Desert of Wheat. 1919.
The Man of the Forest. 1920.
The Mysterious Rider. 1921.
To the Last Man. 1922.
The Day of the Beast. 1922.
Wanderer of the Wasteland. 1923.
The Call of the Canyon. 1924.
Roping Lions in the Grand Canyon. 1924.
The Thundering Herd. 1925.
The Vanishing American. 1925; as *The Vanishing Indian*, 1926.
Under the Tonto Rim. 1926.
Forlorn River. 1927.
Nevada. 1928.
Wild Horse Mesa. 1928.
Fighting Caravans. 1929.
The Shepherd of Guadaloupe. 1930.
Sunset Pass. 1931.
Arizona Ames. 1932.
Robbers' Roost. 1932; abridged edition, as *Thieves' Canyon*, 1965.
The Drift Fence. 1933.
The Hash Knife Outfit. 1933.
Code of the West. 1934.
Thunder Mountain. 1935.
The Trail Driver. 1936.
The Lost Wagon Train. 1936.
West of the Pecos. 1937.
Tex Thorne Comes Out of the West. 1937.
Majesty's Rancho. 1938.
Raiders of the Spanish Peaks. 1938.
Western Union. 1939.
Knights of the Range. 1939.
30,000 on the Hoof. 1940.
Twin Sombreros. 1941.
Stairs of Sand. 1943.
Wilderness Trek. 1944.
Shadow of the Trail. 1946.
Valley of Wild Horses. 1947.
Rogue River Feud. 1948.
The Deer Stalker. 1949.
The Maverick Queen. 1950.
The Dude Ranger. 1951.
Captives of the Desert. 1952.

Wyoming. 1953.
Lost Pueblo. 1954.
Black Mesa. 1955.
Stranger from the Tonto. 1956.
The Fugitive Trail. 1957.
The Arizona Clan. 1958.
Horse Heaven Hill. 1959.
Boulder Dam. 1963.
Grey, Outdoorsman: Best Hunting and Fishing Tales, edited by George Reiger. 1972.
Greatest Western [Indian, Animal] Stories, edited by Loren Grey. 3 vols., 1975.
The Big Land, edited by Loren Grey. 1976.
Yaqui and Other Great Indian Stories, edited by Loren Grey. 1976.
Shark! Tales of Man-Eating Sharks, edited by Loren Grey. 1976.
The Reef Girl, edited by Loren Grey. 1977.
The Buffalo Hunter, edited by Loren Grey. 1977.
The Westerner, edited by Loren Grey. 1977.
Savage Kingdom. 1979.
The Undiscovered Fishing Stories, edited by George Reiger. 1983.

Plays

Screenplays: *The Vanishing Pioneer*, with others, 1928; *Rangle River*, with Charles and Elsa Chauvel, 1936.

Other (for children)

The Short-Stop. 1909.
The Young Forester. 1910.
The Young Pitcher. 1911.
The Young Lion Hunter. 1911.
Ken Ward in the Jungle. 1912.
The Red-Headed Outfield and Other Baseball Stories. 1920.
Tappan's Burro and Other Stories. 1923.
Don: The Story of a Lion Dog. 1928.
The Wolf Tracker. 1930.
Book of Camps and Trails. 1931.
King of the Royal Mounted [and the Northern Treasure, in the Far North, Gets His Man, Policing the Far North, and the Great Jewel Mystery, and the Ghost Guns of Roaring River]. 7 vols., 1936–46.
The Ranger and Other Stories. 1960.
Blue Feather and Other Stories. 1961.

Other

Nassau, Cuba, Yucatan, Mexico: A Personal Note of Appreciation of These Nearby Foreign Lands. 1909.
Tales of Fishes [Lonely Trails, Southern Rivers, Fishing Virgin Seas, The Angler's Eldorado—New Zealand, Swordfish and Tuna, Fresh-Water Fishing, Tahitian Waters]. 8 vols., 1919–31; augmented edition of *Tales of the Angler's El Dorado*, as *Angler's El Dorado: Grey in New Zealand*, 1982.
An American Angler in Australia. 1936.
Adventures in Fishing, edited by Ed Zern. 1952.
Tales from a Fisherman's Log. 1978.
Grey: A Photographic Odyssey (Zane Grey's photographs), text by Loren Grey. 1985.

*

Bibliography: *Grey, Born to the West: A Reference Guide* by Kenneth W. Scott, 1979; *Grey, A Documented Portrait: The Man, The Bibliography, The Filmography* by G.M. Farley, 1985.

Critical Studies: *Grey: A Biography* by Frank Gruber, 1970; *Grey* by Carlton Jackson, 1973; *Grey* by Ann Ronald, 1975; *Grey, Story Teller* by Carol Gay, 1979; *Grey's Arizona* by Candace C. Kant, 1984.

* * *

Zane Grey's literary career typifies the American Horatio Alger success story, and Grey helped to perpetuate the Alger myth, using striking settings in the American west. At the beginning of his career Grey struggled for several years in New York City and near Lackawaxen, Pennsylvania, writing essays on fishing and a trilogy based on the Zane family history in the settlement of the Ohio Valley. But he received little encouragement, save from his wife, and gathered rejection slips until he found his subject in the American west as a result of a visit to Arizona at the request of C.J. "Buffalo" Jones, a business entrepreneur.

Grey's own taste in literature was for the romantic, and he realized that the west was still close enough to frontier conditions for him to use it as a splendid testing ground of a man's worth. Owen Wister had discovered the cowboy as romantic hero with *The Virginian* (1902), and Grey was quick to capitalize on Wister's discovery. He paid his debt to Wister by using the subtitle of Wister's famous novel as the title for his first book about the west, *The Last of the Plainsmen*.

That book was largely a narrative of travel and was followed by his first proper novel of the west, *The Heritage of the Desert*. The success in sales was moderate, but in the story of the rise to manhood of an eastern misfit, John Hare, Grey had found those elements of adventure, suspense, and history that were to make him the most popular writer of his time. *Riders of the Purple Sage*, his next western, was to insure that Grey's struggles to establish himself as a writer were at an end. From then on he easily outdistanced other American writers in sales and popular, although not critical, appreciation.

Grey was bothered by the reaction of critics to his work. There is, however, much of the formula in his work. He is often melodramatic and sentimental, and his style is stilted or awkward. But his fiction has emphasized the importance of the West to the American psyche, and embodied values in American life that those given critical acclaim frequently scoffed at or ignored. Grey was concerned about changing mores in American society. His *The Call of the Canyon*, for example, is contemporary in its concern for the plight of the returned soldier and in its objection to the "new woman." Grey's views, obviously, reflected a large segment of popular opinion in the 1920's, when he was frequently at or near the top of the best-seller lists.

Although Grey also wrote many books for boys and books about the outdoors, he will continue to be known for his western fiction. His energies were so great that new Grey titles were published for years after his death. His work is perennially popular.

—Joseph M. Flora

GUINEY, Louise Imogen. Born in Roxbury, Boston, Massachusetts, 7 January 1861. Educated at the Convent of the Sacred Heart, Elmhurst, Rhode Island. Worked for a time as a journalist; postmistress, Auburndale, Massachusetts; worked in the cataloging department, Boston Public Library; editor, with Alice Brown, *Pilgrim Scrip*; moved to England, 1895. *Died 2 November 1920.*

PUBLICATIONS

Verse

Songs at the Start. 1884.
The White Sail and Other Poems. 1887.
A Roadside Harp. 1893.
Nine Sonnets Written at Oxford. 1895.
England and Yesterday: A Book of Short Poems. 1898.
The Martyrs' Idyl and Shorter Poems. 1899.
Happy Ending: Collected Lyrics. 1909; revised edition, 1927.

Fiction

Lovers', Saint Ruth's, and Three Other Tales. 1895.

Other

Goose-Quill Papers. 1885.
Brownies and Bogles (for children). 1888.
Monsieur Henri: A Foot-Note to French History. 1892.
A Little English Gallery. 1894.
Three Heroines in New England Romance: Their True Stories, with Harriet Prescott Spoffard and Alice Brown. 1894.
Patrins, To Which Is Added an Inquirendo into the Wit and Other Good Parts of His Late Majesty King Charles the Second. 1897.
Robert Emmet: A Survey of His Rebellion and of His Romance. 1904.
Blessed Edmund Campion. 1908.
Letters, edited by Grace Guiney. 2 vols., 1926.
Colonel Guiney and the Ninth Massachusetts: A Filial Appreciation. 1932.

Editor, *James Clarence Mangan: His Selected Poems.* 1897.
Editor, *Sohrab and Rustum and Other Poems*, by Matthew Arnold. 1899.
Editor, *The Mount of Olives and Primitive Holiness*, by Henry Vaughan. 1902.
Editor, *Selected Poems*, by Katherine Philips. 2 vols., 1904–05.
Editor, *Hurrell Froude: Memoranda and Comments.* 1904.
Editor, *Thomas Stanley: His Original Lyrics, Complete.* 1907.
Editor, *Some Poems of Lionel Johnson.* 1912.
Editor, *Arthur Laurie Thomas: A Memoir*, by F.E. Thomas. 1920.
Editor, with Geoffrey Bliss, *Recusant Poets.* 1938.

Translator, *The Sermon to the Birds and the Wolf of Gubbio.* 1898.
Translator, *The Secret of Fougereuse: A Romance of the Fifteenth Century*, by Louise Morvan. 1898.

*

Bibliography: in *Bibliography of American Literature* by Jacob Blanck, 1959.

Critical Studies: *Guiney* by Alice Brown, 1921; *Guiney: Her Life and Works* by E.M. Tenison, 1923; *Guiney: Laureate of the Lost* by Henry G. Fairbanks, 1972.

* * *

Although she published nearly thirty books and a hundred articles, Louise Imogen Guiney is relatively forgotten today. Her best volume of verse, *A Roadside Harp*, brings to maturity the themes and attitudes which she introduced in two previous collections, *Songs at the Start* and *The White Sail and Other Poems*, and which were to preoccupy her throughout her career: an attachment to the past, a fondness for nature, and a love for religion and learning. Technically, Guiney's poetry is conservative and genteel. Its carefully measured rhythms and conventional forms earned her the admiration of Oliver Wendell Holmes, who called her his "little golden guinea," and the disapproval of the editor and critic Horace Scudder, who found her work excessively "oblique and allusive."

For her models, Guiney looked toward the classics, in which she was extraordinarily well instructed, and the Renaissance, in which she was an acknowledged expert. Guiney was particularly fond of sonnets and elegies. *Nine Sonnets Written at Oxford* was considered by many to be one of the finest collections of sonnets published during the 19th century. So precise was her attention to form and so classical were her tastes that several of Guiney's poems were mistaken for translations of Greek originals. Guiney's longer narrative poetry, which she herself disparaged for its lack of unity, was less successful. At its best Guiney's poetry sparkles with wit and allusion; at its worst it is imitative and artificial.

Later in life, Guiney found it increasingly more difficult to write poetry, and she turned instead toward scholarship. A poorly written collection of stories, *Lovers', St. Ruth's, and Three Other Tales*, early convinced her that the essay, not fiction, was the form of prose most suited to her talents. Her most famous book of essays, *Patrins*, avoids the stylistic pitfalls of an earlier collection, *Goose-Quill Papers*, which bordered on the precious and even, at times, the euphuistic. In *Patrins* she summarizes her critical theory, articulated previously in her preface to a translation of Mérimée's *Carmen* and in the introduction to her edition of the poetry of James Clarence Mangan, that literature should be emphatically humanistic and that it should express "joy" rather than what she termed "willful sadness." But Guiney's critical theories, while pronounced, were by no means intolerant. Although she disapproved of realism and naturalism, she was not beyond appreciating the artistry and talent of someone like Harold Frederic, whom she called a "country boy of genius."

Guiney's many biographical works, which include *A Little English Gallery*, *Robert Emmet*, and *Blessed Edmund Campion*, display the painstaking exactitude and genuine devotion to learning that characterize nearly everything she wrote. A knowledgeable editor, Guiney published selections from the works of Henry Vaughan, Matthew Arnold, Hurrell Froude, Thomas Stanley, and Lionel Johnson, among others. Many of her essays express her lifelong commitment to Roman Catholicism, and at the time of her death, she was working on a collection, with copious biographical and bibliographical notes, of poetry written by Catholics in England from 1535 to 1735, posthumously published as *Recusant Poets*.

—James A. Levernier

GUTHRIE, Ramon. Born in New York City, 14 January 1896. Educated at Mt. Hermon, 1912–14; University of Toulouse, Docteur en Droit, 1922; the Sorbonne, Paris, 1919, 1922–23. Served in the American Field Service, 1916–17; U.S. Army Air Corps, 1917–19; Office of Strategic Services, 1943–45: Silver Star. Married Marguerite Maurey in 1922. Assistant Professor of Romance Languages, University of Arizona, Tucson, 1924–26; Professor of French, 1930–63, and Professor Emeritus, 1963–73, Dartmouth College, Hanover, New Hampshire. Recipient: National Endowment for the Arts grant, 1969, 1971; Marjorie Peabody Waite Award, 1970. M.A., 1939, and D.Litt., 1971, Dartmouth College. *Died 22 November 1973*.

PUBLICATIONS

Collections

Maximum Security Ward and Other Poems, edited by Sally M. Gall. 1984.

Verse

Trobar Clus. 1923.
A World Too Old. 1927.
The Legend of Ermengarde. 1929.
Scherzo, From a Poem to be Entitled "The Proud City." 1933.
Graffiti. 1959.
Asbestos Phoenix. 1968.
Maximum Security Ward 1964–1970. 1970.

Fiction

Marcabrun. 1926.
Parachute. 1928.

Other

Editor, with George E. Diller, *French Literature and Thought since the Revolution*. 1942.
Editor, with George E. Diller, *Prose and Poetry of Modern France*. 1964.

Translator, *The Revolutionary Spirit in France and America*, by Bernard Faÿ. 1927.
Translator, *The Other Kingdom*, by David Rousset. 1947.
Translator, *The Republic of Silence*, edited by A.J. Liebling. 1947.

*

Critical Studies: *Guthrie Kaleidoscope*, 1963 (includes bibliography by Alan Cooke); *Guthrie's Maximum Security Ward* by Sally M. Gall, 1984.

* * *

Ramon Guthrie's last and most important work, *Maximum Security Ward*, appeared when he was 74. Indeed, although he was a contemporary of Cummings and Crane, most of his significant work belongs to the late 1950's and 1960's and is collected in *Graffiti*, *Asbestos Phoenix*, and *Maximum Security Ward*. All three books contain striking poems, but the cumulative force of the last, which derives from its dramatic center, is by far Guthrie's most sustained success. The speaker, a critically ill and suffering old man, uses all the resources of his imagination, memory, intellect, and humor to overcome his bewildering isolation and disappointment in himself and his fellow human beings. The book is a particularly valuable addition to the genre of the modern lyric sequence.

The best introduction to the poet and his style comes in the first of the 49 poems of *Maximum Security Ward*:

> So name her Vivian. I, scarecrow Merlin—
> our Broceliande this frantic bramble of
> glass and plastic tubes and stainless steel—
> could count off such illusions as I have
> on a quarter of my thumbs.

Here are all the hallmarks of Guthrie's mature verse: the passionate immediacy of the speaking voice; the subtle internal rhymes and skilful assonance, alliteration, and colliteration (the use of related consonants); the unpretentious, humorous, colloquial tone combined with a scholarly range of reference and romantic wistfulness; and the recurrent reference to French art and literature, particularly medieval romance, as a psychological touchstone.

Guthrie was bilingual and a Francophile, and his intimate knowledge of France is reflected in his poetry. He lived, studied, and wrote in France during most of the 1920's and sporadically thereafter and knew the expatriate community of artists well. He served in France in two wars, married a Frenchwoman, and taught French literature throughout his academic career. His earliest important literary influences were French, and Proust was his philosophical mentor. But he was an eminently American poet, writing out of the traditions of American verse and at times satirizing his country's hypocrisies and cruelties—particularly its role in Vietnam—for the good of the body politic. Of course, his great subject in *Maximum Security Ward* is supranational: the meaning of the whole human enterprise—what it is to be fully human psychologically, socially, politically—and the role of any artist, whether writer, painter, musician, or sculptor, in uncovering what is essentially a sacred meaning.

A good amateur painter, Guthrie had a visual imagination that matched and reinforced his great love for the texture of language and that enhanced the exquisitely tactile sensuousness of some of his most evocative passages:

> this smooth knoll of your shoulder,
> this cwm of flank, this moss-delineated quite
> un-Platonic cave. . . .
>
> Everywhere about is landscape as far as foot can feel
> lamps exude their light on flagstones
> there are quaint quiet trains in
> corridors of pure perspective

Guthrie's poems are filled with concrete, memorable phrases and imagery; he moves skilfully from tone to tone, from the most jarring to the most lyrical; wit, intelligence, and a deep sympathy and humanity inform his work. It is a pity it is not better known.

—Sally M. Gall

H.D. See **DOOLITTLE, Hilda.**

HALLECK, Fitz-Greene. Born in Guilford, Connecticut, 8 July 1790. Educated at public schools in Guilford. Worked in a store in Guilford, 1806–11; clerk in the banking house of Jacob Barker, New York, 1812–30; toured Europe, 1822; confidential clerk in the banking house of John Jacob Astor, 1832 until he retired to Guilford on an annuity left him by Astor, 1849. Leading member of the Knickerbocker Group, New York; Vice-President, Authors Club, New York, 1837. *Died 19 November 1867.*

PUBLICATIONS

Collections

Poetical Writings, edited by James Grant Wilson. 1868.

Verse

Poems, with Joseph Rodman Drake. 1819; revised edition, as *The Croakers*, 1860.
Fanny. 1819; revised edition, 1821.
Alnwick Castle with Other Poems. 1827.
The Recorder with Other Poems. 1833.
Fanny with Other Poems. 1839.
Poetical Works. 1847.
Young America. 1865.

Other

A Letter Written to Joel Lewis Griffing in 1814. 1921.

Editor, *The Works of Lord Byron in Verse and Prose*. 1833.
Editor, *Selections from the British Poets*. 2 vols., 1840.

*

Bibliography: in *Bibliography of American Literature* by Jacob Blanck, 1959.

Critical Studies: *Life and Letters of Halleck* by James Grant Wilson, 1869; *Some Notices of the Life and Writings of Halleck* by William Cullen Bryant, 1869; *Halleck: An Early Knickerbocker Wit and Poet* by Nelson Frederick Adkins, 1930.

* * *

With the exception of William Cullen Bryant, Fitz-Greene Halleck was, among his contemporaries, the most popular of the Knickerbocker poets, and although such once-famous Knickerbockers as Samuel Woodworth, Robert Sands, and George Pope Morris have long been forgotten by virtually everyone except literary historians, Halleck is still remembered as a minor poet and satirist of New York society in the early 19th century.

Poetry was for Halleck, as for other Knickerbockers, an avocation, a pleasant diversion for gentlemen. His poetry is also exceedingly derivative. Campbell, Scott, and Moore are among those who most influenced him, but no poet's influence was greater then Byron's—an influence that Halleck freely acknowledged. (Indeed Halleck repaid the debt in his memoir and collected edition of Bryon's works, the first such edition to be published on either side of the Atlantic.)

Although Halleck published little poetry of consequence, its range was large, including the heroic ("Marco Bozzaris"), the pastoral ("Wyoming"), the sentimental ("Alnwick Castle"), the elegiac ("On the Death of Joseph Rodman Drake"), and the satiric (*Fanny*). His reputation was established in 1819 with the publication of "The Croaker Papers," written jointly with Joseph Rodman Drake. These poems, widely read and praised in their day, satirize prominent figures in the financial, political, and social life of New York. *Fanny*, Halleck's most sustained literary effort and his best, is a pointed but delicate satire of fashionable New York society, a world which Halleck knew well. During the last four decades of his life, Halleck, who died in 1867, published little of interest.

Despite his satires of fashionable New York, it was in that New York that Halleck was most at home. As personal secretary to John Jacob Astor, he was assured of access to the social realm he most admired. Here literature was a pastime, a diversion. Astor's world was the ideal setting for the accomplished but amateur poet that Halleck indisputably was.

—Edward Halsey Foster

HAMMETT, (Samuel) Dashiell. Born in St. Mary's County, Maryland, 27 May 1894. Educated at Baltimore Polytechnic Institute to age 13. Served in the Motor Ambulance Corps of the U.S. Army, 1918–19: Sergeant; also served in the U.S. Army Signal Corps in the Aleutian Islands, 1942–45. Married Josephine Annas Dolan in 1920 (divorced, 1937); two daughters. Worked as a clerk, stevedore, and advertising manager; private detective, Pinkerton Agency, 1908–22; full-time writer from 1922: book reviewer, *Saturday Review of Literature*, New York, 1927–29, and New York *Evening Post*, 1930; lived in Hollywood, 1930–42; began long relationship with Lillian Hellman, *q.v.*, in 1930; teacher of creative writing, Jefferson School of Social Science, New York, 1946–56. Convicted of contempt of Congress and sentenced to six months in prison, 1951. President, League of American Writers, 1942, and Civil Rights Congress of New York, 1946–47; member of the Advisory Board, *Soviet Russia Today*. *Died 10 January 1961.*

PUBLICATIONS

Collections

The Big Knockover: Selected Stories and Short Novels, edited by Lillian Hellman. 1966; as *The Hammett Story Omnibus*, 1966; as *The Big Knockover* and *The Continental Op*, 2 vols., 1967.

Fiction

Red Harvest. 1929.
The Dain Curse. 1929.

The Maltese Falcon. 1930.
The Glass Key. 1931.
The Thin Man. 1934.
$106,000 Blood Money. 1943; as *Blood Money*, 1943; as *The Big Knockover*, 1948.
The Adventures of Sam Spade and Other Stories, edited by Ellery Queen. 1944; as *They Can Only Hang You Once*, 1949; selection, as *A Man Called Spade*, 1945.
The Continental Op, edited by Ellery Queen. 1945.
The Return of the Continental Op, edited by Ellery Queen. 1945.
Hammett Homicides, edited by Ellery Queen. 1946.
Dead Yellow Women, edited by Ellery Queen. 1947.
Nightmare Town, edited by Ellery Queen. 1948.
The Creeping Siamese, edited by Ellery Queen. 1950.
Woman in the Dark, edited by Ellery Queen. 1951.
A Man Named Thin and Other Stories, edited by Ellery Queen. 1962.
The Continental Op, edited by Steven Marcus. 1974.

Plays

Watch on the Rhine (screenplay), with Lillian Hellman, in *Best Film Plays of 1943–44*, edited by John Gassner and Dudley Nichols. 1945.

Screenplays: *City Streets*, with Oliver H.P. Garrett and Max Marcin, 1931; *Woman in the Dark*, with others, 1934; *After the Thin Man*, with Frances Goodrich and Albert Hackett, 1936; *Another Thin Man*, with Frances Goodrich and Albert Hackett, 1939; *Watch on the Rhine*, with Lillian Hellman, 1943.

Other

Secret Agent X-9 (cartoon strip), with Alex Raymond. 2 vols., 1934.
The Battle of the Aleutians, with Robert Colodny. 1944.

Editor, *Creeps by Night*. 1931; as *Modern Tales of Horror*, 1932; as *The Red Brain*, 1961; as *Breakdown*, 1968.

*

Bibliography: *Hammett: A Descriptive Bibliography* by Richard Layman, 1979.

Critical Studies: "The Black Mask School" by Philip Durham and "The Poetics of the Private-Eye: The Novels of Hammett" by Robert I. Edenbaum, both in *Tough Guy Writers of the Thirties* edited by David Madden, 1968; *Hammett: A Casebook*, 1969, and *Hammett: A Life at the Edge*, 1983, both by William F. Nolan; *An Unfinished Woman*, 1969, *Pentimento*, 1973, and *Scoundrel Time*, 1976, all by Lillian Hellman; *Beams Falling: The Art of Hammett* by Peter Wolfe, 1980; *Shadow Man: The Life of Hammett* by Richard Layman, 1981; *Hammett* by Dennis Dooley, 1983; *Hammett: A Life* by Diane Johnson, 1983, as *The Life of Hammett*, 1984; *Hammett* by William Marling, 1983; *Private Investigations: The Novels of Hammett* by Sinda Gregory, 1984; *Hammett* by Julian Symons, 1985.

* * *

In the same year (1923) that he began publishing his stories of the Continental Op in *Black Mask*, the monthly pulp magazine founded by H.L. Mencken and George Jean Nathan, Dashiell Hammett contributed to their more sophisticated *Smart Set* a collection of terse observations about his career as a Pinkerton agent under a title echoing the writings of his former employer: "From the Memoirs of a Private Detective." In form these "memoirs" play against familiar conventions of detective literature. A wry remark such as "I know a forger who left his wife because she had learned to smoke cigarettes while he was serving a term in prison" diminishes the categorical morality of crime literature, and other comments on the inadequacy of fingerprints as clues or the number of unsolved cases in a detective's files disparage all accounts of infallible detective procedures. Since the stories of the Continental Op, Ned Beaumont, Sam Spade, and Nick Charles similarly transgress familiar conventions, it is not hard to see why readers, like Raymond Chandler in his famous essay "The Simple Art of Murder," consider Hammett to have added realism to a form grown effete by its emphasis on the myths of ratiocinative detection.

Hammett is notable for the versimilitude in his use of criminal argot and the description of underworld life, but that cannot be confused with imitation of *the real world*. And his use of American vernacular speech in the first-person narrations of the Continental Op or Nick Charles and the density of action and dialogue in the futile quest for the Maltese falcon or the political crimes of *The Glass Key* should be seen as the requirement of the contract between author and reader of fiction that there be a specific world within the fiction. The extraordinarily complicated, and unlikely, plotting even in the novelettes about the Op, are as incongruent with the reader's known world as the private detectives are unlike their real-life counterparts who occupy themselves with tawdry divorce cases or employee theft.

What, then, is Hammett's achievement, if it is not in mimetic narrative? The answer seems to be that he supplants the mystery puzzle and idealized heroes of earlier detective fiction with themes that codify a modern sense of urban disorder. He achieves this, first of all, by creation of a milieu of pervasive corruption. In his novels—all but *The Thin Man* originally serialized in *Black Mask*—and short stories the socially reputable are as criminal as the gangsters with whom they often collaborate. The action of plot necessarily follows. Everyone becomes involved in crime, while the force of violence is the common expression of will for those who recognize no law but their own domination, and for the detective because his reason is insufficient alone. When the systems of our social and political myths cannot account for the feel of confusion and menace in urban life, the caricature of a naturalistic world in Hammett's fiction becomes a plausible image.

Similarly, Hammett's stylized representation of hard-boiled detectives offers an appropriate common-sense theme of behavior. Sam Spade repressing sentiment, Ned Beaumont acting on motives that are unclear even to himself, the Continental Op just doing his job, and Nick Charles affecting sophistication are all masked figures. Behind the tough and cool face they maintain before their world, as though there were no such thing as subjective psychology, we sense a vulnerability that becomes justification for wariness and a disposition to violence. We are intrigued by the thought that Hammett's detectives are what Huck Finn would have become when he found that the Territory in which he hoped to escape civilization was dotted with cities, and in adulthood converted his sense of complicity in events beyond his control into a principle of behavior.

—John M. Reilly

HANSBERRY, Lorraine (Vivian). Born in Chicago, Illinois, 19 May 1930. Educated at the Art Institute, Chicago; University of Wisconsin, Madison, 1948–50. Married Robert Nemiroff in 1953 (divorced, 1964). Journalist, 1950–51, and associate editor after 1952, *Freedom*, New York. Recipient: New York Drama Critics Circle award, 1959. *Died 12 January 1965.*

PUBLICATIONS

Collections

Les Blancs: The Collected Last Plays (includes *Les Blancs, The Drinking Gourd, What Use Are Flowers?*), edited by Robert Nemiroff. 1972.

Plays

A Raisin in the Sun (produced 1959). 1959.
The Sign in Sidney Brustein's Window (produced 1964). 1965.
To Be Young, Gifted, and Black: A Portrait of Hansberry in Her Own Words, adapted by Robert Nemiroff (produced 1969). 1971.
Les Blancs, edited by Robert Nemiroff (produced 1970). In *Les Blancs* (collection), 1972.

Screenplay: *A Raisin in the Sun*, 1961.

Other

The Movement: Documentary of a Struggle for Equality. 1964; as *A Matter of Colour*, 1965.
To Be Young, Gifted, and Black: A Portrait of Hansberry in Her Own Words, edited by Robert Nemiroff. 1969.

*

Critical Studies: "Hansberry Issue" of *Freedomways 19*, 1979; *Hansberry* by Anne Cheney, 1984.

* * *

The importance of Lorraine Hansberry as an American dramatist rests with two plays, *A Raisin in the Sun* and *The Sign in Sidney Brustein's Window*, both produced during her tragically short life of 34 years. The first, by all measurements, was a major success. The second was a commercial failure, meeting only limited critical support. There were two posthumous productions, the effective but somewhat pasted-up collection presented as *To Be Young, Gifted, and Black* and *Les Blancs*, more or less complete but obviously still unfinished.

Hansberry is an important, though minor, figure in American drama if for no more than the fact that she wrote an outstanding play of substantial popular and critical success as a black writer contributing to an essentially white-oriented commercial theatre during a period when the black identity in American letters was at a very delicate stage. It was a period when a strong pull existed between those blacks who preferred to stand on their achievements as artists, irrespective of race, and those who preferred to take a stand, artistic as well as social or political, because of the very fact of their blackness. This dichotomy is clear in the opinions of critics who evaluate Hansberry as a black writer. While she herself was completely uncontroversial and avoided the pointedly racial-political involvements associated with black writers of her era, there is some controversy as to whether or not her two major plays were merely outstanding, relatively conventional, dramatic works of a fine young American playwright of promising talent who happened to be black, or were the works of a dedicated black playwright treating subjects directly involved in the causes espoused by the writers overtly conscious of their race.

A Raisin in the Sun at first glance would suggest that Hansberry is allied to those black writers who choose to place onstage the social issue of the ghetto-trapped family. The specifications are there, from the exasperated young black male, fumbling and frustrated in The Man's world, to the matriarch holding the fatherless family together. But Hansberry actually composed a solid, almost conventional "well-made" play, centering upon a theme which could have at one time as easily been Irish, Jewish, or Oriental, but which happens, given the time it was written and the knowledge of its creator, to be black. True, the plight of the Youngers, a serious and prevalent American theme, exists almost entirely *because* they are black, but the confrontations, save for that with the rather pitiful Linder, who brings the outside forces briefly into the Youngers' living room, remain offstage or are postponed until after the curtain falls. Audience interest in the Youngers is in their human, not their racial, qualities.

The Sign in Sidney Brustein's Window is a sensitive comedy far removed in subject and intent from *Raisin*. The world of a white Jewish flat in Greenwich Village, visited by attractive, if not always "normal" characters and centered upon a strictly local political campaign, is not the usual subject associated with a black writer intent on attacks against the social injustices of a racist society. Hansberry attacks petty individual prejudices, those against Black or sexual deviant, as well as personal selfishness which can be fatal to those one ought to love.

It is impossible to know where Hansberry might have gone. Perhaps she would have become "radicalized," or perhaps she was already more radicalized than we recognize. It hardly matters. Judgment of her two important plays shows that she was a writer of singular promise, a very important voice in an uncertain historical and social period.

—Jordan Y. Miller

HARRIGAN, Edward. Born in New York City, 26 October 1844. Received little schooling. Married Annie T. Braham in 1876; seven children. Left home for San Francisco, and appeared in vaudeville in the west, 1867–70; returned to New York, and appeared on stage, with Sam Rickey, as a vaudeville comic team, 1870; first appeared with Anthony J. Cannon (stage name: Tony Hart), as Harrigan and Hart, 1871, and with him managed and appeared at the Theatre Comique, New York, 1871 until the theatre was torn down, 1881: during this period wrote more than 80 sketches, music by David Braham, which developed into the complete plays of his later career in which he always acted the leading part; with Hart, opened the New Theatre Comique, 1881, and managed it until it was destroyed by fire, 1884; partnership with Hart ended, 1885; leased Harrigan's Park Theatre, 1884–88; built Harrigan's, later the Garrick, Theatre, 1891–95; retired, 1908. *Died 6 June 1911.*

PUBLICATIONS

Collections

The Famous Songs of Harrigan and Hart, edited by Edward B. Marks. 1938.

Plays and Sketches

The Mulcahey Twins (produced 1870). Songs published 1872.
The Little Fraud (produced 1871). Songs published 1870.
The Big and Little of It (produced 1871).
The Day We Went West (produced 1871).
The German Emigrants (produced 1871).
The Irish Emigrant (produced 1871).
You 'spute Me (produced 1871).
Ireland vs. Italy (also called *Who Owns the Line?*) (produced 1872).
Shamus O'Brien at Home (produced 1872).
Sing Sing (produced 1872).
The Mulligan Guard (produced 1873). Songs published 1873.
St. Patrick's Day Parade (also called *The Day We Celebrate*) (produced 1873; revised 1874 and thereafter). Songs published 1884.
The Absent-Minded Couple (produced 1873).
An Editor's Troubles (produced 1873). 1875.
The Mixed Couple (produced 1873).
Eureka, with John Woodard (produced 1874).
Muldoon, The Solid Man (produced 1874).
The Raffle for Mrs. Hennessey's Clock (produced 1874).
The Regular Army, O! (produced 1874).
A Terrible Example (produced 1874).
Who Stole the Monkey? (produced 1874).
The Skidmores (produced 1874).
The Invalid Corps (produced 1874).
Going Home Again (produced 1874).
The Night Clerk's Troubles; or, The Fifth Avenue Hotel (also called *The Porter's Troubles*) (produced 1875). 1875.
The Blue and the Gray (produced 1875). 1875.
Fee-Gee (produced 1875).
The Doyle Brothers, with John Woodard (produced 1875).
April Fool (produced 1875).
Innocence at Home (produced 1875).
No Irish Wanted Here (produced 1875).
The Donovans (produced 1875).
King Calico's Body Guard (produced 1875).
The Two Awfuls (produced 1875).
Behind the Scenes (produced 1875).
Slavery Days (produced 1875). Songs published 1875.
Down Broadway; or, From Central Park to the Battery (produced 1875). Songs published 1878.
The Bradys (produced 1876).
The Italian Ballet Master (produced 1876).
Malone's Night Off (produced 1876).
The Bold Hibernian Boys (produced 1876).
S.O.T. (Sons of Temperance) (produced 1876). Songs published 1876.
Iascaire (produced 1876).
Walkin' for Dat Cake (produced 1876). Songs published 1877.
Bar Ber Ous (produced 1876).
Down in Dixie (produced 1876).
Matrimonial Ads (produced 1877).
The Rising Star (produced 1877).
The Telephone (produced 1877).
Christmas Joys and Sorrows (produced 1877). 1877.
The Grand Duke's Opera House (produced 1877).
Old Lavender (also called *Old Lavender Water* and *Around the Docks*) (produced 1877; revised version, 1878, 1885). 1877.
My Wife's Mother (produced 1878). 1877.
Callahan the Detective (produced 1877).
The Crushed Actors (produced 1877).
The Pillsbury Muddle (produced 1877).
Sullivan's Christmas (produced 1877).
Our Irish Cousins (produced 1877).
The Two Young Fellows and Her Majesty's Marines (produced 1877).
Love vs. Insurance (produced 1878).
A Celebrated Hard Case (produced 1878). 1878.
The Lorgaire (produced 1878; revised 1888). 1878.
The Mulligan Guard Picnic (produced 1878). 1880.
Coloured Baby Show (produced 1878).
The Italian Junkman (produced 1878).
The Lady of Lions (produced 1878).
Our Law Makers (produced 1878).
O'Brien, Counselor-at-Law (produced 1879).
The Great In-Toe-Natural Walking Match (produced 1879).
The Mulligan Guard Ball (produced 1879). 1879.
The Mulligan Guard Chowder (produced 1879). 1879.
The Mulligan Guards' Christmas (produced 1879). 1879.
The Mulligan Guard Nominee (produced 1880). 1880.
The Mulligan Guards' Surprise (produced 1880). 1880.
The Major (produced 1881). 1881.
The Mulligans' Silver Wedding (produced 1881). 1881.
Squatter Sovereignty (produced 1882). 1881.
Our Cranks, with G.L. Stout (produced 1881).
Mordecai Lyons (produced 1882). 1882.
McSorley's Inflation (produced 1882). 1882.
The Muddy Day (also called *Bunch o' Berries*) (produced 1883). Songs published 1883.
Cordelia's Aspirations (produced 1883).
Dan's Tribulations (also called *Tribulations*) (produced 1884). Songs published 1893.
Investigation (produced 1884). Songs published 1884.
McAllister's Legacy (produced 1885).
Are You Insured? (produced 1885).
The Grip (produced 1885).
The O'Reagans (produced 1886).
The Leather Patch (produced 1886). Songs published 1886.
McNooney's Visit (produced 1887).
Pete (produced 1887).
Waddy Googan (produced 1888). Songs published 1893.
Reilly and the Four Hundred (produced 1890). Songs pub-

lished 1890.
The Last of the Hogans (produced 1891; shortened version, as *Sergeant Hickey*, produced 1897). Songs published 1891.
The Woollen Stocking (produced 1893). Songs published 1893.
Notoriety (produced 1894). Songs published 1894.
The Blue Ribbon (produced 1894).
My Son Dan (produced 1896).
Marty Malone (produced 1896).
Low Life (produced 1897).
An Old New Yorker (produced 1899).
Under Cover (produced 1903).
The Simple Life (produced 1905).
In the North Woods (produced 1907).
The Lord Mayor of Dublin (produced 1908).

Fiction

The Mulligans. 1901.

Verse

Songs for the Banjo. 1888.
Songs. 1893.

Other

Comique Joker, with Tony Hart. 1870(?).
Pictorial History of the Mulligan Guard Ball. 1879.

*

Critical Studies: *The Merry Partners: The Age of Harrigan and Hart* by E.J. Kahn, Jr., 1955; *Harrigan: From Corlear's Hook to Herald Square* by Richard Moody, 1980.

* * *

The enthusiastic comparisons which critics applied to Edward Harrigan's plays would seem to have assured him an international reputation. William Dean Howells (in *Harper's*, July 1886) described him as the American Goldoni and a playwright who created "the spring of a true American Comedy." Others compared him to Hogarth, Balzac, Zola, and Dickens. At a time when American literature and art were firmly caught up in the rise of realism Harrigan deserved this critical attention through his successful depiction of Lower East Side New York life. As a comedian and a playwright he believed in "Holding the Mirror Up to Nature," as he explained it in an essay in *Pearson's Magazine* (November 1903), and providing a "series of photographs of life today in the Empire City" (*Harper's Weekly*, 2 February 1889). By using authentic scenes, character types, speech, dress, and gestures he provided realistic farce-comedy in which he infused his own belief in the kindness and good nature of the majority of people. As riotous fun, his plays and performances were both a reflection of the serious artistic and social movements of his generation and an antidote to the grimness which they frequently unveiled.

Harrigan, after several years in vaudeville, formed a comedy team with Anthony J. Cannon, who soon changed his name to Hart. As "Harriganandhart" they performed for fourteen years, and Harrigan began writing the sketches, with music by David Braham, that often developed into full-length plays. Many of the most memorable take place in Mulligan's Alley in New York's Sixth Ward. It was a part of New York that Harrigan researched and knew very well—a jumbled population of Germans, Italians, Chinese, blacks, and Irish who took their ward politics seriously as well as their social activities which seemed always haunted by the "battle of the sexes." There was the Wee Drop Saloon run by Walfingham McSweeny, an Italian junk shop, a Chinese laundry-lodging combination, Lochmuller's butcher shop, and a black social club called the Full Moon Union. It was an international community which Harrigan brought to life with elaborate stage-business, meticulous attention to realistic detail, and a comedian's enthusiasm for the "general melee" which characterized his plays.

Harrigan's most famous plays involved the Mulligans—*The Mulligan Guard*, *The Mulligan Guard Ball*, *The Mulligan Guard Nominee*, and so on—through which he satirized contemporary military organization, social life on the Lower East Side, and politics. *Cordelia's Aspirations* and *Dan's Tribulations* also involve Dan Mulligan and his wife. His other important plays include *Old Lavender*, *Waddy Googan*, and *Reilly and the Four Hundred*. The people and their ideas were real if slight, and the spectators came to see something of themselves on stage. Trying always to be "truthful to the laws that govern society," Harrigan also confessed to being provincial and optimistic. Although he did not fulfill the potentiality that some critics saw or stimulate followers for his theory of American comedy, he was a major favorite for a generation or more of New York theatre-goers.

—Walter J. Meserve

HARRIS, George Washington. Born in Allegheny City, Pennsylvania, 20 March 1814; grew up in Knoxville, Tennessee. Educated in local schools; apprenticed to a metalworker, Knoxville, 1826–33. Married 1) Mary Emeline Nance in 1835 (died, 1867), six children; 2) Jane E. Pride in 1869. Captain of the *Knoxville*, a Tennessee River boat, 1833–38; farmer, Tucaleeche Cove, Tennessee, 1839–43; opened a metalworking shop in Knoxville, 1843; superintendent, Holston Glass Works, 1849; captain of the steamboat *Alida*, Tennessee River, 1854; coppermine surveyor, Ducktown, Tennessee, 1854; alderman, Fourth Ward of Knoxville, 1856; postmaster, Knoxville, 1857–58; conductor, 1859, and freight agent, 1860–61, Nashville and Chattanooga Railroad; lived in Nashville, 1862, and in various parts of the south during the Civil War, 1862–65; worked for the Wills Valley Railroad, Chattanooga, Tennessee, 1866–69. Delegate to the secessionist Southern Commercial Convention, Savannah, Georgia, 1856; member, Democratic State Central Committee, Tennessee, 1859. *Died 11 December 1869*.

PUBLICATIONS

Collections

Sut Lovingood's Yarns, and *High Times and Hard Times*, edited by M. Thomas Inge. 2 vols., 1966–67.

Prose

Sut Lovingood: Yarns Spun by a "Nat'ral Born Durn'd Fool: Warped and Wove for Public Wear." 1867.
Sut Lovingood: Travels with Old Abe Lincoln. 1937.

*

Bibliography: in *Bibliography of American Literature* by Jacob Blanck, 1959.

Critical Studies: *The Lovingood Papers* edited by Ben Harris McClary, 4 vols., 1962–65; *Harris* by Milton Rickels, 1966; *The Frontier Humorists: Critical Views* edited by M. Thomas Inge, 1975.

* * *

George Washington Harris was neither a writer by trade nor a southerner by birth. Yet he contributed to American literature one of its most distinctively southern comic figures in Sut Lovingood and brought the American literary vernacular to its highest level of achievement before Mark Twain.

Harris had been brought as a child to Knoxville, Tennessee, by his half-brother from the place of his birth in Allegheny City, Pennsylvania, and he adapted to the attitudes and mores of the ante-bellum South with spirited enthusiasm. With little education in the formal sense, he had learned from a wide range of occupations, including metal working, captaining a steamboat, farming, running a glass works and a sawmill, surveying, running for political office, serving as a postmaster, and working for the railroad. Such diverse experience gave Harris a large reservoir of material from which to draw in his writing.

Writing was a leisure time activity for Harris, who began as an author of political sketches for local newspapers and sporting epistles for the New York *Spirit of the Times*. He quickly developed a facility for local color and dialect and a skill for bringing backwoods scenes and events to life on the printed page. When he contributed the first Sut Lovingood sketch to the *Spirit* (4 November 1854), he outdistanced all the other humorists of the Old Southwest by allowing one central character to tell his own stories in his own vernacular and by granting him (without authorial comment) a lease on life according to the integrity and consistency of that character's independence in thought and action. Mark Twain would learn this lesson well from Harris, whose one collection of stories, *Sut Lovingood: Yarns*, he reviewed, and put it to effective use in *Adventures of Huckleberry Finn*.

While authors and critics such as William Dean Howells and Edmund Wilson have found Sut Lovingood repugnant, others such as Mark Twain, William Faulkner, and F.O. Matthiessen have paid tribute to Harris's genius. What makes Sut distinctive is the combination in his character of such human failings as bigotry, vulgarity, cowardice, brutality, and offensive behavior, along with a steadfast opposition to hypocrisy, dishonesty, and all limitations set on personal and social freedom. Many readers find it difficult to like Sut, but few find it possible to resist his appeal, especially evident when he reveals hypocritic sins and recounts the brutal punishment of those who take advantage of innocence. Sut is a minister of justice in coarse southern homespun whose wildly funny pranks and incorrigible attitudes make him one of the most intriguing characters in American literary history.

—M. Thomas Inge

HARRIS, Joel Chandler. Born near Eatonton, Georgia, 9 December 1848. Educated at Eatonton Academy for Boys. Married Esther LaRose in 1873; nine children. Printer's devil and typesetter, *Countryman* weekly, published at the Turnwold Plantation, 1862–66; staff member, Macon *Telegraph*, Georgia, 1866, *Crescent Monthly*, New Orleans, 1866–67, *Monroe Advertiser*, Forsyth, Georgia, 1867–70, Savannah *Morning News*, Georgia, 1870–76, and Atlanta *Constitution*, 1876–1900; founder, with his son Julian, *Uncle Remus's* magazine, Atlanta, 1907–08. L.H.D.: Emory College, Oxford, Georgia, 1902. Member, American Academy, 1905. *Died 2 July 1908.*

PUBLICATIONS

Collections

The Complete Tales of Uncle Remus, edited by Richard Chase. 1955.

Fiction

Uncle Remus: His Songs and His Sayings: The Folklore of the Old Plantation. 1880; as *Uncle Remus and His Legends of the Old Plantation*, 1881; as *Uncle Remus; or, Mr. Fox, Mr. Rabbit, and Mr. Terrapin*, 1881; revised edition, 1895.
Nights with Uncle Remus: Myths and Legends of the Old Plantation. 1883.
Mingo and Other Sketches in Black and White. 1884.
Free Joe and Other Georgian Sketches. 1887.
Daddy Jake the Runaway and Short Stories Told after Dark. 1889.
Balaam and His Master and Other Sketches and Stories. 1891.
A Plantation Printer: The Adventures of a Georgia Boy During the War. 1892; as *On the Plantation*, 1892.
Uncle Remus and His Friends: Old Plantation Stories, Songs, and Ballads, with Sketches of Negro Character. 1892.
Little Mr. Thimblefinger and His Queer Country: What the Children Saw and Heard There. 1894.
Mr. Rabbit at Home. 1895.
The Story of Aaron (So Named), The Son of Ben Ali, Told by His Friends and Acquaintances. 1896.
Sister Jane, Her Friends and Acquaintances. 1896.
Stories of Georgia. 1896; revised edition, 1896.
Aaron in the Wildwoods. 1897.
Tales of the Home Folks in Peace and War. 1898.
Plantation Pageants. 1899.
The Chronicles of Aunt Minervy Ann. 1899.
On the Wing of Occasions. 1900.
Gabriel Tolliver: A Story of Reconstruction. 1902.
The Making of a Statesman and Other Stories. 1902.
Wally Wanderoon and His Story-Telling Machine. 1903.
A Little Union Scout: A Tale of Tennessee During the Civil War. 1904.

Told by Uncle Remus: New Stories of the Old Plantation. 1905.
Uncle Remus and Brer Rabbit. 1907.
The Bishop and the Boogerman. 1909; as *The Bishop and the Bogie-Man*, 1909.
The Shadow Between His Shoulder-Blades. 1909.
Uncle Remus and the Little Boy. 1910.
Uncle Remus Returns. 1918.
The Witch Wolf: An Uncle Remus Story. 1921.
Qua: A Romance of the Revolution, edited by Thomas H. English. 1946.

Verse

The Tar-Baby and Other Rhymes of Uncle Remus. 1904.

Other

Harris, Editor and Essayist: Miscellaneous Literary, Political, and Social Writings, edited by Julia C. Harris. 1931.

Editor, *Life of Henry W. Grady, Including His Writings and Speeches: A Memorial Volume.* 1890.
Editor, *The Book of Fun and Frolic.* 1901; as *Merrymaker*, 1902.
Editor, *World's Wit and Humor.* 1904.

Translator, *Evening Tales*, by Frédéric Ortoli. 1893.

*

Bibliography: in *Bibliography of American Literature* by Jacob Blanck, 1959; *Harris: A Reference Guide* by R. Bruce Bickley, Jr., and others, 1978.

Critical Studies: *The Life and Letters of Harris* by Julia Collier Harris, 1918; *Harris, Folklorist* by Stella Brewer Brookes, 1950; *Harris: A Biography* by Paul M. Cousins, 1968; *Harris* by R. Bruce Bickley, Jr., 1978, and *Critical Essays on Harris* edited by Bickley, 1981; *Sources and Analogues of the Uncle Remus Tales* by Florence E. Baer, 1980.

* * *

Joel Chandler Harris's reputation as a writer of the Uncle Remus stories for children is somewhat misplaced. His first book, though deliberately illustrated and published as a volume in the publisher's "humorous" catalogue, was introduced by Harris as having a "perfectly serious" intention. He wanted to preserve the legends in their "original simplicity, and to wed them permanently to the quaint dialect . . . through the medium of which they have become a part of the domestic history of every Southern family." He had heard them originally on the Turnwold Plantation from storytellers similar to Uncle Remus himself, and he was careful to present the dialect accurately. Indeed, the original publication of the tales in the Atlanta *Constitution* (and reprinted in northern newspapers) had aroused anthropological interest even before they were published in book form. Harris's introduction also emphasizes the universality of the tales, and the African origin of the adventures of the rabbit, terrapin, fox, tortoise, bear, deer used by Uncle Remus. In a later volume, Harris introduced another black character, African Jack, who sometimes tells the same stories as Uncle Remus has told, but in different versions and in a different (Gullah) dialect.

What is often remembered by later readers of the tales is the picture, perhaps overly sweetened by various illustrators of the stories, of the white-haired 80-year-old ex-slave, Uncle Remus, and the little 7-year-old white boy (never named) to whom he tells his stories. Perhaps Uncle Remus is patching his coat, or blowing the ashes off a yam roasted in some hot coals to share with the boy, as he introduces his story. The stories are often used to point up a moral lesson for the boy (he shouldn't be stingy, or disturb others' property), but the tales themselves are always amusing, and often witty, and even the moral lessons are sometimes tart. Harris, in short, is not merely a transcriber of folklore, but an artist. Mark Twain, in fact, realized the tales' oral potentialities, and successfully used them in his own readings; he even suggested a joint reading tour with Harris.

But Harris wrote other things besides the Uncle Remus stories. Though his literary views demanded that proper "American" writing should deal with common people, preferably in a rural setting, he created a wide range of white and black characters, from the mountains and the lowlands. And the story "Free Joe and the Rest of the World" shows something of the harshness of slavery. Free Joe is a free black in a small community of slaves and masters, simple and friendless, a misfit, in fact. His wife is a slave, and, once her owner realizes that Joe has been visiting her, she is sold to a distant master. Joe is described as "the embodiment of that vague and mysterious danger that seemed to be forever lurking on the outskirts of slavery, . . . a danger always threatening, and yet never assuming shape; intangible, and yet real; impossible, and yet not improbable," suggesting something of the unspoken fears of the southern slave-owning society. Harris also championed a spirit of reconciliation of North and South after the Civil War: he more than once used the motif of a southern girl marrying a northern man who had fought against the South. These writings, along with the Uncle Remus tales, show Harris as perhaps the first writer to present a comprehensive view of the southern black "befo' the war, endurin' the war, en atterwards."

—George Walsh

See the essay on *Uncle Remus*.

HART, Moss. Born in New York City, 24 October 1904. Educated in New York public schools to 7th grade. Married the actress Kitty Carlisle in 1946; one son and one daughter. Delivery boy, clerk, and furrier in New York, late 1910's and early 1920's; worked for theatrical agent Augustus Pitou, 1923; actor and director on little theatre circuit, and resort camp social director, later 1920's; full-time playwright from 1930, often in collaboration with George S. Kaufman; also produced and directed for the Broadway stage. President, Dramatists Guild, 1947–55, and Authors League, 1955–61. Recipient: Megrue Prize, 1930; Pulitzer Prize, 1937; New York Drama Critics Circle award, for directing, 1955; Tony award, for directing, 1957. *Died 21 December 1961.*

PUBLICATIONS

Plays

The Hold-Up Man (produced 1923).
Jonica, with Dorothy Heyward, music by Joseph Meyer, lyrics by William Moll (produced 1930).
No Retreat (produced 1930).
Once in a Lifetime, with George S. Kaufman (produced 1930). 1930.
Face the Music, music by Irving Berlin (produced 1932).
As Thousands Cheer, with Irving Berlin, music and lyrics by Edward Heyman and Richard Myers (produced 1933).
The Great Waltz, from a play by Ernst Marischka and others, music by Johann Strauss (produced 1934).
Merrily We Roll Along, with George S. Kaufman (produced 1934). 1934.
The Paperhanger, with George S. Kaufman. 1935(?).
Jubilee, music by Cole Porter (produced 1935).
The Show Is On (revue), with others (produced 1936).
You Can't Take It with You, with George S. Kaufman (produced 1936). 1937.
I'd Rather Be Right, with George S. Kaufman, music by Richard Rodgers, lyrics by Lorenz Hart (produced 1937). 1937.
The Fabulous Invalid, with George S. Kaufman (produced 1938). 1938.
The American Way, with George S. Kaufman, music by Oscar Levant (produced 1939). 1939.
The Man Who Came to Dinner, with George S. Kaufman (produced 1939). 1939.
George Washington Slept Here, with George S. Kaufman (produced 1940). 1940.
Lady in the Dark, music by Kurt Weill, lyrics by Ira Gershwin (produced 1941). 1941.
Winged Victory (produced 1943). 1943.
Christopher Blake (produced 1946). 1947.
Light Up the Sky (produced 1948). 1949.
The Climate of Eden, from the novel *Shadows Move among Them* by Edgar Mittelholzer (produced 1952). 1953.

Screenplays: *Flesh*, with Edmund Goulding, 1932; *Broadway Melody of 1936*, with Jack McGowan and Sid Silvers, 1935; *Frankie and Johnny*, with Jack Kirkland, 1936; *Winged Victory*, 1944; *Gentleman's Agreement*, 1947; *Hans Christian Andersen*, with Myles Connolly, 1952; *A Star Is Born*, 1954; *Prince of Players*, 1954.

Other

Act One: An Autobiography. 1959.

* * *

Moss Hart's first play, *The Hold-Up Man*, written when he was 19, folded in Chicago. But his *Once in a Lifetime* caught Sam Harris's eye, he was given George S. Kaufman as a collaborator (a story wittily told in Hart's autobiography, *Act One*), and the rest is history. Their play *Once in a Lifetime* was a success and the team continued with *Merrily We Roll Along*, the classic *You Can't Take It With You, The Man Who Came to Dinner*, and *George Washington Slept Here*.

Then Hart, never secure alone, sought other collaborators and produced more important work. Having written *Face the Music* and *As Thousands Cheer* with Irving Berlin, *Jubilee* with Cole Porter, and *I'd Rather Be Right* with Kaufman and Rodgers and Lorenz Hart, he carried on his musical success in 1941 with Kurt Weill and Ira Gershwin: *Lady in the Dark*. This was probably the highlight of his own musical work though he directed such hits by others as Irving Berlin's *Miss Liberty* (1949) and the Lerner and Loewe blockbusters *My Fair Lady* (1956) and *Camelot* (1960). In 1943 he created a "spectacle in two acts and seventeen scenes" for the U.S. Air Force called *Winged Victory*, starring 300 servicemen, including Red Buttons and Lee J. Cobb. "The Army Emergency Relief Fund needs the money," was Lewis Nichols's review in the New York *Times*, but he patriotically if not critically added that it was "a wonderful show." After World War II Hart gave us *Christopher Blake*—which can be forgotten. *Light Up the Sky*, however, is a fine play about theatre folk—slick, sentimental, simplistic, and very funny. It is a delightful expansion of real life. In *The Climate of Eden*, "Eden" turns out to be the British Guiana mission of Gregory Hawke's uncle, and there our hero, feeling guilty for his wife's death, is obsessed with various problems. More interesting are Hart's films such as *Gentleman's Agreement* and *A Star Is Born*.

Hart was always the innovative sort of theatre man who could call for four revolving stages where no one had ever used more than two before—and the dependent sort of theatre man that leaned on collaborators but also got four times as much out of them, and himself, as had ever been obtained before. He was also the sort who could submit *Once in a Lifetime* to six managers (all of whom accepted it) and then sell it to Sam Harris with the understanding that Kaufman would collaborate.

That collaboration produced one of the best comedies of the American theatre, *The Man Who Came to Dinner*. Of course, "real life" made them a gift of the inimitable Alexander Woollcott, but *they* knew what to do with him. It also takes a crack at Noël Coward, one of the Marx Brothers, the Lizzie Borden story (which is rather ineptly worked in), and the midwest, would-be writers, fussy nurses, "the most chic actress on the New York or London stage," etc. The plot (largely Hart's?) is carpentry, but the wisecracks (mostly Kaufman's) are pure gold.

—Leonard R.N. Ashley

HARTE, (Francis) Bret(t). Born in Albany, New York, 25 August 1836; lived with his family in various cities in the northeast, then in New York City after 1845. Educated in local schools to age 13. Married Anna Griswold in 1862; four children. Worked in a lawyer's office, then a merchant's counting room, New York; moved to Oakland, California, 1854; teacher, LaGrange, apothecary's clerk, Oakland, and expressman in various California towns, 1854–55; private tutor, 1856; guard on Wells Fargo stagecoach, 1857; printer and reporter, Arcata *Northern Californian*, 1858–60; moved to San Francisco: typesetter, *Golden Era*, 1860–61; clerk, Surveyor-General's office, 1861–63; secretary, U.S. branch mint, 1863–69; contributor and occasional acting editor, *Californian*, 1864–66; first editor, *Overland Monthly*, 1868–71; lived in New Jersey and New York, 1871–78; went on lecture tours, 1872–74; tried unsuccessfully to establish *Capitol* magazine, 1878; U.S. commercial agent, Krefeld, Germany, 1878–80;

U.S. Consul, Glasgow, 1880–85; lived in London, 1885–1902. *Died 5 May 1902.*

PUBLICATIONS

Collections

Writings. 20 vols., 1896–1914.
Letters, edited by Geoffrey Bret Harte. 1926.
Representative Selections, edited by Joseph B. Harrison. 1941.
The Best Short Stories, edited by Robert N. Linscott. 1967.

Fiction

Condensed Novels and Other Papers. 1867; revised edition, 1871.
The Lost Galleon and Other Tales. 1867.
The Luck of Roaring Camp and Other Sketches. 1870; revised edition, 1871.
Stories of the Sierras and Other Sketches. 1872.
The Little Drummer; or, The Christmas Gift That Came to Rupert: A Story for Children. 1872.
Mrs. Skaggs's Husbands and Other Sketches. 1873.
An Episode of Fiddletown and Other Sketches. 1873.
Idyls of the Foothills. 1874.
Tales of the Argonauts and Other Sketches. 1875.
Wan Lee, The Pagan and Other Sketches. 1876.
Gabriel Conroy. 1876.
Thankful Blossom: A Romance of the Jerseys 1779. 1877.
Thankful Blossom and Other Tales. 1877.
My Friend, The Tramp (stories). 1877.
The Story of a Mine. 1877.
The Man on the Beach (stories). 1878.
Jinny (stories). 1878.
Drift from Two Shores. 1878; as *The Hoodlum Bard and Other Stories*, 1878.
An Heiress of Red Dog and Other Sketches. 1879.
The Twins of Table Mountain (stories). 1879.
Jeff Briggs's Love Story and Other Sketches. 1880.
Flip and Other Stories. 1882.
In the Carquinez Woods. 1883.
California Stories. 1884.
On the Frontier (stories). 1884.
By Shore and Sedge. 1885.
Maruja. 1885.
Snow-Bound at Eagle's. 1886.
The Queen of the Pirate Isle. 1886.
A Millionaire of Rough-and-Ready, and Devil's Ford. 1887.
The Crusade of the Excelsior. 1887.
A Phyllis of the Sierras, and A Drift from Redwood Camp. 1888.
The Argonauts of North Liberty. 1888.
Cressy. 1889.
Captain Jim's Friend, and The Argonauts of North Liberty. 1889.
The Heritage of Dedlow Marsh and Other Tales. 1889.
A Waif of the Plains. 1890.
A Ward of the Golden Gate. 1890.
A Sappho of Green Springs and Other Tales. 1891.
A First Family of Tasajara. 1891.
Colonel Starbottle's Client and Some Other People. 1892.
Susy: A Story of the Plains. 1893.
Sally Dows, Etc. (stories). 1893.
A Protegee of Jack Hamlin's and Other Stories. 1894.
The Bell-Ringer of Angel's and Other Stories. 1894.
Clarence. 1895.
In a Hollow of the Hills. 1895.
Barker's Luck and Other Stories. 1896.
Three Partners; or, The Big Strike on Heavy Tree Hill. 1897.
The Ancestors of Peter Atherly and Other Tales. 1897.
Tales of Trail and Town. 1898.
Stories in Light and Shadow. 1898.
Mr. Jack Hamlin's Mediation and Other Stories. 1899.
From Sand Hill to Pine. 1900.
Under the Redwoods. 1901.
Openings in the Old Trail. 1902; as *On the Old Trail*, 1902.
Condensed Novels: Second Series: New Burlesques. 1902.
Trent's Trust and Other Stories. 1903.

Plays

Two Men of Sandy Bar, from his story "Mr. Thompson's Prodigal." 1876.
Ah Sin, with Mark Twain (produced 1877). Edited by Frederick Anderson, 1961.
Sue, with T. Edgar Pemberton, from the story "The Judgment of Bolinas Plain" by Harte (produced 1896). 1902; as *Held Up* (produced 1903).

Verse

The Heathen Chinee. 1870.
Poems. 1871.
That Heathen Chinee and Other Poems, Mostly Humorous. 1871.
East and West Poems. 1871.
Poetical Works. 1872; revised edition, 1896, 1902.
Echoes of the Foot-Hills. 1874.
Some Later Verses. 1898.
Unpublished Limericks and Cartoons. 1933.

Other

Complete Works. 1872.
Prose and Poetry. 2 vols., 1872.
Lectures, edited by Charles Meeker Kozlay. 1909.
Stories and Poems and Other Uncollected Writings, edited by Charles Meeker Kozlay. 1914.
Sketches of the Sixties by Harte and Mark Twain from The Californian 1864–67. 1926; revised edition, 1927.
San Francisco in 1866, Being Letters to the Springfield Republican, edited by George R. Stewart and Edwin S. Fussell. 1951.

Editor, *Outcroppings, Being Selections of California Verse*. 1865.
Editor, *Poems*, by Charles Warren Stoddard. 1867.

*

Bibliography: in *Bibliography of American Literature* by Jacob Blanck, 1959; *Harte: A Reference Guide* by Linda D. Barnett, 1980.

Critical Studies: *Harte, Argonaut and Exile* by George R. Stewart, 1931; *Mark Twain and Harte* by Margaret Duckett,

1964; *Harte: A Biography* by Richard O'Connor, 1966; *Harte*, 1972, and *Harte, Literary Critic*, 1979, both by Patrick Morrow.

* * *

Because of the nature of his fiction and the timing of his publication of "The Luck of Roaring Camp" (1868), Bret Harte is often remembered as the earliest of American local colorists. Insofar as his craftsmanship is concerned, however, Harte may be considered the logical extension of earlier southern humorists like Augustus Baldwin Longstreet, William Tappan Thompson, Johnson Jones Hooper, and Joseph Glover Baldwin, all of whom were realists writing with broad humor of the more primitive moments of southern frontier life.

Critics have consistently pointed out the influence of Dickens on Harte's work. Joseph B. Harrison in his introduction to *Bret Harte: Representative Selections*, has pinpointed several Dickens influences, e.g., the mixture of humor and sentiment, the exploitation of unique characters in unique situations and environment, the simplification of character to the point of caricature, extravagant dialect and names (Hash, Starbottle, Rats), the love of stupid but good people, opposition to the hypocritical, and satire on injustice.

Harte's literary career lends itself to easy if not simplistic geographic division, i.e., stories composed while the author was living in California, in New York, and in Europe. Scholars consistently point out the gradual deterioration of the artist as he moved further and further from California. In any event, the scholarly consensus is that Harte's literary reputation rests largely on his work completed before the end of 1871, when he returned to the East to write for magazines. Work completed after 1878, when Harte sailed to Europe to be a consul in Prussia, is generally considered hack work and is all but ignored today.

The use of contrast is perhaps the most genuine hallmark of Harte's fiction. Arthur Hobson Quinn, for example, noted Harte's use of "moral contrast," and John Erskine attributed Harte's successful humor to his perception of contrast in American life itself. "The Outcasts of Poker Flat," which vies with "The Luck of Roaring Camp" for the honor of Harte's best work, centers on use of contrasts: four degenerates are juxtaposed with two innocents, a harlot starves herself to death in order to save a virgin, the gambler Oakhurst gives up his chance for safety to the Innocent and then commits suicide. Erskine notes that Harte perceives the good qualities in the life of the lowly as in "Tennessee's Partner" and that his use of parody in *Condensed Novels*, which satirizes popular sentimental and idealistic novels, is comparable to that of Swinburne.

Local color stories, because of their nature, depend to a large extent upon their fidelity to detail. Harte's stories like "The Outcasts of Poker Flat" or "Miggles," are, therefore, frequently praised for their meaningful use of detail. Some of the best short stories Harte ever wrote were written for the *Overland:* "The Outcasts of Poker Flat," "Miggles," "Tennessee's Partner," "The Idyl of Red Gulch," and "Brown of Calaveras." Scholars generally agree that Harte never again equalled their freshness, spontaneity, compression, and unity.

"Tennessee's Partner" is the third most frequently anthologized Harte story. Here, Harte makes chance, fate, and accident the normal, the customary. The sentimentality in the story satisfied the taste of the reading audience of the late 19th century.

Of the more than 200 poems in the standard edition of Harte, more than one half are narrative, one third humorous or satirical, and one third entirely or partially dialect. Although the great strength of Harte's poetry is brevity, he fails to unite this brevity with symbolism and emotional implication, a unity necessary to successful poetry. Harte's best poetry is always his satirical and humorous verse; the two best—and most frequently reprinted—poems are "Plain Language from Truthful James" and "The Society upon the Stanislaus." As a novelist, Harte has generally been judged superficial, for his characters, like many of Dickens's poorer characters, are wooden and puppet-like. The characters, for example, in *Gabriel Conroy, A Waif of the Plains*, and *In the Carquinez Woods* have neither ideas nor passions to be sustained or complicated.

Harte's real achievement, then, is to be found in his local color stories written, for the most part, before 1871, stories which bear his hallmarks of brevity, dramatic action reporting, the new morality of the far west, humor, contrast, and uncluttered style. G.K. Chesterton observed that Harte's fiction serves, realistically, to remind us that "while it is very rare indeed in the world to find a thoroughly good man, it is rarer still, rare to the point of monstrosity, to find a man who does not either desire to be one or imagine that he is one already."

—George C. Longest

See the essay on "The Luck of Roaring Camp."

HAWKES, John (Clendennin Burne, Jr.). Born in Stamford, Connecticut, 17 August 1925. Educated at Trinity School, 1940–41; Pawling High School, 1941–43; Harvard University, Cambridge, Massachusetts, 1943–49, A.B. 1949. Served as an ambulance driver in the American Field Service in Italy and Germany, 1944–45. Married Sophie Goode Tazewell in 1947; three sons and one daughter. Assistant to the production manager, Harvard University Press, 1949–55; Visiting Lecturer, 1955–56, and Instructor in English, 1956–58, Harvard University; Assistant Professor, 1958–62, Associate Professor, 1962–67, Professor of English, 1967–73, and since 1973 T.B. Stowell University Professor, Brown University, Providence, Rhode Island. Visiting Assistant Professor, Massachusetts Institute of Technology, 1959; special guest, Aspen Institute for Humanistic Studies, Colorado, 1962; staff member, Utah Writers Conference, summer 1962, and Bread Loaf Writers Conference, Middlebury College, Vermont, summer 1963; Visiting Professor of Creative Writing, Stanford University, California, 1966–67; Visiting Distinguished Professor of Creative Writing, City College, New York, 1971–72. Member, Panel on Educational Innovation, Washington, D.C., 1966–67. Recipient: American Academy grant, 1962; Guggenheim fellowship, 1962; Ford fellowship, 1964; Rockefeller fellowship, 1968; Foreign Book Prize (France), 1974. Member, American Academy of Arts and Sciences, 1973, and American Academy, 1980. A.M.: Brown University, 1962. Lives in Providence, Rhode Island.

PUBLICATIONS

Fiction

The Cannibal. 1949.
The Beetle Leg. 1951.

The Goose on the Grave, and The Owl: Two Short Novels. 1954; *The Owl* published separately, 1977.
The Lime Twig. 1961.
Second Skin. 1964.
Lunar Landscapes: Stories and Short Novels 1949–1963. 1969.
The Blood Oranges. 1971.
Death, Sleep, and the Traveler. 1974.
Travesty. 1976.
The Universal Fears (story). 1978.
The Passion Artist. 1979.
Virginie: Her Two Lives. 1982.
Innocence in Extremis (story). 1985.
Adventures in the Alaskan Skin Trade. 1985.

Plays

The Wax Museum (produced 1966). In *The Innocent Party*, 1966.
The Questions (produced 1966). In *The Innocent Party*, 1966.
The Innocent Party: Four Short Plays. 1966.
The Undertaker (produced 1967). In *The Innocent Party*, 1966.
The Innocent Party (produced 1968). In *The Innocent Party*, 1966.

Verse

Fiasco Hall. 1943.

Other

Humors of Blood and Skin: A Hawkes Reader. 1984.

Editor, with others, *The Personal Voice: A Contemporary Prose Reader.* 1964.
Editor, with others, *The American Literary Anthology 1: The 1st Annual Collection of the Best from the Literary Magazines.* 1968.

*

Bibliography: *Three Contemporary Novelists: An Annotated Bibliography* by Robert M. Scotto, 1977; *Hawkes: An Annotated Bibliography* by Carol A. Hryciw, 1977, revised edition, as *Hawkes: A Research Guide*, 1986.

Critical Studies: *Hawkes: A Guide to His Fictions* by Frederick Busch, 1973; *Comic Terror: The Novels of Hawkes*, 1973, revised edition, 1978, and *Understanding Hawkes*, 1985, both by Donald J. Greiner; *Hawkes and the Craft of Conflict* by John Kuehl, 1975; *A Hawkes Symposium* edited by Anthony C. Santore and Michael N. Pocalyko, 1977; *A Poetry of Force and Darkness: The Fiction of Hawkes* by Eliot Berry, 1979; *John Fowles, Hawkes, Claude Simon: Problems of Self and Form in the Post-Modernist Novel* by Robert Burden, 1980; *Hawkes* by Patrick O'Donnell, 1982; "Hawkes Issue" of *Review of Contemporary Fiction*, vol. 3, no. 3, 1983.

* * *

American letters has not, on the whole, been particularly receptive to the cultivation of truly esoteric talents, probably because some appeal to a general audience is almost morally as well as commercially compulsory in American culture. John Hawkes, however, comes close to being a writer whose intransigent dedication to a special conception of art provides the exception to this rule. But if he has colonized for himself a separate place in contemporary fiction, he has done so not through the promulgation of an exotic or cultist philosophy, nor through the projection of a public personality that cuts against the grain of conventional mores, but pre-eminently as a prose stylist. In his first novel, *The Cannibal*, he staked out the literary area which he would make uniquely his own: the creation of an uncompromising verbal artifice that aims at rendering sensuously and in the modern idiom the melodramatic atmosphere of traditional gothic materials in a manner designed to implicate the reader in ambivalent sado-masochistic responses. That is, Hawkes has deliberately conceived of his fiction as a premeditated assault against a victimized reader. The establishment of a powerful tension between the outrageously unacceptable behavior of the plot and characters and the equally undeniable visceral reactions of the individual reader results in that impasse of aesthetic distortion that is usually assumed to be within the provenance of "the grotesque." And in Hawkes's work the largest part of the burden in achieving this goal is entrusted to his style—a lean, elusive, visual-kinetic succession of images that alternately beguiles, frustrates, and shocks the reader's expectations.

Set in a fantastic post-World War II Occupied Germany, *The Cannibal* ignores conventional time-sequences, character development, and cause-effect probabilities to describe the triumphant uprising of the defeated nation in the persons of a crippled handful of mutated life-forms tortuously emerging from the debris of their own corruption. Belying its own stoic bitterness, the novel moves casually back and forth through time, dispassionately issuing a series of vividly etched vignettes of murder, betrayal, cannibalism, and destructive perversions of love. And although the work occasionally suggests the experimentalism of Dada and Surrealism, its rigorous stylistic attachment to the matter-of-fact conventions of realism forces it on the reader with the imperative of a personal nightmare.

After *The Cannibal*, Hawkes experimented with a bleak parody of the Western (*The Beetle Leg*) and a grim excursion in archaism (*The Goose on the Grave*) before producing the masterful *The Lime Twig*. Partly indebted to *Brighton Rock* and the post-war British movies, and partly a sardonic parody of the detective novel, *The Lime Twig* depicts brilliantly the ironic confluence of banal bourgeois fantasies (Hencher, Margaret and Michael Banks) and a ruthless underworld gang that brings those fantasies to terrible realization as it endeavors to make a fortune on a horse-race. Hawkes's uncanny evocation of the seedy atmosphere of the British demi-monde and his persuasive characterization of the twisted loneliness of Hencher and the semi-voluntary brutalization of the Bankses give this novel a quality of sadistic and yet poetic grotesquerie remarkable in its integrity to its own cruel aesthetic purposes.

With *Second Skin* Hawkes inaugurates a new direction in narrative focus, restricting himself to the consciousness of the first-person point of view (the Skipper's), throwing some doubt on the reliability of that point of view, and adding an element of playfulness to the chronicle of the horrible events (rape, sodomy, suicide) that mark the Skipper's journey toward ambiguous self-understanding. And in the trilogy of novels that followed (*The Blood Oranges, Death, Sleep, and the Traveler*, and *Travesty*), this use of an increasingly unreliable narrator and a playfulness that sometimes borders on the frivolous have become even more marked. But if these novels show a falling off from the concentrated purity of Hawkes's earlier excursions in seductive horror, his prose style has remained as sensuous, supple, and shocking as it was in the beginning.

His most recent books show Hawkes continuing to refine and extend his range. *The Passion Artist* returns to the bleak fictional world of *The Cannibal. Virginie* is a Nabokovian tour de force that started as a novel based on the life of the Marquis de Sade, but the erotic bliss it presents exists in the realm of poetic artifice. *Adventures in the Alaskan Skin Trade* is the longest of Hawkes's fictions, and the most realistic in method; it employs such surprising (for Hawkes) material as the tall tale.

Hawkes remains well outside the mainstream of contemporary fiction, but he has settled a small but solid island of stylistic rigor which stands as a kind of navigational guide for his contemporaries and those who are voyaging after him.

—Earl Rovit

HAWTHORNE, Nathaniel. Born Nathaniel Hathorne in Salem, Massachusetts, 4 July 1804. Educated at Samuel Archer's School, Salem, 1819; Bowdoin College, Brunswick, Maine, 1821–25. Married Sophia Peabody in 1842; two daughters and one son. Lived with his mother in Salem, writing and contributing to periodicals, 1825–36; editor, *American Magazine of Useful and Entertaining Knowledge*, Boston, 1836; weigher and gager, Boston Customs House, 1839–41; invested in the Brook Farm Commune, West Roxbury, Massachusetts, and lived there, 1841–42; lived in Concord, Massachusetts, 1842–45, 1852, and 1860–64; surveyor, Salem Customs House, 1846–49; lived in Lenox, 1850–51, and West Newton, 1851, both Massachusetts; U.S. Consul, Liverpool, England, 1853–57; lived in Italy, 1858–59, and London, 1859–60. *Died 19 May 1864.*

PUBLICATIONS

Collections

Complete Writings. 22 vols., 1900.
Complete Novels and Selected Tales, edited by Norman Holmes Pearson. 1937.
The Portable Hawthorne, edited by Malcolm Cowley. 1948; revised edition, 1969; as *Hawthorne: Selected Works*, 1971.
Works (Centenary Edition), edited by William Charvat and others. 1963—
Poems, edited by Richard E. Peck. 1967.
Tales and Sketches (Library of America), edited by Roy Harvey Pearce. 1982.
Novels (Library of America), edited by Millicent Bell. 1983.

Fiction

Fanshawe: A Tale. 1828.
Twice-Told Tales. 1837; revised edition, 1842.
The Celestial Rail-Road. 1843.
Mosses from an Old Manse. 1846.
The Scarlet Letter: A Romance. 1850.
The House of the Seven Gables: A Romance. 1851.
The Snow-Image and Other Twice-Told Tales. 1851.
The Blithedale Romance. 1852.
Transformation; or, The Romance of Monte Beni. 1860; as *The Marble Faun*, 1860.
Pansie: A Fragment. 1864.
Septimius: A Romance, edited by Una Hawthorne and Robert Browning. 1872; as *Septimius Felton; or, The Elixir of Life*, 1872.
The Dolliver Romance and Other Pieces, edited by Sophia Hawthorne. 1876.
Fanshawe and Other Pieces. 1876.
Dr. Grimshaw's Secret: A Romance, edited by Julian Hawthorne. 1883; edited by Edward H. Davidson, 1954.
The Ghost of Dr. Harris. 1900.

Other

Grandfather's Chair: A History for Youth. 1841; *Famous Old People, Being the Second Epoch of Grandfather's Chair*, 1841; *Liberty Tree, with the Last Words of Grandfather's Chair*, 1841, revised edition, 1842.
Biographical Stories for Children. 1842.
True Stories from History and Biography. 1851.
A Wonder-Book for Girls and Boys. 1851.
Life of Franklin Pierce (campaign biography). 1852.
Tanglewood Tales for Girls and Boys, Being a Second Wonder-Book. 1853.
Our Old Home: A Series of English Sketches. 1863; in *Works*, 1970.
Passages from the American Note-Books, edited by Sophia Hawthorne. 2 vols., 1868.
Passages from the English Note-Books, edited by Sophia Hawthorne. 2 vols., 1870.
Passages from the French and Italian Note-Books, edited by Una Hawthorne. 2 vols., 1871.
Twenty Days with Julian and Little Bunny: A Diary. 1904.
Love Letters. 2 vols., 1907.
Letters to William D. Ticknor. 2 vols., 1910.
The Heart of Hawthorne's Journal, edited by Newton Arvin. 1929.
The American Notebooks, edited by Randall Stewart. 1932; in *Works*, 1972.
The English Notebooks, edited by Randall Stewart. 1941.
Hawthorne as Editor: Selections from His Writings in the American Magazine of Useful and Entertaining Knowledge, edited by Arlin Turner. 1941.
Hawthorne's Lost Notebook 1835–1841, edited by Barbara S. Mouffe. 1978.

Editor, with Elizabeth Hawthorne, *Peter Parley's Universal History*. 2 vols., 1837; as *Peter Parley's Common School History*, 1838.
Editor, *Journal of an African Cruiser*, by Horatio Bridge. 1845.
Editor, *The Yarn of a Yankee Privateer*, by Benjamin Frederick Browne(?). 1926.

*

Bibliography: *Hawthorne: A Descriptive Bibliography* by C.E. Frazer Clark, Jr., 1978; *Hawthorne and the Critics: A Checklist of Criticism 1900–1978* by Jeanetta Boswell, 1982.

Critical Studies: *Hawthorne* by Henry James, 1879; *Hawthorne: A Biography* by Randall Stewart, 1948; *Hawthorne* by Mark Van Doren, 1949; *Hawthorne's Fiction: The Light and the Dark*, 1952, revised edition, 1964, and *Hawthorne's Imagery*, 1969, both by Richard Harter Fogle; *Hawthorne: A Critical Study*, 1955, revised edition, 1963, and *The Presence of Hawthorne*, 1979, both by Hyatt H. Waggoner; *Hawthorne's Tragic Vision* by Roy R. Male, 1957; *Hawthorne, Man and Writer* by Edward Wagenknecht, 1961; *Hawthorne: An Introduction and Interpretation*, 1961, and *Hawthorne: A Biography*, 1980, both by Arlin Turner; *Hawthorne Centenary Essays* edited by Roy Harvey Pearce, 1964; *Hawthorne* by Terence Martin, 1965, revised edition, 1983; *The Sins of the Fathers: Hawthorne's Psychological Themes* by Frederick Crews, 1966; *Hawthorne: A Collection of Critical Essays* edited by A.N. Kaul, 1966; *Twentieth-Century Interpretations of The Scarlet Letter* edited by John C. Gerber, 1968; *Plots and Characters in the Fiction and Sketches of Hawthorne* by Robert L. Gale, 1968; *Hawthorne, Transcendental Symbolist* by Marjorie Elder, 1969; *The Recognition of Hawthorne: Selected Criticism since 1828* edited by B. Bernard Cohen, 1969; *Hawthorne as Myth-Maker: A Study in Imagination* by Hugo McPherson, 1969; *Hawthorne: The Critical Heritage*, 1970, and *Hawthorne: A Collection of Criticism*, 1975, both edited by J. Donald Crowley; *The Pursuit of Form: A Study of Hawthorne and the Romance* by John Caldwell Stubbs, 1970; *Hawthorne's Early Tales: A Critical Study* by Neal F. Doubleday, 1972; *Hawthorne's Career* by Nina Baym, 1976; *Hawthorne: The Poetics of Enchantment* by Edgar A. Dryden, 1977; *Rediscovering Hawthorne* by Kenneth Dauber, 1977; *Hawthorne and the Truth of Dreams* by Rita K. Gollin, 1979; *A Reader's Guide to the Short Stories of Hawthorne* by Lea B.V. Newman, 1979; *Hawthorne: The English Experience 1853–1864* by Raymona E. Hull, 1980; *Hawthorne in His Times* by James R. Mellow, 1980; *The Productive Tension of Hawthorne's Art* by Claudia D. Johnson, 1981; *Hawthorne: New Critical Essays* edited by A. Robert Lee, 1982; *Family Themes in Hawthorne's Fiction* by Gloria C. Erlich, 1984; *The Province of Piety: Moral History in Hawthorne's Early Tales* by Michael J. Colacurcio, 1984, and *New Essays on The Scarlet Letter* edited by Colacurcio, 1985; *Hawthorne's Secret: An Un-told Tale* by Philip Young, 1984.

* * *

Nathaniel Hawthorne's fiction is unique in two important respects. He was the first major novelist in English to combine high moral seriousness with transcendent dedication to art. He was also the first major novelist in English to insist upon the basic unreality of his works. An imaginative genius gifted with considerable linguistic skill, he opened a path in literature that few have followed with comparable success. Like all great writers he was original in that fundamental sense in which the work resists duplication because it remains identified with the creative individuality of the author. George Eliot followed Hawthorne in the attempt to wed morality to art, but she attempted the fusion within a framework of realistic verisimilitude. Most writers since Hawthorne who have worked outside of the framework of realism have been less concerned than he with the moral seriousness of their works.

Isolation stands at the heart of his development as an artist. For twelve years after his graduation from Bowdoin College he lived in his mother's house in Salem, publishing *Fanshawe* at his own expense and numerous tales and sketches in magazines and gift annuals at rates so low that the income from the 27 tales he published in the *Token* amounted to less than $350. Since all of this early material was published either anonymously or under pseudonyms, he achieved no reputation and acquired no literary friends. In terms of financial success, indeed, it probably would not have mattered much if he had acquired friends and a reputation early. Like other American writers of his time he suffered even during the years of his greatest popularity from the lack of an international copyright law; he could neither compete at home with cheap editions of famous English authors nor reap much income from his sales in England. Although *The Scarlet Letter* made him a name, it earned him a pitifully small income (probably not more than $1,500 from the American sales during his lifetime). Under the circumstances, it is not surprising that he developed a literary aesthetic in which mass appeal had no place. He wrote to please himself and also that occasional isolated reader who would share with him his aesthetic and moral sensibilities.

He early formed the habit of working from the inside outward. Unlike his friend Melville he possessed no well of exotic experience from which to draw his subject matter. His material came from his thoughts, his reading, his brooding upon New England and its history. Coming to believe that all the truth that matters is inner ("the truth," as he expressed it, "of the human heart"), he considered externalities to be inherently deceptive. Consequently he considered verisimilitude, in the sense of faithfulness to the world of actuality, to be a highly questionable merit in fiction. Much more important to him was the construction of a fictive world that remained faithful to the artist's inmost vision. Hence his insistence that his works were to be judged as romances rather than novels. Hence, too, the considerable drive toward symbol and allegory.

He is a romantic writer, but not because his material is distant in time and place. Among his longer fictions, *The House of the Seven Gables*, *The Blithedale Romance*, and *The Marble Faun* are contemporary with his own time. *The Scarlet Letter* and many of the tales are set in that Puritan New England that he knew so intimately. He is romantic in the more important sense of considering verifiable fact to be a less important commodity in the world than the unverifiable discoveries of imagination and intuition. He is also romantic in the particularly American sense of possessing a visionary idea of a society in which perfect freedom, equality, and justice might one day prevail, though no such society has yet appeared on earth. It is against such a vision that *The Scarlet Letter* especially must be read; it is the vision that places Hawthorne, for all his idiosyncrasy, in the direct line of American novelists from Cooper through Melville, Twain, and James.

His most frequent themes revolve around the sanctity of the individual, the necessity for warm human relationships, the nature of sin, a distrust of science and the intellect, and a belief in the fundamental ambiguity of earthly phenomena. All are closely related in his work, with an exploration of the nature of sin the tie that binds the others together. Thus the characters of Rappaccini ("Rappaccini's Daughter"), Ethan Brand ("Ethan Brand"), and Roger Chillingworth (*The Scarlet Letter*) mix their sin from the same ingredients: all are coldly intellectual, scientifically detached individuals who possess no effectively warm human relationships, are willing and even eager to intrude upon the privacy of others, and are convinced of the possibility of ultimate triumph over the mysteries of the phenomenal world. The sin of adultery that Hester Prynne of *The Scarlet Letter* has committed is much less sweeping than this. The result of a natural need for human warmth, it is clothed in ambiguity. There are sins and sins. In a more perfect society Hester's act would be no sin. If there exists, however, the unpardonable sin that Ethan Brand seeks it is very close to that attributed to Roger Chillingworth by Arthur Dimmesdale in *The Scarlet Letter*: "He has violated, in cold blood, the sanctity of a human heart."

The terrific "power of blackness" that Melville saw in Hawthorne begins in the isolation of the artist and ends in the ambiguity of his work. As artist he must break through the isolation or remain self-incased and unread. His artistry drives him inward, away from the human contact that is necessary for survival both as a writer and as a man. In his works he must remain true to his deepest vision, including for Hawthorne an abiding sense of the world's unshakeable ambiguities, but he must also make this vision accessible to others. In "The Minister's Black Veil" and "Young Goodman Brown" the touchstones of isolation and ambiguity are given splendid emphasis, but they remain important to the effect of large numbers of other works as well, from deceptively simple sketches such as "Wakefield" or "The Ambitious Guest" through the relative lightness of *The House of the Seven Gables* to the dark complexities of *The Marble Faun*.

In the end, the peculiar conditions of his creative life served him well. Steeped in the New England that he depicted so effectively in the majority of his works, he created masterly short fiction because the form came naturally to him. He probed beneath the surfaces of his subjects because he saw so little in the outward appearances that was of lasting interest. Without the financial support of the British three-decker tradition, he wrote much shorter novels than Dickens or Eliot, but his works gain in impact through compression. Few novelists in English have accomplished so much in so few words as is accomplished in *The Scarlet Letter*. Few have displayed better than Hawthorne does in his best works the power of romance, or, by inference, the limitations of superficial realism. Seldom have the modes of symbol and allegory been so effectively rendered in prose.

—George Perkins

See the essays on "Ethan Brand" and *The Scarlet Letter*.

HAY, John (Milton). Born in Salem, Indiana, 8 October 1838. Educated at a private school in Pittsfield, and a college in Springfield, both Illinois; Brown University, Providence, Rhode Island, 1855–58, graduated, 1858; studied law in the office of Milton Hay, Springfield; admitted to Illinois bar, 1861. Served with the Union forces during the Civil War: Colonel. Married Clara Louise Stone in 1874. Secretary to President Abraham Lincoln, Washington, D.C., 1861–64; in the U.S. Diplomatic Service: First Secretary of the Legation in Paris, 1865–67; Chargé d'Affaires, Vienna, 1867–68; First Secretary of the Legation in Madrid, 1868–70; First Assistant Secretary of State, Washington, D.C., 1879–81; Ambassador to Great Britain, 1897–98; Secretary of State, to President McKinley, 1898–1901, and to President Theodore Roosevelt, 1901–05. Worked in business, Cleveland, 1875–79. Staff member, 1870–75, and editor, 1881, New York *Tribune*. LL.D.: Western Reserve University, Cleveland; Princeton University, New Jersey; Dartmouth College, Hanover, New Hampshire; Yale University, New Haven, Connecticut; Harvard University, Cambridge, Massachusetts. Member, American Academy, 1904. *Died 1 July 1905.*

PUBLICATIONS

Collections

Complete Poetical Works, edited by Clarence L. Hay. 1916.
Hay's Pike County, edited by George Monteiro. 1984.

Verse

Jim Bludso of the Prairie Belle, and Little Breeches. 1871.
Pike County Ballads and Other Pieces. 1871; as *Little Breeches and Other Pieces*, 1871.
Poems. 1890.

Fiction

The Bread-Winners: A Social Study. 1884.
The Blood Seedling and Other Tales: The Uncollected Fiction of Hay, edited by George Monteiro. 1972.

Other

Castilian Days. 1871; revised edition, 1890; revised abridgement, 1903.
Abraham Lincoln: A History, with John G. Nicolay. 10 vols., 1890.
Addresses. 1906.
Letters and Extracts from Diary, edited by Henry Adams and Clara Louise Hay. 3 vols., 1908.
A Poet in Exile: Early Letters, edited by Caroline Ticknor. 1910.
A College Friendship: A Series of Letters to Hannah Angell. 1938.
Lincoln and the Civil War in the Diaries and Letters of Hay, edited by Tyler Dennett. 1939.
Henry James and Hay: The Record of a Friendship, edited by George Monteiro. 1965.
The Hay-Howells Letters: The Correspondence of Hay and William Dean Howells 1861–1905, edited by George Monteiro and Brenda Murphy. 1980.

Editor, with John G. Nicolay, *Complete Works*, by Abraham Lincoln. 2 vols., 1894.

*

Bibliography: in *Bibliography of American Literature* by Jacob Blanck, 1963.

Critical Studies: *Life and Letters of Hay* by William Roscoe Thayer, 2 vols., 1915; *Hay: From Poetry to Politics* by Tyler Dennett, 1933; *Hay as a Man of Letters* by Kelly Thurman, 1974; *Hay: The Gentleman as Diplomat* by Kenton J. Clymer, 1975; *Hay: The Union of Poetry* by Howard I. Kushner and Anne Hummel Sherrill, 1977; *Hay* by Robert L. Gale, 1978.

* * *

In 1904 John Hay was numbered among the first seven individuals elected to the American Academy of Arts and Letters.

He was given this honor as the famous author of *Castilian Days*, essays on Spain; *Pike County Ballads and Other Pieces; Poems*, a collected edition; and *Abraham Lincoln: A History*, ten volumes written in collaboration with John G. Nicolay. Forgotten were the essays and stories he had published in the 1860's and 1870's in *Putnam's*, *Harper's*, and the *Atlantic*. It had not yet been established, moreover, that Hay was also the author of *The Bread-Winners*, an anti-labor novel that so closely reflected Hay's alarm over the growing threats to society posed by the violent strikes of 1877 and their aftermath, and one that so obviously drew upon his own sense of himself as a beleaguered member of the establishment, that the prudent author chose to publish his novel anonymously. Its authorship, a closely guarded secret for decades, was acknowledged only after his death. *The Bread-Winners* lives today, less for its reactionary argument, than for its sharp portrait of Maud Matchin, a self-made girl. In this pert and impertinent high-school graduate Hay created a portrait of American girlhood to stand beside those of James's Daisy Miller and Howells's Lydia Blood.

Hay's short fiction antedates *The Bread-Winners*, some of it by more than twenty years. Even though the stories constitute early work, they continue to warrant serious attention, both for their intrinsic merit and for their surprisingly skilful anticipation of many of the major technical and thematic interests of the American realists. The principal concerns of his fiction can be described as the dangers awaiting innocent and not-so-innocent Americans trying to make their way in Paris ("Shelby Cabell" and "Kane and Abel"), the duties of those who would be faithful to the Union ("Red, White and Blue"), the wages of love and miscegenation ("The Foster-Brothers") and the murderous proclivities in the heart of the midwestern farmer ("The Blood Seedling").

The last of these stories presents the Golyers, a family that figures as well in the Pike County ballads, the first three of which, "Banty Tim," "Jim Bludso, of the Prairie Belle," and "Little Breeches," catapulted Hay to immediate fame. Contemporary arguments over whether Hay or his friend Bret Harte had been the first to exploit the dialects of the American West served both to promote their fame and to delay the assessment of Hay's achievement. If there was no doubt that his poems captured the rhythmic speech of the Pike County Man, the notion that such speech did not provide fit substance for poetry would long plague Hay. It was not immediately recognized that the poems were not primarily attacks on common poetic speech, but rather sly barbs aimed at the conventional morality of his day. In Jim Bludso he presents a hard-talking bigamist who is nevertheless capable of Christian self-sacrifice. This rude practitioner of a religion of humanity, according to the poet, could hardly suffer retribution from a true Christian God. If this poetically unconventional statement did not receive unanimous approval, it did tap a vein of largely unexpressed feelings. With tears in her eyes, George Eliot frequently recited by heart "Jim Bludso," and in *Ulysses* Joyce has Leopold Bloom, on his way to the brothel, ruminate: "I did alla white man could . . . Jim Bludso. Hold her nozzle again the bank."

At other times Hay wrote more conventional poems that continue to appeal, among them the political "A Triumph of Order," the skilfully devised "Una," and the witty, self-ironic "A Dream of Bric-à-Brac." But when poets are again permitted to tell stories in verse, Hay's spirited ballads will recover something of the favor they enjoyed in 1897 when, on the occasion of Hay's appointment as Ambassador to the Court of St. James's, English publishers, passing up *Castilian Days* and *Abraham Lincoln*, brought out an edition of Hay's poems, ignoring his properly understated title in 1890 for his collected *Poems* in favor of *Pike County Ballads and Other Poems*, one harking back to his first collection.

—George Monteiro

HAYDEN, Robert (Earl). Born in Detroit, Michigan, 4 August 1913. Educated in Detroit public schools; at Detroit City College (now Wayne State University), 1932–36, B.A. 1942; University of Michigan, Ann Arbor (Hopwood award, 1938, 1942) part-time 1938–40, full-time 1941–44, M.A. in English 1944. Married Erma Inez Morris in 1940; one daughter. Writer and researcher, Federal Writers Project (Works Progress Administration), Detroit, 1936–40; Teaching Assistant in English, University of Michigan, 1944–46; Assistant Professor, 1946–53, Associate Professor, 1954–66, and Professor of English, 1967–69, Fisk University, Nashville, Tennessee; Visiting Professor, 1968, and Professor of English, 1969–80, University of Michigan. Poet-in-Residence, Indiana State University, Terre Haute, Summer 1967; Bingham Professor, University of Louisville, Kentucky, Spring 1969; Poet-in-Residence, University of Washington, Seattle, Summer 1969, Denison University, Granville, Ohio, 1971, and Connecticut College, New London, 1974; staff member, Bread Loaf Writers Conference, Middlebury College, Vermont, 1972. Joined Baha'i Faith, 1942: poetry editor of Baha'i magazine *World Order* from 1967. Consultant, Scott Foresman, publishers, Glenview, Illinois, from 1970; Consultant in Poetry, Library of Congress, Washington, D.C., 1976–78. Recipient: Rosenwald fellowship, 1947; Ford Foundation grant, 1954; World Festival of Negro Arts (Dakar, Senegal) poetry prize, 1966; American Academy Loines Award, 1970; Academy of American Poets Fellowship, 1975. D.Litt.: Grand Valley State College, Allendale, Michigan, 1975; D.H.L.: Brown University, Providence, Rhode Island, 1976; Benedict College, Columbia, South Carolina, 1977; Wayne State University, 1977. Member, American Academy, 1979. *Died 25 February 1980.*

PUBLICATIONS

Collections

Collected Prose, edited by Frederick Glaysher. 1984.

Verse

Heart-Shape in the Dust. 1940.
The Lion and the Archer, with Myron O'Higgins. 1948.
Figure of Time. 1955.
A Ballad of Remembrance. 1962.
Selected Poems. 1966.
Words in the Mourning Time. 1970.
The Night-Blooming Cereus. 1972.
Angle of Ascent: New and Selected Poems. 1975.
American Journal. 1978; revised edition, 1982.

Other

How I Write 1, with Judson Philips and Lawson Carter. 1972.

Nine Black American Doctors (for children), with Jacqueline Harris. 1976.

Editor, *Kaleidoscope: Poems by American Negro Poets*. 1967.
Editor, with David J. Burrows and Frederick R. Lapides, *Afro-American Literature: An Introduction*. 1971.
Editor, with James E. Miller, Jr., and Robert O'Neal, *The United States in Literature*. 1973.

*

Critical Study: *From the Auroral Darkness: The Life and Poetry of Hayden* by John Hatcher, 1984.

* * *

Much in the manner of Countée Cullen, the Harlem Renaissance poet, though more comfortable experimenting with free forms of verse, Robert Hayden steadfastly claimed his refusal to write racial poetry but was quite consistently at his poetic best precisely when he used the material of the black American experience. He warned in *Kaleidoscope* against placing the black writer in "a kind of literary ghetto," where he would be "not considered a writer but a species of race-relations man, the leader of a cause, the voice of protest." It must be said that even when Hayden employs racial material and themes, he usually molds them into interesting and often exquisite universal shapes that make him far more than a mere "race-relations man." If there is a criticism to be levelled at him, it would be that he is occasionally too academic (indeed, he has spent much of his life in academe), occasionally lapsing into preciousness (e.g., in "Veracruz": "Thus reality / bedizened in the warring colors / or a dream . . .").

Mostly, however, Hayden composes with notable power and beauty. For example, his evocation, in "The Ballad of Nat Turner," of the 19th-century leader of a slave uprising is perhaps the most succinct and spiritually true in all of imaginative literature. Such poems as "The Diver" capture the essence of the moment or act (in this case the descent of a sea diver "through easeful azure" to the time when "somehow began the measured rise") with the felicitous marriage of sound and sense that is quintessential poetry.

—Alan R. Shucard

HAYNE, Paul Hamilton. Born in Charleston, South Carolina, 1 January 1830. Educated at Cotes's School, Charleston; College of Charleston, graduated 1850; studied law but abandoned practice for a literary career, 1852. Served on Governor Pickens's staff, 1861–62. Married Mary Middleton Michel in 1852; one son. Associate editor, 1852, 1854–55, and editor, 1852–54, *Southern Literary Gazette*, Charleston; founding editor, *Russell's Magazine*, Charleston, 1857–60; made homeless and bankrupt by Civil War: moved to Grovetown, near Augusta, Georgia; news editor, Augusta *Constitutionalist*, 1865; farmer and free-lance writer from 1866. LL.D.: Washington and Lee College, Lexington, Virginia, 1882. *Died 6 July 1886.*

PUBLICATIONS

Collections

The Southern Poets, with Sidney Lanier and Henry Timrod, edited by J.W. Abernethy. 1904.

Verse

Poems. 1854.
Sonnets and Other Poems. 1857.
Avolio: A Legend of the Island of Cos, with Poems Lyrical, Miscellaneous, and Dramatic. 1859.
Legends and Lyrics. 1872.
The Mountain of the Lovers, with Poems of Nature and Tradition. 1875.
Poems, Complete Edition. 1882.
The Broken Battalions. 1885.

Other

Lives of Robert Young Hayne and Hugh Swinton Legaré. 1878.
A Collection of Hayne Letters, edited by Daniel Morley McKeithan. 1944.
The Correspondence of Bayard Taylor and Hayne, edited by Charles Duffy. 1945.
A Man of Letters in the Nineteenth-Century South: Selected Letters of Hayne, edited by Rayburn S. Moore. 1982.

Editor, *The Poems of Henry Timrod*. 1873.

*

Bibliography: in *Bibliography of American Literature* by Jacob Blanck, 1963; by Rayburn S. Moore, in *A Bibliographical Guide to Southern Literature* edited by Louis D. Rubin, Jr., 1969; *Sidney Lanier, Henry Timrod, and Hayne: A Reference Guide* by Jack De Bellis, 1978.

Critical Study: *Hayne* by Rayburn S. Moore, 1972.

* * *

Paul Hamilton Hayne began publishing poems at the age of fifteen, and by 1861 his poetry had appeared in *Graham's Magazine*, the *Atlantic Monthly*, and the *Southern Literary Messenger* and he had collected three volumes of romantic verse based chiefly on the examples of Keats, Hunt, Poe, Tennyson, and Longfellow. His work attracted the critical attention of Lowell and Whipple, but the Civil War temporarily interrupted his development.

After the war Hayne's muse continued to develop in the mainstream of the Anglo-American tradition. He became a versatile versifier and employed a wide range of forms, metrical schemes, and techniques. His short poems—sonnets and nature lyrics in particular—demonstrate his work at its best. In fact, as his career progressed, Hayne became a leading American sonneteer, and such pieces as "Aspects of the Pines," "The Voice in the Pines," "To a Bee," "The First Mocking-Bird in Spring," "Hints of Spring," and "Midsummer (on the Farm)" reflect his achievement as a lyricist on nature.

At the same time Hayne could also write successful long

poems, narratives like "The Wife of Brittany," an interpretation of Chaucer's "Franklin's Tale" and Hayne's most ambitious and fully realized long poem; "Cambyses and the Macrobian Bow," succinct, with a minimum of sentimentality, and, according to Sidney Lanier, a "fearful tale beautifully told" in blank verse; and irregular odes like "Muscadines," a sensuous piece whose verbal melody derives from Keats and the "liquid magic" of the southern grape, and "Unveiled," an ode whose tone and view of nature suggest a philosophical kinship with Wordsworth's "Tintern Abbey." Even late in his career Hayne continued to write long poems, frequently celebrating occasions or commemorating events such as the centennials of the battles of King's Mountain and Yorktown in 1881 or the sesquicentennial of the founding of Georgia in 1883, among others. The ode on Georgia, it should be noted, and the production of his last four years, including three additional long poems, a fine sonnet on Robert E. Lee, and a handful of lyrics that are among the best he ever wrote on his own locale, were never collected.

After Simms's death in 1870, Hayne became the "representative" poet and literary spokesman for the South. Indeed, in the scope, versatility, and bulk of his production, he remains a substantial minor American poet of the period, even though a sizable proportion of his output is ephemeral magazine verse. Admittedly, few of his poems come near the perfection of, say, Poe's "To Helen," for he lacked Poe's sense of art and critical acumen. Moreover, he accepted, without challenge the conventions of the 19th-century Anglo-American poetic tradition, and many of his poems embody certain aspects of its weakest features—ornate and artificial language, empty abstractions, unalloyed bookishness and monotonous metrical regularity. But these standards of time and taste cannot change the fact that Hayne's canon reflects the full scope of a striving for expression in a spectrum of poetic types and structures nor should they in any way detract from the devotion he rendered his muse despite discouraging and distressing conditions of poverty and ill health during the last part of his life. His accomplishment was modest, but his dedication to literature was exemplary.

—Rayburn S. Moore

HEARN, (Patricio) Lafcadio (Tessima Carlos). Born on the island of Santa Maura, Greece, 27 June 1850; brought up in Dublin; became Japanese citizen, 1891. Educated at St. Cuthbert's College, Ushaw, County Durham, England, 1863–66; Petits Précepteurs, Yvetot, near Rouen, France, 1867. Married Setsuko Koizumi in 1891; three sons. Lived in Paris, 1869, and New York, 1869–71; worked at various jobs in Cincinnati, 1872; proofreader, Robert Clarke Company, then staff member, *Trade List* weekly, and reporter, Cincinnati *Enquirer*, 1873–76, and Cincinnati *Commercial*, 1876–77; co-founder, *Ye Giglampz* satirical journal, Cincinnati, 1874; assistant editor, New Orleans *Item*, 1877–81; staff member, New Orleans *Times-Democrat*, 1881–87; lived in Martinique and wrote for *Harper's*, 1887–89; moved to Japan, 1890; teacher, Ordinary Middle School, Matsue, 1890–91, and Government College, Kumamoto, 1891–94; worked for Kobe *Chronicle*, 1894–95; Professor of English Literature, Imperial University, Tokyo, 1896–1903; English teacher, Waseda University, 1904. *Died 26 September 1904.*

PUBLICATIONS

Collections

Writings. 16 vols., 1922.
Selected Writings, edited by Henry Goodman. 1949.
Manuscripts and Letters, edited by Hojin Yano and others. 1974—

Fiction

Chita: A Memory of Last Island. 1889.
Youma: The Story of a West-Indian Slave. 1890.
Barbarous Barbers and Other Stories, edited by Ichiro Nishizaki. 1939.

Other

Stray Leaves from Strange Literature. 1884.
Some Chinese Ghosts. 1887.
Two Years in the French West Indies. 1890.
Glimpses of Unfamiliar Japan. 2 vols., 1894.
Out of the East: Reveries and Studies in New Japan. 1895.
Kokoro: Hints and Echoes of Japanese Inner Life. 1896.
Gleanings in Buddha-Fields: Studies of Hand and Soul in the Far East. 1897.
Exotics and Retrospectives. 1898.
In Ghostly Japan. 1899.
Shadowings. 1900.
A Japanese Miscellany. 1901.
Kotto, Being Japanese Curios, with Sundry Cobwebs. 1902.
Kwaidan: Stories and Studies of Strange Things. 1904.
Japan: An Attempt at Interpretation. 1904.
The Romance of the Milky Way and Other Studies and Stories. 1905.
Letters from the Raven, Being the Correspondence of Hearn with Henry Watkin, edited by Milton Bronner. 1907.
The Japanese Letters, edited by Elizabeth Bisland. 1910.
Leaves from the Diary of an Impressionist: Early Writings, edited by Ferris Greenslet. 1911.
Editorials from the Kobe Chronicle, edited by Merle Johnson. 1913; edited by Makoto Sangu, 1960.
Fantastics and Other Fancies, edited by Charles Woodward Hutson. 1914.
Karma, edited by Albert Mordell. 1918.
Essays in European and Oriental Literature, edited by Albert Mordell. 1923.
Creole Sketches, edited by Charles Woodward Hutson. 1924.
An American Miscellany: Articles and Stories Now First Collected, edited by Albert Mordell. 2 vols., 1924; as *Miscellanies*, 1924.
Occidental Gleanings: Sketches and Essays Now First Collected, edited by Albert Mordell. 2 vols., 1925.
Some New Letters and Writings, edited by Sanki Ichikawa. 1925.
Editorials, edited by Charles Woodward Hutson. 1926.
Facts and Fancies, edited by R. Tanabé. 1929.
Essays on American Literature, edited by Sanki Ichikawa. 1929.
Gibbeted: Execution of a Youthful Murderer, edited by P.D. Perkins. 1933.
Spirit Photography, edited by P.D. Perkins. 1933.
Letters to a Pagan, edited by R.B. Powers. 1933.
Letters from Shimane and Kyushu. 1935.

American Articles, edited by Ichiro Nishizaki. 4 vols., 1939.
Buying Christmas Toys and Other Essays, edited by Ichiro Nishizaki. 1939.
Literary Essays, edited by Ichiro Nishizaki. 1939.
The New Radiance and Other Scientific Sketches, edited by Ichiro Nishizaki. 1939.
Oriental Articles, edited by Ichiro Nishizaki. 1939.
An Orange Christmas. 1941.
Children of the Levee, edited by O.W. Frost. 1957.
Japan's Religions: Shinto and Buddhism, edited by Kazumitsu Kato. 1966.
The Buddhist Writings, edited by Kenneth Rexroth. 1977.
Writings from Japan, edited by Francis King. 1984.

Editor, *La Cuisine Creole: A Collection of Recipes*. 1885.

Translator, *One of Cleopatra's Nights*, by Gautier. 1882.
Translator, *Gombo Zhèbes: Little Dictionary of Creole Proverbs*. 1885.
Translator, *The Crime of Sylvestre Bonnard*, by Anatole France. 1890.
Translator, *Japanese Fairy Tale* series. 5 vols., 1898–1922.
Translator, *The Temptation of St. Anthony*, by Flaubert. 1910.
Translator, *Japanese Lyrics*. 1915.
Translator, *Saint Anthony and Other Stories*, by de Maupassant, edited by Albert Mordell. 1924.
Translator, *The Adventures of Walter Schnaffs and Other Stories*, by de Maupassant, edited by Albert Mordell. 1931.
Translator, *Stories*, by Pierre Loti, edited by Albert Mordell. 1933.
Translator, *Stories*, by Zola, edited by Albert Mordell. 1935.
Translator, *Sketches and Tales from the French*, edited by Albert Mordell. 1935.

Lecture notes of Hearn's Japanese students published: *Interpretations of Literature*, 2 vols., 1915, *Appreciations of Poetry*, 1916, *Life and Literature*, 1917, and *Pre-Raphaelite and Other Poets*, 1922, all edited by John Erskine; *A History of English Literature*, 2 vols., 1927, supplement, 1927, revised edition, 1941, *Complete Lectures on Art, Literature, and Philosophy*, 1932, *On Poetry*, 1934, and *On Poets*, 1934, all edited by R. Tanabé; *Lectures on Shakespeare*, edited by Sanki Ichikawa, 1928; *Lectures on Prosody*, 1929; *Victorian Philosophy*, 1930; *Lectures on Tennyson*, edited by Shigetsugu Kishi, 1941.

*

Bibliography: *Hearn: A Bibliography of His Writings* by F.R. and Ione Perkins, 1934; in *Bibliography of American Literature* by Jacob Blanck, 1963.

Critical Studies: *Life and Letters* by Elizabeth Bisland, 2 vols., 1906; *Hearn* by Marcel Robert, 2 vols., 1950–51; *Young Hearn* by O.W. Frost, 1958; *Hearn* by Elizabeth Stevenson, 1961; *An Ape of Gods: The Art and Thought of Hearn* by Beongcheon Yu, 1964; *Discoveries: Essays on Hearn* by Albert Mordell, 1964; *Hearn* by Arthur E. Kunst, 1969.

* * *

Parental desertion and a rootless, restless childhood left Lafcadio Hearn with a heart "like a bird fluttering impatiently for the migrating season," spurning the "egotistical individualism," "constitutional morality," and scientific positivism of an Anglo-Saxon world from which he "considered (him)self ostracized, tabooed, outlawed." Initially he sought in creole New Orleans ("the paradise of the South") and the tropical Caribbean that "sensuous life . . ., the life desire" which would favour "the development of a morbid nervous sensibility to material impressions, . . . absolute loss of thinking, . . . numbing and clouding of memory." But it was the less languid, more ascetic culture of the Orient which finally offered him the refuge of "feelings, so strangely far away from all the nineteenth century part of me, that the faint blind stirrings of them make one afraid—deliciously afraid."

At his best, Hearn evokes both in form and content an ethos "as gentle as the light of dreams," "the all-temperate world," "soft serenity" and "passionless tenderness" and "the vague but immeasurable emotion of Shinto" of his adoptive homeland. "Depth does not exist in the Japanese soulstream," he observed, and the evocative, picturesque surfaces of his essays seem to gain from his own ocular deficiency: "a landscape necessarily suggests less to the keen-sighted man than to the myope. The keener the view the less depth in the impression produced." His penchant, derived from a journalistic training, was for the quick sketch and fleeting *aperçu; Two Years in the French West Indies* he described as "simple note-making," "impressions of the moment," a method disclosed by the very titles of his later work: *Glimpses of Unfamiliar Japan, Gleanings in Buddha-Fields, Stray Leaves from Strange Literature*, the latter being "reconstructions of what impressed me as most fantastically beautiful in the most exotic literature." *Some Chinese Ghosts, Shadowings, In Ghostly Japan* likewise retell a society through its most impalpable manifestations. Herbert Spencer's evolutionary vitalism taught him "a new reverence for all kinds of faith" which Hearn transferred to the cult of ancestor-worship. Seeking to reconcile his western sense of fragmentary but unique identity with oriental quietism and self-abnegation, he came to believe that "We are, each and all, infinite compounds of anterior lives" (*Gleanings*), and that "the thoughts and acts of each being, projected beyond the individual existence, shape other lives unborn" (*Out of the East*). He saw the past as subliminal echoes investing the present, and in the Japanese Festival of the Dead found a ceremonious symbolism of the human condition: "Are we not ourselves as lanterns launched upon a deeper and a dimmer sea, and ever separating further and further one from another as we drift to the inevitable dissolution?" (*In Ghostly Japan*).

Hearn's style, like that he admired in Poe and Gautier, is an "engraved gem-work of words," rich with "voluptuous delicacy"—exquisite, precious, given to elaborate catalogues of isolated details and a self-conscious, sesquipedalian cadence which can overwhelm the sense ("mesmeric lentor," "the stridulous telegraphy of crickets," "a limpid magnificence of light indescribable"). In his sympathy for the intangible and evanescent he can also rise to poignancy and at times a sharp, racy vigour.

—Stan Smith

HECHT, Ben. Born in New York City, 28 February 1894; moved with his family to Chicago, then to Racine, Wisconsin. Educated at Racine High School, graduated 1910. Married

1) Marie Armstrong in 1915 (divorced, 1925), one daughter; 2) Rose Caylor in 1925, one daughter. Reporter, Chicago *Journal*, 1910–14; reporter, 1914–18, correspondent in Berlin, 1918–19, and columnist, 1919–23, Chicago *News*; founding editor and publisher, Chicago *Literary Times*, 1923–24; thereafter a full-time writer for the stage, and for films from 1933; formed a production company with Charles MacArthur, 1934–36; columnist ("1001 Afternoons in Manhattan") *PM* newspaper, Long Island, New York, 1940–41. Active Zionist from 1946: Co-Chairman, American League for a Free Palestine. Recipient: Oscar, 1928, 1936. *Died 18 April 1964.*

PUBLICATIONS

Plays

The Wonder Hat: A Harlequinade, with Kenneth Sawyer Goodman (produced 1916). 1920.
The Hero of Santa Maria, with Kenneth Sawyer Goodman (produced 1917). 1920.
The Master Poisoner, with Maxwell Bodenheim, in *Minna and Myself*, by Bodenheim. 1918.
The Hand of Siva, with Kenneth Sawyer Goodman. 1920.
The Egoist (produced 1922).
The Wonder Hat and Other One-Act Plays (includes *The Two Lamps, An Idyll of the Shops, The Hand of Siva, The Hero of Santa Maria*), with Kenneth Sawyer Goodman. 1925.
The Stork, from a play by Laszlo Fodor (produced 1925).
Man Eating Tiger (produced 1927).
Christmas Eve: A Morality Play (produced 1939). 1928.
The Front Page, with Charles MacArthur (produced 1928). 1928.
Twentieth Century, with Charles MacArthur (produced 1932). 1932.
The Great Magoo, with Gene Fowler (produced 1932). 1933.
Jumbo, with Charles MacArthur, music by Richard Rodgers, lyrics by Lorenz Hart (produced 1935). 1935.
To Quito and Back (produced 1937). 1937.
Ladies and Gentlemen, with Charles MacArthur, from a play by Ladislas Bus-Fekete (produced 1939). 1941.
Fun to Be Free: Patriotic Pageant, with Charles MacArthur (produced 1941). 1941.
Lily of the Valley (produced 1942).
We Will Never Die (produced 1943). 1943.
Wuthering Heights (screenplay), with Charles MacArthur, in *Twenty Best Film Plays*, edited by John Gassner and Dudley Nichols. 1943.
A Tribute to Gallantry, in *The Best One-Act Plays of 1943*, edited by Margaret Mayorga. 1943.
Miracle on the Pullman (broadcast 1944). In *The Best One-Act Plays of 1944*, edited by Margaret Mayorga, 1945.
The Common Man (produced 1944).
Swan Song, with Charles MacArthur, from a story by Ramon Romero and Harriett Hinsdale (produced 1946). In *Stage Works of MacArthur*, 1974.
A Flag Is Born, music by Kurt Weill (produced 1946). 1946.
Spellbound (screenplay), with Angus MacPhail, in *Best Film Plays 1945*, edited by John Gassner and Dudley Nichols. 1946.
Hazel Flagg, music by Jule Styne, lyrics by Bob Hilliard, from a story by James Street and the screenplay *Nothing Sacred* (produced 1953). 1953.
Winkelberg (produced 1958). 1958.
Simon, from play by Bertolt Brecht and Lion Feuchtwanger (produced 1962).

Screenplays: *Underworld* (*Paying the Penalty*), with others, 1927; *The Big Noise*, with George Marion, Jr., and Tom Geraghty, 1928; *The Unholy Night*, with others, 1929 (also French version, *Le Spectre vert*, 1930); *The Great Gabbo*, with Hugh Herbert, 1929; *Roadhouse Nights* (*The River Inn*), with Garrett Fort, 1930; *The Unholy Garden*, with Charles MacArthur, 1931; *Scarface, The Shame of the Nation*, with others, 1932; *Turn Back the Clock*, with Edgar Selwyn, 1933; *Design for Living*, 1933; *Hallelujah, I'm a Bum* (*Hallelujah, I'm a Tramp, Lazy Bones*), with S.N. Behrman, 1933; *Viva Villa!*, with Howard Hawks, 1934; *Twentieth Century*, with Charles MacArthur, 1934; *Crime Without Passion*, with Charles MacArthur, 1934; *Upperworld*, with others, 1934; *The Scoundrel*, with Charles MacArthur, 1935; *Barbary Coast*, with Charles MacArthur, 1935; *Once in a Blue Moon*, with Charles MacArthur, 1935; *Soak the Rich*, with Charles MacArthur, 1936; *Nothing Sacred*, 1937; *The Goldwyn Follies*, with others, 1938; *Gunga Din*, with others, 1939; *Lady of the Tropics*, 1939; *Wuthering Heights*, with Charles MacArthur, 1939; *It's a Wonderful World*, with Herman J. Mankiewicz, 1939; *Let Freedom Ring* (*Song of the West*), 1939; *Angels over Broadway*, 1940; *Comrade X*, with Charles Lederer and Walter Reisch, 1940; *Lydia*, with others, 1941; *Tales of Manhattan*, with others, 1942; *The Black Swan*, with Seton I. Miller, 1942; *China Girl*, with Melville Crossman, 1942; *Spellbound*, with Angus MacPhail, 1945; *Watchtower over Tomorrow* (short), 1945; *Specter of the Rose*, 1946; *Notorious*, 1946; *Her Husband's Affairs*, with Charles Lederer, 1947; *Kiss of Death*, with Charles Lederer and Eleazar Lipsky, 1947; *Ride the Pink Horse*, with Charles Lederer, 1947; *The Miracle of the Bells*, with Quentin Reynolds, 1948; *Whirlpool*, with Andrew Solt, 1950; *Where the Sidewalk Ends*, with others, 1950; *Actors and Sin*, 1951; *Monkey Business*, with Charles Lederer and I.A.L. Diamond, 1952; *The Indian Fighter*, with Frank Davis and Ben Kadish, 1955; *Ulisse* (*Ulysses*), with others, 1955; *Miracle in the Rain*, 1956; *The Iron Petticoat*, 1956; *Legend of the Lost*, with Robert Presnell, Jr., 1957; *A Farewell to Arms*, 1957; *Queen of Outer Space*, with Charles Beaumont, 1958; *Circus World* (*The Magnificent Showman*), 1964; uncredited collaborations (selection)—*The Front Page*, 1931; *Back Street*, 1932; *Topaze*, 1933; *The President Vanishes* (*The Strange Conspiracy*), 1934; *The Hurricane*, 1937; *His Girl Friday*, 1939; *The Shop Around the Corner*, 1940; *Roxie Hart*, 1942; *Gilda*, 1946; *Dishonored Lady*, 1947; *Rope*, 1948; *Love Happy*, 1949; *The Thing* (*The Thing from Another World*), 1951; *The Secret of Convict Lake*, 1951; *Roman Holiday*, 1953; *John Paul Jones*, 1959; *Mutiny on the Bounty*, 1962; *Casino Royale*, 1967.

Radio Plays: *Miracle on the Pullman*, 1944; *Miracle of a Bum*, 1945.

Television Plays: *Light's Diamond Jubilee*, 1954; *Hello Charlie*, from his book *Charlie*, 1959; *The Third Commandment*, 1959.

Fiction

Erik Dorn. 1921.
Fantazius Mallare: A Mysterious Oath. 1922.
A Thousand and One Afternoons in Chicago (stories). 1922.

Gargoyles. 1922.
The Florentine Dagger. 1923.
Humpty Dumpty. 1924.
The Kingdom of Evil: A Continuation of the Journal of Fantazius Mallare. 1924.
Cutie, A Warm Mamma, with Maxwell Bodenheim. 1924.
Broken Necks and Other Stories. 1924.
Tales of Chicago Streets. 1924.
Broken Necks, Containing More 1001 Afternoons (stories). 1926.
Count Bruga. 1926.
Infatuation and Other Stories of Love's Misfits. 1927.
Jazz and and Other Stories of Young Love. 1927.
The Unlovely Sin and Other Stories of Desire's Pawns. 1927.
The Policewoman's Love-Hungry Daughter and Other Stories of Chicago Life. 1927.
The Sinister Sex and Other Stories of Marriage. 1927.
A Jew in Love. 1931.
The Champion from Far Away (stories). 1931.
Actor's Blood (stories). 1936.
A Book of Miracles (stories). 1939.
1001 Afternoons in New York. 1941.
Miracle in the Rain. 1943.
I Hate Actors! 1944; as *Hollywood Mystery!*, 1946.
The Collected Stories. 1945.
Concerning a Woman of Sin and Other Stories. 1947.
The Cat That Jumped Out of the Story (for children). 1947.
The Sensualists. 1959.
In the Midst of Death. 1964.

Other

A Guide for the Bedevilled. 1944.
A Child of the Century (autobiography). 1954.
Charlie: The Improbable Life and Times of Charles MacArthur. 1957.
A Treasury of Hecht. 1959.
Perfidy. 1961.
Gaily, Gaily (autobiography). 1963.
Letters from Bohemia. 1964.

Film director: *Crime Without Passion*, 1934, *The Scoundrel*, 1935, *Once in a Blue Moon*, 1935, and *Soak the Rich*, 1936, all with Charles MacArthur; *Angels over Broadway*, 1940, *Specter of the Rose*, 1946, and *Actors and Sin*, 1951, all with Lee Garmes.

*

Critical Studies: *The Five Lives of Hecht* by Doug Fetherling, 1977; *Hecht, Hollywood Screenwriter* by Jeffrey Brown Martin, 1985.

* * *

Ben Hecht began his writing career before the evolution of "play lovers" into "play decipherers," the "audience renaissance" which he analysed in a 1963 *Theatre Arts* article. By this evolution the status of the theatre as "our most ancient bridgehead of lucidity" was undermined. Hecht's earliest literary values, influenced by his career in journalism, taught him that "whatever confusions possessed the other arts, the art of the theatre remained basically that of a Western Union telegram—terse and informative." These principles were to govern most of his dramatic output, and partially explain why such a disciplined, intelligent, and prolific writer has only intermittently attracted critical attention.

The journalist's attention to incident and detail, the "katatonic armor" that shields him in daily contact with life's severities, and the craft of shaping these into a "story" are all prominent factors in his plays. Hecht's most famous collaboration with Charles MacArthur, *The Front Page*, has often been dismissed as a romantic melodrama about journalism; however, it also generates a poignant dilemma between public and private values, articulated with a vigorous realism that was all but unique on Broadway in 1928. *To Quito and Back*, considered by many to be the best play that Hecht wrote alone, also introduces a journalist as a secondary character to sift out a situation in Ecuador not unlike that of the Spanish Civil War. However, the diversity of content and style in Hecht's drama is almost as great as in his screenplays. His early one-act plays (written between 1914 and 1918) show experimentation with various types of stylisation then fashionable in "art theatres," a tendency which declines after the death of his first collaborator, the more experienced playwright Kenneth Sawyer Goodman, in 1918. Working with MacArthur, Hecht produced the Hollywood satire *Twentieth Century*, the musical extravaganza *Jumbo*, and the murder melodrama *Swan Song*; with Gene Fowler, he wrote the "dramatic cartoon" *The Great Magoo*; with Kurt Weill, he collaborated in the pageant of Jewish history *A Flag Is Born*, which gave a starring part to the young Marlon Brando, and netted nearly one million dollars for the Zionist cause in 1946. Several of Hecht's later plays are also graveyard dramas: *Lily of the Valley* is a purgatorial allegory, and *Winkelberg* is a work of expressionistic nostalgia. The stylistic eclecticism of Hecht's drama is reflected in the range of collaborators with whom he proved compatible, but his claim to a place in American dramatic history must rest on his tough, anecdotal realism.

Antedating Hecht's "audience renaissance" was the "Chicago Renaissance" to which he was a central contributor, and which provided the context of *Winkelberg*. Assessments of Hecht's novels have been increasingly unfavourable since the 1950's, and criticism of the "clever saccharinity" of the Chicago school is substantiated by a reading of his earliest prose fiction, from *Erik Dorn* to *Gargoyles*. Hecht's role as founding editor of the Chicago *Literary Times* (which he also printed, published, managed, proofed, and helped distribute) was a watershed in his career, and it was a much less pretentious Hecht who emerged to write *The Front Page*; his original purpose in that play was to reflect his "intellectual disdain of and superiority to the Newspaper," but a much more honest, frontal attitude to his writing developed, resulting in his finest novel, *A Jew in Love*, as well as the best of his short stories.

Ironically, it was only late in his career that Hecht found a commitment that would have given cohesive solidity to his central output. Jews and journalists abound in his early novels and plays, but it is only in his later autobiographical writings that he deliberately anatomises his own identity as an American Jew.

—Howard McNaughton

HELLER, Joseph. Born in Brooklyn, New York, 1 May 1923. Educated at Abraham Lincoln High School, New York, graduated 1941; University of Southern California, Los Angeles, 1945–46; New York University, 1946–48, B.A. in English 1948 (Phi Beta Kappa); Columbia University, New York, M.A. 1949; Oxford University (Fulbright Scholar), 1949–50. Served in the U.S. Army Air Force, 1942–45: Lieutenant. Married Shirley Held in 1945; one son and one daughter. Instructor in English, Pennsylvania State University, University Park, 1950–52; advertising writer, *Time* magazine, New York, 1952–56, and *Look* magazine, New York, 1956–58; promotion manager, *McCall's* magazine, New York, 1958–61. Recipient: American Academy grant, 1963; Médicis prize (France), 1985; Interallie prize (France), 1985. Member, American Academy, 1977.

PUBLICATIONS

Fiction

Catch-22. 1961.
Something Happened. 1974.
Good as Gold. 1979.
God Knows. 1984.

Plays

We Bombed in New Haven (produced 1967). 1968.
Catch-22, from his own novel (produced 1971). 1973.
Clevinger's Trial, from chapter 8 of his novel *Catch-22* (produced 1974). 1973.

Screenplays: *Sex and the Single Girl*, with David R. Schwartz, 1964; *Casino Royale* (uncredited), 1967; *Dirty Dingus Magee*, with Tom and Frank Waldman, 1970.

Other

No Laughing Matter (autobiographical), with Speed Vogel. 1986.

*

Bibliography: *Three Contemporary Novelists: An Annotated Bibliography* by Robert M. Scotto, 1977; *Heller: A Reference Guide* by Brenda M. Keegan, 1978.

Critical Studies: *A Catch-22 Casebook* edited by Frederick T. Kiley and Walter McDonald, 1973; *Critical Essays on Catch-22*, 1974, and *Critical Essays on Heller*, 1984, both edited by James Nagel; *From Here to Absurdity: The Moral Battlefields of Heller* by Stephen W. Potts, 1982.

* * *

Joseph Heller is not only regarded as a major contemporary novelist, but also as one who has achieved the rare distinction of balancing academic plaudits with widespread popular success. Even more impressive, the title of his first novel, *Catch-22*, has become a household phrase, one defined by *Webster's New World Dictionary of the American Language* as "a paradox in law, regulation, or practice that makes one a victim of its provisions no matter what one does." In Heller's novel it is the deadly "catch" which specified "that a concern for one's safety in the face of dangers that were real and immediate was the process of a rational mind." Flyers designated as "crazy" are relieved of combat duty; to fly missions designed to produce "tight bombing patterns" and little else is *crazy*. But therein lies *Catch-22*'s deadly rub: flyers who recognize the absurdity of their situation are, by definition, sane—and, of course, they must continue to fly missions.

Catch-22 is nominally a World War II novel, but with important differences. Set in Italy at the tag-end of the war, it focuses on a group of American flyers who discover that the bureaucratic double-shuffle can be as deadly as enemy gunfire. In this sense, it *begins* where World War I novels like Hemingway's *A Farewell to Arms* or Erich Maria Remarque's *All Quiet on the Western Front* end. Gallows humor replaces innocence, and staying alive counts for more than saving the world for democracy.

In short, the novel addressed itself to a generation coming of age in the 1960's. It had exactly the right mix of black humor and satiric bite to speak for those bent on kicking the System in its slats. Yossarian, Heller's protagonist, is the classical Outsider, the man who cannot quite shake the image of a fellow flyer (significantly enough, named Snowden) freezing to death as his insides seep through a flak jacket. For all of *Catch-22*'s hijinks, its brilliantly comic asides, and its fractured chronology, the narrative always arcs back to the image of the dying Snowden.

Heller's next novel, *Something Happened*, transported the nervous energy and the abiding paranoia of *Catch-22* to corporate America and the "willies" Bob Slocum gets when he sees a closed door: ". . . something horrible is happening behind it, something that is going to affect me adversely . . . Something must have happened to me sometime." Slocum—surely a neurotic among contemporary American literature's vast array of neurotics—picks away at the scab that has become his life, trying to figure out where things went wrong. Slocum is a middling man caught in the world of middle management. But, unlike Yossarian, he prefers wringing his hands to tilting at windmills.

Something Happened is, among other things, an extended study in moral bankruptcy. Slocum's first-person narration makes for a draining read. One looks at Slocum with nearly equal doses of fascination and dread. If, as some critics have suggested, he is our Everyman, the portrait Heller holds up to the nature of corporate life is a chilling one indeed. Nonetheless, there are good reasons for supposing that *Something Happened* is the tortoise that will one day overtake *Catch-22*'s hare.

By contrast, Heller's most recent novels—*Good as Gold* and *God Knows*—are not likely candidates to survive the cold eye of subsequent readings. *Good as Gold* is, in effect, three books masquerading as one: a Jewish family comedy in the mode of Philip Roth; a satire of academic life; and a piece of political invective. Unfortunately, the parts are not equal, and, more to the point, they do not mesh. The family dinner scenes, for example, are wonderfully funny, but the lop-sided harangues directed against Henry Kissinger are sophomoric and, even now, terribly dated.

God Knows is yet another extended (i.e., undisciplined) exercise—this time a Borscht Belt version of the King David story with Heller, rather than George Burns, playing God. Heller mixes biblical text and contemporary detail with what he hopes will be wild abandon, but the sad truth is that writers have been mining this particular vein of humor for some time. Juxtapositions of this sort—Yiddish inflections stuffed into the mouths of biblical giants—can work in a short story (one thinks, for example, of Isaac Rosenfeld's "King Solomon"), but the thread is too slender by far to sustain a novel.

Given the slippery nature of literary success in America, it is unlikely that Heller will write a novel that could joint *Catch-22* in that select circle reserved for "contemporary classics." On the other hand, Heller clearly has too much talent for us to imagine that he will continue to turn out "disappointments." He is, after all, a major contemporary writer, and not only because he happened to be the author of *Catch-22*.

—Sanford Pinsker

See the essay on *Catch-22*.

HELLMAN, Lillian (Florence). Born in New Orleans, Louisiana, 20 June 1905 (some sources give 1906). Educated at New York University, 1924–25; Columbia University, New York, 1925. Married the writer Arthur Kober in 1925 (divorced, 1932). Reader, Horace Liveright, publishers, New York, 1924–25; reviewer, New York *Herald-Tribune*, 1925–28; theatrical play reader, 1927–30; reader, Metro-Goldwyn-Mayer, 1930–32; began long relationship with Dashiell Hammett, *q.v.*, in 1930; teacher at Yale University, New Haven, Connecticut, 1966, and at Harvard University, Cambridge, Massachusetts, Massachusetts Institute of Technology, Cambridge, and University of California, Berkeley. Recipient: New York Drama Critics Circle award, 1941, 1960; Brandeis University Creative Arts Award, 1960; American Academy Gold Medal, 1964; National Book Award, for non-fiction, 1970; Paul Robeson Award, 1976; MacDowell Medal, 1976. M.A.: Tufts College, Medford, Massachusetts, 1940; Litt.D.: Wheaton College, Norton, Massachusetts, 1961; Rutgers University, New Brunswick, New Jersey, 1963; Brandeis University, Waltham, Massachusetts, 1965; Yale University, 1974; Smith College, Northampton, Massachusetts, 1974; New York University, 1974; Franklin and Marshall College, Lancaster, Pennsylvania, 1975; Columbia University, 1976. Vice-President, National Institute of Arts and Letters, 1962; Member, American Academy of Arts and Sciences, 1960, and American Academy, 1963. *Died 30 June 1984.*

PUBLICATIONS

Plays

The Children's Hour (produced 1934). 1934.
Days to Come (produced 1936). 1936.
The Little Foxes (produced 1939). 1939.
Watch on the Rhine (produced 1941). 1941.
Four Plays (includes *The Children's Hour, Days to Come, The Little Foxes, Watch on the Rhine*). 1942.
The North Star: A Motion Picture about Some Russian People. 1943.
The Searching Wind (produced 1944). 1944.
Watch on the Rhine (screenplay), with Dashiell Hammett, in *Best Film Plays of 1943–44*, edited by John Gassner and Dudley Nichols. 1945.
Another Part of the Forest (produced 1946). 1947.
Montserrat, from a play by Emmanuel Roblès (produced 1949). 1950.
Regina, music by Marc Blitzstein (produced 1949).
The Autumn Garden (produced 1951). 1951.
The Lark, from a play by Jean Anouilh (produced 1955). 1956.
Candide, music by Leonard Bernstein, lyrics by Richard Wilbur, John LaTouche, and Dorothy Parker, from the novel by Voltaire (produced 1956). 1957.
Toys in the Attic (produced 1960). 1960.
Six Plays. 1960.
My Mother, My Father and Me, from the novel *How Much?* by Burt Blechman (produced 1963). 1963.
The Collected Plays (includes *The Children's Hour, Days to Come, The Little Foxes, Watch on the Rhine, The Searching Wind, Another Part of the Forest, Montserrat, The Autumn Garden, The Lark, Candide, Toys in the Attic, My Mother, My Father and Me*). 1972.

Screenplays: *The Dark Angel*, with Mordaunt Shairp, 1935; *These Three*, 1936; *Dead End*, 1937; *The Little Foxes*, with others, 1941; *Watch on the Rhine*, with Dashiell Hammett, 1943; *The North Star*, 1943; *The Searching Wind*, 1946; *The Children's Hour* (*The Loudest Whisper*), with John Michael Hayes, 1961; *The Chase*, 1966.

Other

Three. 1979.
An Unfinished Woman: A Memoir. 1969.
Pentimento: A Book of Portraits. 1973.
Scoundrel Time. 1976.
Maybe: A Story. 1980.
Eating Together: Recollections and Recipes, with Peter Feibleman. 1984.
Conversations with Hellman (interviews), edited by Jackson R. Bryer. 1986.

Editor, *Selected Letters*, by Chekhov, translated by Sidonie K. Lederer. 1955.
Editor, *The Big Knockover: Selected Stories and Short Novels*, by Dashiell Hammett. 1966; as *The Hammett Story Omnibus*, 1966; as *The Big Knockover* and *The Continental Op*, 2 vols., 1967.

*

Bibliography: *Hellman: An Annotated Bibliography* by Steven H. Bills, 1979; *Hellman: Plays, Films, Memoirs: A Reference Guide* by Mark W. Estrin, 1980; *Hellman: A Bibliography 1926–1978* by Mary Marguerite Riordan, 1980.

Critical Studies: *Hellman* by Jacob Adler, 1969; *Hellman, Playwright* by Richard Moody, 1972; *Hellman* by Doris V. Falk, 1978; *Hellman* by Katherine Lederer, 1979; *Hellman in Hollywood* by Bernard F. Dick, 1982; *Hellman: A Life* by William Wright, 1986.

* * *

Lillian Hellman is one of America's major dramatists. She entered a male-dominated field when she was nearly thirty and wrote some dozen plays in three decades. Her early model was Ibsen, and she shared his love of tightly knit plots and emphasis on sociological and psychological forces. Her best plays, like Ibsen's, are those in which a powerful character cuts loose and transcends the limitations of the play's rigid symmetry and plot contrivance. Along with Clifford Odets, the other significant writing talent of the 1930's, Hellman showed a keen interest in Marxist theory and explored the relationship between the nuclear family and capitalism. Hellman, more than Odets, held ambiguous views of man and society. Her antagonists are not wholly the products of environment but seem at times innately malicious. The quest for power fascinated the author and her characters became famous for their ruthlessness and cunning. Most of her plays verge on melodrama but are admired for their energetic protagonists and swift-moving plots.

In her first play, *The Children's Hour*, Hellman showed how the capricious wielding of power could ruin innocent people. Two young women at a girl's school are falsely accused of having a lesbian relationship by a disturbed child. They are brought to trial by outraged parents and eventually lose their case—and their school. One of the teachers commits suicide and, too late, the child's treachery is discovered. The homosexual motif, though discreetly handled, accounted for the play's notoriety in 1934; but the abuse of power by an arrogant elite is its enduring theme.

Usurping power is also the motivating force in Hellman's best-known play, *The Little Foxes*, at once a political statement and a complex study of family dynamics. The rapacious Hubbard family represents a new brand of southern capitalist who subordinates all traditions and human values to the goal of acquiring wealth and property. The strength of the play lies in Hellman's implicit comparison of the Hubbard siblings' rivalries with the competitiveness of Americans in the free enterprise system. The role of Regina Hubbard, who withholds her dying husband's heart medicine and who outwits her equally greedy brothers in a major business coup, has become a favorite vehicle for American actresses.

At the beginning of World War II Hellman wrote *Watch on the Rhine* and *The Searching Wind* which both dealt with the fascist menace. The former play contains some witty repartee and suspenseful moments; but its solutions to the international crisis are simplistic, and it is better described as an adventure story than a thesis play.

When the war ended, Hellman returned to the easy-to-hate Hubbard family in *Another Part of the Forest*. Unfortunately the exaggerated spitefulness and hysteria of the characters and the unrelieved high-tension atmosphere of this play become nearly ludicrous. The concept of personal manipulation had become an obsession with the author, and a correlation seemed to have developed between her studies of social and societal exploitation and her own excessive control over plot characterization and stage effects. Perhaps the playwright realized this, because in her last plays she turned from Ibsen to Chekhov for inspiration. Both *The Autumn Garden* and *Toys in the Attic* recall the mood and ambiguous moral judgments of Chekhov. Neither of these plays has a truly pernicious villain, and most of the characters seem to be suffering from a Chekhovian paralysis of will. The atmosphere is deterministic and the plots are truer to life. What has changed is that all bids for personal power prove self-defeating—the predatory are caught in traps of their own making and hardly struggle before acknowledging defeat. Nevertheless these plays also include sharp, amusing verbal exchanges and the famous blackmail scenes associated with Hellman. Blackmail, present in all of her plays, is Hellman's favorite metaphor for personal manipulation; but in the later works she uses blackmail and other devices with greater sublety, and presents a somewhat blurred but more convincing vision of stumbling modern man and his society.

Hellman's dramatic mode, based on her adherence to continental models, is bound to an earlier era. Most of her experiments with screenwriting proved frustrating. Her best later works were autobiographical sketches: in *An Unfinished Woman*, *Pentimento*, and *Scoundrel Time* she reveals her penetrating intelligence but tacitly acknowledges that her insights and talents are better suited to the historical memoir.

—Kimball King

See the essay on *The Little Foxes*.

HEMINGWAY, Ernest (Miller). Born in Oak Park, Illinois, 21 July 1899. Educated at Oak Park High School, graduated 1917. Served as a Red Cross ambulance driver in Italy, 1918; also served on the western front with the Italian Arditi: wounded in action: Medaglia d'Argento al Valore Militare; Croce de Guerra; involved in anti-submarine patrol duty off the coast of Cuba, 1942–44. Married 1) Hadley Richardson in 1921 (divorced, 1927), one son; 2) Pauline Pfeiffer in 1927 (divorced, 1940), two sons; 3) the writer Martha Gellhorn in 1940 (divorced, 1946); 4) Mary Welsh in 1946. Reporter, Kansas City *Star*, 1917; reporter, then foreign correspondent, Toronto *Star* and *Star Weekly*, 1920–23: covered the Greco-Turkish War, 1922; moved to Paris, 1921, and became associated with the expatriate community, including Gertrude Stein and Ezra Pound; correspondent in Paris for Hearst newspapers, 1924–27; settled in Key West, Florida, 1928; moved to Cuba, 1940, and to Idaho, 1958; war correspondent for North American Newspaper Alliance, in Spain, 1937–38, and for *Collier's* in Europe, 1944–45: Bronze Star. Recipient: Bancarella Prize (Italy), 1953; Pulitzer Prize, 1953; Nobel Prize for Literature, 1954; American Academy Award of Merit Medal, 1954. *Died (suicide) 2 July 1961*.

PUBLICATIONS

Collections

A Hemingway Selection, edited by Dennis Pepper. 1972.
The Enduring Hemingway, edited by Charles Scribner, Jr. 1974.
88 Poems, edited by Nicholas Gerogiannis. 1979; as *Complete Poems*, 1983.
Selected Letters 1917–1961, edited by Carlos Baker. 1981.

Fiction

Three Stories and Ten Poems. 1923.
In Our Time (sketches). 1924.
In Our Time: Stories. 1925; revised edition, 1930.
The Torrents of Spring: A Romantic Novel in Honor of the Passing of a Great Race. 1926.
The Sun Also Rises. 1926; as *Fiesta*, 1927.
Men Without Women (stories). 1927.
A Farewell to Arms. 1929.
God Rest You Merry Gentlemen (stories). 1933.
Winner Take Nothing (stories). 1933.
To Have and Have Not. 1937.

The Fifth Column and the First Forty-Nine Stories (includes play). 1938.
For Whom the Bell Tolls. 1940.
The Portable Hemingway, edited by Malcolm Cowley. 1944.
The Essential Hemingway. 1947.
Across the River and into the Trees. 1950.
The Old Man and the Sea. 1952.
Hemingway in Michigan (stories), edited by Constance Cappel Montgomery. 1966.
The Fifth Column and Four Stories of the Spanish Civil War. 1969.
Islands in the Stream. 1970.
The Nick Adams Stories, edited by Philip Young. 1972.
A Divine Gesture: A Fable. 1974.
The Garden of Eden. 1986.

Plays

Today Is Friday. 1926.
The Spanish Earth (screenplay). 1938.
The Fifth Column (produced 1940). In *The Fifth Column . . .*, 1938.

Screenplays (documentaries): *Spain in Flames*, with others, 1937; *The Spanish Earth*, 1937.

Verse

Collected Poems. 1960.

Other

Death in the Afternoon. 1932.
Green Hills of Africa. 1935.
The Hemingway Reader, edited by Charles Poore. 1953.
Hemingway: The Wild Years (newspaper articles), edited by Gene Z. Hanrahan. 1962.
A Moveable Feast (autobiography). 1964.
By-Line: Hemingway, Selected Articles and Dispatches of Four Decades, edited by William White. 1967.
Hemingway: Cub Reporter: "Kansas City Star" Stories, edited by Matthew J. Bruccoli. 1970.
The Faithful Bull (for children). 1980.
Hemingway on Writing, edited by Larry W. Phillips. 1984.
The Dangerous Summer. 1985.
Dateline: Toronto: The Complete Toronto Star Dispatches 1920 to 1924, edited by William White. 1985.

Editor, *Men at War: The Best War Stories of All Time*. 1942.

*

Bibliography: *Hemingway: A Comprehensive Bibliography* by Audre Hanneman, 1967, supplement, 1975; *Hemingway: A Reference Guide* by Linda W. Wagner, 1977.

Critical Studies: *Hemingway: The Writer as Artist*, 1952, revised edition 1972, and *Hemingway: A Life Story*, 1969, both by Carlos Baker, and *Hemingway and His Critics: An International Anthology* edited by Baker, 1961; *Hemingway* by Philip Young, 1952, revised edition, as *Hemingway: A Reconsideration*, 1966; *Hemingway* by Stewart F. Sanderson, 1961; *Hemingway: A Collection of Critical Essays* edited by Robert P. Weeks, 1962; *Hemingway* by Earl Rovit, 1963; *Hemingway: An Introduction and Interpretation* by Sheridan Baker, 1967; *Hemingway and the Pursuit of Heroism* by Leo Gurko, 1968; *Hemingway's Nonfiction: The Public Voice* by Robert O. Stephens, 1968, and *Hemingway: The Critical Reception* edited by Stephens, 1977; *Hemingway: The Inward Terrain* by Richard B. Hovey, 1968; *Hemingway's Heroes* by Delbert E. Wylder, 1969; *Hemingway: The Writer's Art of Self-Defense* by Jackson R. Benson, 1969, and *The Short Stories of Hemingway: Critical Essays* edited by Benson, 1975; *A Reader's Guide to Hemingway* by Arthur Waldhorn, 1972; *Hemingway's Craft* by Sheldon Norman Grebstein, 1973; *Hemingway: Five Decades of Criticism* edited by Linda W. Wagner, 1974, and *Hemingway and Faulkner: Inventors/Masters* by Wagner, 1975; *By Force of Will: The Life and Art of Hemingway* by Scott Donaldson, 1977; *Scott and Ernest: The Authority of Failure and the Authority of Success* by Matthew J. Bruccoli, 1978, and *Conversations with Hemingway* (interviews) edited by Bruccoli, 1986; *Hemingway and His World* by Anthony Burgess, 1978; *The Tragic Art of Hemingway* by Wirt Williams, 1981; *Hemingway: The Critical Heritage* edited by Jeffrey Meyers, 1982, and *Hemingway: A Biography* by Meyers, 1985; *Hemingway's Nick Adams* by Joseph M. Flora, 1982; *Hemingway* by Samuel Shaw, 1982; *Hemingway: New Critical Essays* edited by A. Robert Lee, 1983; *The Hemingway Women* by Bernice Kert, 1983; *Hemingway and The Sun Also Rises: The Crafting of a Style* by Frederic J. Svoboda, 1983; *Hemingway: The Writer in Context* edited by James Nagel, 1984; *Concealments in Hemingway's Work* by Gerry Brenner, 1984; *Hemingway: Life and Works* (chronology) by Gerald B. Nelson and Glory Jones, 1984; *Cassandra's Daughters: Women in Hemingway* by Roger Whitlow, 1984; *The Young Hemingway* by Michael Reynolds, 1986.

* * *

When Ernest Hemingway was awarded the Nobel Prize for Literature the Swedish Academy commented on the central themes of his work. Courage and compassion in a world of violence and death were seen as the distinguishing marks of "one of the great writers of our time . . . who, honestly and undauntedly, reproduces the genuine features of the hard countenance of the age." These comments sum up perceptively the characteristic preoccupations of Hemingway's fiction and of the heroic code of behaviour which it explores. But they do less than justice to another aspect of his writing. Hemingway was also a deliberate and careful artist, for whom every book was, in his own words, "a new beginning" in which the writer "should always try for something that has never been done."

Hemingway started his working life as a newspaper reporter, an excellent training in writing graphic declaratory prose. Covering crime stories was one introduction to a violent world, service with a Red Cross ambulance unit in Italy another. Severely wounded just before his nineteenth birthday, he received further emotional wounds when rejected by an American nurse with whom he fell in love. These experiences epitomise themes he was to explore in his short stories and novels, in prose which he deliberately stripped bare of adjectival colouring and rhetorical flourishes.

His first books, *Three Stories and Ten Poems* and *In Our Time*, were slim volumes which attracted coterie attention. The second of them consisted of twelve stark vignettes—scenes of war, bull-fighting, murder—which in a later edition were interleaved between lengthier short stories in which the Hemingway hero, and the heroic code of grace under pressure, first appear.

Seven of the stories are episodes in the experience of a young man whose sensitivity has been violated in various ways, physically, emotionally, and spiritually. One day, he knows, his traumata will be healed; but this will take time, courage, and an effort of will. In the meantime he holds on stoically.

The Torrents of Spring, an uncharacteristic burlesque, is unimportant except as an indication of Hemingway's considerable skill as a comic satirist: it foreshadows the very funny ironical humour in, for instance, passages of *Death in the Afternoon* and *A Moveable Feast*. *In Our Time*, however, is the matrix from which the rest of his fiction is cast, both the later volumes of short stories and the succession of brilliantly finished, though occasionally flawed, novels.

The Sun Also Rises established Hemingway beyond question as a significant new novelist. Narrated in the first person, it deals with the predicament of the hero, emasculated by an unlucky war wound, in his frustrated love for an Englishwoman whom time and misfortune have driven into alcoholism, promiscuity, and self-destructive irresponsibility. Charting the mores of Paris cafe society playboys and would-be artists, Hemingway for some readers obscured the moral seriousness of his novel through the brilliance of his writings, especially in the scenes at the fiesta in Pamplona. But the message is there. The hero has learnt to accept his plight with honesty and courage; and even the heroine, though morally ruined, is honest with herself and in her own fashion also honourable. The hero's own moral strength allows him to treat her with compassion.

In his next novel Hemingway settled for third-person narration. A romantic tragedy of love and war, *A Farewell to Arms* shows considerable technical development. Formally constructed in five acts, it is closely knit by complex sub-structure beneath the surface of the story. Symbols of weather and topography unobtrusively counterpoint the action, while contrasts of profane and sacred love are made both overtly and covertly in the evolving relationship between the hero and the novel's innocent tragic heroine. In this novel, too, Hemingway tried to communicate directly his own experience of being wounded by trench mortar fire, in a cardinal passage which supports his occasionally expressed view that writing is a kind of self-therapy.

Hemingway's views on fiction, which incidentally show how closely he had studied the English, French, and Russian novelists, are for the most part woven into his classic study of bullfighting, *Death in the Afternoon*. In brief, his aim was to write simply and directly about directly received experience. The more precisely a writer can express the essential impact of experience, the more precisely he will impress that experience on his readers. His task is to set down "the sequence of motion and fact which made the emotion," which "with luck and if you stated it purely enough" should remain valid always. By concentrating on describing his characters in action a writer should be able to communicate unwritten emotional reverberations, whereas to write as an omniscient commentator is to spoil his fiction by adding what is structurally unnecessary and undesirable. In a famous comparison, Hemingway likens the artist's work to the tip of an iceberg, whose dignity of movement is due to only one-eighth of it being above water. It is an austere approach to the writer's craft, but one whose discipline gives Hemingway's work unmistakable authority and strength.

While many writers in the early 1930's were as much concerned with political as with literary preoccupations, Hemingway fed his experience and his literary production by big-game hunting, fishing, and shooting. This is the period of some of his best short stories, including "The Snows of Kilimanjaro," technically superb in its accumulated moves from reality to illusory vision. His novel *To Have and Have Not* is less satisfying. An attempt to portray characters under economic stress in the depression, it was cobbled together from two earlier short stories and was written hastily between visits to Spain during the Civil War. This also is the period of *The Fifth Column*, an undistinguished venture into the theatre.

The Spanish Civil War, however, provided Hemingway with the theme of another outstanding novel, *For Whom the Bell Tolls*, in which again he extended his techniques. The story is built around twin themes, the dynamiting of a bridge by a guerrilla group and the love affair of an American partisan and a girl in the group. The action is restricted to some seventy hours, the location to a single valley, the personae to a handful; but by dipping into the stream of the hero's thoughts about his former life and by having various characters recount their memories, Hemingway works beyond these confines to create an ample but tightly organised novel of epic dimensions. There is an optimistic shift, too, in the heroic code, in that the hero is now in command of himself and meets death alone but fearless. Contemporary judgments of this novel were often politically coloured, ranging from allegations that Hemingway had "largely sloughed off his Stalinism" to accusations of Fascist sympathies: today these variant views reflect clearly the success of Hemingway's sympathetic treatment of the complexity of political and human predicaments. Of the novel's literary quality there has never been any doubt.

His next two novels, *Across the River and into the Trees* and *The Old Man and the Sea*, take the heroic code further. The latter's message that a man can be destroyed but not defeated carries a suggestion of Christian salvation. Though *Across the River and into the Trees* contains some of Hemingway's most intense writing (e.g., the description of the duck-shoot with which the novel opens), it is flawed by occasional obtrusions of the author's own personality and by his as yet incomplete mastery of new modes of symbolism operating at multiple levels. These are under perfect control in *The Old Man and the Sea*, a work of flawless craftsmanship that can be read literally, or as an allegory of human life, or of the Crucifixion, or of the artist's struggle to dominate his material.

The posthumous publication of the long, uneven *Islands in the Stream* and *The Garden of Eden*, unrevised by his skilled hand, neither adds to nor detracts from the reputation of a dedicated and sensitive artist, one of the greatest and most influential prose writers of the 20th century.

—Stewart F. Sanderson

See the essays on "Big Two-Hearted River" and *The Sun Also Rises*.

HENRY, O. Pseudonym for William Sydney, or Sidney, Porter. Born in Greensboro, North Carolina, 11 September 1862. Educated at his aunt's private school in Greensboro to age 7; apprentice pharmacist in Greensboro, 1878–81; licensed by the North Carolina Pharmaceutical Association, 1881. Married 1) Athol Estes Roach in 1887 (died, 1897), one son and one daughter; 2) Sara Lindsay Coleman in 1907. Moved to Texas, 1882, and worked on a ranch in LaSalle County, 1882–84;

bookkeeper in Austin, 1884–86; contributed to Detroit *Free Press*, 1887; draftsman, Texas Land office, Austin, 1887–91; teller, First National Bank, Austin, 1891–94; founding editor, *Iconoclast*, later *Rolling Stone* magazine, Houston, 1894–95; columnist ("Tales of the Town," later "Some Postscripts"), Houston *Post*, 1895–96; accused of embezzling funds from his previous employers, First National Bank, Austin, 1895; fled to Honduras to avoid trial, 1896–97; returned to Austin because of wife's illness, 1897; jailed for embezzling in the Federal Penitentiary, Columbus, Ohio, 1898–1901 (5-year sentence reduced to 3): while in prison began publishing stories as O. Henry; moved to Pittsburgh, 1901, and New York, 1902; thereafter a full-time writer; regular contributor, New York *Sunday World*, 1903–05. O. Henry Memorial Award established by the Society of Arts and Sciences, 1918. *Died 5 June 1910.*

PUBLICATIONS

Collections

Complete Works. 1926.
Stories, edited by Harry Hansen. 1965.

Fiction (stories)

Cabbages and Kings. 1904.
The Four Million. 1906.
The Trimmed Lamp and Other Stories of the Four Million. 1907.
Heart of the West. 1907.
The Voice of the City: Further Stories of the Four Million. 1908.
The Gentle Grafter. 1908.
Roads of Destiny. 1909.
Options. 1909.
Strictly Business: More Stories of the Four Million. 1910.
Whirligigs. 1910.
Let Me Feel Your Pulse. 1910.
The Two Women. 1910.
Sixes and Sevens. 1911.
Rolling Stones. 1912.
Waifs and Strays. 1917.
Selected Stories, edited by C. Alphonse Smith. 1922.
The Best of O. Henry. 1929.
More O. Henry. 1933.
The Best Short Stories of O. Henry, edited by Bennett Cerf and Van H. Cartmell. 1945.
The Pocket Book of O. Henry, edited by Harry Hansen. 1948.
Cops and Robbers, edited by Ellery Queen. 1948.
O. Henry Westerns, edited by Patrick Thornhill. 1961.

Play

Lo, with Franklin P. Adams, music by A. Baldwin Sloane (produced 1909).

Other

Complete Writings, 14 vols., 1918.
O. Henryana: Seven Odds and Ends: Poetry and Short Stories. 1920.
Letters to Lithopolis from O. Henry to Mabel Wagnalls. 1922.
Postscripts (from Houston *Post*), edited by Florence Stratton. 1923.
O. Henry Encore: Stories and Illustrations (from Houston *Post*), edited by Mary Sunlocks Harrell. 1939.

*

Bibliography: *A Bibliography of Porter (O. Henry)* by Paul S. Clarkson, 1938; *Porter (O. Henry): A Reference Guide* by Richard C. Harris, 1980; in *Bibliography of American Literature* by Jacob Blanck, edited by Virginia L. Smyers and Michael Winship, 1983.

Critical Studies: *O. Henry Biography* by C. Alphonse Smith, 1916; *The Caliph of Bagdad* by Robert H. Davis and Arthur B. Maurice, 1931; *O. Henry: The Man and His Work*, 1949, and *O. Henry, American Regionalist*, 1969, both by Eugene Hudson Long; *The Heart of O. Henry* by Dale Kramer, 1954; *Alias O. Henry: A Biography* by Gerald Langford, 1957; *O. Henry from Polecat Creek* by Ethel Stephens Arnett, 1962; *O. Henry (Porter)* by Eugene Current-Garcia, 1965; *O. Henry: The Legendary Life of Porter* by Richard O'Connor, 1970; *From Alamo Plaza to Jack Harris's Saloon: O. Henry and the Southwest He Knew* by Joseph Gallegly, 1970; *O. Henry: A Biography* by David Stuart, 1986.

* * *

William Sydney Porter's first story to appear in a national magazine was published in September 1898 while he was in prison, and it was in prison that he began writing in earnest. Following his release, Porter moved to New York where he wrote prodigiously; during 1904 and 1905 he is said to have produced a story a week for the New York *World*. Fame and notoriety, which he shunned, came to him quickly, as did money, which he spent lavishly and usually unwisely. *Cabbages and Kings*, his first collection of stories, established him as an author to be taken seriously. By 1908, with the publication of *The Voice of the City*, he was hailed as having "breathed new life into the short story; the stigma of the genre is wearing off, and for its rehabilitation . . . (Porter) is responsible"; and in 1914, in a symposium conducted by the New York *Times*, "A Municipal Report" was voted "the greatest American short story ever written."

By 1920, ten years after his death, five million volumes of Porter's stories had been sold, but the current of critical opinion had turned against them and their author: not uncharacteristic is H.L. Mencken's pronouncement that "in the whole canon of O. Henry's work you will not find a single recognizable human character." A just estimate of Porter's fiction lies somewhere between such extremes. O. Henry brought verve, excitement, and humor to the genre. Enormously interested in people, he is capable of swift and compassionate insights into the average person, and his sympathy for the underdog, the little man or woman dwarfed in the maze of contemporary life, to a degree accounted for his enormous popularity. He was a good reporter with a keen eye for the significant detail, and he had a feeling for setting unmatched by most of his contemporaries. His brisk openings and the engrossing narrative pace of even his least successful stories are perhaps the major reasons for his instant appeal. Perhaps most important of all, he influenced an entire generation of writers and helped provide an enthusiastic audience for their work.

Porter's faults are as conspicuous as his assets—contrivance, sentimentality, repetition, and melodrama; his trick endings, particularly, seemed patently dated in the context of the new realism of the 1920's. He wrote rapidly—"once I begin a yarn I must finish it without stopping or it kinda goes dead on me"—and revised seldom. Haunted by memories of the past, increasingly engulfed in alcohol, Porter had no illusions about his literary shortcomings. "I'm a failure," he wrote to a friend. "My stories? No, they don't satisfy me. It depresses me to have people point me out as 'a celebrated author.' It seems such a big label for such picayune goods."

Porter's work, as one of his contemporaries commented, never did justice to his talents. Perhaps the soundest estimate of his contribution has been made by one of the most important modern English writers of fiction, H.E. Bates. However one belittles O. Henry, Bates wrote in *The Modern Short Story*, "he still emerges, by his huge achievement and the immense popularity of his particular method, as an astonishingly persistent influence on the short story of almost every decade since his day."

—William Peden

See the essay on "Gifts of the Magi."

HERGESHEIMER, Joseph. Born in Philadelphia, Pennsylvania, 15 February 1880. Educated at a Quaker school in Germantown, Philadelphia; studied painting at Pennsylvania Academy of Fine Arts, Philadelphia. Married Dorothy Hemphill in 1907. Settled in Virginia, 1900; regular contributor to *Saturday Evening Post*, 1915–38; lived in West Chester, Pennsylvania, and Stone Harbor, New Jersey, after 1945. Member, American Academy, 1921. *Died 25 April 1954.*

PUBLICATIONS

Fiction

The Lay Anthony. 1914; revised edition, 1919.
Mountain Blood. 1915; revised edition, 1930.
The Three Black Pennys. 1917.
Gold and Iron. 1918.
The Happy End (stories). 1919.
Linda Condon. 1919.
Java Head. 1919.
Cytherea. 1922.
The Bright Shawl. 1922.
Tol'able David (stories). 1923.
Balisand. 1924.
Merry Dale. 1924.
Tampico. 1926.
Quiet Cities (stories). 1928.
Triall by Armes (stories). 1929.
The Party Dress. 1930.
The Limestone Tree. 1931.
Love in the United States, and The Big Shot. 1932.
Tropical Winter (stories). 1933.
The Foolscap Rose. 1934.

Play

Screenplay: *Flower of Night*, with Willis Goldbeck, 1925.

Other

Hugh Walpole: An Appreciation. 1919.
San Cristóbal de la Habana. 1920.
The Presbyterian Child (autobiography). 1923.
From an Old House (autobiography). 1925.
Swords and Roses. 1929.
Sheridan: A Military Narrative. 1931.
Berlin. 1932.

*

Bibliography: "Hergesheimer: A Selected Bibliography 1913–1945" by James J. Napier, in *Bulletin of Bibliography 24*, 1963–64.

Critical Studies: *Hergesheimer: The Man and His Books* by Llewellyn Jones, 1920; *Hergesheimer* by James Branch Cabell, 1921; *The Fiction of Hergesheimer* by Ronald E. Martin, 1965; *Ingenue among the Lions: Letters of Emily Clark to Hergesheimer* edited by Gerald Langford, 1965; *Hergesheimer* by Victor E. Gimmestad, 1984.

* * *

James Branch Cabell called Joseph Hergesheimer "the most insistently superficial of writers" and meant it as a compliment; sixty years later the remark speaks unintentionally for his detractors. Writing from "aspiration hopelessly in advance of accomplishment," as Hergesheimer described his endeavors, he was reputed one of America's foremost novelists; today he is almost forgotten, and many readers would think deservedly so. After several quasi-historical novels, Hergesheimer turned to his immediate milieu—the American 1920's—and made the subject glossily his own. Later, his attempts at *belles lettres*—travel books and descriptions of old houses in fancy prose—blurred into his fiction, and flesh and blood disappeared into the architecture.

Of his early books, *Java Head* is an excellent adventure story of clipper ships and miscegenation in 18th-century Salem, with a Manchu princess as catalyst. *The Three Black Pennys* is an underrated novel about a Pennsylvania coal mining family, tracing an emotional decline from the eldest, sober and hard-working, to the youngest, a dilettante; finely written, even moving, it is undeserving of its present neglect.

The later novels "flash and glitter like so many fricaseed rainbows," according to George Jean Nathan. *Linda Condon* and *Cytherea* trace the hedonism of the 1920's—prohibition, permanent waves, "extraordinary quantities of superlative jewels and superfine textures"—with ironic detachment. In *The Party Dress*, however, written at the end of the decade, Hergesheimer detailed the mystique of golf—not only the shots in a game but the look of the greens and the quality of the clubs—in deadly earnest, and he lavished as much attention on his characters' houses, clothing, table manners, including the silver and crystal, as he did on their love affairs. Later historical novels, *Balisand* and *The Limestone Tree*, for example, had not even the glamour of the 1920's to enliven them.

Alfred Kazin spotted the quintessential Hergesheimer passage in *Cytherea*: " 'I want to be outraged!' Her low ringing cry seemed suppressed, deadened as though the damasked and florid gilt and rosewood, now inexpressibly shocked, had combined to muffle the expression, the agony, of her body." Kazin called Hergesheimer's passion "vulgar"; Wilson Follett called it an "aristocratic distinction" although "a distinctly un-American trait."

Readers in an audio-visual age may grow impatient with Hergesheimer's tales of beautiful women and wise men stifled by sybaritic description; but many of the novels accurately reflect their own time, however meretricious that time was. Hergesheimer still has much to say, by the fact of his reputation during the 1920's, to a later period preoccupied with pop culture.

—Bruce Kellner

HERNE, James A. Born James Ahern in Cohoes, New York, 1 February 1839. Educated in local schools to age 13. Married 1) Helen Western in 1866 (divorced); 2) the actress Katherine Corcoran in 1878, three daughters. Debut as an actor, in repertory, Troy, New York, 1859; appeared with John Ford's company in Baltimore and Washington, D.C., during the Civil War; leading man in the Lucille Western Company, touring the U.S., 1865–67; thereafter managed the Grand Opera House, New York; stage director, Lucky Baldwin's Academy of Music, San Francisco, 1875–80; began writing for the stage by collaborating with his associate David Belasco in 1879; starred in *Hearts of Oak* for the next seven years, a success which allowed him to retire to Dorchester, Massachusetts, and become full-time writer; lost his fortune on his next play: forced to move back to New York and work as stage manager for Klaw and Erlanger, 1891; appeared in *Shore Acres*, 1892–98, the success of which restored his fortunes; retired to Southampton, Long Island. *Died 2 June 1901.*

PUBLICATIONS

Collections

Shore Acres and Other Plays (includes *Sag Harbor, Hearts of Oak*), edited by Mrs. James A. Herne. 1928.
The Early Plays (includes *The Minute Men of 1774–1775, Drifting Apart, The Reverend Griffith Davenport, Within an Inch of His Life*), edited by Arthur Hobson Quinn. 1940.

Plays

Within an Inch of His Life, with David Belasco, from a play by Emile Gaboriau (produced 1879). In *The Early Plays*, 1940.
Marriage by Moonlight, with David Belasco, from the play *Camilla's Husband* by Watts Phillips (produced 1879).
Hearts of Oak, with David Belasco (as *Chums*, produced 1879; as *Hearts of Oak*, produced 1879). In *Shore Acres and Other Plays*, 1928; revised version by Herne, as *Sag Harbor* (produced 1900), in *Shore Acres and Other Plays*, 1928.
The Minute Men of 1774–1775 (produced 1886). In *The Early Plays*, 1940.
Drifting Apart (produced 1888). In *The Early Plays*, 1940.
Margaret Fleming (produced 1890). Edited by Myron Matlaw, in *The Black Crook and Other 19th-Century American Plays*, 1967.
My Colleen (produced 1892).
Shore Acres (produced 1893). In *Shore Acres and Other Plays*, 1928.
The Reverend Griffith Davenport, from the novel *An Unofficial Patriot* by Helen H. Gardener (produced 1899). In *The Early Plays*, 1940; Act III edited by Arthur Hobson Quinn, in *American Literature 24*, 1952.

*

Bibliography: "Selected Bibliography of Herne" by John Perry, in *Bulletin of Bibliography 31*, 1974.

Critical Studies: *Herne: The Rise of Realism in the American Drama* by Herbert J. Edwards and Julie A. Herne, 1964; *Herne, The American Ibsen* by John Perry, 1978.

* * *

Most of the plays by the accomplished actor James A. Herne remain in the limbo of strictly minor American drama. *The Minute Men of 1774–1775, Drifting Apart, My Colleen*, or *The Reverend Griffith Davenport*, and even those written in collaboration with David Belasco, including *Within an Inch of His Life, Marriage by Moonlight*, or *Hearts of Oak*, redone by Herne as *Sag Harbor*, are now so obscure as to be virtually unobtainable save in limited library collections. But with *Margaret Fleming* and *Shore Acres* Herne has survived as the most important pivotal American playwright of the late 19th century. In these two plays, particularly the former, Herne took the most significant steps of any American dramatist of his time away from the well-made artificialities of 19th-century romance and melodrama toward the development of effective dramatic realism.

Margaret Fleming abounds in 19th-century conventions and artifices: the wronged young girl who must bear her child in shame and die; the threatened vengeance of the shamed girl's sister, a servant in the home of the seducer; the angelic wife struck blind as she learns of her husband's faithlessness. But the play goes well beyond the surface clichés. The seducer is no caddish rogue, but a successful manufacturer, Philip Fleming, obviously well-respected within the community, and deeply in love with his wife. He is no villain, but neither is he a hero. He is in truth, a "fallen man," and it is his suffering and redemption which motivate a good part of the action, not the fate of the fallen woman who, in life and death, remains offstage, merely a point of reference. The problem of Philip Fleming's infidelity is strictly a domestic matter to be recognized and discussed by husband, wife, and family physician. Margaret Fleming, stunned by her husband's inadequately explained deed, refuses to be martyred and she survives through firmness and conviction evolving out of common sense and rational behavior. Her own behavior as an offended human being, not merely a stereotyped wronged woman, renders her far superior to her husband, whom she permits to return to her but only on her conditions. Reconciliation remains solely a dim hope in the indefinite future.

Thus Herne's skill in giving his central characters the strengths, weaknesses, and motivations of recognizable human individuals well developed within a recognizable contemporary society keeps *Margaret Fleming* from collapse into sentimental bathos. The last act, which survives today through Herne's daughter's reconstruction, refuses to tie up the threads in conventionally neat fashion. There will be a life together for Philip and Margaret Fleming, but the ending, rather than "happy," is believable and eminently satisfactory. The wall remains between husband and wife, but, as Herne acknowledges in this ending (he apparently experimented with several) so shocking to 19th-century audiences, men and women, do, in reality, survive such traumas. They continue their lives; the world does not end; the drama does not conclude with the descent of the final curtain. The "ever after," as in life, is uncertain, possibly dangerous, and even terrifying.

Shore Acres, a lesser play, has too many outdated melodramatics. Still, Herne permits no heroes, no heroines, and no villains. There are logic and sound reason behind the businessman who would foreclose and subdivide the homestead. The love affair and its complications, if we ignore the dark and stormy night syndrome, are understandable. Uncle Nat, the prime mover, talks and acts with reasonable believability. The minor characters, relatively well-developed, enter and depart with clear motivation. For all the frequent transparent arbitrariness, there is a realistic aura in setting, action, and language.

Neither play is a great work of dramatic art. Both, however, are significant. To criticize the creaks and groans of structure is to miss the point of their artistic advances. Though *Margaret Fleming* may have been quite literally driven from the stage by adverse reaction to its daring theme and shocking ending, the courage of the playwright in creating it is recognized for the exceptional deed that it was. The significance of the play, together in a lesser degree with *Shore Acres*, in providing the substantial push behind the American drama's movement toward full-fledged artistic participation in 20th-century world theatre is abundantly apparent.

—Jordan Y. Miller

HERRICK, Robert (Welch). Born in Cambridge, Massachusetts, 26 April 1868. Educated at Cambridge High School, 1881–85; Harvard University, Cambridge (editor, *Harvard Monthly*, 1888), 1885–90, graduated 1890. Married Harriet Emery in 1894 (divorced, 1916), two daughters and one son. Instructor in Rhetoric, Massachusetts Institute of Technology, Cambridge, 1890–93; member of the faculty from 1893, and Professor of English, 1905–23, University of Chicago; teacher, Rollins College, Winter Park, Florida, 1931; secretary to the Governor of the Virgin Islands, 1935–38. *Died 23 December 1938.*

PUBLICATIONS

Fiction

Literary Love-Letters and Other Stories. 1897.
The Man Who Wins. 1897.
The Gospel of Freedom. 1898.
Love's Dilemmas (stories). 1898.
The Web of Life. 1900.
The Real World. 1901; as *Jock o' Dreams*, 1908.
Their Child (stories). 1903.
The Common Lot. 1904.
The Memoirs of an American Citizen. 1905; edited by Daniel Aaron, 1963.
The Master of the Inn (stories). 1908.
Together. 1908.
A Life for a Life. 1910.
The Healer. 1911.
His Great Adventure. 1913.
One Woman's Life. 1913.
Clark's Field. 1914.
The Conscript Mother (stories). 1916.
Homely Lilla. 1923.
Waste. 1924.
Wanderings (stories). 1925.
Chimes. 1926.
The End of Desire. 1932.
Sometime. 1933.

Other

Composition and Rhetoric for Schools, with Lindsay Todd Damon. 1899; revised edition, 1902, 1911, 1922.
Teaching English, with May Estelle Cook and Lindsay Todd Damon. 1899.
The World Decision. 1916.
Little Black Dog. 1931.

*

Critical Studies: *Herrick: The Development of a Novelist* by Blake Nevius, 1962; *Herrick* by Louis J. Budd, 1971.

* * *

In his first novelette, *The Man Who Wins*, Robert Herrick dealt with the question which was to be central to his entire work: what is success? A dedicated medical researcher is diverted into a lucrative practice, but late in life he sees his mistake and encourages young men not to seek material gain. Similarly, in *The Web of Life* a doctor samples and rejects the luxurious life of a society physician and refuses to marry the daughter of a capitalist until she renounces her wealth. *The Master of the Inn* presents a doctor who heals with simple methods in a rural hospital although he commands a knowledge of modern medicine. *The Healer* deals with a Canadian doctor who is traduced by his wife into leaving his spiritually rewarding life in the wild for a financially rewarding practice in Chicago. Disgusted by the avarice of city doctors, the doctor recommends that the professions all become "great monastic orders," and returns to his home.

Other novels contrast the proper use of technical knowledge to help mankind with the use of knowledge for selfish gain. An architect in *The Common Lot* exploits his profession until his shady practices cause several people to be killed in a fire. Business executives climb to the top in their fields before realizing the hollowness of their triumphs in *The Real World, A Life for a Life*, and *Waste*. All the executives atone by working for small, struggling businesses and crusading against trusts. Only the central character of *The Memoirs of an American Citizen*, a meat-packer named Van Harrington who claws his way to a fortune and a seat in the Senate, seems to have few regrets. Herrick was more proud of this characterization than any other, and it is doubtless his best. Herrick enlivened these novels with interesting details from the worlds of business and the professions, freighting them with symbolic weight which skillfully clarified the conflict between the central figures. However, it is not always clear why small businesses in the West are more moral and rewarding than large ones in the East.

In all these novels Herrick buttressed the main plot with a sub-plot contrasting the sordid family relationships of the rich and the more loving and simple ones of the working classes. In *Together, One Woman's Life, Homely Lilla*, and *The End of Desire*, he placed his main emphasis on the problem of women's rights, sexual liberation, and modern marriage. Advanced for his day in these matters, Herrick recommended that women share men's work and that men relieve women from the drudgery of housework and child-rearing. As with business, Herrick finds greed the enemy of good marriages.

Clark's Field shows why private property should not be allowed to restrict urban growth; *Chimes* deals with academic life. Herrick's views on many subjects are summarized in his Utopian novel of the future, *Sometime*.

Even if his novels are occasionally resolved by flimsy devices such as earthquakes or fires, Herrick deserves serious attention for his incisive criticism of his culture and his accurate picture of it.

—William Higgins

HEYWARD, (Edwin) DuBose. Born in Charleston, South Carolina, 31 August 1885. Educated in local schools to age 14. Married Dorothy Hartzell Kuhns (i.e., the playwright Dorothy Heyward) in 1923; one daughter. Worked from 1899 in a hardware store, as clerk with a Charleston steamboat line, and as checker in a cotton shed, 1905–06; partner in an insurance business, 1906–23; founder, with Hervey Allen, Poetry Society of South Carolina, 1920, and subsequently lectured and read his works for the Society throughout the South; full-time writer from 1924. Recipient: Pulitzer Prize, for drama, 1927. Litt.D.: University of North Carolina, Chapel Hill, 1928; College of Charleston, 1929. Honorary member, Phi Beta Kappa; member, American Academy. *Died 16 June 1940.*

PUBLICATIONS

Fiction

Porgy. 1925.
Angel. 1926.
The Half Pint Flask (story). 1929.
Mamba's Daughters. 1929.
Peter Ashley. 1932.
Lost Morning. 1936.
Star Spangled Virgin. 1939.

Plays

Porgy, with Dorothy Heyward, from the novel by DuBose Heyward (produced 1927). 1927.
Brass Ankle (produced 1931). 1931.
Porgy and Bess (libretto), lyrics with Ira Gershwin, music by George Gershwin (produced 1935). 1935.
Mamba's Daughters, with Dorothy Heyward, from the novel by DuBose Heyward (produced 1939). 1939.

Screenplay: *The Emperor Jones*, 1933.

Verse

Carolina Chansons: Legends of the Low Country, with Hervey Allen. 1922.
Skylines and Horizons. 1924.
Jasbo Brown and Selected Poems. 1931.

Other

Fort Sumter, with Herbert Ravenel Sass. 1938.
The Country Bunny and the Little Gold Shoes (for children). 1939.

Editor, with others, *Year Book of the Poetry Society of South Carolina, 1921–24*. 4 vols., 1921–24.

*

Critical Studies: *Heyward: A Critical and Biographical Sketch* by Hervey Allen, 1927; *Heyward, The Man Who Wrote Porgy*, 1954, and *Heyward's Use of Folklore in His Negro Fiction*, 1961, both by Frank Durham; *Heyward* by William H. Slavick, 1981.

* * *

Novelist, storywriter, playwright, and poet, DuBose Heyward was a sensitive romantic artist whose earnest but realistic humanitarianism, sympathetic understanding of blacks, and lyrical evocations of the landscape, folklore, and legends of his region made him a forerunner of the southern literary movement which the Poetry Society of South Carolina, under his leadership, helped to initiate among writers' groups and little magazines in the 1920's. His poetry, dealing mainly with the grim battle for survival on the mountains, nostalgic descriptions of low country life, and the mystery and vitality of the black personality, brought him early recognition and served as a crucible for experimenting with the settings, themes, incidents, and tones he was to exploit later in his fiction and drama. It is not hard to see how crucially his novel *Angel* and short story "Brute"—to think of two instances—depend on poems such as "A Mountain Woman" and "A Yoke of Steers" for their vivid scenic particulars, characterization, and treatment of the innate strength and resilience of the human spirit engaged in a fierce and near-impossible struggle with a hostile environment.

Porgy, Heyward's most popular and accomplished novel (which he later adapted into a play, and then into the musical *Porgy and Bess*), makes full use of his poetic and narrative gifts. Heyward subtly intertwines the developing stages of his narrative with the cycle of seasons to provide symbolic elevation to his story of a beggar-murderer whose futile search for stability and peace eventually leads to the recognition that the inexorable pressure of a contrary, even malevolent, fate can be withstood, if not substantially reduced, by an attitude of acceptance. In *Mamba's Daughters*, a more ambitious though less competently executed novel, a variant of the same theme is employed in recounting the trials of three generations of a black family in their upward climb toward security and prosperity.

But, to Heyward, the black was more than a symbol of resistance against overwhelming odds: he was, in most events, conceived as an emissary from an enchanting world of exotic customs and beliefs, possessing an inimitable primitive aura and energy that are vulnerable to the forces of modernization. This view of blacks is given eloquent expression in "The Half-Pint Flask," a haunting story about the erosion of rational and scientific attitudes in the face of time-honoured superstitions. Approaching the same issue in an altered context in *Star Spangled Virgin*, Heyward uses entertaining but biting satire to expose the inadequacy of all reformist measures that ignore the intractable rhythms and perceptions of black life. Such views are also symptomatic of his whole-hearted agreement with a primary assumption of southern writing that art belongs more to the realm of the heart than of the head.

An uneven writer whose later performance, despite occasional enthusiastic responses, never really measured up to the expectations aroused by his early promise, Heyward wrote at his best when he employed dramatic contrivances such as violence and natural calamities to lend pace to his narratives. His treatment of ideas generally tended to be feeble and often regressed to the level of dull pontification. *Porgy* is the single work for which he is likely to be remembered, for it has become, in Frank Durham's words, "a part of native folklore, its characters and their romantic story having gradually so embedded themselves into the group consciousness that the name of their creator is almost forgotten. Not many authors have gained such enduring, if increasingly anonymous, immortality."

—Chirantan Kulshrestha

HOFFMAN, Charles Fenno. Born in New York City, 7 February 1806. Educated at schools in New York and New Jersey; Columbia University, New York, 1821–23; studied law with Harmanus Bleecker, Albany, New York; admitted to New York bar, 1827. Lawyer in New York City, 1827–30; editor with Charles King, New York *American*, 1829–33; editor, *Knickerbocker* magazine, New York, 1833; toured the midwest, 1833–34; editor *American Monthly*, New York, 1835–37, and New York *Mirror*, 1837; full-time writer, 1838–39; associate editor, with Horace Greeley, *New Yorker*, 1840; third chief clerk, 1841–43, and deputy surveyor, 1843–44, Office of the Surveyor of Customs of the Port of New York; full-time writer, 1844–47; editor, *Literary World*, New York, 1847–49; became insane: confined to the State Hospital, Harrisburg, Pennsylvania, 1849–84. A.M.: Columbia University, 1837. *Died 7 June 1884.*

PUBLICATIONS

Verse

The Vigil of Faith and Other Poems. 1842; revised edition, as *Songs and Other Poems*, 1846.
The Echo; or, Borrowed Notes for Home Circulation. 1844.
Love's Calendar, Lays of the Hudson, and Other Poems. 1847.
Poems, edited by Edward F. Hoffman. 1873.

Fiction

Wild Scenes in the Forest and Prairie. 1839.
Greyslaer: A Romance of the Mohawk. 1840.

Other

A Winter in the West. 2 vols., 1835.
The Pioneers of New-York. 1848.

Editor, *The New-York Book of Poetry*. 1837; as *The Gems of American Poetry*, 1840.

*

Bibliography: in *Bibliography of American Literature* by Jacob Blanck, 1963.

Critical Studies: *Hoffman* by Homer F. Barnes, 1930.

* * *

During the 1830's and 1840's, Charles Fenno Hoffman was among the more influential of a group of "literati," as Edgar Allan Poe referred to them, who called themselves the "Knickerbockers," a term made famous by Washington Irving's *A History of New-York* (written as Diedrich Knickerbocker) and by the *Knickerbocker* (1833–65), which Hoffman helped to found. This group, which included James Fenimore Cooper, William Cullen Bryant, and Irving, among others, tried to shape the literary tastes of the nation and to make New York the literary center of the day. It especially encouraged the writing of literature on American themes, and it was dedicated to improving the quality and variety of American literature as it then existed.

Hoffman's works reflect the concerns and preoccupations of the Knickerbocker group. His best poems are those which romanticize the splendor and potentiality of the American landscape. Of these, the most memorable include "To the Hudson River," "The Morning Hymn," "Forest Musings," and "Moonlight on the Hudson." Skilled in the art of prosody, Hoffman injected a lyrical quality into his verse which made many of his poems extremely popular, especially those which were set to music. "Monterey," for example, was for many years one of the most popular ballads written in America, and it is still sung today.

Hoffman's prose, like his verse, was strongly nationalistic in its intentions and themes. His best known novel, *Greyslaer: A Romance of the Mohawk*, was a fictional adaptation of the infamous Beauchamp-Sharp murder case. Critics appreciated *Greyslaer*; it went into two editions, and for a time competed successfully with the frontier romances of Cooper and Simms. The result of an excursion on horseback through Ohio, Illinois, Michigan, Iowa, and Pennsylvania, *A Winter in the West* provided may Americans with their first detailed account of life on the western frontier as it existed in the early 1830's. A skilled observer, Hoffman mastered the genre of travel literature. His discrimination and learning allowed him to select and describe incidents and characters which transcend regional particularities and which, even today, provide insight into whatever part of America he visited.

As a critic and editor for some of the most influential literary magazines of his day, Hoffman encouraged the writing and publication of books and literature on American subjects. He believed that it was the critic's function to encourage excellence rather than to denigrate needlessly. He especially encouraged young writers who he felt might profit from some degree of public recognition, even if undeserved. About *Typee*, Herman Melville's first novel, Hoffman wrote: "One of the most delightful and well written narratives that ever came from an

American pen." He was also instrumental in helping such then unknown writers as Francis Parkman, whose classic account of overland adventure, *The California and Oregon Trail*, was recommended by Hoffman for publication.

Regrettably, Hoffman's literary career was cut short by illness and financial worries. Unable to support himself by writing, he was forced to take a position in a New York customs office. For several years he had been working on an historical novel to be called *Red Spur of the Ramapo* which he hoped would be his greatest literary success but which was accidentally destroyed by his maid, who used it as kindling. This unfortunate mishap proved too much for Hoffman. With nerves already weakened from excessive toil and worry, he began treatment for a mental disorder which eventuated in his incarceration at the state hospital in Harrisburg, Pennsylvania, where he spent the remaining 35 years of his life, contented but hopelessly insane.

—James A. Levernier

HOLMES, Oliver Wendell. Born in Cambridge, Massachusetts, 29 August 1809. Educated at Phillips Academy, Andover, Massachusetts; Harvard University, Cambridge, Massachusetts, graduated 1829; studied law for one year; studied medicine in Paris, 1834–35, and at Harvard Medical School, M.D. 1836. Married Amelia Lee Jackson in 1840; two sons (including the jurist Oliver Wendell Holmes, Jr.) and one daughter. Practised medicine in Boston; Professor of Anatomy and Physiology, Dartmouth College, Hanover, New Hampshire, 1839–40; discovered that puerperal fever is contagious, 1843; Parkman Professor of Anatomy, Harvard Medical School, 1847–82. Recipient: Boylston Prize, for medical essays, 1836, 1837. Honorary degrees: Edinburgh University, 1886; Oxford University, 1887; Cambridge University, 1887. *Died 7 October 1894.*

PUBLICATIONS

Collections

Complete Poetical Works, edited by Horace E. Scudder. 1895.
Representative Selections, edited by S. I. Hayakawa and Howard Mumford Jones. 1939.
Poetical Works, edited by Eleanor M. Tilton. 1975.

Verse

The Harbinger: A May-Gift. 1833.
Poems. 1836; revised edition, 1846, 1848, 1849.
Urania: A Rhymed Lesson. 1846.
Astraea: The Balance of Illusions. 1850.
Poetical Works. 1852.
Songs and Poems of the Class of 1829, second edition. 1859; revised edition, 1868.
Songs in Many Keys. 1861.
Poems. 1862.
Humorous Poems. 1865.
Songs of Many Seasons 1862–1874. 1874.
Poetical Works. 1877.
The Iron Gate and Other Poems. 1880.
Poetical Works. 2 vols., 1881.
Illustrated Poems. 1885.
Before the Curfew and Other Poems, Chiefly Occasional. 1888.
At Dartmouth: The Phi Beta Kappa Poem 1839. 1940.

Fiction

Elsie Venner: A Romance of Destiny. 1861.
The Guardian Angel. 1867.
A Mortal Antipathy: First Opening of the New Portfolio. 1885.

Other

Boylston Prize Dissertations for 1836 and 1837. 1838.
Homoeopathy and Its Kindred Delusions (lectures). 1842.
The Autocrat of the Breakfast-Table. 1858.
The Professor at the Breakfast-Table, with the Story of Iris. 1860.
Currents and Counter-Currents in Medical Science, with Other Addresses and Essays. 1861.
Soundings from the Atlantic. 1863.
Mechanism in Thought and Morals. 1871.
The Poet at the Breakfast-Table: His Talks with His Fellow-Boarders and the Reader. 1872.
John Lothrop Motley: A Memoir. 1878.
The School-Boy. 1879.
Poems and Prose Passages, edited by Josephine E. Hodgdon. 1881.
Medical Essays 1842–1882. 1883.
Pages from an Old Volume of Life: A Collection of Essays 1857–1881. 1883.
Ralph Waldo Emerson. 1884.
Our Hundred Days in Europe. 1887.
Over the Teacups. 1890.
Writings. 14 vols., 1891–92.
A Dissertation on Acute Pericarditis. 1937.
The Autocrat's Miscellanies, edited by Albert Mordell. 1959.

Editor, with Jacob Bigelow, *Principles of the Theory and Practice of Medicine*, by Marshall Hall. 1839.
Editor, with Donald Grant Mitchell, *The Atlantic Almanac 1868*. 1867.

*

Bibliography: *Bibliography of Holmes* by Thomas Franklin Currier and Eleanor M. Tilton, 1953; in *Bibliography of American Literature* by Jacob Blanck, 1963.

Critical Studies: *Life and Letters of Holmes* by John T. Morse, Jr., 2 vols., 1896; *Holmes of the Breakfast-Table* by M. A. De Wolfe Howe, 1936; *Amiable Autocrat: A Biography of Holmes* by Eleanor M. Tilton, 1947; *Holmes* by Miriam R. Small, 1963; *The Improper Bostonian* by Edwin P. Hoyt, 1979.

* * *

The great popular reputation of Oliver Wendell Holmes in the 19th century receded with the eclipse of New England preeminence. Except for the rural Whittier, Holmes was the most provincial of the New England writers, and unlike the others he did not espouse causes. The Boston of his occasional verse and genial essays was not (according to the editors of *Representative Selections*) "the rebellious Boston, out of which came the anti-slavery societies, transcendentalism, and the feminist movement." In the opening chapter of his first novel (*Elsie Venner*) Holmes describes and provides a lasting label for cultured, mercantile Bostonians with Bulfinch houses, Beacon Street addresses, and ancestral portraits. He became the spokesman for this "Brahmin Caste of New England" when his *The Autocrat of the Breakfast-Table* began to appear in the *Atlantic Monthly* in 1857. Although his public had read his occasional poems even since he was a Harvard undergraduate, his new image as "the Autocrat" established Holmes's reputation as a major American writer.

There had been little time for writing prose between 1830 and 1857, for Holmes had become an M.D. and held professorships of anatomy at Dartmouth and Harvard. But Holmes was a brilliant and incessant talker, and when he hit upon the scheme of jotting down his own talk, he had the matter for his essay series. Literary historians agree that his personality imposed itself upon and gave unity to his writing—poetry, essays, and fiction alike. There is a consistent mental set in his writing also: he was a clear-headed rationalist who disliked even the "bullying" of science and abhorred the dogmatism of theology. His attacks on Calvinism were his closest approximation to taking up a cause, but it seems strange now that Boston thought of him as an American Voltaire. However, Holmes liked to point out the parallels between his own life and Dr. Johnson's. Johnson was born in 1709, Holmes in 1809; both were urban beings, and Holmes's devotion to Boston matched Johnson's love of London. Both were great talkers and were devoted to common sense; and, though his wit has not survived as well as Johnson's, one, at least, of Holmes's remarks is remembered: "Boston State-House is the hub of the solar system. You couldn't pry that out of a Boston man if you had the tire of all creation straightened out for a crowbar."

The *Atlantic Monthly* version of *The Autocrat of the Breakfast-Table* begins, "I was just going to say, when I was interrupted." After the twelve *Atlantic* installments had become a book in 1858, the author explains that the interruption had lasted a quarter of a century, since two articles entitled "The Autocrat of the Breakfast Table" had appeared in the *New England Magazine* in 1831 and 1832. He had matured and gained confidence in the 25-year interval: along with his medical practice and professorships, he had published important medical essays—and a volume of poems. His Harvard lectures were as celebrated for their wit as for their learning, and from 1841 to 1857 he was a sought-after lyceum lecturer on literary as well as medical subjects. But Dr. Holmes was becoming even better known in Boston and Cambridge as a genial humorist and master of conversation.

His fellow-Brahmin, James Russell Lowell, accepted the editorship of the *Atlantic Monthly* on the condition that Holmes become a regular contributor. Holmes had suggested the name for the new magazine; and there were Holmes's poems, essays, articles, and reviews or installments of novels in the magazine every year until 1893. The *Atlantic* published 65 Holmes poems, each of his three novels, three series of *Autocrat* sequels—*The Professor at the Breakfast-Table*, *The Poet at the Breakfast-Table*, and *Over the Teacups*—and *Our Hundred Days in Europe*.

It is difficult to evaluate Holmes's writing on medical subjects, or determine how his role as a doctor and professor of anatomy related to his literary career. Scientific medicine was just beginning a phenomenal advance in Holmes's day, but it is generally agreed that his own chief claim to medical distinction was his excellence as a teacher. Most interest in recent years has focused on his three "medicated novels" (Holmes accepted the term of a "dear old lady" who refused to read them): *Elsie Venner, The Guardian Angel*, and *A Moral Antipathy* has been judged "so absurd that it hardly bears repetition." Psychologists and psychiatrists have found validity and importance in the neuroses pictured in these novels, some of them profoundly shocking to Holmes's readers a hundred years ago.

To the 20th century, Oliver Wendell Holmes was a writer of verse, not poetry—which even his contemporaries might have conceded. Significantly, both "The Deacon's Masterpiece" (or "One Hoss Shay"—sometimes interpreted as an allegory of New England Calvinism) and "The Chambered Nautilus," his acknowledged masterpiece, were both "recited" by the Autocrat of the Breakfast Table.

To the generations growing up in the first half of the 20th century, the name Oliver Wendell Holmes meant the distinguished jurist whom Franklin Roosevelt had hailed in 1933 as "the greatest living American." This son and namesake, the only member of his family to outlive Dr. Holmes, had his father's clear-headed rationalistic turn of mind—but none of his other traits. Fifty years after the son's death, the elder Holmes is again emerging as a distinct figure: the conservative but clear-sighted, talkative Brahmin, who liked mill-owners better than abolitionists and transcendentalists, and who lived long enough to write graceful poetic tributes to nearly all of the nineteenth-century New England worthies.

—Clarence A. Glasrud

HOOPER, Johnson Jones. Born in Wilmington, North Carolina, 9 June 1815. Educated in local schools. Married Mary Mildred Brantley in 1842; two sons and one daughter. Printer's devil on newspapers, Charleston, South Carolina, 1826–32; read law with his brother in La Fayette, Alabama, 1835–37: admitted to Alabama bar, 1838; census taker for Tallapoosa County, Dadeville, Alabama, 1840; lawyer from 1841, (in practice with his brother from 1842); editor, La Fayette *East Alabamian*, 1843–45, and Wetumpka *Whig*, Alabama, 1845–46; member of the editorial staff, *Alabama Journal*, Montgomery, 1846–49; editor and part owner, *Chambers County Tribune*, La Fayette, 1850–53; solicitor, 9th Alabama Judicial Circuit, 1849–53; editor, Montgomery *Mail*, 1854–61; secretary, Allegheny Mining Company, 1859; secretary, Provisional Congress of the Southern States, Richmond, 1861–62. *Died 7 June 1862.*

PUBLICATIONS

Fiction and Sketches

Some Adventures of Captain Simon Suggs, Late of the Tallapoosa Volunteers, Together with Taking the Census and Other Alabama Sketches. 1845; augmented edition, 1848.

A Ride with Old Kit Kuncker and Other Sketches and Scenes of Alabama. 1849.

The Widow Rugby's Husband, A Night at the Ugly Man's, and Other Tales of Alabama. 1851.
Dog and Gun: A Few Loose Chapters on Shooting. 1856.

Other

Editor, *Reminiscences of the Creek, or Muscogee Indians*, by Thomas S. Woodward. 1859.

*

Critical Studies: *The Southern Poor-White from Lubberland to Tobacco Road* by Shields McIlwaine, 1939; *Alias Simon Suggs: The Life and Times of Hooper* by W. Stanley Hoole, 1952; *Hooper: A Critical Study* by Howard Winston Smith, 1963; introduction by Manly Wade Wellman to *Adventures of Captain Simon Suggs*, 1969.

* * *

The achievement of Johnson Jones Hooper is rooted in his contributions to 19th-century southwest humor, a broadly realistic, often satiric, sometimes cold-blooded, oral-vernacular taletelling revealing a near absence of civilized standards of conduct. Some establishment critics of the early 20th century tended virtually to dismiss Hooper's art as "discomfiture"—an "ancient, primitive, anti-social kind of merry-making." Despite such narrow judgment, Hooper's work was well received in its own day, appearing in such popular American humor anthologies as *The Big Bear of Arkansas* and *Polly Peablossom's Wedding and Other Tales*. Moreover, within an eighteen year period 21 editions of Hooper's books appeared, eleven editions of his masterpiece, *Some Adventures of Captain Simon Suggs*, appearing between 1845 and 1856.

In form, the work has long been viewed as campaign biography, and hence tied to the political machinations of frontier folk. The work, however, can be taken as a burlesque of campaign biography, with specific events based on Andrew Jackson's military career.

Suggs himself is perhaps the "bad boy" of American literature, a man proficient in the art of drinking, joking, and staying just a step ahead of his creditors. Hooper's biographer, W. Stanley Hoole, cites Bird Young of Tallapoosa County as the historical model for Suggs. As fictional creation, Suggs, however, is the epitome of the poor-white. Shields McIlwaine notes that the adventurer has a "long nose hung above a mouth stained by the filthy weed . . .," his family living in "woolhat poverty." As a cultural-sociological phenomenon, Suggs originates perhaps in the Lubberland of William Byrd.

More than any other character from frontier humor, however, Suggs is indebted to the European tradition of the picaresque. As Howard Winston Smith has noted in his helpful critical study, both Suggs and Don Quixote undergo imitation promotions (Suggs to captaincy and Quixote to knighthood), and both works are episodic in nature. The general picaresque trait of the "picaro and the priest," moreover, originating in *Lazarillo de Tormes*, accounts in large part for Hooper's greatest moment in his most frequently anthologized chapter, "The Captain Attends a Camp Meeting." That particular chapter ultimately became the source for chapter twenty of *Huckleberry Finn*. Hooper ties together the many episodes by having each end in the triumph of frontier rascality over both innocence and sophistication.

None of Hooper's later writings has been judged equal to his first book. Both *The Widow Rugby's Husband, A Night at the Ugly Man's, and Other Tales of Alabama* and *Dog and Gun* attest to the author's love of the life he knew, but neither work reveals the real Hooper that Thackeray judged the "most promising writer of his day."

—George C. Longest

HOPKINSON, Francis. Born in Philadelphia, Pennsylvania, 2 October 1737. Educated at the Academy of Philadelphia (now University of Pennsylvania), 1751–57, A.B. 1757, A.M. 1760; studied law with Benjamin Chew, 1757–61: admitted to Pennsylvania bar, 1761, and New Jersey bar, 1775. Married Ann Borden in 1768; one son. Began study of harpsichord, 1754; gave first public performance, 1757, and later set poems and psalms to music: first American-born composer of secular songs, 1759; developed improved method of quilling harpsichords; collector of customs, Port of Salem, New Jersey, 1763, and New Castle, Delaware, 1772; lawyer in Philadelphia and Bordentown, New Jersey, in 1760's and 1770's; also ran a store in Philadelphia; member, New Jersey Governor's Council, 1774, and New Jersey Provincial Congress, 1774–76; delegate from New Jersey, Second Continental Congress, 1775–76; signed the Declaration of Independence; subsequently served the new U.S. Government as chairman of the Continental Navy Board, 1776–78, and treasurer of the Continental Loan Office, 1778–81; Judge of Admiralty for Pennsylvania, 1779–89; member, Pennsylvania convention to ratify the Constitution, 1787; judge, U.S. District Court for Pennsylvania, 1789–91. Founding member, American Philosophical Society; a designer of the Great Seal of New Jersey, 1776; credited with the design of the American flag, 1777; secretary of the convention that organized the Protestant Episcopal Church, 1789. *Died 9 May 1791.*

PUBLICATIONS

Collections

The First American Composer, edited by Harold V. Milligan. 1919.
Comical Spirit of Seventy-Six: The Humor of Hopkinson, edited by P.M. Zall. 1976.

Verse

An Exercise. 1761.
Science. 1762.
A Collection of Psalm Tunes. 1762.
A Psalm of Thanksgiving. 1766.
The Psalms of David in Metre. 1767.
The Battle of the Kegs. 1779.
An Ode. 1788.
A Set of Eight Songs. 1788.
Ode from Ossian's Poems. 1794.

Play

The Temple of Minerva (oratorio), music by Hopkinson (produced 1781).

Fiction

A Pretty Story, Written in the Year of Our Lord 2774. 1774; as *The Old Farm and the New Farm: A Political Allegory*, 1857.

Other

Errata; or, The Art of Printing Incorrectly. 1763.
Account of the Grand Federal Procession. 1788.
Judgments in the Admiralty of Pennsylvania. 1789.
Miscellaneous Essays and Occasional Writings. 3 vols., 1792.

*

Critical Studies: *The Life and Works of Hopkinson* by George E. Hastings, 1926 (includes bibliography); "Hopkinson and Franklin" by Dixon Wecter, in *American Literature 12*, 1940.

* * *

Poet, politician, musician, judge, scientist, and artist, Francis Hopkinson excelled in so many activities that his contributions to American culture defy easy classification. A friend while in college of the Philadelphia writers Nathaniel Evans, Thomas Godfrey, and Jacob Duché, Hopkinson early showed an interest in a literary career. More than any other event, however, the Revolutionary War shaped Hopkinson's interests, and it is with the war that he is associated today. As a member of the Second Continental Congress, Hopkinson signed the Declaration of Independence, an action which alone was enough to guarantee him a place in history.

Not the least of his accomplishments were the many poems and essays he wrote in support of his country's decision to separate from Great Britain. His verses, most of which satirized the British and praised the Americans, were light, humorous, and deft. While not the stuff of great poetry, they accomplished what they were intended to do. Easily set to music, they lifted the spirits of American soldiers who sang them at the front, and they helped to demoralize the British by good naturedly ridiculing their cause. Hopkinson's most famous poem, *The Battle of the Kegs*, recounts in ballad form how the British, unfamiliar with explosives, battled relentlessly with a flotilla of mines which American patriots had ingeniously floated in kegs down the Delaware River toward their camp. Other famous poems written by Hopkinson during the Revolutionary War include "A Camp Ballad," "The Toast," and "Tory Medley." Together these poems made Hopkinson one of the most popular American poets of his day—"penman of the Revolution."

Equally popular were the prose essays and tracts which Hopkinson directed against the British. From Arbuthnot, Swift, Addison, and Steele, Hopkinson developed a fondness for satire, particularly when it was couched in the form of allegory or a fabricated letter. Like his verse, Hopkinson's prose was extremely effective anti-British propaganda. Written in the form of a humorous allegory, and inspired by Arbuthnot's *History of John Bull*, *A Pretty Story* depicts the events which led the Colonies to declare their independence. In "A Prophecy," also an allegory, Hopkinson uses the persona of a biblical prophet who predicts the establishment of a new and prosperous government in North America.

Although Hopkinson frequently contributed poems and essays to such periodicals as the *American Magazine*, the *Columbian Magazine*, and the *Pennsylvania Packet*, his writing before and after the war lacked the vigor which the conflict itself inspired in him. With the possible exception of "My Days Have Been So Wondrous Free" (1759), a work which is thought to be the oldest American song known, his early and late poetry, for the most part dull and uninteresting, is rarely read today. His letters are more profitable because he corresponded with the most important statesmen of his day, including George Washington, Benjamin Franklin, and Thomas Jefferson. *Miscellaneous Essays and Occasional Writings*, collected by Hopkinson himself, contains only a small portion of his total literary output. Many of his writings, particularly those written for periodicals, have yet to be collected.

—James A. Levernier

HOVEY, Richard. Born in Normal, Illinois, 4 May 1864. Educated at Dartmouth College, Hanover, New Hampshire (editor, *Aegis*), 1881–85, B.A. (cum laude) 1885; Episcopal Seminary, New York, 1886. Married Henrietta Russell in 1894; one son. Teacher, Thomas Davidson's Summer School of Philosophy, 1888; actor, 1890; lived in England, 1894, and France, 1895–96; teacher, Barnard College, New York, 1899–1900. *Died 24 February 1900.*

PUBLICATIONS

Verse

Poems. 1880.
The Laurel: An Ode to Mary Day Lanier. 1889.
Harmonics. 1890.
Seaward: An Elegy on the Death of Thomas William Parsons. 1893.
Songs from Vagabondia, with Bliss Carman. 1894; *More Songs*, 1896; *Last Songs*, 1900.
Along the Trail: A Book of Lyrics. 1898.
To the End of the Trail, edited by Mrs. Richard Hovey. 1908.
Dartmouth Lyrics, edited by Edwin Osgood Grover. 1924.
A Poem and Three Letters. 1935.

Plays

Launcelot and Guenevere: A Poem in Dramas (includes *The Quest of Merlin* and *The Marriage of Guenevere*). 1891; revised versions of *The Marriage of Guenevere*, 1895, and of *The Quest of Merlin*, 1898.
The Birth of Galahad. 1898.
Taliesin: A Masque. 1899.
The Holy Graal and Other Fragments, Being the Uncompleted Parts of the Arthurian Dramas, edited by Mrs. Richard Hovey. 1907.

Other

Hanover by Gaslight; or, Ways That Are Dark, Being an Exposé of the Sophomoric Career of '85. 1883(?).

Translator, *The Plays of Maurice Maeterlinck: Princess Maleine, The Intruder, The Blind, The Seven Princesses.*

1894; second series (includes *Alladine and Palomides, Pelleas and Melisande, Home, The Death of Tintagiles*), 1896.

*

Bibliography: in *Bibliography of American Literature* by Jacob Blanck, 1963.

Critical Studies: *Hovey, Man and Craftsman* by Allan Houston Macdonald, 1957 (includes bibliography by Edward Connery Lathem); *Hovey* by William R. Linneman, 1976.

* * *

Like his contemporary Stephen Crane, Richard Hovey died tragically young, before he could fulfill the artistic promise he demonstrated, before he could make himself felt as a major force in modern poetry. But unlike Crane, Hovey did not seek to confront the turbulence and brutality of his age; yet he rebelled against it in *fin de siècle* aestheticism, in the spirit of bohemianism, of carefree youth, cheerful pleasures, and hearty fellowship. This spirit ruled his life and his poetry.

After graduating in 1885 from Dartmouth College, where he was active in campus literary life (Hovey celebrates the college in many poems, including "Men of Dartmouth," "Hanover Winter Song," and "Our Liege Lady, Dartmouth"), he studied to become an Episcopal priest, but left the seminary after one year. In 1887, he met the artist Tom Meteyard and the Canadian poet Bliss Carman, with both of whom he collaborated on the *Vagabondia* books. The dominant theme in these little volumes is that of the bold and energetic young man, "Wandering with the wandering wind, / Vagabond and unconfined!" ("The Wander-Lovers"); these short lyrics describe Hovey's world, one of adventurous, genteel Bohemianism, dedicated to comradeship and a love of Art. Hovey and Carman each wrote about half the number of poems in the books, which were popular, especially among college students, around the turn of the century.

Hovey was also a serious dramatic poet, planning (but never finishing) a series of verse plays on the Arthurian legends (a world popular with much escapist art and literature of the late 19th century).

A major influence acknowledged by Hovey is that of the American poet Sidney Lanier. Hovey's ode *The Laurel* (dedicated to Mrs. Lanier) and his serious lyric poetry, notably the elegy *Seaward*, reflect Lanier's rhythms and images. Hovey was also influenced by the French *symbolistes*, and translated Mallarmé and Maeterlinck. But he did not have enough time in which to develop his own lyrical talent into a unique or influential poetic voice.

—Jane S. Gabin

HOWARD, Bronson (Crocker). Born in Detroit, Michigan, 7 October 1842. Educated at schools in Detroit, and at Russell's Institute, New Haven, Connecticut. Married Alice Wyndham in 1880. Staff member, Detroit *Free Press*; began writing for the stage, 1864; moved to New York, 1865, and worked as a reporter for *Evening Mail, Tribune*, and *Evening Post*, until his first dramatic success, 1870; thereafter a full-time playwright. Founder, 1891, and first President, American Dramatists Club (later the Society of American Dramatists and Composers). *Died 4 August 1908.*

PUBLICATIONS

Collections

The Banker's Daughter and Other Plays (includes *Old Love Letters, One of Our Girls, Hurricanes, Knave and Queen, Baron Rudolph*), edited by Allan G. Halline. 1941.

Plays

Fantine (produced 1864).

Saratoga; or, Pistols for Seven (produced 1870). 1870.

Ingomar the Idiotic; or, The Miser, The Maid, and the Mangle, with Oswald Allen (produced 1871).

Diamonds (produced 1872).

The Banker's Daughter (as *Lilian's Lost Love*, produced 1873; revised version as *The Banker's Daughter*, produced 1878; as *The Old Love and the New*, produced 1879). 1878; in *The Banker's Daughter and Other Plays*, 1941.

Moorcroft; or, The Double Wedding (produced 1874).

Knave and Queen, with Charles L. Young (as *Ivers Dean*, produced 1877). In *The Banker's Daughter and Other Plays*, 1941.

Old Love Letters (produced 1878). 1897; in *The Banker's Daughter and Other Plays*, 1941.

Hurricanes (produced 1878; as *Truth*, produced 1878). In *The Banker's Daughter and Other Plays*, 1941.

Wives, from a play by Molière (produced 1879).

The Amateur Benefit. 1881.

Baron Rudolph (produced 1881; revised version, with David Belasco, produced 1887). In *The Banker's Daughter and Other Plays*, 1941.

Fun in a Green Room (produced 1882).

Young Mrs. Winthrop (produced 1882). 1899.

One of Our Girls (produced 1885; as *Cousin Kate*, produced 1889). 1897; in *The Banker's Daughter and Other Plays*, 1941.

Camping Out (produced 1886).

Met by Chance (produced 1887).

The Henrietta (produced 1887). 1901; edited by Allan G. Halline, in *American Plays*, 1935.

Shenandoah (produced 1888). 1897; edited by Arthur Hobson Quinn, in *Representative American Plays*, 1917.

Aristocracy (produced 1892). 1898.

Peter Stuyvesant, with Brander Matthews (produced 1899).

Fiction

Kate. 1906.

Other

The Autobiography of a Play (on *The Banker's Daughter*). 1914.

*

Critical Study: *In Memoriam Bronson Howard* (addresses), 1910.

* * *

The contribution to American drama which inspired some critics to describe Bronson Howard as the "Dean of American Drama" derives largely from his ability to support himself as a dramatist, the first American to achieve this distinction. As a professional dramatist he founded the American Dramatists Club in 1891, lectured at Harvard on what he termed "The Laws of Dramatic Composition," established himself firmly as the major playwright to deal with the American businessman, and brought to American drama the international social scene which was then being exploited in fiction with considerable success by Henry James and William Dean Howells.

The fact that Howard could make a career as a playwright suggests something about his abilities. A a good craftsman of the stage, he understood and accepted the commercially oriented conventions and limiting requirements of the late 19th-century American theatre. Although he was markedly more farsighted than his contemporaries in terms of his chosen themes and materials, he carefully adhered to his own outline of a well-constructed play which must be "satisfactory" to an audience and reach a properly moral and happy conclusion. Toward the end of his career he weakened his position as a man of independent thought by joining the stable of playwrights of the Theatrical Syndicate. He was always a man of the theatre, sometimes belligerently so, and it was never his intention to pull together the established rift in America between theatre and drama. Indeed, his expressed antagonism toward dramatic literature and literary people probably further delayed a developing American drama.

A major characteristic of his playwriting was the carefully crafted and commercially successful work which suggested a direction for future dramatists whose careers among theatre managers would be more secure after Howard's efforts. His first success was a play called *Saratoga*, for which he embroidered the usual farce action with better than average farce dialogue and used a favorite American resort as his scene. The fact that the play was transferred successfully to English circumstances by Frank Marshall as *Brighton* (1874) suggests something of his style. More significant are his business plays. *Young Mrs. Winthrop* showed the difficulties which the demands of the business world may bring to married life. *The Henrietta* satirized life on the New York Stock Exchange. *Aristocracy* combined Howard's interest in the American businessman and the socially intriguing international scene by revealing that the obvious route by which new wealth of the American west might unite with New York traditional society was through London aristocracy. In an earlier play, *One of Our Girls*, Howard contrasted American and French social conventions. His single play—a very successful one—which remains outside his usual society-oriented work is *Shenandoah*, a romantic tale of the Civil War.

Basically a transitional dramatist in American theatre, Howard helped to diminish the popularity of foreign plays on the American stage and give the American dramatist greater importance in the theatre. This is his real contribution. Otherwise, he was a generally skillful dramatist for his time who could write entertaining and sentimental social melodrama.

—Walter J. Meserve

HOWARD, Sidney (Coe). Born in Oakland, California, 26 June 1891. Educated at the University of California, Berkeley (editor, *Occident*), 1911–15, B.A. 1915; studied with George Pierce Baker at Harvard University, Cambridge, Massachusetts, 1915–16, A.M. 1916. Served in the American Ambulance Corps, and later in the U.S. Army Air Corps, during World War I: Captain; Silver Star. Married 1) the actress Clare Jenness Eames in 1922 (divorced, 1930), one daughter; 2) Leopoldine Blaine Damrosch in 1931, one daughter and one son. Member of the editorial staff, 1919–22, and literary editor, 1922, *Life* magazine, New York; special investigator and feature writer, *New Republic* and *Hearst's International Magazine*, New York, 1923; full-time playwright from 1923; founder, with Robert E. Sherwood, Elmer Rice, Maxwell Anderson, S.N. Behrman, and John F. Wharton, Playwrights Company, 1938. Member, Board of Directors, American Civil Liberties Union; President, Dramatists Guild, 1935–37. Recipient: Pulitzer Prize, 1925; Oscar, for screenplay, 1940. Litt.D.: Washington and Jefferson College, Washington, Pennsylvania, 1935. Member, American Academy. *Died 23 August 1939.*

Publications

Plays

The Sons of Spain (produced 1914).
Swords (produced 1921). 1921.
S.S. Tenacity, from work by Charles Vildrac (produced 1922).
Sancho Panza, from play by Melchior Lengyel (produced 1923).
Casanova, from a play by Lorenzo de Azertis (produced 1923). 1924.
They Knew What They Wanted (produced 1924). 1925.
Bewitched, with Edward Sheldon (produced 1924).
Lexington (produced 1925). 1924(?).
Michel Auclair (produced 1925). In *Plays for College Theater*, edited by Garrett H. Leverton, 1932.
The Last Night of Don Juan, from a play by Edmond Rostand (produced 1925).
Morals, from a play by Ludwig Thoma (produced 1925).
Lucky Sam McCarver (produced 1925). 1926.
Ned McCobb's Daughter (produced 1926). 1926.
The Silver Cord (produced 1926). 1927.
Salvation with Charles MacArthur (produced 1928). In *Stage Works of MacArthur*, 1974.
Olympia, from a play by Ferenc Molnar (produced 1928). 1928.
Half Gods (produced 1929). 1930.
Lute Song, with Will Irwin (as *Pi-Pa-Ki*, produced 1930); revised version, as *Lute Song*, music by Raymond Scott, lyrics by Bernard Hanighen (produced 1946). 1955.
President, from a play by Ferenc Molnar (as *One, Two, Three* produced 1930). In *Romantic Comedies*, by Molnar, 1952.
Marseilles, from a work by Marcel Pagnol (produced 1930).
The Late Christopher Bean, from a play by René Fauchois (produced 1932). 1933.
Alien Corn (produced 1933). 1933.
Gather Ye Rosebuds, with Robert Littell (produced 1934).
Ode to Liberty, from a play by Michel Duran (produced 1934).
Dodsworth, from the novel by Sinclair Lewis (produced 1934). 1934.
Yellow Jack, with Paul de Kruif, from a work by de Kruif (produced 1934). 1934.

Paths of Glory, from the novel by Humphrey Cobb (produced 1935). 1935.
The Ghost of Yankee Doodle (produced 1937). 1938.
Madam, Will You Walk? (produced 1953). 1955.
GWTW [Gone with the Wind]: *The Screenplay*, edited by Richard Harwell. 1980.

Screenplays: *Bulldog Drummond*, with Wallace Smith, 1929; *Condemned*, 1929; *A Lady to Love*, 1930; *Raffles*, 1930; *One Heavenly Night*, with Louis Bromfield, 1930; *Arrowsmith*, 1931; *The Greeks Had a Word for Them*, 1932; *Dodsworth*, 1936; *Gone with the Wind*, 1939; *Raffles*, with John van Druten, 1940.

Fiction

Three Flights Up (stories). 1924.

Other

The Labor Spy: A Survey of Industrial Espionage, with Robert Dunn. 1921; revised edition, 1924.
Professional Patriots, with John Hearley, edited by Norman Hapgood. 1927.

*

Critical Study: *Howard* by Sidney H. White, 1977.

* * *

The first major writer of social drama after American drama approached the age of maturity following World War I, Sidney Howard mixed melodrama and comedy with the established mode of realism in literature to reflect a dominant social idea of the 1920's—*They Knew What They Wanted*. As the title of one of his best plays, it presented the positive individualism of his generation, which other playwrights (Philip Barry, S.N. Behrman, Maxwell Anderson, Paul Green) soon emphasized. In contrast to some of his outstanding contemporaries, Howard was not an innovator in dramatic form nor a particularly profound writer. He readily admitted such shortcomings, if indeed, they were that. Instead, he was a substantial playwright of considerable theatrical skill and imagination who stepped into the ongoing stream of social drama in America and produced at least two major plays in that genre.

They Knew What They Wanted is a modern version of the Paolo-Francesca love story but with a modern twist that none of those who told the story form Dante to Wagner would have accepted. But Howard's intelligently expedient people, battling the exigencies of the modern world, know what they want, and his hero. Tony, can become, as Frank Loesser's musical adaptation made him, "The Most Happy Fella." In *The Silver Cord* Howard took advantage of ideas propounded by Strindberg and Freud. With a diabolic cunning worthy of Strindberg's Laura, Howard's protagonist fights for the control of her sons in an emotion-packed drama that remains one of America's best thesis plays. Emotion and spectacle are always major aspects of a Howard play. He wrote about people, frequently with a strong sense of irony, and all of his plays held at least one spectacular scene which he handled with a craftsmanship critics have admired. The best include *Lucky Sam McCarver, Ned McCobb's Daughter*, and *The Late Christopher Bean*; he also adapted Sinclair Lewis's *Dodsworth* for the stage.

During a life cut short by a farm accident in 1939 Howard wrote some twenty plays, most of them either adaptations or collaborations. But his reputation in American drama rests solidly upon the plays he wrote by himself, the best of which appeared during the 1920's. He seemed unable to relate successfully to the social atmosphere of the Depression years which followed.

—Walter J. Meserve

HOWE, E(dgar) W(atson). Born near Treaty, Wabash County, Indiana, 3 May 1853. Educated at local schools in Missouri. Married Clara L. Frank in 1873 (divorced, 1901); five children. Apprentice printer on his father's newspaper, *Union of States*, Bethany, Missouri, 1864–65; printer in Missouri, Iowa, Illinois, Nebraska, Wyoming, and Utah, 1866–72; publisher, *Globe*, Golden, Colorado, 1873–75; founder with his brother James, and editor, 1877–1910, Atchison *Globe*, Kansas; editor and publisher, *E.W. Howe's Monthly*, Atchison, 1911–33. Litt.D.: Rollins College, Winter Park, Florida, 1926; Washburn College, Topeka, Kansas, 1927. *Died 3 October 1937.*

PUBLICATIONS

Fiction

The Story of a Country Town. 1883; edited by Brom Weber, 1964.
The Mystery of The Locks. 1885.
A Moonlight Boy. 1886.
A Man Story. 1889.
An Ante-Mortem Statement. 1891.
The Confession of John Whitlock, Late Preacher of the Gospel. 1891.
Dying Like a Gentleman and Other Stories. 1926.
The Covered Wagon and the West (stories). 1928.
Her Fifth Marriage and Other Stories. 1928.
When a Woman Enjoys Herself and Other Tales of a Small Town. 1928.

Other

Mark Antony De Wolfe Howe 1808–1895: A Brief Record of a Long Life. 1897.
Daily Notes of a Trip Around the World. 2 vols., 1907.
The Trip to the West Indies. 1910.
Country Town Sayings: A Collection of Paragraphs from the Atchison Globe. 1911.
Travel Letters from New Zealand, Australia, and Africa. 1913.
Success Easier Than Failure. 1917.
The Blessing of Business. 1918.
Ventures in Common Sense, edited by H.L. Mencken. 1919; as *Adventures in Common Sense*, 1922.
The Anthology of Another Town. 1920.
Notes for My Biographer: Terse Paragraphs on Life and Letters. 1926.
Preaching from the Audience: Candid Comments on Life. 1926.

Sinner Sermons: A Selection of the Best Paragraphs of Howe. 1926.
Plain People (autobiography). 1929.
The Indignations of Howe. 1933.

*

Critical Studies: *Howe, Country Town Philosopher* by Calder M. Pickett, 1968; *Howe* by S.J. Sackett, 1972; *Howe* by Martin Bucco, 1977.

* * *

"I come of a long line of plain people," E.W. Howe writes at the beginning of his autobiography *Plain People*, but as a famous editor in the days of personal journalism and as a minor novelist of the late 19th century, Howe achieved a measure of distinction in his own day and a small niche in the history of American life and culture. He is the author of one novel that continues to be reprinted and read, and his autobiography, long out of print, deserves to be better known. Howe is an authentic bit of Americana woven into the fabric of national experience—a figure to be compared in this respect with Benjamin Franklin, Horatio Alger, H.L. Mencken, and Will Rogers.

After establishing himself as a newspaper editor, Howe turned toward literature. For months in the early 1880's he worked over the manuscript of *The Story of a Country Town* at the kitchen table after finishing a long day in the newspaper office. When commercial publishers turned down his book, he published it himself. The novel was an immediate success and encouraged him to write several more, all of which were failures and never have been reprinted. Eventually he resigned himself to filling his newspaper columns with aphoristic paragraphs that attracted national attention. He continued to write books for the rest of his life, but they are mostly forgotten travel letters, tracts on business, and collections of his newspaper and magazine paragraphs. One other, however, is worth reading: *The Anthology of Another Town*, a prose version of and answer to Edgar Lee Masters's *Spoon River Anthology*.

The Story of a Country Town draws on the life of Howe's father and Howe's own experience growing up in northwest Missouri where the novel takes place. It is basically a melodramatic tragedy of a backwoods Othello who becomes insanely jealous when he discovers that his wife was once in love with another man. As a work of art, it is full of crudities, but the story is told with such a passionate intensity by Howe's persona, young Ned Westlake, who observes the action, that readers are swept along by it.

Both Howells and Twain, who received copies from the author, wrote flattering letters about the novel. Howells thought it a "very remarkable piece of realism" and praised the fidelity of the country town setting although he objected to the sentimentality of the tragic romance. The novel generally has been classed with early examples of realism, but it is only partly realistic, and Howe's later novels demonstrated that he was really a sentimental romancer at heart. *The Story of a Country Town* can be seen, with its bitter memories of the narrator's youth, as a forerunner of the revolt-from-the-village literature of Sinclair Lewis, Sherwood Anderson, and Masters, but Howe during his later years filled his newspaper columns with the most blatant Chamber-of-Commerce puffery and really believed that all virtue resided in the small town and in rural life.

—James Woodress

HOWELLS, William Dean. Born in Martinsville (later Martins Ferry), Ohio, 1 March 1837. Educated at schools in Hamilton and Dayton, Ohio. Married Elinor Gertrude Mead in 1862 (died, 1910); two daughters and one son. Compositor, 1851–60, *Ohio State Journal*, Columbus; contributor to his father's newspaper, Jefferson *Sentinel*, Ohio, from 1852; columnist ("Letter from Columbus," 1857–58, and "Letter from New York," 1866), Cincinnati *Gazette*; columnist, Cleveland *Herald*, 1858; reader, Follett and Foster, publishers, Columbus, 1860; U.S. Consul, Venice, 1861–65; columnist ("Letter from Venice"), Boston *Daily Advertiser*, 1862–64; columnist ("Minor Topics"), *The Nation*, New York, 1865–66; assistant editor, 1866–71, and editor-in-chief, 1871–81, *Atlantic Monthly*, Boston; University Lecturer in Modern Literature, Harvard University, Cambridge, Massachusetts, 1869–71; Lowell Lecturer, Boston, 1870; free-lance writer, 1881–85; columnist ("Editor's Study," 1886–92, and "Editor's Easy Chair," from 1900), *Harper's* monthly, New York, ("Life and Letters"), *Harper's Weekly*, New York, 1895–98, and ("American Letter"), *Literature*, 1898–99; lived in New York after 1891; co-editor, *Cosmopolitan*, New York, 1892. Recipient: American Academy Gold Medal, 1915. M.A.: Harvard University, 1867; Litt.D.: Yale University, New Haven, Connecticut, 1901; Oxford University, 1904; Columbia University, New York, 1905; L.H.D.: Princeton University, New Jersey, 1912. Honorary Fellow, Royal Society of Literature, 1901; President, American Academy, 1908–20. *Died 11 May 1920.*

PUBLICATIONS

Collections

Representative Selections, edited by Clara Marburg Kirk and Rudolf Kirk. 1950.
Selected Writings, edited by Henry Steele Commager. 1950.
Complete Plays, edited by Walter J. Meserve. 1960.
Selected Edition, edited by Ronald Gottesman and others. 1968—
Novels 1875–1886 (Library of America), edited by Edwin H. Cady. 1982.

Fiction

Their Wedding Journey. 1872; edited by John K. Reeves, in *Selected Edition*, 1968.
A Chance Acquaintance. 1873; edited by Ronald Gottesman, David J. Nordloh, and Jonathan Thomas, in *Selected Edition*, 1971.
A Foregone Conclusion. 1874.
The Lady of the Aroostook. 1879.
The Undiscovered Country. 1880.
A Fearful Responsibility and Other Stories. 1881; as *A Fearful Responsibility and Tonnelli's Marriage*, 1882.
Doctor Breen's Practice. 1881.
A Modern Instance. 1882; edited by David J. Nordloh and David Kleinman, in *Selected Edition*, 1977.
A Woman's Reason. 1883.
The Rise of Silas Lapham. 1885; edited by Don L. Cook, 1982.
Indian Summer. 1886; edited by Scott Bennett and David J. Nordloh, in *Selected Edition*, 1971.
The Minister's Charge; or, The Apprenticeship of Lemuel Barker. 1886; edited by David J. Nordloh and David

Kleinman, in *Selected Edition*, 1978.
April Hopes. 1887.
Annie Kilburn. 1888.
A Hazard of New Fortunes. 1889; edited by David J. Nordloh, in *Selected Edition*, 1976.
The Shadow of a Dream. 1890; with *An Imperative Duty*, edited by Martha Banta, Ronald Gottesman, and David J. Nordloh, in *Selected Edition*, 1970.
An Imperative Duty. 1891; with *The Shadow of a Dream*, edited by Martha Banta, Ronald Gottesman, and David J. Nordloh, in *Selected Edition*, 1970.
Mercy. 1892; as *The Quality of Mercy*, 1892; edited by James P. Elliott, in *Selected Edition*, 1979.
The World of Chance. 1893.
The Coast of Bohemia. 1893.
A Traveler from Altruria. 1894; complete edition, edited by Clara Marburg Kirk and Rudolf Kirk, as *Letters of an Altrurian Traveller (1893–1894)*, 1961; with *Between the Dark and the Daylight*, in *Selccted Edition*, 1968.
The Day of Their Wedding. 1896.
A Parting and a Meeting. 1896; with *The Day of Their Wedding*, as *Idyls in Drab*, 1896.
The Landlord at Lion's Head. 1897.
An Open-Eyed Conspiracy: An Idyl of Saratoga. 1897.
The Story of a Play. 1898.
Ragged Lady. 1899.
Their Silver Wedding Journey. 1899; abridged edition, as *Hither and Thither in Germany*, 1920.
A Pair of Patient Lovers (stories). 1901.
The Kentons. 1902; in *Selected Edition*, 1971.
The Flight of Pony Baker: A Boy's Town Story. 1902.
Questionable Shapes. 1903.
Letters Home. 1903.
The Son of Royal Langbrith. 1904; edited by David Burrows, Ronald Gottesman, and David J. Nordloh, in *Selected Edition*, 1969.
Miss Bellard's Inspiration. 1905.
Through the Eye of the Needle. 1907.
Between the Dark and the Daylight: Romances. 1907; with *A Traveler from Altruria*, in *Selected Edition*, 1968.
Fennel and Rue. 1908.
New Leaf Mills: A Chronicle. 1913.
The Leatherwood God. 1916; in *Selected Edition*, 1976.
The Vacation of the Kelwyns: An Idyl of the Middle Eighteen-Seventies. 1920.
Mrs. Farrell. 1921.

Plays

Samson, from the play by Ippolito D'Aste (produced 1874). 1889.
The Parlor Car. 1876.
Out of the Question. 1877.
A Counterfeit Presentment (produced 1877; revised version, produced 1877). 1877.
Yorick's Love, from a play by Manuel Tamayo y Baus (as *A New Play*, produced 1878; as *Yorick's Love*, produced 1880). In *Complete Plays*, 1960.
The Sleeping-Car (produced 1887). 1883.
The Register. 1884.
The Elevator (produced 1885). 1885.
The Garroters (produced 1886). 1886.
A Foregone Conclusion, with William Poel, from the novel by Howells (produced 1886). In *Complete Plays*, 1960.
Colonel Sellers as a Scientist, with Mark Twain, from the novel *The Gilded Age* by Twain and Charles Dudley Warner (produced 1887). In *Complete Plays*, 1960.
The Mouse-Trap (produced 1887–88?). In *The Mouse-Trap and Other Farces*, 1889.
A Sea-Change; or, Love's Stowaway: A Lyricated Farce, music by George Henschel. 1888.
The Mouse-Trap and Other Farces (includes *A Likely Story, Five O'Clock Tea, The Garroters*). 1889.
The Sleeping-Car and Other Farces (includes *The Parlor Car, The Register, The Elevator*). 1889.
The Albany Depot. 1891.
A Letter of Introduction. 1892.
The Unexpected Guests. 1893.
Evening Dress (produced 1894). 1893.
Bride Roses (produced 1894). 1900.
A Dangerous Ruffian (produced 1895).
A Previous Engagement. 1897.
Room Forty-Five. 1900.
An Indian Giver. 1900.
The Smoking Car. 1900.
Minor Dramas. 2 vols., 1907.
The Mother and the Father. 1909.
Parting Friends. 1911.
The Night Before Christmas, and Self-Sacrifice, in *The Daughter of the Storage and Other Things in Prose and Verse*, 1916.

Verse

Poems of Two Friends, with John J. Piatt. 1860.
No Love Lost: A Romance of Travel. 1869.
Poems. 1873; revised edition, 1886.
Stops of Various Quills. 1895.
The Mulberries in Pay's Garden. 1907.

Other

Lives and Speeches of Abraham Lincoln and Hannibal Hamlin, with J. L. Hayes. 1860.
Venetian Life. 1866; revised edition, 1867, 1872; 2 vols., 1907.
Italian Journeys. 1867; revised edition, 1872, 1901.
Suburban Sketches. 1871; revised edition, 1872; abridged edition, as *A Day's Pleasure*, 1876.
Sketch of the Life and Character of Rutherford B. Hayes. 1876.
A Little Girl among the Old Masters. 1884.
Three Villages. 1884.
Tuscan Cities. 1885.
Modern Italian Poets: Essays and Versions. 1887.
A Boy's Town (for children). 1890.
Criticism and Fiction. 1891.
A Little Swiss Sojourn. 1892.
Christmas Every Day and Other Stories Told for Children. 1892.
My Year in a Log Cabin. 1893.
My Literary Passions. 1895.
Impressions and Experiences. 1896.
Stories of Ohio. 1897.
Doorstep Acquaintance and Other Sketches. 1900.
Literary Friends and Acquaintance: A Personal Retrospect of American Authorship. 1900; edited by David F. Hiatt and Edwin H. Cady, in *Selected Edition*, 1968.

Heroines of Fiction. 2 vols., 1901.
Literature and Life: Studies. 1902.
London Films. 1905.
Certain Delightful English Towns. 1906.
Roman Holidays and Others. 1908.
Seven English Cities. 1909.
My Mark Twain: Reminiscences and Criticisms. 1910; edited by Marilyn Austin Baldwin, 1967.
Imaginary Interviews. 1910.
Familiar Spanish Travels. 1913.
The Seen and Unseen at Stratford-on-Avon: A Fantasy. 1914.
The Daughter of the Storage and Other Things in Prose and Verse. 1916.
Years of My Youth (autobiography). 1916; in *Selected Edition*, 1975.
Life in Letters of Howells, edited by Mildred Howells. 2 vols., 1928.
Prefaces to Contemporaries (1882–1920), edited by George Arms, William M. Gibson, and Frederic C. Marston, Jr. 1957.
Criticism and Fiction and Other Essays, edited by Clara Marburg Kirk and Rudolf Kirk. 1959.
Mark Twain-Howells Letters: The Correspondence of Samuel L. Clemens and Howells 1872–1910, edited by Henry Nash Smith and William M. Gibson. 2 vols., 1960; abridged edition, as *Selected Mark Twain-Howells Letters*, 1967.
Discovery of a Genius: Howells and Henry James, edited by Albert Mordell. 1961.
Howells as Critic, edited by Edwin H. Cady. 1973.
Interviews with Howells, edited by Ulrich Halfmann. 1973.
The John Hay-Howells Letters: The Correspondence of John Milton Hay and Howells 1861–1905, edited by George Monteiro and Brenda Murphy. 1980.
The Editor's Study: A Comprehensive Edition of Howells's Column, edited by James W. Simpson. 1983.

Editor, *Three Years in Chili*, by Mrs. C.B. Merwin. 1861; as *Chili through American Spectacles*, n.d.
Editor, *Choice Autobiographies*. 8 vols., 1877–78.
Editor, with Thomas Sergeant Perry, *Library of Universal Adventure by Sea and Land*. 1888.
Editor, *Mark Twain's Library of Humor*. 1888.
Editor, *Poems of George Pellew*. 1892.
Editor, *Recollections of Life in Ohio from 1813 to 1840*, by William Cooper Howells. 1895.
Editor, with Russell Sturgis. *Florence in Art and Literature*. 1901.
Editor, with Henry Mills Alden, *Harper's Novelettes*. 8 vols., 1906–08.
Editor, *The Great Modern American Short Stories: An Anthology*. 1920.
Editor, *Don Quixote*, by Cervantes, translated by Charles Jarvis. 1923.

Translator, *Venice, Her Art-Treasures and Historical Associations: A Guide*, by Adalbert Müller. 1864.

*

Bibliography: *A Bibliography of Howells* by William M. Gibson and George Arms, 1948; in *Bibliography of American Literature* by Jacob Blanck, 1963; *Howells: A Bibliography* by Vito J. Brenni, 1973; *Published Comment on Howells Through 1920: A Research Bibliography* by Clayton L. Eichelberger, 1976.

Critical Studies: *Howells and Italy* by James Woodress, 1952; *The Road to Realism: The Early Years, 1837–1885, of Howells* and *The Realist at War: The Mature Years, 1885–1920, of Howells* by Edwin H. Cady, 2 vols., 1956–58, and *Critical Essays on Howells 1866–1920* edited by Edwin H. and Norma W. Cady, 1983; *Howells: The Development of a Novelist*, 1959, and *The Realism of Howells 1889–1920*, 1973, both by George N. Bennett; *Howells: His Life and World* by Van Wyck Brooks, 1959; *Howells: A Century of Criticism* edited by Kenneth E. Eble, 1962, and *Howells* by Eble, 1982; *Howells, Traveler from Altruria 1889–1894*, 1962, and *Howells and Art in His Time*, 1965, both by Clara Marburg Kirk, and *Howells* by Clara Marburg Kirk and Rudolf Kirk, 1962; *The Immense Complex Drama: The World and Art of the Howells Novel* by George C. Carrington, Jr., 1966, and *Plots and Characters in the Fiction of Howells*, by George C. Carrington, Jr., and Ildiko Carrington, 1976; *The Literary Realism of Howells* by William McMurray, 1967; *Howells* by William M. Gibson, 1967; *The Achievement of Howells: A Reinterpretation* by Kermit Vanderbilt, 1968; *Howells: The Friendly Eye* by Edward Wagenknecht, 1969; *Howells: An American Life* by Kenneth S. Lynn, 1971; *Critics on Howells* edited by Paul A. Escholz, 1975; *The Circle of Eros: Sexuality in the Work of Howells* by Elizabeth Stevens Prioleau, 1983; *The Black Heart's Truth: The Early Career of Howells* by John W. Crowley, 1985.

* * *

William Dean Howells's literary career was remarkable not only for its length and variousness but for its continuous and conscientious productivity. For more than fifty years, extending from the 19th well into the 20th century, Howells appeared in print as a journalist, a poet, a sensitively observant but unsentimental traveler, a novelist, a playwright, a critic and a polemicist in the cause of realism (these last two functions merging in *Criticism and Fiction*), a publicist and explicator of foreign writers for an ill-informed American public, and the educator of that same public to the greatness of its own writers like James and Twain.

The experience behind this writing was also rich and varied, directly furnishing much of the material for the immense productivity. Moreover, it was an experience that had its public occasions, most notably Howells's outspoken opposition to the treatment of the Chicago anarchists in the Haymarket affair. Beneath the surface of a life that moved from midwestern printshops and newspapers through the consulship at Venice and the editorship of the *Atlantic* to the new center of literary activity in New York, and brought varied relationships with the literary giants of New England and deep literary and personal friendships with the new giants of American literature, James and Twain, there was profound personal experience: the challenge of Darwinian science to religious faith, and an increasing awareness of cultural dislocations, political corruptions, and economic inequities. Thus, Howells's writing became a permanently valuable record of a broad spectrum of the American literary, social, economic, religious, and moral experience. Even more importantly, in an impressive number of his fictions Howells achieved the transmutation of actual and vicarious experience into realistic art, and met his own criterion of "dispersing the conventional acceptations by which men live on easy terms with themselves" without falling into the error of claiming thereby to have solved "the riddle of the painful earth."

Howells's relatively late decision to become a novelist kept him close to his own experience and led to the unsophisticated literary devices in the early novels. The tentatively novelistic *Their Wedding Journey* stated his intention to deal with "poor Real life." But the pronouncement stemmed more from his distrust of his ability to manage a sustained narrative and his desire to employ the methods of the travel book than from a theory of realism. *A Chance Acquaintance* also employed the narrative structure of the journey, but it also developed a situation in which the moral spontaneity of an unsophisticated American girl (a portrait highly praised by James) served to reveal the stultifying snobbishness of a proper Bostonian, and, to the dissatisfaction of many, chose the "realistic" mode of an "unhappy" ending in which the girl rejected the ungentlemanly gentleman. Throughout this apprenticeship period, Howells continued to exploit the kind of confrontation labelled by Edwin H. Cady the "conventional-unconventional formula." He also put to use his own experience in summer boarding-houses in *Mrs. Farrell* (serialized as *Private Theatricals*) and in pre-Jamesian versions of the international novel in *A Foregone Conclusion* and *The Lady of the Aroostook*. The former is often cited as a benchmark in the terrain of Howells's early novels because of its skillful dramatic development (a lesson learned from Turgenev) of a "tragic" involvement of an Italian priest and another of Howells's radically innocent American girls.

Beginning in 1880 with *The Undiscovered Country*, Howells's fiction began to take account of issues not easily confined within the limits of the novel of manners (the terminology most frequently applied to the pre- and post-"economic" fiction). That novel has begun to receive deserved attention as an original transformation of Hawthornian themes into a probing study of the problem of religious faith and as Howells's first major attempt to achieve a reconciliation of the American present with its past through a pastoral vision. It was followed by *A Modern Instance*, in any accounting, including Howells's own, one of his most penetrating studies of American life. In spite of general contemporary misunderstanding, it was a contemporary reviewer who noted that the novel was not an anti-divorce tract but "a demonstration of a state of society of which divorce was the index." As the novel expands from a brilliant study of the disintegration of a marriage through a failure of moral discipline, that state of society is depicted as one marked by the decay of vital religious faith, of family solidarity as the nexus of social stability, of the social ethic which is being displaced by purely commercial principles. *The Rise of Silas Lapham* also involves a questioning of American commercial society as Lapham's moral rise is achieved by the sacrifice of the materialistic success for which he very nearly sold his soul. Moreover, it was so far from being a mere comedy of manners—as many readers have termed it because of Lapham's attempts to gain entrance into Boston society and because of the apparent submergence of the moral issue to the romantic sub-plot (the relationship of the plots is a point of extensive critical debate)—that Howells suffered some kind of psychic breakdown in being confronted with the issues it raised: the degree and nature of his commitment to a democracy which included the Irish and Jews; his own relationship with proper Bostonians and New England literati, most of whom had little appreciation for the realistic art to which he had committed himself. The increasing doubts about the America about which he had once been thoroughly optimistic but which he came to feel, as he told James, was "coming out all wrong in the end" made him ripe for the reading of Tolstoy (begun in 1885) and for the expression of a newly open radicalism in the novels of the 1890's which Everett Carter distinguished as works of "critical realism."

The most important of these was *A Hazard of New Fortunes*. It was preceded by *Annie Kilburn*, a demonstration of the Tolstoyan lesson of the necessity for "*justice* not *alms*" as the corrective for the economic and social ills of the polity. It was followed by *The Quality of Mercy*, an accusation of a system of which embezzlers were merely symptomatic, and *The World of Chance*, an examination of the malfunctioning or absence of causality in not only the business world but in all human involvements. Howells then abandoned the realistic novel as the vehicle of his socialistic ideas and turned to an openly dialectical form in two Altrurian (Utopian) romances.

The recovery of a "usable" Howells after a period in which he was the largely unread touchstone of timid gentility and Victorian morality for writers and critics like Sinclair Lewis and H.L. Mencken was directly due to the rediscovery of these two Utopias, with their socio-economic criticisms of American life. Critical debate continues today concerning their artistic quality and their significance to the totality of Howells's career: they have often been seen, even in approaches modified from the doctrinaire criticism of the 1930's, as marking the limit of Howells's artistic growth, and as evidencing a "tragic vision" absent from his other work (and shaped not only by Tolstoy but a number of profound personal experiences, including the hazard of his career in defense of the Haymarket anarchists and the protracted illness and agonizing death of his daughter). Consequently, his career has been seen as a growth through the comedy of manners to social realism to a unique critical realism and then a falling away. That falling away has been variously explained as simply an exhaustion of the creative impulse; as a failure of nerve in questioning the values and value of American society; as a recognition of his inability to provide solutions to the problems he examined; as a deliberate return to the intellectually and financially safe fiction of his earlier career. The complications of Howells's reputation can be seen in the various interpretations of *A Hazard of New Fortunes*, a key novel. It has been seen variously as a comedy of manners, a symbolic myth of Christian atonement, a realistic tragedy, a treatise on aesthetics, and a combined "psychological" and "economic" novel.

After 1893, Howells still had 27 years of productive life during which he published a dozen or so novels. Of these, almost half—*The Landlord at Lion's Head, The Kentons, The Son of Royal Langbrith, The Leatherwood God*, and the posthumous *The Vacation of the Kelwyns*—have, from various critical perspectives, been judged worthy to be included in the permanent Howells canon. If that canon is initiated by *A Modern Instance*—indeed, a case may be made for the earlier *A Foregone Conclusion* or *The Undiscovered Country*—the continuous excellence of Howells's realistic fiction throughout his career assures him an important place in the history of the development of American fiction. And, if there is added to that assessment his also continuous and influential role in his associations with the *Atlantic, Harper's*, and other journals, his importance as a *force* in American literature is difficult to overstate.

—George N. Bennett

See the essay on *The Rise of Silas Lapham*.

HUGHES, (James) Langston. Born in Joplin, Missouri, 1 February 1902. Educated at Central High School, Cleveland, 1916–20; Columbia University, New York, 1921–22; Lincoln University, Pennsylvania (Witter Bynner Award, 1926), 1926–29, B.A. 1929. During World War II, member of the Music and Writers war boards. English teacher in Mexico, 1920–21; seaman, 1923–24; busboy, Wardman Park Hotel, Washington, D.C., 1925; Madrid correspondent, Baltimore *Afro-American*, 1937; columnist ("Simple"), Chicago *Defender*, 1943–67, and New York *Post*, 1962–67; lived in Harlem, New York, after 1947. Founder Harlem Suitcase Theatre, New York, 1938, New Negro Theatre, Los Angeles, 1939, and Skyloft Players, Chicago, 1941. Visiting Professor of Creative Writing, Atlanta University, 1947; Poet-in-Residence, University of Chicago Laboratory School, 1949. Recipient: Harmon Gold Medal, 1931; Rosenwald fellowship, 1931, 1940; Guggenheim fellowship, 1935; American Academy grant, 1946; Anisfield-Wolf Award, 1953; Spingarn Medal, 1960. D.Litt: Lincoln University, 1943; Howard University, Washington, D.C., 1963; Western Reserve University, Cleveland, 1964. Member, American Academy, 1961, and American Academy of Arts and Sciences. *Died 22 May 1967.*

PUBLICATIONS

Verse

The Weary Blues. 1926.
Fine Clothes to the Jew. 1927.
Dear Lovely Death. 1931.
The Negro Mother and Other Dramatic Recitations. 1931.
The Dream-Keeper and Other Poems. 1932.
Scottsboro Limited: Four Poems and a Play in Verse. 1932.
A New Song. 1938.
Shakespeare in Harlem. 1942.
Jim Crow's Last Stand. 1943.
Lament for Dark Peoples and Other Poems, edited by H. Driessen. 1944.
Fields of Wonder. 1947.
One-Way Ticket. 1949.
Montage of a Dream Deferred. 1951.
Selected Poems. 1959.
Ask Your Mama: 12 Moods for Jazz. 1961.
The Panther and the Lash: Poems of Our Times. 1967.
Don't You Turn Back (for children), edited by Lee Bennett Hopkins. 1969.

Plays

The Gold Piece, in *Brownies' Book*, July 1921.
Mulatto (produced 1935; original version produced 1939). In *Five Plays*, 1963.
Little Ham (produced 1935). In *Five Plays*, 1963.
Troubled Island (produced 1935; revised version, music by William Grant Still, produced 1949). 1949.
When the Jack Hollers, with Arna Bontemps (produced 1936).
Joy to My Soul (produced 1937).
Soul Gone Home (produced 1937?). In *Five Plays*, 1963.
Don't You Want to Be Free?, music by Carroll Tate (produced 1937). In *One Act Play Magazine*, October 1938.
Front Porch (produced 1938).
The Organizer, music by James P. Johnson (produced 1939).
The Sun Do Move (produced 1942).
Freedom's Plow (broadcast 1943). 1943.
Pvt. Jim Crow (radio script), in *Negro Story*, May-June 1945.
Booker T. Washington at Atlanta (broadcast 1945). In *Radio Drama in Action*, edited by Eric Barnouw, 1945.
Street Scene (lyrics only), book by Elmer Rice, music by Kurt Weill (produced 1947). 1948.
The Barrier, music by Jan Meyerowitz (produced 1950).
Just Around the Corner (lyrics only), book by Abby Mann and Bernard Drew, music by Joe Sherman (produced 1951).
Simply Heavenly, music by David Martin (produced 1957). 1959.
Esther, music by Jan Meyerowitz (produced 1957).
Shakespeare in Harlem, with James Weldon Johnson (produced 1959).
Port Town, music by Jan Meyerowitz (produced 1960).
The Ballad of the Brown King, music by Margaret Bonds (produced 1960).
Black Nativity (produced 1961).
Gospel Glow (produced 1962).
Let Us Remember Him, music by David Amram (produced 1963).
Tambourines to Glory, music by Jobe Huntley, from the novel by Hughes (produced 1963). In *Five Plays*, 1963.
Five Plays (includes *Mulatto, Soul Gone Home, Little Ham, Simply Heavenly, Tambourines to Glory*), edited by Webster Smalley. 1963.
Jerico-Jim Crow (produced 1963).
The Prodigal Son (produced 1965).

Screenplay: *Way Down South*, with Clarence Muse, 1939.

Radio Scripts: *Jubilee*, with Arna Bontemps, 1941; *Brothers*, 1942; *Freedom's Plow*, 1943; *John Henry Hammers It Out*, with Peter Lyons, 1943; *In the Service of My Country*, 1944; *The Man Who Went to War*, 1944 (UK); *Booker T. Washington at Atlanta*, 1945; *Swing Time at the Savoy*, with Noble Sissle, 1949.

Television Scripts: *The Big Sea*, 1965; *It's a Mighty World*, 1965; *Strollin' Twenties*, 1966.

Fiction

Not Without Laughter. 1930.
The Ways of White Folks (stories). 1934.
Simple Speaks His Mind. 1950.
Laughing to Keep from Crying (stories). 1952.
Simple Takes a Wife. 1953.
Simple Stakes a Claim. 1957.
Tambourines to Glory. 1958.
The Best of Simple. 1961.
Something in Common and Other Stories. 1963.
Simple's Uncle Sam. 1965.

Other (for children)

Popo and Fifina: Children of Haiti, with Arna Bontemps. 1932.
The First Book of Negroes. 1952.
The First Book of Rhythms. 1954.
Famous American Negroes. 1954.
Famous Negro Music-Makers. 1955.
The First Book of Jazz. 1955; revised edition, 1962.
The First Book of the West Indies. 1956; as *The First Book of*

the Caribbean, 1965.
The Hughes Reader. 1958.
Famous Negro Heroes of America. 1958.
The First Book of Africa. 1960; revised edition, 1964.

Other

The Big Sea: An Autobiography. 1940.
The Sweet Flypaper of Life (on Harlem), with Roy De Carava. 1955.
A Pictorial History of the Negro in America, with Milton Meltzer. 1956; revised edition, 1963, 1968.
I Wonder as I Wander: An Autobiographical Journey. 1956.
The Hughes Reader. 1958.
Fight for Freedom: The Story of the NAACP. 1962.
Black Magic: A Pictorial History of the Negro in American Entertainment, with Milton Meltzer. 1967.
Black Misery. 1969.
Good Morning, Revolution: Uncollected Social Protest Writings, edited by Faith Berry. 1973.
Hughes in the Hispanic World and Haiti, edited by Edward J. Mullen. 1977.
Arna Bontemps-Hughes: Letters 1925–1967, edited by Charles H. Nichols. 1980.

Editor, *Four Lincoln University Poets*. 1930.
Editor, with Arna Bontemps, *The Poetry of the Negro 1746–1949: An Anthology*. 1949; revised edition, 1970.
Editor, with Waring Guney and Bruce M. Wright, *Lincoln University Poets*. 1954.
Editor, with Arna Bontemps, *The Book of Negro Folklore*. 1958.
Editor, *An Africa Treasury: Articles, Essays, Stories, Poems by Black Africans*. 1960.
Editor, *Poems from Black Africa*. 1963.
Editor, *New Negro Poets: USA*. 1964.
Editor, *The Book of Negro Humor*. 1966.
Editor, *La Poésie Negro-Américaine* (bilingual edition). 1966.
Editor, *Anthologie Africaine et Malgache*. 1966.
Editor, *The Best Short Stories by Negro Writers: An Anthology from 1899 to the Present*. 1967.

Translator, with Mercer Cook, *Masters of the Dew*, by Jacques Roumain. 1947.
Translator, with Ben Frederic Carruthers, *Cuba Libre*, by Nicolás Guillén. 1948.
Translator, *Gypsy Ballads*, by Federico García Lorca. 1951.
Translator, *Selected Poems of Gabriela Mistral*. 1957.

*

Bibliography: *A Bio-Bibliography of Hughes 1902–1967* by Donald C. Dickinson, 1967, revised edition, 1972; *Hughes and Gwendolyn Brooks: A Reference Guide* by R. Baxter Miller, 1978.

Critical Studies: *Hughes* by James A. Emanuel, 1967; *Hughes: A Biography* by Milton Meltzer, 1968; *Hughes, Black Genius: A Critical Evaluation* edited by Therman B. O'Daniel, 1971 (includes bibliography); *Hughes: An Introduction to the Poetry* by Onwuchekwa Jemie, 1976; *Hughes: The Poet and His Critics* by Richard K. Barksdale, 1977; *Hughes: Before and Beyond Harlem* by Faith Berry, 1983; *I, Too, Sing America* (vol. 1 of *The Life of Hughes*) by Arnold Rampersad, 1986.

* * *

As impressive as Langston Hughes is for his versatility and productivity, his claim to enduring literary importance rests chiefly on his poetry and his Simple sketches. In his poetry his sure lyric touch, his poignant insight into the urban black folk soul rendered with remarkable fidelity to a variety of black idioms, his negative capability of subordinating his own personality so as to convey a vivid impression of scene or incident or mood or character, and his willingness to experiment are his richest endowments, though one also often finds in his verse the comic sense (often ironic or bittersweet), the broad democratic faith, and the total understanding of character which so irradiate the Simple tales.

Although Hughes wrote some verse without specific racial reference, the three major categories of his poetry comprise poems related to black music, poems of racial protest, and poems of racial affirmation. These categories naturally overlap, but it is convenient to discuss them separately. For the entire course of his literary career, Hughes was fascinated by black music: blues, jazz in its several varieties, and gospel. The classic blues stanzaic form, consisting of a statement of a problem or situation in the first line repeated in the second (often with a slight variation) followed by a third line resolving, interpreting, or commenting on the first two, appears frequently in Hughes, as in the following from "Red Sun Blues":

Gray skies, gray skies, won't you let the sun shine through?
Gray skies, gray skies, won't you let that sun shine through?
My baby's left me, I don't know what to do.

Elsewhere, as in the title poem of *The Weary Blues*, Hughes uses the blues and bluesmen as subject in a poem which may incorporate blues stanzas but has its own larger structure. His poems deriving from jazz are more complicated in their experimentation. Taken together, they provide a kind of poetic graph of developments in jazz from the Harlem cabaret life of the exuberant 1920's, through the boogie-woogie of the 1930's and the bebop of the 1940's, to the progressive jazz of the 1950's. From such early examples as "Jazzonia" and "The Cat and the Saxophone" to the ambitious later works *Montage of a Dream Deferred* and *Ask Your Mama*, Hughes used the varieties of jazz as both subject and style, designing the last-named work for musical accompaniment and often reading his poetry on tour to a jazz background. Though less prominently than blues and jazz, spirituals and gospel music figure also in Hughes's poetry (for example, the "Feet of Jesus" section in *Selected Poems*), as well as in his numerous song-plays.

As a poet of racial protest Hughes was less strident than some other well-known black writers, but not necessarily less trenchant or effective. Such poems as "I, Too" and "Let America Be America Again" express a wistful longing for racial equality. Others, such as "Brass Spittoons" and "Ballad of the Landlord" develop miniature dramas of the hardships and injustices of black life in a racist society. Some of the later poems included in the "Words on Fire" section of *The Panther and the Lash* sound notes of rising militancy. Surely among Hughes's best poems in this category are "American Heartbreak," whose laconic understatement achieves a sense of bitter finality, and "Song for a Dark Girl," a starkly tragic and strangely beautiful lyric about a girl's response to the lynching of her lover. Whether wistful, dramatic, angry, or tragic in mood, Hughes was always alive throughout his career to the oppression of his people.

He was equally sensitive to the dignity with which they endured or resisted that oppression. "Mother to Son" and "The Negro Mother" are among his many poems celebrating the black quest for freedom and social justice. Hughes was one of the first writers to use "soul" in a special racial sense, as in his very early poem "The Negro Speaks of Rivers." Color itself delights the poet in the carefully crafted "Dream Variation" and the delicious "Harlem Sweeties." And his comic vision to be developed in such loving detail in the Simple sketches is prefigured in "Sylvester's Dying Bed" and the Madam Alberta K. Johnson poems. Lowlife and working-class blacks, shunned by bourgeois spokesmen of the Harlem Renaissance, often receive special tribute in Hughes's poems of racial affirmation.

Hughes's interest in fiction developed later than his instinct for poetry. The novels *Not Without Laughter* and *Tambourines to Glory* are highly readable if somewhat weak in structure. The best of his 66 published short stories are proficient in technique and perceptive in their treatment of a variety of human situations. The most striking achievement in fiction is the creation of Jesse B. Semple. As Richard K. Barksdale has noted, Simple "had just the right blend of qualities to be Black America's new spokesman—just enough urban humor, cynicism, and sardonic levity and just enough down-home simplicity, mother-wit, innocence, and naiveté" (*Black Writers of America*, edited by Richard K. Barksdale and Keneth Kinnamon). The marvelous talk elicited from this fully realized black working man by the middle-class, intellectual narrator of the sketches constitutes one of the most valuable treasures of American literary humor.

In drama Hughes is perhaps more important for the extent of his activity and the stimulus he gave to black theater than for the intrinsic artistic merit of his own plays. As translator, anthologist, historian, and biographer he played a major role in popularizing Afro-American, Afro-Caribbean, and African subjects. As devoted friend and sponsor of generations of aspiring writers he was at the center of black literary activity for more than four decades. Together with his own accomplishments as poet and humorist, these efforts constitute a total contribution to literature matched by that of few writers in this century.

—Keneth Kinnamon

See the essay on *The Weary Blues*.

HUGO, Richard (Franklin). Born in Seattle, Washington, 21 December 1923. Educated at the University of Washington, Seattle, B.A. 1948, M.A. 1952. Served in the U.S. Army Air Corps during World War II: bombardier. Married and divorced. Worked for Boeing Company, Seattle, 1951–63; member of the English Department, then Professor of English, University of Montana, Missoula. Editor, Yale Younger Poets series, from 1977. Recipient: Northwest Writers award, 1966; Rockefeller fellowship, 1967; Guggenheim fellowship, 1977; Academy of American Poets fellowship, 1981. *Died 22 October 1982.*

PUBLICATIONS

Collections

Making Certain It Goes On: The Collected Poems. 1983.

Verse

A Run of Jacks. 1961.
Five Poets of the Pacific, with others, edited by Robin Skelton. 1964.
Death of the Kapowsin Tavern. 1965.
Good Luck in Cracked Italian. 1969.
The Lady in Kicking Horse Reservoir. 1973.
What Thou Lovest Well, Remains American. 1975.
Rain Five Days and I Love It. 1975.
Duwamish Head. 1976.
31 Letters and 13 Dreams. 1977.
Selected Poems. 1979.
White Center. 1980.
The Right Madness on Skye. 1980.

Other

The Triggering Town: Lectures and Essays on Poetry and Writing. 1979.
The Real West Marginal Way: A Poet's Autobiography, edited by Ripley S. Hugo and others. 1986.

*

Critical Studies: *We Are Called Human: The Poetry of Hugo* by Michael S. Allen, 1982; *A Trout in the Milk: A Composite Portrait of Hugo* edited by Jack Myers, 1982; *Hugo* by Donna Gerstenberger, 1983.

* * *

The last poem in *Making Certain It Goes On*, Richard Hugo's collected poems, ends with a speculation that the community, which has emerged as the subject of the poem, will be "going strong another hundred years." The simple, almost naive, affirmation strikes the reader with conviction and inspires confidence in its probability. That reaction is all the more notable because the poem begins with a drunk fisherman at an unpromising trout stream steadfastly refusing to engage any of the positive opportunities which surround him. Hugo's concerns in his poetry move between these contraries of the isolated, often alienated individual and the communities of people whose bonds and relationships lie beyond the understanding of the casual observer or the curious newcomer. In the late poems, especially *White Center* and *The Right Madness on Skye*, Hugo characteristically poses as a traveller or refugee happening into a new place or situation which at first seems only vaguely interesting, but which finally reveals a sense of connection with other places and other people. The speaker, always very conscious of being an outsider, thrills to the new knowledge and often invites or challenges the reader to join in the delights and the responsibilities which the insight offers. The concern and focus of many of the later poems revolve around this simultaneous presence of individuality and self-awareness and access to the deep and mysterious cohesion of communities. "Distances," one of Hugo's last poems, opens with "Driving a prairie," thus establishing the fluid, tentative relationship between the speaker and his setting and the low-definition of the landscape which almost taunts an observer to try to make a point. When the speaker can manage the confidence needed to observe that "Whole symphonies live between / here and a distant whatever-we-look-at," Hugo has won the struggle to celebrate self, community, and place in his poetry.

The early poems in *A Run of Jacks* and *Death of the Kapowsin Tavern* usually focused on places. Indeed, Hugo is often identified with the American northwest because he so often uses specific places as occasions for his poems. Perhaps this sense of identification with place is more understandable in the early poems because Hugo's speakers often elaborate on an experience in a place and in the process of elaboration reveal a significant aspect of the experience. A poem such as "G.I. Graves in Tuscany" begins with the speaker, although also a traveller, involved in his reaction to the graves and in the course of elaborating that experience finding a sense of his own meaning in the scene. These early poems are regional only in the sense that Hugo, like most poets, draws on personal experiences. The early poems show a modernist cast in their preference for leaving much of the revelation unstated or only suggested. While the speaker clearly has a change during the course of the experience, the reader must fill in the gaps to develop a sense of meaning.

In the burst of work Hugo published between 1973 and 1977 the stance of the poet and his speakers shifts to a greater concern that the communication initiated by the speaker's utterance work on the reader. In *The Lady in Kicking Horse Reservoir* and *What Thou Lovest Well, Remains American* Hugo regularly brings the speaker's concerns around to issues recognizable as important to larger groups of fellow citizens. He wants the poems to identify a connection between the collective personal experiences and discoveries of groups of people. This process of increasing concern for community culminates in the 1977 volume *31 Letters and 13 Dreams* which established Hugo as a master of the very difficult form of the letter poem. These letter poems play off the tension and challenges of the dependable, accessible format of the letter against the lyric and ritualized forms of poetry. The musical and stylized language which calls attention to itself in so much of Hugo's poetry always lurks behind the comfortable, casual prose forms of the letter. At a moment, the very pleasant letter enfolds into a tightly organized and powerful poetic utterance. The flow back and forth between the two forms justifies the focus on common and ordinary subjects and points out the origins and historical functions of poems.

Hugo's search for and interest in simple concerns such as innocence, sincerity, and beauty at first glance seem naive and sentimental. But his care in establishing appropriate postures and his mastery of language create the justification for his concerns and the conditions under which his search succeeds.

—Richard C. Turner

HUNEKER, James (Gibbons). Born in Philadelphia, Pennsylvania, 31 January 1857. Educated at Roth's Military Academy, Philadelphia; subsequently studied law; studied piano in Paris with Georges Mathias, and in New York with Rafael Joseffy. Music critic and editor, *Musical Courier*, 1887–1902; teacher of piano, National Conservatory, 1888–98; music critic, 1900–02, drama critic, 1902–04, and art critic, 1906–12, New York *Sun*; foreign correspondent on the arts, 1912–13, and music critic, 1918–19, New York *Times*; music critic, New York *World*, 1919–21. *Died 9 February 1921.*

PUBLICATIONS

Collections

Letters and *Intimate Letters*, edited by Josephine Huneker. 2 vols., 1922–24.
Essays, edited by H.L. Mencken. 1929.
Americans in the Arts 1890–1920: Critiques by Huneker, edited by Arnold T. Schwab. 1985.

Fiction

Melomaniacs (stories). 1902.
Visionaries (stories). 1905.
Painted Veils. 1920.

Other

Mezzotints in Modern Music. 1899.
Chopin: The Man and His Music. 1900.
Overtones: A Book of Temperaments. 1904.
Iconoclasts: A Book of Dramatists. 1905.
Egoists: A Book of Supermen. 1909.
Promenades of an Impressionist. 1910.
Franz Liszt. 1911.
The Pathos of Distance: A Book of a Thousand and One Moments. 1913.
Old Fogy: His Musical Opinions and Grotesques. 1913.
New Cosmopolis: A Book of Images. 1915.
Ivory, Apes, and Peacocks. 1915.
Unicorns. 1917.
The Philharmonic Society of New York and Its Seventy-Fifth Anniversary: A Retrospect. 1917(?).
The Steinway Collection of Paintings by American Artists. 1919.
Bedouins (essays and stories). 1920.
Steeplejack (autobiography). 2 vols., 1920.
Variations. 1921.

Music editions: *Forty Piano Compositions* by Chopin, 1902; *Forty Songs* by Brahms, 1903; *The Greater Chopin*, 1908; *Forty Songs* by Strauss, 1910; *Forty Songs* by Tchaikovsky, 1912; *Romantic Preludes and Studies for Piano*, 1919.

*

Bibliography: in *Bibliography of American Literature* by Jacob Blanck, 1963.

Critical Studies: *Huneker* by Benjamin DeCasseres, 1925; *Huneker, Critic of the Seven Arts* by Arnold T. Schwab, 1963.

* * *

James Huneker is probably America's most versatile critic. Beginning in the late 1880's as a music critic, he acquired an international reputation in the next fifteen years, especially for his writings on Chopin, Liszt, and Richard Strauss. The musical associations of Baudelaire, Gautier, Huysmans, George

Moore, and others led him to their non-musical books and thus into literary criticism, of which his best book was *Egoists*. His deep interest in the new psychology quickly attuned him to the work of Ibsen, Strindberg, Shaw, Maeterlinck, Hauptmann, and Sudermann, and his *Iconoclasts* was the most brilliant study of these playwrights to appear in America.

Best known for popularizing contemporary or near-contemporary Continental writers, Huneker also singled out the best American novelists of his day—James, Howells, Wharton, Norris, Dreiser—and called attention to Whitman, Poe, Dickinson, and Robinson at a time when these poets were either vilified or ignored by many other critics. But his talent in detecting the most enduring of early 20th-century American artists (thoroughly revealed only recently in his *Americans in the Arts*) was most notably reflected, perhaps, in his praise of painters such as Bellows, Davies, Henri, Luks, Marin, Maurer, Prendergast, Shinn, and Sloan.

As a critic, Huneker was probably most comfortable, technically, in music (he had studied and taught piano) and least secure, despite his perspicacity, in art. Fond of anecdotes, puns, and parodies, he produced essays admired for their wit, humor, urbanity, and range. His tendency to dart from topic to topic, idea to idea, name to name, paying little attention to connecting links and logical development, sometimes made him seem superficial or irritating to those who valued clear sustained reasoning above the picturesque phrase and the evocative association. But the staccato manner and the incessant allusions sprang from a mind richly loaded with gleanings from life and literature and quick with intuitive perception and sympathy. Not hesitating to pass judgment, in an undogmatic way, on artists of his own day, he was usually right: few of his swans turned out to be geese.

In his short stories—collected in *Melomaniacs, Visionaries*, and *Bedouins*—and in his one novel, *Painted Veils*, Huneker displayed the wide reading, powerful curiosity about the artist as a human being, the fascination with sexual or sensory abnormality, and the colorful, epigrammatic style reflected in his criticism. If the stories smack a bit too much of the grotesqueries of Hoffmann and Poe, they achieve some originality in Huneker's attempt to penetrate and portray the emotional life of the musician. In coming to grips with sexual themes, he was clearly ahead of his time in his fiction as well as his criticism. His plots reveal his flair for the humorously bizarre, and touches of comic description accompany his lively imagination. If his skill in execution—especially in characterization and dialogue—had matched his inventive facility, Huneker might have become the outstanding writer of fiction he always wanted to be.

—Arnold T. Schwab

HURSTON, Zora Neale. Born in Eatonville, Florida, 7 January 1901 (?). Educated at Robert Hungerford School, Eatonville, and a school in Jacksonville, Florida; Morgan Academy, Baltimore, 1917–18; Howard Preparatory School, 1918–19, and Howard University, part-time 1920–24, Washington, D.C.; Barnard College, New York, 1925–28, B.A. 1928. Married 1) Herbert Sheen in 1927 (divorced, 1931); 2) Albert Price III in 1939 (divorced, 1943). Maid with traveling repertory company, 1915–16; waitress while at Howard Preparatory School and University, 1918–24; folklore researcher in Alabama, Florida, and Louisiana, 1927–32, and in Haiti and the British West Indies, 1936–38; drama instructor, Bethune Cookman College, Daytona, Florida, 1933–34; editor, Federal Writers Project, Florida, 1938–39; member of the Drama Department, North Carolina College for Negroes, Durham, 1939–40; story consultant, Paramount, Hollywood, 1941–42; part-time teacher, Florida Normal College, St. Augustine, 1942; maid in Florida, 1949–50; reporter, Pittsburgh *Courier*, 1952; librarian, Patrick Air Force Base, Florida, 1956–57; reporter, Fort Pierce *Chronicle*, Florida, 1957–59; substitute teacher, Lincoln Park Academy, Fort Pierce, 1958–59. Recipient: Rosenwald fellowship, 1934; Guggenheim fellowship, 1936, 1937; Anisfield Wolf Award, 1942; Howard University award, 1943. Litt.D.: Morgan State College, Baltimore, 1939. *Died 28 January 1960.*

PUBLICATIONS

Collections

I Love Myself When I am Laughing . . . and Then Again When I am Looking Mean and Impressive: A Hurston Reader, edited by Alice Walker. 1979.

Fiction

Jonah's Gourd Vine. 1934.
Their Eyes Were Watching God. 1937.
Moses, Man of the Mountain. 1939.
Seraph on the Suwanee. 1948.

Plays

Color Struck, in *Fire!!*, November 1926.
The First One, in *Ebony and Topaz*, edited by Charles S. Johnson. 1927.
The Great Day (produced 1932).
Singing Steel (produced 1934).

Other

Mules and Men. 1935.
Tell My Horse. 1938; as *Voodoo Gods: An Inquiry into Native Myths and Magic in Jamaica and Haiti*, 1939.
Dust Tracks on a Road: An Autobiography. 1942.

Editor, *Caribbean Melodies*. 1947.

*

Critical Studies: *In A Minor Chord* (on Hurston, Cullen and Toomer) by Darwin T. Turner, 1971; *Hurston: A Literary Biography* by Robert E. Hemenway, 1977; *Hurston* by Lillie P. Howard, 1980.

* * *

The leading fact about Zora Neale Hurston is her identification with black folklore. She spent her childhood in the black town of Eatonville, Florida. As a student in anthropology, she recorded the oral literature of the black South and Caribbean, and her best writing employs the intangible artifacts of traditional culture. Yet the preoccupation with folk life had ambivalence. As Robert E. Hemenway has shown, she experienced conflict between her role as a scientific observer of culture and the need to express her feelings as an intuitive participant. She never denied the value of science, but eventually art alone claimed her talents.

Art, however, had its own ambivalence. For, while the substance of Hurston's work derived from spontaneous folk life, she was, of course, a deliberate literary writer. *Mules and Men* represents an early effort to resolve the consequent aesthetic problem. In it Hurston adapts folklore to the requirements of written literature by creating a persona and framing folktales in the context of a return home. This structure provides readers with a sense of entry into the community. One feels a privileged listener, but it must be remembered that one actually heard Hurston's selectively condensed version of the tales. Several years later, in *Moses, Man of the Mountain*, Hurston's confidence in her ability to reshape folk matter permitted her to assume the role openly. Taking as her premise the traditional parallel between the children of Israel and enslaved Africans she synthesizes legends and images to establish Moses as a humanized Afro-American.

Still more literary ways of using folk life appear in *Jonah's Gourd Vine* and *Their Eyes Were Watching God*. The first book presents as its central figure a preacher endowed with magnificent command of poetic language who thereby typifies the creativity of folk culture. At the same time he is morally flawed by a sexual drive that continually brings him low. Possibly through this flaw Hurston meant to create a tragic figure, but there can be no doubt that with the preacher's wife she touched the theme of her most distinguished book. *Their Eyes Were Watching God*, a novel about Janie Crawford's disappointing marriages and exhilarating love affair with the ebullient Tea Cake fully merges author and folk subject. The theme of a woman struggling to realize herself was inevitable for a female artist as independent as Hurston. That Janie becomes free within the culture of the black South, however, represents both a social and an aesthetic resolution. The social resolution appears as preference for black cultural values despite shortcomings, the aesthetic resolution as the assimilation of folk to the consciousness of a modern artist.

—John M. Reilly

INGE, William (Motter). Born in Independence, Kansas, 3 May 1913. Educated at Montgomery County High School, Independence, graduated 1930; University of Kansas, Lawrence, 1930–35, A.B. 1935; Peabody Teachers College, Nashville, Tennessee, 1935–36, M.A. 1938; Yale University, New Haven, Connecticut, 1940. Announcer, KFH Radio, Wichita, Kansas, 1936–37; teacher at Columbus High School, Kansas, 1937–38, Stephens College, Columbia, Missouri, 1938–43, and Washington University, St. Louis, 1946–49; arts critic, St. Louis *Star-Times*, 1943–46; story consultant, *Bus Stop* television series, 1961–62; Lecturer, University of North Carolina, Chapel Hill, 1969, and University of California, Irvine, 1970. Recipient: George Jean Nathan Award, 1951; Pulitzer Prize, 1953; New York Drama Critics Circle award, 1953; Donaldson Award, 1953; Oscar, for screenplay, 1962. *Died (suicide) 10 June 1973.*

PUBLICATIONS

Plays

The Dark at the Top of the Stairs (as *Farther Off from Heaven*, produced 1947; revised version, as *The Dark at the Top of the Stairs*, produced 1957). 1958.
Come Back, Little Sheba (produced 1949). 1950.
Picnic: A Summer Romance (produced New York, 1953). 1953; revised version, as *Summer Brave* (produced 1962), in *Summer Brave and Eleven Short Plays*, 1962.
Bus Stop (produced 1955). 1955.
Four Plays (includes *Come Back, Little Sheba; Picnic; Bus Stop; The Dark at the Top of the Stairs*). 1958.
Glory in the Flower (produced 1959). In *24 Favorite One-Act Plays*, edited by Bennett Cerf and Van H. Cartmell, 1958.
The Tiny Closet (produced 1959). In *Summer Brave and Eleven Short Plays*, 1962.
A Loss of Roses (produced 1959). 1960.
Splendor in the Grass: A Screenplay. 1961.
Natural Affection (produced 1962). 1963.
Summer Brave and Eleven Short Plays (includes *To Bobolink, For Her Spirit; A Social Event; The Boy in the Basement; The Tiny Closet; Memory of Summer; The Rainy Afternoon; The Mall; An Incident at the Standish Arms; People in the Wind; Bus Riley's Back in Town; The Strains of Triumph*). 1962.
Where's Daddy? (as *Family Things, Etc.*, produced 1965; as *Where's Daddy?*, produced 1966). 1966.
The Disposal (as *Don't Go Gentle*, produced 1968; as *The Last Pad*, produced 1972). In *Best Short Plays of the World Theatre, 1958–1967*, edited by Stanley Richards, 1968; revised version, as *The Disposal*, music by Anthony Caldarella, lyrics by Judith Gero (produced 1973).
Two Short Plays: The Call, and A Murder. 1968.
Midwestern Manic, in *Best Short Plays 1969*, edited by Stanley Richards. 1969.
Overnight (produced 1969).
Caesarian Operations (produced 1972).
Love Death Plays: Dialogue for Two Men, Midwestern Music, The Love Death, Venus and Adonis, The Wake, The Star (produced 1975).

Screenplays: *Splendor in the Grass*, 1961; *All Fall Down*, 1962; *Bus Riley's Back in Town*, 1965.

Television Play: *Out on the Outskirts of Town*, 1964.

Fiction

Good Luck, Miss Wyckoff. 1971.
My Son Is a Splendid Driver. 1972.

*

Bibliography: *Inge: A Bibliography* by Arthur F. McClure, 1982.

Critical Study: *Inge* by R. Baird Shuman, 1966.

* * *

William Inge remains an interesting phenomenon in American drama. His impact upon critic and public alike demands that he be included in any serious consideration of the postwar theatre, but in subject matter and in style he was so counter to the patterns of his contemporaries as to seem to belong to quite another generation. Leaving behind a minimal impression upon the development of recent American drama, his name rapidly fading, he was nonetheless a major figure for almost a decade and wrote some of the most appealing dramatic pieces of the late 1940's and 1950's.

Inge's significance in American drama is limited to four plays: *Come Back, Little Sheba*, *Picnic*, *Bus Stop*, and *The Dark at the Top of the Stairs*. His first, *Farther Off from Heaven*, produced by Margo Jones in Dallas, got to New York only in a much-revised version. *A Loss of Roses* failed completely, as did *Natural Affection* and *Family Things, Etc.* His screenplays, though they were made into notable films, brought no added fame, and his prose fiction is limited in appeal.

While Tennessee Williams, Arthur Miller, and Eugene O'Neill dwelt upon the tragic nature of their often inauspicious characters, Inge chose to emphasize his characters' fundamentally pathetic and frequently comic nature. The tragic fates are nowhere in evidence. Inge's appeal lies in a compassionate understanding of and a great sensitivity toward his petty little people, as he conveys successfully to his audiences the universally amusing and simultaneously agonizing quality of ordinary human nature under very ordinary circumstances. Furthermore, at a time when his major contemporaries favored impressionistic stagings, stylized settings, politico-historical themes, and regional emphases, Inge remained consistently a writer of straightforward, single-set plays of Ibsenesque realism. His characters, straight from the unprepossessing streets and towns of the vast mid-section of contemporary America, moved within settings, both geographical and theatrical, remarkable for their unobtrusive, innocuous nature. Inge is one of the most regional of dramatists, but he is emphatically not a "regionalist"; that is, his chosen locale is so lacking in specific regional association and importance, and hence influence upon his characters, as to be virtually neutral. The importance of the surroundings into which Inge places his characters lies precisely in their lack of any importance at all.

Nor does Inge permit the many individual problems of his characters to become the central "problem" of the plays as a whole. His first success, *Come Back, Little Sheba*, is a fine case in point. For instance, we learn a great deal about A.A. and alcoholism, but it is not a play *about* alcoholism. Sexual restraints, taboos, and frustrations, past and present, cause serious personal problems for Doc and Lola, but the play is in no way *about* sex. The air of pessimistic hopelessness surrounding the Delaneys may be the strongest theme, but the play refuses to dwell upon the subject and, in fact, displays a considerable awareness of the positive aspect of human resilience *and* ultimate hope. *Come Back, Little Sheba*, is, then, a play which sends out strong shock waves from all of these problems, permitting none of them to dominate the action. The audience finds itself attracted to these wholly undistinguished people in this undistinguished small town by bonds of mutual sympathy and understanding, together with an appreciation of Inge's outstanding ability to demonstrate what human love, patience, and endurance really mean to virtually all of us. Much has been lost by Doc and Lola in the course of the action, but much has been gained in return. Everybody, at the final curtain, is back at the beginning, more or less, and that, in the end, is far more the way of the world than otherwise. Inge's characters, here and elsewhere, will move no mountains in their lifetimes, but they are, as one critic has said, the salt of the earth, their importance lying almost entirely in the fact of their being human.

Picnic, as one opening night critic observed, is still "basic Inge." The sensation of the season, the play won a Pulitzer Prize and remains probably Inge's most famous play. Adding a few characters and moving them from kitchen to back yard, Inge proved that his formula for the dramatic impact of *Sheba* had been no fluke. "Affectionate, understanding, interesting, engagingly funny, emotionally touching, with fascinating characters" were the critical terms that greeted the play's portrayal of what happens on a Labor Day weekend in a Kansas back yard among a group of almost embarrassingly stock stage figures from clucking-hen mother to sexually frustrated old-maid schoolteacher. Highly emotional things happen in *Picnic*, as they do in *Sheba*, caused mainly by the intrusion of the handsome semi-clad drifter who causes a general loosening of assorted libidos, culminating in fornication, drunkenness, and elopement. But none of these things in themselves, any more than in *Sheba*, is the point. What matters is Inge's highly skilled and absolutely convincing portrayal of the driving human forces of underlying desires, frustrations, fears, and joys of these routinely bland people in an equally bland environment.

In *Bus Stop* Inge falls back on a device that worked for Shakespeare on Prospero's island, for Melville aboard the *Pequod*, and for James Jones in his pre-Pearl Harbor army. Into Grace's microcosmic lunchroom, driven by the unalterable force of a prairie blizzard, the playwright sends a group of individuals as stereotyped and undistinguished as anything he or many another artist has attempted. What emerges, for all that, is a wholly delightful human comedy with an underlying drama of deep human pathos. The pursuit and capture of the pitifully floozy "chantoosie" by the frantically infatuated, rambunctious but innocent cowboy is superbly comic, beautifully controlled. Simultaneously, the parallel affair of the decadent professor and the naive waitress, while ever on the edge of the pit of gratuitous sensation, carries the more serious theme with touching effectiveness. Before he is through with us, Inge has made us care a great deal about Bo, Cherie, Lyman, Elma, and Virgil. Normally we, as well as the rest of the world, would take little note of them, but Inge has shown us that they are highly important people to themselves and in many ways to each other. Cherie, hopelessly tarnished, artistically a fiasco, has stood her ground with dignity while vigorously defending her womanly honor against the onrushing Bo. He in turn, literally forced to bow before her, has learned, to his wondering astonishment, that women are not calves to be bulldogged, hogtied, and subdued. Elma has come dangerously close to the total destruction of her innocence, but that very innocence has given the aging sensualist pause enough to permit both of them, for the time, to escape. By the time Inge returns all on stage to equilibrium and sends his bus on its journey, we have encountered a touching human experience of lasting impressiveness.

In his final and least noteworthy "success," *The Dark at the Top of the Stairs*, Inge unfortunately surrenders to artificialities of plot, less than subtle symbolism, gratuitous violence, and remarkably unconvincing characters. There is much of the "basic Inge" to be seen and, upon occasion, praised, but the strong human appeal of the first three plays is lost amid generally unsatisfactory handling of marital problems, racial prejudices, and parent-child relationships. We may still understand some of the reasons for Rubin Flood's infidelity and Sonny's mamma's boy behavior, as well as little Sammy's suicide, but, on the whole, there is too much of the trite and unimaginative to be as convincing as we would like.

The ultimate appeal of Inge seems to lie in his ability to transform the lives and behavior of drab people in drab surroundings into a significant drama of human experience. Taking us inside and outside the houses most of us pass every day down the block and around the corner, he reveals some rather profound human truths, and he grips us in fascination as he does so.

—Jordan Y. Miller

See the essay on *Picnic*.

INGRAHAM, Joseph Holt. Born in Portland, Maine, 26 January 1809. Educated at Hallowell Academy, Maine; Yale University, New Haven, Connecticut, 1828–29. Married Mary Brookes in 1849; three daughters and one son. Teacher, Jefferson College, Washington, Mississippi, after 1830; writer of romances from 1835; established a girls school in Nashville, Tennessee, 1849; began theological studies: ordained deacon, 1851, and priest, 1852, in the Protestant Episcopal Church, and thereafter wrote books with religious themes; missionary in Aberdeen, Mississippi, 1852–53; rector, St. John's Church, Mobile, Alabama, 1853–57, a church in Riverside, Tennessee, 1857–58, and Christ Church, Holly Springs, Mississippi, 1858–60. *Died 18 December 1860.*

PUBLICATIONS

Fiction

Lafitte, The Pirate of the Gulf. 1836; as *The Pirate*, 1839.
Burton; or, The Sieges. 1838; as *Quebec and New York; or, The Three Beauties*, 1839.
Captain Kyd; or, The Wizard of the Sea. 1839; as *Kyd the Buccaneer*, 1839.
The American Lounger; or, Tales, Sketches, and Legends Gathered in Sundry Journeyings. 1839.
The Quadroone; or, St. Michael's Day. 1840.
The Dancing Feather; or, The Amateur Freebooters: A Romance of New York. 1842; as *The Pirate Schooner*, 1877.
Edward Austin; or, The Hunting Flask: A Tale of the Forest and Town. 1842.
The Gipsy of the Highlands; or, The Jew and the Heir. 1843.
Jemmy Daily; or, The Little News Vender. 1843.
Morris Graeme; or, The Cruise of the Sea-Slipper: A Sequel to The Dancing Feather. 1843.
Fanny H—; or, The Hunchback and the Roué. 1843.
Mark Manly; or, The Skipper's Lad: A Tale of Boston in the Olden Times. 1843.
Frank Rivers; or, The Dangers of the Town. 1843.
The Young Genius; or, Trials and Triumphs. 1843.
Howard; or, The Mysterious Disappearance: A Romance of the Tripolitanian War. 1843.
Black Ralph; or, The Helmsman of Hurlgate. 1844.
Theodore; or, The Child of the Sea, Being a Sequel to Lafitte. 1844.
Rodolphe in Boston! 1844.
Billy Woodhull; or, The Pretty Haymaker. 1844.
The Corsair of Casco Bay; or, The Pilot's Daughter. 1844.
Ellen Hart; or, The Forger's Daughter. 1844.
The Miseries of New York; or, The Burglar and Counsellor. 1844.
Steel Belt; or, The Three Masted Goleta: A Tale of Boston Bay. 1844.
Arnold; or, The British Spy! (includes *The Bold Insurgent*). 1844; as *The Treason of Arnold*, 1847.
The Midshipman; or, The Corvette and Brigantine. 1844.
La Bonita Cigarera; or, The Beautiful Cigar Vendor: A Tale of New York. 1844.
The Spanish Galleon; or, The Pirate of the Mediterranean: A Romance of the Corsair Kidd. 1844.
Estelle; or, The Conspirator of the Isle: A Tale of the West Indian Seas. 1844.
The Silver Bottle; or, The Adventures of Little Marlboro in Search of His Father. 1844.
Herman de Ruyter; or, The Mystery Unveiled: A Sequel to The Beautiful Cigar Vendor. 1844.
The Diary of a Hackney Coachman. 1844.
Santa Claus; or, The Merry King of Christmas. 1844.
Caroline Archer; or, The Milliner's Apprentice. 1844.
Eleanor Sherwood, The Beautiful Temptress! 1844.
The Clipper-Yacht; or, Moloch the Money-Lender: A Tale of London and the Thames. 1845.
Marie; or, The Fugitive: A Romance of Mount Benedict. 1845.
Freemantle; or, The Privateersman! A Nautical Romance of the Last War. 1845.
Scarlet Feather; or, The Young Chief of the Abenaquies: A Romance of the Wilderness of Maine. 1845.
Forrestal; or, The Light of the Reef. 1845.
Rafael. 1845.
The Knights of Seven Lands. 1845; as *The Seven Knights*, 1845.
Montezuma, The Serf; or, The Revolt of the Mexitili: A Tale of the Last Days of the Aztec Dynasty. 1845.
Will Terril; or, The Adventures of a Young Gentleman Born in a Cellar. 1845.
Norman; or, The Privateersman's Bride: A Sequel to Freemantle. 1845.
Neal Nelson; or, The Siege of Boston: A Tale of the Revolution. 1845; as *Sons of Liberty*, 1887.
A Romance of the Sunny South; or, Feathers from a Traveller's Wing. 1845.
Paul Deverell; or, Two Judgments for One Crime: A Tale of the Present Day. 1845.
Paul Perril, The Merchant's Son; or, The Adventures of a New-England Boy Launched upon Life. 2 vols., 1845–46(?).
The Adventures of Will Wizard! Corporal of the Saccarapa Volunteers. 1845.
Alice May, and Bruising Bill (stories). 1845.
Bertrand; or, The Story of Marie de Heywode, Being a Sequel to Marie. 1845.
Charles Blackford; or, The Adventures of a Student in Search of a Profession. 1845.
The Cruiser of the Mist. 1845.
Fleming Field; or, The Young Artisan: A Tale of the Days of the Stamp Act. 1845.
Grace Weldon; or, Frederica the Bonnet-Girl: A Tale of Boston and Its Bay. 1845.
Harry Harefoot; or, The Three Temptations: A Story of City Scenes. 1845.

Henry Howard; or, Two Noes Make One Yes (includes *Trout-Fishing*). 1845.
Mary Wilbur; or, The Deacon and the Widow's Daughter. 1845.
The Mast-Ship; or, The Bombardment of Falmouth. 1845.
The Wing of the Wind. 1845.
Arthur Denwood; or, The Maiden of the Inn: A Tale of the War of 1812. 1846.
The Lady of the Gulf. 1846; as *Josephene*, 1853(?).
Leisler; or, The Rebel and the King's Man: A Tale of the Rebellion of 1689. 1846.
Ramero; or, The Prince and the Prisoner! 1846.
Bonfield; or, The Outlaw of the Bermudas. 1846.
The Silver Ship of Mexico. 1846.
Berkeley; or, The Lost and Redeemed. 1846.
Mate Burke; or, The Foundlings of the Sea. 1846.
The Mysterious State-Room: A Tale of the Mississippi. 1846.
The Odd Fellow; or, The Secret Association, and Foraging Peter (stories). 1846.
Pierce Fenning; or, The Lugger's Chase. 1846; as *The Rebel Coaster*, 1867.
The Ringdove; or, The Privateer and the Cutter. 1846(?); as *A Yankee Blue-Jacket*, 1888.
The Slave King; or, The Triumph of Liberty. 1846.
The Spectre Steamer and Other Tales. 1846.
The Young Artist, and The Bold Insurgent (stories). 1846.
The Surf Skiff; or, The Heroines of the Kennebec (includes *Captain Velasco*). 1847.
The Truce; or, On and Off Soundings: A Tale of the Coast of Maine. 1847.
Blanche Talbot; or The Maiden's Hand: A Romance of the War of 1812 (includes *Henry Temple*). 1847.
The Brigantine; or, Guitierro and the Castilian: A Tale Both of Boston and Cuba (includes *The Old Bean*). 1847.
Edward Manning; or, The Bride and the Maiden. 1847.
Beatrice, The Goldsmith's Daughter: A Story of the Reign of the Last Charles. 1847.
Ringold Griffitt; or, The Raftsman of the Susquehannah: A Tale of Pennsylvania. 1847.
The Free-Trader; or, the Cruiser of Narragansett Bay. 1847.
The Texan Ranger; or, The Maid of Matamoras (includes *Alice Brandon*). 1847.
Wildash; or, The Cruiser of the Capes. 1847.
Jennette Alison; or, The Young Strawberry Girl. 1848.
Nobody's Son; or, The Life and Adventures of Percival Mayberry. 1851.
The Arrow of Gold; or, The Shell Gatherer. 1854(?).
The Prince of the House of David; or, Three Years in the Holy City. 1855.
Rivingstone; or, The Young Ranger Hussar: A Romance of the Revolution. 1855.
The Pillar of Fire; or, Israel in Bondage. 1859.
The Throne of David: From the Consecration of the Shepherd of Bethlehem to the Rebellion of Prince Absalom. 1860.
The Sunny South; or, The Southerner at Home. 1860; as *Not "A Fool's Errand,"* 1880; as *Kate's Experiences*, 1880.
Mortimer; or, The Bankrupt's Heiress. 1865.
Wildbird; or, The Three Chances. 1869.
The Avenging Brother; or, The Two Maidens. 1869.
The Pirate Chief; or, The Cutter of the Ocean. N.d.

Other

The South-West. 2 vols., 1835.
Pamphlets for the People, in Illustration of the Claims of the Church and Methodism. 1854.

*

Bibliography: in *Bibliography of American Literature* by Jacob Blanck, 1963.

Critical Study: *Ingraham* by Robert W. Weathersby II, 1980.

* * *

Joseph Holt Ingraham was one of the first Americans to try to make a living by writing fiction, and his career provides a paradigm of the forms to which early would-be professionals turned in their efforts to meet the destructive competition from imported works in the days before international copyright.

After achieving success with his non-fiction account of his travels in Louisiana and Mississippi (*The South-West*), he turned to the then favorite two-volume historical novel after the manner of Scott and Cooper. His first, *Lafitte, The Pirate of the Gulf*, a conventional romance about a patriotic Louisiana pirate who turns out to have been highborn, was his most successful and remained in print well into the 20th century. *Burton* (which is about the Canadian campaign of Aaron Burr during the American Revolution) and *Captain Kyd* (another fantasy about a famous pirate) were less successful; despite the appeal of the subjects, the stories were too preposterous and chaotically constructed even for readers accustomed to gothic fiction. A fourth double-decker, *The Quadroone*, another tale of baby-switching during the Spanish occupation of New Orleans in the 18th century, was coldly received; and a projected fifth, *The Dancing Feather*, an unlikely tale of contemporary piracy in New York harbor, had to be ended abruptly after the tenth chapter of a planned fifty and published as a cheap paperback.

During the next five years, Ingraham led in productivity a pack of hungry writers churning out the hundred-page pamphlets that new high-speed printing presses made it possible to sell for 25 cents. Ingraham wrote at least sixty; most were stories of pirates and other nautical adventurers, though some were early tales of the shady side of big city life. Typical and most interesting are *The Beautiful Cigar Vendor* and its sequel *Herman de Ruyter*, in which Ingraham provides his own solution to the mystery of the disappearance of Mary Cecilia Rogers, a New York girl who inspired also Poe's "The Mystery of Marie Roget."

When Ingraham entered the work of the Protestant Episcopal church in 1847, what the *Knickerbocker* magazine called his "cheap and nasty," "immoral" stories ceased to flow from his pen, although in 1851 he produced a final short work, *Nobody's Son*, protesting the mistreatment of orphans in the manner of Dickens's popular fictions.

Ingraham's greatest success and major contribution to literature came late in his life, however, when, as he was engaged in the ministry, he began to write a life of Christ in the form of a series of letters from an impressionable young Egyptian girl visiting the Holy Land in Christ's time. These developed into *The Prince of the House of David*, the first religious bestseller, and the prototype of a vein that has flourished through the works of Lew Wallace, Lloyd Douglas, and others to the present day. Further attempts, however, to tell the story of Moses (*The Pillar of Fire*) and the founding of the Hebrew kingdom (*The Throne of David*) were less successful because the novels became too long-winded and were clumsily constructed. He failed to find a publisher for a projected fourth novel, *St. Paul, The Roman Citizen*, before his sudden and still mysterious death.

—Warren French

IRVING, Washington. Born in New York City, 3 April 1783. Educated in local schools; studied law in the offices of Henry Masterton, 1799, Brockholst Livingstone, 1801, and Josiah Ogden Hoffman, 1802; admitted to New York bar, 1806, but practised only intermittently. Served as military aide to New York Governor Tompkins in the U.S. Army during the War of 1812. Travelled in Europe, 1804–06; became partner, with his brothers, in family hardware business, New York and Liverpool, 1810; representative of the business in England, 1815 until the firm collapsed, 1818; editor, *Analectic* magazine, Philadelphia and New York, 1812–14; lived in Dresden, 1822–23, London, 1824, Paris, 1825, and Madrid, as member of the U.S. Legation, 1826–29; Secretary, U.S. Legation, London, 1829–32; returned to New York, then toured the southern and western U.S., 1832; lived at the manor house "Sunnyside," Tarrytown-on-Hudson, New York, 1836–42; U.S. Ambassador to Spain, in Barcelona and Madrid, 1842–45; then returned to Tarrytown. President, Astor Library (later New York Public Library), 1848–59. Recipient: Royal Society of Literature medal, 1830. LL.D.: Oxford University, 1831; honorary degree: Columbia University, New York; Harvard University, Cambridge, Massachusetts. Corresponding Member, Royal Academy of History (Spain), 1829. *Died 28 November 1859.*

PUBLICATIONS

Collections

Works (Author's Revised Edition). 15 vols., 1848–51.
Representative Selections, edited by Henry A. Pochmann. 1934.
Complete Works, edited by Richard Dilworth Rust and others. 1969—
Complete Tales, edited by Charles Neider. 1975.
History, Tales and Sketches (Library of America), edited by James W. Tuttleton. 1983.

Fiction and Sketches

Salmagundi; or, The Whim-Whams and Opinions of Launcelot Langstaff, Esq., and Others, with James Kirke Paulding and William Irving. 2 vols., 1807–08; revised (by Washington Irving only), 1824.
The Sketch Book of Geoffrey Crayon, Gent. 7 vols., 1819–20; revised edition, 2 vols., 1820.
Bracebridge Hall; or, The Humourists: A Medley. 1822; edited by J.D. Colclough, 1898.
Letters of Jonathan Oldstyle, Gent. 1824.
Tales of a Traveller. 1824.
The Alhambra: A Series of Tales and Sketches of the Moors and Spaniards. 1832.
Essays and Sketches. 1837.
Chronicles of Wolfert's Roost and Other Papers. 1855.

Plays

Charles the Second; or, The Merry Monarch, with John Howard Payne, from a play by Alexandre Duval (produced 1824). 1824; edited by Arthur Hobson Quinn, in *Representative American Plays*, 1917.
Richelieu: A Domestic Tragedy, with John Howard Payne, from a play by Alexandre Duval (produced 1826; as *The French Libertine*, produced 1826). 1826.
Abu Hassan. 1924.
The Wild Huntsman, from a play by Friedrich Kind. 1924.
An Unwritten Play of Lord Byron. 1925.

Verse

The Poems, edited by William R. Langfeld. 1931.

Other

A History of New-York from the Beginning of the World to the End of the Dutch Dynasty. 2 vols., 1809; revised edition, 1812, 1848.
A History of the Life and Voyages of Christopher Columbus. 4 vols., 1828; edited by Winifred Hulbert, as *The Voyages of Columbus*, 1931.
A Chronicle of the Conquest of Granada. 2 vols., 1829.
Voyages and Discoveries of the Companions of Columbus. 1831.
Miscellanies (*A Tour on the Prairies, Abbotsford and Newstead Abbey, Legends of the Conquest of Spain*). 3 vols., 1835; *A Tour on the Prairies* edited by John Francis McDermott, 1956.
Astoria; or, Anecdotes of an Enterprise Beyond the Rocky Mountains. 2 vols., 1836; edited by Edgeley W. Todd, 1964.
Adventures of Captain Bonneville; or, Scenes Beyond the Rocky Mountains of the Far West, based on journals of B.L.E. Bonneville. 3 vols., 1837; as *The Rocky Mountains*, 1837.
The Life of Oliver Goldsmith, with Selections from His Writings. 2 vols., 1840; revised edition, as *Oliver Goldsmith: A Biography*, in *Works II*, 1849; edited by G.S. Blakely, 1916.
Biography and Poetical Remains of the Late Margaret Miller Davidson. 1841.
A Book of the Hudson. 1849.
Mahomet and His Successors, in *Works*. 2 vols., 1850.
Life of George Washington. 5 vols., 1855–59; abridged and edited by Charles Neider, 1976.
Spanish Papers and Other Miscellanies, edited by Pierre M. Irving. 2 vols., 1866.
Letters to Mrs. William Renwick and to Her Son James Renwick. 1915.
Letters to Henry Brevoort, edited by George S. Hellman. 2 vols., 1915.
The Journals (Hitherto Unpublished), edited by William P. Trent and George S. Hellman. 3 vols., 1919.
Notes and Journal of Travel in Europe 1804–1805. 3 vols., 1921.
Diary: Spain 1828–1829, edited by Clara Louisa Penney. 1926.
Notes While Preparing Sketch Book 1817, edited by Stanley T. Williams. 1927.

Tour in Scotland 1817, and Other Manuscript Notes, edited by Stanley T. Williams. 1927.
Letters from Sunnyside and Spain, edited by Stanley T. Williams. 1928.
Journal (1823–1824), edited by Stanley T. Williams. 1931.
Irving and the Storrows: Letters from England and the Continent 1821–1828, edited by Stanley T. Williams. 1933.
Journal 1803, edited by Stanley T. Williams. 1934.
Journal 1828, and Miscellaneous Notes on Moorish Legend and History, edited by Stanley T. Williams. 1937.
The Western Journals, edited by John Francis McDermott. 1944.
Contributions to the Corrector, edited by Martin Roth. 1968.
Irving and the House of Murray (letters), edited by Ben Harris McClary. 1969.

Editor, *The Miscellaneous Works of Goldsmith*. 4 vols., 1825.
Editor, *Poems* (London edition), by William Cullen Bryant. 1832.
Editor, *Harvey's Scenes of the Primitive Forest of America*. 1841.

Translator, with Peter Irving and Georges Caines, *A Voyage to the Eastern Part of Terra Firma; or, The Spanish Main*, by F. Depons. 3 vols., 1806.

*

Bibliography: *A Bibliography of the Writings of Irving* by Stanley T. Williams and Mary Allen Edge, 1936; in *Bibliography of American Literature* by Jacob Blanck, 1969; *Irving: A Reference Guide* by Haskell Springer, 1976.

Critical Studies: *Life and Letters of Irving* by Pierre M. Irving, 4 vols., 1862–64; *The Life of Irving* by Stanley T. Williams, 2 vols., 1935; *The World of Irving* by Van Wyck Brooks, 1944; *Irving and Germany* by Walter A. Reichart, 1957; *Irving: Moderation Displayed* by Edward Wagenknecht, 1962; *Irving* by Lewis Leary, 1963; *Irving: An American Study 1802–1835* by William L. Hedges, 1965; *Irving Reconsidered: A Symposium* edited by Ralph Aderman, 1969; *The Worlds of Irving*, 1974, and *A Century of Commentary on the Works of Irving*, 1976, both edited by Andrew B. Myers; *Comedy and America: The Lost World of Irving* by Martin Roth, 1976; *Pierre M. Irving and Washington Irving: A Collaboration in Life and Letters* by Wayne R. Kime, 1977; *Irving* by Mary Weatherspoon Bowden, 1981.

* * *

Born in 1783, the year in which the American Revolution ended, Washington Irving, son of a prosperous New York hardware merchant, became the first author of the new country to be acclaimed in England. Although he never wrote a novel—indeed, his chief achievement resides in perhaps a dozen sketches and short stories—he must be acknowledged as the first man of letters in the United States. He lived until 1859, much admired by Poe and Hawthorne, whose grapplings with the darker side of human nature were as foreign to his own sanguine temperament as were their respective interests in ideas and in the extended development of plot and character. Yet Irving had managed to win not only their admiration but also that of Scott, Coleridge, and Byron. By the time he published *The Sketch Book of Geoffrey Crayon, Gent*. in 1819–20, his best work had been done. In the succeeding forty years he, like his contemporary William Cullen Bryant, became enshrined as a living figurehead of literary culture in America, though the conditions of American life rapidly outstripped his preparation or inclination to treat them in his writing.

In the event, however, Irving did bring to his vocation a belletristic sensibility, and a style that combined grace and poise with an inimitable pictorial quality. This style seems a fusion of Augustan balance with the sentiments of early Romanticism; it is among the first purely literary artifacts in the culture of the new republic. Irving's stylistic influence is visible in Hawthorne, in the tales of Bret Harte set in Spanish California, and even in Henry James (e.g., the description of Gardencourt in *The Portrait of a Lady*). But a decade before achieving the grace and strength of this style in *The Sketch Book*, Irving had scored a literary triumph of a different stripe with *A History of New-York* (as the pseudonymous Diedrich Knickerbocker). This burlesque, Hudibrastic in its energy, is a satiric debunking of the Colonial history of Dutch New York, published in 1809; its author's and its country's 26th year. Although Irving was not to be so boldly satirical again, this youthful extravagance exhibits also another aspect of his sensibility which stayed with him to the end: his fascination with the past.

Not one to stay tied to the family hardware business, he served in the War of 1812 as a staff colonel, and in 1815 returned to Europe (he had taken a grand tour in 1804)—little knowing that he would not see New York again for seventeen years. Arriving in England, he sought out Scott, who had admired his *History*. Irving quickly became Scott's disciple, and, as is seen in *The Sketch Book*, he turned, in his most memorable stories, to the local settings and legends of the same Dutch ancestors whose political figures he had, as Diedrich Knickerbocker, lampooned a decade earlier. But Irving, although he anticipates by half a century the local color movement in fiction, was not merely a local colorist. He used the color of his native locale the Hudson Valley, to impart the tinge of native realism to fables he deftly appropriated from European literature. "Rip Van Winkle," the tale which would bring Irving world-wide fame, is in part a nearly literal rendering from Otmar's *Volkssagen*. "The Legend of Sleepy Hollow," Irving's other masterpiece, is similarly based on Bürger's *Der Wilde Jäger* and one of the Rübezahl tales. Yet Irving did more than give these Germanic folk motifs a local habitation and a name. He infused them with subliminal universal significance, and at the same time, by an authorial alchemy no doubt unconscious on his part, expressed in them the very spirit of his nation and of his time.

In "Rip Van Winkle" the localization of the ancient German tale is perfect. Rip, a shrewbedevilled husband, is a stock comic figure seeking regressive freedom in his bottle and in the wilderness of the mountaintop. There, encountering the ghosts of Hendrik Hudson's crew, he drinks their magical draught—and awakens as an old man, his fowling gun rusted beside him. In the meantime, however, life had gone on in the village below: that life included the American Revolution. So Rip's return from the blessed otherworld of the irretrievable past is to a new, busy, bustling nation he cannot understand, or enter. Irving's pervasive theme of nostalgia for the unrecoverable past is here at once mythologized and made unforgettable.

In "The Legend of Sleepy Hollow" Irving again appropriates a comic stereotype, for his Ichabod Crane, the Yankee schoolmaster, is akin to satirical versions of the Puritan character—calculating, narrow-gauged, lacking in spontaneity—found in the popular culture of the time. With intuitive prescience Irving puts Ichabod in opposition to Brom Bones, a brawny, forthright Dutchman whose character resembles that of such frontier folk heroes yet to come as Mike Fink or Davy Crockett. Thus at the beginning of American literature Irving anticipates the regional conflict between East and West, between the Puritan, urban, prudential character and the freedom of the natural man. He further imbeds this story in the expressive energies of popular culture by making the plot hinge on a tall tale that is also the frontiersman's hoax. Ichabod, known to be superstitious, is run out of town by the headless horseman. Brom Bones, in the saddle with the pumpkinhead in his lap, stays in Kinderhook to marry the girl. Thus Irving bestows his favor on an American of the coming century. In his own life, however, Irving was not as lucky as Brom Bones. His fiancée, Matilda Hoffman, daughter of a judge, died, and it may be that this early loss colored Irving's Romantic nostalgia.

Elsewhere in *The Sketch Book* Irving wrote at lower levels of intensity, exploring the folk customs of English Christmas, describing "A Country Church," "A Sunday in London," and the like. These at best are gentle impressionistic evocations of nostalgic moods. In *Bracebridge Hall* and *Tales of a Traveller* he reiterated similar subjects: *Chronicles of Wolfert's Roost* draws on Irving's travels in Germany and Spain, but the best tales are "Kidd the Pirate" and "The Devil and Tom Walker," the one an American legend, the other a native adaptation of the Faustian theme. Little in these books has lived, though in their time they doubtless enriched American literature with an antiquarian's love of the vanished or vanishing folkways of Europe.

Irving spent the winter of 1825 in Dresden, the next three years in Madrid, and then served from 1829 until his return in 1832 as Secretary of the American legation in London. His Spanish sojourn led to his writing the tales in *The Alhambra* and to his lengthy biographies of Mahomet and Columbus. These, as Stanley Williams has observed, are really romances rather than factual accounts of their subjects. After returning to America Irving, aware of the public's desire for fictional treatments of the west, took a tour of the wilds and provided them with *A Tour on the Prairies*, *Astoria* (an account of John Jacob Astor's success in the fur trade) and *Adventures of Captain Bonneville*. Thus the famous writer tried to obviate suspicion of his long exile, but these writings bring to the west only the pictorialist's eye trained in London and Madrid. Irving could not romanticize such subjects.

It was characteristic of this genial author's temperament that he chose as his private vehicle the sketch during the decades when the short story was supplanting it in popularity. In fact his own tales served as models for Poe, Hawthorne, and other authors whose fictions hurried the genre of the sketch into oblivion. If Irving's works of lasting value are but few and those few brief, his career is nonetheless significant; not only did he write some incomparable tales, and prove that authorship was a possible profession in a new country, but at the very moment when American literary consciousness was first developing he enriched his nation's culture with his cosmopolitan reflection of the themes and modes of British and continental Romanticism.

—Daniel Hoffman

See the essay on "The Legend of Sleepy Hollow."

JACKSON, Helen (Maria) Hunt (née Fiske). Born in Amherst, Massachusetts, 15 October 1830. Educated at Ipswich Female Seminary, Massachusetts, and Spingler Institute, New York. Married 1) Edward Bissell Hunt in 1852 (died, 1863), two sons; 2) William Sharpless Jackson in 1875. Neighbor and schoolmate of Emily Dickinson, who remained her life-long friend; after her first marriage, traveled throughout the United States with her husband, an officer in the Army Corps of Engineers; lived in Newport, Rhode Island, 1866–74; traveled in Europe, 1868–70; lived in Colorado Springs, 1875–85; commissioner, Bureau of Indian Affairs, to investigate conditions of the Mission Indians of California, 1882–83. *Died 12 August 1885.*

Publications

Fiction

Saxe Holm's Stories. 2 vols., 1874–78.
The Story of Boon. 1874.
Mercy Philbrick's Choice. 1876.
Hetty's Strange History. 1877.
Nelly's Silver Mine: A Story of Colorado Life. 1878.
The Hunter Cats of Connorloa. 1884.
Ramona. 1884.
Zeph: A Posthumous Story. 1885.
Pansy Billings and Popsy: Two Stories of Girl Life. 1898.

Verse

Verses. 1870; revised edition, 1871, 1874.
Easter Bells. 1884.
Pansies and Orchids, edited by Susie B. Skelding. 1884.
Sonnets and Lyrics. 1886.

Other

Bits of Travel. 1972.
Bits of Talk about Home Matters. 1873.
Bits of Talk, in Verse and Prose, for Young Folks. 1876.
Bits of Travel at Home. 1878.
A Century of Dishonor: A Sketch of the United States Government's Dealings with Some of the Indian Tribes. 1881; edited by Andrew F. Rolle, 1965.
Mammy Tittleback and Family: A True Story of Seventeen Cats. (for children). 1881.
The Training of Children. 1882.
Report on the Condition and Needs of the Mission Indians of California, with Abbot Kinney. 1883; *Father Junipero and His Work* edited by Richard B. Yale, 1966.
Glimpses of Three Coasts. 1886.
Between Whiles. 1887.

Editor, *Letters from a Cat*, by Deborah Fiske. 1879.

Translator, *Bathmendi*, by J.P.C. de Florian. 1867.

*

Bibliography: in *Bibliography of American Literature* by Jacob Blanck, 1963.

Critical Studies: *Jackson* by Ruth Odell, 1939; "Jackson, Sentimentalist vs. Realist" by Allan Nevins, in *American Scholar*, Summer 1941; *Jackson* by Evelyn I. Banning, 1973.

* * *

When Helen Hunt Jackson died in 1885 Emily Dickinson promised her immortality: "Helen of Troy will die, but Helen of Colorado, never." At the time of her death her reputation was at its height as the result of two works, *A Century of Dishonor* and *Ramona*, both produced partly in consequence of Jackson's move to Colorado and the west after her second marriage in 1875. Thomas Wentworth Higginson compared her to George Eliot; another critic thought her verse in some respects superior to that of Elizabeth Barrett Browning. *A Century of Dishonor* went out of print in 1885 and remained so until 1965 but *Ramona* went through over 300 printings in the intervening years and was transferred to both stage and screen.

Paradoxically these two works alone do not give much understanding of either the writer's background or of her cultural and literary drives. In essence she was a New Englander whose closest friends and influences included not only Dickinson and Higginson but Nathaniel Hawthorne, Horace Greeley, and the sculptors Horace Greenough and William Wetmore Story. Much of her verse and prose was filled by preoccupations with sin and morality, with the evil in man and the need for moral struggle. Allan Nevins argued in *American Scholar* (1941) that *A Century of Dishonor* is too sentimental, and he is correct in that its purpose was polemical rather than literary or historical. But there is far less sentimentality in the main body of Jackson's work. Though her descriptions are often close to cosy, her sympathies are defined by a rationalism and an individualism that make her characters in the end fully responsible for their fates, and she does not bring excess emotion to the telling of their destinies. Her characters survive and struggle on after what in other novelists of the day would have been the final and crippling climax, as can be seen in both *Hetty's Strange History* and *Mercy Philbrick's Choice*.

Such a modern sounding quality is linked to what some of her contemporary critics felt needed apology: a devaluing of narrative in some of her work. At times the results are anticlimactic, for it is difficult to sustain the dramatic tension once the central focus of the plot has been passed. The difference in the characters' lives before and after this point is often too extremely presented, but the great advantage is escape from dénouement. It is possible that Jackson's emphasis on the continuity of life was one aspect of an outlook partly formed by a vigorous and intelligent sense of humour, though this quality is to be found more in her ephemeral writings like *Bits of Travel at Home* than in the more formal works.

Modern readers would be attracted not only by her sympathy for the Native American but also by her strong feminism. Her heroines are the prime movers of her plots; the men revolve about them. Her women tend to be socially committed, fulfilling themselves through the exercise of their talents in the world, and, if introspective, only in a way that strengthens them when in contact with others. The women she describes would not have been at home among the New England millworkers; their freedom of action depended on their freedom from poverty. Her lack of interest in this connection prevented her being swamped by naturalism and has deprived her of readers in a century that demands it.

In life Jackson was vivacious, articulate, intelligent, and active. Her work deserves respect as that of a modern woman in the thirty years after the Civil War.

—R.A. Burchell

JACKSON, Laura (Riding). See **RIDING, Laura.**

JACKSON, Shirley (Hardie). Born in San Francisco, California, 14 December 1919. Educated at Burlingame High School, California; Brighton High School, Rochester, New York; University of Rochester, 1934–36; Syracuse University, New York, 1937–40, B.A. 1940. Married the writer Stanley Edgar Hyman in 1940; two sons and two daughters. Lived in North Bennington, Vermont, after 1945. Recipient: Mystery Writers of America Edgar Allan Poe Award, 1961. *Died 8 August 1965.*

PUBLICATIONS

Collections

The Magic of Jackson, edited by Stanley Edgar Hyman. 1966.

Fiction

The Road Through the Wall. 1948; as *The Other Side of the Street*, 1956.
The Lottery; or, The Adventures of James Harris (stories). 1949.
Hangsaman. 1951.
The Bird's Nest. 1954; as *Lizzie*, 1957.
The Sundial. 1958.
The Haunting of Hill House. 1959.
We Have Always Lived in the Castle. 1962.

Plays

The Lottery, from her own story, in *Best Television Plays 1950–1951*, edited by William I. Kauffman. 1952.
The Bad Children: A Play in One Act for Bad Children. 1959.

Other

Life among the Savages. 1953.
The Witchcraft of Salem Village (for children). 1956.
Raising Demons. 1957.
Special Delivery: A Useful Book for Brand-New Mothers. 1960; as *And Baby Makes Three*, 1960.
9 Magic Wishes (for children). 1963.
Famous Sally (for children). 1966.
Come Along with Me: Part of a Novel, Sixteen Stories, and Three Lectures, edited by Stanley Edgar Hyman. 1968.

*

Critical Study: *Jackson* by Lenemaja Friedman, 1975.

* * *

Throughout her work Shirley Jackson focuses on incongruities in an everyday setting, whether for comic or sinister effect. This is as true of her "disrespectful memoir" of her children, *Life among the Savages*, and its equally hilarious sequel, *Raising Demons*, as of the dark psychological explorations of her novels and short stories. In her later fiction she wrote about extraordinary characters and situations, but these were always located in an ordinary setting, the juxtaposition providing her staple ingredient of incongruity.

Much of Jackson's work is concerned with an attempt to gain, or regain, an identity. *The Bird's Nest* concerns a mentally disturbed girl who has four different voices and identities. It is triumphantly structured, but, like the earlier *Hangsaman*, the positive note on which it ends fails to remove our doubts about the future of the main character. In *The Sundial* Jackson focuses on an eccentric group of characters in the Halloran family house, where, directed by a dead relative, they await the end of the world in the belief that they alone will be saved. Allegorical relationships emerge between the characters, and the narrative, characteristically both comic and macabre, develops baroque motifs of sundial and maze.

Like *The Sundial* and her famous spine-chiller *The Haunting of Hill House* (with its "clashing disharmonies"), *We Have Always Lived in the Castle* centres on a house. Even more than *The Sundial* the reader is induced to identify with its inhabitants—eccentric or criminal though they may be—against "them" in the world outside. Eighteen-year-old "Merricat" describes her life with her sister Constance after the latter's acquittal from a charge of poisoning the rest of the family—a charge of which the local police believe her to be guilty. The destructive invasion of the world outside parallels the set-piece of the peaceable invasion of the locals invited to the final barbeque in *The Sundial*. The portrayal of the sisters' loving relationship, albeit in macabre circumstances, makes *We Have Always Lived in the Castle* the most remarkable of Jackson's books.

A few of Jackson's short stories delight in the incongruous for its own sake; however, most of her stories, including the title story of *The Lottery* (which caused a sensation on its publication in the *New Yorker* in 1948), are informed by a genuine sense of evil. The stories generally centre on an isolated female, often the inadequate victim of a daemon lover (such as James Harris in *The Lottery*). These characters are lost in the concrete jungle of the Kafkaesque city or are on long-distance journeys "to the end of the night." This theme is habitually announced by laughter, lines from songs and poems, or nursery rhymes, transmuted to sinister leitmotifs.

To portray the fragmented personality Jackson resorted to a kind of zany verbal logic and semantic irony. Yet though there are passages in her work reminiscent of Borges, she kept any experimental tendency in her writing subordinated to the demands of storytelling, her prime consideration, as the lectures in *Come Along with Me* make clear.

—Val Warner

JAMES, Henry. Born in New York City, 15 April 1843; brother of William James, *q.v.*; emigrated to England; became British citizen, 1915. Educated at the Richard Pulling Jenks School, New York; traveled with his family in Europe from an early age: studied with tutors in Geneva, London, Paris, and Boulogne, 1855–58, Geneva, 1859, and Bonn, 1860; lived with his family in Newport, Rhode Island, 1860–62; attended Harvard Law School, Cambridge, Massachusetts, 1862–63. Lived with his family in Cambridge and wrote for *Nation* and *Atlantic Monthly*, 1866–69; toured Europe, 1869–70; returned to Cambridge, 1870–72; wrote art criticism for *Atlantic Monthly*, 1871–72; lived in Europe, 1872–74, Cambridge, 1875, and Paris, 1875–76; writer for New York *Tribune*, Paris, 1875–76; moved to London, 1876, and lived in England for the rest of his life; settled in Rye, Sussex, 1896; traveled throughout the U.S., 1904–05. L.H.D.: Harvard University, 1911; Oxford University, 1912. Order of Merit, 1916. *Died 28 February 1916.*

PUBLICATIONS

Collections

Novels and Stories, edited by Percy Lubbock. 35 vols., 1921–24.
Complete Plays, edited by Leon Edel. 1949.
Complete Tales, edited by Leon Edel. 12 vols., 1962–64.
Representative Selections, revised edition, edited by Lyon N. Richardson. 1966.
Tales, edited by Maqbool Aziz. 1973—
Letters, edited by Leon Edel. 4 vols., 1974–84.
Novels 1871–1880 and *1881–1886* (Library of America), edited by William T. Stafford. 2 vols., 1983–85.
Literary Criticism (Library of America), edited by Leon Edel. 2 vols., 1984.
Tales, edited by Christof Wegelin. 1984.

Fiction

A Passionate Pilgrim and Other Tales. 1875.
Roderick Hudson. 1875; revised edition, 1879.
The American. 1877.
Watch and Ward. 1878.
The Europeans: A Sketch. 1878.
Daisy Miller: A Study. 1878.
An International Episode. 1879.
The Madonna of the Future and Other Tales. 1879.
Confidence. 1879.
A Bundle of Letters. 1880.
The Diary of a Man of Fifty, and A Bundle of Letters. 1880.
Washington Square. 1881.
The Portrait of a Lady. 1881.
The Siege of London, The Pension Beaurepas, and The Point of View. 1883; revised edition, 1884.
Novels and Tales. 14 vols., 1883.
Tales of Three Cities. 1884.
The Author of Beltraffio, Pandora, Georgina's Reasons, The Path of Duty, Four Meetings. 1885.
Stories Revived. 1885.
The Bostonians. 1886.
The Princess Casamassima. 1886.
The Reverberator. 1888.
The Aspern Papers, Louisa Pallant, The Modern Warning. 1888.

A London Life, The Patagonia, The Liar, Mrs. Temperly. 1889.
The Tragic Muse. 1890.
The Lesson of the Master, The Marriages, The Pupil, Brooksmith, The Solution, Sir Edmund Orme. 1892.
The Real Thing and Other Tales. 1893.
The Private Life, The Wheel of Time, Lord Beaupré, The Visits, Collaboration, Owen Wingrave. 1893.
Terminations: The Death of the Lion, The Coxon Fund, The Middle Years, The Altar of the Dead. 1895.
Embarrassments: The Figure in the Carpet, Glasses, The Next Time, The Way It Came. 1896.
The Other House. 1896.
The Spoils of Poynton. 1897; edited by Bernard Richards, 1982.
What Maisie Knew. 1897; edited by Douglas Jefferson, 1966.
In the Cage. 1898; edited by Morton Dauwen Zabel, 1958.
The Two Magics: The Turn of the Screw, Covering End. 1898; *The Turn of the Screw* edited by Robert Kimbrough, 1966.
The Awkward Age. 1899; edited by Vivien Jones, 1984.
The Soft Side (stories). 1900.
The Sacred Fount. 1901; edited by Leon Edel, 1953.
The Wings of the Dove. 1902; edited by Peter Brooks, 1984.
The Better Sort (stories). 1903.
The Ambassadors. 1903; edited by Christopher Butler, 1985.
The Golden Bowl. 1904; edited by Virginia Llewellyn Smith, 1983.
Novels and Tales (New York Edition), revised by James. 26 vols., 1907–17.
Julia Bride. 1909.
The Finer Grain. 1910.
The Outcry. 1911.
The Ivory Tower, edited by Percy Lubbock. 1917.
The Sense of the Past, edited by Percy Lubbock. 1917.
Gabrielle de Bergerac, edited by Albert Mordell. 1918.
Travelling Companions (stories), edited by Albert Mordell. 1919.
A Landscape Painter (stories), edited by Albert Mordell. 1919.
Master Eustace (stories). 1920.
Eight Uncollected Tales, edited by Edna Kenton. 1950.

Plays

Daisy Miller, from his own story. 1883.
The American, from his own novel (produced 1891). 1891.
Guy Domville (produced 1895). 1894.
Theatricals (includes *Tenants, Disengaged*) (produced 1909). 1894.
Theatricals: Second Series (includes *The Album, The Reprobate*) (produced 1919). 1894.
The High Bid (produced 1908). In *Complete Plays*, 1949.
The Saloon (produced 1911). In *Complete Plays*, 1949.
The Outcry (produced 1917). In *Complete Plays*, 1949.

Other

Transatlantic Sketches. 1875; revised edition, as *Foreign Parts*, 1883.
French Poets and Novelists. 1878; revised edition, 1883; edited by Leon Edel, 1964.
Hawthorne. 1879; edited by William M. Sale, Jr., 1956.
Portraits of Places. 1883.
Notes on a Collection of Drawings by George du Maurier. 1884.
A Little Tour in France. 1884; revised edition, 1900.
The Art of Fiction, with Walter Besant. 1885 (?); edited by Leon Edel, in *The House of Fiction*, 1957.
Partial Portraits. 1888.
Picture and Text. 1893.
Essays in London and Elsewhere. 1893.
William Wetmore Story and His Friends. 2 vols., 1903.
The Question of Our Speech, The Lesson of Balzac: Two Lectures. 1905.
English Hours. 1905; edited by Alma Louise Lowe, 1960.
The American Scene. 1907; edited by Leon Edel, 1968.
View and Reviews. 1908.
Italian Hours. 1909.
The Henry James Year Book, edited by Evelyn Garnaut Smalley. 1911.
Autobiography, edited by F.W. Dupee. 1956.
A Small Boy and Others. 1913.
Notes of a Son and Brother. 1914.
The Middle Years, edited by Percy Lubbock. 1917.
Notes on Novelists and Some Other Notes. 1914.
Letters to an Editor. 1916.
Within the Rim and Other Essays 1914–1915. 1919.
Letters, edited by Percy Lubbock. 2 vols., 1920.
Notes and Reviews. 1921.
A Most Unholy Trade, Being Letters on the Drama. 1923.
Three Letters to Joseph Conrad, edited by Gerard Jean-Aubry. 1926.
Letters to Walter Berry. 1928.
Letters to A.C. Benson and Auguste Monod, edited by E. F. Benson. 1930.
Theatre and Friendship: Some James Letters, edited by Elizabeth Robins. 1932.
The Art of the Novel: Critical Prefaces, edited by R. P. Blackmur. 1934.
Notebooks, edited by F. O. Matthiessen and Kenneth B. Murdock. 1947.
The Art of Fiction and Other Essays, edited by Morris Roberts. 1948.
James and Robert Louis Stevenson: A Record of Friendship and Criticism, edited by Janet Adam Smith. 1948.
The Scenic Art: Notes on Acting and the Drama 1872–1901, edited by Allan Wade. 1948.
Daumier, Caricaturist. 1954.
The American Essays, edited by Leon Edel. 1956.
The Future of the Novel: Essays on the Art of the Novel, edited by Leon Edel. 1956; as *The House of Fiction*, 1957.
The Painter's Eye: Notes and Essays on the Pictorial Arts, edited by John L. Sweeney. 1956.
Parisian Sketches: Letters to the New York Tribune 1875–1876, edited by Leon Edel and Ilse Dusoir Lind. 1957.
Literary Reviews and Essays on American, English, and French Literature, edited by Albert Mordell. 1957.
James and H.G. Wells: A Record of Their Friendship, Their Debate on the Art of Fiction, and Their Quarrel, edited by Leon Edel and Gordon N. Ray. 1958.
The Art of Travel: Scenes and Journeys in America, England, France, and Italy, edited by Morton Dauwen Zabel. 1958.
French Writers and American Women: Essays, edited by Peter Buitenhuis. 1960.
Selected Literary Criticism, edited by Morris Shapira. 1963.
James and John Hay: The Record of a Friendship, edited by

George Monteiro. 1965.

Switzerland in the Life and Work of James: The Clare Benedict Collection of Letters from James, edited by Jörg Hasler. 1966.

James: Interviews and Recollections, edited by Norman Page. 1984.

The Art of Criticism: James on the Theory and Practice of Fiction, edited by William Veeder and Susan M. Griffin. 1986.

The Complete Notebooks, edited by Leon Edel and Lyall H. Powers. 1986.

Translator, *Port Tarascon*, by Alphonse Daudet. 1891.

*

Bibliography: *A Bibliography of James* by Leon Edel and Dan H. Laurence, 1957, revised edition, 1961, 1982; *James: A Bibliography of Secondary Works* by Beatrice Ricks, 1975; *James 1917–1959: A Reference Guide* by Kristin Pruitt McColgan, 1979; *James 1960–1974: A Reference Guide* by Dorothy M. Scura, 1979; *James 1866–1916: A Reference Guide* by Linda J. Taylor, 1982; *James: A Bibliography of Criticism 1975–1981* by John Budd, 1983.

Critical Studies: *James: The Major Phase*, 1944, and *The James Family*, 1947, both by F. O. Matthiessen; *James* (biography) by Leon Edel, 5 vols., 1953–72, revised edition, 2 vols., 1978; *The American James* by Quentin Anderson, 1957; *The Comic Sense of James: A Study of the Early Novels* by Richard Poirier, 1960; *The Novels of James* by Oscar Cargill, 1961; *The Ordeal of Consciousness in James* by Dorothea Krook, 1962; *James and the Jacobites* by Maxwell Geismar, 1963, as *James and His Cult*, 1964; *The Expense of Vision: Essays on the Craft of James* by Laurence B. Holland, 1964; *The Imagination of Loving: James's Legacy to the Novel* by Naomi Lebowitz, 1965; *Plots and Characters in the Fiction of James* by Robert L. Gale, 1965; *An Anatomy of The Turn of the Screw* by Thomas Mabry Cranfill and Robert Lanier Clark, Jr., 1965; *James* by Bruce McElderry, 1965; *James: A Reader's Guide* by S. Gorley Putt, 1966, as *A Reader's Guide to James*, 1966; *Search for Form: Studies in the Structure of James's Fiction* by J. A. Ward, 1967; *James and the Children: A Consideration of James's The Turn of the Screw* by Eli Siegel, edited by Martha Baird, 1968; *James: The Critical Heritage* edited by Roger Gard, 1968; *James*, 1968, and *James: The Writer and His Work*, 1985, both by Tony Tanner; *The Negative Imagination: Form and Perspective in the Novels of James* by Sallie Sears, 1969; *The Early Tales of James* by James Kraft, 1969; *James and the Visual Arts* by Viola Hopkins Winner, 1970; *The Ambiguity of James* by Charles Thomas Samuels, 1971; *James and the Occult* by Martha Banta, 1972; *Reading James* by Louis Auchincloss, 1975; *Language and Knowledge in the Late Novels of James* by Ruth Bernard Yeazell, 1976; *Who's Who in James* by Glenda Leeming, 1976; *Person, Place and Thing in James's Novels* by Charles R. Anderson, 1977; *The Crystal Cage: Adventures of the Imagination in the Fiction of James* by Daniel J. Schneider, 1978; *A Rhetoric of Literary Character: Some Women of James* by Mary Doyle Springer, 1978; *Eve and James: Portraits of Women and Girls in His Fiction*, 1978, *The Novels of James*, 1983, and *The Tales of James*, 1984, all by Edward Wagenknecht; *James and the Experimental Novel* by Sergio Perosa, 1978; *The Novels of James: A Study of Culture and Consciousness* by Brian Lee, 1978; *James: The Later Novels* by Nicola Bradbury, 1979; *Love and the Quest for Identity in the Fiction of James* by Philip Sicker, 1980; *Writing and Reading in James* by Susanne Kappeler, 1980; *Culture and Conduct in the Novels of James* by Alwyn Berland, 1981; *The Literary Criticism of James* by Sarah B. Daugherty, 1981; *James and the Structure of the Romantic Imagination* by Daniel M. Fogel, 1981; *James: The Early Novels* by Robert Emmet Long, 1983; *Studies in James* by R.P. Blackmur, edited by Veronica A. Makowsky, 1983; *James the Critic* by Vivien Jones, 1984; *James and the Art of Power* by Mark Seltzer, 1984; *A Woman's Place in the Novels of James* by Elizabeth Allen, 1984; *The Ambassadors* by Alan W. Bellringer, 1984; *James and the Darkest Abyss of Romance* by William R. Goetz, 1986; *The Museum World of James* by Adeline R. Tintner, 1986.

* * *

Few who accord the novels and short stories of Henry James the attention they deserve come away from the experience unmoved by the subject matter and unenlightened by the artistry, yet it is probably true that James would be little read today if it were not for the continuing enthusiasm of individuals who discover him first as a reading assignment in a college or university course. More than almost any other great novelist, James is a writer whose best works require a sympathetic power of attention that the casual reader is not disposed to give. For most people James is an acquired taste. Unless they approach him in the right spirit they never acquire the taste at all. Yet he is certainly one of the great writers in English, one of those artists of another era who nevertheless seems perennially modern.

His dedication to literature for fifty years from the Civil War until his death in 1916 produced a body of work of monumental scope. He never married, never carried on anything resembling a conventional courtship. His friendships were virtually all rooted in shared literary or artistic enthusiasms. He travelled—often, it seems, merely to reinvigorate himself for a new assault upon his artistic problems. With less talent and similar dedication he might have produced novels and tales that consisted mainly of the same stories retold, the same techniques exploited again and again in order to recapture prior successes. Something of this tendency resides in his work as it does in the work of all masters, but there is also an extraordinary continual development that reaches its peak in three late masterpieces: *The Wings of the Dove, The Ambassadors*, and *The Golden Bowl*. The late work of some poets can best be read largely in the light of the education gained by studying their earlier efforts: James is one of a relatively few novelists whose work cries out to be approached in a similar manner.

"It's a complex fate being an American," James once wrote, "and one of the responsibilities it entails is fighting against a superstitious valuation of Europe." Herein is expressed the essence of the "international theme" that runs through much of his work. In a time when more than a few novelists were making capital out of the social complications that arise when individuals from one side of the Atlantic confront the natives of the other side upon their home ground, James made this subject peculiarly his own by returning to it in work after work. So doing, he lifted it outside the confines of drawing room comedy and placed it squarely at the crossroads of the two great traditions of the 19th-century novel in English. Among the best of James's international novels and tales are *The American, The Europeans, Daisy Miller, The Portrait of a Lady, The Wings of the Dove, The Ambassadors,* and *The Golden Bowl*. In these works the central concerns of previous novelists in English come together in a confrontation almost mythic in its implications. Simply expressed, the central concern of English novelists from Austen through Scott, Dickens, and Eliot was the accommodation of individual aspirations within the sheltering embrace of the social framework; both their social view and their art were shaped by a realistic vision of compromise. Just as simply expressed, the central concern of American novelists from Cooper through Hawthorne, Melville, and Twain, was with those individual aspirations that are incapable of accommodation within any social framework except the as-yet-unrealized American dream of perfect freedom, equality, and justice; their social view and their art were shaped by a vision that looked toward a world considerably more ideal than the world they lived in. James brought these visions together in an amalgamation inherently tragic. His best works express in metaphor how much the condition of modern man hangs continually in the balance between the European dream of social accommodation and the American dream of perfect freedom.

Closely related to the international theme is James's continual emphasis upon partial perspectives. Human knowledge, he insists, and consequently human action, is sharply limited by inescapable conditions of time and place. From Christopher Newman to Lambert Strether his Americans achieve their destiny because the perspectives forced upon them by birth and education allow them no choices except the ones they inevitably make. From Madame de Cintré to Madame de Vionnet his Europeans are similarly limited. This at least is the theory: the novel is realistic, as James most often intended it should be, when the fates of the characters follow inevitably from the conditions that surround them; it is romantic, as James sometimes allowed, when the fates evolve from conditions imposed by the author that are quite distinct from the facts of observable reality. The realistic effect that he intended for most of his novels derives from the success with which he developed techniques for objectifying the partial perspectives from which humans direct their lives.

An important part of his work is also the theme of awareness that comes too late. His people are concerned above all with the question of how to live, but most of them have not any clear idea of how to begin. Sometimes they are wealthy, like Christopher Newman in *The American*, Millie Theale in *The Wings of the Dove*, and Maggie Verver in *The Golden Bowl*. Sometimes they become wealthy, like Isabel Archer in *The Portrait of a Lady*. Sometimes they live in expectation of wealth, like Kate Croy in *The Wings of the Dove*. In most instances they have at least, like Lambert Strether in *The Ambassadors*, enough to enable them to live comfortably, though it is often true of the less attractive figures that they suppose themselves in need of more than they possess. In any event they are mostly free of the more mundane cares of life and have nearly total leisure in which to pursue happiness through courtship, marriage, liaisons, social activity, travel, the search for culture: whatever, in short, seems most attractive to them. To live most fully, James makes clear in a number of places, is to be most fully aware of one's possibilities so that one may make the best of them. Since, however, the most interesting possibilities come from human relationships which are inherently a tissue of subtle complexities, to be most fully aware is to possess a depth of sympathetic insight that comes to few people until it is too late to take advantage of it. Total freedom for James's characters involves the freedom to make social commitments different from those that all too often they make, wrongly, in bondage to some mistaken understanding, or do not make at all because, sadly, they fail to perceive the opportunity that lies before them.

A great critic, James is also a great technical experimenter. The best of his criticism is preserved in individual essays such as "The Art of Fiction" and in his *Notebooks* and the prefaces that he wrote for the New York edition of his works. All are read most profitably in conjunction with the example of his fiction. His technical experiments are most readily approached through those many fictions in which he enforces the theme of partial perspectives by contriving severely limited perspectives from which to narrate. Some of the easier works in which this theme and this method are important are the early *Daisy Miller* and the late "The Beast in the Jungle." Because Daisy is never seen except from the partial view that Winterbourne enjoys, the reader remains in danger of sharing Winterbourne's misunderstanding of her character. Because May Bartram, in "The Beast in the Jungle," is never seen except in a view accessible to Marcher, the same potential exists. Fundamentally simple in these works, both theme and technique become more complex in "The Aspern Papers," *The Turn of the Screw*, and *The Sacred Fount*. In all three the careful reader is aware that there may be some aspect of the truth that remains dark to the central vision of the narrator; in *The Turn of the Screw* there are good reasons to suppose both that the ghosts do and do not exist; in *The Sacred Fount* the puzzle that begins the novel becomes not less but more of a puzzle as it ends. In *The Portrait of a Lady, The Wings of the Dove, The Ambassadors*, and *The Golden Bowl*, the theme of partial perspectives (which involves often the theme of too late awareness) merges with the international theme to provide the substance of James's most lasting achievement.

Many of James's fictions conclude upon a sense of loss. In his deepest vision human life is fundamentally tragic because of the eternal tension between the individual's sense of his vast human opportunities and his frequently inadequate awareness of his personal limitations. Like Isabel Archer or Lambert Strether, 20th-century readers, too, are possessed by dreams of boundless freedom. Like both, they make in the end the choices that they *can* make—which are often not all the choices that they would make if they lived in a world in which a just and equal perfect freedom came less insistently into conflict with the requirements of social accommodation.

—George Perkins

See the essays on *The Ambassadors, The Portrait of a Lady,* and *The Turn of the Screw*.

JAMES, William. Born in New York City, 11 January 1842; brother of Henry James, *q.v.* Educated in Europe, 1857–60; studied art with William Morris Hunt, Newport, Rhode Island, 1860–61; attended Lawrence Scientific School, 1861–63, and Harvard Medical School, M.D. 1869, both Cambridge, Massachusetts. Married Alice Howe Gibbens in 1878; four sons and one daughter. Member of the Thayer Expedition to Brazil (led by Louis Agassiz), 1865–66; traveled and studied in Germany, 1867–68; Instructor in Anatomy and Physiology, 1873–76, Assistant Professor of Physiology, 1876–80, Assistant Professor of Psychology, 1880–85, and Professor of Physiology, 1885–1907, Harvard University. Gifford Lecturer, University of Edinburgh, 1901–02; Lowell Institute Lecturer, Boston, 1906; Hibbert Lecturer, Manchester College, Oxford, 1908. LL.D.: Harvard University. *Died 26 August 1910.*

PUBLICATIONS

Collections

Letters, edited by Henry James (William's son). 2 vols., 1920.
Selected Letters, edited by Elizabeth Hardwick. 1961.
Works, edited by Frederick H. Burkhardt, Fredson Bowers, and Ignas K. Skrupskelis. 1975—
Writings, edited by John J. McDermott. 1977.

Prose

The Principles of Psychology. 2 vols., 1890; chapter *Habit* published separately, 1914.
Psychology (Briefer Course). 1892; as *Text-Book of Psychology*, 1892.
Is Life Worth Living? 1896.
The Will to Believe, and Other Essays in Popular Philosophy. 1897.
Human Immortality: Two Supposed Objections to the Doctrine. 1898.
Talks to Teachers on Psychology, and to Students on Some of Life's Ideals. 1899; selection, as *On Some of Life's Ideals*, 1912.
The Varieties of Religious Experience: A Study in Human Nature. 1902.
Pragmatism: A New Name for Some Old Ways of Thinking. 1907.
The Energies of Men. 1908.
The Meaning of Truth: A Sequel to "Pragmatism." 1909.
A Pluralistic Universe: Hibbert Lectures at Manchester College on the Present Situation in Philosophy. 1909.
Some Problems of Philosophy: A Beginning of an Introduction to Philosophy, edited by Henry James (William's son). 1911.
Memories and Studies, edited by Henry James (William's son). 1911.
Essays in Radical Empiricism, edited by Ralph Barton Perry. 1912.
Selected Papers on Philosophy, edited by C.M. Bakewell. 1917.
Collected Essays and Reviews, edited by Ralph Barton Perry. 1920.
The Philosophy of James. 1925.
As James Said: Extracts from the Published Writings, edited by Elizabeth Perkins Aldrich. 1942.
Essays on Faith and Morals, edited by Ralph Barton Perry. 1943.
James on Psychical Research, edited by Gardner Murphy. 1960.
Letters of James and Théodore Flournoy, edited by Robert C. LeClair. 1966.
The Moral Equivalent of War and Other Essays, and Selections from Some Problems of Philosophy, edited by John K. Roth. 1971.
The Moral Philosophy of James, edited by John K. Roth. 1971.
The Essential Writings, edited by Bruce W. Wilshire. 1971.
A James Reader, edited by Gay Wilson Allen. 1972.
Selected Unpublished Correspondence 1885–1910, edited by Frederick J.D. Scott. 1986.

Editor, *The Literary Remains of the Late Henry James* (William's father). 1885.
Editor, *The Foundation of Ethics*, by John Edward Maude. 1887.

*

Bibliography: in *Writings* edited by John J. McDermott, 1977; *James: A Reference Guide* by Ignas K. Skrupskelis, 1977.

Critical Studies: *The Thought and Character of James* by Ralph Barton Perry, 2 vols., 1935; *The James Family* by F.O. Matthiessen, 1947; *The Thirteen Pragmatisms and Other Essays* by Arthur O. Lovejoy, 1963; *James* by Edward Carter Moore, 1965; *Introduction to James* by Andrew J. Reck, 1967; *James: A Biography*, 1967, and *James*, 1970, both by Gay Wilson Allen; *James* by Bernard P. Brennan, 1968; *Freedom and the Moral Life: The Ethics of James* by John K. Roth, 1969; *The Radical Empiricism of James* by John Wild, 1969; *Henry James and Pragmatistic Thought: A Study in the Relationship Between the Philosophy of William James and the Literary Art of Henry James* by Richard A. Hocks, 1974; *Purpose and Thought: The Meaning of Pragmatism* by John E. Smith, 1978; *Chaos and Context: A Study in James* by Charlene H. Seigfried, 1978; *A Stroll with James* by Jacques Barzun, 1983; *Becoming James* by Howard M. Feinstein, 1984; *James: His Life and Thought* by Gerald E. Meyers, 1986.

* * *

It was once said that William James was not really a philosopher: his excursions into philosophy were more "in the nature of raids." This is something of an exaggeration. Nevertheless, those viewing James only from the vantage points of his pragmatism and radical empiricism, or who consider him meaningful only because he anticipated various philosophic courses, underestimate his contribution. James wrote mainly for the public mind and his skill in the presentation of ideas was consummate. His journals and letters are a charming insight into the life of a famous 19th-century family, and his witty, eloquent and heavily metaphorical style has much appeal even today. His qualities and cast of mind are dateless. With James, the philosophic enterprise begins again. He attempted to provide a method of inquiry which would mediate between the evolutive procession of nature and the realization of uniquely human concerns. This attempt can best be seen in the contexts of 19th-century evolutionary theory, James's belief in an intelligible, continuous, but unfinished universe, and his personal confrontation with nihilism.

In 1869 and 1870 James underwent a personal crisis of despair which culminated in a rejection of suicide in favour of a possibly creative life unsupported by certitude. Reading Renouvier's second *Essais*, he saw no reason why that definition of free will, "the sustaining of a thought because I choose to when I might have other thoughts," need be the definition of an illusion. He writes in his diary of 30 April 1870: "My first act of free will shall be to believe in free will." This promethean quality pervades his work. The dramatic and active role of belief is asserted in *The Will to Believe*. In the physical world a belief that a certain task is possible can contribute to its being achieved. In the spiritual or moral realm belief in potential goodness may help a person achieve it. To refuse belief until viewing all the evidence is irrational. Decisions, even in science, are the product of human selectivity, so, James suggests, we have a right to belief, when it accords with our "passional nature." This is particularly true of religious and moral beliefs as their worth lies not in their source, but in the effects they are capable of promoting.

James, however, was not a subjectivist. He did not deny humanity's inextricable bond with nature, but, in view of evolutionary theory, neither could he imbue nature with meaning, as did Emerson. In *Pragmatism*, which insists that the truth of an assertion be estimated solely by its bearing on practical human interests, he pronounces: "Woe to him whose beliefs play fast and loose with the order which realities follow in his experience; they will lead him nowhere. . . ." Belief was not to be perpetrated beyond its ability to generate supporting evidence, but was, rather, to provide a liberating dimension in life, while acknowledging that facts are both stubborn and irreducible. James was profoundly aware of the need to affirm a view of the world which would allow for such a doctrine. Throughout life he argued that the universe was open and pluralistic. It was neither a monastic whole, nor a number of independent parts. "There can be no difference anywhere," says James, "that doesn't make a difference elsewhere." The universe then is open to initiative from the human mind.

The Principles of Psychology was published in 1890 to great acclaim, and the chapter "Habit" remains a classic statement on that aspect of human life. "Habit is the enormous fly-wheel of society, its most precious conservative agent," James says with typical exuberance. He had rejected the idea of becoming a painter early in life, but his painter's sensitivity and eye for vivid portrayal remained with him. The work is a storehouse of human experience, and is James's endeavour to explain mind in terms of evolution. He took psychology out of metaphysics, and into science, creating a work which explored possibilities and indicated directions. John Dewey remarks that it forms a junction between the traditional methods of psychology: behaviourism and introspection. Behaviourism was foreshadowed by the James-Lange theory, which suggested that emotion was nothing but the subjective feelings engendered by body changes or action. We do not cry because we feel sorry, rather ". . . we feel sorry because we cry." On the other hand, consciousness could be known only through introspection. James discovered that no one "ever had a simple sensation by itself." His notion of a stream of consciousness continues to inspire new literary techniques even today. Further, consciousness behaved like an organism with interests. It would favour some interests over others. "The knower is an actor," James says.

The insights of James refuse to be localized. He provided initiatives for existentialism, phenomenism, and the operational philosophy of science. For the ordinary reader he provides a way of thinking which is creative and honest. His *Pragmatism* has become a part of popular consciousness. Philosophy, he once said, is the habit of always seeing an alternative. "My belief, to be sure, can't be optimistic—but I will posit life (the real, the good) in the self-governing resistance of the ego to the world. Life shall be built in doing and suffering and creating."

—Jan Pilditch

JARRELL, Randall. Born in Nashville, Tennessee, 6 May 1914. Educated at Vanderbilt University, Nashville (editor, *Masquerader*), B.S. in psychology 1936 (Phi Beta Kappa), M.A. in English 1939. Served as a celestial navigation tower operator in the U.S. Army Air Corps, 1942–46. Married 1) Mackie Langham in 1940; 2) Mary Eloise von Schrader in 1952. Instructor in English, Kenyon College, Gambier, Ohio, 1937–39, University of Texas, Austin, 1939–42, and Sarah Lawrence College, Bronxville, New York, 1946–47; Associate Professor, 1947–58, and Professor of English, 1958–65, Woman's College of the University of North Carolina (later University of North Carolina at Greensboro). Lecturer, Salzburg Seminar in American Civilization, 1948; Visiting Fellow in Creative Writing, Princeton University, New Jersey, 1951–52; Fellow, Indiana School of Letters, Bloomington, Summer 1952; Visiting Professor of English, University of Illinois, Urbana, 1953; Elliston Lecturer, University of Cincinnati, Ohio, 1958. Acting literary editor, *The Nation*, New York, 1946–47; poetry critic, *Partisan Review*, New Brunswick, New Jersey, 1949–53, and *Yale Review*, New Haven, Connecticut, 1955–57; member of the Editorial Board, *American Scholar*, Washington, D.C., 1957–65. Consultant in Poetry, Library of Congress, Washington, D.C., 1956–58. Recipient: Guggenheim fellowship, 1946; American Academy grant, 1951; National Book Award, 1961; University of North Carolina Gardner Award, 1962; American Association of University Women award, 1964; Ingram Merrill Award, 1965. D.H.L.: Bard College, Annandale-on-Hudson, New York, 1962. Member, American Academy, 1961; Chancellor, Academy of American Poets, 1965. *Died 14 October 1965.*

PUBLICATIONS

Collections

The Complete Poems. 1969.
The Achievement of Jarrell: A Comprehensive Selection of His Poems, edited by Frederick J. Hoffman. 1970.
Jarrell's Letters: An Autobiographical and Literary Selection, edited by Mary Jarrell. 1985.

Verse

Five Young American Poets, with others. 1940.
Blood for a Stranger. 1942.
Little Friend, Little Friend. 1945.
Losses. 1948.
The Seven-League Crutches. 1951.
Selected Poems. 1955.
Uncollected Poems. 1958.
The Woman at the Washington Zoo: Poems and Translations. 1960.
Selected Poems. 1964.
The Lost World: New Poems. 1965.
Jerome: The Biography of a Poem. 1971.

Play

The Three Sisters, adaptation of a play by Chekhov (produced 1964). 1969.

Fiction

Pictures from an Institution: A Comedy. 1954.

Other (for children)

The Rabbit Catcher and Other Fairy Tales of Ludwig Bechstein. 1962.
The Golden Bird and Other Fairy Tales by the Brothers Grimm. 1962.
The Gingerbread Rabbit. 1964.
The Bat-Poet. 1964.
The Animal Family. 1965.
Snow-White and Other Fairy Tales from the Brothers Grimm. 1972.
The Juniper Tree and Other Tales from Grimm, with Lore Segal. 1973.
Fly by Night. 1976.
A Bat is Born. 1978.
The Fisherman and His Wife. 1980.

Other

Poetry and the Age. 1953.
Poets, Critics, and Readers (address). 1959.
A Sad Heart at the Supermarket: Essays and Fables. 1962.
The Third Book of Criticism. 1969.
Kipling, Auden & Co.: Essays and Reviews 1935–1964. 1980.

Editor, *The Anchor Book of Stories*. 1958.
Editor, *The Best Short Stories of Rudyard Kipling*. 1961; as *In the Vernacular: The English in India* and *The English in England*, 2 vols., 1963.
Editor, *Six Russian Short Novels*. 1963.

Translator, with Moses Hadas, *The Ghetto and the Jews of Rome*, by Ferdinand Gregorovius. 1948.
Translator, *Goethe's Faust, Part One*. 1976.

*

Bibliography: "Jarrell: A Bibliographical Checklist" by Robert A. Wilson, in *American Book Collector*, May-June 1982; "Jarrell: A Bibliography of Criticism 1941–1981" by Jeffrey Meyers, in *Bulletin of Bibliography*, December 1982; *Jarrell: A Descriptive Bibliography 1929–1983* by Stuart Wright, 1986.

Critical Studies: *Jarrell 1914–1965* edited by Robert Lowell, Peter Taylor, and Robert Penn Warren, 1967; *Jarrell* by Karl Shapiro, 1967; *Jarrell* by Suzanne Ferguson, 1971, and *Critical Essays on Jarrell* edited by Ferguson, 1983; *Jarrell* by M.L. Rosenthal, 1972; *Jarrell* by Bernetta Quinn, 1981; *Worlds and Lives: The Poetry of Jarrell* by Charlotte H. Beck, 1983; *Jarrell's Children's Books* by Jerry Griswold, 1984.

* * *

Shortly after his death the elegant, brilliant, and quixotic Randall Jarrell was eulogized by Karl Shapiro as the greatest poet-critic since T. S. Eliot. At a memorial service at Yale, such men as Robert Lowell, Robert Penn Warren, and Richard Eberhart came to honor their dead friend as a master among men of their craft. Lowell called him "the most heartbreaking English poet of his generation." Celebrated as well was Jarrell's literary criticism, for in work like *Poetry and the Age*, he had altered dominant critical trends and tastes. He had brought Walt Whitman into prominence, and he had brought into focus Frost, Stevens, Williams, and Marianne Moore, among others; he had attacked the New Critics, and he had affirmed the relevance of art to life. Not unlike Ezra Pound, Jarrell was one of those truly committed critics who, although a poet himself, had helped the writers around him to define 20th century art.

As Walter Rideout in his essay in *Poets in Progress* (edited by Edward Hungerford, 1962) noted, when Jarrell published his *Selected Poems* in 1955, he grouped them in such a way as to obscure the rather marked delineations in central subject matter that had distinguished volume after volume. The style of his first book *Blood for a Stranger*, however, is noticeably derivative, and shows the influence of Allen Tate, John Crowe Ransom, and particularly W. H. Auden in its experiments with villanelles, sestinas, and unusual rhyming patterns, as well as in its intellectual brilliance and metaphysical questionings. The volume cries out against a world politically heaving itself toward catastrophe. Jarrell's tone is one of existential loneliness and despair.

Little Friend, Little Friend and *Losses* are less formal; Jarrell establishes a more direct and characteristic tone; the poet seems, in fact, personally more attracted to death. Jarrell's ambiguous view of humanity, man as murderer and victim, innocent and guilty, ultimately like the child facing the "capricious infinite" parental power, found its perfect expression in these war poems. But Jarrell's war poems treat the human condition, their central image, man as soldier/prisoner. Jarrell dramatizes man's guilt and suffering upon a stage of worldwide struggle. *Losses* treats all sorts of prisoners—children, black Americans, DP's at Haifa, Jews in concentration camps—and focuses upon how each is a victim within "the necessities that governed every act." Even the enemy contains the child, who, called upon to commit a terrible violence, is himself an innocent. Using the perspective of the child, Jarrell makes the outcome of war the product of innocence:

> The other murderers troop in yawning;
> Three of them play Pitch, one sleeps, and one
> Lies counting missions, lies there sweating
> Till even his heart beats: One; One; One.
> O *murderers*! . . . Still, this is how it's done.

Reality is defined as nightmare, "experience" before and after life as the dream. In "The Death of the Ball Turret Gunner," he writes: "From my mother's sleep I fell into the State / . . . I woke to black flak and the nightmare fighters." Jarrell supports no conventional political position, no "program for chance." Instead, the man-child is "a ticket / Someone bought and lost on, a stray animal / . . . Bewildered . . . / What have you understood, to die?" His compassion extends even to the enemy; the powerful also suffer: "Who will teach the Makers how to die?" he writes.

Jarrell's great and fertile period concluded with *The Seven-League Crutches*. The early works focused upon lost childhood and innocence, the terrible shock of awareness of adult hypocrisy and social disintegration. Jarrell now moved away from more public concerns to private life; his poems are more relaxed. Although the theme of illness remains in the poems about children, his work is more psychological, more dream-filled. One senses now, in addition, "a way out," in the face of "Necessity": "Man you must learn to live / though you want nothing but to die." Stoical, compassionate, and even at times capable of a bittersweet humor, some of Jarrell's most mature work now appeared. Man may perhaps even transcend Necessity through the imaginative life, the creation and perception of art.

After this Jarrell turned to fairy tale and became preoccupied with children's stories, with German Romanticism. The fairy tale offered him the innocent's victory over the potent and evil forces of the universe. In "The Märchen" (Grimm's Tales), he wrote, for example:

> We felled our islands there, at last, with iron.
> The sunlight fell to them, according to our wish,
> And we believed, till nightfall, in that wish;
> And we believed, till nightfall, in our lives.

The title poem of *The Woman at the Washington Zoo*, a return to Jarrell's more formal style of the 1940's, crystallizes the poet's concern with aging and loneliness. The woman cries out for relief, for transformation again, from her empty life: "the world goes by my cage and never sees me." She cries: "You know what I was, / You see what I am: change me, change me!"

In *The Lost World*, published after a nervous breakdown, many of his recurrent themes appear: loneliness, lovelessness, age, lost youth, the world's hypocrisy, and, as Lowell put it, childhood, "above all childhood!" *The Lost World* fails to exhibit the brilliance, power, elegance, and diversity that characterize his earlier work. More importantly, there is about it too much of a confessional quality; the poems are awkward and read like revelations on the analyst's couch. The speaker appears filled with a sense of guilt and helplessness. He tries to forgive, especially, his parents, but he is unsuccessful. In "The Piano Player," for example, he confesses: "I go over, hold my hands out, play I play— / If only, somehow, I had learned to live!" His childhood football hero, Daddy Lipscomb, admits: "I've been scared / Most of my life. You wouldn't think so to look at me. / It gets so bad I cry myself to sleep." Many of these poems contain a female persona, a woman sometimes unfaithful to her lover, often cruel to people and animals to the point of murder, but, most frequently, unmitigatingly unkind to her child. Although one senses Jarrell's attempt to understand and forgive these people, the poet remains in despair: "I identify myself, as always / With something that there's something wrong with."

One feels a debt toward Jarrell for his enormous encouragement and advice to the poets of his time. But one must regard him as well as an important poet with a brilliant intelligence, elegance, and humor. Jarrell's uniqueness remains in his special combination of sophistication with undiminished yearnings for childhood, that bittersweet faith that through art, or dreams, or fairy tales, one could regain childhood innocence and joy and negate the inevitable processes of aging, isolation, and death.

—Lois Gordon

JEFFERS, (John) Robinson. Born in Pittsburgh, Pennsylvania, 10 January 1887. Tutored by his father; educated at private schools in Switzerland and Germany; University of Western Pennsylvania (now University of Pittsburgh), 1902–03; Occidental College, Los Angeles (editor, *Aurora*), 1903–05, B.A. 1905; University of Southern California, Los Angeles, 1905–06, 1907–10, M.A.; University of Zurich, 1906–07; studied forestry at University of Washington, Seattle, 1910–11. Married Una Call Kuster in 1913 (died, 1950); one daughter and twin sons. Lived near Carmel, California, from 1914. Recipient: Academy of American Poets fellowship, 1958; Shelley Memorial Award, 1961. D.H.L.: Occidental College, 1937; University of Southern California, 1939. Member, American Academy; Chancellor, Academy of American Poets, 1945–56. *Died 20 January 1962.*

PUBLICATIONS

Collections

Selected Poems. 1965.
Selected Letters 1897–1962, edited by Ann N. Ridgeway. 1968.

Verse

Flagons and Apples. 1912.
Californians. 1916.
Tamar and Other Poems. 1924.
Roan Stallion, Tamar, and Other Poems. 1925.
The Women at Point Sur. 1927.
Poems. 1928.
An Artist. 1928.
Cawdor and Other Poems. 1928.
Dear Judas and Other Poems. 1929.
Stars. 1930.
Apology for Bad Dreams. 1930.
Descent to the Dead: Poems Written in Ireland and Great Britain. 1931.
Thurso's Landing and Other Poems. 1932.
Give Your Heart to the Hawks and Other Poems. 1933.
Return. 1934.
Solstice and Other Poems. 1935.
The Beaks of Eagles. 1936.
Such Counsels You Gave to Me and Other Poems. 1937.
The Selected Poetry. 1938.
Two Consolations. 1940.
Be Angry at the Sun. 1941.
The Double Axe and Other Poems. 1948.
Hungerfield and Other Poems. 1954.
The Loving Shepherdess. 1956.
The Beginning and the End and Other Poems. 1963.
The Alpine Christ and Other Poems, edited by William Everson. 1973.
Brides of the South Wind: Poems 1917–1922, edited by William Everson. 1974.
Granite and Cypress, edited by William Everson. 1975.
The Women at Point Sur and Other Poems. 1977.
The Double Axe and Other Poems, edited by William Everson. 1977.
What Odd Expedients and Other Poems, edited by Robert Ian Scott. 1981.

Plays

Medea, from a play by Euripides (produced 1947). 1946.
The Cretan Women, from a play by Euripides (produced 1954 ?). In *From the Modern Repertoire 3*, edited by Eric Bentley, 1956.

Other

Poetry, Gongorism, and a Thousand Years. 1949.
Themes in My Poems. 1956.
Tragedy Has Obligations. 1973.

*

Bibliography: *A Bibliography of the Works of Jeffers* by S.S. Alberts, 1933; *The Critical Reception of Jeffers: A Bibliographical Study* by Alex A. Vardamis, 1972.

Critical Studies: *Jeffers: The Man and His Works* by Lawrence Clark Powell, 1940; *The Loyalties of Jeffers* by Radcliffe Squires, 1956; *Jeffers* by Frederic I. Carpenter, 1962; *The Stone Mason of Tor House: The Life and Work of Jeffers* by Melba B. Bennett, 1966; *Jeffers: Fragments of an Older Fury* by Brother Antoninus (William Everson), 1968; *Jeffers, Poet of Inhumanism* by Arthur B. Coffin, 1971; *Jeffers: Myth, Ritual, and Symbol in His Narrative Poems*, 1973, revised edition, 1976, and *Jeffers*, 1975, both by Robert J. Brophy; *In This Wild Water: The Suppressed Poems of Jeffers* by James Shebl, 1976; *Shining Clarity: God and Man in the Works of Jeffers* by Marlan Beilke, 1977; *Rock and Hawk: Jeffers and the Romantic Agony* by William H. Nolte, 1978; *The Cliffs of Solitude: A Reading of Jeffers* by Robert Zaller, 1983.

* * *

In 1925 *Roan Stallion, Tamar, and Other Poems* established Robinson Jeffers as one of the major poets of his generation. But beginning in 1927 with *The Women at Point Sur* his repeated use of forbidden themes alienated many readers, and in 1941 his opposition to American participation in World War II all but destroyed his reputation. Since his death in 1962 a better perspective has been achieved, and now he is recognized as one of the most powerful—if also most controversial—of modern poets.

Most of his volumes include one or more long narrative poems, together with many shorter lyrics. And these longer poems all deal, either implicity or explicitly, with the materials of myth. His *Medea*, for instance, is a free adaptation of the play of Euripides, but *Solstice* attempts to domesticate the violent Greek myth in a realistic California setting. His most successful narrative poems, such as "Roan Stallion" which describes a woman's passionate adoration of a horse, use mythical materials and most unobtrusively. But the aura of myth and the forbidden passions which the old myths described, such as incest, parricide, and the love of man for beast, all trouble the narrative poetry of Jeffers.

Besides these myths, his poetry gives vivid expression to an extraordinary sense of place. The wild coast of the country south of Carmel, where he lived all his creative life, provides both actual setting and the conviction of immediate reality for all his poems, both narrative and lyric. But most significant of all is the symbolic nature of this actual country. Here is "Continent's End," both in fact and in idea, "the long migrations' end," where human civilization now faces "the final Pacific" and looks westward toward its first beginnings in "mother Asia."

In his poetry this realistic sense of place combines with a consciousness of the symbolic significance of this place and a remembrance of the prehistoric origins of civilization suggested by the ancient myths. At its best this poetry realizes a vision of human history unique in its temporal scope and its imaginative power. It is small wonder if it sometimes fails to unify these disparate elements and to realize this all-inclusive vision.

The volume which first established Jeffers's reputation probably remains his best, and the three narrative poems which it includes illustrate the various combinations of narrative realism with mythical symbolism which his later poetry developed. "Roan Stallion" is most completely realistic, and perhaps for this reason has remained the favorite of traditional minded readers. "Tamar" is most extreme, both in plot and in technique, although the strange story of incest plays itself out in a California setting. "The Tower Beyond Tragedy" retells the story of the Oresteia in its original Greek setting, but with modern characterization.

The heroine of "Roan Stallion" is named "California," and both name and plot recall the Greek myth of Europa. But the god-like stallion remains simply an animal, and the woman's adoration for him remains psychological. Meanwhile the mythical dimensions of the naturalistic story are emphasized by poetic suggestion:

> The fire threw up figures
> And symbols meanwhile, racial myths formed and
> dissolved in it, the phantom rulers of humanity
> That without being are yet more real than what
> they are born of, and without shape, shape that
> which makes them.

"Tamar" is a very different poem, perhaps unique in literature. Its incestuous heroine rejects all the inhibitions of civilization, but her seemingly realistic actions are motivated by passages of dream, vision, and racial memory until the modern story seems to reenact the earliest creation myths of the incestuous union of Coelus and Terra, of gods and men. The heroine's absolute rejection of morality is paralleled only by that of the later *The Women at Point Sur*. But here the repeated use of dream and vision transforms the realistic story into the realm of timeless myth.

"The Tower Beyond Tragedy" narrates the plot of the Oresteia in realistic terms, but focuses on the character of Cassandra and her predictions of doom. Midway through the poem these enlarge into an all-embracing prophecy of the ultimate destruction of future empires, ending with "a mightier to be cursed and a higher for malediction," America. The poem concludes with the refusal of Orestes to inherit Mycenae, or imperial power, and an eloquent poetic statement of his philosophy of total detachment in a "tower beyond tragedy."

This denunciation of imperial power and this celebration of human detachment is also the theme of many of Jeffers's best shorter poems, such as "Shine, Perishing Republic" and "Continent's End." Other lyrics celebrate simply the beauty of nature, such as "Night" and "Boats in a Fog." Perhaps the best of his short poems is "To the Stone Cutters," which treats the ancient theme of mutability.

After the *Roan Stallion* volume, *The Women at Point Sur* narrated a story of the total rejection of traditional morality by a renegade Christian minister. But this longest of Jeffers's poems was also most realistic, so that the mythical and instinctual incest of "Tamar" became calculated and explicit. Actually the poem recalls the story of Euripides's *Bacchae*, which Jeffers also used in his short poem "The Humanist's Tragedy," but the longer poem abandoned all reference to myth and symbol. Although most contemporary readers rejected it, Jeffers's chief modern disciple, William Everson (Brother Antoninus), has praised it highly in *Jeffers: Fragments of an Older Fury*.

In *Dear Judas* Jeffers retold the gospel story with new characterization, as he had retold the Oresteia in "The Tower Beyond Tragedy." The striking originality of his conception and the soaring poetry with which he clothed it make the poem memorable. But his rejection of Christian orthodoxy seemed blasphemous to many readers. "The Loving Shepherdess," a companion narrative poem, created a character of such beauty that her story seems unique among Jeffers's dark tragedies.

In the 1930's Jeffers turned to a series of more realistic long poems with contemporary California settings, without mythical overtones. "Cawdor," "Thurso's Landing," and "Give Your Heart to the Hawks" all take place in "Jeffers Country" south of Carmel, and all develop their tragic stories effectively. Only some names and passages of poetic commentary suggest larger themes. Near the end of "Thurso's Landing" the poet comments:

> The platform is like a rough plank theatre-stage
> Built on the brow of the promontory: as if our blood had labored all around the earth from Asia
> To play its mystery before strict judges at last, the final ocean and sky, to prove our nature
> More shining than that of the other animals. It is rather ignoble in its quiet times, mean in its pleasures,
> Slavish in the mass; but at stricken moments it can shine terribly against the dark magnificence of things.

After 1935 Jeffers published new volumes every few years, but only a few of the narrative poems achieved excellence. "At the Birth of an Age" develops incidents from the Niblung Saga, but the poetry overshadows the story, and the mythical and philosophic elements which it illustrates find powerful expression. The second narrative poem in *The Double Axe*, "The Inhumanist," creates a hermit-hero who gives expression to Jeffers's philosophy both in speech and in action. Finally, "Hungerfield" creates a brief modern myth recalling that of Herakles.

Many readers prefer Jeffers's shorter poems to his long narratives. His "Apology for Bad Dreams" offers both illustration and explanation of the violent imagery and pessimistic philosophy which characterize all his poetry. A later poem, "The Bloody Sire," gives perfect expression to this philosophy of violence, ending: "Who would remember Helen's face / Lacking the terrible halo of spears?"

Much of the difficulty of his poetry stems from his insistence upon the philosophy of "Inhumanism," which he attempted to define in his later writing. His opposition both to human self-importance and to the classical tradition of humanism emphasized instead the modern search for objective truth. In contrast to T. S. Eliot's traditional classicism, Jeffers celebrated the values of science and discovery.

—Frederic I. Carpenter

JEFFERSON, Thomas. Born in Shadwell, Goochland (now Albemarle) County, Virginia, 13 April 1743. Educated by tutors at his uncle's estate, Tuckahoe, 1748–51; at William Douglas's Latin School, 1752–57; James Maury's School, 1758–59; College of William and Mary, Williamsburg, Virginia, 1760–62, graduated 1762; studied law with George Wythe, 1762–67: admitted to bar, 1767, and practiced law until 1774. Served as commander of the Albemarle militia, 1775. Married Martha Wayles Skelton in 1772 (died, 1782); five daughters and one son. Member, Virginia House of Burgesses, 1769–75: held strongly anti-British views; Lieutenant, 1770, and surveyor, 1773, Albemarle County; delegate, Second Continental Congress, 1775–76; member of the drafting committee, principal author, and signatory, Declaration of Independence, 1776; member, Virginia House of Delegates, 1776–79, 1782: wrote preamble to Virginia's Constitution and drew up a statute establishing religious freedom (which became model for the First Amendment of the U.S. Constitution); Governor of Virginia, 1779–81, re-elected 1781, but resigned when British forces captured Richmond and raided his home Monticello, near Charlottesville; appointed to peace commission to Europe, 1782 (commission withdrawn); delegate, 1783, and chairman, 1784, Continental Congress; foreign minister to negotiate commercial treaties, 1784–87 (successful treaty with Prussia, 1785; unsuccessful negotiations with Britain, 1786, and Morocco, 1787); minister to France, 1785–89: negotiated consular convention, 1788; first U.S. Secretary of State in administration of George Washington, New York, 1790, and Philadelphia, 1791–93: considerable policy differences with Secretary of the Treasury Alexander Hamilton led to formation of Republican (Jefferson) and Federalist (Hamilton) parties; lived at Monticello, 1794–96; U.S. Vice-President in Federalist administration of John Adams, Philadelphia, 1797–1800: main duty was to preside over Senate; U.S. President, Washington, D.C., 1801–09 (initially tied in election with Aaron Burr, who became his first administration Vice-President; re-elected 1805, with George Clinton as Vice-President); during presidency: Louisiana Purchase, 1803, Lewis and Clark expedition, 1804–05, treaty with Tripoli and Morocco over Barbary pirates, 1805, trial of Aaron Burr, 1807, embargo against Britain, 1807–09; lived at Monticello, 1809–26 (began work on the estate, 1768). Trustee, Albemarle Academy, from 1814; member of the Board of Visitors, Central College, Charlottesville, 1817 (chartered as University of Virginia, 1819; opened, 1825); Rector, University of Virginia, 1819–26: designed and supervised construction of many campus buildings. President, American Philosophical Society, 1797–1815; Associate, Institute of France, 1801. *Died 4 July 1826.*

PUBLICATIONS

Collections

Writings, edited by Paul Leicester Ford. 10 vols., 1892–99.
Papers, edited by Julian P. Boyd. 1950—
The Portable Jefferson, edited by Merrill D. Peterson. 1975.
Writings (Library of America), edited by Merrill D. Peterson. 1984.

Prose

A Summary View of the Rights of British America. 1774.
The Declaration of Independence, with others. 1776.
Notes on the State of Virginia. 1785.
An Act for Establishing Religious Freedom. 1786.
An Appendix to the Notes on Virginia Relative to the Murder of Logan's Family. 1800.

A Manual of Parliamentary Practice for Use in the Senate of the United States. 1801.
Early History of the University of Virginia, as Contained in the Letters of Jefferson and Joseph C. Cabell, edited by Nathaniel Francis Cabell. 1856.
The Life and Morals of Jesus of Nazareth (The Jefferson Bible). 1902; complete edition, 1904; edited by Henry Wilder Foote, 1951.
The Complete Anas, edited by Franklin B. Sawvel. 1903.
Germantown Letters, edited by Charles Francis Jenkins. 1906.
The Confidential Letters to William Wirt. 1912.
Autobiography, edited by Paul Leicester Ford. 1914.
Correspondence, Printed from the Originals in the Collections of William K. Bixby, edited by Worthington Chauncey Ford. 1916.
The Best Letters, edited by Joseph G. de Roulhac Hamilton. 1926.
The Commonplace Book of Jefferson: A Repertory of His Ideas on Government, edited by Gilbert Chinard. 1928.
The Literary Bible of Jefferson: His Commonplace Book of Philosophers and Poets, edited by Gilbert Chinard. 1928.
Jeffersonian Principles, edited by James Truslow Adams. 1928.
The Letters of Lafayette and Jefferson, edited by Gilbert Chinard. 1929.
Jefferson and Education in a Republic, edited by Charles Flinn Arrowood. 1930.
Correspondence Between Jefferson and Pierre Samuel du Pont de Nemours 1798–1817, edited by Dumas Malone. 1930.
The Correspondence of Jefferson and du Pont de Nemours, edited by Gilbert Chinard. 1931; revised edition, 1970.
Alexander Hamilton and Jefferson: Representative Selections, edited by Frederick C. Prescott. 1934.
Democracy, edited by Saul K. Padover. 1939; as *Jefferson on Democracy*, 1954.
The Living Thoughts of Jefferson, edited by John Dewey. 1940.
The Wisdom of Jefferson, edited by Edward Boykin. 1941.
Jefferson Himself: The Personal Narrative, edited by Bernard Mayo. 1942.
Jefferson and His Unknown Brother Randolph: Twenty-Eight Letters 1807 to 1815, edited by Bernard Mayo. 1942.
The Complete Jefferson, edited by Saul K. Padover. 1943.
Jefferson's Garden Book 1766–1824, with Relevant Extracts from His Other Writings, edited by Edwin Morris Betts. 1944.
The Life and Selected Writings of Jefferson, edited by Adrienne Koch and William Peden. 1944.
Basic Writings, edited by Philip S. Foner. 1944.
Correspondence of Jefferson and Francis Walker Gilmer 1814–1826, edited by Richard Beale Davis. 1946.
Jefferson's Ideas on a University Library: Letters from the Founder of the University of Virginia to a Boston Bookseller, edited by Elizabeth Cometti. 1950.
Farm Book, edited by Edwin Morris Betts. 1953.
The Political Writings: Representative Selections, edited by Edward Dumbauld. 1955.
A Jefferson Profile as Revealed in His Letters, edited by Saul K. Padover. 1956.
The Adams-Jefferson Letters: The Complete Correspondence Between Jefferson and Abigail and John Adams, edited by Lester J. Cappon. 2 vols., 1959.
The Jefferson-Dunglison Letters, edited by John M. Dorsey. 1960.
Architectural Drawings, edited by Frederick Doveton Nichols. 1960; revised edition, 1961.
Crusade Against Ignorance: Jefferson on Education, edited by Gordon C. Lee. 1961.
The Essential Jefferson, edited by Albert Fried. 1963.
To the Girls and Boys (letters), edited by Edward Boykin. 1964.
Jefferson and the Foundations of American Freedom, edited by Saul K. Padover. 1965.
The Family Letters, edited by Edwin Morris Betts and James Adam Bear, Jr. 1966.

Translator, with Joel Barlow, *Volney's Ruins; or, Meditations on the Revolution of Empires*. 2 vols., 1802.

*

Bibliography: *Jefferson: A Reference Guide* by Eugene L. Huddleston, 1982; *Jefferson: A Comprehensive, Annotated Bibliography of Writings About Him (1926–1980)* by Frank Shuffleton, 1983.

Critical Studies: *The Jefferson Cyclopedia* by John P. Foley, 1900; *The Philosophy of Jefferson* by Adrienne Koch, 1943; *The Declaration of Independence: The Evolution of the Text* by Julian P. Boyd, 1945; *Jefferson among the Arts: An Essay in Early American Esthetics* by Eleanor Davidson Berman, 1947; *Jefferson and His Time* by Dumas Malone, 6 vols., 1948–81; *The Head and Heart of Jefferson* by John Dos Passos, 1954; *The Jefferson Image in the American Mind*, 1960, and *Jefferson and the New Nation*, 1970, both by Merrill D. Peterson, and *Jefferson: A Profile* edited by Peterson, 1967; *A Casebook on the Declaration of Independence* edited by Robert Ginsberg, 1967; *Jefferson: An Intimate History* by Fawn M. Brodie, 1974; *Inventing America: Jefferson's Declaration of Independence* by Garry Wills, 1978; *Jefferson* by William K. Bottorff, 1979; *Jefferson's Monticello* by W. Howard Adams, 1983.

* * *

Thomas Jefferson is without doubt one of the great writers of the Revolutionary and Early National eras, and among American Presidents who wrote with distinction his only rivals are Abraham Lincoln and Woodrow Wilson. The ideas of the founding fathers of the American republic are nowhere better articulated than in the writings of Jefferson, in his public papers, in his one book, and in his letters. He was extremely conscious of the great events taking place in America in the last quarter of the 18th century, and his writings are wise and lucid, felicitously phrased, and continuously important for anyone wishing to understand the foundations of the republic, its ideological underpinning, and its development during its first half century.

Jefferson was born the son of a self-made, little educated man, Peter Jefferson, who became a prosperous landowner and member of the Virginia House of Burgesses, and Jane Randolph, who came from one of the most prominent families of the colony. As a member of a distinguished and affluent family, Jefferson was given the best education available. His years of study culminated in his graduation from the College of William and Mary and post-graduate work reading law with the celebrated George Wythe. The classical education that he received, which is reflected in his writings, was a shaping influence on his life. He wrote Joseph Priestley in 1800 that to read the Latin and Greek authors in their original is a sublime luxury: "I thank Him who directed my early education, for having put into my possession this rich source of delight; and I would not exchange it for anything which I could then have acquired."

Jefferson was a member of the Virginia Assembly when events were moving inexorably towards the Revolution, and his first important writing was *A Summary View of the Rights of British America*, a strong plea for natural rights for the British colonies and a stern indictment of British tyranny. It was read at the Virginia convention in Williamsburg in August 1774 but it was considered too revolutionary and was not adopted. The resolutions it contained, however, were widely circulated, and Jefferson acquired a reputation as an eloquent spokesman for the developing American point of view. This document led to his appointment to the committee, containing John Adams and Benjamin Franklin, charged by Congress to write the Declaration of Independence. The Declaration, though edited somewhat by Adams, Franklin, and Congress, is almost entirely the work of Jefferson and states brilliantly the social contract theory of government then gaining currency during the Enlightenment.

When the Revolution was in its final days, Jefferson retired as Governor of Virginia and returned to his home at Monticello. There he wrote the one book published during his lifetime: *Notes on the State of Virginia*, still a remarkably interesting volume after 200 years. It was cast in the form of answers to queries posed by the secretary of the French legation in Philadelphia, and it covers every aspect of the state, its history, government, ethnology, religion, geology, flora, and fauna. It shows Jefferson as an 18th-century polymath, a man intensely interested in ideas, curious about all sides of human nature and science, and widely read in authors ancient and modern.

During the years that Jefferson was actively engaged in government on the national level, as Washington's Secretary of State, Vice-President under John Adams, and then as President for two terms, he wrote many state papers which are notable for their cogency and clarity. After his years in Europe as American minister to France, he returned with a knowledge of world affairs and statecraft far beyond most Americans, who on the whole were provincial in outlook. His state papers reflect this broad experience and vision. His First Inaugural Address, one of his most memorable statements, was delivered after the turmoil of the Adams years and the intense partisan struggle that ended in his election as President. It is an eloquent call for unity and harmony: "We are all republicans—we are all Federalists. If there be any among us who would wish to dissolve the Union or to change its republican form, let them stand undisturbed as monuments of the safety with which error of opinion may be tolerated where reason is left to combat it."

After Jefferson retired from the Presidency, he continued his intellectual interests and carried on a distinguished correspondence with important scientists, philosophers, and statesmen in America and Europe. The hundreds of letters he wrote went, to name a few, to Lafeyette, Kosciusko, Priestley, and Thomas Cooper in Europe, to Madison and Monroe, his successors in the Presidency, and to Benjamin Rush and Benjamin Waterhouse in the United States. The list is legion, and the subjects discussed are innumerable; but perhaps the most interesting is the extensive correspondence with his old political rival Adams. These letters constitute an important exchange of ideas between two of the founding fathers as they reflect back on their careers from the perspective of old age. Jefferson also in his last years wrote a partial autobiography that is an important record of his career down to 1790.

In Jefferson's declining years he devoted much of his attention to education, and the opening of the University of Virginia the year before he died was the culmination of years of planning. He believed passionately that education was an end in itself, the way to happiness, and the foundation on which self-government rested. He planned the university, chose the books for the library, selected the faculty, drew up the curriculum, designed the buildings, and oversaw their construction. He even wrote "An Essay on the Anglo-Saxon Language," one of his many interests, for his new university. When he died fifty years to the day following the signing of the Declaration of Independence, he directed that his tombstone record the three accomplishments of which he was most proud: author of the Statute of Virginia for Religious Freedom and the Declaration of Independence and the founder of the University of Virginia.

—James Woodress

JEWETT, (Theodora) Sarah Orne. Born in South Berwick, Maine, 3 September 1849. Educated as Miss Raynes's School, 1855, and Berwick Academy, 1861–66, graduated 1866. Full-time writer in Berwick from 1866: contributed to *Atlantic Monthly* from 1869. Litt.D.: Bowdoin College, Brunswick, Maine, 1901. *Died 24 June 1909*.

PUBLICATIONS

Collections

Stories and Tales. 7 vols., 1910.
The Best Stories, edited by Willa Cather. 2 vols., 1925.
Letters, edited by Richard Cary. 1956; revised edition, 1967.
The Country of the Pointed Firs and Other Stories, edited by Mary Ellen Chase. 1968.

Fiction

Deephaven. 1877; edited by Richard Cary, with other stories, 1966.
Old Friends and New (stories). 1879.
Country By-Ways. 1881.
The Mate of the Daylight, and Friends Ashore (stories). 1883.
A Country Doctor. 1884.
A Marsh Island. 1885.
A White Heron and Other Stories. 1886.
The King of Folly Island and Other People. 1888.
Strangers and Wayfarers. 1890.
Tales of New England. 1890.
A Native of Winby and Other Tales. 1893.
The Life of Nancy (stories). 1895.
The Country of the Pointed Firs. 1896.
The Queen's Twin and Other Stories. 1899.
The Tory Lover. 1901.
An Empty Purse: A Christmas Story. 1905.
Uncollected Short Stories, edited by Richard Cary. 1971.

Verse

Verses, edited by M. A. De Wolfe Howe. 1916.

Other

Play Days: A Book of Stories for Children. 1878.
The Story of the Normans (for children). 1887.
Betty Leicester: A Story for Girls. 1890.
Betty Leicester's English Xmas (for children). 1894; as *Betty Leicester's Christmas*, 1899.
Letters, edited by Annie Fields. 1911.
Letters Now in Colby College Library, edited by Carl J. Weber. 1947.

Editor, *Stories and Poems for Children*, by Celia Thaxter. 1895.
Editor, *The Poems of Celia Thaxter*. 1896.
Editor, *Letters of Sarah Wyman Whitman*. 1907.

*

Bibliography: *A Bibliography of the Published Writings of Jewett* by Clara Carter Weber and Carl J. Weber, 1949; in *Bibliography of American Literature* by Jacob Blanck, 1969; *Jewett: A Reference Guide* by Gwen L. and James Nagel, 1978.

Critical Studies: *Jewett* by F.O. Mattheissen, 1929; *Acres of Flint: Writers of New England 1870–1900* by Perry D. Westbrook, 1951, revised edition, as *Acres of Flint: Jewett and Her Contemporaries*, 1981; *Jewett* by John Eldridge Frost, 1960; *Jewett* by Richard Cary, 1962, and *Appreciation of Jewett: 29 Interpretive Essays* edited by Cary, 1973; *Jewett* by Margaret Farrand Thorp, 1966; *Jewett* by Josephine Donovan, 1980; *Critical Essays on Jewett* edited by Gwen L. Nagel, 1984.

* * *

Willa Cather ranked Sarah Orne Jewett's *The Country of the Pointed Firs* with Nathaniel Hawthorne's *The Scarlet Letter* and Mark Twain's *Huckleberry Finn* as one of the three American prose literary works most likely to endure. The estimate is probably overenthusiastic; yet *The Country of the Pointed Firs*, a loosely constructed episodic novel set on the Maine coast, is at least a minor classic and will continue to be read for many years to come. Jewett was an eminently successful literary regionalist—a depicter of setting and character in the area where she had been born and brought up in a patrician family whose sympathies had been Loyalist during the Revolutionary War. Yet her somewhat aristocratic viewpoint—she was inordinately proud of her Anglo-Norman ancestry—in no way affected her understanding and admiration of the fishing and farming people about whom she wrote in her best work.

Her first book, *Deephaven*, fashioned from sketches that had previously appeared in the *Atlantic Monthly*, deals with life among all classes in a typical Maine seaport, with emphasis upon social and economic decay as commerce and shipping became more and more concentrated in the larger ports like Boston and New York. Jewett's tone in this volume, as in much of her writing, is one of nostalgia for a time when her region had figured vitally in the maritime life of the nation and had nurtured a population of hardy seafarers who sailed their vessels to all the great ports of the world. These days, regrettably, were past, but Jewett still found much to praise among the Maine folk of her time. *The Country of the Pointed Firs* is her major tribute to these quiet, resourceful, hard-working people, the significance of whose lives, now that the adventurous seafaring days were gone, Jewett found to be in the success with which they had adjusted to a harsh environment. The women especially (and most of Jewett's strong characters are women) had learned to live in harmony with their native region—a rocky, island-studded coast with steep pastures and forested mountains rising close back from the water. The most notable of these women, the widow Almira Todd, subsisted as a herbalist, thus personifying the Maine folks' ability to draw life-giving strength from a seemingly sterile land.

Jewett, in her Preface to *Deephaven*, stated that she considered one of her functions as a regional writer was to make the rest of the nation acquainted with the lives and characteristics of a little-known segment of the population. But more important, taking her cue from a statement by George Sand regarding the French peasantry, Jewett believed that the scrutiny to which she, as a writer, subjected her Maine neighbors would reveal a human worth and gentle heroism rarely found elsewhere. Jewett, indeed, saw a physical resemblance between the Maine Coast and the coast and isles of Greece, and she saw classical qualities in her Maine characters. Thus Mrs. Todd, standing on an Atlantic headland and mourning her husband drowned in shipwreck, reminds Jewett of Antigone "alone on the Theban plain." Elsewhere Mrs. Todd as an herbalist reminds Jewett of the enchantress Medea. Such allusions, inserted in passing, underline Jewett's point in this and other books: that the simplest persons can attain a dignity, even a tragic grandeur, essentially the same as that found in the great classical works. She did not always find these qualities only among maritime people. The persons in her fiction include up-country farmers, elderly ladies in elm-shaded inland towns, and Irish maid-servants, and almost invariably she presents them as possessing, and exhibiting, a potential for the full range of human experience from tragedy to ecstasy.

Jewett's prose is notable for its purity and variety. Her descriptions of land and sea are lyrically evocative. Her narrative style is direct and flowing. In her dialogue she succeeds better than any other New England writer in reproducing the accents and, especially, the rhythms of the speech of her region. Unlike many local-colorists, she does not strive for phonetic renderings of dialect—efforts that usually result in grotesque and nearly unintelligible manglings of spelling. Jewett emphasizes regional diction, idiom, and cadence with only minor alterations in spelling. The result is not only readable but authentic.

Jewett in her lifetime was an admired and popular writer, publishing a sizable number of novels and collections of tales and sketches. Among the novels *A Country Doctor*, which draws from her experiences in accompanying her physician father on his rounds, deserves mention, as does *A Marsh Island*, an idyllic celebration of life on a coastal farm. Among her volumes of short fiction and sketches three of the richest are *Country By-Ways, A White Heron and Other Stories* (the title piece being her most famous story), and *The King of Folly Island and Other People*, containing the superb story "Miss Tempy's Watchers."

Though born and brought up in a small Maine town and always fiercely loyal to the place of her birth, Jewett was very much in touch with, and an influence in, the literary life of her times. A close friend of Mrs. James Fields, wife of the prominent Boston publisher, she was active in Boston literary circles and met many of the nation's and world's great writers as they visited the publisher's home. Eventually she became recognized as the author who carried local color, or regionalism, to the highest artistic level it has attained in America. Her writing has served as a model for other American authors, not all of them local-colorists, especially women of her and later generations. For example, Cather, following Jewett's example and personal advice, redirected her early efforts from rather mediocre fiction in the manner of Henry James to the writing of highly successful novels based on life in the midwestern farmlands where she had been brought up. Jewett always held that an author's chief source of materials should be his or her own locale and personal experience. To this conviction she remained faithful throughout her writing career.

—Perry D. Westbrook

See the essay on *The Country of the Pointed Firs*.

JOHNSON, James Weldon. Born in Jacksonville, Florida, 17 June 1871. Educated at Atlanta University, A.B. 1894, A.M. 1904; also studied at Columbia University, New York, for three years. Married Grace Nail in 1910. Principal, Stanton Central Grammar School for Negroes, Jacksonville; helped found Jacksonville *Daily American*; admitted to Florida bar, and practised in Jacksonville, 1897–1901; moved to New York, to collaborate with his brother, the composer J. Rosamond Johnson, in writing popular songs and light opera, 1901–06; U.S. Consul, Puerto Cabello, Venezuela, 1906–09, and Corinto, Nicaragua, 1909–12; Executive Secretary, National Association for the Advancement of Colored People, 1916–30; Spence Professor of Creative Literature, Fisk University, Nashville, Tennessee, 1930–38; Visiting Professor of Creative Literature, New York University, 1934. Columnist, New York *Age*. Director, American Fund for Public Service; trustee, Atlanta University. Recipient: Spingarn Medal, 1925; Du Bois Prize for Negro Literature, 1933. Litt.D.: Talladega College, Alabama, 1917; Howard University, Washington, D.C., 1923. Member, Academy of Political Science. *Died 26 June 1938.*

PUBLICATIONS

Verse

Fifty Years and Other Poems. 1917.
God's Trombones: Seven Negro Sermons in Verse. 1927.
Saint Peter Relates an Incident of the Resurrection Day. 1930.
Saint Peter Relates an Incident: Selected Poems. 1935.

Plays

Goyescas; or, The Rival Lovers, from a play by Fernando Periquet, music by Enrique Granados (produced 1915). 1915.
Shakespeare in Harlem, with Langston Hughes (produced 1959).

Fiction

The Autobiography of an Ex-Colored Man. 1912.

Other

The Changing Status of Negro Labor. 1918.
Africa in the World Democracy, with Horace M. Kallen. 1919.
Self-Determining Hayti. N.d.
Lynching: America's National Disgrace. 1924.
The Race Problem and Peace. 1924.
Fundamentalism Versus Spiritualism: A Layman's Viewpoint. 1925.
Native African Races and Culture. 1927.
Legal Aspects of the Negro Problem. N.d.
Black Manhattan. 1930.
The Shining Life. 1932.
Along This Way (autobiography). 1933.
Negro Americans, What Now? 1934.

Editor, *The Book of American Negro Poetry*. 1922; revised edition, 1931.
Editor, *The Book of American Negro Spirituals*. 1925; *Second Book*, 1926.

*

Bibliography: *Johnson and Arna Wendell Bontemps: A Reference Guide* by Robert E. Fleming, 1978.

Critical Studies: *Johnson* by Sterling A. Brown, Carl Van Vechten, and A. B. Spingarn, 1941(?); *Roots of Negro Racial Consciousness: Three Harlem Renaissance Authors* by Stephen H. Bronz, 1964; *Johnson, Black Leader, Black Voice* by Eugene D. Levy, 1973 (includes bibliography); *Black Poets of the United States* by Jean Wagner, 1973.

* * *

James Weldon Johnson's literary output was slight but it is a solid achievement and one that proves crucial when viewed as that of a black American aspiring to a literary career in the early 20th century. In *God's Trombones: Seven Negro Sermons in Verse* Johnson achieved a considerable success in melding Afro-American folk and Euro-American sophisticated modes of expression to gain the kind of artistic synthesis he hoped would assist in confirming the right to full citizenship for peoples of African descent in the United States, by virtue of a demonstrated capacity (which their detractors would argue they did not possess) to contribute significantly to the formation of a new national culture. This task of recuperation became a theme in Johnson's influential picaresque novel, now regarded as a classic, *The Autobiography of an Ex-Colored Man*, first published anonymously in 1912. The novel's "tragic mulatto" protagonist is a trained musician who earns his way as an inspired ragtime pianist. He professes, however ironically (and it is to Johnson's skillful manipulation of irony that the novel owes the greater part of its success), to bring "glory and honour to the Negro race." This he intends to achieve through compositions in the European classical tradition incorporating elements of Afro-American folk music, the projected field research for which, however, never gets done. Further insight into Johnson's aims is available in the important Prefaces to two editions of his equally influential and classic anthology, *The Book of American Negro Poetry*. In these he compares the Afro-American poet's need to achieve a distinct mode of expression rooted in and supportive of Afro-American life ("a form that will express the racial spirit by symbols from within" rather than from without) to that recognized by the Irish poet-playwright J. M. Synge which led to the assimilation of indigenous folk material into his works.

Johnson's accidental death cut short his efforts, but his poems in *God's Trombones* mark a significant step in the direction of his goal. This work has continued to serve as an inspiration and a model for Afro-American writers. Stylistically inspired by the folk preaching Johnson observed in Afro-American churches, the poems assume the form and essential rhythm of the sermons and prayers he heard. As such they are a marked stylistic departure from the prevailing Anglo-American poetic tradition of the day. Also, they constitute a corrective to the artificial and, as Johnson saw it, denigrating folk speech of the stereotype-fostering dialect mode that had been grafted onto that tradition, including its use in Johnson's own early dialect poetry. On the Euro-American side, the poems in *God's Trombones* are biblical-Whitmanesque, gaining an appeal at once sophisticated and folk-oriented. Similarly, *The Autobiography of an Ex-Colored Man* delineates the artistic defusing of various stereotypes that Afro-American writers were coming to recognize as an obligatory function of their works. Toward that end, Johnson imbues his protagonist with the superficialities of the "tragic mulatto" stereotype but portrays him with a psychological verisimilitude and with irony, thus enabling the stereotypical aspect to achieve a virtual self-destruction. He thus carried forward a tradition of corrective aesthetics pioneered by his predecessors, Charles W. Chesnutt and, to a lesser degree, Paul Laurence Dunbar.

—Alvin Aubert

JONES, James. Born in Robinson, Illinois, 6 November 1921. Educated at the University of Hawaii, Honolulu, 1942; New York University, 1945. Served in the U.S. Army, 1939–44: Bronze Star; Purple Heart. Married Gloria Mosolino in 1957; one son and one daughter. Lived in Paris, 1958–74; Writer-in-Residence, Florida International University, Miami, 1974–77. Recipient: National Book Award, 1952. *Died 9 May 1977.*

PUBLICATIONS

Fiction

From Here to Eternity. 1951.
Some Came Running. 1957.
The Pistol. 1959.
The Thin Red Line. 1962.
Go to the Widow-Maker. 1967.
The Ice-Cream Headache and Other Stories. 1968.
The Merry Month of May. 1971.
A Touch of Danger. 1973.
Whistle: A Work-in-Progress. 1974; complete version, as *Whistle*, 1978.

Play

Screenplay: *The Longest Day*, with others, 1962.

Other

Viet Journal. 1974.
WWII, with Art Weithas. 1975.

*

Bibliography: *Jones: A Checklist* by John R. Hopkins, 1974.

Critical Studies: *Jones: A Friendship* by Willie Morris, 1978; *Jones* by James R. Giles, 1981; *Jones* by George Garrett, 1984; *Into Eternity: Jones: The Life of an American Writer* by Frank MacShane, 1985.

* * *

Generally regarded as the most successful "war-novelist" to emerge from World War II, James Jones, at his best, writes the way a good combat infantryman serves out a campaign. His prose is direct, muscular, prepared to take advantage of tactical opportunities, efficient, cynical without being pessimistic, and cannily aware of the ambiguous areas where fear mingles with bravery, and self-interest and self-sacrifice shade together. One of the few modern writers to depict the character of man-as-warrior sympathetically and without romantic illusions, Jones will probably be remembered for *From Here to Eternity, The Thin Red Line*, and his acute nonfictional study, *WWII: A Chronicle of Soldiering*.

In *From Here to Eternity*, Jones found a story perfectly adequate to his thematic interests: the heroic struggle of the warrior-individual trying to maintain his sense of self against the pressures of the very system that provides him with his cherished identity. Prewitt, the doomed protagonist, becomes an indelible figure in the gallery of American fictional soldiers that runs from Crane's Henry Fleming through Hemingway's Frederic Henry to Joseph Heller's Yossarian. Unlike the others, however, Prewitt is a soldier by choice and devotion; he is neither a rebel against, nor a victim of, the institution in which he finds his fullest realization. Jones's non-military fiction—including *Some Came Running, Go to the Widow-Maker*, and *The Merry Month of May*—tends to lack the controlled narrative focus of his war novels; characteristically, the prose is much looser, the action moves toward the melodramatic and sensational, and the novels suffer from a combination of verbosity and sentimentality.

—Earl Rovit

JONES, LeRoi. See **BARAKA, Amiri.**

KAUFMAN, George S. Born in Pittsburgh, Pennsylvania, 16 November 1889. Educated at Liberty School, New Castle School, and Central High School, Pittsburgh, graduated 1907; Western University of Pennsylvania Law School (now University of Pittsburgh), 1907. Married 1) Beatrice Bakrow in 1917 (died, 1945), one adopted daughter; 2) the actress Leueen

MacGrath in 1949 (divorced, 1957). Worked as a surveyor, clerk in the Allegheny County Tax Office, and stenographer for the Pittsburgh Coal Company; traveling salesman, Columbia Ribbon Company, Paterson, New Jersey, 1909–12; columnist, Washington *Times*, 1912–13; drama critic, New York *Tribune*, 1914–15; columnist, New York *Evening Mail*, 1915; drama critic, later drama editor, New York *Times*, 1917–30. Writer for the stage from 1918, often in collaboration; stage director from 1928; panelist, *This Is Show Business* radio and TV program, 1948–52. Chairman of the Board, Dramatists Guild 1927. Recipient: Megrue Prize, 1931; Pulitzer Prize, 1932, 1937; Tony award, for directing, 1951. *Died 2 June 1961.*

PUBLICATIONS

Collections

By George: A Kaufman Collection, edited by Donald Oliver. 1979.

Plays

Among Those Present, with Larry Evans and Walter C. Percival (produced 1918; as *Someone in the House*, produced 1918).
Jacques Duval, from play by Hans Miller (produced 1919).
Dulcy, with Marc Connelly (produced 1921). 1921.
To the Ladies!, with Marc Connelly (produced 1922). 1923.
No, Sirree!, with Marc Connelly (produced 1922).
The 49ers, with Marc Connelly (produced 1922).
West of Pittsburgh, with Marc Connelly (produced 1922; revised version, as *The Deep Tangled Wildwood*, produced 1923).
Merton of the Movies, with Marc Connelly, from the story by Harry Leon Wilson (produced 1922). 1925.
A Christmas Carol, with Marc Connelly, from the story by Dickens, in *Bookman*, December 1922.
Helen of Troy, New York, with Marc Connelly, music and lyrics by Harry Ruby and Bert Kalmar (produced 1923).
Beggar on Horseback, with Marc Connelly, music by Deems Taylor, from a play by Paul Apel (produced 1924). 1925.
Sketches, in *'Round the Town* (produced 1924).
Be Yourself, with Marc Connelly, music and lyrics by Lewis Genzler and Milton Schwarzwald, additional lyrics by Ira Gershwin (produced 1924).
Minick, with Edna Ferber, from the story "Old Man Minick" by Ferber (produced 1924). In *Old Man Minick: A Short Story . . . Minick: A Play*, 1924.
The Butter and Egg Man (produced 1925). 1926.
The Cocoanuts, music by Irving Berlin (produced 1925). 1925.
Business Is Business, with Dorothy Parker (produced 1925).
If Men Played Cards Like Women Do. 1926.
The Good Fellow, with Herman J. Mankiewicz (produced 1926). 1931.
The Royal Family, with Edna Ferber (produced 1927). 1928; as *Theatre Royal* (produced 1935), 1936.
Animal Crackers, with Morrie Ryskind, music and lyrics by Harry Ruby and Bert Kalmar (produced 1928).
The Still Alarm (sketch), in *The Little Show* (produced 1929). 1930.
June Moon, with Ring Lardner, from the story "Some Like Them Cold" by Lardner (produced 1929). 1930.
The Channel Road, with Alexander Woollcott (produced 1929).
Strike Up the Band, book by Morrie Ryskind from a libretto by Kaufman, music by George Gershwin, lyrics by Ira Gershwin (produced 1930).
Once in a Lifetime, with Moss Hart (produced 1930). 1930.
The Band Wagon, with Howard Dietz, music by Arthur Schwartz (produced 1931).
Eldorado, with Laurence Stallings (produced 1931).
Of Thee I Sing, with Morrie Ryskind, music by George Gershwin, lyrics by Ira Gershwin (produced 1931). 1932.
Dinner at Eight, with Edna Ferber (produced 1932). 1932.
Let 'em Eat Cake, with Morrie Ryskind, music by George Gershwin, lyrics by Ira Gershwin (produced 1933). 1933.
The Dark Tower, with Alexander Woollcott (produced 1933). 1934.
Merrily We Roll Along, with Moss Hart (produced 1934). 1934.
Bring on the Girls, with Morrie Ryskind (produced 1934).
Prom Night. 1934.
Cheating the Kidnappers. 1935.
The Paperhanger, with Moss Hart. 1935(?).
First Lady, with Katharine Dayton (produced 1935). 1935.
Stage Door, with Edna Ferber (produced 1936). 1936.
You Can't Take It with You, with Moss Hart (produced 1936). 1937.
I'd Rather Be Right, with Moss Hart, music by Richard Rodgers, lyrics by Lorenz Hart (produced 1937). 1937.
The Fabulous Invalid, with Moss Hart (produced 1938). 1938.
The American Way, with Moss Hart, music by Oscar Levant (produced 1939). 1939.
The Man Who Came to Dinner, with Moss Hart (produced 1939). 1939.
George Washington Slept Here, with Moss Hart (produced 1940). 1940.
The Land Is Bright, with Edna Ferber (produced 1941). 1941.
Six Plays, with Moss Hart. 1942.
The Late George Apley, with John P. Marquand, from the novel by Marquand (produced 1944). 1946.
Local Boy Makes Good, in *The Seven Lively Arts* (produced 1944).
Hollywood Pinafore (produced 1945).
Park Avenue, with Nunnally Johnson, music by Arthur Schwartz, lyrics by Ira Gershwin (produced 1946).
Bravo!, with Edna Ferber (produced 1948). 1949.
The Small Hours, with Leueen MacGrath (produced 1951). 1951.
Fancy Meeting You Again, with Leueen MacGrath (produced 1952). 1952.
The Solid Gold Cadillac, with Howard Teichmann (produced 1953). 1954.
Silk Stockings, with Leueen MacGrath and Abe Burrows, music by Cole Porter, suggested by Melchior Lengyel (produced 1955). 1955.
Amicable Parting, with Leueen MacGrath (produced 1957). 1957.

Screenplays: *Roman Scandals*, with others, 1933; *A Night at the Opera*, with Morrie Ryskind and James Kevin McGuinness, 1935; *Star Spangled Rhythm*, with others, 1942.

Film director: *The Senator Was Indiscreet* (*Mr. Ashton Was Indiscreet*), 1947.

*

Critical Studies: *Act One* by Moss Hart, 1959; *Kaufman: An Intimate Portrait*, by Howard Teichmann, 1972; *Kaufman and His Friends* by Scott Meredith, 1974, abridged version, as *Kaufman and the Algonquin Round Table*, 1977; *Kaufman: His Life, His Theater* by Malcolm Goldstein, 1979.

* * *

George S. Kaufman was a devastating wit and a serious satirist who worked, almost always in collaboration, on successful plays, musicals, and films. He was especially effective with Moss Hart, a productive blend of talents much studied and admired: "Their most distinguished works, *You Can't Take It with You* and *The Man Who Came to Dinner*, reveal Kaufman and Hart," says Milton Levin (in *The Reader's Encyclopedia of World Drama*), "as the best satirists in American drama."

Kaufman's first play was with the team of Larry Evans and Walter C. Percival. Then he and Marc Connelly (another newspaperman from Pennsylvania active in New York) entered on a series of collaborations: *Dulcy, To the Ladies!, Merton of the Movies, The Deep Tangled Wildwood,* and *Beggar on Horseback*. Of these only *The Deep Tangled Wildwood* (a satire "upon the Winchell-Smith type of play") was a failure. *Merton of the Movies*, the story of a movie-struck clerk who achieves success because he, unconsciously, burlesques serious roles, was a delight. The dream sequence of *Beggar on Horseback* (a penniless composer, Neil McRae is given a sedative and has nightmares about having to work in a "widget" factory and then a Consolidated Art Factory, where he has to write music for songs like: "You've broken my heart like you broke my heart / So why should you break it again?") was considered "a fine expression of the resentment of the artist" for those who are "contemptuous of those who show originality" (A. H. Quinn). *Beggar on Horseback* is considered a milestone in American expressionism. The team broke up and Kaufman wrote his one unaided work, *The Butter and Egg Man* (1925), and Connelly tried an original also, *The Wisdom Tooth* (1926). Neither was much good, for Kaufman's farce and Connelly's fantasy did not seem to work separately.

"I have always been smart enough to attach myself to the most promising lad that came along in the theater," said Kaufman, and he joined forces with a number of burgeoning, bright talents. With Edna Ferber he wrote *Minick, The Royal Family, Dinner at Eight, Stage Door*, and *The Land is Bright*. With Herman J. Mankiewicz, another journalist and wit, he wrote *The Good Fellow*, which flopped (Mankiewicz went on to success as a screenwriter, probably writing most of *Citizen Kane* though that is still argued), but Kaufman had a hit with Ring Lardner, that "wonderful man" with such a great ear for American speech, in an hilarious take-off of Tin-Pan Alley, *June Moon*. About the same time Kaufman began to work with one of the madcap writers behind the Marx Brothers, the too-little-acknowledged zany genius, Morrie Ryskind. With Ryskind Kaufman entered the world of Broadway musicals, starting with *Animal Crackers*. Their collaboration was later to produce *Of Thee I Sing* (with the Gershwins; Pulitzer Prize 1932) and *Let 'em Eat Cake* (with the Gershwins), satires of politics and revolutionaries. With Alexander Woollcott, Kaufman wrote *The Channel Road* and, not much better, *The Dark Tower*. With Katharine Dayton he did a comedy of Washington politics and social life, *First Lady*. In the 1930's he was at his best with Moss Hart. *Once in a Lifetime* was a facile but funny satire on Hollywood. *Merrily We Roll Along* cleverly told its story backwards, taking the middle-aged failure back to the promise of his youth. *I'd Rather Be Right* took its title from a Henry Clay speech of 1850 ("I would rather be right than be President"), but attacked the administration of Franklin Delano Roosevelt. *You Can't Take It with You* well deserved its Pulitzer Prize, for the crazy Sycamore family creates one of the fastest, most furious, funniest farces ever and manages to effect a sweet, sentimental ending as well. The musicals *Strike Up the Band* and *The Band Wagon* (with Howard Dietz) were fun—but *The Man Who Came to Dinner*, with Hart, was fabulous. At the center of the chaos stands (or sits, in a wheelchair) Sheridan Whiteside, described by Monty Woolley in the film biography of Cole Porter as "an intolerable ass." As Woolley played him on stage and screen, this caricature of Alexander Woollcott was irresistible and, though the play is cluttered with other matters (such as cartoons of Noël Coward, one of the Marx Brothers, and a Lizzie Borden character), he delightfully dominates the action as he dominates the poor family who were unlucky enough to have him break a hip on their premises. The play contains some of the best single lines in American comedy.

The Man Who Came to Dinner may be the high spot of Kaufman's career. *George Washington Slept Here* was accurately reviewed as "George Kaufman slipped here" and later work such as *The Late George Apley* (with novelist John P. Marquand) and *The Solid Gold Cadillac* (with Howard Teichmann) were a part of Kaufman's long career as a play doctor, though much of their success was no doubt due to his expertise. He also worked with other play doctors (such as Abe Burrows) and with Nunnally Johnson, Leueen MacGrath and others.

Kaufman gained various strengths from various collaborators—farce, fantasy, satire, structure—but, to put it briefly, he can best be understood if one thinks of him as a Jewish comedian. He was a leader among the "Broadway intellectuals" (with Hart, Dorothy Parker, S. N. Behrman, George Jean Nathan) and a master of the wisecrack. His is the *echt* Jewish humor that plays with language (as in Goodman Ace); often sees the world as *ash und porukh* (ashes and dust) but will hang on to see what happens ("You might as well live"—Dorothy Parker); deals in insult; sometimes takes off into nonsense, intoxicated by words (S. J. Perelman), and sometimes into sentimentality (Sam Levine), attracted to nostalgia for better times; is repelled by pretension and more than a little attracted to cynicism (though not at Kaufman's time going as far as Lenny Bruce) and always loves to tinker with logic until it explodes. In *World of Our Fathers* (1977), Irving Howe dissects this Jewish humor which chooses laughter as the alternative to tears and often uses satire as both a defensive and an offensive weapon. Howe quotes Gilbert Seldes, who claimed that the Jewish entertainers' "daemonic" approach was traceable to "their fine carelessness about our superstitions of politeness and gentility . . . contempt for artificial notions of propriety."

Kaufman was businessman enough to know that an all-out assault on the Establishment would not pay off. His pose was that of the hero of *The Butter and Egg Man*, the naïf in the big city. His targets were the obvious, safe ones that are best suited to musical comedy and farce. When he tried something "positive" like *The American Way* (a patriotic panorama), he was at his weakest. A wisecrack has to be a *zinger*, not a compliment. He never let himself get bitter; *that* was the kind of satire, as he said, which "closes on Sunday night." He wasn't a *kvetch* or a nag or a moralist, just a very funny wisecracking wit, one of the best.

—Leonard R. N. Ashley

KELLY, George (Edward). Born in Schuykill Falls, Pennsylvania, 16 January 1887. Educated privately. Served in the U.S. Army, 1917. Debut as actor, 1908; subsequently acted in touring companies and vaudeville. Recipient: Pulitzer Prize, 1926; Brandeis University Creative Arts Award, 1959. A.F.D.: LaSalle College, Philadelphia, 1962. *Died 18 June 1974.*

PUBLICATIONS

Plays

One of Those Things (produced 1913). In *One-Act Plays for Stage and Study*, 3rd series, 1927.
Finders-Keepers (produced 1916). 1923.
Mrs. Ritter Appears (produced 1917; revised version, as *The Torchbearers: A Satirical Comedy* produced 1922). 1923; revised version of Act III, as *Mrs. Ritter Appears*, 1964.
The Flattering Word (produced 1919). In *The Flattering Word and Other One-Act Plays*, 1925.
The Weak Spot (produced 1922). In *The Flattering Word and Other One-Act Plays*, 1925.
Poor Aubrey (produced 1922). In *The Flattering Word and Other One-Act Plays*, 1925; revised version, as *The Show-Off: A Transcript of Life* (produced 1924), 1924.
Mrs. Wellington's Surprise (produced 1922).
Smarty's Party (produced 1923). In *The Flattering Word and Other One-Act Plays*, 1925.
The Flattering Word and Other One-Act Plays. 1925.
Craig's Wife (produced 1925). 1926.
Daisy Mayme (produced 1926). 1927.
Behold the Bridegroom (produced 1927). 1928.
A La Carte (sketches and lyrics only; produced 1927).
Maggie the Magnificent (produced 1929).
Philip Goes Forth (produced 1931). 1931.
Reflected Glory (produced 1936). 1937.
The Deep Mrs. Sykes (produced 1945). 1946.
The Fatal Weakness (produced 1946). 1947.

Screenplay: *Old Hutch*, 1936.

*

Bibliography: "Kelly: An Eclectic Bibliography" by Paul A. Doyle, in *Bulletin of Bibliography*, September-December 1965.

Critical Studies: in *Theatre Chronicles 1937–1962* by Mary McCarthy, 1963; *Kelly* by Foster Hirsch, 1975.

* * *

George Kelly had a lot of brothers and sisters and he followed his older brother Walter ("The Virginia Judge" of vaudeville) into the theatre. In those days it was not quite so unusual a place to find a moralist, even an anti-romantic, deeply puritanical one.

Kelly played juveniles on the Keith and Orpheum circuits and began to write sketches such as *One of Those Things*, *Finders-Keepers*, *The Flattering Word*, and *Poor Aubrey*. They were light little satires on character flaws such as vanity and bragging. People who overstepped the accepted moral code were given their comeuppance, like the adventuress who outsmarts herself in *Smarty's Party*. They were popular enough: really trenchant satire (as George S. Kaufman remarked) "closes on Saturday night," but audiences like to see obvious targets hit skilfully and wittily.

But then Kelly expanded *Poor Aubrey* into the full-length play of *The Show-Off*, in which vanity Aubrey Piper's bragging and bluffing are exposed and his lies and pretensions exploded. It was Kelly's first success, for *The Torchbearers*, a rather gentle send-up of the pretensions of Little Theatres with even littler talent in them, did not catch on at first, though it later was to achieve some recognition.

Kelly achieved the height of his career (and the Pulitzer Prize) with *Craig's Wife*. The vanity of *The Flattering Word* and the manipulator defeated of *Smarty's Party* combine in the well-constructed but rather grimly determined story of a woman whose concern with appearances and control of her sterile environment give "Good Housekeeping" a bad name. But character study is confused with the problem play and Kelly is no Ibsen. Mrs. Craig was unforgettable but essentially just revealed, not developed. A revival of the play in the 1970's made the theatrical success of a half century before look too theatrical and the character of Mrs. Craig too static and that of her long-suffering husband too trivial.

After *Craig's Wife*, Kelly was on the slide. He had four failures in a row: *Daisy Mayme* was talky; *Behold the Bridegroom* was worse, preachy; *Maggie the Magnificent* and *Philip Goes Forth* convinced the dramatist to give up Broadway, though he returned with *Reflected Glory*, and *The Deep Mrs. Sykes*. After the poor reception of *The Fatal Weakness* in 1946, Kelly seemed to recognize his own fatal weaknesses as a playwright—getting in the way of the characters, imposing himself and his views on the situation and using the stage as a soapbox without the brilliance of Shaw or the cleverness of Brecht—and retired. Today he is known as the author of *Craig's Wife* and *The Torchbearers*.

—Leonard R. N. Ashley

KENNEDY, John Pendleton. Born in Baltimore, Maryland, 25 October 1795. Educated at the Sinclair Academy, Baltimore, and Baltimore College, graduated 1812; studied law: admitted to Maryland bar, 1816. Served in the U.S. Army during the War of 1812. Married 1) Mary Tennant in 1824 (died, 1824); 2) Elizabeth Gray in 1829. Lawyer in Baltimore from 1816; Member, Maryland House of Delegates, 1820–23; inherited large income from an uncle c. 1830 and increasingly gave up the law for literature and politics; member from Maryland, U.S. House of Representatives, 1838, 1840–44; Chairman of the Congressional Committee on Commerce; member of the Maryland House of Delegates, and Speaker of the House, 1846–48; Secretary of the Navy, under President Millard Fillmore, 1852–53; organized Commodore Perry's expedition to Japan, 1852. Provost, University of Maryland; President, Board of Trustees, Peabody Institute, Baltimore; member, American Philosophical Society. *Died 18 August 1870.*

PUBLICATIONS

Collections

Collected Works. 10 vols., 1871–72.

Fiction

Swallow Barn; or, A Sojourn in the Old Dominion. 1832; edited by Jay B. Hubbell, 1929.
Horse-Shoe Robinson: A Tale of the Tory Ascendency. 1835; edited by Ernest E. Leisy, 1937.
Rob of the Bowl: A Legend of St. Inigoe's. 1838; edited by William S. Osborne, 1965.
Quodlibet, Containing Some Annals Thereof. 1840.

Other

The Red Book, with Peter Hoffman Cruse. 2 vols., 1820–21.
Defence of the Whigs. 1844.
Memoirs of the Life of William Wirt, Attorney General of the United States. 2 vols., 1849; revised edition, 1850.
The Border States. 1860.
Mr. Ambrose's Letters on the Rebellion. 1865.

Editor, with Alexander Bliss, *Autograph Leaves of Our Country's Authors.* 1864.

*

Bibliography: in *Bibliography of American Literature* by Jacob Blanck, 1969.

Critical Studies: *The Life of Kennedy* by Henry T. Tuckerman, in *Collected Works,* 1871; *Kennedy, Gentleman from Baltimore* by Charles H. Bohner, 1961; *Kennedy* by J. V. Ridgely, 1966.

* * *

Only two of John Pendleton Kennedy's four works of fiction can really be called novels. Much like Washington Irving's *Bracebridge Hall,* which it both resembles and satirizes, *Swallow Barn* is hardly more than a series of sketches loosely held together by common characters and a pair of shadowy plot lines, and *Quodlibet* is a satire on Jacksonian politics and policies of the 1830's projected through a history of the imaginary borough of Quodlibet. *Horse-Shoe Robinson* and *Rob of the Bowl* are thus his only true novels. Both are historical romances of the kind made popular by Scott and Cooper.

Swallow Barn is in many ways his most attractive book. Hardly the realistic work it has sometimes been called, it makes good-natured fun of a group of Virginia planters in the early 19th century, burlesques their chivalric ideals and pretensions, yet also treats with respect many of the gentlemanly values they attempt to preserve. *Quodlibet,* by contrast, attacks the leveling democrats through one of their number. Solomon Secondthoughts recounts the history of Quodlibet in such a way as to damn the very policies and practices he thinks he is upholding. The work is a clever, if dated, piece of satire.

Horse-Shoe Robinson and *Rob of the Bowl,* on the other hand, develop their themes through the use of history. Kennedy sought to maintain historical accuracy in both, but like other historical romances, the books are concerned not so much with demonstrable fact as with the meaning to be found in the events of the past. Thus, *Horse-Shoe Robinson* portrays the American Revolution as a desperate struggle by young patrician leaders and their yeoman supporters to establish a free society, and *Rob of the Bowl* depicts the successful defense of 17th-century Maryland against both Puritan rebels and lawless buccaneers as the maintenance of established order against the threat of disruption.

Kennedy's four books would thus seem to work at cross purposes: *Horse-Shoe Robinson* affirming the need for progressive social change, and *Rob of the Bowl* upholding the value of social stability; *Swallow Barn* satirizing Virginia aristocrats, and *Quodlibet* attacking leveling democrats. Yet the books are not so diverse in meaning as they may seem. The issues they present are those that troubled American thinking during the 1830's, and Kennedy seems to suggest that some kind of balance among the conflicting ideas should be maintained: though American society must progress, it should not change so radically as to destroy the personal and social values that had come to it from the past. Taken together, then, his four works of fiction indicate the skill with which Kennedy, who did not think of himself as a professional man of letters, was able to develop a complex social theme.

—Donald A. Ringe

KEROUAC, Jack. Born Jean Louis Lebris de Kerouac in Lowell, Massachusetts, 12 March 1922. Educated at Lowell High School; Horace Mann School, New York, 1939–40; Columbia University, New York, 1940–41, 1942. Served in the U.S. Merchant Marine, 1942, 1943, and U.S. Navy, 1943. Married 1) Edie Parker in 1944 (annulled, 1945); 2) Joan Haverty in 1950 (divorced), one daughter; 3) Stella Sampas in 1966. Sports reporter, Lowell *Sun,* 1942; worked at various jobs from 1944; brakeman, Southern Pacific Railroad, San Francisco, 1952–53; traveled throughout the U.S. and Mexico, 1953–56; fire lookout for U.S. Agricultural Service in Washington State, 1956; full-time writer from 1957. *Died 21 October 1969.*

PUBLICATIONS

Fiction

The Town and the City. 1950.
On the Road. 1957; edited by Scott Donaldson, 1978.
The Subterraneans. 1958.
The Dharma Bums. 1958.
Doctor Sax: Faust Part Three. 1959.
Maggie Cassidy. 1959.
Excerpts from Visions of Cody. 1959.
Tristessa. 1960.
Book of Dreams. 1960.

Big Sur. 1962.
Visions of Gerard. 1963.
Desolation Angels. 1965.
Satori in Paris. 1966.
Vanity of Duluoz: An Adventurous Education 1935–46. 1968.
Pic. 1971.
Visions of Cody. 1973.
Two Early Stories. 1973.

Play

Pull My Daisy (screenplay). 1961.

Screenplay: *Pull My Daisy*, 1959.

Verse

Mexico City Blues. 1959.
Hymn—God Pray for Me. 1959.
Rimbaud. 1960.
The Scripture of the Golden Eternity. 1960.
Poem. 1962.
A Pun for Al Gelpi. 1966.
Hugo Weber. 1967.
Someday You'll Be Lying. 1968.
A Last Haiku. 1969.
Scattered Poems. 1971.
Trip, Trap: Haiku along the Road from San Francisco to New York 1959, with Albert Saijo and Lew Welch. 1973.
Heaven and Other Poems, edited by Donald Allen. 1977.

Other

Lonesome Traveler, drawings by Larry Rivers. 1960.
Old Angel Midnight. N.d.
Dear Carolyn (letters to Carolyn Cassady), edited by Arthur and Kit Knight. 1983.

*

Bibliography: *A Bibliography of Works by Kerouac 1939–1967* [*1939–1975*] by Ann Charters, 1967, revised edition, 1975; *Kerouac: An Annotated Bibliography of Secondary Sources 1944–1979* by Robert J. Milewski, 1981.

Critical Studies: *No Pie in the Sky: The Hobo as American Cultural Hero in the Works of Jack London, John Dos Passos, and Kerouac* by Frederick Feied, 1964; *Kerouac: A Biography* by Ann Charters, 1973; *Kerouac's Town* by Barry Gifford, 1973, revised edition, 1977, and *Jack's Book: An Oral Biography* by Gifford and Lawrence Lee, 1978; *Visions of Kerouac* by Charles E. Jarvis, 1974; *The Visions of the Great Rememberer* by Allen Ginsberg, 1974; *Heart Beat: My Life with Jack and Neal* by Carolyn Cassady, 1976; *Kerouac, Prophet of the New Romanticism: A Critical Study* by Robert A. Hipkiss, 1976; *Kerouac: The New Picaroon* by Luc Gaffié, 1977; *Kerouac* by Harry Russell Huebel, 1979; *Desolate Angel: Kerouac, The Beats, and America* by Dennis McNally, 1979; *Kerouac's Crooked Road: The Development of a Fiction* by Tim Hunt, 1981; *The Kerouac We Knew: Unposed Portraits, Action Shots* edited by John Montgomery, 1982; *Memory Babe: A Critical Biography of Kerouac* by Gerald Nicosia, 1983; "Kerouac Issue" of *Review of Contemporary Fiction*, vol. 3, no. 2, 1983; *Kerouac* by Tom Clark, 1984; *Quest for Kerouac* by Chris Challis, 1984; *Kerouac* by Warren French, 1986.

* * *

Along with Gary Snyder, Allen Ginsberg, William Burroughs, Neal Cassady, and their compatriots, Jack Kerouac was an unlikely cultural hero. Each, in his own very different way, was a thread in the vast social ethnic called the United States. Kerouac was rooted more than most in a traditional American mythos. Raised in a working-class Catholic family in Lowell, Massachusetts, given to normal boyhood fantasies of early greatness as a football star (he very nearly recognized them in his brief stay at Columbia University), he later became the leading prose writer of the Beat movement. His group and its substantial youthful following sparked a cultural renaissance in the mid-century United States—in literature, music, painting, and the larger realms of society and politics—that will not soon be forgotten.

Kerouac's favorite early nickname was "memory babe," suggestive of his own prodigious memory and the accompanying later desire to preserve, in a weakly fictionalized pickle, the experiences of childhood and youth in Lowell, his days on the road in the heart of America, and particularly his friends and exploits along the way. From his first and most conventional work, *The Town and the City*, he sought to preserve in their essences: himself (as Peter Martin, Sal Paradise, and Jack Duluoz), Snyder (as Japhy Ryder), Ginsberg (as Carlo Marx and Irwin Garden), Burroughs (as Old Bull Lee and Bull Hubbard), and Neal Cassady (as Dean Moriarity and Cody Pomeray). He had hoped, in later life, to collect his works—uniformly bound as multi-volumes of a single gigantic work, with real names and places restored.

Kerouac, the man and the writer, represented a revitalization of the romantic spirit in America. He idealized a return to a more essential and authentic life and intense existence in the present, be it in the streets of his fictional Lowell (*The Town and the City, Doctor Sax*), along the streams and firetrails of his fictional Oregon (*The Dharma Bums*), in the barrios of his fictional California and Mexico (*On the Road, Big Sur, Mexico City Blues*), or in subterranean clubs of New York, Denver, San Francisco, and points along the way. His biographers, particularly Ann Charters and Charles Marcus, document his own fierce and often troubled individualism, recurrent optimism, and reverence for sentient life, and the tragedy of his later years—virtually alone in Florida and finally Lowell.

Kerouac's work depicted both the ideals of the "hot" beats—those like Neal Cassady who burned their lives as filaments in a quest for "IT!," "kicks," pure ecstatic existence in what Norman Mailer calls "the enormous present"—and the "cool" beats—Gary Snyder and kindred spirits who sought a return to essence in the more Eastern detached, ascetic realms of Zen and allied philosophies. A keynote of his fiction and poetry is the notion that the act of creating literature is in itself a performance, an authentic act testifying to intensely felt experience. (We should recall the great popularity of poetry as a *declaimed* form, a *song* as well as a text, often combined with jazz, during the Beat years.) Thus Kerouac's work rarely responds well to the techniques of close textual reading. He claimed to have written *On the Road* "at white heat" in several weeks on an unbroken roll of teletype paper; his later work was rarely revised, very loose in form, episodic and lyrical at best, improvised like the jazz the Beats so admired, given to humor and nostalgia and the crests and valleys of romantic fiction.

Like many of his fellow Beats (a predominantly masculine group), Kerouac was widely lauded and damned—in his own day and in the present. Like Burroughs and Cassady and Ginsberg, Kerouac lived his life as a kind of work of art, an action painting, a jazz riff. Their experiments in sexuality, with drugs, with the many and often frightening potentialities of psychic and social order and disorder, their bold and often naive desires to re-awaken dormant chords in American life and writing—these have rarely been met with balanced opinions. And Kerouac, as the central figure of the most well-defined literary movement in 20th-century America, like most truly revolutionary figures, found no final peace in his life and will not soon rest easily in mass thought or literary history.

—Jack Hicks

See the essay on *On the Road*.

KINGSLEY, Sidney. Born Sidney Kirshner in New York City, 22 October 1906. Educated at Townsend Harris Hall, New York, 1920–24; Cornell University, Ithaca, New York (state scholarship), 1924–28, B.A. 1928. Served in the U.S. Army, 1941–43: Lieutenant. Married the actress Madge Evans in 1939. Actor in the Tremont Stock Company, Bronx, New York, 1928–29; thereafter play-reader and scenario writer for Columbia Pictures; full-time writer and stage director from 1934. President, Dramatists Guild, 1961–69. Recipient: Pulitzer Prize, 1934; New York Theatre Club medal, 1934, 1936, 1943; New York Drama Critics Circle award, 1943, 1951; New York Newspaper Guild Front Page Award, 1943, and Page One Citation, 1949; Mystery Writers of America Edgar Allan Poe Award, 1950; Donaldson Award, 1951; American Academy Award of Merit Medal, 1951; Yeshiva University award, 1965. D.Litt.: Monmouth College, West Long Branch, New Jersey, 1978; Ramapo College, Mahwah, New Jersey, 1978. Lives in New Jersey.

PUBLICATIONS

Plays

Men in White (produced 1933). 1933.
Dead End (produced 1935). 1936.
Ten Million Ghosts (produced 1936).
The World We Make, from the novel *The Outward Room* by Millen Brand (produced 1939). 1939.
The Patriots (produced 1943). 1943.
Detective Story (produced 1949). 1949.
Darkness at Noon, from the novel by Arthur Koestler (produced 1951). 1951.
Lunatics and Lovers (produced 1954). Condensed version in *Theater 1955*, 1955.
Night Life (produced 1962). 1966.

Screenplay: *Homecoming*, with Paul Osborn and Jan Lustig, 1948.

* * *

Sidney Kingsley was one of "the young radicals our colleges are said to be full of nowadays" (as S. N. Behrman put it in *End of Summer*). His agit-prop approach to theatre was a bit less strident than that of some other proletarian dramatists, but sufficient to endear him to the famous Group Theater, whose financial life he saved early in its career with the success of his first play, *Men in White*.

The story of the Group Theater is brilliantly told by Harold Clurman in *The Fervent Years*. The story of *Men in White* is accurately told by John Mason Brown (*Two on the Aisle*, 1938): it "is a piffling script, mildewed in its hokum, childishly sketchy in its characterization, and so commonplace in its every written word that it in no way justifies its own unpleasantness." Moreover, "the finished result, as Arthur Hopkins once observed when Mr. [David] Belasco converted his stage into a Childs Restaurant, is *only remarkable because it is not real*." Very just; but just also to add that Kingsley's approach has since been copied, in its dab-hand dramaturgy and somewhat fuzzy concern with ethical standards, in Paddy Chayefsky's *The Hospital* and *Network* and in many television soap operas and feature films.

Also seminal was *Dead End*, establishing for the cinema many of the clichés of slum-life sociology, "a raucous tone-poem of the modern city" (Brooks Atkinson), a shaky melodrama set down in a handsome set (by Norman Bel Geddes) with a pier-head jutting right into the orchestra pit. The contrived plot brings the Dead End kids and other poor folk into contact with some rich East Siders in New York: the facade of the wealthy apartment house is under repair, which brings the rich people round to the back and right on stage. Unfortunately for Kingsley, he does not seem to remember poverty without sentimentality and, at least before the considerable success of *Dead End*, seems never to have met anyone rich. His sociology is superficial and his dramaturgy profoundly pedestrian.

Ten Million Ghosts is a confused discussion of munitions magnates. Kingsley was well out of his intellectual depth. *The World We Make* was not much better, although for once in the 1930's the emphasis is upon character rather than upon "The System" and environment. *The Patriots* is about a decade in the life of Thomas Jefferson. In none of these plays did Kingsley have the advantages he had in *Dead End*. He desperately needed stars and set designers and a whole team to "make something" of his scripts. He once half perceived this when he said: "When two people have a baby, the baby is a bit of a surprise. In the theater we have a marriage of many people. I can't really tell how the baby will come out."

Kingsley was once a leading Broadway playwright. He became known to wider audiences through such films as *Men in White*, *Dead End*, and *Detective Story*. He was at his best whenever he had help: the committed cast of *Men in White*, the street arabs and street scene of *Dead End*, Millen Brand's novel *The Outward Room* as a basis for *The World We Make*, Madge Evans to help with *The Patriots*, Arthur Koestler's novel behind *Darkness at Noon*. *Crowell's Handbook of Contemporary Drama* (1971) give as fair an estimate as any: "In most of his work Kingsley relies on a sense of atmosphere generated by realistic re-creation of a particular world—hospitals, slums, police stations, prisons—a vivid mileiu that supplies much of the vivid impact of the play and also constitutes its limitation. The plays are frequently melodramatic in plot and sketchy in characterization; timely issues have made them at first appear more substantial than they later are seen to be."

—Leonard R. N. Ashley

KIRKLAND, Joseph. Born in Geneva, New York, 7 January 1830; grew up in Michigan and Illinois. Received little formal education; studied law, 1873–80: admitted to Illinois bar, 1880. Served in the Civil War, in the Illinois 12th Regiment, 1861, as aide-de-camp, Adjutant-General's Department, Washington, D.C., 1861, and on the staff of Generals Fitz-John Porter and George McClellan, 1862–63: Major. Married Theodosia Burr Wilkinson in 1863; four children. Sailor on packet ship to Europe, 1847; clerk, New York City, 1848–52; clerk and reader, *Putnam's Monthly*, New York, 1852–55; auditor, Illinois Central Railroad, Chicago, 1855–58; supervisor, Carbon Coal Company, Tilton, Illinois, 1858–61 and 1863–64; co-founder, *Prairie Chicken* literary journal, Tilton, 1864–65; established coal mining business in Tilton, 1865, and a retail coal business in Chicago, 1868 (business destroyed in Chicago fire, 1871); worked for U.S. Revenue Service 1873–80; lawyer, in partnership with Mark Bangs, Chicago, 1880–90; special correspondent and literary editor, Chicago *Tribune*, 1889–93. Member, Committee on the World's Columbian Exposition in Chicago, 1893. *Died 28 April 1894.*

PUBLICATIONS

Fiction

Zury, The Meanest Man in Spring County: A Novel of Western Life. 1887; revised edition, 1888.
The McVeys (An Episode). 1888.
The Captain of Company K. 1891.

Play

Sidonie, The Married Flirt, with James B. Runnion, from a novel by Alphonse Daudet (produced 1877).

Other

The Story of Chicago, completed by Caroline Kirkland. 2 vols., 1892–94; revised edition of vol. 1, 1892.
The Chicago Massacre of 1812. 1893.

Editor, *Lily Pearl and the Mistress of Rosedale*, by Ida Glenwood. 1892.
Editor, with John Moses, *The History of Chicago.* 2 vols., 1895.

*

Bibliography: in *Bibliography of American Literature* by Jacob Blanck, 1969.

Critical Study: *Kirkland* by Clyde E. Henson, 1962.

* * *

Joseph Kirkland's claim to fame rests entirely on one book, *Zury*, and a superficial reading of it is likely to be misleading. Literary historians have been too quick to classify Kirkland with other "agrarian realists" and "protest novelists." It is true that *Zury* contains many details conveying the narrowness, brutality, and deprivation of midwestern farm life in the middle of the 19th century. *Zury* (the name is short for Usury) has a beloved sister who dies as a result of the primitive conditions on the farm, and the family has no coins with which to weight her eyelids. Since she dies in mid-winter, the family has no choice but to let the body freeze and wait for the spring thaw to bury her.

The novel also forcefully describes the cruelty and niggardliness Zury must possess to accumulate his modest fortune. Having been made selfish by his environment, he seeks to avoid his responsibility for making pregnant Anne Sparrow, the young and innocent schoolteacher from the east. He arranges to marry her to a local idler, John McVey.

However, to emphasize these details is to neglect the end of *Zury* and the entirety of the sequel, *The McVeys*. The second volume followed soon after the first, and in it Zury sees his error and takes an interest in his and Anne's twin children (McVey has conveniently died). Although she at first rejects him, Zury and Anne eventually marry and symbolically combine the vitality and toughness of Zury's West with the culture and refinement of Anne's East, and the last scene of *The McVeys* finds them cozy and happy in a prosperous farmhouse. One might suggest that Kirkland was ultimately more "realistic" than some of his more bitter contemporaries, and certainly more entertaining.

After writing *The Captain of Company K*, an episodic but vivid story of the Civil War, Kirkland showed little interest in artistic creation, and devoted himself to editorial and historical work.

—William Higgins

KOPIT, Arthur (Lee). Born in New York City, 10 May 1937. Educated at Lawrence High School, New York, graduated 1955; Harvard University, Cambridge, Massachusetts, A.B. (cum laude) 1959 (Phi Beta Kappa). Married to Leslie Ann Garis; two sons and one daughter. Playwright-in-Residence, Wesleyan University, Middletown, Connecticut, 1975–76; CBS Fellow, 1976–77, and Adjunct Professor of Playwriting, 1977–80, Yale University, New Haven, Connecticut; taught playwriting workshop at City College, New York, from 1982. Council member, Dramatists Guild, from 1982. Recipient: Vernon Rice Award, 1962; Outer Circle award, 1962; Guggenheim fellowship, 1967; Rockefeller grant, 1968; American Academy award, 1971; National Endowment for the Arts grant, 1974; Wesleyan University Center for the Humanities fellowship, 1974; Italia prize, for radio play, 1979. Lives in Connecticut.

PUBLICATIONS

Plays

The Questioning of Nick (produced 1957). In *The Day the Whores Came Out to Play Tennis and Other Plays*, 1965.
Gemini (produced 1957).
Don Juan in Texas, with Wally Lawrence (produced 1957).
On the Runway of Life, You Never Know What's Coming Off Next (produced 1958).
Across the River and into the Jungle (produced 1958).
To Dwell in a Place of Strangers, Act I published in *Harvard Advocate*, May 1958.

Aubade (produced 1959).
Sing to Me Through Open Windows (produced 1959; revised version, produced 1965). In *The Day the Whores Came Out to Play Tennis and Other Plays*, 1965.
Oh Dad, Poor Dad, Mamma's Hung You in the Closet and I'm Feelin' So Sad: A Pseudoclassical Tragifarce in a Bastard French Tradition (produced 1960). 1960.
Mhil'daim (produced 1963).
Asylum; or, What the Gentlemen Are Up To, And As for the Ladies (produced 1963; *And As for the Ladies* produced, as *Chamber Music*, 1971). *Chamber Music* in *The Day the Whores Came Out to Play Tennis and Other Plays*, 1965.
The Conquest of Everest (produced 1964). In *The Day the Whores Came Out to Play Tennis and Other Plays*, 1965.
The Hero (produced 1964). In *The Day the Whores Came Out to Play Tennis and Other Plays*, 1965.
The Day the Whores Came Out to Play Tennis (produced 1965). In *The Day the Whores Came Out to Play Tennis and Other Plays*, 1965.
The Day the Whores Came Out to Play Tennis and Other Plays. 1965; as *Chamber Music and Other Plays*, 1969.
Indians (produced 1968). 1969.
An Incident in the Park, in *Pardon Me, Sir, But Is My Eye Hurting Your Elbow?*, edited by Bob Booker and George Foster. 1968.
What's Happened to the Thorne's House (produced 1972).
Louisiana Territory; or, Lewis and Clark—Lost and Found (produced 1975).
Secrets of the Rich (produced 1976). 1978.
Wings (produced 1978). 1978.
Nine (libretto), music and lyrics by Maury Yeston, from an adaptation by Mario Fratti of the screenplay *8½* by Federico Fellini (produced 1981). 1983.
Good Help Is Hard to Find (produced 1981). 1982.
Ghosts, from a play by Ibsen (produced 1982).
End of the World (With a Symposium to Follow) (produced 1984; as *The Assignment*, produced 1985). 1984.

Television Plays: *The Conquest of Television*, 1966; *Promontory Point Revisited*, 1969.

*

Critical Study: *Sam Shepard, Kopit, and the Off-Broadway Theater* by Doris Auerbach, 1982.

* * *

"Do I exaggerate?" asks Michael Trent in his first speech in *End of the World*. "Of course. That is my method. I am a playwright." The line is a comic one which becomes ironic in the face of a theme—the prospect of global annihilation—which turns even the grandest theatrical exaggeration into austere understatement. Out of context, the words provide a suitable description of the way Arthur Kopit works.

At 23, fresh out of Harvard, Kopit escaped—or appeared to escape—the cocoon of university production when *Oh Dad, Poor Dad, Mamma's Hung You in the Closet and I'm Feelin' So Sad* was published by a house that specializes in serious drama and went on to production in London and New York. A fashionable success, it established Kopit as a dramatist, but it also saddled him with the label "undergraduate playwright" which stayed with him long after the playfulness of *Oh Dad* had given way to the mixed-genre method that marks his best and most complex plays. One reason the epithet stuck is that the work that immediately followed *Oh Dad* lacked the flash of that play and offered little substance in consolation. *The Day the Whores Came Out to Play Tennis and Other Plays*, which contained some of his student work along with his post-*Oh Dad* efforts, seemed to confirm the critics who saw him simply as a clever young man noodling around.

Such a judgment is far too dismissive. Although some of *Oh Dad*'s games—the parody references to Tennessee Williams, for instance—seem too cute in retrospect, it is an early indication of the dramatic virtues that have become increasingly apparent in Kopit's work: a facility with language, an ear for the clichés of art and life, an eye for the effective stage image (the waltz scene in which Madame Rosepettle breaks Commodore Roseabove, for instance), a strategic use of caricature, the talent for being funny about a subject that is not at all comic. All of these are in evidence in *Oh Dad* and all of them are in the service of a serious theme (or one that seemed serious in 1960)—the emasculation of the American male by the too protective mother, the iron-maiden temptress and the little girl as seducer.

In an interview in *Mademoiselle* (August 1962), Kopit said, "Comedy is a very powerful tool . . . You take the most serious thing you can think of and treat it as comically as you can." Although he invoked Shaw, *Oh Dad* is the immediate reference. Since then, he has thought of more serious things—war, death, nuclear destruction—and has treated them seriously. And comically, as *Indians* and *End of the World* indicate. The Bantam edition of *Indians* (1971) prints a long interview with John Lahr in which Kopit identifies his play as a response to "the madness of our involvement in Vietnam," but he chose to approach the subject obliquely, going back to the eviction of the American Indian from his land. The play shows the distance between official words and deeds, the power of platitude and the way in which myths are made and used. The central figure is Buffalo Bill, who begins as a friend of the Indians and ends—a star of his own show—as an apologist for slaughter. The play moves back and forth between comic and serious scenes, from the broad farce of the play within the play and the cartoon Ol' Time President to the powerful accusatory ending in which the Wild West Show is invaded by the dead Indians. For some, the funny scenes fit uncomfortably with the solemn subject matter, but they are not simply entertaining decoration. The comedy is thematic. The disastrous production of the Ned Buntline melodrama at the White House is both an instance of the creation of myth and a critique of it.

End of the World is a similar fusion of genres. It concerns a playwright who is commissioned to write a play about the dangers of nuclear proliferation—as Kopit was, in fact—and finds that he can only do so by writing a play about a playwright who . . . The parody private-eye frame of the play (the playwright as detective), the agents' lunch at the Russian Tea Room and the three interviews in which the rationale of nuclear stockpiling and scenarios of destruction are presented as comic turns are all central to the play's assumption that there are personal, artistic, and official ways of not facing up to the impending horror. When Michael Trent learns in the play that all the nuclear strategists know the situation is hopeless but do not believe what they know, and that he was chosen to write the play because, like the men he interviews, he has an attraction to evil and destruction. A painful and funny play, it provides no solution, only an insistence on the probability of catastrophe and, unlike the conventional post-bomb melodrama, no promise of rebirth.

If *Indians* and *End of the World* share dramatic method, *Wings* is an indication of Kopit's unpredictability. There are funny lines in the play, but is primarily a lyric exploration of death. It is about a woman who suffers a stroke, struggles to make her fragmented speech fit her still coherent thoughts and, after a second stroke, becomes eloquent as she sees herself flying into the unknown. A wing-walker in her youth, her profession/art provides the main metaphor for her final sense of exhilarating discovery. The play evokes both the concerned narrowness of medicine's perception of the woman and the imagination that continues to carry her above her stammering exasperation with herself and those around her. It is an indication—along with *Indians* and *End of the World*—that Kopit is wing-walking far above the bravura flight of *Oh Dad*.

—Gerald Weales

KOSINSKI, Jerzy (Nikodem). Born in Lodz, Poland, 14 June 1933; emigrated to the U.S. in 1957; became citizen, 1965. Educated at the University of Lodz, 1950–55, M.A. in political science 1953, M.A. in history 1955; Columbia University, New York (Ford Foundation Fellow), 1958–64; New School for Social Research, New York, 1962–65. Married Mary Hayward Weir in 1962 (died, 1968). Ski instructor, Zakopane, Poland, winters 1950–56; Aspirant (graduate assistant), Polish Academy of Science, Warsaw, 1955–57; visiting researcher, Lomosov University, Moscow, 1957; laborer, truck driver, chauffeur, and projectionist on arriving in U.S.; Fellow, Center for Advanced Studies, Wesleyan University, Middletown, Connecticut, 1968–69; Senior Fellow, Council for the Humanities, and Visiting Lecturer, Princeton University, New Jersey, 1969–70; Professor of English Prose and Criticism, School of Drama, and Resident Fellow, Davenport College, Yale University, New Haven, Connecticut, 1970–73. Photographer: individual show—Crooked Circle Gallery, Warsaw, 1957. President, PEN American Center, 1973–75. Member of the Executive Board, National Writers Club; director, International League for Human Rights, 1973–79. Recipient: Polish Academy of Science grant, 1955; Foreign Book Prize (France), 1966; Guggenheim fellowship, 1967; National Book Award, 1969; American Academy award, 1970; Yale University John Golden Fellowship in Playwriting, 1970; Brith Sholom Humanitarian Freedom Award, 1974; American Civil Liberties Union First Amendment Award, 1978; Writers Guild of America award, for screenplay, 1979; Polonia Media award, 1980; BAFTA award, for screenplay, 1981; Spertus College Humanitarian Award, 1982. Doctor of Hebrew Letters: Spertus College, Chicago, 1982. Lives in New York City.

PUBLICATIONS

Fiction

The Painted Bird. 1965; revised edition, 1970.
Steps. 1968.
Being There. 1971.
The Devil Tree. 1973; revised edition, 1981.
Cockpit. 1975.
Blind Date. 1977.
Passion Play. 1979.
Pinball. 1982.
The Hermit. 1986.

Plays (screenplays)

Being There. 1973; revised edition, 1980.
Passion Play. 1982.

Screenplay: *Being There*, 1980.

Other

Dokumenty walki o czlowieka (Documents of the Struggle for Man). 1955.
Program rewolucji Ludowej Jakoba Jaworskiego (Jakob Jaworski's Program of People's Revolution). 1955.
The Future is Ours, Comrade: Conversations with Russians. 1960.
No Third Path. 1962.
Notes of the Author on The Painted Bird 1965. 1965.
The Art of the Self: Essays à propos Steps. 1968.

Editor, *Socjologia Amerykánska* (American Sociology). 1962.

*

Bibliography: *John Barth, Kosinski, and Thomas Pynchon: A Reference Guide* by Thomas P. Walsh and Cameron Northouse, 1977.

Critical Studies: *Kosinski: Literary Alarm Clock* by Byron L. Sherwin, 1981; *Kosinski* by Norman Lavers, 1982.

* * *

In Jerzy Kosinski's first novel, *The Painted Bird*, there is an incident that not only sums up the thrust of the novel in which it appears, but points to the core of the great variety of experiences that appear in Kosinski's later novels. A peasant catches a raven, paints it with brilliant colors, and releases it to return to its fellows. But the other birds will not accept it and tear it to pieces. This image is a metaphor which expresses the experience of the narrator in the novel, a child of dark aspect ("gypsy" or "Jewish" by turns) who wanders through Poland, deprived of his parents and depending on the ungentle mercies of the peasants he encounters; the peasants, blond and stupid, regard the child as full of evil magic. And the "painted" child learns to survive by duplicity; he endures a solitude that he has not chosen; the only morality he knows is that of survival.

It is a morality which, with appropriate alterations, the central figures of the other novels sense; just so do they define and experience their existences. Such a morality is tested—admired from several angles—in *Steps*, a collection of narrative fragments and mostly unlocalized amorous dialogues. Much of this material is linked with the education and migration to a foreign country of a young man who is, like the child in *The Painted Bird*, on the run, exploited and exploiting wherever he goes. To him every new acquaintance is both an affront and an opportunity.

For a change of pace, the hero of *Being There* is no person displaced by war; rather, he is an orphan without identity, unable to read, skillful only as a gardener. But when he leaves the

Eden where he has learned his only skills, his oddity and peculiar vulnerability arouse wonder and respect, rather than antipathy as in *The Painted Bird*. His trivial remarks about gardening are taken as profound and enigmatic insights by those he encounters; businessmen, TV reporters, and others surround him with an aura of ultimate authority. In *The Devil Tree*, a young man named Jonathan James Whalen wanders through another landscape of solitude, this one created by his great inherited wealth. There is practically nothing that he cannot purchase and manipulate, and the absolute control he can exercise separates him from other persons as fully as does, for example, the "gypsy" aspect of the child in *The Painted Bird*. Whatever can be purchased can also be thrown away; this is the core of Whalen's experience.

The wanderings presented in *Cockpit* are those of a secret agent named Tarden. Born in a Communist country, he soon learns what *his* precious endowment is: intelligence and guile that surpass the intelligence and guile of all other persons. Every person he meets is a predestined victim whom Tarden can mislead and abuse, all with the intent of showing that Tarden is one "painted bird" whom his hostile peers cannot destroy.

Blind Date unites, within the confines of one novel, intense realizations of themes dispersed elsewhere. There is the solitude of a man, George Levanter, who has left his native Russia, has succeeded as an investment broker, and can afford the luxury of satisfying all his whims. He travels, he has many sexual encounters, and (a little odd in this context) he is an occasional enforcer of justice in an unjust world. In short, Levanter is both a knight errant and, more often, just an exile errant, all in a luxurious world which only superlatives can describe.

Two other novels—*Pinball* and *Passion Play*—are also variations on basic themes, ornamented with special attention to materials not treated elsewhere. Both novels present human beings incommunicado. In *Pinball* a girl seeks to find a rock star, and in *Passion Play* a polo player wants to discover competitors who are his equals. Each novel has its individual note: rock versus traditional music in *Pinball* and horsemanship in *Passion Play*.

Each of Kosinski's novels is a demonstration of one variety of solipsism. Community of any kind is a figment that misleads inferior imaginations. Each of Kosinski's novels dissolves such illusions. Innocence, wealth, and guile are alternate strategies, but they have a common goal. All confirm that each human being is alone, and those who have a degree of wisdom recognize their solitude and enforce it.

—Harold H. Watts

KUNITZ, Stanley (Jasspon). Born in Worcester, Massachusetts, 29 July 1905. Educated at Classical High School, Worcester, graduated 1922; Harvard University, Cambridge, Massachusetts (Garrison Medal, 1926), A.B. (summa cum laude) 1926 (Phi Beta Kappa), A.M. 1927. Served in the U.S. Army Air Transport Command, 1943–45: Sergeant. Married 1) Helen Pearce in 1930 (divorced, 1937); 2) Eleanor Evans in 1939 (divorced, 1958), one daughter; 3) Elise Asher in 1958. Editor, *Wilson Library Bulletin*, New York, 1928–43; member of the faculty, Bennington College, Vermont, 1946–49; Professor of English, Potsdam State Teachers College (now State University of New York), 1949–50, and summers, 1949–53; Lecturer, New School for Social Research, New York, 1950–57; Visiting Professor, University of Washington, Seattle, 1955–56, Queens College, Flushing, New York, 1956–57, Brandeis University, Waltham, Massachusetts, 1958–59, Yale University, New Haven, Connecticut, 1970–72, Rutgers University, Camden, New Jersey, 1974, Princeton University, New Jersey, 1978, and Vassar College, Poughkeepsie, New York, 1981. Director, YM-YWHA Poetry Workshop, New York, 1958–62; Danforth Visiting Lecturer, 1961–63; Lecturer, 1963–67, and Adjunct Professor of Writing, 1967–85, Columbia University, New York; since 1968 associated with the Fine Arts Work Center, Provincetown, Massachusetts; Senior Fellow in Humanities, Princeton University, 1978. Editor, Yale Younger Poets series, Yale University Press, New Haven, Connecticut, 1969–77. Consultant in Poetry, Library of Congress, Washington, D.C., 1974–76. Cultural exchange lecturer, U.S.S.R., Poland, Senegal, Ghana, Israel, and Egypt. Recipient: Guggenheim fellowship, 1945; Amy Lowell traveling fellowship, 1953; Harriet Monroe Award, 1958; Pulitzer Prize, 1959; Ford grant, 1959; American Academy grant, 1959; Brandeis University Creative Arts Award, 1964; Academy of American Poets fellowship, 1968; Lenore Marshall Award, 1980; National Endowment for the Arts senior fellowship, 1984. Litt.D.: Clark University, Worcester, Massachusetts, 1961; Anna Maria College, Paxton, Massachusetts, 1977; L.H.D.: Worcester State College, Massachusetts, 1980. Fellow, Yale University, 1969; member, American Academy; Chancellor, Academy of American Poets, 1970. Lives in New York City.

PUBLICATIONS

Verse

Intellectual Things. 1930.
Passport to the War: A Selection of Poems. 1944.
Selected Poems 1928–1958. 1958.
The Testing-Tree. 1971.
The Terrible Threshold: Selected Poems 1940–1970. 1974.
The Coat Without a Seam: Sixty Poems 1930–1972. 1974.
The Lincoln Relics. 1978.
The Poems 1928–1978. 1979.
The Wellfleet Whale and Companion Poems. 1983.
Next-to-Last Things (includes essays). 1985.

Other

Robert Lowell, Poet of Terribilità (lecture). 1974.
A Kind of Order, A Kind of Folly: Essays and Conversations. 1975.
From Feathers to Iron (lecture). 1976.

Editor, *Living Authors: A Book of Biographies*. 1931.
Editor, with Howard Haycraft and Wilbur C. Hadden, *Authors Today and Yesterday: A Companion Volume to Living Authors*. 1933.
Editor, with others, *The Junior Book of Authors*. 1934; revised edition, 1961.
Editor, with Howard Haycraft, *British Authors of the Nineteenth Century*. 1936.

Editor, with Howard Haycraft, *American Authors 1600–1900: A Biographical Dictionary of American Literature*. 1938.
Editor, with Howard Haycraft, *Twentieth Century Authors: A Biographical Dictionary of Modern Literature*. 1942; *First Supplement*, with Vineta Colby, 1955.
Editor, with Howard Haycraft, *British Authors Before 1800: A Biographical Dictionary*. 1952.
Editor, *Poems*, by John Keats. 1964.
Editor, with Vineta Colby, *European Authors 1000–1900: A Biographical Dictionary of European Literature*. 1967.
Editor and Translator, with Max Hayward, *Poems of Akhmatova*. 1973.
Editor and Co-Translator, *Orchard Lamps*, by Ivan Drach. 1978.

Translator, with others, *Stolen Apples*, by Yevgeny Yevtushenko. 1972.
Translator, with others, *Story under Full Sail*, by Andrei Voznesensky. 1974.

*

Critical Studies: *Kunitz* by Marie Hénault, 1980; "Kunitz Issue" of *Antaeus*, Spring 1980; *Kunitz: An Introduction to the Poetry* by Gregory Orr, 1985; *A Celebration for Kunitz on His Eightieth Birthday*, 1986.

* * *

Stanley Kunitz's *Selected Poems 1928–1958* offers us a good standard of the classic forms and modes of poetry that largely governed American poets of these three decades. Kunitz has more often fought the form imposed on his sometimes extravagant lyrical language than given in to it, and where this creative conflict between a restless content and a rigid, enveloping form is sustained the result has unusual vigor and freshness. The effect is of loosely woven statements held under intense pressure of symmetry and repeated rhythm, as in this nervous, jaggedly expressed love lyric, "Green Ways":

Let me not say it, let me not reveal
How like a god my heart begins to climb
The trellis of the crystal
In the rose-green moon;
Let me not say it, let me leave untold
This legend, while the nights snow emerald.

Let me not say it, let me not confess
How in the leaflight of my green-celled world
In self's pre-history
The blind moulds kiss;
Let me not say it, let me but endure
This ritual like feather and like star.

Let me proclaim it—human be my lot!—
How from my pit of green horse-bones
I turn, in a wilderness of sweat,
To the moon-breasted sibylline,
And lift this garland, Danger, from her throat
To blaze it in the foundries of the night.

But "Green Ways" is the balance that Kunitz has not always been able to strike in his poetry; here passion and form give way to each other, but in some of his work the feeling has been too thoroughly subdued by order and conscious craft, creating a lyric that is too dry and rehearsed in its utterance. But even in the severest of his poems, the reader is aware of the intensity of the poet's mind, the irrepressible energy of his imagination.

Often called the poet's poet, a term he has tended to dismiss more vigorously in later years, Kunitz has himself defended the unruly side of the poetic medium. As editor of the Yale Younger Poets series, Kunitz has been enthusiastic in his advocacy of poetry of process and impulsive strategies. In his occasional and critical prose, he has also tended to favor the ungoverned muse: in his essay "A Kind of Order" he says: "With young writers I make a nuisance of myself talking about order, for the good reason that order is teachable; but in my bones I know that only the troubled spirits among them, those who recognize the disorder without and within, have a chance to become poets."

In the strictest balance, however, Kunitz's *Selected Poems* conveys, even in its most rigid formulations of lyric, a stubbornly individual mind that has known all the extremes of feeling and mood. "Night-Piece," "The Man Upstairs" with its Eliotic strain of irony and wit, the poems gathered under the section "The Terrible Threshold," and much else in this collection are provocative and vital.

In the new edition of his selected poems (*The Poems 1928–1978*), which covers fifty years of poetry, Kunitz follows the bent of his disorderly side, not only in breaking up the thematic order of the older edition, but in putting first his new poems, and then arranging the rest in chronological order. The new poems are livelier, fresher, and freer in tone and method. Kunitz is fortunately one of those in whom age is an access to one's youth, as he reports in his opening poem, "The Knot," with its image of the "obstinate bud, / sticky with life." *Next-to-Last Things* contains new poems and essays, which bears as part of its epigraph a line that reads, "that he might risk his soul in the streets." Though few, these are some of his most charming poems; the prose section following is a reckoning with age and his changed views: "A poem is at once the most primitive and most sophisticated use of language, but my emphasis is on the former," he writes in "The Wisdom of the Body."

—Paul Christensen

LA FARGE, Oliver (Hazard Perry). Born in New York City, 19 December 1901. Educated at the Groton Academy, Lowell, Massachusetts, graduated 1920; Harvard University, Cambridge, Massachusetts (editor, *Harvard Lampoon*; President, *Advocate*; class poet), 1920–24, B.A. 1924, then did graduate work in anthropology (Hemenway Fellow), M.A. 1929. Served in the U.S. Army, 1942–46: Lieutenant-Colonel; Legion of Merit, 1946. Married 1) Wanden E. Mathews in 1929 (divorced, 1937), one son and one daughter; 2) Consuelo Otille C. de Baca in 1939, one son. Anthropologist: involved in expeditions for the Peabody Museum, Harvard, in Arizona, 1921, 1922, 1924; Assistant in Ethnology, Department of Middle American Research, Tulane University, New Orleans, 1925–26; involved in research expeditions to Mexico and Guatemala, 1926–28; Research Associate in Ethnology, Columbia University, New York, 1931; director of the Columbia University expedition to Guatemala, 1932; thereafter a full-time writer and historian; columnist, Santa Fe *New Mexican*, 1950–63. President, Association on American Indian Affairs, 1932–

41, 1948. Recipient: Pulitzer Prize, 1930; O. Henry Award, 1931; Guggenheim fellowship, 1941. A.M.: Brown University, Providence, Rhode Island, 1932. Fellow, American Association for the Advancement of Science, 1938, American Anthropological Association, 1947, and American Academy of Arts and Sciences, 1953; member, American Academy, 1957. *Died 2 August 1963*.

PUBLICATIONS

Fiction

Laughing Boy. 1929.
Sparks Fly Upward. 1931.
Long Pennant. 1933.
All the Young Men (stories). 1935.
The Enemy Gods. 1937.
The Copper Pot. 1942.
A Pause in the Desert (stories). 1957.
The Door in the Wall (stories). 1965.

Play

Screenplay: *Behold My Wife*, with William R. Lipman, 1934.

Other

Tribes and Temples: A Record of the Expedition to Middle America Conducted by the Tulane University of Louisiana in 1925, with Frans Blom. 2 vols., 1926–27.
The Year Bearer's People, with Douglas Byers. 1931.
An Alphabet for Writing the Navajo Language, with J.P. Harrington. 1936.
As Long as the Grass Shall Grow, photographs by Helen M. Post. 1940.
War below Zero: The Battle for Greenland, with Bernt Balchen and Corey Ford. 1944.
Raw Material (autobiography). 1945.
Santa Eulalia: The Religion of a Cuchumatán Indian Town. 1947.
The Eagle in the Egg. 1949.
Cochise of Arizona: The Pipe of Peace Is Broken (for children). 1953.
The Mother Ditch (for children). 1954.
A Pictorial History of the American Indian. 1956; edition for children, as *The American Indian*, 1960.
Behind the Mountains. 1956.
Santa Fe: The Autobiography of a Southwestern Town, with Arthur N. Morgan. 1959.
The Man with the Calabash Pipe: Some Observations, edited by Winfield Townley Scott. 1966.

Editor, *Introduction to American Indian Art*. 1931.
Editor, with Jay Bryan Nash, *The New Day for the Indians: A Survey of the Working of the Indian Reorganization Act of 1934*. 1938.
Editor, *The Changing Indian*. 1942.

Translator, *A Man's Place*, by Ramón Sender. 1940.

*

Critical Studies: *La Farge* by Everett A. Gillis, 1967; *Indian Man: A Life of La Farge* by D'Arcy McNickle, 1971; *La Farge* by T.M. Pearce, 1972.

* * *

Of the more than twenty books by Oliver La Farge, nearly half are scientific or historical, and a third are fiction. Yet he is generally known as the author of but one book, his first novel, *Laughing Boy*.

It is not surprising that his histories are virtually unknown. Of those concerning Indians, his most important is *A Pictorial History of the American Indian*, which offers a wealth of material about the various tribes to a public aware of the minority question. Other histories, however—about World War II, the city of Santa Fe, the events of La Farge's own life—are too specialized to be of general interest.

For a similar reason, his scientific work is all but unknown. Not only has the subsequent accumulation of knowledge dwarfed his contributions to ethnology, but as he notes in his personal history, *Raw Material*, the details that absorb the scientist are unlikely to interest more than a handful of fellow scientists. The accounts of his expeditions to Central America—*Tribes and Temples*, *The Year Bearer's People*, *Santa Eulalia*—are highly readable, but too narrowly concerned with the Indian to interest the public for which they were intended.

On the other hand his second novel, *Sparks Fly Upward*, using the same Indian material, was a bestseller. This and *The Enemy Gods*, dealing with the Navajos in the southwest, reveal the plight of the Indian caught between two cultures. The theme is also explored in a collection of short stories, *All the Young Men*.

With his fifth novel, *The Copper Pot*, La Farge attempted to avoid being typecast as a writer about Indians. This story of an artist in New Orleans is more an affectionate memoir, however, than a novel. Two short story collections, *A Pause in the Desert* and *The Door in the Wall*, use other than Indian material, as does *The Long Pennant*, a novel about the aftermath of piracy by a New England vessel.

Yet it is La Farge's knowledgeable use of Indian material that distinguishes his fiction. A symbiotic relationship exists between the scientific and the creative in his work, the former providing it with substance and originality. Although a first-rate storyteller, he exhibits no particularly original turn of mind. He breaks no new ground in his use of language or fictional techniques. As he makes plain in his newspaper columns, collected in *The Man with the Calabash Pipe*, he wished to preserve traditional values, in language and elsewhere—an attitude reflected in his lifelong involvement with the Indian.

This attitude and his unique material are most happily met in his two finest novels, *Laughing Boy* and *The Enemy Gods*. The latter is considered superior, presenting more information and dealing with weightier problems. Yet it is unremittingly melancholy and gray compared with *Laughing Boy*, whose young lovers in an Indian Eden are likely to continue to make it the book by which La Farge will be known.

—Robert F. Richards

LANIER, Sidney. Born in Macon, Georgia, 3 February 1842. Educated at a private academy in Macon, and at Oglethorpe University, near Milledgeville, Georgia, 1857–60, graduated 1860. Served with the Macon Volunteers in the Confederate forces during the Civil War, 1861–65: prisoner-of-war, 1864–65. Married Mary Day in 1867; four sons. Worked in his father's law office, and as a hotel clerk and teacher, Macon, 1865–73; musician from an early age: flute player in the Peabody Orchestra, Baltimore, from 1873; Lecturer in English, Johns Hopkins University, Baltimore, 1879–81. *Died 7 September 1881.*

PUBLICATIONS

Collections

The Works (includes letters), edited by Charles R. Anderson and others. 10 vols., 1945.
Selected Poems, edited by Stark Young. 1947.

Verse

The Centennial Meditation of Columbia, music by Dudley Buck. 1876.
Poems. 1877.
Poems, edited by Mary Day Lanier. 1884; revised edition, 1891, 1916.
Poem Outlines. 1908.

Fiction

Tiger-Lilies. 1867.

Other

Florida: Its Scenery, Climate, and History. 1875.
Some Highways and Byways of American Travel, with others. 1878.
The Science of English Verse. 1880.
The English Novel and the Principle of Its Development, edited by William Hand Browne. 1883; edited by Mary Day Lanier, 1897.
Music and Poetry: Essays upon Some Aspects and Inter-Relations of the Two Arts, edited by Henry Wysham Lanier. 1898.
Retrospects and Prospects: Descriptive and Historical Essays, edited by Henry Wysham Lanier. 1899.
Letters of Lanier: Selections from His Correspondence 1866–1881, edited by Henry Wysham Lanier. 1899.
Bob: The Story of Our Mocking-Bird, edited by Henry Wysham Lanier. 1899.
Shakespeare and His Forerunners: Studies in Elizabethan Poetry and Its Development from Early English, edited by Henry Wysham Lanier. 2 vols., 1902.

Editor, *The Boy's Froissart, Being Sir John Froissart's Chronicles*. 1879.
Editor, *The Boy's King Arthur, Being Sir Thomas Malory's History of King Arthur and His Knights of the Round Table*. 1880.
Editor, *The Boy's Mabinogion*. 1881.
Editor, *The Boy's Percy, Being Old Ballads of War, Adventure, and Love*. 1882.

*

Bibliography: in *Bibliography of American Literature* by Jacob Blanck, 1969; *Lanier, Henry Timrod, and Paul Hamilton Hayne: A Reference Guide* by Jack De Bellis, 1978.

Critical Studies: *Lanier: A Biographical and Critical Study* by Aubrey H. Starke, 1933; *Lanier, Poet and Prosodist* by Richard Webb and Edwin R. Coulson, 1941; *Lanier: The Man, The Poet, The Critic* by Edd Winfield Parks, 1968; *Lanier* by Jack De Bellis, 1972; *A Living Minstrelsy: The Poetry and Music of Lanier* by Jane S. Gabin, 1985.

* * *

The life of Sidney Lanier is an odyssey from a small southern city to the great cultural centers of America; from a law desk in a Georgia office to a prominent place in a major professional orchestra; from an aesthetically restrictive tradition to an existence totally imbued with the arts. Throughout his career, from the time he was deciding whether to defy southern tradition in favor of art, through the period in which he was totally devoted to art, music seems to have been in competition with poetry for his time and attention. But there was never any conflict in the negative sense, for without his musical experiences Lanier could never have arrived at the type of poetry he was finally to create.

The story of Lanier is both inspiring and pathetic. It is a series of thwarted plans, shattered hopes, incomplete projects. Lanier spent most of his life dreaming of entering artistic circles, but when he finally decided to devote himself wholeheartedly to this end he was able to reach only slightly beyond the periphery. He was forever not quite reaching his goals. He aimed for the *Atlantic Monthly*, the country's arbiter of literary taste, but reached *Lippincott's*; he vowed to play only for Theodore Thomas's orchestra in New York, but instead worked with Asger Hamerik at the Peabody Conservatory; he craved acclaim in New York City, but had to find it in Baltimore. True, what he did accomplish was of no little consequence—*Lippincott's* was also one of the nation's leading publications, Hamerik a conductor of international reputation, and Baltimore a thriving and respected center of culture. But they were all second choices for Lanier, and represent the disappointment that underlay all his successes.

Yet considering Lanier's background, he accomplished miracles. He came from a genteel southern tradition which scorned the arts as a profession. His education was removed from the main currents of American academic life, and he had very little formal musical training. Constantly hounded by poverty after the Civil War, he was forced to write pot-boilers in order to support his family, wasting precious creative energy. Tuberculosis had attacked him when he was 22; by the time he finally determined to pursue an artistic career, he had only seven years to live, and of this time had to spend weeks and months away from his work in desperate search of a cure.

It is remarkable that Lanier managed to do so much in so little time. He played first flute in a conservatory orchestra; delivered successful and popular lectures on Shakespeare and on the English novel; wrote numerous essays on music and about literature; edited collections of legends and tales for children; produced a guidebook to Florida which is still popular in that state; composed numerous musical works; wrote one of the best studies of English prosody (*The Science of English Verse* is a musical analysis of poetry); and in the midst of all these activities wrote dozens of poems, some of which are the most beautifully original in American literature.

His poetic style is a unique result of an attempt to convey musical impression in verse; this stems from his lifelong interest in the unity of poetry and music. His creative technique is original, and Lanier arrived at it through music. One has only to compare the early, naive, and sentimental lyrics of his 1868 song "Little Ella" and the intricately textured poem of 1880, "Sunrise," to see the revolutionary development of Lanier's verse. This change was brought about by music, and it is music which made Lanier a poet. Without it, his verse would have remained pretty and lyrical, but simple in structure, texturally unimaginative, and tied to the limiting song-concept. But Lanier's best works, his later poems, reflect the influence of larger musical forms, the blending of voices, lines, and timbre characteristic of the symphony. If he had never played Berlioz's *Symphonie Fantastique*, he might never have written his best poem, "The Marshes of Glynn." To Lanier, music and poetry were two different, but intimately related, media through which he expressed one ideal. This ideal is most notably expressed at the end of the poem "The Symphony": "Music is Love in search of a word." Lanier believed that man could come to terms with the problems of his civilization only through the redeeming powers of faith and love of art.

The most creative periods of Lanier's life—and the happiest—were those in which he was musically most active. Lanier's friends were, in the main, musical, not literary. He found enthusiastic applause for his flute-playing—which is supposed to have been of astonishing virtuosity—a compensation for the rejection-slips he received for his poetry. His writing, because it was so original, often came under harsh attack, but his musical performances never earned an unfavorable review.

Lanier is a unique figure—or rather phenomenon—in American literature; and since he is one of the rare American poets who was also a professional musician, his poetry's qualities are determined by practical experience. Lanier was an innovator whose possible further accomplishments can only be subjects of wistful speculation; but he is generally acknowledged by today's critics to be a significant figure in early modern literature.

—Jane S. Gabin

LARDNER, Ring(gold Wilmer). Born in Niles, Michigan, 6 March 1885. Educated at Niles High School, graduated 1901; Armour Institute of Technology (now Illinois Institute of Technology), Chicago, 1901–02. Married Ellis Abbott in 1911; four sons. Freight clerk, bookkeeper, and employee of Niles Gas Company, 1902–05; reporter, South Bend *Times*, Indiana, 1905–07; sportswriter, *Inter Ocean*, Chicago, 1907, Chicago *Examiner*, 1908, and Chicago *Tribune*, 1908–10; managing editor, *Sporting News*, St. Louis, 1910–11; sports editor, Boston *American*, 1911, Chicago *American*, 1911–12, and Chicago *Examiner*, 1912–13; columnist ("In the Wake of the News"), Chicago *Tribune*, 1913–19; moved to Long Island, New York, 1919; columnist ("Weekly Letter"), 1919–27, and wrote *You Know Me Al* comic strip, 1922–25, both for the Bell Syndicate; radio reviewer, *New Yorker*, 1932–33. *Died 25 September 1933.*

PUBLICATIONS

Collections

The Lardner Reader, edited by Maxwell Geismar. 1963.
The Best of Lardner, edited by David Lodge. 1984.

Fiction

You Know Me Al: A Busher's Letters. 1916.
Gullible's Travels (stories). 1917.
Own Your Own Home. 1919.
The Real Dope. 1919.
The Big Town. 1921.
How to Write Short Stories (with Samples). 1924.
The Love Nest and Other Stories. 1926.
Round Up: The Stories. 1929; as *Collected Short Stories*, 1941.
Some Champions: Sketches and Fiction, edited by Matthew J. Bruccoli and Richard Layman. 1976.

Plays

Zanzibar, music and lyrics by Harry Schmidt (produced 1903). 1903.
Elmer the Great (produced 1928).
June Moon, with George S. Kaufman, from the story "Some Like Them Cold" by Lardner (produced 1929). 1930.

Screenplay: *The New Klondike*, with Tom Geraghty, 1926.

Verse

Bib Ballads. 1915.

Other

My Four Weeks in France. 1918.
Treat 'em Rough: Letters from Jack the Kaiser Killer. 1918.
Regular Fellows I Have Met. 1919.
The Young Immigrunts. 1920.
Symptoms of Being 35. 1921.
Say It with Oil: A Few Remarks about Wives, with *Say It with Bricks: A Few Remarks about Husbands*, by Nina Wilcox Putnam. 1923.
What of It? 1925.
The Story of a Wonder Man. 1927.
Lose with a Smile. 1933.
First and Last. 1934.
Shut Up, He Explained, edited by Babette Rosmond and Henry Morgan. 1962.
Ring Around Max: The Correspondence of Lardner and Max Perkins, edited by Clifford M. Caruthers. 1973.
Letters from Ring, edited by Clifford M. Caruthers. 1979.
Lardner's You Know Me Al: The Comic Strip Adventures of Jack Keefe. 1979.

Editor, with Edward G. Heeman, *March 6th, 1914: The Home Coming of Charles A. Comisky, John J. McGraw, James J. Callahan*. 1914.

*

Bibliography: *Lardner: A Descriptive Bibliography* by Matthew J. Bruccoli and Richard Layman, 1976.

Critical Studies: *Lardner: A Biography* by Donald Elder, 1956; *Lardner* by Walton R. Patrick, 1963; *Lardner* by Otto A. Friedrich, 1965; *Lardner and the Portrait of Folly* by Maxwell Geismar, 1972; *The Lardners: My Family Remembered* by Ring Lardner, Jr., 1976; *Ring: A Biography of Lardner* by Jonathan Yardley, 1977; *Lardner* by Elizabeth Evans, 1979; *Small Town Chicago: The Comic Perspective of Finley Peter Dunne, George Ade, and Lardner* by James DeMuth, 1980.

* * *

Ring Lardner wrote in the tradition of a long line of American popular journalists and humourists who exploited slang and the illiteracies of vernacular speech for comic ends. In doing so, he transmuted what was initially a stock comic device into something much more, an instrument of satire. At the same time, he was, however unwittingly, one of those writers, of whom Mark Twain is the great exemplar, whose sensitivity to the value of the spoken word helped to liberate American prose from the artificial diction that marked so much 19th-century writing.

Beginning as a sports writer on an Indiana paper, in 1913 he took over the "In the Wake of the News" column in the Chicago *Tribune*. The Jack Keefe letters were meanwhile appearing in magazines, purporting to be written by an oafish, semi-literate baseball player who through his own words unconsciously exposes himself in all his obnoxiousness. Published as an epistolary novel, *You Know Me Al*, the letters brought Lardner the attention of a wider public and *How to Write Short Stories*, the title of which has been seen as typical of Lardner's inability to believe that he was a serious writer, brought critical acclaim. Edmund Wilson, for example, commenting on the discrepancy between the matter of the book and the jokey way in which it was presented, wrote, "what one finds in *How to Write Short Stories* is a series of studies of American types almost equal in importance to those of Sherwood Anderson and Sinclair Lewis."

Among the stories appearing in the volume were "Some Like Them Cold," an exchange of letters, wonderfully funny in their dead-pan way, between an aspiring popular song-writer on the make in New York City and a girl he has met by chance in the LaSalle Street railway station in Chicago, and "The Golden Honeymoon," in which an aging middle-class man from Trenton, New Jersey, father-in-law of "John H. Kramer, the real estate man," recounts the holiday he and his wife spent in Florida to celebrate their golden wedding.

These stories illustrate two things. The first is that Lardner, as Wilson pointed out in his *Dial* review, had "an unexcelled, a perhaps unrivalled, mastery" of the American language, that he knew equally well the language of the popular-song writer and the "whole vocabulary of adolescent clichés of the middle-aged man from New Jersey," and that he understood the difference between the spoken language of these types and the language they used for writing. The other thing is that, as all his critics have pointed out, Lardner's is nothing if not a reductive art. His characters expose themselves unerringly in their speech and letters in all the grossness of their complacency and self-regard. No element of affection or compassion is allowed to creep into their delineation. It measures the difference between Lardner's art and Sinclair Lewis's on the one hand and Sherwood Anderson's on the other.

In other words, Lardner was essentially a satirist, and increasingly since his death he has been seen as one of the major American satirists. In this respect he has, perhaps, been overrated. In his 1924 review Wilson, who had put Lardner forward as in some sense a latter-day Mark Twain, asked: "Will Ring Lardner then, go on to his *Huckleberry Finn* or has he already told all he knows?" The appearance of *The Love Nest and Other Stories* two years later, though it contained the merciless "Haircut," showed in effect that he had already told us all he knew. Admirable as his satire is, it seems time once again to emphasise the part he played in the liberation of American prose by bringing back into it the rhythms of native speech.

—Walter Allen

See the essay on "Haircut."

LAURENTS, Arthur. Born in Brooklyn, New York, 14 July 1918. Educated at Cornell University, Ithaca, New York, B.A. 1937. Served in the U.S. Army, 1940–45: Sergeant; radio playwright, 1943–45 (Citation, Secretary of War, and *Variety* radio award, 1945). Stage director. Director, Dramatists Play Service, New York, 1961–66. Council member, Dramatists Guild, from 1955. Recipient: American Academy award, 1946; Sidney Howard Memorial Award, 1946; Tony award, for play, 1967, for directing, 1984; Vernon Rice Award, 1974; Golden Globe award, 1977; Screenwriters Guild award, 1978; Sydney Drama Critics award, for directing, 1983. Lives in Quogue, New York.

PUBLICATIONS

Plays

Now Playing Tomorrow (broadcast 1939). In *Short Plays for Stage and Radio*, edited by Carless Jones, 1939.
Western Electric Communicade (broadcast 1944). In *The Best One-Act Plays of 1944*, edited by Margaret Mayorga, 1944.
The Last Day of the War (broadcast 1945). In *Radio Drama in Action*, edited by Erik Barnouw, 1945.
The Face (broadcast 1945). In *The Best One-Act Plays of 1945*, edited by Margaret Mayorga, 1945.
Home of the Brave (produced 1945; as *The Way Back*, produced 1949). 1946.
Heartsong (produced 1947).
The Bird Cage (produced 1950). 1950.
The Time of the Cuckoo (produced 1952). 1953.
A Clearing in the Woods (produced 1957). 1957; revised edition, 1960.
West Side Story, music by Leonard Bernstein, lyrics by Stephen Sondheim (produced 1957). 1958.
Gypsy, music by Jule Styne, lyrics by Stephen Sondheim, from a book by Gypsy Rose Lee (produced 1959). 1960.
Invitation to a March (produced 1960). 1961.
Anyone Can Whistle, music by Stephen Sondheim (produced 1964). 1965.
Do I Hear a Waltz?, music by Richard Rodgers, lyrics by Stephen Sondheim (produced 1965). 1966.

Hallelujah, Baby!, music and lyrics by Jule Styne, Betty Comden, and Adolph Green (produced 1967). 1967.
The Enclave (produced 1973). 1974.
Scream (produced 1978).
The Madwoman of Central Park West, with Phyllis Newman, music by Peter Allen and others, from the play *My Mother Was a Fortune Teller* by Newman (produced 1979).
A Loss of Memory (produced 1981).

Screenplays: *The Snake Pit*, with Frank Partos and Millen Brand, 1948; *Rope*, with Hume Cronyn, 1948; *Anna Lucasta*, with Philip Yordan, 1949; *Caught*, 1949; *Anastasia*, 1956; *Bonjour Tristesse*, 1958; *The Way We Were*, 1973; *The Turning Point*, 1977.

Radio Plays: *Now Playing Tomorrow*, 1939; *Hollywood Playhouse*, *Dr. Christian*, *The Thin Man*, *Manhattan at Midnight*, and other series, 1939–40; *The Last Day of the War*, *The Face*, *Western Electric Communicade*, and other plays for *The Man Behind the Gun, Army Service Force Presents* and *Assignment: Home* series, 1943–45; *This Is Your FBI* series, 1945.

Television Script: *The Light Fantastic*, 1967.

Fiction

The Way We Were. 1972.
The Turning Point. 1977.

* * *

Brooklyn-born, Hollywood-bred, Arthur Laurents is best known for his work in the two most successful American art forms, the Broadway musical and the Hollywood film.

His films include *Caught* and *The Snake Pit* and versions of two of his stage plays, *Home of the Brave* and *The Time of the Cuckoo* (filmed as *Summertime*). All tend to prove Samuel Beckett's thesis: "We are all born mad. Some remain so." Psychology, especially self-realization, is Laurent's major interest and it runs through all of his serious work, even getting into musicals.

His musicals are *West Side Story* (*Romeo and Juliet* updated), *Gypsy* (based on the life of stripper Gypsy Rose Lee), *Do I Hear a Waltz?* and *Hallelujah, Baby!* These musicals show all the inventiveness and commercial savvy one would expect from a writer whose work ranges from adapting Marcel Maurette's TV play *Anastasia* for Ingrid Bergman's return to the screen to a modern version of the Sleeping Beauty legend in which the heroine refuses to tread boring conventional paths and takes off with a plumber (*Invitation to a March*). Laurents attempted to make Broadway musicals in some way more serious. He didn't always succeed. As Walter Kerr put it in *Thirty Plays Hath November*, "if a musical is going to be as serious as *Do I Hear a Waltz?* it has got to be more serious than *Do I Hear a Waltz?* . . . Half measures taken toward sobriety tend to leave us all halfhearted, torn between an elusive passion on the one hand and a lost playfulness on the other." Shall we settle for the ersatz, typically Broadway idea of the serious (especially in diversions such as *A Chorus Line*) and not strive for reality?

Laurents's plays do make a serious effort at seriousness: in a sense they are religious, if psychology is the New Religion. In *The Bird Cage* downtrodden employees of a dictatorial employer fly their nightclub cage. We sense Symbolism and are tempted to ask, What Does That Mean? In *A Clearing in the Woods* a woman yearns "to rise in the air just a little, to climb, to reach a branch, even the lowest" and this bird learns to accept herself as "an imperfect human being," thus escaping the cage of her past. Can it be that Laurents, for all his interest in psychology, is telling us that we should avoid all the psychiatrists who want to adjust us, and achieve "mental health" just by learning to be happy with our craziness, accepting ourselves as "imperfect human beings"? In *Home of the Brave* (which Kenneth Tynan found pat but promising), an Army shrink copes with Coney, a soldier who learns that though he is Jewish he is just another "imperfect human being" like Mingo and everyone else who is secretly glad that it was The Other Guy who got killed, regardless of race, color, or creed. In *The Time of the Cuckoo* the uptight New England spinster Leona Samish has to work out for herself the appropriate reactions to a brief encounter in Venice with a dashing (but married) Italian. Predictably, "those louses / Go back to their spouses" (as *Diamonds Are a Girl's Best Friend* teaches) and Leona realizes, reviewing her Puritan code, that he wasn't such a nice man, after all. This psychologizing may not be as broad as a barn door, nor so deep as a well, but it will serve in the theatre, where Thornton Wilder once got away with summing up all of Freud in a single sentence: "We're all just as wicked as we can be."

—Leonard R.N. Ashley

LAWSON, John Howard. Born in New York City, 25 September 1894. Educated at the Halstead School, Yonkers, New York; Cutler School, New York, graduated 1910; Williams College, Williamstown, Massachusetts, 1910–14, B.A. 1914. Served in the American Ambulance Service in France and Italy during World War I. Married 1) Kathryn Drain in 1919 (divorced, 1923), one son; 2) Susan Edmond in 1925, one son and one daughter. Cable editor, Reuters Press, New York, 1914–15; lived in Paris for two years after the war; director, New Playwrights Theatre, New York, 1927–28; film writer in Hollywood, 1928–47. Council member, Authors League of America, 1930–40; founding President, 1933–34, and member of the Executive Board, 1933–40, Screen Writers Guild. One of the Hollywood Ten: served a one-year sentence for contempt of the House Un-American Activities Committee, 1950–51. *Died 11 August 1977.*

PUBLICATIONS

Plays

Servant-Master-Lover (produced 1916).
Standards (produced 1916).
Roger Bloomer (produced 1923). 1923.
Processional: A Jazz Symphony of American Life (produced 1925). 1925.
Nirvana (produced 1926).
Loudspeaker (produced 1927). 1927.
The International (produced 1928). 1928.
Success Story (produced 1932). 1932.
The Pure in Heart (produced 1934). In *With a Reckless Preface*, 1934.

Gentlewoman (produced 1934). In *With a Reckless Preface*, 1934.
With a Reckless Preface: Two Plays. 1934.
Marching Song (produced 1937). 1937.
Algiers (screenplay), with James M. Cain, in *Foremost Films of 1938*, edited by Frank Vreeland. 1939.
Parlor Magic (produced 1963).

Screenplays: *Dream of Love*, with others, 1928; *The Pagan*, with Dorothy Farnum, 1929; *Dynamite*, with Jeanie Macpherson and Gladys Unger, 1929; *The Sea Bat*, with others, 1930; *Our Blushing Brides*, with Bess Meredyth and Helen Mainard, 1930; *The Ship from Shanghai*, 1930; *Bachelor Apartment*, with J. Walter Rubin, 1931; *Success at Any Price*, with others, 1934; *Blockade*, 1938; *Algiers*, with James M. Cain, 1938; *They Shall Have Music*, with Irmgard Von Cube, 1939; *Four Sons*, with Milton Sperling, 1940; *Earthbound*, with Samuel C. Engel, 1940; *Sahara*, with others, 1943; *Action in the North Atlantic*, with others, 1943; *Counter-Attack* (*One Against Seven*), 1945; *Smash-Up—The Story of a Woman*, with others, 1947.

Other

Theory and Technique of Playwriting. 1936; revised edition, as *Theory and Technique of Playwriting and Screenwriting*, 1949.
The Hidden Heritage: A Rediscovery of the Ideas and Forces That Link the Thought of Our Time with the Culture of the Past. 1950.
Film in the Battle of Ideas. 1953.
Film: The Creative Process: The Search for an Audio-Visual Language and Structure. 1964; revised edition, 1967.

*

Critical Studies: *Drama and Commitment: Politics in the American Theatre of the Thirties* by Gerald Rabkin, 1964; *The Left Side of Paradise: The Screenwriting of Lawson* by Gary Carr, 1984.

* * *

John Howard Lawson was one of the Hollywood Ten who went to jail rather than implicate others before the House Un-American Activities Committee. HUAC need not have summoned him; they could have read his plays or seen his movies. Whether he belonged to the Communist Party or not is basically none of our business. That his work is imbued with Marxism and that he is characteristic of a period in which (as the garment workers' musical *Pins and Needles* put it) many sang "Sing Me a Song of Social Significance," is abundantly clear. In his time, it gave him strength. Now it makes all but a few of his film works look impossibly dated.

Servant-Master-Lover, *Standards*, and *Roger Bloomer* gave him his start, and with *Processional* his left-wing sympathies were expressed in the story of "the West Virginia coal fields during a strike" told in "this new technique . . . essentially vaudevillesque in character." The theory is adumbrated in a preface (more of his interesting ideas appear in prefatory material to *The Pure in Heart* and *Gentlewoman* and in the excellent textbook *Theory and Technique of Playwriting*) and illustrated in a series of scenes which recall the Living Newspaper of the depression, the propaganda techniques of agitprop, and other attempts at "an immediate emotional response across the footlights." All the force and all the faults of the left-wing theatre tracts of the 1920's and 1930's, "the fervent years" (as Harold Clurman calls them), are here: the party-line dogmatism and narrow vision; the confusion of tragedy and pathos; the axe-to-grind earnestness, where comedy (and everything else that relates to a sense of proportion) perishes; and so on, down to the stereotyped characters: Cohen the Jewish comedian, Rastus the minstrel clown, the hard-boiled Sheriff, the city-slicker newspaperman Phillpots, the woman called Mrs. Euphemia Stewart Flimmins, even a Man in a Silk Hat.

George Abbott played Dynamite Jim in *Processional*, but only in the last act did he soar for a moment above what Stark Young called "antagonisms, bad taste and crass thinking." The critics thought it basically an amateur play "conceived with varying degrees of taste, intelligence, insight and imagination." When it is good it is very, very good—Stark Young risked "streaked with genius"—and when it is bad it's as foolish as Odets without his primitive charm. It is not that the characters are unrealistic—"Mr. Lawson," reported *Contemporary Drama*, "says that he can find vaudeville characters on every street corner, whereas the so-called realistic characters he sees on the stage he never meets in life"—but that the politics distort the truth.

Processional was produced by the Theatre Guild and ran 96 performances in 1925 and 81 more when the Federal Theatre revived it in 1937. Today it would not run any more than would *Nirvana*, *Loudspeaker*, *The International* (a musical), *Success Story*, *Marching Song*, or other Lawson efforts. "All great art and literature," boomed Shaw, "is propaganda," but that does not mean that all propaganda is great art.

Some of Lawson's films have survived better. Very typical are, say, *Blockade* and *Smash-Up*. The cinema was more congenial to Lawson's talents, though *Theory and Technique of Playwriting* amply demonstrates that, as Théophile Gautier said of drama critics and eunuchs in harems, those who see it done every night may know all about it but be quite unable to do it themselves.

—Leonard R.N. Ashley

LEE, Manfred B. See **QUEEN, Ellery.**

LEVERTOV, Denise. Born in Ilford, Essex, England, 24 October 1923; moved to the U.S. in 1948; became citizen, 1955. Educated privately. Served as a civilian nurse at St. Luke's Hospital, London, during World War II. Married the writer Mitchell Goodman in 1947 (divorced, 1972); one son. Worked in antique shop and bookshop, London, 1946; nurse at British Hospital, Paris, Spring 1947; teacher at the YM-YWHA Poetry Center, New York, 1964, City College of New York, 1965, and Vassar College, Poughkeepsie, New York, 1966–67; Visiting Professor, Drew University, Madison, New Jersey, 1965, University of California, Berkeley, 1969, Massachusetts Institute of Technology, Cambridge, 1969–70, Kirkland College, Clinton, New York, 1970–71, University of

Cincinnati, Spring 1973, and Tufts University, Medford, Massachusetts, 1973–79; Fannie Hurst Professor (Poet-in-Residence), Brandeis University, Waltham, Massachusetts, 1981–83; since 1982 Professor of English, Stanford University, California. Poetry editor, *The Nation*, New York, 1961, 1963–65, and *Mother Jones*, San Francisco, 1975–78. Honorary Scholar, Radcliffe Institute for Independent Study, Cambridge, Massachusetts, 1964–66. Recipient: Longview award, 1961; Guggenheim fellowship, 1962; American Academy grant, 1966, 1968; Lenore Marshall Prize, 1976; Bobst Award, 1983; Shelley Memorial Award, 1984. D.Litt.: Colby College, Waterville, Maine, 1970; University of Cincinnati, 1973; Bates College, Lewiston, Maine, 1984; St. Lawrence University, Canton, New York, 1984. Member, American Academy, 1980; Corresponding Member, Mallarmé Academy, 1983. Lives in West Somerville, Massachusetts.

PUBLICATIONS

Verse

The Double Image. 1946.
Here and Now. 1956.
Overland to the Islands. 1958.
5 Poems. 1958.
With Eyes at the Back of Our Heads. 1960.
The Jacob's Ladder. 1961.
O Taste and See: New Poems. 1964.
City Psalm. 1964.
Psalm Concerning the Castle. 1966.
The Sorrow Dance. 1967.
Penguin Modern Poets 9, with Kenneth Rexroth and William Carlos Williams. 1967.
A Tree Telling of Orpheus. 1968.
A Marigold from North Viet Nam. 1968.
Three Poems. 1968.
The Cold Spring and Other Poems. 1969.
Embroideries. 1969.
Relearning the Alphabet. 1970.
Summer Poems 1969. 1970.
A New Year's Garland for My Students, MIT 1969–1970. 1970.
To Stay Alive. 1971.
Footprints. 1972.
The Freeing of the Dust. 1975.
Chekhov on the West Heath. 1977.
Modulations for Solo Voice. 1977.
Life in the Forest. 1978.
Collected Earlier Poems 1940–1960. 1979.
Pig Dreams: Scenes from the Life of Sylvia. 1981.
Wanderer's Daysong. 1981.
Candles in Babylon. 1982.
Poems 1960–1967. 1983.
Oblique Prayers: New Poems with 14 Translations from Jean Joubert. 1984.
El Salvador—Requiem and Invocation. 1984.
The Menaced World. 1984.
Selected Poems. 1986.

Fiction

In the Night. 1968.

Other

The Poet in the World (essays). 1973.
Conversation in Moscow. 1973.
Levertov: An Interview, with John K. Atchity. 1980.
Light Up the Cave (essays). 1981.

Editor, *Out of the War Shadow: An Anthology of Current Poetry*. 1967.
Editor and Translator, with Edward C. Dimock, Jr., *In Praise of Krishna: Songs from the Bengali*. 1967.

Translator, *Selected Poems*, by Guillevic. 1969.

*

Bibliography: *A Bibliography of Levertov* by Robert A. Wilson 1972.

Critical Studies: *Levertov* by Linda W. Wagner, 1967, and *Levertov: In Her Own Province* edited by Wagner, 1979; *The Imagination's Tongue: Levertov's Poetic* by William Slaughter, 1981; *Revelation and Revolution in the Poetry of Levertov* by Peter Middleton, 1981.

* * *

By her own admission, Denise Levertov began writing as a "British Romantic with almost Victorian background" and has since become one of the powerful probing voices of contemporary American poetry. Her outspoken advocacy of the women's movement, her opposition to the Vietnam War, her adherence generally to the values of the political left came about through the gradual transformations of awareness since publishing *Here and Now* in 1957.

Raised and educated in a literary household in England, she published a first book of poems, *The Double Image*, in 1946. In 1948 she emigrated to the United States with her American husband, the novelist Mitchell Goodman, whose friendship with Robert Creeley led to her association with the Black Mountain movement and the journal *Origin*, which began publishing her work. Her early poems show the influence of Williams and Olson in their diction and form, but by the middle of the 1950's, Robert Duncan encouraged her to experiment more boldly with mythic perception of her identity and circumstances. She has since explained her own poetic in the essay "Organic Form," which distinguishes between a free verse of disjointed statements and organic poetry, where "form," all facets of technique, is "a revelation of content." But her poems retain traditional verse conventions, and she has occasionally attacked the improvisatory mode of other poets.

In her first substantial work, *With Eyes at the Back of Our Heads*, her poems moved to frank self-disclosures, in an effort to grasp a personal identity underlying sexual stereotype. In "The Goddess," one of the finest poems of the volume, she dramatizes her awakening to an inner nature after her expulsion from "Lie Castle," where she has been flung

across the room, and
room after room (hitting the walls, re-
bounding—to the last
sticky wall—wrenching away from it
pulling hair out!)
til it lay
outside the outer walls!

There in the cold air
lying still where her hand had thrown me,
I tasted the mud that splattered my lips
the seeds of a forest were in it,
asleep and growing! I tasted
her power!

O Taste and See pursues the implications of "The Goddess" by boldly reaching into the feminine psyche to discover its raw vitality, as in this startling image of appetite:

In the black of desire
we rock and grunt, grunt and
shine

Beginning with *Relearning the Alphabet*, she moved beyond purely personal issues to larger political concerns, war resistance, women's rights, poverty and oppression in the Third World. The poems of *To Stay Alive* and *Footprints*, many taking a longer, serial form, follow her increasingly activist participation in various social movements of the last three decades.

Life in the Forest represents a deflation of all the intensity of Levertov's earlier political poetry during the Vietnam war years; as its title implies, the focus has shifted to the not-I, to the languors and diffusions of lyric focus to be found in "Cesar Pavese's poems of the '30s," according to her prefatory note. The poems are not as dense or electric here, but show the poet's flexibility with new subjects and rhythms, as she makes sense of her middle life and of peacetime. But in *Candles in Babylon* Levertov returns to the main theme of her canon, alienation in the modern age, and her poems are defenses against the torpor and discord of contemporary reality. These tighter, more argumentative poems are the true voice of the poet; her candor and perspicuity as a critic are to be found in the critical collection *Levertov: In Her Own Province* and in *Light Up the Cave*, which collects her recent essays and occasional prose.

—Paul Christensen

LEWIS, (Harry) Sinclair. Born in Sauk Centre, Minnesota, 7 February 1885. Educated at Sauk Centre High School; Oberlin Academy, Ohio, 1902–03; Yale University, New Haven, Connecticut (editor, *Yale Literary Magazine*), 1903–06, 1907–08, A.B. 1908. Married 1) Grace Livingstone Hegger in 1914 (divorced, 1928), one son; 2) the journalist Dorothy Thompson in 1928 (separated, 1937; divorced, 1942), one son. Janitor at Upton Sinclair's socialist community Helicon Home, Englewood, New Jersey, 1906–07; assistant editor, *Transatlantic Tales*, New York, 1907; reporter, Waterloo *Daily Courier*, Iowa, 1908; worked for charity organization, New York, 1908; secretary to Alice MacGowan and Grace MacGowan Cooke, Carmel, California, 1909; writer, San Francisco *Evening Bulletin*, 1909, and Associated Press, San Francisco, 1909–10; staff member, *Volta Review*, Washington, D.C., 1910; manuscript reader, Frederick A. Stokes, publishers, 1910–12, assistant editor, *Adventure*, 1912, editor for Publishers' Newspaper Syndicate, 1913–14, and editorial assistant and advertising manager, George H. Doran, publishers, 1914–15, all New York; full-time writer from 1916; columnist ("Book Week"), *Newsweek*, New York, 1937–38, and *Esquire*, New York, 1945. Writer-in-Residence, University of Wisconsin, Madison, Autumn 1942. Recipient: Pulitzer Prize, 1926 (refused); Nobel Prize for Literature, 1930. Litt.D.: Yale University, 1936. Member, 1935, and Vice-President, 1944, National Institute of Arts and Letters; member, American Academy, 1938. *Died 10 January 1951.*

PUBLICATIONS

Collections

The Man from Main Street: Selected Essays and Other Writings 1904–1950, edited by Harry E. Maule and Melville H. Cane. 1953.

Fiction

Hike and the Aeroplane (for children). 1912.
Our Mr. Wrenn. 1914.
The Trail of the Hawk. 1915.
The Job. 1917.
The Innocents. 1917.
Free Air. 1919.
Main Street. 1920.
Babbitt. 1922.
Arrowsmith. 1925; as *Martin Arrowsmith*, 1925.
Mantrap. 1926.
Elmer Gantry. 1927.
The Man Who Knew Coolidge. 1928.
Dodsworth. 1929.
Ann Vickers. 1933.
Work of Art. 1934.
Selected Short Stories. 1935.
It Can't Happen Here. 1935.
The Prodigal Parents. 1938.
Bethel Merriday. 1940.
Gideon Planish. 1943.
Cass Timberlane. 1945.
Kingsblood Royal. 1947.
The God-Seeker. 1949.
World So Wide. 1951.
I'm a Stranger Here Myself and Other Stories, edited by Mark Schorer. 1962.

Plays

Hobohemia, from his own story (produced 1919).
Jayhawker, with Lloyd Lewis (produced 1934). 1935.
It Can't Happen Here, from his own novel (produced 1936). 1938.
Angela Is Twenty-Two (produced 1938).
Storm in the West (screenplay), with Dore Schary. 1963.

Other

John Dos Passos' "Manhattan Transfer." 1926.
Cheap and Contented Labor: The Picture of a Southern Mill Town in 1929. 1929.
The American Fear of Literature. 1931.
From Main Street to Stockholm: Letters of Lewis 1919–1930, edited by Harrison Smith. 1952.

*

Bibliography: *The Merrill Checklist of Lewis* by James Lundquist, 1970; *Lewis: A Reference Guide* by Robert E. Fleming, 1980.

Critical Studies: *Lewis: An American Life*, 1961, and *Lewis*, 1963, both by Mark Schorer, and *Lewis: A Collection of Critical Essays* edited by Schorer, 1962; *Lewis* by Sheldon Norman Grebstein, 1962; *Dorothy and Red* by Vincent Sheean, 1963; *The Art of Lewis* by D.J. Dooley, 1967; *Lewis* by James Lundquist, 1973; *The Quixotic Vision of Lewis* by Martin Light, 1975; *A Lewis Lexicon* by Hiroshige Yoshida, 1976; *Critical Essays on Lewis* edited by Martin Bucco, 1986.

* * *

Sinclair Lewis, the first American Nobel Laureate in Literature, was recognized with justice by the Nobel Prize committee for the accuracy and the detail with which he portrayed American life. He applied the concepts of critical realism as they had been developed in the 19th century to the subject of the American midwest, and, using a gift for satiric caricature and a remarkable skill at mimicry, created a vivid picture of middle-class America and its values, ideals, and assumptions in the early 20th century. He portrayed with devastating satiric power and sardonic force the lack of beauty, dignity, and value in America's materialistic culture. Lewis, although he was hailed in his own day as the spokesman of a new literary movement, was actually a culmination of the movement of critical realism which had begun in the decades immediately after the Civil War. He came as the summarizing expression of moods and methods typical of the midwestern "revolt from the village" that had produced such writers as Hamlin Garland, E.W. Howe, and Edgar Lee Masters. Like many other midwest writers, Lewis moved from the west to the east—in his case from Minnesota to Connecticut and New York—and then used the land of his childhood as his chief subject and often his principal target.

Between 1914 and 1920 he published five novels, the best being *The Job* and *Free Air*, and a number of short stories in popular periodicals. Critical hindsight now shows us that these early works, although clearly in the tradition of the popular fiction of their time, also adumbrated in theme, treatment, and character the major work which was to come. In 1920 he published *Main Street*, a corruscating picture of the dullness, drabness, conformity, and materialism of a small, midwestern town. With it his career was brilliantly launched to the acclaim of the nation and the world. He followed it with *Babbitt*, a portrayal of a petit-bourgeois businessman in a middle-sized midwestern city, a weak man who vainly attempts to break out of the pattern of conformity which shapes his days and to understand himself and achieve his own freedom. This plot pattern was to be recurrent in most of Lewis's work. *Babbitt*, perhaps his most satisfactory single work, was the first of a long series of novels each of which examined a specific business or profession. After publishing it, he started collecting material for a novel on the labor movement, but that book was never written. *Arrowsmith*, written with the aid of the biologist Paul DeKruif, and in its own time regarded by many as his finest work, studied the profession of medicine and contrasted it with the idealized view of scientific research. Lewis pointed his satiric guns at the Protestant ministry in *Elmer Gantry*, a howling comedy of extravagant and slashing satire; and he sympathetically portrayed the American businessman abroad and satirized the cultural pretensions of his wife in *Dodsworth*. This novel begins Lewis's significant shift from the harsh treatment of his middle-class American subjects to a steadily growing sympathy for them.

In 1930, he received the Nobel Prize for literature and in his acceptance speech attacked Howells, whose critical movement he was himself the product of, and praised a group of young writers, such as Thomas Wolfe and Ernest Hemingway, who were soon to be important in advancing novelistic innovations that quickly dated his own work. In the 1920's Lewis had defined America, or at least important aspects of it, for itself and had produced vital, lively, original, and important satiric portraits of America's middle-class failings. The Nobel Prize crowned one of the major accomplishments in the social novel ever achieved by an American. But it came when that accomplishment was virtually complete. For following 1930, Lewis's career seems almost to be a search for subject matter.

In *Ann Vickers*, a book much influenced by his admiration for and exasperation with his second wife, the famous journalist Dorothy Thompson, Lewis examined the career woman, but with clearly mixed feelings. He turned his attention to the hotel industry in *Work of Art*, the first of his "major" works which was, as Mark Schorer declared, "completely without distinction." *It Can't Happen Here* re-established an important position for him with the American public. This study of the potentiality for American fascism seemed to be a political warning that spoke directly and responsibly to major issues in American life. Today, however, it seems thin and surprisingly conservative. That Lewis was indeed becoming increasingly conservative despite his attacks upon fascism was evident in *The Prodigal Parents*, a book about radical and irresponsible children, in which he draws what is almost a comic strip view of communism. Its protagonist, Fred Cornplow, whom Lewis admires, is essentially the same middle-class businessman he had earlier satirized as Babbitt and the denizens of *Main Street*. *Bethel Merriday* is the story of the education of a young actress in summer stock and touring companies. It is embarrassingly sentimental. *Gideon Planish* is an attack on organized philanthrophy. More like *Elmer Gantry* than any book Lewis had written since 1927, it is angry and intemperate, an example of slashing satire and violent comedy; yet it is so overdrawn that it seems almost a parody of Lewis's earlier work. *Cass Timberlane* is an account of American marriage. *Kingsblood Royal* takes up the issue of race in a mechanical and unconvincing parable. *The God-Seeker* is a historical novel set in Minnesota in the days of its early settlement. Although it can be considered the first novel in an unfinished panel of labor books, it is too much like costume romance to be taken seriously. In *World So Wide*, published posthumously in 1951, the year of his death, Lewis returns to the theme of the American in Europe in a book which is virtually a rewriting of *Dodsworth*, though now the satiric edge is gone, and the European culture that he once supported has become the target of his attack. The characters in this last sad work seemed, as Malcolm Cowley said, "survivors from a vanished world."

Lewis's work falls easily into three periods—the early apprenticeship work, followed by the great accomplishment of the 1920's in which in five novels he gives a vigorous and emphatic picture of his world, followed by a long, sad, groping toward suitable subjects. Few American writers have had a greater impact on their world than Lewis during his ten great years, 1920–29. As Schorer said, "He gave us a vigorous, perhaps unique thrust into the imagination of ourselves." But after this great success he was increasingly removed from the materials which were his primary subject matter, and he wrote out of memory rather than direct experience, so that his later novels were increasingly the memorials to a world and an age that was past. He was a very good social novelist but not a truly great writer. Nevertheless, it was appropriate that the first American Nobel Laureate in Literature should have been a man intimately committed to using literature to portray his fellow countrymen and to instruct them through satiric portraiture.

—C. Hugh Holman

See the essay on *Main Street*.

LINDSAY, (Nicholas) Vachel. Born in Springfield, Illinois, 10 November 1879. Educated at Hiram College, Ohio, 1897–1900; studied for the ministry; studied art at Chicago Art Institute, 1901, and New York Art School, 1905. Married Elizabeth Conner in 1925; one son, one daughter. Pen and ink designer, 1900–10; lecturer on art history, 1905–10; also traveled through the U.S. living by reciting his poems, 1906–12; after 1912 became known for his verses and was thereafter in demand as lecturer and reader; teacher, Gulf Park College, Mississippi, 1923–24. Litt.D.: Hiram College, 1930. Member, American Academy. *Died (suicide) 5 December 1931.*

PUBLICATIONS

Collections

Selected Poems, edited by Mark Harris. 1963.
Letters, edited by Marc Chénetier. 1979.
The Poetry, edited by Dennis Camp. 2 vols., 1984–85.

Verse

The Tramp's Excuse and Other Poems. 1909.
Rhymes to Be Traded for Bread. 1912.
General William Booth Enters into Heaven and Other Poems. 1913.
The Congo and Other Poems. 1914.
The Chinese Nightingale and Other Poems. 1917.
The Golden Whales of California and Other Rhymes in the American Language. 1920.
The Daniel Jazz and Other Poems. 1920.
Going-to-the-Sun. 1923.
Collected Poems. 1923; revised edition, 1925.
Going-to-the-Stars. 1926.
The Candle in the Cabin: A Weaving Together of Script and Singing. 1926.
Johnny Appleseed and Other Poems (for children). 1928.
Every Soul Is a Circus. 1929.
Selected Poems, edited by Hazelton Spencer. 1931.

Other

The Village Magazine. 1910.
Adventures While Preaching the Gospel of Beauty. 1914.
The Art of the Moving Picture. 1915; revised edition, 1922.
A Handy Guide for Beggars, Especially Those of the Poetic Fraternity. 1916.
The Golden Book of Springfield, Being a Review of a Book That Will Appear in 2018. 1920.
The Litany of Washington Street (miscellany). 1929.
Letters to A. Joseph Armstrong, edited by Armstrong. 1940.

*

Critical Studies: *Lindsay: A Poet in America* by Edgar Lee Masters, 1935; *The West-Going Heart: A Life of Lindsay* by Eleanor Ruggles, 1959; *Lindsay* by Raymond Purkey, 1968; *Lindsay: Fieldworker for the American Dream* by Ann Massa, 1970; *The Vision of This Land: Studies of Lindsay, Edgar Lee Masters, and Carl Sandburg* edited by John E. Hallwas and Dennis J. Reader, 1976.

* * *

Vachel Lindsay was a man out of phase with his time. He was also a writer who had the misfortune to be judged solely on the basis of his poetry, even though he produced a sizeable corpus of prose, work which he felt to be ultimately more important than his poetry. While it is true that he has recently begun to receive the critical appreciation and interpretation he deserves, it is equally true that he is still considered by many to be a writer (and reciter) of verse—a 20th-century troubadour who toured the country reciting his poems to hugely enthusiastic audiences, a propagandist for America whose exhortations were clothed in bombast, naivety, sentimentality, and theatrics a phenomenon whose time had already come and gone. His role as social critic was unrecognized and such prose works as *Adventures While Preaching the Gospel of Beauty*, *The Art of the Moving Picture*, *A Handy Guide for Beggars*, and *The Golden Book of Springfield* were virtually ignored.

Lindsay's early books of verse, *General William Booth Enters into Heaven and Other Poems* and *The Congo and Other Poems*, established his reputation as a herald of the New Poetry. They mark a dramatic break with the genteel, derivative verse that then dominated the American literary scene, while marking a continuity with the Whitmanesque mode. His best poems ring with genuine music and vibrate with energy, and Lindsay's theatrical recitation of them established his reputation as an entertainer. But the latter reputation eclipsed the former and clung to him throughout the remainder of his life. His problem was two-fold: his superb qualities as an entertainer and the public's refusal to accept his definition of the role of the poet.

Lindsay felt poetry should serve the masses; that art for art's sake had no place on the American scene; that elitism in poetry was a negative and destructive force; and that Americans had to be awakened to the fact that they were allowing their country's true destiny to slip away. Lindsay considered his poetry to be the best means by which he could jolt the people into an awareness of what was happening; when they were made aware of it they would then fall in line behind him and join his efforts to recapture and restore to America its original promise.

But Lindsay's vision of America was not the vision of the American majority. Moreover, his pessimism and fundamentalist viewpoint (both of America's problems and of the solutions to them) were anathema to political, social, and literary arbiters of the day. And finally, since Lindsay believed poetry to be a social as opposed to artistic instrument (content should take precedence over style), he was not part of the imagist movement which influenced the course of 20th-century American poetry from his day to the present.

Lindsay never recovered from the realization that the people wanted only entertainment from him and that his crusade for "religion, equality and beauty," his "gospel," was doomed. He died by his own hand, a bitter and psychotic man, "Staking his last strength and his final fight / That cost him all, to set the old world right" (Litany of the Heroes").

—Catherine Seelye

LOCKE, David Ross. See **NASBY, Petroleum V.**

LOCKRIDGE, Ross. Born in Bloomington, Indiana, 25 April 1914. Educated at Indiana University, Bloomington, 1931–35, B.A. (summa cum laude) in English 1935 (Phi Beta Kappa); post-graduate study, Harvard University, Cambridge, Massachusetts, 1940–41. Married Vernice Baker in 1937; four children. Instructor in English, Indiana University, 1936–40, and Simmons College, Boston, 1941–45. *Died (suicide) 6 March 1948.*

PUBLICATIONS

Fiction

Raintree County. 1948.

*

Critical Study: *Ross and Tom: Two American Tragedies* by John Leggett, 1974.

* * *

Ross Lockridge's one published work, the sprawling thousand-page novel *Raintree County*, was a huge popular and critical success in 1948. Praised as "a novel of rare stature," the first American epic since *Moby-Dick*, then increasingly disparaged as "an amalgam of undigested Wolfe, murky Faulkner, and watery Whitman," it is now rarely read or mentioned. Periodically literary historians try to restore it to prominence, even eminence, but with lean results, perhaps because the novel's sunny optimism, frontier humor, and abiding faith in the American dream are not congenial to contemporary readers. On all its many layers, *Raintree County* is an exuberant Fourth of July festival of Americana.

On the Fourth of July, 1892, in the small town of Waycross, Indiana, the townspeople join together for a holiday of celebration, oratory, and reminiscence, as observed by John Wickliff Shawnessy, a 53-year-old schoolteacher reunited with his boyhood friends—a sleek senator, an ailing railroad tycoon, a wry journalist. Flashbacks re-create their common past, which eventuates in montage: structurally, events in John's life contrast with national events (his wedding is counterpointed with John Brown's execution, the birth of his son with the firing on Fort Sumter), and stylistically each event is viewed in the contrasting styles of fictitious newspaper accounts, old diaries and letters, blustering gossips and salty frontiersmen. The montages build into a panoramic view of American history and a critique of the 19th-century corrosion of the Declaration of Independence. The omniscient, disillusioned, but still hopeful narrator implies that the second American Revolution was the Civil War, epic atonement for slavery, and that the third was the Rail Strike of 1877, epic industrialism and enslavement of the poor. The urbane, witty journalist (a fine comic character) is the hero's Darwinian alter ego, cosmopolitan theoretician of the American experiences that Hoosier Johnny must undergo and struggle to understand—such as soldiering against the South, watching the first trains arrive in the midwest. The hero himself, a Jeffersonian idealist, is also America's fledgling poet, the modern Johnny Appleseed restoring the national earth with his words, his ideals, and his faith. Ringed with comic Bunyanesque characters and somber Lincolnesque tragedies, Johnny is in many ways the uncorruptible soul of epic America, and his life documents the century's "contest for my soul." On multiple levels of historical and literary allusion, each level complete with its contrapuntal movements of personal and national life, Lockridge weaves a kaleidoscopic epic, striving to be myth, that owes obvious debts to Joyce, Melville, Whitman. Lockridge's America is "mancreated," "greatchested," "buntinghung." Though the symbolism is sometimes muddled, and the sentiment sometimes saccharine, Lockridge's gigantesque conception and his technical virtuosity were perhaps unparalleled in America until Pynchon's *Gravity's Rainbow*. There is ample reason to consider *Raintree County* an important novel for its era and a substantial achievement.

—Jan Hokenson

LONDON, Jack (John Griffith London). Born in San Francisco, California, 12 January 1876. Educated at a grammar school in Oakland, California; Oakland High School, 1895–96; University of California, Berkeley, 1896–97. Married 1) Bessie Maddern in 1900 (separated, 1903; divorced, 1905), two daughters; 2) Charmian Kittredge in 1905, one daughter. Worked in a cannery in Oakland, 1889–90; oyster "pirate," then member of the California Fisheries Patrol, 1891–92; sailor on the *Sophia Sutherland*, sailing to Japan and Siberia, 1893; returned to Oakland, wrote for the local paper, and held various odd jobs, 1893–94; tramped the U.S. and Canada, 1894–96; arrested for vagrancy in Niagara Falls, New York; joined the gold rush to the Klondike, 1897–98, then returned to Oakland and became a full-time writer; visited London, 1902; war correspondent in the Russo-Japanese War for the San Francisco *Examiner*, 1904; moved to a ranch in Sonoma County, California, 1906; attempted to sail round the world on a 45-foot yacht, 1907–09; war correspondent in Mexico, 1914. *Died 22 November 1916.*

PUBLICATIONS

Collections

Short Stories, edited by Maxwell Geismar. 1960.
(*Works*; Fitzroy Edition), edited by I.O. Evans. 18 vols., 1962–68.

The Bodley Head London, edited by Arthur Calder-Marshall. 4 vols., 1963–66; as *The Pan London*, 2 vols., 1966–68.
Novels and Stories (Library of America), edited by Donald Pizer. 1982.
Novels and Social Writings (Library of America), edited by Donald Pizer. 1984.

Fiction

The Son of the Wolf: Tales of the Far North. 1900; as *An Odyssey of the North*, 1915.
The God of His Fathers and Other Stories. 1901; as *The God of His Fathers: Tales of the Klondike*, 1902.
Children of the Frost (stories). 1902.
The Cruise of the Dazzler. 1902.
A Daughter of the Snows. 1902.
The Kempton-Wace Letters, with Anna Strunsky. 1903.
The Call of the Wild. 1903.
The Sea-Wolf. 1904.
The Faith of Men and Other Stories. 1904.
Tales of the Fish Patrol. 1905.
The Game. 1905.
White Fang. 1906.
Moon-Face and Other Stories. 1906.
The Apostate (story). 1906.
Love of Life and Other Stories. 1907.
Before Adam. 1907.
The Road (stories). 1907.
The Iron Heel. 1908.
Martin Eden. 1909.
Burning Daylight. 1910.
Lost Face (stories). 1910.
When God Laughs and Other Stories. 1911.
South Sea Tales. 1911.
Adventure. 1911.
The Strength of the Strong (story). 1911.
The House of Pride and Other Tales of Hawaii. 1912.
A Son of the Sun (stories). 1912; as *The Adventures of Captain Grief*, 1954.
Smoke Bellew (stories). 1912; as *Smoke and Shorty*, 1920.
The Dream of Debs (story). 1912(?).
The Night-Born. . . . 1913.
The Abysmal Brute. 1913.
John Barleycorn. 1913; as *John Barleycorn; or, Alcoholic Memoirs*, 1914.
The Valley of the Moon. 1913.
The Mutiny of the Elsinore. 1914.
The Strength of the Strong (collection). 1914.
The Scarlet Plague. 1915.
The Jacket (The Star Rover). 1915; as *The Star Rover*, 1915.
The Little Lady of the Big House. 1916.
The Turtles of Tasman (stories). 1916.
The Human Drift. 1917.
Jerry of the Islands. 1917.
Michael, Brother of Jerry. 1917.
Hearts of Three. 1918.
The Red One (stories). 1918.
On the Makaloa Mat. 1919; as *Island Tales*, 1920.
Dutch Courage and Other Stories. 1922.
Tales of Adventure, edited by Irving Shepard. 1956.
The Assassination Bureau Ltd., completed by Robert L. Fish. 1963.
Stories of Hawaii, edited by A. Grove Day. 1965.
Great Short Works, edited by Earle Labor. 1965.
Goliah: A Utopian Essay. 1973.
Curious Fragments: London's Tales of Fantasy Fiction, edited by Dale L. Walker. 1975.
The Science Fiction of London, edited by Richard Gid Powers. 1975.
The Unabridged London, edited by Lawrence Teacher and Richard E. Nicholls. 1981.
London's Yukon Women. 1982.
Young Wolf: The Early Adventure Stories, edited by Howard Lachtman. 1984.
In a Far Country: London's Western Tales, edited by Dale L. Walker. 1986.

Plays

The Great Interrogation, with Lee Bascom (produced 1905).
Scorn of Women. 1906.
Theft. 1910.
The Acorn-Planters: A California Forest Play. . . . 1916.
Daughters of the Rich, edited by James E. Sisson. 1971.
Gold, with Herbert Heron, edited by James E. Sisson. 1972.

Other

The People of the Abyss. 1903.
The Tramp. 1904.
The Scab. 1904.
London: A Sketch of His Life and Work. 1905.
War of the Classes. 1905.
What Life Means to Me. 1906.
The Road. 1907.
London: Who He Is and What He Has Done. 1908(?).
Revolution. 1909.
Revolution and Other Essays. 1910.
The Cruise of the Snark. 1911.
London by Himself. 1913.
London's Essays of Revolt, edited by Leonard D. Abbott. 1926.
London, American Rebel: A Collection of His Social Writings. . . ., edited Philip S. Foner. 1947.
Letters from London, Containing an Unpublished Correspondence Between London and Sinclair Lewis, edited by King Hendricks and Irving Shepard. 1965.
London Reports: War Correspondence, Sports Articles, and Miscellaneous Writings, edited by King Hendricks and Irving Shepard. 1970.
London's Articles and Short Stories in the (Oakland) High School Aegis, edited by James E. Sisson. 1971.
No Mentor But Myself: A Collection of Articles, Essays, Reviews, and Letters on Writing and Writers, edited by Dale L. Walker. 1979.
Revolution: Stories and Essays, edited by Robert Barltrop. 1979.
London on the Road: The Tramp Diary and Other Hobo Writings, edited by Richard W. Etulain. 1979.
Sporting Blood: Selections from London's Greatest Sports Writing, edited by Howard Lachtman. 1981.
London's California: The Golden Poppy and Other Writings, edited by Sal Noto. 1986.

*

Bibliography: *London: A Bibliography* by Hensley C. Woodbridge, John London, and George H. Tweney, 1966, supplement by Woodbridge, 1973; in *Bibliography of American Literature* by Jacob Blanck, 1969; *The Fiction of London: A Chronological Bibliography* by Dale L. Walker and James E. Sisson, 1972; *London: A Reference Guide* by Joan R. Sherman, 1977.

Critical Studies: *London: A Biography* by Richard O'Connor, 1964; *London and the Klondike: The Genesis of an American Writer* by Franklin Walker, 1966; *The Alien Worlds of London* by Dale L. Walker, 1973; *London* by Earle Labor, 1974; *White Logic: London's Short Stories* by James I. McClintock, 1975; *London: The Man, The Writer, The Rebel* by Robert Barltrop, 1976; *Jack: A Biography of London* by Andrew Sinclair, 1977; *London: Essays in Criticism* edited by Ray Wilson Ownbey, 1978; *London: An American Myth* by John Perry, 1981; *Solitary Comrade: London and His Work* by Joan D. Hedrick, 1982; *The Novels of London: A Reappraisal* by Charles N. Watson, Jr., 1983; *Critical Essays on London* edited by Jacqueline Tavernier-Courbin, 1983; *London* by Gorman Beauchamp, 1984; *London: An American Radical?* by Carolyn Johnston, 1984.

* * *

Jack London was a talented writer so caught up in certain myths that they were part of what destroyed him. The illegitimate son of an impoverished spiritualist, Flora Wellman, he early learned self-reliance. Although he attended high school and, briefly, college, he was largely self-educated. London's university was the world he experienced and subsequently wrote about: San Francisco Bay, first as an oyster pirate and then as a member of the State Fish Patrol; the Pacific, the Orient, and the Bering Sea as an able seaman on a schooner hunting seals; the nation, across which he tramped as a vagabond; Alaska, where he prospected for gold; and California, where eventually he was a wealthy landowner burdened by the problems of maintaining a large ranch. London saw himself as an exemplar of the rags-to-riches story, an Anglo-Saxon superman who succeeded because of his superior intelligence and physical prowess, who took pride in his individualism, yet sympathized with the masses and believed that some form of socialism was the cure for the inequities of capitalist society.

To assert that his deprived childhood and his personal adventures were central to his development is not to deny that he was profoundly influenced by what he read as a young man. Early in his adolescence he delved into the seminal thinkers of the 19th century; his biographer Andrew Sinclair writes that during a winter in the Alaskan Klondike London absorbed "the books that became the bedrock of his thought and writing, underlying even the socialism which was his faith." Among London's readings that winter were the works of Darwin, Thomas Huxley, Spencer, and Kipling. "Charles Darwin and Herbert Spencer, messiahs of the new creed, became his intellectual mentors, along with Frederich Nietzsche and Karl Marx," Charles Child Walcutt wrote in a pamphlet about London, declaring that the author's struggles came to seem to himself "an epitome of the Darwinian Struggle for Existence, his success an example of the Spencerian Survival of the Fittest." Natural laws governed everything, London decided, so his problem became to reconcile the unimportance of the individual in a Darwinian universe and the Marxist certainty of social revolution with his equal certainty that he had the force and intelligence to rise above his fellow men.

His writing constantly reflects these contradictory beliefs, sometimes emphasizing one, sometimes another. In a succession of essays, short stories, novels, plays, travels books, and autobiographical tracts—during his forty years of life he wrote more than fifty books, too many for them all to be good—he portrayed the immutable laws of nature and man's need for community, while at the same time creating heroic figures who dominated both people and environment. As London's success grew, he heeded his socialist beliefs less, ultimately in his fiction painting what he liked to think were self-portraits of supermen defying the forces of nature and the demands of capitalism or of the masses. At his best London was able to hold these contradictions in balance; and technically his work, as H.L. Mencken wrote in *Prejudices: First Series*, contained "all the elements of sound fiction: clear thinking, a sense of character, the dramatic instinct, and, above all, the adept putting together of words—words charming and slyly significant, words arranged, in the French phrase, for the respiration and the ear." But finally his techniques could not sustain work that had lost its thematic equilibrium. He was an individualist, not a socialist. His lip service to socialism, wrote Walcutt, was a "protest against his early poverty"; London, he added, never dwelled on what might be the benefits of socialism.

London's heroes and heroines are individualists who survive the challenges of nature and society if they are strong enough, or are defeated if they are not—or, one might add, if London was pained by his socialist conscience. Thus in what is perhaps his best and best known story, *The Call of the Wild*, the powerful dog Buck, snatched from an easy life and submitted to brutal treatment and a harsh environment in the Klondike, survives because he is the superior individual. Buck, returned to the world of his ancestors, eventually runs with a pack of wolves, but he is at their head, where his intelligence and strength have put him. Wolf Larsen, the superman figure of *The Sea-Wolf*, both attracts and repels the beautiful, fragile poetess Maud Brewster and the effete Humphrey Van Weyden, whom Larsen rescues aboard his ship, the *Ghost*. Antagonized by Larsen, the two escape to an island, only to have him reappear aboard the wrecked *Ghost*. The arrogant individualist Larsen eventually dies, but it is his strength and skill that are admirable; the other two survive because they become strong like Wolf, yet lack his utter egotism. London would later assert that his point had been that a Wolf Larsen could not survive in modern society; but clearly he empathized with the arch-individualist, and Van Weyden's victory comes only after he has assimilated Larsen's qualities.

Another of London's heroes, Martin Eden, would die because of his individualism, but his death by suicide seems gratuitous, not, as London claimed, the result of Eden's believing in nothing and not accepting the socialism the author professed to favor. London could not portray a socialist state even before he abandoned socialism, which he did in his fiction when—as in the novels *Burning Daylight*, *The Valley of the Moon*, and *The Little Lady of the Big House*—he blatantly espoused Aryan superman and escape from the urban masses. His socialist novel *The Iron Heel* takes the form of a text discovered long after socialism has triumphed. What the novel describes, however, is not a socialist utopia, but the violent rise of a repressive totalitarian state opposed by small cadres of insurgents led by a blond superman, Ernest Everhard. By 1914, when London reported for *Collier's* magazine on the revolution in Mexico, he "no longer spoke as the compassionate revolutionary," notes Andrew Sinclair, "but as the racist and jingoist supporter of the American oil interests—a man of property, a man used to servants, who was echoing the views of other men used to property and servants."

London died in 1916, by then severely ill and depressed by the recognition that he could not live out the myths he portrayed in his fiction. Still, he had not failed; his best work is vivid and dramatic; and his hyperbole, if annoying, nevertheless tells the reader much about United States culture.

—Townsend Ludington

See the essay on *The Call of the Wild*.

LONGFELLOW, Henry Wadsworth. Born in Portland, Maine, 27 February 1807. Educated at Bowdoin College, Brunswick, Maine, 1822–25, graduated 1825. Married 1) Mary Potter in 1831 (died, 1835); 2) Frances Appleton in 1843 (died, 1861), two sons and four daughters. Appointed to new Chair of Modern Languages, Bowdoin College, on condition he study abroad for a further three years: sent by trustees to Europe, 1826–29; taught at Bowdoin College, 1829–35; sent to Germany by Harvard University, Cambridge, Massachusetts, 1835, and Smith Professor of Modern Languages, Harvard University, 1836–54; visited Europe, 1842 and 1868–69. Honorary degrees: Cambridge University, 1868; Oxford University, 1869. *Died 24 March 1882.*

PUBLICATIONS

Collections

The Works and *Final Memorials*, edited by Samuel Longfellow. 14 vols., 1886–87.
Works. 10 vols., 1909.
The Essential Longfellow, edited by Lewis Leary. 1963.
Letters, edited by Andrew Hilen. 6 vols., 1966–83.

Verse

Voices of the Night. 1839.
Ballads and Other Poems. 1842.
Poems on Slavery. 1842.
Poems. 1845.
The Belfry of Bruges and Other Poems. 1845.
Evangeline: A Tale of Acadie. 1847.
Poems, Lyrical and Dramatic. 1848.
The Seaside and the Fireside. 1849.
The Golden Legend. 1851.
The Song of Hiawatha. 1855.
Poetical Works. 1858.
The Courtship of Miles Standish and Other Poems. 1858.
Tales of a Wayside Inn. 1863.
Noël (in French). 1864.
Household Poems. 1865.
Flower-de-Luce. 1867.
The New-England Tragedies. 1868.
Poetical Works. 1868.
The Divine Tragedy. 1871.
Three Books of Song. 1872.
Christus: A Mystery (includes *The Divine Tragedy, The Golden Legend, The New-England Tragedies*). 1872.
Poetical Works. 1872; revised edition, 1875, 1880, 1883.
Aftermath. 1873.
The Hanging of the Crane. 1874.
The Masque of Pandora and Other Poems. 1875.
Kéramos and Other Poems. 1878.
The Early Poems, edited by Richard Herne Shepherd. 1878.
Ultima Thule. 1880; *In the Harbor: Ultima Thule—Part II*, 1882.
Michael Angelo. 1884.
Boyhood Poems, edited by Ray W. Pettengill. 1925.

Play

The Spanish Student (produced 1895). 1843.

Fiction

Hyperion: A Romance (includes verse). 1839.
Kavanagh: A Tale. 1849.

Other

Syllabus de la Grammaire Italienne. 1832.
Outre-Mer: A Pilgrimage Beyond the Sea, numbers 1-2. 2 vols., 1833–34; vol. 2, 1835; revised edition, 1851.
Prose Works. 2 vols., 1857.
Complete Works, revised edition. 7 vols., 1866.

Editor, *Manuel de Proverbes Dramatiques*. 1830; revised edition, 1830, 1832.
Editor and Translator, *Elements of French Grammar*, by Lhomond. 1830.
Editor, *French Exercises*. 1830.
Editor, *Novelas Españolas*. 1830.
Editor, *Le Ministre de Wakefield*, by Oliver Goldsmith, translated by T.E.G. Hennequin. 1831.
Editor, *Saggi de' Novellieri Italiani d'Ogni Secolo*. 1832.
Editor, *The Waif: A Collection of Poems*. 1845.
Editor, *The Poets and Poetry of Europe*. 1845; revised edition, 1871.
Editor, *The Estray: A Collection of Poems*. 1846.
Editor, with George Nichols and John Owen, *The Works of Charles Sumner*. 10 vols., 1870–83.
Editor, *Poems of Places: England*, 4 vols.; *Ireland*, 1 vol.; *Scotland*, 3 vols.; *France*, 2 vols.; *Italy*, 3 vols.; *Spain*, 2 vols.; *Switzerland*, 1 vol.; *Germany*, 2 vols.; *Greece*, 1 vol.; *Russia*, 1 vol.; *Asia*, 3 vols.; *Africa*, 1 vol.; *America*, 6 vols.; *Oceanica*, 1 vol. 31 vols., 1876–79.

Translator, *Coplas de Don Jorge Manrique*. 1833.
Translator, *The Divine Comedy*, by Dante. 3 vols., 1867.

*

Bibliography: in *Bibliography of American Literature* by Jacob Blanck, 1969.

Critical Studies: *The Life of Longfellow, with Extracts from His Journals and Correspondence* by Samuel Longfellow, 2 vols., 1886; *Young Longfellow (1807–1843)* by Lawrance Thompson, 1938; *Longfellow and Scandinavia: A Study of the Poet's Relationship with the Northern Languages and Literature* by Andrew Hilen, 1947; *Longfellow: A Full-Length Portrait*, 1955, *Longfellow: Portrait of an American Humanist*, 1966, and

Longfellow, 1985, all by Edward Wagenknecht; *Longfellow: His Life and Work* by Newton Arvin, 1963; *Longfellow* by Cecil B. Williams, 1964; *Longfellow* by Edward L. Hirsch, 1964; *Longfellow Reconsidered: A Symposium* edited by J. Chesley Mathews, 1970.

* * *

Some writers survive for the wrong reasons, like nostalgia or derision; some survive despite their defects, like prolixity or sentimentality; some survive—or deserve to—because of a small body of modest work culled long after the fact of popularity. Henry Wadsworth Longfellow belongs in all three categories.

No American writer was so admired, even revered, during his life; no writer has been so ridiculed subsequently. From 1839, when "A Psalm of Life" first moved his readers—as heavily influenced as the poem itself by Victorian and Puritan attitudes—to embrace its homilies ("Heart within, and God o'erhead!"), until his death in 1882, the decorous optimism of Longfellow's lyrics and the monotonous drone of his narrative poems stood him in high esteem. Oliver Wendell Holmes may have best defined Longfellow's appeal to his contemporaries: "a soft voice, a sweet and cheerful temper, a receptive rather than aggressive intelligence. . . ." This may, however, be a more damning indictment of the limitations of popular taste than of the poet's achievement. Longfellow's sympathetic biographer, Newton Arvin, proposed that we "agree, once for all that he was a minor writer." Still, in the classroom at least, the myth of Longfellow's significance persists, and probably rather more than fewer students have turned away from poetry because of some educator's insistence on perpetuating the lie.

Longfellow's lack of variety and seeming inability either to escape conventional metrics or to bring any originality to them always hampered him; moreover, he did not easily judge the prosody best suited to his materials. At the age of thirteen, he had published his first poem in the Portland *Gazette*, "The Battle of Lovell Pond," hammered out in anapestic couplets with mathematical regularity. He never really advanced far in technical proficiency after that. His earliest successes—"The Skeleton in Armour," "The Wreck of the Hesperus," and the quintessential "Excelsior" suffer from this limitation. When, as in the last poem, the subject is "inspirational," he invites derision; and "higher" in its Latin comparative form is easily translated into shredded packing material—and not only by schoolboys who do not know their Latin. Longfellow was technically endowed to write light verse, had he possessed the sense of humor to do so, for he is not without extraordinary invention in manipulating syntax to suit his rhythms; and his inexhaustible command of rhyme, if employed for amusement, might not so easily undermine the content. At the zenith of his career, Longfellow beat his *Evangeline* into submission in jiggling dactyllic hexameters. This popular narrative traces the wanderings of a girl from Acadia (Nova Scotia) in search of her lost lover. Finally, after many remarkable adventures, she becomes a kind of nun in Pennsylvania in her old age, only to meet her lover on his death bed. This "first genuine . . . fount which burst from the soil of America," called by one critic "one of the decisive poems of the world," sold 36,000 copies in its first ten years. *The Song of Hiawatha* did even better: 30,000 copies in six months. This pseudo-epic traces the development of an American Indian from birth to immortality: fathered by the West Wind; educated by nature and animals; loved by the beautiful Minnehaha; given mythic significance in his killing of an underwater monster, with the assistance of a helpful squirrel; sobered and matured by the deaths of Minnehaha (for whom he mourns seven days and seven nights) and his best friend (for whom he mourns seven times longer); and, finally, brought to a kind of metaphysical suicide—he simply gets in his canoe and starts paddling west—by the inevitable coming of the white race. Longfellow cramped this really promising material into 164 pages of four-trochee lines, likened by Oliver Wendell Holmes to the "normal rhythm of breathing" and by more than one high school student to tomtoms. At least *Hiawatha* didn't rhyme.

Longfellow wrote two inferior novels, *Hyperion* and *Kavanagh*, which offer some insight into his private life and attitudes toward religion, politics and literature. His single play, *The Spanish Student*, about a gypsy dancer named Preciosa (who turns out to be the long-lost daughter of a wealthy nobleman) and her chaste beau, suffers all the usual limitations of 19th-century melodrama. Although Longfellow had a successful career in education—he was one of the first modern language teachers, first as Bowdoin, then for 18 years at Harvard—his critical prose is distinguished by clarity rather than ingenuity or originality.

In spite of these several reservations, however, Longfellow wrote a number of valuable poems. In the sparse landscape of 19th-century American poetry, they grow sturdily. "Mezzo Camin," written in 1842 but not published until after his death, is a fine sonnet in which he laments his lack of significant poetic accomplishment. "The Cross of Snow," also unpublished during his life, and also a sonnet, is a touching tribute to his wife after her early death. Despite an insufferable circuitous dependent clause taking up all of its octet, the sonnet "Nature" ends superbly. A mother puts her child to bed: "So nature deals with us, and takes away / Our playthings one by one, and by the hand / Leads us to rest so gently, that we go / Scarce knowing if we wish to go or stay, / Being too full of sleep to understand / How far the unknown transcends the what we know." Its sustained imagery invites comparison with Whitman's "Goodbye, My Fancy," Emerson's "Terminus," and other epitaphic poems of the period. His ode to old age, "Morituri Salutamus," is especially valuable during the recent movement in America to recognize the oldest generation. "The Tide Rises, The Tide Falls" clearly anticipates Robert Frost's "Stopping by Woods on a Snowy Evening," even if less powerful a poem. Finally, his less well-known "The Jewish Cemetery at Newport" deserves attention. Its inhabitants, "Taught in the school of patience to endure / The Life of anguish and the death of fire," now abide in American soil, "not neglected; for a hand unseen, / Scattering its bounty, like a summer rain, / Still keeps their graves and their remembrance green." Probably there are other poems as well by this mild man which reflect, not without some distinction, the age of restraint and decorum for which they were written. Further, a skeleton in armour, a village smithy, a midnight ride by Paul Revere, even an arrow shot into the air, may introduce some beginning readers to some of the pleasures in poetry.

—Bruce Kellner

See the essay on *The Song of Hiawatha*.

LONGSTREET, Augustus Baldwin. Born in Augusta, Georgia, 22 September 1790. Educated at Waddell Academy,

Willington, South Carolina, 1808–11; Yale University, New Haven, Connecticut, 1811–13, graduated 1813; studied law in Litchfield, Connecticut, 1813–14: admitted to Virginia bar, 1815. Married Frances Eliza Parke in 1817 (died, 1867); one son and two daughters. Lawyer, Greensboro, Georgia, from 1817; member, Georgia Legislature, 1821; circuit judge, Superior Court of Georgia, 1822–25; moved to Augusta, Georgia, 1827; contributor, *Southern Recorder*, Milledgeville, Georgia, and various other newspapers, 1827–30; founding editor, *States Rights Sentinel*, Augusta, 1834–36; ordained Methodist minister, 1838; President, Emory College, Oxford, Georgia, 1839–48, Centenary College, Jackson, Louisiana, 1849, University of Mississippi, Oxford, 1849–56, and South Carolina College (now University of South Carolina), Columbia, 1857–65; lived in Mississippi after 1865. LL.D.: Yale University, 1841; D.D.: University of Mississippi. *Died 9 July 1870.*

PUBLICATIONS

Fiction and Sketches

Georgia Scenes, Characters, and Incidents, etc. 1835.
Master William Mitten; or, A Youth of Brilliant Talents Who Was Ruined by Bad Luck. 1864.
Stories with a Moral, Humorous and Descriptive of Southern Life a Century Ago, edited by Fitz. R. Longstreet. 1912.

Other

A Voice from the South (letters). 1847.

*

Bibliography: in *Bibliography of American Literature* by Jacob Blanck, 1973.

Critical Studies: *Judge Longstreet: A Life Sketch* by O.P. Fitzgerald, 1891 (includes letters and unpublished material); *Longstreet: A Study of the Development of Culture in the South* by John Donald Wade, 1924, edited by M. Thomas Inge, 1969; *Longstreet* by Kimball King, 1984.

* * *

Augustus Baldwin Longstreet's reputation rests primarily on *Georgia Scenes*, a collection of sketches and tales about life in Middle Georgia in the early 19th century. *Georgia Scenes* contrasted with the plantation literary tradition which focused on wealthy slaveholding landowners. As a circuit-court judge, Longstreet visited many rural communities and collected humorous stories and anecdotes of rough but colorful country people. Their simple amusements such as barn dances, horse-swapping, and shooting matches are affectionately recorded, along with a slightly more brutal side of life (gander-pulling, fights, and political disputes). Overt cruelty and violence are generally overlooked. For example, in "The Fight" the maiming of the combatants is treated in an almost slapstick vein. In his close attention to physical details and settings and in his attempts to write colloquial dialogue, Longstreet anticipated the local color writers of the post-Civil War period. His best works, such as "Turn-Out," in which unruly country boys playfully "force" their schoolmaster to give them a day's vacation, are based on folk traditions and rituals and possess an archetypal power. Poe praised Longstreet because he was anxious to see American writers use native materials in their stories.

Longstreet was forty before he turned his hand to fiction. First his legal career, then his work as newspaper owner and editor, and later his ministry in the Methodist church took precedence over authorship. He sometimes feared his comic sketches were undignified; in fact, everything he wrote expressed firm religious beliefs and conservative political views. In *Georgia Scenes* his narrator, Hall, describes rural escapades, while the character Baldwin ridicules the affectations of newly rich townspeople. Both are aloof and frequently disapproving, like the author. Blacks, although they seldom appear in the stories, are treated comically or with contempt. Later essays, such as those collected in *A Voice from the South*, were devoted to defending slavery.

In his own day Longstreet was best known as the president of four different southern universities. Some of his experiences with students are included in his only novel, *Master William Mitten*. As a record of the times this neglected work is as informative as *Georgia Scenes*; and the author's characterizations of William and William's mother and uncle reveal a surer sense of satire and of the dynamics of family life than one finds in the earlier work. His essays on religious and political subjects and the posthumously collected tales in *Stories with a Moral* are elegantly phrased but discursive and tedious. He eventually considered himself more of a moral guide or social historian than a storyteller. Although some critics consider Longstreet a frontier humorist, he is primarily a southern writer, highly didactic, constructing a value system unique to his region.

—Kimball King

LOVECRAFT, H(oward) P(hillips). Born in Providence, Rhode Island, 20 August 1890. Educated by tutors at home, and at a local elementary school and Hope Street High School, Providence, 1904–05, 1907–08. Married Sonia Greene in 1924 (divorced, 1929). Free-lance writer from 1908, working as a ghostwriter and, after 1918, a revisionist; astrology columnist, Providence *Evening News*, 1914–18; active in the amateur journalism movement from 1914: published *The Conservative*, 1915–19, 1923, and President of the United Amateur Press Association, 1917–18, 1923; regular contributor to *Weird Tales* after 1923. *Died 15 March 1937.*

PUBLICATIONS

Collections

Collected Poems. 1963; abridged edition, as *Fungi from Yuggoth and Other Poems*, 1971.
Selected Letters 1911–1937, edited August Derleth and Donald Wandrei. 5 vols., 1965–76.

Fiction (stories)

The Shunned House. 1928.
The Battle That Ended the Century. 1934.
The Cats of Ulthar. 1935.

The Shadow over Innsmouth. 1936.
The Outsider and Others, edited by August Derleth and Donald Wandrei. 1939.
The Weird Shadow over Innsmouth and Other Stories of the Supernatural. 1944.
The Best Supernatural Stories of Lovecraft, edited by August Derleth. 1945; revised edition, as *The Dunwich Horror and Others*, 1963.
The Dunwich Horror. 1945.
The Dunwich Horror and Other Weird Tales. 1945.
The Lurker at the Threshold (novel), with August Derleth. 1945.
The Lurking Fear and Other Stories. 1947; as *Cry Horror!*, 1958.
The Haunter of the Dark and Other Tales of Horror. 1951.
The Case of Charles Dexter Ward. 1952.
The Curse of Yig. 1953.
The Dream Quest of Unknown Kadath. 1955.
The Survivor and Others, with August Derleth. 1957.
The Lurking Fear and Other Stories (not same as 1947 book). 1964.
At the Mountains of Madness and Other Novels. 1964.
The Colour Out of Space. 1964.
Dagon and Other Macabre Tales, edited by August Derleth. 1965.
The Dark Brotherhood and Other Pieces, with others, edited by August Derleth. 1966.
3 Tales of Horror. 1967.
The Shadow Out of Time and Other Tales of Horror, with August Derleth. 1968; abridged edition, as *The Shuttered Room and Other Tales of Horror*, 1970.
Ex Oblivione. 1969.
The Tomb and Other Tales. 1969.
The Horror in the Museum and Other Revisions (ghostwriting), edited by August Derleth. 1970; abridged edition, 1975.
Nyarlathotep. 1970.
What the Moon Brings. 1970.
The Dream-Quest of Unknown Kadath (not same as 1955 book), edited by Lin Carter. 1970.
Memory. 1970.
The Shadow over Innsmouth and Other Tales of Horror. 1971.
The Shuttered Room and Other Tales of Terror, with August Derleth. 1971.
The Doom That Came to Sarnath, edited by Lin Carter. 1971.
The Lurking Fear and Other Stories (not same as 1947 and 1964 books). 1971.
The Watchers Out of Time and Others, with August Derleth. 1974.
The Horror in the Burying Ground and Other Tales. 1975.
Herbert West Reanimator. 1977.
Collapsing Cosmoses. 1977.
Bloodcurdling Tales of Horror and the Macabre: The Best of Lovecraft. 1982.
The Dunwich Horror and Others (original versions), edited by S.T. Joshi. 1985.

Verse

The Crime of Crimes. 1915.
A Sonnet. 1936.
H.P.L. 1937.
Fungi from Yuggoth. 1941.
A Winter Wish, edited by Tom Collins. 1977.

Other

Looking Backward. 1920(?).
The Materialist Today. 1926.
Further Criticism of Poetry. 1932.
Charleston. 1936.
Some Current Motives and Practices. 1936(?).
A History of The Necronomicon. 1938.
The Notes and Commonplace Book, edited by R.H. Barlow. 1938.
Beyond the Wall of Sleep, edited by August Derleth and Donald Wandrei. 1943.
Marginalia, edited by August Derleth and Donald Wandrei. 1944.
Supernatural Horror in Literature. 1945; revised edition, 1975.
Something about Cats and Other Pieces, edited by August Derleth. 1949.
The Lovecraft Collector's Library, edited by George T. Wetzel. 5 vols., 1952–55.
The Shuttered Room and Other Pieces, with others, edited by August Derleth. 1959.
Dreams and Fancies. 1962.
Autobiography: Some Notes on a Nonentity. 1963.
Hail, Klarkash-Ton! 1971.
Ec'h-Pi-El Speaks: An Autobiographical Sketch. 1972.
Medusa: A Portrait. 1975.
The Occult Lovecraft. 1975.
Lovecraft at Last (correspondence with Willis Conover). 1975.
To Quebec and the Stars, edited by L. Sprague de Camp. 1976.
Writings in The United Amateur 1915–1925, edited by Marc A. Michaud. 1976.
First Writings: Pawtuxet Valley Gleaner 1906, edited by Marc A. Michaud. 1976.
The Conservative: Complete 1915–1923, edited by Marc A. Michaud. 1977.
Memoirs of an Inconsequential Scribbler. 1977.
Writings in The Tryout, edited by Marc A. Michaud. 1977.
The Californian 1934–1938. 1977.
Uncollected Prose and Poetry, edited by S.T. Joshi and Marc A. Michaud. 1978.
Science versus Charlatanry: Essays on Astrology, with J.F. Hartmann, edited by S.T. Joshi and Scott Connors. 1979.

Editor, *The Poetical Works of Jonathan E. Hoag*. 1923.
Editor, *White Fire*, by John Ravenor Bullen. 1927.
Editor, *Thoughts and Pictures*, by Eugene B. Kuntz. 1932.

*

Bibliography: *The New Lovecraft Bibliography* by Jack L. Chalker, 1962, revised edition, with Mark Owings, as *The Revised Lovecraft Bibliography*, 1973; *A Catalog of Lovecraftiana* by Mark Owings and Irving Binkin, 1975; *Lovecraft and Lovecraft Criticism: An Annotated Bibliography* by S.T. Joshi, 1981; *Lovecraft: The Books, Addenda and Auxiliary* by Joseph Bell, 1983.

Critical Studies: *In Memoriam Lovecraft: Recollections, Appreciations, Estimates* edited by W. Paul Cook, 1941; *H.P.L: A Memoir*, 1945, and *Some Notes on Lovecraft*, 1959, both by August Derleth; *Rhode Island on Lovecraft* edited by Donald M. Grant and Thomas P. Hadley, 1945; "Lovecraft Issue" of *Fresco*, Spring 1958; *Lovecraft: A Look Behind the Cthulhu Mythos* by Lin Carter, 1972; *Lovecraft: Dreamer on the Nightside* by Frank Belknap Long, 1975; *Essays Lovecraftian* edited by Darrell Schweitzer, 1976, and *The Dream Quest of H.P. Lovecraft*, 1978, and *Discovering Lovecraft*, 1986, both by Schweitzer; *The Lovecraft Companion* by Philip A. Schreffler, 1977; *The Major Works of Lovecraft* by John Taylor Gatto, 1977; *The Roots of Horror in the Fiction of Lovecraft* by Barton Levi St. Armand, 1977; *Lovecraft: Four Decades of Criticism* edited by S.T. Joshi, 1980, and *Lovecraft* by Joshi, 1982; *Lovecraft: A Critical Study* by Donald R. Burleson, 1983.

* * *

H.P. Lovecraft's reputation depends not so much on any particular one of the more than sixty fantastic stories that he published, mostly in the pulp magazine *Weird Tales*, but rather on the way in which most of these stories contribute to what has become known since the author's death as the "Cthulhu Mythos." Although the stories are not consistent with each other and although Lovecraft never codified his cosmology (he was a visionary, not a blueprint-maker), the basic construct of the Mythos is that, in the days before mankind, this planet was inhabited by a group of fish-like beings called the "Old Ones," who worshipped Cthulhu, represented in "The Call of Cthulhu" as a gigantic, gelatinous form. Apparently because their culture decayed, the "Old Ones" were driven from the earth by man; but they were not destroyed. Led by the apparently immortal Yog-Sothoth, they retreated to the remote, dark planet Yogguth, where they still conspire to regain control of the earth. Sometimes, as in "The Whisperer in Darkness," they contemplate an attack on a decadent mankind; but more often, as in Lovecraft's longest work, "The Case of Charles Dexter Ward," they seek, through unspeakable rites of black magic, to mate with human beings through the connivance of dissolute human collaborators.

The generally suppressed knowledge of the Cthulhuites is hinted at only in the forbidden *Necronomicon* of the mad Arab Abdul Alhazred, one Latin copy of which is preserved at Miskatonic University in Arkham, a mouldering New England seaport that is the setting of many of Lovecraft's tales. When the plots of the "Old Ones" are foiled, the earthly invaders or fishy-looking halfbreeds dissolve leaving behind only a pool of noxious-smelling, jelly-like material. Characters who are willfully or inadvertently involved in the conspiracies—like those in "The Dunwich Horror" and "The Color Out of Space"—usually face madness and inevitable destruction. The Mythos, despite vagueness and inconsistencies, is a remarkable fictional manifestation of the mentality that has produced many conspiratorial theories about local and extra-terrestrial threats to human societies. At first Lovecraft had difficulty finding readers, but he found his advocate to the world in 1926 when he attracted the attention of August Derleth. Derleth expanded and regularized the mythos, kept it in print, and even invited others to contribute to it; and Lovecraft attracted a small but fanatical band of cultists in the United States and abroad, especially in France.

Ordinary critical standards are irrelevant to such an enterprise. Lovecraft's fables were often awkwardly plotted and obscurely worded, but so are many "scriptures." Critics complained that he did not write novels, but, like Poe, his visions were best suited to shorter forms. Although many find his fantasies preposterous, he did create one of the most remarkable imaginative constructs of the 20th century—an original myth that arises from a child's enormous fascination with sex and his repressive fear of it. Lovecraft's uniqueness lies in his ability to preserve—if perhaps only through dreams—and to articulate in adulthood the fantasies that provide a child's internal defense against inscrutable threats.

—Warren French

LOWELL, Amy (Lawrence). Born in Brookline, Massachusetts, 9 February 1874. Educated privately. Lived in Europe for several years; associated with the Imagists in London, 1913, and thereafter promoted their work in America. Lecturer, Brooklyn Institute of Arts and Sciences, 1917–18. Recipient: Pulitzer Prize, 1926. Litt.D.: Baylor University, Waco, Texas, 1920. *Died 12 May 1925.*

PUBLICATIONS

Collections

The Complete Poetical Works. 1955.
A Shard of Silence: Selected Poems, edited by Glenn Richard Ruihley. 1957.

Verse

A Dome of Many-Coloured Glass. 1912.
Sword Blades and Poppy Seed. 1914.
Men, Women, and Ghosts. 1916.
Can Grande's Castle. 1918.
Pictures of the Floating World. 1919.
Legends. 1921.
Fir-Flower Tablets: Poems Translated from the Chinese by Florence Ayscough, English Versions by Lowell. 1921.
A Critical Fable. 1922.
What's O'Clock, edited by Ada Dwyer Russell. 1925.
East Wind, edited by Ada Dwyer Russell. 1926.
The Madonna of Carthagena. 1927.
Ballads for Sale, edited by Ada Dwyer Russell. 1927.

Play

Weeping Pierrot and Laughing Pierrot, music by Jean Hubert, from a work by Edmond Rostand. 1914.

Fiction

Dream Drops; or, Stories from Fairy Land, with Elizabeth Lowell and Katherine Bigelow Lowell. 1887.

Other

Six French Poets: Studies in Contemporary Literature. 1915.
Tendencies in Modern American Poetry. 1917.

John Keats. 2 vols., 1925.
Poetry and Poets: Essays, edited by Ferris Greenslet. 1930.
Florence Ayscough and Lowell: Correspondence of a Friendship, edited by Harley Farnsworth MacNair. 1946.

Editor, *Some Imagist Poets*. 3 vols., 1915–17.

*

Critical Studies: *Lowell: A Critical Appreciation* by Bryher, 1918; *Lowell: A Chronicle, with Extracts from Her Correspondence* by S. Foster Damon, 1935; *Lowell: Portrait of the Poet in Her Time* by Horace Gregory, 1958; *Lowell* by Frank C. Flint, 1969; *The Thorn of a Rose: Lowell Reconsidered* by Glenn Richard Ruihley, 1975; *Amy: The World of Lowell and the Imagist Movement* by Jean Gould, 1975; *American Aristocracy: The Lives and Times of James Russell, Amy, and Robert Lowell* by C. David Heymann, 1980; *Lowell* by Richard Benvenuto, 1985.

* * *

Even more than is commonly the case with rebel poets and personalities, Amy Lowell was subjected to heavy-handed abuse as well as uncritical admiration in her own lifetime. But there was little or no understanding of the nature of her work, and, following her untimely death in 1925, a shift in poetic fashions all but obliterated the memory of her unusual achievements. The reasons for that eclipse lie both in the poet and in her audience. Lowell was very prolific and very uneven. Because so much of her poetry was bad, it was easy to judge her harshly. Moreover, her best and most characteristic poetry was very puzzling to conventional readers and remains so to this day. The language of these poems is chiefly pictorial, with the result that she was dismissed as a writer who touched only the physical surfaces of the world and so failed to illuminate any of its deeper meanings. As for the defects in her audience, the misreading of the poet was due to the ignorance and superficiality of the literary journalists of her day. After her death, the misunderstanding was perpetuated by the "new critics" who scorned writers who fell outside the pale of the poetry of wit and cultural memory promoted by T.S. Eliot and Ezra Pound. Though Lowell, at her best, is a writer of extraordinary verve, freshness, and beauty of expression, she is little better understood sixty years after her death than she was in 1912 when she published her first book of poems, *A Dome of Many-Coloured Glass*.

This book was rightly criticized for its feebleness and conventionality of expression; but it has one merit unnoticed by the interpreters of her poetry. The poems are written in a late Romantic style of direct statement and they chart with unusual thoroughness all of the facets of Lowell's idealistic and mystical thought. After 1912, as suggested above, Lowell expressed herself imagistically. To a poet concerned with extra-rational areas of experience, the new style was a great advance over the confines of logical statement, but it also led to failures of communication. However, study of the poems in *A Dome* enables us to know precisely the content of her thought and the beliefs she had adopted, as a substitute for Christianity, to explain her own insights into reality.

The most important of these concerns the existence of a transcendent power that permeates the world and accounts for the divinity that Lowell sensed in all created things. In her poem "Before the Altar," a lonely and penniless worshipper offers his life and being as sacrifice to this Power, which Lowell also celebrated in "The Poet," another early poem. Moved by the awesome splendors of creation, the poet is urged, she says, to forsake the ordinary pleasures of life to pursue the ideality symbolized by the "airy cloudland palaces" of sunset. Such a person, she says, "spurns life's human friendships to profess / Life's loneliness of dreaming ecstasy." In much of Lowell's most admirable imagistic poetry, this mystical conception of reality is rendered by means of her "numinous landscape" or scene, as in the poems "Ombre Chinoise" or "Reflections" where the physical objects concerned are presented with a kind of divine nimbus.

The realm of ideality envisioned in these four poems is sometimes perceived as a solution to the painful incompletions of life. This is the second major theme in Lowell's poetry, and the incompletion is most tragic in the case of the denial of love. Such denial is a spiritual malaise, in her view, because she identifies love not with sex but with inner emotional development. "Patterns," Lowell's most famous poem, dramatizes the withering of spirit resultant on the death of the heroine's lover. The poem is highly voluptuous and insists on the physical beauties of lover and lady and the formal, spring-time garden where the poem is set, but the heroine's decision to live a loveless, celibate life calls attention to the deeper meaning of the relationship.

The spirituality that is implicit in romantic attachments includes recognition of an element of divinity in the beloved. The achievement of love as sacred rite is a third principal theme in Lowell's writings and it occurs in many of her most striking poems, beginning with a loose effusion in *A Dome* but ending with the sublimity of "In Excelsis" and her six sonnets written to Eleonora Duse. The loved one as sacred presence or, at the least, a part of an all-encompassing Divinity is consistent with the poet's preoccupation with a transcendent reality and completes the circle of her themes by returning her thought to its starting place. In terms of individual poems, Lowell's treatment of these themes is so varied and intermixed with nearly all the other issues of life that only a long survey can do them justice. But it is important to note that Lowell approached life *as a mystic* at a profound, intuitive level, and the imagistic mode in which she cast her poems was the one best suited to her gifts and the visionary character of her poetry. As poet her contribution is a revivification of the human sense of the beauties and mysteries of existence.

In addition to the solitary, contemplative role of poet that she adopted for herself, Lowell fulfilled another dynamic "political" role in the far-reaching effort she made to obtain public acceptance of the "new poetry" that appeared in America in 1912. The role she played was political in that the new poetry, seemingly odd and irregular in its form, challenged nearly all established social norms and ideals. Through her critical writings as well as her countless public appearances as lecturer and reader, Lowell assumed leadership of this movement and was responsible for a large measure of its success in creating a new poetic taste and awareness in America.

—Glenn Richard Ruihley

LOWELL, James Russell. Born in Cambridge, Massachusetts, 22 February 1819. Educated at Harvard College, Cambridge, 1834–38, A.B. 1838, and Harvard Law School, 1838–40, LL.B. 1840; admitted to Massachusetts bar, 1840.

Married 1) Maria White in 1844 (died, 1853), three daughters and one son; 2) Frances Dunlap in 1857 (died, 1885). Editor, with Robert Carter, *The Pioneer: A Literary and Critical Magazine*, Boston, 1843; editorial writer, *Pennsylvania Freeman*, Philadelphia, 1845; corresponding editor, *National Anti-Slavery Standard*, 1848; lived in Europe, 1851–52; delivered Lowell Lectures, Boston, 1855; Smith Professor of Modern Languages, 1855–86, and Professor Emeritus, 1886–91, Harvard University; first editor, *Atlantic Monthly*, Boston, 1857–61; editor, with Charles Eliot Norton, *North American Review*, Boston, 1864–72; visited Europe, 1872–75; delegate, Republican National Convention, and member of the Electoral College, 1876; U.S. Ambassador to Spain, 1877–80, and to Great Britain, 1880–85. D.C.L.: Oxford University, 1872; LL.D.: Cambridge University, 1874; University of Edinburgh, 1884. *Died 12 August 1891.*

PUBLICATIONS

Collections

Poetical Works, edited by Horace E. Scudder. 1897; revised edition, edited by Marjorie R. Kaufman, 1978.
The Complete Writings, edited by Charles Eliot Norton. 16 vols., 1904.
Essays, Poems, and Letters, edited by William Smith Clark II. 1948.

Verse

Class Poem. 1838.
A Year's Life and Other Poems. 1841.
Poems. 1844.
Poems: Second Series. 1848.
A Fable for Critics. 1848.
The Biglow Papers. 1848; edited by Thomas Wortham, 1977.
The Vision of Sir Launfal. 1848.
Poems. 2 vols., 1849.
The Biglow Papers, Second Series. 3 vols., 1862.
Ode Recited at the Commemoration of the Living and Dead Soldiers of Harvard University. 1865.
Under the Willows and Other Poems. 1869.
Poetical Works. 1869.
The Cathedral. 1870.
Three Memorial Poems. 1877.
Under the Old Elm and Other Poems. 1885.
Heartsease and Rue. 1888.
Last Poems, edited by Charles Eliot Norton. 1895.
Four Poems. 1906.
Uncollected Poems, edited by Thelma M. Smith. 1950.
Undergraduate Verses: Rhymed Minutes of the Hasty Pudding Club, edited by Kenneth Walter Cameron. 1956.

Play

Il Pesceballo: Opera Seria, with Francis J. Child. 1862; edited by Charles Eliot Norton, 1899.

Other

Conversation on Some of the Old Poets. 1845.
Fireside Travels. 1864.
Among My Books. 2 vols., 1870–76.
My Study Windows. 1871.
Democracy and Other Addresses. 1887.
Political Essays. 1888.
The English Poets, Lessing, Rousseau: Essays. 1888.
Books and Libraries and Other Papers. 1889.
The Writings. 10 vols., 1890; 2 additional vols. edited by Charles Eliot Norton, 1891–92.
American Ideas for English Readers (lectures). 1892.
Letters, edited by Charles Eliot Norton. 2 vols., 1894.
Lectures on English Poets, edited by S.A. Jones. 1897.
Impressions of Spain, edited by Joseph B. Gilder. 1899.
Early Prose Writings. 1902.
The Anti-Slavery Papers, edited by William Belmont Parker. 2 vols., 1902.
The Round Table. 1913.
The Function of the Poet and Other Essays, edited by Albert Mordell. 1920.
New Letters, edited by M.A. De Wolfe Howe. 1932.
The Pioneer (magazine), edited by Sculley Bradley. 1947.
Representative Selections, edited by Harry Hayden Clark and Norman Foerster. 1947.
The Scholar-Friends: Letters of Francis James Child and Lowell, edited by M.A. De Wolfe Howe and G.W. Cottrell, Jr. 1952.
Literary Criticism, edited by Herbert F. Smith. 1969.

Editor, *The Poems of Maria Lowell*. 1855.
Editor, *The Poetical Works of Dr. John Donne*. 1855.
Editor, *The Poetical Works of Andrew Marvell*. 1857.

*

Bibliography: in *Bibliography of American Literature* by Jacob Blanck, 1973.

Critical Studies: *Lowell: A Biography* by Horace E. Scudder, 2 vols., 1901; *Lowell* by Richmond Croom Beatty, 1942; *Victorian Knight-Errant: A Study of the Early Literary Career of Lowell* by Leon Howard, 1952; *Lowell* by Martin Duberman, 1966; *Lowell* by Claire McGlinchee 1967; *Lowell: Portrait of a Many-Sided Man* by Edward Wagenknecht, 1971; *American Aristocracy: The Lives and Times of James Russell, Amy, and Robert Lowell* by C. David Heymann, 1980.

* * *

Of all the schoolroom poets James Russell Lowell was easily the most talented, clearly the most versatile, and probably the one who strove hardest to achieve poetic excellence. Yet today his poetry is less critically valued and read than the verses of his contemporaries Holmes, Longfellow, and Whittier. Some explanation for the disparity between his ability and accomplishments resides in the very nature of his life and talents. Among other things he was poet, essayist, journalist, editor, critic, linguist, teacher, reformer, and diplomat. In 1848, before his thirtieth birthday, he published *A Fable for Critics*, *The Biglow Papers*, and *The Vision of Sir Launfal* to secure his poetic reputation. Ten years later he assumed the first editorship of the *Atlantic Monthly* and by his critical judgment and taste made it into the finest literary journal in America. In his later years he became ambassador to Spain, and from 1880–85 he served as ambassador to Britain. To highlight these few achievements from so many illustrates part of Lowell's problem: his brilliance, erudition, and versatility constantly led him to new tasks and dissipated the control and self-discipline needed for artistic excellence. In addition his responsiveness to the tradition of public oratory and imitations of older writers made his serious verse declamatory and derivative. Dated by now forgotten issues and lacking a significant form, much of his longer poetry remains unreadable today.

Despite these critical problems, Lowell wrote good poetry and in selected pieces well deserves his place among American poets. His *A Fable for Critics* occupies a central place among the few critical pronouncements written by 19th-century American authors. Its mocking, casual humor perfectly balances shrewd critical insights, while its taut epigrams still surprise and delight. Lowell called Poe "two-fifths sheer fudge," depicted Byrant as "quiet, as cool, and as dignified, / As a smooth, silent iceberg, that never is ignified," and noted that Cooper's females were "All sappy as maples and flat as a prairie." Even his own shortcomings were catalogued: "There is Lowell, who's striving Parnassus to climb / With a whole bale of *isms* tied together with rhyme." Both series of his Biglow Papers display a mastery of Down East Humor, Yankee dialect and caricature. Though their contemporary subject matter and grotesque mixture of moral aphorisms with political observations render them uneven, individual pieces like "The Courtin' " and "Sumthin' in the Pastoral Line" demonstrate Lowell's rare gift for native idiom and folk humor. His exploration of these New England materials produced his finest poem, "Fitz Adam's Story," a 632-line saga about the essential traits of a Yankee world. Though its central story concerns the attempts of a crusty Deacon Bitters to outsmart the devil, the poem's rich digressions on religion, back-country types, and rural descriptions constitute its main pleasure.

Among his longer, more serious poems, "Agassiz," *Ode Recited at the Commemoration of the Living and Dead Soldiers of Harvard University*, *The Cathedral*, and a few others deserve continued reading and examination. In these poems Lowell's deeply felt thoughts were elaborately and skillfully presented, while the form, that of the familiar verse essay, perfectly suited his penchant for rhymed declamation and long digressions. "Agassiz," a moving tribute to the great Harvard scientist, cleverly blends the tradition of the pastoral elegy with contemporary images as the telegraph wire announces Agassiz's death. Throughout the poem Lowell balances his personal sorrow with a tenuous, yet affirmative, hope that such a nature as Agassiz's must exist somewhere "perfected and conscious." In the *Ode* Lowell uses the occasion of the Civil War to present a rhymed meditation on the complex oppositions of song and deed, war and truth, death and the ideal. The poem's conclusion and didactic tone prove acceptable because of the poem's careful development of basic images and firm structure. Perhaps Lowell's most successful longer poem is *The Cathedral*. Like Tennyson's *In Memoriam* it deals with a quest for religious certainty by a man imbued with his age's disbelief. The magnificent stone monument of Chartres Cathedral serves as the focus for the poem's imagery and structure. Its four main sections examine natural, religious, and even democratic responses to the spiritual, and build to the hesitant but honest suggestion that the commonplace of miracles is available for every age.

What Lowell achieved is best seen in a poem like *The Cathedral*. If his verse lacked the mighty choral power of Whitman and only fitfully imitated Emerson's grandeur, it deserves its own place among the American traditions of vernacular poetry, satiric verse, and rhymed public oratory. As Henry James once noted upon rereading Lowell" "He looms, in such a renewed impression, very large and ripe and sane. . . . He was strong without narrowness; he was wise without bitterness and bright without folly. That appears for the most part the clearest ideal of those who handle the English form, and he was altogether in the straight tradition."

—John B. Pickard

See the essay on *The Cathedral*.

LOWELL, Robert (Traill Spence, Jr.). Born in Boston, Massachusetts, 1 March 1917. Educated at schools in Washington, D.C., and Philadelphia; Brimmer School, Boston; Rivers School; St Mark's School, Southboro, Massachusetts, 1930–35; Harvard University, Cambridge, Massachusetts, 1935–37; Kenyon College, Gambier, Ohio, 1938–40, A.B. (summa cum laude) 1940 (Phi Beta Kappa); Louisiana State University, Baton Rouge, 1940–41. Conscientious objector during World War II: served prison sentence, 1943–44. Married 1) Jean Stafford, *q.v.*, in 1940 (divorced, 1948); 2) the writer Elizabeth Hardwick in 1949 (divorced, 1972), one daughter; 3) the writer Caroline Blackwood in 1972, one son. Editorial assistant, Sheed and Ward, publishers, New York, 1941–42; teacher at the University of Iowa, Iowa City, 1950, 1953, and Kenyon School of Letters, Gambier, Ohio, 1950, 1953; lived in Europe, 1950–52; teacher at Salzburg Seminar on American Studies, 1952, University of Cincinnati, 1954, Boston University, 1956, Harvard University, 1958, 1963–70, 1975, 1977, and New School for Social Research, New York, 1961–62; Professor of Literature, University of Essex, Wivenhoe, Colchester, 1970–72. Consultant in Poetry, Library of Congress, Washington, D.C., 1947–48; Visiting Fellow, All Souls College, Oxford, 1970. Recipient: Pulitzer Prize, 1947; American Academy grant, 1947; Guggenheim fellowship, 1947, 1974; Harriet Monroe Poetry Award, 1952; Guinness prize, 1959; National Book Award, 1960; Ford grant, for poetry, 1960, for drama, 1964; Bollingen Poetry Translation Prize, 1962; New England Poetry Club Golden Rose, 1964; Obie award, for drama, 1965; Sarah Josepha Hale Award, 1966; Copernicus Award, 1974; National Medal for Literature, 1977. Member, American Academy. *Died 12 September 1977.*

PUBLICATIONS

Collections

The Collected Prose, edited by Robert Giroux. 1987.

Verse

Land of Unlikeness. 1944.
Lord Weary's Castle. 1946.
Poems 1938–1949. 1950.
The Mills of the Kavanaughs. 1951.
Life Studies. 1959; augmented edition, 1959.
Imitations. 1961.
For the Union Dead. 1964.
Selected Poems. 1965.

The Achievement of Lowell: A Comprehensive Selection of His Poems, edited by William J. Martz. 1966.
Near the Ocean. 1967.
The Voyage and Other Versions of Poems by Baudelaire. 1968.
Notebook 1967–1968. 1969; augmented edition, as *Notebook*, 1970.
The Dolphin. 1973.
For Lizzie and Harriet. 1973.
History. 1973.
Poems: A Selection, edited by Jonathan Raban. 1974.
Selected Poems. 1976; revised edition, 1977.
Day by Day. 1977.

Plays

Phaedra, from the play by Racine (produced 1961). In *Phaedra and Figaro*, 1961.
The Old Glory (*Benito Cereno* and *My Kinsman, Major Molineux*) (produced 1964). 1964; expanded version, including *Endecott and the Red Cross* (produced 1968), 1966.
Prometheus Bound, from a play by Aeschylus (produced 1967). 1969.
The Oresteia of Aeschylus. 1978.

Other

Editor, with Peter Taylor and Robert Penn Warren, *Randall Jarrell 1914–1965*. 1967.

Translator, *Poesie*, by Eugenio Montale. 1960.

*

Bibliography: *Lowell: A Reference Guide* by Steven Gould Axelrod and Helen Doese, 1982.

Critical Studies: *The Achievement of Lowell 1939–1959*, 1960, and *The Poetic Themes of Lowell*, 1965, both by Jerome Mazzaro, and *Profile of Lowell* edited by Mazzaro, 1971; *Lowell: The First Twenty Years* by Hugh B. Staples, 1962; *Lowell: A Collection of Critical Essays* edited by Thomas Parkinson, 1968; *Lowell* by Richard J. Fein, 1970, revised edition, 1979; *The Autobiographical Myth of Lowell* by Phillip Cooper, 1970; *The Public Poetry of Lowell* by Patrick Cosgrove, 1970; *Lowell: A Portrait of the Artist in His Time* edited by Michael London and Robert Boyers, 1970; *Lowell* by Jay Martin, 1970; *Critics on Lowell* edited by Jonathan Price, 1972; *The Poetic Art of Lowell* by Marjorie G. Perloff, 1973; *The Poetry of Lowell* by Vivian Smith, 1974; *Lowell* by John Crick, 1974; *Pity the Monsters: The Political Vision of Lowell* by Alan Williamson, 1974; *Circle to Circle: The Poetry of Lowell* by Stephen Yenser, 1975; *Lowell: Life and Art* by Steven Gould Axelrod, 1978; *American Aristocracy: The Lives and Times of James Russell, Amy, and Robert Lowell* by C. David Heymann, 1980; *Lowell* by Burton Raffel, 1981; *Lowell: A Biography* by Ian Hamilton, 1982; *Lowell: Nihilist as Hero* by Vereen M. Bell, 1983; *Lowell: An Introduction to the Poetry* by Mark Rudman, 1983; *Lowell: The Poet and His Critics* by Norma Procopiow, 1984.

* * *

Robert Lowell has been described as "a poet of restlessness without repose" (John Crick). His career is a history of violent changes in subject matter, and in manner, which often annoyed and confused his critics. Even now, after his death, there is little general agreement about his stature. But perhaps, even in this, Lowell is a *representative* figure: the years in which Lowell was publishing (1944–77) witnessed a fragmentation of culture that denies us the sorts of certainty about the status that it was once possible to accord to Eliot, or to Yeats. This period will never, one suspects, be accepted as "The Age of Lowell." Individual poets seem no longer capable of this sort of centrality of significance.

But if any poet in this period—perhaps sometimes with too earnest a deliberateness—lived through, proved upon his pulses, the central concerns, preoccupations, and pains of his time, it was Lowell. The career may, conveniently, be seen in three parts: the early poetry of Lowell's Catholicism that embraces *Land of Unlikeness*, *Lord Weary's Castle*, and *The Mills of the Kavanaughs*; the mid-period poetry of personal breakdown and political concern that includes *Life Studies*, *For the Union Dead*, and *Near the Ocean*; and the final period that saw the various attempts to create a larger, freer form through the subsequent stages of *Notebook*, *History*, *For Lizzie and Harriet*, and *The Dolphin*, a period concluding with the sustained elegiac note of *Day by Day*.

On the face of it, the three phases of the career seem to have little in common, apart from certain stylistic tics—most notably, and often irritatingly, Lowell's penchant for the triple adjective and the attention-seeking oxymoron. Some insight into an underlying continuity in Lowell's "one life, one writing" may be provided by remarking on his exceptional insistence on revising himself in public. One of the most upsetting aspects of *Notebook*, for many of its reviewers, was the shock of coming across familiar Lowell lines either in very different contexts, or procrusteanly racked into the uniform regularity of the book's "sonnets." Lowell's apparently cavalier freedom with his own published work suggests not so much a desire to do a little better what he has done brilliantly before, but rather a deep-seated impatience with his own enormous talent and with poetry itself. In the poem "Tired Iron" in *The Dolphin*, there is an almost Beckettian dismissal of the work, even as he is engaged on it—"I can't go on with this, the measure is gone." It is possible to see in Lowell, as in some of the greatest artists of the second half of the 20th century, a radical dissatisfaction with art itself, with its consolations, its sense of order, its morality. What gives Lowell's dissatisfaction its unique savour is his refusal of the obvious alternative of a bleak nihilism in favour of a worried, guilty commitment to a traditional New England liberalism. The oddity of Robert Lowell's sensibility is perhaps suggested in a shorthand way by pointing to the poems in *Notebook* and *History* dedicated to Eugene McCarthy and Robert Kennedy: and existential absurdist clinging precariously to sanity celebrates the pragmatic politics of liberal capitalism.

Dissatisfaction, restlessness, unease: these are the signatures of Lowell's work. The early formalist poetry nominally takes its cue from Allen Tate and the southern Fugitives. In fact, the formal majesty of the poems is everywhere disturbed by a raucous alliterative bellowing; the Catholicism is everywhere collapsed into savage heresy and blasphemy:

> O Mother, I implore
> Your scorched, blue thunderbreasts of love to pour
> Buckets of blessings on my burning head.

If this is rhetoric, it is a rhetoric of desperation. Even in the more tender poems—"The Quaker Graveyard in Nantucket" and "Mother Marie Therese"—Lowell's sonic boom threatens his formal perfection. His dissatisfaction compels him almost to wring the neck of his magnificent rhetoric. Such dissatisfactions led to a long silence during "the tranquillized Fifties," a silence during which the dissatisfactions of his personal life involved periods in mental hospitals. The silence was broken only at the end of the decade by the publication of *Life Studies*, a book in an entirely different mode and manner; Lowell was now so dissatisfied with his earlier work that he attempted almost its polar opposite, a poetry close to Chekhovian prose. This is the one work of Lowell's about which almost all critics agree: it was *the* book of its time, following, with total assurance, a direction more hesitantly beginning to be taken by some of his contemporaries, profoundly influential in its discovery of a new sort of personal voice. It signals, in "Beyond the Alps," Lowell's break with Catholicism, and it proceeds to worry out, "confessionally," the psychic disturbances and extremities of his harrowing personal experience. This is a poetry resolutely committed to walking naked; but the voice is moving and desperate and rises to a unique and instantly recognizable "Lowellian" pathos:

> A car radio bleats,
> 'Love, O careless Love . . . I hear
> my ill-spirit sob in each blood cell,
> as if my hand were at its throat . . .
> I myself am hell,
> nobody's here—.

But, unlike that of some poets who crawled in under the mantle of "confessional" poetry, Lowell's writing refuses the temptations of an easy solipsism. Christopher Ricks, in a *New Statesman* review of *For the Union Dead* (26 March 1965), maintained that "The singular strength of Robert Lowell's poetry has always been a matter of his power to enforce a sense of context." The work after *Life Studies* evidences a desire to speak, out of personal pain and catastrophe, about society and politics, and about literature, religion, and history, the sustaining "outer contexts" of our lives. Restlessly moving away from the "prose" style of *Life Studies*, Lowell wrote, in the central poems of *Near the Ocean*—especially, perhaps, in "Walking Early Sunday Morning"—the greatest elegies for a generation that suffered the Vietnam war and the threat of nuclear extinction, and he wrote them, with his casually characteristic refusal of the obvious, in a finely judged, perfectly achieved neoclassical form that recalls that other poet of the barbarities of which a "civilised" society is capable, Andrew Marvell:

> Pity the planet, all joy gone
> from this sweet volcanic cone;
> peace to our children when they fall
> in small war on the heels of small
> war—until the end of time
> to police the earth, a ghost
> orbiting forever lost
> in our monotonous sublime.

In *For the Union Dead*, the forms are again free, though the relatively uncluttered simplicity of these poems belies a carefully crafted subtlety of association, allusion, and symbolism. These haunted, nostalgic poems begin in a consideration of the joys and pains of personal relationship but extend themselves into the troubles of political life. The volume's title-poem relates private and public breakdown in a muted poetry of understatement, working by implication and suggestion. The poem's final stanza is as devastating as anything in Lowell, but the devastation comes across quietly, hesitantly, thrown off almost parenthetically compared to the aggressive climaxes of the poems in *Lord Weary's Castle*:

> The Aquarium is gone. Everywhere,
> giant finned cars nose forward like fish;
> a savage servility
> slides by on grease.

The ability to relate his own trouble to the trouble of his times is the impulse behind *Notebook*. This, and the works that grew out of it, are the most ambitious of Lowell's writing: he is attempting a large, inclusive form, a form for all occasions, in the manner of Pound's *Cantos*, of Berryman's *Dream Songs*. In the poems in the sequence—all irregular fourteen-liners—that deal with "history," there is too often the feeling of formal monotony, rhythmic inertia, a tired, mechanical repetitiveness. The lack of a real voice, and the absence of anything but the most straightforward chronology to serve as "plot," render *History* a generally wearying experience. The failure derives, perhaps, from Lowell's refusal to admit that a sonnet sequence, or its equivalent, is really capable of handling only limited types of material. The larger successes of *For Lizzie and Harriet* and *The Dolphin* are perhaps the result of their being more traditionally plotted around the themes and occasions of personal love and marriage. The idea of writing "history" as a sequence of sonnets has an almost wilful perversity about it, as though Shakespeare had decided to put the material of the history plays, as well as the story of his "two loves," into a sonnet sequence.

But such perversity, and the overall failure of a single book, are perhaps the inevitable price of an heroic refusal to repeat himself, a nervous, restless desire to define and re-define the protean self. "We are words," Lowell insists in a poem in *History* addressed to Berryman, "John, we used the language as if we made it." The claim is large; it is characteristic of Lowell's proud ambition that he should make it for himself; but in the formal variety, the technical ingenuity, and the inventiveness of his poems—and of his translations and plays—he comes, at the very least, close to justifying it.

—Neil Corcoran

See the essay on *Life Studies*.

LYTLE, Andrew (Nelson). Born in Murfreesboro, Tennessee, 26 December 1902. Educated at Sewanee Military Academy, Tennessee; Exeter College, Oxford, 1920; Vanderbilt University, Nashville, 1921–25, B.A. 1925 (Phi Beta Kappa); Yale University School of Drama, New Haven, Connecticut, 1927–28. Married Edna Langdon Barker in 1938 (died, 1963); three daughters. Actor in and around New York, 1929–30; Professor of History, Southwestern College, Memphis, Tennessee, 1936; Professor of History, University of the South, Sewanee, Tennessee, and managing editor, *Sewanee Review*, 1942–43; Lecturer, 1946–48, and Acting Head, 1947–48, University of Iowa School of Writing, Iowa City; Lecturer in Creative Writing, University of Florida, Gainesville, 1948–61; Lecturer in English, 1961–67, and Professor of English, 1968–73, University of the South, and editor, *Sewanee Review*, 1961–73; teacher at University of Kentucky, Lexington, 1977. Recipient: Guggenheim fellowship, 1940, 1941, 1960; National Endowment for the Arts grant, 1966; Lyndhurst Foundation prize, 1985. Litt.D.: Kenyon College, Gambier, Ohio, 1965; University of Florida, 1970; University of the South, 1973; D.H.L.: Hillsdale College, Michigan, 1985. Lives in Monteagle, Tennessee.

PUBLICATIONS

Fiction

The Long Night. 1936.
At the Moon's Inn. 1941.
A Name for Evil. 1947.
The Velvet Horn. 1957.
A Novel, A Novella and Four Stories. 1958.
Alchemy. 1979.
Stories: Alchemy and Others. 1984.

Other

I'll Take My Stand: The South and the Agrarian Tradition, with others. 1930.
Bedford Forrest and His Critter Company (biography). 1931; revised edition, 1960.
Who Owns America? A New Declaration of Independence, with others, edited by Herbert Agar and Allen Tate. 1936.
The Hero with the Private Parts: Essays (literary criticism). 1966.
A Wake for the Living: A Family Chronicle. 1975.

Editor, *Craft and Vision: The Best Fiction from The Sewanee Review*. 1971.

*

Bibliography: *A Lytle Checklist* by Jack De Bellis, 1960; *Lytle: A Bibliography 1920–1982* by Stuart Wright, 1982; *Lytle, Walker Percy, Peter Taylor: A Reference Guide* by Victor A. Kramer, 1983.

Critical Studies: "Lytle Issue" of *Mississippi Quarterly*, Fall 1970; *The Form Discovered: Essays on the Achievement of Lytle* edited by M.E. Bradford, 1973.

* * *

Andrew Lytle's family on both sides was prominent in middle Tennessee, and in fact Murfreesboro, the town where he was born, was founded on land given by his ancestor. His family chronicle, *A Wake for the Living*, traces the course of their history for almost two centuries. Lytle's movement into the writing of fiction was gradual. His undergraduate years at Vanderbilt University coincided with the heyday of the Fugitive group, and the friendships he formed with these poets led him into his own literary career. His main interest during the 1920's, however, was theater; he studied playwriting at the Yale School of Drama, and in New York he had a brief career as an actor.

Even before he left New York he had begun the research on his first book, *Bedford Forrest and His Critter Company*. He thus followed his friends Allen Tate and Robert Penn Warren, whose first prose works were likewise Civil War biographies. In 1930 these men and nine of their friends, led by their former teacher John Crowe Ransom, published *I'll Take My Stand*. This famous symposium inaugurated the Agrarian movement, to which Lytle was passionately committed. He was indeed about the only Agrarian who actually practiced farming during the 1930's, and for a few years he attempted to combine this with the literary profession. His great interest in the history of his region led to his first novel, *The Long Night*, a tragedy of revenge set against the background of the Civil War.

Although Lytle is usually identified with Tennessee, where three of his four novels are set, he is keenly aware of the larger clash of cultures. *At the Moon's Inn* brings the Spanish explorer De Soto to his fate in North America as he attempts to overcome the vast wilderness through an act of will. The short novel "Alchemy" likewise has Pizarro confronting the Inca world of Peru. In the foreword to *A Novel, A Novella, and Four Stories* Lytle comments that "The westward movement of Europeans, beginning with Columbus, not only shattered the narrow physical boundaries of Christendom but, like all extension, weakened it by reducing a union composite of spiritual and temporal parts to the predominance of material ends." This statement might serve as the theme that links all of Lytle's books. His third novel, *A Name for Evil*, is about a modern southerner who brings ruin upon himself and his family in an abortive effort to restore the past; the fictional convention here is the ghost story, *The Velvet Horn*, which is set in the Cumberland Mountains soon after the Civil War, involves a boy's initiation into manhood and an extraordinary tangle of family relationships. It is the richest of Lytle's books and one of the masterpieces of southern fiction.

—Ashley Brown

MacARTHUR, Charles (Gordon). Born in Scranton, Pennsylvania, 5 November 1895. Educated at Wilson Memorial Academy, Nyack, New York. Served as a trooper in the 1st Illinois Cavalry, on the Mexican border, 1916; in the 149th Field Artillery, U.S. Army, 1917–19: Private; assistant to the Chief of the Chemical Warfare Service, Washington, D.C., 1942–45: Lieutenant Colonel. Married 1) Carol Frink in 1920 (divorced, 1926); 2) the actress Helen Hayes in 1928, one daughter and one adopted son, the actor James MacArthur. Reporter, *Oak Leaves*, Oak Park, Illinois, 1915, Chicago *City Press*, 1915–16, Chicago *Examiner*, 1919–21, and Chicago *Tribune*, 1921–24; writer, New York *American*, 1924–27, and for *New Yorker* and *International Magazine*; screenwriter, producer, and director from 1929; formed a production company with Ben Hecht, 1934–36; editor, *Theatre Arts* magazine, New York, 1948–50. Recipient: Oscar, 1936. *Died 21 April 1956.*

PUBLICATIONS

Collections

The Stage Works (includes *Lulu Belle; Salvation; The Front Page; Twentieth Century; Ladies and Gentlemen; Swan Song; Johnny on a Spot; Stag at Bay*, with Nunnally Johnson), edited by Arthur Dorlag and John Irvine. 1974.

Plays

My Lulu Belle, with Edward Sheldon (as *Lulu Belle*, produced 1926). 1925; in *Stage Works*, 1974.
Salvation, with Sidney Howard (produced 1928). In *Stage Works*, 1974.
The Front Page, with Ben Hecht (produced 1928). 1928; in *Stage Works*, 1974.
Twentieth Century, with Ben Hecht (produced 1932). 1932; in *Stage Works*, 1974.
Jumbo, with Ben Hecht, music by Richard Rodgers, lyrics by Lorenz Hart (produced 1935). 1935.
Ladies and Gentlemen, with Ben Hecht, from a play by Ladislas Bus-Fekete (produced 1939). 1941; in *Stage Works*, 1974.
Fun to Be Free: Patriotic Pageant, with Ben Hecht (produced 1941). 1941.
Johnny on a Spot, from a story by Parke Levy and Alan Lipscott (produced 1942). In *Stage Works*, 1974.
Wuthering Heights (screenplay), with Ben Hecht, in *Twenty Best Film Plays*, edited by John Gassner and Dudley Nichols. 1943.
Swan Song, with Ben Hecht, from a story by Ramon Romero and Harriett Hinsdale (produced 1946). In *Stage Works*, 1974.
Stag at Bay, with Nunnally Johnson (produced 1976). In *Stage Works*, 1974.

Screenplays: *Billy the Kid*, with Wanda Tuchock and Laurence Stallings, 1930; *The King of Jazz*, with others, 1930; *Way for a Sailor*, with others, 1930; *The Girl Said No*, with Sarah Y. Mason and A.P. Younger, 1930; *Paid*, with Lucien Hubbard, 1931; *The Unholy Garden*, with Ben Hecht, 1931; *The New Adventures of Get-Rich-Quick Wallingford*, 1931; *The Sin of Madelon Claudet* (*The Lullaby*), 1931; *Rasputin and the Empress*, 1932; *Twentieth Century*, with Ben Hecht, 1934; *Crime Without Passion*, with Ben Hecht, 1934; *The Scoundrel*, with Ben Hecht, 1935; *Barbary Coast*, with Ben Hecht, 1935; *Once in a Blue Moon*, with Ben Hecht, 1935; *Soak the Rich*, with Ben Hecht, 1936; *Wuthering Heights*, with Ben Hecht, 1939; *Gunga Din*, with others, 1939; *I Take This Woman*, with James Kevin McGuinness, 1940; *The Senator Was Indiscreet*, with Edwin Lanham, 1947; *Lulu Belle*, with Everett Freeman, 1948; uncredited collaborations—*The Front Page*, 1931; *The President Vanishes* (*The Strange Conspiracy*), 1934.

Other

A Bug's-Eye View of the War. 1919.
War Bugs. 1929.

Film Director: *Crime Without Passion*, 1934, *The Scoundrel*, 1935, *Once in a Blue Moon*, 1935, and *Soak the Rich*, 1936, all with Ben Hecht.

*

Critical Studies: *Charlie: The Improbable Life and Times of MacArthur* by Ben Hecht, 1957; *Front Page Marriage: Helen Hayes and Charles MacArthur* by Jhan Robbins, 1984.

* * *

The young Charles MacArthur was a reporter in Chicago, worked on the New York *American*, and contributed to Hearst's *International Magazine* and other journals. From their Chicago journalism experience, but chiefly from Jed Harris traditions of Broadway melodrama, MacArthur and Ben Hecht created the famous play *The Front Page*. The New York *Times* (15 August 1928) liked this sensational and sentimental, if somewhat raucous and callous hymn to the antics of the working press. It said the play opened the season "noisily": "By superimposing a breathless melodrama upon a good newspaper play the authors and directors [actually George S. Kaufman] of 'The Front Page' . . . have packed an evening with loud, rapid, coarse and unfailing entertainment . . . have told a racy story with all the tang of front-page journalism . . . [and] convey the rowdy comedy of the pressroom, the whirr of excitement, of nerves on edge . . . in the hurly-burly of a big newspaper yarn."

MacArthur's unaided work (such as the forced farce of *Johnny on a Spot*) was undistinguished, but in collaboration he did well: he wrote *Lulu Belle* with Edward Sheldon, *Salvation* with Sidney Howard, and *Twentieth Century* with Hecht. All were solid Broadway vehicles. With Hecht he also wrote the spectacular *Jumbo*, *Ladies and Gentlemen*, *Swan Song*, and several film scripts.

MacArthur married as his second wife Helen Hayes, later to be queen of the legitimate stage, but professionally after 1928 he was more or less married to the movies. He began with several scripts in 1930, but hit the jackpot with a vehicle for Helen Hayes, *The Sin of Madelon Claudet*. Later films include *Rasputin and the Empress* (with the Barrymores), *Crime Without Passion* (writer, producer, director), *The Scoundrel*, *Gunga Din*, and *Wuthering Heights*. When he died he was working with Anita Loos on a vehicle for Hayes. He was by then one of Hollywood's most respected writers.

His service with the Rainbow Division in France in World War I led to *A Bug's-Eye View of the War* and *War Bugs*. It is too bad he did not do more humorous prose. He brought together a nice combination of sentiment and wit and a touch of irony with a raucous sense of fun and irreverence. All these elements are at their best in *The Front Page*. Brooks Atkinson wrote that "*The Front Page* is to journalism what *What Price Glory?* is to the marines—rudely realistic in style but romantic in its loyalties, and also audaciously profane." Actually, the "baldest profanity and most slatternly jesting as has ever been heard on the public stage" (as the New York *Times* had it in 1928) today sounds rather tame—and the play is not as realist as it seemed then. But some reporters still at least attempt to sound like MacArthur-Hecht characters (for nature imitates art), and *The Front Page* still has life in it, while *Five Star Final*, *Press Time*, *The Squeaker*, *Freedom of the Press*, and *Kiss the Boys Goodbye*, and a host of other newspaper plays are long dead.

—Leonard R.N. Ashley

MACDONALD, Ross. Pseudonym for Kenneth Millar. Born in Los Gatos, California, 13 December 1915; brought up in Canada. Educated at the Kitchener-Waterloo Collegiate Institute, Ontario, graduated 1932; University of Western Ontario, London, 1933–38, B.A. (honors) 1938; University of Toronto, 1938–39; University of Michigan, Ann Arbor, 1941–44, 1948–49 (Graduate Fellow, 1941–42; Rackham Fellow, 1942–

43), M.A. 1942, Ph.D. in English 1951. Served in the U.S. Naval Reserve, in the Pacific, 1944–46: Lieutenant Junior Grade. Married Margaret Sturm (i.e., the writer Margaret Millar) in 1938; one daughter. Teacher of English and history, Kitchener-Waterloo Collegiate Institute, 1939–41; Teaching Fellow, University of Michigan, 1942–44, 1948–49. Book reviewer, San Francisco *Chronicle*, 1957–60. Member, Board of Directors, 1960–61, 1964–65, and President, 1965, Mystery Writers of America. Recipient: Crime Writers Association Silver Dagger, 1965; University of Michigan Outstanding Achievement Award, 1972; Mystery Writers of America Grand Master Award, 1973; Popular Culture Association Award of Excellence, 1973; Private Eye Writers of America Life Achievement Award, 1981. *Died 11 July 1983.*

PUBLICATIONS

Fiction

The Dark Tunnel. 1944; as *I Die Slowly*, 1955.
Trouble Follows Me. 1946; as *Night Train*, 1955.
Blue City. 1947.
The Three Roads. 1948.
The Moving Target. 1949; as *Harper*, 1966.
The Drowning Pool. 1950.
The Way Some People Die. 1951.
The Ivory Grin. 1952; as *Marked for Murder*, 1953.
Meet Me at the Morgue. 1953; as *Experience with Evil*, 1954.
Find a Victim. 1954.
The Name Is Archer (stories). 1955.
The Barbarous Coast. 1956.
The Doomsters. 1958.
The Galton Case. 1959.
The Ferguson Affair. 1960.
The Wycherly Woman. 1961.
The Zebra-Striped Hearse. 1962.
The Chill. 1964.
The Far Side of the Dollar. 1965.
Black Money. 1966.
The Instant Enemy. 1968.
The Goodbye Look. 1969.
The Underground Man. 1971.
Sleeping Beauty. 1973.
The Blue Hammer. 1976.
Lew Archer, Private Investigator (stories). 1977.

Other

On Crime Writing. 1973.
A Collection of Reviews. 1979.
Self-Portrait: Ceaselessly into the Past, edited by Ralph B. Sipper. 1981.

Editor, *Great Stories of Suspense*. 1974.

*

Bibliography: *Millar/Macdonald: A Descriptive Bibliography* by Matthew J. Bruccoli, 1983.

Critical Studies: *Dreamers Who Live Their Dreams: The World of Macdonald's Novels* by Peter Wolfe, 1976; *Macdonald* by Jerry Speir, 1978; *Macdonald/Millar* by Matthew J. Bruccoli, 1984.

* * *

Ross Macdonald is one of the central authors of his time and place. Inheriting a wide variety of influences from a number of different sources, his works provide an accurate and fascinating chronicle of the major preoccupations of contemporary America; it seems likely that future generations will read his fiction as we read, for example, Conan Doyle—to discover some important facts and truths about a bygone age. The complicated elements of his complicated books reveal a spider web of connections with literature and history, with the cultures of past and present, and with some timeless themes and patterns of human behavior.

As all readers of detective fiction must know, Macdonald's novels initially grew out of the hard-boiled fiction of the 1920's and 1930's, more specifically, from the powerful traditions established by Dashiell Hammett and Raymond Chandler. He named his private detective Lew Archer, after Sam Spade's murdered partner in *The Maltese Falcon*, and endowed him with some of the wit and compassion of Chandler's Philip Marlowe. Although his early books displayed some interesting prose, a sure sense of scene and atmosphere, and an ability to sketch out character, Macdonald came into his own when he stopped trying merely to improve upon Hammett and Chandler and began to stake out new territory in detective fiction. His humor and toughness always had the forced, false ring of a toy telephone and his style sometimes bordered on the self-consciously literary; what changed Macdonald was his own recognition of his real strengths—complexity and sorrow.

Starting—by his own reckoning—with *The Galton Case*, Macdonald began Lew Archer's long and troubled exploration of the tangled wilderness of the human heart that he embodies in the landscape of southern California. (In reality, his themes are at least roughly adumbrated in such early books as *Blue City* and *The Three Roads*.) His novels began to depart radically from the tough fiction of his original inspiration in their curiously static sense of action; instead of representing human behavior in moments of sequential violence, they generally demonstrate the continuing mysteries of the past. The most notable element in all of Macdonald's fiction is its obsessive preoccupation with the sources of human evil. Lew Archer invariably discovers that whatever crime or problem he confronts in the present has its real meaning in some previous—almost always perverse or shocking—event many years before. The immensely complicated plots of the Macdonald novels are not so much chronicles of actions as retracings of interlocking histories and personalities.

In their profuse ramifications, the plots—along with other important aspects of his fiction—demonstrate the author's significant links with a variety of writers and modes far removed from the usual backgrounds of detective stories. Like his illustrious predecessors in the form, he creates yet another version of the chivalric romance, which has always been submerged but visible beneath the dark waters of the private-eye novel. Like that of previous American writers, Hawthorne and Melville in particular, his chief concern is not so much with the fact of crime as with its causes and effects. Like Dickens, whom he resembles in his penchant for intricate stories and surprising connections, he frequently builds his work around the image and reality of a betrayed, neglected, abandoned, and suffering child.

Out of his knowledge of psychology, his scholar's training in literature, and his interest in such figures as Homer, Sophocles, Coleridge, and Freud, and out of the painful personal life that he occasionally discussed with interviewers, Macdonald made perhaps the most powerful use of the normal materials of detective fiction. With a structure and texture derived from folklore, fairy tale, romance, and myth, he confronts the age-old problems that also, quite unsurprisingly, turn out to be the major difficulties of our time: paternity, identity, the iron chains forged by violence, by sex, by blood, by guilt. The body of his fiction forms a complex picture, then, of our world and its tensions and anxieties.

Those who see his work as a sort of southern California pop sociology miss the point; that is merely the location where his subject surfaces. Those who consider him a useful reporter of the rapid changes in contemporary American society catch a bit more, but all the descriptions of aimless youths, drug users, the decadent rich and the corrupted bourgeoisie, the destruction of the environment, and so forth provide only the necessary context for more permanent concerns. Those who read his works in the future may find some accurate creation of a special time and place, but it is more likely that in Macdonald's fiction they will be instructed in the harsh lessons of an inner reality. They will discover in the novel of crime, violence, and detection a sense of the mystery and sadness of human action, a dark and troubled picture of a dark and troubled age. Macdonald not only inherited a form and a central figure from Hammett and Chandler; he also acquired the sense of mission to continue and improve their advances in making the detective novel a significant and powerful literary form.

Macdonald's own place in the continuum of American detective fiction is as solid as that of Hammett and Chandler. His influence on later writers, beyond the superficial levels of the host of writers who imitate some of his mannerisms and themes, is more difficult to determine. Though contemporary detective fiction is littered with sensitive private eyes, it remains to be seen if the form will truly learn from Macdonald's work in the ways he learned from that of Hammett and Chandler; his present imitators do not seem promising. What cannot be doubted is that Macdonald's greatest influence has been to add to the literary richness and possibility of his form.

—George Grella

MacKAYE, Percy (Wallace). Born in New York City, 16 March 1875; son of the dramatist Steele MacKaye. Educated at Harvard University, Cambridge, Massachusetts, A.B. 1897; University of Leipzig, 1898–1900. Married Marion Homer Morse in 1898 (died, 1939), two daughters and one son. Teacher, Craigie School for Boys, New York, 1900–04; full-time writer from 1904; Fellow in Poetry, Miami University, Ohio, 1920–24; advisory editor, *Folk-Say* journal, from 1929; teacher of poetry and folk backgrounds, Rollins College, Winter Park, Florida, 1929–31; Visiting Professor of Drama, Sweet Briar College, Virginia, 1932–33; director, White Top Mountain Folk Festival, Virginia, 1933; folklore researcher in the Appalachian Mountains, 1933–35, and in Switzerland and the British Isles, 1936–37. Founding member, Phi Beta Kappa Associates, 1941; President, Pan American Poets League of North America, 1943; founder, Marion Morse-Percy MacKaye Collection at Harvard University Library, 1943. Recipient: Shelley Memorial Award, 1943; Academy of American Poets fellowship, 1948. M.A.: Dartmouth College, Hanover, New Hampshire, 1914; Litt.D.: Miami University, 1924. Member, American Academy. *Died 31 August 1956.*

PUBLICATIONS

Plays

Kinfolk of Robin Hood (as *Inhabitants of Carlyle*, produced 1901). 1924.
The Canterbury Pilgrims (produced 1903). 1903; revised version, music by Reginald DeKoven, 1916.
Fenris the Wolf. 1905.
St. Gaudens Masque-Prologue (produced 1905). 1910.
Jeanne d'Arc (produced 1906). 1906.
Sappho and Phaon (produced 1907). 1907.
Mater: An American Study in Comedy (produced 1908). 1908.
The Scarecrow, from the story "Feathertop" by Hawthorne (produced 1908). 1908.
A Garland to Sylvia: A Dramatic Reverie. 1910.
Anti-Matrimony (produced 1910). 1910.
Hannele, with Mary Safford, from a play by Gerhart Hauptmann (produced 1910).
A Masque of Labor. 1912.
Tomorrow (produced 1913). 1912.
Yankee Fantasies (includes *Chuck, Gettysburg, The Antick, The Cat-Boat, Sam Average*). 1912.
Chuck (produced 1912). In *Yankee Fantasies*, 1912.
Sam Average (produced 1912). In *Yankee Fantasies*, 1912.
Gettysburg (produced 1912). In *Yankee Fantasies*, 1912.
The Antick (produced 1915). In *Yankee Fantasies*, 1912.
Sanctuary: A Bird Masque (produced 1913). 1914.
A Thousand Years Ago: A Romance of the Orient (produced 1913). 1914.
St. Louis: A Civic Pageant, with Thomas Wood Stevens (produced 1914). 1914.
The Immigrants, music by Frederick Converse. 1915.
The New Citizenship: A Civic Ritual (produced 1916). 1915.
Caliban, By the Yellow Sands (produced 1916). 1916.
The Evergreen Tree (produced 1917). 1917.
Sinbad the Sailor. 1917.
The Roll Call: A Masque of the Red Cross (produced 1918). 1918.
The Will of Song: A Dramatic Service of Community Singing, music by Harry Barnhart (produced 1919). 1919.
Washington, The Man Who Made Us (produced 1920). 1919; shortened versions published, as *George Washington*, 1920, *Washington and Betsy Ross*, 1927, and *Young Washington at Mt. Vernon*, 1927.
Rip Van Winkle, music by Reginald DeKoven (produced 1920). 1919.
The Pilgrim and the Book. 1920.
This Fine-Pretty World (produced 1923). 1924.
Kentucky Mountain Fantasies (includes *Napoleon Crossing the Rockies, The Funeralizing of Crickneck, Timber*). 1928; revised edition, 1932.
The Sphinx. 1929.

Wakefield: A Folk-Masque of America, music by John Tasker Howard (produced 1932). 1932.
The Mystery of Hamlet, Prince of Denmark; or, What We Will: A Tetralogy (produced 1949). 1950.

Fiction

Tall Tales of the Kentucky Mountains. 1926.
Weathergoose Woo! 1929.

Verse

Johnny Crimson: A Legend of Hollis Hall. 1895.
Ode on the Centenary of Abraham Lincoln. 1909.
Poems. 1909; as *The Sistine Eve and Other Poems*, 1915.
Uriel and Other Poems. 1912.
The Present Hour. 1914.
Dogtown Common. 1921.
The Skippers of Nancy Gloucester. 1924.
April Fire. 1925.
Winged Victory. 1927.
The Gobbler of God: A Poem of the Southern Appalachians. 1928.
Songs of a Day. 1929.
William Vaughn Moody, Twenty Years After. 1930.
Moments en Voyage: Nine Poems for the Harvard Class of 1897. 1932.
In Another Land, with Albert Steffen. 1937.
The Far Familiar. 1938.
Poem-Leaflets in Remembrance of Marion Morse MacKaye. 1939.
My Lady Dear, Arise! Songs and Sonnets in Remembrance of Marion Morse MacKaye. 1940.
What Is She? A Sonnet of Sonnets to Marion Morse. 1943.
Rememberings 1895–1945: Four Poems. 1945.
The Sequestered Shrine. 1950.
Discoveries and Inventions: Victories of the American Spirit. 1950.

Other

The Playhouse and the Play, and Other Addresses Concerning the Theatre and Democracy in America. 1909.
The Civic Theatre in Relation to the Redemption of Leisure. 1912.
A Substitute for War. 1915.
Poems and Plays. 2 vols., 1916.
Epoch: The Life of Steele MacKaye. 2 vols., 1927.
American Theatre-Poets. 1935.
Poesia Religio. 1940.
Poog's Pasture: The Mythology of a Child: A Vista of Autobiography. 1951.
Poog and the Caboose Man: The Mythology of a Child: A Vista of Autobiography. 1952.

Editor, *Letters to Harriet*, by William Vaughn Moody. 1935.
Editor, *An Arrant Knave and Other Plays*, by Steele MacKaye. 1941.

Translator, *The Canterbury Tales of Chaucer: A Modern Rendering into Prose of the Prologue and Ten Tales*. 1904.
Translator, with John S.P. Tatlock, *The Modern Reader's Chaucer: Complete Poetical Works Now First Put into Modern English*. 1912; selection as *Canterbury Tales*, edited by Carl W. Ziegler, 1923.

*

Critical Studies: *MacKaye: A Sketch of His Life with Bibliography of His Works*, 1922; *Dipped in Sky* by Frank A. Doggett, 1930; *Annals of an Era: Percy MacKaye and the MacKaye Family* edited by E.O. Grover, 1932.

* * *

As the son of Steele MacKaye, Percy MacKaye might have been expected to show an interest in experimental drama. And he did, beginning with his graduation speech from Harvard in 1897 entitled "The Need of Imagination in the Drama of Today." Early in his career he added his efforts to the work of a small group of poetic dramatists—William Vaughn Moody, Josephine Peabody Marks, George Cabot Lodge—who were attempting to offset the excess of realism on the American stage with something of the artistry which Yeats and Maeterlinck were creating abroad. MacKaye's poetic dramas, however—*The Canterbury Pilgrims, Jeanne d'Arc, Sappho and Phaon*—were minor contributions to the genre.

It was with pageant drama and community theatre that MacKaye trod most successfully in the steps of his father, generally celebrating America's heritage on the grand scale his father envisioned. As a crusader for community theatre he wrote several books and numerous articles—*The Playhouse and the Play*, *The Civic Theatre*. One of his most successful pageants—allegorical masques is a more accurate descriptive term: he called his work "poetry for the masses; the drama of democracy"—was *St. Louis: A Civic Pageant* which had a cast of 7,500 and attracted over half a million people to its five performances. *Caliban, By the Yellow Sands*, produced on the 300th anniversary of Shakespeare's death, was an elaborate pageant using various scenes from Shakespeare's plays to humanize Caliban, to suggest, as MacKaye explained, "the slow education of mankind through the influences of cooperative art." His other pageants included *The Roll Call*, requested by the American Red Cross, and *Wakefield*, in which he attempted to dramatize the effect of "the Folk-Spirit of America" on American freedom.

For the historian of American drama one of MacKaye's particular contributions is *Epoch*, his definitive two-volume biography of his father, a man Percy worshipped and with whom he shared the dream of creating drama for the people. As a poet and a dramatist, MacKaye's best and most enduring work was his dramatization of Nathaniel Hawthorne's "Feathertop" which he called *The Scarecrow*. Created before the audience's eyes with a display of imagination and theatrical skill, the scarecrow comes to life as Lord Ravensbane and achieves a considerable sense of humanity before it succumbs to the wiles of mankind and its own artificial construction. It is a fine example of MacKaye's commentary on the "need of imagination" and still retains its theatrical magic for modern audiences.

—Walter J. Meserve

MacLEISH, Archibald. Born in Glencoe, Illinois, 7 May 1892. Educated at schools in Glencoe; Hotchkiss School, Lakeville, Connecticut, 1907–11; Yale University, New Haven, Connecticut (editor, *Yale Literary Magazine*), 1911–15, A.B. 1915 (Phi Beta Kappa); Harvard Law School, Cambridge, Massachusetts, 1915–17, 1919, LL.B. 1919. Served in the U.S. Army, 1917–19: Captain. Married Ada Hitchcock in 1916; one daughter and three sons. Lecturer in Government, Harvard University, 1919–21; attorney, Choate Hall and Stewart, Boston, 1920–23; lived in Paris, 1923–28; editor, *Fortune* magazine, New York, 1929–38; curator, Niemann Foundation, Harvard University, 1938; Librarian of Congress, Washington, D.C., 1939–44; director, U.S. Office of Facts and Figures, 1941–42, assistant director, Office of War Information, 1942–43, and Assistant Secretary of State, 1944–45, Washington, D.C.; Chairman of the U.S. Delegation to the Unesco drafting conference, London, 1945, and member of the executive Board, Unesco, 1946. Rede Lecturer, Cambridge University, 1942; Boylston Professor of Rhetoric and Oratory, Harvard University, 1949–62; Simpson Lecturer, Amherst College, Massachusetts, 1963–67. Recipient: Shelley Memorial Award, 1932; Pulitzer Prize, for verse, 1933, 1953, for drama, 1959; New England Poetry Club Golden Rose, 1934; Bollingen Prize, 1952; National Book Award, 1953; Sarah Josepha Hale Award, 1958; Tony award, 1959; National Association of Independent Schools award, 1959; Academy of American Poets fellowship, 1965; Oscar, for documentary, 1966; Presidential Medal of Freedom, 1977; National Medal for Literature, 1978; American Academy Gold Medal for Poetry, 1979. M.A.: Tufts University, Medford, Massachusetts, 1932; Litt.D.: Wesleyan University, Middletown, Connecticut, 1938; Colby College, Waterville, Maine, 1938; Yale University, 1939; University of Pennsylvania, Philadelphia, 1941; University of Illinois, Urbana, 1947; Rockford College, Illinois, 1952; Columbia University, New York, 1954; Harvard University, 1955; Carleton College, Northfield, Minnesota, 1956; Princeton University, New Jersey, 1965; University of Massachusetts, Amherst, 1969; York University, Toronto, 1971; LL.D.: Dartmouth College, Hanover, New Hampshire, 1940; Johns Hopkins University, Baltimore, 1941; University of California, Berkeley, 1943; Queen's University, Kingston, Ontario, 1948; University of Puerto Rico, Rio Piedras, 1953; Amherst College, Massachusetts, 1963; D.C.L.: Union College, Schenectady, New York, 1941; L.H.D.: Williams College, Williamstown, Massachusetts, 1942; University of Washington, Seattle, 1948. Commander, Legion of Honor (France); Commander, el Sol del Peru; President American Academy, 1953–56. *Died 20 April 1982.*

PUBLICATIONS

Collections

Letters 1907–1982, edited by R.H. Winnick. 1983.

Verse

Songs for a Summer's Day (A Sonnet-Cycle). 1915.
Tower of Ivory. 1917.
The Happy Marriage and Other Poems. 1924.
The Pot of Earth. 1925.
Streets in the Moon. 1926.
The Hamlet of A. MacLeish. 1928.
Einstein. 1929.
New Found Land: Fourteen Poems. 1930.
Before March. 1932.
Conquistador. 1932.
Frescoes for Mr. Rockefeller's City. 1933.
Poems 1924–1933. 1933; abridged edition, as *Poems*, 1935.
Public Speech. 1936.
Land of the Free—U.S.A. 1938.
Dedication: Motet for Six Voices, music by Douglas Stuart. 1938.
America Was Promises. 1939.
Freedom's Land, music by Roy Harris. 1942.
Actfive and Other Poems. 1948.
Collected Poems 1917–1952. 1952.
Songs for Eve. 1954.
New York. 1958.
Collected Poems. 1963.
The Wild Old Wicked Man and Other Poems. 1968.
The Human Season: Selected Poems 1926–1972. 1972.
New and Collected Poems 1917–1976. 1976.
On the Beaches of the Moon. 1978.

Plays

Nobodaddy. 1926.
Union Pacific (ballet scenario), music by Nicholas Nabokoff (produced 1934). In *The Book of Ballets*, 1939.
Panic: A Play in Verse (produced 1935). 1935.
The Fall of the City: A Verse Play for Radio (broadcast 1937). 1937.
Air Raid: A Verse Play for Radio (broadcast 1938). 1938.
The States Talking (broadcast 1941). In *The Free Company Presents*, edited by James Boyd, 1941.
The American Story: Ten Broadcasts (includes *The Admiral; The American Gods; The American Name; Nat Bacon's Bones; Between the Silence and the Surf; Discovered; The Many Dead; The Names for the Rivers; Ripe Strawberries and Gooseberries and Sweet Single Roses; Socorro, When Your Sons Forget*) (broadcast 1944). 1944.
The Trojan Horse (broadcast 1952). 1952.
This Music Crept by Me upon the Waters (broadcast 1953). 1953.
J.B.: A Play in Verse (produced 1958). 1958.
The Secret of Freedom (televised 1959). In *Three Short Plays*, 1961.
Three Short Plays: The Secret of Freedom, Air Raid, The Fall of the City. 1961.
Our Lives, Our Fortunes, and Our Sacred Honor (as *The American Bell*, music by David Amram, produced 1962). In *Think*, July-August 1961.
Herakles: A Play in Verse (produced 1965). 1967.
An Evening's Journey to Conway, Massachusetts: An Outdoor Play (produced 1967). 1967.
The Play of Herod (produced 1968).
Scratch, from *The Devil and Daniel Webster* by Stephen Vincent Benét (produced 1971). 1971.
The Great American Fourth of July (produced 1975). 1975.
Six Plays (includes *Nobodaddy*, *Panic*, *The Fall of the City*, *Air Raid*, *The Trojan Horse*, *This Music Crept by Me upon the Waters*). 1980.

Screenplays (documentaries): *Grandma Moses*, 1950; *The Eleanor Roosevelt Story*, 1965.

Radio Plays: *The Fall of the City*, 1937; *King Lear*, from the play by Shakespeare, 1937; *Air Raid*, 1938; *The States Talking*, 1941; *The American Story* series, 1944; *The Son of Man*, 1947; *The Trojan Horse*, 1952; *This Music Crept by Me upon the Waters*, 1953.

Television Play: *The Secret of Freedom*, 1959.

Other

Housing America, with others. 1932.
Jews in America, with others. 1936.
The Irresponsibles: A Declaration. 1940.
The Next Harvard, As Seen by MacLeish. 1941.
A Time to Speak: The Selected Prose. 1941.
The American Cause. 1941.
American Opinion and the War: The Rede Lecture. 1942.
A Time to Act: Selected Addresses. 1943.
Poetry and Opinion: The Pisan Cantos of Ezra Pound: A Dialog on the Role of Poetry. 1950.
Freedom Is the Right to Choose: An Inquiry into the Battle for the American Future. 1951.
Art Education and the Creative Process. 1954.
Poetry and Journalism. 1958.
Emily Dickinson: Three Views, with Louise Bogan and Richard Wilbur. 1960.
Poetry and Experience. 1961.
The Dialogues of MacLeish and Mark Van Doren, edited by Warren V. Bush. 1964.
The Eleanor Roosevelt Story. 1965.
A Continuing Journey. 1968.
The Great American Frustration. 1968.
Champion of a Cause: Essays and Addresses on Librarianship, edited by Eva M. Goldschmidt. 1971.
Riders on the Earth: Essays and Recollections. 1978.
Reflections, edited by Bernard A. Drabeck and Helen E. Ellis. 1986.

Editor, with E.F. Prichard, Jr., *Law and Politics: Occasional Papers of Felix Frankfurter 1913–1938*. 1962.

Other journalism pieces, lectures, and pamphlets published.

*

Bibliography: *A Catalogue of the First Editions of MacLeish* by Arthur Mizener, 1938; *MacLeish: A Checklist* by Edward J. Mullaly, 1973.

Critical Studies: *MacLeish* by Signi Lenea Falk, 1965; *MacLeish* by Grover Smith, 1971; "MacLeish Revisited" by William H. Pritchard, in *Poetry*, February 1983.

* * *

By 1940 Archibald MacLeish had written numerous books of poems, and was a well-known writer. He was also the target of adverse criticism. His early work is too derivative. It abounds with the distracting influence of Eliot and Pound, among others. MacLeish writes on the same subjects as Eliot and Pound and from exactly their point of view, but his early long poems proved very weak. His most famous one is *Conquistador*, which won him the first of three Pulitzer Prizes. It is a verbose, unqualified glorification of Spain's slaughter and enslavement of Mexican natives, and is, at best, unthinkingly adolescent. Other works in this period are marred by the confusing about-face MacLeish executes concerning the role of the poet. In his "Invocation to the Social Muse," he criticizes those who would urge the poet to concentrate on social issues. These issues, however, soon become central to his own work. MacLeish proceeds to sermonize, harangue—and produce much poor poetry, especially in *Public Speech* and his plays for radio.

Yet, despite the inferior work written in these decades, MacLeish was beginning to compile an outstanding body of lyric poetry. Some of the short poems in *Streets in the Moon* and *New Found Land* hold up very well. "L'an trentiesme de mon âge" is a superior presentation on the subject of the lost generation. Other fine poems include "Eleven," "Immortal Autumn," and "Memorial Rain." "Ars poetica" develops the stimulating idea that "A poem should not mean / But be." Perhaps the best of all is "The End of the World," a dramatization of the belief that the universe is basically meaningless. *Poems 1924–1933* brought together such superior lyrics as "Pony Rock," "Unfinished History," and "Lines for an Interment."

What became increasingly apparent in the 1940's and thereafter was that MacLeish's primary strength as a writer resided in the lyric form. In fact, MacLeish did most of his best work after the age of fifty.

Even some of MacLeish's later plays and long poems, two genres he never really excelled at, rise above the mediocre. The full-length play *J.B.*, despite its bland poetry and tepid main character, effectively dramatizes the tragedies that engulf that character and offers a frequently rousing debate between Mr. Zuss (representing orthodox religion) and Nickles (representing a pragmatic outlook). The one-act play *This Music Crept by Me upon the Waters* is also successful. The main characters, Peter and Elizabeth, are interesting; the plot builds in suspense; and the poetry and the theme (a preference for the present over the past) are powerful. *Actfive* is MacLeish's best long poem. The first section, which delineates modern man's basic predicament, is quite absorbing.

Still, it is MacLeish's lyric poetry that will be remembered the longest. Starting with the poems collected in 1948, the number of excellent lyrics mounts steadily, rendering unjust the critical neglect of MacLeish in recent years. These later lyrics center on three sometimes overlapping subjects. One presents the poet's increasing awareness of the mystery that permeates human experience. Earlier in his life, MacLeish wrote several poems that spoke confidently, if not cockily about setting out on explorations; now he writes "Voyage West," a sensitive expression of the uncertainty involved in a journey. Significantly, "Poet's Laughter" and "Crossing" are full of questions, while "The Old Man to the Lizard" and "Hotel Breakfast" end with questions, not answers. MacLeish sums up his sense of the mysterious in "Autobiography" when he says, "What do I know of the mystery of the universe? / Only the mystery."

He also wrote several tender eulogies and epitaphs. Two such poems about his mother are "The Burial" and "For the Anniversary of My Mother's Death." A pair of even finer poems, "Poet" and "Hemingway," have Ernest Hemingway for their subject. Other outstanding poems in this vein include "Edwin Muir," "Cummings," and "The Danger in the Air."

Finally, MacLeish wrote a host of fine poems about old age. The difficulty of creativity when one is no longer young is described in "They Come No More, Those Words, Those Finches." Tiredness is poignantly depicted in "Walking" and "Dozing on the Lawn." "Ship's Log" records the narrowing awareness of the old: "Mostly I have relinquished and forgotten / Or grown accustomed, which is a way of forgetting." Yet " 'The Wild Old Wicked Man' " presents an old person's wisdom and passion. In the two poems concerning "The Old Gray Couple," MacLeish offers the reader a moving portrait of the final, deepest stage of human love. Lastly, using Odysseus as narrator, MacLeish chooses human love (symbolized by the aging wife) and mortal life over love for the abstract (symbolized by the goddess Calypso) and the metaphysical in his lovely poem "Calypso's Island": "I long for the cold, salt, / Restless, contending sea and for the island / Where the grass dies and the seasons alter."

—Robert K. Johnson

MAILER, Norman (Kingsley). Born in Long Branch, New Jersey, 31 January 1923. Educated at Boys' High School, Brooklyn, New York, graduated 1939; Harvard University, Cambridge, Massachusetts (associate editor, *Harvard Advocate*), 1939–43, S.B. (cum laude) in aeronautical engineering 1943; the Sorbonne, Paris, 1947. Served in the U.S. Army, 1944–46: Sergeant. Married 1) Beatrice Silverman in 1944 (divorced, 1951), one daughter; 2) Adèle Morales in 1954 (divorced, 1961), two daughters; 3) Lady Jeanne Campbell in 1962 (divorced, 1963), one daughter; 4) Beverly Bentley in 1963 (divorced, 1979), two sons; 5) Carol Stevens in 1980 (divorced, 1980); 6) Norris Church in 1980, one son. Cofounder, 1955, and columnist, 1956, *Village Voice*, New York; columnist ("Big Bite"), *Esquire*, New York, 1962–63, and *Commentary*, New York, 1962–63. Member of the Executive Board, 1968–73, and since 1984, President, PEN American Center. Independent Candidate for Mayor of New York City, 1969. Recipient: American Academy grant, 1960; National Book Award, for non-fiction, 1969; Pulitzer Prize, for nonfiction 1969, 1980; MacDowell Medal, 1973; National Arts Club Gold Medal, 1976. D.Litt.: Rutgers University, New Brunswick, New Jersey, 1969. Member, American Academy, 1985. Lives in Brooklyn, New York.

PUBLICATIONS

Fiction

The Naked and the Dead. 1948.
Barbary Shore. 1951.
The Deer Park. 1955.
New Short Novels 2, with others. 1956.
Advertisements for Myself (includes essays and verse). 1959.
An American Dream. 1965.
The Short Fiction. 1967.
Why Are We in Vietnam? 1967.
A Transit to Narcissus, edited by Howard Fertig. 1978.
The Short Fiction (not same as 1967 book). 1981.
Ancient Evenings. 1983.
Tough Guys Don't Dance. 1984.

Plays

The Deer Park, from his own novel (produced 1960; revised version, produced 1967). 1967.
A Fragment from Vietnam (as *D.J.*, produced 1967). In *Existential Errands*, 1972.
Maidstone: A Mystery (screenplay and essay). 1971.

Screenplays: *Wild 90*, 1968; *Beyond the Law*, 1968; *Maidstone*, 1971; *The Executioner's Song*, 1982.

Verse

Deaths for the Ladies and Other Disasters. 1962.

Other

The White Negro. 1957.
The Presidential Papers. 1963.
Cannibals and Christians. 1966.
The Bullfight. 1967.
The Armies of the Night: The Novel as History, History as a Novel. 1968.
Miami and the Siege of Chicago: An Informal History of the Republican and Democratic Conventions of 1968. 1968.
The Idol and the Octopus: Political Writings on the Kennedy and Johnson Administrations. 1968.
Of a Fire on the Moon. 1971; as *A Fire on the Moon*, 1971.
The Prisoner of Sex. 1971.
The Long Patrol: 25 Years of Writing, edited by Robert F. Lucid. 1971.
King of the Hill: On the Fight of the Century. 1971.
Existential Errands. 1972.
St. George and the Godfather. 1972.
Marilyn: A Novel Biography (on Marilyn Monroe). 1973.
The Faith of Graffiti, with Mervyn Kurlansky and Jon Naar. 1974; as *Watching My Name Go By*, 1975.
The Fight. 1975.
Some Honorable Men: Political Conventions 1960–1972. 1976.
Genius and Lust: A Journey Through the Major Writings of Henry Miller, with Henry Miller. 1976.
The Executioner's Song: A True Life Novel (on Gary Gilmore). 1979.
Of Women and Their Elegance, photographs by Milton H. Greene. 1980.
The Essential Mailer. 1982.
Pieces and Pontifications (essays and interviews). 1982.

Film director: *Wild 90*, 1968; *Beyond the Law*, 1968; *Maidstone*, 1971.

*

Bibliography: *Mailer: A Comprehensive Bibliography* by Laura Adams, 1974.

Critical Studies: *Mailer* by Richard Foster, 1968; *The Structured Vision of Mailer* by Barry H. Leeds, 1969; *Sexual Politics* by Kate Millett, 1970; *Mailer: The Man and His Work* edited by Robert F. Lucid, 1971; *Mailer* by Richard Poirier, 1972; *Mailer: A Collection of Critical Essays* edited by Leo Braudy, 1972; *Down Mailer's Way* by Robert Solotaroff, 1974; *Mailer: A Critical Study* by Jean Radford, 1975; *Existential Battles: The Growth of Mailer* by Laura Adams, 1976; *Mankind in Barbary: The Individual and Society in the Novels of Mailer* by Stanley T. Gutman, 1976; *Mailer* by Philip Bufithis, 1978; *Mailer* by Robert Merrill, 1978; *Mailer: The Radical as*

Hipster by Robert Ehrlich, 1978; *Mailer's Novels* by Sandy Cohen, 1979; *Mailer, Quick-Change Artist* by Jennifer Bailey, 1979; *Acts of Regeneration: Allegory and Archetype in the Work of Mailer* by Robert J. Begiebing, 1980; *An American Dreamer: A Psychoanalytic Study of the Fiction of Mailer* by Andrew M. Gordon, 1980; *Mailer: A Biography* by Hilary Mills, 1982; *Mailer: His Life and Times* by Peter Manso, 1985.

* * *

Norman Mailer's career embraces the whole of what we might call contemporary American literature—from his brilliant debut with *The Naked and the Dead* to the long-awaited, much ballyhooed *Ancient Evenings*. Indeed, it would be hard to think of another American writer who has so dominated "the scene" by his words and by his presence. If he is the *enfant terrible* personified, as exasperating as he is controversial, he is also *central*. For better or worse, his private obsessions have become our cultural facts.

Mailer's themes—whether they express themselves in his novels or his non-fiction, on television or the lecture circuit—remain the same: violence, sex, power. The configurations may change, but Mailer remains convinced that these are the dark threads of America's cultural tapestry.

The Naked and the Dead, a mercilessly realistic World War II novel set in the Pacific, was at one and the same time a breathtaking debut for 25-year-old Mailer and an albatross of expectation he has had to wear ever since. Great wars ought to produce great literature—World War I (e.g., Hemingway's *A Farewell to Arms*; e.e. cummings's *The Enormous Room*; Erich Maria Remarque's *All Quiet on the Western Front*) certainly did. Until Joseph Heller's *Catch-22* came along in 1961, *The Naked and the Dead* had virtually no competition as *the* World War II novel.

In retrospect, the very realism that had so impressed its first, and second, generation of readers—the decaying corpses, the nearly overpowering sense of jungle stench—seems as strained as its aesthetics seems dated. But in the confrontations between General Cummings and Lieutenant Hearn—as well as those that pit one GI against another—Mailer was pointing to concerns that would continue to riddle him, and us, in the decades after World War II: the fate of the individual in a world increasingly filled with crushing institutions; the price of courage vs. the costs of cowardice; and perhaps most important of all, what power game will prevail in contemporary America.

For Mailer, this quest took the shape of novels—or more correctly, the grand vision of novels—that would test out how a hero fit for our time might look and, more important, *act*. As Mailer imagined it, the "Napoleonic" plan—consisting of an eight-part epic work—would carry his mythic hero, Sergius O'Shaugnessy, through the eight stages of his dream life. It was an ambitious scheme, but Mailer proved himself no James Joyce, nor was his novel likely to be mentioned in the same breath as *Finnegans Wake*. The best Mailer could do by way of O'Shaugnessy—after devoting nearly all of the 1950's to the project—was *The Deer Park* (essentially a Hollywood novel, in the mold of Nathanael West's *The Day of the Locust*) and two short stories: "The Man Who Studied Yoga" and "The Time of Her Time."

What Mailer discovered, however, is that nothing succeeds in American letters like "failure." In 1959, he published *Advertisements for Myself*, a collection of reprinted material and candid, even "confessional," introductions that were as revealing, and as riveting, about Mailer as F. Scott Fizgerald's "Crack-Up" essays had been about him.

That Mailer did not develop as a novelist *per se* began to seem less important than his roles as national dreamer, public gadfly, talk show "personality." *An American Dream* represented Mailer's capacity for dream at its novelistic best. Stephen Rojack, yet another of Mailer heroes who is destined to push against all limitations, all that would repress, and then deaden the psyche. It is a novel of tests, and of extremes, but for all its dizzying heights of violence and absurdity, there was a disturbing sense that Mailer had seen contemporary American life steady and whole.

Nonetheless, the Novel seemed more limited in the 1960's than it did when Mailer, writing *The Naked and the Dead*, imagined the genre capable of enormous power. Increasingly, Mailer turned his attention to that hybrid form known as the "New Journalism," and in works like *The Armies of the Night* and *The Prisoner of Sex* and most spectacularly in *The Executioner's Song* he was able to bring his formidable skills as a novelist to the turf usually occupied by newspaper reporters. Along with Truman Capote and Tom Wolfe, Mailer revolutionized the ground rules, and our expectations. Not surprisingly, there were those who felt that such works ducked the imaginative requirements of fiction, as well as the responsibilities of journalism.

Ancient Evenings was the Big Novel Mailer had been promising for some three decades. If T.S. Eliot mined the anthropology of Frazer's *The Golden Bough* for eventual use in a Christian view of tragedy, Mailer used the mythology surrounding Isis and Osiris as a testing ground for his pet theories about existential hipness (see, for example, "The White Negro" in *Advertisements for Myself*) and further investigations into the polymorphous perverse. *Ancient Evenings* is an extended odyssey through the Land of the Dead (indeed, Mailer's principle piece of research seems to be *The Egyptian Book of the Dead*), with all its terrors and violence and general unpleasantness.

To be sure, Mailer means to use this material as both an instruction manual on behalf of a healthy Ka, or shadow self, and as a cautionary tale for those whose lives are not yet worthy of reincarnation. Menenhetet, the novel's protagonist, is a wanderer, a quester of his elusive identity through four lifetimes. The result makes for a complicated plot, full of wooden talk about "how an existential man should live." At bottom, though, what Mailer tries mightily to beat is the Death Question. Earlier in his controversial career, he had claimed that cancer signified a life badly lived; with *Ancient Evenings*, he seems to suggest that death itself is what happens to those who are afraid of Life.

About Mailer nobody is neutral. But even those who do not count themselves among his ardent supporters must admit that he will figure prominently when the history of contemporary American letters is written. He has all the elements that make for sticking power: ambition, scope, and a willingness to explore the darker side of the psyche's uncharted vistas.

—Sanford Pinsker

See the essay on *The Naked and the Dead*.

MALAMUD, Bernard. Born in Brooklyn, New York, 26 April 1914. Educated at Erasmus Hall High School, New

York; City College of New York, 1932–36, B.A. 1936; Columbia University, New York, 1937–38, M.A. 1942. Married Ann de Chiara in 1945; one son and one daughter. Teacher, New York high schools, evenings 1940–49; Instructor to Associate Professor of English, Oregon State University, Corvallis, 1949–61; Member of the Division of Languages and Literature, Bennington College, Vermont, 1961–86. Visiting Lecturer, Harvard University, Cambridge, Massachusetts, 1966–68. President, PEN American Center, 1979–81. Recipient: Rosenthal Award, 1958; Daroff Memorial Award, 1958; Ford fellowship, 1959, 1960; National Book Award, 1959, 1967; Pulitzer Prize, 1967; O. Henry Award, 1969, 1973; Jewish Heritage Award, 1977; Vermont Council on the Arts award, 1979; Brandeis University Creative Arts Award, 1981; American Academy Gold Medal, 1983; Bobst Award, 1983; Mondello prize (Italy), 1985. Member, American Academy, 1964, and American Academy of Arts and Sciences, 1967. *Died 18 March 1986.*

PUBLICATIONS

Fiction

The Natural. 1952.
The Assistant. 1957.
The Magic Barrel (stories). 1958.
A New Life. 1961.
Idiots First (stories). 1963.
The Fixer. 1966.
Pictures of Fidelman: An Exhibition. 1969.
The Tenants. 1971.
Rembrandt's Hat (stories). 1973.
Two Fables. 1978.
Dubin's Lives. 1979.
God's Grace. 1982.
The Stories. 1983.

Other

A Malamud Reader. 1967.

*

Bibliography: *Malamud: An Annotated Checklist* by Rita N. Kosofsky, 1969; *Malamud: A Reference Guide* by Joel Salzburg, 1985.

Critical Studies: *Malamud* by Sidney Richman, 1967; *Malamud and Philip Roth: A Critical Essay* by Glenn Meeter, 1968; *Malamud and the Critics*, 1970, and *Malamud: A Collection of Critical Essays*, 1975, both edited by Leslie A. and Joyce W. Field; *Art and Idea in the Novels of Malamud* by Robert Ducharme, 1974; *Malamud and the Trial by Love* by Sandy Cohen, 1974; *The Fiction of Malamud* edited by Richard Astro and Jackson J. Benson, 1977 (includes bibliography); *Rebels and Victims: The Fiction of Richard Wright and Malamud* by Evelyn Gross Avery, 1979; *Malamud* by Sheldon J. Hershinow, 1980; *The Good Man's Dilemma: Social Criticism in the Fiction of Malamud* by Iska Alter, 1981; *Understanding Malamud* by Jeffrey Helterman, 1985.

* * *

Bernard Malamud, one of the most popular contemporary writers of Jewish-American fiction, contributed significantly to the growth in ethnic consciousness in American letters. He raised serious questions about the wpopulate his fiAmerican dream and the American tradition. The luckless and bungling heroes ction are 20th-century replies to the supernatural powers of Natty Bumppo, the heroic stature of Captain Ahab, and the moral development of Isabel Archer.

Malamud's short stories and novels derived from two essential aspects of his life: his Jewish upbringing and his secular education. The Jewish past provided Malamud with much surface detail (setting, dialect) and with the ironic tone and biting humor of much of his fiction. But Malamud was also a careful student of the Western Christian literary tradition which was often a source for symbols and literary parallels. It even colored his theme of redemption through suffering to the extent that his characters appear more as Christian martyrs than as Yiddish-speaking immigrants.

Malamud's first novel, *The Natural*, is his most ingenious adaptation of Christian legend. The story of the baseball hero, Roy Hobbs, it is a conflation of the American myth of the sports hero, specifically the baseball hero, and the medieval legends of the Fisher King and the Grail. A natural athlete, Roy is plagued by false goddesses and unworthy goals. In the end, when promised the opportunity to redeem the dry land, the unsuccessful team, Roy fails morally. He helps fix the game.

The Assistant, also a novel of striving after new gods, is one of Malamud's most oppressive: but it is not a story of hopelessness. Frank Alpine, a Gentile who participates in the robbery of Morris Bober's grocery and rapes Helen Bober, learns to repent. An admirer of St. Francis, Frank is redeemed through his suffering—he becomes a Jew like his former employer Morris Bober. One of the most effective aspects of this novel is its vividly evoked setting. The Bobers are living a life of poverty and desperation, but into this darkened vision beams the light of Frank's love for Helen and his gradual salvation through the laws of self-sacrifice.

A New Life, a barely disguised *roman à clef* of Malamud's years at Oregon State University, chronicles the growth of Sam Levin from loser to family man. He arrives at a first teaching position; he is approaching thirty, anxious to please, filled with aspirations. Only after he arrives at Cascadia College does he discover that it is not a liberal arts school but a technical institute. This is only the first of a series of disappointments and reversals. In his first year he has an affair with the wife of the chairman of the English Department and is forced to leave Cascadia and the profession of teaching. He takes with him a pregnant woman whom he no longer loves, her two adopted children, and a mature vision of the responsibility of the individual.

In *The Fixer* Malamud turns from the American landscape to the Russian countryside. The plot is based on the Mendel Belis case of the early 20th century, but the character Yakov Bok is wholly Malamud's creation. A simple, irreligious Jew, Yakov attempts to escape the *shtetl*, Jewishness, and an unfaithful wife by slipping out of the Pale of Settlement. He is discovered living in a Christian area and accused of the ritual murder of a Gentile boy. The development of his Jewish and humanitarian consciousness is a direct result of his torture in the Russian prison. His victory over disease, death, and insanity is more than a physical one and more than an individual one.

In *Pictures of Fidelman*, a picaresque novel, Arthur Fidelman travels to Italy, first to study art, then to paint, finally simply to become human. Three of the episodes collected in this novel had been previously published as short stories. By collecting them into a single volume and adding new episodes, Malamud rounds out the bungling and lost character that is Fidelman. In this foreign setting, an American innocent, like many American innocents before him, learns what Europe has to offer. But, more than that, he learns what his own inadequacies are.

The Tenants, an experimental novel, suggests some of the complexities of the relationship between blacks and Jews in mid-20th-century America. Malamud's ambivalence about this relationship is apparent in the three suggested endings to the novel. Added to the problems of black-white interaction are the deprived atmosphere of the setting (an abandoned tenement house) and the jealousy of competitors (both main characters are novelists). As the conflict intensifies between Harry Lesser and Willie Spearmint, Malamud develops the social, sexual, political, and even aesthetic implications of their argument. In the end, they represent also the struggle between the formalist writer and the Marxist writer. Another writer—this time a biographer—is the central character of *Dubin's Lives*.

Malamud's tales run the gamut from painful reality to sheer fantasy. (Fantasy, surprisingly, is the tone of his final novel, *God's Grace*, an apocalyptic and allegorical beast fable.) The short stories are most often peopled by the Jews of Malamud's experience—immigrants and second-generation Americans. Even in the most fantastic of the tales, the quality of the Yiddish past filters through—in the turn of a phrase, detail of a setting, background of a character, or in a thematic concern with the holiness of intellectuality.

In the best of Malamud's short fiction the main characters share more with the Yiddish past than do their counterparts in the novels. Whether the hero be an unfeeling yeshiva student ("Magic Barrel"), a father protecting an idiot son ("Idiots First"), a modern-day Job confronted by a black Jewish angel ("Angel Levine"), a talking bird ("The Jewbird"), a guilty son duped by a fake miracle rabbi ("The Silver Crown"), a frightened American in Russia accosted by a censored writer ("Man in the Drawer"), or a talking horse ("The Talking Horse"), each of these individuals is clearly indebted to the Jewish past in the Diaspora. Each is specifically indebted to the ambivalent feelings of chosenness that has been the lot of the Jew in Europe since the first century.

—R. Barbara Gitenstein

See the essay on *The Assistant*.

MARKHAM, Edwin. Born Charles Edward Anson Markham in Oregon City, Oregon, 23 April 1852. Educated at San Jose Normal School, California; Christian College, Santa Rosa, California. Married 1) Annie Cox in 1875 (divorced, 1884); 2) Carolyn E. Bailey in 1887; 3) Anna Catherine Murphy in 1898; one son. Schoolteacher: headmaster, University Observation School, Oakland, California, for 10 years. Lived in New York and New Jersey from c. 1900: lecturer and editor. Recipient: Academy of American Poets prize. Honorary degrees: Baylor University, Waco, Texas; Syracuse University, New York; New York University. Honorary President, Poetry Society of America. Member, American Academy, 1930. *Died 7 March 1940.*

PUBLICATIONS

Collections

Poems, edited by Charles L. Wallis. 1950.

Verse

The Man with the Hoe and Other Poems. 1899.
Lincoln and Other Poems. 1901.
The Shoes of Happiness and Other Poems. 1915.
Gates of Paradise and Other Poems. 1920.
Funeral of Adam Willis Wagnalls. 1924.
New Poems: Eighty Songs at Eighty. 1932.
The Star of Araby. 1937.

Other

Modern Poets and Christian Teaching, with Richard Watson Gilder and E.R. Sill. 1906.
The Burt-Markham Primer: The Nature Method, with Mary Burt. 1907.
Children in Bondage: A Presentation of the Anxious Problem of Child Labor, with Benjamin B. Lindsey and George Creel. 1914.
California the Wonderful. 1914.
Archibald Henderson: An Appreciation of the Man. 1918.
Campbell Meeker. 1925.

Editor, *The Real America in Romance*. 15 vols., 1909–27.
Editor, *Foundation Stones of Success*. 10 vols., 1917.
Editor, *The Book of Poetry*. 3 vols., 1926.
Editor, *Songs and Stories of California*. 1931.
Editor, *The Book of English Poetry*. 1934.
Editor, *Poetry of Youth*. 1935.

*

Critical Studies: *Markham* by William L. Stidger, 1933; *The Unknown Markham: His Mystery and Its Significance* by Louis Filler, 1966; *Markham: The Poet for Preachers* by George Truman Carl, 1977.

* * *

Edwin Markham, best known for a single poem, "The Man with the Hoe," produced five published collections of verse in his lifetime, as well as a few other poetic attempts, and in addition a series of articles on the injustices of child labor and on various other Progressive/Reform causes. As a poet he was an unsophisticated traditionalist (hence, a mainstream writer, as Dickinson, Whitman, Wallace Stevens, E.E. Cummings, and W.C. Williams could never be). He strove, generally with the aid of regular rhythms and conventional rhymes, to promote brotherhood, love, and all the other standard virtues. A strong sense of Christian "awareness" runs throughout his work, which reflects not only his sensitive conscience in the face of man's inhumanity to man, but his spiritual commitment: an ongoing manifesto of the need for *good works* and the security of *faith*.

A series of unlikely circumstances combined to make "The Man with the Hoe" (based on the painting by the Barbizon artist Jean-François Millet) one of America's most famous poems of all time: deeper and more suggestive than its subject, in almost a subliminal, inexpressible way. Millet's painting of course must be kept in mind here; then the opening lines of the poem: "Bowed by the weight of centuries he leans / Upon his hoe and gazes on the ground, / The emptiness of ages in his face, / And on his back the burden of the world." That this poem and no other quite like it could profoundly affect an entire nation, was proven by the general neglect accorded Markham's comparable poem (likewise predicated on a Millet painting of a poor peasant), "The Sower" (in *Lincoln and Other Poems*): "He is the stone rejected, yet the stone / Whereon is built metropolis and throne."

Markham's "Lincoln, The Man of the People" was well received, with its image of the fallen President suggesting the fall of "a lordly cedar," leaving "a lonesome place against the sky." A good deal of comment and speculation were provoked by his poem "Virgilia" (in *The Shoes of Happiness and Other Poems*). With its companion-piece, "The Crowning Hour," it spoke of a mysterious lost love and the poet's determination to undertake a cosmic quest in order to find her; here again one can sense, despite all the changes in fashion and style since the poem was written, the basis for strong reader identification: "Our ways go wide and I know not whither, / But my song will search through the worlds for you, / Till the Seven Seas waste and the Seven Stars wither / And the dream of the heart comes true."

Staid, ultra-conventional though Markham's poems were, he himself was a deeply passionate man and a much more complicated person than he is generally regarded as being. School superintendent and principal, writer of popular poems and verses, public lecturer and anthologist of popular verse—these job designations do not begin to explain him, any more than do the facts of his unhappy childhood and his tormented relationship with his neurotic mother, or his being a product of the Oregon-California coastal region. A restless, driven man, he lived an inner life quite at variance with his outward appearance of majestic, assured, bearded dignity; this is borne out, for example, by the nightmare poem "The Ballad of the Gallows Bird" (printed originally in 1926).

—Samuel Irving Bellman

MARQUAND, John P(hillips). Born in Wilmington, Delaware, 10 November 1893. Educated at Newburyport High School, Massachusetts; Harvard University, Cambridge, Massachusetts, 1912–15, A.B. 1915. Served in the Massachusetts National Guard in the Mexican Border Service, 1916; student, Camp Plattsburg, 1917; commissioned 1st Lieutenant in the U.S. Field Artillery, and served in the 4th Brigade in France, 1917–18; special consultant to the Secretary of War, Washington, D.C., 1944–45; war correspondent for the U.S. Navy, 1945. Married 1) Christina Davenport Sedgwick in 1922 (divorced, 1935), one son and one daughter; 2) Adelaide Hooker in 1937 (divorced, 1958), two sons and one daughter. Assistant magazine editor, Boston *Transcript*, 1915–17; with the Sunday magazine department, New York *Tribune*, 1919–20; advertising copywriter, J. Walter Thompson Company, New York, 1920–21. Member, Board of Overseers, Harvard University; member of the Editorial Board, Book-of-the-Month Club, 1944–60. Recipient: Pulitzer Prize, 1938; Sarah Josepha Hale Award, 1957. Litt.D.: University of Maine, Orono, 1941; Rochester University, Rochester, New York, 1944; Yale University, New Haven, Connecticut, 1950; D.H.L.: Bates College, Lewiston, Maine, 1954. Member, American Academy. *Died 16 July 1960.*

PUBLICATIONS

Fiction

The Unspeakable Gentleman. 1922.
Four of a Kind (stories). 1923.
The Black Cargo. 1925.
Do Tell Me, Doctor Johnson. 1928.
Warning Hill. 1930.
Haven's End. 1933.
Ming Yellow. 1935.
No Hero. 1935; as *Mr. Moto Takes a Hand*, 1940; as *Your Turn, Mr. Moto*, 1963.
Thank You, Mr. Moto. 1936.
The Late George Apley: A Novel in the Form of a Memoir. 1937.
Think Fast, Mr. Moto. 1937.
Mr. Moto Is So Sorry. 1938.
Wickford Point. 1939.
Don't Ask Questions. 1941.
H.M. Pulham, Esquire. 1941.
Last Laugh, Mr. Moto. 1942.
So Little Time. 1943.
Repent in Haste. 1945.
B.F.'s Daughter. 1946; as *Polly Fulton*, 1947.
Point of No Return. 1949.
It's Loaded, Mr. Bauer. 1949.
Melville Goodwin, USA. 1951.
Sincerely, Willis Wayde. 1955.
North of Grand Central (omnibus). 1956.
Mr. Moto's Three Aces (omnibus). 1956.
Stopover: Tokyo. 1957; as *The Last of Mr. Moto*, 1963; as *Right You Are, Mr. Moto*, 1977.
Life at Happy Knoll (stories). 1957.
Women and Thomas Harrow. 1958.

Play

The Late George Apley, with George S. Kaufman, from the novel by Marquand (produced 1944). 1946.

Other

Prince and Boatswain: Sea Tales from the Recollections of Rear-Admiral Charles E. Clark, with James Morris Morgan. 1915.
Lord Timothy Dexter of Newburyport, Mass. 1925.
Federalist Newburyport; or, Can Historical Fiction Remove a Fly from Amber? 1952.
Thirty Years (miscellany). 1954.
Timothy Dexter Revisited. 1960.

*

Critical Studies: *Marquand* by John J. Gross, 1963; *Marquand* by C. Hugh Holman, 1965; *The Late John Marquand* by

Stephen Birmingham, 1972 (includes bibliography); *Marquand: An American Life* by Millicent Bell, 1979.

* * *

John P. Marquand was a popular professional writer who whetted his skills of realistic and gently satiric writing to a very fine edge in several popular novels and scores of short stories in the mass circulation magazines before, in 1937, he set out to employ these skills with affectionate irony and gentle satire on the society of affluent upper-middle-class America in its seats of influence and power. For the twenty years that followed he was not only a practiced portrayer of American life but also one of the most popular novelists that America has produced.

The Late George Apley, which in 1937 broke the pattern of Marquand's popular fiction, is a parody of "collected letters with commentary" of distinguished people. It is a satiric picture of a very proper Bostonian and the ways in which the constraints of his society kept him in line and made him a good but stuffy and frustrated man. It received the Pulitzer Prize and launched Marquand's career as an important American social novelist. It was the first of three novels in which Marquand explored in contrasting panels aspects of the life of Boston. *Wickford Point* is the story of a decaying family loosely bound to the Transcendentalists, a comic picture of the diminishment of greatness and the sadness of the Indian summer of the spirit, and *H.M. Pulham, Esquire* is a self-portrait by a contemporary Bostonian, a post-World War I businessman, and the account of his ineffectual revolt against his class and its customs. These three novels form a triptych of New England life and use a variety of satiric skills, largely resulting from ironic points of view and the extensive use of flashbacks.

Like Sinclair Lewis, whom he greatly admired, Marquand moved on, after his complex portrait of Boston, to other cities and other professions in his growing list of studies of American life. *So Little Time* explores the vulgarly opulent world of west coast moviemakers. It is set during World War II, and suggests the inexorable passage of time. His other wartime novel, *B.F.'s Daughter*, deals with big business and the Washington bureaucracy, and is only a limited success. (A short novel *Repent in Haste* also deals with the war, but it is very slight.) *Point of No Return* is, after *The Late George Apley*, Marquand's best novel. It is the story of a banker who explores his New England small-town roots in an effort to find bases for a decision he must make, only to discover that all the decisions had already been made without his being aware of it, and that he has passed "the point of no return," a conclusion that most Marquand protagonists reach after painfully reviewing their lives. In addition to many amusing social caricatures, the book contains a serious examination of the sociology of New England towns, and to some degree of New York City. It and the Boston trilogy are Marquand's works which seem most likely to survive.

Melville Goodwin, USA is a portrayal of a General seen through the admiring eyes of a popular journalist. The journalist is a devastating portrait of the shallowness of the view of man held by the popular media, but, at the time the book was published, few critics recognised that it was an ironic novel that cut both ways, and they made the mistake of assuming that Marquand approved of the military officer and his decisions. It represents, after *The Late George Apley*, Marquand's most complex use of narrative point of view for satire, and indicates that his use of technical devices and his skill as a satiric novelist continued to grow through much of his long career. *Sincerely, Willis Wayde* is that Marquand novel most obviously like the Sinclair Lewis of the 1920's. It is a devastating portrait of a big business promoter, a man utterly without character. In 1958 Marquand published what he declared in advance would be his last novel, *Women and Thomas Harrow*, the story of a very successful playwright and his three marriages. This novel is a kind of self-consciously ironic *Tempest* to John P. Marquand's career.

Marquand is particularly notable for the double vision through which he could be in his world and still see it and himself from the vantage point of a detached onlooker. The result was that his portraits of American citizens, their frustrations, the extent to which their lives had already been determined by a structure of social decisions made by others without their awareness, and the sort of quiet desperation in which they lived out their days was particularly powerful. The reader who sees himself in some of his more absurd actions and postures in Marquand's novels has the feeling that he is also seeing Marquand as well. Like Sinclair Lewis he is the chronicler of men who make ineffectual revolts, of men who lack the stature of character and mind to be in any significant sense heroes; thus his ultimate view is comic. He examined the social conditions of American lives with irony and grace, and his "badgered American male" captures in his recurrent problems and poses not only how we behave, but also how hollow our lives often are at the core. He speaks both to our social-historical sense and to an unslaked spiritual thirst which our aridity creates. He never was capable of poetic soaring, but to his own age, at least, he spoke with ease and skill, with irony and wit, but, above all, with the authority of unsentimental knowledge.

—C. Hugh Holman

MARQUIS, Don(ald Robert Perry). Born in Walnut, Illinois, 29 July 1878. Educated at Walnut High School to age 15; Knox College, Galesburg, Illinois, 1 term; Corcoran School of Art, Washington, D.C., 1899–1900. Married 1) Reina Melcher in 1909 (died, 1923), one son and one daughter; 2) the actress Marjorie Vonnegut in 1926 (died, 1936). Worked in a pharmacy, on a chicken farm, on the railroad, and as a schoolteacher, late 1890's; clerk, U.S. Census Bureau, and reporter, Washington *Times*, 1900–02; journalist in Philadelphia, 1902; associate editor, Atlanta *News*, 1902–04; editorial writer, Atlanta *Journal*, 1904–07; associate editor to Joel Chandler Harris, *Uncle Remus's* magazine, Atlanta, 1907–09; reporter, New York *American*, and Brooklyn *Daily Eagle*, 1909–12; staff member, 1912, and columnist ("The Sun Dial"), 1912–22, New York *Sun*; columnist ("The Lantern"), New York *Tribune* (later *Herald Tribune*), 1922–25; screenwriter in Hollywood, 1928–29 and intermittently, 1931–36; founding publisher, *Column*, 1933. Member, American Academy, 1923. *Died 29 December 1937.*

PUBLICATIONS

Collections

The Best of Marquis, edited by Christopher Morley. 1946.

Fiction

Danny's Own Story. 1912.
The Cruise of the Jasper B. 1916.
Carter and Other People (stories). 1921.
Pandora Lifts the Lid, with Christopher Morley. 1924.
When the Turtles Sing and Other Unusual Tales. 1928.
A Variety of People (stories). 1929.
Off the Arm. 1930.
Chapters for the Orthodox (stories). 1934.
Sun Dial Time (stories). 1936.
Sons of the Puritans (unfinished novel). 1939.

Plays

The Old Soak (produced 1922). 1926.
The Dark Hours: Five Scenes from a History (produced 1932). 1924.
Words and Thoughts. 1924.
Out of the Sea (produced 1927). 1927.
Everything's Jake (produced 1930). 1978.
Master of the Revels. 1934.

Screenplay: *Skippy*, with others, 1931.

Verse

Dreams and Dust. 1915.
Noah an' Jonah an' Cap'n John Smith. 1921.
Poems and Portraits. 1922.
Sonnets to a Red-Haired Lady (from a Gentleman with a Blue Beard) and Famous Love Affairs. 1922.
The Awakening and Other Poems. 1924.
The Lives and Times of Archy and Mehitabel. 1940.
Archy and Mehitabel. 1927.
Archys Life of Mehitabel. 1933.
Archy Does His Part. 1935.
Love Sonnets of a Cave Man and Other Verses. 1928.
An Ode to Hollywood. 1929.

Other

Hermione and Her Little Group of Serious Thinkers. 1916.
Prefaces. 1919.
The Old Soak, and Hail and Farewell. 1921.
The Revolt of the Oyster. 1922.
Mr. Hawley Breaks into Song. 1923.
The Old Soak's History of the World. 1924.
The Almost Perfect State (essays). 1927.
Her Foot Is on the Brass Rail. 1935.

*

Critical Studies: *O Rare Don Marquis: A Biography* by Edward Anthony, 1962; *Marquis* by Lynn Lee, 1981.

* * *

Don Marquis is remembered as a humorist, but he wrote both humorous and serious plays, poetry, and fiction. His last novel, *Sons of the Puritans*, is serious. Although unfinished, this autobiographical narrative about a boy who grows to manhood in a small midwestern town presents greater depth of feeling and complexity of character and situation than Marquis's earlier, lighter novels. Like most of his work, it is well written and interesting. Like his serious short stories, plays, and poetry, however, it is unique without being very different from good books by other authors on the same subject.

His serious poetry in particular sounds like the well written, graceful verse of other poets on the same well-worn themes. Yet his first collection of serious poems, *Dreams and Dust*, served a purpose; for the effect of much of his later comic verse—*Love Sonnets of a Cave Man*, for example—depends upon his sure knowledge of such themes in just such terms. Even his parodies of free verse, over the name of "Archy the Cockroach," occasionally contain poems that are comic largely on account of their sprightly elegant meter and rhyme.

Marquis is remembered chiefly for his creation of Archy, whose ideas and adventures first filled his newspaper columns and then were collected in books. Other columns, collected in *The Almost Perfect State*, deal lightly, humorously, sometimes seriously, with Marquis's notions concerning that State. Still other columns resulted in books about "The Old Soak," who became the central character in Marquis's only successful play.

The Old Soak, Archy the Cockroach, and Mehitabel the Cat reveal Marquis's comic capabilities at their best. As Archy, Marquis views life from the underside that is, the side from which it appears ridiculous and therefore not to be taken seriously. So the incongruities, discrepancies, paradoxes, involved in this view—whether of man's morality and politics, Mehitabel's social and artistic pretensions, or any other matter—strike the reader as comic. Further, Archy's literary efforts make him ridiculous in turn, both because he is a cockroach and because he has the quite human soul of a free verse poet. For his broken typographic lines, without punctuation or capital letters, could not have been written by a cockroach and should not have been written by a poet. The comic effect is increased by the mockery of free verse and its maker.

Similarly, the Old Soak cannot be taken seriously. His views of history, the Good Book, and prohibition, together with his misspellings and malapropisms, expose his ignorance and turn him into a figure of fun. For good reason, the play about him succeeded, banal as it is, whereas Marquis's more serious plays—mainly derived from legend and history—failed. Marquis was constantly depressed because he had to do what he called hack work for a living, and believed his serious work had greater literary value. Yet his strength lies not in development of character, but in "characters," not in suspenseful action, but in absurd situations. These express his real gift, rare and rewarding in literature, the truly comic angle of vision.

—Robert F. Richards

MARVEL, Ik. See **MITCHELL, Donald Grant.**

MASTERS, Edgar Lee. Born in Garnett, Kansas, 23 August 1868; brought up in Lewistown, Illinois. Educated at schools in Lewistown; Knox College, Galesburg, Illinois, 1889; studied law in his father's law office; admitted to Illinois bar, 1891. Married 1) Helen M. Jenkins in 1898 (divorced, 1925), three children; 2) Ellen Coyne in 1926. Lawyer in Chicago, 1891–1921; then full-time writer in New York. Recipient: Twain Medal, 1927; Academy of American Poets fellowship, 1946. *Died 5 March 1950.*

PUBLICATIONS

Collections

Selected Poems, edited by Denys Thompson. 1972.

Verse

A Book of Verses. 1898.
The Blood of the Prophets. 1905.
Songs and Sonnets. 2 vols., 1910–12.
Spoon River Anthology. 1915; revised edition, 1916.
The Great Valley. 1916.
Songs and Satires. 1916.
Toward the Gulf. 1918.
Starved Rock. 1919.
Domesday Book. 1920.
The Open Sea. 1921.
The New Spoon River. 1924.
Selected Poems. 1925.
The Fate of the Jury: An Epilogue to Domesday Book. 1929.
Lichee Nuts. 1930.
The Serpent in the Wilderness. 1933.
Invisible Landscapes. 1935.
The Golden Fleece of California. 1936.
Poems of People. 1936.
The New World. 1937.
More People. 1939.
Illinois Poems. 1941.
Along the Illinois. 1942.
The Harmony of Deeper Music: Posthumous Poems, edited by Frank K. Robinson. 1976.

Plays

Maximilian. 1902.
Althea. 1907.
The Trifler. 1908.
The Leaves of the Tree. 1909.
Eileen. 1910.
The Locket. 1910.
The Bread of Idleness. 1911.
Lee: A Dramatic Poem. 1926.
Jack Kelso: A Dramatic Poem. 1928.
Gettysburg, Manila, Acoma. 1930.
Godbey: A Dramatic Poem. 1931.
Dramatic Duologues (includes *Henry VIII and Ann Boleyn, Andrew Jackson and Peggy Eaton, Aaron Burr and Madam Jumel, Rabelais and the Queen of Whims*). 1934.
Richmond: A Dramatic Poem. 1934.

Fiction

Mitch Miller. 1920.
Children of the Market Place. 1922.
Skeeters Kirby. 1923.
The Nuptial Flight. 1923.
Mirage. 1924.
Kit O'Brien. 1927.
The Tide of Time. 1937.

Other

The New Star Chamber and Other Essays. 1904.
Levy Mayer and the New Industrial Era: A Biography. 1927.
Lincoln, The Man. 1931.
The Tale of Chicago. 1933.
Vachel Lindsay: A Poet in America. 1935.
Across Spoon River: An Autobiography. 1936.
Whitman. 1937.
Mark Twain: A Portrait. 1938.
The Sangamon (on the Sangamon River). 1942.

Editor, *The Living Thoughts of Emerson*. 1940.

*

Bibliography: *Masters: Catalogue and Checklist* by Frank K. Robinson, 1970.

Critical Studies: *The Chicago Renaissance in American Letters* by Bernard Duffey, 1954; *The Vermont Background of Masters* by Kimball Flaccus, 1955; in *America's Literary Revolt* by Michael Yatron, 1959; *Spoon River Revisited* by Lois Hartley, 1963; *Masters: The Spoon River Poet and His Critics* by John T. Flanagan, 1974; *The Vision of This Land: Studies of Vachel Lindsay, Masters, and Carl Sandburg* edited by John E. Hallwas and Dennis J. Reader, 1976; *Masters: A Biographical Sketchbook* by Hardin Wallace Masters, 1978; *Beyond Spoon River: The Legacy of Masters* by Ronald Primeau, 1981; *Last Stands: Notes from Memory* by Hilary Masters, 1982; *Masters* by John H. and Margaret M. Wrenn, 1983.

* * *

One of the ancient Greek poets has written: "No man knows happiness; all men / Learn misery who live beneath the sun," thereby anticipating the spirit of Edgar Lee Masters's *Spoon River Anthology*. Though the book was brilliantly successful, the road to it was a long and arduous one. Seventeen years earlier Masters's first book of poems was an ignominious failure. The next few books were also unsuccessful. By this date the poet was a well-known lawyer, a robust man about town in Chicago who had made an unsuitable marriage but never allowed matrimony to interfere with his libertine instincts. The contrast between the poems, classic in form and hackneyed in thought, and their lusty author led one literary friend of Masters, the editor of *Reedy's Mirror*, to nudge him in the direction of a more original subject-matter. In any case, at the age of 45, Masters had failed at poetry, the one great passion of his life, and in his personal life. His one transcendent gift, fascination with human nature and insight into its workings, had found expression only in his legal career where he had espoused the cause of working-class victims of capitalist greed.

This was the situation in May 1914, when the poet's mother arrived to visit him. According to Masters, this lady was witty, acutely observant, and "full of divinations" into the lives of the townspeople they had known in Petersburg and Lewistown, Illinois. Mother and son reviewed these lives, reviving emotions and interests that had long been dormant in the poet's mind. The result was the sudden eruption of his latent gifts as chronicler of a whole community of inter-related lives. Between May and December, though under heavy pressure from his legal duties, Masters composed the 214 epitaphs that were published that year in *Reedy's Mirror*. Other than the memory of his neighbors, the chief sources of inspiration were the polished epigrams of the *Greek Anthology* and the stimulus of the American free verse revolt that had just burst on a startled, genteel reading public. These three sources, along with the sobering reflections on human mortality induced by his mother's visit, produced "the most read and talked of volume of poetry that has ever been written in America."

Five years after the publication of *Spoon River*, Masters retired from the law and devoted himself to the writing of thirty or more books of poetry, novels, biographies, and Illinois history and geography. Though he showed a dogged determination to succeed, he never caught fire again. His first great achievement was his last, and the remaining 35 years of his life were an embarrassing anticlimax as his first 45 were a despairing preparation. Masters's own life, which he includes in his book under the name Webster Ford, was one of the most curious and ironical of the tales he tells there.

The anthology, as expanded and republished in 1916, contains a short prologue, "The Hill," and 243 individual epitaphs. The verses, of a marvelous conciseness and vitality, relate only the most essential features of the speakers' lives. Each soul, speaking for himself from the grave, bares his innermost nature and the secrets of his life, his own self-portrait being qualified by the words of those with whom his fate was interlocked, so that nineteen separate story lines are developed. Each epitaph has its own tone and style; each speaker treats the climactic experiences or insights of his life. Depending on the character of the speaker, the language varies from mystical utterance downwards to sonorous rhetoric and racy colloquialism. The criticism that the style is prosy and flat, made by Floyd Dell and others when the book first appeared, is traceable to the lack of conventional prettiness in meter and rhyme. Though rarely "pretty," many of the poems are written in a highly imaginative metaphoric style, all are freshly conceived on the basis of a unifying rhetorical design with ample use of every form of verbal patterning, many are haunting, and some contain images of real beauty.

Without the power of its language, *Spoon River* would never have aroused its readers as it did. But its essence is in its portraiture. As few other authors have done, and no other author, perhaps, in the compass of a single book, Masters produced a "summation" and "universal depiction of life." Every variety of human nature is represented: celebrants at life's feast and neurasthenics, rowdies and lovers, pious Christians and atheists, rapists and whores, society women and laundresses, scientists and factory hands, clairvoyants, preachers, and a stable boy who sees the face of God. One of the largest groups is the philosophers. Masters was a zealous scholar and had read widely in several languages. Along with the anti-Christian and libertarian elements in his make-up, there was also the social idealist, the cosmic optimist, and the mystic that he counted as his essential self. The epitaphs of the philosophers are usually limited to one strand of thought from which one may infer their life and character, and their reflections are framed in such a way that they are as dramatic as the life histories.

Two criticisms of Masters should be considered here. The first is that the poet is preoccupied with sex, and much of the anthology is sordid and obscene. This charge, originating with Amy Lowell and others, is curious because there are only a dozen poems that are chiefly concerned with sex, none of these is salacious, and they tend to show that the wages of sin are death. The basis of the complaint lies in the candor with which Masters treats sex wherever it appears in life. Readers had been conditioned to literature in which the subject-matter was not actual life but a given writer's conception of it so that much of the earth and roots had been removed—as well as the uppermost reaches of branches that were beyond the interests of a workaday world. One of the novelties of Masters's treatment was to eliminate authorial censorship and to allow his characters, based as they were on real-life persons, to speak honestly of their lives. Though this was not his intention, the result was the fist exposé of village life, which set a new pattern for literature, while the poet's views are said to have influenced subsequent writing between the two world wars.

According to the second objection, the poet falsified the American midwestern town by presenting an overly sensationalistic and pessimistic account of its life. It is true that the incidence of crime and sudden death is greater than one would normally find, but Masters was not writing a sociological report. The epitaphs taken together form a highly patterned comical tragedy that represents life as it works on the human imagination. At some moment all of these disasters actually happen to someone, but the book, as Alice Henderson remarked, is also steeped in a "flaming idealism." There are many heroes and noble souls, and the final impression that it makes is of the dignity, stoic courage, and resilience of humanity in its hapless "fool's errand" to the grave. In writing these portraits, Masters creates the bond of understanding and sympathy with a many-faced humanity that motivated his own legal work for luckless victims of circumstances.

—Glenn Richard Ruihley

MATHER, Cotton. Born in Boston, Massachusetts, 12 February 1663; son of the clergyman and writer Increase Mather. Educated at home and at Boston Latin School; Harvard University, Cambridge, Massachusetts, 1675–78, A.B. 1678; studied medicine, 1679–80, M.A. 1681. Married 1) Abigail Phillips in 1686 (died, 1702), nine children; 2)Elizabeth Clark Hubbard in 1703 (died, 1713), six children; 3) Lydia Lee George in 1715. Assistant, 1680–85 (ordained, 1685), teacher, 1685–1723, and minister, 1723–28, 2nd Congregational Church (Old North Church), Boston. A leader in colony's rebellion against British governor Sir Edmund Andros, 1689. Fellow, Harvard University, 1690–1703: appointed president of Harvard, 1703, but appointment overruled; involved with Connecticut College (later Yale University): appointed president, 1721 (declined). D.D.: University of Glasgow, Scotland, 1710. Member, Royal Society (London), 1713 (first American-born member). *Died 13 February 1728.*

PUBLICATIONS

Collections

Selections, edited by Kenneth B. Murdock. 1926.
Selected Letters, edited by Kenneth Silverman. 1971.

Works (selection)

A Poem Dedicated to the Memory of Urian Oakes. 1682.
The Boston Ephemeris: An Almanack. 1683.
An Elegy on Nathaniel Collins. 1685.
The Call of the Gospel. 1686.
Military Duties Recommended to an Artillery Company. 1687.
Early Piety Exemplified. 1689.
The Declaration of the Gentlemen. 1689.
Work upon the Ark. 1689.
Memorable Providences, Relating to Witchcrafts and Possessions. 1689; in *Narratives of the Witchcraft Cases 1648–1706*, edited by George Lincoln Burr, 1914.
The Present State of New-England. 1690.
A Companion for Communicants. 1690.
The Way to Prosperity. 1690.
The Wonderful Works of God Commemorated. 1690.
Little Flocks Guarded Against Grievous Wolves. 1691.
Some Considerations on the Bills of Credit. 1691.
The Triumphs of the Reformed Religion in America. 1691; as *The Life and Death of the Renowned Mr. John Eliot*, 1691.
Blessed Unions. 1692.
Fair Weather. 1692.
A Midnight Cry. 1692.
Preparatory Meditations upon the Day of Judgment, with *Great Day of Judgment*, by Samuel Lee. 1692.
Ornaments for the Daughters of Zion. 1692.
The Return of Several Ministers (on the Salem witchcraft trials). 1692.
The Wonders of the Invisible World (on the Salem witchcraft trials). 1692; in *Narratives of the Witchcraft Cases 1648–1706*, edited by George Lincoln Burr, 1914.
Winter-Meditations. 1693.
The Short History of New-England. 1694.
Early Religion Urged. 1694.
Durable Riches. 1695.
Brontologia Sacra. 1695.
Johannes in Eremo. 1695.
Piscator Evangelicus; or, The Life of Mr. Thomas Hooker. 1695.
Things for a Distressed People to Think Upon. 1696.
Songs of the Redeemed: A Book of Hymns. 1697.
Humiliations Followed with Deliverances. 1697.
Pietas in Patriam: The Life of His Excellency Sir William Phips. 1697; as *The Life of Sir William Phips*, edited by Mark Van Doren, 1929.
The Bostonian Ebenezer: Some Historical Remarks on the State of Boston. 1698.
Eleutheria; or, An Idea of the Reformation in England. 1698.
Decennium Luctuosum. 1699; in *Narratives of the Indian Wars 1675–1699*, edited by Charles Henry Lincoln, 1913.
Pillars of Salt: An History of Some Criminals Executed in This Land for Capital Crimes. 1699.
A Family Well-Ordered. 1699.
A Pillar of Gratitude. 1700.
The Everlasting Gospel. 1700.
The Religious Mariner. 1700.
An Epistle to the Christian Indians. 1700.
A Monitory and Hortatory Letter to Those English Who Debauch the Indians by Selling Strong Drink unto Them. 1700.
A Warning to the Flocks. 1700.
Reasonable Religion. 1700.
A Collection of Some of the Many Offensive Matters Contained in The Order of the Gospel Revived. 1701.
An Advice to the Churches of the Faithful. 1702.
Christianus per Ignem. 1702.
Proposals for the Preservation of Religion in the Churches. 1702.
Magnalia Christi Americana; or, The Ecclesiastical History of New-England. 1702; edited by Thomas Robbins, 2 vols., 1853–55; books 1–2 edited by Kenneth B. Murdock, 1977.
Wholesome Words. 1702(?).
A Faithful Man Described and Rewarded (on Michael Wigglesworth). 1705.
Family-Religion Excited and Assisted. 1705.
Hatchets to Hew Down the Tree of Sin. 1705.
A Letter about the Present State of Christianity among the Christianized Indians. 1705.
Lex Mercatoria; or, Just Rules of Commerce Declared. 1705.
The Negro Christianized. 1706.
Good Fetched Out of Evil (captivity narratives). 1706.
The Best Ornaments of Youth. 1707.
A Memorial of the Present Deplorable State of New-England. 1707.
Frontiers Well-Defended. 1707.
A Golden Curb for the Mouth. 1707.
The Soldier Told What He Shall Do. 1707.
Corderius Americanus: An Essay upon the Good Education of Children. 1708.
The Deplorable State of New-England. 1708.
Winthropi Justa. 1708.
The Sailor's Companion. 1709.
Nehemiah: A Brief Essay on Divine Consolations. 1710.
Theopolis Americana. 1710.
Bonifacius: An Essay upon the Good. 1710; as *Essays to Do Good*, edited by George Burder, 1807; edited by David Levin, 1966.
Christianity Demonstrated. 1710.
Dust and Ashes: An Essay upon Repentance. 1710.
Elizabeth in Her Holy Retirement. 1710.
The Heavenly Conversation. 1710.
Orphanotrophium; or, Orphans Well-Provided For. 1711.
Persuasions from the Terror of the Lord. 1711.
A Letter about Good Management under the Distemper of Measles. 1713.
Duodecennium Luctuosum. 1714.
A New Offer to the Lovers of Religion and Learning. 1714(?).
The Stone Cut Out from the Mountain/Lapis e Monte Excisus. 1716.
Fair Dealing Between Debtor and Creditor. 1716.
Malachi. 1717.
Victorina. 1717.
Psalterium Americanum. 1718.
A Voice from Heaven. 1719.
Concio ad Populum. 1719.
Virgilius. 1719.
Mirabilia Dei. 1719.
News from Robinson Cruso's Island (possibly not by Mather). 1720.
The Christian Philosopher. 1720.
The Accomplished Singer. 1721.
Silentiarius. 1721.
India Christiana. 1721.
Some Account of Inoculating the Small Pox, with Zabdiel Boylston. 1721.
The Angel of Bethesda. 1722; edited by Gordon W. Jones,

1972.
Friendly Debate, with Isaac Greenwood. 1722.
A Father Departing. 1723.
Coelestinus: A Conversation in Heaven. 1723.
The Voice of God in a Tempest. 1723.
Parentator (on Increase Mather). 1724.
The Words of Understanding. 1724.
Une Grande Voix du Ciel à la France. 1725.
The Palm-Bearers. 1725.
El-Shaddai. 1725.
Vital Christianity. 1725.
A Proposal for an Evangelical Treasury. 1725.
Zalmonah. 1725.
Manuductio ad Ministerium. 1726.
Fasciculus Viventium. 1726.
Ratio Disciplinae Fratrum Nov Anglorum: A Faithful Account of the Discipline Professed and Practiced in the Churches of New-England. 1726.
The Vial Poured Out upon the Sea: A Remarkable Relation of Certain Pirates. 1726.
A Good Old Age. 1726.
Hatzar-Maveth. 1726.
The Instructor. 1726.
Some Seasonable Advice unto the Poor. 1726.
Suspiria Vinctorum. 1726.
Terra Beata. 1726.
Agricola; or, The Religious Husbandman. 1727.
The Terror of the Lord: Some Account of the Earthquake That Shook New-England. 1727.
Boanerges: A Short Essay to Preserve and Strengthen the Good Impressions Produced by Earthquakes. 1727.
Christian Loyalty. 1727.
The Balance of the Sanctuary. 1727.
Baptismal Piety. 1727.
Hor-Hagidgad. 1727.
Signatus. 1727.
The Mystical Marriage. 1728.
Diluvium Ignis. 1730.
Diary 1681–1724, edited by Worthington Chauncey Ford. 2 vols., 1911–12.
The Diary for the Year 1712, edited by William R. Manierre II. 1964.
Paterna: The Autobiography, edited by Ronald A. Bosco. 1976.

*

Bibliography: *Mather: A Bibliography of His Works* by Thomas J. Holmes, 3 vols., 1940.

Critical Studies: *The Mathers: Three Generations of Puritan Intellectuals 1596–1728* by Robert Middlekauff, 1971; *Mather: The Young Life of the Lord's Remembrancer 1663–1703* by David Levin, 1978; *Mather* by Babette Levy, 1979; *The Life and Times of Mather* by Kenneth Silverman, 1984; *Mather and Benjamin Franklin: The Price of Representative Personality* by Mitchell Robert Breitwieser, 1984.

* * *

Cotton Mather was viewed as a stereotyped New England puritan before the stereotype existed. A Harvard student at age eleven, already proficient in Latin, Greek, and Hebrew, he was regarded as a prig by his fellow students. His congregants and acquaintances in later life were largely in agreement with this early assessment of his character, for while respected as a worthy and learned heir to New England's most illustrious dynasty of scholars and divines, that dynasty's mission of creating in New England a New Jerusalem was fading in the light of new commercial concerns and 18th-century rationalism. More receptive to the new thinking than is usually recognized, Mather was still very much aware of what was expected of him and strove, perhaps too hard, to compensate for a speech impediment, a melancholy disposition, and a number of personal tragedies, in carrying out the role in which God had cast him.

As one on whom heredity had placed the mantle of a prophet to the chosen in the new Israel of Massachusetts, Mather spoke with a prophet's self-assurance, and he spoke often. He published over 400 works and left volumes of manuscripts that have never seen print. Indeed, some critics have suggested that his position in American letters is owed less to the quality of his work than to the quantity; so much from so famous a name could not but have some effect on colonial American culture and therefore at least an indirect influence on the generations that followed. Recent criticism has treated him somewhat more kindly. To be sure, most readers still remember the infamous *The Wonders of the Invisible World*, a treatise on witchcraft largely supportive of the Salem witch trials. The last gasp of the superstitious horror that had plagued Europe for centuries, Mather's book should at least be credited for its insistence on careful evidence rather than torture in such proceedings.

Certainly the work that has received the most critical attention is *Magnalia Christi Americana*, a monumental history of the first century of the Massachusetts colony. Even this, his major literary effort, has attracted such adjectives of critical praise as bigoted, ponderous, pompous, and superstitious. It is all of these, but its flaws are somewhat less glaring if approached as something other than history. As a historian, Mather did not weigh the significance of his material. Witches, church leaders, even criminals appear in equal prominence; folklore bleeds into fact, and the facts are too often just plain wrong. Moreover, the whole is an expression of the long-ago discarded theory of history as the working out of God's will. As a reliable record of the American puritan theocracy, the *Magnalia* fails. Modern critics, then, have had to consider whether it can stand, as a few supposedly factual narratives can, as a work of imaginative literature. Viewed as an allegorical epic on the theme of a new dispensation, a divine covenant with a new Israel that will prepare the world for the Messiah's reappearance, the *Magnalia* fares better. The elements of the narrative need not be weighed on the scale of mundane human significance; the episodes are not significant as facts. The *Magnalia* is a cloud of exempla revolving around the single, grand theme of the old covenant renewed.

Mather liked the ornate style popular in the 17th century, and often he is pompous for pomposity's sake, but the high style of the *Magnalia* seems less inappropriate when heard as an epic rather than historical voice. Mather was a great appreciator of Milton; passages from *Paradise Lost* are quoted and adapted for the *Magnalia*. Critics have had trouble with Milton's style too, but considering the grandeur of the theme, decorum has argued for the forgiveness of his linguistic excesses. However, Milton's theme, on close scrutiny protestant and puritan to be sure, was still catholic enough to fit into the context of general Christianity. Mather's theme of a new Israel in America, while grand too, was tied to the destiny of a particular people in a particular time and place. Milton dealt with God in the universe; Mather put Him in New England, and in narrowing the thematic focus, so diminished the need for the style he chose that in the view of most critics intended magnificence still rings as pomposity and even bombast.

Some mention should be made of Mather as a writer of sermons, for two-thirds of his published works are of this genre. Considerably less baroque than the *Magnalia*, they are now all but unread. While reflective of traditional puritan themes, the sermons read in the context of Mather's own diary are more personal than might at first be suspected and depict the same earthly concerns in conflict with spiritual aspirations that the moody and imaginative author experienced throughout his life. As he coped with his own doubts by deliberately accentuating in thought and conduct the puritan ideals of which he was the last and greatest spokesman, so the sermons echo with a conscious and too often dull self-righteousness that renders them even less readable as literature than the histories.

In 1963 the *Magnalia* was chosen as one of 1800 books from America's literary history to make up a White House library for Presidents. It sits there, one supposes, not so much as a book really to be read as a monument to a period in American history that modern students view with very mixed feelings. The literary career of that book's author is itself a monument to enormous effort on behalf of an ideal that was fading even then and like most monuments is acknowledged now only in passing.

—William J. Heim

McCARTHY, Mary (Therese). Born in Seattle, Washington, 21 June 1912; sister of the actor Kevin McCarthy. Educated at Forest Ridge Convent, Seattle; Annie Wright Seminary, Tacoma, Washington; Vassar College, Poughkeepsie, New York, A.B. 1933 (Phi Beta Kappa). Married 1) Harold Johnsrud in 1933 (divorced, 1936); 2) Edmund Wilson *q.v.*, in 1938 (divorced, 1946), one son; 3) Bowden Broadwater in 1946 (divorced, 1961); 4) James Raymond West in 1961. Editor, Covici Friede, publishers, New York, 1936–38; editor, 1937–38, and drama critic, 1937–62, *Partisan Review*, New York, and New Brunswick, New Jersey; Instructor, Bard College, Annandale-on-Hudson, New York, 1945–46, and Sarah Lawrence College, Bronxville, New York, 1948; Northcliffe Lecturer, University College, London, 1980; President's Distinguished Visitor, Vassar College, 1982. Recipient: Guggenheim fellowship, 1949, 1959; American Academy grant, 1957; National Medal for Literature, 1984; MacDowell Medal, 1984. D.Let.: Syracuse University, New York, 1973; Bard College, 1976; D.Litt.: University of Hull, Yorkshire, 1974; Bowdoin College, Brunswick, Maine, 1981; University of Maine, Orono, 1982. Member, American Academy. Lives in Castine, Maine.

PUBLICATIONS

Fiction

The Company She Keeps. 1942.
The Oasis. 1949; as *A Source of Embarrassment*, 1950.
Cast a Cold Eye (stories). 1950.
The Groves of Academe. 1952.
A Charmed Life. 1955.
The Group. 1963.
Birds of America. 1971.
Cannibals and Missionaries. 1979.
The Hounds of Summer and Other Stories. 1981.

Other

Sights and Spectacles 1937–1956. 1956; as *Sights and Spectacles: Theatre Chronicles 1937–1958*, 1959; augmented edition, as *Theatre Chronicles 1937–1962*, 1963.
Venice Observed: Comments on Venetian Civilization. 1956.
Memories of a Catholic Girlhood. 1957.
The Stones of Florence. 1959.
On the Contrary (essays). 1961.
The Humanist in the Bathtub (essays). 1964.
Vietnam. 1967.
Hanoi. 1968.
The Writing on the Wall and Other Literary Essays. 1970.
Medina. 1972.
The Mask of State: Watergate Portraits. 1974.
The Seventeenth Degree. 1974.
Can There Be a Gothic Literature? (lecture). 1975.
Ideas and the Novel. 1980.
La Traviata (story adaptation), music by Verdi. 1983.
Occasional Prose. 1985.

Translator, *The Iliad; or, the Poem of Force*, by Simone Weil. 1948.
Translator, *On the Iliad*, by Rachel Bespaloff. 1948.

*

Bibliography: *McCarthy: A Bibliography* by Sherli Goldman, 1968.

Critical Studies: *McCarthy* by Barbara McKenzie, 1966; *The Company She Kept* by Doris Grumbach, 1967; *McCarthy* by Irvin Stock, 1968; *McCarthy* by Willene Schaefer Hardy, 1981.

* * *

Mary McCarthy belongs to that set of modern American authors who appear at first to be circumscribed by their own times. Her first novel, *The Company She Keeps*, is the most charming and vigorous of her novels in spite of being almost too conscious of the political and social milieu of Greenwich Village. *The Company She Keeps* is light reading, but, in terms of plot, a daring experiment. It contains six chapters, each differing from the others in time and place, with one personality to hold the stories together. The strength of the personality, of the viewing eye, and the consistency of outlook which that eye provides, form the only cohesion in the "novel." It has about it the feel of the early experiments in surrealist fiction and at the same time the freshness and youthful vitality in the early stories of Fitzgerald. McCarthy has captured, through details, the spirit of her generation just as surely. In the historical-social context, one learns more from writers like McCarthy and Fitzgerald than from our more "literary" writers. *The Company She Keeps* also offers a fascinating glimpse of McCarthy's powers as a journalist. Her critical essays are collected in *On the Contrary*, *The Writing on the Wall*, *Ideas and the Novel*, and *Occasional Prose*. Her *Theatre Chronicles*, begun in the 1930's, offer the same strong command and vigor, as well as a truly original understanding and analysis of the theatre. The essay on *Macbeth* in *The Writing on the Wall* is a perfect example of the ways McCarthy perceives connections and modern relevancy that startle and enlighten the reader.

Her essays show what kind of professor she must have been: funny, inventive, clever, determined to catch at the sparkling threads of every idea. With *The Groves of Academe*, she created a small scandal with a biting portrait of a college President struggling with the politics of his English Department. *The Groves of Academe* and her fourth novel, *A Charmed Life*, are probably meant to be allegories—the former of Senator Joseph McCarthy's communist witch-hunts, and the latter of a moral and philosophical sort where generalizations meant to apply to all of us are drawn out of a small community. *A Charmed Life* is a magnificent book—unlimited by time or distracting political concepts, it concerns what happens to people who retire from the world to devote themselves to something, in this case Art. It is a gentle but shocking reminder to modern man that he cannot hide from the world out of sensibility or devotion to an unworldly goal; life remains dangerous. The characters in this novel come to life more thoroughly than the eight heroines of *The Group*, McCarthy's most famous novel. *The Group* was a great success when it appeared: its vision of life affected an entire generation. McCarthy's autobiography, *Memories of a Catholic Girlhood*, is a beautiful, classic, searching piece of writing. Along with *A Charmed Life*, *Memories* is the best showcase for her prose.

McCarthy has always walked a very delicate line between her knowledge that the modern novel is plotless and between her love for the world and its myriad details. *The Company She Keeps* is a very carefully plotted novel, but it does not follow a time-line; *The Groves of Academe* has a traditional novelistic conception but, lacking the freewheeling movement of *Company*, is less successful; *A Charmed Life* is positioned insecurely but brilliantly on the line between the Dickensian novel of action and detail and the plotless modern impressionistic novel: it is in some senses a play in which the dramatic conflict is between clashing ideas and philosophies; *The Group* returns to a novel form that is more disjointed but richer of plot. *Birds of America* was an interesting idea that somehow did not take form, but it is sweet, funny, and very clever.

—Brady Nordland

McCULLERS, (Lula) Carson (née Smith). Born in Columbus, Georgia, 19 February 1917. Educated at Columbus High School, graduated 1933; attended classes at Columbia University, New York, and New York University, 1934–36. Married James Reeves McCullers, Jr., in 1937 (divorced, 1941); remarried in 1945 (died, 1953). Lived in Charlotte, 1937–38, and Fayetteville, 1938–39, both North Carolina, and in New York City, 1940–44, and Nyack, New York after 1944. Recipient: Bread Loaf Writers Conference fellowship, 1940; Guggenheim fellowship, 1942, 1946; American Academy grant, 1943; New York Drama Critics Circle award, 1950; Donaldson Award, for drama, 1950; Theatre Club Gold Medal, 1950; University of Mississippi grant, 1966; Bellamann Award, 1967. Member, American Academy, 1952. *Died 29 September 1967.*

PUBLICATIONS

Fiction

The Heart Is a Lonely Hunter. 1940.
Reflections in a Golden Eye. 1941.
The Member of the Wedding. 1946.
The Ballad of the Sad Café: The Novels and Stories of McCullers. 1951; as *Collected Short Stories*, 1961; as *The Shorter Novels and Stories of McCullers*, 1972.
Seven (stories). 1954.
Clock Without Hands. 1961.

Plays

The Member of the Wedding, from her own novel (produced 1949). 1951.
The Square Root of Wonderful (produced 1957). 1958.

Television Plays: *The Invisible Wall*, from her story "The Sojourner," 1953; *The Sojourner*, from her own story, 1964.

Verse

The Twisted Trinity, music by David Diamond. 1946.
Sweet as a Pickle and Clean as a Pig (for children). 1964.

Other

The Mortgaged Heart (uncollected writings), edited by Margarita G. Smith. 1971.

*

Bibliography: *Katherine Anne Porter and McCullers: A Reference Guide* by Robert F. Kiernan, 1976; *McCullers: A Descriptive Listing and Annotated Bibliography of Criticism* by Adrian M. Shapiro, Jackson R. Bryer, and Kathleen Field, 1980.

Critical Studies: *McCullers: Her Life and Work* by Oliver Evans, 1965, as *The Ballad of McCullers*, 1966; *McCullers* by Lawrence Graver, 1969; *McCullers* by Dale Edmonds, 1969; *The Lonely Hunter: A Biography of McCullers* by Virginia Spencer Carr, 1975; *McCullers* by Richard M. Cook, 1975; *McCullers' The Member of the Wedding: Aspects of Structure and Style* by Eleanor Wikborg, 1975; *McCullers* by Margaret B. McDowell, 1980.

* * *

Although severe illness—strokes, heart disease, paralysis, and eventually cancer—limited Carson McCullers's productivity after the age of thirty, she had already achieved both critical and popular acclaim in several genres—the novel, the novella, the short story, and the drama. Her first three novels appeared in six years, each selling over half a million copies. Her play based on *The Member of the Wedding* ran for over a year on Broadway and then became a successful film, as did her first two novels.

McCullers regarded all her major works as southern, maintaining that authors always reflect the place of their birth and cannot escape from its "voices and foliage and memory." All her novels are set in Georgia. Though she repeatedly returned to the south, she retained an antagonism toward it as a region where one might be regarded as worth "no more than a load of hay": her treatment of southern life, thus, is never sentimental. Her most effective use of southern folklore occurs in the blending of realism and fantasy in *The Ballad of the Sad Café*. Problems of unemployed transients and of workers in southern textile mills loom in the background of *The Heart Is a Lonely Hunter* and *The Ballad of the Sad Café*. Richard Wright praised her treatment of southern blacks in *The Heart Is a Lonely Hunter*. Her portrayal of Berenice and her black friends and relatives in *The Member of the Wedding* brought wide acclaim. In her last novel, *Clock Without Hands*, she less effectively portrayed Sherman Pew, a blue-eyed black homosexual. However, even in this novel, her depiction of Sherman Jones's execution; the police action in the death of Grown Boy, a retarded adolescent; and the plight of the legless beggar, Wagon, provide a striking contrast between the struggles of southern blacks and the mindlessness of segregationist Judge Clane.

Because she is southern, some have assumed that the bizarre situations and grotesque characters in *Reflections in a Golden Eye* and *The Ballad of the Sad Café* categorize McCullers as a writer of sensational and comic southern gothic. Actually her serious implications of uncontrollable evil link these works instead with the gothic tales of the Danish Isak Dinesen, greatly admired by McCullers, and with the fiction of D.H. Lawrence which explores the psychic origins of deviant or irrational behavior. In McCullers's novels, military regimentation, athletic prowess, police cruelty, imprisonment, and even executions cannot change the course of perverse human nature or mindless fate.

Though a master of the realistic, McCullers moved always toward symbolic, allegorical, and philosophical ramifications as she analyzed the elemental realities confronting her characters. She repeats a few central themes: the individual's frustrated love for a less worthy person; the universality of loneliness; love pursued as the only cure for loneliness; love as the intensifier of loneliness; the rare existence of selfless love; the evanescence of even the most affectionate relationship; and the connection between isolation and evil. In nearly every work conflict occurs within an individual who longs for close identification with others, but at the same time struggles for freedom, lack of responsibility, and self-centered control of outside forces. Such conflict is most forcefully presented in Frankie Addams in *The Member of the Wedding* and Miss Amelia in *The Ballad of the Sad Café*. Related to this conflict is the agonizing loneliness that most of McCullers's characters experience and their inability to communicate their deep feelings. In *The Heart Is a Lonely Hunter*, two deaf-mutes symbolize such inability in all the other characters. Elgee Williams, the silent soldier in *Reflections in a Golden Eye*, functions similarly as he lurks in the night staring in the window at the sleeping wife of an army officer. In *The Member of the Wedding*, Frankie looks toward a perfect intuitive and wordless understanding in the three-person wedding she envisions that will unite her with her brother and his bride. Berenice looks back toward her perfect marriage, with the now dead Ludie, where words of love were not needed. Frankie and Berenice have occasional moments of perfect wordless communication but ordinarily speak in parallel monologues rather than to one another. In *Clock Without Hands*, Malone suffers needlessly alone for months because he cannot share the news of his impending death with his family.

Ultimately, the universality of music pervasively informs metaphor and background in McCullers's work more than does a sense of her geographical region. Her eight hours of daily piano practice in childhood and adolescence surely intensified McCullers's persistent sense of being different from others, as it isolated her from her peers. She clearly implies this in her first story, "Wunderkind," written when she was sixteen. The other two young girls in her novels—Mick Kelly in *The Heart Is a Lonely Hunter* and Frankie in *The Member of the Wedding*—lack McCullers's prodigious musical talent, but both are almost obsessively preoccupied with music. Mick hides under windows in the dark to hear music from her neighbors' radios and listens to the phonograph owned by a tenant in her mother's boarding house. She builds a violin from a cigar box, and she grieves about having to quit school, mainly because she can no longer try to play the piano in the empty gym. Frankie complains about "sweet sleazy music" on the kitchen radio; she fears she will go mad when the piano tuner fails to finish a scale and when a trombonist in a neighboring house interrupts a compelling phrase in a blues song. She finds comfort in the rhythm of a small motor she has salvaged for her room. McCullers assumed a connection between her work and her musical understanding. Her first novel was outlined for the publisher completely in musical, rather than literary, terms, as if it were a symphony. She insisted that *The Member of the Wedding*—both as novel and stage play—had to possess "precision and harmony." Because of this, she was able to present effectively the subtleties of the separate personalities warring within both Frankie and Berenice and project the internal action and philosophical implications demanded by the drama for which Tennessee Williams had paved the way in the theaters of the 1950's.

—Margaret B. McDowell

See the essay on *The Member of the Wedding*.

McKAY, Claude. Born Festus Claudius McKay in Sunny Ville, Clarendon Parish, Jamaica, 15 September 1889. Educated at a grammar school in Jamaica; Tuskegee Institute, Alabama, 1912; Kansas State College, Manhattan, 1913–14. Married Eulalie Imelda Edwards in 1914 (separated, 1914); one daughter. Apprentice cabinet-maker and wheelwright, 1907–08; joined Jamaican Constabulary, 1909, and policeman in Spanish Town, Jamaica, 1911–12; moved to New York, worked at various jobs and opened a restaurant, 1914; staff member, *Workers' Dreadnought* communist newspaper, London, 1919–20; associate editor, 1921–22, and co-editor, 1922, *Liberator*, New York; lived in the Soviet Union, 1922–23, and Europe (mainly France) and Tangier, 1923–34; laborer in welfare camp, New York, 1934–35; writer for the Works Progress Administration until 1939; worked in a shipbuilding yard, 1943; joined Catholic Church, 1944, and worked for National Catholic Youth Organization, Chicago, 1944–48. Recipient: Harmon prize, 1929. *Died 22 May 1948.*

PUBLICATIONS

Collections

Selected Poems. 1953.
The Passion of McKay: Selected Poetry and Prose 1912–1948, edited by Wayne Cooper. 1973.

My Green Hills of Jamaica, and Five Jamaican Short Stories, edited by Mervyn Morris. 1979.

Verse

Constab Ballads. 1912.
Songs of Jamaica. 1912.
Spring in New Hampshire and Other Poems. 1920.
Harlem Shadows. 1922.
The Dialect Poetry. 1972.

Fiction

Sud Linchom (in Russian). 1925; translated as *Trial by Lynching: Stories about Negro Life in North America*, edited by A.L. McLeod, 1977.
Home to Harlem. 1928.
Banjo: A Story Without a Plot. 1929.
Gingertown (stories). 1932.
Banana Bottom. 1933.

Other

Negry v Amerike (in Russian). 1923; translated as *The Negroes in America*, edited by A.L. McLeod, 1979.
A Long Way from Home (autobiography). 1937.
Harlem: Negro Metropolis. 1940.

*

Bibliography: by Manuel D. Lopez, in *Bulletin of Bibliography*, October-December 1972.

Critical Studies: *Roots of Negro Racial Consciousness: Three Harlem Renaissance Authors* by Stephen H. Bronz, 1964; *The West Indian Novel and Its Background* by Kenneth Ramchand, 1970; *McKay: The Black Poet at War* by Addison Gayle, Jr., 1972; *McKay* by James R. Giles, 1976; *McKay: Rebel Sojourner in the Harlem Renaissance* by Wayne F. Cooper, 1987.

* * *

Claude McKay attempted throughout his career to resolve the complexities surrounding the black man's paradoxical situation. A widely travelled man, he lived for twelve years (1922–1934) in Britain, Russia, Germany, France, Spain, and Morocco. It is during these years that a new wave of Afro-American writing, now widely known as the Harlem Renaissance, spread across America. McKay is generally credited with having inspired the Renaissance with his militant poem "If We Must Die" (1919) when the nation was gripped with a red scare and race riots in the northern cities. Later, however, the self-exiled McKay developed an ambivalent relationship with the New Negroes of the 1920's; he did not share the "social uplift" philosophy of Alain Locke and W.E.B. DuBois although he had affinities as writer with Jean Toomer, Langston Hughes and Zora Neale Hurston. McKay is also considered a pioneer in the development of West Indian fiction, though he never returned to the land of his birth, Jamaica, having left it at age 23. Today, many regard his fiction as his most valuable contribution, but McKay also published four collections of poems, an autobiography, many essays, and a sociological study of Harlem.

It is as a poet that McKay first won attention in both the West Indies and the United States. In 1912, before he went to Kansas as an agriculture student (hoping to become the prophet of scientific farming on his return home!), he had published two volumes of dialect verse, *Songs of Jamaica* and *Constab Ballads*, and won himself a reputation as "the Jamaican Bobby Burns." Soon, he was made aware of the intricacies of American racial prejudice and he decided to cast his lot with working-class Afro-Americans. McKay was both stimulated and angered by the American environment—"Although she feeds me bread of bitterness / . . . I love this cultured hell that tests my youth!" ("America"). His background in the Jamaican society where the blacks formed a majority often gave him an edge as poet-observer over black American artists whose careers were sometimes wrecked by a debilitating bitterness. In his poems of personal love and racial protest, McKay gave strong expression to joy and anger, pride and stoicism. "If We Must Die," although not his best poem, won him great popularity because it powerfully evoked, in lines charged with emotion, the militant mood of Afro-American communities over the treatment meted out to black soldiers returning from World War I. The poem achieved a kind of universality in spite of its trite diction, as was well-demonstrated when Winston Churchill related it to the Allied cause by reading it to the House of Commons during World War II.

McKay's influence on later black poetry is measured better by the power of his sentiment than by any innovations in form, style or diction. McKay empathises with the sufferings of working-class blacks in the many poems of *Harlem Shadows*, but he succeeds best when he focusses on an individual's tragedy to protest against the forces of oppression. This is evident in poems such as "The Harlem Dancer," where a young female dancer is surrounded by a crowd of "wine-flushed, bold-eyed boys" which has no inkling of her soulful pride. In "Baptism," he express a Victorian stoicism that asserts the individual's victory through the harshest of tests. McKay often tried his hand at the sonnet form, using irregular rhyme and metre to achieve his own poetic ends. "One Year After," dealing with inter-racial love in a two-sonnet sequence, anticipates contemporary black attitudes in attributing the failure of a black-white relationship not to society's pressures but to the lover's black pride: "Not once in all our days of poignant love / Did I a single instant give to thee / My undivided being wholly free." McKay also wrote many poems about love and sex that had little to do with racial conflict and in some of these (e.g., "Flower of Love" and "A Red Flower")—as often in his fiction, especially in *Home to Harlem*—he creates erotic effects through suggestive portrayals of sexual pleasure. Yet McKay's link to more recent black literature is based primarily on his protest poems and his three novels.

McKay wrote both short stories and novels. *Gingertown*, his only collection of short stories, is important mainly as a source of clues and parallels to his development as novelist-thinker. The three novels—*Home to Harlem*, *Banjo*, and *Banana Bottom*—together form a thematic trilogy exploring the black man's special situation against the Manichean opposition between "instinct" and "intellect." *Home to Harlem* and *Banjo*, both essentially plotless novels, raise issues relating to the black's alleged primitivism, and its possible uses in an age when the fear of standardization is obsessive. The two protagonists—Jake and Banjo respectively—are rollicking roustabouts, taking life and women as they come. Their life of instinctive simplicity is, however, not without a Hemingway-like code. If they would not scab against a fellow worker, they would not be gullible enough to join a union either. As lovers, they do not permit themselves to become pimps or demean themselves to satisfy their women's masochistic desires. In the sexual metaphor that is McKay's lens in all the three novels, sexual deviations and perversions symbolize the pernicious influence of white values on black lives. In *Banana Bottom* there is a tentative resolution of these conflicts in the character of Bita Plant who (like McKay himself) despite self-hatred cannot reject native traditions completely even as she continues to find uses in her life for Western thought. Bita is, in some ways, a dramatization of the tangled thoughts on the significance of race and heritage in modern life that McKay filtered through the character of Ray, who appears in both *Home to Harlem* and *Banjo*.

There is no hint in either his autobiography, *A Long Way from Home*, or his sociological study, *Harlem: Negro Metropolis*, of McKay's conversion in 1944 to Roman Catholicism, an astonishing turnabout by any standards. McKay's autobiography is unusual in not giving any details of his personal life, although useful as a mirror to his independence in the midst of stimulating encounters with issues, places, and people (including Frank Harris, H.G. Wells, Isadora Duncan, Sinclair Lewis). The section on his Russian visit is particularly valuable in determining a phase of his uneasy relationship with the leftist movement, from the days of his association with Max Eastman and *The Liberator* to the anti-Communist sentiments of his final years. *Harlem: Negro Metropolis* offers a scathing view of Harlem's community life and the obsessive fight of its leaders against segregation. The reviewers criticized the book justifiably for its frequent failures in objectivity. Although McKay never became an apologist for capitalist imperialism, he did try in his last years to vindicate his conversion to Catholicism in his essay "On Becoming a Roman Catholic" and in many letters to his life-long friend, Max Eastman. One cannot, however, help feeling that a tired McKay surrendered his difficult search for the positive meanings of black life by giving in to the traditional discipline of the Roman Church. As he himself put it in a letter (16 October 1944) to Eastman: "It seems to me that to have a religion is very much like falling in love with a woman. You love her for her . . . Beauty, which cannot be defined."

—Amritjit Singh

MELVILLE, Herman. Born in New York City, 1 August 1819. Educated at New York Male School; Albany Academy to age 12. Married Elizabeth Knapp Shaw in 1847; two sons and two daughters. Worked from age 12 as clerk, farmhand, and schoolteacher; ship's boy on the *St. Lawrence*, bound for Liverpool, 1839–40; traveled in midwest, 1840; ordinary seaman on the whaler *Achushnet*, 1841 until he jumped ship in the Marquesas, 1842; left the islands on the Sydney whaling barque *Lucy Ann*, and jumped ship in Tahiti, 1842; harpooner on whaler *Charles and Henry*, from Nantucket, in southern Pacific, 1842–43; clerk and bookkeeper in general store, Honolulu, 1843; shipped back to Boston on U.S. Navy frigate *United States*, 1843–44; writer from 1844; lived in New York, 1847–50, and Pittsfield, Massachusetts, 1850–63; traveled in Near East and Europe, 1856–57; on lecture circuits in the U.S., 1857–60; lived in Washington, D.C., 1861–62, and in New York after 1863; district inspector of customs, New York, 1866–85. *Died 28 September 1891.*

PUBLICATIONS

Collections

Works. 16 vols., 1922–24.
Collected Poems, edited by Howard P. Vincent. 1947.
The Portable Melville, edited by Jay Leyda. 1952.
Letters, edited by Merrell R. Davis and William H. Gilman. 1960.
Selected Poems, edited by Hennig Cohen. 1964.
Great Short Works, edited by Warner Berthoff. 1966.
Writings, edited by Harrison Hayford, Hershel Parker, and G. Thomas Tanselle. 1968—
Selected Poems, edited by Robert Penn Warren. 1970.
Typee, Omoo, Mardi (Library of America), edited by G. Thomas Tanselle. 1982.
Redburn, White-Jacket, Moby-Dick (Library of America), edited by G. Thomas Tanselle. 1983.
Pierre, Israel Potter, The Confidence-Man, Tales and Billy Budd (Library of America), edited by Harrison Hayford. 1985.

Fiction

Narrative of Four Months' Residence among the Natives of a Valley in the Marquesas Islands; or, A Peep at Polynesian Life. 1846; as *Typee*, 1846; revised edition, 1846.
Omoo: A Narrative of Adventures in the South Seas. 1847.
Mardi, and a Voyage Thither. 1849.
Redburn, His First Voyage. 1849.
White Jacket; or, The World in a Man-of-War. 1850; as *White-Jacket*, 1850.
The Whale. 1851; as *Moby-Dick; or, The Whale*, 1851.
Pierre; or, The Ambiguities. 1852.
Israel Potter, His Fifty Years of Exile. 1855.
The Piazza Tales. 1856.
The Confidence-Man, His Masquerade. 1857.
The Apple-Tree Table and Other Sketches. 1922.
Billy Budd and Other Prose Pieces, edited by Raymond M. Weaver, in *Works*. 1924.

Verse

Battle-Pieces and Aspects of the War. 1866; edited by Hennig Cohen, 1963.
Clarel: A Poem, and Pilgrimage in the Holy Land. 1876; edited by Walter E. Bezanson, 1960.
John Marr and Other Sailors, with Some Sea-Pieces. 1888.
Timoleon Etc. 1891.

Other

Journal up the Straits October 11, 1856–May 5, 1857, edited by Raymond M. Weaver. 1935; edited by Howard C. Horsford, as *Journal of a Visit to Europe and the Levant*, 1955.
Journal of a Visit to London and the Continent 1849–1850, edited by Eleanor Melville Metcalf. 1948.

*

Bibliography: *The Merrill Checklist of Melville* by Howard P. Vincent, 1969; in *Bibliography of American Literature* by Jacob Blanck, 1973; *Melville: An Annotated Bibliography 1:*

1846–1930 by Brian Higgins, 1979; *Melville and the Critics: A Checklist of Criticism 1900–1978* by Jeanetta Boswell, 1981.

Critical Studies: *Melville: The Tragedy of Mind* by William E. Sedgwick, 1944; *Call Me Ishmael: A Study of Melville* by Charles Olson, 1947; *The Trying-Out of Moby-Dick* by Howard Vincent, 1949; *Melville* by Richard Chase, 1949; *Melville* by Newton Arvin, 1950; *The Melville Log: A Documentary Life of Melville 1819–1891* by Jay Leyda, 2 vols., 1951, revised edition, 1969; *Melville: A Biography* by Leon Howard, 1951; *Melville's Quarrel with God* by Lawrance Thompson, 1952; *The Fine-Hammered Steel of Melville* by Milton R. Stern, 1957; *Melville's Billy Budd and the Critics* edited by William T. Stafford, 1961, revised edition, 1968; *The Example of Melville* by Warner Berthoff, 1962; *A Reader's Guide to Melville* by James E. Miller, Jr., 1962; *Melville* by Tyrus Hillway, 1963, revised edition, 1979; *Ishmael's White World: A Phenomenological Reading of Moby-Dick* by Paul Brodtkorb, Jr., 1965; *Melville's Thematics of Form: The Great Art of Telling the Truth* by Edgar A. Dryden, 1968; *Plots and Characters in the Fiction and Narrative Poetry of Melville* by Robert L. Gale, 1969; *Melville: The Ironic Diagram* by John D. Seelye, 1970; *Moby-Dick as Doubloon: Essays and Extracts 1851–1970* edited by Hershel Parker and Harrison Hayford, 1970; *An Artist in the Rigging: The Early Works of Melville*, 1972, *Melville's Short Fiction*, 1977, and *Melville's Later Novels*, 1986, all by William B. Dillingham; *Melville: The Critical Heritage* edited by W.G. Branch, 1974; *The Early Lives of Melville* by Merton M. Sealts, Jr., 1974, and *Pursuing Melville 1940–1980* edited by Sealts, 1982; *Melville* (biography) by Edwin Haviland Miller, 1975; *The Method of Melville's Short Fiction* by R. Bruce Bickley, Jr., 1975; *Twentieth-Century Interpretations of Moby-Dick* edited by Michael T. Gilmore, 1977; *New Perspectives on Melville* edited by Faith Pullin, 1978; *The Body Impolitic: A Reading of Four Novels by Melville* by R.M. Blau, 1979; *Melville* by Edward H. Rosenberry, 1979; *Exiled Waters: Moby-Dick and the Crisis of Allegory* by Bainard Cowan, 1982; *Subversive Genealogy: The Politics and Art of Melville* by Michael Paul Rogin, 1983; *Melville: Reassessments* edited by A. Robert Lee, 1984; *A Companion to Melville Studies* edited by John Bryant, 1986.

* * *

What characterizes Herman Melville's novels from *Typee* through *Moby-Dick* is the sense of an immanent personality, the author through his narrator, examining himself, his experiences, and the world about him. This personality seeks categorical answers and finds none, and, when his quest fails, seeks ways to survive in an inscrutable universe. In these novels the theme of the autobiographical quest is signalled by the presence of a first-person narrator and by the easy identification of setting and events with the facts of Melville's life as a sailor. If the writings after *Moby-Dick* seem less autobiographical, it is because Melville places more distance between himself and his stories. Their subjects are more obviously interior, spiritual voyages to less romantic places, and an omniscient author, skeptical though compassionate, has displaced the roving, questing youth who spins high-spirited tales of his travels.

Soon after he returned from his voyage to the Pacific, Melville began to write. His first books, *Typee* and *Omoo*, are sailor's yarns based on his adventures in the Marquesas Islands and Tahiti after he jumped ship to sojourn with cannibals, to comb the beaches, and, when his Polynesian paradise began to pall, to go back to the sea. Hindsight reveals hints of themes which were to preoccupy him later, such as man's capacity for evil, appearance and reality, or the dubious blessings of both civilization and its opposite, primitivism; for it was typical of Melville to present another side of the question as a way of stating the complexity and uncertainty of things. They also show a capacity for quiet comedy, delight in word play, and penchant for social criticism. But in the main these books are light-hearted, colorful adventure, mildly fictionalized. Actually, *Typee* follows the facts closely, exploiting the potentiality for suspense in the uncertainty of the Typee's eating habits, the temptations of the narrator's situation as their petted prisoner, and the accumulating pressure to escape from being culturally if not physically consumed by them. An Australian whaler in need of hands rescues him, and he sails off toward the horizon. At this point the sequel, *Omoo* (the name means "wanderer"), begins. The captain proves incompetent and the mate a drunkard, so the sailors refuse duty. They are confined to a casually kept jail in Tahiti from which the young narrator wanders to a nearby island. After more wanderings of a picaresque sort, he goes back to sea.

Such open-endedness suggests uncertainty, or at least open-mindedness, and it encourages sequels. By this time Melville had been taken up by Evert and George Duyckinck, influential New York editors. He began to imbibe their ideas on literary nationalism and liberal politics and to borrow from their extensive collection of Renaissance books, reading Rabelais, Montaigne, Burton, Browne, and the Renaissance dramatists. This was heady stuff, and along with the chagrin he felt because publishers and critics questioned the authenticity of his realistic narratives, it caused him to try another tack. His third narrative, *Mardi*, begins realistically. On board a whaler in the South Seas two sailors contemplate desertion. However, theirs soon becomes "a chartless voyage" among allegorical islands of a mythical archipelago. The sailor-narrator rescues a symbolically provocative white captive, loves her, loses her, and pursues her beyond the ends of the earth. He is as relentless as Ahab in quest of the white whale and as self-destructive, but the search is put aside from time to time for intervals of philosophizing, rhapsodizing, and satirizing on topics of contemporary political, theological, artistic, and scientific interest. *Mardi* is a thing of patches, some of which presage the bravura passages of *Moby-Dick* and *The Confidence-Man*. Melville's family and friends advised that he forego his mental travelling, and to the accompaniment of grumbling about financial necessities, he restrained himself in *Redburn* and *White Jacket*.

Redburn recalls Melville's first voyage, a summer's service on a trader carrying cotton to Liverpool. *White Jacket* reflects his experiences as an ordinary seaman on a "homeward bound" American frigate. They contributed to his bank account and reputation. In *Redburn* the titular narrator is a callow lad who grows up, discarding his social pretension, encountering misery and evil about which he can do little, yet learning to stand on his own. *White Jacket* is likewise an initiation story, but more. Its titular character is named for a non-regulation pea jacket he is issued, which distinguishes him in a way that he first finds flattering yet proves so disadvantageous that the plot concerns his efforts to rid himself of it. His ship is treated as a microcosm of his nation, a professedly democratic state but one sustained by an authoritarian hierarchy which abuses "the people," as the ratings are called, and which is corrupt or inept. Despite this irony, *White Jacket*, with its emphasis on the brotherhood of the common seaman and the prospect that "Our Lord Admiral" above will right earthly wrongs, is

Melville's most optimistic book.

Apparently *Moby-Dick* was conceived in the pattern of its predecessors—a sailor recalling, in a realistic and casual way, his experiences aboard a whaler on a Pacific cruise. But it grew from narrative to novel, encompassing drama and epic and a number of lesser genres (e.g., sermon, natural history, tall tale, technical manual); expanding its tonal range to include low comedy, high wit, and lofty tragedy; and posing questions both metaphysical and pragmatic. If the theme of this leviathanic book must be simplistically stated, one could say that it is a quest for a way to live with dignity in a world in which the only certainty is uncertainty. Superficially, it is the melodramatic tale of the search for an albino whale by a mad sea captain whom it had maimed, but the book is so rich that it encourages many interpretations. Indeed this seems the intention of the author, supporting its essential nature as an epistemological quest.

Pierre is a departure from Melville's six sea narratives. It opposes an Edenic countryside and a postlapsarian city, settings in which Pierre, an idealistic young patrician, attempts to attack the evil he discovers, the sin of his father, with the weapons of Christian rectitude. In a memorable analogy, Melville suggests that clocks on earth are only relatively accurate because they must be made applicable to earthly contours. Absolutely perfect time obtains in heaven alone. Pierre's attempt to apply celestial time to earth is disastrously out of joint. Badly received, *Pierre* compels, in the words of its subtitle, by means of "the ambiguities" laid bare through its psychological and ethical probing.

Melville now turned magazinist. *Israel Potter*, the fictionalized biography of a soldier during the Revolutionary War and later adrift in London, explores the endurance of the common man. The magazine stories were collected in *Piazza Tales*. It is distinguished for "Bartleby," an account of the response of a worldly lawyer whose copyist gently declines to exist; "Benito Cereno," the gothic adventure of a goodnatured American sea captain who encounters a ship deviously controlled by its cargo of slaves; and "The Encantadas," sketches of the Galápagos Islands, a volcanic waste in the thrall of an evil spell. The last prose fiction Melville published, *The Confidence-Man*, is a darkly comic work of such originality of concept, technique, and verbal dexterity that it seems a prototype of the modern American novel. The setting is a Mississippi River steamboat on April Fool's Day. The action is a series of confidence men (though perhaps only one, variously guised) in ritualistic confrontation with their marks who are vulnerable because of their faith, hope, and charity. The book satirizes American types and deflates American beliefs through the device of the confidence man who preaches trust apparently for some selfish reason. But one is never sure. This, Melville's most ingenious book, was a failure. Thereafter he never attempted to write for a popular audience.

Always a self-taught student, Melville studied poetry. Near the end of the Civil War he undertook a verse sequence, *Battle-Pieces*, which sought to comprehend this national tragedy. It begins with "The Portent," on the hanging of the abolitionist firebrand John Brown, and ends with elegies to the dead of both sides. Walt Whitman's *Drum-Taps* is the only comparable body of verse. A decade later he published *Clarel*, an ambitious narrative poem about a party of "pilgrims" of diverse background and persuasion who tour the Holy Land. The framework permits discussions of science, religion, and the future of the New World. While on the whole they do not lift the spirits and the tetrameter couplets grow wearisome, the poem has a stony integrity and curious, digressive cantos on such subjects as Piranesi's prison etchings and the Hindu god Rama. His shorter verses, issued privately, draw from his early life as a sailor, his travels in Europe and the Levant, and his literary explorations. They are uneven, but the most flawed are not without interest for their tensions, juxtapositions, and sense of tragedy, for what they attempt rather than what they achieve.

Melville's last work is a short novel, *Billy Budd*. A handsome sailor on a warship strikes down a petty officer. There are mitigating circumstances, but he is hanged so that the discipline of the crew might be assured. The tale is sensitive to every complexity and delicately controlled, but as always with Melville its emphasis is on questions rather than answers.

—Hennig Cohen

See the essays on *Billy Budd* and *Moby-Dick*.

MENCKEN, H(enry) L(ouis). Born in Baltimore, Maryland, 12 September 1880. Educated at Knapp's Institute, Baltimore; Baltimore Polytechnic Institute, 1892–96. Married Sara Powell Haardt in 1930 (died, 1935). Reporter, *Herald*, 1899–1901; editor, *Sunday Herald*, 1901–03; city editor, *Morning Herald*, 1903–04, and *Evening Herald*, 1904–05; editor-in-chief, *Herald*, 1906; news editor, *Evening News*, 1906; editor, *Sunday Sun*, 1906–10, and editor and columnist ("The Free Lance"), *Evening Sun*, 1910–16, all in Baltimore; war correspondent in Germany, 1916–18; columnist, New York *Evening Mail*, 1917–18; columnist and political correspondent, *Baltimore Sunpapers*, 1919–41, 1948. Literary critic, 1908–23, and editor with George Jean Nathan, 1914–23, *Smart Set*, New York; founder, with Nathan, *Parisienne*, *Saucy Stories*, and *Black Mask* pulp magazines, late 1910's; founder, with Nathan, 1923, co-editor, 1924–25, and sole editor, 1925–33, *American Mercury*, New York; contributor, Chicago *Tribune*, 1924–28, and New York *American*, 1934–35; contributing editor, *The Nation*, New York, 1931–32. Literary adviser, Knopf publishers, New York, from 1917. Recipient: American Academy Gold Medal, 1950. *Died 29 January 1956.*

PUBLICATIONS

Collections

Letters, edited by Guy J. Forgue. 1961.
The American Scene: A Reader, edited by Huntington Cairns. 1965.

Fiction

Christmas Story. 1946.

Plays

The Artist (produced 1927). 1912.
Heliogabalus: A Buffoonery, with George Jean Nathan. 1920.

Verse

Ventures into Verse. 1903.

Other

George Bernard Shaw: His Plays. 1905.
The Philosophy of Friedrich Nietzsche. 1908.
What You Ought to Know about Your Baby, with Leonard Keene Hirshberg. 1910.
Men Versus the Man: A Conversation Between Robert Rives La Monte, Socialist, and Mencken, Individualist. 1910.
Europe after 8:15, with George Jean Nathan and Willard Huntington Wright (travel). 1914.
A Little Book in C Major. 1916.
A Book of Burlesques. 1916; revised edition, 1920.
A Book of Prefaces. 1917.
Pistols for Two, with George Jean Nathan. 1917.
Damn! A Book of Calumny. 1918; as *A Book of Calumny*, 1918.
In Defense of Women. 1918; revised edition, 1922.
The American Language: A Preliminary Inquiry into the Development of English in the United States. 1919; revised edition, 1921, 1923, 1936; supplement, 1945, 1948.
Prejudices, First Series. 1919; *Second Series*, 1920; *Third Series*, 1922; *Fourth Series*, 1924; *Selected Prejudices*, 2 vols., 1926–27; *Fifth Series*, 1926; *Sixth Series*, 1927; *Prejudices: A Selection*, edited by James T. Farrell, 1958.
The American Credo, with George Jean Nathan. 1920.
Notes on Democracy. 1926.
James Branch Cabell. 1927.
Treatise on the Gods. 1930; revised edition, 1946.
Making a President: A Footnote to the Saga of Democracy. 1932.
Treatise on Right and Wrong. 1934.
The Sunpapers of Baltimore 1837–1937, with others. 1937.
A Choice of Days (selections from autobiography), edited by Edward L. Galligan. 1980.
Happy Days 1880–1892. 1940.
Newspaper Days 1899–1906. 1941.
Heathen Days 1890–1936. 1943.
A Mencken Chrestomathy. 1949.
The Vintage Mencken, edited by Alistair Cooke. 1955.
Minority Report: Mencken's Notebooks. 1956.
A Carnival of Buncombe (essays), edited by Malcolm Moos. 1956; as *On Politics*, 1960.
The Bathtub Hoax and Other Blasts and Bravos from the Chicago Tribune, edited by Robert McHugh. 1958.
Mencken on Music, edited by Louis Cheslock. 1961.
Smart Set Criticism, edited by William H. Nolte. 1968.
The Young Mencken: The Best of His Work, edited by Carl Bode. 1973.
A Gang of Pecksniffs and Other Comments on Newspaper Publishers, Editors, and Reporters, edited by Theo Lippman, Jr. 1975.
Mencken's Last Campaign: Mencken on the 1948 Election, edited by Joseph C. Goulden. 1976.
The New Mencken Letters, edited by Carl Bode. 1977.
Letters from Baltimore: The Mencken-Cleator Correspondence, edited by P.E. Cleator. 1982.

Editor, *A Doll's House, Little Eyolf*, by Ibsen. 2 vols., 1909.
Editor, *The Gist of Nietzsche*. 1910.
Editor, *The Free Lance Books*. 5 vols., 1919–21.
Editor, *Americana*. 1925.
Editor, *Menckeniana: A Schimpflexicon*. 1928.
Editor, *Essays*, by James Huneker. 1929.
Editor, *The American Democrat*, by James Fenimore Cooper. 1931.
Editor, *Southern Album*, by Sara Haardt. 1936.
Editor, *A New Dictionary of Quotations on Historical Principles*. 1942.

Translator, *The Antichrist*, by Nietzsche. 1920.

*

Bibliography: *H.L.M.: The Mencken Bibliography* by Betty Adler and Jane Wilhelm, 1961, and *The Mencken Bibliography: A Ten-Year Supplement 1962–1971*, by Adler, 1971.

Critical Studies: *Life of Mencken* by William Manchester, 1951, revised edition, 1986, as *The Sage of Baltimore*, 1952; *Mencken: A Portrait from Memory* by Charles Angoff, 1956; *Mencken: Literary Critic* by William H. Nolte, 1966; *Mencken* by Philip Wagner, 1966; *The Constant Circle: Mencken and His Friends* by Sara Mayfield, 1968; *Mencken* by Carl Bode, 1969; *Mencken: Iconoclast from Baltimore* by Douglas C. Stenerson, 1971; *Serpent in Eden: Mencken and the South* by Fred C. Hobson, Jr., 1974; *Mencken* by W.H.A. Williams, 1977; *Mencken: A Study of His Thought* by Charles A. Fecher, 1978; *Mencken: Critic of American Life* by George H. Douglas, 1978; *On Mencken* edited by John Dorsey, 1980; *The Sage in Harlem: Mencken and the Black Writers of the 1920's* by Charles Scruggs, 1984; *Mencken and the Debunkers* by Edward A. Martin, 1984.

* * *

H.L. Mencken's reputation was etched by the acidic wit that characterized his commentary on the American culture of his day. Trained as a newspaperman, Mencken reached the height of his powers in the 1920's when, as an associate of the *Sun* papers in Baltimore and an editor first of the *Smart Set* and then of the *American Mercury*, he became one of the nation's most influential critics.

A prodigious writer, he published some 25 books—not to mention literally thousands of articles, essays, stories, editorials, book reviews—during the course of his career, beginning curiously with the now-forgotten *Ventures into Verse* in 1903 and moving in 1905 and 1908 respectively to the more representative *George Bernard Shaw: His Plays* and *The Philosophy of Friedrich Nietzsche*. Throughout, however, his style and his messages were those found in *Prejudices*, his most representative work, a six-volume collection of opinion published between 1919 and 1927. The messages were intensely iconoclastic: American culture had become stultified by its rigid adherence to a peculiarly "Puritan" form of Christian morality, and the quality of American politics—and, indeed, of American life—was being compromised by a foolish but persistent belief in egalitarianism. These messages and their many corollaries he published again and again, employing a style which became his particular signature, a style whose ingredients were the acerbic allusion, the caustic joke, the unusual word, the irreverent comparison. However, a story like "The Girl from Red Lion, P.A." is essentially a good-natured look at an ignorant country girl, with more than a hint of compassion.

With the advent of the 1930's Depression, the popularity of

Mencken's social commentary waned. In 1919, however, he had published *The American Language*, a book which he revised and supplemented at various times until 1948. In *The American Language* Mencken sought, as he said in his subtitle, to inquire "into the development of English in the United States." The volume was quickly accepted by linguists, and continues today as a standard reference work in the field. Indeed, it may well account for Mencken's fame long after his other work has become dated and been forgotten.

—Bruce A. Lohof

MERRILL, James (Ingram). Born in New York City, 3 March 1926. Educated at Lawrenceville School; Amherst College, Massachusetts, B.A. 1947. Served in the U.S. Army, 1944–45. Recipient: National Book Award, 1967, 1979; Bollingen Prize, 1973; Pulitzer Prize, 1977; National Book Critics Circle award, 1984; Bobst Award, 1984. Member, American Academy, 1971. Lives in Stonington, Connecticut.

PUBLICATIONS

Verse

Jim's Book: A Collection of Poems and Short Stories. 1942.
The Black Swan and Other Poems. 1946.
First Poems. 1951.
Short Stories. 1954.
A Birthday Cake for David. 1955.
The Country of a Thousand Years of Peace and Other Poems. 1959; revised edition, 1970.
Selected Poems. 1961.
Water Street. 1962.
The Thousand and Second Night. 1963.
Violent Pastoral. 1965.
Nights and Days. 1966.
The Fire Screen. 1969.
Two Poems. 1972.
Braving the Elements. 1972.
Yannina. 1973.
The Yellow Pages: 59 Poems. 1974.
Divine Comedies. 1976.
Metamorphosis of 741. 1977.
Mirabell: Books of Number. 1978.
Ideas, etc. 1980.
Scripts for the Pageant. 1980.
The Changing Light at Sandover. 1982.
Marbled Paper. 1982.
Santorini: Stopping the Leak. 1982.
From the First Nine: Poems 1947–1976. 1982.
Souvenirs. 1984.
Bronze. 1984.
Late Settings. 1985.

Plays

The Bait (produced 1953). In *Artists' Theatre: Four Plays*, edited by Herbert Machiz, 1960.
The Immortal Husband (produced 1955). In *Playbook: Plays for a New Theatre*, 1956.

Fiction

The Seraglio. 1957.
The (Diblos) Notebook. 1965.

Other

Recitative, edited by J.D. McClatchy. 1986.

*

Bibliography: by Jack W.C. Hagstrom and George Bixby, in *American Book Collector*, November-December 1983.

Critical Studies: *Alone with America* by Richard Howard, 1969, revised edition, 1980; *Merrill: Essays in Criticism* edited by David Lehman and Charles Berger, 1983; *Merrill: An Introduction to the Poetry* by Judith Moffett, 1984.

* * *

James Merrill's books of poems are like the rings of a tree: each extends beyond the content, expression, outlook, and craft of the previous work. Merrill has patiently, even doggedly, pursued his craft, giving each poem, however short or terse or ephemeral, a certain lapidary sheen and hardness. Merrill's complete output of verse, fiction, and plays is characterized by an absorption with technique and difficulty.

But his earliest poems are overworked with rhyme scheme, metric pattern, enamelled diction. Merrill came onto the literary scene during the vogue of revived metaphysical poetry, verse wrought in a traditional manner with high polish and much verbal flourishing under formal restraint. Such is the poetry of his first major book, *The Country of a Thousand Years of Peace*, with its elegant experiences, its widely cultivated tastes, its voice of leisured travel and gracious living—the poetry, in other words, of an American aristocrat. *Water Street* continues this elegant discourse on the vicissitudes of life, love, travel, the perennially chilly rooms and beds of his daily life.

But with *The Fire Screen* a new dimension to the persona comes into view: his life in Greece, where the warm sun, the old culture, the intimacy of life release a deeper self-awareness into his poems. Instead of the isolated, inward existence of New England, here the speaker is thrust into a more primal and assertive culture where his passions and convictions are awakened. There are also poems of return to the northeastern United States, lyrics of resignation and quiet regrets. In the American edition is the too-long verse narrative "The Summer People," with its heavy-handed irony; Robert Lowell said more about the vacation culture in his one page poem "Skunk Hour." *Braving the Elements* is both freer in its verse forms and more open and intimate in its content. Instead of the choppy quality of his earlier, too tightly wrought lines, there is now a smooth, conversational rhythm in his three or four line stanza structures. "Days of 1935," "18 West 11th Street" (which laments the death of young anti-war radicals), and "Days of 1971" are open, intimate revelations of the poet's mind.

Merrill's progress is toward a compromise between rigid formalism and the open poem, where craft would continue to discipline the choice and assembly of language but where the content would be free to take its own course. That balance is reached in the long sequence "The Book of Ephraim" in *Divine Comedies*. The 26 alphabetically ordered parts are interwoven through a leisurely plot where the poet and his lover communicate, through the Ouija board, with the spirit of Ephraim, whose insight and wit make life seem a mere changing room in a vast spiritual universe. In discovering this broader realm, Merrill is dazzling as a conversational poet. Ephraim's reckless honesty about the other side enables the speaker to unravel a complex plot of lives and after-lives, including his own father's, in a humorous, novel-like progression of poems. The verse never impedes the narrative; it enhances it with its exuberance of puns, amazing condensations of ideas and observations, feats of beautiful lyric sound.

With the appearance in 1982 of *The Changing Light at Sandover* an ambitious project begun in *Divine Comedies* came to completion. Though critical assessments are still only preliminary on this newest of the century's long poems, it is indisputable that this 560-page verse narrative must be ranked among the epical masterworks of the modern age. Though its range and intellectual intentions are smaller than those of earlier long poems, Merrill's opus is a tour de force of technical virtuosity comparable to Lowell's sonnet cycle, *History*. Its central device of a Ouija board, through which to weave many arguments connecting spiritual and material realms, puts it in the mainstream of contemporary art. *Late Settings* is a small gathering of poems written after the ardors of *The Changing Light at Sandover*, and is a quiet, gentle series of reflections on mortality.

—Paul Christensen

MERWIN, W(illiam) S(tanley). Born in New York City, 30 September 1927. Educated at Princeton University, New Jersey, A.B. in English 1947. Married Diana Whalley in 1954. Tutor in France and Portugal, 1949, and to Robert Graves's son in Mallorca, 1950; free-lance translator, London, 1951–54; Playwright-in-Residence, Poets' Theatre, Cambridge, Massachusetts, 1956–57; poetry editor, *The Nation*, New York, 1962; associate, Théâtre de la Cité, Lyons, France, 1964–65. Recipient: American Academy grant, 1957; Arts Council of Great Britain bursary, 1957; Rabinowitz research fellowship, 1961; Ford grant, 1964; Chapelbrook Award, 1966; PEN translation prize, 1969; Rockefeller grant, 1969; Pulitzer Prize, 1971; Academy of American Poets fellowship, 1973; Shelley Memorial Award, 1974; National Endowment for the Arts grant, 1978; Bollingen Prize, 1979. Member, American Academy.

PUBLICATIONS

Verse

A Mask for Janus. 1952.
The Dancing Bears. 1954.
Green with Beasts. 1956.
The Drunk in the Furnace. 1960.
The Moving Target. 1963.
The Lice. 1967.
Three Poems. 1968.
Animae. 1969.
The Carrier of Ladders. 1970.
Signs: A Poem. 1971.
Writings to an Unfinished Accompaniment. 1974.
The First Four Books of Poems. 1975.
Three Poems. 1975.
The Compass Flower. 1977.
Feathers from the Hill. 1978.
Finding the Islands. 1982.
Opening the Hand. 1983.

Plays

Darkling Child, with Dido Milroy (produced 1956).
Favor Island (produced 1957).
Eufemia, from the play by Lope de Rueda, in *Tulane Drama Review*, December 1958.
The Gilded West (produced 1961).
Turcaret, from the play by Alain Lesage, in *The Classic Theatre 4*, edited by Eric Bentley. 1961.
The False Confession, from a play by Marivaux (produced 1963). In *The Classic Theatre 4*, edited by Eric Bentley, 1961.
Yerma, from the play by García Lorca (produced 1966).
Iphigenia at Aulis, with George E. Dimock, Jr., from a play by Euripides (produced 1982). 1982.

Other

A New Right Arm (essay). N.d.
Selected Translations 1948–1968. 1968.
The Miner's Pale Children. 1970.
Houses and Travellers. 1977.
Selected Translations 1968–1978. 1979.
Unframed Original: Recollections. 1982.

Editor, *West Wind: Supplement of American Poetry*. 1961.

Translator, *The Poem of the Cid*. 1959.
Translator, *The Satires of Persius*. 1961.
Translator, *Some Spanish Ballads*. 1961; as *Spanish Ballads*, 1961.
Translator, *The Life of Lazarillo de Tormes: His Fortunes and Adversities*. 1962.
Translator, *The Song of Roland*, in *Medieval Epics*. 1963; published separately, 1970.
Translator, *Transparence of the World: Poems of Jean Follain*. 1969.
Translator, *Products of the Perfected Civilization: Selected Writings*, by Sebastian Chamfort. 1969.
Translator, *Voices: Selected Writings of Antonio Porchia*. 1969.
Translator, *Twenty Love Poems and A Song of Despair*, by Pablo Neruda. 1969.
Translator, with others, *Selected Poems: A Bilingual Edition*, by Pablo Neruda, edited by Nathaniel Tarn. 1969.
Translator, *Chinese Figures: Second Series*. 1971.
Translator, *Japanese Figures*. 1971.
Translator, *Asian Figures*. 1973.
Translator, with Clarence Brown, *Selected Poems of Osip Mandelstam*. 1973.
Translator, *Vertical Poems*, by Roberto Juarroz. 1977.
Translator, with J. Moussaieff Masson, *Sanskrit Love Poetry*. 1977; as *The Peacock's Egg: Love Poems from Ancient India*, 1981.

Translator, *Four French Plays*. 1984.
Translator, *From the Spanish Morning*. 1984.

*

Bibliography: "Seven Princeton Poets," in *Princeton Library Chronicle*, Autumn 1963.

Critical Studies: "Merwin Issue" of *Hollins Critic*, June 1968; *The Quest for Being: Theodore Roethke, Merwin, and Ted Hughes* by Daniel Liberthson, 1977.

* * *

W.S. Merwin's writing career erupted suddenly in 1952 with the publication of *A Mask for Janus*. Both it and *The Dancing Bears* are books of traditional poetry, stressing short, consciously crafted lines that move with densely worded statement. *The Dancing Bears*, slightly freer in form and showing more confidence in composition, is dry and bookish, but Merwin exercised his skill in these earliest volumes, and his intelligence and promise were evident throughout.

In *Green with Beasts* and *The Drunk in the Furnace* Merwin is in greater control of his imagination, and the experience in his lyrics is suddenly intense and compelling. The mythic content of *Green with Beasts* anticipates the bold explorations of subjectivity of later volumes. But sheer variety of tone and diction, clarity of image, leaps of thought and perception give *Green with Beasts* surges of power. *The Drunk in the Furnace* retreats slightly from the daring pursuit of the earlier volume, but the ordinary world is rediscovered here, especially in the title poem, in which the poet discovers a man living contentedly in an abandoned furnace. The landscape of these mature works is charged with magic and the fabulous, and the drunk rattling his bottle of liquor against the iron walls of his home is typical of the uncanny world in which Merwin has rooted his lyric.

By 1960, Merwin appears to have exhausted his interest in traditional English poetry, for in translating certain Spanish poets he discovered surrealist techniques that continue to affect his unique, wistfully lyrical style. The problem with *The Moving Target*, however, is the emphasis given to a disembodied voice whose lyric statements arise from unstated situations and have little or no core of argument. There is a sameness to this poetry as each poem passes into the other with its silky array of words touching briefly on the particulars of life.

In his more recent volumes, Merwin has written what appears to be the stages of a spiritual progress. Each volume is intent to mine a deeper layer of the subjective mind, to test the limits of perception where it borders on fantasy and archetypal thought, to let merge the states of dream and waking. *The Lice* is composed in the soft, remote language of surrealist lyrics and offers a distant reflection of the turbulence of the 1960's, without indictment or direct reference to actual events. A sense of political terror and unrest pervades these sombre poems. *The Carrier of Ladders* broods on absence of meaning, on death, on spiritual transcendence of the objective and alien landscape. In *Writings to an Unfinished Accompaniment*, Merwin comes to an end of the disjunctive, loosely imagistic poem. A noticeable change of attention takes over in *The Compass Flower* where the quotidian is suddenly fresh and vital, and his poems come to crisp focus on objects of immediate experience.

Opening the Hand, Merwin's latest book, is a reckoning with his personal past, particularly the memory of his father, and of his own youth. Like other poets of his generation, Merwin is struggling to make reconciliations after the tumultuous and often rebellious work of youth; some of these poems make peace with a contentious nature, and seek to discover value in what was once dismissed as an arid sentimentality. The language abounds in images of light, mirrors, memories, as the past is relived and revalued.

—Paul Christensen

MILLAR, Kenneth. See **MACDONALD, Ross.**

MILLAY, Edna St. Vincent. Born in Rockland, Maine, 22 February 1892. Educated at Camden High School, Maine, graduated 1909; Barnard College, New York, 1913; Vassar College, Poughkeepsie, New York, 1914–17, graduated 1917. Married Eugen Boissevain in 1923 (died, 1949). Free-lance writer, and occasionally actress, New York, 1917–21; associated with the Provincetown Players; contributor, 1920, and European correspondent, 1921–23, *Vanity Fair*, New York; lived in Austerlitz, New York, after 1925. Recipient: Pulitzer Prize, 1923. Litt.D.: Tufts University, Medford, Massachusetts, 1925; Colby College, Waterville, Maine; University of Wisconsin, Madison; L.H.D.: New York University. Member, American Academy. *Died 19 October 1950.*

PUBLICATIONS

Collections

Letters, edited by Allan Ross Macdougall. 1952.
Collected Poems, edited by Norma Millay. 1956.

Verse

Renascence and Other Poems. 1917.
A Few Figs from Thistles. 1920.
Second April. 1921.
The Ballad of the Harp-Weaver. 1922.
The Harp-Weaver and Other Poems. 1923; as *Poems*, 1923.
(*Poems*), edited by Hughes Mearns. 1927.
The Buck in the Snow and Other Poems. 1928.
Poems Selected for Young People. 1929.
Fatal Interview: Sonnets. 1931.
Wine from These Grapes. 1934.
Vacation Song. 1936.
Conversation at Midnight. 1937.
Huntsman, What Quarry? 1939.
Make Bright the Arrows: 1940 Notebook. 1940.
There Are No Islands Any More. 1940.
Collected Sonnets. 1941.
The Murder of Lidice. 1942.
Collected Lyrics. 1943.
Mine the Harvest: A Collection of New Poems, edited by Norma Millay. 1954.

Plays

Aria da Capo (produced 1920). 1921.
The Lamp and the Bell (produced 1921). 1921.
Two Slatterns and a King: A Moral Interlude (produced 1921). 1921.
Three Plays. 1926.
The King's Henchman (opera libretto), music by Deems Taylor (produced 1927). 1927.
The Princess Marries the Page. 1932.

Other

Distressing Dialogues. 1924.
Fear. 1927(?).

Translator, with George Dillon, *Flowers of Evil*, by Baudelaire. 1936.

*

Bibliography: *A Bibliography of the Works of Millay* by Karl Yost, 1937; *Millay: A Reference Guide* by Judith Nierman, 1977.

Critical Studies: *The Indigo Bunting: A Memoir of Millay* by Vincent Sheean, 1957; *Restless Spirit: The Life of Millay* by Miriam Gurko, 1962; *Millay* by Norman A. Brittin, 1967, revised edition, 1982; *Millay* by James Gray, 1967; *The Poet and Her Book: A Biography of Millay* by Jean Gould, 1969; *Millay in Greenwich Village* by Anne Cheney, 1975.

* * *

If it is true that "You cannot touch a flower without disturbing a star," then the whole firmament must have been tremulous at the birth of Edna St. Vincent Millay. A woman of pronounced and strongly held convictions, she was catapulted to fame in 1920 by her book *A Few Figs from Thistles*, and became the prototype of the "new, emancipated woman." The unheard of freedom which Millay demanded—freedom in love, freedom of thought in matters of morality and religion, equality with men, and, above all, the freedom to act out her own individuality unhampered by outworn social codes—was one that was needed to counteract the deadening effects of Victorian proprieties. The rebellion that Millay promoted opened many new paths for the adventuresome human spirit and she is not to be blamed if the new freedoms are often abused. As she noted in one of her finest sonnets, "What rider spurs him," civilization is a contest fought in the dark against tremendous obstacles and requires a continuous forward motion to counteract the destructive and stultifying tendencies in human nature. It is curious that Millay, the proponent of new, creative designs for life, clothed her verse in traditional forms and language, while T.S. Eliot, who harked to the past and worshipped authority as the solution to the world's ills, developed a new language and style for poetry. His contribution was also a forward motion for poetry, but the great admiration for Eliot among academics served for many years to minimize the recognition of the achievements of lyrical poets such as Millay.

More, perhaps, than any other poet in English, Millay's stance vis-à-vis the universe was one of a human being almost totally absorbed in her own human situation, whose reactions to that situation, including, of course, the condition of the whole human race, are nearly always of an immediate, personal character. She does not stand outside herself but reports all the tumults of existence as they reverberate in her own being. Since she was a personality more than life-size and was gifted with "a high sense of drama," her personalist approach created poetry of great vitality and conviction. On the other hand, being caught in the cage of personal, individual existence becomes suffocating, and, in her case, largely excluded awareness of the strange Otherness of things, or any transcendent order of reality.

Such as it was, however, Millay's outlook produced a large body of lyrical works of the highest distinction and expressiveness. It is easy to understand Louis Untermeyer's hyperbolic statement in 1923 that "Renascence," written when Millay was nineteen years old, was "possibly the most astonishing performance of this generation." Sentiments of great verve and freshness are given classic expression in a style that is always concise and musical. As James Gray says, the content of her poetry is equally attractive since it consists of her own version of the ageless contest between life and death, in both the physical and spiritual senses, the raptures and failures of love, and the ever-present struggle between the processes of decay and rebirth. There are times, as suggested above, when the reader may feel oppressed by the weight of Millay's tortured self-absorption, but this is a price worth paying for the sharply etched and poignant account of her soul's turnings.

—Glenn Richard Ruihley

MILLER, Arthur. Born in New York City, 17 October 1915. Educated at Abraham Lincoln High School, New York, graduated 1932; University of Michigan, Ann Arbor (Hopwood Award, 1936, 1937), 1934–38, A.B. 1938. Married 1) Mary Slattery in 1940 (divorced, 1956), one son and one daughter; 2) the actress Marilyn Monroe in 1956 (divorced, 1961); 3) Ingeborg Morath in 1962, one daughter. Worked in automobile supply warehouse, 1932–34; member of the Federal Theatre Project, 1938; writer for CBS and NBC Radio Workshops; Associate Professor of Drama, University of Michigan, 1973–74. International President, PEN, London and New York, 1965–69. Recipient: Theatre Guild award, 1938; New York Drama Critics Circle award, 1947, 1949; Tony award, 1947, 1949, 1953; Pulitzer Prize, 1949; National Association of Independent Schools award, 1954; American Academy Gold Medal, 1959; Brandeis University Creative Arts Award, 1969; Peabody Award, for television play, 1981; Bobst Award, 1983. D.H.L.: University of Michigan, 1956; Litt.D.: University of East Anglia, Norwich, 1984. Member, American Academy, 1981. Lives in Connecticut.

PUBLICATIONS

Plays

Honors at Dawn (produced 1936).
No Villains (*They Too Arise*) (produced 1937).
The Pussycat and the Expert Plumber Who Was a Man, and *William Ireland's Confession*, in *100 Non-Royalty Radio Plays*, edited by William Kozlenko. 1941.

The Man Who Had All the Luck (produced 1944). In *Cross-Section 1944*, edited by Edwin Seaver, 1944.
That They May Win (produced 1944). In *Best One-Act Plays of 1944*, edited by Margaret Mayorga, 1945.
Grandpa and the Statue, in *Radio Drama in Action*, edited by Erik Barnouw. 1945.
The Story of Gus, in *Radio's Best Plays*, edited by Joseph Liss. 1947.
The Guardsman, radio adaptation of a play by Ferenc Molnar, and *Three Men on a Horse*, radio adaptation of the play by George Abbott and John Cecil Holm, in *Theatre Guild on the Air*, edited by William Fitelson. 1947.
All My Sons (produced 1947). 1947.
Death of a Salesman: Certain Private Conversations in Two Acts and a Requiem (produced 1949). 1949.
An Enemy of the People, from a play by Ibsen (produced 1950). 1951.
The Crucible (produced 1953). 1953.
A View from the Bridge, and A Memory of Two Mondays: Two One-Act Plays (produced 1955). 1955; revised version of *A View from the Bridge* (produced 1956), 1957.
Collected Plays (includes *All My Sons*, *Death of a Salesman*, *The Crucible*, *A Memory of Two Mondays*, *A View from the Bridge*). 1957.
After the Fall (produced 1964). 1964.
Incident at Vichy (produced 1964). 1965.
The Price (produced 1968). 1968.
Fame, and The Reason Why (produced 1970). *Fame* in *Yale Literary Magazine* March 1971.
The Creation of the World and Other Business (produced 1972). 1973; revised version, as *Up from Paradise*, music by Stanley Silverman (produced 1974).
The Archbishop's Ceiling (produced 1977; revised version, produced 1984). 1984.
The American Clock, from the work *Hard Times* by Studs Terkel (produced 1979). 1980.
Playing for Time, from a work by Fania Fenelon (televised 1980; produced 1986). In *Collected Plays 2*, 1981.
Collected Plays 2 (includes *The Misfits*, *After the Fall*, *Incident at Vichy*, *The Price*, *The Creation of the World and Other Business*, *Playing for Time*). 1981.
Two-Way Mirror (includes *Elegy for a Lady* and *Some Kind of Love Story*) (produced 1982). 1984.
Danger! Memory! (produced 1987). 1986.

Screenplays: *The Story of G.I. Joe* (uncredited), 1945; *The Witches of Salem*, 1958; *The Misfits*, 1961.

Radio Plays: *The Pussycat and the Expert Plumber Who Was a Man*, *William Ireland's Confession*, *Grandpa and the Statue*, *The Story of Gus*, *The Guardsman*, *Three Men on a Horse*, early 1940's.

Television Play: *Playing for Time*, 1980.

Fiction

Focus. 1945.
The Misfits (novelization of screenplay). 1961.
I Don't Need You Any More: Stories. 1967.

Other

Situation Normal. 1944.
Jane's Blanket (for children). 1963.
In Russia, photographs by Inge Morath. 1969.
The Portable Miller, edited by Harold Clurman. 1971.
In the Country, photographs by Inge Morath. 1977.
The Theatre Essays of Miller, edited by Robert A. Martin. 1978.
Chinese Encounters, photographs by Inge Morath. 1979.
"Salesman" in Beijing. 1984.

*

Bibliography: "Miller: The Dimension of His Art: A Checklist of His Published Works," in *The Serif*, June 1967, and *Miller Criticism (1930–1967)*, 1969, revised edition, as *An Index to Miller Criticism*, 1976, both by Tetsumaro Hayashi; *Miller: A Reference Guide* by John H. Ferres, 1979.

Critical Studies: *Miller*, 1961, and *Miller: A Study of His Plays*, 1979, revised edition, as *Miller the Playwright*, 1983, both by Dennis Welland; *Miller* by Robert Hogan, 1964; *Miller: The Burning Glass* by Sheila Huftel, 1965; *Miller: Death of a Salesman: Text and Criticism* edited by Gerald Weales, 1967; *Miller* by Leonard Moss, 1967, revised edition, 1980; *Miller, Dramatist* by Edward Murray, 1967; *Miller: A Collection of Critical Essays* edited by Robert W. Corrigan, 1969; *Psychology and Miller* by Richard I. Evans, 1969; *The Merrill Guide to Miller* by Sidney H. White, 1970; *Miller: Portrait of a Playwright* by Benjamin Nelson, 1970; *Miller* by Ronald Hayman, 1970; *Twentieth-Century Interpretations of The Crucible* edited by John H. Ferres, 1972; *Studies in Death of a Salesman* edited by Walter J. Meserve, 1972; *Critical Essays on Miller* edited by James J. Martine, 1979; *Miller: New Perspectives* edited by Robert A. Martin, 1982; *Miller* by Neil Carson, 1982; *Twentieth-Century Interpretations of Death of a Salesman* edited by Helene Wickham Koon, 1983.

* * *

In "On Social Plays," the introduction to the 1955 edition of *A View from the Bridge*, Arthur Miller expressed his dissatisfaction with the subjective play so popular on Broadway in the 1950's. At the same time, he rejected the customary definition of the social play ("an arraignment of society's evils") and identified his own work as "the drama of the whole man," an inextricable mixture of the social and the psychological. The emphasis on one side or the other varied over the years and his conception of the nature of man underwent a change in the 1960's, but his 1955 sense of his work is a useful description of the whole career of Miller as a social playwright.

In his student plays, his wartime one-acters, his early radio plays, even his first Broadway offering, *The Man Who Had All the Luck*, Miller can be seen working his way toward the theme that was to dominate his early plays. From *All My Sons* through *A View from the Bridge*, Miller places his protagonist in a setting in which society functions as a creator of images, and the hero-victim is destroyed because, as he says in the essay quoted above, "the individual is doomed to frustration when once he gains a consciousness of his own identity." Ironically, the destruction comes whether a man accepts or rejects the role that society asks or demands that he play. Joe Keller, in *All My Sons*, is a good man, a loving husband and father, a successful businessman who believes that his responsibility ends "at the building line"; when his son teaches him that neither the welfare of his family nor the self-protective impulse of conventional business ethics can excuse a shipment of faulty airplane parts, he commits suicide. Willy Loman, in *Death of a Sales-*

man, embraces the American dream, assumes that success is not only possible, but inevitable, and, faced with his failure, kills himself; the irony of the final suicide and the strength of the play is that Willy goes to his death, his dream still intact, convinced that the elusive success will be visited on his son, Biff, a man already crippled by society's neatly packaged ideas. In *The Crucible*, the victim becomes a romantic hero. John Proctor, guilty of adultery, confuses his accusing wife with an accusing society and admits to practicing witchcraft, but, finally unwilling to sign his name, he rejects society's demand for ritual confession, regains his identity, and dies, purely, in an act of defiance. Eddie Carbone, in *A View from the Bridge*, dies crying out for his name, too, but he wants a lie, the pretense that he has not violated the neighborhood ethic; like Joe Keller and Willy Loman, he accepts his society, but he breaks its rules when his desire for his niece and his attraction to her sweetheart threaten him with labels more frightening than informer. The explicit assumption of all these plays is that, win or lose, in contemporary society you can't win; the implicit assumption is that the individual is at his strongest, philosophically and dramatically, when the tensions between self and society are made manifest by a revealing crisis. The artistic result of the twin assumptions is a group of remarkably effective plays, reflecting Miller's theatrical skill as clearly as they do his moral concerns. In the best of them, *Death of a Salesman*, Miller's social-psychological mix has given birth, in Willy Loman, to one of the richest characters in American drama.

Between 1956, when the revised version of *A View from the Bridge* appeared, and 1964, Miller was inactive in the theater. During those years he published a number of short stories, later collected in *I Don't Need You Any More*, including "The Misfits," which was the basis for the short novel and screenplay, written for his wife Marilyn Monroe. The most startling thing about the work is that in it Miller seems to be accepting the concept of the curative power of love in a way that recalls the prevailing cliché of Broadway in the 1950's; he had already given the idea explicit statement in two essays published a few years before the story-novel-film—the introduction to *Collected Plays* and "Bridge to a Savage World" (*Esquire*, October 1958).

When Miller returned to the theater with *After the Fall* and *Incident at Vichy*, he had put aside the momentary softness of *The Misfits*, but he had also discarded the concept of man as an admirable loser which marked his earlier plays. "The first problem," he wrote in "Our Guilt for the World's Evil" (*New York Times Magazine*, 3 January 1965), "is . . . to discover our own relationship to evil, its reflection of ourselves." Quentin in *After the Fall* learns to live and Von Berg in *Vichy* to die by the process of self-discovery already familiar in Miller's work, but identity is no longer individual. Miller, like the Salem of *The Crucible*, is now forcing an image of guilt on his characters. Finally in 1972, with *The Creation of the World and Other Business*, Miller makes obvious what has already been stated in the title *After the Fall*, that his post-1964 subject is original sin translated into the psychological commonplace that makes everyone responsible for "the World's Evil." Miller does not try to dramatize the corollary, that when everyone is guilty no one is, but it is possible—or so the autobiographical elements in *After the Fall* suggest—that the idea is working on the author if not within the play. One result of Miller's new concept of man is that the later plays have a schematic look to them; the characters lack the vitality of Miller's early protagonists and often appear to be simply figures in an exemplum. *The Price* is the only one of the later plays that escapes the look of drama as demonstration. Ideologically one with the other post-1964 plays, it returns to the domestic setting familiar with Miller as far back as the time of his student work *They Too Arise*. Whether it is the inherent drama of two brothers at odds or the presence of the old furniture dealer, Miller's only successful comic figure, *The Price* escapes Significance with a capital S and finds theatrical validity. In *The Archbishop's Ceiling* Miller seems to have moved away from the ideological concerns that marked his drama from *After the Fall* to *The Creation of the World*, but the play is more intellectual than dramatic and the characters are more complex in conception than in presentation. In recent years his work has reflected diversity of material and form. This work includes *The American Clock*, which grew out of Studs Terkel's *Hard Times*; a number of short plays; *Playing for Time*, a television adaptation of Fania Fenelon's book about an orchestra composed of prisoners in a concentration camp; and still another revision of *Up from Paradise*, the musical version of *The Creation of the World* which he and Stanley Silverman have been working on since 1974.

Since Miller is a playwright of ideas, it is perhaps fitting that I have largely stuck to his themes in discussing his work, stopping occasionally to suggest that the ideational content of a play can interfere with the dramatic action or dehumanize character. These strictures are valid only to the extent that Miller is a realistic playwright in the American tradition, a dramatist who wants to create psychologically valid characters with whom audiences can identify directly. That is Miller's tradition, although he is one of a number of postwar American playwrights who recognize that that kind of character can exist outside a conventional realistic play. *Death of a Salesman* and *After the Fall* are examples of domesticated American Expressionism in which realistic scenes are played in an anti-realistic context. *The Crucible* is a romantic history play with a consciously artificial language, and Alfieri's stilted speeches in *A View from the Bridge*, which turn into free verse in the original version, are an attempt to impose the label *tragedy* on the play. *The Creation of the World* is an unhappy mixture of philosophical drama and Jewish low comedy. *Incident at Vichy* is a roundtable discussion and *The Price* is a debate of sorts with exits and entrances so artificially conceived that Miller surely means them to be seen as devices. The playwright's nearest approaches to traditional realism are *All My Sons* and the affectionate short play *A Memory of Two Mondays*.

Aside from his plays, Miller's work includes not only the short stories and screenplay mentioned above, but a novel, *Focus*; a report on Americans in training during World War II, *Situation Normal*; a children's book, *Jane's Blanket*; three volumes in which his text shares space with photographs by his wife Inge Morath, *In Russia*, *In the Country* and *Chinese Encounters*; his most impressive recent work, *"Salesman" in Beijing*, an account of his directing *Death of a Salesman* in China; and a great many articles and essays, most of them about the theater. The chief value of these works lies less in their specific generic virtues than in those analogies—in theme, in method—that heighten our appreciation of the plays. After all, Miller is pre-eminently a playwright, one of the best the American theater has produced.

—Gerald Weales

See the essay on *Death of a Salesman*.

MILLER, Henry (Valentine). Born in Yorkville, New York City, 26 December 1891. Educated at P.S. 85, Brooklyn, graduated 1907; City College, New York, 1909. Married 1) Beatrice Sylvas Wickens in 1917 (divorced, 1924), one daughter; June Edith Smith in 1924 (divorced, 1934); 3) Janina Martha Lepska in 1944 (divorced, 1952), one daughter and one son; 4) Eve McClure in 1953 (divorced, 1961); 5) Hiroko Tokuda in 1967 (separated, 1970). Had many jobs: worked for Atlas Portland Cement Company, New York, 1909; reporter in Washington, D.C., 1917; worked for Bureau of Economic Research, New York, 1919; employment manager, Western Union Telegraph Company, 1920–24; lived in Europe, mainly in France, 1930–40; proofreader, Chicago *Tribune* Paris edition, 1932; teacher, Lycée Carnot, Dijon, 1932; psychoanalyst, New York, 1935; editor, with Lawrence Durrell and Alfred Perlès, *The Booster* (later *Delta*), Paris, 1937–38; European editor, *Volontes*, Paris, 1938–39, and *Phoenix*, Woodstock, New York, 1938–39; returned to the U.S., 1940; lived in California from 1942. Also an artist: exhibitions of watercolors in New York, 1927, London, 1944, and Los Angeles, 1966. Member, American Academy, 1958; Officer, Legion of Honor (France), 1975. *Died 7 June 1980.*

PUBLICATIONS

Collections

A Miller Reader, edited by John Calder. 1985.

Fiction

Tropic of Cancer. 1934.
Black Spring. 1936.
Tropic of Capricorn. 1939.
The Smile at the Foot of the Ladder. 1948.
The Rosy Crucifixion:
Sexus. 1949.
Plexus. 1953.
Nexus. 1960.
Nights of Love and Laughter (stories). 1955.
Quiet Days in Clichy. 1956.
Opus pistorum. 1983; as *Under the Roofs of Paris*, 1985.

Plays

Scenario: A Film with Sound. 1937.
Just Wild about Harry: A Melo-Melo in Seven Scenes (produced 1963). 1963.

Verse

Reflections, edited by Twinka Thiebaud. 1981.

Other

What Are You Going to Do About Alf? 1935.
Aller Retour New York. 1935; selection, as *Reunion in Barcelona*, 1959.
Money and How It Gets That Way. 1938.
Max and the White Phagocytes. 1938.
Hamlet, with Michael Fraenkel. 2 vols., 1939–41; vol. 1 revised, 1943; both vols. revised, as *The Michael Fraenkel-Miller Correspondence*, 1962.
The Cosmological Eye. 1939.
The World of Sex. 1940; revised edition, 1957.
The Colossus of Maroussi; or, The Spirit of Greece. 1941.
Wisdom of the Heart (short stories and essays). 1941.
Murder the Murderer: An Excursus on War. 1944.
Varda: The Master Builder. 1944.
The Angel Is My Watermark. 1944.
Sunday after the War. 1944.
The Plight of the Creative Artist in the United States of America. 1944.
Semblance of a Devoted Past. 1944; unexpurgated edition, with *To Paint Is to Love Again*, 1968.
Echolalia: Reproductions of Water Colors by Miller. 1945.
Why Abstract?, with Hilaire Hiler and William Saroyan. 1945.
Miller Miscellanea. 1945.
The Air-Conditioned Nightmare. 1945; vol. 2, *Remember to Remember*, 1947.
Obscenity and the Law of Reflection. 1945.
The Amazing and Invariable Beauford De Laney. 1945.
Maurizius Forever. 1946; abridged edition, as *Reflections on the Maurizius Case*, 1974.
Patchen: Man of Anger and Light, with *A Letter to God*, by Kenneth Patchen. 1947.
Of, By and About Miller: A Collection of Pieces by Miller, Herbert Read, and Others. 1947.
Portrait of General Grant. 1947.
The Waters Reglitterized: The Subject of Water Color in Some of Its More Liquid Phases (includes reproductions of pictures). 1950.
The Books in My Life. 1952.
A Devil in Paradise: The Story of Conrad Moricand, Born Paris, 7 or 7:15pm, January 17, 1887, Died Paris, 10:30pm, August 31, 1954. 1956.
Argument about Astrology. 1956.
The Time of the Assassins: A Study of Rimbaud. 1956.
Big Sur and the Oranges of Hieronymus Bosch. 1957.
The Red Notebook. 1958.
Art and Outrage: A Correspondence about Miller Between Alfred Perlès and Lawrence Durrell, with an Intermission by Miller. 1959.
A Miller Reader, edited by Lawrence Durrell. 1959; as *The Best of Miller*, 1960.
The Intimate Miller. 1959.
Defence of the Freedom to Read. 1959.
To Paint Is To Love Again (includes reproductions of pictures). 1960.
Stand Still like the Hummingbird. 1962.
Watercolors, Drawings and His Essay "The Angel Is My Watermark." 1962.
Lawrence Durrell and Miller: A Private Correspondence, edited by George Wickes. 1963.
Books Tangent to Circle: Reviews. 1963.
Greece. 1964.
Miller on Writing, edited by Thomas H. Moore. 1964.
Letters to Anaïs Nin, edited by Gunther Stuhlmann. 1965.
Selected Prose. 2 vols., 1965.
Order and Chaos chez Hans Reichel. 1966.
Writer and Critic: A Correspondence, with William A. Gordon. 1968.
Collector's Quest: The Correspondence of Miller and J. Rives Childs, edited by Richard Clement Wood. 1968.
Entretiens de Paris, with Georges Belmont. 1970; translated as *Face to Face with Miller: Conversations with Georges*

Belmont, 1971; as *Miller in Conversation*, 1972.
Insomnia; or, The Devil at Large. 1970.
My Life and Times, edited by Bradley Smith. 1971.
Reflections on the Death of Mishima. 1972.
On Turning Eighty, and Journey to an Antique Land. 1972.
The Immortal Bard (on John Cowper Powys). 1973.
First Impressions of Greece. 1973.
This Is Henry—Henry Miller from Brooklyn: Conversations, with Robert Snyder. 1974.
Letters of Miller and Wallace Fowlie 1943–1972, edited by Fowlie. 1975.
The Nightmare Notebook. 1975.
J'suis pas plus con qu'un autre. 1976; as *Je ne suis pas plus con qu'un autre*, 1980.
Genius and Lust: A Journey Through the Major Writings of Miller, with Norman Mailer. 1976.
Flash Back: Entretiens à Pacific Palisades, with Christian de Bartillat. 1976.
Miller's Book of Friends (memoirs). 1976; vol. 2, *My Bike and Other Friends*, 1978; vol. 3, *Joey: A Loving Portrait of Alfred Perlès, Together with Some Bizarre Episodes Relating to the Other Sex*, 1979.
Four Visions of America, with others. 1977.
Sextet: Six Essays. 1977.
Mother, China, and the World Beyond. 1977.
Gliding into the Everglades and Other Essays. 1977.
An Open Letter to Stroker! 1978.
Miller: Years of Trial and Triumph 1962–1964: The Correspondence of Miller and Elmer Gertz, edited by Gertz and Felice Flanery Lewis. 1978.
The Theatre and Other Pieces. 1979.
The World of Lawrence: A Passionate Appreciation, edited by Evelyn J. Hinz and John J. Teunissen. 1980.
Notes on "Aaron's Rod" and Other Notes on Lawrence from the Paris Notebooks, edited by Seamus Cooney. 1980.
Correspondance privée 1935–1978, with Joseph Delteil, edited by F.-J. Temple. 1980.
The Paintings of Miller (includes essays), edited by Noel Young. 1982.
From Your Capricorn Friend: Miller and the Stroker 1978–1980 (letters). 1984.
Dear, Dear Brenda: The Love Letters of Miller to Brenda Venus, edited by Gerald Seth Sindell. 1986.

*

Bibliography: *Miller: A Chronology and Bibliography* by Bern Porter, 1945; *Bibliography of Miller* by Thomas H. Moore, 1961; *A Bibliography of Miller 1945–1961* by Maxine Renken, 1962; *Miller: A Bibliography of Secondary Sources* by Lawrence J. Shifreen, 1979.

Critical Studies: *Miller* by Nicholas Moore, 1953; *My Friend Miller: An Intimate Biography* by Alfred Perlès, 1956; *Miller, Expatriate* by Annette Kar Baxter, 1961; *Miller and the Critics* edited by George Wickes, 1963, and *Miller* by Wickes, 1966; *Miller* by Kingsley Widmer, 1963; *Miller* by F.-J. Temple, 1965; *The Mind and Art of Miller* by William A. Gordon, 1967; *The Literature of Silence: Miller and Samuel Beckett* by Ihab Hassan, 1968; *Miller: Three Decades of Criticism* edited by Edward B. Mitchell, 1971; *Orpheus in Brooklyn: Orphism, Rimbaud and Miller* by Bertrand Mathieu, 1976; *Always Merry and Bright: The Life of Miller* by Jay Martin, 1978; *Miller* by J.D. Brown, 1986; *Miller: Full of Life* by Kathryn Winslow, 1986.

* * *

Henry Miller's name became known to a wider public than that of a fashionable, rather trendy literary elite largely as an unexpected result of the Allied forces in Paris after 1944. The soldiers and the civilians who accompanied them discovered his books—*Tropic of Cancer*, *Black Spring*, *Tropic of Capricorn*—most of which had been refused publication in English-speaking countries because of their blatantly sexual matter. But they were available in Paris published by Girodias's Obelisk Press, and were eagerly seized on by Americans and Britons, many of whom succeeded in smuggling their finds into their home countries.

Too often the books were large, inchoate, rambling works with an autobiographical thread. They passed rapidly, like a rushing, uncontrolled stream, from the rhapsodic to the sordid to the pornographic. Miller's freedom of language and subject had a deep influence on the thousands of writers who benefitted from the literary emancipation from censorship. Miller himself may have been influenced by much of the erotica of the ages. But he was influenced also by such American writers as Whitman and Robinson Jeffers, by the back-to-nature animists such as Thoreau and D.H. Lawrence (about whom he wrote a study), and by all the European writers who in one way or another contributed to such movements as Dadaism and Surrealism. He praises such not always well-known writers as Céline, Cingria, Blaise Cendrars, Milosz, Knut Hamsun, and Rimbaud, whose *Season in Hell* he translated. He has a sort of American-Irish dislike of the British, except for Lawrence Durrell and John Cowper Powys (whose novels he claims to understand, but whose real virtue was that he had written *In Defence of Sensuality*, and sensuality was a habit to which Miller always gave a high priority).

Miller as a writer is for freedom in every possible sense, an indecent Shelley, a Tom Paine with the lid off. He expresses, too, a semi-mystical belief that everything links with everything else and that the Creator will arrange that "If there is a genuine need it will be met." Miller, indeed, himself had amazing luck in becoming a highly saleable writer. He always suffered from logorrhea—and, when he realized that he could earn real money by writing, from appalling over-production. He can be funny in a boisterous sort of way; he is a farceur; he can even convince one from time to time that he is genuinely perceptive, though the conviction seldom lasts long. He had a gift for assimilating trendy names and attitudes; Zen, Hokusai, the Essenes, Restif de la Bretonne, astrology, the occult, Milarepa the Tibetan monk. But paradoxically he can still react salutarily against the fashionable, against the claims, for example, of American medicine and the endless, self-defeating "don'ts" of urban Western societies—don't over-eat, don't walk if you can run, don't listen to the radio or watch television, don't get vaccinated or inoculated, don't get frightened if you are over or under weight. And, he concludes: "The great hoax which we are perpetuating every day of our lives is that we are making life easier, more comfortable, more enjoyable, more profitable. We are doing just the contrary. We are making life stale, flat and unprofitable every day in every way. . . ." His attitude is far from new. It is certainly as old as the time of the Romantic poets. Nor does it advance our perceptions to keep on saying these things. Miller is not a great writer, and he can en masse be a great bore.

His best literary work, written with skill and brio, is *The Colossus of Maroussi*, for it carries to us the whole flavour of Athens in the months immediately preceding World War II, and the sense of the Greek-ness of Greeks. In general his early works are much the best, for he was then really trying. *Tropic of Cancer* is a light-hearted, racy account of his life as a poor, often hungry, always lustful, writer in the Paris suburbs, just as *Sexus* (part of *The Rosy Crucifixion* trilogy) does give a picture of the lower-middle-class, working-class, and prostitutes' life in New York in the years before World War I. There are some rather fine passages in these books—"Easter came in like a frozen hare—but it was fairly warm in bed." Nor can one deny that he achieves at least novelty in his descriptions, sometimes quite comic, of sexual organs and of varieties of the sexual act. But the characters in his long autobiographical reminiscences are seldom visualised, except occasionally as extreme oddities when we see them like comic caricatures. There is little consideration of motives and less of psychology. The men and women move and act but we know only that it is because of the prime, crude instincts—sexual desire, and the desire for food of which Miller makes a great deal.

Miller was a copious letter writer all his life and an entertaining one. The correspondence between him and Durrell makes excellent reading, and there are vast stores of Miller letters in the archives of the University of California at Los Angeles.

—Kenneth Young

MILLER, Joaquin. Pseudonym for Cincinnatus Hiner Miller. Born in Liberty, Indiana, 10 March 1839; moved with his parents to Oregon, 1852. Studied law in Oregon; admitted to Oregon bar, 1861. Messenger in the gold mining district of Idaho, 1856–59; manager, Eugene *Democratic Register*, Oregon, 1863; lawyer in Canon City, Oregon, 1863–66; county court judge, Grant County, Oregon, 1866–70; lived in London and gained notoriety as the "frontier poet," 1870–71; returned to the U.S. and subsequently became a fruit grower: lived on his estate in Oakland, California, after 1887; Klondike correspondent, New York *Journal*, 1897–98. *Died 17 February 1913.*

PUBLICATIONS

Collections

Poetical Works, edited by Stuart P. Sherman. 1923.
Selections (verse), edited by Juanita Joaquina Miller. 1945.
Selected Writings, edited by Alan Rosenus. 1977.

Verse

Specimens. 1868.
Joaquin, et al. 1869.
Pacific Poems. 1871.
Songs of the Sierras. 1871.
Songs of the Sun-Lands. 1873.
The Ship in the Desert. 1875.
Songs of Italy. 1878.
Songs of Far-Away Lands. 1878.
Songs of the Mexican Seas. 1887.
In Classic Shades and Other Poems. 1890.
Songs of the Soul. 1896.
Complete Poetical Works. 1897; revised edition, 1902.
Chants for the Boer. 1900.
As It Was in the Beginning: A Poem Dedicated to the Mothers of Men. 1903.
Light: A Narrative Poem. 1907.
Panama: Union of the Oceans. 1912.

Plays

The Baroness of New York. 1877.
First Fam'lies in the Sierras. 1875; revised version, as *The Danites in the Sierras* (produced 1880), 1881.
Forty-Nine: A California Drama. 1882.
The Silent Man. 1883.
Tally-Ho!, music by John Philip Sousa. 1883.
An Oregon Idyll, in *Collected Works*. 1910.

Fiction

The One Fair Woman. 1876.
Shadows of Shasta. 1881.
'49: The Gold-Seeker of the Sierras. 1884.
The Destruction of Gotham. 1886.

Other

Life Amongst the Modocs: Unwritten History. 1873; as *Paquita, The Indian Heroine*, 1881; revised edition, as *My Own Story*, 1890; as *Romantic Life Amongst the Red Indians: An Autobiography*, 1890; as *Unwritten History*, edited by Alan Rosenus, 1972.
The Danites and Other Choice Selections, edited by A.V.D. Honeyman. 1878.
Memorie and Rime. 1884.
The Building of the City Beautiful. 1893.
An Illustrated History of the State of Montana. 2 vols., 1894.
The Battle of Castle Crags. 1894.
True Bear Stories. 1900.
Japan of Sword and Love, with Yone Noguchi. 1905.
Collected Works. 6 vols., 1909–10.
Trelawney with Shelley and Byron. 1922.
Overland in a Covered Wagon: An Autobiography, edited by Sidney G. Firman (based on Introduction to *Collected Works*). 1930.
California Diary 1855–1857, edited by John S. Richards. 1936.

*

Bibliography: in *Bibliography of American Literature* by Jacob Blanck, 1973; *Three Writers of the Far West: A Reference Guide* by Ray C. Longtin, 1980.

Critical Studies: *Miller: Literary Frontiersman* by Martin S. Peterson, 1937; *Splendid Poseur: Miller, American Poet* by M. Marion Marberry, 1953; *Miller* by O.W. Frost, 1967; *Miller* by Benjamin S. Lawson, 1980.

* * *

Were it not for the outlandish image of himself which he deliberately cultivated, Cincinnatus Hiner Miller, better known as Joaquin Miller, after the Mexican bandit Joaquin Murietta, whose exploits he helped to popularize, would probably be forgotten today. Dressed in western sombrero, boots, and buckskin britches, Miller proclaimed himself the poetic spokesman for the American west, and during his lifetime he came to symbolize, both in America and abroad, the spirit of freedom, adventure, and bravado which characterized the west in the popular imagination.

Ironically, Miller rose to fame not in America but in England, where he went to find a publisher for his book, *Pacific Poems*, and to make his presence felt in more sophisticated literary circles than those which America offered him. His earlier collections of poetry, *Specimens* and *Joaquin et al.*, had received scant recognition in America, and Miller shrewdly understood that he and his works might best appeal to a foreign audience unfamiliar with the stereotypes which he projected. Although Americans simply refused to take him seriously, Miller became something of a celebrity in Britain, where his rustic dress and primitive manners endeared him to the public and brought him to the attention of the leading literary figures of the day. From Britain, Miller's fame spread to America. His most famous book, *Songs of the Sierras*, first published in London, was issued the same year in Boston.

Most of Miller's works are vaguely autobiographical. He drew his themes from his own experiences, which he embellished or exaggerated according to the effects he wished to achieve. Nearly all of Miller's works are about the west. *Life Amongst the Modocs* and *Memorie and Rime* are prose accounts of his early adventures in the mines and among the Indians of California. *Shadows of Shasta*, Miller's most successful novel, draws attention to the injustices done to the Indians, with whom Miller greatly sympathized. When he writes about the west, Miller is generally passionate and bold. He possessed the ability to make legend seem real and the real seem legendary. Miller possessed a flair for the dramatic and was especially effective as a playwright. His most popular play, *The Danites in the Sierras*, was acted before packed audiences, much to the chagrin of Bret Harte and Mark Twain, who envied Miller's dramatic talents. When he departed from western themes, however, as he did in the novels *The One Fair Woman* and *The Destruction of Gotham*, Miller's writing becomes forced and unconvincing.

Miller's poetry, while lacking in intrinsic merit, had a profound effect on the development of western American literature. For forms and techniques, Miller studied the British romantics and the American fireside poets. Like Longfellow, Miller was especially fond of rhymed iambic pentameter, and his western heroes bear a marked resemblance to those of Byron. In those poems where form matches content, Miller's verse possesses a haunting, rhythmic quality, reminiscent of Indian chants, and captures the spirit and vitality of his western themes. Miller is especially noted for his attempts to write poetry in the American vernacular. His most famous poem, "Columbus," has become a classic and is still recited by American schoolchildren, who see in it a primitive expression of the American Dream.

—James A. Levernier

MITCHELL, Donald Grant. Pseudonym: Ik Marvel. Born in Norwich, Connecticut, 12 April 1822. Educated at John Hall's School, Ellington, Connecticut, 1830–37; Yale University, New Haven, Connecticut (editor, *Yale Literary Magazine*), 1837–41, graduated 1841. Married Mary Frances Pringle in 1853. Farmer and writer, New London County, Connecticut, 1841–43; clerk to the U.S. Consul, Liverpool, England, 1844–45; toured Europe, 1845–46; wrote for *Morning Courier and New York Enquirer* (correspondent in Paris, 1848), also studied law in the offices of John Osborne Sargent, New York, 1846–50; editor, *Lorgnette*, New York, 1850; full-time writer from 1850; U.S. Consul, Venice, 1853–54; lived in Paris, 1855; returned to the U.S. and settled on a farm, later called Edgewood, near New Haven, Connecticut. Recipient: New York Agricultural Society silver medal, 1843; New England Association of Park Superintendents silver cup, 1904. *Died 15 December 1908.*

PUBLICATIONS

Fiction

The Lorgnette; or, Studies of the Town by an Opera Lover. 1850; as *The Opera Goer*, 1852.
Reveries of a Bachelor; or, A Book of the Heart. 1850.
Dream Life: A Fable of the Seasons. 1851.
Fudge Doings, Being Tony Fudge's Record of the Same. 1855.
Seven Stories, with Basement and Attic. 1864.
Dr. Johns, Being a Narrative of Certain Events in the Life of an Orthodox Minister of Connecticut. 1866.

Other

Fresh Gleanings; or, a New Sheaf from the Old Fields of Continental Europe. 2 vols., 1847.
The Battle Summer, Being Transcripts from Personal Observation in Paris 1848. 1849.
My Farm of Edgewood: A Country Book. 1863.
Wet Days at Edgewood, with Old Farmers, Old Gardeners, and Old Pastorals. 1865.
Rural Studies, with Hints for Country Places. 1867; as *Out-of-Town Places*, 1884.
Pictures of Edgewood, photographs by Rockwood. 1868.
About Old Story-Tellers, of How and When They Lived, and What Stories They Told. 1878.
A Report to the Commissioners on Lay-Out of East Rock Park. 1882.
Bound Together: A Sheaf of Papers. 1884.
English Lands, Letters, and Kings. 4 vols., 1889–97.
American Lands and Letters. 2 vols., 1897–99.
Looking Back at Boyhood. 1906.
Works. 15 vols., 1907.
Louis Mitchell: A Sketch, edited by Waldo H. Dunn. 1947.

Editor, with Oliver Wendell Holmes, *The Atlantic Almanac 1868.* 1867.
Editor, *The Atlantic Almanac 1869.* 1868.
Editor, with Alfred Mitchell, *The Woodbridge Record, Being an Account of the Descendants of the Rev. John Woodbridge.* 1883.
Editor, *Daniel Tyler: A Memorial Volume.* 1883.

*

Bibliography: in *Bibliography of American Literature* by Jacob Blanck, 1973.

Critical Study: *The Life of Mitchell* by Waldo H. Dunn, 1922.

* * *

There was perhaps no writer in 19th-century America who could more appropriately be labelled "genteel" than Donald Grant Mitchell. There was also perhaps no writer who more fully expressed the ambitions and mores of middle-class Americans. Like his contemporaries Richard Watson Gilder, Thomas Bailey Aldrich, and Richard Henry Stoddard, Mitchell addressed a middle-class audience that in both public and private life gave priority to "respectability," and nowhere was respectability more firmly entrenched than in the home. In a series of "country books" that included *My Farm of Edgewood*, *Wet Days at Edgewood*, and *Rural Studies*, Mitchell detailed an ideal respectable domestic life based on his own life at Edgewood, his home in rural Connecticut. The "country books" are long out of print, but for half a century they were highly regarded. At the time of Mitchell's death in 1908, surely few of his readers could have guessed that within a generation both Edgewood and its genial master would be forgotten.

Mitchell established his reputation in 1850 with the publication of *Reveries of a Bachelor*—a book utterly without original ideas but with a wealth of sentimental observations that gave it especial appeal for young women. Mitchell never disappointed his original audience; in book after book, they (and their husbands) found abundant sentiment and gentle advice. The formula extended even to his literary criticism, collected in, among other volumes, *American Lands and Letters*. Strictly speaking, it was not literary criticism but literary appreciation that he wrote.

Mitchell's genial, invariably pleasing writings deserve greater attention than they usually receive. As literature, they are of minor interest, yet as expositions of the aspirations and values of the genteel American they are invaluable. If a reader wishes to discover the ideal perimeters of life in middle-class America a century ago, Mitchell's books can show him.

—Edward Halsey Foster

MITCHELL, Langdon (Elwyn). Born in Philadelphia, Pennsylvania, 17 February 1862; son of S. Weir Mitchell, *q.v.* Educated at St. Paul's School, Concord, New Hampshire; studied for three years in Dresden and Paris, then studied law at Harvard Law School, Cambridge, Massachusetts, and Columbia University, New York; admitted to New York bar, 1886, but did not practice. Married the actress Marion Lea in 1892; one son and two daughters. Playwright and author from mid-1880's; Lecturer in English, George Washington University, Washington, D.C., 1918–20; Professor of Playwriting, University of Pennsylvania, Philadelphia, 1928–30. Member, American Academy. *Died 21 October 1935.*

PUBLICATIONS

Plays

Sylvian, in *Sylvian: A Tragedy, and Poems*. 1885.
George Cameron (produced 1891).
In the Season (produced 1892). 1898.
Ruth Underwood (produced 1892).
Deborah (produced 1892; as *The Slave Girl*, produced 1893).
Don Pedro (produced 1892).
Becky Sharp, from the novel *Vanity Fair* by Thackeray (produced 1899). Edited by J.B. Russak, in *Monte Cristo and Other Plays*, 1941.
The Adventures of Françoise, from a novel by S. Weir Mitchell (produced 1900).
The Kreutzer Sonata, from a work by Jacob Gordin based on novel by Tolstoy (produced 1906). 1907.
The New York Idea (produced 1906). 1908.
The New Marriage (produced 1911).
Major Pendennis, from the novel by Thackeray (produced 1916).

Fiction

Love in the Backwoods (stories). 1897.

Verse

Sylvian: A Tragedy, and Poems. 1885.
Poems. 1894.

Other

Understanding America. 1927.

* * *

Langdon Mitchell's reputation in American theatre rests almost completely on one play—*The New York Idea*. His first published play, *Sylvian*, a tragedy written partly in verse and more for the closet than the stage, appeared in a volume of verse in 1885. Among his ten other plays, *Becky Sharp*, a dramatization of Thackeray's *Vanity Fair*, was a successful vehicle for the American actress Minnie Madden Fiske. But only *The New York Idea* which Arthur Hobson Quinn, the drama historian, termed a "sterling comedy," could be considered a contribution to the developing American drama. It also helped spread the work of American dramatists abroad, for it played in London, was produced in Germany as *Jonathans Tochter* under the direction of Max Reinhardt, and was translated into other European languages.

Something of a landmark in the progress of social comedy in America, *The New York Idea*—"New York is bounded on the North, South, East and West by the state of Divorce"—mixes farce-comedy with melodrama in delightful portions while Mitchell reveals his rather probing insights into the "state of Divorce" through witty and satirical comments. As a satire on marriage in New York society, the play defines marriage as "three parts love and seven parts forgiveness of sin." The fast-moving plot is determined by two divorced women each of whom plans to marry the other's ex-husband until one of them decides she really loves the man she has just divorced. Most of the characters are one-dimensional foils for the author's quick wit—the stuffy husband, the insipid clergyman, the English fop intriguer. Contrived situations such as the wedding scene and the clubhouse episode make the play successful and show Mitchell's particular skills as a dramatist. With wit, irony, and carefully created incongruities, the play treats a serious issue with a modern touch that provides some distinction to early

20th-century American drama.

Mitchell never repeated his success and, in fact, made only two more attempts to write for the theatre, neither one successful. In related work he became, in 1928, the first occupant of the Chair of Playwriting founded by the Mask and Wig Club at the University of Pennsylvania, a position he held for two years. For the student or historian of American drama he remains primarily the author of a single memorable play.

—Walter J. Meserve

MITCHELL, Margaret (Munnerlyn). Born in Atlanta, Georgia, 8 November 1900. Educated at Washington Seminary, Atlanta, 1914–18; Smith College, Northampton, Massachusetts, 1918–19. Married 1) Berrien Kinnard Upshaw in 1922 (divorced); 2) John R. Marsh in 1925. Feature writer and reporter, Atlanta *Journal and Constitution* and *Sunday Journal Magazine*, 1922–26. Recipient: Pulitzer Prize, 1937. M.A.: Smith College, 1939. *Died 16 August 1949.*

PUBLICATIONS

Fiction

Gone with the Wind. 1936.

Other

Mitchell's "Gone with the Wind" Letters 1936–1949, edited by Richard Harwell. 1976.
Mitchell, A Dynamo Going to Waste: Letters to Allen Edee 1919–1921, edited by Jane Peacock. 1985.

*

Critical Studies: *Mitchell of Atlanta* by Finis Farr, 1965; *The Road to Tara: The Life of Mitchell* by Anne Edwards, 1983; *Gone with the Wind as Book and Film* edited by Richard Harwell, 1983.

* * *

Margaret Mitchell wrote only one novel, *Gone with the Wind*, but it proved to be the most popular novel of her generation. At the time of her death in 1949, 3,800,000 copies were in print, and it continues to attract a large number of readers. *Gone with the Wind* was also made into a motion picture that at the time broke all box-office records and has since been regularly revived.

The continuing popularity of *Gone with the Wind* is not hard to account for. The tempestuous love affair of Scarlett O'Hara and Rhett Butler is in the great popular tradition. The Civil War background, the pathos of the South's defeat, the poverty and suffering (with its clear parallels to the 1930's depression) and eventual economic triumph of Scarlett, so cheering to readers with little to feel cheerful about, and then the "realistic" ending with its bitter-sweet parting of Rhett and Scarlett, contained more excitement than a dozen lesser novels. When one adds to the plethora of homely details about southern life, the humor, the dozens of colorful minor characters all presented in competent if somewhat florid prose, one understands how even a writer as discriminating as F. Scott Fitzgerald would be impressed with what Mitchell had been able to pull off.

Literary critics also found things to admire in *Gone with the Wind*; some even felt it deserved the Pulitzer prize it won in 1937 by nosing out George Santayana's *The Last Puritan*. In *Cavalcade of the American Novel*, Edward Wagenknecht praised it for undercutting the "futilitarianism" and "deflation of values" that had been so smart in the 1920's. One can see how a political message could be extracted from Scarlett O'Hara's willingness to do anything (exploit convict labor, seduce her sister's fiancé) to get the money to save the family plantation. Even more significant, however, is the contrast afforded between Mitchell's vision of southern history and William Faulkner's, particularly Mitchell's pragmatism and Faulkner's traditionalism. If one considers Faulkner's Flem Snopes one side of the moral coin, on the other side of which is Scarlett O'Hara, Mitchell's pragmatic history takes on an even deeper significance.

—W.J. Stuckey

MITCHELL, S(ilas) Weir. Born in Philadelphia, Pennsylvania, 15 February 1829. Educated at the University Grammar School, Philadelphia; University of Pennsylvania, Philadelphia, 1844–48, left because of illness without taking a degree, awarded a B.A. for Class of 1848, 1906; Jefferson Medical College, Philadelphia, M.D. 1850; studied medicine in Europe, 1850–51. Served as a surgeon in the Union Army during the Civil War. Married 1) Mary Middleton Elwyn in 1858 (died, 1862), two sons, including Langdon Mitchell, *q.v.*; 2) Mary Cadwalader in 1875. Practised medicine in Philadelphia, initially as an assistant to his father, from 1851; staff member, Philadelphia Orthopaedic Hospital and Infirmary for Nervous Diseases for forty years, and Professor at the Philadelphia Polyclinic and College for Graduates in Medicine; also a researcher: published extensively on pharmacological, physiological, and toxicological subjects, and, most notably, on his research into nervous diseases: pioneered the application of psychology to medicine; renowned for developing the theory of the "rest cure" as treatment for various mental diseases. Trustee, University of Pennsylvania, from 1875; trustee, Carnegie Institution, Washington, D.C.; first President, Franklin Inn (writer's club of Philadelphia), 1902–14. M.D.: University of Bologna, 1888; LL.D.: Harvard University, Cambridge, Massachusetts, 1886; University of Edinburgh, 1895; Princeton University, New Jersey, 1896; University of Toronto, 1906; Jefferson Medical College, 1910. Fellow, American Academy of Arts and Sciences. *Died 4 January 1914.*

PUBLICATIONS

Fiction

The Children's Hour (for children), with Elizabeth Stevenson. 1864.
The Wonderful Stories of Fuz-Buz and Mother Grabem the Spider (for children). 1867.

Hephzibah Guinness, Thee and You, and A Draft on the Banks of Spain. 1880.
In War Time. 1885.
Roland Blake. 1886.
Prince Little Boy and Other Tales Out of Fairy-Land. 1888.
Far in the Forest. 1889.
Characteristics. 1892.
Mr. Kris Kringle: A Christmas Tale. 1893.
When All the Woods Are Green. 1894.
Philip Vernon: A Tale in Prose and Verse. 1895.
A Madeira Party. 1895.
Hugh Wynne, Free Quaker. 1897.
The Adventures of François, Foundling, Thief, Juggler, and Fencing-Master During the French Revolution. 1898.
The Autobiography of a Quack, and The Case of George Dedlow. 1900.
Dr. North and His Friends. 1900.
Circumstance. 1901.
The Autobiography of a Quack and Other Stories. 1901.
A Comedy of Conscience. 1903.
Little Stories. 1903.
New Samaria, and The Summer of St. Martin. 1904.
The Youth of Washington, Told in the Form of an Autobiography. 1904.
Constance Trescot. 1905.
A Diplomatic Adventure. 1906.
A Venture in 1777 (for children). 1908.
The Red City: A Novel of the Second Administration of President Washington. 1908.
The Guillotine Club and Other Stories. 1910.
John Sherwood's Ironmaster. 1911.
Westways: A Village Chronicle. 1913.

Play

Francis Drake: A Tragedy of the Sea. 1893.

Verse

The Hill of Stones and Other Poems. 1883.
A Masque and Other Poems. 1888.
The Cup of Youth and Other Poems. 1889.
A Psalm of Deaths and Other Poems. 1891.
The Mother. 1891.
The Mother and Other Poems. 1893.
Collected Poems. 1896.
Ode on a Lycian Tomb. 1899.
The Wager and Other Poems. 1900.
Selections from the Poems. 1901.
Pearl, Rendered into Modern English Verse. 1906.
The Comfort of the Hills. 1909.
The Comfort of the Hills and Other Poems. 1910.
Complete Poems. 1914.

Other

Researches upon the Venom of the Rattlesnake. 1861.
Gunshot Wounds and Other Injuries of Nerves, with George R. Morehouse and William W. Keen. 1864.
Wear and Tear; or, Hints for the Overworked. 1871.
Injuries of Nerves and Their Consequences. 1872.
Fat and Blood, and How to Make Them. 1877; revised edition, 1878, 1884.
Lectures on Diseases of the Nervous System, Especially in Women. 1881; revised edition, 1885.
Researches upon the Venom of Poisonous Serpents, with Edward T. Reichert. 1886.
Doctor and Patient. 1888.
Two Lectures on the Conduct of the Medical Life. 1893.
The Composition of Expired Air and Its Effects upon Animal Life, with J.S. Billings and D.H. Bergey. 1895.
Clinical Lessons on Nervous Diseases. 1897.
A Brief History of Two Families: The Mitchells of Ayrshire and the Symons of Cornwall. 1912.
Some Recently Discovered Letters of William Harvey, with Other Miscellanea. 1912.
Works. 13 vols., 1913.

Editor, *Five Essays*, by John Kearsley Mitchell. 1859.

*

Bibliography: in *Bibliography of American Literature* by Jacob Blanck, 1973.

Critical Studies: *Mitchell: His Life and Letters* by Anna Robeson Burr, 1929; *Mitchell: Novelist and Physician* by Ernest Earnest, 1950; *Mitchell as a Psychiatric Novelist* by David M. Rein, 1952; *Mitchell, M.D.—Neurologist: A Medical Biography* by Richard D. Walker, 1970; *Mitchell* by Joseph P. Lovering, 1971.

* * *

S. Weir Mitchell enjoyed during his lifetime almost as wide an acclaim for his work as a physician as for his writing. The hand that produced hundreds of scientific medical treatises was no less prolific in this *other* imaginative area, as Mitchell viewed it, and he voluminously turned out novels, short fiction, and poetry. "He's a world-doctor for sure," but "I can't say that he's a world-author," said Walt Whitman. Contemporary praise that ranked one Mitchell novel with *The Scarlet Letter*, two others as superior to *Henry Esmond* and *A Tale of Two Cities*, and one of his poems as finer than "Lycidas" was sincere but excessive.

Preceding and then accompanying his novel writing, Mitchell's short fiction is noteworthy mainly for its foreshadowing and typifying. The tales of fantasy, a few O. Henryish pieces, and several Poe-esque stories of supernatural mystery are more distinctive, but traditional trappings prevail in others. Probably most memorable is "The Case of George Dedlow," the autobiography of a quadruple amputee whose legs return during a climactic séance.

Mitchell's primary success as a storyteller came from his "summer-born books," the thirteen novels which were largely vacation products of his last thirty years. More accurately labeled romances, these works reveal a pioneer physician but a literary conservative during the rise of American Realism. Mitchell made three distinct contributions to American fiction, each with important realistic implications but none with significant realistic achievement. Characterization grounded in the psychological knowledge of his clinical experience was first in time and remains first in import. His coup here, the obsessed, neurotic woman with a marked capacity for evil, is best seen in *Roland Blake*, *Circumstance*, and *Constance Trescot*. Mitchell chose his names carefully: Octopia Darnell is octopus-like in her demanding hold upon the Wynnes, Lucretia Hunter is an unscrupulous seeker of lucre, and Constance Trescot is relentless in driving her husband's killer to suicide. Mitchell rightly thought *Constance Trescot* the best of his novels. A second contribution was the creation of a convincing atmosphere of a definite past. His long works of historical fiction—*Hugh Wynne, Free Quaker*, a best-seller about the American Revolution; *The Adventures of François*, set during the French Revolution; and *The Red City*, a novel of Philadelphia in Washington's second administration—manifest the extensive research and historical immersion with which Mitchell prepared himself for their writing. His third contribution, like his first, is more suggestive than fully realized. *Characteristics* and its sequel, *Dr. North and His Friends*, have been called "conversation novels" and lauded for their experimental originality. Plainly autobiographical, they continue the tradition of Oliver Wendell Holmes's autocratic *Breakfast-Table* series but look toward the more sophisticated use of conversation and complex interpersonal relationships in more serious fiction.

Mitchell was always serious about his poetry, but the judgment he hoped it would be given by time has not been forthcoming. His own nomination for immortality was the "Ode on a Lycian Tomb," inspired by the *Les Pleureuses* monument and his deep grief for the death of a daughter.

—Bert Hitchcock

MOODY, William Vaughn. Born in Spencer, Indiana, 8 July 1869. Educated at New Albany High School, Indiana, graduated 1885; Riverview Academy, Poughkeepsie, New York, 1887–89; Harvard University, Cambridge, Massachusetts (editor, *Harvard Monthly*), 1889–94, A.B. 1893, A.M. 1894. Married Harriet Tilden Brainard in 1909. High school teacher, Corydon Pike, 1886, and Spencer, 1886–89, Indiana; Instructor in English, Harvard University and Radcliffe College, Cambridge, Massachusetts, 1894–95; Instructor in English and Rhetoric, 1895–99, and non-teaching Assistant Professor of English, 1901–08, University of Chicago; full-time writer after 1908. Litt.D.: Yale University, New Haven, Connecticut, 1908. Member, American Academy, 1908. *Died 17 October 1910.*

PUBLICATIONS

Collections

Selected Poems, edited by Robert Morss Lovett. 1931.

Plays

The Masque of Judgment: A Masque-Drama. 1900.
The Fire-Bringer. 1904.
The Great Divide (as *A Sabine Woman*, produced 1906; revised version, as *The Great Divide*, produced 1906). 1909.
The Faith Healer. 1909; revised version (produced 1910), 1910.

Verse

Poems. 1901; as *Gloucester Moors and Other Poems*, 1909.

Other

A History of English Literature, with Robert Morss Lovett. 1902; revised edition, 1918; simplified edition, as *A First View of English Literature*, 1905; as *A First View of English and American Literature*, 1909.
Poems and Plays, edited by John M. Manly. 2 vols., 1912.
Some Letters, edited by Daniel Gregory Mason. 1913.
Letters to Harriet, edited by Percy MacKaye. 1935.

Editor, *The Pilgrim's Progress*, by Bunyan. 1897.
Editor, *The Rime of the Ancient Mariner by Coleridge and The Vision of Sir Launfal by Lowell*. 1898.
Editor, *The Lady of the Lake*, by Scott. 1899.
Editor, with Wilfred Wesley Cressy, *The Iliad of Homer*, books 1, 6, 22, 24, translated by Alexander Pope. 1899.
Editor, *The Complete Poetical Works of Milton*. 1899.
Editor, with George Cabot Lodge and John Ellerton Lodge, *The Poems of Trumbull Stickney*. 1905.
Editor, *Selections from De Quincey*. 1909.

*

Bibliography: in *Bibliography of American Literature* by Jacob Blanck, 1973.

Critical Studies: *Moody: A Study* by David D. Henry, 1934; *Moody* by Martin Halpern, 1964; *Estranging Dawn: The Life and Works of Moody* by Maurice F. Brown, 1973.

* * *

After William Vaughn Moody's early death, Edwin Arlington Robinson, his close friend and literary ally, wrote Harriet Moody, "Thank God he lived to do his work—or enough of it to place him among the immortals." While that assessment now seems exaggerated, Moody's work, as a scholar, poet, and dramatist, is sufficient to give him a firm place in literary history. As the author of *The Great Divide*, he is considered the first playwright to provide the American stage with a serious, realistic, modern drama, thus ushering in the new age in American theatre. Critics have speculated that had he lived to realize his full potential, his only rival would have been Eugene O'Neill.

Martin Halpern, in his critical biography of Moody, has suggested that his literary career falls into two periods: from 1890 until the publication of *The Masque of Judgment* and *Poems*, in 1900 and 1901 respectively, his primary interest was poetry; from then until his final illness debilitated him in 1909 he worked consciously as a practicing dramatist. Although *The Masque of Judgment* is the first part of a projected dramatic trilogy, it is a closet drama in verse. And while two of the four plays he wrote during the last decade of his life are also verse dramas, they were intended for the stage.

Moody's poems have few admirers today, largely because they seem imitative of the English romantics in inflated diction and archaic subject matter. Some of his poems are innovative, however, notably his poems that involve social commentary or those that are conscious attempts to use the vernacular. "On a Soldier Fallen in the Philippines," for instance, is an ironic attack on American foreign policy. Perhaps his most celebrated poem today is "The Menagerie," a comic soliloquy in which the inebriated speaker speculates on how the animals in the zoo regard the putative fulfillment of the evolutionary process, man. The psychologically honest "The Daguerreotype," a tribute to his mother, and the ambiguous "I Am the Woman" are two disparate treatments of the symbolic and psychic implications of the feminine principle, an interest that informs "The Death of Eve." Generally his poems, like his poetic trilogy, are full of high seriousness, frequently devolving upon theological, especially eschatological, matters.

Moody's two prose plays successfully combine realistic and symbolic dramatic techniques. Originally produced as *A Sabine Woman* in Chicago, *The Great Divide* was a commercial as well as a critical success, playing for two years in New York. The play deals with the conflicting cultures of the eastern and western United States, symbolized by the abduction and eventual marriage of a woman from Massachusetts to a rough but honest man from Arizona. The less well-received *The Faith Healer* deals with the conflict between human and spiritual passions; the conflict is resolved when the protagonist discovers that his religious work is effective only when he has accepted human love.

Although *The Fire-Bringer*, Moody's verse play based on the Prometheus legend, and the fragment, *The Death of Eve*, were not produced commercially, critics have found them to be more artistically interesting than the prose plays. Moody was able to complete only one act of *The Death of Eve*, but the poem by the same title and his recorded plans for the play suggest that with it he might have achieved his dream of making verse drama a viable theatrical experience. Even so, his contribution to American drama and poetry is considerable.

—Nancy Carol Joyner

MOORE, Marianne (Craig). Born in Kirkwood, Missouri, 15 November 1887. Educated at Metzger Institute, Carlisle, Pennsylvania, 1896–1905; Bryn Mawr College, Pennsylvania, 1905–09, A.B. 1909; Carlisle Commercial College, Pennsylvania, 1909–10, diploma 1910. Head of the Commercial Studies Department, U.S. Industrial Indian School, Carlisle, 1911–15; lived in Chatham, New Jersey, 1916–17; private tutor and secretary, New York, 1918–21; part-time librarian, Hudson Park Branch of New York Public Library, 1921–25; acting editor, 1925, and editor, 1926–29, *The Dial*, New York; lived in Brooklyn, 1929–65, and Manhattan after 1966; teacher, Cummington School, Massachusetts, 1942; Visiting Lecturer, Bryn Mawr College, 1953; Ewing Lecturer, University of California, 1956. Recipient: Hartsock Memorial Prize, 1935; Shelley Memorial Award, 1941; Harriet Monroe Poetry Award, 1944; Guggenheim fellowship, 1945; American Academy grant, 1946, and Gold Medal, 1953; Pulitzer Prize, 1952; National Book Award, 1952; Bollingen Prize, 1953; Poetry Society of America Gold Medal, 1960, 1967; Brandeis University Creative Arts Award, 1962; Academy of American Poets fellowship, 1965; MacDowell Medal, 1967; National Medal for Literature, 1968. Litt.D.: Wilson College, Chambersburg, Pennsylvania, 1949; Mount Holyoke College, South Hadley, Massachusetts, 1950; Rochester University, Rochester, New York, 1951; Dickinson College, Carlisle, 1952; Rutgers University, New Brunswick, New Jersey, 1955; New York University, 1967; St. John's University, Jamaica, New York, 1968; Princeton University, New Jersey, 1968; Harvard University, Cambridge, Massachusetts, 1969; L.H.D.: Smith College, Northampton, Massachusetts, 1950; Pratt Institute, Brooklyn, 1958; D.Litt.: Washington University, St. Louis, 1967. Member, American Academy, 1955. *Died 5 February 1972.*

PUBLICATIONS

Collections

Complete Prose, edited by Patricia C. Willis. 1986.

Verse

Poems. 1921.
Marriage. 1923.
Observations. 1924; revised edition, 1925.
Selected Poems. 1935.
The Pangolin and Other Verse. 1936.
What Are Years. 1941.
Nevertheless. 1944.
Collected Poems. 1951.
Like a Bulwark. 1956.
O to Be a Dragon. 1959.
Eight Poems. 1962.
The Arctic Ox. 1964.
Tell Me, Tell Me: Granite, Steele, and Other Topics. 1966.
The Complete Poems. 1967; revised edition, 1981.
Selected Poems. 1969.
Unfinished Poems. 1972.

Play

The Absentee, from a story by Maria Edgeworth. 1962.

Other

Predilections. 1955.
Idiosyncrasy and Technique: Two Lectures. 1958.
Letters from and to the Ford Motor Company, with David Wallace. 1958.
A Moore Reader. 1961.
Dress and Kindred Subjects. 1965.
Poetry and Criticism. 1965.
Answers to Some Questions Posed by Howard Nemerov (essay). 1982.

Translator, with Elizabeth Mayer, *Rock Crystal: A Christmas Tale*, by Adalbert Stifter. 1945; revised edition, 1965.
Translator, *The Fables of La Fontaine*. 1954; *Selected Fables*, 1955.
Translator, *Puss in Boots, The Sleeping Beauty, and Cinderella: A Retelling of Three Classic Fairy Tales*, by Charles Perrault. 1963.

*

Bibliography: *Moore: A Descriptive Bibliography*, 1977, and *Moore: A Reference Guide*, 1978, both by Craig S. Abbott.

Critical Studies: *The Achievement of Moore: A Biography 1907–1957* by Eugene P. Sheehy and Kenneth A. Lohf, 1958; *Moore* by Bernard F. Engel, 1964; *Moore* by Jean Garrigue, 1965; *Moore: An Introduction to the Poetry* by George W. Nitchie, 1969; *Moore* by Sister Mary Thérèse, 1969; *Moore: A Collection of Critical Essays* edited by Charles Tomlinson, 1969; *Moore: The Cage and the Animal* by Donald Hall, 1970; *Moore: Poet of Affection* by Pamela White Hadas, 1977; *Moore: The Poet's Advance* by Laurence Stapleton, 1978; *Moore: Imaginary Possessions* by Bonnie Costello, 1981; *Moore* by Elizabeth Phillips, 1982.

* * *

Marianne Moore seems the best woman poet to have written in the United States during this century. Her poetry is richer and more inclusive than that of H.D. or of Elizabeth Bishop, to name two who resemble her in their fastidious interest in natural history—Moore's predilection and habitual material. Herself of the modernist generation of Stevens, Williams, Pound, and Eliot, she knew Williams, Pound, and H.D. in her days at Bryn Mawr College; and in the 1920's she was associated with the New York magazine *The Dial*, becoming its editor from 1926 to 1929. Like Williams, she was a naturalist in her subject-matter, and would not have disagreed with Pound's programme for Imagism. Many of the American modernist poets learned to purge their beams at her empirical eye. Yet Eliot, who could not have accepted Williams's dictum "No ideas but in things," also admired Moore's poetry for the distinction of its language. In his preface to her *Selected Poems*, he judged that she was "one of those few who have done the language some service in my lifetime."

Moore appears at first an idiosyncratic writer. She chooses odd subjects and sees them from odd angles; she is miscellaneous in her subject matter and unpredictable in her reflections; she writes in a chopped prose in lines of spectacular irregularity, but with metrical distinctness and, surprisingly often, rhyme. Yet her style, for all its asymmetry, is rapid, clear, unself-concerned, flexible, and accurate, and her work gradually discloses her exceptional sanity, intelligence, and imaginative depth. Unmistakably modern, she has no modernist formlessness; curious and precise, she is too brave in her vision to be an old maid. Some of these paradoxical qualities appear in her openings, which demand attention by their directness, as in "The Steeple-Jack":

> Dürer would have seen a reason for living
>   in a town like this, with eight stranded whales
> to look at; with the sweet sea air coming into your house
> on a fine day, from water etched
>   with waves as formal as the scales
> on a fish.

or "Silence":

> My father used to say,
> "Superior people never make long visits,
> have to be shown Longfellow's grave
> or the glass flowers at Harvard.
> Self-reliant like the cat—
> that takes its prey to privacy,
> the mouse's limp tail hanging like a shoelace from its mouth—
> they sometimes enjoy solitude . . ."

or "To a Snail":

> If "compression is the first grace of style,"
> you have it. Contractility is a virtue
> as modesty is a virtue.

or "Poetry":

> I, too, dislike it.
>   Reading it, however, with a perfect contempt for it, one discovers in
> it, after all, a place for the genuine.

This last is a complete poem, and unusually brief, although most of her poems are meditations of this characteristic briskness. "The Steeple-Jack" is a classic among her longer poems, as is "A Grave," which begins:

> Man looking into the sea,
> taking the view from those who have as much right to it as you have to it yourself,
> it is human nature to stand in the middle of a thing,
> but you cannot stand in the middle of this;
> the sea has nothing to give but a well excavated grave.

The resonance of that last line states openly, with "an elegance of which the source is not bravado," the essential seriousness which Moore often took pains to bury deep in her bright-eyed concern with the external world, of which she was such a connoisseur. Like La Fontaine, whose *Fables* she translated, she was fundamentally a humane moralist, however passionate and fine her observation of animals, baseball players, and nature's remoter aspects; and she was fundamentally serious despite her turn for the smacking epigram.

Her career illuminated the American scene for an exceptionally long time, and to increasing recognition. Her powers did not diminish, but her idiosyncrasy and allusiveness intensified. Thoroughly American and modern, she demonstrated the possibility of a highly civilised and eclectic mind operating with discrimination and unsentimental enjoyment on the premise basic to so much modern American poetry, that everything that is human is material for poetry. "Whatever it is, let it be without / affectation" ("Love in America").

—M.J. Alexander

See the essay on "Poetry."

MORLEY, Christopher (Darlington). Born in Haverford, Pennsylvania, 5 May 1890. Educated at Haverford College, 1906–10, B.A. 1910; New College, Oxford (Rhodes Scholar), 1910–13. Married Helen Booth Fairchild in 1914; one son and three daughters. Staff member, Doubleday, Page and Company, publishers, New York, 1913–17, *Ladies Home Journal*, New York, 1917–18, Philadelphia *Evening Public Ledger*, 1918–20, and New York *Evening Post*, 1920–23; a founder, 1924, and columnist ("The Bowling Green"), 1924–41, *Saturday Review of Literature*, New York. D.Litt.: Haverford College, 1933. Member, American Academy. *Died 28 March 1957*.

PUBLICATIONS

Collections

Bright Cages: Selected Poems and Translations from the Chinese, edited by John Bracker. 1965.

Fiction

Parnassus on Wheels. 1917.
In the Sweet Dry and Dry, with Bart Haley. 1919.
The Haunted Bookshop. 1919.
Kathleen. 1920.
Tales from a Rolltop Desk. 1921.
Where the Blue Begins. 1922.
Pandora Lifts the Lid, with Don Marquis. 1924.
Thunder on the Left. 1925.
Pleased to Meet You. 1927.
The Arrow. 1927; augmented edition, as *The Arrow and Two Other Stories*, 1927.
Rudolph and Amina; or, the Black Crook. 1930.
Human Being. 1932.
Swiss Family Manhattan. 1932.
The Trojan Horse. 1937.
Kitty Foyle. 1939.
Thorofare. 1942.
The Man Who Made Friends with Himself. 1949.

Plays

Thursday Evening (produced 1921). 1922.
Rehearsal. 1922.
One Act Plays (includes *Thursday Evening, Rehearsal, Bedroom Suite, On the Shelf, Walt, East of Eden*). 1924.
Where the Blue Begins, with E.S. Colling. 1925.
Good Theatre. 1926.
Really, My Dear. . . . 1928.
In Modern Dress. 1929.
The Blue and the Gray; or, War Is Hell, from the play *Allatoona* by Judson Kilpatrick and J. Owen Moore. 1930.
The Rag-Picker of Paris; or, The Modest Modiste, from the play by Edward Stirling. 1937.
Soft Shoulders (produced 1940).
The Trojan Horse. 1941.

Screenplay: *You Will Remember*, with Lydia Hayward and Sewell Stokes, 1941.

Verse

The Eighth Sin. 1912.
Songs for a Little House. 1917.
The Rocking Horse. 1919.
Hide and Seek. 1920.
Chimneysmoke. 1921.
Translations from the Chinese. 1922.
Parsons' Pleasure. 1923.
Toulemonde. 1928.
Poems. 1929.
Mandarin in Manhattan: Further Translations from the Chinese. 1933.
The Apologia of the Ampersand. 1936.
Footnotes for a Centennial. 1936.
The Middle Kingdom: Poems 1929–1944. 1944.
Spirit Level and Other Poems. 1946.
The Old Mandarin: More Translations from the Chinese. 1947.
Poetry Package, with William Rose Benét. 1950.
The Ballad of New York, New York, and Other Poems 1930–1950. 1950.
A Pride of Sonnets. 1951.
Gentlemen's Relish. 1955.

Other

Shandygaff. 1918.
Mince Pie: Adventures on the Sunny Side of Grub Street. 1919.
Travels in Philadelphia. 1920.
Pipefuls (essays). 1920.
Plum Pudding. 1921.
An Apology for Boccaccio. 1923.
Conrad and the Reporters. 1923.
Inward Ho! 1923.
The Powder of Sympathy. 1923.
Outward Bound. 1924.
Religio Journalistici. 1924.
Hostages to Fortune (miscellany). 1925.
Forty-four Essays. 1925; as *Safety Pins and Other Essays*, 1925.
Paumanok. 1926.
The Romany Stain. 1926.
I Know a Secret (for children). 1927.
The Case of Bouck White. 1927.
(*Works*). 12 vols., 1927.
The Tree That Didn't Get Trimmed. 1927.
Essays. 1928.
A Letter to Leonora. 1928.
Off the Deep End. 1928.
A Ride in the Cab of the Twentieth Century Limited. 1928.
The House of Dooner, with T.A. Daly. 1928.
The Worst Christmas Story. 1928.
Seacoast of Bohemia. 1929.
The Goldfish under the Ice (for children). 1930.
Apologia pro Sua Preoccupatione. 1930.
Born in a Beer Garden; or, She Troupes to Conquer: Sundry Ejaculations, with Ogden Nash and Cleon Throckmorton. 1930.
On the Nose. 1930.
Blythe Mountain, Vermont. 1931.
When We Speak of a Tenth—. 1931.
John Mistletoe (reminiscences). 1931.
Notes on Bermuda. 1931.
Ex Libris Carissimis (lectures). 1932.
Fifth Avenue Bus (miscellany). 1933.
Shakespeare and Hawaii (lectures). 1933.
Internal Revenue (essays). 1933.
"Effendi," Frank Nelson Doubleday 1862–1934. 1934.
Hasta la Vista; or, A Postcard from Peru. 1935.
Old Loopy: A Love Letter for Chicago. 1935.
Rare Books: An Essay. 1935.
Streamlines (essays). 1936.
Morley's Briefcase. 1936.
Morley's Magnum. 1938.
History of an Autumn. 1938.
No Crabb, No Christmas. 1938.
Letters of Askance. 1939.
Another Letter to Lord Chesterfield. 1945.

The Ironing Board (essays). 1949.
Barometers and Bookshops. 1952.
Prefaces Without Books: Prefaces and Introductions to Thirty Books, edited by Herman Abromson. 1976.

Editor, *Record of the Class of 1910 of Haverford College*. 1910.
Editor, *American Rhodes Scholars, Oxford 1910–1913*. 1913.
Editor, *The Booksellers' Blue Book*. 2 vols., 1914.
Editor, *Making Books and Magazines*. 1916.
Editor, *Modern Essays*. 2 vols., 1921–24.
Editor, *The Bowling Green: An Anthology of Verse*. 1924.
Editor, *A Book of Days*. 1930.
Editor, *Ex Libris: A Small Anthology*. 1936.
Editor, with Louella D. Everett, *Bartlett's Familiar Quotations*, 11th edition. 1937; 12th edition, 1948.
Editor, *Walt Whitman in Camden: A Selection of Prose from Specimen Days*. 1938.
Editor, *Leaves of Grass*, by Walt Whitman. 1940.
Editor, *Sherlock Holmes and Dr. Watson: A Textbook of Friendship*. 1944.
Editor, *The Best of Don Marquis*. 1946.

Translator, *Two Fables*, by Alfred de Musset and Wilhelm Hauff. 1925.
Translator, *Max and Moritz*, by Wilhelm Busch. 1932.

*

Bibliography: *A Bibliography of Morley* by Guy R. Lyle and H. Tatnall Brown, Jr., 1952.

Critical Studies: *Morley* by Mark I. Wallach and Jon Bracker, 1976; *Three Hours for Lunch: The Life and Times of Morley* by Helen McK. Oakley, 1976.

* * *

Christopher Morley was a distinguished and popular novelist, essayist, and poet, whose intense literary passions and promotions, such as his sponsorship of the writings of Joseph Conrad and his organization (with his brothers) of the Baker Street Irregulars, combine with his writings to make him one of the few genuine American "men of letters."

Morley's earliest novels, *Parnassus on Wheels* and *The Haunted Bookshop*, are brief, simple stories of booksellers in World War I America, yet they set the tone for the more sophisticated works to follow, many of which also revolve around characters involved in the literary world. *Where the Blue Begins*, an allegory about the human quest for meaning in life, is written as a dog story and enjoyed considerable success in a children's edition, but is actually a profoundly and successfully serious book. *Thunder on the Left*, which followed, is a thoughtful and controversial fantasy about the problems of children trying to come to terms with adulthood.

Kitty Foyle, Morley's best-selling novel, is an ambitious interior monologue told by a working-class girl from Philadelphia. Kitty is an atypical Morley protagonist, neither intellectual nor literary, yet *Kitty Foyle* represents Morley at the peak of his style. Derived from Morley's experiences with the "new generation" of New York career girls in the 1920's and 1930's, Kitty nonetheless displays a striking degree of individuality. Although *Kitty Foyle* largely abandons Morley's usual "mission" of bringing literature to the common man, it paradoxically comes closest of all of Morley's works to being great literature itself.

Morley's last novel, *The Man Who Made Friends with Himself*, embodies much of what is weakest and strongest in his fiction: it is intensely personal, extravagantly allusive, and rich with quotation. Somewhat autobiographical, it is a complex and demanding book to read, but worth the effort for lovers of prose style.

While Morley is best remembered as a novelist, his frequent and polished essays in the *Saturday Review*, which he helped found in 1920, were perhaps as important in establishing his distinctive reputation among his contemporaries as a "man of letters." Collected into published volumes, such as *Streamlines* and *The Ironing Board*, many of these discuss people, places, and events with literary ties. While most are meant to be informative, Morley's essays always undertake the additional task of entertaining the reader, and are among his most enjoyable works.

Much of Morley's poetry reflects his predominant concern with literature. His earliest poems, however, following his marriage in 1914, are both domestic in subject and sentimental in tone, a blend Morley (with the concurrence of his critics) coined "dishpantheism." Perhaps his most important poetry is an original genre he called "Translations from the Chinese," which Morley first conceived as a burlesque of free verse, but later developed into a shrewd, ironic vehicle for social commentary. These "Translations" are among the most readable works of a writer who, while not of the first rank, was one of his era's most versatile and interesting literary figures.

—Mark I. Wallach

MORRIS, Wright (Marion). Born in Central City, Nebraska, 6 January 1910. Educated at Lakeview High School, Chicago; Crane College, Chicago; Pomona College, Claremont, California, 1930–33. Married 1) Mary Ellen Finfrock in 1934 (divorced, 1961); 2) Josephine Kantor in 1961. Lecturer at Haverford College, Pennsylvania, Sarah Lawrence College, Bronxville, New York, and Swarthmore College, Pennsylvania; Professor of English, California State University, San Francisco, 1962–75. Also a photographer. Recipient: Guggenheim fellowship, 1942, 1946, 1954; National Book Award, 1957; American Academy grant, 1960; Rockefeller grant, 1967; National Endowment for the Arts fellowship, 1976; Western Literature Association award, 1979; American Book Award, 1981; Common Wealth award, 1982; Whiting Award, 1985. Honorary degrees: Westminster College, Fulton, Missouri, 1968; University of Nebraska, Lincoln, 1968; Pomona College, 1973. Member, American Academy, 1970. Lives in Mill Valley, California.

PUBLICATIONS

Fiction

My Uncle Dudley. 1942.
The Man Who Was There. 1945.
The World in the Attic. 1949.

Man and Boy. 1951.
The Works of Love. 1952.
The Deep Sleep. 1953.
The Huge Season. 1954.
The Field of Vision. 1956.
Love among the Cannibals. 1957.
Ceremony in Lone Tree. 1960.
What a Way to Go. 1962.
Cause for Wonder. 1963.
One Day. 1965.
In Orbit. 1967.
Green Grass, Blue Sky, White House (stories). 1970.
Fire Sermon. 1971.
War Games. 1972.
A Life. 1973.
Here Is Einbaum (stories). 1973.
The Cat's Meow (stories). 1975.
Real Losses, Imaginary Gains (stories). 1976.
The Fork River Space Project. 1977.
Plains Song: For Female Voices. 1980.
The Origin of Sadness (story). 1984.
Collected Stories 1948–1986. 1986.

Other

The Inhabitants (photo-text). 1946.
The Home Place (photo-text). 1948.
The Territory Ahead (essays). 1958.
A Bill of Rites, A Bill of Wrongs, A Bill of Goods (essays). 1968.
God's Country and My People (photo-text). 1968.
Morris: A Reader. 1970.
Love Affair: A Venetian Journal (photo-text). 1972.
About Fiction: Reverent Reflections on the Nature of Fiction with Irreverent Observations on Writers, Readers, and Other Abuses. 1975.
Structure and Artifacts: Photographs 1933–1954. 1975.
Conversations with Morris: Critical Views and Responses, edited by Robert E. Knoll. 1977.
Earthly Delights, Unearthly Adornments: American Writers as Image Makers. 1978.
Will's Boy: A Memoir. 1981.
Morris (portfolio of photographs). 1981.
Picture America, photographs by Jim Alinder. 1982.
Photographs and Words, edited by Jim Alinder. 1982.
The Writing of My Uncle Dudley (address). 1982.
Solo: An American Dreamer in Europe 1933–34. 1983.
Time Pieces: The Photographs and Words of Morris (exhibition catalogue). 1983.
A Cloak of Light: Writing My Life. 1985.

Editor, *The Mississippi River Reader*. 1962.

*

Critical Studies: *Morris* by David Madden, 1965; *Morris* by Leon Howard, 1968; *The Novels of Morris: A Critical Interpretation* (includes bibliography) by G.B. Crump, 1978; *Morris* by Roy K. Bird, 1985.

*   *   *

Wright Morris, who has been called "the most major minor novelist in America," has had greater success with the critics than with the novel-reading public. He is also an important photographer: his "photo-text" books are interspersed among the many novels he has published since 1942. In addition, Morris's critical essays on the art of fiction, and its relation to life and the modern reader, are unusually candid and stimulating. In all of his fiction the characters are vivid Americans, their talk salty and often funny; but these people also struggle with the issues and problems that beset the modern world. Morris recognizes his estrangement from other novelists and novel readers, and the reasons for it: "In my use of language there is an element that the narrative novelist has no interest in, might even find obstructive. He would say, 'One of the things that is wrong with this novel is that it holds the reader up. He has to read too carefully.' I would agree."

The Nebraska plains of Morris's first nine years haunt his imagination, and his first five books (novels and photo-texts) all take him "home" again. Then, in his novels of the early 1950's, Morris portrays people cut off from the past (and often from love): they are monsters (like Mrs. Ormsby of *Man and Boy*), or suicidal (like Will Brady of *The Works of Love*). In *The Deep Sleep* the Porter house in suburban Philadelphia becomes a symbol of America, and the events in the novel become American experience in miniature. In the three "major" Morris novels that followed—*The Huge Season, The Field of Vision*, and *Ceremony in Lone Tree*—past and present are transformed through heroism, love, and the creative imagination.

In most of his fiction Morris contrasts old and young, and the revolution of the 1960's gave him exciting new matter. New frontiers of sex are explored in *Love among the Cannibals* and *What a Way to Go*: in both erotic love is overtly important. Although the action is focused upon the animal pound in a small California town in *One Day*, the day is November 22, 1963: Morris suggests, as he also does elsewhere, that nature might well abandon human civilization and make a new start with an animal (like the chipmunk in *The Huge Season*). In typical Morris fashion, too, the intellectual pessimism is leavened by his fascination with life, revealed most clearly through the hundreds of grotesque but vital characters that crowd his novels. *In Orbit* reveals age looking at youth: age sees the horrible but hopeful, living new day, envies and even admires. The prototypical motorcycle hoodlum rapes and pillages, albeit in a sometimes burlesque way; the victims, who are "upright citizens" of a small town, are unable—apparently unwilling—to identify the culprit. Then a tornado sweeps through the village, and the townspeople have no more hope of stopping the marauding youth than of halting the devastating wind storm. Both seem awful natural forces.

In *Fire Sermon* Morris returns to the picaresque auto trip of his first novel, *My Uncle Dudley*; the journey is still from California to the midwest, but the time has moved forward from the 1920's to the 1960's. Using a familiar Morris pair-up, *Fire Sermon* takes an old man and a boy back to Nebraska, plus two hitch-hikers picked up on the way. This young hippie couple, totally free, inspire admiration in both the man and the boy; though it means the end of his day for the old man, he accepts the inevitable, natural succession of youth. *A Life* completes the story of the old man, who now seeks and achieves death at the hands of an Indian and thus fulfills a ritual requirement of nature.

Characters recur in Morris novels, sometimes (but not always) retaining the same names. Thus, Tom Scanlon first appears in *The World in the Attic*, is one of the central figures in *The Field of Vision*, and survives as the remaining inhabitant of

Lone Tree, Nebraska, in *Ceremony in Lone Tree*. Taken together (and including his most recent novels, *The Fork River Space Project* and *Plains Song: For Female Voices*), Morris's works are intent on seeking out a usable past and its impact on the present, asserting the continuity of the American character, and positing the creative and vital forces in nature.

—Clarence A. Glasrud

MOTLEY, Willard (Francis). Born in Chicago, Illinois, 14 July 1912. Educated at elementary and high schools in Chicago. Married; two sons. Transient laborer, waiter, cook, ranch hand, etc., throughout the U.S. during the 1930's: served jail sentence for vagrancy, Cheyenne, Wyoming; writer from 1939; photographer, interviewer for Chicago Housing Authority, and writer for Office of Civilian Defense, Chicago, 1940's; moved to Mexico, 1951. *Died 5 March 1965.*

PUBLICATIONS

Collections

Diaries, edited by Jerome Klinkowitz. 1979.

Fiction

Knock on Any Door. 1947.
We Fished All Night. 1951.
Let No Man Write My Epitaph. 1958.
Let Noon Be Fair. 1966.

*

Critical Study: "Motley and the Sociological Novel" by Alfred Weissgärber, in *Studi Americani 7*, 1961.

* * *

A middle-class black writer, Willard Motley refused to confine his work to racial subjects, deliberately moving into the Chicago slums in order to live in an amalgam of the backgrounds, religions, and races that later appear in his books. Sometimes called superior to Dreiser's novels or Terkel's nonfiction studies, his novels are naturalist panoramas of slum conditions. He orchestrates a dozen lives together in the same appalling career from idealistic youth to death in defeat as "cop-killer," "junkie," "whore," society's labels for its weakest victims, Motley's protagonists. There are many echoes of Zola in Motley's Chicago, the devouring Beast. Few American social realists have written with Motley's angry brilliance on ghetto immigrants, drug addiction, jack-rolling, racketeering. In his finest novel, *We Fished All Night*, Motley widens his focus on social and economic conditions in the slum—the cycle of poverty and oppression that slowly transforms his gentle adolescent heroes into "punks"—to include corporate and political structures, indeed the gangsterism at the root of World War II which leaves the slum depopulated, its few "heroes" mutilated or insane. Motley's youths (Italian, Polish, Mexican, black) are driven from home by brutality and squalor onto the streets for companionship and understanding; if they stay on the streets (in "the leer of the neon light") they end as hunted criminals; and if they try to move on, they claw their way among bribe-taking police and vote-buying politicians, ending just as hunted by their political enemies and just as criminal.

Every reader notes the flaws in Motley's work, the simplistic thesis of determinant slum environment, and the flaccidity of the last two novels where the artistic rigor relaxes and the vibrant anger often dissolves into bathos. But no reader denies Motley's astonishing ability to depict the pained squalor of life in the tenement, the poolroom, the bookie joint, the bar, the death-row cell, the addict's gibbered revery. Traditional in form, using flashback and narrated monologue within a tight chronological frame, the novels inter-relate through recurring characters, including successive generations, underscoring the sameness, the suffocating immutability of their world.

—Jan Hokenson

MOWATT, Anna Cora (née Ogden). Born in Bordeaux, France, 5 March 1819, to American parents; lived in or near Bordeaux as a child; moved with her family to New York City, 1826. Educated at Mrs. Okill's School, New York, 1826–28, and at a school in New Rochelle, New York, 1828–31. Married 1) James Mowatt in 1834 (died, 1851), three adopted children; 2) William Foushee Ritchie in 1854. Travelled abroad for her health, 1837–38; returned to New York and began writing for the stage, 1839; appeared in recitals of poetry, New York and Boston, 1841–42, and thereafter wrote under the pseudonym Helen Berkley for *Godey's Lady's Book*, *Graham's*, and other magazines, and compiled books on cooking, etiquette, etc., for various publishers; made debut as actress, New York, 1845, and appeared, with E.L. Davenport as leading man, in New York and other American cities, London, and Dublin, 1846 until she retired in 1854; full-time writer from 1854; lived abroad after 1861, mainly in Florence. Active in the campaign to preserve Mount Vernon: Vice-Regent, Mount Vernon Ladies Association of the Union, 1858–66. *Died 21 July 1870.*

PUBLICATIONS

Plays

Gulzara; or, The Persian Slave (produced 1840). In *The New World*, 1840.
Fashion; or, Life in New York (produced 1845). 1849.
Armand; or, The Peer and the Peasant (produced 1847). 1849.

Fiction

The Fortune Hunter; or, The Adventures of a Man about Town: A Novel of New York Society. 1842.
Evelyn; or, A Heart Unmasked. 1845.
Mimic Life; or, Before and Behind the Curtain (stories). 1856.
Twin Roses. 1857.
Fairy Fingers. 1865.
The Mute Singer. 1866.
The Clergyman's Wife and Other Sketches. 1867.

Verse

Pelayo; or, The Cavern of Covadonga. 1836.
Reviewers Reviewed: A Satire. 1837.

Other

Life of Goethe. 1844.
Etiquette of Courtship and Marriage. 1844.
The Management of the Sick Room. 1844.
The Memoirs of Madame d'Arblay. 1844.
Autobiography of an Actress; or, Eight Years on the Stage. 1853.
Italian Life and Legends. 1870.

*

Critical Studies: *Life and Letters* by Marius Blesi, 1952; *Anna Cora: The Life and Theatre of Mowatt* by Eric Wollencott Barnes, 1954, as *The Lady of Fashion*, 1955.

* * *

Mid-19th-century American stage history records no more engaging figure than author-actress Anna Cora Mowatt, whose performances in her own and others' plays delighted audiences throughout the United States and Britain. Though known today chiefly for her comedy, *Fashion*, an amusing satire on middle-class pretentiousness, Mowatt's popularity during the 1850's derived from numerous other writings, but primarily from the many successful roles she brought to life in both English and American theatres. Her dual career marked a turning point, demonstrating that an American woman of genteel birth, given talent, perseverance, family support, and hard work, could achieve professional recognition in theatrical circles without sacrificing social respectability.

As her autobiography reveals, the story of Mowatt's dramatic experiences is still fascinating. Born in Bordeaux, the ninth of sixteen children of wealthy Americans, she enjoyed from early childhood such cultural advantages as extensive European travel; entrée into the world of art, literature, and theatre; familial stimulus and encouragement toward creative effort; and, above all, the guidance and support of her husband, James Mowatt, whom she married at fifteen. At sixteen she published a juvenile poetic romance entitled *Pelayo; or, The Cavern of Covadonga*, and then wrote an operetta, "The Gypsy Wanderer." These youthful effusions led to more mature essays, stories, and sketches appearing in leading American periodicals, and to her three plays, *Gulzara; or, The Persian Slave*, *Fashion*, and *Armand*. Other publications included three novels, two romantic tales of theatrical life under the title *Mimic Life; or, Before and Behind the Curtain*, and the detailed account of her experiences in *Autobiography of an Actress*—in all, an impressive collection, written mainly between frequent illnesses and extended theatrical engagements.

Although Mowatt's stage performances were more widely heralded than her writings in the 1850's, throughout ensuing decades her reputation as the author of *Fashion* superseded that of her acting career. For the play not only scored immediate hits and enjoyed repeated, long-run performances in both England and America; it has continued, even within recent times, to attract more attention from producing groups than any other 19th-century American play except *Uncle Tom's Cabin*. Its enduring appeal is well deserved because no other play of its period captured so accurately or spoofed with such buoyant, satiric humor, characterization, and sprightly dialogue, the bourgeois aspirations of mid-century New York society.

—Eugene Current-Garcia

MURFREE, Mary Noailles. Pseudonym: Charles Egbert Craddock. Born at Grantland, the family estate near Murfreesboro, Tennessee, 24 January 1850; became lame as a child; moved with her family to Nashville, Tennessee, 1856. Educated at Nashville Female Academy; Chegary Institute, Philadelphia, 1867–69. Writer from 1874; lived in St. Louis, 1881–90, and thereafter in Nashville. Honorary degree: University of the South, Sewanee, Tennessee, 1922. *Died 31 July 1922.*

PUBLICATIONS

Fiction

In the Tennessee Mountains (stories). 1884.
Where the Battle Was Fought. 1884.
Down the Ravine. 1885.
The Prophet of the Great Smoky Mountains. 1885.
In the Clouds. 1886.
The Story of Keedon Bluffs. 1887.
The Despot of Broomsedge Cove. 1889.
In the "Stranger People's" Country. 1891.
His Vanished Star. 1894.
The Phantoms of the Foot-Bridge and Other Stories. 1895.
The Mystery of Witch-Face Mountain and Other Stories. 1895.
The Young Mountaineers: Short Stories. 1897.
The Juggler. 1897.
The Story of Old Fort Loudon. 1899.
The Bushwhackers and Other Stories. 1899.
The Champion. 1902.
A Spectre of Power. 1903.
The Frontiersmen (stories). 1904.
The Storm Centre. 1905.
The Amulet. 1906.
The Windfall. 1907.
The Fair Mississippian. 1908.
The Raid of the Guerilla and Other Stories. 1912.
The Ordeal: A Mountain Romance of Tennessee. 1912.
The Story of Duciehurst: A Tale of the Mississippi. 1914.

*

Bibliography: in *Bibliography of American Literature* by Jacob Blanck, 1973; "Murfree: An Annotated Bibliography" by Reese M. Carleton, in *American Literary Realism 1870–1910*, Autumn 1974.

Critical Studies: *Craddock (Murfree)* by Edd Winfield Parks, 1941; *Murfree* by Richard Cary, 1967.

* * *

Mary Noailles Murfree gained a deserved reputation in her day as an accurate and graphic local colorist. Her short stories and novels set in the mountains of Tennessee are distinguished for their accurate transcription of dialect and their vivid depictions of scenery. "I love to be particular," she stated, and in her attention to the detail of mountain background and speech she was indeed "particular."

The eight stories of *In the Tennessee Mountains*, published under the pseudonym of Charles Egbert Craddock, won immediate popularity and came to be regarded as significant contributions to the short story genre. In the books that followed, notably *Where the Battle Was Fought*, *The Prophet of the Great Smoky Mountains*, and *In the "Stranger People's" Country*, the meticulous portrayal of landscape and local color continued to be her forte.

Murfree's characterizations were sometimes stylized, and her lengthy descriptions occasionally impeded the flow of the narrative, especially in her novels. Her themes were in general restricted to a handful of set situations involving the legal tussles of mountainfolk and townspeople, the impact of the sophisticated stranger upon the mountain girl and her jealous lover, the complications that follow in the wake of the superstitious religious fanatic. None the less, many of her characters achieved a high degree of verisimilitude: her beauties and crones, her fugitives from justice, her blacksmiths and preachers. In narrating their frustrated lives against the picturesque setting of the Tennessee Mountains, Murfree captured the public imagination and gained for herself a niche in regional literature.

Her style matched her vigorous themes. It was straightforward, forceful, and robust. Thus the revelation that Charles Egbert Craddock was the pseudonym of a woman astounded not merely her readers but her editor, Thomas Bailey Aldrich of the *Atlantic Monthly*.

Although Murfree experimented with other literary genres, including the historical novel and the romance, she is remembered primarily for these local color stories. Her work has been compared, in respect of its general portrayal of scenery and people, with that of other regional writers such as Bret Harte, George Washington Cable, and Sarah Orne Jewett.

—Madeleine B. Stern

NABOKOV, Vladimir. Pseudonym (for works in Russian): V. Sirin. Born in St. Petersburg (now Leningrad), Russia, 23 April 1899; left U.S.S.R. in 1919; became U.S. citizen, 1945. Educated at the Prince Tenishev School, St. Petersburg, 1910–17; Trinity College, Cambridge, 1919–22, B.A. (honours) 1922. Married Véra Slonim in 1925; one son. Lived in Berlin, 1922–37, and Paris, 1937–40; moved to the U.S., 1940; Instructor in Russian Literature and Creative Writing, Stanford University, California, Summer 1941; Lecturer in Comparative Literature, Wellesley College, Massachusetts, 1941–48; part-time research fellow, Museum of Comparative Zoology, Harvard University, Cambridge, Massachusetts, 1942–48; Professor of Comparative Literature, Cornell University, Ithaca, New York, 1948–59; Visiting Lecturer, Harvard University, Spring 1952; lived in Montreux, Switzerland, 1961–77. Recipient: Guggenheim fellowship, 1943, 1953; American Academy grant, 1951, and Award of Merit Medal, 1969; Brandeis University Creative Arts Award, 1953; National Medal for Literature, 1973. *Died 2 July 1977.*

PUBLICATIONS

Fiction

Mashen'ka. 1926; translated by the author and Michael Glenny as *Mary*, 1970.
Korol', Dama, Valet. 1928; translated by the author and Dmitri Nabokov as *King, Queen, Knave*, 1968.
Zashchita Luzhina (The Luzhin Defense). 1930; translated by the author and Michael Scammell as *The Defense*, 1964.
Vozvrashchenie Chorba: Rasskazy i Stikhi (The Return of Chorba: Stories and Poems). 1930.
Kamera Obskura. 1932; translated by W. Roy as *Camera Obscura*, 1936; revised and translated by the author as *Laughter in the Dark*, 1938.
Podvig' (The Exploit). 1933; translated by the author and Dmitri Nabokov as *Glory*, 1971.
Otchayanie. 1936; translated by the author as *Despair*, 1937; revised edition, 1966.
Soglyadataj (The Spy). 1938; translated by the author and Dmitri Nabokov as *The Eye*, 1965.
Priglashenie na Kazn'. 1938; translated by the author and Dmitri Nabokov as *Invitation to a Beheading*, 1959.
The Real Life of Sebastian Knight. 1941.
Bend Sinister. 1947.
Nine Stories. 1947.
Dar. 1952; translated by the author and Michael Scammell as *The Gift*, 1963.
Lolita. 1955; translated by the author into Russian, 1967; *The Annotated Lolita*, edited by Alfred Appel, Jr., 1970.
Vesna v Fial'te i Drugie Rasskazi (Spring in Fialta and Other Stories). 1956.
Pnin. 1957.
Nabokov's Dozen: A Collection of 13 Stories. 1958.
Pale Fire. 1962.
Nabokov's Quartet (stories). 1966.
Ada; or Ardor: A Family Chronicle. 1969.
Transparent Things. 1972.
A Russian Beauty and Other Stories, translated by Dmitri Nabokov. 1973.
Look at the Harlequins! 1974.
Tyrants Destroyed and Other Stories, translated by the author and Dmitri Nabokov. 1975.
Details of a Sunset and Other Stories. 1976.
The Enchanter (novella), translated by Dmitri Nabokov. 1986.

Plays

Smert' (Death) 1923, *Dedushka* (Grandad) 1923, *Agaspher* (Agasfer) 1923, *Tragediya Gospodina Morna* (The Tragedy of Mr. Morn) 1924, and *Polyus* (The South Pole) 1924, all in *Rul'* (The Rudder) magazine.
Skital'tsy (The Wanderers), in *Grani II* (Facets II) magazine, 1923.
Chelovek lz SSSR (The Man from the USSR) (produced 1926). In *Rul'* (The Rudder) magazine, 1927.
Sobytie (The Event) (produced 1938). In *Russkiya Zapiski*, 1938.
Izobretenie Val'sa (produced 1968). In *Russkiya Zapiski*, 1938; translated as *The Waltz Invention* (produced 1969), 1966.
Lolita: A Screenplay. 1974.

The Man from the USSR and Other Plays, translated by Dmitri Nabokov. 1984.

Screenplay: *Lolita*, 1962.

Verse

Stikhi (Poems). 1916.
Dva Puti: Al'manakh (Two Paths: An Almanac). 1918.
Gornij Put' (The Empyrean Path). 1923.
Grozd' (The Cluster). 1923.
Stikhotvoreniya 1929–1951 (Poems). 1952.
Poems. 1959.
Poems and Problems. 1971.
Stikhi (Poems). 1979.

Other

Nikolai Gogol. 1944.
Conclusive Evidence: A Memoir. 1951; as *Speak, Memory: A Memoir*, 1952; revised edition, as *Speak, Memory: An Autobiography Revisited*, 1966.
Nabokov's Congeries: An Anthology, edited by Page Stegner. 1968; as *The Portable Nabokov*, 1977.
Strong Opinions (essays). 1973.
The Nabokov-Wilson Letters: Correspondence Between Nabokov and Edmund Wilson 1940–1971, edited by Simon Karlinsky. 1979.
Lectures on Literature, edited by Fredson Bowers. 1980.
Lectures on "Ulysses": A Facsimile of the Manuscript. 1980.
Lectures on Russian Literature, edited by Fredson Bowers. 1981.
Nabokov's Fifth Arc: Nabokov and Others on His Life's Work, edited by J.E. Rivers and Charles Nicol. 1982.
Lectures on Don Quixote, edited by Fredson Bowers. 1983.

Editor and Translator, *Eugene Onegin*, by Alexander Pushkin. 4 vols., 1964; revised edition, 4 vols., 1976.

Translator, *Nikolka Persik* (Colas Breugnon), by Romain Rolland. 1922.
Translator, *Anya v Strane Chudes* (Alice in Wonderland), by Lewis Carroll. 1923.
Translator, *Three Russian Poets: Verse Translations from Pushkin, Lermontov and Tyutchev*. 1945; as *Poems by Pushkin, Lermontov and Tyutchev*, 1948.
Translator, with Dmitri Nabokov, *A Hero of Our Time*, by Mikhail Lermontov. 1958.
Translator, *The Song of Igor's Campaign: An Epic of the Twelfth Century*. 1960.

*

Bibliography: *Nabokov: Bibliographie des Gesamtwerks* by Dieter E. Zimmer, 1963, revised edition, 1964; *Nabokov: A Bibliography* by Andrew Field, 1973; *Nabokov: A Reference Guide* by Samuel Schuman, 1979.

Critical Studies: *Escape into Aesthetics: The Art of Nabokov* by Page Stegner, 1966; *Nabokov: His Life in Art: A Critical Narrative*, 1967, *Nabokov: His Life in Part*, 1977, and *VN: The Life and Art of Nabokov*, 1986, all by Andrew Field; *Nabokov: The Man and His Work* edited by L.S. Dembo, 1967; *Keys to Lolita* by Carl R. Proffer, 1968, and *A Book of Things about Nabokov* edited by Proffer, 1974; *Nabokov: Criticism, Reminiscences, Translations, and Tributes* edited by Alfred Appel, Jr., and Charles Newman, 1970, and *Nabokov's Dark Cinema* by Appel, 1974; *Nabokov* by Julian Moynahan, 1971; *Nabokov's Deceptive World* by W. Woodlin Rowe, 1971; *Crystal Land: Artifice in Nabokov's English Novels* by Julia Bader, 1972; *Nabokov's Garden: A Guide to Ada* by Bobbie Ann Mason, 1974; *Nabokov* by Donald E. Morton, 1974; *Reading Nabokov* by Douglas Fowler, 1974; *Nabokov* by L.L. Lee, 1976; *The Real Life of Nabokov* by Alex de Jonge, 1976; *Nabokov Translated: A Comparison of Nabokov's Russian and English Prose* by Jane Grayson, 1977; *Nabokov: America's Russian Novelist* by George Malcolm Hyde, 1977; *Fictitious Biographies: Nabokov's English Novels* by Herbert Grabes, 1977; *Nabokov: The Dimensions of Parody* by Dabney Stuart, 1978; *Blue Evenings in Berlin: Nabokov's Short Stories of the 1920's* by Marina Naumann, 1978; *Nabokov: His Life, His Work, His World: A Tribute* edited by Peter Quennell, 1979; *Nabokov and the Novel* by Ellen Pifer, 1980; *Nabokov: The Critical Heritage* edited by Norman Page, 1982; *Nabokov's Novels in English* by Lucy Maddox, 1983; *The Novels of Nabokov* by Laurie Clancy, 1984; *Nabokov: A Critical Study of the Novels* by David Rampton, 1984; *Critical Essays on Nabokov* edited by Phyllis A. Roth, 1984; *Worlds in Regression: Some Novels of Nabokov* by D. Barton Johnson, 1985; *A Nabokov Who's Who* by Christine Rydel, 1986.

* * *

The most fruitful way to approach the extensive and varied Vladimir Nabokov canon (verse, plays, short stories, autobiography, translations, critical articles, and works on chess and lepidoptery) is undoubtedly through the novels, particularly the earlier Russian ones which are frequently overlooked but which contain the fundamental themes and devices of the later works. For what is striking about Nabokov's art is the consistency with which it develops, structurally and thematically, from the initial exploration of nostalgia and émigré life of Berlin in *Mary* to the celebration of language and artifice and the treatment of time in *Ada*.

Nabokov's second novel, *King, Queen, Knave*, is the first to juxtapose crime and art for parodic purposes and leaves its hero, Franz, a myopic character (literally and figuratively), stranded outside the bliss of his criminal fictions. *The Eye*, a novella whose émigré narrator is beset with split perceptions of his self, is, according to Nabokov, the first work where he develops that "involute abode" of his later fiction. Of the other novels of this Berlin/Paris period, *Despair* is the most important, since Herman Karlovich is a recognizable (though very different) predecessor to *Lolita*'s Humbert Humbert. Herman is a wily, self-conscious villain who devises a complex crime involving the murder of his double, who, however, does not resemble Herman at all. Herman's "perfect crime," and his journal which records that crime, are flawed by the same misconception; he fails to realize that contingent reality cannot be manipulated and that "the invention of art contains far more truth than life's reality."

The Gift is important for its exploration of biography as a fictional form, an exploration which is also prominent in Nabokov's first English novel, *The Real Life of Sebastian Knight*. V., the narrator, attempts to write the biography of his brother, Sebastian Knight, but is foiled at every turn since Knight's life moves with that same obliqueness as the chess piece after which he is named. Ultimately, however, V.'s narrative approximates Sebastian's life by virtue of the dynamic character of the unfulfilled quest which uses parody as "a kind of springboard for leaping into the highest region of serious emotion."

Pnin is a warmly witty but sad portrait of Professor Timofey Pnin, an aging Russian exile attempting to master American language and culture at a New England university; the professorial politicking finally defeats him. Besides its preoccupation with cultural exile, the novel shows a self-consciousness of language, though never to the extent that we find in Nabokov's best-known novel, *Lolita*. In fact, given that Humbert Humbert, the narrator and hero, writes about his nympholeptic escapades with the twelve-year-old Lolita in prison where he has "only words to play with," language frames the entire novel and is the vehicle through which Humbert and Lolita are finally relegated to the "bliss of fiction." Humbert's sexual desire becomes a metaphor for the artistic desire to create, though not until Humbert learns the hard lesson that it is desire and not possession which is the transcendent reality. So when Humbert possesses Lolita in part I of the novel (the crime), he is forced to protect her jealously in a motel trek across America in part II (the getaway). He has violated the "intangible island of entranced time" which is established early in the novel with his childhood love, Annabel Lee. It is Annabel Lee in her "kingdom by the sea" who establishes the initial rift between desire and possession. Ultimately, Lolita is abducted from Humbert by Quilty, Humbert's double, and the final chase scene culminates in Quilty's murder, a comic, grotesque exorcism that allows Humbert some measure of grace in the "bliss of fiction."

Pale Fire is the most experimental and enigmatic of Nabokov's novels, since its structure entails a 999-line poem by John Shade and a foreword, commentary with footnotes, and index by Charles Kinbote, the poet's homosexual neighbour who is really an exile from the distant northern land of Zembla (Russia). Beyond the obvious parody of pedantic scholarship, the novel explores the interdependencies of multi-layered worlds, each reflecting and refracting the other: Shade tells his story in verse; Kinbote uses Shade's poem to reveal his Zemblan past; Gradus, a secret agent intent on killing Kinbote, murders Shade by mistake; and of course, stalking through the work there is Nabokov, the arch-inventor of them all. Because the narrative of each layer is invented and sustained by the other, the final effect is a spiral of artifice.

Ada, Nabokov's most ambitious fiction (although its status among critics remains uncertain), fuses the novelist's earlier themes and techniques with greater scope and linguistic dexterity. The opening three chapters present a baroque invocation, a fanfare of language for the core of the novel which chronicles the incestuous love affair of the precocious hero, Van Veen, and his sister, Ada. Van's obsession with the past and the novel's eroticism culminate in part IV in a long lecture on time and space. Here the past becomes an inseparable link to the present, making a "glittering 'now' that is the only reality of Time's texture." Erotic desire, the art of inventing, and the butterfly's life cycle are metaphors for the constant metamorphosis of the present, while the future is relegated to an unknowable realm of space. The narrative moves across an imaginary geography of overlapping Russian, European, and American landscapes, with an equally overlaid texture of language. All the familiar Nabokovian motifs and devices are heaped against the aristocratic setting of the "ardors and arbors of Ardis Hall": butterflies and botany, dreams and doubles, puns, word games, nostalgia, false leads, and eroticism. It is undoubtedly Nabokov's most festive celebration of language, artifice, and, what should not be overlooked, love.

Transparent Things is a novella bordering on the metaphysical as it deals with the transparency of objects in the present, and finally of life itself, as death, abetted by chance, brings Hugh Person to a characteristic Nabokovian ending. *Look at the Harlequins!* is a first-person memoir of a writer whose life and works have disguised parallels with Nabokov's own. It is a fiction created out of fiction, a deepening of the labyrinth of inventing. And while these two works never surpass *Ada*, they do illustrate what has been evident in Nabokov from the start, namely, that fiction becomes the only sustained reality beyond contingent existence—even, no doubt, the sustenance of self.

—Brent MacLaine

See the essay on *Lolita*.

NASBY, Petroleum V(esuvius). Pseudonym for David Ross Locke. Born in Vestal, near Binghamton, New York, 20 September 1833. Educated at schools in Marathon, New York, 1840–45. Married Martha Hannah Bodine in 1855; three sons. Apprentice printer, Cortland *Democrat*, Cortland, New York, 1845–50; printer, Corning *Journal*, Corning, New York, 1850–51, and Cleveland *Herald* and *Plain Dealer*, 1852; co-owner and editor, Plymouth *Advertiser*, Ohio, 1853–55; publisher, Mansfield *Herald*, 1855–56, and Bucyrus *Journal*, 1856–61, both Ohio; publisher and editor, *Hancock Jeffersonian*, Findlay, Ohio, 1861–65 (wrote first Nasby letter for the paper, 1862); worked for a drug firm in Findlay, 1864–65; owner, Bellefontaine *Republican*, Ohio, 1864; editor, Toledo *Blade*, Ohio, 1865–88 (wrote Nasby letters for the paper until 1887); on lecture circuit in U.S., 1867–73; publisher and treasurer, New York *Evening Mail*, 1871–78; partner in advertising business, New York, 1873–75. Alderman from third ward, Toledo, 1886–88. *Died 15 February 1888.*

PUBLICATIONS

Fiction and Sketches

The Nasby Papers. 1864.
Divers Views, Opinions, and Prophecies of Yours Trooly, Petroleum V. Nasby. 1866; abridged edition, as *Let's Laugh*, edited by Lloyd E. Smith, 1924.
Androo Johnson, His Life. 1866.
Swingin' round the Cirkle. 1867.
Ekkoes from Kentucky. 1868.
The Impendin Crisis uv the Democracy. 1868.
The Struggles (Social, Financial and Political) of Petroleum V. Nasby. 1872; revised edition, 1888; abridged edition, edited by Joseph Jones, 1963.
The Morals of Abou Ben Adhem. 1875.
Inflation at the Cross Roads. 1875.
The President's Policy. 1877.
A Paper City (novel). 1879.
The Democratic John Bunyan. 1880.
The Diary of an Office Seeker. 1881.
Nasby in Exile; or, Six Months of Travel. 1882.
The Demagogue (novel). 1891.
The Nasby Letters. 1893.
Civil War Letters, edited by Harvey S. Ford. 1962.

Plays

Inflation, with Charles Gayler (produced 1876).
Widow Bedott (produced 1879).

Verse

Hannah Jane. 1882.

Other (temperance pamphlets)

Beer and the Body. 1884.
Prohibition. 1886.
High License Does Not Diminish the Evil. 1887.

*

Bibliography: by James C. Austin, in *American Literary Realism 4*, 1971.

Critical Studies: *Nasby* by James C. Austin, 1965; *The Man Who Made Nasby, David Ross Locke* by John M. Harrison, 1969.

* * *

Petroleum V. Nasby was the creation of David Ross Locke, one of America's greatest newspapermen. Beginning as a printer at the age of twelve and progressing successfully as writer, editor, and publisher of several New York and Ohio newspapers, he took over the Toledo, Ohio, *Blade* in 1865, and made it one of the most widely read papers in the midwest. He had very little schooling, but he developed a rough but powerful editorial style that contributed to the course of American history. He supported the Republican Party from its beginnings. His opposition to the Confederacy during the Civil War encouraged the Union cause and President Lincoln personally. His insistence on the rights of blacks helped lead public opinion toward the Emancipation Proclamation and the Thirteenth, Fourteenth, and Fifteenth Amendments to the Constitution. His attacks on political corruption promoted Civil Service reform and the exposure of political fraud in the Gilded Age. He aided the causes of prohibition and women's rights which led long after his death to the Eighteenth and Nineteenth Amendments.

But his greatest and most lasting fame came from the Nasby letters—a series of newspaper columns written from 1862 until shortly before Locke's death in 1888. Petroleum Vesuvius Nasby, the fictitious writer of the letters, stood for everything that Locke was against. Nasby was an illiterate, drunken, bigoted, racist Democrat. The Nasby letters are considered part of the American tradition of crackerbox humor—journalistic humor expressed in a lowbrow, rustic dialect and with a common-sense philosophy. But they are not humorous in a strict sense of the term; they are bitterly satirical, violently partisan, grossly concrete pictures of the American political scene. With the exception of Benjamin Franklin, Locke was probably America's greatest political satirist.

The best-known Nasby letters were collected in various books beginning in 1864. The best of these is *Divers Views*, which exposed blatantly the pro-Southern views of the Ohio Copperhead, Nasby, during the Civil War. But each collection included parts of the earlier material, and *The Nasby Letters* is the most complete, comprising a panorama of Republican thought and action during the most critical quarter-century of United States history.

The Nasby letters were but a part of Locke's literary activities. He was one of the most popular lecturers in America in an age when public lecturing was as important as television is today. His three famous lectures, delivered throughout the country under the pseudonym of Nasby, were small masterpieces on the issues of civil rights for blacks, women's rights, and political corruption. He was the author of two excellent political novels, *A Paper City* and *The Demagogue*, two plays, *Inflation* and *Widow Bedott*, the latter being performed continually into the 20th century; a very popular, very sentimental poem, *Hannah Jane*; a number of quite creditable hymns; and an untold number of articles, editorials, stories, novels, verses, and essays in newspapers, magazines, and pamphlets.

Locke did not pretend to be a literary artist. He wrote for his times, and he believed that politics was the most important concern of a democracy. He was a significant editor and publisher. And his Nasby letters and his lectures deserve continued attention.

—James C. Austin

NASH, (Frederick) Ogden. Born in Rye, New York, 19 August 1902. Educated at St. George's School, Newport, Rhode Island, 1917–20; Harvard University, Cambridge, Massachusetts, 1920–21. Married Frances Rider Leonard in 1931; two daughters. Teacher, St. George's School, 1922–23; bond salesman on Wall Street, New York, 1924; worked in advertising department of Doubleday, publishers, New York, 1925–31; editorial staff member, *New Yorker*, 1932, and regular contributor thereafter; screenwriter in Hollywood, 1936–42; panelist, *Masquerade* radio program, 1950's. Recipient: Sarah Josepha Hale Award, 1964. Member, American Academy. *Died 19 May 1971*.

PUBLICATIONS

Collections

I Wouldn't Have Missed It: Selected Poems, edited by Linell Smith and Isabel Eberstadt. 1975.

Verse

Hard Lines. 1931.
Free Wheeling. 1931.
Hard Lines and Others. 1932.
Happy Days. 1933.
Four Prominent So and So's, music by Robert Armbruster. 1934; as *Four Prominent Bastards Are We*, 1934.
The Primrose Path. 1935.
The Bad Parent's Garden of Verse. 1936.
Bon Voyage. 1936.
I'm a Stranger Here Myself. 1938.
The Face Is Familiar: Selected Verse. 1940; revised edition, 1954.
Good Intentions. 1942; revised edition, 1956.
The Nash Pocket Book. 1944.

Many Long Years Ago. 1945.
Selected Verse. 1946.
Nash's Musical Zoo, music by Vernon Duke. 1947.
Versus. 1949.
Family Reunion. 1950.
The Private Dining Room and Other New Verses. 1953.
You Can't Get There from Here. 1957.
Verses from 1929 On. 1959; as *Collected Verse from 1929 On*, 1961.
Scrooge Rides Again. 1960.
Everyone But Thee and Me. 1962.
Marriage Lines: Notes of a Student Husband. 1964.
The Mysterious Ouphe. 1965.
A Nash Omnibook. 1967.
Santa Go Home: A Case History for Parents. 1967.
There's Always Another Windmill. 1968.
Funniest Verses, edited by Dorothy Price. 1968.
Bed Riddance: A Posy for the Indisposed. 1970.
The Old Dog Barks Backwards. 1972.

Plays

One Touch of Venus, with S.J. Perelman, music by Kurt Weill, from *The Tinted Venus* by F. Anstey (produced 1943). 1944.
Sweet Bye and Bye (lyrics only), book by S.J. Perelman and Al Hirschfeld, music by Vernon Duke (produced 1946).
Two's Company (lyrics only; revue) (produced 1952).
The Littlest Revue, with others (produced 1956).

Screenplays: *The Firefly*, with Frances Goodrich and Albert Hackett, 1937; *The Shining Hour*, with Jane Murfin, 1938; *The Feminine Touch*, with George Oppenheimer and Edmund L. Hartmann, 1941.

Other (for children)

The Cricket of Carador, with Joseph Alger. 1925.
Parents Keep Out: Elderly Poems for Youngerly Readers. 1951.
The Christmas That Almost Wasn't. 1957.
The Boy Who Laughed at Santa Claus. 1957.
Custard the Dragon. 1959.
A Boy Is a Boy: The Fun of Being a Boy. 1960.
Custard the Dragon and the Wicked Knight. 1961.
The New Nutcracker Suite and Other Innocent Verses. 1962.
Girls Are Silly. 1962.
The Adventures of Isabel. 1963.
A Boy and His Room. 1963.
The Untold Adventures of Santa Claus. 1964.
The Animal Garden. 1965.
The Cruise of the Aardvark. 1967.
The Scroobious Pip, by Edward Lear (completed by Nash). 1968.

Other

Born in a Beer Garden; or, She Troupes to Conquer: Sundry Ejaculations, with Christopher Morley and Cleon Throckmorton. 1930.

Editor, *Nothing But Wodehouse*. 1932.
Editor, *The Moon Is Shining Bright as Day: An Anthology of Good-Humored Verse*. 1953.
Editor, *I Couldn't Help Laughing: Stories* (for children). 1957.
Editor, *Everybody Ought to Know: Verses Selected and Introduced*. 1961.

*

Critical Study: *An Index to the Poems of Nash* by Lavonne B. Axford, 1972.

* * *

Ogden Nash's career as a writer of light verse began in the 1930's when he accepted defeat as a poet. Realizing that his serious verses were tongue-tied and sentimental, he began constructing a peculiar form of doggerel which broke all rules of symmetry and harmony in poetry. Lines grew as long as subway trains, capped by rhymes as outrageous as cocktail party chatter; philosophical questions were mocked by horse-sensical conclusions. "What is life? Life is stepping down a step or sitting on a chair, / And it isn't there." Though it wasn't great poetry, it made Nash America's most popular comic poet.

With these techniques, Nash was able to express poetically the plain-spoken American's frustration with poetic complication, as well as the conviction that, really, poetry is just prose that rhymes. (Or should be, Nash hints: "One thing that literature would be greatly the better for / Would be a more restricted use of simile and metaphor.") In the Introduction to the 1975 Nash collection *I Wouldn't Have Missed It*, Archibald MacLeish gave away the secret: "Nothing . . . suggests the structure of verse but the rhymes" which are used baldly to shoehorn sentences into what looked like verse. Basing his poems not on the poetic line, but on the sentence, Nash became (in his work) a "wersifier" painting men, women, and society from their poetic backsides.

Like his wersification, Nash's subjects come straight out of everyday life: summer colds and Monday mornings, leaky faucets and crashing bores. He is assailed by the mundane torments of living, perplexed by the oddities and failings of human nature, and mystified by women, just as they are by men. Yet no matter how disastrous life may be, Nash reassures us that perhaps it isn't so bad after all: "When I consider how my life is spent, / I hardly ever repent."

—Walter Bode

NEAL, John. Born in Falmouth (now Portland), Maine, 25 August 1793. Educated at local schools. Married Eleanor Hall in 1828; five children. Clerk in a succession of shops in Portland, then itinerant teacher of penmanship and drawing in various towns along the Kennebec River; settled in Baltimore: co-owner of dry goods store, 1814–16; studied law, while writing for a living (briefly editor of Baltimore *Telegraph*; contributed to *Portico*; assisted Paul Allen in compiling *A History of the American Revolution*; published novels), 1816–23: admitted to bar, 1819; lived in England, 1823–27: contributor to *Blackwood's* and other periodicals, and secretary to Jeremy Bentham; returned to the U.S., 1827, settled in Portland, and practised law there; editor, *Yankee*, 1828–29; later briefly editor of *New England Galaxy*, Boston, and a Portland newspaper; editor, *Brother Jonathan* (comic), New York, 1843; contributor to *North American Review, Harper's*, and *Atlantic Monthly*, from 1850. M.A.: Bowdoin College, Brunswick, Maine, 1836. *Died 20 June 1876.*

PUBLICATIONS

Collections

Observations on American Art: Selections from the Writings, edited by Harold Edward Dickson. 1943.
The Genius of Neal: Selections, edited by Benjamin Lease and Hans-Joachim Lang. 1978.

Fiction

Keep Cool: A Novel, Written in Hot Weather. 1817.
Logan: A Family History. 1822.
Errata; or, The Works of Will Adams. 1823.
Randolph. 1823.
Seventy-Six. 1823.
Brother Jonathan; or The New Englanders. 1825.
Rachel Dyer: A North American Story. 1828.
Authorship: A Tale. 1830.
The Down-Easters. 1833.
True Womanhood: A Tale. 1859.
The White-Faced Pacer; or, Before and After the Battle. 1863.
The Moose-Hunter; or, Life in the Maine Woods. 1864.
Little Mocassin; or, Along the Madawaska: A Story of Life and Love in the Lumber Region. 1866.

Play

Otho. 1819.

Verse

The Battle of Niagara. 1818; revised edition, 1819.

Other

One Word More: Intended for the Reasoning and Thoughtful among Unbelievers. 1854.
Account of the Great Conflagration in Portland. 1866.
Wandering Recollections of a Somewhat Busy Life: An Autobiography. 1869.
Great Mysteries and Little Plagues. 1870.
Portland Illustrated. 1874.
American Writers, edited by Fred Lewis Pattee. 1937.

*

Bibliography: in *Bibliography of American Literature* by Jacob Blanck, 1973.

Critical Studies: *A Down-East Yankee from the District of Maine* by Windsor Pratt Daggett, 1920; *That Wild Fellow Neal and the American Literary Revolution* by Benjamin Lease, 1972; *Neal* by Donald A. Sears, 1978; *A Right View of the Subject: Feminism in the Works of Charles Brockden Brown and Neal* by Fritz Fleischmann, 1983.

* * *

Strongly influenced by American nationalism following the War of 1812, John Neal developed a theory of literature that, put into practice in a series of unusual novels, has helped to win him a minor place in American literary history. Concerned that American writers like Charles Brockden Brown, Washington Irving, and James Fenimore Cooper were not sufficiently "American" in their writing, Neal sought to create an original body of fiction that would imitate no foreign models, and would accurately depict American persons and places and faithfully reproduce the American language. He constructed his works, moreover, on a psychological theory that placed great stress on the "heart" and the "blood," as opposed to the mind, a theory that led him to write rather formless fictions that frequently lapse into incoherence.

He turned to the American past for some of his novels—Indian conflicts in *Logan*, the American Revolution in *Seventy-Six* and *Brother Jonathan*, and the Salem witch trials in *Rachel Dyer*—and he drew American characters and reproduced American speech with considerable skill. At his best, Neal achieved a degree of realism uncommon in his time and occasionally reached a depth of psychological penetration suggestive of Poe. At his worst, however, he strained too much for effect, descended to Byronic posturing, indulged in both gothic and sentimental absurdities, and fell into melodrama. All of Neal's books suffer to some degree from his excesses, and from his unwillingness—or inability—to give form to his novels. Only *Rachel Dyer*, perhaps his best book, exhibits a sustained authorial control, but even it has a long and digressive passage in one of the courtroom scenes.

Neal's one significant contribution to American fiction is his style. Derived from the cadences of American speech, it ranges from local dialect through the more general vernacular to the biblical or prophetic. At its best, it gives a sense of immediacy to his work, whether the story is told, like *Seventy-Six*, by a common man who uses his natural language, or, like *Rachel Dyer*, by a narrative voice appropriately attuned to the seriousness of the action and theme. Neal was especially skillful in moving his story forward through the speech of his characters, and in some of his works, the reader will find page after page containing little more than conversation. In both style and narrative technique, therefore, Neal stands near the head of the vernacular tradition in American literature and dimly foreshadows the language of Mark Twain.

—Donald A. Ringe

NEMEROV, Howard (Stanley). Born in New York City, 1 March 1920; brother of the photographer Diane Arbus. Educated at Fieldston School, New York, graduated 1937; Harvard University, Cambridge, Massachusetts (Bowdoin Prize, 1940), A.B. 1941. Served in the Royal Canadian Air Force, 1942–44: Flying Officer; and the U.S. Air Force, 1944–45: First Lieutenant. Married Margaret Russell in 1944; three sons. Instructor in English, Hamilton College, Clinton, New York, 1946–48; member of the Literature Faculty, Bennington College, Vermont, 1948–66; Professor of English, Brandeis University, Waltham, Massachusetts, 1966–69; Hurst Professor of English, 1969–76, and since 1976 Edward Mallinckrodt Distinguished University Professor, Washington University, St. Louis. Visiting Lecturer, University of Minnesota, Minneapolis, 1958–59; Writer-in-Residence, Hollins College, Virginia, 1962–64; Consultant in Poetry, Library of Congress, Washington, D.C., 1963–64. Associate editor, *Furioso*, Madison, Connecticut, later Northfield, Minnesota, 1946–51. Recipient: American Academy grant, 1961; New England Poetry Club Golden Rose, 1962; Brandeis University Creative Arts Award, 1962; National Endowment for the Arts grant, 1966; Theodore Roethke Award, 1968; Guggenheim fellowship, 1968; St. Botolph's Club prize, 1968; Academy of American Poets fellowship, 1970; Pulitzer Prize, 1978; National Book Award, 1978; Bollingen Prize, 1981. D.L.: Lawrence University, Appleton, Wisconsin, 1964; Tufts University, Medford, Massachusetts, 1969; Washington and Lee University, Lexington, Virginia, 1976; University of Vermont, Burlington, 1979; Cleveland State University; Hamilton College, Clinton, New York; McKendree College, Lebanon, Illinois. Fellow, American Academy of Arts and Sciences, 1966; member, American Academy, 1976; Chancellor, Academy of American Poets, 1977. Lives in St. Louis.

PUBLICATIONS

Verse

The Image and the Law. 1947.
Guide to the Ruins. 1950.
The Salt Garden. 1955.
Small Moment. 1957.
Mirrors and Windows. 1958.
New and Selected Poems. 1960.
The Next Room of the Dream: Poems and Two Plays. 1962.
Five American Poets, with others, edited by Ted Hughes and Thom Gunn. 1963.
Departure of the Ships. 1966.
The Blue Swallows. 1967.
A Sequence of Seven. 1967.
The Winter Lightning: Selected Poems. 1968.
The Painter Dreaming in the Scholar's House. 1968.
Gnomes and Occasions. 1972.
The Western Approaches: Poems 1973–1975. 1975.
The Collected Poems. 1977.
By Al Lebowitz's Pool. 1979.
Sentences. 1980.
Inside the Onion. 1984.

Play

Endor. 1962.

Fiction

The Melodramatists. 1949.
Federigo; or, The Power of Love. 1954.
The Homecoming Game. 1957.
A Commodity of Dreams and Other Stories. 1959.
Stories, Fables, and Other Diversions. 1971.

Other

Poetry and Fiction: Essays. 1963.
Journal of the Fictive Life. 1965.
Reflexions on Poetry and Poetics. 1972.
Figures of Thought: Speculations on the Meaning of Poetry and Other Essays. 1978.
New and Selected Essays. 1985.

Editor, *Longfellow*. 1959.
Editor, *Poets on Poetry*. 1966.

*

Bibliography: *Elizabeth Bishop and Nemerov: A Reference Guide* by Diana E. Wyllie, 1983.

Critical Studies: *Nemerov* by Peter Meinke, 1968; *The Critical Reception of Nemerov: A Selection of Essays and a Bibliography* edited by Bowie Duncan, 1971; *The Shield of Perseus: The Vision and Imagination of Nemerov* by Julia A. Bartholomay, 1972; *The Stillness in Moving Things: The World of Nemerov* by William Mills, 1975; *Nemerov* by Ross Labrie, 1980.

* * *

Although Howard Nemerov has written a journal, two collections of short stories, three novels, and much fine criticism (including exceptionally insightful essays on Wallace Stevens, Dylan Thomas, and Vladimir Nabokov), his primary importance as a writer stems from his poetry. He is a superior craftsman, particularly skilled at blank verse. Moreover, the content of his poetry is quite penetrating. Perhaps the foremost reason for this richness in content is that Nemerov believes that a major function of the poet is to try to perceive reality precisely as it is. "The Private Eye" makes it clear that the artist should strip himself of preconceptions. In "Vermeer" Nemerov praises this painter for taking "what is, and seeing it as it is."

Despite the fact that reality contains patterns, Nemerov finds that, fundamentally, reality is primitive and chaotic. "The Town Dump" and "The Quarry" stress the relentless chaotic decay occurring in our world, while raw primitiveness is emphasized in "Lobsters." "The Goose Fish" reports that nature is also impenetrably enigmatic. No Dionysian oneness fusing man and nature is possible. Instead, nature is apt to paralyze man's will, as it does the speaker's in "Death and the Maiden."

Man, then, is a very limited creature, a main point in both of Nemerov's verse plays, *Endor* and *Cain*. For Nemerov the other major function of the artist is to create some kind of comforting order, even though this order is only temporary and subjective. Nemerov stresses this point in such poems as "Elegy for a Nature Poet" and "Lines and Circularities." He also reminds us, in "Monet" for example, that nature's beauty can stir us to create works of art celebrating that beauty. However, we must never think that human creations can "replace" reality—the warning given in "Projection." So, too, after meditating on reality, we must return to it, a theme in "The Sanctuary."

Because nature is ceaselessly changing, Nemerov suggests that man, too, should be flexible. "Lot Later" dramatizes this point. Man should not let the past imprison him; for even sanctified history can later be proven false, the point in "To Clio, Muse of History." Nevertheless, man should not let himself be crippled by cynicism, as is the Minister in *Endor*.

Nemerov's poetry is valuable because it incisively presents us with a no-nonsense view of the world, a view that is stark, but not entirely negative. In "The View from an Attic Window" he declares that we live amid chaos, that our individual lives are short, and that, as a result, "life is hopeless," yet "beautiful"—and we should try to endure and to grow. We can summon the strength to cope with what haunts us late in life (described in "Insomnia I") and with our own death ("Last Things"). Finally, Nemerov maintains that our love of the physical world is not a foolish emotion. We gain sustenance from it and, as "Autumnal" states, from the love that can exist between two people.

—Robert K. Johnson

NIN, Anaïs. Born in Paris, France, 21 February 1903; moved to the U.S. in 1914; later became U.S. citizen. Educated at John Jasper Elementary School, New York, 1914–18. Married Hugh Guiler (also called Ian Hugo) in 1924(?). Fashion and artist's model, 1918–20; lived in Paris, 1930–40; established Siana Editions, Paris, 1935; moved to New York, 1940, and established Gemor Press. Member, American Academy. *Died 14 January 1977.*

PUBLICATIONS

Fiction

The House of Incest. 1936.
The Winter of Artifice. 1939.
Under a Glass Bell. 1944; augmented edition, as *Under a Glass Bell and Other Stories*, 1948.
This Hunger. 1945.
Ladders to Fire. 1946.
Children of the Albatross. 1947.
The Four-Chambered Heart. 1950.
A Spy in the House of Love. 1954.
Solar Barque. 1958.
Cities of the Interior. 1959.
Seduction of the Minotaur. 1961.
Collages. 1964.
Cities of the Interior (collection). 1974.
Waste of Timelessness and Other Early Stories. 1977.
Delta of Venus: Erotica. 1977.
Little Birds: Erotica. 1979.
The White Blackbird and Other Writings, with *The Tale of an Old Geisha and Other Stories* by Kanoko Okamoto. 1985.

Other

D.H. Lawrence: An Unprofessional Study. 1932.
Realism and Reality. 1946.
On Writing. 1947.
The Diary, edited by Gunther Stuhlmann. 6 vols., 1966–76; as *The Journals*, 6 vols., 1966–77; *A Photographic Supplement*, 1974.
The Novel of the Future. 1968.
Unpublished Selections from the Diary. 1968.
Nuances. 1970.
An Interview with Nin, by Duane Schneider. 1970.
Paris Revisited. 1972.
Nin Reader, edited by Philip K. Jason. 1973.
A Woman Speaks: The Lectures, Seminars, and Interviews of Nin, edited by Evelyn J. Hinz. 1975.
In Favor of the Sensitive Man and Other Essays. 1976.
Aphrodisiac, with John Boyce. 1978.
Linotte: The Early Diary 1914–1920, translated by Jean Sherman. 1978; *The Early Diary 1920–1931*, 3 vols., 1982–85.
Henry and June: From the Unexpurgated Diary. 1986.

*

Bibliography: *Nin: A Bibliography* by Benjamin Franklin V, 1973; *Nin: A Reference Guide* by Rose Marie Cutting, 1978.

Critical Studies: *Nin* by Oliver Evans, 1968; *The Mirror and the Garden: Realism and Reality in the Writings of Nin* by Evelyn J. Hinz, 1971; *A Casebook on Nin* edited by Robert Zaller, 1974; *Collage of Dreams: The Writings of Nin* by Sharon Spencer, 1977; *Nin: An Introduction* by Benjamin Franklin V and Duane Schneider, 1979; *Nin* by Bettina L. Knapp, 1979; *Nin* by Nancy Scholar, 1984.

* * *

Anaïs Nin's fiction may best be described as symphonic tone poems in prose, with their programmatic intermingling of similar themes and characters from one novel to another. Her characters are dancers, actresses, artists, musicians, and writers, all impelled by inner visions, illusions, or frustrations, who play their solo parts contrapuntally and always return as in the rondo form to the central female protagonist, with whom they all interact. Also characteristic of tone poems, Nin's style is psychologically discursive and impressionistic, with dreams and interior monologues substituting for the realism, dialogue, and clearly delineated plots of more traditional narratives. And her language is rhythmic, rich in sensuous imagery, and symbolic.

Nin's interests and opinions weave in and out of her novels like leitmotifs as contrapuntally as her characters do. Haunting all her fiction are evocations of music—jazz, opera, symphony—which Nin views as the inevitable preserver of memory and thus a barrier to all efforts to escape the past. Her faith in psychoanalysis as a tool for plumbing that past for constructive creative resources pervades all the novels, as does her belief in the permanency of art in contrast to the ephemerality of politics. Her fiction is totally apolitical; it focuses instead on the intricacies of intense physical and emotional relationships. Through these relationships, Nin also manifests her strong conviction in the fundamentally different sensibilities of men and women. Her men are usually unable to accept emotional responsibilities, are frustrated by their inability to act, and are drawn to the vision and sensitivity of nurturing women. Her women are seductive, submissive, and vulnerable because of their need for men; at the same time, they struggle to overcome this dependency on authority figures and to develop into independent human beings. Nin's depiction of women's search for a synthesis of these contrary facets of their personality along with her explicit rendering of female responses to sexual and emotional encounters—traditionally described from the male perspective—have made her novels attractive to a wide audience.

While her fiction need not be read in any particular order, there is a gradual evolution of control over the structure and language of her novels during the thirty years of their composition. Her craft developed from the earliest, *The House of Incest*, a random collection of poetic impressions, to later ones like *Collages* which are more complex in characterization and more ambitious in structure, artistically shaped cycles of portraits radiating from a central figure. If Nin's fiction is read chronologically and concurrently with her diaries of the same period, the essential function of the latter to her fictional mode becomes strikingly evident. It was from her experiences and the portraits delineated in her diaries that Nin drew the material for all her novels, sometimes rewritten, often lifted intact into them. And the characteristics of her diaries parallel those in her fiction: musically counterpointed themes and characters; mystical, sensual, and poetic prose; and an enduring faith in the artistic life, psychoanalysis, and the differing sensibilities of the male and the female.

—Estelle C. Jelinek

NORRIS, (Benjamin) Frank(lin, Jr.). Born in Chicago, Illinois, 5 March 1870; moved with his family to San Francisco, 1884. Educated at Belmont Academy, California, 1885–87; Boys' High School, San Francisco; studied art at Atelier Julien, Paris, 1887–89; attended University of California, Berkeley, 1890–94, and Harvard University, Cambridge, Massachusetts, 1894–95. Married Jeannette Black in 1900; one daughter. War correspondent for San Francisco *Chronicle* in South Africa during the Uitlander insurrection, 1895–96; editorial staff member, San Francisco *Wave*, 1896–97; Spanish-American War correspondent in Cuba for *McClure's* magazine, New York, 1898; reader for Doubleday, publishers, New York, 1899–1902; moved to San Francisco, 1902. *Died 25 October 1902.*

PUBLICATIONS

Collections

Collected Writings. 10 vols., 1928.
The Letters, edited by Franklin Walker. 1956.
Novels and Essays (Library of America), edited by Donald Pizer. 1986.

Fiction

Moran of the Lady Letty: A Story of Adventure off the California Coast. 1898; as *Shanghaied*, 1899.
McTeague: A Story of San Francisco. 1899; edited by Donald Pizer, 1977.
Blix. 1899.
A Man's Woman. 1900.
The Epic of Wheat:
The Octopus: A Story of California. 1901; edited by Kenneth S. Lynn, 1958.
The Pit: A Story of Chicago. 1903.
A Deal in Wheat and Other Stories of the New and Old West. 1903.
The Joyous Miracle. 1906.
The Third Circle (stories). 1909.
Vandover and the Brute, edited by Charles G. Norris. 1914.

Verse

Yvernelle: A Legend of Feudal France. 1891.

Other

The Responsibilities of the Novelist and Other Literary Essays. 1903.
The Surrender of Santiago: An Account of the Historic Surrender of Santiago to General Shafter, July 17, 1898. 1917.
Two Poems and "Kim" Reviewed. 1930.
Norris of The Wave: Stories and Sketches from the San Francisco Weekly 1893 to 1897, edited by Oscar Lewis. 1931.
The Literary Criticism, edited by Donald Pizer. 1964.
A Novelist in the Making: A Collection of Student Themes and the Novels Blix and Vandover and the Brute, edited by James D. Hart. 1970.

*

Bibliography: *Norris: A Bibliography* by Kenneth A. Lohf and Eugene P. Sheehy, 1959; *The Merrill Checklist of Norris* by John S. Hill, 1970; in *Bibliography of American Literature* by Jacob Blanck, 1973; *Norris: A Reference Guide* by Jesse S. Crisler and Joseph R. McElrath, Jr., 1974.

Critical Studies: *Norris: A Biography* by Franklin Walker, 1932; *Norris: A Study* by Eugene Marchand, 1942; *Norris* by Warren French, 1962; *The Novels of Norris* by Donald Pizer, 1966; *Norris* by Wilbur M. Frohock, 1969; *Norris: Instinct and Art* by William D. Dillingham, 1969; *The Fiction of Norris: The Aesthetic Context* by Don Graham, 1978, and *Critical Essays on Norris* edited by Graham, 1980; *Norris: The Critical Reception* edited by Joseph R. McElrath, Jr., and Katherine Knight, 1979.

* * *

Although Frank Norris never wrote a work that could be considered a masterpiece, he occupies an important place in American literary history. He is an early practitioner of naturalism, along with his contemporaries Crane and Dreiser; he is an example of the French influence on American letters; and he is a noteworthy creator of the fictional landscape of California. Norris was a very uneven writer and capable of writing both popular magazine romance as well as serious fiction in the realistic/naturalistic tradition. Only two or three of his novels have demonstrated survival power.

As a young man Norris studied art in Paris, but there is no evidence that he read the French realists/naturalists at that time. He then was interested in romance, and his first work was a narrative poem, *Yvernelle: A Legend of Feudal France*, published while he was a student at the University of California. In 1894, when he entered Harvard as a special student of writing under Lewis Gates, he discovered Balzac, Flaubert, and especially Zola. He worked on his first novel *McTeague* during that year but didn't finish it until later after returning to California.

McTeague is a remarkable first novel, the most important piece of naturalism produced in America up to that time. It shows a strong Zola influence but is thoroughly naturalized in the United States. It is the story of a San Francisco dentist who is victimized by his inability to cope with marriage and complex social relationships. McTeague is a man of great strength but under the influence of alcohol loses his self-control. He is too stupid to cope with his wife, who becomes a miser, and a former friend, who causes him to lose his dental practice. The San Francisco locale is well done, and the disintegration of

McTeague under the impact of forces he cannot control makes this a powerful naturalistic novel. The ending, unfortunately, is melodramatic and the symbolism far too obvious.

The Octopus, however, is a more mature work and is generally regarded as Norris's best achievement. It was the first of a projected trilogy to be called *The Epic of Wheat. The Octopus* deals with the growing of the wheat and is laid in the San Joaquin Valley of California. The ranching scenes, especially the planting of the wheat, are rendered with a good eye for local color. Although there are many characters and several subplots, the story basically concerns the struggle between the ranchers and the railroad (the octopus) over shipping rates and land prices. It is an unequal battle because the railroad holds all the trump cards, and in the climactic episode of the novel the ranchers are defeated in an armed confrontation with the railroad deputies. There are a good many romantic elements in the novel and it ends on a note of cosmic optimism, but the work falls mainly in the category of naturalism. After the railroad has won the struggle, the President of the company argues that the railroad is a "force born out of certain conditions." No man can stop or control it any more than anyone can stop the wheat from growing.

The second novel in the trilogy was *The Pit*, completed just before Norris's fatal appendectomy and published posthumously. It depicts the trading of the wheat on the Chicago grain exchange, and while it is inferior to *The Octopus*, it tells an absorbing story of the protagonist's unsuccessful efforts to corner the wheat market. The third volume in the trilogy, which was to have been called *The Wolf* and was to deal with the distribution of the wheat in a famine-stricken Europe, was never written.

Another of Norris's novels that also deserves attention is *Vandover and the Brute*, a work that he wrote before *McTeague* but never could get published. It was issued with some cuts and perhaps some additions by his brother Charles, in 1914. The novel, a powerful study of disintegrating character, was too advanced for Doubleday, McClure and Co. in 1899. Vandover is weak-willed, indolent, badly brought up, and after his father dies, leaving him a handsome legacy, he squanders his money, is victimized by a friend, and ends in abject degradation.

Norris is perhaps the most notable disciple of Zola in American literature. He praised Zola passionately and often reread his favorite novels, *L'Assommoir, La Terre, Germinal, La Bête humaine*. He researched his novels as Zola did, studying a manual of dentistry before writing *McTeague*, visiting a wheat farm while planning *The Octopus*. So pervasive was the influence that he joked about it in the inscription he wrote in the flyleaf of his wife's copy of *The Octopus*: "To my boss, Jeannette Norris, most respectfully . . . Mr. Norris (The Boy Zola)."

Although he was influenced by Zola, Norris never got over the original impulse towards romance. His critical views as outlined in *The Responsibilities of the Novelist* favor the spontaneous, improvising storyteller. He cites Dumas as an excellent example. He also believed that all good novels must have some significant pivotal event—such as the battle between the ranchers and the railroad deputies in *The Octopus*. It is no wonder that Norris is not a thorough-going naturalist. In addition, Norris never took himself very seriously. He wrote too fast and between *McTeague* and *The Octopus* there is much trash. He was torn between the Kipling-Richard Harding Davis tradition and Zola.

—James Woodress

See the essay on *The Octopus*.

O'BRIEN, (Michael) Fitz-James. Born in Ireland, probably in County Limerick, in 1828; emigrated to the U.S., 1852. Served in the Civil War in the 7th New York Regiment, 1861–62: aide-de-camp to General Lander; commissioned Lieutenant, 1862; died of wounds. Left Ireland for London, 1849: editor, *Parlour Magazine*, 1851; moved to New York, 1852: staff member, New York *Daily Times*, 1852–53; regular contributor to *Harper's Monthly*, 1853–62, and assistant editor and columnist ("Man about Town"), *Harper's Weekly*, 1857; drama critic, New York *Saturday Press*, 1858–59; press agent for actress Matilda Heron, 1859; columnist ("Here and There"), *Vanity Fair*, 1860. *Died 6 April 1862*.

PUBLICATIONS

Collections

The Poems and Stories, edited by William Winter. 1881.
The Golden Ingot, The Diamond Lens, A Terrible Night, What Was It? 1921.
Collected Stories, edited by Edward J. O'Brien. 1925.
The Fantastic Tales, edited by Michael Hayes. 1977.

Plays

My Christmas Dinner (produced 1852).
A Gentleman from Ireland (produced 1854).
The Sisters, from a French play (produced 1854).
Duke Humphrey's Dinner (produced 1856).
The Tycoon; or, Young America in Japan, with Charles G. Rosenberg (produced 1860).

Verse

Sir Brasil's Falcon. 1853.

*

Bibliography: in *Bibliography of American Literature* by Jacob Blanck, 1973.

Critical Study: *O'Brien: A Literary Bohemian of the Eighteen-Fifties* by Francis Wolle, 1944 (includes bibliography).

* * *

After education in Ireland, and a short stint in London on the literary fringes, Fitz-James O'Brien emigrated to the United States and soon became a prominent member of New York's literary bohemia that frequented Pfaff's, the old Hone House, and Windust's. O'Brien contributed lavishly to a number of American periodicals over the next six years among them the *American Whig Review*, *Putnam's*, *Harper's Weekly* and *Monthly*, *Vanity Fair*, the *Atlantic Monthly*, the New York *Times*. O'Brien was also the author of several plays, one, *A Gentleman from Ireland*, being presented successfully as late as 1895. His most imaginative story, "The Diamond Lens," appeared in 1858, winning him some fame, but at that point O'Brien's career as dandy author and bohemian faltered. He had acted as literary agent to M.L. Bateman, a theatrical director, and became involved with Matilda Heron, who appears to have had some responsibility for the collapse of O'Brien's fortunes. His splendid clothes, extensive library, elegant furnishings, soon disappeared; even his attractive personal appearance suffered a change for the worse with a broken nose from a professional pugilist. But he retained all his ebullience, and his end was brilliant. When the Civil War broke out, he joined the 7th Regiment of the National Guard of New York and won special mention for gallantry at the Battle of Bloomery Gap. A few days later he was wounded in the shoulder, indifferently nursed, and died of tetanus in 1862.

The general judgment on O'Brien is that he is more significant as personality than as author. Certainly, he wrote with unfortunate facility, and his verse is jaunty and negligible. Several of his stories, however, suggest a minor Poe with a dash of Hoffmann. O'Brien had an undisciplined but powerful gothic imagination that ranged over such topics as abnormal psychology, mesmerism, magic, alchemy, revenants, along with sharp flashes of prophetic imagination. "The Diamond Lens," a study of a mad microscopist, "The Wondersmith," with its aggressive manikin robots, and the ectoplasmic visitor of "What Was It?" retain some power to "electrify" the reader.

—Ian Fletcher

O'CONNOR, (Mary) Flannery. Born in Savannah, Georgia, 25 March 1925. Educated at Peabody High School, Milledgeville, Georgia, graduated 1942; Georgia State College for Women (now Georgia College at Milledgeville), 1942–45, A.B. 1945; University of Iowa, Iowa City, 1945–47, M.F.A. 1947. Suffered from disseminated lupus after 1950. Recipient: American Academy grant, 1957; O. Henry Award, 1957, 1963, 1964; Ford Foundation grant, 1959; National Catholic Book Award, 1966; National Book Award, 1972. D.Litt.: St. Mary's College, Notre Dame, Indiana, 1962; Smith College, Northampton, Massachusetts, 1963. *Died 3 August 1964.*

PUBLICATIONS

Collections

Complete Stories. 1971.
The Habit of Being: Letters, edited by Sally Fitzgerald. 1979.

Fiction

Wise Blood. 1952.
A Good Man Is Hard to Find and Other Stories. 1955; as *The Artificial Nigger and Other Tales*, 1957.
The Violent Bear It Away. 1960.
Everything That Rises Must Converge (stories). 1965.

Other

Mystery and Manners: Occasional Prose, edited by Sally and Robert Fitzgerald. 1969.
The Presence of Grace and Other Book Reviews, edited by Carter W. Martin and Leo J. Zuber. 1983.
The Correspondence of O'Connor and Brainard Cheneys, edited by C. Ralph Stephens. 1986.

Editor, *A Memoir of Mary Ann.* 1961; as *Death of a Child*, 1961.

*

Bibliography: *O'Connor and Caroline Gordon: A Reference Guide* by Robert E. Golden and Mary C. Sullivan, 1977; *O'Connor: A Descriptive Bibliography* by David Farmer, 1981.

Critical Studies: *O'Connor: A Critical Essay* by Robert Drake, 1966; *O'Connor* by Stanley Edgar Hyman, 1966; *The Added Dimension: The Art and Mind of O'Connor* edited by Melvin J. Friedman and Lewis A. Lawson, 1966, and *Critical Essays on O'Connor* edited by Friedman and Beverly L. Clark, 1985; *The True Country: Themes in the Fiction of O'Connor* by Carter W. Martin, 1969; *The World of O'Connor* by Josephine Hendin, 1970; *The Eternal Crossroads: The Art of O'Connor* by Leon Driskell and Joan T. Brittain, 1971; *The Christian Humanism of O'Connor* by David Eggenschwiler, 1972; *Nightmares and Visions: O'Connor and the Catholic Grotesque* by Gilbert Muller, 1972; *O'Connor: Voice of the Peacock* by Kathleen Feeley, 1972, revised edition, 1982; *Invisible Parade: The Fiction of O'Connor* by Miles Orvell, 1972; *O'Connor* by Dorothy Walters, 1973; *The Question of O'Connor* by Martha Stephens, 1973; *O'Connor* by Preston M. Browning, Jr., 1974; *O'Connor* by Dorothy Tuck McFarland, 1976; *The Pruning Word: The Parables of O'Connor* by John R. May, 1976; *O'Connor's Dark Comedies: The Limits of Inference* by Carol Shloss, 1980; *O'Connor: Her Life, Library, and Book Reviews*, 1980, and *Nature and Grace in O'Connor's Fiction*, 1982, both by Lorine M. Getz; *O'Connor's South* by Robert Coles, 1980; *O'Connor's Georgia* by Barbara McKenzie, 1980; *The O'Connor Companion* by James A. Grimshaw, Jr., 1981; *O'Connor: The Imagination of Extremity* by Frederick Asals, 1982; *O'Connor: Images of Grace* by Harold Fickett and Douglas Gilbert, 1986; *O'Connor's Religion of the Grotesque* by Marshall Bruce Gentry, 1986.

* * *

Flannery O'Connor belongs to a small group of 20th-century writers whose work is profoundly religious, not through direct statement or preachment but because its informing theme and structure are theological. O'Connor was raised as a Roman Catholic in the Protestant south, and she found in the "Christ-haunted" fundamentalist religious beliefs of that region much that awoke responsive chords in her, despite her basic theological differences with the Protestant faith. She brought to the portrayal of the people of her region a clear, hard, witty style, an unblinking eye, and a sense of both the divine and the ridiculous; and she used her violent portrayals of grotesque people to express a deep and unsentimental religious faith. Fairly early in her career, she developed lupus, an incurable disease that progressed inexorably to its conclusion in her death at the age of 39. Much of her work was produced after this disease had initially struck, and a great deal of her best fiction is concerned with death, and often with death as a release or means of salvation. Although this is a limited theme, and the range of her work often seems distressingly narrow, Flannery O'Connor worked within the limits of her art with great commitment, artistic integrity, high technical skill, and frequent success.

She is primarily a writer of short stories. The collection *A Good Man Is Hard to Find* and the posthumous *Everything That Rises Must Converge* contained nineteen examples of her best work in this form. *The Complete Stories* added twelve more. Her first novel, *Wise Blood*, is a weaving together of material originally written in short story form. Her only other novel was *The Violent Bear It Away.* (She was working on a third novel at the time of her death but apparently without the expectation of ever completing it.) Despite excellent elements in both her novels, O'Connor will survive as a master of the short story form. Her stories were based on what she called "anagogical vision . . . the kind of vision that is able to see different levels of reality in one image or one situation." It is this anagogical element which has led to very extensive examination of levels of meaning in her stories by many critics.

Wise Blood is the story of the preacher Hazel Motes, called, he believed, to preach "the Church without Christ," a man who is driven by acts of violent grace finally to accept the Jesus whom he had denied, to blind himself, and to die, and in his death to achieve a kind of salvation. *The Violent Bear It Away* is the record of the efforts of a boy, Francis Marion Tarwater, to escape the prophetic calling bequeathed to him by his dead great-uncle. A much more tightly organized work than *Wise Blood*, *The Violent Bear It Away* is really the harrowing chronicle of the struggle of cosmic forces, represented by the religious great-uncle and a very modern uncle, for the soul of Francis Tarwater. The great-uncle ultimately triumphs.

O'Connor's short stories deal with simple Georgia people, hungry with a passionate desire for a spiritual dimension which the nature of their lives and their beliefs deny them. The usual pattern in these stories is that of a desperate search through extreme, violent, and grotesque actions that usually culminate in the entry of divine grace through some instrumentality that bestows salvation in the moment of death. The frantic and misdirected struggles of these human beings result in a violent but comic representation that seems in many ways to reflect the long tradition of American southwestern humor, with its extreme portrayals of grotesque people in violent and unusual situations. Her work is most like that of Erskine Caldwell in terms of the grotesqueness of her characters, the extravagance of her actions, the sharp and vigorous starkness of her prose, and her kind of pervasive comic sense. However, where Caldwell presents his characters as people distorted as a result of economic deprivation, O'Connor's world is the world of people rendered grotesque by their inability to satisfy their spiritual hungers. All of her characters can be explained in one sense in St. Augustine's phrase, "Our souls are restless till they find rest in Thee." Among her short stories of particular distinction are "A Good Man Is Hard to Find," "Good Country People," "The Artificial Nigger," "The Lame Shall Enter First," "Revelation," "Greenleaf," and the short novel "The Displaced Person."

In her short life O'Connor accomplished much in her intense art. Narrow though her range and subjects are, they are pursued with great distinction and great force. Ultimately she will remain a minor figure in American letters, but a minor figure of enormous challenge, subtlety, and accomplishment.

—C. Hugh Holman

See the essay on *Wise Blood*.

ODETS, Clifford. Born in Philadelphia, Pennsylvania, 18 July 1906; grew up in the Bronx, New York. Educated at Morris High School, New York, 1921–23. Married 1) the actress Luise Rainer in 1937 (divorced, 1941); 2) Bette Grayson in 1943 (divorced, 1951), one son and one daughter. Actor on radio and on Broadway, 1923–28, and with Theatre Guild Productions, New York, 1928–30; co-founder, Group Theatre, New York, 1930; wrote for the stage from 1933; joined Communist Party, 1934 (resigned 1934); film writer and director. Recipient: New Theatre League prize, 1935; Yale drama prize, 1935; American Academy Award of Merit Medal, 1961. *Died 14 August 1963.*

PUBLICATIONS

Plays

Waiting for Lefty (produced 1935). In *Three Plays*, 1935.
Awake and Sing! (produced 1935). In *Three Plays*, 1935.
Till the Day I Die (produced 1935). In *Three Plays*, 1935.
I Can't Sleep: A Monologue (produced 1935). In *New Theatre 3*, 1936.
Paradise Lost (produced 1935). 1936.
Golden Boy (produced 1937). 1937.
Rocket to the Moon (produced 1938). 1939.
Six Plays. 1939.
Night Music (produced 1940). 1940.
Clash by Night (produced 1941). 1942.
The Russian People, from a play by Konstantin Simonov (produced 1942). In *Seven Soviet Plays*, edited by H.W.L. Dana, 1946.
None But the Lonely Heart (screenplay), in *Best Film Plays 1945*, edited by John Gassner and Dudley Nichols. 1946.
The Big Knife (produced 1949). 1949.
The Country Girl (produced 1950). 1951; revised version, as *Winter Journey* (produced 1952), 1955.
The Flowering Peach (produced 1954). 1954(?).
The Silent Partner (produced 1972).

Screenplays: *The General Died at Dawn*, 1936; *Black Sea Fighters*, 1943; *None But the Lonely Heart*, 1944; *Deadline at Dawn*, 1946; *Humoresque* with Zachary Gold, 1946; *Sweet Smell of Success*, with Ernest Lehman, 1957; *The Story on Page One*, 1960; *Wild in the Country*, 1961.

Television Plays: *Big Mitch*, 1963, and *The Mafia Man*, 1964 (both for *The Richard Boone Show*).

Other

Rifle Rule in Cuba, with Carleton Beals. 1935.
1940 Journal. 1987.

*

Critical Studies: *Odets* by R. Baird Shuman, 1963; *Odets: The Thirties and After* by Edward Murray, 1968; *Odets, Humane Dramatist* by Michael J. Mendelsohn, 1969; *Odets the Playwright* by Gerald Weales, 1971, revised edition, 1985; *Odets, Playwright-Poet* by Harold Cantor, 1978; *Odets, American Playwright: The Years from 1906 to 1940* by Margaret Brenman-Gibson, 1981.

* * *

Clifford Odets's first produced play was *Waiting for Lefty*, a one-act agitprop drama based on the New York City taxi strike of 1934. It is uncharacteristic Odets in both form and intention. A group of naturalistic dramatic sketches set within a union meeting, still visible while the more intimate scenes are being played, *Waiting for Lefty* is non-realistic theater that breaks the conventional frame to invite the audience to join in the final call for a strike. Aside from this play, Odets remained within the American realistic tradition even when he attempted to open the form with cinematic techniques (*Golden Boy*), visual and musical devices (*Night Music*) and Yiddish-biblical fantasy (*The Flowering Peach*). Although most of his plays, particularly the early ones like *Awake and Sing!* and *Paradise Lost*, have the mandatory optimistic ending decreed by the American Left in the 1930's, *Waiting for Lefty* is the only overt propaganda play Odets wrote, except for *Till the Day I Die*, an ineffective anti-fascist piece hastily written to fill out the bill when *Lefty* moved to Broadway. He did do a few sketches, like "I Can't Sleep," for benefit performances and he worked at two political plays, *The Cuban Play* and *The Silent Partner*, which he never got into final form. If *Waiting for Lefty* is uncharacteristic in some ways, it is also unmistakable Odets. Scenes like "Joe and Edna" and "The Young Hack and His Girl" show that Odets's political and social concerns look their best transformed into domestic conflict, and the language of those scenes set the tone for the Odets work to come. When Edna says, "Get out of here!" meaning "I love you" and Sid, in affectionate exasperation, calls his brother, "that dumb basketball player," we get a first taste of the Odets obliquity—the wisecrack as lament, slang as lyricism—that, trailing its Yiddish and urban roots, enriches *Awake and Sing!* and *Paradise Lost* before it peters out in the self-parody of some of the lines in the screenplay *Sweet Smell of Success*.

Although *Waiting for Lefty* introduced Odets to audiences and critics, it was not his first play. *Awake and Sing!* was already written and about to open when *Lefty* was produced. *Awake and Sing!*, Odets's most enduring work, is *the* American depression play, a still vital example of the 1930's conviction that, however terrible the situation, it could be rectified by an infusion of idealistic rhetoric administered at the final curtain. Although Odets was a Communist when he wrote it (and the play carries a few verbal indications of that fact), its optimism is more generalized, tied into the historical American penchant for possibility which, battered by the first years of the depression, had begun to revive with the election of Franklin D. Roosevelt in 1932. Not only is Odets hooked into the American ideational mainstream in *Awake and Sing!* but he recalls earlier American drama in his choice of a family setting for his play and in his willing employment of melodramatic commonplaces—the suicide of Jacob, the pregnancy of Hennie. He transcends the structural weaknesses in the play with the creation of a milieu so real that an audience feels it can be touched; this texture—partly verbal, partly emotional—is probably a product not simply of Odets's talent but of the context in which the play was written. Odets was a member of the Group Theatre, an acting company that was a family of sorts, and his Bergers are an echo of the loving, quarreling Group company which was a home for Odets, one that—reacting like Ralph and Hennie to Bessie Berger's Bronx—he sometimes saw as a trap. All of his plays through *Night Music* were written for the Group actors, but *Paradise Lost*, which Odets once correctly described as "a beautiful play, velvety . . . gloomy and rich," and *Rocket to the Moon* come closest in texture to *Awake and Sing!*

When the success of *Awake and Sing!* was followed by the failure of *Paradise Lost*, Odets went to Hollywood to work on *The General Died at Dawn*. After that, he vacillated between Hollywood and New York, commerce and art, guilt and regeneration. These terms suit his view of the matter as reflected in *The Big Knife*, in which the Odets surrogate, the actor Charlie Castle, is destroyed as man and artist by the movie business. Despite this gloomy view of Hollywood Odets constantly returned to a suspicion that the movies too were an art, all the more attractive for the size of the audience. Ironically, the movies he worked on were conventional Hollywood products; even the two he directed as well as wrote, *None But the Lonely Heart* and *The Story on Page One*, are interesting primarily for their attempt at poetic verisimilitude, the visual equivalent of the sense of milieu created by other means in *Awake and Sing!* and *Paradise Lost*.

Odets's greatest commercial successes were *Golden Boy*, a parable in boxing gloves about the destructiveness of the American success ethic, and *The Country Girl*, an effective sentimental melodrama about an alcoholic actor's attempt to recover his career and his life. Both plays show Odets's theatrical skill, but his most attractive failures, *Paradise Lost* and *Night Music*, display a bumbling sweetness that is as important a part of Odets's talent as his technical proficiency. Both the staccato dialogue of *Golden Boy* and the rambling non sequiturs of *Paradise Lost* are aspects of the authentic Odets voice which can still be heard at its purest in *Awake and Sing!*

—Gerald Weales

See the essay on *Awake and Sing!*

O'HARA, Frank (Francis Russell O'Hara). Born in Baltimore, Maryland, 27 June 1926. Educated privately in piano and musical composition, 1933–43; at New England Conservatory of Music, Boston, 1946–50, A.B. in English 1950; University of Michigan, Ann Arbor (Hopwood Award, 1951), M.A. 1951. Served in the U.S. Navy, 1944–46. Staff member, 1951–54, fellowship curator, 1955–64, associate curator, 1965, and curator of the International Program, 1966, Museum of Modern Art, New York. Editorial associate, *Art News* magazine, New York, 1954–56; art editor, *Kulchur* magazine, New York, 1962–64. Recipient: Ford fellowship, for drama, 1956. *Died 25 July 1966.*

PUBLICATIONS

Collections

Collected Poems, edited by Donald Allen. 1971.
Selected Poems, edited by Donald Allen. 1974.
Selected Plays. 1978.

Verse

A City Winter and Other Poems. 1952.
Oranges. 1953.
Meditations in an Emergency. 1956.
Harrigan and Rivers with O'Hara: An Exhibition of Pictures, with Poems. 1959.
Second Avenue. 1960.
Odes. 1960.
Featuring O'Hara. 1964.

Lunch Poems. 1964.
Love Poems: Tentative Title. 1965.
In Memory of My Feelings: A Selection of Poems, edited by Bill Berkson. 1967.
Two Pieces. 1969.
Odes. 1969.
Belgrade, November 19, 1963. 1973.
Hymns of St. Bridget, with Bill Berkson. 1974.
Early Poems 1946–1951, edited by Donald Allen. 1976.
Poems Retrieved 1951–1966, edited by Donald Allen. 1977.

Plays

Try! Try! (produced 1951; revised version, produced 1952). In *Artists' Theatre*, edited by Herbert Machiz, 1960.
Change Your Bedding (produced 1951).
Love's Labor: An Eclogue (produced 1960). 1964.
Awake in Spain (produced 1960). 1960.
The General Returns from One Place to Another (produced 1964). In *Eight Plays from Off-Off Broadway*, edited by Nick Orzel and Michael Smith, 1966.
Surprising J.A., with Larry Rivers, in *Tracks 1*, November 1974.
Kenneth Koch: A Tragedy, with Larry Rivers (produced 1982).

Screenplay: *The Last Clean Shirt*.

Other

Jackson Pollock. 1959.
Standing Still and Walking in New York, edited by Donald Allen. 1975.
Art Chronicles 1954–1966. 1975.
Early Writing, edited by Donald Allen. 1977.

Editor, *Robert Motherwell: A Catalogue with Selections from the Artist's Writings*. 1966.

*

Bibliography: *O'Hara: A Comprehensive Bibliography* by Alexander Smith, Jr., 1980.

Critical Studies: *O'Hara, Poet among Painters* by Marjorie G. Perloff, 1977; *Homage to O'Hara* edited by Bill Berkson and Joe LeSueur, 1978; *O'Hara* by Alan Feldman, 1979.

* * *

Frank O'Hara's status as an important poet of the post-World War II era has only recently been established. During his lifetime he was known only to a circle of friends, many of them painters in New York whom he knew from his work as an Associate Curator of the Museum of Modern Art. But his canon is large and runs to more than five hundred pages of text in Donald Allen's edition of *The Collected Poems*.

O'Hara was cavalier about his reputation as a poet and reluctant to have his poetry in print. As a result, his work largely went unnoticed in the review columns; when his name did surface, he was taken lightly. Only recently has his work received serious critical attention; Marjorie Perloff's book vigorously argues his major status as an innovator of lyrical poetry. Perloff and others consider O'Hara to have had an influence on younger poets comparable to that of Charles Olson, Robert Creeley, and Allen Ginsberg.

O'Hara's poetry from 1951 to 1954 shows the influence of Pound, William Carlos Williams, and Auden. His early poems, collected in *A City Winter and Other Poems*, are lyrical and strive very deliberately for surprising effects. His friend the poet John Ashbery once commented that this was O'Hara's "French Zen period," which is an astute observation of the lushly surrealistic language of these poems. As he commented in an early poem, "Poetry":

> The only way to be quiet
> is to be quick, so I scare
> you clumsily, or surprise
> you with a stab. A praying
> mantis knows time more
> intimately than I and is
> more casual.

Auden once wrote to caution O'Hara against tiring the reader with an excess of surreal statements, and he appears to have heeded his counsel, for in the poetry of the later 1950's, gathered in *Meditations in an Emergency* and *Lunch Poems*, he exerted greater control over the structure of his poems and gave himself more intense freedom in brief, dazzling displays of lyrical exuberance.

In *Second Avenue* and other longer poems—"Easter," "In Memory of My Feelings," "Ode to Michael Goldberg('s Birth and Other Births)" and the late "Biotherm (for Bill Berkson)"—O'Hara, like Pushkin and Byron before him, created perhaps the essential hero of urban cultural life, a sophisticated romantic who thrives on the city's alien and exotic elements. His many shorter poems are briefer expressions of this same captivating persona.

O'Hara also succeeds in rendering consciousness and its fringe states with intense accuracy and daring in a style partly influenced by the methods and experiments of the Abstract Expressionist painters. O'Hara wrote several plays, and essays on contemporary painting collected in *Standing Still and Walking in New York* and *Art Chronicles 1954–1966*. Although not a theorist or trained critic of painting, his eye was sensitive to technique and his instinct sharp in discerning the great works of his time.

—Paul Christensen

O'HARA, John (Henry). Born in Pottsville, Pennsylvania, 31 January 1905. Educated at Fordham Preparatory School; Keystone State Normal School; Niagara Preparatory School, Niagara Falls, New York, 1923–24. Married 1) Helen Petit in 1931 (divorced, 1933); 2) Belle Mulford Wylie in 1937 (died, 1954), one daughter; 3) Katharine Barns Bryan in 1955. Reporter, Pottsville *Journal*, 1924–26, and Tamaqua *Courier*, Pennsylvania, 1927; reporter, New York *Herald-Tribune*, and *Time* magazine, New York, 1928; rewrite man, New York *Daily Mirror*, radio columnist (as Franey Delaney), New York *Morning Telegraph*, and managing editor, *Bulletin Index* magazine, Pittsburgh, 1928–33; full-time writer from 1933; film writer, for Paramount and other studios, from 1934; columnist ("Entertainment Week"), *Newsweek*, New York, 1940–42; Pacific war correspondent, *Liberty* magazine, New York, 1944; columnist ("Sweet and Sour"), Trenton *Sunday Times-Adviser*, New Jersey, 1953–54; lived in Princeton, New Jersey, from

1954; columnist ("Appointment with O'Hara"), *Collier's*, New York, 1954–56, ("My Turn"), *Newsday*, Long Island, New York, 1964–65, and ("The Whistle Stop"), *Holiday*, New York, 1966–67. Recipient: New York Drama Critics Circle award, 1952; Donaldson Award, for play, 1952; National Book Award, 1956; American Academy Award of Merit Medal, 1964. Member, American Academy, 1957. *Died 11 April 1970.*

PUBLICATIONS

Collections

Selected Letters, edited by Matthew J. Bruccoli. 1978.
Collected Stories, edited by Frank MacShane. 1985.

Fiction

Appointment in Samarra. 1934.
BUtterfield 8. 1935.
The Doctor's Son and Other Stories. 1935.
Hope of Heaven. 1938.
Files on Parade (stories). 1939.
Pal Joey (stories). 1940.
Pipe Night (stories). 1945.
Here's O'Hara (omnibus). 1946.
Hellbox (stories). 1947.
All the Girls He Wanted (stories). 1949.
A Rage to Live. 1949.
The Farmers Hotel. 1951.
Ten North Frederick. 1955.
A Family Party. 1956.
The Great Short Stories of O'Hara. 1956.
Selected Short Stories. 1956.
From the Terrace. 1958.
Ourselves to Know. 1960.
Sermons and Soda Water (includes *The Girl on the Baggage Truck*, *Imagine Kissing Pete*, *We're Friends Again*). 3 vols., 1960.
Assembly (stories). 1961.
The Cape Cod Lighter (stories). 1962.
The Big Laugh. 1962.
Elizabeth Appleton. 1963.
49 Stories. 1963.
The Hat on the Bed (stories). 1963.
The Horse Knows the Way (stories). 1964.
The Lockwood Concern. 1965.
Waiting for Winter (stories). 1966.
The Instrument. 1967.
And Other Stories. 1968.
Lovey Childs: A Philadelphian's Story. 1969.
The O'Hara Generation (stories). 1969.
The Ewings. 1972.
The Time Element and Other Stories, edited by Albert Erskine. 1972.
Good Samaritan and Other Stories, edited by Albert Erskine. 1974.
The Second Ewings. 1977.

Plays

Pal Joey (libretto), music by Richard Rodgers, lyrics by Lorenz Hart, from the stories by O'Hara (produced 1940). 1952.
Five Plays (includes *The Farmers Hotel*, *The Searching Sun*, *The Champagne Pool*, *Veronique*, *The Way It Was*). 1961.
Two by O'Hara (includes *The Man Who Could Not Lose* and *Far from Heaven*). 1979.

Screenplays: *I Was an Adventuress*, with Karl Tunberg and Don Ettlinger, 1940; *He Married His Wife*, with others, 1940; *Moontide*, 1942; *On Our Merry Way* (episode), 1948; *The Best Things in Life Are Free*, with William Bowers and Phoebe Ephron, 1956.

Other

Sweet and Sour (essays). 1954.
My Turn (newspaper columns). 1966.
A Cub Tells His Story. 1974.
An Artist Is His Own Fault: O'Hara On Writers and Writings, edited by Matthew J. Bruccoli. 1977.

*

Bibliography: *O'Hara: A Checklist*, 1972, and *O'Hara: A Descriptive Bibliography*, 1978, both by Matthew J. Bruccoli.

Critical Studies: *The Fiction of O'Hara* by Russell E. Carson, 1961; *O'Hara* by Sheldon Norman Grebstein, 1966; *O'Hara* by Charles C. Walcutt, 1969; *O'Hara: A Biography* by Finis Farr, 1973; *The O'Hara Concern: A Biography* by Matthew J. Bruccoli, 1975; *The Life of O'Hara* by Frank MacShane, 1980; *O'Hara* by Robert Emmet Long, 1983.

* * *

John O'Hara's 374 short stories and 18 novels record the changing habits and values of the United States from World War I to the Vietnam war. O'Hara began writing as a reporter, editor, press agent, and script writer; he worked first in his native Eastern Pennsylvania coal region (Pottsville—his fictional Gibbsville), and later in New York and Hollywood. His short stories began appearing in the *New Yorker* in 1928, and his first novel, *Appointment in Samarra*, identified him as a first-rate writer. His short stories range from short monologues, reminiscent of Ring Lardner (whose influence he acknowledged), to hundred-page novellas that may be his finest work: O'Hara has been called America's best short-story writer. Through his involvement with the New York theatrical world—plus an acknowledged mastery of dialogue—he tried to write for the stage. Even though his *Pal Joey* became a hit Rodgers and Hart musical, his *Five Plays* is a testament to his lack of success as a playwright.

As O'Hara's fame grew, it was often asserted that his first novel, *Appointment in Samarra*, was also his best. The fast pace and shifting point of view holds the reader until the suicide of Julian English at the end, which is still being debated: did Gibbsville drive him to it (just after the Great Crash in 1929), or did the compulsion come from within him? Nearly all of O'Hara's stories hold the reader's interest in the same way: how will the characters develop and what will happen to them? O'Hara said he was picturing, as honestly as he could, how 20th-century Americans were driven by money, sex, and a struggle for status—often to their own destruction. In 1935 O'Hara published *BUtterfield 8*, his only *roman à clef*. The heroine, Gloria Wandrous, is much like the Jazz Age celebrity Starr Faithfull, whose body was washed up on a Long Island beach in 1931. The novel was a popular success and extended O'Hara's fictional domain from Pennsylvania to New York City. *Hope of Heaven* pushed his range much farther, to Hollywood. But there is a link between all three of the first novels: the protagonist-narrator (and Hollywood scriptwriter) of *Hope of Heaven* is Jimmy Malloy, a former Gibbsville reporter who has covered the Gloria Wandrous murder / suicide / accident.

More than a hundred short stories and sketches were published in *The Doctor's Son and Other Stories*, *Files on Parade*, and *Pipe Night*. These tightly written stories present character and situation satirically, but O'Hara is not callous about the loneliness, misery, and degradation he reveals—on Broadway or in Gibbsville. The best-known of these stories are the heavily ironic monologues (in the form of letters) of Joey Evans, a night club master of ceremonies. *Pal Joey*, a collection of fourteen stories, became a Rodgers and Hart musical. Joey is a heel, an anti-hero, and the sexual innuendo was shocking in 1940; but *Pal Joey* also had a strong plot line and has been called the first realistic American musical.

A Rage to Live is the first of O'Hara's long and elaborately documented novels. The period is 1900 to 1920 and the locale Fort Penn (Harrisburg, Pennsylvania), but the serious social history was obscured for many readers by his heroine's lack of sexual control. In *Ten North Frederick* O'Hara moved the setting back to Gibbsville, where Joe Chapin earns great wealth and prestige with the help of his family name, a Yale law degree, and considerable intelligence. But Chapin aspires to be President of the United States: he attempts to buy the lieutenant governorship, is duped by an Irish politician, and drinks himself to death in "the quiet, gentlemanly, gradual way in which he had lived his life," as one critic wrote. *From the Terrace* is an even larger and more ambitious work: O'Hara tells the story of Alfred Eaton, a small-town Pennsylvania boy who goes to New York and Washington, becomes a great financier and government official, and finally discovers that his life is empty and meaningless. O'Hara regarded it as his masterpiece.

O'Hara wrote prodigiously in the last fifteen years of his life. *Ourselves to Know*, a big novel set in eastern Pennsylvania, uses a circular technique and shifting perspective in trying to understand and explain Robert Millhouser, who killed his wife and was acquitted in a murder trial. In the Foreword to *Sermons and Soda Water*, three novellas all filtered through the consciousness of Jimmy Malloy, O'Hara explains why he used this unpopular and unprofitable form instead of expanding each of the stories into a 350-page novel:

> I want to get it all down on paper while I can. I am now fifty-five years old and I have lived with as well as in the Twentieth Century from its earliest days. The United States in this Century is what I know, and it is my business to write about it to the best of my ability, with the sometimes special knowledge I have. The Twenties, the Thirties, and the Forties are already history, but I cannot be content to leave their story in the hands of the historians and the editors of picture books. I want to record the way people talked and thought and felt, and to do it with complete honesty and variety.

The Big Laugh is O'Hara's second Hollywood novel: his monologues of classic Hollywood types are bawdy, funny, and authentic. *Elizabeth Appleton* is an academic novel, focused on a weekend when the dean's wife sees her husband passed over for the presidency of a small Pennsylvania college. *The Lockwood Concern*, O'Hara's last major novel, is "a condensed big book" (400 pages): four generations of the family have lived in a small town near Gibbsville since 1840, but third-generation George Lockwood compulsively destroys the dynasty by driving his only son to a criminal career in California. Critics charged that O'Hara's protagonists often destroy themselves and their social fabric without explicable motivation.

There were three more novels to come. *The Instrument* explores the parasitism of playwright Yank Lucas: he deserts the star actress on opening night, writes a new play on their relationship, and she commits suicide. *Lovey Childs: A Philadelphian's Story* deals with a Main Line heiress and her playboy husband (Sky Childs), who became 1920's celebrities; after divorce she achieves a stable marriage with her proper Philadelphia cousin. This is O'Hara's weakest novel, but it aroused speculation about his interest in lesbianism. At his death in 1970 O'Hara had completed *The Ewings* and was at work on a sequel: better than the two previous novels, it is the story of a young Cleveland lawyer and his wife in the booming economy of World War I. Six short story collections appeared in the 1960's, and two more after O'Hara's death.

Before World War II an "official" view of O'Hara had been established. John Peale Bishop (1937) found him skillful but cynical, a post-Jazz Age follower of Hemingway and Fitzgerald. Edmund Wilson (1940) recognized that O'Hara was a social commentator and that his writing was "of an entirely different kind from Hemingway's." O'Hara resembles Fitzgerald more than any writer, and their friendship—O'Hara proof-read Fitzgerald's *Tender Is the Night*—was renewed during Fitzgerald's last bitter days in Hollywood. O'Hara was a staunch Fitzgerald champion when that was not a popular cause, and wrote the introduction to *The Portable F. Scott Fitzgerald* (1945). When the big O'Hara novels became best sellers in the 1950's and 1960's, critics objected to the "mere accuracy" of his dialogue and detail, to the "surface reality" of his American scenes, and to the social climbing and sexual conduct of his characters. But, even when they found him "a hack writer," critics continued to review his books, and John Steinbeck called O'Hara the most underrated writer in America. His work lives, no matter how unfashionably. Though some critics object that his characters are not worth writing about, O'Hara's readers do not agree; and they admire the clarity of his style even though the critics would like more complexity and ambiguity. The academic world objects to O'Hara's view of life and literature, but if future generations seek an American Balzac to lay bare life in the United States from 1900 to 1970, they will find John O'Hara the most complete, the most accurate, and the most readable chronicler.

—Clarence A. Glasrud

OLSON, Charles (John). Born in Worcester, Massachusetts, 27 December 1910. Educated at Classical High School, Worcester, graduated 1928; Wesleyan University, Middletown, Connecticut, 1928–32, B.A. 1932 (Phi Beta Kappa), M.A. 1933; Harvard University, Cambridge, Massachusetts, 1936–38. Assistant Chief of Foreign Language Division, Office of War Information, Washington, D.C., during World War II. Teacher, Clark University, Worcester, and Harvard University, 1936–39; worked for Democratic Party, 1939–44, and adviser, Democratic National Committee, late 1940's; Instructor and

Rector, Black Mountain College, North Carolina, 1948, 1951–56; teacher at State University of New York, Buffalo, 1963–65, and University of Connecticut, Storrs, 1969. Recipient: Guggenheim grant (twice); Wenner-Gren Foundation grant, 1952; American Academy grant, 1966, 1968. *Died 10 January 1970.*

PUBLICATIONS

Verse

Corrado Cagli March 31 Through April 19 1947. 1947.
Y & X. 1948.
Letter for Melville 1951. 1951.
This. 1952.
In Cold Hell, in Thicket. 1953.
The Maximus Poems 1-10. 1953.
Ferrini and Others, with others. 1955.
Anecdotes of the Late War. 1955.
The Maximus Poems 11-22. 1956.
O'Ryan 2 4 6 8 10. 1958; expanded edition, as *O'Ryan 12345678910*, 1965.
The Maximus Poems. 1960.
The Distances. 1960.
Maximus, From Dogtown I. 1961.
Signature to Petition on Ten Pound Island Asked of Me by Mr. Vincent Ferrini. 1964.
West. 1966.
Olson Reading at Berkeley, edited by Zoe Brown. 1966.
Before Your Very Eyes!, with others. 1967.
The Maximus Poems, IV, V, VI. 1968.
Reading about My World. 1968.
Added to Making a Republic. 1968.
Clear Shifting Water. 1968.
That There Was a Woman in Gloucester, Massachusetts. 1968.
Wholly Absorbed into My Own Conduits. 1968.
Causal Mythology. 1969.
Archaeologist of Morning: The Collected Poems Outside the Maximus Series. 1970.
Maximus, to Himself. 1970.
New Man and Woman. 1970.
May 20, 1959. 1970.
The Maximus Poems, Volume Three, edited by Charles Boer and George F. Butterick. 1975.
The Horses of the Sea. 1976.
Some Early Poems. 1978.
Spearmint and Rosemary. 1979.
The Maximus Poems, edited by George F. Butterick. 1983.

Plays

The Fiery Hunt and Other Plays. 1977.

Fiction

Stocking Cap: A Story. 1966.

Other

Call Me Ishmael: A Study of Melville. 1947.
Apollonius of Tyana: A Dance, with Some Words, for Two Actors. 1951.
Mayan Letters, edited by Robert Creeley. 1953.
Projective Verse. 1959.
A Bibliography on America for Ed Dorn. 1964.
Human Universe and Other Essays, edited by Donald Allen. 1965.
Proprioception. 1965.
Selected Writings, edited by Robert Creeley. 1966.
Pleistocene Man: Letters from Olson to John Clarke During October 1965. 1968.
Letters for Origin 1950-1956, edited by Albert Glover. 1969.
The Special View of History, edited by Ann Charters. 1970.
Poetry and Truth: The Beloit Lectures and Poems, edited by George F. Butterick. 1971.
Additional Prose: A Bibliography on America, Proprioception, and Other Notes and Essays, edited by George F. Butterick. 1974.
The Post Office: A Memoir of His Father. 1974.
In Adullam's Lair (lecture). 1975.
Olson in Connecticut: Last Lectures as Heard by John Cech, Oliver Ford, Peter Rittner. 1975.
Olson and Ezra Pound: An Encounter at St. Elizabeths, edited by Catherine Seelye. 1975.
Muthologos: The Collected Lectures and Interviews of Olson, edited by George F. Butterick. 2 vols., 1976–79.
Olson/Den Boer: A Letter. 1979.
D.H. Lawrence and the High Temptation of the Mind. 1980.
Olson and Robert Creeley: The Complete Correspondence, edited by George F. Butterick. 5 vols., 1980–83.

*

Bibliography: *A Bibliography of Works by Olson* by George F. Butterick and Albert Glover, 1967.

Critical Studies: *What I See in the Maximus Poems* by Ed Dorn, 1960; *Olson/Melville: A Study in Affinity*, 1968, and *Olson: The Special View of History*, 1970, both by Ann Charters; *Olson in Connecticut* by Charles Boer, 1975; *A Guide to the Maximus Poems of Olson* by George F. Butterick, 1978; *Olson's Push: "Origin," Black Mountain, and Recent American Poetry* by Sherman Paul, 1978; *Olson: The Scholar's Art* by Robert von Hallberg, 1978; *Olson: Call Him Ishmael* by Paul Christensen, 1979; *Olson's Maximus* by Don Byrd, 1980; *To Let Words Swim into the Soul: An Anniversary Tribute to the Art of Olson* by Gavin Selerie, 1980; *Olson and Edward Dahlberg: A Portrait of a Friendship* by John Cech, 1982; *The Poetry of Olson: A Primer* by Thomas F. Merrill, 1982.

* * *

Although any final judgment regarding the work and influence of Charles Olson remains controversial, he must nevertheless be regarded as a seminal force in the reshaping of American poetry written since World War II. Olson showed little inclination to be a poet until his mid-thirties. Shortly after the death of Roosevelt, however, Olson left government and committed himself to a literary career. By then he had written only the draft of a short book on Melville, *Call Me Ishmael*, and several conventional poems published in popular magazines. From these unpromising beginnings, Olson began writing in earnest in the late 1940's. With the help of Edward Dahlberg, a completely revised *Call Me Ishmael* was published in 1947; two years later, Olson composed "The Kingfishers," among the most innovative poems to have emerged since World

War II. And in 1950, largely from the example of the techniques employed in "The Kingfishers," and ideas taken from a variety of sources, including William Carlos Williams, Pound, Dahlberg and his close friend Robert Creeley, Olson synthesized the provocative and highly influential manifesto, "Projective Verse."

This essay established a new set of conventions for the short poem. In place of the old rules of repetitive measure, rhyme, and fixed stanza, Olson introduced the principle that "form is an extension of content," or that form is the result of allowing content to assume its own partly accidental shape during composition. Around this main principle are certain technical corollaries: for example, the poet, rather than treating his theme in an orderly progression of ideas, should instead rush from "perception to perception" until his argument is exhausted. The poet should allow the rhythm of his breath during composition to determine the length of each line, so that he has scored it for the reading voice. And in fitting words together in the line itself, the poet should let sound, rather than sense, determine syntax. A logic of the ear should take precedence over intellect in the fashioning of language.

Olson suggested that all of these new conventions were dependent on a new stance to experience, which he called Objectism. The poet should no longer consider his mind a clearing house of data, from which to select bits of information for his poems. Rather, the poet should include the rest of his organism in the act of perception and awareness, and should feel himself rush out of his private emotion into the realms of phenomena free of self-consciousness and inhibition. Objectism called for the poet to accept himself as merely another object inhabiting the phenomenal welter making up the world. The techniques advised in the first half of the essay, then, are all the means of making experience direct and unmediated for the poet who plunges fully into the phenomena around him.

"The Kingfishers" satisfies most of the conditions of composition set forth in the "Projective Verse" essay. Its form is the result of a rush of discourse on a series of loosely related topics, of experiments in combinations of sounds, and of the arrangement of words in clusters to show the changing shape of his thinking moment by moment. This striking poem creates the feeling of having kept pace with the random and shifting content of the poet's awareness.

Olson's projective methodology and the example of "The Kingfishers" are clearly efforts to explore and even to track the behavior of the imagination. More significant is the fact that Olson's poetic brings poetry into the general current of free-forming methods then being applied to the other arts: atonal, free-form jazz composition, abstract expressionism, improvisational theater, and kinetic sculpture.

Olson went on to refine the doctrine now known as Objectism in subsequent essays and lectures, but his several collections of short poems and the long, sequential work *The Maximus Poems* are the basis of his reputation and influence as a poet. In 1953 Creeley published Olson's first full-length volume of poems, *In Cold Hell, in Thicket*, which contains not only "The Kingfishers" but many of Olson's boldest shorter poems. Many, but by no means all, of these shorter poems are composed in the projective mode; others are written in a more leisurely-paced free verse style. The whole work is concerned with the burdens of tradition and influence the poet must cast off to pursue his own direction. The poet argues, often petulantly, against Ezra Pound, whom Olson identifies as his spiritual father and arch rival.

Creeley later edited Olson's *Selected Writings*, further establishing Olson's reputation as a key figure of the new poetry. A more finished and elaborate poetry emerges in *The Distances*, but there is less bold experiment in these maturer lyrical poems. Olson had moved to less defined ares of awareness; many of the poems are startling reenactments of dreams, in which the supralogical narratives are skillfully and persuasively dramatized, and there is a greater interest in myth and the content and forms of consciousness.

But the primary text for judging Olson as poet rests with his central work, the long, epical *Maximus* sequence, begun in the late 1940's and sustained to the last months of his life. The work remains unfinished, although the final volume, found among the poet's papers, has been edited and published. The work in one way is a celebration of the seacoast town of Gloucester, Massachusetts, where communal spirit among the fishermen thrived before industry was established; in another, it is close scrutiny of life in America and a search for an alternative ideology rooted in new spiritual awareness.

In the first volume, *The Maximus Poems*, Olson's persona, Maximus, named after an itinerant Phoenician mystic of the fourth century A.D., surveys contemporary Gloucester and finds its citizenry in disarray and the local culture ugly and alien. This judgment prompts a systematic inquiry into the origins of Gloucester and of America, which takes up the remainder of the volume. In the second volume, *Maximus IV, V, VI*, the speaker widens his interests to include mythological lore, the history of human migration, religious literature, and the finer details of Gloucester's past, which seem to Maximus to re-enact certain of the myths and fables of the ancient world. The final volume, more somber in mood and subject, continues Maximus's intense survey of Gloucester and himself. A vision of a new cosmos is summoned in these poems, in the hope of redeeming and possibly reconstituting the communal ethos of Gloucester's past. But that hope gives way to remorse and disparagement of the reckless present and its deadening commercial enterprises.

The poem is among the more ambitious experiments in sustained narrative in the post-war period; it ranks in conception and execution with other verse epics of the modern period, including Pound's *Cantos*, Williams's *Paterson*, and Hart Crane's *The Bridge*. Although Olson is less musical in his language, and at times a dry poet given to long quotation from historical documents, the sweep of his thought and the scope of his imaginative arguments distinguish him as a major American poet of the Whitman tradition.

—Paul Christensen

See the essay on *The Maximus Poems*.

O'NEILL, Eugene (Gladstone). Born in New York City, 16 October 1888; son of the actor James O'Neill. Toured with his father as a child, and educated at Catholic boarding schools, and at Betts Academy, Stamford, Connecticut; attended Princeton University, New Jersey, 1906–07, and George Pierce Baker's "47 Workshop" at Harvard University, Cambridge, Massachusetts, 1914–15. Married 1) Kathleen Jenkins in 1909 (divorced, 1912), one son; 2) Agnes Boulton in 1918 (divorced, 1929), one son and one daughter; 3) the actress Carlotta Monterey in 1929. Worked for New York-Chicago

Supply Company, mail order firm, New York, 1907–08; gold prospector in Honduras, 1909; seaman on a Norwegian freighter to Buenos Aires, and advance agent and box-office man for his father's company, 1910–11; reporter, New London *Telegraph*, Connecticut, 1912; patient in a tuberculosis sanitarium, 1912–13; full-time writer from 1914; associated with the Provincetown Players, New York, and Provincetown, Massachusetts, as actor and writer, 1916–20; wrote for the Theatre Guild; manager, with Kenneth Macgowan and Robert Edmond Jones, Greenwich Village Theatre, New York, 1923–27; a founding editor, *American Spectator*, 1934; in ill-health from 1934: in later years suffered from Parkinson's Disease. Recipient: Pulitzer Prize, 1920, 1922, 1928, 1957; American Academy of Arts and Letters Gold Medal, 1922; Nobel Prize for Literature, 1936; New York Drama Critics Circle award, 1957. Litt.D.: Yale University, New Haven, Connecticut, 1926. Member, American Academy, 1923, and Irish Academy of Letters. *Died 27 November 1953.*

PUBLICATIONS

Plays

Thirst and Other One Act Plays (includes *The Web, Warnings, Fog, Recklessness*). 1914.
Thirst (produced 1916). In *Thirst and Other Plays*, 1914.
Fog (produced 1917). In *Thirst and Other Plays*, 1914.
Bound East for Cardiff (produced 1916). In *The Moon of the Caribbees . . .*, 1919.
Before Breakfast (produced 1916). 1916.
The Sniper (produced 1917). In *Lost Plays*, 1950.
In the Zone (produced 1917). In *The Moon of the Caribbees . . .*, 1919.
The Long Voyage Home (produced 1917). In *The Moon of the Caribbees . . .*, 1919.
Ile (produced 1917). In *The Moon of the Caribbees . . .*, 1919.
The Rope (produced 1918). In *The Moon of the Caribbees . . .*, 1919.
Where The Cross Is Made (produced 1918). In *The Moon of the Caribbees . . .*, 1919.
The Moon of the Caribbees (produced 1918). In *The Moon of the Caribbees . . .*, 1919.
The Moon of the Caribbees and Six Other Plays of the Sea. 1919.
The Dreamy Kid (produced 1919). In *Complete Works 2*, 1924.
Beyond the Horizon (produced 1920). 1920.
Anna Christie (as *Chris*, produced 1920; revised version, as *Anna Christie*, produced 1921). With *The Hairy Ape, The First Man*, 1922.
Exorcism (produced 1920).
The Emperor Jones (produced 1920). With *Diff'rent, The Straw*, 1921.
Diff'rent (produced 1920). With *The Emperor Jones, The Straw*, 1921.
The Straw (produced 1921). With *The Emperor Jones, Diff'rent*, 1921.
Gold (produced 1921). 1921.
The First Man (produced 1922). With *The Hairy Ape, Anna Christie*, 1922.
The Hairy Ape (produced 1922). With *The First Man, Anna Christie*, 1922.
Welded (produced 1924). With *All God's Chillun Got Wings*, 1924.
The Ancient Mariner: A Dramatic Arrangement of Coleridge's Poem (produced 1924).
S.S. Glencairn: Four Plays of the Sea (includes *Bound East for Cardiff, In the Zone, The Long Voyage Home, The Moon of the Caribbees*) (produced 1924). 1926.
All God's Chillun Got Wings (produced 1924). With *Welded*, 1924.
Desire under the Elms (produced 1924). In *Complete Works 2*, 1924.
Complete Works. 2 vols., 1924.
The Fountain (produced 1925). With *The Great God Brown, The Moon of the Caribbees*, 1926.
The Great God Brown (produced 1926). With *The Fountain, The Moon of the Caribbees*, 1926.
Marco Millions (produced 1928). 1927.
Lazarus Laughed (produced 1928). 1927.
Strange Interlude (produced 1928). 1928.
Dynamo (produced 1929). 1929.
Mourning Becomes Electra: A Trilogy (produced 1931). 1931.
Ah, Wilderness! (produced 1933). 1933.
Days Without End (produced 1934). 1934.
The Iceman Cometh (produced 1946). 1946.
A Moon for the Misbegotten (produced 1947). 1952.
Lost Plays (includes *Abortion, The Movie Man, The Sniper, Servitude, A Wife for a Life*), edited by Lawrence Gellert. 1950.
Long Day's Journey into Night (produced 1956). 1956.
A Touch of the Poet (produced 1957). 1957.
Hughie (produced 1958). 1959.
More Stately Mansions (produced 1962). 1964.
Ten "Lost" Plays. 1964.
Children of the Sea and Three Other Unpublished Plays (includes *Bread and Butter, Now I Ask You, Shell Shock*), edited by Jennifer McCabe Atkinson. 1972.
The Calms of Capricorn (scenario by O'Neill, with completion by Donald Gallup). 1982.
Chris Christophersen (original version of *Anna Christie*). 1982.

Verse

Poems 1912–1944, edited by Donald Gallup. 1980.

Other

Inscriptions: O'Neill to Carlotta Monterey O'Neill, edited by Donald Gallup. 1960.
O'Neill at Work: Newly Released Ideas for Plays, edited by Virginia Floyd. 1981.
The Theatre We Worked For: The Letters of O'Neill to Kenneth Macgowan, edited by Jackson R. Bryer. 1982.

*

Bibliography: *O'Neill and the American Critic: A Bibliographical Checklist* by Jordan Y. Miller, 1973; *O'Neill: A Descriptive Bibliography* by Jennifer McCabe Atkinson, 1974.

Critical Studies: *The Haunted Heroes of O'Neill* by Edwin A. Engel, 1953; *O'Neill and the Tragic Tension* by Doris V. Falk, 1958, revised edition, 1982; *O'Neill and His Plays: Four Dec-*

ades of Criticism edited by Oscar Cargill and others, 1961; *O'Neill* (biography) by Arthur and Barbara Gelb, 1962, revised edition, 1973; *The Tempering of O'Neill* by Doris Alexander, 1962; *O'Neill* by Frederic I. Carpenter, 1964, revised edition, 1979; *O'Neill: A Collection of Critical Essays* edited by John Gassner, 1964; *The Plays of O'Neill* by John Henry Raleigh, 1965; *Playwright's Progress: O'Neill and the Critics* by Jordan Y. Miller, 1965; *O'Neill* by John Gassner, 1965; *O'Neill's Scenic Images* by Timo Tiusanen, 1968; *O'Neill: Son and Playwright*, 1968, and *O'Neill: Son and Artist*, 1973, both by Louis Sheaffer; *A Drama of Souls: Studies in O'Neill's Super-Naturalistic Techniques* by Egil Törnqvist, 1969; *O'Neill* by Horst Frenz, 1971, and *O'Neill's Critics: Voices from Abroad* edited by Frenz and Susan Tuck, 1984; *Contour in Time: The Plays of O'Neill* by Travis Bogard, 1972; *O'Neill: A Collection of Criticism* edited by Ernest Griffin, 1976; *Ritual and Pathos: The Theater of O'Neill* by Leonard Chabrowe, 1976; *Forging a Language: A Study of the Plays of O'Neill* by Jean Clothia, 1979; *O'Neill: A World View* edited by Virginia Floyd, 1980, and *The Plays of O'Neill: A New Assessment* by Floyd, 1984; *O'Neill's New Language of Kinship* by Michael Manheim, 1982; *O'Neill* by Normand Berlin, 1982; *The O'Neill Companion* by Margaret Loftus Ranald, 1984; *Critical Essays on O'Neill* edited by James J. Martins, 1984; *Final Acts: The Creation of Three Late O'Neill Plays* by Judith E. Barlow, 1985.

* * *

Now recognized as America's greatest dramatist, Eugene O'Neill stumbled through several styles and subjects in his will to resurrect tragedy for the modern stage. In 1912, at age 24, having survived a suicide attempt and a bout with tuberculosis, he determined to become a playwright, and he spent the next three decades in dedication to that mission. Starting with variants on melodrama, he steered into realistic sea plays, then to expressionist agons, and finally to sprawling realistic plays with an epic dimension. O'Neill was haunted by death, but he gave dramatic life to America's history and geography, men and women, poets and stutterers, illusion and disillusion. Earnest of purpose, contemptuous of facility, O'Neill shaped his thought and torment into 46 (published) plays, destroying those that illness prevented him from completing.

O'Neill's early melodramas have survived by accident, and they are of interest mainly by contrast with *Bound East for Cardiff*, the first of the *S. S. Glencairn* sea plays. Astonishing is young O'Neill's graduation from literary imitation to experiential authenticity, from stilted dialogue to salty colloquialism, from exotic settings to the minutely observed ship, from climactic violence to aimless drifting, for already O'Neill converted his seagoing experience into a long day's dramatic journey into night.

Beyond the Horizon brought O'Neill beyond the horizon of Provincetown to New York. Spanning a decade in the lives of two brothers in love with the same woman, the play traces the irony of their fate; marriage yokes the dreamer Robert to domesticity, whereas practical Andrew goes to sea. The three major characters succumb to their destiny, but O'Neill's three-act tragedy was his first triumph. Such irony within and outside his plays colors O'Neill's whole career.

No sooner did O'Neill find his sealegs in realism than he reached out toward expressionism. In 1920 he worked almost simultaneously upon the experimental *The Emperor Jones* and the realistic *Ole Davil* (which became *Anna Christie*). The two dissimilar plays not only confirmed O'Neill's position as America's leading dramatist at that time; they also endure in many non-commercial productions to this day. O'Neill later said that he had attempted to create "original rhythms of beauty, where beauty apparently isn't" in four plays written between 1920 and 1924—*The Emperor Jones*, *The Hairy Ape*, *All God's Chillun Got Wings*, and *Desire under the Elms*.

The Emperor Jones is at once a gripping drama about an oppressed American black, a modern tragedy about a hero with a flaw, an expressionist quest play probing to the racial roots of the protagonist; above all, it is more highly theatrical than its European analogues, gradually quickening the tom-tom from normal pulse-rhythm, stripping away colorful costume to the naked man beneath, subordinating dialogue to innovative lighting in order to illuminate an individual and his racial heritage.

Another expressionist play, *The Hairy Ape* dramatizes the quest of natural man in a mechanized world. And again the quest is a failure, ending in death. More ambitious scenically and symbolically, *The Hairy Ape* has not weathered as well as *The Emperor Jones*, and *All God's Chillun* is no longer performed at all. *Desire under the Elms*, by contrast, is not only frequently revived, it set O'Neill's feet firmly on hard realistic ground. Like the other three plays in which O'Neill felt he had created "original rhythms of beauty," *Desire under the Elms* dramatizes people at the bottom of the social ladder—in this case 19th-century New England farmers. In O'Neill's hands, however, these characters loom large—in part because the plot follows the Phaedra-Hippolytus-Theseus myth, in part because the indoor-outdoor setting permits visualization of the private-public resonances of that plot. Although marred by turgid dialogue and abuse of repetition, *Desire under the Elms* nevertheless achieves moments of passionate intensity which predict O'Neill's wholly functional final tragedies.

O'Neill, ever productive though he was, only gradually worked up to that summit. From the mid-1920's to the mid-1930's he cast about for non-realistic forms to contain his tragic vision. *Desire under the Elms*'s American background for Greek tragedy climbs the social ladder in *Mourning Becomes Electra*—a post-Civil War *Oresteia* in which the many specific details are credible at both the realistic and mythic levels. *Marco Millions* stages a picaresque and satirized Babbitt. O'Neill used masks to theatricalize an Apollonian-Dionysian conflict in *The Great God Brown*. Shortly afterwards O'Neill wrote his most ambitious play, *Lazarus Laughed*, which draws upon the Bible, Greek choruses, Elizabethan expansiveness, expressionist masks, crowd scenes with over a hundred actors, and orchestrated laughter that damns materialism. Then, reverting to the 20th century for *Strange Interlude*, O'Neill in his "woman play" resurrects the stage aside to reveal repressed desires. *Dynamo* deifies a dynamo in its final apocalyptic scene. Although it is customary to consider these plays unplayable today, a recent staging of *Strange Interlude* (with Glenda Jackson a memorable Nina Leeds) gives the lie to this custom. During O'Neill's lifetime, he never magnetized a consistently loyal director, but José Quintero faithfully directed the late realistic tragedies after the playwright's death.

In 1932, at age 44, O'Neill conceived the idea of a cycle of plays about several generations of an American family—"A Tale of Possessors Self-Dispossessed." By 1941, he noted in his Work Diary: "Idea was first 5 plays, then 7, then 8, then 9, now 11!—will never live to do it—but what price anything but a dream these days!" His prediction was accurate. Ill and unable to write, he salvaged only *A Touch of the Poet*, and *More*

Stately Mansions was salvaged in spite of his wishes. Ironically, O'Neill's extra-cycle, extra-dream plays are his greatest—*The Iceman Cometh* and *Long Day's Journey into Night*. The two plays are similar in their return to surface realism, their concentration and specificity of place and time (the year 1912), their tender comedy that intensifies the tragic drive, their memorable characters that do not strain for, yet somehow attain mythic dimension. The differences between the two plays testify to O'Neill's final range and depth: a working-class saloon and an upper-middle-class country home; nineteen characters of diverse origin and four members of an Irish-American family; a plot that derives from the Bible and a bawdy joke and a plot grounded in O'Neill's own autobiography; the gentle savoring of illusory hope and the merciless exposure of pernicious illusion.

Finally, O'Neill lives in contradictions. The sheer bulk of his achievement is undermined by a relative paucity of contemporary production; his restless experimentation is subdued to realism; his obsession with tragedy is eroded by productions that stress comedy, stasis, or existential absurdity. The tragic fate that O'Neill pursues in play after play crystallizes at last in palpable moments of grace.

—Ruby Cohn

See the essays on *Long Day's Journey into Night* and *Strange Interlude*.

PAGE, Thomas Nelson. Born on Oakland Plantation, Hanover County, Virginia, 23 April 1853. Educated in local schools, and at Washington College (later Washington and Lee University), Lexington, Virginia, 1869–72; read law with his father, 1872–73; studied law at the University of Virginia, Charlottesville, 1873–74, LL.B. 1874. Married 1) Annie Seddon Bruce in 1886 (died, 1888); 2) Florence Lathrop Field in 1893 (died, 1921). Lawyer in Richmond, Virginia, 1874–93; writer, 1884–1910; lived in Washington, D.C., after 1893; U.S. Ambassador to Italy, 1913–19. Litt.D.: Washington and Lee University, 1887; Yale University, New Haven, Connecticut, 1901; Harvard University, Cambridge, Massachusetts, 1913; LL.D.: Tulane University, New Orleans, 1899; College of William and Mary, Williamsburg, Virginia, 1906; Washington and Lee University, 1907. Member, American Academy, 1908. *Died 1 November 1922.*

PUBLICATIONS

Fiction

In Ole Virginia; or, Marse Chan and Other Stories. 1887.
Two Little Confederates. 1888.
On Newfound River. 1891; revised edition, 1906.
Among the Camps; or, Young People's Stories of the War. 1891.
Elsket and Other Stories. 1891.
The Burial of the Guns. 1894.
Pastime Stories. 1894.
Unc' Edinburg: A Plantation Echo. 1895.
The Old Gentleman of the Black Stock. 1897.
Two Prisoners. 1898; revised edition, 1903.
Red Rock: A Chronicle of Reconstruction. 1898.
Santa Claus's Partner. 1899.
Gordon Keith. 1903.
Bred in the Bone (stories). 1904.
Under the Crust (stories). 1907.
Tommy Trot's Visit to Santa Claus. 1908.
John Marvel, Assistant. 1909.
The Land of the Spirit (stories). 1913.
The Stranger's Pew (story). 1914.
The Red Riders. 1924.

Verse

Befo' de War: Echoes in Negro Dialect, with A.C. Gordon. 1888.
The Coast of Bohemia. 1906.

Other

The Old South: Essays Social and Political. 1892.
Social Life in Old Virginia Before the War. 1897.
The Negro: The Southerner's Problem. 1904.
The Novels, Stories, Sketches, and Poems (Plantation Edition). 18 vols., 1906–12.
Robert E. Lee: The Southerner. 1908; as *General Lee*, 1909.
The Old Dominion: Her Making and Her Manners. 1908.
Mount Vernon and Its Preservation. 1910.
Robert E. Lee: Man and Soldier. 1911.
Italy and the World War. 1920.
Dante and His Influence: Studies. 1922.
Washington and Its Romance. 1923.
Mediterranean Winter—1906: Journal and Letters, edited by Harriet R. Holman. 1971.

Editor, *The Old Virginia Gentleman and Other Sketches*, by George W. Bagby. 1910.

*

Bibliography: by Theodore L. Gross, in *American Literary Realism 1*, 1967; in *Bibliography of American Literature* by Jacob Blanck, 1973; *Three Virginia Writers: A Reference Guide* by George C. Longest, 1978.

Critical Studies: *Page: A Memoir of a Virginia Gentleman* by Rosewell Page, 1923; *Patriotic Gore: Studies in the Literature of the American Civil War* by Edmund Wilson, 1962; *Page* by Theodore L. Gross, 1967; *The Literary Career of Page 1884–1910* by Harriet R. Holman, 1978.

* * *

Thomas Nelson Page owed his popularity to the local color movement, the interest of Northern readers in the defeated South following the Civil War, and the growth of the family magazine. Although there were writers in the deep South and the mountain areas, the dominant literary image of the region was provided by accounts of life in the tidewater. Page and other writers in the plantation literary tradition increased the Southerner's pride in his past and dramatized his sense of victimization and self-sacrifice. Page's essays and dialect stories, published first in such magazines as *Scribner's* and *Century*, eulogized a civilization in which landlords abided by an almost medieval sense of *gentilesse*, women were exalted, and all the chivalric virtues prevailed. Sir Walter Scott's romances and stories by the Virginia writers George Bagby and Armistead Gordon influenced Page's style and themes. His protagonists were typically those who had survived the war and were faced with the task of adjusting to a new and alien culture. He attempted to evoke a world that lived only in memory, and nostalgia was, therefore, the dominant mood of his most successful work.

The favorable reception in both North and South of "Marse Chan," "Meh Lady," and the other stories of *In Ole Virginia* convinced Page that authorship would prove a surer path to fame than the legal profession. Consequently, after his first wife died and he married a wealthy widow. Page devoted himself to full-time writing. He wrote several novels in which he experimented with urban settings and satirical dialogue. Even in these works, however, Page described the impact of Southern values on the rest of the nation. Each of the major novels written in his middle years (*Red Rock*, *Gordon Keith*, and *John Marvel, Assistant*) concerns southern "missionaries," Virginia gentlemen who preach their southern ideals and convert Yankees in the process. Part of their doctrine was a distrust of industrialization, a belief that aristocratic paternalism could still combat the grosser aspects of democracy, and a wistful agrarianism. It was the first decade of the new century that brought Page to the peak of his literary fame. After 1910 he all but retired from writing and devoted his time to political affairs in Washington, D.C.; he was a personal friend of Theodore Roosevelt, and eventually became ambassador to Italy.

Few writers after Page described southern institutions so uncritically. Of the later writers Margaret Mitchell came closer than most to sharing the elegant Virginian's views, while Glasgow, Cabell, Faulkner, and their contemporaries perceived the ironies and injustices of the system Page had defended. At his best Page epitomized the plantation literary tradition, and the strengths and weaknesses of his prose provide an excellent illustration of a once popular literary genre.

—Kimball King

PAINE, Thomas. Born in Thetford, Norfolk, England, 29 January 1737. Educated at grammar school to age 13; then apprenticed in his father's trade of staymaker (corsets, or possibly ship's cables). Served in the Pennsylvania militia, 1776. Married 1) Mary Lambert in 1759 (died, 1760); 2) Elizabeth Ollive in 1771 (legally separated, 1774; died, 1808). Went to sea on privateer, 1756; staymaker, London, 1756–57, and Dover, 1758, Sandwich, 1759, and Margate, 1760, all Kent; supernumerary excise officer, Thetford, 1761, Grantham, Lincolnshire, 1762–64, and Alford, Lincolnshire, 1764–65 (dismissed for neglect of duty); staymaker, Diss, Norfolk, 1766; usher, London, 1766–68; excise officer, Lewes, Sussex, 1768–74 (dismissed after leading move to gain pay rise); went to Philadelphia, 1774, with letters of introduction from Benjamin Franklin; journalist: editor, *Pennsylvania Magazine*, Philadelphia, 1775–76; secretary, Continental Congress committee to negotiate treaty with the Indians, 1777, and committee on foreign affairs, 1777–79; clerk, Pennsylvania Assembly, 1779–81; secretary on a mission to France to raise money for George Washington's army, 1781; lived in Bordentown, New Jersey, and on farm (confiscated from loyalists) given to him near New Rochelle, New York, and worked on design for single arch iron bridge (design approved by French Academy, 1787), 1783–87; lived in England and France from 1787; tried in absentia for treason (over *The Rights of Man*), and outlawed from England, 1792; made French citizen by Assembly, 1792; member of National Convention, for Pas de Calais, 1792, as part of Gironde group (supported banishment, not execution, of Louis XVI); at fall of Girondists deprived of French citizenship and imprisoned, 1793–94; resumed seat in Convention, 1795, and lived in Paris until 1802; lived in New Jersey, New Rochelle, and New York City, 1802–09. M.A. University of Pennsylvania, Philadelphia, 1780. *Died 8 June 1809*.

PUBLICATIONS

Collections

Life and Works, edited by William M. Van der Weyde. 10 vols., 1925.
Representative Selections, edited by Harry Hayden Clark. 1944; revised edition, 1961.
Complete Writings, edited by Philip S. Foner. 2 vols., 1945.

Works

Common Sense. 1776; revised edition, 1776.
The American Crisis. 13 vols., 1776–83; *The Crisis Extraordinary*, 1780; *A Supernumerary Crisis*, 2 vols., 1783.
Public Good. 1780.
Letter Addressed to the Abbé Raynal on the Affairs of North America. 1782.
Dissertations on Government: The Affairs of the Bank; and Paper-Money. 1786.
Prospects on the Rubicon. 1787; as *Prospects on the War and Paper Currency*, 1793.
The Rights of Man. 2 vols., 1791–92; edited by Henry Collins, 1969.
Letter Addressed to the Addressers. 1792.
The Writings. 1792 (?).
The Case of the Officers of Excise. 1793.
Reasons for Wishing to Preserve the Life of Louis Capet (i.e., Louis XVI). 1793.
The Age of Reason. 2 vols., 1794–95.
Dissertation on First Principles of Government. 1795.
The Decline and Fall of the English System of Finance. 1796.
Letter to George Washington. 1796.
La justice agraire. 1797; as *Agrarian Justice*, 1797.
Letter to the People of France and the French Armies. 1797.
Discourse at the Society of Theophilanthropists. 1798; as *Atheism Refuted*, 1798.
Compact Maritime. 1801.
Letters to the Citizens of the United States. 1803.
To the Citizens of Pennsylvania, on the Proposal for Calling a Convention. 1805.
Examination of the Passages in the New Testament, Quoted from the Old, and Called Prophecies Concerning Jesus Christ. 1807.
Of the Causes of Yellow Fever, and the Means of Preventing It. 1807.
On the Origins of Free-masonry. 1810.
Miscellaneous Poems. 1819.
Six New Letters, edited by Harry Hayden Clark. 1939.
Selected Work, edited by Howard Fast. 1946.

Common Sense and Other Political Writings, edited by Nelson F. Adkins. 1953.

*

Critical Studies: *The Life of Paine* by Moncure Daniel Conway, 2 vols., 1892; *Man of Reason: The Life of Paine*, 1959, and *Paine's American Ideology*, 1984, both by Alfred Owen Aldridge; *Paine: His Life, Work, and Times* by Audrey Williamson, 1973; *Paine* by David Freeman Hawke, 1974; *Paine and Revolutionary America* by Eric Foner, 1976; *Paine* by Jerome D. Wilson and William F. Ricketson, 1978; *Paine, The Greatest Exile* by David Powell, 1985.

* * *

Few American writers have generated as much controversy as that surrounding Thomas Paine and his works. Revered as a folk hero during the American Revolution, Paine died in ignominy, an embarrassment to his former friends and an object of ridicule in the very country that his writings had done so much to establish. Nonetheless, his works are, as one critic explains, "unique as an example of English in action," placing him among the most successful persuasive writers of all times. Even Paine's most strident adversaries have been forced to admit that without him there may very well have never been an American Revolution.

Paine first rose to public prominence as a writer of pamphlets during the time of the Revolutionary War. Published anonymously in early January 1776, his essay *Common Sense* sold literally hundreds of thousands of copies and is credited with almost single-handedly convincing the American colonies to enter into armed rebellion against Great Britain. In this work Paine popularized the Enlightenment concept that government is a "social contract" that exists by consent of the people for the protection of their "natural rights." Attacking the idea of monarchy, Paine catalogued the abuses that the British king had imposed upon his American subjects, and he called for the establishment of a new government, independent of Britain. Equally popular and equally effective was *The American Crisis*, an essay series published in thirteen parts (including an addendum) between 1776 and 1783. Issued at periods during the war when the patriot cause seemed desperate, *The American Crisis* lifted the morale of soldiers and civilians alike and helped secure the revenues and determination needed to see the conflict through to a successful conclusion. According to one scholar, the very history of the war "may be read in the blazing light of these mighty pamphlets." The first part opens:

> These are the times that try men's souls. The summer soldier and the sunshine patriot will, in this crisis, shrink from the service of their country; but he that stands it *now* deserves the love and thanks of man and woman. Tyranny, like hell, is not easily conquered; yet we have this consolation with us, that the harder the conflict, the more glorious the triumph.

After the war, in such works as *The Rights of Man* and *The Age of Reason*, Paine set out to accomplish for the world what he had already accomplished for America. Written in two parts, *The Rights of Man* defends the French Revolution against the attacks lodged against it by Edmund Burke in his *Reflections on the Revolution in France* and even goes so far as to call for a democratic revolution against the British monarchy. So fearful was the British crown that this work might indeed inspire rebellion that an order was issued for Paine's arrest, and he was forced to leave the country for France, where he was initially received as a hero but later imprisoned for his denunciation of the execution of Louis XVI.

Abandoned by three countries and embittered, Paine wrote *The Age of Reason* in the hopes of enlightening mankind concerning matters of religion. Far from the atheism that it was labelled by Paine's political detractors, *The Age of Reason* consists of little more than an educated attempt to popularize the ideas of scientific deism widely held during the late 18th century by individuals as respected as Benjamin Franklin, Thomas Jefferson, and George Washington. "My country is the world," wrote Paine, "and my religion is to do good." Nonetheless, it was this work, along with a letter critical of Washington, that led to Paine's vilification in the American popular imagination and that earned him the title of "filthy little atheist."

Although scholars have debated the exact nature of Paine's indebtedness to other writers, it is generally conceded that with few exceptions most of Paine's ideas were not original. His social and political theories, for example, are borrowed from such writers as Rousseau, Montesquieu, Locke, and Hobbes, and his religious views owe their origin to the theories set in motion by Newton and Diderot. Likewise, it is generally conceded that what distinguishes Paine from other writers of his time is his tremendous talent for persuasion.

Indeed, Paine has been called "one of the world's truly great practitioners of the art of persuasive writing," and although he sometimes ignored the niceties of conventional grammar and was capable of subverting logic to suit his ends, in the works of Paine can be seen a truly extraordinary grasp of the principles of effective rhetoric. Speaking with conviction as a common man in the idiom of the common man, Paine at his best could generate a unique sense of identification between himself and his audience. He is, as Quintilian would have said, an admirable man speaking to an equally admirable group of people.

Disavowing the complex neoclassical rhetoric of his day, Paine espoused instead a style that was forceful, direct, clear, and simple. Easily understood, his prose was carefully structured to move his audience to action. A master at the use of such rhetorical devices as parallelism, repetition, the apostrophe, the invective, the rhetorical question, the summary, and the ethical appeal, Paine was able, as one scholar has explained, to awaken "the lukewarm, hesitating, and indifferent, and turn them in great numbers to the support of the cause." As a result, lines such as those quoted above and "The sun never shined on a cause of greater worth" remain, as one analyst has pointed out, "as vibrant today as they were 200 years ago."

—James A. Levernier

See the essay on *Common Sense*.

PARKER, Dorothy (née Rothschild). Born in West End, New Jersey, 22 August 1893. Educated at Blessed Sacrament Convent, New York; Miss Dana's School, Morristown, New Jersey, 1907–11, graduated 1911. Married 1) Edwin Pond Parker II in 1917 (divorced, 1928); 2) Alan Campbell in 1933 (divorced, 1947; remarried, 1950; died, 1963). Played piano at a dancing school, New York, 1912–15; editorial staff member,

Vogue, New York, 1916–17; staff writer and drama critic, *Vanity Fair*, New York, 1917–20; theatre columnist, *Ainslee's*, 1920–33; book reviewer ("Constant Reader" column), *New Yorker*, 1925–27; columnist, *McCall's*, New York, late 1920's; book reviewer, *Esquire*, New York, 1957–62. Founder, with Robert Benchley, Robert E. Sherwood, and others, Algonquin Hotel Round Table, 1920. Recipient: O. Henry Award, 1929; Marjorie Peabody Waite Award, 1958. *Died 7 June 1967.*

PUBLICATIONS

Fiction

Laments for the Living. 1930.
After Such Pleasures. 1933.
Here Lies: The Collected Stories. 1939.
Collected Stories. 1942.

Plays

Chauve-Souris (revue), with others (produced 1922).
Round the Town (lyrics only; revue) (produced 1924).
Close Harmony; or, The Lady Next Door, with Elmer Rice (produced 1924). 1929.
Business Is Business, with George S. Kaufman (produced 1925).
Sketches, in *Shoot the Works* (revue) (produced 1931).
The Coast of Illyria, with Ross Evans (produced 1949).
The Ladies of the Corridor, with Arnaud d'Usseau (produced 1953). 1954.
Candide (lyrics only, with Richard Wilbur and John La-Touche), book by Lillian Hellman, music by Leonard Bernstein, from the novel by Voltaire (produced 1956). 1957.

Screenplays: *Here Is My Heart* (uncredited), with others, 1934; *One Hour Late*, with others, 1935; *The Big Broadcast of 1936*, with others, 1935; *Mary Burns, Fugitive*, with others, 1935; *Hands Across the Table*, with others, 1935; *Paris in Spring*, with others, 1935; *The Moon's Our Home*, with others, 1936; *Lady Be Careful*, with others, 1936; *Three Married Men*, with Alan Campbell and Owen Davis, Sr., 1936; *Suzy*, with others, 1936; *A Star Is Born*, with others, 1937; *Sweethearts*, with Alan Campbell, 1938; *Trade Winds*, with others, 1938; *The Little Foxes*, with others, 1941; *Weekend for Three*, with Alan Campbell and Budd Schulberg, 1941; *Saboteur*, with Peter Viertel and Joan Harrison, 1942; *Smash-Up—The Story of a Woman*, with others, 1947; *The Fan*, with Walter Reisch and Ross Evans, 1949.

Television Plays: *The Lovely Leave*, *A Telephone Call*, and *Dusk Before Fireworks*, from her own stories, 1962.

Verse

Enough Rope. 1926.
Sunset Gun. 1928.
Death and Taxes. 1931.
Collected Poems: Not So Deep as a Well. 1936; as *Collected Poetry*, 1944.

Other

High Society, with George S. Chappell and Frank Crowninshield. 1920.
Men I'm Not Married To, with *Women I'm Not Married To*, by Franklin P. Adams. 1922.
The Portable Parker. 1944; as *The Indispensable Parker*, 1944; as *Selected Short Stories*, 1944; revised edition, as *The Portable Parker*, 1973; as *The Collected Parker*, 1973.
Constant Reader. 1970; as *A Month of Saturdays*, 1971.

Editor, *The Portable F. Scott Fitzgerald*. 1945.
Editor, with Frederick B. Shroyer, *Short Story: A Thematic Anthology*. 1965.

*

Critical Studies: *An Unfinished Woman: A Memoir* by Lillian Hellman, 1969; *You Might as Well Live: The Life and Times of Parker* by John Keats, 1970; *Parker* by Arthur F. Kinney, 1978; *The Late Mrs. Parker* by Leslie Frewin, 1987.

* * *

Dorothy Parker's writings were aptly characterized by Alexander Woollcott as "a potent distillation of nectar and wormwood, of ambrosia and deadly nightshade." This assessment covers her perennially popular volumes of short stories, *Laments for the Living* and *After Such Pleasures*. It also encompasses her three best-selling volumes of wry, bittersweet verse (not serious "poetry," she claimed), *Enough Rope*, *Sunset Gun*, and *Death and Taxes*—mostly love lamentations. It could also apply to her crisp, tart book reviews for the *New Yorker*; she dismissed Milne's *The House at Pooh Corner* with "Tonstant Weader fwowed up."

Her book reviews for *Esquire* (1957–62) are skimpier and less successful. Her major play, *The Ladies of the Corridor* (with Arnaud d'Usseau), a slice-of-life portrayal of aging, pathetic women who have lost their central purpose for living (through departures of husbands, lovers, children) is better as dialogue than as drama.

Many of Parker's well-crafted short stories focus on upper-class Manhattan women of the 1920's and 1930's. The economic comfort of these women, whether young, middle-aged, or old, is counteracted by their superficial, pointless lives, barren of goals, meaningful activities, and inner resources. Although they are often physically attractive and elegantly dressed ornaments at the parties they live for, without such external social props they collapse.

Other people in Parker's stories do the *real* work; the men earn the money, the maids rear the children. So these women are bored, neurotic, unhappy, pampered parasites. Their fate is the fate of those who live through others, excessive emotional dependency: "Please, God, let him telephone me now." This cripples their potentiality for gaiety and charm and transforms them into shrill, malicious shrews who drink too much, talk too much, think too shallowly, and do too little. These characters are their own most pathetic victims; they seldom deceive others as they delude themselves.

Parker excels in economically incisive descriptions of personalities, settings, costumes: a honeymooning bride "looked as new as a peeled egg." Her dramatic monologues are devastating, ironic characterizations. Thus the hypocritical "Lady with a Lamp" offers cold comfort to her alleged friend, jilted and unhappily recuperating from a clandestine abortion: "I worry so about you, living in a little furnished apartment, with nothing that belongs to you, no roots, no nothing." Parker's dialogues capture the cadences of real speech and the subtle nuances of personality and values: "Good night, useless," says the spoiled mother to her firstborn infant.

The essence of such social satire is the author's implicit desire to reform these empty lives into significant existences. Her best story, "Big Blonde," which won the O. Henry Award in 1929, epitomizes Parker's mixture of love and anger, coalesced into an enduring work of art. Indeed, many of Parker's stories are memorable cameos, etched in acid and polished to gemlike lustre.

—Lynn Z. Bloom

PARKMAN, Francis (Jr.). Born in Boston, Massachusetts, 16 September 1823. Educated at John Angier's school, Medford, Massachusetts, 1831–35; Gideon Thayer's school, Boston, 1835–40; Harvard University, Cambridge, Massachusetts, 1840–44, A.B. 1844 (Phi Beta Kappa); Dane Law School, Harvard University, 1844–46, LL.B. 1846. Married Catherine Scollay Bigelow in 1850 (died 1858); two daughters and one son. Traveled from St. Louis along Oregon Trail and spent some weeks with Sioux Indians, 1846. Suffered from series of nervous ailments after 1846. Professor of Horticulture, Harvard University, 1871. Overseer, 1868–71 and 1874–76, and Fellow of the Corporation, 1875–88, Harvard University. President, Massachusetts Horticultural Society, 2 years; founder, Archeological Institute of America, 1879; founder and first President, St. Botolph Club, Boston. LL.D.: McGill University, Montreal, 1879; Harvard University, 1889. *Died 8 November 1893.*

PUBLICATIONS

Collections

Works, edited by John Fiske. 20 vols., 1897–98.
The Parkman Reader, edited by Samuel Eliot Morison. 1955; as *France and England in North America*, 1956.
Letters, edited by Wilbur R. Jacobs. 2 vols., 1960.

Fiction

Vassall Morton. 1856.

Other

The California and Oregon Trail, Being Sketches of Prairie and Rocky Mountain Life. 1849; revised edition, as *The Oregon Trail*, 1872; edited by David Levin, 1982.
History of the Conspiracy of Pontiac and the War of the North American Tribes Against the English Colonies. 2 vols., 1851; revised edition, 1868, 1870.
France and England in North America (Library of America), edited by David Levin. 2 vols., 1983.
Pioneers of France in the New World. 1865; revised edition, 1886.
The Jesuits in North America in the Seventeenth Century. 1867.
The Discovery of the Great West. 1869; revised edition, as *La Salle and the Discovery of the Great West*, 1879.
The Old Régime in Canada. 1874; revised edition, 1894.
Count Frontenac and New France under Louis XIV. 1877.
Montcalm and Wolfe (part 7). 1884.
A Half-Century of Conflict (part 6). 1892.
The Book of Roses. 1866.
Some of the Reasons Against Woman Suffrage. 1883.
Our Common Schools. 1890.
Letters from Parkman to E.G. Squier, edited by Don C. Seitz. 1911.
Representative Selections, edited by Wilbur L. Schramm. 1938.
The Journals, edited by Mason Wade. 2 vols., 1947.

*

Bibliography: in *Bibliography of American Literature* by Jacob Blanck, 1973.

Critical Studies: *Parkman, Heroic Historian* by Mason Wade, 1942; *Parkman's History: The Historian as Literary Artist* by Otis A. Pease, 1953; *History as Romantic Art: Bancroft, Motley, Prescott, and Parkman* by David Levin, 1959; *Parkman* by Howard Doughty, 1962; *Parkman* by Robert L. Gale, 1973; *The American Compromise: Theme and Method in the Histories of Bancroft, Parkman, and Adams* by Richard C. Vitzthum, 1974.

* * *

Francis Parkman began his literary career in 1845 with four short stories and a poem, all published in *Knickerbocker Magazine*. All dealt with one of the themes of his writing, the conflict between whites and Indians in North America. He had dedicated himself at eighteen to write what he called "a history of the American forest" and these were the first literary results. Parkman was primarily a historian whose one attempt at a major literary work, the novel *Vassall Morton*, was not successful. But his history survives because of its literary qualities.

His most well-known work, *The Oregon Trail*, went through nine editions in his lifetime and remains in print. Its qualities explain Parkman's survival while fellow historians like Motley or Prescott have long since disappeared from publishers' lists. Parkman paid great attention to atmosphere, to introducing the reader to all the sights, sounds, and smells of described landscapes. He worked to integrate his historical characters into their worlds. His imaginative reconstructions have survived all attempts to question their authenticity, bearing witness to his qualities both as historian and literary figure.

Parkman's major literary influences were Cooper, Scott, and Byron. He shared Scott's delight in reconstructing historical episodes and transforming them into literary vehicles though he took no liberties with the facts. He responded to Cooper's fascination with the west and to Byron's interest in character especially as drawn out in *Childe Harold's Pilgrimage* which Parkman re-read throughout his life. Parkman's education introduced him to the literatures of Germany, France, and Spain, as well as that of ancient Greece which had a particular influence on him. His *La Salle and the Discovery of the Great West* presents a man who would be familiar to all readers of Greek tragedy, brave, purposeful, self-absorbed—so fatally flawed, and in the end destroyed. Similarly the description of Pontiac, the central figure in *History of the Conspiracy of Pontiac* owes much to Greek models.

Parkman was also influenced by French writers like Chateaubriand who showed his fascination with man's interaction with Nature. Parkman is read today partly because of the influence on him of another Frenchman, the ethnologist Joseph-François Lafitau who saved him from contemporary stereotypes of Indians. Parkman was no cultural relativist but he did see the Indian in his own terms and disapproval only followed after understanding. Likewise Parkman was able to reject much of his Protestantism (he was a Mather on his mother's side) when dealing with the Jesuits of New France. A tour of Italy (1843–44) led him, he felt, to understand the functional importance of the Catholic Church and to be able to deal with it even-handedly on the North American continent. He did, however, feel that Catholicism and despotism were closely connected, as were Protestantism and liberty, and, like many another teleologically-minded 19th-century observer, that the triumph of secularism was inevitable. This underlying process helped explain the triumph of Great Britain and the fall of France in North America, dealt with climactically in *Montcalm and Wolfe*.

Parkman's fascination with the heroic and with the individual has been criticised by a more democratically minded age. He was, like Cooper, fearful of democratic excess and believed in beneficent leadership by the educated. Too much should not be made of the social attitudes exhibited in *The Oregon Trail* which is the work of a young man. It does not seem sensible to reject Parkman's west because he fails to dwell on frontiersmen. Frederick Jackson Turner admired Parkman's work though he did see him as "even greater as an artist than as an historian" because of his "dramatic insight." Parkman was fascinated by leadership, its demands and its destructiveness and therefore generally ignored those who merely followed. The accent on the individual makes him seem old-fashioned in contemporary historiographical circles but does not detract from his literary merits. Since contemporary historiographical preoccupations are unlikely to be permanent it may be that such criticisms will in time become outdated.

Parkman understood the need to balance "dramatic interest" and "historic proportion," as he put it. His success in doing so explains his attractiveness to historian and literary critic alike. It is possible that his partial blindness made him particularly aware of the power of good descriptive writing, but it is also true that in the end his imagination was a limited one. Perhaps because of his historical training Parkman wrote best when he fleshed out historical incident, best of all when he decorated his own experiences as in those depicted in *The Oregon Trail*. Parkman needed sources before he could begin to write successfully, but this limitation brought rewards. Not many writers could expect to be praised by Henry James as both "solid and artistic."

—R.A. Burchell

PATCHEN, Kenneth. Born in Niles, Ohio, 13 December 1911. Educated at East Junior High School, 1924–26, and Warren G. Harding High School, 1926–29, both Warren, Ohio; Experimental College, University of Wisconsin, Madison, 1929–30; Commonwealth College, Mena, Arkansas, 1930. Married Miriam Oikemus in 1934. Farm worker, gardener, and janitor, throughout the U.S. and Canada, 1930–33; free-lance writer from 1934; staff member, New Directions, publishers, Norfolk, Connecticut, 1939–40; moved to San Francisco, 1951, and to Palo Alto, California, 1956. Artist: individual show of books, graphics, and paintings, Corcoran Gallery, Washington, D.C., 1969. Recipient: Guggenheim fellowship, 1936; Shelley Memorial Award, 1954; National Endowment for the Arts grant, 1967. *Died 8 January 1972.*

PUBLICATIONS (illustrated by the author)

Verse

Before the Brave. 1936.
First Will and Testament. 1939.
The Teeth of the Lion. 1942.
The Dark Kingdom. 1942.
Cloth of the Tempest. 1943.
An Astonished Eye Looks Out of the Air, Being Some Poems Old and New Against War and in Behalf of Life. 1945.
Outlaw of the Lowest Planet, edited by David Gascoyne. 1946.
Selected Poems. 1946; revised edition, 1958, 1964.
Pictures of Life and Death. 1947.
They Keep Riding Down All the Time. 1947.
Panels for the Walls of Heaven. 1947.
A Letter to God, with *Patchen: Man of Anger and Light*, by Henry Miller. 1947.
CCCLXXIV Poems. 1948.
To Say If You Love Someone and Other Selected Love Poems. 1948.
Red Wine and Yellow Hair. 1949.
Fables and Other Little Tales. 1953.
The Famous Boating Party and Other Poems in Prose. 1954.
Poems of Humor and Protest. 1954.
Orchards, Thrones and Caravans. 1955.
Glory Never Guesses. 1956.
A Surprise for the Bagpipe Player. 1956.
When We Were Here Together. 1957.
Hurrah for Anything: Poems and Drawings. 1957.
Two Poems for Christmas. 1958.
Poem-scapes. 1958.
Pomes Penyeach. 1959.
Poems of Humor and Protest. 1960.
Because It Is: Poems and Drawings. 1960.
A Poem for Christmas. 1960.
The Love Poems. 1960.
Patchen Drawing-Poem. 1962.
Picture Poems. 1962.
Doubleheader. 1966.
Hallelujah Anyway. 1966.
Where Are the Other Rowboats? 1966.
But Even So (includes drawings). 1968.
Love and War Poems, edited by Dennis Gould. 1968.
Selected Poems. 1968.
The Collected Poems. 1968.
Aflame and Afun of Walking Faces: Fables and Drawings. 1970.
There's Love All Day, edited by Dee Danner Barwick. 1970.
Wonderings. 1971.
In Quest of Candlelighters. 1972.
Still Another Pelican in the Breadbox, edited by Richard G. Morgan. 1980.

Plays

The City Wears a Slouch Hat (broadcast 1942). In *Lost Plays*, 1977.
Don't Look Now (produced 1959; as *Now You See It*, produced 1966). In *Lost Plays*, 1977.
Lost Plays, edited by Richard G. Morgan. 1977.

Radio Play: *The City Wears a Slouch Hat*, 1942.

Fiction

The Journal of Albion Moonlight. 1941.
The Memoirs of a Shy Pornographer: An Amusement. 1945.
Sleepers Awake. 1946.
See You in the Morning. 1948.

Other

Patchen: Painter of Poems (exhibition catalogue). 1969.
The Argument of Innocence: A Selection from the Arts of Patchen, edited by Peter Veres. 1976.
Patchen: The Last Interview, edited by Gene Detro. 1976.
What Shall We Do Without Us? The Voice and Vision of Patchen. 1984.

*

Bibliography: *Patchen: An Annotated, Descriptive Bibliography* by Richard G. Morgan, 1978.

Critical Studies: *Patchen: A Collection of Critical Essays* edited by Richard G. Morgan, 1977; *Tribute to Patchen*, 1977; *Patchen* by Larry Smith, 1978; *Patchen and American Mysticism* by Raymond Nelson, 1984.

* * *

Kenneth Patchen is in the tradition of American poets that descends from Walt Whitman through William Carlos Williams to the Black Mountain poets, and beyond them to such younger writers as Galway Kinnell. That is to say, Patchen is a "redskin" poet as opposed to a "paleface." His poems do not make use of European-inspired formal devices; his language is deliberately a "barbaric yawp" (Whitman's famous phrase from *Song of Myself*); and his subject matter is drawn from his own very American experiences. He is a poet of the open air and the open road, a hunter after experience, claiming a kind of mystical connection with the animals he kills (in this he is very like Hemingway, James Dickey, and, perhaps, Robinson Jeffers); his style is free-ranging, colloquial, wise-cracking, but also unembarrassedly ready with the big word, the huge emotion. In short, he sounds very like Carl Sandburg.

Yet Patchen is a self-conscious poet. He may *play* the cracker-barrel philosopher, but as Thomas Hardy said of William Barnes, "He sings his native woodnotes wild with a great deal of art." Look, for example, at so small a poem as "In Memory of Kathleen":

> How pitiful is her sleep.
> Now her clear breath is still.
> There is nothing falling tonight,
> Bird or man,
> As dear as she.
>
> Nowhere that she should go
> Without me. None but my calling.
>
> O nothing but the cold cry of the snow.

It is a very finely written poem of grief, and a subtle one. The play on "pitiful" is perhaps obvious; but the way in which "falling" anticipates the cry of the snow is not so obvious, yet entirely just; as is the extraordinary compacted "None but my calling." "None" comes from the earlier "nowhere," and it means that Patchen finds himself utterly alone: she has gone where he can't follow, there is only *his* calling, *his* voice to be heard. That, and the cry of the snow: whiteness, death, its falling reminding him that she, too, has fallen in death. Glanced casually over, this little poem may seem hopelessly slight; looked at more carefully, it emerges as the work of considerable poet.

Patchen doesn't always write with this degree of tense urgency. It is characteristic of his kind of poetry that there should be a great deal of sprawl about it; and while one may salute the energy that led him to produce so many volumes of verse—he must be one of the most unflaggingly fertile of 20th-century American poets—it is also possible to wish that some of his work had been more intensively worked over. There is, for instance, a wonderful idea, partly spoiled, in *First Will and Testament* which has at its core a play for voices, featuring a Mr. Kek and his brothel, to which come, in turn, a group of famous poets, Donne, Marvell, Jonson, etc.; and then jazzmen Beiderbecke, Armstrong, Allen; gangsters, sportsmen—all outsiders, all seeking warmth and love and a good time, and trying to escape "the enemy." Much of this is obviously borrowed from Auden, but it has some fizzing wit and a great deal of hard-hitting panache that are Patchen's own. The trouble is that it degenerates into Cummings-like sentimentality; all picaros are better than all lawmen; to be an artist you have to be on the outside, a society reject, a bum. In other words the play is written out of cliché, so that although it has local life it is finally soggy.

This criticism applies to a good deal of Patchen's work. Yet nothing said here is intended to detract from the vitality of his best writing, which can crop up anywhere, and is just as likely to show itself in a late volume, like *When We Were Here Together*, as in an early one, such as *Before the Brave*.

—John Lucas

PAULDING, James Kirke. Born in Great Nine Partners, now Putnam County, New York, 22 August 1778; grew up in Tarrytown, New York. Educated at a local school. Served in the New York militia, 1814: Major. Married Gertrude Kemble in 1818 (died, 1841); several children. Settled in New York City c. 1796, worked in a public office, and continued his studies on his own; writer from c. 1805; contributor, *Analectic Magazine*, 1812; secretary, Board of Navy Commissioners, Washington, D.C., 1815–23; navy agent, Port of New York, 1823–38; Secretary of the Navy, in the administration of Martin Van Buren, 1838–41; lived on a country estate near Hyde Park, New York, after 1846. *Died 6 April 1860.*

PUBLICATIONS

Collections

Collected Works, edited by William I. Paulding. 4 vols., 1867–68.
The Letters, edited by Ralph M. Aderman. 1962.

Fiction

Salmagundi; or, The Whim-Whams and Opinions of Launcelot Langstaff, Esq., and Others, with Washington and William Irving. 2 vols., 1807–08; in *History, Tales and Sketches* (Library of America) by Washington Irving, edited by James W. Tuttleton, 1983; *Second Series* (by Paulding only), 2 vols., 1819–20.
The Diverting History of John Bull and Brother Jonathan. 1812; revised edition, 1813.
Koningsmarke: The Long Finne: A Story of the New World. 1823.
John Bull in America; or, The New Munchausen. 1825.
The Merry Tales of the Three Wise Men of Gotham. 1826.
Tales of the Good Woman. 1829.
Chronicles of the City of Gotham, from the Papers of a Retired Common Councilman. 1830.
The Dutchman's Fireside. 1831.
Westward Ho! 1832; as *The Banks of the Ohio*, 1833.
The Book of Saint Nicholas. 1836.
A Christmas Gift from Fairy Land. 1838; as *A Gift from Fairy Land*, n.d.
The Old Continental; or, The Price of Liberty. 1846.
The Puritan and His Daughter. 1849.
A Book of Vagaries (selections), edited by William I. Paulding. 1868.

Plays

The Lion of the West, revised by John Augustus Stone and William Bayle Bernard (produced 1831; as *The Kentuckian; or, A Trip to New York*, produced 1833). Edited by James N. Tidwell, 1954.
The Bucktails; or, Americans in England. In *American Comedies* by William I. Paulding, 1847.

Verse

The Lay of the Scottish Fiddle: A Tale of Havre de Grace, Supposed to Be Written by Walter Scott, Esq. 1813.
The Backwoodsman. 1818.

Other

The United States and England. 1815.
Letters from the South. 2 vols., 1817.
A Sketch of Old England by a New England Man. 2 vols., 1822.
The New Mirror for Travellers, and Guide to the Springs. 1828.
Sketch of the Early Life of Joseph Wood, Artist. 1834.
Works. 15 vols., 1834–39.
A Life of Washington. 2 vols., 1835(?).
Slavery in the United States. 1836.

*

Bibliography: in *Bibliography of American Literature* by Jacob Blanck, edited by Virginia L. Smyers and Michael Winship, 1983.

Critical Studies: *Literary Life of Paulding* by William I. Paulding, 1867; *Paulding: Versatile American* by Amos L. Herold, 1926; *Paulding* by Larry J. Reynolds, 1984.

* * *

Through the 1830's James Kirke Paulding's popularity with American readers rivalled that of his somewhat younger contemporaries Irving and Cooper. His name was also well known not only in Britain, but on the continent, where two of his novels—*The Dutchman's Fireside* and *Westward Ho!*—appeared in numerous translations. Although his audience dwindled sharply after 1845, he is still remembered as perhaps the most versatile, if not the most graceful, American author of the generation that matured between the two wars with Britain. During his long career Paulding won fame as a poet, novelist, essayist, biographer, playwright, and critic. He also wrote scores of short stories and sketches for both American and British periodicals. Most of his writing was done while he followed another career as public servant that culminated with his appointment in 1838 as Secretary of the Navy by President Martin Van Buren, a long-time friend whose ancestral roots were, like Paulding's, in the Dutch-American Hudson River valley.

Paulding was always more concerned with ideas than with art. Unlike his friend Irving (to whom he was related by marriage and with whom he collaborated on *Salmagundi*) he never made peace with either England or the romantic movement, which he scorned as a British conspiracy designed to sap the fiber of sturdy new-world republicanism. In a series of satires, commencing with *The Diverting History of John Bull and Brother Jonathan* and concluding with *John Bull in America*, he vigorously defended his young country against printed attacks by British travelers and reviewers. During the same period he wrote *The Lay of the Scottish Fiddle*, a book-length parody of *The Lay of the Last Minstrel*, burlesquing not only Scott's verse but his copious notes, and *The Backwoodsman*, another lengthy, often clumsy poem in heroic couplets designed, according to Paulding, to inform young American writers of the "rich poetic resources" available to them on their native ground. His call for American literary independence continued in his best-remembered essay, "National Literature," which appeared in *Salmagundi, Second Series*.

Prompted by the success of Cooper's *The Spy* and *The Pioneers*, Paulding turned to the novel in 1823, with *Koningsmarke*. Here he continued his satirical attack on Scott and what he considered to be the excesses of romanticism. In this first novel, Paulding hoped to demonstrate that Fielding, rather than Scott, was the proper model for American novelists. When *Koningsmarke* was misread and praised for the wrong reasons, Paulding abandoned satire and modified his attitude toward romanticism. *The Dutchman's Fireside*, set in the 1750's and in an area (upstate New York) that Cooper had already celebrated, was widely praised—not only by Cooper himself but by British readers, including an anonymous critic for the *West-*

minister Review who praised Paulding for being "neither too elaborate like Irving, nor too diffuse like Cooper." Paulding's third novel, *Westward Ho!*, captured the sense of adventure that urged many of his contemporaries to move from a settled east to an unsettled and still dangerous west. A fourth novel, *The Old Continental*, is based on the Benedict Arnold episode of the American Revolution. This and *The Puritan and His Daughter* were poorly planned and awkwardly written; they deserve the neglect they received even in Paulding's time.

Although Paulding had great ambitions as a playwright, he wrote only two plays of note, both comedies that dramatized social tensions between England and America. The second of them, *The Lion of the West*, won him a national prize, and was successfully produced in America and in London. It is most memorable for the character of Nimrod Wildfire, who closely resembles the American frontier hero, Davy Crockett.

Paulding's greatest success as a biographer came with his *A Life of Washington*, a work that appeared in numerous editions until it was superseded by Washington Irving's.

—Thomas F. O'Donnell

PAYNE, John Howard. Born in New York City, 9 June 1791. Educated at Berry Street Academy, Boston, to 1805; Union College, Schenectady, New York, 1806–08. Clerk in the counting house of Grant and Bennet Forbes, New York, 1805–06; editor, *Thespian Mirror*, New York, 1805–06, and *Pastime*, Schenectady, 1807–08; began writing for the stage, 1806; made debut as an actor in New York in 1809 and enjoyed an immediate success throughout the U.S.; moved to England, 1813; acted in the provinces, 1814; thereafter earned his living in London by dramatic hackwork; secretary at Covent Garden, 1818–19; leased Sadler's Wells Theatre, to produce his own plays, 1820, but went bankrupt: imprisoned for debt, Fleet Prison, 1820–21; moved to Paris to escape his creditors, 1821; lived in London, 1823–25 and 1826–32; editor and publisher of the weekly theatrical paper *Opera Glass*, 1826–27; returned to the U.S. 1832; U.S. Consul, Tunis, 1842–45 and 1851–52. *Died 9 April 1852.*

PUBLICATIONS

Collections

Life and Writings, edited by Gabriel Harrison. 1875; revised edition, as *Payne, His Life and Writings*, 1885.
Trial Without Jury and Other Plays (includes *Mount Savage*, *The Boarding School*, *The Two Sons-in-Law*, *Mazeppa*, *The Spanish Husband*), edited by Codman Hislop and W.R. Richardson. 1940.
The Last Duel in Spain and Other Plays (includes *Woman's Revenge*, *The Italian Bride*, *Romulus the Shepherd King*, *The Black Man*), edited by Codman Hislop and W.R. Richardson. 1940.

Plays

Julia; or, The Wanderer (as *The Wanderer*, produced 1806). 1806.
Lovers' Vows, from versions by Mrs. Inchbald and Benjamin Thompson of a play by Kotzebue (produced 1809?). 1809.
The Magpie or the Maid?, from a play by L.C. Caigniez and J. Baudouin d'Aubigny (produced 1815). 1815; as *Trial Without Jury; or, The Magpie and the Maid*, in *Trial Without Jury and Other Plays*, 1940.
Accusation; or, The Family D'Anglade, from a play by Fréderic du Petit-Méré (produced 1816). 1817.
Brutus; or, The Fall of Tarquin, music by Hayward (produced 1818). 1818.
Thérèse, The Orphan of Geneva, from a play by Victor Ducange (produced 1821). 1821.
Adeline, The Victim of Seduction, from a play by Pixérécourt (produced 1822). 1822.
Love in Humble Life, from a play by Scribe and Dupin (produced 1822). 1825.
Ali Pacha; or, The Signet-Ring, adapted by J.R. Planché (produced 1822). 1823.
Peter Smink; or, The Armistice (produced 1822; revised version, produced 1826). N.d.
The Two Galley Slaves, music by Tom Cooke and C.E. Horn (produced 1822). 1825.
Mount Savage, from a play by Pixérécourt (as *The Solitary of Mount Savage; or, The Fate of Charles the Bold*, produced 1822). In *Trial Without Jury and Other Plays*, 1940.
Clari; or, The Maid of Milan, music by Henry Bishop (produced 1823). 1823.
Mrs. Smith; or, The Wife and the Widow (produced 1823). N.d.
Charles the Second; or, The Merry Monarch, with Washington Irving, from a play by Alexandre Duval (produced 1824). 1824; edited by Arthur Hobson Quinn, in *Representative American Plays*, 1917.
'Twas I; or, The Truth a Lie, from a French play (produced 1825). 1827.
The Fall of Algiers, music by Henry Bishop (produced 1825). 1825.
Richelieu: A Domestic Tragedy, with Washington Irving, from a play by Alexandre Duval (produced 1826; as *The French Libertine*, produced 1826). 1826.
The White Maid, from a play by Scribe, music by Adrien Boieldieu (produced 1827; also produced as *The White Lady*).
The Lancers (produced 1827). 1828(?).
Procrastination (produced 1829).
The Spanish Husband; or, First and Last Love, from a play by La Beaumelle (produced 1830). In *Trial Without Jury and Other Plays*, 1940.
Fricandeau; or, The Coronet and the Cook (produced 1831).
Oswali at Athens (produced 1831).
Woman's Revenge (produced 1832). In *The Last Duel in Spain and Other Plays*, 1940.
Virginia (produced 1834).

Verse

Juvenile Poems. 1813; revised edition, as *Lispings of the Muse*, 1815.

Other

Indian Justice: A Cherokee Murder Trial, edited by Grant Foreman. 1934.

Payne to His Countrymen, edited by Clemens de Baillou. 1961.

Editor, *Addresses Delivered Before the Boston Federal Band*. 1805.

*

Bibliography: in *Bibliography of American Literature* by Jacob Blanck, edited by Virginia L. Smyers and Michael Winship, 1983.

Critical Studies: *The Early Life of Payne* by Willis T. Hanson, Jr., 1913; *Payne* by Rosa Pendleton Chiles, 1930; *America's First Hamlet* by Grace Overmyer, 1957.

* * *

During the first half of the 19th century, theatre audiences in both England and America enjoyed the strong, romantic rhetoric of poetic drama. In America the earliest dramatist to achieve success in this genre, and the most prolific, was John Howard Payne. A youthful prodigy, he attracted attention as an actor, a critic, and an editor of the *Thespian Mirror*, and as a playwright whose first work *Julia; or, The Wanderer*, was performed at New York's Park Theatre in 1806. When his career as an actor did not reach the success he anticipated, however, he embarked in 1813 for what he felt would be the greener theatrical fields of England. In this he was seriously mistaken for his acting engagements were few and soon relegated to the provinces. But chance and necessity offered him a new career.

In 1809, before going to England, Payne had published *Lovers' Vows*, a version of August von Kotzebue's *Das Kind der Liebe* which he had adapted from two English translations. Six years later while in Paris he translated the current French hit, *La Pie Voleuse*, as *The Magpie or the Maid?* for the Drury Lane management. This was the beginning of a career—adapting and translating comedy, melodrama, and romantic tragedy—in which his particular forte was his ability to recognize dramatic material and create a successful play from various sources. Like other prolific dramatists of his time, his talent was not in writing original plays, but he soon became the first American dramatist to enjoy a substantial reputation abroad.

Among his best works is *Brutus; or, The Fall of Tarquin*. Using five major sources he created a major acting vehicle for Edmund Kean; the subsequent cry of plagiarism was particularly ironic at a time when play pirating was a common sport. Another popular adaptation was *Clari; or, The Maid of Milan*, which contains the song for which most Americans will, if at all, remember Payne—"Home, Sweet Home." They would, however, readily recognize the name of his collaborator in his most successful comedy, *Charles the Second; or, The Merry Monarch*—Washington Irving. Before Irving tired of the drama they worked on six plays together.

Returning to America in 1832 Payne epitomized the plight of the dramatist during America's formative years. With considerable skill and abundant energy, he had created many successful plays and made money for everyone—actors, managers—but himself. Recognized by theatre-goers and critics as a major contributor to American drama, he was never financially secure and became increasingly bitter over the treatment of American dramatists during the final years of his life which were separated from the theatre. His position in the history of American drama, however, is unquestionably secure.

—Walter J. Meserve

PERCY, Walker. Born in Birmingham, Alabama, 28 May 1916. Educated at the University of North Carolina, Chapel Hill, B.A. 1937; Columbia University, New York, M.D. 1941; intern at Bellevue Hospital, New York, 1942. Married Mary Bernice Townsend in 1946; two daughters. Contracted tuberculosis, gave up medicine, and became a full-time writer, 1943. Recipient: National Book Award, 1962; American Academy grant, 1967; National Catholic Book Award, 1972; St. Louis Literary award, 1985. Fellow, American Academy of Arts and Sciences; member, American Academy. Lives in Covington, Louisiana.

PUBLICATIONS

Fiction

The Moviegoer. 1961.
The Last Gentleman. 1966.
Love in the Ruins: The Adventures of a Bad Catholic at a Time Near the End of the World. 1971.
Lancelot. 1977.
The Second Coming. 1980.

Other

The Message in the Bottle: How Queer Man Is, How Queer Language Is, and What One Has to Do with the Other. 1975.
Lost in the Cosmos: The Last Self-Help Book. 1983.
Novel-Writing in an Apocalyptic Time. 1984.
Conversations with Percy (interviews), edited by Lewis A. Lawson and Victor A. Kramer. 1985.

*

Bibliography: *Andrew Lytle, Percy, Peter Taylor: A Reference Guide* by Victor A. Kramer, 1983.

Critical Studies: *The Sovereign Wayfarer: Percy's Diagnosis of the Malaise* by Martin Luschei, 1972; *Percy: An American Search* by Robert Coles, 1978; *The Art of Percy: Stratagems for Being* edited by Panthea Reid Broughton, 1979; *Percy: Art and Ethics* edited by Jac Tharpe, 1980, and *Percy* by Tharpe, 1983; *Percy's Heroes: A Kierkegaardian Self* by L. Jerome Taylor, 1984; *Percy and the Old Modern Age: Reflections on Language, Argument, and the Telling of Stories* by Patricia Lewis Poteat, 1985; *Percy: A Southern Wayfarer* by William Rodney Allen, 1986.

* * *

Walker Percy belongs to the movement in modern southern writing that derives from T.S. Eliot and includes, among others, Allen Tate, Caroline Gordon, Robert Penn Warren, and

William Faulkner. Percy is a traditionalist in reaction against what is perceived as the decay of moral standards, the loss of a sense of community and of shared values. His ideas are given rather full intellectual scope in his work of non-fiction, *The Message in the Bottle*. In his novels the issue is focused on sexuality, and the problem, as expressed in his fiction, is how to square sexual desire with traditional ideas of love and responsibility, complicated by the modern confusion of love and sex. What used to be regarded as sin and perversion is now acceptable to, even sanctioned by, church and state. The traditional concept of love is too idealistic to provide Percy's protagonists with a satisfactory pattern of behavior. Inevitably his novels involve the setting up of the problem and the working out of a solution, the protagonist wrestling with his moral confusion, then, finally, creating for himself a synthesis in which love and lust—giving and taking—are appropriately balanced.

His first novel, *The Moviegoer*, concludes with the protagonist, a lusty bachelor, failing in his latest sexual escapade and marrying a young woman of his own class, partly out of affection, but also because they share a sense of experienced responsibility. In *The Last Gentleman*, the hero, who suffers emotional detachment (which Percy sees as the chief modern malady) cures himself through his personal devotion to a dying youth and in turn helps cure a confused young woman and her cynical older brother. *Love in the Ruins*, set in the future "at a time near the end of the world," deals with the collapse of modern technology and concludes with the responsible marriage of the protagonist who tries to save his doomed world but, failing that, gives himself over to whiskey and lust for three beautiful women. At the novel's close he marries the most responsible and moral of the three and begins to live a simple, natural, and properly lustful life in the shadow of the remnants of the old Catholic Church. In *Lancelot* the pessimism is deeper, the solution more tenuous. The hero, at first tolerant of his wife's sexual infidelity, finally kills her and her lover, is confined to a mental institution, is "cured" and then released into the world. For a time, he takes on responsibility for a young woman who has been raped and maimed by a gang of thugs, but is rebuffed by her in the language of radical feminism. This protagonist, then, stands alone against a world shown to be corrupt beyond redemption. A slight ray of final hope is that the woman may eventually join him in his exile. *The Second Coming* has the familiar problem and resolution: Will Barrett's death-in-life existence is resolved by a lusty love affair with a schizophrenic girl, and Barrett, a non-believer, nevertheless concludes that the girl, a "gift," must be a sign of the Lord, "the giver."

Percy's rendering of characters and scenes is striking, vivid, and bitingly satirical. He is a moral and, ultimately, a religious writer, but a perceptive novelist of manners as well. His sensitive and poetic style elevates material that less subtly treated might appear contrived and moralistic.

—W.J. Stuckey

PERELMAN, S(idney) J(oseph). Born in Brooklyn, New York, 1 February 1904. Educated at schools in Providence, Rhode Island; Brown University, Providence, 1921–25, B.A. 1925. Married Laura West (sister of Nathanael West) in 1929 (died, 1970); one son and one daughter. Writer and cartoonist, *Judge* magazine, 1925–29, and *College Humor* magazine, 1929–30; contributor to *New Yorker* from 1934; host of radio quiz show *Author, Author!*, 1939; lived in London, 1970–72. Recipient: New York Film Critics award, 1956; Oscar, for screenplay, 1957; Writers Guild West award, for screenplay, 1957; Special National Book Award, 1978. Member, American Academy. *Died 17 October 1979.*

PUBLICATIONS

Prose

Dawn Ginsbergh's Revenge. 1929.
Parlor, Bedlam and Bath, with Q.J. Reynolds. 1930.
Strictly from Hunger. 1937.
Look Who's Talking! 1940.
The Dream Department. 1943.
Crazy Like a Fox. 1944.
Keep It Crisp. 1946.
Acres and Pains. 1947.
The Best of Perelman. 1947.
Westward Ha! or, Around the World in Eighty Clichés. 1948.
Listen to the Mocking Bird. 1949.
The Swiss Family Perelman. 1950.
A Child's Garden of Curses (omnibus). 1951.
The Ill-Tempered Clavicord. 1952.
Hold That Christmas Tiger! 1954.
Perelman's Home Companion: A Collector's Item (the Collector Being S.J. Perelman) of 36 Otherwise Unavailable Pieces by Himself. 1955.
The Road to Miltown; or, Under the Spreading Atrophy. 1957; as *Bite on the Bullet*, 1957.
The Most of Perelman. 1958.
The Rising Gorge. 1961.
Chicken Inspector No. 23. 1966.
Baby, It's Cold Inside. 1970.
Monkey Business. 1973.
Vinegar Puss. 1975.
Eastward Ha! 1977.
The Last Laugh. 1981.

Plays

Sketches in *The Third Little Show* (produced 1931).
Sketches, with Robert MacGunigle, in *Walk a Little Faster* (produced 1932).
All Good Americans, with Laura Perelman (produced 1933).
Sketches in *Two Weeks with Pay* (produced 1940).
The Night Before Christmas, with Laura Perelman (produced 1941). 1942.
One Touch of Venus, with Ogden Nash, music by Kurt Weill, from *The Tinted Venus* by F. Anstey (produced 1943). 1944.
Sweet Bye and Bye, with Al Hirschfeld, music by Vernon Duke, lyrics by Ogden Nash (produced 1946).
The Beauty Part (produced 1962). 1963.
Monkey Business (screenplay), with Will B. Johnstone, in *The Four Marx Brothers in Monkey Business and Duck Soup*, 1972.

Screenplays: *Monkey Business*, with Will B. Johnstone, 1931; *Horse Feathers*, with others, 1932; *The Miracle Man*, with others, 1932; *Sitting Pretty*, with Jack McGowan and Lou

Breslow, 1933; *Florida Special*, with others, 1936; *Boy Trouble*, with others, 1939; *Ambush*, with Laura Perelman and Robert Ray, 1939; *The Golden Fleecing*, with others, 1940; *Around the World in Eighty Days*, with James Poe and John Farrow, 1956.

Television Scripts: for *Omnibus* series, 1957–59; *The Changing Ways of Love*, 1957; *Elizabeth Taylor's London*, 1963.

*

Bibliography: *Perelman: An Annotated Bibliography* by Steven H. Gale, 1985.

Critical Studies: *Perelman* by Douglas Fowler, 1983; *Perelman: A Life* by Dorothy Herrmann, 1986.

* * *

As screenwriter, playwright, and, primarily, essayist, S.J. Perelman spent fifty years perfecting a unique and surrealistic style of humor marked by an uncontrollable imagination and an enormous, arcane vocabulary. Perhaps best described as a mixture of Groucho Marx (with whom he worked) and James Joyce (whom he called "the comic writer of the century"). Perelman is a roman candle of language, firing off metaphors where the untrained eye might see only an unloaded verb: "Carstairs exchanged a quizzical glance with his manservant, fitted it into an ivory holder, and lit it abstractedly." At the extreme, Perelman's sentences leap from pillar to post with a sheerly linguistic logic, sneering at cliché: "On her dainty egg-shaped head was massed a crop of auburn curls; the cucumbers she had grown there the previous summer were forgotten in the pulsing rhythm of the moment." Perelman's distinguishing characteristic is his total imaginative control of the work, and consequently neither his film scripts nor his stage plays have the comic intensity of the meticulously crafted essays.

Perelman's distaste for the mediocrity of the everyday world manifested itself in a complete disdain for broad political and social satire. A large number of his essays take aim at popular movies, magazines, and novels, at newspapers, at advertising—soft prose and soft thinking of all stripes. Increasingly, however, he turned inward, spinning off exotic tales from the merest personal anecdotes. Perelman was pleased to call himself a *feuilletoniste*, a writer of lapidary prose, and a crank who wrote only when sufficiently enraged. He once summed up his interest in humor with these words (*New York Times Magazine*, 26 January 1969): "For me, its chief merit is the use of the unexpected, the glancing allusion, the deflation of pomposity, and the constant repetition of one's helplessness in a majority of situations."

—Walter Bode

PHILLIPS, David Graham. Born in Madison, Indiana, 31 October 1867. Educated at Madison High School, graduated 1882; Asbury College (now DePauw University), Greencastle, Indiana, 1882–85; Princeton University, New Jersey, 1885–87, A.B. 1887. Reporter, Cincinnati *Star Times*, 1888, and Cincinnati *Commercial Gazette*, 1889–90; editorial staff member, New York *Sun*, 1890–93; London correspondent, 1893, general reporter, 1893–95, feature writer, 1895–97, and editorial department member, 1897–1902, New York *World*; full-time writer from 1902; frequent contributor to various national magazines, especially *Saturday Evening Post*, Philadelphia, and *Cosmopolitan*, New York. *Died (murdered) 24 January 1911.*

PUBLICATIONS

Fiction

The Great God Success. 1901.
Her Serene Highness. 1902.
A Woman Ventures. 1902.
Golden Fleece: The American Adventures of a Fortune Hunting Earl. 1903.
The Master-Rogue: The Confessions of a Croesus. 1903.
The Cost. 1904.
The Mother-Light. 1905.
The Plum Tree. 1905.
The Social Secretary. 1905.
The Deluge. 1905.
The Fortune Hunter. 1906.
The Second Generation. 1907.
Light-Fingered Gentry. 1907.
Old Wives for New. 1908.
The Fashionable Adventures of Joshua Craig. 1909.
The Hungry Heart. 1909.
White Magic. 1910.
The Husband's Story. 1910.
The Grain of Dust. 1911.
The Conflict. 1911.
The Price She Paid. 1912.
George Helm. 1912.
Degarmo's Wife and Other Stories. 1913.
Susan Lenox: Her Fall and Rise. 1917.

Play

The Worth of a Woman: A Play, Followed by A Point of Law: A Dramatic Incident (produced 1908). 1908.

Other

The Reign of Gilt. 1905.
The Treason of the Senate (essays). 1953.
Contemporaries: Portraits in the Progressive Era, edited by Louis Filler. 1981.

*

Bibliography: in *Bibliography of American Literature* by Jacob Blanck, edited by Virginia L. Smyers and Michael Winship, 1983.

Critical Studies: *Phillips: His Life and Times* by Isaac F. Marcosson, 1932; *Phillips* by Abe C. Ravitz, 1966; *Voice of Democracy: A Critical Biography of Phillips, Journalist, Novelist, Progressive* by Louis Filler, 1978.

* * *

David Graham Phillips's first novel, *The Great God Success*, concerns a newspaperman who gains fortune and power by championing the cause of the people against "the interests," but who sells out when he begins to identify with the rich. In *The Deluge*, *Light-Fingered Gentry*, *The Master-Rogue*, and *The Grain of Dust* Phillips also dealt with the corrupting influence of capitalism on essentially good men.

While in college, Phillips roomed with Albert Beveridge, who was later to serve as Senator from Indiana. They remained good friends for the rest of their lives, and Phillips used Beveridge as a model for his paragon of political virtues, Hampden Scarborough. In *The Cost*, Scarborough's career is contrasted with his rival in love, an evil industrialist named Dumont. Scarborough's legislation ultimately triumphs over the capitalist's trusts. In *The Plum Tree*, Scarborough becomes a foil to a dishonest political power-broker. In these, as in his other political novels, *The Fashionable Adventures of Joshua Craig* and *George Helm*, Phillips recommends a vague populism and a return to honesty as the answer to the enormous social and economic problems facing America. His interest seems to be in exposing corruption, not in solving problems.

In his two "economic" novels, Phillips was somewhat bolder. Victor Dorn, the hero of *The Conflict*, is a revolutionary who contends that Marx will dominate the next two thousand years as Christ has dominated the last two thousand. In *The Second Generation*, Phillips seems to recommend the abolition of inherited property because of the harm done to both society and property-owners themselves.

Yet Phillips's greatest achievement was in his novels dealing with women's place in modern society. In *A Woman Ventures*, *Old Wives for New*, *The Price She Paid*, and in his only play, *The Worth of a Woman*, he ridiculed the stereotypical weak, soft home-bodies and extolled the virtues of women who competed on equal terms with men. In *The Hungry Heart* he defended the rights of neglected women to seek sexual satisfaction outside of marriage. Phillips's most impressive novel, *Susan Lenox: Her Fall and Rise*, published posthumously, chronicles the life of a girl who is condemned by social forces beyond her control to a life of vice and crime. Nothing in Dreiser or Sinclair can match the brutality of Phillips's pictures of slum life and the horrors of white slavery. Through all her degradation, Susan maintains her essential dignity. When she overcomes her poverty, she still rejects all offers of respectability and marriage.

When Roosevelt applied the term "Muckraker" to a certain kind of investigative reporting, he was specifically referring to Phillips and his *The Treason of the Senate*, and it is for his reporting, not his literary work, that history will remember him. Yet his novels provide a valuable insight into the hopeful, optimistic America of his era.

—William Higgins

PLATH, Sylvia. Born in Boston, Massachusetts, 27 October 1932. Educated at schools in Wellesley, Massachusetts; Smith College, Northampton, Massachusetts (Glasscock Prize, 1955), B.A. (summa cum laude) in English 1955 (Phi Beta Kappa); Newnham College, Cambridge (Fulbright Scholar), 1955–57, M.A. 1957. Married the poet Ted Hughes in 1956 (separated, 1962); one daughter and one son. Guest editor, *Mademoiselle* magazine, New York, Summer 1953; Instructor in English, Smith College, 1957–58; moved to England in 1959. Recipient: Yaddo fellowship, 1959; Cheltenham Festival award, 1961; Saxon fellowship, 1961. *Died (suicide) 11 February 1963.*

PUBLICATIONS

Collections

Collected Poems, edited by Ted Hughes. 1981.
Selected Poems, edited by Ted Hughes. 1985.

Verse

A Winter Ship. 1960.
The Colossus. 1960.
Ariel, edited by Ted and Olwyn Hughes. 1965.
Uncollected Poems. 1965.
Wreath for a Bridal. 1970.
Million Dollar Month. 1971.
Fiesta Melons. 1971.
Crossing the Water, edited by Ted Hughes. 1971.
Crystal Gazer. 1971.
Lyonnesse: Hitherto Uncollected Poems. 1971.
Winter Trees, edited by Ted Hughes. 1971.
Child. 1971.
Pursuit. 1973.
Two Poems. 1980.
Two Uncollected Poems. 1980.

Play

Three Women: A Monologue for Three Voices (broadcast 1962; produced 1973). 1968.

Radio Play: *Three Women*, 1962.

Fiction

The Bell Jar. 1963.

Other

Letters Home: Correspondence 1950–1963, edited by Aurelia Schober Plath. 1975.
The Bed Book (for children). 1976.
Plath: A Dramatic Portrait (miscellany), edited by Barry Kyle. 1976.
Johnny Panic and the Bible of Dreams, and Other Prose Writings, edited by Ted Hughes. 1977; augmented edition, 1979.
The Journals, edited by Ted Hughes and Frances McCullough. 1982.

Editor, *American Poetry Now: A Selection of the Best Poems by Modern American Writers*. 1961.

*

Bibliography: *A Chronological Checklist of the Periodical Publications of Plath* by Eric Homberger, 1970; *Plath and Anne Sexton: A Reference Guide* by Cameron Northouse and Thomas P. Walsh, 1974; *Plath: A Bibliography* by Gary Lane and Maria Stevens, 1978; *Plath: An Analytical Bibliography* by Stephen Tabor, 1986.

Critical Studies: *The Art of Plath: A Symposium* edited by Charles Newman, 1970; *The Savage God: A Study of Suicide* by A. Alvarez, 1971; *The Poetry of Plath: A Study of Themes* by Ingrid Melander, 1972; *A Closer Look at Ariel: A Memory of Plath* by Nancy Hunter Steiner, 1973; *Plath* by Eileen M. Aird, 1973; *Plath: Method and Madness* by Edward Butscher, 1976, and *Plath: The Woman and the Work* edited by Butscher, 1977; *Plath: Poetry and Existence* by David Holbrook, 1976; *Chapters in a Mythology: The Poetry of Plath* by Judith Kroll, 1976; *Plath* by Caroline King Barnard, 1978; *Plath and Ted Hughes* by Margaret Dickie Uroff, 1979; *Plath: New Views on the Poetry* edited by Gary Lane, 1979; *Plath: The Poetry of Initiation* by Jon Rosenblatt, 1979; *Protean Poetics: The Poetry of Plath* by Mary Lynn Broe, 1980; *Plath's Incarnations: Woman and Creative Process* by Lynda K. Bundtzen, 1983; *Critical Essays on Plath* edited by Linda W. Wagner, 1984, and *Plath: A Literary Biography* by Wagner, 1986; *Ariel Ascending: Writings about Plath* edited by Paul Alexander, 1985; *The Dialectics of Art and Life: A Portrait of Plath as Woman and Poet* by Sylvia Lehrer, 1985.

* * *

The adolescent heroine of Sylvia Plath's only novel, *The Bell Jar*, has looked into her grave and seen a sobering and a maddening truth. Her suicidal hysteria, like that which finally took Plath herself, is the anguish of a being who has realized her own gratuitousness, "Factitious, artificial, sham." What she has called her "self," that unique and coddled ego, is no more than a nexus of donated being, a field of battle where the conflicting forces of her environment, her familial and social experience, clash, divide, and coalesce. Plath wrote of the poem "Daddy" as "spoken by a girl with an Electra complex. Her father died while she thought he was God. Her case is complicated by the fact that her father was also a Nazi and her mother very possibly Jewish. In the daughter the two strains marry and paralyze each other—she has to act out the awful little allegory before she is free of it." While the details hardly correspond accurately to Plath's own biography, their symbolic function in the emotional ecology of her work is clear. The title poem of *The Colossus* acknowledges such a condition: addressed to her dead father ("I shall never get you put together entirely") it is self-consciously post-Freudian and pre-Christian: "A blue sky out of the Oresteia / Arches above us"; if her father is now no more than a "Mouthpiece of the dead," this is equally true of all selves, whose "hours are married to shadow," the marionettes of an unconscious in whose formation they had no hand. "Poem for a Birthday" is a complex dramatic monologue in which a psyche struggles towards birth, in "the city of spare parts" which is the world. Its voice is a Cinderella or Snow-White princess in nightmare exile among incomprehensible and uncomprehending powers, feeling herself "Duchess of Nothing," "housekeep[ing] in Time's gut end" and "married [to] a cupboard of rubbish." It is a representative text.

The imagery of Plath's poems undergoes endless transformations, in which the links are often suppressed or arbitrary: sudden shifts of tack and emotion lead off in unexpected directions. Her poetic narratives fork and proliferate in this way because, in unfolding the implications of a sequence of images, she uncovers the complex and contradictory possibilities condensed within them, the infantile traumas lying treacherously beneath the surface of adult experience. The same image can be charged with quite contradictory emotional valencies. The bee, for example, a recurring motif (her father was an apiculturalist), stirs rich, ambiguous feelings. It is a female, a source of honey and creativity, but it has a male sting; the hive includes drudges and drones, but also that dark leonine queen at the core; in "The Swarm" and "The Arrival of the Bee-Box", bees are the collective "black, intractable mind" of a genocidal Europe and the "swarmy," "angrily clambering" impulsions of the individual unconscious. Such transitions express her own sense of the self, not as a hierarchically ordered pyramid, but as an ensemble of possibilities, in which none usurps precedence for long, and to which only a provisional coherence can be given, in the specifying of a name and image ("The Arrival of the Bee-Box," after toying with the starvation or release of the bees which threaten and fascinate, concludes, "The box is only temporary"). Self for Plath is either a rigid, false persona or an amorphous, uncongealed, and fluid congeries, like the bee-swarm itself, undergoing constant metamorphosis, continually dying and being reborn in the mutations of the imagery. In "Elm," the social self speaks as a tree, rooted in its context, wrenched violently by a wind that "will tolerate no bystanding." But such fixity is an illusion, for its roots reach down to the dissolute sea, its branches "break up in pieces that fly about like clubs," it is dragged by the moon (usually the image of a sterile maternal force), and it contains subversive lives which are part of itself yet frighteningly independent:

> I am inhabited by a cry.
> Nightly it flaps out
> Looking, with its hooks, for something to love.
>
> I am terrified by this dark thing
> That sleeps in me;
> All day I feel its soft, feathery turnings, its malignity.

Plath repeatedly sees relationships as predatory, exploitative, and destructive, yet desired and necessary, as in "The Rabbit-Catcher" ("And we too had a relationship, / Tight wires between us, / Pegs too deep to uproot, and a mind like a ring / Sliding shut on some quick thing, / The constriction killing me also"). In "Tulips," even the smiles of husband and children, in a photograph, "catch onto my skin, little smiling hooks," while identity itself, in "The Applicant," is seen as a collection of functions, answers to others' questions, a poultice for their wounds, apple for their eyes, "A living doll" which is the accretion of artificial limbs and artificial commitments.

This aspect of her verse has made her co-option by the women's movement inevitable. But it is also just. Plath is, in fact, a profoundly political poet, who has seen the generic nature of these private catastrophes of the self, their public origin in a civilization founded on mass-manipulation and collective trickery. Esther Greenwood, in *The Bell Jar*, links her electric shock treatment with the electrocution which is the Rosenbergs' punishment for rebellion against the American way of life: she fears most of all being consigned to the charity wards, "with hundreds of people like me, in a big cage in the basement. The more hopeless you were, the further away they hid you." In a century which has shut away millions, in hospitals, concentration camps, and graveyards, where the self can be "wiped out . . . like chalk on a blackboard" by administrative diktat, Plath sees a deep correspondence between the paternal concern of the psychiatrist and the authority of the modern state, even in its most extreme variants: both presuppose the self as the victim, passive and compliant, as *sine qua non* of any "final solution." For Plath, concerned that "personal experience shouldn't be a kind of shut box and mirror-looking narcissistic experience," but "should be generally relevant, to such things as Hiroshima and Dachau and so on," the refusal to collaborate was a profoundly positive act, the assertion not of the nihilism of which she has been accused but of a more exacting and scrupulous conscience. If, in poems such as "Daddy" and "Lady Lazarus," she veers close to disintegration, she also promises a breakthrough into a resurrection which sheds the constricting husks of the past, a vengeful return which is only justice:

So, so. Herr Doktor.
So, Herr Enemy.
I am your opus,
I am your valuable,
The pure gold baby

That melts to a shriek.
I turn and burn,
Do not think I underestimate your great concern. . . .

Herr God, Herr Lucifer
Beware
Beware.

Out of the ash
I rise with my red hair
And I eat men like air.

—Stan Smith

See the essay on *Ariel*.

POE, Edgar Allan. Born in Boston, Massachusetts, 19 January 1809; orphaned, and given a home by John Allan, 1812. Educated at the Dubourg sisters' boarding school, Chelsea, London, 1816–17; Manor House School, Stoke Newington, London, 1817–20; Joseph H. Clarke's School, Richmond, 1820–23; William Burke's School, Richmond, 1823–25; University of Virginia, Charlottesville, 1826; U.S. Military Academy, West Point, New York, 1830–31 (court-martialled and dismissed). Served in the U.S. Army, 1827–29: Sergeant-Major. Married his 13-year-old cousin Virginia Clemm in 1836 (died, 1847). Lived in Baltimore, 1831–35; assistant editor, 1835, and editor, 1836–37, *Southern Literary Messenger*, Richmond; lived in New York, 1837 and after 1843, and Philadelphia, 1838–43; assistant editor, *Gentleman's Magazine*, 1839–40, and editor, *Graham's Magazine*, 1841–42, both Philadelphia; sub-editor, New York *Evening Mirror*, 1844; editor and briefly proprietor, *Broadway Journal*, New York, 1845–46. Lecturer after 1844. *Died 7 October 1849*.

PUBLICATIONS

Collections

Complete Works (Virginia Edition), edited by James A. Harrison. 17 vols., 1902.
Letters, edited by John Ward Ostrom. 2 vols., 1948; revised edition, 2 vols., 1966.
Poems, edited by Floyd Stovall. 1965.
Collected Works, edited by Thomas Ollive Mabbott. 3 vols., 1969–78.
Short Fiction, edited by Stuart and Susan Levine. 1976.
Collected Writings, edited by Burton R. Pollin. 1981—
Poetry and Tales (Library of America), edited by Patrick F. Quinn. 1984.
Essays and Reviews (Library of America), edited by G.R. Thompson. 1984.

Verse

Tamerlane and Other Poems. 1827.
Al Aaraaf, Tamerlane, and Minor Poems. 1829.
Poems. 1831.
The Raven and Other Poems. 1845.

Plays

Politian: An Unfinished Tragedy, edited by Thomas Ollive Mabbott. 1923.

Fiction

The Narrative of Arthur Gordon Pym of Nantucket. 1838.
Tales of the Grotesque and Arabesque. 1840.
The Prose Romances 1: The Murders in the Rue Morgue, and The Man That Was Used Up. 1843.
Tales. 1845.
The Literati: Some Honest Opinions about Autorial Merits and Demerits. 1850.

Other

The Conchologist's First Book; or, A System of Testaceous Malacology (textbook; revised by Poe). 1839; revised edition, 1840.
Eureka: A Prose Poem. 1848; edited by Richard P. Benton, 1973(?).
Literary Criticism, edited by Robert L. Hough. 1965.
The Unknown Poe: An Anthology of Fugitive Writings, edited by Raymond Foye. 1980.
The Annotated Poe, edited by Stephen Peithman. 1981.
The Other Poe: Comedies and Satires, edited by David Galloway. 1983.

*

Bibliography: *Bibliography of the Writings of Poe* by John W. Robertson, 1934; *A Bibliography of First Printings of the Writings of Poe* by Charles F. Heartman and James R. Canny, 1940, revised edition, 1943; *Poe: A Bibliography of Criticism 1827–1967* by J. Lesley Dameron and Irby B. Cauthen, Jr., 1974; *Poe: An Annotated Bibliography of Books and Articles in English 1827–1973* by Esther F. Hyneman, 1974; in *Bibliography of American Literature* by Jacob Blanck, edited by Virginia L. Smyers and Michael Winship, 1983.

Critical Studies: *Poe: A Critical Biography* by Arthur Hobson Quinn, 1941; *Poe as a Literary Critic* by John Esten Cooke, edited by N. Bryllion Fagin, 1946; *Life of Poe* by Thomas Holley Chivers, edited by Richard Beale Davis, 1952; *Poe: A*

Critical Study by Edward H. Davidson, 1957; *The French Face of Poe* by Patrick F. Quinn, 1957; *Poe* by Vincent Buranelli, 1961, revised edition, 1977; *Poe: A Biography* by William Bittner, 1962; *Poe: The Man Behind the Legend* by Edward Wagenknecht, 1963; *Poe's Literary Battles: The Critic in the Context of His Literary Milieu* by Sidney P. Moss, 1963; *Poe as Literary Critic* by Edd Winfield Parks, 1964; *Poe* by Geoffrey Rans, 1965; *The Recognition of Poe: Selected Criticism since 1829* edited by Eric W. Carlson, 1966; *Poe: A Collection of Critical Essays* edited by Robert Regan, 1967; *Poe, Journalist and Critic* by Robert D. Jacobs, 1969; *Poe the Poet: Essays New and Old on the Man and His Work* by Floyd Stovall, 1969; *Plots and Characters in the Fiction and Poetry of Poe* by Robert L. Gale, 1970; *Twentieth-Century Interpretations of Poe's Tales* edited by William L. Howarth, 1971; *Poe Poe Poe Poe Poe Poe Poe* by Daniel Hoffman, 1972; *Poe: A Phenomenological View* by David Halliburton, 1973; *Poe's Fiction: Romantic Irony in the Gothic Tales* by G.R. Thompson, 1973; *Poe* by David Sinclair, 1977; *Building Poe Biography* by John Carl Miller, 1977; *The Tell-Tale Heart: The Life and Works of Poe* by Julian Symons, 1978; *The Extraordinary Mr. Poe* by Wolf Mankowitz, 1978; *The Rationale of Deception in Poe* by David Ketterer, 1979; *A Psychology of Fear: The Nightmare Formula of Poe* by David R. Saliba, 1980; *A Poe Companion: A Guide to the Short Stories, Romances, and Essays* by J.R. Hammond, 1981; *Poe* by Bettina L. Knapp, 1984; *Poe: The Critical Heritage* edited by I.M. Walker, 1986; *Poe, Death and the Life of Writing* by J. Gerald Kennedy, 1987.

* * *

Although Edgar Allan Poe wrote that for him "poetry has been not a purpose but a passion," he wrote only some fifty poems (excluding his album verses, jingles, and acrostics). Obliged to work at drudging journalism, he never realized his dream of founding a literary magazine of his own. While grinding out scores of reviews of some of the most forgettable books of the 19th century he wrote the tales, poems, and essays on which his posthumous renown is based. Aiming his work "not above the popular, nor below the critical, taste," he made use, as a professional magazinist must, of the fictional conventions of his day, turning to his own obsessive needs the gothic horror story ("Ligeia," "The Fall of the House of Usher," "Berenice") and the tale of exploration ("A Descent into the Maelstrom," *The Narrative of Arthur Gordon Pym*). In "The Gold Bug," "The Murders in the Rue Morgue," and "The Purloined Letter' he virtually invented the modern detective story, and he set the mold upon science fiction with "Mesmeric Revelations," "The Facts in the Case of Monsieur Valdemar," and "The Balloon Hoax." He also wrote dozens of satirical sketches. His critical writings were the most systematic and intelligent produced in America until his time.

Despite the paucity of his productions as a poet, he proved a major influence upon Baudelaire, who translated several of his tales and wrote that if Poe had not existed, he would have had to invent him. Through Baudelaire, Poe's critical theories influenced the entire French Symbolist movement. Although Poe believed, with Tennyson, that imprecision of meaning was necessary for the creation of beauty, he also believed that the poet is a deliberate maker who devises all of his effects to contribute to the single aim of his poem. "The Philosophy of Composition," an essay purporting to demonstrate how Poe wrote "The Raven," presents the creative process as an interlocked series of conscious choices. Although this would seem the opposite of the Romantic view of the poet as inspired seer, Poe's systematic process is in fact determined by Romantic necessity and is derived from Coleridge's aesthetic. That necessity is the excitation of the soul through the contemplation of the most melancholy of subjects—the death of a beautiful woman. The complex interaction in this theory between obsessive emotional need and what Poe in his detective stories called "ratiocination" is characteristic of all of his best work.

It seems ironic and cruel that a writer whose tales of guilt and terror won him the admiration of Dostoevsky had to live a hand-to-mouth existence and, after his death, was defamed by a hostile editor and reviled by readers who took as autobiographical the characters in his tales who were opium fiends and necrophiliacs. Allen Tate (in his essay "The Angelic Imagination") identifies what it is in Poe's work that really set on edge Victorian sensibility: the lack of any God save impersonal force, a fictive world without Christian morality. Far more evocatively than in the naturalistic novels of fifty years later, Poe imagined the nightmare of a universe without the consolations of faith.

This visionary author's life was unmitigatedly wretched. His parents were itinerant actors; the alcoholic father deserted, leaving Elizabeth Arnold Poe with three infant children. A brother and sister of Edgar's were adopted by connections in Baltimore but she kept young Eddie by her as she acted the heroine in plays no more melodramatic than his life would be. Stricken by tuberculosis, she died a lingering death in Richmond, Virginia, attended by kindly local matrons, when Edgar was only three. The boy was taken into the home of John Allan, a prosperous tobacco factor who brought Edgar to England when his business took him there and sent the boy to the school so vividly remembered in "William Wilson." Allan sent Poe to the new University of Virginia where, on a niggardly allowance among the scions of wealthy families, he ran up gambling debts and was expelled. Mrs. Allan, like Poe's natural mother, died of tuberculosis, and Poe, who had no inclination for the tobacco business, quarreled with his "Pa" (he had discovered Allan's infidelities while his wife was still alive). Allan withheld love from Edgar and never adopted him, so Poe was cast adrift penniless to make his way as an author. Not even a hitch in the army or a later enlistment in the military academy at West Point mollified Allan. Poe, deciding to leave West Point, could not persuade "Pa" to intercede for his release and had to feign illness until he was expelled. By this time he had published two volumes of poems. One is dedicated to the Corps of Cadets.

Poe's career henceforth was as assistant or principal editor on several magazines in Richmond, Philadelphia, and New York. While so engaged, he wrote nearly 90 tales and sketches, countless critical columns and reviews, two novellas, and an astrophysical treatise on the nature of the universe, entitled *Eureka*, which he described as a poem.

Poe married his first cousin Virginia Clemm when she was thirteen and lived with her and her mother (his aunt) until Virginia, too, died of tuberculosis at 23. Thereafter Poe conducted frenzied courtships of several poetesses; at this time he well may have been mad with grief. He died in delirium, under unexplained circumstances, on a trip to Baltimore. Poe's biographers agree that he idealized women, and that sexual desire seems not to have had an overt part in any of his relationships.

Poe classified his own fiction into the categories of "Tales of the Grotesque and Arabesque." Borrowing these terms from Scott, Poe meant by them to describe satirical, bizarre, jocose writings on the one hand, and on the other the fictional equivalents of poems. These were his prose efforts to excite his readers' souls by the contemplation of beauty and terror. His review of Hawthorne outlines his theory of fiction. The tale, like the poem, must be all of a piece, each detail contributing to the desired unity of effect; symbolism (Poe in the nomenclature of the day calls it allegory) must be present as a "profound undercurrent" in the tale. His fiction will work by indirection.

In Poe's work there is a mysterious interpenetrability of the soul's excitation with subterranean dread. A *frisson* of horror runs through his most impassioned tales. The clue of Poe's contradictions may be in his sketch "The Imp of the Perverse," for the fiction frequently dramatizes its theme of man's irresistible urge toward self-destruction (a man is driven to commit a terrible crime, then to reveal his guilt). This connects also with the theme of double identity ("William Wilson," "The Cask of Amontillado") and Poe's strain of hoaxing, not entirely confined to his jocular productions. Poe delighted in tricking his readers. He would make them believe that his mesmerizer had really hypnotized a dying man so that the soul lingered and answered questions for months after the death of the body; or that his balloonists had actually crossed the Atlantic in three days, arriving in South Carolina. So too with fantastic descents into the maelstrom and journeys to the end of the earth and back. "The Philosophy of Composition" is in one respect such a hoax. Like his detective genius Monsieur Dupin, Poe demonstrates his intuitive intellectual superiority.

Although only in *Pym* did he write a successful fiction of more than thirty pages, Poe's significance is multifold. He is a systematic critic and theorist predictive of the Symbolist movement. His best poems and fictions embody his aesthetic intention that every part of the literary artifact must contribute to the unifying effect of the whole. His mastery of popular genres made him the unwitting godfather of much popular literature in the present century, as well as a major influence on films. His poetic theory passed from the Symbolists back into American poetry through T.S. Eliot and its influence continues in Allen Tate and Richard Wilbur, among others. His fiction is widely translated and widely read. Poe's work indeed has reached both the popular and the critical taste.

—Daniel Hoffman

See the essays on "The Fall of the House of Usher" and "The Murders in the Rue Morgue."

PORTER, Katherine Anne. Born Callie Russell Porter in Indian Creek, Texas, 15 May 1890. Educated at Thomas School, San Antonio, Texas. Married 1) John Henry Koontz in 1906 (separated, 1914; divorced, 1915); 2) Ernest Stock in 1925; 3) Eugene Dove Pressly in 1933 (divorced, 1938); 4) Albert Russell Erskine, Jr., in 1938 (divorced, 1942). Journalist and film extra in Chicago, 1911–14; tuberculosis patient, Dallas, San Angelo, Texas, and Carlsbad, New Mexico, 1915–17; worked with tubercular children in Dallas, 1917; staff member, Fort Worth *Critic*, Texas, 1917–18; reporter, 1918, and drama critic, 1919, *Rocky Mountain News*, Denver; lived in New York, 1919, and mainly in Mexico, 1920–31, and Europe in 1930's; copy editor, Macauley and Company, publishers, New York, 1928–29; taught at Olivet College, Michigan, 1940; contract writer for M.G.M., Hollywood, 1945–46; Lecturer in Writing, Stanford University, California, 1948–49; Guest Lecturer in Literature, University of Chicago, Spring 1951; Visiting Lecturer in Contemporary Poetry, University of Michigan, Ann Arbor, 1953–54; Fulbright Lecturer, University of Liège, Belgium, 1954–55; Writer-in-Residence, University of Virginia, Charlottesville, Autumn 1958; Glasgow Professor, Washington and Lee University, Lexington, Virginia, Spring 1959; Lecturer in American Literature for U.S. Department of State, in Mexico, 1960, 1964; Ewing Lecturer, University of California, Los Angeles, 1960; Regents' Lecturer, University of California, Riverside, 1961. Library of Congress Fellow in Regional American Literature, 1944; U.S. delegate, International Festival of the Arts, Paris, 1952; member, Commission on Presidential Scholars, 1964; Consultant in Poetry, Library of Congress, 1965–70. Recipient: Guggenheim fellowship, 1931, 1938; New York University Libraries Gold Medal, 1940; Ford Foundation grant, 1959, 1960; O. Henry Award, 1962; Emerson-Thoreau Medal, 1962; Pulitzer Prize, 1966; National Book Award, 1966; American Academy Gold Medal, 1967; Mystery Writers of America Edgar Allan Poe Award, 1972. D.Litt.: University of North Carolina Woman's College, Greensboro, 1949; Smith College, Northampton, Massachusetts, 1958; Maryville College, St. Louis, 1968; D.H.L.: University of Michigan, Ann Arbor, 1954; University of Maryland, College Park, 1966; Maryland Institute, 1974; D.F.A.: La Salle College, Philadelphia, 1962. Vice-President, National Institute of Arts and Letters, 1950–52; member, American Academy, 1967. *Died 18 September 1980.*

Publications

Fiction

Flowering Judas. 1930; augmented edition, as *Flowering Judas and Other Stories*, 1935.
Hacienda: A Story of Mexico. 1934.
Noon Wine (story). 1937.
Pale Horse, Pale Rider: Three Short Novels. 1939.
The Leaning Tower and Other Stories. 1944.
Selected Short Stories. 1945.
The Old Order: Stories of the South. 1955.
A Christmas Story. 1958.
Ship of Fools. 1962.
Collected Stories. 1964; augmented edition, 1967.

Other

My Chinese Marriage. 1921.
Outline of Mexican Popular Arts and Crafts. 1922.
What Price Marriage. 1927.
The Days Before: Collected Essays and Occasional Writings. 1952; augmented edition, as *The Collected Essays and Occasional Writings*, 1970.
A Defense of Circe. 1955.
The Never-Ending Wrong (on the Sacco-Vanzetti case). 1977.
Conversations with Porter, Refugee from Indian Creek, with Enrique Hank Lopez. 1981.

Translator, *French Song-Book*. 1933.
Translator, *The Itching Parrot*, by Fernandez de Lizárdi. 1942.

*

Bibliography: *A Bibliography of the Works of Porter and A Bibliography of the Criticism of the Works of Porter* by Louise Waldrip and Shirley Ann Bauer, 1969; *Porter and Carson McCullers: A Reference Guide* by Robert F. Kiernan, 1976; *Porter: A Bibliography* by Kathryn Hilt, 1985.

Critical Studies: *The Fiction and Criticism of Porter* by Harry John Mooney, Jr., 1957, revised edition, 1962; *Porter* by Ray B. West, Jr., 1963; *Porter and the Art of Rejection* by William L. Nance, 1964; *Porter* by George Hendrick, 1965; *Porter: The Regional Sources* by Winifred S. Emmons, 1967; *Porter: A Critical Symposium* edited by Lodwick Hartley and George Core, 1969; *Porter's Fiction* by M.M. Liberman, 1971; *Porter* by John Edward Hardy, 1973; *Porter: A Collection of Critical Essays* edited by Robert Penn Warren, 1979; *Porter: A Life* by Joan Givner, 1982; *Porter's Women: The Eye of Her Fiction* by Jane Krause DeMouy, 1983; *Truth and Vision in Porter's Fiction* by Darlene H. Unrue, 1985.

* * *

Katherine Anne Porter was probably the finest writer of short stories and novellas of her time in the United States. Her last work of fiction, *Ship of Fools*, suggests either that the novel as such was not her form or that the hatred and contempt aroused in her by German behaviour under the Nazis had robbed her both of her usual skill and of her usual sense that life, in all its sadness and frustrations, is incurably poetic. Her collections of essays, *The Days Before*, however, is fascinating both in the excellence of its criticism and in the light it throws on her own work: "I am passionately involved with those individuals who populate all these enormous migrations, calamities, who fight wars and furnish life for the future." We see such an individual in Porter's own stories (in *The Leaning Tower*, for instance) as a quiet, imaginative, sad girl of old southern family, aware of the past because of her grandmother and her old black servant, aware of the grotesque because of a visit to a circus whose clowns frighten her, and aware of death and horror because of a brother who kills a pregnant rabbit and shows her the baby rabbits, who will now never be born in its womb. We see Miranda (in *Pale Horse, Pale Rider*) as a young girl who has married to flee from her family and yet in some ways emotionally dried up. Other stories, like *Noon Wine*, evoke a sense of fatality, violence springing from heat and bewilderment.

Porter's great gift as a storyteller is to take material, particularly a wistfulness for the past, a sense of the strangeness, loneliness, cruelty, and treachery of life, the decay of love, or the failure to be able to love, and to avoid the twin temptations of treating this material with either sentimentality or a cheap cynicism. She evokes gravely and gracefully both the potential beauty and the bewildering lurking betrayal of life. Born in Texas in 1890, but maturing as a writer in the 1930's, she combined in an unusual way a solid sense of the past and the atmosphere of place with a fine sense of that ambivalence or complexity of attitude that we have in mind when we talk of "modernity" in fiction. Her proper readers will have the sense of reading in two ages at once, and of being presented with two possible standards of judgment, one the firm, exact, and unargued standard of the Old South, the other the modern standard which, more frighteningly, hands over the task of judgment to the reader.

—G.S. Fraser

See the essay on "Old Mortality."

PORTER, William Sydney. See **HENRY, O.**

POUND, Ezra (Weston Loomis). Born in Hailey, Idaho, 30 October 1885. Educated at Chelten Hills School, Cheltenham Military Academy, and Cheltenham Township High School, all Philadelphia; University of Pennsylvania, Philadelphia, 1901–03 and 1907–08, M.A. in Romance languages 1906; Hamilton College, Clinton, New York, 1903–05, Ph.B. 1905. Married Dorothy Shakespear in 1914; one daughter (by Mary Rudge) and one son. Traveled in Spain, Italy, and France, 1906–07; member of the Department of Romance Languages, Wabash College, Crawfordsville, Indiana, 1907; lived in Venice, 1908, London, 1908–21, Paris, 1921–24, and Rapallo, Italy, 1924–46; regular reviewer, *New Age*, London, from 1911; English editor, *Poetry*, Chicago, 1912–19; literary editor, *New Freewoman* (later *The Egoist*), London, 1913–14; founder, with Wyndham Lewis, *Blast*, London, 1914; English editor, *Little Review*, 1917–19; drama and ballet critic, *Athenaeum*, London, 1920; Paris correspondent, *The Dial*, 1920–23; founding editor, *The Exile*, 1927–28; contributor, *Il Mare*, Rapallo, 1932–40, and *New English Weekly*, London, 1932–35; promoted "social credit" economic theories from late 1920's; met Mussolini, 1933, and visited his Salò Republic, 1943; broadcast over Rome Radio from 1940, and was arrested and jailed for these broadcasts by the U.S. Army, 1945; imprisoned near Pisa, found unfit to stand trial for treason, and committed to St. Elizabeths Hospital, Washington, D.C., 1946–58; returned to Italy, and lived mainly in Venice, 1958–72. Recipient: Bollingen Prize, 1949; Harriet Monroe Award, 1962; Academy of American Poets fellowship, 1963; National Endowment for the Arts grant, 1966. Honorary degree: Hamilton College, 1939. *Died 1 November 1972.*

PUBLICATIONS

Collections

Selected Prose 1909–1965, edited by William Cookson. 1973.
Selected Poems 1908–1959. 1975.

Verse

A Lume Spento. 1908.
A Quinzaine for This Yule. 1908.
Personae. 1909.
Exultations. 1909.
Provença: Poems Selected from Personae, Exultations, and Canzoniere. 1910.
Canzoni. 1911.
Ripostes. 1912.
Lustra. 1916.
Lustra, with Earlier Poems. 1917.
The Fourth Canto. 1919.
Quia Pauper Amavi. 1919.
Hugh Selwyn Mauberley. 1920.
Umbra: The Early Poems. 1920.
Poems, 1918–21, Including Three Portraits and Four Cantos. 1921.

A Draft of XVI Cantos. 1925.
Personae: The Collected Poems. 1926; revised edition, 1949; as *Personae: Collected Shorter Poems*, 1952; as *Collected Shorter Poems*, 1968.
A Draft of the Cantos 17–27. 1928.
Selected Poems, edited by T.S. Eliot. 1928.
A Draft of XXX Cantos. 1930.
Eleven New Cantos: XXXI-XLI. 1934; as *A Draft of Cantos XXXI-XLI*, 1935.
Homage to Sextus Propertius. 1934.
Alfred Venison's Poems, Social Credit Themes. 1935.
The Fifth Decad of Cantos. 1937.
Cantos LII-LXXI. 1940.
A Selection of Poems. 1940.
The Pisan Cantos. 1948.
The Cantos. 1948; revised edition, 1965; revised edition, as *Cantos No. 1-117, 120*, 1970.
Selected Poems. 1949.
Seventy Cantos. 1950; revised edition, as *The Cantos*, 1954, 1964, 1976.
Section: Rock-Drill: 86-95 de los cantares. 1955.
Thrones: 96-109 de los cantares. 1959.
Versi prosaici. 1959.
A Lume Spento and Other Early Poems. 1965.
Canto CX. 1965.
Selected Cantos. 1967; revised edition, 1970.
Cantos, 110-116. 1967.
Drafts and Fragments of Cantos CX-CXVII. 1969.
Collected Early Poems, edited by Michael John King. 1976.

Other

The Spirit of Romance. 1910; revised edition, 1953.
Gaudier-Brzeska: A Memoir. 1916; revised edition, 1960.
"Noh" or Accomplishment: A Study of the Classical Stage of Japan, with Ernest Fenollosa. 1917; as *The Classical Noh Theatre of Japan*, 1959.
Pavannes and Divisions. 1918.
Instigations. 1920.
Indiscretions; or, Une Revue de Deux Mondes. 1923.
Antheil, and The Treatise on Harmony. 1924.
Imaginary Letters. 1930.
How to Read. 1931.
ABC of Economics. 1933.
ABC of Reading. 1934.
Make It New: Essays. 1934.
Social Credit: An Impact. 1935.
Jefferson and/or Mussolini. 1935; revised edition, as *Jefferson e Mussolini*, 1944.
Polite Essays. 1937.
Guide to Kulchur. 1938; as *Culture*, 1938.
What Is Money For? 1939.
Carta da visita. 1942; translated by John Drummond, as *A Visiting Card*, 1952.
L'America, Roosevelt, e le cause della guerra presente. 1944; translated by John Drummond, as *America, Roosevelt, and the Causes of the Present War*, 1951.
Oro e lavoro. 1944; translated by John Drummond, as *Gold and Labour*, 1952.
Introduzione alla natura economica degli S.U.A. 1944; translated by Carmine Amore, as *An Introduction to the Economic Nature of the United States*, 1950.
Orientamenti. 1944.
If This Be Treason. 1948.
Patria Mia. 1950; with *The Treatise on Harmony*, 1962.
The Letters of Pound 1907–1941, edited by D.D. Paige. 1950.
The Translations of Pound. 1953; revised edition, 1970.
Secondo biglietto da visita. 1953.
Literary Essays, edited by T.S. Eliot. 1954.
Lavoro ed usura. 1954.
Pavannes and Divagations. 1958.
Impact: Essays on Ignorance and the Decline of American Civilization, edited by Noel Stock. 1960.
Nuova economia editoriale. 1962.
EP to LU: Nine Letters Written to Louis Untermeyer, edited by J. Albert Robbins. 1963.
Être Citoyen Romain. 1965.
Pound/Joyce: The Letters of Pound to James Joyce, edited by Forrest Read. 1967.
The Caged Panther: Pound at St. Elizabeths (includes 53 letters), by Harry M. Meachum. 1967.
Rondondillas; or, Something of That Sort. 1968.
Dk: Some Letters of Pound, edited by Louis Dudek. 1975.
Certain Radio Speeches of Pound: From the Recordings and Transcriptions of His Wartime Broadcasts, Rome 1941–1943, edited by William Levy. 1975.
Sulla moneta. 1977.
Pound and Music: The Complete Criticism, edited by R. Murray Schaefer. 1977.
Pound Speaking: Radio Speeches of World War II, edited by Leonard W. Doob. 1978.
Letters to Ibbotson 1935–1952 (letters to Joseph Darling Ibbotson), edited by Vittoria I. Mondolfo and Margaret Hurley. 1979.
Pound and the Visual Arts, edited by Harriet Zinnes. 1980.
Lettere 1907–1958, edited by Aldo Tagliaferri. 1980.
From Syria: The Worksheets, Proofs, and Text, edited by Robin Skelton. 1981.
Pound's Cavalcanti: An Edition of the Translations, Notes and Essays, edited by David Anderson. 1982.
Pound/Ford: The Story of a Literary Friendship (letters to Ford Madox Ford), edited by Brita Lindberg-Seyersted. 1982.
Letters to John Theobald, edited by Donald Pearce and Herbert Schneidau. 1984.
Pound and Dorothy Shakespear: Their Letters 1909–1914, edited by Omar Pound and A. Walton Litz. 1985.
Pound/Lewis: The Letters of Pound and Wyndham Lewis, edited by Timothy Materer. 1985.
Letters to Tom Carter, edited by Andrew Kappel. 1985.
Pound and Japan, edited by Sanehide Kodama. 1986.

Editor, *Des Imagistes: An Anthology*. 1914.
Editor, *Poetical Works of Lionel Johnson*. 1915.
Editor, *Catholic Anthology 1914–1915*. 1915.
Editor, *Passages from the Letters of John Butler Yeats*. 1917.
Editor, *Rime*, by Guido Cavalcanti. 1932.
Editor, *Profile: An Anthology*. 1932.
Editor, *Active Anthology*. 1933.
Editor, *The Chinese Written Character as a Medium for Poetry: An Ars Poetica*, by Ernest Fenollosa. 1936.
Editor, *De Moribus Brachmanorum, Liber Sancto Ambrosio Falso Adscriptus*. 1956.
Editor, with Marcella Spann, *Confucius to Cummings*. 1964.

Translator, *The Sonnets and Ballate of Guido Cavalcanti*. 1912; as *Pound's Cavalcanti Poems*, 1966.
Translator, *Cathay: Translations*. 1915.

Translator, with Ernest Fenollosa, *Certain Noble Plays of Japan*. 1916.
Translator, *Dialogues of Fontenelle*. 1917.
Translator, *The Natural Philosophy of Love*, by Rémy de Gourmont. 1922.
Translator, *The Call of the Road*, by Edouard Estaunié. 1923.
Translator, *Ta Hio: The Great Learning*, by Confucius. 1928.
Translator, *Digest of the Analects*, by Confucius. 1937.
Translator, *Italy's Policy of Social Economics 1939–1940*, by Odon Por. 1941.
Translator, with Alberto Luchini, *Ta S'en Dai Gaku, Studio Integrale*, by Confucius. 1942.
Translator, *Ciung Iung, l'Asse che non vacilla*, by Confucius. 1945.
Translator, *The Unwobbling Pivot and The Great Digest*, by Confucius. 1947.
Translator, *Confucian Analects*. 1951.
Translator, *The Classic Anthology Defined by Confucius*. 1954; as *Shih-ching*, 1976.
Translator, *Moscardino*, by Enrico Pea. 1956.
Translator, *Women of Trachis*, by Sophocles. 1956.
Translator, *Rimbaud* (5 poems). 1957.
Translator, with Noel Stock, *Love Poems of Ancient Egypt*. 1962.
Translator, *Fancy Goods, and Open All Night*, by Paul Morand, edited by Breon Mitchell. 1984.

*

Bibliography: *Pound: A Bibliography* by Donald Gallup, 1983.

Critical Studies: *Pound: His Metric and Poetry* by T.S. Eliot, 1918; *Poetry and Opinion: The Pisan Cantos of Pound: A Dialog on the Role of Poetry* by Archibald MacLeish, 1950; *Pound: A Collection of Essays* edited by Peter Russell, 1950, as *An Examination of Pound*, 1950; *The Poetry of Pound*, 1951, and *The Pound Era*, 1971, both by Hugh Kenner; *Pound and the Cantos* by Harold H. Watts, 1952; *Motive and Method in the Cantos of Pound* edited by Lewis Leary, 1954; *A Primer of Pound* by M.L. Rosenthal, 1960; *Pound* by G.S. Fraser, 1960; *Pound* by Charles Norman, 1960, revised edition, 1969; *The Confucian Odes of Pound: A Critical Appraisal* by L.S. Dembo, 1963; *Pound: Poet as Sculptor*, 1964, and *Pound*, 1975, both by Donald Davie; *Pound's Poetics and Literary Tradition* by N. Christoph De Nagy, 1966; *The Influence of Pound* by K.L. Goodwin, 1966; *The Rose in the Steel Dust: An Examination of the Cantos of Pound* by Walter Baumann, 1967; *The Early Poetry of Pound* by Thomas H. Jackson, 1968; *The Poetry of Pound: Forms and Renewal 1908–1920* by Hugh Witemeyer, 1969; *New Approaches to Pound* edited by Eva Hesse, 1969; *The Barb of Time: On the Unity of Pound's Cantos* by Daniel Pearlman, 1969; *The Life of Pound* by Noel Stock, 1970, revised edition, 1982; *A ZBC of Pound* by Christine Brooke-Rose, 1971; *Pound* by Jeannette Lander, 1971; *Discretions* by Mary de Rachewiltz, 1971; *Pound and the Troubadour Tradition* by Stuart McDougal, 1972; *Pound: The Critical Heritage* edited by Eric Homberger, 1972; *Pound: An Introduction to the Poetry* by Bernetta Quinn, 1973; *Pound: A Collection of Critical Essays* edited by Grace Schulman, 1974; *Pound, The Last Rower: A Political Profile* by C. David Heymann, 1976; *The Genesis of Pound's Cantos* by Ronald Bush, 1976; *Time in Pound's Work* by William Harmon, 1977; *The Later Cantos of Pound*, 1977, and *The American Roots of Pound*, 1985, both by James J. Wilhelm; *Pound* by James F. Knapp, 1979; *Pound's Cantos: The Story of the Text* by Barbara Eastman, 1979; *A Student's Guide to the Selected Poems of Pound* by Peter Brooker, 1979; *End to Torment: A Memoir of Pound* by H.D., edited by Norman Holmes Pearson and Michael King, 1979 (includes poems by Pound); *The Poetic Achievement of Pound* by M.J. Alexander, 1979; *A Light from Eleusis: A Study of Pound's Cantos* by Leon Surette, 1979; *Pound and the Cantos: A Record of Struggle* by Wendy Stallard Flory, 1980; *A Companion to the Cantos of Pound* by Carroll F. Terrell, 2 vols., 1980–85; *The Formèd Trace: The Later Poetry of Pound* by Massimo Bacigalupo, 1980; *The Tale of the Tribe: Pound and the Modern Verse Epic* by Michael Andé Bernstein, 1980; *Pound and the Pisan Cantos* by Anthony Woodward, 1980; *Pound and His World* by Peter Ackroyd, 1981; *Critic as Scientist: The Modernist Poetics of Pound* by Ian Bell, 1981, and *Pound: Tactics for Reading* edited by Bell, 1982; *Pound and William Carlos Williams* edited by Daniel Hoffman, 1983; *A Guide to Pound's Selected Poems*, 1983, and *To Write Paradise: Style and Error in Pound's Cantos*, 1985, both by Christine Froula; *Cities on Hills: A Study of I-XXX of Pound's Cantos* by Guy Davenport, 1983; *The Roots of Treason: Pound and the Secret of St. Elizabeths* by E. Fuller Torrey, 1984; *Pound: The Prime Minister of Poetry* by Burton Raffel, 1984; *Pound and History* by Marianne Korn, 1985; *Pound's Cantos* by Peter Makin, 1985; *A Guide to the Cantos of Pound* by William Cookson, 1985; *Pound* by P.N. Furbank, 1985; *The Modernism of Pound: The Science of Poetry* by Martin Kayman, 1986.

* * *

Ezra Pound is conventionally regarded as one of the fathers of modernism, the man who discovered Eliot and Joyce and got them into print, and was in the vanguard of the modernist movement with his own poetic experiments before 1914, and his *Cantos* in the years following World War I. The reality was somewhat different. Pound was first and foremost a showman, an impresario who was expert (in his early years) at managing his own performance and that of his contemporaries. He championed and promoted modernism because it was the current movement, rather than because he had any deep-rooted modernist inclinations. Later he got bored with it, turned to an eccentric branch of economics, and drifted into political propaganda. In most people's eyes, he made a fool of himself in so doing; but at least he retained public attention until the end of his life, and this is probably what he wanted most of all.

He was descended from two old-established American families who had come down in the world. Brought up in a suburb of Philadelphia and educated at the University of Pennsylvania and at Hamilton College, he displayed no marked talent at anything except self-advertisement until, having failed to hold down a teaching job in a small midwestern college, he departed precipitously for Europe in the spring of 1908, aged 22. During a summer in Venice he had his first book of poems, *A Lume Spento*, printed privately, and then set off for London, where he managed to attract the sympathetic notice of various figures in the British literary establishment, including W.B. Yeats. Only a matter of months after his arrival, *Punch* was guying him jocularly, and many reviewers felt they could perceive that an important new voice had arrived in poetry.

His early poems did have a lot of life in them, but it was the vigour of an antiquarian, an enthusiastic literary historian, rather than of a poet writing from personal experience and feeling. His first major passion was for the medieval French troubadours, and he wrote in what he believed to be their manner, though it usually came out as Pre-Raphaelite pastiche. Now and then he achieved a brilliant little poem of his own, such as "Portrait d'une Femme," or "The Return" (1912), which Yeats thought was the most accomplished piece of *vers libre* written to that date. But he made more splash as the leader of a new poetic movement, Imagism (typically, he invented the name before he knew what it really meant); and arguably he achieved more by championing the causes of others—James Joyce, the sculptor Gaudier-Brzeska, Wyndham Lewis, and the young T.S. Eliot—than in his own writing. His best work before 1920 did include the brilliant little *Cathay*, a set of loose translations from the Chinese, but his ambitious *Homage to Sextus Propertius* was widely pilloried for its erroneous renderings from the Latin (though it is a fine poem in itself), and his mannered, obscure *Hugh Selwyn Mauberley* is metrically brilliant but scarcely manages to communicate more than a set of nuances.

Pound's rebarbative character soon alienated him from London's editors and publishers, and by the end of 1920 he decided, with his English wife Dorothy, to abandon the British capital for the Continent, taking with him the beginnings of an "endless poem" that was to be all about everything, the *Cantos*. It emerged into print, section by section, from 1925 until the end of his life, eventually numbering somewhat over a hundred cantos (a precise figure cannot be given as it ends in fragments). The *Cantos* contain many passages of beauty, but only Pound's most convinced admirers can manage to persuade themselves that the work possesses any real structure, or is more than a fairly random set of statements about what happened to be interesting its author at a particular moment—subjects ranging from ancient Chinese history to American Presidents and contemporary economic theory. Unfortunately Pound chose to write no other form of poetry once he had begun the *Cantos*, burying his tremendous lyric gift (William Carlos Williams said his was the finest ear ever born to listen to language) beneath a mass of redundant, irrelevant detail.

Immensely long as the work is, the *Cantos* only represents a comparatively small part of Pound's literary output from the 1920's onwards. Towards the end of that decade, he became obsessed with the eccentric economic theories of one Major C.H. Douglas, and devoted most of the 1930's to evangelising Douglas's doctrine of "Social Credit"—which few people have clearly understood, and of which (it may be suspected) Pound himself had only a shaky grasp. At times he seemed to have grown bored with literary activities. At other moments he would rush into print, in such books as *ABC of Reading* and *Guide to Kulchur*, telling the world what it should read and think—usually basing his instructions on an alarmingly narrow and esoteric range of ideas; he rejected most major poets (Shakespeare, Milton, Wordsworth, to name a few), exhorted his readers to study Confucius, and praised such obscure thinkers as Leo Frobenius (a German anthropologist) and Sylvio Gesell (another unorthodox economist). Much of *Guide to Kulchur* is devoted to proving that Aristotle's ethics are rubbish.

By the mid-1930's Pound had become an admirer of Mussolini (though he scarcely had any idea what Fascism meant), and he began to indulge in anti-semitism, first in private letters, and then more openly in the newspaper columns of the British Union of Fascists. He was now living in Italy—Paris, his first Continental port of call, had proved as disappointing as London, and he shifted to Rapallo—and when war broke out he was content to remain behind enemy lines, and broadcast on the "American Hour" of the official Fascist radio. His radio talks were eccentric explosions of rage against Roosevelt, for being supposedly duped into a meaningless war; the real war, said Pound, was against the "usurers." The broadcasts are often—intentionally—comic; he read his scripts in a variety of exaggerated American crackerbarrel accents, and one might argue that there is more poetry in his performance at the microphone than in many stretches of the *Cantos*. But the American government did not take kindly to it, and when Italy was liberated in May 1945 Pound found himself under interrogation, on a treason charge. He was confined for several weeks in a cage in the open air, an experience which prompted the writing of *The Pisan Cantos* (his detention camp was at Pisa), the only section of the work in which personal experience and feeling is allowed to penetrate and bring to life the jumbled fragments in Pound's storehouse of literary memory.

His trial (in Washington, D.C.) was abandoned when a jury found him insane, a judgment which took no account of the fact that his behaviour at the microphone was no different from how he had always behaved; he was no more (or less) insane in 1945 than he had been in 1908. But he was incarcerated in the Federal mental asylum (St. Elizabeths Hospital, Washington), and it took his friends and supporters more than twelve years to get him out. During his internment he worked at two further sections of the *Cantos*, but failed to bring the enterprise towards any sort of conclusion; and when he left St. Elizabeths in 1958 and returned to Italy he began to suffer severe depression. Eventually, after bouts of illness, he sank into near-silence—though typically he made himself the centre of attention by so doing.

Terms like "flawed" or "patchy" are totally inadequate for the whole body of Pound's poetry. It is scarcely credible that the man who wrote *Cathay* could descend to some of the near-meaningless jumble of the John Adams Cantos (written at the end of the 1930's); and all through his *oeuvre* there are indications of laziness and total disregard for normal standards. Yet at his best, there is no one better. His good work has probably been more influential than Eliot's, for (as Yeats said) he was the first person in English to make free verse sound natural. But it is unwise to take him seriously (as some critics have done, at enormous length); rather, one should relish the whole absurd variety of the man and his work, and wonder at the spectacle of such a talented poet becoming bored, so quickly, with his own talent, and choosing instead to be what Dudley Fitts called "the bad boy, strutting and shocking."

—Humphrey Carpenter

See the essay on the *Cantos*.

POWERS, J(ames) F(arl). Born in Jacksonville, Illinois, 8 July 1917. Educated at Quincy College Academy, Illinois; Northwestern University, Chicago campus, 1938–40. Married Betty Wahl in 1946; three daughters and two sons. Worked in Chicago, 1935–41; editor, Illinois Historical Records Survey, 1938; hospital orderly during World War II; teacher at St. John's University, Collegeville, Minnesota, 1947 and after 1975, Marquette University, Milwaukee, 1949–51, and University of Michigan, Ann Arbor, 1956–57; Writer-in-Residence, Smith College, Northampton, Massachusetts, 1965–66. Recipient: American Academy grant, 1948; Guggenheim fellowship, 1948; Rockefeller fellowship, 1954, 1957, 1967; National Book Award, 1963. Member, American Academy.

PUBLICATIONS

Fiction

Prince of Darkness and Other Stories. 1947.
The Presence of Grace (stories). 1956.
Morte d'Urban. 1962.
Look How the Fish Live (stories). 1975.

Critical Studies: *Powers* by John F. Hagopian, 1968; *Powers* edited by Fallon Evans, 1968.

* * *

J.F. Powers was frustrated trying to find work in Chicago during the depression years 1935–41. In the early years of World War II he met many social rebels in Chicago—workers, blacks, and European exiles—and became a pacifist: he was appalled equally by the destructive war and patriotic propaganda. Early in 1943 he was the only lay person to attend a priests' retreat at St. John's Abbey in Collegeville, Minnesota. Following a period of reading and introspection Powers wrote "Lions, Harts, Leaping Does," in which Father Didymus attains true holiness as he dies, holding to his faith along with a strong sense of unworthiness. Three Powers sketches appeared in the *Catholic Worker* in 1943: "the upholstery of Christianity has held up better than the idea and practice. . . . Anyone who is not a saint is spiritually undersized—the world is full of spiritual midgets."

In *Prince of Darkness and Other Stories*, the best pieces have priest protagonists: the title story, "The Forks," "The Valiant Woman," and "Lions, Harts, Leaping Does." Among the eleven stories are three bitter tales about the plight of Chicago Blacks; "Jamesie," a story of adolescence that is probably autobiographical; and "Renner," a story of anti-Semitism. The critical reception of Powers's stories—especially among his fellow writers—was impressive. *The Presence of Grace* has nine stories, all but two of them about priests. The prevailing mood is mellow in these stories, and some reviewers found his clerical scenes deplorably picturesque instead of astringent.

Except for the story of Father Didymus, Powers used both humor and irony to expose priestly venality in his earlier stories: they reveal the dark side of "the endless struggle between religious idealism and selfish, worldly interests." Wit and subtle irony are still at work on priestly foibles in the nine stories of *The Presence of Grace*, but the absurdities seem less vicious and more forgivable. "Zeal" is a fair example: obtuse and bungling Father Early provokes his sophisticated bishop into a redeeming examination of his own soul.

Powers has published only one novel, *Morte d'Urban*, which grew out of a short story he had begun 15 years earlier. In "The Devil Was the Joker," the Order of St. Clement is a central concern; and some minor figures in the novel—Father Udovic, Monsignor Renton, and their Bishop—are the chief characters in "Dawn." For his novel Powers sets up two Minnesota dioceses, Great Plains and Ostergothenburg. Powers's own words best describe his intention: "The story is about Father Urban being sent to this foundation of the Order (Clementines) in Minnesota. He had been a big-time speaker, a poor man's Fulton Sheen. He was suddenly sent up here to this white elephant . . . as one of the boys. . . . That's my story . . . how he tried to put the place on its feet. . . . I thought it would be a nice little nut-brown novel, all kinds of irony." Though the critics reviewed *Morte d'Urban* favorably, most of them missed some levels of irony and even misinterpreted the point. Perhaps because parts of the novel had appeared in journals and Powers had an impressive reputation as a writer of short stories, many reviewers found *Morte d'Urban* episodic and lacking in unity as novel. Powers's ironic unifying devices were possibly too subtle.

Look How the Fish Live is uneven: half of the stories are clearly below Powers's usual high quality. Several of these inferior pieces, including the title story and "Tinkers," are new in subject matter and technique; but they fall far short of five stories in this collection that match Powers's best. These are stories of young, emancipated curates devoted to their creature comforts and with callow notions of how the Church should modernize; middle-aged priestly operators who specialize in efficiency, PR, and good housekeeping; elderly priests and dying bishops who clearly belong to another era but survive preposterously and precariously in an alien world. Through the agency of such Roman Catholic clerics, Powers views the modern world humorously and seriously at the same time—but always ironically.

Powers has always been a painstaking writer, and critics often praised his "structural finesse and verbal sensitivity," his "remarkable ear for the dialects and idioms of midwestern speech," and "the perfect fluency, realism, and economy" of his dialogue. The brilliant satire and subtle humor of *Morte d'Urban* have been recognized—though not widely enough; and Powers's use of the Arthurian matter has been variously interpreted and assessed. But one aspect of this and other Powers fiction has not been properly appreciated, perhaps because his Roman Catholic matter is probed so deeply and detailed so accurately. He uses the dilemma of Roman Catholicism in the middle years of the 20th century to dramatize the impact of rampant materialism on a society trying to save—or find—its soul and sanity.

—Clarence A. Glasrud

PURDY, James (Otis). Born near Fremont, Ohio, 14 July 1923. Educated at the University of Chicago, 1941, 1946; University of Puebla, Mexico; University of Madrid. Worked as an interpreter in Latin America, France, and Spain; teacher at Lawrence College, Appleton, Wisconsin, 1949–53; since 1953 full-time writer. Visiting Professor, University of Tulsa, Oklahoma, 1977. Recipient: American Academy award, 1958; Guggenheim fellowship, 1958, 1962; Ford fellowship, for drama, 1961. Lives in Brooklyn, New York.

PUBLICATIONS

Fiction

Don't Call Me by My Right Name and Other Stories. 1956.
63: Dream Palace (stories). 1956.
Color of Darkness: Eleven Stories and a Novella. 1957.

Malcolm. 1959.
The Nephew. 1960.
Children Is All (stories and plays). 1961.
Cabot Wright Begins. 1964.
Eustace Chisholm and the Works. 1967.
An Oyster Is a Wealthy Beast (story and poems). 1967.
Mr. Evening: A Story and Nine Poems. 1968.
On the Rebound: A Story and Nine Poems. 1970.
Sleepers in Moon-Crowned Valleys:
Jeremy's Version. 1970.
The House of the Solitary Maggot. 1974.
I Am Elijah Thrush. 1972.
In a Shallow Grave. 1976.
A Day after the Fair: A Collection of Plays and Stories. 1977.
Narrow Rooms. 1978.
Lessons and Complaints (story). 1978.
Sleep Tight (story). 1979.
Mourners Below. 1981.
On Glory's Course. 1984.
The Candles of Your Eyes (story). 1985.
In the Hollow of His Hand. 1986.

Plays

Mr. Cough Syrup and the Phantom Sex, in *December*, vol. 8, no. 1, 1960.
Cracks (produced 1963).
Wedding Finger, in *New Directions 28*. 1974.
Two Plays (includes *A Day after the Fair* and *True*). 1979.
Proud Flesh: Four Short Plays. 1980.
Scrap of Paper, and The Berry-Picker: Two Plays. 1981.
The Berry-Picker (produced 1985). In *Scrap of Paper, and The Berry-Picker*, 1981.

Verse

The Running Sun. 1971.
Sunshine Is an Only Child. 1973.
I Will Arrest the Bird That Has No Light. 1977.
The Brooklyn Branding Parlors. 1986.

*

Bibliography: by Jay Ladd, in *American Book Collector*, September–October 1981.

Critical Studies: *The Not-Right House: Essays on Purdy* by Bettina Schwarzchild, 1968; *City of Words* by Tony Tanner, 1971; *Purdy* by Henry Chupack, 1975; *Purdy* by Stephen D. Adams, 1976.

* * *

"We're all alike, inside, and we're all connected."

"You can't run away from yourself. You can run to the ends of the earth, but you'll be waiting for yourself there."

James Purdy is a much neglected writer who stands firm against the literary establishment which, as he has said, rejects his unconventional and often scalding portrayals of American society: "From the beginning my work has been greeted with a persistent and even passionate hostility." "The theme of American commercial culture," he adds, is "that man can be adjusted . . . that to be 'in' is to exist. My work is the furthest from this definition of reality." Despite the difficulties in gaining publication ("Had it not been for Dame Edith Sitwell, who prevailed upon a British publisher," states Purdy, "I would never have been published in America and never heard of"), when *Color of Darkness* and, later, *Malcolm* appeared, Purdy was recognized as a writer of extraordinary imagination, a fantasist who, while concerned with matters common to the beats and the dramatists of the absurd—the isolation of youth from peers, parents, and society—brought to his form a unique style. Purdy combined surrealism with a meticulously rhetoric-free prose. He mixed realism, fairy tale, and allegory, and created an entirely new form; he transcribed and often poeticized native American speech within brutal satiric forms; he illustrated the exquisite varieties of suffering that society imposes upon the innocent, the nonconformist. In *63: Dream Palace, Color of Darkness, The Nephew*, and, perhaps his best-known work, *Malcolm*, he portrayed the inevitable and lethal possessiveness within both heterosexual and homosexual love; the need and yet fear of human companionship; man's failure in his struggle toward identity. Malcolm, typical of Purdy's orphaned heroes and prototype of all Purdy's men-children longing to belong and embrace an identity, becomes instead an appendage, an object—to be used, manipulated, brutalized, and ultimately discarded by the so-called caring people of his world. In *Children Is All, Cabot Wright Begins* and *Eustace Chisholm and the Works*, Purdy remains for his readers frightening—indeed deeply troubling—as he treats in detail taboo subjects like homosexuality, abortion, rape, and incest, within ingenious frames. *Cabot Wright Begins*, which portrays an American automaton who can assert a human identity only through acts of rape, is one of America's most savage and grotesque comedies. Purdy's tone remains defiant. As one of his earliest critics, Warren French, later wrote of *Eustace Chisholm*, in *A Season of Promise*: "I was scarcely prepared for the violently compressed power, the exhausting vehemence, the almost superhuman exorcism of the wanton evil that destroys many innocents that sets Purdy's new effort far apart from the whining and cocktail chatter that often passes for serious fiction."

Jeremy's Version and *The House of the Solitary Maggot*, the first two parts of Purdy's trilogy, *Sleepers in Moon-Crowned Valleys*, combine his gift for realism with the erotic phantasmagorias of his more elliptical works. Again, scathing humor and caustic wit indict a society and its efforts to neuterize the human spirit. Purdy abandons the symbolic concretizations of the erotic, in order to draw more palpably flesh-and-blood characters, people with whom one identifies more immediately. Somewhat like Faulkner in *The Sound and the Fury*, Purdy here creates in a post-bellum family a parable of fallen America. He portrays in incredible and vivid detail a family whose growth and decline is underscored by excruciating pride and pain, where parents and children (in all combinations) visit once one another an occasional kindness, but more often a persistent cruelty. Purdy's subject again is, on the one hand, man's struggle for love—specifically in the context of birthright and family—and on the other, the inevitable selfishness, violence, and destruction that are played out in parent (especially the mother) and child in payment for the bonds of incest.

In a Shallow Grave, about a war veteran whose incredibly disfigured body is both the grave from which he must daily survive and the world in which he must submit himself, was described by the New York *Times* reviewer as "a modern Book of Revelation," a gripping, imaginative, "powerful" novel "with prophecies, vision and demonic landscapes." The remarkable *Mourners Below* combines Purdy's investigation into the fragile distance between the living and the dead with the initiation theme. After the delicate and young Duane Bledsoe learns that his two adored brothers have been killed, he retreats into a world of isolation and mourning. Their ghosts, especially Justin's, visit him, and he becomes the victim of their commands, participating in a series of violent and grotesque sexual acts, while retaining his innocence. *On Glory's Course* further explores the pain of lovelessness, along with the power of guilt and greed, in a meticulously detailed 1930's midwestern community. Comparing Purdy's work with that of his respected American contemporaries, a reviewer in the *Spectator* wrote: "Although he strikes me as a writer of far greater originality and power, . . . Purdy has only rarely received his due in his native America . . . I have always felt that a small, perpetually radioactive particle of genius irradiates the mass of the work he has produced . . . [in] his attempts to create a private American mythology."

In fact, what has been called Purdy's unremitting bitterness and grotesqueness of vision is ultimately transcended by an exquisite poetic prose and by the author's deep feeling for mankind. Purdy's style, based upon, as he has said, "the rhythms and accents of American speech," has about it, as the New York *Times* reviewer well noted, "briers in his voice, as if he meant to tear at his readers with a kind of harsh music . . . [a] deliberate scratching of the reader's ear" enabling the author "to mix evil and naiveté without spilling over into melodrama and tedious morality plays." Remarkable, in addition, is Purdy's richly textured, compressed, seemingly simple and direct prose, which weaves together level upon level of symbol—often from nature (especially birds, flowers, animals, and light and dark), as well as from classical and biblical sources.

Finally, one is left with the author's profound compassion. One may often feel anger, horror, and even repulsion towards Purdy's sadistic, licentious, and greedy people, but at the same time, one is haunted and overwhelmed by their loneliness and innocence. Purdy touches his readers on the deepest level, as he portrays, in everything he writes, man's courage, dignity, and ultimate victory in the act of mere survival.

—Lois Gordon

PYNCHON, Thomas. Born in Glen Cove, New York, 8 May 1937. Educated at Cornell University, Ithaca, New York, 1954–58, B.A. 1958. Served in the U.S. Naval Reserve. Former editorial writer, Boeing Aircraft, Seattle. Recipient: Faulkner Award, 1964; Rosenthal Memorial Award, 1967; National Book Award, 1974; American Academy Howells Medal, 1975.

PUBLICATIONS

Fiction

V. 1963.
The Crying of Lot 49. 1966.
Gravity's Rainbow. 1973.
Mortality and Mercy in Vienna (story). 1976.
Low-lands (story). 1978.
The Secret Integration (story). 1980.
The Small Rain (story). 1980(?).
Slow Learner: Early Stories. 1984.

*

Bibliography: *Three Contemporary Novelists: An Annotated Bibliography* by Robert M. Scotto, 1977; *John Barth, Jerzy Kosinski, and Pynchon: A Reference Guide* by Thomas P. Walsh and Cameron Northouse, 1977.

Critical Studies: *Pynchon* by Joseph V. Slade, 1974; *Mindful Pleasures: Essays on Pynchon* edited by George Levine and David Leverenz, 1976; *The Grim Phoenix: Reconstructing Pynchon* by William M. Plater, 1978; *Pynchon: A Collection of Critical Essays* edited by Edward Mendelson, 1978; *Pynchon: Creative Paranoia in Gravity's Rainbow* by Mark Richard Siegel, 1978; *Pynchon: The Art of Allusion* by David Cowart, 1980; *The Rainbow Quest of Pynchon* by Douglas A. Mackey, 1980; *Pynchon's Fictions: Pynchon and the Literature of Information* by John O. Stark, 1980; *A Reader's Guide to Gravity's Rainbow* by Douglas Fowler, 1980; *Critical Essays on Pynchon* edited by Richard Pearce, 1981; *Pynchon: The Voice of Ambiguity* by Thomas H. Schaub, 1981; *Pynchon* by Tony Tanner, 1982; *Signs and Symptoms: Pynchon and the Contemporary World* by Peter L. Cooper, 1983; *Approaches to Gravity's Rainbow* edited by Charles Clerc, 1983; *Ideas of Order in the Novels of Pynchon* by Molly Hite, 1983.

* * *

Thomas Pynchon's novels *V.*, *The Crying of Lot 49*, and *Gravity's Rainbow* have in common qualities that attract some readers and repel others. Both companies of readers are, however, likely to agree on what it is that they respond to in the work of Pynchon. It is an unremitting brilliance of invention, accompanied by a wide range of knowledge. The knowledge embraces the major course of European history over the past century, and it often deviates into nooks and crannies of the entire course of Western experience. In this respect, Pynchon has a novelist's plenty that makes him the peer of John Barth, William Gaddis, and others of his time. The consequence is that one has the sense of reading not only a novel but of progressing through pages from the *Britannica*, torn out at random.

The phrase "at random" is not entirely just. The assorted slices of erudition—scientific as well as cultural—are linked with Pynchon's often mad narrative sequences in ways that lead a reader to think, at a certain turn of a Pynchon novel, that he has come to the beating heart of the narrative. For throughout the tales are scattered clues that seem to lead from the witch's house of a particular novel—a place of confinement à la Hansel and Gretel—back to comprehension and mastery. But the clues to meaning—to the intent and often the animus of the novels—are scattered so generously that each reader is likely to follow a solitary path from the witch's hut (the novel as experienced) to some safe edge of a forest (the act of personal judgment).

Yet certain judgments are not wholly solitary. Each novel has a strand of interest that threads through scenes of great comic and satiric effect. There is, in *V.*, a decades-long pursuit of a mysterious being; one can hardly call this being a woman since her eyes are glass, her dentures precious metal, and her feet detachable. And there is, in *The Crying of Lot 49*, the effort of Mrs. Oedipa Maas to discover whether an ancient European secret society for distributing mail is still alive and functioning in today's California. In *Gravity's Rainbow* events in England and Germany during the closing years of World War II are concerned with English efforts to frustrate buzz bombs and other missiles and with German efforts to launch those missiles. (A young American named Slothrop has a sexual activity that seems linked with the arrival of the bombs. But this is only a small part of a variegated story.)

Such strands are obviously purloined from popular and facile tales of intrigue. In Pynchon's novels the strands become enmeshed in displays of brilliant language and events both grotesque and, if one has missed a clue or so, gratuitous. The clues—if that is what certain passages come to—sometimes do point to the identity of V., or the workings of the society that competes with the public mail systems of the world in *The Crying of Lot 49*, or that crisis of world order in *Gravity's Rainbow*. At other times, the clues are—or seem to be—self-subsistent rather than centers about which one can gather the motley contents of a novel. *V.*, for example, ranges from the 1910's to about 1956. European-based characters are touched by V. and "her" progress from being a human person to an assemblage of inanimate elements wondrously animated. In contrast, the American characters are known only in an immediate present; this is "The Crew," a collection of people united by their drinking and whoring and also by an uneasy but quite intermittent questioning of all they do. What is the relation between these two strands? Is the V. experience an account of the decadence that reached its terminus in Pynchon's boozy crew of young "Nueva Yorkers"? Similarly, is the Trystero group that Oedipa Maas pursues, come weal come woe, one that allures the heroine because it speaks, unclearly, of firm purpose asserting itself in a world where there is none? And is the action of the German rocket chief in *Gravity's Rainbow*—the launching of the body of his young lover inside one of the last rockets—a scream of despair for civilization or just one more comic incident among many such?

Pynchon, satiric and ironic at most times, moralistic in rare but intense passages, creates textures of narrative that distort—but do not much misrepresent—the society they mirror. Back and forth over this texture Pynchon's mind darts. It sometimes expresses an intellect that is disembodied and uninvolved. At other times, there is acknowledgement of a link between the novelist and what he sets down. But such a link is no sooner noted than it is severed.

—Harold H. Watts

See the essay on *Gravity's Rainbow*.

QUEEN, Ellery. Pseudonym for the cousins Frederic Dannay and Manfred B. Lee. **DANNAY, Frederic:** Born Daniel Nathan in Brooklyn, New York, 20 October 1905; grew up in Elmira, New York. Educated at Boys' High School, Brooklyn. Married 1) Mary Beck in 1926 (died), two sons; 2) Hilda Wisenthal in 1947 (died, 1972), one son; 3) Rose Koppel in 1975. Writer and art director for advertising agency, New York, prior to 1931; full-time writer, with Lee, 1931–71, and on his own from 1971. Visiting Professor, University of Texas, Austin, 1958–59. *Died 3 September 1982*. **LEE, Manfred B(ennington):** Born Manford Lepofsky in Brooklyn, New York, 11 January 1905. Educated at Boys' High School, Brooklyn; New York University. Married the actress Kaye Brinker (second wife), in 1942; four daughters and four sons. Publicity writer for film companies, New York, prior to 1931; full-time writer, with Dannay, 1931–71. Justice of the Peace, Roxbury, Connecticut, 1957–58. *Died 3 April 1971*. Dannay and Lee were under contract to film companies in the 1930's; they edited *Mystery League* magazine, 1933–34, and *Ellery Queen's Mystery Magazine*, from 1941 (Dannay the active editor); they wrote *The Adventures of Ellery Queen* radio series, 1939–48. Co-Founders and Co-Presidents, Mystery Writers of America. Recipients: Mystery Writers of America Edgar Allan Poe Award, for radio play, 1945, for story, 1947, 1949, special award, 1951, 1968, and Grand Master Award, 1960.

PUBLICATIONS

Fiction

The Roman Hat Mystery. 1929.
The French Powder Mystery. 1930.
The Dutch Shoe Mystery. 1931.
The Egyptian Cross Mystery. 1932.
The Greek Coffin Mystery. 1932.
The Tragedy of X: A Drury Lane Mystery. 1932.
The Tragedy of Y: A Drury Lane Mystery. 1932.
The Tragedy of Z: A Drury Lane Mystery. 1933.
Drury Lane's Last Case: The Tragedy of 1599. 1933.
The Siamese Twin Mystery. 1933.
The American Gun Mystery. 1933; as *Death at the Rodeo*, 1951.
The Chinese Orange Mystery. 1934.
The Adventures of Ellery Queen (stories). 1934.
The Spanish Cape Mystery. 1935.
Halfway House. 1936.
The Door Between. 1937.
The Four of Hearts. 1938.
The Devil to Pay. 1938.
The Dragon's Teeth. 1939; as *The Virgin Heiresses*, 1954.
The New Adventures of Ellery Queen (stories). 1940; with varied contents, as *More Adventures of Ellery Queen*, 1940.
Calamity Town. 1942.
There Was an Old Woman. 1943; as *The Quick and the Dead*, 1956.
The Case Book of Ellery Queen. 1945.
The Murderer Is a Fox. 1945.
Ten Days' Wonder. 1948.
Cat of Many Tails. 1949.
Double Double. 1950; as *The Case of the Seven Murders*, 1958.
The Origin of Evil. 1951.
Calendar of Crime (stories). 1952.
The King Is Dead. 1952.
The Scarlet Letters. 1953.
The Golden Summer (by Dannay only). 1953.
The Glass Village. 1954.
Q.B.I.: Queen's Bureau of Investigation. 1954.
Inspector Queen's Own Case: November Song. 1956.
The Finishing Stroke. 1958.
The Player on the Other Side. 1963.
And on the Eighth Day. 1964.

The Fourth Side of the Triangle. 1965.
Queens Full (stories). 1965.
A Study in Terror (novelization of screenplay). 1966; as *Sherlock Holmes Versus Jack the Ripper*, 1967.
Face to Face. 1967.
The House of Brass. 1968.
QED: Queen's Experiments in Detection. 1968.
Cop Out. 1969.
The Last Woman in His Life. 1970.
A Fine and Private Place. 1971.
The Best of Queen: Four Decades of Stories from the Mystery Masters, edited by Francis M. Nevins, Jr., and Martin H. Greenberg. 1985.

Plays

Danger, Men Working, with Lowell Brentano (produced 1936?).

Screenplays: *Closed Gates*, by Manfred B. Lee and Frances Guihan, 1927; *Ellery Queen, Master Detective*, with Eric Taylor, 1940.

Radio Plays: most scripts for *The Adventures of Ellery Queen* series, 1939–48.

Other

The Detective Short Story: A Bibliography. 1942.
Queen's Quorum: A History of the Detective-Crime Short Story as Revealed by the 106 Most Important Books Published in This Field Since 1845. 1951; revised edition, 1969.
In the Queen's Parlor, and Other Leaves from the Editors' Notebook. 1957.
Queen's International Case Book (true crime). 1964.
The Woman in the Case (true crime). 1966; as *Deadlier Than the Male*, 1967.

Editor, *Challenge to the Reader*. 1938.
Editor, *101 Years' Entertainment: The Great Detective Stories, 1841–1941*. 1941; revised edition, 1946.
Editor, *Sporting Blood: The Great Sports Detective Stories*. 1942; as *Sporting Detective Stories*, 1946.
Editor, *The Female of the Species: The Great Woman Detectives and Criminals*. 1943; as *Ladies in Crime: A Collection of Detective Stories by English and American Writers*, 1947.
Editor, *The Misadventures of Sherlock Holmes*. 1944.
Editor, *Best Stories from Ellery Queen's Mystery Magazine*. 1944.
Editor, *The Adventures of Sam Spade and Other Stories*, by Dashiell Hammett. 1944; as *They Can Only Hang You Once*, 1949; selection, as *A Man Called Spade*, 1945.
Editor, *Rogues' Gallery: The Great Criminals of Modern Fiction*. 1945.
Editor, *The Continental Op*, by Dashiell Hammett. 1945.
Editor, *The Return of the Continental Op*, by Dashiell Hammett. 1945.
Editor, *To the Queen's Taste: The First Supplement to 101 Years' Entertainment, Consisting of the Best Stories Published in the First Five Years of Ellery Queen's Mystery Magazine*. 1946.
Editor, *Hammett Homicides*, by Dashiell Hammett. 1946.
Editor, *The Queen's Awards*, later *Mystery Annuals* and *Anthologies* (from *Ellery Queen's Mystery Magazine*). 34 vols., 1946–81.
Editor, *Murder by Experts*. 1947.
Editor, *Dead Yellow Women*, by Dashiell Hammett. 1947.
Editor, *The Riddles of Hildegarde Withers*, by Stuart Palmer. 1947.
Editor, *Dr. Fell, Detective, and Other Stories*, by John Dickson Carr. 1947.
Editor, *The Department of Dead Ends*, by Roy Vickers. 1947.
Editor, *The Case Book of Mr. Campion*, by Margery Allingham. 1947.
Editor, *20th Century Detective Stories*. 1948; revised edition, 1964.
Editor, *Nightmare Town*, by Dashiell Hammett. 1948.
Editor, *Cops and Robbers*, by O. Henry. 1948.
Editor, *The Literature of Crime: Stories by World-Famous Authors*. 1950; as *Queen's Book of Mystery Stories*, 1957.
Editor, *The Creeping Siamese*, by Dashiell Hammett. 1950.
Editor, *The Monkey Murder and Other Hildegarde Withers Stories*, by Stuart Palmer. 1950.
Editor, *Woman in the Dark*, by Dashiell Hammett. 1951.
Editor, *Queen's 1960 Anthology*, and later volumes, including *Mid-Year*, *Spring-Summer*, and *Fall-Winter* editions. 43 vols., 1959–81.
Editor, *A Man Named Thin and Other Stories*, by Dashiell Hammett. 1962.
Editor, *12*. 1964.
Editor, *Lethal Black Book*. 1965.
Editor, *Poetic Justice: 23 Stories of Crime, Mystery and Detection by World-Famous Poets from Geoffrey Chaucer to Dylan Thomas*. 1967.
Editor, *The Case of the Murderer's Bride and Other Stories*, by Erle Stanley Gardner. 1969.
Editor, *Minimysteries: 70 Short-Short Stories of Crime, Mystery and Detection*. 1969.
Editor, *Murder—In Spades!* 1969.
Editor, *Shoot the Works!* 1969.
Editor, *Mystery Jackpot*. 1970.
Editor, *P as in Police*, by Lawrence Treat. 1970.
Editor, *The Golden 13: 13 First Prize Winners from Ellery Queen's Mystery Magazine*. 1971.
Editor, *The Spy and the Thief*, by Edward D. Hoch. 1971.
Editor, *Queen's Best Bets*. 1972.
Editor, *Amateur in Violence*, by Michael Gilbert. 1973.
Editor, *Kindly Dig Your Grave and Other Stories*, by Stanley Ellin. 1975.
Editor, *How to Trap a Crook and 12 Other Mysteries*, by Julian Symons. 1977.
Editor, *Japanese Golden Dozen: The Detective Story World in Japan*. 1978.
Editor, *Secrets of Mystery*. 1979.
Editor, *The Amazing Adventures of Lester Leith*, by Erle Stanley Gardner. 1981.
Editor, *Eyes of Mystery*. 1981.
Editor, *Eyewitnesses*. 1981.
Editor, *Maze of Mysteries*. 1982.
Editor, with Eleanor Sullivan, *Book of First Appearances*. 1982.
Editor, with Eleanor Sullivan, *Lost Ladies*. 1983.
Editor, with Eleanor Sullivan, *Lost Men*. 1983.
Editor, with Eleanor Sullivan, *Prime Crimes*. 1984.

*

Critical Studies: *Queen: A Double Profile* by Anthony Boucher, 1951; *Royal Bloodline: Queen, Author and Detective* by Francis M. Nevins, Jr., 1974 (includes bibliography).

* * *

Ellery Queen is both the pseudonym and the detective creation of two Brooklyn-born first cousins, Frederic Dannay and Manfred B. Lee. At the time they created Ellery Queen, Dannay was a copywriter and art director for a Manhattan advertising agency and Lee a publicity writer for the New York office of a film studio. The announcement of a $7500 prize contest for a detective novel catalyzed the cousins into literary action in 1928, and Ellery's first adventure was published the following year. Dannay's experience in advertising may have inspired the innovation of using the same name for the cousins' deductive protagonist and for their own joint byline—a device that, along with the excellence of the books themselves, turned Ellery Queen into a household name and his creators into wealthy men.

In the late 1920's the dominant figure in American detective fiction was S.S. Van Dine (Willard Huntington Wright), an erudite art critic whose novels about the impossibly intellectual aesthete-sleuth Philo Vance were consistent best-sellers. The early Ellery Queen novels, with their patterned titles and their scholarly dilettante detective forever dropping classical quotations, were heavily influenced by Van Dine, though superior in plotting, characterization, and style. Ellery is a professional mystery writer and amateur sleuth who assists his father, Inspector Richard Queen, whenever a murder puzzle becomes too complex for ordinary police methods. His first-period cases, from *The Roman Hat Mystery* (1929) through *The Spanish Cape Mystery* (1935), are richly plotted specimens of the Golden Age deductive puzzle at its zenith, full of bizarre circumstances, conflicting testimony, enigmatic clues, alternative solutions, fireworks displays of virtuoso reasoning, and a constant crackle of intellectual excitement. All the facts are presented, trickily but fairly, and the reader is formally challenged to solve the puzzle ahead of Ellery. Most of Queen's distinctive story motifs—the negative clue, the dying message, the murderer as Iagoesque manipulator, the patterned series of clues deliberately left at scenes of crimes, the false answer followed by the true and devastating solution—originated in these early novels. Perhaps the best works of the first period are *The Greek Coffin Mystery* and *The Egyptian Cross Mystery*, which both appeared in 1932, the same year in which, under the second pseudonym of Barnaby Ross, Dannay and Lee published the first and best two novels in the tetralogy dealing with actor-detective Drury Lane: *The Tragedy of X* and *The Tragedy of Y*.

By 1936 the Van Dine touches had left Queen's work and been replaced by the influence of the slick-paper magazines and the movies, to both of which the cousins had begun to sell. In second-period Queen the patterned titles vanish and Ellery gradually becomes less priggish and more human. In several stories of the period he is seen working as a Hollywood screenwriter, reflecting the cousins' brief stints at Columbia, Paramount, and MGM. Most of Queen's work in the late 1930's is thinly plotted, overburdened with "love interest," and too obviously written with film sales in mind, but the best book of the period, *The Four of Hearts*, is an excellent detective story as well as a many-faceted evocation of Hollywood in its peak years.

At the start of the new decade most of the cousins' energies went into writing a script a week for the long-running *The Adventures of Ellery Queen* radio series (1939–48) and accumulating a vast library of detective short stories. Out of this collection came Queen's *101 Years' Entertainment*, the foremost anthology of the genre, and *Ellery Queen's Mystery Magazine*, which from 1941 until his death was edited solely by Dannay. In 1942 the cousins returned to fiction with the superbly written and characterized *Calamity Town*, a semi-naturalistic detective novel in which Ellery solves a murder in the "typical small town" of Wrightsville, U.S.A. Their third and richest period as mystery writers lasted sixteen years and embraced twelve novels, two short story collections and Dannay's autobiographical novel *The Golden Summer* (1953), published as by Daniel Nathan. In third-period Queen the complex deductive puzzle is fused with in-depth character studies, magnificently detailed evocations of place and mood, occasional ventures into a topsy-turvy Alice in Wonderland otherworld reflecting Dannay's interest in Lewis Carroll, and explorations into historical, psychiatric, and religious dimensions. The best novels of this period are *Calamity Town* itself; *Ten Days' Wonder*, with its phantasmagoria of biblical symbolism; *Cat of Many Tails*, with its unforgettable images of New York City menaced by a heat wave, a mad strangler of what seem to be randomly chosen victims, and the threat of World War III; and *The Origin of Evil*, in which Darwinian motifs underlie the clues and deductions. Finally, in *The Finishing Stroke*, the cousins nostalgically recreated Ellery's young manhood in 1929, just after the publication of "his" first detective novel, *The Roman Hat Mystery*.

The cousins apparently meant to retire as active writers after *The Finishing Stroke*. Five years later, however, they launched a fourth and final group of Ellery Queen novels, from *The Player on the Other Side* (1963), the best book of the period, to *A Fine and Private Place* (1971), published in the year of Manfred Lee's death. The novels and short stories of period four retreat from all semblance of naturalistic plausibility and rely on what Dannay has called "fun and games"—heavily stylized plots and characterizations and the repetition of dozens of motifs from the earlier periods. But the reputation of Ellery Queen, author and detective, has long been assured. Of all America's mystery writers Queen is the supreme practitioner of that noble but now dying genre, the classic formal detective story.

—Francis M. Nevins, Jr.

RANSOM, John Crowe. Born in Pulaski, Tennessee, 30 April 1888. Educated at Bowen School, Nashville, Tennessee, graduated 1903; Vanderbilt University, Nashville, 1903–04 and 1907–09, A.B. 1909 (Phi Beta Kappa); Christ Church, Oxford (Rhodes Scholar), 1910–13, B.A. 1913. Served in the U.S. Army, 1917–19. Married Robb Reavill in 1920; three children. Schoolteacher in Mississippi, 1905, and Tennessee, 1906, in a private school, 1909–10, and at Hotchkiss School, Lakeville, Connecticut, 1913–14; Instructor, 1914–16, Assistant Professor, 1919–26, and Professor of English, 1927–37, Vanderbilt University; Carnegie Professor of Poetry, 1937–58, and Professor Emeritus, 1958–74, Kenyon College, Gambier, Ohio. Visiting Lecturer in English, Chattanooga University, Tennessee, 1938; Visiting Lecturer in Language and Criticism, University of Texas, Austin, 1956. Member of the Fugitive group of poets: co-founder, *The Fugitive*, Nashville, 1922–25;

editor, *Kenyon Review*, Gambier, Ohio, 1937–59. Honorary Consultant in American Letters, Library of Congress, Washington, D.C. Recipient: Guggenheim fellowship, 1931; Bollingen Prize, 1951; Loines Award, 1951; Brandeis University Creative Arts Award, 1958; Academy of American Poets fellowship, 1962; National Book Award, 1964; National Endowment for the Arts award, 1966; Emerson-Thoreau Medal, 1968; American Academy Gold Medal, 1973. Member, American Academy, and American Academy of Arts and Sciences. *Died 3 July 1974.*

PUBLICATIONS

Collections

Selected Essays, edited by Thomas Daniel Young and John J. Hindle. 1984.
Selected Letters, edited by Thomas Daniel Young and George Core. 1985.

Verse

Poems about God. 1919.
Armageddon, with *A Fragment* by William Alexander Percy, and *Avalon* by Donald Davidson. 1923.
Chills and Fever. 1924.
Grace after Meat. 1924.
Two Gentlemen in Bonds. 1927.
Selected Poems. 1945; revised edition, 1963, 1969.

Other

I'll Take My Stand: The South and the Agrarian Tradition, with others. 1930.
God Without Thunder: An Unorthodox Defense of Orthodoxy. 1930.
Shall We Complete the Trade? A Proposal for the Settlement of Foreign Debts to the United States. 1933.
Who Owns America? A New Declaration of Independence, with others, edited by Herbert Agar and Allen Tate. 1936.
The World's Body. 1938; revised edition, 1968.
The New Criticism. 1941.
A College Primer of Writing. 1943.
Poems and Essays. 1955.
Exercises on the Occasion of the Dedication of the New Phi Beta Kappa Hall (in Williamsburg, Virginia). 1958.
American Poetry at Mid-Century, with Delmore Schwartz and John Hall Wheelock. 1958.
Beating the Bushes: Selected Essays 1941–1970. 1972.

Editor, *Topics for Freshman Writing: Twenty Topics for Writing, with Appropriate Materials for Study*. 1935.
Editor, *The Kenyon Critics: Studies in Modern Literature from the "Kenyon Review."* 1951.
Editor, *Selected Poems*, by Thomas Hardy. 1961.

*

Bibliography: *Ransom: An Annotated Bibliography* by Thomas Daniel Young, 1982.

Critical Studies: *Ransom* by John L. Stewart, 1962; *The Poetry of Ransom: A Study of Diction, Metaphor, and Symbol* by Karl F. Knight, 1964; *The Equilibrist: A Study of Ransom's Poems 1916–1963* by Robert Buffington, 1967; *Ransom: Critical Essays and a Bibliography* edited by Thomas Daniel Young, 1968, and *Ransom*, 1971, and *Gentleman in a Dustcoat: A Biography of Ransom*, 1976, both by Young; *Ransom* by Thornton H. Parsons, 1969; *Ransom: Critical Principles and Preoccupations* by James E. Morgan, 1971; *The Poetry of Ransom* by Miller Williams, 1972.

* * *

As poet, teacher, critic, and editor, John Crowe Ransom was one of the most influential men of his generation. Although scholars and critics have agreed that Ransom commands an eminent position, they have disagreed on the precise nature of his contribution. The priorities Ransom established for his literary career displeased some of his friends. He was, as Allen Tate once said, "one of the great elegiac poets of the English language," who produced ten or twelve almost perfect lyrics which will be read as long as poetry is regarded as a serious art. Yet the major portion of his creative energies were devoted to the writing of poetry only for a very brief period. During the remainder of a long and active literary career, much of his thought and most of his effort were expended on speculations on the nature and function of poetic discourse; on the significance of religious myth, the need for an inscrutable God; and on discussions of the proper relations that should exist between man, God, and nature.

Most of the poetry for which Ransom will be remembered was written between 1922 and 1925 and published in *Chills and Fever* and *Two Gentlemen in Bonds*. During the winter of 1922 Ransom read at one of the Fugitive meetings his poem "Necrological," which convinced Allen Tate that almost "overnight he had left behind him the style of his first book [*Poems about God*] and, without confusion, had mastered a new style." All of his best poems are written in this "new style," what critics have come to refer to as his "mature manner": the subtle irony, the nuanced ambiguities, the wit, and the cool detached tone. In these poems Ransom uses a simple little narrative as a means of presenting the "common actuals"; an innocent character is involved in a common situation and through this involvement he comes to have a fuller understanding of his own nature. Few poets of his generation have been able to represent with greater accuracy and precision the inexhaustible ambiguities, the paradoxes and tensions, the dichotomies and ironies that make up the life of modern man. His poetry reiterates a few themes: man's dual nature and the inevitable misery and disaster that accompany the failure to recognize and accept this basic truth; mortality and the fleetingness of youthful vigor and grace, the inevitable decay of feminine beauty; the disparity between the world as man would have it and as it actually is, between what people want and need emotionally and what is available for them, between what man desires and what he can get; the necessity of man's simultaneous apprehension of nature's indifference and mystery and his appreciation of nature's sensory beauties; the inability of modern man to experience love.

Throughout his career Ransom maintained that human experience can be fully realized only through art. In many of his critical essays—some of which are collected in *The World's Body, The New Criticism*, and *Beating the Bushes*—Ransom tries to define the unique nature of poetic discourse, which functions to "induce the mode of thought that is imaginative rather than logical," to recover "the denser and more refractory original world which we know loosely through our perceptions and memories." That which we may learn from poetry is "ontologically distinct" because it is the "kind of knowledge by which we must know what we have arranged that we cannot know otherwise." Only through poetry, which is composed of a "loose logical structure with a good deal of local texture," can man recover the "body and solid substance of the world." The basic kind of data which science can collect reduces the "world to a scheme of abstract conveniences." Whereas science is interesting only in *knowing*, art has a double function; it wants both to *know* and to *make*.

In many of his later essays Ransom attempts to demonstrate how the critic should react in his efforts to define the nature of poetic discourse and to justify its existence in a society becoming more and more enamored of the quasi-knowledge and the false promises of science. In essay after essay he insists that the truths that poetry contains can be obtained only through a detailed analytical study of the poems themselves, and he repeats one theme: without poetry man's knowledge of himself and his world is fragmentary and incomplete.

—Thomas Daniel Young

RAWLINGS, Marjorie Kinnan. Born in Washington, D.C., 8 August 1896. Educated at Western High School, Washington, D.C.; University of Wisconsin, Madison, 1914–18, B.A. 1918 (Phi Beta Kappa). Married 1) Charles Rawlings in 1919 (divorced, 1933); 2) Norton Sanford Baskin in 1941. Editor, YWCA National Board, New York, 1918–19; assistant service editor, *Home Sector* magazine, 1919; staff member, Louisville *Courier Journal*, Kentucky, and Rochester *Journal*, Rochester, New York, 1920–28; syndicated verse writer ("Songs of a Housewife"), United Features, 1926–28; full-time writer in Florida from 1928. Recipient O. Henry Award, 1933; Pulitzer Prize, 1939. LL.D.: Rollins College, Winter Park, Florida, 1939; L.H.D.: University of Florida, Gainesville, 1941. Member, American Academy, 1939. *Died 14 December 1953*.

PUBLICATIONS

Collections

The Rawlings Reader, edited by Julia Scribner Bigham. 1956.
Selected Letters, edited by Gordon E. Bigelow and Laura V. Monti. 1983.

Fiction

South Moon Under. 1933.
Golden Apples. 1935.
The Yearling. 1938.
When the Whippoorwill— (stories). 1940.
Jacob's Ladder. 1950.
The Sojourner. 1953.

Other

Cross Creek. 1942.
Cross Creek Cookery. 1942; as *The Rawlings Cookbook*, 1961.
The Secret River (for children). 1955.

*

Critical Studies: *Frontier Eden: The Literary Career of Rawlings* by Gordon E. Bigelow, 1966; *Rawlings* by Samuel Irving Bellman, 1974.

* * *

Marjorie Kinnan Rawlings is a regional writer. Her work is inhabited by the simple people and natural settings of the Florida backwoods which she adopted as her home. Often paramount in her novels is the struggle against the vicissitudes of an uncertain existence by the poor white—the Florida cracker—commonly epitomized in an archetypical young protagonist with frontier virtues. These patterns are evident in her first four novels and in much of her short fiction.

South Moon Under depicts the difficulties of a hunter scratching out a living as a moonshiner in the Florida scrub country. The novel combines vividly descriptive scenes of rural existence with strong characterizations and an eventful plot. *Golden Apples* recounts the efforts of an orphaned and impoverished brother and sister to survive in late 19th-century northern Florida. They "squat" on the estate of an exiled and embittered young Englishman whom they patiently regenerate. The resourceful protagonist is a more convincing figure than the vaguely sketched Englishman in this flawed but dramatically forceful novel. In the novella *Jacob's Ladder* a rootless and destitute young cracker couple encounter adversities in luckless attempts to wrest a living from a bounteous but treacherous environment. The pair's deep mutual reliance and indomitable spirit are poignant and emotionally powerful.

Rawlings's internationally acclaimed novel *The Yearling* is her finest achievement. The hero is 12-year-old Jody Baxter who lives with his parents in the Florida hammock country in the 1870's. As his family undergoes severe economic setbacks, Jody tames a fawn which becomes his forest-roaming companion. When, however, his pet cannot be restrained from eating the precious crops, it must be killed. The anguished boy feels betrayed by his father and severs their close relationship. Eventually they are reconciled. Tragedy has made a man of Jody. Throughout the story weave such themes as man's need to belong to the land which, in turn, belongs to those who lovingly cultivate it, and the inevitability of unfair and unexpected betrayal by man and nature. Rawlings's compellingly truthful portrait of a boy and his tender relationships is universally appealing. Her striking description of nature's elemental forces and the simple but significant events in the lives of people close to the land enrich an absorbingly ingenuous story. *The Yearling* is a classic of both adult and children's literature.

When the Whippoorwill—, a collection of Rawlings's major short fiction, is highlighted by three richly amusing cracker comedies often told in the vernacular ("Benny and the Bird Dogs," "Cocks Must Crow," and "Varmints"), and also contains a serious portrayal of a wife exploited by a shiftless backwoods bootlegger ("Gal Young 'Un") as well as the novella "Jacob's Ladder." While the remaining stories are undistinguished, the overall collection displays the hand of an able storyteller. *The Sojourner*, an ambitious but imperfect novel, is a wooden family chronicle centering on a Job-like farmer toiling on a New York State farm owned by an unloving mother reserving her affection for his wandering elder brother. Notably absent are the Florida locales of her earlier fiction, which were also detailed with verve and warmth in the autobiographical *Cross Creek*.

Rawlings is a pastoral writer of percipience and power whose blaze on the tree of American regional literature has been cut deep enough to last.

—Christian H. Moe

REXROTH, Kenneth. Born in South Bend, Indiana, 22 December 1905. Educated at Englewood High School, and the Art Institute, both Chicago; Art Students' League, New York. Married 1) Andrée Dutcher in 1927 (died, 1940); 2) Marie Kass in 1940 (divorced, 1948); 3) Marthe Larsen in 1949 (divorced, 1961), two daughters; 4) Carol Tinker in 1974. Conscientious objector during World War II. Forest Service patrolman in Washington State, farm worker, factory hand, and seaman, 1920's; moved to San Francisco, 1927, and was active in libertarian and anarchist movements of 1930's and 1940's; orderly, San Francisco County Hospital, 1939–45; painter: individual shows in Los Angeles, New York, Chicago, San Francisco, and Paris; San Francisco correspondent, *The Nation*, New York, from 1953; columnist, San Francisco *Examiner*, 1958–68, *San Francisco Magazine*, and *San Francisco Bay Guardian*, from 1968; teacher, San Francisco State College, 1964, and University of Wisconsin, Madison; part-time lecturer, University of California, Santa Barbara, from 1968. Recipient: Guggenheim fellowship, 1948; Shelley Memorial Award, 1958; Amy Lowell Fellowship, 1958; American Academy grant, 1964; Fulbright fellowship, 1974; Copernicus Award, 1975; National Endowment for the Arts grant, 1977. Member, American Academy. *Died 6 June 1982.*

PUBLICATIONS

Collections

Selected Poems, edited by Bradford Morrow. 1984.

Verse

In What Hour. 1940.
The Phoenix and the Tortoise. 1944.
The Art of Worldly Wisdom. 1949.
The Signature of All Things: Poems, Songs, Elegies, Translations, and Epigrams. 1950.
The Dragon and the Unicorn. 1952.
A Bestiary for My Daughters Mary and Katharine. 1955.
Poems. 1955.
In Defense of the Earth. 1956.
The Homestead Called Damascus. 1963.
Natural Numbers: New and Selected Poems. 1963.
Collected Shorter Poems. 1967.
Penguin Modern Poets 9, with Denise Levertov and William Carlos Williams. 1967.
The Heart's Garden, The Garden's Heart. 1967.
Collected Longer Poems. 1968.
The Spark in the Tinder of Knowing. 1968.
Sky Sea Birds Trees Earth House Beasts Flowers. 1970.
New Poems. 1974.
On Flower Wreath Hill. 1976.
The Silver Swan: Poems Written in Kyoto 1974–75. 1976.
The Morning Star: Poems and Translations. 1979.
Between Two Wars: Selected Poems Written Prior to the Second World War. 1982.

Plays

Beyond the Mountains (includes *Phaedra, Iphigenia, Hermaios, Berenike*) (produced 1951). 1951.

Other

Bird in the Bush: Obvious Essays. 1959.
Assays (essays). 1961.
An Autobiographical Novel. 1966.
Classics Revisited. 1968.
The Alternative Society: Essays from the Other World. 1970.
With Eye and Ear (literary criticism). 1970.
American Poetry in the Twentieth Century. 1971.
The Rexroth Reader, edited by Eric Mottram. 1972.
The Elastic Retort: Essays in Literature and Ideas. 1973.
Communalism: From Its Origins to the Twentieth Century. 1975.

Editor, *Selected Poems*, by D.H. Lawrence. 1948.
Editor, *The New British Poets: An Anthology*. 1949.
Editor, *Four Young Women: Poems*. 1973.
Editor, *Tens: Selected Poems 1961–1971*, by David Meltzer. 1973.
Editor, *The Selected Poems of Czeslaw Milosz*. 1973.
Editor, *The Buddhist Writings*, by Lafcadio Hearn. 1977.
Editor, *Seasons of Sacred Lust*, by Kazuko Shiraishi. 1978.

Translator, *Fourteen Poems*, by O.V. de L.-Milosz. 1952.
Translator, *100 Poems from the Japanese*. 1955.
Translator, *100 Poems from the Chinese*. 1956.
Translator, *30 Spanish Poems of Love and Exile*. 1956.
Translator, *100 Poems from the Greek and Latin*. 1962.
Translator, *Poems from the Greek Anthology*. 1962.
Translator, *Selected Poems*, by Pierre Reverdy. 1969.
Translator, *Love and the Turning Earth: 100 More Classical Poems*. 1970.
Translator, *Love and the Turning Year: 100 More Chinese Poems*. 1970.
Translator, *100 Poems from the French*. 1970.
Translator, with Ling O. Chung, *The Orchid Boat: Women Poets of China*. 1972.
Translator, *100 More Poems from the Japanese*. 1976.
Translator, with Ikuko Atsumi, *Burning Heart: The Women Poets of Japan*. 1977.
Translator, with Ling O. Chung, *Complete Poems*, by Li Ch'ing-chao. 1979.

*

Critical Studies: *Rexroth* by Morgan Gibson, 1972; "Rexroth Issue" of *Ark 14*, 1982.

* * *

Kenneth Rexroth must now be counted among the last of a distinguished and vanishing rank of writers in America, the true man of letters. He was acutely perceptive as a literary critic and historian; he was an active force in the San Francisco Renaissance through his editorial and teaching roles; he was an able translator and anthologist; above all, he possessed the enviable acuity of the polymath, with his attention focused on many centers of cultural activity at once, which he then brought to his poetry and various other writings. He has left his profound influence upon the quality and variety of literature produced in California since World War II. Final assessments of his contributions to American literary life will have to include his efforts in bridging the literature of modernism (1910–1925), especially the poetry of Ezra Pound, with that of post-modernism, the surge of experimental writing that began in the 1950's. Rexroth championed the work of America's primary innovators and taught their uses to younger writers. His work as a translator brought to American readers the international currents of modernism, thus helping to end the literary provinciality that had persisted well into the midcentury.

Rexroth's longer poems resemble the casual narrative style of Auden, although comparisons should not be taken too far. In his polemic essays, his style and approach to the basic issues of American culture, industrial economy, depersonality in the mass population, and commerciality, are reminiscent of the early essays of Edmund Wilson, Paul Goodman, and Edward Dahlberg. Rexroth's poems on nature anticipated by many years the accurate, sensitive naturalist poems of Gary Snyder, who later in turn influenced Rexroth.

It is therefore difficult to isolate Rexroth from the stream of literature and ideas in which he fashioned his work. But an essential Rexroth is perceptible in his elegant love poems and landscape meditations, gathered in *Collected Shorter Poems*. These reveries and amorous lyrics present an unguarded, visionary persona unlike any in American poetry, as in "Camargue":

> Green moon blaze
> Over violet dancers
> Shadow heads catch fire
> Forget forget
> Forget awake aware dropping in the well
> Where the nightingale sings
> In the blooming pomegranate
> You beside me
> Like a colt swimming slowly in kelp
> In the nude sea
> Where ten thousand birds
> Move like a waved scarf
> On the long surge of sleep

The shorter poetry is brief, lyrical, touching on love, travels, occasionally social comment. The strain of the didactic is strong in Rexroth's work, especially in the long travelogue poem, *The Dragon and the Unicorn*.

Rexroth's polemical criticism of American literature and ideology is contained in a number of volumes, *With Eye and Ear, The Alternative Society, Communalism*, and *American Poetry in the Twentieth Century*, in which he is intensely perceptive and iconoclastic. In the last he argued persuasively that American poetry should be traced not from Europe but from Native Indian cultures. As a figure central to most of the major phases of American writing throughout the century, Rexroth was a watershed of literary ideas and principles, and a writer who communicated a stubborn, wilful intellect in a century of increasing squeamishness and doubt.

—Paul Christensen

RICE, Elmer. Born Elmer Leopold Reizenstein in New York City, 28 September 1892. Educated at a high school in New York to age 14; earned high school diploma and studied law in night school, LL.B. (cum laude), New York Law School, 1912; admitted to New York bar, 1913. Married 1) Hazel Levy in 1915 (divorced, 1942), one son and one daughter; 2) the actress Betty Field in 1942 (divorced, 1956), two sons and one daughter; 3) Barbara A. Marshall in 1966. Claims clerk, Samstag and Hilder Brothers, New York, 1907; law clerk, 1908–14; began writing and producing for the theatre, 1914; dramatic director, University Settlement, 1915–16, and Chairman, Inter-Settlement Dramatic Society, New York; scenarist, Samuel Goldwyn Pictures Corporation, Hollywood, 1918–20; free-lance writer for Famous Players, the Lasky Corporation, and Real Art Films, Hollywood, 1920; lived in Paris, 1928–30; returned to New York and organized the Morningside Players, with Hatcher Hughes; purchased and operated the Belasco Theatre, New York, 1934–37; regional director, Federal Theatre Project (Works Progress Administration), New York, 1935–36; founder, with Robert E. Sherwood, Maxwell Anderson, S.N. Behrman, Sidney Howard, and John F. Wharton, Playwrights Company, 1938; Lecturer in English, University of Michigan, Ann Arbor, 1954; Adjunct Professor of English, New York University, 1957–58. President, Dramatists Guild, 1939–43, and Authors League of America, 1945–46; International Vice-President, and Vice-President of the New York Center, PEN, 1945–46. Recipient: Pulitzer Prize, 1929. Litt.D.: University of Michigan, 1961. Member, American Academy. *Died 8 May 1967.*

PUBLICATIONS

Plays

On Trial (produced 1914). 1919.
The Iron Cross (produced 1917). 1965.
The Home of the Free (produced 1917). 1934.
For the Defense (produced 1919).
Wake Up, Jonathan, with Hatcher Hughes (produced 1921). 1928.
It Is the Law, from a novel by Hayden Talbot (produced 1922).
The Adding Machine (produced 1923). 1923.
The Mongrel, from a play by Hermann Bahr (produced 1924).
Close Harmony; or, The Lady Next Door, with Dorothy Parker (produced 1924). 1929.
Is He Guilty?, from play *The Blue Hawaii* by Rudolph Lothar (produced 1927).
Cock Robin, with Philip Barry (produced 1928). 1929.
Street Scene (produced 1929). 1929; revised version, music by Kurt Weill, lyrics by Langston Hughes (produced 1947), 1948.
The Subway (produced 1929). 1929.
A Diadem of Snow, in *One-Act Plays for Stage and Study 5*, edited by Rice. 1929.

See Naples and Die (produced 1929). 1930.
The Left Bank (produced 1931). 1931.
Counsellor-at-Law (produced 1931). 1931.
The House in Blind Alley. 1932.
Black Sheep (produced 1932). 1938.
We, The People (produced 1933). 1933.
The Gay White Way, in *One-Act Plays for Stage and Study 8*. 1934.
Judgment Day (produced 1934). 1934.
The Passing of Chow-Chow (produced 1934). 1934(?).
Three Plays Without Words (includes *Landscape with Figures, Rus in Urbe, Exterior*). 1934.
Between Two Worlds (produced 1934). In *Two Plays*, 1935.
Two Plays: Not for Children, and Between Two Worlds. 1935.
Not for Children (produced 1935; as *Life Is Real*, produced 1937). In *Two Plays*, 1935; revised version (produced 1951), 1951.
American Landscape (produced 1938). 1939.
Two on an Island (produced 1940). 1940.
Flight to the West (produced 1940). 1941.
A New Life (produced 1943). 1944.
Dream Girl (produced 1945). 1946.
Seven Plays. 1950.
The Grand Tour (produced 1951). 1952.
The Winner (produced 1954). 1954.
Cue for Passion (produced 1958). 1959.
Love among the Ruins (produced 1963). 1963.
Court of Last Resort. 1985.

Screenplays: *Help Yourself*, with others, 1920; *Rent Free*, with Izola Forrester and Mann Page, 1922; *Doubling for Romeo*, with Bernard McConville, 1922; *Street Scene*, 1931; *Counsellor-at-Law*, 1933; *Holiday Inn*, with Claude Binyon and Irving Berlin, 1942.

Fiction

A Voyage to Purilia. 1930.
Imperial City. 1937.
The Show Must Go On. 1949.

Other

The Supreme Freedom. 1949.
The Living Theatre. 1959.
Minority Report: An Autobiography. 1963.

Editor, *One-Act Plays for Stage and Study 5*. 1929.

*

Bibliography: "Rice: A Bibliography" by Robert Hogan, in *Modern Drama*, February 1966.

Critical Studies: *The Independence of Rice* by Robert Hogan, 1965; *Rice* by Frank Durham, 1970; *Rice: A Playwright's Vision of America* by Anthony F. Palmieri, 1980.

* * *

Elmer Rice was one of the most prolific and technically proficient of modern American dramatists, as well as, in many of his plays, an eclectic experimenter and an outspoken social critic. Although he graduated from law school cum laude and was admitted to the New York bar, he gave up law to write plays; and one of his early pieces, a deftly constructed thriller entitled *On Trial*, achieved a rather spectacular success in 1914. For the next nine years, Rice wrote two kinds of plays—commercial potboilers, some of which were produced, and experimental plays with social themes, which were generally not produced. In 1923, however, he had a critical success when the Theatre Guild staged his expressionistic satire about the automated modern world, *The Adding Machine*. This play is one of Rice's few to retain its popularity and effectiveness over the years, and is considered one of the significant modern American plays. A companion piece, *The Subway*, did not receive a production until 1929; although somewhat dated, it has some remarkable strengths and has been unfairly neglected. Rice's other plays until 1929 were either adaptations or collaborations (one with Dorothy Parker and one with Philip Barry) of little importance.

In 1929, after much difficulty in finding a producer, Rice's *Street Scene* opened in New York, ran for 602 performances, and won the Pulitzer Prize. The play is a realistic depiction of life on a segment of a New York street, with something of a melodramatic plot to tie its many diverse strands together. Its powerful impact was that of a "shock of recognition"; and only a huge cast requirement (more than eighty characters) has prevented its more frequent revival. Rice also directed this play, and was thereafter to direct all of his New York productions, as well as some by Behrman and Sherwood. Also in 1929 Rice produced a trivial light comedy, *See Naples and Die*, and, in 1931, a somewhat more substantial study of American expatriates in Paris, *The Left Bank*. The same year saw one of Rice's most durable pieces, *Counsellor-at-Law*. Somewhat akin in tone and pace to *The Front Page*, the play is full of hectic activity and makes an excellent vehicle for a strong actor.

Three other plays of the 1930's show Rice's preoccupation with social issues. *We, The People* is a sprawling "panoramic presentation" of American life, specifically critical but generally affirmative. Its large cast and many issues make it thin in characterisation and rather more akin to a film scenario than to a play: in the novels *Imperial City* and *The Show Must Go On* Rice was able to be fuller and more effective. In 1934 Rice acquired the Belasco Theatre in New York, intending to produce a season of his own work. The first play, *Judgment Day*, a serious melodrama based somewhat on the Reichstag fire trial, was an indictment of fascism; it was a failure in New York, but a distinct success in London. Rice's second play at the Belasco, *Between Two Worlds*, was even less successful with the New York critics, though a better play. It is a thickly drawn Chekhovian drama of ideas, containing some of Rice's best work. Set on an ocean liner and with the usual large cast, the play contrasts the values of capitalistic and communistic societies, and suggests that the best of two worlds must somehow be welded together. Rice was to have produced a third play, *Not for Children*, at the Belasco, but, disheartened by the critical response to the first two plays, he announced his disenchantment with the commercial stage and turned to travel and to writing a novel. The unproduced play (done some years later in an inferior revised version) is a richly droll, technically dazzling attack on the inadequacies and superficialities of the drama as an artistic form. Successful really only in its Dublin production at the Gate Theatre, the play remains a seriously neglected tour de force.

In 1938 Rice returned to the theatre as a partner in the Playwrights Company. Most of the plays he wrote for the company were patriotic social commentaries, such as *American Landscape* and *Flight to the West*, and thin work compared to the Belasco plays. One comedy, *Dream Girl*, which starred his second wife, Betty Field, was successful theatre; and his panoramic paean to New York City, *Two on an Island*, contains some excellent satiric writing in a rather trite plot.

Rice's last commercially produced plays were less ambitious in scope, but more thoughtful in content. *The Grand Tour* and *The Winner* were about the relation of morality to money, and, although not his most memorable work and set on a much smaller scale, both were quite craftsmanlike. *Cue for Passion* was a psychoanalytic version of the Hamlet story, set in California, and is really too weak in characterization to be successful. *Love among the Ruins* is a thoughtful contemplation of the contemporary world, in which a group of American tourists in Lebanon look back on America. Rather more ambitious than *The Winner*, the play is also somewhat dull.

When Rice died in 1967, he had written over fifty plays (of which about forty were published or produced), two long novels, a satire on the early movies, a knowledgeable book about the professional theatre, and a long autobiography. He will, however, be remembered primarily as a playwright, as one of the men who transformed the American theatre from the gentility of Clyde Fitch and the entertainment of David Belasco into a form for the serious depiction of life, the critical social statement, and the broadening of technique. Not as powerful as Eugene O'Neill, sometimes deficient in character drawing, and often simplistic in statement, Rice nevertheless left a handful of plays which must be considered part of the permanent American repertory.

—Robert Hogan

RICH, Adrienne (Cecile). Born in Baltimore, Maryland, 16 May 1929. Educated at Roland Park Country School, Baltimore, 1938–47; Radcliffe College, Cambridge, Massachusetts, A.B. (cum laude) 1951 (Phi Beta Kappa). Married Alfred H. Conrad in 1953 (died, 1970); three sons. Lived in the Netherlands, 1961–62; teacher at the YM—YWHA Poetry Center Workshop, New York, 1966–67; Visiting Poet, Swarthmore College, Pennsylvania, 1966–68; Adjunct Professor, Graduate Writing Division, Columbia University, New York, 1967–69; Lecturer, 1968–70, Instructor, 1970–71, Assistant Professor of English, 1971–72, and Professor, 1974, City College of New York; Fannie Hurst Visiting Professor, Brandeis University, Waltham, Massachusetts, 1972–73; Professor of English, Douglass College, Rutgers University, New Brunswick, New Jersey, 1976–78; since 1981 A.D. White Professor-at-Large, Cornell University, Ithaca, New York. Recipient: Guggenheim fellowship, 1952, 1961; Ridgely Torrence Memorial Award, 1955; American Academy award, 1960; Amy Lowell traveling scholarship, 1962; Bollingen Poetry Translation Prize, 1962; National Translation Center grant, 1968; National Endowment for the Arts grant, 1969; Shelley Memorial Award, 1971; Ingram Merrill Foundation grant, 1973; National Book Award, 1974; Fund for Human Dignity award, 1981. D.Litt.: Wheaton College, Norton, Massachusetts, 1967; Smith College, Northampton, Massachusetts, 1979.

PUBLICATIONS

Verse

A Change of World. 1951.
(*Poems*). 1952.
The Diamond Cutters and Other Poems. 1955.
The Knight, after Rilke. 1957.
Snapshots of a Daughter-in-Law: Poems 1954–1962. 1963.
Necessities of Life: Poems 1962–65. 1966.
Focus. 1966.
Selected Poems. 1967.
Leaflets: Poems 1965–1968. 1969.
The Will to Change: Poems 1968–1970. 1971.
Diving into the Wreck: Poems 1971–1972. 1973.
Poems Selected and New 1950–1974. 1975.
Twenty-One Love Poems. 1976.
The Dream of a Common Language: Poems 1974–1977. 1978.
A Wild Patience Has Taken Me This Far: Poems 1978–1981. 1981.
Sources. 1983.
The Fact of a Doorframe: Poems Selected and New 1950–1984. 1984.
Your Native Land, Your Life. 1986.

Plays

Ariadne. 1939.
Not I, But Death. 1941.

Other

Of Woman Born: Motherhood as Experience and Institution. 1976.
Women and Honor: Some Notes on Lying. 1977.
On Lies, Secrets, and Silence: Selected Prose 1966–1978. 1979.
Compulsory Heterosexuality and Lesbian Existence. 1981.
Blood, Bread, and Poetry: Selected Prose 1979–1985. 1986.

*

Critical Studies: *Rich's Poetry* edited by Barbara Charlesworth Gelpi and Albert Gelpi, 1975; *Reconstituting the World: The Poetry and Vision of Rich* by Judith McDaniel, 1979; *American Triptych: Anne Bradstreet, Emily Dickinson, Rich* by Wendy Martin, 1984; *The Transforming Power of Language: The Poetry of Rich* by Miriam Díaz-Diocaretz, 1984.

* * *

Adrienne Rich's comments on her early poems offer the best insight into the shape of her career. In "When We Dead Awaken: Writing as Re-Vision" (1971) she notices that "Beneath the conscious craft are glimpses of the split I even then experienced between the girl who wrote poems, who defined herself in writing poems, and the girl who defined herself by her relationships with men." In other contexts Rich extends her use of the term "splits" to explain the structure of all contemporary problems—artistic, psychological, and social. Insofar as she defines her poetry in terms of a response to splits within and without, Rich accepts the modernist premise that the poet begins his or her work in a fragmented world.

Her early poems in *A Change of World* and *The Diamond Cutters* use their mastery of formal elements to control and order the splits. The poems in *Snapshots of a Daughter-in-Law* continue the intense examination of experience, but they no longer insist on bringing all tensions under control by the end of the poem and risk very dearly bought defenses in order to get closer to the actual dynamics of experience. With this change of stance, her poems begin to confront the tensions she finds in the world with an eye towards changing the world, or changing that part of herself which formerly had been intimidated by the tensions. Rather than protecting the self or the poet's voice from the tensions in the world, these poems begin the process of integrating the self in order to encounter the world in a full and direct attempt to overcome the limitations of experience, or of that intimidating experience of the early poems. So, while speakers in the early poems took comfort and defined success in closing shutters and other protective habits developed by experience, the speaker in "The Phenomenology of Anger" (1972) finds the simmering frustrations and tensions a source of energy, and enjoys speculating on the shape of future experiences when the force of the anger breaks out from its containment.

Having begun this intense exploration of self and world, she finds a sense of wholeness in poems such as "Planetarium" (1971) and "Diving into the Wreck" (1973) which develop images that respect the integrity of conflicts within and without and still enable a holistic view of self and world. In one of Rich's longest poems, "From an Old House in America," she extends the possibilities of her sense of an integrated identity to social and political contexts. She finds not only a positive definition of self, as she had in "Diving into the Wreck," but she also finds a place in which the self can work and interact in a positive and effective fashion. The poems in *The Dream of a Common Language* extend the positive sense of self and world to social, political, and personal relationships, especially with other women, contemporaries and predecessors, and with all women in all places. The problems of epistemological consistency and psychological comfort become occasions for discovery and new information in *The Dream of a Common Language* and in *A Wild Patience Has Taken Me This Far*. In her recent poetry Rich not only finds a wholeness but she establishes a platform from which to move the world.

—Richard C. Turner

RICHTER, Conrad (Michael). Born in Pine Grove, Pennsylvania, 13 October 1890. Educated at the Susquehanna Academy and Tremont High School, Pennsylvania, graduated 1906. Married Harvena Achenbach in 1915; one daughter. Teamster, farm laborer, bank clerk, and journalist, in Pennsylvania, 1906–08; editor, *Weekly Courier*, Patton, Pennsylvania, 1909–10; reporter, Johnstown *Leader*, Pennsylvania, and Pittsburgh *Dispatch*, 1910–11; private secretary in Cleveland, 1911–13; free-lance writer, in Pennsylvania, 1914–27; settled in New Mexico, 1928. Recipient: New York University Society of Libraries Gold Medal, 1942; Pulitzer Prize, 1951; American Academy grant, 1959; National Book Award, 1960. Litt.D.: Susquehanna University, Selinsgrove, Pennsylvania, 1944; University of New Mexico, Albuquerque, 1958; Lafayette College, Easton, Pennsylvania, 1966; LL.D.: Temple University, Philadelphia, 1966; L.H.D.: Lebanon Valley College, Annville, Pennsylvania, 1966. Member, American Academy. *Died 30 October 1968.*

PUBLICATIONS

Fiction

Brothers of No Kin and Other Stories. 1924.
Early Americana and Other Stories. 1936.
The Sea of Grass. 1937.
The Awakening Land. 1966.
  The Trees. 1940.
  The Fields. 1946.
  The Town. 1950.
Tacey Cromwell. 1942.
The Free Man. 1943.
Smoke over the Prairie and Other Stories. 1947.
Always Young and Fair. 1947.
The Light in the Forest. 1953.
The Lady. 1957.
The Waters of Kronos. 1960.
A Simple Honorable Man. 1962.
The Grandfathers. 1964.
A Country of Strangers. 1966.
The Wanderer. 1966.
The Aristocrat. 1968.
The Rawhide Knot and Other Short Stories. 1978.

Other

Human Vibration: The Mechanics of Life and Mind. 1925.
Principles in Bio-Physics. 1927.
The Mountain on the Desert: A Philosophical Journey. 1955.
Over the Blue Mountain (for children). 1967.

*

Critical Studies: *Richter* by Edwin W. Gaston, Jr., 1965; *Richter* by Robert J. Barnes, 1968; *Richter's Ohio Trilogy: Its Ideas, Themes, and Relationship to Literary Tradition* by Clifford D. Edwards, 1970; *Richter's America* by Marvin J. LaHood, 1975.

* * *

Conrad Richter is the latest and one of the best novelists of the American frontier, in the tradition of James Fenimore Cooper and Willa Cather. To this tradition he brings a deeper perspective and a more self-conscious artistry, as suggested by his choice of titles: his first novel was *The Sea of Grass*, and his second volume of short stories, *Early Americana*. But his best fiction, by far, is the trilogy *The Trees*, *The Fields*, and *The Town*. These three novels narrate the growth of an American family from its early struggle with the wilderness and the Indians, through its settlement and clearing of the fields, to the beginnings of an industrial America in the new town.

Perhaps the best and certainly the most original of these novels is *The Trees*, which follows the migration of Sayward Luckett and her family through the forests of western Pennsylvania to the Ohio frontier. But more powerful than any human protagonist is the brooding presence of the primeval trees, which shadow the lives of all those beneath, until "the woodsies" adopt their dark and often savage ways in order to survive. In this world tragedy is inevitable: Sayward's mother dies of fever, her huntsman father deserts (or disappears), and she is left to bring up her younger siblings. There is no room in this world for romance, and the novel ends with Sayward's strange marriage to a drunken young lawyer, a fugitive from his New England past. The later two novels of the trilogy continue the story of the new family into the modern world.

After this Ohio trilogy Richter's most interesting novels are two which use autobiographical material to describe the conflict between a preacher father and his son. *The Waters of Kronos* tells of an early pioneer town which has been condemned to make way for a new reservoir, whose waters—like the waters of time—will drown the memory of its pioneer past. Underlying this is the ancient myth of Kronos, the titan father conquered by the son. A second novel, *A Simple Honorable Man*, describes the infinite complexity of the conflicts which create the "simple" character of the titular hero.

Richter's best early novel, *The Sea of Grass*, tells of the pioneer southwest, as do many of his short stories. *The Light in the Forest* narrates the tragic conflict of a white boy, kidnapped and brought up by Indians, who tries to return to his own people. This same conflict informs *A Country of Strangers*, whose heroine had also been raised by Indians. Three novels, *Tacey Cromwell*, *Always Young and Fair*, and *The Lady*, describe heroines of different types who cope in different ways with the male-dominated society of the frontier. Finally, several volumes of non-fiction develop the philosophy which gives form to all Richter's creative writing. The best of these is *The Mountain on the Desert*.

—Frederic I. Carpenter

RIDING, Laura. Born Laura Reichenthal in New York City, 16 January 1901; took the surname Riding in 1926. Educated at Girls' High School, Brooklyn; Cornell University, Ithaca, New York, 1918–21. Married 1) Louis Gottschalk in 1920 (divorced, 1925); 2) Schuyler B. Jackson in 1941 (died, 1968). Associated with the Fugitive group of poets; lived in Europe, 1926–39: with Robert Graves established the Seizin Press, 1928, and *Epilogue* magazine, 1935. Recipient: Guggenheim fellowship, 1973; National Endowment for the Arts fellowship, 1979. Lives in Wabasso, Florida.

PUBLICATIONS

Verse

The Close Chaplet. 1926.
Voltaire: A Biographical Fantasy. 1927.
Love As Love, Death As Death. 1928.
Poems: A Joking Word. 1930.
Twenty Poems Less. 1930.
Though Gently. 1930.
Laura and Francisca. 1931.
The Life of the Dead (in French and English), illustrated by John Aldridge. 1933.
The First Leaf. 1933.
Poet: A Lying Word. 1933.
Americans. 1934.
The Second Leaf. 1935.
Collected Poems. 1938.
Selected Poems: In Five Sets. 1970.
The Poems. 1980.

Fiction

Experts Are Puzzled (stories). 1930.
No Decency Left, with Robert Graves. 1932.
14A, with George Ellidge. 1934.
Progress of Stories. 1936; revised edition, 1982.
Convalescent Conversations. 1936.
A Trojan Ending. 1937.
Lives of Wives (stories). 1939.
Description of Life. 1980.

Other

A Survey of Modernist Poetry, with Robert Graves. 1927.
A Pamphlet Against Anthologies, with Robert Graves. 1928; as *Against Anthologies*, 1928.
Contemporaries and Snobs. 1928.
Anarchism Is Not Enough. 1928.
Four Unposted Letters to Catherine. 1930.
Pictures (pamphlet on painting). 1933.
Len Lye and the Problem of Popular Films. 1938.
The Covenant of Literal Morality. 1938.
The Telling. 1972.
From the Chapter "Truth" in "Rational Meaning: A New Foundation for the Definition of Words" (Not Yet Published), with Schuyler B. Jackson. 1975.
It Has Taken Long (selected writings), in "Riding Issue" of *Chelsea 35*, 1976.

Editor, *Everybody's Letters*. 1933.
Editor, *Epilogue 1–3*. 3 vols., 1935–37.
Editor, *The World and Ourselves: Letters about the World Situation from 65 People of Different Professions and Pursuits*. 1938.

Translator, *Anatole France at Home*, by Marcel Le Goff. 1926.
Translator, with Robert Graves, *Almost Forgotten Germany*, by Georg Schwarz. 1936.

*

Bibliography: *Riding: A Bibliography* by Joyce Piell Wexler, 1981.

Critical Study: *Riding's Pursuit of Truth* by Joyce Piell Wexler, 1979.

* * *

Laura Riding is, according to Kenneth Rexroth in *American Poetry in the Twentieth Century*, "the greatest lost poet in American literature." The inaccessibility of her poetry, both in the literal and figurative sense, partially accounts for this lack of attention. Since the publication of her substantial *Collected Poems* in 1938, she has published sparingly and has rarely allowed her poems to be anthologized. Hence her poetry is hard to find, and, once found, hard to follow. Her brief poem, "Grace," illustrates her obscurity:

This posture and this manner suit
Not that I have an ease in them
But that I have a horror
And so stand well upright—
Lest, should I sit and, flesh-conversing, eat,
I choke upon a piece of my own tongue-meat.

Characteristic of other poems by Riding, this one is virtually unadorned, with the single concrete image withheld until the last two lines. The subject matter is, typically and paradoxically, an examination of an interior feeling, a topic that one does not expect to find treated with this austerity.

Riding's definition of a poem in the preface to the *Collected Poems* is "an uncovering of truth of so fundamental and general a kind that no other name besides poetry is adequate except truth." This definition, if tautological, is indicative of Riding's strong commitment to purity in the language. This strong belief impelled her eventually to abandon the writing of poetry, for she found that she could not reconcile the necessity to keep the language pure with the desirability of making the poems sensuously appealing to the readers.

Riding's undeservedly neglected fiction has received even less attention than her poetry. Her *Progress of Stories*, a collection marked by impressive variety and a somewhat flamboyant wit, is unlike her poetry in tone although it treats similar themes. The comic sketch, "Eve's Side of It," for instance, complements such feminist poems as "Divestment of Beauty" and "Auspice of Jewels." She has deliberately adopted a lighter vein for these stories, she explains in the preface, because she is tired of the accusation of obscurity and being made "a scape goat for the incapacity of people to understand what they only pretend to want to know."

Of her numerous theoretical studies, the two she wrote in collaboration with Robert Graves are best known. Compared to her other works, *A Survey of Modernist Poetry* is a model of lucidity. It suggests a method of textual scrutiny that possibly influenced William Empson's *Seven Types of Ambiguity*. While the work of E.E. Cummings most often provides examples for the book, Riding's poem "The Rugged Back of Anger" is also examined. To apply Riding's critical method to her poetry is helpful in understanding this austere and significant poet.

—Nancy Carol Joyner

RILEY, James Whitcomb. Born in Greenfield, Indiana, 7 October 1849. Educated at local schools, and at Greenfield Academy, 1870. House- and sign-painter, 1870–71; itinerant entertainer, giving readings and lectures, 1872–75, 1876; worked in his father's law office, 1875–76; lived in Indianapolis from 1879; journalist, Indianapolis *Journal*, 1879–88; gave annual reading tour of the U.S., 1882–1903. Recipient: American Academy Gold Medal, 1911. M.A.: Yale University, New Haven, Connecticut, 1902; D.Litt.: University of Pennsylvania, Philadelphia, 1904; D.L.: Indiana University, Bloomington, 1907. Member, American Academy, 1911. *Died 22 July 1916.*

PUBLICATIONS

Collections

Letters, edited by William Lyon Phelps. 1930.
The Best of Riley, edited by Donald C. Manlove. 1982.

Verse

The Old Swimmin'-Hole and 'leven More Poems. 1883; revised edition, as *Neghborly Poems*, 1891.
Afterwhiles. 1887.
Nye and Riley's Railway Guide, with Edgar W. Nye. 1888.
Old-Fashioned Roses. 1888.
Pipes o' Pan at Zekesbury. 1888.
Rhymes of Childhood. 1890.
The Flying Islands of the Night. 1891.
Green Fields and Running Brooks. 1893.
Poems Here at Home. 1893.
Armazindy. 1894.
The Days Gone By and Other Poems. 1895.
A Tinkle of Bells and Other Poems. 1895.
A Child-World. 1896.
Rubáiyát of Doc Sifers. 1897.
The Golden Year, edited by Clara E. Laughlin. 1898.
Love-Lyrics. 1899.
Home-Folks. 1900.
The Book of Joyous Children. 1902.
Nye and Riley's Wit and Humor, with Edgar W. Nye. 1902.
His Pa's Romance. 1903.
Out of Old Aunt Mary's. 1904.
A Defective Santa Claus. 1904.
Songs o' Cheer. 1905.
While the Heart Beats Young. 1906.
Morning. 1907.
The Boys of the Old Glee Club. 1907.
The Riley Baby Book. 1913; as *Baby Ballads*, 1914.
Songs of Friendship. 1915.
The Old Soldier's Story: Poems and Prose Sketches. 1915.

Fiction

Character Sketches: The Boss Girl: A Christmas Story, and Other Sketches. 1886; as *Sketches in Prose and Occasional Verses*, 1891.

Other

Poems and Prose Sketches (Homestead Edition). 16 vols., 1897–1914.
Complete Works (Biographical Edition), edited by Edmund Henry Eitel. 6 vols., 1913.

*

Bibliography: *A Bibliography of Riley* by Anthony J. and Dorothy R. Russo, 1944; in *Bibliography of American Literature* by Jacob Blanck, edited by Virginia L. Smyers and Michael Winship, 1983.

Critical Studies: *Commemorative Tribute to Riley* by Hamlin Garland, 1922; *Riley, Hoosier Poet* by Jeannette Covert Nolan, 1941, and *Poet of the People: An Evaluation of Riley* by Nolan, Horace Gregory, and James T. Farrell, 1951; *Hoosier Boy: Riley* by Minnie B. Mitchell, 1942; *Those Innocent Years: The Legacy and Inheritance of a Hero of the Victorian Era, Riley* by Richard H. Crowder, 1957; *Riley* by Peter Revell, 1970.

* * *

Although James Whitcomb Riley occasionally committed prose, he was pre-eminently a poet—one of the most famous in turn-of-the-century America. Not exactly the household word he once was, Riley remains an important figure in American popular culture; schoolchildren continued to learn "Little Orphan Annie" and "The Raggedy Man" well through the 1930's and more than seventy years after his death his work stays in print. He began to write verse in the 1870's, contributing primarily to Indiana newspapers, particularly the Indianapolis *Journal*, on the staff of which he served for years. His verse was widely reprinted and, as his reputation spread, new poems began to appear in newspapers and magazines far from his Indiana base. His first book *The Old Swimmin'-Hole and 'leven More Poems* was published in 1883 and new collections of his periodical verse quickly followed. He issued book-length poems only twice—*The Flying Islands of the Night*, a verse drama so uncharacteristic that his readers rejected it, and the more acceptable *Rubáiyát of Doc Sifers*, written in the Hoosier dialect used in his most popular poems.

He occasionally tried set forms—sonnets, for instance—but he ordinarily worked in rhymed couplets or quatrains, and the subject matter dictated the length of the poems. The stanza forms sometimes vary, and the meter is sometimes irregular, but in most cases these are designed to fit the speaking voice. Riley was as much performer as poet, traveling the country to give readings, and his admirers have always known that his verse fits better in the mouth than on the page. His dialect poems are much more effective than his other verse, which too easily succumbs to conventional poetic diction, as a comparison of "Knee-deep in June" with the sonnet beginning "O queenly month of indolent repose!" will show.

Riley wrote many happy poems—evocations of nature and recollections of childhood—but popular taste has always been as lugubrious as it is sentimental, and Riley, whose own despondency found an answering chord in his audience, fills his work with broken toys and broken hearts, dead children and cheerful cripples, lost days, lost joys, "lost sunshine / Of youth." He offers the consolation of Heaven or of time which lets one taste "the sweet / Of honey in the saltest tear." It is pain not comfort, however, that gives Riley his best images, as in the old man who wants to "strip to the soul, / And dive off in my grave like the old swimmin'-hole" or the speaker in "A Summer's Day" who longs to "spread / Out like molasses on the bed, / And jest drip off the aidges in / The dreams that never comes ag'in." Riley's triumph as a popular poet is that he gave a great deal of pleasure to a great many people over a great many years, but all his readers know, as they wink back the happy tears, that

> the Gobble-uns'll git you
> Ef you
> Don't
> Watch
> Out!

—Gerald Weales

RINEHART, Mary Roberts. Born in Pittsburgh, Pennsylvania, 12 August 1876. Educated at elementary and high schools in Pittsburgh; Pittsburgh Training School for nurses, graduated 1896. Married Stanley Marshall Rinehart in 1896 (died, 1932); three sons. Full-time writer from 1903. Correspondent, *Saturday Evening Post*, during World War I; reported Presidential nominating conventions. Lived in Pittsburgh until 1920, in Washington, D.C., 1920–32, and in New York from 1932. Recipient: Mystery Writers of America Special Award, 1953. Litt.D.: George Washington University, Washington, D.C., 1923. *Died 22 September 1958.*

PUBLICATIONS

Fiction

The Circular Staircase. 1908.
The Man in Lower Ten. 1909.
When a Man Marries. 1909.
The Window at the White Cat. 1910.
The Amazing Adventures of Letitia Carberry. 1911.
Where There's a Will. 1912.
The Case of Jennie Brice. 1913.
The After House. 1914.
The Street of Seven Stars. 1914.
K. 1915.
Tish. 1916.
Bab, A Sub-Deb. 1917.
Long Live the King! 1917.
The Altar of Freedom. 1917.
The Amazing Interlude. 1918.
Twenty-Three and a Half Hours' Leave. 1918.
Dangerous Days. 1919.
Love Stories. 1919.
A Poor Wise Man. 1920.
The Truce of God. 1920.
Affinities and Other Stories. 1920.
More Tish. 1921.
Sight Unseen, and The Confession. 1921.
The Breaking Point. 1922.
The Out Trail. 1923.
Temperamental People (stories). 1924.
The Red Lamp. 1925; as *The Mystery Lamp*, 1925.
Tish Plays the Game. 1926.
Nomad's Land (stories). 1926.
The Bat (novelization of play). 1926.
Lost Ecstasy. 1927; as *I Take This Woman*, 1927.
Two Flights Up. 1928.
This Strange Adventure. 1929.
The Romantics (stories). 1929.
The Door. 1930.
Miss Pinkerton. 1932; as *The Double Alibi*, 1932.
The Album. 1933.
Mr. Cohen Takes a Walk. 1934.
The State Versus Elinor Norton. 1934; as *The Case of Elinor Norton*, 1934.
The Doctor. 1936.
Married People (stories). 1937.
Tish Marches On. 1937.
The Wall. 1938.
The Great Mistake. 1940.
Familiar Faces: Stories of People You Know. 1941.
Haunted Lady. 1942.
Alibi for Isabel and Other Stories. 1944.
The Yellow Room. 1945.
The Curve of the Catenary. 1945.

A Light in the Window. 1948.
Episode of the Wandering Knife: Three Mystery Tales. 1950; as *The Wandering Knife*, 1952.
The Swimming Pool. 1952; as *The Pool*, 1952.
The Frightened Wife and Other Murder Stories. 1953.
The Best of Tish (stories). 1955.

Plays

Double Life (produced 1906).
Seven Days, with Avery Hopwood (produced 1909). 1931.
Cheer Up (produced 1912).
Spanish Love, with Avery Hopwood (produced 1920).
The Bat, with Avery Hopwood, from novel *The Circular Staircase* by Rinehart (produced 1920). 1932.
The Breaking Point (produced 1923).

Screenplay: *Aflame in the Sky*, with Ewart Anderson, 1927.

Other

Kings, Queens, and Pawns: An American Woman at the Front. 1915.
Through Glacier Park: Seeing America First, with Howard Eaton. 1916.
The Altar of Freedom. 1917.
Tenting Tonight: A Chronicle of Sport and Adventure in Glacier Park and the Cascade Mountains. 1918.
Isn't That Just Like a Man! 1920.
My Story (autobiography). 1931; revised edition, 1948.
Writing Is Work. 1939.

*

Critical Study: *Improbable Fiction: The Life of Rinehart* by Jan Cohn, 1980.

* * *

Mary Roberts Rinehart, a successful writer of thrillers and of comic novels about the travels and adventures of a spinster, "Tish," modelled on herself and her friends, is one of the founder figures of the American novel of mystery and suspense. From her successful first novel, *The Circular Staircase*, to a late work like *The Album*, she used the same pattern. The setting is usually in a more-or-less enclosed house, often a lodging house or block of houses deliberately shut off from the outer world. The heroine is usually either an inexperienced but bright young woman or a shrewd but eccentric spinster. By overhearing odd conversations or mysterious footsteps the heroine slowly tracks down a murderer, whose identity comes as a shock to her. But then a real detective, a minor character (he may have been posing as one of the lodgers), rescues her in time. Rinehart's novels are still popular, especially in America, and their period and oddly wholesome flavour (one never really believes that the heroine will suffer the fate looming over her) make them agreeable reading: they were jocularly christened novels of the "Had I but known . . ." school (they were always told in the first person). Mignon G. Eberhart was Rinehart's most distinguished successor.

—G.S. Fraser

ROBERTS, Elizabeth Madox. Born in Perryville, Kentucky, 30 October 1881. Educated at Covington Institute, Springfield, Kentucky; Covington High School, Kentucky, 1896–1900; University of Chicago (Fiske Prize, 1921), 1917–21, Ph.B. in English, 1921 (Phi Beta Kappa). Private tutor and teacher in public schools, Springfield, 1900–10. Recipient: O. Henry Award, 1930. L.H.D.: Russell Sage College, Troy, New York, 1933. Member, American Academy, 1940. *Died 13 March 1941*.

PUBLICATIONS

Fiction

The Time of Man. 1926.
My Heart and My Flesh. 1927.
Jingling in the Wind. 1928.
The Great Meadow. 1930.
A Buried Treasure. 1931.
The Haunted Mirror: Stories. 1932.
He Sent Forth a Raven. 1935.
Black Is My Truelove's Hair. 1938.
Not by Strange Gods: Stories. 1941.

Verse

In the Great Steep's Garden. 1915.
Under the Tree (for children). 1922; revised edition, 1930.
Song in the Meadow. 1940.

*

Critical Studies: *Roberts: A Personal Note* by Glenway Wescott, 1930; *Roberts: An Appraisal* by J. Donald Adams and others, 1938; *Roberts, American Novelist* by Harry Modean Campbell and Ruel E. Foster, 1956; *Herald to Chaos: The Novels of Roberts* by Earl Rovit, 1960; *Roberts* by Frederick P.W. McDowell, 1963 (includes bibliography).

* * *

The philosophic idealism of Bishop Berkeley, the realistic conventions of regional fiction, and a poetic talent for rendering sensuous impressions are the unlikely ingredients that conjoin in the making of Elizabeth Madox Roberts's novels. Her characteristic way of harmonizing these disparate materials is through the focus of an introspective woman who serves as narrator-protagonist—a controlling consciousness that shapes the contours of her own growing personality and those of the outside world, interactively and simultaneously. Two of Roberts's novels, *The Time of Man* and *The Great Meadow*, attained considerable success when they were originally published. The first chronicles the sensibility of a Kentucky girl, Ellen Chesser, whose experience as a migrant farm wife is measured by the eternal cycles of poverty, labor, and the universal portions of grief, pain, joy, and love. Deliberately conceived on the model of the *Odyssey*, *The Time of Man* aims at a kind of epic quality in its unsentimental depiction of the struggle between creative life instincts and the implacable limitations of the human condition. *The Great Meadow* reworks this theme, but its heroine, Diony, is a more sophisticated consciousness; she is aware of herself and her role, and the journey motif is not the twenty-year wanderings of an impoverished farm family, but the great western trek from Virginia to the founding of Kentucky in the late 18th century. Both novels allowed Roberts to develop and display her strengths as a novelist: a supple, lyrical prose style, admirably suited to the particular feminine sensibility that she espoused; a sense of rhythmical narrative structure that moves in slow, undramatic accretions of episodic action; and an unforced, natural symbolism infusing the texture of events.

Although these two novels are regarded as Roberts's major achievements, *My Heart and My Flesh* and *He Sent Forth a Raven* are scarcely less accomplished. The first was meant to be an antithetical sequel to *The Time of Man*, the protagonist, in this case, being stripped of all buffers against adversity only to assert an indomitable will to live. The second is Roberts's most ambitious effort; *He Sent Forth a Raven* invokes the allegorical grandeur of the biblical story of Noah and of *Moby-Dick*, and, although the novel is not entirely able to control its materials, it is rich in meaning and strangely powerful. Roberts also wrote three other novels, two collections of short stories, and three volumes of poetry. Her poems—fresh, vivid, and marked by their capacity to record a direct sensuous immediacy—are frequently anthologized in collections of verse for children.

—Earl Rovit

ROBERTS, Kenneth (Lewis). Born in Kennebunk, Maine, 8 December 1885. Educated at schools in Malden, Massachusetts; Stone's School, Boston; Cornell University, Ithaca, New York (editor, *Cornell Widow*), 1904–08, A.B. 1908. Served in the U.S. Army, in the intelligence section of the Siberian Expeditionary Force, 1918–19: Captain. Married Anna Seiberling Mosser in 1911. Worked in leather business in Boston, 1908–09; reporter and columnist, Boston *Post*, 1909–18, and editor of *Sunday Post* humor page, 1915–18; editorial staff member, *Life* magazine, New York, 1915–18; correspondent, in Washington, D.C., and Europe, *Saturday Evening Post*, Philadelphia, 1919–28; thereafter a full-time writer; lived in Italy, 1928–37, then in Kennebunkport, Maine. Recipient: special Pulitzer Prize, 1957. Litt.D.: Dartmouth College, Hanover, New Hampshire, 1934; Colby College, Waterville, Maine, 1935; Bowdoin College, Brunswick, Maine, 1937; Middlebury College, Vermont, 1938; Northwestern University, Evanston, Illinois, 1945. Member, American Academy. *Died 21 July 1957.*

PUBLICATIONS

Fiction

Arundel. 1930.
The Lively Lady. 1931.
Rabble In Arms. 1933.
Captain Caution: A Chronicle of Arundel. 1934.
Northwest Passage. 1937.
Oliver Wiswell. 1940.
Lydia Bailey. 1947.
Boon Island. 1956.

Plays

Panatella, with Romeyn Berry, music by T.J. Lindorff and others (produced 1907). 1907.
The Brotherhood of Man, with Robert Garland. 1934.

Other

Europe's Morning After. 1921.
Sun Hunting: Adventures and Observations among the Native and Migratory Tribes of Florida. 1922.
Why Europe Leaves Home. 1922.
The Collector's Whatnot, with Booth Tarkington and Hugh Kahler. 1923.
Black Magic. 1924.
Concentrated New England: A Sketch of Calvin Coolidge. 1924.
Florida Loafing. 1925.
Florida. 1926.
Antiquamania. 1928.
For Authors Only and Other Gloomy Essays. 1935.
It Must Be Your Tonsils. 1936.
Trending into Maine. 1938; revised edition, 1944.
The Roberts Reader. 1945.
I Wanted to Write. 1949.
Don't Say That about Maine! 1951.
Henry Gross and His Dowsing Rod. 1951.
The Seventh Sense. 1953.
Cowpens: The Great Morale-Builder. 1957; as *The Battle of Cowpens*, 1958.
Water Unlimited. 1957.

Editor, *March to Quebec: Journals of the Members of Arnold's Expedition*. 1938; revised edition, 1940, 1953.
Editor and Translator, with Anna M. Roberts, *Moreau de St. Méry's American Journey (1793–1798)*. 1947.

*

Bibliography: *Roberts: A Bibliography* by P. Murphy, 1975.

Critical Study: *A Century of American History in Fiction: Roberts' Novels* by Janet Harris, 1976.

* * *

Kenneth Roberts's reputation rests on his historical novels dealing with American history from the time of the French and Indian War to the War of 1812. These are long, character-and-action-packed novels that succeed admirably in bringing history to life. Roberts brought to the writing of fiction two decades of newspaper and magazine journalism and a passion for accurate detail, and his novels are noteworthy for their historical accuracy. His interest in historical fiction began with a curiosity about his own Maine ancestors who had been involved in the American Revolution.

Roberts researched his novels as though he were writing history. He borrowed trunkloads of books from the Library of Congress and historical societies and ransacked the shelves of antiquarian book dealers. When he could not find what he wanted in printed sources, he went to the archives. In researching *Northwest Passage*, for example, he found in the British Public Record Office a large collection of previously unused letters, petitions, and reports written by Major Robert Rogers himself, who was to be the protagonist of the novel. When he was writing *The Lively Lady* at his winter home off the coast of Tuscany he spent hours with Bowditch's *Navigator* and binoculars watching sailing ships in the harbor in order to master the details of sailing a brig.

Without the help of Booth Tarkington, his summer neighbor in Kennebunkport, Maine, however, Roberts might not have become a novelist. In 1928 Tarkington persuaded him to drop his journalism and begin his first novel. For the next fifteen years Tarkington talked over plans, encouraged him and then, when the novels were in rough draft, acted as adviser and editor. Night after night Roberts read aloud from manuscripts and gratefully accepted suggestions for deletions and revisions. Roberts's diary shows that in one three-month period in 1936 he spent 58 nights reading the first 51 chapters of *Northwest Passage*.

Arundel is the story of Benedict Arnold's disastrous expedition against Quebec in 1775, narrated by a Richard Nason from Arundel, Maine. Nason's son is the protagonist of Roberts's next novel, *The Lively Lady*, which deals with the operations of a privateer in the War of 1812. *Rabble in Arms* is also about men from Arundel who fight with Arnold, the hero of the novel, and ends with the Battle of Saratoga. *Captain Caution* is another sea story set at the time of the War of 1812. *Northwest Passage* is Roberts's most memorable work and depicts the fascinating career of Major Rogers, Indian fighter during the French and Indian War, who dreamed of finding the Northwest Passage to the Pacific, was governor of Michilimackinac and later court-martialed. *Oliver Wiswell* is a novel of particular interest because it tells the story of the American Revolution from the viewpoint of a loyalist.

—James Woodress

ROBINSON, Edwin Arlington. Born in Head Tide, Maine, 22 December 1869; grew up in Gardiner, Maine. Educated at Gardiner High School, graduated 1888; Harvard University, Cambridge, Massachusetts, 1891–93. Free-lance writer in Gardiner, 1893–96; lived in New York City, 1897; secretary to the President of Harvard University, 1899; moved to New York, 1899, settled in Greenwich Village, and held various jobs, including subway-construction inspector, 1903–04; through patronage of Theodore Roosevelt, who admired his poetry, became clerk in the U.S. Customs House, New York, 1904–09; spent summers at the MacDowell Colony, Peterborough, New Hampshire, 1911–34. Recipient: Pulitzer Prize, 1922, 1925, 1928; American Academy Gold Medal, 1929. Honorary degrees: Yale University, New Haven, Connecticut, 1922; Bowdoin College, Brunswick, Maine. Member, American Academy. *Died 6 April 1935.*

PUBLICATIONS

Collections

Collected Poems. 1937.
Selected Letters, edited by Ridgely Torrence and others. 1940.
Tilbury Town: Selected Poems, edited by Lawrance Thompson. 1953.
Selected Early Poems and Letters, edited by Charles T. Davis. 1960.
Selected Poems, edited by Morton Dauwen Zabel. 1965.
Uncollected Poems and Prose, edited by Richard Cary. 1975.

Verse

The Torrent and the Night Before. 1896; revised edition, as *The Children of the Night*, 1897.
Captain Craig. 1902; revised edition, 1915.
The Town Down the River. 1910.
The Man Against the Sky. 1916.
Merlin. 1917.
Lancelot. 1920.
The Three Taverns. 1920.
Avon's Harvest. 1921.
Collected Poems. 1921.
Roman Bartholow. 1923.
The Man Who Died Twice. 1924.
Dionysus in Doubt. 1925.
Tristram. 1927.
Collected Poems. 5 vols., 1927.
Sonnets 1889–1927. 1928.
Fortunatus. 1928.
Three Poems. 1928.
Modred: A Fragment. 1929.
The Prodigal Son. 1929.
Cavender's House. 1929.
The Glory of the Nightingales. 1930.
Matthias at the Door. 1931.
Poems, edited by Bliss Perry. 1931.
Nicodemus. 1932.
Talifer. 1933.
Amaranth. 1934.
King Jasper. 1935.
Hannibal Brown: Posthumous Poem. 1936.

Plays

Van Zorn. 1914.
The Porcupine. 1915.

Other

Letters to Howard George Schmitt, edited by Carl J. Weber. 1940.
Untriangulated Stars: Letters to Harry de Forest Smith 1890–1905, edited by Denham Sutcliffe. 1947.
Letters to Edith Brower, edited by Richard Cary. 1968.

Editor, *Selections from the Letters of Thomas Sergeant Perry*. 1929.

*

Bibliography: *A Bibliography of Robinson* by Charles Beecher Hogan, 1936; *Robinson: A Supplementary Bibliography* by William White, 1971; *Robinson: A Reference Guide* by Nancy Carol Joyner, 1978.

Critical Studies: *Robinson* by Mark Van Doren, 1927; *Robinson: A Biography* by Hermann Hagedorn, 1938; *Robinson* by

Yvor Winters, 1946, revised edition, 1971; *Robinson* by Ellsworth Barnard, 1952, and *Robinson: Centenary Essays* edited by Barnard, 1969; *Robinson: The Literary Background of a Traditional Poet* by Edwin S. Fussell, 1954; *Where the Light Falls: A Portrait of Robinson* by Chard Powers Smith, 1965; *Robinson: A Poetry of the Act* by W.R. Robinson, 1967; *Robinson: A Critical Introduction* by Wallace L. Anderson, 1967; *Robinson: The Life of Poetry* by Louis O. Coxe, 1968; *Robinson* by Hoyt C. Franchere, 1968; *Appreciation of Robinson* (essays) edited by Richard Cary, 1969, and *The Early Reception of Robinson: The First Twenty Years* by Cary, 1974; *Robinson: A Collection of Critical Essays* edited by Francis Murphy, 1970.

* * *

More than any other poet of his time, Edwin Arlington Robinson made poetry his career. He neither travelled nor taught, married nor made public appearances. Aside from a handful of prose pieces and two unsuccessful plays, he devoted himself exclusively to the writing of poetry, publishing many volumes of verse in a forty-year period. He suffered during the first half of his career from neglect and near impoverishment; he suffered during his last years from an excess of adulation. After the signal success of *Tristram*, for which he won his third Pulitzer Prize, he was hailed as America's foremost poet. Although his reputation has diminished since his death, he is nevertheless established as the most important poet writing in America at the turn of the century and has a firm place as one of the major modern poets.

He was, as Robert Frost noted in his preface to *King Jasper*, "content with the old way to be new." The old way was his unwavering insistence on traditional forms. His poems demonstrate his facility in an impressive variety of verse forms, from blank verse in most of the long narratives to Petrarchan sonnets and villanelles in his shorter work, but he was positively reactionary in his dismissal of the then current *vers libre* movement. In a letter, he once placed free verse along with prohibition and moving pictures as "a triumvirate from hell, armed with the devil's instructions to abolish civilization."

Robinson was new in his attitudes in and toward his poetry. He may be called an impersonal romantic, breaking with the 19th-century tradition by objectifying and dramatizing emotional reactions while at the same time emphasizing sentiment and mystical awareness. His combination of compassion and irony has become a familiar stance in modern poetry, and his celebrated advocacy of triumphant forbearance in the face of adversity anticipates the existentialist movement. In a letter to the *Bookman* in 1897, responding to the charge that he was pessimistic, he wrote, "This world is not a 'prison house,' but a kind of spiritual kindergarten where millions of bewildered infants are trying to spell God with the wrong blocks." While he was reluctant to be classified as an exponent of any formal philosophical or theological stance, he was entirely willing, in and out of his poetry, to condemn materialistic attitudes. Robinson's use of humor within his serious poetry, in *Amaranth* for instance, placed a new importance on the comic.

While Robinson frequently wrote poems on conventional topics, his subject matter was new in his heavy emphasis on people. Unlike other romantic poets, he generally avoided the celebration of natural phenomena, bragging to a friend about his first volume that one would not find "a single red-breasted robin in the whole collection." Many of his short poems are character sketches of individuals, anticipating Edgar Lee Masters's *Spoon River Anthology*. All of the long narratives deal with complicated human relationships. Frequently they explore psychological reactions to a prior event, such as *Avon's Harvest*, Robinson's "ghost story" about a man destroyed by his own hatred, and *Cavender's House*, a dialogue between a man and his dead wife which deals with questions of jealousy and guilt. The people inhabiting Robinson's books include imaginary individuals; characters modeled on actual acquaintances, such as Alfred H. Louis in *Captain Craig*; figures from history, as in "Ben Jonson Entertains a Gentleman from Stratford," "Rembrandt to Rembrandt," and "Ponce de Leon"; and mythic figures, notably characters from the Bible and Arthurian legend.

Edwin S. Fussell, in his book on Robinson's literary background, devotes separate chapters to the English Bible and the Greek and Roman classics as significant influences on Robinson's work. English poets of particular importance to him are Shakespeare, Wordsworth, Kipling, Tennyson, and Robert Browning, although Robinson objected to the inevitable comparison between his character analyses and those of Browning. Among American poets Robinson found Emerson to be his most significant precursor. Because of his narrative impulse, Robinson's work is also compared to the fiction of Hawthorne and Henry James.

Robinson is best known today for his earliest work, the short sketches of characters, chiefly failures, who reside in Tilbury Town, the name he uses for Gardiner, Maine. Partially because of their frequent appearance in anthologies, "Richard Cory," "Miniver Cheevy," and "Mr. Flood's Party" are his most famous poems. "Eros Turannos" has been singled out by Louis O. Coxe as the most impressive Tilbury poem. Also highly regarded are a few of the poems of medium length, notably "Isaac and Archibald" and "Aunt Imogen."

Not all of Robinson's poems are narratives, and some of the symbolic lyrics have been highly praised, particularly "For a Dead Lady" and the poem about which Theodore Roosevelt wrote, "I am not sure I understand 'Luke Havergal,' but I am sure that I like it." "The Man Against the Sky," the title poem of the first volume that received widespread critical approval, is an ironic meditation on the possibilities of adopting various philosophical attitudes. It has received a great deal of critical attention from both admirers and detractors. Robinson said that the poem "comes as near as anything to representing my poetic vision."

Critics have tended to neglect Robinson's long narratives, those thirteen book-length poems that occupied most of his attention during the second half of his career. According to his earliest biographer, Hermann Hagedorn, the difficulty Robinson had with *Captain Craig*, first in getting a publisher and then in the adverse critical reaction, was a devastating experience for the young poet. Until he issued his first *Collected Poems* in 1921, Robinson alternated his long poems with volumes of shorter, more readily accessible pieces. After he was thoroughly established, however, he concentrated on the long narratives. Though these poems are sometimes verbose and repetitious, they nevertheless provided Robinson with his most congenial form, allowing him to unite his talents of narration, characterization, and symbolic discursiveness.

—Nancy Carol Joyner

ROETHKE, Theodore (Huebner). Born in Saginaw, Michigan, 25 May 1908. Educated at John Moore School, 1913–21, and Arthur Hill High School, 1921–25, Saginaw; University of Michigan, Ann Arbor, 1925–29, B.A. 1929 (Phi Beta Kappa), M.A. 1936; Harvard University, Cambridge, Massachusetts, 1930–31. Married Beatrice O'Connell in 1953. Instructor in English, 1931–35, director of public relations, 1934, and varsity tennis coach, 1934–35, Lafayette College, Easton, Pennsylvania; Instructor in English, Michigan State College, East Lansing, Fall 1935; Instructor, 1936–40, Assistant Professor, 1940–43, and Associate Professor of English Composition, 1947, Pennsylvania State University, University Park; Instructor, Bennington College, Vermont, 1943–46; Associate Professor, 1947–48, Professor of English, 1948–62, and Honorary Poet-in-Residence, 1962–63, University of Washington, Seattle. Recipient: Yaddo fellowship, 1945; Guggenheim grant, 1945, 1950; American Academy grant, 1952; Fund for the Advancement of Education fellowship, 1952; Ford grant, 1952, 1959; Pulitzer Prize, 1954; Fulbright fellowship, 1955; Borestone Mountain award, 1958; National Book Award, 1959, 1965; Bollingen Prize, 1959; Poetry Society of America prize, 1962; Shelley Memorial Award, 1962. D.H.L.: University of Michigan, 1962. *Died 1 August 1963.*

PUBLICATIONS

Collections

On the Poet and His Craft: Selected Prose, edited by Ralph J. Mills, Jr. 1965.
Collected Poems. 1966.
Selected Letters, edited by Ralph J. Mills, Jr. 1968.
Selected Poems, edited by Beatrice Roethke. 1969.

Verse

Open House. 1941.
The Lost Son and Other Poems. 1948.
Praise to the End! 1951.
The Waking: Poems 1933–1953. 1953.
Words for the Wind: The Collected Verse. 1957.
The Exorcism. 1957.
Sequence, Sometimes Metaphysical. 1963.
The Far Field. 1964.
Two Poems. 1965.
The Achievement of Roethke: A Comprehensive Selection of His Poems, edited by William J. Martz. 1966.

Other

I Am! Says the Lamb (for children). 1961.
Party at the Zoo (for children). 1963.
Straw for the Fire: From the Notebooks 1943–1963, edited by David Wagoner. 1972.
Dirty Dinky and Other Creatures: Poems for Children, edited by Beatrice Roethke and Stephen Lushington. 1973.

*

Bibliography: *Roethke: A Bibliography* by James R. McLeod, 1973; *Roethke's Career: An Annotated Bibliography* by Keith R. Moul, 1977.

Critical Studies: *Roethke* by Ralph J. Mills, Jr., 1963; *Roethke: Essays on the Poetry* by Arnold S. Stein, 1965; *Roethke: An Introduction to the Poetry* by Karl Malkoff, 1966; *The Glass House: The Life of Roethke* by Allan Seager, 1968; *Profile of Roethke* edited by William Heyen, 1971; *The Wild Prayer of Longing: Poetry and the Sacred* by Nathan A. Scott, 1971; *A Concordance to the Poems of Roethke* by Gary Lane, 1972; *Roethke's Dynamic Vision* by Richard Allen Blessing, 1974; *Roethke: The Garden Master* by Rosemary Sullivan, 1975; *The Echoing Wood of Roethke* by Jenijoy La Belle, 1976; *The Edge Is What I Have: Roethke and After* by Harry Williams, 1976; *Roethke: An American Romantic* by Jay Parini, 1979; *Roethke: Poetry of the Earth, Poet of the Spirit* by Lynn Ross-Bryant, 1981; *Roethke* by George Wolff, 1981; *Roethke: The Poetics of Wonder* by Norman Chaney, 1982; *Roethke: The Journey from I to Otherwise* by Neal Bowers, 1983; *Roethke's Meditative Sequences: Contemplation and the Creative Process* by Ann T. Foster, 1985.

* * *

Theodore Roethke's posthumous collection, *The Far Field*, is a résumé and retrospect of a lifetime's preoccupations, acknowledging its debt to those poets who have confronted the mystery of personal extinction—the later Eliot and Yeats and that "Whitman, maker of catalogues" whose "terrible hunger for objects" is repeated in these writings of a man who has "moved closer to death, lived with death." Roethke always felt "the separateness of all things," the fragility of being. In "The Dream" he had written "Love is not love until love's vulnerable"; "The Abyss" adds a new, desperate urgency to the theme, poised on a dark stair that "goes nowhere," knowing the abyss is "right where you are— / A step down the stair." Yet if this last volume broods over childhood initiations into mortality, it also celebrates the spontaneous impulse towards life, light, growth in which he shares:

> Many arrivals make us live: the tree becoming
> Green, a bird tipping the topmost bough,
> A seed pushing itself beyond itself. . . .
>
> What does what it should do needs nothing more.
> The body moves, though slowly, towards desire.
> We come to something without knowing why.

Summoned once more to the field's end, in old age Roethke returned to "the first heaven of knowing," that second-childhood of radical innocence which has always been the American visionary's home. If "Old men should be explorers," he replies to the Eliot of *Four Quartets*, "I'll be an Indian. / Iroquois," thus unashamedly assuming the role of the noble savage in retreat, whose "journey into the interior," into the heart of the continent, is also a "long journey out of the self," into the unconscious and preconscious, the elemental life of the planet.

There is a paradoxical resolution of stasis and motion throughout Roethke's work. "The Sententious Man" claims to "know the motion of the deepest stone"; in "The Far Field," imagery of dwindling, darkening, and decline shifts into sudden surges and spurts of life, as not only air, fire, and water but even earth take on the fluidity which leaves no ground secure: "the shale slides dangerously," dust blows, rubble falls, the arroyo cracks, the swamp is "alive with quicksand." Amid this movement the self floats unperturbed: "I rise and fall in the slow sea of a grassy plain" (the theological punning here recurs throughout his verse); "And all flows past. . . . I am not moving but they are," for the soul, preparing itself for death, has finally found that longed-for "imperishable quiet at the heart of form." Throughout his verse, the *field* is a complex metaphor: it is the green field of nature, the field of perception, and, at their intersection, a heraldic field in which matter blazons forth spirit, where "All finite things reveal infinitude," disclosing, in the words of one of his earliest poems, "skies of azure / The pagentry of wings the eyes' right treasure."

Movement from closure to openness, finitude to immensity, has been the characteristic rhythm of all Roethke's poetry. The title poem of *Open House* proclaims this:

> My secrets cry aloud. . . .
> My heart keeps open house,
> My doors are widely swung. . . .
> I'm naked to the bone
> With nakedness my shield.
> Myself is what I wear.

The Lost Son pokes around in origins, under stones, in drains and subsoil, to find the answer to his most basic question: "Where do the roots go?" Roethke felt himself at home amidst the abundant verminous life of a vegetable nature which (as in "Cuttings, *later*") strains like a saint to rise anew in "This urge, wrestle, resurrection of dry sticks"—a world to which he was introduced in his florist father's greenhouses, where he learnt to "study the lives on a leaf: the little / Sleepers, numb nudgers"; and not only to study, but to find in them, as in the "Shoots [which] dangled and drooped, / Lolling obscenely" in "Root Cellar," an imagery of his own instinctual life. He was impressed by the stubborn persistence of this residual realm: "Nothing would give up life: / Even the dirt kept breathing a small breath."

His poems are rites of passage, exits and entrances where "the body, delighting in thresholds, / Rocks in and out of itself." *Praise to the End!* employs the bouncy rhythms and inconsequential surrealism of nursery rhyme and baby talk, used to such effect in his poems for children, to enact the birth or rebirth of the scattered psyche (Roethke suffered from periodic mental illness) out of a tangle of instinctual impulses—eating, touching, snuffling, sucking, licking—in all of which identity is constituted as *lack* ("I Need, I Need"), a fall from innocence into disenchantment which brings us to our proper selfhood, aware of time and consequence, and able to announce "I'm somebody else now." In "Give Way, Ye Gates," one line of six verbs charts the whole pilgrimage through need, mutuality, and loss into separated being: "Touch and arouse. Suck and sob. Curse and mourn." The technique of this volume is a riddling, exclamatory questioning, like that of an insistent child who neither expects nor receives an answer, wanting only confirmation of its own puzzling existence. Yet this catechism of the "happy asker" reveals a world of correspondences where everything *is* an answer to everything else, and the creatures sing their own richness and diversity: "A house for wisdom. A field for revelation. / Speak to the stones and the stars answer."

In his love poems this most physical of poets assumes a metaphysical lightness and delicacy, a clarity of syntax and almost allegoric translucence of imagery which recall Renaissance neo-platonism and the courtly love of the troubadours. His women (even the "woman lovely in her bones") are the Beatrices of a rarefied sensuality, "know[ing] the speech of light" and "cry[ing] out loud the soul's own secret joy"; but even here Roethke's playfulness is preserved in sudden unexpected carnalities of language ("pure as a bride . . . / And breathing hard, as that man rode / Between those lovely tits"). "The Renewal" shows love to be the force that moves the stars, reducing to a oneness knowing and motion, the dualities of his universe, just as "Words for the Wind," which provided the title for his collected verse, sees it as both the journey and the destination of the soul:

> I cherish what I have
> Had of the temporal:
>
> I am no longer young
> But the wind and waters are;
> What falls away will fall;
> All things bring me to love.

—Stan Smith

RØLVAAG, O(le) E(dvart). Born on Dönna Island, Helgeland, Norway, 22 April 1876; emigrated to the U.S., 1896; became citizen, 1908. Educated at Dönna schools to age 14; Augustana College, Canton, South Dakota, 1899–1901; St. Olaf College, Northfield, Minnesota, 1901–05, B.A. 1905, M.A. 1910; University of Oslo, 1905–06. Married Jennie Marie Berdahl in 1908; three sons and one daughter. Fisherman in Norway, 1891–95; worked on his uncle's farm in South Dakota, 1896–99; Professor of Norwegian Language and Literature, 1906–31, and Head of the Norwegian Department, 1916–31, St. Olaf College. Secretary, Norwegian-American Historical Association, 1925–31. Honorary degree: University of Wisconsin, Madison, 1929. Knight of the Order of St. Olaf, Norway, 1926. *Died 5 November 1931.*

PUBLICATIONS

Fiction

Amerika-breve (Letters from America). 1912; translated by Ella Tweet and Solveig Zempel, as *The Third Life of Per Smevik*, 1971.

Paa Glemte Veie (On Forgotten Paths). 1914.

To Tullinger: Et Billede fra Idag (Two Fools: A Picture of Our Time). 1920; revised edition, translated by Sivert Erdahl and Rølvaag, as *Pure Gold*, 1930.

Laengselens Baat. 1921; translated by Nora O. Solum, as *The Boat of Longing*, 1933.

Giants in the Earth, translated by Lincoln Colcord and Rølvaag. 1927.

- *I de Dage: Fortaelling om Norske Nykommere i Amerika* (In Those Days: A Story of Norwegian Pioneering in America). 1924.
- *Ricket Grundlaegges* (The Founding of the Kingdom). 1925.

Peder Seier. 1928; translated by Rølvaag and Nora O. Solum, as *Peder Victorious*, 1929.

Den Signede Dag (The Blessed Day). 1931; translated by Trygve M. Ager, as *Their Fathers' God*, 1931.

Other

Ordforklaring til Nordahl Rolfsens Laesebok for Folkeskolen II. 1909.
Haandbok i Norsk Retskrivning og uttale til Skolebruk og Selvstudium, with P.J. Eikeland. 1916.
Norsk Laesebok, with P.J. Eikeland. 3 vols., 1919–25.
Omkring Faedrearven (essays). 1922.

Editor, *Deklamationsboken*. 1918.

*

Critical Studies: *Rølvaag: A Biography* by Theodore Jorgenson and Nora O. Solum, 1939; *Rølvaag: His Life and Art* by Paul Reigstad, 1972.

* * *

O.E. Rølvaag's great achievement is *Giants in the Earth*, first published in Norway in 1924 and 1925, then translated into English by Rølvaag and Lincoln Colcord in 1927. The result is remarkable: to a bi-lingual reader the characters seem to be thinking and speaking in Norwegian patterns and cadence, even though the words are English and few Norwegian expressions are left untranslated. By common agreement, *Giants in the Earth* is America's best immigrant story, its great pioneering novel, and a towering documentary of the middle west.

The events Rølvaag describes in *Giants in the Earth* occurred 25 years before he arrived in America. But the setting is the South Dakota he came to in 1896 at the age of twenty, the characters his own kind of Norwegian immigrants, and the events a composite of many accounts he had heard from Dakota pioneers. Writing the book in the 1920's, Rølvaag relied especially on the memory of his father-in-law, Andrew Berdahl. Although the prairie he describes is a formidable adversary for his pioneers, Rølvaag's characters are even more remarkable, especially the hard-driving, inventive, and irrepressible Per Hansa: he is the very type of the ideal American pioneer, yet also very Norwegian. An even more moving character is Per's wife, Berit, who is neurotic, backward-looking, and fanatically religious. Rølvaag's pioneer has a dual struggle: against the unbroken prairie and a wife who thinks she has sinned unforgivably in disobeying her parents, in marrying Per Hansa, and in leaving Norway.

Per Hansa's story is heroic and tragic, rare qualities in 20th century fiction. Berit lives on through the two sequels Rølvaag wrote—*Peder Victorious* and *Their Fathers' God*—and achieves a greatness of her own. The struggle to retain her Norwegian heritage in the new American settlements was a cause Rølvaag supported whole-heartedly. But the essential themes of the two later novels—assimilation and cultural clashes—lack the power and drama of the pioneering struggle. Of more interest is *Pure Gold*, a reworking of Rølvaag's 1920 novel *To Tullinger* (Two Fools): it is the stark tale of a pioneering couple who become monsters of greed. Rølvaag's own favorite was *Laengselens Baat*, which appeared in English translation as *The Boat of Longing* after his death. The strong note of pathos (perhaps pessimism) in this novel has two sources: Nils, a sensitive, artistic, young immigrant, encounters a materialistic America; and his Norwegian parents wait in vain for letters from their son.

Even though the greatness of *Giants in the Earth* was recognized at once, scholars and critics have been uneasy about assigning Ole Rølvaag a place in American literature: he wrote in Norwegian, not English. His psychological realism might owe something to Sherwood Anderson, but a greater influence stemmed from Knut Hamsun and Arne Garborg. As his correspondence reveals, Rølvaag wrote as fluently in English as in Norwegian. Working with translators in turning his novels into English, he weighed and considered each word and phrase. But Rølvaag taught Norwegian language and literature during most of his life in America. Despite Conrad's achievement in the English novel, Rølvaag thought that giving up his native language would require "a remaking of soul." Such a "spiritual readjustment" he would not undertake.

—Clarence A. Glasrud

ROTH, Henry. Born in Tysmenica, Austria-Hungary, 8 February 1906; brought to New York City, 1908. Educated at DeWitt Clinton High School, New York, graduated 1924; City College, New York, 1924–28, B.S. 1928. Married Muriel Parker in 1939; two sons. Worked for the Works Progress Administration (WPA), 1939; teacher, Roosevelt High School, New York, 1939–41; precision metal grinder in New York, Providence, Rhode Island, and Boston, 1941–46; teacher in Montville, Maine, 1947–48; attendant, Augusta State Hospital, Maine, 1949–53; waterfowl farmer, 1953–62; private tutor, 1956–65. Recipient: American Academy grant, 1965; City College of New York Townsend Harris Medal, 1965; University of New Mexico D.H. Lawrence Fellowship, 1968. Has lived in Albuquerque, New Mexico, since 1968.

PUBLICATIONS

Fiction

Call It Sleep. 1934.

Other

Nature's First Green (memoir). 1979.

*

Critical Studies: *World of Our Fathers* by Irving Howe, 1976, as *The Immigrant Jews of New York 1881 to the Present*, 1976; *Roth* by Bonnie Lyons, 1977.

* * *

The author of a single novel of intense power, Henry Roth has a minor but vital position in 20th-century American writing. *Call It Sleep*, published in 1934 but neglected until reprinted in 1960, concentrates immigrant life, childhood experience, and Freudian theory in a striking, stream-of-consciousness narrative. Although Roth has never published another novel—some short stories have appeared in periodicals—*Call It Sleep* remains an important work for its blending of Jewish myth, psychological symbol, and urban reality. A writer of the depression and part of a group to emerge in the 1930's in New York and Chicago (Michael Gold, Daniel Fuchs, Meyer Levin), Roth nonetheless remains unique in his creation of a young hero caught between the foulness of life and the purity of dreams.

Call It Sleep appeared in the same year as the first American edition of *Ulysses*, and Roth, who was influenced by Joyce, employed the techniques of interior monologue, free association, and stylistic experimentation. Developing the myths of redemption and rebirth, Roth enlarged his novel from an autobiographical account of Jewish immigrants in Brooklyn and the Lower East Side to a dramatic exploration of childhood, family conflict, and Oedipal aggression. Four symbols dominate the novel: a cellar connoting dark, sexual fears, a picture with overtones of illicit sex, a piece of coal that is the key to flaming redemption and a trolley rail that is the means to a blinding, almost mystical power.

Language in the novel becomes a fascinating interweaving of English narrative, Yiddish speech, and idioms of the street. Emulating the tale of Isaiah and the burning coal of redemption, the young hero, David Schearl, in the climactic scene of the book virtually kills himself by forcing a milk ladle into the third rail of a trolley track. This act is the symbolic culmination of the hero's desperate effort to redeem himself and his world. His act of purification achieves his need for transcending the sordidness of everyday life—the family quarrels, beatings by his father, poverty of his neighborhood, mistreatment of his mother—that has plagued him.

Call It Sleep, for all its accuracy in portraying immigrant life and economic injustice, cannot be labeled a proletarian or radical novel. It is, rather, a work of vivid, imaginative power that surpasses the stereotypes of such fiction. But why has Roth written no other major work? He explains this failure as not having to mature: "In *Call It Sleep* I stuck with the child, so I didn't have to mature. . . . I think I just failed at maturity, at adulthood." Shunning the life of a writer, Roth has been a laborer, teacher, psychiatric attendant, and waterfowl farmer. But his distaste for literary life and small output does not detract from the value of his novel, which remains one of the most affecting works of American prose fiction.

—I.B. Nadel

ROTH, Philip (Milton). Born in Newark, New Jersey, 19 March 1933. Educated at Weequahic High School, New Jersey, 1946–50; Newark College, Rutgers University, 1950–51; Bucknell University, Lewisburg, Pennsylvania, 1951–54, A.B. 1954 (Phi Beta Kappa); University of Chicago, 1954–55, M.A. 1955. Served in the U.S. Army, 1955–56. Married Margaret Martinson in 1959 (separated, 1962; died, 1968). Instructor in English, University of Chicago, 1956–58; Visiting Writer, University of Iowa, Iowa City, 1960–62; Writer-in-Residence, Princeton University, New Jersey, 1962–64; Visiting Writer, State University of New York, Stony Brook, 1966, 1967, and University of Pennsylvania, Philadelphia, 1967–80. General editor, Writers from the Other Europe series, Penguin, publishers, London, 1975–80. Member of the Corporation of Yaddo, Saratoga Springs, New York. Recipient: Guggenheim fellowship, 1959; National Book Award, 1960; Daroff Award, 1960; American Academy grant, 1960; O. Henry Award, 1960; Ford foundation grant, for drama, 1965; Rockefeller fellowship, 1966. Member, American Academy, 1970.

PUBLICATIONS

Fiction

Goodbye, Columbus, and Five Short Stories. 1959.
Letting Go. 1962.
When She Was Good. 1967.
Portnoy's Complaint. 1969.
Our Gang (Starring Tricky and His Friends). 1971.
The Breast. 1972; revised edition in *A Roth Reader*, 1980.
The Great American Novel. 1973.
My Life as a Man. 1974.
The Professor of Desire. 1977.
Zuckerman Bound (includes *The Prague Orgy*). 1985.
  The Ghost Writer. 1979.
  Zuckerman Unbound. 1981.
  The Anatomy Lesson. 1983.
Novotny's Pain (story). 1980.
The Prague Orgy. 1985.
The Counterlife. 1987.

Play

Television Play: *The Ghost Writer*, with Tristram Powell, from the novel by Roth, 1983.

Other

Reading Myself and Others. 1975.
A Roth Reader. 1980.

*

Bibliography: *Roth: A Bibliography* by Bernard F. Rodgers, Jr., 1974; revised edition, 1984.

Critical Studies: *Bernard Malamud and Roth: A Critical Essay* by Glenn Meeter, 1968; *The Fiction of Roth* by John N. McDaniel, 1974; *The Comedy That "Hoits": An Essay on the Fiction of Roth* by Sanford Pinsker, 1975, and *Critical Essays on Roth* edited by Pinsker, 1982; *Roth* by Bernard F. Rodgers, Jr., 1978; *Roth* by Judith Paterson Jones and Guinevera A. Nance, 1981; *Roth* by Hermione Lee, 1982.

* * *

"Sheer Playfulness and Deadly Seriousness are my closest friends," Philip Roth has remarked in interview; "I am also on friendly terms with Deadly Playfulness, Serious Playfulness, Serious Seriousness, and Sheer Sheerness. From the last, however, I get nothing; he just wrings my heart and leaves me speechless." Roth's early work explored with a tense and exasperated earnestness "the whole range of human connections . . . between clannish solidarity . . . and exclusion or rejection," the struggle of what he has called "the determined self" (in a double sense) against its contingent identity and environment. *When She Was Good* surprised his critics by delineating the self-deception and hypocrisy of small-town Gentile America with the same acid sharpness he brought to the anxieties, pieties, and suppressed hysteria of middle-class and metropolitan Jewry in *Goodbye, Columbus* and *Letting Go*. Roth's characters are usually painfully alert to the insistent and insidious dialogue of conscience with the unconscious: beneath the innocent and upright text of conversation and event lurks a subtext of amoral impulsions, disclosed through Freudian slips and misprisions, by displacement, gesture, and "unintended" innuendo. With *Portnoy's Complaint* the libido came into its own, redefining the ironic, self-conscious wit which enlivened the earlier works as the evasive strategy of "people [who] wear the old unconscious on their *sleeves*." Portnoy complains that he is "the son in the Jewish joke—*only it ain't no joke!*", and the book mischievously ends with a "punch line" ("So. Now vee may perhaps to begin. Yes?") which brackets the whole confessional text as a pre-analysis warm-up on Dr. Spielvogel's couch. (This same psychoanalyst returns in *My Life as a Man* as representative of a grey, reassuring normalcy which frames the novelist-hero's outrageously self-dramatizing "life.")

Portnoy's compulsive onanism, fêted with Rabelaisian panache, provides a constant analogy for the art of fiction itself (a "complaint" is both physical disorder and literary device). Story-telling is also an autotelic act, a self-sufficient and finally inconsequential spilling of the beans; and the theme is extended in *The Breast*, where Kepesh wakes to find himself translated into the literary tradition he has been teaching, metamorphosed into a huge, almost self-enclosed mammary gland—"Beyond sublimation. I made the word flesh. I have outKafkaed Kafka." *The Great American Novel* (its very title self-reflexive) is a tissue of parody and pastiche which suggests that baseball is not only *a* theme but *the* supreme fiction of American culture (as Roth remarked in an essay, "The Literature of My Boyhood"). *My Life as a Man* has as its main text the "True Story" of the novelist Peter Tarnopol, preceded by two "Useful Fictions" which are his short-story variations on the crisis of marital breakdown and blocked creativity which dominates his in-any-case fictitious "Life." Roth plays further games with the reader, alluding to previous writings of Tarnopol's that inevitably and teasingly recall his own earlier work. But if here narcissism in "life" (i.e., "content") becomes reflected in the auto-referentiality of the "text" (i.e., "form"), the sheer exuberance of Roth's invention makes it clear that he is not fixated in the dead-end "Sheer Sheerness" of his fictive analogue. If Tarnopol is only tangentially affected by the great historic events of his era, Roth has written of them at length in *Our Gang* (settling accounts in advance with the Nixon mafia) and in the essays collected as *Reading Myself and Others*.

Kepesh, apparently normal, returns in *The Professor of Desire* (though we don't know whether this American abroad has escaped the dilemma of *The Breast*, has yet to face it, or exists in some parallel and unconnected life). Here too he perpetually balances anxious libido and angst-ridden literature, in a final grotesque dream sequence, set in the Prague of police repression and silenced writers, visiting Kafka's whore, who offers to show him her withered cunt in the interests of art (and money). The paralleling of textuality and sexuality from now on takes a darker turn, and Kafka is the lugubrious master of the later works.

In the 1973 essay "Looking at Kafka" Roth imagined being taught Hebrew as a boy by a Kafka who had escaped death and persecution in America. A similar fantasy animates *The Ghost Writer*. It is cast as the reminiscence, twenty years on, by the now successful Nathan Zuckerman, of a one-night visit to the aging novelist E.I. Lonoff, ensconced in the snow-bound Berkshires with a mysterious young woman. Nathan fantasizes that she is really Anne Frank, the diarist of Nazi persecution, accidentally surviving the death camps to find a new life and father-figure in America. Contrasted with her frank and artless narratives, Zuckerman's later artful novel *Carnovsky* (clearly a literary double of Roth's *Portnoy*), seems almost to himself the anti-semitic tract it was accused of being by a scandalised Jewish middle class, who saw him doing the dirt on 4000 years of respectable suffering. *Zuckerman Unbound*, thirteen years on from the fictional time of *The Ghost Writer*, carries on this guilt-ridden post-mortem. Everywhere Zuckerman is mistaken for his fictional alter-ego Carnovsky, lionised, reviled, and accosted in the streets, a prisoner of his own success. Even his own father's last word from his death-bed is "bastard." *The Anatomy Lesson* extends these tribulations. Here, his mother too is "gone," never recovering from the shock of his book, dying from a brain tumour which, when she is asked her name, causes her to write down the word "holocaust." Though she returns to haunt him not out of vengeance but only to check that he hasn't lost weight, a Jewish mother even in death, she perplexes Zuckerman with this inscription, from someone who only ever wrote down recipes and knitting patterns. As he says ambiguously of word or tumour: "it must have been there all the time without their even knowing." He broods about escaping "suffering that isn't semi-comical, the world of massive historical pain" symbolised by the Warsaw Ghetto.

Instead, he is afflicted by "this pain in the neck" that makes writing almost impossible and love-making complicated, generating novel (and novelish) forms of intercourse. The "anatomy lesson" itself is both Rembrandt's coldly clinical painting of a dissection and the chronic back pain that "teaches us who is boss" (just as Portnoy's sexual fixation had). Deciding to free himself from his "graphomania" he seeks "Everything the word's in place of. The lowest of genres—life itself" by trying to redeploy as an obstetrician: "a new perspective on an old obsession . . . he owed it to women." And he finds his guilt assuaged by assuming the persona of a professional pornographer in casual conversations with strangers; for once he professes his obsession as a crusading (and profitable) all-American business enterprise, he is accepted as a respectable citizen. His ultimate anatomy lesson is, however, the living death's head of an old woman who has for four years treated herself for face cancer, her jaw half eaten away and the bone exposed. The book's last sentence leaves him about to begin his initiation, its macabre pun on "corpus" as both book and body defining Roth's perennial dilemma: "as though he still believed that he could unchain himself from a future as a man apart and escape the corpus that was his."

For Roth the introversions of contemporary fiction reflect a wider, social dilemma: "Defying a multitude of bizarre projections, or submitting to them," he has said, "would seem to me at the heart of everyday living in America." Adapting Philip Rahv's division of American writers into "redskins" and "palefaces"—the one rumbustious and anarchic, the other stiff and priggish—he has proposed his own third category, a subversive synthesis of the two, the "redface." Roth's is the poetry of embarrassment and exposure; by making *unease* both theme and narrative technique, he has fused play and seriousness into a style inimitably his own, which is not easily rendered "speechless."

—Stan Smith

ROWLANDSON, Mary (White). Born, probably in England, c. 1637; moved with her family to Lancaster, Massachusetts. Married 1) Joseph Rowlandson c. 1656 (died, 1678), three daughters and one son; 2) Samuel Talcott in 1679. Captured (with three of her children, one of whom died) in raid on Lancaster by Wampanoag Indians during King Philip's War, 1676: held for 11 weeks, then ransomed. Lived in Boston, 1676, and Wethersfield, Connecticut, after 1677. *Died 5 January 1711.*

PUBLICATIONS

Prose

The Soveraignty and Goodness of God, Together with the Faithfulness of His Promises Displayed; Being a Narrative of the Captivity and Restauration of Mrs. Mary Rowlandson. 1682; in *Narratives of the Indian Wars 1675–1699*, edited by Charles Henry Lincoln, 1913.

*

Critical Studies: *Flintlock and Tomahawk: New England in King Philip's War* by Douglas Edward Leach, 1958; *Regeneration Through Violence: The Mythology of the American Frontier 1600–1860* by Richard Slotkin, 1973; *The Indian Captivity Narrative: An American Genre* by Richard VanDerBeets, 1984; "New Light on Rowlandson" by David L. Greene, in *Early American Literature*, 1985.

* * *

Although she wrote only one book—*The Soveraignty and Goodness of God, Together with the Faithfulness of His Promises Displayed; Being a Narrative of the Captivity and Restauration of Mrs. Mary Rowlandson*—Mary Rowlandson is nonetheless remembered as one of the major writers of early America and one of only four women (the other three being Anne Bradstreet, Phillis Wheatley, and Sarah Kemble Knight) from the period to achieve prominence for their writings.

As the subtitle of her narrative indicates, *The Soveraignty and Goodness of God* is an account of its author's captivity among the Indians of New England at the time of King Philip's War (1675–78). Living with her family in the frontier outpost of Lancaster, Massachusetts, Rowlandson, along with her three children, was captured by a confederacy of Indians during a raid on her town in February 1676. Her youngest child, a girl of six, died shortly thereafter of wounds received during the attack. Although she had herself been wounded, Rowlandson remained with the Indians for nearly twelve weeks. Approximately thirty years old at the time of her capture, she was forced to march more than 150 miles in frigid weather and snow, and she was made to endure the privations of an Indian lifestyle during wartime.

On the day of the attack, Rowlandson's husband, a Harvard-educated Congregationalist minister, had been in Boston seeking military assistance for Lancaster. Eventually, he and the citizens of Massachusetts negotiated with Indian leaders for the release of his wife in early May 1676. Their remaining two children—a fourteen-year-old son, named Joseph after his father, and an eleven-year-old daughter, named Mary after her mother—were released within the next few weeks. While it was once thought that Rowlandson had died within a few years of her release, it is now known that after the death of her husband in 1678 she married Captain Samuel Talcott, a leading citizen of Wethersfield, Connecticut, where she resided in prosperity until her death in 1711, more than thirty years later than had once been assumed.

Published in 1682, *The Soveraignty and Goodness of God* immediately became what has been termed America's first bestseller. In the first year of its publication alone, it went through four editions, including one published in England, and since then it has been reprinted more than forty times. Only four pages from the first edition survive because, as has been suggested, it was probably "read to pieces." The lasting popularity of the narrative is easy to understand. Written in a plain but vigorous style, it is an outstanding example of adventure writing at its best. During colonial times, when fear of Indian captivity was an imminent frontier reality, Rowlandson's captivity appealed to the emotions of generations of Americans interested in Indians and what Washington Irving later called "border romance." In more modern times, the vivid realism of Rowlandson's prose, the complexity of her psychology, and the heroism of her ordeal have kept her narrative alive.

In addition to the glimpse that it provides into the lifestyle of the Indians of New England before the wholesale invasion of their culture by the European colonists, Rowlandson's narrative provides insight into the workings of the Puritan American imagination, particularly with regards to the Indian, the wilderness, and the meaning of personal and cultural affliction. Interpreted within a typological context, the Indians are depicted as "murtherous wretches," "Barbarous Creatures," "merciless Enemies," and "hell-hounds," and the wilderness is described as "a lively resemblance of hell." Accordingly, Rowlandson's captivity is seen as a combination punishment and trial at the hands of God's enemies, whom he ultimately uses to instruct his servant and her contemporaries about the mysterious workings of providence.

Artfully written, *The Soveraignty and Goodness of God* is structured according to a series of what Rowlandson terms "Removes." Literally, these "removes" correspond to her physical removal, at the hands of the Indians, away from British civilization and the securities of culture and home. Psychologically and metaphorically, they create an aesthetic perspective not unlike the movement through hell in Dante's *Divine Comedy*, to which Rowlandson's narrative has been compared. Other literary analogues include John Bunyan's *Pilgrim's Progress* and the sermons, histories, and spiritual autobiographies of the day. While Rowlandson was probably not a highly educated woman, she possessed an instinctive grasp of literary structure and language, and she had no doubt read and internalized many of the staples of 17th-century Puritan literature.

Coming as it did at the beginning of a tradition of captivity stories that led in the 19th century to the novels of James Fenimore Cooper, William Gilmore Simms, Robert Montgomery Bird, and Mark Twain, *The Soveraignty and Goodness of God* is nonetheless considered the finest example of the form before it became appropriated by belletristic writers, and it should certainly be read by anyone interested in the literature and culture of early America.

—James A. Levernier

ROWSON, Susanna (née Haswell). Born in Portsmouth, Hampshire, England, c. 1762; taken to Massachusetts, where her father, a naval officer, was stationed, c. 1767; deported with her Loyalist father to England, 1778. Educated privately. Married William Rowson in 1786. Governess to children of Duchess of Devonshire, 1780's; actress, appearing with her husband, in Edinburgh, 1792-93; acted and wrote for New Theatre Company of Philadelphia, in Philadelphia, Baltimore, and Annapolis, Maryland, 1793-96, and Federal Street Theatre Company, Boston, 1796-97; founder and teacher, Young Girls' Academy, Boston, 1797-1822; editor, Boston *Weekly Magazine*, 1802-05. President, Boston Fatherless and Widows Association. *Died 2 March 1824.*

PUBLICATIONS

Fiction

Victoria. 1786.
The Inquisitor; or, Invisible Rambler. 1788.
The Test of Honour. 1789.
Charlotte: A Tale of Truth. 1791; as *Charlotte Temple*, 1794; edited by Clara M. and Rudolf Kirk, 1964; edited by William S. Kable, in *Three Early American Novels*, 1970.
Mentoria; or, The Young Lady's Friend. 1791.
The Fille de Chambre. 1792; as *Rebecca*, 1814.
Trials of the Human Heart. 1795.
Reuben and Rachel; or, Tales of Old Times. 1798.
Sarah; or, The Exemplary Wife. 1813.
Charlotte's Daughter; or, The Three Orphans. 1828; as *Lucy Temple: One of the Three Orphans*, 1842(?).

Plays

Slaves in Algiers; or, A Struggle for Freedom, music by Alexander Reinagle. 1794.
The Female Patriot; or, Nature's Rights, from the play *The Bondman* by Philip Massinger (produced 1795).
The Volunteers: A Musical Entertainment, music by Alexander Reinagle (produced 1795).
Americans in England; or, Lessons for Daughters (produced 1797). 1796; as *The Columbian Daughter; or, Americans in England* (produced 1800), 1800.
The American Tar (produced 1796).
Hearts of Oak, from the work by John Till Allingham (produced 1810-11?).

Verse

A Trip to Parnassus; or, The Judgment of Apollo on Dramatic Authors and Performers. 1788.
Poems on Various Subjects. 1789.
The Standard of Liberty: A Poetical Address. 1795.
Miscellaneous Poems. 1804.

Other

An Abridgement of Universal Geography, Together with Sketches of History. 1806.
A Spelling Dictionary. 1807.
A Present for Young Ladies (miscellany). 1811.
Youth's First Step in Geography. 1818.
Biblical Dialogues Between a Father and His Family. 2 vols., 1822.
Exercises in History, Chronology, and Biography, in Question and Answer. 1822.

*

Bibliography: *Rowson, The Author of Charlotte Temple: A Bibliographical Study* by R.W.G. Vail, 1933; in *Bibliography of American Literature* by Jacob Blanck, edited by Virginia L. Smyers and Michael Winship, 1983.

Critical Studies: *Rowson, America's First Best-Selling Novelist* by Ellen B. Brandt, 1975; *In Defense of Women: Rowson* by Dorothy Weil, 1976.

* * *

Because of the popularity, variety, and number of Susanna Rowson's books, she may properly be considered the foremost woman of letters of her generation in the United States. The phenomenal success on both sides of the Atlantic of her novel *Charlotte Temple* has tended to obscure her other considerable accomplishments, but she also wrote other novels and a large number of plays, poetry, textbooks, and miscellanies which defy classification. Her literary career is even more remarkable in light of her prominence in her other occupations, those of actress and educator. She has the distinction of being not only one of America's first professional women but also one of the first advocates of women's rights in the United States.

Charlotte: A Tale of Truth has gone through over 200 editions since it was first published in 1791 and was, according to R.W.G. Vail, "the most popular of all early American novels." While detractors have dismissed it as being sentimental and formulaic, supporters have accounted for its popularity by insisting on its forthright realism within the sentimental convention. Rowson herself claimed that the story of seduction and betrayal is an actual one, and in the early 1800's the gravestone of the purported model, Charlotte Stanley, was changed to "Charlotte Temple." It still may be seen in Trinity Churchyard in New York City. No other novel by Rowson approaches the popularity of this bestseller, but others were highly regarded, notably *The Fille de Chambre* and *Reuben and Rachel*.

One of her few extant plays, *Slaves in Algiers* is the first successfully produced play by a woman in America. A musical comedy, written in collaboration with Alexander Reinagle, it is of topical interest in that it was a protest against the capture of American ships off the Barbary coast from 1785 to 1794. The play is notable for its fervent nationalism and the insistence upon the equality of women in the new nation. Although it was well-received by playgoers, William Cobbett roundly attacked it for its feminist sentiments.

Rowson's poems and songs were not critically well-received, and today they seem florid and derivative. Nevertheless many of them were immensely popular, especially "America, Commerce, and Freedom." Her textbooks and miscellanies are of only historical interest today. In spite of her significant contributions to American letters, little critical attention was paid her until the final quarter of the 20th century, nearly 200 years after her career began. This recent attention is testimony to the enduring quality of her work.

—Nancy Carol Joyner

RUKEYSER, Muriel. Born in New York City, 15 December 1913. Educated at Fieldston School, New York, 1919–30; Vassar College, Poughkeepsie, New York; Columbia University, New York, 1930–32. Had one son. Vice-President, House of Photography, New York, 1946–60; teacher at Sarah Lawrence College, Bronxville, New York, 1946, 1956–57. Member, Board of Directors, Teachers–Writers Collaborative, New York, from 1967; President PEN American Center, 1975–76. Recipient: Harriet Monroe Award, 1941; American Academy award, 1942; Guggenheim fellowship, 1943; American Council of Learned Societies fellowship, 1963; Swedish Academy translation award, 1967; Copernicus Award, 1977; Shelley Memorial Award, 1977. D.Litt.: Rutgers University, New Brunswick, New Jersey, 1961. Member, American Academy. *Died 12 February 1980.*

PUBLICATIONS

Verse

Theory of Flight. 1935.
Mediterranean. 1937(?).
U.S. 1. 1938.
A Turning Wind. 1939.
The Soul and Body of John Brown. 1940.
Wake Island. 1942.
Beast in View. 1944.
The Children's Orchard. 1947.
The Green Wave. 1948.
Orpheus. 1949.
Elegies. 1949.
Selected Poems. 1951.
Body of Waking. 1958.
Waterlily Fire: Poems 1932–62. 1962.
The Outer Banks. 1967.
The Speed of Darkness. 1968.
29 Poems. 1972.
Breaking Open. 1973.
The Gates. 1976.
The Collected Poems. 1978.

Plays

The Middle of the Air (produced 1945).
The Colors of the Day (produced 1961).
Houdini (produced 1973).

Fiction

Orgy. 1965.

Other (for children)

Come Back Paul. 1955.
I Go Out. 1961.
Bubbles. 1967.
Mazes. 1970.
More Night. 1981.

Other

Willard Gibbs (biography). 1942.
The Life of Poetry. 1949.
One Life (biography of Wendell Wilkie). 1957.
Poetry and Unverifiable Fact: The Clark Lectures. 1968.
The Traces of Thomas Hariot. 1971.

Translator, with others, *Selected Poems of Octavio Paz*. 1963; revised edition, 1973.
Translator, *Sun Stone*, by Octavio Paz. 1963.
Translator, with Leif Sjöberg, *Selected Poems of Gunnar Ekelöf*. 1967.
Translator, *Three Poems by Gunnar Ekelöf*. 1967.
Translator, with others, *Early Poems 1935–1955*, by Octavio Paz. 1973.

*

Critical Study: *The Poetic Vision of Rukeyser* by Louise Kertesz, 1980.

* *

Much has been said about the feminine voice in poetry, usually by critics. No one seems to know exactly what the "true" feminine voice is, except that somewhere between the despair and the joy of woman's second-class existence, a kind of experience is finally being written. Sylvia Plath wrote from this sensibility and a number of more recent women poets have missed the joy expressed between the lines, where Plath had made words that work together. The assumption that despair should somehow outweigh joy in serious poetry by women results from the Dickinson (and now, Plath) tradition.

Reading the work of Muriel Rukeyser, one quickly learns that feminism is not so easily defined. Once again, the near-answer is revealed for what it is, and we are thrown back to the poem itself. Rukeyser's work can be despairing, but her responses have larger potential. Even in moments of sad recollection, as in "Effort at Speech Between Two People," Rukeyser's voice is not entirely despondent:

> When I was three, a little child read a story about a rabbit
> who died, in the story, and I crawled under a chair :
> a pink rabbit : it was my birthday, and a candle
> burnt a sore spot on my finger, and I was told to be happy.

Here, Rukeyser has successfully combined the elements of mature narrative with a verbal sense of what it was like to live through that third birthday. The poem is not cute, in any of its aspects, and in spite of succeeding lines ("I am unhappy. I am lonely. Speak to me.") never indulges in outright despondency. The hope for communication initially caused the poem and it survives, echoed by lively images, and imbues the poem ultimately with a sense of optimism.

Rukeyser's work is always tough, however, and never assumes the false authority that is so often mistaken for wisdom. She investigates nearly every aspect of life, from the desperate haircutting of a boy who needs work to "The Power of Suicide," one of her tight, excellent four-line poems:

> The potflower on the windowsill says to me
> In words that are green-edged red leaves:
> Flower flower flower flower
> Today for the sake of all the dead Burst into flower.

The simplicity of such a poem makes explication impossible: what gimmicks of "style" has the poet employed? One knows only that the poem is bound by a natural rhythm, and seems to relate a part of the poet's experience.

Some of Rukeyser's long poems, in particular "The Speed of Darkness," are among the finest we'll have to carry with us into the next century. Her vocabulary is truly of our generation, but she wrote poems of a longer endurance:

> Whoever despises the clitoris despises the penis
> Whoever despises the penis despises the cunt
> Whoever despises the cunt despises the life of the child.
>
> Resurrection music, silence, and surf.

In "Waterlily Fire," she curiously mixes hard consonant sounds with a softer, feminine voice:

> We pray : we dive into each other's eyes
> Whatever can come to a woman can come to me.
> This the long body : into life from the beginning. . . .

The toughness of these poems suggests that "feminine," with all its present connotations, is not the correct adjective for Rukeyser's work. The frankness of her love poems (read "What I See") combined with her muted optimism also makes for memorable poetry.

Rukeyser's poetry *is* feminine, but only because the poet is a woman. It is enduring because the poet retained all of her "seventeen senses," and used every one of them in her work.

—Geof Hewitt

RUNYON, (Alfred) Damon. Born in Manhattan, Kansas, 4 October 1880. Educated at schools in Pueblo, Colorado. Served in the U.S. Army during the Spanish-American War, 1898–99: contributed to forces newspapers Manila *Freedom* and *Soldier's Letter*. Married 1) Ellen Egan in 1911 (died), one son and one daughter; 2) Patrice del Grande in 1932 (divorced, 1946). Reporter, *Evening Press* and *Evening Post*, 1896–98, and *Chieftain*, 1900, all Pueblo; Colorado Springs *Gazette*, Denver *Post*, 1905–06, *Rocky Mountain News*, Denver, 1906–10, and San Francisco *Post*, 1910; sportswriter and columnist, New York *American* and *Sunday American*, 1911–37; correspondent for Hearst newspapers in Mexico, 1912, and in Europe, 1917–18; columnist and feature writer for King Features/International News Service, from 1918; columnist, New York *Daily Mirror*, late 1930's; producer at RKO and 20th Century-Fox studios, Hollywood, 1942–43. Recipient: National Headliners Club prize, for journalism, 1939. *Died 10 December 1946.*

PUBLICATIONS

Collections

A Treasury of Runyon, edited by Clark Kinnaird. 1958.

Fiction (stories)

Guys and Dolls. 1931.
Blue Plate Special. 1934.
Money From Home. 1935.
More Than Somewhat, edited by E.C. Bentley. 1937.
Furthermore, edited by E.C. Bentley. 1938.
The Best of Runyon, edited by E.C. Bentley. 1938.
Take It Easy. 1938.
My Old Man. 1939.
My Wife Ethel. 1939; as *The Turps*, 1951.
Runyon Favorites. 1942.
Runyon à la Carte. 1944.
The Three Wise Guys and Other Stories. 1946.
In Our Town. 1946.
Short Takes. 1946.
Trials and Other Tribulations. 1948.
Runyon First and Last. 1949; as *All This and That*, 1950.
Runyon on Broadway. 1950.
Runyon from First to Last. 1954.
Romance in the Roaring Forties and Other Stories. 1986.

Play

A Slight Case of Murder, with Howard Lindsay (produced 1935). 1940.

Verse

The Tents of Trouble. 1911.
Rhymes of the Firing Line. 1912.
Poems for Men. 1947.

Other

Captain Eddie Rickenbacker, with Walter Kiernan. 1942.

*

Critical Studies: *Father's Footsteps* by Damon Runyon, Jr., 1954; *A Gentleman of Broadway* by Edwin P. Hoyt, 1964; *Runyonese: The Mind and Craft of Runyon* by Jean Wagner, 1965; *The World of Runyon* by Tom Clark, 1978; *The Men Who Invented Broadway: Runyon, Walter Winchell, and Their World* by John Mosedale, 1981; *Runyon* by Patricia Ward D'Itri, 1982.

* * *

Damon Runyon belongs to that long line of American journalists who make copy out of the comic potentiality of life around them. Much of that comedy derives from the rich variety of speech patterns among the various immigrant communities spread across the U.S.: German, Dutch, Polish, Irish; and, in Runyon's case, the Jewish-Italian speech of the Bronx and other areas of New York. For what gives Runyon his special distinction is that he wrote about life in the big city, whereas previous journalist/fiction-writers in his mould had largely confined themselves to small-town midwestern communities.

Runyon's world is that of the seedy mafiosa, barflies, compulsive gamblers, womanisers, men who sport names such as "Society Max," "Harry the Horse," "Rusty Charlie," "Feet Samuels," "Dancing Dan." All the stories about these characters are written in the continuous present tense, as though Runyon himself is one of the barflies, spinning a yarn into his neighbour's ear, making a chuckly anecdote out of his friends' misfortunes and misadventures. For example: "This Heine Schmitz is a very influential citizen of Harlem, where he has large interests in beer, and it is by no means violating any confidence to tell you that Heine Schmitz will just as soon blow your brains out as look at you. In fact, I hear sooner."

Once he had discovered this raffishly, down-at-heels, yet defiantly stylish world (or sub-world), and had discovered a style of narrating its doings, Runyon had no reason not to go on and on recounting anecdotes about it (much as Wodehouse, having invented Wooster and Jeeves, could set them in motion time after time). Runyon was, in fact, a prolific author. Quite apart from volumes of light verse, there were numerous collections of his short stories and a play. The verse and play need not detain us. They are lightweight, the verse reminiscent of poets like James Whitcomb Riley and Eugene Field, in that they tell folksy tales of lovable low-life characters, although in Runyon's case the characters were often of the city rather than of the country.

Of the volumes of short stories, perhaps the pick are *More Than Somewhat*, *Take It Easy*, *Furthermore*, and *My Old Man*. The best of the stories are hilarious, and Runyon manages effortlessly to capture a style of speech which, in its aping of "polite" or "standard" American English, tells one only too graphically of the difficulties immigrant communities had in learning a new tongue, while desperately—or naturally—keeping to modes of expression that belonged to their mother-tongue. Who can forget Nathan Detroit's anxious questioning of ever-loving Adelaide: "Would you say that some doll might fall for some guy which you would not think she would do so?" Or Joe the Joker's remark that "Only last night, Frankie Ferocious sends for Ropes and tells him he will appreciate it as a special favor if Ropes will bring me to him in a sack"?

One could, of course, object that the real world of the Mafia is so cynically immoral that laughter about it is indefensible. Perhaps. But against that it has to be said that Runyon's world is no more real than the world of the Woosters, or of Blandings. In its own way, however, it is just as funny.

—John Lucas

SALINGER, J(erome) D(avid). Born in New York City, 1 January 1919. Educated at McBurney School, New York; Valley Forge Military Academy, Pennsylvania (editor, *Crossed Sabres*), 1934–36, graduated 1936; New York University, 1937; Ursinus College, Collegetown, Pennsylvania, 1938; Columbia University, New York, 1939. Served in the 4th Infantry Division of the U.S. Army, 1942–45: Staff Sergeant. Married Claire Douglas in 1955 (second marriage; divorced, 1967); one daughter and one son. Has lived in New Hampshire since 1953.

PUBLICATIONS

Fiction

The Catcher in the Rye. 1951.
Nine Stories. 1953; as *For Esmé—With Love and Squalor and Other Stories*, 1953.
Franny and Zooey. 1961.
Raise High the Roof Beam, Carpenters, and Seymour: An Introduction. 1963.

*

Bibliography: *Salinger: A Thirty Year Bibliography 1938–1968* by Kenneth Starosciak, 1971; *Salinger: An Annotated Bibliography 1938–1981* by Jack R. Sublette, 1984.

Critical Studies: *The Fiction of Salinger* by Frederick L. Gwynn and Joseph Blotner, 1958; *Salinger: A Critical and Personal Portrait* edited by Henry Anatole Grunwald, 1962; *Salinger and the Critics* edited by William F. Belcher and James W. Lee, 1962; *Salinger* by Warren French, 1963, revised edition, 1976; *Studies in Salinger* edited by Marvin Laser and Norman Fruman, 1963; *Salinger* by James E. Miller, Jr., 1965; *Salinger: A Critical Essay* by Kenneth Hamilton, 1967; *Zen in the Art of Salinger* by Gerald Rosen, 1977; *Salinger* by James Lundquist, 1979; *Salinger's Glass Stories as a Composite Novel* by Eberhard Alsen, 1984; *Salinger: A Writing Life* by Ian Hamilton, 1986.

* * *

Of his writings, J.D. Salinger has so far wished to preserve only a novel and thirteen short stories, all published between 1948 and 1959, mostly in the *New Yorker*. Despite this limited body of work, Salinger was, at least between 1951 and 1963, the most popular American fiction writer among serious young persons and many alienated adults because of the way in which he served as a spokesman for the feelings of his generation. Thus his work is of unique interest as evidence of the sensibility of those times.

Salinger had taken a short-story writing course under Whit Burnett, the influential editor of *Story*, which gave many important American fiction writers their start. Salinger's first published work, "The Young Folks," appeared there in 1940. Like much of his later work, this slight piece contrasted the behavior of, on one hand, shy, sensitive and, on the other, tough, flippant, unfeeling young upper-middle-class urbanites. During the 1940's, Salinger published (in *Story* and most of the popular slick magazines like *Collier's*) another nineteen stories that he has not allowed to be collected. Some of these, like "This Sandwich Has No Mayonnaise," are of interest for introducing a character named Holden Caulfield, who resembles the later protagonist of *The Catcher in the Rye*, but who dies during World War II. Most are very short, heavily ironic tales about troubled young people defeated by what Holden Caulfield would call "the phony world." The only one of great interest in the light of Salinger's later achievement is the longest, "The Inverted Forest," a cryptic tale about an artist's relationship to society. The lines quoted from the poetry of the central figure, Raymond Ford—"Not wasteland, but a great inverted forest / with all the foliage underground"—suggest that all beauties are internal, so that the artist is exempt from external responsibilities.

The question of the sensitive individual's responsibility to the world remains the focal question in all of Salinger's better known fiction. *The Catcher in the Rye* is the comically grotesque account of Holden Caulfield's two-and-a-half-day odyssey through the waste land of New York City at Christmas time after he decides to quit his fashionable prep school. Holden dreams of escaping the city and going out west where he could build "a little cabin somewhere . . . and live there for the rest of my life . . . near the woods, but not right in them" (a description that foreshadows almost exactly the New England retreat where Salinger himself has lived for the past thirty years). In the speech that gives the novel its title, he tells his little sister Phoebe that the one thing he would like to do is stand guard over "all these little kids playing some game in this big field of rye and all" and "catch everybody if they start to go over the cliff." But Holden learns, when he sees obscenities scratched on the walls of Phoebe's elementary school, that "You can't ever find a place that's nice and peaceful, because there isn't any." And watching Phoebe ride the Central Park carousel, he realizes, "The thing with kids is, if they want to grab for the gold ring, you have to let them do it, and not say anything." Wiser but sadder, he decides that he must return home rather than take the responsibility for leading Phoebe astray.

Although Salinger is most often identified as the author of this novel, Holden Caulfield, who finally compromises with his social responsibilities, is not the typical hero in Salinger's work. The stories that the author has chosen to preserve begin and end with accounts of the suicide of Seymour Glass, oldest son and spiritual guide to his six siblings of a New York Irish-Jewish theatrical family. In "A Perfect Day for Bananafish," the first story in the collection *Nine Stories*, we learn only the circumstances of Seymour's suicide in a Miami Beach hotel. In "Seymour: An Introduction," his brother and interpreter Buddy offers at last the explanation for the event: "The true artist-seer . . . is mainly dazzled to death by his own scruples, the blinding shapes and colors of his own sacred human conscience."

The eleven stories published between these two carry us from the account of the suicide to the illumination of its significance, and reflect along the way Salinger's increasing absorption in oriental philosophies, especially Zen Buddhism. Four stories in *Nine Stories*—"Uncle Wiggily in Connecticut," "The Laughing Man," "Just Before the War with the Eskimos," and "Pretty Mouth and Green My Eyes"—offer, like *The Catcher in the Rye*, depressing pictures of people trapped in the "phony" world, but dreaming of a "nice" world. In four of the later stories, however, Salinger suggests that the grim situation might be ameliorated—"Down at the Dinghy" portrays Seymour's sister reconciling her small son to a threatening world; "For Esmé—With Love and Squalor" is a triumphant epithalamion for a young girl who has done meaningful good in a warring world; "DeDaumier-Smith's Blue Period" is an amazingly successful description of a mystical experience that leads a young man to forsake aggressive ambitions; and the famous concluding story, "Teddy," presents a boy who has truly absorbed the Buddhist concept of the illusoriness of material life and is prepared to move serenely beyond it.

In the longer "Glass Saga" stories, Salinger focuses on Seymour's siblings and presents, in "Franny," the story of the youngest child's breakdown when confronted with the "ego" of the squalid world of college and theater. In "Zooey," her brother literally talks her out of her breakdown by assuming the voice of the departed Seymour, and counselling, "An artist's only concern is to shoot for some kind of perfection, and *on his own terms*, not anyone else's." "Raise High the Roof Beam, Carpenters" prefaces "Seymour: An Introduction" with Buddy's fond recollection of Seymour's violent responses to beauty and his supreme affront to the rituals of his urban caste when he persuades his intended to run off with him on their wedding day instead of submitting to a fancy ceremony.

Since these stories were collected in 1963, Salinger has published only "Hapworth 16, 1924," a labored account of seven-year-old Seymour's prodigious sexual and intellectual proclivities as revealed by a letter home from summer camp. In the one interview he has granted in recent years—to object to an unauthorized edition of his uncollected stories—Salinger protested that he is still writing constantly, but he denounced publication as "a terrible invasion" of his privacy.

—Warren French

See the essay on *The Catcher in the Rye*.

SALTUS, Edgar (Evertson). Born in New York City, 8 October 1855. Educated at St. Paul's School, Concord, New Hampshire; studied at Yale University, New Haven, Connecticut, the Sorbonne, Paris, University of Heidelberg, and University of Munich, 1872–76; Columbia University Law School, New York, 1876–80, LL.B. 1880, but never practised law. Married 1) Helen Sturgis Read in 1883 (divorced, 1891); 2) Elsie Welsh Smith in 1895 (separated, 1901; died, 1911), one daughter; 3) Marie Giles in 1911. Lived in New York; writer from 1884; editor and compiler for P.F. Collier and Son, publishers, late 1890's. *Died 31 July 1921.*

PUBLICATIONS

Fiction

Mr. Incoul's Misadventure. 1887.
The Truth about Tristrem Varick. 1888.
Eden. 1888.
A Transaction in Hearts. 1889.
The Pace That Kills. 1889.
A Transient Guest and Other Episodes. 1889.
Mary Magdalen. 1891; as *Mary of Magdala*, 1903.
Imperial Purple. 1892.
The Facts in the Curious Case of H. Hyrtl, Esq. 1892.
Madam Sapphira: A Fifth Avenue Story. 1893.
Enthralled: A Story of International Life. 1894.
When Dreams Come True: A Story of Emotional Life. 1895(?).
Purple and Fine Women. 1903.
The Perfume of Eros: A Fifth Avenue Incident. 1905.
Vanity Square: A Story of Fifth Avenue Life. 1906.
Daughters of the Rich. 1909.
The Monster. 1913.
The Paliser Case. 1919.
The Ghost Girl, edited by Marie Saltus. 1922.

Verse

Poppies and Mandragora: Poems, with Twenty-Three Additional Poems by Marie Saltus, edited by Marie Saltus. 1926.

Other

Balzac. 1884.
The Philosophy of Disenchantment. 1885.
The Anatomy of Negation. 1886; revised edition, 1889.
Love and Lore. 1890.
Spain and Her Colonies. 1898.
Wit and Wisdom from Saltus, edited by G.F. Monkshood and George Gamble. 1903.

The Pomps of Satan (essays). 1904.
Historia Amoris: A History of Love Ancient and Modern. 1906; as *Love Throughout the Ages*, 1908.
The Lords of the Ghostland: A History of the Ideal. 1907.
Oscar Wilde: An Idler's Impression. 1917.
The Gardens of Aphrodite. 1920.
The Imperial Orgy: An Account of the Tsars from the First to the Last. 1920.
Parnassians Personally Encountered, edited by Marie Saltus. 1923.
The Uplands of Dream (essays and poems), edited by Charles Honce. 1925.
Victor Hugo, and Golgotha: Two Essays, edited Marie Saltus. 1925.

Editor, *The Capitals of the Globe.* 1893.
Editor, *The Lovers of the World.* 3 vols., 1896(?).
Editor, *The Great Battles of All Nations from Marathon to Santiago.* 2 vols., 1898.

Translator, *After-Dinner Stories from Balzac.* 1885; as *Tales from Balzac*, 1909.
Translator, *Tales Before Supper from Théophile Gautier and Prosper Mérimée.* 1887.
Translator, *The Story Without a Name*, by Jules Barbey d'Aurevilly. 1891.

*

Bibliography: in *The Uplands of Dream* by Saltus, edited by Charles Honce, 1925; in *Bibliography of American Literature* by Jacob Blanck, edited by Virginia L. Smyers and Michael Winship, 1983.

Critical Studies: *Saltus, The Man* by Marie Saltus, 1925; *Saltus* by Claire Sprague, 1968.

* * *

In 1884 Edgar Saltus began his literary career with *Balzac*, an introductory study which witnesses to his predominantly European interests. This was followed by his elegant popularisations of German contemporary pessimists, Schopenhauer and Hartmann, in *The Philosophy of Disenchantment* and *The Anatomy of Negation*. His first novel, *Mr. Incoul's Misadventure*, inaugurates the first, most successful phase of his fiction.

In 1891 Saltus published *Mary Magdalen*, reportedly originating in conversations with Oscar Wilde, the first of his impressionist quasi-histories. *Imperial Purple*, high-coloured portraits of the Roman emperors from Caesar to Heliogabalus, was deservedly popular, but the attempted emulation in *Imperial Orgy*, which presented the Russian Czars from Ivan the Terrible to Nicholas "the last," is considerably less achieved.

Mr. Incoul's Misadventure, in fact, is typical of Saltus's novels, with its pessimism, self-conscious style, occasional authentic glimpses of upper-class life, melodramatic themes, and loose plotting: a millionaire coldly and ingeniously revenges himself on his wife and the man who loves her. *The Truth about Tristrem Varick*, is more lucid in structure, with a "point of view" presented by the hero, though the incidents are hardly less melodramatic. *Eden* is less successful, but introduces us to what was to become Saltus's standard types of women: blonde Eve and darkly passionate, "fatal" Lilith. *A Transaction in Hearts* has an interesting "new" woman and a powerful story line. *The Pace That Kills* has a suicidal villain-hero who is a less attractive version of Incoul, while *Enthralled* is an extravaganza owing something to Hugo and to Wilde's *The Picture of Dorian Gray*. In *When Dreams Come True*, a *Bildungsroman* of sorts, Saltus breaks through his own stereotypes—the "fatal woman" emerges as a witty and balanced wife—and produces his best novel. The relationship with his first wife, from whom he was divorced in 1891, underlies his virulent novel *Madam Sapphira*.

The later novels are less satisfying. *The Perfume of Eros*, the best of them, memorably portrays a slum child for whom the wages of sin are success; a charming flapper is killed off when her moral situation threatens to become too complex. *Vanity Square* promises that critique of a cultured and bored society Saltus was well endowed to write, but, though embodying entertaining discussion of ideas, disintegrates into fable. In *Daughters of the Rich* Saltus moves from New York to southern California, but it is inhabited by the familiar Saltus types and situations: "new" women, murder, and misunderstandings in love. Incest, duels, two unconsummated marriages, theosophy, and mildly Wildean wit hardly redeem *The Monster*. *The Paliser Case* is a faded version of *The Perfume of Eros*, and *The Ghost Girl* a mediocre gothic novel.

Saltus's sometimes amusing short stories were written largely for popular consumption and are more melodramatic in plot and exotic in setting than the novels. The poetry was collected in *Poppies and Mandragora*; chiselled in a Parnassian manner, it faintly recalls Hérédia. The brief essay *The Gardens of Aphrodite*, which discusses the god of love as Eros-Don Juan, is interesting in itself and for the light it casts on Saltus's fiction. *The Lords of the Ghostland* examines the major religions of the world, introducing theosophy for the first time. *Oscar Wilde: An Idler's Impression* agreeably records a friendship, mainly through reported conversations. French literature is the subject of *Parnassians Personally Encountered* and *Victor Hugo, and Golgotha*; Saltus also translated Balzac, Merimée, and Gautier.

Saltus's importance is largely that of populariser of European *fin de siècle* modes and topics in the United States. He produced no masterpiece, but his pessimism, determinism, use of fable, allegory, and paradox suggest a poor man's Oscar Wilde, a Wilde without the drama, but a dweller in a high, slightly flashy Bohemia.

—Ian Fletcher

SANDBURG, Carl. Born in Galesburg, Illinois, 6 January 1878. Educated at Lombard College, Galesburg (editor, *Lombard Review*), 1899–1902. Served in the 6th Illinois Volunteers during the Spanish-American War, 1899: Private. Married Lilian Steichen in 1908; three daughters. Staff member, *Tomorrow* magazine, Chicago, 1906; associate editor, *Lyceumite*, Chicago, 1907–08; district organizer, Social-Democratic Party, Appleton, Wisconsin, 1908; city hall reporter, Milwaukee *Journal*, 1909–10; secretary to Mayor of Milwaukee, 1910–12; city editor, Milwaukee *Social Democratic Herald*, 1911; staff member, Milwaukee *Leader* and Chicago *World*, 1912, and *Day Book*, Chicago, 1912–17; associate editor, *System: The Magazine of Business*, Chicago, 1913; Stockholm correspondent, 1918, and manager of the Chicago office, 1919, Newspaper Enterprise Association; reporter, editorial writer, and motion picture editor, 1917–30, and syndicated columnist, 1930–32, Chicago *Daily News*; Lecturer, University of Hawaii, Honolulu, 1934; Walgreen Foundation Lecturer, University of Chicago, 1940; weekly columnist, syndicated by the Chicago *Daily Times*, from 1941. Recipient: Poetry Society of America award, 1919, 1921; Friends of Literature award, 1934; Roosevelt Memorial Association prize, for biography, 1939; Pulitzer Prize, for history, 1940, and for poetry, 1951; American Academy Gold Medal, 1952; National Association for the Advancement of Colored People Award, 1965. Litt.D.: Lombard College, 1928; Knox College, Galesburg, Illinois, 1929; Northwestern University, Evanston, Illinois, 1931; Harvard University, Cambridge, Massachusetts, 1940; Yale University, New Haven, Connecticut, 1940; New York University, 1940; Wesleyan University, Middletown, Connecticut, 1940; Lafayette College, Easton, Pennsylvania, 1940; Syracuse University, Syracuse, New York, 1941; Dartmouth College, Hanover, New Hampshire, 1941; University of North Carolina, Chapel Hill, 1955; Uppsala College, New Jersey, 1959; LL.D.: Hollins College, Virginia, 1941; Augustana College, Rock Island, Illinois, 1948; University of Illinois, Urbana, 1953. Member, American Academy, 1940; Commander, Order of the North Star (Sweden), 1953. *Died 22 July 1967*.

PUBLICATIONS

Collections

The Letters, edited by Herbert Mitgang. 1968.

Verse

In Reckless Ecstasy. 1904.
The Plaint of the Rose. 1904(?).
Incidentals. 1904.
Joseffy. 1910.
Chicago Poems. 1916.
Cornhuskers. 1918.
Smoke and Steel. 1920.
Slabs of the Sunburnt West. 1922.
(*Poems*), edited by Hughes Mearns. 1926.
Selected Poems, edited by Rebecca West. 1926.
Good Morning, America. 1928.
The People, Yes. 1936.
Bronze Wood. 1941.
Complete Poems. 1950; revised edition, 1970.
Harvest Poems 1910–1960. 1960.
Six New Poems and a Parable. 1961.
Honey and Salt. 1963.
Breathing Tokens, edited by Margaret Sandburg. 1978.

Fiction

Remembrance Rock. 1948.

Other (for children)

Rootabaga Stories. 1922.
Rootabaga Pigeons. 1923.
Rootabaga Country. 1929.
Early Moon. 1930.
Potato Face. 1930.
Wind Song. 1960.

Other

You and Your Job. 1908.
The Chicago Race Riot, July 1919. 1919.
Abraham Lincoln:
The Prairie Years. 2 vols., 1926; selection (for children), as *Abe Lincoln Grows Up*, 1928.
The War Years. 4 vols., 1939; revised abridgement, as *Storm over the Land*, 1942.
The Prairie Years and The War Years (selection). 1 vol., 1954.
Steichen, The Photographer. 1929.
Mary Lincoln, Wife and Widow, with Paul M. Angle. 1932.
Home Front Memo. 1943.
The Photographs of Abraham Lincoln, with Frederick Hill Meserve. 1944.
Lincoln Collector: The Story of Oliver R. Barrett's Great Private Collection. 1949.
Always the Young Strangers (autobiography). 1953; selection (for children), as *Prairie-Town Boy*, 1955.
The Sandburg Range (miscellany). 1957.
Ever the Winds of Chance (autobiography). 1983.
Sandburg at the Movies: A Poet in the Silent Era 1920–1927 (film reviews), edited by Dale and Doug Fetherling. 1985.

Editor, *American Songbag*. 1927; *New American Songbag*, 1950.
Editor, *A Lincoln and Whitman Miscellany*. 1938.

Screen documentary: *Bomber*, 1945.

*

Bibliography: *Sandburg: A Bibliography* by Thomas S. Shaw, 1948.

Critical Studies: *Sandburg: A Study in Personality and Background* by Karl W. Detzer, 1941; *Sandburg* by Harry Golden, 1961; *Sandburg* by Richard H. Crowder, 1964; *The America of Sandburg* by Hazel Durnell, 1965; *Sandburg* by Mark Van Doren, 1969 (includes bibliography); *Sandburg: Lincoln of Our Literature* by North Callahan, 1970; *Sandburg, Yes* by W.G. Rogers, 1970; *Sandburg* by Gay Wilson Allen, 1972; *The Vision of This Land: Studies of Vachel Lindsay, Edgar Lee Masters, and Sandburg* edited by John E. Hallwas and Dennis J. Reader, 1976; *A Great and Glorious Romance: The Story of Sandburg and Lilian Steichen* by Helga Sandburg, 1978; *Sandburg Remembered* by William A. Sutton, 1979; *My Friend Sandburg: The Biography of a Friendship* by Lilla S. Perry, 1981.

* * *

Harriet Monroe's magazine *Poetry* in 1914 gave conspicuous position to Carl Sandburg's early poems. Readers were drawn by his Whitman-like quality, now vigorous and rugged, now gentle and compassionate. His books *Chicago Poems* and *Cornhuskers* set the pace and established him as a leading American poet. His free verse lines were, at their best, musical and varied. His subject matter was generally quarried from the cities and countryside of the midwest. His themes were built on concern for the common man, concomitant with his interest in socialism. Out of the Depression came his book *The People, Yes*, consisting of folk sayings cemented together by optimistic prophecies to the effect that the ordinary man would eventually receive his due. Sandburg's last book of poems, *Honey and Salt*, continued to substantiate his thesis that the life of "the family of man" is not all sweet, that it is tempered by the sobering experience of everyday existence and even by tragedy. In this book the old poet, through his reliance on a proliferation of color images unusual in a writer at the end of his career, proved to be as vigorous as a tyro one-third his age.

The People, Yes had been a product of Sandburg's interest in folklore. His two edited collections of the songs of the people established him as something of an authority: *The American Songbag* and the expanded *New American Songbag*. In fact, for the twenty years preceding World War II Sandburg traveled widely singing these songs to large audiences, accompanying himself on the guitar.

In prose biography Sandburg showed a skillful hand. He wrote of his wife's brother in *Steichen, The Photographer* and of the wife of his life-long hero in *Mary Lincoln, Wife and Widow*. His most famous prose work remains his 6-volume biography of Lincoln. If in this monumental work (without footnotes and index) he occasionally rearranged the chronology and indeed embroidered the facts, he nevertheless produced a rich and sensitive portrait, filled with incident, pointed up with insight, and made brilliant with poetic truth. His *Always the Young Strangers* tells the story of his own growing-up with a remarkable analytical objectivity in an enchanting style as engrossing as a novel.

Remembrance Rock was something else again. Commissioned by Metro-Goldwyn-Mayer to write a "great American novel" later to be made into a scenario for a moving picture, Sandburg turned out a wooden, repetitive piece of fiction, not only very long, but very tiresome. Like *The People, Yes* the book is packed with songs, proverbs, anecdotes, folk customs. Effective in a Depression poem, this subject matter was ill suited to the novel form. In spite of the book's ineptness, however, Sandburg was continuing to show his integrity and generosity, his hatred of bigotry, his consuming love for his native country.

He was popular with children; his *Rootabaga Stories, Rootabaga Pigeons*, and *Potato Face* enjoyed wide readership. The fantasy, inventiveness, humor, and light-heartedness in these stories were similar to many of the traits in his poems, selections from which, indeed, were collected in anthologies intended for children.

Sandburg will long be remembered for his Lincoln biography and for many of his poems. The reader can recall the alternating robustness and pathos of "Chicago," the delicate imagism of "Fog," the loud anger of "To a Contemporary Bunkshooter," the wholesome aspiration of *The People, Yes*. Even though one cannot place him in the very top rank of American poets, it is possible to say that to have read Sandburg is to have been the companion of a deeply rooted and dedicated citizen of the United States and of a conscious craftsman skilled in communicating the basic emotions, especially as felt by the "ordinary" person. It must be emphasized that Sandburg was moved not just by the masses, what he lovingly called "the mob." True, he was sympathetic with his "people' as they struggled toward the stars (one of his early poems chanted, "I am the people, the mob"), but his many poems about individuals showed him to be actively aware of the inescapable fact that every man and woman experiences troubles and ecstasies (e.g., "The Hangman at Home," "Helga," "Ice Handler," "Mag"). Furthermore, though Sandburg is linked with Vachel Lindsay and Edgar Lee Masters as an Illinois poet, he is seen to be, on careful study, a poet of universals. If his most frequent subjects are the little people of his home state, his themes are nonetheless the concerns of all people everywhere.

—Richard H. Crowder

SANTAYANA, George (Agustin de). Born in Madrid, Spain, 16 December 1863; emigrated with his family to the U.S., 1872, but retained Spanish nationality. Educated at the Brimmer School and the Latin School, both Boston; Harvard University, Cambridge, Massachusetts, 1882-86, A.B. 1886, A.M. (Walker Fellow in Germany and England), 1888, Ph.D. 1889; King's College, Cambridge, 1896–97. Instructor, 1889–98, Assistant Professor, 1898–1907, and Professor of Philosophy, 1907–12, Harvard University; lived in England, France, and Rome, 1912–52. Hyde Lecturer, the Sorbonne, Paris, 1905–06; Spencer Lecturer, Oxford University, 1923. Recipient: Royal Society of Literature (London) Benson Medal, 1928; Columbia University Butler Gold Medal, 1945. Honorary degree: University of Wisconsin, Madison, 1911. Member, American Academy. *Died 26 September 1952.*

PUBLICATIONS

Collections

Letters, edited by Daniel Cory. 1955.
Complete Poems, edited by William G. Holzberger. 1979.

Fiction

The Last Puritan: A Memoir in the Form of a Novel. 1935.

Plays

Lucifer: A Theological Tragedy. 1899; revised edition, 1924.
The Marriage of Venus, and *Philosophers at Court*, in *The Poet's Testament*. 1953.

Verse

Sonnets and Other Verses. 1894; 2nd series, 1896.
A Hermit of Carmel and Other Poems. 1901.
Poems. 1923.
The Poet's Testament: Poems and Two Plays. 1953.

Other

Platonism in the Italian Poets. 1896.
The Sense of Beauty, Being the Outlines of Aesthetic Theory. 1896.
Interpretations of Poetry and Religion. 1900.
The Life of Reason; or, The Phases of Human Progress. 5 vols., 1905–06; revised edition, with Daniel Cory, 1954.
Three Philosophical Poets: Lucretius, Dante, and Goethe. 1910.
Winds of Doctrine: Studies in Contemporary Opinion. 1913.

Egotism in German Philosophy. 1915; as *The German Mind*, 1968.
Character and Opinion in the United States. 1920.
Little Essays, edited by Logan Pearsall Smith. 1920.
Soliloquies in England and Later Soliloquies. 1922.
Scepticism and Animal Faith. 1923.
The Unknowable. 1923.
Dialogues in Limbo. 1925; revised edition, 1948.
Platonism and the Spiritual Life. 1927.
The Realms of Being. 1942.
The Realm of Essence. 1927.
The Realm of Matter. 1930.
The Realm of Truth. 1937.
The Realm of Spirit. 1940.
The Genteel Tradition at Bay. 1931.
Some Turns of Thought in Modern Philosophy: Five Essays. 1933.
Obiter Scripta: Lectures, Essays, and Reviews, edited by Justus Buchler and Benjamin Schwartz. 1936.
Works (Triton Edition). 15 vols., 1936–40.
Philosophy of Santayana, edited by Irwin Edman. 1936; revised edition, 1953.
Persons and Places (autobiography). 1963.
The Background of My Life. 1944.
The Middle Span. 1945.
My Host the World. 1953.
The Idea of Christ in the Gospels; or, God in Man. 1946.
Atoms of Thought: An Anthology of Thoughts, edited by Ira D. Cardiff. 1950; as *The Wisdom of Santayana*, 1964.
Dominations and Powers: Reflections on Liberty, Society, and Government. 1951.
Essays in Literary Criticism, edited by Irving Singer. 1956.
The Idler and His Works, and Other Essays, edited by Daniel Cory. 1957.
Ten Letters and a Foreword. 1960.
Vagabond Scholar (letters and dialogues with Bruno Lind). 1962.
Animal Faith and Spiritual Life: Previously Unpublished and Uncollected Writings, edited by John Lachs. 1967.
The Genteel Tradition: Nine Essays, edited by Douglas L. Wilson. 1967.
Santayana's America: Essays on Literature and Culture, edited by James Ballowe. 1967.
Santayana on America, edited by Richard Colton Lyon. 1968.
Selected Critical Writings, edited by Norman Henfrey. 2 vols., 1968.
The Birth of Reason and Other Essays, edited by Daniel Cory. 1968.
Physical Order and Moral Liberty: Previously Unpublished Essays, edited by John and Shirley Lachs. 1969.
Lotze's System of Philosophy (1889 doctoral dissertation), edited by Paul Grimley Kuntz. 1971.

Translator, with others, *The Writings of Alfred de Musset*, revised edition, vol. 2. 1907.

*

Bibliography: *Santayana: A Bibliographical Checklist 1880–1980* by Herman J. Saatkamp, Jr., and John Jones, 1982.

Critical Studies: *The Philosophy of Santayana* edited by Paul Arthur Schilpp, 1940 (includes bibliography by Shonig Terzian); *Santayana and the Sense of Beauty* by Richard Butler, 1956; *Santayana's Aesthetics: A Critical Introduction* by Irving Singer, 1957; *Santayana: The Laters Years* by Daniel Cory, 1963; *Santayana, Art, and Aesthetics* by Jerome Ashmore, 1966; *Santayana* by Willard E. Arnett, 1968; *Santayana* by Newton P. Stallknecht, 1971; *Santayana: An Examination of His Philosophy* by Timothy L.S. Sprigge, 1974; *Thresholds of Reality: Santayana and Modernist Poetics* by Lois Hughson, 1977.

* * *

Born in Spain of a Roman Catholic family, George Santayana was a philosopher, an atheist and a materialist, but retained a deep affection for the Roman Catholic Church, and died in his old age, as an invalid, cared for by nuns in a convent hospital in Rome. His working life was spent at Harvard where his colleague, the optimistic pragmatist William James, disliked Santayana intensely and felt that his dry, cynical sadness was corrupting. Few philosophers of his time, if any (the possible rivals are F.H. Bradley and Henri Bergson) wrote with more charm and elegance. The defect of such a style in a philosopher, however, is that it lulls the reader who should be alert for logical flaws; as a result, it would be hard to summarise Santayana's thought. He might be described, perhaps, as a Platonising materialist; only matter was eternal, man was mortal, but man could abstract from matter intellectual essences which (except that they were final products, not sources of being) resembled Plato's world of forms and ideas. Santayana is perhaps at his best as a thinker when he steps away from abstract thinking and applies his mind to literature, as in *Three Philosophical Poets*, or to a place that appealed to him, as in *Soliloquies in England*. In his novel, *The Last Puritan*, based on his knowledge of young Americans through his teaching at Harvard, he tries to do justice to the best sides of that American tradition that, with his innately hierarchical and conservative attitude, he on the whole rejected.

—G.S. Fraser

SAROYAN, William. Born in Fresno, California, 31 August 1908. Educated at public schools in Fresno to age 15. Served in the U.S. Army, 1942–45. Married Carol Marcus in 1943 (divorced, 1949; remarried, 1951; divorced, 1952); one son (the writer Aram Saroyan) and one daughter. Worked as grocery clerk, vineyard worker, post office employee; clerk, telegraph operator, then office manager, Postal Telegraph Company, San Francisco, 1926–28; co-founder, Conference Press, Los Angeles, 1936; founder and director, Saroyan Theatre, New York, 1942; Writer-in-Residence, Purdue University, Lafayette, Indiana, 1961. Recipient: New York Drama Critics Circle award, 1940; Pulitzer Prize, 1940 (refused); Oscar, for screenplay, 1944. Member, American Academy, 1943. *Died 18 May 1981*.

PUBLICATIONS

Collections

My Name Is Saroyan, edited by James H. Tashjian. 1983.

Fiction

The Daring Young Man on the Flying Trapeze and Other Stories. 1934.
Inhale and Exhale (stories). 1936.
Three Times Three (stories). 1936.
Little Children (stories). 1937.
The Gay and Melancholy Flux: Short Stories. 1937.
Love, Here Is My Hat (stories). 1938.
A Native American (stories). 1938.
The Trouble with Tigers (stories). 1938.
Peace, It's Wonderful (stories). 1939.
3 Fragments and a Story. 1939.
My Name Is Aram (stories). 1940.
Saroyan's Fables. 1941.
The Insurance Salesman and Other Stories. 1941.
48 Saroyan Stories. 1942.
Best Stories. 1942.
Thirty-One Selected Stories. 1943.
Some Day I'll Be a Millionaire: 34 More Great Stories. 1943.
The Human Comedy. 1943.
Dear Baby (stories). 1944.
The Adventures of Wesley Jackson. 1946.
The Saroyan Special: Selected Short Stories. 1948.
The Fiscal Hoboes (stories). 1949.
The Twin Adventures: The Adventures of Saroyan: A Diary; The Adventures of Wesley Jackson: A Novel. 1950.
The Assyrian and Other Stories. 1950.
Rock Wagram. 1951.
Tracy's Tiger. 1951.
The Laughing Matter. 1953; as *A Secret Story*, 1954.
The Whole Voyald and Other Stories. 1956.
Mama I Love You. 1956.
Papa You're Crazy. 1957.
Love (stories). 1959.
Boys and Girls Together. 1963.
One Day in the Afternoon of the World. 1964.
After Thirty Years: The Daring Young Man on the Flying Trapeze (includes essays). 1964.
Best Stories of Saroyan. 1964.
My Kind of Crazy Wonderful People: 17 Stories and a Play. 1966.
An Act or Two of Foolish Kindness: Two Stories. 1977.

Plays

The Man with the Heart in the Highlands, in *Contemporary One-Act Plays*, edited by William Kozlenko. 1938; revised version, as *My Heart's in the Highlands* (produced 1939), 1939.
The Time of Your Life (produced 1939). In *The Time of Your Life* (miscellany), 1939.
The Hungerers (produced 1945). 1939.
A Special Announcement (broadcast 1940). 1940.
Love's Old Sweet Song (produced 1940). In *Three Plays*, 1940.
Three Plays: My Heart's in the Highlands, The Time of Your Life, Love's Old Sweet Song. 1940.
Subway Circus. 1940.
Something about a Soldier (produced 1940).
Hero of the World (produced 1940).
The Great American Goof (ballet scenario; produced 1940). In *Razzle Dazzle*, 1942.
Radio Play (broadcast 1940). In *Razzle Dazzle*, 1942.
The Ping-Pong Game (produced 1945). 1940; as *The Ping Pong Players*, in *Razzle Dazzle*, 1942.
Sweeney in the Trees (produced 1940). In *Three Plays*, 1941.
The Beautiful People (produced 1941). In *Three Plays*, 1941.
Three Plays: The Beautiful People, Sweeney in the Trees, Across the Board on Tomorrow Morning. 1941.
Across the Board on Tomorrow Morning (produced 1941). In *Three Plays*, 1941.
The People with Light Coming Out of Them (broadcast 1941). In *The Free Company Presents*, 1941.
There's Something I Got To Tell You (broadcast 1941). In *Razzle Dazzle*, 1942.
Hello, Out There, music by Jack Beeson (produced 1941). In *Razzle Dazzle*, 1942.
Jim Dandy (produced 1941). 1941; as *Jim Dandy: Fat Man in a Famine*, 1947.
Talking to You (produced 1942). In *Razzle Dazzle*, 1942.
Razzle Dazzle; or, The Human Opera, Ballet, and Circus; or, There's Something I Got to Tell You: Being Many Kinds of Short Plays As Well As the Story of the Writing of Them (includes *Hello, Out There, Coming Through the Rye, Talking to You, The Great American Goof, The Poetic Situation in America, Opera, Opera, Bad Men in the West, The Agony of Little Nations, A Special Announcement, Radio Play, The People with Light Coming Out of Them, There's Something I Got to Tell You, The Hungerers, Elmer and Lily, Subway Circus, The Ping Pong Players*). 1942; abridged edition, 1945.
Opera, Opera (produced 1955). In *Razzle Dazzle*, 1942.
Bad Men in the West (produced 1971). In *Razzle Dazzle*, 1942.
Get Away Old Man (produced 1943). 1944.
Sam Ego's House (produced 1947). In *Don't Go Away Mad and Two Other Plays*, 1949.
Don't Go Away Mad (produced 1949). In *Don't Go Away Mad and Two Other Plays*. 1949.
Don't Go Away Mad and Two Other Plays: Sam Ego's House; A Decent Birth, A Happy Funeral. 1949.
The Son (produced 1950).
The Oyster and the Pearl: A Play for Television (televised 1953). In *Perspectives USA*, Summer 1953.
A Lost Child's Fireflies (produced 1954).
Once Around the Block (produced 1956). 1959.
The Cave Dwellers (produced 1957). 1958.
Ever Been in Love with a Midget (produced 1957).
The Slaughter of the Innocents (produced 1957). 1958.
Cat, Mouse, Man, Woman and *The Accident*, in *Contact 1*, 1958.
The Dogs; or, The Paris Comedy (as *The Paris Comedy; or, The Secret of Lily*, produced 1960; as *Lily Dafon*, produced 1960). In *The Dogs; or, The Paris Comedy and Two Other Plays*, 1969.
Settled Out of Court, with Henry Cecil, from the novel by Cecil (produced 1960). 1962.
Sam, The Highest Jumper of Them All; or, The London Comedy (produced 1960). 1961.
High Time along the Wabash (produced 1961).
Ah Man, music by Peter Fricker (produced 1962).
Four Plays: The Playwright and the Public, The Handshakers, The Doctor and the Patient, This I Believe, in *Atlantic*, April 1963.
The Time of Your Life and Other Plays. 1967.
Dentist and Patient and *Husband and Wife*, in *The Best Short*

Plays 1968, edited by Stanley Richards. 1968.
The Dogs; or, The Paris Comedy and Two Other Plays: Chris Sick; or, Happy New Year Anyway, Making Money, and Nineteen Other Very Short Plays. 1969.
The New Play, in *The Best Short Plays 1970*, edited by Stanley Richards. 1970.
Armenians (produced 1974).
The Rebirth Celebration of the Human Race at Artie Zabala's Off-Broadway Theatre (produced 1975).
Two Short Paris Summertime Plays of 1974 (includes *Assassinations* and *Jim, Sam, and Anna*). 1979.
Play Things (produced 1980).

Screenplays: *The Good Job* (documentary), 1942; *The Human Comedy*, with Howard Estabrook, 1943.

Radio Plays: *Radio Play*, 1940; *A Special Announcement*, 1940; *There's Something I Got to Tell You*, 1941; *The People with Light Coming Out of Them*, 1941.

Television Plays: *The Oyster and the Pearl*, 1953; *Ah Sweet Mystery of Mrs. Murphy*, 1959; *The Unstoppable Gray Fox*, 1962; *Making Money and Thirteen Other Very Short Plays*, 1970.

Ballet Scenario: *A Theme in the Life of the Great American Goof*, 1940.

Verse

A Christmas Psalm. 1935.
Christmas 1939. 1939.

Other

Those Who Write Them and Those Who Collect Them. 1936.
The Time of Your Life (miscellany). 1939.
Harlem as Seen by Hirschfeld. 1941.
Hilltop Russians in San Francisco. 1941.
Why Abstract?, with Henry Miller and Hilaire Hiler. 1945.
The Bicycle Rider in Beverly Hills (autobiography). 1952.
The Saroyan Reader. 1958.
Here Comes, There Goes, You Know Who (autobiography). 1962.
A Note on Hilaire Hiler. 1962.
Me (for children). 1963.
Not Dying (autobiography). 1963.
Short Drive, Sweet Chariot (autobiography). 1966.
Look at Us: Let's See: Here We Are: Look Hard: Speak Soft: I See, You See, We all See; Stop, Look, Listen; Beholder's Eye; Don't Look Now But Isn't That You? (us? U.S.?). 1967.
Horsey Gorsey and the Frog (for children). 1968.
I Used to Believe I Had Forever; Now I'm Not So Sure. 1968.
Letters from 74 rue Taitbout. 1969; as *Don't Go But If You Must Say Hello to Everybody*, 1970.
Days of Life and Death and Escape to the Moon. 1970.
Places Where I've Done Time. 1972.
The Tooth and My Father (for children). 1974.
Famous Faces and Other Friends: A Personal Memoir. 1976.
Morris Hirshfield. 1976.
Sons Come and Go, Mothers Hang In Forever (memoirs). 1976.
Chance Meetings. 1978.
Obituaries. 1979.
Births. 1983.

Editor, *Hairenik 1934–1939: An Anthology of Short Stories and Poems*. 1939.

*

Bibliography: *A Bibliography of Saroyan 1934–1964* by David Kherdian, 1965.

Critical Studies: *Saroyan* by Howard R. Floan, 1966; *Last Rites: The Death of Saroyan*, 1982, and *Saroyan*, 1983, both by Aram Saroyan; *Saroyan: My Real Work Is Being* by David Stephen Calonne, 1983; *Saroyan* by Edward Halsey Foster, 1984; *Saroyan: A Biography* by Lawrence Lee and Barry Gifford, 1984.

* * *

William Saroyan is one of the striking paradoxes in 20th-century American literature. Dismissed by some for being non-literary, he was praised by Edmund Wilson for his uncanny gift for creating atmosphere: "Saroyan takes you to the bar, and he creates for you there a world which is the way the world would be if it conformed to the feeling instilled by drinks. In a word, he achieves the feat of making and keeping us boozy without the use of alcohol and purely by the action of art."

Saroyan never went beyond high school and exemplifies the successful homespun writer. *The Daring Young Man on the Flying Trapeze and Other Stories* was his first collection of short fiction, and many consider it to be his finest. A breath-takingly prolific writer (he produced about 500 stories between 1934 and 1940), Saroyan wrote in several genres, but his claim to greatness rests essentially on his plays like *My Heart's in the Highlands* and *The Time of Your Life* and on his short stories. He has been criticized for excessive sentimentality, but he replied that it is a very sentimental thing to be a human being. And to the charge that his style is careless and sloppy, he responded: "I do not know a great deal about what the words come to, but the presence says, Now don't get funny; just sit down and say something: it'll be all right. Say it wrong; It'll be all right anyway. Half the time I *do* say it wrong, but somehow or other, just as the presence says, it's right anyway. I am always pleased about this."

One of his best stories, "The Daring Young Man on the Flying Trapeze," is an interior monologue revealing the recollections of a poor young writer who lives in the troubled present while achieving distance from it by reaching back into the past. Mostly unperturbed on the conscious level by his problems, occasionally the writer is embittered by his need to sell his books to buy food. Finally, one afternoon he returns to his room from his wanderings and dies a sudden and painless death. Saroyan's identification with his young protagonist is evident, despite the disclaimers. The story is suffused with pathos, though there is clearly an attempt to hold the sentimentality in check. Among his plays, *The Time of Your Life* probably most fully reveals Saroyan the artist. It received both the Drama Critics Circle award and the Pulitzer Prize, but Saroyan refused the latter as an expression of his contempt for commercial patronage of art. Despite its melodramatic plot, the play, as Howard R. Floan admirably sums up, is "about a state of mind, illusive but real, whose readily recognizable components are, first, an awareness of America's youth—its undisciplined swaggering, unregulated early life—and, secondly, a pervasive sense of America in crisis: an America of big business, of labor strife, of depersonalized government, and, above all, of imminent war."

Saroyan's interest in the comedy-tragedy of life remained undiminished to the end of his writing career: "Living is the only thing. It is an awful pain most of the time, but this compels comedy and dignity." What made Saroyan stand out—especially among American writers—was his optimism about life despite the world's evidence to the contrary. His buoyancy certainly worked with his considerable reading public, but the major appeal of his writing comes from his characters, who are common people, and from his heavily romantic emphasis on the individuality of human beings.

—J.N. Sharma

SCHWARTZ, Delmore (David). Born in Brooklyn, New York, 8 December 1913. Educated at Townsend Harris High School; George Washington High School, New York, graduated 1931; University of Wisconsin, Madison, 1931–32; New York University (editor, *Mosaic*), 1933–35, B.A. in philosophy 1935; Harvard University, Cambridge, Massachusetts (Bowdoin Prize, 1936), 1935–37. Married 1) Gertrude Buckman in 1938 (separated, 1943; divorced, 1944); 2) Elizabeth Pollet in 1949 (separated, 1955). Briggs-Copeland Instructor in English Composition, 1940, Instructor in English, 1941–45, and Assistant Professor of English, 1946–47, Harvard University; lecturer, New School for Social Research and New York University, late 1940's; Gauss Lecturer, 1949, and Visiting Professor, 1952, Princeton University, New Jersey; fellow, Kenyon School of English, Gambier, Ohio, Summer 1950; Visiting Professor, Indiana School of Letters, Bloomington, 1951, University of Chicago, 1954, and University of California, Los Angeles, 1961; Professor of English, Syracuse University, Syracuse, New York, 1962–66. Poetry editor, 1939, editor, 1943–47, and associate editor, 1947–55, *Partisan Review*, New York, later New Brunswick, New Jersey; associated with *Perspectives* magazine, New York, 1952–53; literary consultant, New Directions, publishers, New York, 1952–53; poetry editor and film critic, *New Republic*, Washington, D.C., 1953–57. Recipient: Guggenheim fellowship, 1940; American Academy grant, 1953; Bollingen Prize, 1960; Shelley Memorial Award, 1960. *Died 11 July 1966.*

PUBLICATIONS

Collections

Selected Essays, edited by Donald A. Dike and David H. Zucker. 1970.
What Is to Be Given: Selected Poems, edited by Douglas Dunn. 1976.
Letters, edited by Robert Phillips. 1984.

Verse

In Dreams Begin Responsibilities (includes short story, and play *Dr. Bergen's Belief*). 1938.
Genesis: Book One (includes prose). 1943.
Vaudeville for a Princess and Other Poems (includes prose). 1950.
Summer Knowledge: New and Selected Poems 1938–1958. 1959.
Last and Lost Poems, edited by Robert Phillips. 1979.

Plays

Choosing Company, in *The New Caravan*, edited by Alfred Kreymborg. 1936.
Shenandoah; or, The Naming of the Child. 1941.

Fiction

The World Is a Wedding and Other Stories. 1948.
Successful Love and Other Stories. 1961.
In Dreams Begin Responsibilities and Other Stories, edited by James Atlas. 1978.

Other

American Poetry at Mid-Century, with John Crowe Ransom and John Hall Wheelock. 1958.
I Am Cherry Alive, The Little Girl Sang (for children). 1979.
Portrait of Delmore: Journals and Notes 1939–1959, edited by Elizabeth Pollet. 1986.
The Ego Is Always at the Wheel: Bagatelles, edited by Robert Phillips. 1986.

Editor, *Syracuse Poems 1964*. 1965.

Translator, *A Season in Hell* (bilingual edition), by Arthur Rimbaud. 1939; revised edition, 1940.

*

Bibliography: in *Selected Essays*, 1970.

Critical Studies: *Schwartz* by Richard McDougall, 1974; *Schwartz: The Life of an American Poet* by James Atlas, 1977.

* * *

It is difficult, reading Delmore Schwartz, to disentangle the poetry from the legend. The darling of the group of American intellectuals associated with the *Partisan Review* in the 1930's and 1940's—to which he contributed as poet, critic, and short story writer, eventually becoming co-editor—Schwartz had a career worthy of the last *poète maudit*. A precociously brilliant first book, *In Dreams Begin Responsibilities*, was followed by a tragic decline into alcohol, insanity, and an early death, alone, in a seedy Manhattan hotel. Posthumously, Schwartz has undergone a literary "canonisation" in one of the most heartbreaking sequences of John Berryman's *Dream Songs* and as the eponymous "hero" of Saul Bellow's *Humboldt's Gift*. The life forbiddingly close to stereotyped, "romantic" conceptions of "the Poet."

And Schwartz almost certainly saw himself in something like this role. The titles alone of some of his best known poems—"Do Others Speak of Me Mockingly, Maliciously?," "All of Us Always Turning Away for Solace"—suggest his fundamental view of the poet as one isolated from his tribe, cut off, as in the marvellous "The Heavy Bear Who Goes with Me," from contact even with his own body. The characteristic Schwartzian stance is apparent in his "Sonnet: O City, City": we live

> Where the sliding auto's catastrophe
> Is a gust past the curb, where numb and high
> The office building rises to its tyranny,
> Is our anguished diminution until we die.

In the same poem, however, he longs for an alternative human sympathy, "the self articulate, affectionate and flowing." Between these terms the course of his poetry runs.

It is a poetry that rarely loses touch with political and historical realities: "The Ballad of the Children of the Czar" and the verse play *Shenandoah* poignantly express Schwartz's understanding of his family's experience as Jewish immigrants to America. There is the larger feeling, in many poems, of human beings *imprisoned* in time, bearing the guilt of generations, and Schwartz probes at his guilts and anxieties in a way that occasionally, as in "Prothalamion," points forward to the "confessional" poetry to be written by his more famous contemporaries Berryman and Lowell. The guardian angels of these poems, figures which haunt Schwartz's imagination and are returned to with obsessive insistence, are the heroic solitaries—Faust, Socrates, "Tiger Christ," "Manic-depressive Lincoln," and, above all, Hamlet.

But there is also in Schwartz, if less insistently, an energetically vibrant language and feeling, a kind of robust dandyism, as in "Far Rockaway":

> The radiant soda of the seashore fashions
> Fun, foam, and freedom. The sea laves
> The shaven sand. And the light sways forward
> On the self-destroying waves.

Douglas Dunn, in his introduction to *What Is to Be Given*, referred to Schwartz's "sometimes dispiriting ebullience," and it is this that many critics have objected to in the later work. A poem like "Seurat's Sunday Afternoon along the Seine" certainly needs to be read without the expectation of those judicious ironies on which most modern poetry thrives. But, *relaxed into*, the stretch and sweep, the sheer verbal intoxication of the poem, carry persuasive power.

Schwartz is a poet, and a critic, too little read and too little understood. Recent republications, however, suggest that his work will survive, along with the best of his generation.

—Neil Corcoran

SEDGWICK, Catharine Maria. Born in Stockbridge, Massachusetts, 28 December 1789. Educated at the district school, and at boarding schools in Boston and Albany, New York; also received private instruction in several languages. Lived in Albany and New York City, 1807–13; returned to Stockbridge, 1813; later lived in Lenox, Massachusetts, and New York; traveled in Europe, 1839–40, and in the midwest, 1854. Active in the work of the Unitarian Church, and the Women's Prison Association of New York. *Died 31 July 1867.*

PUBLICATIONS

Fiction

A New-England Tale; or, Sketches of New-England Character and Manners. 1822; revised edition, as *A New England Tale, and Miscellanies*, 1852.
Mary Hollis. 1822.
Redwood. 1824; revised edition, 1850.
The Travellers (for children). 1825.
The Deformed Boy. 1826.
Hope Leslie; or, Early Times in the Massachusetts. 1827; revised edition, 1842.
Clarence; or, A Tale of Our Own Times. 1830; revised edition, 1849.
Home. 1835.
The Linwoods; or, "Sixty Years Since" in America. 1835.
Tales and Sketches. 2 vols., 1835–44.
The Poor Rich Man, and the Rich Poor Man. 1836.
Live and Let Live; or, Domestic Service Illustrated. 1837.
Stories for Young Persons. 1840.
The Boy on Mount Rhigi (for children). 1848.
Tales of City Life. 1850; as *The City Clerk and His Sister, and Other Stories*, 1851.
The Irish Girl and Other Tales. 1853.
The Mysterious Story-Book; or, The Good Stepmother. 1856.
Married or Single? 1857.

Other

A Short Essay to Do Good. 1828.
Means and Ends; or, Self-Training (for children). 1839.
Letters from Abroad to Kindred at Home. 2 vols., 1841; revised edition, 1 vol., 1841.
Morals of Manners; or, Hints for Our Young People. 1846.
Facts and Fancies for School-Day Reading. 1847.
Memoir of Joseph Curtis, A Model Man. 1858.

Editor, with Katharine Sedgwick Minot, *Letters from Charles Sedgwick to His Family and Friends*. 1870.

*

Bibliography: in *Bibliography of American Literature* by Jacob Blanck, edited by Virginia L. Smyers and Michael Winship, 1983.

Critical Studies: *Life and Letters* edited by Mary E. Dewey, 1871; *Sedgwick* by Sister Mary Michael Welsh, 1937; *Three Wise Virgins* by Gladys Brooks, 1957; *Sedgwick* by Edward Halsey Foster, 1974.

* * *

The novels of Catharine Maria Sedgwick, the best of which include *Redwood* and *Hope Leslie*, are distinguished by close attention to realistic detail, especially regional customs and manners. They use American scenery, manners, customs, and materials, and are usually centered on moral circumstances of especially American interest. *Redwood*, for example, contrasts a Northern and a Southern family. *Hope Leslie* is set in Puritan New England, and aspects of New England history, scenery, and manners are finely detailed. In *The Linwoods*, the tensions that resulted in the American Revolution are dramatized in the conflicts between a family of colonists and a family of royalists. *Clarence* demonstrates the value of a natural aristocracy, an aristocracy of talent and virtue such as projected by Thomas Jefferson, over an aristocracy based solely on birth and wealth. *A New-England Tale*, the first of Sedgwick's novels, is partially a religious tract attacking the remnants of Calvinism in New England, and *Married or Single?* is one of the earliest feminist American pleas for socially equitable treatment of women.

Sedgwick's moral preoccupations are largely tied to the social and political concerns of her day, and while these moral concerns are in many instances now of little interest (as well as obscure to readers without training in American social and political history), her novels have continuing literary value, being among the earliest and the best examples of regionalism in American writing. Sedgwick had an acute ear for American dialect and a fine sense of regional customs and manners. As a literary stylist, she was not especially remarkable, although superior to most of her contemporaries in America, but she was capable of detailing with precision regional characteristics, landscapes, and dialect. Furthermore, alone among American novelists of her time she created credible women in fiction. While it was common for American novelists to portray women as ideally (if improbably) passive and unambitious, Sedgwick's heroines are morally superior; all of her novels center on women whose superior moral judgment places them far above others—particularly men.

—Edward Halsey Foster

SEWALL, Samuel. Born in Bishopstoke, Hampshire, England, 28 March 1652; emigrated with his family to Boston, 1661. Educated at Harvard University, Cambridge, Massachusetts, 1667–71, A.B. 1671, A.M. in theology 1674. Married 1) Hannah Hull in 1676 (died, 1717), 14 children; 2) Abigail Tilley in 1719 (died, 1720); 3) Mary Gibbs in 1722. Resident fellow (tutor), Harvard University, 1673–74; merchant and banker; made a freeman of the Massachusetts Bay Colony, 1679, and began political career; manager of Boston's printing press, 1681–84; deputy to General Court for Westfield, Hampden County, and President of the General Court, 1683; member of the colony's council, 1684–86, and (under new charter), 1691–1725; justice, Superior Court, 1692; appointed by Governor Sir William Phips as one of 9 judges in Salem witchcraft cases, 1692 (19 persons were executed; Sewall publicly admitted errors of judgment, 1697, the only judge to do so); probate judge, Suffolk County, 1715–18; Chief Judge, Superior Court, 1718–28. Member, 1679, and Captain, 1701, Ancient and Honorable Artillery Company; commissioner, Society for the Propagation of the Gospel in New England, 1699. *Died 1 January 1730.*

PUBLICATIONS

Prose

Phaenomena quaedam Apocalyptica; or, Some Few Lines Towards a Description of the New Heaven. 1697.
The Selling of Joseph. 1700; edited by Sidney Kaplan, 1969.
Proposals Touching the Accomplishment of Prophecies. 1713.
Diary 1674–1729. 3 vols., 1878–82; edited by M. Halsey Thomas, 2 vols., 1973.
Letter-Book. 2 vols., 1886–88.
Letters of Samuel Lee and Sewall Relating to New England and the Indians, edited by George Lyman Kittredge. 1912.

*

Critical Studies: *Sewall and the World He Lived In* by Nathan H. Chamberlain, 1897; *Sewall of Boston* by Ola Elizabeth Winslow, 1964; *Sewall: A Puritan Portrait* by T.B. Strandness, 1967.

* * *

Samuel Sewall, whose nearly four score years bridged the 17th and 18th centuries, was a man of consequence in his New England Puritan world. Moses Coit Tyler's assertion that he was "great by almost every measure of greatness" suggests the legendary aura which continues to surround the Sewall name, even though the judgment invites qualification. Rejecting a call to the ministry for which he had prepared, Sewall's principal activities were in the secular world. Upon marrying into great wealth, he became an astute merchant and man of property and is sometimes judged critically for his questionable accommodation of religious ideas to pragmatic business procedures. It is true that he was a worldly and mercenary man; but he was also a man with intense religious convictions and a deep sense of justice, and he loyally served community, province, and colony.

Born in England in 1652, Samuel Sewall arrived in Boston at the age of nine. Under the tutelage of a local minister, he prepared for admission to Harvard College and was enrolled in the class of 1671. He stayed on following graduation to complete requirements for the master's degree in theology, and although he chose not to enter the ministry, his interest in theology pervaded his entire life. His public service was extensive. For a few years he managed the colony's printing press; one year in England he assisted Increase Mather in an unsuccessful effort to restore the colony's charter (1688–89); in 1683 he was elected to the Massachusetts General Court, and although he lacked formal legal training, he was appointed a judge of the Superior Court and later served as Chief Justice. More widely remembered is the fact that he was one of the magistrates selected to conduct the Salem witch trials in 1692. Later, in his personal petition of penitence read before his home congregation, he was the only magistrate to admit error in judgment.

Obviously, the role of Sewall as public servant cannot be separated from history, but that temporal role pales when placed beside the lingering importance of Sewall as writer. Two works have special significance. In 1700, "dissatisfied with the Trade of fetching Negros from Guinea" and stimulated by the reading of biblical commentary, Sewall hastily prepared a statement, *The Selling of Joseph*, for presentation to the Council and General Court. The compelling piece, one of the earliest anti-slavery tracts published in America, continues to have historical interest. It is his remarkable diary, however, covering somewhat irregularly the years 1673 to 1729, for which Sewall is principally remembered. Often compared to the diary of the Englishman Samuel Pepys, but covering a longer span of time and lacking the "under the stairs" detail offered by Pepys, Sewall's diary is a major source of information not only of Sewall the man but also of the shifting texture of life among second- and third-generation Puritans in New England. Sewall's clearly secular tendencies, which he shared with the powerful men of his time, are tempered by the stern and honorable demeanor then conventional; his interest in material achievement and standing is juxtaposed against his devotion to the teachings of Calvin and his own almost obsessive interest in the sermons and religious writings of his day; the piety of his respected contemporaries is qualified by his casual notation of their eccentricities; his devotion to his beloved first wife, Hannah Hull, to whom he was married for 41 years and whom he describes as "my most Constant Lover, my most laborious Nurse, a most tender mother," stands in sharp contrast to his meditated pursuit after her death of eligible widows whom he sought to attract with incongruous gifts such as sermons, shoebuckles, and raisins. At times the diary is an emotional record, responding to the joy of birth and the sadness of death; it is "edged in black," wrote T.B. Strandness, "illness and death on almost every page"—a factual reflection of the high mortality rate in both family and community, for Sewall himself lived to witness the deaths of two of his wives and all but three of his fourteen children. But it also exhibits the rational and sometimes troubled inquiry into the nature of justice and the necessity of reconciling Calvinistic dogma and secular advantage.

The highly personal diary remains vital reading, for it is a rich repository of vivid detail not only about the life of one man but also about the historical milieu which he in large measure epitomizes.

—Clayton L. Eichelberger

SEXTON, Anne (Gray, née Harvey). Born in Newton, Massachusetts, 9 November 1928. Educated at schools in Wellesley, Massachusetts, 1934–45; Rogers Hall, Lowell, Massachusetts, 1945–47; Garland Junior College, Boston, 1947–48; Radcliffe Institute, Cambridge, Massachusetts (Scholar), 1961–63. Married Alfred M. Sexton in 1948 (divorced, 1974); two daughters. Fashion model, Boston, 1950–51; teacher, Wayland High School, Massachusetts, 1967–68; Lecturer, 1970–71, and Professor of Creative Writing, 1972–74, Boston University; Crawshaw Professor of Literature, Colgate University, Hamilton, New York, 1972. Recipient: Bread Loaf Writers Conference Robert Frost Fellowship, 1959; American Academy traveling fellowship, 1963; Ford grant, 1964; Shelley Memorial Award, 1967; Pulitzer Prize, 1967; Guggenheim fellowship, 1969. Litt.D.: Tufts University, Medford, Massachusetts, 1970; Regis College, Weston, Massachusetts, 1971; Fairfield University, Connecticut, 1971. Fellow, Royal Society of Literature (London). *Died (suicide) 4 October 1974.*

PUBLICATIONS

Collections

The Heart of Sexton's Poetry, edited by Linda Gray Sexton and Lois Ames. 1977.
Complete Poems. 1981.

Verse

To Bedlam and Part Way Back. 1960.
All My Pretty Ones. 1962.
Selected Poems. 1964.
Live or Die. 1966.
Poems, with Douglas Livingstone and Thomas Kinsella. 1968.
Love Poems. 1969.
Transformations. 1971.
The Book of Folly. 1972.
O Ye Tongues. 1973.
The Death Notebooks. 1974.
The Awful Rowing Toward God. 1975.
Words for Dr. Y.: Uncollected Poems with Three Stories, edited by Linda Gray Sexton. 1978.

Play

45 Mercy Street (produced 1969). Edited by Linda Gray Sexton, 1976.

Other

Eggs of Things (for children), with Maxine Kumin. 1963.
More Eggs of Things (for children), with Maxine Kumin. 1964.
Joey and the Birthday Present (for children), with Maxine Kumin. 1971.
The Wizard's Tears (for children), with Maxine Kumin. 1975.
Sexton: A Self-Portrait in Letters, edited by Linda Gray Sexton and Lois Ames. 1977.
No Evil Star: Selected Essays, Interviews, and Poems, edited by Steven E. Colburn. 1985.

*

Bibliography: *Sylvia Plath and Sexton: A Reference Guide* by Cameron Northouse and Thomas P. Walsh, 1974.

Critical Studies: *Sexton: The Artist and Her Critics* edited by J.D. McClatchy, 1978.

* * *

Anne Sexton is known primarily for her remarkable imagery and apparent personal honesty in poems ranging from the formally structured early work (*To Bedlam and Part Way Back*) to the quasi-humorous prose poems of *Transformations* and the evocative free form poetry of *Love Poems*. Sexton had published much of her most mature work in the years immediately preceding her evident suicide, and her critical reputation has yet to acknowledge that last productive period.

Sexton was a model who married, reared two daughters, and came to poetry through a workshop at Boston University conducted by Robert Lowell. Influenced by Lowell and the writing of W.D. Snodgrass to break the restraint and intellectualism common to American poetry during the 1950's, Sexton wrote such moving personal poems as "The Double Image." Her consideration here of the relationship among a mother, daughter, and grandchild is important not only for the technical prowess with which she handled a possibly sentimental subject, but for the genuine insight into the women's condition. Encouraged by her friendship with Sylvia Plath, who also was a student in the Lowell workshop, Sexton mined areas of theme and image that were virtually unknown to contemporary poetry. "Those Times" re-creates her own childhood as a time of torment; "Little Girl, My String Bean, My Lovely Woman" celebrates her joy in her daughter; "Flee on Your Donkey" plumbs the depths of personal despair; "Menstruation at Forty" questions the mortality image from a feminine view—most of Sexton's poems are adventurous in that she is writing not only about unconventional subjects, but her quick progression from image to image lends an almost surreal effect to the poetry.

Rather than simply describing Sexton's work as "confessional," the over-used label that attached itself to any writing that seemed autobiographical in origin (as what poetry is, finally, not?), readers should be aware that her work manages to distill the apparently autobiographical details into an imagistic whole which convinces any reader of its authenticity. The life in Sexton's poems is the life of the imagination, regardless of whether or not she has used the facts from her own existence in the re-creation of that life. Once the poems from the late collections have been assimilated with the earlier work, her continuous interest in religious themes and images will become as noticeable as her use of feminine psychology and concerns. Sexton's importance to American poetry will not rest simply on her mental stability or instability, her suicide, or her use of personal detail in her work; her importance will rest, finally, on her ability to craft poems that moved the reader to the act of understanding.

—Linda W. Wagner

SHAPIRO, Karl (Jay). Born in Baltimore, Maryland, 10 November 1913. Educated at the University of Virginia, Charlottesville, 1932–33; Johns Hopkins University, Baltimore, 1937–39; Pratt Library School, Baltimore, 1940. Served in the U.S. Army, 1941–45. Married 1) Evalyn Katz in 1945 (divorced, 1967), two daughters and one son; 2) Teri Kovach in 1967 (died, 1982); 3) Sophie Wilkins in 1985. Clerk in family business, mid-1930's; Associate Professor, Johns Hopkins University, 1948–50; Visiting Professor, University of Wisconsin, Madison, 1948, and Loyola University, Chicago, 1951–52; Visiting Professor, University of California, Berkeley and Davis, 1955–56, and University of Indiana, Bloomington, 1956–57; Professor of English, University of Nebraska, Lincoln, 1956–66, University of Illinois, Chicago Circle, 1966–68, and University of California, Davis, 1968–84. Editor, *Poetry*, Chicago, 1950–56, *Newberry Library Bulletin*, Chicago, 1953–55, and *Prairie Schooner*, Lincoln, Nebraska, 1956–66. Consultant in Poetry, 1946–47, and Whittall Lecturer, 1964, 1967, Library of Congress, Washington, D.C.; Lecturer, Salzburg Seminar in American Studies, 1952; State Department Lecturer, India, 1955; Elliston Lecturer, University of Cincinnati, 1959. Recipient: American Academy grant, 1944; Guggenheim fellowship, 1944, 1953; Pulitzer Prize, 1945; Shelley Memorial Award, 1946; Kenyon School of Letters fellowship, 1956, 1957; Bollingen Prize, 1969. D.H.L.: Wayne State University, Detroit, 1960; D.Litt.: Bucknell University, Lewisburg, Pennsylvania, 1972. Fellow in American Letters, Library of Congress; member, American Academy of Arts and Sciences, and American Academy, 1959. Lives in New York City.

PUBLICATIONS

Verse

Poems. 1935.
Five Young American Poets, with others. 1941.
The Place of Love. 1942.
Person, Place and Thing. 1942.
V-Letter and Other Poems. 1944.
Essay on Rime. 1945.
Trial of a Poet and Other Poems. 1947.
Poems 1940–1953. 1953.
The House. 1957.
Poems of a Jew. 1958.
The Bourgeois Poet. 1964.
Selected Poems. 1968.
There Was That Roman Poet Who Fell in Love at Fifty-Odd. 1968.
White-Haired Lover. 1968.
Auden (1907–1973). 1974.
Adult Bookstore. 1976.
Collected Poems 1940–1977. 1978.
Love and War, Art and God. 1984.

Plays

The Tenor, with Ernst Lert, from a play by Wedekind, music by Hugo Weisgall (produced 1952). 1957.
The Soldier's Tale, from a libretto by C.F. Ramuz, music by Stravinsky (produced 1968). 1968.

Fiction

Edsel. 1971.

Other

English Prosody and Modern Poetry. 1947.
A Bibliography of Modern Prosody. 1948.
Poets at Work, with others, edited by Charles D. Abbott. 1948.
Beyond Criticism. 1953; as *A Primer for Poets*, 1965.
In Defense of Ignorance (essays). 1960.
Start with the Sun: Studies in Cosmic Poetry, with James E. Miller, Jr., and Bernice Slote. 1960.
The Writer's Experience, with Ralph Ellison. 1964.
A Prosody Handbook, with Robert Beum. 1965.
Randall Jarrell. 1967.
To Abolish Children and Other Essays. 1968.
The Poetry Wreck: Selected Essays 1950–1970. 1975.

Editor, with Louis Untermeyer and Richard Wilbur, *Modern American and Modern British Poetry*, revised shorter edition. 1955.
Editor, *American Poetry*. 1960.
Editor, *Prose Keys to Modern Poetry*. 1962.
Editor, *Tryne*, by Cynthia Bates, Steve Ellzey, and Bill Lynch. 1976.

*

Bibliography: *Shapiro: A Descriptive Bibliography 1933–1977* by Lee Bartlett, 1979.

Critical Study: *Shapiro* by Joseph Reino, 1981.

* * *

Karl Shapiro is a poet of great versatility who has a sophisticated command of prosody and a sharp ear for speech rhythms and verbal harmonies. He is a man of considerable erudition, though he never finished college, and a serious though good-humored social critic. Since his first volume of poems in 1935, he has published continuously. As poet and critic he always has taken an iconoclastic stance. He attacks with great vigor intellectual poetry, poseurs, stuffed shirts, and the establishment, and as a result has been a controversial figure. As editor of *Poetry* and the *Prairie Schooner* for 16 years, he was a significant force in contemporary poetry, and as a professor he taught three decades of aspiring writers.

When Shapiro published *Selected Poems*, he ignored his first volume, about which he writes in "Recapitulations":

> My first small book was nourished in the dark,
> Secretly written, published, and inscribed.
> Bound in wine-red, it made no brilliant mark.
> Rather impossible relatives subscribed.

His first recognition came in 1941 when he appeared in *Five Young American Poets*. His next volume, *Person, Place and Thing*, contains excellent poems of social comment in traditional form. "The Dome of Sunday" comments in sharp, clear imagery cast in blank verse on urban "Row houses and row-lives"; "Drug Store" observes youth culture satirically in unrhymed stanzas; "University [of Virginia]" mounts a low-keyed attack: "To hurt the Negro and avoid the Jew / Is the curriculum."

V-Letter and Other Poems contains some of the best poems to come out of World War II, some of which are "V-Letter," "Elegy for a Dead Soldier," "Troop Train," "The Gun," "Sunday: New Guinea," and "Christmas Eve: Australia." The form usually is rhymed stanzas, even *terza rima*, and here Shapiro's social comment finds a wider context. There also begin to be foreshadowings of later preoccupations: religious themes and attacks on intellectualism. "The Jew" anticipates *Poems of a Jew*, and "The Intellectual" ("I'd rather be a barber and cut hair / Than walk with you in gilt museum halls") looks toward attacks on Pound and Eliot in *In Defense of Ignorance*.

Although Shapiro does not write long poems (the exception is *Essay on Rime*, a youthful treatise on the art of poetry in which "Everything was going to be straightened out"), *Poems 1940–1953* contains an evocative, seven-part sequence telling the story of Adam and Eve. (This interest in myth reasserts itself in *Adult Bookstore* in a poignant version in 260 lines of "The Rape of Philomel.") This volume also contains "Israel," occasioned by the founding of that country: "When I see the name of Israel high in print / The fences crumble in my flesh. . . ." As a boy Shapiro grew up in a Russian-Jewish family not particularly religious, and after his bar mitzvah "I lost all interest in what I had learned." But *Poems of a Jew* explores his Jewishness with pride, wit, and irony, beginning with "The Alphabet" ("letters . . . strict as flames," "black and clean" and bristling "like barbed wire").

As early as 1942 Shapiro had published a prose-poem, "The Dirty Word," but in 1964 he turned to this form exclusively in *The Bourgeois Poet*, dropping the kind of verses he previously had thought best, "the poem with a beginning, a middle, and an end . . . that used literary allusion and rhythmic structuring and intellectual argument." He wanted a medium in which he could say anything he pleased—ridiculous, nonsensical, obscene, autobiographical, pompous. The individual pieces cover a wide variety of topics and, as earlier, they comment on persons, places, things. The longest (14 pages), "I Am an Atheist Who Says His Prayers," which reminds one of Shapiro's enthusiasm for Whitman, could have been called "Song of Myself." These prose poems (or free verse set as prose paragraphs) had a mixed reception. But Adrienne Rich noted that in his new style Shapiro was going through a "constant revising and purifying of his speech," as all poets must, and she thought parts of this volume were "a stunning success."

In *White-Haired Lover*, a cycle of middle-aged love poems, Shapiro returned to traditional forms, often the sonnet. This also is true of *Adult Bookstore*, a collection that ranges widely in subject. "The Humanities Building," "A Parliament of Poets," and the title poem show that Shapiro has not lost the wit, irony, and technique that have always characterized his work. "The Heiligenstadt Testament" is a splendid dramatic monologue of Beethoven's deathbed delirium, and among the poems occasioned by his move to California are "Garage Sale" ("This situation . . . / Strikes one as a cultural masterpiece") and a perfect Petrarchan sonnet on freeways and California suburbia.

The Poetry Wreck, which contains Shapiro's most important critical statements, throws light on his poetry, his sources, his beliefs. The derogatory essays on Pound and Eliot are reprinted along with admiring appraisals of W.H. Auden ("Eliot and Pound had rid the poem of emotion completely . . . Auden reversed the process"), William Carlos Williams, "whose entire literary career has been dedicated to the struggle to preserve spontaneity and immediacy of experience," Whitman, Dylan Thomas, Henry Miller, and Randall Jarrell. Jarrell, whose "poetry I admired and looked up to most after William Carlos Williams," once said in a passage Shapiro quotes: "Karl Shapiro's poems are fresh and young and rash and live; their hard clear outline, their flat bold colors create a world like that of a knowing and skillful neo-primitive painting, without any of the confusion or profundity of atmosphere, or aerial perspective, but with notable visual and satiric force."

—James Woodress

SHAW, Henry Wheeler. Pseudonym: Josh Billings. Born in Lanesboro, Massachusetts, 21 April 1818. Educated at Lenox Preparatory School, Massachusetts; Hamilton College, Clinton, New York, 1833–34. Married Zilpha Bradford in 1845; two daughters. Worked at odd jobs in the midwest, 1835–45, and in the east, 1845–54; auctioneer and realtor in Poughkeepsie, New York, 1854–66: Alderman, 1858; contributor, Poughkeepsie *Daily Press* from 1860; lecturer, 1863–80; moved to New York, 1867; contributor, New York *Weekly*, 1867–85, and *Century Magazine*, 1884–85. *Died 14 October 1885.*

Publications

Collections

Uncle Sam's Uncle Josh, edited by Donald Day. 1953.

Fiction

Josh Billings, Hiz Sayings. 1866; as *Josh Billings, His Book of Sayings*, 1866.
Josh Billings on Ice, and Other Things. 1868.
Josh Billings' Farmer's Allminax for the Year 1870. 1869 (and later volumes to 1879); 1 vol. edition, as *Old Probability: Perhaps Rain—Perhaps Not*, 1879; as *Josh Billings' Old Farmer's Allminax 1870–1879*, 1902.
Josh Billings' Wit and Humor. 1874; as *Everybody's Friend; or, Josh Billing's* (sic) *Encyclopedia and Proverbial Philosophy of Wit and Humor*, 1874.
Josh Billings: His Works, Complete. 1876.
Josh Billings' Trump Kards: Blue Grass Philosophy. 1877.
Josh Billings' Cook Book and Picktorial Proverbs. 1880; revised edition, as *Josh Billings Struggling with Things*, 1881.
Life and Adventures of Josh Billings. 1883.

Editor, *Josh Billings' Spice Box*. 1881(?).

*

Bibliography: in *Bibliography of American Literature* by Jacob Blanck, edited by Virginia L. Smyers and Michael Winship, 1983.

Critical Studies: *Billings, Yankee Humorist* by Cyril Clemens, 1932; *Shaw (Billings)* by David B. Kesterson, 1973.

* * *

Farmer, boatman, explorer, real-estate salesman, auctioneer, Henry Wheeler Shaw turned to writing in his middle age and leapt into national prominence in America with an "Essa on the Muel bi Josh Billings" ("The Muel is haf hoss and haf Jackass, and then kums to a full stop, natur diskovering her mistake"). He took a pen name but avoided the topical subjects of his contemporaries. Unfortunately for the modern reader, he did adopt the comic device of atrocious spelling, then considered in America to be a sure-fire laugh-getter. As with the Irish dialect of Finley Peter Dunne's "Mr. Dooley," however, it is often worth the extra effort in reading for Josh Billings's cracker-barrel philosophy and "trump-kard" aphorisms are frequently hilarious. It's worth the trouble to meet characters such as Mehitable Saffron, "the virgin-hero ov wimmins' rights . . . she spoke without notes, at arms' length."

Max Eastman declared that Josh Billings was "the father of imagism" and found nothing in New England poetry before Billings's time "quite comparable to his statement that goats 'know the way up a rock as natural as woodbine,' which is Homeric." Certainly Billings is a primitive La Bruyère, a rustic La Rochefoucauld, and an aphorist with a moralistic rather than a cynical streak. "Most people repent ov their sins bi thanking God they ain't so wicked as their nabers." He stressed that "yu hav tew be wise before yu kan be witty" and there is plenty of wisdom in such comments as "There may cum a time when the Lion and the Lamb will lie down together—i shall be as glad to see it as enny body—but i am still betting on the Lion."

—Leonard R.N. Ashley

SHEPARD, Sam. Born Samuel Shepard Rogers in Fort Sheridan, Illinois, 5 November 1943. Educated at Duarte High School, California, graduated 1960; Mount San Antonio Junior College, Walnut, California, 1960–61. Married O-Lan Johnson in 1969, one son; one daughter by the actress Jessica Lange. Worked as hot walker at the Santa Anita Race Track, stable hand, Connolly Arabian Horse Ranch, Duarte, herdsman, Huff Sheep Ranch, Chino, orange picker in Duarte, and sheep shearer in Pomona, all in California; actor with Bishop's Company Repertory Players, Burbank, California, and U.S. tour, 1962; car wrecker, Charlemont, Massachusetts; bus boy, Village Gate, 1963–64, waiter, Marie's Crisis Café, 1965, and musician with the Holy Modal Rounders, 1968, all in New York; lived in England, 1971–74, and in California since 1974; director of many of his own plays; film actor: roles in *Brand X*, 1970, *Days of Heaven*, 1978, *Resurrection*, 1981, *Raggedy Man*, 1981, *Frances*, 1982, *The Right Stuff*, 1983, *Country*, 1984, and *Fool for Love*, 1985. Recipient: Obie award, 1967, 1970, 1973, 1975, 1978 (twice), 1980, 1984; Yale University fellowship, 1967; Rockefeller grant, 1967; Guggenheim grant, 1968; American Academy grant, 1974; Brandeis University Creative Arts Award, 1976; Pulitzer Prize, 1979.

PUBLICATIONS

Plays

Cowboys (produced 1964).
The Rock Garden (produced 1964; excerpt produced in *Oh! Calcutta!*, 1967). In *The Unseen Hand and Other Plays*, 1971.
Up to Thursday (produced 1965).
Dog (produced 1965).
Rocking Chair (produced 1965).
Chicago (produced 1965). In *Five Plays*, 1967.
Icarus's Mother (produced 1965). In *Five Plays*, 1967.
4-H Club (produced 1965). In *The Unseen Hand and Other Plays*, 1971.
Fourteen Hundred Thousand (produced 1966). In *Five Plays*, 1967.
Red Cross (produced 1966). In *Five Plays*, 1967.
La Turista (produced 1967). 1968.
Melodrama Play (produced 1967). In *Five Plays*, 1967.
Five Plays. 1967; as *Chicago and Other Plays*, 1982.
Cowboys #2 (produced 1967). In *Mad Dog Blues and Other Plays*, 1971.
Forensic and the Navigators (produced 1967). In *The Unseen Hand and Other Plays*, 1971.
The Holy Ghostly (produced 1969). In *The Unseen Hand and Other Plays*, 1971.
The Unseen Hand (produced 1969). In *The Unseen Hand and Other Plays*, 1971.
Operation Sidewinder (produced 1970). 1970.
Shaved Splits (produced 1970). In *The Unseen Hand and Other Plays*, 1971.
Mad Dog Blues (produced 1971). In *Mad Dog Blues and Other Plays*, 1971.
Cowboy Mouth, with Patti Smith (produced 1971). In *Mad Dog Blues and Other Plays*, 1971.
Back Bog Beast Bait (produced 1971). In *The Unseen Hand and Other Plays*, 1971.
The Unseen Hand and Other Plays. 1971.
Mad Dog Blues and Other Plays. 1971.

The Tooth of Crime (produced 1972). In *The Tooth of Crime, and Geography of a Horse Dreamer*, 1974.
Blue Bitch (televised 1972; produced 1973).
Nightwalk, with Megan Terry and Jean-Claude van Itallie (produced 1973).
Little Ocean (produced 1974).
Geography of a Horse Dreamer (produced 1974). In *The Tooth of Crime, and Geography of a Horse Dreamer*, 1974.
The Tooth of Crime, and Geography of a Horse Dreamer. 1974.
Action (produced 1974). In *Action, and The Unseen Hand*, 1975.
Action, and The Unseen Hand. 1975.
Killer's Head (produced 1975). In *Angel City and Other Plays*, 1976.
Angel City (produced 1976). In *Angel City and Other Plays*, 1976.
Angel City and Other Plays. 1976.
Suicide in B Flat (produced 1976). In *Buried Child and Other Plays*, 1979.
The Sad Lament of Pecos Bill on the Eve of Killing His Wife (produced 1976). In *Fool for Love, and The Sad Lament of Pecos Bill on the Eve of Killing His Wife*, 1983.
Curse of the Starving Class (produced 1977). In *Angel City and Other Plays*, 1976.
Inacoma (produced 1977).
Buried Child (produced 1978). In *Buried Child and Other Plays*, 1979.
Seduced (produced 1978). In *Buried Child and Other Plays*, 1979.
Tongues, with Joseph Chaikin, music by Shepard, Skip LaPlante, and Harry Mann (produced 1978). In *Seven Plays*, 1981.
Buried Child and Other Plays. 1979; as *Buried Child, and Seduced, and Suicide in B Flat*, 1980.
Savage/Love, with Joseph Chaikin, music by Shepard, Skip LaPlante, and Harry Mann (produced 1979). In *Seven Plays*, 1981.
True West (produced 1980). 1981.
Jackson's Dance, with Jacques Levy (produced 1980).
Four Two-Act Plays (includes *La Turista, The Tooth of Crime, Geography of a Horse Dreamer, Operation Sidewinder*). 1980.
Seven Plays (includes *Buried Child, Curse of the Starving Class, The Tooth of Crime, La Turista, True West, Tongues, Savage/Love*). 1981.
Superstitions (produced 1983).
Fool for Love (produced 1983). 1984.
Fool for Love, and The Sad Lament of Pecos Bill on the Eve of Killing His Wife. 1983.
Fool for Love and Other Plays. 1984.
Paris, Texas (screenplay), with Wim Wenders, edited by Chris Sievernich. 1984.
A Lie of the Mind (produced 1985). 1987.

Screenplays: *Me and My Brother*, with Robert Frank, 1969; *Zabriskie Point*, with others, 1970; *Ringaleevio*, 1971; *Paris, Texas*, 1984; *Fool for Love*, 1985.

Television Play: *Blue Bitch*, 1972.

Other

Hawk Moon: A Book of Short Stories, Poems, and Monologues. 1973.
Rolling Thunder Logbook. 1977.
Motel Chronicles. 1982.

*

Critical Studies: *American Dreams: The Imagination of Shepard* edited by Bonnie Marranca, 1981; *Shepard, Arthur Kopit, and the Off-Broadway Theater* by Doris Auerbach, 1982; *Inner Landscapes: The Theater of Shepard* by Ron Mottram, 1984; *Shepard* by Vivian M. Patraka and Mark Siegel, 1985; *Shepard* by Don Shewey, 1985; *Shepard: The Life and Work of an American Dreamer* by Ellen Oumano, 1986.

* * *

Sam Shepard is the pre-eminent mythmaker in a country that elected another Illinois-born actor from California as its president. Like Ronald Reagan comfortable living out a western-ranch fantasy and capitalizing on Americans' obsession with father images, Shepard differs from the White House cowpoke in at least one respect: the playwright is an imaginative original.

Possibly wedded to paradox, Shepard is a movie star so suspicious of commercial theatre he won't let his scripts be mounted on Broadway, a Pulitzer Prize winner whose plays are so outside the mainstream they often eschew development of consistent characters or a coherent plot, and a creator of distinctively crafted monologues and dialogues acclaimed for their verbal skill who nevertheless puts words together improvisationally, with a spontaneity akin to the surrealists' "automatic writing." Although a writer especially concerned with father/son relationships, Shepard offended his father by dropping their surname (Rogers) and has left his son in the care of his ex-wife. Many of his plays mock the movies, yet Shepard has been nominated for a performance Oscar and is a big Hollywood box-office attraction. Although he debunks the American Dream in his drama, Shepard has fulfilled that dream in his life. Whereas the author grew up on a ranch, dresses like a cowboy, and is at home on a horse, the plays disparage far more than they celebrate the macho Western type who is so often their subject.

A formative influence on Shepard's style was his early association with Joseph Chaikin's Open Theater, where he was exposed to acting exercises of sudden, mid-scene character transformation. Cody in *Geography of a Horse Dreamer* becomes an Irishman, the New Yorkers in *Cowboys #2* move in and out of cowboy roles, Stu in *Chicago* periodically talks like an old lady, the characters in *Back Bog Beast Bait* turn into animals, and the boy in *La Turista* becomes both Kent's son and Kent himself before Kent escapes from the play as a movie monster. Another escape through transformation occurs when the Lobster Man in *Cowboy Mouth* is transmogrified into the rock-'n'-roll savior.

In *Curse of the Starving Class*, Emma shifts from an A student to a delinquent while Weston alters from a violent drunk to a model househusband and Wesley, by donning his father's clothes, becomes Weston. In *Angel City* the contagion of Hollywood fantasy turns the drummer into a child and a chef, the writer into a medicine man, a child, a newscaster, and a native, the secretary into an Irish nun and a teenager, one producer into a boxer and a teenager, and the other producer into a lizard—until he and the writer switch roles, suggesting that the writer is the disaster in this own disaster movie. Blue Morphan and Sycamore likewise switch characters in *The Unseen Hand*, as do Pop and Ice in *The Holy Ghostly*. In *The Tooth of Crime* character transformations are a dueling technique, and in *Suicide in B Flat* they serve as a vehicle for murder.

Shifts in who a given character may be are part of the dramatist's interest in the mutability of individual identity and indeed in the larger issue of ontology, or the nature of being. Shepard characters worry about disappearing or they seem to be part of duplicated characters, as when two people in *Forensic and the Navigators* answer to the name Forensic, Drake and Cisco dress like Duke in *Melodrama Play*, or Niles identifies with Pablo and Louis in *Suicide in B Flat*. Human duality is also represented by opposites like Lee and Austin in *True West* or Jake and Frankie in *A Lie of the Mind*. Both sets of brothers trade places, as Lee becomes a writer and Austin a thief who wants to escape to the desert, and Frankie replaces Jake in Beth's affections. Lies of the mind, Shepard suggests, distort our identities, our natures, our beings.

Other subjects which recur in Shepard are the Old West, the family, and the plight of the creative artist. Shepard expresses ambivalent fascination with romantic myths of the frontier beginning with his first play, *Cowboys*, and extending right up to such recent critiques as *The Sad Lament of Pecos Bill on the Eve of Killing His Wife*, *True West*, *Fool for Love*, and *A Lie of the Mind*. Sometimes he kills off the mythic West—as in *Pecos Bill*, *Suicide*, and *The Holy Ghostly*'s patricide—but his heritage returns repeatedly to haunt him. The importance of father/son relations, though it surfaced in the early *The Rock Garden* and *The Holy Ghostly*, was not apparent until his five big family plays of recent years (together with his film *Paris, Texas*). These constitute a devastating examination of the Greek theme of philos-aphilos, or love mixed with hatred, as incest, bigamy, violence, murder, and Oedipal and sibling rivalries stalk the stage. Finally, the plays which dramatize the artist facing commercial pressures to produce another hit are, with the exception of *True West*, not the domestic dramas but the more fanciful *Melodrama Play*, *The Tooth of Crime*, *Geography of a Horse Dreamer*, *Angel City*, and *Suicide in B Flat*.

Shepard as a pioneer in form is even more intriguing than Shepard as a commentator on our times, or as Edward Albee says, "What Shepard's plays are about is a great deal less interesting than how they are about it." In addition to character transformations, absurdist disjunctions in the action, and Pinteresque menace (repeatedly evident), Shepard excels at visual theatricality, humor, and distinctive language.

Shepard's spectators carry away memorable images: Lobster Man cracking open in *Cowboy Mouth*; the headlights and fire and characters bouncing off the walls in *Fool for Love*; Stu clothed but sitting in a bathtub in *Chicago*; the giant catfish in *Pecos Bill*; Kent smashing through the set's back wall in *La Turista*; the two-headed pig-beast in *Back Bog Beast Bait*; monster scales and green ooze in *Angel City*; Hackamore covering himself with Kleenex in *Seduced*; the ghost, the witch and the huge fire in *The Holy Ghostly*; or the Hopi costumes and ritual, the flashing blue lights and the giant rattlesnake in *Operation Sidewinder*. Food imagery is plentiful, especially in the recent plays. Who can forget, along with the muddy corpse in *Buried Child*, the piles of corn and carrots? Food farce occurs with Rice Krispies in *Forensic and the Navigators*, with apples in *4-H Club*, and later in two more plays set in kitchens: toast popping out of a row of toasters in *True West* rivals the refrigerator stuffed with artichokes in *Curse of the Starving Class* as the archetypal Shepard symbols for both the raw hunger of libido and Americans' spiritual malnutrition.

Shepard's humor is nearly all non-verbal. Laughs grow from sight gags (Louis trying to kill himself with one hand and to save himself with the other in *Suicide* or Becky making a pass at herself with one hand and trying to stop it with the other in *The Tooth of Crime*) or from situations (Mom walking into her house filled with debris and dead plants in *True West*; Shelly and later Father Dewis stranded with weirdos in *Buried Child*; Sycamore bewildered by the 20th century in *The Unseen Hand*). Yet the dialogue, particularly in *Mad Dog Blues* and *Fool for Love*, yields a few delicious jokes.

Shepard's language is the argot of assorted male subcultures, including sports, outlaws, the wild west, music and movie makers, power brokers, and ornery middle Americans. He often interpolates long monologues into the action, and these speeches can be more narrative, expository, or descriptive than dramatic. Some speeches interrupt the action on the model of a jazz solo, a prose poem, or a tap dance tour de force. Characters may seem not to be addressing one another, replying to what has gone before—or even listening. Yet the rhythms are insistent, the not surprising product of a writer who is also a rock drummer and often constructs his plays around music.

—Tish Dace

See the essay on *The Tooth of Crime*.

SHERWOOD, Robert E(mmet). Born in New Rochelle, New York, 4 April 1896. Educated at Milton Academy, Massachusetts, 1909–14; Harvard University, Cambridge, Massachusetts (editor, *Harvard Lampoon*), 1914–17, A.B. 1918. Served in the Canadian Black Watch, 1917–19: wounded in action, 1918; served as special assistant to the Secretary of War, Washington, D.C., 1939–42; director, Overseas Branch, Office of War Information, 1942–44; special assistant to the Secretary of the Navy, Washington, D.C., 1945. Married 1) Mary Brandon in 1922 (divorced, 1934), one daughter; 2) Madeline Hurlock Connelly in 1935. Drama editor, *Vanity Fair*, New York, 1919–20; film reviewer and associate editor, 1920–24, and editor, 1924–28, *Life* magazine, New York; literary editor, *Scribner's*, New York, 1928–30; full-time playwright from 1930; founder, with Elmer Rice, Sidney Howard, Maxwell Anderson, S.N. Behrman, and John F. Wharton, Playwrights Company, 1938. Founder, with Robert Benchley, Dorothy Parker, and others, Algonquin Hotel Round Table, 1920. Secretary, 1935, and President, 1937–40, Dramatists Guild; President, American National Theatre and Academy, 1940. Recipient: Megrue Prize, 1932; Pulitzer Prize, 1936, 1939, 1941, and, for biography, 1949; American Academy Gold Medal, 1941; Oscar, for screenplay, 1946; Bancroft Prize, for history, 1949; Gutenberg Award, 1949. D.Litt.: Dartmouth College, Hanover, New Hampshire, 1940; Yale University, New Haven, Connecticut, 1941; Harvard University, 1949; D.C.L.: Bishop's University, Lennoxville, Quebec, 1950. *Died 14 November 1955.*

PUBLICATIONS

Plays

A White Elephant (produced 1916).
Barnum Was Right (produced 1918).

The Road to Rome (produced 1927). 1927.
The Love Nest, from the story by Ring Lardner (produced 1927).
The Queen's Husband (produced 1928). 1928.
Waterloo Bridge (produced 1930). 1930.
This Is New York (produced 1930). 1931.
Reunion in Vienna (produced 1931). 1932.
Acropolis (produced 1933).
The Petrified Forest (produced 1935). 1935.
Idiot's Delight (produced 1936). 1936.
The Ghost Goes West (screenplay), with Geoffrey Kerr, in *Successful Film Writing* by Seton Margrave. 1936.
Tovarich, from a play by Jacques Deval (produced 1936). 1937.
The Adventures of Marco Polo (screenplay), in *How to Write and Sell Film Stories* by Frances Marion. 1937.
Abe Lincoln in Illinois (produced 1938). 1939.
There Shall Be No Night (produced 1940). 1940.
An American Crusader (broadcast 1941). In *The Free Company Presents*, edited by James Boyd, 1941.
Rebecca (screenplay), with others, in *Twenty Best Film Plays*, edited by John Gassner and Dudley Nichols. 1943.
The Rugged Path (produced 1945). Shortened version in *The Best Plays of 1945–46*, edited by Burns Mantle, 1946.
Miss Liberty, music by Irving Berlin (produced 1949). 1949.
Second Threshold, completion of a play by Philip Barry (produced 1951). 1951.
Small War on Murray Hill (produced 1957). 1957.

Screenplays: *The Hunchback of Notre Dame*, with others, 1924; *The Lucky Lady*, with James T. O'Donohoe and Bertram Bloch, 1926; *The Age for Love*, 1931; *Around the World in Eighty Minutes with Douglas Fairbanks*, 1931; *Cock of the Air*, with Charles Lederer, 1932; *Roman Scandals*, with others, 1933; *The Scarlet Pimpernel*, with others, 1935; *The Ghost Goes West*, with Geoffrey Kerr, 1936; *Over the Moon*, with others, 1937; *Thunder in the City*, with others, 1937; *The Adventures of Marco Polo*, 1938; *The Divorce of Lady X*, with Lajos Biro, 1938; *Idiot's Delight*, 1939; *Abe Lincoln in Illinois*, 1940; *Rebecca* with others, 1940; *The Best Years of Our Lives*, 1946; *The Bishop's Wife*, with Leonardo Bercovici, 1947; *Man on a Tightrope*, 1953; *Main Street to Broadway*, with Samson Raphaelson, 1953.

Radio Play: *An American Crusader*, 1941.

Television Writing: *The Backbone of America*, 1954.

Fiction

The Virtuous Knight. 1931; as *Unending Crusade*, 1932.

Other

Roosevelt and Hopkins: An Intimate History. 1948; revised edition, 1950; as *The White House Papers of Harry L. Hopkins*, 2 vols., 1948–49.

Editor, *The Best Moving Pictures of 1922–23, Also Who's Who in the Movies and the Yearbook of the American Screen*. 1923.

*

Critical Studies: *The Worlds of Sherwood: Mirror to His Times 1896–1939*, 1962, and *The Ordeal of a Playwright: Sherwood and the Challenge of War*, edited by Norman Cousins, 1970, both by John Mason Brown; *Sherwood* by R. Baird Shuman, 1964; *Sherwood: Reluctant Moralist* by Walter J. Meserve, 1970.

* * *

Though of a generation often described as "rootless" and "lost," Robert E. Sherwood was a romantic idealist with a liberal outlook whose plays embodied assumptions underlying the political philosophy of the Roosevelt administration and gave those assumptions powerful artistic expression. Alive to the need for creating an art imbued with a social and moral fervour, Sherwood believed that the one determining consideration for the future of the theatre was "its ability to give its audiences something they can't obtain, more cheaply and conveniently, in the neighboring cinema palaces." The artist's lack of social purpose, he pointed out in his address to the PEN International Congress in 1950, gave him a guilty sense of inadequacy—the uneasy knowledge that reform, though needed, was not taking place. The supreme task of "all writers, young and old" was, therefore, to achieve a reconciliation of the "problems of the human heart with a world state of mind that appears to become increasingly inhuman."

Sherwood's apprehension of the threats posed by a world situation indifferent to finer human sentiments dominates his dramatic art. His realistic problem plays—whether set in Finland under Russian attack (*There Shall Be No Night*) or in a hotel in the Alps (*Idiot's Delight*) or in a gasoline station and lunch room in the Arizona desert (*The Petrified Forest*)—often relied on an extreme situation, a background of war or violence, to highlight the protagonist's search for ethical values. Sherwood's pacifism, though attuned to the feeling of many liberals during the Roosevelt era, was never parochial or chauvinistic and displayed dynamic, even militant, modulations over the years. His first play, *The Road to Rome*, dealing comically with Hannibal's decision to defer his march on Rome, represents a plea for absolute peace; his last important play, *There Shall Be No Night*, is characterised by the realisation that freedom has to be defended even at the cost of endangering peace temporarily. In fighting the Russians in Finland, the scientist-protagonist of *There Shall Be No Night* fights for the emancipation of all men from oppression. *The Rugged Path* can be read, at one level, as an idealist's resolve to join the war in defence of peace and human dignity.

Several of Sherwood's plays exemplify his belief that the willingness to make personal sacrifice is the main moral test. In *The Petrified Forest* sacrifice appears as a necessary means of preventing Nature from "taking the world away from the intellectuals and giving it back to the apes." On the other hand, *Abe Lincoln in Illinois*, chronicling Lincoln's difficult years before his election to the presidency, sensitively focuses on the relationship between an individual's sacrifice and national interest. *There Shall Be No Night* returns to the same moral issue and implies, through the fate of its protagonist, that "There is no coming to consciousness without pain."

Sherwood is vulnerable to the charge of didacticism, but he understood his age and rarely suggested daring departures from opinions then current. As a result, the moralistic intentions behind his plays were so static that their appeal seldom extended beyond the topical. But it should be recognised that Sherwood's didacticism often became integral to the dramatic form: in *Abe Lincoln in Illinois*, for example, the curtain drops just as the farewell crowd, which is singing "John Brown's Body," reaches the line "His soul goes marching on." Also, Sherwood's use of comedy, as in *The Road to Rome* and *The Queen's Husband*, helps relieve the moralistic solemnity. Sherwood's ironic consciousness would not let him overlook the flaws in his own plays, flaws he recorded with rare candour. For instance, he found *The Road to Rome* defective because it employed "the cheapest sort of device—making historical characters use modern slang."

Sherwood wrote in other genres with mixed results. *The Virtuous Knight*, his early historical novel about the Third Crusade, was generally regarded as a failure, though in retrospect it does provide useful insights into the themes and techniques of his plays. His screenplay *The Best Years of Our Lives* won an Oscar in 1946, but his television show, *The Backbone of America*, was a dismal flop. The greatest success of his nondramatic writing was his biography *Roosevelt and Hopkins*, based on his experience as special assistant to the Secretary of War, director of the Overseas Branch of the Office of War Information, and, most important, as Roosevelt's favourite speech writer and unofficial adviser. This book ranks among the finest histories of World War II written in the United States, and certainly deserved its Pulitzer Prize.

Immensely popular in his own lifetime, Sherwood is no O'Neill, Miller, or Williams. As time passes his plays seem increasingly dated. Still, his realistic problem plays, inspired as they were by his passion for freedom and peace, faithfully reflected the urges and anxieties of the American 1920's and 1930's and thereby have made a significant contribution to American drama.

—Chirantan Kulshrestha

SIMMS, William Gilmore. Born in Charleston, South Carolina, 17 April 1806. Educated at public and private schools in Charleston; apprenticed to pharmacist, 6 years; studied law: admitted to South Carolina bar, 1827. Married 1) Anna Malcolm Giles in 1826 (died, 1832), one daughter; 2) Chevillette Roach in 1836 (died, 1863), 13 children. Lawyer in Charleston, 1827–29; editor, *Southern Literary Gazette*, 1828, and Charleston *City Gazette*, 1830–32; visited the North, 1832, and formed friendship with William Cullen Bryant; lived in the North, 1833–34; returned to Charleston, 1835; lived at wife's family home, Woodlands Plantation, Barnwell County, and in Charleston, from 1836, and made annual trips to the North to look after his publishing interests; editor, *Magnolia*, 1842–43, *Southern and Western Magazine* (later *Simms's Magazine*), 1845, and *Southern Quarterly Review*, 1849–54; advocate of slavery: lectured in New York, 1856; editor of the newspapers Columbia *Phoenix*, 1865, *Daily South Carolinian*, 1865–66, and *Courier*, 1870; wrote serials for magazines in New York and Philadelphia from 1865. *Died 11 June 1870.*

PUBLICATIONS

Collections

The Letters, edited by Mary C. Simms Oliphant, Alfred Taylor Odell, and T.C. Duncan Eaves. 5 vols., 1952–56; supplement, 1982.

Writings (Centennial Edition), edited by John C. Guilds. 1969—

Fiction

Martin Faber: The Story of a Criminal. 1833; in *Writings 5*, 1974.

The Book of My Lady: A Melange (stories). 1833.

Guy Rivers: A Tale of Georgia. 1834.

The Yemassee: A Romance of Carolina. 1835; edited by J.V. Ridgely, 1964.

The Partisan: A Tale of the Revolution. 1835.

Mellichampe: A Legend of the Santee. 1836.

Martin Faber and Other Tales. 1837.

Richard Hurdis; or, The Avenger of Blood. 1838.

Pelayo: A Story of the Goth. 1838.

Carl Werner: An Imaginative Story, with Other Tales. 1838; as *Matilda*, 1846; in *Writings 5*, 1974.

The Damsel of Darien. 1839.

Border Beagles: A Tale of Mississippi. 1840.

The Kinsmen; or, The Black Riders of Congaree. 1841; as *The Scout*, 1854.

Confession; or, The Blind Heart: A Domestic Story. 1841.

Beauchampe; or, The Kentucky Tragedy. 1842; vol. 1 revised, as *Charlemont; or, The Pride of the Village*, 1856; vol. 2 revised, as *Beauchampe; or, The Kentucky Tragedy*, 1856.

The Prima Donna: A Passage from City Life. 1844; in *Writings 5*, 1974.

Castle Dismal; or, The Bachelor's Christmas: A Domestic Legend. 1844.

Helen Halsey; or, The Swamp State of Conelachita: A Tale of the Borders. 1844; as *The Island Bride*, 1869.

The Wigwam and the Cabin (stories). 2 vols., 1845–46; as *Life in America*, 1848.

Count Julian; or, The Last Days of the Goth. 1845.

The Lily and the Totem; or, The Huguenots in Florida. 1850; as *The Huguenots in Florida*, 1884.

Flirtation at the Moultrie House. 1850; in *Writings 5*, 1974.

Katharine Walton; or, The Rebel of Dorchester. 1851.

The Golden Christmas: A Chronicle of St. John's, Berkeley. 1852.

As Good as a Comedy; or, The Tennesseean's Story. 1852; in *Writings 3*, 1972.

The Sword and the Distaff; or, "Fair, Fat and Forty." 1852; as *Woodcraft; or, Hawks about the Dovecote*, 1854; edited by Charles S. Watson, 1983.

Marie De Berniere (stories). 1853; as *The Maroon: A Legend of the Caribbees, and Other Tales*, 1855; as *The Ghost of My Husband*, 1866; in *Writings 5*, 1974.

Vasconselos: A Romance of the New World. 1853.

Southward Ho! A Spell of Sunshine. 1854.

The Forayers; or, The Raid of the Dog-Days. 1855.

Eutaw: A Sequel to The Forayers. 1856.

The Cassique of Kiawah. 1859.

Cavalier of Old South Carolina: Simms's Captain Porgy (selections), edited by Hugh W. Hetherington. 1966.

Voltmeier; or, The Mountain Men, edited by Donald Davidson and Mary C. Simms Oliphant, in *Writings 1.* 1969.

Paddy McGann; or, The Demon of the Stump, edited by Robert Bush, in *Writings 3.* 1972.

Joscelyn: A Tale of the Revolution, edited by Stephen Meats and Keen Butterworth, in *Writings 16.* 1975.

Plays

Norman Maurice; or, The Man of the People. 1851.
Michael Bonham; or, The Fall of Bexar. 1852.

Verse

Monody on the Death of Gen. Charles Cotesworth Pinckney. 1825.
Lyrical and Other Poems. 1827.
Early Lays. 1827.
The Vision of Cortes, Cain, and Other Poems. 1829.
The Tri-Color; or, The Three Days of Blood in Paris. 1830.
Atalantis: A Story of the Sea. 1832; revised edition, 1848.
Southern Passages and Pictures. 1839.
Donna Florida. 1843.
Grouped Thoughts and Scattered Fancies: A Collection of Sonnets. 1845.
Areytos; or, Songs of the South. 1846.
Lays of the Palmetto. 1848.
Charleston and Her Satirists: A Scribblement. 2 vols., 1848.
The Cassique of Accabee, A Tale of Ashley River, with Other Pieces. 1849.
Sabbath Lyrics; or, Songs from Scripture. 1849.
The City of the Silent. 1850.
Poems: Descriptive, Dramatic, Legendary and Contemplative. 2 vols., 1854.
Poems: Areytos; or, Songs and Ballads of the South, with Other Poems. 1860.

Other

Slavery in America, Being a Brief Review of Miss Martineau on That Subject. 1838; revised version, in *The Pro-Slavery Argument*, 1852.
The History of South Carolina. 1840; revised edition, 1842, 1860.
The Geography of South Carolina (for children). 1843.
The Social Principle: The True Source of National Permanence. 1843.
The Life of Francis Marion. 1844.
The Sources of American Independence. 1844.
Views and Reviews in American Literature, History and Fiction. 1846; 2nd series, 1847; 1st series edited by C. Hugh Holman, 1962.
The Life of Captain John Smith. 1847.
Self-Development. 1847.
The Life of Chevalier Bayard. 1848.
Father Abbot; or, The Home Tourist. 1849.
South-Carolina in the Revolutionary War. 1853.
Egeria; or, Voices of Thought and Counsel for the Woods and Wayside. 1853.
Works (Uniform Edition). 20 vols., 1853–59.
The Spartanburg Female College. 1855.
Sack and Destruction of the City of Columbia, S.C. 1865; edited by A.S. Salley, 1937.
The Sense of the Beautiful. 1870.

Editor, *The Remains of Maynard Davis Richardson*. 1833.
Editor, *The Charleston Book: A Miscellany in Prose and Verse*. 1845.
Editor, *A Supplement to the Plays of William Shakspeare*. 1848.
Editor, *The Life of Nathanael Greene*. 1849.
Editor, *War Poetry of the South*. 1866.

*

Bibliography: *A Bibliography of the Separate Writings of Simms* by Oscar Wegelin, revised edition, 1941; *Pseudonymous Publications of Simms* by James E. Kibler, Jr., 1976, and *Simms: A Reference Guide* by Kibler and Keen Butterworth, 1980; in *Bibliography of American Literature* by Jacob Blanck, edited by Virginia L. Smyers and Michael Winship, 1983.

Critical Studies: *Simms* by William P. Trent, 1892; *Simms as Literary Critic* by Edd Winfield Parks, 1961; *Simms* by J.V. Ridgely, 1962; *The Politics of a Literary Man: Simms* by Jon L. Wakelyn, 1973; *The Poetry of Simms: An Introduction and Bibliography* by James E. Kibler, Jr., 1979.

* * *

The most versatile and representative southern writer of the 19th century and one of the more talented American writers of his period, William Gilmore Simms tried his hand at many literary forms and tasks. He published at least four biographies, the best of which, *The Life of Francis Marion*, is a consideration of sources and materials also used in several of his long fictions on the Revolution. He also wrote books on the geography and history of South Carolina.

Simms was early and late a journalist. He edited both newspapers and magazines and eventually possessed considerable influence, especially in the south, as editor and contributor of essays and criticism to such journals as the *Southern Literary Gazette*, *Southern Literary Messenger*, *Southern Literary Journal*, *Southern Quarterly Review*, and *Russell's Magazine*. He also contributed to many of the most consequential northern magazines, including the *Knickerbocker*, *Democratic Review*, *Graham's*, *Harper's New Monthly*, and *Lippincott's*. Some of his best periodical criticism is collected in *Views and Reviews*, but, as Edd Winfield Parks noted in *William Gilmore Simms as Literary Critic*, there is also important criticism in his prefaces and advertisements to the novels and in his letters. In the Advertisement to *The Yemassee* in 1835, for example, Simms elaborated on a distinction between the romance and the novel that allowed the writer of the former considerable latitude in the treatment of the possible and the probable; in long critical essays he discoursed learnedly on Cooper's writings in 1842 (and gave his chief American rival every bit of his due), and in 1845 he dealt effectively with "Americanism in Literature"; and in letters in 1842 and thereafter he discussed perceptively the place of realism in fiction and fairly characterized Poe as magazinist, story writer, and poet. Simms's letters have recently assumed their rightful place in any study of his canon as a result of their publication in five volumes, with a sixth supplementary volume.

Simms also wrote a number of plays, including two in blank verse (*Norman Maurice* and *Michael Bonham*), and his view of his own merit as a poet is indicated in a remark in a letter of 24 November 1853 that his "poetical work exhibits the highest phase of the Imaginative faculty which this Country has yet exhibited, and the most philosophical in connection with it." Few, including his friends Paul Hamilton Hayne and Henry Timrod, agreed with him then or subsequently, but with *The Poetry of Simms* James E. Kibler, Jr., began laying the groundwork for a reappraisal of Simms's verse.

Over the years, however, most critics have agreed that Simms's chief contribution was to the novel. This is still largely the case when one considers the size and scope of his accomplishment in the seven books of the Revolutionary Romances (1835–56) or observes carefully the achievement in such individual works as *The Yemassee, Border Beagles, Katharine Walton, Woodcraft*, or *The Cassique of Kiawah*. But Simms was also a significant writer of short fiction, as John C. Guilds and Betty J. Strickland have demonstrated. Guilds maintains in his introduction to *Stories and Tales* (Volume 5 of the Centennial Edition) that the "short story or tale" is Simms's "best genre," and the contents of this edition plus the better-known tales of *The Wigwam and the Cabin* show that Simms did indeed make a consequential and varied contribution to short fiction.

Simms's versatility and prolixity, to say nothing of the adverse reaction of northern readers to his political views during the Civil War and its aftermath, assuredly contributed to the decline in his literary reputation, which reached its nadir during World War II. However, with the studies of C. Hugh Holman in the late 1940's and thereafter, the edition of letters in the 1950's (including especially the critical evaluation of Simms's best work by Donald Davidson), the publication of the Centennial Edition, and the recent critical studies by Kibler and Mary A. Wimsatt, Simms's work is receiving some of the attention it has long merited.

—Rayburn S. Moore

SIMPSON, Louis (Aston Marantz). Born in Jamaica, British West Indies, 27 March 1923. Educated at Munro College, Jamaica, 1933–40, Cambridge Higher Schools Certificate, 1939; Columbia University, New York, B.S. 1948, A.M. 1950, Ph.D. 1959. Served in the U.S. Army, 1943–45: Purple Heart and Bronze Star. Married 1) Jeanne Claire Rogers in 1949 (divorced, 1954), one son; 2) Dorothy Roochvarg in 1955 (divorced, 1979), one son and one daughter. Editor, Bobbs-Merrill Publishing Company, New York, 1950–55; Instructor, Columbia University, 1955–59; Professor of English, University of California, Berkeley, 1959–67; since 1967, Professor of English, State University of New York, Stony Brook. Recipient: American Academy in Rome fellowship, 1957; Edna St. Vincent Millay Award, 1960; Guggenheim fellowship, 1962, 1970; American Council of Learned Societies grant, 1963; Pulitzer Prize, 1964; Columbia University Medal for Excellence, 1965; American Academy award, 1976; Institute of Jamaica Centenary Award, 1980; National Jewish Book Award, 1981. D.H.L.: Eastern Michigan University, Ypsilanti, 1977. Lives in Port Jefferson, New York.

PUBLICATIONS

Verse

The Arrivistes: Poems 1940–1949. 1949.
Good News of Death and Other Poems. 1955.
A Dream of Governors. 1959.
At the End of the Open Road. 1963.
Five American Poets, with others, edited by Thom Gunn and Ted Hughes. 1963.
Selected Poems. 1965.
Adventures of the Letter I. 1971.
Tondelayo. 1971.
The Mexican Woman. 1973.
The Invasion of Italy. 1976.
Searching for the Ox: New Poems and a Preface. 1976.
Armidale: Poems and a Prose Memoir. 1979.
Out of Season. 1979.
Caviare at the Funeral. 1980.
The Best Hour of the Night. 1983.
People Live Here: Selected Poems 1949–1983. 1983.

Plays

The Father Out of the Machine: A Masque, in *Chicago Review*, Winter 1950.
Good News of Death, in *Hudson Review*, Summer 1952.
Andromeda, in *Hudson Review*, Winter 1956.
The Breasts of Tiresias, from a play by Apollinaire, in *Modern French Theatre*, edited by Michael Benedikt and George E. Wellwarth. 1964; as *Modern French Plays*, 1965.

Fiction

Riverside Drive. 1962.

Other

James Hogg: A Critical Study. 1962.
Air with Armed Men (autobiography). 1972; as *North of Jamaica*, 1972.
Three on the Tower: The Lives and Works of Ezra Pound, T.S. Eliot, and William Carlos Williams. 1975.
A Revolution in Taste: Studies of Dylan Thomas, Allen Ginsberg, Sylvia Plath, and Robert Lowell. 1978; as *Studies of Dylan Thomas, Allen Ginsberg, Sylvia Plath, and Robert Lowell*, 1979.
A Company of Poets. 1981.

Editor, with Donald Hall and Robert Pack, *The New Poets of England and America*. 1957.

*

Bibliography: *Simpson: A Reference Guide* by William H. Roberson, 1980.

Critical Studies: *Louis Simpson* by Ronald Moran, 1972, and *Four Poets and the Emotive Imagination* by Moran and George S. Lensing, 1976.

* * *

Always more of a "paleface" than a "redskin" (to adopt Philip Rahv's famous categorization of American writers), Louis Simpson took some time to find his own poetic voice. His early poetry is heavily dependent on John Crowe Ransom, and much of the work of his first two volumes, *The Arrivistes* and *Good News of Death*, seems to derive from art rather than life. The exception comes with a remarkable group of war poems, especially "Carentan O Carentan" and "The Battle," which, with the exception of Randall Jarrell's, are the best poems to have come from an American poet's confrontation with World War II.

A Dream of Governors is a tired, "literary" volume, full of echoes of such poets as Nemerov, Hecht, and Wilbur, all of them more polished performers than Simpson himself. Reading it, you feel than Simpson's talent is all but dead. But *At the End of the Open Road* achieves a remarkable breakthrough. Gone are the formal posturings, the conventional subjects, the making of poems out of poems, that featured so heavily in the earlier volumes. It is as though Simpson has suddenly found his true subject, and with it an answerable style. Instead of trying to be like other poets, he is now content to be himself: he lets his Jewishness into the poetry, his sense of being something of an outcast, but an outcast who nevertheless knows he belongs to America, and who therefore sets out to celebrate his country, whenever he can find it and whatever it may prove to be. As the title of the volume hints, Simpson turns, as so many American poets have found themselves turning, to Walt Whitman. The Whitman he responds most deeply to is the poet who could embrace multitudes, engage contradictions, responsibly accept irresponsibility: whose gigantic achievement was to perceive the noble folly of American dreams. "All the grave weight of America / Cancelled! Like Greece and Rome. / The future in ruins." Those lines come from "Walt Whitman at Bear Mountain," one of Simpson's best poems.

Most of the poems of *At the End of the Open Road* are written in an informal, loose-limbed manner, which frees them to convey a more powerful and convincing personal voice than the earlier poems had managed to do. And where Simpson does return to a more formal mode, as in the extraordinarily fine, wittily melancholic "My Father in the Night Commanding No," he does it without leaning on any other poet. Some of the finest poems in this remarkable volume are ones in which Simpson broods on the inescapable fact of his Jewishness. He prods at it like an aching tooth, fascinated by it, yet fearing the pain it causes. The best of these is undoubtedly "A Story about Chicken Soup."

In *Adventures of the Letter I* Simpson attempts to make further use of the style he had discovered for himself: musing, wryly observant, quizzical, contemplative; it is a volume marking time. There are no poems in it as good as the best in *At the End of the Open Road*; and yet it is an utterly readable, enjoyable piece of work by a poet who, having found his own voice, can be relied on not to bore. Like Whitman, Simpson has become at the very least a good companion.

—John Lucas

SINCLAIR, Upton. Born in Baltimore, Maryland, 20 September 1878; moved with his family to New York, 1888. Educated at City College, New York, 1893–97, A.B. 1897; Columbia University, New York, 1897–1901. Married 1) Meta H. Fuller in 1900 (divorced, 1911); 2) Mary Craig Kimbrough in 1913 (died, 1961); 3) Mary Elizabeth Willis in 1961 (died, 1967). Writer from 1893; wrote Clif Faraday stories (as Ensign Clarke Fitch) and Mark Mallory stories (as Lieutenant Frederick Garrison) for various boys' weeklies, 1897–98; founded socialist community, Helicon Home, Englewood, New Jersey, 1906–07; Socialist candidate for Congress, from New Jersey, 1906; settled in Pasadena, California, 1915; Socialist candidate for Congress, 1920, for U.S. Senate, 1922, and for Governor of California, 1926, 1930; moved to Buckeye, Arizona, 1953. Recipient: Pulitzer Prize, 1943; American Newspaper Guild award, 1962. *Died 25 November 1968.*

PUBLICATIONS

Fiction

Springtime and Harvest: A Romance. 1901; as *King Midas*, 1901.
Prince Hagen. 1903.
The Journal of Arthur Stirling. 1903.
Manassas. 1904; revised edition, as *Theirs Be the Guilt*, 1959.
The Jungle. 1906.
A Captain of Industry. 1906.
The Industrial Republic. 1907.
The Metropolis. 1908.
The Moneychangers. 1908.
Samuel the Seeker. 1910.
Love's Pilgrimage. 1911.
Sylvia. 1913.
Damaged Goods. 1913.
Sylvia's Marriage. 1914.
King Coal. 1917.
Jimmie Higgins. 1918.
The Spy. 1919; as *100%: The Story of a Patriot*, 1920; excerpt, as *Peter Gudge Becomes a Secret Agent*, 1930.
They Call Me Carpenter. 1922.
The Millennium: A Comedy of the Year 2000. 1924.
Oil! 1927.
Boston. 1928; abridged edition, as *August 22nd*, 1965.
Mountain City. 1929.
The Wet Parade. 1931.
Roman Holiday. 1931.
Co-op: A Novel of Living Together. 1936.
The Gnomobile. 1936.
Little Steel. 1938.
Our Lady. 1938.
Marie Antoinette. 1939; as *Marie and Her Lover*, 1948.
World's End. 1940.
Between Two Worlds. 1941.
Dragon's Teeth. 1942.
Wide Is the Gate. 1943.
Presidential Agent. 1944.
Dragon Harvest. 1945.
A World to Win. 1946.
Presidential Mission. 1947.
One Clear Call. 1948.
O Shepherd, Speak! 1949.
Another Pamela; or, Virtue Still Rewarded. 1950.
The Return of Lanny Budd. 1953.
What Didymus Did. 1954; as *It Happened to Didymus*, 1958.
The Cup of Fury. 1956.
Affectionately Eve. 1961.
The Coal War: A Sequel to King Coal. 1976.

Plays

Prince Hagen, from his own novel (produced 1909). 1909.
Plays of Protest (includes *Prince Hagen*, *The Naturewoman*, *The Machine*, *The Second-Story Man*). 1912.
Hell: A Verse Drama and Photo-Play. 1923.
The Pot Boiler. 1924.
Singing Jailbirds (produced 1930). 1924.
Bill Porter. 1924.
Wally for Queen! The Private Life of Royalty. 1936.
A Giant's Strength. 1948.

The Enemy Had It Too. 1950.
Three Plays (includes *The Second-Story Man, John D., The Indignant Subscriber*). 1965.

Verse

Songs of Our Nation. 1941.

Other

The Toy and the Man. 1904.
Our Bourgeois Literature. 1905.
Colony Customs. 1906.
The Helicon Home Colony. 1906.
A Home Colony: A Prospectus. 1906.
What Life Means to Me. 1906.
The Overman. 1907.
Good Health and How We Won It, with Michael Williams. 1909; as *The Art of Health*, 1909; as *Strength and Health*, 1910.
War: A Manifesto Against It. 1909.
Four Letters About "Love's Pilgrimage." 1911.
The Fasting Cure. 1911.
The Sinclair-Astor Letters: Famous Correspondence Between Socialist and Millionaire. 1914.
The Social Problem as Seen from the Viewpoint of Trade Unionism, Capital, and Socialism, with others. 1914.
Sinclair: Biographical and Critical Opinions. 1917.
The Profits of Religion. 1918.
Russia: A Challenge. 1919.
The High Cost of Living (address). 1919.
The Brass Check. 1919; excerpt, as *The Associated Press and Labor*, 1920.
Press-titution. 1920.
The Crimes of the "Times": A Test of Newspaper Decency. 1921.
Mind and Body. 1921; revised edition, 1950.
The McNeal-Sinclair Debate on Socialism. 1921.
Love and Society. 1922; revised edition, 4 vols., n.d.
The Book of Life. 1922.
The Goose-Step: A Study of American Education. 1922; revised edition, n.d.
Biographical Letter and Critical Opinions. 1922.
The Goslings. 1924; excerpt, as *The Schools of Los Angeles*, 1924.
Mammonart. 1925.
Letters to Judd. 1926; revised edition, as *This World of 1949 and What to Do about It*, 1949.
The Spokesman's Secretary. 1926.
Money Writes! 1927.
The Pulitzer Prize and "Special Pleading." 1929.
Mental Radio. 1930; revised edition, 1962.
Socialism and Culture. 1931.
Upton Sinclair on "Comrade" Kautsky. 1931.
American Outpost. 1932; as *Candid Reminiscences: My First Thirty Years*, 1932.
I, Governor of California, and How I Ended Poverty. 1933.
Upton Sinclair Presents William Fox. 1933.
The Way Out—What Lies Ahead for America? 1933; revised edition as, *Limbo on the Loose: A Midsummer Night's Dream*, 1948.
EPIC Plan for California. 1934.
EPIC Answers: How to End Poverty in California. 1934.
Immediate EPIC. 1934.
The Lie Factory Starts. 1934.
A Sinclair Anthology, edited by I.O. Evans. 1934; revised edition, 1947.
Sinclair's Last Will and Testament. 1934.
We, People of America, and How We Ended Poverty: A True Story of the Future. 1934.
Depression Island. 1935.
I, Candidate for Governor, and How I Got Licked. 1935; as *How I Got Licked and Why*, 1935.
What God Means to Me: An Attempt at a Working Religion. 1936.
The Flivver King. 1937.
No Pasoran! (They Shall Not Pass). 1937.
Terror in Russia: Two Views, with Eugene Lyons. 1938.
Sinclair on the Soviet Union. 1938.
Expect No Peace! 1939.
Telling the World. 1939.
What Can Be Done about America's Economic Troubles? 1939.
Your Million Dollars. 1939; as *Letters to a Millionaire*, 1939.
Is the American Form of Capitalism Essential to the American Form of Democracy? 1940.
Peace or War in America? 1940.
Index to the Lanny Budd Story, with others. 1943.
To Solve the German Problem—A Free State? 1943.
A Personal Jesus: Portrait and Interpretation. 1952; as *Secret Life of Jesus*, 1962.
Radio Liberation Speech to the Peoples of the Soviet Union. 1955.
My Lifetime in Letters. 1960.
The Autobiography of Sinclair. 1962.

Editor, *The Cry for Justice: An Anthology of the Literature of Social Protest*. 1915.

*

Bibliography: *Sinclair: An Annotated Checklist* by Ronald Gottesman, 1973.

Critical Studies: *Sinclair: A Study in Social Protest* by Floyd Dell, 1927; *This Is Sinclair* by James Harte Lambert, 1938; *The Literary Manuscripts of Sinclair* by Ronald Gottesman and Charles L.P. Silet, 1972; *Sinclair* by Jon A. Yoder, 1975; *Sinclair, American Rebel* by Leon Harris, 1975; *Critics on Upton Sinclair* edited by Abraham Blinderman, 1975; *Sinclair* by William A. Bloodworth, 1977.

* * *

No American author has produced more writing, had a greater influence on society, and received less serious critical attention than Upton Sinclair. The depository of Sinclair manuscripts, books, and letters at the Lilly Library, Indiana University, weighs more than eight tons. More than 250,000 letters are included in the collection, letters to Shaw, Gandhi, Trotsky, Roosevelt, Kennedy, and countless letters to readers and critics concerning his own work and that of others. The material is available for work that might lead to a reassessment of Sinclair similar to that which the discovery of the Malahide papers brought about in critical opinion concerning James Boswell.

Upton Sinclair wrote on more subjects than we can catalogue; he was interested in extrasensory perception, religion, economics, alcoholism, and much more. He wrote ninety books and many pamphlets, and without his work the social world in which we live would probably lack many of the benefits we take for granted. But of those books, only one, *The Jungle*, has survived as an American classic, and critics are divided as to whether it is a classic of imaginative literature or a classic work of propaganda. Even the once popular Lanny Budd series (eleven novels, 1940–53), one of which, *Dragon's Teeth*, won the Pulitzer Prize, is all but forgotten. The key critical issue apparent in the rather limited Sinclair scholarship is whether Upton Sinclair is a genuine novelist or a very skilled and effective propagandist for social and socialist reform. Most critics think the latter.

Van Wyck Brooks, in *The Confident Years*, acknowledged *The Jungle* as an outstanding example of muckraking literature; however, muckraking literature operates only on a level of social effect and falls short of serious art. *The Jungle* tells of the Lithuanian emigrant family of Jurgis Rudkus. Seeking the realization of the American Dream, the family settles in the Chicago of the early 20th century. Jurgis goes to work in the stockyards (which provides Sinclair the opportunity to describe the filthy practices of the meat-packing industry) and the family moves into a ramshackle house, deceptively painted by the agent to appear new. There follows a series of tragedies and horrors as members of the family are killed or debased by a social system that cares nothing for the helpless people it exploits. Jurgis's futile attempts to strike back are rewarded with prison sentences. Finally, he learns of the socialist movement. He finds a job in a hotel managed by a socialist, and recaptures a sense of hope.

Despite certain well-constructed scenes of genuinely human life, such as the Lithuanian wedding of Jurgis and Ona, it is evident to most readers that Jurgis's family exists primarily as a means by which to gauge the failures of the social system that destroys them. They are acted upon; they do not act. Indeed, all we learn about human nature from *The Jungle*'s characters is that human nature can be perverted and debased by society. On the other hand, we learn a very great deal about the society. Readers in 1906 learned more than they imagined, and the conditions in the meat-packing industry, so well described by Sinclair, attracted the attention of reformers and presidents. The world of *The Jungle* is a naturalistic world, a world in which only the economically fit survive. Here, human lives are manipulated by an indifferent, if not hostile, scheme of things. But Sinclair's message is that the scheme can change. We have created or at least permitted the existence of the thing that oppresses us, and if enough are made aware of the full horror of that thing, the few who control and profit from it will have to surrender.

In *Upton Sinclair, American Rebel* Leon Harris observes that successful propaganda must disappear. It seeks to make its ideas commonplace; it causes us to accept its message as the product of our own clear perception of the way things are. Then the actual organ of the propaganda fades in the glow of our self-satisfaction. Most of Sinclair's literature was intended to be, and was, just this kind of successful propaganda. Only on a very rare occasion does a piece of propaganda strike us with such impact that the work itself becomes part of the history that we study and remember, for it is dangerous to forget history. The result, as in the case of *The Jungle*, is a puzzle for critics who know that propaganda should fade away and novels should concern themselves with character development. Paradoxically, than, Sinclair at his best fails in both genres and creates a work that the literate world insists is a classic.

—William J. Heim

See the essay on *The Jungle*.

SINGER, Isaac Bashevis. Born Icek-Hersz Zynger in Leoncin, Poland, 14 July 1904; emigrated to the U.S., 1935; became citizen, 1943. Educated at the Tachkemoni Rabbinical Seminary, Warsaw, 1921–22. Married Alma Haimann in 1940; one son from earlier marriage. Proofreader and translator, *Literarishe Bleter*, Warsaw, 1923–33; associate editor, *Globus*, Warsaw, 1933–35; journalist, *Vorwärts* (*Jewish Daily Forward*) Yiddish newspaper, New York, from 1935. Recipient: Louis Lamed Prize, 1950, 1956; American Academy grant, 1959; Daroff Memorial Award, 1963; Foreign Book Prize (France), 1965; two National Endowment for the Arts grants, 1966; Bancarella Prize (Italy), 1968; Brandeis University Creative Arts Award, 1969; National Book Award, for children's literature, 1970, and for fiction, 1974; Nobel Prize for Literature, 1978. D.H.L.: Hebrew Union College, Los Angeles, 1963; D.Lit.: Colgate University, Hamilton, New York, 1972; D.Litt.: Texas Christian University, Fort Worth, 1972; Ph.D.: Hebrew University, Jerusalem, 1973; Litt.D.: Bard College, Annandale-on-Hudson, New York, 1974; Long Island University, Greenvale, New York, 1979. Member, American Academy, 1965; American Academy of Arts and Sciences, 1969; Jewish Academy of Arts and Sciences; Polish Institute of Arts and Sciences. Lives in New York City.

PUBLICATIONS

Fiction

Der sotn in Goray. 1935; translated by Jacob Sloan, as *Satan in Goray*, 1955.
The Family Moskat, translated by A.H. Gross. 1950.
Gimpel the Fool and Other Stories, translated by Saul Bellow and others. 1957.
The Magician of Lublin, translated by Elaine Gottlieb and Joseph Singer. 1960.
The Spinoza of Market Street and Other Stories, translated by Elaine Gottlieb and others. 1961.
The Slave, translated by the author and Cecil Hemley. 1962.
Short Friday and Other Stories, translated by Ruth Whitman and others. 1964.
Selected Short Stories, edited by Irving Howe. 1966.
The Manor, translated by Elaine Gottlieb and Joseph Singer. 1967.
The Séance and Other Stories, translated by Ruth Whitman and others. 1968.
The Estate, translated by Elaine Gottlieb, Joseph Singer, and Elizabeth Shub. 1969.
A Friend of Kafka and Other Stories, translated by the author and others. 1970.
Enemies: A Love Story, translated by Alizah Shevrin and Elizabeth Shub. 1972.
A Crown of Feathers and Other Stories, translated by the author and others. 1973.
Passions and Other Stories. 1975.
Shosha, translated by Joseph Singer. 1978.
Old Love (stories). 1979.
Reaches of Heaven. 1980.
The Collected Stories. 1982.
The Penitent. 1983.
The Image and Other Stories. 1985.

Fiction (for children; translated by the author and Elizabeth Shub)

Zlateh the Goat and Other Stories. 1966.

Mazel and Shlimazel; or, The Milk of a Lioness. 1967.
The Fearsome Inn. 1967.
When Shlemiel Went to Warsaw and Other Stories, translated by Channah Kleinerman-Goldstein and others. 1968.
Joseph and Koza; or, The Sacrifice to the Vistula. 1970.
Alone in the Wild Forest. 1971.
The Topsy-Turvy Emperor of China. 1971.
The Fools of Chelm and Their History. 1973.
A Tale of Three Wishes. 1976.
Naftali the Storyteller and His Horse, Sus, and Other Stories, translated by the author and others. 1976.
The Power of Light: Eight Stories for Hanukkah. 1980.
The Golem. 1982.
Stories for Children. 1985.

Plays

The Mirror (produced 1973).
Shlemiel the First (produced 1974).
Yentl, The Yeshiva Boy, with Leah Napolin, from a story by Singer (produced 1974). 1979.
Teibele and Her Demon, with Eve Friedman (produced 1978). 1984.

Other (for children; translated by the author and Elizabeth Shub)

A Day of Pleasure: Stories of a Boy Growing Up in Warsaw (autobiographical), translated by Channah Kleinerman-Goldstein and others, photographs by Roman Vishniac. 1969.
Elijah the Slave: A Hebrew Legend Retold. 1970.
The Wicked City. 1972.
Why Noah Chose the Dove. 1974.

Other

In My Father's Court (autobiography), translated by Channah Kleinerman-Goldstein and others. 1966.
A Singer Reader. 1971.
The Hasidim: Paintings, Drawings, and Etchings, with Ira Moskowitz. 1973.
Love and Exile: The Early Years: A Memoir. 1984.
A Little Boy in Search of God: Mysticism in a Personal Light, illustrated by Ira Moskowitz. 1976.
A Young Man in Search of Love, translated by Joseph Singer. 1978.
Lost in America, translated by Joseph Singer. 1981.
Nobel Lecture. 1979.
Singer on Literature and Life: An Interview, with Paul Rosenblatt and Gene Koppel. 1979.
Conversations with Singer, with Richard Burgin. 1985.

Editor, with Elaine Gottlieb, *Prism 2*. 1965.

Translator (into Yiddish):

Pan, by Knut Hamsun. 1928.
Di Vogler (The Vagabonds), by Knut Hamsun. 1928.
In Opgrunt Fun Tayve (In Passion's Abyss), by Gabriele D'Annunzio. 1929.
Mete Trap (Mette Trap), by Karin Michaëlis. 1929.
Roman Rolan (Romain Rolland), by Stefan Zweig. 1929.
Viktorya (Victoria), by Knut Hamsun. 1929.
Oyfn Mayrev-Front Keyn Nayes (All Quiet on the Western Front), by Erich Maria Remarque. 1930.
Der Tsoyberbarg (The Magic Mountain), by Thomas Mann. 4 vols., 1930.
Der Veg oyf Tsurik (The Road Back), by Erich Maria Remarque 1931.
Araber: Folkstimlekhe Geshikhtn (Arabs: Stories of the People), by Moshe Smilansky. 1932.
Fun Moskve biz Yerusholayim (From Moscow to Jerusalem), by Leon S. Glaser. 1938.

*

Bibliography: by Bonnie Jean M. Christensen, in *Bulletin of Bibliography 26*, January–March 1969; *Bibliography of Singer 1924–1949* by David Neal Miller, 1983.

Critical Studies: *Singer and the Eternal Past* by Irving Buchen, 1968; *The Achievement of Singer* edited by Marcia Allentuck, 1969; *Critical Views of Singer* edited by Irving Malin, 1969, and *Singer* by Malin, 1972; *Singer* by Ben Siegel, 1969; *Singer and His Art* by Askel Schiotz, 1970; *Singer, The Magician of West 86th Street* by Paul Kresh, 1979; *Singer* by Edward Alexander, 1980; *The Brothers Singer* by Clive Sinclair, 1983; *Fear of Fiction: Narrative Strategies in the Works of Singer* by David N. Miller, 1985.

* * *

Isaac Bashevis Singer is an example of a strange phenomenon in American Jewish literature—a Yiddish writer who in his later years gained international fame through the English translation of his novels and short stories. The Yiddish audience for which Singer wrote was never a very large one; he did not cater for the nostalgic yearnings of one school of Yiddishists, or the socialistic diatribes of the other.

Distancing himself from the latter group was especially difficult for the young Singer, for it implied a separation from his older brother, Israel Joshua, also an accomplished writer. This older brother was the first to open the door to secular education and to the questions which inevitably awakened Isaac to the narrowness of his father's world of Hasidism and the inadequacy of his mother's more rational, but nevertheless medieval, normative Judaism. But, unlike his brother, Isaac Bashevis was unwilling to discard his past altogether; he was unwilling to choose between mysticism and rationality, between past and present, or even between gothicism and realism. Singer's art is a marriage of these diverse elements in his past; they are what afford his fiction both its charm and its sophistication.

In his early years, Singer wrote solely for the Yiddish press, under several pseudonyms—for example, Varshavsky and Segal. Even his name Bashevis is a pseudonym in honor of his mother, Bathsheba. These early pieces included feuilletons, autobiographical sketches, short fiction, and novels. Some of these have been translated into English, but many remain unknown to the non-Yiddish-reading public. By 1950, Singer had begun the process which was to lead to his great fame in the next twenty years; he began to publish in English translation as well as in the original Yiddish.

The first major venture in this double publication was his epic novel *The Family Moskat*, which appeared simultaneously in English and Yiddish. The significant differences between the Yiddish original and the English translation reveal the problematic nature of Singer's identity as an English writer. In the

English version, the main characters are left to their doom in Warsaw on the eve of the Nazi takeover. In the Yiddish version, a youthful remnant escapes to Israel. The symbolic significance of their escape and tenuous existence is not lost on the Yiddish writer Singer, nor the Yiddish reader.

As defined by Irving Malin, Singer's novels can be divided into two groups, open and closed. *The Family Moskat* is probably the best example of his open novels. It is an historical family chronicle; the scope of the tale is large and has significant sociological implication; the style is primarily realistic. For Singer, these chronicles are most often set in a time during which the confined *shtetl* life of the East European Jew is being questioned. Other novels in this manner include *The Manor* and *The Estate*.

Of the second (closed) type of Singer novel, *Satan in Goray* is probably the purest example. It is short, condensed in time; there is an aura of mystery and irrationality; the style, the characters, the setting are all symbolic. Set in the distressing era of the anti-semitic pogromist Chmielnicki and the false messiah Shabbatai Zevi, this novel relates the disintegration of personality and community that resulted from these horrors of the Jewish past. Other closed novels include *The Magician of Lublin* and *The Slave*. (*Enemies: A Love Story* is hard to classify, but it is more closed than open.)

Singer's use of symbolism, which owes much to the structure and style of *kaballah*, is prominent in many of his short stories as well as the closed novels. In the best of the stories Singer suggests the complex dichotomies, the multiple levels of human existence, and the ambivalent nature of life itself by the use of name symbolism, the supernatural, and multiple narrators. Before the reader can with assurance interpret a story, he must note who tells that story. The reader of "The Destruction of Kreshev" overlooks at his peril the fact that the narrator is Satan. If he reads the superstitious tale "Zeitl and Rickel," he must note that an uneducated old woman is speaking. The events in these tales are filtered through a perspective that colors subject, tone, and conclusion. Even in the masterpiece "Gimpel the Fool," we must recognize that Gimpel himself tells the tale; his naivety and good nature determine the conclusion.

Another important type of narrator in Singer's fiction is semi-autobiographical. In the more belletristic of the tales, Singer uses this portrait of himself as a mirror reflecting another's story. In "A Friend of Kafka," Jacques Kohn tells the history of his peculiar life. But we do not hear the tale directly; rather we hear it from a man bearing many similarities to the young Isaac Singer. He knew Jacques; Jacques told him a story, and he tells us.

The more simply autobiographical pieces are collected in two books (*In My Father's Court* and *A Day of Pleasure*). These sketches give a clear impression of the life of the young Singer, of his awakening experiences in life, love, and education, and his movement away from his father's narrow past. However, it is the more recent *A Little Boy in Search of God* that most tellingly reveals the intellectual ferment that troubled the young Singer and led him to the development of his 20th-century mysticism.

Singer is modern in his vision of humanity: his treatment of sexuality and insanity alienated him from many of his Yiddish readers while enhancing his stature in the modern American mind. This rift has caused many English-language critics to overemphasize Singer's modernity. In so doing, they have overlooked the medieval method of symbolism which adds much of the depth and beauty to Singer's work. But such confusion is only a natural consequence of Singer's position as a Jewish-American writer, a man born in Poland but writing in New York, a man writing in Yiddish but being read in English, and a man looking toward the past to tell of the future.

—R. Barbara Gitenstein

SMITH, Seba. Pseudonym: Major Jack Downing. Born in Buckfield, Maine, 14 September 1792; moved with his family to Bridgton, Maine, 1799. Educated at a school in Bridgton; Bowdoin College, Brunswick, Maine, 1815–18, B.A. (honors) 1818. Married Elizabeth Oakes Prince (the writer Elizabeth Oakes Smith) in 1823; five children. Schoolteacher in Bridgton, 1811–15, and Portland, Maine, 1818–19; traveled in the southern U.S. and in Europe, 1819–20; assistant editor and part owner, *Eastern Argus*, Portland, 1820–26; founding editor, Portland *Courier*, 1829–34 (contributed Downing letters from 1830); publisher, *Family Reader*, 1830–36, and *Downing Gazette*, Portland, 1834–36; moved to New York, 1842; editor, *Bunker Hill* and *Rover*, 1844–45; contributed Downing letters to *National Intelligencer*, Washington, D.C., 1847–56; editor, *United States Magazine*, 1854–59; founder, *Great Republic* magazine, 1859; lived in Patchogue, Long Island, from 1860. *Died 28 July 1868.*

PUBLICATIONS

Fiction

The Life and Writings of Major Jack Downing, of Downingville. 1833; revised edition, 1834.
Letters Written During the President's Tour "Down East" (some letters not by Smith). 1833.
The Select Letters of Major Jack Downing (some letters not by Smith). 1834.
John Smith's Letters, with "Picters" to Match. 1839.
May-Day in New-York; or, House-Hunting and Moving. 1845; as *Jack Downing's Letters*, 1859(?).
'Way Down East; or, Portraitures of Yankee Life. 1854.
My Thirty Years Out of the Senate. 1859.
Speech of John Smith, Not Delivered at Smithville Sept. 15th, 1864. 1864.

Verse

Powhatan: A Metrical Romance. 1841.

Other

New Elements of Geometry. 1850.

Editor, *Dew-Drops of the Nineteenth Century.* 1846; as *The Gift of Friendship*, n.d.; as *The Keepsake*, n.d.

*

Bibliography: in *Bibliography of American Literature* by Jacob Blanck, edited by Virginia L. Smyers and Michael Winship, 1983.

Critical Studies: *Two American Pioneers: Seba Smith and Elizabeth Oakes Smith* by Mary Alice Wyman, 1927; *Smith* by Milton and Patricia Rickels, 1977.

* * *

Jack Downing, the creation of Seba Smith, is the prototype of the Yankee critic and humorist, a racy character set against the rustic and picturesque New England background, yet clever enough to serve as confidant of an American President. This pattern of humor paved the way for such homey critics and philosophers as Sam Slick, Hosea Biglow, and Will Rogers.

Smith launched his Jack Downing in the Portland *Courier*, his own newspaper, the first daily to be issued in Maine, in 1830. Jack takes on the guise of a Yankee adventurer who left his native village of Downingville to trade in Portland. From bartering and bargaining, Jack turned to politics and wrote humorous accounts of his career and partners to the family back home. The Downing letters enjoyed a wide circulation in New England, which encouraged Smith to widen his horizons, so he sent Jack to Washington where he becomes counselor to the President. What poured from his pen was a scathing but humorous satire of Jacksonian democracy. Singled out for criticism was the horde of job seekers that descended on Washington as well as the folly and disaster of land speculation and the national bank. One of the prime targets for Jack's sarcastic venom was the Mexican War. Jack bitingly remarks to General Pierce: "Uncle Joshua always says, in nine cases out of ten, it costs more to rob an orchard than it would be to buy the apples."

His last series of Downing letters appeared under the title *My Thirty Years Out of the Senate*, a parody of Thomas Hart Benton's *Thirty Years' View*. He also wrote a collection of tales on Yankee customs, *'Way Down East*.

—Dominic J. Bisignano

SNODGRASS, W(illiam) D(eWitt). Born in Wilkinsburg, Pennsylvania, 5 January 1926. Educated at Geneva College, Beaver Falls, Pennsylvania, 1943–44, 1946; University of Iowa, Iowa City, 1946–55, B.A. 1949, M.A. 1951, M.F.A. 1953. Served in the U.S. Navy, 1944–46. Married 1) Lila Jean Hank in 1946 (divorced, 1953), one daughter; 2) Janice Wilson in 1954 (divorced, 1966), one son; 3) Camille Rykowski in 1967 (divorced, 1978). Instructor in English, Cornell University, Ithaca, New York, 1955–57, University of Rochester, New York, 1957–58, and Wayne State University, Detroit, 1959–67; Professor of English and Speech, Syracuse University, New York, 1968–77. Visiting Teacher, Morehead Writers Conference, Kentucky, Summer 1955, Antioch Writers Conference, Yellow Springs, Ohio, summers 1958–59, Narrative Poetry Workshop, State University of New York, Binghamton, 1977, Old Dominion University, Norfolk, Virginia, 1978–79, and University of Delaware, Newark, since 1979. Recipient: Ingram Merrill Foundation award 1958; Longview Award, 1959; Poetry Society of America Special Citation, 1960; Yaddo grant, 1960, 1961, 1965, 1976, 1977; American Academy grant, 1960; Pulitzer Prize, 1960; Guinness Award (UK), 1961; Ford fellowship, for drama, 1963; Miles Award, 1966; National Endowment for the Arts grant, 1966; Guggenheim fellowship, 1972; Academy of American Poets fellowship, 1973; Centennial Medal (Romania), 1977. Member, American Academy, 1972; Fellow, Academy of American Poets, 1973. Lives in Newark, Delaware.

PUBLICATIONS

Verse

Heart's Needle. 1959.
After Experience: Poems and Translations. 1968.
Remains. 1970.
The Führer Bunker: A Cycle of Poems in Progress. 1977.
If Birds Build with Your Hair. 1979.
The Boy Made of Meat. 1983.
Magda Goebbels. 1983.
Owls: A Poem. 1983.
D.D. Byrde Callyng Jennie Wrenn. 1984.

Play

The Führer Bunker (produced 1980).

Other

In Radical Pursuit: Critical Essays and Lectures. 1975.

Editor, *Syracuse Poems 1969*. 1969.

Translator, with Lore Segal, *Gallows Songs*, by Christian Morgenstern. 1967.
Translator, *Six Troubadour Songs*. 1977.
Translator, *Traditional Hungarian Songs*. 1978.
Translator, *Six Minnesinger Songs*. 1983.
Translator, *The Four Seasons*. 1984.

*

Bibliography: *Snodgrass: A Bibliography* by William White, 1960.

Critical Study: *Snodgrass* by Paul L. Gaston, 1978.

* * *

In his essay "A Poem's Becoming" (*In Radical Pursuit*), W.D. Snodgrass charts the evolution of his verse from the the densely composed, ambiguous lyrics of his early years at the University of Iowa to a style of "becoming," in which a dramatic action unfolds through the speaker's intimate disclosures and self-revelations. But throughout his transition to a freer mode of lyric delivery, he has remained a technically conservative poet, writing mostly in tightly rhymed patterns and in set metrical rhythms.

Although the craftsmanship of *Heart's Needle* and *After Experience* is at once lustrous and immaculate, Snodgrass is chiefly to be noted for having given voice to the inner life of the average middle-class American who came to maturity during World War II. Like Robert Lowell, whom he studied under, Snodgrass bases the speaker in his poems on his own life, from service in the war to graduate student days in Iowa to teaching posts around the country. His poems, however, are a careful selection of experiences that capture the disappointments, vicissitudes, and angst of a whole generation of Americans. The most emphatic theme of *Heart's Needle* and *After Experience* is a sense of an increasingly depersonalized identity as social life grows more rationalized.

Heart's Needle begins with the disenchantments of returning veterans, who, in "Returned to Frisco, 1946," reenter civilian life

free to prowl all night
Down streets giddy with lights, to sleep all day,

Pay our own way and make our own selections;
Free to choose just what they meant we should. . . .

With this hint at authoritarianism, Snodgrass chronicles the life of the post-war American who carries pent-up, even violent, emotions under a carefully trained surface. Some of these poems have their speaker worry that he has grown too fearful and timid, as in "Home Town," where he has pursued, then eluded a bold young girl:

Pale soul, consumed by fear
of the living world you haunt,
have you learned what habits lead you
to hunt what you don't want;
learned who does not need you;
learned you are no one here?

The lovely, complex music of the final sequence, "Heart's Needle," captures this likeable, confused new Everyman as he struggles to remain parent to his young daughter. Snodgrass gives these ten poems his richest, most daringly metaphorical speech.

After Experience continues the Everyman chronicle of *Heart's Needle*, but this volume is less carefully structured and often less resonant in its language. Many of the poems take up themes of captivity, terror, potential violence, and disaster. Typical is "Lobsters in the Window," with its moving depiction of the near-frozen lobster seen through a restaurant window:

He's fallen back with the mass
Heaped in their common trench
Who stir, but do not look out
Through the rainstreaming glass,
Hear what the newsboys shout,
Or see the raincoats pass.

The closing section of the volume features skilful translations of a number of poets, particularly Rilke.

The violence and turmoil that are subtexts of much of Snodgrass's poetry come to the surface in *The Führer Bunker*, which recreates the last days of Hitler in his tunnels below the Reich Chancellory. Some of the scenes are harrowing indeed, and there are bold efforts to widen the poet's technical repertoire to include dramatic strategies, many of which are successfully deployed in the poem.

—Paul Christensen

SNYDER, Gary (Sherman). Born in San Francisco, California, 8 May 1930. Educated at Lincoln High School, Portland, Oregon, graduated 1947; Reed College, Portland, 1947–51, B.A. in anthropology 1951; Indiana University, Bloomington, 1952–53; University of California, Berkeley, 1953–56; studied Buddhism in Japan 1956, 1959–64, 1965–68. Married 1) Alison Gass in 1950 (divorced, 1952); 2) the poet Joanne Kyger in 1960 (divorced, 1965); 3) Masa Uehara in 1967, two sons. Seaman 1957–58; Lecturer in English, University of California, Berkeley, 1964–65. Recipient: Bollingen grant, for Buddhist studies, 1965; American Academy prize, 1966; Guggenheim fellowship, 1968; Pulitzer Prize, 1975; Before Columbus Foundation award, 1984. Lives in California.

PUBLICATIONS

Verse

Riprap. 1959.
Myths and Texts. 1960.
Hop, Skip, and Jump. 1964.
Nanao Knows. 1964.
The Firing. 1964.
Across Lamarack Col. 1964.
Riprap, and Cold Mountain Poems. 1965.
Six Sections from Mountains and Rivers Without End. 1965; augmented edition, 1970.
Dear Mr. President, with Philip Whalen. 1965.
Three Worlds, Three Realms, Six Roads. 1966.
A Range of Poems. 1966.
The Back Country. 1967.
The Blue Sky. 1969.
Sours of the Hills. 1969.
Regarding Wave. 1969; augmented edition, 1970.
Anasazi. 1971.
Manzanita. 1971.
Clear Cut. N.d.
Manzanita (collection). 1972.
The Fudo Trilogy: Spell Against Demons, Smokey the Bear Sutra, The California Water Plan. 1973.
Turtle Island. 1974.
All in the Family. 1975.
True Night, illustrated by Bob Giorgio. 1980.
Axe Handles. 1983.
Left Out in the Rain: Poems 1947–1984. 1986.

Other

Earth House Hold: Technical Notes and Queries to Fellow Dharma Revolutionaries. 1969.
Four Changes. 1969.
On Bread and Poetry: A Panel Discussion, with Lew Welch and Philip Whalen. 1977.
The Old Ways: Six Essays. 1977.
He Who Hunted Birds in His Father's Village: The Dimensions of a Haida Myth. 1979.
The Real Work: Interviews and Talks 1964–1979, edited by Scott McLean. 1980.
Passage Through India. 1984.

Editor, with Gutetsu Kanetsuki, *The Wooden Fish: Basic Sutras and Gathas of Rinzai Zen*. 1961.

*

Bibliography: *Snyder* by Katherine McNeil, 1983.

Critical Studies: "Snyder Issue" of *In Transit*, 1969; *The Tribal Dharma: An Essay on the Work of Snyder* by Kenneth White, 1975; *Snyder* by Bob Steuding, 1976; *Snyder* by Bert Almon, 1979.

* * *

Gary Snyder's writing is the chronicle of an itinerant visionary naturalist. His poetry contains few technical innovations, but consolidates the Imagist ideas of Pound and Williams and the free forms of Olson and the Beat poets. The poetry is wholly absorbed in the chronicle of the poet's wanderings, his religious training in Japan, and his mythic and cultural perception of nature and experience.

Snyder organizes most of his poetry according to experience rather than theme. In *Riprap*, the crisp, taciturn Imagist poems narrate his days as "look out" and "choker" in the remote reaches of the American northwest, and then his first trip to Japan on merchant tankers. The charm of these poems lies in the frank, modest, often tender lyric nature of the young observer, as in "Piute Creek":

> No one loves rock, yet we are here.
> Night chills. A flick
> In the moonlight
> Slips into Juniper shadow:
> Back there unseen
> Cold proud eyes
> Of cougar and Coyote
> Watch me rise and go.

Cold Mountain Poems contains translations of the Chinese poet, Han-shan, in which Snyder shows skill as an interpreter and cunning in the choice of a poet like himself in vision and inclination. Han-shan was a mountain recluse, whose regard for the mystery of nature is intense but not ponderous.

Myths and Texts, written before *Riprap* but not published until 1960, is the best orchestrated and developed of his works. By dividing the book into three parts, "Logging," "Hunting," and "Burning," Snyder creates an initiation ritual for his persona, who enters nature as destroyer (working for logging companies), then as hunter, who must understand his prey to succeed, and who returns from these encounters awed by the power and will of nature. The themes of Snyder's early books establish the lines of development of his succeeding works. In *The Back Country*, he narrates experience from early years in Washington and Oregon, his departure for Japan in 1956, his later return to California. The volume has some notational lyrics, but the concision and intensity of most of the poems are deeply effective and dramatic.

Earth House Hold, a collection of prose, powerfully states the depth of his regard for the natural world and shows the maturing intellectual and spiritual subtlety of his mind over the twenty years it records. Snyder, who became a cult figure of the ecology movement, carefully traces the evolution of his thought from jottings of natural phenomena to notes for the making of tribal culture in the post-industrial era. An able prose writer, Snyder is in command of both the facts and the theories of a new pastoral ideology.

Regarding Wave and *Turtle Island* continue the chronicle of the poet through family life and residence in the United States, where environmental abuse has stirred him to a lyricism of greater and greater activism. The final passages of *Turtle Island* are a series of prose tracts on conservation addressed directly to the reader. Snyder's latest book of poems, *Axe Handles*, pushes his poetic position to its limit of simplicity and directness of address. The language is shorn of all but the essential speech of daily life, and depends for its poetic effects strictly upon the assumptions and conclusions that are implicit in its delicate brevity. The title refers to the fact that one fashions the new handle from the old, and the human tool from the natural object, principles which Snyder himself exhibits with cunning throughout this collection.

—Paul Christensen

STAFFORD, Jean. Born in Covina, California, 1 July 1915. Educated at the University of Colorado, Boulder, B.A. 1936, M.A. 1936; University of Heidelberg, 1936–37. Married 1) Robert Lowell, *q.v.*, in 1940 (divorced, 1948); 2) Oliver Jensen in 1950 (divorced, 1953); 3) the writer A.J. Liebling in 1959 (died, 1963). Instructor, Stephens College, Columbia, Missouri, 1937–38; secretary, *Southern Review*, Baton Rouge, Louisiana, 1940–41; Lecturer, Queens College, Flushing, New York, Spring 1945; Fellow, Center for Advanced Studies, Wesleyan University, Middletown, Connecticut, 1964–65; Adjunct Professor, Columbia University, New York, 1967–69. Recipient: American Academy grant, 1945; Guggenheim fellowship, 1945, 1948; National Press Club award, 1948; O. Henry Award, 1955; Ingram-Merrill grant, 1969; Chapelbrook grant, 1969; Pulitzer Prize, 1970. Member, American Academy, 1970. *Died 26 March 1979.*

PUBLICATIONS

Fiction

Boston Adventure. 1944.
The Mountain Lion. 1947.
The Catherine Wheel. 1952.
Children Are Bored on Sunday (stories). 1953.
New Short Novels, with others, edited by Mary Louise Aswell. 1954.
Stories, with others. 1956; as *A Book of Stories*, 1957.
Bad Characters (stories). 1964.
Selected Stories. 1966.
The Collected Stories. 1969.

Other

Elephi: The Cat with the High I.Q. (for children). 1962.
The Lion and the Carpenter and Other Tales from the Arabian Nights Retold (for children). 1962.
A Mother in History (on Marguerite C. Oswald). 1966.

*

Bibliography: *Stafford: A Comprehensive Bibliography* by Wanda Avila, 1983.

* * *

The art of Jean Stafford is the art of the miniaturist—the quickly realized short story, told with economy and control, is her ideal form. Many of her stories were published in the *New*

Yorker and the *Saturday Evening Post*, and it is easy to detect the economy and tautness that come from the pressures of journalistic publication. "Miss Bellamy was old and cold," begins "The Hope Chest," "and she lay quaking under an eiderdown which her mother had given her when she was a girl of seventeen." In a sense, the half-dozen pages which follow merely expand the implications of that sentence. Typically, the story is rooted in the old woman's memories of her childhood and years as a young woman: most of Stafford's writing deals with loneliness perceived by the child who suffers it or by the adult who was once the child.

Her own artistic eye, in fact, is that of the child poised on the brink of adult experience and focusing on the concrete details of surrounding life. Her most successful writing enlarges its range by suggesting wider experience through symbols such as the mountain lion of her second novel, which represents the untamed, authentic power of the natural world into which the two young children of the story are plunged. The horrific violence which concludes the novel comes not from the lion but from man; like many of the stories, the work simmers with a brooding though suppressed sense of the brutality of experience.

Stafford's other novels, *Boston Adventure* and *The Catherine Wheel*, are less successful possibly because they lack such a convincing controlling symbol. As is often the case in Stafford's work, both novels are concerned with young people, but the world these young grow into suggests imprisonment and failure rather than fulfilment and enrichment. But although these are not her best works, their prose is as fine as in any of her stories.

—Patrick Evans

STAFFORD, William (Edgar). Born in Hutchinson, Kansas, 17 January 1914. Educated at the University of Kansas, Lawrence, B.A. 1937, M.A. 1947; University of Iowa, Iowa City, Ph.D. 1954. Conscientious objector during World War II; active in pacifist organizations, and since 1959 member, Oregon Board, Fellowship of Reconciliation. Married Dorothy Hope Frantz in 1944; two daughters and two sons. Member of the English Department, 1948–54, 1957–60, and since 1960 Professor of English, Lewis and Clark College, Portland, Oregon; Assistant Professor of English, Manchester College, Indiana, 1955–56; Professor of English, San Jose State College, California, 1956–57. Consultant in Poetry, Library of Congress, Washington, D.C., 1970–71; U.S. Information Agency Lecturer in Egypt, Iran, Pakistan, India, Nepal, and Bangladesh, 1972. Recipient: Yaddo fellowship, 1955; Oregon Centennial Prize, for poetry and for short story, 1959; National Book Award, 1963; Shelley Memorial Award, 1964; American Academy award, 1966, 1981; Guggenheim fellowship, 1966; Melville Cane Award, 1974. D.Litt.: Ripon College, Wisconsin, 1965; Washington College, Chesterton, Maryland, 1981; L.H.D.: Linfield College, McMinnville, Oregon, 1970. Lives in Lake Oswego, Oregon.

PUBLICATIONS

Verse

Poems. 1959(?).
West of Your City. 1960.
Traveling Through the Dark. 1962.
Five American Poets, with others, edited by Thom Gunn and Ted Hughes. 1963.
Five Poets of the Pacific Northwest, with others, edited by Robin Skelton. 1964.
The Rescued Year. 1966.
Eleven Untitled Poems. 1968.
Weather. 1969.
Allegiances. 1970.
Temporary Facts. 1970.
Poems for Tennessee, with Robert Bly and William Matthews. 1971.
Someday, Maybe. 1973.
That Other Alone. 1973.
In the Clock of Reason. 1973.
Going Places. 1974.
North by West, with John Haines, edited by Karen and John Sollid. 1975.
Late, Passing Prairie Farm. 1976.
Braided Apart, with Kim Robert Stafford. 1976.
Stories That Could Be True: New and Collected Poems. 1977.
The Design in the Oriole. 1977.
Two about Music. 1978.
All about Light. 1978.
Passing a Crèche. 1978.
Tuft by Puff. 1978.
Around You, Your House; and A Catechism. 1979.
The Quiet of the Land. 1979.
Absolution. 1980.
Things That Happen When There Aren't Any People. 1980.
Sometimes Like a Legend. 1981.
A Glass Face in the Rain: New Poems. 1982.
Roving Across Fields: A Conversation and Uncollected Poems 1942–1982, edited by Thom Tammaro. 1983.
Segues: A Correspondence in Poetry, with Marvin Bell. 1983.
Smoke's Way: Poems from Limited Editions (1968–1981). 1983.
Listening Deep. 1984.
Stories, Storms, and Strangers. 1984.

Other

Down in My Heart (experience as a conscientious objector during World War II). 1947.
Friends to This Ground: A Statement for Readers, Teachers, and Writers of Literature. 1967.
Leftovers, A Care Package: Two Lectures. 1973.
Writing the Australian Crawl: Views on the Writer's Vocation. 1978.

Editor, with Frederick Candelaria, *The Voices of Prose*. 1966.
Editor, *The Achievement of Brother Antoninus: A Comprehensive Selection of His Poems with a Critical Introduction*. 1967.
Editor, with Robert H. Ross, *Poems and Perspectives*. 1971.
Editor, with Clinton F. Larson, *Modern Poetry of Western America*. 1975.

*

Critical Studies: "Stafford Issue" of *Northwest Review*, Spring 1974, and of *Modern Poetry Studies*, Spring 1975; *Four Poets and the Emotive Imagination* by George S. Lensing and Ronald Moran, 1976; *The Mark to Turn: A Reading of Stafford's Poetry* by Jonathan Holden, 1976.

* * *

William Stafford's poetry exemplifies the best of what is left of American transcendentalism. Like Emerson and Thoreau, he regards the human imagination as "salvational," and many of his poems are about the capacity of the imagination to derive meaning and awe from the world. Like the transcendentalists Stafford also regards the natural world as a possible model for human behavior:

> The earth says every summer have a ranch
> that's minimum: one tree, one well, a landscape
> that proclaims a universe—sermon
> of the hills, hallelujah mountain,
> highway guided by the way the world is tilted.

But, although in Stafford's poems Nature ("the landscape of justice") evinces both a glimmer of consciousness and a strict propriety of process, it contains few prescriptions definite enough to be useful guides to human behavior. It provides only distant analogues. Nor is Nature a comforting maternal presence. If there be any one lesson which the human species might draw from natural process, it is humility, to know your place, to have local priorities. Stafford has an organic conception of poetry, which also recalls the transcendentalists. For him, poetry is a manifestation of the "deepest [truest] place we have":

> They call it regional, this relevance—
> the deepest place we have: in this pool forms
> the model of our land, a lonely one,
> responsive to the wind. Everything we own
> has brought us here: from here we speak.

Composition is thus, for Stafford, a means of bringing to light the dark processes of the self:

> I do tricks in order to know:
> Careless I dance,
> then turn to see
> the mark to turn God left for me.

The style of Stafford's poems is quiet and colloquial. Few of them are very long. Throughout his poetry, certain words recur with a symbolic meaning. The most prominent of these words are "dark," "deep," "cold," "far," "God," and "home." Many of his earlier poems are rhymed, some heavily, some with slant or touch rhyme. His earlier work shows a fondness for sprung rhythm rather than quantitative metric. Since 1960 his work has grown steadily more relaxed in form and more rhetorically inventive. Typical of such inventiveness is the poem "Important Things":

> Like Locate Knob out west
> of town where maybe the world
> began. Like the rusty wire
> sagged in the river for a harp
> when floods go by.
> Like a way of talking, the slur
> in hello to mean you and God
> still think about justice.
> Like being alone, and you are
> alone, like always.
> You always are.

—Jonathan Holden

STEELE, Wilbur Daniel. Born in Greensboro, North Carolina, 17 March 1886. Educated in Germany, 1889–92, and at schools in Colorado, 1892–1900; University of Denver Preparatory School, 1900–03; University of Denver, 1903–07, B.A. 1907; Boston Museum School of Fine Arts, 1907–08; Académie Julian, Paris, 1908. Married 1) Margaret Thurston in 1913 (died, 1931), two sons; 2) Norma Mitchell in 1932 (died, 1967). Free-lance writer; lived in Provincetown, Massachusetts, until 1929: co-founder, Provincetown Players, 1915; lived in Chapel Hill, North Carolina, 1929–32, Hamburg, Connecticut, 1932–56, and Old Lyme, Connecticut, 1956–64; in rest home and hospital after 1964. D.Litt.: University of Denver, 1932. *Died 26 May 1970.*

PUBLICATIONS

Fiction

Storm. 1914.
Land's End and Other Stories. 1918.
The Shame Dance and Other Stories. 1923.
Isles of the Blest. 1924.
Taboo. 1925.
Urkey Island (stories). 1926.
The Man Who Saw Through Heaven and Other Stories. 1927.
Meat. 1928; as *The Third Generation*, 1929.
Tower of Sand and Other Stories. 1929.
Undertow. 1930.
Sound of Rowlocks. 1938.
That Girl from Memphis. 1945.
The Best Stories. 1945.
Diamond Wedding. 1950.
Full Cargo: More Stories. 1951.
Their Town. 1952.
The Way to the Gold. 1955.

Plays

Contemporaries (produced 1915).
Not Smart (produced 1916). In *The Terrible Woman . . .*, 1925.
The Giants' Stair (produced 1924). 1924.
Ropes, in *The Terrible Woman. . . .* 1925.
The Terrible Woman and Other One Act Plays. 1925.
Post Road, with Norma Mitchell (produced 1934). 1935.
How Beautiful with Shoes, with Anthony Brown, from the story by Steele (produced 1935).
Luck, in *One Hundred Nonroyalty Plays*, edited by William Kozlenko. 1941.

*

Critical Study: *Steele* by Martin Bucco, 1972.

* * *

Between World War I and the Depression Wilbur Daniel Steele was America's recognized master of the popular short story. Many of his nearly 200 published stories (an unschematized history of certain values prevailing in America at the time) transcend the formulas and clichés of mass fiction. Steele submitted to his day's conventions, but, like Poe, created a medley of dazzling variations. By wedding the "New Psychology" to his tight plots, melodramatic adventures, jagged coincidences, and surprise endings, he achieved a particular and celebrated perfection. But as magazines turned increasingly to social realism, sensational confession, and quicksilver style, demand for Steele's intricate stories declined.

Through exotic detail and vivid suggestion, *The Best Stories of Wilbur Daniel Steele* evokes the atmospheres of Cape Cod, the South, the Caribbean, North Africa, and the Middle East. With remarkable purity of concentration Steele exploits the temporality of literature, subordinates part to whole, and makes each yarn a gestalt. "Romantic" themes like suspected innocence, revenge and retribution, power of love and friendship, premonition, and return from the "dead" intertwine with such "realistic" ideas as heredity versus environment, law and conscience, divided self, quest for identity, and awakening. Sophoclean symmetry heightens the commonplace, but sometimes Steele's heavy-handed "chance" destroys his grim illusions. Still, his sinewy twists and shock endings (less meretricious then O. Henry's) force us to *re-see* life's awesome ironies and literature's delightful ones.

"The Man Who Saw Through Heaven," one of his most effective stories, dramatizes the physical and spiritual evolution of mankind in a tour de force of condensation. The classic "How Beautiful with Shoes" (also a Broadway play) renders the emotional awakening of a cloddish Appalachian girl abducted by a runaway psychotic. "When Hell Froze" is a memorable period piece. For sheer ingenuity and suspense "Footfalls," a tale of paternal revenge, has few equals. "Conjuh," "Blue Murder," "Bubbles," "The Body of the Crime," "For They Know Not What They Do"—these stories and many others have received high praise.

Steele's Euclidian logic, detective imagination, and knotty style suited the shorter form far better than the novel. His longer fiction, labored and wooden, displays feeble narrative line, thematic fuzziness, clotted exegesis, and trite detail. Perhaps *Meat*, an early novel which boldly indicts the perpetuation of weakness, is his best.

Today Steele's radiant prize stories crop up in anthologies, and historians of the American short story acknowledge his uniqueness, but he attracts little serious critical attention. An important transitional writer who bridges the Poe-O. Henry and the Anderson-Hemingway traditions, Steele was a marvelous technician who occasionally compelled his stories to the level of high art.

—Martin Bucco

STEIN, Gertrude. Born in Allegheny, Pennsylvania, 3 February 1874; as a child lived in Vienna, Paris, and Oakland, California. Educated at schools in Oakland and San Francisco; Radcliffe College, Cambridge, Massachusetts, 1893–97: studied philosophy under William James, B.A. (Harvard University), 1897; studied medicine at Johns Hopkins Medical School, Baltimore, 1897–1901. Lived in Paris from 1903, with Alice B. Toklas from 1908; center of a circle of artists, including Picasso, Matisse, and Braque, and of writers, including Hemingway and Fitzgerald; lived in Mallorca, 1914–16; worked with American Fund for French Wounded, 1917–18; founder, Plain Edition, Paris, 1930–33; lectured in the U.S., 1934–35. *Died 27 July 1946.*

PUBLICATIONS

Collections

Writings and Lectures 1911–1945 (selection), edited by Patricia Meyerowitz. 1967; as *Look at Me Now and Here I Am*, 1971.

Selected Operas and Plays, edited by John Malcolm Brinnin. 1970.

The Yale Stein: Selections, edited by Richard Kostelanetz. 1980.

Fiction

Three Lives: Stories of the Good Anna, Melanctha, and the Gentle Lena. 1909.

The Making of Americans, Being a History of a Family's Progress. 1925.

A Book Concluding with As a Wife Has a Cow: A Love Story. 1926.

Lucy Church Amiably. 1931.

Ida: A Novel. 1941.

Brewsie and Willie. 1946.

Blood on the Dining Room Floor. 1948.

Things as They Are: A Novel in Three Parts. 1950.

Mrs. Reynolds, and Five Earlier Novelettes, edited by Carl Van Vechten. 1952.

A Novel of Thank You, edited by Carl Van Vechten. 1958.

Plays

Geography and Plays. 1922.

A Village: Are You Ready Yet Not Yet. 1928.

Operas and Plays. 1932.

Four Saints in Three Acts, music by Virgil Thomson (produced 1934). 1934.

A Wedding Bouquet: Ballet, music by Lord Berners (produced 1936). 1936.

In Savoy; or, Yes Is for a Very Young Man (produced 1946). 1946.

The Mother of Us All, music by Virgil Thomson (produced 1947). 1947.

Last Operas and Plays, edited by Carl Van Vechten. 1949.

In a Garden, music by Meyer Kupferman (produced 1951). 1951.

Lucretia Borgia. 1968.

Verse and Prose Poems

Tender Buttons: Objects, Food, Rooms. 1914.

Have They Attacked Mary. He Giggled. 1917.

Before the Flowers of Friendship Faded Friendship Faded. 1931.
Two (Hitherto Unpublished) Poems. 1948.
Stanzas in Meditation and Other Poems (1929–1933), edited by Carl Van Vechten. 1956.

Other

Portrait of Mabel Dodge. 1912.
Composition as Explanation. 1926.
Descriptions of Literature. 1926.
An Elucidation. 1927.
Useful Knowledge. 1928.
An Acquaintance with Description. 1929.
Dix Portraits. 1930.
How to Write. 1931.
The Autobiography of Alice B. Toklas. 1933.
Matisse, Picasso, and Gertrude Stein, with Two Shorter Stories. 1933.
Portraits and Prayers. 1934.
Chicago Inscriptions. 1934.
Lectures in America. 1935.
Narration: Four Lectures. 1935.
The Geographical History of America; or, The Relation of Human Nature to the Human Mind. 1936.
Everybody's Autobiography. 1937.
Picasso. 1938.
The World Is Round (for children). 1939.
Prothalamium. 1939.
Paris France. 1940.
What Are Masterpieces. 1940.
Petits poèmes pour un livre de lecture (for children). 1944; translated as *The First Reader, and Three Plays*, 1946.
Wars I Have Seen. 1945.
Selected Writings, edited by Carl Van Vechten. 1946.
Four in America. 1947.
Kisses Can. 1947.
Literally True. 1947.
Two: Stein and Her Brother and Other Early Portraits (1908–1912), edited by Carl Van Vechten. 1951.
Bee Time Vine and Other Pieces (1913–1927), edited by Carl Van Vechten. 1953.
As Fine as Melanctha (1914–1930), edited by Carl Van Vechten. 1954.
Painted Lace and Other Pieces (1914–1937), edited by Carl Van Vechten. 1955.
Absolutely Bob Brown; or, Bobbed Brown. 1955.
To Bobchen Haas. 1957.
Alphabets and Birthdays, edited by Carl Van Vechten. 1957.
On Our Way (letters). 1959.
Cultivated Motor Automatism, with Leon M. Solomons. 1969.
Stein on Picasso, edited by Edward Burns. 1970.
A Primer for the Gradual Understanding of Stein, edited by Robert Bartlett Haas. 1971.
Fernhurst, Q.E.D., and Other Early Writings, edited by Leon Katz. 1971.
Sherwood Anderson/Stein: Correspondence and Personal Essays, edited by Ray Lewis White. 1972.
Reflection on the Atomic Bomb, edited by Robert Bartlett Haas. 1973.
Money. 1973.
How Writing Is Written, edited by Robert Bartlett Haas. 1974.
Dear Sammy: Letters from Stein to Alice B. Toklas, edited by Samuel M. Steward. 1977.
The Letters of Stein and Carl Van Vechten 1913–1946, edited by Edward Burns. 2 vols., 1986.

*

Bibliography: *Stein: A Bibliography* by Robert A. Wilson, 1974; *Stein: An Annotated Critical Bibliography* by Maureen R. Liston, 1979; *Stein and Alice B. Toklas: A Reference Guide* by Ray Lewis White, 1984.

Critical Studies: *Stein: Form and Intelligibility* by Rosalind S. Miller, 1949; *Stein: A Biography of Her Work* by Donald Sutherland, 1951; *The Flowers of Friendship* (letters to Stein) edited by Donald Gallup, 1953; *Stein: Her Life and Work* by Elizabeth Sprigge, 1957; *The Third Rose: Stein and Her World* by John Malcolm Brinnin, 1959; *Stein* by Frederick J. Hoffman, 1961; *What Is Remembered* by Alice B. Toklas, 1963, and *Staying On Alone: Letters of Alice B. Toklas* edited by Edward Burns, 1973; *The Development of Abstractionism in the Writings of Stein*, 1965, and *Stein*, 1976, both by Michael J. Hoffman; *Stein and the Present* by Allegra Stewart, 1967; *Stein and the Literature of Modern Consciousness* by Norman Weinstein, 1970; *Stein in Pieces* by Richard Bridgman, 1970; *Stein: A Biography* by Howard Greenfield, 1973; *Charmed Circle* by James Mellow, 1974; *Stein: A Composite Portrait* edited by Linda Simon, 1974; *Everybody Who Was Anybody: A Biography of Stein* by Janet Hobhouse, 1975; *Exact Resemblance to Exact Resemblance: The Literary Portraiture of Stein* by Wendy Steiner, 1978; *Stein: Autobiography and the Problem of Narration* by Shirley C. Neuman, 1979; *A Different Language: Stein's Experimental Writing* by Marianne DeKoven, 1983; *The Structure of Obscurity: Stein, Language and Cubism* by Randa Dubnick, 1984; *Stein's Theatre of the Absolute* by Betsy Alayne Ryan, 1984; *The Making of a Modernist: Stein from Three Lives to Tender Buttons* by Jayne L. Walker, 1984.

* * *

If Paul Cézanne, of whom Gertrude Stein wrote a "portrait" in 1911, broke with traditional forms (such as perspective) and traditional modes (such as pictorial replication), he did so by accenting the verticals, horizontals, and diagonals that he saw in nature. He moved painting towards geometric forms, towards the abstract, and developed new spatial patterns in which, by showing an object simultaneously from several viewpoints, planes and surfaces interacted visually on the canvas. His paintings are not of nature, but provide a visualisation of the formal parts of what he saw. Cézanne said that he did not paint pictures; he painted *paint*. Stein does the same thing with words.

Her work is largely a systematic investigation of the formal elements of language (syntax, parts of speech, grammar, etymology, punctuation) or of the formal elements of literature (narrative, poetry, dialogue, fiction, drama), in which we see the skeleton of the writing or of the form rather than the burden it carries. Apparent nonsense, her work has been the subject of much ridicule (yet it has influenced three generations of writers). "Nobody knows what I am trying to do but I do and I know when I succeed," she said, in *As Fine as Melanctha*. William Carlos Williams (*Selected Essays*) praised her for "cleansing" the language, for "tackling the fracture of stupidities bound in thoughtless phrases, in our calcified grammatical constructions, and in the subtle brainlessness of our . . . rhythms which compel words to follow certain others without precision of thought." Her concern is for writing (or reading) as movement; for literature, seen as something other than a body of reference work; for writing (reading) envisioned as the first concern of the immediate and attentive moment.

It is convenient to divide Stein's work into three more-or-less distinct groups. The first consists of such well-known and comparatively straightforward narratives as *The Autobiography of Alice B. Toklas*, *Wars I Have Seen*, and *Three Lives*, which includes the much-anthologized "Melanctha," in which we see (or, more accurately, hear) Melanctha simultaneously from several angles, as in a Cubist painting. Some of the dialogue between Melanctha and Jeff has an effect much like that of Marcel Duchamp's painting *Nude Descending a Staircase*. Richard Wright records reading the story to "a group of semi-literate Negro stockyard workers" who "slapped their thighs, howled, laughed, stomped, and interrupted me constantly to comment on the characters" (*PM*, 11 March 1945). It is the language of speech.

The second group contains Stein's critical and exegetical work, such as *Composition as Explanation*, *Narration*, *What Are Masterpieces*, and the celebrated *Lectures in America*, in which she discusses her own writing, and, offering general reflections on the forms, genres, modes, and periods of English literature, explains the principles on which much of her own work is based. The fruit of protracted meditation on language, her exegeses are at times difficult to follow; as Thornton Wilder observed, "Miss Stein pays her listeners the high compliment of dispensing for the most part with that apparatus of illustrative simile and anecdote that is so often employed to recommend ideas." And when, in *Lectures in America*, she says "more and more one does not use nouns," she is pointing to the very plasticity of language one finds in the third group of her work, the overtly experimental and difficult writing.

Work in this group, such as *Tender Buttons*, *Stanzas in Meditation*, *An Acquaintance with Description*, or *How to Write*, may properly be thought of as "exemplary," since it demonstrates the principles enunciated in the exegetical work. While composing *How to Write* Stein called *Tender Buttons* "my first conscious struggle with the problem of correlating sight, sound and sense, and eliminating rhythm;—now I am trying grammar and eliminating sight and sound" (*Transition 14*, 1928), while in *Lectures in America* she said that in *Tender Buttons* "I struggled with the ridding of myself of nouns. I knew that nouns must go in poetry as they had gone in prose if anything that is everything was to go on meaning something." A noun is the name of a thing, and "if you feel what is inside that thing you do not call it by the name by which it is known"; instead, like Whitman, you "mean names without naming them." Breaking syntax, forcing words into multiple grammatical functions, in *Tender Buttons* or *Stanzas in Meditation* Stein seeks to write a poem which, taken as a whole, becomes itself a noun. For example, as Meredith Yearsley points out, under the title "A Box" the poem acts a box out linguistically by the quadruple repetition of a particular construction. The closedness of the box is caught by use of grammatical constructions which force the reader to re-scan the sentence. Here, most clearly, Stein uses words the way Cézanne uses paint.

How to Write, originally entitled *Grammar, Paragraphs, Sentences, Vocabulary, Etcetera*, works similarly, through exploring the effect of semantic and syntactic anomalies in a prose which demands of the reader the expectation that words, the part of speech, will hold their conventional position and function in the sentence. In a sentence like "It is very well a date which makes each separate in a leaf in a dismissal," the major source of difficulty is not in the lack of punctuation so much as in the ambiguous functions of words and phrases. In other sentences from "Arthur a Grammar" the reader need only supply punctuation to render the sentence wholly intelligible: "There is a difference between a grammar and a sentence this is grammar in a sentence I will agree to no map with which you may be dissatisfied and therefore beg you to point out what you regard as incorrect in the positions of the troops in my two sentences." In each case, the sentence acts out its meaning.

In such ways Stein's words remove themselves from the context in which they (may have) originated and acquire a new context in which they can assert their meaning by demonstrating it. The world of Stein is one in which things are the cause rather than the content of language, and it is thus an interiorized world, where definitions are held in the process and in the moment of defining: Stein held that poetry is stasis, where the object, be it Melanctha or Roast Beef or Arthur a Grammar, fills all the available space, much as a Cubist object fills a crowded flat surface. The work is dense, and exuberant.

While the strength of Stein's personality might account for her influence on writers like Hemingway or Sherwood Anderson, it does not account for her later influence, or for her friendship with painters like Picasso or Juan Gris. Later readers of her work, like Robert Duncan, George Bowering, or B.P. Nichol, find themselves, imitating her writing, turning to their own childhood. This is in part because Stein's language is devoid of allusion, seems to have no past, and things seem to speak directly, perceived in immediacy.

—Peter Quartermain

STEINBECK, John (Ernst). Born in Salinas, California, 27 February 1902. Educated at Salinas High School, graduated 1919; Stanford University, California, intermittently 1919–25. Married 1) Carol Henning in 1930 (divorced, 1942); 2) Gwyn Conger (i.e., the actress Gwen Verdon) in 1943 (divorced, 1948), two sons; 3) Elaine Scott in 1950. Worked at various jobs, including reporter for New York *American*, apprentice hod-carrier, apprentice painter, chemist, caretaker of an estate at Lake Tahoe, surveyor, and fruit picker, 1925–35; full-time writer from 1935; lived in Monterey, California, then New York City; special writer for U.S. Army Air Force during World War II; correspondent in Europe, New York *Herald Tribune*, 1943. Recipient: New York Drama Critics Circle award, 1938; Pulitzer Prize, 1940; King Haakon Liberty Cross (Norway), 1946; O. Henry Award, 1956; Nobel Prize for Literature, 1962; Presidential Medal of Freedom, 1964; U.S. Medal of Freedom, 1964. Member, American Academy, 1939. *Died 20 December 1968.*

PUBLICATIONS

Fiction

Cup of Gold: A Life of Henry Morgan, Buccaneer, with Occasional Reference to History. 1929.
The Pastures of Heaven. 1932.

To a God Unknown. 1933.
Tortilla Flat. 1935.
In Dubious Battle. 1936.
Saint Katy the Virgin (story). 1936.
Of Mice and Men. 1937.
The Red Pony (stories). 1937.
The Long Valley (stories). 1938.
The Grapes of Wrath. 1939; edited by Peter Lisca, 1972.
The Moon Is Down. 1942.
Cannery Row. 1945.
The Wayward Bus. 1947.
The Pearl. 1947.
Burning Bright: A Play in Story Form. 1950.
East of Eden. 1952.
The Short Novels. 1953.
Sweet Thursday. 1954.
The Short Reign of Pippin IV: A Fabrication. 1957.
The Winter of Our Discontent. 1961.

Plays

Of Mice and Men, from his own novel (produced 1937). 1937.
The Forgotten Village (screenplay). 1941.
The Moon Is Down, from his own novel (produced 1942). 1942.
A Medal for Benny, with Jack Wagner and Frank Butler, in *Best Film Plays 1945*, edited by John Gassner and Dudley Nichols. 1946.
Burning Bright, from his own novel (produced 1950). 1951.
Viva Zapata! The Original Screenplay, edited by Robert E. Morsberger. 1975.

Screenplays: *The Forgotten Village* (documentary), 1941; *Lifeboat*, with Jo Swerling, 1944; *A Medal for Benny*, with Jack Wagner and Frank Butler, 1945; *La perla* (*The Pearl*), with Jack Wagner and Emilio Fernandez, 1946; *The Red Pony*, 1949; *Viva Zapata!*, 1952.

Other

Their Blood Is Strong. 1938.
Steinbeck Replies (letter). 1940.
Sea of Cortez: A Leisurely Journal of Travel and Research, with Edward F. Ricketts. 1941.
Bombs Away: The Story of a Bomber Team. 1942.
The Viking Portable Library Steinbeck, edited by Pascal Covici. 1943; abridged edition, as *The Steinbeck Pocket Book*, 1943; revised edition, as *The Portable Steinbeck*, 1946, 1958; revised edition, edited by Pascal Covici, Jr., 1971; 1946 edition published as *The Indispensable Steinbeck*, 1950, and as *The Steinbeck Omnibus*, 1951.
The First Watch (letter). 1947.
Vanderbilt Clinic. 1947.
A Russian Journal, photographs by Robert Capa. 1948.
The Log from the Sea of Cortez. 1951.
Once There Was a War. 1958.
Travels with Charley in Search of America. 1962.
Speech Accepting the Nobel Prize for Literature. . . . 1962(?).
America and Americans. 1966.
Journal of a Novel: The East of Eden Letters. 1969.
Steinbeck: A Life in Letters, edited by Elaine Steinbeck and Robert Wallsten. 1975.
The Acts of King Arthur and His Noble Knights, From the Winchester Manuscripts of Malory and Other Sources, edited by Chase Horton. 1976.
Letters to Elizabeth: A Selection of Letters from John Steinbeck to Elizabeth Otis, edited by Florian J. Shasky and Susan F. Riggs. 1978.

*

Bibliography: *A New Steinbeck Bibliography 1929–1971* and *1971–1981* by Tetsumaro Hayashi, 2 vols., 1973–83; *Steinbeck: A Bibliographical Catalogue of the Adrian H. Goldstone Collection* by Adrian H. Goldstone and John R. Payne, 1974.

Critical Studies: *The Novels of Steinbeck: A First Critical Study* by Harry T. Moore, 1939, as *Steinbeck and His Novels*, 1939; *Steinbeck and His Critics: A Record of Twenty-Five Years* edited by E.W. Tedlock, Jr., and C.V. Wicker, 1957; *The Wide World of Steinbeck*, 1958, and *Steinbeck, Nature, and Myth*, 1978, both by Peter Lisca; *Steinbeck* by Warren French, 1961, revised edition, 1975, and *A Companion to The Grapes of Wrath* edited by French, 1963; *Steinbeck* by F.W. Watt, 1962; *Steinbeck: An Introduction and Interpretation* by Joseph Fontenrose, 1964; Steinbeck Monograph series, from 1972, and *A Study Guide to Steinbeck: A Handbook to His Major Works*, 2 vols., 1974–79, both edited by Tetsumaro Hayashi; *Steinbeck: A Collection of Critical Essays* edited by Robert Murray Davis, 1972; *Steinbeck and Edward F. Ricketts: The Shaping of a Novelist* by Richard Astro, 1973; *The Novels of Steinbeck: A Critical Study* by Howard Levant, 1974; *Steinbeck: The Errant Knight: An Intimate Biography of His California Years* by Nelson Valjean, 1975; *The Intricate Music: A Biography of Steinbeck* by Thomas Kiernan, 1979; *Steinbeck* by Paul McCarthy, 1980; *The True Adventures of Steinbeck, Novelist: A Biography* by Jackson J. Benson, 1984; *Steinbeck: The California Years* by Brian St. Pierre, 1984; *Steinbeck's Revision of America* by Louis Owens, 1985; *Steinbeck's Fiction: The Aesthetics of the Road Taken* by John H. Timmerman, 1986.

* * *

John Steinbeck often puzzled critics during his lifetime because early in his career his style and subject matter seemed to change with each new story, and after World War II there was a generally acknowledged but puzzling decline in his artistic powers. Now, however, in a larger perspective we can see that underlying the apparent diversity of Steinbeck's work is a consistently developing vision of man's relation to his environment. This larger perspective is provided, in part, by the generally acknowledged end of the Age of Modernism, as described in Maurice Beebe's "What Modernism Was" (*Journal of Modern Literature*, July 1974). After offering a longer definition, Beebe approves Philip Stevick's observation that the modernist sensibility might almost be defined by "its irony, its implicit admiration for verbal precision and understatement." Marston LaFrance in *A Reading of Stephen Crane* (1971) traces this characteristic irony to Kierkegaard and describes its possessors as perceiving "a double realm of values where a different sort of mind would perceive only a single realm."

Steinbeck's varying works during the years of his greatest popularity and power in the 1930's were characterized by precisely this kind of irony. It is excellently illustrated by Sir Henry Morgan's speech at the end of Steinbeck's first novel,

Cup of Gold, "Civilization will split up a character, and he who refuses to split goes under." Despite its importance in establishing Steinbeck's viewpoint, this apprentice work is strikingly different from his later books. A flamboyantly written historical costume drama about a Caribbean pirate who sacks the golden city of Panama to capture a legendary woman and then returns her to her husband for a ransom and sells out his piratical cohorts for high government position, *Cup of Gold* exudes the same disenchanted world-weariness as the abundant "Waste Land" literature of the 1920's.

A similar preoccupation with characters of mythical dimensions in a dying world colors one of Steinbeck's strangest novels, *To a God Unknown* (third published, it antedates the second). In this fantasy, Joseph Wayne—the leader among four brothers who allegorize lust, sanctimoniousness, animalism, and martyrdom—sacrifices himself to bring the needed rain to his parched valley. Here, as in the story-cycle called *The Pastures of Heaven*, Steinbeck discovers the beautiful, small valleys of his native California as the settings for his most powerful tales. But whereas *To a God Unknown* employs the same kind of baroque language and bizarre episodes as *Cup of Gold*, *The Pastures of Heaven* offers a lower-keyed, vernacular language and earthy tales of the defeat of good intentions in a naturalistic manner that emphasizes the irony of man's sufferings in a paradisically beautiful setting.

Steinbeck continues to employ this naturalistic viewpoint in his next works. *Tortilla Flat* seems at first glance much different from the others because of the archaic style arising from the effort to translate Malory's *Morte Darthur* into the language and actions of Mexican-American "paisanos" in Monterey, California; but beneath its surface of quaint humor, it, too, is an ironic fable of civilization "splitting up" a person: once the fabulous Danny abandons his "natural life" in the woods to become a property owner, he can never go back again and must die with a gesture of defiant despair. *In Dubious Battle*, which is often justifiably called the best American strike novel, deals realistically with tense labor problems among California apple growers and migrant pickers and ends as grimly as *Tortilla Flat*, with the disappearance of Doc Burton, the one man of objective good will in the story, and a murder that renders faceless a young labor organizer.

In *Of Mice and Men*, Steinbeck's first experiment in writing a play-novelette, Lennie, a tower of physical strength, must die because he has not the mentality to control his behavior and kills the soft things he loves to fondle. His death destroys also his protector George's dream of their some time finding security on a farm of their own. The stories collected in *The Long Valley* record similar helpless defeats—in the most familiar of them, "Chrysanthemums" and "Flight," we see first a love-starved woman exploited by a wily itinerant and then another young man whose mind is not strong enough to control his behavior driven to his death by shadowy pursuers. The collection concludes with one of Steinbeck's most popular and masterful works, *The Red Pony*. This four-story cycle depicts a sensitive boy's growing into maturity through his encounters on his father's ranch with the fallibility of man, the wearing out of man, the unreliability of nature, and the exhaustion of nature that leads to the extinguishing of man's dynamic urge for "Westering."

Steinbeck's next work after his success with *Of Mice and Men* was apparently planned as another ironic, defeatist tale entitled *L'Affaire Lettuceberg*, based on his observation of the outrageous plight of migrant workers who had fled the mid-western Dust Bowl in hope of making a new start in California. During the writing, however, Steinbeck experienced a great change of heart, abandoned what he had written as "a smart-alec book," and, writing feverishly, recast his work as *The Grapes of Wrath*, his most popular and critically most highly acclaimed work.

The Grapes of Wrath alternates the story of the travails of the Joad family, share-croppers tractored out of Oklahoma who find only a hostile reception in the west, with inter-chapters that generalize this family history as a nation's tragedy. Through the inspiration of the martyred ex-preacher Jim Casy, the Joads at last learn the lesson of co-operation summed up by Ma's speech, "Use' ta be the fambly was fust. It ain't so now. It's anybody." Yet the novel is still modernist in sensibility, for the much discussed ending in which daughter Rosasharn offers breast milk intended for her own dead baby to a dying old man is ambiguous. The Joads have found temporary haven, but no security; the national tragedy can only be solved by the readers, not the writer. Steinbeck has, however, turned from characters who are helpless victims to those who learn to heighten their consciousnesses enough to transcend their afflictions.

After reshaping this key novel, Steinbeck would never revert completely to the ironical modernist point of view; but neither was he able consistently to contrive situations convincingly optimistic enough to provide an alternative. His two further play-novelettes, *The Moon Is Down*—written during World War II about the military occupation of a peaceful nation—and *Burning Bright*—a meditation on sterility that pleads that "the species must go staggering on"—suffered from "misplaced universalism." They were populated with two-dimensional allegorical figures from medieval morality plays. Other works like the very popular *The Pearl*, *The Wayward Bus*, and the script for Elia Kazan's film *Viva Zapata!*—like the earlier short film *The Forgotten Village*—take Mexicans from underprivileged backgrounds and turn them into folk-Messiahs, "natural saints." (The driver of *The Wayward Bus* even has the initials J.C.) Kino's gesture in *The Pearl* of casting away the fabulous jewel that has brought only misery rather than promised fortune and the tribute at the end of Kazan's film to Zapata's indomitable spirit have heartened audiences, but they are theatricalized indications that Steinbeck, instead of looking ahead, seeks—as such later non-fiction works as *America and Americans* and the "Letters to Alicia" make clear—a return to simple, folk values of the past.

Only in *Cannery Row*, where Steinbeck again universalizes the comic story he tells through "inter-chapters," does he succeed in creating, in his portrait of Doc (based on his good friend Ed Ricketts), a remarkable figure who has both the selflessness and the sophistication to transcend the trials and temptations of the materialistic world by escaping into "the cosmic Monterey" fragmentarily embodied in deathless art.

Steinbeck attempted to tell such a story of transcendence again in his most ambitious novel, *East of Eden*, by again alternating between two kinds of material, but this time they fail to fuse. The story of his own family returns to the lyrical naturalism of his work of the 1930's, but the narrative is so heavily ironic that it fails to produce an affirmation; he seeks this through the labored fictional pursuit of the meaning of the Hebrew word "Timshel," which animates another allegorical fable—this one spiced up with much sensational material—about a modern Adam, his errant wife, and his twin sons who re-enact the biblical account of man's first family.

Steinbeck's subsequent fiction was trivial. *Sweet Thursday* brought back Doc and other characters from *Cannery Row*, but reduced Doc to a confused sentimentalist ministered to principally by kindly whores. *The Short Reign of Pippin IV* was a very funny, timely attack on French politics and art during the years of Charles de Gaulle, but its sketchiness makes it dated. Finally in *The Winter of Our Discontent*, Steinbeck tried to make a fresh start by writing about a small Long Island town. The novel developed from a very funny short story, "How Mr. Hogan Robbed a Bank," but the humor disappeared in this account of Ethan Allen Hawley's struggles with his conscience about having been betrayed by others and betraying others. While the novel does not quite become simply another revelation of modernist alienation (Hawley makes the affirmative gesture of rejecting suicide in order to help his daughter live) he really makes for less selfish reasons the same kind of compromise that the pirate Henry Morgan makes in Steinbeck's first novel. Thus Steinbeck's fiction returns at last almost full circle to the point where it had begun after achieving but falling away from the triumphant visions of *The Grapes of Wrath* and *Cannery Row*.

—Warren French

See the essay on *The Grapes of Wrath*.

STEVENS, Wallace. Born in Reading, Pennsylvania, 2 October 1879. Educated at Harvard University, Cambridge, Massachusetts, 1897–1900; New York University Law School, 1901–03; admitted to New York bar, 1904. Married Elsie V. Kachel in 1909; one daughter. Reporter, New York *Herald Tribune*, 1900–01; lawyer in New York, 1904–16; joined the Hartford Accident and Indemnity Company, Connecticut, 1916: Vice-President, 1934–55. Recipient: Harriet Monroe Poetry Award, 1946; Bollingen Prize, 1950; National Book Award, 1951, 1955; Pulitzer Prize, 1955. Member, American Academy, 1946. *Died 2 August 1955.*

PUBLICATIONS

Collections

Letters, edited by Holly Stevens. 1967.
The Palm at the End of the Mind: Selected Poems and a Play, edited by Holly Stevens. 1971.

Verse

Harmonium. 1923; revised edition, 1931.
Ideas of Order. 1935.
Owl's Clover. 1936.
The Man with the Blue Guitar and Other Poems. 1937.
Parts of a World. 1942.
Notes Toward a Supreme Fiction. 1942.
Esthétique du Mal. 1945.
Description Without Place. 1945.
Transport to Summer. 1947.
Three Academic Pieces: The Realm of Resemblance, Someone Puts a Pineapple Together, Of Ideal Time and Choice. 1947.
A Primitive Like an Orb. 1948.
The Auroras of Autumn. 1950.
Selected Poems, edited by Dennis Williamson. 1952.
Selected Poems. 1953.
Collected Poems. 1954.

Plays

Carlos among the Candles (produced 1917). In *Opus Posthumous*, 1957.
Three Travelers Watch a Sunrise (produced 1920). In *Opus Posthumous*, 1957.
Bowl, Cat, and Broomstick, in *Quarterly Review of Literature 16*, 1969.

Other

Two or Three Ideas. 1951.
The Relations Between Poetry and Painting. 1951.
The Necessary Angel: Essays on Reality and the Imagination. 1951.
Raoul Dufy: A Note. 1953.
Opus Posthumous (miscellany), edited by Samuel French Morse. 1957.

*

Bibliography: *Stevens: A Descriptive Bibliography* by J.M. Edelstein, 1973.

Critical Studies: *The Shaping Spirit: A Study of Stevens* by William Van O'Connor, 1950; *Stevens: An Approach to His Poetry and Thought* by Robert Pack, 1958; *Stevens* by Frank Kermode, 1960, revised edition, 1967; *The Achievement of Stevens* edited by Ashley Brown and Robert S. Haller, 1962; *The Comic Spirit of Stevens* by Daniel Fuchs, 1963; *The Clairvoyant Eye: The Poetry and Poetics of Stevens* by Joseph N. Riddel, 1965; *The Act of the Mind: Essays on the Poetry of Stevens* edited by Roy Harvey Pearce and J. Hillis Miller, 1965; *Stevens: Musing the Obscure* by Ronald Sukenick, 1967; *The Dome and the Rock: Structure in the Poetry of Stevens* by James Baird, 1968; *On Extended Wings: Stevens' Longer Poems*, 1969, and *Stevens: Words Chosen Out of Desire*, 1984, both by Helen Vendler; *Stevens: Poetry as Life* by Samuel French Morse, 1970; *Stevens: The Poem as Act* by Merle E. Brown, 1970; *Images of Stevens* by Edward Kessler, 1971; *Introspective Voyager: The Poetic Development of Stevens* by A. Walton Litz, 1972; *Stevens* by Lucy Beckett, 1974; *Stevens: The Poems of Our Climate* by Harold Bloom, 1977; *Souvenirs and Prophecies: The Young Stevens* by Holly Stevens, 1977; *Stevens: An Introduction to the Poetry* by Susan B. Weston, 1977; *Stevens: The Poet and His Critics* by Abbie F. Willard, 1978; *Stevens: The Making of the Poem* by Frank Doggett, 1980, and *Stevens: A Celebration* edited by Doggett and Robert Buttel, 1980; *Advance on Chaos: The Sanctifying Imagination of Stevens* by David M. La Guardia, 1983; *Stanza My Stone: Stevens and the Hermetic Tradition* by Leonora Woodman, 1983; *Parts of a World: Stevens Remembered: An Oral Biography* by Peter Brazeau, 1983; *The Transparent Lyric: Reading and Meaning in the Poetry of Stevens and Williams* by David Walker, 1984; *The Long Poems of Stevens: An Interpretative Study* by Rajeev S. Patke, 1985; *Stevens: The Critical Heritage* edited by Charles Doyle, 1985; *Stevens: A Mythology of Self* by Milton J. Bates, 1985; *Forms of Farewell: The Late Poetry of Stevens* by Charles Berger, 1985; *Stevens: The Poetics of Modernism* edited by Albert Gelpi, 1986; *Stevens: The Early Years*

1879–1923 by Joan Richardson, 1986; *Stevens: A Poet's Growth* by George S. Lensing, 1986.

* * *

Wallace Stevens is a poet who combined a long poetic career with another career, as a business executive. The career that concerns us here—that of poet—produced a large body of work that circles around a lifelong consideration from which all his best poems radiate. Each poem is one testimony to an encompassing vision of what Stevens judges to be the prime obligation of a modern poet. That obligation leaves its mark on comparatively brief and early poems like "Peter Quince at the Clavier," "Sunday Morning," and "Thirteen Ways of Looking at a Blackbird" and continues in later and quite extensive works like *Transport to Summer* and *Ideas of Order*. Stevens is, early and late, concerned with a purification of the human intellect and sensibility—in the first place, the intellect and the sensibility of the poet who is writing, and, in the second place, the intellect and sensibility of the reader who responds to what the poet has written.

The purification takes place as service to a set of ideas—"ideas of order" in Stevens's phrase—that are ignored or, at best, served badly and intermittently in the culture to which Stevens belongs. Our sensibility has been corrupted by habits of thought that seduce the poet and his readers from a prime duty. Poet and reader have the chance, if they but respond rightly to the world which constantly surrounds them and indeed bombards them with endless impressions, to take in special sensations (the colors of light on the sea, the taste of cheese and pineapple, a musical cadence) and set them down in words. These sensations are most pure at a special time of the year (summer) and in southern climes where light and color are most intense. The sensations are adulterated by many things, by winter and northern climes, for example. Even more crucial in Stevens's account are the betrayals that are built into human culture, the dogmas and traditions and forms of artistic expression that are conventional and hackneyed. Stevens can speak bitterly of "statues" that dominate public squares and inhibit the innocent and intense sensory responses of the people who walk there.

Implied by this emphasis is a psychology—a theory of human perception—that is basically nominalistic. What is real and worthy of reverence—the poet's reverence and his readers'—is, for example, the contact the eye makes with a certain slant of light which is never the equivalent of some past contact with a slant of light. It is a mistake to move from several such special moments to any general conception about "shades of light." Each moment of perception must be preserved in its uniqueness, and the poet must, ideally, move no further from that moment than the carefully selected set of words that allow him to make a verbal record. Stevens—a poet quite well-informed in such matters—is aware of the traps into which other poets and other human beings have fallen. In *Harmonium*, there is an "Invective Against Swans." Stevens writes: "The soul, o ganders, flies beyond the parks / And far beyond the discords of the wind." Here the "soul" has a vertigo that takes it beyond "parks" (and their clusters of rare and unique sensations) and beyond the manifestly rich "discords of the wind." The "soul" treacherously detaches the human sensibility from its proper and health-giving ground: the never-ending moments of intense sensation. The "soul" carries the human sensibility into a context of religious and social ideas that have at best a tenuous connection with "parks" and "discords of the wind."

The positive aspect of Stevens's reiterated warning appears in such lines as these from "Credences of Summer" in *Transport to Summer*. Here, Stevens suggests, is sound belief: "The rock cannot be broken. It is the truth. / It rises from land and sea and covers them." That is, the rock is—and remains—the source of acute physical perception. It is a natural object, far removed from any piece of stone that human hands have chipped at and made into a "statue," a memorial of some past event or an expression of human dogmas. A few more lines refine this particular statement, one that resembles many others in Stevens's work. The "rock of summer" (a "rock of winter" is apparently inferior) is not "A hermit's truth nor symbol in hermitage." A "hermit's truth" is what the gander soul flutters toward. Stevens continues:

> It is the visible rock, the audible,
> The brilliant mercy of a sure repose,
> On this present ground, the vividest repose,
> Things certain sustaining us in certainty.

Brief annotation—and all of Stevens's work stimulates such effort—would indicate that it is the actual rock that is esteemed, not the idea, Platonic or otherwise, of "rock." From the visible rock the errant "soul" gains a sure and not a treacherous "repose." And the rock is a "present ground" and, as such, the source of the only certainty that a poet and his reader can have confidence in.

Such lines indicate a perspective that extends throughout Stevens's work like a prairie landscape, insistent and unaltering. The lines, elegant in expression and charged with authority, invite each person to be a "center" into which are gathered separate moments of "vividest repose." Not the ersatz "repose" of some religious or political certainty. Not, even, the "repose" that some poets, retreating from politics and dogma, try to discover in personal relations, intense and unshakable. For the fierce outcry which is Matthew Arnold's only comfort on the "darkling plain" of "Dover Beach"—"Ah, love, let us be true / To one another!"—Stevens would have scarcely more patience than he has for "statues." As he observes in *Parts of a World*:

> Words are not forms of a single word.
> In the sum of the parts, there are only the parts.
> The world must be measured by eye . . .

To the villainous "gander soul," the whole is always greater than the sum of its parts and testimony to principle, to some inclusive order that lies in a divine mind or, at least, at the very roots of things. The "single word" (or Word, as Christians would say) is a delusion. Words serve the eye, and the eye takes in what aspect a "rock of summer" has at a particular moment.

As Stevens's large body of work indicates, such labor can be lifelong. It can exclude—and does—elements of existence that have counted for other poets and that, from Stevens's point of view, have corrupted them and those who read them. Stevens's "center" (the poet's awareness and perhaps his readers') is a clear crystal which sensation reaches—reaches and passes through with as little refraction as possible.

—Harold H. Watts

See the essay on "Sunday Morning."

STICKNEY, (Joseph) Trumbull. Born in Geneva, Switzerland, 20 June 1874. Spent his childhood in Europe; tutored by his father; educated at Walton Lodge, Clevedon, Somerset, 1886; Cutler's School, New York, 1890; Harvard University, Cambridge, Massachusetts, 1891–95 (editor, *Harvard Monthly*), A.B. (magna cum laude) 1895; the Sorbonne, Paris, Doctorat ès Lettres, 1903. Instructor in Greek, Harvard University, 1903–04. *Died 11 October 1904.*

PUBLICATIONS

Collections

Homage to Stickney (selected verse), edited by James Reeves and Seán Haldane. 1968.
The Poems, edited by Amberys R. Whittle. 1972.

Verse

Dramatic Verses. 1902.
Poems, edited by George Cabot Lodge, John Ellerton Lodge, and William Vaughn Moody. 1905.

Other

Les Sentences dans la Poésie Grecque d'Homère à Euripide. 1903.

Translator, with Sylvain Lévi, *Bhagavadgita.* 1938.

*

Critical Studies: *The Fright of Time: Stickney* by Seán Haldane, 1970; *Stickney* by Amberys R. Whittle, 1973.

* * *

One of that group of gifted Americans who came to early maturity in the 1890's only to have their lives snuffed out before the first decade of the new century was completed, Trumbull Stickney is memorable on several counts. As an accomplished Greek and Sanskrit scholar and one of the first intellectual cosmopolitans to attempt a career in American letters, he exhibits a cultural impulse which is to be later followed more extensively by writers like Pound and Eliot. Further, along with William Vaughn Moody and George Cabot Lodge, he aimed at resuscitating verse-drama, and his work in this genre (*Prometheus Pyrphoros* and two fragments based on the lives of the Emperor Julian and the young Benvenuto Cellini) points forward to later efforts in the century. And, powerfully under the influence of Browning, he produced a number of "dramatic scenes" ("Kalypso," "Oneiropolos," "Lodovico Martelli," "Requiescam," etc.), although his instincts for dramatic conflict and psychological subtlety seem less vigorous than his evident delight in historical reconstruction.

It is perhaps the lyrical quality of his writing that suggests the most promise in his work. Almost suffocated in the cloying rhetoric of the *fin de siècle*, heavy with twilight and rose-dust and a fatigued embrace of futility, Stickney's lyrics frequently manage a new, if wistful, vitality to the clichés of romantic decadence. In poems like "Chestnuts in November," "At Sainte-Marguerite," "Mt. Lykaion," and in isolated passages from "Eride," Stickney's tempered musicality sustains the conventional formal structures, raising these poems above the level of similar lamentations which the Mauve Decade manufactured in wholesale lots. And in poems like "With thy two eyes look on me once again," "Leave him now quiet by the way," and, especially, "Mnemosyne," a quiet strength joins with a precise sense of rhythmical phrasing to produce verse which possesses an autonomy of statement and genuine eloquence. It is futile to speculate on what might have been, but in half a dozen poems Stickney's success was authentic and undeniable. As graceful as Santayana's verse but more concretely sensual, with an intellectual structure as sturdy as the early Robinson's but more personal and direct in tone, Stickney's achievement illustrates the highest ambitions of his generation, while implying a technique that may compensate for the weaknesses of its gentility.

—Earl Rovit

STOUT, Rex (Todhunter). Born in Noblesville, Indiana, 1 December 1886. Educated at Topeka High School, Kansas; University of Kansas, Lawrence. Served in the U.S. Navy as a Yeoman on President Theodore Roosevelt's yacht, 1906–08. Married 1) Fay Kennedy in 1916 (divorced, 1933); 2) Pola Hoffman in 1933; two daughters. Office boy, store clerk, bookkeeper, and hotel manager, 1916–27; invented the banking system for schoolchildren; full-time writer from 1927. Founding director, Vanguard Press, New York; host, *Speaking of Liberty*, *Voice of Freedom*, and *Our Secret Weapon* radio programs, 1941–43. Chairman of the Writers' War Board, 1941–46, and the World Government Writers Board, 1949–75; President, Friends of Democracy, 1941–51, Authors' Guild, 1943–45, and Society for the Prevention of World War III, 1943–46; President, 1951–55, 1962–69, and Vice-President, 1956–61, Authors League of America; Treasurer, Freedom House, 1957–75; President, Mystery Writers of America, 1958. Recipient: Mystery Writers of America Grand Master Award, 1959. *Died 27 October 1975.*

PUBLICATIONS

Fiction

How Like a God. 1929.
Seed on the Wind. 1930.
Golden Remedy. 1931.
Forest Fire. 1933.
Fer-de-Lance. 1934.
The President Vanishes. 1934.
The League of Frightened Men. 1935.
O Careless Love! 1935.
The Rubber Band. 1936; as *To Kill Again*, 1960.
The Red Box. 1937.
The Hand in the Glove. 1937; as *Crime on Her Hands*, 1939.
Too Many Cooks. 1938.
Mr. Cinderella. 1938.
Some Buried Caesar. 1939; as *The Red Bull*, 1945.
Mountain Cat. 1939; as *The Mountain Cat Murders*, 1943.
Red Threads. 1939.
Double for Death. 1939.
Over My Dead Body. 1940.

Where There's a Will. 1940.
The Broken Vase. 1941.
Alphabet Hicks. 1941; as *The Sound of Murder*, 1965.
Black Orchids (stories). 1942.
Booby Trap (stories). 1944.
Not Quite Dead Enough (stories). 1944.
The Silent Speaker. 1946.
Too Many Women. 1947.
And Be a Villain. 1948; as *More Deaths Than One*, 1949.
The Second Confession. 1949.
Trouble in Triplicate (stories). 1949.
Three Doors to Death (stories). 1950.
In the Best Families. 1950; as *Even in the Best Families*, 1951.
Murder by the Book. 1951.
Curtains for Three (stories). 1951.
Triple Jeopardy (stories). 1951.
Prisoner's Base. 1952; as *Out Goes She*, 1953.
The Golden Spiders. 1953.
Three Men Out (stories). 1954.
The Black Mountain. 1954.
Before Midnight. 1955.
Might as Well Be Dead. 1956.
Three Witnesses (stories). 1956.
Three for the Chair (stories). 1957.
If Death Ever Slept. 1957.
Champagne for One. 1958.
And Four to Go (stories). 1958; as *Crime and Again*, 1959.
Plot It Yourself. 1959; as *Murder in Style*, 1960.
Three at Wolfe's Door (stories). 1960.
Too Many Clients. 1960.
The Final Deduction. 1961.
Gambit. 1962.
Homicide Trinity (stories). 1962.
The Mother Hunt. 1963.
Trio for Blunt Instruments (stories). 1964.
A Right To Die. 1964.
The Doorbell Rang. 1965.
Death of a Doxy. 1966.
The Father Hunt. 1968.
Death of a Dude. 1969.
Please Pass the Guilt. 1973.
A Family Affair. 1975.
Justice Ends at Home and Other Stories, edited by John McAleer. 1977.
Under the Andes. 1985.

Other

The Nero Wolfe Cook Book, with others. 1973.
Corsage (miscellany). 1977.

Editor, *The Illustrious Dunderheads*. 1942.
Editor, with Louis Greenfield, *Rue Morgue 1*. 1946.
Editor, *Eat, Drink, and Be Buried*. 1956; as *For Tomorrow We Die*, 1958.

*

Bibliography: *Stout: An Annotated Primary and Secondary Bibliography* by Guy M. Townsend, 1980.

Critical Studies: *Nero Wolfe of West Thirty-Fifth Street: The Life and Times of America's Largest Private Detective* by William S. Baring-Gould, 1969; *Stout: A Biography* by John McAleer, 1977; *The Brownstone House of Nero Wolfe* by Ken Darby, 1983; *Stout* by David R. Anderson, 1984.

* * *

At the beginning of a career undertaken after he had earned enough money in business to permit full-time devotion to writing, Rex Stout published four critically acceptable but unpopular "straight" novels. Then, in the decade after he had committed himself to the detective genre with the publication of *Fer-de-Lance*, he developed a variety of sleuths: "Dol" Bonner and Sally Colt in *The Hand in the Glove*, Tecumseh Fox who appeared in three novels, Alphabet Hicks in one novel bearing his name, Delia Brand in *Mountain Cat*, and Inspector Cramer of *Red Threads*. Stout is known, however, almost entirely because he was the creator of Nero Wolfe.

Like Sherlock Holmes, Stout's evident model for a Great Detective, Nero Wolfe so dominates the tales in which he appears that enthusiasts refer to them as though they were authorless—they are simply Nero Wolfe stories; and, again like his model and a small handful of other fictional detectives such as Charlie Chan or Sam Spade, Nero Wolfe—the enormously fat, eccentric genius-recluse—has achieved independence of the tales themselves. He is an autonomous figure in the popular imagination, familiar even to those with only the slightest literary knowledge of his exploits.

There can be no doubt it was Stout's intention to create a mythic detective. The constellation of traits attributed to Wolfe coupled with his mental infallibility are the formula of a character who dominates as well as presides, and the narrative voice of Archie Goodwin, though it is quite unlike Dr. Watson's, provides for the distancing that surrounds the solver of mysteries with his own aura of mystery. Moreover, Archie's speech develops the illusion of a case's history with the attendant suspense necessary to deflect our awareness that the only subject of the fiction is the detective.

It would be incorrect, however, to describe Stout only as an imitator of formulas pioneered by Arthur Conan Doyle, for Stout artfully manages the genre of detection fiction in his own way. It is just that his way involves simplification of the genre rather than the transgression of conventions we usually associate with innovation. A striking example of Stout's simplification is in the setting of the stories. Wolfe's household is central to every tale. He never goes abroad to the classic country house or to walk the city's mean streets; thus, in one stroke we get both ambience (W. 35th St. equals Baker St.) and intensification of the detective's prominence, since clients and aides with the guilty and innocent suspects must all subject themselves to the force of his orbit, their thoughts and acts entirely subordinate to Wolfe's interpretations.

Fundamentally, the plot of every tale of detection is epistemological. It progresses through scenes of a detective's methodical expansion of his knowledge of the reality of some mysterious events until it is concluded by a celebration of rationality in which all the secondary characters witness the detective's literal creation of truth through summary analysis of events and motives. In plot, too, Stout has simplified. With Wolfe working on cases in his own study—the consummate armchair detective—each scene prefigures the classical denouement, maintaining a dominance by Wolfe's mind over events that matches the supremacy of his personality.

The result of Stout's simplification of the detection story is to invest the saga of Nero Wolfe with an Augustan formality. The incidents of the stories and novels vary, but each repeats invariable movements extolling the nature of a Great Detective.

—John M. Reilly

STOWE, Harriet (Elizabeth) Beecher. Born in Litchfield, Connecticut, 14 June 1811. Educated at Miss Sarah Pierce's school, Litchfield; Hartford Female Seminary, Connecticut, 1824. Married Reverend Calvin Ellis Stowe in 1836 (died, 1886); three daughters and four sons. Teacher, Hartford Female Seminary, 1829–32, and Western Female Institute, Cincinnati, 1833–35; lived in Brunswick, Maine, 1850–51, Andover, Massachusetts, 1852–63, then in Hartford and Mandarin, Florida; famous and controversial as a writer after publication of *Uncle Tom's Cabin*, 1852; active in abolitionist movement; visited England three times, and toured Europe; friend of Lady Byron, George Eliot, and Ruskin. *Died 1 July 1896.*

PUBLICATIONS

Collections

The Writings. 16 vols., 1896.
Collected Poems, edited by John M. Moran, Jr. 1967.
Uncle Tom's Cabin, The Minister's Wooing, Oldtown Folks (Library of America), edited by Kathryn Kish Sklar. 1982.

Fiction

Prize Tale: A New England Sketch. 1834.
The Mayflower; or, Sketches of Scenes and Characters among the Descendants of the Pilgrims. 1843; augmented edition, 1855.
Uncle Tom's Cabin; or, Life among the Lowly. 1852; edited by Kenneth S. Lynn, 1962.
Uncle Sam's Emancipation (stories). 1853.
Dred: A Tale of the Great Dismal Swamp. 1856; as *Nina Gordon*, 1866.
The Minister's Wooing. 1859.
Agnes of Sorrento. 1862.
The Pearl of Orr's Island: A Story of the Coast of Maine. 1862.
The Daisy's First Winter and Other Stories. 1867.
Queer Little People. 1867; as *Queer Little Folks*, 1886.
Oldtown Folks. 1869; edited by Henry F. May, 1966.
My Wife and I; or, Harry Henderson's History. 1871.
Pink and White Tyranny: A Society Novel. 1871.
Sam Lawson's Oldtown Fireside Stories. 1872.
We and Our Neighbors; or, The Records of an Unfashionable Street. 1875.
Poganuc People: Their Loves and Lives. 1878.

Play

The Christian Slave, from her novel *Uncle Tom's Cabin*. 1855.

Verse

Religious Poems. 1867.

Other

Primary Geography for Children, with Catharine Beecher. 1833; revised edition, as *First Geography for Children*, 1855; as *A New Geography for Children*, 1855.
An Elementary Geography. 1835.
A Key to Uncle Tom's Cabin, Presenting the Original Facts and Documents upon Which the Story Is Founded. 1853.
Sunny Memories of Foreign Lands. 2 vols., 1854.
The Two Altars; or, Two Pictures in One. 1855.
Our Charley and What to Do with Him. 1858.
A Reply in Behalf of the Women of America. 1863.
The Ravages of a Carpet. 1865.
Stories about Our Dogs. 1865.
House and Home Papers. 1865.
Little Foxes. 1866.
The Chimney-Corner. 1868.
Men of Our Times. 1868; as *The Lives and Deeds of Our Self-Made Men*, 1872.
The American Woman's Home; or, Principles of Domestic Science, with Catharine Beecher. 1869; revised edition, as *The New Housekeeper's Manual*, 1873.
Little Pussy Willow (for children). 1870.
Lady Byron Vindicated. 1870.
Woman in Sacred History. 1873; as *Bible Heroines*, 1878.
Palmetto-Leaves. 1873.
Betty's Bright Idea. 1876.
Footsteps of the Master. 1877.
A Dog's Mission (for children). 1881.
Our Famous Women. 1884.

*

Bibliography: *Stowe: A Bibliography* by Margaret Holbrook Hildreth, 1976; *Stowe: A Reference Guide* by Jean Ashton, 1977.

Critical Studies: *Life of Stowe from Her Letters and Journals* edited by Charles Edward Stowe, 1889; *Life and Letters of Stowe* edited by Annie A. Fields, 1897; *Crusader in Crinoline: The Life of Stowe* by Forrest Wilson, 1941; *The Rungless Ladder: Stowe and New England Puritanism* by Charles H. Foster, 1954; *Stowe* by John R. Adams, 1963; *Stowe: The Known and the Unknown* by Edward Wagenknecht, 1965; *The Novels of Stowe* by Alice C. Crozier, 1969; *Stowe: A Biography* by Noel B. Gerson, 1976; *The Building of "Uncle Tom's Cabin"* by E. Bruce Kirkham, 1977; *Stowe and American Literature* by Ellen Moers, 1978; *Critical Essays on Stowe* edited by Elizabeth Ammons, 1980; *The Religious Ideas of Stowe: Her Gospel of Womanhood* by Gayle Kimball, 1982.

* * *

Uncle Tom's Cabin, Harriet Beecher Stowe's masterpiece, has been said to have had a "social impact . . . on the United States . . . greater than that of any book before or since." There is no doubt that it is one of the few books to have changed the climate of public opinion and helped swing the political pendulum. Although recent evaluations of the work tend to reveal in it not less but more literary craftsmanship, any critical analysis must consider this novel not so much as a literary production but as an instrument that led to action.

Stowe grew up in "a kind of moral heaven, replete with moral oxygen—fully charged with intellectual electricity," and much of that "moral oxygen" and "intellectual electricity" was injected into *Uncle Tom's Cabin*. The guiding principles of self-abnegation, spiritual regeneration, and Christian purpose inculcated in her early training filtered into her writing. Coupled with her own high-minded interest in social reform, they were shaped into a powerful ethical weapon. The author had read of the atrocities of slavery, and, when the Fugitive Slave Law spurred her to action, she was finally metamorphosed into the instrument of the Lord who created an "epic of Negro bondage." This powerful narrative of damnation and salvation, with its bold message that slavery destroys both the master and the slave, electrified the nation. While *Uncle Tom's Cabin* is, on the one hand, a domestic novel, it is also a forceful, vital, original, and daring moral instrument.

Although its characters are sometimes symbols and some of its incidents are stylized, the figures of Simon Legree, Eliza, Mr. St. Clare, Little Eva, and Uncle Tom have joined the parade of unforgettable literary characters that have become part of the national consciousness. The author's reliance upon tact did not preclude her recourse to realism. Just how powerfully Mrs. Stowe's timely propaganda stirred the American conscience is revealed by its publishing history. Within a year of publication its sales topped 300,000, and before the Civil War the figure reached three million. It made its author famous overnight, inspired a spate of anti-*Uncle Tom* novels, and won the praise of such diverse critics as Henry Wadsworth Longfellow and Henry James. According to one reviewer: "The mightiest princes of intellect, as well as those who have scarcely harbored a stray thought . . . friends of slavery equally with the haters of that institution . . . all . . . bend with sweating eagerness over her magic pages." Emerson traced its power to the universality of its message when he commented: "We have seen an American woman write a novel of which a million copies were sold in all languages, and which had one merit, of speaking to the universal heart, and was read with equal interest to three audiences, namely, in the parlor, in the kitchen, and in the nursery of every house." *Uncle Tom's Cabin* still has the power of stirring conflicting emotions in its critics. James Baldwin's attribution of racial prejudice to the novel, for example, has met its effective rebutters. Although the novel is no longer widely read, it is unlikely that it will ever be forgotten.

Stowe's earlier work consisted of sentimental and conventional sketches that reflected her belief in the sanctity of the home and woman's place in it. After the success of *Uncle Tom's Cabin* she replied to objectors with *A Key to Uncle Tom's Cabin* and returned to the theme of anti-slavery in *Dred*. Between 1862 and 1884, she produced at least a book a year; most of them consisted of essays on the home, domestic novels, stories of death and redemption, as well as a defense of Lady Byron.

Stowe has recently, and surprisingly, been called "the only major feminine humorist nineteenth-century America produced," an attribution based less upon a sense of the jocular than upon an ear for idiom and an eye for actuality. The books that flowed from her tireless pen often reveal these qualities. They also reveal her dissection of the Calvinist ethic, and despite their sentimentality they provide considerable documentary insight into the moral climate of 19th-century New England.

The aptest description of Stowe was made by the biographer who dubbed her a "Crusader in Crinoline." For the most part, her crinolines have turned into period pieces, and her crusade has become historic. Yet she helped to document and advance that crusade, and in *Uncle Tom's Cabin* she created a book that shook the world.

—Madeleine B. Stern

See the essay on *Uncle Tom's Cabin*.

STRIBLING, T(homas) S(igismund). Born in Clifton, Tennessee, 4 March 1881. Educated at Clifton Masonic Academy; Southern Normal College, Huntingdon, Tennessee, 1898–1900; Normal College, Florence, Alabama, 1902–03, graduated 1903; studied law at the University of Alabama, Tuscaloosa, LL.B. 1905. Married Lou Ella Kloss in 1930. Editor, Clifton *News*, 1900–02; teacher, Tuscaloosa High School, 1903–04; lawyer in Florence, 1906–07; staff member, *Taylor-Trotwood Magazine*, Nashville, Tennessee, 1907–08; full-time writer from 1908; wrote moral stories for Sunday school magazines; lived in South America and Europe, 1908–16; reporter, Chattanooga *News*, 1917; stenographer, Aviation Bureau, Washington, D.C., 1918; Instructor in Creative Writing, Columbia University, New York, 1936, 1940; lived in Clifton after 1959. Recipient: Pulitzer Prize, 1933. LL.D.: Oglethorpe University, Atlanta, 1936. *Died 10 July 1965*.

PUBLICATIONS

Fiction

The Cruise of the Dry Dock. 1917.
Birthright. 1922.
Fombombo. 1923.
Red Sand. 1924.
Teeftallow. 1926.
Bright Metal. 1928.
East Is East. 1928.
Clues of the Caribbees, Being Certain Criminal Investigations of Henry Poggioli, Ph.D. 1929.
Strange Moon. 1929.
Backwater. 1930.
The Forge. 1931.
The Store. 1932.
Unfinished Cathedral. 1934.
The Sound Wagon. 1935.
These Bars of Flesh. 1938.
Best Dr. Poggioli Detective Stories. 1975.

Play

Rope, with David Wallace, from the novel *Teeftallow* by Stribling (produced 1928).

Other

Laughing Stock: The Posthumous Autobiography of Stribling, edited by Randy K. Cross and John T. McMillan. 1982.

*

Critical Study: *Stribling* by Wilton Eckley, 1975.

* * *

T.S. Stribling, who began as a writer of moral adventure tales for Sunday school magazines and then moved on to the pulps and finally to serious fiction, is remembered chiefly for *The Store*, which won him the Pulitzer Prize in 1933. It is the second volume of his trilogy (*The Forge* and *Unfinished Cathedral* are the other two) dealing with the fortunes of the Vaiden family, particularly with the rise of Miltaides Vaiden from poor man to rich landowner and cotton planter in the ante-bellum south. In this trilogy, as in his other serious novels (*Birthright*, *Teeftallow*, *Bright Metal*, *The Sound Wagon*, *These Bars of Flesh*), Stribling is a social satirist and local colorist. His strong point is his gift of observation, of setting down in credible language the look and feel of a natural landscape and the poor whites and blacks who inhabit it. His weaknesses are his themes (which tend to be simplistic), his plots (melodramatic), and his style (often crudely pretentious). Like Sinclair Lewis, Stribling is a social critic and debunker, his locale the middle south (Tennessee, Alabama), and his chief concern prejudice against blacks and the general narrow-mindedness of ingrown southern communities. In *Birthright*, he deals with a Harvard-educated black from Tennessee forced to live the stereotyped role of an uneducated black laborer. But he also debunked the American scene of lawyers and businessmen (*The Sound Wagon*) and the American education college (*These Bars of Flesh*). Much of his fiction is hackwork, quickly turned out melodrama with a slight satirical edge. *Fombombo*, *Red Sand*, and *Strange Moon* mix satire, South American politics, business, and romance. Stribling also wrote detective stories (*Clues of the Caribbees*).

Stribling is an "objective" observer who sees history as a mechanical process, individuals as pawns in the grip of economic and social forces. His fiction is interesting to the literary historian for the way he blends popular stereotypes with old-fashioned liberal political and social ideas, and for the contrast offered between his mechanistic histories of the south and William Faulkner's mythical histories, a contrast that helps make clear not only Stribling's appeal to liberal critics in the 1930's but also the reason Faulkner was disliked and undervalued.

—W.J. Stuckey

STYRON, William. Born in Newport News, Virginia, 11 June 1925. Educated at Christchurch School, Virginia; Davidson College, North Carolina, 1942–43; Duke University, Durham, North Carolina, 1943–44, 1946–47, B.A. 1947 (Phi Beta Kappa); New School for Social Research, New York, 1947. Served in the U.S. Marine Corps, 1944–45, 1951: 1st Lieutenant. Married Rose Burgunder in 1953; three daughters and one son. Associate editor, McGraw Hill, publishers, New York, 1947; since 1952, advisory editor, *Paris Review*, Paris and New York; member of the Editorial Board, *American Scholar*, Washington, D.C., 1970–76. Since 1964, Fellow, Silliman College, Yale University, New Haven, Connecticut; Honorary Consultant in American Letters, Library of Congress, Washington, D.C. Recipient: American Academy Rome Prize, 1952, and Howells Medal, 1970; Pulitzer Prize, 1968; American Book Award, 1980; Connecticut Arts Award, 1984; Cino del Duca Prize, 1985. Litt.D.: Duke University, 1968. Member, American Academy, and American Academy of Arts and Sciences; Commander, Order of Arts and Letters (France). Lives in Roxbury, Connecticut.

PUBLICATIONS

Fiction

Lie Down in Darkness. 1951.
The Long March. 1956.
Set This House on Fire. 1960.
The Confessions of Nat Turner. 1967.
Shadrach (story). 1979.
Sophie's Choice. 1979.

Play

In the Clap Shack (produced 1972). 1973.

Other

The Four Seasons, illustrated by Harold Altman. 1965.
Admiral Robert Penn Warren and the Snows of Winter: A Tribute. 1978.
The Message of Auschwitz. 1979.
Against Fear. 1981.
As He Lay Dead, A Bitter Grief (on William Faulkner). 1981.
This Quiet Dust and Other Writings. 1982.
Conversations with Styron (interviews), edited by James L.W. West III. 1985.

Editor, *Best Short Stories from the Paris Review*. 1959.

*

Bibliography: *Styron: A Descriptive Bibliography* by James L.W. West III, 1977; *Styron: A Reference Guide* by Jackson R. Bryer and Mary B. Hatem, 1978; *Styron: An Annotated Bibliography of Criticism* by Philip W. Leon, 1978.

Critical Studies: *Styron* by Robert H. Fossum, 1968; *Styron* by Cooper R. Mackin, 1969; *Styron* by Richard Pearce, 1971; *Styron* by Marc L. Ratner, 1972; *Styron* by Melvin J. Friedman, 1974; *The Achievement of Styron* edited by Irving Malin and Robert K. Morris, 1975, revised edition, 1981; *Critical Essays on Styron* edited by Arthur D. Casciato and James L.W. West III, 1982; *The Root of All Evil: The Thematic Unity of Styron's Fiction* by John K. Crane, 1985.

* * *

In the three decades of William Styron's fiction to date, from *Lie Down in Darkness* (1951) to *Sophie's Choice* (1979), the Southern Renaissance went into a sad decline, suffering a loss of authority and coherence. To be sure, Robert Penn Warren and Eudora Welty continued to write, and Flannery O'Connor and Walker Percy made substantial contributions to fiction, but the triumphs of the New Criticism, which owed so much to the south, and of the poetry that came from it, and the vision of William Faulkner were not matched. Styron is emblematic of this decline, both in his ambiguous relationship to the south and in the intrinsic quality of his work.

There is no question about a "southern" cast to Styron's fiction. It derives, above all, from the influence of Faulkner, and of Warren and Thomas Wolfe as well. All share an appetite for powerful rhetoric; in Styron's case the rhetoric is often turgid and undisciplined. In *Lie Down in Darkness* and *The*

Confessions of Nat Turner Styron uses the matter of the south and deals with those problems of sin, dissolution, and decadence that southern history has thrust upon the imagination of many southern writers. In this respect he is a traditionalist in subject matter and in values as well. But he is unaware of the cost of the ethical and humanistic orthodoxies that he has accepted. After his first novel, where the principal thrust is nihilistic, his fiction depends upon ideas of a viable self; upon the dignity of man; upon the reality of guilt and the possibility of redemption (religious concepts secularized in his work); upon the recognition and rejection of decadence; upon the need for love; upon the desirability of freedom; and upon the possibility of tragic magnitude and nobility. These constitute the intellectual and ethical furniture of the traditional novelist and seem particularly appropriate to a writer of the south where tradition is cherished.

Like most writers who take these positions in the postwar world, Styron knows that great forces are at work everywhere to destroy them. He senses the morbidity of contemporary life and feels the presence of anarchic murder in the air. He knows that the machine age has damaged the south and attacked Old Testament fundamentalism there. His response to these destructive forces is, paradoxically, to deny allegiance to the south and dissociate himself from the southern school of letters. But analysis of his work will show that he has not escaped the south any more than he has neglected the Bible, which in fact he acknowledges as an influence upon him. Surely, both the south and the Bible helped him to frame those traditional values and attitudes which appear in his fiction.

That confusion about the impact of the south upon his literary consciousness is of a piece with his unselfconscious acceptance of the ideas of truth and reality, which are both metaphysical and technical constituents of his fiction. He agrees, for example, with Georg Lukács's proposition that the writer should reproduce the complex and ramifying totality of the past with historical faithfulness. He seems to think that a single reality existed in the past, that it is "true," and that novelists can capture it, presumably by imitating "reality." He appears unaware of the challenge to literary realism made by the modernists. He appears naive in asserting that he tries to make his characters round, when modernists have called into question the very concept of character. He thinks the progression of time is one of the novelist's difficult problems, but they tend to believe that the idea of linear time may have been shattered by contemporary science. It is acceptable enough that the theory of fiction governing his practice of fiction be old-fashioned and conventional, but it is damaging that he can bring no vitality of deep understanding to the tradition, that he does not make the old new.

Lie Down in Darkness, derived from Faulkner and Freud, dramatizes the collapse into decadence and chaos of ceremony and ritual, of family, marriage, love, and religion. Styron deals here with the dissolution of a Virginia family in such a way as to show that the sins of the father are visited upon the daughter. Styron tries to broaden the impact of his novel by using the Freudian interpretation of the Electra myth and by linking the suicide of his protagonist to the dropping of the atomic bomb on Hiroshima. The novel ends bleakly in an affirmation of nihilism that does not appear in Styron's subsequent work.

The Long March, a largely successful novelette, embraces possibilities in human endurance and of triumph over absurdity. Peyton, naked at the end of the first novel, is nothingness; Mannix, the hero of this book, stripped to the skin at the end, is man, chastened but alive, with a regained sense of his own humanity. This guarded optimism also characterizes *Set This House on Fire*, which ends in a Norman Mailer-like regeneration through violence that restores the protagonist's creative capacities and in a successful quest for expiation. Unfortunately, this novel is pretentious and prolix; it strains for parallels to Greek tragedy, but in its banalities emerges as more like Italian opera.

The Confessions of Nat Turner also treats regeneration through violence, but here Styron's difficulties do not arise from a melodramatic treatment of his materials. Styron has other problems. He cannot reconcile Turner's dedication to both biblical ideals and murderous rebellion, or even create a satisfying and believable tension in these ambivalences. Further, he slights the values of freedom and social justice implicit in these religious ideals and in the issue of slavery itself. Finally, as a white southerner who cannot "know" the black man, he creates more difficulties for himself than he can resolve by making Nat the narrator of the novel. The novel aims at affirmation arising out of tragic failure, but Styron does not render this paradox convincing, and instead *The Confessions of Nat Turner* is a failed affirmation.

In the melodrama of *Sophie's Choice* Styron uses an exaggerated rhetoric to explore the idea of evil. He turns for help, in a not fully successful way, to Hannah Arendt, Simone Weil, and George Steiner, whose notions he does not adequately integrate into his fiction. The novel combines autobiographical and detective story methods. It deals with the terror and madness of the Nazis, which persuade the narrator that absolute evil can never be "extinguished from the world," a conclusion that cannot be squared with the unearned optimism with which Styron ends the book.

—Chester E. Eisinger

SUCKOW, Ruth. Born in Hawarden, Iowa, 6 August 1892. Educated at Grinnell College, Iowa, 1910–13; Curry Dramatic School, Boston, 1914–15; University of Denver, 1915–18, B.A. 1917, M.A. 1918. Married Ferner Nuhn in 1929. Editorial assistant, *The Midland*, Iowa City, 1921–22; owner and manager, Orchard Apiary, Earlville, Iowa, 1920's; spent winters in New York, 1924–34; lived in Cedar Falls, Iowa, 1934–52, and Claremont, California, from 1952. M.A.: Grinnell College, 1931. *Died 23 January 1960.*

PUBLICATIONS

Fiction

Country People. 1924.
The Odyssey of a Nice Girl. 1925.
Iowa Interiors (stories). 1926; as *People and Houses*, 1927.
The Bonney Family. 1928.
Cora. 1929.
The Kramer Girls. 1930.
Children and Older People (stories). 1931.
The Folks. 1934.
Carry-Over. 1936.
New Hope. 1942.
Some Others and Myself: Seven Stories and a Memoir. 1952.
The John Wood Case. 1959.

*

Critical Studies: *Suckow* by Leedice McAnelly Kissane, 1969; *Suckow: A Critical Study of Her Fiction* by Margaret Stewart Omrcanin, 1972; *Suckow* by Abigail Ann Hamblen, 1978.

* * *

In the 1920's Ruth Suckow was considered a major talent, destined to write novels and short stories of distinction, possibly a great American writer. H.L. Mencken published her short fiction in his *Smart Set* and *American Mercury*, and praised her extravagantly. Suckow's stories seemed to fit somewhere between those of Willa Cather and Sinclair Lewis, but to many she was more honest and straightforward than either. Sixty years later Suckow is considered a minor figure: a good Iowa regionalist, an uncompromising, unsentimental realist who wrote about the ordinary, middle-class people of the American heartland at the beginning of the automotive age.

After the 1920's the literary standing of Cather and Lewis was eclipsed by Hemingway, Dos Passos, Steinbeck, Fitzgerald, and Faulkner. Literary fashion turned against Suckow, but more important factors were responsible for her decline in stature. Her quiet, uneventful accounts worked best in short stories, but novels were more profitable and more prestigious. Her most ambitious novel, *The Folks* (727 pages), was a Literary Guild selection in 1934. More than twenty years elapse in this account of an Iowa small-town banker and his wife, and the start in life of their four children. The action extends to New York and San Diego, but the point of view is always Iowa small-town. Departing from her earlier practice, in this novel Suckow interprets and comments on the actions and motivations of her characters. But though people, places, and events ring true, there is too little drama, conflict, or interest in the people to sustain the long story. Two later novels—*New Hope* and *The John Wood Case*—drew little critical attention.

The Folks reveals Suckow's shortcomings. The same weaknesses are found in her earlier novels: *Country People*, *The Odyssey of a Nice Girl*, *The Bonney Family*, *Cora*, and *The Kramer Girls*. The last two of this group reveal her new interest in feminism; the earlier novels reveal the texture of small-town life in Iowa seen through the eyes of a young girl.

The short stories of *Iowa Interiors* and *Children and Older People* are Suckow's best work. The stories in a third volume, *Some Others and Myself*, are admittedly inferior—more reflective and contemplative, less objective. As in her longer fiction, the point of view in these stories is restricted and revealing: as a daughter of a small-town clergyman, Suckow saw many lonely, elderly couples and frustrated spinsters. She describes the countless family gatherings and church affairs she had been a part of, not social, political, and economic machinations. There is no explicit sex, no violence, no drama or suspense.

In his *Midwestern Farm Novel* Roy Meyer finds Suckow unsatisfactory because she sees Iowa farms—their people and problems—from the point of view of a small-town preacher's daughter who occasionally went out to visit those farms. A fellow-Iowan, the socialist Josephine Herbst, objected to Suckow's blindness to social implications. A comparison with her slightly older contemporary, Sherwood Anderson, is revealing: like Suckow's, Anderson's short stories are far better than his novels, but the psychological insights in Anderson's stories contrast sharply with the flatness and simplicity of her honest realism.

—Clarence A. Glasrud

TARKINGTON, (Newton) Booth. Born in Indianapolis, Indiana, 29 July 1869. Educated at Phillips Exeter Academy, New Hampshire; Purdue University, Lafayette, Indiana, 1888–89; Princeton University, New Jersey, 1891–93. Married 1) Laurel Louisa Fletcher in 1902 (divorced, 1911), one daughter; 2) Susannah Robinson in 1912. Writer from 1893; also an artist: illustrated *Character Sketches* by James Whitcomb Riley and other works; member of the Indiana House of Representatives, 1902–03; in later life also lived in Kennebunkport, Maine. Recipient: Pulitzer Prize, 1919, 1922; American Academy Gold Medal, 1933, and Howells Medal, 1945; Boy Scouts of America Silver Buffalo, 1935; Roosevelt Distinguished Service Medal, 1942. A.M.: Princeton University, 1899; Litt.D.: Princeton University, 1918; De Pauw University, Greencastle, Indiana, 1923; Columbia University, New York, 1924; L.H.D.: Purdue University, 1939. Member, American Academy. *Died 19 May 1946.*

PUBLICATIONS

Collections

The Gentleman from Indianapolis: A Treasury of Tarkington, edited by John Beecroft. 1957.

Fiction

The Gentleman from Indiana. 1899.
Monsieur Beaucaire. 1900.
The Two Vanrevels. 1902.
Cherry. 1903.
In the Arena: Stories of Political Life. 1905.
The Beautiful Lady. 1905.
The Conquest of Canaan. 1905.
His Own People. 1907.
The Guest of Quesnay. 1908.
Beasley's Christmas Party. 1909.
The Flirt. 1913.
Penrod: His Complete Story (revised version). 1931.
  Penrod. 1914.
  Penrod and Sam. 1916.
  Penrod Jashber. 1929.
Growth. 1927.
  The Turmoil. 1915.
  The Magnificent Ambersons. 1918.
  The Midlander. 1923.
Seventeen. 1916.
The Spring Concert (story). 1916.
Harlequin and Columbine and Other Stories. 1918.
Ramsey Milholland. 1919.
Alice Adams. 1921.
Gentle Julia. 1922.
The Fascinating Stranger and Other Stories. 1923.
Women. 1925.
Selections from Tarkington's Stories, edited by Lilian Holmes Strack. 1926.
The Plutocrat. 1927.
Claire Ambler. 1928.
Young Mrs. Greeley. 1929.
Mirthful Haven. 1930.
Mary's Neck. 1932.
Wanton Mally. 1932.
Presenting Lily Mars. 1933.

Little Orvie. 1934.
Mr. White, The Red Barn, Hell, and Bridewater. 1935.
The Lorenzo Bunch. 1936.
Rumbin Galleries. 1937.
The Heritage of Hatcher Ide. 1941.
The Fighting Littles. 1941.
Kate Fennigate. 1943.
Image of Josephine. 1945.
The Show Piece (unfinished). 1947.
Three Selected Short Novels (includes *Walterson*, *Uncertain Molly Collicut*, and *Rennie Peddigoe*). 1947.

Plays

The Guardian, with Harry Leon Wilson. 1907; as *The Man from Home* (produced 1908), 1908; revised version, 1934.
Cameo Kirby, with Harry Leon Wilson (produced 1908).
Foreign Exchange (produced 1909).
If I Had Money (produced 1909).
Springtime (produced 1909).
Your Humble Servant, with Harry Leon Wilson (produced 1909).
Beauty and the Jacobin: An Interlude of the French Revolution (produced 1912). 1912.
The Man on Horseback (produced 1912).
The Ohio Lady, with Julian Street. 1916; as *The Country Cousin* (produced 1921), 1921.
Mister Antonio (produced 1916). 1935.
The Gibson Upright, with Harry Leon Wilson (produced 1919). 1919.
Up from Nowhere, with Harry Leon Wilson (produced 1919).
Poldekin (produced 1920). In *McClure's*, March–July 1920.
Clarence (produced 1921). 1921.
The Intimate Strangers (produced 1921). 1921.
The Wren (produced 1922). 1922.
The Ghost Story (for children) (produced 1922). 1922.
Rose Briar (produced 1922).
The Trysting Place (produced 1923). 1923.
Magnolia (produced 1923).
Tweedles, with Harry Leon Wilson (produced 1924). 1924.
Bimbo, The Pirate (produced 1926). 1926.
The Travelers (produced 1927). 1927.
Station YYYY (produced 1927). 1927.
How's Your Health?, with Harry Leon Wilson (produced 1930). 1930.
Colonel Satan (produced 1932).
The Help Each Other Club (produced 1933). 1934.
Lady Hamilton and Her Nelson (produced 1945). 1945.

Screenplays: *Edgar and the Teacher's Pet*, 1920; *Edgar's Hamlet*, 1920; *Edgar's Little Saw*, 1920; *Edgar, The Explorer*, 1921; *Get Rich Quick Edgar*, 1921; *Pied Piper Malone*, with Tom Geraghty, 1924; *The Man Who Found Himself*, with Tom Geraghty, 1925.

Radio Plays: *Maud and Cousin Bill* series, 1932–33 (75 episodes).

Other

Works (Autograph Edition). 27 vols., 1918–32.
Works (Seaweed Edition). 27 vols., 1922–32.
The Collector's Whatnot, with Hugh Kahler and Kenneth Roberts. 1923.
Looking Forward and Others (essays). 1926.
The World Does Move (reminiscences). 1928.
Some Old Portraits: A Book about Art and Human Beings. 1939.
Your Amiable Uncle: Letters to His Nephews. 1949.
On Plays, Playwrights, and Playgoers: Selections from the Letters of Tarkington to George C. Tyler and John Peter Toohey 1918–1925, edited by Alan S. Downer. 1959.

Translator, *Samuel Brohl and Company*, with Victor Cherbuliez. 1902.

*

Bibliography: *A Bibliography of Tarkington* by Dorothy Ritter Russo and Thelma L. Sullivan, 1949, supplement in *Princeton University Library Chronicle 16*, 1955.

Critical Studies: *Tarkington: Gentleman from Indiana* by James Woodress, 1955; *Tarkington* by Keith J. Fennimore, 1974; *My Amiable Uncle: Recollections about Tarkington* by Susanah Mayberry, 1983.

* * *

Although Booth Tarkington was a very popular author during his lifetime, his reputation has dimmed since his death, and today few of his works are read. Yet he was an excellent fictional craftsman and a first-rate storyteller, and his best novels are absorbing. Though there are no sexual titillation and little tragedy in his books, he has a sense of humor and observes and records the human comedy with a clear eye. His significance lies in his depiction of urban, midwestern, middle-class America during the decades of intensely rapid growth in the late 19th and early 20th centuries, and in his stories of children. He writes in the tradition of commonplace realism as pioneered by Howells.

His trilogy published under the collective title *Growth* is important. These novels study the social and economic life of a medium-sized midwestern city that may be identified as Indianapolis. *The Turmoil*, which contains a very contemporary-sounding indictment of air pollution and civic neglect in the pursuit of the dollar, is the story of an ascending family, the first-generation makers of the new industrial wealth. *The Magnificent Ambersons*, winner of a Pulitzer Prize, deals with an old family whose money was made in the Gilded Age. The family is engulfed by the encroaching industrialism of the 20th century, and the wealth is dissipated by the second and third generations. *The Midlander*, which comes as close as Tarkington ever came to tragedy, is the unhappy story of a promoter-developer of urban growth. Similar in subject and theme to the *Growth* trilogy is *Alice Adams*, perhaps Tarkington's best novel. This novel, which deserves to be better known, is a poignant comedy of manners that details the unsuccessful efforts of a girl of modest circumstances to catch a socially prominent husband. Character, plot, and the theme of social mobility are skillfully blended in this novel, which won Tarkington a second Pulitzer Prize.

Tarkington's second major accomplishment lies in his stories of boyhood, *Penrod*, *Penrod and Sam*, and *Penrod Jashber*. These distinguished tales in the realistic tradition begun by Mark Twain in *Tom Sawyer* appeal to both children and adults, are rich in authentic detail and dialogue, and may turn out to be the author's most enduring work. Tarkington also was adroit in depicting adolescents, but the vast change in teen-age mores since *Seventeen* appeared in 1916 makes this once-popular novel a period piece rather than a story of perennial interest.

Tarkington was a playwright as well as a novelist, and any history of American drama must accord him some attention for his two dozen plays. *The Man from Home*, which he wrote with Harry Leon Wilson, enjoyed a long run on Broadway, and *Clarence*, which starred Alfred Lunt and Helen Hayes at the beginning of their careers, was a memorable success. Few American novelists have mastered the play form as well as Tarkington.

—James Woodress

TATE, (John Orley) Allen. Born in Winchester, Kentucky, 19 November 1899. Educated at Georgetown Preparatory School, Washington, D.C.; Vanderbilt University, Nashville, Tennessee, 1918–22, B.A. 1923. Married 1) Caroline Gordon, *q.v.*, in 1924 (divorced and remarried, 1946; separated, 1955; divorced, 1959), one daughter; 2) the poet Isabella Stewart Gardner in 1959 (separated, 1965; divorced, 1966); 3) Helen Heinz in 1966, twin sons. Member of the Fugitive group of poets: co-founder, *The Fugitive*, Nashville, 1922–25; high school teacher, Lumberport, West Virginia, 1924; assistant to the editor, *Telling Tales* magazine, New York, 1925; lived in Patterson, New York, 1926–27, Paris, 1928–29, Clarksville, Tennessee, 1930–31, and France, 1932–33; Lecturer in English, Southwestern College, Memphis, Tennessee, 1934–36; Professor of English, The Woman's College, Greensboro, North Carolina, 1938–39; Poet-in-Residence, Princeton University, New Jersey, 1939–42; Consultant in Poetry, Library of Congress, Washington, D.C., 1943–44; editor, *Sewanee Review*, Tennessee, 1944–46; editor, Belles Lettres series, Henry Holt, publishers, New York, 1946–48; Lecturer in Humanities, New York University, 1948–51; from 1951, Professor of English, University of Minnesota, Minneapolis: Regents' Professor, 1966; Professor Emeritus, 1968. Visiting Professor in the Humanities, University of Chicago, 1949; Fulbright Lecturer, Oxford University, 1953, University of Rome, 1953–54, and Oxford and Leeds universities, 1958–59; Department of State Lecturer at universities of Liège and Louvain, 1954, Delhi and Bombay, 1956, the Sorbonne, Paris, 1956, Nottingham, 1956, and Urbino and Florence, 1961; Visiting Professor of English, University of North Carolina, Greensboro, 1966, and Vanderbilt University, 1967. Fellow, 1948, and Senior Fellow, 1956, Kenyon School of English, Kenyon College, Gambier, Ohio (now Indiana University School of Letters, Bloomington); member, Phi Beta Kappa Senate, 1951–53. Recipient: Guggenheim fellowship, 1928, 1929; American Academy grant, 1948; Bollingen Prize, 1957; Brandeis University Creative Arts Award, 1960; Dante Society Gold Medal (Florence), 1962; Academy of American Poets fellowship, 1963; National Medal for Literature, 1976. Litt.D.: University of Louisville, Kentucky, 1948; Coe College, Cedar Rapids, Iowa, 1955; Colgate University, Hamilton, New York, 1956; University of Kentucky, Lexington, 1960; Carleton College, Northfield, Minnesota, 1963; University of the South, Sewanee, Tennessee, 1970. Member, American Academy, 1964; Chancellor, Academy of American Poets, 1964; Member, American Academy of Arts and Sciences, 1965; President, National Institute of Arts and Letters, 1968. *Died 9 February 1979.*

PUBLICATIONS

Verse

The Golden Mean and Other Poems, with Ridley Wills. 1923.
Mr. Pope and Other Poems. 1928.
Ode to the Confederate Dead, Being the Revised and Final Version of a Poem Previously Published on Several Occasions: To Which Are Added Message from Abroad and The Cross. 1930.
Three Poems. 1930.
Poems 1928–1931. 1932.
The Mediterranean and Other Poems. 1936.
Selected Poems. 1937.
Sonnets at Christmas. 1941.
The Winter Sea: A Book of Poems. 1944.
Poems 1920–1945: A Selection. 1947.
Fragment of a Meditation. 1947.
Poems 1922–1947. 1948.
Two Conceits for the Eye to Sing, If Possible. 1950.
Poems. 1960.
The Swimmers and Other Selected Poems. 1970.
Collected Poems 1919–1976. 1977.

Play

The Governess, with Anne Goodwin Winslow (produced 1962).

Fiction

The Fathers. 1938; revised edition, 1960.
The Fathers and Other Fiction. 1977.

Other

Stonewall Jackson: The Good Soldier: A Narrative. 1928.
Jefferson Davis: His Rise and Fall: A Biographical Narrative. 1929.
I'll Take My Stand: The South and the Agrarian Tradition, with others. 1930.
Who Owns America? A New Declaration of Independence, with others, edited by Herbert Agar and Tate. 1936.
Reactionary Essays on Poetry and Ideas. 1936.
Reason in Madness: Critical Essays. 1941.
Invitation to Learning, with Huntington Cairns and Mark Van Doren. 1941.
Recent American Poetry and Poetic Criticism: A Selected List of References. 1943.
Sixty American Poets 1896–1944: A Preliminary Checklist. 1945.
On the Limits of Poetry: Selected Essays 1928–1948. 1948.
The Hovering Fly and Other Essays. 1948.
The Forlorn Demon: Didactic and Critical Essays. 1953.
The Man of Letters in the Modern World: Selected Essays 1928–1955. 1955.
Collected Essays. 1959.
Christ and the Unicorn: An Address. 1966.
Essays of Four Decades. 1969.

Mere Literature and the Lost Traveller. 1969.
The Translation of Poetry. 1972.
The Literary Correspondence of Donald Davidson and Tate, edited by John Tyree Fain and Thomas Daniel Young. 1974.
Memoirs and Opinions 1926–1974. 1975; as *Memories and Essays: Old and New 1926–1974*, 1976.
The Republic of Letters in America: The Correspondence of John Peale Bishop and Tate, edited by Thomas Daniel Young and John J. Hindle. 1981.
The Poetry Reviews of Tate 1924–1944, edited by Ashley Brown and Frances Neel Cheney. 1983.

Editor, with others, *Fugitives: An Anthology of Verse*. 1928.
Editor, with Herbert Agar, *Who Owns America? A New Declaration of Independence*. 1936.
Editor, with A. Theodore Johnson, *America Through the Essay: An Anthology for English Courses*. 1938.
Editor, *The Language of Poetry*. 1942.
Editor, *Princeton Verse Between Two Wars: An Anthology*. 1942.
Editor, with John Peale Bishop, *American Harvest: Twenty Years of Creative Writing in the United States*. 1942.
Editor, *A Southern Vanguard: The John Peale Bishop Memorial Volume*. 1947.
Editor, *The Collected Poems of John Peale Bishop*. 1948.
Editor, with Caroline Gordon, *The House of Fiction: An Anthology of the Short Story*. 1950; revised edition, 1960.
Editor, with David Cecil, *Modern Verse in English, 1900–1950*. 1958.
Editor, with John Berryman and Ralph Ross, *The Arts of Reading* (anthology). 1960.
Editor, *Selected Poems of John Peale Bishop*. 1960.
Editor, with Robert Penn Warren, *Selected Poems*, by Denis Devlin. 1963.
Editor, *T.S. Eliot: The Man and His Work*. 1966.
Editor, *The Complete Poems and Selected Criticism of Edgar Allan Poe*. 1968.
Editor, *Six American Poets: From Emily Dickinson to the Present: An Introduction*. 1972.

Translator, *The Vigil of Venus/Pervigilium Veneris*. 1943.

*

Bibliography: *Tate: A Bibliography* by Marshall Fallwell, Jr., 1969.

Critical Studies: *The Last Alternatives: A Study of the Works of Tate* by R.K. Meiners, 1962; *Tate* by George Hemphill, 1964; *Tate* by Ferman Bishop, 1967; *Rumors of Morality: An Introduction to Tate* by M.E. Bradford, 1969; *Tate: A Literary Biography* by Radcliffe Squires, 1971, and *Tate and His Work: Critical Evaluations* edited by Squires, 1972; *Tate and the Augustinian Imagination: A Study of the Poetry* by Robert S. Dupree, 1983; *Tate and the Poetic Way* edited by J. Larry Allums, 1984.

* * *

Allen Tate is always associated with the Fugitives, the small group of southern poets who were led by John Crowe Ransom at Vanderbilt University in Nashville during the early 1920's. But Tate was always his own man, and as a young Fugitive he found it necessary to reject much in the south; by 1924 he was living in New York City. Certainly southern literary culture offered nothing that he could imitate directly, though his sense of the age led him to the French symbolists and hence back to Poe, about whom he was to write three of his most important essays. His best poem before 1925 is his version of Baudelaire's "Correspondences." This seems as important as his friendship with his first master, Ransom, because it allowed him access to the mainstream of modern poetry.

In New York City, married to the novelist Caroline Gordon, Tate was on close terms with many writers of his generation, especially Hart Crane, and he could easily be put among the second generation of modernists (if we put Eliot, Pound, and Joyce in the first generation). It may well be that his regional sense was sharpened by his residence in the east and then Paris for six years. At any rate, by 1926 he was writing the first version of his most ambitious early poem, "Ode to the Confederate Dead." The correspondence between Tate and his Fugitive friend Donald Davidson shows him at that time occupying a kind of intermediary position between Davidson, who was writing *The Tall Men*, a long poem about Tennessee, and Crane, who was working on *The Bridge*, a visionary poem about America. Almost by instinct Tate shunned the "epical" treatment of experience. Where his southern quality emerges most convincingly is in the elevation of tone that was characteristic of the rhetoricians of this region. In a sense the Old South was organized by the voices of the preacher and the politician, and this legacy of public speaking descended to many of the writers of the modern Southern Renaissance.

The 1930's was the Agrarian period for the old Fugitive group, and Tate was frequently involved in the controversies that grew out of this movement, which coincided with an extraordinary outburst of literary achievement in the south. But his main energy went into his poetry, and his *Selected Poems* is one of the best collections of poetry in the decade. This volume contains the final version of the "Ode to the Confederate Dead," a distinguished meditative poem called "The Mediterranean," and a dozen shorter poems of great power and considerable range, such as "Emblems," "The Cross," and "The Wolves."

Meanwhile Tate was becoming one of the most important American critics; his first volume, *Reactionary Essays on Poetry and Ideas*, fully established his position. As critic he always took a large view of literary culture, but many of his influential early essays were written about such contemporaries as Crane, Archibald MacLeish, and John Peale Bishop. Certain theoretical essays have become classics of modern criticism: "Tension in Poetry," "Techniques of Fiction," "The Hovering Fly," and "A Southern Mode of the Imagination." These generated as much discussion as anything written during their period in the United States. Perhaps Tate's finest essays are two on Poe and Dante, "The Angelic Imagination" and "The Symbolic Imagination," published in 1951 at a time when he was writing some outstanding poems. Tate's criticism, in fact, is very much the work of a poet and often provides the setting for his verse.

Another work in prose that is closely related to Tate's verse of the 1930's is his novel *The Fathers*, which has been even more admired in recent years than it was when it was first published. Influenced in its technique by Ford Madox Ford's *The Good Soldier* ("the masterpiece of British fiction in this century"), the novel dramatizes with a great poetic intelligence the destruction of a Virginia family at the beginning of the Civil War. Tate's biographer, Radcliffe Squires, has shown the extent to which Tate drew on the history of his own family for the subject.

The last phase of Tate's poetry started during the early 1940's, though it was long anticipated. It includes the splendid satire "Ode to Our Young Pro-Consuls of the Air," an attack on the modern religion of the state; his very title proposes an analogy between America and Rome. This in a sense was preparatory for the long poem "Seasons of the Soul" and a later group of poems in *terza rima*, including "The Swimmers" and "The Buried Lake," his most impressive work of all. In these late poems Tate set his experience (his own, his family's, his region's) against a background of Christian experience represented most fully by Dante, and "imitated" Dante's verse more closely than any other American poet has done. Brilliant and sometimes restless, Tate was more than a fine poet: he helped to set the standards for the literary community in the United States.

—Ashley Brown

TAYLOR, Bayard. Born in Kennett Square, Chester County, Pennsylvania, 11 January 1825. Educated at Bolmar's Academy, West Chester, Pennsylvania, 1837–40; Unionville Academy, Pennsylvania, 1842. Married 1) Mary Agnew in 1850 (died, 1850); 2) Marie Hansen in 1857, one daughter. Teacher, Unionville Academy, 1842; apprenticed to the printer of the West Chester *Village Record*, 1842–44; traveled in Europe, as correspondent for *Saturday Evening Post* and *United States Gazette*, Philadelphia, and New York *Tribune*, 1844–46; publisher, *Pioneer* newspaper, Phoenixville, Pennsylvania, 1846–47; columnist, *Literary World*, New York, 1847–48; manager of the literary department, New York *Tribune*, 1848, and covered the California gold rush for the *Tribune*, 1849; traveled in the Middle and Far East, 1851–53, and lectured on his travels throughout the U.S. 1854–56; traveled in Europe, 1856–58; settled on a farm, Cedarcroft, near Kennett Square, 1858; Washington correspondent, *Tribune*, 1862; secretary, later chargé d'affaires, American Legation, St. Petersburg, Russia, 1862–63; returned to Cedarcroft, and worked on his translation of *Faust*, 1863–70; Non-Resident Professor of German, Cornell University, Ithaca, New York, 1870–77; U.S. Ambassador to Germany, 1878. *Died 19 December 1878.*

PUBLICATIONS

Collections

Dramatic Works. 1880.
Poetical Works. 1880.

Verse

Ximena; or, The Battle of Sierra Morena and Other Poems. 1844.
Rhymes of Travel, Ballads, and Poems. 1848.
A Book of Romances, Lyrics, and Songs. 1851.
Poems of the Orient. 1854.
Poems of Home and Travel. 1855.
Poems. 1856.
The Poet's Journal. 1862.
The Poems. 1864.
The Picture of St. John. 1866.
The Golden Wedding: A Masque. 1868.
The Ballad of Abraham Lincoln (for children). 1870.
Lars: A Pastoral of Norway. 1873.
Home Pastorals, Ballads, and Lyrics. 1875.
The National Ode. 1877.

Plays

The Masque of the Gods. 1872.
The Prophet: A Tragedy. 1874.
Prince Deukalion: A Lyrical Drama. 1878.

Fiction

Hannah Thurston. 1863.
John Godfrey's Fortunes. 1864.
The Story of Kennett. 1866; edited by C.W. La Salle, II, 1973.
Joseph and His Friend. 1870.
Beauty and the Beast, and Tales of Home. 1872.

Other

Views A-Foot; or, Europe Seen with Knapsack and Staff. 1846.
Eldorado; or, Adventures in the Path of Empire. 1850.
A Journey to Central Africa. 1854.
The Lands of the Saracen. 1854.
A Visit to India, China, and Japan in the Year 1853. 1855; revised edition, edited by G.F. Pardon, 1860.
Northern Travel. 1857.
Travels in Greece and Russia. 1859.
At Home and Abroad. 2 vols., 1859–62.
Colorado: A Summer Trip. 1867.
By-Ways of Europe. 1869.
A School History of Germany. 1874.
Egypt and Iceland in the Year 1874. 1874.
The Echo Club and Other Literary Diversions. 1876.
Boys of Other Countries: Stories for American Boys. 1876.
Studies in German Literature. 1879.
Critical Essays and Literary Notes, edited by Marie Hansen-Taylor. 1880.
Life and Letters, edited by Marie Hansen-Taylor and Horace E. Scudder. 2 vols., 1884.
Unpublished Letters in the Huntington Library, edited by John R. Schultz. 1937.
The Correspondence of Taylor and Paul Hamilton Hayne, edited by Charles Duffy. 1945.

Editor, with George Ripley, *Hand-book of Literature and Fine Arts*. 1852.
Editor, *Cyclopaedia of Modern Travel*. 1856.
Editor, *Frithiofs Saga*, by Esaias Teghér, translated by William Lewery Blackley. 1867.
Editor, *Travels in Arabia*. 1871.
Editor, *Japan in Our Day*. 1872.
Editor, *Travels in South Africa*. 1872.
Editor, *The Lake Regions of Central Africa*. 1873.
Editor, *Central Asia*. 1874.
Editor, *Picturesque Europe*. 1877.

Translator, *Faust*, by Goethe. 2 vols., 1870–71; edited by Stuart Atkins, 1972.

Translator, *A Sheaf of Poems*, edited by Mary Taylor Kiliani. 1911.

*

Critical Studies: *Taylor* by Albert H. Smyth, 1896 (includes bibliography); *Taylor: Laureate of the Gilded Age* by Richmond Croom Beatty, 1936; *The Genteel Circle: Taylor and His New York Friends* by Richard Cary, 1952; *Taylor and German Letters* by John T. Krumpelmann, 1959; *Taylor* by Paul C. Wermuth, 1973.

* * *

Although he wished to be remembered for his poetry, Bayard Taylor supported himself by writing travel literature, and it is for these works, as well as for his translation of *Faust*, that we remember him today. The titles of his many travel books, most of which were widely read during the 19th century, reveal the vast extent of Taylor's travels: *A Journey to Central Africa*, *The Lands of the Saracen*, *A Visit to India, China, and Japan*, *Northern Travel*, *Travels in Greece and Russia*, and *Egypt and Iceland*, among numerous other works. Ironically, however, Taylor was at his best when writing about his homeland. His book on the California gold rush, *Eldorado*, which he wrote for Horace Greeley's New York *Times*, is one of the earliest and most engaging accounts of its subject; and *Colorado*, which he wrote while on a summer trip to the west, is a classic of American overland adventure. Rarely controversial, always factual, and seldom boring, Taylor's books appealed to the sensibilities of a largely female 19th-century American audience which was eager to learn more about foreign culture and exotic lands, including the American west.

With the onset of the Civil War, the market for travel literature declined, and, to earn a living, Taylor began writing novels. His models were Dickens and Thackeray, and his plots were overly melodramatic and excessively contrived, but, despite their conventionality, Taylor's novels provide a valuable insight into the tastes and spirit of the times which demanded felicitous endings, purity from its heroines, and a proper respect for social decorum. They also bridge the gap between the romanticism of the first half of the 19th century and the realism of the second. *Hannah Thurston*, for example, is about a bluestocking suffragette turned housewife and mother who finds true happiness and freedom in the values of the home; and *The Story of Kennett*, with its quaint and descriptive portrayal of life in a rural Pennsylvania town, anticipates the local color movement of the 1870's, 1880's and 1890's.

Taylor's poems, like his travel books and novels, demonstrate more than a modicum of literary talent but suffer from a self-conscious desire to please. He had an astute ear for music, and his verse is technically quite proficient, but it lacks the universal tensions which make for good poetry, and it also tends to be overly sentimental, overly ornate, and overly derivative, particularly of Shelley and the British romantics. Nonetheless, his most famous poem, "The Bedouin Song," is far from his best; and such poems as "The Summer Camp," "Hylas," "Daughter of Egypt," and "Hassan and His Mare" deserve more recognition than they have received. *The Poet's Journal* and *The Picture of St. John* are especially deserving of attention because they constitute Taylor's attempt to write long narrative verse about his own experiences, vaguely disguised. His most popular collection of poetry, *Poems of the Orient*, displays a refreshing and aesthetically pleasing sense of the exotic. A collected edition of Taylor's poems was published during his lifetime; his masques and closet dramas were published after his death.

Throughout his life, Taylor maintained a genuine admiration for German culture. His second wife was German, and he was for many years non-resident professor of German literature at Cornell University. Taylor's interest in Germany appears in many of his works, especially in *Studies in German Literature*, which was for many years one of the best introductions to the field, and in his translation of *Faust*, whose copious scholarly annotations and faithful reproduction of the meter of the original make it to this day one of the finest translations of Goethe's masterpiece.

—James A. Levernier

TAYLOR, Edward. Born in Sketchley, Leicestershire, England, in 1642(?). Lost a teaching position in Bagworth, Leicestershire, for failing to subscribe to the Act of Uniformity, 1662; may then have attended Cambridge University; emigrated to Massachusetts Bay Colony, 1668; attended Harvard University, Cambridge, Massachusetts, 1668–71, A.B. 1671. Married 1) Elizabeth Fitch in 1674 (died, 1689), eight children; 2) Ruth Wyllys in 1692, six children. Congregational minister, Westfield, Massachusetts, 1671–1725. A.M.: Harvard University, 1720. *Died 24 June 1729.*

PUBLICATIONS

Collections

The Poetical Works, edited by Thomas H. Johnson. 1939.
The Poems, edited by Donald E. Stanford. 1960; *Selection*, 1963.
Unpublished Writings, edited by Thomas M. and Virginia L. Davis. 3 vols., 1981.

Verse

Metrical History of Christianity (transcript), edited by Donald E. Stanford. 1962.

Other

Christographia (sermons and meditations), edited by Norman S. Grabo. 1962.
The Diary, edited by Francis Murphy. 1964.
Treatise Concerning the Lord's Supper (sermons), edited by Norman S. Grabo. 1966.

*

Bibliography: *Taylor: An Annotated Bibliography 1668–1970* by Constance J. Gefvert, 1971.

Critical Studies: *Taylor* by Norman S. Grabo, 1961; *Taylor* by Donald E. Stanford, 1965; "Taylor Issue" of *Early American Literature*, vol. 4, no. 3, 1969–70; *The Will and the Word: The Poetry of Taylor* by William J. Scheick, 1974; *The Example of*

Taylor by Karl Keller, 1975; *Saint and Singer: Taylor's Typology and the Poetics of Meditation* by Karen E. Rowe, 1986.

* * *

It should be remembered as we read the poetry of Edward Taylor that he was for over fifty years the village parson of a small New England frontier town, Westfield in western Massachusetts. The ministry was his vocation; poetry was his avocation. The religious experience of the Puritan Calvinist was his abiding concern as a preacher and it was the subject matter of all his extant poems. His library, impressive for its time and place, had many religious books, some of them rare and expensive, but only one volume of verse in English, the poems of Anne Bradstreet. Yet Taylor wrote poetry all of his mature life, and today he is considered the major poet of New England Calvinistic Congregationalism just as Jonathan Edwards, who lived two generations later, is considered its paramount preacher, and this position Taylor has attained in spite of the fact that he published nothing during his life time.

Taylor's reputation as a poet rests on (to quote verbatim his own title page as it appears on his undated manuscript) *Gods Determinations touching his Elect: and The Elects Combat in their Conversion, and Coming up to God in Christ together with the Comfortable Effects thereof* and on his (to quote Taylor's manuscript page again) *Preparatory Meditations before my Approach to the Lords Supper. Chiefly upon the Doctrin preached upon the Day of administration*.

The manuscript of *Gods Determinations* was prepared with particular care and may have been intended for publication, a supposition strengthened by the aim and content of the work. *Gods Determinations* is a series of poems in the form of dramatic dialogues interspersed with narrative and expository passages which explain and justify God's ways in bringing a few selected men ("the elect") to salvation. Its purpose, apparently, was to convert those members of the Puritan community who felt themselves unable to accept full communion in the church because they had not experienced the reception of God's saving grace. Hence a great deal of the poem is taken up with a dramatization of the various ways in which God's grace operates among sinning men.

Gods Determinations opens with a "Preface" which describes the creation in Calvinistic terms. The physical universe as well as all its inhabitants, including man, was created out of nothing by an Omnipotent God who may return it to nothing if he pleases. "The Effects of Mans Apostacy" follows, describing the Fall and the terror of natural man when he finds God his enemy. The tone of the verse and the theology are similar to that of Jonathan Edwards's later famous sermon *Sinners in the Hands of an Angry God*. With the third poem, a dialogue between Justice and Mercy, personified attributes of God, the dramatic struggle for the redemption of the elect begins with Justice playing the role of divine avenger who punishes and terrifies man and Mercy playing the role of divine comforter who offers salvation to those who confess their sins and come into the church. Satan and Christ join the struggle and the ensuing action is seen as a series of military engagements in which Satan is eventually defeated by the combined efforts of Justice and Mercy. At the end of the poem the elect are depicted as riding to Glory in Christ's coach.

Much of the poem, in style and content, is "dated." However, Satan's methods of tempting the sinner to abandon hope, methods derived in part from William Ames's *Cases of Conscience*, are subtle and sophisticated, and they reveal an understanding of the psychology of guilt that is still of interest to the modern reader. Also, there are passages written in a vigorous, colloquial, and highly figurative style which are worth noting, particularly the famous query in the opening lines referring to the creation: "Who in this Bowling Alley bowld the Sun?"

The *Preparatory Meditations* is a body of remarkable devotional verse consisting of more than two hundred poems written over a period of more than forty years, from 1682 to 1725. Because of their style, which is reminiscent of the Metaphysical Poets (particularly Herbert but also occasionally Donne, Crashaw, and Vaughan) they have in recent years attracted the attention of scholars, for in the age of Pope Taylor was writing like Donne. But his Meditations are of more than mere historical interest. His recurrent and moving expression of the experience of Saving Grace establishes him as the most important religious poet in American literature and worthy of comparison not only with Donne and Herbert but also with Gerard Manley Hopkins.

The purpose of each Meditation was to prepare the pastor for administering the Lord's Supper, a sacrament by means of which the soul of the participant was united to Christ; therefore a number of the Meditations express the almost mystical exaltation of the union of the human with the divine, as in "The Experience":

> Most strange it was! But yet more strange that shine
> Which filld my Soul then to the brim to spy
> My Nature with thy Nature all Divine
> Together joyn'd in Him thats Thou, and I.

The structure of the poems varies, but more frequently it is three-fold with the opening lines expressing despairing personal awareness of original sin followed by joyful contemplation of Saving Grace made possible through faith in Christ and concluding with the hope that the poet will be one of the elect who will achieve salvation. These poems are in the tradition of the Christian meditative practice of self-examination best exemplified among the Roman Catholics by Loyola, but by the 17th century common among protestant divines such as Richard Baxter, author of *The Saints Everlasting Rest* (1650), a book with which Taylor was probably familiar and which may have influenced his own meditative methods. The meditant fixes his attention on some point of doctrine, analyzes it by means of his understanding, and as a result of comprehending it is moved by feelings of love, hope, joy, etc. The doctrine in Taylor's Meditations is usually stated in a biblical text which is quoted in the title of the poem, the favorite source of quotation for Taylor being the *Song of Songs* or, as Taylor called it, *Canticles*. Taylor frequently makes use of Christian allegory, symbolism, typology, and a figurative style derived chiefly from the Bible (especially from the *Song of Songs* and *Revelation*) and from Herbert. A widely variant vocabulary is employed with words ranging from the humble life of the farmer—"I'le Wagon Loads of Love, and Glory bring" to abstruse theological terminology. Complicated conceits with terms and images from widely disparate fields of experience are juxtaposed and yoked by violence together in the metaphysical style (as defined by Samuel Johnson). At its best the style is direct and forceful, but at its worst bizarre, over-rhetorical, and rhythmically awkward. Yet in reading the *Preparatory Meditations* as a whole, one gains the impression that they were written by a humble, extremely pious, sincere Puritan for whom the experience of God's grace was profound and overwhelming.

Taylor composed and preached innumerable sermons during

his long pastorate but the manuscripts of only a few have survived, the more important being available in *Christographia*, a series of fourteen sermons preached in Westfield from 1701 to 1703 on the mystery of the union of the divine and human natures of Christ, and in *Treatise Concerning the Lord's Supper* (eight sermons preached in 1694), in which he argues that the Lord's Supper should be confined to the regenerate elect only. These sermons are, then, an attack on the practice of Solomon Stoddard (the grandfather of Jonathan Edwards) who in his Northampton Church was using the sacrament as a converting ordinance and inviting all who led a Christian life to partake. In this as in other matters Taylor expressed the views of the conservative faction of the Congregational Church of New England.

Taylor also wrote a number of occasional poems, the most interesting of which are the charming "Upon a Wasp Child with Cold" and the striking "Upon the Sweeping Flood." He composed a long poem of over twenty thousand lines and of doubtful literary merit on the persecutions and martyrdoms of the Christians from the earliest times through the reign of Queen Mary of England, *Metrical History of Christianity*. He also wrote elegies on his contemporaries, the best being those on his first wife and on Samuel Hooker, pastor of the church of Farmington, Connecticut. But by far his best poetry is to be found in *Gods Determinations* and in the *Preparatory Meditations*.

—Donald E. Stanford

See the essay on *Gods Determinations*.

TEASDALE, Sara. Born in St. Louis, Missouri, 8 August 1884. Educated privately. Married Ernst B. Filsinger in 1914 (divorced, 1929). Traveled to Europe, 1912; moved to New York, 1916. Recipient: Columbia Poetry Prize (later Pulitzer Prize), 1918. *Died (suicide) 29 January 1933.*

PUBLICATIONS

Collections

Collected Poems. 1937.
Mirror of the Heart: Poems of Teasdale, edited by William Drake. 1984.

Verse

Sonnets to Duse and Other Poems. 1907.
Helen of Troy and Other Poems. 1911; revised edition, 1922.
Rivers to the Sea. 1915.
Love Songs. 1917.
Vignettes of Italy: A Cycle of Nine Songs for High Voice. 1919.
Flame and Shadow. 1920; revised edition, 1924.
Dark of the Moon. 1926.
Stars To-Night: Verses New and Old for Boys and Girls. 1930.
A Country House. 1932.
Strange Victory. 1933.

Other

Editor, *The Answering Voice: One Hundred Love Lyrics by Women*. 1917; revised edition, 1928.
Editor, *Rainbow Gold: Poems Old and New for Boys and Girls*. 1922.

*

Bibliography: by Vivian Buchan, in *Bulletin of Bibliography 25*, 1967.

Critical Studies: *Teasdale: A Biography* by Margaret Haley Carpenter, 1960; *Teasdale, Woman and Poet* by William Drake, 1979.

* * *

Sara Teasdale, whose verse suggests, in her own phrase, "a delicate fabric of bird song," was one of America's most charming lyrists. Well-received and popular for some fifteen years after *Love Songs* (1917) took the Pulitzer Prize for poetry, she was posthumously, and unjustly, somewhat underrated by the time *Collected Poems* appeared in 1937.

Teasdale's first book of consequence was her third, *Rivers to the Sea*, in which signs of the mature poet became evident. Happily, the best of her early work was incorporated into the body of *Love Songs*, whose seemingly artless musicality informs a lucid lyricism. *Flame and Shadow* marks, if anything, an advance in emotional depth and "natural falterings"; but *Dark of the Moon*, while gracefully competent, appears somewhat anticlimactic in its minor accents: the book of a "woman seemingly poured empty." The first posthumous collection, *Strange Victory*, has, however, some of Teasdale's most memorable pieces—"All That Was Mortal," "Grace Before Sleep," "Advice to a Girl," and others.

Teasdale's verse, repeatedly concerned with the stars, often reflective of her travels, always simple in technique and form and natural in statement, dewlike and fragile in quality, and gentle in its acceptance of sorrow (though never bathetic), poses no intellectual problems. Constantly preoccupied with beauty, as idea and as evocation, it offers instead quietly ironic, but joyful, acceptance of life, exquisiteness of feminine perception, and delicate artistry. All of which does not deny that Teasdale occasionally "reached into the black waters whose chill brings wisdom," poems like "Wood Song" and numerous others being the memorable evidence.

—George Brandon Saul

THOMAS, Augustus. Born in St. Louis, Missouri, 8 January 1857. Educated at local elementary and high schools. Married Lisle Colby in 1890; one son and one daughter. Page in Missouri Assembly, 1868, and in U.S. House of Representatives, Washington, D.C., 1870–71; worked in the freight department of a railway company in St. Louis from 1871; reporter, St Louis *Post-Dispatch*, 1885; worked for Kansas City *Mirror*, 1887–88; began acting and writing for the stage from 1875; moved to New York, 1888, and worked as a theatrical assistant and press agent; full-time playwright after 1891. President, Society of American Dramatists, 1906–12; Executive Chairman, Producing Managers Association, and campaigned unsuccessfully for the establishment of a national theatre, 1922–25. Recipient: American Academy Gold Medal, 1914. M.A.: Williams College, Williamstown, Massachusetts, 1914; Litt.D.: Columbia University, New York, 1921; LL.D.: University of Missouri, Columbia, 1923. President, American Academy, 1914–16. *Died 12 August 1934.*

PUBLICATIONS

Plays

Alone (produced 1875).
The Big Rise (produced 1882).
A Leaf from the Woods (produced 1883).
A New Year's Call (produced 1883).
Editha's Burglar, from the story by Frances Hodgson Burnett (produced 1883). 1932.
A Man of the World (produced 1883).
Combustion (produced 1884).
The Burglar (produced 1889).
A Proper Impropriety (produced 1889). 1932.
Tit for Tat, with Helen Barry, from a German play (produced 1890; as *A Night's Frolic*, produced 1891).
A Woman of the World (produced 1890).
For Money, with Clay M. Greene (produced 1890).
Afterthoughts (produced 1890).
Reckless Temple (produced 1890).
Alabama (produced 1891). 1898.
Colonel Carter of Cartersville, from the novel by F. Hopkinson Smith (produced 1892).
The Holly-Tree Inn (produced 1892).
Surrender (produced 1892).
In Mizzoura (produced 1893). 1916.
New Blood (produced 1894).
The Music Box (produced 1894).
The Man Upstairs (produced 1895). 1918.
The Capitol, from a story by Opie Read (produced 1895).
Chimmie Fadden, from a story by E.W. Townsend (produced 1896).
The Jucklins (produced 1896).
The Hoosier Doctor (produced 1897).
That Overcoat (produced 1898).
Don't Tell Her Husband (produced 1898; as *The Meddler*, produced 1898).
Colonel George of Mount Vernon (produced 1898). 1931.
Arizona (produced 1899). 1899.
Oliver Goldsmith (produced 1900). 1916.
On the Quiet (produced 1901).
Champagne Charley (produced 1901).
Colorado (produced 1901).
Soldiers of Fortune, from the play by R.H. Davies based on a novel by F. Marion Crawford (produced 1902).
The Earl of Pawtucket (produced 1903). 1917.
The Other Girl (produced 1903). 1917.
Mrs. Leffingwell's Boots (produced 1905). 1916.
Beside the Bonnie Briar Bush, with James MacArthur, from a novel by Ian Maclaren (produced 1905).
The Education of Mr. Pipp, from pictures by Charles Dana Gibson (produced 1905).
Delancey (produced 1905).
The Embassy Ball (produced 1905).
A Constitutional Point (produced 1906). 1932.
The Ranger (produced 1907).
The Member from Ozark (produced 1907).
The Witching Hour (produced 1907). 1916.
The Harvest Moon (produced 1909). 1922.
The Matinee Idol, from the play *His Last Legs* by William Bayle Bernard (produced 1909).
As a Man Thinks (produced 1911). 1911.
The Model (produced 1912; also produced as *When It Comes Home*).
Mere Man (produced 1912).
At Liberty (produced 1912).
At Bay, with George Scarborough (produced 1913).
Indian Summer (produced 1913).
Three of Hearts (produced 1913).
The Battle Cry, from a novel by Charles N. Buck (produced 1914). 1914.
The Nightingale (produced 1914). 1914.
Rio Grande (produced 1916).
The Copperhead, from the work *The Glory of His Country* by Frederick Landis (produced 1918). 1922.
David's Adventures, from a novel (produced 1918).
The Cricket of Palmy Days (as *Palmy Days*, produced 1919). 1929.
Under the Bough (produced 1920; also called *The Blue Devil* and *Speak of the Devil*).
The Tent of Pompey (produced 1920).
Nemesis (produced 1921). 1921.
Still Waters (produced 1925). 1926.

Other plays (for amateurs): *Love Will Find a Way; The Dress Suit.*

Other

The Print of My Remembrance (autobiography). 1922.
Commemorative Tribute to Francis Hopkinson Smith. 1922.

*

Critical Studies: *The Wallet of Time* by William Winter, 1913; *Thomas* by Ronald J. Davis, 1984.

* * *

Considered by contemporary critics as one of the half-dozen major American dramatists at the turn of the century, Augustus Thomas achieved some success by dramatizing American subjects that would catch the public interest. Like his contemporaries he was a good craftsman who wrote exciting melodramas and farces, generally with a particular actor or actress in mind. During his long career he wrote some 60 plays (including one-act plays and adaptations), organized and managed a professional theatre company, served as Executive Chairman of the Producing Managers Association and tried to develop a sense of self-censorship in the theatre world, was decorated by the French government, and wrote an autobiography, *The Print of My Remembrance*, which remains a useful if biased source for an appreciation of his plays and his theory of playwriting.

Thomas's playwriting took advantage of such topics of national interest as western regionalism, the labor movement, Washington politics, and new social fads. In *Alabama*, *In Mizzoura*, *Arizona*, and *Colorado* he used local scenery and atmosphere to enhance melodramatic plots. Only *Arizona* had any real success on stage. *New Blood* was sympathetic to the problems of laborers in a large manufacturing company. *The Capitol* revealed the influence of financiers on Washington politics and the lobbying practices of the Catholic Church but in a manner that would offend no one. *As a Man Thinks*, an average play on the double moral standard in marriage that interested playwrights and social reformers of this period, is distinguished by one of Thomas's best characters, the Jewish Dr. Seelig, who functions as a raisonneur in the play. *The Copperhead* achieved reasonable success on stage as a realistic picture of the effect of the Civil War on a midwestern town.

Thomas's best known play and probably his most significant work is *The Witching Hour*. Although a conventional melodrama of sentiment and morality, it exploits a popular interest by dramatizing the story of a young man who, under the influence of hypnotism, has killed a man. Beneath the mystery-laden plot there is the deeper idea of the effect of suggestion upon the human mind, but Thomas was seldom thought-provoking. Mainly he entertained with farces such as *The Earl of Pawtucket* and the thrills of the well-made melodrama.

—Walter J. Meserve

THOREAU, Henry David. Born David Henry Thoreau in Concord, Massachusetts, 12 July 1817. Educated at Miss Wheeler's school, and Center School, both Concord; Concord Academy, 1828–33; Harvard University, Cambridge, Massachusetts, 1833–35 and 1836–37, graduated 1837. Teacher in Canton, Massachusetts, 1835–36, and at Center School, 1837, (resigned); worked in his father's pencil factory, 1837–38, 1844, 1849–50 (in 1853 business changed to supplying lead to printers); took over Concord Academy with his brother, and taught there, 1838–41; secretary and curator, 1838–40, and curator, 1842–43, Concord Lyceum, and regular lyceum lecturer from 1848; contributor to the Transcendentalist periodical *The Dial*, Concord, 1840–44 (editor of April 1843 issue); lived with Ralph Waldo Emerson, 1841–43, and with Emerson's family, 1847; tutor to William Emerson's sons, Staten Island, New York, 1843; lived in a cabin at Walden Pond, near Concord, 1845–47; jailed for refusing to pay poll tax (on anti-slavery and anti-war principles), 1846; visited Maine, 1846, 1853, and 1857, and Canada, 1850; worked at various odd jobs, including gardening and building work; land surveyor from 1848. *Died 6 May 1862*.

PUBLICATIONS

Collections

Complete Works, edited by Harrison G.O. Blake. 5 vols., 1929.
Collected Poems, edited by Carl Bode. 1943; revised edition, 1964.
The Correspondence, edited by Walter Harding and Carl Bode. 1958.
Writings (includes *Journal*, edited by John C. Broderick, 1981—), edited by William L. Howarth. 1971—
Thoreau's Vision: The Major Essays, edited by Charles R. Anderson. 1973.
Selected Works, edited by Walter Harding. 1975.
A Week on the Concord and Merrimack Rivers, Walden, The Maine Woods, Cape Cod (Library of America), edited by Robert Sayre. 1985.

Prose

A Week on the Concord and Merrimack Rivers. 1849.
Walden; or, Life in the Woods. 1854; *The Variorum Walden* edited by Walter Harding, 1962.
Excursions, edited by Ralph Waldo Emerson. 1863.
The Maine Woods, edited by Sophia Thoreau and William Ellery Channing. 1864.
Cape Cod, edited by Sophia Thoreau and William Ellery Channing. 1865.
Letters to Various Persons, edited by Ralph Waldo Emerson. 1865.
A Yankee in Canada, with Anti-Slavery and Reform Papers (includes "Civil Disobedience"), edited by Sophia Thoreau and William Ellery Channing. 1866; *The Variorum Civil Disobedience* edited by Walter Harding, 1967; *Reform Papers* edited by Wendell Clark, in *Writings*, 1973.
Early Spring in Massachusetts. 1881; *Summer*, 1884; *Autumn*, 1888; *Winter*, 1892.
Miscellanies. 1894.
The Service, edited by Frank B. Sanborn. 1902.
Sir Walter Raleigh, edited by Henry Aiken Metcalf. 1905.
The First and Last Journeys of Thoreau, edited by Frank B. Sanborn. 2 vols., 1905.
Journal, edited by Bradford Torrey. 14 vols., 1906; edited by Francis H. Allen, 1949; *Selected Journals* edited by Carl Bode, 1967, as *The Best of Thoreau's Journals*, 1971.
The Moon. 1927.
Consciousness at Concord: The Text of Thoreau's Hitherto Lost Journal (1840–1841), edited by Perry Miller. 1958.
Thoreau's Minnesota Journey: Two Documents, edited by Walter Harding. 1962.
Literary Notebook, edited by Kenneth Walter Cameron. 1964.
Over Thoreau's Desk: New Correspondence 1838–1861, edited by Kenneth Walter Cameron. 1965.
Fact Book, edited by Kenneth Walter Cameron. 2 vols., 1966.
Canadian Notebook, edited by Kenneth Walter Cameron. 1967.
Huckleberries (lecture), edited by Leo Stoller. 1970.
The Indians of Thoreau: Selections from the Indian Notebooks, edited by Richard F. Fleck. 1974.
The Winged Life: The Poetic Voice of Thoreau, edited by Robert Bly. 1986.

Translator, *The Transmigration of the Seven Brahmans*, edited by Arthur E. Christy. 1932.
Translator, *Seven Against Thebes*, by Aeschylus, edited by Leo Max Kaiser. 1960.

*

Bibliography: *A Bibliography of the Thoreau Society Bulletin Bibliographies 1941–1969: A Cumulation and Index* by Jean Cameron Advena, edited by Walter Harding, 1971; *The Literary Manuscripts of Thoreau* by William L. Howarth, 1974; *Thoreau and the Critics: A Checklist of Criticism 1900–1978* by Jeanetta Boswell and Sarah Crouch, 1981; *Thoreau: A Descriptive Bibliography* by Raymond R. Borst, 1982.

Critical Studies: *Thoreau, The Poet-Naturalist* by William Ellery Channing, 1873, revised edition, 1902; *Thoreau: A Critical Study* by Mark Van Doren, 1916; *The Concord Saunterer* by Reginald Cook, 1940, revised edition, as *Passage to Walden*, 1949; "From Emerson to Thoreau" by F.O. Matthiessen, in *American Renaissance: Art and Expression in the Age of Emerson and Whitman*, 1941; *Thoreau* by Joseph Wood Krutch, 1948; *A Thoreau Gazetteer* by Robert F. Stowell, 1948, revised edition, edited by William L. Howarth, 1970; *Thoreau: The Quest and the Classics* by Ethel Seybold, 1951; *The Making of Walden* by J. Lyndon Shanley, 1957; *After Walden: Thoreau's Changing Views on Economic Man* by Leo Stoller, 1957; *The Shores of America: Thoreau's Inward Exploration* by Sherman Paul, 1958, and *Thoreau: A Collection of Critical Essays* edited by Paul, 1962; *A Thoreau Handbook*, 1959 (revised edition, as *The New Thoreau Handbook*, with Michael Meyer, 1980), and *The Days of Thoreau: A Biography*, 1965, revised edition, 1982, both by Walter Harding, and *The Thoreau Centennial* edited by Harding, 1964; *Companion to Thoreau's Correspondence* by Kenneth Walter Cameron, 1964; *Emerson and Thoreau: Transcendentalists in Conflict* by Joel Porte, 1966; *Twentieth-Century Interpretations of Walden* edited by Richard Ruland, 1968; *The Recognition of Thoreau: Selected Criticism since 1848* edited by Wendell Glick, 1969; *Thoreau* by Leon Edel, 1970; *Thoreau as Romantic Naturalist* by James McIntosh, 1974; *Thoreau and the American Indians* by Robert F. Sayre, 1977; *Young Man Thoreau*, 1977, and *Thoreau's Seasons*, 1984, both by Richard Lebeaux; *Thoreau's Redemptive Imagination* by Frederick Garber, 1977; *Several More Lives to Live: Thoreau's Political Reputation in America* by Michael Meyer, 1977; *Thoreau in the Human Community* by Mary E. Moller, 1980; *Thoreau: What Manner of Man?* by Edward Wagenknecht, 1981; *Dark Thoreau* by Richard Bridgman, 1982; *The Book of Concord: Thoreau's Life as a Writer* by William L. Howarth, 1982; *Thoreau: A Naturalist's Liberty* by John Hildebidle, 1983; *Thoreau's Psychology: Eight Essays* edited by Raymond D. Gozzi, 1983; *Writing Nature: Thoreau's Journal* by Sharon Cameron, 1985; *Thoreau: A Life of the Mind* by Robert D. Richardson, Jr., 1986.

* * *

Henry David Thoreau was long remembered in his native town of Concord in Massachusetts as a quirky man, and indeed he was, but he was also a bold economist. "The mass of men," he said, "lead lives of quiet desperation," so intent on earning a living that they have no time to live. How much better, he thought, was one day of work and six days at more profitable occupation than six days of labor and one day of rest. Thoreau's work was for a brief period that of school teacher, for a longer time that of a helper in his father's pencil-making business, and latterly that of a surveyor. His occupation was that of an observer and recorder of nature, and of man's proper relation to the world in which he lived. Punning on the correct pronunciation of his name, he called himself a thorough man, and that he was, thoroughly attentive to his daily task of walking, observing, recording, and then painstakingly transcribing into his journals the profits that each day brought. These journals were his storehouse containing materials from which his writings were drawn, and remain a storehouse in which readers today discover quizzical nudgings toward truths.

For to Thoreau truths were not to be captured by declarative frontal attack. They must be warily approached, as any wild thing must be approached, circled cautiously, lest in fear they take flight, or, if sprung on too suddenly become caged in words which inevitably distort. "In wildness," Thoreau announced, "is the preservation of the world." But wildness did not mean wilderness. He was shocked to fear by wind-swept mountain tops, so like primordial chaos. Nature was better with man in it. Thoreau preferred the woodlands, swamplands, and waterways of a man-centered universe. He thought of himself as a "self-appointed inspector of snow-storms and rainstorms," a "surveyor, if not of highways, then of forest paths and across-lots routes," faithfully minding, he said, "my own business."

He had a large sense of drama. He dramatized himself, and he dramatized the world of nature. Though others have been imprisoned for the cause of conscience, Thoreau is remembered as the one who spent a night in jail for refusal to pay taxes to support a tainted war, and who then wrote the essay "Civil Disobedience" which still remains a handbook for young rebels. When he retired in 1845 to a cabin beside Walden Pond, he chose the 4th of July, the anniversary of America's Declaration of Independence, as the day to take residence there in token of his own independence. He was a supreme egotist, vauntingly unashamed of eccentricities of dress and deportment. His mission was, he said, to crow like Chanticleer, to wake his neighbors up.

He went to his cabin in the woods, not in surly withdrawal from a workaday world. Indeed, he often walked into town, if only to feast on his mother's delicious pies. While officially in residence beside Walden Pond, he took time off for an excursion to Mount Katahdin in Maine. But ordinarily he remained in residence, an eccentric man making daily eccentric pilgrimages around and beyond the still waters of the pond, his evenings spent in recording his daily adventures, culling from them and earlier recordings materials to be made into books or essays. For, like any sensible writer, he sought in his pond-side retreat the quiet and solitude necessary for writing.

While there, again dramatically for exactly two years, two months, and two days, he completed one book and the draft of another. The first was a reminiscent account of a two-week excursion which he and his brother, now deceased, had taken during the summer of 1839, travelling through waterways in a boat of their own construction to the White Mountains in New Hampshire. In composing *A Week on the Concord and Merrimack Rivers*, Thoreau telescoped those two weeks to one and limited himself almost entirely to river adventures. By many, *A Week* is considered Thoreau's most lively book, filled with youthful verve and sombre remembrances, and with observations on men and nature and books, and the livening power of each. "A basket," Thoreau later called it, "of delicate texture," the weaving so fine that, as basket, its strands fall apart to shower a reader with whimsical wisdom and insightful perceptions.

But *A Week* was not well-received when it appeared in 1849. Of an edition of a thousand copies more than seven hundred were returned to him by its publisher unsold. Meanwhile, Thoreau, in residence now in Concord, continued on small excursions, to Cape Cod, again to Maine, but mostly through the outskirts of his native town. He lectured occasionally, but not comfortably nor outstandingly well. He published accounts of his excursions and "Civil Disobedience," first titled "Resistance to Civil Government." But, if not mostly, most importantly, he puttered over revisions of the second book which had occupied him during his residence beside Walden Pond.

When it appeared in 1854, *Walden; or, Life in the Woods* was better received than *A Week* had been, but the reception was not always enthusiastic, indeed was more than often mocking: who is this humbug, pretending to be a hermit, who has the insolence to tell us how we should live? But no book written in the 19th century, except perhaps Karl Marx's *Das Kapital*, has become more of a scripture, a guide, a handbook. Its long first chapter on "Economy" was often reprinted as a tract used by advocates of labor reform on both sides of the Atlantic. Other people built, and still build, secluded small hideaways where work may be done, in art, literature, or contemplation. Many a busy, work-imprisoned person has lived vicariously in an imaginary pond-side retreat of his own. William Butler Yeats is said to have modeled his Innisfree on recollections of *Walden*. W.H. Hudson proclaimed Thoreau "without master or mate . . . in the foremost ranks of the prophets."

Thoreau condenses his more than two-year residence beside Walden Pond into the four seasons of a single year, joyously through New England's brief summer for twelve chapters, then a single chapter on autumn and three more on winter, an exultant penultimate chapter on spring, moving toward a conclusion which gives final coherence to the cycle, which is not only seasonal but diurnal—day, evening, night, and morning—and which also suggests the ages of man through youth, manhood, old age, death, and finally, with spring and morning, resurrection. Though reprimanding people for work-filled sloth, *Walden* is also a compelling, ecstatic book, a manual of affirmation, confidently asserting in its final sentences, "There is more day to dawn. The Sun is but a morning star."

To most people Thoreau is *Walden*, and *Walden* Thoreau, or, if you wish, thorough. But there was more life to live and record, more excursions to make, more writing to be meticulously done. In his journals he made notes for a Book of the Seasons, which remains in embryo, never put together except by other people who have mined the journals for seasonal lore. When Thoreau died in his mid-fifties, he left sheaves of manuscript as his principal worldly legacy. Most of them have been variously edited by friends or admirers. *Excursions* in 1863 was made up of essays, many of them previously published. *The Maine Woods* in 1864 told of three excursions into the northern wilderness. *Cape Cod* in 1865 and *A Yankee in Canada* in 1866, though not without occasional delicately phrased insights, were, like most of *The Maine Woods*, narratives of travel rather than testaments to an ideal. Thoreau's journals have been published, though not in their entirety, and other people have culled books from them; his letters have been gathered, his poems and translations from the Greek, and his juvenile writings, often neither complete nor completely correct, until in 1971 the Princeton University Press inaugurated a new meticulous edition, now in progress, of his writings.

Thoreau represents many things to many people. To some he is the ultimate nonconformist who brings comfort to those who relish nonconformity in lifestyle or dress. To others, he is an escapist, unhindered by familial responsibilities. Still others suspect that his bachelorhood resulted from fear or distrust of women, or of himself. Naturalists have found him inexpert in identification of species. Ecologists claim him as a pioneer. Civil rebels, from Gandhi to Martin Luther King and beyond, have found him a spark igniting them to action. He was perhaps each of these, but was in total more than the sum of them all. He was a writer, a stylist quite equal to any who in his time or since has managed the flexible complexities of our language. The delicacy of the web that his words construct is too fine to provide the comfort of didacticism. His words fly free to allow each reader to pattern them to dimensions of his own. Everyone, it has been said, gets the Thoreau that he deserves.

—Lewis Leary

See the essay on *Walden*.

THORPE, Thomas Bangs. Born in Westfield, Massachusetts, 1 March 1815. Educated at schools in Albany, New York, and New York City; studied painting with John Quidor, New York, 1830–33; attended Wesleyan University, Middletown, Connecticut, 1834–36. Served in the military government of New Orleans, 1862–64: Colonel. Married 1) Anne Maria Hinckley in 1838 (died, 1855), two daughters and one son; 2) Jane Fosdick in 1857. Painter in Louisiana 1837–54; lived in New York, 1840, then moved to St. Francisville, Louisiana; editor, *Southern Sportsman* magazine, 1843, and the Whig newspapers *Concordia Intelligencer*, Vidalia, 1843–45, New Orleans *Commercial Times*, 1845–46, New Orleans *Daily Tropic*, 1846 (war correspondent in Mexico), Baton Rouge *Conservator*, 1846–47, and New Orleans *National*, 1847; postmaster, Vidalia, 1844–45; lived in Baton Rouge, 1848–54; moved to New York, 1854; member of the editorial staff, *Leslie's Illustrated Newspaper*, 1857; lawyer, 1858–60; co-owner and co-editor, *Spirit of the Times*, New York, 1859–61; surveyor, Port of New Orleans, 1862–63; city surveyor, New York, 1865–69; chief of the warehouse department, New York Customs House, 1869–78. Delegate, Louisiana Constitutional Convention, 1864. M.A.: Wesleyan University, 1847. *Died 20 September 1878.*

PUBLICATIONS

Fiction and Sketches

The Mysteries of the Backwoods; or, Sketches of the Southwest. 1845.
The Hive of the Bee-Hunter: A Repository of Sketches. 1854.
The Master's House: A Tale of Southern Life. 1854.

Other

Our Army on the Rio Grande. 1846.
Our Army at Monterey. 1847.
The Taylor Anecdote Book: Anecdotes and Letters of Zachary Taylor. 1848.
Reminiscences of Charles L. Elliott, Artist. 1868.

*

Critical Study: *Thorpe, Humorist of the Old Southwest* by Milton Rickels, 1962.

* * *

Thomas Bangs Thorpe, a northerner who loved the south and lived in Louisiana for many years, is one of the finest writers in the group known as old southwestern humorists. At his best Thorpe was able to relinquish a formal, educated, fashionable mode of writing for an informal, ungrammatical, humorous view of the old southwest. Indeed, Thorpe's great talent was his ability to render frontier speech and humor vividly.

In 1839, Thorpe, a portrait painter by trade, achieved national and international attention with his first essay about the frontier. "Tom Owen, The Bee-Hunter" described an eccentric whom Thorpe had met in the backwoods of Louisiana, a man whose primary interest in life was fearlessly pursuing bees and taking their honey. Unfortunately, in this essay Thorpe used a highly literary language, hardly the language of the frontier, and he thereby held himself and his readers at a considerable distance from his subject.

This problem of authorial distance was completely solved, however, in Thorpe's masterpiece "The Big Bear of Arkansas," published in 1841. Although he began this tale with a predominantly formal description of the "heterogeneous" passengers on a Mississippi steamboat and ended it in an equally formal style, Thorpe permitted a rather uncouth passenger to tell a tall tale within this frame. Jim Doggett, an Arkansas frontiersman, speaks throughout most of "The Big Bear" and his language is far from literary. His pronunciation (as suggested by misspellings), the rhythms of his speech, his grammatical errors, the idioms and metaphors he uses are all appropriate to the Western roarer, and form a purposeful, telling contrast to the relatively dull frame style. This contrast is intensified by the exaggerated nature of Jim's frontier humor: Jim reports that in Arkansas beets grow as large as cedar stumps and wild turkeys grow too fat to fly. But the primary exaggeration in this story is not particularly humorous. Doggett says that the big bear seems to raid his farm at will, to have almost supernatural powers, and to loom as large as a "black mist." None of these details sets one laughing. They do, however, suggest that this "creation bar," like Faulkner's bear, is a symbol of a once vast wilderness which itself is doomed. Indeed, Thorpe's bear seems to recognize his inevitable doom and to die, though at Jim's hands, only because "his time come." There is, nevertheless, a joke embedded within this rather melancholy strain. When the bear decides his time has come, he surprises Doggett at a most inopportune moment—the Arkansas hunter is literally caught with his "inexpressibles" down.

Thorpe never equalled this tale. His "second finest frontier story" (according to Milton Rickels), "Bob Herring, The Arkansas Bear Hunter," is certainly of interest. Though Bob Herring is not the ring-tail roarer that Jim Doggett is, he is a realistic frontiersman, and his language is both amusing and authentic. Yet the structure of this story lacks the technical brilliance of "The Big Bear." While "The Big Bear" encloses Jim's yarn within a frame, "Bob Herring" rather awkwardly juxtaposes two bear hunts told from different perspectives. Moreover, the latter story relies extensively upon an imaginative but gentlemanly narrator, and one longs to hear the voice of Bob Herring more pervasively.

Thorpe subsequently published two collections of stories and essays, edited a number of newspapers, wrote a history of the Mexican War, composed a mediocre reform novel, and contributed many articles to national periodicals. But his single most creative product came early in his career and was not to be matched by later works. "The Big Bear of Arkansas" was Thorpe's greatest achievement, one that abetted the rise of realism, dealt with the nature of the frontier, and guaranteed its author a place in American literary history.

—Suzanne Marrs

THURBER, James (Grover). Born in Columbus, Ohio, 8 December 1894. Educated at Ohio State University, Columbus, 1913–14, 1915–18. Married 1) Althea Adams in 1922 (divorced, 1935), one daughter; 2) Helen Wismer in 1935. Code clerk, American Embassy, Paris, 1918–20; reporter, Columbus *Dispatch*, 1920–24, Paris edition of Chicago *Tribune*, 1925–26, and New York *Evening Post*, 1926–27; editor, 1927, writer, 1927–38, then free-lance contributor, *New Yorker*; also an illustrator from 1929: several individual shows. Litt.D.: Kenyon College, Gambier, Ohio, 1950; Yale University, New Haven, Connecticut, 1953; L.H.D.: Williams College, Williamstown, Massachusetts, 1951. *Died 2 November 1961.*

PUBLICATIONS

Collections

Vintage Thurber: A Collection of the Best Writings and Drawings. 2 vols., 1963.
Selected Letters, edited by Helen Thurber and Edward Weeks. 1981.

Short Stories and Sketches (illustrated by the author)

The Owl in the Attic and Other Perplexities. 1931.
The Seal in the Bedroom and Other Predicaments. 1932.
My Life and Hard Times. 1933.
The Middle-Aged Man on the Flying Trapeze: A Collection of Short Pieces. 1935.
Let Your Mind Alone! and Other More or Less Inspirational Pieces. 1937.
Cream of Thurber. 1939.
The Last Flower: A Parable in Pictures. 1939.
Fables for Our Time and Famous Poems Illustrated. 1940.
My World—and Welcome to It. 1942.
Men, Women, and Dogs: A Book of Drawings. 1943.
The Thurber Carnival. 1945.
The Beast in Me, and Other Animals: A New Collection of Pieces and Drawings about Human Beings and Less Alarming Creatures. 1948.
The Thurber Album: A New Collection of Pieces about People. 1952.
Thurber Country: A New Collection of Pieces about Males and Females, Mainly of Our Own Species. 1953.
Thurber's Dogs: A Collection of the Master's Dogs, Written and Drawn, Real and Imaginary, Living and Long Ago. 1955.
A Thurber Garland. 1955.
Further Fables for Our Time. 1956.
Alarms and Diversions. 1957.
Lanterns and Lances. 1961.
Credos and Curios. 1962.
Thurber and Company. 1966.

Fiction (for children)

Many Moons. 1943.
The Great Quillow. 1944.
The White Deer. 1945.
The 13 Clocks. 1950.
The Wonderful O. 1955.

Plays

The Male Animal, with Elliott Nugent (produced 1940). 1940.
A Thurber Carnival, from his own stories (produced 1960). 1962.

Wrote the books for the following college musical comedies:

Oh My! Omar, with Hayward M. Anderson, 1921; *Psychomania*, 1922; *Many Moons*, 1922; *A Twin Fix*, with Hayward M. Anderson, 1923; *The Cat and the Riddle*, 1924; *Nightingale*, 1924; *Tell Me Not*, 1924.

Other

Is Sex Necessary? or, Why You Feel the Way You Do, with E.B. White. 1929.
Thurber on Humor. 1953.
The Years with Ross. 1959.

*

Bibliography: *Thurber: A Bibliography* by Edwin T. Bowden, 1968.

Critical Studies: *Thurber* by Robert E. Morsberger, 1964; *The Art of Thurber* by Richard C. Tobias, 1969; *Thurber, His Masquerades: A Critical Study* by Stephen A. Black, 1970; *The Clocks of Columbus: The Literary Career of Thurber* by Charles S. Holmes, 1972, and *Thurber: A Collection of Critical Essays* edited by Holmes, 1974; *Thurber: A Biography* by Burton Bernstein, 1975; *Thurber's Anatomy of Confusion* by Catherine McGehee Kenney, 1984.

* * *

James Thurber, who was not destined to be one of America's celebrated poets, first turned up in the pages of the *New Yorker* on 26 February 1927 with two forgettable bits of verse. His third contribution (5 March 1927) was more indicative of what was to come. Called "An American Romance," it is the account of a "little man in an overcoat that fitted him badly," who stations himself in a revolving door, defying a number of authority figures, and stays there until he is rewarded with instant celebrity. An ur-Walter Mitty, then, caught in an American landscape which Thurber would eventually view more sardonically, almost a fable for our time.

Thurber had been a newspaperman on the Columbus *Dispatch* and the Paris edition of the Chicago *Tribune* and a freelance contributor to a number of publications before he arrived at the *New Yorker*, but it was with that magazine that his reputation both as writer and cartoonist was made, a reputation that he sometimes saw as limiting to his artistic aspirations. He served on the staff until 1938 and remained a contributor until 1961; eventually he tried to define the quality of the place and his own ambiguous attachment to it in *The Years with Ross*, which E.B. White called "a sly exercise in denigration, beautifully concealed in words of sweetness and love."

Thurber's first book was a collaboration with White, the parody volume *Is Sex Necessary?* His second, *The Owl in the Attic*, initiated the practice of collecting his magazine pieces which he would follow for the rest of his writing life. Sometimes—*My Life and Hard Times, Let Your Mind Alone!, The Years with Ross*—the group of essays was obviously conceived as a book; in most cases, the mixture is fortuitous, although occasionally, as in *Thurber's Dogs*, held together by a common subject matter. Of his early books, *My Life and Hard Times*, a marvelously funny mock biography, is the most impressive, the more so when one considers that Thurber returned to the same Ohio home ground to do the completely different and equally successful *The Thurber Album*.

There are many Thurbers: the playwright (*The Male Animal*, *A Thurber Carnival*); the author of children's books, of which *The White Deer* and *The 13 Clocks* are the happiest inventions; the adult fabulist of *Fables for Our Time* and *Further Fables*; the canine celebrant (*Thurber's Dogs*); the social observer who could write so well about soap opera ("Soapland" in *The Beast in Me, and Other Animals*); the perceptive critic who could work through parody or direct comment and the concerned artist who defended humor from outside attack and inside timidity in the repressive atmosphere of the 1950's. Through all these, there is a persistent Thurber, the dark humorist who, one way or another, kept asking, as the moral of one of the *Further Fables* puts it, "Oh, why should the shattermyth have to be a crumplehope and a dampenglee?"

—Gerald Weales

See the essay on "The Secret Life of Walter Mitty."

TIMROD, Henry. Born in Charleston, South Carolina, 8 December 1828. Educated at German Friendly Society School and Cotes's School, Charleston, 1836–40; Franklin College (later University of Georgia), 1845–46; read law in the office of James L. Petigru, Charleston, 1847–49. Served in the Confederate Army during the Civil War, 1862 (discharged for health reasons, 1862). Married Kate Goodwin in 1864; one son. Schoolmaster and tutor for various Southern plantation families, 1850–61; assistant editor, Charleston *Mercury*, 1863; associate editor, and part owner, Columbia *South Carolinian*, 1864 until 1865 when Sherman's troops sacked the town; assistant private secretary to Governor J.L. Orr, 1864. *Died 7 October 1867.*

PUBLICATIONS

Collections

The Essays, edited by Edd Winfield Parks. 1942.
The Collected Poems: A Variorum Edition, edited by Edd Winfield Parks and Aileen Wells Parks. 1965.

Verse

Poems. 1859.
The Poems, edited by Paul Hamilton Hayne. 1873.
The Uncollected Poems, edited by Guy A. Cardwell. 1942.

Other

The Last Years of Timrod 1864–1867: Including Letters to Paul Hamilton Hayne and Letters about Timrod by William Gilmore Simms, John R. Thompson, John Greenleaf Whittier, and Others, edited by Jay B. Hubbell. 1941.

*

Bibliography: *Sidney Lanier, Timrod, and Paul Hamilton Hayne: A Reference Guide* by Jack De Bellis, 1978.

Critical Study: *Timrod* by Edd Winfield Parks, 1964.

* * *

Had it not been for the Civil War, Henry Timrod, although the best southern poet of his time except for Poe, could be almost unknown today. In view of his reputation as chief of the southern poets of the War—he is characterized in such rebarbative phrases as "Laureate of the Confederacy" and "Harp of the South"—his life and thought are rich in ironies.

There was nothing of the Cavalier about his ancestry, and he was not a zealous propagandist for the region or for slavery. Like a number of other antebellum Southern writers, he was often at odds with his section and its culture; a strain of astringent candor ran through his excellent essays. Although Charleston was the publishing center of the south, Timrod describes the region as a literary backwater, archaic in taste, unformed in judgment, materialistic, prosaic, uninterested in intellectual and poetic knowledge. He opposed Southernism in literature and emphasized that poetry must belong to the world.

To some of the older generation of Charleston literary men, Timrod seemed extravagantly avant-garde: his principal heroes and models were Wordsworth and Tennyson. His theory and practice were tempered, however, by classicist ideas and habits. He insisted that after inspiration must come artistry; that excessive subjectivity spoils verse; and that poetry must be true and ethical. His apprentice verses show him industriously experimenting in forms and meters, and variant versions of mature poems indicate that he was an assiduous reviser. Sidney Lanier wrongly held that Timrod possessed a dainty artless art but never had time to learn the craft of the poet. His lyricism is most successful when most considered: his verse lacks spontaneity, intensity, and figurative imagination; his ideas and metrics are unoriginal. He was in a large sense an occasional poet whose delight in words and skill with meters could produce simply structured, controlled verses remarkably free of the sentimental verbosity and crudity of form that are characteristic of his southern contemporaries.

Amative and nature poetry make up the bulk of Timrod's verse, but the critical consensus is right in judging his war poetry, most of which stresses the losses and sorrows of the conflict, to be his best. Most memorable are "Ethno-genesis," "The Cotton Boll," "Carolina," "A Cry to Arms," "Charleston," and his Magnolia Cemetery ode.

Nearly all of Timrod's verses were first published in Southern newspapers and magazines, usually for no pay. The *Southern Literary Messenger*, of Richmond, and *Russell's Magazine*, of Charleston, were the most important of the miscellanies to which he made regular contributions. Friends guaranteed the costs of the one slim volume of his verse that appeared during his lifetime. Posthumous collections more than double the number of poems contained in that first volume.

—Guy A. Cardwell

TOLSON, Melvin B(eaunorus). Born in Moberly, Missouri, 6 February 1898. Educated at Lincoln High School, Kansas City, Missouri, graduated 1918; Fisk University, Nashville, Tennessee, 1918–20; Lincoln University, Oxford, Pennsylvania, 1920–23, B.A. 1923; Columbia University, New York, 1930–31, M.A. 1940. Married Ruth Southall in 1922; three sons and one daughter. Teacher at Wiley College, Marshall, Texas, 1924–47; Professor of English and Drama, Langston University, Oklahoma, 1947–66; Avalon Professor of Humanities, Tuskegee Institute, Alabama, 1965. Columnist ("Caviar and Cabbage"), Washington *Tribune*, 1937–44; Mayor of Langston, 1954 (re-elected 1954, 1956, 1958). Recipient: American Academy award, 1966. D.L., 1954, and D.H.L., 1965, Lincoln University. Order of the Star of Africa (Liberia), 1954. *Died 29 August 1966.*

PUBLICATIONS

Verse

Rendezvous with America. 1944.
Libretto for the Republic of Liberia. 1953.
Harlem Gallery: Book I, The Curator. 1965.
A Gallery of Harlem Portraits, edited by Robert M. Farnsworth. 1979.

Play

The Fire in the Flint, from the novel by Walter F. White (produced 1952).

Other

Caviar and Cabbage: Selected Columns from the Washington Tribune 1937–1944, edited by Robert M. Farnsworth. 1982.

*

Critical Studies: introduction by Karl Shapiro to *Harlem Gallery*, 1965; *Tolson* by Joy Flasch, 1972; *Tolson's Harlem Gallery: A Literary Analysis* by Mariann Russell, 1980; *Tolson: Plain Talk and Poetic Prophecy* by Robert M. Farnsworth, 1984.

* * *

On the basis of his first volume of poetry, *Rendezvous with America*, it would hardly have been possible to predict the kind of poet Melvin Tolson was to be a decade later. A poet who writes "I gaze upon her silken loveliness / She is a passion-flower of joy and pain / On the golden bed I came back to possess" does not show particular promise. Likewise the lines "America is the Black Man's country / The Red Man's, the Yellow Man's / The Brown Man's, the White Man's" are not suggestive of the great lines yet to come.

There are, however, certain characteristics of the earlier poetry which were to develop and become hallmarks of the later poetry, more its essence than ornament. The second stanza, for example, of "An Ex-Judge at the Bar" is in style and content very much like a good deal of the later poetry and untypical of the rather commonplace character of much of the first volume. That stanza, "I know, Bartender, yes, I know when the Law / Should wag its tail or rip with fang and claw. / When Pilate washed his hands, that neat event / Set for us judges a Caesarean precedent," is in tone typically Tolsonian. The juxtaposition of the formal and the informal, the classical and the contemporary, the familiar and the unusual accounts in large measure for the unique character of Tolson's best poetry.

Such juxtapositions are more pronounced in *Libretto for the Republic of Liberia*, where, in addition, the "gift for language" noted in Allen Tate's introduction to the volume becomes apparent. The effect of the juxtaposition of the learned encyclopedia references and the most abstruse vocabulary with commonplace references, vocabulary, and rhyme, all managed within a highly traditional form, is pyrotechnic. The occurrence in the same context of French, German, Latin, Hebrew, Swahili, Arabic, Spanish, and Sanskrit references with everyday activities, occupations, and events created a system of tensions not unlike the dynamic of forces holding an atom or a galaxy together. Each element threatens to go off on its own; yet as long as the balance of forces remains constant, the system functions. Tolson, by virtue of an extraordinary mind and intelligence, keeps a vast array of disparate elements in constant relationship. His poetry is, therefore, coherent, and its primary effect is of the containment and control of vast reserves of energy.

This bears on Karl Shapiro's controversial statement in his introduction to *Harlem Gallery*, Tolson's final volume, that "Tolson writes in Negro." It is not at bottom the language which prompted Shapiro's observation. Rather, it is the intellectual disposition of the tension between two worlds that finds its manifestation in the language. Tolson belongs (and this distinguishes him from Eliot, Pound, and Hart Crane, whom he read avidly) to an Afro-American world and an American-European world, and he knows these worlds in intricate detail. The balance he sustains between them is the source of his power. Few understand him because few know both worlds as well, and few are as totally committed as he to such a high universal standard of values.

—Donald B. Gibson

TOOMER, Jean (Nathan Eugene Toomer). Born in Washington, D.C., 26 December 1894. Educated at high schools in Brooklyn, New York, and Washington, D.C.; University of Wisconsin, Madison, 1914; Massachusetts College of Agriculture; American College of Physical Training, Chicago, 1916; New York University, Summer 1917; City College, New York, 1917. Married 1) Margery Latimer in 1931 (died, 1932), one daughter; 2) Marjorie Content in 1934. Taught physical education in a school near Milwaukee, 1918; clerk, Acker Merrall and Conduit grocery company, New York, 1918; shipyard worker, New York; worked at Howard Theatre, Washington, D.C., 1920; studied at Gurdjieff's Institute in Fontainebleau, France, 1924, 1926: led Gurdjieff groups in Harlem, 1925, and Chicago, 1926–33; lived in Pennsylvania after 1934. *Died 30 March 1967.*

PUBLICATIONS

Collections

The Wayward and the Seeking: A Collection of Writings by Toomer, edited by Darwin T. Turner. 1980.

Fiction

Cane (includes verse). 1923.

Play

Balo, in *Plays of Negro Life*, edited by Alain Locke and Montgomery Gregory. 1927.

Other

Essentials (aphorisms). 1931.
An Interpretation of Friends Worship. 1947.
The Flavor of Man. 1949.

*

Bibliography: "Toomer: An Annotated Checklist of Criticism" by John M. Reilly, in *Resources for American Literary Study*, Spring 1974.

Critical Studies: *In a Minor Chord* (on Toomer, Cullen, and Hurston) by Darwin T. Turner, 1971; *The Merrill Studies in Cane* edited by Frank Durham, 1971; *The Grotesque in American Negro Fiction: Toomer, Wright, and Ellison* by Fritz Gysin, 1975; *Toomer* by Brian Joseph Benson and Mabel Mayle Dillard, 1980; *Toomer, Artist: A Study of His Literary Life and Work 1894–1936* by Nellie Y. McKay, 1984.

* * *

In a startling image of fulfillment Jean Toomer likened the descendants of slaves among whom he sought poetic motive to "purple ripened plums," the seed of one becoming "An everlasting song, a singing tree, / Caroling softly souls of slavery, / What they were, and what they are to me." The lyric containing this image, "Song of the Son," serves as one of the impressionistic epigraphs uniting *Cane* into a symbolic account of Toomer's effort to reconcile the technical sophistication of Harlem Renaissance art with folk life. His assertion that black rural life in Georgia provided him with the soil for a living literature ratified the cultural nationalism of the Renaissance, while the experimental form of this book demonstrated its kinship with literary modernism. For contemporaries, then, *Cane* promised a vitally new art.

Each of the stories, sketches, and poems making up *Cane* examines the possibility of intuitive self-fulfillment. In the first part of the book, set in the south, a series of female characters achieve momentary redemption through expression of spontaneous feelings. The second part, set in Washington, D.C., variously represents characters whose feelings are blocked by social artifice. The whole concludes with a story-play in which the central figure, Kabnis, has internalized the violence and repression of caste relations so effectively that he is terrified of opening his senses at all. The complex intermingling of impressionism, expressionism, and generic forms in *Cane*, therefore, constitutes an argument for the spontaneity associated with "primitivism."

The tension between sophistication and spontaneity remained a dynamic source for Renaissance writers, but not for Toomer. Shortly after *Cane* was published he met Gurdjieff, had a mystical experience, and turned his life-long need for meaning toward a search for a transcendent principle of unity. One consequence was denial of the significance of racial identity. Another was production of writing increasingly distant from the sensual style of *Cane*. Toomer, once a harbinger of new art, became an enigmatic historical figure.

Only a small portion of his later writings was published. For critics the most notable piece is "Blue Meridian," a long, visionary poem about a new American race, which at its best resonates with the inspiration of Whitman. One must conclude that in Toomer biographical experience overwhelmed creative imagination. A search for identity became so compelling that he could no longer gain the distance needed to convert the motive of his life into the substance of successful literature.

—John M. Reilly

TOURGÉE, Albion W(inegar). Born in Williamsfield, Ohio, 2 May 1838. Educated at Kingsville Academy, Ohio, 1854–59; Rochester University, Rochester, New York, 1859–61, B.A. 1862; studied law: admitted to Ohio bar, 1864. Served in the 27th New York Volunteers, 1861: wounded at the first Battle of Bull Run, 1861; Lieutenant in the 105th Ohio Regiment, 1862–64: prisoner of war, 1863. Married Emma L. Kilbourne in 1863; one daughter, Assistant principal of a school in Wilson, New York, 1861; taught and wrote for a newspaper in Erie, Pennsylvania, 1864–65; settled in Greensboro, North Carolina, 1865; practised law; entered politics for "carpetbagger" interests, 1866; founded *Union Register*, which failed, 1867; delegate to the "carpetbag" conventions, 1868, 1875; judge, Superior Court of North Carolina, 1868–75; writer from 1874; pension agent, Raleigh, North Carolina, 1876–78; moved to New York, 1879, and settled in Mayville, 1881; editor, *Our Continent*, Philadelphia, 1882–84; regular contributor to the *Daily Inter Ocean*, Chicago, 1885–98; founded *The Basis: A Journal of Citizenship*, Buffalo, New York, 1895–96; U.S. Consul-General, Bordeaux, France, 1897–1905. *Died 21 May 1905.*

PUBLICATIONS

Fiction

Toinette. 1874; as *A Royal Gentleman*, 1881.
Figs and Thistles: A Western Story. 1879.
A Fool's Errand. 1879; revised edition, incorporating *The Invisible Empire*, 1880; edited by John Hope Franklin, 1961.
Bricks Without Straw. 1880; edited by Otto H. Olsen, 1969.
'Zouri's Christmas. 1881.
John Eax and Marmelon; or, The South Without the Shadow. 1882.
Hot Plowshares. 1883.
Button's Inn. 1887.
Black Ice. 1888.
With Gauge and Swallow, Attorneys. 1889.
Murvale Eastmas, Christian Socialist. 1890.
Pactolus Prime. 1890.
'89. 1891.
A Son of Old Harry. 1892.
Out of the Sunset Sea. 1893.
An Outing with the Queen of Hearts. 1894.
The Mortgage on the Hip-Roof House. 1896.
The Man Who Outlived Himself (stories). 1898.

Play

A Fool's Errand, with Steele MacKaye, from the novel by Tourgée, edited by Dean H. Keller. 1969.

Other

The Code of Civil Procedure of North Carolina, with Victor C. Barringer and Will B. Rodman. 1878.
An Appeal to Caesar. 1884.
The Veteran and His Pipe (essays). 1886.
Letters to a King. 1888.
The War of the Standards: Coin and Credit Versus Coin Without Credit. 1896.
The Story of a Thousand, Being a History of the 105th Volunteer Infantry, 1862 to 1865. 1896.
A Civil War Diary, edited by Dean H. Keller. 1965.

*

Bibliography: "A Checklist of the Writings of Tourgée" by Dean H. Keller, in *Studies in Bibliography 18*, 1965.

Critical Studies: *Tourgée* by Roy Floyd Dibble, 1921; *Tourgée* by Theodore L. Gross, 1963; *Carpetbagger's Crusade: The Life of Tourgée* by Otto H. Olsen, 1965.

* * *

Albion W. Tourgée's views on the art of the novel and his own practice as a novelist carry the unmistakable stamp of his active involvement as a journalist, polemicist, and judge in the political and public issues of the Reconstruction period. His unreserved preference for historical veracity and social purpose (as implied in his criticism of Henry James) always took precedence over subtleties of technique and nuances of character. Observing no separation between the role of the novelist and that of the historian, Tourgée conceived of the novel essentially as a frame for "a possible life . . . in a true environment," insisting that the test of artistic success was inevitably the consistency with which such a life related to its milieu and to the dominant predispositions of the age. Interestingly enough, such a conviction did not bring him any closer to the writers of a realist and naturalist persuasion whose treatment of human depravity and poverty he found crude and repulsive. His admiration, sometimes carried to uncritical extremes, was for the realism of James Fenimore Cooper's descriptions, for there he found the ideals of love, truth, and purity that were worthy of emulation by the citizen of a new republic. As the author of *The Code of Civil Procedure of North Carolina* and the editor of the *Union Register*, a newspaper firmly committed to radical reform, he promoted these ideals in practical ways.

Tourgée's best novels, *A Fool's Errand*, recounting a carpetbagger's grim struggle to work for the cause of equality and pacificism in the south, and *Bricks Without Straw*, concerned with an uneducated but enlightened black man's attempt to achieve selfhood, amplify and illustrate his fictional themes and moral concerns—the possibility of social amelioration, the problem of vindicating one's cherished beliefs in a hostile society, the responses evoked by the tender and redemptive sentiment of love, sympathy for blacks, and the selflessness of the Republican set against the cupidity of the southern white supremacist intent on denying political and civil rights to blacks. To these are added a preacher's zeal and intensity, a penchant for melodrama, a forceful style, and a penetrating if occasionally biased reading of the political climate in the south in the 1860's and 1870's. Tourgée's commitment to such themes and values places him securely, in Edmund Wilson's incontestable judgment, in the "second category of writers who aim primarily at social history. His narrative has spirit and movement; his insights are brilliantly revealing, and they are expressed with emotional conviction."

The inwardness of the imagination that Tourgée sought to exploit in his later fiction on his return to the north in 1879 produced disappointing results. The absence of concrete historical, political, and social contexts often led him to write sentimental romantic tales abounding with improbable coincidences and permeated by an impractical ethical and religious humanitarianism: in *Black Ice* a somnambulist, who has climbed to the top of a snowy mountain in search of her baby's grave, is heroically rescued; in *Button's Inn* the hero, an ex-murderer, is redeemed by conversion to Mormonism. The relative success of *'89*, in which Tourgée returned to his earlier themes in the original Southern setting, showed that he obviously was at ease in the comforts of a familiar environment and that he wrote most competently when called upon to provide a kind of fictional *apologia* for Radical Republicanism.

—Chirantan Kulshrestha

TRAVEN, B. Pseudonym for a writer whose identity has not been established. Now most frequently identified with Hermann Albert Otto Maximilian Feige: born in Swiebodzin, Poland, 28 February 1882; worked as apprentice locksmith for 4 years; adopted name Ret Marut and worked as actor in Germany, 1907–15; political activist: published journal *Der Ziegel Brenner*, 1917–22; press minister in brief left-wing government in Munich, 1919; arrested and escaped; left Germany for England, 1923 (jailed as illegal alien, 1923–24); moved to Mexico and adopted name Traven Torsvan; government photographer on expedition to Chiapas, 1926; became Mexican citizen, 1951; married Rosa Elena Luján in 1957; also used name Hal Croves; *died 26 March 1969*.

PUBLICATIONS

Fiction

Das Totenschiff. 1926; as *The Death Ship*, 1934.
Der Wobbly. 1926; as *Die Baumwollpflücker*, 1929; as *The Cotton-Pickers*, 1956.
Der Schatz der Sierra Madre. 1927; as *The Treasure of the Sierra Madre*, 1934.
Der Busch (stories). 1928; revised edition, 1930.
Die Brücke im Dschungel. 1929; as *The Bridge in the Jungle*, 1938.
Die weisse Rose. 1929; as *The White Rose*, 1965.
Der Karren. 1931; as *The Carreta*, 1935.
Regierung. 1931; as *Government*, 1935.
Der Marsch ins Reich der Caoba: Ein Kriegsmarsch. 1933; as *March to Caobaland*, 1961; as *March to the Montería*, 1964.
Die Rebellion der Gehenkten. 1936; as *The Rebellion of the Hanged*, 1952.
Die Troza. 1936.
Ein General kommt aus dem Dschungel. 1940; as *General from the Jungle*, 1954.
Macario (in German). 1950.
Aslan Norval (in German). 1960.
Stories by the Man Nobody Knows: Nine Tales. 1961.
The Night Visitor and Other Stories. 1966.
Maze of Love. 1967.
The Kidnapped Saint and Other Stories, edited by Rosa Elena Luján and Mina C. and H. Arthur Klein. 1975.
Das Frühwerk (by Ret Marut). 1977.
Khundar: Ein deutsches Märchen (by Ret Marut). 1977.
To the Honourable Miss S— and Other Stories (by Ret Marut), translated by Peter Silcock. 1981.

Other

Land des Frühlings (on Mexico). 1928.
Sonnen-Schöpfung: Indianische Legende. 1936; as *The Creation of the Sun and the Moon*, 1968.

*

Bibliography: "A Checklist of the Works of Traven and the Critical Estimates and Biographical Essays on Him" by E.R. Hagemann, in *Papers of the Bibliographical Society of America 53*, 1959.

Critical Studies: *Anonymity and Death: The Fiction of Traven* by Donald O. Chankin, 1975; *Traven: An Introduction* by Michael L. Baumann, 1976; *Das Traven Buch* edited by Johannes Beck and others, 1976; *The Mystery of Traven* by Judy Stone, 1977; *My Search for Traven* by Jonah Raskin, 1980; *The Man Who Was Traven* by Will Wyatt, 1980, as *The Secret of the Sierra Madre*, 1980.

* * *

B. Traven kept his identity a closely guarded secret and never gave interviews to the press. He had Marxist leanings, wrote usually in German, and died in Mexico City. He knew Mexico well: his novel *General from the Jungle* tells the story of a rebellion of Indians against a Mexican dictator. Among adventure writers he deserves a high place—on the same level as Jack London—while some of his themes bring to mind Conrad.

In all his fiction Traven is concerned with the problem of Mammon. "Gold is the devil," says one of the characters in *The Treasure of the Sierra Madre*—a book on which John Huston based the successful film. Traven's most famous novel, and his finest, is *The Death Ship*. When it first came out in the mid-1930's in Germany, it sold over 200,000 copies before it was banned. Sub-titled "The Story of an American Sailor," it might be better described as the story of a hero without a name, for the author regards the sailor on a death ship as a gladiatorial hero whose Emperor is Mammon. Death ships are those which carry contraband, with ammunition and rifles hidden in crates labelled "Toys" or "Cocoa" or "Corned Beef." The crews are enlisted from men on the run—no names, no questions—or from seamen who have lost their papers and so have no status. This is what happens to Traven's hero, who is informed by the American consul in Paris: "I doubt your birth as long as you have no certificate of birth. The fact that you are sitting in front of me is no proof of your birth."

Later the hero, after a series of adventures with the Belgian and Dutch police and a short spell in a prison in Toulouse, finds himself aboard the *Yorikke*, a death ship that has put into Barcelona. Taken on as a fireman, he is made to work as a coal-shoveller. In a ship as old and patched up as the *Yorikke*, there is a constant danger that he may be burnt by the darts of scalding steam which continually escape from the pipes. He has to learn to slither from point to point like a snake. "Only the best snake dancers survived. . . . Others who had tried and failed were no longer alive." (In another novel, *March to Caobaland*, Traven writes: "Indian mahogany workers can be fed as royally as the stokers and oilers of a death ship where, as a rule, the food is of the lowest quality possible.")

The Nazis banned *The Death Ship* because they thought it communist; some critics have said the same about Traven's other books. But this is to misinterpret them. Traven's fiction is as much an attack on bureaucrats, whatever their political creed, as it is a protest against the dictatorial power which money can invest in one man over another. Labour camps, no less than sweated labour, are both a part of the world of Mammon.

—Neville Braybrooke

TRILLING, Lionel. Born in New York City, 4 July 1905. Educated at Columbia University, New York, B.A. 1925, M.A. 1926, Ph.D. 1938. Married Diana Rubin (i.e., the writer Diana Trilling) in 1929; one son. Editorial assistant, *Menorah Journal*, New York, 1923–31; Instructor in English, University of Wisconsin, Madison, 1926–27, and Hunter College, New York, 1927–32; Instructor, 1932–38, Assistant Professor, 1939–45, Associate Professor, 1945–48, Professor of English, 1948–70, Woodberry Professor of Literature and Criticism, 1965–70, University Professor, 1970–74, and University Professor Emeritus, 1974–75, Columbia University. George Eastman Visiting Professor, Oxford University, 1964–65; Norton Visiting Professor of Poetry, Harvard University, Cambridge, Massachusetts, 1969–70; Visiting Fellow, All Souls College, Oxford, 1972–73. Co-founder and Senior Fellow, Kenyon School of English, Kenyon College, Gambier, Ohio (now Indiana University School of Letters, Bloomington). Recipient: Brandeis University Creative Arts Award, 1968. D.Litt.: Trinity College, Hartford, Connecticut, 1955; Harvard University, 1962; Case Western Reserve University, Cleveland, 1968; Durham University, England, 1973; Leicester University, England, 1973; L.H.D.: Northwestern University, Evanston, Illinois, 1963; Brandeis University, Waltham, Massachusetts, 1974; Yale University, New Haven, Connecticut, 1974. Member, American Academy, 1951; American Academy of Arts and Sciences, 1952. *Died 5 November 1975.*

PUBLICATIONS

Collections

Works (Uniform Edition), edited by Diana Trilling. 12 vols., 1978–80.

Fiction

The Middle of the Journey. 1947.
Of This Time, Of That Place and Other Stories, edited by Diana Trilling. 1979.

Other

Matthew Arnold. 1939; revised edition, 1949.
E.M. Forster. 1943; revised edition, 1965.
The Liberal Imagination: Essays on Literature and Society. 1950.
The Opposing Self: Nine Essays in Criticism. 1955.
Freud and the Crisis of Our Culture. 1956; revised version, in *Beyond Culture*, 1965.
A Gathering of Fugitives. 1956.
The Scholar's Caution and the Scholar's Courage. 1962.
Beyond Culture: Essays on Literature and Learning. 1965.
Sincerity and Authenticity. 1972.
Mind in the Modern World. 1973.
Prefaces to The Experience of Literature. 1979.
The Last Decade: Essays and Reviews, edited by Diana Trilling. 1979.
Speaking of Literature and Society, edited by Diana Trilling. 1980.

Editor, *The Portable Matthew Arnold*. 1949; as *The Essential Matthew Arnold*, 1969.
Editor, *Selected Letters of John Keats*. 1951.
Editor, with Steven Marcus, *The Life and Work of Sigmund Freud*, by Ernest Jones. 1961.
Editor, *The Experience of Literature: A Reader with Commentaries*. 1967.
Editor, *Literary Criticism: An Introductory Reader*. 1970.

*

Critical Studies: *Three American Moralists: Mailer, Bellow, Trilling* by Nathan A. Scott, Jr., 1973; *Trilling: Negative Capability and the Wisdom of Avoidance* by Robert Boyers, 1977; *Art, Politics, and Will: Essays in Honor of Trilling* edited by Quentin Anderson and others, 1977; *Three Honest Men: Edmund Wilson, F.R. Leavis, Trilling: A Critical Mosaic* by Philip French, 1980; *Trilling: Criticism and Politics* by William M. Chace, 1980; *Trilling* by Edward Joseph Shoben, Jr., 1981; *Trilling and the Fate of Cultural Criticism* by Mark Krupnick, 1986.

* * *

Lionel Trilling was one of America's most distinguished literary critics. His first two books were on Matthew Arnold and E.M. Forster, and these were followed by a number of essays in which, like Arnold and Forster, he tried to show how liberal cultural values fostered by the study of literature could help civilization. In some of his later works, especially perhaps in *Beyond Culture*, this liberal stance, though aggressively stated, is maintained with a good deal of pessimism.

Keenly interested in politics in the early 1950's, Trilling seemed optimistic then about the fruitful interplay between politics and literature. Later, with the failure of the campus revolts of the 1960's and the retreat of literary criticism into its own peculiar jargon-ridden fortress, he became less confident, although *Sincerity and Authenticity* still maintains a high moral tone and is still written with the same sinewy elegance as the earlier works. The range of Trilling's criticism is very wide; he wrote brilliantly on Keats, and Joyce and Freud, two writers not noted for sweetness or light, are treated at length and with perception. Trilling founded no critical movement, and his wish to see, like Arnold, things steadily and whole, may seem unfashionable, but truth does not cease to be truth merely because people have ceased to believe it.

An early short story, "Of This Time, Of That Place," first published in *Partisan Review* in 1943, is curiously prophetic. It shows how a university teacher, Joseph Howe, deals with two students, the brilliant but mad Tertan, and the amoral and philistine Blackburn. Tertan fails and Blackburn succeeds in spite of Howe's good intentions.

An equal pessimism is found in Trilling's one novel, *The Middle of the Journey*. The central character of this novel, John Laskell, recovering from a serious illness, visits his friends the Crooms in a Connecticut village. He finds himself involved with a woman in the village, Emily Caldwell, whose husband, Duck, works for the Crooms. A fleeting affair with Emily has little chance of success as her daughter Susan dies, attacked by the drunken Duck, though she has a weak heart and her death is accidental. The Crooms, who are presented unsympathetically, maintain that it is society, not Duck, who is responsible, whereas another friend of Laskell's, Gifford Maxim, a renegade communist who has adopted a Christian stance and whose defection is bitterly resented by the Crooms, thinks that Duck is guilty. Laskell takes up an indeterminate position, but does not feel that the rejection of the dogmatism of his friends is particularly effective, any more than his gesture of paying for Susan's funeral achieves anything. Written before the McCarthy witch-hunts had brought the issue of communism in America into the limelight, *The Middle of the Journey* may seem a confusing novel at a time when McCarthy himself is virtually forgotten. But it is not just a novel about communism versus Christianity, as it might seem to be at first sight; it is, perhaps a little too obviously, a novel which strives to assert the liberal values of Forster and Arnold in an unsympathetic world, and as such, should take its place with Trilling's critical works.

—T.J. Winnifrith

TRUMBULL, John. Born in Westbury, Connecticut, 24 April 1750. Educated at Yale University, New Haven, Connecticut (Berkeley Scholar), 1763–70, B.A. 1767, M.A. 1770; studied law in John Adams's office in Boston, 1773; admitted to Connecticut bar, 1773. Married Sarah Hubbard in 1776; seven children. Schoolteacher and law student, Wethersfield, Connecticut, 1770–71; contributed essays (as "The Correspondent") to *Connecticut Journal*, 1770–73; tutor, Yale University, 1772–73; lawyer in New Haven, 1774–77, Westbury, 1777–81, and Hartford, Connecticut, 1781–1825. Treasurer, Yale University, 1776–82; member, Hartford City Council, 1784–93; state attorney for Hartford, 1789–95; member, General Assembly of Connecticut, 1792, 1800–01; judge, Connecticut Superior Court, 1801–19, and Supreme Court of Errors, 1808–19; lived in Detroit, Michigan, 1825–31. Literary leader of the "Hartford Wits" in the 1780's and 1790's. LL.D.: Yale University, 1818. Member, American Academy of Arts and Sciences, 1791. *Died 11 May 1831.*

PUBLICATIONS

Collections

The Works, edited by Theodore Sizer. 1950; supplement, *The Autobiography*, 1953.

The Satiric Poems, edited by Edwin T. Bowden. 1962.

Verse

An Elegy on the Death of Mr. Buckingham St. John. 1771.
The Progress of Dulness. 3 vols., 1772–73.
M'Fingal: A Modern Epic Poem, Canto First. 1775 (?); *M'Fingal in Four Cantos*, 1782; edited by Benson J. Lossing, 1864.
The Poetical Works. 2 vols., 1820.
The Anarchiad: A New England Poem, with others, edited by Luther G. Riggs. 1861.

Other

An Essay on the Use and Advantages of the Fine Arts. 1770.
Biographical Sketch of the Character of Governor Trumbull. 1809.

*

Critical Studies: *Trumbull, Connecticut Wit* by Alexander Cowie, 1936 (includes bibliography); *Trumbull* by Victor E. Gimmestad, 1974.

* * *

John Trumbull is best remembered as spokesman for the group of writers known as the "Connecticut" or "Hartford Wits." This group, which included Joel Barlow, Timothy Dwight, and David Humphreys, among others, was active during the years following the Revolutionary War. Most of its members, Trumbull included, were educated at Yale and were extremely conservative in their political and literary views. They appreciated neoclassical decorum, and, from their center at Hartford, Connecticut, they used their literary talent to exert pressure on the nation to stem the rise of Jeffersonian democracy and to create a strong federal government, themes that the group collaboratively explored in *The Anarchiad*, written in 1786 and 1787.

A lawyer by profession, Trumbull was also devoted to the arts. He composed verses at the age of four and passed the entrance exam to Yale when he was only seven. He possessed a keen mind and a shrewd wit, which he used to his advantage when he wrote satire. He was a master of the octosyllabic line, and delighted in writing hudibrastic verse. For poetic models, Trumbull emulated the works of Pope, Swift, and Dryden. More concerned with ideas than with emotions, Trumbull valued restraint and disliked sentiment. Needless to say, he did not appreciate the Romantics, especially Wordsworth and Coleridge, who he felt placed expression before reason and subjectivity before objectivity.

Trumbull possessed a genuine gift for humor: he was at his best when writing burlesque or satire, and found more serious verse difficult to sustain. Like his contemporaries, he considered the ode and the elegy superior in literary merit to satire, and although he frequently tried to write in these forms, his "Ode to Sleep: An Elegy on the Times," and *An Elegy on the Death of Mr. Buckingham St. John* are among his least interesting poems. More engaging is *The Progress of Dulness*, a three-part satirical epic, written while Trumbull was studying for his master's degree at Yale, which ridicules outmoded educational practices and calls for a more useful system of instruction than that experienced by Trumbull as an undergraduate.

His most famous poem, *M'Fingal*, earned Trumbull the title of "Poet of the Revolution." Written in the tradition of Dryden's *Mac Flecknoe*, it is a mock heroic epic about the raucous adventures of a Tory squire patterned after a British General, Thomas Gage, but named M'Fingal, who tries to prevent a group of patriots from giving further support to the Revolutionary War and is himself tarred and feathered in the process. During the Revolutionary War, *M'Fingal* was used to stir up popular sentiment against the British, and it was even printed in England, where its literary merit drew the praise of critics who were impartial enough to disassociate their political allegiances from their critical pronouncements. In America, the popularity of *M'Fingal* continued long after it ceased to be useful as anti-British propaganda. Today it is recognized as one of the finest political verse satires written in American prior to the Civil War.

Trumbull is also remembered for his essays. Like his verse, they are best when they satirize institutions and events. Favorite targets are education, the clergy, and, of course, the British, whom he never really despised but was always ready to satirize. He patterned his prose style, which is witty and extremely polished, after that of Addison and Steele, whom he very much admired.

—James A. Levernier

TUCKERMAN, Frederick Goddard. Born in Boston, Massachusetts, 4 February 1821. Educated at Bishop Hopkins' School, Burlington, Vermont, 1833–37; Harvard University, Cambridge, Massachusetts, 1837–38, and Harvard Law School, 1839–42; admitted to Suffolk County, Massachusetts bar, 1844. Married Hannah Lucinda Jones in 1847 (died, 1857); three children. Briefly practised law; lived in Greenfield, Massachusetts, 1847–73. *Died 9 May 1873.*

PUBLICATIONS

Collections

The Complete Poems, edited by N. Scott Momaday. 1965.

Verse

Poems. 1860.

*

Critical Studies: *Tuckerman* by Samuel A. Golden, 1966; "Alone with God and Nature: The Poetry of Jones Very and Tuckerman" by David Seed, in *Nineteenth-Century American Poetry* edited by A. Robert Lee, 1985.

* * *

Because Frederick Goddard Tuckerman's poetry was rescued from near-oblivion only fairly recently, a natural temptation for the critic is to fan the excitement generated by that rescue by overstating the value of the poetry. This temptation should be avoided, for much of Tuckerman's poetry is pedestrian.

Tuckerman's narrative poems are often merely inflated anecdotes. Many poems are maimed by tepid sermonizing. Sometimes Tuckerman's diction is ornate and tediously archaic, and his syntax awkward, even puzzling. Several sonnets are poorly constructed; the climax is followed by a number of distractingly anti-climactic lines. In his perceptive book on Tuckerman, Samuel A. Golden summarizes part of Tuckerman's world view. For the poet, "man's certainty rests in God." Unfortunately, Tuckerman's expressions of his religious faith are almost always inadequately documented and, as a result, are verbally bland, and quite unconvincing.

Nonetheless, the excitement caused by the rediscovery of Tuckerman's work is justified. Five sonnet sequences and "The Cricket"—all inspired by the death, after childbirth, of Tuckerman's wife—represent his finest efforts. Both the content and the form of these poems are, at their best, of a high quality.

In the 19th century most American poets regarded nature from a wholly sentimental point of view. Tuckerman tempered this view. As his sonnets make clear, he, too, believed that nature was a part of God's cosmic scheme, but, unlike his contemporaries, he did not proceed to interpret nature for the benefit of his readers. Instead, he admitted that he did not comprehend the ways of nature. Nor did nature provide Tuckerman with an all-encompassing comfort. "The Cricket" and the sonnets report that he gained solace from nature only after severely qualifying the degree of solace he hoped to gain.

Although Tuckerman—like his Transcendentalist peers—sometimes yearned to merge with nature, he chose to resist this impulse. In fact he came to realize that it was impossible to fulfill such an impulse. While the Transcendentalists found nature (indeed, the whole universe) to be wondrously like their own personalities, Tuckerman found nature to be quixotic, contradictory, enigmatic, and fundamentally separate from himself.

In "The Cricket" and the first two sonnet sequences especially, Tuckerman's stylistic weaknesses are far outweighed by many fine phrases, metaphors, and long descriptive passages enhanced by skillful rhythms, and rhyming. In "The Cricket," for instance, Tuckerman speaks of dead friends with "faces where but now a gap must be" and of death as the "crowning vacancy." He describes a night of love in terms of "wringing arms . . . / Closed eyes, and kisses that would not let go." His best sonnets also display a superb blending of form and content.

—Robert K. Johnson

TWAIN, Mark. Pseudonym for Samuel Langhorne Clemens. Born in Florida, Missouri, 30 November 1835; moved to Hannibal, Missouri, 1839. Married Olivia Langdon in 1870 (died, 1904); one son and three daughters. Printer's apprentice and typesetter for Hannibal newspapers, 1847–50; helped brother with Hannibal *Journal*, 1850–52; typesetter and printer in St. Louis, New York, Philadelphia, for Keokuk *Saturday Post*, Iowa, 1853–56, and in Cincinnati, 1857; apprentice river pilot, on the Mississippi, 1857–58; licensed as pilot, 1859–60; went to Nevada as secretary to his brother, then on the staff of the Governor, and also worked as goldminer, 1861; staff member, Virginia City *Territorial Enterprise*, Nevada, 1862–64 (first used pseudonym Mark Twain, 1863); reporter, San Francisco *Morning Call*, 1864; correspondent, Sacramento *Union*,

1866, and San Francisco *Alta California*, 1866–69: visited Sandwich (i.e., Hawaiian) Islands, 1866, and France, Italy, and Palestine, 1867; lecturer from 1867; editor, *Express*, Buffalo, New York, 1869–71; moved to Hartford, Connecticut and became associated with Charles L. Webster Publishing Company, 1884; invested in unsuccessful Paige typesetter and went bankrupt, 1894 (last debts paid, 1898); lived mainly in Europe, 1896–1900, New York, 1900–07, and Redding, Connecticut, 1907–10. M.A.: Yale University, New Haven, Connecticut, 1888; Litt.D.: Yale University, 1901; Oxford University, 1907; LL.D.: University of Missouri, Columbia, 1902. Member, American Academy, 1904. *Died 21 April 1910.*

PUBLICATIONS

Collections

Letters, edited by Albert Bigelow Paine. 2 vols., 1917.
The Writings (Definitive Edition), edited by Albert Bigelow Paine. 37 vols., 1922–25.
The Portable Twain, edited by Bernard De Voto. 1946.
The Complete Short Stories, edited by Charles Neider. 1957.
Selected Shorter Writings, edited by Walter Blair. 1962.
The Complete Novels, edited by Charles Neider. 2 vols., 1964.
Twain Papers, edited by Robert H. Hirst. 1967—
Works (Iowa-California Edition), edited by John C. Gerber and others. 1972—
Mississippi Writings (Library of America), edited by Guy A. Cardwell. 1982.
The Innocents Abroad and Roughing It (Library of America), edited by Guy A. Cardwell. 1984.

Fiction

The Celebrated Jumping Frog of Calaveras County and Other Sketches, edited by Charles Henry Webb. 1867.
The Innocents Abroad; or, The New Pilgrims' Progress. 1869.
The Innocents at Home. 1872.
The Gilded Age: A Tale of Today, with Charles Dudley Warner. 1873; *The Adventures of Colonel Sellers, Being Twain's Share of The Gilded Age*, edited by Charles Neider, 1965; complete text, edited by Bryant Morey French, 1972.
The Adventures of Tom Sawyer. 1876.
A True Story and the Recent Carnival of Crime. 1877.
Date 1601: Conversation as It Was by the Social Fireside in the Time of the Tudors. 1880; as *1601*, edited by Franklin J. Meine, 1939.
A Tramp Abroad. 1880.
The Prince and the Pauper. 1881.
The Stolen White Elephant. 1882.
The Adventures of Huckleberry Finn (Tom Sawyer's Comrade). 1884; as *Adventures of Huckleberry Finn*, 1885; edited by Sculley Bradley and others, 1977.
A Connecticut Yankee in King Arthur's Court. 1889; as *A Yankee at the Court of King Arthur*, 1889; edited by Allison R. Ensor, 1982.
The American Claimant. 1892.
Merry Tales. 1892.
The £1,000,000 Bank-Note and Other New Stories. 1893.
Pudd'nhead Wilson. 1894; augmented edition, as *The Tragedy of Pudd'nhead Wilson, and The Comedy of Those Extraordinary Twins*, 1894; edited by Sidney E. Berger, 1980.
Tom Sawyer Abroad. 1894.
Tom Sawyer Abroad, Tom Sawyer, Detective, and Other Stories. 1896; as *Tom Sawyer, Detective, as Told by Huck Finn, and Other Tales*, 1896.
Personal Recollections of Joan of Arc. 1896.
The Man That Corrupted Hadleyburg and Other Stories and Essays. 1900.
A Double Barrelled Detective Story. 1902.
Extracts from Adam's Diary. 1904.
A Dog's Tale. 1904.
The $30,000 Bequest and Other Stories. 1906.
Eve's Diary. 1906.
A Horse's Tale. 1907.
Extract from Captain Stormfield's Visit to Heaven. 1909; revised edition, as *Report from Paradise*, edited by Dixon Wecter, 1952.
The Mysterious Stranger: A Romance. 1916; *Mysterious Stranger Manuscripts*, edited by William M. Gibson, 1969.
The Curious Republic of Gondour and Other Whimsical Sketches. 1919.
The Mysterious Stranger and Other Stories. 1922.
A Boy's Adventure. 1928.
The Adventures of Thomas Jefferson Snodgrass, edited by Charles Honce. 1928.
Jim Smiley and His Jumping Frog, edited by Albert Bigelow Paine. 1940.
A Murder, A Mystery, and a Marriage. 1945.
The Complete Humorous Sketches and Tales, edited by Charles Neider. 1961.
Simon Wheeler, Detective, edited by Franklin R. Rogers. 1963.
Satires and Burlesques, edited by Franklin R. Rogers. 1967.
Twain's Hannibal, Huck, and Tom, edited by Walter Blair. 1969.
Twain's Quarrel with Heaven: Captain Stormfield's Visit to Heaven and Other Sketches, edited by Roy B. Browne. 1970.
Early Tales and Sketches, edited by Edgar M. Branch and Robert H. Hirst. 2 vols., 1979–81.
Wapping Alice. 1981.
The Science Fiction of Twain, edited by David Ketterer. 1984.
Twain at His Best, edited by Charles Neider. 1986.

Plays

Ah Sin, with Bret Harte (produced 1877). Edited by Frederick Anderson, 1961.
Colonel Sellers as a Scientist, with William Dean Howells, from the novel *The Gilded Age* by Twain and Charles Dudley Warner (produced 1887). In *Complete Plays of Howells*, edited by Walter J. Meserve, 1960.
The Quaker City Holy Land Excursion: An Unfinished Play. 1927.

Verse

On the Poetry of Twain, with Selections from His Verse, edited by Arthur L. Scott. 1966.

Other

Twain's (Burlesque) Autobiography and First Romance. 1871.
Memoranda: From the Galaxy. 1871.
Roughing It. 1872.
A Curious Dream and Other Sketches. 1872.
Screamers: A Gathering of Scraps of Humour, Delicious Bits, and Short Stories. 1872.
Sketches. 1874.
Sketches, New and Old. 1875.
Old Times on the Mississippi. 1876; as *The Mississippi Pilot*, 1877.
An Idle Excursion. 1878.
Punch, Brothers, Punch! and Other Sketches. 1878.
A Curious Experience. 1881.
Life on the Mississippi. 1883.
Facts for Twain's Memory Builder. 1891.
How to Tell a Story and Other Essays. 1897; revised edition, 1900.
Following the Equator: A Journey Around the World. 1897; as *More Tramps Abroad*, 1897.
Writings (Autograph Edition). 25 vols., 1899–1907.
The Pains of Lowly Life. 1900.
English as She Is Taught. 1900; revised edition, 1901.
To the Person Sitting in Darkness. 1901.
Edmund Burke on Croker, and Tammany. 1901.
My Début as a Literary Person, with Other Essays and Stories. 1903.
Twain on Vivisection. 1905(?).
King Leopold's Soliloquy: A Defense of His Congo Rule. 1905; revised edition, 1906.
Editorial Wild Oats. 1905.
What Is Man? 1906.
On Spelling. 1906.
Writings (Hillcrest Edition). 25 vols., 1906–07.
Christian Science, with Notes Containing Corrections to Date. 1907.
Is Shakespeare Dead? From My Autobiography. 1909.
Speeches, edited by F.A. Nast. 1910; revised edition, 1923.
Queen Victoria's Jubilee. 1910.
Letter to the California Pioneers. 1911.
What Is Man? and Other Essays. 1917.
Moments with Twain, edited by Albert Bigelow Paine. 1920.
Europe and Elsewhere. 1923.
Autobiography, edited by Albert Bigelow Paine. 2 vols., 1924.
Sketches of the Sixties by Bret Harte and Twain . . . from The Californian 1864–67. 1926; revised edition, 1927.
The Suppressed Chapter of "Following the Equator." 1928.
A Letter from Twain to His Publisher, Chatto and Windus. 1929.
Twain the Letter Writer, edited by Cyril Clemens. 1932.
Works. 23 vols., 1933.
The Family Twain (selections). 1935.
The Twain Omnibus, edited by Max J. Herzberg. 1935.
Representative Selections, edited by Fred L. Pattee. 1935.
Notebook, edited by Albert Bigelow Paine. 1935.
Letters from the Sandwich Islands, Written for the Sacramento Union, edited by G. Ezra Dane. 1937.
The Washoe Giant in San Francisco, Being Heretofore Uncollected Sketches, edited by Franklin Walker. 1938.
Twain's Western Years, Together with Hitherto Unreprinted Clemens Western Items, by Ivan Benson. 1938.
Letters from Honolulu Written for the Sacramento Union, edited by Thomas Nickerson. 1939.
Twain in Eruption: Hitherto Unpublished Pages about Men and Events, edited by Bernard De Voto. 1940.
Travels with Mr. Brown, Being Heretofore Uncollected Sketches Written for the San Francisco Alta California in 1866 and 1867, edited by Franklin Walker and G. Ezra Dane. 1940.
Republican Letters, edited by Cyril Clemens. 1941.
Letters to Will Bowen, edited by Theodore Hornberger. 1941.
Letters in the Muscatine Journal, edited by Edgar M. Branch. 1942.
Washington in 1868, edited by Cyril Clemens. 1943.
Twain, Business Man, edited by Samuel Charles Webster. 1946.
The Letters of Quintus Curtius Snodgrass, edited by Ernest E. Leisy. 1946.
Twain in Three Moods: Three New Items of Twainiana, edited by Dixon Wecter. 1948.
The Love Letters, edited by Dixon Wecter. 1949.
Twain to Mrs. Fairbanks, edited by Dixon Wecter. 1949.
Twain to Uncle Remus 1881–1885, edited by Thomas H. English. 1953.
Twins of Genius: Letters of Twain, Cable, and Others, edited by Guy A. Cardwell. 1953.
Twain of the Enterprise, edited by Henry Nash Smith and Frederick Anderson. 1957.
Traveling with the Innocents Abroad: Twain's Original Reports from Europe and the Holy Land, edited by Daniel Morley McKeithan. 1958.
The Autobiography, edited by Charles Neider. 1959.
The Art, Humor, and Humanity of Twain, edited by Minnie M. Brashear and Robert M. Rodney. 1959.
Twain and the Government, edited by Svend Petersen. 1960.
Twain-Howells Letters: The Correspondence of Samuel L. Clemens and William Dean Howells 1872–1910, edited by Henry Nash Smith and William M. Gibson. 2 vols., 1960; abridged edition, as *Selected Twain-Howells Letters*, 1967.
Your Personal Twain. . . . 1960.
Life as I Find It: Essays, Sketches, Tales, and Other Material, edited by Charles Neider. 1961.
The Travels of Twain, edited by Charles Neider. 1961.
Contributions to The Galaxy 1868–1871, edited by Bruce R. McElderry. 1961.
Twain on the Art of Writing, edited by Martin B. Fried. 1961.
Letters to Mary, edited by Lewis Leary. 1961.
The Pattern for Twain's "Roughing It": Letters from Nevada by Samuel and Orion Clemens 1861–1862, edited by Franklin R. Rogers. 1961.
Letters from the Earth, edited by Bernard De Voto. 1962.
Twain on the Damned Human Race, edited by Janet Smith. 1962.
The Complete Essays, edited by Charles Neider. 1963.
Twain's San Francisco, edited by Bernard Taper. 1963.
The Forgotten Writings of Twain, edited by Henry Duskus. 1963.
General Grant by Matthew Arnold, with a Rejoinder by Twain (lecture), edited by John Y. Simon. 1966.
Letters from Hawaii, edited by A. Grove Day. 1966.
Which Was the Dream? and Other Symbolic Writings of the Later Years, edited by John S. Tuckey. 1967.
The Complete Travel Books, edited by Charles Neider. 1967.
Letters to His Publishers 1867–1894, edited by Hamlin Hill. 1967.

Clemens of the Call: Twain in California, edited by Edgar M. Branch. 1969.
Correspondence with Henry Huttleston Rogers 1893–1909, edited by Lewis Leary. 1969.
Man Is the Only Animal That Blushes—or Needs To: The Wisdom of Twain, edited by Michael Joseph. 1970.
Everybody's Twain, edited by Caroline Thomas Harnsberger. 1972.
Fables of Man, edited by John S. Tuckey. 1972.
A Pen Warmed Up In Hell: Twain in Protest, edited by Frederick Anderson. 1972.
What Is Man? and Other Philosophical Writings, edited by Paul Baender, in *Works*. 1973.
The Choice Humorous Works of Twain. 1973.
Notebooks and Journals, edited by Frederick Anderson and others. 1975—
Letters from the Sandwich Islands, edited by Joan Abramson. 1975.
Twain Speaking, edited by Paul Fatout. 1976.
The Mammoth Cod, and Address to the Stomach Club. 1976.
The Comic Twain Reader, edited by Charles Neider. 1977.
Interviews with Clemens 1874–1910, edited by Louis J. Budd. 1977.
Twain Speaks for Himself, edited by Paul Fatout. 1978.
The Devil's Race-Track: Twain's Great Dark Writings: The Best from "Which Was the Dream" and "Fables of Man," edited by John S. Tuckey. 1980.
Selected Letters, edited by Charles Neider. 1982.
Plymouth Rock and the Pilgrims, and Other Salutary Platform Opinions, edited by Charles Neider. 1984.
Twain Laughing: Humorous Stories by and about Clemens, edited by P.M. Zall. 1985.

Translator, *Slovenly Peter (Der Struwwelpeter)*. 1935.

*

Bibliography: *A Bibliography of the Works of Twain* by Merle Johnson, revised edition, 1935; in *Bibliography of American Literature* by Jacob Blanck, 1957; *Twain: A Reference Guide* by Thomas Asa Tenney, 1977; *Twain International: A Bibliography and Interpretation of His Worldwide Popularity* edited by Robert H. Rodney, 1982.

Critical Studies: *My Twain: Reminiscences and Criticisms* by William Dean Howells, 1910, edited by Marilyn Austin Baldwin, 1967; *Twain: A Biography* by Albert Bigelow Paine, 3 vols., 1912, abridged edition, as *A Short Life of Twain*, 1920; *The Ordeal of Twain* by Van Wyck Brooks, 1920, revised edition, 1933; *Twain's America*, 1932, and *Twain at Work*, 1942, both by Bernard De Voto; *Twain: The Man and His Work* by Edward Wagenknecht, 1935, revised edition, 1961, 1967; *Twain: Man and Legend* by De Lancey Ferguson, 1943; *The Literary Apprenticeship of Twain* by Edgar M. Branch, 1950; *Twain as a Literary Artist* by Gladys Bellamy, 1950; *Mark Twain and Huck Finn* by Walter Blair, 1960; *Twain* by Lewis Leary, 1960, and *A Casebook on Twain's Wound* edited by Leary, 1962; *Twain and Southwestern Humor* by Kenneth S. Lynn, 1960; *The Innocent Eye: Childhood in Twain's Imagination* by Albert E. Stone, 1961; *Twain: Social Philosopher*, 1962, and *Our Twain: The Making of a Public Personality*, 1983, both by Louis J. Budd, and *Critical Essays on Twain 1867–1910*, 1982, *Critical Essays on Twain 1910–1980*, 1983, and *New Essays on Adventures of Huckleberry Finn*, 1985, all edited by Budd; *Twain: The Development of a Writer* by Henry Nash Smith, 1962, and *Twain: A Collection of Critical Essays* edited by Smith, 1963; *Discussions of Twain* edited by Guy A. Cardwell, 1963; *Mr. Clemens and Mark Twain: A Biography*, 1966, and *Twain and His World*, 1974, both by Justin Kaplan; *Twain: The Fate of Humor* by James M. Cox, 1966; *Twain as Critic* by Sydney J. Krause, 1967; *Twain: God's Fool* by Hamlin Hill, 1973; *Plots and Characters in the Works of Twain* by Robert L. Gale, 2 vols., 1973; *The Dramatic Unity of Huckleberry Finn* by George C. Carrington, Jr., 1976; *The Art of Twain* by William M. Gibson, 1976; *Twain: A Collection of Criticism* edited by Dean Morgan Schmitter, 1976; *Twain as a Literary Comedian* by David E.E. Sloane, 1979; *Twain's Last Years as a Writer* by William R. Macnaughton, 1979; *Critical Approaches to Twain's Short Stories* edited by Elizabeth McMahan, 1981; *Twain's Escape from Time: A Study of Patterns and Images* by Susan K. Harris, 1982; *Writing Tom Sawyer: The Adventures of a Classic* by Charles A. Norton, 1983; *Twain* by Robert Keith Miller, 1983; *The Authentic Twain: A Biography of Clemens* by Everett Emerson, 1984; *One Hundred Years of Huckleberry Finn* edited by Robert Sattelmeyer and J. Donald Crowley, 1985; *The Making of Twain* by John Lauber, 1985; *Huck Finn among the Critics: A Centennial Selection* edited by M. Thomas Inge, 1985.

* * *

Samuel Langhorne Clemens, better known as Mark Twain, remains one of America's most widely read authors. To a great extent his popularity has rested upon his humor. It would be a mistake, however, to think of him simply as a humorist. To do so is to overlook the sharpness of his observation, the penetration of his social criticism, the depth of his concern for human suffering, and the clarity and extraordinary beauty of his style.

Storytelling came easily to Twain because he grew up in the little town of Hannibal on the Mississippi river where the telling of tall tales was one of the chief pastimes. Even as a boy he developed a reputation for yarnspinning, a reputation he strengthened while a pilot on the Mississippi and a newspaperman in Nevada and California. Before he left California for the East in 1867 he had begun to deliver humorous lectures, a practice that he continued on and off until almost the end of his life. Oral storytelling was immensely useful to him as a writer, for it taught him the value of such stylistic elements as point of view, proportion, timing, climax, concreteness, and dialogue that suggests real talk. He learned that the ear can catch much that the eye will miss; before finishing *Huckleberry Finn*, for example, he read it aloud over and over to make sure that it *sounded* right.

It should not be thought, however, that Twain was an untutored genius who became a fine writer simply because he could tell a good tale. To be sure he had only a few years of formal schooling. But he worked in newspaper offices under some of the finest journalists of the time. More importantly he was a steady reader. A limited list of his reading would include American newspaper humor; popular fiction, as well as juvenile fiction; parodies and burlesques; travel books; the novels of such writers as Cervantes and Dickens (whom he admired) and Austen and Scott (whom he did not admire); history, biography, and autobiography; scientific works; and the writings of such persons as Hobbes, Bentham, Paine, Jefferson, Macaulay, Darwin, Carlyle, and especially W.E.H. Lecky. Most of Twain's important works are a blend of his reading and his personal experience given form by his imagination.

Naturally enough he began his literary career by writing humorous sketches for midwestern and western newspapers. These apprentice pieces are derivative, satiric, and often gamey. About the only one that shows Twain's real promise as a literary figure is "The Celebrated Jumping Frog of Calaveras County." Significantly he wrote it for eastern instead of western publication. Van Wyck Brooks has argued that an eastern wife and eastern literary friends stunted Twain's artistic growth, even emasculated it. But most critics agree with Bernard De Voto that Twain would probably have remained little more than a newspaper humorist without the influence of eastern readers and writers. One fact is certain: once Twain began writing for an eastern audience he dropped the gaminess that had characterized his earlier work. Mrs. Clemens has been criticized for being too much of the moral censor, but the facts seem to indicate that Twain censored himself far more than did his wife or any of his friends. Ribald in some of his speeches at men's banquets and in a few works meant only for men readers (e.g., *1601*) he rarely in his major works alludes even to romance between the sexes except in conventional Victorian ways.

Twain continued to write short humorous sketches all through his life. His first longer works were travel books: *The Innocents Abroad* and *Roughing It*—followed later by *A Tramp Abroad, Life on the Mississippi*, and *Following the Equator*. Actually, the shift from short sketches to travel books was minimal since Twain's travel works were simply series of sketches, tales, and anecdotes strung together by loose chronological threads. Based largely on letters he wrote for the *Alta California, The Innocents Abroad* relates episodes from a trip Twain took to the Holy Land in 1867. It is not a tightly constructed book but a literary vaudeville show in which the reader's pleasure comes from the variety rather than the cohesion. As narrator, Twain shifts his role back and forth from a superior person (e.g., a gentleman or a teacher) to an inferior person (e.g., a simpleton or a sufferer) with unexpected and hilarious results. The appeal of *The Innocents Abroad* lies mainly in its humor, but in its time it also satisfied a growing curiosity in America about foreign lands, and in treating European culture without the customary deference it gave Americans an opportunity to feel less inferior about their own culture. Sold from door to door by agents of the American Publishing Company, a subscription house that published Twain's early books, it was an extraordinary success even though the times were hard.

Roughing It was even more successful and has continued to be one of Twain's best sellers. It is an account of his experiences in Nevada, California, and the Hawaiian Islands from 1861 through 1866. A somewhat more coherent account than *The Innocents Abroad*, it is still primarily a series of sketches, actual and imagined, salted with old anecdotes and folklore. Although as narrator he again plays a variety of roles for comic effect, there is in *Roughing It* a basic consistency as Twain shows himself developing from a callow greenhorn to the experienced old-timer. *A Tramp Abroad* recounts a trip with Joseph Twichell, a Hartford minister, through parts of Germany, Switzerland, and Italy in 1878. It also contains such famous set-pieces as "Baker's Blue-Jay Yarn" and "The Awful German Language." *Life on the Mississippi* is the most disconnected of the travel books. The best portion, chapters IV-XVII, was published in seven installments in the *Atlantic Monthly* in 1875 under the title "Old Times on the Mississippi." These chapters offer comic glimpses of Twain's experience as an apprentice pilot. The remainder of the book, sprinkled with many irrelevancies, tells of a trip down and up the Mississippi from New Orleans to St. Paul taken in 1882. *Following the Equator* narrates the story of the around-the-world lecture tour Twain took in 1895–96 with Mrs. Clemens and his daughter Clara in an attempt to recoup some of the fortune he had just lost. Financially the trip was a success, but it was hard on his health and ended in misery when news came to them in England that their oldest daughter, Susy, was dying of meningitis. The book, Twain said, was written to forget.

Twain collaborated with Charles Dudley Warner in writing his first novel, *The Gilded Age*. The work is poorly constructed and in places reads like the worst of sentimental novels, but it contains one of Twain's most memorable characters—Colonel Sellers, the incurable optimist—and some of his finest satire. His attacks on current get-rich-quick schemes and on political corruption were so trenchant that it is hardly an accident that the post Civil War period in America has been called "the gilded age."

Next came the great books about boys. *The Adventures of Tom Sawyer* is his best constructed work since in it Twain manages to keep three narrative strands carefully interwoven: the family complication involving Tom and Aunt Polly; the love story between Tom and Becky; and the murder plot involving Tom, Huck, and Injun Joe. *Tom Sawyer* has been called "an idyll of boyhood," and as such it has never been surpassed. *The Prince and the Pauper*, the story of a mix-up in identity between Edward VI and the ragamuffin Tom Canty, was a happy addition to the children's literature of the time. *Adventures of Huckleberry Finn*, however, was an addition to the world's classics. This picaresque narrative is a modified frame story with Tom Sawyer being the focal center in the first three chapters and the last ten, and Huck and Jim being the center of interest in the middle 29 chapters dealing with the journey down the river on a raft. Episodic in nature, the story nevertheless holds together because of the river, the constant presence of Huck as narrator, and perhaps especially because of Huck's growing awareness of Jim's humanity. The emotional climax of the book occurs where Huck resolves to save Jim from slavery even if he must go to hell for doing so. Many readers believe that the book goes downhill from that point to the end. Despite its humor and picturesque qualities the work is at bottom an unrelenting indictment of Mississippi river society in the 1840's—and of humanity in general at any time. But probably the most notable aspect of *Huckleberry Finn* is its style. Letting Huck tell the story forced Twain to do what he did best: report concrete happenings in colloquial language. The result is what can properly be called folk poetry. It was this colloquial style that caused Ernest Hemingway to say that modern American literature began with *Huckleberry Finn*.

A Connecticut Yankee in King Arthur's Court begins as a spoof of Malory's *Morte Darthur* but quickly turns into an indictment of human tyranny: political, religious, and economic. As the sixth-century "boss," the 19th-century Yankee mechanic has one comic experience after another, but the work is essentially social satire, not so much of English history as contemporary industrialized society. The Yankee becomes less and less interesting as Twain uses him increasingly as a mouthpiece for his own views, especially the view that we are all the products of our training. The book is prophetic in its suggestion at the end that technology renders us insensitive to human suffering.

In the last twenty years of his life Twain's work fell off artistically though his political and social concerns continued to expand. In a work of potential greatness, *Pudd'nhead Wilson*, he confronted for the first time the more brutal aspects of slavery. His *Personal Recollections of Joan of Arc* is embarrassingly sentimental but more accurate in depicting the political forces at work than many other biographies of Joan. Shorter pieces attack such issues of the time as American imperialism, Christian Science, the role of the Western powers in the Boxer Rebellion, King Leopold's treatment of the Congolese, and the lynching of blacks in the southern states. *The Mysterious Stranger*, a work that Twain started at least three times and never finished, exhibits his philosophy of mechanical determinism and his growing belief that life is only a dream. *What Is Man?*, a dialogue in which an elderly cynic invariably bests a young idealist, argues that man is a machine and that choice is only an illusion. There is no doubt that the pessimism and bitterness, latent in Twain throughout most of his life, finally surfaced in these last twenty years. Financial difficulties and the deaths of his wife and two daughters seemed at times to be more than he could bear. Nevertheless his perceptions remained sharp and his writing controlled. Besides, he was sustained by honors from home and abroad such as no other American writer had ever enjoyed.

Much that Twain wrote was topical and overwrought and is sliding into oblivion. But his best works remain unrivalled in their depiction of the comic and the pathetic in life—and of the inevitable relation between the two. William Dean Howells, Twain's best friend for forty years, composed a fitting epitaph when he wrote that Mark Twain was "sole, incomparable, the Lincoln of our literature."

—John C. Gerber

See the essays on *Adventures of Huckleberry Finn*, *The Adventures of Tom Sawyer*, and "The Man That Corrupted Hadleyburg."

TYLER, Royall. Born William Clark Tyler in Boston, Massachusetts, 18 July 1757. Educated at Harvard University, Cambridge, Massachusetts, 1772–76, A.B. 1776, A.M. 1779; honorary B.A., Yale University, New Haven, Connecticut, 1776; studied law in the office of Francis Dana in Cambridge; admitted to Massachusetts bar, 1780. Commanding Major, Independent Company of Boston, in the Continental Army, serving as aide to General Sullivan in the Battle of Rhode Island, 1778; later served as aide to General Benjamin Lincoln and participated in the suppression of Shays's Rebellion, 1787. Married Mary Hunt Palmer in 1794; eight sons and three daughters. Lawyer in Falmouth, Massachusetts, Portland, Maine, and Braintree, Massachusetts, 1780–85, Boston, 1785–91, and Guilford, Vermont, 1791–1801; collaborated with Joseph Dennie (as Colon and Spondee), 1794, and wrote satirical verse and prose for periodicals; state's attorney, Windham County, Vermont, 1794–1801; associate judge, 1801–07, and Chief Justice, 1807–13, Supreme Court of Vermont; Professor of Jurisprudence, University of Vermont, Burlington, 1811–14; registrar of probate, Brattleboro, Vermont, after 1815. *Died 26 August 1826.*

PUBLICATIONS

Collections

Verse and *Prose*, edited by Marius B. Péladeau. 2 vols., 1968–72.

Plays

The Contrast (produced 1787). 1790; edited by James B. Wilbur, 1920.
May Day in Town; or, New York in an Uproar (produced 1787).
The Georgia Spec; or, Land in the Moon (produced 1797; as *A Good Spec*, produced 1797).
Four Plays (includes *The Island of Barrataria, The Origin of the Feast of Purim, Joseph and His Brethren, The Judgement of Solomon*), edited by Arthur Wallace Peach and George Floyd Newbrough. 1941.

Fiction

The Algerine Captive. 1797.
The Bay Boy; or, The Autobiography of a Youth of Massachusetts Bay: Sketches from an Unpublished Novel, edited by Martha R. Wright. 1978.

Verse

The Origin of Evil. 1793.
The Chestnut Tree; or, A Sketch of Brattleborough at the Close of the Twentieth Century. 1931.

Other

The Trial of Cyrus B. Dean. 1808.
The Yankey in London. 1809.
Reports of Cases Argued and Determined in the Supreme Court of Vermont (for 1800–03). 2 vols., 1809–10.
A Book of Forms (law forms). 1845.

*

Critical Studies: *Tyler* by G. Thomas Tanselle, 1967; *Tyler* by Ada Lou Carson and Herbert L. Carson, 1979.

* * *

With the presentation of *The Contrast* in New York City on 16 April 1787, Royall Tyler, identified by the evening's drama critics as "a man of genius," entered the history of American drama, becoming the first known native American writer of comedy to be professionally produced. At a time when the new nation was struggling for identity, Tyler showed his particular genius in his choice of material and the manner of his expression. Creating a typical Yankee character, and generally fostering the "just pride of patriotism" which Washington would later emphasize in his Farewell Address, Tyler wrote a popular play for his time. He was never able to do it again, and perhaps once was enough. He also had other interests to pursue.

Tyler was that inspired person who could combine the joys of literary creation with a professional career, and as a lawyer he eventually rose in his profession to serve as Chief Justice of Vermont's Supreme Court. As a writer, however, he was attracted by all genres. With Joseph Dennie, essayist, critic, and editor of the *Port Folio*, he wrote a large number of amusing and satirical essays, sketches, and verses. Signing themselves as "Colon & Spondee" they provided light and topical commentary on society, literature, and politics until 1811. Poetry, particularly in a light and satiric vein, interested Tyler throughout his life. His only novel, an episodic work stimulated by the activity of the Barbary Coast pirates, was *The Algerine Captive*. Other than *The Contrast*, however, he was at his best in essay or short sketch. The collection called *The Yankey in London* best illustrates his work: a sprightly style, a reverence for America, and a varied subject matter.

It was with *The Contrast* that he gained his reputation as a writer. Although it lacks much of a plot and is a talky play imitative of 18th-century British sentimental comedy, it is clearly distinguished by an originality in thought and character. From the prologue—"Exult each patriot heart!"—to the climax all aspects of the play emphasize the new nationalism. Although they may be caricatures, the characters' distinctive qualities delight the reader and viewer. And everywhere there is satire—on fashion, theatre, the English, gossip—superimposed on the *contrast*—a contrast between the people of England and those of America, between affectation and straightforwardness, between city and country, between hypocrisy and sincerity, between foreign fraud and native worth. It was a play well designed to meet the demands and tastes of the new country.

Tyler continued to write more plays, but without great success. *May Day in Town; or, New York in an Uproar* appeared in a New York theatre a month after *The Contrast* but was not repeated. Four of Tyler's plays are published in the *America's Lost Plays* series. *The Island of Barrataria* is based on an episode in *Don Quixote*; the others have biblical sources. Only *The Island of Barrataria* deserves more critical attention than it has received. All, as might be expected of a lawyer, treat concepts of law, government, and justice. For Tyler, however, playwriting was only an avocation, though a pleasant one; he earned his living as a lawyer and justice. For the historian of American letters he is remembered mainly as the author of a single play.

—Walter J. Meserve

UPDIKE, John (Hoyer). Born in Shillington, Pennsylvania, 18 March 1932. Educated at public schools in Shillington; Harvard University, Cambridge, Massachusetts, A.B. (summa cum laude) 1954; Ruskin School of Drawing and Fine Arts, Oxford (Knox Fellow), 1954–55. Married 1) Mary Pennington in 1953 (marriage dissolved), two daughters and two sons; 2) Martha Bernhard in 1977. Staff reporter, *New Yorker*, 1955–57. Recipient: Guggenheim fellowship, 1959; Rosenthal Award, 1960; National Book Award, 1964; O. Henry Award, 1966; Foreign Book Prize (France), 1966; New England Poetry Club Golden Rose, 1979; MacDowell Medal, 1981; Pulitzer Prize, 1982; American Book Award, 1982; National Book Critics Circle award, for fiction, 1982, for criticism, 1984; Union League Club Abraham Lincoln Award, 1982; National Arts Club Medal of Honor, 1984. Member, American Academy, 1976. Lives in Beverly Farms, Massachusetts.

PUBLICATIONS

Fiction

The Poorhouse Fair. 1959.
The Same Door (stories). 1959.
Rabbit, Run. 1960.
Pigeon Feathers and Other Stories. 1962.
The Centaur. 1963.
Olinger Stories: A Selection. 1964.
Of the Farm. 1965.
The Music School (stories). 1966.
Couples. 1968.
Bech: A Book (stories). 1970.
Rabbit Redux. 1971.
The Indian (story). 1971.
Museums and Women and Other Stories. 1972.
Warm Wine: An Idyll (story). 1973.
A Month of Sundays. 1975.
Picked-Up Pieces (stories). 1975.
Couples: A Short Story. 1976.
Marry Me: A Romance. 1976.
The Coup. 1978.
Too Far to Go: The Maples Stories. 1979; as *Your Lover Just Called: Stories of Joan and Richard Maple*, 1980.
Problems and Other Stories. 1979.
Three Illuminations in the Life of an American Author (story). 1979.
The Chaste Planet (story). 1980.
Rabbit Is Rich. 1981.
The Beloved (story). 1982.
Bech Is Back (stories). 1983.
The Witches of Eastwick. 1984.
Roger's Version. 1986.

Plays

Three Texts from Early Ipswich: A Pageant. 1968.
Buchanan Dying. 1974.

Verse

The Carpentered Hen and Other Tame Creatures. 1958; as *Hoping for a Hoopoe*, 1959.
Telephone Poles and Other Poems. 1963.
Verse. 1965.
Dog's Death. 1965.
The Angels. 1968.
Bath after Sailing. 1968.
Midpoint and Other Poems. 1969.
Seventy Poems. 1972.
Six Poems. 1973.
Query. 1974.
Cunts (Upon Receiving the Swingers Life Club Membership Solicitation). 1974.
Tossing and Turning. 1977.
Sixteen Sonnets. 1979.
An Oddly Lovely Day Alone. 1979.
Five Poems. 1980.
Spring Trio. 1982.
Jester's Dozen. 1984.
Facing Nature. 1985.

Other

The Magic Flute (for children), with Warren Chappell. 1962.
The Ring (for children), with Warren Chappell. 1964.
Assorted Prose. 1965.
A Child's Calendar. 1965.
On Meeting Authors. 1968.

Bottom's Dream: Adapted from William Shakespeare's "A Midsummer Night's Dream" (for children). 1969.
A Good Place. 1973.
Picked-Up Pieces. 1975.
Hub Fans Bid Kid Adieu. 1977.
Talk from the Fifties. 1979.
Ego and Art in Walt Whitman. 1980.
People One Knows: Interviews with Insufficiently Famous Americans. 1980.
Invasion of the Book Envelopes. 1981.
Hawthorne's Creed. 1981.
Hugging the Shore: Essays and Criticism. 1983.

Editor, *Pens and Needles*, by David Levine. 1970.
Editor, with Shannon Ravenel, *The Best American Short Stories 1984*. 1984; as *The Year's Best American Short Stories*, 1985.

*

Bibliography: *Updike: A Bibliography* by C. Clarke Taylor, 1968; *An Annotated Bibliography of Updike Criticism 1967–1973, and a Checklist of His Works* by Michael A. Olivas, 1975; *Updike: A Comprehensive Bibliography with Selected Annotations* by Elizabeth A. Gearhart, 1978.

Critical Studies: *Updike* by Charles T. Samuels, 1969; *The Elements of Updike* by Alice and Kenneth Hamilton, 1970; *Pastoral and Anti-Pastoral Elements in Updike's Fiction* by Larry E. Taylor, 1971; *Updike: Yea Sayings* by Rachael C. Burchard, 1971; *Updike* by Robert Detweiler, 1972, revised edition, 1984; *Rainstorms and Fire: Ritual in the Novels of Updike* by Edward P. Vargo, 1973; *Fighters and Lovers: Theme in the Novels of Updike* by Joyce B. Markle, 1973; *Updike: A Collection of Critical Essays* edited by David Thorburn and Howard Eiland, 1979; *Updike* by Suzanne H. Uphaus, 1980; *The Other Updike: Poems / Short Stories / Prose / Play*, 1981, and *Updike's Novels*, 1984, both by Donald J. Greiner; *Updike's Images of America* by Philip H. Vaughan, 1981; *Married Men and Magic Tricks: Updike's Erotic Heroes* by Elizabeth Tallent, 1982; *Critical Essays on Updike* edited by William R. Macnaughton, 1982.

* * *

The successes of John Updike are linked with the *New Yorker*, a magazine on which he was once a staff member and for which he has remained a frequent contributor. But many of his novels go beyond the limits of interest that are frequently attributed to the journal: a well-bred skepticism as to what is possible for human sensibility in our time. It is true that Updike's novels and, even more, his short stories sometimes conform to these limits which see all human effort as subject to the ironies of cross-purpose. But Updike's sensibility, particularly as it unfolds in his longer works, is not that of a writer who has fully acquiesced in the general decay and uncertainty of an era. Rather Updike takes shape as a writer who keeps circling around the modern detritus with a sharp eye for some fragmented persistence of meaning and order. He is a moralist out of season. The season for confident reading of meaning may be over, but the desire for such activity persists in much of Updike's work.

This may not be immediately apparent to some readers who can doubt that there is any link between a continuing moral curiosity and the many passages in the novels which give explicit accounts of sexual success and sexual impotence. Yet the sexual adventures of the minister in *A Month of Sundays* are no more exactly set down than are the "spiritual" aspirations that lead the minister to compose discourses that link the presence of sexuality with the advent of Grace. For Updike is not the kind of Stoic moralist familiar to us in the 18th century and elsewhere who seeks to detect and defend a purely humanistic code of excellence. The code of excellence that reveals itself intermittently in the Updike novels is one that has its roots in the *O altitudos* that had their traditional expression in the transports of mystics and in the teaching of the New Testament itself. The minister of *A Month of Sundays* thinks of Barth and Tillich when he is not fornicating and sometimes when he is. Updike provides some of his novels with epigraphs from the New Testament and Pascal. Updike provides flickers of light and inchoate illuminations that direct attention beyond traditional common sense and the current doubt that there is any sense whatever to the lives that a novelist may at present describe.

There is, in several of the novels, a central figure who sums up the moral situation in which modern persons live and make their Updike-sponsored effort to enjoy their lives and understand them. In *The Centaur* Updike speaks of a sequence—priest, teacher, and artist—that links the present to the past. The central figure in *The Centaur* is a frustrated teacher of science in a high school; his prototype is the ancient centaur, Chiron, who tried to reveal to *his* recalcitrant pupils the wisdom that had come to the early Greek oracles and the priests of holy places. The ancient centaur was mocked and wounded by his pupils; so also is the high school teacher by *his* students. But the modern centaur's son, Peter, responds to the harassed and comic nobility of his father. And when that son becomes an artist—when he has left his father behind him—the son wonders whether his service of esthetic excellence continues or cancels the pursuits of his father. (Earlier, the father had wondered about the relation of his teaching activity to his father's career as a clergyman.) Is the artist son the last link in a chain that extends backwards in time and moral-religious experience? Or is he a link that is independent of the earlier ones, a servant of a good that has no contact with the earlier excellences that his father and grandfather were devoted to?

This is a question that much of Updike's work raises but does not answer. The question is not asked monotonously. In his first novel, *The Poorhouse Fair*, Updike contrasts the humanitarian Connor, the director of the poor house, with a ninety-year-old man who maintains touch with older sources of moral illumination. In *Rabbit, Run*, *Rabbit Redux*, and *Rabbit Is Rich*, the center of awareness is Harry Angstrom, an ill-educated and adulterous printer and, later, thanks to a useful marriage, a prosperous car salesman. He is a man who would, it seems, be singularly cut off from "priest" and "teacher." Yet Rabbit Angstrom is subject to malaises that have only a feeble source in his parents and that rather rise from his changes of partners, his ill-fulfilled obligations to his son, and his contact with a rebellious black. In the midst of a life that is badly broken up, Angstrom demands not only sexual gratification but moral illumination from persons who are as confused as he is. The illumination is transient and is usually lost in a subsequent catastrophic event. But the event that is more than event—that is illumination—has occurred. This is all that Updike can report in his *Rabbit* narratives and elsewhere. In *Marry Me* Updike leads his chief character, who is about to dissolve a "good" marriage, to observe that we are in the midst of "the twilight of the old morality, and there's just enough to torment us, and not enough to hold us in."

Such are most of Updike's novels: clever narratives that move from narrative to meditation. A book like *The Witches of Eastwick* is a late and excellent example of the usual Updike blend of mockery and seriousness. A company of modern New England witches—women isolated, feckless, and bitter—work their black magic and do little to alter themselves. Only in a book like *The Coup* does Updike make a rare foray beyond usual boundaries and direct his comic intelligence on human beings novel to him; the hero of *The Coup* is the dictator of an African state and falls foul of matters political, marital, and economic in ways that makes him, at the very least, a distant cousin of Rabbit Angstrom.

At first encounter, Updike's work seems to be devoted to the reproduction of textures that are self-evident: textures of the inconsecutive, textures composed by the crass indifference of most men to each other. All this is done with brilliance and is "right." But through this neatly comprehended terrain move "priestly" and academic ghosts, the shades of Updike's "centaur" and the "centaur's" father.

—Harold H. Watts

VAN DOREN, Mark (Albert). Born in Hope, Illinois, 13 June 1894. Educated at elementary and high schools in Urbana, Illinois; University of Illinois, Urbana, A.B. 1914, A.M. 1915; Columbia University, New York, Ph.D. 1920. Served in the U.S. Army Infantry, 1917–18. Married Dorothy Graffe in 1922; two sons. Instructor, 1920–24, Assistant Professor, 1924–35, Associate Professor, 1935–42, and Professor of English, 1942–59, Columbia University; lecturer, St. John's College, Annapolis, Maryland, 1937–57. Literary editor, 1924–42, and film critic, 1935–38, *The Nation*, New York; panelist on the radio program *Invitation to Learning*, 1940–42. Visiting Professor of English, Harvard University, Cambridge, Massachusetts, 1963. Recipient: Pulitzer Prize, 1940; Columbia University Alexander Hamilton Medal, 1959; Hale Award, 1960; National Conference of Christians and Jews Brotherhood Award, 1960; Huntington Hartford award, 1962; Emerson-Thoreau Medal, 1964. Litt.D.: Bowdoin College, Brunswick, Maine, 1944; University of Illinois, 1958; Columbia University, 1960; Knox College, Galesburg, Illinois, 1966; Harvard University, 1966; Jewish Theological Seminary of America, New York, 1970; L.H.D.: Adelphi University, Garden City, New York, 1957; Mount Mary College, Milwaukee, Wisconsin, 1965; Honorary M.D.: Connecticut State Medical Society, 1966. Member, American Academy. *Died 10 December 1972.*

PUBLICATIONS

Collections

Essays, edited by William Claire. 1980.

Verse

Spring Thunder and Other Poems. 1924.
7 P.M. and Other Poems. 1926.
Now the Sky and Other Poems. 1928.
Jonathan Gentry. 1931.
A Winter Diary and Other Poems. 1935.
The Last Look and Other Poems. 1937.
Collected Poems 1922–1938. 1939.
The Mayfield Deer. 1941.
Our Lady Peace and Other War Poems. 1942.
The Seven Sleepers and Other Poems. 1944.
The Country Year. 1946.
The Careless Clock: Poems about Children in the Family. 1947.
New Poems. 1948.
Humanity Unlimited: Twelve Sonnets. 1950.
In That Far Land. 1951.
Mortal Summer. 1953.
Spring Birth and Other Poems. 1953.
Selected Poems. 1954.
Morning Worship. 1960.
Collected and New Poems 1924–1963. 1963.
Narrative Poems. 1964.
That Shining Place: New Poems. 1969.
Good Morning: Last Poems. 1973.

Plays

The Last Days of Lincoln (produced 1961). 1959.
Never, Never Ask His Name (produced 1965). In *Three Plays*, 1966.
Three Plays (includes *Never, Never Ask His Name, A Little Night Music, The Weekend That Was*). 1966.

Fiction

The Transients. 1935.
Windless Cabins. 1940.
Tilda. 1943.
The Short Stories. 1950.
The Witch of Ramoth and Other Tales. 1950.
Nobody Say a Word and Other Stories. 1953.
Home with Hazel and Other Stories. 1957.
Collected Stories. 3 vols., 1962–68.

Other

Henry David Thoreau: A Critical Study. 1916.
The Poetry of John Dryden. 1920; revised edition, 1931; as *John Dryden: A Study of His Poetry*, 1946.
American and British Literature since 1890, with Carl Van Doren. 1925; revised edition, 1939.
Edwin Arlington Robinson. 1927.
Dick and Tom: Tales of Two Ponies (for children). 1931.
Dick and Tom in Town (for children). 1932.
Shakespeare. 1939.
Studies in Metaphysical Poetry: Two Essays and a Bibliography, with Theodore Spencer. 1939.
The Transparent Tree (for children). 1940.
Invitation to Learning, with Huntington Cairns and Allen Tate. 1941.
The New Invitation to Learning. 1942.
The Private Reader: Selected Articles and Reviews. 1942.
Liberal Education. 1943.
The Noble Voice: A Study of Ten Great Poems. 1946; as *Great Poems of Western Literature*, 1966.
Nathaniel Hawthorne. 1949.

Introduction to Poetry. 1951.
Joseph and His Brothers. 1956.
Don Quixote's Profession. 1958.
Autobiography. 1958.
The Happy Critic and Other Essays. 1961.
The Dialogues of Archibald MacLeish and Van Doren, edited by Warren V. Bush. 1964.
Somebody Came (for children). 1966.
Carl Sandburg. 1969.
In the Beginning, Love: Dialogues on the Bible, with Maurice Samuel, edited by Edith Samuel. 1973.
The Book of Praise: Dialogues on the Psalms, with Maurice Samuel, edited by Edith Samuel. 1975.

Editor, *Samuel Sewall's Diary*. 1927.
Editor, *A History of the Life and Death, Virtues and Exploits of General George Washington*, by Mason Locke Weems. 1927.
Editor, *An Anthology of World Poetry*. 1928; revised edition, 1936; selection, as *An Anthology of English and American Poetry*, 1936.
Editor, *The Travels of William Bartram*. 1928.
Editor, *Nick of the Woods; or, The Jibbenainosay: A Tale of Kentucky*, by Robert Montgomery Bird. 1928.
Editor, *A Journey to the Land of Eden and Other Papers*, by William Byrd II. 1928.
Editor, *An Autobiography of America*. 1929.
Editor, *Correspondence of Aaron Burr and His Daughter Theodosia*. 1929.
Editor, with Garibaldi M. Lapolla, *A Junior Anthology of World Poetry*. 1929.
Editor, *The Life of Sir William Phips*, by Cotton Mather. 1929.
Editor, with Garibaldi M. Lapolla, *The World's Best Poems*. 1932.
Editor, *American Poets, 1630–1930*. 1932; as *Masterpieces of American Poets*, 1936.
Editor, *The Oxford Book of American Prose*. 1932.
Editor, with John W. Cunliffe and Karl Young, *Century Readings in English Literature*, 5th edition. 1940.
Editor, *A Listener's Guide to Invitation to Learning, 1940–41, 1941–42*. 2 vols., 1940–42.
Editor, *The Night of the Summer Solstice and Other Stories of the Russian War*. 1943.
Editor, *Walt Whitman*. 1945.
Editor, *The Portable Emerson*. 1946.
Editor, *Selected Poetry*, by William Wordsworth. 1950.
Editor, *Introduction to Poetry*. 1951; as *Enjoying Poetry*, 1951.
Editor, with others, *Riverside Poetry: 48 New Poems by 27 Poets*. 1956.
Editor, with others, *Insights into Literature*. 1965.
Editor, *100 Poems*. 1967.

* * *

Mark Van Doren's poetry, which consists of over a thousand poems in *Collected and New Poems* and other volumes, including a posthumous collection, *Good Morning*, constitutes one of the more prolific and accomplished bodies of work by an American poet in the 20th century. While the sheer bulk has often astonished and sometimes dismayed critics, it represents, as Richard Howard has observed, "not so much an embarrassment as an embodiment of riches."

Van Doren was originally hailed by T.S. Eliot and others as a master of rural verse and conveniently placed in the tradition of Robert Frost. He soon demonstrated, however, a distinctive voice that deepened through a sustained middle period culminating in his first *Collected Poems* (1939) and which grew in variety of subject matter and range for over three more decades after he received the Pulitzer Prize in 1940. Influenced by John Dryden as a young scholar, Van Doren belongs in a group that might include Hardy, early Yeats, Graves and, in specifically American ways, Emily Dickinson, Edwin Arlington Robinson, and Frost. Allen Tate once wisely concluded, after also suggesting "a trace of William Browne (epigrams and *Britannia's Pastorals*, 1613), traces of Ben Jonson, more than a trace of Robert Herrick" that all of them might "add up to Mark Van Doren who is like nobody else."

Singularly devoid of the common French influences in modern verse, Van Doren also eschewed confessional or analytic tendencies. He treated his principal subjects, the cosmos, love, finality, family matters, and particularly children, animals, paradox, and knowledge in a lucid manner that transcends simplistic notions of modernity and personal sensibilities. There is a passionate intelligence lurking behind many of the poems that somehow never intrudes. Indeed, it is a subtle presence that calls forth different interpretations on subsequent readings, though there is never intentional obscurity.

His poetic corpus contains an intricate world of pleasures, observations, and intellectual insights. As a master craftsman, Van Doren would make an excellent case study for the continuity of English lyric and narrative verse. He also personifies a humanistic and metaphysical approach that is American at its core, a kind of Emersonian individualism with contemporary concerns. Taken together, his work over a half-century, which included substantial accomplishments in other literary fields, illustrates the American literary presence at its best with a poetry that, as one critic observed, never having been in fashion, will never go out of fashion.

—William Claire

---

van DRUTEN, John (William). Born in London, England, 1 June 1901; moved to the U.S., 1926; became citizen, 1944. Educated at University College School, London, 1911–17; worked in a law office and studied law: LL.B., University of London, 1922; qualified as solicitor, 1923. Special Lecturer in English Law and Legal History, University College of Wales, Aberystwyth, 1923–26; full-time writer from 1926; also stage director: directed *The King and I*, New York, 1951, and several of his own plays. Recipient: American Academy Award of Merit Medal, 1946; New York Drama Critics Circle award, 1952. Member, American Academy, 1951. *Died 19 December 1957.*

PUBLICATIONS

Plays

The Return Half (produced 1924).
Young Woodley (produced 1925). 1926.
Chance Acquaintance (produced 1927).
Diversion (produced 1928). 1928.

The Return of the Soldier, from the novel by Rebecca West (produced 1928). 1928.
After All (produced 1929; revised version, produced 1930). 1929.
London Wall (produced 1931). 1931.
Sea Fever, with Auriol Lee, from a play by Marcel Pagnol (produced 1931).
There's Always Juliet (produced 1931). 1931.
Hollywood Holiday, with Benn Levy (produced 1931). 1931.
Somebody Knows (produced 1932). 1932.
Behold, We Live (produced 1932). 1932.
The Distaff Side (produced 1933). 1933.
Flowers of the Forest (produced 1934). 1934.
Most of the Game (produced 1935). 1936.
Gertie Maude (produced 1937). 1937.
Leave Her to Heaven (produced 1940). 1941.
Old Acquaintance (produced 1940). 1941.
Solitaire, from the novel by Edwin Corle (produced 1942).
The Damask Cheek, with Lloyd R. Morris (produced 1942). 1943.
The Voice of the Turtle (produced 1943). 1944.
I Remember Mama, from the stories *Mama's Bank Account* by Kathryn Forbes (produced 1944). 1945.
The Mermaids Singing (produced 1945). 1946.
The Druid Circle (produced 1947). 1948.
Make Way for Lucia, from novels by E.F. Benson (produced 1948). 1949.
Bell, Book, and Candle (produced 1950). 1951.
I Am a Camera, from *The Berlin Stories* by Christopher Isherwood (produced 1951). 1952.
I've Got Sixpence (produced 1952). 1953.
Dancing in the Chequered Shade (produced 1955).

Screenplays: *Young Woodley*, with Victor Kendall, 1930; *I Loved a Soldier*, 1936; *Parnell*, with S.N. Behrman, 1937; *Night Must Fall*, 1937; *The Citadel*, with others, 1938; *Raffles*, with Sidney Howard, 1940; *Lucky Partners*, with Allan Scott, 1940; *My Life with Caroline*, with Arnold Belgard, 1941; *Johnny Come Lately* (*Johnny Vagabond*), 1943; *Old Acquaintance*, with Lenore Coffee, 1943; *Forever and a Day*, with others, 1944; *Gaslight*, with Walter Reisch and John L. Balderston, 1944; *The Voice of the Turtle*, 1948.

Fiction

Young Woodley. 1929.
A Woman on Her Way. 1930.
And Then You Wish. 1936.
The Vicarious Years. 1955.

Other

The Way to the Present: A Personal Record. 1938.
Playwright at Work. 1953.
The Widening Circle (autobiography). 1957.

*

Critical Studies: *As They Appear* by John Mason Brown, 1953; *Theatre Chronicles 1937–1962* by Mary McCarthy, 1963.

* * *

A prolific writer—best known for his plays but also recognized as a novelist, screenwriter, and autobiographer—John van Druten delighted audiences for more than thirty years with his polished, urbane comedies. The persistent tone in his works is warm and gentle; his style has been praised for its convincing naturalness and controlled simplicity.

Van Druten's plots are often loosely structured, imitative, and readily forgettable. *I Remember Mama*, one of his most popular works, for example, is structured as a series of vignettes linked together by tone and characters, but scarcely more unified than the collection of Kathryn Forbes's short stories on which it was based.

When there is a developed plot in either his original works or his adaptations, it is usually one of two variations on the same basic action: two people meet, have or contemplate having an affair, discover that they love each other, and then joyfully renounce wantonness and move toward a thoroughly conventional marriage (as in *There's Always Juliet*; *The Distaff Side*; *Bell, Book, and Candle*; *The Damask Cheek*; and *The Voice of the Turtle*); or, sadly, discover that their age, circumstance, or character prevents such a marriage (as in *Young Woodley, Old Acquaintance, The Mermaids Singing*, and *I Am a Camera*). In developing these plots, van Druten moves perilously close to the brink of sentimentality and heavyhanded moralism; but his wit and determination to master "the difficult art of sincerity" keep him, with rare exceptions, from plunging headlong into the abyss.

Indeed, van Druten's plays were consistently praised for their fresh dialogue, their unforced cleverness, and their sophisticated repartée. His fiction and autobiographies, too, are natural and eminently readable.

His awareness of the importance of style and his concern that his works be well-written are reflected both in his commentary on his own works and in his evaluation of the works of others. For example, he criticizes bad writing, which he describes as that which is filled with bathos, facetiousness, and an endless flow of shop-worn phrases that "produce no effect save that of total weariness." He states that only the immature taste can appreciate great sweetness or a "mustard and vinegar sharpness," which the experienced palate would disdain. And in his own works, from the beginning, he attempted to avoid these excesses.

Van Druten's artistry in writing dialogue brings his characters to life. They are unforgettable. Sally Bowles, the complex, misguided, comical, pathetic American expatriate in *I Am a Camera*, who leads the life of the grasshopper as the deadly threat of the Third Reich moves forward; Marta, the warm, clever, protective, stable foundation of her family in *I Remember Mama*; Gillian Holroyd, the thoroughly human witch in *Bell, Book, and Candle*—these are only three who clearly rise above the ordinary to the distinctive.

This ability to create memorable characters, and thus major roles, was early recognized by Hollywood, where van Druten wrote dialogue, adapted his own works and those of others, and collaborated on screenplays for major actors from virtually every important studio. He was largely responsible, for instance, for creating the role of Paula Alquist in *Gaslight*, a role for which Ingrid Bergman won an Oscar in 1944. It is on such success that van Druten's reputation rests.

—Helen Houser Popovich

VAN VECHTEN, Carl. Born in Cedar Rapids, Iowa, 17 June 1880. Educated at Cedar Rapids High School; University of Chicago, 1899–1903, Ph.B. 1903. Married 1) Anna Elizabeth Snyder in 1907 (divorced, 1912); 2) the actress Fania Marinoff in 1914. Composer and journalist: reporter, Chicago *American*, 1903–05; assistant music critic, 1906–07, 1910–13, and Paris correspondent, 1908–10, New York *Times*; author of program notes for the Symphony Society of New York, 1910–11; drama critic, New York *Press*, 1913–14; editor, *Trend*, New York, 1914; portrait photographer from 1932: individual exhibitions from 1942. Member of the Board of the Cosmopolitan Symphony Orchestra, and the W.C. Handy Foundation for the Blind; founder, 1941, and Honorary Curator, 1946, James Weldon Johnson Memorial Collection of Negro Arts and Letters, Yale University Library, New Haven, Connecticut; literary executor of Gertrude Stein, and editor of the Yale University Press Stein Edition, from 1946. Recipient: Yale University Gold Medal, 1955. D.Litt.: Fisk University, Nashville, Tennessee, 1955. Member, American Academy, 1961. *Died 21 December 1964.*

PUBLICATIONS

Fiction

Peter Whiffle, His Life and Works. 1922.
The Blind Bow-Boy. 1923.
The Tattooed Countess. 1924.
Firecrackers. 1925.
Nigger Heaven. 1926.
Spider Boy: A Scenario for a Moving Picture. 1928.
Parties: Scenes from Contemporary New York Life. 1930.

Other

Music after the Great War and Other Studies. 1915.
Music and Bad Manners. 1916.
Interpreters and Interpretations. 1917; revised edition, as *Interpreters*, 1920.
The Merry-Go-Round. 1918.
The Music of Spain. 1918.
In the Garret. 1920.
The Tiger in the House. 1920.
Red: Papers on Musical Subjects. 1925.
Excavations: A Book of Advocacies. 1926.
Feathers. 1930.
Sacred and Profane Memories (essays). 1932.
James Weldon Johnson, with Sterling A. Brown and A.B. Spingarn. 1941(?).
Ex Libris, in *Dance Index* (triple issue). 1942.
Fragments from an Unwritten Autobiography. 2 vols., 1955.
The Dance Writings, edited by Paul Padgette. 1975.
With Formality and Elegance (on photography). 1977.
Portraits (photographs), edited by Saul Mauriber. 1978.
Keep a-Inchin' Along: Selected Writings about Black Art and Letters, edited by Bruce Kellner. 1979.
The Dance Photography, edited by Paul Padgette. 1981.
The Letters of Gertrude Stein and Van Vechten 1913–1946, edited by Edward Burns. 2 vols., 1986.

Editor, *Lords of the Housetops: Thirteen Cat Tales.* 1921.
Editor, *My Musical Life*, by Nikolay Rimsky-Korsakoff, translated by Judah A. Joffe. 1923; revised edition, 1942.
Editor, *Gertrude Stein: Selected Writings.* 1946.
Editor, *Last Operas and Plays*, by Gertrude Stein. 1949.
Editor, *Unpublished Writings of Gertrude Stein.* 8 vols., 1951–58.

*

Bibliography: *Van Vechten: A Bibliography* by Klaus W. Jonas, 1955; *A Bibliography of the Work of Van Vechten* by Bruce Kellner, 1980.

Critical Studies: *Van Vechten and the Twenties*, 1955, and *Van Vechten*, 1965, both by Edward Lueders; *Van Vechten and the Irreverent Decades* by Bruce Kellner, 1968.

* * *

Carl Van Vechten's personal flamboyance in manner and dress, as well as his frequent enthusiasm for both the avant garde and the patently old-fashioned, labelled him a dilettante in his own time. The range and foresight in several distinct careers, however, mark him a unique and underestimated American writer.

A partial list of his discoveries is staggering. As a newspaper critic he endorsed the first performances in America of Isadora Duncan, Anna Pavlova, Mary Garden, Feodor Chaliapin, and Sergei Rachmaninoff, and he was the earliest American admirer of the music of Erik Satie, Richard Strauss, and Igor Stravinsky. In a series of volumes of musical and literary criticism—*Interpreters* and *Excavations* are particularly rewarding—his perceptions are startlingly fresh. He advocated musical scores for films by serious composers, the value of popular music and ragtime, ballet, Spanish music—all far in advance of other writers. He was one of the first to rediscover Herman Melville, and Ronald Firbank and Arthur Machen owe their American reputations to him. Van Vechten's tireless efforts on behalf of Gertrude Stein are well known; he was instrumental in placing the first books of Wallace Stevens and Langston Hughes; he fostered the careers of George Gershwin, Ethel Waters, Paul Robeson among musicians, and James Purdy among writers. His book about cats, *The Tiger in the House*, is seminal. He was largely responsible for the popular recognition of the Negro as a creative artist during the Harlem Renaissance.

Van Vechten is probably too analytical and discursive, too involved with amassing and cataloging outré material, to have written fiction of the first order, although all seven of his novels are variously engaging. Few books catch the charm of New York and Paris before World War I so well as *Peter Whiffle*. None serves as such a good introduction to Harlem during the 1920's as *Nigger Heaven. The Tattooed Countess* criticizes small-town life at the turn of the century with a gently cheerful malice denied more resolute realists. Three novels document Van Vechten's "splendid drunken Twenties," as he called the period: *The Blind Bow-Boy, Firecrackers*, and *Parties* form a serious social trilogy in the disguise of buffoonery and farce, written with slinky elegance and wit.

Van Vechten gave up writing in favor of photography to document the century's celebrities for various collections he established: the James Weldon Johnson Memorial Collection of Negro Arts and Letters, at Yale, and the George Gershwin Memorial Collection of Music and Musical Literature, at Fisk, among others.

His work has dated very little; since he wrote from the perspective of middle age, Van Vechten's evaluations of the 1920's are perhaps more solidly grounded than those of several more celebrated younger writers of the period.

—Bruce Kellner

VERY, Jones. Born in Salem, Massachusetts, 28 August 1813; spent much of his childhood at sea with his father, a ship's captain. Educated at Fisk Latin School, Salem, 1832–34; Harvard University, Cambridge, Massachusetts, 1834–36 (Junior and Senior Bowdoin Prize), A.B. 1836; tutor in Greek at the university 1836–38; entered Harvard Divinity School, 1836; forced to resign because of erratic behavior caused by his mystical experiences, 1838. Spent a month in McLean Asylum, Somerville, Massachusetts, 1838; associate of Emerson, 1838–c. 1840; licensed to preach as Unitarian minister by Cambridge Association of Ministers, 1843: held temporary pastorates in Eastport, Maine, and North Beverly, Massachusetts; lived in Salem after 1848. *Died 8 May 1880.*

PUBLICATIONS

Collections

Selected Poems, edited by Nathan Lyons. 1966.

Other

Essays and Poems, edited by Ralph Waldo Emerson. 1839; revised edition, edited by James Freeman Clarke, as *Poems and Essays*, 1886; edited by Kenneth Walter Cameron, as *Poems*, 1965.

*

Critical Studies: *Very: Emerson's "Brave Saint"* by William Irving Bartlett, 1942 (includes bibliography); *Very: The Effective Years 1833–1840* by Edwin Gittleman, 1967; "Alone with God and Nature: The Poetry of Very and Frederick Goddard Tuckerman" by David Seed, in *Nineteenth-Century American Poetry* edited by A. Robert Lee, 1985.

* * *

A curious example of single-minded Quietism, Jones Very occupies a special place in 19th-century American poetry. He wrote over 700 poems, most of these produced between 1833 and 1840—the tumultuous years in which Very resolved his youthful religious doubts and reconciled himself to the eccentricities of his dominating mother and the loss of his sea-captain father. Dramatically realizing the Transcendentalist equation of self-reliance with God-reliance, Very experienced a transfiguring conversion in which he attained a second birth through the agency of the Holy Spirit. True, most of these poems tend to be repetitive, conventional in thought and expression, tedious, and oblivious to drama, the play of language, humor, or the ambiguities of human experience. In his best poems, however, Very's voice can be as piercing as a knife-blade. Writing from the perspective of one who knows himself to be the passive instrument of a Higher Will, Very triumphs in lean enunciations of Being rather than explorations of Becoming. Characteristically using mild variations on the form of the Shakespearean sonnet and deeply imbued with the diction and syntax of the Bible, his utterance sometimes rises above its own awkwardness and penchant for bland abstractions to achieve an intense purity of religious awareness. Even though his successful poems are overly dependent on the Christian paradox of total submission as a condition of total fulfillment, the results are unsentimental and wholly persuasive.

His "nature poetry" and his literary essays could perhaps have been written by any gifted young man swept up in the enthusiasm of Channing's Unitarianism and Emerson's *Nature*. But some dozen or so meditational sonnets (e.g., "The Hand and Foot," "The Absent," "Morning," "The Presence," "The Journey," "The Eagles") succeeded in translating literally the Transcendentalist exhortations to discover an inner divinity into spiritual declarations of considerable power. At first extravagantly praised by Emerson, Bronson Alcott, Margaret Fuller, and Elizabeth Peabody, Very became something of an embarrassment due to the fanatic rigidity with which he judged all deviations from his way to salvation as well as the monochromatic mediocrity of much of his verse. From 1843 until his death, his literary production was almost entirely restricted to not particularly distinguished sermons.

—Earl Rovit

VIDAL, Gore (Eugene Luther Vidal, Jr.). Born in West Point, New York, 3 October 1925. Educated at Los Alamos School, New Mexico, 1939–40; Phillips Exeter Academy, New Hampshire, 1940–43. Served in the U.S. Army, 1943–46: Warrant Officer. Editor, E.P. Dutton, publishers, New York, 1946; lived in Antigua, Guatemala, 1947–49, and Italy, from 1967. Member, Advisory Board, *Partisan Review*, New Brunswick, New Jersey, 1960–71; Democratic-Liberal candidate for Congress, New York, 1960; member, President's Advisory Committee on the Arts, 1961–63; Co-Chairman, New Party, 1968–71. Recipient: Mystery Writers of America Edgar Allan Poe Award, for television play, 1954; National Book Critics Circle award, for criticism, 1983. Lives in Ravello, near Salerno, Italy.

PUBLICATIONS

Fiction

Williwaw. 1946.
In a Yellow Wood. 1947.
The City and the Pillar. 1948; revised edition, 1965.
The Season of Comfort. 1949.
Dark Green, Bright Red. 1950.
A Search for the King: A Twelfth Century Legend. 1950.
The Judgment of Paris. 1952; revised edition, 1965.
Death in the Fifth Position. 1952.
Death Before Bedtime. 1953.
Death Likes It Hot. 1954.
Messiah. 1954; revised edition, 1965.
A Thirsty Evil: Seven Short Stories. 1956.

Julian. 1964.
Washington, D.C. 1967.
Myra Breckinridge. 1968.
Two Sisters: A Memoir in the Form of a Novel. 1970.
Burr. 1973.
Myron. 1974.
1876. 1976.
Kalki. 1978.
Creation. 1981.
Duluth. 1983.
Lincoln. 1984.

Plays

Visit to a Small Planet (televised 1955). In *Visit to a Small Planet and Other Television Plays*, 1956; revised version (produced 1957), 1957.
Honor (televised 1956). In *Television Plays for Writers: Eight Television Plays*, edited by A.S. Burack, 1957; revised version, as *On the March to the Sea: A Southron Comedy* (produced 1961), in *Three Plays*, 1962.
Visit to a Small Planet and Other Television Plays (includes *Barn Burning, Dark Possession, The Death of Billy the Kid, A Sense of Justice, Smoke, Summer Pavilion, The Turn of the Screw*). 1956.
The Best Man: A Play about Politics (produced 1960). 1960.
Three Plays (includes *Visit to a Small Planet, The Best Man, On the March to the Sea*). 1962.
Romulus: A New Comedy, from a play by Friedrich Dürrenmatt (produced 1962). 1962.
Weekend (produced 1968). 1968.
An Evening with Richard Nixon and . . . (produced 1972). 1972.

Screenplays: *The Catered Affair*, 1956; *I Accuse*, 1958; *The Scapegoat*, with Robert Hamer, 1959; *Suddenly Last Summer*, with Tennessee Williams, 1959; *The Best Man*, 1964; *Is Paris Burning?*, with Francis Ford Coppola, 1966; *Last of the Mobile Hot-Shots*, 1970.

Television Plays: *Barn Burning*, from the story by Faulkner, 1954; *Dark Possession*, 1954; *Smoke*, from the story by Faulkner, 1954; *Visit to a Small Planet*, 1955; *The Death of Billy the Kid*, 1955; *A Sense of Justice*, 1955; *Summer Pavilion*, 1955; *The Turn of the Screw*, from the story by Henry James, 1955; *Honor*, 1956; *The Indestructible Mr. Gore*, 1960.

Other

Rocking the Boat (essays). 1962.
Sex, Death, and Money (essays). 1968.
Reflections upon a Sinking Ship (essays). 1969.
Homage to Daniel Shays: Collected Essays 1952–1972. 1972; as *Collected Essays 1952–1972*, 1974.
Matters of Fact and of Fiction: Essays 1973–1976. 1977.
Sex Is Politics and Vice Versa (essay). 1979.
Views from a Window: Conversations with Vidal, with Robert J. Stanton. 1980.
The Second American Revolution and Other Essays 1976–1982. 1982; as *Pink Triangle and Yellow Star and Other Essays*, 1982.
Vidal in Venice. 1985.

Editor, *Best Television Plays*. 1956.

*

Bibliography: *Vidal: A Primary and Secondary Bibliography* by Robert J. Stanton, 1978.

Critical Studies: *Vidal* by Ray Lewis White, 1968; *The Apostate Angel: A Critical Study of Vidal* by Bernard F. Dick, 1974; *Vidal* by Robert F. Kiernan, 1982.

* * *

Of all the critical overviews of the wide-ranging work of Gore Vidal, his own appraisal may be as straightforward as one could hope for. In a foreword to the 1956 collection *Visit to a Small Planet and Other Television Plays*, he says: "I am at heart a propagandist, a tremendous hater, a tiresome nag, complacently positive that there is no human problem which could not be solved if people would simply do as I advise." There is a determined strain of social criticism—always articulate, often vituperative, and sometimes just bitchy—at the center of most of his fiction, drama, and film scripts, especially in his most recent work. Consumed by American political history, Vidal has fashioned characters and situations that often serve as mouthpieces for his heretical suspicions about the past and his unrelieved cynicism with regard to the future. Fortunately, there is almost always evidence of his considerable literary skill as well.

Since the publication of *Williwaw* when he was 21, Vidal has prompted enthusiasm from critics lauding his "promise." Whether that promise has been fulfilled after forty years of work in popular American literature is still the central question for most Vidal commentators. What is certain is that he has managed to keep his name in contention the whole time. He found popular and critical success in fiction—first with *Williwaw*, then with bestsellers like *The City and the Pillar, Julian, Washington, D.C., Myra Breckinridge, Burr, 1876*, and *Lincoln*. He turned to television in its formative years, in the era of live tele-drama, and produced well received plays for *Omnibus, Studio One*, and *Philco Television Playhouse* (including the highly praised *Visit to a Small Planet*). *The Best Man*, produced on Broadway in 1960, was a major success, encouraging a film adaptation in 1964, followed by other film adaptations (including *Suddenly Last Summer*, written with Tennessee Williams) and original screenplays.

But critics familiar with Vidal's entire range of work seem to think that his real talent lies with the perfection of the essay. Indeed, the 1977 publication of a collection of his essays—*Matters of Fact and Fiction*—was greeted with widespread praise, even if some reviewers had reservations. Vidal's affinity for the essay form may account for the frequently heard criticism that his other work is too polemical. It may well be, as Vidal himself has suggested informally, that at the heart of his dramatic and fictional efforts there beats an essay, which sometimes overwhelms the conventions of the form that seeks to contain it.

The elements of Vidal's creative polemic seem to be characterized by his gift for language, his "wit" (in the classical sense), and his strong reactionary instincts. This last tendency seems puzzling at first, given his well known liberalism in social and political affairs (television networks have used him as a representative "liberal intellectual," and he has run for office on suicidally liberal platforms). But the contradiction might be a natural consequence of being Gore Vidal, grandson of T.P. Gore, respected Senator from Oklahoma, and son of a much admired college athlete who was an instructor at West Point when Vidal was born. The reactionary strain might be a case of his natural predispositions—based upon his aristocratic origins, his attraction to money and power and his unshakeable suspicions about the stupidity of the American public—overwhelming whatever ideological hopes he claims.

What emerges, in the words of P.N. Furbank (in a 1974 piece in the *Listener*), is "a sort of patriotic gloom." Rooted as he was in the schoolbook traditions of American history and its institutions, Vidal seems to have been particularly embittered by the unflattering lessons of his historical scholarship and his personal experience. He is stuck with the residue of his expectations about American innocence and morality, confounded by what he knows about political history. So to do justice to both the dream and the informed reality, he has developed an articulate, even lyrical, cynicism about the direction of modern letters and the final collision of the Republic with the world it has, in part, created.

—Lawrence R. Broer

VONNEGUT, Kurt, Jr. Born in Indianapolis, Indiana, 11 November 1922. Educated at Cornell University, Ithaca, New York, 1940–42, 1945; Carnegie Institute, Pittsburgh, 1943; University of Chicago, 1945–47, M.A. in anthropology 1971. Served in the U.S. Army Infantry, 1942–45: Purple Heart. Married 1) Jane Marie Cox in 1945 (divorced, 1979), one son and two daughters, and three adopted sons; 2) Jill Krementz in 1979. Police reporter, Chicago City News Bureau, 1946; public relations writer, General Electric Company, Schenectady, New York, 1947–51; since 1951, free-lance writer; after 1965 teacher, Hopefield School, Sandwich, Massachusetts. Visiting Lecturer, Writers Workshop, University of Iowa, Iowa City, 1965–67, and Harvard University, Cambridge, Massachusetts, 1970–71; Visiting Professor, City University, New York, 1973–74. Recipient: Guggenheim fellowship, 1967; American Academy grant, 1970. Litt.D.: Hobart and William Smith Colleges, Geneva, New York, 1974. Member, 1973, and Vice-President, 1975, American Academy. Lives in New York City.

PUBLICATIONS

Fiction

Player Piano. 1952; as *Utopia 14*, 1954.
The Sirens of Titan. 1959.
Canary in a Cat House (stories). 1961.
Mother Night. 1962.
Cat's Cradle. 1963.
God Bless You, Mr. Rosewater; or, Pearls Before Swine. 1965.
Welcome to the Monkey House: A Collection of Short Works. 1968.
Slaughterhouse-Five; or, The Children's Crusade. 1969.
Breakfast of Champions; or, Goodbye, Blue Monday. 1973.
Slapstick; or, Lonesome No More! 1973.
Jailbird. 1979.
Deadeye Dick. 1982.
Galápagos. 1985.

Plays

Happy Birthday, Wanda June (as *Penelope*, produced 1960; revised version, as *Happy Birthday, Wanda June*, produced 1970). 1970.
The Very First Christmas Morning, in *Better Homes and Gardens*, December 1962.
Between Time and Timbuktu; or, Prometheus-5: A Space Fantasy (televised 1972; produced 1976). 1972.
Fortitude, in *Wampeters, Foma, and Granfalloons*, 1974.
Timesteps (produced 1979).
God Bless You, Mr. Rosewater, from his own novel (produced 1979).

Television Play: *Between Time and Timbuktu*, 1972.

Other

Wampeters, Foma, and Granfalloons: Opinions. 1974.
Sun Moon Star. 1980.
Palm Sunday: An Autobiographical Collage. 1981.
Fates Worse Than Death. 1982(?).

*

Bibliography: *Vonnegut: A Descriptive Bibliography and Annotated Secondary Checklist* by Asa B. Pieratt, Jr., and Jerome Klinkowitz, 1974.

Critical Studies: *Vonnegut* by Peter J. Reed, 1972; *Vonnegut: Fantasist of Fire and Ice* by David H. Goldsmith, 1972; *The Vonnegut Statement* edited by Jerome Klinkowitz and John Somer, 1973, *Vonnegut in America: An Introduction to the Life and Work of Vonnegut* edited by Klinkowitz and Donald L. Lawler, 1977, and *Vonnegut* by Klinkowitz, 1982; *Vonnegut* by Stanley Schatt, 1976; *Vonnegut* by James Lundquist, 1977; *Vonnegut: A Preface to His Novels* by Richard Giannone, 1977; *Vonnegut: The Gospel from Outer Space* by Clark Mayo, 1977; *Vonnegut's Duty-Dance with Death: Theme and Structure in Slaughterhouse-Five* by Monica Loeb, 1979.

* * *

In *Slaughterhouse-Five*, Kurt Vonnegut summarizes a science-fiction novel by Kilgore Trout in which a time traveler goes back to the Crucifixion and, with a stethoscope, listens to Christ's heart. The Savior, alas, is dead, stone dead. Trout is a character in several of Vonnegut's books, but his novel might well have been written by Vonnegut, for, like it, Vonnegut's novels portray a world in which there is no hope, no purpose, no salvation for the universe. Vonnegut is a moralist, but one who begins with the premise that morality, like civilization, merely expresses wishful thinking and chance. In this universe, divine intention is only imagined; it does not really exist.

Vonnegut's novels describe a deterministic, mechanistic world—a world of cause and effect with no overriding purpose or goal. The major novels and other works center on innocents like Billy Pilgrim (in *Slaughterhouse-Five*) and Dwayne Hoover (in *Breakfast of Champions*) who are victims both of other people, and, more particularly, of an inability meaningfully to affect their own lives. For Vonnegut, civilization's problem is not that people don't, strictly speaking, take responsibility for their lives, but that they can't. *Breakfast of Champions* suggests that art offers at least temporary salvation, but it is more characteristic of Vonnegut's books to suggest that if there is any salvation for men, it lies in their innocence or their stupidity—and consequently their inability to understand how totally they are the product of circumstance, not free will.

Vonnegut's early reputation was largely among readers of science fiction. His books emphasize the obvious, if often overlooked, fact that the elaborate theoretical structures devised by modern technology and science have important moral implications. Since these structures tend to be entirely deterministic, they suggest that objective views of the universe have no room for chance or inspiration: everything has its immediate, ascertainable cause. True moral choice is, therefore, impossible.

In *Slapstick* Vonnegut argues that, at the least, "common decency" should characterize human relations. This conclusion may make his bleak moral view palatable to some readers, but it is also deeply sentimental. Vonnegut can appear sentimental even in his best work, but it may be this, together with his comic sense, that allows his work to escape the bitterness, if not the resignation, that his bleak view of experience would encourage.

Vonnegut's fiction has often centered on "privileged" Americans—i.e., Americans with the right genealogy, connections, or opportunities. But success in Vonnegut's world is without traditional moral dimensions, of course, and even Walter F. Starbuck, the "jailbird" in the novel of that name, eventually acquires respectability. What can one do with such a world? Vonnegut solves that problem in *Deadeye Dick* with a nuclear explosion. However much he may plead for "common decency," one senses a remorseless nihilism throughout his fiction. Vonnegut's most recent novel, *Galápagos*, argues in effect that the universe is too often shaped by chance, sheer randomness, for anyone seriously to accept Darwin's orderly, logical conception of evolution, the survival of the fittest. In *Galápagos* the fittest never survive, and the book is finally as bleak and resigned as any Vonnegut has published.

—Edward Halsey Foster

WALKER, Alice (Malsenior). Born in Eatonton, Georgia, 9 February 1944. Educated at Spelman College, Atlanta, 1961–63; Sarah Lawrence College, Bronxville, New York, B.A. 1965. Married Melvyn R. Leventhal in 1967 (divorced, 1976); one daughter. Voter registration and Head Start program worker, Mississippi, and with New York City Department of Welfare, in mid-1960's; teacher, Jackson State College, 1968–69, and Tougaloo College, 1970–71, both Mississippi; lecturer, Wellesley College, Cambridge, Massachusetts, 1972–73, and University of Massachusetts, Boston, 1972–73; Associate Professor of English, Yale University, New Haven, Connecticut, after 1977. Distinguished Writer, University of California, Berkeley, Spring 1982; Fannie Hurst Professor, Brandeis University, Waltham, Massachusetts, Fall 1982. Recipient: Bread Loaf Writers Conference scholarship, 1966; Merrill fellowship, 1967; MacDowell fellowship, 1967, 1977; Radcliffe Institute fellowship, 1971; Lillian Smith Award, for poetry, 1973; American Academy Rosenthal Award, 1974; National Endowment for the Arts grant, 1977; Guggenheim grant, 1978; American Book Award, 1983; Pulitzer Prize, 1983. Ph.D: Russell Sage College, Troy, New York, 1972; D.H.L.: University of Massachusetts, Amherst, 1983. Lives in San Francisco.

PUBLICATIONS

Fiction

The Third Life of Grange Copeland. 1970.
In Love and Trouble: Stories of Black Women. 1973.
Meridian. 1976.
You Can't Keep a Good Woman Down (stories). 1981.
The Color Purple. 1982.

Verse

Once. 1968.
Five Poems. 1972.
Revolutionary Petunias and Other Poems. 1973.
Good Night, Willie Lee, I'll See You in the Morning. 1979.
Horses Make a Landscape Look More Beautiful. 1984.

Other

Langston Hughes, American Poet (biography for children). 1974.

In Search of Our Mothers' Gardens: Womanist Prose. 1983.

Editor, *I Love Myself When I am Laughing . . . and Then Again When I am Looking Mean and Impressive: A Zora Neale Hurston Reader.* 1979.

* * *

Alice Walker's poems are direct and exuberant, but they are a minor achievement in comparison with her prose. Her main impulse in writing fiction, she has said, is to record history—"and the history of my family, like that of all black Southerners, is one of dispossession."

Dispossession, emotional and material, is the theme of *The Third Life of Grange Copeland*. Grange, in his "first life," is brutalized by his field labour and by the humiliation of his deference to the white overseer. He abandons his son, Brownfield, listlessly named after the autumn colours of the Georgia cottonfields, and Brownfield becomes, in his turn, a sadistic brute. Grange spends his "second life" in New York, and returns to spend his "third life" caring for Brownfield's youngest daughter Ruth, whom he can ultimately protect only by murdering Brownfield, "a beast Grange himself had created." The weakness of the novel is that Grange's crucial spiritual regeneration is unconvincing; its strength is in its vivid evocation of the Georgia countryside, and of the intricate miseries of the suppression of hope and love.

Meridian is the fragmented, unchronological story of Meridian Hill and her political and spiritual development, as she moves through marriage and motherhood at seventeen, a repressive college education, and traumatic experiences as a civil rights worker, into something approaching sainthood. It is also the story of Lynne Rabinowitz, a white girl from the north, married and rejected by Meridian's black civil rights colleague Truman Held. Although Lynne is satirized for her self-indulgent reaction to the life of southern blacks as "the same weepy miracle that Art always was for her," she is presented with great sympathy, and is a far more developed character than Truman. *Meridian* is a series of brilliant episodes rather than a unified whole.

The Color Purple is told through the letters of two black sisters, Celie and Nettie. Nettie's letters, written from Africa where she is a missionary, are tedious and banal, but Celie's letters, at first poignant in their poverty of expression, become marvellously rich as she gradually struggles against the effects of her stepfather's cruelty and against her husband's indictment: "You black, you pore, you ugly, you a woman . . . you nothing at all." The colour purple comes to stand for Celie's affirmation of beauty and happiness; as Shug Avery, the woman who becomes her friend and lover, tells her: "I think it pisses God off if you walk by the color purple in a field somewhere and don't notice it." However, the optimism of the story's resolution still seems contrived and inconsistent, and Sofia, a minor, tragic, figure, is the most impressive character in the novel.

Walker's art is peculiarly suited to the short story. Outstanding are "Everday Use" and "Strong Horse Tea" from *In Love and Trouble*, and "Nineteen Fifty-five" and "The Abortion" from *You Can't Keep a Good Woman Down*.

"Everday Use" is narrated by the mother of Dee, who has become a sophisticated Black Muslim, and Maggie, her awkward and ignorant sister. The story turns on the old family quilts, which Dee wants to hang up to display her "heritage" and which, as she complains, Maggie would put to "everday use." The mother, in a rare surge of feeling for Maggie, gives her the quilts, and Dee drives angrily away. "Strong Horse Tea" describes the pathetic and futile attempts of a poor black woman to save the life of her baby boy. Like "Everday Use," its power is in the subtle economy of its rapidly shifting perspectives.

"The Abortion" is the sharp, witty account of a complex tangle of politics, sexuality and sentimentality. "Nineteen Fifty-five" is Walker's best story. It is narrated by an old blues singer, Gracie Mae Still, who sells one of her songs to Traynor, a character obviously based on Elvis Presley. Over the years, Traynor becomes more and more oppressed by his failure to understand the song, even though he has made it a huge commercial success. He and Gracie Mae also get fatter and fatter. Her bulk is hilariously described, but eventually she realizes that "my fat is the hurt I don't admit, not even to myself." The story ends with Traynor's televised funeral, his ignorantly blubbering fans, and Gracie Mae's comment: "One day this is going to be a pitiful country, I thought."

Some of Walker's stories in *You Can't Keep a Good Woman Down*, "Coming Apart," for example, are very close to essays, and her book of essays, *In Search of Our Mothers' Gardens*, contains many narratives, including several pieces of autobiography. The essays are lively, opinionated, and demonstrate her generous appreciation of other writers.

—Mary Jarrett

WALLACE, Lew(is). Born in Brookville, Indiana, 10 April 1827; moved with his family to Indianapolis, 1837. Studied law in his father's office in Indianapolis: admitted to Indiana bar, 1849. Raised a company, and served as a 2nd Lieutenant in the U.S. Army Infantry, in the Mexican War, 1846–47; appointed Adjutant General of Indiana at the beginning of the Civil War: served as a Colonel in the 11th Indiana Volunteers; promoted to Brigadier General, 1861, and Major General, 1862; prepared the defense of Cincinnati, 1863; given command of the Middle Division and VIII Army Corps, with headquarters at Baltimore, 1863; fought battle of Monocracy, and saved Washington, D.C., from capture, 1864; member of the court that tried Lincoln's assassins, and President of the court that tried the commandant of the Andersonville prison; mustered out, 1865. Married Susan Arnold Elston in 1852. Edited a free soil paper in Indianapolis, 1848; lawyer in Indianapolis, 1849; moved to Covington, 1850: prosecuting attorney, 1850–53; moved to Crawfordsville, 1853; member, Indiana State Senate, 1856; returned to Crawfordsville and his law practice after the Civil War; Republican candidate for U.S. House of Representatives, for Indiana, 1870; writer from 1870, also an illustrator; Governor of the New Mexico Territory, 1878–81; U.S. Minister to Turkey, 1881–85, then returned to Crawfordsville. *Died 15 February 1905.*

PUBLICATIONS

Fiction

The Fair God; or, The Last of the 'Tzins: A Tale of the Conquest of Mexico. 1873.
Ben-Hur: A Tale of the Christ. 1880.
The Boyhood of Christ. 1888.
The Prince of India; or, Why Constantinople Fell. 1893.

Play

Commodus. 1876.

Verse

The Wooing of Malkatoon, Commodus. 1898.

Other

Life of General Ben Harrison. 1888.
An Autobiography. 2 vols., 1906.

Editor, *Famous Paintings of the World*. 1894.

*

Critical Studies: *"Ben-Hur" Wallace* by Irving McKee, 1947; *Wallace: Militant Romantic* by Robert E. and Katharine M. Morsberger, 1980.

* * *

Though famous in his day as a soldier, governor, lawyer, and diplomat, Lew Wallace is mainly remembered as the author of *Ben-Hur*, one of the three best-selling American novels of the 19th century. Indeed, the novel is known by many who could not name the author. *Ben-Hur* occupies a unique place in American cultural history; subtitled "A Tale of the Christ," it was the first and in some cases the only novel to be read by many puritanical fundamentalists who considered other fiction to be a sinful and idle waste of time. Dramatized in 1899 by

William Young, *Ben-Hur* was an immense success for 20 years as a stage spectacle complete with chariot race run on treadmills. The play further broke down puritan inhibitions by introducing many to the theatre, and a colossal 1925 film version accomplished the same thing for the movies. Wallace wrote two other successful historical novels, *The Fair God* and *The Prince of India*; a blank verse drama, *Commodus*; a long narrative poem, *The Wooing of Malkatoon*, about the founder of the Ottoman Empire; a campaign biography of Benjamin Harrison; an account of Fort Donelson for *Battles and Leaders of the Civil War*; and an autobiography completed by his wife after his death in 1905.

Though the reading public considered *Ben-Hur* a supplement to sacred scripture and went to the dramatizations as to a passion play, Wallace was not a churchgoer, and the novel is closer in spirit to Jacobean revenge tragedy than to the New Testament. Wallace claimed, however, that he wrote it in part to refute the agnosticism of Robert Ingersol, and that during its composition he became convinced of the divinity of Jesus. All his novels deal with the clash of religions and cultures: *The Fair God* with the conflict of Aztec and Catholic conquistadors; *The Prince of India* with Moslem and Christian during the fall of Constantinople; and *Ben-Hur* with Jewish, pagan Roman, and Christian. Wallace's heroes are an Aztec prince, a prince of Judea, and a Turkish Sultan—all unusual for a 19th-century Anglo-Saxon to champion. A thorough researcher and a careful stylist, Wallace blended exotic romanticism with realistic detail. Though his own life was as dramatic as any of his fiction, he felt himself in some ways a failure and wrote about the romantic past as an escape from the routine of the law, the army, and political and diplomatic posts.

—Robert E. and Katharine M. Morsberger

WALLANT, Edward Lewis. Born in New Haven, Connecticut, 19 October 1926. Educated at University of Connecticut, Storrs, 1944, 1946; Pratt Institute, New York, 1947–50; studied writing at New School for Social Research, New York, 1954–55. Served in the U.S. Navy, 1944–46. Married Joyce Fromkin in 1948; two daughters and one son. Graphic designer for various advertising agencies, New York, 1950–62; became art director for McCann Erickson Agency. Recipient: Bread Loaf Writers Conference fellowship, 1960; Daroff Memorial Award, 1961; Guggenheim fellowship, 1962. *Died 5 December 1962.*

PUBLICATIONS

Fiction

The Human Season. 1960.
The Pawnbroker. 1961.
The Tenants of Moonbloom. 1963.
The Children at the Gate. 1964.

*

Bibliography: by Nicholas Ayo, in *Bulletin of Bibliography 28*, 1971.

Critical Studies: *The Landscape of Nightmare: Studies in the Contemporary American Novel* by Jonathan Baumbach, 1965; *Wallant* by David Galloway, 1979.

* * *

Edward Lewis Wallant died at 36, just as he was becoming known as a promising novelist. The four novels of his brief career center around two dominant motifs: the quest for family connections and the search for a viable religious-philosophical position. In *The Tenants of Moonbloom*, a spokesman comments, "There is a Trinity of survival, and it consists of Courage, Dream, and Love . . . he who possesses all three, or two, or at least one of these things wins whatever there is to win. . . ." All four of Wallant's protagonists become winners, in these terms, but first they must go through painful rebirths or births.

Joe Berman, a middle-aged plumber whose wife has just died in *The Human Season*, Wallant's first novel, curses his Jewish God for a time but then loses his belief in an anthropomorphic deity. In place of this, he comes to insist on the importance of the human capacity for wonder and love and to accept his own failings in family relationships. Thus he lays the ghosts of his god-like father, whom he loved too well, and his son, whom he feels he did not love enough. *The Pawnbroker*, Wallant's second novel, presents Sol Nazerman, whose wife and children died in a Nazi concentration camp, where he was a subject of experimental surgery. Nazerman affects total cynicism and a harshness comparable to that of his Nazi tormentors, but his protective shell is broken by his young assistant in the pawnshop, Jesus Ortiz, who, with three other black men, plans to rob Sol. During the attempted robbery, Jesus, who has developed a confused filial love for Sol, takes the bullet intended for the pawnbroker, and Sol is spiritually reborn. This is not, however, an easy or sentimental resolution. Nazerman's rebirth is into "the crowding filth" of humanity, wherein he feels "hopeless, wretched, strangely proud."

Though published last due to an arrangement Wallant made before he died, *The Children at the Gate* was written third and is transitional. Here the protagonist, Angelo DeMarco, at eighteen, has never been emotionally alive. The agent of his awakening is a Jewish hospital orderly, a benevolent drug pusher and comic Christ figure whose symbol is the bedpan rather than the cross. The characters in this novel tend to be overdrawn, and the humor is sometimes forced, but the book provides a bridge to *The Tenants of Moonbloom*. Norman Moonbloom is another character in the process of becoming. After a protracted, cocoon-like education, his first job is as rental agent for his brother, owner of four tenement houses. Norman begins to empathize with the miserable tenants, and, though knowing it will do no real good, he sets out to repair everything in the tenements, as an act of personal affirmation. Norman's labors are preparatory to birth, and, as is the case in the other novels, coming to life includes recognition of death's inevitability, but for Norman this is not important. Through ritual initiation he has become identified with humanity and has thus achieved a kind of immortality.

In these novels, Wallant progressed from family concerns and questions of Jewish belief to Moonbloom's identification with the human family and an affirmation of the worldly value of the most inclusive religious ritual, the initiation rite. He progressed, also, from the rather grim acceptance of the first novel through reluctant affirmation in the second and third to joyful and comic belonging in the last, in which Moonbloom, at 33, loses his virginity and learns to laugh. Near that last novel's end, Norman Moonbloom, covered with filth from a bathroom wall he is repairing, shouts, "I'M BORN!"

—James Angle

WARD, Artemus. Pseudonym for Charles Farrar Browne. Born in Waterford, Maine, 26 April 1834. Educated at Norway Liberal Institute, Maine. Apprentice printer, Lancaster *Weekly Democrat*, New Hampshire, 1847–48; free-lance compositor and reporter on various New England newspapers and in Boston, 1850–53; contributor to the humor magazine *Carpet-Bag*, 1852–53; printer in Ohio, 1853–57; local editor and columnist (as Artemus Ward), Cleveland *Plain Dealer*, 1858–60; managing editor, *Vanity Fair*, New York, 1860–62; performed selections of his own works in Ohio, 1860, Boston and New York, 1861, Washington, D.C., 1862, California and Nevada, 1863, New York and Canada, 1864, and London, 1866–67; contributor, *Punch*, London, 1866–67. *Died 6 March 1867.*

PUBLICATIONS

Collections

Complete Works. 1870; revised edition, 1898.
Selected Works, edited by Albert Jay Nock. 1924.

Prose

Artemus Ward, His Book. 1862.
Artemus Ward, His Travels. 1865; revised edition, 1865.
Artemus Ward among the Fenians. 1866.
Artemus Ward in London and Other Papers. 1867.
Artemus Ward's Lecture, edited by T.W. Robertson and E.P. Hingston. 1869; as *Artemus Ward's Panorama*, 1869.
Letters of Artemus Ward to Charles E. Wilson 1858–1861. 1900.

*

Bibliography: in *Bibliography of American Literature* by Jacob Blanck, 1955.

Critical Studies: *Ward: A Biography and Bibliography* by Don C. Seitz, 1919; *Ward* by James C. Austin, 1964; *Comic Relief: The Life and Laughter of Ward* by John J. Pullen, 1983.

* * *

Charles Farrar Browne, better known as Artemus Ward, the Yankee humorist, is a foremost representative of native American humor. During the 1850's and 1860's he was so phenomenally popular that he became the national jester of the Civil War period. He reached national prominence with his Artemus Ward pieces, which first appeared in his column in the Cleveland *Plain Dealer* in 1858, and as editor of *Vanity Fair* he became the unofficial dean of American humor. Finally, he turned to lecturing and founded the comic lecture as an enduring American institution.

Browne's literary reputation rests largely on the humor he published in the *Plain Dealer* and *Vanity Fair*. Basic to the technique of this humor is his use of Artemus Ward, an old side-showman and rascal, as his alter ego. Using the side-showman's point of view and colloquial language, Browne commented on a great variety of subjects, usually by means of the anecdote and the mock letter to the editor. His favorite humorous device was misspelling, and he used it expertly.

The Artemus Ward pieces generally treat national figures, subjects, and issues; few significant aspects of mid-19th-century culture escaped his scrutiny. Reformers and cultists caught Browne's attention early, and he directed some of his most pungent satire at the fanatics among them. He satirized militant feminists, zealous temperance advocates, Mormons, Shakers, and proponents of free love; his biggest guns, however, he reserved for unceasing war on the abolitionists. A strong northern Democrat, Browne commented extensively on national politics. During the Civil War he repeatedly attacked Congress, the inept leadership of the Union Army, draft-dodgers, profiteers, and pseudo-patriots.

Browne also expressed freely his socio-economic views, generally those of the Democratic Party. He was critical of questionable business practices, the mania for making money, speculation, and the excesses of capitalism in general. In all cases his targets were the false ideals of his age. In a number of his burlesques of the popular romance, for example, he satirized not only the style of the genre itself, but also the sentimentality, questionable values, and superficial moralism pervading popular culture.

Basically burlesques of the serious lyceum lecture, Browne's lectures were pure popular entertainment. By careful planning and cautious experimentation he succeeded in appealing to a large segment of the American people, and, at the end of his career, to British audiences as well. By making comic lecturing both respectable and profitable he paved the way for Mark Twain and the numerous other literary comedians who followed him. His best and most famous lecture was "Artemus Ward among the Mormons."

For almost two decades Browne held the attention, affection, and respect of countless Americans, including Abraham Lincoln. He not only entertained his fellow citizens, but, pleading for sanity, common sense, and moderation, he helped to shape public opinion during a critical period in American life. Finally, his success abroad helped to bring about a reappraisal by Americans of their native humorists.

—John Q. Reed

WARNER, Charles Dudley. Born in Plainsfield, Massachusetts, 12 September 1829; moved with his family to Charlemont, Massachusetts, 1837, and Cazenovia, New York, 1841. Educated at the Oneida Conference Seminary, Cazenovia; Hamilton College, Clinton, New York, B.A. 1851; studied law at the University of Pennsylvania, Philadelphia, 1856–58, LL.B. 1858. Married Susan Lee in 1856. Railway surveyor in Missouri, 1853–54; in business partnership, Philadelphia, 1855; lawyer in Chicago, 1858–60; moved to Hartford, Connecticut, 1860, and established partnership with Joseph R. Hawley: assistant editor to Hawley, 1860, then editor, 1861–67, of Hawley's *Evening Press*; editor and proprietor, with

Hawley, of the *Courant* (which consolidated with the *Press*), 1867–1900; columnist ("The Editor's Drawer," 1884–98, and "The Editor's Study," 1894–98), *Harper's* magazine New York; editor, *American Men of Letters* series, from 1881; co-editor, *Library of the World's Best Literature*, 1896–97. Member, Hartford Park Commission, and Connecticut State Commission on Sculpture; Vice-President, National Prison Association; President, American Social Science Association, and American Academy. *Died 20 October 1900.*

PUBLICATIONS

Collections

Complete Writings, edited by Thomas R. Lounsbury. 15 vols., 1904.

Fiction

The Gilded Age: A Tale of Today, with Mark Twain. 1873; edited by Bryant Morey French, 1972.
A Little Journey in the World. 1889.
The Golden House. 1895.
That Fortune. 1899.

Other

My Summer in a Garden. 1871.
Saunterings (travel). 1872.
Backlog Studies. 1873.
Baddeck and That Sort of Thing (travel). 1874.
My Winter on the Nile, Among the Mummies and Moslems. 1876.
In the Levant. 1877.
In the Wilderness. 1878.
Being a Boy. 1878.
Washington Irving (biography). 1881.
Captain John Smith (1579–1631), Sometime Governor of Virginia, and Admiral of New England. 1881.
A Roundabout Journey. 1883.
A Study of Prison Reform. 1886.
Their Pilgrimage. 1887.
On Horseback: A Tour of Virginia, North Carolina, and Tennessee. 1888.
A-Hunting of the Deer and Other Essays. 1888.
Studies in the South and West, with Comments on Canada. 1889.
Our Italy. 1891; as *The American Italy*, 1892.
As We Were Saying. 1891.
As We Go. 1893.
The Relation of Literature to Life. 1896.
The People for Whom Shakespeare Wrote. 1897.
Fashions in Literature and Other Literary and Social Essays and Addresses. 1902.
Charles Dickens: An Appreciation. 1913.

Editor, *The Book of Eloquence*. 1851.
Editor, *The Warner Classics*. 4 vols., 1897.
Editor, *Dictionary of Authors, Ancient and Modern*, and *Synopsis of Books, Ancient and Modern*. 2 vols., 1910.

*

Critical Studies: *Warner* by Annie Fields, 1904; *Nook Farm: Mark Twain's Hartford Circle* by Kenneth R. Andrews, 1950.

* * *

Charles Dudley Warner was a competent essayist and editor whose high reputation from 1870 to 1900 is matched by an equally undeserved neglect in the present century. About half of his books are pot-boilers, especially the ten travel books that dealt first with Europe and the Near East and later with America. For example, *Our Italy* was subsidized to encourage travel to California. Only through his collaboration with Mark Twain in *The Gilded Age* is Warner known to readers today. But his 1904 biographer dismissed *The Gilded Age*: "With all its ingenuities and cleverness, the book can hardly be called a literary success." The three novels Warner published from 1889 to 1899—*A Little Journey in the World, The Golden House*, and *That Fortune*—were also passed over without much attention.

But in recent years these novels have been reprinted as the value of their commentary on American society has been recognized. In the trilogy, a great fortune is built up and finally lost, an indictment of the new American plutocracy which accumulated wealth and sacrificed values. Warner knew the threat posed by the Robber Barons in the period called the "Gilded Age," but he had confidence in the eventual triumph of New England-based morality and middle-class idealism. These novels are the culmination of Warner's observations, and are his most serious studies of American society. As fiction they are less notable: Warner was an essayist, not a novelist.

Warner's literary criticism reflects conservative American cultural attitudes at the end of the 19th century. His two biographies are workmanlike: *Washington Irving* was his own volume in the "American Men of Letters" series which he edited in the 1880's; and *Captain John Smith* was written as a semi-humorous contribution to the abortive "Lives of American Worthies" planned by a rival publisher. With his brother, he edited *Library of the World's Best Literature*, volumes that now serve only to document the literary taste of another day.

Although Warner's literary output was varied, his point of view remained consistent throughout his career. He was genial, idealistic, and temperate, a conservative in morals, literary tastes, and business matters. He was a thoroughly professional journalist-literary man, at his natural best in the personal essay. When his modest newspaper pieces collected into *My Summer in a Garden* made a tremendous success, he published the more elaborate *Backlog Studies* and was called a fit successor to Charles Lamb and Washington Irving. *In the Wilderness* and *Their Pilgrimage* are travel books about the Adirondacks and fashionable resorts, but more notable for their essays on manners. *As We Were Saying* and *As We Go* are collections of Warner's *Harper's* essays: American individuality is threatened by materialism and refinement. *Being a Boy* is his nostalgic memoir of a farm in the Berkshires in the 1830's. This reminiscence and *My Summer in a Garden* are worth seeking out and ought to be reprinted: Warner's unpretentious style and mellow mood are still charming.

—Clarence A. Glasrud

WARREN, Mercy (née Otis). Born in West Barnstable, Massachusetts, 25 September 1728; sister of the political activist James Otis. Educated privately. Married James Warren in

1754 (died, 1808); five sons. Settled in Plymouth, Massachusetts, 1754; became active poet and historical apologist for the American cause in the pamphlet war preceding the Revolutionary War; a friend of John Adams and other American patriots. *Died 19 October 1814.*

PUBLICATIONS

Collections

Plays and Poems, edited by Benjamin Franklin V. 1980.

Plays

The Adulateur. 1773.
The Defeat, in Boston *Gazette*, 1773.
The Group. 1775.
The Sack of Rome and *The Ladies of Castile*, in *Poems*. 1790.

Verse

Poems, Dramatic and Miscellaneous. 1790.

Other

Observations on the New Constitution. 1788.
History of the Rise, Progress, and Termination of the American Revolution. 3 vols., 1805.
A Study in Dissent: The Warren-Gerry Correspondence, edited by C. Harvey Gardiner. 1968.

*

Critical Studies: *Warren* by Alice Brown, 1896; *First Lady of the Revolution: The Life of Warren* by Katharine Anthony, 1958.

* * *

Under normal circumstances, Mercy Warren would probably have restrained her literary impulse to private correspondence, elegant letters with, now and then, a poem enclosed. By birth and marriage, however, she was allied to the anti-Tory faction in Massachusetts and, as a matron in her forties, she emerged as a voice in the pamphlet war which preceded America's Revolutionary War for Independence. Unlike her brother, James Otis, whose passionate but closely reasoned pamphlets were so influential in the 1760's, Warren chose to write satirical dramatic sketches. In *The Adulateur*, to which some other hand added a high-rhetoric account of the Boston Massacre, *The Defeat*, and *The Group*, she introduced caricatures of her political opponents who, in waspish blank verse, condemned themselves and their colleagues. However interesting as 18th-century agitprops, Warren's satires are minimally dramatic and have no characters in the complex sense of the word. Since the plays were published anonymously, as so much of the pamphlet literature was, later scholars decided that Warren was the author of a number of unsigned satirical plays. *The Blockheads; or, The Affrighted Officers* (1776) and *The Motley Assembly* (1779), are still assigned to her by some editors, but they are so different in tone and style from anything else that she published that it is highly unlikely that she wrote them. One anonymous work, the pamphlet *Observations on the New Constitution*, a vigorous statement of the anti-federalist position in the ratification fight of 1787–88, is now rightly recognized as hers.

Aside from her political writings, Warren wrote occasional verse, sometimes satirical, more often philosophic. Written in rhymed couplets, her poems were conventional in sentiment, vocabulary, and imagery, although they often embodied the austere, anti-deist, Christian morality that was so important to Warren's life and thought. She wrote two verse tragedies, *The Ladies of Castile* and *The Sack of Rome*, which used historical material with contemporary overtones; like so many minor British plays of the 18th century, they substituted declamation for dramatic action. Her *History of the Rise, Progress, and Termination of the American Revolution*, thirty years in the making, is her most lasting work, although it is interesting today not as an objective history but for the "Biographical, Political, and Moral Observations" the title page promises. Her work as a whole is less important as a literary *oeuvre* than as a vehicle which gives the reader a glimpse of a tough-minded American woman who reflected and in some ways transcended the political and social context in which she wrote.

—Gerald Weales

WARREN, Robert Penn. Born in Guthrie, Kentucky, 24 April 1905. Educated at Guthrie High School; Vanderbilt University, Nashville, Tennessee, 1921–25, B.A. (summa cum laude) 1925; University of California, Berkeley, M.A. 1927; Yale University, New Haven, Connecticut, 1927–28; Oxford University (Rhodes Scholar), B. Litt. 1930. Married 1) Emma Brescia in 1930 (divorced, 1950); 2) the writer Eleanor Clark in 1952, one son and one daughter. Assistant Professor, Southwestern College, Memphis, Tennessee, 1930–31, and Vanderbilt University, 1931–34; Assistant and Associate Professor, Louisiana State University, Baton Rouge, 1934–42; Professor of English, University of Minnesota, Minneapolis, 1942–50; Professor of Playwriting, 1950–56, Professor of English, 1962–73, and since 1973 Professor Emeritus, Yale University. Member of the Fugitive group of poets: co-founder, *The Fugitive*, Nashville, 1922–25; founding editor, *Southern Review*, Baton Rouge, Louisiana, 1935–42; advisory editor, *Kenyon Review*, Gambier, Ohio, 1942–63. Consultant in Poetry, Library of Congress, Washington, D.C., 1944–45; Jefferson Lecturer, National Endowment for the Humanities, 1974. Recipient: Caroline Sinkler Award, 1936, 1937, 1938; Houghton Mifflin fellowship, 1939; Guggenheim fellowship, 1939, 1947; Shelley Memorial Award, 1943; Pulitzer Prize, for fiction, 1947, for poetry, 1958, 1979; Screenwriters Guild Meltzer Award, 1949; Foreign Book Prize (France), 1950; Sidney Hillman Prize, 1957; Edna St. Vincent Millay Memorial Prize, 1958; National Book Award, for poetry, 1958; Bollingen Prize, for poetry, 1967; National Endowment for the Arts grant, 1968, and lectureship, 1974; Bellamann Award, 1970; Van Wyck Brooks Award, for poetry, 1970; National Medal for Literature, 1970; Emerson-Thoreau Medal, 1975; Copernicus Award, 1976; Presidential Medal of Freedom, 1980; Common Wealth Award, 1981; MacArthur Fellowship, 1981; Brandeis University Creative Arts Award, 1983. D.Litt.: University of Louisville, Kentucky, 1949; Kenyon College, Gambier, Ohio, 1952; Colby College, Waterville, Maine, 1956; University of

Kentucky, Lexington, 1957; Swarthmore College, Pennsylvania, 1959; Yale University, 1960; Fairfield University, Connecticut, 1969; Wesleyan University, Middletown, Connecticut, 1970; Harvard University, Cambridge, Massachusetts, 1973; Southwestern College, 1974; University of the South, Sewanee, Tennessee, 1974; Monmouth College, Illinois, 1979; New York University, 1983; Oxford University, 1983; LL.D.: Bridgeport University, Connecticut, 1965; University of New Haven, Connecticut, 1974; Johns Hopkins University, Baltimore, 1977. Member, American Academy, and American Academy of Arts and Sciences; Chancellor, Academy of American Poets, 1972; U.S. Poet Laureate, 1986. Lives in Fairfield, Connecticut.

PUBLICATIONS

Fiction

Night Rider. 1939.
At Heaven's Gate. 1943.
All the King's Men. 1946.
Blackberry Winter (stories). 1946.
The Circus in the Attic and Other Stories. 1948.
World Enough and Time: A Romantic Novel. 1950.
Band of Angels. 1955.
The Cave. 1959.
Wilderness: A Tale of the Civil War. 1961.
Flood: A Romance of Our Time. 1964.
Meet Me in the Green Glen. 1971.
A Place to Come To. 1977.

Plays

Proud Flesh (in verse, produced 1947; revised [prose] version, produced 1947).
All the King's Men, from his own novel (as *Willie Stark: His Rise and Fall*, produced 1958; as *All the King's Men*, produced 1959). 1960.

Verse

Thirty-Six Poems. 1936.
Eleven Poems on the Same Theme. 1942.
Selected Poems 1923–1943. 1944.
Brother to Dragons: A Tale in Verse and Voices. 1953; revised edition, 1979.
To a Little Girl, One Year Old, in a Ruined Fortress. 1956.
Promises: Poems 1954–1956. 1957.
You, Emperors, and Others: Poems 1957–1960. 1960.
Selected Poems: New and Old 1923–1966. 1966.
Incarnations: Poems 1966–1968. 1968.
Audubon: A Vision. 1969.
Or Else: Poem / Poems 1968–1974. 1974.
Selected Poems 1923–1975. 1977.
Now and Then: Poems 1976–1978. 1978.
Two Poems. 1979.
Being Here: Poetry 1977–1980. 1980.
Love. 1981.
Rumor Verified: Poems 1979–1980. 1981.
Chief Joseph of the Nez Perce. 1983.
New and Selected Poems 1923–1985. 1985.

Other

John Brown: The Making of a Martyr. 1929.
I'll Take My Stand: The South and the Agrarian Tradition, with others. 1930.
Who Owns America? A New Declaration of Independence, with others, edited by Herbert Agar and Allen Tate. 1936.
Understanding Poetry: An Anthology for College Students, with Cleanth Brooks. 1938; revised edition, 1950, 1960, 1976.
Understanding Fiction, with Cleanth Brooks. 1943; revised edition, 1959, 1979; abridged edition, as *The Scope of Fiction*, 1960.
A Poem of Pure Imagination: An Experiment in Reading, in *The Rime of the Ancient Mariner*, by Samuel Taylor Coleridge. 1946.
Modern Rhetoric: With Readings, with Cleanth Brooks. 1949; revised edition, 1958, 1970, 1979.
Fundamentals of Good Writing: A Handbook of Modern Rhetoric, with Cleanth Brooks. 1950.
Segregation: The Inner Conflict in the South. 1956.
Selected Essays. 1958.
Remember the Alamo! (for children). 1958; as *How Texas Won Her Freedom*, 1959.
The Gods of Mount Olympus (for children). 1959.
The Legacy of the Civil War: Meditations on the Centennial. 1961.
Who Speaks for the Negro? 1965.
A Plea in Mitigation: Modern Poetry and the End of an Era (lecture). 1966.
Homage to Theodore Dreiser. 1971.
John Greenleaf Whittier's Poetry: An Appraisal and a Selection. 1971.
A Conversation with Warren, edited by Frank Gado. 1972.
Democracy and Poetry (lecture). 1975.
Warren Talking: Interviews 1950–1978, edited by Floyd C. Watkins and John T. Hiers. 1980.
Jefferson Davis Gets His Citizenship Back. 1980.

Editor, with Cleanth Brooks and John Thibaut Purser, *An Approach to Literature: A Collection of Prose and Verse with Analyses and Discussions*. 1936; revised edition, 1952, 1975.
Editor, *A Southern Harvest: Short Stories by Southern Writers*. 1937.
Editor, with Cleanth Brooks, *An Anthology of Stories from the Southern Review*. 1953.
Editor, with Albert Erskine, *Short Story Masterpieces*. 1954.
Editor, with Albert Erskine, *Six Centuries of Great Poetry*. 1955.
Editor, with Albert Erskine, *A New Southern Harvest*. 1957.
Editor, with Allen Tate, *Selected Poems*, by Denis Devlin. 1963.
Editor, *Faulkner: A Collection of Critical Essays*. 1966.
Editor, with Robert Lowell and Peter Taylor, *Randall Jarrell 1914–1965*. 1967.
Editor, *Selected Poems of Herman Melville*. 1970.
Editor and part author, with Cleanth Brooks and R.W.B. Lewis, *American Literature: The Makers and the Making*. 2 vols., 1973.
Editor, *Katherine Anne Porter: A Collection of Critical Essays*. 1979.

*

Bibliography: *Warren: A Reference Guide* by Neil Nakadate, 1977; *Warren: A Descriptive Bibliography 1922–79* by James A. Grimshaw, Jr., 1981.

Critical Studies: *Warren* (in German) by Klaus Poenicke, 1959; *Warren: The Dark and Bloody Ground* by Leonard Casper, 1960; *Warren* by Charles H. Bohner, 1964, revised edition, 1981; *Warren* by Paul West, 1964; *Warren: A Collection of Critical Essays* edited by John Lewis Longley, Jr., 1965; *A Colder Fire: The Poetry of Warren*, 1965, and *The Poetic Vision of Warren*, 1977, both by Victor Strandberg; *Web of Being: The Novels of Warren* by Barnett Guttenberg, 1975; *Twentieth-Century Interpretations of All the King's Men* edited by Robert H. Chambers, 1977; *Warren: A Vision Earned* by Marshall Walker, 1979; *Warren: A Collection of Critical Essays* edited by Richard Gray, 1980; *Critical Essays on Warren* edited by William B. Clark, 1981; *Warren: Critical Perspectives* edited by Neil Nakadate, 1981; *The Achievement of Warren* by James H. Justus, 1981; *Then and Now: The Personal Past in the Poetry of Warren* by Floyd C. Watkins, 1982; *Homage to Warren* edited by Frank Graziano, 1982; *Warren* by Katherine Snipes, 1983; *A Southern Renascence Man: Views of Warren* edited by Walter B. Edgar, 1984; *In the Heart's Last Kingdom: Warren's Major Poetry* by Calvin Bedient, 1984.

* * *

Robert Penn Warren is a distinguished writer in at least three genres: the novel, poetry, and the essay. Although he has lived outside the south since 1942, he has so consistently written novels, essays, and poetry on southern subjects, in southern settings, and about southern themes that he must be regarded still as a southern writer. Over much of his work there is a typically southern brooding sense of darkness, evil, and human failure, and he employs a gothicism of form and an extravagance of language and technique of a sort often associated with writing in the southeastern United States. Warren is a profoundly philosophical writer in all aspects of his work. Writing of Joseph Conrad, he once said, "The philosophical novelist, or poet, is one for whom the documentation of the world is constantly striving to rise to the level of generalization about values . . . for whom the urgency of experience . . . is the urgency to know the meaning of experience." The description fits him well.

In Warren's principal work in the novel and poetry, there are a persistent obsession with time and with history, a sense of man's imperfection and failure, and an awareness that innocence is always lost in the acts of achieving maturity and growth. His characters are usually men who destroy themselves through seeking an absolute in a relative universe. From John Brown, the subject of his first book, a biography, to Percy Munn, the protagonist of *Night Rider*, to Willie Stark of *All the King's Men*, to Jeremiah Beaumont of *World Enough and Time*, to Lilburn Lewis in the poem-play *Brother to Dragons*, to Jed Tewksbury in *A Place to Come To*—Warren's protagonists repeat this pattern of the obsessive and ultimately self-destructive search for the impossible ideal.

His work usually rests on actual events from history or at least on actual historical situations—*Night Rider* on the Kentucky tobacco wars, *At Heaven's Gate* on a Nashville political murder, *All the King's Men* on the career of Huey Long, *World Enough and Time* on an 1825 Kentucky murder, *Band of Angels* and *Wilderness* on the Civil War, *The Cave* on Floyd Collins's cave entombment, *Flood* on the inundating of towns by the Tennessee Valley Authority, *A Place to Come To* to at least some extent on his own experiences as a college teacher, although the story can hardly be considered autobiographical. The poem *Brother to Dragons* is based on an atrocious crime committed by Thomas Jefferson's nephews. This concern with history and the individual implications of social and political events is also present in his non-fiction, such as *Segregation: The Inner Conflict in the South, The Legacy of the Civil War*, and *Who Speaks for the Negro?* These works, too, deal with fundamental issues of southern history.

In order to present the philosophical meaning of his novels and poems, Warren uses highly individualized narrators, such as Jack Burden in *All the King's Men*; special techniques of narrative point of view, as in *World Enough and Time*; frequently a metaphysical style; the illumination of events through contrast with enclosed and frequently recollected narratives, as in *Night Rider* and *All the King's Men*; and highly melodramatic plots which become elaborate workings out of abstract statements, as in *Band of Angels*.

His poetry reiterates essentially the same view of man. He began as an undergraduate at Vanderbilt University writing poetry with the Fugitive poetry group—John Crowe Ransom, Allen Tate, and Donald Davidson—and he continued to write a relatively fixed form, tightly constructed, ironic lyric verse until about 1943. Between 1943 and 1953 he concentrated predominantly on the novel. With *Brother to Dragons* he returned to poetic expression, and since that time has written extensively in both poetic and novelistic forms. The verse forms that he has used since 1953 have been much looser, marked by broken rhythms, clusters of lines arranged in patterns dictated by emotion, and frequent alternations in the level of diction. Behind his poetry, as behind his fiction, there is usually an implied, if not explicit, narrative pattern. This narrative pattern is often historical, as in "The Ballad of Billy Potts," *Brother to Dragons*, or *Audubon*. In his recent verse, Warren contrasts man's weaknesses and imperfections with the enduring stars, with time, and with eternity.

As a critic and a teacher Warren has had a profound influence on the study and criticism of literature. His textbook *Understanding Poetry*, written with Cleanth Brooks, a presentation of poetry in New Critical terms emphasizing the poem as an independent work of art, went a long way toward creating a revolution in how literature was taught in American colleges. He has written many other textbooks and critical studies such as his *Homage to Theodore Dreiser, John Greenleaf Whittier's Poetry*, and *Democracy and Poetry*.

Warren is still very active, especially as a poet. His work in all genres is marked by a high concern with language, a depth of philosophical statement, a firm and rigorous commitment to a moral-ethical view of man, and a willingness to experiment often beyond the limits of artistic safety with the forms in which he works. Warren is a peculiarly indigenous American writer of great intelligence and of significant accomplishment. He can, with justice, be called our most distinguished living man of letters.

—C. Hugh Holman

See the essay on *All the King's Men*.

WASHINGTON, Booker T(aliaferro). Born on Hale's Ford plantation, Franklin County, Virginia, 5 April 1856. Worked in salt-furnace and coal mine, and attended elementary school, Malden, West Virginia, from 1865; later domestic servant in home of furnace and mine owner; educated at Hampton Institute, Virginia, 1872–75, graduated with honors; Wayland Seminary, Washington, D.C., 1878–79. Married 1) Fannie N. Smith in 1882 (died, 1884), one daughter; 2) Olivia A. Davidson in 1885 (died, 1889), two sons; 3) Margaret James Murray in 1893. Hotel waiter, Connecticut, 1875; schoolteacher, Malden, 1875–78; teacher and secretary to principal, Hampton Institute, 1879–81; founder and first principal, Tuskegee Normal School (Tuskegee Institute from 1893), Alabama, 1881–1915. Frequent speaker on education and race relations from 1884; established numerous rural extention programs at Tuskegee Institute; founder, National Negro Business League, 1900; organizer, National Negro Health Week, 1914. A.M.: Harvard University, Cambridge, Massachusetts, 1896; LL.D.: Dartmouth College, Hanover, New Hampshire, 1901. *Died 14 November 1915.*

PUBLICATIONS

Collections

Papers, edited by Louis R. Harlan. 1972—

Prose

Daily Resolves. 1896.
Black-Belt Diamonds: Gems from the Speeches, Addresses, and Talks to Students, edited by Victoria Earle Matthews. 1898.
The Future of the American Negro. 1899.
A New Negro for a New Century, with N.B. Wood and Fannie Barrier Williams. 1900.
Some European Observations and Experiences. 1900.
Sowing and Reaping. 1900.
The Story of My Life and Work. 1900; as *An Autobiography*, 1901.
Up from Slavery: An Autobiography. 1901.
Character Building. 1902.
Working with the Hands. 1904.
Putting the Most into Life. 1906.
Frederick Douglass (biography). 1907.
The Negro in Business. 1907.
The Negro in the South: His Economic Progress in Relation to His Moral and Religious Development, with W.E.B. Du Bois. 1907; as *The American Negro (Southern States)*, 1909.
The Story of the Negro. 2 vols., 1909.
My Larger Education, Being Chapters from My Experience. 1911.
The Man Farthest Down: A Record of Observation and Study in Europe, with Robert E. Park. 1912.
The Story of Slavery. 1913.
Selected Speeches, edited by E. Davidson Washington. 1932.
Quotations, edited by E. Davidson Washington. 1938.

Editor, *The Negro Problem*. 1903.
Editor, *Tuskegee and Its People: Their Ideals and Achievements*. 1905.

*

Bibliography: in *Eight Negro Bibliographies* by Daniel T. Williams, 1970.

Critical Studies: *Washington, Educator and Interracial Interpreter* by Basil Mathews, 1948; *Washington and His Critics: The Problem of Negro Leadership* edited by Hugh Hawkins, 1962; *Washington* edited by E.L. Thornbrough, 1969; *Washington: The Making of a Black Leader 1856–1901*, 1972, and *Washington: The Wizard of Tuskegee 1901–1915*, 1983, both by Louis R. Harlan.

* * *

A reluctant author, persuaded to write by his admirers, Booker T. Washington is not a natural stylist. His books reflect the main concern of his life in the outside world—namely, the "raising up" of his fellow black Americans by means of land ownership and a thorough education, with emphasis on the mastery of skilled trades. Thrift and industry are the solutions he preaches, the familiar 19th-century gospel of self-help given substance by his own success at Tuskegee, the college largely built and supervised by Washington, his staff, and students. As much propaganda as literature, his works launch themselves at the consciousness of the reader with the immediacy of speech. Polemics, exhortations in writing from one of the greatest public speakers of his time, each of them delves deep into the personal experience of the man who wrote them. This experience sustains their author in the alien terrain of "literature." Washington's books impress by simplicity of utterance, by a telling use of anecdotes in the building of arguments, above all by their grasp of practical detail. As he states, "I have great faith in the power and influence of facts."

The improving intention behind his works is usually self-evident. *Character Building* and *My Larger Education* stress the importance of learning, the latter describing Washington's pioneering efforts in "project" education. *Working with the Hands* reaffirms the significance of manual labouring skills as a means of self-betterment. With the more ambitious *The Story of the Negro*, Washington attempts to correct the established mythology of his day, which regarded the black race as lacking in historic and cultural achievement. Some of his findings are questionable, and the book itself somewhat pedestrian, but if Washington knows little of his ancestry, he was surely right to trust the instinct that told him "A race which could produce as good and gentle and loving a woman as my mother must have some good in it that the geographers had failed to discover."

More impressive in many respects is *The Man Farthest Down*, inspired by a tour of Europe not long before the writer's death. In this detailed study Washington examines the lifestyles of European peasants and compares their lot with that of his black fellow-countrymen. It is typical of his positive vision that he claims his compatriots to be more fortunate than their white labouring counterparts. The great populariser of industrial education also sees in the prosperity of Danish farmers proof of his own maxims in support of land ownership and agricultural labour. While his view of the black American's position at the turn of the century is perhaps over-optimistic, *The Man Farthest Down* remains a valid and intriguing social document.

Up from Slavery is Washington's masterpiece, outlining in simple but effective words the magnitude of the achievement that led him from childhood on a slave plantation to leadership of his people. Considering the random, fragmentary manner in which it was compiled, the work retains a remarkable unity and coherence. Laced with stories and humorous aphorisms,

Up from Slavery embodies the broad vision of its author, together with his insistence on neatness and personal hygiene. It also stresses that policy of co-operation with the southern whites that Washington campaigned for all his life, and for which he was so often criticised by his fellow blacks.

Washington's famous speech at the Atlanta Exposition of 1895, contained in the book, remains the most controversial and quotable of all his public utterances. His conciliatory approach, urging both sides to "Cast down your bucket where you are!" and work together, has been construed by some as a betrayal of his own people. Washington's claim that "In all things purely social we can be as separate as the fingers, yet one as the hand in all things essential to mutual progress" certainly implies acceptance of the black's inferior status, and he appears willing to forfeit political rights in return for blacks owning their own land. Nevertheless, it must be remembered that his gradualist message gained more for black Americans in his time than racial protest by his critics. Nor should his conciliatory efforts be misread as cowardice. *Up from Slavery* contains numerous examples of Washington speaking out against racial injustice, notably his impassioned outbursts condemning the Ku Klux Klan and the white lynch mobs. His written work bears witness to a cautious, but shrewd pragmatism, based on an awareness of what could be accomplished. This quality, together with the sincerity of its author, helps to make *Up from Slavery* one of the classic American autobiographies.

Throughout his writings, one is made aware of Washington's humanity, the genuine concern for his fellows that informs every page. Undoubtedly a man of strongly held opinions, he seems incapable of malice ("No man shall drag me down by making me hate him"). Self-taught himself, he never loses his close affinity with the black working man, whose respect he clearly retained. While it can be argued that his books give insufficient emphasis to higher education and political rights, there is truth in his claim that "No race can prosper till it learns that there is as much dignity in tilling a field as in writing a poem . . . Nor should we permit our grievances to overshadow our opportunities."

Washington was not a great writer; what is beyond doubt is that he was a great man. The best of his works are fitting testimony to the heroic nature of his achievement.

—Geoff Sadler

WELTY, Eudora (Alice). Born in Jackson, Mississippi, 13 April 1909. Educated at Mississippi State College for Women, Columbus, 1925–27; University of Wisconsin, Madison, B.A. 1929; Columbia University School for Advertising, New York, 1930–31. Part-time journalist, 1931–32; publicity agent, Works Progress Administration (WPA), 1933–36; staff member, *New York Times Book Review*, during World War II. Honorary Consultant in American Letters, Library of Congress, Washington, D.C., 1958. Recipient: Bread Loaf Writers Conference fellowship, 1940; O. Henry Award, 1942, 1943, 1968; Guggenheim fellowship, 1942, 1948; American Academy grant, 1944, Howells Medal, 1955, and Gold Medal, 1972; Ford fellowship, for drama; Brandeis University Creative Arts Award, 1965; Edward MacDowell Medal, 1970; Pulitzer Prize, 1973; National Medal for Literature, 1980; Presidential Medal of Freedom, 1980; American Book Award, for paperback, 1983; Bobst Award, 1984; Common Wealth Award, 1984; Mystery Writers of America award, 1985. D.Litt.: Denison University, Granville, Ohio, 1971; Smith College, Northampton, Massachusetts; University of Wisconsin, Madison; University of the South, Sewanee, Tennessee; Washington and Lee University, Lexington, Virginia. Member, American Academy, 1971. Lives in Jackson, Mississippi.

PUBLICATIONS

Fiction

A Curtain of Green and Other Stories. 1941.
The Robber Bridegroom. 1942.
The Wide Net and Other Stories. 1943.
Delta Wedding. 1946.
Music from Spain (story). 1948.
The Golden Apples (stories). 1949.
Selected Stories. 1954.
The Ponder Heart. 1954.
The Bride of Innisfallen and Other Stories. 1955.
Thirteen Stories, edited by Ruth M. Vande Kieft. 1965.
Losing Battles. 1970.
The Optimist's Daughter. 1972.
The Collected Stories. 1980.
Moon Lake and Other Stories. 1980.
Retreat (story). 1981.

Verse

A Flock of Guinea Hens Seen from a Car. 1970.

Other

Short Stories (essay). 1949.
Place in Fiction. 1957.
Three Papers on Fiction. 1962.
The Shoe Bird (for children). 1964.
A Sweet Devouring (on children's literature). 1969.
One Time, One Place: Mississippi in the Depression: A Snapshot Album. 1971.
A Pageant of Birds. 1975.
Fairy Tale of the Natchez Trace. 1975.
The Eye of the Storm: Selected Essays and Reviews. 1975.
Ida M'Toy (memoir). 1979.
Miracles of Perception: The Art of Willa Cather, with Alfred Knopf and Yehudi Menuhin. 1980.
Conversations with Welty (interviews), edited by Peggy Whitman Prenshaw. 1984.
One Writer's Beginnings. 1984.

*

Bibliography: by Noel Polk, in *Mississippi Quarterly*, Fall 1973; *Welty: A Reference Guide* by Victor H. Thompson, 1976; *Welty: A Critical Bibliography 1936–1958* by Bethany C. Swearington, 1984.

Critical Studies: *Welty* by Ruth M. Vande Kieft, 1962, revised edition, 1986; *A Season of Dreams: The Fiction of Welty* by Alfred Appel, Jr., 1965; *Welty* by Joseph A. Bryant, Jr., 1968; *The Rhetoric of Welty's Short Stories* by Zelma Turner Howard, 1973; *A Still Moment: Essays on the Art of Welty* edited by John F. Desmond, 1978; *Welty: Critical Essays* edited by Peggy Whitman Prenshaw, 1979; *Welty: A Form of Thanks* edited by Ann J. Abadie and Louis D. Dollarhide, 1979; *Welty's Achievement of Order* by Michael Kreyling, 1980; *Welty* by Elizabeth Evans, 1981; *A Tissue of Lies: Eudora Welty and the Southern Romance* by Jennifer L. Randisi, 1982; *Welty's Chronicle: A Story of Mississippi Life* by Albert J. Devlin, 1983; *With Ears Opening Like Morning Glories: Welty and the Love of Storytelling* by Carol S. Manning, 1985.

*   *   *

Eudora Welty is a party to the great outpouring of fiction that is often referred to as the Southern Renaissance, the discovery of solid traditions and uneasy tensions that color the work of William Faulkner, Katherine Anne Porter, Caroline Gordon, William Styron, and others. Welty's terrain overlaps that of Faulkner—the State of Mississippi. But it offers a contrasting appearance—indeed, a predominantly sunny one despite the shadows of ancient pain, present injustice, and future uncertainty that both Faulkner and Welty discover in their part of the South. But Welty's imaginative world maintains its special rules: rules of civility and of affection that protect the continuance of human meaning and human dignity. It is a continuance that may well be a "losing battle," but it is never really a lost battle. The majority of Welty's characters reel under blows that chance, inheritance, and environment deal them, but they rise to hope and love another day. The compulsions they face and partly master as less awesome than those many a Faulkner character meets. True, there is guilt, but the guilt is personal rather than one which several generations have piled up. There are also authoritative patterns of life. But these patterns, in contrast to those of Faulkner, are familiar and easily identifiable rather than occult and mysterious. There is no "bear" or any other symbol of aboriginal compulsion moving back and forth in the delta and the hill country which Welty recollects and recreates in her short stories and her novels. The minds of her characters—rednecks, cotton aristocrats, and the "just folks" of small county seats—are indeed challenged by the events that overtake them. But the contests between minds and events issues in a draw, and sometimes better than a draw.

This can be seen in the many short stories, simple of surface but calculating in their approach to a revelatory conclusion. The story "Keela, The Outcast Indian Maiden" (in *A Curtain of Green*) seems, for most of its course, to be a study of the guilt a young man feels for his share in the exploitation of a little black man who has been kidnapped and exhibited as a freak in a sideshow. But by the end of the story the young man has made a sort of expiation of his share of guilt; this is a draw. But suddenly attention shifts to the little black man, *he* is only amused by the antics of his visitor and sits down to supper with his children; out of abasement the black man has won a minor victory.

The reverses and complexities that Welty meditates on are the stuff of her many stories. Such reverses and complexities also furnish out the longer works, with the possible exception of the early tale, *The Robber Bridegroom*, which is a pious salute to the violent times when Mississippi land was being invaded by white men, farmers, riverboat men, and robbers who attacked travellers on the Natchez Trace. This narrative has the willed simplicity of folk tale, as indeed do many of the short stories. But it is a simplicity that appears only intermittently in the longer novels, where the writer's imagination engages itself with a more or less contemporary milieu and the sensibilities educated there. *Delta Wedding* is a salute to the cotton aristocrats and their experience of power and complacency in the 1920's. Some characters in the novel enjoy their privileges, and others try to measure them and test them. The careless "lose" their battle; the thoughtful attain to an uneasy survival: a comprehension of their situation. It is a comprehension that, unfortunately, has to be recast from day to day.

This recasting is, in *Delta Wedding*, complex and difficult to express in a phrase. So it continues to be in shorter novels like *The Ponder Heart* and *The Optimist's Daughter*, two tales of matrimonial misadventures which are observed and studied by women—centers of awareness—who are sufficient vehicles for Welty's own discriminations. A more difficult book is *Losing Battles*. In this long account of a family reunion up in the Mississippi hills, the novelist for the most part dispenses with the fairly refined and privileged observers of her other novels. She also gives up the comic discriminations of *Delta Wedding* and *The Ponder Heart*. *Losing Battles* is, in sheer event, not far removed from the farce of Li'l Abner's Dogpatch; there are mad car accidents, watermelon fights, and gargantuan feastings. Nor does Welty allow her own prose to reproduce the thoughts of her mostly back-country characters. The interminable conversations, fashioned from rural clichés, nevertheless become transparent envelopes through which appear the "contents" of each red-neck existence with a range of sensitivity almost as complex as that which is represented in *Delta Wedding*.

In short, Welty has a wide range of strategies. But these all serve a concern that is strict, narrow, and unwavering: how persons respond to their opportunity to live, what comment they are able to make, the deep interest that lies in almost any such comment when it is carefully reproduced and charitably understood.

—Harold H. Watts

See the essay on *Losing Battles*.

WESCOTT, Glenway. Born in Kewaskum, Wisconsin, 11 April 1901. Educated at the University of Chicago (President of the Poetry Society), 1917–19. Full-time writer from 1921; lived in France and Germany, 1925–33. D.Litt.: Rutgers University, New Brunswick, New Jersey, 1963. Member, 1947, and President, 1959–62, National Institute of Arts and Letters. *Died 22 February 1987.*

PUBLICATIONS

Fiction

The Apple of the Eye. 1924.
. . . *Like a Lover* (stories). 1926.
The Grandmothers: A Family Portrait. 1927; as *A Family Portrait*, 1927.
Good-bye Wisconsin (stories). 1928.
The Babe's Bed (story). 1930.
The Pilgrim Hawk: A Love Story. 1940.
Apartment in Athens. 1945; as *Household in Athens*, 1945.

Verse

The Bitterns: A Book of Twelve Poems. 1920.
Native of Rock: XX Poems 1921–1922. 1925.

Other

Elizabeth Madox Roberts: A Personal Note. 1930.
Fear and Trembling (essays). 1932.
A Calendar of Saints for Unbelievers. 1932.
12 Fables of Aesop, Newly Narrated. 1954.
Images of Truth: Remembrances and Criticism. 1962.

Editor, *The Maugham Reader*. 1950.
Editor, *Short Novels of Colette*. 1951.

*

Bibliography: by Sy Myron Kahn, in *Bulletin of Bibliography* 22, 1956.

Critical Studies: *Wescott* by William H. Rueckert, 1965; *Wescott: The Paradox of Voice* by Ira Johnson, 1971.

* * *

Glenway Wescott, a classmate of Yvor Winters and Vincent Sheean, was President of the Poetry Society at the University of Chicago. His imagist lyrics appeared in *Poetry* and were later printed privately in two small volumes. Then he turned away from poetry, and because of ill health left the university in 1919; for six restless years he lived briefly in New Mexico, the Berkshires, New York City, England, and Germany, usually with his lifelong friend Monroe Wheeler. Wescott's precocity, striking appearance (tall, blond), and cultivated British accent marked him during his expatriate years from 1925 to 1933, when he lived in Paris, at Villefrance-sur-Mer, and in Germany. In *The Autobiography of Alice B. Toklas*, Gertrude Stein records his first visit: "Glenway impressed us with his English accent. Hemingway explained. He said, when you matriculate at the University of Chicago, you write down just what accent you will have and they give it to you when you graduate." In the 1920's Wescott published impressive critical reviews (chiefly in the *Dial* and the *New Republic*), two novels, and a collection of short stories, though he has published very little in the succeeding 50 years.

Wescott was 23 when *The Apple of the Eye* was published. The story of Hannah Madoc, a Wisconsin farm woman, is told from various perspectives. It is a novel of initiation and of revolt against the hostile environment of farm and town—especially against repressive Puritanism. *The Grandmothers* was Wescott's greatest popular success. Alwyn Tower, reliving in France his Wisconsin childhood, is "a participating narrator, identical to the author's second (artistic) self" (Ira Johnson). His curiosity aroused by an old family album, the young man pieces together the story of his three grandmothers (one grandfather married twice). Cadenced prose and high sensitivity present the pioneer experience, always focused on Wescott's major themes of love and the self.

An introductory essay lent its title to *Good-bye Wisconsin*, a short story collection. The ten stories, and *The Babe's Bed*, a slightly longer short story published in a limited Paris edition, show Wisconsin as hostile to the realization of the self. Wescott published only five more short stories, from 1932 to 1942, none of them noteworthy. He is often classified as a midwestern realist and regionalist, and these stories obviously connect him with the "Revolt from the Village" writing of Edgar Lee Masters, Sherwood Anderson, and Sinclair Lewis. But Wescott's fiction also demonstrates his abandonment of realism, regionalism, and the provincial midwest for a European aesthetic existence and artistic ideal. Among his friends were Ford Madox Ford, Jean Cocteau, Elly Ney, and Rebecca West.

Westcott's current reputation as a stylist is based primarily on *The Pilgrim Hawk: A Love Story*, which first appeared in two issues of *Harper's* and has been reprinted and anthologized. Alwyn Tower, now in America, recounts a day's incident in France in 1940 which involves Irish and American expatriates and their servants. Tower's nostalgic reminiscence is heavily ironic, and the falcon is central to the love story Tower narrates. In addition to the two physical love triangles, a third appears to perceptive readers, a subtle examination of the conflict between appetite and control; as James Korges puts it (in *Contemporary Novelists*), "The reader is not told about the conflict of love and art; instead he receives it, as a powerful undercurrent in the story of an Irish couple and a hawk, which is also a story about love and art, freedom and captivity."

Wescott considered *Apartment in Athens* his contribution to the war effort. A German officer is billeted in the apartment of a Greek middle-class intellectual. "The cramped physical and moral conditions, the readjustments in the relationships of the family, the whole distortion of the social organism by the unassimilable presence of the foreigner—all this is most successfully created" (Edmund Wilson). The novel, however, is marred by its ending, a long letter smuggled out of the prison cell of the condemned Greek father, and the anti-Nazi editorializing violates the fictional illusion.

Images of Truth collects the critical essays Westcott had published since 1939. His long essays on Katherine Anne Porter, Elizabeth Madox Roberts, Mann, Colette, Maugham, and Wilder are highly personal expressions of Wescott's own idiosyncratic views on life and literature. Wescott's imagist poetry, which he abandoned early, has been long forgotten. His essentially lyric talent finds expression in his prose.

—Clarence A. Glasrud

WEST, Nathanael. Born Nathan Weinstein in New York City, 17 October 1903; changed name, 1926. Educated at DeWitt Clinton High School, New York; Tufts College, Medford, Massachusetts, 1921; Brown University, Providence, Rhode Island, 1922–24, Ph.B. 1924. Married Eileen McKenney in 1940. Worked for his father in real estate business, 1924–25; lived in Paris, 1926–27; night manager, Kenmore Hall Hotel and Suffolk Club Hotel, New York, 1927–31; associate editor, to William Carlos Williams, *Contact: An American Quarterly*, 1931–32; writer for Columbia, 1933, 1938, Republic, 1936–38, Universal, 1938, and RKO, 1938–40, all Hollywood. *Died 22 December 1940.*

PUBLICATIONS

Collections

Complete Works. 1957.

Fiction

The Dream Life of Balso Snell. 1931.
Miss Lonelyhearts. 1933.

A Cool Million: The Dismantling of Lemuel Pitkin. 1934.
The Day of the Locust. 1939.

Plays

Good Hunting: A Satire, with Joseph Shrank (produced 1938).

Screenplays: *The President's Mystery*, with Lester Cole, 1936; *Follow Your Heart*, with others, 1936; *Ticket to Paradise*, with others, 1936; *It Could Happen to You*, with Samuel Ornitz, 1937; *Rhythm in the Clouds*, with others, 1937; *Gangs of New York* (uncredited), 1938; *Orphans of the Street* (uncredited), 1938; *Born to Be Wild*, 1938; *Five Came Back*, with others, 1939; *I Stole a Million*, with Lester Cole, 1939; *Spirit of Culver*, with others, 1939; *Men Against the Sky*, with John Twist, 1940; *Let's Make Music*, 1940.

*

Bibliography: *West: A Comprehensive Bibliography* by William White, 1975; *West: An Annotated Bibliography of the Scholarship and Works* by Dennis P. Vannatta, 1976.

Critical Studies: *West: An Interpretive Study* by James F. Light, 1961, revised edition, 1971; *West* by Stanley Edgar Hyman, 1962; *West: The Ironic Prophet* by Victor Comerchero, 1964; *The Fiction of West* by Randall Reid, 1967; *West: The Art of His Life* by Jay Martin, 1970, and *West: A Collection of Critical Essays* edited by Martin, 1971; *West: A Critical Essay* by Nathan A. Scott, 1971; *West's Novels* by Irving Malin, 1972; *West: The Cheaters and the Cheated* edited by David Madden, 1973; *West* by Kingsley Widmer, 1982; *West* by Robert Emmet Long, 1985.

* * *

While many of the writers of the 1930's found in the naturalistic tradition a form which would directly express their protest at what seemed to be the collapse or corruption of the American Dream, Nathanael West developed an oblique vision that may prove more lasting than the products of many of his contemporaries. A statement by his painter-protagonist, Tod Hackett (*The Day of the Locust*), provides a reasonable thematic definition of West's artistic intentions: "It is hard to laugh at the need for beauty and romance, no matter how tasteless, even horrible, the results of that are. But it is easy to sigh. Few things are sadder than the truly monstrous." Focusing relentlessly on the radical disparity between the romantic expectations pandered to by the mass media and the actual limited portion which is the human lot, West's talent is to delineate "the truly monstrous" in a grotesque world that hovers ambiguously between the hilarious and the heartbreaking. Accepting more or less the same premises that underlie Eliot's *The Waste Land*, West's work is equally hallucinatory and probably more pessimistic, as well as more comic. It is partly indebted to the techniques of surrealism that West absorbed in a brief post-college sojourn in Paris where he wrote his first novel (*The Dream Life of Balso Snell*), and its energy derives from a deep moral exasperation that could be a result of his youthful training in Judaism. Relatively overlooked when it was published, West's fiction brought the sub-genre of "Black Humor" into prominence after World War II when it served as a model of encouragement for such writers as Carson McCullers, James Purdy, Flannery O'Connor, and John Hawkes.

Although West wrote four novels in his abruptly ended career, he is remembered primarily for *Miss Lonelyhearts* and *The Day of the Locust*. In both novels West cultivates a stripped cinematic style, advancing his narrative in a spastic sequence of intense and fragmented scenes. As a Hollywood screenwriter for the last years of his life, West clearly found the discipline of the film compatible with his own penchant for constructing stories out of dominantly visual images, and *The Day of the Locust* is generally regarded as the premiere "Hollywood novel" in American fiction.

In *Miss Lonelyhearts*, the un-named protagonist is a bachelor newspaper columnist assigned to the job of giving advice to the lovelorn. Worn down by the barrage of unabated and insoluble misery that pours in on him and bedeviled by the savage nihilism of his city editor, Shrike, he finds himself unable even to imagine palliative possibilities for those who write to him. Further, his defensive cynicism and detachment erode as he begins to recognize his own condition in the broken human beings who are his suppliants. Killed finally in a ludicrous comedy of errors, he becomes a futile immolated Christ whose death is merely another addition to the crumpled heap of frustrated hopes that the novel assembles. West's dark mockery is pointed in all directions. The manipulators are as crippled and impotent as the manipulated; nor does the novel permit any socio-political resolution of the problems it presents. Lacking a sane religious option for satisfying "the need for beauty and romance," the frenetic improvisations of the spiritually dispossessed can only be freakishly monstrous and sad.

The Day of the Locust displaces a greater imaginative volume, just as its setting—Hollywood at the time when it was dream-factory to the world—is a larger milieu than the newspaper office and bars of *Miss Lonelyhearts*. Here West places his artist-protagonist on the margins of the action and structures the novel on what might be termed the principle of "an image within an image." Tod Hackett is engaged in painting *The Burning of Los Angeles*, a giant canvas that he intends to be prophetic in the Old Testament sense; and the novel as a whole duplicates on a greatly magnified screen his apocalyptic vision of a holocaust. Unlike the multitude of victims in *Miss Lonelyhearts*, the grotesques of *The Day of the Locust*, mindless as lemmings, purposeless as falling rain, seek vengeance for the rootlessness, disappointment, and excruciating boredom of their lives in random unprovoked destruction. If the keynote of *Miss Lonelyhearts* is a profound sadness wrested out of grotesque comedy, *The Day of the Locust* re-orchestrates that sadness with chords of terror. And the bitter humor of the earlier novel takes on accents of insane laughter in the later one.

—Earl Rovit

See the essay on *The Day of the Locust*.

WHARTON, Edith (Newbold, née Jones). Born in New York City, 24 January 1862. Traveled in Italy, Spain, and France as a child; educated privately. Married Edward Wharton in 1885 (divorced, 1913). Lived in Newport, Rhode Island, after her marriage, and in Europe from 1907; close friend of Henry James; helped organize the American Hostel for Refugees, and the Children of Flanders Rescue Committee, during World War I. Recipient: Pulitzer Prize, 1921; American Academy Gold Medal, 1924. Litt.D.: Yale University, New Haven, Connecticut, 1923. Chevalier, Legion of Honor (France), 1916, and Order of Leopold (Belgium), 1919; member, American Academy, 1930. *Died 11 August 1937.*

PUBLICATIONS

Collections

A Wharton Reader, edited by Louis Auchincloss. 1965.
Collected Short Stories, edited by R.W.B. Lewis. 1968.
Novels (Library of America), edited by R.W.B. Lewis. 1986.

Fiction

The Greater Inclination (stories). 1899.
The Touchstone. 1900; as *A Gift from the Grave*, 1900.
Crucial Instances (stories). 1901.
The Valley of Decision. 1902.
Sanctuary. 1903.
The Descent of Man and Other Stories. 1904.
The House of Mirth. 1905.
Madame de Treymes. 1907.
The Fruit of the Tree. 1907.
The Hermit and the Wild Woman, and Other Stories. 1908.
Tales of Men and Ghosts. 1910.
Ethan Frome. 1911; edited by Blake Nevius, 1968.
The Reef. 1912.
The Custom of the Country. 1913.
Xingu and Other Stories. 1916.
Summer. 1917.
The Marne. 1918.
The Age of Innocence. 1920.
The Glimpses of the Moon. 1922.
A Son at the Front. 1923.
Old New York: False Dawn (The 'forties), The Old Maid (The 'fifties), The Spark (The 'sixties), New Year's Day (The 'seventies). 1924.
The Mother's Recompense. 1925.
Here and Beyond (stories). 1926.
Twilight Sleep. 1927.
The Children. 1928; as *The Marriage Playground*, 1930.
Hudson River Bracketed. 1929.
Certain People (stories). 1930.
The Gods Arrive. 1932.
Human Nature (stories). 1933.
The World Over (stories). 1936.
Ghosts (stories). 1937.
The Buccaneers. 1938.
Fast and Loose: A Novelette, edited by Viola Hopkins Winner. 1977.

Plays

The Joy of Living, from a play by Hermann Sudermann (produced 1902). 1902.
The House of Mirth, with Clyde Fitch, from the novel by Wharton (produced 1906). Edited by Glenn Loney, 1981.

Verse

Verses. 1878.
Artemis to Actaeon and Other Verse. 1909.
Twelve Poems. 1926.

Other

The Decoration of Houses, with Ogden Codman, Jr. 1897.
Italian Villas and Their Gardens. 1904.
Italian Backgrounds. 1905.
A Motor-Flight Through France. 1908.
Fighting France: From Dunkerque to Belfort. 1915.
Wharton's War Charities in France. 1918.
L'Amérique en Guerre. 1918.
French Ways and Their Meaning. 1919.
In Morocco. 1920.
The Writing of Fiction. 1925.
A Backward Glance (autobiography). 1934.

Editor, *Le Livre des sans-foyer*. 1915; as *The Book of the Homeless: Original Articles in Verse and Prose*, 1916.
Editor, with Robert Norton, *Eternal Passion in English Poetry*. 1939.

*

Bibliography: *Wharton: A Bibliography* by Vito J. Brenni, 1966; *Wharton and Kate Chopin: A Reference Guide* by Marlene Springer, 1976.

Critical Studies: *Wharton: A Study of Her Fiction* by Blake Nevius, 1953; *Wharton: Convention and Morality in the Work of a Novelist* by Marilyn Jones Lyde, 1959; *Wharton*, 1961, and *Wharton: A Woman in Her Time*, 1971, both by Louis Auchincloss; *Wharton: A Collection of Critical Essays* edited by Irving Howe, 1962; *Wharton and Henry James: The Story of Their Friendship* by Millicent Bell, 1965; *Wharton: A Critical Interpretation* by Geoffrey Walton, 1971, revised edition, 1982; *Wharton: A Biography* by R.W.B. Lewis, 1975; *Wharton and the Novel of Manners* by Gary Lindberg, 1975; *Wharton* by Margaret B. McDowell, 1976; *Wharton* by Richard H. Lawson, 1977; *A Feast of Words: The Triumph of Wharton* by Cynthia Griffin Wolff, 1977; *The Frustrations of Independence: Wharton's Lesser Fiction* by Brigitta Lüthi, 1978; *Wharton's Argument with America* by Elizabeth Ammons, 1980; *The Female Intruder in the Novels of Wharton* by Carol Wershoven, 1982; *Wharton: Orphancy and Survival* by Wendy Gimbel, 1984.

* * *

Edith Wharton was a versatile as well as a prolific writer. She published over forty books, including some twenty novels, ten collections of short stories, books of verse, a pioneer work in interior design (with Ogden Codman, Jr.) *The Decoration of Houses*, several books of travel, an autobiography, and books on Italian villas, France, and fictional theory. It is by her fiction, however, that her importance as a writer must be judged. Wharton was an admirer and close friend of Henry James. Because of that friendship and because of certain parallels between their lives (both New Yorkers, both expatriates) and between their fictions (both with an interest in the manners of the rich, and in Americans living abroad), as well as the aesthetic principles Wharton appears to have got from "the master," she has been called a disciple of James, a judgment that has obscured significant differences between them. James was a metaphysical writer, Wharton a novelist of manners. James's method was to remove his characters from the effects of social forces and to locate his story in the minds of his characters, Wharton's was to deal with the impact of social and moral forces on the lives of her protagonists. Conflict in James is usually internal. In Wharton, it is almost always external, involving a superior individual in a struggle with the representatives of a social world with which the individual is fundamentally at odds.

The grand exception is *The Reef*, Wharton's most Jamesian novel. Here the action is confined almost exclusively to a chateau in France and the issue narrowed to a psychological struggle in the mind of the heroine, Anna Leath, who discovers that the man she has agreed to marry has had an affair with the young woman who is about to marry her step-son. Despite the economy, the tightness, the remoteness from the usual social forces that move through Wharton's pages, the conflict is much like that to be found in other Wharton novels, except that here it is treated as a psychological problem rather than a social and moral struggle. Anna Leath, the protagonist, cannot accept her fiancé's promiscuity nor can she give him up; and so, at the end of the novel, she is reduced to a state of tormented indecision.

In the first of her major novels, *The House of Mirth*, Lily Bart, a young woman from an old New York family ruined by financial reverses and extravagance, is caught between her love of beauty and luxury and her moral fastidiousness. If she should marry the man she loves she would live in what to her would be physical squalor; if she marries a man she does not love in order to get the material things essential to her sense of well being, she would violate her deepest nature. She manages to salvage her moral integrity but slides into poverty and, then, death, and a pathetic moral triumph.

Ethan Frome, a short novel that differs in some ways (a New England setting, impoverished rural characters) from Wharton's typical fiction, nonetheless deals with an issue similar to the one that confronts Lily Bart: the conflict between social and moral conventions and the deep desires of the individual. Ethan Frome, married to a homely neuresthenic woman several years older than himself, falls in love with his wife's pretty cousin. Although he contemplates eloping with the girl, Mattie Wills, social pressures win out. Ethan and Mattie's attempt to escape their fate through suicide ends with them maimed for life and left in the care of the grim woman they had tried to foil.

Both *Ethan Frome* and *Summer*, another short New England novel, give fuller rein to sexual passion than other Wharton novels. Ethan and Mattie have to pay for their passion in a cruelly ironic way; Charity Royal, protagonist of *Summer*, is allowed a kind of idyllic bliss in the arms of her lover before the score is reckoned and she is obliged to marry her elderly guardian, a good, solid man who will give her a respectable place in the town of North Dormer and a name for her unborn child, but a passionless marriage.

In *The Age of Innocence*, the last of Wharton's important novels, the same issue is dealt with in a lightly ironic way. Newland Archer has two choices: he can marry the conventional young woman to whom he is engaged or he can break with her and live with Ellen Olenska, a Europeanized American shown to be emotionally and aesthetically more attractive to Archer. The choice is between what is socially acceptable to old New York society and what most engages Archer's deepest feelings. Again, convention triumphs. Archer marries May. Ellen returns to Europe. Years later, in a kind of wistful epilogue, Archer visits Europe and, with his wife dead, might reestablish his relationship with Ellen. Archer fails to visit Ellen, however, and takes comfort from the knowledge that his life with May has had its compensations. Thus, it seems, Wharton has made a kind of peace with the vexing conflict between personal desire and social obligation.

The Custom of the Country, which appeared in 1913, strikes a note that was to be echoed increasingly after 1920. It is Wharton's major satire on American life and its lays out in a manner that anticipates the cruder satires of Sinclair Lewis the rise of vulgar Americans from the west. Undine Sprague is the feminine version, Elmer Moffat the male. With neither taste nor moral scruple, they assail the old monied New York aristocracy, conquer it, and move on to Europe and repeat their triumph. Undine marries and divorces Ralph Marvel of New York, marries and divorces a French aristocrat and, then, marries Elmer Moffat who is now a multi-millionaire settled in Europe and buying up rare antique art. In this novel Wharton's usual theme—the impingement of social and economic forces on the lives of sensitive individuals—is relegated to a minor role. Ralph Marvel's suicide (precipitated by Undine's greed) is but one of the brutal blows inflicted by Undine during her upward scramble.

After 1920 the satirical note predominated in novels such as *Twilight Sleep, The Children, Hudson River Bracketed*, and *The Gods Arrive*. In all of these novels there was a decided falling off both of artistic integrity and of imaginative energy. The brilliant, lucid style of the early work was scarcely visible now, except in *The Mother's Recompense* and in the nonsatirical parts of *The Children. The Glimpses of the Moon* was not much above the level of soap opera, and *Twilight Sleep* was a broader and less convincing satire on current representatives of American women than *The Custom of the Country. Hudson River Bracketed* and *The Gods Arrive* deal with the career of an American novelist, Vance Weston, tracing his rise from obscurity in Euphoria, Illinois, to international fame in London and Paris, but they fail to bring his story into significant focus. In *The Buccaneers* Wharton returned once more to the scene of her earlier and best triumphs, old New York before the turn of the century, but the novel remained unfinished at her death.

Among Wharton's seventy or so published short stories at least a dozen appear to have enduring quality, including "The Other Two," "Xingu," "Kerfol," "The Bunner Sisters," "The Triumph of Night," "Bewitched," "A Bottle of Perrier," "After Holbein," "Mr. Jones," "Pomegranate Seed," "Roman Fever," and "Joy in the House," and "The Eyes."

In 1934 Wharton published her autobiography, an engaging though carefully selective account of her life, which referred only briefly to her disastrous marriage and dealt humorously and ironically with her eminent friend Henry James. Even before her death in 1937 Wharton's literary reputation had begun to decline. It is only recently that interest in her work has revived, partly as the result of the new feminist consciousness. Still, even now, her novels and stories are not so highly regarded as they once were nor as seriously treated by literary critics as they deserve to be. What were once regarded as her strengths—her firm grasp of the social realities of her time and place, and her ready accessibility—now appear to be her chief limitations. However, her two novels about New England life, *Ethan Frome* and *Summer*, along with *The House of Mirth, The Reef* and *The Age of Innocence* are among the best novels of their time and constitute an impressive body of work.

—W.J. Stuckey

See the essay on *The House of Mirth*.

WHEATLEY, Phillis. Born in Africa, possibly Senegal, c. 1753–54; sold as a slave to the John Wheatley family in Boston, 1761. Educated by the Wheatley family. Married John Peters, a freed slave, in 1778; three children. Sent to England for her health, 1773, and was received in London society; returned to Boston to care for Mrs. Wheatley, 1773; manumitted by the Wheatleys, 1774, and separated from the loyalist Wheatleys by the Revolutionary War; lived in Wilmington, Massachusetts, 1779–83, and Boston after 1783. *Died 5 December 1784.*

PUBLICATIONS

Collections

Poems (includes letters), edited by Julian D. Mason, Jr. 1966.
Wheatley and Her Writings, edited by William H. Robinson. 1984.

Verse

On Messrs. Hussey and Coffin. 1767.
An Elegiac Poem on the Death of George Whitfield. 1770.
To Mrs. Leonard. 1771.
To the Rev. Mr. Pitkin. 1772.
To Thomas Hubbard. 1773.
Poems on Various Subjects, Religious and Moral. 1773.
An Elegy to Mary Moorhead. 1773.
Phillis's Reply to the Answer in Our Last by the Gentleman in the Navy. 1775.
An Elegy to Samuel Cooper. 1784.
Liberty and Peace. 1784.
To Mr. and Mrs.—, on the Death of Their Infant Son. 1784.

*

Bibliography: *Wheatley: A Bio-Bibliography* by William H. Robinson, 1981.

Critical Studies: *Wheatley: A Critical Attempt and Bibliography* by Charles F. Heartman, 1915; *Bid the Vassal Soar* (on Wheatley and George Moses Horton) by Merle A. Richmond, 1974; *Wheatley in the Black American Beginnings* by William H. Robinson, 1975, and *Critical Essays on Wheatley* edited by Robinson, 1982.

* * *

Phillis Wheatley's poetry is characterized by its adherence to form, in particular the heroic couplet, and conformity to neoclassical ritual in language and content. Thematically, she wrote to God's goodness, as opposed to His wrath, and she stressed that salvation is the most important goal in life. Her exposure to history, classical literature, and myths is obvious in her poetry.

Wheatley's verses were didactic, pious, conventional, and predictable in that she wrote a significant number of occasional poems—for commemorating an event, perhaps, or for lamenting a death. Her tone fits the poems, however, and there is revealed in them a genuine adaptation to the subject-at-hand. She incorporates the Popean politeness into her verses as well as other features of his style—antithesis, the mid-line pause, and apostrophe. Underneath the instructive tone and religious themes is the note of genuine religious joy based on her salvation from "The land of errors . . . those dark abodes." Some critics have argued that Wheatley lost contact with her blackness; rather, she accommodated her blackness to a form she selected freely to use for expressing herself artistically—the heroic couplet.

She did, however, condemn the hypocrisy of liberals who professed Christian charity towards blacks but also held slaves. In the 11 March 1774 *Connecticut Gazette* Wheatley published a letter that would be reprinted many times. She wrote: ". . . in every human Breast, God has implanted a Principle, which we call Love of Freedom . . . God grant Deliverance in his own Way and Time, and get him honour upon all those whose Avarice impels them to countenance and help forward the Calamities of their fellow Creatures. This I desire not for their Hurt, but to convince them of the strange Absurdity of their Conduct whose Words and Actions are so diametrically opposite."

In nearly all of Wheatley's poetry, however, there rings affirmation of life, even when she clearly identifies her race in what seems shame for her past enslavement. Her efforts to project herself away from the individual to the universal was part of the artistic detachment imposed by the form of poetry she loved, and the Puritan world in which she lived and believed. She paid close attention to the requirements of good manners that were a part of the upper-class milieu in which she lived during her first fourteen years in America (she was about 7 when she came with other slaves in 1761).

Wheatley's total output seems small only if one forgets her origins, her brief life, and the possibility that her husband sold or lost many of her works after her death. From poverty and slavery emerged a remarkable poet who sang "What songs should rise, how constant, how divine!"

—Margaret Perry

WHEELWRIGHT, John (Brooks). Born in Boston, Massachusetts, 9 September 1897. Educated at St. George's School, Newport, Rhode Island; Harvard University, Cambridge, Massachusetts, 1916–20; studied architecture at Massachusetts Institute of Technology, Cambridge, late 1920's. Briefly worked in architectural partnership in Boston; joined Socialist Party of Massachusetts, 1932, and poetry editor of the party journal *Arise*; founding member of Trotskyist Socialist Workers Party, 1937; editor, *Poems for a Dime* series, Boston, 1934–37. Officer, New England Poetry Society. *Died 15 September 1940.*

PUBLICATIONS

Collections

Collected Poems, edited by Alvin H. Rosenfeld. 1972.

Verse

North Atlantic Passage. 1925.
Rock and Shell: Poems 1923–1933. 1933.
Masque with Clowns. 1936.

Mirrors of Venus: A Novel in Sonnets 1914–1938. 1938.
Political Self-Portrait. 1940.
Selected Poems. 1941.

Other

Editor, *A History of the New England Poetry Club 1915–1931*. 1932.

*

Critical Studies: *New England Saints* by Austin Warren, 1956; *The Revolutionary Imagination: The Poetry and Politics of Wheelwright and Sherry Mangan* by Alan M. Wald, 1983.

* * *

John Wheelwright published three collections during his lifetime, but none received sufficient notice to give him a reputation while alive. Wheelwright was not the average socialist scribbler of the Depression era, but a "proper Bostonian" of impeccable ancestry: on his father's side, he claimed his radical blood from the first Wheelwright, an emigré from England in 1636, who preached religious tolerance until he was banished from the Bay Colony. On his mother's side, he descended from John Brooks, an early governor of Massachusetts.

The contradictions explicit in such ancestry, radicalism and political authority, were manifest in Wheelwright's own character and poetry. He taunted Boston Brahmins with his eccentric behavior in public and declared his allegiance to the proletariat, whose Depression plight he championed in many poems. All the while he accepted his upper-class status and remained much of his life an official of the doughty New England Poetry Society.

Wheelwright was an erratic craftsman in his poems, even though he emphasized his technique in long prose commentaries that accompanied his three published books. Many poems are long-winded, prosaic, and loosely framed. But occasionally his poems spring out with unanticipated lyric genius, as in "Train Ride" (*Political Self-Portrait*). His "sonnet novel" *Mirrors of Venus*, generally over-wrought, includes his masterful elegy "Father":

Come home. Wire a wire of warning without words.
Come home and talk to me again, my first friend. Father,
come home, dead man, who made your mind my home.

Wheelwright's work often takes the form of rambling poetic tracts, where he is an interpreter of what he felt to be the reshaping of America. As he wrote at the end of *Political Self-Portrait*, "The main point is not what noise poetry makes, but how it makes you think and act,—not what you make of it; but what it makes of you." Although this is unfair to the musical grace of much of his language, it is pointed and correct essentially about his intentions for his poetry.

His first book, *Rock and Shell*, shows the poet searching for some premise of unity in his experience, especially in the powerful opening poem, "North Atlantic Passage," which joins prose and poetry together. Spiritual loneliness is followed by sexual loneliness in this carefully plotted book. *Mirrors of Venus* is, as one critic described it, his *In Memoriam* to his friend Ned Couch, but sags generally from its weight of technical embellishments.

Political Self-Portrait is Wheelwright's best book; here he has found a balance between the wrought textures of language and loosely plotted ideological arguments. The poems are longer, more discursive, but intensely dramatic as they register a diffident, sensitive conscience faced with social upheaval and coming war. The poems are rich in imagery, raw in angry, direct language, but dignified overall by the depth of the speaker's convictions. Some of these poems have lost their edge now, but many, including "Collective Collect," "Bread-Word Giver," and "Train Ride" are lasting expressions of faith in humanity. "Dusk to Dusk," included in *Collected Poems*, has an even shriller tone of indignation than *Political Self-Portrait*, and its structure is fragmented by the unleashed energies of this unusual poet.

—Paul Christensen

WHITE, E(lwyn) B(rooks). Born in Mount Vernon, New York, 11 July 1899. Educated at Mount Vernon High School, graduated 1917; Cornell University, Ithaca, New York (editor, *Cornell Daily Sun*, 1920–21), 1917–21, A.B. 1921. Served in the U.S. Army, 1918: Private. Married Katharine Sergeant Angell in 1929 (died, 1977); one son. Reporter, Seattle *Times*, 1922–23; advertising copywriter, Frank Seaman Inc. and Newmark Inc., New York, 1924–25; contributing editor, *New Yorker*, from 1926; columnist ("One Man's Meat"), *Harper's* magazine, New York, 1938–43. Recipient: National Association of Independent Schools award, 1955; American Academy Gold Medal, for essays, 1960; Presidential Medal of Freedom, 1963; American Library Association Wilder Award, for children's books, 1970; National Medal for Literature, 1971; Pulitzer Special Citation, 1978. Litt.D.: Dartmouth College, Hanover, New Hampshire, 1948; University of Maine, Orono, 1948; Yale University, New Haven, Connecticut, 1948; Bowdoin College, Brunswick, Maine, 1950; Hamilton College, Clinton, New York, 1952; Harvard University, Cambridge, Massachusetts, 1954; L.H.D.: Colby College, Waterville, Maine, 1954. Fellow, American Academy of Arts and Sciences, 1973; Member, American Academy. *Died 1 October 1985.*

PUBLICATIONS

Sketches and Prose

Is Sex Necessary? or, Why You Feel the Way You Do, with James Thurber. 1929.
Alice Through the Cellophane. 1933.
Every Day Is Saturday. 1934.
Farewell to Model T. 1936.
Quo Vadimus? or, The Case for the Bicycle. 1939.
One Man's Meat. 1942; augmented edition, 1944.
World Government and Peace: Selected Notes and Comment 1943–1945. 1945.
The Wild Flag: Editorials from the New Yorker on Federal World Government and Other Matters. 1946.
Here Is New York. 1949.
The Second Tree from the Corner. 1954.
The Elements of Style, by William Strunk, Jr., revised by White. 1959; revised edition, 1972, 1979.

The Points of My Compass: Letters from the East, The West, The North, The South. 1962.
A White Reader, edited by William W. Watt and Robert W. Bradford. 1966.
Essays. 1977.

Fiction (for children)

Stuart Little. 1945.
Charlotte's Web. 1952.
The Trumpet of the Swan. 1970.

Verse

The Lady Is Cold. 1929.
The Fox of Peapack and Other Poems. 1938.
Poems and Sketches. 1981.

Other

Letters, edited by Dorothy Lobrano Guth. 1976.

Editor, *Ho Hum: Newsbreaks from the New Yorker*. 1931.
Editor, *Another Ho Hum: More Newsbreaks from the New Yorker*. 1932.
Editor, with Katharine S. White, *A Subtreasury of American Humor*. 1941.
Editor, *Onward and Upward in the Garden*, by Katharine S. White. 1979.

*

Bibliography: *White: A Bibliography* by A.J. Anderson, 1978; *White: A Bibliographic Catalogue of Printed Materials in the Department of Rare Books, Cornell University Library* by Katherine R. Hall, 1979.

Critical Studies: *White* by Edward C. Sampson, 1974; *White: A Biography* by Scott Elledge, 1984.

* * *

In an editorial headnote in *Letters*, E.B. White refers to the "squibs and poems" that he began submitting to the *New Yorker* shortly after it was founded in 1925. He joined the staff of the magazine two years later and retained a real, if sometimes tenuous, connection with it for the rest of his writing life. His poems are conventional light verse, rather weak examples of a genre that tends toward wry sentiment, easy irony, and even easier rhyme. His important literary work is the care and feeding of the "squib," its transformation from fragile sketch to full-bodied essay. One of the tools in effecting that change was the discipline involved in writing the unsigned editorials, the "Notes and Comments" that he once called "my weekly sermon," samples of which have been collected in *Every Day Is Saturday* and *The Wild Flag*. It was the signed pieces, the "casuals" to use the *New Yorker* term, for which White became best known. As with most of the *New Yorker* humorists, he worked in a variety of styles (including the parody volume *Is Sex Necessary?* that he wrote with James Thurber), but he is at his most characteristic sketching ordinary incidents with affection and mild surprise, colored occasionally by outright fantasy. Most of his early work never escaped the pages of the magazine for which it was written, but the best of these pieces can be found in *Quo Vadimus?*

As early as 1929, in a letter to his brother, he wrote, "I discovered a long time ago that writing of the small things of the day, the trivial matters of the heart, the inconsequential but near things of this living, was the only kind of creative work which I could accomplish with any sincerity or grace." Although he never ceased to be concerned with "the small occasions," as he once called them, he came to know that the trivial and the inconsequential are inextricably bound with the vital, to write about everyday life with the awareness that it involved everyday death. The deepening tone in White's work began with "One Man's Meat," the monthly essay he started contributing to *Harper's* in 1937; it can be heard in later volumes like *The Second Tree from the Corner* and *The Points of My Compass*. In *Essays*, a retrospective gathering of more than forty years, White can be found at his saddest, his richest, his finest.

There is another White, but the author of the books for children is simply a gentler variation on the man who wrote *Essays*, as can be seen in the death of Charlotte and the rebirth made explicit in the arrival of all those baby spiders. *Charlotte's Web* is the most complex of White's children's books, placing a fantasy rescue in a realistic setting, using artifice to celebrate natural processes. Both *Stuart Little* and *The Trumpet of the Swan* are quest stories; the first of these is probably White's most enduring book for children, not simply for the charm of its hero, but because it has an ending that does not end, a close that leaves Stuart—like White, like any good writer—still in search of beauty.

—Gerald Weales

WHITMAN, Walt(er). Born in West Hills, Huntington, Long Island, New York, 31 May 1819. Educated at schools in Brooklyn, New York, 1825–39. Office boy/clerk in a lawyer's office, a doctor's office, and, in 1830, a printing office; worked on *Long Island Patriot* and for printers Worthington, 1831, and Spooner, 1832–34; schoolteacher on Long Island, 1836–41; founding editor, *Long Islander*, Huntington, 1838–39; compositor, *Long Island Democrat*, 1839; journalist in New York from 1841; editor, *Aurora*, 1842, *Evening Tattler*, 1842, *Statesman*, 1843, and *Democrat*, 1844; staff member, *Long Island Star*, 1845; editor, Brooklyn *Daily Eagle*, 1846–48, New Orleans *Crescent*, 1848, and Brooklyn *Freeman* (Free Soil Party paper), 1848–49; lived with his parents, writing poetry and working part-time as carpenter, 1850–54; free-lance journalist, 1855–62; editor, Brooklyn *Daily Times*, 1857–59; served as a nurse in the Civil War, at hospitals in Washington, D.C., 1862–65; clerk, army paymaster's office, 1863, and Bureau of Indian Affairs, 1865, and staff member, Attorney-General's office, 1865–73, all in Washington, D.C.; suffered paralytic stroke, 1873, and lived with his brother in Camden, New Jersey; traveled in the western U.S. and Canada, 1879–80; lived in Camden after 1884. *Died 26 March 1892.*

PUBLICATIONS

Collections

Complete Writings, edited by Richard Maurice Bucke and others. 10 vols., 1902.

Collected Writings, edited by Gay Wilson Allen and Sculley Bradley. 1961—
Complete Poems, edited by Francis Murphy. 1975.
Poetry and Prose (Library of America), edited by Justin Kaplan. 1982.

Verse

Leaves of Grass. 1855; revised edition, 1856, 1860, 1866, 1871, 2 vols. 1876, 1881, 1889, 1892, 1897; manuscripts edited by Fredson Bowers, 1955, and Arthur Golden, 2 vols., 1968; *A Textual Variorum of the Printed Poems* edited by Sculley Bradley, 3 vols., 1980.
Drum-Taps. 1865; with *Sequel to Drum-Taps*, 1865.
Poems, edited by W.M. Rossetti. 1868.
Passage to India. 1871.
After All, Not to Create Only. 1871.
As a Strong Bird on Pinions Free. 1872.
November Boughs (includes prose). 1888.
Good-Bye My Fancy. 1891.
Pictures: An Unpublished Poem, edited by Emory Holloway. 1927.

Fiction

Franklin Evans: or, The Inebriate. 1842; edited by Emory Holloway, 1929.
The Half-Breed and Other Stories, edited by Thomas Ollive Mabbott. 1927.

Other

Democratic Vistas. 1870.
Memoranda During the War. 1876; edited by Roy P. Basler, 1962.
Specimen Days and Collect. 1882; revised edition, as *Specimen Days in America*, 1887.
Complete Poems and Prose 1855–1888. 1888.
Complete Prose Works. 1892.
Autobiographia. 1892.
In Re Walt Whitman, edited by Horace L. Traubel and others. 1893.
Calamus (letters), edited by Richard Maurice Bucke. 1897.
The Wound Dresser (letters), edited by Richard Maurice Bucke. 1898.
Notes and Fragments, edited by Richard Maurice Bucke. 1899.
An American Primer, edited by Horace L. Traubel. 1904.
Diary in Canada, edited by William Sloane Kennedy. 1904.
Lafayette in Brooklyn. 1905.
Criticism: An Essay. 1913.
The Gathering of the Forces (journalism and essays), edited by Cleveland Rodgers and John Black. 2 vols., 1920.
Uncollected Poetry and Prose, edited by Emory Holloway. 2 vols., 1921.
Rivulets of Prose: Critical Essays, edited by Carolyn Wells and Alfred F. Goldsmith. 1928.
Whitman's Workshop, edited by Clifton Joseph Furness. 1928.
A Child's Reminiscence, edited by Thomas Ollive Mabbott and Rollo G. Silver. 1930.
I Sit and Look Out (editorials), edited by Emory Holloway and Vernolian Schwarz. 1932.
Whitman and the Civil War: A Collection of Original Articles and Manuscripts, edited by Charles I. Glicksberg. 1933.
New York Dissected (essays), edited by Emory Holloway and Ralph Adimari. 1936.
Backward Glances, edited by Sculley Bradley and John A. Stevenson. 1947.
Faint Clews and Indirections: Manuscripts of Whitman and His Family, edited by Clarence Gohdes and Rollo G. Silver. 1949.
Whitman Looks at the Schools, edited by Florence Bernstein Freedman. 1950.
Whitman of the New York Aurora, edited by Joseph Jay Rubin and Charles H. Brown. 1950.
The Eighteenth Presidency!, edited by Edward F. Grier. 1956.
Whitman's Civil War, edited by Walter Lowenfels. 1960.
Whitman's New York: From Manhattan to Montauk (essays), edited by Henry M. Christman. 1963.
Camden Conversations, edited by Walter Teller. 1973.

*

Bibliography: by Oscar Lovell Triggs, in *Complete Writings 10*, 1902; *A Concise Bibliography of the Works of Whitman* by Carolyn Wells and Alfred Goldsmith, 1922; *Whitman's Journalism: A Bibliography* by William White, 1969; *Whitman and the Critics: A Checklist of Criticism 1900–1978* by Jeanetta Boswell, 1980; *Whitman 1838–1939: A Reference Guide* by Scott Giantvalley, 1981; *Whitman 1940–1975: A Reference Guide* by Donald D. Kummings, 1982.

Critical Studies: *Whitman* by Frederik Schyberg, translated by Evie Allison Allen, 1951; *The Solitary Singer: A Critical Biography*, 1955, revised edition, 1967, *A Reader's Guide to Whitman*, 1970, and *The New Whitman Handbook*, 1975, all by Gay Wilson Allen; *Whitman Reconsidered*, 1955, and *Whitman*, 1961, both by Richard Chase; *Leaves of Grass One Hundred Years After*, 1955, and *Whitman: The Critical Heritage*, 1971, both edited by Milton Hindus; *The Evolution of Whitman* by Roger Asselineau, 2 vols., 1960–62; *The Presence of Whitman* edited by R.W.B. Lewis, 1962; *Whitman: A Collection of Critical Essays* edited by Roy Harvey Pearce, 1962; *Whitman*, 1962, and *The American Quest for a Supreme Fiction: Whitman's Legacy in the Personal Epic*, 1979, both by James E. Miller, Jr.; *A Century of Whitman Criticism* edited by Edwin H. Miller, 1969, and *Whitman's Poetry: A Psychological Journey* by Miller, 1969; *The Structure of Leaves of Grass* by Thomas E. Crawley, 1971; *The Historic Whitman* by Joseph Jay Rubin, 1973; *The Foreground of Leaves of Grass* by Floyd Stovall, 1974; *Whitman's Journeys into Chaos: A Psychoanalytic Study of the Poetic Process* by Stephen Ames Black, 1975; *Whitman: A Life* by Justin Kaplan, 1980; *Whitman and the Body Beautiful* by Harold Aspiz, 1980; *Emerson, Whitman, and the American Muse* by Jerome Loving, 1982; *Language and Style in Leaves of Grass* by C. Carroll Hollis, 1983; *Critical Essays on Whitman* edited by James Woodress, 1983; *Whitman: The Making of a Poet* by Paul Zweig, 1984.

* * *

The life and work of Walt Whitman are in some measure a metaphor for America. Whitman began sounding his "barbaric yawp" over the roofs of the world when the youthful United States was a power of little consequence among nations. He was scorned or ignored at first, but gradually his *Leaves of*

Grass compelled attention to its democratic message. By the time Whitman died his poetry had become a force to reckon with in the world.

Whitman's considerable apprenticeship as a newspaper writer and editor before 1855 gives no warning of a major poet in the making. His early poetry is undistinguished, and his prose is only competent journalism. But somehow Whitman found his inspiration and his vocation as poet. Emerson was probably the dominant influence, for in his essay "The Poet" he had called for a great American poet: "I look in vain for the poet whom I describe." And he added that "we have yet had no genius in America" who "knew the value of our incomparable materials." Whitman, for his part, later said: "I was simmering, simmering, simmering; Emerson brought me to a boil."

In response to a presentation copy of the first edition of *Leaves of Grass* in 1855 Emerson wrote Whitman: "I find it the most extraordinary piece of wit and wisdom that America has yet contributed . . . I greet you at the beginning of a great career." The first edition was a slender volume of 95 pages that Whitman had had to publish himself, but it contained one of the great poems of the English language, the long, untitled poem that later, after revisions and additions, was called "Song of Myself." What Emerson had read when he opened the volume to the beginning of the poetry was

> I celebrate myself,
> And what I assume you shall assume,
> For every atom belonging to me as good belongs to you.

Thus began Whitman's mystic vision of equality, national purpose, and international brotherhood, "hoping to cease not till death," as he added in a line written later. The work did go on as long as he lived, and preparations for the final edition of his lifetime, arranged in the way he wanted his literary executors to print future editions, were in progress at the time he died.

The first edition is the work of the somewhat brash, 36-year-old Brooklyn carpenter-poet. But by the time the third edition appeared in 1860, Whitman had matured and deepened his human sympathies. Also the book had grown from the original 12 poems to 100 and contained the so-called "sex poems" that made Whitman anathema to proper Victorians. These are the "Children of Adam" poems dealing with heterosexual love and the "Calamus" poems treating homosexual affection. Many of them are tender, beautiful poems worth close study. But the most important new poem was "Out of the Cradle Endlessly Rocking," one of Whitman's greatest lyrics. It blends theme, symbol, and reminiscence in a free-verse form that Whitman had absolutely mastered. This edition, moreover, gives us a clear insight into Whitman's growth as a poet. It is an articulated whole, with a beginning, middle, and end, and one can begin to see the shape of *Leaves of Grass* in its final form. The most prominent themes of the third edition are love and death; both appear in the first two editions, but here they take on a tragic significance, and in Whitman's struggle with these themes he becomes a major poet.

Whitman's experiences in Washington as a volunteer nurse and his visits to Virginia battlefields during the Civil War provided the material for *Drum-Taps*, later incorporated into *Leaves of Grass*. This is the best collection of war poetry produced by any American writer on the Civil War. "Come Up from the Fields, Father" and "Vigil Strange I Kept on the Field One Night" are vivid, poignant examples. Shortly after *Drum-Taps* appeared, Lincoln's assassination inspired Whitman's memorable elegy "When Lilacs Last in the Dooryard Bloom'd." This poem employs the symbols of star (Lincoln), lilac (love), and bird (poet's soul) in 16 stanzas of beautiful free verse and begins:

> When lilacs last in the dooryard bloom'd,
> And the great star early droop'd in the western sky in the
> night,
> I mourn'd, and yet shall mourn with ever-returning spring.

But at the end the poet is reconciled to the loss of the wartime leader. The star, the lilac, and the bird singing in the swamp will remind him annually of "the dead I loved so well."

The fifth edition of *Leaves of Grass* came out in 1871, and in it the main order of the book became settled. It opens with the "Inscriptions," follows with "Starting from Paumanok," and ends with "Songs of Parting." Published as an annex to this edition was another of Whitman's best-known poems, "A Passage to India," a poem in which his vision of universal fraternity is clearly shown. It begins by celebrating the joining of east and west by the transcontinental railroad, the Suez Canal, and the Atlantic cable and goes on to envision these engineering feats as part of "God purpose" for "The people to become brothers and sisters."

An edition of 1881 was to have been brought out by James R. Osgood and Co. of Boston, but the district attorney of Boston threatened prosecution and Whitman was forced to find another publisher. A bolder Philadelphia firm issued the book without incident, for by this time Whitman, "The good gray poet," as his friend William O'Connor had dubbed him during the Washington years, was becoming a national figure and living down the early notoriety. In this edition the poems received their final revisions and titles ("Song of Myself" appears here for the first time) and permanent positions. Whitman continued to write until he died, but later editions print the later poems as annexes.

Although Whitman's poetry is the reason for his literary stature, he also wrote a considerable body of prose. The preface to the 1855 edition is an important statement; also noteworthy is the preface to *As a Strong Bird. Democratic Vistas*, however, is his major prose work. It is a collection of essays that are more a glimpse into the future of democracy than an analysis of the present. It tempers Whitman's usual buoyant optimism with a frank admission that the American democracy of 1871 (the period of the Grant Administration and the "Gilded Age") was not perfect. But he did not lose his faith in the ultimate success of the American experiment. Another prose work of interest is the informal autobiography that he published under the title *Specimen Days*.

Whitman was the first American poet to achieve a truly international reputation. Although Baudelaire discovered Poe before anyone had ever heard of Whitman, the Pre-Raphaelites in England soon discovered Whitman, and William Michael Rossetti edited an edition of *Leaves of Grass* in 1868. British interest in Whitman helped to convince Americans that the poet was not a charlatan, and from that modest beginning his reputation has spread like eddies from a rock dropped in still water. Jan Christian Smuts wrote a book on him in 1895, a study of his prosody was published in Italy in 1898, and an important French study appeared in 1908.

Although Whitman claimed he was not interested in technique, the sizable number of extant manuscripts show that he labored over his poems, making many cuts, additions, emendations. The variant readings of successive editions likewise reveal the poet as reviser. His form, however, has given critics trouble over the years. He said: "My form has strictly grown from my purports and facts, and is the analogy of them." His purpose was to present his vision and his experience, and it is not surprising that some readers have seen in his work the raw material of poetry rather than finished poems. The chief structural device is parallelism: repetition of idea, repetition of syntax, repetition of sound. Some 41% of the 10,500 lines of *Leaves of Grass* contain initial reiteration. One notes also that run-on lines are a rarity, and the first person singular is used extensively.

The influences on Whitman's free verse seem to have been public address, the Bible, and music. Not only was Emerson an inspiration in Whitman's finding his vocation as poet, but Emerson's essays, written as lectures, contain many of the same rhetorical devices that Whitman uses. Whitman as a young man wrote speeches and at one time had thought of making a career as a public speaker. The parallelism and coordinate structure of the Bible, which Whitman knew well, also may have influenced his style, though this is hard to document. Finally, the impact of music must be accorded a place in Whitman's development. The repetition of themes, the use of *recitative* and *aria* support Whitman's own statement: "But for the opera I could never have written *Leaves of Grass*."

—James Woodress

See the essay on *Leaves of Grass*.

WHITTIER, John Greenleaf. Born near Haverhill, Massachusetts, 17 December 1807. Educated at local schools; studied art at Haverhill Academy, 1827. Editor of various country newspapers, 1826–32, and of *American Manufacturer*, Boston, 1829–31; teacher, Haverhill Academy, 1827–28; delegate to the founding convention of the American Anti-Slavery Society, 1833, and edited and wrote for abolitionist and reform journals, 1833–60; representative for Haverhill in Massachusetts Legislature, 1835; editor, *Pennsylvania Freeman*, Philadelphia, 1838; contributing editor, *National Era*, Washington, D.C., 1847–57; regular contributor, *Atlantic Monthly*, Boston, after 1857. Lived in Amesbury after 1836, and Danvers after 1876, both Massachusetts. *Died 7 September 1892*.

PUBLICATIONS

Collections

The Writings, edited by Horace E. Scudder. 7 vols., 1888–89; revised edition, 1894.
The Poetical Works, edited by W. Garrett Horder. 1919.
Letters, edited by John B. Pickard. 3 vols., 1975.

Verse

Moll Pitcher. 1831; revised edition, 1840.
Mogg Megone. 1836.
Poems Written During the Progress of the Abolition Question, 1830–1838. 1837.
Poems. 1838.
Moll Pitcher, and The Minstrel Girl. 1840.
Lays of My Home and Other Poems. 1843.
The Song of the Vermonters. 1843.
Miscellaneous Poems. 1844.
Ballads and Other Poems. 1844.
The Stranger in Lowell. 1845.
Voices of Freedom. 1846.
Poems. 1849.
Songs of Labor and Other Poems. 1850.
Poetical Works. 1853.
The Chapel of the Hermits and Other Poems. 1853.
A Sabbath Scene. 1854.
The Panorama and Other Poems. 1856.
The Sycamores. 1857.
The Poetical Works. 2 vols., 1857.
Home Ballads and Other Poems. 1860.
In War Time and Other Poems. 1864.
National Lyrics. 1865.
Snow-Bound: A Winter Idyl. 1866.
The Tent on the Beach and Other Poems. 1867.
Among the Hills and Other Poems. 1869.
Poetical Works. 2 vols., 1870.
Ballads of New England. 1870.
Miriam and Other Poems. 1871.
The Pennsylvania Pilgrim and Other Poems. 1872.
Hazel-Blossoms. 1875.
Mabel Martin: A Harvest Idyl. 1876.
Favorite Poems. 1877.
The Vision of Echard and Other Poems. 1878.
The King's Missive and Other Poems. 1881.
The Bay of Seven Islands and Other Poems. 1883.
Early Poems. 1885.
Saint Gregory's Guest and Recent Poems. 1886.
Poems of Nature. 1886.
Narrative and Legendary Poems. 1888.
At Sundown. 1890.
Legends and Lyrics. 1890.
A Legend of the Lake. 1893.
The Demon Lady. 1894.

Fiction

Leaves from Margaret Smith's Journal. 1849.

Other

Legends of New-England. 1831.
Justice and Expediency. 1833.
Narrative of James Williams, An American Slave. 1838.
The Supernaturalism of New England. 1847; edited by Edward Wagenknecht, 1969.
Old Portraits and Modern Sketches. 1850.
Literary Recreations and Miscellanies. 1854.
Prose Works. 2 vols., 1866.
Works. 1874.
Complete Works. 1876.
Whittier on Writers and Writing: The Uncollected Critical Writings, edited by Edwin Cady and Harry Hayden Clark. 1950.

Editor, *The Journal of John Woolman*. 1871.
Editor, *Child Life: A Collection of Poems*. 1873.
Editor, *Child Life in Prose*. 1874.
Editor, *Songs of Three Centuries*. 1876; revised edition, 1877.

*

Bibliography: *A Bibliography of Whittier* by Thomas Franklin Currier, 1937; *Whittier: A Comprehensive Annotated Bibliography* (secondary works) by Albert J. von Frank, 1976.

Critical Studies: *Life and Letters of Whittier* by Samuel T. Pickard, 1894, revised edition, 2 vols., 1907; *A Study of Whittier's Apprenticeship as a Poet* (includes uncollected poetry) by Frances M. Pray, 1930; *Quaker Militant* by Albert Mordell, 1933; *Whittier: Bard of Freedom* by Whitman Bennett, 1941; *Whittier: Friend of Man* by John A. Pollard, 1949; *Whittier* by Lewis Leary, 1961; *Whittier: An Introduction and Interpretation* by John B. Pickard, 1961, and *Memorabilia of Whittier* edited by Pickard, 1968; *Whittier: A Portrait in Paradox* by Edward Wagenknecht, 1967; *Whittier's Poetry: An Appraisal and a Selection* by Robert Penn Warren, 1971; *Critical Essays on Whittier* edited by Jayne K. Kribbs, 1980.

* * *

In the "Proem," a poem which introduced his collected works, John Greenleaf Whittier scrutinized his life and poetic achievement in these lines:

> The rigor of a frozen clime,
> The harshness of an untaught ear,
> The jarring words of one whose rhyme
> Beat often Labor's hurried time,
> Or Duty's rugged march, through storm and strife,
> are here.

The honesty of these sparse lines is characteristic. Raised as a poor farm boy in a non-conformist Quaker faith, he had little education and was primarily a sectional romantic poet in his early years. Fortunately his enlistment in the abolitionist cause in 1833 converted the aspiring young lyricist into a radical propagandist, politician, and part-time editor whose verses championed the rights of slaves and democratic principles. The twenty years of abolitionist work reforged Whittier's vapid sentimentalism into a powerful weapon for the oppressed and strengthened his regard for moral action. By the 1850's Whittier's reform work was over, and in his remaining years his writing showed him as a religious humanist, striving for moral perfection and inner spirituality rather than social and political reform.

Like those of most of the "schoolroom" poets, Longfellow, Lowell, Holmes, and others, Whittier's themes were few and limited: the value of domestic emotions, the innocence of childhood, the necessity of social equality, and the nobility of ethical action. However, unlike these other popular poets, Whittier drew upon his native roots for inspiration. In his best poems Whittier displayed a mastery of local color techniques, a competent use of rural imagery, and the everyday language of the Merrimack farmer. His instinctive handling of native materials conveyed his inner love for the environment that molded, and his understanding of the traditions that inspired, him. Still his poetry suffered from the diffusion and sentimentality inherent in the tradition of public rhetoric in which he wrote. Perhaps no other established 19th-century American poet wrote so much poor verse, but the miracle is that by the most exacting poetical standards his best remains so good.

Aside from a few nature poems like "The Last Walk in Autumn," an occasional abolitionist poem like "Ichabod," and selections from his religious poems, Whittier's ballads and genre pieces represent his finest poetical achievement. They contain some of the best examples of native folklore written in America. His ballads, especially, express his lifelong interest in colonial history, the Quakers, local legends, and folk superstitions; and they are remarkably true to the graphic realism and dramatic intensity of traditional folk balladry. His best ballads take incidents like a skipper who had betrayed his own townspeople, a witch who prophesied death, or the terrifying actions of specter warriors, bed-rocks them with exact physical detail, and then concentrates on the dramatic moment of conflict. "Telling the Bees" skillfully handles a local superstition with childlike detail to hide the chilling reality of nature's destruction; "The Garrison of Cape Anne," "The Palatine," and "The King's Missive" rework historical incidents; "Amy Wentworth," "The Countess," and "The Witch of Wenham" narrate pastoral romances; while the often-parodied "Barbara Frietchie" was accepted by a war-wearied nation as an expression of their personal conviction that the Union must be preserved. Whittier's finest ballad, "Skipper Ireson's Ride," was based on an old Marblehead song about women tarring and feathering a fishingboat captain. The ballad opens *in medias res*, plunging directly into the wild tumult and chaos of mob action as the skipper is pushed through Marblehead. Finally Ireson cries out his remorse, and with "half scorn, half pity" the women free him. The final refrain changes "Old" Floyd Ireson to "Poor" Floyd Ireson and becomes a mournful dirge forever accusing and dooming Ireson, besides emphasizing the hollowness of the women's revenge.

Similarly, Whittier's genre poems elevated the ordinary details of Essex County life into a universal expression of boyhood innocence, agrarian simplicity, and pastoral romance that caught the pathos and beauty of a dying rural tradition. In poems like "Maud Muller," "In School-Days," "Among the Hills," and "Memories," Whittier idealized and typified the district school days, the harvest-filled autumn days, and the barefoot-boy days to capture the romantic aspirations of a responsive American public. "Cobbler Keezar's Vision," "Abraham Davenport," "To My Old Schoolmaster," and others contain some of Whittier's best rustic anecdotes as well as realistic and humorous sketches of the Yankee character. Whittier's particular skill in recreating the past is seen most fully in his one sustained triumph, *Snow-Bound*. In this poem Whittier expresses the value of family affections by the symbolic development of a fire-snow contrast and by the skillful interweaving of present reality with past memories. His artistic handling of structure, careful development of the fire image, and graphic depiction of the family and outside visitors make this a minor masterpiece of 19th-century poetry. In this poem Whittier captured the essence of the New England mind and placed himself in the direct line of American expression that stretches from Anne Bradstreet to Robert Frost.

Although Whittier's poems fall far short of the poetic imagination and philosophical depth of major American poets such as Whitman, Poe, Dickinson, and Emerson, his verses exhibit more spiritual illumination and downright "grit" than the polished verses of Longfellow and the other minor poets. Despite the severe criticism of his poetry in the 20th century, Whittier's place in American literature seems secure. He will continue to be read and enjoyed as long as people respond to their traditions and demand honest expression of their fundamental democratic and religious feelings.

—John B. Pickard

See the essay on *Snow-Bound*.

WIGGLESWORTH, Michael. Born in England, probably in Yorkshire, 18 October 1631; emigrated with his parents to the Massachusetts Bay Colony, 1638, and settled in New Haven, Connecticut. Educated at Harvard University, Cambridge, Massachusetts, A.B. 1651, A.M. 1653. Married 1) Mary Reyner in 1655 (died, 1659), one daughter; 2) Martha Mudge in 1679 (died, 1690), five daughters and one son; 3) Sybil Sparhawk Avery in 1691, one son. Tutor, Harvard University, 1652–54; ordained minister of Puritan church, 1656; minister to the church at Malden, Massachusetts, 1656–63 and with assistants because of ill-health, 1663–86; sole minister again after 1686; also studied and practised medicine. Freeman, Massachusetts Bay Colony, 1680; Fellow, Harvard University, 1697–1705. *Died 10 June 1705.*

PUBLICATIONS

Collections

The Day of Doom with Other Poems, edited by Kenneth B. Murdock. 1929.

Verse

The Day of Doom. 1662(?); revised edition, 1666.
Meat Out of the Eater. 1670; revised edition, with *Riddles Unriddled*, 1689.
Riddles Unriddled; or, Christian Paradoxes. 1689.

Other

The Diary 1653–1657, edited by Edmund S. Morgan. 1965.

*

Critical Studies: *Sketch of the Life of Wigglesworth, to Which Is Appended a Fragment of His Autobiography, Some of His Letters, and a Catalogue of His Library* by John W. Dean, 1863, revised edition, as *Memoir of Wigglesworth*, 1871; *No Featherbed to Heaven: A Biography of Wigglesworth* by Richard H. Crowder, 1962.

* * *

Michael Wigglesworth's first major publication, *The Day of Doom*—a bestseller for a century—was a jeremiad of 224 eight-line stanzas presenting in vivid detail the Calvinist notion of the events of the Final Judgment. The writer's purpose was not to write fine poetry but to provide uncomplicated facts in easy rhyme. For generations children recited from memory the entire poem, which devotes a few stanzas to the rewards of the saved but many more to the pleas, sentencing, and punishment of the damned. In the same volume with *The Day of Doom* Wigglesworth published several other poems setting forth Puritan doctrine, pleading with the reader to turn from wickedness and avoid everlasting punishment (e.g., "A Short Discourse on Eternity" and "Vanity of Vanities"), verses couched in sermonic phrases, jogging along in well-worn meters without much variety. The imagery, already familiar to his church-going readers, was nevertheless vigorously pictorial as the poet strove to convert the sinners.

Another jeremiad, "God's Controversy with New-England," showed the reader that because of the general evil-doing of the colonists God was right in inflicting illness and drought on the region. The verse forms here change from ballad structure ("fourteeners") to six-line iambics to quatrains as Wigglesworth pleads the cause for spiritual renewal.

The other large work he called *Meat Out of the Eater*, a series of ten meditations and "A Conclusion Hortatory" demonstrating "the Necessity, End, and Usefulness of Afflictions." "Riddles Unriddled," clusters of verses constituting nine paradoxes, uses a little more variety in verse form in an attempt to fit structure to meaning. For example, the first paradox, "Light in Darkness," consists of ten "Songs," some in the form of medieval debates. The poet moves from ballad form in one "Song" to six-syllable lines in couplet rhyme in another. The other paradoxes likewise are composed of a number of separate poems, illustrating such themes as "Strength in Weakness" and "In Confinement Liberty."

In a twelve-year span (1662–1673)—during a period when he was physically too weak to preach from his Malden pulpit—Wigglesworth wrote nearly all his extant poetry, and in a surprising variety of forms: lyric, dramatic, narrative, descriptive, didactic and hortatory, and autobiographical. Though not a major poet, he made a serious contribution to Puritan Calvinist doctrine, preserving in not unreadable verse the ideas that his readers were hearing from the pulpit Sunday after Sunday.

Wigglesworth's diary was edited by Edmund S. Morgan. He transcribed and made available to modern readers the frequent passages in shorthand. The diary fully discloses the poet's constant struggle with his conscience, his soul warring against powerful drives inside his frail flesh. A couple of college orations (including "The Praise of Eloquence") have been preserved and are sometimes anthologized. Written in "plain style," they are obviously class assignments discussing the elements of effective oratory.

—Richard H. Crowder

WILBUR, Richard (Purdy). Born in New York City, 1 March 1921. Educated at Amherst College, Massachusetts, B.A. 1942; Harvard University, Cambridge, Massachusetts, A.M. 1947. Served in the U.S. Army, 1943–45: Sergeant. Married Charlotte Ward in 1942; one daughter and three sons. Member of the Society of Fellows, 1947–50, and Assistant Professor of English, 1950–54, Harvard University; Associate Professor of English, Wellesley College, Massachusetts, 1955–57; Professor of English, Wesleyan University, Middletown, Connecticut, 1957–77; since 1977 Writer-in-Residence, Smith College, Northampton, Massachusetts. General editor, Laurel Poets series, Dell Publishing Company, New York. State Department cultural exchange representative to the U.S.S.R., 1961. Recipient: Guggenheim fellowship, 1952, 1963; American Academy in Rome fellowship, 1954; Pulitzer Prize, 1957; National Book Award, 1957; Edna St. Vincent Millay Memorial Award, 1957; Ford fellowship, for drama, 1960; Melville Cane Award, 1962; Bollingen Prize, for translation, 1963, and for verse, 1971; Sarah Josepha Hale Award, 1968; Brandeis University Creative Arts Award, 1970; Henri Desfeuilles Prize, 1971; Shelley Memorial Award, 1973; Harriet Monroe Award, 1978; PEN translation award, 1983; Drama Desk award, for translation, 1983. L.H.D.: Lawrence College, Appleton, Wisconsin, 1960; Washington University, St. Louis,

1964; Williams College, Williamstown, Massachusetts, 1975; Rochester University, Rochester, New York, 1976; Carnegie Mellon University, Pittsburgh, 1980; D.Litt.: Amherst College, 1967; Clark University, Worcester, Massachusetts, 1970; American International College, Springfield, Massachusetts, 1974; Marquette University, Milwaukee, 1977; Wesleyan University, 1977; Lake Forest College, Illinois, 1982. Member, American Academy of Arts and Sciences; President, 1974–77, and Chancellor, 1977–78, 1981, American Academy; Chancellor, Academy of American Poets; Chevalier, Ordre National des Palmes Académiques, 1983. Lives in Cummington, Massachusetts.

PUBLICATIONS

Verse

The Beautiful Changes and Other Poems. 1947.
Ceremony and Other Poems. 1950.
Things of This World. 1956; one section reprinted as *Digging to China*, 1970.
Poems 1943–1956. 1957.
Advice to a Prophet and Other Poems. 1961.
The Poems. 1963.
The Pelican from a Bestiary of 1120. 1963.
Prince Souvanna Phouma: An Exchange Between Wilbur and William Jay Smith. 1963.
Complaint. 1968.
Walking to Sleep: New Poems and Translations. 1969.
Seed Leaves: Homage to R.F. 1974.
The Mind-Reader: New Poems. 1976.
Verses on the Times, with William Jay Smith. 1978.
Seven Poems. 1981.

Plays

The Misanthrope, from the play by Molière (produced 1955). 1955; revised version, music by Margaret Pine (produced 1977).
Candide (lyrics only, with Dorothy Parker and John LaTouche), book by Lillian Hellman, music by Leonard Bernstein, from the novel by Voltaire (produced 1956). 1957.
Tartuffe, from the play by Molière (produced 1964). 1963.
School for Wives, from a play by Molière (produced 1971). 1971.
The Learned Ladies, from a play by Molière (produced 1977). 1978.
Andromache, from the play by Racine. 1982.

Other

Emily Dickinson: Three Views, with Louise Bogan and Archibald MacLeish. 1960.
Loudmouse (for children). 1963.
Opposites (for children), drawings by the author. 1973.
Responses: Prose Pieces 1953–1976. 1976.
The Whale and Other Uncollected Translations. 1982.
On My Own Work. 1983.

Editor, with Louis Untermeyer and Karl Shapiro, *Modern American and Modern British Poetry*, revised shorter edition. 1955.
Editor, *A Bestiary* (anthology). 1955.
Editor, *Complete Poems of Poe*. 1959.
Editor, with Alfred B. Harbage, *Poems of Shakespeare*. 1966; revised edition, as *The Narrative Poems, and Poems of Doubtful Authenticity*, 1974.
Editor, *Selected Poems*, by Witter Bynner. 1978.

Translator, *The Funeral of Bobo*, by Joseph Brodsky. 1974.

*

Bibliography: *Wilbur: A Bibliographical Checklist* by John P. Field, 1971.

Critical Studies: *Wilbur* by Donald L. Hill, 1967; *Wilbur* by Paul F. Cummins, 1971; *Wilbur's Creation* edited by Wendy Salinger, 1983.

* * *

Richard Wilbur's first volume of poems surprised its early readers in 1947: there was none of the standard theorizing about history or large "modern" issues and only occasional reflections of the poet's experiences in the war; instead, the poet of *The Beautiful Changes* spoke openly of beauty, unabashedly expressing his delight in the sights and sounds and movements of the world and demonstrating a dazzling virtuosity at recreating them in his verse. He also revealed his delight in wit, imaginative play, and even games. One of the poems was entitled simply "&," and his delights are joined in some lines from "Grace":

> One is tickled again, by the dining-car waiter's absurd
> Acrobacy—tipfingered tray like a wind-besting bird
> Plumblines his swinging shoes, the sole things sure
> In the shaken train.

In addition to the high spirits, the poems often almost exemplified elegance, poise, and good manners.

A number of those qualities and subjects came to seem even more startling in the years which followed. From the beginning Wilbur's poetry has shown notable continuities. He has remarked that in his later poems he tends to move towards "a plainer and more straightforward" way of writing and, also, from poems that use a "single meditative voice balancing argument and counter-argument, feeling and counter-feeling" to more "dramatic" ones (such as "Two Voices in a Meadow" or "The Aspen and the Stream") that may use two opposing voices. Readers may also detect a general deepening of feeling and a clearer personal voice as well as some unpredictable developments. But most of the earlier qualities remain, and there continue to be signal exclusions: no confessional poetry and no free verse (Wilbur wrote that in the fairy story about the genie which could be summoned out of a bottle, he had always assumed that the genie gained his strength from being *in* the bottle).

It is unlikely that anyone could have predicted, however, that the poet who showed an almost Keatsian responsiveness to the sensuous should become the translator of Molière into extraordinary English couplets. In retrospect, it is clearer that Molière represents part of what Wilbur is, as well as what he admires: a humane voice of uncommonly rational commonsense; a user of language that is both familiar and chaste; a witty enemy of the pompous, the gross, and the fanatic; and a juggler, a master of poise and point. (That he later became the translator of

Racine—*Andromache* and the forthcoming *Phèdre*—may still seem surprising.) Nor could one have anticipated "Junk," the liveliest recreation of Anglo-Saxon meters and feeling since Pound, or the scathing Miltonic sonnet to Lyndon Johnson, or the tenderness of the translations from Charles d'Orléans, Voltaire, and Francis Jammes, or the effectiveness of "A Christmas Hymn," or the moving elegy for Dudley Fits.

Neither could one have quite anticipated "Walking to Sleep," an extraordinary exploration of the paths, stratagems, surprises, and terrors that lie between waking and sleep, nor "The Mind-Reader," although both long poems extend one of Wilbur's most persistent themes in his more obviously personal lyrics: the processes, reflections, and creations of the mind. Wilbur once remarked, "A good part of my work could, I suppose, be understood as a public quarrel with the aesthetics of Edgar Allan Poe." His continuous concern is evidenced by his edition of Poe's poems and a number of substantial essays on both the prose and the verse: three of the sixteen provocative and lucid essays in *Responses: Prose Pieces 1953–1976* concern Poe. He once wrote, "There has never been a grander conception of poetry [than Poe's], nor a more impoverished one." As that sentence suggests, the quarrel continues because Wilbur finds it so difficult to make a decision once for all. His ambivalence is the theme of a number of his best poems. At its simplest level this ambivalence arises from his fascination with the intellectual, the perfectly beautiful and purely harmonious, and his almost simultaneous reaction away from such an ideal in an acceptance and love for the imperfect human and material reality that we can know here and now. "A World Without Objects Is a Sensible Emptiness" is one of many that move from a moment of the soul's ascension towards the empyrean to a rejoicing in the body and its world. Wilbur's poetry often seems that of a natural Platonist who keeps learning to accept the Incarnation. "The Writer" movingly recognizes that the literary "flight" has its origins as well as final resting place in human suffering and love.

If Robert Frost has an authentic living heir, it is probably Wilbur—particularly as the poet of the short lyric in strict and familiar meters who speaks in the middle voice, wittily and movingly, to a wide audience. There are, however, important differences: Wilbur's voice is usually more obviously that of an urban man in contrast to the characteristic voice of the countryman which Frost so carefully crafted; and Frost never devoted such care to the attempt to translate, self-effacingly, the poetry of others, nor did he write for the public theater. But the most important difference is probably in their spirits. Frost did not share with anything like Wilbur's conviction the notion that "Love Calls Us to the Things of This World." It may have been, in part at least, that conviction which enabled Wilbur to make imaginatively convincing his "Advice to a Prophet" concerning how we might be persuaded not to destroy our earth.

—Joseph H. Summers

WILDER, Thornton (Niven). Born in Madison, Wisconsin, 17 April 1897. Educated at Thacher School, Ojai, California, 1912–13; Berkeley High School, California, graduated 1915; Oberlin College, Ohio, 1915–17; Yale University, New Haven, Connecticut, 1917, 1919–20, A.B. 1920; American Academy in Rome, 1920–21; Princeton University, New Jersey, 1925–26, A.M. 1926. Served in the U.S. Coast Artillery Corps, 1918; in the U.S. Army Air Intelligence, rising to the rank of Lieutenant-Colonel, 1942–45: honorary M.B.E. (Member, Order of the British Empire), 1945. French teacher, 1921–25, and house master, 1927–28, Lawrenceville School, New Jersey. Full-time writer from 1928. Part-time Lecturer in Comparative Literature, University of Chicago, 1930–36; Visiting Professor, University of Hawaii, Honolulu, 1935; Charles Eliot Norton Professor of Poetry, Harvard University, Cambridge, Massachusetts, 1950–51. U.S. Delegate: Institut de Cooperation Intellectuelle, Paris, 1937; International PEN Club Congress, England, 1941; Unesco Conference of the Arts, Venice, 1952. Recipient: Pulitzer Prize, for fiction, 1928, for drama, 1938, 1943; American Academy Gold Medal, 1952; Freedom prize (Frankfurt), 1957; Brandeis University Creative Arts Award, 1959; MacDowell Medal, 1960; Presidential Medal of Freedom, 1963; National Medal for Literature, 1965; National Book Award, for fiction, 1968. D.Litt.: New York University, 1930; Yale University, 1947; Kenyon College, Gambier, Ohio, 1948; College of Wooster, Ohio, 1950; Northeastern University, Boston, 1951; Oberlin College, 1952; University of New Hampshire, Durham, 1953; Goethe University, Frankfurt, 1957; University of Zurich, 1961; LL.D.: Harvard University, 1951. Chevalier, Legion of Honor (France), 1951; member, Order of Merit (Peru); Order of Merit (Germany), 1957; honorary member, Bavarian Academy of Fine Arts; Mainz Academy of Science and Literature; member, American Academy. *Died 7 December 1975.*

PUBLICATIONS

Fiction

The Cabala. 1926.
The Bridge of San Luis Rey. 1927.
The Woman of Andros. 1930.
Heaven's My Destination. 1934.
The Ides of March. 1948.
The Eighth Day. 1967.
Theophilus North. 1973.

Plays

The Trumpet Shall Sound (produced 1926). In *Yale Literary Magazine*, October-December 1919, January 1920.
The Angel That Troubled the Waters and Other Plays (includes *Nascuntur Poetae, Proserpina and the Devil, Fanny Otcott, Brother Fire, The Penny That Beauty Spent, The Angel on the Ship, The Message and Jehanne, Childe Roland to the Dark Tower Came, Centaurs, Leviathan, And the Sea Shall Give Up Its Dead, Now the Servant's Name Was Malchus, Mozart and the Gray Steward, Hast Thou Considered My Servant Job?, The Flight into Egypt*). 1928.
The Long Christmas Dinner (produced 1931). In *The Long Christmas Dinner and Other Plays*, 1931; libretto for opera version, as *Das Lange Weihnachtsmal*, music by Paul Hindemith (produced 1961), libretto published, 1961.
The Happy Journey to Trenton and Camden (produced 1931). In *The Long Christmas Dinner and Other Plays*, 1931; revised version, as *The Happy Journey*, 1934.
Such Things Only Happen in Books (produced 1931). In *The Long Christmas Dinner and Other Plays*, 1931.
Love and How to Cure It (produced 1931). In *The Long*

Christmas Dinner and Other Plays, 1931.
The Long Christmas Dinner and Other Plays in One Act. 1931.
Queens of France (produced 1932). In *The Long Christmas Dinner and Other Plays*, 1931.
Pullman Car Hiawatha (produced 1962). In *The Long Christmas Dinner and Other Plays*, 1931.
Lucrèce, from a play by André Obey (produced 1932). 1933.
A Doll's House, from a play by Ibsen (produced 1937).
Our Town (produced 1938). 1938.
The Merchant of Yonkers, from a play by Johann Nostroy, based on *A Well-Spent Day* by John Oxenford (produced 1938). 1939; revised version, as *The Matchmaker* (produced 1954), in *Three Plays*, 1957.
The Skin of Our Teeth (produced 1942). 1942.
Our Century (produced 1947). 1947.
The Victors, from a play by Sartre (produced 1949).
Die Alkestiade (as *A Life in the Sun*, produced 1955; as *Die Alkestiade*, music by Louise Talma, produced 1962). 1960; as *The Alcestiad; or, A Life in the Sun, and The Drunken Sisters: A Satyr Play*, 1977.
The Drunken Sisters (produced 1970). 1957.
Three Plays. 1957.
Bernice, and The Wreck of the 5:25 (produced 1957).
Plays for Bleecker Street (includes *Infancy*, *Childhood*, and *Someone from Assisi*) (produced 1962). *Childhood* and *Infancy* published, 2 vols., 1960–61.

Screenplays: *We Live Again*, with others, 1934; *Our Town*, with Frank Craven and Harry Chandlee, 1940; *Shadow of a Doubt*, with others, 1943.

Other

The Intent of the Artist, with others. 1941.
Kultur in einer Demokratie. 1957.
Goethe und die Weltliteratur. 1958.
American Characteristics and Other Essays, edited by Donald Gallup. 1979.
The Journals 1939–1961 (includes unfinished play *The Emporium*), edited by Donald Gallup. 1985.

*

Bibliography: *Wilder: A Bibliographical Checklist of Works by and About Wilder* by Richard Goldstone and Gary Anderson, 1982.

Critical Studies: *Wilder* by Rex Burbank, 1961, revised edition, 1978; *Wilder* by Helmut Papajewski, 1961, translated by John Conway, 1968; *Wilder* by Bernard Grebanier, 1964; *The Art of Wilder* by Malcolm Goldstein, 1965; *The Plays of Wilder: A Critical Study* by Donald Haberman, 1967; *Wilder: The Bright and the Dark* by Mildred Christophe Kuner, 1972; *Wilder: An Intimate Portrait* by Richard Goldstone, 1975; *Wilder: His World* by Linda Simon, 1979; *A Vast Landscape: Time in the Novels of Wilder* by Mary Ellen Williams, 1979; *Wilder and His Public* by Amos Wilder, 1980; *The Enthusiast: A Life of Wilder* by Gilbert A. Harrison, 1983; *Wilder* by David Castronovo, 1986.

* * *

Many recent American writers have written both plays and fiction, but no other has achieved such a distinguished reputation for both as Thornton Wilder. He is distinguished also for the uniqueness of his works: each is a fresh formal experiment that contributes to his persistent conception of the artist's reinventing the world by revivifying our preceptions of the universal elements of human experience.

Wilder's earliest published works in *The Angel That Troubled the Waters and Other Plays* are short pieces presenting usually fantastic situations in an arch, cryptic style employed by such favored writers of the 1920's as Elinor Wylie. A number of the plays deal with the special burden that falls upon persons who discover that they possess artistic gifts, and most of them demand staging too complex for actual performance.

Before he became a successful playwright, Wilder was a novelist. His first novel *The Cabala*, displays much the same preciosity as the early plays. It describes through loosely linked episodes the effort of an aspiring young American writer to be accepted by the Cabala, "members of a circle so powerful and exclusive that . . . Romans refer to them with bated breath." These elegant figures turn out to be contemporary embodiments of the ancient Roman gods, and the veiled point of the work is that the U.S. is to succeed a decaying Rome as the next abiding place of these gods.

This fantasy did not attract many readers, but Wilder achieved an astonishing success with his next short novel, *The Bridge of San Luis Rey*, which became a surprise bestseller. This episodic story about the perishability of material things and the endurance of love is exquisitely structured. It tells the stories of the five persons who die in the collapse of a famous Peruvian bridge. The framework of the novel is provided by the narrative of a Brother Juniper, who investigates the accident to learn whether "we live by accident and die by accident, or live by plan and die by plan." For his efforts, both he and his book are publicly burned. The last sentence stresses that the only bridge that survives is love.

Wilder's third novel, *The Woman of Andros*, was attacked by socially-minded critics of the 1930's for evading present realities and retreating to the classical world; but this subtle fictionalization of Terence's *Andria* actually relates closely to Wilder's own seemingly dying world through its presentation of the death of the Greek world at the time of the coming of Christ because its commercial and artistic communities had become alienated. With his next novel, *Heaven's My Destination*, Wilder returned to contemporary America to create one of his most beguiling characters, George Brush, a high-school textbook salesman in the midwest, who fails comically and pathetically in his constant efforts to uplift other people and who recovers his faith only when he realizes that he must remain an isolated wanderer, happy only in the world that he makes for himself.

The world that we make for ourselves is the subject again of one of Wilder's most admired works and his major contribution to a myth of American community, the play *Our Town*. Wilder explained in *The Intent of the Artist* that he turned from the novel to the stage in the 1930's because "the theater carries the art of narration to a higher power than the novel or the epic poem." He was impatient, however, with the elaborate stage settings of the naturalistic theater, and he had already sought in short plays like *The Long Christmas Dinner* to tell a fundamental human story with only the simplest of props. His culminating experiment with this technique was *Our Town*, a chronicle of the value of "the smallest events in our daily life" in a traditional New England village.

Wilder next experimented with updating a 19th-century farce that had been popular in both English and German versions as *The Merchant of Yonkers*. Unsuccessful when first ponderously presented by Max Reinhardt, the play in a revised version entitled *The Matchmaker* was a popular success that subsequently provided the basis for the enormously popular musical comedy, *Hello, Dolly!* Wilder did enjoy great immediate success with his third major play, *The Skin of Our Teeth*, an expressionist fantasy about man's struggles for survival through the Ice Age, the Flood, and the Napoleonic Wars as symbolized by the travails of the Antrobus family. Again Wilder's timing was superb. A world reduced to doubt and despair by World War II responded enthusiastically to this affirmative vision of man's possible survival despite his destructive propensities.

Wilder served with American Intelligence units in Italy during World War II, and for his first post-war work returned to the novel and to a classical Roman setting for *The Ides of March*. This pseudo-history, which Malcolm Goldstein compares to "a set of bowls placed one within another," centers on the assassination of Julius Caesar, but traces through four overlapping sections an ever widening circle of events in order to present "the tragic difference between Caesar's idealistic visions and the sordid events for which they are finally responsible"—a subject fraught with implications for the mid-20th century.

After the comparatively cool reception of this work, Wilder published little for twenty years. Although his plays remained popular, he was generally too lightly regarded after World War II when existential *angst* dominated literary criticism. His writings were felt to be too affirmative and optimistic, and his long silence caused him to be regarded as an artist whose time had passed. Literary mandarins were startled, therefore, by the appearance in 1967 of his longest and most complex work, *The Eighth Day*. This novel jumps back and forth in time as it resurrects the events relating to a murder in a southern Illinois coal town early in the 20th century, the false conviction of a man who escapes, and the eventual solution of the cunning crime. This mystery plot, however, provided only a backdrop for Wilder's observation that all history is one "enormous tapestry" and that "there are no Golden Ages and no Dark Ages. There is the oceanlike monotony of the generations of men under the alternations of fair and foul weather." At the center of the work stands the falsely accused John Ashley, who avoids succumbing to despair over this inescapable cycle by "inventing" afresh such fossilized institutions as marriage and fatherhood as he also invents small practical objects to make man's work easier. An old woman whom he meets sums up the sensibility that informs the novel, "The human race gets no better. Mankind is vicious, slothful, quarrelsome, and self-centered . . . [But] you and I have a certain quality that is rare as teeth in a hen. We work. And we forget ourselves in our work."

The Eighth Day triumphantly capped Wilder's "re-invention" of mankind, but he had one final delight for readers. Perhaps to complement James Joyce's and others' portraits of the artist as a young man *by* a young man, Wilder presented in his last published work, *Theophilus North*, an episodic novel about the artist as a young man *by* an old man. The seemingly loosely connected tales are actually—as in his other works—parts of an intricate mosaic that discloses against a background of the "nine cities" of Newport, Rhode Island, the nine career possibilities that a young man explores before discovering that being a writer will encompass all of them.

—Warren French

See the essay on *Our Town*.

WILLIAMS, Tennessee (Thomas Lanier Williams). Born in Columbus, Mississippi, 26 March 1911. Educated at the University of Missouri, Columbia, 1929–31; Washington University, St. Louis, 1936; University of Iowa, Iowa City, 1938, A.B. 1938. Clerical worker and manual laborer, International Shoe Company, St. Louis, 1934–35; held various jobs, including waiter and elevator operator, New Orleans, 1939; teletype operator, Jacksonville, Florida, 1940; worked at odd jobs, New York, 1942, and as screenwriter for MGM, Hollywood, 1943; full-time writer from 1944; Distinguished Writer-in-Residence, University of British Columbia, Vancouver, 1980. Recipient: Rockefeller fellowship, 1940; American Academy grant, 1944, and Gold Medal, 1969; New York Drama Critics Circle award, 1945, 1948, 1955, 1962; Sidney Howard Award, 1945; Donaldson Award, 1945, 1948; Pulitzer Prize, 1948, 1955; London *Evening Standard* award, 1958; Brandeis University Creative Arts Award, 1964; Medal of Freedom, 1980. L.H.D.: Harvard University, Cambridge, Massachusetts, 1982. Member, American Academy, 1976. *Died 25 February 1983*.

PUBLICATIONS

Collections

Collected Stories. 1985.

Plays

Cairo, Shanghai, Bombay!, with Doris Shapiro (produced 1935).
The Magic Tower (produced 1936).
Headlines (produced 1936).
Candles to the Sun (produced 1937).
Fugitive Kind (produced 1937).
Spring Song (produced 1938).
The Long Goodbye (produced 1940). In *27 Wagons Full of Cotton*, 1946.
Battle of Angels (produced 1940). 1945; revised version, as *Orpheus Descending* (produced 1957), published as *Orpheus Descending, with Battle of Angels*, 1958.
At Liberty (produced 1968). In *American Scenes*, edited by William Kozlenko, 1941.
This Property Is Condemned (produced 1942). In *27 Wagons Full of Cotton*, 1946.
You Touched Me!, with Donald Windham, from the story by D.H. Lawrence (produced 1943). 1947.
The Glass Menagerie (produced 1944). 1945.
27 Wagons Full of Cotton and Other One-Act Plays (includes *The Purification*, *The Lady of Larkspur Lotion*, *The Last of My Solid Gold Watches*, *Portrait of a Madonna*, *Auto-da-Fé*, *Lord Byron's Love Letter*, *The Strangest Kind of Romance*, *The Long Goodbye*, *Hello from Bertha*, and *This Property Is Condemned*). 1946; augmented edition (includes *Talk to Me Like the Rain and Let Me Listen* and *Something Unspoken*), 1953.
Portrait of a Madonna (produced 1946). In *27 Wagons Full of Cotton*, 1946.
The Last of My Solid Gold Watches (produced 1947). In *27 Wagons Full of Cotton*, 1946.
Lord Byron's Love Letter (produced 1947). In *27 Wagons Full of Cotton*, 1946; revised version, music by Raffaello de Banfield (produced 1964); libretto published, 1955.

Auto-da-Fé (produced 1947). In *27 Wagons Full of Cotton*, 1946.
The Lady of Larkspur Lotion (produced 1947). In *27 Wagons Full of Cotton*, 1946.
The Purification (produced 1954). In *27 Wagons Full of Cotton*, 1946.
27 Wagons Full of Cotton (produced 1955). In *27 Wagons Full of Cotton*, 1946.
Hello from Bertha (produced 1961). In *27 Wagons Full of Cotton*, 1946.
The Strangest Kind of Romance (produced 1969). In *27 Wagons Full of Cotton*, 1946.
Moony's Kid Don't Cry (produced 1946). In *American Blues*, 1948.
Stairs to the Roof (produced 1947).
A Streetcar Named Desire (produced 1947). 1947.
Summer and Smoke (produced 1947). 1948; revised version, as *The Eccentricities of a Nightingale* (produced 1964), published as *The Eccentricities of a Nightingale, and Summer and Smoke*, 1965; revised version (produced 1976).
American Blues: Five Short Plays (includes *Moony's Kid Don't Cry*; *The Dark Room*; *The Case of the Crushed Petunias*; *The Long Stay Cut Short; or, The Unsatisfactory Supper*; and *Ten Blocks on the Camino Real*). 1948.
Ten Blocks on the Camino Real, in *American Blues*, 1948; revised version, as *Camino Real* (produced 1953). 1953.
The Case of the Crushed Petunias (produced 1957). In *American Blues*, 1948.
The Dark Room (produced 1966). In *American Blues*, 1948.
The Long Stay Cut Short; or, The Unsatisfactory Supper (produced 1971). In *American Blues*, 1948.
The Rose Tattoo (produced 1951). 1951.
I Rise in Flame, Cried the Phoenix: A Play about D.H. Lawrence (produced 1959). 1951.
Something Unspoken (produced 1955). In *27 Wagons Full of Cotton*, 1953.
Talk to Me Like the Rain and Let Me Listen (produced 1958). In *27 Wagons Full of Cotton*, 1953.
Cat on a Hot Tin Roof (produced 1955). 1955; revised version (produced 1973), 1975.
Three Players of a Summer Game (produced 1955).
Sweet Bird of Youth (produced 1956). 1959.
Baby Doll: The Script for the Film, Incorporating the Two One-Act Plays Which Suggested It: 27 Wagons Full of Cotton and The Long Stay Cut Short; or, The Unsatisfactory Supper. 1956.
Garden District: Something Unspoken, Suddenly Last Summer (produced 1958). 1958.
The Fugitive Kind: Original Play Title: Orpheus Descending (screenplay). 1958.
Period of Adjustment: High Point over a Cavern: A Serious Comedy (produced 1958). 1960.
A Perfect Analysis Given by a Parrot (produced 1976). 1958.
The Enemy: Time, in *Theatre*, March 1959.
The Night of the Iguana (produced 1959; revised version, produced 1961). 1962.
To Heaven in a Golden Coach (produced 1961).
The Milk Train Doesn't Stop Here Anymore (produced 1962; revised versions, produced 1963, 1964, 1968). 1964.
Slapstick Tragedy (*The Mutilated* and *The Gnädiges Fräulein*) (produced 1966). 2 vols., 1967; revised version of *The Gnädiges Fräulein*, as *The Latter Days of a Celebrated Soubrette* (produced 1974).
Kingdom of Earth, in *Esquire* (New York), February 1967; (revised version, as *The Seven Descents of Myrtle*, produced 1968), published as *Kingdom of Earth (The Seven Descents of Myrtle)*. 1968.
The Two-Character Play (produced 1967; revised version, produced 1969). 1969; revised version, as *Out Cry* (produced 1971), 1973; revised version (produced 1974).
In the Bar of a Tokyo Hotel (produced 1969). 1969.
I Can't Imagine Tomorrow (televised 1970; produced 1976). In *Dragon Country*, 1970.
Confessional (produced 1970). In *Dragon Country*, 1970; revised version, as *Small Craft Warnings* (produced 1972), 1972.
The Frosted Glass Coffin (produced 1970). In *Dragon Country*, 1970.
Dragon Country: A Book of Plays (includes *In the Bar of a Tokyo Hotel*; *I Rise in Flame, Cried the Phoenix*; *The Mutilated*; *I Can't Imagine Tomorrow*; *Confessional*; *The Frosted Glass Coffin*; *The Gnädiges Fräulein*; *A Perfect Analysis Given by a Parrot*). 1970.
Tennessee Laughs: Three One-Act Plays (*Some Problems for the Moose Lodge; A Perfect Analysis Given by a Parrot; The Frosted Glass Coffin*) (produced 1980; revised version of *Some Problems for the Moose Lodge*, as *A House Not Meant to Stand*, produced 1981, revised version, 1982). *The Frosted Glass Coffin* and *A Perfect Analysis Given by a Parrot* in *Dragon Country*, 1970.
Senso, with Paul Bowles, in *Two Screenplays*, by Luigi Visconti. 1970.
A Streetcar Named Desire (screenplay), in *Film Scripts 1*, edited by George Garrett, O.B. Hardison, Jr., and Jane Gelfman. 1971.
The Theatre of Williams:
1. *Battle of Angels*, *A Streetcar Named Desire*, *The Glass Menagerie*. 1972.
2. *The Eccentricities of a Nightingale*, *Summer and Smoke*, *The Rose Tattoo*, *Camino Real*. 1972.
3. *Cat on a Hot Tin Roof*, *Orpheus Descending*, *Suddenly Last Summer*. 1972.
4. *Sweet Bird of Youth*, *Period of Adjustment*, *Night of the Iguana*. 1972.
5. *The Milk Train Doesn't Stop Here Anymore; Kingdom of Earth*, revised version; *Small Craft Warnings; The Two-Character Play*, revised version. 1976.
6. *27 Wagons Full of Cotton and Other One Act Plays* (includes *The Unsatisfactory Supper*, *Steps Must Be Gentle*, *The Demolition Downtown: Count Ten in Arabic*). 1981.
7. *Dragon Country*, *Lifeboat Drill*, *Now the Cats with Jewelled Claws*, *Now the Peaceable Kingdom*. 1981.

The Red Devil Battery Sign (produced 1975; revised version, produced 1976).
Demolition Downtown: Count Ten in Arabic—Then Run (produced 1976). In *The Theatre of Williams 6*, 1981.
This Is an Entertainment (produced 1976).
Vieux Carré (produced 1977). 1979.
Tiger Tail (produced 1978).
A Lovely Sunday for Creve Coeur (as *Creve Coeur*, produced 1978; as *A Lovely Sunday for Creve Coeur*, produced 1979). 1980.
Lifeboat Drill (produced 1979). In *The Theatre of Williams 7*, 1981.
Kirche, Küchen, und Kinder (produced 1980).
Clothes for a Summer Hotel (produced 1980). 1983.
Will Mr. Merriwether Return from Memphis? (produced 1980).

Something Cloudy, Something Clear (produced 1981).
Stopped Rocking and Other Screenplays. 1984.

Screenplays: *Senso* (*The Wanton Countess*; English dialogue, with Paul Bowles), 1949; *The Glass Menagerie*, with Peter Berneis, 1950; *A Streetcar Named Desire*, with Oscar Saul, 1951; *The Rose Tattoo*, with Hal Kanter, 1955; *Baby Doll*, 1956; *Suddenly Last Summer*, with Gore Vidal, 1959; *The Fugitive Kind*, with Meade Roberts, 1960; *Boom*, 1968.

Television Plays: *I Can't Imagine Tomorrow*, 1970; *Stopped Rocking*, 1975.

Fiction

One Arm and Other Stories. 1948.
The Roman Spring of Mrs. Stone. 1950.
Hard Candy: A Book of Stories. 1954.
Three Players of a Summer Game and Other Stories. 1960.
Grand (stories). 1964.
The Knightly Quest: A Novella and Four Short Stories. 1967; augmented edition, as *The Knightly Quest: A Novella and Twelve Short Stories*, 1968.
Eight Mortal Ladies Possessed: A Book of Stories. 1974.
Moise and the World of Reason. 1975.
It Happened the Day the Sun Rose and Other Stories. 1982.

Verse

Five Young American Poets, with others. 1944.
In the Winter of Cities. 1956.
Androgyne, Mon Amour. 1977.

Other

Memoirs. 1975.
Letters to Donald Windham 1940–1965, edited by Windham. 1976.
Where I Live: Selected Essays, edited by Christine R. Day and Bob Woods. 1978.
Conversations with Williams (interviews), edited by Albert J. Devlin. 1986.

*

Bibliography: *Williams: A Bibliography* by Drewey Wayne Gunn, 1980; *The Critical Reputation of Williams: A Reference Guide* by John S. McCann, 1983.

Critical Studies: *Williams* by Signi Lenea Falk, 1961, revised edition, 1978; *Williams: The Man and His Work* by Benjamin Nelson, 1961; *Williams, Rebellious Puritan* by Nancy Tischler, 1961; *The Dramatic World of Williams* by Francis Donahue, 1964; *Williams and Friends* by Gilbert Maxwell, 1965; *The Broken World of Williams* by Esther Jackson, 1965; *Williams* by Gerald Weales, 1965; *A Look at Williams* by Mike Steen, 1969; *Williams: A Moralist's Answer to the Perils of Life* by Ingrid Rogers, 1976; *Williams: A Tribute* edited by Jac Tharpe, 1977; *Williams: A Collection of Critical Essays* edited by Stephen S. Stanton, 1977; *The World of Williams* edited by Richard Freeman Leavitt, 1978; *Williams: The Tragic Tension* by Emmanuel B. Asibong, 1978; *A Portrait of the Artist: The Plays of Williams* by Foster Hirsch, 1979; *Williams* by Felicia H. Londré, 1980; *Williams: An Intimate Biography* by Dakin Williams and Shepherd Mead, 1983; *The Glass Menagerie: A Collection of Critical Essays* edited by R.B. Parker, 1983; *Dictionary of Literary Biography Documentary Series 4* edited by Margaret A. Van Antwerp and Sally Johns, 1984; *Tennessee: Cry of the Heart: An Intimate Memoir of Williams* by Dotson Rader, 1985; *The Kindness of Strangers: The Life of Williams* by Donald Spoto, 1985; *Williams on File* edited by Catherine M. Arnott and Simon Trussler, 1985; *As If: A Personal View of Williams* by Donald Windham, 1985; *Williams* by R. Boxill, 1986; *Williams: A Portrait in Laughter and Lamentation* by Harry Rasky, 1986.

* * *

Shortly before *Vieux Carré* opened on Broadway in 1977, Tennessee Williams wrote an article for the New York *Times* which began, "Of course no one is more acutely aware than I that I am widely regarded as the ghost of a writer." So, at that time, he was. The name Tennessee Williams still conjures up the flamboyant plays of the 1940's and 1950's—*A Streetcar Named Desire*, *Cat on a Hot Tin Roof*, *Suddenly Last Summer*. But except for a period in the mid-1960's when he suffered mental and physical collapse, Williams was a remarkably busy ghost. In the mid-1970's new plays were staged in London, San Francisco, and New York and he published a novel (*Moise and the World of Reason*), a book of short stories (*Eight Mortal Ladies Possessed*) a book of poems (*Androgyne, Mon Amour*) and *Memoirs*. Artistically and personally, he became an advertisement for the theme that obsessed him ever since Amanda Wingfield tried to hold her disintegrating family together in *The Glass Menagerie*—survival.

When *Vieux Carré* opened, the critics did treat it as a ghost play, a nostalgic look at the New Orleans of Williams's youth, full of echoes of characters, situations, themes relentlessly familiar to Williams admirers. In the *Times* article, in *Memoirs*, in any number of interviews, Williams attempted to explain how he was transformed from America's most popular serious playwright into an historical figure, inexplicably still active in the real world. His plays through *The Night of the Iguana*, he suggested, shared a similarity of style—"poetic naturalism" he called it—which became so identified with him that when he made a shift into new styles, his audiences could not or would not follow him. It is true that there are great stylistic similarities among the Williams plays through *The Night of the Iguana* and it is also true that he lost the large audiences that had once flocked to this work, but the new styles had their roots in his earlier work.

He was never a realistic playwright, which may be what the phrase *poetic naturalism* is supposed to suggest, but he was always capable of writing a psychologically valid scene in the American realistic tradition—the breakfast scene in *The Glass Menagerie*, for instance, or the birthday dinner in *A Streetcar Named Desire*. His characters are able to claim the allegiance of audiences who continue to identify with them even after they become larger than life (Big Daddy in *Cat on a Hot Tin Roof*, Alexandra Del Lago in *Sweet Bird of Youth*) or when the use of significant names (Val Xavier in *Orpheus Descending*, Alma in *Summer and Smoke*) turn them into myth or symbol. However grounded in realistic surface, the events in Williams's plays, particularly the violent events, take on meaning that transcends psychological realism ("Here is your God, Mr. Shannon," says Hannah when the storm breaks in *The Night of the Iguana*), and when the violence moves off stage—the cannibalism in *Suddenly Last Summer*, the castration in *Sweet Bird of Youth*—

the nonrealistic implications of the event are heightened by its transformation into narrative (*Summer and Smoke*) or promise (*Sweet Bird of Youth*). From the glass menagerie through the dressmaker's dummies in *The Rose Tattoo* to the costumes, ritually donned by Shannon and Hannah in *The Night of the Iguana*, Williams always used sets, props, dress as devices whose significance runs deeper than the verisimilitude required by realism. When Williams deserted old forms—or thought he did—he brought two decades of nonrealistic theater with him. *Slapstick Tragedy* may have suggested absurdist drama to some of its viewers, but Polly and Molly, the grotesque comedy team whose voices sustain *The Gnädiges Fräulein*, are variations on Dolly and Beulah, who introduce *Orpheus Descending*, and Flora and Bessie, the "female clowns" of *The Rose Tattoo* and *A Perfect Analysis Given by a Parrot*. When each of the characters in *Small Craft Warnings* takes his place in the spotlight to sound his sorrow—a mechanism which suggests that the title of an earlier version of the play, *Confessional*, is more apt—we have at most an intensification of the device Williams used extensively in his earlier plays, most notably in Maggie's opening speech in *Cat on a Hot Tin Roof* and the soliloquies of Chance and Alexandra in *Sweet Bird of Youth*.

Stylistically, then, the later Williams plays grow out of the early ones. Nor are there surprising shifts in theme. The similarities between the pre- and post-*The Night of the Iguana* plays can best be seen in the recurrence of characters. The Blanche of *A Streetcar Named Desire*, whose variants people *Summer and Smoke*, *Camino Real*, *Sweet Bird of Youth*, and *The Night of the Iguana*, is still visible in Isabel in *Period of Adjustment*, Miriam in *In the Bar of a Tokyo Hotel*, and bizarrely, in the fish-trapping heroine of *The Gnädiges Fräulein*. Amanda—or at least her comic toughness—is apparent in Flora Goforth in *The Milk Train Doesn't Stop Here Anymore*, Myrtle in *Kingdom of Earth*, and Leona in *Small Craft Warnings*, and Laura, the frightened daughter of *The Glass Menagerie*, is present in characters as different as One in *I Can't Imagine Tomorrow* and Clare in *Out Cry*. Blanche, Amanda, Laura, three aspects of the perennial Williams character, the fugitive kind, who, male and female, was the playwright's concern from his very early one-act plays to *Vieux Carré*. At first, his characters were simply outsiders, set off from the rest of society by a recognizable difference of one kind or another—Laura's limp, Blanche's defensive sexuality, Alma's pseudo-artistic sensitivity. It became increasingly clear—even as the forces that opposed his protagonists became more violent—that all men are outsiders. The murderous Jabe in *Orpheus Descending* is set apart by the disease that is killing him as obviously as Val is by his priapic aura, his guitar, and his snakeskin jacket, as Lady is by being Italian, as Carol Cutrere is by her unconsoling wealth and self-lacerating sex, as Vee Talbot is by her painting and her religious visions. Chance calls Alexandra "nice monster" in *Sweet Bird of Youth*, and she calls him "pitiful monster," and both are "Lost in the beanstalk country . . . the country of the flesh-hungry, blood-thirsty ogre," but the play's ogre, Boss Finley, is supposed to be monster-ridden too and Williams kept revising the play in the hopes that that point would emerge. The enemy is no longer the ugly other, but a surrogate self, or time (note all those age-obsessed Williams characters, like Mrs. Stone who wanted a Roman spring), or a godless universe. This last is presented most clearly in two plays, *Suddenly Last Summer* and *The Night of the Iguana*, which come closest to making specific theological statements. Man, as Williams sees him—as Williams embodies him—is a temporary resident in a frightening world in an indifferent universe. The best he can hope is the transitory consolation of touching and the best he can do is hang on for dear (and only) life.

In the *Times* article quoted above Williams mentioned his "private panic," his dreams "full of alarm and wild suspicion" that made him want to "cry . . . out to all who will listen," and his continued revision of *Out Cry* emphasized his urgency. But that cry always echoed through his work—his novels, his short stories, his poetry, his autobiography, and all his plays. In the hope that the cry would come through more clearly, he continually revised and rewrote, turning short stories into plays, short plays into long ones, full-length plays into other full-length plays, as *Battle of Angels* became *Orpheus Descending*, and *Summer and Smoke* became *The Eccentricities of a Nightingale*. Audiences withdrew from Williams, I suspect, not because his style changed or his concerns altered, but because in his desperate need to cry out he turned away from the sturdy dramatic containers which once gave the cry resonance and settled for pale imitations of familiar stage images; he built on the direct address of the early soliloquies and the discursiveness of plays like *The Night of the Iguana* and substituted lyric argument for dramatic language. It is a measure of his stature as a playwright and the importance of his central theme that each new play carried the promise of old vigor in new disguise. If that promise was not fulfilled for audiences when Williams's later plays were first performed, new strengths may still be discovered with the revaluations which are sure to come now that the playwright has died. In the meantime, admirers of Williams will continue to turn back to his more celebrated works, works that have now become contemporary classics.

—Gerald Weales

See the essays on *The Glass Menagerie* and *A Streetcar Named Desire*.

WILLIAMS, William Carlos. Born in Rutherford, New Jersey, 17 September 1883. Educated at a school in Rutherford, 1889–96; Chateau de Lancy, near Geneva, Switzerland, and Lycée Condorcet, Paris, 1897–99; Horace Mann High School, New York, 1899–1902; University of Pennsylvania, Philadelphia, 1902–06, M.D. 1906; intern at hospitals in New York City, 1906–08; post-graduate work in pediatrics, University of Leipzig, 1908–09. Married Florence Herman in 1912; two sons. Practised medicine in Rutherford, 1910 until he retired in the mid-1950's. Editor, *Others*, 1919; editor, with Robert McAlmon, *Contact*, 1920–23; editor, *Contact: An American Quarterly*, 1931–33. Appointed Consultant in Poetry, Library of Congress, Washington, D.C., 1952, but did not serve. Recipient: Loines Award, 1948; National Book Award, 1950; Bollingen Prize, 1952; Academy of American Poets fellowship, 1956; Brandeis University Creative Arts Award, 1958; American Academy Gold Medal, 1963; Pulitzer Prize, 1963. LL.D.: State University of New York, Buffalo, 1956; Fairleigh Dickinson University, Teaneck, New Jersey, 1959; Litt.D.: Rutgers University, New Brunswick, New Jersey, 1948; Bard College, Annandale-on-Hudson, New York, 1948; University of Pennsylvania, 1952. Member, American Academy. *Died 4 March 1963*.

PUBLICATIONS

Collections

The Williams Reader, edited by M.L. Rosenthal. 1966.
Selected Poems, edited by Charles Tomlinson. 1976.
Collected Poems, edited by A. Walton Litz and Christopher MacGowan. 1987—

Verse

Poems. 1909.
The Tempers. 1913.
Al Que Quiere! 1917.
Kora in Hell: Improvisations. 1920.
Sour Grapes. 1921.
Spring and All. 1923.
Go Go. 1923.
The Cod Head. 1932.
Collected Poems, 1921–1931. 1934.
An Early Martyr and Other Poems. 1935.
Adam & Eve & the City. 1936.
The Complete Collected Poems 1906–1938. 1938.
The Broken Span. 1941.
The Wedge. 1944.
Paterson, Book One. 1946; *Book Two*, 1948; *Book Three*, 1949; *Book Four*, 1951; *Book Five*, 1958; *Books I-V*, 1963.
The Clouds. 1948.
The Pink Church. 1949.
Selected Poems. 1949.
The Collected Later Poems. 1950; revised edition, 1963.
The Collected Earlier Poems. 1951.
The Desert Music and Other Poems. 1954.
Journey to Love. 1955.
Pictures from Brueghel and Other Poems. 1962.
Penguin Modern Poets 9, with Denise Levertov and Kenneth Rexroth. 1967.

Plays

Betty Putnam (produced 1910).
A Dream of Love (produced 1949). 1948.
Many Loves (produced 1958). In *Many Loves and Other Plays*, 1961.
Many Loves and Other Plays: The Collected Plays (includes *A Dream of Love*; *Tituba's Children*; *The First President*, music by Theodore Harris; *The Cure*). 1961.

Fiction

A Voyage to Pagany. 1928.
A Novelette and Other Prose 1921–1931. 1932.
The Knife of the Times and Other Stories. 1932.
Trilogy:
White Mule. 1937.
In the Money. 1940.
The Build-Up. 1952.
Life along the Passaic River (stories). 1938.
Make Light of It: Collected Stories. 1950.
The Farmers' Daughters: The Collected Stories. 1961.

Other

The Great American Novel. 1923.
In the American Grain. 1925.
The Autobiography. 1951.
Williams' Poetry Talked About, with Eli Siegel. 1952; revised edition, edited by Martha Baird and Ellen Reiss, as *The Williams-Siegel Documentary*, 1970, 1974.
Selected Essays. 1954.
John Marin, with others. 1956.
Selected Letters, edited by John C. Thirlwall. 1957.
I Wanted to Write a Poem: The Autobiography of the Works of a Poet, edited by Edith Heal. 1958.
Yes, Mrs. Williams: A Personal Record of My Mother. 1959.
Imaginations: Collected Early Prose, edited by Webster Schott. 1970.
The Embodiment of Knowledge, edited by Ron Loewinsohn. 1974.
Interviews with Williams: Speaking Straight Ahead, edited by Linda W. Wagner. 1976.
A Recognizable Image: Williams on Art and Artists, edited by Bram Dijkstra. 1978.
Something to Say: Williams on Younger Poets, edited by James E.B. Breslin. 1985.

Translator, *Last Nights of Paris*, by Philippe Soupault. 1929.
Translator, with others, *Jean sans terre/Landless John*, by Yvan Goll. 1944.
Translator, with Raquel Hélène Williams, *The Dog and the Fever*, by Francisco de Quevedo. 1954.

*

Bibliography: *A Bibliography of Williams* by Emily Wallace Mitchell, 1968; *Williams: A Reference Guide* by Linda W. Wagner, 1978.

Critical Studies: *Williams* by Vivienne Koch, 1950; *Williams: A Critical Study* by John Malcolm Brinnin, 1963; *The Poems of Williams*, 1964, and *The Prose of Williams*, 1970, both by Linda W. Wagner; *The Poetic World of Williams* by Alan Ostrom, 1966; *Williams: A Collection of Critical Essays* edited by J. Hillis Miller, 1966; *An Approach to Paterson* by Walter Scott Peterson, 1967; *The Music of Survival* by Sherman Paul, 1968; *Williams' Paterson: Language and Landscape* by Joel Connarroe, 1970; *Williams: An American Artist* by James E.B. Breslin, 1970; *Williams: The American Background* by Mike Weaver, 1971; *A Companion to Williams's Paterson* by Benjamin Sankey, 1971; *Williams: The Later Poems* by Jerome Mazzaro, 1973; *The Inverted Bell: Modernism and the Counterpoetics of Williams* by Joseph N. Riddel, 1974; *Williams* by Kenneth Burke and Emily H. Wallace, 1974; *Williams: The Knack of Survival in America* by Robert Coles, 1975; *Williams: Poet from Jersey* by Reed Whittemore, 1975; *Williams: The Poet and His Critics*, 1975, and *Williams: A New World Naked*, 1981, both by Paul L. Mariani; *The Early Poetry of Williams* by Rod Townley, 1976; *Williams and the American Scene 1920–1940* by Dickran Tashjian, 1978; *Williams's Paterson: A Critical Reappraisal* by Margaret Glynne Lloyd, 1980; *Williams: The Critical Heritage* edited by Charles Doyle, 1980, and *Williams and the American Poem* by Doyle, 1982; *Williams and the Painters 1909–1923* by William Marling, 1982; *Williams: Man and Poet* by Carroll F. Terrell, 1983; *Williams: A Poet in the American Theatre* by David A. Fedo, 1983; *Ezra Pound and Williams* edited by Daniel Hoffman, 1983; *Williams and Romantic Idealism* by Carl Rapp, 1984; *The Visual Text of Williams* by Henry M. Sayre, 1984; *Ameri-*

can Beauty: Williams and the Modernist Whitman by Stephen Tapscott, 1984; *The Transparent Lyric: Reading and Meaning in the Poetry of Stevens and Williams* by David Walker, 1984; *Williams and the Meanings of Measure* by Stephen Cushman, 1985; *A Poetry of Presence: The Writing of Williams* by Bernard Duffey, 1986.

* * *

William Carlos Williams is one of the leading figures of American modernist poetry whose recent recognition critically supports the impact his poems and fiction had throughout the modern and contemporary periods. Williams was a writer's writer in that his reputation existed chiefly among other writers—Ezra Pound, H. D., Marianne Moore, Hart Crane, Wallace Stevens, John Dos Passos, Ernest Hemingway—at least until New Directions began publishing his work in the late 1930's. Most of Williams's first dozen books were privately printed or subsidized. Some were collections of poems; others were an innovative mixture of poetry and prose, or of prose-poem form. Regardless of apparent genre, Williams wrote consistently in a mode based on the rhythms of the speaking voice, complete with idiomatic language, colloquial word choice, organic form and structure, and an intense interest in locale as both setting and subject.

This most American of poets was born of mixed parentage, and part of his fascination with the identification of—even the definition of—the American character may have stemmed from his own feeling of dislocation. His short early poems as well as his collection of essays on American historical figures, *In the American Grain*, present personae and scenes germane to the United States: "a young horse with a green bed-quilt / on his withers shaking his head," "A big young bareheaded woman / in an apron," "Flowers through the window / lavender and yellow / changed by white curtains." The fact that these scenes and characters are presented with neither apology nor psychological justification emphasized the aesthetic position that the thing was its own justification. Whether echoing John Dewey, Henri Bergson, or William James, Williams's innate pragmatism led him to a concentration on the unadorned image (as a means to universal understanding, truth) that opened many new directions in modern poetry. Williams did not use the image as symbol, a substitute for a larger idea; he was content to rest with the assumption that the reader could duplicate his own sense of importance for the red wheelbarrows and green glass between hospital walls, and thereby dismiss the equivocation of symbolism. As he said so succinctly in *Paterson*, "no ideas but in things."

Allied with the notion of presentation was the corollary that the author was to be as invisible as possible, so as not to dilute the effect of the concrete object or character. Not until his later poems did Williams change that tenet, but the strikingly personal "The Desert Music" and "Asphodel, That Greeny Flower" benefit from his use of a more personal stance toward the materials. Through the writing of his five-book epic poem, *Paterson*, from the 1940's to 1958, Williams was moving toward a kind of self-revelation, albeit unevenly. The epic concerns a poet-doctor-city persona named Paterson, tracing some events of the poet-doctor's life through an intense juxtaposition of scene, image, and memory. The technique of placing one image or scene against another, often without verbal transition, resembled the montage effect in the art contemporary with Williams; troubling as it was to his readers thirty years ago, it became the *modus operandi* for many contemporary writers, a way of increasing speed, of covering more images and sources of imagery, in the context of a rapidly-moving poem.

Williams established many new principles in the writing of his poetry—his confidence that the common American was an apt source of character, his joy in re-creating natural speech, his experimentation with a structure and line that would allow the flexible and fluid pace of speech to be presented—but his prose was also influential. From the 1923 *Spring and All*, when he combined aesthetic theory with such famous poems as "The Red Wheelbarrow," "To Elsie," and "At the Ballgame," to the trilogy of a family establishing itself in American business culture (the Stetchers in *White Mule*, *In the Money*, and *The Build-Up*), Williams turned away from the established conventions in order to present sharply, idiomatically, the gist of his drama. Much of his prose is carried through dialogue that makes Hemingway's seem contrived and redundant; most of his fiction has no ostensible plot. Moving as far from artifice as possible, his prose was criticized repeatedly for being artless; but contemporary readers have found the organic emphasis on language-structure-character an important direction for their own writing. "The Burden of Loveliness," "Jean Beicke," "The Use of Force" are stories often anthologized, provocative in their presentation of convincing characters whose human conditions proceed without drama, but—in Williams's handling—always with sympathy.

That Williams was a practicing physician until the mid-1950's adds some interest to his use of apparently real people in his fiction and poetry. The authenticity of his knowledge about people is undeniable, and he speaks movingly in his autobiography about the reciprocity between being a doctor (a pediatrician by specialization, but a general practitioner for all intents) and a writer. Working from insights that a more reclusive person might not have had, Williams was able to portray accurately many elements of the American culture that had not been treated in the literature of the 20th century (Eliot's Prufrock would not have come to Williams's New Jersey office). Disturbed as he often was about his lack of time to write, he nevertheless acknowledged that his busy life was a rich one; and his writing after his retirement (chiefly because of a severe stroke) frequently returned to subjects and characters from that more active life. The stories about Williams's writing during his rushed days as physician are apocryphal: pulling his car off the road while on his way to make a house call so that he could scribble a poem on a prescription blank; equipping his office desk with a hidden typewriter so that he could flip the machine in place between patients. His production as writer in the midst of his full days as doctor is amazing, but what made that production possible was his personal intent: he considered himself primarily a poet; his aim and direction in life were toward success in writing. No hurried schedule could prevent his implementing that dream.

Williams's poems are not all affirmative pictures of American character and scene; in fact, much of his writing during the 1930's and 1940's is bleak and despairing, and the early books of *Paterson* reflect that disillusionment with what had earlier appeared to be inexhaustible American promise. The late books of *Paterson*, however, supply Williams's own hard-won answers: love, even if foolhardy; virtue; knowing oneself; doing what one can; creating. These are hardly new answers, but their lack of innovation does not lessen their impact. Like Dante traveling through the Inferno, Paterson-Williams takes us into blind alleys (his poems are realistic because we see wrong answers as well as right ones, and sometimes no answers at all), only to move up through Limbo to a kind of modern-day heaven, a place with the answers at least implied in passages like:

> Through this hole
> at the bottom of the cavern
> of death, the imagination
> escapes intact.
> It is the imagination
> which cannot be fathomed.
> It is through this hole
> we escape. . . .

From this resolution, it is only a step to the gentle poise of the last poems. One of the most striking poems of his Pulitzer Prize-winning book, *Pictures from Brueghel*, is "Asphodel," the love poem to his wife of nearly fifty years, which speaks of "love, abiding love." "Death / is not the end of it," Williams writes, comparing love to "a garden which expands . . . a love engendering / gentleness and goodness." Williams contrasts the quiet assurance of this love with "Waste, waste! / dominates the world. It is the bomb's work." And his love is broadened to include his total response to life, as he declares proudly toward the end of the poem:

> Only the imagination is real!
> I have declared it
> time without end.
>
> If a man die
> it is because death
> has first
> possessed his imagination. . . .
> But love and the imagination
> are of a piece
> swift as the light
> to avoid destruction. . . .

Williams's impact on modern American poetics might appear to have been largely technical, for all the discussion of his use of the local, the triadic line, the idiom; but ultimately readers and fellow writers probably respond as well to the pervasive optimism of the doctor-poet's view, and to the openness with which he shared his life and his reactions with his readers. One may forget the rationale for Williams's triadic line division; but one does not forget his candor and his affirmation.

—Linda W. Wagner

See the essay on *Paterson*.

WILLIS, Nathaniel Parker. Born in Portland, Maine, 20 January 1806. Educated at Boston Latin School; Phillips Academy, Andover, Massachusetts; Yale University, New Haven, Connecticut, 1823–27, graduated 1827. Married 1) Mary Stace in 1835 (died, 1845); 2) Cornelia Grinnell in 1846, three daughters and two sons. Became known as a writer while still an undergraduate; edited 2 issues of *The Legendary*, 1828, and an annual *The Token*, 1829; founding editor, *American Monthly Magazine*, Boston, 1829–31; co-editor, 1831–33, and correspondent in Europe, 1833–36, and the U.S., 1836–39, New York *Mirror*; founding co-editor, *Corsair*, New York, 1839; co-owner and editor, *New Mirror*, 1843, and *Weekly* and *Evening Mirror*, 1844–45; visited Europe, 1845; co-owner and editor, *National Press* (later *Home Journal*), 1846–64, and sole owner and editor, 1864–67; lived in Idlewild, New York, after 1853. *Died 20 January 1867.*

PUBLICATIONS

Collections

Prose Writings, edited by Henry A. Beers. 1885.
Poetical Works. 1888.

Fiction

Inklings of Adventure. 1836.
Loiterings of Travel. 1840.
Romance of Travel (stories). 1840.
Dashes at Life with a Free Pencil. 1845.
People I Have Met (stories). 1850.
Life Here and There (stories). 1850.
Fun-Jottings; or, Laughs I Have Taken a Pen To (stories). 1853.
Paul Fane; or, Parts of a Life Else Untold. 1857.

Plays

Bianca Visconti; or, The Heart Overtasked (produced 1837). 1839.
Tortesa; or, The Usurer Matched (produced 1839). 1839.

Verse

Sketches. 1827.
Fugitive Poetry. 1829.
Poem Delivered Before the Society of the United Brothers, with Other Poems. 1831.
Melanie and Other Poems. 1835.
The Sacred Poems. 1843.
Poems of Passion. 1843.
The Lady Jane and Other Poems. 1843.
Poems Sacred, Passionate, and Humorous. 1845; revised edition, 1849.
Poems of Early and After Years. 1848.

Other

Pencillings by the Way. 3 vols., 1835; revised edition, 1844; reprinted in part as *Summer Cruise in the Mediterranean*, 1853.
A l'Abri; or, The Tent Pitched. 1839; revised edition, as *Letters from under a Bridge, and Poems*, 1840.
American Scenery, drawings by W.H. Bartlett. 2 vols., 1840.
Canadian Scenery Illustrated, drawings by W.H. Bartlett. 2 vols., 1842.
The Scenery and Antiquities of Ireland, with J. Stirling Coyne, drawings by W.H. Bartlett. 2 vols., 1842.
Lectures on Fashion. 1844.
Complete Works. 1846.
Prose Works. 1849.
Rural Letters and Other Records of Thought at Leisure. 1849.
Hurry-Graphs; or, Sketches of Scenery, Celebrities, and Soci-

ety. 1851.
Memoranda of the Life of Jenny Lind. 1853.
Health Trip to the Tropics. 1854.
Famous Persons and Places. 1854.
Out-Doors at Idlewild. 1855.
The Rag-Bag: A Collection of Ephemera. 1855.
The Convalescent. 1859.

Editor, *The Legendary*. 1828.
Editor, *Trenton Falls, Picturesque and Descriptive*. 1851.
Editor, with George Pope Morris, *The Prose and Poetry of Europe and America*. 1857.

*

Critical Studies: *Willis* by Henry A. Beers, 1885 (includes bibliography); *The World of Washington Irving* by Van Wyck Brooks, 1944; *Willis* by Cortland P. Auser, 1969.

* * *

Nathaniel Parker Willis was in his day the most famous recorder of the details of social life and customs in America. In a sense, he was to his age what Tom Wolfe is to ours, but he was, in a way that Wolfe is not, sympathetic to most of the signs of status that he found around him—the resorts, homes, clothes, and so forth.

Willis seldom dealt with old established families. He generally concerned himself with the newly rich in search of the means through which they could express their status. He provided them with newspaper and magazine columns describing exactly the things they wanted to know and collected his observations in a series of volumes that were quite popular at the time. His books about fashionable life can be divided into three categories: books dealing with fashionable life abroad (a subject of endless fascination for newly rich Americans who, as a measure of their recently acquired status, adopted European standards, customs, and even diction—although few such people had crossed the Atlantic); books concerning fashionable life in America, especially in New York City and in such watering-places as Saratoga Springs, New York; and, most significantly, books detailing rural, middle-class life. *Pencillings by the Way* is an excellent account of his observations abroad, and *Hurry-Graphs* is typical of his volumes on life in America. His books on rural life include *A l'Abri*, *Out-Doors at Idlewild*, and *The Convalescent* and are of major importance to social as well as cultural historians as three of the earliest and most influential expressions of middle-class obsession with rural and suburban life. Willis, together with the essayist and landscape gardener Andrew Jackson Downing, was among the first to popularize this way of life in America. He also worked with the picturesque painter W.H. Bartlett.

Willis was also a poet (albeit a minor one), a playwright, a novelist, and a short story writer. His short stories, such as those collected in *Dashes at Life with a Free Pencil*, have from time to time attracted critical attention, and his novel *Paul Fane* has been considered a forerunner of Henry James's international novels, but it was as a journalist, critics generally agree, that he was most successful: Willis will be remembered for his documents of fashionable life.

—Edward Halsey Foster

WILSON, Edmund. Born in Red Bank, New Jersey, 8 May 1895. Educated at Hill School, Pottstown, Pennsylvania, 1909–12; Princeton University, New Jersey (member of the editorial staff, 1913–15, and managing editor, 1915–16, *Nassau Literary Magazine*), 1912–16, A.B. 1916. Served in the U.S. Army Intelligence Corps, 1917–19. Married 1) Mary Blair in 1923 (divorced, 1928), one daughter; 2) Margaret Canby in 1930 (died, 1932); 3) Mary McCarthy, *q.v.*, in 1938 (divorced, 1946), one son; 4) Elena Thornton in 1946, one daughter. Reporter, New York *Evening Sun*, 1916–17; managing editor, *Vanity Fair*, New York, 1922–23; contributing editor, 1925–26, and associate editor, 1926–31, *New Republic*, New York; book reviewer, *New Yorker*, 1944–47, and occasionally thereafter. Recipient: Guggenheim fellowship, 1935; American Academy Gold Medal, for non-fiction, 1955; Presidential Medal of Freedom, 1963; MacDowell Medal, 1964; Emerson-Thoreau Medal, 1966; National Medal for Literature, 1966; Aspen Award, 1968; Nice Book Festival Golden Eagle, 1971. *Died 12 June 1972.*

PUBLICATIONS

Collections

Letters on Literature and Politics 1912–1972, edited by Elena Wilson. 1977.
The Portable Wilson, edited by Lewis M. Dabney. 1983.

Fiction

I Thought of Daisy. 1929; revised edition, with *Galahad*, 1967.
Memoirs of Hecate County (stories). 1946; revised edition, 1958.
Galahad, with I Thought of Daisy. 1967.

Plays

The Evil Eye, lyrics by F. Scott Fitzgerald, music by P.B. Dickey and F. Warburton Guilbert (produced 1915). 1915.
The Crime in the Whistler Room (produced 1924). In *This Room and This Gin and These Sandwiches*, 1937.
Discordant Encounters: Plays and Dialogues. 1926.
This Room and This Gin and These Sandwiches: Three Plays (includes *The Crime in the Whistler Room*, *A Winter in Beech Street*, and *Beppo and Beth*) (produced 1978). 1937.
The Little Blue Light (produced 1950). 1950.
Five Plays: Cyprian's Prayer, The Crime in the Whistler Room, This Room and This Gin and These Sandwiches, Beppo and Beth, The Little Blue Light. 1954.
The Duke of Palermo and Other Plays, with an Open Letter to Mike Nichols (includes *Dr. McGrath* and *Osbert's Career; or, The Poet's Progress*). 1969.

Verse

The Undertaker's Garland, with John Peale Bishop. 1922.
Poets, Farewell! (poems and essays). 1929.
Note-Books of Night (poems, essays and stories). 1942.
The White Sand. 1950.
Three Reliques of Ancient Western Poetry Collected by Wilson from the Ruins of the Twentieth Century. 1951.
Wilson's Christmas Stocking: Fun for Young and Old. 1953.

A Christmas Delerium. 1955.
Night Thoughts. 1961.
Holiday Greetings 1966. 1966.

Other

Axel's Castle: A Study in the Imaginative Literature of 1870–1930. 1931.
The American Jitters: A Year of the Slump (essays). 1932; as *Devil Take the Hindmost*, 1932.
Travels in Two Democracies (dialogues, essays, and story). 1936.
The Triple Thinkers: Ten Essays on Literature. 1938; augmented edition, as *The Triple Thinkers: Twelve Essays on Literary Subjects*, 1948.
To the Finland Station: A Study in the Writing and Acting of History. 1940.
The Boys in the Back Room: Notes on California Novelists. 1941.
The Wound and the Bow: Seven Studies in Literature. 1941.
Europe Without Baedeker: Sketches among the Ruins of Italy, Greece, and England. 1947; revised edition, 1966.
Classics and Commercials: A Literary Chronicle of the Forties. 1950.
The Shores of Light: A Literary Chronicle of the Twenties and Thirties. 1952.
Eight Essays. 1954.
The Scrolls from the Dead Sea. 1955; revised edition, as *The Dead Sea Scrolls 1947–1969*, 1969; as *Israel and the Dead Sea Scrolls*, 1978.
A Literary Chronicle 1920–1950. 1956.
Red, Black, Blond, and Olive: Studies in Four Civilizations: Zuñi, Haiti, Soviet Russia, Israel. 1956.
A Piece of My Mind: Reflections at Sixty. 1956.
The American Earthquake: A Documentary of the Twenties and Thirties. 1958.
Apologies to the Iroquois. 1960.
Patriotic Gore: Studies in the Literature of the American Civil War. 1962.
The Cold War and the Income Tax: A Protest. 1963.
The Bit Between My Teeth: A Literary Chronicle of 1950–1965. 1965.
O Canada: An American's Notes on Canadian Culture. 1965.
A Prelude: Landscapes, Characters, and Conversations from the Earlier Years of My Life. 1967.
The Fruits of the MLA. 1968.
Upstate: Records and Recollections of Northern New York. 1971.
A Window on Russia for the Use of Foreign Readers. 1972.
The Devils and Canon Barham: Ten Essays on Poets, Novelists, and Monsters. 1973.
The Twenties [*The Thirties, The Forties, The Fifties*]: *From Notebooks and Diaries of the Period*, edited by Leon Edel. 4 vols., 1975–86.
The Nabokov-Wilson Letters: Correspondence Between Vladimir Nabokov and Wilson 1940–1971, edited by Simon Karlinsky. 1979.

Editor, *The Last Tycoon: An Unfinished Novel by F. Scott Fitzgerald, Together with The Great Gatsby and Selected Writings*. 1941.
Editor, *The Shock of Recognition: The Development of Literature in the United States Recorded by the Men Who Made It*. 1943; enlarged edition, 1955.
Editor, *The Crack-Up, with Other Uncollected Pieces, Note-Books, and Unpublished Letters*, by F. Scott Fitzgerald. 1945.
Editor, *The Collected Essays of John Peale Bishop*. 1948.
Editor, *Peasants and Other Stories*, by Chekhov. 1956.

*

Bibliography: *Wilson: A Bibliography* by Richard David Ramsey, 1971.

Critical Studies: *Wilson: A Study of the Literary Vocation in Our Time* by Sherman Paul, 1965; *Wilson* by Warner Berthoff, 1968; *Wilson* by Charles P. Frank, 1970; *Wilson* by Leonard Kriegel, 1971; *A Wilson Celebration* edited by John Wain, 1978, as *Wilson: The Man and His Work*, 1978; *Three Honest Men: Wilson, F.R. Leavis, Lionel Trilling: A Critical Mosaic* by Philip French, 1980; *Wilson's America* by George H. Douglas, 1983; *Wilson* by David Castronovo, 1984.

* * *

The life and work of Edmund Wilson place him in a quintessentially American literary tradition, somewhere between the pragmatic tinker role of Benjamin Franklin and the omnivorous man of letters stance of Henry James. While the concept of an author who works in many genres may seem quite European—only a few contemporary Americans such as Thornton Wilder, Robert Penn Warren, Norman Mailer, or John Updike fit such a definition—Wilson's literary craft is not as broad or deep as it may seem. True, he wrote literary criticism, poetry, drama, short stories, novels, reportage, anthropological studies, history, memoirs, diaries. Also true, he mastered many languages and political positions, from Russian to Hebrew, from cool mandarin to engaged leftist. But Wilson was fundamentally a writer fascinated by a sort of prose narrative one might call critical characterizations. He wrote a great, continuing novel about figures in the cultural landscape, characters in action—as poets, soldiers, religious thinkers, novelists, ethnics, revolutionaries. But all his subjects share one quality with their chronicler: they all create.

Although Wilson commenced his career as an occasional poet—his first published book, written with John Peale Bishop, *The Undertaker's Garland*, appeared in 1922, and he continued to write light verse and modestly introspective short poems throughout his career until *Night Thoughts* (1961)—and short story writer as well as closet dramatist, his formally creative efforts seem to strike a minor chord. The novel *I Thought of Daisy* does evoke a sense of being young and in lust in the New York of the 1920's; the notorious (banned in Boston) *Memoirs of Hecate County* is remarkable mostly for the lyric power of "The Princess with the Golden Hair" and the story *à clef* "The Man Who Shot Snapping Turtles." And Wilson wrote nearly a dozen plays from *The Crime in the Whistler Room* (produced by Provincetown Players in New York) to his apocalyptic *The Little Blue Light*. His creative efforts, however, unlike those of other artist-critics such as T.S. Eliot or Ezra Pound, serve largely to exemplify Wilson's willingness to attempt a variety of genres and his skills in writing adequate and intelligent poems, stories, and plays.

Wilson's reputation as a literary critic, as opposed to journalist or reviewer, depends on three seminal books that—as was most often the case—collect essays first published in journals such as the *New Republic* or the *New Yorker*. *Axel's Castle: A Study in the Imaginative Literature of 1870–1930* treats in a combination of concise biography and richly inspired readings the basic works of those authors now enshrined as the giants of modernism: Yeats, Valéry, Eliot, Proust, Joyce, Stein, and Rimbaud. Unabashedly describing writer and text with the confidence of a firm biographer and superb reader, Wilson releases his genuinely creative talent; these portraits are clear and tough-minded, not vague and impressionistic, studies of complexly vital characters and forcefully difficult texts. While he never condescends to his readers, still, Wilson has the popularizer's zest as he energetically describes symbolism and stream of consciousness as if they are parts of the contemporary reader's cultural baggage, and enlivens the authors as if they are psychologically valid characters. *The Triple Thinkers* is more wide-ranging, more a collection of occasional pieces on Pushkin, Housman, Flaubert, Butler, and Shaw; two of the essays, on John Jay Chapman and on the ambiguity of Henry James, are among Wilson's finest, and the last, "Marxism and Literature," points the way to his socially involved writing. *The Wound and the Bow* may be Wilson's critical masterpiece. Taking as a point of departure the myth of Philoctetes who compensated for a wound by his fine archery, Wilson in a Freudian mode attends to Casanova and Wharton, Hemingway ("The Gauge of Morale," a brilliant early appreciation) and Joyce ("The Dream of H.C. Earwicker"); and in Wilson's views of Dickens ("The Two Scrooges") and the "unknown" Kipling for the first time establishes the ways the childhood wounds of blacking factory and parental desertion, when understood, help to account for the anger in the novels and stories. Generations of scholars have drawn on these insights. Wilson's strength comes from his novelistic ability to make the real figures of Dickens and Kipling appealing and remarkable as characters without reducing their works to psychological exempla.

As the United States moved into social and political traumas during the 1930's, Wilson turned his attention first to documentary writing then to historical studies. *The American Jitters* gathers his reportage on travels through Depression-stunned America before the Roosevelt era's attempts to help the poor and jobless: the book is angry, informed, topical, radical, and personalized. Both Wilson the reporter and American working- and middle-class figures become embittered characters in a starkly realized landscape. Much of the book is superbly evoked description, ordered and impassioned. Also travelling to the Soviet Union, studying the history of socialist thought, Wilson started to publish his major historical work *To the Finland Station* as chapters in the *New Republic* in 1934. By the time the book appeared in 1940, it combined most of Wilson's literary gifts: it is a report on how socialism grew as an idea from the 19th century to the moment in 1917 when Lenin made his dramatic return to Russia; the book is very much a literary study, describing and commenting on key texts from Michelet, Vico, and Marx; and *To the Finland Station* bids fair to gain consideration as an historical epic, peopled with marvelously drawn characterizations of Marx, Lenin, and Trotsky, among others. Here Wilson the journalist, the literary critic, the social historian, and the creator of character joins his techniques in a manner established by Thomas Carlyle's best writing in *The French Revolution*.

The next thirty years of Wilson's writing career followed the pattern defined in the first two decades. He continued to attend to literature, most steadily in his role as book reviewer for the *New Yorker*, from whence came *Classics and Commercials: A Literary Chronicle of the Forties*. Wilson also kept up his special brand of travel writing—on Italy, Greece, and England after the war (*Europe Without Baedeker*); on the Zuñi and Iroquois tribes, on Haiti, on Israel (*Red, Black, Blond, and Olive*). At times anthropological, at times scholarly and historical, Wilson remained a popularizer, largely because of his flexible and persuasive narrative style; thus, *The Scrolls from the Dead Sea* (for which he mastered Hebrew) was both fare for *New Yorker* readers and acceptable to biblical scholars.

Finally, Wilson concentrated on American literature and history. In 1943 he edited *The Shock of Recognition*, a brilliantly articulated collection of writers' responses to each other's achievements that highlights American authors as personalities; he also edited his friend F. Scott Fitzgerald's literary remains in *The Crack-Up*. This looking backward inspired Wilson to follow three strands of American writing that took up his later career. First, he began to collect and rework his own previous writings; *The Shores of Light*, for example, is subtitled "A Literary Chronicle of the Twenties and Thirties." Even posthumously, under the dedicated editing of Leon Edel, Wilson's letters and journals of the decades continue to provide revisits to his published essays. Second, he become more fascinated with his own life and that of his family, as well as his home in Talcottville, New York, culminating in a powerful memoir, *Upstate*. And third, for over ten years he worked on what many consider his greatest achievement, *Patriotic Gore*, certainly a valuable American companion to his earlier work on European history. A remarkable study, part literary criticism, part a reading of history, part character analysis, the book responds to Wilson's lifelong need to draw, in ways that eluded him as writer of formal fiction or drama, American characters. By using the great fratricidal moment in American history, the Civil War, as foreground and watershed, Wilson provided portraits of American political and literary heroes and heroines that are concise yet probing. By critically understanding their rhetoric, Wilson enlivens old names such as Harriet Beecher Stowe and Julia Ward Howe, such as the fiction writers John William De Forest and Ambrose Bierce, such as the anti-heroes Jefferson Davis and Alexander Stephens, such as Wilson's heroes, Abraham Lincoln and Oliver Wendell Holmes, and many other figures. Evocative and concerned, *Patriotic Gore* displays Wilson at his creative best, a novelist as historian, a lyricist as critic.

—Eric Solomon

WINTERS, (Arthur) Yvor. Born in Chicago, Illinois, 17 October 1900; grew up in Eagle Rock, California. Educated at the University of Chicago, 1917–18; University of Colorado, Boulder, 1923–25, B.A. and M.A. in Romance languages 1925; Stanford University, California, Ph.D. 1934. Married the writer Janet Lewis in 1926; one daughter and one son. Patient in tuberculosis sanatorium, Santa Fe, New Mexico, 1919–21; schoolteacher, Madrid and Los Cerillos, New Mexico, 1921–22; Instructor in French and Spanish, University of Idaho, Pocatello, 1925–27; Instructor, 1927–37, Assistant Professor, 1937–40, Associate Professor, 1941–48, Professor, 1948–51, and Albert Guerard Professor, 1961–66, Stanford University. Founding editor, with Howard Baker and Janet Lewis, *Gyroscope*, Palo Alto, California, 1929–30; regional editor, *Hound and Horn*, Portland, Maine, 1932–34; Fellow,

Kenyon School of English, Gambier, Ohio, 1948–50. Recipient: American Academy grant, 1952; Brandeis University Creative Arts Award, 1959; Harriet Monroe Poetry Award, 1960; Bollingen Prize, 1961; National Endowment for the Arts grant, 1967. Member, American Academy of Arts and Sciences. *Died 25 January 1968.*

PUBLICATIONS

Collections

Collected Poems, edited by Donald Davie. 1978.

Verse

The Immobile Wind. 1921.
The Magpie's Shadow. 1922.
The Bare Hills: A Book of Poems. 1927.
The Proof. 1930.
The Journey and Other Poems. 1931.
Before Disaster. 1934.
Poems. 1940.
The Giant Weapon. 1943.
To the Holy Spirit: A Poem. 1947.
Three Poems. 1950.
Collected Poems. 1952; revised edition, 1960.
The Early Poems 1920–28. 1966.

Fiction

The Brink of Darkness (story). 1947.

Other

The Case of David Lamson: A Summary, with Frances Theresa Russell. 1934.
Primitivism and Decadence: A Study of American Experimental Poetry. 1937.
Maule's Curse: Seven Studies in the History of American Obscurantism. 1938.
The Anatomy of Nonsense. 1943.
Edwin Arlington Robinson. 1946; revised edition, 1971.
In Defense of Reason. 1947; revised edition, 1960.
The Function of Criticism: Problems and Exercises. 1957.
On Modern Poets. 1959.
The Poetry of W.B. Yeats. 1960.
The Poetry of J.V. Cunningham. 1961.
Forms of Discovery: Critical and Historical Essays on the Forms of the Short Poem in English. 1967.
Uncollected Essays and Reviews, edited by Francis Murphy. 1973.
Hart Crane and Winters: Their Literary Correspondence, edited by Thomas Parkinson. 1978.

Editor, *Twelve Poets of the Pacific*. 1937.
Editor, *Selected Poems*, by Elizabeth Daryush. 1948.
Editor, *Poets of the Pacific, Second Series*. 1949.
Editor, with Kenneth Fields, *Quest for Reality: An Anthology of Short Poems in English*. 1969.

Translator, *The Last Sonnets of Pierre de Ronsard*, with *Diadems and Fagots*, by Olavo Bilac, translated by John Meem. 1921(?).

*

Bibliography: *Winters: An Annotated Bibliography 1919–1982* by Grosvenor Powell, 1983.

Critical Studies: *The Complex of Winters' Criticism* by Richard Sexton, 1973; *Language as Being in the Poetry of Winters* by Grosvenor Powell, 1980; *An Introduction to the Poetry of Winters* by Elizabeth Isaacs, 1981; "Winters Issue" of *Southern Review*, October 1981; *Wisdom and Wilderness: The Achievement of Winters* by Dick Davis, 1983; *Revolution and Convention in Modern Poetry* by Donald E. Stanford, 1983; *In Defense of Winters* by Terry Comito, 1986.

* * *

The poetry of Yvor Winters falls into two phases, the imagist phase (1920–28), and the post-symbolist phase (1929–68). During the first period Winters was writing markedly cadenced, imagistic free verse under the influence of William Carlos Williams, Ezra Pound, Glenway Wescott, H.D., and American Indian poetry. The influence was technical: that is, Winters learned to write his free verse by studying carefully selected poems he admired by these authors, but his own poems were not merely imitative. He developed a style of his own of great emotional intensity, brilliantly perceptive and even hypersensitive to the point of being hallucinatory. The literary and autobiographical background of these early years is described by Winters in his introduction to *The Early Poems*, in which he states that his philosophical position at that time was solipsistic and deterministic, a position which he later rejected. Some of the most remarkable of these verses are evocative of the life and landscape of New Mexico where Winters was recuperating from tuberculosis. At the same time, Winters was studying the mechanics of the image and how it was most effectively employed not only by the imagists but by Coleridge, Browning, Hopkins, Robinson, Stevens, Emerson, and the French Symbolists.

In his late twenties Winters became impatient with the limitations of so-called free verse; he began to suspect that he could gain a greater emotional and intellectual range by the employment of the conventional iambic line as it occurs in the heroic couplet, the sonnet, in tetrameter and pentameter quatrains, and in other forms. *The Proof*, though it opens with poems written in the imagist manner, contains in the closing pages a number of verses in traditional iambic meters. The eight poems in *The Journey* are all in heroic couplets which show the influence not only of Dryden and Pope but also of the freely run-over couplets of Charles Churchill. One of the best of these, "On a View of Pasadena from the Hills," was directly influenced by Robert Bridges's 1899 poem in iambic pentameter couplets, "Elegy: The Summer-House on the Mound."

In his early thirties Winters was re-reading the poetry of Bridges, Hardy, Robinson, Stevens, Paul Valéry, and T. Sturge Moore with increasing admiration. All these poets (including Stevens in his best poem, "Sunday Morning") wrote in conventional prosody, a fact which strengthened Winters's conviction that free verse and imagism were temporary aberrations from the main tradition of Anglo-American verse. At this time he was forming the tastes and principles to be found in his critical essays, which were to attract considerably more attention than his poetry. In *Primitivism and Decadence* he analyzed the technical innovations of the "new poetry," and, although he admired a few free verse poems by H.D., Williams, Stevens, and Marianne Moore, he concluded that on the whole the experimentalist movement had been a failure. By the time he was writing the poetry that appeared in *The Giant Weapon* and in the *Collected Poems* of 1952 he had developed his critical theory concerning the nature of poetry, applied in a series of essays eventually published under the titles *In Defense of Reason*, *The Function of Criticism*, and *Forms of Discovery*. The gist of his theory is that a successful poem is a statement in words about human experience which communicates by means of verse—as distinct from prose, which is less precisely rhythmical than verse and therefore less effective in expressing emotion—appropriate feeling motivated by an understanding of the experience. In this kind of poetry full use is made of both the denotative and connotative significance of words. This theory is obviously operating in all the poetry of Winters's mature years.

Late in his career Winters began referring to what he called the post-symbolist style of the best American poetry of the 20th century. In his essay "Poetic Styles Old and New" (1959), after a discussion of the two major styles of the Renaissance, the plain and the ornamental, he said in describing post-symbolism, "It ought to be possible to embody our sensory experience in our poetry in an efficient way, not as ornament, and with no sacrifice of rational intelligence." Sensory experience communicated by fresh and original imagery charged with rational significance occurs in Winters's best poems from about 1930 on, including "The Slow Pacific Swell" (1931), "Sir Gawaine and the Green Knight" (1937), and "A Summer Commentary" (1938).

A few dominant and closely related themes, explored in Winters's verse from the beginning of his career until the end, give to his work a remarkable coherence and unity. Among these are a recurrent examination of the relationship between the rational mind and the poetic sensibility which may enrich it or destroy it, a theme which derives from his own experience and also from the poetry of T. Sturge Moore. In his earliest verse the sensibility is dominant to the point of rational disintegration, and even as late as 1955 Winters was writing in his "At the San Francisco Airport": "The rain of matter upon sense / Destroys me momently." Achievement of balance between intellect and sensibility is the subject of "A Summer Commentary" and "Sir Gawaine and the Green Knight"; it is implicit in his allegorical poems on Greek subjects such as "Heracles," "Theseua," "Orpheus," and others. His concern with threats to the preservation of one's identity motivated a number of poems on death and the ravages of time, the most powerful of which are "For My Father's Grave," "To the Holy Spirit," "The Cremation," "A Leave-Taking," and "Prayer for My Son."

Winters is considered one of the most intellectual of all American poets. Yet he was keenly alive to the beauties of the sensory world as well as to its dangers. His purpose was "To steep the mind in sense / Yet never lose the aim." Consequently much of his poetry is remarkable for its freshly perceived descriptive detail of the natural world as in "The California Oaks" and "Time and the Garden." Finally it should be noted that Winters is the only 20th-century poet of consequence who mastered the technique of free verse as practised by the imagists and then abandoned it for conventional prosody, although he did not abandon what he had learned about the effective use of imagery. His poetry and his criticism present a significant case history of revolution and counter-revolution in modern poetry.

—Donald E. Stanford

WISTER, Owen. Born in Germantown, Philadelphia, Pennsylvania, 14 July 1860. Educated at schools in Hofwyl, Switzerland, 1870–71, and England, 1871–72; Germantown Academy, 1872; St. Paul's School, Concord, New Hampshire, 1873–78; Harvard University, Cambridge, Massachusetts, 1878–82, B.A. (summa cum laude) in music 1882; studied music in Paris, 1882–83; attended Harvard Law School, 1885–88, LL.B. 1888; admitted to Pennsylvania bar, 1889. Married his second cousin Mary Channing Wister in 1898 (died, 1913); three sons and three daughters. Worked at Union Safe Deposit Vaults, Boston, 1884–85; lawyer in Philadelphia, 1889–91; thereafter a full-time writer; moved to Charleston, South Carolina, 1902. Overseer, Harvard University, 1912–18, 1919–25. Member, American Academy; Honorary Member, Society of Letters (Paris); Honorary Fellow, Royal Society of Literature (London). *Died 21 July 1938.*

PUBLICATIONS

Collections

The West of Wister: Selected Short Stories, edited by Robert L. Hough. 1972.

Fiction

The New Swiss Family Robinson. 1882.
The Dragon of Wantley. 1892.
Red Men and White (stories). 1896.
Lin McLean. 1897.
The Jimmyjohn Boss and Other Stories. 1900.
The Virginian: A Horseman of the Plains. 1902.
Philosophy 4: A Story of Harvard University. 1903.
A Journey in Search of Christmas (story). 1904.
Lady Baltimore. 1906.
How Doth the Simple Spelling Bee. 1907.
Mother. 1907.
Members of the Family. 1911.
Padre Ignacio (stories). 1911.
When West Was West. 1928.

Plays

Dido and Aeneas, music by Wister (produced 1882).
Watch Your Thirst: A Dry Opera. 1923; revised version, as *The Honeymoon Shiners*, in *Writings*, 1928.
The Vain, with Kirke La Shelle. 1958.

Verse

Done in the Open, illustrated by Frederic Remington. 1903.
Indispensable Information for Infants; or, Easy Entrance to Education. 1921.

Other

Ulysses S. Grant. 1900.
Musk-Ox, Bison, Sheep, and Goat, with Caspar W. Whitney and George Bird Grinnell. 1904.
The Seven Ages of Washington: A Biography. 1907.
The Pentecost of Calamity (essay). 1915.
A Straight Deal; or, The Ancient Grudge (essay). 1920.
Neighbors Henceforth. 1922.

Writings. 11 vols., 1928.
Roosevelt: The Story of a Friendship 1880–1919. 1930; as *Theodore Roosevelt*, 1930.
Two Appreciations of John Jay Chapman. 1934.
My Father, Owen Wister, and Ten Letters . . . to His Mother During His First Trip to Wyoming in 1885, by Frances Kemble Wister Stokes. 1952.
Wister Out West: His Journals and Letters, edited by Fanny Kemble Wister. 1958.
My Dear Wister: The Frederic Remington–Wister Letters, edited by Ben Vorpahl. 1972.
That I May Tell You: Journals and Letters of the Wister Family, edited by Fanny Kemble Wister. 1979.

*

Bibliography: by Dean Sherman, in *Bulletin of Bibliography 28*, 1971; "Wister: An Annotated Bibliography of Secondary Material" by Sanford E. Morovitz, in *American Literary Realism 7*, 1974.

Critical Studies: *The Eastern Establishment and the Western Experience: The West of Frederic Remington, Theodore Roosevelt, and Wister* by G. Edward White, 1968; *Wister* by Richard W. Etulain, 1973; *Wister* by John J. Cobbs, 1984; *Wister: Chronicler of the West, Gentleman of the East* by Darwin Payne, 1985.

*   *   *

Although he never gave himself fully to the American west, the west was the making of Owen Wister as a man and as a writer. Born into an aristocratic Philadelphia family, educated in eastern schools and abroad, Wister initially sought a career in music. His practical father encouraged a business career, then law. Uncertain of himself, Wister took the advice of his physician in 1885 and went to Wyoming for the summer. Then and in succeeding summers in the west, he found health, and a frontier and cowboy milieu that he knew was about to end and deserved to be put into fiction. Wister saw great romantic possibilities in the cowboy, at that time known to fiction only in dime novels.

Wister had published a burlesque of *Swiss Family Robinson* the year he graduated from Harvard. Shortly thereafter he and a cousin wrote a novel, but he took the advice of William Dean Howells, who found the book too bold, and did not submit it for publication. Wister's instinct was for the actual and the concrete, and he might have been a better writer had he not acquiesced repeatedly to the genteel tradition. The habit of writing ingrained, he kept detailed journal entries on his western summers—the factual basis for many of his stories. The journals, published twenty years after Wister's death, are well worth reading.

In 1891 Wister wrote "Hank's Woman," his first western story. *Harper's* accepted it and encouraged Wister to write about the west. His stories were full of local color interest when the local color movement was still important in American literature. *Red Men and White*, his first short story collection, was published in 1896, followed by *Lin McLean*. The cowboy McLean gave some unity to the book, but it is hardly a novel. *The Virginian*, the novel that is Wister's most important achievement, was likewise based on earlier published stories. It, too, has problems of point of view. The eastern tenderfoot who arrives in Wyoming and "grows up" there could not possibly know all the material he relates. The novel's structure is episodic. The contrast of east and west, however, gave embodiment to Wister's sense of the romantic possibility of the cowpuncher, possibilities that became legion in western novels and movies. Wister's hero is a natural aristocrat who is capable of showing his inner fiber in a land with its own rules for law and order. Wister was not particularly interested in portraying the inside of ranch life; rather he wished to show his hero grow and adjust to the closing frontier, proving himself worthy of the aristocratic Molly Stark Wood of Vermont, who has come to Wyoming to teach school. Later, Wister described the Virginian as the embodiment of "the best thing the Declaration of Independence ever turned out."

However attractive the west might be for summer hunting and adventure, Wister became increasingly pulled to the east and to Europe, and to the south. He had moved to Charleston, South Carolina, in 1902, where the southern aristocratic codes were congenial to his temperament. *Lady Baltimore* is Wister's Jamesian comedy of manners. The Jamesian narrator comes from the north to Kings Port (Charleston) to engage in genealogical research. The love story he narrates, and plays a part in, enables Wister to juxtapose culture against culture. The novel is pleasant reading, convincing in its portrayal of southern attitudes of the time, and indicative of the reservations Wister had about the cruder west. Thereafter, Wister wrote other stories about the west, but he ceased to visit it, and by the time of World War I his main concern was his family, Europe, and politics.

—Joseph M. Flora

See the essay on *The Virginian*.

WOLFE, Thomas (Clayton). Born in Asheville, North Carolina, 3 October 1900. Educated at the Orange Street grade school, Asheville, 1905–12; North State Fitting School, Asheville, 1912–16; University of North Carolina, Chapel Hill (editor, *Tar Heel* magazine), 1916–20, B.A. 1920; Harvard University, Cambridge, Massachusetts, where he studied playwriting in George Pierce Baker's "47 Workshop", 1920–23, M.A. in English 1922. Part-time Instructor in English, Washington Square College, New York University, 1924–30; full-time writer from 1930; made several trips to Europe and lived briefly in London; traveled in the Pacific Northwest, 1938: contracted pneumonia. Recipient: Guggenheim fellowship, 1930. Member, American Academy. *Died 15 September 1938*.

PUBLICATIONS

Collections

The Letters, edited by Elizabeth Nowell. 1956; selection, 1958.
The Wolfe Reader, edited by C. Hugh Holman. 1962.
Complete Short Stories, edited by Francis E. Skipp. 1987.

Fiction

Look Homeward, Angel: A Story of the Buried Life. 1929.
Of Time and the River: A Legend of Man's Hunger in His Youth. 1935.

From Death to Morning (stories). 1935.
The Web and the Rock, edited by Edward C. Aswell. 1939.
You Can't Go Home Again, edited by Edward C. Aswell. 1940.
The Hills Beyond (stories), edited by Edward C. Aswell. 1941.
The Short Novels, edited by C. Hugh Holman. 1961.
A Prologue to America, edited by Aldo P. Magi. 1978.
K-19: Salvaged Pieces, edited by John L. Idol, Jr. 1983.
The Train and the City, edited by Richard S. Kennedy. 1984.

Plays

The Return of Buck Gavin (produced 1919). In *Carolina Folk-Plays*, second series, 1924.
The Third Night (produced 1919). In *The Carolina Play-Book*, September 1938.
The Mountains (produced 1921). Edited by Pat M. Ryan, 1970.
Welcome to Our City (produced 1923). Edited by Richard S. Kennedy, 1983.
Gentlemen of the Press (produced 1928). 1942.
Mannerhouse. 1948; edited by Louis D. Rubin, Jr., and John L. Idol, Jr., 1985.
The Streets of Durham, edited by Richard Walser. 1982.

Verse

A Stone, A Leaf, A Door, edited by John S. Barnes. 1945.

Other

The Crisis in Industry. 1919.
The Story of a Novel. 1936.
A Note on Experts: Dexter Vespasian Joyner. 1939.
Wolfe's Letters to His Mother, Julia Elizabeth Wolfe, edited by John Skally Terry. 1943.
The Years of Wandering in Many Lands and Cities. 1949.
A Western Journal: A Daily Log of the Great Parks Trip, June 20–July 2, 1938. 1951.
The Correspondence of Wolfe and Homer Andrew Watt, edited by Oscar Cargill and Thomas Clark Pollock. 1954.
Wolfe's Purdue Speech, "Writing and Living," edited by William Braswell and Leslie A. Field. 1964.
The Letters of Wolfe to His Mother, Newly Edited from the Original Manuscripts, edited by C. Hugh Holman and Sue Fields Ross. 1968.
The Notebooks, edited by Richard S. Kennedy and Paschal Reeves. 2 vols., 1970.
My Other Loneliness: Letters of Wolfe and Aline Bernstein, edited by Suzanne Stutman. 1983; supplement, as *Holding On for Heaven: The Cables and Postcards of Wolfe and Aline Bernstein*, edited by Stutman, 1985.
The Autobiography of an American Novelist (includes *The Story of a Novel* and *Writing and Living*), edited by Leslie Field. 1983.
Beyond Love and Loyalty: The Letters of Wolfe and Elizabeth Nowell, edited by Richard S. Kennedy. 1983.
Wolfe Interviewed 1929–1938, edited by Aldo P. Magi and Richard Walser. 1985.

*

Bibliography: *Of Time and Thomas Wolfe: A Bibliography with a Character Index*, 1959, and *Wolfe: A Checklist*, 1970, both by Elmer D. Johnson; *Wolfe: A Reference Guide* by John S. Phillipson, 1977.

Critical Studies: *Wolfe* by Herbert J. Muller, 1947; *Thomas Wolfe: A Critical Study* by Pamela Hansford Johnson, 1947, as *Hungry Gulliver: An English Critical Appraisal of Wolfe*, 1948, as *The Art of Wolfe*, 1963; *The Enigma of Wolfe* edited by Richard Walser, 1953, and *Wolfe: An Introduction and Interpretation*, 1961, and *Wolfe, Undergraduate*, 1977, both by Walser; *Wolfe: The Weather of His Youth* by Louis D. Rubin, Jr., 1955, and *Wolfe: A Collection of Critical Essays* edited by Rubin, 1973; *Wolfe's Characters* by Floyd C. Watkins, 1957; *Wolfe: A Biography* by Elizabeth Nowell, 1960; *Wolfe*, 1960, and *The Loneliness at the Core: Studies in Wolfe*, 1975, both by C. Hugh Holman, and *The World of Wolfe* edited by Holman, 1962; *The Window of Memory: The Literary Career of Wolfe* by Richard S. Kennedy, 1962; *Wolfe as I Knew Him and Other Essays* by Vardis Fisher, 1963; *Wolfe* by Bruce R. McElderry, Jr., 1964; *Wolfe* by Andrew Turnbull, 1968; *Wolfe: Three Decades of Criticism* edited by Leslie A. Field, 1968; *Wolfe's Albatross: Race and Nationality in America* by Paschal Reeves, 1969, and *Wolfe: The Critical Reception* edited by Reeves, 1974; *Wolfe* by Elizabeth Evans, 1984; *Critical Essays on Wolfe* edited by John S. Phillipson, 1985; *Look Homeward: A Life of Wolfe* by David Herbert Donald, 1987.

* * *

With the publication in 1929 of Thomas Wolfe's *Look Homeward, Angel*, American fiction was invested with a fresh talent quite unlike that of any writer of the past. On its narrative level, it was a story of maturation, covering the first twenty years in the life of a youth in conflict with his family and his small North Carolina town, but it was no novel in the usual sense, rather a loose chronicle held together with an assemblage of some memorable characters. Noticeable throughout were vestiges of thwarted careers in playwriting and poetry, careers he would have preferred. Availing himself of the titanism then permitted in American fiction, and gifted with a Proustian power of nearly total recall of sights and sounds, Wolfe lacquered the narrative of *Look Homeward, Angel* with dithyrambic luxuriance and a sensuous Whitmanesque prose, twisting easily from the rhetorical to the dramatic. At his command, too, was a gift for caricature, even burlesque, and satire. His comic exaggeration in depicting characters was never understood by those acquainted with the models on whom they were based. Symbols—the angel, the ghost, trains, mountains, and those images in the haunting refrain "a stone, a leaf, an unfound door"—underscored Wolfe's intent in characterization and meaning.

A sequel, *Of Time and the River*, took Wolfe's autobiographical hero, Eugene Gant, to Harvard, New York, and Europe. For his thesis, Wolfe appropriated the Joycean wanderer's search for the father, and imposed an epic framework upon the narrative by intoning names from Greek legends. In such a novel as this, Wolfe became, according to one ecstatic comment, "our closest approach to Homer." Allied with the search for the father was an attempt to discover America's greatness through the intensity of one man's experience, and to reveal to Americans as totally as possible the loneliness and transiency of their lives. In order to accomplish this, the hero was provided with a Faustian hunger, an obsessive and unquenchable desire for achievement and knowledge. There must be, he proclaimed, "*never* an end to curiosity! . . . I must think. I must mix it all with myself and with America." *The Story of a Novel*, Wolfe's confessional monograph of how *Of Time and the River* was written, tells of a "great black cloud" within him which poured forth "a torrential and ungovernable flood" about "night and darkness in America." The result was a novel of apparent formlessness, but it was an intentional formlessness, symbolically parallel to the formlessness of life itself and of his native land.

Though Wolfe's second book was a great success, so sensitive was he to charges of excessive emotional energy and lyricism that for his third, *The Web and the Rock*, he promised to write an "objective" account of his hero, now named George Webber. Webber was given a somewhat different background and young manhood, but in midstream Webber took on the familiar traits of Eugene Gant—that is to say, Thomas Wolfe himself. A love affair with a woman much older than Webber led directly into *You Can't Go Home Again*, by the end of which Wolfe's promise of objectivity was realized, his understanding of social problems effected, and his transformation completed: from romantic egocentricity to a clearer vision of the realities of life, from chaos to order, from uncertainty to assurance, from self, in short, to mankind. In the development of a social consciousness, Wolfe's hero was propelled into a rejection of a number of youthful ambitions. No longer sufficient were success and fame and romantic love; of ultimate primacy was one's belief "that America and the people in it are deathless, undiscovered, and immortal, and must live."

After the publication of *Look Homeward, Angel* Wolfe lived only another nine years. Since he was resolved on a one-man vision of life, everything was part of the "single" book, including his early plays, two volumes of letters, his notebooks, two collections of short stories, the excerpts and essays, and *A Western Journal*. That he produced such an abundance in so short a time was due to a compulsion to write almost continuously. He rarely took vacations, was annoyed by intrusions, and was committed wholly to his "work," as he called it. It has been argued that Wolfe's works should be read in isolated segments, as tone poems perhaps, or as short novels where his control can easily be observed. His books, according to another view, were rather a "fictional thesaurus," composed of many diverse elements—theatrical dialogue, choral ode, essay, travelogue, biography, oratory, lyric poetry, dramatic episode. Though his four major books were no more autobiographical than many single works by Melville and Twain, Fitzgerald and Hemingway, his persistent chronological continuum affronted some readers and critics in a way the practices of other novelists had not.

As an American writer—and he may turn out to be the most American writer—Wolfe was in the tradition of Emerson, Thoreau, Melville, Twain, Dreiser, Sandburg, and Sherwood Anderson. He shared the idealism of Jefferson and Whitman, especially in their projection of the American Dream in which lay the hopes of young men and women everywhere to do the best that was within them to do. His pages were often a sheer symbolic poetry of time and the river, of the web and the rock. Yet his greatest attainment was a fiction of scenes and characters remarkably vital, bountiful, and rich.

—Richard Walser

See the essay on *Look Homeward, Angel*.

WOOLSON, Constance Fenimore. Born in Claremont, New Hampshire, 5 March 1840; while still an infant moved with her family to Cleveland. Educated at Miss Hayden's School, Cleveland, and the Cleveland Female Seminary; Madame Chegaray's School, New York, graduated 1858. Lived in Cleveland after 1858, and for part of each year in the Carolinas and Florida, 1873–79; regular contributor to *Harper's*, *Atlantic Monthly*, and other periodicals; lived in Italy, 1879–83, England, 1883–86, Florence, 1887–89, Oxford, 1891–93, and Venice, 1893–94. Close friend of Henry James from 1880. *Died 24 January 1894.*

PUBLICATIONS

Collections

(*Selection*), in *Five Generations*, edited by Clare Benedict. 1930; revised edition, published separately, 1932.

For the Major and Selected Short Stories, edited by Rayburn S. Moore. 1967.

Fiction

The Old Stone House (for children). 1872.
Castle Nowhere: Lake-Country Sketches. 1875.
Rodman the Keeper: Southern Sketches. 1880.
Anne. 1882.
For the Major. 1883.
East Angels. 1886.
Jupiter Lights. 1889.
Horace Chase. 1894.
The Front Yard and Other Italian Stories. 1895.
Dorothy and Other Italian Stories. 1896.

Verse

Two Women: 1862. 1877.

Other

Mentone, Cairo, and Corfu. 1895.

*

Bibliography: by Rayburn S. Moore, in *A Bibliographical Guide to Midwestern Literature* edited by Gerald Nemanic, 1981.

Critical Studies: *Woolson: Literary Pioneer* by John D. Kern, 1934; *Henry James: The Conquest of London 1870–1881*, and *Henry James: The Middle Years 1882–1895* both by Leon Edel, 1962; *Woolson* by Rayburn S. Moore, 1963.

* * *

Although Constance Fenimore Woolson contributed verse to magazines and published a long poem, wrote a children's story, and collected some of her travel sketches for a volume that appeared posthumously, she was best known in her own day as a writer of fiction, and to one Boston critic at least as the "novelist laureate" of America. Such a characterization is likely to strike present-day readers as a bit off the mark, but in the late 19th century her stories and novels struck many reviewers and critics, including Henry James, as important contributions to literature.

Even today's readers must concede that Woolson made a contribution to the short fiction of her period. Her best stories—"The Lady of Little Fishing," "Rodman the Keeper," "King David," "The Front Yard," and "A Transplanted Boy," among others—demonstrate her capacity to deal with scenes as varied as the Great Lakes country, the South, and Europe and with universally valid characters. She was not an innovator in technique, but her best tales suggest that she was mindful of the work of George Eliot, Turgenev, and Henry James.

As a novelist she was less successful. Though the scenes and characters are, as in the short stories, handled ably, the structure of her novels (except *Horace Chase*) seems episodic and infrequently functional. This weakness in structure is ironically pointed up by her success with *For the Major*, her only novella, a minor classic in many ways, and her most successful sustained piece of fiction. Still, each novel has its individual merits and *East Angels*, as James maintained in *Harper's Weekly* in 1887, "is a performance which does Miss Woolson the highest honour."

Her best work belongs to the development of realism in America, as regards both local color and the psychological analysis of character, and it offers, as I have noted in *Constance Fenimore Woolson*, "a sympathetic understanding and treatment of character in authentic surroundings by one whose vision was broad enough and whose insight was deep enough to include not only her own country but Europe as well."

—Rayburn S. Moore

WRIGHT, James (Arlington). Born in Martins Ferry, Ohio, 13 December 1927. Educated at Kenyon College, Gambier, Ohio, B.A. 1952; University of Vienna (Fulbright Fellow), 1953; University of Washington, Seattle, M.A. 1954, Ph.D. 1959. Married Edith Anne Runk; two sons from previous marriage. Teacher at University of Minnesota, Minneapolis, 1957–64, Macalaster College, St. Paul, Minnesota, 1963–65, and Hunter College, New York, 1966–80. Recipient: American Academy grant, 1959; Guggenheim fellowship, 1964, 1978; Brandeis University Creative Arts Award, 1970; Academy of American Poets fellowship, 1971; Melville Cane Award, 1972; Pulitzer Prize, 1972. Member, American Academy, 1974. *Died 25 March 1980.*

PUBLICATIONS

Collections

Collected Prose, edited by Annie Wright. 1982.

Verse

The Green Wall. 1957.
Saint Judas. 1959.
The Lion's Tail and Eyes: Poems Written Out of Laziness and Silence, with Robert Bly and William Duffy. 1962.
The Branch Will Not Break. 1963.
Shall We Gather at the River. 1968.
Collected Poems. 1971.
Two Citizens. 1974.
Moments of the Italian Summer. 1976.
Old Booksellers and Other Poems. 1976.
To a Blossoming Pear Tree. 1977.
The Journey. 1981.
This Journey. 1982.
The Temple in Nimes. 1982.

Other

The Summers of James and Annie Wright. 1980.
With the Delicacy and Strength of Lace: Letters Between Leslie Marmon Silko and Wright, edited by Annie Wright. 1986.

Editor and Translator, *Poems*, by Hermann Hesse. 1970.

Translator, with Robert Bly, *Twenty Poems of Georg Trakl*. 1961.
Translator, with Robert Bly and John Knoepfle, *Twenty Poems of César Vallejo*. 1962.
Translator, *The Rider on the White Horse*, by Theodor Storm. 1964.
Translator, with Robert Bly, *Twenty Poems of Pablo Neruda*. 1968.
Translator, with Robert Bly and John Knoepfle, *Neruda and Vallejo: Selected Poems*. 1971.

*

Bibliography: "Wright: A Checklist" by Belle M. McMaster, in *Bulletin of Bibliography 31*, 1974.

Critical Studies: *Four Poets and the Emotive Imagination* by George S. Lensing and Ronald Moran, 1976; "Wright Issue" of *Ironwood 10*, 1977; *The Pure Clear Word: Essays on the Poetry of Wright* edited by Dave Smith, 1982.

* * *

James Wright's poems are notable for their range of intense emotions and for the way both form and theme develop in the work. Wright's early style was characteristic of the 1950's in its rhetorical literariness and use of traditional English metres, often with exact rhymes. Titles such as "A Girl in a Window," "To the Ghost of a Kite" were formal too, almost announcing themselves as technical exercises and part of Wright's apprenticeship as a poet. His first book, *The Green Wall*, included the notable and characteristic "On the Skeleton of a Hound":

> Nightfall, that saw the morning-glories float
> Tendril and string against the crumbling wall,
> Nurses him now, his skeleton for grief,
> His locks for comfort curled among the leaf.

That skilfully formed poem, exhibiting a near perfect surface elegance and finish helped Wright in his next book, *Saint Judas*, to advance his impressive range of techniques in order to express the reality of human suffering. "In Shame and Humiliation," "Old Man Drunk," and "At the Executed Murderer's Grave" all express powerful emotions. The biblical Judas, in the title poem of the collection, heading off to commit suicide, runs to the help of a man set on by a mob:

> Banished from heaven, I found this victim beaten,
> Stripped, kneed, and left to cry. Dropping my rope

Aside, I ran, ignored the uniforms:
Then I remembered bread my flesh had eaten,
The kiss that ate my flesh. Flayed without hope,
I held the man for nothing in my arms.

A profound, somewhat tortured humanity is to be found throughout Wright's poetry. This was its first appearance and perhaps the most moving of all.

When Wright published his *Collected Poems* in 1971 he interposed a number of translations from Juan Ramón Jiménez, Jorge Guillén, Pablo Neruda, Georg Trakl, César Vallejo, Pedro Salinas, and Goethe between the poems of *Saint Judas* and those of his next book to indicate the introduction of something new in the progression. Wright's knowledge of other languages and his translations from the Spanish of Neruda and Vallejo introduced new rhythms into his poems, extending their tone and feel far beyond the technical restraint of his earlier iambic metres. Robert Bly, himself an important translator and a friend of Wright's, published these influential translations during the 1960's. Wright was also to publish a selection from the poems of Hermann Hesse in 1970. The extent to which these translations opened up the forms of American poetry has never properly been acknowledged.

Wright, Bly, and William Duffy each contributed poems to *The Lion's Tail and Eyes*. This book demonstrated the development brought about in Wright's poems by his translations and also his use of the so-called "deep-image" style of writing, whereby each poem focused solely on one central image. The poems, reprinted with others in Wright's next book—and surely his very best—*The Branch Will Not Break*, are spare, delicate, original, and sensitive in their use of the new rhythm. As in "Lying in a Hammock at William Duffy's Farm in Pine Island, Minnesota" where the poet meditates on the natural life around him concluding: "I lean back, as the evening darkens and comes on. / A chicken hawk floats over, looking for home. / I have wasted my life." The mood creates the rhythm and, as a consequence, convinces the reader that the final line is a natural associative conclusion to what has gone before. The poem has what Herbert Read called "organic unity," a quality enabling Wright unobtrusively to express personal feeling, as again in the second part of "Two Hangovers":

In a pine tree,
A few yards away from my window sill,
A brilliant blue jay is springing up and down, up and down,
On a branch.
I laugh, as I see him abandon himself
To entire delight, for he knows as well as I do
That the branch will not break.

Nothing could be further from the formal grandeur of Wright's first book. Wright had learned how to pare away inessential verbiage to arrive at the heart of the poem, the essence of what should be expressed. The book includes poems of subtle political comment, and also poems on the suffering of individuals; but it is chiefly memorable for an overall acceptance of life, whereby suffering is complemented by happiness.

If *The Branch Will Not Break* is about acceptance and the possibility of happiness, *Shall We Gather at the River*, Wright's next book, returns anew to the theme of isolation and unhappiness, expressed this time in more fluid organic rhythms. Old people, the poor, mourners, prostitutes, an illiterate black soldier hiding in a church, lone animals such as a brown cricket, a dead swan, are the subjects of the poems. The book seems to come out of a period of trouble, and it expresses isolation honestly, without selfconsciousness and in a profoundly moving way. Suffering is accepted with equanimity, even quiet humour, in the title "In Terror of Hospital Bills" a poem containing the affirmation "But my life was never so precious / To me as now."

Wright's *Collected Poems* marked him out as one of the most original contemporary American poets. His ability to express the deepest emotions in a simple manner was a welcome antidote to the shrill imitators of "confessional poetry" much in evidence at the time. The books after the *Collected Poems*: *Two Citizens*, *To a Blossoming Pear Tree*, and *This Journey* (posthumously published after his early death in 1980), continued to express in fluid rhythms and deceptively unadorned language the deepest human emotions. But, although each contained fine poems, it is true to say that none exceeded the all round excellence of *The Branch Will Not Break*. This is not to say that Wright's powers declined. To the end his poems celebrate beauty, the animal kingdom, landscape, places, people: Wright's warmth and empathy for isolated individuals or animals are continually present.

One other posthumous publication which should not be overlooked is Wright's *Collected Prose* edited by his widow Annie Wright. This book is essential reading for anyone who wants to find out more about the man who wrote the poems. It reveals Wright as a first-rate critical intelligence, and contains essays and reviews on Dickens, Whitman, Gary Snyder, Robert Penn Warren, Thomas Hardy, Georg Trakl, Robert Frost, and many other writers. It also includes "Some Notes on Chinese Poetry," the text of a sermon, and four interviews. In the interview with Michael Andre of 1972 Wright talks of the poet Edward Thomas: "A holy man, I believe, a saintly man, Edward Thomas, without any great public reputation, but one of the secret spirits who help keep us alive . . . This is all we have, is it not? We have our internal life. Our external life is usually asinine. . . ." Words which we may equally well apply to the poetry of Wright himself, cutting, as it so often does, through all the niceties of literature to speak on our behalf of the essential things of life.

—Jonathan Barker

WRIGHT, Richard (Nathaniel). Born near Natchez, Mississippi, 4 September 1908; brought up in an orphanage. Educated at local schools through junior high school. Married 1) Rose Dhima Meadman in 1938; 2) Ellen Poplar; two daughters. Worked in a post office in Memphis, Tennessee, at age 15; later moved to New York; worked for Federal Writers Project, 1937, and Federal Negro Theatre Project; member, Communist Party, 1932–44; Harlem editor, *Daily Worker*, New York; lived in Paris from 1947. Recipient: Guggenheim fellowship, 1939; Spingarn Medal, 1941. *Died 28 November 1960.*

PUBLICATIONS

Collections

The Wright Reader, edited by Ellen Wright and Michel Fabre. 1978.

Fiction

Uncle Tom's Children: Four Novellas. 1938; augmented edition, 1940.
Native Son. 1940.
The Outsider. 1953.
Savage Holiday. 1954.
The Long Dream. 1958.
Eight Men (stories), 1961.
Lawd Today. 1963.
The Man Who Lived Underground (story; bilingual edition), translated by Claude Edmonde Magny, edited by Michel Fabre. 1971.

Plays

Native Son (The Biography of a Young American), with Paul Green, from the novel by Wright (produced 1941). 1941; revised version, 1980.
Daddy Goodness, from a play by Louis Sapin (produced 1968).

Screenplay: *Native Son*, 1951.

Other

How Bigger Was Born: The Story of "Native Son." 1940.
The Negro and Parkway Community House. 1941.
12 Million Black Voices: A Folk History of the Negro in the United States. 1941.
Black Boy: A Record of Childhood and Youth. 1945.
Black Power: A Record of Reactions in a Land of Pathos. 1954.
Bandoeng: 1.500.000.000 Hommes, translated by Hélène Claireau. 1955; as *The Color Curtain: A Report on the Bandung Conference*, 1956.
Pagan Spain. 1957.
White Man, Listen! 1957.
Letters to Joe C. Brown, edited by Thomas Knipp. 1968.
American Hunger (autobiography). 1977.

*

Bibliography: *Wright: A Primary Bibliography* by Charles T. Davis and Michel Fabre, 1982.

Critical Studies: *Wright: A Biography* by Constance Webb, 1968; *Wright* by Robert Bone, 1969; *The Art of Wright* by Edward Margolies, 1969; *The Most Native of Sons: A Biography of Wright* by John A. Williams, 1970; *Twentieth-Century Interpretations of Native Son* edited by Houston A. Baker, Jr., 1972; *The Emergence of Wright: A Study of Literature and Society* by Keneth Kinnamon, 1972; *Wright* by David Bakish, 1973; *The Unfinished Quest of Wright* by Michel Fabre, translated by Isabel Barzun, 1973, and *The World of Wright* by Fabre, 1985; *Wright: Impressions and Perspectives* edited by David Ray and Robert M. Farnsworth, 1973; *Wright's Hero: The Faces of a Rebel-Victim* by Katherine Fishburn, 1977; *Wright: The Critical Reception* edited by John M. Reilly, 1978; *Rebels and Victims: The Fiction of Wright and Bernard Malamud* by Evelyn Gross Avery, 1979; *Wright* by Robert Felgar, 1980; *Wright: Ordeal of a Native Son* by Addison Gayle, Jr., 1980; *The Daemonic Genius of Wright* by Margaret Walker, 1982; *Critical Essays on Wright* edited by Yoshinobu Hakutani, 1982; *Wright: A Collection of Critical Essays* edited by Richard Macksey and Frank E. Moorer, 1984.

* * *

Richard Wright's career can be described in terms of three reputations he has earned: the realist protesting racial oppression, the typifier of the experience of entry into modern history, and the author who makes his themes seem inevitable by his artistry. In the best recent criticism these three reputations coalesce, and the different levels of significance in his writing are explored. But while Wright was alive the fact of his race and his dissent from the culture of his native land, first as radical, then as expatriate, concentrated attention upon the thematic burden of his works.

Wright served a literary apprenticeship made harsh because of his poverty and the restrictions of Jim Crow laws but otherwise similar to other American authors'; yet he seemed to leap into literary prominence when his collection of stories, *Uncle Tom's Children*, won first prize in a contest sponsored by *Story* magazine for writers on the Federal Writers Project. The four novellas in that volume are arranged to depict the struggles of southern black peasants in resistance to a caste system dependent upon lynch violence for its sanction and efficacy. For most reviewers the book was a shocking rendition of the facts of racial conflict in an affecting narrative, its distinction not so much that the author was black, though reviews made as much of that as they did of the prize the book had won, but rather that *Uncle Tom's Children* told its stories from within the black experience. The book brought news that blacks could effectively articulate their victimization.

As though to match horror with horror, Wright's first published novel, *Native Son*, carried the story of racial conflict to the North where Bigger Thomas, Chicago-born and bred, acts out his role in the American racial drama by his murder of a white woman. At the risk of fulfilling racist expectations in his portrayal of Bigger, Wright completed his inversion of the stereotype of the black victim by showing violence as the necessary prelude to self-realization for his protagonist. Again Wright had written a book that brought news to its audience; *Native Son* was a cautionary tale for whites.

With the popular success of *Native Son* Wright became a public figure called upon to lecture and write as a spokesman for the American Negro. He was qualified for the role not only by literary success but also by a childhood in Mississippi and an adulthood in northern cities similar in pattern to the life of thousands of other black migrants, so it was appropriate that he organize that experience in literature: first with *12 Million Black Voices*, a documentary history of black peasants transplanted into urban life told in the poetic prose of a collective first-person narration, and then with his own autobiography, *Black Boy*.

It is unusual for a person not yet forty to write an autobiography and to end the story even before he had established himself in adulthood, but Wright justifies his book by presenting it as at once his own and his people's story. For many other blacks this latter point was dubious. They charged that he had been extremely selective by omitting any positive portrayal of black cultural and family life. The point has justice, but *Black Boy* enhanced Wright's reputation as the realist who showed more profoundly than anyone before him the human waste that is the heritage of North American slavery.

There can be no doubt Wright felt personally threatened by racism in a way that literary success could not alleviate. It was the motive for his move to Paris in 1947. Though objectively different, Wright's experience in the Communist Party (described in a portion of the original manuscript of *Black Boy*, cut from the book on advice of editors, published separately in 1944, and issued in the excised section of autobiography titled *American Hunger* in 1977) seems to have been psychologically as problematic as racism, so that when he exiled himself from America he was also without the political committment that had informed his work until 1944.

The first book he wrote in exile enhanced Wright's second reputation. *The Outsider* portentously invites reading as philosophical fiction. Cross Damon seizes upon the accident of a false report of his death to embark upon a life free of contingency, where action is self-sanctioned and alienation grants a perception of mankind in a world of dead myths. Cross, however, can neither escape anguish nor achieve disalienation in his version of freedom. In that respect his problem reflects the author's. Wright described himself in publicity for the novel as a man without ideological burdens for the first time in his life, but his own characteristic feeling of alienation produced an interesting novel undermined by its nihilism.

Wright needed new premises for his writing and found them in the Third World. The four non-fictional books he published from 1954 to 1957 derive from Wright's belief that his own experience was being repeated in the history of Africans and Asians moving from a pre-industrial, traditional society into a modern, mass world. Out of this felt congruity he wrote accounts of Ghana, the Bandung Conference, Spain—which represented the world not yet touched by modernism—and the lectures published as *White Man, Listen!* All blend reportage and subjective response to show Wright looking at, feeling with the world in change, and defining himself again as typical, though this time on a world-wide stage.

Wright's exile has sometimes been described as though it were the fag end of his career. In fact, it was a creative period twice as long as he had in the United States. Besides his non-fictional reports, he published three novels and compiled a collection of short stories, *Eight Men*, issued posthumously. One of the novels, *Savage Holiday*, extends Wright's interest in extreme narrative situations to the plight of a white man trapped by psychosis and an accidental death for which he feels responsible. *The Long Dream*, meant to open a trilogy tracing the movement of a young man from Mississippi into life in Europe, is a tightly written *Bildungsroman* neatly synthesizing Wright's conception of the psychological trauma of social experience in the person of "Fish" Tucker.

None of Wright's exile writings, however, received the critical or popular acclaim of his first works. There may be a number of explanations for this, besides the possibility of their lesser quality, but a leading reason for the slump in his popular reputation must be that he no longer wrote as the realistic bringer of news about America and that his performance in the rolc of typifier of modern life had less authority than the writing by acknowledged "experts." Nevertheless, the exile works alert us to the importance of Wright as an artist.

Examining *The Outsider* and *Savage Holiday*, for instance, we find that their structures are inversions and parodies of the thriller genre, that the expressionistic parable "The Man Who Lived Underground," as well as the stories in *Eight Men*, include experiments in narrative stripped down to bare dialogue. Intrigued by these findings, we return to the early writings and find that they, too, are constructed so that transgression of the conventions of genre constitute meaning, with imagery and controlled narrative voice accounting for the impact of such stories as *Native Son* which we read at first without awareness of literary craft, and that the mediations of ideology in *Uncle Tom's Children* and the portrait of the artist in *Black Boy* are masterfully subordinated in character and plot. In short, we complete the survey of Wright's career by recognizing that the themes which won him fame as a realist and attention as an intellectual are the products of art. So, now we are ready to study Richard Wright in earnest.

—John M. Reilly

See the essay on *Native Son*.

WYLIE, Elinor (Morton, née Hoyt). Born in Somerville, New Jersey, 7 September 1885. Educated at Miss Baldwin's School, Bryn Mawr, Pennsylvania, 1893–97; Mrs. Flint's School, 1897–1901, and Holton-Arms School, 1901–04, both Washington, D.C. Married Philip Hichborn in 1906 (died, 1912), one son; 2) Horace Wylie in 1916 (separated, 1921; divorced, 1923), one son; 3) William Rose Benét, *q.v.*, in 1923. Eloped with Horace Wylie in 1910, and moved with him to England as Mr. and Mrs. Waring; returned to the U.S. in 1915; moved to New York, 1921; poetry editor, *Vanity Fair*, New York, 1923–25; editor, Literary Guild, New York, 1926–28; contributing editor, *New Republic*, New York, 1926–28. Recipient: Julia Ellsworth Ford Prize, 1921. *Died 16 December 1928.*

PUBLICATIONS

Collections

Collected Poems, edited by William Rose Benét. 1932.
Collected Prose. 1933.

Verse

Incidental Numbers. 1912.
Nets to Catch the Wind. 1921.
Black Armour. 1923.
(*Poems*), edited by Laurence Jordan. 1926.
Trivial Breath. 1928.
Angels and Earthly Creatures: A Sequence of Sonnets. 1928.
Angels and Earthly Creatures (collection). 1929.
Nadir. 1937.
Last Poems, edited by Jane D. Wise. 1943.

Fiction

Jennifer Lorn: A Sedate Extravaganza. 1923.
The Venetian Glass Nephew. 1925.
The Orphan Angel. 1926; as *Mortal Image*, 1927.
Mr. Hodge and Mr. Hazard. 1928.

*

Critical Studies: *Wylie: The Portrait of an Unknown Lady* by Nancy Hoyt, 1935; *Wylie* by Thomas A. Gray, 1969; *Wylie, A*

Life Apart: A Biography by Stanley Olson, 1979; *The Life and Art of Wylie* by Judith Farr, 1983.

* * *

Elinor Wylie's prestigious social background, striking personality, beauty, elegance, and conversational gifts, with the romantic aura of her daring break with conventional society when she eloped with Horace Wylie, made her a symbolic figure to many persons caught up in the "American poetic renaissance." Consequently, judgments of her writings were for some years infused with feelings about the writer. Thomas A. Gray's monograph of 1969 discusses widely differing views of her achievement.

In the essay "Jewelled Bindings" (1923), Wylie saw herself and a few other contemporary lyric poets as "enchanted by a midas-touch or a colder silver madness into workers in metal and glass . . . in crisp and sharp-edged forms." They choose "short lines, clear small stanzas, brilliant and compact." Such standards produced her most widely known poems: the 3-quatrain "Let No Charitable Hope" that climaxes with "In masks outrageous and austere / The years go by in single file; / But none has merited my fear, / And none has quite escaped my smile"; "The Eagle and the Mole," with its fastidious trimeter: "Avoid the reeking herd . . ."; the art-for-art's-sake poem "Say not of Beauty she is good, / Or aught but beautiful"; and the exquisite "Velvet Shoes": "Let us walk in the white snow / In a soundless space. . . ."

This preference for the delicately sensuous or even impalpable characterized many of her poems—"I love the look, austere, immaculate, / Of landscapes drawn in pearly monotones"—and her first two "novels." *Jennifer Lorn: A Sedate Extravaganza* appealed to a public that was seeking relief from the ugly realities. Set in the late 18th century in the realms of aristocracy and wealth in England and India, it is a long catalogue of lovely, delicate objects; what plot it has concerns the fragile, fainting Jennifer and—the spine of the story—her husband Gerald, the exact, cool aesthete. It has been compared to a tapestry, and among the *mille fleurs* are many phrases and lines from 18th-century literature. Wylie's wide reading in this period showed itself also in the amusing *The Venetian Glass Nephew*. Her long and perhaps abnormal admiration for Shelley brought about *The Orphan Angel*, in which the libertarian poet is rescued from drowning and accompanies a Yankee sailor to America and across the continent. This trend toward more realistic treatment continued in *Mr. Hodge and Mr. Hazard*, a satirical allegory on the stifling of the late romantics by the Victorians.

Mary Colum, who described Wylie as "one of the few important women poets in any literature," observes, "She seemed to write little out of a mood or out of a passing emotion . . . but nearly always out of complex thought. . . ." (*Life and the Dream*, 1947). Many found her poems cold; the fastidious speaker seeks isolation and death. A last group of sonnets, however, shows a capacity for love: "And so forget to weep, forget to grieve, / And wake, and touch each other's hands, and turn / Upon a bed of juniper and fern." Another critic found her not a "great" poet but a "rare" poet: "Refinement is her essential characteristic as an artist."

—Alice R. Bensen

YERBY, Frank (Garvin). Born in Augusta, Georgia, 5 September 1916. Educated at Paine College, Augusta, A.B. 1937; Fisk University, Nashville, Tennessee, M.A. 1938; University of Chicago, 1939. Married 1) Flora Helen Claire Williams in 1941 (divorced), two sons and two daughters; 2) Blanca Calle Pérez in 1956. Instructor, Florida Agricultural and Mechanical College, Tallahassee, 1938–39, and Southern University and A. and M. College, Baton Rouge, Louisiana, 1939–41; laboratory technician, Ford Motor Company, Dearborn, Michigan, 1941–44; Magnaflux inspector, Ranger (Fairchild) Aircraft, Jamaica, New York, 1944–45; full-time writer from 1945; moved to Madrid, 1954. Recipient: O. Henry Award, 1944.

PUBLICATIONS

Fiction

The Foxes of Harrow. 1946.
The Vixens. 1947.
The Golden Hawk. 1948.
Pride's Castle. 1949.
Floodtide. 1950.
A Woman Called Fancy. 1951.
The Saracen Blade. 1952.
The Devil's Laughter. 1953.
Benton's Row. 1954.
Bride of Liberty. 1954.
The Treasure of Pleasant Valley. 1955.
Captain Rebel. 1956.
Fairoaks. 1957.
The Serpent and the Staff. 1958.
Jarrett's Jade. 1959.
Gillian. 1960.
The Garfield Honor. 1961.
Griffin's Way. 1962.
The Old Gods Laugh: A Modern Romance. 1964.
An Odor of Sanctity. 1965.
Goat Song: A Novel of Ancient Greece. 1967.
Judas, My Brother: The Story of the Thirteenth Disciple. 1969.
Speak Now. 1969.
The Dahomean. 1971; as *The Man from Dahomey*, 1971.
The Girl from Storyville: A Victorian Novel. 1972.
The Voyage Unplanned. 1974.
Tobias and the Angel. 1975.
A Rose for Ana María. 1976.
Hail the Conquering Hero. 1977.
A Darkness at Ingraham's Crest. 1979.
Western: A Saga of the Great Plains. 1982.
Devilseed. 1984.
McKenzie's Hundred. 1985.

*

Critical Study: "The Guilt of the Victim: Racial Themes in Some Yerby Novels" by Jack B. Moore, in *Journal of Popular Culture*, Spring 1975.

* * *

Readers of his many bestselling romances are still amazed to discover that Frank Yerby began his career as a militant writer of black protest fiction. Perhaps a more surprising activity of his early years was his poetry writing. The careful and painstaking construction of sonnets does not seem a practice this supposedly inartistic teller of racy, swashbuckling tales would spend much time on. But Yerby is a writer and a person filled with curious complexities, and the more one studies his career the more one observes a fascinating and paradoxical phenomenon.

His first published short stories in the 1940's were outspoken and bitter works about the predicament of contemporary black Americans. "Homecoming" (*Common Ground*, 1946) ironically portrays the return to his home in the rural south of a young black veteran who has lost a leg defending democracy. His white neighbors view him as just another uppity nigger too big for his britches, and instead of receiving a hero's welcome he is almost lynched. "Health Card" (*Harper's*, May 1944), another early story, won an O. Henry Award. The work relates the humiliation a black soldier and his wife are forced to face in the south during World War II: it is assumed in the camp town where the protagonist is stationed that any black woman seen with a black man is probably a whore needing a "health card."

Around the time World War II ended, Yerby's life as a writer took a totally unpredictable turn. He had written an apparently realistic novel about black life but no publisher was interested in it. And so, according to a very cynical article he wrote for *Harper's* in 1959, he set out quite coolly and rationally to become a popular author. He studied those novels that had high sales over a period of years, and derived from them what almost amounts to a formula to ensure popularity. He would create escapist costume novels containing no dominating social problems. He would construct relatively tightly plotted stories about strong sexy men and vivacious sexy women.

Obviously, few writers who attempt to write racy adventurous novels become bestsellers. But Yerby succeeded in an unprecedented fashion. Since his first published novel and first smash popular success, *The Foxes of Harrow*, Yerby has written hit after hit, many of which have been made into films. Around the mid-1950's his very high popularity began to decline. It has been claimed that eight of his novels made bestseller lists, a record that at one time placed him second only to Mary Roberts Rinehart. This achievement seems even more remarkable when it is considered that since the 1960's his novels have rarely been reviewed in the major mass-circulation magazines. The audience he has built up apparently needs no stimulation beyond his books themselves.

The few critics who have taken his work seriously point out that he writes something closer to anti-romance than romance. Both his heroes and heroines are more apt to be cunning opportunists than virtuous aristocrats. The fantasy worlds in which his characters operate—the Spanish Main, the Holy Land, the reconstruction south—are rather dirty and unglamorous places as Yerby describes them. Moreover, the frequently restated charge that he has turned his back on his race (in *Anger and Beyond*, for example, Saunders Redding claimed that in ignoring his racial heritage Yerby was revealing "pathological overtones" in his fiction) is absolutely false. In many of his most popular novels, such as *Griffin's Way* or *A Woman Called Fancy*, Yerby dealt quite accurately with the oppressive treatment of blacks in the south. More recently, *A Darkness at Ingraham's Crest* not only attacks slavery but presents an aristocratic African hero, Hwesu ("Wes"), who views and treats most southern whites as uncivilized savages. *McKenzie's Hundred* upends a number of Civil War myths, depicting many members of the southern gentry as cowards or louts with barnyard sexual appetites, and reports in detail on the infamous New York City Draft Riots of 1863, in which free blacks including women and children were hounded and slaughtered by rampaging whites. The novel's hero, Rose McKenzie, rambles far from the traditional pedestal of southern womanhood, and romps lustily like a picaro from battlecamp to bedroom with great spirit though not too much intelligence among mainly doltish or brutal males. Yerby now differentiates between his serious works (such as *Speak Now*) and his entertainments (practically any of his early hits) and claims that he is going to concentrate on serious fiction. Certainly his sardonic and academic "A Note to the Reader" prefacing *A Darkness at Ingraham's Crest* openly declares the book's political message that slavery in the south was more an absolute evil than the crimes of Nazi Germany. The distinction between his serious and entertaining work seems something of an apology, however, and perhaps an unnecessary one. Though his characterizations are rarely subtle, and sometimes it is difficult to determine what is parodic and what is tritely formulaic in his dialogue and plotting, for several decades Yerby has been the most popular novelist in America addressing the racial theme.

—Jack B. Moore

ZUKOFSKY, Louis. Born in New York City, 23 January 1904. Educated at Columbia University, New York, M.A. 1924. Married Celia Thaew in 1939; one son. Teacher at University of Wisconsin, Madison, 1930–31; Colgate University, Hamilton, New York, 1947, and Polytechnic Institute of Brooklyn, New York, 1947–66. Recipient: Longview Foundation award, 1961; National Endowment for the Arts grant, 1966, 1968; American Academy award, 1976. Honorary degree: Bard College, Annandale-on-Hudson, New York, 1977. *Died 12 May 1978.*

PUBLICATIONS

Verse

First Half of "A"-9. 1940.
55 Poems. 1941.
Anew. 1946.
Some Time: Short Poems. 1956.
Barely and Widely. 1958.
"A" 1-12. 1959.
16 Once Published. 1962.
I's Pronounced "Eyes." 1963.
After I's. 1964.
Found Objects 1962–1926. 1964.
An Unearthing: A Poem. 1965.
Iyyob. 1965.
I Sent Thee Late. 1965.
Finally a Valentine. 1965.
"A" Libretto. 1965.
All: The Collected Short Poems 1923–1958 and *1956–1964*. 2 vols., 1965–66.
"A"-9. 1966.
"A"-14. 1967.
"A" 13-21. 1969.

The Gas Age: A Poem. 1969.
Initial. 1970.
"A"-24. 1972.
"A"-22 and 23. 1975.
"A" (complete version). 1978.
80 Flowers. 1978.

Play

Arise, Arise. 1973.

Fiction (stories)

It Was. 1961.
Little: A Fragment for Careenagers. 1967; complete version, 1970.
Ferdinand, Including It Was. 1968.

Other

Le Style Apollinaire. 1934.
5 Statements for Poetry. 1958.
Bottom: On Shakespeare. 1963.
Prepositions: The Collected Critical Essays. 1967; revised edition, 1981.
Autobiography. 1970.

Editor, *An Objectivists Anthology*. 1932.
Editor, *A Test of Poetry*. 1948.

Translator, *Albert Einstein*, by Anton Reiser. 1930.
Translator, with Celia Zukofsky, *Catullus: Fragmenta*, music by Paul Zukofsky. 1969.
Translator, with Celia Zukofsky, *Catullus*. 1969.

*

Bibliography: *Bibliography of Zukofsky*, 1969, and "Year by Year Bibliography of Zukofsky," in *Paideuma 7*, Winter 1978, both by Celia Zukofsky; *A Catalogue of the Zukofsky Manuscript Collection* edited by Marcella Booth, 1975.

Critical Studies: *At: Bottom* by Cid Corman, 1966; "Zukofsky Issue" of *Grosseteste Review* Winter 1970, *Maps 5* 1974, and *Paideuma 7* Winter 1978; article by Peter Quartermain, in *Open Letter*, second series, Fall 1973; *Zukofsky, Man and Poet* edited by Carroll F. Terrell, 1979; *Zukofsky's "A": An Introduction* by Barry Ahearn, 1983.

* * *

If William Carlos Williams, by writing about roses as though no-one had written about them before, freed the American language from its heavy dependence on English antecedents and associations, Louis Zukofsky, by stripping words of their meaning or by overloading them so that no single meaning comes through, showed writers such as Robert Creeley and Robert Duncan (and others) how to let the movement of words generate a play and discovery of meaning by paying attention to their music so that the language might *sing*. It is a trick he learned from Apollinaire (about whom he wrote a book) and from Spinoza, who insisted that a thing is said to be free if it "exists by the mere necessity of its own nature and is determined in its actions by itself alone." For Zukofsky, the poem is an object.

Here is one of his poems:

FOR
Four tubas
or
two-by-four's.

Zukofsky's Brooklyn accent emphasises the palindromic echoes of "four tubas" and "tuba-fours"; the aural rhyme of "or" with "four" and the visual rhyme of "or" with the title, and the ambiguity of the apostrophe, all reflect a mind which not only delights in puns but also takes absolutely literally Pound's dictum that poetry is made up of sight, sound, intellection, and rhythm. The complexities of meaning are established through tentative possibilities of relationship which are never fully realised in the poem: the romantic, lyric implications of the title, the mundane quality of the last line, the ambiguity of the prepositions, all of whose meanings have relevance to the structure of a poem which, highly comic yet at the same time moving, draws attention to the neglected minutiae of the language: prepositions, conjunctions, articles. The poetry is in the words, rather than in the ideas.

Thus, in "*A*," his long poem in 24 movements which explore most traditional verse forms ("A"-7 is a sonnet-cycle, "A"-9 is a double canzone, "A"-21 is a Roman comedy), Zukofsky plays on the possibilities of the indefinite article (as, earlier—in 1926—he had written "Poem Beginning 'The' ") while interweaving personal, political and aesthetic themes round two central figures: Bach and Shakespeare (music and poetry). If themes are stated, they are stated so that they may play against one another ("Words rangeless, melody forced by writing," in "A"-6), and much of the poem's complex play occurs as the result of pitting one specialised vocabulary or context against another—as, in "A"-9, modern physics is pitted against Marx, Cavalcanti, and Spinoza. Similarly, Zukofsky may pit one language against another, as in the opening of "A"-15 (English echoing the Hebrew sound of passages from the Book of Job), or in his "translation" of *Catullus*, where the English, repeating the sound of the Latin, comes to be seen, in its knotted turbulence, from "outside itself." Such work, innovative, difficult, often bewildering, and controversial, has nevertheless been influential: some readers, many of them poets, consider Zukofsky to rank with Pound and Joyce among 20th-century writers.

—Peter Quartermain

WORKS

ABSALOM, ABSALOM!
Novel by William Faulkner, 1936.

Although often considered William Faulkner's best novel, *Absalom, Absalom!* is also his most involved. First of all, the narrative is related by mostly unreliable narrators years after the events described. The basic details upon which the story is based are few and easily related, but as they pass through the consciousnesses of the narrators who relate them, they become not only complicated and involved but at many points contradictory. Each narrator has a different version of what happened and often varying opinions of the effects of what occurred on the inhabitants of Jefferson.

In 1833 Thomas Sutpen came to Jefferson riding a thoroughbred horse and wearing two well-oiled and carefully cared-for pistols. After a few days at the hotel, he left and returned a few weeks later, bringing with him a wagon, a few tools, some half-wild slaves, and a French architect. The rumor spread that Sutpen had acquired some land from the Chickasaws, and he was doing no less than establishing the largest and best plantation in Yoknapatawpha County. After his return little was seen or heard of Sutpen, although he did occasionally invite some of the men from Jefferson out to hunt. On these outings he would often join several of his slaves in a pit about twenty feet wide and five feet deep where they would "fight, stomp, and gouge" until there was only one man left conscious and standing, and that man was usually Sutpen. The visitors would always note the progress Sutpen was making as he attempted to bring his wilderness under control and how the mansion the French architect was building for him was developing.

One day Sutpen passed through the town again. When he returned this time he brought with him furniture and furnishings finer than anyone in Yoknapatawpha County had ever seen. He was making the mansion into a showplace. Then he began his quest for the accoutrements that would make him a southern gentleman in one generation, a station the Compsons, Sartorises, and McCaslin had reached only after many years. First, he named his place Sutpen's Hundreds and married Ellen Coldfield, daughter of one of the leading families in Jefferson. In due time he had the required son and heir, Henry, and a daughter, Juliet.

Henry eventually entered the law school of the University of Mississippi, the law being one of the acceptable professions for a southern gentleman. There he met Charles Bon, who was rumored to be Sutpen's son by his first marriage, which he had dissolved as soon as he discovered his wife was part black. Henry and Charles become good friends and Henry brings Charles home with him. Charles and Juliet fall in love, but before they can marry, Henry, Charles, and Sutpen go off to the Civil War, Sutpen as second in command of the cavalry unit raised by Colonel John Sartoris. Soon the men in the unit become convinced Colonel Sartoris is exposing them to unnecessary danger and elect Sutpen as their commanding officer. Charles and Henry fight side-by-side throughout the war. During their years together Henry has learned of Charles's true identity, and all the way home he begs Charles to tell him what he is going to do about the engagement. Charles will not reveal his intentions. As they come in sight of the house, Henry says, you cannot marry my sister because you are my half-brother. "No, I'm not," Charles replies, "I'm the nigger that's going to marry your sister." Almost before the words are out of his mouth, Henry kills him and leaves home. (He later returns half-crazy and Juliet hides him in the house.) Sutpen returns to find his slaves gone, his buildings ruined, and his land grown up in weeds. His "design" is destroyed. He is later killed by Wash Jones because Sutpen mistreats his daughter, Millie, because the illegitimate child he has by her is a girl. He wants a boy so that he can reestablish his "design" and become an aristocrat.

Like many other great novels, this one has been subjected to many interpretations. The reading I offer is based upon the following hypothesis: 1) there is no reliable narrator, so except for a few basic facts we don't know what happened and why it occurred; 2) the Quentin Compson who appears as a character and narrator in *Absalom, Absalom!* is the same youth who had the disturbing and destroying experiences related in *The Sound and the Fury*; and 3) the narrative he "creates" in *Absalom* is mostly influenced by the experience of that novel (to understand fully *Absalom*, one must first read *The Sound and the Fury*). Quentin is the principal agent in the creation of a legend that gives him temporary relief from the powerful emotional disturbances (found in *The Sound and the Fury*) that will destroy him: his inability to punish Dalton Ames, his sister's seducer (as Henry punished "the nigger" who was going to marry *his* sister), his failure to accept the incestuous feelings he has for his sister (as Thomas is able to accept his feeling toward Judith). The "real legend" of Thomas Sutpen is the one Quentin creates because in relating it to his roommate he receives the strength that allows him to bear for a short time his own overwhelming burdens.

—Thomas Daniel Young

ADVENTURES OF HUCKLEBERRY FINN.
Novel by Mark Twain, 1884.

Mark Twain conceived of what became *Adventures of Huckleberry Finn* in the summer of 1875, began to write the following summer, and after long interruptions completed a manuscript with a rush in 1883. It was to be a boys' book, a sequel to *The Adventures of Tom Sawyer*; yet even the first reviewers saw some ambiguity about its proper audience. What Twain himself seems never fully to have understood is the extent to which the book moved during composition towards the adult and the serious or how superior it is to his other works.

Appealing to a broad spectrum of readers, the book gained an immediate popular success. Although several reviewers objected to its violence and to the bad models it set for boys, most liked it for his comedy, characters, and pictures of life in the Mississippi Valley of about 1840. It was easy to feel sympathy in the mid-1880's for Twain's praise of freedom and condemnation of slavery. Industrial capitalism had brought tensions; images of peace, individual liberty, dozing villages, and harmony with Nature had general appeal. The myth of the West was potent everywhere.

More recently, optimistic readings have declined, and emphasis has been placed on themes and thematic images that run counter to primary American ideologies and *mentalités* of the past century. The book now appears to imply more than a distaste for a slave society: the Old South is metonymic. All society is coercive; men are greedy. The novel subverts the assumptions of all religion and of all socially inspired morality.

A certain gravity was built into the novel from its first conception: it had to do with slavery and hypocrisy. The southwestern humorists whom Twain learned from wished to do more than amuse; they intended to capture for posterity regional oddities of life and speech, to record manners, customs, and characters. They did not, however, write jeremiads. Twain's book as published is crowded with images of fog and night, violent death, difficult rebirth, unfreedom, and shifting identity. Counter images of peace, freedom, generosity, loving companionship, and cosmicity tend to blur.

Twain's chief characters have maintained their appeal. As Twain wrote later, in Huck "a sound heart & a deformed conscience come into collision & conscience suffers defeat." By passing a series of moral tests, Huck, a Rousseauistic Child of Nature, separates himself from a tainted society. Tom, who helps open the book with his childish fantasizing, reappears in Chapter 33, and Huck slips back into something resembling his original state. Sophisticated readers often judge Tom to be the novelistic villain of the piece: he lives by false conventions; he diminishes the book's seriousness. The treatment accorded Jim has repeatedly raised the issue of racism. Jim begins and ends as a minstrel-show darkey; but in the book's center he furnishes authentic pathos, achieves full humanity, and joins Huck as an archetypal figure. In this central section the River becomes (in T.S. Eliot's phrase) "a strong brown god" and the equivalent of a character. A gallery of lesser figures who provide comedy and tragedy populate the Shore or irrupt upon the majestic River.

The structure of the novel has been much discussed. That the book is, to an extent, picaresque has always been recognized. It has also been described as a romance, a social novel, a realistic novel, a symbolic novel, and a psychological novel. Polysemous possibilities encourage hermeneutic fecundity. Loose organization and awkward, mechanical plotting are typical of Twain; but more subtle unifying elements than plot have been found. The voice of Huck as narrator is of first importance: his moral development gives the book the configuration of a *Bildungsroman*. The River, too, plays an organizing role; and rhythmic patterns develop, as in shifts from burlesque to genre passages to tragedy, from low-vernacular to vernacular-sublime. Contrapuntal themes (life-death; freedom-slavery; individual-society) are elaborated and fortified by illustrative symbols and images.

The principal flaw in the novel is reputed to be its final section, beginning with Chapter 33, where Tom Sawyer reappears; but even that section has distinguished champions. Lionel Trilling and Eliot have defended the ending on technical grounds: it has a formal aptness, is appropriate for a romance and for Huck—a hero who by his nature can have no beginning and no end.

Adverse criticism charges the last chapters with destroying the credibility of Huck's moral maturation; he loses sight of his discovery that men are often vicious and hypocritical, and he fails to demonstrate any reasonable accommodation with society. Just as Huck loses his grasp of the realities of the human condition, so Jim loses his dignity, accepts degradation, and becomes again the eye-rolling pawn that he was in the beginning. The major theme of freedom is thus obscured and made trivial. The imagination of Tom, who supplants Huck as hero, seems conventional and puerile, the comedy that he initiates to be interminably, tediously slapstick. The two much-praised final sentences, in which Huck proposes to "light out for the Territory" so that Aunt Sally cannot adopt and "sivilize" him, yield only a glint of hope. Civilization and community may not, it is felt, be dismissed so lightly.

In praising the novel critics have often isolated one or two of its aspects as responsible for its greatness. Eliot wrote that "the Boy and the River" gave the book distinction. Others have concentrated attention on Twain's choice of the first-person point of view and on Huck, a speaker of richly colloquial English, as his narrative persona. Yet it may be observed that although Twain used approximately the same formula later, he was notably unable to repeat his triumph.

It is to grant to *Huckleberry Finn* too much novelty and influence to suggest, as have Trilling and others, that in this volume Twain established for writers the virtues of American colloquial speech. Twain has, nevertheless, been exceptionally influential through his effective representation of the colloquial. Contrary to the opinion of many critics, Huck's voice does not carry without lapse throughout the book, nor does Twain give us with exactness the colloquial and dialectal speech of the Missouri region. The author's mask slips at many places; Huck's voice falters. It may well be argued, however, that Twain improved on conventional renderings and did what was artistically necessary to give the impression of living speech.

Critics see Huck's vernacular as true to the culture, vivid, and flexible—a touchstone for exposing the falsities of "genteel" speech and "literary" rhetoric. This impression may be enhanced for readers by their acceptance of the pervasive image of Twain as a hero of the folk. Huck's presence as narrator placed useful constraints on Twain's tendencies towards excess in the direction of buffoonery and sentimentality and forced the writer to dramatize. But no matter how important, Huck is not the sole savior of the book: its towering reputation is properly attributable to the combination of many elements, some planned, some fortuitous. At this time, it would seem that no other American novel has been so suspected and so controverted, and perhaps that no other has maintained its eminence so well.

—Guy A. Cardwell

THE ADVENTURES OF TOM SAWYER.
Novel by Mark Twain, 1876.

In his preface to *The Adventures of Tom Sawyer* Mark Twain writes that "most of the adventures recorded in this book really occurred; one or two were experiences of my own, the rest of boys who were schoolmates of mine." Twain's memories of his boyhood in Hannibal, Missouri, form the basis of the novel and give it its idyllic, often nostalgic tone of celebration of lost childhood; Twain called the book "simply a hymn, put into prose form to give it a worldly air."

Tom Sawyer is not the complex masterpiece that its successor *Adventures of Huckleberry Finn* is, but it is well worth reading in its own right. The novel lives on because of its humor and its memorable evocation of the world of childhood. The novel takes place in a transformed, eternal-summer version of Hannibal called St. Petersburg (Saint Peter's burg, a kind of Heaven). *Tom Sawyer* is full of lavish lyrical descriptions of the summer world as it is experienced by those who can appreciate it best—children. The novel also remembers the nightmare side of childhood; grave-robbing, murder, revenge, and grisly death are also part of St. Petersburg.

As he wrote and revised the book, Twain could not make up his mind whether he was writing a book for children or adults. In his preface, Twain expresses a double purpose: "Although my book is intended mainly for the entertainment of boys and girls, I hope it will not be shunned by men and women on that account, for part of my plan has been to try to pleasantly remind adults of what they once were themselves." Although the point of view is Tom's most of the time, the narrator leading us into Tom's experience is clearly an adult—amused, superior, and nostalgic by turns—who expects readers to see more than Tom does, to laugh at him and admire him from a perspective of adulthood.

Tom Sawyer is in part a reaction against the "Sunday-school literature" abounding in 19th-century America, which featured relentlessly good children who were rewarded and naughty children who came to bad ends. Comic writers like Thomas Bailey Aldrich and B.P. Shillaber parodied this moralistic school. Before *Tom Sawyer* Twain wrote burlesques entitled "The Story of the Bad Little Boy Who Didn't Come to Grief" and "The Story of the Good Little Boy Who Did Not Prosper," but in *Tom Sawyer* he went a step further and told the story of a "bad" (i.e., normal) boy who will clearly become a good man.

In the opening chapters of the novel, Tom displays all the faults of the "bad child" of the moralists: he lies, plays hooky, steals, and generally considers the respectable adult world his natural enemy. He cannot learn a single Bible verse, but he can memorize the most minute details of the adventures of Robin Hood. It never occurs to him to apply himself in school, but he can be patient, careful, and untiringly diligent in pursuit of childhood arts like whistling and in his sentimental courtship of Becky Thatcher. Like that earlier Tom, Tom Jones, this imprudent boy is naturally good-hearted; in *Tom Sawyer* Twain is willing to believe in a natural goodness of heart, however much he may distrust such a notion elsewhere.

Tom lives in a private world of gorgeous theatrical dreams, sagas of pirates, robbers, and buried treasure, all starring himself. He successfully transforms dusty everyday life in St. Petersburg into dramas in which he holds center stage, most spectacularly when he attends his own funeral. He is an inspired schemer and entrepreneur, as readers learn in one of the first incidents in the book, the famous whitewashing scene.

Twain himself said that the book had "no plot" and critics since his time have called *Tom Sawyer* everything from "utterly formless and shapeless" to "a most ingeniously plotted novel." Three related plotlines intertwine. The first is Tom's relationship with Aunt Polly, and by extension with the confining "respectable" adult world; this relationship is loving but elaborately hedged with comic plotting on both sides. The second strand is Tom's courtship of Becky Thatcher, and the third is his involvement with the murder, the buried treasure, and the horrific Injun Joe. During the course of these adventures Tom begins to mature; at the end, while Huck remains the natural and innocent escapee from "civilization," Tom edges closer to it.

But is "civilized" St. Petersburg worth joining? From the narrator's wider perspective, we can perceive the narrowness and hypocrisy of the worthies of the little country town. Much of the book's humor comes from the disparity between what the inhabitants of St. Petersburg "officially" think and feel and what they actually think and feel. But Twain does not condemn this world as he condemns the river society of *Huck Finn*, and *Tom Sawyer* does not taste of the bitter pessimism of Twain's later works. Tom's increasing "civilization" is not a cause for alarm; he will be a good man in a good if parochial world.

—Mollie Sandock

ALL THE KING'S MEN.
Novel by Robert Penn Warren, 1946.

Robert Penn Warren's *All the King's Men* was published in 1946 and received the Pulitzer Prize. It is the most celebrated of a series of novels that was initiated by *Night Rider* and that continues through such books as *The Cave* and *Flood*. In general, the novels are centered on an awareness that is more sensitive and discriminating than those which surround it; it is an awareness that would like to make sense of the mixture of good and evil in society and in each person but is usually unable to do so. One could say that Warren's alter egos in the novels—Jack Burden in *All the King's Men*—aspire to philosophic utterance but are often distracted by the diversity and sheer disorder of the life in which they are immersed. The result—in *All the King's Men*, at least—is a series of arresting insights, but insights the outlines of which are recurrently made obscure by the malice of other persons and the sheer jumble of event, of chance, that makes a thinker doubt the general relevance of an insight he has just framed. An early comment by Diana Trilling noted this "largeness of intention." "Mr. Warren's study of a political leader is intended to investigate the moral relativism inherent in the historical process. One might describe it as a fictional demonstration of Hegel's philosophy of history."

As just noted, the "thinker" in *All the King's Men* is a middle-aged man named Jack Burden, product of a privileged southern environment and a good education. At one point Burden had tried to base a university dissertation on the journal of a Civil War ancestor named Cass Mastern. But Burden abandoned this work to become a newspaperman. It was work that moved him away from the assessment of human values that, perhaps, comes naturally to a student of history. And Jack Burden—of Burden's Landing—moves still further away from thought and often becomes lost in the sheer welter of event when he becomes an administrative assistant to a southern politician named Willie Stark.

It is Willie Stark from whom radiates the confusion that haunts Burden. It is Willie Stark, incidentally, who assured the contemporary celebrity of the novel. Any reader of the mid-1940's could recognize that Willie Stark was at least suggested to Warren by the career of the Louisiana governor of the 1930's, Huey Long, to some an unscrupulous rabble-rouser and plunderer of the public till, and to others (chiefly the poor and the uneducated) a knight on a white horse.

With Long as a point of departure (but no more) Warren elaborates the figure that holds Jack Burden in bondage; the guile of Stark exerts esthetic fascination at the same time that it arouses moral repugnance. Burden again and again tries to tear himself loose from the low-brow corruption of Willie but is set free only when Willie is shot to death. Only then is Burden—Warren's assessor of meaning—able to embrace his true loves: a woman named Anne Stanton and the life of thought and analysis that is natural to him.

A film version of the novel and popular discussion of it of course placed Willie Stark at the center of the stage. But the book is more justly read with Jack Burden's preoccupations in command, as indeed they are in Warren's book. For Burden is actually surrounded by many other persons just as essential to him as Willie. One and all these persons compose the seed-bed of evil which, as Burden sees the matter, is the only terrain from which good can grow. Among the persons are Willie's hangers-on, as corrupt as Willie but less clever, less charismatic. There is Sadie Burke, Willie's secretary and one-time mistress; she is the ultimate planner of Willie's death. There is Tiny Duffy, a venal operator who helps set up the actual slaying of Willie to protect his own interests. And from outside the State House circle comes the actual assassin, Adam Stanton, a noble scientist whom Willie outrages on two counts: Willie's new mistress is Adam's sister Anne (she is also Jack Burden's ultimate beloved), and Willie also seems to be using Adam Stanton as a respectable "front" in the construction of a hospital.

When Jack Burden often draws away from all this—to catch his breath, as it were—he finds Burden's Landing no purer in fact than Willie Stark's State House. For human betrayal is also endemic in Jack's childhood town, and he is often more aware of the seed-bed of evil there than he is of the love and affection he has met in the village.

A great interest in the novel is Burden's alternation between resigned connivance with corruption and his passionate revolt against it: a revolt made in the name of goodness, purity of intent, and all those traditional values lost in the southern shuffle of the novel. Two long sections of the novel are typical withdrawals from the unending depiction of the "real world."

First, there is Burden's study of his ancestor's Civil War journal. Cass Mastern emerges from that record as a man antique and curious: curious at least to Burden. For Mastern is a man who breaks the moral code and can say clearly to himself that he has broken the code that holds society together. In contrast, Jack Burden his descendant wants to pass similar judgments on himself and others, but is often unable to do so. So Burden's study of the ancestral journal puts before him a noble sinner whom he cannot imitate.

Then there is Burden's auto trip to California, during which he has a revelation that is cynical and easier for him to appropriate. At moments of course. For no appropriation of Burden's is final. Two phrases dominate the Burden mind at times. There is the Great Sleep, which amounts to a resignation from the entire human project, evil or good. And there is the annunciation of an alternate deity: alternate to the one ancestor Cass Mastern knew. This deity is the Great Twitch: briefly, reflex and conditioning as shaping forces in human life. (The novel was written at the time when Pavlov and his dogs were barking.)

Readers who wish to make final sense of *All the King's Men* will move beyond the limits of the novel itself and will leave Burden behind enjoying the only security he can trust: the arms of his boyhood sweetheart, Anne Stanton, once the mistress of Willie Stark and, at the end of the novel, Burden's solace—if not his key to inclusive meaning. As Diana Trilling observed in 1946, it is perhaps "the low quality of Burden's moral awareness" that qualifies the impact of *All the King's Men*. Jack Burden (if not Warren himself) cannot really rise above his version of the Hegelian ebb-and-flow.

—Harold H. Watts

THE AMBASSADORS.
Novel by Henry James, 1903.

The Ambassadors was the first written of Henry James's three late "major phase" novels. James himself regarded it "as, frankly, quite the best, 'all round,' of my productions" (Preface). After the shorter "experimental" fiction of the 1890's, experimenting with technique and treating English themes, James returns here to a large-scale novel treating the theme of international confrontation with which he originally established his reputation. His middle-aged hero, Lambert Strether, is a recognizable Jamesian type sometimes referred to as "the poor sensitive gentleman," who combines sensibility, integrity, and a capacity for growth, with naivety and relative powerlessness in worldly terms. Strether is the first of the ambassadors designated in the title, and the novel concerns the gradual evolution of his insights and attitudes.

He arrives in Europe from Woollett, Massachusetts, as the representative of his patron and provisional fiancée, Mrs. Newsome, assuming that it is his unequivocal duty to rescue her son Chad from a French mistress and from the dissipations of Paris. But he discovers an immensely improved and civilized Chad, and a lady, Madame de Vionnet, whose gentility is unquestionable and whose sophistication and grace both captivate and intimidate Strether himself. Strether's gradual awakening to the pleasures, beauty, style, and nuance of Paris is epitomized in the first of the two great recognition scenes of the novel, that of the sculptor Gloriani's garden party in Book V. Here Madame de Vionnet makes her first appearance in her representative character of *femme du monde*, accompanied by her exquisite young daughter Jeanne, as quintessential *jeune fille*. Strether must now speculate anew on what holds Chad in Paris. Moreover, he is overwhelmed by the sense of his own social ineptitude, middle age, and lost opportunities, and this sense culminates in the speech which James designates in his Preface as the origin of the novel, Strether's enjoinder to a young man present to "Live all you can; it's a mistake not to."

In this ecstatic embrace of Parisian possibilities Strether finds himself altogether at odds with the Woollett point of view, and by the end of Book VI, the exact midpoint of the novel, he reverses his original position. It would be wrong for Chad to desert a world and a person who have recreated him as a civilized man. Hence the need for Mrs. Newsome to despatch the second ambassador alluded to in the title, her thin-lipped, humorless, narrowly judgmental daughter, Sarah Pocock, accompanied by Sarah's husband Jim, who thinks that Paris is the Folies Bergère. The arrival of the Pocock ménage therefore sets off the imaginative distance Strether has traversed, his spiritual evolution from the moralistic Woollett pole of values toward the aesthetic Parisian pole of values. But the structure of the novel was devised by James as that of an hourglass, and its second half now reverses the first. Having cast all his allegiance with Madame de Vionnet and Paris, and effectively resigned his Woollett ambassadorship, Strether is now gradually subjected to a more intimate view of Paris, the seamy underside of his own original impression. Chad, he discovers, is superficially refined but not intrinsically changed and is, therefore, susceptible to the bait of a pretty girl back home and an advertising career in Woollett. Madame de Vionnet and not Jeanne fears for the loss of him. In the second great recognition scene of the novel, in Book XI, Strether accidentally discovers Chad and Madame de Vionnet boating together in the countryside during a week-end excursion and must recognize, after all, that this is the old Parisian story of an adulterous love affair.

This moment of discovery indisposes his moral stomach and he must retreat to Woollett to maintain his own integrity, yet his vision of a richer, more beautiful life in Paris and his own affection and pity for Madame de Vionnet have unfitted him for Woollett, too.

The Ambassadors is representative of James in this sort of unresolved, bleak ending in which loss figures largely; in its counterpointing of aesthetic and moral values, sophistication and naivety, against one another in association with European and American points of view; and in its suggestion that the fusion of aesthetic and moral sensibility exists as an ideal bought at great price by his supersubtle protagonists. *The Ambassadors* is also representative in technique, for example in its architectonic crafting, manifest in the hourglass structure and in the counterbalancing of the recognition scenes in Books V and XI, and also in its dramatization of intense inward subjective experience. To this end James utilizes functional characters ("*ficelles*") such as Maria Gostrey, a Europeanized American resident in Paris, and Waymarsh, a staunch New Englander and Mrs. Newsome's spy, to engage and challenge Strether and thereby to draw out and dramatize his states of mind. Likewise, settings and symbolic metaphors project character and mental attitudes, for the story is primarily one of inward evolution rather than outer events.

—Jean Frantz Blackall

ARIEL.
Poems by Sylvia Plath, 1965.

Sylvia Plath's best-known collection of poetry, *Ariel*, was published posthumously in 1965. It was assembled from the work left at her death in early 1963, and included most of the poems written during the fall of 1962 (the so-called "October" poems such as "Lady Lazarus," "Daddy," "Cut," and the bee sequence) and those from early 1963, "Edge," "Words," "Totem," and "Kindness." The poems from *Ariel* have more recently been published in *The Collected Poems*, which appeared in 1981 and was awarded the Pulitzer Prize for Poetry in 1982. In that book, they are arranged by the date in which they were written, according to Plath's records.

The effect of this slim volume of poetry—both in England, where it first appeared, and then in the United States, where it carried an introduction by Robert Lowell—was one of shock mingled with admiration for the strange brilliance of the poetry. The shock stemmed from the seemingly harsh anger underlying many of the poems, sometimes treated with comedy, again expressed as vituperation. Except for Allen Ginsberg's long poem *Howl* in the mid-1950's, very few American poems had treated such powerful emotion; to find such feeling in poetry by a woman was especially surprising. From the beginning, Plath's work was considered an anomaly, as well as a conundrum: what was the furor behind her writing? what was a well-educated American woman living in London doing writing poems such as these?

Readers quickly adopted her as an important poet, and—perhaps more central to many lives—a representative of a culture where unspoken anger was understood: the women's movement quoted her work, people interested in depression and suicide, other poets whose lives had also been spent trying for new effects in a highly competitive art. She quickly became a staple of poetry anthologies, and a few key poems became the Plath poems that everyone recognized. It was as if she had managed to express the social angers and angst that was to become pervasive a few years later, in the disillusioned 1960's and 1970's.

Plath's poem "Lady Lazarus" was a mocking monologue, spoken by a woman who divided her lifetime into suicide attempts: "I have done it again. / One year in every ten / I manage it—" The wry comedy of this poem, punctuated with horrifying comments like "Dying / Is an art, like everything else. / I do it exceptionally well," was set in surprising juxtaposition to the raw seriousness of its theme. Her poem "Daddy" worked in the same manner: to move the reader from an expected response (in this case, a perhaps maudlin but certainly sentimental evocation of the daughter's memories of her father) to a sharply contrasted mood. The venom of the speaker's reminiscence in "Daddy" seems inexplicable, until the key psychological fusion—that the husband who has recently left her and the father figure are one and the same, the authoritative male—is clarified:

> I made a model of you,
> A man in black with a Meinkampf look
>
> And a love of the rack and the screw.
> And I said I do, I do. . . .

Marriage fares badly in *Ariel*, most bitterly in "The Applicant," a funny poem about a woman's qualifications for the lifework of marrying a man, but motherhood is caught vividly and with sympathy. "You're," the series of metaphors describing the unborn child, is a sprightly and winning poem; "The Night Dances," the beautiful "Morning Song" ("Love set you going like a fat gold watch"), "Balloons," and "Kindness," with its poignant "The blood jet is poetry, / There is no stopping it. / You hand me two children, two roses," are each masterful poems expressing the mother's enjoyment in her children.

The majority of Plath's *Ariel* poems, however, are darkly foreboding, from the 1961 "Tulips" with its long, weary lines to the sinister "A Birthday Present," "Elm," "Getting There," and "Death & Co." The oppressive weight of the knowledge of death recurs in poems like "Berck-Plage" and "The Bee Meeting," even though the other four poems in what is known as the "bee sequence" are more affirmative. "Stings," for example, pictures the achieving woman as the old, wily queen bee, still in control, still winning ("They thought death was worth it, but I / Have a self to recover"). Many of Plath's late poems set this image of victory against the omnipresent tone of defeat: "Wintering," "Little Fugue," "Fever 103°," and especially the title poem, "Ariel," in which the speaker rides a triumphant horse into the sun, "the red / Eye, the cauldron of morning." Throughout these striking poems, Plath has managed to weave imagery from anthropology and dream, as well as from women's lives, to evoke truly wide-ranging responses. The *Ariel* poems must not be read as rational statements. They are the best of contemporary poetry, drawing on all the poet's resources, and demanding that panoply of resources as well from the reader.

Because Plath's estranged husband, Ted Hughes, edited the book *Ariel* for its publication, changing it dramatically from the manuscript Plath had left ready for the press, readers should check the information about the book as Plath had planned it in *The Collected Poems*, where all the late poems now appear. There, its identity as the words of the androgynous, and ultimately triumphant, spirit from Shakespeare's *The Tempest* rises above the sense of depression that dominates the collection as it was published in 1965. In Plath's own arrangement, the book began with the word "Love" and ended with "Spring," and was a memorable progression of emotion, from affirmation through depression to further affirmation.

—Linda W. Wagner

THE ASSISTANT.
Novel by Bernard Malamud, 1957.

Alfred Kazin has written of Bernard Malamud's fiction: "The scene is always the down-at-heel grocery, the winter street, the irreversible hardness of the modern city. Malamud has caught at once the guttural toughness of big city speech and the classic bitterness of Jewish dialogue" (*Contemporaries*, 1962). But, he goes on, this harshness is always linked with another quality: "the otherworldly feeling." Nowhere is this truer than of *The Assistant*.

Malamud, Kazin says, gives us "the talk of people who are not merely on edge but who live really on the edge." In *The Assistant* this is not merely the edge of economic marginality. Philip Roth observed of Malamud in "Writing American Fiction" that "his people live in a timeless depression and a placeless Lower East Side," and indeed it would be difficult, without comparing commodity prices in Morris Bober's store, to work out in which of several decades in this century the novel is set. Bober's grocery store is certainly down at heel, in a declining neighbourhood. The Jewish idiom of his wife Ida catches the irony of his perpetual bad-timing: "You should sell long ago the store." But if Bober's luck is always wrong, "he could not escape his honesty, it was bedrock; to cheat would cause an explosion in him, yet he trusted cheaters." He gets up every morning at six a.m. for a single customer, the old anti-semitic Polish woman who buys a three cent roll—not just for the money but out of a sense of obligation. One of the people who cheats him is Frank Alpine, the young Italo-American down-and-out and drifter, another anti-semite, who first with a friend mugs and robs Bober for a few dollars from the till and then, found starving and unrecognized by Bober in his cellar, comes to work as his assistant. Another person whose luck has always evaded him, Frank obscurely hopes to pay Morris back by stinting himself, falling in love with Bober's daughter Helen while barely daring to speak to her, but weakly unable to resist spying on her in the shower, until he finds himself once more with his hand in the till.

Frank transgresses another margin, between love and lust, when he first rescues Bober's daughter Helen from a rapist and then rapes her himself. Both these crimes, of robbery and rape, in a sense actually consummate the blood relation between Alpine and the Bober family. Like so many of Malamud's characters, Alpine is on edge with a spiritual restlessness and anxiety, a sense of failure before even starting out, and, an orphan, he feels that his true, authentic life, has eluded him. "Life renews itself," Helen says to him after he tells her of his failure in one earlier attempt to "look for a better life": "My luck stays the same," he replies. It is this belief in an external "luck" which is the heart of his problem. What Alpine comes to realise is that "his luck had so often curdled, because he had the wrong idea of what he really was and had spent all his energy trying to do the wrong things." But finding who he really is is not so easy. For Frank, it involves conversion to that Jewishness he once despised as a religion of suffering and acquiescence.

The edge these characters finally approach is that between life and death. Bober dies after falling while, still sick, he insists on clearing snow outside the store. Frank, losing his footing on the crumbling edge of Bober's grave, actually tumbles in, but in doing so he begins his rebirth, taking on himself for the first time the weight of responsibilities Bober has now renounced.

In the end, the edge of which Kazin speaks is that between two dimensions of moral being—the this-worldly cynicism and brutality in which Alpine has been reared, and the other-worldly realm towards which he aspires, represented by his patron saint, St. Francis, whose self-chosen poverty becomes the symbol of a different way of living. This other world makes itself felt in Frank's repeated moral urge towards atonement, his desire to justify and redeem himself in the eyes of some surrogate for the father he never had, which is the deepest impulse of his being. Frank had confused renewal with running away. Like all Malamud's heroes, he learns in the end that the new life is found where he is, in a new mode of relation to his life and those around him. Struggling to make himself worthy of Helen, he takes over Morris's role after his death, working to make the shop profitable and send Helen to college. Helen, still keeping him at a distance in the closing pages of the book, nevertheless notices the change:

> She had despised him for the evil he had done, without understanding the why or aftermath, or admitting that there could be an end to the bad and a beginning of good. It was a strange thing about people—they could look the same but be different. He had been one thing, low, dirty, but because of something in himself—something she couldn't define, a memory perhaps, an ideal he might have forgotten and then remembered—he had changed into somebody else, no longer what he had been. . . . What he did to me was wrong, she thought, but since he has changed in his heart he owes me nothing.

Helen has changed, too, moving towards Christian forgiveness as he moves towards a Jewish sense of atonement (the language of debt and credit common to both religions). In the last moments of the book he consummates this change by undergoing circumcision ("The pain enraged and inspired him. After Passover he became a Jew") thereby redeeming his own casual anti-semitism and accidental criminality by an act of deliberate choice and commitment. Alpine's conversion is not the renunciation of one religion for another—a kind of flight. Rather it is the bringing to fruition of the messianic hope concealed in both: the rebirth of the other-worldly within the flesh of this world. It is a token of that release from historical contingency which is also a release into his own true life and identity, finding a new life and testament within the old. Significantly, Malamud prefaces this symbolic gift of the foreskin to Jehovah with a different gift, conceived of in terms of Frank's Catholicism. In a reverie, Frank dreams of St. Francis retrieving from the garbage where Helen had thrown it the wooden rose Frank had carved for her. In the saint's hands, it turns into a real flower and, from him, Helen accepts the gift. The sexual symbolism is as real and as persuasive as the spiritual one. For Malamud, the "different life" all the characters seek is to be found, at last, not in some other-worldly place, but by making the sordid and actual world they inhabit flower with a human, and humane, significance.

—Stan Smith

AWAKE AND SING!
Play by Clifford Odets, 1935.

The social and economic environment of the Depression dominates Clifford Odets's classic play *Awake and Sing!* in a curiously ambiguous way. The survival ethic that, in one way or other, governs all members of the Bronx Jewish family means that in places a heroic defiance enshrines human stature, even in some of its meanest gestures. On the other hand, the Depression context also operates like the melodramatic hand of fate, arbitrarily making and breaking, so that individuality seems a transitory commodity. Economic survival becomes a lottery, cushioning some characters, driving others to suicide, and a similar pattern of arbitrary causation invades other aspects of characters' lives, as when the daughter finds she is pregnant to a (non-appearing) commercial traveller. Microcosmically, the family absorbs the national fraud, through the father's faith that "the government ain't gonna allow everything to be a fake." The naivety of this view is exposed by the lodger, who has learned a line of pragmatism from his experience as a war cripple: "It's all a racket—from horse racing down. Marriage, politics, big business—everybody plays cops and robbers." For some characters, the lesson is picaresque: they learn what their mother has known from the start, that they cannot afford morality. But, however vague, the principles of regeneration and transcendence echo from the title to lift other characters through adversity towards a better (revolutionary) future.

Because most of the events are presented as the product not of personality, but rather of superhuman forces, the mechanics of the action may seem contrived or propagandist. The play, however, is quite distinct from the mainstream of melodrama because the characters' existence is quite remote from audience norms. The Berger family seems to be lower middle class (Odets may even have conceived them as proletarian), and so the characters' mobility is actually in the direction of the audience. This means that not only does an upper-middle-class theatre audience fail to share the Bergers' dreams, but an intense irony is generated because the characters' fantasies fall short of audience commonplace. When Jacob, the economic messiah, commits suicide so that his grandson may inherit his insurance money, $3,000, the audience simply shudders at a drama that is pivoting on principles of extrinsic value. His life's worth seems to correlate precisely with the Caruso records which, broken, drain much of the lyricism out of the title.

The first version of the play, entitled *I Got the Blues*, was found by the Group Theatre's director, Harold Clurman, to have a "masochistically pessimistic ending." This was partially remedied in the produced version by the substitution of an ambivalent ending (in which pessimism is an available interpretation), and by an enormous reduction in the explicit Yiddishkeit in the dialogue. No close study of any version of the play, however, can ignore the fact that all the characters suffer from an intense feeling of cultural dislocation, and are groping for a 20th-century promised land. In need of a liberator in the mold of Gideon, one character pins his hopes on Teddy Roosevelt, another on Popeye the Sailor—who, eating spinach and knocking out "four bums," seems the closer to the legendary judges of Israel. Similarly, several characters articulate a notion of paradise, within the sordid constraints of 20th-century life. Cultural dislocation also generates a nervous assertiveness. As a settled American Jew, with a matriducal empire tentatively established, Bessie feels an intense antagonism towards a recently arrived "foreigner" who, though also Jewish, lacks her expertise in American English. It is, similarly, important to her husband to lecture his son on "an American father's duty."

The brittleness of a family structure grounded on such premises is considerable, especially when both female characters perjure themselves in their dealings with their men, without being pushed to an extreme situation. That at least some of the characters have some constancy is shown when the grandfather, a Marxist Jew who quotes the title passage from *Isaiah*, commits suicide by jumping from the tenement roof; this is generally interpreted as a means of exploiting an insurance company, but it may also imply a realisation of that eschatological section of the *Isaiah* prophecy (ch. 26–7). Such matters were alluded to extensively in the first version, but in the final text are reduced to stage directions as vague as "Quotes two lines of Hebrew."

Awake and Sing! is unquestionably important for its political and cultural content, and the terms of its social realism are striking beside other plays which Group audiences were at the time responding warmly to, such as Sidney Kingsley's absurd medical melodrama, *Men in White*. Odets's play, however, also has a strong claim for critical attention on dramaturgic grounds, in that it exploits subtextual energies much more extensively than any other American play of the 1930's. Partly, this is through Yiddish mannerisms, but it also emerges through "wiseguy" talk from characters whose insecurity in human relationships leads them to a sonorous commercial rhetoric, the basis of which in reality is often impossible to determine.

—Howard McNaughton

THE AWAKENING.
Novel by Kate Chopin, 1899.

Like most of Kate Chopin's stories, *The Awakening*, set in the late 19th-century Creole society of the New Orleans area, features a strong local ambiance and a richly symbolic texture; but thematically it transcends regional writing. Critics have frequently noted its close connections to the French work of Maupassant and Flaubert, especially Flaubert's *Madame Bovary. The Awakening* is the story of a young woman's quest for freedom; and the discoveries she makes along the way, including the ultimate realization that the complete freedom for which she yearns is not available to her in mortal life, constitute her awakening.

During her summer dalliance with one Robert Lebrun, Edna Pontellier becomes increasingly aware of the restrictiveness of her conventional marriage, and almost by chance discovers, simultaneously with her learning to swim, that the drive toward self-determination should be just as appropriate for women as it traditionally has been for men. It occurs to her that tradition has placed restraints on women by establishing societal modes (the structure of the family, patterns of social conduct) and by dictating concepts of morality (primarily through the church). Acting on her new realization that since tradition has been created by people it can also be set aside by people, she defies her husband and her father, sends her children to the country, moves out of the family home into her own small cottage, and in an illicit relationship with one Alcée Arobin flaunts her rebellion against moral propriety.

At first pleased with her escape from tradition, she soon discovers that she is less free than she had expected to be. Her sensual attraction to Arobin teaches her that sex and love are not equivalent, that sex is a separate, instinctive, fundamental force of nature that attracts men and women to each other and, as Per Seyersted asserts in his Chopin biography, "spurs us blindly on toward procreation." Edna's relationship with Arobin, combined with her smoldering love for Robert and her presence at the travail of her friend Adèle, the conventional biblical mother, leads Edna to understand that free love is not free, that the connection between love-making and the pain of childbirth is firmly established within the context of natural law by which all people are bound and from which there is no escape. But although she understands all this and although she feels intensely the loneliness and the sense of separation which inevitably accompany the attempt to create one's own destiny, Edna is not willing to relinquish her quest.

Still driven by the need for self-determination, by the urgent longing for total freedom, and unwilling to accept the natural role which she sees as an inevitable succession of lovers before her, she returns to the gulf to recapture the sense of freedom that exhilarated her by signalling her independence when, early in the novel, she learned to swim. Alone, ignoring warnings intended for her well-being, she swims out too far and tires. Flawed by her own mortality, like the bird with the broken wing, she falters—"her strength was gone." Kaleidoscopic images of the past flash through her mind reminding her of cast-off traditional connections, but they do not draw her back. Informed by her recent discoveries, she realizes it is too late for all that—"the shore was far behind her." Assuming the role of the courageous soul, one who "dares and defies," she indicates no desire to return or to be rescued. Like Taji in Melville's *Mardi*, when he was unable to find ultimate beauty in this world, Edna moves out through "the circumvallating reef" into the unknown regions beyond, thus extending her search into eternity. Her realization that the ideal she so desperately desires is not available to her as a mortal is her final discovery, the final phase of her awakening.

Whether the denouement of the novel is read literally as the renunciation of the unacceptable restrictions of mortal life or interpreted as a symbolic extension of the quest for ultimate freedom, the existential choice of self-determination is implicit.

—Clayton L. Eichelberger

BECAUSE I COULD NOT STOP FOR DEATH.
Poem by Emily Dickinson, written 1863.

According to Thomas H. Johnson, whose indispensable 1955 edition of Emily Dickinson's poetry established both canon and chronology, "Because I could not stop for Death" (J.712) was written in 1863, one of the three of those astonishingly prolific years in which she produced over one-third of the 1775 poems in the collection. Also included in the first collection of the poems in 1890, it was given a title, "The Chariot," and suffered other emendations by Thomas Wentworth Higginson, who deleted stanza four entirely and made such changes in diction as substituting "played" for "strove" in line nine: "where Children strove / At Recess—in the Ring—." It is the most famous of her proleptic poems (i.e., the persona speaks beyond the grave) and is typical of her work in that it fuses two of her most prevalent themes, death and courtship, and represents her major strategy, using the simple ballad stanza and natural or domestic images for elliptical and complex statement.

The six quatrains can be summarized as follows: 1) Death in the personification of a suitor calls on the speaker and takes her for a carriage ride, along with one other passenger named Immortality; 2) they ride slowly because Death is not in a hurry and the speaker has politely put aside both her work and play in order to go with him; 3) they pass familiar sights: schoolchildren, a field of grain, the sunset; 4) the temperature drops and the speaker becomes aware of her inadequate clothing; 5) they pause near an underground dwelling; 6) the centuries that have passed since then seem less long than the day the carriage ride began.

Neither this nor any other paraphrase can do justice to the multiplicity of interpretations inherent in the poem. Death may be construed as a courtly lover or a false seducer. Similarly, the speaker may be understood to be a willing or unwilling partner. The clothes imagery of the fourth stanza, a gown made of gossamer and a tippet of tulle, suggests both a bridal dress and a nun's habit. Most intriguing of all are the concluding lines:

> Since then—'tis Centuries—and yet
> Feels shorter than the Day
> I first surmised the Horse's Heads
> Were toward Eternity—

These might imply that the speaker is remembering the day of her death from beyond the grave, or that her escort has betrayed her by keeping her riding in limbo, or that she is expressing a death wish, or that she merely distinguishes between finitude ("the Day") and timelessness, or that she finds the human's lot of the realization of death to be so overwhelming that it makes time stand still.

Interpreters have remained constant in focusing attention on this poem, even as critical styles and emphases have changed. A 1932 essay by Allen Tate, calls it "one of the perfect poems in English" and praises it for its ambiguity. In 1960 Charles R. Anderson concentrated on the necessarily metaphoric language to express the inexpressible and saw the poem "flawless to the last detail." Sharon Cameron, in her 1979 study, *Lyric Time*, provides a post-structural reading, emphasizing the shifting back and forth between temporality and timelessness. Vivian R. Pollak (*Dickinson: The Anxiety of Gender*, 1984) and Jane Donahue Eberwein (*Dickinson: Strategies of Limitation*, 1985) offer feminist readings, one arguing that the speaker represents the poet, the other that the speaker is imaginary. According to

Richard B. Sewall's highly respected biography, the impulse for this poem might derive from Dickinson's hearing that an acquaintance, Olivia Coleman, died suddenly of tuberculosis while riding in a carriage. Eberwein reminds us that Dickinson wrote Abiah Root in 1846: "I almost wish there was no Eternity. To think that we must live forever and never cease to be." These biographical hints shed some light on the provenance and philosophical stance of the poem.

Technically, the poem is typical of Dickinson's eccentric style. Within the ballad form she is presumed to have adopted from familiar hymns, she incorporates here slant rhyme, unconventional capitalization, punctuation consisting almost entirely of dashes, syntactical peculiarities, puns ("Civility" and "gazing grain"), and elaborate personification. One atypical attribute is the colorlessness of its imagery. Ordinarily Dickinson uses color lavishly, as she does in the "Blue—uncertain, stumbling Buzz" of a companion proleptic poem, "I heard a Fly buzz—when I died" (J.465). The lack of color in J.712 is underscored by the filmy, ghost-like quality of "gossamer" and "tulle," and in turn underscores the cool, detached tone of one of the several masterpieces of this extraordinary poet.

—Nancy Carol Joyner

THE BIG SLEEP.
Novel by Raymond Chandler, 1939.

In "The Simple Art of Murder" Raymond Chandler poured scorn on the stylised decadence of "logic-and-deduction" detective stories, all exhibiting "the same old fussing around with timetables and bits of charred paper and who trampled the jolly old flowering arbutus under the library window." During the 1930's, beginning in the hard-boiled fiction of the pulp magazines, the crime novel was displacing the detective story. When at fifty Chandler wrote *The Big Sleep*, his first novel, he cannibalised whole chunks from several of the twenty short stories he had already written for the pulps.

Chandler, with literary ambitions, wanted to shift the emphasis from plot to character and style. Character sketches, not plot, make the opening hook for the reader. But character remains largely stereotype; style is Chandler's triumph. Out went ratiocination and the body in the library, in came tough talk, mean streets, fast violent action, and—in Marlowe—a hero whose idealism and sentimentality hides behind self-deprecating irony and wit. Marlowe is the man with a code of behaviour, the familiar figure of the frontier translated to the modern city. Originally called Mallory, he remained a knight: his search for damsels to rescue is figured in the stained-glass entrance of the Sternwood house on *The Big Sleep*'s first page. But Carmen, the novel's naked damsel, is to Chandler not worth saving. The irony is aimed not at knights but at a world which doesn't deserve them: "it wasn't a game for knights," Marlowe admits later.

Eddie Mars is the god behind most of the private wars. Marlowe cannot stop him, fails to clean up society, and in that sense is an anti-hero. There is also an absent hero, Rusty Regan, dead before the narrative begins, emphasizing the futility of Marlowe's quest. Regan and Marlowe brought joy and salvation to the Sternwoods and were to be thanked by being dumped in the sump, the source of their oil-rich wealth. In the depression of 1932 Chandler had been sacked from his oil company job for alcoholism; in the novel Carmen, not Marlowe, has the exotic drink problem. Marlowe and his oil-millionaire employer get on well when they meet man to man. This is Chandler's fantasy of revenge and self-justification. It is also a parable of the individualistic ethic and its contradictions. By living on his wits Marlowe escapes wage-slavery, yet must still seek employment: "I'm selling what I have to sell to make a living." Ideology as much as style makes for Chandler's appeal to intellectuals.

"Down these mean streets a man must go who is not himself mean, who is neither tarnished nor afraid," wrote Chandler of his hero. Marlowe may throw more wisecracks than punches, but in one way he is worse than mean: "Women made me sick." Part baby, part sexual predator, Carmen is the familiar schizoid stereotype of romanticism. Her "small corrupt body," her threatening sexuality, are the novel's signs of murderous insanity. Her sister Vivian ("She'd make a jazzy weekend, but she'd be wearing for a steady diet") is little better, for Chandler equates them when they both offer themselves to Marlowe in quick succession. There must be more to hate than this, but Marlowe's loves are no more plausible. Mona Mars, his obsession at the end, is a metal woman, with a wig "so platinumed that her hair shone like a silver fruit bowl" and a "silvery voice" with a "tiny tinkle" in it. He calls her "Silver-Wig," never using her name. In complete contrast, when Bogart played Marlowe his easy empathy with women became the driving force of the film. But in the book male attractiveness throws Marlowe as much as female, and the strident disgust at "fags," "queens," and "pansies," plus the mistrust of women, have led some to discern a savage repression of the homosexual element in Marlowe-Chandler. Going to bed with women is "letting them down." Chandler's English public-school attitudes are showing. Thankfully some of the women get their own back in kind: when Marlowe asks the dumb blonde Agnes whether he hurt her head, she replies, "You and every other man I ever met."

This novel's "mean streets" are hardly mean at all. Chandler loved the city, and Marlowe evokes it memorably as the coffee shop smell and the soot from the oil burners of the hotel drift in at his window. The streets are never cosier than when drenched by Chandler's insistent rain. Marlowe snuggles down in his car and watches the policemen in their rubber slickers which "shone like gun barrels" having fun carrying giggling girls through puddles. It is the suburbs, canyons, and empty country beyond the city which are this Marlowe's heart of darkness. Houses lurk low down behind their trees and shrubs. The imaginative deaths happen out of the city: Regan rotting in the lonely sump, Owen Taylor drowned off Lido pier, Geiger in his dark exotic house with the square box hedge masking the door completely and "no solid ground" around it. The book's two climaxes, the confrontations with Canino and with Carmen, have equally lonely settings. This jungle, not urban but "natural," is prefigured in the opening chapters with the "uncomfortable" line of the foothills and the orchids of Sternwood's conservatory, "nasty things" with flesh "too much like the flesh of men." Nature becomes comfortable only when tamed like the "flawless lines of the orange trees" which go "wheeling away like endless spokes into the night" as Marlowe drives to face Canino.

Later Chandler works were sometimes more perfect, sometimes more hesitant, than this fast-paced first novel. Though it is memorable for its action and for Marlowe talking out of the left side of his heart, it is this other aspect of style—the imagery of nature, the city, mirrors, rain, and the images of colour in the opening chapters—which truly constitutes the novel's imaginative intensity.

—R.J.C. Watt

BIG TWO-HEARTED RIVER.
Story by Ernest Hemingway, 1925.

"Big Two-Hearted River" is one of the great American short stories, although long by Ernest Hemingway's standards. It relates a single day's fishing excursion by a young man in Michigan's secluded upper peninsula. Nick Adams is the only character, and, as the reader comes to recognize, the real drama takes place in his psyche. Nevertheless, while Hemingway creates a memorable landscape (he had Cézanne in mind) of the far north country, he appeals to all of our senses (sight, touch, smell, taste, and sound) as he relates Nick's walk to the river, his preparation of camp, and his fishing for trout.

Often anthologized, the story is the first Hemingway writing that many readers encounter. Such readers will find much to admire and to intrigue them, but they will discover more of the story's complexity if they read it in the context of *In Our Time* (1925, revised 1930), Hemingway's first major book, an experimental work that confirmed his genius. Hemingway conceived of the story as the culmination to that work, which he thought of as much more than a gathering of his short stories. The book has, he insisted, a special unity.

"Big Two-Hearted River" returns the reader to Nick Adams, the character who figures prominently in the first several stories of *In Our Time*, stories that carry Nick in chronological order from his boyhood to the risky time when he lights out on his own, as he does in "The Battler," a story written especially for *In Our Time*. After that story Nick *seems* to disappear from the work. Then Hemingway boldly focuses attention on him in "Cross-Country Snow," the last in a group of four stories about young married people; there we learn that Nick has taken his place among the married, though earlier his friend Bill advised that marrying meant that a man was "absolutely bitched."

But no wives are mentioned in "Big Two-Hearted River." If Nick is not married in "Big Two-Hearted River," then that story departs from the chronological pattern that governs *In Our Time*. It is important to remember that although there are parallels between Nick's life and Hemingway's, there are also many differences. Though this story is based on a trip Hemingway took the year before his marriage to Hadley Richardson, material that he excised from "Big Two-Hearted River" indicates that he had thought of Nick there as a married man. In any case, memories of women are, by design, kept minimal. Women mean complexities, Nick learned, and his fishing trip is an effort to simplify his life. Despite a shaky beginning to his journey, things begin to go better simply because he is a disciplined traveler. "Nick felt he had left everything behind, the need for thinking, the need to write, other needs." Although the story is pronouncedly a male affair (even the trout Nick catches are male), the context of *In Our Time* suggests that Nick has to work through numerous problems, many of them having to do with women. There is the mother he rejects ("The Doctor and the Doctor's Wife"), the ruined romance with Marge ("The End of Something"), and possibly a greater trauma suggested by the rejection of the unnamed protagonist by Luz in "A Very Short Story" near the middle of *In Our Time*. This experience suggests the turning point, perhaps the most important loss Nick had yet experienced.

Interchapter VI, juxtaposed tightly against "A Very Short Story," suggests another major trauma. The chapter commences "Nick sat against the wall of the church," where he has been carried after being badly wounded in shelling on the Italian front. The interchapters of the first half of *In Our Time*, all concerned with war, have acted as counterpart to the cluster of stories about Nick's youth that begin the book. Although the book contains no stories about Nick's war experiences, "Big Two-Hearted River" reveals a young man still coming to terms with the destruction of the war and his own close brush with death. In "Big Two-Hearted River" Nick returns to a place removed from the late conflict, but he remembers it as he passes through the ruins of Seney, Michigan, burned to the ground. Life contains many destructions.

For a time Nick is stunned as he surveys the burnt-out country in and around Seney. But he slowly rallies, finding in nature abiding values that enable him to carry a heavy load to a well-earned rest as night falls. He rises refreshed the next morning to test his nerves in the drama of trout fishing, not wishing to rush his sensations or even to catch many fish. He looks to make small gains so that he can later make big gains—perhaps even to write the stories about the war that are not found in *In Our Time*. We catch a vision of the challenge Nick faces through the image of the dark swamp. Nick wisely refrains from entering it now: "In the swamp fishing was a tragic adventure. Nick did not want it. He did not want to go down the stream any further today." He will save that psychic journey for another time.

The "Big Two-Hearted River" comes to symbolize the stream-of-life—its challenges, its affirmations and its denials, finally the reality of death. Although the Nick who goes fishing in it has a specific history (evoked most concretely in the story through memories of his friend Hopkins near the end of the first part of the two-part story), Nick also becomes archetypal. As he walks through the forest toward "the good place" that he seeks, he is like John Bunyan's Pilgrim, who shoulders a heavy load before finding a satisfactory rest. And Nick Adams is never more Adamic than he is in this story. He experiences anew the innocence he had earlier lost, finds the primal energy that will enable him to pursue again the challenge of creation. Although many of Hemingway's stories deal with loss, he ended *In Our Time* with a story of affirmation and hope, but not of false promise. "There were plenty of days when he could fish the swamp."

—Joseph M. Flora

BILLY BUDD.
Novel by Herman Melville, 1924 (written 1888–91).

Billy Budd is a classic because it deals with universal themes with the insight and artistry of a great writer. The themes are the timeless questions: What is the source of evil? Is there ultimate justice? What is the worth of the individual? What philosophy can an honest man accept? In his masterpiece, *Moby-Dick* (1851), Herman Melville explored these issues through the first-person narrator, Ishmael (symbol of all the spiritually disinherited). In the end everyone except the philosophizing narrator goes down with the whale (symbol of a cruelly impersonal universe). Thus the author judges Romanticism's "noble savage," Humanism's "superman," and Christianity's "first mate" inadequate. He is left clinging to partial truths drifting on an ocean of doubt. Forty years later, in a style equally rich in symbolism and allusion, Melville reduces the scale of setting and characters but deepens his perceptions of the major truths.

In *Billy Budd*, instead of primeval forces or a megalomaniac, tragedy is introduced through the credible villainy of a petty officer. The "noble savage" is no longer a Pacific Island prince with power over life and death but an illiterate British seaman. The Christian is no longer the cautious first mate of a New England whaler but the noble captain of a British man-o'-war and a learned gentleman. The author no longer speaks through a youthful critic of society but as the author, sympathetic to all facets of the drama. Thus he finds Claggart's evil baffling but concedes the man is powerless to resist it. He acknowledges the brutality of war but approves the character of the naval chaplain and justifies Vere's decision to sacrifice one for the good of all.

By historical incident, reasoned argument, symbolism, and allusion Melville argues that this life is an ironic mixture of good and evil that will be set right by the "Last Assizes" (Final Judgment). The Great Mutiny was a "monstrous" evil, but it led to good. Vere (truth) reminds the drumhead court that a decision based on compassion for Billy risks mutiny, a tragedy for many. When the ship (society) engages the enemy, the *Athéiste* (atheist), it defeats it but at terrible cost, for Vere is mortally wounded. However, he dies with Billy's name on his lips, not in remorse but in the conviction that they are to be reunited. Other allusions support this basically Christian position. Of Claggart's death Vere exclaims, "It is the divine judgment of Ananias" (Acts 5:1–5). Vere's farewell to Billy is likened to that of Abraham about to sacrifice his son, Isaac, a test of obedience to God. Billy and the crew call out "God bless Captain Vere"; Billy's hanging becomes an Ascension (victory over death), and chips of the spar from which he was hanged become as pieces of the Cross to his shipmates (lasting influence for good).

Attention to the wealth of allusion and symbolism reveals Melville's perception of the complexity of this life and the spiritual universe it imperfectly reflects. For example, Billy is described as "young Adam before the Fall," but is, of course, living in the world after the Fall. His appearance implies that his mother was "eminently favored by Love and the Graces," but these gifts were used to produce a "foundling." Billy's tan (sea-going experience) has subdued the lily (purity) but not the rose (passion) in him. The Dansker, an "old sea-Chiron" (tutor to Achilles and Hercules) names Billy "Baby Budd," identifying his fatal immaturity. Captain Graveling calls him a "peacemaker," saying a "virtue went out of him" (as in Jesus's healing); Lieutenant Ratcliffe replies, "blessed are the peacemakers [Matt. 5:9], especially the fighting peacemakers." The *Rights of Man* loses Billy to the demands of society's survival, but while he loses some of his rights, he gains opportunity to prove his worth (Vere was about to recommend him to the captaincy of the mizentop).

Perhaps the most significant symbol is speech, a paramount achievement of civilized man. Its skillful use is essential to most of society's functions. It is also a major indicator of the individual's mental, emotional, and spiritual condition. Thus Vere uses it successfully to command his ship and to win the trust and affection of Billy. He perceives its misuse by Claggart, urges its careful use upon Billy. Billy's failure to use it under inner stress is the crucial evidence of his immaturity.

Melville wrote his earlier sea tales during a period of rapid expansion in America's size, wealth, and power, but, like his friend Hawthorne, he challenged the popular optimism by portraying the tragic aspects of Nature, Society, and Individualism. As the biographical nature of his material gave way to his increasingly painful spiritual struggles, his work grew richer but darker. In this final work the gloom is dissipated by acceptance of concepts that restore beauty to youth, honor to leadership, value to society, victory to goodness.

—Esther Marian Greenwell Smith

THE BRIDGE.
Poem by Hart Crane, 1930.

In his essay "Modern Poetry" (1930) Hart Crane argued that ". . . unless poetry can absorb the machine, i.e., *acclimatize* it as naturally and casually as trees, cattle, galleons, castles and all other human associations of the past, then poetry has failed of its full contemporary function." In fact Crane seems to have done more than simply "acclimatize" the machine as a subject for poetry. It would seem that in a sense he created poems as machines are created, and perhaps in turn the machine is useful as a metaphor to understand how Crane's poem achieves its objective.

The Bridge, like the structure it celebrates, is a work of creative engineering. In a remarkable letter which Crane wrote to his patron Otto Kahn while *The Bridge* was in progress, he discusses his work on the poem as dryly and objectively as an engineer might detail his plans for a new kind of engine or a new road. It is clear that Crane quite consciously developed his metrical and symbolic patterns and strategies for the poem on the basis of his close study of French symbolism and the metrics of the Elizabethans, Donne, and other early English poets. Traditional prosody was as immutable to his poetic sensibility as the laws of physics which dictated the essential form of the Brooklyn Bridge. Crane used that prosody to realize his poem in much the way that John Fitch, John Stevens, and other early American engineers used the steam engine to make new forms of transportation: one adapted one's vision to whatever means—metrical or mechanical—were available.

The poetic vision at the center of *The Bridge*—a vision of the American spirit as endowed with quasi-divine strength and purpose—came largely from Whitman, but Crane seems to have had little interest in, or at least understanding of, Whitman's prosody. For Whitman it was essential to develop a new poetics, a new way of speaking, in order to express his special vision of the American spirit; the language and the vision are not in fact separate or separable. For Crane, however, prosody and vision were not at all the same; the second was in effect a device at the service of the first.

Crane's very conservative poetics obviously set off *The Bridge* from the work of older modernist poets such as William Carlos Williams and Marianne Moore, and the Whitmanesque optimism which much of the poem embodies was largely at odds with much serious poetry being published. (It was at this time, after all, that Eliot's *The Waste Land* was having its impact on the sensibilities of new poets.) But if the great optimism of *The Bridge* is seldom found in the work of subsequent poets, the influence of Crane's synthesis of traditional English poetics, French symbolism, and American subjects can be clearly seen in the work of such "academic" poets as Robert Lowell, notably in "The Quaker Graveyard in Nantucket."

The Bridge is divided into eight sections, preceded by "To Brooklyn Bridge," eleven tightly shaped, metrically precise, rhymed quatrains which show Crane's symbolist technique at its most intense and in which the bridge is poetically raised to divine significance: "Unto the lowliest sometime sweep, descend / And of the curveship lend a myth to God." With its powerful mixture of sublime conviction and absolute metrical control, "To Brooklyn Bridge" is among Crane's most impressive achievements, and several of the poems which follow are also of an equally high order. Among the best certainly are "Atlantis," "The River," "Ave Maria," and "Cape Hatteras," in which the poet confronts his mentor, Whitman.

In "Cape Hatteras" the airplane serves Crane as the equivalent of the railroad in "Passage to India," Whitman's celebration of technology. Later in "The Tunnel," the poet meets Poe ("Your eyes like agate lanterns") in the dark, violent world of the subway—also, of course, a railroad but, unlike Whitman's, one suggesting discord, anger, and fear. Crane takes Whitman's vision but expands it with moral and emotional complexities that his predecessor could not, or would not, acknowledge. Poe's nightmare sensibility cannot be excluded from Crane's America, but it does not finally weaken or damage the sublime Whitmanesque optimism that is at the center of *The Bridge*. The poem ends with the same ecstatic affirmation of its vision as that with which it began.

In spite of that ecstatic affirmation, however, one senses that it is less the Whitmanesque vision itself than the poet's own will which fuses his poem into a single effective unit. Read separately, parts of *The Bridge*, particularly "Indiana," seem weak and sentimental. But behind even the weakest parts, Crane's determination to unify *The Bridge* can be felt. It is that determination and fixed delight in making things, in engineering things, that may be seen as the ultimate motivating power in *The Bridge* and perhaps the chief reason it continues to astonish us.

—Edward Halsey Foster

THE CALL OF THE WILD.
Novel by Jack London, 1903.

In the Soviet Union, Jack London is regarded as one of the greatest of American writers, chiefly because of such sentiments as are found in now-obscure works of his such as "A Night with the Philomaths." There he has a firebrand orating about a revolution of the proletariat

> twenty-five millions strong . . . to make rulers and ruling classes pause and consider. The cry of this army is: No quarter! We want all that you possess. We want in our hands the reins of power and the destiny of mankind. . . . We are going to take your governments, your palaces, and all your purpled ease away from you, and in that day you shall work for your bread even as the peasant in the field or the starved and runty clerk in your metropolises. . . . You have failed in your management of society, and your management is to be taken away from you. . . . This is the revolution, my masters. Stop it if you can.

However, the early poverty and struggle that drew London to Marx and to communist or socialist ideology as he read books in the Klondike winter were followed by success and belief, according to Charles Child Walcutt, in himself as "an epitome of the Darwinian Struggle for Existence, his success an example of the [Herbert] Spencerian Survival of the Fittest." He had also read Nietzsche, and he came to people his prolific output of fiction with supermen, heroes who could succeed without or in spite of either communism or democracy, heroes that were not so much self-sacrificing socialists as rapacious capitalists of the spirit. They conquered by force of will and indomitable courage rather than by cleverness. In the great American tradition, they "hung in there"; and when the going got tough, they got tougher. London liked to think of himself as one of these semi-divine heroes. A newspaper reporter once noticed that his Korean houseboy called London "Mr. God." The reporter added, "Jack liked it."

In London's most popular novel, *The Call of the Wild*, the hero is a dog—the story is told entirely from the dog Buck's point of view—and even when ill treatment causes him to revert to the "dominant primordial beast" he is a symbol of what man can do to overcome obstacles and become the leader of his fellows. A mongrel, a cross between a German Shepherd and a St. Bernard, Buck is uprooted, stolen from his comfortable California home, and sold for work as a sled dog in the Gold Rush of 1897. Then he becomes the companion and eventually the savior of a young prospector. Finally he becomes the leader of a wild pack, and the book ends with these triumphant and famous words:

> When the long winter nights come on and the wolves follow their meat into the lower valleys, he may be seen running at the head of the pack through the pale moonlight or glimmering borealis, leaping gigantic above his fellows, his great throat a-bellow as he sings a song of the younger world, which is the song of the pack.

In some sense Buck is a representation of the author as he would like to see himself. An illegitimate child of a spiritualist (who later married John London, not his father), London quit school at 14, worked in a cannery, became a pirate on the ship *Razzle Dazzle* in San Francisco Bay at 16 and a sailor to Siberia and Japan at 17, tramped around, and went to the Klondike in 1897. There he found more adventure, opportunity for the will to power, risk and challenge and self-fulfillment, freedom from civilization's restraints—the life suited to a man who once said "morality is only an evidence of low blood pressure."

London returned from the Klondike without gold but with a rich vein of wilderness experiences which he industriously mined thereafter. *The Call of the Wild* is but one of his tales of heroism and violence in circumstances of danger. Where Bret Harte told the story of "A Yellow Dog" that became a snob in the gold fields and Eric Knight was to sentimentalize canine faithfulness in *Lassie Come-Home*, London told the tale of a dog who went from snob to superdog. London's was a rousing tale that had a message as well as a love for mankind.

London, who always had more drive than deftness in writing, was extremely clever to focus on Buck rather than on the human world around him. Judge Miller, by whose Santa Clara, California, fireside the young Buck lay in innocence and peace before he was "dognapped," has more of a function than a character in the book. John Thornton, the strong, silent, noble type to whom Buck becomes attached in the Yukon, is a stereotype: we provide his qualities from other reading rather than discover them in the novel. "Black" Burton and other bad guys are also stock characters. So are the greenhorns and the French-Canadians and the other humans. The animals, however, are sufficiently humanized, and if they, too, are stereotypes we are more impressed with the personalities they are given than with their lack of depth. Pike (the thief), Dub (the clumsy one), Dave and Sol-leks (the sled dogs who are dedicated "professionals"), Curly (the amiable Newfoundland dog) who "made advances to a husky dog the size of a full-grown wolf" and was "ripped open from eye to jaw" in an instant—these animals each have their place in the story and can be said to be characters in the fiction in a sense in which the humans are not. Among the dogs are the "bully" personalities so beloved of the Teddy Roosevelt period of American history. Among them is clearly shown "the law of club and fang": "So that was the way. No fair play. Once down, that was the end of you." Among them, also, there are treachery and nobility, faithfulness unto death, and a conviction that moral nature is "a vain thing and a handicap in the ruthless struggle for existence." They learn that "kill or be killed, eat or be eaten, was the law. . . ." Towering above all is Buck. "When he was made, the mould was broke," says Pete. And in awkward dialect Hans affirms: "Py jingo! I t'ink so mineself."

That a good deal of the book is given to describing the feelings of the animals is an advantage in the light of London's clumsiness with cliché ("Every animal was motionless as though turned to stone") and dialogue ("Plumb tuckered out, that's what's the matter"). The action moves swiftly; we are seldom aware of the "stoppages" of the sleds or that characters are "lessoned," of the awkward prolepsis or the literary infelicities, as the melodramatic tale unfolds of how Buck "put his name many notches higher on the totem pole of Alaskan fame." We discover that sentiment can exist without a love story; Mercedes, the only woman in the book, is a shadow. Popular writers discover that a riveting story, as of the "kidnapped king" tried in the furnace and emerging pure gold (or "a yellow metal," as London would say), is enough.

Those who want more can see London as a racist, fascist, Social Darwinist; as a predecessor of Kerouac and other "on the road" writers; as a tough-guy writer in the tradition developed by Dos Passos, Hemingway, Mailer, though perhaps best exemplified in Dashiell Hammett and other writers of crime fiction; as a writer about animals (such as Buck and the wolf-dog that seeks civilization in *White Fang*) foreshadowing Orwell's *Animal Farm* in using them as metaphors of humanity; as a giant in his time—in 1913 the most popular and best-paid writer in the world—who was denigrated in later times; as (to note Andrew Sinclair's argument) a path-finder in areas as different as the boxing novel and sociobiology of the school of Lorenz, Ardrey, Desmond Morris.

In the biography *Jack* (1977), Sinclair makes a gallant effort to rescue London from too close identification with the message that "a man with a club was a law-giver, a master to be obeyed" and the view of "nature red in tooth and claw." Sinclair does much to bring him to serious consideration as much more than a once-popular author, an author of juvenile literature, the master of the dog story. Nonetheless, London's place in literary history depends now and always will depend on the appeal of *The Call of the Wild*.

—Leonard R.N. Ashley

THE CANTOS.
Poems by Ezra Pound, from 1925.

The *Cantos* of Ezra Pound are a work of 802 pages in the current Faber 1975 edition (reprinted from the earlier New Directions editions). They are the chief product of the author's very active writing life, the continuous though not the sole project of the years 1909–59. He always wanted to write an epic ("a poem containing history" and "the tale of the tribe"); the result is his greatest achievement, *pace* those who prefer his earlier poems or even his criticism. The ostensible purpose of the *Cantos* is to show the history of the West from its mythical origins in the world of the *Odyssey*, through various ideal societies, through its eventual perversion in the triumph of mercantile avarice in an industrial society run by presbyterian bankers—to its final crash in 1914. There are 117 cantos, issued in ten volumes between 1925 and 1969, a canto being a sequence of between two and twenty pages in length. Each is devoted to a single subject often presented dramatically and from sharply opposed angles. The mode of presentation is dramatic and lyrical rather than discursive or analytic, and the author's views are not stated, though it is clear, for example, that he is against usury (Canto 45) and in favour of the founding fathers of the American republic. The technique is frequently of a moving tableau or montage of images, a concentrated style developed for shorter poems in the period of imagism.

The result is full of historical "piths and gists," of magically evocative landscapes and crucial moments. The lack of a unified narrative and of an explicit discourse makes the reading of the *Cantos* a disconnected experience, especially after *The Pisan Cantos* (1948), a dramatic monologue from the poet's cell in the U.S. Army camp outside Pisa in 1945: "from the ruins of Europe, *ego scriptor*." Thereafter the poem, though chiefly concerned with periods of pre-modern history, becomes increasingly, though sometimes unwittingly, an intellectual autobiography, as the guide nears the end of his guided tour. As well as an Odyssean exploration of cultural experience, the *Cantos* are intermittently modelled on a Dante-like ascent from hell through purgatory to heaven, though the steps are not obvious and Aquinas's map useless to a humanist. Hell and purgatory are full of usurers, war-profiteers, and newspapers, heaven is a mythical Mediterranean landscape of ideal city states run by just rulers and full of cafés, nymphs, temples, and goddesses, where farmers, craftsmen, and artists can flourish. Pound preferred Italy to Philadelphia, the old world to the new, and being looked at by Beatrice to listening to Virgil. His own political ideals are various, from the Confucius who in Canto

XIII says "When the prince has gathered about him / All the savants and artists, his riches will be fully employed," to the lawgivers of Byzantium and mediaeval England, to the reformist founders Jefferson and Napoleon, and to unorthodox men of will and destiny such as Sigismundo Malatesta of Rimini and Benito Mussolini. Pound wants a just society by good government in the interests of the more productive of the people, in a curious combination of a Ruskinian mediaeval organic society (such as one sees in Ambrogio Lorenzetti's fresco of Good Government in the Palazzo Pubblico at Siena), with a free American individualism which seems at odds with so harmonious a vision. Though Pound advocated Social Credit economics in the middle cantos, practical political contradictions do not have to be resolved because the *Cantos* work by the juxtaposition of fragments in a way Pound called "ideogrammic," contrasting various kinds of good government or individual conduct with their opposites rather than by articulating the relations of various social goods. Though full of actualities and documented facts, the *Cantos* are primarily concerned with these as instances of ideals in action. Their moments of splendid coherence are lyrical rather than systematic. Pound's *Cantos* are the greatest, as well as the longest, long poem in English of this century; only David Jones's *The Anathemata* bears comparison. Pound's epic is greatest in ambition and in achievement, and in its radical challenge to received cultural history; in scope, range, and variety, and in voice, image, music, and finesse. The chief disadvantage of the poem is not its difficulty of reference but its scale and structure, and its serial production. In their ventriloquism, allusiveness, and multicultural fragmentariness the *Cantos* resemble *The Waste Land* (for which the first seven cantos prepared the way). Pound, having cut *The Waste Land* severely, described it as "19 pages, and let us say the longest poem in the English langwidge" (sic). The *Cantos* are 40 times as long as *The Waste Land*, and organized less visibly. Joyce's *Ulysses* eventually becomes more unreadable than the *Cantos*, but it did appear in one volume.

The first thirty cantos centre on the individualist world of Italian Renaissance princes, their lust for beauty and order in art in contrast with their lust for power in their lives; here the successful rebel Sigismundo Malatesta is Pound's hero. A second contrast, between the Quattrocento and a perverted modern world, is insisted upon; and the economic theme becomes strident in the middle cantos, counterpointed with paradisal visions of Chinese and Mediterranean historical epochs and landscapes. From Canto 42 onwards the enlightened 18th-century republics of Siena and the United States are presented, with a Confucian digest of the history of China. Cantos 71–2, in Italian, defending the Italian republic of Mussolini, do not appear in English editions. The Pisan cantos articulate a seared vision of a world seen from the "death cells" at Pisa. Thereafter the personal and visionary parts of the poem are markedly more successful than the chunks of "objective" historical celebration of ideal states and just cities. The fragmentariness of the units of composition increases as the poem goes on, but so does the poet's refinement of skill in creating a vocal weave and a musical organisation for his perceptions, his nuggets of historical and actual fact, and his memories. The *Cantos* are not, as extracts may suggest, a lecture with a machine-gun, but a sustained conversation with the reader. Pound is a great talker in verse, often with a self-ironic or interrogative note, as well as a lyric celebrant of the world of eye and ear.

—M.J. Alexander

THE CATCHER IN THE RYE.
Novel by J.D. Salinger, 1951.

When J.D. Salinger published *The Catcher in the Rye* in 1951, it met with mixed reviews but soon became a tremendous success among young people, who felt that Salinger was speaking to them directly. The novelist Joan Didion reports meeting a typical Salinger fan in 1956, a young woman from Sarah Lawrence who declared that Salinger was the only person in the world capable of understanding her. In the 1960's members of the youth culture who read Salinger's later stories hoping to find enlightenment in the conversations of the Glass family continued to read *Catcher* as a testament to the emptiness of the "establishment." Today the novel is more often assigned in English courses than passed from friend to friend, but it continues to find a number of enthusiastic readers outside the classroom.

The Catcher in the Rye has been read both as the story of a neurotic who cannot make the "adjustments" necessary to adult life and as the story of an outsider who can see clearly, with the vision of a child or a saint, the horrors of mid-century American life which are not visible to those comfortably ensconced within it. The novel is a long monologue by Holden Caulfield, who tells the story of "this madman stuff that happened to me around last Christmas," the events of three days in a bleak, loveless New York City, where Holden has fled after flunking out of his third prep school. He is in flight from what he sees as the unbearably "phony" world of prep school snobbery, stupidity, and cruelty, and from a future in which he can do no more than "make a lot of dough and play golf and play bridge and buy cars and drink Martinis and look like a hotshot."

Holden is an outcast like Huck Finn, and like Huck he tells his story in his own idiom. Holden's voice is not merely a virtuoso re-creation of contemporary adolescent speech. His profanity reflects his experience of a "goddam"-ed life, a "hell." He repeatedly insists that he is telling the truth ("I really did," "It really is") because in his experience and by his rigorous standards, most people do *not* speak the truth. He prefaces his revelations with "if you really want to hear about it," "if you really want to know," and "if you want to know the truth," because he has found that few people *do* want to know the truth.

Holden feels a scathing, harrowing disgust for the "phoniness" he senses so acutely all around him. It makes him literally ill. He is repulsed not only by the insincerity and self-promotion of the "phonies," "hot-shots," "jerks," "bastards," and "morons," but by the phoniness that is excellence corrupted: Holden's brother D.B., the Lunts, and Ernie the piano player are corrupted by the success of what they do well. Holden himself is implicated in the pretense that so disgusts him; we see him do those things for which he castigates others, and he is half-aware of the fact. But in the midst of his revulsion he is moved by pity and forgiving love for the people who appall him.

His story is full of failed attempts to communicate, messages never delivered, uncompleted phone calls, overtures not taken up, appeals repulsed. William Faulkner, who praised the novel, said that when Holden "attempted to enter the human race, there was no human race there." In his great trouble, Holden attempts to address serious questions to Mr. Spencer, to Sally Hayes, to Carl Luce, to Mr. Antolini; no one can really hear him. All interchanges prove sour and barren. When Holden despairs of ever getting through to anybody, he decides in furious disgust to run away and stop trying: "I thought what I'd do was, I'd pretend I was one of those deaf-mutes. That way I wouldn't have to have any goddam stupid useless conversations with anybody."

One literal message does get delivered: Holden's note to his little sister Phoebe, significantly, does reach her. Phoebe receives the message, and she is the only one who listens to him. And it is Phoebe, finally, who brings Holden back to some unresolved relationship with the world he is fleeing. At his lowest point in the novel, alone in the defaced mummies' tomb in the museum, he ascends to find her dragging a heavy suitcase, begging to run away with him; he finds that he cannot be responsible for taking her away from what she finds hopeful and good even in the world he so distrusts.

Holden wishes that Phoebe could remain safe in beautiful and innocent childhood; this feeling is allied to his grief for his brother Allie who died at ten, Phoebe's age. He wants what is "nice" to be proof against change; he dreams of saving children from falling "over the cliff" into the adult world, so much of which disgusts him. Phoebe's redeeming love makes him realize that he cannot keep her from "falling": "The thing with kids is, if they want to grab for the gold ring, you have to let them do it. . . . If they fall off, they fall off. . . ." It is not at all clear whether Holden can (or should) compromise with the life expected of him, but he will not lure Phoebe into total retreat, and she saves him from it.

—Mollie Sandock

CATCH-22.
Novel by Joseph Heller, 1961.

Joseph Heller's *Catch-22* is essentially a postmodern war novel. It recreates and mocks, simultaneously, the tradition of ironic and grim war fiction that culminated in the separate peace sought by Ernest Hemingway's characters. And Heller's book deconstructs all wars and establishments: ostensibly about World War II, but written after Korea, and published during Vietnam, *Catch-22* parodies the American business, religious, and political hegemonies that the military echelons reflect.

The humor of *Catch-22* appeared to Philip Toynbee to resemble a Marx brothers film as Kafka might have conceived it. The novel is apocalyptic and lunatic, illogical and post-Christian. And very funny. A work also of black humor, *Catch-22* has a hero in Yossarian who not only perceives the system's venality and corruption but ultimately makes an existential choice for freedom. To leave the insane war—where men are suborned to bomb their own units for business purposes, where pilots are sacrificed for their superior officers' records, where the good and the innocent become victims—is not to desert in the face of the enemy but to refuse to help this enemy within; as Walt Kelly's Pogo remarked, "We have met the enemy, and he is us."

Heller has admitted that his novel is "about the contemporary regimented business society" and satirizes oil claims, public relations, psychiatry, racism, loyalty oaths, and security trials as well as larger American idealistic constructs such as sportsmanship, success, patriotism, and abstract morality: the Protestant Ethic and the American Dream. Heller writes of war in terms of contemporary philosophy, raising matters of time's indeterminacy, phenomenology, alienation, and illogic. Like a Swift, Heller apologizes for his soldiers' revolts because in the absurd world of war, the men revolt against what *is* revolting. And Heller's vision is such that in doing so they convert revolutionary anger into sardonic comedy.

There are four basic character divisions in this novel that traces a bomber squadron's missions during the Italian campaign; their drunken and sex-obsessed leaves in Rome; their absorption into the business enterprises of the madly corrupt mess officer Milo Minderbinder who cheats and steals to the motto "What's good for M & M Enterprises is good for the country," even to the extent of arranging to bomb American bases and steal their morphine; their attempts to stop the ever-increasing numbers of missions to be flown before the pilots can go home; their disappearances and deaths. First there are the purely corrupt, ambitious men who use their fellow humans: the Colonels Cathcart and Korn, Generals Dreedle and Peckham, and officers who accept the system, Cargill, Scheisskopf, Black, Whitcomb, Aarfy; they are all, like Aarfy, murderers. At the opposite end of the spectrum are the outsiders, good men trapped in and mostly wiped out by this system: Nately, Chief White Halfoat (whose family history as a Native American is appallingly awful and humorous), Hungry Joe, McWatt, Danby, Dunbar, the Chaplain. Yossarian is one of them, and momentarily their leader, for in refusing to fly any more missions, he saves the remnant. While the third character group is predatory, too, each is so outrageously comic and so self-aware of rapacity, that the individuals are only evil in the sense of a Groucho Marx or W.C. Fields persona: Milo, ex-Pfc Wintergreen, Doc Daneeka, even Clevinger, Major Major Major, and Major ________ de Coverly. Fourth, there are those who carry the novel's serious subtext, the dead who never were alive in the book: the unknown soldier Mudd who did not officially get on the roster, Kraft, the invisible soldier in the hospital, and, crucially, Snowden, whose ghastly death in Yossarian's arms over Avignon recurs again and again in a T.S. Eliot-like litany that raises the overwhelming question, What is Man? (Just matter, entrails.) In categories of their own are the women nurses who are only objects of lust, and Orr, the wise squirrel of a pragmatist who tries to teach Yossarian how to crash and escape by raft to Sweden.

In many important ways the novel is deeply religious as it moves from portraying Yossarian as a mock-savior eschewing false gods of violence and business—Heller stated that he was depicting business society "against the background of universal sorrow and inevitable death"—to showing his paranoia become valid when he makes a terrible night journey through a devastated Rome where "The night was filled with horrors, and he thought he knew how Christ must have felt as he walked through the world. . . ." Heller asserts that the comic world of American bomber squadrons is a function of the tragic world of beaten children and murdered whores. Thus, Yossarian's refusal to be tempted by the Colonels who would save him at the price of betrayal of his fellow pilots, his commitment to himself, to the young sister of a dead whore, to Sweden—freedom—turn *Catch-22* from a war novel of despair to a universal fiction that ends in hope, in the admission of the protagonist's humanity, into a leap for freedom and responsibility (just as Ralph Ellison's Invisible Man will rise from underground), in the acceptance of contingency and a war against war. All this and marvelous comic writing too make *Catch-22* one of the great war novels of this century.

—Eric Solomon

THE CATHEDRAL.
Poem by James Russell Lowell, 1870.

James Russell Lowell's *The Cathedral* is a neglected major American poem. First printed in 1869 and given final revised form for an edition of Lowell's collected works in 1890, it is richly representative of Lowell as poet, and profoundly reflective of his historical time and nationality. It is no less revealingly and impressively the product of a timeless human struggle.

How God is to be defined or man to fix his relationship to Him—the old question of faith—is the burden of *The Cathedral*. Consisting of 813 lines of blank verse in 21 unnumbered sections, it is an extended meditation, a verse essay. Historically it is important as a transitional work between romanticism and modernism. While its diction, syntax, and rhetoric may sometimes convey the flavor of a static 19th-century poetic product, its dominant, modernist impact is of a shared process, of experiencing an individual mind in search of answers.

The Cathedral was inspired by a visit to Chartres when Lowell was in France in the summer of 1855. The day of his visit was "clear and lucent," truly "superb," he reported to a friend at the time, and the Chartres cathedral was "wonderful," "very grand." Never, he wrote, had he "heard finer music than the wind made among the stone chords of the spire"; the cathedral "was almost enough in itself for a lifetime." Fourteen years later a poem based upon the experience "wrote itself"—just "all of a sudden it was *there*," Lowell claimed. "I hope it is good," he said in a letter just after the intense period of the poem's creation, "for it fairly trussed me at last and bore me up as high as my poor lungs will bear into the heaven of invention." "It is a kind of religious poem. . . ."

Its original title of *A Day at Chartres* indicates the germinal, concentrated personal experience out of which *The Cathedral* was written and which remains a powerful emotional factor and the narrative, structural framework of the finished poem. It is with the memory of this particular day that the poem opens—a day "Cloudless of care, down-shod to every sense, / And simply perfect from its own resource"—but transition is quickly made through other "such days" to general philosophical considerations, classically Romantic in concept and Transcendental in assertion ("I find my own complexion everywhere"). In this concern with memory and experience, thought and Fancy, Nature and Self, the presence of a distinct individual is strong, and is straightforwardly accounted for: "I know not how it is with other men / Whom I but guess, deciphering myself." Introduced into the poem, then, before the return to "a day at Chartres" in line 179 are the themes of loss and doubt, and a sense of individual struggle with questions that are personal because they are universal.

Visiting the cathedral, which is "Imagination's very self in stone," the poet is visited by major questions about supernatural faith. Although he tries to believe himself "a happy Goth," he realizes that he is a "child of an age that lectures, not creates," of an "age that blots out life with question-marks." "Ancient faith" is "irrecoverable," he concludes; "each age must worship its own thought of God." In the cathedral and elsewhere "where others worship," the poet can "but look and long," and yet, reaching a tentative resolution, he is thankful that "seeing where God *has* been," it may be possible to "trust in Him."

Such respite from doubt is short-lived, however, for Time and Change and an overwhelming sense of the present return to dominate the poet's thoughts. An American, he seizes upon Democracy and its New World Man as perhaps the hope, the answer, of the future. But this belief, this hope, cannot be sustained either. The poet walks saddened from the cathedral, and in his turning, parting look gets a hint of a solution from seeing sparrow-hawks above sparrows on the cathedral. Moving from interpreting this sight to another natural analogy of root and tree-top, the poet finds consoling "evidence of Thee so far above / Yet in and of me!" His final fear, the expression of which concludes *The Cathedral*, is not of God's non-existence or His withdrawal from man, but of "seeing, to know Thee not," of himself and other men's failing to recognize God "in the commonplace of miracle." This conclusion, as a modern commentator has noted, should be "seen as hope rather than as homily," "an appropriate and valiant ending to a challenging poem."

The Cathedral invites comparison, looking back, to Tennyson's *In Memoriam* and Matthew Arnold's "Stanzas from the Grande Chartreuse" and, looking forward, to Henry Adams's *Mont-Saint-Michel and Chartres* and *The Education of Henry Adams* and T.S. Eliot's *Four Quartets*. John Ruskin found its "main substance" "most precious," "its separate lines sometimes unbetterable."

The change of title to *The Cathedral* is significant, adding to the poem's meaning and emphasizing inspired human art. Lowell wrote that in his work he could see "a bit of clean carving here and there, a solid buttress or two, and perhaps a gleam through painted glass." Indeed there are parallels between what he created and the building that inspired it, including the grotesque that results in the poem from co-existence of the humorous, down-to-earth, very-consciously-American Lowell and the learned Harvard-professor, very-consciously-European Lowell. But Lowell's craftsmanship often impresses itself upon a reader, particularly in individual lines. And if, philosophically and spiritually, solid buttresses are harder to come by, they do exist in *The Cathedral*. About, metaphorically, its providing at least "a gleam through painted glass," there can be no doubt.

—Bert Hitchcock

COMMON SENSE.
Essay by Thomas Paine, 1776.

Thomas Paine's little pamphlet *Common Sense* is one of those books that changed the world. Like *Uncle Tom's Cabin, The Communist Manifesto*, or *The Origin of Species*, it had the effect of altering men's minds with consequences that were far-reaching and long-lasting. No one could have predicted such a work from the pen of Paine, who had come to America only in 1774 at the age of 37 after a very undistinguished career in England. He was a born propagandist, however, and the cause of American independence fueled his imagination and inspired his writing. Of all the thousands of political pamphlets that have been forgotten since the invention of printing this is one that has survived. Written as an ephemeral tract, it has remained one of the important documents of American history.

The pamphlet appeared on 10 January 1776, less than six months before the signing of the Declaration of Independence. At the time it was published Americans were very much divided in their attitude towards Britain. The struggle for home rule had been going on for years and was gradually intensifying, but only a few Americans then favored separation from England. The Continental Congress was called in 1774 in an effort to head off a radical solution. Franklin in London said in March 1775 that he had never heard anyone in America, drunk or sober, advocate independence. Washington told a friend in May 1775 that if the friend ever heard of his joining the movement for separation, he had his leave to set him down for everything wicked. Jefferson wrote in July 1775 that he was looking with fondness towards reconciliation with Great Britain.

Then the next January Paine's pamphlet, with title supplied by Benjamin Rush, burst on the colonies, and nothing was ever the same afterwards. Although leaders like Washington, Samuel Adams, Franklin, Richard Henry Lee, and others were beginning to work quietly for independence by that time, no one before Paine had come out flatly in print for separation. Paine's pamphlet swept through the colonies, and since there was no copyright law, anyone could reprint it. Perhaps 100,000 copies were in circulation by the time the Declaration was signed, and it has been estimated that probably every literate person in the thirteen colonies had read it. While most writers of political pamphlets were intellectuals writing for other intellectuals, Paine wrote a prose that anyone could read, farmers, mechanics, tradesmen, laborers. Paine committed every logical fallacy in his argument, but the brilliance of his journalism was overwhelming, and it had a catalytic effect in moving public opinion in favor of independence.

Washington wrote to Joseph Reed: "By private letters which I have lately received from Virginia, I find *Common Sense* is working a powerful change there in men's minds." Charles Lee, who became a general in the continental army, wrote Washington: "I never saw such a masterly, irresistible performance. It will . . . give the *coup-de-grace* to Great Britain." Franklin and others also testified to the prodigious effects of the pamphlet, and the *American Annual Register . . . for the Year 1796* recalled: "When the first copies arrived in the American camp at Cambridge, they were perused with transport. An officer in that army observed lately that a reinforcement of five thousand men would not have inspired the troops with equal confidence as this pamphlet did." Of course, the Revolution would have occurred whether or not Paine had existed, but *Common Sense* did prepare people's minds for the break with England.

Where Paine got the ideas that he put into his pamphlet is moot. He was not a reader, and he no doubt picked up his notions here and there, perhaps from conversations with friends like Franklin and Rush. He always prided himself on the originality of his ideas, but his thoughts on government and natural rights were widely current in the Enlightenment, as perhaps are the ideas of Freud today among people who never have read him. The idea with which Paine opened his pamphlet, that "government, even in its best state, is but a necessary evil; in its worst state an intolerable one" was held by many liberal theorists of the time. After this preliminary statement, Paine went for the jugular in attacking the British Constitution and undermining American loyalty to the Crown. Americans already were at odds with Parliament over the issue of taxation without representation, but they did not blame the king for their grievances. Paine attacked monarchy, hereditary succession, and the divine right of kings with eminently quotable language. As for the divine right of William the Conqueror to rule England: "A French bastard, landing with an armed banditti and establishing himself king of England against the consent of the natives is in plain terms a very paltry rascally original."

Then Paine moved on to "Thoughts on the Present State of American Affairs," in which he offered "nothing more than simple facts, plain arguments, and common sense." He answered the argument that because America had flourished under British rule it should remain under it by saying: "We may as well assert that because a child has thrived on milk, that it is never to have meat." And later he even called on astronomy to buttress his case: ". . . there is something absurd in supposing a continent to be perpetually governed by an island. In no instance hath nature made the satellite larger than its primary planet." So he went on, arguing sometimes logically, sometimes illogically, arguing by analogy, begging the question, but always phrasing his brief in memorable language. He ended this section with a peroration for freedom: "O ye that love mankind! Ye that dare oppose not only the tyranny but the tyrant, stand forth! Every spot of the old world is overrun with oppression. . . . Europe regards her [freedom] like a stranger, and England hath given her warning to depart. O receive the fugitive, and prepare in time an asylum for mankind." Then he ended the final chapter of the pamphlet with a call for a DECLARATION FOR INDEPENDENCE.

—James Woodress

THE COUNTRY OF THE POINTED FIRS.
Novel by Sarah Orne Jewett, 1896.

Sarah Orne Jewett's *The Country of the Pointed Firs*, which many fellow writers (Kipling was one, Willa Cather, less surprisingly, another) have considered a small masterpiece, belongs not so much to a genre as to a certain infrequent kind which seems, by its nature, to have a curious lasting appeal. Its nearest English likeness is Mrs. Gaskell's *Cranford* (1853): but more on this presently. Not quite autobiography (the narrator is nameless, uninvolved), neither novel nor nouvelle (it has linked episodes rather than central plot), *The Country of the Pointed Firs* recreates a scene and a people at a late point in their own time. Each character might be a painting (Dutch master? American primitive?) suddenly touched into life. Strange personal tales are there, sometimes partly caught, in teasing or haunting fragments—but so it is in life. The strong wild landscape, dark woods and cliffs, the rocky shore, the sweet-smelling herbs and grasses, the abiding sea and wind, are present on every page.

"One evening in June a single passenger landed upon the steamboat wharf." So the narrator (a writer wanting rustic quiet) steps into the orderly frugal life of this dwindling, aging community on the coast of Maine. The people she comes to know are solitaries, widows of seamen, seamen widowers, with their working days and emotional upheavals behind them; but memories and secrets can be summoned for the narrator's hearing. The visitor—she is an event, and welcome—is the medium through which we know these people. But—good listener, observer, and companion as she is sometimes called on to be—she is deliberately underplayed in the book; we know nothing of her name, her looks, and this is as it should be. Her story, if any, lies elsewhere.

In one sense, then, we are in a haven of ordered peace, where the smallest event has quality, and the only wildness is in the elements. We meet no rebellious or troubled adolescents. The child inhabitants of the little schoolhouse that the narrator rents as a workplace in the vacation are nowhere visible in the book. But no character is without a private drama, something not so tranquil. Mrs. Almira Todd, with whom the narrator lodges, herb-gatherer and herbal healer, spirit of goodness, the book's central figure indeed, still feels sharp grief not only for her drowned young husband Nathan, but for the real love of her youth, prevented from marrying by his parents. "My heart was gone out o' my keeping before ever I saw Nathan; though he loved me well and made me real happy." It was, in the narrator's words, "an absolute archaic grief. She might have been Antigone alone on the Theban plain." We hear of "Poor Joanna," who felt that she had "committed the unpardonable sin" (jilted just before her marriage, she had allowed herself to feel a wrath towards God), and had spent the rest of her life totally alone on a little island several miles from the coast. We also meet the dignified old woman whose hard life had been cheered by the thought that she was Queen Victoria's twin, born on the same day, giving her children the same names. We share the narrator's pleasure in discovering the secret courtship of quiet William and his shepherdess, both in their sixties and toilworn, seeing each other scarcely once a year.

Most memorable of all, though, is the story told to the narrator by Captain Littlepage, a man of worn and troubled refinement with a head full of classical poetry and a tale of Coleridgean awe. Wrecked in the arctic regions, he was given rough shelter by an old seaman, Gaffett, lone survivor of a polar exploring expedition. "There is a strange sort of country," Gaffett told him, "way up north beyond the ice, and strange folks living in it . . . shapes of folks, all blowing gray figures."

> Gaffett believed that it was the next world to this. He said that he and another man came near one of the fog-shaped men that was going along slow with the look of a pack on his back, among the rocks, an' they chased him; but, Lord! he flittered away out o' sight like a leaf the wind takes with it, or a piece of cobweb. They would make as if they talked together, but there was no sound of voices.

"Say what you like," Gaffett assured him, " 'twas a kind of waiting place between this world and the next."

Did Jewett know *Cranford*? It hardly matters; each of the works is essentially of its author's kind. Still, the likenesses and differences are of interest. Both use an under-stressed narrator as viewer and recorder. Both are episodic. Both are based on long-known places and people. Both centre affectionately on the middle-aged and old. You can't really choose between them. But the Jewett book has the tremendous asset of the natural scene itself. This scene is an essential part of the book's fabric. So is the meticulous and moving detail (Joanna's gingham dress, for instance; the bonnet of the angry old woman, paralysed by a stroke); so too is the speech of its characters with its quaint, almost Elizabethan turn of phrase. As for the story element, you would call the work open-ended; no tale is brought to a final close. If the test of a book's quality is that it can be read again and again with unfailing interest, there is no doubt of this book's high place.

—Naomi Lewis

THE DAMNATION OF THERON WARE.
Novel by Harold Frederic, 1896.

The literary sensation of 1896 was Harold Frederic's *The Damnation of Theron Ware*, published in England as *Illumination*. One of the oddities in this book about a Methodist minister who strays from the fundamentals of his religion is that no one, neither Theron Ware himself nor the Catholic priest Father Forbes, seems to believe in God. Religion is, rather, a profession and a social institution, and the motto of the book might well be Alice Ware's disappointed remark when her husband is not awarded the pastorate he had longed for: "Don't talk to me about the Lord to-night; I can't bear it!" The novel concerns just such petty people unable to bear (surely that verb has a mock heroic ring to it in the context of Alice's petulance) petty disappointments, empty men and women who yearn for the status symbols of the middle class. In materialistic America at the end of the 19th century, with old-time religion under attack as never before by the new science, damnation no longer signifies alienation from God and the good, as it had for Jonathan Edwards or Lorenzo Dow. Now damnation means the failure to achieve wealth, success, and power, or, from Frederic's point of view, the failure to achieve true self-knowledge. Theron Ware is indeed cursed by his own self-deception, by alienation from himself.

When the Methodist elders deny Theron Ware the pulpit at Tecumseh he had so much coveted and assign him instead to Octavius ("render unto Caesar the things that are Caesar's"), he finds himself the minister of a tight-fisted fundamentalist congregation. His salvation, like Hester Prynne's in *The Scarlet Letter* (a book upon which Frederic drew heavily, as he did also upon "Young Goodman Brown" and "Ethan Brand," among other stories), involves accepting a point of view initially presented as unattractive in the extreme. Certain that no one in his new audience will appreciate the oratorical powers upon which he had built his hopes for the Tecumseh pastorate, Theron rejects the townspeople's fundamentalism and gravitates instead toward the Darwinian Doctor Ledsmar, the comparative mythology of Father Forbes, and, above all, the self-styled Hellenism of Celia Madden, spoiled daughter of the richest Roman Catholic in town. Theron's religious training identifies all Catholics with the Antichrist, while his ideas about the Irish come largely from the political cartoons of Thomas Nast. He sees them as bestial and sensual, but will not acknowledge to himself that for just those reasons—that is, for her sensuality and supposed accessibility—he is attracted toward Miss Madden. That his prurience is altogether of an adolescent or even infantile variety becomes clear in the scene in the forest during the Catholic picnic when he buries his head in the folds of Celia's clothes and imagines himself a small boy again, being mothered. Later he follows Celia and Father Forbes to New York, stalking them like a detective he remembers from a favorite juvenile fiction and hoping to detect them in a re-enactment of the primal scene, thereby establishing (in his own mind) their absolute guilt and his own unimpeachable innocence and integrity.

Celia Madden is not the only woman in the novel with whom Theron Ware fantasizes an ambiguous relationship, part infantile and part sexual. Both his own wife, Alice, and the debt-raiser Sister Soulsby serve also as surrogate mothers (and symbols of power and influence), and both also inspire Theron's sexual curiosity. He sees himself as a figure of irresistible virility, like the circuit riders from the early days of muscular Christianity, and there is more than a little irony involved in Levi Gorringe's comparing him with Henry Ward Beecher, central figure in a notorious scandal and trial for adultery. For adultery is what, in his darkest heart, Theron dreams of committing with Celia and Sister Soulsby, even as he seems incapable of entering into any normal sexual relationship with women.

In addition to such psychological themes centering on Theron's sexuality but possessing as well implications for 19th-century American culture, there are numerous other themes in *The Damnation of Theron Ware* that command the interest of the reader. These include the book's treatment of the impact of Darwinian thought upon articles of basic religious faith; the city (New York) and the country (Theron's boyhood home, among other rustic locales) as symbols of America's past and future; and European complexity (the Roman Catholic culture and religion) in conflict with American simplicity. These themes are treated ambiguously, as, indeed, are all the major ideas in the novel. But the book is most engaging, finally, in its portrayal of Theron's inability to understand his own motivations, to take himself at anything other than face value and as anything other than the finest of fellows, cruelly misunderstood and betrayed. The great future that he sees before him at the end of the novel is, like so much of the rest of his life as chronicled in the book, a fictional construction, a grand illusion, but Theron never loses faith in his own fictions.

—Robert D. Arner

THE DAY OF THE LOCUST.
Novel by Nathanael West, 1939.

Nathanael West's *The Day of the Locust* is a realistic novel about an unreal city. Centered in Hollywood and the world of movie-making, the story avoids the glitter of stardom to concentrate on the life of the disenchanted. It presents the disillusioned, those who find themselves cheated of the glamour their fantasies promised and the movies provided. The novel emphasizes the spiritual and moral death of the city, symptomatic of the condition within the country as a whole. Focusing on the despair of out-of-work bit actors, the illusions of romantic but untalented actresses, the unhappiness of once-successful vaudeville comics, the paralysis of those who journey to the coast, the novel stresses the death of dreams and culminates in a fiery riot of frenzied movie fans at a Hollywood premiere. This scene, which ends the novel, embodies the efforts of the protagonist, Tod Hackett, to finish his panoramic painting recording life in the city which he titles *The Burning of Los Angeles*. With the Old Testament allusions of its title and its apocalyptic ending by fire, the novel stands as a unique indictment of romance and its destruction in modern America. This intensely moral work, displaying characters entrapped between their idealism and corruption, initiates a series of Hollywood novels which extend West's satire. F. Scott Fitzgerald's *The Last Tycoon*, Budd Schulberg's *What Makes Sammy Run?*, and Joan Didion's *Play It As It Lays* are three distinguished examples.

The principal themes of *The Day of the Locust* are the tension between disillusionment and romance and the reaction to recognizing the absurdity of everyday life. The clearest demonstration of the conflict occurs in chapter 18 when Tod Hackett wanders about a studio lot in quest of Faye Greener, the lustful but elusive *femme fatale* he has met earlier in the book. Believing she is an extra in an epic entitled *Waterloo*—the title itself symbolic of the imminent downfall of Hollywood—he follows a group of *cuirassiers* heading for the set in search of her. He quickly loses them but encounters in succession a painted ocean liner, a papier-mâché sphinx, a desert, a western saloon, a jungle, a Paris street, a Romanesque courtyard, a waterfall, a campy resort, and a Greek temple where the god of Eros "lay face downward in a pile of old newspapers and bottles." Such is the fate of love in the novel—lost, discarded, and impotent. Before he actually witnesses the literal collapse of a cardboard Mont St. Jean when hundreds of soldiers enter a mock battle but unexpectedly crash through canvas, cardboard, and plaster, Tod glimpses an adobe fort, a wooden horse of Troy, a set of baroque palace stairs, a Dutch windmill, and the bones of a dinosaur. In this pivotal chapter, West emphasizes the riot of scenes and fraudulent quality of history when placed in the hands of the image makers. But the chapter also echoes the illusionary lives all the characters lead in a city that is itself a jumble of architectural and life styles and which values masquerade over authenticity. In Hollywood, West emphasizes, the natural is the artificial.

The unusual characters in the novel parallel the melange of styles and values depicted. A dwarf, a painter, a bookkeeper, a family of Eskimos, a cowboy, a vaudeville comedian, and an untalented actress/prostitute are the principals. But their mixture expresses the frustration rather than achievement of talents. The life of these extras, movie fans, would-be stars, screenwriters, and hangers-on is one of boredom, suffering, and impotence repeated thematically and symbolically throughout the novel. Sordid rooms, sterile landscapes, and dead-end streets project the empty lives in Los Angeles. Promised romance and stardom, adventures and sex, the figures discover only the artificial world of make-believe. And for West's characters, resentment at this discovery unleashes violence. Not surprisingly, the original title of the novel was *The Cheated*.

Faye Greener, the heroine, embodies many of the contradictions of the city. Pursued by all, obtained by none, she is a kind of bitch goddess (like success) who will be possessed only by those who can pay for her. But like the image on a screen, she remains untouchable, a fantasy. She becomes a phantom bride not only for Tod Hackett and Homer Simpson, the retired bookkeeper, but also for the seedy cowboy actor Earle Shoop and the brutal but sexual Mexican Miguel. Faye remains elusive, the dream of love that is unattainable for the nation but which it continues to desire. "Her invitation wasn't to pleasure," West writes, "but to struggle, hard and sharp, closer to murder than to love."

The Day of the Locust is relentless in its exposure of the decay and violence that comes from the betrayal of dreams. Yet West exhibits supreme control in the telling of his story, despite the continued division between the idealism and actuality of Hollywood life. Adjusting to the discrepancy between the imagined and the real, Hackett becomes both an artist fashioning a new future and a Jeremiah predicting doom. The novel is a remarkable satire of America and its dreams, providing a disturbing portrait of its fantasies evoked through language, symbol, and character. And at the core of these desires is violence which for West is idiomatic in America. When the masses discover that "they haven't the mental equipment for leisure, the money nor the physical equipment for pleasure," their only recourse is to destroy. Boredom and disappointment make them savage, as Hackett experiences when he is caught in the mob scene at Kahn's Persian Palace Theatre which ends the novel. But the event paradoxically allows him a vision of his completed painting which he has been unable to finish until that moment.

Just before the climactic riot, Hackett remarks that "at the sight of their heroes and heroines, the crowd would turn demonic." The frustrations beneath the surface of wish-fulfillment and dream-seeking sharpen the theme of middle-class dissatisfaction, creating a startling work of fiction. In its presentation of divided characters, split between their desires and actions, in its rendering of anguish-ridden romantics surrounded by indifferent pragmatists, the work conveys the dilemma of the modern American psyche. And in its accuracy in showing "all those poor devils who can only be stirred by the promise of miracle and then only to violence," the novel has a remarkable contemporary quality. For West, life as illusion masks discontent, although awareness of this condition ironically intensifies the need for fantasy. Difficult to control and uncertain in their goals, the masses feel threatened by their idols and are prepared to destroy them when they fail to gratify their dreams. In the neo-Gothic world of his California, West creates a riveting but profoundly disturbing fiction.

—I.B. Nadel

DEATH OF A SALESMAN.
Play by Arthur Miller, 1949.

Published and first produced in 1949, Arthur Miller's *Death of a Salesman* won the Pulitzer Prize and other major awards, and in 1985 demonstrated its continuing dramatic power in Dustin Hoffman's extraordinary made-for-television production. Critics have differed widely over whether the play is a tragedy or not, whether it is chiefly social criticism, and if so about what, whether Linda or Willy should be considered the chief character, and whether Willy has or lacks the stature to be a tragic hero. Some see it in the classical Marxist, or existential tradition, while others see it as Biff's story, or an Oedipal ritual. Then is the "Requiem" tearful or not, is it intended as such by Miller, and what does its ironic nature say about the rest of the play? Is Willy Everyman, or merely shallow?

Phyllis Hartnoll states the play depicts the destructive power of illusion (related to Ibsen's conception of the "saving lie" in reverse?) shown in Willy Loman's refusal to face the failure of his own career as a salesman or the failure of his family relationships. Family and friends, in the play, declare him a "prince," yet surely not Machiavelli's, who never lets emotion interfere with reason, who does only that which works. Lee A. Jacobus contends that the play concerns Willy's acceptance of the idea that his success as a person must be measured in terms of his success as a businessman, and should be read as an attack on the "commercialization of society . . . and the confusion of human and monetary values"; this critic also feels the play can indeed be classified as a tragedy—the only one written by a contemporary dramatist.

Miller himself ("Tragedy and the Common Man") declared that "the common man is as apt a subject for tragedy in its highest sense as kings were," a point likely to be granted by most, but not meeting, necessarily, the two criteria generally held to be needed for achieving tragic status: 1) a hero with enough stature to make his suffering significant; and 2) a course of action that produces enlightenment. Other critics declare the play an indictment following the American Marxist line of the 1930's, undermining the "idyll of suburbia." The play becomes the tragedy of a man with noble traits inarticulately expressed; his choice of "the appointed death" makes it his own no less truly than Othello's or Antony's, though there is exultation—perhaps not shared by the audience—in Willy's preparing to join Ben in that dark land loaded with diamonds, so Biff can once more pass Bernard with the $20,000 in the mail from Willy's life insurance, "the last deception" (Allison, Carr, and Eastman, *Masterpieces of the Drama*).

Defining Willy's pathetic faith, "that he is beloved of buyers and that to be loved is to be a success," the *New York Times* wrote that Miller seized an essential feature of American psychology but felt that England, despite its national taste for games, would continue to believe that it took more than being well liked to gain diamonds, especially since Willy's worshipfully encouraged "sports" of sons became "seedy seducer" and "drifting lawbreaker." Perhaps Beckett's Vladimir and Estragon while waiting for Godot, and Camus's Sisyphus rolling that rock in hell, would have understood about games as opposed to reality, the need to stay busy so you don't realize your responsibilities to others, or the torment demolishing you, or, in Willy's case, the real world about you. Perhaps we have an existential negative parable, a modern day rendering of dramatic irony worsened by Willy's lack of spiritual values and/or his unwillingness to examine those he might have. Existentially speaking, man is free but responsible, required to try to lift the quality of life not only for himself but also for everyone else every time he acts—and he must act. He is not free to run because compassionate actions may be difficult or dangerous, or to die to escape responsibility. Willy appears to see death as a means of avoiding the consequences of actions with which he can no longer cope, a means of escaping difficult decision-making, in addition to benefiting Biff financially. He spells "success" $uCCe$$, is extremely image-conscious, determined to succeed "out front with a shine and a smile," and is going through motions no longer effective, with strength he no longer has. Lonely on the road, with no spiritual vision to sustain him, he is vulnerable to predatory Boston females, some of those "good people" in his "New England paradise."

The Marxist view of an old worker tossed away when he no longer produces cannot fully explain the catastrophe. What we do see in Act II is Willy's being torn apart right before our eyes, figuratively speaking, an excruciatingly painful blend of his Boston adultery exposure scene and his crushing defeat in New York City immediately following his being fired and Biff's failure to get a loan from Oliver for the latest fairy tale get-rich-and-famous-quickly project. The boys leave Willy babbling in a toilet while they plan and leave for an evening's sex orgy, even denying at one point he's their father. As the Boston scene crushes Biff, and the New York scene Willy, the limp audience, drained of pity and terror, falls strangely quiet during the "Requiem." Charley survived because "I never took any interest in anything," doubtless playing the benevolent Machiavel, and offered Willy a paying job, which he refused. Willy, crushed, was no high-tragedy glorious failure—glorious because of spiritual victory, failure because of death. "Enter

Here Only the Well-Liked" was not inscribed over his gate to heaven. Personality has lost the day. All he wanted was love and respect, freedom to work with his hands, success based on popularity in business . . . and Biff's love.

—Louis Charles Stagg

THE DEATH OF THE HIRED MAN.
Poem by Robert Frost, 1914.

Robert Frost's "The Death of the Hired Man" vividly illustrates a primary feature of his poetry: his preoccupation with conflict. As the poem opens, we learn that Silas, a now feeble old man who periodically worked for Warren and Mary, has returned to their farm. Mary has fed him and left him in the kitchen. When Warren comes home, she informs him of Silas's return and makes one of the key thematic statements in the poem; she says to Warren, "Be kind." Warren gruffly protests that he has never been anything but kind to Silas.

This exchange leads to the major development in the poem. Pressured to decide what to do about Silas, Mary and Warren present their outlooks on life. These viewpoints, like those of the two men in "Mending Wall," are distinctly different, but do not prove to be antipodal. Because Silas has failed to live up to Warren's high standards, Warren declares he will not allow Silas to remain on the farm. Warren bases his judgment on the fact that in the past Silas was undependable, going off when Warren needed him the most and (an important point with Warren) going off not even for the purpose of bettering himself. Significantly, Mary does not dispute what Warren says. Her reply makes it clear, though, that due to Silas's weak physical condition, she believes that any discussion about him must center not on usefulness, but on life and death. Because Silas, like Warren, judges men primarily according to their value as workers, he had insisted to Mary that he could still help with farm chores. Mary knows this illusion springs from Silas's attempt to maintain a modicum of self-respect—for which she admires him. When Mary tells Warren that Silas rambled on regretfully about his quarrels with the temperamentally different Harold Wilson, who also used to work on the farm, we realize this conflict counterpoints the one between Mary and Warren.

Mary's report about Silas stirs Warren to praise Silas's skill at building a load of hay and, so, to soften his attitude toward the old man. In this same sequence, Mary's summation of Silas's present situation indicates that Frost has created an Everyman figure in Silas. She describes him as someone with "nothing to look backward to with pride, / And nothing to look forward to with hope." Mary herself becomes an archetypal mother figure. Frost writes that Mary stares at the moon, which pours its light "softly in her lap." She touches the "morning-glory strings" hanging above the "garden bed." As Fritz H. Oehlschlaeger points out in his article in *Essays in Literature*, "The passage links Mary to three symbols of fertility" and shows she is "in touch with the cosmic rhythms of birth and death." Warren represents many fathers. When Mary tells him that Silas "has come home to die," Warren stresses justice and duty in his definition of home as a "place where, when you have to go there, / They have to take you in." Mary's definition of home as "Something you somehow haven't to deserve" stresses mercy, compassion, and an acceptance of man as frail.

Mary's words do not, however, end the debate. Warren states that Silas's brother could help out. Mary agrees, just as she tacitly agreed earlier with Warren that Silas was often irresponsible. Mary, then, is by no means non-judgmental. She is merely a kinder judge than her husband is. Warren resists Mary's viewpoint in another way—a way that saves the poem from any taint of mawkishness. When Mary risks saying that Silas's "working days are done," Warren quickly replies, "I'd not be in a hurry to say that." He does not want to surrender the hope that he can still get some practical use out of Silas. Mary simply tells him to go see Silas. Warren does and discovers that Silas is dead.

Silas and Harold Wilson always remained at odds. So, too, in many of Frost's other poems, such as "Home Burial," "The Hill Wife," and "A Servant to Servants," reconciliations to conflicts are not achieved. Indeed, human conflicts could cause the end of civilization, as Frost points out in "Fire and Ice." But in "The Death of the Hired Man," Warren and Mary finally come closer to each other. When Warren returns to say Silas is dead, he gently takes Mary's hand in his.

Reconciliations are of central importance to Frost because they provide one of the few sources of sustenance in a stark world where God is inscrutable and not always benevolent. Despite his scepticism regarding society and government, Frost did not believe people could stand alone and thrive. Although they should maintain their individuality, people need each other. And they can live together successfully—but only if they are not completely unyielding and allow their individuality to be subsumed by love. As Frost states in "Birches," earth is "the right place for love"—because that is where love is needed the most.

—Robert K. Johnson

DEMOCRACY.
Novel by Henry Adams, 1880.

Democracy is a novel of considerable interest without being a great work of art. Taking place in Washington during the 1870's, it is a *roman à clef* in which contemporary readers were able to recognize several prominent political figures. The novel caused a sensation when it appeared in 1880, and tea tables and receptions buzzed with speculation about both the characters in the novel and the author. Henry Adams had published the book anonymously and told only three of his closest friends that he had written it. They kept the secret, and it was not until 1915, three years before Adams died, that his authorship became known, but even then the fact was not confirmed until after his death.

No one suspected Adams probably because he was known primarily as an historian and biographer. He had taught history at Harvard until three years before publishing *Democracy*, which was the first of only two novels he wrote. The book is what one might call a performance with the left hand, for Adams's purpose in going to Washington was to write history, and he later produced the monumental *History of the United*

States of America During the Administration of Thomas Jefferson and James Madison in nine volumes (1889–91). But he also was a close observer of Washington politics, and the character of Madeleine Lee, the young affluent widow who goes to the national capital to study political life, is in part Adams himself. In addition, Marian Hooper, the daughter of a wealthy Boston family, whom Adams married in 1872, also sat for the portrait. Her role as a Washington hostess paralleled Madeleine Lee's.

Adams is justly famous for his history and his great autobiography, *The Education of Henry Adams*, but he was only a mediocre novelist. Madeleine Lee, her younger sister Sybil, Carrington, the former Confederate officer and Washington lawyer, and other minor characters never come to life. There is far too much exposition and too little dramatic action in the story to make the novel first rate, and it becomes a little too melodramatic at the end when Madeleine finally decides not to marry Senator Ratcliffe; but after all these flaws are noted, the novel still has an appeal and is worth reading.

Adams's great achievement is the creation of Senator Silas P. Ratcliffe from Illinois, the dominant figure in the Senate and the dominant character in the novel. He was modeled after James G. Blaine, senator from Ohio, who was defeated for the Presidency by Grover Cleveland in 1884. Blaine, as Ratcliffe, had been narrowly defeated for the nomination to head the Republican ticket in 1876 when Rutherford B. Hayes carried away the prize. Adams makes a great deal of the enmity of these two men in the novel, though he creates a caricature of "Old Granite," as the President is called in the novel. Yet the picture of an inexperienced midwestern politician overwhelmed by Washington and forced to let Ratcliffe, his enemy, distribute patronage is very well done.

Ratcliffe is portrayed as a shrewd, calculating, unscrupulous politician. He almost manages to marry Madeleine, who is motivated by a desire for power and is nearly seduced by the conviction that Ratcliffe will be the next President. The sharp conflict within Madeleine over the temptation of power and her own moral code provides a measure of drama in the concluding chapters. There seems little doubt that Adams despised Ratcliffe, as his character Carrington does in the novel, but Adams does not make the Illinois senator a monster. Ratcliffe puts loyalty to his country first, his party second, and his own integrity third. During the war he had taken part in a vote fraud to keep the peace party from winning an Illinois election. He honestly believed that the peace party's victory would have been fatal to the Union cause. The bribe that he later accepted, the plot device that Adams uses to finish Ratcliffe with Madeleine, turns out to be a secret contribution to pay off campaign debts, a quid pro quo for legislation, to be sure, but not personal gain for Ratcliffe.

Two other characters who ought to be mentioned are also based on real people: Count Jacobi and the historian Gore. The former, who is a Bulgarian diplomat in the novel, was drawn from the Turkish ambassador, in real life a friend of Adams; the latter was suggested by John L. Motley, the Massachusetts historian, who had in fact served in diplomatic posts in Europe. In the novel he wants to be ambassador to Spain, but the President doesn't like Eastern intellectuals. He has a friend from Indiana who wants to be postmaster at Indianapolis, but the local politicians will not have him; so he is given Spain. There is much satire of the patronage system in the novel, in bits like this, and though the civil service protects most bureaucrats today, top-level jobs still go to cronies and the party faithful.

Adams is critical of democracy, but he believes it is the best system so far devised. The historian Gore probably speaks for Adams on this subject: "I believe in democracy. I accept it. I will faithfully serve and defend it. . . . it appears to me the inevitable consequence of what has gone before it. Democracy asserts the fact that the masses are now raised to higher intelligence than formerly. . . . I grant it is an experiment, but it is the only direction society can take that is worth taking. . . . Every other possible step is backward, and I do not care to repeat the past."

—James Woodress

THE DREAM SONGS.
Poems by John Berryman, from 1964.

John Berryman began writing his "dream songs" in 1955 and continued—by habit, he said—until his death 17 years later. They are his principal achievement as a poet. 432 have been published, and hundreds more are in manuscript. *77 Dream Songs* was published in 1964, and an additional 308 appeared in *His Toy, His Dream, His Rest* in 1968. Two were included in *Delusions, Etc.* (1972) and another 45 in *Henry's Fate and Other Poems* (1977). The last of these volumes was not edited by Berryman, and there is some feeling that many of the songs published in it are inferior to the general level of those which had appeared earlier.

Most of the songs contain three stanzas of six lines, variously rhymed and metered. Berryman created a special language for his songs, in part formal and in part idiomatic and vernacular. They are marked as well by sudden syntactical inversions and nervous, jagged, clipped, at times frantic rhythms that reflect the tensions of their principal speaker and subject.

That speaker is "Henry" (not, as some have insisted, the poet himself), a man who, in Berryman's words, "has suffered an irreversible loss" (apparently the death of his father by suicide). Henry's personality is complex but marked essentially by anger, self-loathing, depression, fear, and other black moods and emotions. At times he can be very amusing, but the humor is ironic, bitter, or self-defensive. Although he is apparently a man of considerable learning, he has few passionate interests—or at least few that satisfy him. He travels widely, is obsessed with women, and has achieved some fame or celebrity as a writer, but nothing, except his children, seems to make him happy, and there are few songs that are not deeply touched by his private anguish.

Henry's private hell is made worse by the failure of any traditional means of release—spiritual, intellectual, emotional, sexual—to help him in any final way. He looks for salvation of any kind and finally finds it in anger, which allows him at least to speak with intensity and to find, for the moment, a source for his pain—something he can point to and name rather than live always in a swirl of seemingly causeless anguish. The most powerful of the songs are those in which Henry's emotional turbulence suddenly resolves itself into a redemptive, righteous anger—153 and 384 are among the best of these—or at least into sudden terrifying insight into the nature of his condition such as happens in the unnumbered dream song "Henry's Understanding," published in *Delusions*.

As John Haffenden's biography of Berryman (1982) demonstrated, there are considerable similarities between the facts of Henry's life and what we know of Berryman's, but Robert Phillips and others who have read the songs as autobiographical confession have missed the essential point. Berryman was writing songs, not autobiography, and his task was to force music out of a modern sensibility trapped in the psychological hell of anguish, depression, and despair. In the best of the dream songs, there is a lyric intensity that moves with precision and grace in spite of the depressive weight. Henry finds redemption in anger, but a much greater redemption lies in the fact that, in the midst of his personal horror, he is still able to sing.

The Dream Songs, according to 293, are structured "according to / Henry's / nature," but any sense of progression from one to the next is on occasion difficult or impossible to locate. Berryman insisted that the songs were not independent units but parts of a larger conception though "admittedly more independent than parts usually are." One way to approach them is as a series of modulations of sensibility and tone, but even so, at points the ordering seems entirely haphazard. The poem is also open-ended; it appears to lead to no inevitable conclusion, and had Berryman lived, he might well have continued writing songs as long as he wished. The variations which his subject and method allow seem infinite.

In many ways, *The Dream Songs* may remind us of Walt Whitman's "Song of Myself"—also a series of modulations of sensibility and tone seemingly capable of infinite expansion. Whitman's poem ends essentially because the poet says it does, certainly not because it has said all that it has to say; if that were the case, Whitman would not have felt the need repeatedly to revise and expand it or, for that matter, add to *Leaves of Grass* such poems as "Song of the Open Road," which are in effect extended footnotes to the original poem. Berryman's Henry shares Whitman's infinite expansiveness and inclusiveness, but while the ability to accept everything and not bring things to an end is a source of much power for Whitman's poetic vision, it is another source of Henry's anguish: he is in pain because the past will not let him go, because he cannot ignore what is happening and what has happened to him, because he cannot forget. Whitman's expansiveness led to a new poetic line, a new kind of singing, free from the restrictions of traditional prosody. Henry, on the other hand, can transform his hell into song only by electing a formal and altogether arbitrary verse pattern. If his songs were to expand with the grand, arching lines of Whitman's verse, the pain would expand unbearably with them. It is only by keeping the poetic form constrained and tight that Henry is able to hold in his pain, survive it, and transform it into redemptive song. *The Dream Songs*, begun exactly a hundred years after the first edition of *Leaves of Grass*, is Berryman's dark inversion of Whitman's "Song of Myself."

—Edward Halsey Foster

THE EDUCATION OF HENRY ADAMS: AN AUTOBIOGRAPHY. 1907.

When the Massachusetts Historical Society published *The Education of Henry Adams* in 1918 it gave the world a work that had been written in 1905 and privately printed in 1907, intended for a small band of readers, one hundred in number. The publishers added the subtitle *An Autobiography*, something that decreases the intimacy of the original and suggests both an end and a beginning, whereas Adams had deliberately failed to bring the work to a conclusion. Two questions may be asked, first, whether *The Education* is to be read as the record of the historical Henry Adams, and second, whether it is to be taken as merely pursuing one theme.

Adams's preface speaks not of the man but of the "manikin" "on which the toilet of education is to be dropped." What he terms "the Ego," he says, has steadily tended to efface itself over 150 years. It would be easier to see *The Education* as the autobiography of a disappointed man were it not for the introduction of this passive, lifeless figure and the extent to which Adams suggests his supposed sense of failure. Many critics have argued that this had a single origin, the failure to achieve high political office, yet it is difficult to find any definition of success within the work, while neither his friends for whom he wrote nor the less well connected reader would find it easy to see his life as lacking in achievement. Indeed the author may protest too much.

The Education proceeds chronologically but does not cover the twenty years between 1871 and 1892. Some critics have maintained that even Adams could not detach himself from the events leading up to and following on the suicide of his wife Marian in 1885. Whatever the reason the result is to emphasise that this is a record of a search for intellectual not emotional stability. It may be that Boston and Quincy, to use Adams's own figures, would not have allowed him to discuss feeling, the Puritan heritage demanding self-control, but whatever the reason this is an autobiography omitting much that is dear to 20th-century curiosity.

The search for intellectual stability becomes more marked, even more frantic, as *The Education* proceeds. Adams, as befits a man who complained that the formal education at Harvard gave him no knowledge of either Comte or Marx, hoped as they did to find some general explanation, particularly as a historian, for a meaning behind the passage of time. Unlike most historians he felt that this might come through an understanding of natural science and its rules, and the final chapters of *The Education* show his attempts to use its units of measurement to discover what he terms the "formula." This, as he argued, would not be possible without establishing a point of origin which led him, even as he was conceiving *The Education*, to publish *Mont-Saint-Michel and Chartres: A Study of Thirteenth-Century Unity*. He intended to fix a point from which he might better see his own position. According to Adams, the subtitle to *The Education* would have been *A Study of Twentieth-Century Multiplicity* and his purpose thus to see how multiplicity had grown from unity.

The Education, however, appears less interested in multiplicity than unity. Though it is debatable how much unity Adams believed the European mind of the period 1150–1250 possessed, it is clear that he would have welcomed the chance to resurrect its integrity. His desire was so strong that it led him to the paradox that unity was chaos at one point. It is arguable that all of *The Education*, even the earlier, more historical chapters, exhibits the drive to comprehend, to discover "some great generalization which would finish one's clamor to be educated," as he said, and that even the episode in England during the Civil War, fascinating as it is as an insider's account of the travails of the Northern delegation, might best be seen in terms of the lesson it taught Adams the historian that there was no single way of properly interpreting the actions of the British cabinet.

In this sense *The Education* was not the record of a disappointed man, for Adams felt able in the end to give a meaning to the passage of time, described in the chapter "A Law of Acceleration (1904)." The problem with the idea was the cataclysmic undertone, for as he said, "Prolonged one generation longer, it would require a new social mind." This followed from his assumption that there was an integral process stretching from 1200 to 1900, something that might suggest that the Ego was not as effaced as he said it was, for it is at least remarkable that he used all the past to explain his own present. Nonetheless the failure to provide the one great truth scarcely damns the account of one of the great intellectual odysseys of not merely the 19th century but also of the American mind. Adams begins by referring to Rousseau and Franklin as models; he ends by joining their select company.

—R.A. Burchell

ETHAN BRAND.
Story by Nathaniel Hawthorne, 1850.

"Ethan Brand" by Nathaniel Hawthorne is an imperfect work of art about an extremely potent idea. Subtitled "A Chapter from an Abortive Romance," it does not develop its title character in much depth and merely synopsizes most of his life. Ethan is seen from the perspective of a lime-burner and his son; from their kiln, he had started on his search for the Unpardonable Sin, and to it he has returned, having found that the sin resides in his own heart. To the lime-burner, he defines it with perverse pride as "The sin of an intellect that triumphed over the sense of brotherhood with man and reverence for God, and sacrificed everything to its own mighty claims!"

Much of the story consists of conversation among the rustics about the mysterious Ethan Brand, and we learn that one of his activities was the ruin of a young girl and perhaps the annihilation of her soul in a cold and remorseless psychological experiment. Brooding in despair, Ethan recalls the tenderness, love, and sympathy for humanity with which he had begun his experiments, during the course of which "ensued that vast intellectual development which . . . disturbed the counterpoise between his mind and heart." In consequence, "He had lost his hold on the magnetic chain of humanity. . . . he was now a cold observer, looking on mankind as the subject of his experiment. . . . from the moment that his moral nature had ceased to keep the pace of improvement with his intellect," he had become a fiend.

Despite his proud statement that he would unshrinkingly reenact the sin, Brand is in such torment that he leaps into the lime-kiln, embracing the "deadly element of Fire," and is consumed, all but his hard heart.

As a story, "Ethan Brand" strains credulity and is guilty of what Poe called "the heresy of the didactic." One problem is that we see only the consequences of the Unpardonable Sin, not the sin itself. It is defined clearly enough, but Hawthorne does not dramatize it. His concept of the Unpardonable Sin is extremely perceptive and timeless, but readers may fail to grasp its significance because the author has not embodied it in an adequate narrative. Like many of Hawthorne's tales, "Ethan Brand" resembles a legend or fairy tale. On one level this quality gives the tales a timelessness, but it also removes such stories as "The Bosom Serpent," "The Man of Adamant," "Rappaccini's Daughter," and "The Birthmark" from reality. We read them as allegories rather than as plausible events. Hawthorne has to spell out for us what the sin is, because he has not dramatized it in Ethan. The crime of having experimented upon a young girl and ruined her life is too vague and is tossed off in a sentence.

Thus D.H. Lawrence's statement in his essay on Hawthorne is particularly applicable to "Ethan Brand": "You *must* look through the surface of American art and see the inner diabolism of the symbolic meaning. Otherwise it is all mere childishness." Likewise, Melville wrote that "Young Goodman Brown" sounds like "a simple little tale. . . . Whereas it is as deep as Dante; nor can you finish it, without addressing the author in his own words: 'It is yours to penetrate, in every bosom, the deep mystery of sin.' " This statement applies equally to "Ethan Brand."

Since the story fails to incarnate the Unpardonable Sin in a sufficiently sinister form, we must apply Hawthorne's definition of it to history. There it is more than amply exemplified, in any figures for whom ideas are more important than individuals, abstractions, orthodoxies, and ideologies count for more than people, who for the sake of some elusive utopia or idea of purity will torture, brainwash, purge, enslave, or execute the individual. Examples before Hawthorne's time include the Spanish Inquisition, which tormented the bodies of alleged heretics in order to purify their souls and burned them at the stake to keep them from infecting the orthodox community; the revolutionary French ideologues who enacted a reign of terror to bring about liberty, equality, and fraternity via the guillotine; witch hunting in Hawthorne's own birthplace, Salem; and even the Puritan god of wrath and vengeance who, according to Calvinism, was so pure that He considered humans totally depraved and damned most of them to everlasting torment for being less pure than Himself.

Many other characters in Hawthorne's fiction are guilty of the Unpardonable Sin and suffer its punishment of solitary alienation from the chain of humanity. Roger Chillingworth falls into it in his obsessive revenge upon Dimmesdale; Aylmer, in "The Birthmark," commits it when he brings about his wife's death rather than tolerate the birthmark that symbolizes her imperfect humanity; Dr. Rappaccini commits it when he makes his daughter the subject of a poisonous experiment; and Hollingsworth in *The Blithedale Romance* is guilty of it when he puts his obsession with prison reform ahead of love and friendship: "By and by, you . . . grew drearily conscious that Hollingsworth had a closer friend than ever you could be; and this friend was the cold, spectral monster which he had himself conjured up, and on which he was wasting all the warmth of his heart, and of which at last . . . he had grown to be the bond slave. It was his philanthropic theory."

Profoundly influenced by Hawthorne, Melville rewrote *Moby-Dick* under that influence, transforming it from a fairly simply narrative into a complex symbolic work that explores the "mystery of iniquity." In it, Captain Ahab is guilty of the Unpardonable Sin in being so obsessed with revenge that he has withdrawn from human fellowship and risks the bodies and souls of his crew to fulfill his obsession.

Writers after Hawthorne did not use the term the Unpardonable Sin, but many of them expressed the same idea, and subsequent history certainly illustrated it. Several of Dostoevsky's characters are guilty of it. Raskolnikov, murdering an expendable old pawnbroker so her money can start him on the road to being a great humanitarian, learns that unless every life has value, no life does. Ivan, the intellectual Karamazov brother, argues a syllogistic amorality that if there is no God, all things are lawful, including murder, which the terrorists of *The Possessed* commit for political ideology. Terrorism and totalitarian regimes perfectly exemplify the Unpardonable Sin, whereby ideology is more important than humanity. One could go on multiplying examples—the Nazi doctors and scientists, the politicians and scientists who make chemical weapons and other horrors of modern warfare: and most of Hawthorne's unpardonable sinners are scientists. The point is that Hawthorne's seemingly simple tale is acutely perceptive, and its central concept has a long pedigree and an extensive progeny.

—Robert E. Morsberger

THE FALL OF THE HOUSE OF USHER.
Story by Edgar Allan Poe, 1839.

Generally acknowledged as Edgar Allan Poe's finest tale, "The Fall of the House of Usher" has attracted a good deal of negative criticism from some of the major literary figures of the 20th century, including T.S. Eliot, Cleanth Brooks, Robert Penn Warren, and Allen Tate. Most commonly, objections have been raised to Poe's heavily ornamented style and lack of concern for action and character development. The story has but one character, Roderick; Madeline, the narrator, the house are simply other versions of him, and Roderick does nothing. He neither acts nor is acted upon but merely exists for a few pages in an atmosphere created by style. Of course, these are the objections of post-World War I realism to romanticism in general.

Much, much more has been said about Poe's few pages of characterless inaction; indeed, in variety and volume of critical response, "The Fall of the House of Usher" is one of the most interpreted stories in the English language. Critics like to make precise what artists make vague, and Poe's tale is a masterpiece of ambiguity and imprecision. The story might be read as the reliable account of an encounter with a madman who buried his sister alive. It may be a quite literal account of a brush with the supernatural, a vampire tale perhaps, for certainly Madeline's escape from the vault described by the narrator could be accomplished by nothing human. "The Fall of the House of Usher" has inspired several film versions. Jean Epstein won acclaim with a French production in 1929; most famous is Roger Corman's American International version of 1960. The literal interpretation obviously works best for the filmmakers. The strength of their medium is its power to establish visual reality, but this it gains at the expense of the ambiguity available to the writer. Audiences will believe their eyes, but they may well doubt what they are told by an unreliable source, and here the literal interpretation meets a problem. There is little question but that Roderick Usher is mad, but as events unfold, the narrator, impressionable from the start, comes increasingly under Roderick's influence and even admits to the weakening of his own capacity for rational objectivity. He comes to accept without critical comment Roderick's impression of what is happening. As Madeline approaches, Roderick deliriously talks seemingly to himself and applies the epithet "madman," which ironically might now address the only other person present, the narrator. Thus, "The Fall of the House of Usher" can be read as the effusion of an irrational mind not only about the loss of sanity but itself an example of that theme.

With the narrator rejected as a reliable relater of facts, the way is opened for a variety of critical approaches that seek symbolic significance for characters and events. Perhaps Poe has written an allegory on the artistic process. Roderick, after all, is not really inactive, as some critics have charged. Whatever the real nature of the events that have led him to his present state, Roderick has painted them as abstractions so fantastic and powerful as to cause the narrator to reject his own senses and reason and accept the artist's vision as a truer account of reality. André Malraux said, "The modern artist's supreme aim is to subdue all things to his style." Roderick certainly does this in his paintings, in his "Haunted Palace" poem, and, in a larger sense, in the story itself. Of course, Malraux's "all things" must include the darker elements of the universe that the artist cannot explore without risk of passing a point of no return to reason. Roderick passed that point.

Poe's tale also lends itself very well to Freudian interpretation. Here, the entire story—just like the "Haunted Palace" poem it frames—is a symbolic image of a human mind. Roderick is the ego or consciousness which attempts to bury the primitive impulses of the id, Madeline. The narrator in this reading functions as the superego, an awareness of standards and conventions that mediates between the twins. The attempt to repress the force of the id is unsuccessful; Madeline breaks out of her tomb and emerges to the level of the waking consciousness precipitating the total mental breakdown of the organism.

Critics have commonly remarked on the tight unity of the tale; character, setting, and action are bound into a single image of ruin by a style carefully wrought for the purpose. Unity, however, is more than an effect in "The Fall of the House of Usher"; it is actually a theme, a central theme in Poe's work that found its definitive expression in *Eureka* (1848). Poe theorized that all creation emanated from a single point, and, despite cosmic diffusion, it is still a part of the Godhead. Ultimately this universe will cease to expand and bend back upon itself in a cycle of contraction resulting in final reunification with the source that must annihilate things as they now exist. Such ideas, long present in several mystical systems, resemble the Big Bang theory of modern theoretical physics. Poe's story is about fragments coming together. The narrator is drawn to the house; Roderick and Madeline, both at one with the house, are at last drawn violently and fatally together, and all is sucked into the black hole of the tarn. Poe's finest tale, then is about the end of things, which D.H. Lawrence, writing on Poe, remarked is part of the dual rhythm of "American art-activity" and prerequisite to the "forming of a new consciousness underneath."

—William J. Heim

THE FEDERALIST.
Essays by Alexander Hamilton, James Madison, and John Jay, 1788.

Written by Alexander Hamilton, James Madison, and John Jay, *The Federalist* consists of 85 essays (later combined and numbered as 84), most of which were originally published in New York newspapers between 27 October 1787 and 16 August 1788.

Initially, at least, these essays were intended for immediate ends and, it is believed, were meant only for local distribution. According to current scholarship, most of the essays were hurriedly written and only hastily revised. As one scholar has explained, although it now enjoys the status of "a great political classic," at the time of its publication "*The Federalist* was at bottom an electioneering pamphlet written to persuade contemporary New Yorkers to vote right." Responding to a groundswell of anti-Federalist sentiment in the New York press, Hamilton thought it necessary to generate additional popular support for the Constitution in New York. Pressed by numerous other commitments, he enlisted the assistance of his colleagues, John Jay and James Madison, and writing under the pseudonym of "Publius," they announced the publication of "a series of papers" in support of the Constitution. William Duer, Gouverneur Morris, and possibly Rufus King are also thought to have been approached, but they either declined or their work was rejected.

Roughly half the essays (1–36) that followed deal with the inadequacy of the Confederation of States as it then existed; the other half (37–85) deal with the need for a strong, centralized, federal government such as that proposed in the Constitution recently drafted at the convention for that purpose in Philadelphia. After the publication of these essays in two volumes in 1788, *The Federalist*, as the project then came to be called, received relatively wide circulation throughout the states even after ratification of the Constitution was assured, and it eventually became almost as important among early analysts of the Constitution as that document itself.

Even today *The Federalist* is generally considered "the most significant contribution Americans have made to political philosophy," and it is read and studied by scholars and students of both literature and history as "the classic interpretation of the American Constitution." As one commentator has explained, "Taken singly many of the papers still invite close study for what they say about federalism, representative government, checks and balances, judicial reviews, and guarantees of human rights. Altogether they have been taken as seminal writings of the founders, ranking just after the Declaration of Independence and the Constitution itself as explanations of the shape of American politics and institutions." Particularly singled out for analysis in this regard is *Federalist* 10, in which it is argued that an extended republic of the kind presented in the Constitution would preserve individual liberties by encouraging so many factions that no single group could ever gain an advantage over the others.

Regrettably, because *The Federalist* was published pseudonymously, the exact nature of the collaboration among its authors remains difficult to reconstruct, and despite vigorous scholarly efforts to do so, no one has been able successfully to identify the precise authorship of many of the essays in the project. In general, scholars concur that Hamilton assumed responsibility for writing 1, 6–9, 11–13, 21–36, 59–61, and 65–85; Madison for 10, 14, and 37–48; and Jay for 2–5 and 64. At issue are 18–20, 49–58, and 62–63, with internal evidence supporting Madison as the primary author for all but 49 and 53, which are generally attributed to Hamilton. Because of the furious pace at which the essays were published, there was probably little time for the authors to circulate their work among themselves. Most certainly, however, they discussed at the onset the ideas they intended to develop in their parts of the project, and evidence exists to suggest that the authors may have exchanged notes and research. Jay wrote the fewest of the essays because shortly after undertaking the endeavor he became incapacitated by illness.

It is, however, the general opinion of scholars that the success and overall brilliance of *The Federalist* reside less with any individual writer than with the combined expertise and goodwill that all three authors brought to the series. At the conclusion of the Constitutional Convention, both Hamilton and Madison emerged with profound doubts about the efficacy of the document they had helped to create, and, moreover, each objected to it for radically different reasons. Distrustful of the laboring classes, Hamilton wanted a far stronger federal government than that proposed by the Constitution. Madison, on the other hand, feared that the Constitution gave too much centralized power to a federal authority, and he worried about the possibilities of tyranny and the loss of regional control by the states. In later life, Hamilton and Madison would once again come to odds over these issues, but at the time when they wrote *The Federalist* they realized that without some type of effective federal union anarchy and dissolution would inevitably erupt among the states and that the consequences for the future of North America would indeed be dire. For this reason, they put aside their differences, joined forces under the banner of "Publius," and in a spirit of unique goodwill argued the prospective merits of a federal union of the kind outlined in the Constitution. The result of this decision was what one scholar has termed a richly textured interplay of opinion and a model of decorum that the readers of *The Federalist*, who themselves were divided by suspicions and factional interests, could appreciate, emulate, and eventually embrace.

In dividing up the essays, each writer took primary responsibility for those areas he was most suited to discuss. Jay, for example, with his extensive diplomatic experience, focused on the subject of foreign relations. As a former military officer, Hamilton devoted much of his attention to military and executive concerns. By far the most scholarly of the three, Madison is considered to have been the world's foremost expert on the strengths and weaknesses of historical republics, and hence he directed much of his energy to analyzing the potential advantages and disadvantages of the proposed union. All three writers brought to their discussions a familiarity with the most current political and social theorists of the day, including Locke, Hobbes, Montesquieu, and Hume.

As a literary artifact, *The Federalist* deserves attention for its remarkable clarity of expression, precision of argument, lucidity of style, and mastery of organization. Although it belongs in that genre of literature known as the "political pamphlet," a form that in America can be traced back to the published debates between Roger Williams and John Cotton, *The Federalist* avoids the excesses of vituperation so often found in such works during the 18th century. For their style and tone the writers of *The Federalist* turned to the essays of Joseph Addison, but they nonetheless managed to avoid the cleverness of phrasing and rhetorical embellishments popular among many 18th-century essayists. In many ways, the style of *The Federalist* is unique. As one critic has pointed out, in writing *The Federalist* the authors seemed to have adhered to the very modern theory of rhetoric that they articulated in *Federalist* 37: "The use of words is to express ideas. Perspicuity, therefore, requires not only that the ideas should be distinctly formed, but that they should be expressed by words distinctly and exclusively appropriate to them." By applying this theory to their own writing, the authors of *The Federalist* fashioned "a literary monument to one of [their] country's greatest achievements." In the words of one commentator, "a literary craftsman can hardly do more."

—James A. Levernier

FOUR QUARTETS.
Poems by T.S. Eliot, 1943.

Twenty years separate *The Waste Land* from *Little Gidding*, the last of T.S. Eliot's *Four Quartets*. In spite of the interval, important signs of continuity unite the two works: most obviously the division of the poems into "movements" which reflect a "musical" conception of structure and the alternation of lyrical and discursive passages. Even the direct recourse to religious concepts in the *Quartets* is less innovative than might appear. The poems do not require the previous acceptance of any doctrinal formulation, but invite us rather to share in the exploration of a fully contemporary experience in which doubt, the difficulty of affirmative commitment, has a necessary part to play.

The first quartet, *Burnt Norton*, is concerned to establish a conceptual basis on which the later development may rest. After the initial tentative proposal of a possible convergence between time lived and time remembered—"What might have been and what has been / Point to one end, which is always present"—the first "movement" addresses itself to a past moment of personal illumination which might seem to confirm it. "Round the corner," "through the first gate" which seems, on reflection, to have opened into a "first world" of pure simplicity, the poem strives to recapture an experience which may indeed have been a "deception," but which might also offer the fleeting glimpse of a timeless reality. The fragments of past experience are held in precarious unity until the pressure of present reality returns them to their separate elements: "Go, go, go, said the bird: human kind / Cannot bear very much reality." Vision or illusion? In our incapacity, as time-conditioned beings, to hold fast to these moments of illumination only reflection, speculation on what has irretrievably vanished, can hope to tell.

To speculation, accordingly, we turn in the remainder of the first quartet. The experience in the garden seemed to suggest, while it lasted, that "To be conscious is not to be in time"; but, since only in time can it be remembered, the temporal element is inseparable from any continuing significance it may have. "Involved with past and future, / Only through time, time is conquered." To accept time as an ultimate reality is to risk turning our moments of timeless insight into illusions; but to deny the reality of the temporal is to render our experience, within its human limits, impossible.

The dilemma has particular application to the poet's creative endeavour. Language, the material of his art, shares in the necessary fragility of the temporal: "Words move, music moves / Only in time; but that which is only living / Can only die." Words "strain," "crack," continually "break" in the effort to express the timeless core of experience; and yet it is towards such expression, through a search for the "stillness," the achievement of the subsistent "pattern," that the deepest intuitions of art tend. To approach the timeless through the temporal, obtaining through the elements given by temporal experience the form that is the limited expression of a timeless reality, is at once the task of the artist and the obligation imposed upon him by his intermediate condition—poised "between being and un-being"—as a man.

Upon these conceptual foundations the following quartets build an expanding succession of meanings. The point of departure for *East Coker* is the disillusionment inspired, at a time of personal stress and collapsing certainties, by the approach of old age. "The long hoped for calm, the autumnal serenity" which we have been taught to expect as the reward of a lifetime's effort seems to have turned into a comfortless delusion. The disappointment, however, can be seen to contain a salutary warning against the temptation, inseparable from old age, to seek finality in an illusory "wisdom" based exclusively on past experience. "Home" may indeed be "where one starts from," and the end of the human journey in time may be sought, as the illuminating moment in the garden seemed to suggest, through a return; but between "beginning" and "end," the birth and death of each individual life, the degree of insight achieved necessarily changes and acceptance of this necessity is a condition of continuing life in the present. "Old men ought to be explorers": and again, "We must be still, and still moving." *Still*: ready, that is, to refrain from premature self-assertion in relation to a reality that is at each moment new, unpredictable, uniquely challenging; but equally *still moving*, ready to move with the current, rejecting the temptation to evade the dangerous challenge of the present by falling back upon judgments relevant only in the past.

The third quartet—*The Dry Salvages*—relates this doctrine of necessary renewal to a wider human context. Comparing the course of life—both that of the individual and that of the race to which he belongs—to the progress of a great river as it runs into the sea, the poem has recourse, more directly than at any previous point, to concepts which reflect the distilled experience of the poet's own Christian tradition. The only conceivable answer to "the bone's prayer to Death its God" is to be found in "the hardly, barely prayable / Prayer of the one Annunciation." What is "announced," presented as a redeeming possibility, is the related concept of "Incarnation": the spirit revealed through flesh, "The point of intersection of the timeless / With time": the possibility of a fresh approach to the "meaning," one which "restores the experience / In a different form, beyond any meaning / We can assign to happiness." This leads to a re-statement of the traditional notion of the "good death." Since, as we have already seen, the "pattern" of each human life is at any given point in time incomplete, its final sense can emerge only at the moment of death, when time ceases to be relevant and when the destiny of the individual is incorporated into that of the generations which have shaped the tradition to which his own efforts have now added their contribution. The moment of death becomes not an isolated point but one which covers the entire course of human existence. The end of the journey is present in its beginning, and experience becomes an invitation to confidence: "Not farewell, but fare forward, voyagers."

The last poem in the series, *Little Gidding*, is, theologically speaking, the most explicit. The acceptance of Incarnation leads naturally to an anticipation of the descent of the Spirit in tongues of fire. Once again, the poem proposes no short cut to spiritual peace. Its second "movement" offers, through a deeply personal meditation on "the gifts reserved for age," a conclusion as dismissive of easy consolation as anything in the sequence. The prevailing image of fire has a double significance, penitential and purgatorial, before it becomes the illuminating flame of Pentecost.

As the sequence moves to its conclusion, however, the doctrine of detachment developed in the earlier quartets becomes an "expanding" one of love beyond "desire": a reconciling condition in which even those who were divided during their life-times by sincerely held convictions—such as those which separated committed men during the religious conflicts of 17th-century England—can be seen from the perspective of history as "United in the strife which divided them," gathered in the unity of "a single party." In a related way the poet's own struggle, sustained through a life-time, to find a medium adequate to express his meanings bears fruit in an instrument which has been perfected through succeeding generations and to which he is now making his personal contribution: that of a language

> where every word is at home,
> Taking its place to support the others,
> The word neither diffident nor ostentatious,
> An easy commerce of the old and the new,
> The common word exact without vulgarity,
> The formal word precise but not pedantic,
> The complete consort dancing together.

The end of the poem, and of the series, returns to its beginning, but in a form clarified by the intervening development. It is true that "we die with the dying," accepting the necessary death implied in our temporal condition; but it is true also that "we are born with the dead" and may aspire to a state in which seeming opposites are brought together, reconciled in the lover's knot, the "rose" woven from the element of purifying and transfiguring "fire."

—Derek A. Traversi

GIFTS OF THE MAGI.
Story by O. Henry, 1905.

Considered from a non-traditional perspective, O. Henry's best-loved story, "Gifts of the Magi," published in the 10 December 1905 issue of the New York *Sunday World Magazine*, is much more than a sentimental Christmas morality. Though it has often been taken as the latter and is tagged with one of his conspicuous, ironic twists of plot, it is actually one of the strangest and most haunting stories he ever wrote. (The story is more familiar as "The Gift of the Magi," the title given it for its book publication in *The Four Million*.)

There is a succession of curious, provocative features, a layered pattern of fact and implication, relating to the story's composition and to the author's obscure intentions. First, the feature of subject matter and writer: "Gifts of the Magi" emphasizes the felicity of domestic relations and the sacramental nature of a married couple's exchange of Christmas presents. But it was written by a man who cared neither for marriage nor for religion. His two attempts at matrimony were egregious failures, largely because of his individualistic lifestyle and his lack of concern for the spouse. As for religion, his pagan outlook had been remarked on in his own day. Commenting on this, his biographer Richard O'Connor states, "He wasn't against religion, he simply ignored it."

Next there is the business of literary creation. Hobbled by bad work habits and a helter-skelter mode of bohemian-bachelor existence, O. Henry ground out his fiction pieces under the nagging pressure of crowding editorial deadlines and (what were for him) skimpy finances. He always found writing to order difficult, and the brief that led to "Gifts of the Magi" was especially irksome: he was to produce a newspaper fiction work scheduled for the Christmas issue, and having "something to do with Christmas, something at least faintly religious." His initial problem was lack of inspiration regarding the assignment; this was compounded by repeated delays in just getting down to work; but the result was a literary gem hurriedly conveyed to the newspaper office shortly before the paper went to press.

A young, struggling couple in an eight-dollar-per-week furnished flat have sold their most prized possessions—Jim Young, the gold watch that had come down from his father and his grandfather; his wife Della, her long beautiful tresses—so each could buy an appropriate Christmas gift for the other: a set of combs for Della and a watch fob-chain for Jim. Significantly, "Gifts of the Magi" evokes the biblical account of Samson and Delilah; in this instance the woman, whose name clearly suggests "Delilah," ravishes her own hair. This brings us to the biblical magi referred to by O. Henry, and to the gifts they bring to the Babe in the manger—gold, frankincense, and myrrh—gifts which O. Henry regards somewhat dubiously.

When Della tells Jim what she has done to her hair and why, she asks him to understand, saying that no one could ever measure her love for him. The author indicates that there is no way to put a monetary value on the rental of their flat—presumably because of the love it holds. In his illustration, neither mathematicians nor wits nor magi could explain the difference between what the Youngs pay for rent, and a million a year. Valuable as the magi's gifts to the Babe in the manger were, the ability to reduce love to monetary figures was not one of their gifts. This leads O. Henry to conclude that the magi doubtless gave the Babe wise gifts, possibly *exchangeable* "in case of duplication." But these "two foolish children" were the wisest of all giftgivers and receivers—because for their gifts they had "most unwisely sacrificed" their "greatest treasures"; people like them are the wisest of all—the (real-life) magi. Still, there is an elusive something in this strange amalgam of tenement romance and Bible sampler that nags at the reader's mind.

The last curious feature of "Gifts of the Magi" has to do with Jim Young, his watch, and conventional time. Before he sold his paternal heirloom watch, Jim had been accustomed to taking it out and admiring it. Della, before she learned that he had sold the watch, had told him that he would presently have to look at it a hundred times each day—in wifely fashion anticipating the effect of her gift, and reinforcing O. Henry's point that Jim had been very conscious of time. But with Jim's Christmas sacrifice of his timepiece, the old order of time ended. Yet, though he and Della will not be living under a new temporal order—symbolically, a timeless limbo—the possibility of redemption in an ultimate order of time remains. Jim, to Della: "let's put our Christmas presents away and keep 'em a while. They're too nice to use just at present." Thus, with *her* hair slowly beginning to grow back, and the (implied) possibility that Jim's watch might somehow, someday be bought back, there is good reason for these two self-sacrificing "magi" so deeply in love to await the glorious birth of a new age of unlimited possibility.

If O. Henry's ironic story-line suggests irony beyond irony, it may be stated in the form of a question: had he been a devout churchgoer and a good and proper husband, could O. Henry have written a more effective, meaningful story with the same original ingredients?

—Samuel Irving Bellman

THE GLASS MENAGERIE.
Play by Tennessee Williams, 1944.

Tennessee Williams first developed the characters and situation of *The Glass Menagerie* in a short story, "Portrait of a Girl in Glass" (published later in 1948), and an unproduced screenplay, *The Gentleman Caller*, before his first major success came with its award-winning Broadway stage production starring Laurette Taylor as Amanda. The autobiographical nature of his characters is evident. The playwright dramatizes his youthful self in Tom Wingfield, a would-be poet trapped by family obligations with a dull Depression-days job in a shoe factory, and in the maturing merchant seaman-narrator recalling for the audience with a mixture of guilt and sentimentality the memory of a mother, whom he self-tormentingly appreciates; an absent father (represented only by a grinning photograph which lights up on cue) from whom he is estranged; and a sister to whom he is strongly attached. Amanda, the charmingly overbearing mother, clings to the memory of being a southern belle in a genteel past that conflicts unkindly with her present straitened circumstances in a dingy city apartment. She neither understands her son's need for adventure and self-fulfillment nor accepts the extent of her daughter's reclusiveness. Tom's painfully shy and physically crippled sister Laura hides in a fantasy world of tiny glass animals. The characters are variations, excepting a younger brother, of Williams's own family: his mother, a Mississippi minister's daughter who experienced difficult circumstances while raising a family and forced a separation from the playwright's mostly absent father, a hard-drinking salesman not understanding of his quiet and bookish older son; his schizophrenic sister Rose; and the playwright himself whose experience parallels that of Tom Wingfield.

More significant, however, than the play's autobiographical base is its demonstration of Williams's early ability to write theatrically effective scenes that artfully intermixed the comic and the tragic and made telling use of symbolism (the drama's title is a prime example) to evoke mood and meaning, to compose lyrically rich dialogue reflecting a gifted poetic temperament and an ear for the rhythmic speech patterns of his native south, and to create finely sculpted characters who anticipate both his emerging view of the human condition and the nature of major characters yet to walk in subsequent works. Persons with the streak of sensitivity, gentility, or romanticism in Williams's world are confronted with a harsh, unkind reality which either destroys them as victims, rejects them as outcasts, or serves as a battleground on which they tenaciously struggle to emerge as survivors. While Amanda Wingfield clutches the romantic recollection of a gentle era when she entertained 17 gentlemen callers in one afternoon she also resiliently and feistily copes with life's stern reality for her own survival and that of her family. Laura, after abortive encounters with life including a climactic one with a "gentleman caller," reveals herself as too fragile—like her glass unicorn whose horn is broken by the caller's clumsiness—to pursue outside reality and thus becomes instead its victim retreating into her own fantasy world. Tom Wingfield refuses to accept commonplace life's proscriptive obligations and strictures and becomes therefore an outcast and wanderer. These figures are images that will appear again on the playwright's other dramatic canvases. Unusual in Williams's work is this tender family portrait, in sharp contrast to the far less gentle works which followed.

The play presents its people within the framework of eight scenes, essentially realistic in style but augmented by symbolic overtones and nonrealistic theatrical devices. Strong in theatricality and emotional power, the scenes, summoned up by the narrator who steps in and out of them as observer and participant, lead to the action's major incident: the arrival and aftermath of the gentleman caller, the unimaginative warehouse worker Jim O'Connor whom Laura recognizes as a secretly loved former high school hero. In a poignant scene, the caller unwittingly raises romantic expectations in Laura only to dash them when he confesses his engagement to another girl. His swift departure leaves a desolate Laura who retreats back with finality to her world of figurines, and an angry Amanda whose unfair upbraiding of Tom drives him to a pre-planned final departure. The action's climax and resolution are both moving and compelling. The play limns a portrait of the poet as a young man who must be free to follow his art and commemorates his escape from a family, the memory of which will pursue him on his journey as a writer.

Generally accepted as one of Williams's masterpieces, this work represents the start of his strongest creative period, lasting to *The Night of the Iguana* in 1961. Since its first New York production, *The Glass Menagerie* has been continually produced throughout the world. Its long-lasting success is well deserved.

—Christian H. Moe

GO TELL IT ON THE MOUNTAIN.
Novel by James Baldwin, 1953.

On occasion in his fiction James Baldwin wears the mask of the passionate priest, a medieval monk who has seized the pen in order to inscribe the legends, the chronicles, and the martyrdoms of his people. Indeed, his first novel, *Go Tell It on the Mountain*, reveals Baldwin in this role as monkish chronicler, setting forth in miniature the history of his people as they move from bondage and seek the promised land. And the religious ambience of this novel is consistent with a view of it as a formalized version of black legend.

It is not systematic or intellectual history, but folk history, episodic in character, made up of typical and representative actions which rest upon a commonly held body of belief and assumption and so carry wide-ranging implications. Minor examples will quickly illustrate this kinship with medieval literature. Florence, the aunt of John Grimes, the protagonist, flees the south when her employer threatens to make her his concubine. Deborah, the first wife of Gabriel, John's father, was raped by white men when she was sixteen years old. A nameless black soldier is mutilated and killed by a white mob. These actions are presented as typical, not unique, experiences. Baldwin is fulfilling a pattern for a literary exercise as highly stylized as the sermon or the legend: he is treating what might be called, after the medieval practice, the matter of the south. The reader in tune with Baldwin understands his heuristic purpose and can construct from his suggestive episodes the whole history of a suffering race.

Much of the novel deals with the emergence of the Grimes family from the south and especially with the struggle of Gabriel, the father and a preacher, to reach a state of grace, despite the obstacles that society puts in his way and despite his own violent and sinning nature. His marriage to Deborah, made in good part because she had been raped, and his marriage to Elizabeth, who had had an illegitimate son, are actions taken deliberately in search of expiation for his own sins. His hopes for Roy, the only living son of his loins, are the hopes of a patriarch for a successor who shall fulfill the destiny of his people. Baldwin persuades the reader to feel the weight of Gabriel's anguish as he makes his fateful choices and struggles with his exaggerated sense of sin. Gabriel is a more human figure than any other character in the chronicle, a man in whom passion and faith collide. And, as the lineaments of humanity appear in him, he is removed from his conventional role as Patriarch, Leader of his Tribe. Nevertheless, in the largest sense, the story of the Grimes family as Baldwin conceives it is a formalized chronicle, a history of escape from a land of oppression to a new place where, after suffering, freedom and salvation may come, some time in the future, as deserved rewards.

This account of the suffering of the black people and the search for salvation, capsulized in the career of Gabriel Grimes, is treated in a series of flashbacks in the novel, while the action in the present takes place at a service in the Temple of the Fire Baptized church in Harlem. The flashback technique gives that sense of distance in time which creates the aura appropriate to legend, and in the singing and praying, the service lends ritual amplitude to the legend.

Baldwin plays his role as monkish chronicler well, in the sense that he faithfully records stereotypical characters and situations. He brings some originality and vitality to the other important aspect of this novel, the maturation of John Grimes, Gabriel's stepson and bastard of Elizabeth. The fourteen-year-old John is clearly an autobiographical figure, as Baldwin has said elsewhere, who is seeking to find his way out of adolescence. He must cope with a tyrannical father, an evangelical and puritanical religion, and exaggerated sense of sin, and a Harlem environment pregnant with violence as he seeks the road to maturity and identity. In the crucial experience of his life thus far, he frees himself from all the tyrannies in his life—the father, the guilt over his sins, the ghetto—by embracing religion and being embraced by it, by knowing that he must climb the mountain of faith and place his destiny in the hands of the Lord. John, the rejected son—it has been argued that he is Ishmael to Gabriel's Abraham—frees himself from his father, partly by rising above him in purity and zeal, when he gives himself into bondage to faith; at least some of the tensions between them are washed away in the new moral and spiritual assurance that comes to John after his ecstatic experience. Like Gabriel, John had suffered from a conflict between the narrow morality of his church and the awakening sexual demands of his body. This conflict is submerged if not resolved in that access of spirit which comes to John. The church also offers a refuge from the violence and degeneracy of Harlem which represent both the conditions of black life and the conception of it held by others. The church frees John from his father's tyranny and self-righteousness, from guilt over sin, from shame and terror at being black in the midst of black corruption. At the same time it defines the conditions of his search for maturity and identity. At the end of *Go Tell It on the Mountain* John accepts religion and Christianity because they free him from the problems he faces in the world; they free him to grow within the limits they set.

—Chester E. Eisinger

GODS DETERMINATIONS.
Poem by Edward Taylor, written 1680's (?).

Gods Determinations touching his Elect: and The Elects Combat in their Conversion, and Coming up to God in Christ together with the Comfortable Effects thereof, which was probably written in the 1680's when the Stoddard controversy was just beginning, is the first of two major works by the American puritan poet and congregationalist minister Edward Taylor, the other being the *Preparatory Meditations* (1682–1725), a series of over 200 poems written as spiritual preparation for the pastor's administration of the Lord's Supper to his congregation in the church at Westfield, a small town in the western part of the Massachusetts Bay Colony. Although in fact only two stanzas of all of Taylor's poetic works were published in the poet's lifetime, Taylor may have at one time intended to publish *Gods Determinations*. The single extant manuscript of this poem of 2,101 lines was written in a very careful hand on numbered pages (the other pages in the Yale manuscript of the collected poems are not numbered) and placed just before the series of meditations. One has the impression that before he bound up *Gods Determinations* with other poems, he considered it as an independent work which he may well have carried with him to read from the pulpit or at prayer meetings. The poem is hortatory in nature. It is written with a definite audience in mind—first, perhaps, the members of his own congregation and by extension (if published) to any Christian reader who needed assurance that he was one of God's predestined elect and therefore eligible to be a full church member and participate in the sacred communion of the Lord's Supper. In the 1680's there was need of a spiritual awakening, for many puritans were under the so-called Half Way Covenant and uncertain of their spiritual fitness to become full members. At this time Solomon Stoddard, pastor of the church in the neighboring town of Northampton, was beginning to promulgate the doctrine that the Lord's Supper was a converting ordinance and that those who doubted their election might be converted to full assurance by accepting communion. Taylor attacked Stoddard in his letters, sermons, and poems. His position, the "orthodox" one, was that a person must be a converted "saint" before accepting communion. His task as a minister and (perhaps) as a poet was to convince the backward members of his congregation *before* communion that they were of the elect and could come to the communion table without fear of damnation. In *Gods Determinations* Taylor dramatically presents and explains God's mysterious ways in bringing his few chosen saints to salvation.

The doctrine of the poem is the orthodox Calvinism of the leading colonial ministers of Taylor's period including Increase and Cotton Mather and Michael Wigglesworth, author of the notorious poem *The Day of Doom*: predestination, the salvation of the elect few, the damnation of the many, the perseverance of the saints, the inefficacy of works to attain saving grace, justification and salvation by faith alone. Heaven and hell are seen as definite locations, not symbolic states of mind, and God, Christ, Satan, angels, and demons may take on the attributes of real persons. *Gods Determinations* is made up of a group of 35 poems in various meters and stanza forms. The poem as a whole has a three-fold structure: 1) The creation of the world and man, the fall of man, the damnation of the many, the salvation of the elect few through God's saving grace; 2) Satan's powerful attack on the elect and his failure to destroy them; 3) the joys of salvation.

Some of the best writing occurs in the Preface of part one. Taylor describes the beauties of the earth which God created out of "Nothing":

> Who made the Sea's its Selvedge, and it locks
> Like a Quilt Ball within a Silver Box?
> Who Spread its Canopy? Or Curtains Spun?
> Who in this Bowling Alley bowld the Sun?

God who is seen as all powerful ("Whose single Frown will make the Heavens shake / Like as an aspen leafe the Winde makes quake") creates "Nothing Man," giving him an eternal soul to glorify Him, but because of man's fall, this "Brightest Diamond" is "grown / Darker by far than any Coalpit stone." The next four poems describe in detail man's fall and God's foresight in planning how, through the intervention of Christ's mercy, the elect will be saved. Part two, consisting of 23 individual poems, dramatically presents the spiritual combat between Satan and the elect. A very few of the elect escape the rigors of combat and are converted immediately by God into saints. The rest are divided into three ranks to face the terrors of Satan's temptations. Satan becomes the most colorful character in the drama—a raging roaring beast intent on destroying his enemies at first by physical terror. The first rank, however, are soon comforted by Christ's intervention and, escaping Satan, begin their journey to heaven. Satan now, in a series of poems, but most interestingly in "Satan's Sophestry," attacks the remaining ranks with psychological warfare. In the most subtle of all his arguments he claims that if man is certain he is saved he (a poor sinner) is guilty of "presumption," that is, pride, which is a cardinal sin, and therefore he is damned. At last, however, the second and third ranks, with the help of God acting through saints already saved, become convinced they are truly of the elect and so escape Satan's wiles. Part three, which consists of seven poems, describes the ecstasy of the saints "while in Christs Coach they sweetly sing / As they to Glory ride therein."

The poem is in the spiritual combat tradition with scenes of martial warfare reminiscent of the Old Testament, and one is reminded also at times of Bunyan and Milton as well as of the medieval morality plays. Judged by literary standards, *Gods Determinations* cannot be compared with Milton's *Paradise Lost* which also was written to "justify the ways of God to men." Nevertheless, because of its metrical and stylistic variety ranging from the colloquial diction of the colonial farmer to the exalted diction of such poets as Vaughan and Crashaw, it is far superior to Wigglesworth's *The Day of Doom* and more dramatic and intense than any of the longer poems of Anne Bradstreet. It is the best long poem of the 17th century written on what was to become United States soil.

—Donald E. Stanford

THE GRAPES OF WRATH.
Novel by John Steinbeck, 1939.

Today the *New York Review of Books* comments on social change: the roads are clogged with "retired farmers" who "leave for Florida in their fancy campers." John Steinbeck's *The Grapes of Wrath* records an earlier time, depression days of Dust Bowl farmers, their farms blown away, heading in jalopies for California's golden groves. If modern America has any idea of Okies and hard times, it is largely due to Steinbeck's greatest work.

In it, Steinbeck's "voice over" and vivid episodes create a kind of newsreel of a period when times got tough and the tough got going, westward as ever in their very American and indomitable flight to something better. It is that courage and determination "in the presence of this continent" that has made the book a classic of our literature, that gained it in its own day a great success despite its ignorant Okies (with their accents and even their customs all wrong), and its nasty union men (either venal or fanatic), and its sordid language, as some thought. ("Take the vulgarity out of this book," a shocked Oklahoma congressman told the House of Representatives in 1940, "and it would be blank from cover to cover.") Steinbeck outdid himself as he wrote about what some representative Americans of his time "are doing, thinking, wanting." He said: "It's all a writer knows. I have set down what a large section of our people are doing and wanting, and symbolically what all people of all time are doing and wanting. The migration is the outward sign of the want. . . ." He intensely admired the Okies "because they are brave, although the technique of their life is difficult and complicated, they meet it with increasing strength, because they are kind, humorous and wise, because their speech has the metaphor and flavor and imagery of poetry, because they can resist and fight back, and because I believe that out of these qualities will grow a new system and a new life which will be better than anything we have had before."

Steinbeck's faith seems to have been in something more like a Life Force than the strident socialism of his day; he had a sort of mystical belief in people, not a political belief in the proletariat. And so he wrote a work of art that went beyond the propaganda novel of police brutality and proletarian strikes, an angry and unorthodox New Testament of a religion of mankind. Critics differ as to whether Jim Casy is the Christ or the John the Baptist of this gospel and whether Tom Joad is the Christ or the St. Paul, but all must agree with the critic who wrote that what we have is "a re-enactment in modern times of events which occurred centuries ago," a story of man evicted from his garden that is far more successful as an allegory than *East of Eden*. The trials and tribulations show the sacrifice of a child to remove the curse of barrenness, the testing and the promise of salvation in the end, as well as the desert of despair and the water of life. God who provided the turtle with a shell can offer man no less protection. Run over, he will survive. Changes will have to come, but if brave Ma perishes then Rose of Sharon will be our Blessed Mother. This is a religious novel, not merely a socialist one, not merely a bitter comment on the sentimental "wagons westward" epics and the sociological diatribes. Steinbeck is more artist than activist, and he has woven of actual events and biblical allusions what has been rightly identified as "a pattern of dispossession; of nobility achieved by sacrifice necessitated by suffering; of wandering in the wilderness of exile; of struggle, defeat, hope, and eventual victory; of decadence and renewed struggles—here is an allegory of humanity itself."

This is the kind of message, if not exactly the kind of writing, that wins the Nobel Prize for Literature. This is the kind of theme that for once exactly fitted one of Steinbeck's basic limitations: he is not a great thinker and his characters are not, either. He specializes, our best American critic (Edmund Wilson) quickly noted, "not in those aspects of humanity in which it is most thoughtful, imaginative, constructive" but in simple human beings, "almost at the animal level," enduring or fighting to survive. His best subject is "the processes of life itself."

Steinbeck at his best, as in *The Grapes of Wrath*, writes of basic plights of mankind. Warren French perceptively writes: "If the Joads had not been caught up in the events of a particular time and place that had profoundly affected Steinbeck and troubled his public, we might more easily recognize that their story belongs with Shakespeare's *The Tempest* and other masterpieces of the travail and triumph of the human spirit."

That is why Peter Lisca (who edited the 1972 edition of *The Grapes of Wrath*, in which the text appears with about a dozen essential critical documents of great value to the serious student) could write this at the beginning of his preface:

> Very few of those who read *The Grapes of Wrath* in 1939 could have foreseen that this book, which dramatized the headlines and newsreels of the day, which seemed so intimately connected with them that its merits were debated not in literary terms but in those of sociological research and political ideology, would continue to be read long after the headlines had been forgotten. . . . What distinguishes this one novel is not only its greater authenticity of detail but also the genius of its author, who, avoiding mere propaganda, was able to raise those details and themes to the level of lasting art, while muting none of the passionate human cry against injustice. . . . In fact, the response of students leaves no doubt that as literature *The Grapes of Wrath* is generally experienced more completely today than it was in 1939, when it was much more difficult to dissociate the novel from current events or to see Steinbeck's bold technical experiments as something more than what one critic called "calculated crudities."

The novel also reads better today because many college students are, quite frankly, almost as unfamiliar with fine writing as they are with socialist theories or biologism or regional Oklahoma dialect (all of which take a beating in the book). They are moved by the tragedy of the Joads and the lilt of a "song of social significance" and they do not notice that this is one of those great American masterpieces (along with *Moby-Dick* and *An American Tragedy*, not to get too close to living writers) which is very awkwardly written. Edmund Wilson again: in 1948 he shrewdly summed up Steinbeck's novels, of which this is indisputably the most powerful, as marking "precisely the borderline between work that is definitely superior and work that is definitely bad."

The strong story line is well-known. The Joad family is driven from the Dust Bowl farm "house broke." Hardworking Grampa and religious Granma and lonely Uncle John join Ma (she's the one in charge) and Pa (he's a trifle confused by it all), stupid Noah, hotheaded Tom, Connie and Rose of Sharon (carrying a child), Al, Ruthie and Winfield—a motley crew joined in desperation and in hope. The trek will also involve Jim Casy (a sort of mix of the traditional preacher and the traditional village atheist). Some are lost on the way. Some desert. But the rest keep on: "There ain't nothin' else you can do." California is their dream but turns out to be a nightmare of evil sheriffs and worse. The caravan winds up in a kind of concentration camp and the able-bodied are forced to pick fruit in a black-listed orchard, where they run into angry strikers. Leading the strikers is socialist Casy. He is killed, and Tom kills Casy's murderer and has to lie low. The others guard him, and pick cotton, and finally Ma sends Tom away. He goes to take up Casy's cudgels as a labor organizer, with a credo of helping the Little Man in need wherever he may be. Rose of Sharon's baby is born dead, but there is a hope of life going on: she suckles a starving man who "ain't et for six days." The men will organize and fight and the women will succour and bring new life. A little food, a dry place. Things will get better, somehow, some time. "We ain't gonna die out," says Ma. "People is goin' on . . . goin' right on." As the novel ends what is left of the group is hard-pressed indeed, but we are meant to believe that they will survive. It is, in fact, impossible to think otherwise.

This upbeat philosophy—and *The Grapes of Wrath* is bold to mix philosophy or even a secular theology with facts—is what the Nobel Prize chiefly honored in Steinbeck in 1962 when the Swedish Academy said:

> His sympathies always go out to the oppressed, the misfits, and the distressed; he likes to contrast the simple joy of life with the brutal and cynical craving for money. But in him we find the American temperament also expressed in his great feeling for nature, for the tilled soil, the waste land, the mountains and the ocean coasts, all an inexhaustible source of inspiration to Steinbeck in the midst of, and beyond, the world of human beings.

Steinbeck liked the title *The Grapes of Wrath* "Because it is a march, because it is in our revolutionary tradition and because in reference to this book it has a large meaning." He added: "And I like it because people know the Battle Hymn [of the Republic] who don't know the Stars and Stripes." Others like the book because it is quintessentially American, and all the more so (perhaps) because though not "literary" it is one of our literary classics.

—Leonard R.N. Ashley

GRAVITY'S RAINBOW.
Novel by Thomas Pynchon, 1973.

Gravity's Rainbow, which *Time* found "funny, disturbing, exhausting, mind-fogging in its range and permutations," is

Thomas Pynchon's masterpiece, the absurdist and apocalyptic story of the last days of World War II with dire significance for what we hope are not the last days of our nuclear age. It is the product of the rarest kind of American writer, the intellectual who keeps away from literary fads and pays no attention to contemporary authors or critical theories. It is that typically American everything-but-the-kitchen-sink construction and that almost unheard of American thing, the hilarious intellectual meditation. (Few Americans realize the truth of Borges's dictum that intellectual activity is always essentially ludicrous.) Critics, in the habit of reviewing personalities rather than real books, have hardly known how to react to a 900-page tome by an author who is practically anonymous, who (says *Saturday Review*) "has caught the inward movement of our time," and who writes about the most important things of our age in a way that is both dazzling and didactic.

The book is often overwhelming in language and structure. Not since James Joyce's *Finnegans Wake*, perhaps, has there been a major novel so extraordinary in its cinematographic construction and its mixtures and manipulation of languages. *Gravity's Rainbow*, too, is worthy of a "key" or a "key to the key" (or even an abridgement by Anthony Burgess, for it is as self-indulgent and extravagant in length as it is in everything else). Meanwhile we have to work it out for ourselves, supplying the history of the end of the Third Reich, brushing up on our German, Russian, French, Spanish, basic sciences, and more, picking our way through the intellectual minefields of the book and looking up lots of literary allusions, cheered by the fact that this is not "work in progress" but a finished product, loosely but carefully put together, depressing in its descriptions of war and pessimistic in its predictions of doom but laugh-out-loud funny and ultimately a hymn to man's ability to survive, even to survive the technological disasters he brings upon himself. Also, if man did not destroy himself, God would have to invent a destruction for him; *c'est son métier*, destroying as well as creating, and if The Firm or the military-industrial complex or some other bogeyman doesn't get you (or, as more often happens, you don't like the way you have been getting yourself all along), then God and entropy, justice and gravity will.

And what meaning does this complexity strive to express? As man rose from the clay, so he will end in it. God Who made the universe made this rule as well: everything that goes up must come down, whether priapic or ballistic. Life is your trajectory and your glory, the temporary triumph over extinction, the being that beats nothingness for five minutes with a rocket and maybe a little longer with an erection or an accomplishment. But Society if not God Himself wants to use and to use up anyone potent, especially the artist, and only for a brief span can one be "a system *won*," a burning (self-consuming) meteor or rocket "away from the feminine darkness, held against the entropies of lovable but scatterbrained Mother Nature." Women make babies to carry things on; men make technology to *get it up*, but neither time nor gravity waits for any woman or man. Rather, they lie in wait. So live while you can, and enjoy your arc. Gravity makes a nice parabolic rainbow in the sky of a destruction-laden V-2 rocket.

The plot resembles a detective or, better, espionage story: the antihero is in flight as in some John Buchan adventure, trying to make discoveries while he himself is being sought. It is also something of a political act, as all good novels are. Something of an anti-technology document, but written by a realist well aware that we can't blame our science for ourselves, because we made it before it started to remake us. Something of a love story, there being at least one character "in love, in sexual love, with his own death." Central in this picaresque and sometimes grotesque collection of (mostly) stereotypes with fictive names and firm functions in the book is the protagonist, Lt. Tyrone Slothrop, who can enjoy no excess of sloth because PISCES (Psychological Intelligence Scheme for Expediting Surrender) is after him. They have discovered that between his erections and the firing of German V-2s on London there is a "mean lag time" of four and a half days. He could be an instrument in the war effort! He wants to be a human being, not a tool, and he runs from Furies disguised as "The Firm," from the Authorities, from the ubiquitous Them—and he becomes just the runaway, the target, the Rocketman: another abstraction. He also is on an Orphic search in the Underworld: he has lost his harmonica down the toilet—the whole world is down the tubes, really—at Roseland. He meets a comic cast that would have done Fellini proud. (*Gravity's Rainbow* is also something of a Keystone Cop or Star Wars chase movie.)

In *Gravity's Rainbow* there is mention of Poisson's Distribution; it governs the random pattern of rocket strikes. Ours is a universe of laws (like gravity); so is the world of the novel. An iron rule of cohesion governs the wild and brilliant combinations of words, persons, places, things, ideas and digressions from them, in *Gravity's Rainbow*. As fully as in *Finnegans Wake*, as things fall apart the center holds, the author's personal genius keeps it all together. Perhaps not so much like a novelist as traditionally viewed, but more like that modern juggler who convulses and scares audiences as he juggles a weird assortment of bowling balls, sharp axes, oranges, and maybe a buzzsaw. It has the desire at once to entertain and to inculcate into audiences pride in humanity's skill in performance, acceptance of challenge, and final basic triviality. We run in search of ourselves and pursued by Them and in the long run it's the brief game that counts and not the victory.

There were few sensible reactions to *Gravity's Rainbow* when it was published some fifteen years ago, but there were some; and over the years the book that *Newsweek* greeted with caution ("it isn't plausible to call a novel great the week it's published, because the future will decide that") has become a classic, though that may mean simply a book everyone respects but has never read. Richard Poirier reviewed it elatedly: "the book is . . . a profound (and profoundly funny) historical meditation on the humanity sacrificed to a grotesque delusion—the Faustian illusion of the inequality of lives and the inequality of the nature of signs."

At the very worst, earth could start all over. If it cannot, at least it is *not a major planet*. And we had our innings, our brilliant "gravity's rainbow," or should have done, and if we haven't we have no one to blame but you-know-who, and it's not God.

—Leonard R.N. Ashley

THE GREAT GATSBY.
Novel by F. Scott Fitzgerald, 1925.

Influenced by Joseph Conrad, F. Scott Fitzgerald convinced his editor Maxwell Perkins, and most readers since, that *The*

Great Gatsby, though barely fifty thousand words long, includes everything necessary to tell Gatsby's story. One reason Fitzgerald is able to accomplish this feat is his choice of point of view. The angle of narration is that of Nick Carraway, Gatsby's next-door neighbor on Long Island, who, like Gatsby, is a transplanted midwesterner. Nick can tell the story effectively and dramatically because he has information the reader does not have and since he is telling the story after the fact he realizes which of the events are important and the significance of each event. As he informs the reader on the second page of the novel: "When I came back from the East last Autumn I felt that I wanted to be in uniform and at a sort of moral attention forever; I wanted no more riotous excursions with privileged glimpses into the human heart." Jay Gatsby is the only character he wants exempted from his reaction because in Gatsby there was "something gorgeous . . . some heightened sensitivity to the promises of life."

The other reason Fitzgerald can get so much into such a compact novel, Perkins wrote him, is that "a vast amount is said by implication." Fitzgerald not only eliminates all unnecessary details but he maintains a unity of tone and texture: the reader knows all he needs to know of Tom Buchanan, the villain of the novel, from two or three lines of dialogue, including his Nazi-like theories of race. The spiritless inertia of the age is revealed by an abandoned dentist's sign and the wasteland environment around it, the rootlessness of the characters by the climactic action's occurring in an anonymous hotel room (almost as if none of the characters belongs anywhere). Gatsby's parties fall into perspective by the "old sports" he uses to recognize everyone, by the anonymous "long distance" telephone calls, by the "blue" cocktail music, the books in the library with their uncut pages, the unabashed pride with which he displays his vast horde of shirts. The values of Gatsby's world are indicated by the fact that almost all the images in the novel are sight images. Sounds, tastes, smells—those images more subtly associated with deep feelings—are conspicuously absent.

The story Nick tells is a version of the rags-to-riches tale so popular in American since Franklin's *Autobiography*, except in this case the hero does not get the girl. Jay Gatsby, whose real name is Gatz, comes from a poor midwestern family. As a young man he leaves home, becomes a protégé of a wealthy goldminer and lives with him until the miner dies. Then, with some wealth of his own for the first time, he dreams of having more, but before he can get well underway, war is declared and he goes into the army. In uniform it is difficult to tell the rich from the poor so Gatsby begins to see the most popular girl in the town near his army post. From that time on he is determined to have the girl, Daisy. After the war he becomes involved in a drug ring and quickly gains wealth. When he next sees Daisy, however, she is married to Tom Buchanan and lives near him on Long Island. Gatsby begins to give parties, to which everyone is invited, in the hope Daisy will come to one of them. He discovers that Nick is a distant cousin of Tom's, and gets Nick to take him to see Daisy. He foolishly expects to resume his romance with Daisy exactly at the point where he had left it several years before. This is impossible, of course. In the end Gatsby is murdered by the man who thinks he has killed his wife, though actually Daisy has accidentally run over the woman in Gatsby's car.

Gatsby learns that he can neither recall the past nor shape the future. After Gatsby's death Nick comes to realize that, despite his unsavory reputation, he was the best of the lot. He was willing to take the blame for the death of Myrtle Wilson, Tom's mistress, even though Daisy had been driving the car. And Tom is responsible for Gatsby's death because he makes Wilson believe that Myrtle was Gatsby's mistress. At the end of the book Nick muses on the changes that have come to this "land of promise," since it had "flowered . . . for Dutch sailors' eyes—a fresh green breast of the new world."

—Thomas Daniel Young

HAIRCUT.
Story by Ring Lardner, 1925.

Ring Lardner's devastating attacks on big cities (and, especially, resorts where you spend too much money to hobnob with people who at first snub you and then make you wish you had never met them) should give no one the expectation that he thought life in the boondocks was more beautiful. He was born in provincial America—in Niles, Michigan—and he knew it for what it was. It is devastated in such stories as "The Maysville Minstrel" (in which a bucolic bard perpetrates such couplets as "The Maysville Gas Co. has eight hundred meters / The biggest consumer in town is Mrs. Arnold Peters"), "The Facts" (of a broken engagement, broken off before announced, "So only a thousand or so of the intimate friends and relatives of the parties knew anything about it," getting that wrong in the bargain), "The Anniversary" (in a little town where the Carnegie Library had "very few 'hot' books and the few were nearly always out"), and "Gullible's Travels" (among what the hilariously hick narrator calls "the *high polloi*"). But perhaps most famous of all of Lardner's tales of Rube America, equal to his masterpieces "Alibi Ike" and "The Golden Honeymoon," is "Haircut." This is a short story that ranks, in its revelation of unpleasant secrets in small towns, with Faulkner's "A Rose for Emily." Its masterful use of the narrator recalls such triumphs as Chekhov's "Ninotchka," Sherwood Anderson's "I'm a Fool," and Eudora Welty's "Why I Live at the P.O."

If one looks at the tables of contents of those massive anthologies of the American short story recently published for college classes (and, maybe, a few "common readers"), Lardner's name is missing; he is not fashionable. But his brilliant technique and the serious satire behind all the fun, sometimes even a gaga (or dada) whimsy, make him a far more important writer than many writers now so earnestly studied. Perhaps even more significant, his sharp eye for American foible and his acute ear for American speech will in time establish Lardner (along with other authors now rather unappreciated, such as John O'Hara) as one to read in order to see what this nation was like in his time. Humorists have always been somewhat downgraded by American critics and seldom get the recognition they deserve, James Thurber being one notable exception. And Lardner is a more "serious" writer than Thurber usually is. Lardner is more subtle and substantial than that darling of the critics, the acerbic Dorothy Parker. The targets of his satire are often unusual (a rookie pitcher in baseball stories, a dumb detective in "Own Your Own Home"), but he also covers the standard city slickers and country bumpkins with a characteristic trick of pushing them forward to tell their own stories in their own words, avoiding editorial intrusion and yet never abrogating the writer's responsibility to let the acute reader know not only what he is "getting" but "how to take it." His best stories, in such collections as *How to Write Short Stories* and *The Round Up*, show him to be an even better reporter of the 1920's than his friend Fitzgerald and one of the principal American authors of the 20th century.

Take "Haircut." It is not much longer than this note on it. Much depends in the story on Whitey, the narrator. On first reading, the narrator seems to be a loquacious and not very bright tanktown barber; subsequent readings suggest that there may be a lot more to him than that. Like many talkative humorous characters in earlier American literature, hayseed farmers, fools on the frontier, oafs in the sticks, he may be smarter than he looks. Does Whitey tell the tale of a deliberate murder that he is stupid enough, along with others in his small town, perhaps, to take for an accident? Or does he know exactly what happened to Jim Kendall, but think that the victim deserved his fate and that nothing useful would be accomplished by making an issue of it? Or is Whitey putting us all on with a typically backwoods yarn created to get some fun out of horrifying the gullible stranger?

True, there was some person named James H. Kendall in the town. The shaving mug with his name on it in the barbershop is proof of that. But for all we know Whitey took one look at the naive visitor, glanced around his shop for inspiration, saw the mug (and the mug who would believe a tall tale), and made the whole thing up—perhaps even worrying that the real, live Jim Kendall would walk in and blow the whole thing sky-high. Maybe it's pure fabrication, and Whitey is an artist who needs only a few twigs of fact (the shaving mug, for one) to which to attach the spiderweb of story he makes from filaments of his imagination. Maybe his reward is the rapt attention and the unwarranted belief of the listener. Maybe it's an aria, unprompted, uninterrupted by the listener, a fictional achievement.

Whitey's listener, like the reader, really has no way to check on facts. This is, like Henry James's "The Real Thing" and a number of other stories, a short story about the art of short fiction: it asks us about the difference between fact and fiction. There is something essentially Jamesian, for example, in the explanation of what happened when Paul went to Doc Stair with the story of a trick on Julie that had cruelly been played—we are told—by Jim Kendall, who was "all right at heart" but a "character" and "just bubblin' over with mischief":

> It's a cinch Doc went up in the air and swore he'd make Jim suffer. But it was kind of a delicate thing, because if it got out that he had beat Jim up, Julie was bound to hear of it and then she'd know that Doc knew and of course knowin' that he knew would make it worse for her than ever. He was goin' to do somethin', but it took a lot of figurin'.

This is a kind of detective story, but to the sophisticated the problem is not who killed Jim Kendall or even the motive or the outcome of the murder but this: "Is Whitey to be trusted?"

I think not. He quotes dialogue verbatim and then uses similar phrases in his own narration, which suggests the dialogue is invented by him. He makes a few wild jumps in the story; one, for instance, is the sudden change in Doc Stair. The Doc, Whitey tells us, decides to punish Jim Kendall for his mischief, though that is not going to be easy. I think Whitey is rather telling himself what his task and his challenge will be as he continues to spin a story, and that Doc is going to have to be as vengeful and nasty as Jim at his worst—worse, really, because Jim is just a "card" and Doc is far more devious and dangerous.

Well, "Jim and Paul had went shootin' " and Jim gave the gun to the half-wit Paul (why?) and Paul "was shakin' so hard he couldn't control the gun" and shot Jim dead. Then Doc, the coroner, was called, and presumably was delighted to discover what had happened to someone he had once said "ought not to be let live." Moreover, no one was going to blame poor Paul for it, so the case was closed and Justice was done. It's true that Doc was "nervous" when he heard that Jim and Paul had taken off for the lake on John Scott's farm to go hunting ducks with a gun, but then why didn't he rush out there before the "accident," not jump into Frank Abbott's flivver and rush out there when he knew Jim was already dead?

Of course we are able to examine the details of the story in a way in which Whitey's audience of one in the barbershop—where there is, says Whitey, "a reserved seat like they have sometimes in a theayter"—could not. Does that give us a chance to see through his faults as storyteller, in dialogue, in character, in plot, in point of view (as when he narrates a detail he could not possibly have known because he was not present and it was not later reported)? We certainly discover that Lardner himself is a genius of narration, a true artist, a creator of a persona that is skillfully and secretly manipulated to present us with a story that bears reading and re-reading, that should arouse our awe.

—Leonard R.N. Ashley

HERZOG.
Novel by Saul Bellow, 1964.

In *Herzog*, one of the finest novels of ideas written by a 20th-century American, Saul Bellow makes serious use of comedy while demonstrating that human existence has value and worth. In the course of the novel Moses Herzog, a Jewish-American professor with a powerful intellectual attachment to Europe, analyzes and discards various intellectual formulations of pessimism or crisis ethics fashionable in the post-war period and comes in the end to a dependence upon faith in reason and intuitive feeling. Thus Bellow opts, as he had in earlier books, for a celebration of mind and life, even in the face of overwhelming evidence that "reality" is brutal, depraved, corrupt, violent. This defense of humanism, an unlikely blend of 18th-century rationalism and 19th-century Transcendentalism, is in the hands of an unheroic protagonist on the edge of psychic breakdown, an innocent like Candide who, for all his intelligence, acts like a schlemiel. The form of *Herzog* is an adaptation of the epistolary novel, a vehicle beautifully appropriate for the self-communing protagonist in a book which is largely a meditation; the story of an alienated intellectual imprisoned in the self needs a medium that promises privacy and turns in upon itself. The result is a book alive with ideas but deficient in action, written in a flexible, breathless, lively, energetic style which at the same time is restrained by the wry, skeptical, sometimes bitter expression with which Bellow endows Herzog.

These latter qualities are associated with what are regarded as typically Jewish modes of discourse. The "Jewish" aspects of the novel are also to be seen in the pattern of the alienated man and the Wandering Jew to which Herzog, like Joyce's Bloom, conforms. It can be argued that the strong family feeling; the schooling in grief; the ethnocentrism; the high value placed on education, intellectual achievement, and art; and even the rejection of despair and nihilism in favor of a humanistic faith in life, all present in the novel, do give the book, when taken together, a discernible Jewish flavor.

While Herzog's Jewish identity is clear enough, he is troubled because people do not perceive him as an American as well. But he had made a claim on his American heritage in high school, when he showed that he sprang from the faith and exuberance of Transcendentalism. As class orator, he had taken his text from Emerson, whose voice instructs and inspires him in the way of optimism, individualism, and the divinity of man.

This Jewish-American commands the intellectual riches of the European past as well. His model is the *philosophe*; he cares about creative reason, wisdom, the problems of belief, moral principles. He is also attached by lines of sympathetic understanding to the terrible plight of World War II Europe. He is a cosmopolitan, this new man, this American, and as such a distillation of the modern experience and a symbol of the modern condition, a man superbly and painfully conscious of the difficulties of being alive in our time. He teeters between sanity and destruction and carries the burden of his life precariously, and ineptly.

Opposed to 18th-century humanism, Transcendentalism, and the Jewish heritage, as Herzog conceives these, are the realities of the contemporary world and the philosophies of decline and negativism fashionable in his world. The disasters of his personal life bring him into the sordid company of lawyers, who represent themselves to him as Reality-Instructors and who regard him as an innocent whose troubles spring from a romantic conception of the world. Facts are nasty, they say; ergo, life is nasty. They open to Herzog the stunning power of corruption and cynicism in the "reality" of the external world and in human nature.

That notion of reality is confirmed by those intellectuals who believe in the disintegration and evil of mankind: Spengler and his decline of the West; Eliot and the spiritual aridities of the wasteland; Marx and others in their notions of alienation; Kierkegaard and the despair and absurdity of existentialism. But Herzog rejects all this, rejects the inauthenticity of despair, the passivity and humility of religion, the praise of suffering, the hopelessness of nihilism. Mankind, he asserts, is a subject too great for such weakness and cowardice. Herzog is a victim of history, of cultural disorder, of other people (and of his own ineptitude), who refuses to reconcile himself to victimhood. Everybody nowadays believes that man is a sick animal, he says, but he himself cannot feel spectacularly sick. He has experienced evil but he refuses to bow to it. He knows the limitations of reason, but he acts on faith and calls it reason. Obeying the deepest needs of his being, Herzog chooses an affirmative stance in life.

At the end, Herzog retires to his farm in the Berkshires, as Candide to his garden. He has brought himself under control. His psychic health is returning. Bellow does not suggest that Herzog has succeeded in making that synthesis of ideas which will yield him a final triumph over the intellectual, religious, and psychic fragmentations of contemporary life. But he has survived to deal with them, and at that point Bellow brings his story to a close. The ending is both abrupt and tentative, but Bellow is firmly clear about what he stands for and stands against. He is less sure about the coherence of his position or the eventual triumph of his ideas and values.

—Chester E. Eisinger

THE HOUSE OF MIRTH.
Novel by Edith Wharton, 1905.

The House of Mirth, Edith Wharton's first major novel of manners, reflects her intimate knowledge of the elitist New York society into which she was born and her judgment of that society. Wharton draws her title from *Ecclesiastes* 7:4, "the heart of fools is in the house of mirth." It may be understood as a judgment either on her heroine, Lily Bart, or on Lily's social milieu, that of fashionable upper-middle-class New York City in the early 1900's. For Lily alternately succumbs to the materialistic values and empty lifestyle of her social world and, in fits of restiveness or moral recoil, despises the very things she aspires to. She is at once subject to and superior to her social environment.

The orphaned Lily's beauty and *savoir faire* are her working capital, together with the possibility of an inheritance. She has only to project agreeable images and to be useful to female patrons. This entails being a decorative object, an entertaining companion, an obliging social secretary, and an ingenue in the presence of likely suitors. Thus Lily should be able to make a marriage for place and for money, on which social power and a luxurious lifestyle depend. But Lily is unable to follow the prescribed course singlemindedly, and she is vulnerable as an unmarried and impecunious woman. Hence *The House of Mirth* becomes a naturalistic tragedy documenting a painful downward trajectory through socio-economic strata culminating in Lily's ambiguous death, a presumptive suicide.

"Inherited tendencies had combined with early training to make her the highly specialized product she was: an organism as helpless out of its narrow range as the sea-anemone torn from the rock. She had been fashioned to adorn and delight. . . . And was it her fault that the purely decorative mission is less easily and harmoniously fulfilled among social beings than in the world of nature? That it is apt to be hampered by material necessities or complicated by moral scruples? These last were the two antagonistic forces which fought their battle in her breast." The social Darwinism manifest in this passage, the detached scrutiny of Lily as an organism at the mercy of forces both hereditary and environmental, is characteristic of Wharton's attitudes and language. And yet like George Eliot, whom she greatly admired, Wharton holds her characters responsible for their behavior even as she documents their social entrapment and vulnerability as creatures.

Moral sentiment in Lily expresses itself in aesthetic terms. She is repelled by crudity and ugliness manifested either in physical objects, in a drab lifestyle, or in conduct. But she is capable under the duress of economic necessity and social ambition of postponing scrutiny of her own behavior. She accepts "loans" from Gus Trenor, a married man, without reckoning the potential cost. She allows herself to become a social intermediary for Simon Rosedale, a Jewish *nouveau riche*. And she allows Bertha Dorset to use her to entertain her husband while

Bertha has an affair with Neddy Silverton. It is Lawrence Selden, whom Lily would love if circumstances permitted, who forces her into confrontations with herself. Selden enjoins Lily to be free in spirit, to extricate herself "from all the material accidents." To others he celebrates her beauty, and claims to believe that "the real Lily" is superior to her trivial world. Yet Selden is himself a male counterpart to Lily in his spiritual dividedness. They are products of the same society. If Lily cannot discard its economic norms, Selden is bound by the fiction that unmarried women must be ideal. He cannot trust his own judgment over the tarnished image reflected in the social mirror. Selden kneels at Lily's deathbed believing that, had she lived, they would have found each other, but the reader need not think so. Selden's aloof attitude of spectatorship, be it amused, admiring, or judgmental, is representative of various male figures in Wharton's fiction who stop short of full commitment to the women they profess to love. With characteristic irony Wharton makes Lily's last unambiguously willed act the burning of letters documenting Selden's own love affair with Bertha Dorset. Lily could have used these letters to blackmail Bertha into renewed social patronage and thereby cleared the way for her own social rehabilitation.

The closing scenes reflect a social terrain less familiar to Wharton, but equally characteristic of her interest. Destitute at last and living in a slum, Lily comes upon a working-class girl whom she had once patronized. Nettie has survived ill-health and a seduction because the man she later married accepted her as she was, another ironic reflection on Selden. Nettie comforts Lily and places her infant child in Lily's arms. Such empathic depiction of the very poor and the child as a symbol of hope are recurrent motifs in Wharton's fiction, as if she were reaching out imaginatively to worlds beyond her own experience.

—Jean Frantz Blackall

HOWL.
Poem by Allen Ginsberg, 1956.

What Jack Kerouac hailed in *The Dharma Bums* as the beginning of the San Francisco Renaissance was a reading on 13 October 1955 at Six Gallery on Fillmore Street in the Marina that featured the west coast poets subsequently most prominently identified with the Beat Generation—Philip Lamantia, Michael McClure, Gary Snyder, and Philip Whalen. The high point of the evening, however, was the first public performance of a recently written long poem by a visitor from the east, Allen Ginsberg. His poem *Howl* was to provide the keynote for a growing countercultural movement. Respectable society at first ignored the outburst, but in March 1957 a second printing arriving from London was confiscated by U.S. Customs as obscene. These copies were released in May when a U.S. Attorney refused to proceed with the case, but the juvenile department of the San Francisco police took over and made the poem famous by arresting Lawrence Ferlinghetti for publishing and selling the work at his City Lights bookstore. A parade of famous reviewers and critics who testified for the defense attracted international attention to the work that trial judge Clayton Horn agreed he did not believe was "without the slightest redeeming social importance." His verdict for the defense inspired subsequent trials involving banned books and films that by 1969 virtually abolished governmental censorship in the United States.

Judge Horn's opinion—strongly influenced by Mark Schorer's testimony—still provides the most lucid and sensitive brief explication of the poem: "*Howl* presents a picture of a nightmare world; the second part is an indictment of those elements in modern society destructive of the best qualities of human nature. . . . The third part presents a picture of an individual who is a specific representation of what the author conceives as a general condition. . . . 'Footnote to *Howl*' seems to be a declaration that everything in the world is holy, including parts of the body by name. It ends in a plea for holy living. . . ."

Howl has indeed turned out to be, as some early reviewers predicted, *The Waste Land* of its generation; but an even more significant parallel, as Robert Duncan maintained during Ferlinghetti's trial, is with Whitman's *Leaves of Grass*, which had appeared exactly a century earlier. Ginsberg's feeling for Whitman is shown in "A Supermarket in California," one of five new poems collected with *Howl*, in which he addresses his predecessor as "dear father, graybeard, lonely old courage-teacher." A centennial regeneration of Whitman's style and sentiments in language even he wouldn't have dared use, *Howl* proves that the most vital inspiration of the American bard remains Whitman's still unfulfilled vision of democracy, spirituality, and brotherhood.

Indeed, a problem that Ginsberg has posed his successors is that the opening line of *Howl* preempts the outraged charge that animates successive American countercultures: "I saw the best minds of my generation destroyed by madness, starving hysterical naked . . . angelheaded hipsters burning for the ancient heavenly connection." The rest of the long opening section follows Whitman's practice of reiterating initial reference pronouns to accumulate a graphic catalogue that many readers find shocking, identifying the practices by which the "best minds" would during the next two decades dramatically alter the American lifestyle through racial and sexual liberation movements.

The second section of the poem has been most aptly described by Judge Horn's listing of the destructive forces in modern culture as "materialism, conformity, and mechanization leading toward war," attributed by the repetition at the beginning of nearly every line to the Philistine god Moloch, whose worship involved the human sacrifice of children by the power hungry.

The third section is specifically addressed to Carl Solomon, whom Ginsberg had met while being treated at a psychiatric institution and to whom the whole poem is dedicated. The repeated lines beginning "I'm with you in Rockland" stress the point frequently made in many other modern social protests that those inside today's asylums are saner than their jailers, and the poem concludes—like Ginsberg's related "America"—by showing that the poet, again like Whitman, has not lost an affectionate faith in his often misguided native land: "we hug and kiss the United States under our bedsheets the United States that coughs all night and won't let us sleep."

Finally Judge Horn perceived better than many anthologists who have doubly missed *Howl*'s message by simply climbing on its bandwagon that "Footnote to Howl" is an inseparable part of the whole, which changes and counters the generally apocalyptic tone by evoking Whitman's vision of the holiness of a world that should glow with "the supernatural extra brilliant intelligent kindness of the soul!"

—Warren French

INVISIBLE MAN.
Novel by Ralph Ellison, 1952.

Anyone challenging Ralph Ellison's position in American literature because he has completed only one novel must recognize that *Invisible Man* is a hard act to follow. Arguably the most comprehensive fictional probing of the 20th-century American psyche, it is entitled to a place beside the 19th-century *Moby-Dick*. It is fitting that the novel is the work of a member of the nation's most consequential ethnic minority; yet its connection with the fashionable discovery of black writing has been a principal reason for often inadequate readings. Although deeply rooted in black experience, the implications of the unnamed narrator's tribulations are not basically racial in origin.

The invisible man's closing sentence addresses readers of any race, sex, or class: "Who knows but that, on the lower frequencies, I speak for you?" This is the story of anyone striving to establish a personal identity with dignity who learns that selfish forces seek to exploit others to advance themselves. When at the beginning of the novel the invisible man observes, "All my life I had been looking for something, and everywhere I turned someone tried to tell me what it was," he speaks for the human condition.

Another reductive error is viewing the novel as a modern picaresque, in which the protagonist's loosely linked misadventures parody Horatio Alger's myth of poor but honest and ambitious youngsters making their way to respectability in an America that offers unbounded opportunities. *Invisible Man* projects a far more complex and sophisticated vision of forces thwarting self-fulfillment.

Its structure resembles a series of nested boxes that an individual, trapped in the constricting center, seeks to escape, only to find each box within a bigger one that is more difficult to escape because it presents problems for which the captive figure's previous successes have not at all prepared him. Any summary of such a work must be oversimplified, but outlining the principal stages indicates the growing challenges each successively poses.

Ellison confines his shocking version of southern white middle-class exploitation of blacks to a brilliant first chapter in which the recent high school graduate, after being physically and intellectually humiliated, is condescendingly rewarded with a scholarship to a black college where he can learn to serve his people in a way approved by white supremacists. This melodramatic episode does nothing to prepare the naive youth for the tragedy to follow. He loves the college and daydreams of succeeding the Booker T. Washington-type President Bledsoe in this sanctuary, but his illusions are cruelly shattered when, in a controversial deviation from the conventions of black American fiction, Ellison shows how oppressed blacks can sometimes innocently and sometimes deceitfully exploit white benefactors. The narrator receives the most painful of many wounds when Bledsoe expels him permanently for not knowing how to lie to whites in order to protect the tiny empire Bledsoe has obsequiously created. Exiled to New York without recommendations, the narrator finally locates a menial job in a paint factory through a rich, sympathetic homosexual, whose more generous offers the narrator apparently does not comprehend. In his first encounter with industrial culture, he is trapped between the implacably opposed forces of an old-fashioned craftsman who fantasizes that *he* controls the business and a union seeking to organize the anonymous corporation. Expelled by a literal explosion, the narrator wakes up in the factory hospital, the subject of experiments by doctors who treat their patients the same way southern bigots did an "inferior" race.

The invisible man finds temporary refuge with Mary, the only person who treats him with genuine affection; but he must run out on her when her oversolicitousness might threaten the promising new career he accidentally launches when he makes an impassioned speech in support of an elderly black family that is being dispossessed. His talents bring him to the attention of two groups whose threats he fails to recognize until he is literally marked for execution. A white-controlled Brotherhood (resembling not just the Communist Party but any thought-control group) seeks to transform him into an unquestioning mouthpiece for its party line, but this work is resented by the black nationalist Ras, who vows to kill the narrator for betraying his race. The narrator tries to protect himself by emulating Rinehart, who successfully leads a double life as a numbers runner and "Spiritual Technologist" for a revivalist church; but the invisible man is never able to test the efficacy of this cynical pose, for while being pursued by Ras's assassins, he is literally swallowed up by the earth to become truly an invisible man living parasitically in an underground cavern illuminated by 1369 blazing electric lights.

Those who question the optimism of the narrator's final speculation that "there's a possibility that even an invisible man has a socially responsible role to play" should consider that Ellison's failure to produce a sequel to *Invisible Man* may mean that he has not been able to work out the nature of such a role in a society that has not changed much since the 1930's and 1950's that he mirrored.

—Warren French

JOHN BROWN'S BODY.
Poem by Stephen Vincent Benét, 1928.

"This poem is the most ambitious ever undertaken by an American on an American theme," Allen Tate wrote of *John Brown's Body* (*Nation*, 19 September 1928), although he did not believe that Stephen Vincent Benét's 1500 lines of verse about the Civil War constituted an epic. Yet for many reviewers and for thousands of readers, *John Brown's Body* was an American *Iliad*. Benét himself in his opening invocation to the American Muse said modestly that he had called "unsurely, from a haunted ground, / Armies of shadows and the shadow-sound." Later in the poem he lamented his inability to write the "black-skinned epic" of the liberated slaves as well.

In spite of his very real humility, however, Benét was not unconscious of the genre, as shown by his invocation, his epic catalogue of ships (romantic sails metaphorically sunk by the iron-clad "Monitor"), and his ride-past of the Southern chiefs and of the Northern regiments. Long metaphors fulfill the function of Homeric similes, and there are many allusions to the tale of Troy, sometimes ironic or satiric. For instance, Benét tells us that if Sarpedon fell in the Civil War, his limbs would not be laved in Scamander's streams, but buried in a "cumbered pit." Picnicking Congressmen watch the Battle of Bull Run "Like Iliad gods, wrapped in the sacred cloud" of bay-rum and cigars. A Southern soldier thinks "This is Virginia's *Iliad*. . . .' " Lee's young aide-de-camp imagines his general in the chariot-rank with Agamemnon and Achilles, while Benét himself asks how to humanize this "marble man . . . / The head on the Greek coin." But humanize him he does, in what critics praised as the best historical portrait in the poem, although that of Stonewall Jackson is as effective.

For these and other historical characters and episodes, Benét read extensively, with a thirst for accuracy of detail. In certain passages, such as John Brown's last message or Lincoln's soliloquy, he quoted or adapted the man's own words. He showed realistically the terrible minutiae of army life and death, often with an implied analogy between the Civil War and World War I.

Critics such as Tate found *John Brown's Body* too episodic, told in "motion picture flashes," but Benét employed the film technique of montage to demonstrate America's diversity, already epitomized in his invocation. He eschewed panoramic effects except in the set battle pieces such as the "three long double miles / Of men and guns and horses . . ." at Gettysburg. Instead, he focussed briefly and vividly on successive characters, cutting rapidly from north to south, east to west, from owner to slave, "hider" to volunteer, from Jefferson Davis to Abraham Lincoln. These are all connected by the war itself, by recurrent images of star, stone, and grain, and of Time and Phaeton, the letter also being the private symbol of Jack Ellyat, who represents the North. His Southern counterpart, Clay Wingate of Virginia, is characterized by his home Wingate Hall, which, like the South it represents, must tumble down, "a dream dissolving."

Wingate and Ellyat are the fictional centers of *John Brown's Body*, providing both insight and conventional romantic interest. Wingate hesitates between Sally, a French dancing-master's daughter, and Lucy, a proto-Scarlett O'Hara. Ellyat, escaping from his Southern captors, finds Melora Vilas, whose father has followed the wilderness stone. After an idyllic episode Ellyat is recaptured, and when Melora's child is born, she and her father go in search of him. To those who watch them pass by Vilas is the Wandering Jew or John Brown's ghost; Melora becomes a folksong.

Indeed, legend and folksong are important motifs running through the poem. Benét refers to, quotes from, or adapts ballads, spirituals, and popular songs such as "Lord Randall," "Go Down, Moses," "Dixie," and "Jubilo." Their rhythms and those of Benét's own interpolated lyrics are part of the metrical variety of *John Brown's Body*, which consists primarily of unrhymed and irregularly iambic pentameters and hexameters, with occasional sections of much shorter or much longer lines. The Wingate episodes, however, dance and dash in a bouncing mixture of shorter couplets and quatrains. Sometimes there are even prose passages to link battle scenes and to paint a vignette of Walt Whitman, whose *Leaves of Grass* had a significant influence on Benét.

Yet it is John Brown who made this epic happen and who moves through it with his song as a shepherd, a fanatic, a ghost, and a legend, until, at the end of Book Eight, the bygone South and "the America we have not been" are buried in John Brown's grave. From his body grow, not the red rose of folk ballad, but "revolving steel, / . . . . / Rivet and girder, motor and dynamo. . . ." Originally Benét had intended to write a poem of twelve books (the number of the *Aeneid*), but he felt it had come to an end with eight. In a strangely low-key conclusion, he asks us neither to condemn nor adore the new America, but to say only, " 'It is here.' " Perhaps these lines are also applicable to Benét's poem itself, over-valued and over-condemned by critics, but here—as 20th-century America's closest approach to an epic.

—Jane W. Stedman

THE JUNGLE.
Novel by Upton Sinclair, 1906.

The Jungle, Upton Sinclair's one claim to a place in literary history, was not so much a novel as it was a tract for the times. Sinclair intended it not as a work of art but as an instrument for changing people's minds. He thought of it as an expendable round of ammunition in the battle for social justice. The novel is better judged as propaganda than as literature, but it has compelling power and interests readers today long after the circumstances under which it was written passed into history. Sinclair's considerable ability as a storyteller, coupled with the fierce indignation of a born reformer, made *The Jungle* perhaps the most memorable document of the muckraking movement. He was incensed by the appalling conditions he observed among the workers in the Chicago stockyards and was determined to do something to improve them.

Sinclair recalled the novel's provenance in 1946 when he wrote an introduction for a new edition. He remembered being sent in 1904 by the *Appeal to Reason*, a socialist magazine, to investigate conditions in the meat-packing industry. This was at a time when American business answered to no one for safety, sanitary conditions, product reliability, or working conditions. Unions were weak or non-existent, and business squeezed as much profit as it could from low wages. A good many magazines, chief of which was *McClure's*, were then busily publishing exposés of corruption and malpractice in both industry and government. After the scandal of lethal "embalmed beef" sold to the army during the Spanish-American War, the meat-packing industry seemed a prime subject for investigative reporting.

Sinclair spent seven weeks in Chicago living among and interviewing the stockyard workers and studying conditions in the packing plants. He found that he could go anywhere in the stockyards provided he wore old clothes and carried a lunch pail. One day outside the slaughter-houses he chanced upon a Lithuanian wedding supper and dance, spent the afternoon and evening watching and talking to the newly married couple and their relations, and realized that this immigrant group could provide his point of view for his propaganda novel. He invented Jurgis Rudkus and his family and depicted their lives in and about the stockyards. The story, which begins with the happy wedding scene, moves from joy to ever-increasing misery, as the Lithuanians are exploited inside the packing plant and cheated outside of it. The novel is never dull, at least the early chapters that involve the slaughter-house and life behind the stockyards are not. Here the novel has all the melodrama of a soap opera, and Jurgis suffers more disasters than the early Christian martyrs. Later Sinclair couldn't resist writing a polemic for the Socialist Party, and the novel even ends with a speech that Sinclair had delivered himself at a mass meeting in Chicago on behalf of Eugene V. Debs, the perennial socialist candidate for President in that era.

The Jungle was written in a one-room cabin outside Princeton, New Jersey. He offered the book to Macmillan, publisher of the romances he had written earlier, but that firm would not publish it unless some of the more lurid details about the packing industry were deleted. Meantime, it had been appearing in the *Appeal to Reason* where it was creating a sensation. Sinclair published the book himself with aid from Jack London and others, following which Doubleday Page took it over. Sinclair's purpose in writing the book was to improve the lot of the packinghouse workers, but his account of the lack of proper sanitation, the processing of spoiled and diseased meat, particularly the report of men who fell into the lard vats and were rendered into lard, shocked the public. Sinclair said of his book: "I aimed at the public's heart and by accident I hit it in the stomach."

No book ever published in the United States produced such an immediate response. Sinclair remembered being summoned to the White House by Theodore Roosevelt to tell his story, after which the President ordered an investigation of the Chicago slaughterhouses. Consumers shuddering over what they might be eating bombarded their senators and representatives with demands for action. Before the year was out Congress passed its first law to regulate the meat, food, and drug industries. No politician could ignore the outcry for reform produced by *The Jungle*.

The contemporary reader finds the socialist propaganda ladled generously into the novel hard to get through, and even the most dramatic chapters are written in a pedestrian style. The organization of the story, moreover, is loose and rambling. But despite its faults the novel has the air of truth and conveys a sense of terrible urgency. This, of course, is the result of its being true. Sinclair was writing a kind of work that might be called the reportorial novel or the novel of social protest, of which there have been many more recent examples. There is relatively little work of the creative imagination in *The Jungle*, for the bulk of it consists of closely observed detail and innumerable facts. Today the same material probably would be cast in the form of non-fiction, the sort of multi-part documentary that often appears in the *New Yorker*. Any student of American history and culture owes it to himself to read *The Jungle* in order to understand more clearly the impulse behind the labor movement, the drive for regulatory agencies, and the need for social conscience on the part of all citizens.

—James Woodress

THE LAST OF THE MOHICANS.
Novel by James Fenimore Cooper, 1826.

For more than a century after its publication in 1826, *The Last of the Mohicans* was by far the most widely read of any of the novels of James Fenimore Cooper. Nonetheless, while praised for its strong narrative interest, *The Last of the Mohicans* was generally disparaged as the least substantive of the Leatherstocking Tales, with *The Prairie, The Pioneers, The Pathfinder*, and *The Deerslayer* receiving far greater critical acclaim. According to its 19th-century critics, *The Last of the Mohicans* satisfied the popular demands of audiences that craved adventure, but it did so at the expense of both content and realism. Particularly objectionable was Cooper's depiction of Indians, whom reviewers found hopelessly romanticized and not at all historical. As one commentator explained, Cooper's Indians "have no living prototype in our forests. They may wear leggins and moccasins, and be wrapped in a blanket or a buffalo skin, but they are civilized men, not Indians." Even Francis Parkman, who found worth in Cooper's mythic dimensions, felt that the Indians of the Leatherstocking Tales were "either superficially or falsely drawn." As a result, *The Last of the Mohicans* was for the most part dismissed as "almost pure adventure with slight social import."

Ironically, only in the 20th century, when the novel began to decline in popularity, did critical distinctions between novels of realism and novels of romance pave the way for scholars to discern in *The Last of the Mohicans* depths that had gone unnoticed for decades. To begin with, scholars attacked the notion that the novel lacked historical veracity. Research into Cooper's sources indicated that although he wrote the book in approximately four months he had researched his materials quite carefully. Among the many historical and anthropological sources attributed to the novel are Alexander Henry's *Travels and Adventures* (1809), Jonathan Carver's *Travels Through the Interior Parts of North-America* (1778), David Humphrey's *Life of Israel Putnam* (1788), Alexander Mackenzie's *Voyages from Montreal* (1802), and *The History . . . of Captains Lewis and Clark* (1814).

Additional research further determined that the Indian materials in the novel were derived from a careful reading of such works as John Heckewelder's *History, Manners, and Customs of the Indian Nations* (1818) and Cadwallader Colden's *History of the Five Indian Nations* (1727). Literary sources include *The Iliad, The Odyssey*, and *The Aeneid*, as well as *Paradise Lost* and the novels of Scott and Austen. Leatherstocking himself is thought to be based on John Filson's "Adventures of Col. Daniel Boone" (1784), and mistakes in historical accuracy, including the eloquent language of Cooper's Indians, are in general attributable to Cooper's sources, who at the time when they wrote were considered the foremost experts on the subjects they addressed. Even Cooper's landscape portraits, once thought to be hopelessly romantic backdrops to his fiction, came to be seen as complex symbolic structures that provide insight into the metaphysical foundations for a pre-Conradian analysis of the relationship between the wilderness and civilization.

Cooper himself said, however, that in writing *The Last of the Mohicans* he created a novel "essentially Indian in character," and it is in exploring what one analyst described as "the question of the relations between men of different races in the New World" that critics have found in the book a theme of "national, even hemispheric significance." Within this context, Cooper's vision of historical progress is seen as profoundly pessimistic and astutely prophetic. Extended into the wilderness setting of the novel, the rivalries between the French and English for control of the North American continent continue to propagate racial and nationalistic prejudices that the events of the narrative violently display. At the same time, the brutality of the Indians undercuts the romantic myth that in the wilderness of the New World the civilizations of the past will undergo a pastoral revitalization. Of the three characters in the novel capable of offering the possibility for moral renewal through a blending of the virtues of the Old and New Worlds, Cora and Uncas die, and Leatherstocking, described as a "man without a cross"—in other words, someone without preconceived prejudices who is open to the possibility of a new kind of moral order—remains childless and eventually vanishes into the wilderness. According to one critic, "In the bloodshed of William Henry the determining power of history is affirmed." People are seen as "incapable of change," and history becomes nothing more than "an endlessly repeating decimal" in which America's future will "necessarily recapitulate the European and the tribal past."

—James A. Levernier

LEAVES OF GRASS.
Poems by Walt Whitman, 1855 (and later revisions).

In 1872, Walt Whitman wrote: "*Leaves of Grass* is, in its intentions, the song of a great composite *Democratic Individual*, male or female"; and this individual, he stated, was to be the prototype of a superlative "*Democratic Nationality*"; for the pre-eminent subject of Whitman's verse is the United States, which he considered to be "the greatest poem." His intentions were already evident in the opening poem (later named "Song of Myself") in the first (1855) edition of *Leaves of Grass*. The subject of this poem is much larger than one person; it deals, rather, with the human spirit in its relations with the physical and historical environment, the destiny of the race, and ultimately God. Discerning critics have recognized that "Song of Myself," like many other poems in *Leaves of Grass*, is a record of a mystical experience and the insights and visions that are revealed during it. Early in the poem, the poet describes how one "transparent summer morning" there

> Swiftly arose and spread around me the peace and
> knowledge that pass all the argument of the earth,
> And I know that the hand of God is the promise of
> my own,
> And I know that the spirit of God is the brother of
> my own. . . .

By definition a mystical experience involves the merging of the individual's soul, or consciousness, with some entity outside itself—God, the cosmos, all humanity, nature. Obviously, Whitman was not perpetually in a mystical state, but much of his writing was stimulated and colored by the lasting effects of an occasional mystical transport. The conviction that the mind under favorable conditions may have access to vast and unaccustomed areas of understanding and certainty has been held by some in all ages. In Whitman's day, the American transcendentalists (notably Emerson and Thoreau), among whom Whitman must be numbered, shared this conviction.

Leaves of Grass, beginning with the slim 1855 volume, underwent a steady growth in breadth and depth of content, as well as in size, through nine editions, the last (the so-called "deathbed edition") appearing in 1891–92. Over the years, Whitman added new poems, occasionally removed old ones, changed the position of some of them, and revised and rewrote extensively. If he published a set of poems separately, as with *Drum-Taps* (1865) or *Passage to India* (1871), he would soon incorporate its contents in the larger volume. The growth of *Leaves of Grass*, then, was organic; though continuously changing and expanding, it nevertheless remained the same entity.

Critics have attempted, with questionable success, to outline the structure of *Leaves of Grass*. There are, however, certain clusters of poems with similar themes. Among these are the groups titled "Children of Adam," celebrating "amativeness" or sexual love; "Calamus," celebrating "cohesiveness" or comradely love; "Sea-Drift," containing poems inspired by the sea. Most impressive of all the clusters are "Drum-Taps" and the related "Memories of President Lincoln." Among these poems are vivid renderings of war scenes ("By the Bivouac's Fitful Flame"); expressions of tender sympathy for wartime suffering ("Come Up from the Fields Father"); and the greatest of all of Whitman's poems, his elegy on Lincoln, "When Lilacs Last in the Dooryard Bloom'd." Whitman's experience as a volunteer in the military hospitals in Washington during the Civil War exerted a spiritualizing influence on him and his writing for the rest of his life.

"I am the poet of the body and I am the poet of the soul," Whitman wrote; and he wrote of the body with a frankness that shocked most readers of his day. Again, he declared, "I am not the poet of goodness only, I do not decline to be the poet of wickedness also," and thus alienated even more readers and set himself apart from most of his fellow transcendentalists, who were reluctant to admit the existence of evil, except perhaps in its political expressions. Yet Whitman shared the transcendentalists' optimism concerning the future of humanity. The preponderance of his verse is a celebration of life in all its aspects as lived in the United States in his times. But he was a poet of death too, and had at one time planned to write, as a companion volume to *Leaves of Grass*, a book of poems in which he would "exhibit the problem and paradox of the same ardent and fully appointed personality entering the sphere of the resistless gravitation of Spiritual Law, and with a cheerful face estimating Death . . . as the entrance upon by far the greatest part of existence, and something that Life is at least as much for, as for itself." But Whitman did not need to produce this second volume; he had already done the job in *Leaves of Grass*. As early as 1855 he had written:

> And I know I am deathless,
> I know this orbit of mine cannot be swept by a carpenter's
> compass,
> I know I shall not pass like a child's carlacue with a
> burnt stick at night.

"The knowledge of death" and "the thought of death," to use Whitman's phrases, pervade *Leaves of Grass* like leitmotivs and are the subject of several of his major poems. In "Out of the Cradle Endlessly Rocking" the poet, in some of his finest lyrical verse, recounts how as a boy he heard on the seashore alone at night a bird lamenting in song its dead mate, heard the waves lisping "the low and delicious word death," and knew years later that his "songs awakened from that hour." In "When Lilacs Last in the Dooryard Bloom'd" the hermit thrush sings of "*lovely and soothing death . . . dark mother . . . strong deliveress*." In "Passage to India" a journey to that land of "budding bibles" via the newly built Suez Canal becomes a "Passage to more than India," a passage even to more than "primal thought," a passage, indeed, into death, as the poet exhorts:

O my brave soul!
O farther farther sail!
O daring joy, but safe! are they not all the seas of God?
O farther, farther, farther sail!

Though Whitman deplored organized religion as he knew it, he clearly shared belief in the immortality of the soul with most of the world's faiths.

Whitman, indeed, called for a "New Theology" and insisted that *Leaves of Grass* had a religious purpose. The "New Theology" apparently was to be based not only on a belief in the immortality of the soul but also on a conviction of a divine element in human beings and the consequent sacredness of life. Influenced by Emerson's essays "The Poet" and "The American Scholar," Whitman in the Preface to the 1855 edition of *Leaves of Grass* envisaged poets rather than priests as the spiritual leaders of the future. Again taking a cue from Emerson, he called for a poetry liberated from traditional rules and customs regarding subject matter and meter and rhyme. A new religion, a new people needed a new mode of literary expression. Thus Whitman developed a prosody suggestive of the *vers libre* of the next century. He eschewed rhyme and regular meter, letting, he hoped, the subject determine the form of the verse. As Emerson urged, he wrote of commonplace things and everyday events and situations, often resorting to pages-long lists in his effort to include in a poem a segment of life in America. In his style there are echoes of the Bible, Ossian, Shakespeare, oratory, and even opera, but he did create a style unprecedented in the poetry of the English language and one that has since found many admirers and imitators. For Whitman, largely scorned while alive, has long since gained the status of a world poet, perhaps the only one that America has produced.

—Perry D. Westbrook

THE LEGEND OF SLEEPY HOLLOW.
Story by Washington Irving, 1820.

"The Legend of Sleepy Hollow," Washington Irving's classic tale of the Hudson River Valley, with its late 18th-century Dutch villagers and its ghost legends (particularly that of the "headless horseman," the decapitated Hessian soldier left over from the Revolutionary War), has had an unusually wide appeal for readers of all ages. Spindly Ichabod Crane, hell-raising Brom Bones, and "plump as a partridge" Katrina Van Tassel are supposed to be comic figures. Ichabod's getting knocked off his borrowed nag Gunpowder by the pumpkin Brom throws at him is taken as a high point in early American humor. Scholars have pointed out the story's various Germanic literary sources (Bürger, Musäus, Otmar, etc.), in discussing Irving's sculpting and reworking a mass of folklore and legend, *and Americanizing it*. They have also considered the environmental influence of the Hudson River Valley on the imagination, Irving's joking and spoofing tendency, and his penchant (intensified by his travels in the German states, it would seem) for gothic tales and ghosts stories. Like youngsters exposed to the Walt Disney cartoon version of "The Legend of Sleepy Hollow," some of these much older readers have been smitten with the sensational plot element of the headless horseman, and they have traced its origins in Irving's reading, from Robert Burns's "Tam O'Shanter," back into obscure Germanic lore. An opinion often found in this latter group of academicians and critics is that there is a kind of regional-ethnic-ideological conflict in the case of Ichabod and his opponent. There is a suggestion that the Tarrytown-Sleepy Hollow region is well rid of Ichabod, and fortunate in having such a *hero* (Irving uses the word a number of times) in Brom Bones.

A different view of the story may be offered, but first it is necessary to state the bases given in the critical literature for the conventional view of the schoolmaster's and the bully's differences. Briefly, Ichabod is seen as the invading (Connecticut) Yankee, bringing his smart-aleckiness, book-learning, gluttony, and fortune-hunting opportunism into the peaceful agrarian Dutch community of industrious farm folk. Ichabod is also seen as having a kind of "imagination of disaster," with his head crammed full of Cotton Mather's wonders of the invisible world as well as a plethora of other spook stories and superstitions. In contrast to this oddball outlander, Brom is seen as *belonging*: a rough but good-natured local boy just having a little fun now and then with his buddies, while ripening toward the state of a proper Dutch farmer and landowner.

In fact, Irving's tale points up a viewpoint at variance with the conventional readings. It is odd that Ichabod, merely trying to get on in the world by means of his numerous talents (and what if he *is* a Yankee "handy-andy"?), seems by his very existence to arouse ridicule if not outrage in a number of the commentators, who resent his later prosperity in "a distant part of the country," through schoolteaching, practicing law, entering politics, and becoming a petty magistrate. Brom, so well accepted by the critics, is actually a lawless psychopath, a vandal, like many a village bully since time immemorial. Herculean and arrogant, he rules by force of might. Irving's description of the effect on the villagers when Brom and his crew ride into their midst reminds one of Ku Klux Klan doings or the western story in which the Bad Man and his gang periodically gallop into the helpless frontier town and shoot it up—for sport. Is there anything intrinsically funny about any of Brom's destructive capers, including the pumpkin-throw?

As for Katrina and her overall desirability as a wife: Irving's jocularity and playfulness (especially in his Postscript) cannot hide his feelings in the matter. Katrina is described archly (and repeatedly) as a coquette. While this is a natural enough condition for such a spoiled little rich girl in a sleepy Dutch village, clearly she would not make the kind of wife Ichabod visualizes: a pioneer woman westering with her husband and a wagonload of children and belongings. Rather, she is one to lead any man a merry chase—unless he physically tames her and then intimidates her to keep her down. Irving mentions Brom's having selected her "for the object of his uncouth gallantries," compares Brom's "amorous toyings" with "the gentle caresses and endearments of a bear," and indicates that she somewhat encourages Brom's hopes. Did they live happily ever after? But then Katrina is affiliated with two groups that Irving openly disparages: women and the Dutch. The latter group is pictured as a simple, empty-headed lot (Brom Bones as *hero* is a playful contradiction in terms) living an utterly static existence. The former group is composed of creatures who cause "more perplexity to mortal man than ghosts, goblins, and the whole race of witches put together. . . ." Irving is telling us, finally: Ichabod is well out of it, and deucedly lucky not to have linked up with a girl of Katrina's tastes and inclinations.

Conventional readings of the story notwithstanding, the above view is set forth by Irving in the moral offered in the Postscript. Far from being a mere joke or jest, the moral (stated by the story-teller) is true not only to the events of this story but to the meaning that a reasonable person would derive from the evidence in the text. It is stated as a pseudo-syllogism: a) every situation can be taken advantage of, if we accept a joke on its own terms; b) running a race with a goblin trooper will mean rough riding; c) therefore, "for a country schoolmaster to be refused the hand of a Dutch heiress is a certain step to high preferment, in the state." One gathers that if Irving had any trickery in mind when he wrote this last, it was to so apply his gift of drollery that unwary readers (whose number has always been legion) would find truth, and mistake it for frolic.

—Samuel Irving Bellman

LIFE STUDIES.
Poems by Robert Lowell, 1959.

Robert Lowell's *Life Studies* is the best single volume of poetry in a movement known as confessional poetry, now regarded as an important contribution to the postmodernist rebellion against the impersonality of modernism. The name was first applied to *Life Studies* by M.L. Rosenthal, who, though praising Lowell, voiced a reservation: "it is hard not to think of *Life Studies* as a series of personal confidences, rather shameful, that one is honor-bound not to reveal." Lowell's pioneering in this direction was a surprise, since as the author of Pulitzer Prize winning *Lord Weary's Castle*, he had been seen as an important new voice in the impersonal literary modernism in vogue since the 1920's. What only Lowell's friends knew was that by 1953 he was seeking to break away, not only from a style that he had come to regard as symbol-ridden and unnecessarily obscure but from personal emotional restraints.

Lowell had developed a healthy respect for the sound of conversation in the poetry of Robert Frost and William Carlos Williams and sought to loosen up his own poetry by getting it closer to prose. But the specific model for a new subject matter was the poetry of a student at the Iowa Creative Writing Programs, W.D. Snodgrass, who was chronicling his divorce and painful separation from his daughter, later published as *Heart's Needle* (1959). Lowell began turning to the subject of four generations of his own family, existential versions of the social portraits in the early premodernist Boston poetry of T.S. Eliot. Following Williams, he provided for these family poems a "sense of place," Boylston Street, Dunbarton, Cap Cod, both to illuminate character and to portray the rapidly disintegrating world of the blueblooded Lowells and Winslows.

Life Studies is divided into four parts. In part I only "Beyond the Alps" is personal, describing a train ride from Rome to Paris, but metaphorically evoking Saint Augustine in order to see Lowell's own life journey as progressing from the "City of God" to Augustine's "Earthly City." Instead of continuing to confess to the clergy of God, Lowell will now address a laity of strangers.

Part II is Lowell's only long prose piece, "91 Revere Street," introducing his own unhappy childhood, focusing on the quarrels between his mother and his father but also evoking a sense of the decline of Boston society as the social register yielded to the cash register. Part III consists of four poems about tormented and spiritually exiled fellow artists—Ford Madox Ford, George Santayana, Delmore Schwartz, and Hart Crane.

Part IV is the "Life Studies" proper, eight time-obsessed poems marking a family sequence. The long poem "My Last Afternoon with Uncle Devereux Winslow" centers on Uncle Devereux, "dying of the incurable Hodgkin's disease," but Lowell also seeks to establish continuity with the past through remembered things. Two poems, "Dunbarton" and "Grandparents," dramatize the old order of his grandparents, "altogether otherworldly now." Three poems, "Commander Lowell," "Terminal Days at Beverly Farm," and "Father's Bedroom," further the account in "91 Revere Street" by reporting his father's last days and his death from a coronary. The last of these poems, "Sailing Home from Rapallo," records the death of his mother in Europe, shipped back home in the hold of the ship with her name on her coffin, misspelled "LOVEL."

The concluding poems, those on Lowell's own manic-depressive illness and on marriage, are the most personally confessional and the most emotionally intense. "During Fever" covers four generations of Lowells, his daughter in fever, his memories of conversations with his mother about his father, and her memories of her own father, "that old life of decency / without unseemly / intimacy or quarrels." The final six poems feature Lowell as mental patient. "Waking in the Blue" views a mental hospital as a prison; in it Lowell confesses his fears of madness and death and presents a microcosm of the sickness of Boston society. "Home after Three Months Away" is an ironic poem of return—"Cured, I am frizzled, stale, and small." "Memories of West Street and Lepke" revisits the past once more to begin an evaluation of what it is to live "in the tranquilized fifties," a time "of lost connections," reminding him of the lobotomized Czar Lepke of Murder Inc.

The last poem, "Skunk Hour," is one of Lowell's best. Its setting evoking the loneliness and decadence at a resort area off season is appropriate for Lowell's frankest description of madness, an attempt to portray both a "dark night" of the soul and the hell of Milton's Satan—"I am myself hell"—while finding in a mother skunk searching for food for her children a reminder of the continuing will to live.

The controversy about the confessional nature of Lowell's *Life Studies* is long forgotten. The poems are rooted in the past and present of Lowell's personal life, contemplating the dark night of man's soul, never reaching any sort of transcendence, yet affirming painful endurance in Eliot's still present "waste land" of modern society. *Life Studies* is truly of its own time, the existential 1950's, but his aristocratic Boston Lowells and Winslows are as still relevant as Faulkner's Mississippi Sartorises and Compsons.

—Richard J. Calhoun

THE LITTLE FOXES.
Play by Lillian Hellman, 1939.

Lillian Hellman freely admitted that she was a moral writer, that she could not deny herself that final summing up, and in this play she made a resounding statement about "the little foxes that spoil the vines." Called an adult horror play, this study of consuming greed focuses that horror within the trappings of carefully structured romantic melodrama to illuminate Hellman's biting social commentary and determined warning.

The ebb and flow of action are deftly contrived to reveal the psychological position of the major character, Regina Giddens, who connives with or against her brothers, Ben and Oscar Hubbard, to barter southern culture for northern industrial money. First, she must control Horace, her sick and dying husband—and his money. Once the business deal with Mr. Marshall of Chicago is completed and Regina has requested and received a 40% share, she reigns supreme in her own estimation. Meanwhile the greed and vulgarity which she and her brothers represent are theatrically underscored by the slap Oscar gives Birdie just before the end of Act One. When Horace arrives home from the hospital and refuses to become party to the business venture, Regina's sense of power begins to deteriorate. Unable to change Horace's mind, she finds herself abandoned by her brothers who have sent Leo to Chicago with Horace's bonds to help insure the deal with Marshall. Ostensibly defeated in her objective, Regina can only strike back with characteristic venom. "I hope you die soon," she tells Horace.

In Act Three, having discovered what happened to his bonds, Horace purposely helps the brothers manipulate and control Regina. The anger she feels at this infuriating situation and the personal humiliation of being laughed at by her brothers are tempered for Regina only by Horace's statement that he will do nothing about the theft as long as he lives. Willfully tormenting her sick husband, Regina calmly remains seated, watching as he dies. In control of the bonds and her brothers as well, Regina then demands 75% as her share of the business deal. Once more on top of the world, she "puts her arms above her head, stretches, laughs." There is, however, something tenuous about her victory; questions remain unanswered. "What is a man in a wheel chair doing on a staircase?" Ben wants to know. "Are you afraid, Mama?" asks Alexandra.

In characterization and plotting devices *The Little Foxes* ranks among the best of American social melodramas. The bonds and the medicine along with the constantly changing situations and the sharp contrasts, poignant and sentimental, are expertly employed to excite audience emotions. How ironic it is that the glory of Lionnet must someday be represented by a most unregal Leo who beats horses, steals, chases after women, and reveals the weakest aspects of both parents. Oscar, his father, is cruel, cowardly, slow-witted, and degenerate. Music makes him nervous. His primary pleasure is to shoot birds. Birdie, Leo's mother, epitomizes the naive, tender, and inept but sweet aristocrat. She adores music and the gentle culture her parents enjoyed but could not maintain, and she drinks to keep from watching what is going on around her—a beautiful but weak bird. Crafty, unscrupulous, but patient, Ben secretly envies the southern aristocracy and brags that he could not send his old cook away. Far from queenly, Regina exhibits dangerous insecurities. These are the Hubbards whose pretense toward gentility through a close family relationship is fiercely satirized in their repeated giggling. Responding to Oscar's argument with reference to Leo's marriage to Alexandra that their grandmother and grandfather were first cousins, Regina and Ben giggle; "And look at us," says Regina.

Alexandra is the strongest character in the play, well created to bear Hellman's moral summing up. It is she who learns and matures. Her sensibilities assaulted by Leo's beating the horses, Alexandra begins to suggest her independence when Birdie warns that she will be made to marry Leo. Formally released from the protective instincts of southern gentility in the opening scene of Act Three, her awareness and assertiveness grow as she listens to Horace and Birdie reminisce and hears Addie talk about "the people who eat the earth and all the people on it." It is Addie's confession—"Sometimes I think it ain't right to stand and watch them do it"—that stimulates Alexandra's final decisions in the play. "Mama," she says, now fully cognizant of the meaning in Addie's and her father's comments, "I'm not going to stand around and watch you do it." Rather than go to Chicago with her mother, she is off "to some place where people don't just stand around and watch." With this determination by her young heroine, Hellman asserted a philosophy that directed her life and colored all of her plays, the same idea she stated with memorable eloquence before the House UnAmerican Activities Committee: "I cannot and will not cut my conscience to fit this year's fashions."

—Walter J. Meserve

LITTLE WOMEN.
Novel by Louisa May Alcott, 1868–69.

The most famous work of Louisa May Alcott, *Little Women* (in two parts, 1868 and 1869), has remained a classic, in the sense that it has demonstrated remarkable staying power as a popular book, for nearly twelve decades. Although it does not command the wide audience it once did (for instance, in a 1927 survey American high school students listed *Little Women* as the book of most interest to them), it remains in print in several editions, and is considered a major work both in 19th-century fiction and in children's literature. From the outset *Little Women* was recognized as more than a children's book, however; in reviewing the first part of the novel the *Nation* wrote (October 1868): "Miss Alcott's new juvenile is an agreeable little story, which . . . may also be read with pleasure by older people." *Harper's* (August 1869) called the second part of *Little Women* "a rather mature book for the little women, but a capital one for their elders."

Alcott's purpose in writing *Little Women* was not to create a nostalgic portrait of an idyllic childhood, though the book is often read as such. She wrote it to make money. At first reluctant to agree to her publisher's wish for a "girl's book," she relented, and the writing became a cathartic process through which she could re-create her own difficult early years. At the time Alcott began this task she was 35 but looked older, and in constant pain as a result of the mercury poisoning she suffered while serving as a volunteer nurse during the Civil War. Her father, the philosopher Bronson Alcott, was lost in his own abstractions, as absent from his family mentally as Mr. March is absent physically during much of *Little Women*. Abigail May Alcott, the strong and long-suffering model for Marmee, had by now retreated into a preoccupation with her family history. For more than a decade Alcott had been augmenting the family income through writing, but most of her works were lurid "gothic" romances written under pseudonyms and filled with angry and tormented women. But in *Little Women* she created the loving March family whose four daughters—Meg, Jo, Beth, and Amy—were modelled after the Alcott girls. Though many elements in the story are based on actual events—family theatricals, the rebellious daughter's literary aspirations, the death of a beloved sister—*Little Women* transformed the troubling into the ideal. The Marches are not rich, but are much more prosperous than the Alcotts. Feast scenes in the book seem to compensate for the fact that at times the young Alcott did not have enough to eat. Jo cuts off her long hair to raise money to bring home her father, wounded in the war; in reality, Alcott lost her hair due to illness and poor medical treatment during her own wartime nursing experience.

Little Women therefore represents a psychologically helpful process for Alcott, a shift in her writing focus, and a clever response to the desires of the reading public. Her contemporary readers wanted tales of adventure, romance, piety, temperance, reform, travel, and the Civil War; Alcott gave them a stew of everything, but with her own flavoring. She was no hack, cranking out a simple plot with predictable characters. A number of statements in the book would have been considered unusual for the day, and illustrate Alcott's interest in unconventional ideas. For instance, Mrs. March removes Amy from a school in which there is corporal punishment, quite a departure in the "spare the rod and spoil the child" era. In a Protestant society, the book expresses an appreciation and approval of Catholic practices. The importance of dividing domestic labor is stressed; though the women do all the work in the March household, as in the Alcott home, peace comes to Meg and her husband John only after they divide housework and child care. *Little Women* also emphasizes the value of women working outside the home; Jo's lifestyle—up to a point—is a departure from the traditional feminine role, and she is happy and successful in her endeavors as a writer. She enjoys an exciting life because she refuses to fit the conventional mold of a "little woman," but eventually she does conform in some ways to the expected norms. Although Alcott herself would have preferred Jo to remain single, she allowed herself to be pressured by public opinion into having her marry. Still, Alcott demonstrates her strength: she insists upon expressing her own opinions while simultaneously keeping within the mainstream of popular thought. Books that alienated the reader, of course, would not sell, and *Little Women*, from the very first, sold exceptionally well. One mark of its success is that it was followed by several sequels, including *Little Men* and *Jo's Boys*.

In many ways *Little Women* is markedly superior to other books of its genre. While almost every other popular 19th-century novel had heavy-handed sermonizing, *Little Women* kept its homilies short and, appearing at natural intervals in the story, unobtrusive. In other books, villains were plainly villains and the virtuous were always clearly so. Alcott, more sophisticated, realized the complexities of the human character, and so created personalities with whose shortcomings and internal struggles readers could identify. Characters who are basically good do or contemplate things that are blameworthy: Jo, foreseeing an accident, still ignores Amy's cries for help when they are ice-skating; Amy burns Jo's books; Laurie embarrasses Meg by forging a note from John. In *Little Women* human frailty is apparent—and believable. Descriptions are not overly sentimentalized and, again, readers could identify with many of the situations—comic, tragic, and tender—occurring in this story of a warm family dealing with realistic situations in a loving and positive way.

Although many of the events and circumstances are obviously dated, enough universality remains so that readers are still intrigued by the book. To the young reader of the 19th century, *Little Women* was a manual of social grace, illustrating how to overcome one's faults and problems on the pilgrimage toward maturity. To the modern reader, it is a charming portrayal of family relationships as well as a palatable study of 19th-century lifestyle, mores, and social structure.

—Jane S. Gabin

LOLITA.
Novel by Vladimir Nabokov, 1955.

The apparent subject of Vladimir Nabokov's *Lolita* is the titillating perversion of a madman who virtually kills his wife in order to make captive and lasciviously possess her 12-year-old daughter; and when the child, who has in fact seduced him, escapes him, running off with another man, he apparently kills that man. This lurid tale would seem to invite either a sensational or a moral response. The problem Nabokov deliberately sets for himself, however, is to persuade the reader to transcend the erotic content and eschew moral judgment in order to perceive his novel as an artistic creation and not as a reflection or interpretation of reality. *Lolita* is not immoral or didactic, he has said; it has no moral. It is a work of art. The apparent subject of the novel is Humbert Humbert's perverted passion for a nymphet. But we come closer to the real subject if we perceive that his passion is his prison and his pain, his ecstasy and his madness. His release from the prison of his passion and the justification of his perversion is in art, and that is the real subject of the novel: the pain of remembering, organizing, and telling his story is a surrogate for the pain of his life and a means of transcending and triumphing over it; art, as it transmutes the erotic experience, becomes the ultimate experience in passion and madness.

Late in the book Humbert says that unless it can be proved to him that it does not matter that Lolita had been deprived of her childhood by a maniac, then he sees nothing for the treatment of his misery but the palliative of articulate art. At the end of the novel, addressing Lolita, he says, I am thinking of angels, the secret of durable pigments, prophetic sonnets, the refuge of art. Here is the only immortality he and Lolita may share. Here is the only balm that will soothe. Here, in art, are the forms that will control the passionate furies while the music of the words cloaks it all in saving beauty.

Not that "reality" doesn't intrude. Nabokov sought and captured the way schoolgirls talk; he conveys the feel and the smell of American motel rooms in all their philistine vulgarity. But a major thrust of the novel is toward undermining and mocking the concepts of fact, reality, and truth in fiction, toward destroying, in short, the very bases of literary realism. Nabokov undercuts a firm conception of reality by involving Nabokov the "author," Humbert the "narrator," and John Ray the supposititious editor in the making of the book, creating an ambiguity and uncertainty about authorship, reliability, and authority which attack the validity of fact, reality, and truth: can we trust the criminally insane Humbert as the primary source of our knowledge of events and people, especially since "Humbert Humbert" is Humbert's own invention? And more especially since his diary, presumably the original source of the narrative, has been destroyed? Or the pompous Ray, who speaks of newspapers which carry the story of Humbert "For the benefit of old-fashioned readers who wish to follow the destinies of the 'real' people beyond the 'true' story . . .," a man who asserts that the tale tends toward a moral apotheosis? The factitious factual character of the story that Ray emphasizes is only a device for encouraging our conventional expectations as readers of traditionally realistic fictions which make traditional moral judgments. Nabokov will disappoint these expectations just as he has deliberately confused the point of view and the identity and relationship of the characters. The techniques of the novel are forms of play for him, as art itself is play.

Writing his memoirs in prison, Humbert says, Oh, my Lolita, I have only words to play with. It is the case that word play and pure sound are one source of the wit and joy of the novel, as Humbert imagines the nymphet he would coach in French and fondle in Humbertish. Nabokov uses language so that it draws attention to itself. It is frequently more important than the action of the novel. It is thus possible to argue that if Humbert had only words to play with, he never had a flesh and blood 12-year-old girl at all. She is a fantasy, imagined by a madman imprisoned as much in his cell as he is in his lust. Indeed the entire book may be a fantasy. When Humbert kills Clare Quilty, the playwright who abducted Lolita, the characters move as though they were under water or with that heavily retarded motion common to nightmare. Quilty may be as unreal as Lolita, Humbert's alter ego haunting him for his guilt in relation to the child. Lolita is thus an occasion for Humbert's fantasy of sex and Quilty for his fantasy of violence and revenge. It is as necessary to transmute the pain of one's fantasy life into art as it is the pain of one's conscious and quotidian life. Whether Lolita and Quilty are "real" or not, language will serve as a means of dealing with them.

It is not only through language that Lolita is removed from the "real" world. As a nymphet, she is nymphic, that is, daemonic. A nympholept like Humbert instantly recognizes and always burns for such a creature. When he gets her into bed, in an inn called appropriately enough for a magical, mythical experience The Enchanted Hunters, he thinks of her as an immortal daemon disguised as a female child. Thus it is possible to read Lolita as a daemonic spirit residing in the human id, that is, as an irrational, self-destructive force related to the primitive in man that will overwhelm his rationality with the frenzy of its appetite. The price of this ecstasy is its inevitable pain. And so we return to language, because only it, only art, will bring these demonic energies under control. And that is the essence of the entire novel: its primary if not its sole reality is language.

—Chester E. Eisinger

LONG DAY'S JOURNEY INTO NIGHT.
Play by Eugene O'Neill, 1956.

Composed in 1940, first produced in Stockholm in 1956, then in New York in 1957 and London in 1958, Eugene O'Neill's *Long Day's Journey into Night* won the Drama Critics Circle Award as well as the first Pulitzer Prize ever awarded posthumously, and has been revived several times, notably with Laurence Olivier at London's National Theatre in 1971. It has been made into two excellent films—one with an all black cast starring Ruby Dee, and the other with an all white cast with Jason Robards and Katharine Hepburn. O'Neill dramatizes the "psychological trap in which his characters are caught by diminishing . . . the area of light in which his characters are permitted to move," beginning "in morning sunlight, but gradually, as the night comes and fog surrounds the house, the stage is reduced to a dim circle of light surrounded by darkness." O'Neill's last plays present "a bitter, uncompromising indictment of the failure of vision in a land of hope . . . the world beyond the fog, the unlighted cities, the source of terror that finally causes men to seek their reason for being, if not their salvation, by withdrawing into darkness, journeying into night" (Travis Bogard). James Tyrone's penuriousness intensifies the situation further as he forbids the family to burn more than one light bulb at a time, deepening the fog-induced darkness, so they will not make the electric company rich, as he all but turned out the light of Mary's and Edmund's lives by denying them crucial medical care, because of his intense fear of poverty, as he had "turned off" Mary's desire even to try to break the morphine addiction because he refuses to make his house a home where a wife can be happy and children can develop normally. At best Mary Tyrone watches the family watch her, with little or no compassionate support offered to anyone by anyone.

Usually preferring expressionism, the language of poetic symbolism, and a faith in the dignity of man, O'Neill also enriched his art by an understanding of the "new psychology," an enlarged awareness of all conscious and unconscious realities—not merely Freudian—resulting in a "new depth of seriousness, a new vitality . . . and the free use, in stagecraft and acting, of experimental techniques which completely ignored the 'well-made' conventions, and called directly upon the subconscious responses of the audience" (*The American Tradition in Literature*). His analysis of the inner workings of human emotions in his characters, and the terror they can impose, has been compared to the best work of John Webster and Cyril Tourneur, 17th-century masters of terror. Such analysis, for O'Neill, constituted the essence of the dramatic, since he believed emotions, not the Greek gods of old, caused much of man's behavior, emotions which in most O'Neill plays produce a violent explosion by play's end. In addition to sound—the foghorn in *Long Day's Journey into Night*—to emphasize the hostile environment condemning man to loneliness, O'Neill also uses dialogue, especially that between Edmund and James Tyrone in Act IV. O'Neill's characters seem, frequently, to be making private, solitary utterances, not attempts to communicate, whether they use dialogue, monologue, soliloquy, or aside. Since no topic is "off limits" for the family members, and few, if any, wish to face the realities of daily life, especially the painful realities, the encounters are at times savage. Yet O'Neill tried to treat the characters—"his own dead"—with compassion and forgiveness. John Henry Raleigh contends that "old country" customs—part of Irish Catholic family culture—can account for much in characterization and action in *Long Day's Journey into Night*: Irish love poetry, the Judas-complex (a pathological obsession with it, in fact), national commitment to Roman Catholicism (with religious-blasphemous interaction), preoccupation with rhetoric and eloquence (loquaciousness), family relationships being non-communal, sexual chastity (specifically defined as not bothering good women), turbulence, drunkenness, sentimental and ironical feelings about love held simultaneously, tendency toward later marriage and young men living at home longer, and the difficult process of assimilating the Irish into American life.

The four haunted Tyrones reach spiritual self-realization seldom, and then only in the depths of despair: Mary who, if she dared, would take a lethal overdose, has now given up and decided to use morphine to send herself back to the safe, pure, and simplistic romantic time, before she met James Tyrone, when she thought she was either about to become a nun or a concert pianist; or James who realizes that he will never become the superior Shakespearean actor he could be because the possibility of making an incredible amount of money, plus the terror of devastating poverty, makes him prostitute his art and refuse to care for his family; or Jamie, who, in the depths of an incredibly intense drunk, warns Edmund of the love-hate feeling he has had for him all along, and states that he "taught him all he knew" merely to bring him down to his own level: the same Jamie who could not corrupt a pure woman and was as dedicated to the Virgin Mary as was Mary Tyrone, though the "Cynara" to whom he was faithful was Fat Violet, the prostitute about to be fired for being undesirable; or Edmund, who must have in terror and anger perceived what his family was doing to him, and admits he might have done better as a sea gull or a fish since his most memorable moments came when he was drunk with the beauty and singing rhythm of the sea, with no humans present.

Then there are the loneliness, and the alienation from nature, themselves, God, everything: Mary being forced to wait in cheap hotels or country houses for the drunken James Tyrone, Edmund waiting for death, James Tyrone waiting for poverty, Jamie waiting to conquer drink when Mary conquers dope, in a household run by a murderous Richard-III-at-Tewkesbury-father, and an Ophelia-run-mad-mother . . . as night deepens.

—Louis Charles Stagg

LOOK HOMEWARD, ANGEL.
Novel by Thomas Wolfe, 1929.

"Genius is Not Enough," the catchy title of Bernard De Voto's negative review of Thomas Wolfe's essay *The Story of a Novel*, was not written of *Look Homeward, Angel: A Story of the Buried Life*. Ever since the publication of Wolfe's first and unarguably best novel, it has been a target for critical attack and encomium. But the severest attacks Wolfe suffered were in reaction to his subsequent work. If Wolfe had never written anything else, *Look Homeward, Angel* would have more stature today. It has been dismissed as a "novel of youth," attractive only to teenagers; it has been excoriated as formless, verbose, shallow, and altogether too personal. While there is some truth in all of those accusations, the novel stands as a unique, perdurable monument of American literature. Richard Walser has called it "the most lyric novel ever written by an American," while Wolfe's principal British champion, Pamela Hansford Johnson, finds it the most "clear-sighted" of his novels, portraying his world "with an objectivity altogether remarkable." These traits of lyricism and realism, along with a Joycean complexity and exuberant good humor, are the most compelling qualities of the work.

An unabashedly autobiographical *Bildungsroman*, the book recounts the inner and outer life of the first twenty years (1900–20), of Eugene Gant. Eugene is the youngest of seven children of W.O. and Eliza Gant, a couple who live in the mountain village of Altamont. W.O., a Pennsylvanian with a penchant for rhetoric, alcohol, and prostitutes, owns a stonecutter's shop; his wife is a native of the area with a well-developed head for business and an interest in real estate. After a brief stint in 1904 in St. Louis, where one of her twins dies, she opens a boarding house in Altamont named Dixieland. The precocious Eugene starts school, aged five, against his mother's wishes. He spends his high school years in a private academy and at 15 enrolls in the university at Pulpit Hill. On his first summer vacation he has a brief romance with Laura James, a boarder at Dixieland. During the next summer he works as a laborer in Norfolk and that fall his favorite brother, Ben, dies of influenza. He graduates from college and leaves Altamont to study in the north.

All of the events of the preceding paragraph are exactly parallel to Thomas Wolfe's life. Only the names of the living characters and some place names have been changed. Altamont is the fictitious name for Asheville, North Carolina; Pulpit Hill is Chapel Hill. Floyd C. Watkins, after identifying 250 or 300 names of characters and places in *Thomas Wolfe's Characters*, maintains that there is not a single entirely fictional character or incident in the novel.

Anticipating negative reactions from the easily identifiable characters he portrays, Wolfe explains in a prefatory note that "all serious work in fiction is autobiographical" and that "he meditated no man's portrait here." Many of his readers did not accept that disclaimer, however, and were enraged when the book appeared (coincidentally in the same month as the stock market crash). That reaction is incorporated into his later work in two ways: fictionally in *You Can't Go Home Again* and factually in *The Story of a Novel*.

In *The Story of a Novel* Wolfe observed that "the quality of my memory is characterized . . . in a more than ordinary degree by the intensity of its sense impressions, its power to evoke and bring back the odors, sounds, colors, shapes, and feel of things with concrete vividness." Wolfe's special talent, then, is not a reportorial one but one which exercises almost total recall of sensory images. It is important to remember that he produced the bulk of his enormous manuscript, originally 350,000 words, while he was living in London during 1926–28. That he was far removed in space and time from the events he describes makes the sense of immediacy in his writing all the more impressive.

In spite of charges of formlessness, *Look Homeward, Angel* is carefully constructed. It attains unity and shape through the focus on Eugene, the chronological sequence of events, the preservation of the theme of the search for identity, and the balance, in Chapters 5 and 35, of the death scenes of the twins.

The tombstone in the form of an angel is a significant unifying device. "An angel poised upon cold phthisic feet, with a smile of soft stone idiocy" is first mentioned on the second page of the novel. It is the focus of Chapter 19, "The Angel on the Porch," an excellent vignette published in slightly different form in the August 1929 issue of *Scribner's Magazine*. A similar angel is present in the last scene of the book when Eugene has a conversation with his dead brother, Ben. As all symbols must, this one holds a multitude of meanings: death, remembrance, existence on a spiritual plane, W.O. Gant, and the stone-like quality of people in their inability to communicate with each other. When the original title of the novel, *O Lost*, was changed to the inspired borrowing from Milton's "Lycidas," the angel imagery was further strengthened.

Finally, one should not overlook the pervading humor of the novel. Bruce R. McElderry, Jr., in fact, has found it to be the funniest book in American literature since *Huckleberry Finn*. One manifestation of the humor may be seen in the comedic appeal of the characterizations—W.O.'s bombast, Luke's stuttering, Eliza's habit of pursing her lips and nodding her head. Another element of humor is found in the tone and timing. One instance involves the scene early on when the baby Eugene's face is stepped on by a dray-horse, Eugene having escaped from his yard into an adjoining alley and the driver of the encroaching wagon having fallen asleep. A physician is called: " 'This looks worse than it is,' observed Dr. McGuire, laying the hero upon the lounge. . . . Nevertheless, it took two hours to bring him round. Everyone spoke highly of the horse."

Look Homeward, Angel was published in the same year as Faulkner's *The Sound and the Fury* and Hemingway's *A Farewell to Arms*. While it does not currently enjoy the prestige of those other landmarks of American letters, it has never been out of print and continues to attract popular and critical attention. If Wolfe's genius was not enough to sustain a universally acclaimed writing career, it was ample for the creation of a genuine literary achievement.

—Nancy Carol Joyner

LOOKING BACKWARD 2000–1887.
Novel by Edward Bellamy, 1888.

The political and social impact of *Looking Backward 2000–1887* has been so great, the merits and deficiencies of the planned state it proposed so often and intensely debated, that the work's value as a product of the imagination has perhaps been unfairly minimized. Had not Edward Bellamy's novel been wrought with a craft appropriate to his polemical purposes it is doubtful that his idealistic document would have received such unusual attention. In Russia, Lenin's wife read it and Tolstoy made certain it was translated; in England the Fabians, including Bernard Shaw, discussed it; both Charles Beard and John Dewey listed it as second only to *Das Kapital* in its significance. Revealingly, it was a bestseller and within a decade of its publication more than a million copies were in circulation in the United States. Most of its readers were probably of the middle class, whose civic dreams the book's schemes so powerfully embodied that citizens formed over 150 political clubs inspired by Bellamy's plans, seeking to make them a fact not a fantasy of American life.

The character Ike in John Dos Passos's *The 42nd Parallel* suggests the hope many gleaned from Bellamy's solid-seeming vision in a not completely accurate but heartfelt résumé of the book's plot: "It's about a galoot that goes asleep an' wakes up in the year two thousand and the social revolution's all happened and everything's socialistic an' there's no jails or poverty and nobody works for themselves an there's no way anybody can get to be a rich bondholder or capitalist and life's pretty slick for the working class."

The central problems for which Bellamy sought solutions—unequal distribution of wealth, conflicts between classes, ruthless commercial competition, all those conditions that make life nasty, brutish, and short for so many and less rich and fulfilling for most—were of course not limited to any particular region. But his attack was rooted in the particular condition of post-Civil War America, a time according to historian Russel Nye embodying "a great paradox. The nation's material prosperity was the envy of all Europe yet most of its social, cultural, and political institutions lagged far behind those of the advanced western countries. . . . In almost every sphere except the technological the nation's institutions cried out for modernization." Farmers found their profits drying up, powerful corporations in the oil, steel, coal, cotton, and sugar industries (to name a few) were turning into monopolies and trusts that corrupted politicians and controlled the lives of millions but with comparatively little control placed on them—indeed many businesses were larger in employees, revenues, and resources than some state governments. Gaps between workers, managers, and owners seemed to stretch into abysses, and industrial strife was increasingly common and violent. Daniel Boorstin refers to the time as "an age of revolution" in American life where "traditional politics could not cope with" the commercial institutions causing the revolution, "nor could traditional law harness them to social welfare."

Bellamy's Utopia in many ways flowed with the direction of force in America rather than opposed it. He presented an urban, industrial, technologically advanced society counter to the bucolic Brook Farms of earlier radicals. He imagined rather than one great union, one great trust. All monopolies merge into one, which blends into the state, run presumably for the equitable benefit of all. This state clearly resembles a socialist or welfare state, though it is neither, precisely, at least according to Bellamy who studiously avoided using any form of the word socialism in explaining what he aimed at.

According to Bellamy the advanced state is achieved not through violent conflict or social Darwinian competition, but through humanity's increased awareness of its needs for cooperation. Underlying the social and political change in *Looking Backward* is Bellamy's "religion of solidarity," which declared that while an individual's badness was manifest in greed and selfishness, human goodness was a potentially greater counterforce leading toward a "passion for losing ourselves in others" and attaining a sense of "true self-interest" which was rational, and unselfish. The personal and selfish in humankind constituted a centrifugal force, whereas the willingness to join with others for common good was centripetal, drawing individuals together in communal harmony, not driving them apart and causing violence.

As the very reasonable Dr. Leete and sometimes his daughter Edith explain the good society of 2000 to Julian West, a 19th-century dilettante, its main features become crystal clear. Bellamy showed in his novels (for example, *The Duke of Stockbridge*) and his short stories that he was quite capable of adjusting the techniques of art to achieve various ends. Thus the book's undoubted success possibly results more from the craft of his seemingly simple narration than critics have generally admitted. However, it is the fullness of his picture and its clarity together with the many glimpses of a better life *that is attainable* that most compel interest. Describing a nation where all are employed, have access to good housing, can obtain a good and appropriate education, where none can accumulate or hoard or bequeath excessive profits, Bellamy can be very convincing. Less satisfactory are his reliance on a simplistic (though laudable) view of the essential goodness and reasonableness of mankind, and his failure to deal with some prickly contemporary problems such as minority rights. That he failed to perceive the dangers of state bureaucracies and the potentially dehumanizing effects of scientific management is lamentable but understandable.

Late in the book Julian dreams he has returned to Boston in 1887, and in a stunning, depressing passage the misery and woe of a degrading society are revealed to him as a nightmare which readers often recognize, cruelly enough, as their own real world. Henry George called *Looking Backward* "a castle in the air, with clouds for its foundation," but if so, it is also a construct that inspired utopian thinkers and common people alike to search for a better life in humanely conceived communities.

—Jack B. Moore

LOSING BATTLES.
Novel by Eudora Welty, 1970.

Eudora Welty has never belonged to any literary school. Her fiction explores life's mysteries rather than espousing any ideology, and it seldom falls into predictable patterns. The most distinguishing characteristics of Welty's fiction are its great variety and its consistent virtuosity—two qualities epitomized by the long novel *Losing Battles*. In this novel Welty deals with complex human relationships and a changing era, does so in both comic and tragic terms, and in the process fuses narrative method and her major concerns into a powerful whole.

Set in the 1930's during a family reunion in northeast Mississippi, *Losing Battles* presents two attitudes toward social change. On the one hand, the reunion participants—Granny Vaughn, her grandsons surnamed Beecham and granddaughter Beulah Beecham Renfro, their spouses, children, grandchildren, and in-laws—want to continue leading the traditional life of subsistence farmers. They worship the land on which they live, even when that land is parched and barren; they participate in a close-knit family life that "involves both a submerging and a triumph of the individual"; and they value the past—they know that the remembering and recounting of family stories are essential to a family's vitality. The retired schoolteacher Julia Mortimer, on the other hand, is a modernist who has never been a member of any reunion: she has faith in man's ability to harness or control nature; she emphasizes individual freedom and social duty as more desirable than family loyalty; and she believes in a philosophy of progress. Granny Vaughn and her descendants stand in sharp contrast to Julia Mortimer, but Welty does not choose between these viewpoints. Instead she presents two modes of survival in a world that resists systematization of any sort.

These unresolved conflicts between traditionalists and modernists follow both comic and tragic lines of development. Part 2 of *Losing Battles*, for instance, is the stuff of farce; Jack Renfro sets out to obey the will of his family reunion and to wreak vengeance on Judge Oscar Moody, the man who sentenced him to two years in Parchman Penitentiary. Jack hopes to force Moody's "luxurious" Buick into a ditch; instead when Jack's wife and daughter appear inopportunely in front of Moody's auto, Moody swerves to avoid hitting them and drives up Banner Top, the highest hill in Boone County. Jack, in gratitude, resolves to become Moody's savior, not his tormentor. Jack's love for his wife and child, his ability to defy his extended family without estranging himself from it, and his heart-felt recognition of human transience are all evident in his decision to save Moody. The plot is comic, but its import is quite serious. Yet not all of *Losing Battles*'s serious concerns are conveyed through comedy. Julia Mortimer's individualistic battles with ignorance, her many losses, and the abuse which plagues her final years reveal her heroic devotion to progress and the horrifying isolation to which such a life can lead. To label Julia's dark tale as tragic, however, is not to say it is nihilistic. Julia has known failure, but she has also produced many successful students. And Julia has come to realize that "From flat on your back you may not be able to lick the world, but at least you can keep the world from licking you. I haven't spent a lifetime fighting my battle to give up now. I'm ready for all they send me. There's a measure of enjoyment in it."

Whether the subject of *Losing Battles* is tragic or comic, Welty's method of narration and her major themes are complementary. *Losing Battles* consists primarily of short tales told by the Beechams and Renfros who have gathered to celebrate Granny Vaughn's 90th birthday, and their typically southern story-telling is central to the novel's deepest meaning. Welty has written that in the American south

> . . . stories could be watched in the happening—lifelong and generation-long stories watched and participated in, first by one member of the family and then without a break by another, allowing the continuous and never-ending recital to be passed along in full course and to grow. The event and the memory and the comprehension of it and taking a role in it were scarcely marked off from the other in the glow of hearing it again, telling it anew, anticipating, knowing the whole thing by heart—and all right here where it happened.

The reunion of *Losing Battles* certainly is part of a "continuous and never-ending recital." The past is not gone for the clan. It comes alive at least once a year on Granny's birthday. Then the old stories are told, new stories are added to be retold in the future, and everyone participates in the telling—Percy with his "thready" voice, Etoyle who "embroiders," Aunt Beck with her "mourning dove's" voice, everyone. The death of Grandpa Vaughn is the reunion's newest story, and it is recounted with great sadness. Jack's rescue of the Moody's Buick will be a story that the next reunion can tell in high humor. The family members thus know that their lives are and will be part of the enduring family story, a story that seems to come alive in the telling. They feel a real continuity with the past. Yet this tendency to look backward in time also leads the family to resist or ignore innovative ideas, to refuse to plan for the future, and to face helplessly the decline of the agrarian south. The family is both blessed and encumbered by its reverence for the past, a reverence embodied in the storytelling which constitutes *Losing Battles*.

In *Losing Battles* Welty explores profoundly significant concepts and emotions, she refuses to simplify them, and she makes her method of narration a metaphor for her novel's central issues. As a result, Welty's description of great fiction seems a precise description of her own. "Great fiction," she writes, "is given to sprawling and escaping from bounds, is capable of contradicting itself, and is not impervious to humor. There is absolutely everything in great fiction but a clear answer. Humanity itself seems to matter more to the novelist than what humanity thinks it can prove." Though *Losing Battles* clearly investigates divergent ideas, no clear answers emerge from this investigation. And that fact may best explain the novel's powerful impact upon readers. The complexity, the humor and tragedy, the craftsmanship, the humanity of *Losing Battles* combine to make it a major achievement in the rich and varied career of a major American writer.

—Suzanne Marrs

THE LUCK OF ROARING CAMP.
Story by Bret Harte, 1868.

Bret Harte's later career, his rejection by the American reading public and self-imposed exile in Britain, supports the view that he was a writer of limited abilities, one who found a brief moment of glory when form, content, and public interest came together. Yet there have been critics willing to argue that he maintained his quality throughout, that he fell victim to changes in public tastes. "The Luck of Roaring Camp" could support either view.

Detractors would notice the lack of realism. Harte, it is well known, had no firsthand knowledge of the California Gold Rush and only began writing about it two decades after its inception. Certainly no mining camp resembled Roaring Camp, with its closed, static community, its sense of centre and of social roles. Miners were a peripatetic lot and if they were not they worked in gangs, even in the early days, often for wages, and a much more common pastime than gambling or drinking was writing home to their wives, sweethearts, friends, and relations. They were more literate than the average American, many were wealthier even before they arrived, and few developed a loyalty to any one spot or community. If they banded they congregated with those from their locality back east.

The story implies an inaccurate environmentalism, too. It needs to suggest prior cultural regression in order to make its point of moral regeneration. The miners, barbarised by their life of toil, their absolute separation from wives, families, church, and school, are reminded of their fall from grace by the arrival of innocence in the form of a child. Point is added in that the child is both illegitimate and, probably, non-white. Contemporaries would not have expected to read of a white "husband" for Cherokee Sal. Regeneration is thus all the more remarkable in the lowly origins of the first cause. There are echoes of Bethlehem stables here. A cynic might also notice that the child's early death disposed of the problem of its future in a highly ethnocentric if not racist world.

Yet there are enough reverberations from historical reality to sustain belief. There were prostitutes in the mines; they were very largely non-white. There were few women and children in the early days and the camps did contain members from all parts of the Union and abroad. There was some social homogeneity in that men could not be distinguished by their consumption, there being little to consume. In any case the Harte world, the democracy in the wilderness, was what the American public expected existed.

But if the world described was unreal so were its characters. As usual Harte defined those in the story through a set of paradoxes that in the end left them almost as shadowy as before. Equally his paradoxical approach only served to delineate the extremes: if the gambler "had the melancholy air and intellectual abstraction of a Hamlet," and "the strongest man had but three fingers on his right hand," what of the vast majority of the usual? Harte's defence might be that in his fiction there is no ordinariness, but the paradoxical approach highlights unreality.

Like so much of his work, "The Luck of Roaring Camp" swims in sentimentality. Hearts of gold abound, evil is conspicuous by its absence, and the reader is implicitly assured that the near-vicious will be punished. The reader is led to sympathise with the morally flawed but need not worry about long-term commitment to their regeneration. Stumpy and Kentuck who have retrieved themselves somewhat through their kindness to the child are both drowned, but presumably in a state of grace. It is the lack of any moral chaos in Harte's work that makes it difficult to read in any great amount.

Yet the stories had a large impact when they were first printed. They were lively, direct, unornamented, good-natured, and witty. "The Luck of Roaring Camp" can still amuse in its description of the attempt to send the child to sleep: "Either through the peculiar rocking of Jack or the length of his song—it contained ninety stanzas, and was continued with conscientious deliberation to the bitter end—the lullaby had the desired effect." "Conscientious" strikes forcibly. Stumpy's assertion "Me and that ass has been father and mother to him" is cruder but still to be enjoyed.

Critics have not tended to see much irony in Harte, yet to do so may be to retrieve something of his reputation. The very title of the story is ironic, unless the reader assumes regeneration outlasted the flood that carries off Kentuck, Stumpy, and the babe. The miners of Roaring Camp may have roared but they may not have grown richer. Nature may have been the "nurse and playfellow" but she later destroys. This is not to argue for a strong ironic voice, but to suggest that such ironic elements as there are may explain why this and other stories are saved from being swamped by their sentimentalities.

Wallace Stegner has pointed out how Harte's creations have survived and become stereotypes because they do approximate myths. American readers in particular wanted the goldfields described in certain ways and populated by predefined figures. the characterisation in "The Luck of Roaring Camp" is slight but it bears out this point. Rough, unshaven, dirty miners have noble souls, retrievable, and given the right circumstances will regenerate. Readers should not despair of the miners; they should never despair of America. Such a message may not have attracted Americans in the anxious 1890's but it is embedded in basic American cultural attitudes.

—R.A. Burchell

MAIN STREET.
Novel by Sinclair Lewis, 1920.

"The history of a nation," Woodrow Wilson declared in 1900, "is only the history of its villages written large." Twenty years later, Sinclair Lewis infected millions with his large novelistic dose of the Village Virus in *Main Street: The Story of Carol Kennicott*. "Main Street" came to mean the smug, intolerant, dull conformity of the American small town. The book sold sensationally—nearly 300,000 copies the first year, another 100,000 copies before cheaper editions reached the masses—and provided timely ammunition for the cynical postwar generation. Lewis's apprenticeship novels—*Our Mr. Wrenn, The Trail of the Hawk, The Job, The Innocents, Free Air*—reveal the realistic touches, satiric flashes, and smalltown tintypes developed in *Main Street*. An heir of Charles Dickens and Mark Twain, of H.G. Wells and H.L. Mencken, Lewis wrote his explosive novel in the grubby-village tradition of Edward Eggleston, E.W. Howe, Joseph Kirkland, Hamlin Garland, Harold Frederic, Edgar Lee Masters, Sherwood Anderson, Floyd Dell, and Zona Gale. He first sketched his "Village Virus" exposé in Sauk Centre, Minnesota, in 1905, when, a Yale sophomore home on vacation, he read Garland's *Main-Travelled Roads*. Knowing that magazine editors would expunge his slashing satire and gargantuan detail, Lewis 15 years later refused to subject *Main Street*—as he had subjected his previous two novels—to serialization.

His panoramic novel of provincial life in the northern midwest from 1912 to 1920 documents in nearly 200 episodes the war between Carol Kennicott and Gopher Prairie. We first see Lewis's protagonist as a flighty Blodgett College idealist in Minneapolis in 1906, then as an earnest library student at a Chicago studio party, and later as a slightly weary librarian in St. Paul. Here beauty-minded Carol Milford meets competent, boyish Dr. Will Kennicott, who shows her photographs of his "darn pretty town." At year's end they marry, honeymooning in Colorado. On the gritty train to Gopher Prairie, Carol foresees in the scrawny trackside settlements the ugliness awaiting her. Seeking relief from her bridal home (a mildewed Victorian horror), Carol strolls around the whole disjointed hamlet in 32 minutes. Later, at dull parties in her honor, she raises prairie eyebrows by overplaying the Clever Little Bride from the Cities. Hikes, new furniture, her Oriental housewarming party, winter sports, and a few confidants mitigate her unease, but young matrons of the Jolly Seventeen bridge club, among others, regard her as an affected snob. Her yearning to enlighten Will about poetry and to idealize his surgical dexterity prove as futile as her naive gestures to improve the town's architecture and culture through the la-di-da Thanatopsis Club. As the stagnant years pass, Carol, though devoted to her baby, draws further from her husband, imagining herself in love with a faun-like tailor. Thoroughly disillusioned with the peeping town, Carol decides to flee with her son to Washington, D.C. There she attains the empty freedom of a government clerk. After thirteen months Will visits, begging her to return home. Having failed to transform her husband into Sir Launcelot and her town into the Vale of Arcady, Carol Kennicott—more mature and resigned after nearly two years in the capital (and feeling Will's second child stirring within her) returns to Main Street.

Even then, Carol, refusing to admit that her rebellion was wrong, resolves to continue questioning—with sympathy, not sarcasm. Leaving little unsaid, the discursive narrator explains that Carol "was a woman with a working brain and no work." No tragic figure, the high-strung Carol Kennicott, like Emma Bovary, is the type of the unfulfilled dreamer, the failed romantic, the female Quixote. Peopling Gopher Prairie are "humors" like the Good Influence, the Village Radical, the Big Cheese, the Gentleman Hen, the Loyal Servant, and the Street-corner Roué. Further, the novel is a guidebook of the seedy and the meretricious, a grammar of sectional slang and immigrant dialect. In truth, *Main Street* illustrates the author's own life-long ambivalence toward the Middle West and the Middle Class, the unsettled juxtaposition of the fantastic-pragmatic, the Carol-Will in himself.

Indeed, this inconsistency—Lewis's now uplifting, now undercutting of his main characters—bothered many critics. Yea-sayers saw Carol's battle as balanced, whole, and hallowed, but nay-sayers saw it as unfair, incomplete, and profane. Satire, of course, is never "fair." Like the caricaturist, the satirist startles us into recognition. Nor is he required to prescribe a "real" program of reform. So natural to Lewis were serial and slick-story engineering that even in *Main Street* he relies on a long series of contracted flights, installmentesque cliffhangers, and a swift, nervous style, flexible enough for popular fiction but never adequately rendering interior nuance. *Main Street*'s loose-jointed structure allowed the author to insert or delete his relentless catalogs of Gopher Prairieana. Lewis cut out 20,000 words before his manuscript went to press, but *Main Street* is still too long, its story simply too slender to support the freight of Lewis's around-the-clock carping.

Still, American popular fiction encouraged Lewis to look at the contemporary American scene. Sauk Centre, the town that once raged against its native son, raves about him now. Though *Main Street* might read like a period piece today, many young women still can identify with Carol—and some small towns with Gopher Prairie. For good or ill, many city people first learned to see the small town through Lewis's blazing camera-eyes. After *Main Street*, its author gained a reputation as more than a popular storyteller. After *Babbitt, Arrowsmith, Elmer Gantry*, and *Dodsworth*, this "fabulist" in 1930 was the first American to win the Nobel Prize in Literature. But for every reader who would elevate Lewis above George Eliot, no doubt there is another who would consign him to a place below James Whitcomb Riley. The influence of *Main Street* on major American writers like Thomas Wolfe, Richard Wright, and William Faulkner has been less direct than its impact on such important regional writers as Edith Summers, T.S. Stribling, and Frederick Manfred.

—Martin Bucco

MAIN-TRAVELLED ROADS.
Stories by Hamlin Garland, 1891.

After three years reading, writing, and lecturing in Boston, Hamlin Garland in 1887 (after six years away from home) traveled to the old homestead in Iowa and then to South Dakota to visit his parents. Although Garland had grown up on frontier farms and rebelled against their drudgery, never before had he realized so fully their wretchedness. Guilt-ridden, depressed, and bitter about "the system," young Garland—disciple of William Dean Howells, Herbert Spencer, Henry George, and Eugène Véron—began a series of stories in the anti-idyllic tradition of Edward Eggleston's *The Hoosier School-Master* (1871), E.W. Howe's *The Story of a Country Town* (1883), and Joseph Kirkland's *Zury* (1887). Four of the original six Mississippi valley stories in *Main-Travelled Roads* first appeared in the magazines *Harper's Weekly* and *Arena*. Garland added three stories to the 1899 edition and two more to the 1922 edition, but the first collection is historically the most important.

In "A Branch-Road," jealous Will Hannon, misunderstanding his sweetheart, flees his rural home. He returns seven years later, learns the truth, and begs her to abandon her bleak life with his former rival. In the end, Will leads mother and child out of their rustic hell. The last part of this story dramatically reverses the happy-to-sad structure of the first three parts. With his argument rising "to the level of Browning's philosophy," Garland's strong man does indeed sound like the great poet proposing to Elizabeth Barrett; as well, Will's early conviction that his sweetheart "gave herself too freely" echoes "My Last Duchess." Garland's impressionistic method recreates country scenes effectively, but his naive admixture of high-toned French and border dialect (" 'biled chickun' formed the *pièce de résistance*") is as bathetic as his lisping urchins.

Like "A Branch-Road," the next story is about return, but "Up the Coulé" ends despondently. After successfully managing and acting in a theater troupe, elegant Howard McLane of New York returns to Wisconsin to discover that his mother, his brother, and his brother's family toil in poverty. Admitting his neglect, Howard heroically plans to buy back the old homestead for them, but his embittered brother, sensing that it is too late, refuses his brother's help. Garland describes well Howard's nostalgic mind, the images that rise up between the artificial world of his success and the natural world of his brother's failure. The dinner of milk, bread, and honey; the neighbors' surprise party; and the sister-in-law's revelations of despair are convincing. Less so is Howard's recital of a paragraph—indented—by the French painter Jean François Millet about domestic tragedy surrounded by natural glory.

The return home in "Among the Corn Rows" ends happily for Rob Rodemaker, a young outlander in need of a wife. An idealistic newspaperman looks upon Rodemaker ("roadmaker") as an expanding Whitmanesque personality. Leaving his thriving South Dakota wheat field and joshing companions, Rob briefly back-trails to Wisconsin, where girls are "thicker 'n huckleberries." Among the hot corn rows there Julia Peterson, coincidentally, daydreams of a Yankee coming to rescue her. Although no particular tenderness existed between the former schoolmates, Rob now is affected "massively" by the swaying of Julia's powerful body. The eroticism, though oblique, is palpable. Julia's decision to escape from her hard Norwegian father triggers in her a flood of feeling for Rob. Late that night the pair come together like Romeo ("Rob!") and Juliet ("Julyie!"). To the song of katydids Rob indeed steals a hand, with only the harsher companion stories intimating their probable future.

"The Return of a Private" elevates Garland's father into the type of the Civil War veteran. His war with the south over, he must daily fight nature and injustice. Each scenic episode—the weary soldier's return, the wife's loneliness and dinner at Widder Gray's, the family reunion—builds to a dramatic resolution, only to be marred by Garland's metaphorical sentimentality: "They are fighting a hopeless battle, and must fight till God gives them furlough."

Also proud is Timothy Haskins, the moiling farmer in the highly compressed "Under the Lion's Paw," Garland's best-known story. Driven out of Kansas by grasshoppers, the Haskins family is befriended by an older farm couple. Haskins, however, is trapped by a speculator into paying double for the land that Haskins himself had doubled in value. Appropriately, the story ends abruptly, Haskins's head "sunk in his hands." Not *forced* to squeeze the luckless Haskins, the greedy Butler is more the villain of melodrama than himself the victim of economic determinism. The thumbnail sketch of Haskins's nine-year-old son slogging through his chores is Garland himself at that age.

The last story, "Mrs. Ripley's Trip," is flinty but less grim. Frugal Gran'ma Ripley fulfills her 23-year promise to herself to visit her eastern birthplace—but not without feeling guilty for leaving her husband and young grandson even for a short time. The simple two-part story treats only what happens before and after the trip. The old couple's bittersweet b'gosh squabbling right down to the wife's last-minute instructions at the depot leads directly into Garland's sober picture of her trudging back home through the snow drifts. In response to her grandson's effusive welcome and her husband's restrained greeting, "She took up her burden again, never more thinking to lay it down."

In spite of obvious faults, *Main-Travelled Roads* is inherently and historically valuable. The author's combination of realism and impressionism effectively recreated the west of a particular time, place, and self. His essays in *Crumbling Idols* define his idea of *veritism*—"passion for truth and individual expression." Later, in his Rocky Mountain romances, Garland nourished rather than dispelled the myth of the west, but even in *Main-Travelled Roads*, as we have seen, Garland's ambivalence is obvious. But in both *Main-Travelled Roads* and the book which *Main-Travelled Roads* inspired Sinclair Lewis to write—*Main Street* (1920)—negative feelings predominate. Howard McLane's impressions of La Crosse could be Carol Kennicott's impressions of Gopher Prairie: "How poor and dull and sleepy and squalid it seemed! The one main street ended at the hillside at his left and stretched away to the north, between two rows of the usual village stores, unrelieved by a tree or a touch of beauty."

—Martin Bucco

THE MAN THAT CORRUPTED HADLEYBURG.
Story by Mark Twain, 1899.

In 1898, while living in Vienna, Mark Twain wrote "The Man That Corrupted Hadleyburg." First published in *Harper's Magazine* in 1899 and in book form in 1900, this story drew relatively little notice at the time of its publication. In recent years, however, it has been anthologized as the embodiment of themes and issues that preoccupied Twain during the last two decades of his life. It has also spurred vigorous critical debate while gathering praise as one of Twain's greatest achievements in short fiction, with some scholars naming it among the greatest short stories ever written.

In "The Man That Corrupted Hadleyburg" Twain depicts a self-righteous American town nationally renowned for its honest reputation. To gain revenge for an unnamed offence suffered at the hands of a Hadleyburg citizen, a stranger presents to the town an elaborate scheme whereby he exposes the community as a bastion of hypocrisy and greed. The stranger brings about the fall of Hadleyburg by tempting with prospects of wealth its nineteen principal inhabitants, including an elderly couple named Mary and Edward Richards, who become the focus of the narrative. Ironically, the temptation that the stranger introduces, a sack of gilded lead coins, is as false as the hypocritical facade of piety that he exposes. Disgraced, the town changes its name and motto, and its inhabitants vow never to be caught "napping again."

The plot of this carefully structured story breaks into four distinct sequences of action, each sequence initiated by a letter from the scheming stranger. As one critic notes, the result is a unity of plot more reminiscent of Poe than of a man who said, "Narrative should flow as the brook down through the hills and the leafy woodlands." Inspiration for Twain's plot has been traced to such disparate sources as Dante's *Inferno*, Milton's *Paradise Lost*, and Poe's "The Cask of Amontillado," as well as to the classical myth of Baucis and Philomen. While Twain offers no clear geographical reference whereby the actual identity of Hadleyburg can be determined, scholars have argued persuasively for Fredonia, New York, where Twain's mother and sister once lived and where Twain himself became embroiled in several disputes and in a business venture that contributed to his bankruptcy.

Although critics divide over whether "The Man That Corrupted Hadleyburg" should be read as a deterministic allegory or a moralistic parable, the story clearly reflects themes that Twain repeated in most of his later works. In this narrative, as in many of these works, Twain attacks mankind, and America in particular, with a characteristically cruel satiric condemnation of the idealistic, romantic themes of democracy, religion, free will, and honesty prevalent in the popular culture and literature of his day. Developing these themes, Twain unmasks the ritual hypocrisy he saw in mankind, motivated by greed, ignorance, and vacuous pride. Virtually always read as satanic, the stranger in the tale echoes Twain's fascination in later life with Satan, who also functions prominently in such works as *The Mysterious Stranger* and *Letters from the Earth*.

On its most general level "The Man That Corrupted Hadleyburg" illustrates the maxims that money is the "root of all evil" and that "everyone has a price." On a deeper level, Twain attacks the concept of democracy. Instead of nurturing the common good, the citizens of Hadleyburg care only for their individual welfares, and at the end of the story, after their supposed regeneration from self-delusion and pride into virtue and moral responsibility, they elect Harkness (i.e., "Darkness"), the most sinister of the town's leaders, to the United States Congress, where he can practice his graft not just on Hadleyburg but on the nation as a whole. Moreover, there seems little indication that the citizens of Hadleyburg have come to revere the memory of Goodson, who is typically read as a Christ figure (i.e., "God's son"). Instead, they change the town motto from "Lead Us Not Into Temptation" to "Lead Us Into Temptation," thereby, as one critic has noted, rewriting Christ's words on how to pray and thus placing their own prideful confidence in themselves above the Bible and God.

Underscoring both these levels of meaning is a re-enactment of the myth of Eden in the environment of post-Enlightenment America. In Hadleyburg, where the town hall is "clothed," "festooned," and "swathed" with flags, where the nineteen leading citizens are known as "the incorruptibles," and where babies from the cradle are shielded from all temptation, Twain creates an ironic American Eden, an Eden founded on the Calvinistic principles of privilege and hypocrisy that Twain so reviled, one whose outward reputation was more important than its underlying values. Into this New World Eden again comes Satan, who, in the hopes of settling an ancient grudge, tempts mankind to sin anew.

According to Twain, people are always destined to choose evil over good because, as the stranger in the tale surmises, it is in both the nature of humanity and in the scheme of things for them to do so. Greed, selfishness, and pride—qualities engrained, Twain tells us, in the very essence of mankind since the beginning—are the motivating factors that determine the outcome of events in Hadleyburg, as they do in most of Twain's later fiction. Nonetheless, it should be noted that some critics view the story as a "sober affirmation" of free will. They point out that at each juncture in the narrative the citizens have the opportunity to make moral choices and that if they would choose to abide by the honest principles they profess the stranger's plan would fail. Within this context, Satan is seen as an ironic savior who forces the town to examine its sin and withstand future temptations.

In any event, in "The Man That Corrupted Hadleyburg" Twain pokes a cruel thorn in the side of humanity as a needling reminder that appearance is almost never reality. This fine story provides considerable insight into the workings of Twain's imagination during the final phase of his remarkable career.

—Thomas E. Hockersmith and James A. Levernier

MARGRET HOWTH.
Novel by Rebecca Harding Davis, 1862.

Pioneer realist and sociological fiction writer, Rebecca Harding Davis was ahead of her times. But her times caught up with her. With sincerest intentions, she succumbed to prevailing literary tastes, and she is read today as a piece of literary history. An examination of her writing is a study of the unresolved conflict between well-wrought intentions and popular expediency. Her first and best-known novel, *Margret Howth*, is the key to the dilemma.

When originally published in the *Atlantic Monthly* (October 1861 to March 1862) the novel was entitled *A Story of To-Day*. It was meant to be timely. The action takes place within three consecutive days in October 1860 plus a conclusion of a few weeks in December. "Let me tell you a story of To-Day" are the opening words of the novel. "You want something," she says to her readers, "to lift you out of this crowded, tobacco-stained commonplace, to kindle and chafe and glow in you. I want you to dig into this commonplace, this vulgar American life, and see what is in it. Sometimes I think it has a new and awful significance that we do not see." "This vulgar American life" entails the drudgery of factory labor, unemployment, racism, economic inequality, anti-feminism, and class prejudice. These are the issues that were fermenting in the time of the election of Abraham Lincoln, November 1860, and the secession of South Carolina in December. Rebecca Blaine Harding (she married L. Clarke Davis in 1863) observed the issues with unsurpassed foresight and understanding.

Her setting too is timely—a mill town on the Wabash River in southwestern Indiana, where the industry of the east meets the feudalism of the south in the experimental democracy of the west. The author describes abundantly the sounds and smells of the woolen mills and the contrasting woods and prairies of the environs.

Further, the author shows an awareness of contemporary Republican, Socialist, Communist, Comtean, Federalist, Fourierite, Fichtean social philosophies—as well as American Transcendentalism and Democracy. These she presents through the mouths of her characters. Most of the story is seen through the minds of these characters, as the author moves skillfully from the point of view of one to that of another. Margret Howth is the sweet but strong American woman; Stephen Holmes is the self-reliant individualist; Dr. Knowles is the would-be philanthropic reformer; old Mr. Howth is the southern conservative but pathetically weak; Joe Yare is the renegade ex-slave, gone wrong because of his social environment. And little Lois, Joe's daughter—patterned after Charles Dickens's Little Nell and Harriet Beecher Stowe's Little Eva—is the catalytic model of innocent Christian charity in a deformed body and retarded mind. These characters are authentic American types, but they become humanly real through their reactions to their time and place.

But there is more than specific time and place to *Margret Howth*—more than local color. The ideological and social backgrounds that the author belabors are meant to show the Yesterday of which "To-Day" is the result. Not only through the characters and settings does the author show the influence of the past on the present; she also speaks directly as omniscient author to the reader. Furthermore, she is concerned not only with Yesterday and To-Day but with Tomorrow: its "new and awful significance that we do not see." Creeds, ideologies, and programs notwithstanding, we are too often "blind to the prophecy written on the earth since God first bade it tell thwarted man of the great To-morrow." The human lot in life is to suffer, with the only hope being in heavenly salvation.

Such is the gloomy message of *Margret Howth*. But the message is diluted and sentimentalized by the feminine novelistic manner that the author felt compelled to follow. In fact, she was literally compelled by her editor, James T. Fields, to provide an ending more "sunny" than that she had originally submitted. After the climactic fire that burns down the mill at the end of Chapter VII, the novel deteriorates into authorial apologies and liberal Christian explanations. Stephen Holmes has a change of heart; Lois dies but with a profusion of tears and blessings; Joe Yare is not prosecuted for his villainy and remains free; and Margret marries her Stephen.

—James C. Austin

THE MAXIMUS POEMS.
By Charles Olson, from 1953.

Charles Olson was perhaps more admired during the 1950's and 1960's for "Projective Verse" and his other essays on poetic theory than for *The Maximus Poems*, increasingly regarded now as one of the principal achievements of postmodernist American poetry. But, as Marjorie Perloff and others have shown, those essays owe more to the theories of other writers than Olson's supporters may have realized or at least were willing to admit. (Perloff found echoes of Pound, Williams, and others in "Projective Verse.") Furthermore, Olson's poetry at times seems to have very little to do with the theories. He insisted, for example, that the breath should somehow provide the measure for the line, but whose breath he had in mind is a mystery—certainly in any case not his own as his recorded readings repeatedly testify.

Olson's supporters have felt that *Maximus* exemplifies the theories given in the essays and that in effect the essays are an introduction to the poems. In fact, it may be better to see essays and poems as complementing each other: both are the expressions of one of the most intense, assured, and compelling voices in contemporary American poetry. What matters is not whether the ideas in the essays *and*, for that matter, *Maximus* are derivative, poorly developed, or simply wrong: the voice which speaks them is what is interesting, and it has a fire, conviction, and apparent sophistication that experimental poets among Olson's generation rarely possessed.

Poets have, of course, traditionally sustained a poetic voice within self-imposed prosodic limits and the limits of the language itself, its vocabulary, syntax, and so forth. Olson in effect asserted the power of the voice over the language and the right to reject such limits. That he tried to bolster what he was doing poetically by arguing that these limits reduce language to a flat, linear process that denies the actual nature of experience is beside the point. The problem was not theoretical but practical: a poetic voice which, like Whitman's, required possibilities with language greater than, or at least very different from, any required by his predecessors. In his essays, Olson spoke as if he were reinventing poetry for the future, but that is simply another expression of his sublimely self-confident, expansive voice. In fact, the poetry he was reinventing was largely for himself.

In *Maximus* from time to time Olson simply suppresses traditional grammar, particularly connectives (something he had learned to do from Pound), and tries to establish new relationships between words. Within the English language, of course, only certain relationships—"and," "is," "seems," and so forth—can be indicated. The placement of words on the page—their proximity to, or distance from, each other—takes on special importance in *Maximus* as a way of suggesting the degree or the nature of relationship between terms. Even when the syntax looks most conventional, it is tempered by this visual fact, and *Maximus* cannot be read as Olson intended it should unless it is seen in the format, even in the particular typeface, in which the book appeared when its three sections were published in 1960, 1968, and 1975, respectively, and which they retain in the complete single-volume edition published in 1983. Clearly Olson rejected one set of prosodic and grammatical limits only to encumber himself with another, but within those new limits he was able to unleash a fury of linguistic invention that makes reading *Maximus* as exciting as any other masterwork of postmodernist poetry.

Much of Olson's book is dense with antiquarian knowledge about Gloucester, Massachusetts (in which the poem is set), as well as with references to Olson's rather esoteric and exotic readings in archeology, anthropology, and mythology, George F. Butterick's *A Guide to the Maximus Poems of Charles Olson* is an important companion to the work for that reason, but it is by no means essential to share Olson's antiquarian and scholarly interests in order to read *Maximus*. The book, like the essays, moves essentially according to the power of the poet's voice, not his interests. Indeed the interests seem fundamentally excuses for the poet to keep talking. Whatever it was Olson had to say in his essays and in *Maximus*, it was never as interesting as the voice with which it was said.

In the best way, good talk is what makes *Maximus* a great work. As "Letter 3" near the very beginning of the work concludes:

Isolated person in Gloucester, Massachusetts, I, Maximus,
address you
you islands
of men and girls

—Edward Halsey Foster

THE MEMBER OF THE WEDDING.
Novel by Carson McCullers, 1946.

The Member of the Wedding reflects such central Carson McCullers themes as the universality of isolation and the desperation arising from the unavailability of love and belonging. These themes are suggested, stated, and restated in the fashion of a sonata throughout the three distinct parts of the novella, a simple third-person story of a precocious and lonely girl's four-day initiatory journey from uneasy adolescence to young adulthood.

Akin to a sonata's first movement, Part I introduces the primary theme. Frankie Addams is a gawky, motherless, 12-year-old tomboy rejected by her girlish friends, little attended to by a preoccupied father, and thrown on her own incoherent resources during school-less August days in a Georgia town near the end of World War II. Feeling like an "unjoined person," Frankie has spent the summer moping around the kitchen with her two sole companions, the only other major characters: John Henry, her six-year-old cousin, and Berenice Sadie Brown, the black cook. These two represent different refrains of Frankie's separateness. Frankie broodingly yearns to be a member of something, a "we" person. When her brother returns on wartime furlough to marry a local girl, Frankie seizes the notion of leaving and staying with them after the wedding. "They," she exclaims, "are the we of me." Thus Part I's ending rhythmically changes to a tempo of joyfulness.

McCullers perceptively details the three major characters with sympathy, humor, and detachment. Articulate, quick-witted Frankie uses language revealing her quality of mind and sensibility: words like "puzzling" and "curious," and literary affectations like "I am sick unto death." She longs for the future, impatient with John Henry's concern for the present and Berenice's for the past. She scrutinizes the human condition and yet also fantasizes fulsomely. Berenice, who claims to be 35, speaks with a deliberate cadence suggesting stoical wisdom earned from hard experience and uses an array of folk-sayings ("I believe the sun has fried your brains"), combining commonsensical earthiness with flowery metaphorical language. She fails with her loving, firm attempts to recall Frankie to the limitations of reality. Her four-marriage history and her blue false eye symbolize attempts at flight from the predestined conditions of her birth and betray a yet indefatigable romantic strain. She loved her first husband Ludie until his death and then married three worthless men in turn because each reminded her of "pieces" of Ludie. Berenice has learned that love cannot be repeated and hesitates to marry an importunate suitor because he does not make her "shiver." John Henry, the trio's third loving member, is still a child and cannot yet comprehend Frankie's feelings nor articulate his own. The trio's relationship is epitomized at one point when they join different songs in a wailing harmony suggesting the "we" of their separate lives, and exemplifying one of many moments when musical references are used to express the characters' often unarticulated emotions.

In Part II, the main theme further develops in a changed rhythm. Convinced that she is to be a member of the wedding and thereby "connected" to others, Frankie formally declares herself as "F. Jasmine Addams." The day before the wedding, she announces it in town to strangers and feels a kinship with the world. Her exuberant mood changes when she returns to her unchanged friends in the kitchen. Then she voices her problem: that everyone has a "caught" condition of spiritual isolation despite the urgent desire to be related to others: ". . . what is it all about? People loose and at the same time caught. Caught and loose. All these things and you don't know what ties them up." Berenice, being black and knowing life, responds that all of us are caught: "We born this way or that way and we don't know why." Confessing that with Ludie she didn't feel so "caught," Berenice accentuates the thesis: that love while it endures enables a person to escape the isolation of self and, paradoxically, to acquire self-identity by connecting with something outside.

In Part III, the novel's last "movement," are the climax and denouement. After the wedding, Frankie's dream of joining the couple ends predictably: she is pulled from the wedding car and hauled home. A "coda" concludes: some weeks later, Frankie (now called Frances) has turned 13, acquired a girlfriend, and forgotten her disillusionment. She has also forgotten John Henry, now dead from meningitis, and seems unconcerned that Berenice is leaving to marry a man who does not remind her of Ludie. Despite her new feelings of membership, Frankie remains an unjoined person out of touch with those who were closest to her. Yet the novella ends on a positive note: as adolescence passes, our individual aloneness is leavened by the recognition that human kinship is a fact of life.

This small, affecting portrait of adolescent angst skillfully recreates its compelling protagonist's mind and emotions through a simple plot and highly evocative poetical style. McCullers employs strong powers of narrative description and characterization to examine her theme, and communicates her vision directly, honestly, and lyrically.

—Christian H. Moe

MOBY-DICK.
Novel by Herman Melville, 1851.

"Is it I, God, or who, that lifts this arm," cries the mighty and suffering Ahab in his fearless pursuit of the white whale that has mutilated both his body and spirit. In Herman Melville's *Moby-Dick* Ahab would deprive himself of all human comfort and travel to the ends of the earth if he could just confront the seeming inscrutability of evil, that "malign thing that has plagued and frightened man since time began," that "mauls" and "destroys" and leaves man with half a body or half a soul. He is incapable of accepting the injustice of a godless and purposeless universe in which man plays no role in the distribution of good and evil.

Less noble yet courageous men accuse him of madness, egotism, and godlessness ("God, God is against thee, old man," cries the decent but prosaic Starbuck). Like his namesake, the wicked Old Testament king, and like Jonah, Ahab has defied the traditional godhead in his rejection of what is presumably the natural order. And early on, the character Elijah predicts a cursed voyage. But Ahab is not to be judged by ordinary standards or local superstition; he is already a man of exemplary reputation when the book begins, having enlisted an excellent crew from every corner of the world; later, under the greatest of extremities, each man remains loyal to him. Throughout, Melville describes him as spiritual heir of the greatest mythic and historical figures—Prometheus, Agamemnon, Oedipus, Job, Lear, Satan, Faust, Perseus, Adonis, and Jesus. Now, "old and bowed" and like "Adam, staggering beneath the piled centuries since Paradise," Ahab is magnificent in his rage for truth. He must understand his place in the scheme of things and demonstrate that man may indeed assert his will in the vast cosmos:

> All visible objects . . . are but as pasteboard masks. But in each event . . . some unknown but still reasoning thing puts forth the moulderings of its features from behind the unreasoning mask. If man will strike, strike through the mask! How can the prisoner reach outside except by thrusting through the wall? To me, the white whale is that wall. . . . Sometimes I think there's naught beyond. But 'tis enough. He tasks me; he heaps me; I see in him outrageous strength, with an inscrutable malice sinewing it. That inscrutable thing is chiefly what I hate; and be the White Whale agent, or be the white whale principal, I will wreak that hate upon him. Talk not to me of blasphemy man; I'd strike the sun if it insulted me. . . . Fair play. . . . Who's over me? Truth hath no confines.

What Ahab comes to see, of course, is the "naught beyond."

The narrator with whom, interestingly, the reader also identifies, provides the means by which issues of evil, power, responsibility, and control—all the ethical issues relevant to Ahab's acts and the universe at large—are evaluated; he is the obsessively moral and thinking mind, the meditative foil against which Ahab acts out his grand compulsion. From Ishmael come speculations on many subjects, and like his captain and the sea itself, Ishmael lives in a state of eternal transformation, in his own quest for truth. (His final vision must have been blasphemous to both the transcendental and orthodox views of Melville's day: "I have written a wicked book," Melville confessed to Hawthorne, "and feel as spotless as a lamb.")

An outsider and a loner, not unlike Ahab, Ishmael has his own quest. Is there, as he initially says, a pattern in the universe, where every act has a corresponding significance in nature, as well as in the higher realm of ultimates and absolutes: "O Nature, and O Soul of man! how far beyond all utterance are your linked analogies! Not the smallest atom stirs or lives on matter, but has its cunning duplicate in mind." We witness the love and trust Ishmael gives to the cannibal Queequeg and are seduced by his honesty and magical recordings of the plenitude and significance of life around him and, most importantly, his adoration of the captain. Always counterpointing his innocence and discourse, of course, are Ahab's increasing passion and singleminded goal. Melville maintains a subtle balance between Ishmael's book knowledge and Ahab's intuitive and experiential wisdom. Ishmael's small tome on the natural history of the genus whale is merely the formal classification of Ahab's vast understanding of the sea, including, for example, even the white whale's most secret swimming patterns.

What Ishmael comes to learn, or at least observe, and what Ahab will not accept is that evil and good, like order and disorder, exist both in man and in nature; furthermore, no purposive or malicious force marks the individual for either. Moby Dick, ubiquitous and eternal, scarred like Ahab and similarly majestic and terrible, is in fact the colorless neutrality of nature—beautiful, indifferent, massive, brutal, erotic, and protean, the color of death and atheism but also the color of purity and innocence, at one time all colors and a tabula rasa, the benign indifference of the universe, the universe without man or God, the rainbow without color, the absence of meaning. ("Is it that by its indefiniteness it shadows forth the heartless voids and immensities of the universe and stabs us from behind with the thought of annihilation, when beholding the white depths of the milky way?") To Ahab, this is unacceptable. There *must* be some way man may assert himself and touch or restore order to this world. To accept nature's moral neutrality is to rob it of both its majesty and terror. One ought to be able to place God on trial.

How, then, does one deal with Ahab's increasing madness, with his sacrifice of the crew, and with his willing denial of humanity—with, as Lewis Mumford expresses it, his battle against evil with "power instead of love," whereby he becomes the image of the thing he hates? Has Ahab actually lost his humanity in the very act of vindicating it? Or may one argue that Ahab is all the more magnificent for rejecting his humanity in order to fulfill his task?

Clearly, Ahab does not renounce all human connectedness, and the impersonality which he affects is accompanied by great pain. Melville makes it clear that he suffers for all mankind, "with crucifixion in his face," barely sleeping "with clenched hands . . . with his own bloody nails in his palms." At one of several points, when his feelings overwhelm his control, he "dropped a tear into the sea," about which Ishmael remarks, "nor did all the Pacific contain such wealth as that one wee drop."

Yet when Starbuck warns him to desist—"See Moby Dick seeks thee not. It is thou, thou that madly seekest him!"—Ahab acknowledges that renunciation of all human claims will alone serve his purpose. He speaks of the loneliness of his sacrifice, and he *would* save Starbuck and the ship:

> When I think of this life I have led; the desolation of solitude it has been; the . . . exclusiveness . . . oh weariness! heaviness! . . . Aye, I widowed that poor girl when I married her. . . . And then the madness, the frenzy. . . . Old Ahab has furiously, foamingly chased his prey. . . . Why this strife of the chase? . . . Hear, brush this old hair aside; it blinds me, that I seem to weep. . . . I feel deadly faint, bowed, and humped. . . . God! God!—crack my heart!—stave my brain!—mockery! mockery! bitter, bitter, biting mockery of grey hairs . . . Close! stand close to me. . . . I see my wife and my child in thine eye. No, no; stay on board, on board!—lower not when I do. . . ."

Like Jesus, Oedipus, Prometheus, and the many other figures with whom he is compared, Ahab knows that he cannot dissipate what must be superhuman will with human emotion. Neither can he reconcile himself to a fate he cannot understand, avoid, or control; he must fight every consolation if he is to retain the courage of his task and face that which he most fears. That he knows this claims his humanity and that he fully understands its consequences makes him superior to his fate: "I know that of me which thou knowest not of thyself, oh, thou omnipotent. . . . Through thee, thy flaming self, my scorched eyes do dimly see."

Ahab dies with self-knowledge and unmitigated hatred at the horror he has touched. He also knows that there is a pattern beyond human comprehension and that all of man's acts finally end in meaningless death: "We are turned round and round in this world, like yonder windlass, and Fate is the handspike. . . . We all sleep at last on the field . . . [and] rust amid greenness, as last year's scythes flung down, and left in the half-cut swaths."

There is a despair at the end of the novel, a sense of hopelessness beyond pain and feeling. As at the end of *The Sound and the Fury*, there is a kind of mindless serenity as the "orphan" Ishmael is picked up by the mourning-mother emblem, the ship *Rachel*, having borne witness to the majestic and demonic, to the futile effort of man's trying to understand his world, and the tale signifying nothing. Ishmael has seen Job in the whirlwind and will return victorious only in an art which, like that of the Ancient Mariner or Conrad's Marlow, will haunt and transfix his audience in some of our most magnificent language. Ishmael must forever relate Ahab's majestic reflections:

> But if the great sun move not of himself; but is as an errand-boy in heaven; nor one single star can revolve, but by some invisible power; how then can this one small heart beat; this one small brain think thoughts; unless God does that beating, does that thinking, does that living, and not I. . . . Look! see yon Albacore! who put it into him to chase and fang that flying fish! Where do murderers go, man! Who's to doom, when the judge himself is dragged to the bar! But it is a mild, mild wind, and a mild looking sky; and the air smells now, as if it blew from a far-away meadow. . . .

—Lois Gordon

MODERN CHIVALRY.
Fiction by Hugh Henry Brackenridge, 1792–1805 (and later revisions).

Hugh Henry Brackenridge's *Modern Chivalry* is generally called a novel, but it stretches any accepted definition of that genre. Rather, it is a rambling, fictive diary of the development of democracy in the United States from the administration of George Washington to that of James Madison. It is also fine and sometimes raucous satire.

The structure of *Modern Chivalry* is simple on the one hand but loose and endless on the other. Simply, it is the story of the picaresque adventures of Captain John Farrago and his Irish servant Teague O'Regan. Patterned after Don Quixote and Sancho Panza, they travel geographically, politically, and socially around Brackenridge's western Pennsylvania. Teague gets into scrapes that the Captain has to help him out of. This leads to moral philosophizing by Farrago, followed by "reflections" and "observations" by the author Brackenridge himself. Such episodes, complete in themselves, are the format that the author repeated for 23 years. "Sir," Brackenridge is reported to have said in 1790, "I could set down and write a piece of humour for fifty-seven years without being in the least exhausted."

It is a matter of textual and bibliographical judgment even to establish the body of work that we can call *Modern Chivalry*. The best modern text (edited by Claude Milton Newlin, 1937) "is an exact reproduction of the first editions of the various parts of *Modern Chivalry*, except that it has been checked against the revised text of 1815 for the correction of misprints in the first editions." The "first editions" include seven volumes published separately between 1792 and 1815. The 1815 text is a collection containing revisions, deletions, and additions. The repetitive plot is similar to that of the comic strip or the soap opera. It can go on forever—a shaggy-dog story.

The formula permits the author to deal with all the topics of the times: law, education, religion, Indian treaties, marriage, romantic love, universities, racism, ethnicity, medicine, philosophical societies, the theater, popular oratory, social snobbery. He also deals with the mud and muck of the highways and the taverns of the everyday life of the times.

The consistent thesis is Madisonian democracy. Brackenridge was a classmate of James Madison at Princeton. *Modern Chivalry* should be required reading, after *The Federalist* papers, for any student of American government. "There is in every government a patrician class, against whom the spirit of the multitude naturally militates: And hence a perpetual war; the aristocrats endeavouring to detrude the people, and the people contending to obtrude themselves. And it is right it should be so; for by this fermentation, the spirit of democracy is kept alive."

Perhaps Brackenridge's greatest claim to fame is his literary style. In the Introduction to the first volume of *Modern Chivalry*, he boasts, with self-irony:

> It has always appeared to me, that if some great master of stile should arise, and without regarding sentiment, or subject, give an example of good language in his composition, which might serve as a model for future speakers and writers, it would do more to fix the orthography, choice of words, idiom of phrase, and structure of sentence, than all the Dictionaries and Institutes that have been ever made.

Brackenridge's style is brilliant. It is based on the classical Greek and Roman authors with whom he was proudly familiar, but even more it is based on the styles of Swift, Addison, and Fielding. "It may be said of satire, what was said of anger by some philosopher, It never pays the service it requires. It is your scratching, rump-tickling people, that get into place and power. I never knew any good come of wit and humour yet." It may be said of Brackenridge that his wit and humor are good today if we can take it.

—James C. Austin

MURDER IN THE CATHEDRAL.
Play by T.S. Eliot, 1935.

When, in the 1930's, T.S. Eliot decided to become a poet in (if not really of) the theatre, he started first with an "Aristophanic" fragment and a pageant. The relevance of *Sweeney Agonistes* (1932) and *The Rock* (1934) to *Murder in the Cathedral* has not been as much addressed as it ought to have been in the masses of criticism that have greeted *Murder in the Cathedral*, as (in fact) almost everything else by Eliot. In the long run his place in theatrical history will be for the children's book that served as the inspiration for the smash musical *Cats* and not for his imitation drawing-room comedies (*The Family Reunion, The Cocktail Party, The Confidential Clerk, The Elder Statesman*)—and for *Murder in the Cathedral*, which well may outlast all the rest of his drama because of its poetic rhythms (like *Sweeney Agonistes*) and for its pageantry (like *The Rock*).

First, rhythm. In 1936 Eliot gave a lecture in Dublin (not published until 1985 in the *Southern Review*), "The Tradition and the Practice of Poetry." It centered on the subject of rhythm and asserted that "the great revolutions of poetry are revolutions in the sense of rhythm." He said that "Wordsworth and Coleridge initiated a new age—not because their ideas were original, but because their rhythms were a departure from tradition." In *Sweeney Agonistes* he had given jazzy, modern, syncopated rhythms to his satirical comments on the lives of apenecks. In *Murder in the Cathedral* he perfected a kind of cadence of reason, a theatrical but philosophical-sounding rhythm of what one might call poetic-philosophical conversation. It gives a power to his play which puts it head and shoulders over *The Family Reunion* in theatrical effectiveness. Having experienced *Murder in the Cathedral* in performance, even those more or less baffled by the message will inevitably recall some of the impressive cadences of its great arias and exchanges. The rhythms lend it a kind of majesty, a quieter but also more dignified and intellectual evocativeness on the stage than even Marlowe's famous "mighty line." The verse gives a shape and a sound to the speeches (and they are speeches more than dialogue) that make the speakers larger and more memorable than ordinary people. Charwomen turn into Greek choruses, soldiers into philosophers, an archbishop into Everyman. It is all in the noble rhythms of their words. The play has a music that functions rather like the sound track of a film. It colors the words and interprets for us the situations. It assists in putting ideas into emotional contexts. As movie music often can make non-actors look as if they are acting, so the rhythms of the poetry often make *Murder in the Cathedral* seem to be happening, rather than simply being presented. The rhythms make a grand subject and grand historical figures grander, just as the archbishop in cope and mitre looks like more than a man. Afraid of Eliot's reputation for profundity (or obscurity), audiences went to performances of *Murder in the Cathedral* dutifully and came away delighted. The rhythm of the verse, even more than any of the ideas, entranced audiences. They discovered *Murder in the Cathedral* is a musical. Like *Cats*, it has a vast and spectacular set and plenty of stimulating music.

The second point concerns not audiences but spectators. *Murder in the Cathedral* was initially meant to celebrate a church festival at Canterbury, to be a kind of super village pageant. What Eliot offered was far more than anyone could have expected, but it was and remains essentially more an historical pageant than a play. Like a High Mass, *Murder in the Cathedral* conveys messages through ritual and celebrates a martyrdom and salvation. It has a priest and acolytes, poetic chants and responses, and a sermon (Thomas à Becket's Christmas sermon, in prose). The sanctuary is the stage for a liturgical drama and all the Christian symbols are used to work on our visual sense while the poetry excites what Eliot called our "auditory imagination." Like an opera, the play has recitatives and arias, even verbal *leitmotifs*.

But is is more than a ceremony or a musical extravaganza. It is a well-ordered combination, within the overall religious setting which underlines the centrality of Christianity in western culture, of diverse dramatic traditions. It is a Greek tragedy, and the *hubris* of the hero is a central concern. It reminds us how the liturgy gave birth to the drama in Christian churches and later on pageant wagons. It resembles a medieval Morality play; its theme is the search for sainthood, and among its participants are embodiments of abstractions such as Worldly Pleasure, Temporal Power, Spiritual Power, and Eternal Glory, while St. Thomas is a more than usually self-examining Everyman, superior to other Morality protagonists in that he is no mere passive and unthinking victim. It is a problem play, with conflicted persons and reasons and rationalizations and a social message. It is a psychological drama that rises above mere didacticism or case study; at its center is a man torn between pride and humility, driven in some sense to suicide while of unsound mind and in another sense fully understanding even such subtleties as how one can do "the right deed for the wrong reason." It is a political play and a significant advance over closet drama in a direction more like that of Yeats than of such later proponents of the verbal pyrotechnic as (say) Christopher Fry. It is a true milestone in the poetic drama and also the drama of ideas, arguably the *locus classicus* of Eliot as "classicist in literature, royalist in politics, Anglo-Catholic in religion."

Murder in the Cathedral grapples with moral and spiritual values in a world where doubt has replaced dogma, in an Age of Anxiety which has replaced an Age of Faith. In this play Eliot is as Stephen Spender reports he always was in personal conversation: dogged and diffident at once, "gravely insistent." For once he seems able to be more outspoken as (to use Eric Thompson's phrase) a "philosophical poet in an age of disbelief," and, perhaps because his subject is a man examining his own belief and misgivings, he speaks out more clearly than he does in that marvelous poetry which (E.M. Forster once trenchantly remarked) Eliot wrote with his cards held too close to his chest, like a man who has seen something terrible but is not going to tell us, who will not let us "in" lest our presence increase the "barrenness" and desolation he suffers. Many of Eliot's other poetic works say to us that "that is not it, that is not it at all," and even when he promises to come back and tell us all, he does not. Harry Puckett, writing of Eliot's poetry in *New England Quarterly* (June 1971) says: "His people are surrounded by a world of talking birds, cryptic messages, telling images, and words unheard . . . knowledge latent, veiled, or hovering, often in some sense silent or unheeded, commonly available only through images."

For once, in his first important verse play, Eliot is able to deliver complex but clear messages to the eye and the ear, to improve the static into a tableau and make even the ancient fabric of Canterbury cathedral, or any church in whose sanctuary the play is mounted, speak to us. His own conflicts instead of preventing him from expressing himself straightforwardly rather contribute to the deep psychological soul-searching his characters undergo, and their attitudes toward self and certainty enrich the drama.

It is quite possible that J.B. Priestley was right when he criticized Eliot's devotion to a "Church that is timid and time-serving," but at least it produced in *Murder in the Cathedral* an honest and bold, timely and useful discussion of the place of faith in the modern world. If Shaw was right, we may not be ready for our saints. But in Becket as Eliot presents him we have as modern a man as anyone could wish, and questions that are timeless.

—Leonard R.N. Ashley

THE MURDERS IN THE RUE MORGUE.
Story by Edgar Allan Poe, 1841.

"The Murders in the Rue Morgue," published in *Graham's Magazine* in April 1841, was the first of what Edgar Allan Poe called his tales of ratiocination. It is now generally regarded as the first detective story. Both descriptions are somewhat misleading.

Poe fathered the detective story while engaged in something slightly different. Reading the tale in the light of subsequent detective fiction, we see so many features which were to become staples of the later genre—the locked-room mystery, the bungling police, the amateur investigator with his brilliant deductions and his marvelling companion—that it needs an effort to see that detection is almost a by-product of Poe's scheme, the point where two of his interests happen to coincide. The essential ingredients of "The Murders in the Rue Morgue" are an interest in logic and ratiocination on the one hand, and a fascination with the violent, sensational, and macabre on the other. When they combine, a mystery gets solved. But Poe's hero, Dupin, is not a detective as such, nor is that term used since detectives did not exist when the tale was written. And the elements which Poe called "grotesque and arabesque" contribute at least as much to the tale's impact as the element of ratiocination.

Poe begins with a disquisition on the analytical faculty which, though the "very soul and essence of method," brings about results so astonishing that they have the "air of intuition." In fact the tale which follows is the exact reverse: though the essence of imaginative invention, it has, as Poe cheerfully admitted elsewhere, an "*air* of method." Already we are being elaborately bamboozled.

More philosophical irony follows, and logic becomes the medium of mystification. Juggling with terms, the narrator argues the near-absurdity that chess taxes merely the attention, whereas draughts challenges the "higher powers of the reflective intellect." (The "higher powers" turn out to be the ability to fool an opponent.) We see the trick, but not how it is done; it has been well said that Poe's address to the reader is that of a hypnotist or a stage magician. Then comes an account of whist-playing, again in terms of gamesmanship. Central to all these—chess, draughts, whist—is the idea of a contest. Though they are offered as analogies for the tale which follows, nothing could be less appropriate: Dupin, the hero, will face no battle of wits with an antagonist. The analogies really point to the contest between Poe and his reader—a contest in which Poe holds all the cards as he dupes us into a sense of the uncanny and then springs his surprise explanation. Poe is aware of all this more acutely than some later practitioners of the story-written-backwards. As he said elsewhere, "where is the ingenuity of unravelling a web which you yourself (the author) have woven for the purpose of unravelling?" The tale mocks its readers' credulity and its own dubious methods.

After softening us up with discourse, Poe turns to narration. The scene shifts to Paris, the goal of many an American reader's cultural ambitions. The philosophical adept to whom we have listened now becomes a tyro dumbfounded by the brilliance of Dupin. And the familiar properties of gothic begin to take shape. Dupin and the narrator live in darkened rooms in their "grotesque" mansion and emerge at night, emphasising their alienation from the social world. Interestingly, the murder victims, Madame L'Espanaye and her daughter, also live "an exceedingly retired life" in darkened rooms, and these parallels between hero and victims have encouraged allegorical and Freudian interpretations.

The episode where Dupin follows his silent companion's train of thought and then breaks in upon it is crucial in its appeal: what seems at first to be preternatural power of insight, compelling the reader's admiration, turns out when explained to be so simple that we all feel capable of it. Thus the promise of God-like power through the exercise of pure mind is held out to us all. But Dupin is called a "Bi-Part Soul . . . a double Dupin—the creative and the resolvent." The analytical rationalist is also the intuitive, visionary artist: in that sense Dupin is Poe himself, though a Poe translated into a fantasy society where his talents become all-powerful instead of superfluous.

The rest of the tale—the discovery of the mutilated corpses in the locked room, the evidence of witnesses, and Dupin's reasoning that the "criminal" is an escaped orang-outang—is a study in the refinements of the macabre. Poe used the orang-outang elsewhere. Here it is satisfying and necessary because when Dupin triumphantly reveals his deduction of its presence the grotesque and the rational coincide perfectly. The formal language of the inquest ("The head of the deceased was entirely separated from the body") and Dupin's appearance of inhuman rationality (he undertakes the investigation for "amusement") give a new twist to horror by narrating it deadpan. Critics have variously detected flaws in the details and logic of the story, but none of them matters much, especially when logic itself has already been so ironised: the illusion is all. Poe took pains to perfect it, revising details so as to make the ape's feat of swinging itself in at the window more credible.

Dupin was a central conception and Poe used him in further stories. Aristocratic, Romantic, alienated, Dupin was the progenitor of all those figures whose attraction to the intellectual reader consists in flattering the illusion that the reclusive thinking man can set the world to rights in occasional forays and can become what Conan Doyle calls Holmes, society's last court of appeal. And the choice of orang-outang as "villain" reduces crime to "natural" behaviour, an irruption into an otherwise stable social order: violence is explained only to the extent of detecting the details of its occurrence, and any further social enquiry is closed off before it can begin. Poe's legacy to detective fiction was not taken up for three decades, but then, for good and ill, it became ubiquitous.

—R.J.C. Watt

MY ÁNTONIA.
Novel by Willa Cather, 1918.

The dual character of Willa Cather's *My Ántonia* is suggested by its title, for it is at once the story of Ántonia Shimerda, a Bohemian émigré to the state of Nebraska in the 1880's, and the story of the narrator character, who creates his own image of Ántonia. The novel is cast as Jim Burden's reminiscent re-creation of his childhood and youth. Ántonia figures both as a childhood companion and as a symbol of values that Jim retrospectively associates with the frontier experience that he has left behind. The novel changes character somewhat depending on whether one reads it as Ántonia's story or as Jim Burden's, but these threads merge initially in the depiction of the pioneering life shared by easterners removed to the frontier and by Scandinavian, Russian, and Bohemian émigrés.

Jim Burden, orphaned in Virginia, arrives at Black Hawk (a fictional counterpart to Red Cloud, Nebraska) by the same train that brings the Shimerda family. The superb Book I of the novel counterpoints the more stable, established homesteading lifestyle of Burden's grandparents, a patriarchal lifestyle, against the animalistic grovelling struggle for survival of the penniless Shimerdas during their first winter in a sod hut. Cather depicts the hardships of the struggle to endure the weather and to master the land. She renders characters in silhouette against vast landscapes of undulating red grass and limitless horizons, or tunneling through snow to feed livestock. Animals are both competitors and companions to human beings in their solitude. Human and animal predators operate by the same rules. Suicide, murder, and madness are the lot of those least fit to survive. The quintessential grotesque image of the cost of the struggle is that of Ántonia's father's corpse, frozen to the ground in his own blood after he has shot himself, his coat and neckcloth and boots removed beforehand and carefully laid by for the survivors. Cather frequently uses a vivid episode or image such as this one to establish the mood of her story.

The dividedness between Jim's and Ántonia's fortunes becomes more explicit after their early childhood because of their disparate places in the social hierarchy. Removed from the farm to Black Hawk, the Burdens enter the establishment community, respectable, conventional, and dull in Jim's esteem, but the immigrants are hired girls, waitresses, and laundresses. It is characteristic of Cather to perceive the small-minded small town as the antagonist of individual enterprise and initiative, so that in Books II–IV the impulse to escape is a central motif of the novel. Jim flees to the university at Lincoln and eventually to Harvard and law school. Lena Lingard, a Norwegian girl, denigrates the farm and the family, and becomes a successful and celibate dressmaker in Lincoln. Tiny Soderball, who had worked in the hotel, makes her fortune feeding prospectors during the Klondike gold rush, and later invites Lena to join her in San Francisco. Even Ántonia has the prospect of escaping drudgery on the farm and domestic servitude in town through her romance with a railway conductor, but deceived and deserted in Denver, she returns to the farm and her taskmaster brother Ambrosch.

The land mastered, she must now overcome social opprobrium. Her success in doing so is celebrated by Jim in the concluding Book V of the novel, where he makes a nostalgic visit home and heroizes Ántonia as a sort of earth mother or fertility goddess. Twenty years have passed. Married within the Bohemian community, Ántonia has produced ten or eleven children and presides over a flourishing household: "She lent herself to immemorial human attitudes which we recognize by instinct as universal and true," Jim muses. "She was a battered woman now, not a lovely girl; but she still had that something which fires the imagination, could still stop one's breath for a moment by a look or a gesture that somehow revealed the meaning in common things. She had only to stand in the orchard, to put her hand on a little crab tree and look up at the apples, to make you feel the goodness of planting and tending and harvesting at last. . . . It was no wonder that her sons stood tall and straight. She was a rich mine of life, like the founders of early races." The adulatory retrospective attitude displayed here is typical of Jim's voice throughout the novel. Romantic, nostalgic, and unfulfilled in life, he celebrates the vitality and fruitfulness of the pioneering era as a lost Edenic world. In both the impulse to flee Black Hawk and the nostalgic retrospect, in his enduring reverence for the pioneers, Jim's career and attitudes are indicative of Cather's own. But as a male character he has been perceived as being sexually ambivalent in his attitude toward the immigrant girls, escapist and regressive in the romanticizing of his own childhood.

—Jean Frantz Blackall

THE NAKED AND THE DEAD.
Novel by Norman Mailer, 1948.

Norman Mailer's *The Naked and the Dead* is a naturalistic novel remarkable for its critical examination of liberal-leftist ideology, and, oddly, for Mailer's discovery, as he wrote, that violence was more deeply appealing to him than politics. It is an impressive war novel, one to be grouped with the best written by Americans: *Guard of Honor, From Here to Eternity, Catch-22*.

The structure of the novel reveals more art than one might expect from a naturalistic writer's first book. As we know, the theory of naturalism dictates random movement governed by chance and inclusion of the totality of experience, but the practice of fiction imposes the task of selection and emphasis. Mailer shrewdly holds these mutually exclusive demands in equilibrium. He gives the appearance of random movement while at the same time imposing limitations that make for order. The accidental imperatives of combat seem to govern movement of the troops in the book; the focus shifts back and forth from men to officers for no apparent reason; and time shifts are abrupt. All this conveys the impression of planlessness. Yet the entire action takes place on an island, which means that, confined this way, the action is self-limiting. The story begins with the invasion of the Japanese-held island and ends with the defeat of the enemy and conquest of the island. This successfully completed campaign constitutes an action of classical unity. The random freedom of movement within the story turns out to be in fact movement defined and controlled by the setting and by the directed progress of the story from the beginning to the preordained end. That end is achieved not only in the ironic victory of General Cummings, in command of the American forces, but also in the victory of Cummings and Sergeant Croft over Lieutenant Hearn and Red Valsen. These pairings give us the ideological conflict in the novel which also provides a structural principle, the first two men representing militarism and proto-fascism and the second two liberalism and anti-authoritarianism. In his treatment of this conflict Mailer shows how thematic statement and an idea of order are mutually interdependent.

The naturalistic bias in the novel appears early in Mailer's conventional view of Mount Anaka, on the island, as indifferent to the designs of men. And throughout the novel nature is a barrier and obstacle to human purposes simply because it is indifferent. It is the motiveless malignancy of nature, in the form of jungle, hornets, mountain that frustrates man's will and action, as the failed effort to climb Mount Anaka illustrates. This natural intransigence seems to indicate Mailer's belief in the absence of any benevolent guiding power in the cosmos.

Mailer's view of man, influenced by Marxist thought, is likewise naturalistic. Man in the mass, as in the army, is typical not individual man upon whom social forces exert determining and conditioning forces. Martinez, the Mexican-American sergeant specifically likened to Pavlov's dog, is conditioned to insecurity and fear by his status in American society. For Mailer, the quality of human existence produced by that society is rich in racial and religious tensions, haunted by the possibilities for fascism, scarred by economic insecurity, and rife with sexual frustrations.

These views, applied to the island war, give us a world in which nobody wins. General Cummings's victory is not the result of his brilliance but of the blundering effort of a stupid subordinate and of unanticipated Japanese weakness; in short, of accident. Effort, will, skill, mind, life itself are made to appear meaningless. But Cummings and Croft, the instrument of the General's theories, do win the ideological conflict. The General's army represents the concentration and apotheosis of power which kills individualism and arranges all men on the fear ladder. It induces anxieties, depersonalizes all men, and robs them of their beings. It is a paradigm for the authoritarian, stratified society that will emerge as postwar fascism in America. Opposed to these two are Hearn, whose liberalism is a compound of guilt and hesitation over commitment; whose egalitarianism is sentimental; and whose thinking is confused; and Valsen, who has only a romantic, rebellious anarchism to fall back upon. The organization of power represented by fascism first corrupts and then kills Hearn, and it breaks Valsen.

Mailer began the novel as a Marxist-influenced liberal-leftist who discovered, as he wrote, that he was responding to his characters at some point beneath the level of ideology. Sensing that his political ideology is bankrupt, he discovers in himself a terrifying appetite for violence. He faces the possibility that the worshipers of force, like Croft the war lover, will triumph in our world and that he may acquiesce in their victory. Thus Mailer engages in self-discovery, as he writes the novel, coming to terms with the deepest imperatives of his own being and anticipating the themes of his later books.

—Chester E. Eisinger

NAKED LUNCH.
Novel by William S. Burroughs, 1959.

In the course of *Naked Lunch* (originally published as *The Naked Lunch*) William S. Burroughs tells us that this particular passage or that was written under the influence of a specific drug. In an interview some ten years after the publication of the novel, he said that he owes many scenes in it to cannabis. Certainly drugs have contributed both to the hallucinatory substance and to the apparently disorganized form of the book. Burroughs discusses these matters as he goes along in the novel itself. The book spilled off the page in all directions, he says; it is a kaleidoscope of vistas and a medley of tunes and street noises. He professes to respond directly to sense stimulation: "There is only one thing a writer can write about: what is in front of his senses at the moment of writing. . . . I am a recording instrument. . . . Insofar as I succeed in *Direct* recording of certain areas of psychic process I may have limited function. . . . I am not an entertainer. . . ." It is not surprising, then, that much of the writing is the product of random or free association and that Burroughs uses the stream-of-consciousness method. The book is apparently fragmentary and formless, without plot or story line. It consists, according to the "Introduction" that Burroughs wrote for the Grove Press edition, of notes on his sickness and delirium as a junkie. The title, which Jack Kerouac suggested, means a "frozen moment when everyone sees what is on the end of every fork." That notion gives unity to the book as a whole, which Allen Ginsberg is supposed to have shaped, and to the style. The essence of the style is in the images of nausea which are pervasive in the book. These are the images that convey total revulsion, images of sexual perversion or the eating of excrement. They are the essence of the nightmare in which the victim is entwined. He takes in all that is loathsome and then vomits up all that he has taken in. These images are at the heart of the imaginary universe that Burroughs said he proposed to map in this book.

That universe is dominated by drugs, sex, and death. It is presented in the form of sadistic-masochistic fantasies of the most violent and revolting sort. Perhaps the most extreme example comes in a section called "Hassan's Rumpus Room," where Burroughs works up a gruesome stew of murder, pederasty, fellatio, and disease in which youths are violated in an atmosphere pervaded by excrement. The use of sex as violence and punishment seems to be a deliberate effort to point up the potential for extremes of nastiness and degradation in human beings. It is not simply that Burroughs wishes to rub his readers' noses in what he claims is their own filth, although he wants that. He wants to humiliate and degrade us, because he believes that we want it. He sees contemporary men as infected with guilt; they want to be violated in order to expiate the guilt and he, like the untouchable Sollubi of his book, "perform[s] a priestly function in taking on [himself] all human vileness." This widespread guilt arises from an acceptance of the official culture and from participation in the given structure of reality.

But when Burroughs drives the imagination to depicting scenes of perverted forms of intercourse while a hanging takes place or scenes of intercourse with a dead body which end with the eating of that body, then it seems he has shifted away from the themes of humiliation and expiation and blindly turned toward a form of therapy. R.D. Laing has posited a psychoanalytical cure on the proposition that it is necessary for the patient to plunge to the abysmal bottom where the utterly naked psyche gives in to every atavistic violation of the body. Such a sinking is the necessary prelude to a rise to eventual health. Burroughs's sickness in *Naked Lunch* goes beyond drug addiction. It is the sickness of a soul made ill by the vision of a diseased and unreal culture that has infected helpless humanity. Burroughs seeks the bottom as a way of treating his own condition and ours as well. But in vain.

Burroughs has said that the carny world, the sub-culture of the carnival, is "one I exactly intended to create. . . ." The carnival is only a superficial, externalized version of Burroughs's world. Underneath it, the liquefaction of protoplasm as he describes it proceeds inexorably. The final vision in *Naked Lunch* is that of total dissolution. The absolute that Burroughs confronts ultimately denies the possibility of life itself. It is, of course, death, when, in the entropic nightmare, everything melts away. This black, nihilistic vision is what the book finally conveys.

—Chester E. Eisinger

NATIVE SON.
Novel by Richard Wright, 1940.

If, as the black activist and educator W.E.B. Du Bois asserted, "the problem of the Twentieth Century is the problem of the color line," Richard Wright's *Native Son* is the central novel of the time—at least in the United States—for it remains after its first, explosive appearance, the most powerful novel on the subject yet written. Writing of the book's social impact, the critic Irving Howe claimed in a well-known pronouncement that because of *Native Son* "American culture was changed forever. . . . It made impossible a repetition of the old lies." Wright had "brought out into the open, as no one ever had before, the hatred, fear and violence that have crippled and may yet destroy our culture."

Not that the book has received unanimous critical approval. In fact, its enduring vitality is nowhere better demonstrated than by the critical controversy it still engenders along artistic and ideological lines: it has been attacked as being unfair to whites, and it has been criticized for its inadequacies in treating black life—though most frequently it is praised for the honesty and penetration of its vision of racial polarities. Some accused Wright of infusing the book too greatly with a left-wing perspective, while Ben Davis, Jr., an official of the Communist Party of America, wrote in a party publication that communism in the book was represented by atypical members with distorted ideas "which far from adequately" expressed Communist Party policy. Seemingly endless debate has focused on the merits (or shortcomings) of Wright's art, though increasingly few serious commentators question the novel's compelling drive and force.

Bigger Thomas represents in *Native Son* a black man (ultimately any human being) trapped under the oppressive weight of a history of cruelty, oppression, and violence that he had no role in creating. His ignorant, cowardly, hostile and ultimately murderous behavior seems completely determined by the history of inequality and mutilated opportunity into which he is born. He is the worst-case product of an unjust society, and he seems as stuck in his character as a person's body would be fixed by something like a mine cave-in. Yet Bigger escapes his trap in the most shocking of ways: he kills two women (though tried only for the murder of the first, who is white), flees the police, is captured and convicted in racist proceedings—and accepts the responsibility for his acts. He does this because he discovers that they have liberated him from his passive, unknowing acceptance of fate. Therefore, he says, what he did must have been good. The killings, and what they came to mean to him, brought him to life.

Naturally this conclusion, its philosophic implications and worth, its suitability as a means of self-knowledge and assertion, have been examined from many angles. Wright was not, of course, crudely advocating murder as invariably a legitimate means of self-expression. But he did seem to advocate the necessity of violence after certain instances of extreme oppression to break the steel grip of determinism. It should be noted carefully, however, that Bigger's liberation, in terms of his finally coming to see who he was in the world and to take responsibility for his behavior, comes only after he has not just experienced but *contemplated* his crimes. His lawyer, Boris Max (patterned partly after Clarence Darrow, partly after the lawyer in Theodore Dreiser's *An American Tragedy*, clearly one of Wright's major literary sources, along with Dostoevsky's *Crime and Punishment*), in a summation sometimes condemned as excessively rambling and vague, attempts to save Bigger's life through denying his responsibility and by pleading in effect that only by a shockingly nonviolent act—not destroying Bigger for the murder Max admits his client committed—can the cycle of oppression, violence, mutual fear, and counter violence be broken. But Bigger is executed. He goes to his death perhaps for the first time in his life seeing himself as a man, a human being, assuring Max he is "all right."

Though few critics have claimed that *Native Son* is tightly wrought, it is carefully conceived and forcefully orchestrated. Divided into three sections headed "Fear," "Flight," and "Fate," its texture and tone evolve as Bigger becomes at first more, then less and less of an animal. Crammed with realistic detail from its opening when an alarm clock's harsh clang and angry voices awaken Bigger's body (but not his mind), it proceeds relentlessly to another clang at the book's end when a steel door on death row shuts in Bigger but does not jail his now emancipated spirit. Particularly in the first two sections the book abounds in painfully real, and concurrently effectively symbolic scenes of black ghetto life, for example in the sequence where Bigger traps a panicked, vicious black rat as his mother prays to God for deliverance. Soon Bigger will be the rat. When in the street Bigger sees a plane, a symbol of impossible hope and futile escape, he wishes he could fly it so he could drop bombs. Other interwoven images of blindness, walls, and whiteness show how little people know of each other's realities, how thwarted and stifled life can be, how submerged black existence is in white society.

The book's last section is more discursive and less documentary as characters parade before Bigger like allegorical representations in a medieval drama, sometimes becoming less real people than representations of ideas. Wright also here employs expressionistic distortion of certain probabilities of life, the number and kinds of people who would be allowed in Bigger's cell, for example, to depict truths beneath the surface of reality. Flawed though it may be, *Native Son* is an inescapable accomplishment in American literature, and a revelation unbounded by time or region of what can happen when the human spirit is trapped.

—Jack B. Moore

NATURE.
Essay by Ralph Waldo Emerson, 1836.

Ralph Waldo Emerson's essay *Nature*, appearing in 1836 as a little booklet, is a landmark in American thought and literature. It is the archetypal statement of transcendentalism, one of the more extreme forms which European romanticism took in America. As one commentator has written, Emerson's "real purpose in *Nature* . . . was to find a scheme of unity into which God, the soul, and nature . . . could be fitted." In this ambitious purpose Emerson had been aided importantly by German idealist philosophy as interpreted to the English-speaking peoples by Samuel Taylor Coleridge in his *Aids to Reflection* (1825). Emerson was especially impressed by Coleridge's elucidation of the Kantian distinction between the Reason and the Understanding—a distinction basic not only in Emerson's writing but in transcendentalist thought generally. Coleridge explains the distinction as follows: "Reason is the power of universal and necessary conviction, the source and substance of truths above sense, and having their evidence in themselves. . . . Understanding is discursive"; it arrives at truth step by step and "in all its judgments refers to some other faculty (e.g., the senses) as its ultimate authority." Reason, then, closely resembles intuition. Understanding resembles what in everyday parlance is called reason. But as Emerson stated, Reason "never reasons; never proves, it simply perceives; it is vision."

Emerson used this distinction as a starting point in formulating his concept of nature and its relation to humankind. Yet Emerson realized that his views and those of the idealist and transcendentalist philosophers had their origins far back in the history of human thought. As an epigraph in the first edition of *Nature*, he quoted from Plotinus: "Nature is but an image or imitation of wisdom, the last thing of the soul"; and as early as 1830 he included in his *Journals* this quotation from the *Mahabharata*: "The senses are nothing but the soul's instruments of action; no knowledge can get to the soul by this channel," and he noted that idealism (i.e., transcendentalism) is "a primeval theory."

Nature is one of the most carefully organized of Emerson's writings. He begins with a definition: Nature is that "great apparition that shines so peacefully around us." It is "the NOT ME," everything including one's body and human artifacts. Next, as an illustration of how truth may come to one, he describes a personal experience: "Crossing a bare common . . . at twilight . . . I become a transparent eyeball; I am nothing; I see all; the currents of Universal Being circulate through me." The Reason, or intuition, floods him with the profoundest of insights, as was the case with Wordsworth during moments of mystical revelation near Tintern Abbey.

Nature, Emerson continues, serves humanity in four ways: as commodity, as beauty, as language, as discipline. As commodity, it serves the body's needs. But "a nobler want is served by nature, namely, the love of Beauty"—especially moral beauty, which appeals to the sense of right and wrong as apprehended by the Reason. Nature also provides mankind with a language—all language, to Emerson, derives from the metaphorical use of natural objects—not only for everyday communication but for the loftiest poetic or philosophic utterances. Finally, nature serves as a teacher, or as discipline, most fundamentally in the exercise of the moral sense in the decisions and demands of daily life. "All things are moral," Emerson wrote, ". . . all things with which we deal preach to us. What is a farm but a mute gospel?"

Emerson speculates whether nature actually exists outside the mind, but reaches no conclusion. Yet he does insist that nature stands "as the apparition of God. It is the organ through which the universal spirit speaks to the individual as a plant upon the earth, so a man rests upon the bosom of God." Indeed the Reason is akin to the divine; Man, then, is actually a God, but "a God in ruins . . . the dwarf of himself." Once humans come to recognize the divinity within them, their potential for goodness and growth will prove to be infinite. Emerson's optimism was limitless.

Emerson in *Nature* and all his writings depended on striking epigrams and startling metaphors to goad his readers into thinking. The foregoing quotations illustrate this stylistic device. Other examples are: "A fact is the end or last issue of spirit"; or, ". . . the whole of nature is a metaphor of the human mind." Whether one accepts or rejects such sweeping statements, they give one pause and, at least momentarily, stimulate thought.

—Perry D. Westbrook

THE OCTOPUS.
Novel by Frank Norris, 1901.

The Octopus was the sixth of the seven novels that Frank Norris wrote before his sudden death, at 32, in 1902. It is in most respects his best. In writing it, Norris was determinedly filling a gap in American literature: America had no adequate non-imitative "American novel" and no epic of the winning of the west.

By 1899 Norris had conceived an adequate subject: "the Wheat." Raised in the vast San Joaquin Valley of southern central California, it involved the labor of inhabitants of every ethnic and economic group. Then in "the Pit" in Chicago it was bought and resold to "the People" of the world. Finally, this product of American soil and labor sustained populaces of the farthest countries. *The Octopus* would be the first volume of a trilogy; *The Pit*, the second; and there would be a third, to have been called *The Wolf*, which Norris did not live to write.

The title *The Octopus* refers not, of course, to the wheat, but to the spoiling force, the railroad. The valley's fecundity gave rise to the railroad and made possible the abuses perpetrated by it. By the mid-1890's Norris had come to value and use various aspects of Zola's realism and naturalism—contemporary topics, careful documentation, close observation, recognition of natural forces—after a rather prolonged youthful period of captivation with medieval romance. The "Mussel Slough Massacre," the armed battle that had taken place between the agents of the Southern Pacific Railroad and the wheat farmers of Tulare County in May 1880, was the documented fact on which the action of *The Octopus* was based. In choosing to treat of the abuses of the railroad company, Norris was not taking a daring stand or even breaking new ground. The "unanimous hatred of the people of California toward the Southern Pacific Railway" already existed. The novel is more an epic than a work of propaganda.

The wheat and the need to transport it organize almost all of the action. The wheat grows on the new soil in generous abundance, ready to be used, but the railroad tycoons require farm machines to be moved by circuitous routes, raise rates prohibitively for small producers, cut wages despite high profits, fire those who protest, govern the local newspapers, and finally renege on the contracts made with the ranchers who have leased and improved the land. The company has bought the state government and the courts; the valley people are too disorganized to make a stand. Norris follows Zola in seeing the railroad as a living monster; it is a gigantic octopus with its tentacles clutching all.

Presley, an educated outsider and a poet, who has come to the west with the hope of writing a vaguely conceived grand romantic epic of the Indian and Spanish epochs, follows Norris's own development in jettisoning this plan and studying to depict the present valley situation. This observer is a friend of the young ranchers, drawn from friends of Norris: Harran Derrick, whose stately father Magnus had lost his bid for governorship rather than engage in corrupt politics; Annixter—truculent but admirable—the most fully presented character; the sophisticated Osterman. And there is Vanamee, an educated man, a strange mystic rover, temporarily a farm laborer, whose etherial sweetheart, Angèle, raped by an intruder, had died in childbirth; his friendship with the old Spanish priest at the mission church sustains in the novel the Spanish background of the region. Many of the workmen are of Spanish or Portuguese descent. And there is the old German farmer, the anarchist bar-owner, and a scattering of womenfolk.

Memorable set scenes, Norris's forte, dramatize the life of those who tend the wheat: the big barn dance, the jackrabbit drive, the annual plowing: "The ploughs, thirty-five in number, each drawn by its team of ten, stretched in an interminable line, nearly a quarter of a mile in length. . . . Each of these ploughs held five shears, so that when the entire company was in motion, one hundred and seventy-five furrows were made at the same instant. At a distance, the ploughs resembled a great column of field artillery." Further animating the meticulous details of the scene is the metaphor of the earth—"the uneasy agitation of its members, the hidden tumult of its womb, demanding to be made fruitful, to reproduce, to disengage the eternal renascent germ of Life that stirred and struggled in its loins."

The wheat is the living witness of the evolutionary force. When Annixter, after a night of internal struggle, finally recognizes his total love for Hilma—herself a type of Love—he sees in the dawn light the young wheat that has burst through the ground: "the Wheat, the Wheat . . . an exulting earth gleaming transcendent with the radiant significance of an inviolable pledge."

Though the struggle with the corrupt railroad causes the loss of Magnus Derrick's honor and the lives of Annixter, Harran, several other ranchers, and Hilma's baby, the promise of "life out of death" is sustained by the coming of the dead Angèle's daughter the night of the first wheat, and by the unusually splendid harvest of the wheat itself. The book ends with an ambiguous passage in which the leading railroad tycoon justifies the railroad as itself being ruled by forces beyond it. Unambiguously, the railroad's local petty tyrant, S. Behrman, as he is exulting at seeing his wheat rushing down the chute into a ship for India, is himself caught into the downward rush.

Norris's exact descriptions, his recording, like Zola's, of scenes, sounds, and smells, produced a vibrant and memorable novel, despite some overwriting and unclear logic.

—Alice R. Bensen

OLD MORTALITY.
Story by Katherine Anne Porter, 1938.

"Old Mortality," like most of Katherine Anne Porter's fiction, is deeply rooted in its time. This is not to say that her stories lack originality or that they will fail to be of interest in the future, but rather, like the fiction of Hemingway and others of that generation, her stories grew out of and reflect the social and cultural upheavals that took place during and after World War I. There is a harking back to an earlier, innocent, more romantic time, but also simultaneously a fierce insistence on seeing life from what is felt to be a more honest modern point of view.

Part I: 1885–1902 of "Old Mortality" deals with the legends of the older generations; it captures the air of nostalgia and romance engendered by those legends while to some extent undercutting them by an ironic tone and by subjecting them, at times, to the doubtful questioning of two little girls, Miranda and her sister Maria. The girls are enchanted by their elders' stories, whether of a visit to the theater or of the larger than life actions of Aunt Amy and Uncle Gabriel, and they grow up with a sense of "a life beyond a life in this world" and have confirmed for them "the nobility of human feeling, the divinity of man's vision of the unseen, the importance of life and death, the depths of the human heart, the romantic value of tragedy." But even as they are charmed, Miranda and Maria have difficulty matching their grandmother's decaying keepsakes and the absurdly old-fashioned photographs of the dead heroes and heroines with the tales of high deeds and romantic adventure. These doubts and the pervasive tone of gentle mockery anticipate the disillusioning that is to come in Parts II and III.

Part I has an anecdotal richness; it ranges over several years and includes numerous episodes and characters, suggesting in method an old-fashioned way of storytelling. Part II: 1904, by contrast, has a decidedly modern ring. Whereas Part I recounted in leisurely fashion the legends of the old order, Part II narrowly focuses on the lives of two members of the younger generation, Maria and Miranda: it is limited to the events of one day during and after a visit to the racetrack. The limited scope, the constricted time and space, and, above all, the sordidness of detail and general air of deflation and repressed hope all give Part II a quality of modern "truth-telling" rather like that to be found in the stories of James Joyce's *Dubliners*. The point of this method of narration, however, is not merely modern truth-telling; it is a strategy for developing the theme of the story. The sordidness of Part II, which is in marked contrast to the romantic quality of Part I, is occasioned by the appearance at the racetrack of the girls' Uncle Gabriel who figured so prominently in Part I in the romantic legend of their Aunt Amy. The man the girls had been brought up to associate with gallant and romantic adventure turns out to be a "shabby fat man with bloodshot blue eyes, sad beaten eyes, and a big melancholy laugh, like a groan." Uncle Gabriel is a revelation the meaning of which looks forward to Part III and to a fuller, more devastating revelation.

In Part III: 1912, Miranda is confronted by another figure out of the past, Cousin Eva Parrington, who, even in the stories told by Miranda's father, appeared as an unromantic, chinless spinster, suffragette, and teacher of Latin. Now, on the train carrying them both to Gabriel's funeral, she presents Miranda with her own myth of the past which, on the face of it, sounds plausible enough, perhaps even scientific. Cousin Eva dismisses all of the legendary claims about Amy's beauty and tragic nobility and provides a kind of economic and Freudian version of the past. All of those dances and parties, Cousin Eva claims, were a kind of marketplace for girls like Amy who were trying to cut the ground out from under each other. "It was just sex,' " Cousin Eva says, "in despair, 'their minds dwell on nothing else. They didn't call it that, it was all smothered under pretty names, but that's all it was, sex.' " Miranda briefly considers this new version of the past and then, wisely dismisses it. " 'Of course it was not like that. This is no more true than what I was told before, it's every bit as romantic.' "

Later, off the train, Miranda observes her father and cousin with their heads together, the old-fashioned romantic and the new Freudian, in cahoots over their common past, and she envies them their naturalness, their freedom from playing the role of son or daughter to an aged person. Then she rejects them and their love which requires that she see the world through their eyes "and yet could not tell her the truth, not in the smallest thing." Later, she thinks that although she can never know the truth about "the legend of the past, other people's memory of the past," she can at least know "the truth about what happens to" her. At that point the author steps in to comment: "making a promise to herself, in her hopefulness, her ignorance."

Although some readers may regard this comment as an unwarranted intrusion into the story, this final phrase provides a crucial insight. Miranda is able to recognize the falseness of the myths told by her father and her cousin, but she fails to understand the larger implications of the bond between them. Their easy acceptance of their past, despite their different versions of it, is the result of shared experience. For the truth about life, the conclusion of this story suggests, is not to be found in any words about it; such formulations are legends shaped by individual feeling and memory; the only reliable version of the past is the experience itself, the actual living of it.

—W.J. Stuckey

ON THE ROAD.
Novel by Jack Kerouac, 1957.

On the Road remains after thirty years not only the most popular novel by Jack Kerouac, but also the best-known prose work of the Beat Generation. It was not, however, Kerouac's personal favorite among his writings. He preferred *Visions of Cody* and considered *On the Road* as a superseded preliminary version of his efforts to transform his life "on the road" with Neal Cassady between 1947 and 1950 into part of the "Duluoz Legend," a projected fictionalization of his life. *On the Road* was, in fact, the first of four such preliminary efforts to be completed.

These attempts began in 1948, immediately after the completion of Kerouac's first novel, *The Town and the City*, while the events used in the new work were still in progress. Kerouac's estate has denied access to the manuscripts of the first two versions, but Tim Hunt has managed in *Kerouac's Crooked Road* (1981) to reconstruct them from Kerouac's correspondence and other unpublished materials. The third version, narrated by a teenaged black boy from North Carolina, provides most of the text for the posthumously published *Pic*.

The 175,000-word fourth version, typed on a single scroll of paper during three weeks in April 1951, was rejected by many publishers while it circulated with the title "The Beat Generation"; but finally, through the persistence of Malcolm Cowley, who suggested cuts and revisions, it was published by the prestigious Viking Press in 1957. As early as 1951, however, Kerouac, inspired by his discovery of "spontaneous prose," had begun to displace this text with the very different and much more experimental "Neal Book," which was not published in its entirety as *Visions of Cody* until after Kerouac's death. In it, the story line of *On the Road* is drastically condensed into the final fifth and its downbeat ending is replaced by a more optimistic one in which Ti-Jean Duluoz (Kerouac's alter ego) finally transcends the influence of Cody Pomeray (Neal Cassady's final avatar).

The formally traditional *On the Road* is thus a supplanted version of a work in progress that the author allowed to be published for financial reasons when even his friends considered the Joycean final version of his masterwork unmarketable. Possibly as a result of changes Malcolm Cowley suggested, *On the Road* is a much more carefully structured work than the published components of the "Duluoz Legend." Each of the four parts of this novel based on the experiences of Kerouac (Sal Paradise) and Cassady (Dean Moriarity) during their life on the road follows a repeated narrative pattern that foreshadows the brief fifth section. Each begins with Sal depressed by his sheltered life at home as he is writing his first novel. Energized by the example of Dean, Sal takes to the road four times and each time the action accelerates manically. As each frenzied episode reaches its climax, however, a disillusioning experience dashes Sal's hopes; and he slinks home, dejected and again depressed.

In Part One, Sal makes his first trip to San Francisco (largely by bus), where he ends up as a frustrated guard in a menacing security camp, "at the end of America" with "nowhere to go." During his trip home, Sal establishes with a Mexican girl the one satisfying romantic relationship depicted in the novel; but he abandons her because of what he later laments as his "white expectations." A year later in Part Two he travels with Dean to New Orleans and again San Francisco, where he envisions Dean, standing naked by a window, as someday "the pagan mayor" of the city; but Dean's energies run out, and Sal goes home not caring whether they ever meet again.

By the next Spring, however, in Part Three, Sal is drawn back to San Francisco, where he offers to take his "brother" Dean to Italy and support them both, but on this, their wildest cross-country junket, in a borrowed car, Sal ruminates morbidly about his "raggedy travelings," and Dean becomes involved with so many wives and children that the trip abroad is called off. By Spring 1950, however, Sal can still generate enthusiasm for a trip to Mexico City as "the most fabulous" one of all; but when Sal becomes seriously ill in Mexico, Dean deserts him and Sal realizes "what a rat" Dean is. The novel ends with a tableau that symbolizes the transparent but impenetrable wall between Sal and Dean. Back in New York Sal rides off to a Duke Ellington concert in a bookmaker friend's Cadillac, while Dean is left outside in the rain. Sal can only wave wordlessly through the back window before brooding that he can see no future but "the forlorn rags of growing old."

Thus far from being the seductive promotional tract for an irresponsible threat to the traditional American way of life that it has been condemned as, *On the Road* is rather a defeatist cautionary tale about the "endless and beginningless emptiness" of what Sal calls "the senseless nightmare road." Its downbeat ending foreshadows better than Kerouac's preferred works his subsequent rejection of any responsibility for the counterculture that this novel helped inspire.

—Warren French

ONE OF THE MISSING.
Story by Ambrose Bierce, 1888.

In Ambrose Bierce's Civil War story "One of the Missing" Private Jerome Searing of General Sherman's army is instructed to get as near Rebel lines as possible and "learn all he could" about enemy strength, armament, and movements. Sherman's army is "confronting the enemy at and about Kennesaw Mountain, Georgia," and Jerome ends up quite soon beneath the debris of a small building struck by a shell; his own rifle is pointed at him. Certain immediate circumstances have led to his predicament: his surrender to the impulse to linger long enough to kill one of the retreating Rebels, matched by the impulse of a Confederate captain of artillery to fire one last shell. Assuming erroneously that his rifle is still cocked and loaded and that having thrust the board against the trigger he has released a bullet aimed at his forehead, Searing literally scares himself to death. Bierce prepares for this denouement with several references to fear, especially: "he screamed with fear. He was not insane—he was terrified." Certain that something would eventually trip the hammer, Jerome, to release himself from the no longer bearable terror of prolonged anticipation, chooses suicide. In a monstrously ironic way, he is master of his fate.

The omniscient narrator sees everything, within a somewhat cosmic framework, while Jerome and his brother Adrian and the artillery captain often act on fallacies of human perception. To Jerome, it "looked as if the whole edifice would go down at the touch of a finger." Ironically, the shell brings it down. Later, "in the perception of this circumstance" (that the rifle is aimed at the exact center of his forehead), he remembers that he "set the trigger so that a touch would discharge it." Jerome, the "incomparable marksman," takes aim, then hears "a rushing sound in the air," perceiving it to be "like that made by the wings of a great bird swooping down on its prey." The artillery officer has sighted his field piece at "what he took to be some Federal officers on the crest of a hill" (if what he saw really were Federal officers, Lt. Adrian Searing may have been one of them; but the shell accidentally hits the building where Adrian's brother Jerome is just getting a Confederate in his rifle sights). The artillery captain may have been his target, for sharpshooters usually aim at officers.

As he listens with "attentive ears," Adrian hears a rumble that is "like the clatter of a falling building translated by distance"; the reader knows, through the omniscient point of view, that a shell has caused a building to collapse on Adrian's brother, Jerome. The shell brings "down the crazy edifice with a loud clatter, in clouds of blinding dust!" Bierce returns at the end to the faulty perceptions of the dead man's brother. Passing on both sides of the wrecked building, the skirmishers observe nothing. But Adrian sees a dead body; dust makes it appear to be clad in Confederate gray. "From his point of view the officer does not observe" the rifle, which the omniscient author has shown the reader. Adrian deduces that "the man was apparently killed by the fall of the building." "Dead a week" is his erroneous conclusion. In fact, Adrian's brother has been dead only minutes, perhaps seconds. Thus the ironies of fallacious human perceptions trigger ironic physical events, all of which are interrelated in various ways.

But the larger ironies are predetermined. Blatant contrivances in a work of fiction usually earn the reader's contempt, but Bierce's tales show, from various perspectives, ways in which the nature of life itself is contrived to victimize us all. Given Bierce's pessimistically ironic vision of life, the contrived, coincidental convergence of faulty character perception and character action is justified. And the omniscient point of view is uniquely appropriate for the vision of life to which Bierce subjects his readers. The passage in the opening section that begins "But it was decreed from the beginning of time that Private Searing was not to murder anybody" is a typical example of the kind of omniscient authorial intrusion modern readers find irritatingly overbearing, but Bierce is one of those writers whose sensibility, temperament, and vision of life compel him to delineate an unusually overt omniscient perspective.

"One of the Missing" is a more overt and complete expression of Bierce's ironic vision of life than his most famous story, "An Occurrence at Owl Creek Bridge." That vision suffuses the entire story, beginning with the title. We are reading about "One of the Missing" until we realize a major implication of Bierce's vision: that all of us are missing; the reader becomes "one" of the missing, and the author is another (whether or not the reader knows that Bierce became literally one of the world's most famous missing persons).

The following lines become ironic: Jerome stepped "across a light line of earthworks, and disappeared into a forest" (a typical first move in the action pattern of a Bierce story); "an incomparable marksman" is juxtaposed to "insensible to fear"; " 'That is the last of him,' said one of the men. 'I wish I had his rifle . . .' " Jerome's "eyes penetrated everywhere"; "he had rightly interpreted the signs. . . ." He "was not without a certain kind of ambition" is juxtaposed ironically to "he heard a rushing sound in the air. . . ." "They'll find me." *They* do not; his brother does, mistaking him for an enemy corpse. Jerome escapes into sleep, into "pleasant memories of childhood," but the opening of the haunted Dead Man's Cave becomes the "ring of metal" aimed at his head. One time he beat an enemy soldier to death with his rifle, discovering later that it was cocked. The memory of that discovery ironically causes him to remember that he had cocked his rifle just before the shell struck and to assume it is still cocked and loaded. He calls himself a rat in a trap but the rats who threaten to set off his rifle are survivors of the same trap. This "trap" becomes his "sole universe"—and, Bierce insists, ours.

—David Madden

OUR TOWN.
Play by Thornton Wilder, 1938.

One of the most successful American plays of the 20th century, Thornton Wilder's *Our Town* owes its fame chiefly to the skill with which its author dramatizes the age-old theme of the importance of ordinary day-to-day human existence: namely, by means of a daring rearrangement of conventional stagecraft. To depict the supreme worth of savoring life fully while we possess it, Wilder drew upon such classic models as Homer's *Odyssey* and Dante's *Purgatorio*, both of which offer poignant contrasts between the fleeting beauty of the living and the dreary permanence of the dead, as in Achilles's dour comment in Hades that he would rather be a living slave than a dead king. In *Our Town* Wilder converted the universal message implicit in this scene into an allegory involving birth, marriage, and death in the United States of the 1930's. By his bold methods of staging his drama, his artful manipulation of time and place, he related the here and now of an insignificant New England village to the timeless concerns of human nature everywhere. His aim, he wrote, was "an attempt to find a value above all price for the smallest events in our daily life. I have made the claim as preposterous as possible, for I have set the village against the largest dimensions of time and place."

Wilder's two major innovations enabling him to fulfill his aim were the use of a bare stage and a centralizing character, the Stage Manager, a throwback to both the Chorus in classic Greek drama and the Property Man in Chinese theatre. As a stand-in for author and director, he not only arranges stage props, but also initiates, controls, and interprets setting and action, explaining directly to the audience from the outset that they are going to witness a play about life in an ordinary little town in New Hampshire, Grover's Corners, beginning just before dawn on 7 May 1901. After pointing to some of its notable imaginary features, including the cemetery, he gives a brief history of the town, identifies some of its leading citizens, focusing on several members of the two neighboring families, the Webbs and the Gibbses, whose interrelationships will dominate the action from there on. As the Stage Manager develops their typical encounters with one another that day throughout Act One, he also offers further commentary from time to time, which illustrates the commonplaceness of routine in the Webb and Gibbs households, but also suggests its broader metaphysical significance. The blessed tie that binds Grover's Corners to the Universe and the Mind of God is then circuitously expressed in the colloquy between young George Gibbs and his sister Rebecca at the end of the first act.

Similar techniques are employed in the second and third acts to strengthen and clarify the union of theme and action. In Act II, which deals with the courtship and marriage of George Gibbs and Emily Webb three years later, the Stage Manager serves as both the minister who weds them and the commentator who disparages the glamour of the ceremony, which, he says, is interesting only "once in a thousand times." Nevertheless, as he muses on the fact that millions of folk since the dawn of time have celebrated such marriage rites as these, it becomes clear that the wedding of this particular young couple, however commonplace it appears, symbolizes a universal "fusion of nature's physical and spiritual purposes."

Again, in Act III Wilder boldly extends his basic analogy by literally juxtaposing life and death on the stage. Nine more years have elapsed, and some of the town's recent dead who were alive in Act II are now seated on chairs representing their graves in the cemetery, where they are witnessing the burial of Emily, who has just died in childbirth. As she joins them in the vacant chair next to her mother-in-law, she becomes the catalyst for the swift evocation of Wilder's deepest meaning. The granting of her desire to relive just a single day of her former life, her twelfth birthday, leads to her discovery that the living can neither appreciate nor understand the beauty of life till they have lost it. Crying "Oh, earth you're too wonderful for anybody to realize you," she is ready to return to the passionless Dead, whom the Stage Manager had described at the opening of the act as "waitin' for something they feel is comin'. Something important and great." The action has built up steadily throughout the play toward the dramatic revelation that human life, however painful, dreary, or inconsequential its quotidian events, is both a precious gift in itself as well as part of a mysterious plan that rests in the "Mind of God."

—Eugene Current-Garcia

PATERSON.
Poem by William Carlos Williams, 1946–63.

Paterson is among the half dozen or so long poems, including Ezra Pound's *Cantos*, T.S. Eliot's *Four Quartets*, Hart Crane's *The Bridge*, Charles Olson's *Maximus Poems*, and Louis Zukofsky's *A*, that mark a resurgence of epic writing in the 20th century. Unlike their European counterparts of the middle ages, these American epics celebrate the unity of culture by means other than kings, heroes, saints, or religions, and speak of history in terms of ordinary life and personal experience, instead of wars, conquests, or high adventure. Walt Whitman's *Leaves of Grass* (1855) was an early indication of the possibility of extended poetry in the industrial age, and subsequent long poems have drawn from it. But a more direct influence upon the modern long poem was James Joyce's *Ulysses* (1922), an Irish novel which draws parallels between Dublin life and the world of Homer's *Odyssey*. Joyce's novel seized upon the seeming disarray of contemporary life and thought and discerned principles of unity that not only related modernity to the past, but synthesized the fruits of the intellectual revolution of Darwin, Marx, Freud, and Einstein, from which a new vision of life was emerging.

William Carlos Williams did not conceive the project of a long poem until 1942, though *Kora in Hell* (1920) marks an early effort at writing an extended work, which his friend Pound liked but judged an imitation of the French poet Arthur Rimbaud. Williams's autobiographical novel *A Voyage to Pagany* portrays a writer seeking the experience that would lead him to a bold new form of writing, but who rejects the European culture other American writers had embraced as their subject. While Pound and Eliot wrote about European capitals in their own long poems, Hart Crane broke new ground in *The Bridge* (1930) with an extended verse treatment of the Brooklyn Bridge and of American life.

Paterson is divided into five books, which serve to structure the poem into a five-act drama in which a central figure, Mr. Paterson, seeks to dissolve boundaries between self and the city around him. His purpose is to incorporate the hidden nature of the city into his thought, to join the so-called objective or external world to his identity, and thus bring to mind an otherwise separate, alien reality. No one had tried to treat the American city from this vantage before—to make it an extension of self, an aspect of one's own nature, though in Whitman's "Song of Myself" a similar incorporation of the world to self is celebrated, but on a grander scale and without the struggle here dramatized. Indeed, the difficulties and reconciliations between Dedalus and Bloom in *Ulysses*, between lofty and sensuous extremes, is closer to the plotting of Williams's poem. In Book I of *Paterson* many things are set against each other, including the giant figures of Mr. Paterson, masculine intellect, and the feminine energies of the hills on which he stretches. Polarity must be overcome by patient dismantling of the closed self; each step gained is marked by a flow of sensuous identity and sympathy with the outside world. Book II contains the famous passage in which the central figure enters and liberates his own unconscious, with its confusion of experience resembling the vast stretches of terrain constituting Paterson. The Passaic river, which flows through Paterson, comes to represent the "stream of consciousness" of its citizenry, which the narrator articulates as his own voice. Various letters inserted in the text either accuse the protagonist of narcissism and self-indulgence, or praise his goals and intentions, thus monitoring the difficulties of his journey into the world.

Though conceived as early as 1942, the first four books of *Paterson* were not published as a single volume until 1958; the complete poem of five books, with notes and sketches for a sixth, was issued in 1963. Thus, the poem was written late in the author's life, but it marks Williams's richest period of composition, in which he also completed *Journey to Love* and *Pictures from Brueghel*, and such remarkable extended lyrics as "The Desert Music," written in 1951, and "Asphodel, That Greeny Flower," included in *Journey to Love*. The late work is characterized by greater frankness and intimacy, and by a more fluid phrasing, positioned on the page to suggest the pauses and rushes of thought during composition. These technical developments follow directly from the intentions of *Paterson*, in which a figure struggles to transcend his inhibitions and have free exchange with the life around him.

Paterson marks the point at which American poetry turned its attention away from Europe to its own culture, to domestic life and the travails of selfhood at home. Its treatment of a city as a living thing, in which a central intelligence articulates its character, pointed the way for subsequent treatments, most notably in the work of Robert Lowell, Charles Olson, and Allen Ginsberg, who made the cities of Boston, Gloucester, Massachusetts, and New York the subject of their poetry. Moreover, Williams's various strategies in *Paterson* for showing the interaction between personal and collective realms, a highly original program of devices that breaks up the flow of thought with intrusions from the outside, soon became the conventions of postmodern poetry. *Paterson*, together with Pound's *The Pisan Cantos* (1948), opened the way for a second surge of experiment in American poetry.

—Paul Christensen

PICNIC.
Play by William Inge, 1953.

Although originally set in the 1930's, written in the late 1940's, and finally reproduced in a new version on Broadway in 1973, *Picnic* epitomizes the American 1950's and the small-town midwest in which William Inge was born and bred.

In *Picnic* Inge creates a female world—insular, insecure, parochial, lonely, sexually unfulfilled—and agitates it by injecting a virile male presence. Set in two adjoining back yards during the end-of-summer Labor Day weekend—a time symbolizing fading youth and hopes for spinster teacher Rosemary, who boards with Madge, her sister Millie, and mother Flo—this realistic play employs as catalyst the sensual Hal Carter, who, while doing chores for Flo's neighbor Helen, sheds his shirt and arouses all the women, even tomboy Millie. Each of the women is carefully selected both for her potential vulnerability to Hal's charms and for the 1950's inhibitions likely to keep her forever sexually frustrated. Inge gives us varied portraits of tumescence curbed by propriety, for the 1950's presupposed the prohibition of sex outside marriage, and women took seriously their obligations to chastity—or guilt.

Inge's sympathies are entirely with this poignant female assortment: Helen Potts, doomed to care for the invalid mother who prevented Helen from consummating her marriage and had it annulled; Flo Owens, whose marriage was short and unfulfilling; Rosemary Sydney, whose hypocritical prudishness is designed to mask her longing for a man; young Millie, who feels too unattractive and ill at ease to try to please a man; and beautiful Madge, who, under maternal pressure to conform to social norms, has been doing what's expected of her in going out with a rich boy. Yet Madge—created by Janice Rule in her stage debut—also is a dreamer who wonders what the world might have in store for her if Alan—a sexually uncompelling fellow who, amazingly, was played by the young Paul Newman—weren't in her future and she took a train for someplace other than Kansas.

Inge constructs his second act around growing sexual excitement which builds in an impromptu, pre-picnic backyard dance. This mating ritual first foreshadows Hal and Madge's passion, then finds Rosemary (Eileen Heckart's role) throwing herself at Hal and, after her explosive disappointment has wounded Hal and provided Madge plenty of motive to comfort him, prompts Rosemary to demand romantic fulfillment from her own boyfriend: "I want to drive into the sunset, Howard! I want to drive into the sunset!" Left alone to bring the picnic baskets in their car, Hal instead lifts Madge in his arms and—in the culmination of the scene's erotic progression—announces "We're not goin' on no God-damn picnic."

Having thrust his two major women in forbidden sexual relations during the break between Acts II and III, Inge dramatizes the consequences of virgins yielding to their sexual needs. Rosemary may have given herself to Howard in order to trap him. Feeling trapped herself, stuck in her job teaching high school typing and shorthand and too old to have any more "chances," Rosemary repeatedly begs Howard to marry her. Responding to social pressures himself, Howard does what he "should" and accedes. Their marriage is the socially acceptable choice. The much younger Madge responds differently to a night of sexual and emotional fulfillment. Although she refuses Hal's importuning her to run off with him, once he's hopped a freight and she's had a few minutes to contemplate life without him, she hurries after her stud, jilting the man who offers a secure life in favor of her primal urges.

From their first meeting, Madge and Hal are strongly attracted to each other. Their eventually acting on their desire seems inevitable. Nevertheless, Inge himself was uncomfortable with Madge's following Hal—an ending which apparently evolved under director Joshua Logan's influence. He therefore reworked *Picnic* into *Summer Brave*.

Making many incidental and sometimes harmful changes,

Inge particularly alters Hal's character. Some months before the action begins, in his efforts to go to Hollywood, Hal has stolen Alan's car, a precursor to his stealing Alan's girl. Inge improves his dramaturgy in one instance by giving Madge clearer choices in the third act. Despite Madge's having been bedded by his rival, Alan is still asserting his right to her when Madge refuses to go with Hal, saying she's going to marry Alan. Yet she does not bother to disguise from Alan her love for Hal, so she loses Alan. Madge regrets Hal's departure (but not Alan's), but she doesn't follow Hal. As the play ends, she appears resilient, already thinking of accepting a date from yet another fellow.

These changes have the curious effect of strengthening Madge (say, from a feminist viewpoint) yet trivializing all that has gone before, especially Madge and Hal's attraction—and their pain. The original inspires considerable compassion as well as admiration for Madge's courage in flouting convention and following her heart. *Summer Brave* substitutes for that a portrait—depending on how it is directed—either of impending sexual degeneracy or of a woman's maturation and independence.

In both versions, Inge created bittersweet roles for women, characters who live lives of not so quiet desperation. The older women are object lessons in female denial, suppression and repression, and the younger women—Millie who hopes to be a novelist and Madge who plans to be a wife and then surprises herself—become archetypes of 1950's women resisting the models their mothers set for them.

—Tish Dace

POETRY.
Poem by Marianne Moore, 1919 (and later revisions).

"I, too, dislike it" is the startling opening statement of "Poetry," Marianne Moore's most famous poem. This landmark of 20th-century literature illustrates Moore's practice of extensive revision, her precision in language and syllabic consistency, her observation of zoological phenomena, her predilection for aesthetic enquiry and the work of contemporaneous poets, and her contrariness in her use of "anti-poetic" and paradoxical statements.

Bonnie Costello, in her 1981 *Marianne Moore: Imaginary Possessions*, says that revision "is a central part of Moore's aesthetic." Certainly the numerous revisions of "Poetry" are impossible to ignore. The original 30 lines of 1919 were reduced to 13 in 1924, but almost all of the original version, 29 lines, was restored in 1935. George W. Nitchie, in his comparison of the versions in his 1969 introduction to Moore's poetry, notes that this most often anthologized version is flawed technically in that the truncation destroys the consistency of the syllabic verse, which, in Moore's use, was a repetition of the number and arrangement of syllables in each stanza. The most drastic revision occurred in 1967, in what Moore whimsically chose to call *The Complete Poems*:

I, too, dislike it.
  Reading it, however, with a perfect contempt for it, one
    discovers in
it, after all, a place for the genuine.

In "To a Snail" Moore says that "contractility is a virtue." Apparently Moore found a virtue in presenting an imageless poem on poetry, but most of her critics have regarded this final "fiddling" a mistake, as does Donald Hall (*Marianne Moore: The Cage and the Animal*, 1970). At least the mistake is somewhat mitigated by her including the 1935 version in the notes to her final volume.

The argument of the poem is that poetry, though not especially important, is nevertheless "useful" insofar as it is intelligible and not restricted in subject matter, but that it must be written with skill and imagination. Poetry can only be worthwhile if it is written by " 'literalists of the imagination' " who provide " 'imaginary gardens with real toads in them'."

In her notes Moore identifies the first of the above quoted statements as Yeats's comment on Blake in *Ideas of Good and Evil*. "Imaginary gardens with real toads in them," the most notable image in the poem, also is enclosed in quotations, but it is not identified. Stanley Lourdeaux has written a note in the 1982 *Modern Philology* suggesting that the toad image comes from William Carlos Williams's "Romance Moderne," published in *Others* six months before "Poetry" appeared in that journal. Whatever the source, the line compellingly illustrates the theme of the poem and has attracted frequent explorations into the precise meaning of the metaphor.

The poem is amplified by other memorable and disjointed images, such as bats and baseball fans, statisticians and schoolbooks. It proceeds through a series of contradictions and implications, raising both ontological and pragmatic questions about the worth of poetry. The apparent irony of the initial statement dissolves eventually to a consideration of its ambiguity, until the reader is finally convinced of the author's passionate restraint in dealing on both the abstract and concrete levels with the subject to which she devoted her life.

—Nancy Carol Joyner

THE PORTRAIT OF A LADY.
Novel by Henry James, 1881.

The Portrait of a Lady is the culminating work of Henry James's early period, a quintessential Victorian novel that yet adumbrates those particular qualities, architectonic and narrative, that James contributed to the development of the 20th-century novel.

The reader can perceive the older and newer impulses at work by comparing chapters 6 and 42. In chapter 6 a confidential narrator offers an analytic verbal portrait of Isabel Archer, enjoining the reader's indulgence and sympathy for a young heroine in whom theories may take the place of knowledge of the world, whose self-esteem may cause her to believe too much in her own opinion, and whose idealism and innocence may lead her into complexities she little anticipates. In short, "her errors and delusions were frequently such as a biographer interested in preserving the dignity of his subject must shrink from specifying." Not only the narrative manner in such a passage, but also James's theme is Victorian, the marriage market and the relationship of money to marital options. Will money bring Isabel freedom of choice or make her an object of social predators? What effect has money upon her own imagination? In chapter 42, which James notes in his retrospective Preface as "obviously the best thing in the book," Isabel sits by the fire pondering what her husband has asked of her this evening, examining her marriage: "It was very well to undertake to give him a proof of loyalty; the real fact was that the knowledge of his expecting a thing raised a presumption against it. It was as if he had had the evil eye; as if his presence were a blight and his favour a misfortune. Was the fault in himself or only in the deep mistrust she had conceived for him? This mistrust was now the clearest result of their short married life; a gulf had opened between them over which they looked at each other with eyes that were on either side a declaration of the deception suffered." Here the action has moved inward, the point of view focused in the heroine's own consciousness, and the range of vision narrowed to what she herself can see and interpret. Question replaces answer, metaphor supersedes explicit statement, as Isabel searches for the similitude that will convey her intuitions and feelings. Such a passage is nearer to the late James in point of view and figurative language, and anticipates the 20th-century psychological novel which his own subtler experimentation fostered at the turn of the century.

The carefully crafted structure also looks to the later James. In his celebrated Preface to *The Portrait of a Lady*, written for the definitive New York Edition of his works, James has much to say about the architectonics of his novel, how he laid it brick by brick, building it outward from the initial perception of the character of Isabel Archer by devising those relations with other characters and those settings which would best reveal his heroine. "Such is the aspect that to-day *The Portrait* wears for me: a structure reared with an *'architectural'* competence . . . that makes it, to the author's own sense, the most proportioned of all my productions after *The Ambassadors*."

The Portrait of a Lady is also the crowning work, from his early period, in James's development of his theme of international contrast. Its plot is very simple and has been recognized as that of a fairy tale, in which the heroine must choose among three suitors; her fortunes must depend thereafter upon the wisdom of her choice. The first two suitors, Caspar Goodwood, an American businessman, and Lord Warburton, an English aristocrat, manifest national as well as personal characteristics, the dangers of ruthless self-assertiveness and of hereditary forms and obligations. Isabel's chosen suitor, Gilbert Osmond, is an American living abroad, who has absorbed effete and corrupt aspects of European civilization together with European aestheticism and sophistication. He becomes the principal foil for Isabel's new-world virtues of enthusiasm, innocence, and aspiration. Secondary characters, Mme. Merle, who betrays Isabel into this marriage, and Henrietta Stackpole, who remains her friend despite it, define similar polarities. Isabel's fate is left in the balance at the end. Having chosen wrongly, will she desert her husband or slavishly perpetuate the form of an empty marriage? Will she live by the memory of her deceased cousin Ralph Touchett, whom she now perceives as beloved? Or for the sake of her stepdaughter Pansy Osmond, to preclude a similar fate for her?

"The obvious criticism," James wrote in his *Notebooks*, "will be that it is not finished—that I have not seen the heroine to the end of her situation. . . . That is both true and false. The *whole* is never told; you can only take what groups together." Here again James analyzes his own salient qualities, his concern with form and the characteristic open-endedness of his fictions.

—Jean Frantz Blackall

THE RECOGNITIONS.
Novel by William Gaddis, 1955.

Contemplating one of the richest tapestries of character relationships in modern literature, readers of William Gaddis's *The Recognitions* may become confused. But it is not impossible to disentangle the numerous nexuses of relationships among the more than fifty characters, ten of whom are major, and to trace and link up the disconnected strands of narrative.

Once the reader begins to perceive—at once emotionally and intellectually—the complex ways Wyatt Gwyon affects each of the characters, the confusion will begin to dissolve. Wyatt grows up in a small New England village, shaped mind and soul by his father, a Calvinist minister, his Aunt May, and his mother's father, the town carpenter. Wyatt goes to Paris to paint. Then he marries Esther, a novelist, and settles in New York. The mysterious fever he had as a child still burns in his eyes; in nightmares, his hair catches fire. His torment, manifested in his unfinished paintings, is more spiritual than artistic.

The figure of Wyatt looms over the intertwining stories of four other characters in segments that focus alternately on each: Basil Valentine, a spoiled priest, now art critic; Esme, Wyatt's model and mistress; Otto, a young playwright, a parody of Wyatt, his hero; Stanley, a simple, intensely devout Catholic, whom Gaddis places, in a seriocomic, sometimes almost farcical spectrum, between tortured Wyatt and ridiculous Otto.

Five other characters counterpoint aspects of those five: Sinisterra, a master counterfeiter; Otto's father, Mr. Pivner, a sentimental true-believer; Anselm, who obsessively uses perverted sex and obscene blasphemies to disrupt Stanley's spiritual serenity; Recktall Brown, who markets Wyatt's forgeries; Agnes Deigh, a literary agent, a betrayer betrayed. Galaxies of minor characters cluster around and enhance the major figures, providing a many-faceted series of parallels and contrasts. Numerous characters wander in and out of the novel with no direct relationship to the others.

Wyatt leaves Esther and becomes a forger of old masters; possessed by an image of himself as a master painter in the Guild in Flanders, he says, "I don't live, I'm lived." He returns to New York. Seeing his own depravity in Basil, he stabs him, and flees to San Swingli, the little Spanish town where his mother is buried. Anonymous throughout most of the middle of the novel, Wyatt is reborn as Stephen (another source of reader bewilderment). Wyatt stays in the monastery at San Swingli, working patiently with a knife to restore old masterworks that have been painted over.

Like Joyce's *Ulysses, The Recognitions* is a necessarily, profoundly encyclopedic novel, full of expertise on a wide range of subjects, many of them arcane. Gaddis's omniscient commentary, sometimes as aggressive as Thackeray's or Fielding's but more aesthetically justified, enables him to suggest the pagan origins of modern Christian beliefs and to evoke every major era of man's history, with an emphasis on medieval times. He omits no kind of sex, normal or perverted; many kinds of crime are committed, although there are more instances of suicide (about ten) than of murder. The reader becomes intricately involved with all the arts and with practitioners and critics of each. The novel swarms with references to books, most of them real, some made up. Incongruously juxtaposed, popular and classical music assault the characters. Gaddis demonstrates many ways in which popular culture intersects high culture through camp and parallels serious and avant-garde culture. In America, it is business that keeps art and literature going, as seen in the ads that permeate the novel. Wherever they go, most of the characters carry either a book or a magazine. Gaddis composes medleys of newspaper items and radio voices.

The main subject and theme of *The Recognitions* is religion. The novel is full of early Christian lore, which is constantly contrasted to religion today. The question "Is God watching?" haunts the book. Gaddis deliberately exaggerates the Christ symbolism, which was at the height of popularity in the 1950's. It is a prophetic book, depicting horrors of the 1950's that, rooted in the past, anticipate realities of the 1980's.

The artist as criminal, the criminal as artist, Thomas Mann's recurrent theme, is one of the most fascinating concepts dramatized in *The Recognitions*. The technical and philosophical conversations between Wyatt and Basil about art forgery are absorbing. The final futility of forgery as a means of "recognizing patterns already there" and redeeming time is demonstrated in life as well as in art. Imitative, forged, counterfeit people—impostors—populate Gaddis's novel. Delusions, mistaken identity, masquerading result in separation. Gaddis demonstrates that we are damned to experience familiar patterns and people over and over.

The blessing is that all these coincidences and resemblances can result in *recognitions*—a word repeated in every possible context and variation. And grace comes when these recognitions result in *revelation*, a word seldom used, but always implied as the reader's responsibility. The high incidence of chance, coincidence, accident, and repetition in the book is a compulsive consequence of Gaddis's vision and aesthetic. In the method and organization of *The Recognitions*, Gaddis enables us to "redeem time"—if we will. Poetic juxtaposition is his most effective technique, and, with the reader's complicity, he comes as close as any writer ever has to pulling his fragments together, to shoring them against his, and our, ruins. The achievement of the orchestration of Gaddis's technical devices is the creation, for the attentive reader, of a sense of simultaneity, cohering not, as for most works of art, in a compressed, poetic image, but in a mental, and perhaps spiritual, state of recognition.

—David Madden

THE RED BADGE OF COURAGE.
Novel by Stephen Crane, 1895.

The Red Badge of Courage is the most famous of all novels written about the Civil War. It is even more remarkable as the work of a young journalist of 24 who was not even born until six years after the conflict ended. When the novel appeared in 1895 it made Stephen Crane the most visible writer of his generation. The novel came at a time when the Civil War was a subject of great public interest. As the agonies of the war were forgotten and the bitter years of Reconstruction faded into memory, old soldiers began writing their memoirs, and historians found a public for their accounts of the old campaigns. There was, in addition, a great demand for historical romance in the 1890's, and Crane's novel appeared at an opportune time.

The Red Badge of Courage, however, is not historical romance, but rather a notable piece of realism with a certain amount of literary naturalism added. It belongs in the tradition of realism, such as William Dean Howells was urging on American novelists, and it anticipates the naturalism of Theodore Dreiser and Frank Norris inspired by the novels of Zola. Crane's novel also is notable for its impressionistic use of color, its streamlined unity (the story is told in 45,000 words), and its use of irony.

Crane worked very carefully from sources, though he manages to conceal background detail, and it takes close analysis to tie the novel to a specific engagement of the Civil War. Yet Crane used the three-day Battle of Chancellorsville, which took place 1–3 May 1863, as his setting. This was a Northern defeat that occurred just before the tide of war turned in favor of the Union armies. Crane may have heard about this battle when he was a boy, because some of the men who fought in it were from Port Jervis, New York, where he spend his childhood, but he also used *Battles and Leaders of the Civil War*, a book published in 1886, as a source.

Crane's chief interest in the novel is in the psychology of battle. He keep a steady focus on his protagonist, Henry Fleming, the youth who enlists in the Union Army against his mother's wishes and leaves his New York farm. All unessential detail is pared away, and the reader stays constantly with Henry as his unit prepares for battle. There are no broad panoramas and no digressions. What takes place is what one private soldier can see and know from one small corner of the battlefield.

The three days of the Battle of Chancellorsville enabled Crane to examine Henry during three different phases. In the first part, which takes place before the battle and during the light fighting of the first day, Henry is tortured by doubt, wondering if he will run in the face of the enemy. During the second day when the fighting is heavy, he loses his nerve, drops his rifle, and bolts in panic towards the rear. Crane does a convincing job of creating a sense of terror, depicting the chaos and confusion of battle, during Henry's headlong flight. In this nightmarish scene Henry is hit on the head with a rifle butt by a crazed soldier and receives, ironically, his red badge of courage. When the confusion dies down, he returns sheepishly to his unit and receives the solicitous comfort of his buddies. The third and final day is Henry's triumph, as he leads the charge, captures the enemy flag, and becomes a hero.

Several aspects of Crane's style are of considerable interest. His use of epithets instead of names gives the illusion of universal war experience. He refers to Henry as the youth repeatedly, and it is not until the end of chapter 11 that the reader learns his name. Other soldiers are referred to similarly: the loud soldier, the tattered soldier, the tall soldier. To gain the psychological realism he wanted, Crane stays within the consciousness of his protagonist through much of the novel: Henry thinks, Henry feels, Henry contemplates. The reader experiences the war through Henry's mind. The technique is a sort of edited stream of consciousness, as opposed to the unedited sort that James Joyce uses in *Ulysses*.

Crane's use of color provides sharp, visual imagery, and the reader at the very outset sees the army camped along an amber-tinted river, and at night the red campfires of the enemy across the stream glow in the dark. When the army begins to march in the morning, their uniforms "glowed a deep purple hue." In the eastern sky "there was a yellow patch like a rug laid for the feet of the coming sun; and against it and patternlike, loomed the gigantic figure of the colonel on a gigantic horse." Besides the use of color, which has suggested to many readers a technique with words analogous to the brushwork of the impressionistic painters of Crane's day, Crane's novel abounds in animal imagery. The campfires of the enemy are not just red points across the river, they are red eyes shining in the dark, like those of predatory animals. When the battle begins Henry fights like a pestered animal worried by dogs, and on the third day he plunges like a mad horse at the Confederate flag.

The use of animal imagery helps convey the deterministic point of view of the literary naturalist, the idea that men are caught like animals in a world they cannot control. The naturalism is particularly clear in the flight chapters when Henry is running away in terror. When he retreats behind the lines and is no longer in danger, he rationalizes his act. Any creature has the right to self-preservation, he thinks. He throws a pine cone at a squirrel, which runs frightened up a tree. Henry feels exonerated: "Nature had given him a sign." The squirrel "did not stand stolidly baring his furry belly to the missile."

Crane, who is usually ironic, plants ironic barbs throughout the novel. The title, of course, is the supreme irony, but the battle itself is ironic, for after Henry's great display of bravery on the third day of battle, the army retreats and all the ground won at great cost is given up. Crane makes the sacrifices of war seem futile and the suffering not worth the cost. The moral, however, is implicit, for as the novel ends Henry feels great pride in himself: "He was a man."

—James Woodress

THE RISE OF SILAS LAPHAM.
Novel by William Dean Howells, 1885.

The Rise of Silas Lapham, the most widely read of William Dean Howells's many novels, is an excellent example of its author's theory of literary realism, which he set forth in his essay *Criticism and Fiction* (1891). Strongly influenced by such continental writers as Flaubert, Tolstoy, and Turgenev, Howells insisted on a distinction between the novel and the romance as two separate genres. The romance, in his view, serves for entertainment only, though its influence at times can be harmful. But the novel, he thought, is by definition serious, purposeful, and *realistic*; its emphasis is less on plot than on motivation, character, and ethical and social problems, though, he warned, it should not concern itself with what he called "illicit" love. It must, of course, be plausible in its presentation of events and situations. Howells, in his own realistic novels, was most successful in his close and accurate observation of the superficies of human behavior in the circumstances and interrelationships of everyday living. He was less effective when he attempted psychological or sociological analysis of motives and attitudes. He liked to place his characters in commonplace situations like a journey, an environment unfamiliar to them, or some social event, and examine their conduct, and he was fond of bringing together persons of different classes or backgrounds and describing their interaction.

The Rise of Silas Lapham is the story of a Vermont farmer who has discovered on his land minerals highly suitable for the manufacture of paint. Becoming wealthy, he moves to Boston with his wife and two daughters, Penelope and Irene, and there he struggles for acceptance by the upper, so-called Brahmin class. When Tom Corey, the son of an elite family, falls in love with one of the daughters and takes a position in Lapham's paint business, the goal of acceptance seems to have been reached, even though Lapham gets drunk and makes a fool of himself at a dinner party at the Coreys. In the meantime, Lapham has been having a house built in a section of the city appropriate for a family with social standing.

But Lapham's luck does not hold. His business is threatened with failure, and his beloved house, almost completed, burns to the ground uninsured. His only chance to recoup his business losses is by involving himself in a deal that would financially injure many innocent persons. His real "rise," as opposed to the social one, occurs when, after protracted agonizing, he turns down the deal, accepts failure, and returns to Vermont, where the ethical sense that prompted his honorable decision had presumably been bred into him. Howells implies that, in his crisis, Lapham's behavior is realistic in that it stems from a basic quality in his character—a decency that sets him apart from many, perhaps most, businessmen in a similar dilemma.

Howells employs a subplot in the novel to make another statement of his philosophy of realism, which he insists is applicable to actual living as well as to the writing of fiction. The Laphams have assumed that Tom Corey has been in love with the pretty but rather dull daughter, Irene; but it turns out that he actually loves the rather plain but witty Penelope. Irene is devastated by the discovery, and Penelope is prepared to sacrifice her happiness so that Irene may marry Tom after all. The problem is solved by a liberal clergyman, who points out that the choice is whether three people will be miserable, if Penelope rejects Tom, or only one, if she accepts Tom. The latter, realistic course is followed. The problem arose, according to Howells, because the girls had been reading romances, in which needless self-sacrifice is often presented as a supreme virtue. Had they been reading "realistic" novels, we are led to assume, the situation would never have occurred.

Thus, the novel is a vehicle for Howells's ideas on the value of realism both in literature and in life. But not to be overlooked is Howells's realism in the creation of character and physical and social setting. Howells knew his Boston well, and he acquaints his readers with many parts and aspects of it. His description of Lapham's sleigh rides through the city on brisk winter days are a delight. His account of the dinner party at which the Coreys entertain the Laphams to the restrained amusement of the former and the selfconsciousness of the latter is a masterpiece of the observation of manners. The characterization of brash, boastful, at times foolish, yet ultimately honest Lapham places him as one of the memorable figures in American fiction—a forebear of Babbitt, perhaps, but more likable. The unobtrusive sophistication of Tom and his dilettantish father, the grace with which they carry their wealth and their culture, softens any snobbishness that lies beneath the surface and makes them appear something more than mere representatives of their exclusive social class.

—Perry D. Westbrook

THE SCARLET LETTER.
Novel by Nathaniel Hawthorne, 1850.

There are reasons to call *The Scarlet Letter* the first modern novel. Certainly it has ancestors in the classic English gothic novel, in the popular sentimental novel, and in the divergent realism of Defoe and Fielding. Even more, it is a descendant of the historical romance of Walter Scott. But the heritage of these British models is transformed in the American offspring of Nathaniel Hawthorne. *The Scarlet Letter* is a modern novel in 1) its unity of plot, characterization, space, time, tone, and imagery; 2) its conscious use of symbolism; and 3) its serious moral-psychological theme.

The unity of *The Scarlet Letter* derives from the fact that Hawthorne was a short story writer and that he found an editor who realized that he had material for a self-sustaining book. Before 1850, Hawthorne had achieved a respectable reputation as a writer of short fiction. In fact, he made the short story an art form. *The Scarlet Letter* began as an extended short story, further expanded by editor James T. Fields's encouragement to a little over 250 uncrowded pages, not counting the 54-page introduction on the Salem, Massachusetts, Custom House (where Hawthorne worked as surveyor from 1846 to 1849). It was far shorter than the two- or three-volume English novels of the time. There was none of their rambling loquaciousness, designed to pass the hours of the bored upper-middle-class women and men who read novels both in England and America.

But Hawthorne's brevity is loaded. Though he could be chatty and timely in his essayistic style—as in the introductory "The Custom-House"—he exhibits the height of concentration in *The Scarlet Letter*. While Hawthorne followed Scott in style and in the romantic use of history, there are, in *The Scarlet Letter*, no subplots and no intrigues that require complicated explanations at the end. In fact, the physical action in the novel is minimal, most of it taking place before the novel begins. The opening and closing scenes at the scaffold are the only outwardly dramatic ones. Otherwise, the action proceeds in the minds and the words of the characters—with sufficient authorial narration and comment to direct the reader.

There are only four significant characters: Hester Prynne, Arthur Dimmesdale, Roger Chillingworth, and little Pearl. They are simplified types—indeed, archetypes—of American character. But they develop morally and psychologically through the novel, and are not, as they would be in a short story, transformed by a single event.

Each episode of *The Scarlet Letter* is set concretely and dramatically. The scenes move almost imperceptibly from chapter to chapter, and they are all within walking distance of the prison, the scaffold, the market-place, and the meeting-house in the early town of Boston between 1645 and 1653. References to the wide world, before and after the main action of the plot, are enough to suggest that Hester—and Hawthorne—transcend the place and time.

The whole drama is done in black and red, but with the quite important green and partly sunny Chapters XIV to XIX, where Hester confronts each of the other characters in the natural settings of the seaside and the forest. Except for that pivotal interlude, the final tone of the novel is tragically bleak: "so sombre is it, and relieved only by one ever-glowing point of light gloomier than the shadow:—'ON A FIELD SABLE, THE LETTER A, GULES.' "

Hawthorne's use of symbolism is simplistic on the one hand, yet infinitely complex. The letter *A* stands for adultery, the violation of the Seventh Commandment in the code of Puritan New England. But the letter *A* had more significance for Hawthorne and for subsequent readers. The letter *A* is the first letter of the alphabet. In the *New England Primer*, familiar to Hawthorne and to every schoolboy in New England since the 17th century, the letter was represented by the words: "In Adam's Fall / We sinned all"—with a woodcut of Adam and Eve on either side of a fruitful tree (of knowledge). We are all guilty, not of adultery, but of Adam's sin.

And the letter *A* can stand for more than adultery or Adam's fall. Hawthorne was not unaware of its implications, however much modern imagination may carry them to extremes. For example, *A* represents *amour, art, ambiguity, allegory, America*, and as far-fetched as these attributions appear, Hawthorne's open imagination would welcome them.

It is true that the letter *A* is overworked in the book, and the moral symbolism becomes wearisome. By the time the letter appears in the sky (or doesn't appear) in Chapter XII, we have had enough of it, and its appearance (or non-appearance) on Dimmesdale's naked breast in the penultimate chapter is more than enough. Hawthorne was working with something that had not been fully exploited, and he felt compelled to make it clear to his readers—whether Puritan prudes or devourers of sentimental love stories—that he was concerned with more than surface.

By the time the letter appears in the sky, Hawthorne has evolved what has been called his "ambiguity device." Did the letter appear in the sky or was it an apparition of those who chose to believe? Was Hester guilty of anything beyond the transgression of the parochial beliefs of her immediate environment? Was her "sin" Christian and human love? Was she the noble heroine of a love story ordained in Heaven? Such ideas would be shocking—and were shocking—to many 19th-century readers. Hawthorne left them as questions.

The first chapter of *The Scarlet Letter*, entitled "The Prison-Door," portends the whole. In the three short paragraphs of this chapter Hawthorne establishes the place and time of his narrative, fixing it in historical fact as well as in folklore. He sets the social-psychological mood of the people, the men in "sad-colored garments" assembled before the prison. He makes it visually real with concrete detail: "the wooden jail . . . already marked with weather-stains" and with "rust on the ponderous iron-work of its oaken door." The prevailing color imagery of the novel is forecast in reference to the prison as "the black flower of civilized society," one of the "earliest practical necessities" in the settlement of a new colony. The black is in contrast with the implied, but unstated, red of the wild rose bush next to the prison door.

> This rose-bush, by a strange chance, has been kept alive in history; but whether it had merely survived out of the stern old wilderness, so long after the fall of the gigantic pines and oaks that originally overshadowed it,—or whether, as there is fair authority for believing, it had sprung up under the footsteps of the sainted Ann Hutchinson, as she entered the prison-door,—we shall not take upon us to determine. Finding it so directly on the threshold of our narrative, which is now about to issue from that inauspicious portal, we could hardly do otherwise than to pluck one of its flowers and present it to the reader. It may serve, let us hope, to symbolize some sweet moral blossom, that may be found along the track, or relieve the darkening close of a tale of human frailty and sorrow.

That concluding paragraph of Chapter I states the symbolic intent of the author. Yet it is carefully ambiguous. The "sweet moral blossom" of *The Scarlet Letter* is that good grows out of evil. Hester's sin was a violation of contemporary social values. Recognizing this, she rose to a humble heroism.

Hawthorne did not say that she ascended to heavenly bliss, nor did he say that she was condemned to the fiery hell of Puritan damnation. He was too aware of his own human frailty to arrogate final judgment. He left it to his readers to recognize their own sinful humanity and their redeeming brotherhood—and sisterhood—with their fellow humans.

—James C. Austin

THE SECRET LIFE OF WALTER MITTY.
Story by James Thurber, 1939.

Originally published in the *New Yorker* on 18 March 1939, "The Secret Life of Walter Mitty" is far and away James Thurber's most famous piece of fiction. The story features two themes, the war between men and women and the theme of psychological fantasy, long identified with Thurber, but in no other story has he brought them so successfully together. Though he was to write essays, stories, and casuals (those brief, anecdotal, and often autobiographical pieces favored by the *New Yorker* over formal short stories) for more than twenty years after this story appeared, in many ways "The Secret Life of Walter Mitty" represents the culmination of his career.

The war between men and women is fought on many fronts in Thurber's fiction: during cocktail parties and courtships; in bars, speakeasies, and saloons—wherever men and women come into each other's company. But it is waged most bitterly and insidiously by couples who are married, and for good reason. The special curse of marriage as an institution is that the prolonged intimacy it demands too often ends by estranging people from one another, reducing character to caricature and denying all privacies of personality. Over the years, husband and wife begin to believe that each knows the mind and spirit of the other, knows what and why the other thinks regardless of what words are being said. The process is essentially a fictionalizing one, substituting synecdoche and metonymy for the whole complex being, and it fictionalizes the self as well in response to the fiction of the other that has been created. " 'I was thinking,' " Walter Mitty declares when his wife interrupts his fantasy for the fourth or fifth time. " 'Does it ever occur to you that I am sometimes thinking?' " In marriages that have deteriorated into mere form, as the Mittys' marriage has, the answer to that question is, of course, that such an idea would never occur to Mrs. Mitty; it does not belong to the character of Mitty she has created, any more than the notion that Mitty's behavior is, indeed, a genuine cause for concern belongs to the image of his wife or himself with which Mitty lives. Mitty's astonished stare at his wife when she interrupts his first fantasy—she seemed, Thurber tells us, "grossly unfamiliar, like a strange woman who had yelled at him in a crowd"—may stand as a metaphor for the peculiar sense of estrangement that too often goes with marriages.

All of Mitty's fantasies involve gestures of renunciation and simple, unambiguous actions in a world of men, machines, and warfare. Mrs. Mitty responds with fictions of her own that cast her into the role of self-sacrificing, long-suffering mother of a sick child (the Mittys, significantly, appear to have no children): " 'I'm going to take your temperature when I get you home.' " As much as her husband, in other words, though less obviously than he, Mrs. Mitty leads a fantasized existence, one that compensates for her husband's abdication of male responsibility and rewards her with his traditional power for having endured so cruel a mismatch.

The form of Thurber's story implicitly argues that no comfortable and absolute distinctions can be drawn between such mental constructions as Mitty's and his wife's and the supposed "real" world of physical events and activities. Mitty's first fantasy, for example, elaborates upon a few ascertainable facts (ascertainable, that is, within the context of a work of fiction): he is driving a car in weather that may be a bit inclement (recall Mrs. Mitty's command that he buy overshoes). But the fantasy also triumphantly transforms Mrs. Mitty's words, " 'You're not a young man any longer,' " into an heroic image of the naval commander, the "Old Man" idolized by the crew. Increasingly, moreover, one fantasy fertilizes another, and the "facts" upon which each new fantasy is built become more and more ambiguous. Mitty's broken arm in the courtroom fantasy, for instance, originates in his earlier determination to "wear my right arm in a sling" to prove that he couldn't possibly remove his own tire chains, and the melodrama of the trial itself comes from a newsboy's hawking cry about the "Waterbury trial." (As usual, Mitty's imagination transmutes this trial into something rich and strange, for the historical Waterbury trial was about political corruption and bribery, not murder.) The most poignant remark in the story, Mitty's vague and dream-like " 'Things close in,' " is likewise born of two worlds, one conveniently labelled reality (Mrs. Mitty's sudden striking of his shoulder) and the other just as conveniently and arbitrarily called fantasy (the box-barrage as it closes in during Mitty's experiences as a World War I flying ace).

It is customary to regard Thurber's attitude toward Mitty as, finally, critical of the banal fantasies. Perhaps so. That, after all, is an aesthetic judgment with which most readers would concur. But they need also to admit that they, too, can become involved in the clichés of adventure literature, as they inevitably do when the story opens, and that they are unpleasantly awakened with Mitty to a different textual world from the one they thought they had entered: " 'Not so fast! You're driving too fast!' " Such readers need also to recognize that, as habitual consumers of fiction, they regularly grant ontological status to works of sheer fantasy. Like all good parody, in short, Thurber's story subtly satirizes the reader, but out of that satire comes an increased awareness of the omnipresence of fantasy at the boundaries of any active mental life.

—Robert D. Arner

SISTER CARRIE.
Novel by Theodore Dreiser, 1900.

In *Sister Carrie* Theodore Dreiser went beyond the Hoosier romanticism of Meredith Nicholson's "Alice of Old Vincennes" (1900) and the genteel realism of Booth Tarkington's *The Gentleman from Indiana* (1899). Growing up poor in Indiana, the daydreamy Dreiser envied the escape to the metropolis of his older brothers and sisters. Later, he drifted from one newspaper to another—Chicago, St. Louis, Pittsburgh. Charged with Balzac's *Comédie humaine*, Herbert Spencer's

First Principles, and his own vivid memories, Dreiser began *Sister Carrie* in New York in 1899. The author based his first novel partly on his sister, Emma, who in 1886 had fled from the law with a saloon clerk. Because of the novel's sexual frankness, Dreiser's own publisher (Doubleday Page) did not promote it; but the senior reader, the writer Frank Norris, zealously sent out review copies. When B.W. Dodge (in 1907) and Grosset and Dunlap (in 1908) reissued the controversial book, *Sister Carrie* reached a larger public.

The novel has an hourglass structure. Carrie Meeber—pretty, eighteen, penniless, full of illusions—leaves her dull Wisconsin home in 1889 for Chicago. On the train Charles Drouet, a jaunty traveling salesman, impresses her with his worldliness and affluence. In Chicago, Carrie lives in a cramped flat with her sister and brother-in-law. Her job at a shoe factory is physically and spiritually crushing. After a period of unemployment, she allows Drouet to "keep" her. During his absences, however, she falls under the influence of Drouet's friend, a suave, middle-aged bar manager. George Hurstwood deserts his family, robs his employers, and elopes with Carrie, first to Montreal and then, after returning most of the money, to New York, where they live together for several years. As Hurstwood declines, Carrie develops. To earn money, she goes on stage, rising from chorus girl to minor acting parts. When Hurstwood, failing to find decent work, becomes too great a burden, Carrie deserts him. In time, she becomes a star of musical comedies. Meanwhile, Hurstwood sinks into beggary and suicide. In spite of her freedom and success, Carrie is lonely and unhappy.

Critics have labeled the novel's biological-environmental determinism, graphic fidelity, and compassionate point of view as the work of, respectively, a "naturalist," a "realist," a "romanticist." Consistently, Dreiser intermingles the world-as-it-is, -seems, and -should-be. Like Stephen Crane, Frank Norris, and Jack London, he creates characters caught in the web of causation and chance. In one of his numerous philosophical asides, the narrator informs us that physico-chemical laws underlie all activity: "Now it has been shown experimentally that a constantly subdued frame of mind produces certain poisons in the blood called katastates, just as virtuous feelings of pleasure and delight produce helpful chemicals called anastates." To evoke the illusion of mechanical motion and spiritual drift, Dreiser relies on metaphor and symbol—Carrie attracted to the magnetic city, Carrie tossed about in the sea of humanity, Carrie rocking in a chair. Against baffling forces, she is a "half-equipped little knight," a "little soldier of fortune." And as fortune propels Carrie upward, so it spins Hurstwood downward. Though the narrator avows glorious reason at the end of human evolution, at the end of the novel he pictures a discontented Carrie—fated to remain in the clutch of her powerful opportunistic instincts.

Dreiser's network of dramatic contrasts, parallels, foreshadowings, and ironies (not to mention the cryptic chapter-headings his publishers requested) help unify this episodic novel. The sheer mass of detail obscures the chiasmic symmetry of Carrie's rise and Hurstwood's fall, as it screens somewhat the improbability of Hurstwood's "accidental" theft of money and his calculated "abduction" of Carrie. Still, Hurstwood's destitution and matter-of-fact death seem less melodramatic than the tacked on apostrophe sentimentalizing Carrie as no Saved Sinner or Lost Soul but rather as the Beautiful Dreamer. The awkwardness, repetition, and clichés of Dreiserian prose often grate on fine-tuned sensibilities—as when the narrator informs us that Carrie had "four dollars in money" or when a chapter begins: "The, to Carrie, very important theatrical performance was to take place at the Avery on conditions which were to make it more noteworthy than was at first anticipated." For all this, the author retains the power to endow his factories, hotels, department stores, slums, theaters, and restaurants with an extraordinary sense of life.

At first, *Sister Carrie* (in the 1901 abridged Heinemann edition) was better received in Britain than in America, though the myth of its "suppression" contributed to later interest both in America and abroad. Through *Sister Carrie* Dreiser led socio-literary novelists in the first decade of the 20th century into the creation of closer ties between American life and American literature. Although Dreiser did not receive the Nobel Prize, *Sister Carrie* and *An American Tragedy* are among the truly important novels in American literature. *Sister Carrie* is now available in the Pennsylvania edition (1981), which restores the novel as closely as possible to the author's more complex original manuscript. Whatever one might say about Dreiser's graceless genius, the raw integrity of *Sister Carrie* helped pave the way for the more candid, more crafted American masterpieces of the 1920's.

—Martin Bucco

SNOW-BOUND.
Poem by John Greenleaf Whittier, 1866.

The opening sequence of John Greenleaf Whittier's *Snow-Bound* introduces one of the poem's finest features—its descriptive details. Presenting the dreariness of the weather, these details make it clear that the poem will not be an overly sentimental depiction of New England in winter. The "cheerless" December sun gives the noon hour a "sadder light" than the "waning moon" would. The "thickening sky" warns of a storm; the bitter cold creates a "chill no coat" can "quite shut out." Early that evening comes "the swarm / And whirl-dance of the blinding storm." It will snow for two days and three nights. Yet even before the poet, a young lad at the time this storm occurred, goes to bed, he notes that the snowfall has already turned the clothes-line posts into "tall and sheeted ghosts." This detail introduces a major theme: the intermingling of the commonplace and the marvelous. Thus, the next morning the narrator remarks that "old familiar sights" took "marvellous shapes," that "strange domes and towers / Rose up where sty or corn-crib stood."

The "shrieking of the mindless wind" increases the isolation of the farmhouse inhabitants—a family and its boarders. Yet each "blast" makes the group feel more unified and more secure. The poet reports later that although snowflakes sifted through his bedroom's unplastered walls, he soon fell sound asleep. The sense of isolation builds to such an emotional intensity that the reader is not startled by the poem's sudden lyrical interludes. These outpourings, as Winfield Townley Scott remarks in "Something about *Snow-Bound*," rise "like songs from the narrative while remaining indigenous to the mood of the poem." The first "song" centers on the poet's acute awareness of time and change. A later, more effective one focuses on the poet's dead sisters. A good indication of

Whittier's personality, this interlude's expression of hope for a familial reunion in the after-life is not based on theological reasoning, but on the poet's felt convictions, on truths "to flesh and sense unknown."

The pace of the action slows considerably at the end of the second day when the farmhouse inhabitants gather around the hearth to talk. The quality of the poem, however, does not decrease; for Whittier uses this scene to present vivid character delineations and interesting themes. Although the inhabitants are snow-bound, they roam far through their reminiscences. Yet intertwined with these realistic remembrances are reminders that physical reality also contains the mysterious. The father speaks of "witchcraft"; the mother, of a "gray wizard's conjuring book." These speakers illustrate Whittier's belief that physical reality is rich and multifold. So, too, the hearthside monologues stress the power of the imagination. The poet exclaims, "Forgotten was the outside cold."

The striking inclusiveness of the poet's view of the world becomes apparent. The world simultaneously contains the commonplace and the extraordinary, time present, past and future, and physical reality and an eternal realm. Further, by means of his depiction of his uncle, a "simple" and "childlike" person, Whittier applauds traits that Wordsworth also honored. However, by means of his favorable portrait of the scholarly schoolteacher boarding at the farm, Whittier—unlike many Romantics—also praises the intellectual, seeing in him the justification for high hopes for America's future.

Then, just as the poem begins to sag toward sentimentality, Whittier introduces the other boarder—Harriet Livermore, a "half-welcome guest." His compelling portrait of this prickly, volatile woman evokes the darker, more dangerous side of life's mysterious forces. Indeed, the term "half-welcome" conveys the ambivalent feelings this powerful personality stirred in others. Because Whittier never understood this woman, she makes him humbly aware how complicated human beings can be.

By the third morning, the storm has ceased, and the poem moves toward its conclusion. Awakened by shouts from teamsters breaking through the snow, the poet realizes that the storm has quickened human life in the whole region. In this lively section, variations of themes are offered. Inclusiveness, to cite one example, is celebrated again when the newspaper arrives with its fascinating world news. The intense isolation ends, and the poet declares that "all the world was ours once more!"

This would have been the best place for Whittier to end the poem. Instead, before concluding, he abandons his narrative base to sermonize. Still, the overall strengths of the poem decisively outweigh its weaknesses. Whittier took one pastoral incident, a snow storm, and skillfully used it to offer a vibrant variety of themes. As Edward Wagenknecht states in his book on the poet, Whittier also vividly recaptured past experiences and "revealed the beauty of common things." The result is a poem that easily passes the test of time.

—Robert K. Johnson

SOMEWHERE I HAVE NEVER TRAVELLED, GLADLY BEYOND.
Poem by E.E. Cummings, 1931.

The bulk of E.E. Cummings's poetry falls into three major categories. He is perhaps most famous for his satirical poems, such as "Plato told" and "My sweet old etcetera." "All ignorance toboggans into know" is one of his many pieces that feature sweeping assertions. The third category consists of his poems of praise. He celebrates, for instance, the individualist in "My father moved through dooms of love"; the natural world in "This is the garden: colours come and go" and "In Just-"; the metaphysical world in "I will wade out"; and man's complexity in poems beginning "so many selves" and "but / he' i." Finally, "Somewhere i have never travelled, gladly beyond" exemplifies Cummings's many poems in praise of love. Because this poem also outlines Cummings's basic view of reality, it merits special attention.

The main reason the speaker in this love lyric values and praises his beloved so highly is introduced at the start of the poem when he states: "somewhere i have never travelled . . . your eyes have their silence." For this "silence" leads the speaker to a richer knowledge of reality than his previous experiences did. Because this knowledge is wholly positive, both the speaker and the woman he loves react to it "gladly" or joyously. A fundamental feature of this deeper reality is gentleness—but a gentleness far more powerful than brute force. For this reason the beloved's "most frail gesture" spurs the speaker to seek being enclosed within the realm of love. Though the woman is physically attractive, the gentleness her beauty embodies also spurs the speaker beyond the solely sensual—beyond what he could "touch"—to "things" essentially metaphysical. Yet the metaphysical permeates physical reality. As Norman Friedman points out, the true world for Cummings is both "the natural world" and "a timeless world of the eternal present."

Stanza two makes it clear that the love awakened in the speaker is inclusive as well as exclusive. Although the speaker, it is implied, had previously closed himself off from a corrupt and hostile society, the woman he loves, symbolized by "Spring," opens him (a "rose") "petal by petal"—sexually, emotionally, spiritually. "Spring," the only word capitalized in the poem, not only stands for the beloved, but also connotes the most important characteristics of the material world—life and resurrection (connoting, in turn, eternity). Furthermore, the springtime is described as skillful and mysterious, indicating that love and nature have enormous, but unfathomable powers. In the third stanza's last two lines it is suggested again that the speaker's desire for exclusiveness is prompted by society's cruelty and crassness, represented by the snow "everywhere descending."

The penultimate stanza begins, "nothing which we are to perceive in this world equals / the power of your intense fragility." This fragility proves multifold, containing many "countries" or layers. The stanza's last line declares what was alluded to earlier. The power that resides within the woman renders "death and forever with each breathing." That is to say, quickened by love, the speaker intuits that physical reality and metaphysical reality are intertwined, and that the human spirit is immortal. Employing synesthesia in the last stanza, the speaker re-emphasizes that although it permeates the material world, the timeless world is beyond rational comprehension. The speaker can say only that "something in me understands / the voice of your eyes is deeper than all roses." In the poem's last line, rain is personified. But "nobody, not even the rain," has hands as "small" as his beloved's. For the speaker, nothing on earth matches the mysterious, delicate beauty of his beloved and of love.

"Somewhere i have never travelled, gladly beyond" is not a perfect representation of Cummings's poetry. It does not showcase the one original characteristic of his work, his experiments in word-coinage, punctuation, and typography—though he does in this poem use unconventional devices to prevent the punctuation from slowing down the rhythmic intensity. It is also true that Cummings's finest poems cannot hide the fact that his outlook on life became increasingly simplistic and intolerant. (In one poem he declares, "Humanity / i hate you.") However, "Somewhere i have never travelled, gladly beyond" does present Cummings's phrasing at its evocative best. Its content acknowledges life's painfulness, but promises that if people open themselves to love, they will gain the courage to withstand cruelty and will perceive the universe's immeasurably positive richness. Lastly, the poem contains Cummings's typical dynamic intensity, an intensity that pulls the reader along line by line.

—Robert K. Johnson

THE SONG OF HIAWATHA.
Poem by Henry Wadsworth Longfellow, 1855.

Henry Wadsworth Longfellow's narrative poem of Indian mythology, *The Song of Hiawatha*, is a reworking of the legends and folklore of the Ojibway (Chippewa) living in the Lake Superior region. He depended heavily on the authoritative materials collected by Henry R. Schoolcraft, but had also read other valuable accounts such as those of John Heckewelder and John Tanner, and had been somewhat influenced by Indian visitors to the Boston area. Though Schoolcraft's protagonist had been called Manabozho, Longfellow gave his culture hero the ancient, traditional name Hiawatha. Longfellow tried hard to project something of a universal-benefactor quality into his quasi-historic figure who united five (or six) of the Indian tribes into the Iroquois alliance, but to a close reader Hiawatha remains a shadowy, enigmatic construct described via a memorable poetic medium.

Restating the familiar fact of Longfellow's adapting the trochaic tetrameter rhythm (strongly suggesting the beat of an Indian tom-tom) from the Kalevala epic of the Finns does not convey the mesmeric, even maddening, effect of reading a poem of 5200 lines (more or less) in this exclusive prosodic pattern. Longfellow himself, reading proofs of the printed work, thought it was making him idiotic, and he no longer could tell if it was bad or good. His wife justifiably anticipated harsh treatment by the critics because the poem had this kind of unrhymed rhythm. One superb response, Lewis Carroll's wonderfully amusing poem (with the same unrhymed trochaic tetrameter), "Hiawatha's Photographing" (1857), seems at once a joke and a tribute of sorts.

The Song of Hiawatha is embellished with the moralistic piety and ethnic prejudice of Longfellow's social class (for example, the narrator's opening remarks to his supposedly superior readers about the people in the poem, and near the end, the missionaries' language in touching on the story of Jesus). In the beginning, the mighty Gitche Manito, "Master of Life," convened all the Indian tribes and announced that he would send them a Prophet, a Deliverer, to guide and teach them, suffer and toil with them. If they obeyed his teachings they would "multiply and prosper"; if they did not heed his warnings they would "fade away and perish!" Hiawatha's supernatural birth is described. Nokomis, Daughter of the Moon, his grandmother, had a daughter, Wenonah, who was wooed one evening by Mudjekeewis the West-Wind; then "she bore a son in sorrow" and "In her anguish died deserted . . ." Later the young Hiawatha sought out his father and engaged in battle with him but could not kill the immortal. For his valor in the ordeal by combat the lad was promised by Mudjekeewis a share in his kingdom, but after death: Hiawatha would rule the Northwest-Wind.

Hiawatha "Prayed and fasted in the forest"—not for personal gain, "but for the profit of the people, / For advantage of the nations." In the course of his fasting, a youth appeared to him—Mondamin, the corn deity—and they entered into a series of wrestling matches. Hiawatha acquitted himself well and was taught by Mondamin how to bury him and care for his interred body, so that he might rise from the earth: in other words how to plant and cultivate corn. Hiawatha entered upon other deadly contests of courage and strength. He killed the huge sturgeon Nahma, King of Fishes, and then dispatched the great Pearl-Feather Megissogwon (mightiest of magicians).

A high point of the narrative is Hiawatha's wooing of the Dacotah maid Minnehaha, Laughing Water (was the hard-working Longfellow resorting to punning here?)—and the ceremonials of the Wedding Feast. As commentators have remarked, there *is* beautiful language in the poem, if we excuse the hypnotizing metrics, and it is to be found in Longfellow's treatment of the love that binds man and woman together. Hiawatha then taught Minnehaha how to insure the corn crop's safety: by walking nude in a magic circle around the cornfields. Hiawatha taught his people many, many useful things, including picture-writing, the healing arts, and improved funeral practices. He eventually lost his good friends Chibiabos the musician and Kwasind (the very strong man), and engaged in a series of deadly combats with the mischief-maker Pau-Puk-Keewis (the Storm Fool).

Then a fearful famine came upon the land, taking a heavy toll; Minnehaha suffered and died as a result. In those dark days Hiawatha had a vision of the coming of the white men and of the filling up of the land with "the unknown, crowded nations" marching westward, and the remnants of his people "Sweeping westward, wild and woeful . . ." The first whites were the Catholic missionaries coming to convert the Indians, and Hiawatha listened respectfully, telling his people to be courteous to them. After that he "Launched his birch canoe for sailing . . . Whispered to it, 'Westward! westward!' " and departed "To the Islands of the Blessed . . . and the land of the Hereafter."

Though the outcome of the Hiawatha narrative does not seem dramatically logical, considering the initial arrangements involving Hiawatha as Deliverer and his people as obedient followers, and though Longfellow preserved the "Lo! the poor Indian" tradition in dealing with his materials, his poetic talents still stood him in good stead when he wrote the poem. Even in these rapidly changing times the work will continue to have more than a little reader appeal.

—Samuel Irving Bellman

SOULS OF BLACK FOLK.
Essays by W.E.B. Du Bois, 1903.

Souls of Black Folk, a collection of socio-political essays from the turn of the century, ranks among the great primal texts of black American literature. If Booker T. Washington may be seen as prefiguring Martin Luther King, W.E.B. Du Bois in these writings continues and intensifies a legacy of protest begun by Frederick Douglass and stretching forward to the present day. Both in form and content *Souls of Black Folk* stands as archetypal ancestor to works as disparate as James Baldwin's *Notes of a Native Son*, Eldridge Cleaver's *Soul on Ice*, and some of the feminist essays of Angela Davis. The writer's attempt to penetrate the "Veil" of racial prejudice and show to his readers "the strange meaning of being black here at the dawning of the twentieth century" makes imaginative use of the essay form, welding a variety of short fragments into a coherent whole, whose theme is the black experience.

From beginning to end, the writing is impressive. Unlike his great rival Washington, Du Bois has a natural literary talent, and his force of expression is backed by a corresponding depth of thought. His prose style, occasionally ornate and high-flown in the manner of the day, is a potent weapon which manages to appear at once passionate and reasoned, its sober dignity matched by a fiery eloquence. It serves him well in *Souls of Black Folk*, ranging freely over the myriad aspects of black American life, and the barriers of discrimination that deny fulfillment to his people. Du Bois forces much into a short compass, sketching a brief history of his race's struggles since Emancipation, and the connivance of prejudice and political expedience that thwarted them of freedom. The section best known to most readers is that in which he launches an attack upon Washington, then the most respected black leader in the country. Du Bois's criticism of his great contemporary, while carefully balanced, is remorseless in its logic, justly ridiculing the incompatible vision of a landowner who is also a second-class citizen shorn of voting rights. His thrusts are rendered more telling by the dignified restraint of his argument, honouring Washington's achievements while exposing the flaws in his "gospel of Work and Money." In this Du Bois clearly represents the voice of a growing black intelligentsia, based mainly in the north, who had come to regard Washington as an obstacle to progress.

If the attack on Washington is the best known of Du Bois's writings, it is by no means the most impressive. Some of the factual essays describing Du Bois's tours of the south, and in particular his work as a teacher there, blend literary mastery with the keen eye of the sociologist to bring a "problem" alive, the dry statistics taking on human form in a memorable and touching way. His searching analysis of a Georgia county laid waste by its reliance on the cotton crop is a brilliant piece of work, the breadth of the overview neatly balanced by thumbnail character sketches. Strong and penetrating in a different way are Du Bois's investigations of black religion and especially music as embodying the spiritual core of his people, their finest essence and at that time their sole means of fulfillment. If there is a weak point in the book, it comes towards the end, in the harrowing account of his child's death, and the grim—presumably fictional—parable, "Of the Coming of John." Understandably, period sentiment weighs rather too heavily in the former, while the latter cannot escape a certain touch of melodrama. Freed from the constraints of social analysis, Du Bois tends to grow self-indulgent, with the result that these essays impress themselves less upon the reader than their excellent companion pieces. Such minor flaws, however, serve only to highlight the virtues of the work as a whole, and to render it more striking.

Above all, *Souls of Black Folk* is a cry against injustice, the demand of a maligned race for its rights. The Du Bois of this period may be a world away from the Marxism of his later years—at one point he deplores "a cheap and dangerous socialism"—but his message is straightforward, and admits of no compromise. "For this much all men know," he claims, "the Negro is not free," and concludes that: "the problem of the Twentieth Century is the problem of the color line." Du Bois asserts the qualities of his race, praising the elite of university graduates from a people thought incapable of learning, to which "Talented Tenth" he looks for future leadership. He exults in the cultural richness of black America, the supreme gift of the music of slave songs and spirituals. ("The Negro folk-song . . . stands not simply as the sole American music, but as the most beautiful expression of human experience born this side of the seas.") Recognizing this vast potential, he demands that the white world acknowledge it. The barriers which deny the black man his humanity must be dismantled, and he and his contemporaries will accomplish it. Invoking the Declaration of Independence, Du Bois declares: "By every civilized and peaceful method we must strive for the rights which the world accords to men."

As a social and political testament, *Souls of Black Folk* impresses; as a work of literature, it merits its classic status. A creation of vigorous youth which ensured the reputation of its author, it remains a landmark in American writing. Formerly, as with Washington, the black man made polite requests. Here, in memorable language, he stands proudly to demand the birthright that is his.

—Geoff Sadler

THE SOUND AND THE FURY.
Novel by William Faulkner, 1929.

When *The Sound and the Fury* was published in 1929, it was William Faulkner's fourth novel to see print, and sold the least well of any. Critical acclaim was loud, however, and the novelist Evelyn Scott was so moved by the convoluted story of the Compson family that she wrote a major essay for use in publicizing the book. It was, according to Faulkner in an unpublished preface to the book, an experience of great emotional intensity, unparalleled in his writing career. "One day I seemed to shut a door between me and all publishers' addresses and book lists. I said to myself, Now I can write. Now I can make myself a vase like that which the old Roman kept at his bedside and wore the rim slowly away with kissing it."

Like other American modernists, Faulkner believed in the supreme value of the art object—whether it was a vase or a novel. He would be judged by his work; that was his only identity (and many of the tales he invented when asked about his personal life were evidence of that belief that his only existence rested in his fiction). The rare technical prowess of *The Sound and the Fury* attracted the admiration of writers, but it just as frequently confused the general reader.

Faulkner tells the story of the decaying Compson family and its southern home in a four-part structure. The first, told by the retarded Benjy, the youngest of the four children, recounts scenes and emotional understandings from the childhood of the four children—Quentin, Candace, Jason, and Benjy (formerly named Maury after his maternal uncle). Water fights in the branch, the death of their grandmother, Caddy's wedding, Benjy's castration, and Jason's misbehavior are woven into a modern-day narration that includes losing a quarter, celebrating Benjy's 33rd birthday, and arguments between the niece Quentin (Caddy's child) and her uncle, Jason. To simulate the flow of Benjy's consciousness, Faulkner used a remarkable stream-of-consciousness device. He asked that the text be set in eight different colors of type. Because the cost of doing this would have been prohibitive, the publisher used italic type, but to move into and out of italics does not do justice to the layers of narrative caught in Benjy's memory. One aid to placing events in time is the Gibson family, whose mother, Dilsey, has worked for the Compson family throughout their history; her children and grandchildren have, through the years, been responsible for caring for Benjy and their varying names aid the reader considerably.

The first part of the novel occurs on 7 April 1928, the Saturday of Easter weekend. The third, Jason's recounting, occurs the day before, on 6 April; and the fourth, told by a limited omniscient narrator, on Sunday, 8 April. The second, a striking counterpoint to the on-going 1928 story, is Quentin's monologue on the day of his suicide, 2 June 1910, as he plans his death by drowning and mulls over the various conflicts within his family. Moving back into the time of many of the events in Benjy's section intensifies the reader's reaction to those conflicts between mother and children, Caddy's sexuality and Quentin's modesty, Mr. Compson's cynicism and the need for innocence in children, and other of the dominant family patterns. Focus throughout is on Quentin's inability to deal with the realities of life, imaged in the character of his younger sister, Caddy. She, then, although she has no section of the book as her own, becomes a central figure in the development of each of her brothers.

Section three, the 1928 story as recounted by the middle child, Jason, currently a clerk in a local hardware store, is an ironic retelling of a Good Friday betrayal. Jason exemplifies the evil of conscious wrong-doing, and his treatment of his niece Quentin sets up the theft that closes the Easter weekend at the Compson home. That story occupies Easter Sunday, and though Dilsey takes her family and Benjy to a stirring service in the black church, Jason searches futilely, and almost meets his death in macabre fashion, for the last lost member of the Compson family, Quentin. The lineage of the Compson family ends in despair and emptiness, rather than fruition, and—as Faulkner said in the Appendix which he wrote for the reprinting of the novel in 1945—the chief virtue of the tale is that the Gibson family, with its traditional values, including religion and respect for personhood and community, did endure.

Mirroring the tragedy of Shakespeare's *Macbeth*, from which the title is drawn, *The Sound and the Fury* conveys the bleak view of a narrator raised to believe in family, community, and established verities—and only in those values—without being equipped in any way to meet the changes that the modern age brought to southern life. For readers who had lived through World War I and knew the inevitability of change and what Faulkner called "flux," the sorrowful tale of the Compson family was universal rather than regional. It was moving as well as admonitory. It was also a skillful virtuoso performance by a writer whose equal was not to be found in modern American literature.

—Linda W. Wagner

STRANGE INTERLUDE.
Play by Eugene O'Neill, 1928.

The enormous success of Eugene O'Neill's *Strange Interlude* in its premiere season in 1928 astonished many critics almost as much as its popularity in revival right up to Glenda Jackson's performance in 1984, although in its remarkable production history it has also earned the verdict of "the worst play ever written by a major dramatist." As often with O'Neill, such extreme reactions reflect the audacity of his technical experimentation.

The story of this colossal, nine-act play is a Strindbergian saga of the sex war in which the dominant character is Nina, whose predatory sexual behaviour is presented as a reaction to the loss of her fiancé during World War I. Her first act of redemptive compensation consists in nursing crippled soldiers, and sleeping with many of them (her relationship with her fiancé was, she regrets, unconsummated). On the death of her father, a professor, she finds herself surrounded by three men: an oedipal, bisexual novelist, a coolly professional doctor, and a "guileless," boyish hero-worshipper of her fiancé, whom she marries. News of his family's congenital lunacy precipitates a secret abortion and the adulterous conception of a son by the doctor, in a context of (ostensibly) disinterested Darwinian debate. In the second part (final four acts), as in the second part of Strindberg's *Dance of Death*, much of the action is ironically duplicated in the next generation: Nina's son emulates the war hero fiancé on the sports field, but by doing so attracts another Nina (Madeline) who wins the attentions of doctor and novelist and asks the obvious questions about the son's paternity, all of which are left hanging after Nina's husband's death at the end.

The play's chief distinction is in its dramaturgy, in the pervasive use of "thought asides," as O'Neill termed the (spoken) interior monologues which take up nearly half the published script. Obviously influenced to an extent by James Joyce's stream of consciousness and by popular psychoanalytical writings, the asides express thoughts which are often in conflict with dialogue utterances, and through them O'Neill generates more irony on a single page than many whole plays contain. All of the characters have asides (they are a well-established habit for Nina's son by the age of eleven) and so the audience's privileged insight penetrates the whole cast.

As a device for sustaining a contrapuntal tension, for constantly exposing the fabric of lies and half-truths that the characters trade as dialogue, the aside is an obviously valuable instrument. O'Neill, however, deployed it not just for verification, but as a means of dissolving the "masks" which, in his view, shield all behaviour. Although his asides may simply undermine verbal behaviour, they may alternatively corroborate it, embellish it, or reveal a subtextual dilemma which is scarcely hinted at in the dialogue. Their convenience for conveying exposition is evident, and O'Neill also develops them into a highly versatile means of generating momentum and suspense. Characters often ask questions of themselves, and use the aside to articulate their uncertainty, in which case its informative value is nebulous. But, in another sense, every aside is virtually a disguised question, as it inevitably raises the possibility that its content may at some stage be translated into overt dialogue or action. The longer the play develops, the more extensive this subtextual minefield becomes, so that the final two acts are extremely intense, verging on a grand resolution and recognition scene which never quite occurs. It is particularly significant that most of the expressions of aggression and animosity in the play are contained in asides, never achieving realisation.

O'Neill was well aware that various levels of consciousness might be in conflict within his characters, and the asides (to him, the most important part of the play) were deployed largely as a vehicle for this conflict; he judged his attempt successful "in so far as it concerns only surfaces and their immediate subsurfaces, but not where, occasionally, it tries to probe deeper." The stage directions which accompany the asides indicate that the controllability of the thoughts varies greatly; sometimes they are fantasies generated for consolation or self-gratification, at other times they have an antagonistic energy of their own. Sometimes their effect on the thinker is presented as consolidating, but more often it is clearly divisive.

Plausibility is a criterion that has often been used against the characterisation of Nina in particular; the way in which adolescent frustration escalates into a triumphant, Gargantuan voraciousness seems to indicate an authorial obsession about the nature of women. However, the yardstick of plausibility may less easily be applied to the thought asides, and the presentational style used in the theatre since the premiere should dismiss assumptions from realistic premises: throughout the thought asides, the actors freeze. In some productions, this has achieved the effect of embodying poetic crystallisations of fragments of the mind.

—Howard McNaughton

A STREETCAR NAMED DESIRE.
Play by Tennessee Williams, 1947.

What Walter Kerr designated "the finest single work yet created for the American theatre" packs such an emotional punch it can cut through a macho man's defenses. Well cast—as it has been on three occasions with the English actresses Jessica Tandy (Broadway), Vivien Leigh (London and the film), and Rosemary Harris (Broadway revival)—and well directed—as it was by Elia Kazan in a lyric production featuring jazz and a spotlight on Blanche DuBois—Tennessee Williams's *A Streetcar Named Desire* devastates spectators with those feelings engendered by tragedies, pity and fear.

Employing poetic symbolism but a frequently terse prose style, Williams creates compassion for a frightened, lonely, aging, southern belle, daughter of a patrician family, who is visiting her sister Stella and brother-in-law Stanley Kowalski in their cramped apartment in the French Quarter of New Orleans. Romance with a sensitive friend of Stanley's seems headed for marriage. But, as Blanche luxuriates in a hot bath offstage while singing "It wouldn't be make-believe if you believed in me," Stanley gives his wife the lowdown on her big sister who, after a disastrous marriage with a homosexual, has devoted her nights to casual sex. Stanley also tells Blanche's suitor the juicy details, thereby destroying her chance for a healing haven. Later, after he has issued the ultimatum that penniless Blanche must leave her refuge and as her mental stability is tottering, Stanley rapes Blanche. Her future destroyed, Blanche, like Williams's beloved sister Rose, is led off to an asylum.

Cleverly constructed around the seasons, *Streetcar* begins in springtime, a period when Blanche hopes she can salvage her life, progresses through a sweltering summer of explosive passions, and winds down in autumn, when not merely the days but Blanche's dreams will wane. *Streetcar*'s remarkable economy of language is made possible by unobtrusive symbols: Stanley wears virile primary colors; Blanche, whose name means white, is garbed in that color because she's only technically impure. The family plantation, Belle Reve, was not a "beautiful dream" to live on but rather the scene of waking nightmares of death. The characters suggest the past versus the present in a changing south. Blanche soaks in a tub to keep herself dainty, in contrast to Stanley's body soaked in sweat. Streetcars named Desire and Cemeteries have brought Blanche to a road called Elysian Fields. (Previous Williams titles, *Blanche's Chair in the Moon* and *The Poker Night*, were not so evocative.) The colored paper lantern Blanche supplies to cover the light bulb serves to soften unpleasant truths about her age, her nerves, her situation. A Mexican woman sells "flores para los muertos" after we see Blanche's dreams of marriage to Mitch doomed.

Williams reveals Blanche's real prospects gradually. Blanche disguises her desperation with lies—about her drinking, her age, her reasons for coming to New Orleans, her sexual experience. Although she speaks of some of her losses early on—of the plantation and her relatives—only late in the play do we discover that she blames herself for her homosexual husband's suicide and that promiscuity much like his has cost her her reputation and her job.

Williams provides Stanley with many motives for hating Blanche. She drinks his hooch, patronizes him, sponges off him—while complaining because Stella has no maid. She has lost Belle Reve. Her presence interferes with Stanley and Stella's sex life. Blanche competes with Stanley for Stella, offering to rescue her from him. Crucial is Blanche's tirade about Stanley being a subhuman ape. The eavesdropping man is stung by her contempt.

Yet Blanche is rarely rude. Whereas Stanley is no gentleman, Blanche is a gentlewoman—refined, fragile, sensitive. Her sexual purity, like her jewelry, is imitation, but her gentility is genuine. Pitiable, but not pitiful, she is felled by a "common" Polish-American Apollo, a lusty barbarian, captain of the bowling team, an American version of Lady Chatterley's gardener. In part modeled on Williams's father, an aggressive, hard-drinking, poker player who damaged his son's self-respect, Stanley is a stud who appeals to Williams but also repels him; he is not the character with whom the dramatist's greatest sympathies lie.

Williams appreciates Blanche's fears that her sexual "misconduct" will come to light because of his own early days as a closeted homosexual. Like Williams, Blanche has furtive sexual encounters but, though she does not repress her desires, she also cannot suppress her guilt. When she enters the French Quarter, which could accept her earthier side, she is prevented by the values she internalized in her youth from acknowledging the desire which brought her there.

One of the most difficult ways to grow up female in the United States early in this century was to do so in impoverished circumstances in the deep south. Women of aristocratic lineage were expected to refrain from seeking most forms of employment—"A lady doesn't work"—although the teaching profession was an exception. And a lady must neither seek sex nor appear to enjoy it. As a woman of her period and place, Blanche was raised to trade upon her attractiveness. Yet when the marriage with which her allures are rewarded is destroyed by her conventional moral standards and then her own renegade sexuality flouts social strictures, she finds herself in turn the outcast who must deceive to survive. Williams may take a certain delight, of course, in seeing the easily shocked wife of a homosexual follow in his footsteps. On the other hand, *Streetcar*'s original producer, Irene Selznick, as a woman, may have been touched by the power of the double standard to dictate that Blanche's father and grandfather could indulge in "epic fornications" and Stanley could be admired for his sexual prowess but a woman of Blanche's class, once she has slipped off her pedestal, is fair target for rape.

Nowadays we regard rape not as a stud's right but as a reprehensible act of violence. We therefore can appreciate Stanley's attack on Blanche as completing the murder of her soul which he began when he decided to block her marriage to Mitch and throw her out of his home. (Sending her to the booby hatch afterwards is merely carting off the corpse to the cemetery to Stanley, although Stella and Mitch agonize at their complicity.) We can plainly see Blanche is terrified of Stanley, defends her honor with a broken bottle, is overpowered by him, and has a right to refuse him, whatever her sexual history may be.

Not so in December 1947. When *Streetcar* opened it received enthusiastic but misguided reviews from critics—all men, incidentally—who regarded Blanche as a 19th-century fallen woman suffering punishment or, still worse, believed she went to bed with Stanley willingly. They described her as a prostitute or a nymphomaniac—a word not fashionable since women asserted their right to enjoy their sexuality—and spoke of her "affair" with Stanley and of the "strong attraction between them which is satisfied." Twenty-five years later few reviews misconstrued this event, and it was labeled rape.

Streetcar's early critics and its more recent interpreters likewise disagree about Blanche's sanity. Those writing in the late 1940's sometimes saw Blanche as deranged throughout the play. Now we are more likely to believe that until the play's end, when Blanche expects Shep Huntleigh, she does not confuse her pretenses with reality. She knows the difference, but prefers lies to her sordid surroundings and the looming abyss. A victim of romantic clichés about life, Blanche is one of "the fugitive kind," seeking solace in "magic." Her self-image as a lady may be at odds with the sleazier details of her past, but it is also the source of strength which allows her to survive. Knowing she has been raped, having lost her sister's protection because she has told the truth—an ironic downfall for a "fibber"—Blanche maintains dignity in defeat. "Please don't get up," she enjoins the poker players on her exit. She does not delude herself about their rising because a lady has entered the room, for rise they do. Perhaps heroism in a hopeless situation and madness are much the same thing.

An elegy from a chivalrous Mississippi playwright on the "civilized" south menaced by robust barbarians, *Streetcar* demonstrates in Williams's own words, "If we don't watch out, the apes will take over." As the author also remarked, "we are in the jungle with whatever we can work out for ourselves. It seems to me that the cards are stacked against us. The only victory is how we take it." So he sets up Blanche as a heart-wrenching sure loser, every card "stacked against" her, and she "takes it" with dignity as she is thrust once more upon "the kindness of strangers."

—Tish Dace

THE SUN ALSO RISES.
Novel by Ernest Hemingway, 1926.

Ernest Hemingway's first novel created a large and, generally, appreciative readership for the most modern fiction an American had, in 1926, yet produced. Spare dialogue, little description, and even less authorial interference made *The Sun Also Rises* seem an easy book to read, and its story of young Americans living abroad, disillusioned by the aftermath of World War I and people's reaction to it, was also accessible. Hemingway had earlier published poetry and short stories (vignettes or sketches, as some of the magazines that rejected them called them), and his short story collection *In Our Time* had been very well received. Working from these shorter modes, Hemingway brought to this full-length text some of the same techniques: images used to expand meaning, scenes that combined plot movement and characterization, laconic description of characters. The novel was innovative as well as shocking.

For the "hero" of *The Sun Also Rises* was a wounded newspaperman who spent much of his time drinking with his friends and expressing a disillusion with war, patriotism, mainstream American life, and whatever verities middle-class America held dear. Jake Barnes was the center of a group of nomadic expatriates who lived from day to day, bed to bed, and drink to drink—none of his friends showed any more ambition or direction that he supposedly did. Yet *The Sun Also Rises* was, in Hemingway's words, a very moral novel. It showed the human values of friendship, understanding, love in a different context, a different milieu, and convinced most readers that the post-war generation was in no way "lost."

Hemingway's mentor, Gertrude Stein, had quoted the author some words of a French auto mechanic, to the effect that the post-war generation was "lost," and Hemingway places that statement as the first quotation on his epigraph page. But below appears a long passage from Ecclesiastes, from which the novel's title comes, stating that life is cyclic: the sun rises and sets, the earth revolves, life goes on. Affirmation consequently follows negation, just as the values of Hemingway's characters evolve. From their disillusion comes a way to live in the disordered world.

Jake Barnes—despite his impotence from his wound—is the man Brett Ashley would like to spend her life with. Already engaged to Mike Campbell, she falls passionately in love with Pedro Romero, the young and noble Spanish bullfighter. In her decision to leave Romero, rather than ruin his promising career as a matador, Brett comes to understand morality in the post-war world. The active plot of the novel concerns Brett and her decisions; the meditative plot, which is a strong counterpart to the more active, concerns Jake as he fishes with his old friend

Bill Gorton, tries to keep his friends together, and serves as a source of wisdom and comfort throughout the book. Rich with symbolism, *The Sun Also Rises* appears to be a racy account of friends moving from Paris to Spain, going on the holiday that gave the British edition of the book the title *Fiesta*, but Hemingway instead builds in intense meaning at every turn. Random conversations lead to important thoughts about relativity; Jake's visit to the monastery at Roncesvalles evokes the pagentry of past bravery; and the friendship of the aficionado understanding in Spain brings Jake himself to new realizations—among them that he and Brett cannot continue to be intimate.

The stark descriptions and laconic scenes, the heavy irony, and the sense of readers being a part of the sometimes secret meanings of the text mark the novel as particularly modern. Called a *roman à clef* because its characters and plot resembled the summer of 1925 in Spain, *The Sun Also Rises* presented as heroes people who did not live by accepted, middle-class codes of behavior. In doing so, it questioned those codes and values, just as had F. Scott Fitzgerald's novel, *The Great Gatsby*, the year before. The question in both fictions remained, what was valued in American life, and what did the man who wanted to be successful in that culture have to do to be so considered? Very much a part of the 1920's atmosphere, *The Sun Also Rises* was in some ways more affirmative than other texts from that decade—T. S. Eliot's *The Waste Land*, for example, or Sinclair Lewis's *Main Street*. Hemingway showed his characters as acting, thinking human beings (for the most part; there is a heavy strain of antisemitism that is regrettable), who manage to make viable decisions even when faced with calamity, of whatever sort.

For 1926, *The Sun Also Rises* was no small accomplishment. Indeed, it prefigured many of the fictions to come during the 1930's, when all of America was called on to question its values in the midst of the devastating Depression. By that time, Hemingway had become famous, with *A Farewell to Arms*, more stories, and his columns for *Esquire* and other magazines. The nucleus of nearly all of his later work, however, was the tough characterization and the rapid-fire action of *The Sun Also Rises*.

—Linda W. Wagner

SUNDAY MORNING.
Poem by Wallace Stevens, 1923.

"Sunday Morning" by Wallace Stevens was first published by Harriet Monroe in her magazine *Poetry* in November 1915. She impaired the quality of the original poem by omitting three stanzas and by rearranging the remaining five stanzas. Although the poem was not published as Stevens wrote it until the first edition of his first book, *Harmonium*, in 1923, the Monroe version was sufficiently remarkable to establish 1915 as the year in which Stevens began his career as a major poet. "Sunday Morning" is today considered to be one of Stevens's most important poems, and many believe it to be the greatest poem written by an American in the 20th century.

It is a meditation on the loss of Christian faith, on what that loss meant to Stevens and, by implication, on what it meant to the Western world. As Stevens said in a letter in which he refers to the female protagonist of "Sunday Morning," "This is not essentially a woman's meditation on religion and the meaning of life. It is anybody's meditation." Loss of religious faith was a common subject of late Victorian and early 20th-century literature, but the poem itself is far from commonplace. Its importance lies in the power of its language. The beautifully cadenced and controlled blank verse with subtle and unobtrusive echoes of Shakespeare, Keats, Wordsworth, Milton, Bryant, and Christian liturgy and with its significantly charged and freshly perceived imagery has seldom if ever been equalled in modern poetry.

In the opening stanza a woman amid the comfortable "Complacencies of the peignoir, and late / Coffee and oranges in a sunny chair" is disturbed by the thought of death and, because it is Sunday morning, specifically by the recollection of the crucifixion which, as will be made clear in the last stanza, she realizes is an actual physical and spiritual death. There is no resurrection, no transcendence, no immortality. The poem presents modern man face to face with absolute nihilism.

The woman's response to this "dark encroachment" is identical with Stevens's own—an aesthetic hedonism reminiscent of Walter Pater who wrote in his essay "Aesthetic Poetry": "One characteristic of the pagan spirit the aesthetic poetry has . . . the continual suggestion, pensive or passionate, of the shortness of life. This is contrasted with the bloom of the world, and gives new seduction to it." Stevens in a letter commenting on "Sunday Morning" wrote, "The poem is simply an expression of paganism."

In the second stanza the protagonist seeks consolation in the only paradise that for her exists, the earthly paradise:

> Shall she not find in comforts of the sun,
> In pungent fruit and bright green wings, or else
> In any balm or beauty of the earth,
> Things to be cherished like the thought of heaven?

And in this earthly paradise she may hold communion with the only divinity possible for her, her own emotions and the enjoyment of them. "Divinity must live within herself." The third stanza contrasts the hierarchical aristocratic pagan religions of the Graeco-Roman world (here personified by Jove) with the more democratic Christian religion. "The very hinds discerned it, in a star." The final lines look forward to a new paganism which will replace Christianity. This will be more fully defined in stanza seven. Stanza four is a melodious but melancholy (Pater would have called it "pensive") farewell to both the old pagan religions, "the golden underground" and "isle / Melodious where spirits gat them home," and Christianity, "the cloudy palm / Remote on heaven's hill." These are transitory and gone forever. Her own present earthly paradise seems to her more enduring.

In stanza five the thought of death again intrudes. Her response to it, "Death is the mother of beauty," is again reminiscent of Pater who wrote "the sense of death and the desire of beauty: the desire of beauty quickened by the sense of death." As Mario Praz has pointed out, the association of death with beauty is characteristic of what he called "the romantic agony." "Beauty and Death [were] looked upon as sisters by the Romantics . . . a beauty of which, the more bitter the taste, the more abundant the enjoyment." In Stevens's poem, new fruits are brought forth by the perishing of the old, and the maidens enjoy them amid images of death and decay: "The maidens taste / And stray impassioned in the littering leaves." Stanza six is a vision of a paradise similar to the earthly paradise but unchanging and eternal. Such a paradise would become tiresome and produce what Baudelaire called the greatest sin of all, ennui. Stanza seven describes the religion of the future, a new paganism in which men worship the physical universe, "the sun," of which they are a part and in which they had their origin. They shall believe in the brotherhood of man and they shall be aware that the lives of all men are temporary. "And whence they came and wither they shall go / The dew upon their feet shall manifest." Stevens's own gloss on these lines is "Life is as fugitive as dew upon the feet of men dancing in dew. Men do not either come from any direction or disappear in any direction. Life is as meaningless as dew." There is an interesting passage in D. H. Lawrence's *Apocalypse* (published several years after "Sunday Morning") in which Lawrence envisages a future religion exactly like that of Stevens. "We ought to dance with rapture that we should be alive and in the flesh, and part of the living incarnate cosmos. I am part of the sun as my eye is part of me. That I am part of the earth my feet know perfectly."

The beautifully written final stanza states that Jesus (God) is dead and that man must live alone, "unsponsored," on a transitory but lovely planet ("an old chaos of the sun"). In the last four lines the pigeons, symbolizing all life including man, are seen as accidental ("casual") components of a meaningless ("ambiguous") physical universe descending to death "on extended wings."

The structure of the poem is somewhat repetitious. As in music, a theme or an image such as the "wide water" is introduced, dropped, and then repeated, perhaps several times, and developed. It is this repetition, probably, that Monroe was trying to avoid when she first printed the poem with several stanzas deleted and the others re-arranged. Most critics, however, consider the cumulative effect of the repeated themes and images to be successful. The poem as a whole is a striking example of what Yvor Winters defined as the post-symbolist method—the employment of associative rather than logical structure and the use of functional instead of merely ornamental imagery, each image being charged with a significance relevant to the poem as a whole.

—Donald E. Stanford

THE SWIMMER.
Story by John Cheever, 1964.

At the burial service for John Cheever in 1982, he was eulogized as "the leading fabulist of his generation . . . [who] wrote prose fiction in a manner more common with poets and their poetry." The speaker, John Updike, then added that the compactness of Cheever's rich, swift style was "always outracing expectation and keeping the thread between reader and writer taut." "The Swimmer" is a sparkling example of Cheever's best work, for it is a deftly condensed evocation of the classic Odyssean voyage, the heroic but abortive struggle of a modern middle-class wanderer to reach the safe haven of his home. But the story conveys much more than its surface events reveal.

Like most of Cheever's sizable body of fiction—especially his 130 or more short stories—"The Swimmer" presents a desolate yet sympathetic critique of 20th-century middle-class society in America by holding a mirror to the values and limitations of its members. Its emphatic but ominous tone is set in the bibulous scene at the Westerhazys' swimming pool in the opening paragraph: "We all *drank* too much." And as the youthful-looking but "far from young" Neddy Merrill sits beside the pool with one hand "around a glass of gin," both bravado and folly are implicit in the grandiose project he conceives and decides to undertake on this beautiful summer afternoon. He will swim and portage himself through some fourteen other pools at the homes of old friends and neighbors, which are strung out in a southwesterly dogleg direction from the Westerhazys' to his home in Bullet Park eight miles away.

Excitement and anticipation attend Merrill's jaunty take-off and initial progress as he makes his way easily, meeting conviviality and more good cheer along his watery course (now named the Lucinda River in his wife's honor) at the homes of the Grahams, Hammers, Lears, Howlands, and Bunkers, where an uproarious party is in full swing. But from here on gradual atmospheric changes and unexpected developments upset the rhythm of his quest and begin to dampen his enthusiasm for it. The Levys he finds temporarily absent and so drinks alone while sitting out a thunderstorm in their gazebo, but at the Welchers' he finds the house locked up and their pool dry. Then, having crossed his most difficult portage at route 424, where an empty beer can is thrown at him from the passing traffic, his sensibilities suffer increasingly greater indignities. For lack of a proper identification he is ejected from the crowded, stinking public pool at Lancaster; he receives foreboding news of his wife and daughters from their old friend, Mrs. Halloran and still bleaker disclosures from her daughter, Helen Sachs, who can offer no liquor to relieve his chill at her poolside next door; and finally he receives outright insults at the Biswangers' for crashing their party uninvited, as well as a shocking repudiation at the home of his former mistress, Shirley Adams. Wearied, shivering, and unstrung, Merrill can at last barely crawl through the last two pools and stagger under a darkened sky up the driveway to his own home—which he finds totally dark, locked, and empty!

To readers who follow Cheever's deepening tone carefully, this abrupt denouement may come as no great surprise, even though its shock value is unmistakable. They will have noted in the clues he drops progressively that his subtle allusions to discrepancies in time, to those of memory and forgetfulness, and to contrasts between warmth and chill, darkness and light, vigor and fatigue, all combine to form a pattern of meaning that transcends the merely structural account of a single imaginary exploit. Like one of Hawthorne's best tales—let us say "Young Goodman Brown"—"The Swimmer" offers a dream vision of human life itself. The story shows why Saul Bellow, another literary friend at Cheever's memorial service, said that he strove "to give us the poetry of the bewildering and stupendously dream-like world in which we find ourselves."

—Eugene Current-Garcia

TENDER IS THE NIGHT.
Novel by F. Scott Fitzgerald, 1934.

F. Scott Fitzgerald's last completed novel, *Tender Is the Night*, is at once his most ambitious, inchoate, and successful achievement. Nine years in the writing, *Tender Is the Night* went through countless new starts, revisions, structural changes for reasons that may seem biographical, socio-historical, or formal but really concern Fitzgerald's need to grow beyond the lyric or controlled successes of his earlier work. He was adept in the arts of the short story, got away with excesses of spiritual autobiography in his first two novels, and reached artistic culmination in the ordered narrative and viewpoint of *The Great Gatsby*, a novella that employed symbolic resonance to loom as a major statement of the flawed American dream.

The doomed anti-hero of *Tender Is the Night*, Dick Diver, a psychiatrist turned husband/keeper of the beautiful, spoiled, wealthy Nicole, is, in part, a dark version of Fitzgerald's fears for his own crackup into alcoholism and decadence. The sprawling canvas of the novel—set in the south of France, full of echoes of America and equally filled with brilliant cameos of lost American expatriates—catches the tone of the Depression United States both in the personal despair of the Divers and in the social clarity that highlights the waste of spirit and money that leads to a society's collapse. And in his attempt to write a "big" novel, Fitzgerald tries to control his variety of themes, characters, and settings by techniques that are almost, but not quite, triumphant: the use of an innocent eye as narrative viewpoint in the book's opening, through Rosemary, a young, tough but unspoiled Hollywood actress who over-identifies with the glamorous Divers' surface; then a long flashback section to World War I and Dick's psychiatric career as well as Nicole's illness, told from an omniscient viewpoint that concentrates on Dick's thoughts; finally a scattered, staccato ending of drunkenness and violence shown through both Dick's and Nicole's minds.

Tender Is the Night is more than the story of Dick Diver's degeneration and his marriage with Nicole, set against the European background. Like the author, Dick is inextricably caught up in this society that alternately enthralls and revolts him. The rich complexity of the novel stems from the coherent portraits of the characters who attend on the Divers as they create a beach at Antibes, or a glittering and cruel dinner party, or a nostalgic excursion to old battlefields. Abe North the drunken, self-destructive composer, his failed singer wife Mary, Tommy Barban the reckless soldier of fortune who will inherit Nicole, writers and actors, doctors and patients—all contribute to a superb rendering of a lost generation "who had been dissipating all spring and summer, so that now everything they did had a purely nervous inspiration." This world, viewed externally or internally, is guilty and insane. Nicole's psychosis, her role as victim of parental incest, Dick's homosexual and syphilitic patients reflect what seemed then to be an unnatural, ravaged culture.

Fitzgerald creates a potentially tragic figure in Dick Diver, the brilliant doctor who through his love for a lost woman and his own internal weakness, betrays the gifts of perception and warmth to become a party-giver and then a party-destroyer. Diver does not attain full tragic status because, as in all Fitzgerald's fiction, the hero is too close to the author's own needs and doubts. Thus, Fitzgerald protests too much the reasons for Diver's inability to work and create, his misuse of his talents. Diver, like Fitzgerald, misses the better world, an older America of Puritan work values and southern gallantry. ". . . momentarily he sat again on his father's knee, riding with Mosby, while the old loyalties and devotions fought on around him. Almost with an effort . . . he faced the whole new world in which he believed." The fault, Fitzgerald argues, is not in Diver but in the cultural values of the 1920's. The novel is not primarily a social analysis but an inner probing of the reasons for one man's failure. In Dick's collapse, moreover, Fitzgerald intends that we should comprehend Nicole's madness, Tommy's mindless violence, Abe's self-destruction that leads to his drunk's gutter death. Dick's great flaw is not tragic, but tragi-comic: Fitzgerald's own refusal to accept age and maturity. The climax of Dick Diver's deterioration is his inability to perform a youthful trick on an aquaplane. Diver takes this event as seriously as wars and economic collapses. The prose is glowingly poetic, the characterization makes sense, but the motivations ultimately are trivial (which accounts for the novel's poor reception, both in reviews and sales—the novel seemed another superficial Twenties romp, inappropriate for the present dark times). Yet Diver's pain is real: "The manner remains intact for some time after the morale cracks."

Dick Diver never loses his charm for the reader, and at the novel's end, bereft of wife and children, friends and lovers, home and profession, he still retains dignity since Fitzgerald allows for the possibility that Dick willed his collapse, in a self-sacrifice directed by his best instincts that led him into his marriage and his parties, the desire to be used. As he grows weak, Nicole grows strong and independent: Dr. Diver does effect a cure. Although he is perhaps destroyed by Nicole's millions, part of him remains loyal to the memory of his dead father whom Dick buries in Maryland and bids farewell—"Goodbye all my fathers." The novel closes on a typical moment of Fitzgerald's 1920's high symbolic drama—Dick makes the sign of the cross and blesses the beach as he departs, and Tommy prevents Nicole from going to her husband—and 1930's tough-minded social realism—Diver disappears into a degenerating medical practice somewhere in the American landscape: "a very small town, in any case he is almost certainly in that section of the country, in one town or another."

—Eric Solomon

THE TENTH MUSE.
Poems by Anne Bradstreet, 1650.

Anne Bradstreet's *The Tenth Muse Lately sprung up in AMERICA . . . By a Gentlewoman in those parts* is the first book of poems by an American poet and one of the first by a woman writing in English. Had Bradstreet not developed later into a poet of some importance, these would be about the only reasons for reserving a place for *The Tenth Muse* in literary history, for the poetry in this volume is generally undistinguished, with only a few flashes of originality or insight. Indeed, imitation and not originality was uppermost in Bradstreet's mind; she deliberately set herself the task of writing like her father, Thomas Dudley, and the French poet Guillaume du Bartas (as translated by Joshua Sylvester). She conceived of poetry as a vehicle for public rather than private sentiments and, like another of her models, Sir Walter Ralegh, saw the functions of poet and historian as complementary if not identical. The poems in *The Tenth Muse* are what they are largely because of Bradstreet's preconceptions concerning poetry, its nature and uses.

Yet *The Tenth Muse* is also the work of a craftswoman learning her trade, and as such it has a value larger than the merely historical. In it, Bradstreet begins the process of discovering her own voice and themes, both of which originate, finally, in her roles as wife and mother in American Puritan society. The limitations of such roles are obvious, but had her place in society not been so secure—had she not read Spenser and Sidney and maybe even Shakespeare *and* been encouraged in her writing by her family—she might never have written the poems for which she is remembered. By spiriting away her manuscript without her knowledge and arranging for its publication in London, her brother-in-law John Woodbridge may have embarrassed her as an artist, as she complained in a later poem entitled "The Author to Her Book," but that poem also makes clear that Woodbridge's act of benevolent piracy awakened her to a sense of artistic responsibility and self-awareness. She was to take her writing seriously thereafter, even to the extent of revising *The Tenth Muse*.

Following a cluster of dedicatory poems by Nathaniel Ward, Nicholas Henry, Benjamin Woodbridge, and other male writers, all of whom expressed playful (?) astonishment that a woman could write anything worth reading, *The Tenth Muse* commences with a poem inscribed to Bradstreet's father, and alluding to his poem, now lost, on the four parts of the world. It is likely that John Woodbridge got this and the next poem, "The Prologue," mixed up in the manuscript, for "To Her Most Honoured Father Thomas Dudley" clearly introduces "The Foure Elements" and the other Quaternions, while "The Prologue" just as clearly introduces the long "Four Monarchies"—patently a poem about wars and commonwealths and kings. In the book as Woodbridge assembled it, the reader must wait some sixty pages for the subject matter promised in "The Prologue."

It is, unfortunately, a wait without a reward. "The Four Monarchies" is so pedestrian that even Bradstreet grows impatient with it, taking Nathaniel Ward's favorite proverb about cobblers sticking to their lasts as her motto also and rushing through the Roman monarchy in five "tedious brief" pages. "The Prologue" in which she forewarns her readers about this tiresome poem, on the other hand, is probably the best piece in *The Tenth Muse*. In it, Bradstreet deftly contrasts humanistic with Christian and Calvinistic views of the capabilities of women and asserts at least a modest claim for herself as a poet: "Give wholesome Parsley wreath, I aske no Bayes" (this line, by the way, she later improved to "Give thyme or parsley wreath, I ask no bays"). In making her own femininity and the act of poetry itself the themes of this poem, Bradstreet anticipates attitudes that underlie her best and most memorable work.

Although some sprightly lines adorn "The Foure Ages of Man" and "The Foure Seasons of the Yeare," the most interesting of the remaining poems in *The Tenth Muse* are "A Dialogue between Old *England* and New" (for its topical references) and the elegies on Sir Philip Sidney (with whom she appears to claim remote kinship) and Elizabeth I. Elizabeth provides Bradstreet with a persona in whose name to claim worth for women: "Let such, as say our sex is void of reason, / Know 'tis a slander now, but once was treason." The final poem in the volume, "Of the vanity of all worldly creatures," restates as in a coda the themes of mutability, human frailty, and the inevitable demise of all earthly empires, reminding us at the end that Anne Bradstreet, America's first poet of note, produced her poetry in the context of an ideology that held, at best, a limited place for such frivolities.

—Robert D. Arner

THANATOPSIS.
Poem by William Cullen Bryant, 1821.

Anthologized in virtually every major collection of American poetry, "Thanatopsis" is William Cullen Bryant's most famous poem and is today considered a 19th-century American "classic." Begun when Bryant was not yet 18, "Thanatopsis" represents his youthful, yet remarkably sophisticated, attempts to confront his early doubts about life and his persistent fears about death. Taken from the Greek, the term "Thanatopsis" literally means "glimpse or view of death," and death is the subject of the poem.

Although from an early age onward Bryant wished to write a poem that would be remembered by future generations, "Thanatopsis" was originally published anonymously, without his knowledge or consent. While Bryant was away from home studying law, his father discovered unfinished versions of "Thanatopsis" and another poem, "Inscription for the Entrance to a Wood," and he sent both manuscripts to the *North American Review*, where in 1817 they were published together as one poem. Scholars debate the actual date when Bryant began writing the poem, but it is believed that he may have composed a first draft as early as 1811 and certainly not later than 1814. From numerous extant manuscripts we know that Bryant continued revising "Thanatopsis" until 1821, when it was published in its final form, with introductory and concluding stanzas substituting for the poem erroneously published as part of it in the 1817 version.

The complicated textual history of "Thanatopsis" is perhaps one explanation for the poem's tripartite structure. The poem begins with a 17-line introduction, spoken through a persona, who explains that nature's "visible forms" offer a variety of messages to anyone who "holds Communion with her." Specifically, the persona explains, nature offers a "healing sympathy" to those troubled by "bitter" thoughts of death. In the second section of the poem, extending in two stanzas from lines 18 to 72, nature itself speaks, attempting to console the individual who fears loss of personal identity in the general dissolution of the grave.

In response to these fears, nature offers two points of consolation. First, nature explains that death is a universal, if not an essentially democratic experience. Death, says nature, should not be taken personally; all of us are called to its "mysterious realm": "Thou shalt lie down / With patriarchs of the infant world—with kings, / The powerful of the earth— / The wise, the good." Second, nature explains that death is a natural and basically peaceful experience, part of the predictable cycles of life. Through death, explains nature, the individual simply blends forms with the "hills / Rock-ribbed and ancient as the sun,—the vales / Stretching in pensive quietness between," and the "venerable woods" and "rivers that move / In majesty" and "make the meadows green." Finally, in the last section of the poem, which extends for an additional nine lines, nature provides its now famous injunction to approach "the silent halls of death" not "like the quarry-slave at night, / Scourged to his dungeon" but with the "unfaltering trust" of "one who wraps the drapery of his couch / About him, and lies down to pleasant dreams."

While to the 20th-century reader, such ideas as these may seem didactic, sentimental, and even trite, it should be remembered that during the early 19th century, when religion provided the primary framework for any approach to death, they were far from conventional. Bryant's editors at the *North American Review*, for example, found "Thanatopsis" so original that they thought it could not have been written by someone "on this side of the water." Because its stoic approach toward death is totally devoid of religious consolation, one of Bryant's contemporaries publicly labelled "Thanatopsis" a "pagan" poem. Although Bryant was undoubtedly inspired to write "Thanatopsis" by the "graveyard" verses of the British poets Henry Kirke White, Bishop Beilby Porteous, Robert Blair, and Thomas Gray, among others, he refuses to succumb to either their neoclassical verse excesses or their piety. In fact, the language and diction of "Thanatopsis" is so restrained and so poignantly austere that the poem has been likened to a Puritan sermon and its language to the Puritan plainstyle.

Neither, however, does Bryant succumb to the equally facile and tempting romantic conclusion that death is desirable because it offers the harried individual a mystical fusion with nature's sublimity. Despite nature's encouraging message, Bryant views death not with anticipation, only with a stoic's sense of acceptance. While he hopes that death will bring with it "pleasant dreams," he possesses no illusions that death is preferable to life. Throughout the poem and even from the very voice of nature, bleak images of "melancholy waste," "sad abodes," the "sluggish clod," and the "oak" whose "roots" shall "pierce thy mold" remain ominously in the background.

In the end it is perhaps Bryant's stubborn refusal to dismiss the ultimate questions of life and death through conventional conclusions that creates the tensions and ambiguities that have attracted generations of readers to "Thanatopsis." No matter how easy it would be to reduce complex questions to simple answers, Bryant's intuitions inform him that life's more serious problems defy easy solutions. "Thanatopsis" remains true to those intuitions. It appeals to the haunting doubts in everyone that any single system of belief can totally quiet the ever present and unsettling reality "Of the stern agony, and shroud, and pall." If not a great work of art in the 20th-century sense of the term, "Thanatopsis" displays more than a little originality and certainly at least a spark of genius.

—James A. Levernier

TOBACCO ROAD.
Novel by Erskine Caldwell, 1932.

Fifty years ago, the National Council of Teachers of English ranked *God's Little Acre* among the 1000 works of literature an educated person ought to have read. Today neither *God's Little Acre* nor the once equally shocking *Tobacco Road* is on anyone's list of masterworks. But however dated it now appears, *Tobacco Road* will always be with us; it will have a place in the history of the southern novel and (because of a famously successful stage version) in the history of the American stage. It will also inevitably be mentioned as "sensational" every time the American public has one of its recurrent fits of morality.

Today novels far more "sensational" than these two by Erskine Caldwell are routinely published. In some sense Caldwell can claim some credit or responsibility for that, for his picture of degeneracy and degradation among the po' white trash of Georgia acclimatized the reading public to something stronger than it had been used to. Between his crude beginnings with *The Bastard* (1930) and *Tragic Ground* (1944), with the excellent work of *Georgia Boy* and some other books in between, Caldwell contributed significantly to American sociological literature in a period of great advance in far more than frankness. He found an avid popular readership for strong meat about disenfranchised blacks and Depression whites, and his gothic grotesques were not very far from reality itself. His tales were easy reading about hard times. They were enlivened with rough humor and freighted with serious social concern, as well as breaking new ground in what we should now call "permissiveness" or "explicit scenes."

God's Little Acre was a book that people went to for "the good parts," the sex or "adult material" that looks rather restrained now. But *Tobacco Road* is probably the novel by which Caldwell will be remembered in the catalogues of immensely popular writers who hit upon the right combination, in their time, of sex and humor, entertainment and "social significance."

It was Caldwell's obvious (if rather simplistic) social concern that made *Tobacco Road* more than pornography or titillation. If he was shocking, he was also realistic, and he lacked the doctrinaire dullness that was then so common in literature which addressed questions of social justice and the plight of the poor. His humor helped to sugar-coat a pill which, though no panacea, was good for at least a few of the things that ailed America. Those who missed the sugar coating may have found the sensationalism bitter to swallow, but their rage was rather like that of Caliban at seeing his own reflection. Those who attacked Caldwell for his starkly realistic picture of American life disliked what was really going on and somehow thought that lying about bad news could make things better.

Tobacco Road was lighter and better than much writing by the "committed" writers of those days; it remains crudely amusing if garishly graphic and definitely dated. Caldwell's comic talent has been too much neglected because our literary history of that period has been written by critics with more sense of history than sense of humor. Caldwell's humor is strange but never sardonic. Now it seems a trifle less grotesque than before to readers who have read a good deal of southern gothic. *Tobacco Road* is an early and not extreme picture of degeneracy and decay, life and lust among the dirt farmers and not the stereotypes of the Old Plantation and the magnolias.

Tobacco Road tackles incest and tragedy and death. The plot involves a short time in the lives of Jeeter Lester and his dirt-poor, inbred relatives. Jeeter is keeping on as well as he can, trying to scrape a living as a sharecropper in the depths of rural Georgia. He has a starving old mother, a sick wife with some loathsome disease, and a passel of no-account young 'uns that ought to make any modern parent grateful for any but the very worst of adolescent children. Jeeter's son is Dude, more stupid than 16 can account for. The two daughters are Ellie May (younger than Dude but already beginning to feel the sap rising and unlikely to get many offers to run wild, because she has a harelip) and Pearl (who was married off as soon as she reached 12 to Lov Bensey, a poor slob just getting by as a worker on the railroad). Enter Jeeter's widowed Sister Bessie Rice, back from a series of revival meetings. Sister Bessie is looking for a male to help her with her itinerant bible-pounding and, she admits, "for other things," now that her man has gone to his eternal reward.

Sister Bessie hits on Dude—there is not much of a selection available—and bribes him into marrying her by offering a flashy new automobile. What teenager could resist? Dude predictably wrecks the car (just as predictably, perhaps, getting Grandma off the scene for good), and Pearl runs away from Lov Bensey, who complains to her father in the tone one might use with a retailer who had sold one a defective appliance. Ellie May sees her chance and offers to take her sister's place in Lov's household. Unable to do any better, Lov accepts. Back on the farm on Tobacco Road, Jeeter and his wife Ada perish in a fire when the ramshackle dwelling burns to the ground.

All this is very candidly presented and there are some "bits" that no reader today would bother to look up—considering what television and the movies offer so freely—but which in their day kept pages turning and made this, with *Lady Chatterley's Lover* and a few others, the kind of book one waited to get from the public library but then could rush through pretty quickly, the most dog-eared pages clearly being the ones on which to concentrate. A whole generation got ideas about sex in such guilty pastimes but, unlike the current generation, at least had to learn to read.

Tobacco Road's original readers could, had they a mind to, have noted that the treatment of sex in American fiction was undergoing a considerable change, a change to which writers such as Caldwell (and many others; James T. Farrell, for instance) significantly contributed. Moreover, Caldwell's work was not crushed under Freudian symbols or wooden dialogue. He had a certain literary flair and a certain amount of courage to confront the puritanical who, then as now, are always ready to take umbrage at "adult themes and language," trying to make literature suitable for children.

Tobacco Road was loved by the public and hated by the guardians of public morality. Then it became a theatrical bombshell, running 3182 consecutive performances on Broadway after 1933 and setting the long-run record. *Tobacco Road* the play merits its place in the popular pantheon, and *Tobacco Road* the film its place in the work of the renowned director John Ford. And *Tobacco Road* the novel merits its place in the literature of the Depression. If it is essentially as tacky as (say) Depression glassware, it was part of the history of its time, possessed of a certain popular appeal and charm, and is destined to look more quaint and less vulgar as time goes on.

—Leonard R. N. Ashley

THE TOOTH OF CRIME.
Play by Sam Shepard, 1972.

Sam Shepard wrote *The Tooth of Crime* in London in 1972: "It wasn't until I came to England that I found out what it means to be an American." What it meant flowed into the drama as wanderlust, violence, image mania. In their virtuosic verbal sparring two characters, Hoss and Crow, synthesize such dialects of the tribe as rock jargon, crime movies, street slang, science fiction.

Mallarmé's "Angoisse" provides Shepard's arresting title: "A heart that the tooth of crime cannot wound." Mallarmé's sonnet contrasts the vulnerable persona with his invulnerable partner in vice, and Shepard contrasts vulnerable Hoss with invulnerable Crow. Shepard's subtitle is "A play with music in two acts," and music takes the form of eight songs: "I wanted the music in *The Tooth of Crime* so that you could step out of the play for a minute, every time a song comes, and be brought to an emotional comment on what's been taking place in the play."

The *emotional* comment is Shepard's twist on Brechtian estrangement. The stage is comparably bare, "except for an evil-looking black chair with silver studs and a very high back, something like an Egyptian Pharaoh's throne." Like the classical tragedy that Brecht condemned, however, *The Tooth of Crime* opens close to its crisis: Hoss needs a kill in "the game." He fondles the array of guns—"the gear"—proffered by Becky, his servant-mistress-tutor. Wiser than Shakespeare's Caesar who ignores the stars, Hoss consults his Star-Man and also his astrologer Galactic Jack, who reassures him: "A shootin' star, baby. High flyin' and no jivin'. You is off to number nine . . . You're number one with a bullet and you ain't even got the needle in the groove."

Becky reports that a Gypsy has been "sussed," and Hoss sounds out his Chauffeur Cheyenne about "cruising," but that faithful retainer demurs against violating "the code." Hoss then reaches out for an alliance with Little Willard in the East, only to learn of his suicide. Doc's injection does not tranquilize Hoss who reveals his full dread to Becky: "And confidence is just a hype to keep away the open-ended shakes." Then, alone on stage, Hoss bifurcates into a dialogue with his father: "They're all countin' on me. The bookies, the agents, the Keepers. I'm a fucking industry." Once Hoss accepts his father's reply—"You're just a man, Hoss. Just a man"—he can accept the challenge of Crow.

Act II opens with Crow alone on stage, dressed in the hard rock fashion of the 1960's. As Shakespeare's Hal donned his father's crown, Crow momentarily usurps Hoss's throne, violently chewing gum. The Gypsy greets his adversary: "Got the molar chomps. Eyes stitched. You can vision what's sittin'. Very razor to cop z's sussin' me to be on the far end of the spectrum." From Hoss's stellar isolation, he asks Crow for news of the outside world, and the younger man's replies are implied threats: "Image shots are blown, man. No fuse to match the hole. Only power forces weigh the points in our match." Hoss mocks Crow with swift shifts of roles—cowboy, 1920's gangster, his earlier self that Crow imitates: "That's not the way you walk! That's the way I walk!" before summoning a referee to judge their contest.

In Round 1 Crow attacks Hoss with a capsule biography of a coward and a loser, and Ref awards the round to Crow. In Round 2 Hoss accuses Crow of denying his musical origins in the blues of black people—"You'd like a free ride on a black man's back"—but Crow counters: "I got no guilt to conjure! Fence me with the present" and the Ref declares it a draw. In Round 3 Crow ridicules Hoss's outdated music and accuses him of stealing styles; the Ref calls it a T.K.O., so an infuriated Hoss shoots him.

Having thus violated the code, Hoss automatically becomes a Gypsy, needing lessons in survival from Crow. In a digression influenced by the movie *Alphaville*, Becky enacts a rape perpetrated upon her, perhaps by Hoss. In defeat, however, Hoss cannot learn to talk, walk, and sing as a Gypsy. Like classical heroes, he prefers death to dishonor: "It is my life and my death in one clean shot." He falls upon that shot, and

Crow finally pays him homage: "A genius mark" as his own reign begins.

The Tooth of Crime is Shepard's most tightly plotted play, with his most carefully nuanced characters, even while it subsumes many of the themes of his earlier plays—the tenuous position of the American artist, his heritage of wanderlust and violence, his roots in popular culture and his assault by media images, the manic machismo of the 1960's culminating in nationally televised death scenes. At once a competition between two rock stars, a style contest between performers, and a metaphysical bout between generations, *The Tooth of Crime* is the last great play of Shepard's "loners" before he turned to a theater of mythic families. More than themes, however, the bitter bite of *Tooth* springs from a lexical blend of drugs, sports, rock music, crime, astrology, and big business—in short, the contemporary American landscape.

—Ruby Cohn

THE TURN OF THE SCREW.
Story by Henry James, 1898.

Henry James was fascinated by the ghost story. He felt that to be truly effective tales of the supernatural should not simply recount otherworldly "events" but instead should portray the effects of those events upon a sensitive observer. James acted upon this theory in writing *The Turn of the Screw*, and created a tale which has horrified, and mystified, generations of readers. Few works of art have elicited such acerbic, polemical, and often fanciful critical debate.

The debate grows out of the ambiguities imposed by the way James limits point of view. From the moment that the governess's narrative takes over the story, our knowledge is strictly limited: all that we learn of the events at Bly, we learn through her. There is no omniscient narrator who can tell us directly what "really" happened or read the other characters' minds; all we have is the record of what the governess sees, or thinks she sees, and what she determines that others think and feel.

The governess tells a disturbing story. She, an inexperienced young woman, accepts a position as governess to two orphaned children who live on a remote country estate. Their uncle in London demands an unusual condition: she is never to report to him nor communicate with him in any way. She is to be head of the household and manage everything herself. The governess is charmed with her two small charges, eight-year-old Flora and ten-year-old Miles, although she is disturbed to find that Miles has been dismissed from school on mysterious grounds. All apparently goes well until the governess sees an unknown and quite horrifying man in one of the towers of the house and later at a window. She learns that the man she saw was surely Peter Quint, the master's former valet, but that Quint is dead!

It soon becomes clear to her that Quint and the previous governess, Miss Jessel (who is also dead), were "infamous" when alive, corrupted the children, and have now returned for them from beyond the grave; the seemingly innocent children welcome the demonic visitors. The frightened young woman struggles against this apparently invincible evil with no help but that of the unimaginative housekeeper, the aptly-named Mrs. Grose, who cannot see the ghosts herself. The governess repeatedly doubts her own sanity and becomes nearly as eager to vindicate herself as to save the children. She does apparently save little Flora, but she saves Miles only in the most equivocal way: when she wrenches the boy's spirit away from Peter Quint, the "white face of damnation" at the window, he dies of the shock, "dispossessed."

But many readers have claimed that there is a second, hidden story beneath the governess's narrative: the governess is mad, the ghosts are hallucinations, and the true horror of the story is that two innocent children are placed in the sole care of a madwoman, who literally frightens one of them to death.

These readers find support in the governess's nervous anxiety and insomnia, her romantic dreams about her employer, her father's reported "eccentricities," her confessed aptitude for sensing ghostly phenomena, and most of all in the fact that nobody else ever sees (or admits seeing?) the ghosts. These readers explain the children's growing uneasiness as a normal reaction to the peculiar behavior of their governess. And they point to the indisputable fact that the governess draws sweeping and horrifying inferences from very small and ambiguous pieces of evidence.

But, finally, any reader who claims that the evil spirits are merely the governess's hallucinations is left with an inexplicable kernel of "fact": how could the governess describe Peter Quint exactly, point by point, when she had never seen him nor heard of him, unless she really did see his "spirit?" Quint's is an unusual face, with attributes traditionally ascribed to the devil; the governess describes him minutely and Mrs. Grose recognizes the portrait at once. Furthermore, James himself wrote about the tale as a well-crafted ghost story, not simply a case study of madness.

James wrote that he wanted to "give the impression of the communication to the children of the most infernal imaginable evil and danger," and he wisely determined to leave the specifics of that evil to the imagination of each reader, only supplying hints that it was somehow sexual. "Only make the reader's general vision of evil intense enough, I said to myself . . . and his own experience, his own imagination, his own sympathy (with the children) and horror (of their false friends) will supply him quite sufficiently with all the particulars. Make him *think* the evil, make him think it for himself, and you are released from weak specifications." The question of the governess's sanity can be seen in this light: ambiguity is much more disturbing than specificity. The lingering ambiguities give yet another turn of the screw to the disquieting effect of this disturbing story.

—Mollie Sandock

U.S.A.
Novels by John Dos Passos, 1930–36.

John Dos Passos's *U.S.A.* (complete version, 1938) had as its goal the depiction of life and society in the United States during the first thirty years of the 20th century. Actually *U.S.A.* comprises three novels, each published separately—*The 42nd Para-*

llel, 1919, and *The Big Money*. Dos Passos had already attempted a similar project, with considerable success, in *Manhattan Transfer*, a fictional representation of New York in all its complexity during the first two decades of the century. But *U.S.A.* was a vaster undertaking which challenged to the utmost the author's skill in developing new techniques suitable for his purpose. The manner and devices with which he met this challenge make him one of the most remarkable innovators in American literature. But before examining his methods, we need to know his attitude toward his subject.

Dos Passos was an idealistic liberal, if not a radical. As such, he was distressed by the materialism, the greed, the ruthlessness of business that he perceived as violating the promise of America. *U.S.A.* is an angry book. In its first two novels it leans toward Marxism; in the last, *The Big Money*, the influence of Thorstein Veblen is dominant (a brief biography of Veblen, "The Bitter Drink", is included). While writing *U.S.A.* Dos Passos's political and economic philosophy was switching from the far left to the right, though it had not yet reached the conservatism of his later years.

The three novels in *U.S.A.* deal with three stages that Dos Passos discerns in the nation's economic and spiritual life. *The 42nd Parallel* describes pre-World War I confidence, an almost frontier type of brashness; but it also focuses on the labor troubles and other discontents of the period. Indeed the title of the book refers to a frequent meteorological storm path. *1919* has as its theme the moral and political disruptions immediately following the war. *The Big Money* presents a picture of spiritual bankruptcy on a national scale.

Dos Passos employs the same techniques in all three novels. The narrative elements, carried in 52 separate sections, revolve around the lives of twelve main characters who appear and reappear in one or more of the novels. Some of them, but not all, become involved with others of the twelve. These characters differ widely in background, education, goals, values, and competence; and each one may be perceived as a case history. To name several, Fenian McCreary is a printer and a worker in the I.W.W.; Charley Anderson, an ace in the air corps during the war, makes a fortune in business and in stocks, destroys his career and personal life with alcohol, and dies in an automobile crash; Mary French, a Vassar graduate, becomes involved in Communist-supported labor agitation; Margo Dowling is a star in the silent movies and temporarily Charley Anderson's mistress; J. Ward Morehouse, a public relations executive, succeeds in business but fails in his personal life.

Between the narrative sections are so-called Newsreels and Camera Eyes and biographical sketches of famous or notorious men and women of the era. There are biographies of Henry Ford (headed "Tin Lizzie"), William Randolph Hearst ("Poor Little Rich Boy"), Rudolph Valentino ("Adagio Dancer"), Isadora Duncan ("Art and Isadora"), Samuel Insull ("Power Superpower"), and President Wilson ("Meester Veelson"). In these and other sketches Dos Passos freely reveals his own feelings, which range from contempt to admiration. Most bitter of all is his sketch of the Unknown Soldier ("The Body of an American") at the end of *1919*. All of them serve in setting the tone and establishing the background in the sections of the trilogy in which they appear.

So also do the Newsreels, which are montages made up of snatches of newspaper articles, headlines, verses from popular songs, and advertisements. The Camera Eyes also serve the same purpose; but they are more subjective, for they record Dos Passos's own feelings in either private situations or in regard to public events in which he is involved. In a sense the Camera Eyes add an autobiographical dimension to the book. Though written as prose, they may be described as imagistic, impressionistic free verse. Most impressive in style and feeling is the Camera Eye beginning "walking from Plymouth to North Plymouth through the raw air of Massachusetts Bay . . .", in which the author meditates on what he is sure is the wrong done to Bartolomeo Vanzetti, one of two Italian radicals executed in 1927 for a murder that liberals of the time considered unproved.

In writing *U.S.A.* Dos Passos drew to the limit from his talents as literary innovator. Like the Newsreels the entire trilogy (almost 1500 pages) is a montage designed to create an inclusive impression (rather than a chronicle) of thirty years of a nation's and a people's existence. The impression is a disheartening one, which inevitably leaves the reader with the sense of profound loss and of ideals and values betrayed. Yet the fervor with which Dos Passos writes indicates that he believes the loss may not be irretrievable. He wrote from imagination, outrage perhaps, but not total despair.

—Perry D. Westbrook

UNCLE REMUS.
Stories and sketches by Joel Chandler Harris, 1880.

Among the handful of literary characters who have a hold on immortality Joel Chandler Harris's Uncle Remus and Brer Rabbit are unusual, the mythical rabbit ostensibly the creation of the imaginary man. The models for both lay intertwined in the author's teenage experience at Turnwold plantation in the early 1860's, and transmutation into art began fortuitously when he was called on to fill in for a writer of short dialect sketches on the Atlanta *Constitution* in 1876. Uncle Remus evolved into the now familiar Old-South plantation storyteller over the next year and a half, and within another year and a half Harris had discovered the black folktale as subject, presided over supremely if not exclusively by Brer Rabbit. *Uncle Remus: His Songs and His Sayings* might never have appeared if a publisher had not sought out the shy Georgia newspaperman to urge him to collect the stories, songs, and aphorisms that had appeared in the *Constitution*. Despite the subtitle it was the tales of Uncle Remus that would endure. Ultimately the world would be given more than 180 of them in books published throughout and after Harris's lifetime. But Uncle Remus and Brer Rabbit appeared in their essence, became honored citizens of American literature, and were on their way to international embrace by virtue of the 1880 *Uncle Remus*.

"However humorous it may be in effect, its intention is perfectly serious," wrote Harris of his first book. A main purpose was "to preserve . . . legends in their original simplicity, and to wed them permanently to the quaint dialect" which he had tried to capture not merely in form but in essence. Myth and fable were words that Harris knowledgeably employed in his Introduction to the original *Uncle Remus*. He had recognized both art and drama in the oral telling of many tales, and he was aware as well of allegorical interpretation. "No scientific investigation" was required to know why the black American chose "as his hero the weakest and most harmless of animals, and brings him out victorious in contests with the bear, the wolf, and the fox. It is not virtue that triumphs, but helplessness; it is not malice, but mischievousness."

Mischievous Brer Rabbit is, but because he usually triumphs, the famous hero of Uncle Remus's tales does not seem helpless. Confidently alert and serenely smoking a pipe, a golden Brer Rabbit lounges comfortably on the front cover of the first edition of *Uncle Remus*. The first and longest section of the book, "Legends of the Old Plantation," is dominated by Remus's anthropomorphic animals, who are dominated by Brer Rabbit; 31 of the 34 "legends" have animals characters, and Brer Rabbit figures in 25. The cunning trickster able to extricate himself from almost any difficulty and to emerge on top of almost every situation commands immediately the habitual American favoring of the underdog. But Brer Rabbit is more than simply an imaginative and entertaining underdog who triumphs; although not without some exhibitions of cruelty, he is both superficially attractive and deeply lovable. He's a husband and the father of a family; he's both prideful and playful, just "bleedzed fer ter fling back some er his saas" to Brer Fox by shouting "Bred en bawn in a brier-patch!"; and, very important, he too is vulnerable: Buzzard and Fox and Terrapin can and do get the best of him. When Brer Terrapin defeats Brer Rabbit by cheating, as Remus's young auditor "dolefully" recognizes, Uncle Remus speaks forthrightly about normal fairness and honor in human relationships.

If Brer Rabbit reflects the human, and perhaps especially the black human in America, he himself is reflected in Uncle Remus, the teller of the tales who is at the same time a character in another story. In the important fictional frame, the seven-year-old son of a plantation master and mistress is drawn magnetically day after day to Uncle Remus's cabin. Remus's love for the little boy is manifest, but the old man is not above using his power over him for selfish ends. Lovable and entertaining, Uncle Remus is also mischievous and calculating, willing to take advantage of the gullibility of this little white man just as the rabbit does of that of the fox or bear. The teller of the Brer Rabbit tales mirrors his roguish hero.

Neither Harris's disparagement of himself as an unoriginal, unliterary reporter of old stories nor, ironically, the sheer natural delight of the tales themselves must be allowed to blind readers to his accomplished art. The "accuracy" of literary dialect in reproducing or representing actual speech is logically a non-question. Effective written prose style is not. Harris was a careful and consummate craftsman who knew how and when to bring dramatic rise and fall, to give affecting shape, to achieve preternatural, exquisite smoothness in individual sentences as well as in whole tales and cycles of tales. In his seeming artlessness is great art.

Uncle Remus: His Songs and His Sayings is properly described as "a miscellaneous anthology of the Old South." In addition to the 34 "legends" told by Uncle Remus it contains 70 proverbs, ten songs, a story including a Civil War incident related by Remus, and, finally, 21 sketches about another Uncle Remus, a resident of Atlanta. While rooted in some New-South realities, this "other" Remus character is a condescendingly drawn minstrel figure, himself the object of amusement. Not well known as a Harris figure, this Remus is like countless postbellum "darkeys" who appeared in white newspapers and books of the American south until as late as the 1950's. The Uncle Remus who endures is the plantation slave, the master storyteller capable of delighting and instructing the world just as he amused and instructed a little boy. Artfully given warm, full life by his creator, he is made the artful conveyor of stories that draw deep from the universal sources of our humanity.

—Bert Hitchcock

UNCLE TOM'S CABIN.
Novel by Harriet Beecher Stowe, 1852.

If the greatness of a novel were based solely upon its popularity and sociological impact, then Harriet Beecher Stowe's *Uncle Tom's Cabin* would undoubtedly be one of the greatest American novels of all time. Originally published in the *National Era* between 5 June 1851 and 1 April 1852, Stowe's novel achieved unparalleled popularity and attention when it was eventually issued in two volumes by John P. Jewett, a fledgling publisher who worried that the tale might not sell because of its length and content.

Within two days of its release, the entire first edition had sold out, and after one year sales of the novel were estimated at more than 325,000 copies in America alone. Worldwide more than three million copies of the novel are thought to have been printed during Stowe's lifetime. According to one commentator, *Uncle Tom's Cabin* has been "translated into every civilized language from Welsh to Bengali," and it became, during the 19th century, "the world's second best seller, outranked only by the Bible." In terms of its effects on history, *Uncle Tom's Cabin* had equally sensational results. Abraham Lincoln himself is said to have referred to Stowe as "the little lady who wrote the book that made this big war," and Frederick Douglass described the novel as the flame that kindled "a million camp fires in front of the embattled hosts of slavery." No one, however, was more surprised at the success of the book than its author, who it is said had only hoped to earn enough from her first royalties to buy a new silk dress.

While detractors of *Uncle Tom's Cabin* have since the time of its publication been quick to point out its flaws in style, structure, and historicity, it is easy in retrospect to understand why the novel was such a sensation during the 19th century and why even today it continues to generate fierce critical debate. Simply put, it was, in the words of Leslie A. Fiedler, the "greatest of all novels of sentimental protest." Writing in response to the passage of 1850 of the Fugitive Slave Law that forbade citizens of free states from in any way assisting in the flight of runaway slaves, Stowe explained that her primary motive in publishing the book was "to show the institution of slavery just as it existed." This she accomplished, forcefully and effectively, by constructing what she termed "a *living dramatic reality*" that "endeavored to show it [slavery] fairly, in its best and worst phases."

Accordingly, Stowe created some of the most memorable characters in all literature: Uncle Tom, the self-sacrificing slave who truly embodies the spirit of Christianity taught to him but not practiced by his white "masters"; Augustine St. Clare, the well-intentioned but ultimately ineffectual slaveholder who deplores the evils of slavery but despairs of how to remedy them; Topsy, the slave child so miserably abused since birth that she believed herself incapable of doing good; and, of course, Simon Legree, the villainous embodiment of depravity who persists in tormenting and ultimately murdering Tom only because of Tom's goodness.

Although during the 19th century, Stowe was attacked as a rabid, unthinking, and untalented abolitionist who totally failed to research her novels and whose only goal was to villify the south, scholarship has substantiated that most of the incidents and characters in the novel were based on carefully researched historical realities and that she did in fact attempt to provide a relatively "fair" depiction of slavery as it existed in America before the Civil War. Significantly, the southern slaveholder St. Clare is one of the most compassionate characters in the novel while the basest character in the book, Legree, was born and nurtured in the north, as was the New England reformer, Ophelia Sinclare, who outwardly professed an absolute abhorrence of slavery but who inwardly harbored prejudices that prevented her from so much as touching anyone of another race and whose solution to the problem of slavery was simply to transport the slaves back to Africa, out of "sight and smell."

Similarly, 20th-century accusations that the novel encourages racist stereotyping and is devoid of artistry have been largely dispelled by scholars who have illustrated that *Uncle Tom's Cabin* is far more complex that it seems and is far more susceptible to rigorous aesthetic analysis than was once generally thought. Particularly noteworthy in this regard are analyses of Stowe's attitudes toward sexual roles, the law, and religion, as well as her pre-Marxist insights into the nature of class conflict and the millennial politics of her day.

Whatever controversies *Uncle Tom's Cabin* has engendered in the past or will continue to engender in the future, one thing remains certain: it will always be an important work for anyone interested in the literary and cultural development of the United States. As Charley Dudley Warner explained in 1896, "*Uncle Tom's Cabin* has the fundamental qualities, the sure insight into human nature, and the fidelity to the facts of its own time which have from age to age preserved works of genius."

—James A. Levernier

THE VIRGINIAN.
Novel by Owen Wister, 1902.

The Virginian was the novel that made both author, Owen Wister, and the cowboy famous. It has to be said immediately that it is an extremely uneven work. This is largely due to its ancestry. Like all Wister's fictional works save *Lady Baltimore* it was a stitching together of previously published pieces, here some seven short stories that appeared after 1893. One immediate result is an episodic narrative and a number of awkward transitions, another the lack of a central theme.

Three major currents run through the work. There is the love story, the wooing of Molly Stark Wood, with its exploration of what Wister would call quality and equality. There is the feud between the Virginian and Trampas which only enters episodically but ends in a gunfight; and there is the relationship between the Virginian and an unspecified narrator, who has no part to play even as a reporter in much of the novel. There are further episodes in which the Virginian appears alone, not to be further defined but in order that Wister may reuse cannibalised stories. But for all these flaws the novel had great success.

This depended very largely on the character of the Virginian, the cowboy as seen by Wister. Wister was not the first to capitalise on a growing eastern interest in a vanishing west but he was important in further defining its most heroic and mythic character. Countless subsequent western heroes had to be modelled upon the Virginian though it is a mark of Wister's own self-assurance that his hero has an impressive number of quite significant moral flaws, unlike the men in white hats who were to litter the later Hollywood versions of the Virginian's archetypal story. Wister's hero, for instance, has clearly been with other women before he meets Molly Wood. He inspires his fellow cowboys as much by his skill in singing dirty songs as at the poker table. He drinks and he swears. Wister presents all this without apology. But centrally he is the soul of honour.

This was Wister's achievement, to suggest that the west produced a superior type, particularly a man of honour. Modern historians of 19th-century America would stress as important the fact that the Virginian was a southerner, that unconsciously perhaps Wister was introducing antebellum southern values into the west through choosing this birthplace for the hero. Of course it is also clear that the west was not able to produce such paragons automatically. It also produced Trampas and Shorty, Steven and Ed, all of whom steal and are cast out. But the west does help the narrator figure to recover his health and to mature and Wister certainly argues that westerners run rings around easterners by virtue of superior knowledge. Even New York after-dinner speakers can be abashed by the superior native wit of the cowboy.

This superiority is centered on physical self-confidence. The Virginian is, of course, a near-perfect physical specimen, nearly six feet and weighing 173 pounds. Much stems from the resultant high self-regard including a deep respect for the rights of others, particularly of women, though it is not easy to argue that the Virginian sees women as his inferiors. Molly Wood is his superior socially and in terms of education and if she has ever had qualms they are moral and not physical ones. Her rescue of the wounded hero is an example of her courage and ability. Their relationship is thus one of mutual self-respect and survives one or two challenges because of this. The Virginian and Molly are white as are all the other characters except for a band of Indians who are heard off-stage. There are no Mexicans, no blacks, nor even any Chinese though a character does maintain that she would not employ a Chinese cook. Like many of his class and time Wister believed in the superiority of the WASP and like many in New England despaired of its future, besieged as it was not only by Irish but by increasing numbers of southeast Europeans. Easterners thus looked west for a region free from such alien influences but ironically they failed to see that the west was being settled primarily by immigrants and their children. Theodore Roosevelt may have believed of the Dakotas what Wister was saying of Wyoming but he failed to notice that there was as high a percentage of foreigners in Fargo as in New York City. The west was open to the latest version of the courtly Saxon Knight in appearance only.

The Virginian articulates most of the author's prejudices in one way or another, often implicitly since, as a gentleman, he can be rude only indirectly. Thus he dislikes the commercialism of the drummer, the theology of predestination or of damnation, several forms of vulgarity, while praising religious restraint, or episcopalianism, breeding, though not family, aristocracy rather than democracy. The narrator gives voice to most of these, the Virginian's reactions make the point in other ways. The paradox of arguing for aristocracy in a republic is solved by using the concept of the natural aristocrat, suggesting that democracy is what the 18th century would have called mobocracy.

One of the problems Wister faced with *The Virginian* was how to end it. He could hardly argue that his hero, a cowboy at 25, would still be heroic on horseback at 60. Any American worth his salt had to be rich by then. Accordingly Wister slips in the incongruous fact that the Virginian has his own land, though he is someone else's foreman and the novel ends with the Virginian admitting that he has his eye on its coal deposits. At the very end there is news that the deposits have been developed and the Virginian is rich. Thus in a sense, the east has caught up with him and he has lost his identity. But before that happens Wister has recounted the history and character of the archetype western figure as well as further defining his antithesis, Trampas, and his subverter, Molly Wood. The cowboy, the gunman-gambler, and the virtuous schoolmarm were now ready for use by countless imitators.

—R.A. Burchell

WALDEN.
Prose by Henry David Thoreau, 1854.

Walden; or, Life in the Woods by Henry David Thoreau is a major literary expression of New England transcendentalism. It records its author's experiences and thoughts while living for two years and two months in a hut that he had built on the wooded shores of Walden Pond near Concord, Massachusetts. A native of Concord and a graduate of Harvard College, Thoreau as a young man had become the protégé of Ralph Waldo Emerson, the leading figure in transcendentalism and a resident of Concord. Thoreau had access to Emerson's library and for a time lived in the Emerson household, serving as handyman in return for room and board. Thus he became thoroughly imbued with transcendentalist thought and attitudes, equaling his mentor in enthusiasm and surpassing him in his determination to put his ideals and beliefs into practice.

On 4 July 1845 Thoreau moved into his hut at Walden, planning to write *A Week on the Concord and Merrimack Rivers*, but with the added purpose of putting to a test the transcendentalist view of life. "I went to the woods," he wrote in *Walden*, "because I wished to live deliberately, to front only the essential facts of life, and see if I could learn what it had to teach, and not, when I came to die, discover that I had not lived." The basic premise of transcendentalism was that reality lies in the worlds of thought and spirit; yet the world of things reflects intellectual and spiritual truths and hence merits close attention. "There seems to be a necessity in spirit to manifest itself in material forms," Emerson wrote; and Thoreau in one of his essays, echoed Emerson: "Let us not underrate the value of a fact; it will one day flow into a truth." However, both Emerson and Thoreau thought that material things were being vastly *over*rated in the America of their times. Believing that "our life is frittered away by detail," Thoreau at Walden Pond attempted to simplify his own existence to the utmost in order to free it from the conventions and concerns that in his opinion deaden the spirit.

In *Walden* Thoreau devotes his first chapter, titled "Economy," to a description of the way in which he rid his life of all but the most basic material demands. His living expenses for the first eight months at the pond came to exactly $61.99 3/4, including the cost of building his cabin. About half of this sum he had on hand; the rest he earned by day labor and by the sale of farm produce that he raised on a nearby field; his conclusion was that six weeks of physical work annually would maintain him in health; the remainder of the year he could spend in more important ways. Thus *Walden* is in part a repudiation of the Puritan work ethic, which required that one be constantly engaged in some productive occupation, whether for one's own profit or for the benefit of others.

Having arranged his life in this manner, Thoreau was ready for the spiritual "awakening" which he thought to be his due and that of every human being. "Awakening," in fact, is the central theme of *Walden*, and as he developed this theme, Thoreau revealed himself as a true poet both in the imagery and rhythms of his prose and in his use of metaphor. Thoreau agreed with Emerson that a function of nature is to provide language by which spiritual truths may be expressed. Consequently Thoreau's writing is always concrete, and he takes great pleasure in describing what he heard and saw and did at Walden, and he strives to bring his readers to a similar recognition of the beauty and significance of the world of nature. In the second chapter of *Walden*, "Where I Lived and What I Lived For," Thoreau declared, "I do not propose to write an ode to dejection, but to brag as lustily as chanticleer in the morning, standing on his roost, if only to wake my neighbors up"; and in what is virtually a hymn to dawn, he wrote: "The morning wind forever blows, the poem of creation is uninterrupted; but few are the ears that hear it . . . Morning is when I am awake and there is a dawn in me. Moral reform is the effort to throw off sleep." There is a potential dawn in everyone, according to Thoreau. As the day unfolds the fully "awake" person will discern new meanings in things and happenings previously taken for granted.

Thoreau occupied himself in many ways: walking, reading, talking with neighbors, writing, working—but always he was alert for meanings implicit in the objects and scenes and persons around him. The most remarkable of his days were those like the one described in the chapter "Sounds," in which he sat yogi-like (he was deeply read in the sacred books of the East) on the doorstep of his hut, listening to the sounds that impinged on the silence in which he was immersed. The critic Sherman Paul has written: "Silence and sound were Thoreau's grand analogy: silence was the celestial sea of eternity, the general, spiritual, and immutable: sound was the particular and momentary bubble on its surface." Silence was to Thoreau and Emerson a symbol of the Oversoul, or the "soul of the whole, the wise silence" (in Emerson's words), in which each individual person participates. Thus to Thoreau "all sound . . . produces one and the same effect, a vibration of the universal lyre." On days of such acute receptivity he said he grew in spirit "like corn in the night."

In "Sounds" Thoreau was describing what can only be taken as a mystical experience—the only one recorded in *Walden*. Elsewhere he focuses more on his daily life at the pond, always subjecting it to interpretations that go deeper than mere description or narrative. Thus, while the day from dawn to dusk symbolizes the awakening of the spirit to the reality beyond appearances, so too does the year. In *Walden* the succession of chapters follows the seasons from high summer through the spring of the following year—the two years and two months of residence at Walden Pond being telescoped into one year. Summer, of course, is the season of fullest spiritual awakening—the season of the chapter "Sounds."

The day, the year, then, served as symbols of the growth of the spirit to a full realization of itself. Another symbol, Walden Pond, is ever-present almost in symphonic counterpoint with those of the day and the year. First, the pond, which Thoreau had known from earliest childhood, typifies his profoundest self—the self that he shares with all humanity and which rests in the Oversoul. Local residents believed Walden Pond to be bottomless; Thoreau measured the depth and found it to be slightly over one hundred feet—still extraordinary for so small a pond and sufficient to represent the depths of the human spirit. Thus to Thoreau drifting in a boat on the pond's surface, with a fishline in the water, the tug of a biting fish was suggestive of the truths that one might pull from far beneath the surface of consciousness.

Thoreau conducted daily observations of the pond. In winter he made a chart of its depths, cutting holes in the ice through which to drop his leaded cod-line. He was interested when crews of men arrived to harvest ice, and he was delighted with the knowledge that much of the ice would be shipped as ballast to India and that there "the pure Walden water would mingle with the sacred water of the Ganges"—and this was Thoreau's way of saying that the insights and thoughts that his time at Walden had revealed to him were of the profoundest significance for all people and their birthright.

—Perry D. Westbrook

THE WASTE LAND.
Poem by T.S. Eliot, 1922.

When *The Waste Land* first appeared, in 1922, it was widely rejected as arid and incomprehensible, even as a tasteless joke at the expense of its readers. A more perceptive response shows it to be neither. T.S. Eliot's poem works through "a heap of broken images," the reflection of a world of fragments; but the aim is to weave these fragments into a harmony, which however is not to be imposed upon them, but must emerge—if at all—at the end of the creative process.

The first of the poem's five sections—*The Burial of the Dead*—opens with an evocation of springtime memories, in which the month of rebirth becomes the month of deception, "breeding lilacs out of the dead land," tenuous intimations of life in "a heap of stony rubbish." In such a world certainty is sought in the ambiguous revelations of the medium Madame Sosostris, "known to be the wisest woman in Europe, / With a wicked pack of cards." She brings a series of sinister images—"the drowned Phoenician sailor," "Belladonna . . . The lady of situations," the Hanged Man—which will reappear in the course of the poem and which have in common a preoccupation with death under a variety of forms. This opening "movement" ends with a vision of the "Unreal City," where the crowds streaming each morning across London Bridge are seen as so many souls moving into Dante's Hell.

In the second section, *A Game of Chess*, the vision narrows to two sketches of vacancy and boredom in different "situations" of life. Both concern loveless "desire." A woman of leisure alternately addresses herself and her lover in tense staccato rhythms which answer to the emptiness and isolation stressed in an obsessive reiteration of the key word of the episode: "You know *nothing*? Do you see *nothing*? Do you remember / *Nothing*?" At this moment of rising tension a contrasting motif emerges in the form of an evocative echo from *The Tempest*: "Those are pearls that were his eyes." Two possible attitudes to death balance the sordid reality of "rat's alley" against the delicate beauty of Shakespeare's marine symbolism. A possible relationship between them may emerge by the end of the poem; but for the moment the sense of vacancy prevails in the return of the question "Are you alive or not? Is there nothing in your head?" and is underlined in a parallel episode by the gossip of two women in a working-class pub at the expense of a third who lives in fear of old age, unwanted children, and betrayal by her husband in search of "a good time" after demobilization. At the end of the "movement" the obsessive time-theme emerges in the final call of the barman—"Hurry up, please, it's time"—both as an urgent call to responsible choice and as an indication of the bleak reality which threatens to render it meaningless.

The third section, *The Fire Sermon*, is central to the entire conception. Against a background of the Thames, seen both in its commerce-stained modern aspect and in the more romantic light projected by the poets of the past, the pursuit of "desire" is embodied in the loveless seduction of a bored typist by "a small house agent's clerk." Seen through the eyes of a spectator, the blind seer Tiresias whose vision constitutes, as Eliot himself said, the substance of the poem, the episode marks the point at which its separate fragments begin to come together in a possible pattern. The Buddha and St. Augustine, representing ascetic tradition in East and West, are found to agree in presenting fire—the symbol of "desire"—as both consuming and purifying: "Burning burning burning burning / O Lord, thou pluckest me out." The first broken intimation of prayer prepares the way for as much positive resolution as the poem is prepared to offer.

After the short lyrical interlude *Death by Water*, which takes up a theme equivocally announced by Madame Sosostris and confirmed in the Shakespearean echo of *A Game of Chess*, the final "movement," *What the Thunder Said*, proposes a tentative ordering and recapitulation. Once more we are in the desert, the Waste Land; but the arid landscape is now associated with the Passion of Christ—the silence in the orchard, the red light on sweaty faces, the agony in stony places—and from it there emerges the vision (reality or illusion?) of the risen Saviour on the road to Emmaus. The dryness of the desert leads to a descent into delirium as the absent water—symbol of life and restoration—becomes an obsessive presence in the imagination of the suffering pilgrim.

The hoped for relief, however, does not come. The moment of vision is replaced by an impression, equally conceived in delirium, of general ruin. The "falling towers" of the great cities of the past—London, Rome, Athens, Jerusalem—are, like the city of *The Burial of the Dead*, "unreal," and the voices evocative of past beliefs which emerge from them sing "out of empty cisterns and exhausted wells." Yet once again, and at the culminating moment of delirium, the vision changes. The voice of the cock is heard, heralding the long-awaited break in the drought. As a "damp gust" promises rain for the parched soil, the thunder affirms as much positive vision as can be available to those who dwell in the Waste Land.

"Thus spoke the Thunder." Its message is conveyed in a triple Sanskrit exhortation: "Give, Sympathize, Control." The three words answer to a logical progression. What must be "given" is "The awful daring of a moment's surrender": acceptance of the risk involved in the commitment by which alone our lives may become more than empty memories preserved in blank obituaries. To "give," in turn, is to aspire to "sympathize," to relate our isolation to that of our fellow human beings imprisoned in the private worlds of their own experience. Those who have accepted the risk of commitment and projected it into sympathy may, according to the third and final admonition, aspire to exercise "control" over their lives. The "boat" which they steer may be expected to respond "gladly," in joyful affirmation, to the hand now—and only now—"expert with sail and oar."

We note, however, that this sketch of a possible release remains tentative. The "boat" *would have responded*: the statement remains conditional rather than directly affirmative. As the poem ends its shadowy protagonist sits on the shore, with the "arid plain" still in sight, though now behind him, tentatively surpassed. The picture of human endeavour is still dominated by collapse and ruin, but the hope has emerged that the lives of individuals may be redeemed by the effort to achieve such personal order as may be within our reach. "Shall I at least set my lands in order?" To this end the speaker has "shored" certain fragments of tradition against his "ruin": fragments which have been present through the poem in the form of "broken," disconnected images and which he may now aspire to relate positively to his developed experience. Though *The Waste Land* is not to be read as a poem of religious affirmation, it bears within itself implications of further progress.

—Derek A. Traversi

THE WEARY BLUES.
Poems by Langston Hughes, 1926.

Langston Hughes's first book was published in February 1926 almost simultaneous with his 24th birthday. The earliest poem in *The Weary Blues*, "When Sue Wears Red," was written when Hughes was 17 and still in high school. One of the most famous, "The Negro Speaks of Rivers," he composed at 18, shortly after his graduation. Yet this youthful volume contains some of Hughes's best-known and best-loved poetry.

Despite the book's title, it contains very few blues. Indeed, about half the book is lyric poems. Among these are some relatively traditional nature poems and poetry employing western images and conventions, such as *carpe diem* in several poems, the court fool—albeit black—in "The Jester," and the Pierrot figure in two poems. Yet even in such lyrics, Hughes employs amusing or startling imagery; the "March Moon" is joshed "Don't you know / It isn't nice to be naked?" and the "Caribbean Sunset" resembles "God having a hemorrhage, / Blood coughed across the sky."

For every bit of artificial diction such as "thou" in "Poem / To the Black Beloved" and "Song to the Dark Virgin," for every derivative cadence ("We buried him high on a windy hill, / But his soul went out to sea"), there are several verses of effective simplicity, such as the complete text of "Suicide's Note": "The calm, / Cool face of the river / Asked me for a kiss"; the close of "Sea Calm": "It is not good / For water / To be so still that way"; and the close of "Dream Variations": "Night coming tenderly / Black like me." What Hughes can do with the terse, reflective lyric may best be exemplified with one of the pieces known only as "Poem" and dedicated to "F.S.": "I loved my friend. / He went away from me. / There's nothing more to say. / The poem ends, / Soft as it began,— / I loved my friend."

If Hughes sometimes wrote of topics treated by bards of many another clime and time—death, the sea, love, dreams—and was influenced by other poets—particularly Carl Sandburg and Walt Whitman—he still generally chose as his focus his own people. If we have heard before something very like the refrain of "Harlem Night Song,"—"Come, / Let us roam the night together / Singing"—we have not heard this sung about roof tops in the ghetto. And so infused with his race are some of these early Hughes lyrics that they are truly original. The combination of historical perspective—"A queen from some time-dead Egyptian night / Walks once again"—and church shout—"Blow trumpets, Jesus!"—renders the teenage Hughes's tribute to Susanna Jones wearing red far above much verse by older writers.

This early influence of spirituals was only the first of many musical elements in Hughes's free verse. About a dozen of the book's poems reflect the form and mood of black music, the blues or jazz or both. Like most of *The Weary Blues*'s best poems, these love songs to Harlem are dramatic works, characterizing a person, describing a theatrical scene, telling a story, or addressing someone in monologue or dialogue. In "Jazzonia," "Six long-headed jazzers play," in "Danse Africaine" the tom-tom to a jazz beat "Stirs your blood," "Harlem Night Club" adjures the band "Play, PlAY, PLAY!", while the dancers in "Cabaret" whirl to a jazz-band which sobs, belying the form's apparent gaiety. "Lenox Avenue: Midnight" only tells us "The rhythm of life / Is a jazz rhythm," but "Negro Dancers"—one of Hughes's dialect poems—demonstrates this with its "Da da" imitation of the jazz instrumental. The greatest innovation in form, however, occurs in "The Cat and the Saxophone (2 A.M.)," which creates a verbal equivalent to syncopation with its interweaving of a lusty, liquor-swilling couple's conversation and a singer's wail. This extraordinary counterpoint is the poem about which Countée Cullen (who preferred to write and read bourgeois black verse) sneered—after questioning whether it was a poem—"I cannot say *This will never do*, but I feel that it ought never to have been done."

The same rhythmic risk-taking characterizes "Song for a Banjo Dance," an experiment which combines blues form and jazz riffs, one of many Hughes jive poems espousing a live-for-the-moment philosophy. Sexier is the blues "Strut and wiggle" of the "shameless gal" addressed in "To Midnight Nan at Leroy's," whereas the spirit of "Blues Fantasy" ranges from pain to laughter in a repertoire which reminds us that "I laugh to keep from crying" was a classic blues refrain before Hughes adapted it as a title for his fiction.

Most famous is the title poem about a blues pianist whose foot goes "Thump, thump, thump" on the floor, the "musical fool" who takes blues "from a black man's soul." Hughes had heard his Weary Blues refrain as a Kansas teenager, but it was his inner ear which created "Droning a drowsy syncopated tune, / Rocking back and forth to a mellow croon, / I heard a Negro play."

Because he dared to appropriate sensual, spontaneous music as his inspiration and to write about bohemian, urban types—

dancers, lovers, musicians, and, repeatedly, prostitutes—Hughes was castigated by the black bourgeoisie. They would have preferred raceless rhymings of June and moon, and were more tolerant of "Aunt Sue's Stories" for a child than the earthy, hip, often funny blues and jazz poems.

Of Hughes's other specifically race-based poems, several eventually emerged—as it became more respectable for a black poet to acknowledge and even revel in his blackness—as major contributions to American literature. "I, too, sing America. / I am the darker brother," Hughes insisted when, while penniless in Genoa, he watched his white brothers easily hired by ships which denied him employment. "I looked upon the Nile and raised the pyramids above it" he exulted in "The Negro Speaks of Rivers," while contemplating the ancient and enduring black soul "grown deep like the rivers." "The South," his first protest poem, excoriates Ku Klux Klan territory, while "Lament for Dark Peoples" broadens the indictment to encompass white colonialism world-wide and "Cross" speculates on the fate of mulattoes "neither white nor black." In "Proem" (later reprinted as "Negro") and "My People" Hughes praises his race generally, whereas in "Mother to Son" the pride becomes a more personal injunction—in a maternal persona—not to give up when "it's kinder hard. / Don't you fall now— / For I'se still goin', honey, / I'se still climbin', / And life for me ain't been no crystal stair."

—Tish Dace

WHO'S AFRAID OF VIRGINIA WOOLF?
Play by Edward Albee, 1962.

Savage and beautiful, cruel and compassionate, one of the funniest of modern plays yet one of the most devastating, Edward Albee's *Who's Afraid of Virginia Woolf?* has been hailed by some as a tragedy and by others as a comedy; a smaller group—among them the Columbia University Trustees who denied it the 1963 Pulitzer Prize—simply regard it as a dirty play. For that reason, John Chapman's contemporary review was headlined "For Dirty Minded Females Only," while Robert Coleman insisted "No red-blooded American would bring his wife to this shocking play." Contrast these responses to Dorothy Kilgallen's judgment "People who are reluctant to face life will be reluctant to face this play."

What so profoundly divides critics is a disturbing domestic drama which takes place on a sexual battleground. Choosing, like Strindberg as well as the Greek tragedians, the subject of philos-aphilos, or the mixture of love and hatred expressed within families, Albee dissects two academic marriages. The hostilities occur during a long night in which huge quantities of booze are consumed and large numbers of obscenities are hurled about. These and the play's sexuality prompted the Lord Chamberlain to demand extensive changes in the London production, beginning with the play's first words: "Jesus H. Christ" became "Mary H. Magdalen."

Taking his title—with Leonard Woolf's permission—from a Greenwich Village graffito which suggests the possibility of living without dependence on comforting allusions, Albee examines the ways we try to get through life, or at least the part of life involving sex and career. His characters, perhaps named after the Washingtons, are George, a history professor, and Martha, his wife, who return home after a party given by her father, the college president, whom George would one day replace if only he had administrative ability, or even the academic ability to make it to full professor. Soon they are joined by Nick and Honey, a younger academic couple whose revelations about their own marriage prove catalytic to George and Martha and vice versa. After they have had a try at humiliating one another, Martha unsuccessfully tries to seduce Nick, and Honey gets sick in the bathroom. George wins the war with Martha by killing off their imaginary son, and he exorcises a few of Nick and Honey's spooks in the bargain. Feisty Martha is reduced to frightened clinging to George, ironically the only man who ever made her happy, the only man she ever loved.

The play's sado-masochism—which prompted a *New York Times* critic to paraphrase Elizabeth Barrett Browning as "How can I hurt thee? Let me count the ways"—involves everyone wounding and wounded by everyone else. Frequently the weapons are words—what Norman Nadel terms Albee's "acetylene torch dialogue"—yet the immoral choices designed to damage others are far more telling. The "Fun and Games" (as Act I is called) which George sums up as "Good; better; best; bested," are mostly Martha having brutal fun at George's expense, as in her changing into sexy clothes, her "blue games for the guests," her account of George as a "bog" and a "flop," and her telling Honey she and George have a son—the latter a violation of the game-playing rules.

George retaliates first by taking aim at Martha with a short-barreled trick shotgun, second, when hostilities escalate in the "Walpurgisnacht" section, by attempted strangulation when Martha has embarrassed him over his novel, and, still later, by feigned indifference to Martha's seduction of Nick. By that time, however, to Martha's attempts to bed Nick and bag George ("Hump the Hostess" and "Humiliate the Host") has been added George's game of "Get the Guests." His efforts are made easier by Nick's surprising candor regarding his opportunistic marrying for money as well as Honey's honesty about her fear of pregnancy.

Spectators tend to accept the naivety with which Nick and Honey confide in George, along with their failure to leave the party as George and Martha's private war widens to include their guests. Although some critics have questioned the credibility of the younger couple's behavior, during the play's performance the psychological violence seems necessary and the son's symbolic murder in Act III—George's victory—inevitable. The masterful third act, dramatized with economy of words and actions, proves almost as devastating to an audience as to Martha. By the time George counterpoints Martha's speech on maternal protection with the requiem mass's "dies irae," we've inferred that this play—written by an adopted son—is about not one, but two childless couples.

If any thoughts intrude during the searing final minutes, they are likely to be comparisons of George's deliberate destruction of their solace in the fantasy son to the temporary loss of pipe dreams in *The Iceman Cometh* or the permanent replacement of illusion by confrontation with truth in *Long Day's Journey into Night* and *That Championship Season*. Although a few critics have delved for arcane symbols here—finding Khrushchev in Nick's character, representation of the American Dream in the son, or a figurative gay relationship in George and Martha's marriage—so lacerating and real is George and Martha's agonizing mutual dependence that anything which obscures it must be dismissed as extraneous to the play.

—Tish Dace

WINESBURG, OHIO.
Stories by Sherwood Anderson, 1919.

Winesburg, Ohio originated in observations of an actual place. Sherwood Anderson wrote, "I made last year a series of intensive studies of people of my home town, Clyde, Ohio" (letter, 14 November 1916). Yet the stories that comprise the finished work are so selectively developed according to a central theme that Winesburg must be understood as a mythical town populated by imaginary beings. That theme is announced in a prefatory sketch, "The Book of the Grotesque," which preserves the author's original title for his book and intimates his purpose. For *Winesburg* associates characters who resemble one another in being eccentric, ludicrous, absurd, persons who are in some way ridiculous.

In form the work is a cycle of stories, a genre which Anderson may have helped to popularize among American writers. "I have even sometimes thought that the novel form does not fit an American writer," he said, "that it is a form which had been brought in. What is wanted is a new looseness; and in *Winesburg* I had made my own form" (*Memoirs*). Such a form brings together individual stories which yet reflect upon and modify each other so as to create a total effect much richer and more complex than its parts. Anderson integrates his stories most obviously by their shared theme of the grotesque, but also by other insistently recurrent motifs, such as loneliness, isolation, the failure of communication, and frustrated or compromising sexual experience. Out of this reiteration of themes in a minor key a prevailing mood develops, a kind of autumnal mood of resignation, acceptance, reflectiveness: " 'What is the matter with me? I will do something dreadful if I am not careful,' she thought, and turning her face to the wall, began trying to force herself to face bravely the fact that many people must live and die alone, even in Winesburg" ("Adventure").

Another salient connective device is the reappearance of some characters in more than one story: Dr. Reefy, Kate Swift, Elizabeth Willard, and others. Most important among these is George Willard, an adolescent boy, whose work as the sole reporter for the Winesburg *Eagle* weekly newspaper places him in a pivotal position within the community. In this role George both seeks knowledge of the town and, because of his attitudes of curiosity and responsiveness, is sought by the grotesques in their efforts to communicate. Moreover, George aspires to be a writer, and this circumstance permits both the characters and the authorial persona to reflect upon the writer's vocation: " 'You must not become a mere peddler of words. The thing to learn is to know what people are thinking about, not what they say' " ("The Teacher"). " 'He is groping about, trying to find himself,' she thought. 'He is not a dull clod, all words and smartness. Within him is a secret something that is striving to grow. It is the thing I let be killed in myself' " ("The Mother").

The figure of the writer appears first in the prefatory sketch in the guise of an old man who has kept alive "the young thing within him," i.e., the imagination or inspiration or desire that causes him to envision "a long procession of figures before his eyes." This old man would seem to be an alter ego for George, the writer that he aspires to be or that he will become. For both are moved by pity for the grotesques. "The grotesques were not all horrible. Some were amusing, some almost beautiful." Here the voice of the authorial persona, speaking for the aged writer, guides the reader's response. This voice of the persona, which is in some sense that of the author, is yet another of the unifying principles of the book. It is a reflective, sympathetic, interpretive voice, speaking in a style that despite its seemingly colloquial effect, is highly contrived. Motif words and images supersede direct statement. Such motifs are dreams and dreaming, adventure, and, as we see above, words. The movements of hands, and the placing of hands upon the shoulders of another character, are gestures emblematic of the impulse to communicate; and looking out a window is a characteristic attitude of the passive grotesques. George Willard's own alternatives, to stay at home or to venture forth into the world, are intimated by images that masquerade as simple description: "[His room] had a window looking down into an alleyway and one that looked across railroad tracks to Biff Carter's Lunch Room facing the railroad station" ("The Thinker").

As these techniques suggest, Anderson's style has a poetic quality. He has been praised for his capacity to render the lyrical intensity of a captured moment of defiance, self-discovery, resignation, or the like. Stories in *Winesburg* that are particularly admired for this effect, sometimes compared to a Joycean epiphany, include "Hands," "The Strength of God," and "The Untold Lie."

—Jean Frantz Blackall

WINTERSET.
Play by Maxwell Anderson, 1935.

As a verse drama with a contemporary setting, Maxwell Anderson's *Winterset* ranks alongside T.S. Eliot's *The Family Reunion* in its achievement. However, as an American popular play, it also addresses the difficulty of accommodating modern vernacular in verse, the stylistic resistance of poetic tragedy to fast movement across the stage, and the uneasy demarcation between the "sublime" and the pretentious in the theatre. All of these have been advanced as obstacles to Anderson's ambitions in practical terms.

Anderson, who a decade earlier had achieved a pragmatic, down-to-earth realism in his war play *What Price Glory?*, could scarcely have chosen a more difficult story for a modern poetic drama in *Winterset*: the effects on a judge, a wrongfully executed man's son, and the recently released criminal of the emergence of new evidence about a murder. In romantic drama, the odd highwayman or anti-social subversive had occasionally been introduced, but Anderson's whole cast derives from such a milieu; apart from the judge and an old Jewish patriarch, all the characters move within a gangster subculture of "punks."

The story's source in recent history was well known; Anderson had in fact already used it in another play. Consequently, the plausibilities and constraints of realism could be defied from the start. Trock, a terminally ill recidivist with a style of invective that echoes Coriolanus, prowls the stage ominously; Garth, his accomplice whose evidence could have convicted him of murder, appears and is intimidated. In the next scene, Mio, whose father was wrongly executed in Trock's place, arrives, as does the (now demented) Judge. The coincidence of all this, within the first three scenes of the play, should leave audiences and critics in no doubt that behaviour is not being plotted naturalistically. Apart from gestures of contrition, defiance, self-justification, and intimidation, the remaining action primarily consists just of Mio's choosing between his revenge impulse and his growing love for Garth's sister, poignantly terminated when the two of them are gunned down by the gangsters.

Some disparity may be argued between Anderson's intentions and his achievement in this play. Several extensive theoretical works leave no doubt of his serious ambition to create a new poetic drama that would be both modern and popular; in this objective, he stands in the company of W.B. Yeats, Eliot, and Christopher Fry. His work, like theirs, has drawn comparisons with Greek and Elizabethan classics, but he is the only one of this group to have grounded his work within an urban proletarian context. However, the fact that this play was unquestionably popular—with a long initial Broadway run—generated scepticism about the profundity of its thought as well as about the intrinsic value of its poetry.

In terms of achievement, one notes the play's audacious use of a constructivist set; the "poetic" qualities of Jo Mielziner's symbolist design for the premiere were widely praised. Above the tenements on stage, a gigantic span of a bridgehead soars over the characters and the audience, creating a Promethean arena in which the set provides a concrete correlative to the aspirations and frustrations of the collective theatre population (just as the poetry provides a verbal correlative). In the case of a playwright who did not protest so vigorously that his objectives lay elsewhere, this would be termed expressionistic, and related to the theme of transcendence and the dignity of mankind that is asserted so strongly in the play's closing suicide, a common element in continental expressionism (as opposed to the American practice of Eugene O'Neill, Elmer Rice, and others).

Similarly, when the playwright's stated aims are ignored, the play's affinities with the 1940's musical become the more noticeable. Anderson's stage directions, and his management of a large cast, often seem to anticipate this theatrical style, and so does his use of the poetic "solo," deployed to embellish or monumentalise the thought rather than to advance the action; in fact, the chief justification for Esdras, Garth's father, has nothing to do with the story, but offers a line of pragmatic or homiletic commentary in the guise of vatic poetry.

Within three years of *Winterset* Anderson was involved in his first collaboration with Brecht's former composer, Kurt Weill, in *Knickerbocker Holiday*, and after World War II the two would produce *Lost in the Stars*, a remarkable stage musical adaptation of Alan Paton's *Cry, The Beloved Country*; the songs on themes related to the title, to do with man's alienation, injustice, and earth-bound blindness when exposed to celestial light, may all be interpreted as an expansion of Esdras's final speech to his son over his daughter's body in *Winterset*. To suggest the emergence of stage musical from poetic tragedy might, to some, imply trivialisation, but it was a logical development in view of Anderson's commitment to popular culture.

—Howard McNaughton

WISE BLOOD.
Novel by Flannery O'Connor, 1952.

"For the author Hazel's integrity lies in his not being able to get rid of the ragged figure who moves from tree to tree in the back of his mind." According to Flannery O'Connor's interpretation of *Wise Blood* the ragged figure is Christ. She underlines the influence of her own convictions in the writing of the novel in the same note to the second edition: Hazel is a "Christian malgré lui," the novel was written by an author for whom "the belief in Christ is a matter of life and death," and who believes that "free will does not mean one will, but many wills conflicting in one man. Freedom cannot be conceived simply. It is a mystery . . ."

Can a man driven to kill another and to maim himself by his inability to get rid of the ragged figure really be called free? What choice can Hazel make, pursued as he is by the figure, with his back against the wall? He can turn his back to it, but there is only a wall ahead, and the figure is behind, hounding him. He does not have many wills, he has two wills, one for and one against, and he is fighting a Christ who has all the cards in his hands, who can turn coincidence into inevitability, accident into necessity, who can use the world for purposes that are so alien that whoever is being used is perceived as a monster. Even the clouds take shape, "the sky was . . . clear and even, with only one cloud in it, a large blinding white one with curls and a beard," and change shape to underline the pervasiveness of the presence from which Hazel is trying to flee, "the blinding white cloud had turned into a bird with long thin wings and was disappearing in the opposite direction." Hazel is not free, that is the message that comes through loud and clear. Or rather, his only freedom comes from embracing the ragged figure, blinding himself and walking away from the wall hand in hand with it, wearing wire around his chest and stones in his shoes. What kind of freedom is that?

Hazel denies his call to Christianity with the same vehemence with which he would have embraced it, and acts with a violence towards himself and others that echoes in its particularity the violence in every manifestation of religious extremism, be it the primitive sacrificing of a life to the gods or a holy war or any ascetic's life down the ages. That is the mystery that seems to lie at the core of this novel: the mystery of the impulse towards holiness (which a Christian will call grace, but which is not the prerogative of Christianity), and the destructiveness of that impulse when carried to extremes. What is the necessity, in the eyes and in the will of a creative God, for such manifestations? What good do they do? Can it really, profoundly be said that the necessity for such distortions, for what could in many cases be seen as a depravity simply stems from the presence of sin in the world, that it is necessary to have those who act destructively from goodness, from rectitude, from integrity, to balance the mindless destructiveness of those who are evil? What good comes of it?

Certainly in *Wise Blood*, as in Dostoevsky's *The Idiot*, the result of goodness acting in the world is destructiveness, and although it is true that each character in *Wise Blood* has a moment when he or she could acknowledge the gnawing importance of Christ, and that this moment is brought about by Hazel's presence in their life, it is even more true that they all act with conspicuous lack of freedom, and that they seem simply instruments to drive Hazel to recognition and submission to the ragged figure. Who is "saved"? Not Enoch, last seen in a gorilla suit, staring "over the valley at the uneven skyline of the city." Not the false prophet, mowed down by an implacable Hazel, not Hawks or Onnie Jay Holy who disappear back into their lives of exploitation, not Sabbath who ends up in a detention home. Hazel, we suppose, is saved. But his inability to free himself of his religious impulse already guaranteed his salvation, and freedom and grace seem curiously spurious in his case.

There is only one person in the book who retains a human ambiguity in response to the call of religion and of Christianity and yet is transformed and converted by contact with Hazel and by sharing his (apparently) self-imposed martyrdom: the landlady, who on the last page "felt as if she had finally got to the beginning of something she couldn't begin." Can it be that in a world that moves, creates, and destroys itself through the conflict of wills, a God is fashioning human beings (those we call prophets), who have in fact no real choice, but are simply there as instruments to make the possibilities clearer to others? Can it be that Hazel's life and death make sense only to the extent that they led one, and only one, human being to a recognition of the essential mystery of life? Can it be that the apparently absurd convictions of the author of *Wise Blood* make sense to the extent that they lead us, in the reading, to the same recognition, and to gaze, with the landlady, into "the dark tunnel" until we too see "the pinpoint of light," even if it is "so far away that [we cannot] hold it steady in [our] mind"?

—M.J. Fitzgerald

THE WONDERFUL WIZARD OF OZ.
Novel by L. Frank Baum, 1900.

The first of fabulist L. Frank Baum's books in his Oz series, *The Wonderful Wizard of Oz* is strong neither in literary style nor in grand design. Yet it is compelling and multi-layered enough to captivate children and gratify serious adult readers and critics. (For an extensive survey of critical responses to the novel and other Baum works, see *Twentieth-Century Literary Criticism 7*, edited by Sharon K. Hall, 1982.)

Like earlier narratives of travel in exotic lands, *The Wizard of Oz* dispenses with the credible and gives us marvels: talking animals, artificial humans, and sorcerers. However, the protagonist is not the traditional masculine model of courage and enterprise, but a very young girl whose basic concern is finding a way of returning to her family. Whirled away from her home on the Kansas prairie by a cyclone and dumped down in the Eastern region of the Land of Oz, Dorothy must cope with an array of unfamiliar creatures (some hazardous) and with a perilous obstacle course on alien soil before she can have any hope of returning to Kansas. She is aided to an extent by talismanic objects (a pair of magic slippers and a magic cap) and by a protective kiss from a good witch, but her hindrances are many, and the Wizard, on whom she relies for assistance, turns out to be a fraud.

An intriguing feature of *The Wizard of Oz* is its framework of allusions to American life. No one line of reasoning can be pushed very far, but a general if incomplete outline may be suggested. First, a necessary word on topography. The beautiful, jewel-rich Land of Oz, surrounded by an enormous desert, is divided into four zones. The North and South are each presided over by a good witch; the East and West (the latter a yellow-colored country of gold) are each dominated by a wicked witch. In the middle of Oz is the Emerald City, ruled by the Wizard himself, the Great Oz, in solitary splendor.

The cyclone drops Dorothy's house down on the wicked witch of the East killing her instantly. Thus, assuming that Baum was taking a populist view of the political-economic situation, we have the predatory Eastern capitalists ravaging American midwestern farmers, and laborers generally. Dorothy and her companions (Scarecrow, Cowardly Lion, Tin Woodman—symbols of the exploited classes) must follow the Yellow Brick Road (i.e., the current "gold standard") to find the Wizard and ask him to grant their wishes. But Dorothy has the dead witch's silver slippers to wear as amulets (the proposed "free silver" policy which would have brought economic relief to those oppressed by the federal government's single standard of gold for the national currency). These slippers, which will eventually carry her back to Kansas, once she learns the appropriate ritual to use with them, would have taken her back home at any time, had she only known that ritual. The ineffective Wizard may represent one of the Presidents of the 1890's—Benjamin Harrison, Grover Cleveland, William McKinley—or all three or perhaps William Jennings Bryan, the repeatedly unsuccessful Presidential candidate, advocate of "free silver." (A neatly-argued political-economic interpretation that has been useful here is the 1964 study by Henry M. Littlefield.) North and South both appear as good—or at least safe—regions, but East and West suggest evil, until their witches are destroyed. Baum may have had something more in mind regarding the West (whose wicked witch Dorothy annihilates by dousing her with water) than the gold fever of 1849 and thereafter: namely, the ruinous freight rates imposed on western farmers by the railroad "octopus."

Psychological interpretations of *The Wizard of Oz* are also possible; Dorothy is removed from her proper authority figures—aunt and uncle (who remain safely behind in Kansas)—and is thrown among outsize *toy* figures for a strange interlude. Two temporary authority figures (witches) signify harm, but she suffers relatively little on their account; two others (also witches) are benevolent; and the leading authority figure in the land of her temporary exile (the Wizard) is actually a humbug. By the end of the story the small girl has been neither initiated nor transformed, just blissfully restored to her original guardians.

Underlying all other interpretations of *The Wizard of Oz* is a *pattern of substitutions* for coping with life's problems, real and imagined. Dorothy lives with substitute parents. Returning from Oz she finds that the old farmhouse the cyclone carried away has been replaced by a new one. The Wizard of her expectations becomes the con man of her experience, substituting special effects for the manifestations of himself that he wants others to believe in. He offers Dorothy's companions makeshift tokens (which they accept) for the things they want most: courage, brains, a heart. Dorothy's means of transportation back home should be the Wizard's balloon, but instead it is the magic slippers from the wicked witch of the East. Everywhere, forces of good seem to replace forces of evil. Even the Cowardly Lion displaces his evil counterpart—a giant tarantula terrorizing the creatures of the forest—so that he can assume his proper role as King of the Beasts. The one substitution that cannot endure—the desert-locked Land of Oz replacing Dorothy's poor, prairie-locked farm home in Kansas—at least serves a useful function in that it brings Dorothy and her surrogate parents even closer together than they were earlier. In addition it points up the eternal truth of the old adage: "North, South, East, or West—*home*'s the best!"

—Samuel Irving Bellman

CHRONOLOGY

Abbreviations:

- (f) fiction
- (p) play
- (pr) prose
- (v) verse

Chronology prepared by Marshall Walker.

DATE	AUTHOR AND TITLE	EVENT
1492		Christopher Columbus discovers West Indies, landing at San Salvador
1502		Amerigo Vespucci sails down eastern seaboard of South America
1513		Florida discovered for Spain by Ponce de León
1558		Elizabeth I's reign (1558–1603)
1585		Attempt under Sir Walter Ralegh to found colony in North Carolina; abandoned 1586
1588	Harriot, Thomas (c. 1560–1621): *A Brief and True Report of the New Found Land of Virginia* (pr)	Defeat of Spanish Armada by English fleet
1603		James I's reign (1603–25)
1607		Colony of Virginia inaugurated at Jamestown by Captain John Smith
1608	Smith, John (1580–1631): *A True Relation* (pr)	
1611		King James Version of the Bible is published
1616	Smith, John: *A Description of New England* (pr)	
1620	*The Mayflower Compact* (pr)	Voyage of the *Mayflower*; settlement of Plymouth by Pilgrims
1624	Smith, John: *The Generall History of Virginia, New England, and the Summer Isles* (pr)	
1625		Charles I's reign (1625–49)
1626		Dutch colony of New Amsterdam founded on Hudson River; Manhattan Island purchased from Indians for about 60 guilders' worth of cloth and trinkets
1629		Colony of Massachusetts Bay founded
1636		Harvard, first American university, founded
1637	Morton, Thomas (c. 1575–c. 1647): *New English Canaan* (pr)	
1638		First printing press in America established in Cambridge, Massachusetts

DATE	AUTHOR AND TITLE	EVENT
1640	*The Bay Psalm Book* (v) printed in Cambridge, Massachusetts; in use until 1773	
1641	Cotton, John (1584–1652): *The Way of Life* (pr)	
1643		Colonies of New England form New England Federation
1644	Cotton, John: *The Keyes of the Kingdom of Heaven* (pr) Williams, Roger (1603–83): *The Bloudy Tenent of Persecution, for Cause of Conscience* (pr)	
1649	Mather, Richard (1596–1669): *A Platform of Church Discipline* (pr) Winthrop, John (1588–1649): *History of New England* (pr) completed (published 1825–26)	Trial and execution of Charles I Commonwealth (1649–60)
1650	Bradford, William (1590–1657): *History of Plymouth Plantation* (pr) completed (published 1856) Bradstreet, Anne (c. 1612–72): *The Tenth Muse Lately Sprung Up in America* (v)	
1652	Williams, Roger: *The Bloudy Tenent Yet More Bloudy* (pr)	
1659	Hooker, Thomas (1586–1647): "A True Sight of Sin" (pr)	
1660		Restoration of monarchy Charles II's reign (1660–85)
1662	Wigglesworth, Michael (1631–1705): *The Day of Doom* (v)	
1664		English seize New Amsterdam, later renamed New York
1676		War against Indians in New England ends Destruction of Jamestown by Nathaniel Bacon and followers
1678	Bradstreet, Anne: *Severall Poems*	
1682	Rowlandson, Mary (c. 1637–1711): *The Soveraignty and Goodness of God . . . Being a Narrative of the Captivity and Restauration of Mrs. Mary Rowlandson* (pr)	
1685		James II's reign (1685–88)
1689		William III and Mary II's (d. 1694) reign (1689–1702)
1691		Plymouth Colony absorbed by Massachusetts
1692		Witchcraft trials in Salem, Massachusetts
1693	Mather, Increase (1639–1723): *Cases of Conscience Concerning Evil Spirits* (pr)	
1700	Sewall, Samuel (1652–1730): *The Selling of Joseph* (pr)	
1701		Foundation of Collegiate School of America, later Yale University
1702	Mather, Cotton (1663–1728): *Magnalia Christi Americana* (pr)	Anne's reign (1702–14) Asiento Guinea Company formed to develop slave trade between Africa and America

DATE	AUTHOR AND TITLE	EVENT
1704		The *News-Letter*, first continuously published weekly paper, founded by John Campbell of Boston
1708	Cooke (or Cook), Ebenezer (c. 1667–c. 1732): *The Sot-Weed Factor* (v)	
1714		George I's reign (1714–27)
1725	Franklin, Benjamin (1706–90): *A Dissertation on Liberty and Necessity, Pleasure and Pain* (pr)	
1727		George II's reign (1727–60)
1728	Byrd, William, II (1674–1744): *A History of the Dividing Line Run in the Year 1728* (between Virginia and North Carolina; pr; published 1841)	Vitus Bering discovers Straits between Asia and North America
1729	Sewall, Samuel completes his *Diary* (pr; published in 3 vols., 1878–82)	
1731		Building (to 1751) of State House, Philadelphia, later Independence Hall, designed by Alexander Hamilton Benjamin Franklin founds free public library in Philadelphia
1732	Franklin, Benjamin: first issue of *Poor Richard's Almanack* (pr)	Founding of Georgia, last British colony in America
1733	Byrd, William, II: *A Journey to the Land of Eden, A.D. 1733* (pr; published 1841)	Molasses Act: American trade with West Indies forbidden
1740	Edwards, Jonathan (1703–58): *Personal Narrative* (pr)	
1741		Jonathan Edwards preaches sermon *Sinners in the Hands of an Angry God* in Enfield, Connecticut
1745		Foundation of Philadelphia Academy, later (1789) University of Pennsylvania
1746		Princeton University and Library founded
1754		French and Indian War in North America; George Washington defeated at Great Meadows George II founds King's College, New York (Columbia University)
1756		Start of Seven Years War
1760		George III's reign (1760–1820)
1763		Peace of Paris, ending Seven Years War
1764		Sugar Act levied
1765		Stamp Act; Patrick Henry's speech to Virginia House of Burgesses
1766		Stamp Act repealed; withdrawal of British troops from Boston Mason-Dixon Line marks boundaries between Pennsylvania and Maryland, separating free and slave regions

DATE	AUTHOR AND TITLE	EVENT
1767	Dickinson, John (1732–1808): *Letters from a Farmer in Pennsylvania to the Inhabitants of the British Colonies* (pr); first letters printed in Pennsylvania newspapers	
1770		Boston Massacre Repeal of American import duties except for that on tea
1773		Boston Tea Party
1774	Woolman, John (1720–72): *Journal* (pr)	Parliamentary suppression of opposition to tea duty First meeting of Continental Congress in Philadelphia
1775		Revolutionary War; Battle of Bunker's Hill; Paul Revere's ride; Battle of Concord and Lexington
1776	Paine, Thomas (1737–1809): *Common Sense* (pr) and first of 13 pamphlets in *American Crisis* series (pr) Jefferson, Thomas (1743–1826): *Declaration of Independence* (pr) Trumbull, John (1750–1831): *M'Fingal: A Modern Epic Poem*	Declaration of Independence from Britain
1780		American Academy of Sciences founded in Boston
1781	Freneau, Philip (1752–1832): *The British Prison-Ship* (v)	British under Cornwallis surrender to Washington at Yorktown
1782	Crèvecoeur, Hector St. John de (1735–1813): *Letters from an American Farmer* (pr)	Bank of America established in Philadelphia
1783		Treaty of Paris ends Revolutionary War
1785	Dwight, Timothy (1752–1817): *The Conquest of Canaan* (v)	Dollar established as official U.S. currency
1786	Barlow, Joel (1754–1812), John Trumbull, and others: *The Anarchiad* (v; concluded 1787)	Daniel Shays's Rebellion in Massachusetts
1788	Hamilton, Alexander (1757–1804), James Madison (1751–1836), and John Jay (1745–1829): *The Federalist* (pr)	
1789	Brown, William Hill (1765–93): *The Power of Sympathy* (f)	U.S. Constitution adopted George Washington administration (1789–97)
1791	Bartram, William (1739–1823): *Travels Through North and South Carolina, Georgia, East and West Florida* (pr) Franklin, Benjamin: *Autobiography* (pr)	Bill of Rights becomes law
1792	Brackenridge, Hugh Henry (1748–1816): *Modern Chivalry* (f; completed 1815)	Invention of the cotton gin by Eli Whitney U.S. Mint established
1797		John Adams administration (1797–1801)
1798	Brown, Charles Brockden (1771–1810): *Wieland* (f)	
1799	Brown, Charles Brockden: *Ormond* (f), *Edgar Huntly* (f), *Arthur Mervyn* (f; publication completed 1800)	Death of George Washington
1800	Weems, Mason Locke (1759–1825): *The Life and Memorable Actions of George Washington* (pr)	Library of Congress established

DATE	AUTHOR AND TITLE	EVENT
1801		Thomas Jefferson administration (1801–09)
1803		Louisiana Purchase
1804		Alexander Hamilton killed in duel with Aaron Burr
1808		Importing of slaves forbidden by Federal Government
1809	Irving, Washington (1783–1859): *A History of New-York* (pr)	James Madison administration (1809–17) Sequoya (c. 1760–1843) begins to develop writing system for Cherokee Indians
1812		War of 1812
1814	Key, Francis Scott (1779–1843): "The Star-Spangled Banner" (v)	Washington, D.C., burned by British troops
1817		James Monroe administration (1817–25)
1819	Irving, Washington: *The Sketch Book of Geoffrey Crayon, Gent.* (f; publication completed 1820)	
1820	Cooper, James Fenimore (1789–1851): *Precaution* (f)	Founding of Liberian Republic for freed slaves Missouri Compromise
1821	Bryant, William Cullen (1794–1878): *Poems* Cooper, James Fenimore: *The Spy* (f)	*Saturday Evening Post* begins publication
1823	Cooper, James Fenimore: *The Pilot* (f), *The Pioneers* (f)	Monroe Doctrine
1825		John Quincy Adams administration (1825–29)
1826	Cooper, James Fenimore: *The Last of the Mohicans* (f)	
1827	Audubon, John James (1785–1851): first sections of *The Birds of America* (pr; completed 1838) Cooper, James Fenimore: *The Prairie* (f) Poe, Edgar Allan (1809–49): *Tamerlane and Other Poems*	Disciples of Christ founded by Alexander Campbell
1828	Webster, Noah (1758–1843): *An American Dictionary of the English Language* (pr)	Washington Square Park created in New York
1829		Andrew Jackson administration (1829–37)
1830	Smith, Joseph (1805–44): *Book of Mormon* (pr)	Debate in Congress between Daniel Webster and Robert Y. Hayne on the nature of the Union
1831	Bird, Robert Montgomery (1806–54): *The Gladiator* (p) Poe, Edgar Allan: *Poems*	Nat Turner's rebellion
1832	Irving, Washington: *The Alhambra* (f)	Anti-slavery Abolitionist Party founded in Boston
1835	Tocqueville, Alexis de (French; 1805–59): *Democracy in America*, vol. 1 (pr; vol. 2, 1840)	New York *Herald* founded Samuel Colt patents his revolver
1836	Emerson, Ralph Waldo (1803–82): *Nature* (pr)	
1837	Emerson, Ralph Waldo: "The American Scholar" (pr), Phi Beta Kappa address at Harvard Hawthorne, Nathaniel (1804–64): *Twice-Told Tales* (f)	Martin Van Buren administration (1837–41)
1838	Poe, Edgar Allan: *The Narrative of Arthur Gordon Pym* (f)	Underground railway organized by abolitionists

DATE	AUTHOR AND TITLE	EVENT
1839	Audubon, John James: *Ornithological Biography* (pr) Longfellow, Henry Wadsworth (1807–82): *Voices of the Night* (v)	10,000 Mormons settle at Nauvoo, Illinois (formerly Commerce)
1840	Cooper, James Fenimore: *The Pathfinder* (f) Poe, Edgar Allan: *Tales of the Grotesque and Arabesque* (f)	Transcendentalist magazine *The Dial* founded under editorship of Margaret Fuller (1810–50)
1841	Cooper, James Fenimore: *The Deerslayer* (f) Emerson, Ralph Waldo: *Essays* (pr)	William Henry Harrison administration (1841) John Tyler administration (1841–45) New York *Tribune* founded by Horace Greeley
1843	Prescott, William Hickling (1796–1859): *History of the Conquest of Mexico* (pr)	Joseph Smith authorizes Mormon polygamy
1845	Mowatt, Anna Cora (1819–70): *Fashion; or, Life in New York* (p) Poe, Edgar Allan: *Tales* (f), *The Raven and Other Poems*	James K. Polk administration (1845–49) U.S. annexes Texas *Scientific American* begins publication
1846	Hawthorne, Nathaniel: *Mosses from an Old Manse* (f) Melville, Herman (1819–91): *Typee* (f) Whittier, John Greenleaf (1807–92): *Voices of Freedom* (v)	U.S. war with Mexico Mormons under Brigham Young set out for Utah Smithsonian Institution founded in Washington, D.C.
1847	Emerson, Ralph Waldo: *Poems* Longfellow, Henry Wadsworth: *Evangeline* (v) Melville, Herman: *Omoo* (f) Prescott, William Hickling: *History of the Conquest of Peru* (pr)	U.S. troops capture Mexico City Salt Lake City founded by Mormons Gold discovered in California More than 200,000 leave Ireland, many bound for U.S.
1848	Lowell, James Russell (1819–91): *The Biglow Papers*, first series (v/pr)	American Association for the Advancement of Science End of Mexican war
1849	Parkman, Francis (1823–93): *The California and Oregon Trail* (pr) Thoreau, Henry David (1817–62): "Civil Disobedience" (pr), *A Week on the Concord and Merrimack Rivers* (pr)	Zachary Taylor administration (1849–50) William Hunt invents safety pin "Bloomers" introduced by Amelia Jenks Bloomer
1850	Emerson, Ralph Waldo: *Representative Men* (pr) Hawthorne, Nathaniel: *The Scarlet Letter* (f) Melville, Herman: *White-Jacket* (f)	Millard Fillmore administration (1850–53) *Harper's New Monthly Magazine* founded Slave trade forbidden in District of Columbia *Raftsmen Playing Cards* (painting) completed by George Caleb Bingham Building of St. Patrick's Cathedral, New York (completed 1879) by James Renwick
1851	Hawthorne, Nathaniel: *The House of the Seven Gables* (f) Melville, Herman: *Moby-Dick* (f) Parkman, Francis: *The Conspiracy of Pontiac* (pr)	First U.S. state prohibition law voted in Maine
1852	Hawthorne, Nathaniel: *The Blithedale Romance* (f) Melville, Herman: *Pierre; or, The Ambiguities* (f) Stowe, Harriet Beecher (1811–96): *Uncle Tom's Cabin* (f)	Wells, Fargo stagecoach company founded in New York Governor of California seeks land grants to encourage further Chinese immigration
1853		Franklin Pierce administration (1853–57)
1854	Thoreau, Henry David: *Walden* (pr)	Republican Party formally established
1855	Boker, George Henry (1823–90): *Francesca da Rimini* (p) Longfellow, Henry Wadsworth: *The Song of Hiawatha* (v) Whitman, Walt (1819–92): *Leaves of Grass* (v)	John Bartlett publishes his compilation, *Familiar Quotations*

DATE	AUTHOR AND TITLE	EVENT
1856	Melville, Herman: *The Piazza Tales* (f)	Osawatomie Massacre by John Brown
1857		James Buchanan administration (1857–61) *Atlantic Monthly* begins publication
1858	Holmes, Oliver Wendell (1809–94): *The Autocrat of the Breakfast-Table* (pr)	Central Park, New York, opened to the public
1859	Thoreau, Henry David: "A Plea for Captain John Brown" (pr)	*Thunderstorm with Rocky Mountains* (painting) by Albert Bierstadt *Old Kentucky Home* (painting) by Eastman Johnson After raid on federal arsenal at Harper's Ferry, John Brown hanged; song "John Brown's Body" attributed to T.B. Bishop (1835–1905)
1860	Emerson, Ralph Waldo: *The Conduct of Life* (pr)	Abraham Lincoln elected President South Carolina secedes from Union
1861	Holmes, Oliver Wendell: *Elsie Venner* (f)	Abraham Lincoln administration (1861–65) Outbreak of Civil War
1862	Davis, Rebecca Harding (1831–1910): *Margret Howth* (f)	Battles of Shiloh, second Bull Run, Antietam (Sharpsburg), Fredericksburg Sioux rising in Minnesota suppressed
1863	Longfellow, Henry Wadsworth: *Tales of a Wayside Inn* (v)	Lincoln proclaims emancipation of slaves from 1 January Battles of Chancellorsville, Gettysburg, Vicksburg, Chattanooga *Symphony in White* (painting) by James McNeill Whistler
1864		Sherman's march through Georgia Ku Klux Klan organized in Pulaski, Tennessee
1865	Whitman, Walt: *Drum-Taps* (v) and *Sequel to Drum-Taps* including "When Lilacs Last in the Dooryard Bloom'd" (v)	End of Civil War; Thirteenth Amendment abolishes slavery Lincoln assassinated by John Wilkes Booth Andrew Johnson administration (1865–69) *Prisoners from the Front* (painting) by Winslow Homer
1866	Melville, Herman: *Battle Pieces* (v) Whittier, John Greenleaf: *Snow-Bound* (v)	American Equal Rights Association founded
1867		Alaska ceded by Russia to U.S.
1868	Alcott, Louisa May (1832–88): *Little Women* (f; completed 1869) Alger, Horatio (1834–99): *Ragged Dick* (f)	Fourteenth Amendment ratified
1869	Harte, Bret (1836–1902): "The Outcasts of Poker Flat" (f) Twain, Mark (1835–1910): *The Innocents Abroad* (f)	Ulysses S. Grant administration (1869–77) Union Pacific and Central Pacific railroads join in Utah American Woman's Suffrage Association started by Susan B. Anthony
1870	Lowell, James Russell: *The Cathedral* (v) Whitman, Walt: *Democratic Vistas* (pr)	
1873	Twain, Mark, and Charles Dudley Warner (1829–1900): *The Gilded Age* (f)	Financial panic in U.S. caused by speculation and overproduction Remington Company produces typewriter
1875	Eddy, Mary Baker (1821–1910): *Science and Health* (pr) James, Henry (1843–1916): *Roderick Hudson* (f)	*The Gross Clinic* (painting) by Thomas Eakins

DATE	AUTHOR AND TITLE	EVENT
1876	Lanier, Sidney (1842–81): "The Symphony" (v) Twain, Mark: *The Adventures of Tom Sawyer* (f)	Telephone patented by Alexander Graham Bell Phonograph invented by Thomas Edison *Breezing Up* (painting) by Winslow Homer
1877		Rutherford B. Hayes administration (1877–81)
1880	Adams, Henry (1838–1918): *Democracy* (f) Harris, Joel Chandler (1848–1908): *Uncle Remus: His Songs and His Sayings* (f)	
1881	James, Henry: *The Portrait of a Lady* (f)	James A. Garfield administration (1881) Garfield mortally wounded by assassin Chester A. Arthur administration (1881–85) Boston Symphony Orchestra founded
1883	Twain, Mark: *Life on the Mississippi* (pr) Wilcox, Ella Wheeler (1850–1919): *Poems of Passion*	New York Metropolitan Opera founded North Pacific Railroad constructed
1884	Twain, Mark: *The Adventures of Huckleberry Finn* (f; London edition)	Mergenthaler Linotype machine patented
1885	Howells, William Dean (1837–1920): *The Rise of Silas Lapham* (f) Riley, James Whitcomb (1849–1916): "Little Orphant Annie" (v)	Grover Cleveland first administration (1885–89)
1886	Carnegie, Andrew (1835–1919): *Triumphant Democracy* (pr) James, Henry: *The Bostonians* (f), *The Princess Casamassima* (f)	Statue of Liberty, New York, cast in copper: gift from France, designed by Frederick Auguste Bartholdi American Federation of Labor founded
1888	Bellamy, Edward (1850–98): *Looking Backward 2000–1887* (f)	"Kodak" box camera invented by George Eastman
1889		Benjamin Harrison administration (1889–93)
1890	Dickinson, Emily (1830–86): *Poems* James, William (1842–1910): *The Principles of Psychology* (pr) Whittier, John Greenleaf: *At Sundown* (v)	Anti-trust law enacted Mississippi legislature institutes poll tax, literacy tests, etc., designed to restrict voting by blacks; other southern states follow this example
1891	Garland, Hamlin (1860–1940): *Main-Travelled Roads* (f)	
1892	Whitman, Walt: *Leaves of Grass* (v; "Death-Bed Edition")	California earthquake disaster Antonin Dvorak (Czech) accepts directorship of National Conservatory of Music, New York
1893	Crane, Stephen (1871–1900): *Maggie, A Girl of the Streets* (f; revised edition 1896)	Grover Cleveland second administration (1893–97) Chicago World's Columbian Exposition *Struggle of the Two Natures of Man* (sculpture) by George Gray Barnard Symphony No. 9 ("From the New World") by Dvorak
1895	Crane, Stephen: *The Red Badge of Courage: An Episode of the American Civil War* (f)	"Coca-Cola is now sold in every state of the Union"
1896	Frederic, Harold (1856–98): *The Damnation of Theron Ware* (f) Jewett, Sarah Orne (1849–1909): *The Country of the Pointed Firs* (f) Robinson, Edwin Arlington (1869–1935): *The Torrent and the Night Before* (v; revised edition as *The Children of the Night*, 1897)	Louisiana "Jim Crow car law" upheld by Supreme Court William McKinley defeats William Jennings Bryan for presidency

DATE	AUTHOR AND TITLE	EVENT
1897		William McKinley administration (1897–1901)
1898	James, Henry: *The Turn of the Screw* (f)	Spanish-American War
1899	Chopin, Kate (1851–1904): *The Awakening* (f) Dewey, John (1859–1952): *The School and Society* (pr) Norris, Frank (1870–1902): *McTeague* (f)	Scott Joplin's "Original Rag" and "Maple Leaf Rag" are first ragtime piano pieces published in sheet music form
1900	Baum, L. Frank (1856–1919): *The Wonderful Wizard of Oz* (f) Dreiser, Theodore (1871–1945): *Sister Carrie* (f)	Philadelphia Orchestra organized *The Sitwell Family* (painting) by John Singer Sargent
1901	Norris, Frank: *The Octopus* (f)	McKinley assassinated Theodore Roosevelt administration (1901–09)
1902	James, Henry: *The Wings of the Dove* (f) James, William: *The Varieties of Religious Experience* (pr) Keller, Helen (1880–1968): *The Story of My Life* (pr) Robinson, Edwin Arlington: *Captain Craig* (v) Wister, Owen (1860–1938): *The Virginian* (f)	U.S. coal strike (May–October)
1903	Du Bois, W.E.B. (1868–1963): *Souls of Black Folk* (pr) James, Henry: *The Ambassadors* (f) London, Jack (1876–1916): *The Call of the Wild* (f)	New York Stock Exchange building completed
1905	Santayana, George (1863–1952): *The Life of Reason* (pr; completed 1906) Wharton, Edith (1862–1937): *The House of Mirth* (f)	Big oil strike at "Tulsey Town," in Oklahoma, a prelude to "Tulsa" as "Oil Capital of the World" *Wrestlers* (painting) by George Benjamin Luks
1906	Henry, O. (1862–1910): *The Four Million* (f) London, Jack: *White Fang* (f) Sinclair, Upton (1878–1968): *The Jungle* (f)	Pure Food and Drugs Act passed as result of Upton Sinclair's exposure in *The Jungle* of conditions in Chicago stockyards San Francisco earthquake
1907	Adams, Henry: *The Education of Henry Adams* (pr; private printing) James, William: *Pragmatism* (pr)	*The North American Indian*, vol. 1, published by photographer Edward S. Curtis
1909	James, William: *A Pluralistic Universe* (pr) Pound, Ezra (1885–1972): *Personae* (v)	William Howard Taft administration (1909–13) Henry Ford's Model T car Sigmund Freud lectures in U.S. on psychoanalysis Frank Lloyd Wright's prairie-style "Robie House" completed in Chicago
1912	Dreiser, Theodore: *The Financier* (f) Grey, Zane (1872–1939): *Riders of the Purple Sage* (f) Johnson, James Weldon (1871–1938): *The Autobiography of an Ex-Colored Man* (f)	*Poetry* magazine (Chicago) founded by Harriet Monroe F.W. Woolworth Company incorporated by Frank Woolworth Woodrow Wilson defeats William Howard Taft and Theodore Roosevelt for presidency
1913	Cather, Willa (1873–1947): *O Pioneers!* (f) Frost, Robert (1874–1963): *A Boy's Will* (v) Glasgow, Ellen (1873–1945): *Virginia* (f) Lindsay, Vachel (1879–1931): *General William Booth Enters into Heaven* (v) Williams, William Carlos (1883–1963): *The Tempers* (v)	Woodrow Wilson administration (1913–21) Armoury Show of post-Impressionist paintings in New York and Chicago Charlie Chaplin signs contract with filmmaker Mack Sennett Henry Ford pioneers use of conveyor belt
1914	Frost, Robert: *North of Boston* (v) Pound, Ezra (ed.): *Des Imagistes: An Anthology* (v)	World War I begins in Europe

DATE	AUTHOR AND TITLE	EVENT
1915	Masters, Edgar Lee (1868–1950): *Spoon River Anthology* (v) Pound, Ezra: *Cathay: Translations* (v)	D.W. Griffith's film *The Birth of a Nation*
1916	Aiken, Conrad (1889–1973): *The Jig of Forslin* (v) Doolittle, Hilda (H.D.) (1886–1961): *Sea Garden* (v) O'Neill, Eugene (1888–1953): *Bound East for Cardiff* (p) Robinson, Edwin Arlington: *The Man Against the Sky* (v) Sandburg, Carl (1878–1967): *Chicago Poems*	*Saturday Evening Post* buys its first Norman Rockwell illustration Coca-Cola adopts distinctively shaped bottle
1917	Eliot, T.S. (1888–1965): *Prufrock and Other Observations* (v)	U.S. declares war on Germany and Austria-Hungary "The Darktown Strutters' Ball" recorded as first jazz record
1918	Cather, Willa: *My Ántonia* (f)	End of World War I Wilson's Fourteen Points Charlie Chaplin's *Shoulder Arms* (film)
1919	Anderson, Sherwood (1876–1941): *Winesburg, Ohio* (f) Cabell, James Branch (1879–1958): *Jurgen* (f) Mencken, H.L. (1880–1956): *The American Language* (pr)	Commodore Hotel opened in New York—the world's largest
1920	Fitzgerald, F. Scott (1896–1940): *This Side of Paradise* (f) Lewis, Sinclair (1885–1951): *Main Street* (f) Millay, Edna St. Vincent (1892–1950): *A Few Figs from Thistles* (v) O'Neill, Eugene: *The Emperor Jones* (p)	Prohibition of sales of alcoholic beverages (Eighteenth Amendment) Senate blocks U.S. entry into new League of Nations
1921		Warren G. Harding administration (1921–23)
1922	Eliot, T.S.: *The Waste Land* (v) Lewis, Sinclair: *Babbitt* (f)	First issue of *The Fugitive*
1923	Millay, Edna St. Vincent: *The Harp-Weaver and Other Poems* Rice, Elmer (1892–1967): *The Adding Machine* (p) Stevens, Wallace (1879–1955): *Harmonium* (v)	Calvin Coolidge administration (1923–29) First issue of *Time* magazine
1924	Jeffers, Robinson (1887–1962): *Tamar and Other Poems* (v) Melville, Herman: *Billy Budd* (f; written 1888–91) Ransom, John Crowe (1888–1974): *Chills and Fever* (v)	First performance of "Rhapsody in Blue for Jazz Band and Piano" by George Gershwin
1925	Dos Passos, John (1896–1970): *Manhattan Transfer* (f) Dreiser, Theodore: *An American Tragedy* (f) Fitzgerald, F. Scott: *The Great Gatsby* (f) Glasgow, Ellen: *Barren Ground* (f) Pound, Ezra: *A Draft of XVI Cantos* (v)	Tennessee forbids teaching of human evolution in schools "Monkey Trial" of John D. Scopes
1926	Hemingway, Ernest (1899–1961): *The Sun Also Rises* (f) Hughes, Langston (1902–67): *The Weary Blues* (v) Parker, Dorothy (1893–1967): *Enough Rope* (v)	Dancer Martha Graham makes first solo appearance in New York Chicago bootlegger Al Capone's hotel headquarters sprayed with machine-gun fire by rival gang
1927		Execution of Sacco and Vanzetti
1928	Benét, Stephen Vincent (1898–1943): *John Brown's Body* (v) O'Neill, Eugene: *Strange Interlude* (p)	

DATE	AUTHOR AND TITLE	EVENT
1929	Faulkner, William (1897–1962): *Sartoris* (f), *The Sound and the Fury* (f) Hemingway, Ernest: *A Farewell to Arms* (f) Wolfe, Thomas (1900–38): *Look Homeward, Angel* (f)	Herbert Hoover administration (1929–33) Collapse of New York Stock Exchange begins world economic crisis
1930	Crane, Hart (1899–1932): *The Bridge* (v) Hammett, Dashiell (1894–1961): *The Maltese Falcon* (f)	More than four million unemployed in U.S. *American Gothic* (painting) by Grant Wood
1932	Caldwell, Erskine (b. 1903): *Tobacco Road* (f)	
1933	Caldwell, Erskine: *God's Little Acre* (f) Stein, Gertrude (1874–1946): *The Autobiography of Alice B. Toklas* (pr) West, Nathanael (1903–40): *Miss Lonelyhearts* (f)	Franklin D. Roosevelt administration (1933–45) Financial crisis continues; newly inaugurated President Roosevelt says "We have nothing to fear but fear itself" James Joyce's *Ulysses* ruled acceptable for U.S. publication End of Prohibition *Calderberry Bush*, early mobile by Alexander Calder
1934	Fitzgerald, F. Scott: *Tender Is the Night* (f) O'Hara, John (1905–70): *Appointment in Samarra* (f) Saroyan, William (1908–81): *The Daring Young Man on the Flying Trapeze* (f)	*Partisan Review* begins publication First performance of "Symphony: 1933" by Roy Harris Gangster John Dillinger shot dead by F.B.I. agents
1935	Anderson, Maxwell (1888–1959): *Winterset* (p) Eliot, T.S.: *Murder in the Cathedral* (p) Odets, Clifford (1906–63): *Waiting for Lefty* (p), *Awake and Sing!* (p) Santayana, George: *The Last Puritan* (f) Steinbeck, John (1902–68): *Tortilla Flat* (f)	New Deal social security legislation *Porgy and Bess* (opera) by DuBose Heyward and Ira and George Gershwin "Fallingwater" (Kaufmann House) by Frank Lloyd Wright, Bear Run, Pennsylvania
1936	Dos Passos, John: *U.S.A.* trilogy completed (f) Faulkner, William: *Absalom, Absalom!* (f) Mitchell, Margaret (1900–49): *Gone with the Wind* (f) Sandburg, Carl: *The People, Yes* (v)	Ford Foundation established Roosevelt re-elected, carrying 46 states
1937	Marquand, J.P. (1893–1960): *The Late George Apley* (f) Stevens, Wallace: *The Man with the Blue Guitar* (v)	*Newsweek* magazine begins publication *Popular Photography* magazine begins publication *Snow White and the Seven Dwarfs* (film) by Walt Disney
1938	Cummings, E.E. (1894–1962): *Collected Poems* Schwartz, Delmore (1913–66): *In Dreams Begin Responsibilities* (v) Wilder, Thornton (1897–1975): *Our Town* (p)	*Billy the Kid* (ballet) by Aaron Copland
1939	Chandler, Raymond (1888–1959): *The Big Sleep* (f) Hellman, Lillian (1905?–1984): *The Little Foxes* (p) Steinbeck, John: *The Grapes of Wrath* (f) Thurber, James (1894–1961): *Cream of Thurber* (pr) Warren, Robert Penn (b. 1905): *Night Rider* (f) West, Nathanael: *The Day of the Locust* (f)	World War II begins in Europe "Grandma Moses" (Anna M. Robertson) becomes famous in Unknown American Painters Exhibition
1940	Hemingway, Ernest: *For Whom the Bell Tolls* (f) McCullers, Carson (1917–67): *The Heart Is a Lonely Hunter* (f) Wilson, Edmund (1895–1972): *To the Finland Station* (pr) Wright, Richard (1908–60): *Native Son* (f)	U.S. unemployment more than eight million First Social Security payments made U.S. gives Britain 50 destroyers in return for eight bases in the Atlantic Roosevelt re-elected for unprecedented third term
1941	Agee, James (1909–55): *Let Us Now Praise Famous Men* (pr) with photographs by Walker Evans Ferber, Edna (1887–1968): *Saratoga Trunk* (f) Zukofsky, Louis (1904–78): *55 Poems*	Roosevelt and Churchill meet at sea and announce Atlantic Charter U.S. and Germany wage undeclared naval war in the Atlantic Japanese bomb Pearl Harbor; U.S. enters World War II *Citizen Kane* (film) by Orson Welles

DATE	AUTHOR AND TITLE	EVENT
1943	Eliot, T.S.: *Four Quartets* (v)	
1944	Bellow, Saul (b. 1915): *Dangling Man* (f) Williams, Tennessee (1911–83): *The Glass Menagerie* (p) Winsor, Kathleen (b. 1919): *Forever Amber* (f)	Supreme Court rules an American cannot be denied the right to vote because of color
1945	Wright, Richard: *Black Boy* (pr)	Roosevelt dies Harry S. Truman administration (1945–53) World War II ends in Europe U.S. drops atomic bombs on Hiroshima and Nagasaki; Japan surrenders
1946	Hersey, John (b. 1914): *Hiroshima* (pr) Lowell, Robert (1917–77): *Lord Weary's Castle* (v) McCullers, Carson: *The Member of the Wedding* (f) Merrill, James (b. 1926): *The Black Swan* (v) Warren, Robert Penn: *All the King's Men* (f)	Returning veterans swell U.S. college enrollments to more than two million
1947	Miller, Arthur (b. 1915): *All My Sons* (p) Williams, Tennessee: *A Streetcar Named Desire* (p)	Truman Doctrine of aid to countries to combat communism
1948	Mailer, Norman (b. 1923): *The Naked and the Dead* (f) Pound, Ezra: *The Pisan Cantos* (v)	Truman recognizes the State of Israel House Committee on Un-American Activities begins round of anti-communist investigations *Number One* (painting) by Jackson Pollock
1949	Miller, Arthur: *Death of a Salesman* (p)	
1950	Olson, Charles (1910–70): "Projective Verse" (pr)	Korean War begins United Nations Building, New York, completed
1951	Hughes, Langston: *Montage of a Dream Deferred* (v) Jones, James (1921–77): *From Here to Eternity* (f) Lowell, Robert: *The Mills of the Kavanaughs* (v) Salinger, J.D. (b. 1919): *The Catcher in the Rye* (f) Wouk, Herman (b. 1915): *The Caine Mutiny* (f)	First performance of Symphony No. 2 by Charles Ives CBS broadcasts color television U.S. Atomic Energy Commission builds first power-producing nuclear reactor
1952	Ellison, Ralph (b. 1914): *Invisible Man* (f) Hemingway, Ernest: *The Old Man and the Sea* (f) Malamud, Bernard (1914–86): *The Natural* (f) McCarthy, Mary (b. 1912): *The Groves of Academe* (f) Merwin, W.S. (b. 1927): *A Mask for Janus* (v) O'Connor, Flannery (1925–64): *Wise Blood* (f)	General Dwight D. Eisenhower nominated by Republicans to run for presidency against Democratic nominee Adlai Stevenson; Eisenhower wins election
1953	Baldwin, James (b. 1924): *Go Tell It on the Mountain* (f) Bellow, Saul: *The Adventures of Augie March* (f) Inge, William (1913–73): *Picnic* (p) Miller, Arthur: *The Crucible* (p) Olson, Charles: *The Maximus Poems 1–10* (v) Roethke, Theodore (1908–63): *The Waking* (v) Shapiro, Karl (b. 1913): *Poems 1940–1953* Warren, Robert Penn: *Brother to Dragons* (v; revised edition 1979)	Dwight D. Eisenhower administration (1953–61) Ethel and Julius Rosenberg executed for passing atomic secrets to Soviet agents Eisenhower proposes "Atoms for Peace" program Korean War ends *Playboy* magazine begins publication
1954	De Vries, Peter (b. 1910): *The Tunnel of Love* (f) Stevens, Wallace: *Collected Poems* Welty, Eudora (b. 1909): *The Ponder Heart* (f)	Vietnam divided into North and South Lolita Lebron and associates injure congressmen in "Free Puerto Rico" demonstration Senator Joseph R. McCarthy censured by Senate Supreme Court declares segregation in public schools unconstitutional

DATE	AUTHOR AND TITLE	EVENT
1955	Donleavy, J.P. (b. 1926): *The Ginger Man* (f) Gaddis, William (b. 1922): *The Recognitions* (f) Nabokov, Vladimir (1899–1977): *Lolita* (f)	Rosa Parks, of Montgomery, Alabama, refuses to give up her seat on a bus to a white man
1956	Barth, John (b. 1930): *The Floating Opera* (f) Ginsberg, Allen (b. 1926): *Howl and Other Poems* O'Neill, Eugene: *Long Day's Journey into Night* (p)	Supreme Court declares segregated seating in buses unconstitutional *My Fair Lady* (musical) by Alan Jay Lerner and Frederick Loewe
1957	Cheever, John (1912–82): *The Wapshot Chronicle* (f) Kerouac, Jack (1922–69): *On the Road* (f) Malamud, Bernard: *The Assistant* (f) Singer, Isaac Bashevis (b. 1904): *Gimpel the Fool* (f) Stevens, Wallace: *Opus Posthumous* (v/p/pr)	School integration disturbances in Little Rock, Arkansas Civil Rights Commission established First performance of Symphony No. 3 by Roger Sessions *West Side Story* (musical) by Leonard Bernstein, Arthur Laurents, and Stephen Sondheim
1958	Capote, Truman (1924–84): *Breakfast at Tiffany's* (f) Kunitz, Stanley (b. 1905): *Selected Poems 1928–1958*	John Birch Society founded First U.S. earth satellite launched
1959	Albee, Edward (b. 1928): *The Zoo Story* (p) Bellow, Saul: *Henderson the Rain King* (f) Burroughs, William S. (b. 1914): *The Naked Lunch* (f) Faulkner, William: *The Mansion* (f) Gelber, Jack (b. 1932): *The Connection* (p) Hansberry, Lorraine (1930–63): *A Raisin in the Sun* (p) Lowell, Robert: *Life Studies* (v) Purdy, James (b. 1923): *Malcolm* (f) Roth, Philip (b. 1933): *Goodbye, Columbus* (f) Snodgrass, W.D. (b. 1926): *Heart's Needle* (v) Updike, John (b. 1932): *The Poorhouse Fair* (f)	Alaska and Hawaii admitted to U.S. as 49th and 50th states Eisenhower says nation's economy is "on a curve of rising prosperity" Completion of Frank Lloyd Wright's Solomon R. Guggenheim Museum, New York
1960	Barth, John: *The Sot-Weed Factor* (f) Hellman, Lillian: *Toys in the Attic* (p) Kinnell, Galway (b. 1927): *What a Kingdom It Was* (v) O'Connor, Flannery: *The Violent Bear It Away* (f) Plath, Sylvia (1932–63): *The Colossus* (v) Sexton, Anne (1928–74): *To Bedlam and Part Way Back* (v) Singer, Isaac Bashevis: *The Magician of Lublin* (f) Updike, John: *Rabbit, Run* (f)	John F. Kennedy defeats Republican Vice-President Richard M. Nixon for presidency
1961	Baldwin, James: *Nobody Knows My Name* (pr) Heller, Joseph (b. 1923): *Catch-22* (f) Malamud, Bernard: *A New Life* (f) Percy, Walker (b. 1916): *The Moviegoer* (f) Salinger, J.D.: *Franny and Zooey* (f)	U.S. severs relations with Fidel Castro's Cuba John F. Kennedy administration (1961–63) Bay of Pigs invasion; Khrushchev supports Cuba Berlin Wall erected First U.S. manned space expedition by Commander Alan B. Shepard, Jr.
1962	Albee, Edward: *Who's Afraid of Virginia Woolf?* (p) Baldwin, James: *Another Country* (f) Bly, Robert (b. 1926): *Silence in the Snowy Fields* (v) Porter, Katherine Anne (1890–1980): *Ship of Fools* (f)	Cuban missile crisis brings nuclear confrontation with U.S.S.R. U.S. aids South Vietnamese against Vietcong guerrillas
1963	Friedan, Betty (b. 1921): *The Feminine Mystique* (pr) McCarthy, Mary: *The Group* (f) Pynchon, Thomas (b. 1937): *V.* (f) Vonnegut, Kurt, Jr. (b. 1922): *Cat's Cradle* (f) Williams, William Carlos: *Paterson, Books I–V* (v)	Kennedy assassinated in Dallas Lyndon Baines Johnson administration (1963–69) Martin Luther King, Jr., makes "I have a dream" speech at Civil Rights march in Washington, D.C.

DATE	AUTHOR AND TITLE	EVENT
1964	Baraka, Amiri (b. LeRoi Jones, 1934): *Dutchman* (p) Bellow, Saul: *Herzog* (f) Berger, Thomas (b. 1924): *Little Big Man* (f) Berryman, John (1914–72): *77 Dream Songs* (v) Condon, Richard (b. 1915): *An Infinity of Mirrors* (f) Lowell, Robert: *For the Union Dead* (v) Selby, Hubert, Jr. (b. 1926): *Last Exit to Brooklyn* (f) Shepard, Sam (b. 1943): *Cowboys* (p)	U.S. bombs North Vietnamese bases Race riots in Harlem and Philadelphia Student "free speech" demonstrations at University of California, Berkeley Civil Rights Act abolishes segregation in public accommodations throughout the south
1965	Kosinski, Jerzy (b. 1933): *The Painted Bird* (f) Malcolm X (b. Malcolm Little, 1925–65): *The Autobiography of Malcolm X* (pr; with Alex Haley) Plath, Sylvia: *Ariel* (v) Warren, Robert Penn: *Who Speaks for the Negro?* (pr) Wolfe, Tom (b. 1931): *The Kandy-Kolored Tangerine-Flake Streamline Baby* (pr) Zukofsky, Louis: *All: The Collected Short Poems 1923–1958*	U.S. makes formal alliance with South Vietnam Civil Rights demonstrations in Selma, Alabama, and Chicago Race riots in Watts district of Los Angeles Voting Rights Act provides guarantees for black voting in the south Malcolm X shot dead *Early Bird* put into orbit as world's first commercial satellite Painting of a giant Campbell's Tomato Soup Can by Andy Warhol
1966	Baraka, Amiri: *Home: Social Essays* (pr) Capote, Truman: *In Cold Blood* (pr)	James Meredith, University of Mississippi's first black graduate, shot from ambush Race riots in Cleveland, Chicago, and Atlanta
1967	Baraka, Amiri: *Black Magic: Poetry 1961–1967* Bly, Robert: *The Light Around the Body* (v) Brautigan, Richard (1933–84): *Trout Fishing in America* (f) Styron, William (b. 1925): *The Confessions of Nat Turner* (f) Vidal, Gore (b. 1925): *Washington, D.C.* (f)	Anti-Vietnam War demonstrations, notably in New York, San Francisco, and Washington, D.C. Race riots throughout country, worst in Newark and Detroit Stokely Carmichael urges Black Power movement to be more militant
1968	Cleaver, Eldridge (b. 1935): *Soul on Ice* (pr) Dickey, James (b. 1923): *Poems 1957–1967* Giovanni, Nikki (b. 1943): *Black Judgement* (v) Mailer, Norman: *The Armies of the Night* (pr) Updike, John: *Couples* (f) Vidal, Gore: *Myra Breckinridge* (f) Wolfe, Tom: *The Electric Kool-Aid Acid Test* (pr)	My Lai Village massacre in South Vietnam Senator Robert Kennedy assassinated Martin Luther King, Jr., assassinated Demonstrations and riots in Chicago, Boston, Kansas City, and other cities Students for a Democratic Society (SDS) promote strike action on many campuses Richard M. Nixon defeats Hubert Humphrey for presidency
1969	Cheever, John: *Bullet Park* (f) Jarrell, Randall (1914–65): *The Complete Poems* Nabokov, Vladimir: *Ada* (f) Roth, Philip: *Portnoy's Complaint* (f) Vonnegut, Kurt, Jr.: *Slaughterhouse-Five; or, The Children's Crusade* (f)	Richard M. Nixon administration (1969–74) Death of Mary Jo Kopechne at Chappaquiddick Island damages reputation of Senator Edward M. Kennedy U.S. moon landing U.S. economic boom Woodstock Music and Art Festival, New York *Saturday Evening Post* ceases publication
1970	Brown, Dee (b. 1908): *Bury My Heart at Wounded Knee* (pr) Didion, Joan (b. 1934): *Play It as It Lays* (f) Lowell, Robert: *Notebook* (v) Millett, Kate (b. 1934): *Sexual Politics* (pr) Toffler, Alvin (b. 1928): *Future Shock* (pr) Welty, Eudora: *Losing Battles* (f)	National Guardsmen fire on protesting students at Kent State University (Ohio), killing four Arabs blame U.S. for Israel's refusal to give up territory occupied since Six Day War (1967)
1971	Condon, Richard: *The Vertical Smile* (f) Doctorow, E.L. (b. 1931): *The Book of Daniel* (f) O'Hara, Frank (1926–66): *Collected Poems* Wright, James (1927–80): *Collected Poems*	Vietnam War increases rate of inflation Excerpts from Pentagon Papers published in New York *Times*

DATE	AUTHOR AND TITLE	EVENT
1972	Ammons, A.R. (b. 1926): *Collected Poems 1951–1971* Barth, John: *Chimera* (f) Shepard, Sam: *The Tooth of Crime* (p)	Watergate affair begins; Washington *Post* investigates Nixon visits China and U.S.S.R. U.S. signs nuclear arms control agreement with U.S.S.R.
1973	Jong, Erica (b. 1942): *Fear of Flying* (f) Oates, Joyce Carol (b. 1938): *Do with Me What You Will* (f) Pynchon, Thomas: *Gravity's Rainbow* (f) Vidal, Gore: *Burr* (f)	Cease-fire in Vietnam, but bombing of Cambodia continues *Skylab* astronauts photograph Comet "Kohoutek" Senate holds hearings on Watergate affair
1974	Heller, Joseph: *Something Happened* (f) Lurie, Alison (b. 1926): *The War Between the Tates* (f) Mamet, David (b. 1947): *Sexual Perversity in Chicago* (p) Roth, Philip: *My Life as a Man* (f)	World energy crisis deepens Nixon resigns presidency as a result of Watergate affair Gerald Ford administration (1974–77) Ford pardons Nixon
1975	Ashbery, John (b. 1927): *Self-Portrait in a Convex Mirror* (v) Doctorow, E.L.: *Ragtime* (f) Gaddis, William: *JR* (f) Wolfe, Tom: *The Painted Word* (pr)	Puerto Rican militants explode bombs in New York America's *Apollo 16* spacecraft docks in space with Russia's *Soyuz 19* North Vietnam conquers South Vietnam
1976	Gardner, John (1933–82): *October Light* (f) Haley, Alex (b. 1921): *Roots* (pr) Merrill, James: *Divine Comedies* (v)	Bicentennial celebrations Patricia Hearst found guilty of armed robbery *Viking II* spacecraft lands on Mars
1977	Ashbery, John: *Houseboat Days* (v) Cheever, John: *Falconer* (f) Coover, Robert (b. 1932): *The Public Burning* (f) Miller, Arthur: *The Archbishop's Ceiling* (p) Percy, Walker: *Lancelot* (f) Warren, Robert Penn: *Selected Poems 1923–1975* (v), *A Place to Come To* (f)	Jimmy Carter administration (1977–81) Gary Gilmore executed by firing squad Carter pardons draft-dodgers and supports production of neutron bomb Department of Energy created
1978	Cheever, John: *The Stories* Gordon, Mary (b. 1949): *Final Payments* (f) Irving, John (b. 1942): *The World According to Garp* (f) Merrill, James: *Mirabell: Books of Number* (v) Updike, John: *The Coup* (f) Williams, Tennessee: *A Lovely Sunday for Creve Coeur* (p)	More than 1000 Indians walk from California to Washington, D.C., to protest against legislation hostile to their treaty rights U.S. announces intention to end diplomatic relations with Taiwan and to recognize China U.S. agrees to yield control of Panama Canal to Panamanians in year 2000 Carter acts as broker in Camp David agreement between Egypt and Israel
1979	Barth, John: *Letters* (f) Heller, Joseph: *Good as Gold* (f) Mailer, Norman: *The Executioner's Song* (pr) Malamud, Bernard: *Dubin's Lives* (f) Roth, Philip: *The Ghost Writer* (f)	U.S. recognizes new government in Iran Carter supports production of new MX super-missile Sioux Indians awarded $17,500,000 in compensation for Black Hills of Dakota, confiscated in 1877, and judged to be entitled to interest of $105,000,000 U.S. hostages seized in Iran
1980	Doctorow, E.L.: *Loon Lake* (f) Levin, Harry (b. 1912): *Memories of the Moderns* (pr) Toole, John Kennedy (1937–69): *A Confederacy of Dunces* (f)	After U.S.S.R. invades Afghanistan, Carter announces "Carter Doctrine" threatening military retaliation if Soviets invade Persian Gulf region U.S. hostages continue to be held in Iran
1981	De Vries, Peter: *Sauce for the Goose* (f) Forché, Carolyn (b. 1950): *The Country Between Us* (v) Irving, John: *The Hotel New Hampshire* (f) Robinson, Marilynne (b. 1943): *Housekeeping* (f) Updike, John: *Rabbit Is Rich* (f)	Ronald Reagan administration (1981–) U.S. hostages freed by Iranians Reagan hit by shot from would-be assassin *Columbia* space shuttle into orbit Sandra Day O'Connor appointed first woman member of Supreme Court

DATE	AUTHOR AND TITLE	EVENT
1982	Ammons, A.R.: *Worldly Hopes* (v) Bellow, Saul: *The Dean's December* (f) Kosinski, Jerzy: *Pinball* (f) Mamet, David: *Edmond* (p) Merrill, James: *The Changing Light at Sandover* (v) Walker, Alice (b. 1944): *The Color Purple* (f)	Equal Rights Amendment defeated U.S. unemployment more than 11 million (highest figure since 1940) Massive anti-nuclear demonstration in New York
1983	Adler, Renata (b. 1938): *Pitch Dark* (f) Clampitt, Amy (b. 1920): *The Kingfisher* (v) Kennedy, William (b. 1928): *Ironweed* (f) Mailer, Norman: *Ancient Evenings* (f) Malamud, Bernard: *The Stories* Mamet, David: *Glengarry Glen Ross* (p; London production) Oliver, Mary (b. 1935): *American Primitive* (v) Ozick, Cynthia (b. 1928): *The Cannibal Galaxy* (f) Roth, Philip: *The Anatomy Lesson* (f) Warren, Robert Penn: *Chief Joseph of the Nez Perce* (v)	Reagan proposes Strategic Defense Initiative (S.D.I.), which becomes known as "Star Wars" U.S. invades island of Grenada and overthrows leftist regime West European countries begin deployment of U.S.-made Pershing II and Cruise missiles; U.S.S.R. protests by withdrawing from Geneva arms control talks
1984	Ashbery, John: *A Wave* (v) Bellow, Saul: *Him with His Foot in His Mouth and Other Stories* Heller, Joseph: *God Knows* (f) Rich, Adrienne (b. 1929): *The Fact of a Doorframe* (v) Updike, John: *The Witches of Eastwick* (f) Wright, Charles (b. 1935): *The Other Side of the River* (v)	Geraldine Ferraro is first woman to be nominated for the vice-presidency Jesse Jackson is first black to mount serious bid for the presidency Olympic Games held in Los Angeles Reagan re-elected, carrying 49 states
1985	Hersey, John: *The Call* (f) Irving, John: *The Cider House Rules* (f) McMurtry, Larry (b. 1936): *Lonesome Dove* (f) Roth, Philip: *Zuckerman Bound* (f) Shepard, Sam: *A Lie of the Mind* (p) Vonnegut, Kurt, Jr.: *Galápagos* (f)	Reagan and Mikhail Gorbachov hold summit meeting in Vienna U.S.S.R. returns to arms control talks despite Euromissile deployment
1986	Hemingway, Ernest: *The Garden of Eden* (f) Stone, Robert (b. 1937): *Children of Light* (f)	*Challenger* space shuttle explodes; seven astronauts perish U.S. bombs Libya over terrorist links Robert Penn Warren designated America's first official Poet Laureate Reagan-Gorbachov summit at Reykjavik ends in failure to reach agreement on any issue Arms sales to Iran controversy reduces Reagan's popularity

TITLE INDEX

The following index includes the titles of all books listed in the Fiction, Verse, and Plays sections of the Publications lists. These abbreviations are used:

f	fiction
v	verse
p	play
scr	screenplay
radio	radio play
tv	television play

A few titles from other sections (Collections, Other, Prose, etc.) are listed; in these cases no abbreviation appears before the author's name. Titles appearing in **bold** are subjects of individual essays in the Works section.

American Crusader (radio Sherwood), 1941
American Democrat (Cooper), 1838
American Dream (p Albee), 1961
American Dream (f Mailer), 1965
American Dream Girl (f Farrell), 1950
American Duchess (p Fitch), 1893
American Earth (f Caldwell), 1931
American Flag Ritual (p Bullins), 1973
American Gods (p MacLeish), 1944
American Gun Mystery (f Queen), 1933
American Idea (p Cohan), 1908
American Journal (v Hayden), 1978
American Landscape (p Rice), 1938
American Language (Mencken), 1919
American Liberty (v Freneau), 1775
American Lounger (f Ingraham), 1839
American Name (p MacLeish), 1944
American Politician (f Crawford), 1884
American Scene (H. James), 1907
American Scene (Mencken), 1965
American Story series (radio MacLeish), 1944
American Tar (p Rowson), 1796
American Tragedy (f Dreiser), 1925
American Village (v Freneau), 1772
American Way (p Hart, Kaufman), 1939
American Wives and English Husbands (f Atherton), 1898
Americanization of Emily (scr Chayefsky), 1964
Americans (v Riding), 1934
Americans in England (p Rowson), 1797
Amerika-breve (f Rølvaag), 1912
Amicable Parting (p Kaufman), 1957
Among the Camps (f Page), 1891
Among the Hills (v Whittier), 1869
Among the Lost People (f Aiken), 1934
Among the Paths to Eden (tv Capote), 1967
Among Thieves (p Gillette), 1909
Among Those Present (f Ferber), 1923
Among Those Present (p Kaufman), 1918
Amphitryon 38 (p Behrman), 1937
AM/TRAK (v Baraka), 1979
Amulet (f Murfree), 1906
Anaesthetic Revelation (p Dreiser), 1930
Anarchiad (v Barlow, Trumbull), 1861
Anasazi (v Snyder), 1971
Anastasia (scr Laurents), 1956
Anatomy Lesson (f P. Roth), 1983
Ancestors (f Atherton), 1907
Ancestors of Peter Atherly (f Harte), 1897
Ancient Evenings (f Mailer), 1983
Ancient Law (f Glasgow), 1908
Ancient Mariner (p O'Neill), 1924
& (v Cummings), 1925
And As for the Ladies (p Kopit), 1963
And Be a Villain (f Stout), 1948
And Four to Go (f Stout), 1958
And in the Human Heart (v Aiken), 1940
And Now Tomorrow (scr Chandler), 1944
And on the Eighth Day (f Queen), 1964
And Other Stories (f J. O'Hara), 1968
And the Sea Shall Give Up Its Dead (p Wilder), 1928
And Then You Wish (f van Druten), 1936
André (p Dunlap), 1798
Andrew Jackson and Peggy Eaton (p Masters), 1934
Androgyne, Mon Amour (v T. Williams), 1977
Andromache (p Wilbur), 1982
Andromeda (p Simpson), 1956
Androo Johnson, His Life (f Nasby), 1866
Andy Gordon (f Alger), 1905
Andy Grant's Pluck (f Alger), 1902
Anecdotes of the Late War (v Olson), 1955
Anew (v Zukofsky), 1946
Angel (f Heyward), 1926
Angel and the Demon (f Arthur), 1858
Angel Arms (v Fearing), 1929
Angel City (p Shepard), 1976
Angel Intrudes (p Dell), 1917
Angel of the Household (f Arthur), 1854
Angel on the Ship (p Wilder), 1928
Angel That Troubled the Waters (p Wilder), 1928
Angela Is Twenty-Two (p Lewis), 1938
Angels (v Updike), 1968
Angels and Earthly Creatures (v Wylie), 1928
Angels over Broadway (scr Hecht), 1940
Angle of Ascent (v Hayden), 1975
Angry Wife (f Buck), 1947
Animae (v Merwin), 1969
Animal Crackers (p Kaufman), 1928
Animal Kingdom (p Barry), 1932
Animula (v Eliot), 1929
Ankor Wat (v Ginsberg), 1968
Ann Vickers (f Lewis), 1933
Anna Christie (p O'Neill), 1921
Anna Karenina (scr Behrman), 1935
Anna Lee (f Arthur), 1869
Anna Lucasta (scr Laurents), 1949
Anna Milnor (f Arthur), 1845
Annabel (f Baum), 1906
Anne (f Woolson), 1882
Anne Boleyn (p Boker), 1850
Anne of the Thousand Days (p M. Anderson), 1948
Annette (f Caldwell), 1973
Annie Allen (v Brooks), 1949
Annie Kilburn (f Howells), 1887
Another Country (f James Baldwin), 1962
Another Look (v Gregory), 1976
Another Pamela (f Sinclair), 1950
Another Part of the Forest (p Hellman), 1946
Another Thin Man (scr Hammett), 1939
Answered Prayers (f Capote), 1986
Ante-Mortem Statement (f Howe), 1891
Anthropos (p Cummings), 1945
Antick (p MacKaye), 1912
Anti-Matrimony (p MacKaye), 1910
Antiphon (p Barnes), 1958
Anti-Slavery and Reform Papers (Thoreau), 1866
Anyone Can Whistle (p Laurents), 1964
Apache Devil (f E. Burroughs), 1933
Apartment in Athens (f Wescott), 1945
Apologia of the Ampersand (v Morley), 1936
Apology for Bad Dreams (v Jeffers), 1930
Apostate (f London), 1906
Apparition (p Eberhart), 1951
Apple of the Eye (f Wescott), 1924
Apple-Tree Table (f Melville), 1922
Appointment in Samarra (f J. O'Hara), 1934
April (f Fisher), 1937
April Fire (v MacKaye), 1925
April Fool (p Harrigan), 1875

April Hopes (f Howells), 1887
April Twilights (v Cather), 1903
April Weather (p Fitch), 1893
Ara Vos Prec (v Eliot), 1920
Arabian Night in the Nineteenth Century (p Daly), 1879
Archaeologist of Morning (v Olson), 1970
Archbishop's Ceiling (p A. Miller), 1977
Archers (p Dunlap), 1796
Archy and Mehitabel series (v Marquis), from 1927
Arctic Ox (v Moore), 1964
Are You Hungry, Are You Cold (f Bemelmans), 1960
Are You Insured? (p Harrigan), 1885
Arethusa (f Crawford), 1907
Areytos (v Simms), 1846
Argonauts of North Liberty (f Harte), 1888
Aria da Capo (p Millay), 1920
Ariadne (p Rich), 1939
Ariel (v Plath), 1965
Arise, Arise (p Zukofsky), 1973
Aristocracy (p B. Howard), 1892
Aristocrat (f Richter), 1968
Aristocrats (f Atherton), 1901
Arizona (p Thomas), 1899
Arizona Ames (f Grey), 1932
Arizona Clan (f Grey), 1958
Arm Yrself or Harm Yrself (p Baraka), 1967
Armageddon (v Ransom), 1923
Armand (p Mowatt), 1847
Armazindy (v Riley), 1894
Armenians (p Saroyan), 1974
Armidale (v Simpson), 1979
Armies of the Night (Mailer), 1968
Armourer's Escape (p Barker), 1817
Army Alphabet (v Baum), 1900
Army Service Force Presents series (radio Laurents), 1943
Arnold (f Ingraham), 1844
Around the Docks (p Harrigan), 1877
Around the World in Eighty Days (scr Perelman), 1956
Around the World in Eighty Minutes with Douglas Fairbanks (scr Sherwood), 1931
Around You, Your House (v W. Stafford), 1979
Arrivistes (v Simpson), 1949
Arrow (f Morley), 1927
Arrow of Gold (f Ingraham), 1854(?)
Arrowsmith (scr S. Howard), 1931
Arrowsmith (f Lewis), 1925
Art of Fiction (H. James), 1885(?)
Art of Living (f J. Gardner), 1981
Art of Worldly Wisdom (v Rexroth), 1949
Artemis to Actaeon (v Wharton), 1909
Arthur Denwood (f Ingraham), 1846
Arthur Mervyn (f C. Brown), 1799
Article 47 (p Daly), 1872
Artie (f Ade), 1896
Artie (p Ade), 1907
Artificial Nigger (f O'Connor), 1957
Artist (v Jeffers), 1928
Artist (p Mencken), 1912
Arundel (f K. Roberts), 1930
As a Man Thinks (p Thomas), 1911
As a Strong Bird on Pinions Free (v Whitman), 1872
As Good as a Comedy (f Simms), 1852
As Husbands Go (scr Behrman), 1934
As Husbands Go (p Crothers), 1931
As I Lay Dying (f Faulkner), 1930
As It Was in the Beginning (v J. Miller), 1903
As Now It Would Be Snow (v Creeley), 1970
As Thousands Cheer (p Hart), 1933
As We Know (v Ashbery), 1979
As You Like It (p Daly), 1889
As Young as You Feel (scr Chayefsky), 1951
Asbestos Phoenix (v Guthrie), 1968
Ash-Wednesday (v Eliot), 1930
Ask Me Tomorrow (f Cozzens), 1940
Ask Your Mama (v Hughes), 1961
Aslan Norval (f Traven), 1960
Aspern Papers (f H. James), 1888
Aspirant (v Dreiser), 1929
Assassination Bureau Ltd. (f London), 1963
Assassinations (p Saroyan), 1979
Assembly (f J. O'Hara), 1961
Assignment (p Kopit), 1985
Assignment: Home series (radio Laurents), 1943
Assistant (f Malamud), 1957
Assommoir (p Daly), 1879
Assyrian (f Saroyan), 1950
Astonished Eye Looks Out of the Air (v Patchen), 1945
Astoria (Irving), 1836
Astounding Crime on Torrington Road (f Gillette), 1927
Astraea (v Holmes), 1850
Asylum (p Kopit), 1963
At Bay (p Thomas), 1913
At Dartmouth (v Holmes), 1940
At Fault (f Chopin), 1890
At Heaven's Gate (f R. Warren), 1943
At Liberty (p Thomas), 1912
At Liberty (p T. Williams), 1941
At Sundown (v Whittier), 1890
At the Dim'crakr Convention (p Baraka), 1980
At the Earth's Core (f E. Burroughs), 1922
At the End of the Open Road (v Simpson), 1963
At the Moon's Inn (f Lytle), 1941
At the Mountains of Madness (f Lovecraft), 1964
Atalantis (v Simms), 1832
Atlanta (v Chivers), 1853
Atlantis (Donnelly), 1882
Attitudes Towards History (Burke), 1937
Aubade (p Kopit), 1959
Auden (v Shapiro), 1974
Audubon (v R. Warren), 1969
August 22nd (f Sinclair), 1965
Aunt Fanny from Chautauqua (p Ade), 1949
Aunt Jane's Nieces series (f Baum), from 1906
Aunt Jo's Scrap-Bag (f Alcott), from 1872
Aunt Kipp (f Alcott), 1868
Aunt Mary's Preserving Kettle (f Arthur), 1863
Aurora (v Brooks), 1972
Auroras of Autumn (v Stevens), 1950
Author of Beltraffio (f H. James), 1885
Authorship (f Neal), 1830
Autobiography of a Pocket Handkerchief (f Cooper), 1949
Autobiography of an Ex-Colored Man (f Johnson), 1912
Autobiography of a Quack (f S. Mitchell), 1900
Autobiography of Alice B. Toklas (Stein), 1933
Autocrat of the Breakfast-Table (Holmes), 1858
Auto-da-Fé (p T. Williams), 1946
Autonomy (p Barry), 1919
Autumn Garden (p Hellman), 1951

Bay of Seven Islands (v Whittier), 1883
Bayou Folk (f Chopin), 1894
Be Angry at the Sun (v Jeffers), 1941
Be Yourself (p Connelly, Kaufman), 1924
Beacon Lights (f Arthur), 1869
Beaks of Eagles (v Jeffers), 1936
Bean Eaters (v Brooks), 1960
Beasley's Christmas Party (f Tarkington), 1909
Beast in Me (f Thurber), 1948
Beast in View (v Rukeyser), 1944
Beat the Devil (scr Capote), 1953
Beatrice Hallam (f J. Cooke), 1892
Beatrice, The Goldsmith's Daughter (f Ingraham), 1847
Beau Brummell (p Fitch), 1890
Beauchampe (f Simms), 1842
Beautiful and Damned (f Fitzgerald), 1922
Beautiful Changes (v Wilbur), 1947
Beautiful Lady (f Tarkington), 1905
Beautiful People (p Saroyan), 1941
Beautiful Widow (f Arthur), 1847
Beauty and the Beast (f B. Taylor), 1872
Beauty and the Jacobin (p Tarkington), 1912
Beauty Part (p Perelman), 1962
Because I Was Flesh (f Dahlberg), 1964
Because It Is (v Patchen), 1960
Because She Loved Him So (p Gillette), 1898
Bech (f Updike), 1970
Bech Is Back (f Updike), 1983
Beckonings (v Brooks), 1975
Becky Sharp (p L. Mitchell), 1899
Bed Riddance (v Nash), 1970
Bedouins (Huneker), 1920
Bedroom Suite (p Morley), 1924
Bedrooms Have Windows (f E. Gardner), 1949
Bedside Manner (Benchley), 1952
Bedside Manners (p Behrman), 1923
Bee-Hunter (f Cooper), 1848
Beetle Leg (f Hawkes), 1951
Befo' de War (v Page), 1888
Before Adam (f London), 1907
Before and After the Election (f Arthur), 1853
Before Breakfast (p O'Neill), 1916
Before Disaster (v Winters), 1934
Before March (v MacLeish), 1932
Before Midnight (f Stout), 1955
Before the Brave (v Patchen), 1936
Before the Curfew (v Holmes), 1888
Before the Flowers of Friendship Faded Friendship Faded (v Stein), 1931
Before the Gringo Came (f Atherton), 1894
Before Your Very Eyes! (v Olson), 1967
Beggar on Horseback (p Connelly, Kaufman), 1924
Beginning Again (f Alcott), 1875
Beginning and the End (v Jeffers), 1963
Beginning of Wisdom (f S. Benét), 1921
Behind a Mask (f Alcott), 1975
Behind Prison Walls (tv Capote), 1972
Behind the Scenes (p Harrigan), 1875
Behold My Wife (scr La Farge), 1934
Behold the Bridegroom (p Kelly), 1927
Behold, We Live (p van Druten), 1932
Being Here (v R. Warren), 1980
Being There (f Kosinski), 1971
Being There (scr Kosinski), 1980
Belfry of Bruges (v Longfellow), 1845
Belgrade, November 19, 1963 (v F. O'Hara), 1973
Bell, Book,and Candle (p van Druten), 1950
Bell in the Fog (f Atherton), 1905
Bell Jar (f Plath), 1963
Bell Martin (f Arthur), 1843
Belle's Stratagem (p Daly), 1892
Bell-Ringer of Angel's (f Harte), 1894
Beloved (f Updike), 1982
Ben Barclay's Courage (f Alger), 1904
Ben Bruce (f Alger), 1901
Ben Logan's Triumph (f Alger), 1908
Ben Stanton, The Explorer (f Alger), 1887
Ben, The Luggage Boy (f Alger), 1870
Bend Sinister (f Nabokov), 1947
Bending the Bow (v Duncan), 1968
Ben-Hur (f Wallace), 1880
Benito Cereno (p R. Lowell), 1964
Ben's Nugget (f Alger), 1882
Benton's Row (f Yerby), 1954
Beppo and Beth (p Wilson), 1937
Berenike (p Rexroth), 1951
Berkeley (f Ingraham), 1846
Bernard Brook's Adventures (f Alger), 1903
Bernard Carr (f Farrell), 1952
Bernard Clare (f Farrell), 1946
Bernard Clayre (f Farrell), 1948
Bernice (p Glaspell), 1919
Bernice (p Wilder), 1957
Berry-Picker (p Purdy), 1981
Bertha's Christmas Vision (f Alger), 1856
Bertram Cope's Year (f Fuller), 1919
Bertrand (f Ingraham), 1845
Beside the Bonnie Briar Bush (p Thomas), 1905
Best Hour of the Night (v Simpson), 1983
Best Man (p Vidal), 1960
Best Man (scr Vidal), 1964
Best Things in Life Are Free (scr J. O'Hara), 1956
Best Years of Our Lives (scr Sherwood), 1946
Bestiary for My Daughters Mary and Katharine (v Rexroth), 1955
Bethel Merriday (f Lewis), 1940
Betrothal (p Boker), 1850
Better Sort (f H. James), 1903
Betty Putnam (p W. Williams), 1910
Betty Zane (f Grey), 1903
Betty's Finish (p Fitch), 1890
Between the Dark and the Daylight (f Howells), 1907
Between the Silence and the Surf (p MacLeish), 1944
Between Time and Timbuktu (tv Vonnegut), 1972
Between Two Wars (v Rexroth), 1982
Between Two Worlds (p Rice), 1934
Between Two Worlds (f Sinclair), 1941
Beware the Curves (f E. Gardner), 1956
Bewitched (p S. Howard), 1924
Beyond Culture (Trilling), 1965
Beyond Defeat (f Glasgow), 1966
Beyond Desire (f S. Anderson), 1932
Beyond Life (f Cabell), 1919
Beyond the Farthest Star (f E. Burroughs), 1964
Beyond the Horizon (p O'Neill), 1920
Beyond the Law (scr Mailer), 1968
Beyond the Mountains (p Rexroth), 1951
Beyond Thirty (f E. Burroughs), 1955

Bianca Visconti (p Willis), 1837
Bib Ballads (v Lardner), 1915
Bid Me to Live (f Doolittle), 1960
Big and Little of It (p Harrigan), 1871
Big Bonanza (p Daly), 1875
Big Broadcast of 1936 (scr Parker), 1935
Big Clock (f Fearing), 1946
Big Deal (tv Chayefsky), 1953
Big Knife (p Odets), 1949
Big Knockover (f Hammett), 1948
Big Land (f Grey), 1976
Big Laugh (f J. O'Hara), 1962
Big Mitch (tv Odets), 1963
Big Money (f Dos Passos), 1936
Big Noise (scr Hecht), 1928
Big Rise (p Thomas), 1882
Big Sea (tv Hughes), 1965
Big Shot (f Hergesheimer), 1932
Big Sleep (f Chandler), 1939
Big Sleep (scr Faulkner), 1946
Big Sur (f Kerouac), 1962
Big Town (f Lardner), 1921
Big Wave (scr Buck), 1962
Big Woods (f Faulkner), 1955
Bigger They Come (f E. Gardner), 1939
Biglow Papers (v J. Lowell), from 1848
Bill Porter (p Sinclair), 1924
Bill Sturdy (f Alger), 1887
Billie (p Cohan), 1928
Billy Budd (f Melville), 1924
Billy the Kid (scr MacArthur), 1930
Billy Woodhull (f Ingraham), 1844
Bimbo, The Pirate (p Tarkington), 1926
Biography (p Behrman), 1932
Biography of the Life of Manuel (f Cabell), from 1927
Bird Cage (p Laurents), 1950
Bird Center (p Ade), 1904
Bird in the Cage (p Fitch), 1903
Bird's Nest (f S. Jackson), 1954
Birds of America (f McCarthy), 1971
Birth (f Gale), 1918
Birth of Galahad (p Hovey), 1898
Birthday (p Goodman), 1941
Birthday Cake for David (v Merrill), 1955
Birth-Day Song of Liberty (v Chivers), 1856
Birthright (f Stribling), 1922
Bishop and the Bogie-Man (f J. Harris), 1909
Bishop and the Boogerman (f J. Harris), 1909
Bishop's Wife (scr Sherwood), 1947
Bit Between My Teeth (Wilson), 1965
Bite on the Bullet (Perelman), 1957
Bits of Paradise (f Fitzgerald), 1973
Bitter Creek (f Boyd), 1939
Bitter Lotus (f Bromfield), 1944
Bitterns (v Wescott), 1920
Bixby Canyon Ocean Path Word Breeze (v Ginsberg), 1972
Black and White Stories (f Caldwell), 1984
Black Armour (v Wylie), 1923
Black Art (v Baraka), 1966
Black Beetles in Amber (v Bierce), 1892
Black Boy (R. Wright), 1945
Black Cargo (f Marquand), 1925
Black Christ (v Cullen), 1929
Black Commercial No. 2 (p Bullins), 1973
Black Flame (f Du Bois), from 1957
Black Ice (f Tourgée), 1888
Black Is My Truelove's Hair (f E. Roberts), 1938
Black Magic (v Baraka), 1969
Black Man (p Payne), 1940
Black Mass (p Baraka), 1966
Black Mesa (f Grey), 1955
Black Money (f Macdonald), 1966
Black Mountain (f Stout), 1954
Black Nativity (p Hughes), 1961
Black Orchids (f Stout), 1942
Black Oxen (f Atherton), 1923
Black Ralph (f Ingraham), 1844
Black Riders (v S. Crane), 1895
Black Rock (v Fletcher), 1928
Black Sea Fighters (scr Odets), 1943
Black Sheep (p Rice), 1932
Black Spring (f H. Miller), 1936
Black Swan (scr Hecht), 1942
Black Swan (v Merrill), 1946
Blackbeard (p Green), 1922
Blackberry Winter (f R. Warren), 1946
Blackguard (f Bodenheim), 1923
Blackmail (p Richard Harding Davis), 1913
Blade Runner (f W. Burroughs), 1979
Blanche Talbot (f Ingraham), 1847
Blind Bow-Boy (f Van Vechten), 1923
Blind Boy (p Dunlap), 1803
Blind Date (f Kosinski), 1977
Blind Nelly's Boy (f Arthur), 1867
Blindman's World (f Bellamy), 1898
Blithedale Romance (f Hawthorne), 1852
Blix (f Norris), 1899
Blockade (scr Lawson), 1938
Blood for a Stranger (v Jarrell), 1942
Blood Money (f Hammett), 1943
Blood of the Martyr (p S. Crane), 1940
Blood of the Prophets (v Masters), 1905
Blood on the Dining Room Floor (f Stein), 1948
Blood Oranges (f Hawkes), 1971
Blood Seedling (f Hay), 1972
Bloodrites (p Baraka), 1970
Bloody Chasm (f De Forest), 1881
Blue and the Gray (p Harrigan), 1875
Blue and the Gray (p Morley), 1930
Blue Beard (p Dunlap), 1803
Blue Bitch (tv Shepard), 1972
Blue City (f Macdonald), 1947
Blue Dahlia (scr Chandler), 1946
Blue Danube (f Bemelmans), 1945
Blue Devil (p Thomas), 1920
Blue Estuaries (v Bogan), 1968
Blue Grass (p Daly), 1877
Blue Hammer (f Macdonald), 1976
Blue Hotel (p Agee), 1960
Blue Mouse (p Fitch), 1908
Blue Plate Special (f Runyon), 1934
Blue Ribbon (p Harrigan), 1894
Blue Sky (v Snyder), 1969
Blue Sphere (p Dreiser), 1916
Blue Swallows (v Nemerov), 1967
Blue Thunder (p Green), 1928
Blue Voyage (f Aiken), 1927
Blues for Mister Charlie (p James Baldwin), 1964

Bridges of Binding (Benchley), 1928
Brief Moment (p Behrman), 1931
Brief Moment (scr Behrman), 1933
Briefings (v Ammons), 1971
Brigadier and the Golf Widow (f Cheever), 1964
Brigantine (f Ingraham), 1847
Brigham Young—Frontiersman (scr Bromfield), 1940
Bright Cages (Morley), 1965
Bright Metal (f Stribling), 1928
Bright Procession (f Buck), 1952
Bright Shawl (f Hergesheimer), 1922
Bright Star (p Barry), 1935
Bring! Bring! (f Aiken), 1925
Bring It Up from the Dark (v Duncan), 1970
Bring on the Girls (p Kaufman), 1934
Bringing Jazz! (v Bodenheim), 1930
Brink of Darkness (f Winters), 1947
British Prison-Ship (v Freneau), 1781
Broadway Jones (p Cohan), 1912
Broadway Melody of 1936 (scr Hart), 1935
Broken Battalions (v Hayne), 1885
Broken Necks (f Hecht), 1924
Broken Span (v W. Williams), 1941
Broken Vase (f Stout), 1941
Broker of Bogota (p Bird), 1834
Bronze (v Merrill), 1984
Bronze Wood (v Sandburg), 1941
Bronzeville Boys and Girls (v Brooks), 1956
Brook Evans (f Glaspell), 1928
Brooklyn Branding Parlors (v Purdy), 1986
Brooksmith (f H. James), 1892
Brother Fire (p Wilder), 1928
Brother Jonathan (f Neal), 1825
Brother to Dragons (v R. Warren), 1953
Brotherhood of Man (p K. Roberts), 1934
Brotherhood of Men (v Eberhart), 1949
Brothers (radio Hughes), 1942
Brothers of No Kin (f Richter), 1924
Brownstone Eclogues (v Aiken), 1942
Brücke im Dschungel (f Traven), 1929
Bruising Bill (f Ingraham), 1845
Brutus (p Payne), 1818
Buccaneer (p M. Anderson), 1925
Buccaneers (f Wharton), 1938
Buchanan Dying (p Updike), 1974
Buck in the Snow (v Millay), 1928
Buckdancer's Choice (v Dickey), 1965
Bucktails (p Paulding), 1847
Buffalo Hunter (f Grey), 1977
Builders (f Glasgow), 1919
Build-Up (f W. Williams), 1952
Bulldog Drummond (scr S. Howard), 1929
Bullet Park (f Cheever), 1969
Bulwark (f Dreiser), 1946
Bunch o' Berries (p Harrigan), 1883
Bundle of Letters (f H. James), 1880
Bundle of Lies (p Daly), 1895
Burglar (p Thomas), 1889
Burglar of the Zodiac (v W. Benét), 1918
Burial of John Brown (v Channing), 1878
Burial of the Guns (f Page), 1894
Buried Child (p Shepard), 1978
Buried Treasure (f E. Roberts), 1931
Burning Bright (f Steinbeck), 1950
Burning Bright (p Steinbeck), 1950
Burning City (v S. Benét), 1936
Burning Daylight (f London), 1910
Burning Mountain (v Fletcher), 1946
Burning-Glass (f Behrman), 1968
Burnt Norton (v Eliot), 1943
Burr (f Vidal), 1973
Burr Oaks (v Eberhart), 1947
Burton (f Ingraham), 1838
Bus Riley's Back in Town (p Inge), 1962
Bus Riley's Back in Town (scr Inge), 1965
Bus Stop (p Inge), 1955
Busch (f Traven), 1928
Bushwhackers (f Murfree), 1899
Business Is Business (p Kaufman, Parker), 1925
But Even So (v Patchen), 1968
But for Whom Charlie (p Behrman), 1964
Butter and Egg Man (p Kaufman), 1925
Buttered Side Down (f Ferber), 1912
BUtterfield 8 (f J. O'Hara), 1935
Butterfly (f Cain), 1947
Butterfly House (f Freeman), 1912
Button's Inn (f Tourgée), 1887
By Al Lebowitz's Pool (v Nemerov), 1979
By Avon River (v Doolittle), 1949
By George (Kaufman), 1979
By Love Possessed (f Cozzens), 1957
By Shore and Sedge (f Harte), 1885
By the Candelabra's Glare (v Baum), 1898
By the Light of the Soul (f Freeman), 1907
Bylow Hill (f Cable), 1902

Cabala (f Wilder), 1926
Cabbages and Kings (f Henry), 1904
Cabin in the Cotton (scr Green), 1932
Cabot Wright Begins (f Purdy), 1964
Caesarian Operations (p Inge), 1972
Caesar's Column (f Donnelly), 1890
Caesar's Gate (v Duncan), 1955
Cain (v Simms), 1829
Cairo, Shanghai, Bombay! (p T. Williams), 1935
Calamity Town (f Queen), 1942
Calavar (f Bird), 1834
Calaynos (p Boker), 1848
Calendar (v Creeley), 1983
Calendar of Crime (f Queen), 1952
Calhoun (f Algren), 1980
Caliban (p MacKaye), 1916
Calico Shoes (f Farrell), 1934
Calidorf (Bird), 1941
California and Oregon Trail (Parkman), 1849
California Stories (f Harte), 1884
California Water Plan (v Snyder), 1973
Californians (f Atherton), 1898
Californians (v Jeffers), 1916
Call (p Inge), 1968
Call It Sleep (f H. Roth), 1934
Call of the Canyon (f Grey), 1924
Call of the Wild (tv Dickey), 1976
Call of the Wild (f London), 1903
Callahan the Detective (p Harrigan), 1877
Calms of Capricorn (p O'Neill), 1982
Cameo Kirby (p Tarkington), 1908
Camera Obscura (f Nabokov), 1936

Camino Real (p T. Williams), 1953
Camping Out (p B. Howard), 1886
Can All This Grandeur Perish? (f Farrell), 1937
Can Grande's Castle (v A. Lowell), 1918
Can Such Things Be? (f Bierce), 1893
Canary in a Cat House (f Vonnegut), 1961
Candide (p Hellman, Parker, Wilbur), 1956
Candle in the Cabin (v Lindsay), 1926
Candle in the Wind (p M. Anderson), 1941
Candle-Lightin' Time (p Dunbar), 1901
Candles in Babylon (v Levertov), 1982
Candles of Your Eyes (f Purdy), 1985
Candles to the Sun (p T. Williams), 1937
Cane (f Toomer), 1923
Cannery Row (f Steinbeck), 1945
Cannibal (f Hawkes), 1949
Cannibals and Christians (Mailer), 1966
Cannibals and Missionaries (f McCarthy), 1979
Canolles (f J. Cooke), 1877
Canterbury Pilgrims (p MacKaye), 1903
Cantos (v Pound), from 1925
Canzoni (v Pound), 1911
Cape Cod (Thoreau), 1865
Cape Cod Lighter (f J. O'Hara), 1962
Capitol (p Thomas), 1895
Captain Archer's Daughter (f Deland), 1932
Captain Caution (f K. Roberts), 1934
Captain Craig (v Robinson), 1902
Captain Jim's Friend (f Harte), 1889
Captain Jinks of the Horse Marines (p Fitch), 1901
Captain Kyd (f Ingraham), 1839
Captain Macklin, His Memoirs (f Richard Harding Davis), 1902
Captain of Company K (f Kirkland), 1891
Captain of Industry (f Sinclair), 1906
Captain of the Gray-Horse Troop (f Garland), 1902
Captain Ralph (f J. Cooke), 1892
Captain Rebel (f Yerby), 1956
Captain Spike (f Cooper), 1848
Captain Stormfield's Visit to Heaven (f Twain), 1909
Captain Velasco (f Ingraham), 1847
Captains Courageous (scr Connelly), 1937
Captain's Youngest (f Burnett), 1894
Captives of the Desert (f Grey), 1952
Carancro (f Cable), 1887
Career in C Major (f Cain), 1943
Careful and Strict Enquiry into . . . Freedom of Will . . . (Edwards), 1754
Careless Clock (v Van Doren), 1947
Careless Love (v Ginsberg), 1978
Carl Werner (f Simms), 1838
Carlos among the Candles (p Stevens), 1917
Carmen (p Green), 1954
Carolina (scr Green), 1934
Carolina Chansons (v Heyward), 1922
Caroline Archer (f Ingraham), 1844
Carpentered Hen (v Updike), 1958
Carpenter's Gothic (f Gaddis), 1985
Carreta (f Traven), 1935
Carrier of Ladders (v Merwin), 1970
Carry-Over (f Suckow), 1936
Carson of Venus (f E. Burroughs), 1939
Carter and Other People (f Marquis), 1921
Carwin the Biloquist (f C. Brown), 1822
Casa Braccio (f Crawford), 1895
Casanova (p S. Howard), 1923
Case of Charles Dexter Ward (f Lovecraft), 1952
Case of Elinor Norton (f Rinehart), 1934
Case of George Dedlow (f S. Mitchell), 1900
Case of Jennie Brice (f Rinehart), 1913
Case of the . . . series (f E. Gardner), from 1933
Case of the Crushed Petunias (p T. Williams), 1948
Case of the Seven Murders (f Queen), 1958
Casino Royale (scr Hecht, Heller), 1967
Cass Timberlane (f Lewis), 1945
Cassique of Accabee (v Simms), 1849
Cassique of Kiawah (f Simms), 1859
Cast a Cold Eye (f McCarthy), 1950
Cast Adrift (f Arthur), 1873
Cast upon the Breakers (f Alger), 1974
Castaway (f Cozzens), 1934
Castle Dismal (f Simms), 1844
Castle Nowhere (f Woolson), 1875
Cat and the Blackbird (v Duncan), 1967
Cat and the King (f Auchincloss), 1981
Cat, Mouse, Man, Woman (p Saroyan), 1958
Cat of Many Tails (f Queen), 1949
Cat on a Hot Tin Roof (p T. Williams), 1955
Cat That Jumped Out of the Story (f Hecht), 1947
Cat-Boat (p MacKaye), 1912
Catch My Boy on Sunday (tv Chayefsky), 1953
Catcher in the Rye (f Salinger), 1951
Catch-22 (f Heller), 1961
Catch-22 (p Heller), 1973
Catechism (v W. Stafford), 1979
Catered Affair (tv Chayefsky), 1955
Catered Affair (scr Vidal), 1956
Cathedral (v J. Lowell), 1870
Cathedral Singer (f Allen), 1916
Catherine Wheel (f J. Stafford), 1952
Cat's Cradle (f Vonnegut), 1963
Cat's Meow (f Morris), 1975
Cats of Ulthar (f Lovecraft), 1935
Cats Prowl at Night (f E. Gardner), 1943
Caught (scr Laurents), 1949
Caught Wet (p Crothers), 1931
Causal Mythology (v Olson), 1969
Cause for Wonder (f Morris), 1963
Cavalcade (scr Behrman), 1933
Cavalier (f Cable), 1901
Cavalier of Old South Carolina (f Simms), 1966
Cavanagh, Forest Ranger (f Garland), 1910
Cave (f R. Warren), 1959
Cave at Machpelah (p Goodman), 1958
Cave Dwellers (p Saroyan), 1957
Cave Girl (f E. Burroughs), 1925
Cavender's House (v Robinson), 1929
Caviare at the Funeral (v Simpson), 1980
Cawdor (v Jeffers), 1928
Cecilia (f Crawford), 1902
Cecilia Howard (f Arthur), 1844
Cedardale (f Arthur), 1852
Celebrated Hard Case (p Harrigan), 1878
Celebrated Jumping Frog of Calaveras County (f Twain), 1867
Celebrity (f Churchill), 1898
Celestial Rail-Road (f Hawthorne), 1843
Centaur (f Updike), 1963
Centaurs (p Wilder), 1928

Centennial Meditation of Columbia (v Lanier), 1876
Central Motion (v Dickey), 1983
Century's Ebb (f Dos Passos), 1975
Ceremony (v Wilbur), 1950
Ceremony in Lone Tree (f Morris), 1960
Certain Hour (f Cabell), 1916
Certain People (f Wharton), 1930
Certain Women (f Caldwell), 1957
Chainbearer (f Cooper), 1845
Chains (f Dreiser), 1927
Chains of Dew (p Glaspell), 1922
Chains of the Heart (p Dunlap), 1804
Chair Endowed (p Green), 1954
Chalk Face (f Frank), 1924
Chamber Music (p Kopit), 1971
Champagne Charley (p Thomas), 1901
Champagne for One (f Stout), 1958
Champagne Pool (p J. O'Hara), 1961
Champion (f Murfree), 1902
Champion from Far Away (f Hecht), 1931
Chance Acquaintance (f Howells), 1873
Chance Acquaintance (p van Druten), 1927
Change (v Creeley), 1972
Change (v Ginsberg), 1963
Change of World (v Rich), 1951
Change Your Bedding (p F. O'Hara), 1951
Changing Light at Sandover (v Merrill), 1982
Changing Ways of Love (tv Perelman), 1957
Channel Road (p Kaufman), 1929
Chants for the Boer (v J. Miller), 1900
Chapel of the Hermits (v Whittier), 1853
Chapters for the Orthodox (f Marquis), 1934
Character Sketches (f Riley), 1886
Characteristics (f S. Mitchell), 1892
Charity Ball (p Belasco), 1889
Charlemont (f Simms), 1856
Charles Blackford (f Ingraham), 1845
Charles Stuart (p Chivers), 1980
Charles the Second (p Irving, Payne), 1824
Charleston and Her Satirists (v Simms), 1848
Charlie Codman's Cruise (f Alger), 1866
Charlotte (f Rowson), 1791
Charlotte Temple (f Rowson), 1794
Charlotte's Daughter (f Rowson), 1828
Charlotte's Web (f White), 1952
Charm (v Creeley), 1968
Charmed Life (f McCarthy), 1955
Charnel Rose (v Aiken), 1918
Chase (scr Hellman), 1966
Chaste Adventures of Joseph (p Dell), 1914
Chaste Planet (f Updike), 1980
Chatelaine of La Trinité (f Fuller), 1892
Chauve-Souris (p Parker), 1922
Cheating the Kidnappers (p Kaufman), 1935
Cheer Up (p Rinehart), 1912
Cheerful, By Request (f Ferber), 1918
Cheers for Miss Bishop (scr S. Benét), 1941
Chekhov on the West Heath (v Levertov), 1977
Chelovek lz SSSR (p Nabokov), 1926
Chelsea Rooming House (v Gregory), 1930
Cherished and Shared of Old (f Glaspell), 1940
Cherry (f Tarkington), 1903
Chessman of Mars (f E. Burroughs), 1922
Chester Rand (f Alger), 1903
Chestnut Tree (v Tyler), 1931
Chevalier of Pensieri-Vani (f Fuller), 1890
Chicago (p Shepard), 1965
Chicago Poems (v Sandburg), 1916
Chicken Inspector No. 23 (Perelman), 1966
Chief Joseph of the Nez Perce (v R. Warren), 1983
Child (v Plath), 1971
Child is Born (radio S. Benét), 1942
Childe Roland to the Dark Tower Came (p Wilder), 1928
Childhood (p Wilder), 1960
Childhood Is Not Forever (f Farrell), 1969
Childish Jokes (p Goodman), 1938
Children (v Creeley), 1978
Children (f Wharton), 1928
Children and Older People (f Suckow), 1931
Children and Others (f Cozzens), 1964
Children Are Bored on Sunday (f J. Stafford), 1953
Children at the Gate (f Wallant), 1964
Children I Have Known (f Burnett), 1892
Children Is All (f Purdy), 1961
Children of God (f Fisher), 1939
Children of the Albatross (f Nin), 1947
Children of the Frost (f London), 1902
Children of the King (f Crawford), 1893
Children of the Market Place (f Masters), 1922
Children of the Night (v Robinson), 1897
Children of the Sea (p O'Neill), 1972
Children's Hour (p Hellman), 1934
Children's Hour (scr Hellman), 1961
Children's Hour (f S. Mitchell), 1864
Children's Orchard (v Rukeyser), 1947
Child's Garden of Curses (Perelman), 1951
Child-World (v Riley), 1896
Chill (f Macdonald), 1964
Chills and Fever (v Ransom), 1924
Chimera (f Barth), 1972
Chimes (f Herrick), 1926
Chimmie Fadden (p Thomas), 1896
Chimneysmoke (v Morley), 1921
China Flight (f Buck), 1945
China Girl (scr Hecht), 1942
China Sky (f Buck), 1942
China to America (p Buck), 1944
Chinese Nightingale (v Lindsay), 1917
Chinese Orange Mystery (f Queen), 1934
Chita (f Hearn), 1889
Chivalry (f Cabell), 1909
Chocurua (p Eberhart), 1981
Choir Invisible (f Allen), 1897
Choosing Company (p Schwartz), 1936
Chorus for Survival (v Gregory), 1935
Chosen Country (f Dos Passos), 1951
Chris (p O'Neill), 1920
Chris Christophersen (p O'Neill), 1982
Chris Sick (p Saroyan), 1969
Chris'mus Is A-Comin' (p Dunbar), 1905
Christian Slave (p Stowe), 1855
Christine (p Buck), 1960
Christmas (f Gale), 1912
Christmas Carol (tv M. Anderson), 1954
Christmas Carol (p Connelly, Kaufman), 1922
Christmas Comes to Hjalsen (v Clark), 1930
Christmas Delerium (v Wilson), 1955
Christmas Dream (f Alcott), 1886

Christmas Eve (p Hecht), 1928
Christmas Eve Service at Midnight at St. Michael's (v Bly), 1972
Christmas Gift from Fairy Land (f Paulding), 1838
Christmas Joys and Sorrows (p Harrigan), 1877
Christmas: May 10, 1970 (v Creeley), 1970
Christmas Memory (f Capote), 1966
Christmas Memory (tv Capote), 1966
Christmas 1939 (v Saroyan), 1939
Christmas Present, Christmas Presence! (v Duncan), 1967
Christmas Psalm (v Saroyan), 1935
Christmas Story (f Mencken), 1946
Christmas Story (f Porter), 1958
Christmas Tree (v Cummings), 1928
Christopher Blake (p Hart), 1946
Christus (v Longfellow), 1872
Chronicles of Aunt Minervy Ann (f J. Harris), 1899
Chronicles of the City of Gotham (f Paulding), 1830
Chronicles of Wolfert's Roost (f Irving), 1855
Chrysanthemums (v Bly), 1967
Chuck (p MacKaye), 1912
Chums (p Belasco, Herne), 1879
Cigarette-Maker's Romance (f Crawford), 1890
Cimarron (f Ferber), 1930
Cinderella (f Richard Harding Davis), 1896
Cipango's Hinder Door (v Dahlberg), 1965
Circe (v Doolittle), 1917
Circuit Rider (f Eggleston), 1874
Circular Staircase (f Rinehart), 1908
Circumstance (f S. Mitchell), 1901
Circus Day (f Ade), 1903
Circus in the Attic (f R. Warren), 1948
Circus World (scr Hecht), 1964
Citadel (scr van Druten), 1938
Cities of the Interior (f Nin), 1959
Cities of the Red Night (f W. Burroughs), 1981
Citizenship (p Cain), 1926
City (p Fitch), 1909
City and the Pillar (f Vidal), 1948
City Block (f Frank), 1922
City Chap (p Ade), 1910
City Clerk and His Sister (f Sedgwick), 1851
City Life (f Barthelme), 1970
City Looking Glass (p Bird), 1933
City of Illusion (f Fisher), 1941
City of the Silent (v Simms), 1850
City of Trembling Leaves (f Clark), 1945
City Psalm (v Levertov), 1964
City Streets (scr Hammett), 1931
City Wears a Slouch Hat (radio Patchen), 1942
City Winter (v F. O'Hara), 1952
Civil Disobedience (Thoreau), 1866
Civil War Letters (f Nasby), 1962
Claire Ambler (f Tarkington), 1928
Clara Howard (f C. Brown), 1801
Clara's Old Man (p Bullins), 1965
Clarel (v Melville), 1876
Clarence (f Harte), 1895
Clarence (f Sedgwick), 1830
Clarence (p Tarkington), 1921
Clarence Allen (f Ade), 1903
Clari (p Payne), 1823
Clarice (p Gillette), 1905
Clark Gifford's Body (f Fearing), 1942
Clark's Field (f Herrick), 1914
Clash by Night (p Odets), 1941
Class Poem (v J. Lowell), 1838
Classics and Commercials (Wilson), 1950
Claudell (f Caldwell), 1959
Claudelle Inglish (f Caldwell), 1959
Clear Cut (v Snyder), n.d.
Clear Shifting Water (v Olson), 1968
Clearing in the Woods (p Laurents), 1957
Clergyman's Wife (f Mowatt), 1867
Clerk's Journal (v Aiken), 1971
Clevinger's Trial (p Heller), 1973
Clew of the Forgotten Murder (f E. Gardner), 1935
Cliff-Dwellers (f Fuller), 1893
Climate of Eden (p Hart), 1952
Climbers (p Fitch), 1901
Clipper-Yacht (f Ingraham), 1845
Clock Without Hands (f McCullers), 1961
Clorindy (p Dunbar), 1898
Close Chaplet (v Riding), 1926
Close Harmony (p Parker, Rice), 1924
Close the Book (p Glaspell), 1917
Close to Home (f Caldwell), 1962
Closed Gates (scr Queen), 1927
Clotel (f W. Brown), 1853
Clotelle (f W. Brown), 1864
Cloth of the Tempest (v Patchen), 1943
Clothes for a Summer Hotel (p T. Williams), 1980
Cloud Nine (f Cain), 1984
Clouds (p Gale), 1936
Clouds (v W. Williams), 1948
Cloudy with Showers (p Dell), 1931
Club Bedroom (p Auchincloss), 1967
Club Room (f Arthur), 1845
Clue of the Hungry Horse (f E. Gardner), 1947
Clue of the Runaway Blonde (f E. Gardner), 1947
Clues of the Caribbees (f Stribling), 1929
C'mon Back to Heavenly House (p Bullins), 1978
Coal War (f Sinclair), 1976
Coast of Bohemia (f Howells), 1893
Coast of Bohemia (v Page), 1906
Coast of Illyria (p Parker), 1949
Coast of Trees (v Ammons), 1981
Coat Without a Seam (v Kunitz), 1974
Cobwebs from an Empty Skull (f Bierce), 1874
Cock of the Air (scr Sherwood), 1932
Cock Pit (f Cozzens), 1928
Cock Robin (p Barry, Rice), 1928
Cockpit (f Kosinski), 1975
Cocktail Party (p Eliot), 1949
Cocoanuts (p Kaufman), 1925
Cod Head (v W. Williams), 1932
Code of the West (f Grey), 1934
Coelestinus (Mather), 1723
Coffee-House (p Fuller), 1925
Cold Mountain Poems (v Snyder), 1965
Cold Spring (v E. Bishop), 1955
Cold Spring (v Levertov), 1969
Cold Wind and the Warm (p Behrman), 1958
Collaboration (f H. James), 1893
Collages (f Nin), 1964
Collapsing Cosmoses (f Lovecraft), 1977
College Widow (p Ade), 1904
Colonel Carter of Cartersville (p Thomas), 1892

Colonel George of Mount Vernon (p Thomas), 1898
Col. Ross of Piedmont (f J. Cooke), 1893
Colonel Satan (p Tarkington), 1932
Colonel Sellers as a Scientist (p Howells, Twain), 1887
Colonel Starbottle's Client (f Harte), 1892
Colonel's Dream (f Chesnutt), 1905
Color (v Cullen), 1925
Color of Darkness (f Purdy), 1957
Color Purple (f Walker), 1982
Color Struck (p Hurston), 1926
Colorado (f Bromfield), 1947
Colorado (p Thomas), 1901
Colors of the Day (p Rukeyser), 1961
Colossus (v Plath), 1960
Colour Out of Space (f Lovecraft), 1964
Coloured Baby Show (p Harrigan), 1878
Columbia the Gem of the Ocean (p Baraka), 1973
Columbiad (v Barlow), 1807
Columbian Daughter (p Rowson), 1800
Combustion (p Thomas), 1884
Come and Get It (f Ferber), 1935
Come Back, Dr. Caligari (f Barthelme), 1964
Come Back, Little Sheba (p Inge), 1949
Come Here (p Daly), 1870
Come In (v Frost), 1943
Come, My Beloved (f Buck), 1953
Comedian (p Belasco), 1923
Comedy of Conscience (f S. Mitchell), 1903
Comedy of Those Extraordinary Twins (f Twain), 1894
Comfort of the Hills (v S. Mitchell), 1909
Comforted (f Arthur), 1873
Comic Artist (p Glaspell), 1927
Comic Tragedies (p Alcott), 1893
Coming Forth by Day of Osiris Jones (v Aiken), 1931
Coming of Mrs. Patrick (p Crothers), 1907
Coming Through the Rye (p Santayana), 1942
Command the Morning (f Buck), 1959
Commodity of Dreams (f Nemerov), 1959
Commodus (p Wallace), 1876
Common Glory (p Green), 1947
Common Glory Song-Book (v Green), 1951
Common Lot (f Herrick), 1904
Common Man (p Hecht), 1944
Common Sense (Paine), 1776
Company She Keeps (f McCarthy), 1942
Compass Flower (v Merwin), 1977
Complaint (v Wilbur), 1968
Compromise (p Ashbery), 1956
Comrade X (scr Hecht), 1940
Concerning a Woman of Sin (f Hecht), 1947
Conclusive Evidence (Nabokov), 1951
Condemned (scr S. Howard), 1929
Condensed Novels and Other Papers (f Harte), 1867
Conduct of Life (Emerson), 1860
Confederacy (p Green), 1958
Confession (f Rinehart), 1921
Confession (f Simms), 1841
Confession of John Whitlock (f Howe), 1891
Confessional (p T. Williams), 1970
Confessions of a Housekeeper (f Arthur), 1852
Confessions of Nat Turner (f Styron), 1967
Confidence (f H. James), 1879
Confidence Man (scr Ade), 1924
Confidence-Man (f Melville), 1857
Confidential Clerk (p Eliot), 1953
Confidential Service (p Cohan), 1932
Conflict (f Phillips), 1911
Confusion (f Cozzens), 1924
Congo (v Lindsay), 1914
Coniston (f Churchill), 1906
Conjure Woman (f Chesnutt), 1899
Connecticut Yankee in King Arthur's Court (f Twain), 1889
Conqueror (f Atherton), 1902
Conquest (scr Behrman), 1937
Conquest of Canaan (v Dwight), 1785
Conquest of Canaan (f Tarkington), 1905
Conquest of Everest (p Kopit), 1964
Conquest of Television (tv Kopit), 1966
Conquistador (v MacLeish), 1932
Conrad and Eudora (p Chivers), 1834
Conscript Mother (f Herrick), 1916
Considerable Speck (v Frost), 1939
Conspiracy of Kings (v Barlow), 1792
Constab Ballads (v McKay), 1912
Constance Trescot (f S. Mitchell), 1905
Constitutional Point (p Thomas), 1906
Consul (p Richard Harding Davis), 1911
Contemporaries (p Steele), 1915
Continental Op series (f Hammett), from 1945
Contrast (p Tyler), 1787
Convalescent Conversations (f Riding), 1936
Conversation (f Aiken), 1940
Conversation at Midnight (v Millay), 1937
Conversations in Rome (v Channing), 1847
Cool Million (f West), 1934
Co-op (f Sinclair), 1936
Cooper's Ward (f Alger), 1981
Cop Out (f Queen), 1969
Copernican Revolution (v Goodman), 1946
Copper Pot (f La Farge), 1942
Copper Sun (v Cullen), 1927
Copperhead (f Frederic), 1893
Copperhead (p Thomas), 1918
Cops and Robbers (f Henry), 1948
Copy-Cat (f Freeman), 1914
Coquette (f H. Foster), 1797
Cora (f Suckow), 1929
Cordelia's Aspirations (p Harrigan), 1883
Cords of Vanity (f Cabell), 1909
Corleone (f Crawford), 1897
Corn Close (v Creeley), 1980
Corner (p Bullins), 1968
Cornhuskers (v Sandburg), 1918
Coronet of the Duchess (p Fitch), 1904
Corrado Cagli (v Olson), 1947
Corsair of Casco Bay (f Ingraham), 1844
Corsons Inlet (v Ammons), 1965
Cortez (f Bird), 1835
Cost (f Phillips), 1904
Costumes by Eros (f Aiken), 1928
Cotton-Pickers (f Traven), 1956
Counsellor-at-Law (p Rice), 1931
Counsellor-at-Law (scr Rice), 1933
Count Bruga (f Hecht), 1926
Count Frontenac and New France under Louis XIV
(Parkman), 1877
Count Julian (p Chivers), 1980
Count Julian (f Simms), 1845

Count of Nine (f E. Gardner), 1958
Count of Progress (p Dreiser), 1926
Counter-Attack (scr Lawson), 1945
Counterfeit Presentment (p Howells), 1877
Counterlife (f P. Roth), 1987
Counter-Statement (Burke), 1931
Countess Gucki (p Daly), 1895
Counting the Ways (p Albee), 1976
Country By-Ways (f Jewett), 1881
Country Cousin (f Auchincloss), 1978
Country Cousin (p Tarkington), 1921
Country Doctor (f Jewett), 1884
Country Girl (p Daly), 1884
Country Girl (p Odets), 1950
Country House (v Teasdale), 1932
Country of a Thousand Years of Peace (v Merrill), 1959
Country of Strangers (f Richter), 1966
Country of the Pointed Firs (f Jewett), 1896
Country People (f Suckow), 1924
Country Year (v Van Doren), 1946
County Chairman (p Ade), 1903
Coup (f Updike), 1978
Couples (f Updike), 1968
Courage to Be New (v Frost), 1946
Court of Last Resort (E. Gardner), 1952
Court of Last Resort (p Rice), 1985
Court of Love (p Barker), 1836
Courting of Susie Brown (f Caldwell), 1952
Courtship of Miles Standish (v Longfellow), 1858
Cousin Billy (p Fitch), 1905
Cousin Kate (p B. Howard), 1889
Covered Wagon and the West (f Howe), 1928
Covering End (f H. James), 1898
Cowboy and the Lady (scr Behrman), 1938
Cowboy and the Lady (p Fitch), 1899
Cowboy Mouth (p Shepard), 1971
Cowboys (p Shepard), 1964
Cowled Lover (Bird), 1941
Cow's in the Corn (p Frost), 1929
Coxon Fund (f H. James), 1895
Cozy Lion (f Burnett), 1907
Cracks (p Purdy), 1963
Crack-Up (Fitzgerald), 1945
Cradle Song (scr Connelly), 1933
Craig's Wife (p Kelly), 1925
Crater (f Cooper), 1847
Crazy Hunter (f Boyle), 1940
Crazy Like a Fox (Perelman), 1944
Crazy Man (f Bodenheim), 1924
Cream of the Jest (f Cabell), 1917
Creation (f Vidal), 1981
Creation of the World and Other Business (p A. Miller), 1972
Creatures in an Alphabet (v Barnes), 1982
Credos and Curios (f Thurber), 1962
Creeping Siamese (f Hammett), 1950
Creole (p Belasco), 1876(?)
Creoles and Cajuns (Cable), 1959
Cressy (f Harte), 1889
Cretan Women (p Jeffers), 1954
Creve Coeur (p T. Williams), 1978
Cricket of Palmy Days (p Thomas), 1929
Crime and Again (f Stout), 1959
Crime in the Whistler Room (p Wilson), 1924
Crime of Crimes (v Lovecraft), 1915
Crime on Her Hands (f Stout), 1939
Crime Without Passion (scr Hecht, MacArthur), 1934
Crimewatch (tv Capote), 1973
Crisis (f Churchill), 1901
Crisis (Paine), from 1776
Criss-Cross (p Crothers), 1899
Critic (p Daly), 1874
Critical Fable (v A. Lowell), 1922
Critical Year (p Green), 1939
Croakers (v Drake, Halleck), 1860
Cross (v Tate), 1930
Cross and Sword (p Green), 1965
Crossing (f Churchill), 1904
Crossing the Water (v Plath), 1971
Crowded Paradise (scr Connelly), 1956
Crown of Feathers (f Singer), 1973
Crows Can't Count (f E. Gardner), 1946
Crozart Story (f Fearing), 1960
Crucial Instances (f Wharton), 1901
Crucible (p A. Miller), 1953
Cruise of the Dazzler (f London), 1902
Cruise of the Dry Dock (f Stribling), 1917
Cruise of the Jasper B (f Marquis), 1916
Cruiser of the Mist (f Ingraham), 1845
Crusade of the Excelsior (f Harte), 1887
Crushed Actors (p Harrigan), 1877
Cry Horror! (f Lovecraft), 1958
Cry Killer! (f Fearing), 1958
Crying of Lot 49 (f Pynchon), 1966
Crystal Cup (f Atherton), 1925
Crystal Gazer (v Plath), 1971
Cuba and Back (Dana), 1859
Cue for Passion (p Rice), 1958
Culprit Fay (v Drake), 1835
Cultivation of Christmas Trees (v Eliot), 1954
Culture (Pound), 1938
Cunts (v Updike), 1974
Cup of Fury (f Sinclair), 1956
Cup of Gold (f Steinbeck), 1929
Cup of Youth (v S. Mitchell), 1889
Cupid and Chow-Chow (f Alcott), 1872
Curator (v Tolson), 1965
Cure (p W. Williams), 1961
Cure of Flesh (f Cozzens), 1933
Curious Fragments (f London), 1975
Curious Republic of Gondour (f Twain), 1919
Curse of Cain (p Belasco), 1882
Curse of the Starving Class (p Shepard), 1977
Curse of Yig (f Lovecraft), 1953
Curtain of Green (f Welty), 1941
Curtains for Three (f Stout), 1951
Curve of the Catenary (f Rinehart), 1945
Custom of the Country (f Wharton), 1913
Cut Thin to Win (f E. Gardner), 1965
Cutie, A Warm Mamma (f Bodenheim, Hecht), 1924
Cyclist (p Goodman), 1941
Cynic's Word Book (Bierce), 1906
Cyprian's Prayer (p Wilson), 1954
Cyrano de Bergerac (p Daly), 1898
Cytherea (f Hergesheimer), 1922

D.A. series (f E. Gardner), from 1937
D.D. Byrde Callyng Jennie Wrenn (v Snodgrass), 1984
D.J. (p Mailer), 1967

Daddy (p Bullins), 1977
Daddy Goodness (p R. Wright), 1968
Daddy Jake the Runaway (f J. Harris), 1889
Daddy Long Legs (scr Behrman), 1931
Dagger of the Mind (f Fearing), 1941
Dagon (f Lovecraft), 1965
Dahomean (f Yerby), 1971
Dain Curse (f Hammett), 1929
Daisy Mayme (p Kelly), 1926
Daisy Miller (f H. James), 1878
Daisy Miller (p H. James), 1883
Daisy's First Winter (f Stowe), 1867
Dallas Galbraith (f Rebecca Harding Davis), 1868
Damaged Goods (f Sinclair), 1913
Damask Cheek (p van Druten), 1942
Damnation of Theron Ware (f Frederic), 1896
Damned Agitator (f Gold), 1926
Damsel of Darien (f Simms), 1839
Dan, The Detective (f Alger), 1884
Dan the Newsboy (f Alger), 1893
Dance of Death (f Bierce), 1877
Dancing Bears (v Merwin), 1954
Dancing Feather (f Ingraham), 1842
Dancing in the Chequered Shade (p van Druten), 1955
Danger (f Arthur), 1875
Danger! Memory! (p A. Miller), 1986
Danger, Men Working (p Queen), 1936(?)
Dangerous Days (f Rinehart), 1919
Dangerous Ruffian (p Howells), 1895
Dangerous Woman (f Farrell), 1957
Dangling Man (f Bellow), 1944
Daniel Jazz (v Lindsay), 1920
Danites in the Sierras (p J. Miller), 1880
Danny O'Neill series (f Farrell), from 1936
Danny's Own Story (f Marquis), 1912
Dan's Tribulations (p Harrigan), 1884
Dante (p Baraka), 1961
Dante (v Duncan), 1974
Dar (f Nabokov), 1952
Darby's Return (p Dunlap), 1789
Dare's Gift (f Glasgow), 1924
Daring Twins (f Baum), 1911
Daring Young Man on the Flying Trapeze (f Saroyan), 1934
Dark Angel (scr Hellman), 1935
Dark at the Top of the Stairs (p Inge), 1957
Dark Bridwell (f Fisher), 1931
Dark Brotherhood (f Lovecraft), 1966
Dark City! and Its Bright Side (p Daly), 1877
Dark Green, Bright Red (f Vidal), 1950
Dark Hours (p Marquis), 1924
Dark Kingdom (v Patchen), 1942
Dark Lady (f Auchincloss), 1977
Dark Laughter (f S. Anderson), 1925
Dark Mother (f Frank), 1920
Dark of the Moon (v Teasdale), 1926
Dark Possession (tv Vidal), 1954
Dark Princess (f Du Bois), 1928
Dark Room (p T. Williams), 1948
Dark Summer (v Bogan), 1929
Dark Tower (p Kaufman), 1933
Dark Tunnel (f Macdonald), 1944
Darkling Child (p Merwin), 1956
Darkness and the Deep (f Fisher), 1943
Darkness at Ingraham's Crest (f Yerby), 1979
Darkness at Noon (p Kingsley), 1951
Darling of the Gods (p Belasco), 1902
Dartmouth Lyrics (v Hovey), 1924
Dashes at Life with a Free Pencil (f Willis), 1845
Date 1601 (f Twain), 1880
Daughter of the Morning (f Gale), 1917
Daughter of the Philistines (f Boyesen), 1883
Daughter of the Snows (f London), 1902
Daughter of the Storage (Howells), 1916
Daughter of the Vine (f Atherton), 1899
Daughters of Destiny (f Baum), 1906
Daughters of the Rich (p London), 1971
Daughters of the Rich (f Saltus), 1909
David Harum (scr Green), 1934
David's Adventures (p Thomas), 1918
Dawn Ginsbergh's Revenge (Perelman), 1929
Dawn of a To-morrow (f Burnett), 1906
Dawn of a Tomorrow (p Burnett), 1909
Dawn O'Hara (f Ferber), 1911
Day (v Goodman), 1954(?)
Day after the Fair (f Purdy), 1977
Day after the Fair (p Purdy), 1979
Day Book (v Creeley), 1972
Day by Day (v R. Lowell), 1977
Day of Deliverance (v W. Benét), 1944
Day of Doom (v Wigglesworth), 1662(?)
Day of the Beast (f Grey), 1922
Day of the Locust (f West), 1939
Day of Their Wedding (f Howells), 1896
Day the Money Stopped (p M. Anderson), 1958
Day the Pig Fell into the Well (f Cheever), 1978
Day the Whores Came Out to Play Tennis (p Kopit), 1965
Day We Celebrate (p Harrigan), 1873
Day We Went West (p Harrigan), 1871
Day's End (p W. Benét), 1939
Days Gone By (v Riley), 1895
Days to Come (p Hellman), 1936
Days Without End (p O'Neill), 1934
Day's Wooing (f Caldwell), 1944
Dead End (scr Hellman), 1937
Dead End (p Kingsley), 1935
Dead Father (f Barthelme), 1975
Dead Fingers Talk (f W. Burroughs), 1963
Dead Lecturer (v Baraka), 1964
Dead of Spring (f Goodman), 1950
Dead Priestess Speaks (v Doolittle), 1983
Dead Reckoning (v Fearing), 1938
Dead Seal near McClure's Beach (v Bly), 1973
Dead Yellow Women (f Hammett), 1947
Deadeye Dick (f Vonnegut), 1982
Deadline at Dawn (scr Odets), 1946
Deal in Wheat (f Norris), 1903
Dean Dunham (f Alger), 1890
Dean's December (f Bellow), 1982
Dear Adolf (radio S. Benét), 1942
Dear Baby (f Saroyan), 1944
Dear Judas (v Jeffers), 1929
Dear Lovely Death (v Hughes), 1931
Dear Mr. President (v Snyder), 1965
Dear Old Darling (p Cohan), 1935
Dearly Beloved (f Fitzgerald), 1969
Death and Birth of David Markand (f Frank), 1934
Death and Taxes (v Parker), 1931
Death at the Rodeo (f Queen), 1951

Death Before Bedtime (f Vidal), 1953
Death Comes for the Archbishop (f Cather), 1927
Death in the Afternoon (Hemingway), 1932
Death in the Castle (f Buck), 1965
Death in the Family (f Agee), 1957
Death in the Fifth Position (f Vidal), 1952
Death in the Woods (f S. Anderson), 1933
Death Likes It Hot (f Vidal), 1954
Death List (p Bullins), 1970
Death Notebooks (v Sexton), 1974
Death of a Doxy (f Stout), 1966
Death of a Dude (f Stout), 1969
Death of a Man (f Boyle), 1936
Death of a Salesman (p A. Miller), 1949
Death of Bessie Smith (p Albee), 1960
Death of Billy the Kid (tv Vidal), 1955
Death of General Montgomery at the Siege of Quebec (p Brackenridge), 1777
Death of Malcolm X (p Baraka), 1969
Death of Nora Ryan (f Farrell), 1978
Death of the Kapowsin Tavern (v Hugo), 1965
Death of the Lion (f H. James), 1895
Death Ship (f Traven), 1934
Death, Sleep, and the Traveler (f Hawkes), 1974
Death Takes a Holiday (scr M. Anderson), 1934
Death-Dealing Gold (f Arthur), 1890
Deaths for the Ladies (v Mailer), 1962
Deborah (p L. Mitchell), 1892
Debt of Honor (f Alger), 1900
Debtor (f Freeman), 1905
Debtor and Creditor (f Arthur), 1848
Debtor's Daughter (f Arthur), 1850
Decent Birth, A Happy Funeral (p Saroyan), 1949
Declaration of Independence (Jefferson), 1776
Dedication (v Frost), 1961
Dedication (v MacLeish), 1938
Dedushka (p Nabokov), 1923
Deed from the King of Spain (p James Baldwin), 1974
Deep Mrs. Sykes (p Kelly), 1945
Deep Sleep (f Morris), 1953
Deep Tangled Wildwood (p Connelly, Kaufman), 1923
Deephaven (f Jewett), 1877
Deer Park (f Mailer), 1955
Deer Park (p Mailer), 1960
Deer Stalker (f Grey), 1949
Deerslayer (f Cooper), 1841
Defeat (p M. Warren), 1773
Defective Santa Claus (v Riley), 1904
Defense (f Nabokov), 1964
Deformed Boy (f Sedgwick), 1826
Degarmo's Wife (f Phillips), 1913
DeGaulle Story (p Faulkner), 1984
Delancey (p Thomas), 1905
Delicate Balance (p Albee), 1966
Delicate Balance (scr Albee), 1975
Delicate Prey (f Bowles), 1950
Delicious (scr Behrman), 1931
Deliverance (f Dickey), 1970
Deliverance (scr Dickey), 1972
Deliverance (f Glasgow), 1904
Delmonico's (p Daly), 1871
Delta of Venus (f Nin), 1977
Delta Wedding (f Welty), 1946
Deluge (f Phillips), 1905
Delusions, Etc. (v Berryman), 1972
DeLuxe (p Bromfield), 1934
Demagogue (f Nasby), 1891
Democracy (f Adams), 1880
Democratic John Bunyan (f Nasby), 1880
Democratic Vistas (Whitman), 1870
Demolition Downtown (p T. Williams), 1976
Demon Lady (v Whittier), 1894
Den Signede Dag (f Rølvaag), 1931
Denise (p Daly), 1885
Dentist and Patient (p Saroyan), 1968
Departure of the Ships (v Nemerov), 1966
Deplorable State of New-England (Mather), 1708
Deputy Sheriff of Comanche County (f E. Burroughs), 1940
Derivations (v Duncan), 1968
Descendant (f Glasgow), 1897
Descent of Man (f Wharton), 1904
Descent to the Dead (v Jeffers), 1931
Description of Life (f Riding), 1980
Description of the Dismal Swamp (Byrd), 1922
Description Without Place (v Stevens), 1945
Desert Gold (f Grey), 1913
Desert Incident (p Buck), 1959
Desert Music (v W. Williams), 1954
Desert of Wheat (f Grey), 1919
Deserter (f Frederic), 1898
Design in the Oriole (v W. Stafford), 1977
Desire under the Elms (p O'Neill), 1924
Desolation Angels (f Kerouac), 1965
Despair (f Nabokov), 1937
Despot of Broomsedge Cove (f Murfree), 1889
Destruction of Gotham (f J. Miller), 1886
Desultory Days (v Creeley), 1978
Details of a Sunset (f Nabokov), 1976
Detective Story (p Kingsley), 1949
Devil and Daniel Webster (p S. Benét), 1938
Devil and Daniel Webster (f S. Benét), 1937
Devil Catchers (p Bullins), 1971
Devil Is a Woman (scr Dos Passos), 1935
Devil to Pay (f Queen), 1938
Devil Tree (f Kosinski), 1973
Devils and Angels (p Eberhart), 1956
Devil's Dictionary (Bierce), 1911
Devil's Ford (f Harte), 1887
Devil's Laughter (f Yerby), 1953
Devil's Own Dear Son (f Cabell), 1949
Devil's Stocking (f Algren), 1983
Devilseed (f Yerby), 1984
Dharma Bums (f Kerouac), 1958
Diadem of Snow (p Rice), 1929
Dialect Determinism (p Bullins), 1965
Dialect Poetry (v McKay), 1972
Dialogue for Two Men (p Inge), 1975
Diamond Cutters (v Rich), 1955
Diamond Lens (O'Brien), 1921
Diamond Wedding (f Steele), 1950
Diamonds (p B. Howard), 1872
Diana Stair (f Dell), 1932
Diary of a Hackney Coachman (f Ingraham), 1844
Diary of a Man of Fifty (f H. James), 1880
Diary of a Yuppie (f Auchincloss), 1986
Diary of an Office Seeker (f Nasby), 1881
(Diblos) Notebook (f Merrill), 1965
Dictator (p Richard Harding Davis), 1904

Fine Furniture (f Dreiser), 1930
Fine Wagon (p Green), 1959
Finer Grain (f H. James), 1910
Finger (v Creeley), 1968
Finger Man (f Chandler), 1946
Finger Posts on the Way of Life (f Arthur), 1853
Finishing Stroke (f Queen), 1958
Fire and Wine (v Fletcher), 1913
Fire in the Flint (p Tolson), 1952
Fire Next Time (James Baldwin), 1963
Fire on the Moon (Mailer), 1971
Fire Screen (v Merrill), 1969
Fire Sermon (f Morris), 1971
Fire-Bringer (p Moody), 1904
Firecrackers (f Van Vechten), 1925
Firefly (scr Nash), 1937
Fireman's Picnic (p Cohan), 1918
Fireside Angel (f Arthur), 1853
Fir-Flower Tablets (v A. Lowell), 1921
Firing (v Snyder), 1964
First American Gentleman (f Cabell), 1942
First Blues (v Ginsberg), 1975
First Decade (v Duncan), 1968
First Encounter (f Dos Passos), 1945
First Family of Tasajara (f Harte), 1891
First Fam'lies in the Sierras (p J. Miller), 1875
First Flight (p M. Anderson), 1925
First Gentleman of America (f Cabell), 1942
First Gentleman of Europe (p Burnett), 1897
First Lady (p Kaufman), 1935
First Leaf (v Riding), 1933
First Lover (f Boyle), 1933
First Man (p O'Neill), 1922
First One (p Hurston), 1927
First Person Singular (f W. Benét), 1922
First President (p W. Williams), 1961
First Wife (f Buck), 1933
First Wife (p Buck), 1945
First Will and Testament (v Patchen), 1939
Fiscal Hoboes (f Saroyan), 1949
Fish or Cut Bait (f E. Gardner), 1963
Fishing for Snakes (v Eberhart), 1965
Five Came Back (scr West), 1939
$500 Check (f Alger), 1891
$500 (f Alger), 1890
Five Men and Pompey (p S. Benét), 1915
Five Minute Problem Play (p Dell), 1913
Five Murderers (f Chandler), 1944
5 Numbers (v Creeley), 1968
Five O'Clock Tea (p Howells), 1889
Five Sinister Characters (f Chandler), 1945
Fixer (f Malamud), 1966
Fixin's (p Green), 1924
Flag Is Born (p Hecht), 1946
Flagons and Apples (v Jeffers), 1912
Flags in the Dust (f Faulkner), 1973
Flame and Shadow (v Teasdale), 1920
Flappers and Philosophers (f Fitzgerald), 1920
Flash of Lightning (p Daly), 1868
Flattering Word (p Kelly), 1919
Fleming Field (f Ingraham), 1845
Flesh (scr Hart), 1932
Flight into China (p Buck), 1939
Flight into Egypt (p Wilder), 1928
Flight of Pony Baker (f Howells), 1902
Flight to the West (p Rice), 1940
Flip (f Harte), 1882
Flirt (f Tarkington), 1913
Flirtation at the Moultrie House (f Simms), 1850
Floating Opera (f Barth), 1956
Flock of Guinea Hens Seen from a Car (v Welty), 1970
Flood (f R. Warren), 1964
Floodtide (f Yerby), 1950
Florentine Dagger (f Hecht), 1923
Florida Poems (v Eberhart), 1981
Florida Special (scr Perelman), 1936
Flower Fables (f Alcott), 1855
Flower in Her Hair (f Cozzens), 1974
Flower of Night (scr Hergesheimer), 1925
Flower of the Chapdelaines (f Cable), 1918
Flower-de-Luce (v Longfellow), 1867
Flowering Judas (f Porter), 1930
Flowering of the Rod (v Doolittle), 1946
Flowering Peach (p Odets), 1954
Flowers of the Forest (p van Druten), 1934
Flowers of Virtue (p Connelly), 1942
Flush Times of Alabama and Mississippi (f Joseph G. Baldwin), 1853
Flush Times of California (f Joseph G. Baldwin), 1966
Flute and Violin (f Allen), 1891
Flute Player (v Aiken), 1956
Flying Dutchman (p Dunlap), 1827
Flying Girl series (f Baum), from 1911
Flying Islands of the Night (v Riley), 1891
Focus (f A. Miller), 1945
Focus (v Rich), 1966
Fog (p O'Neill), 1914
Foghorn (f Atherton), 1934
Folks (f Suckow), 1934
Folks from Dixie (f Dunbar), 1898
Folline (p Daly), 1874
Follow the Girls (p Connelly), 1915
Follow Your Heart (scr West), 1936
Fombombo (f Stribling), 1923
Fool for Love (p Shepard), 1983
Fool for Love (scr Shepard), 1985
Foolish Notion (p Barry), 1945
Fools Die on Friday (f E. Gardner), 1947
Fool's Errand (f Tourgée), 1879
Fool's Errand (p Tourgée), 1969
Fool's Gold (v Fletcher), 1913
Foolscap Rose (f Hergesheimer), 1934
Footnotes for a Centennial (v Morley), 1936
Footprints (v Levertov), 1972
For Benny and Sabina (v Creeley), 1970
For Betsy and Tom (v Creeley), 1970
For Doyle Fosco (v Ammons), 1977
For Esmé—With Love and Squalor (f Salinger), 1953
For Illinois 1968 (v Brooks), 1968
For Joel (v Creeley), 1966
For Lancelot Andrewes (Eliot), 1928
For Lizzie and Harriet (v R. Lowell), 1973
For Love (v Creeley), 1962
For Money (p Thomas), 1890
For My Mother (v Creeley), 1973
For Passion, For Heaven (f Fisher), 1962
For the Defense (p Rice), 1919
For the Graduation (v Creeley), 1971

For the Major (f Woolson), 1883
For the Union Dead (v R. Lowell), 1964
For Whom the Bell Tolls (f Hemingway), 1940
Foraging Peter (f Ingraham), 1846
Forayers (f Simms), 1855
Force of Calumny (p Dunlap), 1800
Foregone Conclusion (f Howells), 1874
Foregone Conclusion (p Howells), 1886
Foreign Correspondent (scr Benchley), 1940
Foreign Exchange (p Tarkington), 1909
Foreign Language (p Behrman), 1951
Forensic and the Navigators (p Shepard), 1967
Forest Fire (f Stout), 1933
Forest of the South (f Gordon), 1945
Foresters (p Daly), 1892
Forester's Daughter (f Garland), 1914
Forever and a Day (scr van Druten), 1944
Forfeits (p M. Anderson), 1926
Forge (f Stribling), 1931
Forging Ahead (f Alger), 1903
Forgive Us Our Virtues (f Fisher), 1938
Forgotten Village (scr Steinbeck), 1941
Fork River Space Project (f Morris), 1977
Forlorn River (f Grey), 1927
Form of Woman (v Creeley), 1959
Forrestal (f Ingraham), 1845
Fortitude (p Vonnegut), 1974
Fortunatus (v Robinson), 1928
Fortune Heights (p Dos Passos), 1933
Fortune Hunter (f Mowatt), 1842
Fortune Hunter (f Phillips), 1906
Fortunes of Ben Barclay (f Alger), 1896
Fortunes of Philippa Fairfax (f Burnett), 1888
45 Mercy Street (p Sexton), 1969
Forty-Five Minutes from Broadway (p Cohan), 1906
Forty-Nine (p J. Miller), 1882
'49 (f J. Miller), 1884
49ers (p Connelly, Kaufman), 1922
42nd Parallel (f Dos Passos), 1930
Found Objects (v Zukofsky), 1964
Founders (p Green), 1957
Fountain (v Bryant), 1842
Fountain (p O'Neill), 1925
Fountainville Abbey (p Dunlap), 1795
Four Black Revolutionary Plays (p Baraka), 1969
Four Dynamite Plays (p Bullins), 1970
Four Meetings (f H. James), 1885
Four Million (f Henry), 1906
Four of a Kind (f Marquand), 1923
Four of Hearts (f Queen), 1938
Four Prominent Bastards Are We (v Nash), 1934
Four Prominent So and So's (v Nash), 1934
Four Quartets (v Eliot), 1943
Four Ramages (v Bly), 1983
Four Saints in Three Acts (p Stein), 1934
Four Sons (scr Lawson), 1940
Four-Chambered Heart (f Nin), 1950
4-H Club (p Shepard), 1965
Fourteen Hundred Thousand (p Shepard), 1966
14A (f Riding), 1934
Fourth Side of the Triangle (f Queen), 1965
Fox of Peapack (v White), 1938
Foxes of Harrow (f Yerby), 1946
Fragment (v Ashbery), 1969
Fragment from Vietnam (p Mailer), 1967
Fragment of a Meditation (v Tate), 1947
Fragments of a Disordered Devotion (v Duncan), 1952
France and England in North America (Parkman), 1983
Frances Waldeaux (f Rebecca Harding Davis), 1897
Francesca da Rimini (p Boker), 1855
Francesca Da Rimini (p Crawford), 1902
Francis Drake (p S. Mitchell), 1893
Frank and Fearless (f Alger), 1897
Frank Fowler, The Cash Boy (f Alger), 1887
Frank Hunter's Peril (f Alger), 1896
Frank Rivers (f Ingraham), 1843
Frankenstein (p J. Gardner), 1979
Frankie and Johnny (scr Hart), 1936
Franklin and the King (p Green), 1939
Franklin Evans (f Whitman), 1842
Frank's Campaign (f Alger), 1864
Franny and Zoey (f Salinger), 1961
Fraternal Discord (p Dunlap), 1800
Freddy's Book (f J. Gardner), 1980
Frédérick Lemaitre (p Fitch), 1890
Free (f Dreiser), 1918
Free Air (f Lewis), 1919
Free Joe (f J. Harris), 1887
Free Man (f Richter), 1943
Free Wheeling (v Nash), 1931
Freedom of Will (Edwards), 1754
Freedom's a Hard Bought Thing (radio S. Benét), 1941
Freedom's Land (v MacLeish), 1942
Freedom's Plow (radio Hughes), 1943
Freeing of the Dust (v Levertov), 1975
Freeman (v Glasgow), 1902
Freemantle (f Ingraham), 1845
Free-Trader (f Ingraham), 1847
French Girls Are Vicious (f Farrell), 1955
French Governess (f Cooper), 1843
French Libertine (p Irving, Payne), 1826
French Powder Mystery (f Queen), 1930
Frenchman Must Die (f Boyle), 1946
Frescoes for Mr. Rockefeller's City (v MacLeish), 1933
Freshman Love (scr Ade), 1936
Fricandeau (p Payne), 1831
Friend of Kafka (f Singer), 1970
Friends Ashore (f Jewett), 1883
Friendship (p Cohan), 1931
Friendship Village series (f Gale), from 1908
Frightened Wife (f Rinehart), 1953
Frisky Mrs. Johnson (p Fitch), 1903
From Bed to Worse (Benchley), 1934
From Death to Morning (f Wolfe), 1935
From Farm to Fortune (f Alger), 1905
From Flushing to Calvary (f Dahlberg), 1932
From Here to Eternity (f Jones), 1951
From Sand Hill to Pine (f Harte), 1900
From Snow to Snow (v Frost), 1936
From the First Nine (v Merrill), 1982
From the Hidden Way (v Cabell), 1916
From the Other Side (f Fuller), 1898
From the Terrace (f J. O'Hara), 1958
Front Page (p Hecht, MacArthur), 1928
Front Page (scr Hecht, MacArthur), 1931
Front Porch (p Hughes), 1938
Front Yard (f Woolson), 1895
Frontiersmen (f Murfree), 1904

He Married His Wife (scr J. O'Hara), 1940
He Sent Forth a Raven (f E. Roberts), 1935
He Would Be a Mountebank (f Alger), 1888
Head of the Family (p Fitch), 1898
Head of the House of Coombe (f Burnett), 1922
Head-Deep in Strange Sounds (v Dickey), 1979
Headless Horseman (radio S. Benét), 1937
Headlines (p T. Williams), 1936
Headsman (f Cooper), 1833
Healer (f Herrick), 1911
Heart for the Gods of Mexico (f Aiken), 1939
Heart Is a Lonely Hunter (f McCullers), 1940
Heart of Happy Hollow (f Dunbar), 1904
Heart of Hyacinth (f Atherton), 1903
Heart of Maryland (p Belasco), 1895
Heart of Paddy Whack (p Crothers), 1914
Heart of Rome (f Crawford), 1903
Heart of the West (f Henry), 1907
Heart-Histories and Life-Pictures (f Arthur), 1853
Hearts Come Home (f Buck), 1962
Heart's Garden, The Garden's Heart (v Rexroth), 1967
Heart's Highway (f Freeman), 1900
Heart's Kindred (f Gale), 1915
Heart's Needle (v Snodgrass), 1959
Hearts of Oak (p Belasco, Herne), 1879
Hearts of Oak (p Rowson), 1810-11(?)
Hearts of Three (f London), 1918
Heartsease and Rue (v J. Lowell), 1888
Heart-Shape in the Dust (v Hayden), 1940
Heartsong (p Laurents), 1947
Heathcotes (f Cooper), 1854
Heathen Chinee (v Harte), 1870
Heaven (v Kerouac), 1977
Heavenly City, Earthly City (v Duncan), 1947
Heavens and Earth (v S. Benét), 1920
Heaven's My Destination (f Wilder), 1934
Hector's Inheritance (f Alger), 1885
Hedgehog (f Doolittle), 1936
Hedylus (f Doolittle), 1928
Heidenmauer (f Cooper), 1832
Heir of Gaymount (f J. Cooke), 1870
Heiress (f Arthur), 1845
Heiress of Red Dog (f Harte), 1879
Held by the Enemy (p Gillette), 1886
Held Up (p Harte), 1903
Helen: A Courtship (v Faulkner), 1981
Helen Ford (f Alger), 1866
Helen Halsey (f Simms), 1844
Helen in Egypt (v Doolittle), 1961
Helen of Troy (v Teasdale), 1911
Helen of Troy, New York (p Connelly, Kaufman), 1923
Heliodora (v Doolittle), 1924
Heliogabalus (p Mencken), 1920
Hell (p Sinclair), 1923
Hell (f Tarkington), 1935
Hell of a Good Time (f Farrell), 1950
Hellbox (f J. O'Hara), 1947
Hello (v Creeley), 1978
Hello, Broadway! (p Cohan), 1914
Hello Charlie (tv Hecht), 1959
Hello from Bertha (p T. Williams), 1946
Hello, Out There (p Saroyan), 1941
Helmets (v Dickey), 1964
Help Each Other Club (p Tarkington), 1933
Help Yourself (scr Rice), 1920
Helper (p Bullins), 1970
Helping Himself (f Alger), 1886
Hemp (p Cain), 1926
Henderson the Rain King (f Bellow), 1959
Henrietta (p B. Howard), 1887
Henry Howard (f Ingraham), 1845
Henry St. John, Gentleman (f J. Cooke), 1859
Henry Temple (f Ingraham), 1847
Henry VIII and Ann Boleyn (p Masters), 1934
Henry's Fate (v Berryman), 1977
Hephzibah Guinness (f S. Mitchell), 1880
Her (f Doolittle), 1984
Her Fifth Marriage (f Howe), 1928
Her Great Match (p Fitch), 1905
Her Husband's Affairs (scr Hecht), 1947
Her Majesty the Queen (f J. Cooke), 1873
Her Mountain Lover (f Garland), 1901
Her Own Enemy (p Daly), 1884
Her Own Way (p Fitch), 1903
Her Serene Highness (f Phillips), 1902
Her Sister (p Fitch), 1907
Herakles (p MacLeish), 1965
Herb Basket (v Eberhart), 1950
Herbert Carter's Legacy (f Alger), 1875
Herbert Selden (f Alger), 1981
Herbert West Reanimator (f Lovecraft), 1977
Here and Beyond (f Wharton), 1926
Here and Now (v Levertov), 1956
Here Come the Clowns (p Barry), 1938
Here Is Einbaum (f Morris), 1973
Here Is My Heart (scr Parker), 1934
Here Is New York (White), 1949
Here Lies (f Parker), 1939
Here Today and Gone Tomorrow (f Bromfield), 1934
Herfords (p Crothers), 1912
Heritage of Dedlow Marsh (f Harte), 1889
Heritage of Hatcher Ide (f Tarkington), 1941
Heritage of the Desert (f Grey), 1910
Hermaios (p Rexroth), 1951
Herman de Ruyter (f Ingraham), 1844
Hermetic Definition (v Doolittle), 1972
Hermia, An American Woman (f Atherton), 1889
Hermia Suydam (f Atherton), 1889
HERmione (f Doolittle), 1981
Hermit (f Kosinski), 1986
Hermit and Wild Woman (f Wharton), 1908
Hermit of Carmel (v Santayana), 1901
Hero (p Cain), 1926
Hero (v Creeley), 1969
Hero (p Kopit), 1964
Hero of Santa Maria (p Hecht), 1917
Hero of the World (p Saroyan), 1940
Heroes (p Ashbery), 1952
Heroes of the Household (f Arthur), 1869
Heroine in Bronze (f Allen), 1912
Herzog (f Bellow), 1964
Hesper (f Garland), 1903
Hetty's Strange History (f H. Jackson), 1877
Hi There! (v Creeley), 1965
Hiawatha (v Longfellow), 1855
Hidden Flower (f Buck), 1952
Hidden Wings (f Arthur), 1864
Hide and Seek (v Morley), 1920

High Bid (p H. James), 1908
High Place (f Cabell), 1923
High Time along the Wabash (p Saroyan), 1961
High Times and Hard Times (G. Harris), 1967
High Tor (p M. Anderson), 1937
High Window (f Chandler), 1942
Highest Bidder (p Belasco), 1887
Highgate Road (v Ammons), 1977
Highland Call (p Green), 1939
Highland Call Song-Book (v Green), 1941
Hike and the Aeroplane (f Lewis), 1912
Hill of Stones (v S. Mitchell), 1883
Hills Beyond (f Wolfe), 1941
Hilt to Hilt (f J. Cooke), 1869
Him (p Cummings), 1927
Him with His Foot in His Mouth (f Bellow), 1984
Hints and Helps for the Home Circle (f Arthur), 1844
Hippolytus Temporizes (p Doolittle), 1927
Hiram Elwood, The Banker (f Arthur), 1844
His Fortunate Grace (f Atherton), 1897
His Girl Friday (scr Hecht), 1939
His Grace de Grammont (p Fitch), 1894
His Grace of Osmonde (f Burnett), 1897
His Great Adventure (f Herrick), 1913
His Human Majesty (f Boyle), 1949
His Idea (v Creeley), 1973
His Own People (f Tarkington), 1907
His Pa's Romance (v Riley), 1903
His Thought Made Pockets & the Plane Buckt (v Berryman), 1958
His Toy, His Dream, His Rest (v Berryman), 1968
His Vanished Star (f Murfree), 1894
Hist Whist (v Cummings), 1983
History (v R. Lowell), 1973
History of Colonel Nathaniel Bacon's Rebellion in Virginia (v E. Cooke), 1731
History of New-York (Irving), 1809
History of Plymouth Plantation (W. Bradford), 1912
History of the Conspiracy of Pontiac (Parkman), 1851
History of the Work of Redemption (Edwards), 1774
Hither and Thither in Germany (f Howells), 1920
Hit-the-Trail Holliday (p Cohan), 1915
Hive of the Bee-Hunter (f Thorpe), 1854
Hobohemia (p Lewis), 1919
Hoboken Blues (p Gold), 1927
Hockey Poem (v Bly), 1974
Hold That Christmas Tiger! (Perelman), 1954
Hold-Up Man (p Hart), 1923
Holiday (p Barry), 1928
Holiday (f Frank), 1923
Holiday Inn (scr Rice), 1942
Holiday Song (tv Chayefsky), 1952
Holly-Tree Inn (p Thomas), 1892
Hollywood Holiday (p van Druten), 1931
Hollywood Mystery! (f Hecht), 1946
Hollywood Pinafore (p Kaufman), 1945
Hollywood Playhouse series (radio Laurents), 1939
Holy Ghostly (p Shepard), 1969
Holy Graal (p Hovey), 1907
Holy-Cross (f Field), 1893
Homage to Mistress Bradstreet (v Berryman), 1956
Homage to Sextus Propertius (v Pound), 1934
Home (f Sedgwick), 1835
Home as Found (f Cooper), 1838
Home Ballads (v Whittier), 1860
Home Boy (p Bullins), 1976
Home Lights and Shadows (f Arthur), 1853
Home Mission (f Arthur), 1853
Home of the Brave (p Laurents), 1945
Home of the Free (p Rice), 1917
Home on the Range (p Baraka), 1968
Home Pastorals (v B. Taylor), 1875
Home Scenes and Home Influence (f Arthur), 1852
Home to Harlem (f McKay), 1928
Home to My Valley (f Green), 1970
Home with Hazel (f Van Doren), 1957
Homecoming (scr Kingsley), 1948
Homecoming and Departure (v Goodman), 1937
Homecoming Game (f Nemerov), 1957
Home-Folks (v Riley), 1900
Home-Heroes, Saints and Martyrs (f Arthur), 1865
Homely Lilla (f Herrick), 1923
Homespun of Oatmeal Gray (v Goodman), 1970
Homestead Called Damascus (v Rexroth), 1963
Home-Towners (p Cohan), 1926
Homeward Bound (f Cooper), 1838
Homicide Trinity (f Stout), 1962
Honest John O'Brien (p Cohan), 1916
Honest John Vane (f De Forest), 1875
Honey and Salt (v Sandburg), 1963
Honeycomb (p Green), 1972
Honeymoon Shiners (p Wister), 1928
Honeymooners (p Cohan), 1907
Honor (tv Vidal), 1956
Honor of the Family (p Fitch), 1908
Honorable Men (f Auchincloss), 1985
Honors at Dawn (p A. Miller), 1936
Hoodlum Bard (f Harte), 1878
Hoosier Doctor (p Thomas), 1897
Hoosier Hand Book (f Ade), 1911
Hoosier Lyrics (Field), 1905
Hoosier School-Boy (f Eggleston), 1882
Hoosier School-Master (f Eggleston), 1871
Hop, Skip, and Jump (v Snyder), 1964
Hope Leslie (f Sedgwick), 1827
Hope of Heaven (f J. O'Hara), 1938
Hoping for a Hoopoe (v Updike), 1959
Horace Chase (f Woolson), 1894
Horizon (p Daly), 1871
Horn of Life (f Atherton), 1942
Horror in the Burying Ground (f Lovecraft), 1975
Horror in the Museum (f Lovecraft), 1970
Horse Feathers (scr Perelman), 1932
Horse Heaven Hill (f Grey), 1959
Horse Knows the Way (f J. O'Hara), 1964
Horseman in the Sky (f Bierce), 1907
Horses and Men (f S. Anderson), 1923
Horses Make a Landscape Look More Beautiful (v Walker), 1984
Horses of the Sea (v Olson), 1976
Horse's Tale (f Twain), 1907
Horse-Shoe Robinson (f Kennedy), 1835
Hospital (scr Chayefsky), 1971
Hospital (f Fearing), 1939
Hot Iron (p Green), 1926
Hot Plowshares (f Tourgée), 1883
Hotel Universe (p Barry), 1930
Houdini (p Rukeyser), 1973

Hounds of Summer (f McCarthy), 1981
Hour, Gnats (v Eberhart), 1977
Hours after Noon (f Bowles), 1959
House (f Field), 1896
House (v Shapiro), 1957
House Behind the Cedars (f Chesnutt), 1900
House Divided (f Buck), 1935
House in Blind Alley (p Rice), 1932
House in the Uplands (f Caldwell), 1946
House Not Meant to Stand (p T. Williams), 1981
House of Brass (f Queen), 1968
House of Connelly (p Green), 1931
House of Dust (v Aiken), 1920
House of Earth (f Buck), 1935
House of Flowers (p Capote), 1954
House of Incest (f Nin), 1936
House of Lee (f Atherton), 1940
House of Mirth (f Wharton), 1905
House of Mirth (p Fitch, Wharton), 1906
House of Pride (f London), 1912
House of the Five Talents (f Auchincloss), 1960
House of the Prophet (f Auchincloss), 1980
House of the Seven Gables (f Hawthorne), 1851
House of the Solitary Maggot (f Purdy), 1974
House of Women (p Bromfield), 1927
House Party (p Bullins), 1973
Houseboat Days (v Ashbery), 1977
Housebreaker of Shady Hill (f Cheever), 1958
Household in Athens (f Wescott), 1945
Household Poems (v Longfellow), 1865
How Beautiful with Shoes (p Steele), 1935
How Come Christmas (p R. Bradford), 1930
How Do You Do? (p Bullins), 1965
How Doth the Simple Spelling Bee (f Wister), 1907
How His Ship Came Home (f Alger), 1887
How Like a God (f Stout), 1929
How One Friar Met the Devil and Two Pursued Him (f Field), 1900
How to Read (Pound), 1931
How to Try a Lover (p Barker), 1817
How to Write Short Stories (f Lardner), 1924
How Well George Does It! (p Gillette), 1936
Howard (f Ingraham), 1843
Howdy, Honey, Howdy (v Dunbar), 1905
Howl (v Ginsberg), 1956
How's the King? (p Connelly), 1927
How's Your Health? (p Tarkington), 1930
Huckleberry Finn (f Twain), 1884
Hudson River Bracketed (f Wharton), 1929
Huge Season (f Morris), 1954
Hugh Selwyn Mauberley (v Pound), 1920
Hugh Wynne, Free Quaker (f S. Mitchell), 1897
Hughie (p O'Neill), 1958
Hugo, The Deformed (f Alger), 1978
Hugo Weber (v Kerouac), 1967
Huguenots in Florida (f Simms), 1884
Human Being (f Morley), 1932
Human Comedy (f Saroyan), 1943
Human Comedy (scr Saroyan), 1943
Human Drift (f London), 1917
Human Nature (p Dell), 1922
Human Nature (f Wharton), 1933
Human Season (v MacLeish), 1972
Human Season (f Wallant), 1960
Human Zero (f E. Gardner), 1981
Humanity Unlimited (v Van Doren), 1950
Humble Inquiry into . . . Communion (Edwards), 1749
Humble Romance (f Freeman), 1887
Humboldt's Gift (f Bellow), 1975
Humoresque (scr Odets), 1946
Humpty Dumpty (f Hecht), 1924
Hunchback (p Daly), 1892
Hunchback of Notre Dame (scr Sherwood), 1924
Hundred Camels in the Courtyard (f Bowles), 1962
Hungered One (f Bullins), 1971
Hungerers (p Saroyan), 1939
Hungerfield (v Jeffers), 1954
Hungry Heart (f Phillips), 1909
Hunter Cats of Connorloa (f H. Jackson), 1884
Hunter's Moon (p Connelly), 1958
Huntsman, What Quarry? (v Millay), 1939
Hurrah for Anything (v Patchen), 1957
Hurricane (scr Hecht), 1937
Hurricanes (p B. Howard), 1878
Husband and Wife (p Saroyan), 1968
Husband's Story (f Phillips), 1910
Hymen (v Doolittle), 1921
Hymn to the Rising Sun (p Green), 1936
Hymns of St. Bridget (v F. O'Hara), 1974
Hyperion (f Longfellow), 1839

I's Pronounced "Eyes" (v Zukofsky), 1963
I Accuse (scr Vidal), 1958
I Am a Barbarian (f E. Burroughs), 1967
I Am a Camera (p van Druten), 1951
I Am Elijah Thrush (f Purdy), 1972
I Am Lucy Terry (p Bullins), 1976
I Can't Imagine Tomorrow (tv T. Williams), 1970
I Can't Sleep (p Odets), 1935
I Come as a Thief (f Auchincloss), 1972
I de Dage (f Rølvaag), 1924
I Die Slowly (f Macdonald), 1955
I Don't Need You Any More (f A. Miller), 1967
I Greet the Dawn (v Dunbar), 1978
I Hate Actors! (f Hecht), 1944
I Have Moved to Dublin (v Berryman), 1967
I Knew Him When— (f Ade), 1910
I Know My Love (p Behrman), 1949
I Love Myself When I am Laughing (Hurston), 1979
I Love You, I Love You, I Love You (f Bemelmans), 1942
I Loved a Soldier (scr van Druten), 1936
I Married a Witch (scr Connelly), 1942
I Remember Mama (p van Druten), 1944
I Rise in Flame, Cried the Phoenix (p T. Williams), 1951
I See No Sin (f Fisher), 1934
I Sent Thee Late (v Zukofsky), 1965
I Stole a Million (scr West), 1939
I Take This Woman (scr MacArthur), 1940
I Take This Woman (f Rinehart), 1927
I Thought of Daisy (f Wilson), 1929
I Was an Adventuress (scr J. O'Hara), 1940
I Will Arrest the Bird That Has No Light (v Purdy), 1977
I Wouldn't Have Missed It (Nash), 1975
Iascaire (p Harrigan), 1876
Ibsen Revisited (p Dell), 1914
Icarus's Mother (p Shepard), 1965
Ice Palace (f Ferber), 1958
Ice-Cream Headache (f Jones), 1968

In the Suicide Mountains (f J. Gardner), 1977
In the Sweet Dry and Dry (f Morley), 1919
In the Tennessee Mountains (f Murfree), 1884
In the Time of Detachment, In the Time of Cold (v Brooks), 1965
In the Valley (f Frederic), 1890
In the Valley (p Green), 1928
In the Wine Time (p Bullins), 1968
In the Winter of Cities (v T. Williams), 1956
In the Zone (p O'Neill), 1917
In This Our Life (f Glasgow), 1941
In Tragic Life (f Fisher), 1932
In War Time (f S. Mitchell), 1885
In War Time (v Whittier), 1864
In What Hour (v Rexroth), 1940
Inacoma (p Shepard), 1977
Incarnations (v R. Warren), 1968
Incident at the Standish Arms (p Inge), 1962
Incident at Vichy (p A. Miller), 1964
Incident in the Park (p Kopit), 1968
Incidental Numbers (v Wylie), 1912
Incidentals (v Sandburg), 1904
Inconstant (p Daly), 1889
Increasing Purpose (f Allen), 1900
Independence (f Alcott), 1876
Indestructible Mr. Gore (tv Vidal), 1960
Indian (f Updike), 1971
Indian Fighter (scr Hecht), 1955
Indian Giver (p Howells), 1900
Indian Princess (p Barker), 1808
Indian Summer (f Howells), 1886
Indian Summer (p Thomas), 1913
Indians (p Kopit), 1968
Indians in England (p Dunlap), 1799
Indifferent Children (f Auchincloss), 1947
Indignant Subscriber (p Sinclair), 1965
Indiscretion of an American Wife (scr Capote), 1954
Indispensable Information for Infants (v Wister), 1921
Industrial Republic (f Sinclair), 1907
Infancy (p Wilder), 1961
Infatuation (f Hecht), 1927
Infidel (f Bird), 1835
Infidel's Doom (f Bird), 1840
Inflation (p Nasby), 1876
Inflation at the Cross Roads (f Nasby), 1875
Ingomar the Idiotic (p B. Howard), 1871
Inhabitants of Carlysle (p MacKaye), 1901
Inhale and Exhale (f Saroyan), 1936
Inheritance (scr James Baldwin), 1973
Inheritors (p Glaspell), 1921
Initial (v Zukofsky), 1970
Injustice Collectors (f Auchincloss), 1950
Inklings of Adventure (f Willis), 1836
Innocence at Home (p Harrigan), 1875
Innocence in Extremis (f Hawkes), 1985
Innocent Party (p Hawkes), 1966
Innocents (scr Capote), 1961
Innocents (f Lewis), 1917
Innocents Abroad (f Twain), 1869
Innocents at Home (f Twain), 1872
Inquisitor (f Rowson), 1788
Inside of the Cup (f Churchill), 1913
Inside the Onion (v Nemerov), 1984
Instant Enemy (f Macdonald), 1968
Institute (f Cain), 1976
Instrument (f J. O'Hara), 1967
Insubordination (f Arthur), 1841
Insurance Salesman (f Saroyan), 1941
Insurrection (p Baraka), 1969
Intellectual Things (v Kunitz), 1930
International (p Lawson), 1928
International Episode (f H. James), 1879
International Match (p Daly), 1889
Intimate Strangers (p Tarkington), 1921
Intimations of Eve (f Fisher), 1946
Into the Stone (v Dickey), 1960
Introducing Irony (v Bodenheim), 1922
Intruder in the Dust (f Faulkner), 1948
Invaders (f Frank), 1948
Invalid Corps (p Harrigan), 1874
Invasion of Italy (v Simpson), 1976
Investigation (p Harrigan), 1884
Invisible Empire (f Tourgée), 1880
Invisible Landscapes (v Masters), 1935
Invisible Man (f Ellison), 1952
Invisible Swords (f Farrell), 1971
Invisible Wall (tv McCullers), 1953
Invitation to a Beheading (f Nabokov), 1959
Invitation to a March (p Laurents), 1960
Ion (p Doolittle), 1937
Iowa Interiors (f Suckow), 1926
Iowa, O Iowa! (v Garland), 1935
Iphigenia (p Rexroth), 1951
Iphigenia at Aulis (p Merwin), 1982
Ireland vs. Italy (p Harrigan), 1872
Irene the Missionary (f De Forest), 1879
Irish Emigrant (p Harrigan), 1871
Irish Girl (f Sedgwick), 1853
Irish Triangle (p Barnes), 1919
Iron Cross (p Rice), 1917
Iron Gate (v Holmes), 1880
Iron Heel (f London), 1908
Iron Horse (v Ginsberg), 1972
Iron Petticoat (scr Hecht), 1956
Iron Rule (f Arthur), 1853
Iron Woman (f Deland), 1911
Irradiations (v Fletcher), 1915
Is 5 (v Cummings), 1926
Is He Guilty? (p Rice), 1927
Is Paris Burning? (scr Vidal), 1966
Is Sex Necessary? (Thurber, White), 1929
Island (f Creeley), 1963
Island Bride (f Simms), 1869
Island in the Atlantic (f Frank), 1946
Island of Barrataria (p Tyler), 1941
Island of the Innocent (f Fisher), 1952
Island Tales (f London), 1920
Islands in the Stream (f Hemingway), 1970
Isles of the Blest (f Steele), 1924
Israel Potter (f Melville), 1855
It Bees Dat Way (p Bullins), 1970
It Can't Happen Here (f Lewis), 1935
It Can't Happen Here (p Lewis), 1936
It Could Happen to You (scr West), 1937
It Had to Happen (f Bromfield), 1936
It Happened to Didymus (f Sinclair), 1958
It Happened the Day the Sun Rose (f T. Williams), 1982
It Has No Choice (p Bullins), 1966

It Is the Law (p Rice), 1922
It Takes All Kinds (f Bromfield), 1939
It Was (f Zukofsky), 1961
Italian Ballet Master (p Harrigan), 1876
Italian Bride (p Payne), 1940
Italian Father (p Dunlap), 1799
Italian Junkman (p Harrigan), 1878
It's a Mighty World (tv Hughes), 1965
It's a Wonderful World (scr Hecht), 1939
It's Loaded, Mr. Bauer (f Marquand), 1949
It's Nation Time (v Baraka), 1970
Ivan's Homecoming (p Gold), 1917
I've Got Sixpence (p van Druten), 1952
Ivers Dean (p B. Howard), 1877
Ivory Grin (f Macdonald), 1952
Ivory Tower (f H. James), 1917
Iyyob (v Zukofsky), 1965
Izobretenie Val'sa (p Nabokov), 1938

J.B. (p MacLeish), 1958
JR (f Gaddis), 1975
Jack and Jill (f Alcott), 1880
Jack Downing series (Smith), from 1833
Jack Kelso (p Masters), 1928
Jack O'Lantern (Le Feu-Follet) (f Cooper), 1842
Jack Tier (f Cooper), 1848
Jacket (The Star Rover) (f London), 1915
Jackpot (f Caldwell), 1940
Jack's Ward (f Alger), 1875
Jackson's Dance (p Shepard), 1980
Jacob's Ladder (v Levertov), 1961
Jacob's Ladder (f Rawlings), 1950
Jacobowsky and the Colonel (p Behrman), 1944
Jacques Duval (p Kaufman), 1919
Jad-Bal-Ja, The Golden Lion (f E. Burroughs), 1936
Jaglon and the Tiger Fairies (f Baum), 1953
Jailbird (f Vonnegut), 1979
James Shore's Daughter (f S. Benét), 1934
Jamesons (f Freeman), 1899
Jane (p Behrman), 1946
Jane Field (f Freeman), 1892
Jane Talbot (f C. Brown), 1801
Janet Marsh (f Dell), 1923
Japanese Prints (v Fletcher), 1918
Jarl's Daughter (f Burnett), 1879
Jarrett's Jade (f Yerby), 1959
Jasbo Brown (v Heyward), 1931
Jason and Medeia (f J. Gardner), 1973
Jason Edwards (f Garland), 1892
Java Head (f Hergesheimer), 1919
Jayhawker (p Lewis), 1934
Jazz (f Hecht), 1927
Jealous Gods (f Atherton), 1928
Jealous Woman (f Cain), 1950
Jealousy (f Faulkner), 1955
Jean Huguenot (f S. Benét), 1923
Jeanne d'Arc (p MacKaye), 1906
Jed, The Poorhouse Boy (f Alger), 1900
Jeff Briggs's Love Story (f Harte), 1880
Jello (p Baraka), 1965
Jemmy Daily (f Ingraham), 1843
Jennette Alison (f Ingraham), 1848
Jennie Gerhardt (f Dreiser), 1911
Jennifer Lorn (f Wylie), 1923
Jenny by Nature (f Caldwell), 1961
Jeremy's Version (f Purdy), 1970
Jerico-Jim Crow (p Hughes), 1963
Jerome (v Jarrell), 1971
Jerome, A Poor Man (f Freeman), 1897
Jerry of the Islands (f London), 1917
Jerry, The Backwoods Boy (f Alger), 1904
Jes Lak White Fo'ks (p Dunbar), 1900
Jessie Hampton (f Arthur), 1852
Jest of Fate (f Dunbar), 1902
Jester's Dozen (v Updike), 1984
Jesuits in North America in the Seventeenth Century (Parkman), 1867
Jesus Came Again (f Fisher), 1956
Jew in Love (f Hecht), 1931
Jewel Merchants (p Cabell), 1921
Jews Without Money (f Gold), 1930
Jig of Forslin (v Aiken), 1916
Jilts (p Barry), 1923
Jim Black (p Belasco), 1865
Jim Bludso of the Prairie Belle (v Hay), 1871
Jim Crow's Last Stand (v Hughes), 1943
Jim Dandy (p Saroyan), 1941
Jim, Sam, and Anna (p Saroyan), 1979
Jim Smiley and His Jumping Frog (f Twain), 1940
Jimmie Higgins (f Sinclair), 1918
Jimmyjohn Boss (f Wister), 1900
Jimmy's Blues (v James Baldwin), 1983
Jimmy's Cruise in a Pinafore (f Alcott), 1872
Jim's Book (v Merrill), 1942
Jingling in the Wind (f E. Roberts), 1928
Jinny (f Harte), 1878
Jo Anne!!! (p Bullins), 1976
Joan of Arc (scr M. Anderson), 1948
Joan of Lorraine (p M. Anderson), 1946
Joaquin (v J. Miller), 1869
Job (f Lewis), 1917
Jock o' Dreams (f Herrick), 1908
Joe the Hotel Boy (f Alger), 1906
Joe's Luck (f Alger), 1887
Joggin' Erlong (v Dunbar), 1906
John (p Barry), 1927
John Andross (f Rebecca Harding Davis), 1874
John Barleycorn (f London), 1913
John Barry (f Fearing), 1947
John Brown and the Heroes of Harper's Ferry (v Channing), 1886
John Brown's Body (v S. Benét), 1928
John Bull in America (f Paulding), 1825
John Carter of Mars (f E. Burroughs), 1964
John D. (p Sinclair), 1965
John Deth (v Aiken), 1930
John Dough and the Cherub (f Baum), 1906
John Eax and Marmelon (f Tourgée), 1882
John Godfrey's Fortunes (f B. Taylor), 1864
John Gray (f Allen), 1893
John Henry (f R. Bradford), 1931
John Henry (p R. Bradford), 1939
John Henry Hammers It Out (radio Hughes), 1943
John Jackson's Arcady (f Fitzgerald), 1924
John March, Southerner (f Cable), 1894
John Marr and Other Sailors (v Melville), 1888
John Marvel, Assistant (f Page), 1909
John Paul Jones (scr Hecht), 1959

John Sherwood's Ironmaster (f S. Mitchell), 1911
John Smith U.S.A. (v Field), 1905
John Smith's Letters (f Smith), 1839
John Ward, Preacher (f Deland), 1888
John Wood Case (f Suckow), 1959
Johnny Appleseed (v Lindsay), 1928
Johnny Come Lately (scr van Druten), 1943
Johnny Crimson (v MacKaye), 1895
Johnny Johnson (p Green), 1936
Johnny on a Spot (p MacArthur), 1942
Johnny Pye and the Fool-Killer (f S. Benét), 1938
Johnny Vagabond (scr van Druten), 1943
Jonah (p Goodman), 1950
Jonah's Gourd Vine (f Hurston), 1934
Jonathan Gentry (v Van Doren), 1931
Jonica (p Hart), 1930
Jo's Boys (f Alcott), 1886
Joscelyn (f Simms), 1975
Joseffy (v Sandburg), 1910
Joseph and His Brethren (p Tyler), 1941
Joseph and His Friend (f B. Taylor), 1870
Josephene (f Ingraham), 1853(?)
Josh Billings series (f Shaw), from 1866
Journal from Ellipsia (f Calisher), 1965
Journal of Albion Moonlight (f Patchen), 1941
Journal of Arthur Stirling (f Sinclair), 1903
Journey (v Winters), 1931
Journey (v J. Wright), 1981
Journey from Philadelphia to New-York (v Freneau), 1787
Journey in Search of Christmas (f Wister), 1904
Journey of the Magi (v Eliot), 1927
Journey to Jerusalem (p M. Anderson), 1940
Journey to Love (v W. Williams), 1955
Journey to the Land of Eden (Byrd), 1928
Journeyman (f Caldwell), 1935
Joy of Living (p Wharton), 1902
Joy to My Soul (p Hughes), 1937
Joyous Miracle (f Norris), 1906
Joyous Season (p Barry), 1934
Jubilee (p Hart), 1935
Jubilee (radio Hughes), 1941
Jucklins (p Thomas), 1896
Judas, My Brother (f Yerby), 1969
Judd Rankin's Daughter (f Glaspell), 1945
Judgement of Solomon (p Tyler), 1941
Judgment Day (f Farrell), 1935
Judgment Day (p Rice), 1934
Judgment of Paris (f Vidal), 1952
Judith (f Farrell), 1969
Judith, The Daughter of Merari (p Daly), 1864
Juggler (f Murfree), 1897
Julia (p Payne), 1806
Julia Bride (f H. James), 1909
Julia France and Her Times (f Atherton), 1912
Julian (f Vidal), 1964
Julius (f Alger), 1874
Jumbo (p Hecht, MacArthur), 1935
Jumping Out of Bed (v Bly), 1973
June Moon (p Kaufman, Lardner), 1929
Jungle (f Algren), 1957
Jungle (f Sinclair), 1906
Jungle Girl (f E. Burroughs), 1932
Junkie (f W. Burroughs), 1953
Junkies are Full of (SHHH...) (p Baraka), 1970
Junky (f W. Burroughs), 1986
Jupiter Lights (f Woolson), 1889
Jurgen (f Cabell), 1919
Jury of Her Peers (f Glaspell), 1927
Just above My Head (f James Baldwin), 1979
Just and the Unjust (f Cozzens), 1942
Just Around the Corner (p Hughes), 1951
Just Out of College (p Ade), 1905
Just Wild about Harry (p H. Miller), 1963
Justice Ends at Home (f Stout), 1977
Justin Harley (f J. Cooke), 1875
Justine's Lovers (f De Forest), 1878

K (f Rinehart), 1915
K-19 (f Wolfe), 1983
Kaddish (v Ginsberg), 1961
Kaddish (p Ginsberg), 1972
Kalki (f Vidal), 1978
Kamera Obskura (f Nabokov), 1932
Karren (f Traven), 1931
Kate (f B. Howard), 1906
Kate Beaumont (f De Forest), 1872
Kate Fennigate (f Tarkington), 1943
Kate's Experiences (f Ingraham), 1880
Katharine Lauderdale (f Crawford), 1894
Katharine Walton (f Simms), 1851
Kathleen (f Burnett), 1878
Kathleen (f Morley), 1920
Kavanagh (f Longfellow), 1849
Kays (f Deland), 1926
Keep Cool (f Neal), 1817
Keep It Crisp (Perelman), 1946
Keeping Up Appearances (f Arthur), 1847
Kempton-Wace Letters (f London), 1903
Kenneth Koch (p F. O'Hara), 1982
Kenny (f Bromfield), 1947
Kent Hampden (f Rebecca Harding Davis), 1892
Kentons (f Howells), 1902
Kentuckian (p Paulding), 1833
Kentucky Blue Grass Henry Smith (f Dahlberg), 1932
Kentucky Cardinal (f Allen), 1895
Kentucky Mountain Fantasies (p MacKaye), 1928
Kentucky Warbler (f Allen), 1918
Kept Women Can't Quit (f E. Gardner), 1960
Kéramos (v Longfellow), 1878
Key Largo (p M. Anderson), 1939
Khaled (f Crawford), 1891
Khundar (f Traven), 1977
Kid (v Aiken), 1947
Kiddie (p Crothers), 1909
Kidnapped Saint (f Traven), 1975
Kidnapped Santa Claus (f Baum), 1961
Kiki (p Belasco), 1921
Killer in the Rain (f Chandler), 1964
Killer's Head (p Shepard), 1975
Kilmourne (p Baum), 1883
Kincaid's Battery (f Cable), 1908
Kind of Act of (v Creeley), 1953
Kinfolk (f Buck), 1949
Kinfolk of Robin Hood (p MacKaye), 1924
King Arthur's Socks (p Dell), 1916
King Calico's Body Guard (p Harrigan), 1875
King Carrot (p Daly), 1872
King Coal (f Sinclair), 1917

King Coffin (f Aiken), 1935
King David (v S. Benét), 1923
King Is Dead (f Queen), 1952
King Jasper (v Robinson), 1935
King Lear (radio MacLeish), 1937
King Midas (f Sinclair), 1901
King of Folly Island (f Jewett), 1888
King of Jazz (scr MacArthur), 1930
King of Spain (v Bodenheim), 1928
King, Queen, Knave (f Nabokov), 1968
King Was in His Counting House (f Cabell), 1938
Kingdom Coming (f R. Bradford), 1933
Kingdom of Earth (The Seven Descents of Myrtle) (p T. Williams), 1967
Kingdom of Evil (f Hecht), 1924
King's Henchman (p Millay), 1927
King's Indian (f J. Gardner), 1974
King's Jackal (f Richard Harding Davis), 1898
King's Missive (v Whittier), 1881
Kingsblood Royal (f Lewis), 1947
Kinsmen (f Simms), 1841
Kirche, Küchen, und Kinder (p T. Williams), 1980
Kiss of Death (scr Hecht), 1947
Kit Brandon (f S. Anderson), 1936
Kit O'Brien (f Masters), 1927
Kitchen (v Creeley), 1973
Kitty Foyle (f Morley), 1939
Kitty's Choice (f Rebecca Harding Davis), 1874(?)
Kitty's Class Day (f Alcott), 1868
Knave and Queen (p B. Howard), 1941
Kneel to the Rising Sun (f Caldwell), 1935
Knickerbocker Holiday (p Anderson), 1938
Knife of the Times (f W. Williams), 1932
Knight, after Rilke (v Rich), 1957
Knight of Guadalquiver (p Dunlap), 1800
Knighting of the Twins (f Fitch), 1891
Knightly Quest (f T. Williams), 1967
Knight's Adventure (p Dunlap), 1797
Knight's Gambit (f Faulkner), 1949
Knights of Seven Lands (f Ingraham), 1845
Knights of the Range (f Grey), 1939
Knock on Any Door (f Motley), 1947
Knocking the Neighbors (f Ade), 1912
Knot Holes (p Bodenheim), 1917
Königsmark (v Boker), 1869
Koningsmarke (f Paulding), 1823
Kora and Ka (f Doolittle), 1934
Kora in Hell (v W. Williams), 1920
Korol', Dama, Valet (f Nabokov), 1928
Kral Majales (v Ginsberg), 1965
Kramer Girls (f Suckow), 1930
Kreutzer Sonata (p L. Mitchell), 1906
Kurzy of the Sea (p Barnes), 1919
Kyd the Buccaneer (f Ingraham), 1839

La Belle Russe (p Belasco), 1881
La Bonita Cigarera (f Ingraham), 1844
La Salle and the Discovery of the Great West (Parkman), 1879
La Turista (p Shepard), 1967
Lad and the Lion (f E. Burroughs), 1938
Ladders to Fire (f Nin), 1946
Ladies Almanack (Barnes), 1928
Ladies and Gentlemen (p Hecht, MacArthur), 1939
Ladies' Fair (f Arthur), 1843
Ladies of Castile (p M. Warren), 1790
Ladies of the Corridor (p Parker), 1953
Lady (f Richter), 1957
Lady at Home (f Arthur), 1853
Lady Baltimore (f Wister), 1906
Lady Be Careful (scr Parker), 1936
Lady from Dubuque (p Albee), 1980
Lady Hamilton and Her Nelson (p Tarkington), 1945
Lady in Kicking Horse Reservoir (v Hugo), 1973
Lady in the Dark (p Hart), 1941
Lady in the Lake (f Chandler), 1943
Lady Is Cold (v White), 1929
Lady Jane (v Willis), 1843
Lady of Larkspur Lotion (p T. Williams), 1946
Lady of Lions (p Harrigan), 1878
Lady of Luzon (p Connelly), 1914
Lady of Quality (f Burnett), 1896
Lady of Quality (p Burnett), 1897
Lady of Rome (f Crawford), 1906
Lady of the Aroostook (f Howells), 1879
Lady of the Gulf (f Ingraham), 1846
Lady of the Tropics (scr Hecht), 1939
Lady to Love (scr S. Howard), 1930
Lady's Virtue (p Crothers), 1925
Laengselens Baat (f Rølvaag), 1921
Lafitte, The Pirate of the Gulf (f Ingraham), 1836
Lake Effect Country (v Ammons), 1983
Lake Gun (f Cooper), 1932
Lam to the Slaughter (f E. Gardner), 1939
Lament for Dark Peoples (v Hughes), 1944
Laments for the Living (f Parker), 1930
Lamp and the Bell (p Millay), 1921
Lamp for Nightfall (f Caldwell), 1952
Lancelot (f Percy), 1977
Lancelot (v Robinson), 1920
Lancers (p Payne), 1827
Land Is Bright (p Ferber, Kaufman), 1941
Land of Hidden Men (f E. Burroughs), 1963
Land of Nod (f Green), 1976
Land of Terror (f E. Burroughs), 1944
Land of the Blue Flower (f Burnett), 1909
Land of the Free (v MacLeish), 1938
Land of the Pharaohs (scr Faulkner), 1955
Land of the Spirit (f Page), 1913
Land of Unlikeness (v R. Lowell), 1944
Land That Time Forgot (f E. Burroughs), 1924
Landlord at Lion's Head (f Howells), 1897
Landmark (f Allen), 1925
Land's End (f Steele), 1918
Landscape for Wyn Henderson (v Boyle), 1931
Landscape Painter (f H. James), 1919
Landscape West of Eden (v Aiken), 1934
Landscape with Figures (p Rice), 1934
Lange Weihnachtsmal (p Wilder), 1961
Lanterns and Lances (f Thurber), 1961
Lark (p Hellman), 1955
Lars (v B. Taylor), 1873
Last Adam (f Cozzens), 1933
Last Analysis (p Bellow), 1964
Last and Lost Poems (v Schwartz), 1979
Last Carousel (f Algren), 1973
Last Christmas Tree (f Allen), 1914
Last Circle (v S. Benét), 1946

Last Clean Shirt (scr F. O'Hara), n.d.
Last Day of the War (radio Laurents), 1945
Last Days of Lincoln (p Van Doren), 1959
Last Duel in Spain (p Payne), 1940
Last Egyptian (f Baum), 1908
Last Egyptian (scr Baum), 1914
Last Flower (f Thurber), 1939
Last Gentleman (f Percy), 1966
Last Haiku (v Kerouac), 1969
Last Laugh (Perelman), 1981
Last Look (v Van Doren), 1937
Last Night of Don Juan (p S. Howard), 1925
Last Night of Summer (f Caldwell), 1963
Last of My Solid Gold Watches (p T. Williams), 1946
Last of the Dandies (p Fitch), 1901
Last of the Foresters (f J. Cooke), 1856
Last of the Hogans (p Harrigan), 1891
Last of the Lowries (p Green), 1920
Last of the Mobile Hot-Shots (scr Vidal), 1970
Last of the Mohicans (f Cooper), 1826
Last of the Plainsmen (f Grey), 1908
Last Pad (p Inge), 1972
Last Penny (f Arthur), 1852
Last Puritan (f Santayana), 1935
Last Refuge (f Fuller), 1900
Last Ride of Wild Bill (v S. Brown), 1975
Last Trail (f Grey), 1909
Last Trolley Ride (f Calisher), 1966
Last Tycoon (f Fitzgerald), 1941
Last Woman in His Life (f Queen), 1970
Last Word (p Daly), 1890
Last Words (f S. Crane), 1902
Last Words of Dutch Schultz (p W. Burroughs), 1970
Late Christopher Bean (p S. Howard), 1932
Late George Apley (p Kaufman, Marquand), 1944
Late George Apley (f Marquand), 1937
Late, Passing Prairie Farm (v W. Stafford), 1976
Late Settings (v Merrill), 1985
Latent Heterosexual (p Chayefsky), 1967
Later (v Creeley), 1978
Latimer Family (f Arthur), 1877
Latter Days of a Celebrated Soubrette (p T. Williams), 1974
Laugh, Clown, Laugh! (p Belasco), 1923
Laughable Poem (v Freneau), 1809
Laughing Boy (f La Farge), 1929
Laughing Gas (p Dreiser), 1916
Laughing Matter (f Saroyan), 1953
Laughing Pioneer (f Green), 1932
Laughing to Keep from Crying (f Hughes), 1952
Laughter in the Dark (f Nabokov), 1938
Launcelot and Guenevere (p Hovey), 1891
Laura (tv Capote), 1968
Laura and Francisca (v Riding), 1931
Laurel (v Hovey), 1889
Law for the Lion (f Auchincloss), 1953
Law unto Herself (f Rebecca Harding Davis), 1878
Lawd Today (f R. Wright), 1963
Lawton Girl (f Frederic), 1890
Lay Anthony (f Hergesheimer), 1914
Lay of the Scottish Fiddle (v Paulding), 1813
Lay This Body Down (p Green), 1959
Lays of My Home (v Whittier), 1843
Lays of the Hudson (v Hoffman), 1847
Lays of the Palmetto (v Simms), 1848
Lazarus Laughed (p O'Neill), 1927
Lazy Bones (scr Behrman, Hecht), 1933
Le Fou (v Creeley), 1952
Le Mouchoir (f Cooper), 1843
Leaf from the Woods (p Thomas), 1883
Leaflets (v Rich), 1969
League of Frightened Men (f Stout), 1935
Leah the Forsaken (p Daly), 1862
Leaning Tower (f Porter), 1944
Learned Ladies (p Wilbur), 1977
Leather and Silk (f J. Cooke), 1892
Leather Patch (p Harrigan), 1886
Leather Stocking and Silk (f J. Cooke), 1854
Leatherstocking Tales (f Cooper), from 1823
Leatherwood God (f Howells), 1916
Leave Her to Heaven (p van Druten), 1940
Leaves from Margaret Smith's Journal (f Whittier), 1849
Leaves from the Book of Human Life (f Arthur), 1853
Leaves of Grass (v Whitman), 1855
Leaves of the Tree (p Masters), 1909
Leaves, The Lion-Fish and the Bear (f Cheever), 1980
Leavings (p Bullins), 1980
Lee (p Masters), 1926
Lee in the Mountains (v Davidson), 1938
Left Bank (p Rice), 1931
Left Out in the Rain (v Snyder), 1986
Legal Wreck (p Gillette), 1888
Legal Wreck (f Gillette), 1888
Legend (p Dell), 1922
Legend of Ermengarde (v Guthrie), 1929
Legend of "Norwood" (p Daly), 1867
Legend of the Lake (v Whittier), 1893
Legend of the Lost (scr Hecht), 1957
Legends (v A. Lowell), 1921
Legends and Lyrics (v Whittier), 1890
Legends of the Conquest of Spain (Irving), 1835
Leicester (p Dunlap), 1806
Leisler (f Ingraham), 1846
Lemons (p Daly), 1877
Leoni (p Chivers), 1980
Leonor de Guzman (p Boker), 1853
Les Blancs (p Hansberry), 1970
Lesson Number One (scr Benchley), 1929
Lesson of Life (v Boker), 1848
Lesson of the Master (f H. James), 1892
Lessons and Complaints (f Purdy), 1978
Lessons in Life for All Who Will Read Them (f Arthur), 1851
Lester's Luck (f Alger), 1901
Let 'em Eat Cake (p Kaufman), 1933
Let Freedom Ring (scr Hecht), 1939
Let It Come Down (f Bowles), 1952
Let Me Feel Your Pulse (f Henry), 1910
Let Me Hear the Melody (p Behrman), 1951
Let No Man Write My Epitaph (f Motley), 1958
Let Noon Be Fair (f Motley), 1966
Let the Band Play Dixie (f R. Bradford), 1934
Let Us Be Gay (p Crothers), 1929
Let Us Now Praise Famous Men (Agee), 1941
Let Us Remember Him (p Hughes), 1963
Let Your Mind Alone! (f Thurber), 1937
Let's Go Out and Play (radio Fitzgerald), 1935
Let's Laugh (f Nasby), 1924
Let's Make Music (scr West), 1940
Letter for Melville 1951 (v Olson), 1951

Letter from Li Po (v Aiken), 1955
Letter from Peking (f Buck), 1957
Letter of Introduction (p Howells), 1892
Letter to God (v Patchen), 1947
Letter to His Countrymen (Cooper), 1834
Letter to Jackie (p M. Anderson), 1944
Letters (f Barth), 1979
Letters (v Duncan), 1958
Letters Home (f Howells), 1903
Letters of an Altrurian Traveller (f Howells), 1961
Letters of Jonathan Oldstyle, Gent. (f Irving), 1824
Letters Written During the President's Tour "Down East" (f Smith), 1833
Letting Go (f P. Roth), 1962
Leviathan (p Wilder), 1928
Lew Archer, Private Investigator (f Macdonald), 1977
Lewis of Monte Blanco (p Dunlap), 1804
Lexington (p S. Howard), 1924(?)
Liar (p Fitch), 1896
Liar (f H. James), 1889
Liberal Imagination (Trilling), 1950
Liberty and Peace (v Wheatley), 1784
Liberty Jones (p Barry), 1941
Libretto for the Republic of Liberia (v Tolson), 1953
Lice (v Merwin), 1967
Lichee Nuts (v Masters), 1930
Lie Down in Darkness (f Styron), 1951
Lie of the Mind (p Shepard), 1985
Life (p Daly), 1876
Life (f Morris), 1973
Life Adventurous (f Farrell), 1947
Life along the Passaic River (f W. Williams), 1938
Life and Adventures of Santa Claus (f Baum), 1902
Life and Gabriella (f Glasgow), 1916
Life and Morals of Jesus of Nazareth (Jefferson), 1902
Life at Happy Knoll (f Marquand), 1957
Life for a Life (f Herrick), 1910
Life Here and There (f Willis), 1850
Life in America (f Simms), 1848
Life in the Forest (v Levertov), 1978
Life in the Iron Mills (f Rebecca Harding Davis), 1972
Life in the Sun (p Wilder), 1955
Life Is Real (p Rice), 1937
Life of Nancy (f Jewett), 1895
Life of Reason (Santayana), from 1905
Life of the Dead (v Riding), 1933
Life on the Mississippi (Twain), 1883
Life Studies (v R. Lowell), 1959
Lifeboat (scr Steinbeck), 1944
Lifeboat Drill (p T. Williams), 1979
Life's Crosses and How to Meet Them (f Arthur), 1865
Lifted Masks (f Glaspell), 1912
Light (v J. Miller), 1907
Light Around the Body (v Bly), 1967
Light Fantastic (tv Laurents), 1967
Light in August (f Faulkner), 1932
Light in the Forest (f Richter), 1953
Light in the Window (p Dreiser), 1916
Light in the Window (f Rinehart), 1948
Light of Her Countenance (f Boyesen), 1889
Light of the Star (f Garland), 1904
Light of Western Stars (f Grey), 1914
Light on Shadowed Paths (f Arthur), 1864
Light Up the Sky (p Hart), 1948
Light Woman (f Gale), 1937
Light-Fingered Gentry (f Phillips), 1907
Lightnin' (scr Behrman), 1930
Lights and Shadows of Real Life (f Arthur), 1851
Light's Diamond Jubilee (tv Hecht), 1954
Lights in the Valley (v Bodenheim), 1942
Like a Bulwark (v Moore), 1956
. . . Like a Lover (f Wescott), 1926
Likely Story (p Howells), 1889
Li'l' Gal (v Dunbar), 1904
Lilian's Lost Love (p B. Howard), 1873
Liliom (scr Behrman), 1930
Lilli Barr (f Bromfield), 1926
Lily (p Belasco), 1909
Lily and the Totem (f Simms), 1850
Lily Dafon (p Saroyan), 1960
Lily of the Valley (p Hecht), 1942
Lime Twig (f Hawkes), 1961
Limestone Tree (f Hergesheimer), 1931
Lin McLean (f Wister), 1897
Lincoln (v Markham), 1901
Lincoln (f Vidal), 1984
Lincoln Relics (v Kunitz), 1978
Linda Condon (f Hergesheimer), 1919
Line of Love (f Cabell), 1905
Lines Long and Short (f Fuller), 1917
Linwoods (f Sedgwick), 1835
Lion and the Archer (v Hayden), 1948
Lion and the Unicorn (f Richard Harding Davis), 1899
Lion of the West (p Paulding), 1831
Lionel Lincoln (f Cooper), 1825
Lion's Tail and Eyes (v Bly, J. Wright), 1962
Lispings of the Muse (v Payne), 1815
Listen (p Creeley), 1972
Listen to the People (v S. Benét), 1941
Listen to the People (radio S. Benét), 1941
Listen to the Mocking Bird (Perelman), 1949
Listening (radio Albee), 1976
Listening Deep (v W. Stafford), 1984
Literary Love-Letters (f Herrick), 1897
Literati (f Poe), 1850
Litter of Rose Leaves (f S. Benét), 1930
Little (f Zukofsky), 1967
Little Accident (p Dell), 1928
Little Accident (f Dell), 1930
Little Birds (f Nin), 1979
Little Blue Light (p Wilson), 1950
Little Book of Nonsense (v Field), 1901
Little Book of Profitable Tales (f Field), 1889
Little Book of Tribune Verse (v Field), 1901
Little Book of Western Verse (v Field), 1889
Little Bound-Boy (f Arthur), 1858
Little Breeches (v Hay), 1871
Little Children (f Saroyan), 1937
Little City of Hope (f Crawford), 1907
Little David (p Connelly), 1937
Little Drummer (f Harte), 1872
Little Duchess (scr Connelly), 1934
Little Foxes (p Hellman), 1939
Little Foxes (scr Hellman, Parker), 1941
Little Fraud (p Harrigan), 1871
Little Friend, Little Friend (v Jarrell), 1945
Little Gidding (v Eliot), 1942
Little Ham (p Hughes), 1935

Little Hero (p Goodman), 1957
Little Hunchback Zia (f Burnett), 1916
Little Johnny Jones (p Cohan), 1904
Little Journey (p Crothers), 1918
Little Journey in the World (f Warner), 1889
Little Lady of the Big House (f London), 1916
Little Lord Fauntleroy (f Burnett), 1886
Little Men (f Alcott), 1871
Little Millionaire (p Cohan), 1911
Little Miss Million (p Daly), 1892
Little Mr. Thimblefinger and His Queer Country (f J. Harris), 1894
Little Mocassin (f Neal), 1866
Little Nelly Kelly (p Cohan), 1922
Little Night Music (p Van Doren), 1966
Little Norsk (f Garland), 1892
Little Ocean (p Shepard), 1974
Little Orvie (f Tarkington), 1934
Little Pilgrims (f Arthur), 1843
Little Princess (p Burnett), 1903
Little Princess (f Burnett), 1905
Little Regiment (f S. Crane), 1896
Little Saint Elizabeth (f Burnett), 1890
Little Savoyard (f Arthur), 1891
Little Sister (f Chandler), 1949
Little Steel (f Sinclair), 1938
Little Stone (f Bowles), 1950
Little Stories (f S. Mitchell), 1903
Little Unfairy Princess (p Burnett), 1902
Little Union Scout (f J. Harris), 1904
Little Who's Zoo of Mild Animals (v Aiken), 1977
Little Wizard series (f Baum), 1913
Little Women (f Alcott), from 1868
Littlepage series (f Cooper), from 1845
Littlest Revue (p Nash), 1956
Live and Let Live (f Sedgwick), 1837
Live or Die (v Sexton), 1966
Lively Lady (f K. Roberts), 1931
Lives and Times of Archy and Mehitabel (v Marquis), 1940
Lives of Wives (f Riding), 1939
Living for Show (p Daly), 1885
Living Reed (f Buck), 1963
Lizzie (f S. Jackson), 1957
Lizzy Glenn (f Arthur), 1859
Llana of Gathol (f E. Burroughs), 1948
Lo (p Henry), 1909
Local Boy Makes Good (p Kaufman), 1944
Locket (p Masters), 1910
Lockwood Concern (f J. O'Hara), 1965
Logan (f Neal), 1822
Loiterings of Travel (f Willis), 1840
Lolita (p Albee), 1981
Lolita (f Nabokov), 1955
Lolita (scr Nabokov), 1962
London Life (f H. James), 1889
London Wall (p van Druten), 1931
Lone Star (p Green), 1977
Lone Star Ranger (f Grey), 1915
Lone Striker (v Frost), 1933
Loneliest Girl in the World (f Fearing), 1951
Lonely for the Future (f Farrell), 1966
Lonesome Road (p Green), 1926
Long Christmas Dinner (p Wilder), 1931
Long Day's Journey into Night (p O'Neill), 1956
Long Dream (f R. Wright), 1958
Long Goodbye (f Chandler), 1953
Long Goodbye (p T. Williams), 1940
Long Hot Summer (f Faulkner), 1958
Long Hunt (f Boyd), 1930
Long Live the King! (f Rinehart), 1917
Long Love (f Buck), 1949
Long March (f Styron), 1956
Long Night (p Green), 1920
Long Night (f Lytle), 1936
Long Pennant (f La Farge), 1933
Long Reach (v Eberhart), 1984
Long Stay Cut Short (p T. Williams), 1948
Long Street (v Davidson), 1961
Long Time Ago (p Dell), 1917
Long Valley (f Steinbeck), 1938
Long Voyage Home (p O'Neill), 1917
Longest Day (scr Jones), 1962
Look at the Harlequins! (f Nabokov), 1974
Look Homeward, Angel (f Wolfe), 1929
Look How the Fish Live (f Powers), 1975
Look Who's Talking! (Perelman), 1940
Looking Backward 2000-1887 (f Bellamy), 1888
Looking 'em Over (f Farrell), 1960
Loon (v Bly), 1977
Lord Beaupré (f H. James), 1893
Lord Byron's Love Letter (p T. Williams), 1946
Lord Chumley (p Belasco), 1888
Lord Fairfax (f J. Cooke), 1888
Lord Mayor of Dublin (p Harrigan), 1908
Lord Pengo (p Behrman), 1962
Lord Weary's Castle (v R. Lowell), 1946
Lordly Hudson (v Goodman), 1962
Lord's Will (p Green), 1922
Lorenzo Bunch (f Tarkington), 1936
Lorgaire (p Harrigan), 1878
Lorgnette (f D. Mitchell), 1850
Lorlie's Wedding (p Daly), 1864
Los Cerritos (f Atherton), 1890
Losing Battles (f Welty), 1970
Loss of Memory (p Laurents), 1981
Loss of Roses (p Inge), 1959
Losses (v Jarrell), 1948
Lost at Sea (f Alger), 1904
Lost Bride (f Arthur), 1866
Lost Children (f Arthur), 1848
Lost Child's Fireflies (p Saroyan), 1954
Lost Colony (p Green), 1937
Lost Colony Song-Book (v Green), 1938
Lost Continent (f E. Burroughs), 1963
Lost Ecstasy (f Rinehart), 1927
Lost Face (f London), 1910
Lost Galleon (f Harte), 1867
Lost in the Funhouse (f Barth), 1968
Lost in the Stars (p M. Anderson), 1949
Lost Lady (f Cather), 1923
Lost Morning (f Heyward), 1936
Lost on Venus (f E. Burroughs), 1935
Lost Pleiad (v Chivers), 1845
Lost Prince (f Burnett), 1915
Lost Pueblo (f Grey), 1954
Lost Road (f Richard Harding Davis), 1913
Lost Son (v Roethke), 1948
Lost Wagon Train (f Grey), 1936

Lost World (v Jarrell), 1965
Lost Zoo (v Cullen), 1940
Lottery (f S. Jackson), 1949
Lottery (p S. Jackson), 1952
Lottery of Love (p Daly), 1888
Loudest Whisper (scr Hellman), 1961
Loudspeaker (p Lawson), 1927
Louisa Pallant (f H. James), 1888
Louisa's Wonder Book (f Alcott), 1975
Louisiana (f Burnett), 1880
Louisiana Cavalier (p Green), 1976
Louisiana Territory (p Kopit), 1975
Love (f Saroyan), 1959
Love (v R. Warren), 1981
Love among the Cannibals (f Morris), 1957
Love among the Ruins (p Rice), 1963
Love and Death (f Fisher), 1959
Love and Fame (v Berryman), 1970
Love and How to Cure It (p Wilder), 1931
Love and Money (f Caldwell), 1954
Love and War, Art and God (v Shapiro), 1984
Love and War Poems (v Patchen), 1968
Love As Love, Death As Death (v Riding), 1928
Love Conquers All (Benchley), 1922
Love Death (p Inge), 1975
Love Happy (scr Hecht), 1949
Love, Here Is My Hat (f Saroyan), 1938
Love in a Cottage (f Arthur), 1848
Love in Greenwich Village (f Dell), 1926
Love in Harness (p Daly), 1886
Love in High Life (f Arthur), 1849
Love in Humble Life (p Payne), 1822
Love in Idleness (f Crawford), 1894
Love in Tandem (p Daly), 1892
Love in the Backwoods (f L. Mitchell), 1897
Love in the Ruins (f Percy), 1971
Love in the United States (f Hergesheimer), 1932
Love Is Like That (p Behrman), 1927
Love Nest (f Lardner), 1926
Love Nest (p Sherwood), 1927
Love of Landry (f Dunbar), 1900
Love of Life (f London), 1907
Love of Parson Lord (f Freeman), 1900
Love on Crutches (p Daly), 1884
Love Poems (v F. O'Hara), 1965
Love Poems (v Patchen), 1960
Love Poems (v Sexton), 1969
Love Songs (v Teasdale), 1917
Love Sonnets of a Cave Man (v Marquis), 1928
Love Stories (f Rinehart), 1919
Love Story (p Behrman), 1933
Love vs. Insurance (p Harrigan), 1878
Love Will Find a Way (p Thomas), n.d.
Love Without Money (f Dell), 1931
Lovely Leave (tv Parker), 1962
Lovely Shall Be Choosers (v Frost), 1929
Lovely Sunday for Creve Coeur (p T. Williams), 1979
Love-Lyrics (v Riley), 1899
Lovers (f Buck), 1977
Lovers' (f Guiney), 1895
Lovers and Husbands (f Arthur), 1845
Lovers' Lane (p Fitch), 1901
Lovers of Louisiana (Today) (f Cable), 1918
Lover's Revolt (f De Forest), 1898

Lovers' Vows (p Dunlap), 1799
Lovers' Vows (p Payne), 1809
Love's Calendar (v Hoffman), 1847
Love's Dilemmas (f Herrick), 1898
Love's Labor (p F. O'Hara), 1960
Love's Labour's Lost (p Daly), 1891
Love's Lovely Counterfeit (f Cain), 1942
Loves of Pelleas and Etarre (f Gale), 1907
Love's Old Sweet Song (p Saroyan), 1940
Love's Pilgrimage (f Sinclair), 1911
Love's Young Dream (p Daly), 1879
Lovey Childs (f J. O'Hara), 1969
Loving a Woman in Two Worlds (v Bly), 1985
Loving Shepherdess (v Jeffers), 1956
Low Life (p Harrigan), 1897
Low-lands (f Pynchon), 1978
Lucifer (p Santayana), 1899
Luck (p Steele), 1941
Luck and Pluck (f Alger), 1869
Luck of Roaring Camp (f Harte), 1870
Lucky Lady (scr Sherwood), 1926
Lucky Partners (scr van Druten), 1940
Lucky Sam McCarver (p S. Howard), 1925
Lucrèce (p Wilder), 1932
Lucretia Borgia (p Stein), 1968
Lucy Church Amiably (f Stein), 1931
Lucy Gayheart (f Cather), 1935
Lucy Harding (f Cooper), 1844
Lucy Sanford (f Arthur), 1848
Lucy Temple (f Rowson), 1842(?)
Luke Walton (f Alger), 1889
Lullaby (scr MacArthur), 1931
Lulu Belle (p MacArthur), 1926
Lulu Belle (scr MacArthur), 1948
Lulu's Library (f Alcott), from 1886
Lunar Landscapes (f Hawkes), 1969
Lunatics and Lovers (p Kingsley), 1954
Lunch Poems (v F. O'Hara), 1964
Lurker at the Threshold (f Lovecraft), 1945
Lurking Fear (f Lovecraft), 1947
Lustra (v Pound), 1916
Lute Song (p S. Howard), 1946
Lydia (scr Hecht), 1941
Lydia Bailey (f K. Roberts), 1947
Lyonnesse (v Plath), 1971
Lyrics of Love and Laughter (v Dunbar), 1903
Lyrics of Lowly Life (v Dunbar), 1896
Lyrics of Sunshine and Shadow (v Dunbar), 1905
Lyrics of the Hearthside (v Dunbar), 1899

Mabel Martin (v Whittier), 1876
Macario (f Traven), 1950
Machine (p Sinclair), 1912
Mad Dog Blues (p Shepard), 1971
Mad Heiress (f Alger), 1981
Mad King (f E. Burroughs), 1926
Mad Musician (p Eberhart), 1962
Madam Sapphira (f Saltus), 1893
Madam, Will You Walk? (p S. Howard), 1953
Madame Butterfly (p Belasco), 1900
Madame de Treymes (f Wharton), 1907
Madame Delphine (f Cable), 1881
Madeira Party (f S. Mitchell), 1895
Madelaine Morel (p Daly), 1873

Manson, The Miser (f Alger), 1981
Mantrap (f Lewis), 1926
Manuductio ad Ministerium (Mather), 1726
Many Dead (p MacLeish), 1944
Many Long Years Ago (v Nash), 1945
Many Loves (p W. Williams), 1958
Many Marriages (f S. Anderson), 1923
Many Moons (f Thurber), 1943
Many Thousands Gone (f J. Bishop), 1931
Manzanita (v Snyder), 1971
Marble Faun (v Faulkner), 1924
Marble Faun (f Hawthorne), 1860
Marbled Paper (v Merrill), 1982
Marcabrun (f Guthrie), 1926
March Hares (f Frederic), 1896
March to Caobaland (f Traven), 1961
March to Montería (f Traven), 1964
Marching Men (f S. Anderson), 1917
Marching On (f Boyd), 1927
Marching Song (p Lawson), 1937
Marco Millions (p O'Neill), 1927
Mardi (f Melville), 1849
Margaret Fleming (p Herne), 1890
Margret Howth (f Rebecca Harding Davis), 1862
Marie (f Ingraham), 1845
Marie and Her Lover (f Sinclair), 1948
Marie Antoinette (f Sinclair), 1939
Marie Bertrand (f Alger), 1981
Marie De Berniere (f Simms), 1853
Marie Walewska (scr Behrman), 1937
Marietta, A Maid of Venice (f Crawford), 1901
Marigold from North Viet Nam (v Levertov), 1968
Marina (v Eliot), 1930
Marion Darche (f Crawford), 1893
Marionettes (p Faulkner), 1920
Mark Manly (f Ingraham), 1843
Mark Manning's Mission (f Alger), 1905
Mark Mason's Victory (f Alger), 1899
Mark Stanton (f Alger), 1890
Mark, The Match Boy (f Alger), 1869
Marked for Murder (f Macdonald), 1953
Market-Place (f Frederic), 1899
Mark's Reef (f Cooper), 1847
Marlowe series (f Chandler), from 1939
Marmion (p Barker), 1812
Marne (f Wharton), 1918
Maroon (f Simms), 1855
Marquis (p Belasco), 1889
Marriage (p Fitch), 1892
Marriage (v Moore), 1923
Marriage by Moonlight (p Belasco, Herne), 1879
Marriage Game (p Fitch), 1901
Marriage Lines (v Nash), 1964
Marriage of Guenevere (p Hovey), 1891
Marriage of Venus (p Santayana), 1953
Marriage Playground (f Wharton), 1930
Marriages (f H. James), 1892
Married and Single (f Arthur), 1845
Married Life (f Arthur), 1852
Married or Single? (f Sedgwick), 1857
Married People (f Rinehart), 1937
Marrow of Tradition (f Chesnutt), 1901
Marry Me (f Updike), 1976
Marsch ins Reich Caoba (f Traven), 1933
Marse Covington (p Ade), 1906
Marseilles (p S. Howard), 1930
Marsena (f Frederic), 1894
Marsh Island (f Jewett), 1885
Mart Haney's Mate (f Garland), 1922
Martin Arrowsmith (f Lewis), 1925
Martin Eden (f London), 1909
Martin Faber (f Simms), 1833
Marty (tv Chayefsky), 1953
Marty (scr Chayefsky), 1955
Marty Malone (p Harrigan), 1896
Martyr Wife (f Arthur), 1844
Martyrs' Idyl (v Guiney), 1899
Maruja (f Harte), 1885
Mary (f Nabokov), 1970
Mary Burns, Fugitive (scr Parker), 1935
Mary Ellis (f Arthur), 1850
Mary Hollis (f Sedgwick), 1822
Mary Louise series (f Baum), 1916
Mary Magdalen (f Saltus), 1891
Mary Moreton (f Arthur), 1849
Mary of Magdala (f Saltus), 1903
Mary of Scotland (p M. Anderson), 1933
Mary the Third (p Crothers), 1923
Mary Wilbur (f Ingraham), 1845
Maryland Muse (v E. Cooke), 1731
Mary's Fancy (v Creeley), 1970
Mary's Neck (f Tarkington), 1932
Marzio's Crucifix (f Crawford), 1887
Mashen'ka (f Nabokov), 1926
Mask for Janus (v Merwin), 1952
Masked Ball (p Fitch), 1892
Masque (v S. Mitchell), 1888
Masque of Judgment (p Moody), 1900
Masque of Kings (p M. Anderson), 1936
Masque of Labor (p MacKaye), 1912
Masque of Mercy (v Frost), 1947
Masque of Pandora (v Longfellow), 1875
Masque of Pedagogues (p M. Anderson), 1957
Masque of Reason (v Frost), 1945
Masque of the Gods (p B. Taylor), 1872
Masque with Clowns (v Wheelwright), 1936
Master Eustace (f H. James), 1920
Master Key (f Baum), 1901
Master Mind of Mars (f E. Burroughs), 1928
Master of the Inn (f Herrick), 1908
Master of the Revels (p Marquis), 1934
Master Poisoner (p Bodenheim, Hecht), 1918
Master William Mitten (f Longstreet), 1864
Master-Rogue (f Phillips), 1903
Master's House (f Thorpe), 1854
Mast-Ship (f Ingraham), 1845
Matches (p Baum), 1882
Matchmaker (p Wilder), 1954
Mate Burke (f Ingraham), 1846
Mate of the Daylight (f Jewett), 1883
Mater (p MacKaye), 1908
Matilda (f Simms), 1846
Matinee Idol (p Thomas), 1909
Matrimonial Ads (p Harrigan), 1877
Matthias at the Door (v Robinson), 1931
Maud and Cousin Bill series (radio Tarkington), from 1932
Maud Martha (f Brooks), 1953
Maule's Curse (Winters), 1938

Maurice Mystery (f J. Cooke), 1885
Maverick Queen (f Grey), 1950
Maximilian (p Masters), 1902
Maximum Security Ward (v Guthrie), 1970
Maximus Poems (v Olson), from 1953
May Blossom (p Belasco), 1883
May Day in Town (p Tyler), 1787
May Day Sermon (v Dickey), 1981
May 20, 1959 (v Olson), 1970
May-Day in New-York (f Smith), 1845
Mayfield Deer (v Van Doren), 1941
Mayflower (f Stowe), 1843
Mayor and the Manicure (p Ade), 1912
Mazatlan (v Creeley), 1969
Maze of Love (f Traven), 1967
Mazeppa (p Payne), 1940
McAllister's Legacy (p Harrigan), 1885
McKenzie's Hundred (f Yerby), 1985
McLeod's Folly (f Bromfield), 1948
McNooney's Visit (p Harrigan), 1887
McSorley's Inflation (p Harrigan), 1882
McTeague (f Norris), 1899
McVeys (f Kirkland), 1888
Me and My Brother (scr Shepard), 1969
Me and the Colonel (scr Behrman), 1958
Meadow Blossoms (f Alcott), 1879
Meanest Man in the World (radio Chayefsky), 1951
Meat (f Steele), 1928
Meat Out of the Eater (v Wigglesworth), 1670
Medal for Benny (scr Steinbeck), 1945
Meddler (p Thomas), 1898
Medea (v Cullen), 1935
Medea (p Jeffers), 1946
Medea at Kolchis (p Duncan), 1956
Medieval Scenes (v Duncan), 1950
Meditations in an Emergency (v F. O'Hara), 1956
Mediterranean (v Rukeyser), 1937(?)
Mediterranean (v Tate), 1936
Medusa in Gramercy Park (v Gregory), 1961
Meet Me at the Morgue (f Macdonald), 1953
Meet Me in the Green Glen (f R. Warren), 1971
Melanctha (f Stein), 1909
Melanie (v Willis), 1835
Mellichampe (f Simms), 1836
Melodies (S. Foster), 1909
Melodrama Play (p Shepard), 1967
Melodramatists (f Nemerov), 1949
Melomaniacs (f Huneker), 1902
Melville Goodwin, USA (f Marquand), 1951
Member from Ozark (p Thomas), 1907
Member of the Third House (f Garland), 1892
Member of the Wedding (f McCullers), 1946
Member of the Wedding (p McCullers), 1949
Members of the Family (f Wister), 1911
Memoirs of a Shy Pornographer (f Patchen), 1945
Memoirs of an American Citizen (f Herrick), 1905
Memoirs of Hecate County (f Wilson), 1946
Memoirs of Stephen Calvert (f C. Brown), 1978
Memorable Providences, Relating to Witchcrafts and Possessions (Mather), 1689
Memoralia (v Chivers), 1853
Memories (v Creeley), 1984
Memory (f Lovecraft), 1970
Memory Gardens (v Creeley), 1986
Memory of Summer (p Inge), 1962
Memory of Two Mondays (p A. Miller), 1955
Men Against the Sky (scr West), 1940
Men and Brethren (f Cozzens), 1936
Men and Women (p Belasco), 1890
Men and Women (f Caldwell), 1961
Men in White (p Kingsley), 1933
Men Without Women (f Hemingway), 1927
Men, Women, and Dogs (f Thurber), 1943
Men, Women, and Ghosts (v A. Lowell), 1916
Menaced World (v Levertov), 1984
Mentoria (f Rowson), 1791
Mercedes of Castile (f Cooper), 1840
Merchant of Venice (p Belasco), 1922
Merchant of Venice (p Daly), 1898
Merchant of Yonkers (p Wilder), 1938
Merchant's Crime (f Alger), 1888
Merchants from Cathay (v W. Benét), 1913
Mercy (f Howells), 1892
Mercy Philbrick's Choice (f H. Jackson), 1876
Mere Man (p Thomas), 1912
Meridian (f Walker), 1976
Merlin (v Robinson), 1917
Mermaids Singing (p van Druten), 1945
Merrily We Roll Along (p Hart, Kaufman), 1934
Merry Dale (f Hergesheimer), 1924
Merry Gardener (p Dunlap), 1802
Merry Malones (p Cohan), 1927
Merry Month of May (f Jones), 1971
Merry Tales (f Twain), 1892
Merry Tales of the Three Wise Men of Gotham (f Paulding), 1826
Merry Wives of Windsor (p Daly), 1886
Merry-Go-Round (p Fitch), 1898
Merton of the Movies (p Connelly, Kaufman), 1922
Message and Jehanne (p Wilder), 1928
Message for Genevieve (f Caldwell), 1933
Message from Abroad (v Tate), 1930
Message II (v Ginsberg), 1968
Messiah (f Vidal), 1954
Met by Chance (p B. Howard), 1887
Metamorphosis of 741 (v Merrill), 1977
Meteor (p Behrman), 1929
Methods of Lady Walderhurst (f Burnett), 1901
Metrical History of Christianity (v E. Taylor), 1962
Metropolis (f Sinclair), 1908
Mettle of the Pasture (f Allen), 1903
Mexican Woman (v Simpson), 1973
Mexico City Blues (v Kerouac), 1959
M'Fingal (v Trumbull), 1775(?)
Mhil'daim (p Kopit), 1963
Miami and the Siege of Chicago (Mailer), 1968
Michael (p Bullins), 1978
Michael Angelo (v Longfellow), 1884
Michael Bonham (p Simms), 1852
Michael, Brother of Jerry (f London), 1917
Michael Scarlett (f Cozzens), 1925
Michel Auclair (p S. Howard), 1925
Mickelsson's Ghosts (f J. Gardner), 1982
Midcentury (f Dos Passos), 1961
Middle Border series (Garland), from 1917
Middle Kingdom (v Morley), 1944
Middle of the Air (p Rukeyser), 1945
Middle of the Journey (f Trilling), 1947

Middle of the Night (tv Chayefsky), 1954
Middle of the Night (scr Chayefsky), 1959
Middle Years (f H. James), 1895
Middle-Aged Man on the Flying Trapeze (f Thurber), 1935
Midlander (f Tarkington), 1923
Midnight Mass (f Bowles), 1981
Midpoint (v Updike), 1969
Midshipman (f Ingraham), 1844
Midsummer Night's Dream (p Daly), 1888
Midsummer Passion (f Caldwell), 1948
Midwestern Manic (p Inge), 1969
Midwestern Music (p Inge), 1975
Might as Well Be Dead (f Stout), 1956
Mignon (f Cain), 1962
Mildred Pierce (f Cain), 1941
Milk Train Doesn't Stop Here Anymore (p T. Williams), 1962
Mill and the Tavern (f Arthur), 1878
Millennium (f Sinclair), 1924
Miller of Old Church (f Glasgow), 1911
Million Dollar Month (v Plath), 1971
Millionaire of Rough-and-Ready (f Harte), 1887
Millionaire's Daughter (p Belasco), 1879
Mills of the Kavanaughs (v R. Lowell), 1951
Mima (p Belasco), 1928
Mimic Life (f Mowatt), 1856
Mind Breaths (v Ginsberg), 1978
Mind-Reader (v Wilbur), 1976
Mine the Harvest (v Millay), 1954
Ming Yellow (f Marquand), 1935
Mingo (f J. Harris), 1884
Minick (p Ferber, Kaufman), 1924
Minister's Charge (f Howells), 1886
Minister's Wooing (f Stowe), 1859
Minna and Myself (v Bodenheim), 1918
Minor Scene (p Bullins), 1966
Minstrel Girl (v Whittier), 1840
Minute Men of 1774-1775 (p Herne), 1886
Minute Particulars (v J. Bishop), 1935
Mirabell (v Merrill), 1978
Miracle in the Rain (f Hecht), 1943
Miracle in the Rain (scr Hecht), 1956
Miracle Man (p Cohan), 1914
Miracle Man (scr Perelman), 1932
Miracle of a Bum (radio Hecht), 1945
Miracle of the Bells (scr Hecht), 1948
Miracle of the Danube (radio M. Anderson), 1941
Miracle on the Pullman (radio Hecht), 1944
Mirage (f Masters), 1924
Miriam (v Whittier), 1871
Mirror (p Singer), 1973
Mirror of the Heart (Teasdale), 1984
Mirrors (v Creeley), 1983
Mirrors and Windows (v Nemerov), 1958
Mirrors of Venus (v Wheelwright), 1938
Mirthful Haven (f Tarkington), 1930
Misanthrope (p Wilbur), 1955
Miscellanies (Irving), 1835
Miseries of New York (f Ingraham), 1844
Miser's Wedding (p Dunlap), 1793
Misfits (scr A. Miller), 1961
Misfits (f A. Miller), 1961
Miss Bellard's Inspiration (f Howells), 1905
Miss Bonnybel (f J. Cooke), 1892
Miss Civilization (p Richard Harding Davis), 1905
Miss Crespigny (f Burnett), 1878
Miss Helyett (p Belasco), 1891
Miss Hoyden's Husband (p Daly), 1890
Miss Liberty (p Sherwood), 1949
Miss Lonelyhearts (f West), 1933
Miss Ludington's Sister (f Bellamy), 1884
Miss Lulu Bett (f Gale), 1920
Miss Lulu Bett (p Gale), 1920
Miss Mama Aimee (f Caldwell), 1967
Miss McCobb, Manicurist (p Fitch), 1907
Miss Pinkerton (f Rinehart), 1932
Miss Ravenel's Conversion from Secession to Loyalty (f De Forest), 1867
Miss Zilphia Gant (f Faulkner), 1932
Mississippi Poems (v Faulkner), 1979
Mister Antonio (p Tarkington), 1916
Mr. Arcularis (p Aiken), 1949
Mr. Ashton Was Indiscreet (scr MacArthur), 1947
Mr. Blake's Walking-Stick (f Eggleston), 1870
Mister Blue (f Creeley), 1964
Mr. Cinderella (f Stout), 1938
Mr. Cohen Takes a Walk (f Rinehart), 1934
Mr. Cough Syrup and the Phantom Sex (p Purdy), 1960
Mr. Crewe's Career (f Churchill), 1908
Mr. Dooley series (Dunne), from 1898
Mr. Evening (f Purdy), 1968
Mr. Grantley's Idea (f J. Cooke), 1879
Mr. Hodge and Mr. Hazard (f Wylie), 1928
Mr. Incoul's Misadventure (f Saltus), 1887
Mr. Isaacs (f Crawford), 1882
Mr. Jack Hamlin's Mediation (f Harte), 1899
Mr. Keegan's Elopement (f Churchill), 1903
Mr. Kris Kringle (f S. Mitchell), 1893
Mr. Moto series (f Marquand), from 1935
Mister Pitt (p Gale), 1925
Mr. Pope (v Tate), 1928
Mr. Rabbit at Home (f J. Harris), 1895
Mr. Sammler's Planet (f Bellow), 1970
Mr. Smith (f Bromfield), 1951
Mr. Tommy Dove (f Deland), 1893
Mr. White (f Tarkington), 1935
Mr. Wilkinson's Widow (p Gillette), 1891
Mrs. Albert Grundy (f Frederic), 1896
Mrs. Balfame (f Atherton), 1916
Mistress Betty (p Fitch), 1895
Mrs. Farrell (f Howells), 1921
Mrs. Grundy, Jr. (p Fitch), 1893
Mrs. John Hobbs (p Crothers), 1899
Mrs. Leffingwell's Boots (p Thomas), 1905
Mrs. Parkington (f Bromfield), 1943
Mrs. Peckham's Carouse (p Ade), 1908
Mrs. Pendleton's Four-in-Hand (f Atherton), 1903
Mrs. Reynolds (f Stein), 1952
Mrs. Ritter Appears (p Kelly), 1917
Mrs. Skaggs's Husbands (f Harte), 1873
Mrs. Smith (p Payne), 1823
Mrs. Temperley (f H. James), 1889
Mrs. Wellington's Surprise (p Kelly), 1922
Misunderstanding (f Farrell), 1949
Mitch Miller (f Masters), 1920
Mixed Couple (p Harrigan), 1873
Moby-Dick (f Melville), 1851
Moccasin Ranch (f Garland), 1909
Model (p Thomas), 1912

National Ode (v B. Taylor), 1877
Native American (f Saroyan), 1938
Native of Rock (v Wescott), 1925
Native of Winby (f Jewett), 1893
Native Son (f R. Wright), 1940
Native Son (scr R. Wright), 1951
Native Son (The Biography of a Young American) (p Green, R. Wright), 1941
Natural (f Malamud), 1952
Natural Affection (p Inge), 1962
Natural Daughter (p Dunlap), 1799
Natural Numbers (v Rexroth), 1963
Nature (Emerson), 1836
Nature of True Virtue (Edwards), 1765
Naturewoman (p Sinclair), 1912
Naughty Anthony (p Belasco), 1899
Navy Alphabet (v Baum), 1900
Neal Nelson (f Ingraham), 1845
Near Home (v Channing), 1858
Near the Ocean (v R. Lowell), 1967
Necessary Angel (Stevens), 1951
Necessities of Life (v Rich), 1966
Ned McCobb's Daughter (p S. Howard), 1926
Ned Newton (f Alger), 1890
Needles and Pins (p Daly), 1880
Neghborly Poems (v Riley), 1891
Negro Mother (v Hughes), 1931
Neighborhood Stories (f Gale), 1914
Neighbors (radio Gale), 1933
Neighbours (p Gale), 1912
Nelly's Silver Mine (f H. Jackson), 1878
Nelson the Newsboy (f Alger), 1901
Nemesis (p Thomas), 1921
Neon Wilderness (f Algren), 1946
Nephew (f Purdy), 1960
Nero Wolfe series (f Stout), from 1934
Nerves (p S. Benét), 1924
Neshoma Yesorah (f Cahan), 1913
Nest of Ninnies (f Ashbery), 1969
Nets to Catch the Wind (v Wylie), 1921
Nettie (p Ade), 1914
Network (scr Chayefsky), 1975
Nevada (f Grey), 1928
Never Come Morning (f Algren), 1942
Never Despair! (f Alger), 1887
Never, Never Ask His Name (p Van Doren), 1965
Nevertheless (v Moore), 1944
New Adventures of Get-Rich-Quick Wallingford (scr MacArthur), 1931
New Ark's a Moverin (p Baraka), 1974
New Blood (p Thomas), 1894
New Citizenship (p MacKaye), 1915
New Criticism (Ransom), 1941
New England Nun (f Freeman), 1891
New Flag (f Fuller), 1899
New Found Land (v MacLeish), 1930
New Hampshire (v Eberhart), 1980
New Hampshire (v Frost), 1923
New Hope (f Suckow), 1942
New Klondike (scr Lardner), 1926
New Leaf Mills (f Howells), 1913
New Life (f Malamud), 1961
New Life (p Rice), 1943
New Man and Woman (v Olson), 1970
New Marriage (p L. Mitchell), 1911
New Play (p Saroyan), 1970
New Samaria (f S. Mitchell), 1904
New Schoolma'am (f Alger), 1877
New Spirit (v Ashbery), 1970
New Spoon River (v Masters), 1924
New Swiss Family Robinson (f Wister), 1882
New Wizard of Oz (scr Baum), 1915
New Wonderland (f Baum), 1900
New World (v Masters), 1937
New Year (f Buck), 1968
New Year Blues (v Ginsberg), 1972
New Year's Call (p Thomas), 1883
New Year's Day (f Wharton), 1924
New Year's Eve (p Frank), 1929
New Year's Eve/1929 (f Farrell), 1967
New Year's Garland for My Students (v Levertov), 1970
New York (v MacLeish), 1958
New York Boy (f Alger), 1890
New York Idea (p L. Mitchell), 1906
New York Madness (f Bodenheim), 1933
New Yorkers (f Calisher), 1969
New-England Tale (f Sedgwick), 1822
New-England Tragedies (v Longfellow), 1868
News of the Night (p Bird), 1929
Next Room of the Dream (v Nemerov), 1962
Next Time (p Bullins), 1972
Next Time (f H. James), 1896
Next to Nothing (v Bowles), 1976
Next-to-Last Things (v Kunitz), 1985
Nexus (f H. Miller), 1960
Nice People (p Crothers), 1921
Nice Wives (f Alcott), 1875
Nick Adams Stories (f Hemingway), 1972
Nick of the Woods (f Bird), 1837
Nickel Mountain (f J. Gardner), 1973
Nicodemus (v Robinson), 1932
Nigger Heaven (f Van Vechten), 1926
Night among the Horses (f Barnes), 1929
Night at the Opera (scr Kaufman), 1935
Night at the Ugly Man's (f Hooper), 1851
Night Before Christmas (p Howells), 1916
Night Before Christmas (p Perelman), 1941
Night Born (f London), 1913
Night Clerk's Troubles (p Harrigan), 1875
Night in Acadie (f Chopin), 1897
Night in Bombay (f Bromfield), 1940
Night Life (p Kingsley), 1962
Night Music (p Odets), 1940
Night Must Fall (scr van Druten), 1937
Night of the Beast (p Bullins), 1970
Night of the Beast (scr Bullins), 1971
Night of the Fourth (p Ade), 1901
Night of the Hunter (scr Agee), 1955
Night of the Iguana (p T. Williams), 1959
Night Off (p Daly), 1885
Night over Taos (p M. Anderson), 1932
Night Rider (f R. Warren), 1939
Night Thoughts (v Wilson), 1961
Night Train (f Macdonald), 1955
Night Visitor (f Traven), 1966
Night-Blooming Cereus (v Hayden), 1972
Nightingale (p Thomas), 1914
Nightmare at Noon (v S. Benét), 1940

Nightmare at Noon (radio S. Benét), 1942
Nightmare Town (f Hammett), 1948
Nights (f Doolittle), 1935
Nights and Days (v Merrill), 1966
Night's Frolic (p Thomas), 1891
Nights of Love and Laughter (f H. Miller), 1955
Night's Work (p Behrman), 1924
Nightwalk (p Shepard), 1973
Nightwood (f Barnes), 1936
Nina (p Dunlap), 1804
Nina Gordon (f Stowe), 1866
Nine (p Kopit), 1981
Nine Sonnets Written at Oxford (v Guiney), 1895
Nine Stories (f Salinger), 1953
1919 (f Dos Passos), 1932
1939 (f Boyle), 1948
Ninety Days (p Gillette), 1893
Ninth Avenue (f Bodenheim), 1926
Nirvana (p Lawson), 1926
Nixie (p Burnett), 1890
No 'Count Boy (p Green), 1925
No Decency Left (f Riding), 1932
No Hero (f Marquand), 1935
No Irish Wanted Here (p Harrigan), 1875
No Love Lost (v Howells), 1869
No Name (p Daly), 1871
No Name in the Street (James Baldwin), 1972
No News Is Good News (scr Benchley), 1943
No Poems (Benchley), 1932
No Retreat (v Gregory), 1933
No Retreat (p Hart), 1930
No Room at the Inn (f Ferber), 1941
No, Sirree! (p Connelly, Kaufman), 1922
No Star Is Lost (f Farrell), 1936
No T.O. for Love (p Chayefsky), 1945
No Thanks (v Cummings), 1935
No Time for Comedy (p Behrman), 1939
(No Title) (v Cummings), 1930
No Villain Need Be (f Fisher), 1936
No Villains (p A. Miller), 1937
Noa Noa (p Agee), 1960
Noah an' Jonah an' Cap'n John Smith (v Marquis), 1921
Nobodaddy (p MacLeish), 1926
Nobody Knows My Name (James Baldwin), 1961
Nobody Say a Word (f Van Doren), 1953
Nobody's in Town (f Ferber), 1938
Nobody's Son (f Ingraham), 1851
Nocturne of Remembered Spring (v Aiken), 1917
Noël (v Longfellow), 1864
Nomad's Land (f Rinehart), 1926
None But the Lonely Heart (scr Odets), 1944
None Shall Look Back (f Gordon), 1937
Noon Wine (f Porter), 1937
Nora (p Crothers), 1903
Norma Ashe (f Glaspell), 1942
Norman (f Ingraham), 1845
Norman Maurice (p Simms), 1851
Norseman's Pilgrimage (f Boyesen), 1875
North and South (v E. Bishop), 1946
North and South (f Caldwell), 1983
North Atlantic Passage (v Wheelwright), 1925
North by West (v W. Stafford), 1975
North of Boston (v Frost), 1914
North of Grand Central (f Marquand), 1956
North Percy (v Goodman), 1968
North Star (scr Hellman), 1943
Northfield Poems (v Ammons), 1966
Northwest Passage (f K. Roberts), 1937
Not "A Fool's Errand" (f Ingraham), 1880
Not Anything for Peace (f Arthur), 1869
Not by Strange Gods (f E. Roberts), 1941
Not for Children (p Rice), 1935
Not Heaven (f Frank), 1953
Not I, But Death (p Rich), 1941
Not on the Screen (f Fuller), 1930
Not Quite Dead Enough (f Stout), 1944
Not Smart (p Steele), 1916
Not So Deep as a Well (v Parker), 1936
Not Without Laughter (f Hughes), 1930
Notebook (v R. Lowell), from 1969
Note-Books of Night (v Wilson), 1942
Notes after an Evening with William Carlos Williams
(v Ginsberg), 1970
Notes of a Native Son (James Baldwin), 1955
Notes on a Dream (v M. Anderson), 1971
Notes on a Horsethief (f Faulkner), 1950
Notes on the State of Virginia (Jefferson), 1785
Notes Toward a Supreme Fiction (v Stevens), 1942
Notes Towards the Definition of Culture (Eliot), 1948
Nothing But Money (f Arthur), 1865
Nothing Ever Breaks Except the Heart (f Boyle), 1966
Nothing Sacred (scr Hecht), 1937
Nothing to Do (v Alger), 1857
Notoriety (p Harrigan), 1894
Notorious (scr Hecht), 1946
Nova Express (f W. Burroughs), 1964
Novel of Thank You (f Stein), 1958
November Boughs (v Whitman), 1888
Novotny's Pain (f P. Roth), 1980
Now and Then (v R. Warren), 1978
Now I Ask You (p O'Neill), 1972
Now I Lay Me Down to Sleep (f Bemelmans), 1943
Now Playing Tomorrow (radio Laurents), 1939
Now the Cats with Jewelled Claws, Now the Peaceable
Kingdom (p T. Williams), 1981
Now the Servant's Name Was Malchus (p Wilder), 1928
Now the Sky (v Van Doren), 1928
Now with His Love (v J. Bishop), 1933
Now You See It (p Patchen), 1966
Nugget Finders (f Alger), 1894
Nuggets and Dust Panned Out in California (f Bierce), 1873
Number Nine (p Daly), 1897
Number 91 (f Alger), 1887
Number One (f Dos Passos), 1943
Numbers (v Creeley), 1968
Nuptial Flight (f Masters), 1923
Nyarlathotep (f Lovecraft), 1970
Nydia (p Boker), 1929
Nye and Riley's Railway Guide (v Riley), 1888
Nye and Riley's Wit and Humor (v Riley), 1902

O Careless Love! (f Stout), 1935
O Pioneers! (f Cather), 1913
O Shepherd, Speak! (f Sinclair), 1949
O Taste and See (v Levertov), 1964
O, That Way Madness Lies (p Fuller), 1895
O to Be a Dragon (v Moore), 1959
O Ye Tongues (v Sexton), 1973

Oak (v Eberhart), 1957
Oak and Ivy (v Dunbar), 1893
Oak Openings (f Cooper), 1848
Oakdale Affair (f E. Burroughs), 1937
Oasis (f McCarthy), 1949
Oblique Prayers (v Levertov), 1984
O'Brien, Counselor-at-Law (p Harrigan), 1879
Obscure Destinies (f Cather), 1932
Observations (v Moore), 1924
October Light (f J. Gardner), 1976
Octopus (f Norris), 1901
Odd Fellow (f Ingraham), 1846
Oddest of Courtships (f De Forest), 1882
Oddly Lovely Day Alone (v Updike), 1979
Odds Against Him (f Alger), 1890
Ode and Arcadia (v Duncan), 1974
Ode from Ossian's Poems (v Hopkinson), 1794
Ode on a Lycian Tomb (v S. Mitchell), 1899
Ode on the Centenary of Abraham Lincoln (v MacKaye), 1909
Ode Recited at the Commemoration of the Living and Dead Soldiers of Harvard University (v J. Lowell), 1865
Ode to Hollywood (v Marquis), 1929
Ode to Liberty (p S. Howard), 1934
Ode to the Confederate Dead (v Tate), 1930
Odette (p Daly), 1882
Odor of Sanctity (f Yerby), 1965
Odyssey of a Hero (f Fisher), 1937
Odyssey of a Nice Girl (f Suckow), 1925
Odyssey of the North (f London), 1915
Of a Fire on the Moon (Mailer), 1971
Of All Things! (Benchley), 1921
Of Ideal Time and Choice (v Stevens), 1947
Of Mice and Men (f Steinbeck), 1937
Of Mice and Men (p Steinbeck), 1937
Of Plymouth Plantation (W. Bradford), 1896
Of the Farm (f Updike), 1965
Of the War (v Duncan), 1966
Of Thee I Sing (p Kaufman), 1931
Of This Time, Of That Place (f Trilling), 1979
Of Time and the River (f Wolfe), 1935
Off the Arm (f Marquis), 1930
Off-Hand Sketches (f Arthur), 1851
Oh Dad, Poor Dad, Mamma's Hung You in the Closet and I'm Feelin' So Sad (p Kopit), 1960
Oh, What a Paradise It Seems (f Cheever), 1982
O'Halloran's Luck (f S. Benét), 1944
Ohio Lady (p Tarkington), 1916
Oil! (f Sinclair), 1927
Ol' King David and the Philistine Boys (f R. Bradford), 1930
Ol' Man Adam an' His Chillun (f R. Bradford), 1928
Old Acquaintance (p van Druten), 1940
Old Acquaintance (scr van Druten), 1943
Old Astrologer (f Arthur), 1853(?)
Old Bean (f Ingraham), 1847
Old Beauty (f Cather), 1948
Old Booksellers (v J. Wright), 1976
Old Chester series (f Deland), from 1898
Old Christmas (p Green), 1928
Old Continental (f Paulding), 1846
Old Creole Days (f Cable), 1879
Old Dog Barks Backwards (v Nash), 1972
Old Farm and the New Farm (f Hopkinson), 1857
Old Friends and New (f Jewett), 1879
Old Garden (v Deland), 1886
Old Gentleman of the Black Stock (f Page), 1897
Old Glory (p R. Lowell), 1964
Old Gods Laugh (f Yerby), 1964
Old Home Week (scr Ade), 1925
Old Hutch (scr Kelly), 1936
Old Lady 31 (p Crothers), 1916
Old Lavender (p Harrigan), 1877
Old Lavender Water (p Harrigan), 1877
Old Love (f Singer), 1979
Old Love and the New (p B. Howard), 1879
Old Love Letters (p B. Howard), 1878
Old Maid (f Wharton), 1924
Old Man (f Faulkner), 1939
Old Man and the Sea (f Hemingway), 1952
Old Man Minick (p Ferber), 1924
Old Man of Edenton (p Green), 1921
Old Man Rubbing His Eyes (v Bly), 1975
Old Mandarin (v Morley), 1947
Old Man's Bride (f Arthur), 1853
Old Man's Folly (f Dell), 1926
Old New York (f Wharton), 1924
Old New Yorker (p Harrigan), 1899
Old Order (f Porter), 1955
Old Pines (f Boyd), 1952
Old Possum's Book of Practical Cats (v Eliot), 1939
Old Probability (f Shaw), 1879
Old Ragpicker (p Dreiser), 1916
Old Red (f Gordon), 1963
Old Régime in Canada (Parkman), 1874
Old Soak (p Marquis), 1922
Old Soldier's Story (v Riley), 1915
Old Stone House (f Woolson), 1872
Old Swimmin'-Hole (v Riley), 1883
Old Town (p Ade), 1910
Old Wash Lucas (The Miser) (p Green), 1921
Old Wives for New (f Phillips), 1908
Old-Fashioned Girl (f Alcott), 1870
Old-Fashioned Roses (v Riley), 1888
Old-Fashioned Tales (f Gale), 1933
Old-Fashioned Thanksgiving (f Alcott), 1872
Oldtown Folks (f Stowe), 1869
Olinger Stories (f Updike), 1964
Olive and Mary Anne (f Farrell), 1978
Olive of Minerva (f Dahlberg), 1976
Oliver Goldsmith (p Thomas), 1900
Oliver Wiswell (f K. Roberts), 1940
Olivia (p Belasco), 1878
Olympia (p S. Howard), 1928
Ommateum, with Doxology (v Ammons), 1955
Omoo (f Melville), 1847
On Flower Wreath Hill (v Rexroth), 1976
On Glory's Course (f Purdy), 1984
On Keeping Women (f Calisher), 1977
On Newfound River (f Page), 1891
On Our Merry Way (scr J. O'Hara), 1948
On Picket Duty (f Alcott), 1864
On the Beaches of the Moon (v MacLeish), 1978
On the Frontier (f Harte), 1884
On the Makaloa Mat (f London), 1919
On the March to the Sea (p Vidal), 1961
On the Old Trail (f Harte), 1902
On the Plantation (f J. Harris), 1892
On the Quiet (p Thomas), 1901

On the Rebound (f Purdy), 1970
On the Road (f Kerouac), 1957
On the Runway of Life, You Never Know What's Coming Off Next (p Kopit), 1958
On the Shelf (p Morley), 1924
On the Stairs (f Fuller), 1918
On the Wing of Occasions (f J. Harris), 1900
On These I Stand (Cullen), 1947
On Trial (p Rice), 1914
Once (v Walker), 1968
Once Around the Block (p Saroyan), 1956
Once in a Blue Moon (scr Hecht, MacArthur), 1935
Once in a Lifetime (p Hart, Kaufman), 1930
Once upon a Time (p Crothers), 1918
Once upon a Time (f Richard Harding Davis), 1910
One Against Seven (scr Laurents), 1945
One Arm (f T. Williams), 1948
One Basket (f Ferber), 1947
One Clear Call (f Sinclair), 1948
One Day (f Morris), 1965
One Day After Another (v Creeley), 1972
One Day in the Afternoon of the World (f Saroyan), 1964
One Day, When I Was Lost (p James Baldwin), 1972
One Fair Woman (f J.Miller), 1876
One Favored Acorn (v Frost), 1969
One Heavenly Night (scr Bromfield, S. Howard), 1930
One Hour Late (scr Parker), 1935
$106,000 Blood Money (f Hammett), 1943
100% (f Sinclair), 1920
One Man in His Time (f Glasgow), 1922
One Man's Initiation—1917 (f Dos Passos), 1920
One Man's Meat (White), 1942
£1,000,000 Bank-Note (f Twain), 1893
One Minute Please (Benchley), 1945
One More Free Man (p Boyd), 1941
One of Our Girls (p B. Howard), 1885
One of Ours (f Cather), 1922
One of Those Things (p Kelly), 1913
1/20 (v Cummings), 1936
One over Twenty (v Cummings), 1936
$1000 a Week (f Farrell), 1942
1 x 1 (v Cummings), 1944
One Touch of Venus (p Nash, Perelman), 1943
One, Two, Three (p S. Howard), 1930
1.2.3.4.5.6.7.8.9.0. (v Creeley), 1971
One Way to Heaven (f Cullen), 1932
One Woman's Life (f Herrick), 1913
One-Minute Commercial (p Bullins), 1973
One-Way Ticket (v Hughes), 1949
Only a Woman (p Daly), 1882
Only an Irish Boy (f Alger), 1894
Open Boat (f S. Crane), 1898
Open Head (v Ginsberg), 1972
Open House (v Roethke), 1941
Open Sea (v Masters), 1921
Open-Eyed Conspiracy (f Howells), 1897
Opening of the Field (v Duncan), 1960
Opening the Hand (v Merwin), 1983
Openings in the Old Trail (f Harte), 1902
Opera Goer (f D. Mitchell), 1852
Opera, Opera (p Saroyan), 1942
Operation Sidewinder (p Shepard), 1970
Opposing Self (Trilling), 1955
Optimist's Daughter (f Welty), 1972
Options (f Henry), 1909
Opus pistorum (f H. Miller), 1983
Opus Posthumous (Stevens), 1957
Or Else (v R. Warren), 1974
Oralloossa (p Bird), 1832
Orange Blossoms, Fresh and Faded (f Arthur), 1871
Orange Soufflé (p Bellow), 1966
Oranges (v F. O'Hara), 1953
Orchards, Thrones and Caravans (v Patchen), 1955
Ordeal (f Murfree), 1912
Ordeal of Mansart (f Du Bois), 1957
O'Reagans (p Harrigan), 1886
Oregon Idyll (p J. Miller), 1910
Oregon Trail (Parkman), 1872
Oresteia (p R. Lowell), 1978
Organizer (p Hughes), 1939
Orgy (f Rukeyser), 1965
Orient Express (p Daly), 1895
Origin of Evil (f Queen), 1951
Origin of Evil (v Tyler), 1793
Origin of Sadness (f Morris), 1984
Origin of the Feast of Purim (p Tyler), 1941
Ormond (f C. Brown), 1799
Orphan Angel (f Wylie), 1926
Orphan Children (f Arthur), 1850
Orphans in Gethsemane (f Fisher), 1960
Orphans of the Street (scr West), 1938
Orpheus (v Rukeyser), 1949
Orpheus Descending (p T. Williams), 1957
Orpheus Road Company (p Baum), 1917
O'Ruddy (f S. Crane), 1903
O'Ryan (v Olson), 1958
Osbert's Career (p Wilson), 1969
Osceola (p Chivers), 1980
Oswali at Athens (p Payne), 1831
Otchayanie (f Nabokov), 1936
Other Girl (p Thomas), 1903
Other Gods (f Buck), 1940
Other House (f H. James), 1896
Other Main-Travelled Roads (f Garland), 1910
Other Side of the Street (f S. Jackson), 1956
Other Voices, Other Rooms (f Capote), 1948
Other Woman (p Richard Harding Davis), 1893
Otho (p Neal), 1819
Our Blushing Brides (scr Lawson), 1930
Our Century (p Wilder), 1947
Our Children (f Arthur), 1849
Our Cranks (p Harrigan), 1881
Our English Friend (p Daly), 1882
Our Gang (Starring Tricky and His Friends) (f P. Roth), 1971
Our Heroic Themes (v Boker), 1865
Our Irish Cousins (p Harrigan), 1877
Our Lady (f Sinclair), 1938
Our Lady Peace (v Van Doren), 1942
Our Law Makers (p Harrigan), 1878
Our Leading Citizen (scr Ade), 1922
Our Lives, Our Fortunes, and Our Sacred Honor (p MacLeish), 1961
Our Mr. Wrenn (f Lewis), 1914
Our Mrs.McChesney (p Ferber), 1915
Our Neighbors in the Corner House (f Arthur), 1866
Our Neighbour Opposite (f Burnett), 1878
Our Town (p Wilder), 1938
Our Town (scr Wilder), 1940

Our Visit to Niagara (f Goodman), 1960
Ourselves (p Crothers), 1913
Ourselves to Know (f J. O'Hara), 1960
Out Cry (p T. Williams), 1971
Out for Business (f Alger), 1900
Out from Under (p Bellow), 1966
Out in the World (f Arthur), 1864
Out of Old Aunt Mary's (v Riley), 1904
Out of Season (v Simpson), 1979
Out of the Foam (f J. Cooke), 1871
Out of the Question (p Howells), 1877
Out of the Rolling Ocean (v Bly), 1984
Out of the Sea (p Marquis), 1927
Out of the South (p Green), 1939
Out of the Sunset Sea (f Tourgée), 1893
Out of Time's Abyss (f E. Burroughs), 1963
Out on the Outskirts of Town (tv Inge), 1964
Out She Goes (f Stout), 1953
Out Trail (f Rinehart), 1923
Outcry (f H. James), 1911
Outcry (p H. James), 1917
Outer Banks (v Rukeyser), 1967
Outing with the Queen of Hearts (f Tourgée), 1894
Outland Piper (v Davidson), 1924
Outlaw of the Lowest Planet (v Patchen), 1946
Outlaw of Torn (f E. Burroughs), 1927
Outside (p Glaspell), 1917
Outside Looking In (p M. Anderson), 1925
Outsider (f Lovecraft), 1939
Outsider (f R. Wright), 1953
Over My Dead Body (f Stout), 1940
Over the Hump (f E. Gardner), 1945
Over the Moon (scr Sherwood), 1937
Over 21 (radio Chayefsky), 1951
Overland (f De Forest), 1871
Overland to the Islands (v Levertov), 1958
Overnight (p Inge), 1969
Overnight to Many Distant Cities (f Barthelme), 1983
Owen Wingrave (f H. James), 1893
Owl (f Hawkes), 1954
Owl in the Attic (f Thurber), 1931
Owl King (v Dickey), 1977
Owls (v Snodgrass), 1983
Owl's Clover (v Stevens), 1936
Owls Don't Blink (f E. Gardner), 1942
Own Your Own Home (f Lardner), 1919
Ox-Bow Incident (f Clark), 1940
Oyster and the Pearl (tv Saroyan), 1953
Oyster Is a Wealthy Beast (f Purdy), 1967
Oz series (f Baum), from 1900

Paa Glemte Veie (f Rølvaag), 1914
Pace That Kills (f Saltus), 1889
Pacific Poems (v J. Miller), 1871
Pactolus Prime (f Tourgée), 1890
Paddle Your Own Canoe (f Alger), 1887
Paddy McGann (f Simms), 1972
Padre Ignacio (f Wister), 1911
Pagan (scr Lawson), 1929
Pages from Cold Point (f Bowles), 1968
Paid (scr MacArthur), 1931
Painful Predicament of Sherlock Holmes (p Gillette), 1905
Paint Your Wagon (scr Chayefsky), 1969
Painted Bird (f Kosinski), 1965
Painted Veils (f Huneker), 1920
Painter Dreaming in the Scholar's House (v Nemerov)
Pair of Patient Lovers (f Howells), 1901
Pal Joey (f J. O'Hara), 1940
Pal Joey (p J. O'Hara), 1940
Pale Fire (f Nabokov), 1962
Pale Horse, Pale Rider (f Porter), 1939
Palimpsest (f Doolittle), 1926
Paliser Case (f Saltus), 1919
Palm at the End of the Mind (Stevens), 1971
Palmy Days (p Thomas), 1919
Palo Duro (p Green), 1979
Pamela's Prodigy (p Fitch), 1891
Panama (v J. Miller), 1912
Panatella (p K. Roberts), 1907
Pandora (f H. James), 1885
Pandora Lifts the Lid (f Marquis, Morley), 1924
Panels for the Walls of Heaven (v Patchen), 1947
Pangolin (v Moore), 1936
Panic (p MacLeish), 1935
Panorama (v Whittier), 1856
Pansie (f Hawthorne), 1864
Pansies and Orchids (v H. Jackson), 1884
Pansy Billings (f H. Jackson), 1898
Panther and the Lash (v Hughes), 1967
Papa La Fleur (f Gale), 1933
Papa You're Crazy (f Saroyan), 1957
Paper City (f Nasby), 1879
Paperhanger (p Hart, Kaufman), 1935(?)
Parables (v Fletcher), 1925
Parachute (f Guthrie), 1928
Paradise (f Barthelme), 1986
Paradise Lost (p Odets), 1935
Parents Day (f Goodman), 1951
Paris Bound (p Barry), 1927
Paris Comedy (p Saroyan), 1960
Paris in Spring (scr Parker), 1935
Paris, Texas (scr Shepard), 1984
Park Avenue (p Kaufman), 1946
Parlor, Bedlam and Bath (Perelman), 1930
Parlor Car (p Howells), 1876
Parlor Magic (p Lawson), 1963
Parnassus on Wheels (f Morley), 1917
Parnell (scr Behrman, van Druten), 1937
Parricide (p Daly), 1873
Parsons' Pleasure (v Morley), 1923
Parties (f Van Vechten), 1930
Parting and a Meeting (f Howells), 1896
Parting Friends (p Howells), 1911
Partisan (f Simms), 1835
Partners (f Auchincloss), 1974
Partners (f Deland), 1913
Parts of a World (v Stevens), 1942
Party Dress (f Hergesheimer), 1930
Pass the Gravy (f E. Gardner), 1959
Passage to India (v Whitman), 1871
Passing a Crèche (v W. Stafford), 1978
Passing of Chow-Chow (p Rice), 1934
Passing Regiment (p Daly), 1881
Passion Artist (f Hawkes), 1979
Passion of Josef D. (p Chayefsky), 1964
Passion Play (f Kosinski), 1979
Passion Play (p Kosinski), 1982
Passion Within (f Fisher), 1960

Passionate Pilgrim (f H. James), 1875
Passions (f Singer), 1975
Passions Spin the Plot (f Fisher), 1934
Passport to the War (v Kunitz), 1944
Past All Dishonor (f Cain), 1946
Pastime Stories (f Page), 1894
Pastimes of Aleck Maury (f Gordon), 1935
Pastures of Heaven (f Steinbeck), 1932
Pat Hobby Stories (f Fitzgerald), 1962
Patagonia (f H. James), 1889
Patchwork Girl of Oz (scr Baum), 1914
Paterson (v W. Williams), from 1946
Path of Duty (f H. James), 1885
Path of Sorrow (v Chivers), 1832
Pathfinder (f Cooper), 1840
Paths of Glory (p S. Howard), 1935
Patience Sparhawk and Her Times (f Atherton), 1897
Patriot (f Buck), 1939
Patriotic Gore (Wilson), 1962
Patriots (p Kingsley), 1943
Paul Arniff (p Belasco), 1880
Paul Deverell (f Ingraham), 1845
Paul Fane (f Willis), 1857
Paul Patoff (f Crawford), 1887
Paul Perril, The Merchant's Son (f Ingraham), 1845
Paul Prescott the Runaway (f Alger), 1867
Paul Prescott's Charge (f Alger), 1865
Paul the Peddler (f Alger), 1871
Pause in the Desert (f La Farge), 1957
Pavilion of Women (f Buck), 1946
Pawn Ticket 210 (p Belasco), 1887
Pawnbroker (f Wallant), 1961
Pay Dirt (f E. Gardner), 1983
Paying the Penalty (scr Hecht), 1927
Peace, It's Wonderful (f Saroyan), 1939
Peace Like a River (f Fisher), 1957
Peace Manoeuvres (p Richard Harding Davis), 1914
Peacemaker (f Arthur), 1869
Pearl (v S. Mitchell), 1906
Pearl (scr Steinbeck), 1946
Pearl (f Steinbeck), 1947
Pearl of Orr's Island (f Stowe), 1862
Pearls Are a Nuisance (f Chandler), 1953
Peder Seier (f Rølvaag), 1928
Peder Victorious (f Rølvaag), 1929
Peer Gynt (p Green), 1951
Peggy (p Crothers), 1925
Peggy from Paris (p Ade), 1903
Pelayo (v Mowatt), 1836
Pelayo (f Simms), 1838
Pelican from a Bestiary of 1120 (v Wilbur), 1963
Pellucidar (f E. Burroughs), 1923
Pelopidas (Bird), 1919
Pembroke (f Freeman), 1894
Pemmican (f Fisher), 1956
Penelope (p Vonnegut), 1960
Penhally (f Gordon), 1931
Penitent (f Singer), 1983
Pennsylvania Pilgrim (v Whittier), 1872
Penny That Beauty Spent (p Wilder), 1928
Penrod series (f Tarkington), from 1914
Pension Beaurepas (f H. James), 1883
Pentimento (Hellman), 1973
Peony (f Buck), 1948
People (p Glaspell), 1917
People and Houses (f Suckow), 1927
People I Have Met (f Willis), 1850
People in the Wind (p Inge), 1962
People Live Here (v Simpson), 1983
People of Our Neighborhood (f Freeman), 1898
People That Time Forgot (f E. Burroughs), 1963
People with Light Coming Out of Them (radio Saroyan), 1941
People, Yes (v Sandburg), 1936
People You Know (f Ade), 1903
Perch of the Devil (f Atherton), 1914
Père Raphaël (f Cable), 1901
Perfect Analysis Given by a Parrot (p T. Williams), 1958
Perfume of Eros (f Saltus), 1905
Period of Adjustment (p T. Williams), 1958
Perla (scr Steinbeck), 1946
Permanence and Change (Burke), 1935
Permit Me Voyage (v Agee), 1934
Perpetual Light (v W. Benét), 1919
Perry Mason series (f E. Gardner), from 1933
Persecuted Wife (p Ade), 1925
Person, Place and Thing (v Shapiro), 1942
Personae (v Pound), 1909
Personal Recollections of Joan of Arc (f Twain), 1896
Personality Plus (f Ferber), 1914
Persons and Places (Santayana), 1963
Pete (p Harrigan), 1887
Peter Ashley (f Heyward), 1932
Peter Gudge Becomes a Secret Agent (f Sinclair), 1930
Peter Pilgrim (f Bird), 1838
Peter Smink (p Payne), 1822
Peter Stuyvesant (p B. Howard), 1899
Peter the Great (p Dunlap), 1802
Peter Whiffle (f Van Vechten), 1922
Petrified Forest (p Sherwood), 1935
Phaedra (p R. Lowell), 1961
Phaedra (p Rexroth), 1951
Phaenomena quaedam Apocalyptica (Sewall), 1697
Phantasmagoria (p Dreiser), 1926
Phantoms of the Foot-Bridge (f Murfree), 1895
Phases of an Inferior Planet (f Glasgow), 1898
Phil, The Fiddler (f Alger), 1872
Philadelphia Story (p Barry), 1939
Philip and His Wife (f Deland), 1894
Philip Goes Forth (p Kelly), 1931
Philip Marlowe series (f Chandler), from 1939
Philip Stanley (f C. Brown), 1807
Philip Vernon (f S. Mitchell), 1895
Philosopher (p Ashbery), 1978
Philosophers at Court (p Santayana), 1953
Philosophy 4 (f Wister), 1903
Philosophy of Literary Form (Burke), 1941
Phoebe Daring (f Baum), 1912
Phoenix and the Tortoise (v Rexroth), 1944
Phyllis (p Burnett), 1889
Phyllis of the Sierras (f Harte), 1888
Piazza Tales (f Melville), 1856
Pic (f Kerouac), 1971
Piccino (f Burnett), 1894
Picked-Up Pieces (f Updike), 1975
Pick-Up on Noon Street (f Chandler), 1951
Pickwick Papers (p Daly), 1868
Picnic (p Green), 1928
Picnic (p Inge), 1953

Picture of St. John (v B. Taylor), 1866
Picture Poems (v Patchen), 1962
Pictures (v Whitman), 1927
Pictures from an Institution (f Jarrell), 1954
Pictures from Brueghel (v W. Williams), 1962
Pictures of Fidelman (f Malamud), 1969
Pictures of Life and of Death (v Patchen), 1947
Pictures of the Floating World (v A. Lowell), 1919
Pieces (v Creeley), 1968
Pied Piper Malone (scr Tarkington), 1924
Pierce Fenning (f Ingraham), 1846
Pierre (f Melville), 1852
Pierre the Organ-Boy (f Arthur), 1852
Pietro Ghisleri (f Crawford), 1893
Pig Dreams (v Levertov), 1981
Pig Pen (p Bullins), 1970
Pigeon Feathers (f Updike), 1962
Pigeons and People (p Cohan), 1933
Pike County Ballads (v Hay), 1871
Pilgrim and the Book (p MacKaye), 1920
Pilgrim Hawk (f Wescott), 1940
Pilgrimage of Festus (v Aiken), 1923
Pillar of Fire (f Ingraham), 1859
Pillsbury Muddle (p Harrigan), 1877
Pilot (f Cooper), 1823
Pinball (f Kosinski), 1982
Ping Pong Players (p Saroyan), 1942
Ping-Pong Game (p Saroyan), 1940
Pink and White Tyranny (f Stowe), 1871
Pink Church (v W. Williams), 1949
Pink Marsh (f Ade), 1897
Pioneers (f Cooper), 1823
Pioneers of France in the New World (Parkman), 1865
Pi-Pa-Ki (p S. Howard), 1930
Pipe Night (f J. O'Hara), 1945
Pipes o'Pan at Zekesbury (v Riley), 1888
Pique (p Daly), 1875
Pirate (p Behrman), 1942
Pirate (f Ingraham), 1839
Pirate Blood (f E. Burroughs), 1970
Pirate Chief (f Ingraham), n.d.
Pirate Schooner (f Ingraham), 1877
Pisan Cantos (v Pound), 1948
Pistol (f Jones), 1959
Pit (f Norris), 1903
Pizarro in Peru (p Dunlap), 1800
Place Called Estherville (f Caldwell), 1949
Place of Dead Roads (f W. Burroughs), 1983
Place of Love (v Shapiro), 1942
Place to Come To (f R. Warren), 1977
Plagued by the Nightingale (f Boyle), 1931
Plains Song (f Morris), 1980
Plaint of the Rose (v Sandburg), 1904(?)
Planet News (v Ginsberg), 1968
Plantation Melodies (p Dunbar), 1901
Plantation Printer (f J. Harris), 1892
Plantation Pageants (f J. Harris), 1899
Play of Herod (p MacLeish), 1968
Play of the Play (p Bullins), 1973
Play Things (p Saroyan), 1980
Play Time, Pseudo Stein (v Duncan), 1969
Playback (f Chandler), 1958
Player on the Other Side (f Queen), 1963
Player Piano (f Vonnegut), 1952
Playing for Time (tv A. Miller), 1980
Playing the Mischief (f De Forest), 1875
Plays for Bleecker Street (p Wilder), from 1960
Plays of Protest (p Sinclair), 1912
Plays of the Natural and the Supernatural (p Dreiser), 1916
Playwright and the Public (p Saroyan), 1963
Please Pass the Guilt (f Stout), 1973
Pleased to Meet You (f Morley), 1927
Plexus (f H. Miller), 1953
Plot It Yourself (f Stout), 1959
Plots and Counterplots (f Alcott), 1976
Pluck and Luck (Benchley), 1925
Plucky Paul (f Alger), 1888
Plum Tree (f Phillips), 1905
Pluralistic Universe (W. James), 1909
Plutocrat (f Tarkington), 1927
Plutonian Ode (v Ginsberg), 1982
Pnin (f Nabokov), 1957
Pocahontas (p Barker), 1820
Podesta's Daughter (v Boker), 1852
Podvig' (f Nabokov), 1933
Poem Delivered Before the Society of the United Brothers (v Willis), 1831
Poem for Black Hearts (v Baraka), 1967
Poem on Divine Revelation (v Brackenridge), 1774
Poem on the Rising Glory of America (v Brackenridge, Freneau), 1772
Poem Outlines (v Lanier), 1908
Poems: A Joking Word (v Riding), 1930
Poems about God (v Ransom), 1919
Poems All Over the Place (v Ginsberg), 1978
Poems and Problems (v Nabokov), 1971
Poems for Men (v Runyon), 1947
Poems for Tennessee (v Bly, W. Stafford), 1971
Poems from the Margins of Thom Gunn's Moly (v Duncan), 1972
Poems Here at Home (v Riley), 1893
Poems of a Jew (v Shapiro), 1958
Poems of Cabin and Field (v Dunbar), 1899
Poems of Home and Travel (v B. Taylor), 1855
Poems of Humor and Protest (v Patchen), 1954
Poems of Nature (v Whittier), 1886
Poems of People (v Masters), 1936
Poems of the Orient (v B. Taylor), 1854
Poems of the War (v Boker), 1864
Poems of Two Friends (v Howells), 1860
Poems on Slavery (v Longfellow), 1842
Poems Retrieved (v F. O'Hara), 1977
Poems to Poets (v Eberhart), 1976
Poems Written During the Progress of the Abolition Question (v Whittier), 1837
Poems Written in Early Youth (v Eliot), 1950
Poem-scapes (v Patchen), 1958
Poet: A Lying Word (v Riding), 1933
Poet and the Dancer (v Doolittle), 1975
Poetic Disturbances (v Duncan), 1970
Poetic Situation in America (p Saroyan), 1942
Poetry Package (v W. Benét, Morley), 1950
Poets, Farewell! (v Wilson), 1929
Poet's Journal (v B. Taylor), 1862
Poet's Testament (v Santayana), 1953
Poganuc People (f Stowe), 1878
Poggioli series (f Stribling), from 1929
Point of Law (p Phillips), 1908

Point of No Return (f Marquand), 1949
Point of View (p Crothers), 1904
Point of View (f H. James), 1883
Point Reyes Poems (v Bly), 1974
Points of My Compass (White), 1962
Poldekin (p Tarkington), 1920
Police (p Baraka), 1968
Policeman Bluejay (f Baum), 1907
Policeman's Love-Hungry Daughter (f Hecht), 1927
Politian (p Poe), 1923
Political Self-Portrait (v Wheelwright), 1940
Polly Fulton (f Marquand), 1947
Polyus (p Nabokov), 1924
Pomes Penyeach (v Patchen), 1959
Pomps and Vanities (f Frederic), 1913
Ponder Heart (f Welty), 1954
Poodle Springs (f Chandler), 1962
Pool (f Rinehart), 1952
Poor Aubrey (p Kelly), 1922
Poor Fool (f Caldwell), 1930
Poor Harold! (p Dell), 1920
Poor Rich Man, and the Rich Poor Man (f Sedgwick), 1836
Poor Richard: An Almanack (Franklin), from 1732
Poor Richard Improved (Franklin), from 1747
Poor White (f S. Anderson), 1920
Poor Wise Man (f Rinehart), 1920
Poor Wood-Cutter (f Arthur), 1852
Poorhouse Fair (f Updike), 1959
Poppies and Mandragora (v Saltus), 1926
Popsy (f H. Jackson), 1898
Popularity (p Cohan), 1906
Porcupine (p Robinson), 1915
Porgy (f Heyward), 1925
Porgy (p Heyward), 1927
Porgy and Bess (p Heyward), 1935
Port of Saints (f W. Burroughs), 1980
Port Town (p Hughes), 1960
Portable Yenberry (p Connelly), 1962
Porter's Troubles (p Harrigan), 1875
Portion of Labor (f Freeman), 1901
Portnoy's Complaint (f P. Roth), 1969
Portrait in Brownstone (f Auchincloss), 1962
Portrait of a Lady (f H. James), 1881
Portrait of a Madonna (p T. Williams), 1946
Portrait of a Marriage (f Buck), 1945
Portraits (f Chopin), 1979
Portraits of Places (H. James), 1883
Possession (f Bromfield), 1925
"Posson Jone'" and Père Raphaël (f Cable), 1909
Post Road (p Steele), 1934
Postman Always Rings Twice (f Cain), 1934
Postman Always Rings Twice (p Cain), 1936
Pot Boiler (p Sinclair), 1924
Pot of Earth (v MacLeish), 1925
Potter's Field (p Green), 1931
Power of Kindness (f Arthur), 1875
Powers of Attorney (f Auchincloss), 1963
Powhatan (v Smith), 1841
Practical Possum (v Eliot), 1947
Pragmatism (W. James), 1907
Prague Orgy (f P. Roth), 1985
Prairie (f Cooper), 1827
Prairie Folks (f Garland), 1893
Prairie Songs (v Garland), 1893
Praise to the End! (v Roethke), 1951
Prayer Meeting (p Green), 1926
Preacher (Emerson), 1880
Preamble I and II (p Eberhart), 1962
Precaution (f Cooper), 1820
Preface to a Life (f Gale), 1926
Preface to a Twenty Volume Suicide Note (v Baraka), 1961
Prejudices (Mencken), from 1919
Prelude (v Aiken), 1929
Preludes (v Aiken), 1966
Preludes and Symphonies (v Fletcher), 1922
Preludes of Memnon (v Aiken), 1931
Presence of Grace (f Powers), 1956
Present Hour (v MacKaye), 1914
Presenting Lily Mars (f Tarkington), 1933
Presents (f Barthelme), 1980
President (p S. Howard), 1952
President Vanishes (scr Hecht, MacArthur), 1934
President Vanishes (f Stout), 1934
Presidential Agent (f Sinclair), 1944
Presidential Mission (f Sinclair), 1947
Presidential Papers (Mailer), 1963
President's Mystery (scr West), 1936
President's Policy (f Nasby), 1877
Pretty Mrs. Gaston (f J. Cooke), 1874
Pretty Polly Pemberton (f Burnett), 1877
Pretty Sister of José (f Burnett), 1889
Pretty Sister of José (p Burnett), 1903
Pretty Story, Written in the Year of Our Lord 2774 (f Hopkinson), 1774
Previous Engagement (p Howells), 1897
Priapus and the Pool (v Aiken), 1925
Price (p A. Miller), 1968
Price She Paid (f Phillips), 1912
Price Was High (f Fitzgerald), 1979
Pride and Prudence (f Arthur), 1850
Pride of Sonnets (v Morley), 1951
Pride or Principle (f Arthur), 1844
Pride's Castle (f Yerby), 1949
Priest (v Doolittle), 1983
Priglashenie na Kazn' (f Nabokov), 1938
Prima Donna (f Simms), 1844
Primadonna (f Crawford), 1908
Primer for Combat (f Boyle), 1942
Primitive Like an Orb (v Stevens), 1948
Primitive World (p Baraka), 1984
Primitivism and Decadence (Winters), 1937
Primrose Path (v Nash), 1935
Prince and the Pauper (f Twain), 1881
Prince Deukalion (p B. Taylor), 1878
Prince Hagen (f Sinclair), 1903
Prince Hagen (p Sinclair), 1909
Prince Little Boy (f S. Mitchell), 1888
Prince of Darkness (f Powers), 1947
Prince of India (f Wallace), 1893
Prince of Players (scr Hart), 1954
Prince of the House of David (f Ingraham), 1855
Prince Souvanna Phouma (v Wilbur), 1963
Prince There Was (p Cohan), 1918
Princess Aline (p Richard Harding Davis), 1895
Princess Casamassima (f H. James), 1886
Princess Marries the Page (p Millay), 1932
Princess of Mars (f E. Burroughs), 1917
Princess Royal (p Daly), 1877

Rabelais and the Queen of Whims (p Masters), 1934
Rachel Dyer (f Neal), 1828
Racketty-Packetty House (f Burnett), 1906
Racketty-Packetty House (p Burnett), 1912
Radio Play (radio Saroyan), 1940
Rafael (f Ingraham), 1845
Rafael Naarizokh (f Cahan), 1907
Raffle for Mrs. Hennessey's Clock (p Harrigan), 1874
Raffles (scr S. Howard), 1930
Raffles (scr S. Howard, van Druten), 1940
Rage to Live (f J. O'Hara), 1949
Ragged Dick (f Alger), 1868
Ragged Lady (f Howells), 1899
Ragnarok (Donnelly), 1883
Rag-Picker of Paris (p Morley), 1937
Rahab (f Frank), 1922
Raid of the Guerilla (f Murfree), 1912
Raiders of the Spanish Peaks (f Grey), 1938
Railroad of Love (p Daly), 1887
Railway Police (f Calisher), 1966
Rain (scr M. Anderson), 1932
Rain Five Days and I Love It (v Hugo), 1975
Rain from Heaven (p Behrman), 1935
Rainbow (f Buck), 1974
Rainbow Trail (f Grey), 1915
Rainbow's End (f Cain), 1975
Rains Came (f Bromfield), 1937
Raintree County (f Lockridge), 1948
Rainy Afternoon (p Inge), 1962
Rainy Day at Home (f Arthur), 1869
Raise High the Roof Beam, Carpenters (f Salinger), 1963
Raisin in the Sun (p Hansberry), 1959
Raisin in the Sun (scr Hansberry), 1961
Ralph Raymond's Heir (f Alger), 1892
Ralstons (f Crawford), 1895
Ramero (f Ingraham), 1846
Ramona (f H. Jackson), 1884
Ramsey Milholland (f Tarkington), 1919
Randolph (f Neal), 1823
Random Recollections of an Old Doctor (f Arthur), 1846
Randy of the River (f Alger), 1906
Range of Poems (v Snyder), 1966
Ranger (p Thomas), 1907
Rangle River (scr Grey), 1936
Ranson's Folly (f Richard Harding Davis), 1902
Ranson's Folly (p Richard Harding Davis), 1904
Rasputin and the Empress (scr MacArthur), 1932
Ratio Disciplinae Fratrum Nov Anglorum (Mather), 1726
Raven (v Poe), 1845
Ravensnest (f Cooper), 1846
Rawhide Knot (f Richter), 1978
Razzle Dazzle (p Saroyan), 1942
Reaches of Heaven (f Singer), 1980
Reading about My World (v Olson), 1968
Reading the Spirit (v Eberhart), 1936
Real Dope (f Lardner), 1919
Real Life of Sebastian Knight (f Nabokov), 1941
Real Little Lord Fauntleroy (p Burnett), 1888
Real Losses, Imaginary Gains (f Morris), 1976
Real Soldiers of Fortune (f Richard Harding Davis), 1906
Real Thing (f H. James), 1893
Real World (f Herrick), 1901
Reality Sandwiches (v Ginsberg), 1963
Really, My Dear . . . (p Morley), 1928
Realm of Resemblance (v Stevens), 1947
Realms of Being (Santayana), 1942
Reason Why (p A. Miller), 1970
Rebecca (f Rowson), 1814
Rebecca (scr Sherwood), 1940
Rebecca of Sunnybrook Farm (scr Behrman), 1932
Rebel Coaster (f Ingraham), 1867
Rebellion der Gehenkten (f Traven), 1936
Rebellion of the Hanged (f Traven), 1952
Rebirth Celebration of the Human Race (p Saroyan), 1975
Recent Carnival of Crime (f Twain), 1877
Recent Killing (p Baraka), 1973
Reckless Temple (p Thomas), 1890
Recklessness (p O'Neill), 1914
Recognitions (f Gaddis), 1955
Recollections (f Alcott), 1889
Recollections of My Childhood Days (f Alcott), 1890
Reconstructions in Philosophy (Dewey), 1920
Recorder (v Halleck), 1833
Recovery (f Berryman), 1973
Recruiting Officer (p Daly), 1885
Rector (p Crothers), 1902
Rector of Justin (f Auchincloss), 1964
Red Badge of Courage (f S. Crane), 1895
Red Barn (f Tarkington), 1935
Red Box (f Stout), 1937
Red Bull (f Stout), 1945
Red Carpet (p Fuller), 1939
Red City (f S. Mitchell), 1908
Red Cross (p Shepard), 1966
Red Cross Girl (f Richard Harding Davis), 1912
Red Devil Battery Sign (p T. Williams), 1975
Red Harvest (f Hammett), 1929
Red Jacket (v Goodman), 1955
Red Lamp (f Rinehart), 1925
Red Letter Nights (p Daly), 1884
Red Men and White (f Wister), 1896
Red One (f London), 1918
Red Owl (p Gillette), 1924
Red Pony (f Steinbeck), 1937
Red Pony (scr Steinbeck), 1949
Red Ribbon (p Daly), 1870
Red Riders (f Page), 1924
Red Rock (f Page), 1898
Red Roses for Bronze (v Doolittle), 1931
Red Rover (f Cooper), 1827
Red Sand (f Stribling), 1924
Red Scarf (p Daly), 1868
Red Shoes Run Faster (scr Green), 1949
Red Threads (f Stout), 1939
Red, White,and Blue (p Cain), 1926
Red Wind (f Chandler), 1946
Red Wine and Yellow Hair (v Patchen), 1949
Redburn (f Melville), 1849
Redskins (f Cooper), 1846
Redwood (f Sedgwick), 1824
Reef (f Wharton), 1912
Reef Girl (f Grey), 1977
Reflected Glory (p Kelly), 1936
Reflections (v H. Miller), 1981
Reflections in a Golden Eye (f McCullers), 1941
Regarding Wave (v Snyder), 1969
Reggae or Not! (v Baraka), 1982
Regierung (f Traven), 1931

Rock and Shell (v Wheelwright), 1933
Rock Garden (p Shepard), 1964
Rock Wagram (f Saroyan), 1951
Rocket to the Moon (p Odets), 1938
Rocking Chair (p Shepard), 1965
Rocking Horse (v Morley), 1919
Rocky Mountains (Irving), 1837
Roderick Hudson (f H. James), 1875
Rodman the Keeper (f Woolson), 1880
Rodolphe in Boston! (f Ingraham), 1844
Roger Bloomer (p Lawson), 1923
Roger la Honte (p Daly), 1889
Roger's Version (f Updike), 1986
Rogue River Feud (f Grey), 1948
Roland Blake (f S. Mitchell), 1886
Roll Call (p MacKaye), 1918
Roll River (f Boyd), 1935
Roll Sweet Chariot (p Green), 1934
Rolling Stone (f Alger), 1902
Rolling Stones (f Henry), 1912
Rollo Johnson (f Ade), 1904
Roman Bartholow (v Robinson), 1923
Roman Hat Mystery (f Queen), 1929
Roman Holiday (scr Hecht), 1953
Roman Holiday (f Sinclair), 1931
Roman Scandals (scr Kaufman, Sherwood), 1933
Roman Singer (f Crawford), 1884
Roman Spring of Mrs. Stone (f T. Williams), 1950
Romance Island (f Gale), 1906
Romance of a Plain Man (f Glasgow), 1909
Romance of the Sunny South (f Ingraham), 1845
Romance of Travel (f Willis), 1840
Romantic Comedians (f Glasgow), 1926
Romantic Egoists (f Auchincloss), 1954
Romantics (f Rinehart), 1929
Romulus (p Vidal), 1962
Romulus the Shepherd King (p Payne), 1940
Room Forty-Five (p Howells), 1900
Rooming House (v Gregory), 1932
Root of His Evil (f Cain), 1952
Rootabaga series (Sandburg), from 1922
Roots and Branches (v Duncan), 1964
Rope (scr Hecht, Laurents), 1948
Rope (p O'Neill), 1918
Rope (p Stribling), 1928
Ropes (p Steele), 1925
Roping Lions in the Grand Canyon (f Grey), 1924
Rosary (scr Green), 1933
Rose Briar (p Tarkington), 1922
Rose Family (f Alcott), 1864
Rose for Ana María (f Yerby), 1976
Rose in Bloom (f Alcott), 1876
Rose of Dutcher's Coolly (f Garland), 1895
Rose of the Rancho (p Belasco), 1906
Rose of Yesterday (f Crawford), 1897
Rose Tattoo (p T. Williams), 1951
Rose Tattoo (scr T. Williams), 1955
Roseanna McCoy (scr Green), 1949
Rosy Crucifixion (f H. Miller), from 1949
Rough and Ready (f Alger), 1869
Roughing It (Twain), 1872
Roughing It! (p Daly), 1873
Round the Clock (p Daly), 1872
'Round the Town (p Kaufman), 1924
Round the Town (p Parker), 1924
Round Up (f Lardner), 1929
Roving Across Fields (v W. Stafford), 1983
Roxie Hart (scr Hecht), 1942
Roxy (f Eggleston), 1878
Royal Family (p Ferber, Kaufman), 1927
Royal Gentleman (f Tourgée), 1881
Royal Middy (p Daly), 1880
Royal Vagabond (p Cohan), 1919
Royal Youth (p Daly), 1881
Rubáiyát of Doc Sifers (v Riley), 1897
Rubber Band (f Stout), 1936
Rudolph and Amina (f Morley), 1930
Rufus and Rose (f Alger), 1870
Rugged Path (p Sherwood), 1945
Ruined Family (f Arthur), 1843
Ruined Gamester (f Arthur), 1844
Rulers of Kings (f Atherton), 1904
Rules for Reducing a Great Empire to a Small One (Franklin), 1793
Rumbin Galleries (f Tarkington), 1937
Rumination (v Eberhart), 1947
Rumor Verified (v R. Warren), 1981
Rumpelstiltskin (p J. Gardner), 1979
Run of Jacks (v Hugo), 1961
Run, Sheep, Run (f Bodenheim), 1932
Runaway (f Dell), 1925
Running for Office (p Cohan), 1903
Running Sun (v Purdy), 1971
Rupert's Ambition (f Alger), 1899
Rus in Urbe (p Rice), 1934
Ruski (f W. Burroughs), 1984
Russian Beauty (f Nabokov), 1973
Russian People (p Odets), 1942
Rustlers of Pecos County (f Grey), 1914
Ruth Underwood (p L. Mitchell), 1892
Ryder (f Barnes), 1928

S-1 (p Baraka), 1976
S.O.T. (Sons of Temperance) (p Harrigan), 1876
S.S. Glencairn (p O'Neill), 1924
S.S. San Pedro (f Cozzens), 1931
S.S. Tenacity (p S. Howard), 1922
Sabbath Lyrics (v Simms), 1849
Sabbath Scene (v Whittier), 1854
Sabbatical (f Barth), 1982
Sabine Woman (p Moody), 1906
Saboteur (scr Parker), 1942
Sack of Rome (p M. Warren), 1790
Sacred Fount (f H. James), 1901
Sacred Poems (v Willis), 1843
Sacred Wood (Eliot), 1920
Sacrilege of Alan Kent (f Caldwell), 1936
Sad Dust Glories (v Ginsberg), 1975
Sad Lament of Pecos Bill on the Eve of Killing His Wife (p Shepard), 1976
Sadness (f Barthelme), 1972
Safety First (p Fitzgerald), 1916
Sag Harbor (p Herne), 1900
Sagacity (v W. Benét), 1929
Sahara (scr Lawson), 1943
St. Gaudens Masque-Prologue (p MacKaye), 1905
Saint Gregory's Guest (v Whittier), 1886
Saint Judas (v J. Wright), 1959

Saint Katy the Virgin (f Steinbeck), 1936
St. Louis (p MacKaye), 1914
St. Louis Woman (p Cullen), 1946
St. Martin's (v Creeley), 1971
St. Patrick's Day Parade (p Harrigan), 1873
Saint Peter Relates an Incident of the Resurrection Day (v Johnson), 1930
Saint Ruth's (f Guiney), 1895
Sally Dows, Etc. (f Harte), 1893
Salmagundi (v Faulkner), 1932
Salmagundi (f Irving, Paulding), from 1807
Saloon (p H. James), 1911
Salt Garden (v Nemerov), 1955
Salvage (p Belasco), 1925
Salvation (p S. Howard, MacArthur), 1928
Salvation on a String (f Green), 1946
Salvation on a String (p Green), 1954
Sam Average (p MacKaye), 1912
Sam Ego's House (p Saroyan), 1947
Sam Holman (f Farrell), 1983
Sam Lawson's Oldtown Fireside Stories (f Stowe), 1872
Sam Spade series (f Hammett), from 1944
Sam Steele series (f Baum), from 1906
Sam, The Highest Jumper of Them All (p Saroyan), 1960
Sam Tucker (p Green), 1923
Same Door (f Updike), 1959
Sam's Chance, and How He Improved It (f Alger), 1876
Samson (p Howells), 1874
Samson and Delilah (p Daly), 1889
Samuel the Seeker (f Sinclair), 1910
Sancho Panza (p S. Howard), 1923
Sanctuary (f Faulkner), 1931
Sanctuary (p MacKaye), 1913
Sanctuary (f Wharton), 1903
Sandbox (p Albee), 1960
Sant' Ilario (f Crawford), 1889
Santa Claus (p Cummings), 1946
Santa Claus (f Ingraham), 1844
Santa Claus's Partner (f Page), 1899
Santa Go Home (v Nash), 1967
Santorini (v Merrill), 1982
Sapphira and the Slave Girl (f Cather), 1940
Sappho (p Fitch), 1899
Sappho and Phaon (p MacKaye), 1907
Sappho of Green Springs (f Harte), 1891
Sara Crewe (f Burnett), 1887
Saracen Blade (f Yerby), 1952
Saracinesca (f Crawford), 1887
Sarah (f Rowson), 1813
Saratoga (p B. Howard), 1870
Saratoga, Hot (f Calisher), 1985
Saratoga Trunk (f Ferber), 1941
Sardonic Arm (v Bodenheim), 1923
Sartoris (f Faulkner), 1929
Satan in Goray (f Singer), 1955
Satan Never Sleeps (f Buck), 1952
Satanstoe (f Cooper), 1845
Satori in Paris (f Kerouac), 1966
Saturday Night (f Farrell), 1958
Saturday Night (p Green), 1928
Saturday's Children (p M. Anderson), 1927
Savage Holiday (f R. Wright), 1954
Savage Kingdom (f Grey), 1979
Savage/Love (p Shepard), 1979
Savage Pellucidar (f E. Burroughs), 1963
Saved as by Fire (f Arthur), 1881
Saxe Holm's Stories (f H. Jackson), from 1874
Say! Is This the U.S.A.? (Caldwell), 1941
Scapegoat (scr Vidal), 1959
Sçarecrow (p MacKaye), 1908
Scarface (scr Hecht), 1932
Scarlet Car (f Richard Harding Davis), 1907
Scarlet Feather (f Ingraham), 1845
Scarlet Letter (f Hawthorne), 1850
Scarlet Letters (f Queen), 1953
Scarlet Pimpernel (scr Behrman, Sherwood), 1935
Scarlet Plague (f London), 1915
Scattered Poems (v Kerouac), 1971
Scenario (p H. Miller), 1937
Scenes (v Bowles), 1968
Scenes from Humanitas (p Bellow), 1962
Schatz der Sierra Madre (f Traven), 1927
Scherzo, From a Poem to be Entitled "The Proud City" (v Guthrie), 1933
School and Society (Dewey), 1899
School for Scandal (p Daly), 1874
School for Soldiers (p Dunlap), 1799
School for Wives (p Wilbur), 1971
Schoolmaster's Stories for Boys and Girls (f Eggleston), 1874
Science (v Hopkinson), 1762
Scorn of Women (p London), 1906
Scottsboro Limited (v Hughes), 1932
Scoundrel (scr Hecht, MacArthur), 1935
Scoundrel Time (Hellman), 1976
Scout (f Simms), 1854
Scrap Leaves, Hasty Scribbles (v Ginsberg), 1968
Scrap of Paper (p Purdy), 1981
Scratch (p MacLeish), 1971
Scream (p Laurents), 1978
Scripts for the Pageant (v Merrill), 1980
Scripture of the Golden Eternity (v Kerouac), 1960
Scrooge Rides Again (v Nash), 1960
Sea (v Creeley), 1971
Sea Bat (scr Lawson), 1930
Sea Fairies (f Baum), 1911
Sea Fever (p van Druten), 1931
Sea Garden (v Doolittle), 1916
Sea Lions (f Cooper), 1849
Sea of Grass (f Richter), 1937
Sea Wolf (scr Behrman), 1930
Sea-Change (p Howells), 1888
Seacliff (f De Forest), 1859
Seagull on the Step (f Boyle), 1955
Seal in the Bedroom (f Thurber), 1932
Seaman's Friend (Dana), 1841
Seaman's Manual (Dana), 1841
Seamstress (f Arthur), 1843
Séance (f Singer), 1968
Search for the King (f Vidal), 1950
Searching for the Ox (v Simpson), 1976
Searching Sun (p J. O'Hara), 1961
Searching Wind (p Hellman), 1944
Searching Wind (scr Hellman), 1946
Seascape (p Albee), 1975
Seaside and the Fireside (v Longfellow), 1849
Season of Comfort (f Vidal), 1949
Seaward (v Hovey), 1893
Sea-Wife (p M. Anderson), 1932

Sea-Wolf (f London), 1904
Second April (v Millay), 1921
Second Avenue (v F. O'Hara), 1960
Second Chance (f Auchincloss), 1970
Second Coming (f Percy), 1980
Second Confession (f Stout), 1949
Second Ewings (f J. O'Hara), 1977
Second Generation (f Phillips), 1907
Second Leaf (v Riding), 1935
Second Man (p Behrman), 1927
Second Overture (p M. Anderson), 1940
Second Skin (f Hawkes), 1964
Second Threshold (p Barry, Sherwood), 1951
Second Tree from the Corner (White), 1954
Second-Story Man (p Sinclair), 1912
Secret (p Belasco), 1913
Secret Drawer (f Alger), 1981
Secret Garden (f Burnett), 1911
Secret Integration (f Pynchon), 1980
Secret of Convict Lake (scr Hecht), 1951
Secret of Freedom (tv MacLeish), 1959
Secret Service (p Gillette), 1895
Secret Story (f Saroyan), 1954
Secret Way (v Gale), 1921
Secrets of the Heart (f Buck), 1976
Secrets of the Rich (p Kopit), 1976
Section: Rock-Drill (v Pound), 1955
Seduced (p Shepard), 1978
Seduction of the Minotaur (f Nin), 1961
See Naples and Die (p Rice), 1929
See You in the Morning (f Patchen), 1948
Seed Leaves (v Wilbur), 1974
Seed on the Wind (f Stout), 1930
Seed-Time and Harvest (f Arthur), 1851
Seen and the Unseen (f Arthur), 1869
Segues (v W. Stafford), 1983
Seize the Day (f Bellow), 1956
Seizure of Limericks (v Aiken), 1964
Self-Portrait in a Convex Mirror (v Ashbery), 1975
Self-Sacrifice (p Howells), 1916
Selling of Joseph (Sewall), 1700
Senator North (f Atherton), 1900
Senator Was Indiscreet (scr MacArthur), 1947
Senator's Wife (p Belasco), 1887
Senlin (v Aiken), 1918
Sense of Beauty (Santayana), 1896
Sense of Justice (tv Vidal), 1955
Sense of the Past (f H. James), 1917
Senso (scr Bowles, T. Williams), 1949
Sensualists (f Hecht), 1959
Sentences (v Nemerov), 1980
Sepia Star (p Bullins), 1977
Septimius (f Hawthorne), 1872
Septimius Felton (f Hawthorne), 1872
Sequel to Drum-Taps (v Whitman), 1865
Sequence of Seven (v Nemerov), 1967
Sequence, Sometimes Metaphysical (v Roethke), 1963
Sequestered Shrine (v MacKaye), 1950
Seraglio (f Merrill), 1957
Seraph on the Suwanee (f Hurston), 1948
Serena Blandish (p Behrman), 1929
Serenade (f Cain), 1937
Serenata (p Green), 1953
Serge Panine (p Daly), 1883
Sergeant Hickey (p Harrigan), 1897
Serious Doll (v Ashbery), 1975
Sermons and Soda Water (f J. O'Hara), 1960
Serpent and the Staff (f Yerby), 1958
Serpent in the Wilderness (v Masters), 1933
Servant-Master-Lover (p Lawson), 1916
Servitude (p O'Neill), 1950
Set This House on Fire (f Styron), 1960
Seth's Brother's Wife (f Frederic), 1887
Settled Out of Court (p Gillette), 1892
Settled Out of Court (p Saroyan), 1960
Seven Days (p Rinehart), 1909
Seven Descents of Myrtle (p T. Williams), 1968
Seven Keys to Baldpate (p Cohan), 1913
Seven Knights (f Ingraham), 1845
Seven-League Crutches (v Jarrell), 1951
7 P.M. (v Van Doren), 1926
Seven Sleepers (v Van Doren), 1944
7-20-8 (p Daly), 1883
Seventeen (f Farrell), 1959
Seventeen (f Tarkington), 1916
Seventeenth Century Suite (v Duncan), 1973
Seventeenth Star (p Green), 1953
Seventh Daughter (p Richard Harding Davis), 1910
Seventh Son (Du Bois), 1971
Seventy-Six (f Neal), 1823
Several Poems Compiled with Great Variety of Wit and Learning (v Bradstreet), 1678
Sex and the Single Girl (scr Heller), 1964
Sex Life of the Polyp (scr Benchley), 1928
Sexus (f H. Miller), 1949
Seymour: An Introduction (f Salinger), 1963
Shadow Between His Shoulder-Blades (f J. Harris), 1909
Shadow of a Doubt (scr Wilder), 1943
Shadow of a Dream (f Howells), 1890
Shadow of the Trail (f Grey), 1946
Shadow Out of Time (f Lovecraft), 1968
Shadow over Innsmouth (f Lovecraft), 1936
Shadow Train (v Ashbery), 1981
Shadows (f J. Gardner), 1986
Shadows and Sunbeams (f Arthur), 1854
Shadows of Shasta (f J. Miller), 1881
Shadows on the Rock (f Cather), 1931
Shadowy Third (f Glasgow), 1923
Shadrach (f Styron), 1979
Shady Hill Kidnapping (tv Cheever), 1982
Shakespeare in Harlem (v Hughes), 1942
Shakespeare in Harlem (p Hughes, Johnson), 1959
Shall We Gather at the River (v J. Wright), 1968
Shame Dance (f Steele), 1923
Shameless (f Cain), 1958
Shamus O'Brien at Home (p Harrigan), 1872
Shanghaied (f Norris), 1899
Shapes of Clay (v Bierce), 1903
Shard of Silence (A. Lowell), 1957
Shark! (f Grey), 1976
Shattered Idol (p Fitch), 1893
Shaved Splits (p Shepard), 1970
Shawl-Straps (f Alcott), 1872
She (p Gillette), 1887
She Tells Her Daughter (p Barnes), 1923
She Would and Should Not (p Daly), 1883
Sheepfold Hill (v Aiken), 1958
Shell Shock (p O'Neill), 1972

Sheltered Life (f Glasgow), 1932
Sheltering Plaid (p Green), 1965
Sheltering Sky (f Bowles), 1949
Shelty's Travels (p Dunlap), 1794
Shenandoah (p B. Howard), 1888
Shenandoah (p Schwartz), 1941
Shepherd of Guadaloupe (f Grey), 1930
Sheppard Lee (f Bird), 1836
Sherlock Holmes (p Gillette), 1899
Sherlock Holmes Versus Jack the Ripper (f Queen), 1967
Shifting for Himself (f Alger), 1876
Shifts of Being (v Eberhart), 1968
Shills Can't Cash Chips (f E. Gardner), 1961
Shining Hour (scr Nash), 1938
Ship from Shanghai (scr Lawson), 1930
Ship in the Desert (v J. Miller), 1875
Ship of Fools (f Porter), 1962
Shipwreck (p Dunlap), 1805
Shlemiel the First (p Singer), 1974
Shoes of Happiness (v Markham), 1915
Sho-Gun (p Ade), 1904
Shoot the Works (p Parker), 1931
Shop Around the Corner (scr Hecht), 1940
Shore Acres (p Herne), 1893
Shores of Light (Wilson), 1952
Short Friday (f Singer), 1964
Short Play for a Small Theatre (p Bullins), 1973
Short Reign of Pippin IV (f Steinbeck), 1957
Short Takes (f Runyon), 1946
Shosha (f Singer), 1978
Shoulders of Atlas (f Freeman), 1908
Show Boat (f Ferber), 1926
Show Is On (p Hart), 1936
Show Must Go On (f Rice), 1949
Show Piece (f Tarkington), 1947
Showman's Daughter (p Burnett), 1891
Show-Off (p Kelly), 1924
Shroud My Body Down (p Green), 1934
Shunned House (f Lovecraft), 1928
Shuttered Room (f Lovecraft), 1970
Shuttle (f Burnett), 1907
Siamese Twin Mystery (f Queen), 1933
Side Street (f Farrell), 1961
Sidnee Poet Heroical (p Baraka), 1975
Sidney (f Deland), 1890
Sidonie, The Married Flirt (p Kirkland), 1877
Siege of London (f H. James), 1883
Siesta in Xbalba (v Ginsberg), 1956
Sight (v Creeley), 1967
Sight Unseen (f Rinehart), 1921
Sign in Sidney Brustein's Window (p Hansberry), 1964
Signature of All Things (v Rexroth), 1950
Signature to Petition on Ten Pound Island (v Olson), 1964
Signs (v Merwin), 1971
Silas Snobden's Office Boy (f Alger), 1973
Silence (f Freeman), 1898
Silence in the Snowy Fields (v Bly), 1962
Silence of History (f Farrell), 1963
Silent Man (p J. Miller), 1883
Silent Partner (p Odets), 1972
Silent Speaker (f Stout), 1946
Silhouettes of American Life (f Rebecca Harding Davis), 1892
Silk Stockings (p Kaufman), 1955
Silver Bottle (f Ingraham), 1844
Silver Cord (p S. Howard), 1926
Silver Pitchers (f Alcott), 1876
Silver Ship of Mexico (f Ingraham), 1846
Silver Stallion (f Cabell), 1926
Silver Swan (v Rexroth), 1976
Simon (p Hecht), 1962
Simon Suggs series (f Hooper), from 1845
Simon Wheeler, Detective (f Twain), 1963
Simple series (f Hughes), from 1950
Simple Art of Murder (f Chandler), 1950
Simple Honorable Man (f Richter), 1962
Simple Life (p Harrigan), 1905
Simply Heavenly (p Hughes), 1957
Sin of Madelon Claudet (scr MacArthur), 1931
Sinbad the Sailor (p MacKaye), 1917
Sincerely, Willis Wayde (f Marquand), 1955
Sincerity and Authenticity (Trilling), 1972
Sinful Woman (f Cain), 1947
Sing All a Green Willow (p Green), 1969
Sing Sing (p Harrigan), 1872
Sing to Me Through Open Windows (p Kopit), 1959
Singin' Billy (p Davidson), 1952
Singing Jailbirds (p Sinclair), 1924
Singing Steel (p Hurston), 1934
Single Blessedness (f Ade), 1922
Single Hound (v Dickinson), 1914
Sinister Sex (f Hecht), 1927
Sink or Swim (f Alger), 1870
Sinners in the Hands of an Angry God (Edwards), 1741
Sir Brasil's Falcon (v O'Brien), 1853
Sir Edmund Orme (f H. James), 1892
Sirens of Titan (f Vonnegut), 1959
Sister Carrie (f Dreiser), 1900
Sister Jane (f J. Harris), 1896
Sisters (p O'Brien), 1854
Sister's Sacrifice (p Daly), 1891
Sisters-in-Law (f Atherton), 1921
Sistine Eve (v MacKaye), 1915
Sitting Here (v Creeley), 1974
Sitting Pretty (scr Perelman), 1933
Six A.M. (f Bodenheim), 1932
Six Nights with the Washingtonians (f Arthur), 1842
Six to One (f Bellamy), 1878
Six Trees (f Freeman), 1903
Sixes and Sevens (f Henry), 1911
Six-Piece Suite (v Ammons), 1979
1601 (f Twain), 1939
16 Once Published (v Zukofsky), 1962
Sixth Year (tv Chayefsky), 1953
Sixty Seconds (f Bodenheim), 1929
63: Dream Palace (f Purdy), 1956
Skeeters Kirby (f Masters), 1923
Sketch Book of Geoffrey Crayon, Gent. (f Irving), from 1819
Sketches of Life and Character (f Arthur), 1849
Skidmores (p Harrigan), 1874
Skin of Our Teeth (p Wilder), 1942
Skippers of Nancy Gloucester (v MacKaye), 1924
Skippy (scr Marquis), 1931
Skital'tsy (p Nabokov), 1923
Sky Devils (scr Benchley), 1932
Sky Island (f Baum), 1912
Sky Sea Birds Trees Earth House Beasts Flowers (v Rexroth), 1970
Skylight One (v Aiken), 1949

Skylines and Horizons (v Heyward), 1924
Slabs of the Sunburnt West (v Sandburg), 1922
Slapstick (f Vonnegut), 1973
Slapstick Tragedy (p T. Williams), 1966
Slaughter of the Innocents (p Saroyan), 1957
Slaughterhouse-Five (f Vonnegut), 1969
Slave (p Baraka), 1964
Slave (f Singer), 1962
Slave Girl (p L. Mitchell), 1893
Slave King (f Ingraham), 1846
Slave Ship (p Baraka), 1967
Slave Ship (scr Faulkner), 1937
Slavery Days (p Harrigan), 1875
Slaves in Algiers (p Rowson), 1794
Sleep Tight (f Purdy), 1979
Sleepers Awake (f Patchen), 1946
Sleepers in Moon-Crowned Valleys (f Purdy), from 1970
Sleepers Joining Hands (v Bly), 1973
Sleeping Beauty (f Macdonald), 1973
Sleeping Fires (f Atherton), 1922
Sleeping Fury (v Bogan), 1937
Sleeping-Car (p Howells), 1883
Slight Case of Murder (p Runyon), 1935
Slim Princess (f Ade), 1907
Slow and Sure (f Alger), 1872
Slow Learner (f Pynchon), 1984
Slow Vision (f Bodenheim), 1934
Small Craft Warnings (p T. Williams), 1972
Small Hours (p Kaufman), 1951
Small Moment (v Nemerov), 1957
Small Rain (f Pynchon), 1980(?)
Small War on Murray Hill (p Sherwood), 1957
Smart Aleck Kill (f Chandler), 1953
Smarty's Party (p Kelly), 1923
Smash-Up (scr Lawson, Parker), 1947
Smell of Fear (f Chandler), 1965
Smert' (p Nabokov), 1923
Smile at the Foot of the Ladder (f H. Miller), 1948
Smire (f Cabell), 1937
Smirt (f Cabell), 1934
Smith (f Cabell), 1935
Smoke (f Barnes), 1982
Smoke (tv Vidal), 1954
Smoke and Shorty (f London), 1920
Smoke and Steel (v Sandburg), 1920
Smoke Bellew (f London), 1912
Smoke over the Prairie (f Richter), 1947
Smoke's Way (v W. Stafford), 1983
Smokey the Bear Sutra (v Snyder), 1973
Smoking Car (p Howells), 1900
Smoking Mountain (f Boyle), 1951
Smouldering Fires (scr Deland), 1925
Snake Pit (scr Laurents), 1948
Snapshots of a Daughter-in-Law (v Rich), 1963
Snarling Garland of Xmas Verses (v Creeley), 1954
Sniper (p O'Neill), 1917
Snow Mountain (f Bemelmans), 1950
Snow Poems (v Ammons), 1977
Snow White (f Barthelme), 1967
Snow-Bound (v Whittier), 1866
Snow-Bound at Eagle's (f Harte), 1886
Snow-Image (f Hawthorne), 1851
Snowy Owl (v Eberhart), 1984
Snuggle Tales (f Baum), 1916

So Big (f Ferber), 1924
So Little Time (f Marquand), 1943
So Red the Rose (scr M. Anderson), 1935
Soak the Rich (scr Hecht, MacArthur), 1936
Sobytie (p Nabokov), 1938
Social Event (p Inge), 1962
Social Secretary (f Phillips), 1905
Social Strugglers (f Boyesen), 1893
Social Swim (p Fitch), 1893
Society and Solitude (Emerson), 1870
Socorro, When Your Sons Forget (p MacLeish), 1944
Soft Machine (f W. Burroughs), 1961
Soft Shoulders (p Morley), 1940
Soft Side (f H. James), 1900
Soglyadataj (f Nabokov), 1938
Sojourner (tv McCullers), 1964
Sojourner (f Rawlings), 1953
Solar Barque (f Nin), 1958
Soldier (v Aiken), 1944
Soldier of '76 (p Dunlap), 1801
Soldiers of Fortune (f Richard Harding Davis), 1897
Soldiers of Fortune (p Richard Harding Davis), 1902
Soldiers of Fortune (p Thomas), 1902
Soldiers' Pay (f Faulkner), 1926
Soldier's Tale (p Shapiro), 1968
Solid Gold Cadillac (p Kaufman), 1953
Solitaire (p van Druten), 1942
Solitary of Mount Savage (p Payne), 1822
Solstice (v Jeffers), 1935
Solution (f H. James), 1892
Some Account of the Capture of the Ship Aurora (v Freneau), 1899
Some Adventures of Captain Simon Suggs (f Hooper), 1845
Some Buried Caesar (f Stout), 1939
Some Came Running (f Jones), 1957
Some Champions (f Lardner), 1976
Some Day I'll Be a Millionaire (f Saroyan), 1943
Some Kind of Love Story (p A. Miller), 1982
Some of Our Neighbours (f Freeman), 1898
Some Others and Myself (f Suckow), 1952
Some People, Places, and Things That Will Not Appear in My Next Novel (f Cheever), 1961
Some Problems for the Moose Lodge (p T. Williams), 1980
Some Slips Don't Show (f E. Gardner), 1957
Some Time (v Zukofsky), 1956
Some Trees (v Ashbery), 1956
Some Women Won't Wait (f E. Gardner), 1953
Somebody in Boots (f Algren), 1935
Somebody Knows (p van Druten), 1932
Someday, Maybe (v W. Stafford), 1973
Someday You'll Be Lying (v Kerouac), 1968
Someone from Assisi (p Wilder), 1962
Someone in the House (p Kaufman), 1918
Someone Puts a Pineapple Together (v Stevens), 1947
Something about a Soldier (p Saroyan), 1940
Something about Eve (f Cabell), 1927
Something Cloudy, Something Clear (p T. Williams), 1981
Something Happened (f Heller), 1974
Something in Common (f Hughes), 1963
Something Unspoken (p T. Williams), 1953
Sometime (f Herrick), 1933
Sometimes Like a Legend (v W. Stafford), 1981
Somewhere in France (f Richard Harding Davis), 1915
Son (p Saroyan), 1950

Spillway (f Barnes), 1962
Spinning-Wheel Stories (f Alcott), 1884
Spinoza of Market Street (f Singer), 1961
Spirit Level (v Morley), 1946
Spirit of Culver (scr West), 1939
Spirit of Sweetwater (f Garland), 1898
Spirit of the Border (f Grey), 1906
Spirit of the Scene (v W. Benét), 1951
Spirit Reach (v Baraka), 1972
Splendid Idle Forties (f Atherton), 1902
Splendor (scr Crothers), 1935
Splendor in the Grass (scr Inge), 1961
Spoil of Office (f Garland), 1892
Spoils of Poynton (f H. James), 1897
Spoon River Anthology (v Masters), 1915
Sport of the Gods (f Dunbar), 1902
Sport Parade (scr Benchley), 1932
Spring and All (v W. Williams), 1923
Spring and Soforth (v Baraka), 1960
Spring Birth (v Van Doren), 1953
Spring Cleaning (f Burnett), 1908
Spring Concert (f Tarkington), 1916
Spring Dance (p Barry), 1936
Spring in New Hampshire (v McKay), 1920
Spring Recital (p Dreiser), 1916
Spring Song (p T. Williams), 1938
Spring Thunder (v Van Doren), 1924
Spring Trio (v Updike), 1982
Springtime (p Tarkington), 1909
Springtime and Harvest (f Sinclair), 1901
Spy (f Cooper), 1821
Spy (f Sinclair), 1919
Spy in the House of Love (f Nin), 1954
Square Root of Wonderful (p McCullers), 1957
Squatter Sovereignty (p Harrigan), 1881
Stag at Bay (p MacArthur), 1974
Stage Door (p Ferber, Kaufman), 1936
Stagecraft (p Baum), 1914
Stairs of Sand (f Grey), 1943
Stairs to the Roof (p T. Williams), 1947
Stairway of Surprise (v W. Benét), 1947
Stand Up and Fight (scr Cain), 1939
Standard Dreaming (f Calisher), 1972
Standard of Liberty (v Rowson), 1795
Standards (p Lawson), 1916
Stanzas in Meditation (v Stein), 1956
Star (p Inge), 1975
Star Is Born (scr Hart), 1954
Star Is Born (scr Parker), 1937
Star of Araby (v Markham), 1937
Star of Ethiopia (p Du Bois), 1913
Star Rover (f London), 1915
Star Spangled Rhythm (scr Kaufman), 1942
Star Spangled Virgin (f Heyward), 1939
Starry Harness (v W. Benét), 1933
Stars (f Field), 1901
Stars (v Jeffers), 1930
Stars To-Night (v Teasdale), 1930
Start in Life (radio Green), 1941
Starved Rock (v Masters), 1919
Star-Wagon (p M. Anderson), 1937
State Fair (scr Green), 1933
State of Nature (f Goodman), 1946
State Office Bldg. Curse (p Bullins), 1973
State Versus Elinor Norton (f Rinehart), 1934
Statement (v Boyle), 1932
States of Grace (Barry), 1975
States Talking (radio MacLeish), 1941
Station YYYY (p Tarkington), 1927
Stay with Me Flagons (f Ade), 1922
Steel Belt (f Ingraham), 1844
Steeple Bush (v Frost), 1947
Stephen Foster Story (p Green), 1959
Steps (f Kosinski), 1968
Steps Must Be Gentle (p T. Williams), 1981
Sterne's Maria (p Dunlap), 1799
Steve and Velma (p Bullins), 1980
Stewed, Fried and Boiled (scr Benchley), 1929
Still Alarm (p Kaufman), 1929
Still Another Pelican in the Breadbox (v Patchen), 1980
Still Waters (p Thomas), 1925
Stillness (f J. Gardner), 1986
Stitch in Time (p Connelly), 1981
Stocking Cap (f Olson), 1966
Stoic (f Dreiser), 1947
Stolen White Elephant (f Twain), 1882
Stolen Wife (f Arthur), 1843
Stone, A Leaf, A Door (v Wolfe), 1945
Stop at the Red Light (f E. Gardner), 1962
Stop-Light (p Goodman), 1941
Stopover: Tokyo (f Marquand), 1957
Stopped Rocking (tv T. Williams), 1975
Stops of Various Quills (v Howells), 1895
Store (f Stribling), 1932
Store Boy (f Alger), 1887
Stories by the Man Nobody Knows (f Traven), 1961
Stories from History (f Ade), 1896
Stories in Light and Shadow (f Harte), 1898
Stories of China (f Buck), 1964
Stories of Georgia (f J. Harris), 1896
Stories of the Old Dominion (f J. Cooke), 1879
Stories of the Sierras (f Harte), 1872
Stories of the Street and of the Town (f Ade), from 1894
Stories of York State (Frederic), 1966
Stories Revived (f H. James), 1885
Stories, Storms, and Strangers (v W. Stafford), 1984
Stories That Could Be True (v W. Stafford), 1977
Stories Told on a Cellar Door (f Eggleston), 1871
Stork (p Hecht), 1925
Storm (f Steele), 1914
Storm Centre (f Murfree), 1905
Storm in the West (p Lewis), 1963
Storm Operation (p M. Anderson), 1944
Story for Strangers (p Connelly), 1948
Story of a Child (f Deland), 1892
Story of a Country Town (f Howe), 1883
Story of a Mine (f Harte), 1877
Story of a Play (f Howells), 1898
Story of Aaron (So Named) (f J. Harris), 1896
Story of Boon (f H. Jackson), 1874
Story of Duciehurst (f Murfree), 1914
Story of G.I. Joe (scr A. Miller), 1945
Story of Gus (radio A. Miller), 1947
Story of Keedon Bluffs (f Murfree), 1887
Story of Kennett (f B. Taylor), 1866
Story of Old Fort Loudon (f Murfree), 1899
Story on Page One (scr Odets), 1960
Storyville (p Bullins), 1977

Ten Nights in a Bar-Room and What I Saw There (f Arthur), 1854
Ten North Frederick (f J. O'Hara), 1955
Ten Women in Gale's House (v Clark), 1932
Tenants (p H. James), 1894
Tenants (f Malamud), 1971
Tenants of Moonbloom (f Wallant), 1963
Tender Buttons (v Stein), 1914
Tender Is the Night (f Fitzgerald), 1934
Tennessee Laughs (p T. Williams), 1980
Tennis Court Oath (v Ashbery), 1962
Tenor (p Shapiro), 1952
Tent of Pompey (p Thomas), 1920
Tent on the Beach (v Whittier), 1867
Tenth Man (p Chayefsky), 1959
Tenth Muse (v Bradstreet), 1650
Tents of Trouble (v Runyon), 1911
Terminations (f H. James), 1895
Terrible Example (p Harrigan), 1874
Terrible Night (O'Brien), 1921
Terrible Threshold (v Kunitz), 1974
Terrible Woman (p Steele), 1925
Tess of the Storm Country (scr Behrman), 1932
Test Case (p Daly), 1892
Test of Honour (f Rowson), 1789
Testament for My Students (v Boyle), 1970
Testing-Tree (v Kunitz), 1971
Tex Thorne Comes Out of the West (f Grey), 1937
Texan Ranger (f Ingraham), 1847
Texas (p Green), 1966
Texas Forever (v Green), 1967
Texas Song-Book (v Green), 1967
Textiles (p S. Anderson), 1979
Textures of Life (f Calisher), 1963
Thankful Blossom (f Harte), 1877
Thanks (v Creeley), 1977
Thanksgiving Day — 1941 (radio S. Benét), 1941
Thanksgiving Visitor (tv Capote), 1968
That Awful Mrs. Eaton (p S. Benét), 1924
That Fortune (f Warner), 1899
That Girl from Memphis (f Steele), 1945
That Heathen Chinee (v Harte), 1871
That Lass o' Lowrie's (f Burnett), 1877
That Lass o' Lowrie's (p Burnett), 1878
That Little Affair at Boyd's (p Gillette), 1908
That Man and I (p Burnett), 1903
That Other Alone (v W. Stafford), 1973
That Overcoat (p Thomas), 1898
That Shining Place (v Van Doren), 1969
That There Was a Woman in Gloucester, Massachusetts (v Olson), 1968
That They May Win (p A. Miller), 1944
Theatre Royal (p Ferber, Kaufman), 1935
Theatricals series (p H. James), from 1894
Thee (v Aiken), 1967
Thee and You (f S. Mitchell), 1880
Theft (p London), 1910
Their Child (f Herrick), 1903
Their Eyes Were Watching God (f Hurston), 1937
Their Fathers' God (f Rølvaag), 1931
Their Silver Wedding Journey (f Howells), 1899
Their Town (f Steele), 1952
Their Wedding Journey (f Howells), 1872
Theirs Be the Guilt (f Sinclair), 1959
Theme Is Blackness (p Bullins), 1966
Theo (f Burnett), 1877
Theodore (f Ingraham), 1844
Theological Interlude (p Cain), 1926
Theophilus North (f Wilder), 1973
Theory of Flight (v Rukeyser), 1935
Theory of the Moral Life (Dewey), 1960
Theory of Tragedy (p Goodman), 1950
There Are No Islands Any More (v Millay), 1940
There Is Something New under the Sun (p Baum), 1903
There Shall Be No Night (p Sherwood), 1940
There Was an Old Woman (f Queen), 1943
There Was That Roman Poet Who Fell in Love at Fifty-Odd (v Shapiro), 1968
There Were Two Pirates (f Cabell), 1946
There's Always Another Windmill (v Nash), 1968
There's Always Juliet (p van Druten), 1931
There's Love All Day (v Patchen), 1970
There's Something I Got to Tell You (radio Saroyan), 1941
Thérèse, The Orphan of Geneva (p Payne), 1821
These Bars of Flesh (f Stribling), 1938
These 13 (f Faulkner), 1931
These Three (scr Hellman), 1936
They Brought Their Women (f Ferber), 1933
They Burned the Books (radio S. Benét), 1942
They Call Me Carpenter (f Sinclair), 1922
They Can Only Hang You Once (f Hammett), 1949
They Keep Riding Down All the Time (v Patchen), 1947
They Knew What They Wanted (p S. Howard), 1924
They Married Later (p S. Anderson), 1937
They of the High Trails (f Garland), 1916
They Shall Have Music (scr Lawson), 1939
They Stooped to Folly (f Glasgow), 1929
Thicket of Spring (v Bowles), 1972
Thieves' Canyon (f Grey), 1965
Thin Man (f Hammett), 1934
Thin Man series (radio Laurents), 1939
Thin Red Line (f Jones), 1962
Thing (scr Hecht), 1951
Thing from Another World (scr Hecht), 1951
Things as They Are (f Stein), 1950
Things Gone and Things Still Here (f Bowles), 1977
Things of This World (v Wilbur), 1956
Things That Happen When There Aren't Any People (v W. Stafford), 1980
Third Circle (f Norris), 1909
Third Commandment (tv Hecht), 1959
Third Fourth of July (p Cullen), 1946
Third Generation (f Steele), 1929
Third Life of Grange Copeland (f Walker), 1970
Third Life of Per Smevik (f Rølvaag), 1971
Third Little Show (p Perelman), 1931
Third Night (p Wolfe), 1919
Third Violet (f S. Crane), 1897
Thirst (p O'Neill), 1914
Thirsting Heart (p Green), 1959
Thirsty Evil (f Vidal), 1956
13 Clocks (f Thurber), 1950
Thirteen O'Clock (f S. Benét), 1937
39 East (p Crothers), 1919
31 Letters and 13 Dreams (v Hugo), 1977
Thirty Things (v Creeley), 1974
$30,000 Bequest (f Twain), 1906
30,000 on the Hoof (f Grey), 1940

Traveler (p Connelly), 1939
Traveler from Altruria (f Howells), 1894
Travelers (p Tarkington), 1927
Traveling Through the Dark (v W. Stafford), 1962
Travellers (p Barker), 1808
Travellers (f Sedgwick), 1825
Travelling Companions (f H. James), 1919
Travelling Thirds (f Atherton), 1905
Travels with Charley in Search of America (Steinbeck), 1962
Travesty (f Hawkes), 1976
Tread the Green Grass (p Green), 1931
Treason of Arnold (f Ingraham), 1847
Treasure of Pleasant Valley (f Yerby), 1955
Treasure of the Sierra Madre (f Traven), 1934
Treasurer's Report (scr Benchley), 1928
Treasurer's Report (Benchley), 1930
Treatise Concerning Religious Affections (Edwards), 1746
Tree of Life (v Fletcher), 1918
Tree of Night (f Capote), 1949
Tree Telling of Orpheus (v Levertov), 1968
Trees (f Richter), 1940
Trees Die at the Top (f Ferber), 1938
Trent's Trust (f Harte), 1903
Trial and Triumph (f Arthur), 1855
Trial by Jury (p Cain), 1926
Trial by Lynching (f McKay), 1977
Trial of a Poet (v Shapiro), 1947
Trial Without Jury (p Payne), 1940
Triall by Armes (f Hergesheimer), 1929
Trials and Adventures of Herbert Mason (f Alger), 1887
Trials and Confessions of an American Housekeeper (f Arthur), 1854
Trials and Other Tribulations (f Runyon), 1948
Trials of a Neddlewoman (f Arthur), 1853
Trials of the Human Heart (f Rowson), 1795
Tribulations (p Harrigan), 1884
Tribunals (v Duncan), 1970
Tribune Primer (Field), 1881
Tribute (v Doolittle), 1917
Tribute to Gallantry (p Hecht), 1943
Tribute to the Angels (v Doolittle), 1945
Tri-Color (v Simms), 1830
Tried and the Tempted (f Arthur), 1852
Trifler (p Masters), 1908
Trifles (p Glaspell), 1916
Trifles of Thought (v Green), 1917
Trilogy (scr Capote), 1969
Trimmed Lamp (f Henry), 1907
Trio for Blunt Instruments (f Stout), 1964
Trip to Niagara (p Dunlap), 1828
Trip to Parnassus (v Rowson), 1788
Trip, Trap (v Kerouac), 1973
Triple Jeopardy (f Stout), 1951
Triple Thinkers (Wilson), 1938
Triptych (p Eberhart), 1955
Tristessa (f Kerouac), 1960
Tristram (v Robinson), 1927
Triumph of Infidelity (v Dwight), 1788
Triumph of the Egg (f S. Anderson), 1921
Triumphal March (v Eliot), 1931
Trivial Breath (v Wylie), 1928
Trobar Clus (v Guthrie), 1923
Trojan Ending (f Riding), 1937
Trojan Horse (radio MacLeish), 1952
Trojan Horse (f Morley), 1937
Trojan Horse (p Morley), 1941
Troll Garden (f Cather), 1905
Tropic of Cancer (f H. Miller), 1934
Tropic of Capricorn (f H. Miller), 1939
Tropical Winter (f Hergesheimer), 1933
Trouble Follows Me (f Macdonald), 1946
Trouble in July (f Caldwell), 1940
Trouble in Triplicate (f Stout), 1949
Trouble Is My Business (f Chandler), 1951
Trouble with Tigers (f Saroyan), 1938
Troubled Island (p Hughes), 1935
Troubles of Queen Silver-Bell (f Burnett), 1907
Troza (f Traven), 1936
Truce (f Ingraham), 1847
Truce of God (f Rinehart), 1920
Truckline Cafe (p M. Anderson), 1946
True (p Purdy), 1979
True Bills (f Ade), 1904
True Glory (scr Chayefsky), 1945
True Night (v Snyder), 1980
True Riches (f Arthur), 1850
True Story (f Twain), 1877
True to the Core (p Belasco), 1880
True West (p Shepard), 1980
True Womanhood (f Neal), 1859
Trumpet in the Land (p Green), 1970
Trumpet of the Swan (f White), 1970
Trumpet Shall Sound (p Wilder), 1919
Truth (p Fitch), 1907
Truth (p B. Howard), 1878
Truth about Tristrem Varick (f Saltus), 1888
Try and Trust (f Alger), 1873
Try Anything Once (f E. Gardner), 1962
Try! Try! (p F. O'Hara), 1951
Trysting Place (p Tarkington), 1923
Tuft by Puff (v W. Stafford), 1978
Tulips and Chimneys (v Cummings), 1923
Turandot (v Ashbery), 1953
Turcaret (p Merwin), 1961
Turmoil (f Tarkington), 1915
Turn Back the Clock (scr Hecht), 1933
Turn of the Screw (f H. James), 1898
Turn of the Screw (tv Vidal), 1955
Turn On the Heat (f E. Gardner), 1940
Turning Point (f Laurents), 1977
Turning Point (scr Laurents), 1977
Turning Wind (v Rukeyser), 1939
Turns and Movies (v Aiken), 1916
Turps (f Runyon), 1951
Turtle Island (v Snyder), 1974
Turtles of Tasman (f London), 1916
'Twas All for the Best (Bird), 1941
'Twas I (p Payne), 1825
Tweedles (p Tarkington), 1924
Twelfth Night (p Daly), 1893
12 Ethical Sonnets (v Goodman), 1935
$1200 a Year (p Ferber), 1920
Twelve Men (f Dreiser), 1919
Twentieth Century (p Hecht, MacArthur), 1932
Twentieth Century (scr Hecht, MacArthur), 1934
Twenty Poems Less (v Riding), 1930
Twenty-Four Hours (f Bromfield), 1930
Twenty-One Love Poems (v Rich), 1976

Unlovely Sin (f Hecht), 1927
Unmarried Father (f Dell), 1927
Unsatisfactory Supper (p T. Williams), 1981
Unseen (scr Chandler), 1945
Unseen Hand (p Shepard), 1969
Unspeakable Gentleman (f Marquand), 1922
Unspeakable Practices, Unnatural Acts (f Barthelme), 1968
Unstoppable Gray Fox (tv Saroyan), 1962
Until the Day Break (f Bromfield), 1942
Unto Such Glory (p Green), 1928
Unvanquished (f Faulkner), 1938
Unwelcome Man (f Frank), 1917
Unwritten Play of Lord Byron (p Irving), 1925
Up above the World (f Bowles), 1966
Up for Grabs (f E. Gardner), 1964
Up from Nowhere (p Tarkington), 1919
Up from Paradise (p A. Miller), 1974
Up from Slavery (Washington), 1901
Up to Thursday (p Shepard), 1965
Uplands (v Ammons), 1970
Uplift of Lucifer (p Baum), 1915
Uplifters' Minstrels (p Baum), 1916
Upper Berth (f Crawford), 1894
Upperworld (scr Hecht), 1934
Uprising (v Duncan), 1965
Ups and Downs (f Arthur), 1857
Urania (v Holmes), 1846
Uriel (v MacKaye), 1912
Urkey Island (f Steele), 1926
Use of Poetry and the Use of Criticism (Eliot), 1933
Useful Knowledge (Stein), 1928
Ushant (Aiken), 1952
Usual Star (v Doolittle), 1934
Utopia 14 (f Vonnegut), 1954

V. (f Pynchon), 1963
V.V. (f Alcott), 1870
VV (v Cummings), 1931
V-Letter (v Shapiro), 1944
Vacation of the Kelwyns (f Howells), 1920
Vacation Song (v Millay), 1936
Vagabond Tales (f Boyesen), 1889
Vagabondia (f Burnett), 1883
Vagabondia series (v Hovey), from 1894
Vagaries Malicieux (f Barnes), 1974
Vain (p Wister), 1958
Val Vane's Victory (f Alger), 1903(?)
Valerie (p Belasco), 1886
Valiant One (p Crothers), 1937
Valiant Runaways (f Atherton), 1898
Valley Forge (p M. Anderson), 1934
Valley of Decision (f Wharton), 1902
Valley of the Moon (f London), 1913
Valley of the Wild Horses (f Grey), 1947
Valley of Vision (f Fisher), 1951
Van Bibber (f Richard Harding Davis), 1892
Van Der Decken (p Belasco), 1915
Van Zorn (p Robinson), 1914
Vandover and the Brute (f Norris), 1914
Vanishing American (f Grey), 1925
Vanishing Indian (f Grey), 1926
Vanishing Pioneer (scr Grey), 1928
Vanity of Duluoz (f Kerouac), 1971
Vanity Square (f Saltus), 1906
Varieties of Religious Experience (W. James), 1902
Variety of People (f Marquis), 1929
Vasconselos (f Simms), 1853
Vassall Morton (f Parkman), 1856
Vastness and Indifference of the World (v Eberhart), 1965
Vaudeville for a Princess (v Schwartz), 1950
Vegetable (p Fitzgerald), 1923
Vehement Flame (f Deland), 1922
Veil, Turbine, Cord, and Bird (v Duncan), 1979
Vein of Iron (f Glasgow), 1935
Velvet Horn (f Lytle), 1957
Venetian Glass Nephew (f Wylie), 1925
Vengeful Gods (f Atherton), 1928
Venice Poem (v Duncan), 1975
Venture in 1777 (f S. Mitchell), 1908
Ventures into Verse (v Mencken), 1903
Venus (p Crothers), 1927
Venus and Adonis (p Inge), 1975
Venus in Sparta (f Auchincloss), 1958
Vera the Medium (f Richard Harding Davis), 1908
Vera, The Medium (p Richard Harding Davis), 1908
Verge (p Glaspell), 1921
Vermont Notebook (v Ashbery), 1975
Verses on the Times (v Wilbur), 1978
Versi prosaici (v Pound), 1959
Versus (v Nash), 1949
Very First Christmas Morning (p Vonnegut), 1962
Vesna v Fial'te (f Nabokov), 1956
Vesta (p Daly), 1877
Veteran Birth (v Dickey), 1978
Via Crucis (f Crawford), 1899
Vicarious Years (f van Druten), 1955
Victim (f Bellow), 1947
Victor Ollnee's Discipline (f Garland), 1911
Victor Vane, The Young Secretary (f Alger), 1894
Victoria (f Rowson), 1786
Victors (p Wilder), 1949
Vieux Carré (p T. Williams), 1977
View from the Bridge (p A. Miller), 1955
Vigil of Faith (v Hoffman), 1842
Vignettes of Italy (v Teasdale), 1919
Village (p Stein), 1928
Village Doctors (f Arthur), 1843
Village Merchant (v Freneau), 1794
Vinegar Puss (Perelman), 1975
Violent Bear It Away (f O'Connor), 1960
Violent Pastoral (v Merrill), 1965
Virgin Heiresses (f Queen), 1954
Virgin of the Sun (p Dunlap), 1800
Virginalia (v Chivers), 1853
Virginia (f Glasgow), 1913
Virginia (p Payne), 1834
Virginia Bohemians (f J. Cooke), 1880
Virginia Comedians (f J. Cooke), 1854
Virginian (f Wister), 1902
Virginie (f Hawkes), 1982
Virtuous Girl (f Bodenheim), 1930
Virtuous Knight (f Sherwood), 1931
Vision of Columbus (v Barlow), 1787
Vision of Cortes (v Simms), 1829
Vision of Echard (v Whittier), 1878
Vision of Sir Launfal (v J. Lowell), 1848
Vision of Spring (v Faulkner), 1984
Visionaries (f Huneker), 1905

Way of the World (p Fitch), 1901
Way Out (p Frost), 1919(?)
Way Some People Die (f Macdonald), 1951
Way Some People Live (f Cheever), 1943
Way to Peace (f Deland), 1910
Way to Prosper (f Arthur), 1851
Way to the Gold (f Steele), 1955
Way to the House of Santa Claus (f Burnett), 1916
Way to Wealth (Franklin), 1774
Way We Live (p Daly), 1880
Way We Were (f Laurents), 1972
Way We Were (scr Laurents), 1973
Ways of Light (v Eberhart), 1980
Ways of Providence (f Arthur), 1852
Ways of the Hour (f Cooper), 1850
Ways of White Folks (f Hughes), 1934
Wayside Courtships (f Garland), 1897
Wayward and the Seeking (Toomer), 1980
Wayward Bus (f Steinbeck), 1947
We and Our Neighbors (f Stowe), 1875
We Are Betrayed (f Fisher), 1935
We Are the Living (f Caldwell), 1933
We Bombed in New Haven (p Heller), 1967
We Fished All Night (f Motley), 1951
We Have Always Lived in the Castle (f S. Jackson), 1962
We Live Again (scr M. Anderson, Wilder), 1934
We Righteous Bombers (p Bullins), 1969
We Stand United (radio S. Benét), 1940
We the People (p Green), 1976
We, The People (p Rice), 1933
We Will Never Die (p Hecht), 1943
Weak Spot (p Kelly), 1922
Weary Blues (v Hughes), 1926
Weather (v W. Stafford), 1969
Weather Shelter (f Caldwell), 1969
Weathergoose Woo! (f MacKaye), 1929
Web (p O'Neill), 1914
Web and the Rock (f Wolfe), 1939
Web of Life (f Herrick), 1900
Wedding Bouquet (p Stein), 1936
Wedding Day (f Boyle), 1930
Wedding Finger (p Purdy), 1974
Wedge (v W. Williams), 1944
Week on the Concord and Merrimack Rivers (Thoreau), 1849
Weekend (p Vidal), 1968
Weekend for Three (scr Parker), 1941
Weekend That Was (p Van Doren), 1966
Weeping Pierrot and Laughing Pierrot (p A. Lowell), 1914
Weimar 2 (p Baraka), 1981
Weird Shadow over Innsmouth (f Lovecraft), 1944
Weisse Rose (f Traven), 1929
Welcome to Our City (p Wolfe), 1923
Welcome to the Monkey House (f Vonnegut), 1968
Welded (p O'Neill), 1924
Well of Bethlehem (v Goodman), 1957
Wellfleet Whale (v Kunitz), 1983
Wen (p Bellow), 1966
Wept of Wish Ton-Tish (f Cooper), 1829
We're Friends Again (f J. O'Hara), 1960
West (v Olson), 1966
West of Pittsburgh (p Connelly, Kaufman), 1922
West of the Pecos (f Grey), 1937
West of Your City (v W. Stafford), 1960
West Side Story (p Laurents), 1957
Westbrooke Hall (f J. Cooke), 1891
Western (f Yerby), 1982
Western Approaches (v Nemerov), 1975
Western Boy (f Alger), 1878
Western Electric Communicade (radio Laurents), 1944
Western Star (v S. Benét), 1943
Western Union (f Grey), 1939
Westerner (f Grey), 1977
West-Running Brook (v Frost), 1928
Westward Ha! (Perelman), 1948
Westward Ho! (f Paulding), 1832
Westways (f S. Mitchell), 1913
Wet Blanket (p Daly), 1886
Wet Parade (f Sinclair), 1931
Wetherel Affair (f De Forest), 1873
Whale (f Melville), 1851
What a Man Sees Who Goes Away from Home (f Ade), 1896
What a Way to Go (f Morris), 1962
What Advertising Brings (p Cohan), 1915
What Are Years (v Moore), 1941
What Became of Anna Bolton (f Bromfield), 1944
What Came Afterwards (f Arthur), 1865
What Can Woman Do? (f Arthur), 1856
What Didymus Did (f Sinclair), 1954
What Do I Love (v Doolittle), 1943(?)
What Dreams May Come (f Atherton), 1888
What Is Man? (Twain), 1906
What Is She? (v MacKaye), 1943
What Is to Be Given (Schwartz), 1976
What Maisie Knew (f H. James), 1897
What Odd Expedients (v Jeffers), 1981
What Price Glory? (p M. Anderson), 1924
What Should She Do? (p Daly), 1874
What the Moon Brings (f Lovecraft), 1970
What They Think (p Crothers), 1925
What Thou Lovest Well, Remains American (v Hugo), 1975
What Time Collects (f Farrell), 1964
What Use Are Flowers? (Hansberry), 1972
What Was It? (O'Brien), 1921
What Was the Relationship of the Lone Ranger to the Means of Production? (p Baraka), 1979
What's Happened to the Thorne's House (p Kopit), 1972
What's O'Clock (v A. Lowell), 1925
Wheel of Life (f Glasgow), 1906
Wheel of Time (f H. James), 1893
When a Man Marries (f Rinehart), 1909
When a Woman Enjoys Herself (f Howe), 1928
When All the Woods Are Green (f S. Mitchell), 1894
When Boyhood Dreams Come True (f Farrell), 1946
When Dreams Come True (f Saltus), 1895(?)
When God Laughs (f London), 1911
When It Comes Home (p Thomas), 1912
When Ladies Meet (p Crothers), 1932
When Malindy Sings (v Dunbar), 1903
When She Was Good (f P. Roth), 1967
When the Jack Hollers (p Hughes), 1936
When the Turtles Sing (f Marquis), 1928
When the Whippoorwill— (f Rawlings), 1940
When Time Was Born (f Farrell), 1966
When Tomorrow Comes (scr Cain), 1939
When We Were Here Together (v Patchen), 1957
When West Was West (f Wister), 1928
When You Think of Me (f Caldwell), 1959
Where Are the Other Rowboats? (v Patchen), 1966

Where Is He? (p Dunlap), 1801
Where the Battle Was Fought (f Murfree), 1884
Where the Blue Begins (f Morley), 1922
Where the Blue Begins (p Morley), 1925
Where The Cross Is Made (p O'Neill), 1918
Where the Girls Were Different (f Caldwell), 1948
Where the Sidewalk Ends (scr Hecht), 1950
Where There's a Will (f Rinehart), 1912
Where There's a Will (f Stout), 1940
Where's Daddy? (p Inge), 1966
While the Heart Beats Young (v Riley), 1906
Whilomville Stories (f S. Crane), 1900
Whip (v Creeley), 1957
Whirl Asunder (f Atherton), 1895
Whirligigs (f Henry), 1910
Whirlpool (scr Hecht), 1950
Whisper in the Dark (f Alcott), 1889
Whispering Friends (p Cohan), 1928
Whispering Sands (f E. Gardner), 1981
Whispers (scr Connelly), 1920
Whistle (f Jones), 1974
White Blackbird (f Nin), 1985
White Buildings (v H. Crane), 1926
White Center (v Hugo), 1980
White Deer (f Thurber), 1945
White Desert (p M. Anderson), 1923
White Dresses (p Green), 1923
White Elephant (p Sherwood), 1916
White Fang (f London), 1906
White Heron (f Jewett), 1886
White Horses of Vienna (f Boyle), 1936
White Jacket (f Melville), 1850
White Lady (p Payne), 1827
White Magic (f Phillips), 1910
White Maid (p Payne), 1827
White Mane (scr Agee), 1953
White Mice (f Richard Harding Davis), 1909
White Morning (f Atherton), 1918
White Mule (f W. Williams), 1937
White Negro (Mailer), 1957
White Oxen (f Burke), 1924
White People (f Burnett), 1917
White Robe (f Cabell), 1928
White Rose (f Traven), 1965
White Sail (v Guiney), 1887
White Sand (v Wilson), 1950
White Shroud (v Ginsberg), 1986
White Sister (f Crawford), 1909
White Sister (p Crawford), 1937
White Terror and the Red (f Cahan), 1905
White Wings (p Barry), 1926
White-Faced Pacer (f Neal), 1863
White-Footed Deer (v Bryant), 1844
White-Haired Lover (v Shapiro), 1968
White-Jacket (f Melville), 1850
Who Are Happiest (f Arthur), 1852
Who Is Greatest? (f Arthur), 1852
Who Owns America? (Davidson, Lytle, Ransom, Tate, R. Warren), 1936
Who Owns the Line? (p Harrigan), 1872
Who Stole the Monkey? (p Harrigan), 1874
Whole Voyald (f Saroyan), 1956
Wholly Absorbed into My Own Conduits (v Olson), 1968
Who's Afraid of Virginia Woolf? (p Albee), 1962
Who's Who (p Richard Harding Davis), 1913
Whosoever Shall Offend (f Crawford), 1904
Why Are We in Vietnam? (f Mailer), 1967
Why Constantinople Fell (f Wallace), 1893
Why, Daddy? (scr Benchley), 1944
Why Does Nobody Collect Me? (Benchley), 1935
Wichita Vortex Sutra (v Ginsberg), 1966
Wickford Point (f Marquand), 1939
Wide Fields (f Green), 1928
Wide Is the Gate (f Sinclair), 1943
Wide Net (f Welty), 1943
Widow Bedott (p Nasby), 1879
Widow Morrison (f Arthur), 1841
Widow Rugby's Husband (f Hooper), 1851
Widow's Marriage (p Boker), 1852
Widows Wear Weeds (f E. Gardner), 1966
Wieland (f C. Brown), 1798
Wife (f Arthur), 1845
Wife (p Belasco), 1887
Wife for a Life (p O'Neill), 1950
Wife of His Youth (f Chesnutt), 1899
Wife of Two Husbands (p Dunlap), 1804
Wife's Engagement Ring (f Arthur), 1877
Wigwam and the Cabin (f Simms), 1845
Wild Boys (f W. Burroughs), 1971
Wild Country (f Bromfield), 1948
Wild Flag (White), 1946
Wild Horse Mesa (f Grey), 1928
Wild Huntsman (p Irving), 1924
Wild in the Country (scr Odets), 1961
Wild Is the River (f Bromfield), 1941
Wild Man of Borneo (p Connelly), 1927
Wild 90 (scr Mailer), 1968
Wild Old Wicked Man (v MacLeish), 1968
Wild Ones (f Fisher), 1952
Wild Palms (f Faulkner), 1939
Wild Patience Has Taken Me This Far (v Rich), 1981
Wild Scenes in the Forest and Prairie (f Hoffman), 1839
Wildash (f Ingraham), 1847
Wildbird (f Ingraham), 1869
Wilderness (f R. Warren), 1961
Wilderness Road (p Green), 1955
Wilderness Trek (f Grey), 1944
Wildfire (f Grey), 1917
Wild-Goose Chase (p Dunlap), 1800
Will Mr. Merriwether Return from Memphis? (p T. Williams), 1980
Will of Song (p MacKaye), 1919
Will of the People (p Cain), 1926
Will Terril (f Ingraham), 1845
Will This Earth Hold? (p Buck), 1945
Will to Believe (W. James), 1897
Will to Change (v Rich), 1971
William Ireland's Confession (radio A. Miller), 1941
William Vaughn Moody, Twenty Years After (v MacKaye), 1930
William Wilson (p J. Gardner), 1978
Willie Stark (p R. Warren), 1958
Willing Performer (p Ade), 1928
Williwaw (f Vidal), 1946
Will's Wonder Book (f Alcott), 1870
Wind in the Rose-Bush (f Freeman), 1903
Windfall (f Murfree), 1907
Windless Cabins (f Van Doren), 1940

World Over (f Wharton), 1936
World So Wide (f Lewis), 1951
World to Win (f Sinclair), 1946
World Too Old (v Guthrie), 1927
World We Live In (f Bromfield), 1944
World We Make (p Kingsley), 1939
Worldly Hopes (v Ammons), 1982
World's Body (Ransom), 1938
World's End (f Sinclair), 1940
Worlds of Color (f Du Bois), 1961
World-View (v Eberhart), 1941
Worth of a Woman (p Phillips), 1908
Wound and the Bow (Wilson), 1941
Wounded Boy (f Arthur), 1852
Wounds in the Rain (f S. Crane), 1900
Wrack P'int (p Green), 1923
Wreath for a Bridal (v Plath), 1970
Wreath for Margery (v Gregory), 1933
Wreck of the 5:25 (p Wilder), 1957
Wreckage of Agathon (f J. Gardner), 1970
Wrecker (tv Bellow), 1956
Wren (p Tarkington), 1922
Wren Winter's Triumph (f Alger), 1902
Writing, Writing (v Duncan), 1964
Writings to an Unfinished Accompaniment (v Merwin), 1974
Wrong Man (scr M. Anderson), 1957
Wuthering Heights (scr Hecht, MacArthur), 1939
Wyandotté (f Cooper), 1843
Wycherly Woman (f Macdonald), 1961
Wyoming (f Grey), 1953

Xaipe (v Cummings), 1950
Ximena (v B. Taylor), 1844
Xingu (f Wharton), 1916

Y & X (v Olson), 1948
Yank at Oxford (scr Fitzgerald), 1937
Yankee at the Court of King Arthur (f Twain), 1889
Yankee Blue-Jacket (f Ingraham), 1888
Yankee Chronology (p Dunlap), 1812
Yankee Fantasies (p MacKaye), 1912
Yankee in Canada (Thoreau), 1866
Yankee Prince (p Cohan), 1908
Yankee Tourist (p Richard Harding Davis), 1907
Yannina (v Merrill), 1973
Yaqui (f Grey), 1976
Yates Pride (f Freeman), 1912
Year Before Last (f Boyle), 1932
Yearling (f Rawlings), 1938
Years as Catches (v Duncan), 1966
Year's Life (v J. Lowell), 1841
Yekl (f Cahan), 1896
Yellow Gentians and Blue (f Gale), 1927
Yellow Jack (p S. Howard), 1934
Yellow Pages (v Merrill), 1974
Yellow Room (f Rinehart), 1945
Yemassee (f Simms), 1835
Yentl, The Yeshiva Boy (p Singer), 1974
Yerma (p Merwin), 1966
Yesterday's Love (f Farrell), 1948
Yet Other Waters (f Farrell), 1952
Yorick (p Daly), 1874
Yorick's Love (p Howells), 1880
You and I (p Barry), 1923
You Can Die Laughing (f E. Gardner), 1957
You Can't Get There From Here (v Nash), 1957
You Can't Go Home Again (f Wolfe), 1940
You Can't Keep a Good Woman Down (f Walker), 1981
You Can't Take It with You (p Hart, Kaufman), 1936
You, Emperors (v R. Warren), 1960
You Get What You Give (f Bromfield), 1951
You Gonna Let Me Take You Out Tonight, Baby (p Bullins), 1972
You Know Me Al (f Lardner), 1916
You 'spute Me (p Harrigan), 1871
You Touched Me! (p T. Williams), 1943
You Who Have Dreams (v M. Anderson), 1925
You Will Remember (scr Morley), 1941
Youma (f Hearn), 1890
Young Acrobat of the Great North American Circus (f Alger), 1888
Young Adventure (v S. Benét), 1918
Young Adventurer (f Alger), 1878
Young America (v Halleck), 1865
Young Artist (f Arthur), 1850
Young Artist (f Ingraham), 1846
Young Bank Messenger (f Alger), 1898
Young Boatman of Pine Point (f Alger), 1892
Young Book Agent (f Alger), 1905
Young Captain Jack (f Alger), 1901
Young Circus Rider (f Alger), 1883
Young Disciple (p Goodman), 1955
Young Explorer (f Alger), 1880
Young Folks' Ways (p Burnett, Gillette), 1883
Young Genius (f Ingraham), 1843
Young Lady at Home (f Arthur), 1847
Young Lonigan (f Farrell), 1932
Young Manhood of Studs Lonigan (f Farrell), 1934
Young Miner (f Alger), 1879
Young Mrs. Greeley (f Tarkington), 1929
Young Mrs. Winthrop (p B. Howard), 1882
Young Mountaineers (f Murfree), 1897
Young Music Teacher (f Arthur), 1847
Young Musician (f Alger), 1906
Young Outlaw (f Alger), 1875
Young People's Pride (f S. Benét), 1922
Young Ranchman of the Missouri (f Alger), 1888
Young Salesman (f Alger), 1896
Young Washington at Mt. Vernon (p MacKaye), 1927
Young Wisdom (p Crothers), 1913
Young Wolf (f London), 1984
Young Woodley (p van Druten), 1925
Young Woodley (f van Druten), 1929
Young Woodley (scr van Druten), 1930
Younger Son (p Belasco), 1893
Youngest (p Barry), 1924
Your Army (radio S. Benét), 1944
Your Fiery Furnace (p Green), 1926
Your Humble Servant (p Tarkington), 1909
Your Lover Just Called (f Updike), 1980
Your Native Land, Your Life (v Rich), 1986
Your Navy (p M. Anderson), 1942
Your Technocracy and Mine (scr Benchley), 1933
Youth and the Bright Medusa (f Cather), 1920
Youth of Washington (f S. Mitchell), 1904
Yvernelle (v Norris), 1891

NOTES ON CONTRIBUTORS

ALEXANDER, M.J. Berry Professor of English Literature, University of St. Andrews, Scotland. Author of *The Earliest English Poems*, 1966, *Beowulf*, 1973, *Twelve Poems*, 1978, *The Poetic Achievement of Ezra Pound*, 1979, *Old English Riddles from the Exeter Book*, 1980, and *History of Old English Literature*, 1983. **Essays:** Marianne Moore; *The Cantos*.

ALLEN, Walter. Novelist and literary critic. Author of seven novels (the most recent being *Get Out Early*, 1986); several critical works, including *Arnold Bennett*, 1948, *Reading a Novel*, 1949 (revised 1956, 1963), *Joyce Cary*, 1953 (revised 1963, 1971), *The English Novel*, 1954, *Six Great Novelists*, 1955, *The Novel Today*, 1955 (revised 1960), *George Eliot*, 1964, *The Modern Novel in Britain and the United States* (British edition: *Tradition and Dream*), 1964, *Some Aspects of the American Short Story*, 1973, and *The Short Story in English*, 1981; social history, including *The Urgent West: The American Dream and Modern Man*, 1969; and memoirs (*As I Walked Down New Grub Street*, 1981). Has taught at several universities in Britain, the U.S., and Canada. **Essay:** Ring Lardner.

ANDERSON, David D. Professor of American Thought, Michigan State University, East Lansing. Author of *Louis Bromfield*, 1964, *Critical Studies in American Literature*, 1964, *Sherwood Anderson*, 1967, *Anderson's "Winesburg, Ohio,"* 1967, *Brand Whitlock*, 1968, *Abraham Lincoln*, 1970, *Robert Ingersoll*, 1972, *Woodrow Wilson*, 1975, and *Ignatius Donnelly*, 1980. Editor or co-editor of *The Black Experience*, 1969, *The Literary Works of Lincoln*, 1970, *The Dark and Tangled Path*, 1971, and *Sunshine and Smoke*, 1971. **Essay:** Louis Bromfield.

ANGLE, James. Professor of English, Eastern Michigan University, Ypsilanti. Author of poetry and fiction in periodicals, and an article on Edward Lewis Wallant in *Kansas Quarterly*, Fall 1975. **Essay:** Edward Lewis Wallant.

ARNER, Robert D. Professor of English and Comparative Literature, University of Cincinnati. Author of monographs on Kate Chopin, James Thurber, and (forthcoming) the legend of the lost colony in American literature, and numerous articles on early American writers, including Nathaniel Ward, Ebenezer Cooke, Edward Taylor, Anne Bradstreet, Joel Barlow, William Byrd II, Philip Freneau, Nathaniel Hawthorne, and Henry David Thoreau, and introductions to works by Charles Brockden Brown. **Essays:** *The Damnation of Theron Ware*; "The Secret Life of Walter Mitty"; *The Tenth Muse*.

ASHLEY, Leonard R. N. Professor of English, Brooklyn College, City University of New York. Author of *Colley Cibber*, 1965, *Nineteenth-Century British Drama*, 1967, *Authorship and Evidence: A Study of Attribution and the Renaissance Drama*, 1968, *History of the Short Story*, 1968, *George Peele: The Man and His Work*, 1970, *The Wonderful World of Superstition, Prophecy, and Luck*, 1984, *The Wonderful World of Magic and Witchcraft*, 1986, and *The Dictionary of Sex Slang*, 1987. Editor of the *Enriched Classics* series, several anthologies of fiction and drama, and a number of facsimile editions. **Essays:** S. N. Behrman; Ludwig Bemelmans; George M. Cohan; Moss Hart; George S. Kaufman; George Kelly; Sidney Kingsley; Arthur Laurents; John Howard Lawson; Charles MacArthur; Henry Wheeler Shaw; *The Call of the Wild*; *The Grapes of Wrath*; *Gravity's Rainbow*; "Haircut"; *Murder in the Cathedral*; *Tobacco Road*.

AUBERT, Alvin. Professor of English, Wayne State University, Detroit; founding editor and publisher of *Obsidian: Black Literature in Review*. Author of three books of poetry—*Against the Blues*, 1972, *Feeling Through*, 1975, and *South Louisiana: New and Selected Poems*, 1985. **Essay:** James Weldon Johnson.

AUSTIN, James C. Emeritus Professor of English Language and Literature, Southern Illinois University, Edwardsville. Author of *Fields of the Atlantic Monthly*, 1953, *Artemus Ward*, 1964, *Petroleum V. Nasby*, 1965, *Bill Arp*, 1970, *Popular Literature in America*, 1972, *American Humor in France*, 1978, and many articles on American literature, humor, and dialect; also author of the words and lyrics for four musical shows. **Essays:** Petroleum V. Nasby; *Margret Howth*; *Modern Chivalry*; *The Scarlet Letter*.

BARKER, Jonathan. Poetry Librarian, Arts Council Poetry Library, London. Author of articles and reviews in *Agenda*, *PN Review*, *Times Literary Supplement*, and other periodicals. Editor of *The Arts Council Poetry Library Catalogue*, 6th edition, 1981, and *Selected Poems of W. H. Davies*, 1985. **Essay:** James Wright.

BELLMAN, Samuel Irving. Professor of English, California State Polytechnic University, Pomona. Author of *Marjorie Kinnan Rawlings*, 1974, *Constance Rourke*, 1981, *Vaudeville Marriage* (fiction: forthcoming), and articles on John Steinbeck, Nathaniel Hawthorne, and other writers. **Essays:** Kenneth Burke; Edwin Markham; "Gifts of the Magi"; "The Legend of Sleepy Hollow"; *The Song of Hiawatha*; *The Wonderful Wizard of Oz*.

BENNETT, George N. Late Professor of English, Vanderbilt University, Nashville, Tennessee. Author of *William Dean Howells: The Development of a Novelist*, 1959, and *The Realism of William Dean Howells 1889–1920*, 1973. **Essay:** William Dean Howells.

BENSEN, Alice R. Professor of English, Eastern Michigan University, Ypsilanti. Author of *Rose Macaulay*, 1969. **Essays:** Elinor Wylie; *The Octopus*.

BISIGNANO, Dominic J. Associate Professor of English, Indiana University–Purdue University, Indianapolis. **Essays:** Hannah Foster; Seba Smith.

BLACKALL, Jean Frantz. Professor of English, Cornell University, Ithaca, New York; member of the Board of Editors, *Henry James Review*. Author of *Jamesian Ambiguity and the Sacred Fount*, and articles on Harold Frederic, Henry James, Charlotte Brontë, and Edith Wharton. **Essays:** Harold Frederic; *The Ambassadors*; *The House of Mirth*; *My Ántonia*; *The Portrait of a Lady*; *Winesburg, Ohio*.

BLOOM, Lynn Z. Professor of English, Virginia Commonwealth University, Richmond. Author or co-author of *Doctor Spock: Biography of a Conservative Radical*, 1972, *American Autobiography 1945-1980: A Bibliography*, 1982, *Strategic Writing*, 1983, *Fact and Artifact: Writing Nonfiction*, 1985, and articles, reviews, and poetry in periodicals. Co-editor of *Bear*,

Man, and God: Approaches to Faulkner's The Bear, 1964 (revised 1971), *Forbidden Diary: A Record of Wartime Internment 1941–1945* by Natalie Crouter, 1980, *The Essay Connection*, 1983, and *The Lexington Reader*, 1987. **Essay:** Dorothy Parker.

BLOTNER, Joseph. Professor of English, University of Michigan, Ann Arbor. Author of *The Political Novel*, 1955, *The Fiction of J. D. Salinger* (with Frederick L. Gwynn), 1958, *The Modern American Political Novel 1900–1966*, 1966, and *Faulkner: A Biography*, 2 vols., 1974 (revised and condensed edition, 1 vol., 1984). Editor or co-editor of *Faulkner in the University*, 1959, *Faulkner's Library: A Catalogue*, 1964, and *Selected Letters*, 1977, *Uncollected Stories*, 1979, and *Novels 1930–35* (Library of America), 1985, all by Faulkner. **Essay:** William Faulkner.

BODE, Walter. Editor, Grove Press, New York. Editor of *Audition Pieces: Monologues for Student Actors*. **Essays:** Roark Bradford; Ogden Nash; S. J. Perelman.

BOWDEN, Mary Weatherspoon. Member of the Board of Review, National Endowment for the Humanities Public Programs Division; co-ordinator of a scholarly edition of Philip Freneau's works. Author of *Philip Freneau*, 1976, and *Washington Irving*, 1981. **Essay:** Philip Freneau.

BRAYBROOKE, Neville. Writer and editor; contributor to the *Times*, *Times Literary Supplement*, *Guardian*, *New Yorker*, *Saturday Review*, *Sunday Telegraph*, and *Tablet*. Author of three books about London, and *The Idler* (novel), 1961, *The Delicate Investigation* (play), 1969, and *Four Poems for Christmas*, 1986. Editor of *T. S. Eliot: A Symposium*, 1958, *A Partridge in a Pear Tree: A Celebration for Christmas*, 1960, *Pilgrim of the Future: A Teilhard de Chardin Symposium*, 1966, and *The Letters of J. R. Ackerley*, 1975. **Essays:** Djuna Barnes; B. Traven.

BROER, Lawrence R. Associate Professor of English, University of South Florida, Tampa. Author of *Hemingway's Spanish Tragedy*, 1973, and many essays and reviews in periodicals. Editor of *Counter Currents*, 1973, and *The Great Escape of the '20's*, 1977, and co-editor of *The First Time: Initial Sexual Experiences in Literature*, 1974. **Essays:** Stephen Vincent Benét; William Rose Benét; Gore Vidal.

BROWN, Ashley. Professor of English, University of South Carolina, Columbia. Author of articles in *Sewanee Review*, *Southern Review*, *Spectator*, *Virginia Quarterly Review*, and other periodicals. Co-editor of *The Achievement of Wallace Stevens*, 1962, *Modes of Literature*, 1968, *Satire: An Anthology*, 1977, and *The Poetry Reviews of Allen Tate 1924–1944*, 1983. **Essays:** John Peale Bishop; Andrew Lytle; Allen Tate.

BUCCO, Martin. Professor of English, Colorado State University, Fort Collins; Executive Secretary, Western Literature Association. Author of *The Voluntary Tongue* (poetry), 1957, *Frank Waters*, 1969, *Wilbur Daniel Steele*, 1972, *An American Tragedy Notes*, 1974, *E. W. Howe*, 1977, *René Wellek*, 1981, *Western American Literary Criticism*, 1984, and articles in *American Literature*, *Dictionary of Literary Biography*, *Western American Literature*, and *Western Humanities Review*. Editor of *Critical Essays on Sinclair Lewis*, 1986. **Essays:** Wilbur Daniel Steele; *Main Street*; *Main-Travelled Roads*; *Sister Carrie*.

BURCHELL, R. A. Senior Lecturer in American History and Institutions, University of Manchester, England. Author of *Westward Expansion*, 1974, *The San Francisco Irish 1848–80*, 1980, essays in *History of the United States*, 1977, and *Introduction to American Studies*, 1981, and articles in *Journal of American Studies*, *California Historical Quarterly*, and *Immigrants and Minorities*. **Essays:** Helen Hunt Jackson; Francis Parkman; *The Education of Henry Adams*; "The Luck of Roaring Camp"; *The Virginian*.

CALHOUN, Richard J. Alumni Professor of English, Clemson University, South Carolina; co-editor, *South Carolina Review*. Author of *James Dickey* (with Robert W. Hill), 1983. Editor or co-editor of *A Tricentennial Anthology of South Carolina Literature*, 1971, *James Dickey: The Expansive Imagination*, 1973, and *Two Decades of Change*, 1975. **Essays:** James Dickey; *Life Studies*.

CARDWELL, Guy A. Professor of English Emeritus, Washington University, St. Louis. Author of *Der Amerikanische Roman*, 1954, *Charleston Periodicals*, 1960, and articles, poems, and stories in periodicals. Editor of *The Uncollected Poems of Henry Timrod*, 1942, *Readings from the Americas*, 1947, *Twins of Genius: Letters of Mark Twain, George Washington Cable, and Others*, 1953, *Discussions of Mark Twain*, 1963, and *Mississippi Writings* (Library of America), 1982, and *The Innocents Abroad and Roughing It* (Library of America), 1984, by Mark Twain. **Essays:** Henry Timrod; *Adventures of Huckleberry Finn*.

CARPENTER, Frederic I. Author of *Emerson and Asia*, 1930, *Emerson Handbook*, 1953, *American Literature and the Dream*, 1955, *Robinson Jeffers*, 1962, *Eugene O'Neill*, 1964 (revised 1979), and *Laurens van der Post*, 1969. Has taught at the University of Chicago, Harvard University, Cambridge, Massachusetts, and the University of California, Berkeley. **Essays:** Robinson Jeffers; Conrad Richter.

CARPENTER, Humphrey. Free-lance writer. Author of *J. R. R. Tolkien: A Biography*, 1977, *The Inklings*, 1978, *Jesus*, 1980, *W. H. Auden: A Biography*, 1981, the *Mr. Majeika* series (for children), from 1984, *OUDS: A Centenary History of the Oxford University Dramatic Society*, 1985, *Secret Gardens: The Golden Age of Children's Literature*, 1985, and a forthcoming (1987) biography of Ezra Pound. Editor of *The Letters of J. R. R. Tolkien*, 1981, and *The Oxford Companion to Children's Literature* (with Mari Prichard), 1984. **Essay:** Ezra Pound.

CHRISTENSEN, Paul. Professor of Modern Literature, Texas A. & M. University, College Station. Author of several books of poetry and of *Charles Olson: Call Him Ishmael*, 1979. **Essays:** A. R. Ammons; John Ashbery; John Berryman; Robert Bly; Louise Bogan; Robert Creeley; E. E. Cummings; Stanley Kunitz; Denise Levertov; James Merrill; W. S. Merwin; Frank O'Hara; Charles Olson; Kenneth Rexroth; W. D. Snodgrass; Gary Snyder; John Wheelwright; *Paterson*.

CLAIRE, William. President, Washington Resources Inc., Washington, D.C. Author of two books of poetry—*Strange Coherence of Our Dreams*, 1973, and *From a Southern France Notebook*, 1974—and *Publishing in the West: Alan Swallow*, 1975, and articles in *Antioch Review*, *American Scholar*, *The Nation*, *New Republic*, *New York Times*, and other periodicals. Editor of *The Essays of Mark Van Doren*, 1984. Founding editor and publisher, *Voyages: A National Literary Magazine*, 1967–73. **Essay:** Mark Van Doren.

COHEN, Hennig. John Welsh Centennial Professor of History and Literature, University of Pennsylvania, Philadelphia. Author of *The South Carolina Gazette*, 1953, *Articles in American Studies 1954–1968*, 1972, and *The Parade of Heroes: Legendary Figures in American Lore* (with Tristram Potter Coffin), 1978. Editor or co-editor of *Battle Pieces*, 1963, *Selected Poems*, 1964, and *White Jacket*, 1967, all by Herman Melville, and *Humor of the Old Southwest*, 1964, *Folklore in America*, 1966, *The American Culture*, 1968, *Landmarks in American Writing*, 1969, *Folklore from the Working Folk of America*, 1973, *The Indians and Their Captives*, 1977, and *Herman Melville's Malcolm Letter*, 1987. Former editor of *American Quarterly*, and President of the Melville Society. **Essay:** Herman Melville.

COHN, Ruby. Professor of Comparative Drama, University of California, Davis; co-editor of *Modern Drama*, *Theatre Journal*, and *Cambridge Guide to World Drama*. Author of *Samuel Beckett: The Comic Gamut*, 1962, *Currents in Contemporary Drama*, 1969, *Edward Albee*, 1969, *Dialogue in American Drama*, 1971, *Back to Beckett*, 1974, *Modern Shakespeare Offshoots*, 1976, *Just Play: Beckett's Theatre*, 1980, *New American Dramatists 1960–1980*, 1982, and *From Desire to Godot*, 1987. **Essays:** Edward Albee; Ed Bullins; Eugene O'Neill; *The Tooth of Crime*.

COLLINS, William J. Free-lance writer and music critic. **Essay:** Stephen Collins Foster.

CORCORAN, Neil. Lecturer in English, University of Sheffield, England. Author of *The Song of Deeds: A Study of "The Anathemata" of David Jones*, 1982, and reviews in *PN Review* and *Times Literary Supplement*. **Essays:** Conrad Aiken; Robert Lowell; Delmore Schwartz.

COX, Martha Heasley. Professor of English and Director of the Steinbeck Research Center, San Jose State University, California. Author of *Maxwell Anderson Bibliography*, 1958, *A Reading Approach to College Writing*, 1959 (and later editions), *Writing: Form, Process, Purpose*, 1962, *Image and Value: An Invitation to Literature*, 1966, *Nelson Algren* (with Wayne Chatterton), 1975, and articles on Algren, Anderson, and Steinbeck. Editor of *Classic American Short Stories*, 1969. **Essay:** Nelson Algren.

CROWDER, Richard H. Professor Emeritus of English, Purdue University, West Lafayette, Indiana. Author of *Those Innocent Years* (on James Whitcomb Riley), 1957, *No Featherbed to Heaven: A Biography of Michael Wigglesworth*, 1962, and *Carl Sandburg*, 1964. Joint editor of *Frontiers of American Culture*, 1968. **Essays:** Carl Sandburg; Michael Wigglesworth.

CURRENT-GARCIA, Eugene. Hargis Professor Emeritus of American Literature, Auburn University, Alabama; editor of *Southern Humanities Review*, 1967–79. Author of *O. Henry (W. S. Porter): A Critical Study*, 1965, and *The American Short Story Before 1850*, 1985. Editor (with Walton R. Patrick) of *American Short Stories*, 1952 (4th edition 1982), *What Is the Short Story?*, 1961, *Realism and Romanticism in Fiction*, 1962, and *Short Stories of the Western World*, 1969, and of *Shem, Ham, and Japheth: The Papers of W. O. Tuggle*, 1973. **Essays:** Anna Cora Mowatt; *Our Town*; "The Swimmer."

DACE, Tish. Professor of English, Southeastern Massachusetts University, North Dartmouth; theatre critic for *Plays International*, *Stages*, *Village Voice*, *Plays and Players*, *New York Times*, *New York Magazine*, *American Theatre*, *Playbill*, and other publications. Author of *Le Roi Jones (Imamu Amiri Baraka): A Checklist of Works by and about Him*, 1971, and *The Theatre Student: Modern Theatre and Drama*, 1973. **Essays:** Amiri Baraka; Sam Shepard; *Picnic*; *A Streetcar Named Desire*; *The Weary Blues*; *Who's Afraid of Virginia Woolf?*

DAHL, Curtis. Samuel Valentine Cole Professor of English, Wheaton College, Norton, Massachusetts. Author of *Robert Montgomery Bird*, 1963, and articles on Bryant, Bulwer-Lytton, and Disraeli. Editor of *There She Blows: A Narrative of a Whaling Voyage* by Ben-Ezra Ely, 1971. **Essay:** William Cullen Bryant.

DRAYTON, James M. Lecturer, California State University, Sacramento. **Essay:** John Dewey.

DUUS, Louise. Associate Dean and Lecturer in American Studies, Douglass College, Rutgers University, New Brunswick, New Jersey. **Essay:** Rebecca Harding Davis.

EICHELBERGER, Clayton L. Professor of American Literature, University of Texas, Arlington. Author of *A Guide to Critical Reviews of United States Fiction 1870–1910*, 2 vols., 1971–73, and *Published Comment on William Dean Howells Through 1920: A Research Bibliography*, 1976. Editor of *Harper's Lost Reviews: The Literary Notes by Laurence Hutton, John Kendrick Bangs, and Others*, 1976. Editor of the journal *American Literary Realism*, 1967–77. **Essays:** Richard Harding Davis; Samuel Sewall; *The Awakening*.

EISINGER, Chester E. Professor Emeritus of English, Purdue University, West Lafayette, Indiana. Author of *Fiction of the Forties*, 1963, and articles in *Proletarian Writers of the Thirties*, 1968, and *Saturday Review*. Editor of *The 1940's: Profile of a Nation in Crisis*, 1969. **Essays:** Louis Auchincloss; William Styron; *Go Tell It on the Mountain*; *Herzog*; *Lolita*; *The Naked and the Dead*; *Naked Lunch*.

EVANS, Patrick. Senior Lecturer in English and American Studies, University of Canterbury, Christchurch, New Zealand. **Essays:** Paul Bowles; Jean Stafford.

FANNING, Charles. Professor of English, Bridgewater State College, Massachusetts. Author of *Finley Peter Dunne and Mr. Dooley: The Chicago Years*, 1978, and articles on Dunne, the Chicago Irish, James T. Farrell, and Irish American literature. Editor of *Mr. Dooley and the Chicago Irish* (anthology), 1976, and *The Exiles of Erin: Nineteenth-Century Irish American Fiction*, 1987. **Essays:** George Ade; Finley Peter Dunne; James T. Farrell.

FARMER, Philip José. Free-lance writer. Author of more than 45 novels, the most recent being *Dayworld*, 1985, and of *Tarzan Alive: A Definitive Biography of Lord Greystoke*, 1972. **Essays:** L. Frank Baum; Edgar Rice Burroughs.

FITZGERALD, M. J. Free-lance writer. Author of *Rope-Dancer*, 1986, and *Concertina*, 1987 (both fiction). **Essay:** *Wise Blood*.

FLETCHER, Ian. Professor of English, Arizona State University, Tempe; Professor Emeritus, University of Reading, England. Author of poetry and plays, and of *Walter Pater*, 1959 (revised 1971), *Beaumont and Fletcher*, 1967, and *Swinburne*, 1973. Editor of anthologies of poetry and drama, works by Victor Plarr and John Gray, and *The Collected Poems of Lionel Johnson*, 1982. **Essays:** Fitz-James O'Brien; Edgar Saltus.

FLORA, Joseph M. Professor of English, University of North Carolina, Chapel Hill. Author of *Vardis Fisher*, 1965, *William Ernest Henley*, 1974, *Frederick Manfred*, 1974, and *Hemingway's Nick Adams*, 1982. Editor of *Southern Writers: A Biographical Dictionary* (with Robert Bain and Louis D. Rubin, Jr.), 1979, and *The English Short Story 1880–1945*, 1985. **Essays:** James Branch Cabell; Marc Connelly; Vardis Fisher; Zane Grey; Owen Wister; "Big Two-Hearted River."

FOSTER, Edward Halsey. Professor and Director of the American Studies Program, Stevens Institute of Technology, Hoboken, New Jersey. Author of *Catharine Maria Sedgwick*, 1974, *The Civilized Wilderness*, 1975, *Josiah Gregg and Lewis Hector Garrard*, 1977, *Susan and Anna Warner*, 1978, *Richard Brautigan*, 1983, and *William Saroyan*, 1984. Editor of *Hoboken: A Collection of Essays* (with Geoffrey W. Clark), 1976, and *Cummington Poems*, 1982. **Essays:** Richard Henry Dana, Jr.; Fitz-Greene Halleck; Donald Grant Mitchell; Catharine Maria Sedgwick; Kurt Vonnegut, Jr.; Nathaniel Parker Willis; *The Bridge*; *The Dream Songs*; *The Maximus Poems*.

FRASER, G. S. Late Reader in Modern English Literature, University of Leicester, England. Author of several books of poetry (collected as *Poems*, 1981); travel books; critical studies of Yeats, Dylan Thomas, Pound, Durrell, and Pope; and of *The Modern Writer and His World*, 1953, *Vision and Rhetoric*, 1959, *Metre, Rhythm and Free Verse*, 1970, and *A Stranger and Afraid: The Autobiography of an Intellectual*, 1983. Editor of works by Keith Douglas and Robert Burns, and of poetry anthologies. Died 1980. **Essays:** Katherine Anne Porter; Mary Roberts Rinehart; George Santayana.

FRENCH, Warren. Professor of English and Director of the Center for American Studies, Indiana University-Purdue University, Indianapolis, retired 1986; member of the Editorial Board, *American Literature* and *Twentieth-Century Literature*; editor of the American Authors series for Twayne publishers. Author of *John Steinbeck*, 1961 (revised 1975), *Frank Norris*, 1962, *J. D. Salinger*, 1963 (revised 1976), *The Social Novel at the End of an Era*, 1966, *A Season of Promise*, 1968, *The South in Film*, 1981, and *Jack Kerouac*, 1986. Editor of a series on American literature, *The Thirties*, 1967, *The Forties*, 1968, *The Fifties*, 1971, and *The Twenties*, 1975. **Essays:** Timothy Shay Arthur; Joseph Holt Ingraham; H. P. Lovecraft; J. D. Salinger; John Steinbeck; Thornton Wilder; *Howl*; *Invisible Man*; *On the Road*.

GABIN, Jane S. Independent scholar and Instructor, Duke University Office of Continuing Education, Durham, North Carolina. Author of *A Living Minstrelsy: The Poetry and Music of Sidney Lanier*, 1985, and numerous articles in American studies. **Essays:** John Gould Fletcher; Richard Hovey; Sidney Lanier; *Little Women*.

GALL, Sally M. Writer and editor; editor of the journal *EIDOS: The International Prosody Bulletin*. Author of *The Modern Poetic Sequence* (with M. L. Rosenthal), 1983, *Ramon Guthrie's Maximum Security Ward: An American Classic*, 1984, and more than 40 articles in collections and journals. Editor of *Maximum Security Ward and Other Poems* by Guthrie, 1984. **Essay:** Ramon Guthrie.

GERBER, John C. Professor of English, State University of New York, Albany; General Editor of the Iowa–California edition of the works of Mark Twain; member of the Editorial Board, *Resources for American Literary Study*. Author of *Factual Prose* (with Walter Blair), 1945, *Literature*, 1948, *Writers Resource Book*, 1953, and other books on writing and speaking. Editor of *Twentieth-Century Interpretations of The Scarlet Letter*, 1968, and *Studies in Huckleberry Finn*, 1971. **Essays:** Ralph Waldo Emerson; Mark Twain.

GIBSON, Donald B. Professor of English, Rutgers University, New Brunswick, New Jersey. Author of *The Fiction of Stephen Crane*, 1968, and *The Politics of Literary Expression: A Study of Major Black Writers*, 1981. Editor of *Five Black Writers*, 1970, *Black and White: Stories of American Life*, 1971, and *Modern Black Poets*, 1973. **Essay:** Melvin B. Tolson.

GITENSTEIN, R. Barbara. Associate Professor of English, State University of New York, Oswego. Author of articles on Hawthorne, Singer, Bellow, and Cynthia Ozick in *The Comparatist*, *Yiddish*, *Contemporary Jewish-American Poetry*, and other periodicals. **Essays:** Saul Bellow; Abraham Cahan; Bernard Malamud; Isaac Bashevis Singer.

GLASRUD, Clarence A. Professor of English Emeritus, Moorhead State University, Minnesota; advisory editor, *Studies in American Fiction*; member of the Board of Publications, Norwegian–American Historical Association. Author of *Hjalmar Hjorth Boyesen: A Biographical and Critical Study*, 1963. Editor of *The Age of Anxiety*, 1960. **Essays:** H. H. Boyesen; F. Marion Crawford; Oliver Wendell Holmes; Wright Morris; John O'Hara; J. F. Powers; O. E. Rølvaag; Ruth Suckow; Charles Dudley Warner; Glenway Wescott.

GORDON, Lois. Professor and Chair, Department of English and Comparative Literature, Fairleigh Dickinson University, Teaneck and Rutherford, New Jersey. Author of *Stratagems to Uncover Nakedness: The Dramas of Harold Pinter*, 1969, *Donald Barthelme*, 1981, *Robert Coover: The Universal Fictionmaking Process*, 1983, *American Chronicle 1920–1980*, 1987, and articles on Arthur Miller, Tennessee Williams, Samuel Beckett, T. S. Eliot, William Faulkner, Randall Jarrell, Philip Roth, Elizabeth Bishop, William Gaddis, and other modern writers. **Essays:** Richard Eberhart; Jonathan Edwards; Benjamin Franklin; Randall Jarrell; James Purdy; *Moby-Dick*.

GRELLA, George. Associate Professor of English, Rochester University, Rochester, New York. Author of studies of Ian Fleming, Ross Macdonald, and John le Carré in *New*

Republic, and articles on the detective novel, film, and popular culture. **Essay:** Ross Macdonald.

HEATH-STUBBS, John. Writer and lecturer. Author of several books of poetry, the most recent being *The Immolation of Aleph*, 1985, a book of plays, and of *The Darkling Plain: A Study of the Later Fortunes of Romanticism*, 1950, *Charles Williams*, 1955, and studies of the verse satire, the ode, and the pastoral. Editor of anthologies and works by Shelley, Tennyson, Swift, Pope, and Thomas Gray; translator of *The Ruba'iyat of Omar Khayyam*, and works by Giacomo Leopardi, Alfred de Vigny, and others. **Essay:** Hart Crane.

HEIM, William J. Associate Professor of English and Associate Dean of Arts and Letters, University of South Florida, Tampa. Author of articles on Theodore Dreiser, Leigh Hunt, and Sheridan Le Fanu. **Essays:** Cotton Mather; Upton Sinclair; "The Fall of the House of Usher."

HEWITT, Geof. Free-lance writer; founding editor, Kumquat Press. Author of five books of poetry. Editor of the poems of Alfred Starr Hamilton, and of anthologies of poetry. **Essay:** Muriel Rukeyser.

HICKS, Jack. Teacher and free-lance writer; has taught at the University of California, Davis, and the University of Paris. Author of *Cutting Edges: Young American Fiction for the 1970's*, 1973, and *In the Singer's Temple: Prose Fictions of Barthelme, Gaines, Brautigan, Piercy, Kesey, and Kosinski*, 1981. **Essays:** Donald Barthelme; William S. Burroughs; Jack Kerouac.

HIGGINS, William. Member of the Department of English, Western Carolina University, Cullowhee, North Carolina. **Essays:** Winston Churchill; Robert Herrick; Joseph Kirkland; David Graham Phillips.

HITCHCOCK, Bert. Professor and Head of the Department of English, Auburn University, Alabama; member of the bibliography committee, Society for the Study of Southern Literature. Author of *Richard Malcolm Johnston*, 1978. **Essays:** S. Weir Mitchell; *The Cathedral*; *Uncle Remus*.

HOCKERSMITH, Thomas E. Member of the Department of English, Emory University, Atlanta. **Essays:** Reading List (American Literature to 1900); "The Man That Corrupted Hadleyburg" (with James A. Levernier).

HOEFER, Jacqueline. Free-lance writer. Author of articles on Samuel Beckett and other modern writers. **Essay:** Kay Boyle.

HOFFMAN, Daniel. Poet-in-Residence and Felix E. Schelling Professor of English, University of Pennsylvania, Philadelphia. Author of several books of poetry, the most recent being *Brotherly Love*, 1981, and of critical works including *The Poetry of Stephen Crane*, 1957, *Form and Fable in American Fiction*, 1961, *Barbarous Knowledge: Myth in the Poetry of Yeats, Graves, and Muir*, 1967, and *Poe Poe Poe Poe Poe Poe Poe*, 1972. Editor of the *Harvard Guide to Contemporary American Writing*, 1979, and of anthologies and works by Crane. **Essays:** Stephen Crane; Washington Irving; Edgar Allan Poe.

HOGAN, Robert. Free-lance writer; former Professor of English, University of Delaware, Newark. Author or co-author of *The Experiments of Sean O'Casey*, 1960, *Arthur Miller*, 1964, *The Independence of Elmer Rice*, 1965, *The Plain Style*, 1967, *After the Irish Renaissance*, 1967, *Dion Boucicault*, 1969, *The Fan Club*, 1969, *Lost Plays of the Irish Renaissance*, 1970, *Eimar O'Duffy*, 1972, *Mervyn Wall*, 1972, *Conor Cruise O'Brien*, 1974, *The Modern Irish Drama*, 6 vols., 1975–86, and *Since O'Casey*, 1984. **Essay:** Elmer Rice.

HOKENSON, Jan. Associate Professor of Languages and Linguistics, Florida Atlantic University, Boca Raton. Author of articles on Beckett, Céline, and Proust in *James Joyce Quarterly*, *L'Esprit Créateur*, *Far-Western Forum*, and *Samuel Beckett: An Anthology of Criticism* edited by Ruby Cohn, 1975. **Essays:** Ross Lockridge; Willard Motley.

HOLDEN, Jonathan. Professor of English, Kansas State University, Manhattan. Author of *The Mark to Turn: A Reading of William Stafford's Poetry*, 1976, *The Rhetoric of the Contemporary Lyric*, 1980, *Style and Authenticity in Postmodern Poetry*, 1986, and four collections of poetry. **Essay:** William Stafford.

HOLMAN, C. Hugh. Late William Rand Kenan Professor of English, Chairman of the Division of Humanities, and Special Assistant to the Chancellor, University of North Carolina, Chapel Hill; former editor of *Southern Literary Journal*. Author of five detective novels and of several critical books including *The Development of American Criticism*, 1955, *The Southerner as American*, 1960, *Thomas Wolfe*, 1960, *Seven Modern American Novelists*, 1964, *John P. Marquand*, 1965, *The American Novel Through Henry James: A Bibliography*, 1966 (revised 1979), *Three Modes of Modern Southern Fiction*, 1966, *The Roots of Southern Writing*, 1972, *The Loneliness at the Core: Studies in Thomas Wolfe*, 1975, *The Immoderate Past: The Southern Writer and History*, 1977, and *Windows on the World: Essays on American Social Fiction*, 1979. Editor of works by Wolfe, William Gilmore Simms, and others. Died 1981. **Essays:** Ellen Glasgow; Sinclair Lewis; John P. Marquand; Flannery O'Connor; Robert Penn Warren.

HUDSPETH, Robert N. Associate Professor of English, Pennsylvania State University, University Park. Author of *Ellery Channing*, 1973. Editor of *The Letters of Margaret Fuller*, 4 vols., 1983–87. **Essay:** William Ellery Channing.

INGE, M. Thomas. Robert Emory Blackwell Professor of the Humanities, Randolph-Macon College, Ashland, Virginia. Author of studies of southern literature and culture, American humor, ethnic American literature, modern fiction, popular culture, and comic art. Editor of works by George Washington Harris, William Faulkner, and numerous collections including *Agrarianism in American Literature*, 1969, *The Frontier Humorists*, 1975, *Ellen Glasgow: Centennial Essays*, 1976, *Black American Writers*, 2 vols., 1978, *Handbook of American Popular Culture*, 3 vols., 1979–81, *American Women Writers*, 1983, *James Branch Cabell: Centennial Essays*, 1983, *Huck Finn among the Critics*, 1985, and *Truman Capote: Conversations*, 1987. **Essays:** William Byrd II; F. Scott Fitzgerald; George Washington Harris.

JARRETT, Mary. Lecturer in English and American Literature, Westfield College, University of London. **Essay:** Alice Walker.

JELINEK, Estelle C. Writer and editor. Author of *The Tradition of Women's Autobiography: From Antiquity to the Present*, 1986, and articles and reviews in *College English*, *Feminist Criticism*, *Women's Review of Books*, and *Women's Studies International*. Editor of *Women's Autobiography: Essays in Criticism*, 1980. **Essay:** Anaïs Nin.

JOHNSON, Robert K. Professor of English, Suffolk University, Boston. Author of *Neil Simon*, 1983, and articles on Richard Wilbur, Wallace Stevens, T. S. Eliot, and William Carlos Williams. **Essays:** Robert Frost; Archibald MacLeish; Howard Nemerov; Frederick Goddard Tuckerman; "The Death of the Hired Man"; *Snow-Bound*; "Somewhere i have never travelled, gladly beyond."

JOYNER, Nancy Carol. Member of the Department of English, Western Carolina University, Cullowhee, North Carolina. Author of *Edwin Arlington Robinson: A Reference Guide*, 1978. **Essays:** William Vaughn Moody; Laura Riding; Edwin Arlington Robinson; Susanna Rowson; "Because I could not stop for Death"; *Look Homeward, Angel*; "Poetry."

KAPLAN, Zoë Coralnik. Adjunct Assistant Professor of Speech and Theatre, John Jay College of Criminal Justice, City University of New York. **Essay:** Rachel Crothers.

KELLNER, Bruce. Professor of English, Millersville University, Pennsylvania. Author of *Carl Van Vechten and the Irreverent Decades*, 1968, and *A Bibliography of the Work of Carl Van Vechten*, 1980. Editor of *Keep a-Inchin' Along: Selected Writings about Black Art and Letters* by Van Vechten, 1979, and *The Harlem Renaissance: A Historical Dictionary*, 1980. **Essays:** Hortense Calisher; Henry Blake Fuller; Joseph Hergesheimer; Henry Wadsworth Longfellow; Carl Van Vechten.

KING, Kimball. Member of the Department of English, University of North Carolina, Chapel Hill; managing editor of *Southern Literary Journal*. Author of the bibliographies *Ten Modern Irish Playwrights*, 1979, and *Ten Modern American Playwrights*, 1982, and of *Augustus Baldwin Longstreet*, 1984. **Essays:** George Washington Cable; Lillian Hellman; Augustus Baldwin Longstreet; Thomas Nelson Page.

KINNAMON, Keneth. Ethel Pumphrey Stephens Professor of English, and Chairman of the Department, University of Arkansas, Fayetteville. Author of *The Emergence of Richard Wright*, 1972. Editor of *Black Writers of America: A Comprehensive Anthology* (with Richard K. Barksdale), 1972, and *James Baldwin: A Collection of Critical Essays*, 1974. **Essays:** James Baldwin; Ralph Ellison; Langston Hughes.

KUHN, John G. Professor of English and Theater, and Chairman of the Division of English, Theater, and Classics, Rosemont College, Pennsylvania. **Essays:** James Nelson Barker; William Dunlap.

KULSHRESTHA, Chirantan. Teacher and free-lance writer. Author of *The Saul Bellow Estate*, 1976, *Bellow: The Problem of Affirmation*, 1977, chapters in *Considerations*, 1977, and *Through the Eyes of the World: International Essays in American Literature*, 1978, and articles in *Chicago Review*, *American Review*, *Quest*, *Indian Literature*, and other periodicals. Co-editor of *Not by Politics Alone!*, 1978, and editor of *Contemporary Indian English Verse: An Evaluation*, 1982. **Essays:** Michael Gold; DuBose Heyward; Robert E. Sherwood; Albion W. Tourgée.

LEARY, Lewis. William Rand Kenan Professor of English Emeritus, University of North Carolina, Chapel Hill. Author of *Idiomatic Mistakes in English*, 1932, *That Rascal Freneau: A Study in Literary Failure*, 1941, *The Literary Career of Nathaniel Tucker*, 1951, *Articles on American Literature 1900–1975*, 3 vols., 1954–79, *Mark Twain*, 1960, *John Greenleaf Whittier*, 1961, *Washington Irving*, 1963, *Norman Douglas*, 1967, *Southern Excursions*, 1971, *Faulkner of Yoknapatawpha County*, 1973, and *American Literature: A Study and Research Guide*, 1976. Editor of works by Philip Freneau, Henry Wadsworth Longfellow, and Twain, and of several collections of essays. **Essay:** Henry David Thoreau.

LEVERNIER, James A. Associate Professor of English and Director of American Studies, University of Arkansas, Little Rock. Co-author of *Structuring Paragraphs: A Guide to Effective Writing*, 2nd edition 1986, and articles in *ESQ: A Journal of the American Renaissance*, *Research Studies*, *Markham Review*, *Explicator*, and other periodicals. Editor or co-editor of *An Essay for the Recording of Illustrious Providences* by Increase Mather, 1977, *The Indians and Their Captives*, 1977, *Souldiery Spiritualized: Seven Sermons Preached Before the Artillery Companies of New England 1674–1774*, 1979, and *Sermons and Cannonballs*, 1982. **Essays:** Ebenezer Cooke; Frederick Douglass; Kenneth Fearing; Louise Imogen Guiney; Charles Fenno Hoffman; Francis Hopkinson; Joaquin Miller; Thomas Paine; Mary Rowlandson; Bayard Taylor; John Trumbull; *The Federalist*; *The Last of the Mohicans*; "The Man That Corrupted Hadleyburg" (with Thomas E. Hockersmith); "Thanatopsis"; *Uncle Tom's Cabin*.

LEWIS, Naomi. Writer, critic, and broadcaster. Author of *A Visit to Mrs. Wilcox*, 1957, *Fantasy Books for Children*, 1975 (revised 1977), books for children, including *Once Upon a Rainbow*, 1981, and *Come with Us*, 1982, and introductory essays to works on or by Hans Christian Andersen, E. Nesbit, Christina Rossetti, Arthur Waley, and others; contributor to *The Observer*, *New Statesman*, *Times Literary Supplement*, *Listener*, and other periodicals. Editor of *A Peculiar Music: Poems for Young Readers* by Emily Brontë, 1971, and the anthologies *A Footprint on the Air*, 1983, and *Messages*, 1985. **Essay:** *The Country of the Pointed Firs*.

LOHOF, Bruce A. Director of the U.S. Educational (Ful-bright) Foundation in Pakistan, Islamabad. Author of *American Commonplace: Essays on Popular Culture in the United States*, 1983, and articles in *American Quarterly*, *Centennial Review*, *Journal of Popular Culture*, and other periodicals. Former Director of the American Studies Research Centre, Hyderabad, India, and teacher at the University of Miami, and Heidelberg College, Tiffin, Ohio. **Essays:** James Agee; Horatio Alger; George Henry Boker; Margaret Deland; Timothy Dwight; Edward Eggleston; Zona Gale; H. L. Mencken.

LONGEST, George C. Associate Professor of English, Virginia Commonwealth University, Richmond. Author of *Three Virginia Writers: A Reference Guide*, 1978. **Essays:** James Lane Allen; Joseph G. Baldwin; Erskine Caldwell; Truman Capote; Bret Harte; Johnson Jones Hooper.

LUCAS, John. Professor and Head of the Department of English and Drama, Loughborough University, Leicestershire, England; advisory editor, *Victorian Studies*, *Literature and History*, and *Journal of European Studies*. Author of *Tradition and Tolerance in 19th-Century Fiction*, 1966, *The Melancholy Man: A Study of Dickens*, 1970, *Arnold Bennett*, 1975, *Egilssaga: The Poems*, 1975, *The Literature of Change*, 1977, *The 1930's: Challenge to Orthodoxy*, 1978, *Romantic to Modern*, 1982, and *Moderns and Contemporaries*, 1985. Editor of *Literature and Politics in the 19th Century*, 1971, and of works by George Crabbe and Jane Austen. **Essays:** Paul Goodman; Kenneth Patchen; Damon Runyon; Louis Simpson.

LUDINGTON, Townsend. Boshamer Professor of English and American Studies, and Chair, American Studies Curriculum, University of North Carolina, Chapel Hill. Author of *John Dos Passos: A Twentieth Century Odyssey*, 1980. Editor of *The Fourteenth Chronicle: Letters and Diaries of John Dos Passos*, 1973. **Essays:** John Dos Passos; Jack London.

MacLAINE, Brent. Free-lance writer. **Essay:** Vladimir Nabokov.

MacSHANE, Frank. Professor, School of the Arts, and Director of the Translation Center, Columbia University, New York. Author of *Many Golden Ages*, 1963, *The Life and Work of Ford Madox Ford*, 1965, *The Life of Raymond Chandler*, 1976, *The Life of John O'Hara*, 1980, and *Into Eternity: James Jones: The Life of an American Writer*, 1985. Editor of works by Chandler, Ford, O'Hara, and Jorge Luis Borges; translator of several books by Miguel Serrano. **Essays:** Raymond Chandler; Edward Dahlberg.

MADDEN, David. Writer-in-Residence, Louisiana State University, Baton Rouge. Author of novels (*Bijou*, *The Suicide's Wife*), short stories (*The Shadow Knows*, *The New Orleans of Possibilities*), plays, poems, and critical works including *James M. Cain*, 1970, *A Primer of the Novel*, 1980, and *Cain's Craft*, 1985. Editor of *Tough Guy Writers of the Thirties*, 1968, *Proletarian Writers of the Thirties*, 1968, *American Dreams, American Nightmares*, 1970, *Rediscoveries*, 1971, collections of essays on James Agee and Nathanael West, and other works. **Essays:** James M. Cain; "One of the Missing"; *The Recognitions*.

MARRS, Suzanne. Associate Professor of English, State University of New York, Oswego. Author of articles in *American Literature*, *Southern Review*, *Mississippi Quarterly*, and other periodicals. **Essays:** Thomas Bangs Thorpe; *Losing Battles*.

McDOWELL, Margaret B. Professor of Rhetoric and Women's Studies, University of Iowa, Iowa City. Author of *Edith Wharton*, 1976, and *Carson McCullers*, 1980. **Essay:** Carson McCullers.

McNAUGHTON, Howard. Reader in English, University of Canterbury, Christchurch, New Zealand. Author of *Bruce Mason*, 1976, and *New Zealand Drama*, 1981. Editor of *Contemporary New Zealand Plays*, 1976, and *James K. Baxter: Collected Plays*, 1982. **Essays:** Ben Hecht; *Awake and Sing!*; *Strange Interlude*; *Winterset*.

MESERVE, Walter J. Professor of Theatre and Drama, and Director of the Institute for American Theatre Studies, Indiana University, Bloomington. Author of *An Outline History of American Drama*, 1965, *Robert Sherwood: Reluctant Moralist*, 1970, *An Emerging Entertainment: The Drama of the American People to 1828*, 1977, *American Drama* (vol. 8 of the Revels History), with others, 1977, *American Drama to 1900: A Guide to Reference Sources*, 1980, and *Heralds of Promise: The Drama of the American People During the Age of Jackson 1829–1849*, 1986. Editor of *The Complete Plays of William Dean Howells*, 1960, *Discussions of Modern American Drama*, 1966, *American Satiric Comedies*, 1969, *Modern Drama from Communist China*, 1970, *The Rise of Silas Lapham* by Howells, 1971, *Studies in Death of a Salesman*, 1972, and *Modern Literature from China*, 1974. **Essays:** Robert Montgomery Bird; Paddy Chayefsky; Augustin Daly; Clyde Fitch; Susan Glaspell; Edward Harrigan; Bronson Howard; Sidney Howard; Percy MacKaye; Langdon Mitchell; John Howard Payne; Augustus Thomas; Royall Tyler; *The Little Foxes*.

MILLER, Jordan Y. Professor of English, University of Rhode Island, Kingston; now retired. Author of *Playwright's Progress: Eugene O'Neill and the Critics*, 1965, *The War Play Comes of Age*, 1969, and *Eugene O'Neill and the American Critic* (bibliography), 1973. Editor of *American Dramatic Literature*, 1961, and *Twentieth-Century Interpretations of A Streetcar Named Desire*, 1971. **Essays:** Lorraine Hansberry; James A. Herne; William Inge.

MOE, Christian H. Professor of Theatre, Southern Illinois University, Carbondale; member of the Advisory Board, Institute of Outdoor Drama; bibliographer for the American Theatre Association. Author or co-author of *Creating Historical Drama*, 1965, an essay on D. H. Lawrence, and several plays for children. Joint editor of *The William and Mary Theatre: A Chronicle*, 1968, and *Six New Plays for Children*, 1971. **Essays:** Marjorie Kinnan Rawlings; *The Glass Menagerie*; *The Member of the Wedding*.

MONTEIRO, George. Professor of English, Brown University, Providence, Rhode Island. Editor or co-editor of *Henry James and John Hay: The Record of a Friendship*, 1965, *Poems* by Emily Dickinson, 1967, *The Scarlet Letter* by Nathaniel Hawthorne, 1968, *The Poetical Works of Longfellow* (introduction), 1975, *The John Hay–Howells Letters: The Correspondence of John Milton Hay and William Dean Howells*, 1980, and *A Guide to the Atlantic Monthly's Contributors' Club*, 1983. **Essay:** John Hay.

MOORE, Jack B. Professor of English, and Chairman of American Studies, University of South Florida, Tampa. Author of *The Literature of Early America*, 1968, *The Literature of the American Renaissance*, 1969, *Guide to "Idylls of the King,"* 1969, *Maxwell Bodenheim*, 1970, *The Literature of the American Realistic Period*, 1971, *Cooper: The Last of the Mohicans* (study guide), 1971, *W. E. B. Du Bois*, 1981, and

Joe DiMaggio, 1986. **Essays:** Maxwell Bodenheim; Ignatius Donnelly; Frank Yerby; *Looking Backward 2000–1887*; *Native Son*.

MOORE, Rayburn S. Professor of English and Chairman, Division of Language and Literature, Franklin College of Arts and Sciences, University of Georgia, Athens. Author of *Constance Fenimore Woolson*, 1963, *Paul Hamilton Hayne*, 1972, and numerous articles and reviews. Editor of *For the Major and Selected Short Stories of Constance Fenimore Woolson*, 1967, *A Man of Letters in the Nineteenth-Century South: Selected Letters of Paul Hamilton Hayne*, 1982, and *The History of Southern Literature* (with others), 1985. **Essays:** Thomas Holley Chivers; John Esten Cooke; Paul Hamilton Hayne; William Gilmore Simms; Constance Fenimore Woolson.

MORSBERGER, Katharine M. Feature writer, Pitzer College, Claremont, California. Author of *Lew Wallace: Militant Romantic* (with Robert E. Morsberger), 1980, and articles on Hawthorne and Steinbeck. **Essay** (with Robert E. Morsberger): Lew Wallace.

MORSBERGER, Robert E. Professor of English, California State Polytechnic, Pomona. Author of *James Thurber*, 1964, *Commonsense Grammar and Style*, 1965, *Swordplay and the Elizabethan and Jacobean Stage*, 1974, and *Lew Wallace: Militant Romantic* (with Katharine M. Morsberger), 1980. Editor of *Viva Zapata!* by John Steinbeck, 1975. **Essays:** Lew Wallace (with Katharine M. Morsberger); "Ethan Brand."

NADEL, I. B. Professor of English, University of British Columbia, Vancouver. Author of *Biography: Fiction, Fact and Form*, 1984, and articles on Victorian writing and Jewish fiction in *University of Toronto Quarterly*, *Criticism*, *Mosaic*, *Midstream*, *Prose Studies*, and other periodicals. **Essays:** Henry Roth; *The Day of the Locust*.

NEVINS, Francis M., Jr. Professor of Law, St. Louis University School of Law, Missouri. Author of three crime novels and numerous crime short stories, *Royal Bloodline: Ellery Queen, Author and Detective*, 1974, and articles in *Detectionary*, *Journal of Popular Culture*, *Armchair Detective*, and other collections and periodicals. Editor of *The Mystery Writer's Art*, 1971, works by Ellery Queen, Cornell Woolrich, Anthony Boucher, and Christianna Brand, and anthologies. **Essays:** Erle Stanley Gardner; Ellery Queen.

NORDLAND, Brady. Free-lance writer. **Essay:** Mary McCarthy.

O'DONNELL, Thomas F. Late Professor of English, State University of New York, Brockport. Author or co-author of *Harold Frederic*, 1961, *A Bibliography of Harold Frederic*, 1975, and articles on American writers, especially those of New York State, for *American Transcendental Quarterly* and other periodicals. Editor of works by Frederic, James Kirke Paulding, and Adriaen Van Der Donck. Died 1980. **Essays:** Anne Bradstreet; Joseph Rodman Drake; James Kirke Paulding.

PEDEN, William. Professor of English, University of Mis-souri, Columbia. Author of *Night in Funland and Other Stories*, 1968, *Twilight at Monticello* (novel), 1973, and *The American Short Story: Continuity and Change 1940–1975*, 1975. Co-editor of works by Thomas Jefferson, John Adams, and John Quincy Adams, and of *New Writing in South Carolina*, 1971. **Essay:** O. Henry.

PERKINS, Barbara M. Managing editor of *Journal of Narrative Technique*, Eastern Michigan University, Ypsilanti. Author of articles in *Harper Handbook to Literature*, *American Literary Magazines: The Eighteenth and Nineteenth Centuries*, and other books and periodicals. **Essays:** Maxwell Anderson; John William De Forest.

PERKINS, George. Professor of English, Eastern Michigan University, Ypsilanti. Author or editor of *Writing Clear Prose*, 1964, *Varieties of Prose*, 1966, *The Theory of the American Novel*, 1970, *Realistic American Short Fiction*, 1972, *American Poetic Theory*, 1972, *The Practical Imagination* (with others), 1980, *The Harper Handbook to Literature* (with others), 1985, and *The American Tradition in Literature* (with others), sixth edition, 1985. **Essays:** Nathaniel Hawthorne; Henry James.

PERRY, Margaret. Director of Libraries, Valparaiso University, Indiana. Author of *A Bio-Bibliography of Countée P. Cullen*, 1971, *Silence to the Drums: A Survey of the Literature of the Harlem Renaissance*, 1976, *The Harlem Renaissance: An Annotated Bibliography and Commentary*, 1982, and several short stories. **Essays:** Countée Cullen; Phillis Wheatley.

PICKARD, John B. Associate Professor of English, University of Florida, Gainesville. Author of *Whittier: An Introduction and Interpretation*, 1961, the introduction to *Legends of New England* by Whittier, 1965, and *Emily Dickinson: An Introduction and Interpretation*, 1967. Editor of *Memorabilia of Whittier*, 1968, and *The Letters of Whittier*, 3 vols., 1975. **Essays:** James Russell Lowell; John Greenleaf Whittier.

PILDITCH, Jan. Lecturer, University of Waikato, Hamilton, New Zealand. **Essays:** John Gardner; William James.

PINSKER, Sanford. Professor of English, Franklin and Marshall College, Lancaster, Pennsylvania. Author of *The Schlemiel as Metaphor: Studies in the Yiddish and American-Jewish Novel*, 1971, *The Comedy That "Hoits": An Essay on the Fiction of Philip Roth*, 1975, *Still Life and Other Poems*, 1975, *The Languages of Joseph Conrad*, 1978, *Between Two Worlds: The American Novel in the 1960's*, 1978, *Memory Breaks Off and Other Poems*, 1984, *Conversations with Contemporary American Writers*, 1985, and many articles on contemporary fiction. Editor of *Critical Essays on Philip Roth*, 1982, and *America and the Holocaust* (with Jack Fischel), 1984. **Essays:** Joseph Heller; Norman Mailer.

POPOVICH, Helen Houser. President, Florida Atlantic University, Boca Raton. Author of articles on Samuel Beckett and on writing. **Essay:** John van Druten.

QUARTERMAIN, Peter. Associate Professor of English, University of British Columbia, Vancouver. Author of articles on Louis Zukofsky, Robert Creeley, Ezra Pound, Basil Bunting, Guy Davenport, Charles Reznikoff, and other writers. Editor of *American Poets 1880–1945* (Dictionary of Literary Biography), 3 vols., 1986. **Essays:** Robert Duncan; Allen Ginsberg; Gertrude Stein; Louis Zukofsky.

RAY, David. Professor of English, University of Missouri, Kansas City; editor of *New Letters*. Author of several books of poems (the most recent collection being *The Touched Life*, 1982), and a book of short stories. Editor or co-editor of *The Chicago Review Anthology*, 1959, *Richard Wright: Impressions and Perspectives*, 1973, *New Letters Reader*, 2 vols., 1984, and several anthologies of poetry. **Essay:** Horace Gregory.

REED, John Q. Late Chairman of the Department of English, Pittsburg State University, Kansas. Author of *Benjamin Penhallow Shillaber*, 1972, and articles on Artemus Ward, Henry James, William Faulkner, and Mark Twain, in *American Literature*, *Midcontinent American Studies Journal*, *Encyclopaedia Britannica*, *Civil War History*, and *Midwest Quarterly*. Died 1978. **Essay:** Artemus Ward.

REEVES, James. Author of more than 50 books, including poetry (*Collected Poems*, 1974), plays, and books for children; critical works include *The Critical Sense*, 1956, *Understanding Poetry*, 1965, *Commitment to Poetry*, 1969, *Inside Poetry* (with Martin Seymour-Smith), 1970, and *The Reputation and Writings of Alexander Pope*, 1976. Editor of many collections and anthologies, and of works by D. H. Lawrence, Donne, Clare, Hopkins, Robert Browning, Dickinson, Coleridge, Graves, Swift, Johnson, Marvell, Gray, Whitman, Hardy, and others; translator of fairy tales. Died 1978. **Essay:** Emily Dickinson.

REILLY, John M. Professor of English, State University of New York, Albany. Author of many articles on Afro-American literature, popular crime writing and social fiction, and bibliographical essays in *Black American Writers*, 1978, and *American Literary Scholarship*. Editor of *Twentieth-Century Interpretations of Invisible Man*, 1970, *Richard Wright: The Critical Reception*, 1978, and the reference book *Twentieth-Century Crime and Mystery Writers*, 1980 (2nd edition 1985). **Essays:** William Wells Brown; W. E. B. Du Bois; Dashiell Hammett; Zora Neale Hurston; Rex Stout; Jean Toomer; Richard Wright.

RENDER, Sylvia Lyons. Specialist in Afro-American History and Culture, Manuscript Division, Library of Congress, Washington, D.C. Author of *Charles W. Chesnutt*, 1980, the introduction to Chesnutt's *The Marrow of Tradition*, 1969, and of articles in *Encyclopaedia Britannica*, *CLA Journal*, *North Carolina Folklore*, and *Tennessee Folklore Society Bulletin*. Editor of *The Short Fiction of Chesnutt*, 1974. **Essay:** Charles Waddell Chesnutt.

RICHARDS, Robert F. Associate Professor of English, University of Denver, Colorado. Author of articles on esthetics, politics and literature, Ernest Hemingway, F. Scott Fitzgerald, Ralph Hodgson and Thomas Hornsby Ferril, and the introduction to Ferril's *Words for Denver and Other Poems*, 1966. Editor of *Concise Dictionary of American Literature*, 1969. **Essays:** Waldo Frank; Oliver La Farge; Don Marquis.

RINGE, Donald A. Professor of English, University of Kentucky, Lexington. Author of *James Fenimore Cooper*, 1962, *Charles Brockden Brown*, 1966, *The Pictorial Mode: Space and Time in the Art of Bryant, Irving, and Cooper*, 1971, and *American Gothic: Imagination and Reason in Nineteenth-Century Fiction*, 1982. Member of the Editorial Board for *The Writings of James Fenimore Cooper*. **Essays:** Hugh Henry Brackenridge; Charles Brockden Brown; James Fenimore Cooper; John Pendleton Kennedy; John Neal.

ROVIT, Earl. Professor of English, City College of New York. Author of *Herald to Chaos: The Novels of Elizabeth Madox Roberts*, 1960, *Ernest Hemingway*, 1963, *Saul Bellow*, 1967, and three novels—*The Player King*, 1965, *A Far Cry*, 1967, and *Crossings*, 1973. Editor of *Saul Bellow: A Collection of Critical Essays*, 1975. **Essays:** Henry Adams; John Barth; Theodore Dreiser; John Hawkes; James Jones; Elizabeth Madox Roberts; Trumbull Stickney; Jones Very; Nathanael West.

RUIHLEY, Glenn Richard. Member of the Department of English, Eastern Michigan University, Ypsilanti. Author of *The Thorn of a Rose: Amy Lowell Reconsidered*, 1975. Editor of *A Shard of Silence: Selected Poems* by Lowell, 1957. **Essays:** Amy Lowell; Edgar Lee Masters; Edna St. Vincent Millay.

SADLER, Geoff. Assistant Librarian, Local Studies, Chesterfield, Derbyshire, England. Author of western novels (as Jeff Sadler), including, most recently, *Throw of a Rope*, 1984, and *Manhunt in Chihuahua*, 1984, and the *Justus* trilogy of plantation novels (as Geoffrey Sadler), 1982. **Essays:** Booker T. Washington; *Souls of Black Folk*.

SAFFIOTI, Carol Lee. Associate Professor of English, University of Wisconsin—Parkside, Kenosha. **Essay:** Sterling A. Brown.

SANDERSON, Stewart F. Honorary Harold Orton Fellow, University of Leeds, England; Chairman of the Literature Committee, Scottish Arts Council. Author of *Hemingway*, 1961, and of many articles on British and comparative folklore and ethnology, and on modern literature. Editor of *The Secret Common-Wealth* by Robert Kirk, 1970, *The Linguistic Atlas of England* (with others), 1978, and *Studies in Linguistic Geography*, 1985. **Essay:** Ernest Hemingway.

SANDOCK, Mollie. Assistant Professor of English, Valparaiso University, Indiana. Author of articles on 19th-century literature and on librarianship in *Modern Philology*, *Library Quarterly*, *Nineteenth-Century Literature*, and other periodicals. **Essays:** *The Adventures of Tom Sawyer*; *The Catcher in the Rye*; *The Turn of the Screw*.

SAUL, George Brandon. Professor Emeritus of English, University of Connecticut, Storrs; contributing editor, *Journal of Irish Literature*. Author of fiction (*The Wild Queen*, 1967), poetry (*Hound and Unicorn*, 1969, and *Adam Unregenerate*, 1977), and of critical works, including *Prolegomena to the Study of Yeats's Poems* (1957) and *Plays* (1958), *Traditional Irish Literature and Its Backgrounds*, 1970, and *In Praise of the Half-Forgotten: Essays*, 1976. Also a composer. **Essay:** Sara Teasdale.

SCHWAB, Arnold T. Professor of English, California State University, Long Beach. Author of *James Gibbons Huneker: Critic of the Seven Arts*, 1963, and articles on Huneker, George Moore, and Joseph Conrad, in *American Literature*, *Nineteenth-Century Fiction*, and *Modern Philology*. Editor of *Americans in the Arts: Critiques by James Gibbons Huneker*, 1985. **Essay:** James Huneker.

SEELYE, Catherine. Free-lance writer. Editor of *Charles Olson and Ezra Pound: An Encounter at St. Elizabeths*, 1975. **Essays:** Eugene Field; Vachel Lindsay.

SEYERSTED, Per. Professor of American Literature, University of Oslo, Norway; Vice-President of the Nordic Association for Canadian Studies. Author of *Gilgamesj*, 1967, *Kate Chopin: A Critical Biography*, 1969, *Leslie Marmon Silko*, 1980, and *From Norwegian Romantic to American Realist: Studies in the Life and Writings of H. H. Boyesen*, 1984. Editor of *The Complete Works of Kate Chopin*, 1969, and *A Kate Chopin Miscellany* (with Emily Toth), 1979. **Essay:** Kate Chopin.

SHARMA, J. N. Professor and Head of the Department of English, University of Jodhpur, India. **Essays:** Ambrose Bierce; William Saroyan.

SHUCARD, Alan R. Professor of English, University of Wisconsin—Parkside, Kenosha. Author of three books of poetry and *Countée Cullen*, 1984. **Essays:** Gwendolyn Brooks; Walter Van Tilburg Clark; Paul Laurence Dunbar; Robert Hayden.

SINGH, Amritjit. Teacher and free-lance writer. Author of *The Novels of the Harlem Renaissance: Twelve Black Writers*, 1976, and articles in *Indian Journal of American Studies* and other Indian and American periodicals. Co-editor of the bibliographies *Indian Literature in English*, 1977, and *Afro-American Poetry and Drama*, 1977, and of *India: An Anthology of Contemporary Writing*, 1983. **Essay:** Claude McKay.

SMITH, Esther Marian Greenwell. Retired Professor of Language Arts. Author of *William Godwin* (with Elton E. Smith), 1965, *Mrs. Humphry Ward*, 1980, articles on Herman Melville, Nathaniel Hawthorne, Mrs. Humphry Ward, and Olivia Manning, two novels (*The Last Eight Days*, 1985, and *The Cascade Empire*, 1986), and youth fiction for religious publishers. **Essays:** Pearl S. Buck; *Billy Budd*.

SMITH, Stan. Senior Lecturer in English, University of Dundee, Scotland. Author of *A Sadly Contracted Hero: The Comic Self in Post-War American Fiction*, 1981, *Inviolable Voice: History and Twentieth-Century Poetry*, 1982, *W. H. Auden*, 1986, *Edward Thomas*, 1986, the introduction to *Twentieth-Century Poetry*, 1983, and essays in collections and journals. **Essays:** Lafcadio Hearn; Sylvia Plath; Theodore Roethke; Philip Roth; *The Assistant*.

SOLOMON, Eric. Professor of English, San Francisco State University. Author of *Stephen Crane in England*, 1963, *Stephen Crane: From Parody to Realism*, 1966, and many articles on 19th- and 20th-century British and American fiction. Editor of *The Faded Banners*, 1960, and *The Critic Agonistes*, 1985. **Essays:** Edmund Wilson; *Catch-22*; *Tender Is the Night*.

STAGG, Louis Charles. Professor of English and Director of Graduate Studies, Memphis State University, Tennessee. Author or co-author of *Index to Poe's Critical Vocabulary*, 1966, *The Figurative Language of Shakespeare's Chief 17th-Century Contemporaries: An Index*, revised 3rd edition, 1982, *The Figurative Language of the Tragedies of Shakespeare's Chief 16th-Century Contemporaries: An Index*, 1984, and numerous articles and reviews. **Essays:** William Gillette; *Death of a Salesman*; *Long Day's Journey into Night*.

STANFORD, Donald E. Alumni Professor of English Emeritus, Louisiana State University, Baton Rouge; Editor Emeritus of *Southern Review*. Author of two books of poems (*New England Earth*, 1941, and *The Traveler*, 1955), *Edward Taylor*, 1965, *In the Classic Mode: The Achievement of Robert Bridges*, 1978, and *Revolution and Convention in Modern Poetry: Studies in Ezra Pound, T. S. Eliot, Wallace Stevens, Edwin Arlington Robinson, and Yvor Winters*, 1983. Editor of *The Poems of Edward Taylor*, 1960, *Metrical History of Christianity* by Taylor, 1962, *Nine Essays in Modern Literature*, 1965, *Selected Poems of Robert Bridges*, 1974, *Selected Poems of S. Foster Damon*, 1974, *Selected Letters of Robert Bridges*, 2 vols., 1983–84, *Selected Poems of John Masefield*, 1984, and *The Letters of John Masefield to Margaret Bridges 1915–1919*, 1984. **Essays:** Edward Taylor; Yvor Winters; *Gods Determinations*; "Sunday Morning."

STEDMAN, Jane W. Professor of English, Roosevelt University, Chicago. Author of articles and reviews in anthologies of Victorian studies, scholarly journals, and *Opera News*. Editor of *Gilbert Before Sullivan: Six Comic Plays*, 1967. **Essays:** David Belasco; *John Brown's Body*.

STERN, Madeleine B. Free-lance writer; partner in Leona Rostenberg–Madeleine Stern Rare Books, New York. Author of *Louisa May Alcott*, 1950, *Imprints on History: Book Publishers and American Frontiers*, 1956, *We the Women: Career Firsts of 19th-Century America*, 1963, *Heads and Headlines: The Phrenological Fowlers*, 1971, *Old and Rare: Thirty Years in the Book Business* (with Leona Rostenberg), 1975, *Books and Book People in 19th-Century America*, 1978, *Antiquarian Bookselling in the United States: A History from the Origins to the 1940's*, 1985, and several biographies for adults and children. Editor of *Women on the Move*, 1972, *The Victoria Woodhull Reader*, 1974, *Phrenological Dictionary of 19th-Century Americans*, 1982, and *Louisa's Wonder Book*, 1975, *Behind a Mask*, 1975, and *Plots and Counterplots*, 1976, all by Louisa May Alcott. **Essays:** Louisa May Alcott; Mary Noailles Murfree; Harriet Beecher Stowe.

STOUCK, David. Professor of English, Simon Fraser University, Burnaby, British Columbia. Author of *Willa Cather's Imagination*, 1975, *Major Canadian Authors*, 1984, and *The Wardells and the Vosburghs: Records of a Loyalist Family*, 1986. **Essay:** Sherwood Anderson.

STUCKEY, W. J. Professor of English, Purdue University, West Lafayette, Indiana; associate editor of *Journal of Narrative Technique*. Author of *Pulitzer Prize Novels*, 1966 (revised 1981), and *Caroline Gordon*, 1972. **Essays:** Edna Ferber; Caroline Gordon; Margaret Mitchell; Walker Percy; T. S. Stribling; Edith Wharton; "Old Mortality."

SUMMERS, Joseph H. Roswell S. Burrows Professor Emeritus of English, University of Rochester, Rochester, New York. Author of *George Herbert: Religion and Art*, 1954, *The Muse's Method: An Introduction to Paradise Lost*, 1962, and *The Heirs of Donne and Jonson*, 1970. Editor of *Selected Poems* by Andrew Marvell, 1961, *The Lyric and Dramatic Milton*, 1965, and *Selected Poetry* by George Herbert, 1967. **Essays:** Elizabeth Bishop; Richard Wilbur.

TANSELLE, G. Thomas. Vice-President, John Simon Guggenheim Foundation, New York; Adjunct Professor of English, Columbia University, New York; bibliographical editor of *The Writings of Herman Melville* since 1968 (8 vols. so far published). Author of *Royall Tyler*, 1967, *Guide to the Study of United States Imprints*, 2 vols., 1971, *The Editing of Historical Documents*, 1978, *Selected Studies in Bibliography*, 1979, *The History of Books as a Field of Study*, 1981, and articles on descriptive bibliography and scholarly editing. **Essay:** Floyd Dell.

THWAITE, Ann. Free-lance writer; member of the Editorial Board, *Cricket* magazine. Author of 20 books for children and of two biographies—*Waiting for the Party: The Life of Frances Hodgson Burnett*, 1974, and *Edmund Gosse: A Literary Landscape*, 1984. Editor of the *Allsorts* series for children, 1969–75, and *My Oxford*, 1977. **Essay:** Frances Hodgson Burnett.

TRAVERSI, Derek A. Emeritus Professor of English Literature, Swarthmore College, Pennsylvania. Author of *An Approach to Shakespeare*, 1938 (revised 1968), *Shakespeare: The Last Phase*, 1954, *Shakespeare: From Richard II to Henry V*, 1957, *Shakespeare: The Roman Plays*, 1963, *T. S. Eliot: The Longer Poems*, 1976, *The Literary Imagination: Studies in Dante, Chaucer, and Shakespeare*, 1982, and *The Canterbury Tales: A Reading*, 1983. **Essays:** T. S. Eliot; *Four Quartets*; *The Waste Land*.

TURNER, Richard C. Professor and Chair of English, Indiana University–Purdue University, Indianapolis. **Essays:** Richard Hugo; Adrienne Rich.

WAGNER, Linda W. Professor of English, Michigan State University, East Lansing. Author of *The Poems* (1964) and *Prose* (1970) *of William Carlos Williams*, *Denise Levertov*, 1967, *Hemingway and Faulkner: Inventors/Masters*, 1975, *Introducing Poems*, 1976, *Hemingway: A Reference Guide*, 1977, *William Carlos Williams: A Reference Guide*, 1978, *John Dos Passos: Artist as American*, 1979, *Ellen Glasgow: Beyond Convention*, 1982, and *Sylvia Plath: A Literary Biography*, 1986. Editor of works by or about William Faulkner, T. S. Eliot, Ernest Hemingway, William Carlos Williams, Robert Frost, Denise Levertov, and Sylvia Plath. **Essays:** Anne Sexton; William Carlos Williams; *Ariel*; *The Sound and the Fury*; *The Sun Also Rises*.

WALKER, Marshall. Professor of English, University of Waikato, Hamilton, New Zealand. Author of *Robert Penn Warren: A Vision Earned*, 1979, *The Portrait of a Lady: Notes*, 1981, and *The Literature of the United States*, 1983. **Essay:** Chronology.

WALLACH, Mark I. Partner, Calfee Halter and Griswold, Cleveland, Ohio. Author of *Christopher Morley* (with Jon Bracker), 1976, articles on Morley in *Markham Review* and *Dictionary of Literary Biography*, and articles in *Case Western Reserve Law Review* and other periodicals. **Essay:** Christopher Morley.

WALSER, Richard. Professor Emeritus of English, North Carolina State University, Raleigh. Author of *Thomas Wolfe: An Introduction and Interpretation*, 1961, *Literary North Carolina*, 1970, *Thomas Wolfe, Undergraduate*, 1977, and *North Carolina Legends*, 1981. Editor or co-editor of *The Enigma of Thomas Wolfe*, 1953, *The Streets of Durham* by Wolfe, 1982, and *Thomas Wolfe Interviewed*, 1985. **Essays:** James Boyd; Paul Green; Thomas Wolfe.

WALSH, George. Publisher and free-lance writer. **Essay:** Joel Chandler Harris.

WARNER, Val. Free-lance writer. Author of two books of poems (*Under the Penthouse*, 1973, and *Before Lunch*, 1986) and articles and reviews. Editor of *Collected Poems and Prose of Charlotte Mew*, 1981; translator of *Centenary Corbière*, 1974. **Essay:** Shirley Jackson.

WATT, R. J. C. Lecturer in English, University of Dundee, Scotland. Author of articles on contemporary poetry and on textual problems in Shakespeare, and of a forthcoming book on Gerard Manley Hopkins. **Essays:** *The Big Sleep*; "The Murders in the Rue Morgue."

WATTS, Harold H. Professor Emeritus of English, Purdue University, West Lafayette, Indiana. Author of *The Modern Reader's Guide to the Bible*, 1949, *Ezra Pound and the Cantos*, 1952, *Hound and Quarry*, 1953, *The Modern Reader's Guide to Religions*, 1964, and *Aldous Huxley*, 1969. **Essays:** John Cheever; James Gould Cozzens; Hilda Doolittle; William Gaddis; Jerzy Kosinski; Thomas Pynchon; Wallace Stevens; John Updike; Eudora Welty; *All the King's Men*.

WEALES, Gerald. Professor of English, University of Pennsylvania, Philadelphia; drama critic for *The Reporter* and *Commonweal*. Author of *Religion in Modern English Drama*, 1961, *American Drama since World War II*, 1962, *A Play and Its Parts*, 1964, *Tennessee Williams*, 1965, *The Jumping-Off Place: American Drama in the 1960's*, 1969, *Clifford Odets*, 1971 (revised 1985), and *Canned Goods as Caviar: American Film Comedy in the 1930's*, 1985. Editor of several collections of plays and essays and of *The Complete Plays of William Wycherley*, 1966. **Essays:** Philip Barry; Robert Benchley; Arthur Kopit; Arthur Miller; Clifford Odets; James Whitcomb Riley; James Thurber; Mercy Warren; E. B. White; Tennessee Williams.

WEIR, Sybil B. Professor of English and American Studies, San Jose State University, California. Author of articles on Theodore Dreiser, Gertrude Atherton, Constance Fenimore Woolson, and Elizabeth Drew Stoddard. **Essay:** Gertrude Atherton.

WESTBROOK, Perry D. Professor Emeritus of English, State University of New York, Albany. Author of *Acres of Flint: Writers of New England*, 1951 (revised 1981), *Biography of an Island*, 1958, *The Greatness of Man: An Essay on Dostoevsky and Whitman*, 1961, *Mary Ellen Chase*, 1966, *Mary Wilkins Freeman*, 1967, *John Burroughs*, 1974, *William Bradford*, 1978, and *Free Will and Determinism in American Literature*, 1979. Co-editor of *The Writing Women of New England*, 1982, and *The New England Town in Fact and Fiction*, 1982. **Essays:** Edward Bellamy; William Bradford; Mary E. Wilkins Freeman; Sarah Orne Jewett; *Leaves of Grass*; *Nature*; *The Rise of Silas Lapham*; *U.S.A.*; *Walden*.

WINNIFRITH, T. J. Senior Lecturer in English, University of Warwick, Coventry, England. Author or co-author of *The Brontës and Their Background: Romance and Reality*, 1973, *The Brontës*, 1977, *Brontë Facts and Brontë Problems*, 1983, and *1984 and All's Well?*, 1984. Co-editor of *Aspects of the Epic*, 1983, *Greece Old and New*, 1983, *Selected Brontë Poems*, 1983, and works by Charlotte and Branwell Brontë. **Essay:** Lionel Trilling.

WOODRESS, James. Professor of English, University of California, Davis. Author of *Howells and Italy*, 1952, *Booth Tarkington*, 1955, *A Yankee's Odyssey: The Life of Joel Barlow*, 1958, *Dissertations in American Literature*, 1962, *Willa Cather: Her Life and Art*, 1970, *American Fiction 1900–1950: A Guide to Information Sources*, 1975, and *Willa Cather: A Literary Life*, 1987. Editor or co-editor of *Voices from America's Past*, 1961, *Eight American Authors*, 1971, *The Troll Garden* by Cather, 1983, and *Critical Essays on Whitman*, 1983. **Essays:** Joel Barlow; Willa Cather; Hamlin Garland; E. W. Howe; Thomas Jefferson; Frank Norris; Kenneth Roberts; Karl Shapiro; Booth Tarkington; Walt Whitman; *Common Sense*; *Democracy*; *The Jungle*; *The Red Badge of Courage*.

YOUNG, Kenneth. Late literary and political adviser to Beaverbrook Newspapers, London; former editor of the *Yorkshire Post*, England. Author of *D. H. Lawrence*, 1952, *John Dryden*, 1954, *Ford Madox Ford*, 1958, *A. J. Balfour*, 1963, *Churchill and Beaverbrook*, 1966, *The Greek Passion: A Study in People and Politics*, 1969, *Sir Alec Douglas-Home*, 1970, *Stanley Baldwin*, 1976, *A Neighbourhood of Writers*, 1981, and other biographies, literary studies, and political and social histories. Editor of *Diaries of Sir Robert Bruce Lockhart*, 2 vols., 1973–80. Died 1985. **Essay:** Henry Miller.

YOUNG, Thomas Daniel. Gertrude Conway Vanderbilt Professor of English, Vanderbilt University, Nashville, Tennessee. Author or co-author of *The Literature of the South*, 1952, *Donald Davidson: An Essay and a Bibliography*, 1965, *American Literature: A Critical Survey*, 1968, *John Crowe Ransom: Critical Essays and a Bibliography*, 1968, *Ransom*, 1971, *Davidson*, 1971, *Gentleman in a Dustcoat: A Biography of John Crowe Ransom*, 1976, *Tennessee Writers*, 1977, *The Vocation of Letters in America*, 1981, *The Past in the Present*, 1981, *Waking Their Neighbors Up: The Nashville Agrarians Rediscovered*, 1982, and *Ransom: An Annotated Bibliography*, 1982. Editor or co-editor of *The Literary Correspondence of Donald Davidson and Allen Tate*, 1971, *The New Criticism and After*, 1976, *Conversations with Malcolm Cowley*, 1986, and the selected essays and letters of Ransom. **Essays:** Donald Davidson; John Crowe Ransom; *Absalom, Absalom!*; *The Great Gatsby*.